SELECTED CONSUMER STATUTES

2019 Edition

Compiled and Edited by

DEE PRIDGEN
Emeritus Professor of Law
University of Wyoming

JEFF SOVERN
Professor of Law
St. John's University

CHRISTOPHER L. PETERSON
John J. Flynn Endowed Professor of Law
The University of Utah
Director of Financial Services and Senior Fellow
Consumer Federation of America

WEST ACADEMIC PUBLISHING

444 Cedar Street, Suite 700
St. Paul, MN 55101
1-877-888-1330

Printed in the United States of America

ISBN: 978-1-64242-308-2

PREFACE

The volume was created to accompany our casebook, *Consumer Law Cases and Materials* (West Academic 2020), by Dee Pridgen, Jeff Sovern, and Christopher L. Peterson. It is our hope that this book can also serve for other purposes, such as in the practice of consumer law and in clinical courses on consumer issues. We have chosen to call this book *Selected Consumer Statutes* in part because we view it as a companion to *Selected Commercial Statutes* for those working with consumer law.

This is the sixth edition of this book. Since the last edition appeared in 2015, consumer law continues to rapidly evolve. Particularly in the area of financial services both Congress and federal regulators spurred many changes in the law. In 2018 Congress adopted significant revisions to the Dodd-Frank Wall Street Reform and Consumer Protection Act. The Consumer Financial Protection Bureau has issued revisions to the implementing regulations for the Truth in Lending Act, the Real Estate Settlement Procedures Act, and has issued the first proposed regulation implementing the Fair Debt Collection Practices Act. Moreover, state consumer protection law continues to change, including for example, California's recent adoption of a consumer privacy law requiring certain disclosures when businesses collect consumers' personal information These and many other changes are included within this updated volume. Unless otherwise noted, it is current through August 1, 2019.

As with all such compilations of statutes and similar materials, a caveat is in order: While this book is a convenient compilation, it should not be used in lieu of checking the primary sources. Statutes and regulations change quickly. Similarly, uniform statutes may be modified when adopted in a particular jurisdiction.

Although no longer listed as co-authors, Andy Spanogle and Ralph Rohner originated the casebook this book is intended to accompany, and their fingerprints appear throughout that volume and this one. We and the law teachers and students who have used these books have benefited immensely from their wisdom and hard work and we are very grateful to them both for conceiving the companion casebook and allowing us to continue their work.

We wish to thank our research assistants who helped to assemble these and earlier versions of these materials: Jillian A. Gardner, Ruben Huertero, Francis S. Alaimo, Sara Krastins, Christopher Conant, Yelena Gelman, Dana E. Grabiner, Edmund Witter, Ourania Sdogos, Andrew Lipkowitz, Preston J. Postlethwaite, Eric Levine, Daliya Poulose, David F. Knapp, and Jayshree Narendran, all of St. John's University School of Law; Jeremy C. Schwendiman, Dustin J. Richards, Michelle Wimmer, David Hansen, Jeremiah James and Noelle Hill of the University of Wyoming College of Law; and Ben Lehnardt of the University of Utah, S.J. Qunniey College of Law.

We hope you find this volume useful.

DEE PRIDGEN
JEFF SOVERN
CHRISTOPHER L. PETERSON

August 2019

SUMMARY OF MATERIALS IN ALPHABETICAL ORDER

SUMMARY OF CONTENTS

TABLE OF CONTENTS

SELECTED CONSUMER STATUTES

2019 Edition

Part One

FEDERAL MATERIALS

FEDERAL TRADE COMMISSION ACT (FTC ACT)

(Selected Sections)

15 U.S.C.A. §§ 41–58

Table of Sections

§ 41 [FTC Act § 1]. Federal Trade Commission established; membership; vacancies; seal

A commission is created and established, to be known as the Federal Trade Commission (hereinafter referred to as the Commission), which shall be composed of five Commissioners, who shall be appointed by the President, by and with the advice and consent of the Senate. Not more than three of the Commissioners shall be members of the same political party. The first Commissioners appointed shall continue in office for terms of three, four, five, six, and seven years, respectively, from September 26, 1914, the term of each to be designated by the President, but their successors shall be appointed for terms of seven years, except that any person chosen to fill a vacancy shall be appointed only for the unexpired term of the Commissioner whom he shall succeed: *Provided, however*, That upon the expiration of his term of office a Commissioner shall continue to serve until his successor shall have been appointed and shall have qualified. The President shall choose a chairman from the Commission's membership. No Commissioner shall engage in any other business, vocation, or employment. Any Commissioner may be removed by the President for inefficiency, neglect of duty, or malfeasance in office. A vacancy in the Commission shall not impair the right of the remaining Commissioners to exercise all the powers of the Commission.

The Commission shall have an official seal, which shall be judicially noticed.

* * *

§ 44 [FTC Act § 4]. Definitions

The words defined in this section shall have the following meaning when found in this subchapter, to wit:

"Commerce" means commerce among the several States or with foreign nations, or in any Territory of the United States or in the District of Columbia, or between any such Territory and another, or between any such Territory and any State or foreign nation, or between the District of Columbia and any State or Territory or foreign nation.

"Corporation" shall be deemed to include any company, trust, so-called Massachusetts trust, or association, incorporated or unincorporated, which is organized to carry on business for its own profit or that of its members, and has shares of capital or capital stock or certificates of interest, and any company, trust, so-called Massachusetts trust, or association, incorporated or unincorporated, without shares of capital or capital stock or certificates of interest, except partnerships, which is organized to carry on business for its own profit or that of its members.

* * *

"Foreign law enforcement agency" means—

(1) any agency or judicial authority of a foreign government, including a foreign state, a political subdivision of a foreign state, or a multinational organization constituted by and comprised of foreign states, that is vested with law enforcement or investigative authority in civil, criminal, or administrative matters; and

(2) any multinational organization, to the extent that it is acting on behalf of an entity described in paragraph (1).

§ 45 [FTC Act § 5]. Unfair methods of competition unlawful; prevention by Commission

(a) Declaration of unlawfulness; power to prohibit unfair practices; inapplicability to foreign trade

(1) Unfair methods of competition in or affecting commerce, and unfair or deceptive acts or practices in or affecting commerce, are hereby declared unlawful.

(2) The Commission is hereby empowered and directed to prevent persons, partnerships, or corporations, except banks, savings and loan institutions described in section 57a(f)(3) of this title, Federal credit unions described in section 57a(f)(4) of this title, common carriers subject to the Acts to regulate commerce, air carriers and foreign air carriers subject to part A of subtitle VII of Title 49, and persons, partnerships, or corporations insofar as they are subject to the Packers and Stockyards Act, 1921, as amended [7 U.S.C.A. § 181 et seq.], except as provided in section 406(b) of said Act [7 U.S.C.A. § 227(b)], from using unfair methods of competition in or affecting commerce and unfair or deceptive acts or practices in or affecting commerce.

* * *

(4)(A) For purposes of subsection (a) of this section, the term "unfair or deceptive acts or practices" includes such acts or practices involving foreign commerce that—

(i) cause or are likely to cause reasonably foreseeable injury within the United States; or

(ii) involve material conduct occurring within the United States.

(B) All remedies available to the Commission with respect to unfair and deceptive acts or practices shall be available for acts and practices described in this paragraph, including restitution to domestic or foreign victims.

(b) Proceeding by Commission; modifying and setting aside orders

Whenever the Commission shall have reason to believe that any such person, partnership, or corporation has been or is using any unfair method of competition or unfair or deceptive act or practice in or affecting commerce, and if it shall appear to the Commission that a proceeding by it in respect thereof would be to the interest of the public, it shall issue and serve upon such person, partnership, or corporation a complaint stating its charges in that respect and containing a notice of a hearing upon a day and at a place therein fixed at least thirty days after the service of said complaint. The person, partnership, or corporation so complained of shall have the right to appear at the place and time so fixed and show cause why an order should not be entered by the Commission requiring such person, partnership, or corporation to cease and desist from the violation of the law so charged in said complaint. Any person, partnership, or corporation may make application, and upon good cause shown may be allowed by the Commission to intervene and appear in said proceeding by counsel or in person. The testimony in any such proceeding shall be reduced to writing and filed in the office of the Commission. If upon such hearing the Commission shall be of the opinion that the method of competition or the act or practice in question is prohibited by this subchapter, it shall make a report in writing in which it shall state its findings as to the facts and shall issue and cause to be served on such person, partnership, or corporation an order requiring such person, partnership, or corporation to cease and desist from using such method of competition or such act or practice. Until the expiration of the time allowed for filing a petition for review, if no such petition has been duly filed within such time, or, if a petition for review has been filed within such time then until the record in the proceeding has been filed in a court of appeals of the United States, as hereinafter provided, the Commission may at any time, upon such notice and in such manner as it shall deem proper, modify or set aside, in whole or in part, any report or any order made or issued by it under this section. After the expiration of the time allowed for filing a petition for review, if no such petition has been duly filed within such time, the Commission may at any time, after notice and opportunity for hearing, reopen and alter, modify, or set aside, in whole or in part, any report or order made or issued by it under this section, whenever in the opinion of the Commission conditions of fact or of law have so changed as to require such action or if the public interest shall so require, except that (1) the said person, partnership, or corporation may, within sixty days after service upon him or it of said report or order entered after such a reopening, obtain a review thereof in the appropriate court of appeals of the United States, in the manner provided in subsection (c) of this section; and (2) in the case of an order, the Commission shall reopen any such order to consider whether such order (including any affirmative relief provision contained in such order) should be altered, modified, or set aside, in whole or in part, if the person, partnership, or corporation involved files a request with the Commission which makes a satisfactory showing that changed conditions of law or fact require such order to be altered, modified, or set aside, in whole or in part. The Commission shall determine whether to alter, modify, or set aside any order of the Commission in response to a request made by a person, partnership, or corporation under paragraph (2) not later than 120 days after the date of the filing of such request.

(c) Review of order; rehearing

Any person, partnership, or corporation required by an order of the Commission to cease and desist from using any method of competition or act or practice may obtain a review of such order in the court of appeals of the United States, within any circuit where the method of competition or the act or practice in question was used or where such person, partnership, or corporation resides or carries on business, by filing in the court, within sixty days from the date of the service of such order, a written petition praying that the order of the Commission be set aside. A copy of such petition shall be forthwith transmitted by the clerk of the court to the Commission, and thereupon the Commission shall file in the court the record in the proceeding, as provided in section 2112 of Title 28. Upon such filing of the petition the court shall have jurisdiction of the proceeding and of the question determined therein concurrently with the Commission until the filing of the record and shall have power to make and enter a decree affirming, modifying, or setting aside the order of the Commission, and enforcing the same to the extent that such order is affirmed and to issue such writs as are ancillary to its jurisdiction or are necessary in its judgement to prevent injury to the public or to competitors pendente lite. The findings of the Commission as to the facts, if supported by evidence, shall be conclusive. To the extent that the order of the Commission is affirmed, the court shall thereupon issue its own order commanding obedience to the terms of such order of the Commission. If either party shall apply to the court for leave to adduce additional evidence, and shall show to the satisfaction of the court that such additional evidence is material and that there were reasonable grounds for the failure to adduce such evidence in the proceeding before the Commission, the court may order such additional evidence to be taken before the Commission and to be adduced upon the hearing in such manner and upon such terms and conditions as to the court may seem proper. The Commission may modify its findings as to the facts, or make new findings, by reason of the additional evidence so taken, and it shall file such modified or new findings, which, if supported by evidence, shall be conclusive, and its recommendation, if any, for the modification or setting aside of its original order, with the return of such additional evidence. The judgment and decree of the court shall be final, except that the same shall be subject to review by the Supreme Court upon certiorari, as provided in section 1254 of Title 28.

(d) Jurisdiction of court

Upon the filing of the record with it the jurisdiction of the court of appeals of the United States to affirm, enforce, modify, or set aside orders of the Commission shall be exclusive.

* * *

(l) **Penalty for violation of order; injunctions and other appropriate equitable relief**

Any person, partnership, or corporation who violates an order of the Commission after it has become final, and while such order is in effect, shall forfeit and pay to the United States a civil penalty of not more than $10,000 for each violation, which shall accrue to the United States and may be recovered in a civil action brought by the Attorney General of the United States. Each separate violation of such an order shall be a separate offense, except that in a case of a violation through continuing failure to obey or neglect to obey a final order of the Commission, each day of continuance of such failure or neglect shall be deemed a separate offense. In such actions, the United States district courts are empowered to grant mandatory injunctions and such other and further equitable relief as they deem appropriate in the enforcement of such final orders of the Commission.

(m) Civil actions for recovery of penalties for knowing violations of rules and cease and desist orders respecting unfair or deceptive acts or practices; jurisdiction; maximum amount of penalties; continuing violations; de novo determinations; compromise or settlement procedure

(1)(A) The Commission may commence a civil action to recover a civil penalty in a district court of the United States against any person, partnership, or corporation which violates any rule under this chapter respecting unfair or deceptive acts or practices (other than an interpretive rule or a rule violation of which the Commission has provided is not an unfair or deceptive act or practice in violation of subsection (a)(1) of this section) with actual knowledge or knowledge fairly implied on the basis of objective circumstances that such act is unfair or deceptive and is prohibited by such rule. In such action, such person, partnership, or corporation shall be liable for a civil penalty of not more than $10,000 for each violation.

(B) If the Commission determines in a proceeding under subsection (b) of this section that any act or practice is unfair or deceptive, and issues a final cease and desist order, other than a consent order, with respect to such act or practice, then the Commission may commence a civil action to obtain a civil penalty in a district court of the United States against any person, partnership, or corporation which engages in such act or practice—

(1) after such cease and desist order becomes final (whether or not such person, partnership, or corporation was subject to such cease and desist order), and

(2) with actual knowledge that such act or practice is unfair or deceptive and is unlawful under subsection (a)(1) of this section.

In such action, such person, partnership, or corporation shall be liable for a civil penalty of not more than $10,000 for each violation.

(C) In the case of a violation through continuing failure to comply with a rule or with subsection (a)(1) of this section, each day of continuance of such failure shall be treated as a separate violation, for purposes of subparagraphs (A) and (B). In determining the amount of such a civil penalty, the court shall take into account the degree of culpability, any history of prior such conduct, ability to pay, effect on ability to continue to do business, and such other matters as justice may require.

(2) If the cease and desist order establishing that the act or practice is unfair or deceptive was not issued against the defendant in a civil penalty action under paragraph (1)(B) the issues of fact in such action against such defendant shall be tried de novo. Upon request of any party to such an action against such defendant, the court shall also review the determination of law made by the Commission in the proceeding under subsection (b) of this section that the act or practice which was the subject of such proceeding constituted an unfair or deceptive act or practice in violation of subsection (a) of this section.

(3) The Commission may compromise or settle any action for a civil penalty if such compromise or settlement is accompanied by a public statement of its reasons and is approved by the court.

(n) Standard of proof; public policy consideration

The Commission shall have no authority under this section or section 57a of this title to declare unlawful an act or practice on the grounds that such act or practice is unfair unless the act or practice causes or is likely to cause substantial injury to consumers which is not reasonably avoidable by consumers themselves and not outweighed by countervailing benefits to consumers or to competition. In determining whether an act or practice is unfair, the Commission may consider established public policies as evidence to be considered with all other evidence. Such public policy considerations may not serve as a primary basis for such determination.

* * *

§ 45b [FTC Act §5]. Consumer review protection

(a) Definitions

In this section:

(1) Commission

The term "Commission" means the Federal Trade Commission.

(2) Covered communication

The term "covered communication" means a written, oral, or pictorial review, performance assessment of, or other similar analysis of, including by electronic means, the goods, services, or conduct of a person by an individual who is party to a form contract with respect to which such person is also a party.

(3) Form contract

(A) In general

Except as provided in subparagraph (B), the term "form contract" means a contract with standardized terms—

(i) used by a person in the course of selling or leasing the person's goods or services; and

(ii) imposed on an individual without a meaningful opportunity for such individual to negotiate the standardized terms.

(B) Exception

The term "form contract" does not include an employer-employee or independent contractor contract.

(4) Pictorial

The term "pictorial" includes pictures, photographs, video, illustrations, and symbols.

(b) Invalidity of contracts that impede consumer reviews

(1) In general

Except as provided in paragraphs (2) and (3), a provision of a form contract is void from the inception of such contract if such provision—

(A) prohibits or restricts the ability of an individual who is a party to the form contract to engage in a covered communication;

(B) imposes a penalty or fee against an individual who is a party to the form contract for engaging in a covered communication; or

(C) transfers or requires an individual who is a party to the form contract to transfer to any person any intellectual property rights in review or feedback content, with the exception of a non-exclusive license to use the content, that the individual may have in any otherwise lawful covered communication about such person or the goods or services provided by such person.

(2) Rule of construction

Nothing in paragraph (1) shall be construed to affect—

(A) any duty of confidentiality imposed by law (including agency guidance);

(B) any civil cause of action for defamation, libel, or slander, or any similar cause of action;

(C) any party's right to remove or refuse to display publicly on an Internet website or webpage owned, operated, or otherwise controlled by such party any content of a covered communication that—

(i) contains the personal information or likeness of another person, or is libelous, harassing, abusive, obscene, vulgar, sexually explicit, or is inappropriate with respect to race, gender, sexuality, ethnicity, or other intrinsic characteristic;

(ii) is unrelated to the goods or services offered by or available at such party's Internet website or webpage; or

(iii) is clearly false or misleading; or

(D) a party's right to establish terms and conditions with respect to the creation of photographs or video of such party's property when those photographs or video are created by an employee or independent contractor of a commercial entity and solely intended for commercial purposes by that entity.

(3) Exceptions

Paragraph (1) shall not apply to the extent that a provision of a form contract prohibits disclosure or submission of, or reserves the right of a person or business that hosts online consumer reviews or comments to remove—

(A) trade secrets or commercial or financial information obtained from a person and considered privileged or confidential;

(B) personnel and medical files and similar information the disclosure of which would constitute a clearly unwarranted invasion of personal privacy;

(C) records or information compiled for law enforcement purposes, the disclosure of which would constitute a clearly unwarranted invasion of personal privacy;

(D) content that is unlawful or otherwise meets the requirements of paragraph (2)(C); or

(E) content that contains any computer viruses, worms, or other potentially damaging computer code, processes, programs, applications, or files.

(c) Prohibition

It shall be unlawful for a person to offer a form contract containing a provision described as void in subsection (b).

(d) Enforcement by Commission

(1) Unfair or deceptive acts or practices

A violation of subsection (c) by a person with respect to which the Commission is empowered under section 5(a)(2) of the Federal Trade Commission Act (15 U.S.C. 45(a)(2)) shall be treated as a violation of a rule defining an unfair or deceptive act or practice prescribed under section 18(a)(1)(B) of the Federal Trade Commission Act (15 U.S.C. 57a(a)(1)(B)).

(2) Powers of Commission

(A) In general

The Commission shall enforce this section in the same manner, by the same means, and with the same jurisdiction, powers, and duties as though all applicable terms and provisions of the Federal Trade Commission Act (15 U.S.C. 41 et seq.) were incorporated into and made a part of this Act.

(B) Privileges and immunities

Any person who violates this section shall be subject to the penalties and entitled to the privileges and immunities provided in the Federal Trade Commission Act (15 U.S.C. 41 et seq.).

(e) Enforcement by States

(1) Authorization

Subject to paragraph (2), in any case in which the attorney general of a State has reason to believe that an interest of the residents of the State has been or is threatened or adversely affected by the engagement of any person subject to subsection (c) in a practice that violates such subsection, the attorney general of the State may, as parens patriae, bring a civil action on behalf of the residents of the State in an appropriate district court of the United States to obtain appropriate relief.

(2) Rights of Federal Trade Commission

(A) Notice to Federal Trade Commission

(i) In general

Except as provided in clause (iii), the attorney general of a State shall notify the Commission in writing that the attorney general intends to bring a civil action under paragraph (1) before initiating the civil action against a person described in subsection (d)(1).

(ii) Contents

The notification required by clause (i) with respect to a civil action shall include a copy of the complaint to be filed to initiate the civil action.

(iii) Exception

If it is not feasible for the attorney general of a State to provide the notification required by clause (i) before initiating a civil action under paragraph (1), the attorney general shall notify the Commission immediately upon instituting the civil action.

(B) Intervention by Federal Trade Commission

The Commission may—

(i) intervene in any civil action brought by the attorney general of a State under paragraph (1) against a person described in subsection (d)(1); and

(ii) upon intervening—

(I) be heard on all matters arising in the civil action; and

(II) file petitions for appeal of a decision in the civil action.

(3) Investigatory powers

Nothing in this subsection may be construed to prevent the attorney general of a State from exercising the powers conferred on the attorney general by the laws of the State to conduct investigations, to administer oaths or affirmations, or to compel the attendance of witnesses or the production of documentary or other evidence.

(4) Preemptive action by Federal Trade Commission

If the Federal Trade Commission institutes a civil action or an administrative action with respect to a violation of subsection (c), the attorney general of a State may not, during the pendency of such action, bring a civil action under paragraph (1) against any defendant named in the complaint of the Commission for the violation with respect to which the Commission instituted such action.

(5) Venue; service of process

(A) Venue

Any action brought under paragraph (1) may be brought in—

(i) the district court of the United States that meets applicable requirements relating to venue under section 1391 of Title 28; or

(ii) another court of competent jurisdiction.

(B) Service of process

In an action brought under paragraph (1), process may be served in any district in which the defendant—

(i) is an inhabitant; or

(ii) may be found.

(6) Actions by other State officials

(A) In general

In addition to civil actions brought by attorneys general under paragraph (1), any other consumer protection officer of a State who is authorized by the State to do so may bring a civil action under paragraph (1), subject to the same requirements and limitations that apply under this subsection to civil actions brought by attorneys general.

(B) Savings provision

Nothing in this subsection may be construed to prohibit an authorized official of a State from initiating or continuing any proceeding in a court of the State for a violation of any civil or criminal law of the State.

(f) Education and outreach for businesses

Not later than 60 days after December 14, 2016, the Commission shall commence conducting education and outreach that provides businesses with non-binding best practices for compliance with this Act.

(g) Relation to State causes of action

Nothing in this section shall be construed to affect any cause of action brought by a person that exists or may exist under State law.

(h) Savings provision

Nothing in this section shall be construed to limit, impair, or supersede the operation of the Federal Trade Commission Act or any other provision of Federal law.

(i) Effective dates

This section shall take effect on December 14, 2016, except that—

(1) subsections (b) and (c) shall apply with respect to contracts in effect on or after the date that is 90 days after December 14, 2016; and

(2) subsections (d) and (e) shall apply with respect to contracts in effect on or after the date that is 1 year after December 14, 2016.

§ 45c [FTC Act § 5]. Unfair and deceptive acts and practices relating to circumvention of ticket access control measures

(a) Conduct prohibited

(1) In general

Except as provided in paragraph (2), it shall be unlawful for any person—

(A) to circumvent a security measure, access control system, or other technological control or measure on an Internet website or online service that is used by the ticket issuer to enforce posted event ticket purchasing limits or to maintain the integrity of posted online ticket purchasing order rules; or

(B) to sell or offer to sell any event ticket in interstate commerce obtained in violation of subparagraph (A) if the person selling or offering to sell the ticket either-

(i) participated directly in or had the ability to control the conduct in violation of subparagraph (A); or

(ii) knew or should have known that the event ticket was acquired in violation of subparagraph (A).

(2) Exception

It shall not be unlawful under this section for a person to create or use any computer software or system—

(A) to investigate, or further the enforcement or defense, of any alleged violation of this section or other statute or regulation; or

(B) to engage in research necessary to identify and analyze flaws and vulnerabilities of measures, systems, or controls described in paragraph (1)(A), if these research activities are conducted to advance the state of knowledge in the field of computer system security or to assist in the development of computer security product.

(b) Enforcement by the Federal Trade Commission

(1) Unfair or deceptive acts or practices

A violation of subsection (a) shall be treated as a violation of a rule defining an unfair or a deceptive act or practice under section 18(a)(1)(B) of the Federal Trade Commission Act (15 U.S.C. 57a(a)(1)(B)).

(2) Powers of Commission

(A) In general

The Commission shall enforce this section in the same manner, by the same means, and with the same jurisdiction, powers, and duties as though all applicable terms and provisions of the Federal Trade Commission Act (15 U.S.C. 41 et seq.) were incorporated into and made a part of this section.

(B) Privileges and immunities

Any person who violates subsection (a) shall be subject to the penalties and entitled to the privileges and immunities provided in the Federal Trade Commission Act (15 U.S.C. 41 et seq.).

(C) Authority preserved

Nothing in this section shall be construed to limit the authority of the Federal Trade Commission under any other provision of law.

(c) Enforcement by States

(1) In general

In any case in which the attorney general of a State has reason to believe that an interest of the residents of the State has been or is threatened or adversely affected by the engagement of any person subject to subsection (a) in a practice that violates such subsection, the attorney general of the State may, as parens patriae, bring a civil action on behalf of the residents of the State in an appropriate district court of the United States—

(A) to enjoin further violation of such subsection by such person;

(B) to compel compliance with such subsection; and

(C) to obtain damages, restitution, or other compensation on behalf of such residents.

(2) Rights of Federal Trade Commission

(A) Notice to Federal Trade Commission

(i) In general

Except as provided in clause (iii), the attorney general of a State shall notify the Commission in writing that the attorney general intends to bring a civil action under paragraph (1) not later than 10 days before initiating the civil action.

(ii) Contents

The notification required by clause (i) with respect to a civil action shall include a copy of the complaint to be filed to initiate the civil action.

(iii) Exception

If it is not feasible for the attorney general of a State to provide the notification required by clause (i) before initiating a civil action under paragraph (1), the attorney general shall notify the Commission immediately upon instituting the civil action.

(B) Intervention by Federal Trade Commission

The Commission may—

(i) intervene in any civil action brought by the attorney general of a State under paragraph (1); and

(ii) upon intervening—

(I) be heard on all matters arising in the civil action; and

(II) file petitions for appeal of a decision in the civil action.

(3) Investigatory powers

Nothing in this subsection may be construed to prevent the attorney general of a State from exercising the powers conferred on the attorney general by the laws of the State to conduct investigations, to administer oaths or affirmations, or to compel the attendance of witnesses or the production of documentary or other evidence.

(4) Preemptive action by Federal Trade Commission

If the Commission institutes a civil action or an administrative action with respect to a violation of subsection (a), the attorney general of a State may not, during the pendency of such action, bring a civil action under paragraph (1) against any defendant named in the complaint of the Commission for the violation with respect to which the Commission instituted such action.

(5) Venue; service of process

(A) Venue

Any action brought under paragraph (1) may be brought in—

(i) the district court of the United States that meets applicable requirements relating to venue under section 1391 of Title 28; or

(ii) another court of competent jurisdiction.

(B) Service of process

In an action brought under paragraph (1), process may be served in any district in which the defendant—

(i) is an inhabitant; or

(ii) may be found.

(6) Actions by other State officials

(A) In general

In addition to civil actions brought by attorneys general under paragraph (1), any other consumer protection officer of a State who is authorized by the State to do so may bring a civil action under paragraph (1), subject to the same requirements and limitations that apply under this subsection to civil actions brought by attorneys general.

(B) Savings provision

Nothing in this subsection may be construed to prohibit an authorized official of a State from initiating or continuing any proceeding in a court of the State for a violation of any civil or criminal law of the State.

§ 46 [FTC Act § 6]. Additional powers of Commission

The Commission shall also have power—

(a) Investigation of persons, partnerships, or corporations

To gather and compile information concerning, and to investigate from time to time the organization, business, conduct, practices, and management of any person, partnership, or corporation engaged in or whose business affects commerce, excepting banks, savings and loan institutions described in section 57a(f)(3) of this title, Federal credit unions described in section 57a(f)(4) of this title, and common carriers subject to the Act to regulate commerce, and its relation to other persons, partnerships, and corporations.

* * *

(f) Publication of information; reports

To make public from time to time such portions of the information obtained by it hereunder as are in the public interest; and to make annual and special reports to the Congress and to submit therewith recommendations for additional legislation; and to provide for the publication of its reports and decisions in such form and manner as may be best adapted for public information and use: Provided, That the Commission shall not have any authority to make public any trade secret or any commercial or financial information which is obtained from any person and which is privileged or confidential, except that the Commission may disclose such information (1) to officers and employees of appropriate Federal law enforcement agencies or to any officer or employee of any State law enforcement agency upon the prior certification of an officer of any such Federal or State law enforcement agency that such information will be maintained in confidence and will be used only for official law enforcement purposes, and (2) to any officer or employee of any foreign law enforcement agency under the same circumstances that making material available to foreign law enforcement agencies is permitted under section 57b–2(b) of this title.

* * *

(j) Investigative assistance for foreign law enforcement agencies

(1) In general

Upon a written request from a foreign law enforcement agency to provide assistance in accordance with this subsection, if the requesting agency states that it is investigating, or engaging in enforcement proceedings against, possible violations of laws prohibiting fraudulent or deceptive commercial practices, or other practices substantially similar to practices prohibited by any provision of the laws administered by the Commission, other than Federal antitrust laws (as defined in section 6211(5) of this title), to provide the assistance described in paragraph (2) without requiring that the conduct identified in the request constitute a violation of the laws of the United States.

(2) Type of assistance

In providing assistance to a foreign law enforcement agency under this subsection, the Commission may—

(A) conduct such investigation as the Commission deems necessary to collect information and evidence pertinent to the request for assistance, using all investigative powers authorized by this subchapter; and

(B) when the request is from an agency acting to investigate or pursue the enforcement of civil laws, or when the Attorney General refers a request to the Commission from an agency acting to investigate or pursue the enforcement of criminal laws, seek and accept appointment by a United States district court of Commission attorneys to provide assistance to foreign and international tribunals and to litigants before such tribunals on behalf of a foreign law enforcement agency pursuant to section 1782 of Title 28.

(3) Criteria for determination

In deciding whether to provide such assistance, the Commission shall consider all relevant factors, including—

(A) whether the requesting agency has agreed to provide or will provide reciprocal assistance to the Commission;

(B) whether compliance with the request would prejudice the public interest of the United States; and

(C) whether the requesting agency's investigation or enforcement proceeding concerns acts or practices that cause or are likely to cause injury to a significant number of persons.

(4) International agreements

If a foreign law enforcement agency has set forth a legal basis for requiring execution of an international agreement as a condition for reciprocal assistance, or as a condition for provision of materials or information to the Commission, the Commission, with prior approval and ongoing oversight of the Secretary of State, and with final approval of the agreement by the Secretary of State, may negotiate and conclude an international agreement, in the name of either the United States or the Commission, for the purpose of obtaining such assistance, materials, or information. The Commission may undertake in such an international agreement to—

(A) provide assistance using the powers set forth in this subsection;

(B) disclose materials and information in accordance with subsection (f) of this section and section 57b–2(b) of this title; and

(C) engage in further cooperation, and protect materials and information received from disclosure, as authorized by this subchapter.

(5) Additional authority

The authority provided by this subsection is in addition to, and not in lieu of, any other authority vested in the Commission or any other officer of the United States.

(6) Limitation

The authority granted by this subsection shall not authorize the Commission to take any action or exercise any power with respect to a bank, a savings and loan institution described in section 57a(f)(3) of this title, a Federal credit union described in section 57a(f)(4) of this title, or a common carrier subject to the Act to regulate commerce, except in accordance with the undesignated proviso following the last designated subsection of this section.

(7) Assistance to certain countries

The Commission may not provide investigative assistance under this subsection to a foreign law enforcement agency from a foreign state that the Secretary of State has determined, in accordance with section 2405(j) of the Appendix to Title 50, has repeatedly provided support for acts of international terrorism, unless and until such determination is rescinded pursuant to section 2405(j)(4) of the Appendix to Title 50.

(k) Referral of evidence for criminal proceedings

(1) In general

Whenever the Commission obtains evidence that any person, partnership, or corporation, either domestic or foreign, has engaged in conduct that may constitute a violation of Federal criminal law, to transmit such evidence to the Attorney General, who may institute criminal proceedings under appropriate statutes. Nothing in this paragraph affects any other authority of the Commission to disclose information.

(2) International information

The Commission shall endeavor to ensure, with respect to memoranda of understanding and international agreements it may conclude, that material it has obtained from foreign law enforcement agencies acting to investigate or pursue the enforcement of foreign criminal laws may be used for the purpose of investigation, prosecution, or prevention of violations of United States criminal laws.

* * *

§ 52 [FTC Act § 12]. Dissemination of false advertisements

(a) Unlawfulness

It shall be unlawful for any person, partnership, or corporation to disseminate, or cause to be disseminated, any false advertisement—

(1) By United States mails, or in or having an effect upon commerce, by any means, for the purpose of inducing, or which is likely to induce, directly or indirectly the purchase of food, drugs, devices, services, or cosmetics; or

(2) By any means, for the purpose of inducing, or which is likely to induce, directly or indirectly, the purchase in or having an effect upon commerce, of food, drugs, devices, services, or cosmetics.

(b) Unfair or deceptive act or practice

The dissemination or the causing to be disseminated of any false advertisement within the provisions of subsection (a) of this section shall be an unfair or deceptive act or practice in or affecting commerce within the meaning of section 45 of this title.

§ 53 [FTC Act § 13]. False advertisements; injunctions and restraining orders

(a) Power of Commission; jurisdiction of courts

Whenever the Commission has reason to believe—

(1) that any person, partnership, or corporation is engaged in, or is about to engage in, the dissemination or the causing of the dissemination of any advertisement in violation of section 52 of this title, and

(2) that the enjoining thereof pending the issuance of a complaint by the Commission under section 45 of this title, and until such complaint is dismissed by the Commission or set aside by the court on review, or the order of the Commission to cease and desist made thereon has become final within the meaning of section 45 of this title, would be to the interest of the public—

the Commission by any of its attorneys designated by it for such purpose may bring suit in a district court of the United States or in the United States court of any Territory, to enjoin the dissemination or the causing of the dissemination of such advertisement. Upon proper showing a temporary injunction or restraining order shall be granted without bond. Any suit may be brought where such person, partnership, or corporation resides or transacts business, or wherever venue is proper under section 1391 of Title 28. In addition, the court may, if the court determines that the interests of justice require that any other person, partnership, or corporation should be a party in such suit, cause such other person, partnership, or corporation to be added as a party without regard to whether venue is otherwise proper in the district in which the suit is brought. In any suit under this section, process may be served on any person, partnership, or corporation wherever it may be found.

(b) Temporary restraining orders; preliminary injunctions

Whenever the Commission has reason to believe—

(1) that any person, partnership, or corporation is violating, or is about to violate, any provision of law enforced by the Federal Trade Commission, and

(2) that the enjoining thereof pending the issuance of a complaint by the Commission and until such complaint is dismissed by the Commission or set aside by the court on review, or until the order of the Commission made thereon has become final, would be in the interest of the public—

the Commission by any of its attorneys designated by it for such purpose may bring suit in a district court of the United States to enjoin any such act or practice. Upon a proper showing that, weighing the equities and considering the Commission's likelihood of ultimate success, such action would be in the public interest, and after notice to the defendant, a temporary restraining order or a preliminary injunction may be granted without bond: Provided, however, That if a complaint is not filed within such period (not exceeding 20 days) as may be specified by the court after issuance of the temporary restraining order or preliminary injunction, the order or injunction shall be dissolved by the court and be of no further force and effect: Provided further, That in proper cases the Commission may seek, and after proper proof, the court may issue, a permanent injunction. Any suit may be brought where such person, partnership, or corporation resides or transacts business, or wherever venue is proper under section 1391 of Title 28. In addition, the court may, if the court determines that the interests of justice require that any other person, partnership, or corporation should be a party in such suit, cause such other person, partnership, or corporation to be added as a party without regard to whether venue is otherwise proper in the district in which the suit is brought. In any suit under this section, process may be served on any person, partnership, or corporation wherever it may be found.

* * *

§ 54 [FTC Act § 14]. False advertisements; penalties

(a) Imposition of penalties

Any person, partnership, or corporation who violates any provision of section 52(a) of this title shall, if the use of the commodity advertised may be injurious to health because of results from such use under the conditions prescribed in the advertisement thereof, or under such conditions as are customary or usual, or if such violation is with intent to defraud or mislead, be guilty of a misdemeanor, and upon conviction shall be punished by a fine of not more than $5,000 or by imprisonment for not more than six months, or by both such fine and imprisonment; except that if the conviction is for a violation committed after a first conviction of such person, partnership, or corporation, for any violation of such section, punishment shall be by a fine of not more than $10,000 or by imprisonment for not more than one year, or by both such fine and imprisonment: Provided, That for the purposes of this section meats and meat food products duly inspected, marked, and labeled in accordance with rules and regulations issued under the Meat Inspection Act [21 U.S.C.A. § 601 et seq.] shall be conclusively presumed not injurious to health at the time the same leave official "establishments."

(b) Exception of advertising medium or agency

No publisher, radio-broadcast licensee, or agency or medium for the dissemination of advertising, except the manufacturer, packer, distributor, or seller of the commodity to which the false advertisement relates, shall be liable under this section by reason of the dissemination by him of any false advertisement, unless he has refused, on the request of the Commission, to furnish the Commission the name and post-office address of the manufacturer, packer, distributor, seller, or advertising agency, residing in the United States, who caused him to disseminate such advertisement. No advertising agency shall be liable under this section by reason of the causing by it of the dissemination of any false advertisement, unless it has refused, on the request of the Commission, to furnish the Commission the name and post-office address of the manufacturer, packer, distributor, or seller, residing in the United States, who caused it to cause the dissemination of such advertisement.

§ 55 [FTC Act § 15]. Additional definitions

For the purposes of sections 52 to 54 of this title—

(a) False advertisement

(1) The term "false advertisement" means an advertisement, other than labeling, which is misleading in a material respect; and in determining whether any advertisement is misleading, there shall be taken into account (among other things) not only representations made or suggested by statement, word, design, device, sound, or any combination thereof, but also the extent to which the advertisement fails to reveal facts material in the light of such representations or material with respect to consequences which may result from the use of the commodity to which the advertisement relates under the conditions prescribed in said advertisement, or under such conditions as are customary or usual. No advertisement of a drug shall be deemed to be false if it is disseminated only to members of the medical profession, contains no false representation of a material fact, and includes, or is accompanied in each instance by truthful disclosure of, the formula showing quantitatively each ingredient of such drug.

* * *

§ 57 [FTC Act § 17]. Separability clause

If any provision of this subchapter, or the application thereof to any person, partnership, or corporation, or circumstance, is held invalid, the remainder of this subchapter, and the application of such provisions to any other person, partnership, corporation, or circumstance, shall not be affected thereby.

§ 57a [FTC Act § 18]. Unfair or deceptive acts or practices rulemaking proceedings

(a) Authority of Commission to prescribe rules and general statements of policy

(1) Except as provided in subsection (h) of this section, the Commission may prescribe—

(A) interpretive rules and general statements of policy with respect to unfair or deceptive acts or practices in or affecting commerce (within the meaning of section 45(a)(1) of this title), and

(B) rules which define with specificity acts or practices which are unfair or deceptive acts or practices in or affecting commerce (within the meaning of section 45(a)(1) of this title), except that the Commission shall not develop or promulgate any trade rule or regulation with regard to the regulation of the development and utilization of the standards and certification activities pursuant to this section. Rules under this subparagraph may include requirements prescribed for the purpose of preventing such acts or practices.

[**Editor's Note**. §§ 57a(b) to (d) have been omitted. These are the relatively cumbersome "Magnuson-Moss rulemaking" procedures, added to the FTC Act in 1975, that are unique to the FTC. The procedures include advance notice to Congress before rulemaking begins; advance notice of rulemaking must include prior cease and desist orders, and evidence of a widespread pattern of unfair or deceptive practices; informal hearings are open to any interested person and include rebuttal submissions, cross-examinations, verbatim transcripts; statement of basis and purpose must accompany final rule, which is subject to judicial review in the U.S. Court of Appeals upon petition by any interested person within 60 days after promulgation. The Commission's action must be supported by substantial evidence in the rulemaking record. Given the hurdles involved, the FTC has not attempted to use these procedures since the early 1980s. Instead, the FTC promulgates rules using the more streamlined Administrative Procedure Act "notice and comment" provisions in specific areas where the FTC is directed by Congress to promulgate a regulation.]

* * *

§ 57b [FTC Act § 19]. Civil actions for violations of rules and cease and desist orders respecting unfair or deceptive acts or practices

(a) Suits by Commission against persons, partnerships, or corporations; jurisdiction; relief for dishonest or fraudulent acts

(1) If any person, partnership, or corporation violates any rule under this subchapter respecting unfair or deceptive acts or practices (other than an interpretive rule, or a rule violation of which the Commission has provided is not an unfair or deceptive act or practice in violation of section 45(a) of this title), then the Commission may commence a civil action against such person, partnership, or corporation for relief under subsection (b) of this section in a United States district court or in any court of competent jurisdiction of a State.

(2) If any person, partnership, or corporation engages in any unfair or deceptive act or practice (within the meaning of section 45(a)(1) of this title) with respect to which the Commission has issued a final cease and desist order which is applicable to such person, partnership, or corporation, then the Commission may commence a civil action against such person, partnership, or corporation in a United States district court or in any court of competent jurisdiction of a State. If the Commission satisfies the court that the act or practice to which the cease and desist order relates is one which a reasonable man would have known under the circumstances was dishonest or fraudulent, the court may grant relief under subsection (b) of this section.

(b) Nature of relief available

The court in an action under subsection (a) of this section shall have jurisdiction to grant such relief as the court finds necessary to redress injury to consumers or other persons, partnerships, and corporations resulting from the rule violation or the unfair or deceptive act or practice, as the case may be. Such relief may include, but shall not be limited to, rescission or reformation of contracts, the refund of money or return of property, the payment of damages, and public notification respecting the rule violation or the unfair or deceptive act or practice, as the case may be; except that nothing in this subsection is intended to authorize the imposition of any exemplary or punitive damages.

* * *

§ 57b–2b [FTC Act § 21b]. Protection for voluntary provision of information

(a) In general

(1) No liability for providing certain material

An entity described in paragraphs (2) or (3) of subsection (d) of this section that voluntarily provides material to the Commission that such entity reasonably believes is relevant to—

(A) a possible unfair or deceptive act or practice, as defined in section 45(a) of this title; or

(B) assets subject to recovery by the Commission, including assets located in foreign jurisdictions;

shall not be liable to any person under any law or regulation of the United States, or under the constitution, or any law or regulation, of any State, political subdivision of a State, territory of the United States, or the District of Columbia, for such provision of material or for any failure to provide notice of such provision of material or of intention to so provide material.

(2) Limitations

Nothing in this subsection shall be construed to exempt any such entity from liability—

(A) for the underlying conduct reported; or

(B) to any Federal agency for providing such material or for any failure to comply with any obligation the entity may have to notify a Federal agency prior to providing such material to the Commission.

(b) Certain financial institutions

An entity described in paragraph (1) of subsection (d) of this section shall, in accordance with section 5318(g)(3) of Title 31, be exempt from liability for making a voluntary disclosure to the Commission of any possible violation of law or regulation, including—

(1) a disclosure regarding assets, including assets located in foreign jurisdictions—

(A) related to possibly fraudulent or deceptive commercial practices;

(B) related to persons involved in such practices; or

(C) otherwise subject to recovery by the Commission; or

(2) a disclosure regarding suspicious chargeback rates related to possibly fraudulent or deceptive commercial practices.

(c) Consumer complaints

Any entity described in subsection (d) of this section that voluntarily provides consumer complaints sent to it, or information contained therein, to the Commission shall not be liable to any person under any law or regulation of the United States, or under the constitution, or any law or regulation, of any State, political subdivision of a State, territory of the United States, or the District of Columbia, for such provision of material or for any failure to provide notice of such provision of material or of intention to so provide material. This subsection shall not provide any exemption from liability for the underlying conduct.

(d) Application

This section applies to the following entities, whether foreign or domestic:

(1) A financial institution as defined in section 5312 of Title 31.

(2) To the extent not included in paragraph (1), a bank or thrift institution, a commercial bank or trust company, an investment company, a credit card issuer, an operator of a credit card system, and an issuer, redeemer, or cashier of travelers' checks, money orders, or similar instruments.

(3) A courier service, a commercial mail receiving agency, an industry membership organization, a payment system provider, a consumer reporting agency, a domain name registrar or registry acting as such, and a provider of alternative dispute resolution services.

(4) An Internet service provider or provider of telephone services.

* * *

§ 58 [FTC Act § 27]. Short title

This subchapter may be cited as the "Federal Trade Commission Act".

FTC GUIDES AND REGULATIONS

(Selected Sections)

Selections from 16 C.F.R. Parts 233–455

PART 233: GUIDES AGAINST DECEPTIVE PRICING

Table of Sections

§ 233.1. Former price comparisons

(a) One of the most commonly used forms of bargain advertising is to offer a reduction from the advertiser's own former price for an article. If the former price is the actual, bona fide price at which the article was offered to the public on a regular basis for a reasonably substantial period of time, it provides a legitimate basis for the advertising of a price comparison. Where the former price is genuine, the bargain being advertised is a true one. If, on the other hand, the former price being advertised is not bona fide but fictitious—for example, where an artificial, inflated price was established for the purpose of enabling the subsequent offer of a large reduction—the "bargain" being advertised is a false one; the purchaser is not receiving the unusual value he expects. In such a case, the "reduced" price is, in reality, probably just the seller's regular price.

(b) A former price is not necessarily fictitious merely because no sales at the advertised price were made. The advertiser should be especially careful, however, in such a case, that the price is one at which the product was openly and actively offered for sale, for a reasonably substantial period of time, in the recent, regular course of his business, honestly and in good faith—and, of course, not for the purpose of establishing a fictitious higher price on which a deceptive comparison might be based. And the advertiser should scrupulously avoid any implication that a former price is a selling, not an asking price (for example, by use of such language as, "Formerly sold at $______"), unless substantial sales at that price were actually made.

(c) The following is an example of a price comparison based on a fictitious former price. John Doe is a retailer of BrandX fountain pens, which cost him $5 each. His usual markup is 50 percent over cost; that is, his regular retail price is $7.50. In order subsequently to offer an unusual "bargain", Doe begins offering Brand X at $10 per pen. He realizes that he will be able to sell no, or very few, pens at this inflated price. But he doesn't care, for he maintains that price for only a few days. Then he "cuts" the price to its usual level—$7.50—and advertises: "Terrific Bargain: X Pens, Were $10, Now Only $7.50!" This is obviously a false claim. The advertised "bargain" is not genuine.

(d) Other illustrations of fictitious price comparisons could be given. An advertiser might use a price at which he never offered the article at all; he might feature a price which was not used in the regular course of business, or which was not used in the recent past but at some remote period in the past, without making disclosure of that fact; he might use a price that was not openly offered to the public, or that was not maintained for a reasonable length of time, but was immediately reduced.

§ 233.2. Retail price comparisons; comparable value comparisons

(a) Another commonly used form of bargain advertising is to offer goods at prices lower than those being charged by others for the same merchandise in the advertiser's trade area (the area in which he does business). This may be done either on a temporary or a permanent basis, but in either case the advertised higher price must be based upon fact, and not be fictitious or misleading. Whenever an advertiser represents that he is selling below the prices being charged in his area for a particular article, he should be reasonably certain that the higher price he advertises does not appreciably exceed the price at which substantial sales of the article are being made in the area—that is, a sufficient number of sales so that a consumer would consider a reduction from the price to represent a genuine bargain or saving. Expressed another way, if a number of the principal retail outlets in the area are regularly selling Brand X fountain pens at $10, it is not dishonest for retailer Doe to advertise: "Brand X Pens, Price Elsewhere $10, Our Price $7.50".

(b) The following example, however, illustrates a misleading use of this advertising technique. Retailer Doe advertises Brand X pens as having a "Retail Value $15.00, My Price $7.50," when the fact is that only a few small suburban outlets in the area charge $15. All of the larger outlets located in and around the main shopping areas charge $7.50, or slightly more or less. The advertisement here would be deceptive, since the price charged by the small suburban outlets would have no real significance to Doe's customers, to whom the advertisement of "Retail Value $15.00" would suggest a prevailing, and not merely an isolated and unrepresentative, price in the area in which they shop.

(c) A closely related form of bargain advertising is to offer a reduction from the prices being charged either by the advertiser or by others in the advertiser's trade area for other merchandise of like grade and quality—in other words, comparable or competing merchandise—to that being advertised. Such advertising can serve a useful and legitimate purpose when it is made clear to the consumer that a comparison is being made with other merchandise and the other merchandise is, in fact, of essentially similar quality and obtainable in the area. The advertiser should, however, be reasonably certain, just as in the case of comparisons involving the same merchandise, that the price advertised as being the price of comparable merchandise does not exceed the price at which such merchandise is being offered by representative retail outlets in the area. For example, retailer Doe advertises Brand X pen as having "Comparable Value $15.00". Unless a reasonable number of the principal outlets in the area are offering Brand Y, an essentially similar pen, for that price, this advertisement would be deceptive.

§ 233.3. Advertising retail prices which have been established or suggested by manufacturers (or other nonretail distributors)

(a) Many members of the purchasing public believe that a manufacturer's list price, or suggested retail price, is the price at which an article is generally sold. Therefore, if a reduction from this price is advertised, many people will believe that they are being offered a genuine bargain. To the extent that list or suggested retail prices do not in fact correspond to prices at which a substantial number of sales of the article in question are made, the advertisement of a reduction may mislead the consumer.

(b) There are many methods by which manufacturers' suggested retail or list prices are advertised: Large scale (often nationwide) mass-media advertising by the manufacturer himself; preticketing by the manufacturer; direct mail advertising; distribution of promotional material or price lists designed for display to the public. The mechanics used are not of the essence. This part is concerned with any means employed for placing such prices before the consuming public.

(c) There would be little problem of deception in this area if all products were invariably sold at the retail price set by the manufacturer. However, the widespread failure to observe manufacturers' suggested or list prices, and the advent of retail discounting on a wide scale, have seriously undermined the dependability of list prices as indicators of the exact prices at which articles are in fact generally sold at retail. Changing competitive conditions have created a more acute problem of deception than may have existed previously. Today, only in the rare case are all sales of an article at the manufacturer's suggested retail or list price.

(d) But this does not mean that all list prices are fictitious and all offers of reductions from list, therefore, deceptive. Typically, a list price is a price at which articles are sold, if not everywhere, then at least in the principal retail outlets which do not conduct their business on a discount basis. It will not be deemed fictitious if it is the price at which substantial (that is, not isolated or insignificant) sales are made in the advertiser's trade area (the area in which he does business). Conversely, if the list price is significantly in excess of the highest price at which substantial sales in the trade area are made, there is a clear and serious danger of the consumer being misled by an advertised reduction from this price.

(e) This general principle applies whether the advertiser is a national or regional manufacturer (or other non-retail distributor), a mail-order or catalog distributor who deals directly with the consuming public, or a local retailer. But certain differences in the responsibility of these various types of businessmen should be noted. A retailer competing in a local area has at least a general knowledge of the prices being charged in his area. Therefore, before advertising a manufacturer's list price as a basis for comparison with his own lower price, the retailer should ascertain whether the list price is in fact the price regularly charged by principal outlets in his area.

(f) In other words, a retailer who advertises a manufacturer's or distributor's suggested retail price should be careful to avoid creating a false impression that he is offering a reduction from the price at which the product is generally sold in his trade area. If a number of the principal retail outlets in the area are regularly engaged in making sales at the manufacturer's suggested price, that price may be used in advertising by one who is selling at a lower price. If, however, the list price is being followed only by, for example, small suburban stores, house-to-house canvassers, and credit houses, accounting for only an insubstantial volume of sales in the area, advertising of the list price would be deceptive.

(g) On the other hand, a manufacturer or other distributor who does business on a large regional or national scale cannot be required to police or investigate in detail the prevailing prices of his articles throughout so large a trade area. If he advertises or disseminates a list or preticketed price in good faith (i.e., as an honest estimate of the actual retail price) which does not appreciably exceed the highest price at which substantial sales are made in his trade area, he will not be chargeable with having engaged in a deceptive practice. Consider the following example:

(h) Manufacturer Roe, who makes Brand X pens and sells them throughout the United States, advertises his pen in a national magazine as having a "Suggested Retail Price $10," a price determined on the basis of a market survey. In a substantial number of representative communities, the principal retail outlets are selling the product at this price in the regular course of business and in substantial volume. Roe would not be considered to have advertised a fictitious "suggested retail price." If retailer

Doe does business in one of these communities, he would not be guilty of a deceptive practice by advertising, "Brand X Pens, Manufacturer's Suggested Retail Price, $10, Our Price, $7.50."

(i) It bears repeating that the manufacturer, distributor or retailer must in every case act honestly and in good faith in advertising a list price, and not with the intention of establishing a basis, or creating an instrumentality, for a deceptive comparison in any local or other trade area. For instance, a manufacturer may not affix price tickets containing inflated prices as an accommodation to particular retailers who intend to use such prices as the basis for advertising fictitious price reductions.

§ 233.4. Bargain offers based upon the purchase of other merchandise

(a) Frequently, advertisers choose to offer bargains in the form of additional merchandise to be given a customer on the condition that he purchase a particular article at the price usually offered by the advertiser. The forms which such offers may take are numerous and varied, yet all have essentially the same purpose and effect. Representative of the language frequently employed in such offers are "Free," "Buy One—Get One Free," "2-For-1 Sale," "Half Price Sale," "1¢ Sale," "50% Off," etc. Literally, of course, the seller is not offering anything "free" (i.e., an unconditional gift), or ½ free, or for only 1¢, when he makes such an offer, since the purchaser is required to purchase an article in order to receive the "free" or "1¢" item. It is important, therefore, that where such a form of offer is used, care be taken not to mislead the consumer.

(b) Where the seller, in making such an offer, increases his regular price of the article required to be bought, or decreases the quantity and quality of that article, or otherwise attaches strings (other than the basic condition that the article be purchased in order for the purchaser to be entitled to the "free" or "1¢" additional merchandise) to the offer, the consumer may be deceived.

(c) Accordingly, whenever a "free," "2-for-1," "half price sale," "1¢ sale," "50% off" or similar type of offer is made, all the terms and conditions of the offer should be made clear at the outset.

§ 233.5. Miscellaneous price comparisons

The practices covered in the provisions set forth above represent the most frequently employed forms of bargain advertising. However, there are many variations which appear from time to time and which are, in the main, controlled by the same general principles. For example, retailers should not advertise a retail price as a "wholesale" price. They should not represent that they are selling at "factory" prices when they are not selling at the prices paid by those purchasing directly from the manufacturer. They should not offer seconds or imperfect or irregular merchandise at a reduced price without disclosing that the higher comparative price refers to the price of the merchandise if perfect. They should not offer an advance sale under circumstances where they do not in good faith expect to increase the price at a later date, or make a "limited" offer which, in fact, is not limited. In all of these situations, as well as in others too numerous to mention, advertisers should make certain that the bargain offer is genuine and truthful. Doing so will serve their own interest as well as that of the public.

PART 238: GUIDES AGAINST BAIT ADVERTISING

Table of Sections

Sec.

§ 238.0. Bait advertising defined[1]

Bait advertising is an alluring but insincere offer to sell a product or service which the advertiser in truth does not intend or want to sell. Its purpose is to switch consumers from buying the advertised merchandise, in order to sell something else, usually at a higher price or on a basis more advantageous to the advertiser. The primary aim of a bait advertisement is to obtain leads as to persons interested in buying merchandise of the type so advertised.

§ 238.1. Bait advertisement

No advertisement containing an offer to sell a product should be published when the offer is not a bona fide effort to sell the advertised product.

§ 238.2. Initial offer

(a) No statement or illustration should be used in any advertisement which creates a false impression of the grade, quality, make, value, currency of model, size, color, usability, or origin of the product offered, or which may otherwise misrepresent the product in such a manner that later, on disclosure of the true facts, the purchaser may be switched from the advertised product to another.

(b) Even though the true facts are subsequently made known to the buyer, the law is violated if the first contact or interview is secured by deception.

§ 238.3. Discouragement of purchase of advertised merchandise

No act or practice should be engaged in by an advertiser to discourage the purchase of the advertised merchandise as part of a bait scheme to sell other merchandise. Among acts or practices which will be considered in determining if an advertisement is a bona fide offer are:

(a) The refusal to show, demonstrate, or sell the product offered in accordance with the terms of the offer,

(b) The disparagement by acts or words of the advertised product or the disparagement of the guarantee, credit terms, availability of service, repairs or parts, or in any other respect, in connection with it,

(c) The failure to have available at all outlets listed in the advertisement a sufficient quantity of the advertised product to meet reasonably anticipated demands, unless the advertisement clearly and adequately discloses that supply is limited and/or the merchandise is available only at designated outlets,

(d) The refusal to take orders for the advertised merchandise to be delivered within a reasonable period of time,

(e) The showing or demonstrating of a product which is defective, unusable or impractical for the purpose represented or implied in the advertisement,

(f) Use of a sales plan or method of compensation for salesmen or penalizing salesmen, designed to prevent or discourage them from selling the advertised product.

§ 238.4. Switch after sale

No practice should be pursued by an advertiser, in the event of sale of the advertised product, of "unselling" with the intent and purpose of selling other merchandise in its stead. Among acts or practices which will be considered in determining if the initial sale was in good faith, and not a strategem to sell other merchandise, are:

---

[1] For the purpose of this part "advertising" includes any form of public notice however disseminated or utilized.

(a) Accepting a deposit for the advertised product, then switching the purchaser to a higher-priced product,

(b) Failure to make delivery of the advertised product within a reasonable time or to make a refund,

(c) Disparagement by acts or words of the advertised product, or the disparagement of the guarantee, credit terms, availability of service, repairs, or in any other respect, in connection with it,

(d) The delivery of the advertised product which is defective, unusable or impractical for the purpose represented or implied in the advertisement.

NOTE: *Sales of advertised merchandise.* Sales of the advertised merchandise do not preclude the existence of a bait and switch scheme. It has been determined that, on occasions, this is a mere incidental byproduct of the fundamental plan and is intended to provide an aura of legitimacy to the overall operation.

PART 251: GUIDE CONCERNING USE OF THE WORD "FREE" AND SIMILAR REPRESENTATIONS

§ 251.1. The guide

(a) ***General.***

(1) The offer of "Free" merchandise or service is a promotional device frequently used to attract customers. Providing such merchandise or service with the purchase of some other article or service has often been found to be a useful and valuable marketing tool.

(2) Because the purchasing public continually searches for the best buy, and regards the offer of "Free" merchandise or service to be a special bargain, all such offers must be made with extreme care so as to avoid any possibility that consumers will be misled or deceived. Representative of the language frequently used in such offers are "Free", "Buy 1-Get 1 Free", "2-for-1 Sale", "50% off with purchase of Two", "1 ¢ Sale", etc. (Related representations that raise many of the same questions include "____Cents-Off", "Half-Price Sale", "½ Off", etc. See the Commission's "Fair Packaging and Labeling Regulation Regarding 'Cents-Off' and Guides Against Deceptive Pricing.")

(b) ***Meaning of "Free".***

(1) The public understands that, except in the case of introductory offers in connection with the sale of a product or service (See paragraph (f) of this section), an offer of "Free" merchandise or service is based upon a regular price for the merchandise or service which must be purchased by consumers in order to avail themselves of that which is represented to be "Free". In other words, when the purchaser is told that an article is "Free" to him if another article is purchased, the word "Free" indicates that he is paying nothing for that article and no more than the regular price for the other. Thus, a purchaser has a right to believe that the merchant will not directly and immediately recover, in whole or in part, the cost of the free merchandise or service by marking up the price of the article which must be purchased, by the substitution of inferior merchandise or service, or otherwise.

(2) The term regular when used with the term price, means the price, in the same quantity, quality and with the same service, at which the seller or advertiser of the product or service has openly and actively sold the product or service in the geographic market or trade area in which he is making a "Free" or similar offer in the most recent and regular course of business, for a reasonably substantial period of time, i.e., a 30-day period. For consumer products or services which fluctuate in price, the "regular" price shall be the lowest price at which any substantial sales were made during the aforesaid 30-day period. Except in the case of introductory offers, if no substantial sales were made, in fact, at the "regular" price, a "Free" or similar offer would not be proper.

(c) ***Disclosure of conditions.*** When making "Free" or similar offers all the terms, conditions and obligations upon which receipt and retention of the "Free" item are contingent should be set forth clearly and conspicuously at the outset of the offer so as to leave no reasonable probability that the terms of the offer might be misunderstood. Stated differently, all of the terms, conditions and obligations should appear in close conjunction with the offer of "Free" merchandise or service. For example, disclosure of the terms of the offer set forth in a footnote of an advertisement to which reference is made by an asterisk or other symbol placed next to the offer, is not regarded as making disclosure at the outset. However, mere notice of the existence of a "Free" offer on the main display panel of a label or package is not precluded provided that (1) the notice does not constitute an offer or identify the item being offered "Free", (2) the notice informs the customer of the location, elsewhere on the package or label, where the disclosures required by this section may be found, (3) no purchase or other such material affirmative act is required in order to discover the terms and conditions of the offer, and (4) the notice and the offer are not otherwise deceptive.

(d) ***Supplier's responsibilities.*** Nothing in this section should be construed as authorizing or condoning the illegal setting or policing of retail prices by a supplier. However, if the supplier knows, or should know, that a "Free" offer he is promoting is not being passed on by a reseller, or otherwise is being used by a reseller as an instrumentality for deception, it is improper for the supplier to continue to offer the product as promoted to such reseller. He should take appropriate steps to bring an end to the deception, including the withdrawal of the "Free" offer.

(e) ***Resellers' participation in supplier's offers.*** Prior to advertising a "Free" promotion, a supplier should offer the product as promoted to all competing resellers as provided for in the Commission's "Guides for Advertising Allowances and Other Merchandising Payments and Services." In advertising the "Free" promotion, the supplier should identify those areas in which the offer is not available if the advertising is likely to be seen in such areas, and should clearly state that it is available only through participating resellers, indicating the extent of participation by the use of such terms as "some", "all", "a majority", or "a few", as the case may be.

(f) ***Introductory offers.***

(1) No "Free" offer should be made in connection with the introduction of a new product or service offered for sale at a specified price unless the offeror expects, in good faith, to discontinue the offer after a limited time and to commence selling the product or service promoted, separately, at the same price at which it was promoted with the "Free" offer.

(2) In such offers, no representation may be made that the price is for one item and that the other is "Free" unless the offeror expects, in good faith, to discontinue the offer after a limited time and to commence selling the product or service promoted, separately, at the same price at which it was promoted with a "Free" offer.

(g) ***Negotiated sales.*** If a product or service usually is sold at a price arrived at through bargaining, rather than at a regular price, it is improper to represent that another product or service is being offered "Free" with the sale. The same representation is also improper where there may be a regular price, but where other material factors such as quantity, quality, or size are arrived at through bargaining.

(h) ***Frequency of offers.*** So that a "Free" offer will be special and meaningful, a single size of a product or a single kind of service should not be advertised with a "Free" offer in a trade area for more than 6 months in any 12-month period. At least 30 days should elapse before another such offer is promoted in the same trade area. No more than three such offers should be made in the same area in any 12-month period. In such period, the offeror's sale in that area of the product in the size promoted with a "Free" offer should not exceed 50 percent of the total volume of his sales of the product, in the same size, in the area.

(i) ***Similar terms.*** Offers of "Free" merchandise or services which may be deceptive for failure to meet the provisions of this section may not be corrected by the substitution of such similar words and terms as "gift", "given without charge", "bonus", or other words or terms which tend to convey the impression to the consuming public that an article of merchandise or service is "Free".

PART 255: GUIDES CONCERNING USE OF ENDORSEMENTS AND TESTIMONIALS IN ADVERTISING

Table of Sections

§ 255.0. Purpose and definitions

(a) The Guides in this part represent administrative interpretations of laws enforced by the Federal Trade Commission for the guidance of the public in conducting its affairs in conformity with legal requirements. Specifically, the Guides address the application of Section 5 of the FTC Act (15 U.S.C. 45) to the use of endorsements and testimonials in advertising. The Guides provide the basis for voluntary compliance with the law by advertisers and endorsers. Practices inconsistent with these Guides may result in corrective action by the Commission under Section 5 if, after investigation, the Commission has reason to believe that the practices fall within the scope of conduct declared unlawful by the statute. The Guides set forth the general principles that the Commission will use in evaluating endorsements and testimonials, together with examples illustrating the application of those principles. The Guides do not purport to cover every possible use of endorsements in advertising. Whether a particular endorsement or testimonial is deceptive will depend on the specific factual circumstances of the advertisement at issue.

(b) For purposes of this part, an endorsement means any advertising message (including verbal statements, demonstrations, or depictions of the name, signature, likeness or other identifying personal characteristics of an individual or the name or seal of an organization) that consumers are likely to believe reflects the opinions, beliefs, findings, or experiences of a party other than the sponsoring advertiser, even if the views expressed by that party are identical to those of the sponsoring advertiser. The party whose opinions, beliefs, findings, or experience the message appears to reflect will be called the endorser and may be an individual, group, or institution.

(c) The Commission intends to treat endorsements and testimonials identically in the context of its enforcement of the Federal Trade Commission Act and for purposes of this part. The term endorsements is therefore generally used hereinafter to cover both terms and situations.

(d) For purposes of this part, the term product includes any product, service, company or industry.

(e) For purposes of this part, an expert is an individual, group, or institution possessing, as a result of experience, study, or training, knowledge of a particular subject, which knowledge is superior to what ordinary individuals generally acquire.

Example 1: A film critic's review of a movie is excerpted in an advertisement. When so used, the review meets the definition of an endorsement because it is viewed by readers as a statement of the critic's own opinions and not those of the film producer, distributor, or exhibitor. Any alteration in or quotation from the text of the review that does not fairly reflect its substance would be a violation of the standards set by this part because it would distort the endorser's opinion. [See § 255.1(b).]

Example 2: A TV commercial depicts two women in a supermarket buying a laundry detergent. The women are not identified outside the context of the advertisement. One comments to the other how clean her brand makes her family's clothes, and the other then comments that she will try it because she has not been fully satisfied with her own brand. This obvious fictional dramatization of a real life situation would not be an endorsement.

Example 3: In an advertisement for a pain remedy, an announcer who is not familiar to consumers except as a spokesman for the advertising drug company praises the drug's ability to deliver fast and lasting pain relief. He purports to speak, not on the basis of his own opinions, but rather in the place of and on behalf of the drug company. The announcer's statements would not be considered an endorsement.

Example 4: A manufacturer of automobile tires hires a well-known professional automobile racing driver to deliver its advertising message in television commercials. In these commercials, the driver speaks of the smooth ride, strength, and long life of the tires. Even though the message is not expressly declared to be the personal opinion of the driver, it may nevertheless constitute an endorsement of the tires. Many consumers will recognize this individual as being primarily a racing driver and not merely a spokesperson or announcer for the advertiser. Accordingly, they may well believe the driver would not speak for an automotive product unless he actually believed in what he was saying and had personal knowledge sufficient to form that belief. Hence, they would think that the advertising message reflects the driver's personal views. This attribution of the underlying views to the driver brings the advertisement within the definition of an endorsement for purposes of this part.

Example 5: A television advertisement for a particular brand of golf balls shows a prominent and well-recognized professional golfer practicing numerous drives off the tee. This would be an endorsement by the golfer even though she makes no verbal statement in the advertisement.

Example 6: An infomercial for a home fitness system is hosted by a well-known entertainer. During the infomercial, the entertainer demonstrates the machine and states that it is the most effective and easy-to-use home exercise machine that she has ever tried. Even if she is reading from a script, this statement would be an endorsement, because consumers are likely to believe it reflects the entertainer's views.

Example 7: A television advertisement for a housewares store features a well-known female comedian and a well-known male baseball player engaging in light-hearted banter about products each one intends to purchase for the other. The comedian says that she will buy him a Brand X, portable, high-definition television so he can finally see the strike zone. He says that he will get her a Brand Y juicer so she can make juice with all the fruit and vegetables thrown at her during her performances. The comedian and baseball player are not likely to be deemed endorsers because consumers will likely realize that the individuals are not expressing their own views.

Example 8: A consumer who regularly purchases a particular brand of dog food decides one day to purchase a new, more expensive brand made by the same manufacturer. She writes in her personal blog that the change in diet has made her dog's fur noticeably softer and shinier, and that in her opinion, the new food definitely is worth the extra money. This posting would not be deemed an endorsement under the Guides.

Assume that rather than purchase the dog food with her own money, the consumer gets it for free because the store routinely tracks her purchases and its computer has generated a coupon for a free trial bag of this new brand. Again, her posting would not be deemed an endorsement under the Guides.

Assume now that the consumer joins a network marketing program under which she periodically receives various products about which she can write reviews if she wants to do so. If she receives a free bag of the new dog food through this program, her positive review would be considered an endorsement under the Guides.

§ 255.1. General considerations

(a) Endorsements must reflect the honest opinions, findings, beliefs, or experience of the endorser. Furthermore, an endorsement may not convey any express or implied representation that would be deceptive if made directly by the advertiser. [See §§ 255.2(a) and (b) regarding substantiation of representations conveyed by consumer endorsements].

(b) The endorsement message need not be phrased in the exact words of the endorser, unless the advertisement affirmatively so represents. However, the endorsement may not be presented out of context or reworded so as to distort in any way the endorser's opinion or experience with the product. An advertiser may use an endorsement of an expert or celebrity only so long as it has good reason to believe that the endorser continues to subscribe to the views presented. An advertiser may satisfy this obligation by securing the endorser's views at reasonable intervals where reasonableness will be determined by such factors as new information on the performance or effectiveness of the product, a material alteration in the product, changes in the performance of competitors' products, and the advertiser's contract commitments.

(c) When the advertisement represents that the endorser uses the endorsed product, the endorser must have been a bona fide user of it at the time the endorsement was given. Additionally, the advertiser may continue to run the advertisement only so long as it has good reason to believe that the endorser remains a bona fide user of the product. [See § 255.1(b) regarding the "good reason to believe" requirement.]

(d) Advertisers are subject to liability for false or unsubstantiated statements made through endorsements, or for failing to disclose material connections between themselves and their endorsers [see § 255.5]. Endorsers also may be liable for statements made in the course of their endorsements.

Example 1: A building contractor states in an advertisement that he uses the advertiser's exterior house paint because of its remarkable quick drying properties and durability. This endorsement must comply with the pertinent requirements of § 255.3 (Expert Endorsements). Subsequently, the advertiser reformulates its paint to enable it to cover exterior surfaces with only one coat. Prior to continued use of the contractor's endorsement, the advertiser must contact the contractor in order to determine whether the contractor would continue to specify the paint and to subscribe to the views presented previously.

Example 2: A television advertisement portrays a woman seated at a desk on which rest five unmarked computer keyboards. An announcer says, "We asked X, an administrative assistant for over ten years, to try these five unmarked keyboards and tell us which one she liked best." The advertisement portrays X typing on each keyboard and then picking the advertiser's brand. The announcer asks her why, and X gives her reasons. This endorsement would probably not represent that X actually uses the advertiser's keyboard at work. In addition, the endorsement also may be required to meet the standards of § 255.3 (expert endorsements).

Example 3: An ad for an acne treatment features a dermatologist who claims that the product is "clinically proven" to work. Before giving the endorsement, she received a write-up of the clinical study in question, which indicates flaws in the design and conduct of the study that are so serious that they preclude any conclusions about the efficacy of the product. The dermatologist is subject to liability for the false statements she made in the advertisement. The advertiser is also liable for misrepresentations made through the endorsement. [See Section 255.3 regarding the product evaluation that an expert endorser must conduct.]

Example 4: A well-known celebrity appears in an infomercial for an oven roasting bag that purportedly cooks every chicken perfectly in thirty minutes. During the shooting of the infomercial, the celebrity watches five attempts to cook chickens using the bag. In each attempt, the chicken is undercooked after thirty minutes and requires sixty minutes of cooking time. In the commercial, the celebrity places an uncooked chicken in the oven roasting bag and places the bag in one oven. He then takes a chicken roasting bag from a second oven, removes from the bag what appears to be a perfectly cooked chicken, tastes the chicken, and says that if you want perfect chicken every time, in just thirty minutes, this is the product you need. A significant percentage of consumers are likely to believe the celebrity's statements represent his own views even though he is reading from a script. The celebrity is subject to liability for his statement about the product. The advertiser is also liable for misrepresentations made through the endorsement.

Example 5: A skin care products advertiser participates in a blog advertising service. The service matches up advertisers with bloggers who will promote the advertiser's products on their personal blogs. The advertiser requests that a blogger try a new body lotion and write a review of the product on her blog. Although the advertiser does not make any specific claims about the lotion's ability to cure skin conditions and the blogger does not ask the advertiser whether there is substantiation for the claim, in her review the blogger writes that the lotion cures eczema and recommends the product to her blog readers who suffer from this condition. The advertiser is subject to liability for misleading or unsubstantiated representations made through the blogger's endorsement. The blogger also is subject to liability for misleading or unsubstantiated representations made in the course of her endorsement. The blogger is also liable if she fails to disclose clearly and conspicuously that she is being paid for her services. [See § 255.5.]

In order to limit its potential liability, the advertiser should ensure that the advertising service provides guidance and training to its bloggers concerning the need to ensure that statements they make are truthful and substantiated. The advertiser should also monitor bloggers who are being paid to promote its products and take steps necessary to halt the continued publication of deceptive representations when they are discovered.

§ 255.2. Consumer endorsements

(a) An advertisement employing endorsements by one or more consumers about the performance of an advertised product or service will be interpreted as representing that the product or service is effective for the purpose depicted in the advertisement. Therefore, the advertiser must possess and rely upon adequate substantiation, including, when appropriate, competent and reliable scientific evidence, to support such claims made through endorsements in the same manner the advertiser would be required to do if it had made the representation directly, i.e., without using endorsements. Consumer endorsements themselves are not competent and reliable scientific evidence.

(b) An advertisement containing an endorsement relating the experience of one or more consumers on a central or key attribute of the product or service also will likely be interpreted as representing that the endorser's experience is representative of what consumers will generally achieve with the advertised product or service in actual, albeit variable, conditions of use. Therefore, an advertiser should possess and rely upon adequate substantiation for this representation. If the advertiser does not have substantiation that the endorser's experience is representative of what consumers will generally achieve, the advertisement should clearly and conspicuously disclose the generally expected performance in the depicted circumstances, and the advertiser must possess and rely on adequate substantiation for that representation.[105]

(c) Advertisements presenting endorsements by what are represented, directly or by implication, to be "actual consumers" should utilize actual consumers in both the audio and video, or

---

[105] The Commission tested the communication of advertisements containing testimonials that clearly and prominently disclosed either "Results not typical" or the stronger "These testimonials are based on the experiences of a few people and you are not likely to have similar results." Neither disclosure adequately reduced the communication that the experiences depicted are generally representative. Based upon this research, the Commission believes that similar disclaimers regarding the limited applicability of an endorser's experience to what consumers may generally expect to achieve are unlikely to be effective.

Nonetheless, the Commission cannot rule out the possibility that a strong disclaimer of typicality could be effective in the context of a particular advertisement. Although the Commission would have the burden of proof in a law enforcement action, the Commission notes that an advertiser possessing reliable empirical testing demonstrating that the net impression of its advertisement with such a disclaimer is non-deceptive will avoid the risk of the initiation of such an action in the first instance.

clearly and conspicuously disclose that the persons in such advertisements are not actual consumers of the advertised product.

Example 1: A brochure for a baldness treatment consists entirely of testimonials from satisfied customers who say that after using the product, they had amazing hair growth and their hair is as thick and strong as it was when they were teenagers. The advertiser must have competent and reliable scientific evidence that its product is effective in producing new hair growth.

The ad will also likely communicate that the endorsers' experiences are representative of what new users of the product can generally expect. Therefore, even if the advertiser includes a disclaimer such as, "Notice: These testimonials do not prove our product works. You should not expect to have similar results," the ad is likely to be deceptive unless the advertiser has adequate substantiation that new users typically will experience results similar to those experienced by the testimonialists.

Example 2: An advertisement disseminated by a company that sells heat pumps presents endorsements from three individuals who state that after installing the company's heat pump in their homes, their monthly utility bills went down by $100, $125, and $150, respectively. The ad will likely be interpreted as conveying that such savings are representative of what consumers who buy the company's heat pump can generally expect. The advertiser does not have substantiation for that representation because, in fact, less than 20% of purchasers will save $100 or more. A disclosure such as, "Results not typical" or, "These testimonials are based on the experiences of a few people and you are not likely to have similar results" is insufficient to prevent this ad from being deceptive because consumers will still interpret the ad as conveying that the specified savings are representative of what consumers can generally expect. The ad is less likely to be deceptive if it clearly and conspicuously discloses the generally expected savings and the advertiser has adequate substantiation that homeowners can achieve those results. There are multiple ways that such a disclosure could be phrased, e.g., "the average homeowner saves $35 per month," "the typical family saves $50 per month during cold months and $20 per month in warm months," or "most families save 10% on their utility bills."

Example 3: An advertisement for a cholesterol-lowering product features an individual who claims that his serum cholesterol went down by 120 points and does not mention having made any lifestyle changes. A well-conducted clinical study shows that the product reduces the cholesterol levels of individuals with elevated cholesterol by an average of 15% and the advertisement clearly and conspicuously discloses this fact. Despite the presence of this disclosure, the advertisement would be deceptive if the advertiser does not have adequate substantiation that the product can produce the specific results claimed by the endorser (i.e., a 120-point drop in serum cholesterol without any lifestyle changes).

Example 4: An advertisement for a weight-loss product features a formerly obese woman. She says in the ad, "Every day, I drank 2 WeightAway shakes, ate only raw vegetables, and exercised vigorously for six hours at the gym. By the end of six months, I had gone from 250 pounds to 140 pounds." The advertisement accurately describes the woman's experience, and such a result is within the range that would be generally experienced by an extremely overweight individual who consumed WeightAway shakes, only ate raw vegetables, and exercised as the endorser did. Because the endorser clearly describes the limited and truly exceptional circumstances under which she achieved her results, the ad is not likely to convey that consumers who weigh substantially less or use WeightAway under less extreme circumstances will lose 110 pounds in six months. (If the advertisement simply says that the endorser lost 110 pounds in six months using WeightAway together with diet and exercise, however, this description would not adequately alert consumers to the truly remarkable circumstances leading to her weight loss.) The advertiser must have substantiation, however, for any performance claims conveyed by the endorsement (e.g., that WeightAway is an effective weight loss product).

If, in the alternative, the advertisement simply features "before" and "after" pictures of a woman who says "I lost 50 pounds in 6 months with WeightAway," the ad is likely to convey that her experience is representative of what consumers will generally achieve. Therefore, if consumers cannot generally expect to achieve such results, the ad should clearly and conspicuously disclose what they can expect to lose in the depicted circumstances (e.g., "most women who use WeightAway for six months lose at least 15 pounds").

If the ad features the same pictures but the testimonialist simply says, "I lost 50 pounds with WeightAway," and WeightAway users generally do not lose 50 pounds, the ad should disclose what results they do generally achieve (e.g., "most women who use WeightAway lose 15 pounds").

Example 5: An advertisement presents the results of a poll of consumers who have used the advertiser's cake mixes as well as their own recipes. The results purport to show that the majority believed that their families could not tell the difference between the advertised mix and their own cakes baked from scratch. Many of the consumers are actually pictured in the advertisement along with relevant, quoted portions of their statements endorsing the product. This use of the results of a poll or survey of consumers represents that this is the typical result that ordinary consumers can expect from the advertiser's cake mix.

Example 6: An advertisement purports to portray a "hidden camera" situation in a crowded cafeteria at breakfast time. A spokesperson for the advertiser asks a series of actual patrons of the cafeteria for their spontaneous, honest opinions of the advertiser's recently introduced breakfast cereal. Even though the words "hidden camera" are not displayed on the screen, and even though none of the actual patrons is specifically identified during the advertisement, the net impression conveyed to consumers may well be that these are actual customers, and not actors. If actors have been employed, this fact should be clearly and conspicuously disclosed.

Example 7: An advertisement for a recently released motion picture shows three individuals coming out of a theater, each of whom gives a positive statement about the movie. These individuals are actual consumers expressing their personal views about the movie. The advertiser does not need to have substantiation that their views are representative of the opinions that most consumers will have about the movie. Because the consumers' statements would be understood to be the subjective opinions of only three people, this advertisement is not likely to convey a typicality message.

If the motion picture studio had approached these individuals outside the theater and offered them free tickets if they would talk about the movie on camera afterwards, that arrangement should be clearly and conspicuously disclosed. [See § 255.5.]

§ 255.3. Expert endorsements

(a) Whenever an advertisement represents, directly or by implication, that the endorser is an expert with respect to the endorsement message, then the endorser's qualifications must in fact give the endorser the expertise that he or she is represented as possessing with respect to the endorsement.

(b) Although the expert may, in endorsing a product, take into account factors not within his or her expertise (e.g., matters of taste or price), the endorsement must be supported by an actual exercise of that expertise in evaluating product features or characteristics with respect to which he or she is expert and which are relevant to an ordinary consumer's use of or experience with the product and are available to the ordinary consumer. This evaluation must have included an examination or testing of the product at least as extensive as someone with the same degree of expertise would normally need to conduct in order to support the conclusions presented in the endorsement. To the extent that the advertisement implies that the endorsement was based upon a comparison, such comparison must have been included in the expert's evaluation; and as a result of such comparison, the expert must have concluded that, with respect to those features on which he or she is expert and which are relevant and available to an ordinary consumer, the endorsed product is at least equal overall to the competitors' products. Moreover, where the net impression created by the endorsement is that the advertised product is superior to other products with respect to any such feature or features, then the expert must in fact have found such superiority. [See § 255.1(d) regarding the liability of endorsers.]

Example 1: An endorsement of a particular automobile by one described as an "engineer" implies that the endorser's professional training and experience are such that he is well acquainted with the design and performance of automobiles. If the endorser's field is, for example, chemical engineering, the endorsement would be deceptive.

Example 2: An endorser of a hearing aid is simply referred to as "Doctor" during the course of an advertisement. The ad likely implies that the endorser is a medical doctor with substantial experience in the area of hearing. If the endorser is not a medical "doctor" with substantial experience in audiology, the endorsement would likely be deceptive. A non-medical doctor (e.g., an individual with a Ph.D. in exercise physiology) or a physician without substantial experience in the area of hearing can endorse the product, but if the endorser is referred to as "doctor," the advertisement must make clear the nature and limits of the endorser's expertise.

Example 3: A manufacturer of automobile parts advertises that its products are approved by the "American Institute of Science." From its name, consumers would infer that the "American Institute of Science" is a bona fide independent testing organization with expertise in judging automobile parts and that, as such, it would not approve any automobile part without first testing its efficacy by means of valid scientific methods. If the American Institute of Science is not such a bona fide independent testing organization (e.g., if it was established and operated by an automotive parts manufacturer), the endorsement would be deceptive. Even if the American Institute of Science is an independent bona fide expert testing organization, the endorsement may nevertheless be deceptive unless the Institute has conducted valid scientific tests of the advertised products and the test results support the endorsement message.

Example 4: A manufacturer of a non-prescription drug product represents that its product has been selected over competing products by a large metropolitan hospital. The hospital has selected the product because the manufacturer, unlike its competitors, has packaged each dose of the product separately. This package form is not generally available to the public. Under the circumstances, the endorsement would be deceptive because the basis for the hospital's choice—convenience of packaging—is neither relevant nor available to consumers, and the basis for the hospital's decision is not disclosed to consumers.

Example 5: A woman who is identified as the president of a commercial "home cleaning service" states in a television advertisement that the service uses a particular brand of cleanser, instead of leading competitors it has tried, because of this brand's performance. Because cleaning services extensively use cleansers in the course of their business, the ad likely conveys that the president has knowledge superior to that of ordinary consumers. Accordingly, the president's statement will be deemed to be an expert endorsement. The service must, of course, actually use the endorsed cleanser. In addition, because the advertisement implies that the cleaning service has experience with a reasonable number of leading competitors to the advertised cleanser, the service must, in fact, have such experience, and, on the basis of its expertise, it must have determined that the cleaning ability of the endorsed cleanser is at least equal (or superior, if such is the net impression conveyed by the advertisement) to that of leading competitors' products with which the service has had experience and which remain reasonably available to it. Because in this example the cleaning service's president makes no mention that the endorsed cleanser was "chosen," "selected," or otherwise evaluated in side-by-side comparisons against its competitors, it is sufficient if the service has relied solely upon its accumulated experience in evaluating cleansers without having performed side-by-side or scientific comparisons.

Example 6: A medical doctor states in an advertisement for a drug that the product will safely allow consumers to lower their cholesterol by 50 points. If the materials the doctor reviewed were merely letters from satisfied consumers or the results of a rodent study, the endorsement would likely be deceptive because those materials are not what others with the same degree of expertise would consider adequate to support this conclusion about the product's safety and efficacy.

§ 255.4. Endorsements by organizations

Endorsements by organizations, especially expert ones, are viewed as representing the judgment of a group whose collective experience exceeds that of any individual member, and whose judgments are generally free of the sort of subjective factors that vary from individual to individual. Therefore, an organization's endorsement must be reached by a process sufficient to ensure that the endorsement fairly reflects the collective judgment of the organization. Moreover, if an organization is represented as being expert, then, in conjunction with a proper exercise of its expertise in evaluating the product under § 255.3 (expert endorsements), it must utilize an expert or experts recognized as such by the organization or standards previously adopted by the organization and suitable for judging the relevant merits of such products. [See § 255.1(d) regarding the liability of endorsers.]

Example: A mattress seller advertises that its product is endorsed by a chiropractic association. Because the association would be regarded as expert with respect to judging mattresses, its endorsement must be supported by an evaluation by an expert or experts recognized as such by the organization, or by compliance with standards previously adopted by the organization and aimed at measuring the performance of mattresses in general and not designed with the unique features of the advertised mattress in mind.

§ 255.5. Disclosure of material connections

When there exists a connection between the endorser and the seller of the advertised product that might materially affect the weight or credibility of the endorsement (i.e., the connection is not reasonably expected by the audience), such connection must be fully disclosed. For example, when an endorser who appears in a television commercial is neither represented in the advertisement as an expert nor is known to a significant portion of the viewing public, then the advertiser should clearly and conspicuously disclose either the payment or promise of compensation prior to and in exchange for the endorsement or the fact that the endorser knew or had reason to know or to believe that if the endorsement favored the advertised product some benefit, such as an appearance on television, would be extended to the endorser. Additional guidance, including guidance concerning endorsements made through other media, is provided by the examples below.

Example 1: A drug company commissions research on its product by an outside organization. The drug company determines the overall subject of the research (e.g., to test the efficacy of a newly developed product) and pays a substantial share of the expenses of the research project, but the research organization determines the protocol for the study and is responsible for conducting it. A subsequent advertisement by the drug company mentions the research results as the "findings" of that research organization. Although the design and conduct of the research project are controlled by the outside research organization, the weight consumers place on the reported results could be materially affected by knowing that the advertiser had funded the project. Therefore, the advertiser's payment of expenses to the research organization should be disclosed in this advertisement.

Example 2: A film star endorses a particular food product. The endorsement regards only points of taste and individual preference. This endorsement must, of course, comply with § 255.1; but regardless of whether the star's compensation for the commercial is a $1 million cash payment or a royalty for each product sold by the advertiser during the next year, no disclosure is required because such payments likely are ordinarily expected by viewers.

Example 3: During an appearance by a well-known professional tennis player on a television talk show, the host comments that the past few months have been the best of her career and during this time she has risen to her highest level ever in the rankings. She responds by attributing the improvement in her game to the fact that she is seeing the ball better than she used to, ever since having laser vision correction surgery at a clinic that she identifies by name. She continues talking about the ease of the procedure, the kindness of the clinic's doctors, her speedy recovery, and how she can now engage in a variety of activities without glasses, including driving at night.

The athlete does not disclose that, even though she does not appear in commercials for the clinic, she has a contractual relationship with it, and her contract pays her for speaking publicly about her surgery when she can do so. Consumers might not realize that a celebrity discussing a medical procedure in a television interview has been paid for doing so, and knowledge of such payments would likely affect the weight or credibility consumers give to the celebrity's endorsement. Without a clear and conspicuous disclosure that the athlete has been engaged as a spokesperson for the clinic, this endorsement is likely to be deceptive. Furthermore, if consumers are likely to take away from her story that her experience was typical of those who undergo the same procedure at the clinic, the advertiser must have substantiation for that claim.

Assume that instead of speaking about the clinic in a television interview, the tennis player touts the results of her surgery—mentioning the clinic by name—on a social networking site that allows her fans to read in real time what is happening in her life. Given the nature of the medium in which her endorsement is disseminated, consumers might not realize that she is a paid endorser. Because that information might affect the weight consumers give to her endorsement, her relationship with the clinic should be disclosed.

Assume that during that same television interview, the tennis player is wearing clothes bearing the insignia of an athletic wear company with whom she also has an endorsement contract. Although this contract requires that she wear the company's clothes not only on the court but also in public appearances, when possible, she does not mention them or the company during her appearance on the show. No disclosure is required because no representation is being made about the clothes in this context.

Example 4: An ad for an anti-snoring product features a physician who says that he has seen dozens of products come on the market over the years and, in his opinion, this is the best ever. Consumers would expect the physician to be reasonably compensated for his appearance in the ad. Consumers are unlikely, however, to expect that the physician receives a percentage of gross product sales or that he owns part of the company, and either of these facts would likely materially affect the credibility that consumers attach to the endorsement. Accordingly, the advertisement should clearly and conspicuously disclose such a connection between the company and the physician.

Example 5: An actual patron of a restaurant, who is neither known to the public nor presented as an expert, is shown seated at the counter. He is asked for his "spontaneous" opinion of a new food product served in the restaurant. Assume, first, that the advertiser had posted a sign on the door of the restaurant informing all who entered that day that patrons would be interviewed by the advertiser as part of its TV promotion of its new soy protein "steak." This notification would materially affect the weight or credibility of the patron's endorsement, and, therefore, viewers of the advertisement should be clearly and conspicuously informed of the circumstances under which the endorsement was obtained.

Assume, in the alternative, that the advertiser had not posted a sign on the door of the restaurant, but had informed all interviewed customers of the "hidden camera" only after interviews were completed and the customers had no reason to know or believe that their response was being recorded for use in an advertisement. Even if patrons were also told that they would be paid for allowing the use of their opinions in advertising, these facts need not be disclosed.

Example 6: An infomercial producer wants to include consumer endorsements for an automotive additive product featured in her commercial, but because the product has not yet been sold, there are no consumer users. The producer's staff reviews the profiles of individuals interested in working as "extras" in commercials and identifies several who are interested in automobiles. The extras are asked to use the product for several weeks and then report back to the producer. They are told that if they are selected to endorse the product in the producer's infomercial, they will receive a small payment. Viewers would not expect that these "consumer endorsers" are actors who were asked to use the product so that they could appear in the commercial or that they were compensated. Because the advertisement fails to disclose these facts, it is deceptive.

Example 7: A college student who has earned a reputation as a video game expert maintains a personal weblog or "blog" where he posts entries about his gaming experiences. Readers of his blog frequently seek his opinions about video game hardware and software. As it has done in the past, the manufacturer of a newly released video game system sends the student a free copy of the system and asks him to write about it on his blog. He tests the new gaming system and writes a favorable review. Because his review is disseminated via a form of consumer-generated media in which his relationship to the advertiser is not inherently obvious, readers are unlikely to know that he has received the video game system free of charge in exchange for his review of the product, and given the value of the video game system, this fact likely would materially affect the credibility they attach to his endorsement. Accordingly, the blogger should clearly and conspicuously disclose that he received the gaming system free of charge. The manufacturer should advise him at the time it provides the gaming system that this connection should be disclosed, and it should have procedures in place to try to monitor his postings for compliance.

Example 8: An online message board designated for discussions of new music download technology is frequented by MP3 player enthusiasts. They exchange information about new products, utilities, and the functionality of numerous playback devices. Unbeknownst to the message board community, an employee of a leading playback device manufacturer has been posting messages on the discussion board promoting the manufacturer's product. Knowledge of this poster's employment likely would affect the weight or credibility of her endorsement. Therefore, the poster should clearly and conspicuously disclose her relationship to the manufacturer to members and readers of the message board.

Example 9: A young man signs up to be part of a "street team" program in which points are awarded each time a team member talks to his or her friends about a particular advertiser's products. Team members can then exchange their points for prizes, such as concert tickets or electronics. These incentives would materially affect the weight or credibility of the team member's endorsements. They should be clearly and conspicuously disclosed, and the advertiser should take steps to ensure that these disclosures are being provided.

PART 260: GUIDES FOR THE USE OF ENVIRONMENTAL MARKETING CLAIMS

Table of Sections

Sec.

§ 260.1. Purpose, scope, and structure of the guides

(a) These guides set forth the Federal Trade Commission's current thinking about environmental claims. The guides help marketers avoid making environmental marketing claims that are unfair or deceptive under Section 5 of the FTC Act, 15 U.S.C. 45. They do not confer any rights on any person and do not operate to bind the FTC or the public. The Commission, however, can take action under the FTC Act if a marketer makes an environmental claim inconsistent with the guides. In any such enforcement action, the Commission must prove that the challenged act or practice is unfair or deceptive in violation of Section 5 of the FTC Act.

(b) These guides do not preempt federal, state, or local laws. Compliance with those laws, however, will not necessarily preclude Commission law enforcement action under the FTC Act.

(c) These guides apply to claims about the environmental attributes of a product, package, or service in connection with the marketing, offering for sale, or sale of such item or service to individuals. These guides apply to business-to-business transactions. The guides apply to environmental claims in labeling, advertising, promotional materials, and all other forms of marketing in any medium, whether asserted directly or by implication, through words, symbols, logos, depictions, product brand names, or any other means.

(d) The guides consist of general principles, specific guidance on the use of particular environmental claims, and examples. Claims may raise issues that are addressed by more than one example and in more than one section of the guides. The examples provide the Commission's views on how reasonable consumers likely interpret certain claims. The guides are based on marketing to a general audience. However, when a marketer targets a particular segment of consumers, the Commission will examine how reasonable members of that group interpret the advertisement. Whether a particular claim is deceptive will depend on the net impression of the advertisement, label, or other promotional material at issue. In addition, although many examples present specific claims and options for qualifying claims, the examples do not illustrate all permissible claims or qualifications under Section 5 of the FTC Act. Nor do they illustrate the only ways to comply with the guides. Marketers can use an alternative approach if the approach satisfies the requirements of Section 5 of the FTC Act. All examples assume that the described claims otherwise comply with Section 5. Where particularly useful, the Guides incorporate a reminder to this effect.

§ 260.2. Interpretation and substantiation of environmental marketing claims

Section 5 of the FTC Act prohibits deceptive acts and practices in or affecting commerce. A representation, omission, or practice is deceptive if it is likely to mislead consumers acting reasonably under the circumstances and is material to consumers' decisions. See FTC Policy Statement on Deception, 103 F.T.C. 174 (1983). To determine if an advertisement is deceptive, marketers must identify all express and implied claims that the advertisement reasonably conveys. Marketers must ensure that all reasonable interpretations of their claims are truthful, not misleading, and supported by a reasonable basis before they make the claims. See FTC Policy Statement Regarding Advertising Substantiation, 104 F.T.C. 839 (1984). In the context of environmental marketing claims, a reasonable basis often requires competent and reliable scientific evidence. Such evidence consists of tests, analyses, research, or studies that have been conducted and evaluated in an objective manner by qualified persons and are generally accepted in the profession to yield accurate and reliable results. Such evidence should be sufficient in quality and quantity based on standards generally accepted in the relevant scientific fields, when considered in light of the entire body of relevant and reliable scientific evidence, to substantiate that each of the marketing claims is true.

§ 260.3. General principles

The following general principles apply to all environmental marketing claims, including those described in §§ 260.4 through 260.16. [as in original, but should be through 260.17. Ed.] Claims should comport with all relevant provisions of these guides.

(a) Qualifications and disclosures. To prevent deceptive claims, qualifications and disclosures should be clear, prominent, and understandable. To make disclosures clear and prominent, marketers should use plain language and sufficiently large type, should place disclosures in close proximity to the qualified claim, and should avoid making inconsistent statements or using distracting elements that could undercut or contradict the disclosure.

(b) Distinction between benefits of product, package, and service. Unless it is clear from the context, an environmental marketing claim should specify whether it refers to the product, the product's packaging, a service, or just to a portion of the product, package, or service. In general, if the environmental attribute applies to all but minor, incidental components of a product or package, the marketer need not qualify the claim to identify that fact. However, there may be exceptions to this general principle. For example, if a marketer makes an unqualified recyclable claim, and the presence of the incidental component significantly limits the ability to recycle the product, the claim would be deceptive.

Example 1: A plastic package containing a new shower curtain is labeled "recyclable" without further elaboration. Because the context of the claim does not make clear whether it refers to the plastic package or the shower curtain, the claim is deceptive if any part of either the package or the curtain, other than minor, incidental components, cannot be recycled.

Example 2: A soft drink bottle is labeled "recycled." The bottle is made entirely from recycled materials, but the bottle cap is not. Because the bottle cap is a minor, incidental component of the package, the claim is not deceptive.

(c) Overstatement of environmental attribute. An environmental marketing claim should not overstate, directly or by implication, an environmental attribute or benefit. Marketers should not state or imply environmental benefits if the benefits are negligible.

Example 1: An area rug is labeled "50% more recycled content than before." The manufacturer increased the recycled content of its rug from 2% recycled fiber to 3%. Although the claim is technically true, it likely conveys the false impression that the manufacturer has increased significantly the use of recycled fiber.

Example 2: A trash bag is labeled "recyclable" without qualification. Because trash bags ordinarily are not separated from other trash at the landfill or incinerator for recycling, they are highly unlikely to be used again for any purpose. Even if the bag is technically capable of being recycled, the claim is deceptive since it asserts an environmental benefit where no meaningful benefit exists.

(d) Comparative claims. Comparative environmental marketing claims should be clear to avoid consumer confusion about the comparison. Marketers should have substantiation for the comparison.

Example 1: An advertiser notes that its glass bathroom tiles contain "20% more recycled content." Depending on the context, the claim could be a comparison either to the advertiser's immediately preceding product or to its competitors' products. The advertiser should have substantiation for both interpretations. Otherwise, the advertiser should make the basis for comparison clear, for example, by saying "20% more recycled content than our previous bathroom tiles."

Example 2: An advertiser claims that "our plastic diaper liner has the most recycled content." The diaper liner has more recycled content, calculated as a percentage of weight, than any other on the market, although it is still well under 100%. The claim likely conveys that the product contains a significant percentage of recycled content and has significantly more recycled content than its competitors. If the advertiser cannot substantiate these messages, the claim would be deceptive.

Example 3: An advertiser claims that its packaging creates "less waste than the leading national brand." The advertiser implemented the source reduction several years ago and supported the claim by calculating the relative solid waste contributions of the two packages. The advertiser should have substantiation that the comparison remains accurate.

Example 4: A product is advertised as "environmentally preferable." This claim likely conveys that the product is environmentally superior to other products. Because it is highly unlikely that the marketer can substantiate the messages conveyed by this statement, this claim is deceptive. The claim would not be deceptive if the marketer accompanied it with clear and prominent language limiting the environmental superiority representation to the particular attributes for which the marketer has substantiation, provided the advertisement's context does not imply other deceptive claims. For example, the claim "Environmentally preferable: contains 50% recycled content compared to 20% for the leading brand" would not be deceptive.

§ 260.4. General environmental benefit claims

(a) It is deceptive to misrepresent, directly or by implication, that a product, package, or service offers a general environmental benefit.

(b) Unqualified general environmental benefit claims are difficult to interpret and likely convey a wide range of meanings. In many cases, such claims likely convey that the product, package, or service has specific and far-reaching environmental benefits and may convey that the item or service has no negative environmental impact. Because it is highly unlikely that marketers can substantiate all reasonable interpretations of these claims, marketers should not make unqualified general environmental benefit claims.

(c) Marketers can qualify general environmental benefit claims to prevent deception about the nature of the environmental benefit being asserted. To avoid deception, marketers should use clear and prominent qualifying language that limits the claim to a specific benefit or benefits. Marketers should not imply that any specific benefit is significant if it is, in fact, negligible. If a qualified general claim conveys that a product is more environmentally beneficial overall because of the particular touted benefit(s), marketers should analyze trade-offs resulting from the benefit(s) to determine if they can substantiate this claim.

(d) Even if a marketer explains, and has substantiation for, the product's specific environmental attributes, this explanation will not adequately qualify a general environmental benefit claim if the advertisement otherwise implies deceptive claims. Therefore, marketers should ensure that the advertisement's context does not imply deceptive environmental claims.

Example 1: The brand name "Eco-friendly" likely conveys that the product has far-reaching environmental benefits and may convey that the product has no negative environmental impact. Because it is highly unlikely that the marketer can substantiate these claims, the use of such a brand name is deceptive. A claim, such as "Eco-friendly: made with recycled materials," would not be deceptive if: (1) The statement "made with recycled materials" is clear and prominent; (2) the marketer can substantiate that the entire product or package, excluding minor, incidental components, is made from recycled material; (3) making the product with recycled materials makes the product more environmentally beneficial overall; and (4) the advertisement's context does not imply other deceptive claims.

Example 2: A marketer states that its packaging is now "Greener than our previous packaging." The packaging weighs 15% less than previous packaging, but it is not recyclable nor has it been improved in any other material respect. The claim is deceptive because reasonable consumers likely would interpret "Greener" in this context to mean that other significant environmental aspects of the packaging also are improved over previous packaging. A claim stating "Greener than our previous packaging" accompanied by clear and prominent language such as, "We've reduced the weight of our packaging by 15%," would not be deceptive, provided that reducing the packaging's weight makes the product more environmentally beneficial overall and the advertisement's context does not imply other deceptive claims.

Example 3: A marketer's advertisement features a picture of a laser printer in a bird's nest balancing on a tree branch, surrounded by a dense forest. In green type, the marketer states, "Buy our printer. Make a change." Although the advertisement does not expressly claim that the product has environmental benefits, the featured images, in combination with the text, likely convey that the product has far-reaching environmental benefits and may convey that the product has no negative environmental impact. Because it is highly unlikely that the marketer can substantiate these claims, this advertisement is deceptive.

Example 4: A manufacturer's Web site states, "Eco-smart gas-powered lawn mower with improved fuel efficiency!" The manufacturer increased the fuel efficiency by 1/10 of a percent. Although the manufacturer's claim that it has improved its fuel efficiency technically is true, it likely conveys the false impression that the manufacturer has significantly increased the mower's fuel efficiency.

Example 5: A marketer reduces the weight of its plastic beverage bottles. The bottles' labels state: "Environmentally-friendly improvement. 25% less plastic than our previous packaging." The plastic bottles are 25 percent lighter but otherwise are no different. The advertisement conveys that the bottles are more environmentally beneficial overall because of the source reduction. To substantiate this claim, the marketer likely can analyze the impacts of the source reduction without evaluating environmental impacts throughout the packaging's life cycle. If, however, manufacturing the new bottles significantly alters environmental attributes earlier or later in the bottles' life cycle, i.e., manufacturing the bottles requires more energy or a different kind of plastic, then a more comprehensive analysis may be appropriate.

§ 260.5. Carbon offsets

(a) Given the complexities of carbon offsets, sellers should employ competent and reliable scientific and accounting methods to properly quantify claimed emission reductions and to ensure that they do not sell the same reduction more than one time.

(b) It is deceptive to misrepresent, directly or by implication, that a carbon offset represents emission reductions that have already occurred or will occur in the immediate future. To avoid deception, marketers should clearly and prominently disclose if the carbon offset represents emission reductions that will not occur for two years or longer.

(c) It is deceptive to claim, directly or by implication, that a carbon offset represents an emission reduction if the reduction, or the activity that caused the reduction, was required by law.

Example 1: On its web site, an online travel agency invites consumers to purchase offsets to "neutralize the carbon emissions from your flight." The proceeds from the offset sales fund future projects that will not reduce greenhouse gas emissions for two years. The claim likely conveys that the emission reductions either already have occurred or will occur in the near future. Therefore, the advertisement is deceptive. It would not be deceptive if the agency's web site stated "Offset the carbon emissions from your flight by funding new projects that will begin reducing emissions in two years."

Example 2: An offset provider claims that its product "will offset your own 'dirty' driving habits." The offset is based on methane capture at a landfill facility. State law requires this facility to capture all methane emitted from the landfill. The claim is deceptive because the emission reduction would have occurred regardless of whether consumers purchased the offsets.

§ 260.6. Certifications and seals of approval

(a) It is deceptive to misrepresent, directly or by implication, that a product, package, or service has been endorsed or certified by an independent third-party.

(b) A marketer's use of the name, logo, or seal of approval of a third-party certifier or organization may be an endorsement, which should meet the criteria for endorsements provided in the

FTC's Endorsement Guides, 16 CFR Part 255, including Definitions (§ 255.0), General Considerations (§ 255.1), Expert Endorsements (§ 255.3), Endorsements by Organizations (§ 255.4), and Disclosure of Material Connections (§ 255.5).

(c) Third-party certification does not eliminate a marketer's obligation to ensure that it has substantiation for all claims reasonably communicated by the certification.

(d) A marketer's use of an environmental certification or seal of approval likely conveys that the product offers a general environmental benefit (see § 260.4) if the certification or seal does not convey the basis for the certification or seal, either through the name or some other means. Because it is highly unlikely that marketers can substantiate general environmental benefit claims, marketers should not use environmental certifications or seals that do not convey the basis for the certification.

(e) Marketers can qualify general environmental benefit claims conveyed by environmental certifications and seals of approval to prevent deception about the nature of the environmental benefit being asserted. To avoid deception, marketers should use clear and prominent qualifying language that clearly conveys that the certification or seal refers only to specific and limited benefits.

Example 1: An advertisement for paint features a "GreenLogo" seal and the statement "GreenLogo for Environmental Excellence." This advertisement likely conveys that: (1) the GreenLogo seal is awarded by an independent, third-party certifier with appropriate expertise in evaluating the environmental attributes of paint; and (2) the product has far-reaching environmental benefits. If the paint manufacturer awarded the seal to its own product, and no independent, third-party certifier objectively evaluated the paint using independent standards, the claim would be deceptive. The claim would not be deceptive if the marketer accompanied the seal with clear and prominent language: (1) indicating that the marketer awarded the GreenLogo seal to its own product; and (2) clearly conveying that the award refers only to specific and limited benefits.

Example 2: A manufacturer advertises its product as "certified by the American Institute of Degradable Materials." Because the advertisement does not mention that the American Institute of Degradable Materials ("AIDM") is an industry trade association, the certification likely conveys that it was awarded by an independent certifier. To be certified, marketers must meet standards that have been developed and maintained by a voluntary consensus standard body. An independent auditor applies these standards objectively. This advertisement likely is not deceptive if the manufacturer complies with § 260.8 of the Guides (Degradable Claims) because the certification is based on independently-developed and-maintained standards and an independent auditor applies the standards objectively.

Example 3: A product features a seal of approval from "The Forest Products Industry Association," an industry certifier with appropriate expertise in evaluating the environmental attributes of paper products. Because it is clear from the certifier's name that the product has been certified by an industry certifier, the certification likely does not convey that it was awarded by an independent certifier. The use of the seal likely is not deceptive provided that the advertisement does not imply other deceptive claims.

Example 4: A marketer's package features a seal of approval with the text "Certified Non-Toxic." The seal is awarded by a certifier with appropriate expertise in evaluating ingredient safety and potential toxicity. It applies standards developed by a voluntary consensus standard body. Although non-industry members comprise a majority of the certifier's board, an industry veto could override any proposed changes to the standards. This certification likely conveys that the product is certified by an independent organization. This claim would be deceptive because industry members can veto any proposed changes to the standards.

Example 5: A marketer's industry sales brochure for overhead lighting features a seal with the text "EcoFriendly Building Association" to show that the marketer is a member of that organization. Although the lighting manufacturer is, in fact, a member, this association has not evaluated the environmental attributes of the marketer's product. This advertisement would be deceptive because it likely conveys that the EcoFriendly Building Association evaluated the product through testing or other objective standards. It also is likely to convey that the lighting has far-reaching environmental benefits. The use of the seal would not be deceptive if the manufacturer accompanies it with clear and prominent qualifying language: (1) indicating that the seal refers to the company's membership only and that the association did not evaluate the product's environmental attributes; and (2) limiting the general environmental benefit representations, both express and implied, to the particular product attributes for which the marketer has substantiation. For example, the marketer could state: "Although we are a member of the EcoFriendly Building Association, it has not evaluated this product. Our lighting is made from 100 percent recycled metal and uses energy efficient LED technology."

Example 6: A product label contains an environmental seal, either in the form of a globe icon or a globe icon with the text "EarthSmart." EarthSmart is an independent, third-party certifier with appropriate expertise in evaluating chemical emissions of products. While the marketer meets EarthSmart's standards for reduced chemical emissions during product usage, the product has no other specific environmental benefits. Either seal likely conveys that the product has far-reaching environmental benefits, and that EarthSmart certified the product for all of these benefits. If the marketer cannot substantiate these claims, the use of the seal would be deceptive. The seal would not be deceptive if the marketer accompanied it with clear and prominent language clearly conveying that the certification refers only to specific and limited benefits. For example, the marketer could state next to the globe icon: "EarthSmart certifies that this product meets EarthSmart standards for reduced chemical emissions during product usage." Alternatively, the claim would not be deceptive if the EarthSmart environmental seal itself stated: "EarthSmart Certified for reduced chemical emissions during product usage."

Example 7: A one-quart bottle of window cleaner features a seal with the text "Environment Approved," granted by an independent, third-party certifier with appropriate expertise. The certifier granted the seal after evaluating 35 environmental attributes. This seal likely conveys that the product has far-reaching environmental benefits and that Environment Approved certified the product for all of these benefits and therefore is likely deceptive. The seal would likely not be deceptive if the marketer accompanied it with clear and prominent language clearly conveying that the seal refers only to specific and limited benefits. For example, the seal could state: "Virtually all products impact the environment. For details on which attributes we evaluated, go to [a Web site that discusses this product]." The referenced Web page provides a detailed summary of the examined environmental attributes. A reference to a Web site is appropriate because the additional information provided on the Web site is not necessary to prevent the advertisement from being misleading. As always, the marketer also should ensure that the advertisement does not imply other deceptive claims, and that the certifier's criteria are sufficiently rigorous to substantiate all material claims reasonably communicated by the certification.

Example 8: Great Paper Company sells photocopy paper with packaging that has a seal of approval from the No Chlorine Products Association, a non-profit third-party association. Great Paper Company paid the No Chlorine Products Association a reasonable fee for the certification. Consumers would reasonably expect that marketers have to pay for certification. Therefore, there are no material connections between Great Paper Company and the No Chlorine Products Association. The claim would not be deceptive.

§ 260.7. Compostable claims

(a) It is deceptive to misrepresent, directly or by implication, that a product or package is compostable.

(b) A marketer claiming that an item is compostable should have competent and reliable scientific evidence that all the materials in the item will break down into, or otherwise become part of, usable compost (e.g., soil-conditioning material, mulch) in a safe and timely manner (i.e., in approximately the same time as the materials with which it is composted) in an appropriate composting facility or in a home compost pile or device.

(c) A marketer should clearly and prominently qualify compostable claims to the extent necessary to avoid deception if:

(1) the item cannot be composted safely or in a timely manner in a home compost pile or device; or

(2) the claim misleads reasonable consumers about the environmental benefit provided when the item is disposed of in a landfill.

(d) To avoid deception about the limited availability of municipal or institutional composting facilities, a marketer should clearly and prominently qualify compostable claims if such facilities are not available to a substantial majority of consumers or communities where the item is sold.

Example 1: A manufacturer indicates that its unbleached coffee filter is compostable. The unqualified claim is not deceptive, provided the manufacturer has substantiation that the filter can be converted safely to usable compost in a timely manner in a home compost pile or device. If so, the extent of local municipal or institutional composting facilities is irrelevant.

Example 2: A garden center sells grass clipping bags labeled as "Compostable in California Municipal Yard Trimmings Composting Facilities." When the bags break down, however, they release toxins into the compost. The claim is deceptive if the presence of these toxins prevents the compost from being usable.

Example 3: A manufacturer makes an unqualified claim that its package is compostable. Although municipal or institutional composting facilities exist where the product is sold, the package will not break down into usable compost in a home compost pile or device. To avoid deception, the manufacturer should clearly and prominently disclose that the package is not suitable for home composting.

Example 4: Nationally marketed lawn and leaf bags state "compostable" on each bag. The bags also feature text disclosing that the bag is not designed for use in home compost piles. Yard trimmings programs in many communities compost these bags, but such programs are not available to a substantial majority of consumers or communities where the bag is sold. The claim is deceptive because it likely conveys that composting facilities are available to a substantial majority of consumers or communities. To avoid deception, the marketer should clearly and prominently indicate the limited availability of such programs. A marketer could state "Appropriate facilities may not exist in your area," or provide the approximate percentage of communities or consumers for which such programs are available.

Example 5: A manufacturer sells a disposable diaper that states, "This diaper can be composted if your community is one of the 50 that have composting facilities." The claim is not deceptive if composting facilities are available as claimed and the manufacturer has substantiation that the diaper can be converted safely to usable compost in solid waste composting facilities.

Example 6: A manufacturer markets yard trimmings bags only to consumers residing in particular geographic areas served by county yard trimmings composting programs. The bags meet specifications for these programs and are labeled, "Compostable Yard Trimmings Bag for County Composting Programs." The claim is not deceptive. Because the bags are compostable where they are sold, a qualification is not needed to indicate the limited availability of composting facilities.

§ 260.8. Degradable claims

(a) It is deceptive to misrepresent, directly or by implication, that a product or package is degradable, biodegradable, oxo-degradable, oxo-biodegradable, or photodegradable. The following guidance for degradable claims also applies to biodegradable, oxo-degradable, oxo-biodegradable, or photodegradable claims.

(b) A marketer making an unqualified degradable claim should have competent and reliable scientific evidence that the entire item will completely break down and return to nature (i.e., decompose into elements found in nature) within a reasonably short period of time after customary disposal.

(c) It is deceptive to make an unqualified degradable claim for items entering the solid waste stream if the items do not completely decompose within one year after customary disposal. Unqualified degradable claims for items that are customarily disposed in landfills, incinerators, and recycling facilities are deceptive because these locations do not present conditions in which complete decomposition will occur within one year.

(d) Degradable claims should be qualified clearly and prominently to the extent necessary to avoid deception about:

(1) the product or package's ability to degrade in the environment where it is customarily disposed; and (2) the rate and extent of degradation.

Example 1: A marketer advertises its trash bags using an unqualified "degradable" claim. The marketer relies on soil burial tests to show that the product will decompose in the presence of water and oxygen. Consumers, however, place trash bags into the solid waste stream, which customarily terminates in incineration facilities or landfills where they will not degrade within one year. The claim is, therefore, deceptive.

Example 2: A marketer advertises a commercial agricultural plastic mulch film with the claim "Photodegradable," and clearly and prominently qualifies the term with the phrase "Will break down into small pieces if left uncovered in sunlight." The advertiser possesses competent and reliable scientific evidence that within one year, the product will break down, after being exposed to sunlight, and into sufficiently small pieces to become part of the soil. Thus, the qualified claim is not deceptive. Because the claim is qualified to indicate the limited extent of breakdown, the advertiser need not meet the consumer expectations for an unqualified photodegradable claim, i.e., that the product will not only break down, but also will decompose into elements found in nature.

Example 3: A marketer advertises its shampoo as "biodegradable" without qualification. The advertisement makes clear that only the shampoo, and not the bottle, is biodegradable. The marketer has competent and reliable scientific evidence demonstrating that the shampoo, which is customarily disposed in sewage systems, will break down and decompose into elements found in nature in a reasonably short period of time in the sewage system environment. Therefore, the claim is not deceptive.

Example 4: A plastic six-pack ring carrier is marked with a small diamond. Several state laws require that the carriers be marked with this symbol to indicate that they meet certain degradability standards if the carriers are littered. The use of the diamond, by itself, in an inconspicuous location, does not constitute a degradable claim. Consumers are unlikely to interpret an inconspicuous diamond symbol, without more, as an unqualified photodegradable claim.

Example 5: A fiber pot containing a plant is labeled "biodegradable." The pot is customarily buried in the soil along with the plant. Once buried, the pot fully decomposes during the growing season, allowing the roots of the plant to grow into the surrounding soil. The unqualified claim is not deceptive.

§ 260.9. Free-of claims

(a) It is deceptive to misrepresent, directly or by implication, that a product, package, or service is free of, or does not contain or use, a substance. Such claims should be clearly and prominently qualified to the extent necessary to avoid deception.

(b) A truthful claim that a product, package, or service is free of, or does not contain or use, a substance may nevertheless be deceptive if:

(1) the product, package, or service contains or uses substances that pose the same or similar environmental risks as the substance that is not present; or (2) the substance has not been associated with the product category.

(c) Depending on the context, a free-of or does-not-contain claim is appropriate even for a product, package, or service that contains or uses a trace amount of a substance if:

(1) The level of the specified substance is no more than that which would be found as an acknowledged trace contaminant or background level;

(2) The substance's presence does not cause material harm that consumers typically associate with that substance; and

(3) The substance has not been added intentionally to the product.

Example 1: A package of t-shirts is labeled "Shirts made with a chlorine-free bleaching process." The shirts, however, are bleached with a process that releases a reduced, but still significant, amount of the same harmful byproducts associated with chlorine bleaching. The claim overstates the product's benefits because reasonable consumers likely would interpret it to mean that the product's manufacture does not cause any of the environmental risks posed by chlorine bleaching. A substantiated claim, however, that the shirts were "bleached with a process that releases 50% less of the harmful byproducts associated with chlorine bleaching" would not be deceptive.

Example 2: A manufacturer advertises its insulation as "formaldehyde free." Although the manufacturer does not use formaldehyde as a binding agent to produce the insulation, tests show that the insulation still emits trace amounts of formaldehyde. The seller has substantiation that formaldehyde is present in trace amounts in virtually all indoor and (to a lesser extent) outdoor environments and that its insulation emits less formaldehyde than is typically present in outdoor environments. Further, the seller has substantiation that the trace amounts of formaldehyde emitted by the insulation do not cause material harm that consumers typically associate with formaldehyde. In this context, the trace levels of formaldehyde emissions likely are inconsequential to consumers. Therefore, the seller's free-of claim would not be deceptive.

§ 260.10. Non-toxic claims

(a) It is deceptive to misrepresent, directly or by implication, that a product, package, or service is non-toxic. Non-toxic claims should be clearly and prominently qualified to the extent necessary to avoid deception.

(b) A non-toxic claim likely conveys that a product, package, or service is non-toxic both for humans and for the environment generally. Therefore, marketers making non-toxic claims should have competent and reliable scientific evidence that the product, package, or service is non-toxic for humans and for the environment or should clearly and prominently qualify their claims to avoid deception.

Example: A marketer advertises a cleaning product as "essentially non-toxic" and "practically non-toxic." The advertisement likely conveys that the product does not pose any risk to humans or the environment, including household pets. If the cleaning product poses no risk to humans but is toxic to the environment, the claims would be deceptive.

§ 260.11. Ozone-safe and ozone-friendly claims

It is deceptive to misrepresent, directly or by implication, that a product, package, or service is safe for, or friendly to, the ozone layer or the atmosphere.

Example 1: A product is labeled "ozone friendly." The claim is deceptive if the product contains any ozone-depleting substance, including those substances listed as Class I or Class II chemicals in Title VI of the Clean Air Act Amendments of 1990, Pub. L. No. 101–549, and others subsequently designated by EPA as ozone-depleting substances. These chemicals include chlorofluorocarbons (CFCs), halons, carbon tetrachloride, 1,1,1-trichloroethane, methyl bromide, hydrobromofluorocarbons, and hydrochlorofluorocarbons (HCFCs).

Example 2: An aerosol air freshener is labeled "ozone friendly." Some of the product's ingredients are volatile organic compounds (VOCs) that may cause smog by contributing to ground-level ozone formation. The claim likely conveys that the product is safe for the atmosphere as a whole, and, therefore, is deceptive.

§ 260.12. Recyclable claims

(a) It is deceptive to misrepresent, directly or by implication, that a product or package is recyclable. A product or package should not be marketed as recyclable unless it can be collected, separated, or otherwise recovered from the waste stream through an established recycling program for reuse or use in manufacturing or assembling another item.

(b) Marketers should clearly and prominently qualify recyclable claims to the extent necessary to avoid deception about the availability of recycling programs and collection sites to consumers.

(1) When recycling facilities are available to a substantial majority of consumers or communities where the item is sold, marketers can make unqualified recyclable claims. The term "substantial majority," as used in this context, means at least 60 percent.

(2) When recycling facilities are available to less than a substantial majority of consumers or communities where the item is sold, marketers should qualify all recyclable claims. Marketers may always qualify recyclable claims by stating the percentage of consumers or communities that have access to facilities that recycle the item. Alternatively, marketers may use qualifications that vary in strength depending on facility availability. The lower the level of access to an appropriate facility is, the more strongly the marketer should emphasize the limited availability of recycling for the product. For example, if recycling facilities are available to slightly less than a substantial majority of consumers or communities where the item is sold, a marketer may qualify a recyclable claim by stating: "This product [package] may not be recyclable in your area," or "Recycling facilities for this product [package] may not exist in your area." If recycling facilities are available only to a few consumers, marketers should use stronger clarifications. For example, a marketer in this situation may qualify its recyclable claim by stating: "This product [package] is recyclable only in the few communities that have appropriate recycling facilities."

(c) Marketers can make unqualified recyclable claims for a product or package if the entire product or package, excluding minor incidental components, is recyclable. For items that are partially made of recyclable components, marketers should clearly and prominently qualify the recyclable claim to avoid deception about which portions are recyclable.

(d) If any component significantly limits the ability to recycle the item, any recyclable claim would be deceptive. An item that is made from recyclable material, but, because of its shape, size, or some other attribute, is not accepted in recycling programs, should not be marketed as recyclable.

Example 1: A packaged product is labeled with an unqualified claim, "recyclable." It is unclear from the type of product and other context whether the claim refers to the product or its package. The unqualified claim likely conveys that both the product and its packaging, except for minor, incidental components, can be recycled. Unless the manufacturer has substantiation for both messages, it should clearly and prominently qualify the claim to indicate which portions are recyclable.

Example 2: A nationally marketed plastic yogurt container displays the Resin Identification Code (RIC) (which consists of a design of arrows in a triangular shape containing a number in the center and an abbreviation identifying the component plastic resin) on the front label of the container, in close proximity to the product name and logo. This conspicuous use of the RIC constitutes a recyclable claim. Unless recycling facilities for this container are available to a substantial majority of consumers or communities, the manufacturer should qualify the claim to disclose the limited availability of recycling programs. If the manufacturer places the RIC, without more, in an inconspicuous location on the container (e.g., embedded in the bottom of the container), it would not constitute a recyclable claim.

Example 3: A container can be burned in incinerator facilities to produce heat and power. It cannot, however, be recycled into another product or package. Any claim that the container is recyclable would be deceptive.

Example 4: A paperboard package is marketed nationally and labeled either "Recyclable where facilities exist" or "RecyclableB Check to see if recycling facilities exist in your area." Recycling programs for these packages are available to some consumers, but not to a substantial majority of consumers nationwide. Both claims are deceptive because they do not adequately disclose the limited availability of recycling programs. To avoid deception, the marketer should use a clearer qualification, such as those suggested in § 260.12(b)(2).

Example 5: Foam polystyrene cups are advertised as "Recyclable in the few communities with facilities for foam polystyrene cups." A half-dozen major metropolitan areas have established collection sites for recycling those cups. The claim is not deceptive because it clearly discloses the limited availability of recycling programs.

Example 6: A package is labeled "Includes some recyclable material." The package is composed of four layers of different materials, bonded together. One of the layers is made from recyclable material, but the others are not. While programs for recycling the 25 percent of the package that consists of recyclable material are available to a substantial majority of consumers, only a few of those programs have the capability to separate the recyclable layer from the non-recyclable layers. The claim is deceptive for two reasons. First, it does not specify the portion of the product that is recyclable. Second, it does not disclose the limited availability of facilities that can process multi-layer products or materials. An appropriately qualified claim would be "25 percent of the material in this package is recyclable in the few communities that can process multi-layer products."

Example 7: A product container is labeled "recyclable." The marketer advertises and distributes the product only in Missouri. Collection sites for recycling the container are available to a substantial majority of Missouri residents but are not yet available nationally. Because programs are available to a substantial majority of consumers where the product is sold, the unqualified claim is not deceptive.

Example 8: A manufacturer of one-time use cameras, with dealers in a substantial majority of communities, operates a take-back program that collects those cameras through all of its dealers. The manufacturer reconditions the cameras for resale and labels them "Recyclable through our dealership network." This claim is not deceptive, even though the cameras are not recyclable through conventional curbside or drop off recycling programs.

Example 9: A manufacturer advertises its toner cartridges for computer printers as "Recyclable. Contact your local dealer for details." Although all of the company's dealers recycle cartridges, the dealers are not located in a substantial majority of communities where cartridges are sold. Therefore, the claim is deceptive. The manufacturer should qualify its claim consistent with § 260.112(b)(2).

Example 10: An aluminum can is labeled "Please Recycle." This statement likely conveys that the can is recyclable. If collection sites for recycling these cans are available to a substantial majority of consumers or communities, the marketer does not need to qualify the claim.

§ 260.13. Recycled content claims

(a) It is deceptive to misrepresent, directly or by implication, that a product or package is made of recycled content. Recycled content includes recycled raw material, as well as used, reconditioned, and re-manufactured components.

(b) It is deceptive to represent, directly or by implication, that an item contains recycled content unless it is composed of materials that have been recovered or otherwise diverted from the waste stream, either during the manufacturing process (pre-consumer), or after consumer use (post-consumer). If the source of recycled content includes pre-consumer material, the advertiser should have substantiation that the pre-consumer material would otherwise have entered the waste stream. Recycled content claims may—but do not have to—distinguish between pre-consumer and post-consumer materials. Where a marketer distinguishes between pre-consumer and post-consumer materials, it should have substantiation for any express or implied claim about the percentage of pre-consumer or post-consumer content in an item.

(c) Marketers can make unqualified claims of recycled content if the entire product or package, excluding minor, incidental components, is made from recycled material. For items that are partially made of recycled material, the marketer should clearly and prominently qualify the claim to avoid deception about the amount or percentage, by weight, of recycled content in the finished product or package.

(d) For products that contain used, reconditioned, or re-manufactured components, the marketer should clearly and prominently qualify the recycled content claim to avoid deception about the nature of such components. No such qualification is necessary where it is clear to reasonable consumers from context that a product's recycled content consists of used, reconditioned, or re-manufactured components.

Example 1: A manufacturer collects spilled raw material and scraps from the original manufacturing process. After a minimal amount of reprocessing, the manufacturer combines the spills and scraps with virgin material for use in production of the same product. A recycled content claim is deceptive since the spills and scraps are normally reused by industry within the original manufacturing process and would not normally have entered the waste stream.

Example 2: Fifty percent of a greeting card's fiber weight is composed from paper that was diverted from the waste stream. Of this material, 30% is post-consumer and 20% is pre-consumer. It would not be deceptive if the marketer claimed that the card either "contains 50% recycled fiber" or "contains 50% total recycled fiber, including 30% post-consumer fiber."

Example 3: A paperboard package with 20% recycled fiber by weight is labeled "20% post-consumer recycled fiber." The recycled content was composed of overrun newspaper stock never sold to customers. Because the newspapers never reached consumers, the claim is deceptive.

Example 4: A product in a multi-component package, such as a paperboard box in a shrink-wrapped plastic cover, indicates that it has recycled packaging. The paperboard box is made entirely of recycled material, but the plastic cover is not. The claim is deceptive because, without qualification, it suggests that both components are recycled. A claim limited to the paperboard box would not be deceptive.

Example 5: A manufacturer makes a package from laminated layers of foil, plastic, and paper, although the layers are indistinguishable to consumers. The label claims that "one of the three layers of this package is made of recycled plastic." The plastic layer is made entirely of recycled plastic. The claim is not deceptive, provided the recycled plastic layer constitutes a significant component of the entire package.

Example 6: A frozen dinner package is composed of a plastic tray inside a cardboard box. It states "package made from 30% recycled material." Each packaging component is one-half the weight of the total package. The box is 20% recycled content by weight, while the plastic tray is 40% recycled content by weight. The claim is not deceptive, since the average amount of recycled material is 30%.

Example 7: A manufacturer labels a paper greeting card "50% recycled fiber." The manufacturer purchases paper stock from several sources, and the amount of recycled fiber in the stock provided by each source varies. If the 50% figure is based on the annual weighted average of recycled material purchased from the sources after accounting for fiber loss during the papermaking production process, the claim is not deceptive.

Example 8: A packaged food product is labeled with a three-chasing-arrows symbol (a Möbius loop) without explanation. By itself, the symbol likely conveys that the packaging is both recyclable and made entirely from recycled material. Unless the marketer has substantiation for both messages, the claim should be qualified. The claim may need to be further qualified, to the extent necessary, to disclose the limited availability of recycling programs and/or the percentage of recycled content used to make the package.

Example 9: In an office supply catalog, a manufacturer advertises its printer toner cartridges "65% recycled." The cartridges contain 25% recycled raw materials and 40% reconditioned parts. The claim is deceptive because reasonable consumers likely would not know or expect that a cartridge's recycled content consists of reconditioned parts. It would not be deceptive if the manufacturer claimed "65% recycled content; including 40% from reconditioned parts."

Example 10: A store sells both new and used sporting goods. One of the items for sale in the store is a baseball helmet that, although used, is no different in appearance than a brand new item. The helmet bears an unqualified "Recycled" label. This claim is deceptive because reasonable consumers likely would believe that the helmet is made of recycled raw materials, when it is, in fact, a used item. An acceptable claim would bear a disclosure clearly and prominently stating that the helmet is used.

Example 11: An automotive dealer, automobile recycler, or other qualified entity recovers a serviceable engine from a wrecked vehicle. Without repairing, rebuilding, re-manufacturing, or in any way altering the engine or its components, the dealer attaches a "Recycled" label to the engine, and offers it for sale in its used auto parts store. In this situation, an unqualified recycled content claim likely is not deceptive because reasonable consumers in the automotive context likely would understand that the engine is used and has not undergone any rebuilding.

Example 12: An automobile parts dealer, automobile recycler, or other qualified entity purchases a transmission that has been recovered from a salvaged or end-of-life vehicle. Eighty-five percent of the transmission, by weight, was rebuilt and 15% constitutes new materials. After rebuilding the transmission in accordance with industry practices, the dealer packages it for resale in a box labeled "Rebuilt Transmission," or "Rebuilt Transmission (85% recycled content from rebuilt parts)," or "Recycled Transmission (85% recycled content from rebuilt parts)." Given consumer perception in the automotive context, these claims are not deceptive.

§ 260.14. Refillable claims

It is deceptive to misrepresent, directly or by implication, that a package is refillable. A marketer should not make an unqualified refillable claim unless the marketer provides the means for refilling the package. The marketer may either provide a system for the collection and refill of the package, or offer for sale a product that consumers can purchase to refill the original package.

Example 1: A container is labeled "refillable three times." The manufacturer has the capability to refill returned containers and can show that the container will withstand being refilled at least three times. The manufacturer, however, has established no collection program. The unqualified claim is deceptive because there is no means to return the container to the manufacturer for refill.

Example 2: A small bottle of fabric softener states that it is in a "handy refillable container." In the same market area, the manufacturer also sells a large-sized bottle that consumers use to refill the smaller bottles. The claim is not deceptive because there is a reasonable means for the consumer to refill the smaller container.

§ 260.15. Renewable energy claims

(a) It is deceptive to misrepresent, directly or by implication, that a product or package is made with renewable energy or that a service uses renewable energy. A marketer should not make unqualified renewable energy claims, directly or by implication, if fossil fuel, or electricity derived from fossil fuel, is used to manufacture any part of the advertised item or is used to power any part of the advertised service, unless the marketer has matched such non-renewable energy use with renewable energy certificates.

(b) Research suggests that reasonable consumers may interpret renewable energy claims differently than marketers may intend. Unless marketers have substantiation for all their express and reasonably implied claims, they should clearly and prominently qualify their renewable energy claims. For instance, marketers may minimize the risk of deception by specifying the source of the renewable energy (e.g., wind or solar energy).

(c) It is deceptive to make an unqualified "made with renewable energy" claim unless all, or virtually all, of the significant manufacturing processes involved in making the product or package are powered with renewable energy or non-renewable energy matched by renewable energy certificates. When this is not the case, marketers should clearly and prominently specify the percentage of renewable energy that powered the significant manufacturing processes involved in making the product or package.

(d) If a marketer generates renewable electricity but sells renewable energy certificates for all of that electricity, it would be deceptive for the marketer to represent, directly or by implication, that it uses renewable energy.

Example 1: A marketer advertises its clothing line as "made with wind power." The marketer buys wind energy for 50% of the energy it uses to make the clothing in its line. The marketer's claim is deceptive because reasonable consumers likely interpret the claim to mean that the power was composed entirely of renewable energy. If the marketer stated, "We purchase wind energy for half of our manufacturing facilities," the claim would not be deceptive.

Example 2: A company purchases renewable energy from a portfolio of sources that includes a mix of solar, wind, and other renewable energy sources in combinations and proportions that vary over time. The company uses renewable energy from that portfolio to power all of the significant manufacturing processes involved in making its product. The company advertises its product as "made with renewable energy." The claim would not be deceptive if the marketer clearly and prominently disclosed all renewable energy sources. Alternatively, the claim would not be deceptive if the marketer clearly and prominently stated, "made from a mix of renewable energy sources," and specified the renewable source that makes up the greatest percentage of the portfolio. The company may calculate which renewable energy source makes up the greatest percentage of the portfolio on an annual basis.

Example 3: An automobile company uses 100% non-renewable energy to produce its cars. The company purchases renewable energy certificates to match the non-renewable energy that powers all of the significant manufacturing processes for the seats, but no other parts, of its cars. If the company states, "The seats of our cars are made with renewable energy," the claim would not be deceptive, as long as the company clearly and prominently qualifies the claim such as by specifying the renewable energy source.

Example 4: A company uses 100% non-renewable energy to manufacture all parts of its product, but powers the assembly process entirely with renewable energy. If the marketer advertised its product as "assembled using renewable energy," the claim would not be deceptive.

Example 5: A toy manufacturer places solar panels on the roof of its plant to generate power, and advertises that its plant is "100% solar-powered." The manufacturer, however, sells renewable energy certificates based on the renewable attributes of all the power it generates. Even if the manufacturer uses the electricity generated by the solar panels, it has, by selling renewable energy certificates, transferred the right to characterize that electricity as renewable. The manufacturer's claim is therefore deceptive. It also would be deceptive for this manufacturer to advertise that it "hosts" a renewable power facility because reasonable consumers likely interpret this claim to mean that the manufacturer uses renewable energy. It would not be deceptive, however, for the manufacturer to advertise, "We generate renewable energy, but sell all of it to others."

§ 260.16. Renewable materials claims

(a) It is deceptive to misrepresent, directly or by implication, that a product or package is made with renewable materials.

(b) Research suggests that reasonable consumers may interpret renewable materials claims differently than marketers may intend. Unless marketers have substantiation for all their express and reasonably implied claims, they should clearly and prominently qualify their renewable materials claims. For example, marketers may minimize the risk of unintended implied claims by identifying the material used and explaining why the material is renewable.

(c) Marketers should also qualify any "made with renewable materials" claim unless the product or package (excluding minor, incidental components) is made entirely with renewable materials.

Example 1: A marketer makes the unqualified claim that its flooring is "made with renewable materials." Reasonable consumers likely interpret this claim to mean that the flooring also is made with recycled content, recyclable, and biodegradable. Unless the marketer has substantiation for these implied claims, the unqualified "made with renewable materials" claim is deceptive. The marketer could qualify the claim by stating, clearly and prominently, "Our flooring is made from 100 percent bamboo, which grows at the same rate, or faster, than we use it." The marketer still is responsible for substantiating all remaining express and reasonably implied claims.

Example 2: A marketer's packaging states that "Our packaging is made from 50% plant-based renewable materials. Because we turn fast-growing plants into bio-plastics, only half of our product is made from petroleum-based materials." By identifying the material used and explaining why the material is renewable, the marketer has minimized the risk of unintended claims that the product is made with recycled content, recyclable, and biodegradable. The marketer has adequately qualified the amount of renewable materials in the product.

§ 260.17. Source reduction claims

It is deceptive to misrepresent, directly or by implication, that a product or package has been reduced or is lower in weight, volume, or toxicity. Marketers should clearly and prominently qualify source reduction claims to the extent necessary to avoid deception about the amount of the source reduction and the basis for any comparison.

Example 1: An advertiser claims that disposal of its product generates "10% less waste." The marketer does not accompany this claim with a general environmental benefit claim. Because this claim could be a comparison to the advertiser's immediately preceding product or to its competitors' products, the advertiser should have substantiation for both interpretations. Otherwise, the advertiser should clarify which comparison it intends and have substantiation for that comparison. A claim of "10% less waste than our previous product" would not be deceptive if the advertiser has substantiation that shows that the current product's disposal contributes 10%

less waste by weight or volume to the solid waste stream when compared with the immediately preceding version of the product.

PART 424: FTC TRADE REGULATION RULE—RETAIL FOOD STORE ADVERTISING AND MARKETING PRACTICES

§ 424.1. Unfair or deceptive acts or practices

In connection with the sale of offering for sale by retail food stores of food, grocery products or other merchandise to consumers in or affecting commerce as "commerce" is defined in section 4 of the Federal Trade Commission Act, 15 U.S.C. 44, it is an unfair or deceptive act or practice in violation of section 5(a)(1) of the Federal Trade Commission Act, 15 U.S.C. 45(a)(1), to offer any such products for sale at a stated price, by means of an advertisement disseminated in an area served by any stores which are covered by the advertisement, if those stores do not have the advertised products in stock and readily available to customers during the effective period of the advertisement, unless the advertisement clearly and adequately discloses that supplies of the advertised products are limited or the advertised products are available only at some outlets.

§ 424.2. Defenses

No violation of § 424.1 shall be found if:

(a) The advertised products were ordered in adequate time for delivery in quantities sufficient to meet reasonably anticipated demand;

(b) The food retailer offers a "raincheck" for the advertised products;

(c) The food retailer offers at the advertised price or at a comparable price reduction a similar product that is at least comparable in value to the advertised product; or

(d) The food retailer offers other compensation at least equal to the advertised value.

PART 425: FTC TRADE REGULATION RULE—USE OF PRENOTIFICATION NEGATIVE OPTION PLANS

§ 425.1. The rule

(a) In connection with the sale, offering for sale, or distribution of goods and merchandise in or affecting commerce, as "commerce" is defined in the Federal Trade Commission Act, it is an unfair or deceptive act or practice, for a seller in connection with the use of any negative option plan to fail to comply with the following requirements:

(1) Promotional material shall clearly and conspicuously disclose the material terms of the plan, including:

(i) That aspect of the plan under which the subscriber must notify the seller, in the manner provided for by the seller, if he does not wish to purchase the selection;

(ii) Any obligation assumed by the subscriber to purchase a minimum quantity of merchandise;

(iii) The right of a contract-complete subscriber to cancel his membership at any time;

(iv) Whether billing charges will include an amount for postage and handling;

(v) A disclosure indicating that the subscriber will be provided with at least ten (10) days in which to mail any form, contained in or accompanying an announcement identifying the selection, to the seller;

(vi) A disclosure that the seller will credit the return of any selections sent to a subscriber, and guarantee to the Postal Service or the subscriber postage to return such selections to the seller when the announcement and form are not received by the subscriber in time to afford him at least ten (10) days in which to mail his form to the seller;

(vii) The frequency with which the announcements and forms will be sent to the subscriber and the maximum number of announcements and forms which will be sent to him during a 12-month period.

(2) Prior to sending any selection, the seller shall mail to its subscribers, within the time specified by paragraph (a)(3) of this section:

(i) An announcement identifying the selection;

(ii) A form, contained in or accompanying the announcement, clearly and conspicuously disclosing that the subscriber will receive the selection identified in the announcement unless he instructs the seller that he does not want the selection, designating a procedure by which the form may be used for the purpose of enabling the subscriber so to instruct the seller, and specifying either the return date or the mailing date.

(3) The seller shall mail the announcement and form either at least twenty (20) days prior to the return date or at least fifteen (15) days prior to the mailing date, or provide a mailing date at least ten (10) days after receipt by the subscriber, provided, however, that whichever system the seller chooses for mailing the announcement and form, such system must provide the subscriber with at least ten (10) days in which to mail his form.

(b) In connection with the sale or distribution of goods and merchandise in or affecting commerce, as "commerce" is defined in the Federal Trade Commission Act, it shall constitute an unfair or deceptive act or practice for a seller in connection with the use of any negative option plan to:

(1) Refuse to credit, for the full invoiced amount thereof, the return of any selection sent to a subscriber, and to guarantee to the Postal Service or the subscriber postage adequate to return such selection to the seller, when:

(i) The selection is sent to a subscriber whose form indicating that he does not want to receive the selection was received by the seller by the return date or was mailed by the subscriber by the mailing date;

(ii) Such form is received by the seller after the return date, but has been mailed by the subscriber and postmarked at least 3 days prior to the return date;

(iii) Prior to the date of shipment of such selection, the seller has received from a contract-complete subscriber, a written notice of cancellation of membership adequately identifying the subscriber; however, this provision is applicable only to the first selection sent to a canceling contract-complete subscriber after the seller has received written notice of cancellation. After the first selection shipment, all selection shipments thereafter are deemed to be unordered merchandise pursuant to Section 3009 of the Postal Reorganization Act of 1970, as adopted by the Federal Trade Commission in its public notice, dated September 11, 1970;

(iv) The announcement and form are not received by the subscriber in time to afford him at least ten (10) days in which to mail his form.

(2) Fail to notify a subscriber known by the seller to be within any of the circumstances set forth in paragraphs (b)(1)(i) through (iv) of this section, that if the subscriber elects, the subscriber may return the selection with return postage guaranteed and receive a credit to his account.

(3) Refuse to ship within 4 weeks after receipt of an order merchandise due subscribers as introductory and bonus merchandise, unless the seller is unable to deliver the merchandise originally offered due to unanticipated circumstances beyond the seller's control and promptly makes a reasonably equivalent alternative offer. However, where the subscriber refuses to accept alternatively offered introductory merchandise, but instead insists upon termination of his membership due to the seller's failure to provide the subscriber with his originally requested introductory merchandise, or any portion thereof, the seller must comply with the subscriber's request for cancellation of membership, provided the subscriber returns to the seller any introductory merchandise which already may have been sent him.

(4) Fail to terminate promptly the membership of a properly identified contract-complete subscriber upon his written request.

(5) Ship, without the express consent of the subscriber, substituted merchandise for that ordered by the subscriber.

(c) For the purposes of this part:

(1) *Negative option plan* refers to a contractual plan or arrangement under which a seller periodically sends to subscribers an announcement which identifies merchandise (other than annual supplements to previously acquired merchandise) it proposes to send to subscribers to such plan, and the subscribers thereafter receive and are billed for the merchandise identified in each such announcement, unless by a date or within a time specified by the seller with respect to each such announcement the subscribers, in conformity with the provisions of such plan, instruct the seller not to send the identified merchandise.

(2) *Subscriber* means any person who has agreed to receive the benefits of, and assume the obligations entailed in, membership in any negative option plan and whose membership in such negative option plan has been approved and accepted by the seller.

(3) *Contract-complete subscriber* refers to a subscriber who has purchased the minimum quantity of merchandise required by the terms of membership in a negative option plan.

(4) *Promotional material* refers to an advertisement containing or accompanying any device or material which a prospective subscriber sends to the seller to request acceptance or enrollment in a negative option plan.

(5) *Selection* refers to the merchandise identified by a seller under any negative option plan as the merchandise which the subscriber will receive and be billed for, unless by the date, or within the period specified by the seller, the subscriber instructs the seller not to send such merchandise.

(6) *Announcement* refers to any material sent by a seller using a negative option plan in which the selection is identified and offered to subscribers.

(7) *Form* refers to any form which the subscriber returns to the seller to instruct the seller not to send the selection.

(8) *Return date* refers to a date specified by a seller using a negative option plan as the date by which a form must be received by the seller to prevent shipment of the selection.

(9) *Mailing date* refers to the time specified by a seller using a negative option plan as the time by or within which a form must be mailed by a subscriber to prevent shipment of the selection.

PART 429: FTC TRADE REGULATION RULE—RULE CONCERNING COOLING-OFF PERIOD FOR SALES MADE AT HOMES OR AT CERTAIN OTHER LOCATIONS

Table of Sections

§ 429.0. Definitions

For the purposes of this part the following definitions shall apply:

(a) ***Door-to-Door Sale***—A sale, lease, or rental of consumer goods or services in which the seller or his representative personally solicits the sale, including those in response to or following an invitation by the buyer, and the buyer's agreement or offer to purchase is made at a place other than the place of business of the seller (e.g., sales at the buyer's residence or at facilities rented on a temporary or short-term basis, such as hotel or motel rooms, convention centers, fairgrounds and restaurants, or sales at the buyer's workplace or in dormitory lounges), and which has a purchase price of $25 or more if the sale is made at the buyer's residence or a purchase price of $130 or more if the sale is made at locations other than the buyer's residence, whether under single or multiple contracts. The term door-to-door sale does not include a transaction:

(1) Made pursuant to prior negotiations in the course of a visit by the buyer to a retail business establishment having a fixed permanent location where the goods are exhibited or the services are offered for sale on a continuing basis; or

(2) In which the consumer is accorded the right of rescission by the provisions of the Consumer Credit Protection Act (15 U.S.C. 1635) or regulations issued pursuant thereto; or

(3) In which the buyer has initiated the contact and the goods or services are needed to meet a bona fide immediate personal emergency of the buyer, and the buyer furnishes the seller with a separate dated and signed personal statement in the buyer's handwriting describing the situation requiring immediate remedy and expressly acknowledging and waiving the right to cancel the sale within 3 business days; or

(4) Conducted and consummated entirely by mail or telephone; and without any other contact between the buyer and the seller or its representative prior to delivery of the goods or performance of the services; or

(5) In which the buyer has initiated the contact and specifically requested the seller to visit the buyer's home for the purpose of repairing or performing maintenance upon the buyer's personal property. If, in the course of such a visit, the seller sells the buyer the right to receive additional services or goods other than replacement parts necessarily used in performing the maintenance or in making the repairs, the sale of those additional goods or services would not fall within this exclusion; or

(6) Pertaining to the sale or rental of real property, to the sale of insurance, or to the sale of securities or commodities by a broker-dealer registered with the Securities and Exchange Commission.

(b) ***Consumer Goods or Services***—Goods or services purchased, leased, or rented primarily for personal, family, or household purposes, including courses of instruction or training regardless of the purpose for which they are taken.

(c) ***Seller***—Any person, partnership, corporation, or association engaged in the door-to-door sale of consumer goods or services.

(d) ***Place of Business***—The main or permanent branch office or local address of a seller.

(e) ***Purchase Price***—The total price paid or to be paid for the consumer goods or services, including all interest and service charges.

(f) ***Business Day***—Any calendar day except Sunday or any federal holiday (e.g., New Year's Day, Presidents' Day, Martin Luther King's Birthday, Memorial Day, Independence Day, Labor Day, Columbus Day, Veterans' Day, Thanksgiving Day, and Christmas Day.)

§ 429.1. The rule

In connection with any door-to-door sale, it constitutes an unfair and deceptive act or practice for any seller to:

(a) Fail to furnish the buyer with a fully completed receipt or copy of any contract pertaining to such sale at the time of its execution, which is in the same language, e.g., Spanish, as that principally used in the oral sales presentation and which shows the date of the transaction and contains the name and address of the seller, and in immediate proximity to the space reserved in the contract for the signature of the buyer or on the front page of the receipt if a contract is not used and in bold face type of a minimum size of **10** points, a statement in substantially the following form:

> "You, the buyer, may cancel this transaction at any time prior to midnight of the third business day after the date of this transaction. See the attached notice of cancellation form for an explanation of this right."

The seller may select the method of providing the buyer with the duplicate notice of cancellation form set forth in paragraph (b) of this section, provided however, that in the event of cancellation the buyer must be able to retain a complete copy of the contract or receipt. Furthermore, if both forms are not attached to the contract or receipt, the seller is required to alter the last sentence in the statement above to conform to the actual location of the forms.

(b) Fail to furnish each buyer, at the time the buyer signs the door-to-door sales contract or otherwise agrees to buy consumer goods or services from the seller, a completed form in duplicate, captioned either "NOTICE OF RIGHT TO CANCEL" or "NOTICE OF CANCELLATION," which shall (where applicable) contain in ten point bold face type the following information and statements in the same language, e.g., Spanish, as that used in the contract.

Notice of Cancellation

[enter date of transaction]

(Date) ______________

You may CANCEL this transaction, without any Penalty or Obligation, within THREE BUSINESS DAYS from the above date.

If you cancel, any property traded in, any payments made by you under the contract or sale, and any negotiable instrument executed by you will be returned within TEN BUSINESS DAYS following receipt by the seller of your cancellation notice, and any security interest arising out of the transaction will be cancelled.

If you cancel, you must make available to the seller at your residence, in substantially as good condition as when received, any goods delivered to you under this contract or sale, or you may, if you wish, comply with the instructions of the seller regarding the return shipment of the goods at the seller's expense and risk.

If you do make the goods available to the seller and the seller does not pick them up within **20** days of the date of your Notice of Cancellation, you may retain or dispose of the goods without any further obligation. If you fail to make the goods available to the seller, or if you agree to return the goods to the seller and fail to do so, then you remain liable for performance of all obligations under the contract.

To cancel this transaction, mail or deliver a signed and dated copy of this Cancellation Notice or any other written notice, or send a telegram, to [Name of seller], at [address of seller's place of business] NOT LATER THAN MIDNIGHT OF [date].

I HEREBY CANCEL THIS TRANSACTION.

(Date) ______________

(Buyer's signature) ____________

(c) Fail, before furnishing copies of the "Notice of Cancellation" to the buyer, to complete both copies by entering the name of the seller, the address of the seller's place of business, the date of the transaction, and the date, not earlier than the third business day following the date of the transaction, by which the buyer may give notice of cancellation.

(d) Include in any door-to-door contract or receipt any confession of judgment or any waiver of any of the rights to which the buyer is entitled under this section including specifically the buyer's right to cancel the sale in accordance with the provisions of this section.

(e) Fail to inform each buyer orally, at the time the buyer signs the contract or purchases the goods or services, of the buyer's right to cancel.

(f) Misrepresent in any manner the buyer's right to cancel.

(g) Fail or refuse to honor any valid notice of cancellation by a buyer and within 10 business days after the receipt of such notice, to: (i) Refund all payments made under the contract or sale; (ii) return any goods or property traded in, in substantially as good condition as when received by the seller; (iii) cancel and return any negotiable instrument executed by the buyer in connection with the contract or sale and take any action necessary or appropriate to terminate promptly any security interest created in the transaction.

(h) Negotiate, transfer, sell, or assign any note or other evidence of indebtedness to a finance company or other third party prior to midnight of the fifth business day following the day the contract was signed or the goods or services were purchased.

(i) Fail, within 10 business days of receipt of the buyer's notice of cancellation, to notify the buyer whether the seller intends to repossess or to abandon any shipped or delivered goods.

§ 429.2. Effect on State laws and municipal ordinances

(a) The Commission is cognizant of the significant burden imposed upon door-to-door sellers by the various and often inconsistent State laws that provide the buyer the right to cancel a door-to-door sales transaction. However, it does not believe that this constitutes sufficient justification for preempting all of the provisions of such laws and the ordinances of the political subdivisions of the various States. The rulemaking record in this proceeding supports the view that the joint and coordinated efforts of both the Commission and State and local officials are required to insure that consumers who have purchased from a door-to-door seller something they do not want, do not need, or cannot afford, be accorded a unilateral right to rescind, without penalty, their agreements to purchase those goods or services.

(b) This part will not be construed to annul, or exempt any seller from complying with, the laws of any State or the ordinances of a political subdivision thereof that regulate door-to-door sales, except to the extent that such laws or ordinances, if they permit door-to-door selling, are directly inconsistent with the provisions of this part. Such laws or ordinances which do not accord the buyer, with respect to the particular transaction, a right to cancel a door-to-door sale that is substantially the same or greater than that provided in this part, which permit the imposition of any fee or penalty on the buyer for the exercise of such right, or which do not provide for giving the buyer a notice of the right to cancel the transaction in substantially the same form and manner provided for in this part, are among those which will be considered directly inconsistent.

§ 429.3. Exemptions

(a) The requirements of this part do not apply for sellers of automobiles, vans, trucks or other motor vehicles sold at auctions, tent sales or other temporary places of business, provided that the seller is a seller of vehicles with a permanent place of business.

(b) The requirements of this part do not apply for sellers of arts or crafts sold at fairs or similar places.

PART 433: FTC TRADE REGULATION RULE—PRESERVATION OF CONSUMERS' CLAIMS AND DEFENSES

Table of Sections

§ 433.1. Definitions

(a) ***Person.*** An individual, corporation, or any other business organization.

(b) ***Consumer.*** A natural person who seeks or acquires goods or services for personal, family, or household use.

(c) ***Creditor.*** A person who, in the ordinary course of business, lends purchase money or finances the sale of goods or services to consumers on a deferred payment basis; Provided, such person is not acting, for the purposes of a particular transaction, in the capacity of a credit card issuer.

(d) ***Purchase money loan.*** A cash advance which is received by a consumer in return for a "Finance Charge" within the meaning of the Truth in Lending Act and Regulation Z, which is applied, in whole or substantial part, to a purchase of goods or services from a seller who (1) refers consumers to the creditor or (2) is affiliated with the creditor by common control, contract, or business arrangement.

(e) ***Financing a sale.*** Extending credit to a consumer in connection with a "Credit Sale" within the meaning of the Truth in Lending Act and Regulation Z.

(f) ***Contract.*** Any oral or written agreement, formal or informal, between a creditor and a seller, which contemplates or provides for cooperative or concerted activity in connection with the sale of goods or services to consumers or the financing thereof.

(g) ***Business arrangement.*** Any understanding, procedure, course of dealing, or arrangement, formal or informal, between a creditor and a seller, in connection with the sale of goods or services to consumers or the financing thereof.

(h) ***Credit card issuer.*** A person who extends to cardholders the right to use a credit card in connection with purchases of goods or services.

(i) ***Consumer credit contract.*** Any instrument which evidences or embodies a debt arising from a "Purchase Money Loan" transaction or a "financed sale" as defined in paragraphs (d) and (e) of this section.

(j) ***Seller.*** A person who, in the ordinary course of business, sells or leases goods or services to consumers.

§ 433.2 Preservation of consumers' claims and defenses, unfair or deceptive acts or practices

In connection with any sale or lease of goods or services to consumers, in or affecting commerce as "commerce" is defined in the Federal Trade Commission Act, it is an unfair or deceptive act or practice within the meaning of Section 5 of that Act for a seller, directly or indirectly, to:

(a) Take or receive a consumer credit contract which fails to contain the following provision in at least ten point, bold face, type:

NOTICE

ANY HOLDER OF THIS CONSUMER CREDIT CONTRACT IS SUBJECT TO ALL CLAIMS AND DEFENSES WHICH THE DEBTOR COULD ASSERT AGAINST THE SELLER OF GOODS OR SERVICES OBTAINED PURSUANT HERETO OR WITH THE PROCEEDS HEREOF. RECOVERY HEREUNDER BY THE DEBTOR SHALL NOT EXCEED AMOUNTS PAID BY THE DEBTOR HEREUNDER.

or,

(b) Accept, as full or partial payment for such sale or lease, the proceeds of any purchase money loan (as purchase money loan is defined herein), unless any consumer credit contract made in connection with such purchase money loan contains the following provision in at least ten point, bold face, type:

NOTICE

ANY HOLDER OF THIS CONSUMER CREDIT CONTRACT IS SUBJECT TO ALL CLAIMS AND DEFENSES WHICH THE DEBTOR COULD ASSERT AGAINST THE SELLER OF GOODS OR SERVICES OBTAINED WITH THE PROCEEDS HEREOF. RECOVERY HEREUNDER BY THE DEBTOR SHALL NOT EXCEED AMOUNTS PAID BY THE DEBTOR HEREUNDER.

§ 433.3. [Omitted]

PART 435: FTC TRADE REGULATION RULE—MAIL, INTERNET OR TELEPHONE ORDER MERCHANDISE

Table of Sections

Sec.

§ 435.1. Definitions

For purposes of this part:

(a) Mail, internet, or telephone order sales shall mean sales in which the buyer has ordered merchandise from the seller by mail, via the internet, or by telephone, regardless of the method of payment or the method used to solicit the order.

(b) *Prompt refund* shall mean:

(1) Where a refund is made pursuant to paragraph (d)(1), (d)(2)(ii), (d)(2)(iii), or (d)(3) of this section, a refund sent by any means at least as fast and reliable as first class mail within seven (7) working days of the date on which the buyer's right to refund vests under the provisions of this part. Provided, however, that where the seller cannot provide a refund by the same method payment was tendered, *prompt refund* shall mean a refund sent in the form of cash, check, or money order, by any means at least as fast and reliable as first class mail, within seven (7) working days of the date on which the seller discovers it cannot provide a refund by the same method as payment was tendered;

(2) Where a refund is made pursuant to paragraph (d)(2)(i) of this section, a refund sent by any means at least as fast and reliable as first class mail within one (1) billing cycle from the date on which the buyer's right to refund vests under the provisions of this part.

(c) Receipt of a properly completed order shall mean, where the buyer tenders full or partial payment in the proper amount in the form of cash, check, or money order, authorization from the buyer to charge an existing charge account; or other payment methods, the time at which the seller receives both said payment and an order from the buyer containing all of the information needed by the seller to process and ship the order. Provided, however, that where the seller receives notice that a payment by means other than cash or credit as tendered by the buyer has been dishonored or that the buyer does not qualify for a credit sale, receipt of a *properly completed order* shall mean the time at which:

(1) The seller receives notice that a payment by means other than cash or credit in the proper amount tendered by the buyer has been honored,

(2) The buyer tenders cash in the proper amount, or

(3) The seller receives notice that the buyer qualifies for a credit sale.

(d) *Refund* shall mean:

(1) Where the buyer tendered full payment for the unshipped merchandise in the form of cash, check or money order, a return of the amount tendered in the form of cash, check or money order sent to the buyer;

(2) Where there is a credit sale:

(i) And the seller is a creditor, a copy of a credit memorandum or the like or an account statement sent to the buyer reflecting the removal or absence of any remaining charge incurred as a result of the sale from the buyer's account;

(ii) And a third party is the creditor, an appropriate credit memorandum or the like sent to the third party creditor which will remove the charge from the buyer's account and a copy of the credit memorandum or the like sent to the buyer that includes the date that the seller sent the credit memorandum or the like to the third party creditor and the amount of the charge to be removed, or a statement from the seller acknowledging the cancellation of the order and representing that it has not taken any action regarding the order which will result in a charge to the buyer's account with the third party;

(iii) And the buyer tendered partial payment for the unshipped merchandise in the form of cash, check or money order, a return of the amount tendered in the form of cash, check or money order sent to the buyer.

(3) Where the buyer tendered payment for the unshipped merchandise by any means other than those enumerated in paragraph (d)(1) or (2) of this section:

(i) Instructions sent to the entity that transferred payment to the seller instructing that entity to return to the buyer the amount tendered in the form tendered and a statement sent to the buyer setting forth the instructions sent to the entity, including the date of the instructions and the amount to be returned to the buyer; or

(ii) A return of the amount tendered in the form of cash, check, or money order sent to the buyer; or

(iii) A statement from the seller sent to the buyer acknowledging the cancellation of the order and representing that the seller has not taken any action regarding the order which will access any of the buyer's funds.

(e) Shipment shall mean the act by which the merchandise is physically placed in the possession of the carrier.

(f) Telephone refers to any direct or indirect use of the telephone to order merchandise, regardless of whether the telephone is activated by, or the language used is that of human beings, machines, or both.

(g) The *time of solicitation* of an order shall mean that time when the seller has:

(1) Mailed or otherwise disseminated the solicitation to a prospective purchaser,

(2) Made arrangements for an advertisement containing the solicitation to appear in a newspaper, magazine or the like or on radio or television which cannot be changed or cancelled without incurring substantial expense, or

(3) Made arrangements for the printing of a catalog, brochure or the like which cannot be changed without incurring substantial expense, in which the solicitation in question forms an insubstantial part.

§ 435.2. Mail, Internet or telephone order sales

In connection with mail, internet, or telephone order sales in or affecting commerce, as "commerce" is defined in the Federal Trade Commission Act, it constitutes an unfair method of competition, and an unfair or deceptive act or practice for a seller:

(a)(1) To solicit any order for the sale of merchandise to be ordered by the buyer through the mails, via the internet, or by telephone unless, at the time of the solicitation, the seller has a reasonable basis to expect that it will be able to ship any ordered merchandise to the buyer:

(i) Within that time clearly and conspicuously stated in any such solicitation, or

(ii) if no time is clearly and conspicuously stated, within thirty (30) days after receipt of a properly completed order from the buyer. Provided, however, where, at the time the merchandise is ordered the buyer applies to the seller for credit to pay for the merchandise in whole or in part, the seller shall have fifty (50) days, rather than thirty (30) days, to perform the actions required in this paragraph (a)(1)(ii).

(2) To provide any buyer with any revised shipping date, as provided in paragraph (b) of this section, unless, at the time any such revised shipping date is provided, the seller has a reasonable basis for making such representation regarding a definite revised shipping date.

(3) To inform any buyer that it is unable to make any representation regarding the length of any delay unless

(i) the seller has a reasonable basis for so informing the buyer and

(ii) the seller informs the buyer of the reason or reasons for the delay.

(4) In any action brought by the Federal Trade Commission, alleging a violation of this part, the failure of a respondent-seller to have records or other documentary proof establishing its use of systems and procedures which assure the shipment of merchandise in the ordinary course of business within any applicable time set forth in this part will create a rebuttable presumption that the seller lacked a reasonable basis for any expectation of shipment within said applicable time.

(b)(1) Where a seller is unable to ship merchandise within the applicable time set forth in paragraph (a)(1) of this section, to fail to offer to the buyer, clearly and conspicuously and without prior demand, an option either to consent to a delay in shipping or to cancel the buyer's order and receive a prompt refund. Said offer shall be made within a reasonable time after the seller first becomes aware of its inability to ship within the applicable time set forth in paragraph (a)(1) of this section, but in no event later than said applicable time.

(i) Any offer to the buyer of such an option shall fully inform the buyer regarding the buyer's right to cancel the order and to obtain a prompt refund and shall provide a definite revised shipping date, but where the seller lacks a reasonable basis for providing a definite revised shipping date the notice shall inform the buyer that the seller is unable to make any representation regarding the length of the delay.

(ii) Where the seller has provided a definite revised shipping date which is thirty (30) days or less later than the applicable time set forth in paragraph (a)(1) of this section, the offer of said option shall expressly inform the buyer that, unless the seller receives, prior to shipment and prior to the expiration of the definite revised shipping date, a response from the buyer rejecting the delay and cancelling the order, the buyer will be deemed to have consented to a delayed shipment on or before the definite revised shipping date.

(iii) Where the seller has provided a definite revised shipping date which is more than thirty (30) days later than the applicable time set forth in paragraph (a)(1) of this section or where the seller is unable to provide a definite revised shipping date and therefore informs the buyer that it is unable to make any representation regarding the length of the delay, the offer of said option shall also expressly inform the buyer that the buyer's order will automatically be deemed to have been cancelled unless:

(A) The seller has shipped the merchandise within thirty (30) days of the applicable time set forth in paragraph (a)(1) of this section, and has received no cancellation prior to shipment, or

(B) The seller has received from the buyer within thirty (30) days of said applicable time, a response specifically consenting to said shipping delay. Where the seller informs the buyer that it is unable to make any representation regarding the length of the delay, the buyer shall be expressly informed that, should the buyer consent to an indefinite delay, the buyer will have a continuing right to cancel the buyer's order at any time after the applicable time set forth in paragraph (a)(1) of this section by so notifying the seller prior to actual shipment.

(iv) Nothing in this paragraph shall prohibit a seller who furnishes a definite revised shipping date pursuant to paragraph (b)(1)(i) of this section, from requesting, simultaneously with or at any time subsequent to the offer of an option pursuant to paragraph (b)(1) of this section, the buyer's express consent to a further unanticipated delay beyond the definite revised shipping date in the form of a response from the buyer specifically consenting to said further delay. Provided, however, that where the seller solicits consent to an unanticipated indefinite delay the solicitation shall expressly inform the buyer that, should the buyer so consent to an indefinite delay, the buyer shall have a continuing right to cancel the buyer's order at any time after the definite revised shipping date by so notifying the seller prior to actual shipment.

(2) Where a seller is unable to ship merchandise on or before the definite revised shipping date provided under paragraph (b)(1)(i) of this section and consented to by the buyer pursuant to paragraph (b)(1)(ii) or (iii) of this section, to fail to offer to the buyer, clearly and conspicuously and without prior demand, a renewed option either to consent to a further delay or to cancel the order and to receive a prompt refund. Said offer shall be made within a reasonable time after the seller first becomes aware of its inability to ship before the said definite revised date, but in no event later than the expiration of the definite revised shipping date. Provided, however, that where the seller previously has obtained the buyer's express consent to an unanticipated delay until a specific date beyond the definite revised shipping date, pursuant to paragraph (b)(1)(iv) of this section or to a further delay until a specific date beyond the definite revised shipping date pursuant to paragraph (b)(2) of this section, that date to which the buyer has expressly consented shall supersede the definite revised shipping date for purposes of paragraph (b)(2) of this section.

(i) Any offer to the buyer of said renewed option shall provide the buyer with a new definite revised shipping date, but where the seller lacks a reasonable basis for providing a new definite revised shipping date, the notice shall inform the buyer that the seller is unable to make any representation regarding the length of the further delay.

(ii) The offer of a renewed option shall expressly inform the buyer that, unless the seller receives, prior to the expiration of the old definite revised shipping date or any date superseding the old definite revised shipping date, notification from the buyer specifically consenting to the further delay, the buyer will be deemed to have rejected any further delay, and to have cancelled the order if the seller is in fact unable to ship prior to the expiration of the old definite revised shipping date or any date superseding the old definite revised shipping date. Provided, however, that where the seller offers the buyer the option to consent to an indefinite delay the offer shall expressly inform the buyer that, should the buyer so consent to an indefinite delay, the buyer shall have a continuing right to cancel the buyer's order at any time after the old definite revised shipping date or any date superseding the old definite revised shipping date.

(iii) Paragraph (b)(2) of this section shall not apply to any situation where a seller, pursuant to the provisions of paragraph (b)(1)(iv) of this section, has previously obtained consent from the buyer to an indefinite extension beyond the first revised shipping date.

(3) Wherever a buyer has the right to exercise any option under this part or to cancel an order by so notifying the seller prior to shipment, to fail to furnish the buyer with adequate means, at the seller's expense, to exercise such option or to notify the seller regarding cancellation.

(4) Nothing in paragraph (b) of this section shall prevent a seller, where it is unable to make shipment within the time set forth in paragraph (a)(1) of this section or within a delay period consented to by the buyer, from deciding to consider the order cancelled and providing the buyer with notice of said decision within a reasonable time after it becomes aware of said inability to ship, together with a prompt refund.

(c) To fail to deem an order cancelled and to make a prompt refund to the buyer whenever:

(1) The seller receives, prior to the time of shipment, notification from the buyer cancelling the order pursuant to any option, renewed option or continuing option under this part;

(2) The seller has, pursuant to paragraph (b)(1)(iii) of this section, provided the buyer with a definite revised shipping date which is more than thirty (30) days later than the applicable time set forth in paragraph (a)(1) of this section or has notified the buyer that it is unable to make any representation regarding the length of the delay and the seller

(i) Has not shipped the merchandise within thirty (30) days of the applicable time set forth in paragraph (a)(1) of this section, and

(ii) Has not received the buyer's express consent to said shipping delay within said thirty (30) days;

(3) The seller is unable to ship within the applicable time set forth in paragraph (b)(2) of this section, and has not received, within the said applicable time, the buyer's consent to and further delay;

(4) The seller has notified the buyer of its inability to make shipment and has indicated its decision not to ship the merchandise;

(5) The seller fails to offer the option prescribed in paragraph (b)(1) of this section and has not shipped the merchandise within the applicable time set forth in paragraph (a)(1) of this section.

(d) In any action brought by the Federal Trade Commission, alleging a violation of this part, the failure of a respondent-seller to have records or other documentary proof establishing its use of systems and procedures which assure compliance, in the ordinary course of business, with any requirement of paragraphs (b) or (c) of this section will create a rebuttable presumption that the seller failed to comply with said requirement.

§ 435.3. Limited applicability

(a) This part shall not apply to:

(1) Subscriptions, such as magazine sales, ordered for serial delivery, after the initial shipment is made in compliance with this part.

(2) Orders of seeds and growing plants.

(3) Orders made on a collect-on-delivery (C.O.D.) basis.

(4) Transactions governed by the Federal Trade Commission's Trade Regulation Rule entitled "Use of Prenotification Negative Option Plans," 16 CFR part 425.

(b) By taking action in this area:

(1) The Federal Trade Commission does not intend to preempt action in the same area, which is not inconsistent with this part, by any State, municipal, or other local government. This part does not annul or diminish any rights or remedies provided to consumers by any State law, municipal ordinance, or other local regulation, insofar as those rights or remedies are equal to or greater than those provided by this part. In addition, this part does not supersede those provisions of any State law, municipal ordinance, or other local regulation which impose obligations or liabilities upon sellers, when sellers subject to this part are not in compliance therewith.

(2) This part does supersede those provisions of any State law, municipal ordinance, or other local regulation which are inconsistent with this part to the extent that those provisions do not provide a buyer with rights which are equal to or greater than those rights granted a buyer by this part. This part also supersedes those provisions of any State law, municipal ordinance, or other local regulation requiring that a buyer be notified of a right which is the same as a right provided by this part but requiring that a buyer be given notice of this right in a language, form, or manner which is different in any way from that required by this part. In those instances where any State law, municipal ordinance, or other local regulation contains provisions, some but not all of which are partially or completely superseded by this part, the provisions or portions of those provisions which have not been superseded retain their full force and effect.

(c) If any provision of this part, or its application to any person, partnership, corporation, act or practice is held invalid, the remainder of this part or the application of the provision to any other person, partnership, corporation, act or practice shall not be affected thereby.

PART 437: BUSINESS OPPORTUNITY RULE

Table of Sections

Sec.

§ 437.1. Definitions

The following definitions shall apply throughout this part:

(a) *Action* means a criminal information, indictment, or proceeding; a civil complaint, cross claim, counterclaim, or third party complaint in a judicial action or proceeding; arbitration; or any governmental administrative proceeding, including, but not limited to, an action to obtain or issue a cease and desist order, an assurance of voluntary compliance, and an assurance of discontinuance.

(b) *Affiliate* means an entity controlled by, controlling, or under common control with a business opportunity seller.

(c) *Business opportunity* means a commercial arrangement in which:

(1) A seller solicits a prospective purchaser to enter into a new business; and

(2) The prospective purchaser makes a required payment; and

(3) The seller, expressly or by implication, orally or in writing, represents that the seller or one or more designated persons will:

(i) Provide locations for the use or operation of equipment, displays, vending machines, or similar devices, owned, leased, controlled, or paid for by the purchaser; or

(ii) Provide outlets, accounts, or customers, including, but not limited to, Internet outlets, accounts, or customers, for the purchaser's goods or services; or

(iii) Buy back any or all of the goods or services that the purchaser makes, produces, fabricates, grows, breeds, modifies, or provides, including but not limited to providing payment for such services as, for example, stuffing envelopes from the purchaser's home.

(d) *Designated person* means any person, other than the seller, whose goods or services the seller suggests, recommends, or requires that the purchaser use in establishing or operating a new business.

(e) *Disclose or state* means to give information in writing that is clear and conspicuous, accurate, concise, and legible.

(f) *Earnings claim* means any oral, written, or visual representation to a prospective purchaser that conveys, expressly or by implication, a specific level or range of actual or potential sales, or gross or net income or profits. Earnings claims include, but are not limited to:

(1) Any chart, table, or mathematical calculation that demonstrates possible results based upon a combination of variables; and

(2) Any statements from which a prospective purchaser can reasonably infer that he or she will earn a minimum level of income (e.g., "earn enough to buy a Porsche," "earn a six-figure income," or "earn your investment back within one year").

(g) *Exclusive territory* means a specified geographic or other actual or implied marketing area in which the seller promises not to locate additional purchasers or offer the same or similar goods or services as the purchaser through alternative channels of distribution.

(h) *General media* means any instrumentality through which a person may communicate with the public, including, but not limited to, television, radio, print, Internet, billboard, Web site, commercial bulk email, and mobile communications.

(i) *Material* means likely to affect a person's choice of, or conduct regarding, goods or services.

(j) *New business* means a business in which the prospective purchaser is not currently engaged, or a new line or type of business.

(k) *Person* means an individual, group, association, limited or general partnership, corporation, or any other business entity.

(*l*) **Prior business** means:

(1) A business from which the seller acquired, directly or indirectly, the major portion of the business' assets; or

(2) Any business previously owned or operated by the seller, in whole or in part.

(m) *Providing locations, outlets, accounts, or customers* means furnishing the prospective purchaser with existing or potential locations, outlets, accounts, or customers; requiring, recommending, or suggesting one or more locators or lead generating companies; providing a list of locator or lead generating companies; collecting a fee on behalf of one or more locators or lead generating companies; offering to furnish a list of locations; or otherwise assisting the prospective purchaser in obtaining his or her own locations, outlets, accounts, or customers, provided, however, that advertising and general advice about business development and training shall not be considered as "providing locations, outlets, accounts, or customers."

(n) *Purchaser* means a person who buys a business opportunity.

(o) *Quarterly* means as of January 1, April 1, July 1, and October 1.

(p) *Required payment* means all consideration that the purchaser must pay to the seller or an affiliate, either by contract or by practical necessity, as a condition of obtaining or commencing operation of the business opportunity. Such payment may be made directly or indirectly through a third party. A required payment does not include payments for the purchase of reasonable amounts of inventory at bona fide wholesale prices for resale or lease.

(q) *Seller* means a person who offers for sale or sells a business opportunity.

(r) Signature or signed means a person's affirmative steps to authenticate his or her identity. It includes a person's handwritten signature, as well as an electronic or digital form of signature to the extent that such signature is recognized as a valid signature under applicable federal law or state contract law.

(s) Written or in writing means any document or information in printed form or in any form capable of being downloaded, printed, or otherwise preserved in tangible form and read. It includes: type-set, word processed, or handwritten documents; information on computer disk or CD-ROM; information sent via email; or information posted on the Internet. It does not include mere oral statements.

§ 437.2. The obligation to furnish written documents

In connection with the offer for sale, sale, or promotion of a business opportunity, it is a violation of this Rule and an unfair or deceptive act or practice in violation of Section 5 of the Federal Trade Commission Act ("FTC Act") for any seller to fail to furnish a prospective purchaser with the material information required by §§ 437.3(a) and 437.4(a) of this part in writing at least seven calendar days before the earlier of the time that the prospective purchaser:

(a) Signs any contract in connection with the business opportunity sale; or

(b) Makes a payment or provides other consideration to the seller, directly or indirectly through a third party.

§ 437.3. The disclosure document

In connection with the offer for sale, sale, or promotion of a business opportunity, it is a violation of this Rule and an unfair or deceptive act or practice in violation of Section 5 of the FTC Act, for any seller to:

(a) Fail to disclose to a prospective purchaser the following material information in a single written document in the form and using the language set forth in appendix A to this part; or if the offer for sale, sale, or promotion of a business opportunity is conducted in Spanish, in the form and using the language set forth in appendix B to this part; or if the offer for sale, sale, or promotion of a business opportunity is conducted in a language other than English or Spanish, using the form and an accurate translation of the language set forth in appendix A to this part:

(1) Identifying information. State the name, business address, and telephone number of the seller, the name of the salesperson offering the opportunity, and the date when the disclosure document is furnished to the prospective purchaser.

(2) Earnings claims. If the seller makes an earnings claim, check the "yes" box and attach the earnings statement required by § 437.4. If not, check the "no" box.

(3) Legal actions.

(i) If any of the following persons has been the subject of any civil or criminal action for misrepresentation, fraud, securities law violations, or unfair or deceptive practices, including violations of any FTC Rule, within the 10 years immediately preceding the date that the business opportunity is offered, check the "yes" box:

(A) The seller;

(B) Any affiliate or prior business of the seller; or

(C) Any of the seller's officers, directors, sales managers, or any individual who occupies a position or performs a function similar to an officer, director, or sales manager of the seller.

(ii) If the "yes" box is checked, disclose all such actions in an attachment to the disclosure document. State the full caption of each action (names of the principal parties, case number, full name of court, and filing date). For each action, the seller may also provide a brief accurate statement not to exceed 100 words that describes the action.

(iii) If there are no actions to disclose, check the "no" box.

(4) Cancellation or refund policy. If the seller offers a refund or the right to cancel the purchase, check the "yes" box. If so, state all material terms and conditions of the refund or cancellation policy in an attachment to the disclosure document. If no refund or cancellation is offered, check the "no" box.

(5) References.

(i) State the name, state, and telephone number of all purchasers who purchased the business opportunity within the last three years. If more than 10 purchasers purchased the business opportunity within the last three years, the seller may limit the disclosure by stating the name, state, and telephone number of at least the 10 purchasers within the past three years who are located nearest to the prospective purchaser's location. Alternatively, a seller may furnish a prospective buyer with a list disclosing all purchasers nationwide within the last three years. If choosing this option, insert the words "See Attached List" without removing the list headings or the numbers 1 through 10, and attach a list of the references to the disclosure document.

(ii) Clearly and conspicuously, and in immediate conjunction with the list of references, state the following: "If you buy a business opportunity from the seller, your contact information can be disclosed in the future to other buyers."

(6) Receipt. Attach a duplicate copy of the disclosure document to be signed and dated by the purchaser. The seller may inform the prospective purchaser how to return the signed receipt (for example, by sending to a street address, email address, or facsimile telephone number).

(b) Fail to update the disclosures required by paragraph (a) of this section at least quarterly to reflect any changes in the required information, including, but not limited to, any changes in the seller's refund or cancellation policy, or the list of references; provided, however, that until a seller has 10 purchasers, the list of references must be updated monthly.

§ 437.4. Earnings claims

In connection with the offer for sale, sale, or promotion of a business opportunity, it is a violation of this Rule and an unfair or deceptive act or practice in violation of Section 5 of the FTC Act, for the seller to:

(a) Make any earnings claim to a prospective purchaser, unless the seller:

(1) Has a reasonable basis for its claim at the time the claim is made;

(2) Has in its possession written materials that substantiate its claim at the time the claim is made;

(3) Makes the written substantiation available upon request to the prospective purchaser and to the Commission; and

(4) Furnishes to the prospective purchaser an earnings claim statement. The earnings claim statement shall be a single written document and shall state the following information:

(i) The title "EARNINGS CLAIM STATEMENT REQUIRED BY LAW" in capital, bold type letters;

(ii) The name of the person making the earnings claim and the date of the earnings claim;

(iii) The earnings claim;

(iv) The beginning and ending dates when the represented earnings were achieved;

(v) The number and percentage of all persons who purchased the business opportunity prior to the ending date in paragraph (a)(4)(iv) of this section who achieved at least the stated level of earnings;

(vi) Any characteristics of the purchasers who achieved at least the represented level of earnings, such as their location, that may differ materially from the characteristics of the prospective purchasers being offered the business opportunity; and

(vii) A statement that written substantiation for the earnings claim will be made available to the prospective purchaser upon request.

(b) Make any earnings claim in the general media, unless the seller:

(1) Has a reasonable basis for its claim at the time the claim is made;

(2) Has in its possession written material that substantiates its claim at the time the claim is made;

(3) States in immediate conjunction with the claim:

(i) The beginning and ending dates when the represented earnings were achieved; and

(ii) The number and percentage of all persons who purchased the business opportunity prior to the ending date in paragraph (b)(3)(i) of this section who achieved at least the stated level of earnings.

(c) Disseminate industry financial, earnings, or performance information unless the seller has written substantiation demonstrating that the information reflects, or does not exceed, the typical or ordinary financial, earnings, or performance experience of purchasers of the business opportunity being offered for sale.

(d) Fail to notify any prospective purchaser in writing of any material changes affecting the relevance or reliability of the information contained in an earnings claim statement before the prospective purchaser signs any contract or makes a payment or provides other consideration to the seller, directly or indirectly, through a third party.

§ 437.5. Sales conducted in Spanish or other languages besides English

(a) If the seller conducts the offer for sale, sale, or promotion of a business opportunity in Spanish, the seller must provide the disclosure document required by § 437.3(a) in the form and language set forth in appendix B to this part, and the disclosures required by §§ 437.3(a) and 437.4 must be made in Spanish.

(b) If the seller conducts the offer for sale, sale, or promotion of a business opportunity in a language other than English or Spanish, the seller must provide the disclosure document required by

§ 437.3(a) using the form and an accurate translation of the language set forth in appendix A to this part, and the disclosures required by §§ 437.3(a) and 437.4 must be made in that language.

§ 437.6. Other prohibited practices

In connection with the offer for sale, sale, or promotion of a business opportunity, it is a violation of this part and an unfair or deceptive act or practice in violation of Section 5 of the FTC Act for any seller, directly or indirectly through a third party, to:

(a) Disclaim, or require a prospective purchaser to waive reliance on, any statement made in any document or attachment that is required or permitted to be disclosed under this Rule;

(b) Make any claim or representation, orally, visually, or in writing, that is inconsistent with or contradicts the information required to be disclosed by §§ 437.3 (basic disclosure document) and 437.4 (earnings claims document) of this Rule;

(c) Include in any disclosure document or earnings claim statement any materials or information other than what is explicitly required or permitted by this Rule. For the sole purpose of enhancing the prospective purchaser's ability to maneuver through an electronic version of a disclosure document or earnings statement, the seller may include scroll bars and internal links. All other features (e.g., multimedia tools such as audio, video, animation, or pop-up screens) are prohibited;

(d) Misrepresent the amount of sales, or gross or net income or profits a prospective purchaser may earn or that prior purchasers have earned;

(e) Misrepresent that any governmental entity, law, or regulation prohibits a seller from:

(1) Furnishing earnings information to a prospective purchaser; or

(2) Disclosing to prospective purchasers the identity of other purchasers of the business opportunity;

(f) Fail to make available to prospective purchasers, and to the Commission upon request, written substantiation for the seller's earnings claims;

(g) Misrepresent how or when commissions, bonuses, incentives, premiums, or other payments from the seller to the purchaser will be calculated or distributed;

(h) Misrepresent the cost, or the performance, efficacy, nature, or central characteristics of the business opportunity or the goods or services offered to a prospective purchaser;

(i) Misrepresent any material aspect of any assistance offered to a prospective purchaser;

(j) Misrepresent the likelihood that a seller, locator, or lead generator will find locations, outlets, accounts, or customers for the purchaser;

(k) Misrepresent any term or condition of the seller's refund or cancellation policies;

(*l*) Fail to provide a refund or cancellation when the purchaser has satisfied the terms and conditions disclosed pursuant to § 437.3(a)(4);

(m) Misrepresent a business opportunity as an employment opportunity;

(n) Misrepresent the terms of any territorial exclusivity or territorial protection offered to a prospective purchaser;

(*o*) Assign to any purchaser a purported exclusive territory that, in fact, encompasses the same or overlapping areas already assigned to another purchaser;

(p) Misrepresent that any person, trademark or service mark holder, or governmental entity, directly or indirectly benefits from, sponsors, participates in, endorses, approves, authorizes, or is otherwise associated with the sale of the business opportunity or the goods or services sold through the business opportunity;

(q) Misrepresent that any person:

(1) Has purchased a business opportunity from the seller or has operated a business opportunity of the type offered by the seller; or

(2) Can provide an independent or reliable report about the business opportunity or the experiences of any current or former purchaser.

(r) Fail to disclose, with respect to any person identified as a purchaser or operator of a business opportunity offered by the seller:

(1) Any consideration promised or paid to such person. Consideration includes, but is not limited to, any payment, forgiveness of debt, or provision of equipment, services, or discounts to the person or to a third party on the person's behalf; or

(2) Any personal relationship or any past or present business relationship other than as the purchaser or operator of the business opportunity being offered by the seller.

§§ 437.7–.10. [Omitted.]

PART 444: FTC TRADE REGULATION RULE—CREDIT PRACTICES

Table of Sections

§ 444.1. Definitions

(a) ***Lender.*** A person who engages in the business of lending money to consumers within the jurisdiction of the Federal Trade Commission.

(b) ***Retail installment seller.*** A person who sells goods or services to consumers on a deferred payment basis or pursuant to a lease-purchase arrangement within the jurisdiction of the Federal Trade Commission.

(c) ***Person.*** An individual, corporation, or other business organization.

(d) ***Consumer.*** A natural person who seeks or acquires goods, services, or money for personal, family, or household use.

(e) ***Obligation.*** An agreement between a consumer and a lender or retail installment seller.

(f) ***Creditor.*** A lender or a retail installment seller.

(g) ***Debt.*** Money that is due or alleged to be due from one to another.

(h) ***Earnings.*** Compensation paid or payable to an individual or for his or her account for personal services rendered or to be rendered by him or her, whether denominated as wages, salary, commission, bonus, or otherwise, including periodic payments pursuant to a pension, retirement, or disability program.

(i) ***Household goods.*** Clothing, furniture, appliances, one radio and one television, linens, china, crockery, kitchenware, and personal effects (including wedding rings) of the consumer and his or her dependents, provided that the following are not included within the scope of the term household goods:

(1) Works of art;

(2) Electronic entertainment equipment (except one television and one radio);

(3) Items acquired as antiques; and

(4) Jewelry (except wedding rings).

(j) ***Antique.*** Any item over one hundred years of age, including such items that have been repaired or renovated without changing their original form or character.

(k) ***Cosigner.*** A natural person who renders himself or herself liable for the obligation of another person without compensation. The term shall include any person whose signature is requested as a condition to granting credit to another person, or as a condition for forbearance on collection of another person's obligation that is in default. The term shall not include a spouse whose signature is required on a credit obligation to perfect a security interest pursuant to State law. A person who does not receive goods, services, or money in return for a credit obligation does not receive compensation within the meaning of this definition. A person is a cosigner within the meaning of this definition whether or not he or she is designated as such on a credit obligation.

§ 444.2. Unfair credit practices

(a) In connection with the extension of credit to consumers in or affecting commerce, as commerce is defined in the Federal Trade Commission Act, it is an unfair act or practice within the meaning of Section 5 of that Act for a lender or retail installment seller directly or indirectly to take or receive from a consumer an obligation that:

(1) Constitutes or contains a cognovit or confession of judgment (for purposes other than executory process in the State of Louisiana), warrant of attorney, or other waiver of the right to notice and the opportunity to be heard in the event of suit or process thereon.

(2) Constitutes or contains an executory waiver or a limitation of exemption from attachment, execution, or other process on real or personal property held, owned by, or due to the consumer, unless the waiver applies solely to property subject to a security interest executed in connection with the obligation.

(3) Constitutes or contains an assignment of wages or other earnings unless:

(i) The assignment by its terms is revocable at the will of the debtor, or

(ii) The assignment is a payroll deduction plan or preauthorized payment plan, commencing at the time of the transaction, in which the consumer authorizes a series of wage deductions as a method of making each payment, or

(iii) The assignment applies only to wages or other earnings already earned at the time of the assignment.

(4) Constitutes or contains a nonpossessory security interest in household goods other than a purchase money security interest.

(b) [Reserved]

§ 444.3. Unfair or deceptive cosigner practices

(a) In connection with the extension of credit to consumers in or affecting commerce, as commerce is defined in the Federal Trade Commission Act, it is:

(1) A deceptive act or practice within the meaning of Section 5 of that Act for a lender or retail installment seller, directly or indirectly, to misrepresent the nature or extent of cosigner liability to any person.

(2) An unfair act or practice within the meaning of Section 5 of that Act for a lender or retail installment seller, directly or indirectly, to obligate a cosigner unless the cosigner is informed prior to becoming obligated, which in the case of open end credit shall mean prior to the time that the agreement creating the cosigner's liability for future charges is executed, of the nature of his or her liability as cosigner.

(b) Any lender or retail installment seller who complies with the preventive requirements in paragraph (c) of this section does not violate paragraph (a) of this section.

(c) To prevent these unfair or deceptive acts or practices, a disclosure, consisting of a separate document that shall contain the following statement and no other, shall be given to the cosigner prior to becoming obligated, which in the case of open end credit shall mean prior to the time that the agreement creating the cosigner's liability for future charges is executed:

NOTICE TO COSIGNER

You are being asked to guarantee this debt. Think carefully before you do. If the borrower doesn't pay the debt, you will have to. Be sure you can afford to pay if you have to, and that you want to accept this responsibility.

You may have to pay up to the full amount of the debt if the borrower does not pay. You may also have to pay late fees or collection costs, which increase this amount.

The creditor can collect this debt from you without first trying to collect from the borrower. The creditor can use the same collection methods against you that can be used against the borrower, such as suing you, garnishing your wages, etc. If this debt is ever in default, that fact may become a part of your credit record.

This notice is not the contract that makes you liable for the debt.

§ 444.4. Late charges

(a) In connection with collecting a debt arising out of an extension of credit to a consumer in or affecting commerce, as commerce is defined in the Federal Trade Commission Act, it is an unfair act or practice within the meaning of section 5 of that Act for a creditor, directly or indirectly, to levy or collect any delinquency charge on a payment, which payment is otherwise a full payment for the applicable period and is paid on its due date or within an applicable grace period, when the only delinquency is attributable to late fee(s) or delinquency charge(s) assessed on earlier installment(s).

(b) For purposes of this section, collecting a debt means any activity other than the use of judicial process that is intended to bring about or does bring about repayment of all or part of a consumer debt.

§ 444.5. State exemptions

(a) If, upon application to the Federal Trade Commission by an appropriate State agency, the Federal Trade Commission determines that:

(1) There is a State requirement or prohibition in effect that applies to any transaction to which a provision of this rule applies; and

(2) The State requirement or prohibition affords a level of protection to consumers that is substantially equivalent to, or greater than, the protection afforded by this rule;

Then that provision of the rule will not be in effect in that State to the extent specified by the Federal Trade Commission in its determination, for as long as the State administers and enforces the State requirement or prohibition effectively.

(b) [Reserved]

PART 455: FTC TRADE REGULATION RULE—USED MOTOR VEHICLE

Table of Sections

§ 455.1. General duties of a used vehicle dealer; definitions

(a) It is a deceptive act or practice for any used vehicle dealer, when that dealer sells or offers for sale a used vehicle in or affecting commerce as commerce is defined in the Federal Trade Commission Act:

(1) To misrepresent the mechanical condition of a used vehicle;

(2) To misrepresent the terms of any warranty offered in connection with the sale of a used vehicle; and

(3) To represent that a used vehicle is sold with a warranty when the vehicle is sold without any warranty.

(b) It is an unfair act or practice for any used vehicle dealer, when that dealer sells or offers for sale a used vehicle in or affecting commerce as commerce is defined in the Federal Trade Commission Act:

(1) To fail to disclose, prior to sale, that a used vehicle is sold without any warranty; and

(2) To fail to make available, prior to sale, the terms of any written warranty offered in connection with the sale of a used vehicle.

(c) The Commission has adopted this Rule in order to prevent the unfair and deceptive acts or practices defined in paragraphs (a) and (b). It is a violation of this Rule for any used vehicle dealer to fail to comply with the requirements set forth in §§ 455.2 through 455.5 of this part. If a used vehicle dealer complies with the requirements of §§ 455.2 through 455.5 of this part, the dealer does not violate this Rule.

(d) The following definitions shall apply for purposes of this part:

(1) Vehicle means any motorized vehicle, other than a motorcycle, with a gross vehicle weight rating (GVWR) of less than 8500 lbs., a curb weight of less than 6,000 lbs., and a frontal area of less than 46 sq. ft.

(2) Used vehicle means any vehicle driven more than the limited use necessary in moving or road testing a new vehicle prior to delivery to a consumer, but does not include any vehicle sold only for scrap or parts (title documents surrendered to the State and a salvage certificate issued).

(3) Dealer means any person or business which sells or offers for sale a used vehicle after selling or offering for sale five (5) or more used vehicles in the previous twelve months, but does not include a bank or financial institution, a business selling a used vehicle to an employee of that business, or a lessor selling a leased vehicle by or to that vehicle's lessee or to an employee of the lessee.

(4) Consumer means any person who is not a used vehicle dealer.

(5) Warranty means any undertaking in writing, in connection with the sale by a dealer of a used vehicle, to refund, repair, replace, maintain or take other action with respect to such used vehicle and provided at no extra charge beyond the price of the used vehicle.

(6) Implied warranty means an implied warranty arising under State law (as modified by the Magnuson-Moss Act) in connection with the sale by a dealer of a used vehicle.

(7) Service contract means a contract in writing for any period of time or any specific mileage to refund, repair, replace, or maintain a used vehicle and provided at an extra charge beyond the price of the used vehicle, unless offering such contract is "the business of insurance" and such business is regulated by State law.

(8) You means any dealer, or any agent or employee of a dealer, except where the term appears on the window form required by § 455.2(a).

§ 455.2. Consumer sales—window form

(a) General duty. Before you offer a used vehicle for sale to a consumer, you must prepare, fill in as applicable and display on that vehicle the applicable "Buyers Guide" illustrated by Figures 1–2 at the end of this part. Dealers may use remaining stocks of the version of the Buyers Guide in effect prior to the effective date of this Rule for up to one year after that effective date (i.e., until January 27, 2018). Dealers who opt to use their existing stock and choose to disclose the applicability of a non-dealer warranty, must add the following as applicable below the "Full/Limited Warranty" disclosure: "Manufacturer's Warranty still applies. The manufacturer's original warranty has not expired on the vehicle;" "Manufacturer's Used Vehicle Warranty Applies;" or "Other Used Vehicle Warranty Applies," followed by the statement, "Ask the dealer for a copy of the warranty document and an explanation of warranty coverage, exclusions, and repair obligations."

(1) The Buyers Guide shall be displayed prominently and conspicuously in any location on a vehicle and in such a fashion that both sides are readily readable. You may remove the form temporarily from the vehicle during any test drive, but you must return it as soon as the test drive is over.

(2) The capitalization, punctuation and wording of all items, headings, and text on the form must be exactly as required by this Rule. The entire form must be printed in 100% black ink on a white stock no smaller than 11 inches high by 7¼ inches wide in the type styles, sizes and format indicated. When filling out the form, follow the directions in paragraphs (b) through (f) of this section and § 455.4.

Form	Specification
BUYERS GUIDE	28 pt Triumvirate Bold caps
(rule)	2 pt Rule
IMPORTANT: Spoken promises are difficult to enforce. Ask the dealer to put all promises in writing. Keep this form.	10/12 Triumvirate Bold c & lc flush left ragged right maximum line 42 picas
VEHICLE MAKE ____ MODEL ____ YEAR ____ VIN NUMBER ____	10 pt Baseline Rule 8 pt Triumvirate Bold caps
DEALER STOCK NUMBER (Optional) ____	10 pt Baseline Rule 6 pt Triumvirate Bold caps
WARRANTIES FOR THIS VEHICLE:	10 pt Triumvirate Bold caps
(rule)	2 pt Rule
☐ **AS IS - NO WARRANTY**	54 pt Box 42 pt Triumvirate Bold caps
YOU WILL PAY ALL COSTS FOR ANY REPAIRS. The dealer assumes no responsibility for any repairs regardless of any oral statements about the vehicle.	10/10 Triumvirate Bold c & lc flush left ragged right maximum line 42 picas
(rule)	1 pt Rule
☐ **WARRANTY**	54 pt Box 42 pt Triumvirate Bold caps
☐ **FULL** ☐ **LIMITED WARRANTY. The dealer will pay ____% of the labor and ____% of the parts for the covered systems that fail during the warranty period. Ask the dealer for a copy of the warranty document for a full explanation of warranty coverage, exclusions, and the dealer's repair obligations. Under state law, "implied warranties" may give you even more rights.**	10/10 Triumvirate Bold c & lc 4½ picas indent on 2nd line
SYSTEMS COVERED: **DURATION:**	10 pt Triumvirate Bold caps
____ ____ (ten lines each)	10 pt Baseline Rule
☐ **SERVICE CONTRACT. A service contract is available at an extra charge on this vehicle. Ask for details as to coverage, deductible, price, and exclusions. If you buy a service contract within 90 days of the time of sale, state law "implied warranties" may give you additional rights.**	10/10 Triumvirate Bold c & lc maximum line 42 picas
PRE PURCHASE INSPECTION: ASK THE DEALER IF YOU MAY HAVE THIS VEHICLE INSPECTED BY YOUR MECHANIC EITHER ON OR OFF THE LOT.	10/10 Triumvirate Bold caps flush left ragged right maximum line 42 picas
SEE THE BACK OF THIS FORM for important additional information, including a list of some major defects that may occur in used motor vehicles.	10/10 Triumvirate Bold c & lc flush left ragged right maximum line 42 picas

12 pt Thumvirate Bold lc
flush left ragged right
maximum line 42 picas

Below is a list of some major defects that may occur in used motor vehicles.

2 pt Rule

8/9 Thumvirate Bold c & lc
flush left ragged right
maximum line 20 picas
1 em indent on 2nd line

Frame & Body
Frame-cracks, corrective welds, or rusted through
Dogtracks—bent or twisted frame

Engine
Oil leakage, excluding normal seepage
Cracked block or head
Belts missing or inoperable
Knocks or misses related to camshaft lifters and push rods
Abnormal exhaust discharge

Transmission & Drive Shaft
Improper fluid level or leakage, excluding normal seepage
Cracked or damaged case which is visible
Abnormal noise or vibration caused by faulty transmission or drive shaft
Improper shifting or functioning in any gear
Manual clutch slips or chatters

Differential
Improper fluid level or leakage excluding normal seepage
Cracked or damaged housing which is visible
Abnormal noise or vibration caused by faulty differential

Cooling System
Leakage including radiator
Improperly functioning water pump

Electrical System
Battery leakage
Improperly functioning alternator, generator, battery, or starter

Fuel System
Visible leakage

Inoperable Accessories
Gauges or warning devices
Air conditioner
Heater & Defroster

Brake System
Failure warning light broken
Pedal not firm under pressure (DOT spec.)
Not enough pedal reserve (DOT spec.)
Does not stop vehicle in straight (DOT spec.)
Hoses damaged
Drum or rotor too thin (Mfgr. Specs)
Lining or pad thickness less than 1/32 inch
Power unit not operating or leaking
Structural or mechanical parts damaged

Steering System
Too much free play at steering wheel (DOT specs.)
Free play in linkage more than 1/4 inch
Steering gear binds or jams
Front wheels aligned improperly (DOT specs.)
Power unit belts cracked or slipping
Power unit fluid level improper

Suspension System
Ball joint seals damaged
Structural parts bent or damaged
Stabilizer bar disconnected
Spring broken
Shock absorber mounting loose
Rubber bushings damaged or missing
Radius rod damaged or missing
Shock absorber leaking or functioning improperly

Tires
Tread depth less than 2/32 inch
Sizes mismatched
Visible damage

Wheels
Visible cracks, damage or repairs
Mounting bolts loose or missing

Exhaust System
Leakage

2 pt Rule

DEALER

10 pt Baseline Rule
6 pt Thumvirate Bold caps

ADDRESS

SEE FOR COMPLAINTS

2 pt Rule

IMPORTANT: The information on this form is part of any contract to buy this vehicle. Removal of this label before consumer purchase (except for purpose of test-driving) is a violation of federal law (16 C.F.R. 455).

10/12 Thumvirate Bold c & lc
maximum line 42 picas

When filling out the form, follow the directions in (b) through (e) of this section and § 455.4 of this part.

(b) Warranties—

(1) No Implied Warranty—"As Is"/No Dealer Warranty.

(i) If you offer the vehicle without any implied warranty, i.e., "as is," mark the box appearing in Figure 1. If you offer the vehicle with implied warranties only, substitute the IMPLIED WARRANTIES ONLY disclosure specified in paragraph (b)(1)(ii) of this section, and mark the IMPLIED WARRANTIES ONLY box illustrated by Figure 2. If you first offer the vehicle "as is" or with implied warranties only but then sell it with a warranty, cross out the "As Is—No Dealer Warranty" or "Implied Warranties Only" disclosure, and fill in the warranty terms in accordance with paragraph (b)(2) of this section.

(ii) If your State law limits or prohibits "as is" sales of vehicles, that State law overrides this part and this rule does not give you the right to sell "as is." In such States, the heading "As Is—No Dealer Warranty" and the paragraph immediately accompanying that phrase must be deleted from the form, and the following heading and paragraph must be substituted as illustrated in the Buyers Guide in Figure 2. If you sell vehicles in States that permit "as is" sales, but you choose to offer implied warranties only, you must also use the following disclosure instead of "As Is—No Dealer Warranty" as illustrated by the Buyers Guide in Figure 2. See § 455.5 for the Spanish version of this disclosure.

IMPLIED WARRANTIES ONLY

The dealer doesn't make any promises to fix things that need repair when you buy the vehicle or afterward. But implied warranties under your state's laws may give you some rights to have the dealer take care of serious problems that were not apparent when you bought the vehicle.

(2) Full/Limited Warranty. If you offer the vehicle with a warranty, briefly describe the warranty terms in the space provided. This description must include the following warranty information:

(i) Whether the warranty offered is "Full" or "Limited." Mark the box next to the appropriate designation. A "Full" warranty is defined by the Federal Minimum Standards for Warranty set forth in section 104 of the Magnuson-Moss Act, 15 U.S.C. 2304 (1975). The Magnuson-Moss Act does not apply to vehicles manufactured before July 4, 1975. Therefore, if you choose not to designate "Full" or "Limited" for such vehicles, cross out both designations, leaving only "Warranty."

(ii) Which of the specific systems are covered (for example, "engine, transmission, differential"). You cannot use shorthand, such as "drive train" or "power train" for covered systems.

(iii) The duration (for example, "30 days or 1,000 miles, whichever occurs first").

(iv) The percentage of the repair cost paid by you (for example, "The dealer will pay 100% of the labor and 100% of the parts.")

§ 455.3. Window form

(a) Form given to buyer. Give the buyer of a used vehicle sold by you the window form displayed under § 455.2 containing all of the disclosures required by the Rule and reflecting the warranty coverage agreed upon. If you prefer, you may give the buyer a copy of the original, so long as that copy accurately reflects all of the disclosures required by the Rule and the warranty coverage agreed upon."

(b) Incorporated into contract. The information on the final version of the window form is incorporated into the contract of sale for each used vehicle you sell to a consumer. Information on the window form overrides any contrary provisions in the contract of sale. To inform the consumer of these facts, include the following language conspicuously in each consumer contract of sale:

The information you see on the window form for this vehicle is part of this contract. Information on the window form overrides any contrary provisions in the contract of sale.

§ 455.4. Contrary statements

You may not make any statements, oral or written, or take other actions which alter or contradict the disclosures required by §§ 455.2 and 455.3. You may negotiate over warranty coverage, as provided in § 455.2(b) of this part, as long as the final warranty terms are identified in the contract of sale and summarized on the copy of the window form you give to the buyer.

§ 455.5–.7. [Omitted.]

FTC POLICY STATEMENT ON DECEPTION

Appended to *Cliffdale Associates, Inc.*, 103 F.T.C. 110, 174 (1984).

FEDERAL TRADE COMMISSION
WASHINGTON, D.C. 20580

October 14, 1983

The Honorable John D. Dingell
Chairman
Committee on Energy and Commerce
U.S. House of Representatives
Washington, D.C. 20515

Dear Mr. Chairman:

This letter responds to the Committee's inquiry regarding the Commission's enforcement policy against deceptive acts or practices.[1] We also hope this letter will provide guidance to the public.

Section 5 of the FTC Act declares unfair or deceptive acts or practices unlawful. Section 12 specifically prohibits false ads likely to induce the purchase of food, drugs, devices or cosmetics. Section 15 defines a false ad for purposes of Section 12 as one which is "misleading in a material respect."[2] Numerous Commission and judicial decisions have defined and elaborated on the phrase "deceptive acts or practices" under both Sections 5 and 12. Nowhere, however, is there a single definitive statement of the Commission's view of its authority. The Commission believes that such a statement would be useful to the public, as well as the Committee in its continuing review of our jurisdiction.

We have therefore reviewed the decided cases to synthesize the most important principles of general applicability. We have attempted to provide a concrete indication of the manner in which the Commission will enforce its deception mandate. In so doing, we intend to address the concerns that have been raised about the meaning of deception, and thereby attempt to provide a greater sense of certainty as to how the concept will be applied.[3]

I. SUMMARY

Certain elements undergird all deception cases. First, there must be a representation, omission or practice that is likely to mislead the consumer.[4] Practices that have been found misleading or deceptive

---

1 S. Rep. No. 97–451, 97th Cong., 2d Sess. 16; H.R. Rep. No. 98–156, Part I, 98th Cong., 1st Sess. 6 (1983). The Commission's enforcement policy against unfair acts or practices is set forth in a letter to Senators Ford and Danforth, dated December 17, 1980.

2 In determining whether an ad is misleading, Section 15 requires that the Commission take into account "representations made or suggested" as well as "the extent to which the advertisement fails to reveal facts material in light of such representations or material with respect to consequences which may result from the use of the commodity to which the advertisement relates under the conditions prescribed in said advertisement, or under such conditions as are customary or usual." 15 U.S.C. 55. If an act or practice violates Section 12, it also violates Section 5. *Simeon Management Corp.*, 87 F.T.C. 1184, 1219 (1976), *aff'd*, 579 F.2d 1137 (9th Cir. 1978); *Porter & Dietsch*, 90 F.T.C. 770, 873–74 (1977), *aff'd*, 605 P.2d 294 (7th Cir. 1979), *cert. denied*, 445 U.S. 950 (1980).

3 Chairman Miller has proposed that Section 5 be amended to define deceptive acts. Hearing Before the Subcommittee for Consumers of the Committee on Commerce, Science, and Transportation, United States Senate, 97th Cong., 2d Sess. *FTCs Authority Over Deceptive Advertising*, July 22,1982, Serial No. 97–134, p. 9. Three Commissioners believe a legislative definition is unnecessary. *Id.* at 45 (Commissioner Clanton), at 51 (Commissioner Bailey) and at 76 (Commissioner Pertschuk). Commissioner Douglas supports a statutory definition of deception. Prepared statement by Commissioner George W. Douglas, Hearing Before the Subcommittee for Consumers of the Committee on Commerce, Science and Transportation, United States Senate, 98th Cong. 1st Sess. (March 16, 1983) p. 2.

4 A misrepresentation is an express or implied statement contrary to fact. A misleading omission occurs when qualifying information necessary to prevent a practice, claim, representation, or reasonable expectation or belief from being misleading is not disclosed. Not all omissions are deceptive, even if providing the information would benefit

in specific cases include false oral or written representations, misleading price claims, sales of hazardous or systematically defective products or services without adequate disclosures, failure to disclose information regarding pyramid sales, use of bait and switch techniques, failure to perform promised services, and failure to meet warranty obligations.[5]

Second, we examine the practice from the perspective of a consumer acting reasonably in the circumstances. If the representation or practice affects or is directed primarily to a particular group, the Commission examines reasonableness from the perspective of that group.

Third, the representation, omission, or practice must be a "material" one. The basic question is whether the act or practice is likely to affect the consumer's conduct or decision with regard to a product or service. If so, the practice is material, and consumer injury is likely, because consumers are likely to have chosen differently but for the deception. In many instances, materiality, and hence injury, can be presumed from the nature of the practice. In other instances, evidence of materiality may be necessary.

Thus, the Commission will find deception if there is a representation, omission or practice that is likely to mislead the consumer acting reasonably in the circumstances, to the consumer's detriment. We discuss each of these elements below.

II. THERE MUST BE A REPRESENTATION, OMISSION, OR PRACTICE THAT IS LIKELY TO MISLEAD THE CONSUMER.

Most deception involves written or oral misrepresentations, or omissions of material information. Deception may also occur in other forms of conduct associated with a sales transaction. The entire advertisement, transaction or course of dealing will be considered. The issue is whether the act or practice is likely to mislead, rather than whether it causes actual deceptions.[6]

Of course, the Commission must find that a representation, omission, or practice occurred in cases of express claims, the representation itself establishes the meaning. In cases of implied claims, the Commission will often be able to determine meaning through an examination of the representation itself, including an evaluation of such factors as the entire document, the juxtaposition of various phrases in the document, the nature of the claim, and the nature of the transactions.[7] In other

---

consumers. As the Commission noted in rejecting a proposed requirement for nutrition disclosures, "In the final analysis, the question whether an advertisement requires affirmative disclosure would depend on the nature and extent of the nutritional claim made in the advertisement.". ITT Continental Baking Co. Inc., 83 F.T.C. 865, 965 (1976). In determining whether an omission is deceptive, the Commission will examine the overall impression created by a practice, claim, or representation. For example, the practice of offering a product for sale creates an implied representation that it is fit for the purposes for which it is sold. Failure to disclose that the product is not fit constitutes a deceptive omission. [See discussion below at 5–6] Omissions may also be deceptive where the representations made are not literally misleading, if those representations create a reasonable expectation or belief among consumers which is misleading, absent the omitted disclosure.

Non-deceptive emissions may still violate Section 5 if they are unfair. For instance, the R-Value Rule, 16 C.F.R. 460.5 (1983), establishes a specific method for testing insulation ability, and requires disclosure of the figure in advertising. The Statement of Basis and Purpose, 44 FR 50,242 (1979), refers to a deception theory to support disclosure requirements when certain misleading claims are made, but the rule's general disclosure requirement is based on an unfairness theory. Consumers could not reasonably avoid injury in selecting insulation because no standard method of measurement existed.

[5] Advertising that lacks a reasonable basis is also deceptive. *Firestone*, 81 F.T.C. 398, 451–52 (1972), *aff'd*, 481 F.2d 246 (6th Cir.), *cert. denied*, 414 U.S. 1112 (1973). *National Dynamics*, 82 F.T.C. 488, 549–50 (1973); *aff'd and remanded on other grounds*, 492 F.2d 1333 (2d Cir.), *cert. denied*, 419 U.S. 993 (1974), *reissued*, 85 F.T.C. 391 (1976). *National Comm'n on Egg Nutrition*, 88 F.T.C. 89, 191 (1976), *aff'd*, 570 P.2d 157 (7th Cir.), *cert. denied*, 439 U.S. 821, *reissued*, 92 F.T.C. 848 (1978). The deception theory is based on the fact that most ads making objective claims imply, and many expressly state, that an advertiser has certain specific grounds for the claims. If the advertiser does not, the consumer is acting under a false impression. The consumer might have perceived the advertising differently had he or she known the advertiser had no basis for the claim. This letter does not address the nuances of the reasonable basis doctrine, which the Commission is currently reviewing. 48 FR 10,471 (March 11, 1983).

[6] In *Beneficial Corp. v. FTC*, 542 F.2d 611, 617 (3d Cir. 1976), the court noted "the likelihood or propensity of deception is the criterion by which advertising is measured."

[7] On evaluation of the entire document:

situations, the Commission will require extrinsic evidence that reasonable consumers reach the implied claims.[8] In all instances, the Commission will carefully consider any extrinsic evidence that is introduced.

Some cases involve omission of material information, the disclosure of which is necessary to prevent the claim, practice, or sale from being misleading.[9] Information may be omitted from written[10] or oral[11] representations or from the commercial transaction.[12]

In some circumstances, the Commission can presume that consumers are likely to reach false beliefs about the product or service because of an omission. At other times, however, the Commission may require evidence on consumers' expectations.[13]

Marketing and point-of-sales practices that are likely to mislead consumers are also deceptive. For instance, in bait and switch cases, a violation occurs when the offer to sell the product is not a bona fide offer.[14] The Commission has also found deception where a sales representative misrepresented

---

> The Commission finds that many of the challenged Anacin advertisements, when viewed in their entirety, did convey the message that the superiority of this product has been proven [footnote omitted]. It is immaterial that the word "established", which was used in the complaint, generally did not appear in the ads; the important consideration is the net impression conveyed to the public. *American Home Products*, 98 F.T.C. 136, 374 (1981), *aff'd*, 695 F.2d (3d Cir. 1982).

On the juxtaposition of phrases:

> On this label, the statement "Kills Germs By Millions On Contact" immediately precedes the assertion "For General Oral Hygiene Bad Breath, Colds and Resultant Sore Throats" [footnote omitted]. By placing these two statements in close proximity, respondent has conveyed the message that since Listerine can kill millions of germs, it can cure, prevent and ameliorate colds and sore throats [footnote omitted]. *Warner Lambert*, 86 F.T.C. 1398, 1489–90 (1975), *aff'd*, 562 F.2d 749 (D.C. Cir. 1977), *cert. denied*, 435 U.S. 950 (1978) (emphasis in original).

On the nature of the claim, *Firestone* is relevant. There the Commission noted that the alleged misrepresentation concerned the safety of respondent's product, "an issue of great significance to consumers. On this issue, the Commission has required scrupulous accuracy in advertising claims, for obvious reasons." 81 F.T.C. 398, 456 (1972), *aff'd*, 481 F.2d 246 (6th Cir.), *cert. denied*, 414 U.S. IU2 (1973).

In each of these cases, other factors, including in some instances surveys, were in evidence on the meaning of the ad.

[8] The evidence can consist of expert opinion, consumer testimony (particularly in cases involving oral representations), copy tests, surveys, or any other reliable evidence of consumer interpretation.

[9] As the Commission noted in the Cigarette rule, "The nature, appearance, or intended use of a product may create the impression on the mind of the consumer . . . and if the impression is false, and if the seller does not take adequate steps to correct it, he is responsible for an unlawful deception." Cigarette Rule Statement of Basis and Purpose, 29 FR 8324, 8352 (July 2, 1964).

[10] *Porter & Dietsch*, 90 F.T.C. 770, 873–74 (1977), *aff'd*. 605 F.2d 294 (7th Cir. 1979), *cert. denied*, 445 U.S. 950 (1980); *Simeon Management Corp.*, 87 F.T.C. 1184, 1230 (1976), *aff'd*, 579 F.2d 1137 (9th Cir. 1978).

[11] *See, e.g., Grolier*, 91 F.T.C. 315, 480 (1978), *remanded on other grounds*, 615 F.2d 1215 (9th Cir. 1980), *modified on other grounds*, 98 FM 882 (1981), *reissued*, 99 F.T.C. 379 (1982).

[12] In *Peacock Buick*, 86 F.T.C. 1532 (1975), *aff'd*, 553 F.2d 97 (4th Cir. 1977), the Commission held that absent a clear and early disclosure of the prior use of a late model car, deception can result from the setting in which a sale is made and the expectations of the buyer . . .

Even in the absence of affirmative misrepresentations, it is misleading for the seller of late model used cars to fail to reveal the particularized uses to which they have been put . . . When a later model used car is sold at close to list price . . . the assumption likely to be made by some purchasers is that, absent disclosure to the contrary, such car has not previously been used in a way that might substantially impair its value. In such circumstances, failure to disclose a disfavored prior use may tend to mislead. *Id.* at 1557–58.

[13] In *Leonard Porter*, the Commission dismissed a complaint alleging that respondents' sale of unmarked products in Alaska led consumers to believe erroneously that they were handmade in Alaska by natives. Complaint counsel had failed to show that consumers of Alaskan craft assumed respondents' products were handmade by Alaskans in Alaska. The Commission was unwilling, absent evidence, to infer from a viewing of the items that the products would tend to mislead consumers.

By requiring such evidence, we do not imply that elaborate proof of consumer beliefs or behavior is necessary, even in a case such as this, to establish the requisite capacity to deceive. However, where visual inspection is inadequate, some extrinsic testimony evidence must be added. 88 F.T.C. 546, 626, n.5 (1976).

[14] *Bait and Switch Policy Protocol*, December 10, 1975; Guides Against Bait Advertising, 16 C.F.R. 238.0 (1967). 32 PR 15,540.

the purpose of the initial contact with customers.[15] When a product is sold, there is an implied representation that the product is fit for the purposes for which it is sold. When it is not, deception occurs.[16] There may be a concern about the way a product or service is marketed, such as where inaccurate or incomplete information is provided.[17] A failure to perform services promised under a warranty or by contract can also be deceptive.[18]

III. THE ACT OR PRACTICE MUST BE CONSIDERED FROM THE PERSPECTIVE OF THE REASONABLE CONSUMER

The Commission believes that to be deceptive the representation, omission or practice must be likely to mislead reasonable consumers under the circumstances.[19] The test is whether the consumer's interpretation or reaction is reasonable.[20] When representations or sales practices are targeted to a specific audience, the Commission determines the effect of the practice on a reasonable member of that group. In evaluating a particular practice, the Commission considers the totality of the practice in determining how reasonable consumers are likely to respond.

A company is not liable for every interpretation or action by a consumer. In an advertising context, this principle has been well-stated:

> An advertiser cannot be charged with liability with respect to every conceivable misconception, however outlandish, to which his representations might be subject among the foolish or feeble-minded. Some people, because of ignorance or incomprehension, may be misled by even a scrupulously honest claim. Perhaps a few misguided souls believe, for example, that all "Danish pastry" is made in Denmark. Is it therefore an actionable deception to advertise "Danish pastry" when it is made in this country? Of course not, A representation does not become "false and deceptive" merely because it will be unreasonably misunderstood by an insignificant and unrepresentative segment of the class of persons to whom the representation is addressed. Heinz W. Kirchner, 63 F.T.C. 1282, 1290 (1963).

To be considered reasonable, the interpretation or reaction does not have to be the only one.[21] When a seller's representation conveys more than one meaning to reasonable consumers, one of which is false,

---

[15] *Encyclopedia Britannica* 87 F.T.C. 421, 497 (1976), *aff'd*, 605 F.2d 964 (7th Cir. 1979), *cert. denied*, 445 U.S. 934 (1980), *modified*, 100 F.T.C. 500 (1982).

[16] See the complaints in *BayleySuit*, C-3117 (consent agreement) (September 30,1983) [102 F.T.C. 1285]; *Figgie International, Inc.*, D. 9166 (May 17, 1983).

[17] The Commission's complaints in *Chrysler Corporation*, 99 F.T.C. 347 (1982), and *Volkswagen of America*, 99 F.T.C. 446 (1982), alleged the failure to disclose accurate use and care instructions for replacing oil filters was deceptive. The complaint in *Ford Motor Co.*, D. 9154, 96 F.T.C. 362 (1980), charged Ford with failing to disclose a "piston scuffing" defect to purchasers and owners which was allegedly widespread and costly to repair. *See also General Motors*, D. 9145 (provisionally accepted consent agreement, April 26, 1983). [102 F.T.C. 1741]

[18] *See Jay Norris Corp.*, 91 F.T.C. 751 (1978), *aff'd with modified language in order*, 598 P.2d 1244 (2d Cir. 1979), *cert. denied*, 444 U.S. 980 (1979) (failure to consistently meet guarantee claims of "immediate and prompt" delivery as well as money back guarantees); *Southern States Distributing Co.*, 83 F.T.C. 1126 (1973) (failure to honor oral and written product maintenance guarantees, as represented); *Skylark Originals, Inc.*, 80 F.T.C. 337 (1972), *aff'd*, 475 F.2d 1396 (3d Cir. 1973) (failure to promptly honor moneyback guarantee as represented in advertisements and catalogs); *Capitol Manufacturing Corp.*, 73 F.T.C. 872 (1968) (failure to fully, satisfactorily and promptly meet all obligations and requirements under terms of service guarantee certificate).

[19] The evidence necessary to determine how reasonable consumers understand a representation is discussed in Section II of this letter.

[20] An interpretation may be reasonable even though it is not shared by a majority of consumers in the relevant class, or by particularly sophisticated consumers. A material practice that misleads a significant minority of reasonable consumers is deceptive. *See Heinz W. Kirchner*, 63 F.T.C. 1282 (1963).

[21] A secondary message understood by reasonable consumers is actionable if deceptive even though the primary message is accurate. *Sears, Roebuck & Co.*, 95 F.T.C. 406, 511 (1980), *aff'd* 676 F.2d 385 (9th Cir. 1982); *Chrysler*, 87 F.T.C. 749 (1976), *aff'd*, 561 F.2d 357 (D.C. Cir.), *reissued* 90 F.T.C. 606 (1977); *Rhodes Pharmacal Co.*, 208 F.2d 382, 387 (7th Cir. 1953), *aff'd*, 348 U.S. 940 (1955).

the seller is liable for the misleading interpretation.[22] An interpretation will be presumed reasonable if it is the one the respondent intended to convey.

The Commission has used this standard in its past decisions. "The test applied by the Commission is whether the interpretation is reasonable in light of the claim."[23] In the Listerine case, the Commission evaluated the claim from the perspective of the "average listener."[24] In a case involving the sale of encyclopedias, the Commission observed "[i]n determining the meaning of an advertisement, a piece of promotional material or a sales presentation, the important criterion is the net impression that it is likely to make on the general populace."[25] The decisions in *American Home Products, Bristol Myers,* and *Sterling Drug* are replete with references to reasonable consumer interpretations.[26] In a land sales case, the Commission evaluated the oral statements and written representations "in light of the sophistication and understanding of the persons to whom they were directed."[27] Omission cases are no different: the Commission examines the failure to disclose in light of expectations and understandings of the typical buyer[28] regarding the claims made.

When representations or sales practices are targeted to a specific audience, such as children, the elderly, or the terminally ill, the Commission determines the effect of the practice on a reasonable member of that group.[29] For instance, if a company markets a cure to the terminally ill, the practice will be evaluated from the perspective of how it affects the ordinary member of that group. Thus, terminally ill consumers might be particularly susceptible to exaggerated cure claims. By the same token, a practice or representation directed to a well-educated group, such as a prescription drug advertisement to doctors, would be judged in light of the knowledge and sophistication of that group.[30]

---

22 *National Comm'n on Egg Nutrition*, 88 F.T.C. 89, 185 (1976), *enforced in part*, 570 F.2d 157 (7th Cir. 1977); *Jay Norris Corp.*, 91 F.T.C. 751, 836 (1978), *aff'd*, 598 F.2d 1244 (2d Cir. 1979).

23 *National Dynamics*, 82 F.T.C. 488, 524, 548 (1973), *aff'd*, 492 F.2d 1333 (2d Cir.), *cert. denied*, 419 U.S. 993 (1974), *reissued* 85 F.T.C. 39–1 (1976).

24 *Warner-Lambert*, 86 F.T.C. 1398, 1415 n.4 (1975), *aff'd*, 562 F.2d 749 (D.C. Cir. 1977), *cert denied*, 435 U.S. 950 (1978).

25 *Grolier*, 91 F.T.C. 315, 430 (1978), *remanded on other grounds*, 615 F.2d 1215 (9th Cir. 1980), *modified on other grounds*, 98 F.T.C. 882 (1981), *reissued*, 99 F.T.C. 379 (1982).

26 *American Home Products*, 98 F.T.C. 136 (1981), *aff'd* 695 F.2d 681 (3d Cir. 1982). consumers may be led to expect, quite reasonably . . ." (at 386); ". . . consumers may reasonably believe . . ." (*Id.* n.52); ". . . would reasonably have been understood by consumers. . . ." (at 371); "the record shows that consumers could reasonably have understood this language . . ." (at 372). See also, pp. 373, 374, 375. *Bristol-Myers*, D. 8917 (July 5, 1983), appeal docketed, No. 83–4167 (2d Cir. Sept. 12,1983) . . . . . . ads must be judged by the impression they make on reasonable members of the public . . ." (Slip Op. at 4); ". . . consumers could reasonably have understood . . ." (Slip Op. at 7); ". . . consumers could reasonably infer . . ." (Slip Op. at 11) [102 F.T.C. 21 (1983)]. *Sterling Drug, Inc.*, D. 8919 (July 5,1983), appeal docketed, No. 83–7700 (9th Cir. Sept. 14, 1983) . . . . . . consumers could reasonably assume . . ." (Slip Op. at 9); ". . . consumers could reasonably interpret the ads . . ." (Slip Op. at 33). [102 F.T.C. 395 (1983)]

27 *Horizon Corp.*, 97 F.T.C. 464, 810 n.13 (1981).

28 *Simeon Management*, 87 F.T.C. 1184, 1230 (1976).

29 The listed categories are merely examples. Whether children, terminally ill patients, or any other subgroup of the population will be considered a special audience depends on the specific factual context of the claim or the practice.

The Supreme Court has affirmed this approach. "The determination whether an advertisement is misleading requires consideration of the legal sophistication of its audience." *Bates v. Arizona*, 433 U.S. 350, 383 n.37 (1977).

30 In one case, the Commission's complaint focused on seriously ill persons. The ALJ summarized: According to the complaint, the frustrations and hopes of the seriously ill and their families were exploited, and the representation had the tendency and capacity to induce the seriously ill to forego conventional medical treatment worsening their condition and in some cases hastening death, or to cause them to spend large amounts of money and to undergo the inconvenience of traveling for a non-existent "operation." *Travel King*, 86 F.T.C. 715, 719 (1975).

In a case involving a weight loss product, the Commission observed:

> It is obvious that dieting is the conventional method of losing weight. But it is equally obvious that many people who need or want to lose weight regard dieting as bitter medicine. To these corpulent consumers the promises of weight loss without dieting are the Siren's call, and advertising that heralds unrestrained consumption while muting the inevitable need for temperance, if not abstinence, simply does not pass muster. Porter & Dietsch, 90 F.T.C. 770, 864–865 (1977), 605 F.2d 294 (7th Cir. 1979), cert. denied, 445 U.S. 950 (1980).

As it has in the past, the Commission will evaluate the entire advertisement, transaction, or course of dealing in determining how reasonable consumers are likely to respond. Thus, in advertising the Commission will examine "the entire mosaic, rather than each tile separately."[31] As explained by a court of appeals in a recent case:

The Commission's right to scrutinize the visual and aural imagery of advertisements follows from the principle that the Commission looks to the impression made by the advertisements as a whole. Without this mode of examination, the Commission would have limited recourse against crafty advertisers whose deceptive messages were conveyed by means other than, or in addition to, spoken words. American Home Products, 695 F.2d 681, 688 (3d Cir. Dec. 3, 1982).[32]

Commission cases reveal specific guidelines. Depending on the circumstances, accurate information in the text may not remedy a false headline because reasonable consumers may glance only at the headline.[33] Written disclosures or fine print may be insufficient to correct a misleading representations.[34] Other practices of the company may direct consumers' attention away from the qualifying disclosures.[35] Oral statements, label disclosures or point-of-sale material will not necessarily correct a deceptive representation or omission.[36] Thus, when the first contact between a

---

Children have also been the specific target of ads or practices. In *Ideal Toy*, the Commission adopted the Hearing Examiner's conclusion that:

> False, misleading and deceptive advertising claims beamed at children tend to exploit unfairly a consumer group unqualified by age or experience to anticipate or appreciate the possibility that representations may he exaggerated or untrue. *Ideal Toy*, 64 F.T.C. 297, 310 (1964).

See also, *Avalon Industries Inc.*, 83 F.T.C. 1728, 1750 (1974).

[31] *FTC v. Sterling Drug*, 317 F.2d 669, 674 (2d Cir. 1963).

[32] Numerous cases exemplify this point. For instance, in *Pfizer*, the Commission ruled that "the net impression of the advertisement, evaluated from the perspective of the audience to whom the advertisement is directed, is controlling." 81 F.T.C. 23, 58 (1972).

In a subsequent case, the Commission explained that "[i]n evaluating advertising representations, we are required to look at the complete advertisement and formulate our opinions on them on the basis of the net general impression conveyed by them and not on isolated excerpts." *Standard Oil of Calif*, 84 F.T.C. 1401, 1471 (1974), *aff'd as modified*, 577 F.2d 653 (9th Cir. 1978), *reissued*, 96 F.T.C. 380 (1980).

The Third Circuit stated succinctly the Commission's standard. "The tendency of the advertising to deceive must be judged by viewing it as a whole, without emphasizing isolated words or phrases apart from their context." *Beneficial Corp. v. FTC*, 542 F.2d 611, 617 (3d Cir. 1976), *cert denied*, 430 U.S. 983 (1977).

[33] In *Litton Industries*, the Commission held that fine print disclosures that the surveys included only "Litton authorized" agencies were inadequate to remedy the deceptive characterization of the survey population in the headline. 97 F.T.C. 1, 71, n.6 (1981), *aff'd as modified*, 676 F.2d 364 (9th Cir. 1982). Compare the Commission's note in the same case that the fine print disclosure "Litton and one other brand" was reasonable to quote the claim that independent service technicians had been surveyed, "[F]ine print was a reasonable medium for disclosing a qualification of only limited relevance." 97 F.T.C. 1, 70, n.5 (1981).

In another case, the Commission held that the body of the ad corrected the possibly misleading headline because in order to enter the contest, the consumer had to read the text, and the text would eliminate any false impression stemming from the headline. *D.L. Blair*, 82 F.T.C. 234, 255, 256 (1973).

In one case respondent's expert witness testified that the headline (and accompanying picture) of an ad would be the focal point of the first glance. He also told the administrative law judge that a consumer would spend [t]ypically a few seconds at most" on the ads at issue. *Crown Central*, 84 F.T.C. 1493, 1543 nn. 14–15 (1974).

[34] In *Giant Food*, the Commission agreed with the examiner that the fine-print disclaimer was inadequate to correct a deceptive impression. The Commission quoted from the examiner's finding that "very few if any of the persons who would read Giant's advertisements would take the trouble to, or did, read the fine print disclaimer." 61 F.T.C. 326, 348 (1962).

Cf. Beneficial Corp. v. FTC, 542 P.2d 611, 618 (3d Cir. 1976), where the court reversed the Commission's opinion that no qualifying language could eliminate the deception stemming from use of the slogan "Instant Tax Refund."

[35] "Respondents argue that the contracts which consumers signed indicated that credit life insurance was not required for financing, and that this disclosure obviated the possibility of deception. We disagree. It Is clear from consumer testimony that oral deception was employed in some instances to cause consumers to ignore the warning in their sales agreement . . ." *Peacock Buick*, 86 F.T.C. 1532, 1558–59 (1974).

[36] *Exposition Press*, 295 F.2d 69, 873 (2d Cir. 1961); *Gimbel Bros.*, 61 F.T.C. 1051, 1066 (1962); *Carter Products*, 186 F.2d 821, 824 (1951).

By the same token, money-back guarantees do not eliminate deception. In *Sears*, the Commission observed:

seller and a buyer occurs through a deceptive practice, the law may be violated even if the truth is subsequently made known to the purchaser.[37] Pro forma statements or disclaimers may not cure otherwise deceptive messages or practices.[38]

Qualifying disclosures must be legible and understandable. In evaluating such disclosures, the Commission recognizes that in many circumstances, reasonable consumers do not read the entirety of an ad or are directed away from the importance of the qualifying phrase by the acts or statements of the seller. Disclosures that conform to the Commission's Statement of Enforcement Policy regarding clear and conspicuous disclosures, which applies to television advertising, are generally adequate, CCH Trade Regulation Reporter, ¶ 7569.09 (Oct. 21, 1970). Less elaborate disclosures may also suffice.[39]

Certain practices, however, are unlikely to deceive consumers acting reasonably. Thus, the Commission generally will not bring advertising cases based on subjective claims (taste, feel, appearance, smell) or on correctly stated opinion claims if consumers understand the source and limitations of the opinion.[40] Claims phrased as opinions are actionable, however, if they are not honestly held, if they misrepresent the qualifications of the holder or the basis of his opinion or if the recipient reasonably interprets them as implied statements of fact.[41]

The Commission generally will not pursue cases involving obviously exaggerated or puffing representations, *i.e.*, those that the ordinary consumers do not take seriously.[42] Some exaggerated claims, however, may be taken seriously by consumers and are actionable. For instance, in rejecting a

---

A money-back guarantee is no defense to a charge of deceptive advertising. . . . A money-back guarantee does not compensate the consumer for the often considerable time and expense incident to returning a major-ticket item and obtaining a replacement.

Sears, Roebuck and Co., 95 F.T.C. 406, 518 (1980), *aff'd*, 676 F.2d 385 (9th Cir. 1982). However, the existence of a guarantee, if honored, has a bearing on whether the Commission should exercise its discretion to prosecute. *See* Deceptive and Unsubstantiated Claims Policy Protocol, 1975.

37 *See American Home Products*, 98 F.T.C. 136, 370 (1981), *aff'd*, 695 F.2d 681, 688 (3d Cir. Dec. 3, 1982), Whether a disclosure on the label cures deception in advertising depends on the circumstances:

. . . it is well settled that dishonest advertising is not cured or excused by honest labeling [footnote emitted]. Whether the ill-effects of deceptive nondisclosure can be cured by a disclosure requirement limited to labeling, or whether a further requirement of disclosure in advertising should be imposed, is essentially a question of remedy. As such it is a matter within the sound discretion of the Commission [footnote omitted]. The question of whether in a particular case to require disclosure in advertising cannot be answered by application of any hard-and-fast principle. The test is simple and pragmatic: Is it likely that, unless such disclosure is made, a substantial body of consumers will be misled to their detriment? *Statement of Basis and Purpose for the Cigarette Advertising and Labeling Trade Regulation Rule*, 1965, pp. 89–90. 29 FR 8325 (1964).

Misleading "door openers" have also been found deceptive (Encyclopedia Britannica, 87 F.T.C. 421 (1976), *aff'd*, 605 P.2d 964 (7th Cir. 1979), *cert. denied*, 445 U.S. 934 (1980), *as modified*, 100 F.T.C. 500 (1982)), as have offers to sell that are not bona fide offers (*Seekonk Freezer Meats, Inc.*, 82 F.T.C. 1025 (1973)). In each of these instances, the truth is made known prior to purchase.

38 In the Listerine case, the Commission held that pro forma statements of no absolute prevention followed by promises of fewer colds did not cure or correct the false message that Listerine will prevent colds. *Warner Lambert* 86 F.T.C. 1398, 1414 (1975), *aff'd*, 562 F.2d 749 (D.C. Cir. 1977), *cert. denied*, 435 U.S. 950 (1978).

39 *Chicago Metropolitan Pontiac Dealers' Ass'n*, C. 3110 (June 9, 1983). [101 F.T.C. 854 (1983)]

40 An opinion is a representation that expresses only the behalf of the maker, without certainty, as to the existence of a fact, or his judgement as to quality, value, authenticity, or other matters of judgement. American Law Institute, Restatement on Torts, Second ¶ 538 A.

41 *Id.* ¶ 539. At common law, a consumer can generally rely on an expert opinion. *Id.*, ¶ 542(a). For this reason, representations of expert opinion will generally be regarded as representations of fact.

42 "[T]here is a category of advertising themes, in the nature of puffing or other hyperbole, which do not amount to the type of affirmative product claims for which either the Commission or the consumer would expect documentation." *Pfizer, Inc*, 81 F.T.C. 23, 64 (1972).

The term "Puffing" refers generally to an expression of opinion not made as a representation of fact. A seller has some latitude in puffing his goods, but he is not authorized to misrepresent them or to assign to them benefits they do not possess [cite omitted]. Statements made for the purpose of deceiving prospective purchasers cannot properly be characterized as mere puffing. *Wilmington Chemical*, 69 F.T.C. 828, 865 (1966).

respondent's argument that use of the words "electronic miracle" to describe a television antenna was puffery, the Commission stated:

> Although not insensitive to respondent's concern that the term miracle is commonly used in situations short of changing water into wine, we must conclude that the use of "electronic miracle" in the context of respondent's grossly exaggerated claims would lead consumers to give added credence to the overall suggestion that this device is superior to other types of antennae. *Jay Norris*, 91 F.T.C. 751, 847 n.20 (1978), *aff'd*, 598 F.2d 1244 (2d Cir.), *cert. denied*, 444 U.S. 980 (1979).

Finally, as a matter of policy, when consumers can easily evaluate the product or service, it is inexpensive, and it is frequently purchased, the Commission will examine the practice closely before issuing a complaint based on deception. There is little incentive for sellers to misrepresent (either by an explicit false statement or a deliberate false implied statement) in these circumstances since they normally would seek to encourage repeat purchases. Where, as here, market incentives place strong constraints on the likelihood of deception, the Commission will examine a practice closely before proceeding.

In sum, the Commission will consider many factors in determining the reaction of the ordinary consumer to a claim or practice. As would any trier of fact, the Commission will evaluate the totality of the ad or the practice and ask questions such as: how clear is the representation? how conspicuous is any qualifying information? how important is the omitted information? do other sources for the omitted information exist? how familiar is the public with the product or service?[43]

IV. THE REPRESENTATION, OMISSION OR PRACTICE MUST BE MATERIAL

The third element of deception is materiality. That is, a representation, omission or practice must be a material one for deception to occur.[44] A "material" misrepresentation or practice is one which is likely to affect a consumer's choice of or conduct regarding a product.[45] In other words, it is information that is important to consumers. If inaccurate or omitted information is material, injury is likely.[46]

The Commission considers certain categories of information presumptively material.[47] First, the Commission presumes that express claims are material.[48] As the Supreme Court stated recently, "[i]n the absence of factors that would distort the decision to advertise, we may assume that the willingness

---

[43] In *Avalon Industries*, the ALJ observed that the " 'ordinary person with a common degree of familiarity with industrial civilization' would expect a reasonable relationship between the size of package and the size of quantity of the contents. He would have no reason to anticipate slack filling." 83 F.T.C. 1728, 1750 (1974) (I.D.).

[44] "A misleading claim or omission in advertising will violate Section 5 or Section 12, however, only if the omitted information would be a material factor in the consumer's decision to purchase the product." *American Home Products Corp.*, 98 F.T.C. 136, 368 (1981), *aff'd*, 695 F.2d 681 (3d Cir. 1982). A claim is material if it is likely to affect consumer behavior. "Is it likely to affect the average consumer in deciding whether to purchase the advertised product-is there a material deception, in other words?" Statement of Basis and Purpose, *Cigarette Advertising and Labeling Rule*, 1965, pp. 86–87. 29 FR 8325 (1964).

[45] Material information may affect conduct other than the decision to purchase a product. The Commission's complaint in *Volkswagen of America*, 99 F.T.C. 446 (1982), for example, was based on provision of inaccurate instructions for oil filter installation. In its *Restatement on Torts, Second*, the American Law Institute defines a material misrepresentation or omission as one which the reasonable person would regard as important in deciding how to act, or one which the maker knows that the recipient, because of his or her own peculiarities, is likely to consider important. Section 538(2). The Restatement explains that a material fact does not necessarily have to affect the finances of a transaction. "There are many more-or-less sentimental considerations that the ordinary man regards as important." Comment on Clause 2(a)(d).

[46] In evaluating materiality, the Commission takes consumer preferences as given. Thus, if consumers prefer one product to another, the Commission need not determine whether that preference is objectively justified. *See Algoma Lumber*, 291 U.S. 54, 78 (1933). Similarly, objective differences among products are not material if the difference is not likely to affect consumer choices.

[47] The Commission will always consider relevant and competent evidence offered to rebut presumptions of materiality.

[48] Because this presumption is absent for some implied claims, the Commission will take special caution to ensure materiality exists in such cases.

of a business to promote its products reflects a belief that consumers are interested in the advertising."[49] Where the seller knew, or should have known, that an ordinary consumer would need omitted information to evaluate the product or service, or that the claim was false, materiality will be presumed because the manufacturer intended the information or omission to have an effect.[50] Similarly, when evidence exists that a seller intended to make an implied claim, the Commission will infer materiality.[51]

The Commission also considers claims or omissions material if they significantly involve health, safety, or other areas with which the reasonable consumer would be concerned. Depending on the facts, information pertaining to the central characteristics of the product or service will be presumed material. Information has been found material where it concerns the purpose,[52] safety,[53] efficacy,[54] or cost,[55] of the product or service. Information is also likely to be material if it concerns durability, performance, warranties or quality. Information pertaining to a finding by another agency regarding the product may also be material.[56]

Where the Commission cannot find materiality based on the above analysis, the Commission may require evidence that the claim or omission is likely to be considered important by consumers. This evidence can be the fact that the product or service with the feature represented costs more than an otherwise comparable product without the feature, a reliable survey of consumers, or credible testimony.[57]

A finding of materiality is also a finding that injury is likely to exist because of the representation, omission, sales practice, or marketing technique. Injury to consumers can take many forms.[58] Injury

---

49 *Central Hudson Gas & Electric Co. v. PSC*, 447 U.S. 557, 567 (1980).

50 *Cf. Restatement on Contracts, Second* ¶ 162(*l*).

51 In *American Home Products*, the evidence was that the company intended to differentiate its products from aspirin. The very fact that AHP sought to distinguish its products from aspirin strongly implies that knowledge of the true ingredients of those products would be material to purchasers." *American Home Products*, 98 F.T.C. 136, 368 (1981), *aff'd*, 695 F.2d 681 (3d. Cir. 1982).

52 In *Fedders*, the ads represented that only Fedders gave the assurance of cooling on extra hot, humid days. "Such a representation is the raison d'etre for an air conditioning unit-it is an extremely material representation." 85 F.T.C. 38, 61 (1975) (I.D.), *petition dismissed*, 529 F.2d 1398 (2d Cir.), *cert. denied*, 429 U.S. 818 (1976).

53 "We note at the outset that both alleged misrepresentations go to the issue of the safety of respondent's product, an issue of great significance to consumers." *Firestone*, 81 F.T.C. 398, 456 (1972), *aff'd*, 481 P.2d 246 (6th Cir.), *cert. denied*, 414 U.S. 1112 (1973).

54 The Commission found that information that a product was effective in only the small minority of cases where tiredness symptoms are due to an iron deficiency, and that it was of no benefit in all other cases, was material. *J.B. Williams Co.*, 68 F.T.C. 481, 546 (1965), *aff'd*, 381 F.2d 884 (6th Cir. 1967).

55 As the Commission noted in *MacMillan, Inc.*:

In marketing their courses, respondents failed to adequately disclose the number of lesson assignments to be submitted in a course. These were material facts necessary for the student to calculate his tuition obligation, which was based on the number of lesson assignments he submitted for grading. The nondisclosure of these material facts combined with the confusion arising from LaSalle's inconsistent use of terminology had the capacity to mislead students about the nature and extent of their tuition obligation. *MacMillan, Inc.*, 96 F.T.C. 208, 303–304 (1980).

See also, *Peacock Buick*, 86 F.T.C. 1532, 1562 (1975), *aff'd*, 553 F.2d 97 (4th Cir. 1977).

56 *Simeon Management Corp.*, 87 F.T.C. 1184 (1976), *aff'd*, 579 P.2d 1137, 1168, n.10 (9th Cir. 1978).

57 In *American Home Products*, the Commission approved the ALJ's finding of materiality from an economic perspective:

If the record contained evidence of a significant disparity between the prices of Anacin and plain aspirin, it would form a further basis for a finding of materiality. That is, there is a reason to believe consumers are willing to pay a premium for a product believed to contain a special analgesic ingredient but not for a product whose analgesic is ordinary aspirin. *American Home Products*, 98 F.T.C. 136, 369 (1981), *aff'd*, 695 F.2d 681 (3d Cir. 1982).

58 The prohibitions of Section 5 are intended to prevent injury to competitors as well as to consumers. The Commission regards injury to competitors as identical to injury to consumers. Advertising and legitimate marketing techniques are intended to "lure" competitors by directing business to the advertiser. In fact, vigorous competitive advertising can actually benefit consumers by lowering prices, encouraging product innovation, and increasing the specificity and amount of information available to consumers. Deceptive practices injure both competitors and consumers because consumers who preferred the competitor's product are wrongly diverted.

exists if consumers would have chosen differently but for the deception. If different choices are likely, the claim is material, and injury is likely as well. Thus, injury and materiality are different names for the same concept.

V. CONCLUSION

The Commission will find an act or practice deceptive if there is a misrepresentation, omission, or other practice, that misleads the consumer acting reasonably in the circumstances, to the consumer's detriment. The Commission will not generally require extrinsic evidence concerning the representations understood by reasonable consumers or the materiality of a challenged claim, but in some instances extrinsic evidence will be necessary.

The Commission intends to enforce the FTC Act vigorously. We will investigate, and prosecute where appropriate, acts or practices that are deceptive. We hope this letter will help provide you and the public with a greater sense of certainty concerning how the Commission will exercise its jurisdiction over deception. Please do not hesitate to call if we can be of any further assistance.

By direction of the Commission, Commissioners Pertschuk and Bailey dissenting, with separate statements attached and with separate response to the Committee's request for a legal analysis to follow.

/s/James C. Miller III
Chairman

cc: Honorable James T. Broyhill
Honorable James J. Florio
Honorable Norman F. Lent

FTC POLICY STATEMENT REGARDING ADVERTISING SUBSTANTIATION

Appended to *Thompson Medical Co.*, 104 F.T.C. 648, 839 (1984),
aff'd, 791 F.2d 189 (D.C. Cir. 1986), *cert. denied*, 479 U.S. 1086 (1987).

Introduction

On March 11, 1983, the Commission published a notice requesting comments on its advertising substantiation program.[1] To facilitate analysis of the program, the notice posed a number of questions concerning the program's procedures, standards, benefits, and costs, and solicited suggestions for making the program more effective. Based on the public comments and the staff's review, the Commission has drawn certain conclusions about how the program is being implemented and how it might be refined to serve better the objective of maintaining a marketplace free of unfair and deceptive acts or practices. This statement articulates the Commission's policy with respect to advertising substantiation.

The Reasonable Basis Requirement

First, we reaffirm our commitment to the underlying legal requirement of advertising substantiation-that advertisers and ad agencies have a reasonable basis for advertising claims before they are disseminated.

The Commission intends to continue vigorous enforcement of this existing legal requirement that advertisers substantiate express and implied claims, however conveyed, that make objective assertions about the item or service advertised. Objective claims for products or services represent explicitly or by implication that the advertiser has a reasonable basis supporting these claims. These representations of substantiation are material to consumers. That is, consumers would be less likely to rely on claims for products and services if they knew the advertiser did not have a reasonable basis

---

1 48 FR 10471, March 11, 1983.

for believing them to be true.[2] Therefore, a firm's failure to possess and rely upon a reasonable basis for objective claims constitutes an unfair and deceptive act or practice in violation of Section 5 of the Federal Trade Commission Act.

Standards for Prior Substantiation

Many ads contain express or implied statements regarding the amount of support the advertiser has for the product claim. When the substantiation claim is express (e.g., "tests prove", "doctors recommend", and "studies show"), the Commission expects the firm to have at least the advertised level of substantiation. Of course, an ad may imply more substantiation than it expressly claims or may imply to consumers that the firm has a certain type of support; in such cases, the advertiser must possess the amount and type of substantiation the ad actually communicates to consumers.

Absent an express or implied reference to a certain level of support, and absent other evidence indicating what consumer expectations would be, the Commission assumes that consumers expect a "reasonable basis" for claims. The Commission's determination of what constitutes a reasonable basis depends, as it does in an unfairness analysis, on a number of factors relevant to the benefits and costs of substantiating a particular claim. These factors include: the type of claim, the product, the consequences of a false claim, the benefits of a truthful claim, the cost of developing substantiation for the claim, and the amount of substantiation experts in the field believe is reasonable. Extrinsic evidence, such as expert testimony or consumer surveys, is useful to determine what level of substantiation consumers expect to support a particular product claim and the adequacy of evidence an advertiser possesses.

One issue the Commission examined was substantiation for implied claims. Although firms are unlikely to possess substantiation for implied claims they do not believe the ad makes, they should generally be aware of reasonable interpretations and will be expected to have prior substantiation for such claims. The Commission will take care to assure that it only challenges reasonable interpretations of advertising claims.[3]

Procedures for Obtaining Substantiation

In the past, the Commission has sought substantiation from firms in two different ways: through industry-wide "rounds" that involved publicized inquiries with identical or substantially similar demands to a number of firms within a targeted industry or to firms in different industries making the same type of claim; and on a case-by-case basis, by sending specific requests to individual companies under investigation. The Commission's review indicates that "rounds" have been costly to both the recipient and to the agency and have produced little or no law enforcement benefit over a case-by-case approach.

The Commission's traditional investigatory procedures allow the staff to investigate a number of firms within an industry at the same time, to develop necessary expertise within the area of investigation, and to announce our activities publicly in circumstances where public notice or comment is desirable. The Commission intends to continue undertaking such law enforcement efforts when appropriate. However, since substantiation is principally a law enforcement tool and the Commission's concern in such investigations is with the substantiation in the *advertiser's* possession, there is little, if any, information that the public could contribute in such investigations. Therefore, the Commission anticipates that substantiation investigations will rarely be made public before they are completed.

Accordingly, the Commission has determined that in the future it will rely on nonpublic requests for substantiation directed to individual companies via an informal access letter or, if necessary, a formal civil investigative demand. The Commission believes that tailored, firm-specific requests, whether

---

[2] Nor presumably would an advertiser have made such claims unless the advertiser thought they would be material to consumers.

[3] Individual Commissioners have expressed differing views as to how claims should be interpreted so that advertisers are not held to outlandish or tenuous interpretations. Notwithstanding these variations in approach, the focus of all Commissioners on reasonable interpretations of claims is intended to ensure that advertisers are not required to substantiate claims that were not made.

directed to one firm or to several firms within the same industry, are a more efficient law enforcement technique. The Commission cannot presently foresee circumstances under which the past approach of industry-wide rounds would be appropriate in the ad substantiation area.

Relevance of Post-Claim Evidence in Substantiation Cases

The reasonable basis doctrine requires that firms have substantiation before disseminating a claim. The Commission has on occasion exercised its discretion, however, to consider supporting materials developed after disseminations.[4] The Commission has not previously identified in one document the circumstances in which it may, in its discretion, consider post-claim evidence in substantiation cases.[5] Such guidance can serve to clarify the program's actual operation as well as focus consideration of postclaim evidence on cases in which it is appropriate.

The Commission emphasizes that as a matter of law, firms lacking a reasonable basis before an ad is disseminated violate Section 5 of the FTC Act and are subject to prosecution. The goal of the advertising substantiation requirement is to assure that advertising is truthful, however, and the truth or falsity of a claim is always relevant to the Commission's deliberations. Therefore, it is important that the agency retain the discretion and flexibility to consider additional substantiating evidence, not as a substitute for an advertiser's prior substantiation, but rather in the following circumstances:

- When deciding, before issuance of a complaint, whether there is a public interest in proceeding against a firm;
- When assessing the adequacy of the substantiation an advertiser possessed before a claim was made; and
- When deciding the need for or appropriate scope of an order to enter against a firm that lacked a reasonable basis prior to disseminating an advertisement.

First, using post-claim evidence to evaluate the truth of a claim, or otherwise using such evidence in deciding whether there is a public interest in continuing an investigation or issuing a complaint, is appropriate policy. This does not mean that the Commission will postpone action while firms create post-claim substantiation to prove the truthfulness of claims, nor does it mean that subsequent evidence of truthfulness absolves a firm of liability for failing to possess prior substantiation for a claim. The Commission focuses instead on whether existing evidence that claims are true should lead us in the exercise of our prosecutorial discretion to decline to initiate a law enforcement proceeding. If available post-claim evidence proves that the claim is true, issuing a complaint against a firm that may have violated the prior substantiation requirement is often inappropriate, particularly in light of competing demands on the Commission's resources.

Second, post-claim evidence may indicate that apparent deficiencies in the pre-claim substantiation materials have no practical significance. In evaluating the adequacy of prior substantiation, the Commission will consider only post-claim substantiation that sheds light on pre-existing substantiation. Thus, advertisers will not be allowed to create entirely new substantiation simply because their prior substantiation was inadequate.

Finally, the Commission may use post-claim evidence in determining the need for or appropriate scope of an order to be entered against a firm that lacked a reasonable basis. Thus, when additional evidence offered for the first time at trial suggests that the claim is true, the Commission may frame a narrower order than if there had been no post-claim evidence.

The Commission remains committed to the prior substantiation requirement and further believes that these discretionary factors will provide necessary flexibility. The Commission will consider post-claim

---

4 The Commission's evidentiary rule, 16 C.F.R. 3.40, has sometimes been interpreted as precluding introduction of post-claim substantiation. In fact, it does not. Section 3.40 only provides a sanction against the introduction of evidence that should have been produced in response to a subpoena, but was not.

5 The distinction between pre-claim and post-claim evidence is only relevant when the charge is lack of substantiation. For other chases, such as falsity, when evidence was developed is irrelevant to its admissibility at trial.

evidence only in the circumstances listed above. But, whether it will do so in any particular case remains within its discretion.

Self Regulation Groups and Government Agencies

The Commission traditionally has enjoyed a close working relationship with self regulation groups and government agencies whose regulatory policies have some bearing on our law enforcement initiatives. The Commission will not necessarily defer, however, to a finding by a self-regulation group. An imprimatur from a self-regulation group will not automatically shield a firm from Commission prosecution, and an unfavorable determination will not mean the Commission will automatically take issue, or find liability if it does. Rather the Commission will make its judgment independently, evaluating each case on its merits. We intend to continue our useful relationships with self-regulation groups and to rely on the expertise and findings of other government agencies in our proceedings to the greatest extent possible.

By direction of the Commission.

FTC POLICY STATEMENT ON UNFAIRNESS

Appended to *International Harvester Co.*,
104 F.T.C. 949, 1070 (1984).
See 15 U.S.C. § 45(n).

FEDERAL TRADE COMMISSION
WASHINGTON, D. C. 20580

December 17, 1980

The Honorable Wendell H. Ford
Chairman, Consumer Subcommittee
Committee on Commerce, Science, and Transportation
Room 130 Russell Office Building
Washington, D.C. 20510

The Honorable John C. Danforth
Ranking Minority Member, Consumer Subcommittee
Committee on Commerce, Science, and Transportation
Room 130 Russell Office Building
Washington, D.C. 20510

Dear Senators Ford and Danforth:

This is in response to your letter of June 13, 1980, concerning one aspect of this agency's jurisdiction over "unfair or deceptive acts or practices." You informed us that the Subcommittee was planning to hold oversight hearings on the concept of "unfairness" as it has been applied to consumer transactions. You further informed us that the views of other interested parties were solicited and compiled in a Committee Print earlier this year.[1] Your letter specifically requested the Commission's views on cases under Section 5 "not involving the content of advertising," and its views as to "whether the Commission's authority should be limited to regulating false or deceptive commercial advertising." Our response addresses these and other questions related to the concept of consumer unfairness.

We are pleased to have this opportunity to discuss the future work of the agency. The subject that you have selected appears to be particularly timely. We recognize that the concept of consumer unfairness is one whose precise meaning is not immediately obvious, and also recognize that this uncertainty has been honestly troublesome for some businesses and some members of the legal profession. This result is understandable in light of the general nature of the statutory standard. At the same time, though, we believe we can respond to legitimate concerns of business and the Bar by attempting to delineate

1 Unfairness: Views on Unfair Acts and Practices in Violation of the Federal Trade Commission Act (1980) (hereinafter referred to as "Committee Print").

in this letter a concrete framework for future application of the Commission's unfairness authority. We are aided in this process by the cumulative decisions of this agency and the federal courts, which, in our opinion, have brought added clarity to the law. Although the administrative and judicial evolution of the consumer unfairness concept has still left some necessary flexibility in the statute, it is possible to provide a reasonable working sense of the conduct that is covered.

In response to your inquiry we have therefore undertaken a review of the decided cases and rules and have synthesized from them the most important principles of general applicability. Rather than merely reciting the law, we have attempted to provide the Committee with a concrete indication of the manner in which the Commission has enforced, and will continue to enforce, its unfairness mandate. In so doing we intend to address the concerns that have been raised about the meaning of consumer unfairness, and thereby attempt to provide a greater sense of certainty about what the Commission would regard as an unfair act or practice under Section 5.

This letter thus delineates the Commission's views of the boundaries of its consumer unfairness jurisdiction and is subscribed to by each Commissioner. In addition, we are enclosing a companion Commission statement that discusses the ways in which this body of law differs from, and supplements, the prohibition against consumer deception, and then considers and evaluates some specific criticisms that have been made of our enforcement of the law.[2] Since you have indicated a particular interest in the possible application of First Amendment principles to commercial advertising, the companion statement will include discussions relevant to that question. The companion statement is designed to respond to the key questions raised about the unfairness doctrine. However, individual Commissioners may not necessarily endorse particular arguments or particular examples of the Commission's exercise of its unfairness authority contained in the companion statement.

Commission Statement of Policy on the Scope of the Consumer Unfairness Jurisdiction

Section 5 of the FTC Act prohibits, in part, "unfair . . . acts or practices in or affecting commerce."[3] This is commonly referred to as the Commission's consumer unfairness jurisdiction. The Commission's jurisdiction over "unfair methods of competition" is not discussed in this letter.[4] Although we cannot give an exhaustive treatment of the law of consumer unfairness in this short statement, some relatively concrete conclusions can nonetheless be drawn.

The present understanding of the unfairness standard is the result of an evolutionary process. The statute was deliberately framed in general terms since Congress recognized the impossibility of drafting a complete list of unfair trade practices that would not quickly become outdated or leave loopholes for easy evasion.[5] The task of identifying unfair trade practices was therefore assigned to the Commission, subject to judicial review,[6] in the expectation that the underlying criteria would evolve and develop over time. As the Supreme Court observed as early as 1931, the ban on unfairness

---

[2] Neither this letter nor the companion statement addresses ongoing proceedings, but the Commission is prepared to discuss those matters separately at an appropriate time.

[3] The operative sentence of Section 5 reads in full as follows: "Unfair methods of competition in or affecting commerce, and unfair or deceptive acts or practices in or affecting commerce, are declared unlawful." 15 U.S.C. 45(a)(1).

[4] In fulfilling its competition or antitrust mission the Commission looks to the purposes, policies, and spirit of the other antitrust laws and the FTC Act to determine whether a practice affecting competition or competitors is unfair. *See, e.g., FTC v. Brown Shoe Co.*, 384 U.S. 316 (1966). In making this determination the Commission is guided by the extensive legislative histories of those statutes and a considerable body of antitrust case law. The agency's jurisdiction over "deceptive acts or practices" is likewise not discussed in this letter.

[5] *See* H.R. Conf. Rep. No. 1142, 63d Cong., 2d Sess., at 19 (1914) (If Congress "were to adopt the method of definition, it would undertake an endless task"). In 1914 the statute was phrased only in terms of "unfair methods of competition," and the reference to "unfair acts or practices" was not added until the Wheeler-Lee Amendment in 1938. The initial language was still understood as reaching most of the conduct now characterized as consumer unfairness, however, and so the original legislative history remains relevant to the construction of that part of the statute.

[6] The Supreme Court has stated on many occasions that the definition of "unfairness" is ultimately one for judicial determination. *See, e.g., FTC v. Sperry & Hutchinson Co.,* 405 U.S. 233, 249 (1972); *FTC v. R. F. Keppel & Bro.,* 291 U.S. 304, 314 (1934).

"belongs to that class of phrases which do not admit of precise definition, but the meaning and application of which must be arrived at by what this court elsewhere has called 'the gradual process of judicial inclusion and exclusion.' "[7]

By 1964 enough cases had been decided to enable the Commission to identify three factors that it considered when applying the prohibition against consumer unfairness. These were: (1) whether the practice injures consumers; (2) whether it violates established public policy; (3) whether it is unethical or unscrupulous.[8] These factors were later quoted with apparent approval by the Supreme Court in the 1972 case of *Sperry & Hutchinson*.[9] Since then the Commission has continued to refine the standard of unfairness in its cases and rules, and it has now reached a more detailed sense of both the definition and the limits of these criteria.[10]

Consumer injury

Unjustified consumer injury is the primary focus of the FTC Act, and the most important of the three *S & H* criteria. By itself it can be sufficient to warrant a finding of unfairness. The Commission's ability to rely on an independent criterion of consumer injury is consistent with the intent of the statute, which was to "[make] the consumer who may be injured by an unfair trade practice of equal concern before the law with the merchant injured by the unfair methods of a dishonest competitor."[11]

The independent nature of the consumer injury criterion does not mean that every consumer injury is legally "unfair," however. To justify a finding of unfairness the injury must satisfy three tests. It must be substantial; it must not be outweighed by any countervailing benefits to consumers or competition that the practice produces; and it must be an injury that consumers themselves could not reasonably have avoided.

First of all, the injury must be substantial. The Commission is not concerned with trivial or merely speculative harms.[12] In most cases a substantial injury involves monetary harm, as when sellers coerce consumers into purchasing unwanted goods or services[13] or when consumers buy defective goods or services on credit but are unable to assert against the creditor claims or defenses arising from the transaction.[14] Unwarranted health and safety risks may also support a finding of unfairness.[15] Emotional impact and other more subjective types of harm, on the other hand, will not ordinarily make

---

7 *FTC v. Raladam Co.*, 283 U.S. 643, 648 (1931). *See also FTC v. R.F. Keppel & Bro.*, 291 U.S. 304, 310 (1934) ("Neither the language nor the history of the Act suggests that Congress intended to confine the forbidden methods to fixed and unyielding categories").

8 The Commission's actual statement of the criteria was as follows:

> (1) whether the practice, without necessarily having been previously considered unlawful, offends public policy as it has been established by statutes, the common law, or otherwise-whether, in other words, it is within at least the penumbra of some common-law, statutory, or other established concept of unfairness; (2) whether it is immoral, unethical, oppressive, or unscrupulous; (3) whether it causes substantial injury to consumers (or competitors or other businessmen).

Statement of Basis and Purpose, Unfair or Deceptive Advertising and Labeling of Cigarettes in Relation to the Health Hazards of Smoking, 29 Fed. Reg. 8324, 8355 (1964).

9 *FTC v. Sperry & Hutchinson Co.*, 405 U.S. 233, 244–45 n.5 (1972). The Circuit Courts have concluded that this quotation reflected the Supreme Court's own views. *See Spiegel, Inc. v. FTC*, 540 F.2d 287, 293 n.8 (7th Cir. 1976); *Heater v. FTC*, 503 F.2d 321, 323 (9th Cir. 1974). The application of these factors to antitrust matters is beyond the scope of this letter.

10 These standards for unfairness are generally applicable to both advertising and non-advertising cases.

11 83 Cong. Rec. 3255 (1938) (remarks of Senator Wheeler).

12 An injury may be sufficiently substantial, however, if it does a small harm to a large number of people, or if it raises a significant risk of concrete harm.

13 *See, e.g., Holland Furnace Co. v. FTC*, 295 F.2d 302 (7th Cir. 1961) (seller's servicemen dismantled home furnaces and then refused to reassemble them until the consumers had agreed to buy services or replacement parts).

14 Statement of Basis and Purpose, Preservation of Consumers' Claims and Defenses, 40 Fed. Reg. 53,506, 53522–23 (1975).

15 For an example *see Philip Morris, Inc.*, 82 F.T.C. 16 (1973) (respondent had distributed free-sample razor blades in such a way that they could come into the hands of small children) (consent agreement). Of course, if matters involving health and safety are within the primary jurisdiction of some other agency, Commission action might not be appropriate.

a practice unfair. Thus, for example, the Commission will not seek to ban an advertisement merely because it offends the tastes or social beliefs of some viewers, as has been suggested in some of the comments.[16]

Second, the injury must not be outweighed by any offsetting consumer or competitive benefits that the sales practice also produces. Most business practices entail a mixture of economic and other costs and benefits for purchasers. A seller's failure to present complex technical data on his product may lessen a consumer's ability to choose, for example, but may also reduce the initial price he must pay for the article. The Commission is aware of these tradeoffs and will not find that a practice unfairly injures consumers unless it is injurious in its net effects.[17] The Commission also takes account of the various costs that a remedy would entail. These include not only the costs to the parties directly before the agency, but also the burdens on society in general in the form of increased paperwork, increased regulatory burdens on the flow of information, reduced incentives to innovation and capital formation, and similar matters.[18] Finally, the injury must be one which consumers could not reasonably have avoided.[19] Normally we expect the marketplace to be self-correcting, and we rely on consumer choice-the ability of individual consumers to make their own private purchasing decisions without regulatory intervention—to govern the market. We anticipate that consumers will survey the available alternatives, choose those that are most desirable, and avoid those that are inadequate or unsatisfactory. However, it has long been recognized that certain types of sales techniques may prevent consumers from effectively making their own decisions, and that corrective action may then become necessary. Most of the Commission's unfairness matters are brought under these circumstances. They are brought, not to second-guess the wisdom of particular consumer decisions, but rather to halt some form of seller behavior that unreasonably creates or takes advantage of an obstacle to the free exercise of consumer decisionmaking.[20]

Sellers may adopt a number of practices that unjustifiably hinder such free market decisions. Some may withhold or fail to generate critical price or performance data, for example, leaving buyers with insufficient information for informed comparisons.[21] Some may engage in overt coercion, as by dismantling a home appliance for "inspection" and refusing to reassemble it until a service contract is signed.[22] And some may exercise undue influence over highly susceptible classes of purchasers, as by

---

16 *See, e.g.,* comments of Association of National Advertisers, Committee Print at 120. In an extreme case, however, where tangible injury could be clearly demonstrated, emotional effects might possibly be considered as the basis for a finding of unfairness. *Cf.* 15 U.S.C. 1692 *et seq.* (Fair Debt Collection Practices Act) (banning, e.g., harassing late-night telephone calls).

17 *See Pftzer, Inc.*, 81 F.T.C. 23, 62–63 n. 13 (1972); Statement of Basis and Purpose, Disclosure Requirements and Prohibitions Concerning Franchising and Business Opportunity Ventures, 43 Fed. Reg. 59614, 59636 n.95 (1978).

When making this determination the Commission may refer to existing public policies for help in ascertaining the existence of consumer injury and the relative weights that should be assigned to various costs and benefits. The role of public policy in unfairness determinations will be discussed more generally below.

18 For example, when the Commission promulgated the Holder Rule it anticipated an overall lowering of economic costs to society because the rule gave creditors the incentive to police sellers, thus increasing the likelihood that those selling defective goods or services would either improve their practices or leave the marketplace when they could not obtain financing. These benefits, in the Commission's judgment, outweighed any costs to creditors and sellers occasioned by the rule. See Statement of Basis and Purpose, Preservation of Consumers' Claims and Defenses, 40 Fed. Reg. 53506, 53522–23 (1975).

19 In some senses any injury can be avoided—for example, by hiring independent experts to test all products in advance, or by private legal actions for damages-but these courses may be too expensive to be practicable for individual consumers to pursue.

20 This emphasis on informed consumer choice has commonly been adopted in other statutes as well. *See, e.g.,* Declaration of Policy, Fair Packaging and Labeling Act, 15 U.S.C. 1451 ("Informed consumers are essential to the fair and efficient functioning of a free market economy".)

21 *See, e.g.,* Statement of Basis and Purpose, Labeling and Advertising of Home Insulation, 44 Fed. Reg. 50218, 50222–23 (1979); Statement of Basis and Purpose, Posting of Minimum Octane Numbers on Gasoline Dispensing Pumps, 36 Fed. Reg. 23871,23882 (1971). *See also Virginia State Board of Pharmacy v. Virginia Citizens Consumer Council,* Inc., 425 U.S. 748 (1976).

22 *See Holland Furnace Co. v. ETC,* 295 F.2d 302 (7th Cir. 1961); *cf. Arthur Murray Studio, Inc. v.* EW, 458 F.2d 622 (5th Cir. 1972) (emotional high-pressure sales tactics, using teams of salesmen who refused to let the customer leave

promoting fraudulent "cures" to seriously ill cancer patients.[23] Each of these practices undermines an essential precondition to a free and informed consumer transaction, and, in turn, to a well-functioning market. Each of them is therefore properly banned as an unfair practice under the FTC Act.[24]

Violation of public policy

The second *S & H* standard asks whether the conduct violates public policy as it has been established by statute, common law, industry practice, or otherwise. This criterion may be applied in two different ways. It may be used to test the validity and strength of the evidence of consumer injury, or, less often, it may be cited for a dispositive legislative or judicial determination that such injury is present.

Although public policy was listed by the *S & H* Court as a separate consideration, it is used most frequently by the Commission as a means of providing additional evidence on the degree of consumer injury caused by specific practices. To be sure, most Commission actions are brought to redress relatively clear-cut injuries, and those determinations are based, in large part, on objective economic analysis. As we have indicated before, the Commission believes that considerable attention should be devoted to the analysis of whether substantial net harm has occurred, not only because that is part of the unfairness test, but also because the focus on injury is the best way to ensure that the Commission acts responsibly and uses its resources wisely. Nonetheless, the Commission wishes to emphasize the importance of examining outside statutory policies and established judicial principles for assistance in helping the agency ascertain whether a particular form of conduct does in fact tend to harm consumers. Thus the agency has referred to First Amendment decisions upholding consumers' rights to receive information, for example, to confirm that restrictions on advertising tend unfairly to hinder the informed exercise of consumer choice.[25]

Conversely, statutes or other sources of public policy may affirmatively allow for a practice that the Commission tentatively views as unfair. The existence of such policies will then give the agency reason to reconsider its assessment of whether the practice is actually injurious in its net effects.[26] In other situations there may be no clearly established public policies, or the policies may even be in conflict. While that does not necessarily preclude the Commission from taking action if there is strong evidence of net consumer injury, it does underscore the desirability of carefully examining public policies in all instances.[27] In any event, whenever objective evidence of consumer injury is difficult to obtain, the need to identify and assess all relevant public policies assumes increased importance.

Sometimes public policy will independently support a Commission action. This occurs when the policy is so clear that it will entirely determine the question of consumer injury, so there is little need for separate analysis by the Commission. In these cases the legislature or court, in announcing the policy, has already determined that such injury does exist and thus it need not be expressly proved in each

---

the room until a contract was signed). *See also* Statement of Basis and Purpose, Cooling-Off Period for Door-to-Door Sales, 37 Fed. Reg. 22934, 22937–38 (1972).

[23] *See, e.g., Travel King*, Inc., 86 F.T.C. 715, 774 (1975). The practices in this rase primarily involved deception, but the Commission noted the special susceptibilities of such patients as one reason for banning the ads entirely rather than relying on the remedy of fuller disclosure. The Commission recognizes that "undue influence" in advertising and promotion is difficult to define, and therefore exercises its authority here only with respect to substantial coercive-like practices and significant consumer injury.

[24] These few examples are not exhaustive, but the general direction they illustrate is clear. As the Commission stated in promulgating its Eyeglasses Rule, the inquiry should begin, at least, by asking "whether the acts or practices at issue inhibit the functioning of the competitive market and whether consumers are harmed thereby." Statement of Basis and Purpose, Advertising of Ophthalmic Goods and Services, 43 Fed. Reg. 23992,24001 (1978).

[25] *See* Statement of Basis and Purpose, Advertising of ophthalmic Goods and Services, 43 Fed. Reg. 23992,24001 (1978), *citing Virginia State Board of Pharmacy v. Virginia Citizens Consumer Council*, 425 U.S. 748 (1976).

[26] *Cf.* Statement of Basis and Purpose, Advertising of ophthalmic Goods and Services, *supra; see also n.17 supra.*

[27] The analysis of external public policies is extremely valuable but not always definitive. The legislative history of Section 5 recognizes that new forms of unfair business practices may arise which, at the time of the Commission's involvement, have not yet been generally proscribed. See page 4, *supra*. Thus a review of public policies established independently of Commission action may not be conclusive in determining whether the challenged practices should be prohibited or otherwise restricted. At the same time, however, we emphasize the importance of examining public policies, since a thorough analysis can serve as an important check on the overall reasonableness of the Commission's actions.

instance. An example of this approach arose in a case involving a mail-order firm.[28] There the Commission was persuaded by an analogy to the due-process clause that it was unfair for the firm to bring collection suits in a forum that was unreasonably difficult for the defendants to reach. In a similar case the Commission applied the statutory policies of the Uniform Commercial Code to require that various automobile manufacturers and their distributors refund to their customers any surplus money that was realized after they repossessed and resold their customer's cars.[29] The Commission acts on such a basis only where the public policy is suitable for administrative enforcement by this agency, however. Thus it turned down a petition for a rule to require fuller disclosure of aerosol propellants, reasoning that the subject of fluorocarbon safety was currently under study by other scientific and legislative bodies with more appropriate expertise or jurisdiction over the subject.[30]

To the extent that the Commission relies heavily on public policy to support a finding of unfairness, the policy should be clear and well-established. In other words, the policy should be declared or embodied in formal sources such as statutes, judicial decisions, or the Constitution as interpreted by the courts, rather than being ascertained from the general sense of the national values. The policy should likewise be one that is widely shared, and not the isolated decision of a single state or a single court. If these two tests are not met the policy cannot be considered as an "established" public policy for purposes of the *S & H* criterion. The Commission would then act only on the basis of convincing independent evidence that the practice was distorting the operation of the market and thereby causing unjustified consumer injury.

Unethical or unscrupulous conduct

Finally, the third *S & H* standard asks whether the conduct was immoral, unethical, oppressive, or unscrupulous. This test was presumably included in order to be sure of reaching all the purposes of the underlying statute, which forbids "unfair" acts or practices. It would therefore allow the Commission to reach conduct that violates generally recognized standards of business ethics. The test has proven, however, to be largely duplicative. Conduct that is truly unethical or unscrupulous will almost always injure consumers or violate public policy as well. The Commission has therefore never relied on the third element of *S & H* as an independent basis for a finding of unfairness, and it will act in the future only on the basis of the first two.

---

28 *Spiegel, Inc. v. FTC,* 540 F.2d 287 (7th Cir. 1976). In this case the Commission did inquire into the extent of the resulting consumer injury, but under the rationale involved it presumably need not have done so. *See also FTC v. R.F. Keppel & Bro.,* 291 U.S. 304 (1934) (firm had gained a marketing advantage by selling goods through a lottery technique that violated state gambling policies); *cf. Simeon Management Corp.,* 87 F.T.C. 1184, 1231 (1976), *aff'd,* 579 F.2d 1137 (9th Cir. 1978) (firm advertised weight-loss program that used a drug which could not itself be advertised under FDA regulations) (alternative ground). Since these public-policy cases are based on legislative determinations, rather than on a judgment within the Commission's area of special economic expertise, it is appropriate that they can reach a relatively wider range of consumer injuries than just those associated with impaired consumer choice.

29 A surplus occurs when a repossessed car is resold for more than the amount owed by the debtor plus the expenses of repossession and resale. The law of 49 states requires that creditors refund surpluses when they occur, but if creditors systematically refuse to honor this obligation, consumers have no practical way to discover that they have been deprived of money to which they are entitled. *See Ford Motor Co.,* 94 F.T.C. 564, 618 (1979) *appeal pending,* Nos. 79–7649 and 79–7654 (9th Cir.); *Ford Motor Co.,93* F.T.C. 402 (1979) (consent decree); *General Motors Corp.,* D. 9074 (Feb., 1980) (consent decree). By these latter two consent agreements the Commission, because of its unfairness jurisdiction, has been able to secure more than $2 million for consumers allegedly deprived of surpluses to which they were entitled.

30 See Letter from John F. Dugan, Acting Secretary, to Action on Smoking and Health (January 13, 1977). *See* also letter from Charles A. Tobin, Secretary, to Prof. Page and Mr. Young (September 17, 1973) (denying petition to exercise § 6(b) subpoena powers to obtain consumer complaint information from cosmetic firms and then to transmit the data to FDA for that agency's enforcement purposes).

We hope this letter has given you the information that you require. Please do not hesitate to call if we can be of any further assistance. With best regards,

/s/Michael Pertschuk Chairman
/s/Paul Rand Dixon Commissioner
/s/David A. Clanton Commissioner
/s/Robert Pitofsky Commissioner
/s/Patricia P. Bailey Commissioner

CONSUMER FINANCIAL PROTECTION ACT (CFPA)

(Selected Selections)

12 U.S.C.A. §§ 5481 et seq.

Summary

Subtitle A—Bureau of Consumer Financial Protection
Subtitle B—General Powers of the Bureau
Subtitle C—Specific Bureau Authorities
Subtitle D—Preservation of State Law
Subtitle E—Enforcement Powers
Subtitle F—Transfer of Functions and Personnel; Transition Provisions
Subtitle G—Regulatory Improvements
Subtitle H—Conforming Amendments

Table of Sections

§ 5481 [CFPA Act § 1002]. Definitions

(a) Authority. Except as otherwise provided in this subchapter, for purposes of this subchapter, the following definitions shall apply:

(1) Affiliate

The term "affiliate" means any person that controls, is controlled by, or is under common control with another person.

(2) Bureau

The term "Bureau" means the Bureau of Consumer Financial Protection.

(3) Business of insurance

The term "business of insurance" means the writing of insurance or the reinsuring of risks by an insurer, including all acts necessary to such writing or reinsuring and the activities relating to the writing of insurance or the reinsuring of risks conducted by persons who act as, or are, officers, directors, agents, or employees of insurers or who are other persons authorized to act on behalf of such persons.

(4) Consumer

The term "consumer" means an individual or an agent, trustee, or representative acting on behalf of an individual.

(5) Consumer financial product or service

The term "consumer financial product or service" means any financial product or service that is described in one or more categories under—

(A) paragraph (15) and is offered or provided for use by consumers primarily for personal, family, or household purposes; or

(B) clause (i), (iii), (ix), or (x) of paragraph (15)(A), and is delivered, offered, or provided in connection with a consumer financial product or service referred to in subparagraph (A).

(6) Covered person

The term "covered person" means—

(A) any person that engages in offering or providing a consumer financial product or service; and

(B) any affiliate of a person described in subparagraph (A) if such affiliate acts as a service provider to such person.

(7) Credit

The term "credit" means the right granted by a person to a consumer to defer payment of a debt, incur debt and defer its payment, or purchase property or services and defer payment for such purchase.

(8) Deposit-taking activity

The term "deposit-taking activity" means—

(A) the acceptance of deposits, maintenance of deposit accounts, or the provision of services related to the acceptance of deposits or the maintenance of deposit accounts;

(B) the acceptance of funds, the provision of other services related to the acceptance of funds, or the maintenance of member share accounts by a credit union; or

(C) the receipt of funds or the equivalent thereof, as the Bureau may determine by rule or order, received or held by a covered person (or an agent for a covered person) for the purpose of facilitating a payment or transferring funds or value of funds between a consumer and a third party.

(9) Designated transfer date

The term "designated transfer date" means the date established under section 5582 of this title.

(10) Director

The term "Director" means the Director of the Bureau.

(11) Electronic conduit services

The term "electronic conduit services"—

(A) means the provision, by a person, of electronic data transmission, routing, intermediate or transient storage, or connections to a telecommunications system or network; and

(B) does not include a person that provides electronic conduit services if, when providing such services, the person—

(i) selects or modifies the content of the electronic data;

(ii) transmits, routes, stores, or provides connections for electronic data, including financial data, in a manner that such financial data is differentiated from other types of data of the same form that such person transmits, routes, or stores, or with respect to which, provides connections; or

(iii) is a payee, payor, correspondent, or similar party to a payment transaction with a consumer.

(12) Enumerated consumer laws

Except as otherwise specifically provided in section 5519 of this title, subtitle G or subtitle H, the term "enumerated consumer laws" means—

(A) the Alternative Mortgage Transaction Parity Act of 1982 (12 U.S.C. 3801 et seq.);

(B) the Consumer Leasing Act of 1976 (15 U.S.C. 1667 et seq.);

(C) the Electronic Fund Transfer Act (15 U.S.C. 1693 et seq.), except with respect to section 920 of that Act;

(D) the Equal Credit Opportunity Act (15 U.S.C. 1691 et seq.);

(E) the Fair Credit Billing Act (15 U.S.C. 1666 et seq.);

(F) the Fair Credit Reporting Act (15 U.S.C. 1681 et seq.), except with respect to sections 615(e) and 628 of that Act (15 U.S.C. 1681m(e), 1681w);

(G) the Home Owners[1] Protection Act of 1998 (12 U.S.C. 4901 et seq.);

(H) the Fair Debt Collection Practices Act (15 U.S.C. 1692 et seq.);

(I) subsections (b) through (f) of section 43 of the Federal Deposit Insurance Act (12 U.S.C. 1831t(c)–(f))[2];

(J) sections 502 through 509 of the Gramm-Leach-Bliley Act (15 U.S.C. 6802–6809) except for section 505 as it applies to section 501(b);

(K) the Home Mortgage Disclosure Act of 1975 (12 U.S.C. 2801 et seq.);

(L) the Home Ownership and Equity Protection Act of 1994 (15 U.S.C. 1601 note);

(M) the Real Estate Settlement Procedures Act of 1974 (12 U.S.C. 2601 et seq.);

(N) the S.A.F.E. Mortgage Licensing Act of 2008 (12 U.S.C. 5101 et seq.);

(O) the Truth in Lending Act (15 U.S.C. 1601 et seq.);

(P) the Truth in Savings Act (12 U.S.C. 4301 et seq.);

(Q) section 626 of the Omnibus Appropriations Act, 2009 (Public Law 111–8); and

(R) the Interstate Land Sales Full Disclosure Act (15 U.S.C. 1701).

(13) Fair lending

The term "fair lending" means fair, equitable, and nondiscriminatory access to credit for consumers.

(14) Federal consumer financial law

The term "Federal consumer financial law" means the provisions of this title, the enumerated consumer laws, the laws for which authorities are transferred under subtitles F and H, and any rule or order prescribed by the Bureau under this subchapter, an enumerated consumer law, or pursuant to the authorities transferred under subtitles F and H. The term does not include the Federal Trade Commission Act.

(15) Financial product or service

(A) In general

The term "financial product or service" means—

---

1 So in original. Probably should be "Homeowners".

2 So in original.

(i) extending credit and servicing loans, including acquiring, purchasing, selling, brokering, or other extensions of credit (other than solely extending commercial credit to a person who originates consumer credit transactions);

(ii) extending or brokering leases of personal or real property that are the functional equivalent of purchase finance arrangements, if—

(I) the lease is on a non-operating basis;

(II) the initial term of the lease is at least 90 days; and

(III) in the case of a lease involving real property, at the inception of the initial lease, the transaction is intended to result in ownership of the leased property to be transferred to the lessee, subject to standards prescribed by the Bureau;

(iii) providing real estate settlement services, except such services excluded under subparagraph (C), or performing appraisals of real estate or personal property;

(iv) engaging in deposit-taking activities, transmitting or exchanging funds, or otherwise acting as a custodian of funds or any financial instrument for use by or on behalf of a consumer;

(v) selling, providing, or issuing stored value or payment instruments, except that, in the case of a sale of, or transaction to reload, stored value, only if the seller exercises substantial control over the terms or conditions of the stored value provided to the consumer where, for purposes of this clause—

(I) a seller shall not be found to exercise substantial control over the terms or conditions of the stored value if the seller is not a party to the contract with the consumer for the stored value product, and another person is principally responsible for establishing the terms or conditions of the stored value; and

(II) advertising the nonfinancial goods or services of the seller on the stored value card or device is not in itself an exercise of substantial control over the terms or conditions;

(vi) providing check cashing, check collection, or check guaranty services;

(vii) providing payments or other financial data processing products or services to a consumer by any technological means, including processing or storing financial or banking data for any payment instrument, or through any payments systems or network used for processing payments data, including payments made through an online banking system or mobile telecommunications network, except that a person shall not be deemed to be a covered person with respect to financial data processing solely because the person—

(I) is a merchant, retailer, or seller of any nonfinancial good or service who engages in financial data processing by transmitting or storing payments data about a consumer exclusively for purpose of initiating payments instructions by the consumer to pay such person for the purchase of, or to complete a commercial transaction for, such nonfinancial good or service sold directly by such person to the consumer; or

(II) provides access to a host server to a person for purposes of enabling that person to establish and maintain a website;

(viii) providing financial advisory services (other than services relating to securities provided by a person regulated by the Commission or a person regulated by a State securities Commission, but only to the extent that such person acts in a regulated capacity) to consumers on individual financial matters or relating to proprietary financial products or services (other than by publishing any bona fide newspaper, news magazine, or business or financial publication of general and regular circulation, including publishing market data, news, or data analytics or investment information or recommendations that are not tailored to the individual needs of a particular consumer), including—

(I) providing credit counseling to any consumer; and

(II) providing services to assist a consumer with debt management or debt settlement, modifying the terms of any extension of credit, or avoiding foreclosure;

(ix) collecting, analyzing, maintaining, or providing consumer report information or other account information, including information relating to the credit history of consumers, used or expected to be used in connection with any decision regarding the offering or provision of a consumer financial product or service, except to the extent that—

(I) a person—

(aa) collects, analyzes, or maintains information that relates solely to the transactions between a consumer and such person;

(bb) provides the information described in item (aa) to an affiliate of such person; or

(cc) provides information that is used or expected to be used solely in any decision regarding the offering or provision of a product or service that is not a consumer financial product or service, including a decision for employment, government licensing, or a residential lease or tenancy involving a consumer; and

(II) the information described in subclause (I)(aa) is not used by such person or affiliate in connection with any decision regarding the offering or provision of a consumer financial product or service to the consumer, other than credit described in section 5517(a)(2)(A) of this title;

(x) collecting debt related to any consumer financial product or service; and

(xi) such other financial product or service as may be defined by the Bureau, by regulation, for purposes of this subchapter, if the Bureau finds that such financial product or service is—

(I) entered into or conducted as a subterfuge or with a purpose to evade any Federal consumer financial law; or

(II) permissible for a bank or for a financial holding company to offer or to provide under any provision of a Federal law or regulation applicable to a bank or a financial holding company, and has, or likely will have, a material impact on consumers.

(B) Rule of construction

(i) In general

For purposes of subparagraph (A)(xi)(II), and subject to clause (ii) of this subparagraph, the following activities provided to a covered person shall not, for purposes of this subchapter, be considered incidental or complementary to a financial activity permissible for a financial holding company to engage in under any provision of a Federal law or regulation applicable to a financial holding company:

(I) Providing information products or services to a covered person for identity authentication.

(II) Providing information products or services for fraud or identify theft detection, prevention, or investigation.

(III) Providing document retrieval or delivery services.

(IV) Providing public records information retrieval.

(V) Providing information products or services for anti-money laundering activities.

(ii) Limitation

Nothing in clause (i) may be construed as modifying or limiting the authority of the Bureau to exercise any—

(I) examination or enforcement powers authority under this subchapter with respect to a covered person or service provider engaging in an activity described in subparagraph (A)(ix); or

(II) powers authorized by this subchapter to prescribe rules, issue orders, or take other actions under any enumerated consumer law or law for which the authorities are transferred under subtitle F or H.

(C) Exclusions

The term "financial product or service" does not include—

(i) the business of insurance; or

(ii) electronic conduit services.

(16) Foreign exchange

The term "foreign exchange" means the exchange, for compensation, of currency of the United States or of a foreign government for currency of another government.

(17) Insured credit union

The term "insured credit union" has the same meaning as in section 1752 of this title.

(18) Payment instrument

The term "payment instrument" means a check, draft, warrant, money order, traveler's check, electronic instrument, or other instrument, payment of funds, or monetary value (other than currency).

(19) Person

The term "person" means an individual, partnership, company, corporation, association (incorporated or unincorporated), trust, estate, cooperative organization, or other entity.

(20) Person regulated by the Commodity Futures Trading Commission

The term "person regulated by the Commodity Futures Trading Commission" means any person that is registered, or required by statute or regulation to be registered, with the Commodity Futures Trading Commission, but only to the extent that the activities of such person are subject to the jurisdiction of the Commodity Futures Trading Commission under the Commodity Exchange Act.

(21) Person regulated by the Commission

The term "person regulated by the Commission" means a person who is—

(A) a broker or dealer that is required to be registered under the Securities Exchange Act of 1934;

(B) an investment adviser that is registered under the Investment Advisers Act of 1940;

(C) an investment company that is required to be registered under the Investment Company Act of 1940, and any company that has elected to be regulated as a business development company under that Act;

(D) a national securities exchange that is required to be registered under the Securities Exchange Act of 1934;

(E) a transfer agent that is required to be registered under the Securities Exchange Act of 1934;

(F) a clearing corporation that is required to be registered under the Securities Exchange Act of 1934;

(G) any self-regulatory organization that is required to be registered with the Commission;

(H) any nationally recognized statistical rating organization that is required to be registered with the Commission;

(I) any securities information processor that is required to be registered with the Commission;

(J) any municipal securities dealer that is required to be registered with the Commission;

(K) any other person that is required to be registered with the Commission under the Securities Exchange Act of 1934; and

(L) any employee, agent, or contractor acting on behalf of, registered with, or providing services to, any person described in any of subparagraphs (A) through (K), but only to the extent that any person described in any of subparagraphs (A) through (K), or the employee, agent, or contractor of such person, acts in a regulated capacity.

(22) Person regulated by a State insurance regulator

The term "person regulated by a State insurance regulator" means any person that is engaged in the business of insurance and subject to regulation by any State insurance regulator, but only to the extent that such person acts in such capacity.

(23) Person that performs income tax preparation activities for consumers

The term "person that performs income tax preparation activities for consumers" means—

(A) any tax return preparer (as defined in section 7701(a)(36) of the Internal Revenue Code of 1986), regardless of whether compensated, but only to the extent that the person acts in such capacity;

(B) any person regulated by the Secretary under section 330 of Title 31, but only to the extent that the person acts in such capacity; and

(C) any authorized IRS e-file Providers (as defined for purposes of section 7216 of the Internal Revenue Code of 1986), but only to the extent that the person acts in such capacity.

(24) Prudential regulator

The term "prudential regulator" means—

(A) in the case of an insured depository institution or depository institution holding company (as defined in section 3 of the Federal Deposit Insurance Act), or subsidiary of such institution or company, the appropriate Federal banking agency, as that term is defined in section 3 of the Federal Deposit Insurance Act; and

(B) in the case of an insured credit union, the National Credit Union Administration.

(25) Related person

The term "related person"—

(A) shall apply only with respect to a covered person that is not a bank holding company (as that term is defined in section 1841 of this title), credit union, or depository institution;

(B) shall be deemed to mean a covered person for all purposes of any provision of Federal consumer financial law; and

(C) means—

(i) any director, officer, or employee charged with managerial responsibility for, or controlling shareholder of, or agent for, such covered person;

(ii) any shareholder, consultant, joint venture partner, or other person, as determined by the Bureau (by rule or on a case-by-case basis) who materially participates in the conduct of the affairs of such covered person; and

(iii) any independent contractor (including any attorney, appraiser, or accountant) who knowingly or recklessly participates in any—

(I) violation of any provision of law or regulation; or

(II) breach of a fiduciary duty.

(26) Service provider

(A) In general

The term "service provider" means any person that provides a material service to a covered person in connection with the offering or provision by such covered person of a consumer financial product or service, including a person that—

(i) participates in designing, operating, or maintaining the consumer financial product or service; or

(ii) processes transactions relating to the consumer financial product or service (other than unknowingly or incidentally transmitting or processing financial data in a manner that such data is undifferentiated from other types of data of the same form as the person transmits or processes).

(B) Exceptions

The term "service provider" does not include a person solely by virtue of such person offering or providing to a covered person—

(i) a support service of a type provided to businesses generally or a similar ministerial service; or

(ii) time or space for an advertisement for a consumer financial product or service through print, newspaper, or electronic media.

(C) Rule of construction

A person that is a service provider shall be deemed to be a covered person to the extent that such person engages in the offering or provision of its own consumer financial product or service.

(27) State

The term "State" means any State, territory, or possession of the United States, the District of Columbia, the Commonwealth of Puerto Rico, the Commonwealth of the Northern Mariana Islands, Guam, American Samoa, or the United States Virgin Islands or any federally recognized Indian tribe, as defined by the Secretary of the Interior under section 479a–1(a) of Title 25.

(28) Stored value

(A) In general

The term "stored value" means funds or monetary value represented in any electronic format, whether or not specially encrypted, and stored or capable of storage on electronic media in such a way as to be retrievable and transferred electronically, and includes a prepaid debit card or product, or any other similar product, regardless of whether the amount of the funds or monetary value may be increased or reloaded.

(B) Exclusion

Notwithstanding subparagraph (A), the term "stored value" does not include a special purpose card or certificate, which shall be defined for purposes of this paragraph as funds or monetary value represented in any electronic format, whether or not specially encrypted, that is—

(i) issued by a merchant, retailer, or other seller of nonfinancial goods or services;

(ii) redeemable only for transactions with the merchant, retailer, or seller of nonfinancial goods or services or with an affiliate of such person, which affiliate itself is a merchant, retailer, or seller of nonfinancial goods or services;

(iii) issued in a specified amount that, except in the case of a card or product used solely for telephone services, may not be increased or reloaded;

(iv) purchased on a prepaid basis in exchange for payment; and

(v) honored upon presentation to such merchant, retailer, or seller of nonfinancial goods or services or an affiliate of such person, which affiliate itself is a merchant, retailer, or seller of nonfinancial goods or services, only for any nonfinancial goods or services.

(29) Transmitting or exchanging funds

The term "transmitting or exchanging funds" means receiving currency, monetary value, or payment instruments from a consumer for the purpose of exchanging or transmitting the same by any means, including transmission by wire, facsimile, electronic transfer, courier, the Internet, or through bill payment services or through other businesses that facilitate third-party transfers within the United States or to or from the United States.

PART A—BUREAU OF CONSUMER FINANCIAL PROTECTION

§ 5491 [CFPA Act § 1011]. Establishment of the Bureau of Consumer Financial Protection

(a) Bureau established

There is established in the Federal Reserve System, an independent bureau to be known as the "Bureau of Consumer Financial Protection", which shall regulate the offering and provision of consumer financial products or services under the Federal consumer financial laws. The Bureau shall be considered an Executive agency, as defined in section 105 of Title 5. Except as otherwise provided expressly by law, all Federal laws dealing with public or Federal contracts, property, works, officers, employees, budgets, or funds, including the provisions of chapters 5 and 7 of Title 5, shall apply to the exercise of the powers of the Bureau.

(b) Director and Deputy Director

(1) In general

There is established the position of the Director, who shall serve as the head of the Bureau.

(2) Appointment

Subject to paragraph (3), the Director shall be appointed by the President, by and with the advice and consent of the Senate.

(3) Qualification

The President shall nominate the Director from among individuals who are citizens of the United States.

(4) Compensation

The Director shall be compensated at the rate prescribed for level II of the Executive Schedule under section 5313 of Title 5.

(5) Deputy Director

There is established the position of Deputy Director, who shall—

(A) be appointed by the Director; and

(B) serve as acting Director in the absence or unavailability of the Director.

(c) Term

(1) In general

The Director shall serve for a term of 5 years.

(2) Expiration of term

An individual may serve as Director after the expiration of the term for which appointed, until a successor has been appointed and qualified.

(3) Removal for cause

The President may remove the Director for inefficiency, neglect of duty, or malfeasance in office.

(d) Service restriction

No Director or Deputy Director may hold any office, position, or employment in any Federal reserve bank, Federal home loan bank, covered person, or service provider during the period of service of such person as Director or Deputy Director.

(e) Offices

The principal office of the Bureau shall be in the District of Columbia. The Director may establish regional offices of the Bureau, including in cities in which the Federal reserve banks, or branches of such banks, are located, in order to carry out the responsibilities assigned to the Bureau under the Federal consumer financial laws.

§ 5492 [CFPA Act 1012]. Executive and Administrative Powers

(a) Powers of the Bureau

The Bureau is authorized to establish the general policies of the Bureau with respect to all executive and administrative functions, including—

(1) the establishment of rules for conducting the general business of the Bureau, in a manner not inconsistent with this title;

(2) to bind the Bureau and enter into contracts;

(3) directing the establishment and maintenance of divisions or other offices within the Bureau, in order to carry out the responsibilities under the Federal consumer financial laws, and to satisfy the requirements of other applicable law;

(4) to coordinate and oversee the operation of all administrative, enforcement, and research activities of the Bureau;

(5) to adopt and use a seal;

(6) to determine the character of and the necessity for the obligations and expenditures of the Bureau;

(7) the appointment and supervision of personnel employed by the Bureau;

(8) the distribution of business among personnel appointed and supervised by the Director and among administrative units of the Bureau;

(9) the use and expenditure of funds;

(10) implementing the Federal consumer financial laws through rules, orders, guidance, interpretations, statements of policy, examinations, and enforcement actions; and

(11) performing such other functions as may be authorized or required by law.

(b) Delegation of authority

The Director of the Bureau may delegate to any duly authorized employee, representative, or agent any power vested in the Bureau by law.

(c) Autonomy of the Bureau

(1) Coordination with the Board of Governors

Notwithstanding any other provision of law applicable to the supervision or examination of persons with respect to Federal consumer financial laws, the Board of Governors may delegate to the Bureau the authorities to examine persons subject to the jurisdiction of the Board of Governors for compliance with the Federal consumer financial laws.

(2) Autonomy

Notwithstanding the authorities granted to the Board of Governors under the Federal Reserve Act, the Board of Governors may not—

(A) intervene in any matter or proceeding before the Director, including examinations or enforcement actions, unless otherwise specifically provided by law;

(B) appoint, direct, or remove any officer or employee of the Bureau; or

(C) merge or consolidate the Bureau, or any of the functions or responsibilities of the Bureau, with any division or office of the Board of Governors or the Federal reserve banks.

(3) Rules and orders

No rule or order of the Bureau shall be subject to approval or review by the Board of Governors. The Board of Governors may not delay or prevent the issuance of any rule or order of the Bureau.

(4) Recommendations and testimony

No officer or agency of the United States shall have any authority to require the Director or any other officer of the Bureau to submit legislative recommendations, or testimony or comments on legislation, to any officer or agency of the United States for approval, comments, or review prior to the submission of such recommendations, testimony, or comments to the Congress, if such recommendations, testimony, or comments to the Congress include a statement indicating that the views expressed therein are those of the Director or such officer, and do not necessarily reflect the views of the Board of Governors or the President.

(5) Clarification of autonomy of the Bureau in legal proceedings

The Bureau shall not be liable under any provision of law for any action or inaction of the Board of Governors, and the Board of Governors shall not be liable under any provision of law for any action or inaction of the Bureau.

§ 5493 [CFPA Act § 1013]. Administration

(a) Personnel

(1) Appointment

(A) In general

The Director may fix the number of, and appoint and direct, all employees of the Bureau, in accordance with the applicable provisions of Title 5.

(B) Employees of the Bureau

The Director is authorized to employ attorneys, compliance examiners, compliance supervision analysts, economists, statisticians, and other employees as may be deemed necessary to conduct the business of the Bureau. Unless otherwise provided expressly by law, any individual appointed under this section shall be an employee as defined in section 2105 of Title 5 and subject to the provisions of such title and other laws generally applicable to the employees of an Executive agency.

(C) Waiver authority

(i) In general

In making any appointment under subparagraph (A), the Director may waive the requirements of chapter 33 of Title 5, and the regulations implementing such chapter, to the extent necessary to appoint employees on terms and conditions that are consistent with those set forth in section 11(1) of the Federal Reserve Act (12 U.S.C. 248(1)), while providing for—

(I) fair, credible, and transparent methods of establishing qualification requirements for, recruitment for, and appointments to positions;

(II) fair and open competition and equitable treatment in the consideration and selection of individuals to positions;

(III) fair, credible, and transparent methods of assigning, reassigning, detailing, transferring, and promoting employees.

(ii) Veterans preferences

In implementing this subparagraph, the Director shall comply with the provisions of section 2302(b)(11), regarding veterans' preference requirements, in a manner consistent with that in which such provisions are applied under chapter 33 of Title 5. The authority under this subparagraph to waive the requirements of that chapter 33 shall expire 5 years after July 21, 2010.

(2) Compensation

Notwithstanding any otherwise applicable provision of Title 5 concerning compensation, including the provisions of chapter 51 and chapter 53, the following provisions shall apply with respect to employees of the Bureau:

(A) The rates of basic pay for all employees of the Bureau may be set and adjusted by the Director.

(B) The Director shall at all times provide compensation (including benefits) to each class of employees that, at a minimum, are comparable to the compensation and benefits then being provided by the Board of Governors for the corresponding class of employees.

(C) All such employees shall be compensated (including benefits) on terms and conditions that are consistent with the terms and conditions set forth in section 248(*l*) of this title.

(3) Bureau participation in Federal Reserve System Retirement Plan and Federal Reserve System Thrift Plan

(A) Employee election

Employees appointed to the Bureau may elect to participate in either—

(i) both the Federal Reserve System Retirement Plan and the Federal Reserve System Thrift Plan, under the same terms on which such participation is offered to employees of the Board of Governors who participate in such plans and under the terms and conditions specified under section 5584(i)(1)(C) of this title; or

(ii) the Civil Service Retirement System under chapter 83 of Title 5 or the Federal Employees Retirement System under chapter 84 of Title 5, if previously covered under one of those Federal employee retirement systems.

(B) Election period

Bureau employees shall make an election under this paragraph not later than 1 year after the date of appointment by, or transfer under part F to, the Bureau. Participation in, and benefit accruals under, any other retirement plan established or maintained by the Federal Government shall end not later than the date on which participation in, and benefit accruals under, the Federal Reserve System Retirement Plan and Federal Reserve System Thrift Plan begin.

(C) Employer contribution

The Bureau shall pay an employer contribution to the Federal Reserve System Retirement Plan, in the amount established as an employer contribution under the Federal Employees Retirement System, as established under chapter 84 of Title 5 for each Bureau employee who elects to participate in the Federal Reserve System Retirement Plan. The Bureau shall pay an employer contribution to the Federal Reserve System Thrift Plan for each Bureau employee who elects to participate in such plan, as required under the terms of such plan.

(D) Controlled group status

The Bureau is the same employer as the Federal Reserve System (as comprised of the Board of Governors and each of the 12 Federal reserve banks prior to July 21, 2010) for purposes of subsections (b), (c), (m), and (*o*) of section 414 of Title 26.

(4) Labor-management relations

Chapter 71 of Title 5 shall apply to the Bureau and the employees of the Bureau.

(5) Agency ombudsman

(A) Establishment required

Not later than 180 days after the designated transfer date, the Bureau shall appoint an ombudsman.

(B) Duties of ombudsman

The ombudsman appointed in accordance with subparagraph (A) shall—

(i) act as a liaison between the Bureau and any affected person with respect to any problem that such party may have in dealing with the Bureau, resulting from the regulatory activities of the Bureau; and

(ii) assure that safeguards exist to encourage complainants to come forward and preserve confidentiality.

(b) Specific functional units

(1) Research

The Director shall establish a unit whose functions shall include researching, analyzing, and reporting on—

(A) developments in markets for consumer financial products or services, including market areas of alternative consumer financial products or services with high growth rates and areas of risk to consumers;

(B) access to fair and affordable credit for traditionally underserved communities;

(C) consumer awareness, understanding, and use of disclosures and communications regarding consumer financial products or services;

(D) consumer awareness and understanding of costs, risks, and benefits of consumer financial products or services;

(E) consumer behavior with respect to consumer financial products or services, including performance on mortgage loans; and

(F) experiences of traditionally underserved consumers, including un-banked and under-banked consumers.

(2) Community affairs

The Director shall establish a unit whose functions shall include providing information, guidance, and technical assistance regarding the offering and provision of consumer financial products or services to traditionally underserved consumers and communities.

(3) Collecting and tracking complaints

(A) In general

The Director shall establish a unit whose functions shall include establishing a single, toll-free telephone number, a website, and a database or utilizing an existing database to facilitate the centralized collection of, monitoring of, and response to consumer complaints regarding consumer financial products or services. The Director shall coordinate with the Federal Trade Commission or other Federal agencies to route complaints to such agencies, where appropriate.

(B) Routing calls to States

To the extent practicable, State agencies may receive appropriate complaints from the systems established under subparagraph (A), if—

(i) the State agency system has the functional capacity to receive calls or electronic reports routed by the Bureau systems;

(ii) the State agency has satisfied any conditions of participation in the system that the Bureau may establish, including treatment of personally identifiable information and sharing of information on complaint resolution or related compliance procedures and resources; and

(iii) participation by the State agency includes measures necessary to provide for protection of personally identifiable information that conform to the standards for protection of the confidentiality of personally identifiable information and for data integrity and security that apply to the Federal agencies described in subparagraph (D).

(C) Reports to the Congress

The Director shall present an annual report to Congress not later than March 31 of each year on the complaints received by the Bureau in the prior year regarding consumer financial products and services. Such report shall include information and analysis about complaint numbers, complaint types, and, where applicable, information about resolution of complaints.

(D) Data sharing required

To facilitate preparation of the reports required under subparagraph (C), supervision and enforcement activities, and monitoring of the market for consumer financial products and services, the Bureau shall share consumer complaint information with prudential regulators, the Federal Trade Commission, other Federal agencies, and State agencies, subject to the standards applicable to Federal agencies for protection of the confidentiality of personally identifiable information and for data security and integrity. The prudential regulators, the Federal Trade Commission, and other Federal agencies shall share data relating to consumer complaints regarding consumer financial products and services with the Bureau, subject to the standards applicable to Federal agencies for protection of confidentiality of personally identifiable information and for data security and integrity.

(c) Office of Fair Lending and Equal Opportunity

(1) Establishment

The Director shall establish within the Bureau the Office of Fair Lending and Equal Opportunity.

(2) Functions

The Office of Fair Lending and Equal Opportunity shall have such powers and duties as the Director may delegate to the Office, including—

(A) providing oversight and enforcement of Federal laws intended to ensure the fair, equitable, and nondiscriminatory access to credit for both individuals and communities that are enforced by the Bureau, including the Equal Credit Opportunity Act and the Home Mortgage Disclosure Act;

(B) coordinating fair lending efforts of the Bureau with other Federal agencies and State regulators, as appropriate, to promote consistent, efficient, and effective enforcement of Federal fair lending laws;

(C) working with private industry, fair lending, civil rights, consumer and community advocates on the promotion of fair lending compliance and education; and

(D) providing annual reports to Congress on the efforts of the Bureau to fulfill its fair lending mandate.

(3) Administration of office

There is established the position of Assistant Director of the Bureau for Fair Lending and Equal Opportunity, who—

(A) shall be appointed by the Director; and

(B) shall carry out such duties as the Director may delegate to such Assistant Director.

(d) Office of Financial Education

(1) Establishment

The Director shall establish an Office of Financial Education, which shall be responsible for developing and implementing initiatives intended to educate and empower consumers to make better informed financial decisions.

(2) Other duties

The Office of Financial Education shall develop and implement a strategy to improve the financial literacy of consumers that includes measurable goals and objectives, in consultation with the Financial Literacy and Education Commission, consistent with the National Strategy for Financial Literacy, through activities including providing opportunities for consumers to access—

(A) financial counseling, including community-based financial counseling, where practicable;

(B) information to assist with the evaluation of credit products and the understanding of credit histories and scores;

(C) savings, borrowing, and other services found at mainstream financial institutions;

(D) activities intended to—

(i) prepare the consumer for educational expenses and the submission of financial aid applications, and other major purchases;

(ii) reduce debt; and

(iii) improve the financial situation of the consumer;

(E) assistance in developing long-term savings strategies; and

(F) wealth building and financial services during the preparation process to claim earned income tax credits and Federal benefits.

(3) Coordination

The Office of Financial Education shall coordinate with other units within the Bureau in carrying out its functions, including—

(A) working with the Community Affairs Office to implement the strategy to improve financial literacy of consumers; and

(B) working with the research unit established by the Director to conduct research related to consumer financial education and counseling.

(4) Report

Not later than 24 months after the designated transfer date, and annually thereafter, the Director shall submit a report on its financial literacy activities and strategy to improve financial literacy of consumers to—

(A) the Committee on Banking, Housing, and Urban Affairs of the Senate; and

(B) the Committee on Financial Services of the House of Representatives.

* * *

(e) Office of Service Member Affairs

(1) In general

The Director shall establish an Office of Service Member Affairs, which shall be responsible for developing and implementing initiatives for service members and their families intended to—

(A) educate and empower service members and their families to make better informed decisions regarding consumer financial products and services;

(B) coordinate with the unit of the Bureau established under subsection (b)(3), in order to monitor complaints by service members and their families and responses to those complaints by the Bureau or other appropriate Federal or State agency; and

(C) coordinate efforts among Federal and State agencies, as appropriate, regarding consumer protection measures relating to consumer financial products and services offered to, or used by, service members and their families.

(2) Coordination

(A) Regional services

The Director is authorized to assign employees of the Bureau as may be deemed necessary to conduct the business of the Office of Service Member Affairs, including by establishing and maintaining the functions of the Office in regional offices of the Bureau located near military bases, military treatment facilities, or other similar military facilities.

(B) Agreements

The Director is authorized to enter into memoranda of understanding and similar agreements with the Department of Defense, including any branch or agency as authorized by the department, in order to carry out the business of the Office of Service Member Affairs.

(3) Definition

As used in this subsection, the term "service member" means any member of the United States Armed Forces and any member of the National Guard or Reserves.

(f) Timing

The Office of Fair Lending and Equal Opportunity, the Office of Financial Education, and the Office of Service Member Affairs shall each be established not later than 1 year after the designated transfer date.

(g) Office of Financial Protection for Older Americans

(1) Establishment

Before the end of the 180-day period beginning on the designated transfer date, the Director shall establish the Office of Financial Protection for Older Americans, the functions of which shall include activities designed to facilitate the financial literacy of individuals who have attained the age of 62 years or more (in this subsection, referred to as "seniors") on protection from unfair, deceptive, and abusive practices and on current and future financial choices, including through the dissemination of materials to seniors on such topics.

(2) Assistant director

The Office of Financial Protection for Older Americans (in this subsection referred to as the "Office") shall be headed by an assistant director.

(3) Duties

The Office shall—

(A) develop goals for programs that provide seniors financial literacy and counseling, including programs that—

(i) help seniors recognize warning signs of unfair, deceptive, or abusive practices, protect themselves from such practices;

(ii) provide one-on-one financial counseling on issues including long-term savings and later-life economic security; and

(iii) provide personal consumer credit advocacy to respond to consumer problems caused by unfair, deceptive, or abusive practices;

(B) monitor certifications or designations of financial advisors who advise seniors and alert the Commission and State regulators of certifications or designations that are identified as unfair, deceptive, or abusive;

(C) not later than 18 months after the date of the establishment of the Office, submit to Congress and the Commission any legislative and regulatory recommendations on the best practices for—

(i) disseminating information regarding the legitimacy of certifications of financial advisers who advise seniors;

(ii) methods in which a senior can identify the financial advisor most appropriate for the senior's needs; and

(iii) methods in which a senior can verify a financial advisor's credentials;

(D) conduct research to identify best practices and effective methods, tools, technology and strategies to educate and counsel seniors about personal finance management with a focus on—

(i) protecting themselves from unfair, deceptive, and abusive practices;

(ii) long-term savings; and

(iii) planning for retirement and long-term care;

(E) coordinate consumer protection efforts of seniors with other Federal agencies and State regulators, as appropriate, to promote consistent, effective, and efficient enforcement; and

(F) work with community organizations, non-profit organizations, and other entities that are involved with educating or assisting seniors (including the National Education and Resource Center on Women and Retirement Planning).

(h) Application of FACA

Notwithstanding any provision of the Federal Advisory Committee Act (5 U.S.C. App.), such Act shall apply to each advisory committee of the Bureau and each subcommittee of such an advisory committee.

§ 5494. [CFPA Act § 1014]. Consumer Advisory Board

(a) Establishment required

The Director shall establish a Consumer Advisory Board to advise and consult with the Bureau in the exercise of its functions under the Federal consumer financial laws, and to provide information on emerging practices in the consumer financial products or services industry, including regional trends, concerns, and other relevant information.

(b) Membership

In appointing the members of the Consumer Advisory Board, the Director shall seek to assemble experts in consumer protection, financial services, community development, fair lending and civil rights, and consumer financial products or services and representatives of depository institutions that primarily serve underserved communities, and representatives of communities that have been significantly impacted by higher-priced mortgage loans, and seek representation of the interests of covered persons and consumers, without regard to party affiliation. Not fewer than 6 members shall be appointed upon the recommendation of the regional Federal Reserve Bank Presidents, on a rotating basis.

(c) Meetings

The Consumer Advisory Board shall meet from time to time at the call of the Director, but, at a minimum, shall meet at least twice in each year.

(d) Compensation and travel expenses

Members of the Consumer Advisory Board who are not full-time employees of the United States shall—

(1) be entitled to receive compensation at a rate fixed by the Director while attending meetings of the Consumer Advisory Board, including travel time; and

(2) be allowed travel expenses, including transportation and subsistence, while away from their homes or regular places of business.

§ 5495 [CFPA Act § 1015]. Coordination

The Bureau shall coordinate with the Commission, the Commodity Futures Trading Commission, the Federal Trade Commission, and other Federal agencies and State regulators, as appropriate, to promote consistent regulatory treatment of consumer financial and investment products and services.

§ 5496 [CFPA Act § 1016]. Appearances before and reports to Congress

(a) Appearances before Congress

The Director of the Bureau shall appear before the Committee on Banking, Housing, and Urban Affairs of the Senate and the Committee on Financial Services and the Committee on Energy and Commerce of the House of Representatives at semi-annual hearings regarding the reports required under subsection (b).

(b) Reports required

The Bureau shall, concurrent with each semi-annual hearing referred to in subsection (a), prepare and submit to the President and to the Committee on Banking, Housing, and Urban Affairs of the Senate and the Committee on Financial Services and the Committee on Energy and Commerce of the House of Representatives, a report, beginning with the session following the designated transfer date. The Bureau may also submit such report to the Committee on Commerce, Science, and Transportation of the Senate.

(c) Contents

The reports required by subsection (b) shall include—

(1) a discussion of the significant problems faced by consumers in shopping for or obtaining consumer financial products or services;

(2) a justification of the budget request of the previous year;

(3) a list of the significant rules and orders adopted by the Bureau, as well as other significant initiatives conducted by the Bureau, during the preceding year and the plan of the Bureau for rules, orders, or other initiatives to be undertaken during the upcoming period;

(4) an analysis of complaints about consumer financial products or services that the Bureau has received and collected in its central database on complaints during the preceding year;

(5) a list, with a brief statement of the issues, of the public supervisory and enforcement actions to which the Bureau was a party during the preceding year;

(6) the actions taken regarding rules, orders, and supervisory actions with respect to covered persons which are not credit unions or depository institutions;

(7) an assessment of significant actions by State attorneys general or State regulators relating to Federal consumer financial law;

(8) an analysis of the efforts of the Bureau to fulfill the fair lending mission of the Bureau; and

(9) an analysis of the efforts of the Bureau to increase workforce and contracting diversity consistent with the procedures established by the Office of Minority and Women Inclusion.

§ 5496a [CFPA Act § 1016a]. Annual audits

(a) Annual independent audit

The Bureau shall order an annual independent audit of the operations and budget of the Bureau.

(b) Annual GAO audit

The Comptroller General of the United States shall conduct an annual audit of the Bureau's financial statements in accordance with generally accepted government accounting standards.

§ 5496b [CFPA Act § 1016b]. GAO study of financial regulations

(a) Study

Not later than the end of the 180-day period beginning on the date of the enactment of this Act, and annually thereafter, the Comptroller General of the United States shall conduct a study of financial services regulations, including activities of the Bureau. Such study shall include an analysis of—

(1) the impact of regulation on the financial marketplace, including the effects on the safety and soundness of regulated entities, cost and availability of credit, savings realized by consumers, reductions in consumer paperwork burden, changes in personal and small business bankruptcy filings, and costs of compliance with rules, including whether relevant Federal agencies are applying sound cost-benefit analysis in promulgating rules;

(2) efforts to avoid duplicative or conflicting rulemakings, including an evaluation of the consultative process under subparagraphs (B) and (C) of section 5512(b)(2) of this title, information requests, and examinations; and

(3) other matters related to the operations of financial services regulations deemed by the Comptroller General to be appropriate.

(b) Report

Not later than the end of the 30-day period following the completion of a study conducted pursuant to subsection (a), the Comptroller General shall issue a report to the Congress containing a detailed description of all findings and conclusions made by the Comptroller General in carrying out such study, together with such recommendations for legislative or administrative action as the Comptroller General may determine to be appropriate.

§ 5497 [CFPA Act § 1017]. Funding; penalties and fines

(a) Transfer of funds from Board of Governors

(1) In general

Each year (or quarter of such year), beginning on the designated transfer date, and each quarter thereafter, the Board of Governors shall transfer to the Bureau from the combined earnings of the Federal Reserve System, the amount determined by the Director to be reasonably necessary to carry out the authorities of the Bureau under Federal consumer financial law, taking into account such other sums made available to the Bureau from the preceding year (or quarter of such year).

(2) Funding cap

(A) In general

Notwithstanding paragraph (1), and in accordance with this paragraph, the amount that shall be transferred to the Bureau in each fiscal year shall not exceed a fixed percentage of the total operating expenses of the Federal Reserve System, as reported in the Annual Report, 2009, of the Board of Governors, equal to—

(i) 10 percent of such expenses in fiscal year 2011;

(ii) 11 percent of such expenses in fiscal year 2012; and

(iii) 12 percent of such expenses in fiscal year 2013, and in each year thereafter.

(B) Adjustment of amount

The dollar amount referred to in subparagraph (A)(iii) shall be adjusted annually, using the percent increase, if any, in the employment cost index for total compensation for State and local government workers published by the Federal Government, or the successor index thereto, for the 12-month period ending on September 30 of the year preceding the transfer.

(C) Reviewability

Notwithstanding any other provision in this title, the funds derived from the Federal Reserve System pursuant to this subsection shall not be subject to review by the Committees on Appropriations of the House of Representatives and the Senate.

(3) Transition period

Beginning on July 21, 2010, and until the designated transfer date, the Board of Governors shall transfer to the Bureau the amount estimated by the Secretary needed to carry out the authorities granted to the Bureau under Federal consumer financial law, from July 21, 2010 until the designated transfer date.

(4) Budget and financial management

(A) Financial operating plans and forecasts

The Director shall provide to the Director of the Office of Management and Budget copies of the financial operating plans and forecasts of the Director, as prepared by the Director in the ordinary course of the operations of the Bureau, and copies of the quarterly reports of the financial condition and results of operations of the Bureau, as prepared by the Director in the ordinary course of the operations of the Bureau.

(B) Financial statements

The Bureau shall prepare annually a statement of—

(i) assets and liabilities and surplus or deficit;

(ii) income and expenses; and

(iii) sources and application of funds.

(C) Financial management systems

The Bureau shall implement and maintain financial management systems that comply substantially with Federal financial management systems requirements and applicable Federal accounting standards.

(D) Assertion of internal controls

The Director shall provide to the Comptroller General of the United States an assertion as to the effectiveness of the internal controls that apply to financial reporting by the Bureau, using the standards established in section 3512(c) of Title 31.

(E) Rule of construction

This subsection may not be construed as implying any obligation on the part of the Director to consult with or obtain the consent or approval of the Director of the Office of Management and Budget with respect to any report, plan, forecast, or other information referred to in subparagraph (A) or any jurisdiction or oversight over the affairs or operations of the Bureau.

(F) Financial statements

The financial statements of the Bureau shall not be consolidated with the financial statements of either the Board of Governors or the Federal Reserve System.

(5) Audit of the Bureau

(A) **In general**

The Comptroller General shall annually audit the financial transactions of the Bureau in accordance with the United States generally accepted government auditing standards, as may be prescribed by the Comptroller General of the United States. The audit shall be conducted at the place or places where accounts of the Bureau are normally kept. The representatives of the Government Accountability Office shall have access to the personnel and to all books, accounts, documents, papers, records (including electronic records), reports, files, and all other papers, automated data, things, or property belonging to or under the control of or used or employed by the Bureau pertaining to its financial transactions and necessary to facilitate the audit, and such representatives shall be afforded full facilities for verifying transactions with the balances or securities held by depositories, fiscal agents, and custodians. All such books, accounts, documents, records, reports, files, papers, and property of the Bureau shall remain in possession and custody of the Bureau. The Comptroller General may obtain and duplicate any such books, accounts, documents, records, working papers, automated data and files, or other information relevant to such audit without cost to the Comptroller General, and the right of access of the Comptroller General to such information shall be enforceable pursuant to section 716(c) of Title 31.

(B) **Report**

The Comptroller General shall submit to the Congress a report of each annual audit conducted under this subsection. The report to the Congress shall set forth the scope of the audit and shall include the statement of assets and liabilities and surplus or deficit, the statement of income and expenses, the statement of sources and application of funds, and such comments and information as may be deemed necessary to inform Congress of the financial operations and condition of the Bureau, together with such recommendations with respect thereto as the Comptroller General may deem advisable. A copy of each report shall be furnished to the President and to the Bureau at the time submitted to the Congress.

(C) **Assistance and costs**

For the purpose of conducting an audit under this subsection, the Comptroller General may, in the discretion of the Comptroller General, employ by contract, without regard to section 6101 of Title 41, professional services of firms and organizations of certified public accountants for temporary periods or for special purposes. Upon the request of the Comptroller General, the Director of the Bureau shall transfer to the Government Accountability Office from funds available, the amount requested by the Comptroller General to cover the full costs of any audit and report conducted by the Comptroller General. The Comptroller General shall credit funds transferred to the account established for salaries and expenses of the Government Accountability Office, and such amount shall be available upon receipt and without fiscal year limitation to cover the full costs of the audit and report.

(b) **Consumer Financial Protection Fund**

(1) **Separate fund in Federal Reserve established**

There is established in the Federal Reserve a separate fund, to be known as the "Bureau of Consumer Financial Protection Fund" (referred to in this section as the "Bureau Fund"). The Bureau Fund shall be maintained and established at a Federal reserve bank, in accordance with such requirements as the Board of Governors may impose.

(2) **Fund receipts**

All amounts transferred to the Bureau under subsection (a) shall be deposited into the Bureau Fund.

(3) **Investment authority**

(A) Amounts in Bureau Fund may be invested

The Bureau may request the Board of Governors to direct the investment of the portion of the Bureau Fund that is not, in the judgment of the Bureau, required to meet the current needs of the Bureau.

(B) Eligible investments

Investments authorized by this paragraph shall be made in obligations of the United States or obligations that are guaranteed as to principal and interest by the United States, with maturities suitable to the needs of the Bureau Fund, as determined by the Bureau.

(C) Interest and proceeds credited

The interest on, and the proceeds from the sale or redemption of, any obligations held in the Bureau Fund shall be credited to the Bureau Fund.

(c) Use of funds

(1) In general

Funds obtained by, transferred to, or credited to the Bureau Fund shall be immediately available to the Bureau and under the control of the Director, and shall remain available until expended, to pay the expenses of the Bureau in carrying out its duties and responsibilities. The compensation of the Director and other employees of the Bureau and all other expenses thereof may be paid from, obtained by, transferred to, or credited to the Bureau Fund under this section.

(2) Funds that are not Government funds

Funds obtained by or transferred to the Bureau Fund shall not be construed to be Government funds or appropriated monies.

(3) Amounts not subject to apportionment

Notwithstanding any other provision of law, amounts in the Bureau Fund and in the Civil Penalty Fund established under subsection (d) shall not be subject to apportionment for purposes of chapter 15 of Title 31 or under any other authority.

(d) Penalties and fines

(1) Establishment of victims relief fund

There is established in the Federal Reserve a separate fund, to be known as the "Consumer Financial Civil Penalty Fund" (referred to in this section as the "Civil Penalty Fund"). The Civil Penalty Fund shall be maintained and established at a Federal reserve bank, in accordance with such requirements as the Board of Governors may impose. If the Bureau obtains a civil penalty against any person in any judicial or administrative action under Federal consumer financial laws, the Bureau shall deposit into the Civil Penalty Fund, the amount of the penalty collected.

(2) Payment to victims

Amounts in the Civil Penalty Fund shall be available to the Bureau, without fiscal year limitation, for payments to the victims of activities for which civil penalties have been imposed under the Federal consumer financial laws. To the extent that such victims cannot be located or such payments are otherwise not practicable, the Bureau may use such funds for the purpose of consumer education and financial literacy programs.

(e) Authorization of appropriations; annual report

(1) Determination regarding need for appropriated funds

(A) In general

The Director is authorized to determine that sums available to the Bureau under this section will not be sufficient to carry out the authorities of the Bureau under Federal consumer financial law for the upcoming year.

(B) Report required

When making a determination under subparagraph (A), the Director shall prepare a report regarding the funding of the Bureau, including the assets and liabilities of the Bureau, and the extent to which the funding needs of the Bureau are anticipated to exceed the level of the amount set forth in subsection (a)(2). The Director shall submit the report to the President and to the Committee on Appropriations of the Senate and the Committee on Appropriations of the House of Representatives.

(2) Authorization of appropriations

If the Director makes the determination and submits the report pursuant to paragraph (1), there are hereby authorized to be appropriated to the Bureau, for the purposes of carrying out the authorities granted in Federal consumer financial law, $200,000,000 for each of fiscal years 2010, 2011, 2012, 2013, and 2014.

(3) Apportionment

Notwithstanding any other provision of law, the amounts in paragraph (2) shall be subject to apportionment under section 1517 of Title 31 and restrictions that generally apply to the use of appropriated funds in Title 31 and other laws.

(4) Annual report

The Director shall prepare and submit a report, on an annual basis, to the Committee on Appropriations of the Senate and the Committee on Appropriations of the House of Representatives regarding the financial operating plans and forecasts of the Director, the financial condition and results of operations of the Bureau, and the sources and application of funds of the Bureau, including any funds appropriated in accordance with this subsection.

PART B—GENERAL POWERS OF THE BUREAU

§ 5511 [CFPA Act § 1021]. Purpose, objectives, and functions

(a) Purpose

The Bureau shall seek to implement and, where applicable, enforce Federal consumer financial law consistently for the purpose of ensuring that all consumers have access to markets for consumer financial products and services and that markets for consumer financial products and services are fair, transparent, and competitive.

(b) Objectives

The Bureau is authorized to exercise its authorities under Federal consumer financial law for the purposes of ensuring that, with respect to consumer financial products and services—

(1) consumers are provided with timely and understandable information to make responsible decisions about financial transactions;

(2) consumers are protected from unfair, deceptive, or abusive acts and practices and from discrimination;

(3) outdated, unnecessary, or unduly burdensome regulations are regularly identified and addressed in order to reduce unwarranted regulatory burdens;

(4) Federal consumer financial law is enforced consistently, without regard to the status of a person as a depository institution, in order to promote fair competition; and

(5) markets for consumer financial products and services operate transparently and efficiently to facilitate access and innovation.

(c) Functions

The primary functions of the Bureau are—

(1) conducting financial education programs;

(2) collecting, investigating, and responding to consumer complaints;

(3) collecting, researching, monitoring, and publishing information relevant to the functioning of markets for consumer financial products and services to identify risks to consumers and the proper functioning of such markets;

(4) subject to sections 5514 through 5516 of this title, supervising covered persons for compliance with Federal consumer financial law, and taking appropriate enforcement action to address violations of Federal consumer financial law;

(5) issuing rules, orders, and guidance implementing Federal consumer financial law; and

(6) performing such support activities as may be necessary or useful to facilitate the other functions of the Bureau.

§ 5512 [CFPA Act § 1022]. Rulemaking Authority

(a) In general

The Bureau is authorized to exercise its authorities under Federal consumer financial law to administer, enforce, and otherwise implement the provisions of Federal consumer financial law.

(b) Rulemaking, orders, and guidance

(1) General authority

The Director may prescribe rules and issue orders and guidance, as may be necessary or appropriate to enable the Bureau to administer and carry out the purposes and objectives of the Federal consumer financial laws, and to prevent evasions thereof.

(2) Standards for rulemaking

In prescribing a rule under the Federal consumer financial laws—

(A) the Bureau shall consider—

(i) the potential benefits and costs to consumers and covered persons, including the potential reduction of access by consumers to consumer financial products or services resulting from such rule; and

(ii) the impact of proposed rules on covered persons, as described in section 5516 of this title, and the impact on consumers in rural areas;

(B) the Bureau shall consult with the appropriate prudential regulators or other Federal agencies prior to proposing a rule and during the comment process regarding consistency with prudential, market, or systemic objectives administered by such agencies; and

(C) if, during the consultation process described in subparagraph (B), a prudential regulator provides the Bureau with a written objection to the proposed rule of the Bureau or a portion thereof, the Bureau shall include in the adopting release a description of the objection and the basis for the Bureau decision, if any, regarding such objection, except that nothing in this clause shall be construed as altering or limiting the procedures under section 5513 of this title that may apply to any rule prescribed by the Bureau.

(3) Exemptions

(A) In general

The Bureau, by rule, may conditionally or unconditionally exempt any class of covered persons, service providers, or consumer financial products or services, from any provision of this title, or from any rule issued under this title, as the Bureau determines necessary or appropriate to carry out the purposes and objectives of this title, taking into consideration the factors in subparagraph (B).

(B) Factors

In issuing an exemption, as permitted under subparagraph (A), the Bureau shall, as appropriate, take into consideration—

(i) the total assets of the class of covered persons;

(ii) the volume of transactions involving consumer financial products or services in which the class of covered persons engages; and

(iii) existing provisions of law which are applicable to the consumer financial product or service and the extent to which such provisions provide consumers with adequate protections.

(4) Exclusive rulemaking authority

(A) In general

Notwithstanding any other provisions of Federal law and except as provided in section 5581(b)(5) of this title, to the extent that a provision of Federal consumer financial law authorizes the Bureau and another Federal agency to issue regulations under that provision of law for purposes of assuring compliance with Federal consumer financial law and any regulations thereunder, the Bureau shall have the exclusive authority to prescribe rules subject to those provisions of law.

(B) Deference

Notwithstanding any power granted to any Federal agency or to the Council under this title, and subject to section 5581(b)(5)(E) of this title, the deference that a court affords to the Bureau with respect to a determination by the Bureau regarding the meaning or interpretation of any provision of a Federal consumer financial law shall be applied as if the Bureau were the only agency authorized to apply, enforce, interpret, or administer the provisions of such Federal consumer financial law.

(c) Monitoring

(1) In general

In order to support its rulemaking and other functions, the Bureau shall monitor for risks to consumers in the offering or provision of consumer financial products or services, including developments in markets for such products or services.

(2) Considerations

In allocating its resources to perform the monitoring required by this section, the Bureau may consider, among other factors—

(A) likely risks and costs to consumers associated with buying or using a type of consumer financial product or service;

(B) understanding by consumers of the risks of a type of consumer financial product or service;

(C) the legal protections applicable to the offering or provision of a consumer financial product or service, including the extent to which the law is likely to adequately protect consumers;

(D) rates of growth in the offering or provision of a consumer financial product or service;

(E) the extent, if any, to which the risks of a consumer financial product or service may disproportionately affect traditionally underserved consumers; or

(F) the types, number, and other pertinent characteristics of covered persons that offer or provide the consumer financial product or service.

(3) Significant findings

(A) In general

The Bureau shall publish not fewer than 1 report of significant findings of its monitoring required by this subsection in each calendar year, beginning with the first calendar year that begins at least 1 year after the designated transfer date.

(B) Confidential information

The Bureau may make public such information obtained by the Bureau under this section as is in the public interest, through aggregated reports or other appropriate formats designed to protect confidential information in accordance with paragraphs (4), (6), (8), and (9).

(4) Collection of information

(A) In general

In conducting any monitoring or assessment required by this section, the Bureau shall have the authority to gather information from time to time regarding the organization, business conduct, markets, and activities of covered persons and service providers.

(B) Methodology

In order to gather information described in subparagraph (A), the Bureau may—

(i) gather and compile information from a variety of sources, including examination reports concerning covered persons or service providers, consumer complaints, voluntary surveys and voluntary interviews of consumers, surveys and interviews with covered persons and service providers, and review of available databases; and

(ii) require covered persons and service providers participating in consumer financial services markets to file with the Bureau, under oath or otherwise, in such form and within such reasonable period of time as the Bureau may prescribe by rule or order, annual or special reports, or answers in writing to specific questions, furnishing information described in paragraph (4), as necessary for the Bureau to fulfill the monitoring, assessment, and reporting responsibilities imposed by Congress.

(C) Limitation

The Bureau may not use its authorities under this paragraph to obtain records from covered persons and service providers participating in consumer financial services markets for purposes of gathering or analyzing the personally identifiable financial information of consumers.

(5) Limited information gathering

In order to assess whether a nondepository is a covered person, as defined in section 5481 of this title, the Bureau may require such nondepository to file with the Bureau, under oath or otherwise, in such form and within such reasonable period of time as the Bureau may prescribe by rule or order, annual or special reports, or answers in writing to specific questions.

(6) Confidentiality rules

(A) Rulemaking

The Bureau shall prescribe rules regarding the confidential treatment of information obtained from persons in connection with the exercise of its authorities under Federal consumer financial law.

(B) Access by the Bureau to reports of other regulators

(i) Examination and financial condition reports

Upon providing reasonable assurances of confidentiality, the Bureau shall have access to any report of examination or financial condition made by a prudential regulator or other Federal agency having jurisdiction over a covered person or service provider, and to all revisions made to any such report.

(ii) Provision of other reports to the Bureau

In addition to the reports described in clause (i), a prudential regulator or other Federal agency having jurisdiction over a covered person or service provider may, in its discretion, furnish to the Bureau any other report or other confidential supervisory information concerning any insured depository institution, credit union, or other entity examined by such agency under authority of any provision of Federal law.

(C) Access by other regulators to reports of the Bureau

(i) Examination reports

Upon providing reasonable assurances of confidentiality, a prudential regulator, a State regulator, or any other Federal agency having jurisdiction over a covered person or service provider shall have access to any report of examination made by the Bureau with respect to such person, and to all revisions made to any such report.

(ii) Provision of other reports to other regulators

In addition to the reports described in clause (i), the Bureau may, in its discretion, furnish to a prudential regulator or other agency having jurisdiction over a covered person or service provider any other report or other confidential supervisory information concerning such person examined by the Bureau under the authority of any other provision of Federal law.

(7) Registration

(A) In general

The Bureau may prescribe rules regarding registration requirements applicable to a covered person, other than an insured depository institution, insured credit union, or related person.

(B) Registration information

Subject to rules prescribed by the Bureau, the Bureau may publicly disclose registration information to facilitate the ability of consumers to identify covered persons that are registered with the Bureau.

(C) Consultation with State agencies

In developing and implementing registration requirements under this paragraph, the Bureau shall consult with State agencies regarding requirements or systems (including coordinated or combined systems for registration), where appropriate.

(8) Privacy considerations

In collecting information from any person, publicly releasing information held by the Bureau, or requiring covered persons to publicly report information, the Bureau shall take steps to ensure that proprietary, personal, or confidential consumer information that is protected from public disclosure under section 552(b) or 552a of Title 5 or any other provision of law, is not made public under this title.

(9) Consumer privacy

(A) In general

The Bureau may not obtain from a covered person or service provider any personally identifiable financial information about a consumer from the financial records of the covered person or service provider, except—

(i) if the financial records are reasonably described in a request by the Bureau and the consumer provides written permission for the disclosure of such information by the covered person or service provider to the Bureau; or

(ii) as may be specifically permitted or required under other applicable provisions of law and in accordance with the Right to Financial Privacy Act of 1978 (12 U.S.C. 3401 et seq.).

(B) Treatment of covered person or service provider

With respect to the application of any provision of the Right to Financial Privacy Act of 1978,[1] to a disclosure by a covered person or service provider subject to this subsection, the covered person or service provider shall be treated as if it were a "financial institution", as defined in section 1101 of that Act (12 U.S.C. 3401).

(d) Assessment of significant rules

(1) In general

The Bureau shall conduct an assessment of each significant rule or order adopted by the Bureau under Federal consumer financial law. The assessment shall address, among other relevant factors, the effectiveness of the rule or order in meeting the purposes and objectives of this title and the specific goals stated by the Bureau. The assessment shall reflect available evidence and any data that the Bureau reasonably may collect.

(2) Reports

The Bureau shall publish a report of its assessment under this subsection not later than 5 years after the effective date of the subject rule or order.

(3) Public comment required

Before publishing a report of its assessment, the Bureau shall invite public comment on recommendations for modifying, expanding, or eliminating the newly adopted significant rule or order.

§ 5513 [CFPA Act § 1023]. Review of Bureau Functions

(a) Review of Bureau regulations

On the petition of a member agency of the Council, the Council may set aside a final regulation prescribed by the Bureau, or any provision thereof, if the Council decides, in accordance with subsection (c), that the regulation or provision would put the safety and soundness of the United States banking system or the stability of the financial system of the United States at risk.

(b) Petition

(1) Procedure

---

[1] So in original. The comma probably should not appear.

An agency represented by a member of the Council may petition the Council, in writing, and in accordance with rules prescribed pursuant to subsection (f), to stay the effectiveness of, or set aside, a regulation if the member agency filing the petition—

(A) has in good faith attempted to work with the Bureau to resolve concerns regarding the effect of the rule on the safety and soundness of the United States banking system or the stability of the financial system of the United States; and

(B) files the petition with the Council not later than 10 days after the date on which the regulation has been published in the Federal Register.

(2) Publication

Any petition filed with the Council under this section shall be published in the Federal Register and transmitted contemporaneously with filing to the Committee on Banking, Housing, and Urban Affairs of the Senate and the Committee on Financial Services of the House of Representatives.

(c) Stays and set asides

(1) Stay

(A) In general

Upon the request of any member agency, the Chairperson of the Council may stay the effectiveness of a regulation for the purpose of allowing appropriate consideration of the petition by the Council.

(B) Expiration

A stay issued under this paragraph shall expire on the earlier of—

(i) 90 days after the date of filing of the petition under subsection (b); or

(ii) the date on which the Council makes a decision under paragraph (3).

(2) No adverse inference

After the expiration of any stay imposed under this section, no inference shall be drawn regarding the validity or enforceability of a regulation which was the subject of the petition.

(3) Vote

(A) In general

The decision to issue a stay of, or set aside, any regulation under this section shall be made only with the affirmative vote in accordance with subparagraph (B) of 2/3 of the members of the Council then serving.

(B) Authorization to vote

A member of the Council may vote to stay the effectiveness of, or set aside, a final regulation prescribed by the Bureau only if the agency or department represented by that member has—

(i) considered any relevant information provided by the agency submitting the petition and by the Bureau; and

(ii) made an official determination, at a public meeting where applicable, that the regulation which is the subject of the petition would put the safety and soundness of the United States banking system or the stability of the financial system of the United States at risk.

(4) Decisions to set aside

(A) Effect of decision

A decision by the Council to set aside a regulation prescribed by the Bureau, or provision thereof, shall render such regulation, or provision thereof, unenforceable.

(B) Timely action required

The Council may not issue a decision to set aside a regulation, or provision thereof, which is the subject of a petition under this section after the expiration of the later of—

(i) 45 days following the date of filing of the petition, unless a stay is issued under paragraph (1); or

(ii) the expiration of a stay issued by the Council under this section.

(C) Separate authority

The issuance of a stay under this section does not affect the authority of the Council to set aside a regulation.

(5) Dismissal due to inaction

A petition under this section shall be deemed dismissed if the Council has not issued a decision to set aside a regulation, or provision thereof, within the period for timely action under paragraph (4)(B).

(6) Publication of decision

Any decision under this subsection to issue a stay of, or set aside, a regulation or provision thereof shall be published by the Council in the Federal Register as soon as practicable after the decision is made, with an explanation of the reasons for the decision.

(7) Rulemaking procedures inapplicable

The notice and comment procedures under section 553 of Title 5 shall not apply to any decision under this section of the Council to issue a stay of, or set aside, a regulation.

(8) Judicial review of decisions by the Council

A decision by the Council to set aside a regulation prescribed by the Bureau, or provision thereof, shall be subject to review under chapter 7 of Title 5.

(d) Application of other law

Nothing in this section shall be construed as altering, limiting, or restricting the application of any other provision of law, except as otherwise specifically provided in this section, including chapter 5 and chapter 7 of Title 5, to a regulation which is the subject of a petition filed under this section.

(e) Savings clause

Nothing in this section shall be construed as limiting or restricting the Bureau from engaging in a rulemaking in accordance with applicable law.

(f) Implementing rules

The Council shall prescribe procedural rules to implement this section.

§ 5514 [CFPA Act § 1024]. Supervision of nondepository covered persons

(a) Scope of coverage

(1) Applicability

Notwithstanding any other provision of this title, and except as provided in paragraph (3), this section shall apply to any covered person who—

(A) offers or provides origination, brokerage, or servicing of loans secured by real estate for use by consumers primarily for personal, family, or household purposes, or loan modification or foreclosure relief services in connection with such loans;

(B) is a larger participant of a market for other consumer financial products or services, as defined by rule in accordance with paragraph (2);

(C) the Bureau has reasonable cause to determine, by order, after notice to the covered person and a reasonable opportunity for such covered person to respond, based on complaints collected through the system under section 5493(b)(3) of this title or information from other sources, that such covered person is engaging, or has engaged, in conduct that poses risks to consumers with regard to the offering or provision of consumer financial products or services;

(D) offers or provides to a consumer any private education loan, as defined in section 1650 of Title 15, notwithstanding section 5517(a)(2)(A) of this title and subject to section 5517(a)(2)(C) of this title; or

(E) offers or provides to a consumer a payday loan.

(2) Rulemaking to define covered persons subject to this section

The Bureau shall consult with the Federal Trade Commission prior to issuing a rule, in accordance with paragraph (1)(B), to define covered persons subject to this section. The Bureau shall issue its initial rule not later than 1 year after the designated transfer date.

(3) Rules of construction

(A) Certain persons excluded

This section shall not apply to persons described in section 5515(a) or 5516(a) of this title.

(B) Activity levels

For purposes of computing activity levels under paragraph (1) or rules issued thereunder, activities of affiliated companies (other than insured depository institutions or insured credit unions) shall be aggregated.

(b) Supervision

(1) In general

The Bureau shall require reports and conduct examinations on a periodic basis of persons described in subsection (a)(1) for purposes of—

(A) assessing compliance with the requirements of Federal consumer financial law;

(B) obtaining information about the activities and compliance systems or procedures of such person; and

(C) detecting and assessing risks to consumers and to markets for consumer financial products and services.

(2) Risk-based supervision program

The Bureau shall exercise its authority under paragraph (1) in a manner designed to ensure that such exercise, with respect to persons described in subsection (a)(1), is based on the assessment by the Bureau of the risks posed to consumers in the relevant product markets and geographic markets, and taking into consideration, as applicable—

(A) the asset size of the covered person;

(B) the volume of transactions involving consumer financial products or services in which the covered person engages;

(C) the risks to consumers created by the provision of such consumer financial products or services;

(D) the extent to which such institutions are subject to oversight by State authorities for consumer protection; and

(E) any other factors that the Bureau determines to be relevant to a class of covered persons.

(3) Coordination

To minimize regulatory burden, the Bureau shall coordinate its supervisory activities with the supervisory activities conducted by prudential regulators, the State bank regulatory authorities, and the State agencies that licence, supervise, or examine the offering of consumer financial products or services, including establishing their respective schedules for examining persons described in subsection (a)(1) and requirements regarding reports to be submitted by such persons. The sharing of information with such regulators, authorities, and agencies shall not be construed as waiving, destroying, or otherwise affecting any privilege or confidentiality such person may claim with respect to such information under Federal or State law as to any person or entity other than such Bureau, agency, supervisor, or authority.

(4) Use of existing reports

The Bureau shall, to the fullest extent possible, use—

(A) reports pertaining to persons described in subsection (a)(1) that have been provided or required to have been provided to a Federal or State agency; and

(B) information that has been reported publicly.

(5) Preservation of authority

Nothing in this subchapter may be construed as limiting the authority of the Director to require reports from persons described in subsection (a)(1), as permitted under paragraph (1), regarding information owned or under the control of such person, regardless of whether such information is maintained, stored, or processed by another person.

(6) Reports of tax law noncompliance

The Bureau shall provide the Commissioner of Internal Revenue with any report of examination or related information identifying possible tax law noncompliance.

(7) Registration, recordkeeping and other requirements for certain persons

(A) In general

The Bureau shall prescribe rules to facilitate supervision of persons described in subsection (a)(1) and assessment and detection of risks to consumers.

(B) Recordkeeping

The Bureau may require a person described in subsection (a)(1), to generate, provide, or retain records for the purposes of facilitating supervision of such persons and assessing and detecting risks to consumers.

(C) Requirements concerning obligations

The Bureau may prescribe rules regarding a person described in subsection (a)(1), to ensure that such persons are legitimate entities and are able to perform their obligations to consumers. Such requirements may include background checks for principals, officers, directors, or key personnel and bonding or other appropriate financial requirements.

(D) Consultation with State agencies

In developing and implementing requirements under this paragraph, the Bureau shall consult with State agencies regarding requirements or systems (including coordinated or combined systems for registration), where appropriate.

(c) Enforcement authority

(1) The Bureau to have enforcement authority

Except as provided in paragraph (3) and section 5581 of this title, with respect to any person described in subsection (a)(1), to the extent that Federal law authorizes the Bureau and another Federal agency to enforce Federal consumer financial law, the Bureau shall have exclusive authority to enforce that Federal consumer financial law.

(2) Referral

Any Federal agency authorized to enforce a Federal consumer financial law described in paragraph (1) may recommend in writing to the Bureau that the Bureau initiate an enforcement proceeding, as the Bureau is authorized by that Federal law or by this subchapter.

(3) Coordination with the Federal Trade Commission

(A) In general

The Bureau and the Federal Trade Commission shall negotiate an agreement for coordinating with respect to enforcement actions by each agency regarding the offering or provision of consumer financial products or services by any covered person that is described in subsection (a)(1), or service providers thereto. The agreement shall include procedures for notice to the other agency, where feasible, prior to initiating a civil action to enforce any Federal law regarding the offering or provision of consumer financial products or services.

(B) Civil actions

Whenever a civil action has been filed by, or on behalf of, the Bureau or the Federal Trade Commission for any violation of any provision of Federal law described in subparagraph (A), or any regulation prescribed under such provision of law—

(i) the other agency may not, during the pendency of that action, institute a civil action under such provision of law against any defendant named in the complaint in such pending action for any violation alleged in the complaint; and

(ii) the Bureau or the Federal Trade Commission may intervene as a party in any such action brought by the other agency, and, upon intervening—

(I) be heard on all matters arising in such enforcement action; and

(II) file petitions for appeal in such actions.

(C) Agreement terms

The terms of any agreement negotiated under subparagraph (A) may modify or supersede the provisions of subparagraph (B).

(D) Deadline

The agencies shall reach the agreement required under subparagraph (A) not later than 6 months after the designated transfer date.

(d) Exclusive rulemaking and examination authority

Notwithstanding any other provision of Federal law and except as provided in section 5581 of this title, to the extent that Federal law authorizes the Bureau and another Federal agency to issue regulations or guidance, conduct examinations, or require reports from a person described in subsection (a)(1) under such law for purposes of assuring compliance with Federal consumer financial law and any regulations thereunder, the Bureau shall have the exclusive authority to prescribe rules, issue guidance, conduct examinations, require reports, or issue exemptions with regard to a person described in subsection (a)(1), subject to those provisions of law.

(e) Service providers

A service provider to a person described in subsection (a)(1) shall be subject to the authority of the Bureau under this section, to the same extent as if such service provider were engaged in a service relationship with a bank, and the Bureau were an appropriate Federal banking agency under section 1867(c) of this title. In conducting any examination or requiring any report from a service provider subject to this subsection, the Bureau shall coordinate with the appropriate prudential regulator, as applicable.

(f) Preservation of Farm Credit Administration authority

No provision of this title may be construed as modifying, limiting, or otherwise affecting the authority of the Farm Credit Administration.

§ 5515 [CFPA Act § 1025]. Supervision of very large banks, savings associations, and credit unions

(a) Scope of coverage

This section shall apply to any covered person that is—

(1) an insured depository institution with total assets of more than $10,000,000,000 and any affiliate thereof; or

(2) an insured credit union with total assets of more than $10,000,000,000 and any affiliate thereof.

(b) Supervision

(1) In general

The Bureau shall have exclusive authority to require reports and conduct examinations on a periodic basis of persons described in subsection (a) for purposes of—

(A) assessing compliance with the requirements of Federal consumer financial laws;

(B) obtaining information about the activities subject to such laws and the associated compliance systems or procedures of such persons; and

(C) detecting and assessing associated risks to consumers and to markets for consumer financial products and services.

(2) Coordination

To minimize regulatory burden, the Bureau shall coordinate its supervisory activities with the supervisory activities conducted by prudential regulators and the State bank regulatory authorities, including consultation regarding their respective schedules for examining such persons described in subsection (a) and requirements regarding reports to be submitted by such persons.

(3) Use of existing reports

The Bureau shall, to the fullest extent possible, use—

(A) reports pertaining to a person described in subsection (a) that have been provided or required to have been provided to a Federal or State agency; and

(B) information that has been reported publicly.

(4) Preservation of authority

Nothing in this title may be construed as limiting the authority of the Director to require reports from a person described in subsection (a), as permitted under paragraph (1), regarding information owned or under the control of such person, regardless of whether such information is maintained, stored, or processed by another person.

(5) Reports of tax law noncompliance

The Bureau shall provide the Commissioner of Internal Revenue with any report of examination or related information identifying possible tax law noncompliance.

(c) Primary enforcement authority

(1) The Bureau to have primary enforcement authority

To the extent that the Bureau and another Federal agency are authorized to enforce a Federal consumer financial law, the Bureau shall have primary authority to enforce that Federal consumer financial law with respect to any person described in subsection (a).

(2) Referral

Any Federal agency, other than the Federal Trade Commission, that is authorized to enforce a Federal consumer financial law may recommend, in writing, to the Bureau that the Bureau initiate an enforcement proceeding with respect to a person described in subsection (a), as the Bureau is authorized to do by that Federal consumer financial law.

(3) Backup enforcement authority of other Federal agency

If the Bureau does not, before the end of the 120-day period beginning on the date on which the Bureau receives a recommendation under paragraph (2), initiate an enforcement proceeding, the other agency referred to in paragraph (2) may initiate an enforcement proceeding, including performing follow up supervisory and support functions incidental thereto, to assure compliance with such proceeding.

(d) Service providers

A service provider to a person described in subsection (a) shall be subject to the authority of the Bureau under this section, to the same extent as if the Bureau were an appropriate Federal banking agency under section 1867(c) of this title. In conducting any examination or requiring any report from a service provider subject to this subsection, the Bureau shall coordinate with the appropriate prudential regulator.

(e) Simultaneous and coordinated supervisory action

(1) Examinations

A prudential regulator and the Bureau shall, with respect to each insured depository institution, insured credit union, or other covered person described in subsection (a) that is supervised by the prudential regulator and the Bureau, respectively—

(A) coordinate the scheduling of examinations of the insured depository institution, insured credit union, or other covered person described in subsection (a);

(B) conduct simultaneous examinations of each insured depository institution or insured credit union, unless such institution requests examinations to be conducted separately;

(C) share each draft report of examination with the other agency and permit the receiving agency a reasonable opportunity (which shall not be less than a period of 30 days after the date of receipt) to comment on the draft report before such report is made final; and

(D) prior to issuing a final report of examination or taking supervisory action, take into consideration concerns, if any, raised in the comments made by the other agency.

(2) Coordination with State bank supervisors

The Bureau shall pursue arrangements and agreements with State bank supervisors to coordinate examinations, consistent with paragraph (1).

(3) Avoidance of conflict in supervision

(A) Request

If the proposed supervisory determinations of the Bureau and a prudential regulator (in this section referred to collectively as the "agencies") are conflicting, an insured depository institution, insured credit union, or other covered person described in subsection (a) may request the agencies to coordinate and present a joint statement of coordinated supervisory action.

(B) Joint statement

The agencies shall provide a joint statement under subparagraph (A), not later than 30 days after the date of receipt of the request of the insured depository institution, credit union, or covered person described in subsection (a).

(4) Appeals to governing panel

(A) In general

If the agencies do not resolve the conflict or issue a joint statement required by subparagraph (B), or if either of the agencies takes or attempts to take any supervisory action relating to the request for the joint statement without the consent of the other agency, an insured depository institution, insured credit union, or other covered person described in subsection (a) may institute an appeal to a governing panel, as provided in this subsection, not later than 30 days after the expiration of the period during which a joint statement is required to be filed under paragraph (3)(B).

(B) Composition of governing panel

The governing panel for an appeal under this paragraph shall be composed of—

(i) a representative from the Bureau and a representative of the prudential regulator, both of whom—

(I) have not participated in the material supervisory determinations under appeal; and

(II) do not directly or indirectly report to the person who participated materially in the supervisory determinations under appeal; and

(ii) one individual representative, to be determined on a rotating basis, from among the Board of Governors, the Corporation, the National Credit Union Administration, and the Office of the Comptroller of the Currency, other than any agency involved in the subject dispute.

(C) Conduct of appeal

In an appeal under this paragraph—

(i) the insured depository institution, insured credit union, or other covered person described in subsection (a)—

(I) shall include in its appeal all the facts and legal arguments pertaining to the matter; and

(II) may, through counsel, employees, or representatives, appear before the governing panel in person or by telephone; and

(ii) the governing panel—

(I) may request the insured depository institution, insured credit union, or other covered person described in subsection (a), the Bureau, or the prudential regulator to produce additional information relevant to the appeal; and

(II) by a majority vote of its members, shall provide a final determination, in writing, not later than 30 days after the date of filing of an informationally complete appeal, or such longer period as the panel and the insured depository institution, insured credit union, or other covered person described in subsection (a) may jointly agree.

(D) Public availability of determinations

A governing panel shall publish all information contained in a determination by the governing panel, with appropriate redactions of information that would be subject to an exemption from disclosure under section 552 of Title 5.

(E) Prohibition against retaliation

The Bureau and the prudential regulators shall prescribe rules to provide safeguards from retaliation against the insured depository institution, insured credit union, or other covered person described in subsection (a) instituting an appeal under this paragraph, as well as their officers and employees.

(F) Limitation

The process provided in this paragraph shall not apply to a determination by a prudential regulator to appoint a conservator or receiver for an insured depository institution or a liquidating agent for an insured credit union, as the case may be, or a decision to take action pursuant to section 1831*o* of this title or section 1790a of this title, as applicable.

(G) Effect on other authority

Nothing in this section shall modify or limit the authority of the Bureau to interpret, or take enforcement action under, any Federal consumer financial law, or the authority of a prudential regulator to interpret or take enforcement action under any other provision of Federal law for safety and soundness purposes.

§ 5516 [CFPA Act § 1026]. Other banks, savings associations, and credit unions

(a) Scope of coverage

This section shall apply to any covered person that is—

(1) an insured depository institution with total assets of $10,000,000,000 or less; or

(2) an insured credit union with total assets of $10,000,000,000 or less.

(b) Reports

The Director may require reports from a person described in subsection (a), as necessary to support the role of the Bureau in implementing Federal consumer financial law, to support its examination activities under subsection (c), and to assess and detect risks to consumers and consumer financial markets.

(1) Use of existing reports

The Bureau shall, to the fullest extent possible, use—

(A) reports pertaining to a person described in subsection (a) that have been provided or required to have been provided to a Federal or State agency; and

(B) information that has been reported publicly.

(2) Preservation of authority

Nothing in this subsection may be construed as limiting the authority of the Director from requiring from a person described in subsection (a), as permitted under paragraph (1), information owned or under the control of such person, regardless of whether such information is maintained, stored, or processed by another person.

(3) Reports of tax law noncompliance

The Bureau shall provide the Commissioner of Internal Revenue with any report of examination or related information identifying possible tax law noncompliance.

(c) Examinations

(1) In general

The Bureau may, at its discretion, include examiners on a sampling basis of the examinations performed by the prudential regulator to assess compliance with the requirements of Federal consumer financial law of persons described in subsection (a).

(2) Agency coordination

The prudential regulator shall—

(A) provide all reports, records, and documentation related to the examination process for any institution included in the sample referred to in paragraph (1) to the Bureau on a timely and continual basis;

(B) involve such Bureau examiner in the entire examination process for such person; and

(C) consider input of the Bureau concerning the scope of an examination, conduct of the examination, the contents of the examination report, the designation of matters requiring attention, and examination ratings.

(d) Enforcement

(1) In general

Except for requiring reports under subsection (b), the prudential regulator is authorized to enforce the requirements of Federal consumer financial laws and, with respect to a covered person described in subsection (a), shall have exclusive authority (relative to the Bureau) to enforce such laws .

(2) Coordination with prudential regulator

(A) Referral

When the Bureau has reason to believe that a person described in subsection (a) has engaged in a material violation of a Federal consumer financial law, the Bureau shall notify the prudential regulator in writing and recommend appropriate action to respond.

(B) Response

Upon receiving a recommendation under subparagraph (A), the prudential regulator shall provide a written response to the Bureau not later than 60 days thereafter.

(e) Service providers

A service provider to a substantial number of persons described in subsection (a) shall be subject to the authority of the Bureau under section 5515 of this title to the same extent as if the Bureau were an appropriate Federal bank agency under section 1867(c) of this title. When conducting any examination or requiring any report from a service provider subject to this subsection, the Bureau shall coordinate with the appropriate prudential regulator.

§ 5517 [CFPA Act § 1027]. Limitations on authorities of the Bureau; preservation of authorities

(a) Exclusion for merchants, retailers, and other sellers of nonfinancial goods or services

(1) Sale or brokerage of nonfinancial good or service

The Bureau may not exercise any rulemaking, supervisory, enforcement or other authority under this title with respect to a person who is a merchant, retailer, or seller of any nonfinancial good or service and is engaged in the sale or brokerage of such nonfinancial good or service, except to the extent that such person is engaged in offering or providing any consumer financial product or service, or is otherwise subject to any enumerated consumer law or any law for which authorities are transferred under subtitle F or H.

(2) Offering or provision of certain consumer financial products or services in connection with the sale or brokerage of nonfinancial good or service

(A) In general

Except as provided in subparagraph (B), and subject to subparagraph (C), the Bureau may not exercise any rulemaking, supervisory, enforcement, or other authority under this title with respect to a merchant, retailer, or seller of nonfinancial goods or services, but only to the extent that such person—

(i) extends credit directly to a consumer, in a case in which the good or service being provided is not itself a consumer financial product or service (other than credit described in this subparagraph), exclusively for the purpose of enabling that consumer to purchase such nonfinancial good or service directly from the merchant, retailer, or seller;

(ii) directly, or through an agreement with another person, collects debt arising from credit extended as described in clause (i); or

(iii) sells or conveys debt described in clause (i) that is delinquent or otherwise in default.

(B) Applicability

Subparagraph (A) does not apply to any credit transaction or collection of debt, other than as described in subparagraph (C)(i), arising from a transaction described in subparagraph (A)—

(i) in which the merchant, retailer, or seller of nonfinancial goods or services assigns, sells or otherwise conveys to another person such debt owed by the consumer (except for a sale of debt that is delinquent or otherwise in default, as described in subparagraph (A)(iii));

(ii) in which the credit extended significantly exceeds the market value of the nonfinancial good or service provided, or the Bureau otherwise finds that the sale of the nonfinancial good or service is done as a subterfuge, so as to evade or circumvent the provisions of this title; or

(iii) in which the merchant, retailer, or seller of nonfinancial goods or services regularly extends credit and the credit is subject to a finance charge.

(C) Limitations

(i) In general

Notwithstanding subparagraph (B), subparagraph (A) shall apply with respect to a merchant, retailer, or seller of nonfinancial goods or services that is not engaged significantly in offering or providing consumer financial products or services.

(ii) Exception

Subparagraph (A) and clause (i) of this subparagraph do not apply to any merchant, retailer, or seller of nonfinancial goods or services—

(I) if such merchant, retailer, or seller of nonfinancial goods or services is engaged in a transaction described in subparagraph (B)(i) or (B)(ii); or

(II) to the extent that such merchant, retailer, or seller is subject to any enumerated consumer law or any law for which authorities are transferred under subtitle F or H, but the Bureau may exercise such authority only with respect to that law.

(D) Rules

(i) Authority of other agencies

No provision of this title shall be construed as modifying, limiting, or superseding the supervisory or enforcement authority of the Federal Trade Commission or any other agency (other than the Bureau) with respect to credit extended, or the collection of debt arising from such extension, directly by a merchant or retailer to a consumer exclusively for the purpose of enabling that consumer to purchase nonfinancial goods or services directly from the merchant or retailer.

(ii) Small businesses

A merchant, retailer, or seller of nonfinancial goods or services that would otherwise be subject to the authority of the Bureau solely by virtue of the application of subparagraph (B)(iii) shall be deemed not to be engaged significantly in offering or providing consumer financial products or services under subparagraph (C)(i), if such person—

(I) only extends credit for the sale of nonfinancial goods or services, as described in subparagraph (A)(i);

(II) retains such credit on its own accounts (except to sell or convey such debt that is delinquent or otherwise in default); and

(III) meets the relevant industry size threshold to be a small business concern, based on annual receipts, pursuant to section 3 of the Small Business Act (15 U.S.C. 632) and the implementing rules thereunder.

(iii) Initial year

A merchant, retailer, or seller of nonfinancial goods or services shall be deemed to meet the relevant industry size threshold described in clause (ii)(III) during the first year of operations of that business concern if, during that year, the receipts of that business concern reasonably are expected to meet that size threshold.

(iv) Other standards for small business

With respect to a merchant, retailer, or seller of nonfinancial goods or services that is a classified on a basis other than annual receipts for the purposes of section 3 of the Small Business Act (15 U.S.C. 632) and the implementing rules thereunder, such merchant, retailer, or seller shall be deemed to meet the relevant industry size threshold described in clause (ii)(III) if such merchant, retailer, or seller meets the relevant industry size threshold to be a small business concern based on the number of employees, or other such applicable measure, established under that Act.

(E) Exception from State enforcement

To the extent that the Bureau may not exercise authority under this subsection with respect to a merchant, retailer, or seller of nonfinancial goods or services, no action by a

State attorney general or State regulator with respect to a claim made under this title may be brought under subsection 5552(a) of this title, with respect to an activity described in any of clauses (i) through (iii) of subparagraph (A) by such merchant, retailer, or seller of nonfinancial goods or services.

(b) Exclusion for real estate brokerage activities

(1) Real estate brokerage activities excluded

Without limiting subsection (a), and except as permitted in paragraph (2), the Bureau may not exercise any rulemaking, supervisory, enforcement, or other authority under this title with respect to a person that is licensed or registered as a real estate broker or real estate agent, in accordance with State law, to the extent that such person—

(A) acts as a real estate agent or broker for a buyer, seller, lessor, or lessee of real property;

(B) brings together parties interested in the sale, purchase, lease, rental, or exchange of real property;

(C) negotiates, on behalf of any party, any portion of a contract relating to the sale, purchase, lease, rental, or exchange of real property (other than in connection with the provision of financing with respect to any such transaction); or

(D) offers to engage in any activity, or act in any capacity, described in subparagraph (A), (B), or (C).

(2) Description of activities

The Bureau may exercise rulemaking, supervisory, enforcement, or other authority under this title with respect to a person described in paragraph (1) when such person is—

(A) engaged in an activity of offering or providing any consumer financial product or service, except that the Bureau may exercise such authority only with respect to that activity; or

(B) otherwise subject to any enumerated consumer law or any law for which authorities are transferred under subtitle F or H, but the Bureau may exercise such authority only with respect to that law.

(c) Exclusion for manufactured home retailers and modular home retailers

(1) In general

The Director may not exercise any rulemaking, supervisory, enforcement, or other authority over a person to the extent that—

(A) such person is not described in paragraph (2); and

(B) such person—

(i) acts as an agent or broker for a buyer or seller of a manufactured home or a modular home;

(ii) facilitates the purchase by a consumer of a manufactured home or modular home, by negotiating the purchase price or terms of the sales contract (other than providing financing with respect to such transaction); or

(iii) offers to engage in any activity described in clause (i) or (ii).

(2) Description of activities

A person is described in this paragraph to the extent that such person is engaged in the offering or provision of any consumer financial product or service or is otherwise subject to any enumerated consumer law or any law for which authorities are transferred under subtitle F or H.

(3) Definitions

For purposes of this subsection, the following definitions shall apply:

(A) Manufactured home

The term "manufactured home" has the same meaning as in section 5402 of Title 42.

(B) Modular home

The term "modular home" means a house built in a factory in 2 or more modules that meet the State or local building codes where the house will be located, and where such modules are transported to the building site, installed on foundations, and completed.

(d) Exclusion for accountants and tax preparers

(1) In general

Except as permitted in paragraph (2), the Bureau may not exercise any rulemaking, supervisory, enforcement, or other authority over—

(A) any person that is a certified public accountant, permitted to practice as a certified public accounting firm, or certified or licensed for such purpose by a State, or any individual who is employed by or holds an ownership interest with respect to a person described in this subparagraph, when such person is performing or offering to perform—

(i) customary and usual accounting activities, including the provision of accounting, tax, advisory, or other services that are subject to the regulatory authority of a State board of accountancy or a Federal authority; or

(ii) other services that are incidental to such customary and usual accounting activities, to the extent that such incidental services are not offered or provided—

(I) by the person separate and apart from such customary and usual accounting activities; or

(II) to consumers who are not receiving such customary and usual accounting activities; or

(B) any person, other than a person described in subparagraph (A) [1] that performs income tax preparation activities for consumers.

(2) Description of activities

(A) In general

Paragraph (1) shall not apply to any person described in paragraph (1)(A) or (1)(B) to the extent that such person is engaged in any activity which is not a customary and usual accounting activity described in paragraph (1)(A) or incidental thereto but which is the offering or provision of any consumer financial product or service, except to the extent that a person described in paragraph (1)(A) is engaged in an activity which is a customary and usual accounting activity described in paragraph (1)(A), or incidental thereto.

(B) Not a customary and usual accounting activity

For purposes of this subsection, extending or brokering credit is not a customary and usual accounting activity, or incidental thereto.

(C) Rule of construction

---

1 So in original. Probably should be followed by a comma.

For purposes of subparagraphs (A) and (B), a person described in paragraph (1)(A) shall not be deemed to be extending credit, if such person is only extending credit directly to a consumer, exclusively for the purpose of enabling such consumer to purchase services described in clause (i) or (ii) of paragraph (1)(A) directly from such person, and such credit is—

(i) not subject to a finance charge; and

(ii) not payable by written agreement in more than 4 installments.

(D) Other limitations

Paragraph (1) does not apply to any person described in paragraph (1)(A) or (1)(B) that is otherwise subject to any enumerated consumer law or any law for which authorities are transferred under subtitle F or H.

(e) Exclusion for practice of law

(1) In general

Except as provided under paragraph (2), the Bureau may not exercise any supervisory or enforcement authority with respect to an activity engaged in by an attorney as part of the practice of law under the laws of a State in which the attorney is licensed to practice law.

(2) Rule of construction

Paragraph (1) shall not be construed so as to limit the exercise by the Bureau of any supervisory, enforcement, or other authority regarding the offering or provision of a consumer financial product or service described in any subparagraph of section 5481(5) of this title—

(A) that is not offered or provided as part of, or incidental to, the practice of law, occurring exclusively within the scope of the attorney-client relationship; or

(B) that is otherwise offered or provided by the attorney in question with respect to any consumer who is not receiving legal advice or services from the attorney in connection with such financial product or service.

(3) Existing authority

Paragraph (1) shall not be construed so as to limit the authority of the Bureau with respect to any attorney, to the extent that such attorney is otherwise subject to any of the enumerated consumer laws or the authorities transferred under subtitle F or H.

(f) Exclusion for persons regulated by a State insurance regulator

(1) In general

No provision of this title shall be construed as altering, amending, or affecting the authority of any State insurance regulator to adopt rules, initiate enforcement proceedings, or take any other action with respect to a person regulated by a State insurance regulator. Except as provided in paragraph (2), the Bureau shall have no authority to exercise any power to enforce this title with respect to a person regulated by a State insurance regulator.

(2) Description of activities

Paragraph (1) does not apply to any person described in such paragraph to the extent that such person is engaged in the offering or provision of any consumer financial product or service or is otherwise subject to any enumerated consumer law or any law for which authorities are transferred under subtitle F or H.

(3) State insurance authority under Gramm-Leach-Bliley

Notwithstanding paragraph (2), the Bureau shall not exercise any authorities that are granted a State insurance authority under section 6805(a)(6) of Title 15 with respect to a person regulated by a State insurance authority.

(g) Exclusion for employee benefit and compensation plans and certain other arrangements under Title 26

(1) Preservation of authority of other agencies

No provision of this title shall be construed as altering, amending, or affecting the authority of the Secretary of the Treasury, the Secretary of Labor, or the Commissioner of Internal Revenue to adopt regulations, initiate enforcement proceedings, or take any actions with respect to any specified plan or arrangement.

(2) Activities not constituting the offering or provision of any consumer financial product or service

For purposes of this title, a person shall not be treated as having engaged in the offering or provision of any consumer financial product or service solely because such person is—

(A) a specified plan or arrangement;

(B) engaged in the activity of establishing or maintaining, for the benefit of employees of such person (or for members of an employee organization), any specified plan or arrangement; or

(C) engaged in the activity of establishing or maintaining a qualified tuition program under section 529(b)(1) of Title 26 offered by a State or other prepaid tuition program offered by a State.

(3) Limitation on Bureau authority

(A) In general

Except as provided under subparagraphs (B) and (C), the Bureau may not exercise any rulemaking or enforcement authority with respect to products or services that relate to any specified plan or arrangement.

(B) Bureau action pursuant to agency request

(i) Agency request

The Secretary and the Secretary of Labor may jointly issue a written request to the Bureau regarding implementation of appropriate consumer protection standards under this title with respect to the provision of services relating to any specified plan or arrangement.

(ii) Agency response

In response to a request by the Bureau, the Secretary and the Secretary of Labor shall jointly issue a written response, not later than 90 days after receipt of such request, to grant or deny the request of the Bureau regarding implementation of appropriate consumer protection standards under this title with respect to the provision of services relating to any specified plan or arrangement.

(iii) Scope of Bureau action

Subject to a request or response pursuant to clause (i) or clause (ii) by the agencies made under this subparagraph, the Bureau may exercise rulemaking authority, and may act to enforce a rule prescribed pursuant to such request or response, in accordance with the provisions of this title. A request or response made by the Secretary and the Secretary of Labor under this subparagraph shall describe the basis for, and scope of, appropriate consumer protection standards to be implemented under this title with respect to the provision of services relating to any specified plan or arrangement.

(C) Description of products or services

To the extent that a person engaged in providing products or services relating to any specified plan or arrangement is subject to any enumerated consumer law or any law for which authorities are transferred under subtitle F or H, subparagraph (A) shall not apply with respect to that law.

(4) Specified plan or arrangement

For purposes of this subsection, the term "specified plan or arrangement" means any plan, account, or arrangement described in section 220, 223, 401(a), 403(a), 403(b), 408, 408A, 529, 529A, or 530 of Title 26, or any employee benefit or compensation plan or arrangement, including a plan that is subject to Title I of the Employee Retirement Income Security Act of 1974, or any prepaid tuition program offered by a State.

(h) Persons regulated by a State securities commission

(1) In general

No provision of this title shall be construed as altering, amending, or affecting the authority of any securities commission (or any agency or office performing like functions) of any State to adopt rules, initiate enforcement proceedings, or take any other action with respect to a person regulated by any securities commission (or any agency or office performing like functions) of any State. Except as permitted in paragraph (2) and subsection (f), the Bureau shall have no authority to exercise any power to enforce this title with respect to a person regulated by any securities commission (or any agency or office performing like functions) of any State, but only to the extent that the person acts in such regulated capacity.

(2) Description of activities

Paragraph (1) shall not apply to any person to the extent such person is engaged in the offering or provision of any consumer financial product or service, or is otherwise subject to any enumerated consumer law or any law for which authorities are transferred under subtitle F or H.

(i) Exclusion for persons regulated by the Commission

(1) In general

No provision of this title may be construed as altering, amending, or affecting the authority of the Commission to adopt rules, initiate enforcement proceedings, or take any other action with respect to a person regulated by the Commission. The Bureau shall have no authority to exercise any power to enforce this title with respect to a person regulated by the Commission.

(2) Consultation and coordination

Notwithstanding paragraph (1), the Commission shall consult and coordinate, where feasible, with the Bureau with respect to any rule (including any advance notice of proposed rulemaking) regarding an investment product or service that is the same type of product as, or that competes directly with, a consumer financial product or service that is subject to the jurisdiction of the Bureau under this title or under any other law. In carrying out this paragraph, the agencies shall negotiate an agreement to establish procedures for such coordination, including procedures for providing advance notice to the Bureau when the Commission is initiating a rulemaking.

(j) Exclusion for persons regulated by the Commodity Futures Trading Commission

(1) In general

No provision of this title shall be construed as altering, amending, or affecting the authority of the Commodity Futures Trading Commission to adopt rules, initiate enforcement proceedings, or take any other action with respect to a person regulated by the Commodity Futures Trading Commission. The Bureau shall have no authority to exercise any power to enforce this title with respect to a person regulated by the Commodity Futures Trading Commission.

(2) Consultation and coordination

Notwithstanding paragraph (1), the Commodity Futures Trading Commission shall consult and coordinate with the Bureau with respect to any rule (including any advance notice of proposed rulemaking) regarding a product or service that is the same type of product as, or that competes directly with, a consumer financial product or service that is subject to the jurisdiction of the Bureau under this title or under any other law.

(k) Exclusion for persons regulated by the Farm Credit Administration

(1) In general

No provision of this title shall be construed as altering, amending, or affecting the authority of the Farm Credit Administration to adopt rules, initiate enforcement proceedings, or take any other action with respect to a person regulated by the Farm Credit Administration. The Bureau shall have no authority to exercise any power to enforce this title with respect to a person regulated by the Farm Credit Administration.

(2) Definition

For purposes of this subsection, the term "person regulated by the Farm Credit Administration" means any Farm Credit System institution that is chartered and subject to the provisions of the Farm Credit Act of 1971 (12 U.S.C. 2001 et seq.).

(*l*) Exclusion for activities relating to charitable contributions

(1) In general

The Director and the Bureau may not exercise any rulemaking, supervisory, enforcement, or other authority, including authority to order penalties, over any activities related to the solicitation or making of voluntary contributions to a tax-exempt organization as recognized by the Internal Revenue Service, by any agent, volunteer, or representative of such organizations to the extent the organization, agent, volunteer, or representative thereof is soliciting or providing advice, information, education, or instruction to any donor or potential donor relating to a contribution to the organization.

(2) Limitation

The exclusion in paragraph (1) does not apply to other activities not described in paragraph (1) that are the offering or provision of any consumer financial product or service, or are otherwise subject to any enumerated consumer law or any law for which authorities are transferred under subtitle F or H.

(m) Insurance

The Bureau may not define as a financial product or service, by regulation or otherwise, engaging in the business of insurance.

(n) Limited authority of the Bureau

Notwithstanding subsections (a) through (h) and (*l*), a person subject to or described in one or more of such provisions—

(1) may be a service provider; and

(2) may be subject to requests from, or requirements imposed by, the Bureau regarding information in order to carry out the responsibilities and functions of the Bureau and in accordance with section 5512, 5562, or 5563 of this title.

(*o*) No authority to impose usury limit

No provision of this title shall be construed as conferring authority on the Bureau to establish a usury limit applicable to an extension of credit offered or made by a covered person to a consumer, unless explicitly authorized by law.

(p) Attorney General

No provision of this title, including section 5514(c)(1) of this title, shall affect the authorities of the Attorney General under otherwise applicable provisions of law.

(q) Secretary of the Treasury

No provision of this title shall affect the authorities of the Secretary, including with respect to prescribing rules, initiating enforcement proceedings, or taking other actions with respect to a person that performs income tax preparation activities for consumers.

(r) Deposit insurance and share insurance

Nothing in this title shall affect the authority of the Corporation under the Federal Deposit Insurance Act or the National Credit Union Administration Board under the Federal Credit Union Act as to matters related to deposit insurance and share insurance, respectively.

(s) Fair Housing Act

No provision of this title shall be construed as affecting any authority arising under the Fair Housing Act.

§ 5518 [CFPA Act § 1028]. Authority to restrict mandatory pre-dispute arbitration

(a) Study and report

The Bureau shall conduct a study of, and shall provide a report to Congress concerning, the use of agreements providing for arbitration of any future dispute between covered persons and consumers in connection with the offering or providing of consumer financial products or services.

(b) Further authority

The Bureau, by regulation, may prohibit or impose conditions or limitations on the use of an agreement between a covered person and a consumer for a consumer financial product or service providing for arbitration of any future dispute between the parties, if the Bureau finds that such a prohibition or imposition of conditions or limitations is in the public interest and for the protection of consumers. The findings in such rule shall be consistent with the study conducted under subsection (a).

(c) Limitation

The authority described in subsection (b) may not be construed to prohibit or restrict a consumer from entering into a voluntary arbitration agreement with a covered person after a dispute has arisen.

(d) Effective date

Notwithstanding any other provision of law, any regulation prescribed by the Bureau under subsection (b) shall apply, consistent with the terms of the regulation, to any agreement between a consumer and a covered person entered into after the end of the 180-day period beginning on the effective date of the regulation, as established by the Bureau.

§ 5519 [CFPA Act § 1029]. Exclusion for auto dealers

(a) Sale, servicing, and leasing of motor vehicles excluded

Except as permitted in subsection (b), the Bureau may not exercise any rulemaking, supervisory, enforcement or any other authority, including any authority to order assessments, over a motor vehicle dealer that is predominantly engaged in the sale and servicing of motor vehicles, the leasing and servicing of motor vehicles, or both.

(b) Certain functions excepted

Subsection (a) shall not apply to any person, to the extent that such person—

(1) provides consumers with any services related to residential or commercial mortgages or self-financing transactions involving real property;

(2) operates a line of business—

(A) that involves the extension of retail credit or retail leases involving motor vehicles; and

(B) in which—

(i) the extension of retail credit or retail leases are provided directly to consumers; and

(ii) the contract governing such extension of retail credit or retail leases is not routinely assigned to an unaffiliated third party finance or leasing source; or

(3) offers or provides a consumer financial product or service not involving or related to the sale, financing, leasing, rental, repair, refurbishment, maintenance, or other servicing of motor vehicles, motor vehicle parts, or any related or ancillary product or service.

(c) Preservation of authorities of other agencies

Except as provided in subsections (b) and (d), nothing in this title, including subtitle F, shall be construed as modifying, limiting, or superseding the operation of any provision of Federal law, or otherwise affecting the authority of the Board of Governors, the Federal Trade Commission, or any other Federal agency, with respect to a person described in subsection (a).

(d) Federal Trade Commission authority

Notwithstanding section 57a of Title 15, the Federal Trade Commission is authorized to prescribe rules under sections 45 and 57a(a)(1)(B) of Title 15.[1] in accordance with section 553 of Title 5, with respect to a person described in subsection (a).

(e) Coordination with Office of Service Member Affairs

The Board of Governors and the Federal Trade Commission shall coordinate with the Office of Service Member Affairs, to ensure that—

(1) service members and their families are educated and empowered to make better informed decisions regarding consumer financial products and services offered by motor vehicle dealers, with a focus on motor vehicle dealers in the proximity of military installations; and

(2) complaints by service members and their families concerning such motor vehicle dealers are effectively monitored and responded to, and where appropriate, enforcement action is pursued by the authorized agencies.

(f) Definitions

For purposes of this section, the following definitions shall apply:

(1) Motor vehicle

The term "motor vehicle" means—

---

[1] So in original. The period probably should be a comma.

(A) any self-propelled vehicle designed for transporting persons or property on a street, highway, or other road;

(B) recreational boats and marine equipment;

(C) motorcycles;

(D) motor homes, recreational vehicle trailers, and slide-in campers, as those terms are defined in sections 571.3 and 575.103 (d) of title 49, Code of Federal Regulations, or any successor thereto; and

(E) other vehicles that are titled and sold through dealers.

(2) Motor vehicle dealer

The term "motor vehicle dealer" means any person or resident in the United States, or any territory of the United States, who—

(A) is licensed by a State, a territory of the United States, or the District of Columbia to engage in the sale of motor vehicles; and

(B) takes title to, holds an ownership in, or takes physical custody of motor vehicles.

PART C—SPECIFIC BUREAU AUTHORITIES

§ 5531 [CPFA Act § 5531]. Prohibiting unfair, deceptive, or abusive acts or practices

(a) In general

The Bureau may take any action authorized under part E to prevent a covered person or service provider from committing or engaging in an unfair, deceptive, or abusive act or practice under Federal law in connection with any transaction with a consumer for a consumer financial product or service, or the offering of a consumer financial product or service.

(b) Rulemaking

The Bureau may prescribe rules applicable to a covered person or service provider identifying as unlawful unfair, deceptive, or abusive acts or practices in connection with any transaction with a consumer for a consumer financial product or service, or the offering of a consumer financial product or service. Rules under this section may include requirements for the purpose of preventing such acts or practices.

(c) Unfairness

(1) In general

The Bureau shall have no authority under this section to declare an act or practice in connection with a transaction with a consumer for a consumer financial product or service, or the offering of a consumer financial product or service, to be unlawful on the grounds that such act or practice is unfair, unless the Bureau has a reasonable basis to conclude that—

(A) the act or practice causes or is likely to cause substantial injury to consumers which is not reasonably avoidable by consumers; and

(B) such substantial injury is not outweighed by countervailing benefits to consumers or to competition.

(2) Consideration of public policies

In determining whether an act or practice is unfair, the Bureau may consider established public policies as evidence to be considered with all other evidence. Such public policy considerations may not serve as a primary basis for such determination.

(d) Abusive

The Bureau shall have no authority under this section to declare an act or practice abusive in connection with the provision of a consumer financial product or service, unless the act or practice—

(1) materially interferes with the ability of a consumer to understand a term or condition of a consumer financial product or service; or

(2) takes unreasonable advantage of—

(A) a lack of understanding on the part of the consumer of the material risks, costs, or conditions of the product or service;

(B) the inability of the consumer to protect the interests of the consumer in selecting or using a consumer financial product or service; or

(C) the reasonable reliance by the consumer on a covered person to act in the interests of the consumer.

(e) Consultation

In prescribing rules under this section, the Bureau shall consult with the Federal banking agencies, or other Federal agencies, as appropriate, concerning the consistency of the proposed rule with prudential, market, or systemic objectives administered by such agencies.

(f) Consideration of seasonal income

The rules of the Bureau under this section shall provide, with respect to an extension of credit secured by residential real estate or a dwelling, if documented income of the borrower, including income from a small business, is a repayment source for an extension of credit secured by residential real estate or a dwelling, the creditor may consider the seasonality and irregularity of such income in the underwriting of and scheduling of payments for such credit.

§ 5532 [CFPA Act § 1032]. Disclosures

(a) In general

The Bureau may prescribe rules to ensure that the features of any consumer financial product or service, both initially and over the term of the product or service, are fully, accurately, and effectively disclosed to consumers in a manner that permits consumers to understand the costs, benefits, and risks associated with the product or service, in light of the facts and circumstances.

(b) Model disclosures

(1) In general

Any final rule prescribed by the Bureau under this section requiring disclosures may include a model form that may be used at the option of the covered person for provision of the required disclosures.

(2) Format

A model form issued pursuant to paragraph (1) shall contain a clear and conspicuous disclosure that, at a minimum—

(A) uses plain language comprehensible to consumers;

(B) contains a clear format and design, such as an easily readable type font; and

(C) succinctly explains the information that must be communicated to the consumer.

(3) Consumer testing

Any model form issued pursuant to this subsection shall be validated through consumer testing.

(c) Basis for rulemaking

In prescribing rules under this section, the Bureau shall consider available evidence about consumer awareness, understanding of, and responses to disclosures or communications about the risks, costs, and benefits of consumer financial products or services.

(d) Safe harbor

Any covered person that uses a model form included with a rule issued under this section shall be deemed to be in compliance with the disclosure requirements of this section with respect to such model form.

(e) Trial disclosure programs

(1) In general

The Bureau may permit a covered person to conduct a trial program that is limited in time and scope, subject to specified standards and procedures, for the purpose of providing trial disclosures to consumers that are designed to improve upon any model form issued pursuant to subsection (b)(1), or any other model form issued to implement an enumerated statute, as applicable.

(2) Safe harbor

The standards and procedures issued by the Bureau shall be designed to encourage covered persons to conduct trial disclosure programs. For the purposes of administering this subsection, the Bureau may establish a limited period during which a covered person conducting a trial disclosure program shall be deemed to be in compliance with, or may be exempted from, a requirement of a rule or an enumerated consumer law.

(3) Public disclosure

The rules of the Bureau shall provide for public disclosure of trial disclosure programs, which public disclosure may be limited, to the extent necessary to encourage covered persons to conduct effective trials.

(f) Combined mortgage loan disclosure

Not later than 1 year after the designated transfer date, the Bureau shall propose for public comment rules and model disclosures that combine the disclosures required under the Truth in Lending Act and sections 2603 and 2604 of this title, into a single, integrated disclosure for mortgage loan transactions covered by those laws, unless the Bureau determines that any proposal issued by the Board of Governors and the Secretary of Housing and Urban Development carries out the same purpose.

§ 5533 [CFPA Act § 1033]. Consumer rights to access information

(a) In general

Subject to rules prescribed by the Bureau, a covered person shall make available to a consumer, upon request, information in the control or possession of the covered person concerning the consumer financial product or service that the consumer obtained from such covered person, including information relating to any transaction, series of transactions, or to the account including costs, charges and usage data. The information shall be made available in an electronic form usable by consumers.

(b) Exceptions

A covered person may not be required by this section to make available to the consumer—

(1) any confidential commercial information, including an algorithm used to derive credit scores or other risk scores or predictors;

(2) any information collected by the covered person for the purpose of preventing fraud or money laundering, or detecting, or making any report regarding other unlawful or potentially unlawful conduct;

(3) any information required to be kept confidential by any other provision of law; or

(4) any information that the covered person cannot retrieve in the ordinary course of its business with respect to that information.

(c) No duty to maintain records

Nothing in this section shall be construed to impose any duty on a covered person to maintain or keep any information about a consumer.

(d) Standardized formats for data

The Bureau, by rule, shall prescribe standards applicable to covered persons to promote the development and use of standardized formats for information, including through the use of machine readable files, to be made available to consumers under this section.

(e) Consultation

The Bureau shall, when prescribing any rule under this section, consult with the Federal banking agencies and the Federal Trade Commission to ensure, to the extent appropriate, that the rules—

(1) impose substantively similar requirements on covered persons;

(2) take into account conditions under which covered persons do business both in the United States and in other countries; and

(3) do not require or promote the use of any particular technology in order to develop systems for compliance.

§ 5534 [CFPA Act § 1034]. Response to consumer complaints and inquiries

(a) Timely regulator response to consumers

The Bureau shall establish, in consultation with the appropriate Federal regulatory agencies, reasonable procedures to provide a timely response to consumers, in writing where appropriate, to complaints against, or inquiries concerning, a covered person, including—

(1) steps that have been taken by the regulator in response to the complaint or inquiry of the consumer;

(2) any responses received by the regulator from the covered person; and

(3) any follow-up actions or planned follow-up actions by the regulator in response to the complaint or inquiry of the consumer.

(b) Timely response to regulator by covered person

A covered person subject to supervision and primary enforcement by the Bureau pursuant to section 5515 of this title shall provide a timely response, in writing where appropriate, to the Bureau, the prudential regulators, and any other agency having jurisdiction over such covered person concerning a consumer complaint or inquiry, including—

(1) steps that have been taken by the covered person to respond to the complaint or inquiry of the consumer;

(2) responses received by the covered person from the consumer; and

(3) follow-up actions or planned follow-up actions by the covered person to respond to the complaint or inquiry of the consumer.

(c) Provision of information to consumers

(1) In general

A covered person subject to supervision and primary enforcement by the Bureau pursuant to section 5515 of this title shall, in a timely manner, comply with a consumer request for information in the control or possession of such covered person concerning the consumer financial product or service that the consumer obtained from such covered person, including supporting written documentation, concerning the account of the consumer.

(2) Exceptions

A covered person subject to supervision and primary enforcement by the Bureau pursuant to section 5515 of this title, a prudential regulator, and any other agency having jurisdiction over a covered person subject to supervision and primary enforcement by the Bureau pursuant to section 5515 of this title may not be required by this section to make available to the consumer—

(A) any confidential commercial information, including an algorithm used to derive credit scores or other risk scores or predictors;

(B) any information collected by the covered person for the purpose of preventing fraud or money laundering, or detecting or making any report regarding other unlawful or potentially unlawful conduct;

(C) any information required to be kept confidential by any other provision of law; or

(D) any nonpublic or confidential information, including confidential supervisory information.

(d) Agreements with other agencies

The Bureau shall enter into a memorandum of understanding with any affected Federal regulatory agency regarding procedures by which any covered person, and the prudential regulators, and any other agency having jurisdiction over a covered person, including the Secretary of the Department of Housing and Urban Development and the Secretary of Education, shall comply with this section.

§ 5535 [FTCA Act § 1035]. Private Education Loan Ombudsman

(a) Establishment

The Secretary, in consultation with the Director, shall designate a Private Education Loan Ombudsman (in this section referred to as the "Ombudsman") within the Bureau, to provide timely assistance to borrowers of private education loans.

(b) Public information

The Secretary and the Director shall disseminate information about the availability and functions of the Ombudsman to borrowers and potential borrowers, as well as institutions of higher education, lenders, guaranty agencies, loan servicers, and other participants in private education student loan programs.

(c) Functions of Ombudsman

The Ombudsman designated under this subsection shall—

(1) in accordance with regulations of the Director, receive, review, and attempt to resolve informally complaints from borrowers of loans described in subsection (a), including, as appropriate, attempts to resolve such complaints in collaboration with the Department of Education and with institutions of higher education, lenders, guaranty agencies, loan servicers, and other participants in private education loan programs;

(2) not later than 90 days after the designated transfer date, establish a memorandum of understanding with the student loan ombudsman established under section 1018(f) of Title 20, to ensure coordination in providing assistance to and serving borrowers seeking to resolve complaints related to their private education or Federal student loans;

(3) compile and analyze data on borrower complaints regarding private education loans; and

(4) make appropriate recommendations to the Director, the Secretary, the Secretary of Education, the Committee on Banking, Housing, and Urban Affairs and the Committee on Health, Education, Labor, and Pensions of the Senate and the Committee on Financial Services and the Committee on Education and Labor of the House of Representatives.

(d) Annual reports

(1) In general

The Ombudsman shall prepare an annual report that describes the activities, and evaluates the effectiveness of the Ombudsman during the preceding year.

(2) Submission

The report required by paragraph (1) shall be submitted on the same date annually to the Secretary, the Secretary of Education, the Committee on Banking, Housing, and Urban Affairs and the Committee on Health, Education, Labor, and Pensions of the Senate and the Committee on Financial Services and the Committee on Education and Labor of the House of Representatives.

(e) Definitions

For purposes of this section, the terms "private education loan" and "institution of higher education" have the same meanings as in section 1650 of Title 15.

§ 5536 [CFPA Act § 1036]. Prohibited acts

(a) In general

It shall be unlawful for—

(1) any covered person or service provider—

(A) to offer or provide to a consumer any financial product or service not in conformity with Federal consumer financial law, or otherwise commit any act or omission in violation of a Federal consumer financial law; or

(B) to engage in any unfair, deceptive, or abusive act or practice;

(2) any covered person or service provider to fail or refuse, as required by Federal consumer financial law, or any rule or order issued by the Bureau thereunder—

(A) to permit access to or copying of records;

(B) to establish or maintain records; or

(C) to make reports or provide information to the Bureau; or

(3) any person to knowingly or recklessly provide substantial assistance to a covered person or service provider in violation of the provisions of section 5531 of this title, or any rule or order issued thereunder, and notwithstanding any provision of this title, the provider of such substantial assistance shall be deemed to be in violation of that section to the same extent as the person to whom such assistance is provided.

(b) Exception

No person shall be held to have violated subsection (a)(1) solely by virtue of providing or selling time or space to a covered person or service provider placing an advertisement.

§ 5538 [CFPA Act § 1038]. Mortgage loans; rulemaking procedures; enforcement

(a)(1) The Bureau of Consumer Financial Protection shall have authority to prescribe rules with respect to mortgage loans in accordance with section 553 of Title 5. Such rulemaking shall relate to unfair or deceptive acts or practices regarding mortgage loans, which may include unfair or deceptive acts or practices involving loan modification and foreclosure rescue services. Any violation of a rule prescribed under this paragraph shall be treated as a violation of a rule prohibiting unfair, deceptive, or abusive acts or practices under the Consumer Financial Protection Act of 2010 and a violation of a rule under section 18 of the Federal Trade Commission Act (15 U.S.C. 57a) regarding unfair or deceptive acts or practices.

(2) The Bureau of Consumer Financial Protection shall enforce the rules issued under paragraph (1) in the same manner, by the same means, and with the same jurisdiction, powers, and duties, as though all applicable terms and provisions of the Consumer Financial Protection Act of 2010 were incorporated into and made part of this subsection.

(3) Subject to subtitle B of the Consumer Financial Protection Act of 2010 [12 U.S.C. 5511 et seq.], the Federal Trade Commission shall enforce the rules issued under paragraph (1), in the same manner, by the same means, and with the same jurisdiction, as though all applicable terms and provisions of the Federal Trade Commission Act [15 U.S.C. 41 et seq.] were incorporated into and made part of this section.

(b)(1) Except as provided in paragraph (6), in any case in which the attorney general of a State has reason to believe that an interest of the residents of the State has been or is threatened or adversely affected by the engagement of any person subject to a rule prescribed under subsection (a) in practices that violate such rule, the State, as parens patriae, may bring a civil action on behalf of its residents in an appropriate district court of the United States or other court of competent jurisdiction—

(A) to enjoin that practice;

(B) to enforce compliance with the rule;

(C) to obtain damages, restitution, or other compensation on behalf of the residents of the State; or

(D) to obtain penalties and relief provided under the Consumer Financial Protection Act of 2010, the Federal Trade Commission Act [15 U.S.C. 41 et seq.], and such other relief as the court deems appropriate.

(2) The State shall serve written notice to the Bureau of Consumer Financial Protection or the Commission, as appropriate[1] of any civil action under paragraph (1) at least 60 days prior to initiating such civil action. The notice shall include a copy of the complaint to be filed to initiate such civil action, except that if it is not feasible for the State to provide such prior notice, the State shall provide notice immediately upon instituting such civil action.

(3) Upon receiving the notice required by paragraph (2), and subject to subtitle B of the Consumer Financial Protection Act of 2010 [12 U.S.C. 5511 et seq.], the Bureau of Consumer Financial Protection or the Commission, as appropriate[1] may intervene in such civil action and upon intervening—

(A) be heard on all matters arising in such civil action;

(B) remove the action to the appropriate United States district court; and

(C) file petitions for appeal of a decision in such civil action.

(4) Nothing in this subsection shall prevent the attorney general of a State from exercising the powers conferred on the attorney general by the laws of such State to conduct investigations

---

1 So in original. Probably should be followed by a comma.

or to administer oaths or affirmations or to compel the attendance of witnesses or the production of documentary and other evidence. Nothing in this section shall prohibit the attorney general of a State, or other authorized State officer, from proceeding in State or Federal court on the basis of an alleged violation of any civil or criminal statute of that State.

(5) In a civil action brought under paragraph (1)—

(A) the venue shall be a judicial district in which the defendant is found, is an inhabitant, or transacts business or wherever venue is proper under section 1391 of Title 28; and

(B) process may be served without regard to the territorial limits of the district or of the State in which the civil action is instituted.

(6) Whenever a civil action or an administrative action has been instituted by or on behalf of the Bureau of Consumer Financial Protection or the Commission for violation of any provision of law or rule described in paragraph (1), no State may, during the pendency of such action instituted by or on behalf of the Bureau of Consumer Financial Protection or the Commission, institute a civil action under that paragraph against any defendant named in the complaint in such action for violation of any law or rule as alleged in such complaint.

(7) If the attorney general of a State prevails in any civil action under paragraph (1), the State can recover reasonable costs and attorney fees from the lender or related party.

PART D—PRESERVATION OF STATE LAW

§ 5551 [CFPA Act § 1041]. Relation to State law

(a) In general

(1) Rule of construction

This title, other than sections 1044 through 1048, may not be construed as annulling, altering, or affecting, or exempting any person subject to the provisions of this title from complying with, the statutes, regulations, orders, or interpretations in effect in any State, except to the extent that any such provision of law is inconsistent with the provisions of this title, and then only to the extent of the inconsistency.

(2) Greater protection under State law

For purposes of this subsection, a statute, regulation, order, or interpretation in effect in any State is not inconsistent with the provisions of this title if the protection that such statute, regulation, order, or interpretation affords to consumers is greater than the protection provided under this title. A determination regarding whether a statute, regulation, order, or interpretation in effect in any State is inconsistent with the provisions of this title may be made by the Bureau on its own motion or in response to a nonfrivolous petition initiated by any interested person.

(b) Relation to other provisions of enumerated consumer laws that relate to State law

No provision of this title, except as provided in section 1083, shall be construed as modifying, limiting, or superseding the operation of any provision of an enumerated consumer law that relates to the application of a law in effect in any State with respect to such Federal law.

(c) Additional consumer protection regulations in response to State action

(1) Notice of proposed rule required

The Bureau shall issue a notice of proposed rulemaking whenever a majority of the States has enacted a resolution in support of the establishment or modification of a consumer protection regulation by the Bureau.

(2) Bureau considerations required for issuance of final regulation

Before prescribing a final regulation based upon a notice issued pursuant to paragraph (1), the Bureau shall take into account whether—

(A) the proposed regulation would afford greater protection to consumers than any existing regulation;

(B) the intended benefits of the proposed regulation for consumers would outweigh any increased costs or inconveniences for consumers, and would not discriminate unfairly against any category or class of consumers; and

(C) a Federal banking agency has advised that the proposed regulation is likely to present an unacceptable safety and soundness risk to insured depository institutions.

(3) Explanation of considerations

The Bureau—

(A) shall include a discussion of the considerations required in paragraph (2) in the Federal Register notice of a final regulation prescribed pursuant to this subsection; and

(B) whenever the Bureau determines not to prescribe a final regulation, shall publish an explanation of such determination in the Federal Register, and provide a copy of such explanation to each State that enacted a resolution in support of the proposed regulation, the Committee on Banking, Housing, and Urban Affairs of the Senate, and the Committee on Financial Services of the House of Representatives.

(4) Reservation of authority

No provision of this title shall be construed as limiting or restricting the authority of the Bureau to enhance consumer protection standards established pursuant to this subchapter in response to its own motion or in response to a request by any other interested person.

(5) Rule of construction

No provision of this subsection shall be construed as exempting the Bureau from complying with subchapter II of chapter 5 of Title 5.

(6) Definition

For purposes of this subsection, the term "consumer protection regulation" means a regulation that the Bureau is authorized to prescribe under the Federal consumer financial laws.

§ 5552 [CFPA Act § 1042]. Preservation of enforcement powers of States

(a) In general

(1) Action by State

Except as provided in paragraph (2), the attorney general (or the equivalent thereof) of any State may bring a civil action in the name of such State in any district court of the United States in that State or in State court that is located in that State and that has jurisdiction over the defendant, to enforce provisions of this title or regulations issued under this title, and to secure remedies under provisions of this title or remedies otherwise provided under other law. A State regulator may bring a civil action or other appropriate proceeding to enforce the provisions of this title or regulations issued under this title with respect to any entity that is State-chartered, incorporated, licensed, or otherwise authorized to do business under State law (except as provided in paragraph (2)), and to secure remedies under provisions of this title or remedies otherwise provided under other provisions of law with respect to such an entity.

(2) Action by State against national bank or Federal savings association to enforce rules

(A) In general

Except as permitted under subparagraph (B), the attorney general (or equivalent thereof) of any State may not bring a civil action in the name of such State against a national bank or Federal savings association to enforce a provision of this title.

(B) Enforcement of rules permitted

The attorney general (or the equivalent thereof) of any State may bring a civil action in the name of such State against a national bank or Federal savings association in any district court of the United States in the State or in State court that is located in that State and that has jurisdiction over the defendant to enforce a regulation prescribed by the Bureau under a provision of this title and to secure remedies under provisions of this title or remedies otherwise provided under other law.

(3) Rule of construction

No provision of this title shall be construed as modifying, limiting, or superseding the operation of any provision of an enumerated consumer law that relates to the authority of a State attorney general or State regulator to enforce such Federal law.

(b) Consultation required

(1) Notice

(A) In general

Before initiating any action in a court or other administrative or regulatory proceeding against any covered person as authorized by subsection (a) to enforce any provision of this title, including any regulation prescribed by the Bureau under this title, a State attorney general or State regulator shall timely provide a copy of the complete complaint to be filed and written notice describing such action or proceeding to the Bureau and the prudential regulator, if any, or the designee thereof.

(B) Emergency action

If prior notice is not practicable, the State attorney general or State regulator shall provide a copy of the complete complaint and the notice to the Bureau and the prudential regulator, if any, immediately upon instituting the action or proceeding.

(C) Contents of notice

The notification required under this paragraph shall, at a minimum, describe—

(i) the identity of the parties;

(ii) the alleged facts underlying the proceeding; and

(iii) whether there may be a need to coordinate the prosecution of the proceeding so as not to interfere with any action, including any rulemaking, undertaken by the Bureau, a prudential regulator, or another Federal agency.

(2) Bureau response

In any action described in paragraph (1), the Bureau may—

(A) intervene in the action as a party;

(B) upon intervening—

(i) remove the action to the appropriate United States district court, if the action was not originally brought there; and

(ii) be heard on all matters arising in the action; and

(C) appeal any order or judgment, to the same extent as any other party in the proceeding may.

(c) Regulations

The Bureau shall prescribe regulations to implement the requirements of this section and, from time to time, provide guidance in order to further coordinate actions with the State attorneys general and other regulators.

(d) Preservation of State authority

(1) State claims

No provision of this section shall be construed as altering, limiting, or affecting the authority of a State attorney general or any other regulatory or enforcement agency or authority to bring an action or other regulatory proceeding arising solely under the law in effect in that State.

(2) State securities regulators

No provision of this title shall be construed as altering, limiting, or affecting the authority of a State securities commission (or any agency or office performing like functions) under State law to adopt rules, initiate enforcement proceedings, or take any other action with respect to a person regulated by such commission or authority.

(3) State insurance regulators

No provision of this title shall be construed as altering, limiting, or affecting the authority of a State insurance commission or State insurance regulator under State law to adopt rules, initiate enforcement proceedings, or take any other action with respect to a person regulated by such commission or regulator.

* * *

PART E—ENFORCEMENT POWERS

§ 5561 [CFPA Act § 1051]. Definitions

For purposes of this part, the following definitions shall apply:

(1) Bureau investigation

The term "Bureau investigation" means any inquiry conducted by a Bureau investigator for the purpose of ascertaining whether any person is or has been engaged in any conduct that is a violation, as defined in this section.

(2) Bureau investigator

The term "Bureau investigator" means any attorney or investigator employed by the Bureau who is charged with the duty of enforcing or carrying into effect any Federal consumer financial law.

(3) Custodian

The term "custodian" means the custodian or any deputy custodian designated by the Bureau.

(4) Documentary material

The term "documentary material" includes the original or any copy of any book, document, record, report, memorandum, paper, communication, tabulation, chart, logs, electronic files, or other data or data compilations stored in any medium.

(5) Violation

The term "violation" means any act or omission that, if proved, would constitute a violation of any provision of Federal consumer financial law.

§ 5562 [CFPA Act § 1052]. Investigations and administrative discovery

(a) Joint investigations

(1) In general

The Bureau or, where appropriate, a Bureau investigator, may engage in joint investigations and requests for information, as authorized under this title.

(2) Fair lending

The authority under paragraph (1) includes matters relating to fair lending, and where appropriate, joint investigations with, and requests for information from, the Secretary of Housing and Urban Development, the Attorney General of the United States, or both.

(b) Subpoenas

(1) In general

The Bureau or a Bureau investigator may issue subpoenas for the attendance and testimony of witnesses and the production of relevant papers, books, documents, or other material in connection with hearings under this title.

(2) Failure to obey

In the case of contumacy or refusal to obey a subpoena issued pursuant to this paragraph and served upon any person, the district court of the United States for any district in which such person is found, resides, or transacts business, upon application by the Bureau or a Bureau investigator and after notice to such person, may issue an order requiring such person to appear and give testimony or to appear and produce documents or other material.

(3) Contempt

Any failure to obey an order of the court under this subsection may be punished by the court as a contempt thereof.

(c) Demands

(1) In general

Whenever the Bureau has reason to believe that any person may be in possession, custody, or control of any documentary material or tangible things, or may have any information, relevant to a violation, the Bureau may, before the institution of any proceedings under the Federal consumer financial law, issue in writing, and cause to be served upon such person, a civil investigative demand requiring such person to—

(A) produce such documentary material for inspection and copying or reproduction in the form or medium requested by the Bureau;

(B) submit such tangible things;

(C) file written reports or answers to questions;

(D) give oral testimony concerning documentary material, tangible things, or other information; or

(E) furnish any combination of such material, answers, or testimony.

(2) Requirements

Each civil investigative demand shall state the nature of the conduct constituting the alleged violation which is under investigation and the provision of law applicable to such violation.

(3) Production of documents

Each civil investigative demand for the production of documentary material shall—

(A) describe each class of documentary material to be produced under the demand with such definiteness and certainty as to permit such material to be fairly identified;

(B) prescribe a return date or dates which will provide a reasonable period of time within which the material so demanded may be assembled and made available for inspection and copying or reproduction; and

(C) identify the custodian to whom such material shall be made available.

(4) Production of things

Each civil investigative demand for the submission of tangible things shall—

(A) describe each class of tangible things to be submitted under the demand with such definiteness and certainty as to permit such things to be fairly identified;

(B) prescribe a return date or dates which will provide a reasonable period of time within which the things so demanded may be assembled and submitted; and

(C) identify the custodian to whom such things shall be submitted.

(5) Demand for written reports or answers

Each civil investigative demand for written reports or answers to questions shall—

(A) propound with definiteness and certainty the reports to be produced or the questions to be answered;

(B) prescribe a date or dates at which time written reports or answers to questions shall be submitted; and

(C) identify the custodian to whom such reports or answers shall be submitted.

(6) Oral testimony

Each civil investigative demand for the giving of oral testimony shall—

(A) prescribe a date, time, and place at which oral testimony shall be commenced; and

(B) identify a Bureau investigator who shall conduct the investigation and the custodian to whom the transcript of such investigation shall be submitted.

(7) Service

Any civil investigative demand issued, and any enforcement petition filed, under this section may be served—

(A) by any Bureau investigator at any place within the territorial jurisdiction of any court of the United States; and

(B) upon any person who is not found within the territorial jurisdiction of any court of the United States—

(i) in such manner as the Federal Rules of Civil Procedure prescribe for service in a foreign nation; and

(ii) to the extent that the courts of the United States have authority to assert jurisdiction over such person, consistent with due process, the United States District Court for the District of Columbia shall have the same jurisdiction to take any action respecting compliance with this section by such person that such district court would have if such person were personally within the jurisdiction of such district court.

(8) Method of service

Service of any civil investigative demand or any enforcement petition filed under this section may be made upon a person, including any legal entity, by—

(A) delivering a duly executed copy of such demand or petition to the individual or to any partner, executive officer, managing agent, or general agent of such person, or to any agent of such person authorized by appointment or by law to receive service of process on behalf of such person;

(B) delivering a duly executed copy of such demand or petition to the principal office or place of business of the person to be served; or

(C) depositing a duly executed copy in the United States mails, by registered or certified mail, return receipt requested, duly addressed to such person at the principal office or place of business of such person.

(9) Proof of service

(A) In general

A verified return by the individual serving any civil investigative demand or any enforcement petition filed under this section setting forth the manner of such service shall be proof of such service.

(B) Return receipts

In the case of service by registered or certified mail, such return shall be accompanied by the return post office receipt of delivery of such demand or enforcement petition.

(10) Production of documentary material

The production of documentary material in response to a civil investigative demand shall be made under a sworn certificate, in such form as the demand designates, by the person, if a natural person, to whom the demand is directed or, if not a natural person, by any person having knowledge of the facts and circumstances relating to such production, to the effect that all of the documentary material required by the demand and in the possession, custody, or control of the person to whom the demand is directed has been produced and made available to the custodian.

(11) Submission of tangible things

The submission of tangible things in response to a civil investigative demand shall be made under a sworn certificate, in such form as the demand designates, by the person to whom the demand is directed or, if not a natural person, by any person having knowledge of the facts and circumstances relating to such production, to the effect that all of the tangible things required by the demand and in the possession, custody, or control of the person to whom the demand is directed have been submitted to the custodian.

(12) Separate answers

Each reporting requirement or question in a civil investigative demand shall be answered separately and fully in writing under oath, unless it is objected to, in which event the reasons for the objection shall be stated in lieu of an answer, and it shall be submitted under a sworn certificate, in such form as the demand designates, by the person, if a natural person, to whom the demand is directed or, if not a natural person, by any person responsible for answering each reporting requirement or question, to the effect that all information required by the demand and in the possession, custody, control, or knowledge of the person to whom the demand is directed has been submitted.

(13) Testimony

(A) In general

(i) Oath and recordation

The examination of any person pursuant to a demand for oral testimony served under this subsection shall be taken before an officer authorized to administer oaths and affirmations by the laws of the United States or of the place at which the examination is held. The officer before whom oral testimony is to be taken shall put the witness on oath or affirmation and shall personally, or by any individual acting under the direction of and in the presence of the officer, record the testimony of the witness.

(ii) Transcription

The testimony shall be taken stenographically and transcribed.

(iii) Transmission to custodian

After the testimony is fully transcribed, the officer investigator before whom the testimony is taken shall promptly transmit a copy of the transcript of the testimony to the custodian.

(B) Parties present

Any Bureau investigator before whom oral testimony is to be taken shall exclude from the place where the testimony is to be taken all other persons, except the person giving the testimony, the attorney for that person, the officer before whom the testimony is to be taken, an investigator or representative of an agency with which the Bureau is engaged in a joint investigation, and any stenographer taking such testimony.

(C) Location

The oral testimony of any person taken pursuant to a civil investigative demand shall be taken in the judicial district of the United States in which such person resides, is found, or transacts business, or in such other place as may be agreed upon by the Bureau investigator before whom the oral testimony of such person is to be taken and such person.

(D) Attorney representation

(i) In general

Any person compelled to appear under a civil investigative demand for oral testimony pursuant to this section may be accompanied, represented, and advised by an attorney.

(ii) Authority

The attorney may advise a person described in clause (i), in confidence, either upon the request of such person or upon the initiative of the attorney, with respect to any question asked of such person.

(iii) Objections

A person described in clause (i), or the attorney for that person, may object on the record to any question, in whole or in part, and such person shall briefly state for the record the reason for the objection. An objection may properly be made, received, and entered upon the record when it is claimed that such person is entitled to refuse to answer the question on grounds of any constitutional or other legal right or privilege, including the privilege against self-incrimination, but such person shall not otherwise object to or refuse to answer any question, and such person or attorney shall not otherwise interrupt the oral examination.

(iv) Refusal to answer

If a person described in clause (i) refuses to answer any question—

(I) the Bureau may petition the district court of the United States pursuant to this section for an order compelling such person to answer such question; and

(II) if the refusal is on grounds of the privilege against self-incrimination, the testimony of such person may be compelled in accordance with the provisions of section 6004 of Title 18.

(E) Transcripts

For purposes of this subsection—

(i) after the testimony of any witness is fully transcribed, the Bureau investigator shall afford the witness (who may be accompanied by an attorney) a reasonable opportunity to examine the transcript;

(ii) the transcript shall be read to or by the witness, unless such examination and reading are waived by the witness;

(iii) any changes in form or substance which the witness desires to make shall be entered and identified upon the transcript by the Bureau investigator, with a statement of the reasons given by the witness for making such changes;

(iv) the transcript shall be signed by the witness, unless the witness in writing waives the signing, is ill, cannot be found, or refuses to sign; and

(v) if the transcript is not signed by the witness during the 30-day period following the date on which the witness is first afforded a reasonable opportunity to examine the transcript, the Bureau investigator shall sign the transcript and state on the record the fact of the waiver, illness, absence of the witness, or the refusal to sign, together with any reasons given for the failure to sign.

(F) Certification by investigator

The Bureau investigator shall certify on the transcript that the witness was duly sworn by him or her and that the transcript is a true record of the testimony given by the witness, and the Bureau investigator shall promptly deliver the transcript or send it by registered or certified mail to the custodian.

(G) Copy of transcript

The Bureau investigator shall furnish a copy of the transcript (upon payment of reasonable charges for the transcript) to the witness only, except that the Bureau may for good cause limit such witness to inspection of the official transcript of his testimony.

(H) Witness fees

Any witness appearing for the taking of oral testimony pursuant to a civil investigative demand shall be entitled to the same fees and mileage which are paid to witnesses in the district courts of the United States.

(d) Confidential treatment of demand material

(1) In general

Documentary materials and tangible things received as a result of a civil investigative demand shall be subject to requirements and procedures regarding confidentiality, in accordance with rules established by the Bureau.

(2) Disclosure to Congress

No rule established by the Bureau regarding the confidentiality of materials submitted to, or otherwise obtained by, the Bureau shall be intended to prevent disclosure to either House of Congress or to an appropriate committee of the Congress, except that the Bureau is permitted to adopt rules allowing prior notice to any party that owns or otherwise provided the material to the Bureau and had designated such material as confidential.

(e) Petition for enforcement

(1) In general

Whenever any person fails to comply with any civil investigative demand duly served upon him under this section, or whenever satisfactory copying or reproduction of material requested pursuant to the demand cannot be accomplished and such person refuses to surrender such material, the Bureau, through such officers or attorneys as it may designate, may file, in the district court of the United States for any judicial district in which such person resides, is found, or transacts business, and serve upon such person, a petition for an order of such court for the enforcement of this section.

(2) Service of process

All process of any court to which application may be made as provided in this subsection may be served in any judicial district.

(f) Petition for order modifying or setting aside demand

(1) In general

Not later than 20 days after the service of any civil investigative demand upon any person under subsection (b), or at any time before the return date specified in the demand, whichever period is shorter, or within such period exceeding 20 days after service or in excess of such return date as may be prescribed in writing, subsequent to service, by any Bureau investigator named in the demand, such person may file with the Bureau a petition for an order by the Bureau modifying or setting aside the demand.

(2) Compliance during pendency

The time permitted for compliance with the demand in whole or in part, as determined proper and ordered by the Bureau, shall not run during the pendency of a petition under paragraph (1) at the Bureau, except that such person shall comply with any portions of the demand not sought to be modified or set aside.

(3) Specific grounds

A petition under paragraph (1) shall specify each ground upon which the petitioner relies in seeking relief, and may be based upon any failure of the demand to comply with the provisions of this section, or upon any constitutional or other legal right or privilege of such person.

(g) Custodial control

At any time during which any custodian is in custody or control of any documentary material, tangible things, reports, answers to questions, or transcripts of oral testimony given by any person in compliance with any civil investigative demand, such person may file, in the district court of the United States for the judicial district within which the office of such custodian is situated, and serve upon such custodian, a petition for an order of such court requiring the performance by such custodian of any duty imposed upon him by this section or rule promulgated by the Bureau.

(h) Jurisdiction of court

(1) In general

Whenever any petition is filed in any district court of the United States under this section, such court shall have jurisdiction to hear and determine the matter so presented, and to enter such order or orders as may be required to carry out the provisions of this section.

(2) Appeal

Any final order entered as described in paragraph (1) shall be subject to appeal pursuant to section 1291 of Title 28.

§ 5563 [CFPA Act § 1053]. Hearings and adjudication proceedings

(a) In general

The Bureau is authorized to conduct hearings and adjudication proceedings with respect to any person in the manner prescribed by chapter 5 of Title 5 in order to ensure or enforce compliance with—

(1) the provisions of this title, including any rules prescribed by the Bureau under this title; and

(2) any other Federal law that the Bureau is authorized to enforce, including an enumerated consumer law, and any regulations or order prescribed thereunder, unless such Federal law specifically limits the Bureau from conducting a hearing or adjudication proceeding and only to the extent of such limitation.

(b) Special rules for cease-and-desist proceedings

(1) Orders authorized

(A) In general

If, in the opinion of the Bureau, any covered person or service provider is engaging or has engaged in an activity that violates a law, rule, or any condition imposed in writing on the person by the Bureau, the Bureau may, subject to sections 5514, 5515, and 5516 of this title, issue and serve upon the covered person or service provider a notice of charges in respect thereof.

(B) Content of notice

The notice under subparagraph (A) shall contain a statement of the facts constituting the alleged violation or violations, and shall fix a time and place at which a hearing will be held to determine whether an order to cease and desist should issue against the covered person or service provider, such hearing to be held not earlier than 30 days nor later than 60 days after the date of service of such notice, unless an earlier or a later date is set by the Bureau, at the request of any party so served.

(C) Consent

Unless the party or parties served under subparagraph (B) appear at the hearing personally or by a duly authorized representative, such person shall be deemed to have consented to the issuance of the cease-and-desist order.

(D) Procedure

In the event of consent under subparagraph (C), or if, upon the record, made at any such hearing, the Bureau finds that any violation specified in the notice of charges has been established, the Bureau may issue and serve upon the covered person or service provider an order to cease and desist from the violation or practice. Such order may, by provisions which may be mandatory or otherwise, require the covered person or service provider to cease and desist from the subject activity, and to take affirmative action to correct the conditions resulting from any such violation.

(2) Effectiveness of order

A cease-and-desist order shall become effective at the expiration of 30 days after the date of service of an order under paragraph (1) upon the covered person or service provider concerned (except in the case of a cease-and-desist order issued upon consent, which shall become effective at the time specified therein), and shall remain effective and enforceable as provided therein, except to such extent as the order is stayed, modified, terminated, or set aside by action of the Bureau or a reviewing court.

(3) Decision and appeal

Any hearing provided for in this subsection shall be held in the Federal judicial district or in the territory in which the residence or principal office or place of business of the person is located unless the person consents to another place, and shall be conducted in accordance with the provisions of chapter 5 of Title 5.After such hearing, and within 90 days after the Bureau has notified the parties that the case has been submitted to the Bureau for final decision, the Bureau shall render its decision (which shall include findings of fact upon which its decision is predicated) and shall issue and serve upon each party to the proceeding an order or orders consistent with the provisions of this section. Judicial review of any such order shall be exclusively as provided in this subsection. Unless a petition for review is timely filed in a court of appeals of the United States, as provided in paragraph (4), and thereafter until the record in the proceeding has been filed as provided in paragraph (4), the Bureau may at any time, upon such notice and in such manner as the Bureau shall determine proper, modify, terminate, or set aside any such order. Upon filing of the record as provided, the Bureau may modify, terminate, or set aside any such order with permission of the court.

(4) Appeal to court of appeals

Any party to any proceeding under this subsection may obtain a review of any order served pursuant to this subsection (other than an order issued with the consent of the person concerned) by the filing in the court of appeals of the United States for the circuit in which the principal office of the covered person is located, or in the United States Court of Appeals for the District of Columbia Circuit, within 30 days after the date of service of such order, a written petition praying that the order of the Bureau be modified, terminated, or set aside. A copy of such petition shall be forthwith transmitted by the clerk of the court to the Bureau, and thereupon the Bureau shall file in the court the record in the proceeding, as provided in section 2112 of Title 28. Upon the filing of such petition, such court shall have jurisdiction, which upon the filing of the record shall except as provided in the last sentence of paragraph (3) be exclusive, to affirm, modify, terminate, or set aside, in whole or in part, the order of the Bureau. Review of such proceedings shall be had as provided in chapter 7 of Title 5. The judgment and decree of the court shall be final, except that the same shall be subject to review by the Supreme Court of the United States, upon certiorari, as provided in section 1254 of Title 28.

(5) No stay

The commencement of proceedings for judicial review under paragraph (4) shall not, unless specifically ordered by the court, operate as a stay of any order issued by the Bureau.

(c) Special rules for temporary cease-and-desist proceedings

(1) In general

Whenever the Bureau determines that the violation specified in the notice of charges served upon a person, including a service provider, pursuant to subsection (b), or the continuation thereof, is likely to cause the person to be insolvent or otherwise prejudice the interests of consumers before the completion of the proceedings conducted pursuant to subsection (b), the Bureau may issue a temporary order requiring the person to cease and desist from any such violation or practice and to take affirmative action to prevent or remedy such insolvency or other condition pending completion of such proceedings. Such order may include any requirement authorized under this part. Such order shall become effective upon service upon the person and, unless set aside, limited, or suspended by a court in proceedings authorized by paragraph (2), shall remain effective and enforceable pending the completion of the administrative proceedings pursuant to such notice and until such time as the Bureau shall dismiss the charges specified in such notice, or if a cease-and-desist order is issued against the person, until the effective date of such order.

(2) Appeal

Not later than 10 days after the covered person or service provider concerned has been served with a temporary cease-and-desist order, the person may apply to the United States district court for the judicial district in which the residence or principal office or place of business of the person is located, or the United States District Court for the District of Columbia, for an injunction setting aside, limiting, or suspending the enforcement, operation, or effectiveness of such order pending the completion of the administrative proceedings pursuant to the notice of charges served upon the person under subsection (b), and such court shall have jurisdiction to issue such injunction.

(3) Incomplete or inaccurate records

(A) Temporary order

If a notice of charges served under subsection (b) specifies, on the basis of particular facts and circumstances, that the books and records of a covered person or service provider are so incomplete or inaccurate that the Bureau is unable to determine the financial condition of that person or the details or purpose of any transaction or transactions that may have a material effect on the financial condition of that person, the Bureau may issue a temporary order requiring—

(i) the cessation of any activity or practice which gave rise, whether in whole or in part, to the incomplete or inaccurate state of the books or records; or

(ii) affirmative action to restore such books or records to a complete and accurate state, until the completion of the proceedings under subsection (b)(1).

(B) Effective period

Any temporary order issued under subparagraph (A)—

(i) shall become effective upon service; and

(ii) unless set aside, limited, or suspended by a court in proceedings under paragraph (2), shall remain in effect and enforceable until the earlier of—

(I) the completion of the proceeding initiated under subsection (b) in connection with the notice of charges; or

(II) the date the Bureau determines, by examination or otherwise, that the books and records of the covered person or service provider are accurate and reflect the financial condition thereof.

(d) Special rules for enforcement of orders

(1) In general

The Bureau may in its discretion apply to the United States district court within the jurisdiction of which the principal office or place of business of the person is located, for the enforcement of any effective and outstanding notice or order issued under this section, and such court shall have jurisdiction and power to order and require compliance herewith.

(2) Exception

Except as otherwise provided in this subsection, no court shall have jurisdiction to affect by injunction or otherwise the issuance or enforcement of any notice or order or to review, modify, suspend, terminate, or set aside any such notice or order.

(e) Rules

The Bureau shall prescribe rules establishing such procedures as may be necessary to carry out this section.

§ 5564 [CFPA Act § 1054]. Litigation authority

(a) In general

If any person violates a Federal consumer financial law, the Bureau may, subject to sections 5514, 5515, and 5516 of this title, commence a civil action against such person to impose a civil penalty or to seek all appropriate legal and equitable relief including a permanent or temporary injunction as permitted by law.

(b) Representation

The Bureau may act in its own name and through its own attorneys in enforcing any provision of this title, rules thereunder, or any other law or regulation, or in any action, suit, or proceeding to which the Bureau is a party.

(c) Compromise of actions

The Bureau may compromise or settle any action if such compromise is approved by the court.

(d) Notice to the Attorney General

(1) In general

When commencing a civil action under Federal consumer financial law, or any rule thereunder, the Bureau shall notify the Attorney General and, with respect to a civil action against an insured depository institution or insured credit union, the appropriate prudential regulator.

(2) Notice and coordination

(A) Notice of other actions

In addition to any notice required under paragraph (1), the Bureau shall notify the Attorney General concerning any action, suit, or proceeding to which the Bureau is a party, except an action, suit, or proceeding that involves the offering or provision of consumer financial products or services.

(B) Coordination

In order to avoid conflicts and promote consistency regarding litigation of matters under Federal law, the Attorney General and the Bureau shall consult regarding the coordination of investigations and proceedings, including by negotiating an agreement for coordination by not later than 180 days after the designated transfer date. The agreement under this subparagraph shall include provisions to ensure that parallel investigations and proceedings involving the Federal consumer financial laws are conducted in a manner that avoids conflicts and does not impede the ability of the Attorney General to prosecute violations of Federal criminal laws.

(C) Rule of construction

Nothing in this paragraph shall be construed to limit the authority of the Bureau under this title, including the authority to interpret Federal consumer financial law.

(e) Appearance before the Supreme Court

The Bureau may represent itself in its own name before the Supreme Court of the United States, provided that the Bureau makes a written request to the Attorney General within the 10-day period which begins on the date of entry of the judgment which would permit any party to file a petition for writ of certiorari, and the Attorney General concurs with such request or fails to take action within 60 days of the request of the Bureau.

(f) Forum

Any civil action brought under this title may be brought in a United States district court or in any court of competent jurisdiction of a state in a district in which the defendant is located or resides or is doing business, and such court shall have jurisdiction to enjoin such person and to require compliance with any Federal consumer financial law.

(g) Time for bringing action

(1) **In general**

Except as otherwise permitted by law or equity, no action may be brought under this title more than 3 years after the date of discovery of the violation to which an action relates.

(2) **Limitations under other Federal laws**

(A) **In general**

An action arising under this title does not include claims arising solely under enumerated consumer laws.

(B) **Bureau authority**

In any action arising solely under an enumerated consumer law, the Bureau may commence, defend, or intervene in the action in accordance with the requirements of that provision of law, as applicable.

(C) **Transferred authority**

In any action arising solely under laws for which authorities were transferred under subtitles F and H, the Bureau may commence, defend, or intervene in the action in accordance with the requirements of that provision of law, as applicable.

§ 5565 [CFPA Act § 1055]. Relief available

(a) **Administrative proceedings or court actions**

(1) **Jurisdiction**

The court (or the Bureau, as the case may be) in an action or adjudication proceeding brought under Federal consumer financial law, shall have jurisdiction to grant any appropriate legal or equitable relief with respect to a violation of Federal consumer financial law, including a violation of a rule or order prescribed under a Federal consumer financial law.

(2) **Relief**

Relief under this section may include, without limitation—

(A) rescission or reformation of contracts;

(B) refund of moneys or return of real property;

(C) restitution;

(D) disgorgement or compensation for unjust enrichment;

(E) payment of damages or other monetary relief;

(F) public notification regarding the violation, including the costs of notification;

(G) limits on the activities or functions of the person; and

(H) civil money penalties, as set forth more fully in subsection (c).

(3) **No exemplary or punitive damages**

Nothing in this subsection shall be construed as authorizing the imposition of exemplary or punitive damages.

(b) **Recovery of costs**

In any action brought by the Bureau, a State attorney general, or any State regulator to enforce any Federal consumer financial law, the Bureau, the State attorney general, or the State regulator may recover its costs in connection with prosecuting such action if the Bureau, the State attorney general, or the State regulator is the prevailing party in the action.

(c) **Civil money penalty in court and administrative actions**

(1) In general

Any person that violates, through any act or omission, any provision of Federal consumer financial law shall forfeit and pay a civil penalty pursuant to this subsection.

(2) Penalty amounts

(A) First tier

For any violation of a law, rule, or final order or condition imposed in writing by the Bureau, a civil penalty may not exceed $5,000 for each day during which such violation or failure to pay continues.

(B) Second tier

Notwithstanding paragraph (A), for any person that recklessly engages in a violation of a Federal consumer financial law, a civil penalty may not exceed $25,000 for each day during which such violation continues.

(C) Third tier

Notwithstanding subparagraphs (A) and (B), for any person that knowingly violates a Federal consumer financial law, a civil penalty may not exceed $1,000,000 for each day during which such violation continues.

(3) Mitigating factors

In determining the amount of any penalty assessed under paragraph (2), the Bureau or the court shall take into account the appropriateness of the penalty with respect to—

(A) the size of financial resources and good faith of the person charged;

(B) the gravity of the violation or failure to pay;

(C) the severity of the risks to or losses of the consumer, which may take into account the number of products or services sold or provided;

(D) the history of previous violations; and

(E) such other matters as justice may require.

(4) Authority to modify or remit penalty

The Bureau may compromise, modify, or remit any penalty which may be assessed or had already been assessed under paragraph (2). The amount of such penalty, when finally determined, shall be exclusive of any sums owed by the person to the United States in connection with the costs of the proceeding, and may be deducted from any sums owing by the United States to the person charged.

(5) Notice and hearing

No civil penalty may be assessed under this subsection with respect to a violation of any Federal consumer financial law, unless—

(A) the Bureau gives notice and an opportunity for a hearing to the person accused of the violation; or

(B) the appropriate court has ordered such assessment and entered judgment in favor of the Bureau.

§ 5566 [CFPA Act § 1056]. Referrals for criminal proceedings

If the Bureau obtains evidence that any person, domestic or foreign, has engaged in conduct that may constitute a violation of Federal criminal law, the Bureau shall transmit such evidence to the Attorney

General of the United States, who may institute criminal proceedings under appropriate law. Nothing in this section affects any other authority of the Bureau to disclose information.

§ 5567 [CFPA Act § 1057]. Employee protection

(a) In general

No covered person or service provider shall terminate or in any other way discriminate against, or cause to be terminated or discriminated against, any covered employee or any authorized representative of covered employees by reason of the fact that such employee or representative, whether at the initiative of the employee or in the ordinary course of the duties of the employee (or any person acting pursuant to a request of the employee), has—

(1) provided, caused to be provided, or is about to provide or cause to be provided, information to the employer, the Bureau, or any other State, local, or Federal, government authority or law enforcement agency relating to any violation of, or any act or omission that the employee reasonably believes to be a violation of, any provision of this title or any other provision of law that is subject to the jurisdiction of the Bureau, or any rule, order, standard, or prohibition prescribed by the Bureau;

(2) testified or will testify in any proceeding resulting from the administration or enforcement of any provision of this title or any other provision of law that is subject to the jurisdiction of the Bureau, or any rule, order, standard, or prohibition prescribed by the Bureau;

(3) filed, instituted, or caused to be filed or instituted any proceeding under any Federal consumer financial law; or

(4) objected to, or refused to participate in, any activity, policy, practice, or assigned task that the employee (or other such person) reasonably believed to be in violation of any law, rule, order, standard, or prohibition, subject to the jurisdiction of, or enforceable by, the Bureau.

(b) Definition of covered employee

For the purposes of this section, the term "covered employee" means any individual performing tasks related to the offering or provision of a consumer financial product or service.

(c) Procedures and timetables

(1) Complaint

(A) In general

A person who believes that he or she has been discharged or otherwise discriminated against by any person in violation of subsection (a) may, not later than 180 days after the date on which such alleged violation occurs, file (or have any person file on his or her behalf) a complaint with the Secretary of Labor alleging such discharge or discrimination and identifying the person responsible for such act.

(B) Actions of Secretary of Labor

Upon receipt of such a complaint, the Secretary of Labor shall notify, in writing, the person named in the complaint who is alleged to have committed the violation, of—

(i) the filing of the complaint;

(ii) the allegations contained in the complaint;

(iii) the substance of evidence supporting the complaint; and

(iv) opportunities that will be afforded to such person under paragraph (2).

(2) Investigation by Secretary of Labor

(A) In general

Not later than 60 days after the date of receipt of a complaint filed under paragraph (1), and after affording the complainant and the person named in the complaint who is alleged to have committed the violation that is the basis for the complaint an opportunity to submit to the Secretary of Labor a written response to the complaint and an opportunity to meet with a representative of the Secretary of Labor to present statements from witnesses, the Secretary of Labor shall—

(i) initiate an investigation and determine whether there is reasonable cause to believe that the complaint has merit; and

(ii) notify the complainant and the person alleged to have committed the violation of subsection (a), in writing, of such determination.

(B) Notice of relief available

If the Secretary of Labor concludes that there is reasonable cause to believe that a violation of subsection (a) has occurred, the Secretary of Labor shall, together with the notice under subparagraph (A)(ii), issue a preliminary order providing the relief prescribed by paragraph (4)(B).

(C) Request for hearing

Not later than 30 days after the date of receipt of notification of a determination of the Secretary of Labor under this paragraph, either the person alleged to have committed the violation or the complainant may file objections to the findings or preliminary order, or both, and request a hearing on the record. The filing of such objections shall not operate to stay any reinstatement remedy contained in the preliminary order. Any such hearing shall be conducted expeditiously, and if a hearing is not requested in such 30-day period, the preliminary order shall be deemed a final order that is not subject to judicial review.

(3) Grounds for determination of complaints

(A) In general

The Secretary of Labor shall dismiss a complaint filed under this subsection, and shall not conduct an investigation otherwise required under paragraph (2), unless the complainant makes a prima facie showing that any behavior described in paragraphs (1) through (4) of subsection (a) was a contributing factor in the unfavorable personnel action alleged in the complaint.

(B) Rebuttal evidence

Notwithstanding a finding by the Secretary of Labor that the complainant has made the showing required under subparagraph (A), no investigation otherwise required under paragraph (2) shall be conducted, if the employer demonstrates, by clear and convincing evidence, that the employer would have taken the same unfavorable personnel action in the absence of that behavior.

(C) Evidentiary standards

The Secretary of Labor may determine that a violation of subsection (a) has occurred only if the complainant demonstrates that any behavior described in paragraphs (1) through (4) of subsection (a) was a contributing factor in the unfavorable personnel action alleged in the complaint. Relief may not be ordered under subparagraph (A) if the employer demonstrates by clear and convincing evidence that the employer would have taken the same unfavorable personnel action in the absence of that behavior.

(4) Issuance of final orders; review procedures

(A) Timing

Not later than 120 days after the date of conclusion of any hearing under paragraph (2), the Secretary of Labor shall issue a final order providing the relief prescribed by this paragraph or denying the complaint. At any time before issuance of a final order, a proceeding under this subsection may be terminated on the basis of a settlement agreement entered into by the Secretary of Labor, the complainant, and the person alleged to have committed the violation.

(B) Penalties

(i) Order of Secretary of Labor

If, in response to a complaint filed under paragraph (1), the Secretary of Labor determines that a violation of subsection (a) has occurred, the Secretary of Labor shall order the person who committed such violation—

(I) to take affirmative action to abate the violation;

(II) to reinstate the complainant to his or her former position, together with compensation (including back pay) and restore the terms, conditions, and privileges associated with his or her employment; and

(III) to provide compensatory damages to the complainant.

(ii) Penalty

If an order is issued under clause (i), the Secretary of Labor, at the request of the complainant, shall assess against the person against whom the order is issued, a sum equal to the aggregate amount of all costs and expenses (including attorney fees and expert witness fees) reasonably incurred, as determined by the Secretary of Labor, by the complainant for, or in connection with, the bringing of the complaint upon which the order was issued.

(C) Penalty for frivolous claims

If the Secretary of Labor finds that a complaint under paragraph (1) is frivolous or has been brought in bad faith, the Secretary of Labor may award to the prevailing employer a reasonable attorney fee, not exceeding $1,000, to be paid by the complainant.

(D) De novo review

(i) Failure of the Secretary to act

If the Secretary of Labor has not issued a final order within 210 days after the date of filing of a complaint under this subsection, or within 90 days after the date of receipt of a written determination, the complainant may bring an action at law or equity for de novo review in the appropriate district court of the United States having jurisdiction, which shall have jurisdiction over such an action without regard to the amount in controversy, and which action shall, at the request of either party to such action, be tried by the court with a jury.

(ii) Procedures

A proceeding under clause (i) shall be governed by the same legal burdens of proof specified in paragraph (3). The court shall have jurisdiction to grant all relief necessary to make the employee whole, including injunctive relief and compensatory damages, including—

(I) reinstatement with the same seniority status that the employee would have had, but for the discharge or discrimination;

(II) the amount of back pay, with interest; and

(III) compensation for any special damages sustained as a result of the discharge or discrimination, including litigation costs, expert witness fees, and reasonable attorney fees.

(E) Other appeals

Unless the complainant brings an action under subparagraph (D), any person adversely affected or aggrieved by a final order issued under subparagraph (A) may file a petition for review of the order in the United States Court of Appeals for the circuit in which the violation with respect to which the order was issued, allegedly occurred or the circuit in which the complainant resided on the date of such violation, not later than 60 days after the date of the issuance of the final order of the Secretary of Labor under subparagraph (A). Review shall conform to chapter 7 of Title 5. The commencement of proceedings under this subparagraph shall not, unless ordered by the court, operate as a stay of the order. An order of the Secretary of Labor with respect to which review could have been obtained under this subparagraph shall not be subject to judicial review in any criminal or other civil proceeding.

(5) Failure to comply with order

(A) Actions by the Secretary

If any person has failed to comply with a final order issued under paragraph (4), the Secretary of Labor may file a civil action in the United States district court for the district in which the violation was found to have occurred, or in the United States district court for the District of Columbia, to enforce such order. In actions brought under this paragraph, the district courts shall have jurisdiction to grant all appropriate relief including injunctive relief and compensatory damages.

(B) Civil actions to compel compliance

A person on whose behalf an order was issued under paragraph (4) may commence a civil action against the person to whom such order was issued to require compliance with such order. The appropriate United States district court shall have jurisdiction, without regard to the amount in controversy or the citizenship of the parties, to enforce such order.

(C) Award of costs authorized

The court, in issuing any final order under this paragraph, may award costs of litigation (including reasonable attorney and expert witness fees) to any party, whenever the court determines such award is appropriate.

(D) Mandamus proceedings

Any nondiscretionary duty imposed by this section shall be enforceable in a mandamus proceeding brought under section 1361 of Title 28.

(d) Unenforceability of certain agreements

(1) No waiver of rights and remedies

Except as provided under paragraph (3), and notwithstanding any other provision of law, the rights and remedies provided for in this section may not be waived by any agreement, policy, form, or condition of employment, including by any predispute arbitration agreement.

(2) No predispute arbitration agreements

Except as provided under paragraph (3), and notwithstanding any other provision of law, no predispute arbitration agreement shall be valid or enforceable to the extent that it requires arbitration of a dispute arising under this section.

(3) Exception

Notwithstanding paragraphs (1) and (2), an arbitration provision in a collective bargaining agreement shall be enforceable as to disputes arising under subsection (a)(4), unless the Bureau determines, by rule, that such provision is inconsistent with the purposes of this title.

PART F—TRANSFER OF FUNCTIONS AND PERSONNEL; TRANSITIONAL PROVISIONS

§ 5581 [CFPA § 1061]. Transfer of consumer financial protection functions

(a) Defined terms

For purposes of this part—

(1) the term "consumer financial protection functions" means—

(A) all authority to prescribe rules or issue orders or guidelines pursuant to any Federal consumer financial law, including performing appropriate functions to promulgate and review such rules, orders, and guidelines; and

(B) the examination authority described in subsection (c)(1), with respect to a person described in section 5515(a) of this title; and

(2) the terms "transferor agency" and "transferor agencies" mean, respectively—

(A) the Board of Governors (and any Federal reserve bank, as the context requires), the Federal Deposit Insurance Corporation, the Federal Trade Commission, the National Credit Union Administration, the Office of the Comptroller of the Currency, the Office of Thrift Supervision, and the Department of Housing and Urban Development, and the heads of those agencies; and

(B) the agencies listed in subparagraph (A), collectively.

(b) In general

Except as provided in subsection (c), consumer financial protection functions are transferred as follows:

(1) Board of Governors

(A) Transfer of functions

All consumer financial protection functions of the Board of Governors are transferred to the Bureau.

(B) Board of Governors authority

The Bureau shall have all powers and duties that were vested in the Board of Governors, relating to consumer financial protection functions, on the day before the designated transfer date.

(2) Comptroller of the Currency

(A) Transfer of functions

All consumer financial protection functions of the Comptroller of the Currency are transferred to the Bureau.

(B) Comptroller authority

The Bureau shall have all powers and duties that were vested in the Comptroller of the Currency, relating to consumer financial protection functions, on the day before the designated transfer date.

(3) Director of the Office of Thrift Supervision

(A) Transfer of functions

All consumer financial protection functions of the Director of the Office of Thrift Supervision are transferred to the Bureau.

(B) Director authority

The Bureau shall have all powers and duties that were vested in the Director of the Office of Thrift Supervision, relating to consumer financial protection functions, on the day before the designated transfer date.

(4) Federal Deposit Insurance Corporation

(A) Transfer of functions

All consumer financial protection functions of the Federal Deposit Insurance Corporation are transferred to the Bureau.

(B) Corporation authority

The Bureau shall have all powers and duties that were vested in the Federal Deposit Insurance Corporation, relating to consumer financial protection functions, on the day before the designated transfer date.

(5) Federal Trade Commission

(A) Transfer of functions

The authority of the Federal Trade Commission under an enumerated consumer law to prescribe rules, issue guidelines, or conduct a study or issue a report mandated under such law shall be transferred to the Bureau on the designated transfer date. Nothing in this title shall be construed to require a mandatory transfer of any employee of the Federal Trade Commission.

(B) Bureau authority

(i) In general

The Bureau shall have all powers and duties under the enumerated consumer laws to prescribe rules, issue guidelines, or to conduct studies or issue reports mandated by such laws, that were vested in the Federal Trade Commission on the day before the designated transfer date.

(ii) Federal Trade Commission Act

Subject to part B, the Bureau may enforce a rule prescribed under the Federal Trade Commission Act by the Federal Trade Commission with respect to an unfair or deceptive act or practice to the extent that such rule applies to a covered person or service provider with respect to the offering or provision of a consumer financial product or service as if it were a rule prescribed under section 5531 of this title.

(C) Authority of the Federal Trade Commission

(i) In general

No provision of this title shall be construed as modifying, limiting, or otherwise affecting the authority of the Federal Trade Commission (including its authority with respect to affiliates described in section 5515(a)(1) of this title) under the Federal Trade Commission Act or any other law, other than the authority under an enumerated consumer law to prescribe rules, issue official guidelines, or conduct a study or issue a report mandated under such law.

(ii) Commission authority relating to rules prescribed by the Bureau

Subject to part B, the Federal Trade Commission shall have authority to enforce under the Federal Trade Commission Act (15 U.S.C. 41 et seq.) a rule prescribed by the

Bureau under this title with respect to a covered person subject to the jurisdiction of the Federal Trade Commission under that Act, and a violation of such a rule by such a person shall be treated as a violation of a rule issued under section 18 of that Act (15 U.S. C. 57a) with respect to unfair or deceptive acts or practices.

(D) Coordination

To avoid duplication of or conflict between rules prescribed by the Bureau under section 5531 of this title and the Federal Trade Commission under section 18(a)(1)(B) of the Federal Trade Commission Act that apply to a covered person or service provider with respect to the offering or provision of consumer financial products or services, the agencies shall negotiate an agreement with respect to rulemaking by each agency, including consultation with the other agency prior to proposing a rule and during the comment period.

(E) Deference

No provision of this title shall be construed as altering, limiting, expanding, or otherwise affecting the deference that a court affords to the—

(i) Federal Trade Commission in making determinations regarding the meaning or interpretation of any provision of the Federal Trade Commission Act, or of any other Federal law for which the Commission has authority to prescribe rules; or

(ii) Bureau in making determinations regarding the meaning or interpretation of any provision of a Federal consumer financial law (other than any law described in clause (i)).

(6) National Credit Union Administration

(A) Transfer of functions

All consumer financial protection functions of the National Credit Union Administration are transferred to the Bureau.

(B) National Credit Union Administration authority

The Bureau shall have all powers and duties that were vested in the National Credit Union Administration, relating to consumer financial protection functions, on the day before the designated transfer date.

(7) Department of Housing and Urban Development

(A) Transfer of functions

All consumer protection functions of the Secretary of the Department of Housing and Urban Development relating to the Real Estate Settlement Procedures Act of 1974 (12 U.S.C. 2601 et seq.), the Secure and Fair Enforcement for Mortgage Licensing Act of 2008 (12 U.S.C. 5102 et seq.), and the Interstate Land Sales Full Disclosure Act (15 U.S.C. 1701 et seq.) are transferred to the Bureau.

(B) Authority of the Department of Housing and Urban Development

The Bureau shall have all powers and duties that were vested in the Secretary of the Department of Housing and Urban Development relating to the Real Estate Settlement Procedures Act of 1974 (12 U.S.C. 2601 et seq.), the Secure and Fair Enforcement for Mortgage Licensing Act of 2008 (12 U.S.C. 5101 et seq.), and the Interstate Land Sales Full Disclosure Act (15 U.S.C. 1701 et seq.), on the day before the designated transfer date.

(c) Authorities of the prudential regulators

(1) Examination

A transferor agency that is a prudential regulator shall have—

(A) authority to require reports from and conduct examinations for compliance with Federal consumer financial laws with respect to a person described in section 5515(a) of this title, that is incidental to the backup and enforcement procedures provided to the regulator under section 5515(c) of this title; and

(B) exclusive authority (relative to the Bureau) to require reports from and conduct examinations for compliance with Federal consumer financial laws with respect to a person described in section 5516(a) of this title, except as provided to the Bureau under subsections (b) and (c) of section 5516 of this title.

(2) Enforcement

(A) Limitation

The authority of a transferor agency that is a prudential regulator to enforce compliance with Federal consumer financial laws with respect to a person described in section 5515(a) of this title, shall be limited to the backup and enforcement procedures in described in section 5515(c) of this title.

(B) Exclusive authority

A transferor agency that is a prudential regulator shall have exclusive authority (relative to the Bureau) to enforce compliance with Federal consumer financial laws with respect to a person described in section 5516(a) of this title, except as provided to the Bureau under subsections (b) and (c) of section 5516 of this title.

(C) Statutory enforcement

For purposes of carrying out the authorities under, and subject to the limitations of, part B, each prudential regulator may enforce compliance with the requirements imposed under this title, and any rule or order prescribed by the Bureau under this title, under—

(i) the Federal Credit Union Act (12 U.S.C. 1751 et seq.), by the National Credit Union Administration Board with respect to any covered person or service provider that is an insured credit union, or service provider thereto, or any affiliate of an insured credit union, who is subject to the jurisdiction of the Board under that Act; and

(ii) section 1818 of this title, by the appropriate Federal banking agency, as defined in section 1813(q)of this title, with respect to a covered person or service provider that is a person described in section 1813(q) of this title and who is subject to the jurisdiction of that agency, as set forth in sections 1813(q) and 1818 of this title; or

(iii) the Bank Service Company Act (12 U.S.C. 1861 et seq.).

(d) Effective date

Subsections (b) and (c) shall become effective on the designated transfer date.

PART G—REGULATORY IMPROVEMENTS

§ 5601 [CFPA § 1073]. Remittance transfers

(a) Omitted

(b) Automated clearinghouse system

(1) Expansion of system

The Board of Governors shall work with the Federal reserve banks and the Department of the Treasury to expand the use of the automated clearinghouse system and other payment mechanisms for remittance transfers to foreign countries, with a focus on countries that receive significant remittance transfers from the United States, based on—

(A) the number, volume, and size of such transfers;

(B) the significance of the volume of such transfers relative to the external financial flows of the receiving country, including—

(i) the total amount transferred; and

(ii) the total volume of payments made by United States Government agencies to beneficiaries and retirees living abroad;

(C) the feasibility of such an expansion; and

(D) the ability of the Federal Reserve System to establish payment gateways in different geographic regions and currency zones to receive remittance transfers and route them through the payments systems in the destination countries.

(2) Report to Congress

Not later than one calendar year after July 21, 2010, and on April 30 biennially thereafter during the 10-year period beginning on July 21, 2010, the Board of Governors shall submit a report to the Committee on Banking, Housing, and Urban Affairs of the Senate and the Committee on Financial Services of the House of Representatives on the status of the automated clearinghouse system and its progress in complying with the requirements of this subsection. The report shall include an analysis of adoption rates of International ACH Transactions rules and formats, the efficacy of increasing adoption rates, and potential recommendations to increase adoption.

(c) Expansion of financial institution provision of remittance transfers

(1) Provision of guidelines to institutions

Each of the Federal banking agencies and the National Credit Union Administration shall provide guidelines to financial institutions under the jurisdiction of the agency regarding the offering of low-cost remittance transfers and no-cost or low-cost basic consumer accounts, as well as agency services to remittance transfer providers.

(2) Assistance to Financial Literacy Commission[1]

As part of its[2] duties as members of the Financial Literacy and Education Commission, the Bureau, the Federal banking agencies, and the National Credit Union Administration shall assist the Financial Literacy and Education Commission in executing the Strategy for Assuring Financial Empowerment (or the "SAFE Strategy"), as it relates to remittances.

(d) Omitted

(e) Report on feasibility of and impediments to use of remittance history in calculation of credit score

Before the end of the 365-day period beginning on July 21, 2010, the Director shall submit a report to the President, the Committee on Banking, Housing, and Urban Affairs of the Senate, and the Committee on Financial Services of the House of Representatives regarding—

(1) the manner in which the remittance history of a consumer could be used to enhance the credit score of the consumer;

(2) the current legal and business model barriers and impediments that impede the use of the remittance history of the consumer to enhance the credit score of the consumer; and

(3) recommendations on the manner in which maximum transparency and disclosure to consumers of exchange rates for remittance transfers subject to this title and the amendments made by this title may be accomplished, whether or not such exchange rates are known at the time of origination or payment by the consumer for the remittance transfer, including disclosure

---

1 So in original. Probably should be "Financial Literacy and Education Commission".

2 So in original. Probably should be "their".

to the sender of the actual exchange rate used and the amount of currency that the recipient of the remittance transfer received, using the values of the currency into which the funds were exchanged, as contained in sections 1693*o*–1(a)(2)(D) and 1693*o*–1(a)(3) of Title 15 (as amended by this section).

§ 5602 [CFPA § 1076]. Reverse mortgage study and regulations

(a) Study

Not later than 1 year after the designated transfer date, the Bureau shall conduct a study on reverse mortgage transactions.

(b) Regulations

(1) In general

If the Bureau determines through the study required under subsection (a) that conditions or limitations on reverse mortgage transactions are necessary or appropriate for accomplishing the purposes and objectives of this title, including protecting borrowers with respect to the obtaining of reverse mortgage loans for the purpose of funding investments, annuities, and other investment products and the suitability of a borrower in obtaining a reverse mortgage for such purpose1.

(2) Identified practices and integrated disclosures

The regulations prescribed under paragraph (1) may, as the Bureau may so determine—

(A) identify any practice as unfair, deceptive, or abusive in connection with a reverse mortgage transaction; and

(B) provide for an integrated disclosure standard and model disclosures for reverse mortgage transactions, consistent with section 4302(d), that combines the relevant disclosures required under the Truth in Lending Act (15 U.S.C. 1601 et seq.) and the Real Estate Settlement Procedures Act, with the disclosures required to be provided to consumers for Home Equity Conversion Mortgages under section 1715z–20 of this title.

(c) Rule of construction

This section shall not be construed as limiting the authority of the Bureau to issue regulations, orders, or guidance that apply to reverse mortgages prior to the completion of the study required under subsection (a).

CONSUMER CREDIT PROTECTION ACT

---

15 U.S.C. §§ 1601–1693r

Summary

Subchapter	
I-§§ 1601–1677.	Consumer Credit Cost Disclosure (Truth in Lending Act or TILA).
II-§§ 1671–1677.	Restrictions on Garnishment.
II-A-§§ 1679–1679j.	Credit Repair Organizations (Credit Repair Organization Act or CROA).
III-§§ 1681–1681x.	Credit Reporting Agencies (Fair Credit Reporting Act or FCRA, as amended by the Fair and Accurate Credit Transactions Act or FACTA).
IV-§§ 1691–1691f.	Equal Credit Opportunity (Equal Credit Opportunity Act or ECOA).
V-§§ 1692–1692*o*.	Debt Collection Practices (Fair Debt Collection Practices Act or FDCPA).
VI-§§ 1693–1693r.	Electronic Fund Transfers (Electronic Fund Transfer Act or EFTA).

SUBCHAPTER I—CONSUMER CREDIT COST DISCLOSURE (TRUTH IN LENDING ACT OR TILA)

Table of Sections

Part A—General Provisions

Part B—Credit Transactions

Part C—Credit Advertising and Limits on Credit Card Fees

Part D—Credit Billing

[**Editor's Note**. Because of ambiguities in Title XIV of the Dodd-Frank Wall Street Reform and Consumer Protection Act (the Mortgage Reform and Anti-Predatory Lending Act), the effective dates of some provisions in Title XIV are unclear.]

PART A—GENERAL PROVISIONS

§ 1601 [CCPA § 102]. Congressional Findings and Declaration of Purpose

(a) Informed use of credit

The Congress finds that economic stabilization would be enhanced and the competition among the various financial institutions and other firms engaged in the extension of consumer credit would be strengthened by the informed use of credit. The informed use of credit results from an awareness of the cost thereof by consumers. It is the purpose of this subchapter to assure a meaningful disclosure of credit terms so that the consumer will be able to compare more readily the various credit terms available to him and avoid the uninformed use of credit, and to protect the consumer against inaccurate and unfair credit billing and credit card practices.

(b) Terms of personal property leases

The Congress also finds that there has been a recent trend toward leasing automobiles and other durable goods for consumer use as an alternative to installment credit sales and that these leases have been offered without adequate cost disclosures. It is the purpose of this subchapter to assure a meaningful disclosure of the terms of leases of personal property for personal, family, or household purposes so as to enable the lessee to compare more readily the various lease terms available to him, limit balloon payments in consumer leasing, enable comparison of lease terms with credit terms where appropriate, and to assure meaningful and accurate disclosures of lease terms in advertisements.

§ 1602 [CCPA § 103]. Definitions and Rules of Construction

(a) The definitions and rules of construction set forth in this section are applicable for the purposes of this subchapter.

(b) Bureau

The term "Bureau" means the Bureau of Consumer Financial Protection.

(c) The term "Board" refers to the Board of Governors of the Federal Reserve System.

(d) The term "organization" means a corporation, government or governmental subdivision or agency, trust, estate, partnership, cooperative, or association.

(e) The term "person" means a natural person or an organization.

(f) The term "credit" means the right granted by a creditor to a debtor to defer payment of debt or to incur debt and defer its payment.

(g) The term "creditor" refers only to a person who both (1) regularly extends, whether in connection with loans, sales of property or services, or otherwise, consumer credit which is payable by agreement in more than four installments or for which the payment of a finance charge is or may be required, and (2) is the person to whom the debt arising from the consumer credit transaction is initially payable on the face of the evidence of indebtedness or, if there is no such evidence of indebtedness, by agreement. Notwithstanding the preceding sentence, in the case of an open-end credit plan involving a credit card, the card issuer and any person who honors the credit card and offers a discount which is a finance charge are creditors. For the purpose of the requirements imposed under part D of this subchapter and Sections 1637(a)(5), 1637(a)(6), 1637(a)(7), 1637(b)(1), 1637(b)(2), 1637(b)(3), 1637(b)(8), and 1637(b)(10) of this title, the term "creditor" shall also include card issuers whether or not the amount due is payable by agreement in more than four installments or the payment of a finance charge is or may be required, and the Bureau shall, by regulation, apply these requirements to such card issuers, to the extent appropriate, even though the requirements are by their terms applicable only to creditors offering open-end credit plans. Any person who originates 2 or more mortgages referred to in subsection (aa) of this section in any 12-month period or any person who originates 1 or more such mortgages through a mortgage broker shall be considered to be a creditor for purposes of this subchapter. The term "creditor" includes a private educational lender (as that term is defined in section 1650 of this title) for purposes of this subchapter.

(h) The term "credit sale" refers to any sale in which the seller is a creditor. The term includes any contract in the form of a bailment or lease if the bailee or lessee contracts to pay as compensation for use a sum substantially equivalent to or in excess of the aggregate value of the property and services involved and it is agreed that the bailee or lessee will become, or for no other or a nominal consideration has the option to become, the owner of the property upon full compliance with his obligations under the contract.

(i) The adjective "consumer", used with reference to a credit transaction, characterizes the transaction as one in which the party to whom credit is offered or extended is a natural person, and the money, property, or services which are the subject of the transaction are primarily for personal, family, or household purposes.

(j) The terms "open end credit plan" and "open end consumer credit plan" mean a plan under which the creditor reasonably contemplates repeated transactions, which prescribes the terms of such transactions, and which provides for a finance charge which may be computed from time to time on the outstanding unpaid balance. A credit plan or open end consumer credit plan which is an open end credit plan or open end consumer credit plan within the meaning of the preceding sentence is an open end credit plan or open end consumer credit plan even if credit information is verified from time to time.

(k) The term "adequate notice," as used in section 1643 of this title, means a printed notice to a cardholder which sets forth the pertinent facts clearly and conspicuously so that a person against whom it is to operate could reasonably be expected to have noticed it and understood its meaning. Such notice may be given to a cardholder by printing the notice on any credit card, or on each periodic statement of account, issued to the cardholder, or by any other means reasonably assuring the receipt thereof by the cardholder.

(*l*) The term "credit card" means any card, plate, coupon book or other credit device existing for the purpose of obtaining money, property, labor, or services on credit.

(m) The term "accepted credit card" means any credit card which the cardholder has requested and received or has signed or has used, or authorized another to use, for the purpose of obtaining money, property, labor, or services on credit.

(n) The term "cardholder" means any person to whom a credit card is issued or any person who has agreed with the card issuer to pay obligations arising from the issuance of a credit card to another person.

(*o*) The term "card issuer" means any person who issues a credit card, or the agent of such person with respect to such card.

(p) The term "unauthorized use," as used in section 1643 of this title, means a use of a credit card by a person other than the cardholder who does not have actual, implied, or apparent authority for such use and from which the cardholder receives no benefit.

(q) The term "discount" as used in section 1666f of this title means a reduction made from the regular price. The term "discount" as used in section 1666f of this title shall not mean a surcharge.

(r) The term "surcharge" as used in this section and section 1666f of this title means any means of increasing the regular price to a cardholder which is not imposed upon customers paying by cash, check, or similar means.

(s) The term "State" refers to any State, the Commonwealth of Puerto Rico, the District of Columbia, and any territory or possession of the United States.

(t) The term "agricultural purposes" includes the production, harvest, exhibition, marketing, transportation, processing, or manufacture of agricultural products by a natural person who cultivates, plants, propagates, or nurtures those agricultural products, including but not limited to the acquisition of farmland, real property with a farm residence, and personal property and services used primarily in farming.

(u) The term "agricultural products" includes agricultural, horticultural, viticultural, and dairy products, livestock, wildlife, poultry, bees, forest products, fish and shellfish, and any products thereof, including processed and manufactured products, and any and all products raised or produced on farms and any processed or manufactured products thereof.

(v) The term "material disclosures" means the disclosure, as required by this subchapter, of the annual percentage rate, the method of determining the finance charge and the balance upon which a finance charge will be imposed, the amount of the finance charge, the amount to be financed, the total of payments, the number and amount of payments, the due dates or periods of payments scheduled to repay the indebtedness, and the disclosures required by section 1639(a) of this title.

(w) The term "dwelling" means a residential structure or mobile home which contains one to four family housing units, or individual units of condominiums or cooperatives.

(x) The term "residential mortgage transaction" means a transaction in which a mortgage, deed of trust, purchase money security interest arising under an installment sales contract, or equivalent consensual security interest is created or retained against the consumer's dwelling to finance the acquisition or initial construction of such dwelling.

(y) As used in this section and section 1666f of this title, the term "regular price" means the tag or posted price charged for the property or service if a single price is tagged or posted, or the price charged for the property or service when payment is made by use of an open-end credit plan or a credit card if either (1) no price is tagged or posted, or (2) two prices are tagged or posted, one of which is charged when payment is made by use of an open-end credit plan or a credit card and the other when payment is made by use of cash, check, or similar means. For purposes of this definition, payment by check, draft, or other negotiable instrument which may result in the debiting of an open-end credit plan or a credit cardholder's open-end account shall not be considered payment made by use of the plan or the account.

(z) Any reference to any requirement imposed under this subchapter or any provision thereof includes reference to the regulations of the Bureau under this subchapter or the provision thereof in question.

(aa) The disclosure of an amount or percentage which is greater than the amount or percentage required to be disclosed under this subchapter does not in itself constitute a violation of this subchapter.

(bb) High-cost mortgage

(1) Definition

(A) In general

The term "high-cost mortgage", and a mortgage referred to in this subsection, means a consumer credit transaction that is secured by the consumer's principal dwelling, other than a reverse mortgage transaction, if—

(i) in the case of a credit transaction secured—

(I) by a first mortgage on the consumer's principal dwelling, the annual percentage rate at consummation of the transaction will exceed by more than 6.5 percentage points (8.5 percentage points, if the dwelling is personal property and the transaction is for less than $50,000) the average prime offer rate, as defined in section 1639c(b)(2)(B) of this title, for a comparable transaction; or

(II) by a subordinate or junior mortgage on the consumer's principal dwelling, the annual percentage rate at consummation of the transaction will exceed by more than 8.5 percentage points the average prime offer rate, as defined in section 1639c(b)(2)(B) of this title, for a comparable transaction;

(ii) the total points and fees payable in connection with the transaction, other than bona fide third party charges not retained by the mortgage originator, creditor, or an affiliate of the creditor or mortgage originator, exceed—

(I) in the case of a transaction for $20,000 or more, 5 percent of the total transaction amount; or

(II) in the case of a transaction for less than $20,000, the lesser of 8 percent of the total transaction amount or $1,000 (or such other dollar amount as the Board shall prescribe by regulation); or

(iii) the credit transaction documents permit the creditor to charge or collect prepayment fees or penalties more than 36 months after the transaction closing or such fees or penalties exceed, in the aggregate, more than 2 percent of the amount prepaid.

(B) Introductory rates taken into account

For purposes of subparagraph (A)(i), the annual percentage rate of interest shall be determined based on the following interest rate:

(i) In the case of a fixed-rate transaction in which the annual percentage rate will not vary during the term of the loan, the interest rate in effect on the date of consummation of the transaction.

(ii) In the case of a transaction in which the rate of interest varies solely in accordance with an index, the interest rate determined by adding the index rate in effect on the date of consummation of the transaction to the maximum margin permitted at any time during the loan agreement.

(iii) In the case of any other transaction in which the rate may vary at any time during the term of the loan for any reason, the interest charged on the transaction at the maximum rate that may be charged during the term of the loan.

(C) Mortgage insurance

For the purposes of computing the total points and fees under paragraph (4), the total points and fees shall exclude—

(i) any premium provided by an agency of the Federal Government or an agency of a State;

(ii) any amount that is not in excess of the amount payable under policies in effect at the time of origination under section 203(c)(2)(A) of the National Housing Act (12 U.S.C. 1709(c)(2)(A)), provided that the premium, charge, or fee is required to be refundable on a pro-rated basis and the refund is automatically issued upon notification of the satisfaction of the underlying mortgage loan; and

(iii) any premium paid by the consumer after closing.

(2)(A) After the 2-year period beginning on the effective date of the regulations promulgated under section 155 of the Riegle Community Development and Regulatory Improvement Act of 1994, and no more frequently than biennially after the first increase or decrease under this subparagraph, the Bureau may by regulation increase or decrease the number of percentage points specified in paragraph (1)(A), if the Bureau determines that the increase or decrease is—

(i) consistent with the consumer protections against abusive lending provided by the amendments made by subtitle B of title I of the Riegle Community Development and Regulatory Improvement Act of 1994; and

(ii) warranted by the need for credit.

(B) An increase or decrease under subparagraph (A)—

(i) may not result in the number of percentage points referred to in paragraph (1)(A)(i)(I) being less than 6 percentage points or greater than 10 percentage points; and

(ii) may not result in the number of percentage points referred to in paragraph (1)(A)(i)(II) being less than 8 percentage points or greater than 12 percentage points.

(C) In determining whether to increase or decrease the number of percentage points referred to in subparagraph (A), the Bureau shall consult with representatives of consumers, including low-income consumers, and lenders.

(3) The amount specified in paragraph (1)(B)(ii) shall be adjusted annually on January 1 by the annual percentage change in the Consumer Price Index, as reported on June 1 of the year preceding such adjustment.

(4) For purposes of paragraph (1)(B), points and fees shall include—

(A) all items included in the finance charge, except interest or the time-price differential;

(B) all compensation paid directly or indirectly by a consumer or creditor to a mortgage originator from any source, including a mortgage originator that is also the creditor in a table-funded transaction;

(C) each of the charges listed in section 1605(e) of this title (except an escrow for future payment of taxes), unless—

(i) the charge is reasonable;

(ii) the creditor receives no direct or indirect compensation; and

(iii) the charge is paid to a third party unaffiliated with the creditor; and

(D) premiums or other charges payable at or before closing for any credit life, credit disability, credit unemployment, or credit property insurance, or any other accident, loss-of-income, life or health insurance, or any payments directly or indirectly for any debt cancellation or suspension agreement or contract, except that insurance premiums or debt cancellation or suspension fees calculated and paid in full on a monthly basis shall not be considered financed by the creditor;

(E) the maximum prepayment fees and penalties which may be charged or collected under the terms of the credit transaction;

(F) all prepayment fees or penalties that are incurred by the consumer if the loan refinances a previous loan made or currently held by the same creditor or an affiliate of the creditor; and

(G) such other charges as the Bureau determines to be appropriate.

(5) Calculation of points and fees for open-end consumer credit plans

In the case of open-end consumer credit plans, points and fees shall be calculated, for purposes of this section and section 1639 of this title, by adding the total points and fees known at or before closing, including the maximum prepayment penalties which may be charged or collected under the terms of the credit transaction, plus the minimum additional fees the consumer would be required to pay to draw down an amount equal to the total credit line.

(6) This subsection shall not be construed to limit the rate of interest or the finance charge that a person may charge a consumer for any extension of credit.

(cc) The term "reverse mortgage transaction" means a nonrecourse transaction in which a mortgage, deed of trust, or equivalent consensual security interest is created against the consumer's principal dwelling—

(1) securing one or more advances; and

(2) with respect to which the payment of any principal, interest, and shared appreciation or equity is due and payable (other than in the case of default) only after—

(A) the transfer of the dwelling;

(B) the consumer ceases to occupy the dwelling as a principal dwelling; or

(C) the death of the consumer.

(dd) Definitions relating to mortgage origination and residential mortgage loans

(1) Commission

Unless otherwise specified, the term "Commission" means the Federal Trade Commission.

(2) Mortgage originator

The term "mortgage originator"—

(A) means any person who, for direct or indirect compensation or gain, or in the expectation of direct or indirect compensation or gain—

(i) takes a residential mortgage loan application;

(ii) assists a consumer in obtaining or applying to obtain a residential mortgage loan; or

(iii) offers or negotiates terms of a residential mortgage loan;

(B) includes any person who represents to the public, through advertising or other means of communicating or providing information (including the use of business cards, stationery, brochures, signs, rate lists, or other promotional items), that such person can or will provide any of the services or perform any of the activities described in subparagraph (A);

(C) does not include any person who is—

(i) not otherwise described in subparagraph (A) or (B) and who performs purely administrative or clerical tasks on behalf of a person who is described in any such subparagraph, or

(ii) a retailer of manufactured or modular homes or an employee of the retailer, as applicable—

(I) does not received compensation or gain for engaging in activities described in subparagraph (A) that is in excess of any compensation or gain received in a comparable cash transaction;

(II) discloses to the consumer—

(aa) in writing any corporate affiliation with any creditor; and

(bb) if the retailer has a corporate affiliation with any creditor, at least 1 unaffiliated creditor; and

(III) does not directly negotiate with the consumer of lender on loan terms (including rates, fees, and other costs).

(D) does not include a person or entity that only performs real estate brokerage activities and is licensed or registered in accordance with applicable State law, unless such person or entity is compensated by a lender, a mortgage broker, or other mortgage originator or by any agent of such lender, mortgage broker, or other mortgage originator;

(E) does not include, with respect to a residential mortgage loan, a person, estate, or trust that provides mortgage financing for the sale of 3 properties in any 12-month period to purchasers of such properties, each of which is owned by such person, estate, or trust and serves as security for the loan, provided that such loan—

(i) is not made by a person, estate, or trust that has constructed, or acted as a contractor for the construction of, a residence on the property in the ordinary course of business of such person, estate, or trust;

(ii) is fully amortizing;

(iii) is with respect to a sale for which the seller determines in good faith and documents that the buyer has a reasonable ability to repay the loan;

(iv) has a fixed rate or an adjustable rate that is adjustable after 5 or more years, subject to reasonable annual and lifetime limitations on interest rate increases; and

(v) meets any other criteria the Board may prescribe;

(F) does not include the creditor (except the creditor in a table-funded transaction) under paragraph (1), (2), or (4) of section 1639b(c) of this title; and

(G) does not include a servicer or servicer employees, agents and contractors, including but not limited to those who offer or negotiate terms of a residential mortgage loan for purposes of renegotiating, modifying, replacing and subordinating principal of existing mortgages where borrowers are behind in their payments, in default or have a reasonable likelihood of being in default or falling behind.

(3) Nationwide Mortgage Licensing System and Registry

The term "Nationwide Mortgage Licensing System and Registry" has the same meaning as in the Secure and Fair Enforcement for Mortgage Licensing Act of 2008.

(4) Other definitions relating to mortgage originator

For purposes of this subsection, a person "assists a consumer in obtaining or applying to obtain a residential mortgage loan" by, among other things, advising on residential mortgage loan terms (including rates, fees, and other costs), preparing residential mortgage loan packages, or collecting information on behalf of the consumer with regard to a residential mortgage loan.

(5) Residential mortgage loan

The term "residential mortgage loan" means any consumer credit transaction that is secured by a mortgage, deed of trust, or other equivalent consensual security interest on a dwelling or on residential real property that includes a dwelling, other than a consumer credit transaction under an open end credit plan or, for purposes of sections 1639b and 1639c of this title and section 1638(a)(16), (17), (18), and (19) of this title, and sections 1638(f) and 1640(k) of this title, and any regulations promulgated thereunder, an extension of credit relating to a plan described in section 101(53D) of Title 11.

(6) Secretary

The term "Secretary", when used in connection with any transaction or person involved with a residential mortgage loan, means the Secretary of Housing and Urban Development.

(7) Servicer

The term "servicer" has the same meaning as in section 2605(i)(2) of Title 12.

(ee) Bona fide discount points and prepayment penalties

For the purposes of determining the amount of points and fees for purposes of subsection (aa), either the amounts described in paragraph (1) or (2) of the following paragraphs, but not both, shall be excluded:

(1) Up to and including 2 bona fide discount points payable by the consumer in connection with the mortgage, but only if the interest rate from which the mortgage's interest rate will be discounted does not exceed by more than 1 percentage point—

(A) the average prime offer rate, as defined in section 1639c of this title; or

(B) if secured by a personal property loan, the average rate on a loan in connection with which insurance is provided under title I of the National Housing Act (12 U.S.C. 1702 et seq.).

(2) Unless 2 bona fide discount points have been excluded under paragraph (1), up to and including 1 bona fide discount point payable by the consumer in connection with the mortgage, but only if the interest rate from which the mortgage's interest rate will be discounted does not exceed by more than 2 percentage points—

(A) the average prime offer rate, as defined in section 1639c of this title; or

(B) if secured by a personal property loan, the average rate on a loan in connection with which insurance is provided under title I of the National Housing Act (12 U.S.C. 1702 et seq.).

(3) For purposes of paragraph (1), the term "bona fide discount points" means loan discount points which are knowingly paid by the consumer for the purpose of reducing, and which in fact result in a bona fide reduction of, the interest rate or time-price differential applicable to the mortgage.

(4) Paragraphs (1) and (2) shall not apply to discount points used to purchase an interest rate reduction unless the amount of the interest rate reduction purchased is reasonably consistent with established industry norms and practices for secondary mortgage market transactions.

§ 1603 [CCPA § 104]. Exempted Transactions

This subchapter does not apply to the following:

(1) Credit transactions involving extensions of credit primarily for business, commercial, or agricultural purposes, or to government or governmental agencies or instrumentalities, or to organizations.

(2) Transactions in securities or commodities accounts by a broker-dealer registered with the Securities and Exchange Commission.

(3) Credit transactions, other than those in which a security interest is or will be acquired in real property, or in personal property used or expected to be used as the principal dwelling of the consumer and other than private education loans (as that term is defined in section 1650(a) of this title), in which the total amount financed exceeds $50,000.

(4) Transactions under public utility tariffs, if the Bureau determines that a State regulatory body regulates the charges for the public utility services involved, the charges for delayed payment, and any discount allowed for early payment.

(5) Transactions for which the Bureau, by rule, determines that coverage under this subchapter is not necessary to carry out the purposes of this subchapter.

(6) Repealed. Pub.L. 96–221, Title VI, § 603(c) (3), Mar. 31, 1980, 94 Stat. 169

(7) Loans made, insured, or guaranteed pursuant to a program authorized by Title IV of the Higher Education Act of 1965.

§ 1604 [CCPA § 105]. Disclosure Guidelines

(a) Promulgation, contents, etc., of regulations

The Bureau shall prescribe regulations to carry out the purposes of this subchapter. Except with respect to the provisions of section 1639 of this title that apply to a mortgage referred to in section 1602(aa) of this title, such regulations may contain such additional requirements, classifications, differentiations, or other provisions, and may provide for such adjustments and exceptions for all or any class of transactions, as in the judgment of the Bureau are necessary or proper to effectuate the purposes of this subchapter, to prevent circumvention or evasion thereof, or to facilitate compliance therewith.

(b) Model disclosure forms and clauses; publication, criteria, compliance, etc.

The Bureau shall publish a single, integrated disclosure for mortgage loan transactions (including real estate settlement cost statements) which includes the disclosure requirements of this subchapter in conjunction with the disclosure requirements of the Real Estate Settlement Procedures Act of 1974 that, taken together, may apply to a transaction that is subject to both or either provisions of law. The purpose of such model disclosure shall be to facilitate compliance with the disclosure requirements of this subchapter and the Real Estate Settlement Procedures Act of 1974, and to aid the borrower or lessee in understanding the transaction by utilizing readily understandable language to simplify the technical nature of the disclosures. In devising such forms, the Bureau shall consider the use by creditors or lessors of data processing or similar automated equipment. Nothing in this subchapter may be construed to require a creditor or lessor to use any such model form or clause prescribed by the Bureau under this section. A creditor or lessor shall be deemed to be in compliance with the disclosure provisions of this subchapter with respect to other than numerical disclosures if the creditor or lessor (1) uses any appropriate model form or clause as published by the Bureau, or (2) uses any such model form or clause and changes it by (A) deleting any information which is not required by this subchapter, or (B) rearranging the format, if in making such deletion or rearranging the format, the creditor or lessor does not affect the substance, clarity, or meaningful sequence of the disclosure.

(c) Procedures applicable for adoption of model forms and clauses

Model disclosure forms and clauses shall be adopted by the Bureau after notice duly given in the Federal Register and an opportunity for public comment in accordance with section 553 of Title 5.

(d) Effective dates of regulations containing new disclosure requirements

Any regulation of the Bureau, or any amendment or interpretation thereof, requiring any disclosure which differs from the disclosures previously required by this part, part D, or part E or by any regulation of the Bureau promulgated thereunder shall have an effective date of that October 1 which follows by at least six months the date of promulgation, except that the Bureau may at its discretion take interim action by regulation, amendment, or interpretation to lengthen the period of time permitted for creditors or lessors to adjust their forms to accommodate new requirements or shorten the length of time for creditors or lessors to make such adjustments when it makes a specific finding that such action is necessary to comply with the findings of a court or to prevent unfair or deceptive disclosure practices. Notwithstanding the previous sentence, any creditor or lessor may comply with any such newly promulgated disclosure requirements prior to the effective date of the requirements.

(f)[1] Exemption authority

(1) In general

The Bureau may exempt, by regulation, from all or part of this subchapter all or any class of transactions, other than transactions involving any mortgage described in section 1602(aa) of this title, for which, in the determination of the Bureau, coverage under all or part of this subchapter does not provide a meaningful benefit to consumers in the form of useful information or protection.

(2) Factors for consideration

In determining which classes of transactions to exempt in whole or in part under paragraph (1), the Bureau shall consider the following factors and publish its rationale at the time a proposed exemption is published for comment:

(A) The amount of the loan and whether the disclosures, right of rescission, and other provisions provide a benefit to the consumers who are parties to such transactions, as determined by the Bureau.

(B) The extent to which the requirements of this subchapter complicate, hinder, or make more expensive the credit process for the class of transactions.

(C) The status of the borrower, including—

(i) any related financial arrangements of the borrower, as determined by the Bureau;

(ii) the financial sophistication of the borrower relative to the type of transaction; and

(iii) the importance to the borrower of the credit, related supporting property, and coverage under this subchapter, as determined by the Bureau;

(D) whether the loan is secured by the principal residence of the consumer; and

(E) whether the goal of consumer protection would be undermined by such an exemption.

(g) Waiver for certain borrowers

(1) In general

---

1 So in original. No subsection (e) has been enacted.

The Bureau, by regulation, may exempt from the requirements of this subchapter certain credit transactions if—

(A) the transaction involves a consumer—

(i) with an annual earned income of more than $200,000; or

(ii) having net assets in excess of $1,000,000 at the time of the transaction; and

(B) a waiver that is handwritten, signed, and dated by the consumer is first obtained from the consumer.

(2) Adjustments by the Bureau

The Bureau, at its discretion, may adjust the annual earned income and net asset requirements of paragraph (1) for inflation.

(h) Deference

Notwithstanding any power granted to any Federal agency under this subchapter, the deference that a court affords to the Bureau with respect to a determination made by the Bureau relating to the meaning or interpretation of any provision of this subchapter, other than section 1639e or 1639h of this title, shall be applied as if the Bureau were the only agency authorized to apply, enforce, interpret, or administer the provisions of this subchapter.

(i) Authority of the Board to prescribe rules

Notwithstanding subsection (a), the Board shall have authority to prescribe rules under this subchapter with respect to a person described in section 5519(a) of Title 12. Regulations prescribed under this subsection may contain such classifications, differentiations, or other provisions, as in the judgment of the Board are necessary or proper to effectuate the purposes of this subchapter, to prevent circumvention or evasion thereof, or to facilitate compliance therewith.

§ 1605 [CCPA § 106]. Determination of Finance Charge

(a) "Finance charge" defined

Except as otherwise provided in this section, the amount of the finance charge in connection with any consumer credit transaction shall be determined as the sum of all charges, payable directly or indirectly by the person to whom the credit is extended, and imposed directly or indirectly by the creditor as an incident to the extension of credit. The finance charge does not include charges of a type payable in a comparable cash transaction. The finance charge shall not include fees and amounts imposed by third party closing agents (including settlement agents, attorneys, and escrow and title companies) if the creditor does not require the imposition of the charges or the services provided and does not retain the charges. Examples of charges which are included in the finance charge include any of the following types of charges which are applicable:

(1) Interest, time price differential, and any amount payable under a point, discount, or other system of additional charges.

(2) Service or carrying charge.

(3) Loan fee, finder's fee, or similar charge.

(4) Fee for an investigation or credit report.

(5) Premium or other charge for any guarantee or insurance protecting the creditor against the obligor's default or other credit loss.

(6) Borrower-paid mortgage broker fees, including fees paid directly to the broker or the lender (for delivery to the broker) whether such fees are paid in cash or financed.

(b) Life, accident, or health insurance premiums included in finance charge

Charges or premiums for credit life, accident, or health insurance written in connection with any consumer credit transaction shall be included in the finance charges unless

(1) the coverage of the debtor by the insurance is not a factor in the approval by the creditor of the extension of credit, and this fact is clearly disclosed in writing to the person applying for or obtaining the extension of credit; and

(2) in order to obtain the insurance in connection with the extension of credit, the person to whom the credit is extended must give specific affirmative written indication of his desire to do so after written disclosure to him of the cost thereof.

(c) Property damage and liability insurance premiums included in finance charge

Charges or premiums for insurance, written in connection with any consumer credit transaction, against loss of or damage to property or against liability arising out of the ownership or use of property, shall be included in the finance charge unless a clear and specific statement in writing is furnished by the creditor to the person to whom the credit is extended, setting forth the cost of the insurance if obtained from or through the creditor, and stating that the person to whom the credit is extended may choose the person through which the insurance is to be obtained.

(d) Items exempted from computation of finance charge in all credit transactions

If any of the following items is itemized and disclosed in accordance with the regulations of the Bureau in connection with any transaction, then the creditor need not include that item in the computation of the finance charge with respect to that transaction:

(1) Fees and charges prescribed by law which actually are or will be paid to public officials for determining the existence of or for perfecting or releasing or satisfying any security related to the credit transaction.

(2) The premium payable for any insurance in lieu of perfecting any security interest otherwise required by the creditor in connection with the transaction, if the premium does not exceed the fees and charges described in paragraph (1) which would otherwise be payable.

(3) Any tax levied on security instruments or on documents evidencing indebtedness if the payment of such taxes is a precondition for recording the instrument securing the evidence of indebtedness.

(e) Items exempted from computation of finance charge in extensions of credit secured by an interest in real property

The following items, when charged in connection with any extension of credit secured by an interest in real property, shall not be included in the computation of the finance charge with respect to that transaction:

(1) Fees or premiums for title examination, title insurance, or similar purposes.

(2) Fees for preparation of loan-related documents.

(3) Escrows for future payments of taxes and insurance.

(4) Fees for notarizing deeds and other documents.

(5) Appraisal fees, including fees related to any pest infestation or flood hazard inspections conducted prior to closing.

(6) Credit reports.

(f) Tolerances for accuracy

In connection with credit transactions not under an open end credit plan that are secured by real property or a dwelling, the disclosure of the finance charge and other disclosures affected by any finance charge—

(1) shall be treated as being accurate for purposes of this subchapter if the amount disclosed as the finance charge—

(A) does not vary from the actual finance charge by more than $100; or

(B) is greater than the amount required to be disclosed under this subchapter; and

(2) shall be treated as being accurate for purposes of section 1635 of this title if—

(A) except as provided in subparagraph (B), the amount disclosed as the finance charge does not vary from the actual finance charge by more than an amount equal to one-half of one percent of the total amount of credit extended; or

(B) in the case of a transaction, other than a mortgage referred to in section 1602(aa) of this title, which—

(i) is a refinancing of the principal balance then due and any accrued and unpaid finance charges of a residential mortgage transaction as defined in section 1602(w) of this title, or is any subsequent refinancing of such a transaction; and

(ii) does not provide any new consolidation or new advance;

if the amount disclosed as the finance charge does not vary from the actual finance charge by more than an amount equal to one percent of the total amount of credit extended.

§ 1606 [CCPA § 107]. Determination of Annual Percentage Rate

(a) "Annual percentage rate" defined

The annual percentage rate applicable to any extension of consumer credit shall be determined, in accordance with the regulations of the Bureau,

(1) in the case of any extension of credit other than under an open end credit plan, as

(A) that nominal annual percentage rate which will yield a sum equal to the amount of the finance charge when it is applied to the unpaid balances of the amount financed, calculated according to the actuarial method of allocating payments made on a debt between the amount financed and the amount of the finance charge, pursuant to which a payment is applied first to the accumulated finance charge and the balance is applied to the unpaid amount financed; or

(B) the rate determined by any method prescribed by the Bureau as a method which materially simplifies computation while retaining reasonable accuracy as compared with the rate determined under subparagraph (A).

(2) in the case of any extension of credit under an open end credit plan, as the quotient (expressed as a percentage) of the total finance charge for the period to which it relates divided by the amount upon which the finance charge for that period is based, multiplied by the number of such periods in a year.

(b) Computation of rate of finance charges for balances within a specified range

Where a creditor imposes the same finance charge for balances within a specified range, the annual percentage rate shall be computed on the median balance within the range, except that if the Bureau determines that a rate so computed would not be meaningful, or would be materially misleading, the annual percentage rate shall be computed on such other basis as the Bureau may by regulation require.

(c) Allowable tolerances for purposes of compliance with disclosure requirements

The disclosure of an annual percentage rate is accurate for the purpose of this subchapter if the rate disclosed is within a tolerance not greater than one-eighth of 1 per centum more or less than the actual rate or rounded to the nearest one-fourth of 1 per centum. The Bureau may allow a greater tolerance to simplify compliance where irregular payments are involved.

(d) Use of rate tables or charts having allowable variance from determined rates

The Bureau may authorize the use of rate tables or charts which may provide for the disclosure of annual percentage rates which vary from the rate determined in accordance with subsection (a)(1)(A) by not more than such tolerances as the Bureau may allow. The Bureau may not allow a tolerance greater than 8 per centum of that rate except to simplify compliance where irregular payments are involved.

(e) Authorization of tolerances in determining annual percentage rates

In the case of creditors determining the annual percentage rate in a manner other than as described in subsection (d), the Bureau may authorize other reasonable tolerances.

§ 1607 [CCPA § 108]. Administrative Enforcement

(a) Enforcing agencies

Subject to subtitle B of the Consumer Financial Protection Act of 2010, compliance with the requirements imposed under this subchapter shall be enforced under—

(1) section 8 of the Federal Deposit Insurance Act by the appropriate Federal banking agency, as defined in section 3(q) of the Federal Deposit Insurance Act (12 U.S.C. 1813(q)), with respect to—

(A) national banks, Federal savings associations, and Federal branches and Federal agencies of foreign banks;

(B) member banks of the Federal Reserve System (other than national banks), branches and agencies of foreign banks (other than Federal branches, Federal agencies, and insured State branches of foreign banks), commercial lending companies owned or controlled by foreign banks, and organizations operating under section 25 or 25A of the Federal Reserve Act; and

(C) banks and State savings associations insured by the Federal Deposit Insurance Corporation (other than members of the Federal Reserve System), and insured State branches of foreign banks;

(2) the Federal Credit Union Act, by the Director of the National Credit Union Administration, with respect to any Federal credit union;

(3) part A of subtitle VII of Title 49, by the Secretary of Transportation, with respect to any air carrier or foreign air carrier subject to that part;

(4) the Packers and Stockyards Act, 1921 (except as provided in section 406 of that Act), by the Secretary of Agriculture, with respect to any activities subject to that Act;

(5) the Farm Credit Act of 1971, by the Farm Credit Administration with respect to any Federal land bank, Federal land bank association, Federal intermediate credit bank, or production credit association; and

(6) subtitle E of the Consumer Financial Protection Act of 2010, by the Bureau, with respect to any person subject to this subchapter.

(7) sections 21B and 21C in the Securities Exchange Act of 1934, in the case of a broker or dealer, other than a depository institution, by the Securities and Exchange Commission.

(b) Violations of this subchapter deemed violations of pre-existing statutory requirements; additional agency powers

For the purpose of the exercise by any agency referred to in subsection (a) of its powers under any Act referred to in that subsection, a violation of any requirement imposed under this subchapter shall be deemed to be a violation of a requirement imposed under that Act. In addition to its powers under any provision of law specifically referred to in subsection (a), each of the agencies referred to in that subsection may exercise, for the purpose of enforcing compliance with any requirement imposed under this subchapter, any other authority conferred on it by law.

(c) Overall enforcement authority of the Federal Trade Commission

Except to the extent that enforcement of the requirements imposed under this subchapter is specifically committed to some other Government agency under any of paragraphs (1) through (5) of subsection (a), and subject to subtitle B of the Consumer Financial Protection Act of 2010, the Federal Trade Commission shall be authorized to enforce such requirements. For the purpose of the exercise by the Federal Trade Commission of its functions and powers under the Federal Trade Commission Act, a violation of any requirement imposed under this subchapter shall be deemed a violation of a requirement imposed under that Act. All of the functions and powers of the Federal Trade Commission under the Federal Trade Commission Act are available to the Federal Trade Commission to enforce compliance by any person with the requirements under this subchapter, irrespective of whether that person is engaged in commerce or meets any other jurisdictional tests under the Federal Trade Commission Act.

(d) Rules and regulations

The authority of the Bureau to issue regulations under this subchapter does not impair the authority of any other agency designated in this section to make rules respecting its own procedures in enforcing compliance with requirements imposed under this subchapter.

(e) Adjustment of finance charges; procedures applicable, coverage, criteria, etc.

(1) In carrying out its enforcement activities under this section, each agency referred to in subsection (a) or (c), in cases where an annual percentage rate or finance charge was inaccurately disclosed, shall notify the creditor of such disclosure error and is authorized in accordance with the provisions of this subsection to require the creditor to make an adjustment to the account of the person to whom credit was extended, to assure that such person will not be required to pay a finance charge in excess of the finance charge actually disclosed or the dollar equivalent of the annual percentage rate actually disclosed, whichever is lower. For the purposes of this subsection, except where such disclosure error resulted from a willful violation which was intended to mislead the person to whom credit was extended, in determining whether a disclosure error has occurred and in calculating any adjustment, (A) each agency shall apply (i) with respect to the annual percentage rate, a tolerance of one-quarter of 1 percent more or less than the actual rate, determined without regard to section 1606(c) of this title, and (ii) with respect to the finance charge, a corresponding numerical tolerance as generated by the tolerance provided under this subsection for the annual percentage rate; except that (B) with respect to transactions consummated after two years following March 31, 1980, each agency shall apply (i) for transactions that have a scheduled amortization of ten years or less, with respect to the annual percentage rate, a tolerance not to exceed one-quarter of 1 percent more or less than the actual rate, determined without regard to section 1606(c) of this title, but in no event a tolerance of less than the tolerances allowed under section 1606(c) of this title, (ii) for transactions that have a scheduled amortization of more than ten years, with respect to the annual percentage rate, only such tolerances as are allowed under section 1606(c) of this title, and (iii) for all transactions, with respect to the finance charge, a corresponding numerical tolerance as generated by the tolerances provided under this subsection for the annual percentage rate.

(2) Each agency shall require such an adjustment when it determines that such disclosure error resulted from (A) a clear and consistent pattern or practice of violations, (B) gross negligence, or (C) a willful violation which was intended to mislead the person to whom the credit was extended. Notwithstanding the preceding sentence, except where such disclosure error resulted from a willful violation which was intended to mislead the person to whom credit was extended, an agency need not require such an adjustment if it determines that such disclosure error—

(A) resulted from an error involving the disclosure of a fee or charge that would otherwise be excludable in computing the finance charge, including but not limited to violations involving the disclosures described in sections 1605(b), (c) and (d) of this title, in which event the agency may require such remedial action as it determines to be equitable, except that for transactions consummated after two years after March 31, 1980, such an adjustment shall be ordered for violations of section 1605(b) of this title;

(B) involved a disclosed amount which was 10 per centum or less of the amount that should have been disclosed and (i) in cases where the error involved a disclosed finance charge, the annual percentage rate was disclosed correctly, and (ii) in cases where the error involved a disclosed annual percentage rate, the finance charge was disclosed correctly; in which event the agency may require such adjustment as it determines to be equitable;

(C) involved a total failure to disclose either the annual percentage rate or the finance charge, in which event the agency may require such adjustment as it determines to be equitable; or

(D) resulted from any other unique circumstance involving clearly technical and nonsubstantive disclosure violations that do not adversely affect information provided to the consumer and that have not misled or otherwise deceived the consumer.

In the case of other such disclosure errors, each agency may require such an adjustment.

(3) Notwithstanding paragraph (2), no adjustment shall be ordered—

(A) if it would have a significantly adverse impact upon the safety or soundness of the creditor, but in any such case, the agency may—

(i) require a partial adjustment in an amount which does not have such an impact; or

(ii) require the full adjustment, but permit the creditor to make the required adjustment in partial payments over an extended period of time which the agency considers to be reasonable, if (in the case of an agency referred to in paragraph (1), (2), or (3) of subsection (a)), the agency determines that a partial adjustment or making partial payments over an extended period is necessary to avoid causing the creditor to become undercapitalized pursuant to section 38 of the Federal Deposit Insurance Act [12 U.S.C.A. § 1831*o*];

(B) the[1] amount of the adjustment would be less than $1, except that if more than one year has elapsed since the date of the violation, the agency may require that such amount be paid into the Treasury of the United States, or

(C) except where such disclosure error resulted from a willful violation which was intended to mislead the person to whom credit was extended, in the case of an open-end credit plan, more than two years after the violation, or in the case of any other extension of credit, as follows:

(i) with respect to creditors that are subject to examination by the agencies referred to in paragraphs (1) through (3) of subsection (a) of this section, except in connection with violations arising from practices identified in the current examination and only in connection with transactions that are consummated after the date of the

---

1 So in original. Probably should be preceded by "if."

immediately preceding examination, except that where practices giving rise to violations identified in earlier examinations have not been corrected, adjustments for those violations shall be required in connection with transactions consummated after the date of examination in which such practices were first identified;

(ii) with respect to creditors that are not subject to examination by such agencies, except in connection with transactions that are consummated after May 10, 1978; and

(iii) in no event after the later of (I) the expiration of the life of the credit extension, or (II) two years after the agreement to extend credit was consummated.

(4)(A) Notwithstanding any other provision of this section, an adjustment under this subsection may be required by an agency referred to in subsection (a) or (c) only by an order issued in accordance with cease and desist procedures provided by the provision of law referred to in such subsections.

(B) In case of an agency which is not authorized to conduct cease and desist proceedings, such an order may be issued after an agency hearing on the record conducted at least thirty but not more than sixty days after notice of the alleged violation is served on the creditor. Such a hearing shall be deemed to be a hearing which is subject to the provisions of section 8(h) of the Federal Deposit Insurance Act [12 U.S.C.A. § 1818(h)] and shall be subject to judicial review as provided therein.

(5) Except as otherwise specifically provided in this subsection and notwithstanding any provision of law referred to in subsection (a) or (c), no agency referred to in subsection (a) or (c) may require a creditor to make dollar adjustments for errors in any requirements under this subchapter, except with regard to the requirements of section 1666d of this title.

(6) A creditor shall not be subject to an order to make an adjustment, if within sixty days after discovering a disclosure error, whether pursuant to a final written examination report or through the creditor's own procedures, the creditor notifies the person concerned of the error and adjusts the account so as to assure that such person will not be required to pay a finance charge in excess of the finance charge actually disclosed or the dollar equivalent of the annual percentage rate actually disclosed, whichever is lower.

(7) Notwithstanding the second sentence of subsection (e)(1), subsection (e)(3)(C)(i), and subsection (e)(3)(C)(ii), each agency referred to in subsection (a) or (c) shall require an adjustment for an annual percentage rate disclosure error that exceeds a tolerance of one quarter of one percent less than the actual rate, determined without regard to section 1606(c) of this title, with respect to any transaction consummated between January 1, 1977, and March 31, 1980.

§ 1608 [CCPA § 109]. Views of Other Agencies

In the exercise of its functions under this subchapter, the Bureau may obtain upon requests the views of any other Federal agency which, in the judgment of the Bureau, exercises regulatory or supervisory functions with respect to any class of creditors subject to this subchapter.

§ 1609. Repealed. Pub.L. 94–239, § 3(b)(1), Mar. 23, 1976, 90 Stat. 253

§ 1610 [CCPA § 111]. Effect on Other Laws

(a) Inconsistent provisions; procedures applicable for determination

(1) Except as provided in subsection (e), this part and parts B and C, do not annul, alter, or affect the laws of any State relating to the disclosure of information in connection with credit transactions, except to the extent that those laws are inconsistent with the provisions of this subchapter and then only to the extent of the inconsistency. Upon its own motion or upon the request of any creditor, State or other interested party which is submitted in accordance with procedures prescribed in regulations of the Bureau, the Bureau shall determine whether any such inconsistency exists. If the Bureau determines that a State-required disclosure is inconsistent, creditors located in that State may not make disclosures using the inconsistent term or form, and shall incur no liability under the law of that State for failure to use such term or form, notwithstanding that such determination is subsequently amended, rescinded, or determined by judicial or other authority to be invalid for any reason.

(2) Upon its own motion or upon the request of any creditor, State, or other interested party which is submitted in accordance with procedures prescribed in regulations of the Bureau, the Bureau shall determine whether any disclosure required under the law of any State is substantially the same in meaning as a disclosure required under this subchapter. If the Bureau determines that a State-required disclosure is substantially the same in meaning as a disclosure required by this subchapter, then creditors located in that State may make such disclosure in compliance with such State law in lieu of the disclosure required by this subchapter, except that the annual percentage rate and finance charge shall be disclosed as required by section 1632 of this title, and such State-required disclosure may not be made in lieu of the disclosures applicable to certain mortgages under section 1639 of this title.

(b) State credit charge statutes

Except as provided in section 1639 of this title, this subchapter does not otherwise annul, alter or affect in any manner the meaning, scope or applicability of the laws of any State, including, but not limited to, laws relating to the types, amounts or rates of charges, or any element or elements of charges, permissible under such laws in connection with the extension or use of credit, nor does this subchapter extend the applicability of those laws to any class of persons or transactions to which they would not otherwise apply. The provisions of section 1639 of this title do not annul, alter, or affect the applicability of the laws of any State or exempt any person subject to the provisions of section 1639 of this title from complying with the laws of any State, with respect to the requirements for mortgages referred to in section 1602(aa) of this title, except to the extent that those State laws are inconsistent with any provisions of section 1639 of this title, and then only to the extent of the inconsistency.

(c) Disclosure as evidence

In any action or proceeding in any court involving a consumer credit sale, the disclosure of the annual percentage rate as required under this subchapter in connection with that sale may not be received as evidence that the sale was a loan or any type of transaction other than a credit sale.

(d) Contract or other obligations under State or Federal law

Except as specified in sections 1635, 1640, and 1666e of this title, this subchapter and the regulations issued thereunder do not affect the validity or enforceability of any contract or obligation under State or Federal law.

(e) Certain credit and charge card application and solicitation disclosure provisions

The provisions of subsection (c) of section 1632 of this title and subsections (c), (d), (e), and (f) of section 1637 of this title shall supersede any provision of the law of any State relating to the disclosure of information in any credit or charge card application or solicitation which is subject to the requirements of section 1637(c) of this title or any renewal notice which is subject to the requirements of section 1637(d) of this title, except that any State may employ or establish State laws for the purpose of enforcing the requirements of such sections.

§ 1611 [CCPA § 112]. Criminal Liability for Willful and Knowing Violation

Whoever willfully and knowingly

(1) gives false or inaccurate information or fails to provide information which he is required to disclose under the provisions of this subchapter or any regulation issued thereunder,

(2) uses any chart or table authorized by the Bureau under section 1606 of this title in such a manner as to consistently understate the annual percentage rate determined under section 1606(a)(1)(A) of this title, or

(3) otherwise fails to comply with any requirement imposed under this subchapter, shall be fined not more than $5,000 or imprisoned not more than one year, or both.

§ 1612 [CCPA § 113]. Effect on Government Agencies

(a) Consultation requirements respecting compliance of credit instruments issued to participating creditor

Any department or agency of the United States which administers a credit program in which it extends, insures, or guarantees consumer credit and in which it provides instruments to a creditor which contain any disclosures required by this subchapter shall, prior to the issuance or continued use of such instruments, consult with the Bureau to assure that such instruments comply with this subchapter.

(b) Inapplicability of Federal civil or criminal penalties to Federal, state, and local agencies

No civil or criminal penalty provided under this subchapter for any violation thereof may be imposed upon the United States or any department or agency thereof, or upon any State or political subdivision thereof, or any agency of any State or political subdivision.

(c) Inapplicability of Federal civil or criminal penalties to participating creditor where violating instrument issued by United States

A creditor participating in a credit program administered, insured, or guaranteed by any department or agency of the United States shall not be held liable for a civil or criminal penalty under this subchapter in any case in which the violation results from the use of an instrument required by any such department or agency.

(d) Applicability of State penalties to violations by participating creditor

A creditor participating in a credit program administered, insured, or guaranteed by any department or agency of the United States shall not be held liable for a civil or criminal penalty under the laws of any State (other than laws determined under section 1610 of this title to be inconsistent with this subchapter) for any technical or procedural failure, such as a failure to use a specific form, to make information available at a specific place on an instrument, or to use a specific typeface, as required by State law, which is caused by the use of an instrument required to be used by such department or agency.

§ 1613 [CCPA § 114]. Annual Reports to Congress by Bureau

Each year the Bureau shall make a report to the Congress concerning the administration of its functions under this subchapter, including such recommendations as the Bureau deems necessary or appropriate. In addition, each report of the Bureau shall include its assessment of the extent to which compliance with the requirements imposed under this subchapter is being achieved.

§ 1614. Repealed. Pub.L. 96–221, Title VI, 616(b), Mar. 31, 1980, 94 Stat. 182

§ 1615.[1] Prohibition on Use of "Rule of 78's" in Connection with Mortgage Refinancings and Other Consumer Loans

(a) Prompt refund of unearned interest required

(1) In general

[1] Not enacted as part of the Truth in Lending Act.

If a consumer prepays in full the financed amount under any consumer credit transaction, the creditor shall promptly refund any unearned portion of the interest charge to the consumer.

(2) Exception for refund of de minimus amount

No refund shall be required under paragraph (1) with respect to the prepayment of any consumer credit transaction if the total amount of the refund would be less than $1.

(3) Applicability to refinanced transactions and acceleration by the creditor

This subsection shall apply with respect to any prepayment of a consumer credit transaction described in paragraph (1) without regard to the manner or the reason for the prepayment, including—

(A) any prepayment made in connection with the refinancing, consolidation, or restructuring of the transaction; and

(B) any prepayment made as a result of the acceleration of the obligation to repay the amount due with respect to the transaction.

(b) Use of "Rule of 78's" prohibited

For the purpose of calculating any refund of interest required under subsection (a) for any precomputed consumer credit transaction of a term exceeding 61 months which is consummated after September 30, 1993, the creditor shall compute the refund based on a method which is at least as favorable to the consumer as the actuarial method.

(c) Statement of prepayment amount

(1) In general

Before the end of the 5-day period beginning on the date an oral or written request is received by a creditor from a consumer for the disclosure of the amount due on any precomputed consumer credit account, the creditor or assignee shall provide the consumer with a statement of—

(A) the amount necessary to prepay the account in full; and

(B) if the amount disclosed pursuant to subparagraph (A) includes an amount which is required to be refunded under this section with respect to such prepayment, the amount of such refund.

(2) Written statement required if request is in writing

If the customer's request is in writing, the statement under paragraph (1) shall be in writing.

(3) 1 free annual statement

A consumer shall be entitled to obtain 1 statement under paragraph (1) each year without charge.

(4) Additional statements subject to reasonable fees

Any creditor may impose a reasonable fee to cover the cost of providing any statement under paragraph (1) to any consumer in addition to the 1 free annual statement required under paragraph (3) if the amount of the charge for such additional statement is disclosed to the consumer before furnishing such statement.

(d) Definitions

For the purpose of this section—

(1) Actuarial method

The term "actuarial method" means the method of allocating payments made on a debt between the amount financed and the finance charge pursuant to which a payment is applied first to the accumulated finance charge and any remainder is subtracted from, or any deficiency is added to, the unpaid balance of the amount financed.

(2) Consumer, credit

The terms "consumer" and "creditor" have the meanings given to such terms in section 1602 of this title.

(3) Creditor

The term "creditor"—

(A) has the meaning given to such term in section 1602 of this title; and

(B) includes any assignee of any creditor with respect to credit extended in connection with any consumer credit transaction and any subsequent assignee with respect to such credit.

§ 1616 [CCPA § 121]. Board review of consumer credit plans and regulations

(a) Required review

Not later than 2 years after the effective date of this Act and every 2 years thereafter, except as provided in subsection (c)(2), the Board shall conduct a review, within the limits of its existing resources available for reporting purposes, of the consumer credit card market, including—

(1) the terms of credit card agreements and the practices of credit card issuers;

(2) the effectiveness of disclosure of terms, fees, and other expenses of credit card plans;

(3) the adequacy of protections against unfair or deceptive acts or practices relating to credit card plans; and

(4) whether or not, and to what extent, the implementation of this Act and the amendments made by this Act has affected—

(A) cost and availability of credit, particularly with respect to non-prime borrowers;

(B) the safety and soundness of credit card issuers;

(C) the use of risk-based pricing; or

(D) credit card product innovation.

(b) Solicitation of public comment

In connection with conducting the review required by subsection (a), the Board shall solicit comment from consumers, credit card issuers, and other interested parties, such as through hearings or written comments.

(c) Regulations

(1) Notice

Following the review required by subsection (a), the Board shall publish a notice in the Federal Register that—

(A) summarizes the review, the comments received from the public solicitation, and other evidence gathered by the Bureau, such as through consumer testing or other research; and

(B) either—

(i) proposes new or revised regulations or interpretations to update or revise disclosures and protections for consumer credit cards, as appropriate; or

(ii) states the reason for the determination of the Board that new or revised regulations are not necessary.

(2) Revision of review period following material revision of regulations

In the event that the Board materially revises regulations on consumer credit card plans, a review need not be conducted until 2 years after the effective date of the revised regulations, which thereafter shall be treated as the new date for the biennial review required by subsection (a).

(d) Board report to the Congress

The Board shall report to Congress not less frequently than every 2 years, except as provided in subsection (c)(2), on the status of its most recent review, its efforts to address any **issues identified from the review, and any recommendations for legislation.**

(e) Additional reporting

The Federal banking agencies (as that term is defined in section 1813 of Title 12) and the Federal Trade Commission shall provide annually to the Board, and the Board shall include in its annual report to Congress under section 247 of Title 12, information about the supervisory and enforcement activities of the agencies with respect to compliance by credit card issuers with applicable Federal consumer protection statutes and regulations, including—

(1) this Act, the amendments made by this Act, and regulations prescribed under this Act and such amendments; and

(2) section 5 of the Federal Trade Commission Act, and regulations prescribed under the Federal Trade Commission Act, including part 227 of title 12 of the Code of Federal Regulations, as prescribed by the Board (referred to as "Regulation AA").

PART B—CREDIT TRANSACTIONS

§ 1631 [CCPA § 121]. Disclosure Requirements

(a) Duty of creditor or lessor respecting one or more than one obligor

Subject to subsection (b), a creditor or lessor shall disclose to the person who is obligated on a consumer lease or a consumer credit transaction the information required under this subchapter. In a transaction involving more than one obligor, a creditor or lessor, except in a transaction under section 1635 of this title, need not disclose to more than one of such obligors if the obligor given disclosure is a primary obligor.

(b) Creditor or lessor required to make disclosure

If a transaction involves one creditor as defined in section 1602(f) of this title, or one lessor as defined in section 1667(3) of this title, such creditor or lessor shall make the disclosures. If a transaction involves more than one creditor or lessor, only one creditor or lessor shall be required to make the disclosures. The Bureau shall by regulation specify which creditor or lessor shall make the disclosures.

(c) Estimates as satisfying statutory requirements; basis of disclosure for per diem interest

The Bureau may provide by regulation that any portion of the information required to be disclosed by this subchapter may be given in the form of estimates where the provider of such information is not in a position to know exact information. In the case of any consumer credit transaction a portion of the interest on which is determined on a per diem basis and is to be collected upon the consummation of such transaction, any disclosure with respect to such portion of interest shall be deemed to be accurate for purposes of this subchapter if the disclosure is based on information actually known to the creditor at the time that the disclosure documents are being prepared for the consummation of the transaction.

(d) Tolerances for numerical disclosures

The Bureau shall determine whether tolerances for numerical disclosures other than the annual percentage rate are necessary to facilitate compliance with this subchapter, and if it determines that such tolerances are necessary to facilitate compliance, it shall by regulation permit disclosures within such tolerances. The Bureau shall exercise its authority to permit tolerances for numerical disclosures other than the annual percentage rate so that such tolerances are narrow enough to prevent such tolerances from resulting in misleading disclosures or disclosures that circumvent the purposes of this subchapter.

§ 1632 [CCPA § 122]. Form of Disclosure; Additional Information

(a) Information clearly and conspicuously disclosed; "annual percentage rate" and "finance charge"; order of disclosures and use of different terminology

Information required by this subchapter shall be disclosed clearly and conspicuously, in accordance with regulations of the Bureau. The terms "annual percentage rate" and "finance charge" shall be disclosed more conspicuously than other terms, data, or information provided in connection with a transaction, except information relating to the identity of the creditor. Except as provided in subsection (c), regulations of the Bureau need not require that disclosures pursuant to this subchapter be made in the order set forth in this subchapter and, except as otherwise provided, may permit the use of terminology different from that employed in this subchapter if it conveys substantially the same meaning.

(b) Optional information by creditor or lessor

Any creditor or lessor may supply additional information or explanation with any disclosures required under parts D and E and, except as provided in sections 1637a(b)(3) and 1638(b)(1) of this title, under this part.

(c) Tabular format required for certain disclosures under section 1637(c)

(1) In general

The information described in paragraphs (1)(A), (3)(B)(i)(I), (4)(A), and (4)(C)(i)(I) of section 1637(c) of this title shall be—

(A) disclosed in the form and manner which the Bureau shall prescribe by regulations; and

(B) placed in a conspicuous and prominent location on or with any written application, solicitation, or other document or paper with respect to which such disclosure is required.

(2) Tabular format

(A) Form of table to be prescribed

In the regulations prescribed under paragraph (1)(A) of this subsection, the Bureau shall require that the disclosure of such information shall, to the extent the Bureau determines to be practicable and appropriate, be in the form of a table which—

(i) contains clear and concise headings for each item of such information; and

(ii) provides a clear and concise form for stating each item of information required to be disclosed under each such heading.

(B) Bureau discretion in prescribing order and wording of table

In prescribing the form of the table under subparagraph (A), the Bureau may—

(i) list the items required to be included in the table in a different order than the order in which such items are set forth in paragraph (1)(A) or (4)(A) of section 1637(c) of this title; and

(ii) subject to subparagraph (C), employ terminology which is different than the terminology which is employed in section 1637(c) of this title if such terminology conveys substantially the same meaning.

(C) Grace period

Either the heading or the statement under the heading which relates to the time period referred to in section 1637(c)(1)(A)(iii) of this title shall contain the term "grace period".

(d) Additional Electronic Disclosures.

(1) Posting agreements.

Each creditor shall establish and maintain an Internet site on which the creditor shall post the written agreement between the creditor and the consumer for each credit card account under an open-end consumer credit plan.

(2) Creditor to provide contracts to the Bureau.

Each creditor shall provide to the Bureau, in electronic format, the consumer credit card agreements that it publishes on its Internet site.

(3) Record repository.

The Bureau shall establish and maintain on its publicly available Internet site a central repository of the consumer credit card agreements received from creditors pursuant to this subsection, and such agreements shall be easily accessible and retrievable by the public.

(4) Exception.

This subsection shall not apply to individually negotiated changes to contractual terms, such as individually modified workouts or renegotiations of amounts owed by a consumer under an open end consumer credit plan.

(5) Regulations.

The Bureau, in consultation with the other Federal banking agencies (as that term is defined in section 1681a of this title) and the Bureau,[1] may promulgate regulations to implement this subsection, including specifying the format for posting the agreements on the Internet sites of creditors and establishing exceptions to paragraphs (1) and (2), in any case in which the administrative burden outweighs the benefit of increased transparency, such as where a credit card plan has a de minimis number of consumer account holders.

§ 1633 [CCPA § 123]. Exemption for State-Regulated Transactions

The Bureau shall by regulation exempt from the requirements of this part any class of credit transactions within any State if it determines that under the law of that State that class of transactions is subject to requirements substantially similar to those imposed under this part, and that there is adequate provision for enforcement.

§ 1634 [CCPA § 124]. Effect of Subsequent Occurrence

If information disclosed in accordance with this part is subsequently rendered inaccurate as the result of any act, occurrence, or agreement subsequent to the delivery of the required disclosures, the inaccuracy resulting therefrom does not constitute a violation of this part.

§ 1635 [CCPA § 125]. Right of Rescission as to Certain Transactions

(a) Disclosure of obligor's right to rescind

Except as otherwise provided in this section, in the case of any consumer credit transaction (including opening or increasing the credit limit for an open end credit plan) in which a security interest, including any such interest arising by operation of law, is or will be retained or acquired in any property which is used as the principal dwelling of the person to whom credit is extended, the obligor shall have the right to rescind the transaction until midnight of the third business day following the consummation of the transaction or the delivery of the information and rescission forms

[1] So in original.

required under this section together with a statement containing the material disclosures required under this subchapter, whichever is later, by notifying the creditor, in accordance with regulations of the Bureau, of his intention to do so. The creditor shall clearly and conspicuously disclose, in accordance with regulations of the Bureau, to any obligor in a transaction subject to this section the rights of the obligor under this section. The creditor shall also provide, in accordance with regulations of the Bureau, appropriate forms for the obligor to exercise his right to rescind any transaction subject to this section.

(b) Return of money or property following rescission

When an obligor exercises his right to rescind under subsection (a), he is not liable for any finance or other charge, and any security interest given by the obligor, including any such interest arising by operation of law, becomes void upon such a rescission. Within 20 days after receipt of a notice of rescission, the creditor shall return to the obligor any money or property given as earnest money, downpayment, or otherwise, and shall take any action necessary or appropriate to reflect the termination of any security interest created under the transaction. If the creditor has delivered any property to the obligor, the obligor may retain possession of it. Upon the performance of the creditor's obligations under this section, the obligor shall tender the property to the creditor, except that if return of the property in kind would be impracticable or inequitable, the obligor shall tender its reasonable value. Tender shall be made at the location of the property or at the residence of the obligor, at the option of the obligor. If the creditor does not take possession of the property within 20 days after tender by the obligor, ownership of the property vests in the obligor without obligation on his part to pay for it. The procedures prescribed by this subsection shall apply except when otherwise ordered by a court.

(c) Rebuttable presumption of delivery of required disclosures

Notwithstanding any rule of evidence, written acknowledgment of receipt of any disclosures required under this subchapter by a person to whom information, forms, and a statement is required to be given pursuant to this section does no more than create a rebuttable presumption of delivery thereof.

(d) Modification and waiver of rights

The Bureau may, if it finds that such action is necessary in order to permit homeowners to meet bona fide personal financial emergencies, prescribe regulations authorizing the modification or waiver of any rights created under this section to the extent and under the circumstances set forth in those regulations.

(e) Exempted transactions; reapplication of provisions

This section does not apply to—

(1) a residential mortgage transaction as defined in section 1602(w) of this title;

(2) a transaction which constitutes a refinancing or consolidation (with no new advances) of the principal balance then due and any accrued and unpaid finance charges of an existing extension of credit by the same creditor secured by an interest in the same property;

(3) a transaction in which an agency of a State is the creditor; or

(4) advances under a preexisting open end credit plan if a security interest has already been retained or acquired and such advances are in accordance with a previously established credit limit for such plan.

(f) Time limit for exercise of right

An obligor's right of rescission shall expire three years after the date of consummation of the transaction or upon the sale of the property, whichever occurs first, notwithstanding the fact that the information and forms required under this section or any other disclosures required under this part have not been delivered to the obligor, except that if (1) any agency empowered to enforce the provisions of this subchapter institutes a proceeding to enforce the provisions of this section within three years after the date of consummation of the transaction, (2) such agency finds a violation of this section, and (3) the obligor's right to rescind is based in whole or in part on any matter involved in such proceeding, then the obligor's right of rescission shall expire three years after the date of consummation of the transaction or upon the earlier sale of the property, or upon the expiration of one year following the conclusion of the proceeding, or any judicial review or period for judicial review thereof, whichever is later.

(g) Additional relief

In any action in which it is determined that a creditor has violated this section, in addition to rescission the court may award relief under section 1640 of this title for violations of this subchapter not relating to the right to rescind.

(h) Limitation on rescission

An obligor shall have no rescission rights arising solely from the form of written notice used by the creditor to inform the obligor of the rights of the obligor under this section, if the creditor provided the obligor the appropriate form of written notice published and adopted by the Bureau, or a comparable written notice of the rights of the obligor, that was properly completed by the creditor, and otherwise complied with all other requirements of this section regarding notice.

(i) Rescission rights in foreclosure

(1) In general

Notwithstanding section 1649 of this title, and subject to the time period provided in subsection (f), in addition to any other right of rescission available under this section for a transaction, after the initiation of any judicial or nonjudicial foreclosure process on the primary dwelling of an obligor securing an extension of credit, the obligor shall have a right to rescind the transaction equivalent to other rescission rights provided by this section, if—

(A) a mortgage broker fee is not included in the finance charge in accordance with the laws and regulations in effect at the time the consumer credit transaction was consummated; or

(B) the form of notice of rescission for the transaction is not the appropriate form of written notice published and adopted by the Bureau or a comparable written notice, and otherwise complied with all the requirements of this section regarding notice.

(2) Tolerance for disclosures

Notwithstanding section 1605(f) of this title, and subject to the time period provided in subsection (f), for the purposes of exercising any rescission rights after the initiation of any judicial or nonjudicial foreclosure process on the principal dwelling of the obligor securing an extension of credit, the disclosure of the finance charge and other disclosures affected by any finance charge shall be treated as being accurate for purposes of this section if the amount disclosed as the finance charge does not vary from the actual finance charge by more than $35 or is greater than the amount required to be disclosed under this subchapter.

(3) Right of recoupment under State law

Nothing in this subsection affects a consumer's right of rescission in recoupment under State law.

(4) Applicability

This subsection shall apply to all consumer credit transactions in existence or consummated on or after September 30, 1995.

§ 1636. Repealed. Pub.L. 96–221, Title VI, § 614(e)(1), Mar. 31, 1980, 94 Stat. 80

§ 1637 [CCPA § 127]. Open End Consumer Credit Plans

(a) Required disclosures by creditor

Before opening any account under an open end consumer credit plan, the creditor shall disclose to the person to whom credit is to be extended each of the following items, to the extent applicable:

(1) The conditions under which a finance charge may be imposed, including the time period (if any) within which any credit extended may be repaid without incurring a finance charge, except that the creditor may, at his election and without disclosure, impose no such finance charge if payment is received after the termination of such time period. If no such time period is provided, the creditor shall disclose such fact.

(2) The method of determining the balance upon which a finance charge will be imposed.

(3) The method of determining the amount of the finance charge, including any minimum or fixed amount imposed as a finance charge.

(4) Where one or more periodic rates may be used to compute the finance charge, each such rate, the range of balances to which it is applicable, and the corresponding nominal annual percentage rate determined by multiplying the periodic rate by the number of periods in a year.

(5) Identification of other charges which may be imposed as part of the plan, and their method of computation, in accordance with regulations of the Bureau.

(6) In cases where the credit is or will be secured, a statement that a security interest has been or will be taken in (A) the property purchased as part of the credit transaction, or (B) property not purchased as part of the credit transaction identified by item or type.

(7) A statement, in a form prescribed by regulations of the Bureau of the protection provided by sections 1666 and 1666i of this title to an obligor and the creditor's responsibilities under sections 1666a and 1666i of this title. With respect to one billing cycle per calendar year, at intervals of not less than six months or more than eighteen months, the creditor shall transmit such statement to each obligor to whom the creditor is required to transmit a statement pursuant to subsection (b) for such billing cycle.

(8) In the case of any account under an open end consumer credit plan which provides for any extension of credit which is secured by the consumer's principal dwelling, any information which—

(A) is required to be disclosed under section 1637a(a) of this title; and

(B) the Bureau determines is not described in any other paragraph of this subsection.

(b) Statement required with each billing cycle

The creditor of any account under an open end consumer credit plan shall transmit to the obligor, for each billing cycle at the end of which there is an outstanding balance in that account or with respect to which a finance charge is imposed, a statement setting forth each of the following items to the extent applicable:

(1) The outstanding balance in the account at the beginning of the statement period.

(2) The amount and date of each extension of credit during the period, and a brief identification, on or accompanying the statement of each extension of credit in a form prescribed by the Bureau sufficient to enable the obligor either to identify the transaction or to relate it to copies of sales vouchers or similar instruments previously furnished, except that a creditor's failure to disclose such information in accordance with this paragraph shall not be deemed a failure to comply with this part or this subchapter if (A) the creditor maintains procedures reasonably adapted to procure and provide such information, and (B) the creditor responds to and treats any inquiry for clarification or documentation as a billing error and an erroneously billed amount under section 1666 of this title. In lieu of complying with the requirements of the previous sentence, in the case of any transaction in which the creditor and seller are the same person, as defined by the Bureau, and such person's open end credit plan has fewer than 15,000 accounts, the creditor may elect to provide only the amount and date of each extension of credit during the period and the seller's name and location where the transaction took place if (A) a brief identification of the transaction has been previously furnished, and (B) the creditor responds to and treats any inquiry for clarification or documentation as a billing error and an erroneously billed amount under section 1666 of this title.

(3) The total amount credited to the account during the period.

(4) The amount of any finance charge added to the account during the period, itemized to show the amounts, if any, due to the application of percentage rates and the amount, if any, imposed as a minimum or fixed charge.

(5) Where one or more periodic rates may be used to compute the finance charge, each such rate, the range of balances to which it is applicable, and, unless the annual percentage rate (determined under section 1606(a)(2) of this title) is required to be disclosed pursuant to paragraph (6), the corresponding nominal annual percentage rate determined by multiplying the periodic rate by the number of periods in a year.

(6) Where the total finance charge exceeds 50 cents for a monthly or longer billing cycle, or the pro rata part of 50 cents for a billing cycle shorter than monthly, the total finance charge expressed as an annual percentage rate (determined under section 1606(a)(2) of this title), except that if the finance charge is the sum of two or more products of a rate times a portion of the balance, the creditor may, in lieu of disclosing a single rate for the total charge, disclose each such rate expressed as an annual percentage rate, and the part of the balance to which it is applicable.

(7) The balance on which the finance charge was computed and a statement of how the balance was determined. If the balance is determined without first deducting all credits during the period, that fact and the amount of such payments shall also be disclosed.

(8) The outstanding balance in the account at the end of the period.

(9) The date by which or the period (if any) within which, payment must be made to avoid additional finance charges, except that the creditor may, at his election and without disclosure, impose no such additional finance charge if payment is received after such date or the termination of such period.

(10) The address to be used by the creditor for the purpose of receiving billing inquiries from the obligor.

(11)(A) A written statement in the following form: "Minimum Payment Warning: Making only the minimum payment will increase the amount of interest you pay and the time it takes to repay your balance.", or such similar statement as is established by the Bureau pursuant to consumer testing.

(B) Repayment information that would apply to the outstanding balance of the consumer under the credit plan, including—

(i) the number of months (rounded to the nearest month) that it would take to pay the entire amount of that balance, if the consumer pays only the required minimum monthly payments and if no further advances are made;

(ii) the total cost to the consumer, including interest and principal payments, of paying that balance in full, if the consumer pays only the required minimum monthly payments and if no further advances are made;

(iii) the monthly payment amount that would be required for the consumer to eliminate the outstanding balance in 36 months, if no further advances are made, and the total cost to the consumer, including interest and principal payments, of paying that balance in full if the consumer pays the balance over 36 months; and

(iv) a toll-free telephone number at which the consumer may receive information about accessing credit counseling and debt management services.

(C)(i) Subject to clause (ii), in making the disclosures under subparagraph (B), the creditor shall apply the interest rate or rates in effect on the date on which the disclosure is made until the date on which the balance would be paid in full.

(ii) If the interest rate in effect on the date on which the disclosure is made is a temporary rate that will change under a contractual provision applying an index or formula for subsequent interest rate adjustment, the creditor shall apply the interest rate in effect on the date on which the disclosure is made for as long as that interest rate will apply under that contractual provision, and then apply an interest rate based on the index or formula in effect on the applicable billing date.

(D) All of the information described in subparagraph (B) shall—

(i) be disclosed in the form and manner which the Bureau shall prescribe, by regulation, and in a manner that avoids duplication; and

(ii) be placed in a conspicuous and prominent location on the billing **statement.**

(E) In the regulations prescribed under subparagraph (D), the Bureau shall require that the disclosure of such information shall be in the form of a table that—

(i) contains clear and concise headings for each item of such information; and

(ii) provides a clear and concise form stating each item of information required to be disclosed under each such heading.

(F) In prescribing the form of the table under subparagraph (E) the Bureau shall require that—

(i) all of the information in the table, and not just a reference to the table, be placed on the billing statement, as required by this paragraph; and

(ii) the items required to be included in the table shall be listed in the order in which such items are set forth in subparagraph (B).

(G) In prescribing the form of the table under subparagraph (D), the Bureau shall employ terminology which is different than the terminology which is employed in subparagraph (B), if such terminology is more easily understood and conveys substantially the same meaning.

(12) Requirements relating to late payment deadlines and penalties.

(A) Late payment deadline required to be disclosed.

In the case of a credit card account under an open end consumer credit plan under which a late fee or charge may be imposed due to the failure of the obligor to make payment on or before the due date for such payment, the periodic statement required under subsection (b) with respect to the account shall include, in a conspicuous location on the billing statement, the date on which the payment is due or, if different, the date on which a late payment fee will be charged, together with the amount of the fee or charge to be imposed if payment is made after that date.

(B) Disclosure of increase in interest rates for late payments.

If 1 or more late payments under an open end consumer credit plan may result in an increase in the annual percentage rate applicable to the account, the statement required under subsection (b) with respect to the account shall include conspicuous notice of such fact, together with the applicable penalty annual percentage rate, in close proximity to the disclosure required under subparagraph (A) of the date on which payment is due under the terms of the account.

(C) Payments at local branches.

If the creditor, in the case of a credit card account referred to in subparagraph (A), is a financial institution which maintains branches or offices at which payments on any such account are accepted from the obligor in person, the date on which the obligor makes a payment on the account at such branch or office shall be considered to be the date on which the payment is made for purposes of determining whether a late fee or charge may be imposed due to the failure of the obligor to make payment on or before the due date for such payment.

(c) Disclosure in credit and charge card applications and solicitations

(1) Direct mail applications and solicitations

(A) Information in tabular format

Any application to open a credit card account for any person under an open end consumer credit plan, or a solicitation to open such an account without requiring an application, that is mailed to consumers shall disclose the following information, subject to subsection (e) and section 1632(c) of this title:

(i) Annual percentage rates

(I) Each annual percentage rate applicable to extensions of credit under such credit plan.

(II) Where an extension of credit is subject to a variable rate, the fact that the rate is variable, the annual percentage rate in effect at the time of the mailing, and how the rate is determined.

(III) Where more than one rate applies, the range of balances to which each rate applies.

(ii) Annual and other fees

(I) Any annual fee, other periodic fee, or membership fee imposed for the issuance or availability of a credit card, including any account maintenance fee or other charge imposed based on activity or inactivity for the account during the billing cycle.

(II) Any minimum finance charge imposed for each period during which any extension of credit which is subject to a finance charge is outstanding.

(III) Any transaction charge imposed in connection with use of the card to purchase goods or services.

(iii) Grace period

(I) The date by which or the period within which any credit extended under such credit plan for purchases of goods or services must be repaid to avoid incurring a finance charge, and, if no such period is offered, such fact shall be clearly stated.

(II) If the length of such "grace period" varies, the card issuer may disclose the range of days in the grace period, the minimum number of days in the grace period, or the average number of days in the grace period, if the disclosure is identified as such.

(iv) Balance calculation method

(I) The name of the balance calculation method used in determining the balance on which the finance charge is computed if the method used has been defined by the Bureau, or a detailed explanation of the balance calculation method used if the method has not been so defined.

(II) In prescribing regulations to carry out this clause, the Bureau shall define and name not more than the 5 balance calculation methods determined by the Bureau to be the most commonly used methods.

(B) Other information

In addition to the information required to be disclosed under subparagraph (A), each application or solicitation to which such subparagraph applies shall disclose clearly and conspicuously the following information, subject to subsections (e) and (f):

(i) Cash advance fee

Any fee imposed for an extension of credit in the form of cash.

(ii) Late fee

Any fee imposed for a late payment.

(iii) Over-the-limit fee

Any fee imposed in connection with an extension of credit in excess of the amount of credit authorized to be extended with respect to such account.

(2) Telephone solicitations

(A) In general

In any telephone solicitation to open a credit card account for any person under an open end consumer credit plan, the person making the solicitation shall orally disclose the information described in paragraph (1)(A).

(B) Exception

Subparagraph (A) shall not apply to any telephone solicitation if—

(i) the credit card issuer—

(I) does not impose any fee described in paragraph (1)(A)(ii)(I); or

(II) does not impose any fee in connection with telephone solicitations unless the consumer signifies acceptance by using the card;

(ii) the card issuer discloses clearly and conspicuously in writing the information described in paragraph (1) within 30 days after the consumer requests the card, but in no event later than the date of delivery of the card; and

(iii) the card issuer discloses clearly and conspicuously that the consumer is not obligated to accept the card or account and the consumer will not be obligated to pay any of the fees or charges disclosed unless the consumer elects to accept the card or account by using the card.

(3) Applications and solicitations by other means

(A) In general

Any application to open a credit card account for any person under an open end consumer credit plan, and any solicitation to open such an account without requiring an application, that is made available to the public or contained in catalogs, magazines, or other publications shall meet the disclosure requirements of subparagraph (B), (C), or (D).

(B) Specific information

An application or solicitation described in subparagraph (A) meets the requirement of this subparagraph if such application or solicitation contains—

(i) the information—

(I) described in paragraph (1)(A) in the form required under section 1632(c) of this title, subject to subsection (e), and

(II) described in paragraph (1)(B) in a clear and conspicuous form, subject to subsections (e) and (f);

(ii) a statement, in a conspicuous and prominent location on the application or solicitation, that—

(I) the information is accurate as of the date the application or solicitation was printed;

(II) the information contained in the application or solicitation is subject to change after such date; and

(III) the applicant should contact the creditor for information on any change in the information contained in the application or solicitation since it was printed;

(iii) a clear and conspicuous disclosure of the date the application or solicitation was printed; and

(iv) a disclosure, in a conspicuous and prominent location on the application or solicitation, of a toll free telephone number or a mailing address at which the applicant may contact the creditor to obtain any change in the information provided in the application or solicitation since it was printed.

(C) General information without any specific term

An application or solicitation described in subparagraph (A) meets the requirement of this subparagraph if such application or solicitation—

(i) contains a statement, in a conspicuous and prominent location on the application or solicitation, that—

(I) there are costs associated with the use of credit cards; and

(II) the applicant may contact the creditor to request disclosure of specific information of such costs by calling a toll free telephone number or by writing to an address, specified in the application;

(ii) contains a disclosure, in a conspicuous and prominent location on the application or solicitation, of a toll free telephone number and a mailing address at which the applicant may contact the creditor to obtain such information; and

(iii) does not contain any of the items described in paragraph (1).

(D) Applications or solicitations containing subsection (a) disclosures

An application or solicitation meets the requirement of this subparagraph if it contains, or is accompanied by—

(i) the disclosures required by paragraphs (1) through (6) of subsection (a);

(ii) the disclosures required by subparagraphs (A) and (B) of paragraph (1) of this subsection included clearly and conspicuously[1] (except that the provisions of section 1632(c) of this title shall not apply); and

---

1 So in original.

(iii) a toll free telephone number or a mailing address at which the applicant may contact the creditor to obtain any change in the information provided.

(E) Prompt response to information requests

Upon receipt of a request for any of the information referred to in subparagraph (B), (C), or (D), the card issuer or the agent of such issuer shall promptly disclose all of the information described in paragraph (1).

(4) Charge card applications and solicitations

(A) In general

Any application or solicitation to open a charge card account shall disclose clearly and conspicuously the following information in the form required by section 1632(c) of this title, subject to subsection (e) of this section:

(i) Any annual fee, other periodic fee, or membership fee imposed for the issuance or availability of the charge card, including any account maintenance fee or other charge imposed based on activity or inactivity for the account during the billing cycle.

(ii) Any transaction charge imposed in connection with use of the card to purchase goods or services.

(iii) A statement that charges incurred by use of the charge card are due and payable upon receipt of a periodic statement rendered for such charge card account.

(B) Other information

In addition to the information required to be disclosed under subparagraph (A), each written application or solicitation to which such subparagraph applies shall disclose clearly and conspicuously the following information, subject to subsections (e) and (f):

(i) Cash advance fee

Any fee imposed for an extension of credit in the form of cash.

(ii) Late fee

Any fee imposed for a late payment.

(iii) Over-the-limit fee

Any fee imposed in connection with an extension of credit in excess of the amount of credit authorized to be extended with respect to such account.

(C) Applications and solicitations by other means

Any application to open a charge card account, and any solicitation to open such an account without requiring an application, that is made available to the public or contained in catalogs, magazines, or other publications shall contain—

(i) the information—

(I) described in subparagraph (A) in the form required under section 1632(c) of this title, subject to subsection (e) of this section, and

(II) described in subparagraph (B) in a clear and conspicuous form, subject to subsections (e) and (f);

(ii) a statement, in a conspicuous and prominent location on the application or solicitation, that—

(I) the information is accurate as of the date the application or solicitation was printed;

(II) the information contained in the application or solicitation is subject to change after such date; and

(III) the applicant should contact the creditor for information on any change in the information contained in the application or solicitation since it was printed;

(iii) a clear and conspicuous disclosure of the date the application or solicitation was printed; and

(iv) a disclosure, in a conspicuous and prominent location on the application or solicitation, of a toll free telephone number or a mailing address at which the applicant may contact the creditor to obtain any change in the information provided in the application or solicitation since it was printed.

(D) Issuers of charge cards which provide access to open end consumer credit plans

If a charge card permits the card holder to receive an extension of credit under an open end consumer credit plan, which is not maintained by the charge card issuer, the charge card issuer may provide the information described in subparagraphs (A) and (B) in the form required by such subparagraphs in lieu of the information required to be provided under paragraph (1), (2), or (3) with respect to any credit extended under such plan, if the charge card issuer discloses clearly and conspicuously to the consumer in the application or solicitation that—

(i) the charge card issuer will make an independent decision as to whether to issue the card;

(ii) the charge card may arrive before the decision is made with respect to an extension of credit under an open end consumer credit plan; and

(iii) approval by the charge card issuer does not constitute approval by the issuer of the extension of credit.

The information required to be disclosed under paragraph (1) shall be provided to the charge card holder by the creditor which maintains such open end consumer credit plan before the first extension of credit under such plan.

(E) Charge card defined

For the purposes of this subsection, the term "charge card" means a card, plate, or other single credit device that may be used from time to time to obtain credit which is not subject to a finance charge.

(5) Regulatory authority of the Bureau

The Bureau may, by regulation, require the disclosure of information in addition to that otherwise required by this subsection or subsection (d) of this section, and modify any disclosure of information required by this subsection or subsection (d) of this section, in any application to open a credit card account for any person under an open end consumer credit plan or any application to open a charge card account for any person, or a solicitation to open any such account without requiring an application, if the Bureau determines that such action is necessary to carry out the purposes of, or prevent evasions of, any paragraph of this subsection.

(6) Additional notice concerning "introductory rates"—

(A) In general

Except as provided in subparagraph (B), an application or solicitation to open a credit card account and all promotional materials accompanying such application or solicitation for which a disclosure is required under paragraph (1), and that offers a temporary annual percentage rate of interest, shall—

(i) use the term "introductory" in immediate proximity to each listing of the temporary annual percentage rate applicable to such account, which term shall appear clearly and conspicuously;

(ii) if the annual percentage rate of interest that will apply after the end of the temporary rate period will be a fixed rate, state in a clear and conspicuous manner in a prominent location closely proximate to the first listing of the temporary annual percentage rate (other than a listing of the temporary annual percentage rate in the tabular format described in section 1632(c) of this title), the time period in which the introductory period will end and the annual percentage rate that will apply after the end of the introductory period; and

(iii) if the annual percentage rate that will apply after the end of the temporary rate period will vary in accordance with an index, state in a clear and conspicuous manner in a prominent location closely proximate to the first listing of the temporary annual percentage rate (other than a listing in the tabular format prescribed by section 1632(c) of this title), the time period in which the introductory period will end and the rate that will apply after that, based on an annual percentage rate that was in effect within 60 days before the date of mailing the application or solicitation.

(B) Exception

Clauses (ii) and (iii) of subparagraph (A) do not apply with respect to any listing of a temporary annual percentage rate on an envelope or other enclosure in which an application or solicitation to open a credit card account is mailed.

(C) Conditions for introductory rates

An application or solicitation to open a credit card account for which a disclosure is required under paragraph (1), and that offers a temporary annual percentage rate of interest shall, if that rate of interest is revocable under any circumstance or upon any event, clearly and conspicuously disclose, in a prominent manner on or with such application or solicitation—

(i) a general description of the circumstances that may result in the revocation of the temporary annual percentage rate; and

(ii) if the annual percentage rate that will apply upon the revocation of the temporary annual percentage rate—

(I) will be a fixed rate, the annual percentage rate that will apply upon the revocation of the temporary annual percentage rate; or

(II) will vary in accordance with an index, the rate that will apply after the temporary rate, based on an annual percentage rate that was in effect within 60 days before the date of mailing the application or solicitation.

(D) Definitions

In this paragraph—

(i) the terms "temporary annual percentage rate of interest" and "temporary annual percentage rate" mean any rate of interest applicable to a credit card account for an introductory period of less than 1 year, if that rate is less than an annual percentage rate that was in effect within 60 days before the date of mailing the application or solicitation; and

(ii) the term "introductory period" means the maximum time period for which the temporary annual percentage rate may be applicable.

(E) Relation to other disclosure requirements

Nothing in this paragraph may be construed to supersede subsection (a) of section 1632 of this title, or any disclosure required by paragraph (1) or any other provision of this subsection.

(7) Internet-based solicitations

(A) In general

In any solicitation to open a credit card account for any person under an open end consumer credit plan using the Internet or other interactive computer service, the person making the solicitation shall clearly and conspicuously disclose—

(i) the information described in subparagraphs (A) and (B) of paragraph (1); and

(ii) the information described in paragraph (6).

(B) Form of disclosure

The disclosures required by subparagraph (A) shall be—

(i) readily accessible to consumers in close proximity to the solicitation to open a credit card account; and

(ii) updated regularly to reflect the current policies, terms, and fee amounts applicable to the credit card account.

(C) Definitions

For purposes of this paragraph—

(i) the term "Internet" means the international computer network of both Federal and non-Federal interoperable packet switched data networks; and

(ii) the term "interactive computer service" means any information service, system, or access software provider that provides or enables computer access by multiple users to a computer server, including specifically a service or system that provides access to the Internet and such systems operated or services offered by libraries or educational institutions.

(8) Applications from underage consumers.

(A) Prohibition on issuance.

No credit card may be issued to, or open end consumer credit plan established by or on behalf of, a consumer who has not attained the age of 21, unless the consumer has submitted a written application to the card issuer that meets the requirements of subparagraph (B).

(B) Application requirements.

An application to open a credit card account by a consumer who has not attained the age of 21 as of the date of submission of the application shall require—

(i) the signature of a cosigner, including the parent, legal guardian, spouse, or any other individual who has attained the age of 21 having a means to repay debts incurred by the consumer in connection with the account, indicating joint liability for debts incurred by the consumer in connection with the account before the consumer has attained the age of 21; or

(ii) submission by the consumer of financial information, including through an application, indicating an independent means of repaying any obligation arising from the proposed extension of credit in connection with the account.

(C) Safe harbor.

The Bureau shall promulgate regulations providing standards that, if met, would satisfy the requirements of subparagraph (B)(ii).

(d) Disclosure prior to renewal

(1) In general

A card issuer that has changed or amended any term of the account since the last renewal that has not been previously disclosed or that imposes any fee described in subsection (c)(1)(A)(ii)(I) or (c)(4)(A)(i) shall transmit to a consumer at least 30 days prior to the scheduled renewal date of the consumer's credit or charge card account a clear and conspicuous disclosure of—

(A) the date by which, the month by which, or the billing period at the close of which, the account will expire if not renewed;

(B) the information described in subsection (c)(1)(A) or (c)(4)(A) that would apply if the account were renewed, subject to subsection (e) of this section; and

(C) the method by which the consumer may terminate continued credit availability under the account.

(2) Short-term renewals

The Bureau may by regulation provide for fewer disclosures than are required by paragraph (1) in the case of an account which is renewable for a period of less than 6 months.

(3) Redesignated (2)

(e) Other rules for disclosures under subsections (c) and (d)

(1) Fees determined on the basis of a percentage

If the amount of any fee required to be disclosed under subsection (c) or (d) is determined on the basis of a percentage of another amount, the percentage used in making such determination and the identification of the amount against which such percentage is applied shall be disclosed in lieu of the amount of such fee.

(2) Disclosure only of fees actually imposed

If a credit or charge card issuer does not impose any fee required to be disclosed under any provision of subsection (c) or (d), such provision shall not apply with respect to such issuer.

(f) Disclosure of range of certain fees which vary by State allowed

If the amount of any fee required to be disclosed by a credit or charge card issuer under paragraph (1)(B), (3)(B)(i)(II), (4)(B), or (4)(C)(i)(II) of subsection (c) varies from State to State, the card issuer may disclose the range of such fees for purposes of subsection (c) in lieu of the amount for each applicable State, if such disclosure includes a statement that the amount of such fee varies from State to State.

(g) Insurance in connection with certain open end credit card plans

(1) Change in insurance carrier

Whenever a card issuer that offers any guarantee or insurance for repayment of all or part of the outstanding balance of an open end credit card plan proposes to change the person providing that guarantee or insurance, the card issuer shall send each insured consumer written notice of the proposed change not less than 30 days prior to the change, including notice of any increase in the rate or substantial decrease in coverage or service which will result from such change. Such notice may be included on or with the monthly statement provided to the consumer prior to the month in which the proposed change would take effect.

(2) Notice of new insurance coverage

In any case in which a proposed change described in paragraph (1) occurs, the insured consumer shall be given the name and address of the new guarantor or insurer and a copy of the policy or group certificate containing the basic terms and conditions, including the premium rate to be charged.

(3) Right to discontinue guarantee or insurance

The notices required under paragraphs (1) and (2) shall each include a statement that the consumer has the option to discontinue the insurance or guarantee.

(4) No preemption of State law

No provision of this subsection shall be construed as superseding any provision of State law which is applicable to the regulation of insurance.

(5) Bureau definition of substantial decrease in coverage or service

The Bureau shall define, in regulations, what constitutes a "substantial decrease in coverage or service" for purposes of paragraph (1).

(h) Prohibition on certain actions for failure to incur finance charges

A creditor of an account under an open end consumer credit plan may not terminate an account prior to its expiration date solely because the consumer has not incurred finance charges on the account. Nothing in this subsection shall prohibit a creditor from terminating an account for inactivity in 3 or more consecutive months.

(i) Advance Notice of Rate Increase and Other Changes Required

(1) Advance notice of increase in interest rate required

In the case of any credit card account under an open end consumer credit plan, a creditor shall provide a written notice of an increase in an annual percentage rate (except in the case of an increase described in paragraph (1), (2), or (3) of section 1666i–1(b) of this title) not later than 45 days prior to the effective date of the increase.

(2) Advance notice of other significant changes required

In the case of any credit card account under an open end consumer credit plan, a creditor shall provide a written notice of any significant change, as determined by rule of the Bureau, in the terms (including an increase in any fee or finance charge, other than as provided in paragraph (1)) of the cardholder agreement between the creditor and the obligor, not later than 45 days prior to the effective date of the change.

(3) Notice of right to cancel

Each notice required by paragraph (1) or (2) shall be made in a clear and conspicuous manner, and shall contain a brief statement of the right of the obligor to cancel the account pursuant to rules established by the Bureau before the effective date of the subject rate increase or other change.

(4) Rule of construction

Closure or cancellation of an account by the obligor shall not constitute a default under an existing cardholder agreement, and shall not trigger an obligation to immediately repay the obligation in full or through a method that is less beneficial to the obligor than one of the methods described in section 1666i–1(c)(2) of this title, or the imposition of any other penalty or fee.

(j) Prohibition on Penalties for On-Time Payments

(1) Prohibition on double-cycle billing and penalties for on-time payments.

Except as provided in paragraph (2), a creditor may not impose any finance charge on a credit card account under an open end consumer credit plan as a result of the loss of any time period provided by the creditor within which the obligor may repay any portion of the credit extended without incurring a finance charge, with respect to—

(A) any balances for days in billing cycles that precede the most recent billing cycle; or

(B) any balances or portions thereof in the current billing cycle that were repaid within such time period.

(2) Exceptions

Paragraph (1) does not apply to—

(A) any adjustment to a finance charge as a result of the resolution of a dispute; or

(B) any adjustment to a finance charge as a result of the return of a payment for insufficient funds.

(k) Opt-in Required for Over-the-Limit Transactions if Fees Are Imposed

(1) In general

In the case of any credit card account under an open end consumer credit plan under which an over-the-limit fee may be imposed by the creditor for any extension of credit in excess of the amount of credit authorized to be extended under such account, no such fee shall be charged, unless the consumer has expressly elected to permit the creditor, with respect to such account, to complete transactions involving the extension of credit under such account in excess of the amount of credit authorized.

(2) Disclosure by creditor

No election by a consumer under paragraph (1) shall take effect unless the consumer, before making such election, received a notice from the creditor of any over-the-limit fee in the form and manner, and at the time, determined by the Bureau. If the consumer makes the election referred to in paragraph (1), the creditor shall provide notice to the consumer of the right to revoke the election, in the form prescribed by the Bureau, in any periodic statement that includes notice of the imposition of an over-the limit fee during the period covered by the statement.

(3) Form of election

A consumer may make or revoke the election referred to in paragraph (1) orally, electronically, or in writing, pursuant to regulations prescribed by the Bureau. The Bureau shall prescribe regulations to ensure that the same options are available for both making and revoking such election.

(4) Time of election

A consumer may make the election referred to in paragraph (1) at any time, and such election shall be effective until the election is revoked in the manner prescribed under paragraph (3).

(5) Regulations

The Bureau shall prescribe regulations—

(A) governing disclosures under this subsection; and

(B) that prevent unfair or deceptive acts or practices in connection with the manipulation of credit limits designed to increase over-the-limit fees or other penalty fees.

(6) Rule of construction

Nothing in this subsection shall be construed to prohibit a creditor from completing an over-the-limit transaction, provided that a consumer who has not made a valid election under paragraph (1) is not charged an over-the-limit fee for such transaction.

(7) Restriction on fees charged for an over-the-limit transaction

With respect to a credit card account under an open end consumer credit plan, an over-the-limit fee may be imposed only once during a billing cycle if the credit limit on the account is exceeded, and an over-the-limit fee, with respect to such excess credit, may be imposed only once in each of the 2 subsequent billing cycles, unless the consumer has obtained an additional extension of credit in excess of such credit limit during any such subsequent cycle or the consumer reduces the outstanding balance below the credit limit as of the end of such billing cycle.

(*l*) Limit on Fees Related to method of payment

With respect to a credit card account under an open end consumer credit plan, the creditor may not impose a separate fee to allow the obligor to repay an extension of credit or finance charge, whether such repayment is made by mail, electronic transfer, telephone authorization, or other means, unless such payment involves an expedited service by a service representative of the creditor.

(m) Use of Term "Fixed Rate"

With respect to the terms of any credit card account under an open end consumer credit plan, the term "fixed", when appearing in conjunction with a reference to the annual percentage rate or interest rate applicable with respect to such account, may only be used to refer to an annual percentage rate or interest rate that will not change or vary for any reason over the period specified clearly and conspicuously in the terms of the account.

(n) Standards applicable to initial issuance of subprime or "fee harvester" Cards

(1) In general

If the terms of a credit card account under an open end consumer credit plan require the payment of any fees (other than any late fee, over-the-limit fee, or fee for a payment returned for insufficient funds) by the consumer in the first year during which the account is opened in an aggregate amount in excess of 25 percent of the total amount of credit authorized under the account when the account is opened, no payment of any fees (other than any late fee, over-the-limit fee, or fee for a payment returned for insufficient funds) may be made from the credit made available under the terms of the account.

(2) Rule of construction

No provision of this subsection may be construed as authorizing any imposition or payment of advance fees otherwise prohibited by any provision of law.

(*o*) Due dates for credit card accounts

(1) In general

The payment due date for a credit card account under an open end consumer credit plan shall be the same day each month.

(2) Weekend or holiday due dates

If the payment due date for a credit card account under an open end consumer credit plan is a day on which the creditor does not receive or accept payments by mail (including weekends and holidays), the creditor may not treat a payment received on the next business day as late for any purpose.

(p) Parental approval required to increase credit lines for accounts for which parent is jointly liable

No increase may be made in the amount of credit authorized to be extended under a credit card account for which a parent, legal guardian, or spouse of the consumer, or any other individual has assumed joint liability for debts incurred by the consumer in connection with the account before the consumer attains the age of 21, unless that parent, guardian, or spouse approves in writing, and assumes joint liability for, such increase.

(r) College card agreements

(1) Definitions

For purposes of this subsection, the following definitions shall apply:

(A) College affinity card

The term 'college affinity card' means a credit card issued by a credit card issuer under an open end consumer credit plan in conjunction with an agreement between the issuer and an institution of higher education, or an alumni organization or foundation affiliated with or related to such institution, under which such cards are issued to college students who have an affinity with such institution, organization and—

(i) the creditor has agreed to donate a portion of the proceeds of the credit card to the institution, organization, or foundation (including a lump sum or 1-time payment of money for access);

(ii) the creditor has agreed to offer discounted terms to the consumer; or

(iii) the credit card bears the name, emblem, mascot, or logo of such institution, organization, or foundation, or other words, pictures, or symbols readily identified with such institution, organization, or foundation.

(B) College student credit card account

The term "college student credit card account" means a credit card account under an open end consumer credit plan established or maintained for or on behalf of any college student.

(C) College student

The term "college student" means an individual who is a full-time or a part-time student attending an institution of higher education.

(D) Institution of higher education

The term "institution of higher education" has the same meaning as in section[2] 101 and 102 of Title 20.

(2) Reports by creditors

(A) In general

Each creditor shall submit an annual report to the Bureau containing the terms and conditions of all business, marketing, and promotional agreements and college affinity card agreements with an institution of higher education, or an alumni organization or foundation affiliated with or related to such institution, with respect to any college student credit card issued to a college student at such institution.

(B) Details of report

The information required to be reported under subparagraph (A) includes—

(i) any memorandum of understanding between or among a creditor, an institution of higher education, an alumni association, or foundation that directly or indirectly relates to any aspect of any agreement referred to in such subparagraph or

[2] So in original. Probably should be "sections."

controls or directs any obligations or distribution of benefits between or among any such entities;

(ii) the amount of any payments from the creditor to the institution, organization, or foundation during the period covered by the report, and the precise terms of any agreement under which such amounts are determined; and

(iii) the number of credit card accounts covered by any such agreement that were opened during the period covered by the report, and the total number of credit card accounts covered by the agreement that were outstanding at the end of such period.

(C) Aggregation by institution

The information required to be reported under subparagraph (A) shall be aggregated with respect to each institution of higher education or alumni organization or foundation affiliated with or related to such institution.

(D) Initial report

The initial report required under subparagraph (A) shall be submitted to the Bureau before the end of the 9-month period beginning on May 22, 2009.

(3) Reports by Bureau

The Bureau shall submit to the Congress, and make available to the public, an annual report that lists the information concerning credit card agreements submitted to the Bureau under paragraph (2) by each institution of higher education, alumni organization, or foundation.

§ 1637a [CCPA § 127A]. Disclosure Requirements for Open End Consumer Credit Plans Secured by Consumer's Principal Dwelling

(a) Application disclosures

In the case of any open end consumer credit plan which provides for any extension of credit which is secured by the consumer's principal dwelling, the creditor shall make the following disclosures in accordance with subsection (b):

(1) Fixed annual percentage rate

Each annual percentage rate imposed in connection with extensions of credit under the plan and a statement that such rate does not include costs other than interest.

(2) Variable percentage rate

In the case of a plan which provides for variable rates of interest on credit extended under the plan—

(A) a description of the manner in which such rate will be computed and a statement that such rate does not include costs other than interest;

(B) a description of the manner in which any changes in the annual percentage rate will be made, including—

(i) any negative amortization and interest rate carryover;

(ii) the timing of any such changes;

(iii) any index or margin to which such changes in the rate are related; and

(iv) a source of information about any such index;

(C) if an initial annual percentage rate is offered which is not based on an index—

(i) a statement of such rate and the period of time such initial rate will be in effect; and

(ii) a statement that such rate does not include costs other than interest;

(D) a statement that the consumer should ask about the current index value and interest rate;

(E) a statement of the maximum amount by which the annual percentage rate may change in any 1-year period or a statement that no such limit exists;

(F) a statement of the maximum annual percentage rate that may be imposed at any time under the plan;

(G) subject to subsection (b)(3), a table, based on a $10,000 extension of credit, showing how the annual percentage rate and the minimum periodic payment amount under each repayment option of the plan would have been affected during the preceding 15-year period by changes in any index used to compute such rate;

(H) a statement of—

(i) the maximum annual percentage rate which may be imposed under each repayment option of the plan;

(ii) the minimum amount of any periodic payment which may be required, based on a $10,000 outstanding balance, under each such option when such maximum annual percentage rate is in effect; and

(iii) the earliest date by which such maximum annual interest rate may be imposed; and

(I) a statement that interest rate information will be provided on or with each periodic statement.

(3) Other fees imposed by the creditor

An itemization of any fees imposed by the creditor in connection with the availability or use of credit under such plan, including annual fees, application fees, transaction fees, and closing costs (including costs commonly described as "points"), and the time when such fees are payable.

(4) Estimates of fees which may be imposed by third parties

(A) Aggregate amount

An estimate, based on the creditor's experience with such plans and stated as a single amount or as a reasonable range, of the aggregate amount of additional fees that may be imposed by third parties (such as governmental authorities, appraisers, and attorneys) in connection with opening an account under the plan.

(B) Statement of availability

A statement that the consumer may ask the creditor for a good faith estimate by the creditor of the fees that may be imposed by third parties.

(5) Statement of risk of loss of dwelling

A statement that—

(A) any extension of credit under the plan is secured by the consumer's dwelling; and

(B) in the event of any default, the consumer risks the loss of the dwelling.

(6) Conditions to which disclosed terms are subject

(A) Period during which such terms are available

A clear and conspicuous statement—

(i) of the time by which an application must be submitted to obtain the terms disclosed; or

(ii) if applicable, that the terms are subject to change.

(B) Right of refusal if certain terms change

A statement that—

(i) the consumer may elect not to enter into an agreement to open an account under the plan if any term changes (other than a change contemplated by a variable feature of the plan) before any such agreement is final; and

(ii) if the consumer makes an election described in clause (i), the consumer is entitled to a refund of all fees paid in connection with the application.

(C) Retention of information

A statement that the consumer should make or otherwise retain a copy of information disclosed under this subparagraph.

(7) Rights of creditor with respect to extensions of credit

A statement that—

(A) under certain conditions, the creditor may terminate any account under the plan and require immediate repayment of any outstanding balance, prohibit any additional extension of credit to the account, or reduce the credit limit applicable to the account; and

(B) the consumer may receive, upon request, more specific information about the conditions under which the creditor may take any action described in subparagraph (A).

(8) Repayment options and minimum periodic payments

The repayment options under the plan, including—

(A) if applicable, any differences in repayment options with regard to—

(i) any period during which additional extensions of credit may be obtained; and

(ii) any period during which repayment is required to be made and no additional extensions of credit may be obtained;

(B) the length of any repayment period, including any differences in the length of any repayment period with regard to the periods described in clauses (i) and (ii) of subparagraph (A); and

(C) an explanation of how the amount of any minimum monthly or periodic payment will be determined under each such option, including any differences in the determination of any such amount with regard to the periods described in clauses (i) and (ii) of subparagraph (A).

(9) Example of minimum payments and maximum repayment period

An example, based on a $10,000 outstanding balance and the interest rate (other than a rate not based on the index under the plan) which is, or was recently, in effect under such plan, showing the minimum monthly or periodic payment, and the time it would take to repay the entire $10,000 if the consumer paid only the minimum periodic payments and obtained no additional extensions of credit.

(10) Statement concerning balloon payments

If, under any repayment option of the plan, the payment of not more than the minimum periodic payments required under such option over the length of the repayment period—

(A) would not repay any of the principal balance; or

(B) would repay less than the outstanding balance by the end of such period, as the case may be, a statement of such fact, including an explicit statement that at the end of such repayment period a balloon payment (as defined in section 1665b(f) of this title) would result which would be required to be paid in full at that time.

(11) Negative amortization

If applicable, a statement that—

(A) any limitation in the plan on the amount of any increase in the minimum payments may result in negative amortization;

(B) negative amortization increases the outstanding principal balance of the account; and

(C) negative amortization reduces the consumer's equity in the consumer's dwelling.

(12) Limitations and minimum amount requirements on extensions of credit

(A) Number and dollar amount limitations

Any limitation contained in the plan on the number of extensions of credit and the amount of credit which may be obtained during any month or other defined time period.

(B) Minimum balance and other transaction amount requirements

Any requirement which establishes a minimum amount for—

(i) the initial extension of credit to an account under the plan;

(ii) any subsequent extension of credit to an account under the plan; or

(iii) any outstanding balance of an account under the plan.

(13) Statement regarding tax deductibility

A statement that—

(A) the consumer should consult a tax advisor regarding the deductibility of interest and charges under the plan; and

(B) in any case in which the extension of credit exceeds the fair market value (as defined under Title 26) of the dwelling, the interest on the portion of the credit extension that is greater than the fair market value of the dwelling is not tax deductible for Federal income tax purposes.

(14) Disclosure requirements established by Bureau

Any other term which the Bureau requires, in regulations, to be disclosed.

(b) Time and form of disclosures

(1) Time of disclosure

(A) In general

The disclosures required under subsection (a) with respect to any open end consumer credit plan which provides for any extension of credit which is secured by the consumer's principal dwelling and the pamphlet required under subsection (e) shall be provided to any consumer at the time the creditor distributes an application to establish an account under such plan to such consumer.

(B) Telephone, publications, and third party applications

In the case of telephone applications, applications contained in magazines or other publications, or applications provided by a third party, the disclosures required under subsection (a) and the pamphlet required under subsection (e) shall be provided by the creditor before the end of the 3-day period beginning on the date the creditor receives a completed application from a consumer.

(2) Form

(A) In general

Except as provided in paragraph (1)(B), the disclosures required under subsection (a) of this section shall be provided on or with any application to establish an account under an open end consumer credit plan which provides for any extension of credit which is secured by the consumer's principal dwelling.

(B) Segregation of required disclosures from other information

The disclosures required under subsection (a) shall be conspicuously segregated from all other terms, data, or additional information provided in connection with the application, either by grouping the disclosures separately on the application form or by providing the disclosures on a separate form, in accordance with regulations of the Bureau.

(C) Precedence of certain information

The disclosures required by paragraphs (5), (6), and (7) of subsection (a) shall precede all of the other required disclosures.

(D) Special provision relating to variable interest rate information

Whether or not the disclosures required under subsection (a) are provided on the application form, the variable rate information described in subsection (a)(2) may be provided separately from the other information required to be disclosed.

(3) Requirement for historical table

In preparing the table required under subsection (a)(2)(G), the creditor shall consistently select one rate of interest for each year and the manner of selecting the rate from year to year shall be consistent with the plan.

(c) Third party applications

In the case of an application to open an account under any open end consumer credit plan described in subsection (a) which is provided to a consumer by any person other than the creditor—

(1) such person shall provide such consumer with—

(A) the disclosures required under subsection (a) with respect to such plan, in accordance with subsection (b); and

(B) the pamphlet required under subsection (e); or

(2) if such person cannot provide specific terms about the plan because specific information about the plan terms is not available, no nonrefundable fee may be imposed in connection with such application before the end of the 3-day period beginning on the date the consumer receives the disclosures required under subsection (a) with respect to the application.

(d) "Principal dwelling" defined

For purposes of this section and sections 1647 and 1665b of this title, the term "principal dwelling" includes any second or vacation home of the consumer.

(e) Pamphlet

In addition to the disclosures required under subsection (a) with respect to an application to open an account under any open end consumer credit plan described in such subsection, the creditor or other person providing such disclosures to the consumer shall provide-

(1) a pamphlet published by the Bureau pursuant to section 4 of the Home Equity Consumer Protection Act of 1988; or

(2) any pamphlet which provides substantially similar information to the information described in such section, as determined by the Bureau.

§ 1638 [CCPA § 128]. Transactions Other Than Under an Open End Credit Plan

(a) Required disclosures by creditor

For each consumer credit transaction other than under an open end credit plan, the creditor shall disclose each of the following items, to the extent applicable:

(1) The identity of the creditor required to make disclosure.

(2)(A) The "amount financed", using that term, which shall be the amount of credit of which the consumer has actual use. This amount shall be computed as follows, but the computations need not be disclosed and shall not be disclosed with the disclosures conspicuously segregated in accordance with subsection (b)(1):

(i) take the principal amount of the loan or the cash price less downpayment and trade-in;

(ii) add any charges which are not part of the finance charge or of the principal amount of the loan and which are financed by the consumer, including the cost of any items excluded from the finance charge pursuant to section 1605 of this title; and

(iii) subtract any charges which are part of the finance charge but which will be paid by the consumer before or at the time of the consummation of the transaction, or have been withheld from the proceeds of the credit.

(B) In conjunction with the disclosure of the amount financed, a creditor shall provide a statement of the consumer's right to obtain, upon a written request, a written itemization of the amount financed. The statement shall include spaces for a "yes" and "no" indication to be initialed by the consumer to indicate whether the consumer wants a written itemization of the amount financed. Upon receiving an affirmative indication, the creditor shall provide, at the time other disclosures are required to be furnished, a written itemization of the amount financed. For the purposes of this subparagraph, "itemization of the amount financed" means a disclosure of the following items, to the extent applicable:

(i) the amount that is or will be paid directly to the consumer;

(ii) the amount that is or will be credited to the consumer's account to discharge obligations owed to the creditor;

(iii) each amount that is or will be paid to third persons by the creditor on the consumer's behalf, together with an identification of or reference to the third person; and

(iv) the total amount of any charges described in the preceding subparagraph (A)(iii).

(3) The "finance charge", not itemized, using that term.

(4) The finance charge expressed as an "annual percentage rate", using that term. This shall not be required if the amount financed does not exceed $75 and the finance charge does not exceed $5, or if the amount financed exceeds $75 and the finance charge does not exceed $7.50.

(5) The sum of the amount financed and the finance charge, which shall be termed the "total of payments".

(6) The number, amount, and due dates or period of payments scheduled to repay the total of payments.

(7) In a sale of property or services in which the seller is the creditor required to disclose pursuant to section 1631(b) of this title, the "total sale price", using that term, which shall be the total of the cash price of the property or services, additional charges, and the finance charge.

(8) Descriptive explanations of the terms "amount financed", "finance charge", "annual percentage rate", "total of payments", and "total sale price" as specified by the Bureau. The descriptive explanation of "total sale price" shall include reference to the amount of the down payment.

(9) Where the credit is secured, a statement that a security interest has been taken in (A) the property which is purchased as part of the credit transaction, or (B) property not purchased as part of the credit transaction identified by item or type.

(10) Any dollar charge or percentage amount which may be imposed by a creditor solely on account of a late payment, other than a deferral or extension charge.

(11) A statement indicating whether or not the consumer is entitled to a rebate of any finance charge upon refinancing or prepayment in full pursuant to acceleration or otherwise, if the obligation involves a precomputed finance charge. A statement indicating whether or not a penalty will be imposed in those same circumstances if the obligation involves a finance charge computed from time to time by application of a rate to the unpaid principal balance.

(12) A statement that the consumer should refer to the appropriate contract document for any information such document provides about nonpayment, default, the right to accelerate the maturity of the debt, and prepayment rebates and penalties.

(13) In any residential mortgage transaction, a statement indicating whether a subsequent purchaser or assignee of the consumer may assume the debt obligation on its original terms and conditions.

(14) In the case of any variable interest rate residential mortgage transaction, in disclosures provided at application as prescribed by the Bureau for a variable rate transaction secured by the consumer's principal dwelling, at the option of the creditor, a statement that the periodic payments may increase or decrease substantially, and the maximum interest rate and payment for a $10,000 loan originated at a recent interest rate, as determined by the Bureau, assuming the maximum periodic increases in rates and payments under the program, or a historical example illustrating the effects of interest rate changes implemented according to the loan program.

(15) In the case of a consumer credit transaction that is secured by the principal dwelling of the consumer, in which the extension of credit may exceed the fair market value of the dwelling, a clear and conspicuous statement that—

(A) the interest on the portion of the credit extension that is greater than the fair market value of the dwelling is not tax deductible for Federal income tax purposes; and

(B) the consumer should consult a tax adviser for further information regarding the deductibility of interest and charges.

(16) In the case of a variable rate residential mortgage loan for which an escrow or impound account will be established for the payment of all applicable taxes, insurance, and assessments—

(A) the amount of initial monthly payment due under the loan for the payment of principal and interest, and the amount of such initial monthly payment including the monthly payment deposited in the account for the payment of all applicable taxes, insurance, and assessments; and

(B) the amount of the fully indexed monthly payment due under the loan for the payment of principal and interest, and the amount of such fully indexed monthly payment including the monthly payment deposited in the account for the payment of all applicable taxes, insurance, and assessments.

(17) In the case of a residential mortgage loan, the aggregate amount of settlement charges for all settlement services provided in connection with the loan, the amount of charges that are included in the loan and the amount of such charges the borrower must pay at closing, the approximate amount of the wholesale rate of funds in connection with the loan, and the aggregate amount of other fees or required payments in connection with the loan.

(18) In the case of a residential mortgage loan, the aggregate amount of fees paid to the mortgage originator in connection with the loan, the amount of such fees paid directly by the consumer, and any additional amount received by the originator from the creditor.

(19) In the case of a residential mortgage loan, the total amount of interest that the consumer will pay over the life of the loan as a percentage of the principal of the loan. Such amount shall be computed assuming the consumer makes each monthly payment in full and on-time, and does not make any over-payments.

(b) Form and timing of disclosures; residential mortgage transaction requirements

(1) Except as otherwise provided in this part, the disclosures required under subsection (a) shall be made before the credit is extended. Except for the disclosures required by subsection (a)(1) of this section, all disclosures required under subsection (a) and any disclosure provided for in subsection (b), (c), or (d) of section 1605 of this title shall be conspicuously segregated from all other terms, data, or information provided in connection with a transaction, including any computations or itemization.

(2)(A) Except as provided in subparagraph (G), in the case of any extension of credit that is secured by the dwelling of a consumer, which is also subject to the Real Estate Settlement Procedures Act [12 U.S.C. 2601 et seq.], good faith estimates of the disclosures required under subsection (a) shall be made in accordance with regulations of the Bureau under section 1631(c) of this title and shall be delivered or placed in the mail not later than three business days after the creditor receives the consumer's written application, which shall be at least 7 business days before consummation of the transaction.

(B) In the case of an extension of credit that is secured by the dwelling of a consumer, the disclosures provided under subparagraph (A),[1] shall be in addition to the other disclosures required by subsection (a), and shall—

(i) state in conspicuous type size and format, the following: "You are not required to complete this agreement merely because you have received these disclosures or signed a loan application."; and

(ii) be provided in the form of final disclosures at the time of consummation of the transaction, in the form and manner prescribed by this section.

(C) In the case of an extension of credit that is secured by the dwelling of a consumer, under which the annual rate of interest is variable, or with respect to which the regular payments may otherwise be variable, in addition to the other disclosures required by subsection (a), the disclosures provided under this subsection shall do the following:

(i) Label the payment schedule as follows: "Payment Schedule: Payments Will Vary Based on Interest Rate Changes".

(ii) State in conspicuous type size and format examples of adjustments to the regular required payment on the extension of credit based on the change in the interest rates specified by the contract for such extension of credit. Among the examples required to be provided under this clause is an example that reflects the maximum payment amount of the regular required payments on the extension of credit, based on the maximum interest rate allowed under the contract, in accordance with the rules of the Bureau. Prior to issuing any rules pursuant to this clause, the Bureau shall conduct

---

[1] So in original. The comma probably should not appear.

consumer testing to determine the appropriate format for providing the disclosures required under this subparagraph to consumers so that such disclosures can be easily understood, including the fact that the initial regular payments are for a specific time period that will end on a certain date, that payments will adjust afterwards potentially to a higher amount, and that there is no guarantee that the borrower will be able to refinance to a lower amount.

(D) In any case in which the disclosure statement under subparagraph (A) contains an annual percentage rate of interest that is no longer accurate, as determined under section 1606(c) of this title, the creditor shall furnish an additional, corrected statement to the borrower, not later than 3 business days before the date of consummation of the transaction.

(E) The consumer shall receive the disclosures required under this paragraph before paying any fee to the creditor or other person in connection with the consumer's application for an extension of credit that is secured by the dwelling of a consumer. If the disclosures are mailed to the consumer, the consumer is considered to have received them 3 business days after they are mailed. A creditor or other person may impose a fee for obtaining the consumer's credit report before the consumer has received the disclosures under this paragraph, provided the fee is bona fide and reasonable in amount.

(F) Waiver of timeliness of disclosures

To expedite consummation of a transaction, if the consumer determines that the extension of credit is needed to meet a bona fide personal financial emergency, the consumer may waive or modify the timing requirements for disclosures under subparagraph (A), provided that—

(i) the term "bona fide personal emergency" may be further defined in regulations issued by the Bureau;

(ii) the consumer provides to the creditor a dated, written statement describing the emergency and specifically waiving or modifying those timing requirements, which statement shall bear the signature of all consumers entitled to receive the disclosures required by this paragraph; and

(iii) the creditor provides to the consumers at or before the time of such waiver or modification, the final disclosures required by paragraph (1).

(G)(i) In the case of an extension of credit relating to a plan described in section 101(53D) of Title 11—

(I) the requirements of subparagraphs (A) through (E) shall not apply; and

(II) a good faith estimate of the disclosures required under subsection (a) shall be made in accordance with regulations of the Bureau under section 1631(c) of this title before such credit is extended, or shall be delivered or placed in the mail not later than 3 business days after the date on which the creditor receives the written application of the consumer for such credit, whichever is earlier.

(ii) If a disclosure statement furnished within 3 business days of the written application (as provided under clause (i)(II)) contains an annual percentage rate which is subsequently rendered inaccurate, within the meaning of section 1606(c) of this title, the creditor shall furnish another disclosure statement at the time of settlement or consummation of the transaction.

(3) In the case of a credit transaction described in paragraph (15) of subsection (a), disclosures required by that paragraph shall be made to the consumer at the time of application for such extension of credit.

(4) Repayment analysis required to include escrow payments

(A) In general

In the case of any consumer credit transaction secured by a first mortgage or lien on the principal dwelling of the consumer, other than a consumer credit transaction under an open end credit plan or a reverse mortgage, for which an impound, trust, or other type of account has been or will be established in connection with the transaction for the payment of property taxes, hazard and flood (if any) insurance premiums, or other periodic payments or premiums with respect to the property, the information required to be provided under subsection (a) with respect to the number, amount, and due dates or period of payments scheduled to repay the total of payments shall take into account the amount of any monthly payment to such account for each such repayment in accordance with section 10(a)(2) of the Real Estate Settlement Procedures Act of 1974.

(B) Assessment value

The amount taken into account under subparagraph (A) for the payment of property taxes, hazard and flood (if any) insurance premiums, or other periodic payments or premiums with respect to the property shall reflect the taxable assessed value of the real property securing the transaction after the consummation of the transaction, including the value of any improvements on the property or to be constructed on the property (whether or not such construction will be financed from the proceeds of the transaction), if known, and the replacement costs of the property for hazard insurance, in the initial year after the transaction.

(c) Timing of disclosures on unsolicited mailed or telephone purchase orders or loan requests

(1) If a creditor receives a purchase order by mail or telephone without personal solicitation, and the cash price and the total sale price and the terms of financing, including the annual percentage rate, are set forth in the creditor's catalog or other printed material distributed to the public, then the disclosures required under subsection (a) may be made at any time not later than the date the first payment is due.

(2) If a creditor receives a request for a loan by mail or telephone without personal solicitation and the terms of financing, including the annual percentage rate for representative amounts of credit, are set forth in the creditor's printed material distributed to the public, or in the contract of loan or other printed material delivered to the obligor, then the disclosures required under subsection (a) may be made at any time not later than the date the first payment is due.

(d) Timing of disclosure in cases of an addition of a deferred payment price to an existing outstanding balance

If a consumer credit sale is one of a series of consumer credit sales transactions made pursuant to an agreement providing for the addition of the deferred payment price of that sale to an existing outstanding balance, and the person to whom the credit is extended has approved in writing both the annual percentage rate or rates and the method of computing the finance charge or charges, and the creditor retains no security interest in any property as to which he has received payments aggregating the amount of the sales price including any finance charges attributable thereto, then the disclosure required under subsection (a) for the particular sale may be made at any time not later than the date the first payment for that sale is due. For the purposes of this subsection, in the case of items purchased on different dates, the first purchased shall be deemed first paid for, and in the case of items purchased on the same date, the lowest price shall be deemed first paid for.

(e) Terms and disclosure with respect to private education loans

(1) Disclosures required in private education loan applications and solicitations

In any application for a private education loan, or a solicitation for a private education loan without requiring an application, the private educational lender shall disclose to the borrower, clearly and conspicuously—

(A) the potential range of rates of interest applicable to the private education loan;

(B) whether the rate of interest applicable to the private education loan is fixed or variable;

(C) limitations on interest rate adjustments, both in terms of frequency and amount, or the lack thereof, if applicable;

(D) requirements for a co-borrower, including any changes in the applicable interest rates without a co-borrower;

(E) potential finance charges, late fees, penalties, and adjustments to principal, based on defaults or late payments of the borrower;

(F) fees or range of fees applicable to the private education loan;

(G) the term of the private education loan;

(H) whether interest will accrue while the student to whom the private education loan relates is enrolled at a covered educational institution;

(I) payment deferral options;

(J) general eligibility criteria for the private education loan;

(K) an example of the total cost of the private education loan over the life of the loan—

(i) which shall be calculated using the principal amount and the maximum rate of interest actually offered by the private educational lender; and

(ii) calculated both with and without capitalization of interest, if an option exists for postponing interest payments;

(L) that a covered educational institution may have school-specific education loan benefits and terms not detailed on the disclosure form;

(M) that the borrower may qualify for Federal student financial assistance through a program under title IV of the Higher Education Act of 1965 (20 U.S.C. 1070 et seq.), in lieu of, or in addition to, a loan from a non-Federal source;

(N) the interest rates available with respect to such Federal student financial assistance through a program under title IV of the Higher Education Act of 1965 (20 U.S.C. 1070 et seq.);

(O) that, as provided in paragraph (6)—

(i) the borrower shall have the right to accept the terms of the loan and consummate the transaction at any time within 30 calendar days (or such longer period as the private educational lender may provide) following the date on which the application for the private education loan is approved and the borrower receives the disclosure documents required under this subsection for the loan; and

(ii) except for changes based on adjustments to the index used for a loan, the rates and terms of the loan may not be changed by the private educational lender during the period described in clause (i);

(P) that, before a private education loan may be consummated, the borrower must obtain from the relevant institution of higher education the form required under paragraph (3), and complete, sign, and return such form to the private educational lender;

(Q) that the consumer may obtain additional information concerning such Federal student financial assistance from their institution of higher education, or at the website of the Department of Education; and

(R) such other information as the Bureau shall prescribe, by rule, as necessary or appropriate for consumers to make informed borrowing decisions.

(2) Disclosures at the time of private education loan approval

Contemporaneously with the approval of a private education loan application, and before the loan transaction is consummated, the private educational lender shall disclose to the borrower, clearly and conspicuously—

(A) the applicable rate of interest in effect on the date of approval;

(B) whether the rate of interest applicable to the private education loan is fixed or variable;

(C) limitations on interest rate adjustments, both in terms of frequency and amount, or the lack thereof, if applicable;

(D) the initial approved principal amount;

(E) applicable finance charges, late fees, penalties, and adjustments to principal, based on borrower defaults or late payments, including limitations on the discharge of a private education loan in bankruptcy;

(F) fees or range of fees applicable to the private education loan;

(G) the maximum term under the private education loan program;

(H) an estimate of the total amount for repayment, at both the interest rate in effect on the date of approval and at the maximum possible rate of interest offered by the private educational lender and applicable to the borrower, to the extent that such maximum rate may be determined, or if not, a good faith estimate thereof;

(I) any principal and interest payments required while the student for whom the private education loan is intended is enrolled at a covered educational institution and unpaid interest that will accrue during such enrollment;

(J) payment deferral options applicable to the borrower;

(K) whether monthly payments are graduated;

(L) that, as provided in paragraph (6)—

(i) the borrower shall have the right to accept the terms of the loan and consummate the transaction at any time within 30 calendar days (or such longer period as the private educational lender may provide) following the date on which the application for the private education loan is approved and the borrower receives the disclosure documents required under this subsection for the loan; and

(ii) except for changes based on adjustments to the index used for a loan, the rates and terms of the loan may not be changed by the private educational lender during the period described in clause (i);

(M) that the borrower—

(i) may qualify for Federal financial assistance through a program under title IV of the Higher Education Act of 1965 (20 U.S.C. 1070 et seq.), in lieu of, or in addition to, a loan from a non-Federal source; and

(ii) may obtain additional information concerning such assistance from their institution of higher education or the website of the Department of Education;

(N) the interest rates available with respect to such Federal financial assistance through a program under title IV of the Higher Education Act of 1965 (20 U.S.C. 1070 et seq.);

(O) the maximum monthly payment, calculated using the maximum rate of interest actually offered by the private educational lender and applicable to the borrower, to the extent that such maximum rate may be determined, or if not, a good faith estimate thereof; and

(P) such other information as the Bureau shall prescribe, by rule, as necessary or appropriate for consumers to make informed borrowing decisions.

(3) Self-certification of information

(A) In general

Before a private educational lender may consummate a private education loan with respect to a student attending an institution of higher education, the lender shall obtain from the applicant for the private education loan the form developed by the Secretary of Education under section 155 of the Higher Education Act of 1965, signed by the applicant, in written or electronic form.

(B) Rule of construction

No other provision of this subsection shall be construed to require a private educational lender to perform any additional duty under this paragraph, other than collecting the form required under subparagraph (A).

(4) Disclosures at the time of private education loan consummation

Contemporaneously with the consummation of a private education loan, a private educational lender shall make to the borrower each of the disclosures described in—

(A) paragraph (2)(A) (adjusted, as necessary, for the rate of interest in effect on the date of consummation, based on the index used for the loan);

(B) subparagraphs (B) through (K) and (M) through (P) of paragraph (2); and

(C) paragraph (7).

(5) Format of disclosures

(A) Model form

Not later than 2 years after August 14, 2008, the Bureau shall, based on consumer testing, and in consultation with the Secretary of Education, develop and issue model forms that may be used, at the option of the private educational lender, for the provision of disclosures required under this subsection.

(B) Format

Model forms developed under this paragraph shall—

(i) be comprehensible to borrowers, with a clear format and design;

(ii) provide for clear and conspicuous disclosures;

(iii) enable borrowers easily to identify material terms of the loan and to compare such terms among private education loans; and

(iv) be succinct, and use an easily readable type font.

(C) Safe harbor

Any private educational lender that elects to provide a model form developed under this subsection that accurately reflects the practices of the private educational lender shall be deemed to be in compliance with the disclosures required under this subsection.

(6) Effective period of approved rate of interest and loan terms

(A) In general

With respect to a private education loan, the borrower shall have the right to accept the terms of the loan and consummate the transaction at any time within 30 calendar days (or such longer period as the private educational lender may provide) following the date on which the application for the private education loan is approved and the borrower receives the disclosure documents required under this subsection for the loan, and the rates and terms of the loan may not be changed by the private educational lender during that period.

(B) Prohibition on changes

Except for changes based on adjustments to the index used for a loan, the rates and terms of the loan may not be changed by the private educational lender prior to the earlier of—

(i) the date of acceptance of the terms of the loan and consummation of the transaction by the borrower, as described in subparagraph (A); or

(ii) the expiration of the period described in subparagraph (A).

(7) Right to cancel

With respect to a private education loan, the borrower may cancel the loan, without penalty to the borrower, at any time within 3 business days of the date on which the loan is consummated, and the private educational lender shall disclose such right to the borrower in accordance with paragraph (4).

(8) Prohibition on disbursement

No funds may be disbursed with respect to a private education loan until the expiration of the 3-day period described in paragraph (7).

(9) Bureau regulations

In issuing regulations under this subsection, the Bureau shall prevent, to the extent possible, duplicative disclosure requirements for private educational lenders that are otherwise required to make disclosures under this subchapter, except that in any case in which the disclosure requirements of this subsection differ or conflict with the disclosure requirements of any other provision of this subchapter, the requirements of this subsection shall be controlling.

(10) Definitions

For purposes of this subsection, the terms "covered educational institution", "private educational lender", and "private education loan" have the same meanings as in section 1650 of Title 15.

(11) Duties of lenders participating in preferred lender arrangements

Each private educational lender that has a preferred lender arrangement with a covered educational institution shall annually, by a date determined by the Bureau, in consultation with the Secretary of Education, provide to the covered educational institution such information as the Bureau determines to include in the model form developed under paragraph (5) for each type of private education loan that the lender plans to offer to students attending the covered educational institution, or to the families of such students, for the next award year (as that term is defined in section 481 of the Higher Education Act of 1965).

(f) Periodic statements for residential mortgage loans

(1) In general

The creditor, assignee, or servicer with respect to any residential mortgage loan shall transmit to the obligor, for each billing cycle, a statement setting forth each of the following items, to the extent applicable, in a conspicuous and prominent manner:

(A) The amount of the principal obligation under the mortgage.

(B) The current interest rate in effect for the loan.

(C) The date on which the interest rate may next reset or adjust.

(D) The amount of any prepayment fee to be charged, if any.

(E) A description of any late payment fees.

(F) A telephone number and electronic mail address that may be used by the obligor to obtain information regarding the mortgage.

(G) The names, addresses, telephone numbers, and Internet addresses of counseling agencies or programs reasonably available to the consumer that have been certified or approved and made publicly available by the Secretary of Housing and Urban Development or a State housing finance authority (as defined in section 1441a–1 of Title 12).

(H) Such other information as the Board[2] may prescribe in regulations.

(2) Development and use of standard form

The Board shall develop and prescribe a standard form for the disclosure required under this subsection, taking into account that the statements required may be transmitted in writing or electronically.

(3) Exception

Paragraph (1) shall not apply to any fixed rate residential mortgage loan where the creditor, assignee, or servicer provides the obligor with a coupon book that provides the obligor with substantially the same information as required in paragraph (1).

§ 1638a. Reset of Hybrid Adjustable Rate Mortgages

(a) Hybrid adjustable rate mortgages defined

For purposes of this section, the term "hybrid adjustable rate mortgage" means a consumer credit transaction secured by the consumer's principal residence with a fixed interest rate for an introductory period that adjusts or resets to a variable interest rate after such period.

(b) Notice of reset and alternatives

During the 1-month period that ends 6 months before the date on which the interest rate in effect during the introductory period of a hybrid adjustable rate mortgage adjusts or resets to a variable interest rate or, in the case of such an adjustment or resetting that occurs within the first 6 months after consummation of such loan, at consummation, the creditor or servicer of such loan shall provide a written notice, separate and distinct from all other correspondence to the consumer, that includes the following:

(1) Any index or formula used in making adjustments to or resetting the interest rate and a source of information about the index or formula.

(2) An explanation of how the new interest rate and payment would be determined, including an explanation of how the index was adjusted, such as by the addition of a margin.

---

[2] So in original. Probably should be "Bureau."

(3) A good faith estimate, based on accepted industry standards, of the creditor or servicer of the amount of the monthly payment that will apply after the date of the adjustment or reset, and the assumptions on which this estimate is based.

(4) A list of alternatives consumers may pursue before the date of adjustment or reset, and descriptions of the actions consumers must take to pursue these alternatives, including—

(A) refinancing;

(B) renegotiation of loan terms;

(C) payment forbearances; and

(D) pre-foreclosure sales.

(5) The names, addresses, telephone numbers, and Internet addresses of counseling agencies or programs reasonably available to the consumer that have been certified or approved and made publicly available by the Secretary of Housing and Urban Development or a State housing finance authority (as defined in section 1441a–1 of Title 12).

(6) The address, telephone number, and Internet address for the State housing finance authority (as so defined) for the State in which the consumer resides.

(c) Savings clause

The Board may require the notice in paragraph (b) or other notice consistent with this chapter for adjustable rate mortgage loans that are not hybrid adjustable rate mortgage loans.

§ 1639 [CCPA § 129]. Requirements for Certain Mortgages

(a) Disclosures

(1) Specific disclosures

In addition to other disclosures required under this subchapter, for each mortgage referred to in sections 1602(aa)[1] of this title, the creditor shall provide the following disclosures in conspicuous type size:

(A) "You are not required to complete this agreement merely because you have received these disclosures or have signed a loan application."

(B) "If you obtain this loan, the lender will have a mortgage on your home. You could lose your home, and any money you have put into it, if you do not meet your obligations under the loan."

(2) Annual percentage rate

In addition to the disclosures required under paragraph (1), the creditor shall disclose—

(A) in the case of a credit transaction with a fixed rate of interest, the annual percentage rate and the amount of the regular monthly payment; or

(B) in the case of any other credit transaction, the annual percentage rate of the loan, the amount of the regular monthly payment, a statement that the interest rate and monthly payment may increase, and the amount of the maximum monthly payment, based on the maximum interest rate allowed pursuant to section 3806 of Title 12.

(b) Time of disclosures

(1) In general

The disclosures required by this section shall be given not less than 3 business days prior to consummation of the transaction.

---

1 Per redesignation by Pub.L. 111–203, "1602(aa)" probably should read "1602(bb)".

(2) New disclosures required

(A) In general

After providing the disclosures required by this section, a creditor may not change the terms of the extension of credit if such changes make the disclosures inaccurate, unless new disclosures are provided that meet the requirements of this section.

(B) Telephone disclosure

A creditor may provide new disclosures pursuant to subparagraph (A) by telephone, if—

(i) the change is initiated by the consumer; and

(ii) at the consummation of the transaction under which the credit is extended—

(I) the creditor provides to the consumer the new disclosures, in writing; and

(II) the creditor and consumer certify in writing that the new disclosures were provided by telephone, by not later than 3 days prior to the date of consummation of the transaction.

(3) No wait for lower rate

If a creditor extends to a consumer a second offer of credit with a lower annual percentage rate, the transaction may be consummated without regard to the period specified in paragraph (1) with respect to the second offer.

(4) Modifications

The Bureau may, if it finds that such action is necessary to permit homeowners to meet bona fide personal financial emergencies, prescribe regulations authorizing the modification or waiver of rights created under this subsection, to the extent and under the circumstances set forth in those regulations.

(c) No prepayment penalty

(1) In general

(A) Limitation on terms

A mortgage referred to in section 1602(aa) of this title may not contain terms under which a consumer must pay a prepayment penalty for paying all or part of the principal before the date on which the principal is due.

(B) Construction

For purposes of this subsection, any method of computing a refund of unearned scheduled interest is a prepayment penalty if it is less favorable to the consumer than the actuarial method (as that term is defined in section 1615(d) of this title).

(c)(2) Repealed

(d) Limitations after default

A mortgage referred to in section 1602(aa) of this title may not provide for an interest rate applicable after default that is higher than the interest rate that applies before default. If the date of maturity of a mortgage referred to in subsection[1] 1602(aa) of this title is accelerated due to default and the consumer is entitled to a rebate of interest, that rebate shall be computed by any method that is not less favorable than the actuarial method (as that term is defined in section 1615(d) of this title).

(e) No balloon payments

---

1 So in original. Probably should be "section."

No high-cost mortgage may contain a scheduled payment that is more than twice as large as the average of earlier scheduled payments. This subsection shall not apply when the payment schedule is adjusted to the seasonal or irregular income of the consumer.

(f) No negative amortization

A mortgage referred to in section 1602(aa) of this title may not include terms under which the outstanding principal balance will increase at any time over the course of the loan because the regular periodic payments do not cover the full amount of interest due.

(g) No prepaid payments

A mortgage referred to in section 1602(aa) of this title may not include terms under which more than 2 periodic payments required under the loan are consolidated and paid in advance from the loan proceeds provided to the consumer.

(h) Prohibition on extending credit without regard to payment ability of consumer

A creditor shall not engage in a pattern or practice of extending credit to consumers under mortgages referred to in section 1602(aa) of this title based on the consumers' collateral without regard to the consumers' repayment ability, including the consumers' current and expected income, current obligations, and employment.

(i) Requirements for payments under home improvement contracts

A creditor shall not make a payment to a contractor under a home improvement contract from amounts extended as credit under a mortgage referred to in section 1602(aa) of this title, other than—

(1) in the form of an instrument that is payable to the consumer or jointly to the consumer and the contractor; or

(2) at the election of the consumer, by a third party escrow agent in accordance with terms established in a written agreement signed by the consumer, the creditor, and the contractor before the date of payment.

(j) Recommended default

No creditor shall recommend or encourage default on an existing loan or other debt prior to and in connection with the closing or planned closing of a high-cost mortgage that refinances all or any portion of such existing loan or debt.

(k) Late fees

(1) In general

No creditor may impose a late payment charge or fee in connection with a high-cost mortgage—

(A) in an amount in excess of 4 percent of the amount of the payment past due;

(B) unless the loan documents specifically authorize the charge or fee;

(C) before the end of the 15-day period beginning on the date the payment is due, or in the case of a loan on which interest on each installment is paid in advance, before the end of the 30-day period beginning on the date the payment is due; or

(D) more than once with respect to a single late payment.

(2) Coordination with subsequent late fees

If a payment is otherwise a full payment for the applicable period and is paid on its due date or within an applicable grace period, and the only delinquency or insufficiency of payment is attributable to any late fee or delinquency charge assessed on any earlier payment, no late fee or delinquency charge may be imposed on such payment.

(3) Failure to make installment payment

If, in the case of a loan agreement the terms of which provide that any payment shall first be applied to any past due principal balance, the consumer fails to make an installment payment and the consumer subsequently resumes making installment payments but has not paid all past due installments, the creditor may impose a separate late payment charge or fee for any principal due (without deduction due to late fees or related fees) until the default is cured.

(*l*) Acceleration of debt

No high-cost mortgage may contain a provision which permits the creditor to accelerate the indebtedness, except when repayment of the loan has been accelerated by default in payment, or pursuant to a due-on-sale provision, or pursuant to a material violation of some other provision of the loan document unrelated to payment schedule.

(m) Restriction on financing points and fees

No creditor may directly or indirectly finance, in connection with any high-cost mortgage, any of the following:

(1) Any prepayment fee or penalty payable by the consumer in a refinancing transaction if the creditor or an affiliate of the creditor is the noteholder of the note being refinanced.

(2) Any points or fees.

(n) Consequence of failure to comply

Any mortgage that contains a provision prohibited by this section shall be deemed a failure to deliver the material disclosures required under this subchapter, for the purpose of section 1635 of this title.

(*o*) "Affiliate" defined

For purposes of this section, the term "affiliate" has the same meaning as in section 1841(k) of Title 12.

(p) Discretionary regulatory authority of Bureau

(1) Exemptions

The Bureau may, by regulation or order, exempt specific mortgage products or categories of mortgages from any or all of the prohibitions specified in subsections (c) through (i), if the Bureau finds that the exemption—

(A) is in the interest of the borrowing public; and

(B) will apply only to products that maintain and strengthen home ownership and equity protection.

(2) Prohibitions

The Bureau, by regulation or order, shall prohibit acts or practices in connection with—

(A) mortgage loans that the Bureau finds to be unfair, deceptive, or designed to evade the provisions of this section; and

(B) refinancing of mortgage loans that the Bureau finds to be associated with abusive lending practices, or that are otherwise not in the interest of the borrower.

(q) Civil penalties in Federal Trade Commission enforcement actions

For purposes of enforcement by the Federal Trade Commission, any violation of a regulation issued by the Bureau pursuant to subsection (1)(2) shall be treated as a violation of a rule promulgated under section 57a of this title regarding unfair or deceptive acts or practices.

(r) Prohibitions on evasions, structuring of transactions, and reciprocal arrangements

A creditor may not take any action in connection with a high-cost mortgage—

(1) to structure a loan transaction as an open-end credit plan or another form of loan for the purpose and with the intent of evading the provisions of this subchapter; or

(2) to divide any loan transaction into separate parts for the purpose and with the intent of evading provisions of this subchapter.

(s) Modification and deferral fees prohibited

A creditor, successor in interest, assignee, or any agent of any of the above, may not charge a consumer any fee to modify, renew, extend, or amend a high-cost mortgage, or to defer any payment due under the terms of such mortgage.

(t) Payoff statement

(1) Fees

(A) In general

Except as provided in subparagraph (B), no creditor or servicer may charge a fee for informing or transmitting to any person the balance due to pay off the outstanding balance on a high-cost mortgage.

(B) Transaction fee

When payoff information referred to in subparagraph (A) is provided by facsimile transmission or by a courier service, a creditor or servicer may charge a processing fee to cover the cost of such transmission or service in an amount not to exceed an amount that is comparable to fees imposed for similar services provided in connection with consumer credit transactions that are secured by the consumer's principal dwelling and are not high-cost mortgages.

(C) Fee disclosure

Prior to charging a transaction fee as provided in subparagraph (B), a creditor or servicer shall disclose that payoff balances are available for free pursuant to subparagraph (A).

(D) Multiple requests

If a creditor or servicer has provided payoff information referred to in subparagraph (A) without charge, other than the transaction fee allowed by subparagraph (B), on 4 occasions during a calendar year, the creditor or servicer may thereafter charge a reasonable fee for providing such information during the remainder of the calendar year.

(2) Prompt delivery

Payoff balances shall be provided within 5 business days after receiving a request by a consumer or a person authorized by the consumer to obtain such information.

(u) Pre-loan counseling

(1) In general

A creditor may not extend credit to a consumer under a high-cost mortgage without first receiving certification from a counselor that is approved by the Secretary of Housing and Urban Development, or at the discretion of the Secretary, a State housing finance authority, that the consumer has received counseling on the advisability of the mortgage. Such counselor shall not be employed by the creditor or an affiliate of the creditor or be affiliated with the creditor.

(2) Disclosures required prior to counseling

No counselor may certify that a consumer has received counseling on the advisability of the high-cost mortgage unless the counselor can verify that the consumer has received each statement required (in connection with such loan) by this section or the Real Estate Settlement Procedures Act of 1974 with respect to the transaction.

(3) Regulations

The Board may prescribe such regulations as the Board determines to be appropriate to carry out the requirements of paragraph (1).

(v) Corrections and unintentional violations

A creditor or assignee in a high-cost mortgage who, when acting in good faith, fails to comply with any requirement under this section will not be deemed to have violated such requirement if the creditor or assignee establishes that either—

(1) within 30 days of the loan closing and prior to the institution of any action, the consumer is notified of or discovers the violation, appropriate restitution is made, and whatever adjustments are necessary are made to the loan to either, at the choice of the consumer—

(A) make the loan satisfy the requirements of this part; or

(B) in the case of a high-cost mortgage, change the terms of the loan in a manner beneficial to the consumer so that the loan will no longer be a high-cost mortgage; or

(2) within 60 days of the creditor's discovery or receipt of notification of an unintentional violation or bona fide error and prior to the institution of any action, the consumer is notified of the compliance failure, appropriate restitution is made, and whatever adjustments are necessary are made to the loan to either, at the choice of the consumer—

(A) make the loan satisfy the requirements of this part; or

(B) in the case of a high-cost mortgage, change the terms of the loan in a manner beneficial so that the loan will no longer be a high-cost mortgage.

§ 1639a. Duty of Servicers of Residential Mortgages (§ 129A of Truth in Lending Act)

(a) In general

Notwithstanding any other provision of law, whenever a servicer of residential mortgages agrees to enter into a qualified loss mitigation plan with respect to 1 or more residential mortgages originated before May 20, 2009, including mortgages held in a securitization or other investment vehicle—

(1) to the extent that the servicer owes a duty to investors or other parties to maximize the net present value of such mortgages, the duty shall be construed to apply to all such investors and parties, and not to any individual party or group of parties; and

(2) the servicer shall be deemed to have satisfied the duty set forth in paragraph (1) if, before December 31, 2012, the servicer implements a qualified loss mitigation plan that meets the following criteria:

(A) Default on the payment of such mortgage has occurred, is imminent, or is reasonably foreseeable, as such terms are defined by guidelines issued by the Secretary of the Treasury or his designee under the Emergency Economic Stabilization Act of 2008.

(B) The mortgagor occupies the property securing the mortgage as his or her principal residence.

(C) The servicer reasonably determined, consistent with the guidelines issued by the Secretary of the Treasury or his designee, that the application of such qualified loss mitigation plan to a mortgage or class of mortgages will likely provide an anticipated recovery on the outstanding principal mortgage debt that will exceed the anticipated recovery through foreclosures.

(b) No liability

A servicer that is deemed to be acting in the best interests of all investors or other parties under this section shall not be liable to any party who is owed a duty under subsection (a)(1), and shall not be subject to any injunction, stay, or other equitable relief to such party, based solely upon the implementation by the servicer of a qualified loss mitigation plan.

(c) Standard industry practice

The qualified loss mitigation plan guidelines issued by the Secretary of the Treasury under the Emergency Economic Stabilization Act of 2008 shall constitute standard industry practice for purposes of all Federal and State laws.

(d) Scope of safe harbor

Any person, including a trustee, issuer, and loan originator, shall not be liable for monetary damages or be subject to an injunction, stay, or other equitable relief, based solely upon the cooperation of such person with a servicer when such cooperation is necessary for the servicer to implement a qualified loss mitigation plan that meets the requirements of subsection (a).

(e) Reporting

Each servicer that engages in qualified loss mitigation plans under this section shall regularly report to the Secretary of the Treasury the extent, scope, and results of the servicer's modification activities. The Secretary of the Treasury shall prescribe regulations or guidance specifying the form, content, and timing of such reports.

(f) Definitions

As used in this section—

(1) the term "qualified loss mitigation plan" means

(A) a residential loan modification, workout, or other loss mitigation plan, including to the extent that the Secretary of the Treasury determines appropriate, a loan sale, real property disposition, trial modification, pre-foreclosure sale, and deed in lieu of foreclosure, that is described or authorized in guidelines issued by the Secretary of the Treasury or his designee under the Emergency Economic Stabilization Act of 2008; and

(B) a refinancing of a mortgage under the Hope for Homeowners program;

(2) the term "servicer" means the person responsible for the servicing for others of residential mortgage loans (including of a pool of residential mortgage loans); and

(3) the term "securitization vehicle" means a trust, special purpose entity, or other legal structure that is used to facilitate the issuing of securities, participation certificates, or similar instruments backed by or referring to a pool of assets that includes residential mortgages (or instruments that are related to residential mortgages such as credit-linked notes).

(g) Rule of construction

No provision of subsection (b) or (d) shall be construed as affecting the liability of any servicer or person as described in subsection (d) for actual fraud in the origination or servicing of a loan or in the implementation of a qualified loss mitigation plan, or for the violation of a State or Federal law, including laws regulating the origination of mortgage loans, commonly referred to as predatory lending laws.

§ 1639b. Residential mortgage loan origination

(a) Finding and purpose

(1) Finding

The Congress finds that economic stabilization would be enhanced by the protection, limitation, and regulation of the terms of residential mortgage credit and the practices related to such credit, while ensuring that responsible, affordable mortgage credit remains available to consumers.

(2) Purpose

It is the purpose of this section and section 1639c of this title to assure that consumers are offered and receive residential mortgage loans on terms that reasonably reflect their ability to repay the loans and that are understandable and not unfair, deceptive or abusive.

(b) Duty of care

(1) Standard

Subject to regulations prescribed under this subsection, each mortgage originator shall, in addition to the duties imposed by otherwise applicable provisions of State or Federal law—

(A) be qualified and, when required, registered and licensed as a mortgage originator in accordance with applicable State or Federal law, including the Secure and Fair Enforcement for Mortgage Licensing Act of 2008; and

(B) include on all loan documents any unique identifier of the mortgage originator provided by the Nationwide Mortgage Licensing System and Registry.

(2) Compliance procedures required

The Bureau shall prescribe regulations requiring depository institutions to establish and maintain procedures reasonably designed to assure and monitor the compliance of such depository institutions, the subsidiaries of such institutions, and the employees of such institutions or subsidiaries with the requirements of this section and the registration procedures established under section 1507 of the Secure and Fair Enforcement for Mortgage Licensing Act of 2008.

(c) Prohibition on steering incentives

(1) In general

For any residential mortgage loan, no mortgage originator shall receive from any person and no person shall pay to a mortgage originator, directly or indirectly, compensation that varies based on the terms of the loan (other than the amount of the principal).

(2) Restructuring of financing origination fee

(A) In general

For any mortgage loan, a mortgage originator may not receive from any person other than the consumer and no person, other than the consumer, who knows or has reason to know that a consumer has directly compensated or will directly compensate a mortgage originator may pay a mortgage originator any origination fee or charge except bona fide third party charges not retained by the creditor, mortgage originator, or an affiliate of the creditor or mortgage originator.

(B) Exception

Notwithstanding subparagraph (A), a mortgage originator may receive from a person other than the consumer an origination fee or charge, and a person other than the consumer may pay a mortgage originator an origination fee or charge, if—

(i) the mortgage originator does not receive any compensation directly from the consumer; and

(ii) the consumer does not make an upfront payment of discount points, origination points, or fees, however denominated (other than bona fide third party charges not retained by the mortgage originator, creditor, or an affiliate of the creditor or originator), except that the Bureau may, by rule, waive or provide exemptions to this clause if the Bureau determines that such waiver or exemption is in the interest of consumers and in the public interest.

(3) Regulations

The Bureau shall prescribe regulations to prohibit—

(A) mortgage originators from steering any consumer to a residential mortgage loan that—

(i) the consumer lacks a reasonable ability to repay (in accordance with regulations prescribed under section 1639c(a) of this title); or

(ii) has predatory characteristics or effects (such as equity stripping, excessive fees, or abusive terms);

(B) mortgage originators from steering any consumer from a residential mortgage loan for which the consumer is qualified that is a qualified mortgage (as defined in section 1639c(b)(2) of this title) to a residential mortgage loan that is not a qualified mortgage;

(C) abusive or unfair lending practices that promote disparities among consumers of equal credit worthiness but of different race, ethnicity, gender, or age; and

(D) mortgage originators from—

(i) mischaracterizing the credit history of a consumer or the residential mortgage loans available to a consumer;

(ii) mischaracterizing or suborning the mischaracterization of the appraised value of the property securing the extension of credit; or

(iii) if unable to suggest, offer, or recommend to a consumer a loan that is not more expensive than a loan for which the consumer qualifies, discouraging a consumer from seeking a residential mortgage loan secured by a consumer's principal dwelling from another mortgage originator.

(4) Rules of construction

No provision of this subsection shall be construed as—

(A) permitting any yield spread premium or other similar compensation that would, for any residential mortgage loan, permit the total amount of direct and indirect compensation from all sources permitted to a mortgage originator to vary based on the terms of the loan (other than the amount of the principal);

(B) limiting or affecting the amount of compensation received by a creditor upon the sale of a consummated loan to a subsequent purchaser;

(C) restricting a consumer's ability to finance, at the option of the consumer, including through principal or rate, any origination fees or costs permitted under this subsection, or the mortgage originator's right to receive such fees or costs (including compensation) from any person, subject to paragraph (2)(B), so long as such fees or costs do not vary based on the terms of the loan (other than the amount of the principal) or the consumer's decision about whether to finance such fees or costs; or

(D) prohibiting incentive payments to a mortgage originator based on the number of residential mortgage loans originated within a specified period of time.

(d) Liability for violations

(1) In general

For purposes of providing a cause of action for any failure by a mortgage originator, other than a creditor, to comply with any requirement imposed under this section and any regulation prescribed under this section, section 1640 of this title shall be applied with respect to any such failure by substituting "mortgage originator" for "creditor" each place such term appears in each such subsection.[1]

(2) Maximum

The maximum amount of any liability of a mortgage originator under paragraph (1) to a consumer for any violation of this section shall not exceed the greater of actual damages or an amount equal to 3 times the total amount of direct and indirect compensation or gain accruing to the mortgage originator in connection with the residential mortgage loan involved in the violation, plus the costs to the consumer of the action, including a reasonable attorney's fee.

(e) Discretionary regulatory authority

(1) In general

The Bureau shall, by regulations, prohibit or condition terms, acts or practices relating to residential mortgage loans that the Bureau finds to be abusive, unfair, deceptive, predatory, necessary or proper to ensure that responsible, affordable mortgage credit remains available to consumers in a manner consistent with the purposes of this section and section 1639c of this title, necessary or proper to effectuate the purposes of this section and section 1639c of this title, to prevent circumvention or evasion thereof, or to facilitate compliance with such sections, or are not in the interest of the borrower.

(2) Application

The regulations prescribed under paragraph (1) shall be applicable to all residential mortgage loans and shall be applied in the same manner as regulations prescribed under section 1604 of this title.

(f) Timeshare plans

This section and any regulations promulgated thereunder do not apply to extension of credit relating to a plan described in section 101(53D) of Title 11.

§ 1639c. Minimum standards for Residential mortgage Loans

(a) Ability to repay

(1) In general

In accordance with regulations prescribed by the Bureau, no creditor may make a residential mortgage loan unless the creditor makes a reasonable and good faith determination based on verified and documented information that, at the time the loan is consummated, the consumer has a reasonable ability to repay the loan, according to its terms, and all applicable taxes, insurance (including mortgage guarantee insurance), and assessments.

(2) Multiple loans

If the creditor knows, or has reason to know, that 1 or more residential mortgage loans secured by the same dwelling will be made to the same consumer, the creditor shall make a reasonable and good faith determination, based on verified and documented information, that the consumer has a reasonable ability to repay the combined payments of all loans on the same dwelling according to the terms of those loans and all applicable taxes, insurance (including mortgage guarantee insurance), and assessments.

---

1 So in original. Probably should be "in such section."

(3) Basis for determination

A determination under this subsection of a consumer's ability to repay a residential mortgage loan shall include consideration of the consumer's credit history, current income, expected income the consumer is reasonably assured of receiving, current obligations, debt-to-income ratio or the residual income the consumer will have after paying non-mortgage debt and mortgage-related obligations, employment status, and other financial resources other than the consumer's equity in the dwelling or real property that secures repayment of the loan. A creditor shall determine the ability of the consumer to repay using a payment schedule that fully amortizes the loan over the term of the loan.

(4) Income verification

A creditor making a residential mortgage loan shall verify amounts of income or assets that such creditor relies on to determine repayment ability, including expected income or assets, by reviewing the consumer's Internal Revenue Service Form W-2, tax returns, payroll receipts, financial institution records, or other third-party documents that provide reasonably reliable evidence of the consumer's income or assets. In order to safeguard against fraudulent reporting, any consideration of a consumer's income history in making a determination under this subsection shall include the verification of such income by the use of—

(A) Internal Revenue Service transcripts of tax returns; or

(B) a method that quickly and effectively verifies income documentation by a third party subject to rules prescribed by the Bureau.

(5) Exemption

With respect to loans made, guaranteed, or insured by Federal departments or agencies identified in subsection (b)(3)(B)(ii), such departments or agencies may exempt refinancings under a streamlined refinancing from this income verification requirement as long as the following conditions are met:

(A) The consumer is not 30 days or more past due on the prior existing residential mortgage loan.

(B) The refinancing does not increase the principal balance outstanding on the prior existing residential mortgage loan, except to the extent of fees and charges allowed by the department or agency making, guaranteeing, or insuring the refinancing.

(C) Total points and fees (as defined in section 1602(aa)(4) of this title, other than bona fide third party charges not retained by the mortgage originator, creditor, or an affiliate of the creditor or mortgage originator) payable in connection with the refinancing do not exceed 3 percent of the total new loan amount.

(D) The interest rate on the refinanced loan is lower than the interest rate of the original loan, unless the borrower is refinancing from an adjustable rate to a fixed-rate loan, under guidelines that the department or agency shall establish for loans they make, guarantee, or issue.

(E) The refinancing is subject to a payment schedule that will fully amortize the refinancing in accordance with the regulations prescribed by the department or agency making, guaranteeing, or insuring the refinancing.

(F) The terms of the refinancing do not result in a balloon payment, as defined in subsection (b)(2)(A)(ii).

(G) Both the residential mortgage loan being refinanced and the refinancing satisfy all requirements of the department or agency making, guaranteeing, or insuring the refinancing.

(6) Nonstandard loans

(A) Variable rate loans that defer repayment of any principal or interest

For purposes of determining, under this subsection, a consumer's ability to repay a variable rate residential mortgage loan that allows or requires the consumer to defer the repayment of any principal or interest, the creditor shall use a fully amortizing repayment schedule.

(B) Interest-only loans

For purposes of determining, under this subsection, a consumer's ability to repay a residential mortgage loan that permits or requires the payment of interest only, the creditor shall use the payment amount required to amortize the loan by its final maturity.

(C) Calculation for negative amortization

In making any determination under this subsection, a creditor shall also take into consideration any balance increase that may accrue from any negative amortization provision.

(D) Calculation process

For purposes of making any determination under this subsection, a creditor shall calculate the monthly payment amount for principal and interest on any residential mortgage loan by assuming—

(i) the loan proceeds are fully disbursed on the date of the consummation of the loan;

(ii) the loan is to be repaid in substantially equal monthly amortizing payments for principal and interest over the entire term of the loan with no balloon payment, unless the loan contract requires more rapid repayment (including balloon payment), in which case the calculation shall be made (I) in accordance with regulations prescribed by the Bureau, with respect to any loan which has an annual percentage rate that does not exceed the average prime offer rate for a comparable transaction, as of the date the interest rate is set, by 1.5 or more percentage points for a first lien residential mortgage loan; and by 3.5 or more percentage points for a subordinate lien residential mortgage loan; or (II) using the contract's repayment schedule, with respect to a loan which has an annual percentage rate, as of the date the interest rate is set, that is at least 1.5 percentage points above the average prime offer rate for a first lien residential mortgage loan; and 3.5 percentage points above the average prime offer rate for a subordinate lien residential mortgage loan; and

(iii) the interest rate over the entire term of the loan is a fixed rate equal to the fully indexed rate at the time of the loan closing, without considering the introductory rate.

(E) Refinance of hybrid loans with current lender

In considering any application for refinancing an existing hybrid loan by the creditor into a standard loan to be made by the same creditor in any case in which there would be a reduction in monthly payment and the mortgagor has not been delinquent on any payment on the existing hybrid loan, the creditor may—

(i) consider the mortgagor's good standing on the existing mortgage;

(ii) consider if the extension of new credit would prevent a likely default should the original mortgage reset and give such concerns a higher priority as an acceptable underwriting practice; and

(iii) offer rate discounts and other favorable terms to such mortgagor that would be available to new customers with high credit ratings based on such underwriting practice.

(7) Fully-indexed rate defined

For purposes of this subsection, the term "fully indexed rate" means the index rate prevailing on a residential mortgage loan at the time the loan is made plus the margin that will apply after the expiration of any introductory interest rates.

(8) Reverse mortgages and bridge loans

This subsection shall not apply with respect to any reverse mortgage or temporary or bridge loan with a term of 12 months or less, including to any loan to purchase a new dwelling where the consumer plans to sell a different dwelling within 12 months.

(9) Seasonal income

If documented income, including income from a small business, is a repayment source for a residential mortgage loan, a creditor may consider the seasonality and irregularity of such income in the underwriting of and scheduling of payments for such credit.

(b) Presumption of ability to repay

(1) In general

Any creditor with respect to any residential mortgage loan, and any assignee of such loan subject to liability under this subchapter, may presume that the loan has met the requirements of subsection (a), if the loan is a qualified mortgage.

(2) Definitions

For purposes of this subsection, the following definitions shall apply:

(A) Qualified mortgage

The term "qualified mortgage" means any residential mortgage loan—

(i) for which the regular periodic payments for the loan may not—

(I) result in an increase of the principal balance; or

(II) except as provided in subparagraph (E), allow the consumer to defer repayment of principal;

(ii) except as provided in subparagraph (E), the terms of which do not result in a balloon payment, where a "balloon payment" is a scheduled payment that is more than twice as large as the average of earlier scheduled payments;

(iii) for which the income and financial resources relied upon to qualify the obligors on the loan are verified and documented;

(iv) in the case of a fixed rate loan, for which the underwriting process is based on a payment schedule that fully amortizes the loan over the loan term and takes into account all applicable taxes, insurance, and assessments;

(v) in the case of an adjustable rate loan, for which the underwriting is based on the maximum rate permitted under the loan during the first 5 years, and a payment schedule that fully amortizes the loan over the loan term and takes into account all applicable taxes, insurance, and assessments;

(vi) that complies with any guidelines or regulations established by the Bureau relating to ratios of total monthly debt to monthly income or alternative measures of ability to pay regular expenses after payment of total monthly debt, taking into account the income levels of the borrower and such other factors as the Bureau may determine relevant and consistent with the purposes described in paragraph (3)(B)(i);

(vii) for which the total points and fees (as defined in subparagraph (C)) payable in connection with the loan do not exceed 3 percent of the total loan amount;

(viii) for which the term of the loan does not exceed 30 years, except as such term may be extended under paragraph (3), such as in high-cost areas; and

(ix) in the case of a reverse mortgage (except for the purposes of subsection (a) of this section, to the extent that such mortgages are exempt altogether from those requirements), a reverse mortgage which meets the standards for a qualified mortgage, as set by the Bureau in rules that are consistent with the purposes of this subsection.

(B) Average prime offer rate

The term "average prime offer rate" means the average prime offer rate for a comparable transaction as of the date on which the interest rate for the transaction is set, as published by the Bureau.

(C) Points and fees

(i) In general

For purposes of subparagraph (A), the term "points and fees" means points and fees as defined by section 1602(aa)(4) of this title (other than bona fide third party charges not retained by the mortgage originator, creditor, or an affiliate of the creditor or mortgage originator).

(ii) Computation

For purposes of computing the total points and fees under this subparagraph, the total points and fees shall exclude either of the amounts described in the following subclauses, but not both:

(I) Up to and including 2 bona fide discount points payable by the consumer in connection with the mortgage, but only if the interest rate from which the mortgage's interest rate will be discounted does not exceed by more than 1 percentage point the average prime offer rate.

(II) Unless 2 bona fide discount points have been excluded under subclause (I), up to and including 1 bona fide discount point payable by the consumer in connection with the mortgage, but only if the interest rate from which the mortgage's interest rate will be discounted does not exceed by more than 2 percentage points the average prime offer rate.

(iii) Bona fide discount points defined

For purposes of clause (ii), the term "bona fide discount points" means loan discount points which are knowingly paid by the consumer for the purpose of reducing, and which in fact result in a bona fide reduction of, the interest rate or time-price differential applicable to the mortgage.

(iv) Interest rate reduction

Subclauses (I) and (II) of clause (ii) shall not apply to discount points used to purchase an interest rate reduction unless the amount of the interest rate reduction purchased is reasonably consistent with established industry norms and practices for secondary mortgage market transactions.

(D) Smaller loans

The Bureau shall prescribe rules adjusting the criteria under subparagraph (A)(vii) in order to permit lenders that extend smaller loans to meet the requirements of the presumption of compliance under paragraph (1). In prescribing such rules, the Bureau shall consider the potential impact of such rules on rural areas and other areas where home values are lower.

(E) Balloon loans

The Bureau may, by regulation, provide that the term "qualified mortgage" includes a balloon loan—

(i) that meets all of the criteria for a qualified mortgage under subparagraph (A) (except clauses (i)(II), (ii), (iv), and (v) of such subparagraph);

(ii) for which the creditor makes a determination that the consumer is able to make all scheduled payments, except the balloon payment, out of income or assets other than the collateral;

(iii) for which the underwriting is based on a payment schedule that fully amortizes the loan over a period of not more than 30 years and takes into account all applicable taxes, insurance, and assessments; and

(iv) that is extended by a creditor that—

(I) operates predominantly in rural or underserved areas;

(II) together with all affiliates, has total annual residential mortgage loan originations that do not exceed a limit set by the Bureau;

(III) retains the balloon loans in portfolio; and

(IV) meets any asset size threshold and any other criteria as the Bureau may establish, consistent with the purposes of this part.

(3) Regulations

(A) In general

The Bureau shall prescribe regulations to carry out the purposes of this subsection.

(B) Revision of safe harbor criteria

(i) In general

The Bureau may prescribe regulations that revise, add to, or subtract from the criteria that define a qualified mortgage upon a finding that such regulations are necessary or proper to ensure that responsible, affordable mortgage credit remains available to consumers in a manner consistent with the purposes of this section, necessary and appropriate to effectuate the purposes of this section and section 1639b of this title, to prevent circumvention or evasion thereof, or to facilitate compliance with such sections.

(ii) Loan definition

The following agencies shall, in consultation with the Bureau, prescribe rules defining the types of loans they insure, guarantee, or administer, as the case may be, that are qualified mortgages for purposes of paragraph (2)(A), and such rules may revise, add to, or subtract from the criteria used to define a qualified mortgage under paragraph (2)(A), upon a finding that such rules are consistent with the purposes of this section and section 1639b of this title, to prevent circumvention or evasion thereof, or to facilitate compliance with such sections:

(I) The Department of Housing and Urban Development, with regard to mortgages insured under the National Housing Act (12 U.S.C. 1707 et seq.).

(II) The Department of Veterans Affairs, with regard to a loan made or guaranteed by the Secretary of Veterans Affairs.

(III) The Department of Agriculture, with regard[2] loans guaranteed by the Secretary of Agriculture pursuant to 42 U.S.C. 1472(h).

---

2 So in original. Probably should be followed by "to."

(IV) The Rural Housing Service, with regard to loans insured by the Rural Housing Service.

(c) Prohibition on certain prepayment penalties

(1) Prohibited on certain loans

(A) In general

A residential mortgage loan that is not a "qualified mortgage", as defined under subsection (b)(2), may not contain terms under which a consumer must pay a prepayment penalty for paying all or part of the principal after the loan is consummated.

(B) Exclusions

For purposes of this subsection, a "qualified mortgage" may not include a residential mortgage loan that—

(i) has an adjustable rate; or

(ii) has an annual percentage rate that exceeds the average prime offer rate for a comparable transaction, as of the date the interest rate is set—

(I) by 1.5 or more percentage points, in the case of a first lien residential mortgage loan having a original principal obligation amount that is equal to or less than the amount of the maximum limitation on the original principal obligation of mortgage in effect for a residence of the applicable size, as of the date of such interest rate set, pursuant to the 6th sentence of section 1454(a)(2) of Title 12;

(II) by 2.5 or more percentage points, in the case of a first lien residential mortgage loan having a original principal obligation amount that is more than the amount of the maximum limitation on the original principal obligation of mortgage in effect for a residence of the applicable size, as of the date of such interest rate set, pursuant to the 6th sentence of section 1454(a)(2) of Title 12; and

(III) by 3.5 or more percentage points, in the case of a subordinate lien residential mortgage loan.

(2) Publication of average prime offer rate and APR thresholds

The Bureau—

(A) shall publish, and update at least weekly, average prime offer rates;

(B) may publish multiple rates based on varying types of mortgage transactions; and

(C) shall adjust the thresholds established under subclause (I), (II), and (III) of paragraph (1)(B)(ii) as necessary to reflect significant changes in market conditions and to effectuate the purposes of the Mortgage Reform and Anti-Predatory Lending Act.

(3) Phased-out penalties on qualified mortgages

A qualified mortgage (as defined in subsection (b)(2)) may not contain terms under which a consumer must pay a prepayment penalty for paying all or part of the principal after the loan is consummated in excess of the following limitations:

(A) During the 1-year period beginning on the date the loan is consummated, the prepayment penalty shall not exceed an amount equal to 3 percent of the outstanding balance on the loan.

(B) During the 1-year period beginning after the period described in subparagraph (A), the prepayment penalty shall not exceed an amount equal to 2 percent of the outstanding balance on the loan.

(C) During the 1-year period beginning after the 1-year period described in subparagraph (B), the prepayment penalty shall not exceed an amount equal to 1 percent of the outstanding balance on the loan.

(D) After the end of the 3-year period beginning on the date the loan is consummated, no prepayment penalty may be imposed on a qualified mortgage.

(4) Option for no prepayment penalty required

A creditor may not offer a consumer a residential mortgage loan product that has a prepayment penalty for paying all or part of the principal after the loan is consummated as a term of the loan without offering the consumer a residential mortgage loan product that does not have a prepayment penalty as a term of the loan.

(d) Single premium credit insurance prohibited

No creditor may finance, directly or indirectly, in connection with any residential mortgage loan or with any extension of credit under an open end consumer credit plan secured by the principal dwelling of the consumer, any credit life, credit disability, credit unemployment, or credit property insurance, or any other accident, loss-of-income, life, or health insurance, or any payments directly or indirectly for any debt cancellation or suspension agreement or contract, except that—

(1) insurance premiums or debt cancellation or suspension fees calculated and paid in full on a monthly basis shall not be considered financed by the creditor; and

(2) this subsection shall not apply to credit unemployment insurance for which the unemployment insurance premiums are reasonable, the creditor receives no direct or indirect compensation in connection with the unemployment insurance premiums, and the unemployment insurance premiums are paid pursuant to another insurance contract and not paid to an affiliate of the creditor.

(e) Arbitration

(1) In general

No residential mortgage loan and no extension of credit under an open end consumer credit plan secured by the principal dwelling of the consumer may include terms which require arbitration or any other nonjudicial procedure as the method for resolving any controversy or settling any claims arising out of the transaction.

(2) Post-controversy agreements

Subject to paragraph (3), paragraph (1) shall not be construed as limiting the right of the consumer and the creditor or any assignee to agree to arbitration or any other nonjudicial procedure as the method for resolving any controversy at any time after a dispute or claim under the transaction arises.

(3) No waiver of statutory cause of action

No provision of any residential mortgage loan or of any extension of credit under an open end consumer credit plan secured by the principal dwelling of the consumer, and no other agreement between the consumer and the creditor relating to the residential mortgage loan or extension of credit referred to in paragraph (1), shall be applied or interpreted so as to bar a consumer from bringing an action in an appropriate district court of the United States, or any other court of competent jurisdiction, pursuant to section 1640 of this title or any other provision of law, for damages or other relief in connection with any alleged violation of this section, any other provision of this subchapter, or any other Federal law.

(f) Mortgages with negative amortization

No creditor may extend credit to a borrower in connection with a consumer credit transaction under an open or closed end consumer credit plan secured by a dwelling or residential real property that includes a dwelling, other than a reverse mortgage, that provides or permits a payment plan that may, at any time over the term of the extension of credit, result in negative amortization unless, before such transaction is consummated—

(1) the creditor provides the consumer with a statement that—

(A) the pending transaction will or may, as the case may be, result in negative amortization;

(B) describes negative amortization in such manner as the Bureau shall prescribe;

(C) negative amortization increases the outstanding principal balance of the account; and

(D) negative amortization reduces the consumer's equity in the dwelling or real property; and

(2) in the case of a first-time borrower with respect to a residential mortgage loan that is not a qualified mortgage, the first-time borrower provides the creditor with sufficient documentation to demonstrate that the consumer received homeownership counseling from organizations or counselors certified by the Secretary of Housing and Urban Development as competent to provide such counseling.

(g) Protection against loss of anti-deficiency protection

(1) Definition

For purposes of this subsection, the term "anti-deficiency law" means the law of any State which provides that, in the event of foreclosure on the residential property of a consumer securing a mortgage, the consumer is not liable, in accordance with the terms and limitations of such State law, for any deficiency between the sale price obtained on such property through foreclosure and the outstanding balance of the mortgage.

(2) Notice at time of consummation

In the case of any residential mortgage loan that is, or upon consummation will be, subject to protection under an anti-deficiency law, the creditor or mortgage originator shall provide a written notice to the consumer describing the protection provided by the anti-deficiency law and the significance for the consumer of the loss of such protection before such loan is consummated.

(3) Notice before refinancing that would cause loss of protection

In the case of any residential mortgage loan that is subject to protection under an anti-deficiency law, if a creditor or mortgage originator provides an application to a consumer, or receives an application from a consumer, for any type of refinancing for such loan that would cause the loan to lose the protection of such antideficiency law, the creditor or mortgage originator shall provide a written notice to the consumer describing the protection provided by the anti-deficiency law and the significance for the consumer of the loss of such protection before any agreement for any such refinancing is consummated.

(h) Policy regarding acceptance of partial payment

In the case of any residential mortgage loan, a creditor shall disclose prior to settlement or, in the case of a person becoming a creditor with respect to an existing residential mortgage loan, at the time such person becomes a creditor—

(1) the creditor's policy regarding the acceptance of partial payments; and

(2) if partial payments are accepted, how such payments will be applied to such mortgage and if such payments will be placed in escrow.

(i) Timeshare plans

This section and any regulations promulgated under this section do not apply to an extension of credit relating to a plan described in section 101(53D) of Title 11.

§ 1639d. Escrow or Impound Accounts Relating to Certain Consumer Credit Transactions

(a) In general

Except as provided in subsection (b), (c), (d), or (e), a creditor, in connection with the consummation of a consumer credit transaction secured by a first lien on the principal dwelling of the consumer, other than a consumer credit transaction under an open end credit plan or a reverse mortgage, shall establish, before the consummation of such transaction, an escrow or impound account for the payment of taxes and hazard insurance, and, if applicable, flood insurance, mortgage insurance, ground rents, and any other required periodic payments or premiums with respect to the property or the loan terms, as provided in, and in accordance with, this section.

(b) When required

No impound, trust, or other type of account for the payment of property taxes, insurance premiums, or other purposes relating to the property may be required as a condition of a real property sale contract or a loan secured by a first deed of trust or mortgage on the principal dwelling of the consumer, other than a consumer credit transaction under an open end credit plan or a reverse mortgage, except when—

(1) any such impound, trust, or other type of escrow or impound account for such purposes is required by Federal or State law;

(2) a loan is made, guaranteed, or insured by a State or Federal governmental lending or insuring agency;

(3) the transaction is secured by a first mortgage or lien on the consumer's principal dwelling having an original principal obligation amount that—

(A) does not exceed the amount of the maximum limitation on the original principal obligation of mortgage in effect for a residence of the applicable size, as of the date such interest rate set, pursuant to the sixth sentence of section 1454(a)(2) of Title 12, and the annual percentage rate will exceed the average prime offer rate as defined in section 1639c of this title by 1.5 or more percentage points; or

(B) exceeds the amount of the maximum limitation on the original principal obligation of mortgage in effect for a residence of the applicable size, as of the date such interest rate set, pursuant to the sixth sentence of section 1454(a)(2) of Title 12, and the annual percentage rate will exceed the average prime offer rate as defined in section 1639c of this title by 2.5 or more percentage points; or

(4) so required pursuant to regulation.

(c) Exemptions

(1) In General

The Bureau may, by regulation, exempt from the requirements of subsection (a) a creditor that—

(A) operates predominantly in rural or underserved areas;

(B) together with all affiliates, has total annual mortgage loan originations that do not exceed a limit set by the Bureau;

(C) retains its mortgage loan originations in portfolio; and

(D) meets any asset size threshold and any other criteria the Bureau may establish, consistent with the purposes of this subtitle.

(2) Treatment of loans held by smaller institutions

The Bureau shall, by regulation, exempt from the requirements of subsection (a) any loan made by an insured depository institution or an insured credit union secured by a first lien on the principal dwelling of a consumer if—

(A) the insured depository institution or insured credit union has assets of $10,000,000,000 or less;

(B) during the preceding calendar year, the insured depository institution or insured credit union and its affiliates originated 1,000 or fewer loans secured by a first lien on a principal dwelling; and

(C) the transaction satisfies the criteria in sections 1026.35(b)(2)(iii)(A), 1026.35(b)(2)(iii)(D), and 1026.35(b)(2)(v) of title 12, Code of Federal Regulations, or any successor regulation.

(d) Duration of mandatory escrow or impound account

An escrow or impound account established pursuant to subsection (b) shall remain in existence for a minimum period of 5 years, beginning with the date of the consummation of the loan, unless and until—

(1) such borrower has sufficient equity in the dwelling securing the consumer credit transaction so as to no longer be required to maintain private mortgage insurance;

(2) such borrower is delinquent;

(3) such borrower otherwise has not complied with the legal obligation, as established by rule; or

(4) the underlying mortgage establishing the account is terminated.

(e) Limited exemptions for loans secured by shares in a cooperative or in which an association must maintain a master insurance policy

Escrow accounts need not be established for loans secured by shares in a cooperative. Insurance premiums need not be included in escrow accounts for loans secured by dwellings or units, where the borrower must join an association as a condition of ownership, and that association has an obligation to the dwelling or unit owners to maintain a master policy insuring the dwellings or units.

(f) Clarification on escrow accounts for loans not meeting statutory test

For mortgages not covered by the requirements of subsection (b), no provision of this section shall be construed as precluding the establishment of an impound, trust, or other type of account for the payment of property taxes, insurance premiums, or other purposes relating to the property—

(1) on terms mutually agreeable to the parties to the loan;

(2) at the discretion of the lender or servicer, as provided by the contract between the lender or servicer and the borrower; or

(3) pursuant to the requirements for the escrowing of flood insurance payments for regulated lending institutions in section 102(d) of the Flood Disaster Protection Act of 1973.

(g) Administration of mandatory escrow or impound accounts

(1) In general

Except as may otherwise be provided for in this subchapter or in regulations prescribed by the Bureau, escrow or impound accounts established pursuant to subsection (b) shall be established in a federally insured depository institution or credit union.

(2) Administration

Except as provided in this section or regulations prescribed under this section, an escrow or impound account subject to this section shall be administered in accordance with—

(A) the Real Estate Settlement Procedures Act of 1974 and regulations prescribed under such Act;

(B) the Flood Disaster Protection Act of 1973 and regulations prescribed under such Act; and

(C) the law of the State, if applicable, where the real property securing the consumer credit transaction is located.

(3) Applicability of payment of interest

If prescribed by applicable State or Federal law, each creditor shall pay interest to the consumer on the amount held in any impound, trust, or escrow account that is subject to this section in the manner as prescribed by that applicable State or Federal law.

(4) Penalty coordination with RESPA

Any action or omission on the part of any person which constitutes a violation of the Real Estate Settlement Procedures Act of 1974 or any regulation prescribed under such Act for which the person has paid any fine, civil money penalty, or other damages shall not give rise to any additional fine, civil money penalty, or other damages under this section, unless the action or omission also constitutes a direct violation of this section.

(h) Disclosures relating to mandatory escrow or impound account

In the case of any impound, trust, or escrow account that is required under subsection (b), the creditor shall disclose by written notice to the consumer at least 3 business days before the consummation of the consumer credit transaction giving rise to such account or in accordance with timeframes established in prescribed regulations the following information:

(1) The fact that an escrow or impound account will be established at consummation of the transaction.

(2) The amount required at closing to initially fund the escrow or impound account.

(3) The amount, in the initial year after the consummation of the transaction, of the estimated taxes and hazard insurance, including flood insurance, if applicable, and any other required periodic payments or premiums that reflects, as appropriate, either the taxable assessed value of the real property securing the transaction, including the value of any improvements on the property or to be constructed on the property (whether or not such construction will be financed from the proceeds of the transaction) or the replacement costs of the property.

(4) The estimated monthly amount payable to be escrowed for taxes, hazard insurance (including flood insurance, if applicable) and any other required periodic payments or premiums.

(5) The fact that, if the consumer chooses to terminate the account in the future, the consumer will become responsible for the payment of all taxes, hazard insurance, and flood insurance, if applicable, as well as any other required periodic payments or premiums on the property unless a new escrow or impound account is established.

(6) Such other information as the Bureau determines necessary for the protection of the consumer.

(i) Definitions

For purposes of this section, the following definitions shall apply:

(1) Flood insurance

The term "flood insurance" means flood insurance coverage provided under the national flood insurance program pursuant to the National Flood Insurance Act of 1968.

(2) Hazard insurance

The term "hazard insurance" shall have the same meaning as provided for "hazard insurance", "casualty insurance", "homeowner's insurance", or other similar term under the law of the State where the real property securing the consumer credit transaction is located.

(3) Insured credit union

The term "insured credit union" has the meaning given the term in section 1752 of Title 12.

(4) Insured depository institution

The term "insured depository institution" has the meaning given the term in section 1813 of Title 12.

(j) Disclosure notice required for consumers who waive escrow services

(1) In general

If—

(A) an impound, trust, or other type of account for the payment of property taxes, insurance premiums, or other purposes relating to real property securing a consumer credit transaction is not established in connection with the transaction; or

(B) a consumer chooses, and provides written notice to the creditor or servicer of such choice, at any time after such an account is established in connection with any such transaction and in accordance with any statute, regulation, or contractual agreement, to close such account,

the creditor or servicer shall provide a timely and clearly written disclosure to the consumer that advises the consumer of the responsibilities of the consumer and implications for the consumer in the absence of any such account.

(2) Disclosure requirements

Any disclosure provided to a consumer under paragraph (1) shall include the following:

(A) Information concerning any applicable fees or costs associated with either the non-establishment of any such account at the time of the transaction, or any subsequent closure of any such account.

(B) A clear and prominent statement that the consumer is responsible for personally and directly paying the non-escrowed items, in addition to paying the mortgage loan payment, in the absence of any such account, and the fact that the costs for taxes, insurance, and related fees can be substantial.

(C) A clear explanation of the consequences of any failure to pay non-escrowed items, including the possible requirement for the forced placement of insurance by the creditor or servicer and the potentially higher cost (including any potential commission payments to the servicer) or reduced coverage for the consumer in the event of any such creditor-placed insurance.

(D) Such other information as the Bureau determines necessary for the protection of the consumer.

§ 1639e. Appraisal Independence Requirements

(a) In general

It shall be unlawful, in extending credit or in providing any services for a consumer credit transaction secured by the principal dwelling of the consumer, to engage in any act or practice that violates appraisal independence as described in or pursuant to regulations prescribed under this section.

(b) Appraisal independence

For purposes of subsection (a), acts or practices that violate appraisal independence shall include—

(1) any appraisal of a property offered as security for repayment of the consumer credit transaction that is conducted in connection with such transaction in which a person with an interest in the underlying transaction compensates, coerces, extorts, colludes, instructs, induces, bribes, or intimidates a person, appraisal management company, firm, or other entity conducting or involved in an appraisal, or attempts, to compensate, coerce, extort, collude, instruct, induce, bribe, or intimidate such a person, for the purpose of causing the appraised value assigned, under the appraisal, to the property to be based on any factor other than the independent judgment of the appraiser;

(2) mischaracterizing, or suborning any mischaracterization of, the appraised value of the property securing the extension of the credit;

(3) seeking to influence an appraiser or otherwise to encourage a targeted value in order to facilitate the making or pricing of the transaction; and

(4) withholding or threatening to withhold timely payment for an appraisal report or for appraisal services rendered when the appraisal report or services are provided for in accordance with the contract between the parties.

(c) Exceptions

The requirements of subsection (b) shall not be construed as prohibiting a mortgage lender, mortgage broker, mortgage banker, real estate broker, appraisal management company, employee of an appraisal management company, consumer, or any other person with an interest in a real estate transaction from asking an appraiser to undertake 1 or more of the following:

(1) Consider additional, appropriate property information, including the consideration of additional comparable properties to make or support an appraisal.

(2) Provide further detail, substantiation, or explanation for the appraiser's value conclusion.

(3) Correct errors in the appraisal report.

(d) Prohibitions on conflicts of interest

No certified or licensed appraiser conducting, and no appraisal management company procuring or facilitating, an appraisal in connection with a consumer credit transaction secured by the principal dwelling of a consumer may have a direct or indirect interest, financial or otherwise, in the property or transaction involving the appraisal.

(e) Mandatory reporting

Any mortgage lender, mortgage broker, mortgage banker, real estate broker, appraisal management company, employee of an appraisal management company, or any other person involved in a real estate transaction involving an appraisal in connection with a consumer credit transaction secured by the principal dwelling of a consumer who has a reasonable basis to believe an appraiser is failing to comply with the Uniform Standards of Professional Appraisal Practice, is violating applicable laws, or is otherwise engaging in unethical or unprofessional conduct, shall refer the matter to the applicable State appraiser certifying and licensing agency.

(f) No extension of credit

In connection with a consumer credit transaction secured by a consumer's principal dwelling, a creditor who knows, at or before loan consummation, of a violation of the appraisal independence standards established in subsections (b) or (d) shall not extend credit based on such appraisal unless the creditor documents that the creditor has acted with reasonable diligence to determine that the appraisal does not materially misstate or misrepresent the value of such dwelling.

(g) Rules and interpretive guidelines

(1) In general

Except as provided under paragraph (2), the Board, the Comptroller of the Currency, the Federal Deposit Insurance Corporation, the National Credit Union Administration Board, the Federal Housing Finance Agency, and the Bureau may jointly issue rules, interpretive guidelines, and general statements of policy with respect to acts or practices that violate appraisal independence in the provision of mortgage lending services for a consumer credit transaction secured by the principal dwelling of the consumer and mortgage brokerage services for such a transaction, within the meaning of subsections (a), (b), (c), (d), (e), (f), (h), and (i).

(2) Interim final regulations

The Board shall, for purposes of this section, prescribe interim final regulations no later than 90 days after July 21, 2010, defining with specificity acts or practices that violate appraisal independence in the provision of mortgage lending services for a consumer credit transaction secured by the principal dwelling of the consumer or mortgage brokerage services for such a transaction and defining any terms in this section or such regulations. Rules prescribed by the Board under this paragraph shall be deemed to be rules prescribed by the agencies jointly under paragraph (1).

(h) Appraisal report portability

Consistent with the requirements of this section, the Board, the Comptroller of the Currency, the Federal Deposit Insurance Corporation, the National Credit Union Administration Board, the Federal Housing Finance Agency, and the Bureau may jointly issue regulations that address the issue of appraisal report portability, including regulations that ensure the portability of the appraisal report between lenders for a consumer credit transaction secured by a 1–4 unit single family residence that is the principal dwelling of the consumer, or mortgage brokerage services for such a transaction.

(i) Customary and reasonable fee

(1) In general

Lenders and their agents shall compensate fee appraisers at a rate that is customary and reasonable for appraisal services performed in the market area of the property being appraised. Evidence for such fees may be established by objective third-party information, such as government agency fee schedules, academic studies, and independent private sector surveys. Fee studies shall exclude assignments ordered by known appraisal management companies.

(2) Fee appraiser definition

(A) In general

For purposes of this section, the term "fee appraiser" means a person who is not an employee of the mortgage loan originator or appraisal management company engaging the appraiser and is—

(i) a State licensed or certified appraiser who receives a fee for performing an appraisal and certifies that the appraisal has been prepared in accordance with the Uniform Standards of Professional Appraisal Practice; or

(ii) a company not subject to the requirements of section 3353 of Title 12 that utilizes the services of State licensed or certified appraisers and receives a fee for performing appraisals in accordance with the Uniform Standards of Professional Appraisal Practice.

(B) Rule of construction related to appraisal donations

If a fee appraiser voluntarily donates appraisal services to an organization eligible to receive tax-deductible charitable contributions, such voluntary donation shall be considered customary and reasonable for the purposes of paragraph (1).

(3) Exception for complex assignments

In the case of an appraisal involving a complex assignment, the customary and reasonable fee may reflect the increased time, difficulty, and scope of the work required for such an appraisal and include an amount over and above the customary and reasonable fee for non-complex assignments.

(j) Sunset

Effective on the date the interim final regulations are promulgated pursuant to subsection (g), the Home Valuation Code of Conduct announced by the Federal Housing Finance Agency on December 23, 2008, shall have no force or effect.

(k) Penalties

(1) First violation

In addition to the enforcement provisions referred to in section 1640 of this title, each person who violates this section shall forfeit and pay a civil penalty of not more than $10,000 for each day any such violation continues.

(2) Subsequent violations

In the case of any person on whom a civil penalty has been imposed under paragraph (1), paragraph (1) shall be applied by substituting "$20,000" for "$10,000" with respect to all subsequent violations.

(3) Assessment

The agency referred to in subsection (a) or (c) of section 1607 of this title with respect to any person described in paragraph (1) shall assess any penalty under this subsection to which such person is subject.

§ 1639f. Requirements for Prompt Crediting of Home Loan Payments

(a) In general

In connection with a consumer credit transaction secured by a consumer's principal dwelling, no servicer shall fail to credit a payment to the consumer's loan account as of the date of receipt, except when a delay in crediting does not result in any charge to the consumer or in the reporting of negative information to a consumer reporting agency, except as required in subsection (b).

(b) Exception

If a servicer specifies in writing requirements for the consumer to follow in making payments, but accepts a payment that does not conform to the requirements, the servicer shall credit the payment as of 5 days after receipt.

§ 1639g. Requests for Payoff Amounts of Home Loan

A creditor or servicer of a home loan shall send an accurate payoff balance within a reasonable time, but in no case more than 7 business days, after the receipt of a written request for such balance from or on behalf of the borrower.

§ 1639h. Property Appraisal Requirements

(a) In general

A creditor may not extend credit in the form of a higher-risk mortgage to any consumer without first obtaining a written appraisal of the property to be mortgaged prepared in accordance with the requirements of this section.

(b) Appraisal requirements

(1) Physical property visit

Subject to the rules prescribed under paragraph (4), an appraisal of property to be secured by a higher-risk mortgage does not meet the requirement of this section unless it is performed by a certified or licensed appraiser who conducts a physical property visit of the interior of the mortgaged property.

(2) Second appraisal under certain circumstances

(A) In general

If the purpose of a higher-risk mortgage is to finance the purchase or acquisition of the mortgaged property from a person within 180 days of the purchase or acquisition of such property by that person at a price that was lower than the current sale price of the property, the creditor shall obtain a second appraisal from a different certified or licensed appraiser. The second appraisal shall include an analysis of the difference in sale prices, changes in market conditions, and any improvements made to the property between the date of the previous sale and the current sale.

(B) No cost to applicant

The cost of any second appraisal required under subparagraph (A) may not be charged to the applicant.

(3) Certified or licensed appraiser defined

For purposes of this section, the term "certified or licensed appraiser" means a person who—

(A) is, at a minimum, certified or licensed by the State in which the property to be appraised is located; and

(B) performs each appraisal in conformity with the Uniform Standards of Professional Appraisal Practice and title XI of the Financial Institutions Reform, Recovery, and Enforcement Act of 1989, and the regulations prescribed under such title, as in effect on the date of the appraisal.

(4) Regulations

(A) In general

The Board, the Comptroller of the Currency, the Federal Deposit Insurance Corporation, the National Credit Union Administration Board, the Federal Housing Finance Agency, and the Bureau shall jointly prescribe regulations to implement this section.

(B) Exemption

The agencies listed in subparagraph (A) may jointly exempt, by rule, a class of loans from the requirements of this subsection or subsection (a) if the agencies determine that the exemption is in the public interest and promotes the safety and soundness of creditors.

(c) Free copy of appraisal

A creditor shall provide 1 copy of each appraisal conducted in accordance with this section in connection with a higher-risk mortgage to the applicant without charge, and at least 3 days prior to the transaction closing date.

(d) Consumer notification

At the time of the initial mortgage application, the applicant shall be provided with a statement by the creditor that any appraisal prepared for the mortgage is for the sole use of the creditor, and that the applicant may choose to have a separate appraisal conducted at the expense of the applicant.

(e) Violations

In addition to any other liability to any person under this subchapter, a creditor found to have willfully failed to obtain an appraisal as required in this section shall be liable to the applicant or borrower for the sum of $2,000.

(f) Higher-risk mortgage defined

For purposes of this section, the term "higher-risk mortgage" means a residential mortgage loan, other than a reverse mortgage loan that is a qualified mortgage, as defined in section 1639c of this title, secured by a principal dwelling—

(1) that is not a qualified mortgage, as defined in section 1639c of this title; and

(2) with an annual percentage rate that exceeds the average prime offer rate for a comparable transaction, as defined in section 1639c of this title, as of the date the interest rate is set—

(A) by 1.5 or more percentage points, in the case of a first lien residential mortgage loan having an original principal obligation amount that does not exceed the amount of the maximum limitation on the original principal obligation of mortgage in effect for a residence of the applicable size, as of the date of such interest rate set, pursuant to the sixth sentence of section 1454(a)(2) of Title 12;

(B) by 2.5 or more percentage points, in the case of a first lien residential mortgage loan having an original principal obligation amount that exceeds the amount of the maximum limitation on the original principal obligation of mortgage in effect for a residence of the applicable size, as of the date of such interest rate set, pursuant to the sixth sentence of section 1454(a)(2) of Title 12; and

(C) by 3.5 or more percentage points for a subordinate lien residential mortgage loan.

§ 1640 [CCPA § 130]. Civil Liability

(a) Individual or class action for damages; amount of award; factors determining amount of award

Except as otherwise provided in this section, any creditor who fails to comply with any requirement imposed under this part, including any requirement under section 1635 of this title, subsection (f) or (g) of section 1641 of this title, or part D or E of this subchapter with respect to any person is liable to such person in an amount equal to the sum of—

(1) any actual damage sustained by such person as a result of the failure;

(2)(A)(i) in the case of an individual action twice the amount of any finance charge in connection with the transaction, (ii) in the case of an individual action relating to a consumer lease under part E of this subchapter, 25 per centum of the total amount of monthly payments under the lease, except that the liability under this subparagraph shall not be less than $200 nor greater than $2,000, (iii) in the case of an individual action relating to an open end consumer credit plan that is not secured by real property or a dwelling, twice the amount of any finance charge in connection with the transaction, with a minimum of $500 and a maximum of $5,000, or such higher amount as may be appropriate in the case of an established pattern or practice of such failures;[1] or (iv) in the case of an individual action relating to a credit transaction not under

[1] So in original. The semicolon should probably be a comma.

an open end credit plan that is secured by real property or a dwelling, not less than $400 or greater than $4,000; or

(B) in the case of a class action, such amount as the court may allow, except that as to each member of the class no minimum recovery shall be applicable, and the total recovery under this subparagraph in any class action or series of class actions arising out of the same failure to comply by the same creditor shall not be more than the lesser of $1,000,000 or 1 per centum of the net worth of the creditor;

(3) in the case of any successful action to enforce the foregoing liability or in any action in which a person is determined to have a right of rescission under section 1635 or 1638(e)(7) of this title, the costs of the action, together with a reasonable attorney's fee as determined by the court; and

(4) in the case of a failure to comply with any requirement under section 1639 of this title, paragraph (1) or (2) of section 1639b(c) of this title, or section 1639c(a) of this title, an amount equal to the sum of all finance charges and fees paid by the consumer, unless the creditor demonstrates that the failure to comply is not material.

In determining the amount of award in any class action, the court shall consider, among other relevant factors, the amount of any actual damages awarded, the frequency and persistence of failures of compliance by the creditor, the resources of the creditor, the number of persons adversely affected, and the extent to which the creditor's failure of compliance was intentional. In connection with the disclosures referred to in subsections (a) and (b) of section 1637 of this title, a creditor shall have a liability determined under paragraph (2) only for failing to comply with the requirements of section 1635 of this title, 1637(a)[2] of this title, or any of paragraphs (4) through (13) of section 1637(b) of this title, or for failing to comply with disclosure requirements under State law for any term or item that the Bureau has determined to be substantially the same in meaning under section 1610(a)(2) of this title as any of the terms or items referred to in section 1637(a) of this title, or any of paragraphs (4) through (13) of section 1637(b) of this title. In connection with the disclosures referred to in subsection (c) or (d) of section 1637 of this title, a card issuer shall have a liability under this section only to a cardholder who pays a fee described in section 1637(c)(1)(A)(ii)(I) or section 1637(c)(4)(A)(i) of this title or who uses the credit card or charge card. In connection with the disclosures referred to in section 1638 of this title, a creditor shall have a liability determined under paragraph (2) only for failing to comply with the requirements of section 1635 of this title, of paragraph (2) (insofar as it requires a disclosure of the "amount financed"), (3), (4), (5), (6), or (9) of section 1638(a) of this title, or section 1638(b)(2)(C)(ii) of this title, of subparagraphs (A), (B), (D), (F), or (J) of section 1638(e)(2) of this title (for purposes of paragraph (2) or (4) of section 1638(e) of this title), or paragraph (4)(c), (6), (7), or (8) of section 1638(e) of this title, or for failing to comply with disclosure requirements under State law for any term which the Bureau has determined to be substantially the same in meaning under section 1610(a)(2) of this title as any of the terms referred to in any of those paragraphs of section 1638(a) of this title or section 1638(b)(2)(C)(ii) of this title. With respect to any failure to make disclosures required under this part or part D or E of this subchapter, liability shall be imposed only upon the creditor required to make disclosure, except as provided in section 1641 of this title.

(b) Correction of errors

A creditor or assignee has no liability under this section or section 1607 of this title or section 1611 of this title for any failure to comply with any requirement imposed under this part or part E, if within sixty days after discovering an error, whether pursuant to a final written examination report or notice issued under section 1607(e)(1) of this title or through the creditor's or assignee's own procedures, and prior to the institution of an action under this section or the receipt of written notice of the error from the obligor, the creditor or assignee notifies the person concerned of the error and

---

[2] So in original. Probably should be preceded by "section".

makes whatever adjustments in the appropriate account are necessary to assure that the person will not be required to pay an amount in excess of the charge actually disclosed, or the dollar equivalent of the annual percentage rate actually disclosed, whichever is lower.

(c) Unintentional violations; bona fide errors

A creditor or assignee may not be held liable in any action brought under this section or section 1635 of this title for a violation of this subchapter if the creditor or assignee shows by a preponderance of evidence that the violation was not intentional and resulted from a bona fide error notwithstanding the maintenance of procedures reasonably adapted to avoid any such error. Examples of a bona fide error include, but are not limited to, clerical, calculation, computer malfunction and programing, and printing errors, except that an error of legal judgment with respect to a person's obligations under this subchapter is not a bona fide error.

(d) Liability in transaction or lease involving multiple obligors

When there are multiple obligors in a consumer credit transaction or consumer lease, there shall be no more than one recovery of damages under subsection (a)(2) of this section for a violation of this subchapter.

(e) Jurisdiction of courts; limitations on actions; State attorney general enforcement

Except as provided in the subsequent sentence, any action under this section may be brought in any United States district court, or in any other court of competent jurisdiction, within one year from the date of the occurrence of the violation or, in the case of a violation involving a private education loan (as that term is defined in section 1650(a) of this title), 1 year from the date on which the first regular payment of principal is due under the loan. Any action under this section with respect to any violation of section 1639, 1639b, or 1639c of this title may be brought in any United States district court, or in any other court of competent jurisdiction, before the end of the 3-year period beginning on the date of the occurrence of the violation. This subsection does not bar a person from asserting a violation of this subchapter in an action to collect the debt which was brought more than one year from the date of the occurrence of the violation as a matter of defense by recoupment or set-off in such action, except as otherwise provided by State law. An action to enforce a violation of section 1639, 1639b, 1639c, 1639d, 1639e, 1639f, 1639g, or 1639h of this title may also be brought by the appropriate State attorney general in any appropriate United States district court, or any other court of competent jurisdiction, not later than 3 years after the date on which the violation occurs. The State attorney general shall provide prior written notice of any such civil action to the Federal agency responsible for enforcement under section 1607 of this title and shall provide the agency with a copy of the complaint. If prior notice is not feasible, the State attorney general shall provide notice to such agency immediately upon instituting the action. The Federal agency may—

(1) intervene in the action;

(2) upon intervening—

(A) remove the action to the appropriate United States district court, if it was not originally brought there; and

(B) be heard on all matters arising in the action; and

(3) file a petition for appeal.

(f) Good faith compliance with rule, regulation, or interpretation of Bureau or with interpretation or approval of duly authorized official or employee of Federal Reserve System

No provision of this section, section 1607(b) of this title, section 1607(c) of this title, section 1607(e) of this title, or section 1611 of this title imposing any liability shall apply to any act done or omitted in good faith in conformity with any rule, regulation, or interpretation thereof by the Bureau or in conformity with any interpretation or approval by an official or employee of the Federal Reserve System duly authorized by the Bureau to issue such interpretations or approvals under such procedures as the Bureau may prescribe therefor, notwithstanding that after such act or omission has occurred, such rule, regulation, interpretation, or approval is amended, rescinded, or determined by judicial or other authority to be invalid for any reason.

(g) Recovery for multiple failures to disclose

The multiple failure to disclose to any person any information required under this part or part D or E of this subchapter to be disclosed in connection with a single account under an open end consumer credit plan, other single consumer credit sale, consumer loan, consumer lease, or other extension of consumer credit, shall entitle the person to a single recovery under this section but continued failure to disclose after a recovery has been granted shall give rise to rights to additional recoveries. This subsection does not bar any remedy permitted by section 1635 of this title.

(h) Offset from amount owed to creditor or assignee; rights of defaulting consumer

A person may not take any action to offset any amount for which a creditor or assignee is potentially liable to such person under subsection (a)(2) against any amount owed by such person, unless the amount of the creditor's or assignee's liability under this subchapter has been determined by judgment of a court of competent jurisdiction in an action of which such person was a party. This subsection does not bar a consumer then in default on the obligation from asserting a violation of this subchapter as an original action, or as a defense or counterclaim to an action to collect amounts owed by the consumer brought by a person liable under this subchapter.

(i) Class action moratorium

(1) In general

During the period beginning on May 18, 1995, and ending on October 1, 1995, no court may enter any order certifying any class in any action under this subchapter—

(A) which is brought in connection with any credit transaction not under an open end credit plan which is secured by a first lien on real property or a dwelling and constitutes a refinancing or consolidation of an existing extension of credit; and

(B) which is based on the alleged failure of a creditor—

(i) to include a charge actually incurred (in connection with the transaction) in the finance charge disclosed pursuant to section 1638 of this title;

(ii) to properly make any other disclosure required under section 1638 of this title as a result of the failure described in clause (i); or

(iii) to provide proper notice of rescission rights under section 1635(a) of this title due to the selection by the creditor of the incorrect form from among the model forms prescribed by the Bureau or from among forms based on such model forms.

(2) Exceptions for certain alleged violations

Paragraph (1) shall not apply with respect to any action—

(A) described in clause (i) or (ii) of paragraph (1)(B), if the amount disclosed as the finance charge results in an annual percentage rate that exceeds the tolerance provided in section 1606(c) of this title; or

(B) described in paragraph (1)(B)(iii), if—

(i) no notice relating to rescission rights under section 1635(a) of this title was provided in any form; or

(ii) proper notice was not provided for any reason other than the reason described in such paragraph.

(j) Private educational lender

A private educational lender (as that term is defined in section 1650(a) of this title) has no liability under this section for failure to comply with section 1638(e)(3) of this title).[2]

(k) Defense to foreclosure

(1) In general

Notwithstanding any other provision of law, when a creditor, assignee, or other holder of a residential mortgage loan or anyone acting on behalf of such creditor, assignee, or holder, initiates a judicial or nonjudicial foreclosure of the residential mortgage loan, or any other action to collect the debt in connection with such loan, a consumer may assert a violation by a creditor of paragraph (1) or (2) of section 1639b(c) of this title, or of section 1639c(a) of this title, as a matter of defense by recoupment or set off without regard for the time limit on a private action for damages under subsection (e).

(2) Amount of recoupment or setoff

(A) In general

The amount of recoupment or set-off under paragraph (1) shall equal the amount to which the consumer would be entitled under subsection (a) for damages for a valid claim brought in an original action against the creditor, plus the costs to the consumer of the action, including a reasonable attorney's fee.

(B) Special rule

Where such judgment is rendered after the expiration of the applicable time limit on a private action for damages under subsection (e), the amount of recoupment or set-off under paragraph (1) derived from damages under subsection (a)(4) shall not exceed the amount to which the consumer would have been entitled under subsection (a)(4) for damages computed up to the day preceding the expiration of the applicable time limit.

(*l*) Exemption from liability and rescission in case of borrower fraud or deception

In addition to any other remedy available by law or contract, no creditor or assignee shall be liable to an obligor under this section, if such obligor, or co-obligor has been convicted of obtaining by actual fraud such residential mortgage loan.

§ 1641 [CCPA § 131]. Liability of Assignees

(a) Prerequisites

Except as otherwise specifically provided in this subchapter, any civil action for a violation of this subchapter or proceeding under section 1607 of this title which may be brought against a creditor may be maintained against any assignee of such creditor only if the violation for which such action or proceeding is brought is apparent on the face of the disclosure statement, except where the assignment was involuntary. For the purpose of this section, a violation apparent on the face of the disclosure statement includes, but is not limited to (1) a disclosure which can be determined to be incomplete or inaccurate from the face of the disclosure statement or other documents assigned, or (2) a disclosure which does not use the terms required to be used by this subchapter.

(b) Proof of compliance with statutory provisions

Except as provided in section 1635(c) of this title, in any action or proceeding by or against any subsequent assignee of the original creditor without knowledge to the contrary by the assignee when he acquires the obligation, written acknowledgement of receipt by a person to whom a statement is required to be given pursuant to this subchapter shall be conclusive proof of the delivery thereof and, except as provided in subsection (a), of compliance with this part. This section does not affect the rights of the obligor in any action against the original creditor.

[2] So in original. The closing parenthesis probably should not appear.

(c) Right of rescission by consumer unaffected

Any consumer who has the right to rescind a transaction under section 1635 of this title may rescind the transaction as against any assignee of the obligation.

(d) Rights upon assignment of certain mortgages

(1) In general

Any person who purchases or is otherwise assigned a mortgage referred to in section 1602(aa) of this title shall be subject to all claims and defenses with respect to that mortgage that the consumer could assert against the creditor of the mortgage, unless the purchaser or assignee demonstrates, by a preponderance of the evidence, that a reasonable person exercising ordinary due diligence, could not determine, based on the documentation required by this subchapter, the itemization of the amount financed, and other disclosure of disbursements that the mortgage was a mortgage referred to in section 1602(aa) of this title. The preceding sentence does not affect rights of a consumer under subsection (a), (b), or (c) of this section or any other provision of this subchapter.

(2) Limitation on damages

Notwithstanding any other provision of law, relief provided as a result of any action made permissible by paragraph (1) may not exceed—

(A) with respect to actions based upon a violation of this subchapter, the amount specified in section 1640 of this title; and

(B) with respect to all other causes of action, the sum of—

(i) the amount of all remaining indebtedness; and

(ii) the total amount paid by the consumer in connection with the transaction.

(3) Offset

The amount of damages that may be awarded under paragraph (2)(B) shall be reduced by the amount of any damages awarded under paragraph (2)(A).

(4) Notice

Any person who sells or otherwise assigns a mortgage referred to in section 1602(aa) of this title shall include a prominent notice of the potential liability under this subsection as determined by the Bureau.

(e) Liability of assignee for consumer credit transactions secured by real property

(1) In general

Except as otherwise specifically provided in this subchapter, any civil action against a creditor for a violation of this subchapter, and any proceeding under section 1607 of this title against a creditor, with respect to a consumer credit transaction secured by real property may be maintained against any assignee of such creditor only if—

(A) the violation for which such action or proceeding is brought is apparent on the face of the disclosure statement provided in connection with such transaction pursuant to this subchapter; and

(B) the assignment to the assignee was voluntary.

(2) Violation apparent on the face of the disclosure described

For the purpose of this section, a violation is apparent on the face of the disclosure statement if—

(A) the disclosure can be determined to be incomplete or inaccurate by a comparison among the disclosure statement, any itemization of the amount financed, the note, or any other disclosure of disbursement; or

(B) the disclosure statement does not use the terms or format required to be used by this subchapter.

(f) Treatment of servicer

(1) In general

A servicer of a consumer obligation arising from a consumer credit transaction shall not be treated as an assignee of such obligation for purposes of this section unless the servicer is or was the owner of the obligation.

(2) Servicer not treated as owner on basis of assignment for administrative convenience

A servicer of a consumer obligation arising from a consumer credit transaction shall not be treated as the owner of the obligation for purposes of this section on the basis of an assignment of the obligation from the creditor or another assignee to the servicer solely for the administrative convenience of the servicer in servicing the obligation. Upon written request by the obligor, the servicer shall provide the obligor, to the best knowledge of the servicer, with the name, address, and telephone number of the owner of the obligation or the master servicer of the obligation.

(3) "Servicer" defined

For purposes of this subsection, the term "servicer" has the same meaning as in section 2605(i)(2) of Title 12.

(4) Applicability

This subsection shall apply to all consumer credit transactions in existence or consummated on or after September 30, 1995.

(g) Notice of new creditor

(1) In general

In addition to other disclosures required by this subchapter, not later than 30 days after the date on which a mortgage loan is sold or otherwise transferred or assigned to a third party, the creditor that is the new owner or assignee of the debt shall notify the borrower in writing of such transfer, including—

(A) the identity, address, telephone number of the new creditor;

(B) the date of transfer;

(C) how to reach an agent or party having authority to act on behalf of the new creditor;

(D) the location of the place where transfer of ownership of the debt is recorded; and

(E) any other relevant information regarding the new creditor.

(2) Definition

As used in this subsection, the term "mortgage loan" means any consumer credit transaction that is secured by the principal dwelling of a consumer.

§ 1642 [CCPA § 132]. Issuance of Credit Cards

No credit card shall be issued except in response to a request or application therefor. This prohibition does not apply to the issuance of a credit card in renewal of, or in substitution for, an accepted credit card.

§ 1643 [CCPA § 133]. Liability of Holder of Credit Card

(a) Limits on liability

(1) A cardholder shall be liable for the unauthorized use of a credit card only if—

(A) the card is an accepted credit card;

(B) the liability is not in excess of $50;

(C) the card issuer gives adequate notice to the cardholder of the potential liability;

(D) the card issuer has provided the cardholder with a description of a means by which the card issuer may be notified of loss or theft of the card, which description may be provided on the face or reverse side of the statement required by section 1637(b) of this title or on a separate notice accompanying such statement;

(E) the unauthorized use occurs before the card issuer has been notified that an unauthorized use of the credit card has occurred or may occur as the result of loss, theft, or otherwise; and

(F) the card issuer has provided a method whereby the user of such card can be identified as the person authorized to use it.

(2) For purposes of this section, a card issuer has been notified when such steps as may be reasonably required in the ordinary course of business to provide the card issuer with the pertinent information have been taken, whether or not any particular officer, employee, or agent of the card issuer does in fact receive such information.

(b) Burden of proof

In any action by a card issuer to enforce liability for the use of a credit card, the burden of proof is upon the card issuer to show that the use was authorized or, if the use was unauthorized, then the burden of proof is upon the card issuer to show that the conditions of liability for the unauthorized use of a credit card, as set forth in subsection (a), have been met.

(c) Liability imposed by other laws or by agreement with issuer

Nothing in this section imposes liability upon a cardholder for the unauthorized use of a credit card in excess of his liability for such use under other applicable law or under any agreement with the card issuer.

(d) Exclusiveness of liability

Except as provided in this section, a cardholder incurs no liability from the unauthorized use of a credit card.

§ 1644 [CCPA § 134]. Fraudulent Use of Credit Cards; Penalties

(a) Use, attempt or conspiracy to use card in transaction affecting interstate or foreign commerce

Whoever knowingly in a transaction affecting interstate or foreign commerce, uses or attempts or conspires to use any counterfeit, fictitious, altered, forged, lost, stolen, or fraudulently obtained credit card to obtain money, goods, services, or anything else of value which within any one-year period has a value aggregating $1,000 or more; or

(b) Transporting, attempting or conspiring to transport card in interstate commerce

Whoever, with unlawful or fraudulent intent, transports or attempts or conspires to transport in interstate or foreign commerce a counterfeit, fictitious, altered, forged, lost, stolen, or fraudulently obtained credit card knowing the same to be counterfeit, fictitious, altered, forged, lost, stolen, or fraudulently obtained; or

(c) Use of interstate commerce to sell or transport card

Whoever, with unlawful or fraudulent intent, uses any instrumentality of interstate or foreign commerce to sell or transport a counterfeit, fictitious, altered, forged, lost, stolen, or fraudulently obtained credit card knowing the same to be counterfeit, fictitious, altered, forged, lost, stolen, or fraudulently obtained; or

(d) Receipt, concealment, etc., of goods obtained by use of card

Whoever knowingly receives, conceals, uses, or transports money, goods, services, or anything else of value (except tickets for interstate or foreign transportation) which (1) within any one-year period has a value aggregating $1,000 or more, (2) has moved in or is part of, or which constitutes interstate or foreign commerce, and (3) has been obtained with a counterfeit, fictitious, altered, forged, lost, stolen, or fraudulently obtained credit card; or

(e) Receipt, concealment, etc., of tickets for interstate or foreign transportation obtained by use of card

Whoever knowingly receives, conceals, uses, sells, or transports in interstate or foreign commerce one or more tickets for interstate or foreign transportation, which (1) within any one-year period have a value aggregating $500 or more, and (2) have been purchased or obtained with one or more counterfeit, fictitious, altered, forged, lost, stolen, or fraudulently obtained credit cards; or

(f) Furnishing of money, etc., through use of card

Whoever in a transaction affecting interstate or foreign commerce furnishes money, property, services, or anything else of value, which within any one-year period has a value aggregating $1,000 or more, through the use of any counterfeit, fictitious, altered, forged, lost, stolen, or fraudulently obtained credit card knowing the same to be counterfeit, fictitious, altered, forged, lost, stolen, or fraudulently obtained—

shall be fined not more than $10,000 or imprisoned not more than ten years, or both.

§ 1645 [CCPA § 135]. Business Credit Cards; Limits on Liability of Employees

The exemption provided by section 1603(1) of this title does not apply to the provisions of sections 1642, 1643, and 1644 of this title, except that a card issuer and a business or other organization which provides credit cards issued by the same card issuer to ten or more of its employees may by contract agree as to liability of the business or other organization with respect to unauthorized use of such credit cards without regard to the provisions of section 1643 of this title, but in no case may such business or other organization or card issuer impose liability upon any employee with respect to unauthorized use of such a credit card except in accordance with and subject to the limitations of section 1643 of this title.

§ 1646 [CCPA § 136]. Dissemination of Annual Percentage Rates; Implementation, etc.

(a) Annual percentage rates

The Bureau shall collect, publish, and disseminate to the public, on a demonstration basis in a number of standard metropolitan statistical areas to be determined by the Bureau, the annual percentage rates charged for representative types of nonsale credit by creditors in such areas. For the purpose of this section, the Bureau is authorized to require creditors in such areas to furnish information necessary for the Bureau to collect, publish, and disseminate such information.

(b) Credit card price and availability information

(1) Collection required

The Bureau shall collect, on a semiannual basis, credit card price and availability information, including the information required to be disclosed under section 1637(c) of this title, from a broad sample of financial institutions which offer credit card services.

(2) Sample requirements

The broad sample of financial institutions required under paragraph (1) shall include—

(A) the 25 largest issuers of credit cards; and

(B) not less than 125 additional financial institutions selected by the Bureau in a manner that ensures—

(i) an equitable geographical distribution within the sample; and

(ii) the representation of a wide spectrum of institutions within the sample.

(3) Report of information from sample

Each financial institution in the broad sample established pursuant to paragraph (2) shall report the information to the Bureau in accordance with such regulations or orders as the Bureau may prescribe.

(4) Public availability of collected information; report to Congress

The Bureau shall—

(A) make the information collected pursuant to this subsection available to the public upon request; and

(B) report such information semiannually to Congress.

(c) Implementation

The Bureau is authorized to enter into contracts or other arrangements with appropriate persons, organizations, or State agencies to carry out its functions under subsections (a) and (b) and to furnish financial assistance in support thereof.

§ 1647 [CCPA § 137]. Home Equity Plans

(a) Index requirement

In the case of extensions of credit under an open end consumer credit plan which are subject to a variable rate and are secured by a consumer's principal dwelling, the index or other rate of interest to which changes in the annual percentage rate are related shall be based on an index or rate of interest which is publicly available and is not under the control of the creditor.

(b) Grounds for acceleration of outstanding balance

A creditor may not unilaterally terminate any account under an open end consumer credit plan under which extensions of credit are secured by a consumer's principal dwelling and require the immediate repayment of any outstanding balance at such time, except in the case of—

(1) fraud or material misrepresentation on the part of the consumer in connection with the account;

(2) failure by the consumer to meet the repayment terms of the agreement for any outstanding balance; or

(3) any other action or failure to act by the consumer which adversely affects the creditor's security for the account or any right of the creditor in such security.

This subsection does not apply to reverse mortgage transactions.

(c) Change in terms

(1) In general

No open end consumer credit plan under which extensions of credit are secured by a consumer's principal dwelling may contain a provision which permits a creditor to change unilaterally any term required to be disclosed under section 1637a(a) of this title or any other term, except a change in insignificant terms such as the address of the creditor for billing purposes.

(2) Certain changes not precluded

Notwithstanding the provisions of subsection[1] (1), a creditor may make any of the following changes:

(A) Change the index and margin applicable to extensions of credit under such plan if the index used by the creditor is no longer available and the substitute index and margin would result in a substantially similar interest rate.

(B) Prohibit additional extensions of credit or reduce the credit limit applicable to an account under the plan during any period in which the value of the consumer's principal dwelling which secures any outstanding balance is significantly less than the original appraisal value of the dwelling.

(C) Prohibit additional extensions of credit or reduce the credit limit applicable to the account during any period in which the creditor has reason to believe that the consumer will be unable to comply with the repayment requirements of the account due to a material change in the consumer's financial circumstances.

(D) Prohibit additional extensions of credit or reduce the credit limit applicable to the account during any period in which the consumer is in default with respect to any material obligation of the consumer under the agreement.

(E) Prohibit additional extensions of credit or reduce the credit limit applicable to the account during any period in which—

(i) the creditor is precluded by government action from imposing the annual percentage rate provided for in the account agreement; or

(ii) any government action is in effect which adversely affects the priority of the creditor's security interest in the account to the extent that the value of the creditor's secured interest in the property is less than 120 percent of the amount of the credit limit applicable to the account.

(F) Any change that will benefit the consumer.

(3) Material obligations

Upon the request of the consumer and at the time an agreement is entered into by a consumer to open an account under an open end consumer credit plan under which extensions of credit are secured by the consumer's principal dwelling, the consumer shall be given a list of the categories of contract obligations which are deemed by the creditor to be material obligations of the consumer under the agreement for purposes of paragraph (2)(D).

(4) Consumer benefit

(A) In general

For purposes of paragraph (2)(F), a change shall be deemed to benefit the consumer if the change is unequivocally beneficial to the borrower and the change is beneficial through the entire term of the agreement.

(B) Bureau categorization

The Bureau may, by regulation, determine categories of changes that benefit the consumer.

---

1 So in original. Probably should be "paragraph."

(d) Terms changed after application

If any term or condition described in section 1637a(a) of this title which is disclosed to a consumer in connection with an application to open an account under an open end consumer credit plan described in such section (other than a variable feature of the plan) changes before the account is opened, and if, as a result of such change, the consumer elects not to enter into the plan agreement, the creditor shall refund all fees paid by the consumer in connection with such application.

(e) Additional requirements relating to refunds and imposition of nonrefundable fees

(1) In general

No nonrefundable fee may be imposed by a creditor or any other person in connection with any application by a consumer to establish an account under any open end consumer credit plan which provides for extensions of credit which are secured by a consumer's principal dwelling before the end of the 3-day period beginning on the date such consumer receives the disclosure required under section 1637a(a) of this title and the pamphlet required under section 1637a(e) of this title with respect to such application.

(2) Constructive receipt

For purposes of determining when a nonrefundable fee may be imposed in accordance with this subsection if the disclosures and pamphlet referred to in paragraph (1) are mailed to the consumer, the date of the receipt of the disclosures by such consumer shall be deemed to be 3 business days after the date of mailing by the creditor.

§ 1648 [CCPA § 138]. Reverse Mortgages

(a) In general

In addition to the disclosures required under this subchapter, for each reverse mortgage, the creditor shall, not less than 3 days prior to consummation of the transaction, disclose to the consumer in conspicuous type a good faith estimate of the projected total cost of the mortgage to the consumer expressed as a table of annual interest rates. Each annual interest rate shall be based on a projected total future credit extension balance under a projected appreciation rate for the dwelling and a term for the mortgage. The disclosure shall include—

(1) statements of the annual interest rates for not less than 3 projected appreciation rates and not less than 3 credit transaction periods, as determined by the Bureau, including—

(A) a short-term reverse mortgage;

(B) a term equaling the actuarial life expectancy of the consumer; and

(C) such longer term as the Bureau deems appropriate; and

(2) a statement that the consumer is not obligated to complete the reverse mortgage transaction merely because the consumer has received the disclosure required under this section or has signed an application for the reverse mortgage.

(b) Projected total cost

In determining the projected total cost of the mortgage to be disclosed to the consumer under subsection (a), the creditor shall take into account—

(1) any shared appreciation or equity that the lender will, by contract, be entitled to receive;

(2) all costs and charges to the consumer, including the costs of any associated annuity that the consumer elects or is required to purchase as part of the reverse mortgage transaction;

(3) all payments to and for the benefit of the consumer, including, in the case in which an associated annuity is purchased (whether or not required by the lender as a condition of making the reverse mortgage), the annuity payments received by the consumer and financed from the proceeds of the loan, instead of the proceeds used to finance the annuity; and

(4) any limitation on the liability of the consumer under reverse mortgage transactions (such as nonrecourse limits and equity conservation agreements).

§ 1649 [CCPA § 139]. Certain Limitations on Liability

(a) Limitations on liability

For any closed end consumer credit transaction that is secured by real property or a dwelling, that is subject to this subchapter, and that is consummated before September 30, 1995, a creditor or any assignee of a creditor shall have no civil, administrative, or criminal liability under this subchapter for, and a consumer shall have no extended rescission rights under section 1635(f) of this title with respect to—

(1) the creditor's treatment, for disclosure purposes, of—

(A) taxes described in section 1605(d)(3) of this title;

(B) fees described in section 1605(e)(2) and (5) of this title;

(C) fees and amounts referred to in the 3rd sentence of section 1605(a) of this title; or

(D) borrower-paid mortgage broker fees referred to in section 1605(a)(6) of this title;

(2) the form of written notice used by the creditor to inform the obligor of the rights of the obligor under section 1635 of this title if the creditor provided the obligor with a properly dated form of written notice published and adopted by the Bureau or a comparable written notice, and otherwise complied with all the requirements of this section regarding notice; or

(3) any disclosure relating to the finance charge imposed with respect to the transaction if the amount or percentage actually disclosed—

(A) may be treated as accurate for purposes of this subchapter if the amount disclosed as the finance charge does not vary from the actual finance charge by more than $200;

(B) may, under section 1605(f)(2) of this title, be treated as accurate for purposes of section 1635 of this title; or

(C) is greater than the amount or percentage required to be disclosed under this subchapter.

(b) Exceptions

Subsection (a) of this section shall not apply to—

(1) any individual action or counterclaim brought under this subchapter which was filed before June 1, 1995;

(2) any class action brought under this subchapter for which a final order certifying a class was entered before January 1, 1995;

(3) the named individual plaintiffs in any class action brought under this subchapter which was filed before June 1, 1995; or

(4) any consumer credit transaction with respect to which a timely notice of rescission was sent to the creditor before June 1, 1995.

§ 1650 [CCPA § 140]. Preventing Unfair and Deceptive Private Educational Lending Practices and Eliminating Conflicts of Interest

(a) Definitions

As used in this section—

(1) the term "cosigner"—

(A) means any individual who is liable for the obligation of another without compensation, regardless of how designated in the contract or instrument with respect to that obligation, other than an obligation under a private education loan extended to consolidate a consumer's pre-existing private education loans;

(B) includes any person the signature of which is requested as condition to grant credit or to forbear on collection; and

(C) does not include a spouse of an individual described in subparagraph (A), the signature of whom is needed to perfect the security interest in a loan.

(2) the term "covered educational institution"—

(A) means any educational institution that offers a postsecondary educational degree, certificate, or program of study (including any institution of higher education); and

(B) includes an agent, officer, or employee of the educational institution;

(3) the term "gift"—

(A)(i) means any gratuity, favor, discount, entertainment, hospitality, loan, or other item having more than a de minimis monetary value, including services, transportation, lodging, or meals, whether provided in kind, by purchase of a ticket, payment in advance, or reimbursement after the expense has been incurred; and

(ii) includes an item described in clause (i) provided to a family member of an officer, employee, or agent of a covered educational institution, or to any other individual based on that individual's relationship with the officer, employee, or agent, if—

(I) the item is provided with the knowledge and acquiescence of the officer, employee, or agent; and

(II) the officer, employee, or agent has reason to believe the item was provided because of the official position of the officer, employee, or agent; and

(B) does not include—

(i) standard informational material related to a loan, default aversion, default prevention, or financial literacy;

(ii) food, refreshments, training, or informational material furnished to an officer, employee, or agent of a covered educational institution, as an integral part of a training session or through participation in an advisory council that is designed to improve the service of the private educational lender to the covered educational institution, if such training or participation contributes to the professional development of the officer, employee, or agent of the covered educational institution;

(iii) favorable terms, conditions, and borrower benefits on a private education loan provided to a student employed by the covered educational institution, if such terms, conditions, or benefits are not provided because of the student's employment with the covered educational institution;

(iv) the provision of financial literacy counseling or services, including counseling or services provided in coordination with a covered educational institution, to the extent that such counseling or services are not undertaken to secure—

(I) applications for private education loans or private education loan volume;

(II) applications or loan volume for any loan made, insured, or guaranteed under title IV of the Higher Education Act of 1965 (20 U.S.C. 1070 et seq.); or

(III) the purchase of a product or service of a specific private educational lender;

(v) philanthropic contributions to a covered educational institution from a private educational lender that are unrelated to private education loans and are not made in exchange for any advantage related to private education loans; or

(vi) State education grants, scholarships, or financial aid funds administered by or on behalf of a State;

(4) the term "institution of higher education" has the same meaning as in section 102 of the Higher Education Act of 1965 (20 U.S.C. 1002);

(5) the term "postsecondary educational expenses" means any of the expenses that are included as part of the cost of attendance of a student, as defined under section 472 of the Higher Education Act of 1965 (20 U.S.C. 1087*ll*);

(6) the term "preferred lender arrangement" has the same meaning as in section 151 of the Higher Education Act of 1965 [20 U.S.C.A. § 1019];

(7) the term "private educational lender" means—

(A) a financial institution, as defined in section 1813 of Title 12 that solicits, makes, or extends private education loans;

(B) a Federal credit union, as defined in section 1752 of Title 12 that solicits, makes, or extends private education loans; and

(C) any other person engaged in the business of soliciting, making, or extending private education loans;

(8) the term "private education loan"—

(A) means a loan provided by a private educational lender that—

(i) is not made, insured, or guaranteed under of[1] title IV of the Higher Education Act of 1965 (20 U.S.C. 1070 et seq.); and

(ii) is issued expressly for postsecondary educational expenses to a borrower, regardless of whether the loan is provided through the educational institution that the subject student attends or directly to the borrower from the private educational lender; and

(B) does not include an extension of credit under an open end consumer credit plan, a reverse mortgage transaction, a residential mortgage transaction, or any other loan that is secured by real property or a dwelling; and

(9) the term "revenue sharing" means an arrangement between a covered educational institution and a private educational lender under which—

(A) a private educational lender provides or issues private education loans with respect to students attending the covered educational institution;

(B) the covered educational institution recommends to students or others the private educational lender or the private education loans of the private educational lender; and

(C) the private educational lender pays a fee or provides other material benefits, including profit sharing, to the covered educational institution in connection with the private

---

1 So in original. The word "of" probably should not appear.

education loans provided to students attending the covered educational institution or a borrower acting on behalf of a student.

(b) Prohibition on certain gifts and arrangements

A private educational lender may not, directly or indirectly—

(1) offer or provide any gift to a covered educational institution in exchange for any advantage or consideration provided to such private educational lender related to its private education loan activities; or

(2) engage in revenue sharing with a covered educational institution.

(c) Prohibition on co-branding

A private educational lender may not use the name, emblem, mascot, or logo of the covered educational institution, or other words, pictures, or symbols readily identified with the covered educational institution, in the marketing of private education loans in any way that implies that the covered educational institution endorses the private education loans offered by the private educational lender.

(d) Advisory board compensation

Any person who is employed in the financial aid office of a covered educational institution, or who otherwise has responsibilities with respect to private education loans or other financial aid of the institution, and who serves on an advisory board, commission, or group established by a private educational lender or group of such lenders shall be prohibited from receiving anything of value from the private educational lender or group of lenders. Nothing in this subsection prohibits the reimbursement of reasonable expenses incurred by an employee of a covered educational institution as part of their service on an advisory board, commission, or group described in this subsection.

(e) Prohibition on prepayment or repayment fees or penalty

It shall be unlawful for any private educational lender to impose a fee or penalty on a borrower for early repayment or prepayment of any private education loan.

(f) Credit Card Protections for College Students.—

(1) Disclosure required

An institution of higher education shall publicly disclose any contract or other agreement made with a card issuer or creditor for the purpose of marketing a credit card.

(2) Inducements prohibited

No card issuer or creditor may offer to a student at an institution of higher education any tangible item to induce such student to apply for or participate in an open end consumer credit plan offered by such card issuer or creditor, if such offer is made—

(A) on the campus of an institution of higher education;

(B) near the campus of an institution of higher education, as determined by rule of the Bureau; or

(C) at an event sponsored by or related to an institution of higher education.

(3) Sense of the congress.—It is the sense of the Congress that each institution of higher education should consider adopting the following policies relating to credit cards:

(A) That any card issuer that markets a credit card on the campus of such institution notify the institution of the location at which such marketing will take place.

(B) That the number of locations on the campus of such institution at which the marketing of credit cards takes place be limited.

(C) That credit card and debt education and counseling sessions be offered as a regular part of any orientation program for new students of such institution.

(g) Additional protections relating to borrower or cosigner of a private education loan

(1) Prohibition on automatic default in case of death or bankruptcy of non-student obligor

With respect to a private education loan involving a student obligor and 1 or more cosigners, the creditor shall not declare a default or accelerate the debt against the student obligor on the sole basis of a bankruptcy or death of a cosigner.

(2) Cosigner release in case of death of borrower

(A) Release of cosigner

The holder of a private education loan, when notified of the death of a student obligor, shall release within a reasonable timeframe any cosigner from the obligations of the cosigner under the private education loan.

(B) Notification of release

A holder or servicer of a private education loan, as applicable, shall within a reasonable time-frame notify any cosigners for the private education loan if a cosigner is released from the obligations of the cosigner for the private education loan under this paragraph.

(C) Designation of individual to act on behalf of the borrower

Any lender that extends a private education loan shall provide the student obligor an option to designate an individual to have the legal authority to act on behalf of the student obligor with respect to the private education loan in the event of the death of the student obligor.

§ 1651 [CCPA § 140]. Procedure for Timely Settlement of Estates of Decedent Obligors

The Bureau, in consultation with the Bureau[1] and each other agency referred to in section 1607(a) of this title, shall prescribe regulations to require any creditor, with respect to any credit card account under an open end consumer credit plan, to establish procedures to ensure that any administrator of an estate of any deceased obligor with respect to such account can resolve outstanding credit balances in a timely manner.

PART C—CREDIT ADVERTISING AND LIMITS ON CREDIT CARD FEES

§ 1661 [CCPA § 141]. Catalogs and Multiple-Page Advertisements

For the purposes of this part, a catalog or other multiple-page advertisement shall be considered a single advertisement if it clearly and conspicuously displays a credit terms table on which the information required to be stated under this part is clearly set forth.

§ 1662 [CCPA § 142]. Advertising of Downpayments and Installments

No advertisement to aid, promote, or assist directly or indirectly any extension of consumer credit may state

(1) that a specific periodic consumer credit amount or installment amount can be arranged, unless the creditor usually and customarily arranges credit payments or installments for that period and in that amount.

(2) that a specified downpayment is required in connection with any extension of consumer credit, unless the creditor usually and customarily arranges downpayments in that amount.

[1] So in original. Probably a drafting error.

§ 1663 [CCPA § 143]. Advertising of Open End Credit Plans

No advertisement to aid, promote, or assist directly or indirectly the extension of consumer credit under an open end credit plan may set forth any of the specific terms of that plan unless it also clearly and conspicuously sets forth all of the following items:

(1) Any minimum or fixed amount which could be imposed.

(2) In any case in which periodic rates may be used to compute the finance charge, the periodic rates expressed as annual percentage rates.

(3) Any other term that the Bureau may by regulation require to be disclosed.

§ 1664 [CCPA § 144]. Advertising of Credit Other Than Open End Plans

(a) Exclusion of open end credit plans

Except as provided in subsection (b), this section applies to any advertisement to aid, promote, or assist directly or indirectly any consumer credit sale, loan, or other extension of credit subject to the provisions of this subchapter, other than an open end credit plan.

(b) Advertisements of residential real estate

The provisions of this section do not apply to advertisements of residential real estate except to the extent that the Bureau may by regulation require.

(c) Rate of finance charge expressed as annual percentage rate

If any advertisement to which this section applies states the rate of a finance charge, the advertisement shall state the rate of that charge expressed as an annual percentage rate.

(d) Requisite disclosures in advertisement

If any advertisement to which this section applies states the amount of the downpayment, if any, the amount of any installment payment, the dollar amount of any finance charge, or the number of installments or the period of repayment, then the advertisement shall state all of the following items:

(1) The downpayment, if any.

(2) The terms of repayment.

(3) The rate of the finance charge expressed as an annual percentage rate.

(e) Credit transaction secured by principal dwelling of consumer

Each advertisement to which this section applies that relates to a consumer credit transaction that is secured by the principal dwelling of a consumer in which the extension of credit may exceed the fair market value of the dwelling, and which advertisement is disseminated in paper form to the public or through the internet, as opposed to by radio or television, shall clearly and conspicuously state that—

(1) the interest on the portion of the credit extension that is greater than the fair market value of the dwelling is not tax deductible for Federal income tax purposes; and

(2) the consumer should consult a tax adviser for further information regarding the deductibility of interest and charges.

§ 1665 [CCPA § 145]. Nonliability of Advertising Media

There is no liability under this part on the part of any owner or personnel, as such, of any medium in which an advertisement appears or through which it is disseminated.

§ 1665a [CCPA § 146]. Use of Annual Percentage Rate in Oral Disclosures; Exceptions

In responding orally to any inquiry about the cost of credit, a creditor, regardless of the method used to compute finance charges, shall state rates only in terms of the annual percentage rate, except that in the case of an open end credit plan, the periodic rate also may be stated and, in the case of an other than open end credit plan where a major component of the finance charge consists of interest computed at a simple annual rate, the simple annual rate also may be stated. The Bureau may, by regulation, modify the requirements of this section or provide an exception from this section for a transaction or class of transactions for which the creditor cannot determine in advance the applicable annual percentage rate.

§ 1665b [CCPA § 147]. Advertising of Open End Consumer Credit Plans Secured by Consumer's Principal Dwelling

(a) In general

If any advertisement to aid, promote, or assist, directly or indirectly, the extension of consumer credit through an open end consumer credit plan under which extensions of credit are secured by the consumer's principal dwelling states, affirmatively or negatively, any of the specific terms of the plan, including any periodic payment amount required under such plan, such advertisement shall also clearly and conspicuously set forth the following information, in such form and manner as the Bureau may require:

(1) Loan fees and opening cost estimates

Any loan fee the amount of which is determined as a percentage of the credit limit applicable to an account under the plan and an estimate of the aggregate amount of other fees for opening the account, based on the creditor's experience with the plan and stated as a single amount or as a reasonable range.

(2) Periodic rates

In any case in which periodic rates may be used to compute the finance charge, the periodic rates expressed as an annual percentage rate.

(3) Highest annual percentage rate

The highest annual percentage rate which may be imposed under the plan.

(4) Other information

Any other information the Bureau may by regulation require.

(b) Tax deductibility

(1) In general

If any advertisement described in subsection (a) contains a statement that any interest expense incurred with respect to the plan is or may be tax deductible, the advertisement shall not be misleading with respect to such deductibility.

(2) Credit in excess of fair market value

Each advertisement described in subsection (a) that relates to an extension of credit that may exceed the fair market value of the dwelling, and which advertisement is disseminated in paper form to the public or through the Internet, as opposed to by radio or television, shall include a clear and conspicuous statement that—

(A) the interest on the portion of the credit extension that is greater than the fair market value of the dwelling is not tax deductible for Federal income tax purposes; and

(B) the consumer should consult a tax adviser for further information regarding the deductibility of interest and charges.

(C) Certain terms prohibited

No advertisement described in subsection (a) with respect to any home equity account may refer to such loan as "free money" or use other terms determined by the Bureau by regulation to be misleading.

(d) Discounted initial rate

(1) In general

If any advertisement described in subsection (a) includes an initial annual percentage rate that is not determined by the index or formula used to make later interest rate adjustments, the advertisement shall also state with equal prominence the current annual percentage rate that would have been applied using the index or formula if such initial rate had not been offered.

(2) Quoted rate must be reasonably current

The annual percentage rate required to be disclosed under the paragraph (1) rate must be current as of a reasonable time given the media involved.

(3) Period during which initial rate is in effect

Any advertisement to which paragraph (1) applies shall also state the period of time during which the initial annual percentage rate referred to in such paragraph will be in effect.

(e) Balloon payment

If any advertisement described in subsection (a) contains a statement regarding the minimum monthly payment under the plan, the advertisement shall also disclose, if applicable, the fact that the plan includes a balloon payment.

(f) "Balloon payment" defined

For purposes of this section and section 1637a of this title, the term "balloon payment" means, with respect to any open end consumer credit plan under which extensions of credit are secured by the consumer's principal dwelling, any repayment option under which—

(1) the account holder is required to repay the entire amount of any outstanding balance as of a specified date or at the end of a specified period of time, as determined in accordance with the terms of the agreement pursuant to which such credit is extended; and

(2) the aggregate amount of the minimum periodic payments required would not fully amortize such outstanding balance by such date or at the end of such period.

§ 1665c [CCPA § 148.] Interest Rate Reduction on Open End Consumer Credit Plans

(a) In General

If a creditor increases the annual percentage rate applicable to a credit card account under an open end consumer credit plan, based on factors including the credit risk of the obligor, market conditions, or other factors, the creditor shall consider changes in such factors in subsequently determining whether to reduce the annual percentage rate for such obligor.

(b) Requirements

With respect to any credit card account under an open end consumer credit plan, the creditor shall—

(1) maintain reasonable methodologies for assessing the factors described in subsection (a);

(2) not less frequently than once every 6 months, review accounts as to which the annual percentage rate has been increased since January 1, 2009, to assess whether such factors have changed (including whether any risk has declined);

(3) reduce the annual percentage rate previously increased when a reduction is indicated by the review; and

(4) in the event of an increase in the annual percentage rate, provide in the written notice required under section 1637(i) of this title a statement of the reasons for the increase.

(c) Rule of Construction

This section shall not be construed to require a reduction in any specific amount.

(d) Rulemaking

The Bureau shall issue final rules not later than 9 months after May 22, 2009, to implement the requirements of and evaluate compliance with this section, and subsections (a), (b), and (c) shall become effective 15 months after May 22, 2009.

§ 1665d [CCPA § 149.] Reasonable Penalty Fees on Open End Consumer Credit Plans

(a) In General

The amount of any penalty fee or charge that a card issuer may impose with respect to a credit card account under an open end consumer credit plan in connection with any omission with respect to, or violation of, the cardholder agreement, including any late payment fee, over-the-limit fee, or any other penalty fee or charge, shall be reasonable and proportional to such omission or violation.

(b) Rulemaking required

The Bureau, in consultation with the Comptroller of the Currency, the Board of Directors of the Federal Deposit Insurance Corporation, the Director of the Office of Thrift Supervision, and the National Credit Union Administration Board, shall issue final rules not later than 9 months after May 22, 2009, to establish standards for assessing whether the amount of any penalty fee or charge described under subsection (a) is reasonable and proportional to the omission or violation to which the fee or charge relates. Subsection (a) shall become effective 15 months after May 22, 2009.

(c) Considerations

In issuing rules required by this section, the Bureau shall consider—

(1) the cost incurred by the creditor from such omission or violation;

(2) the deterrence of such omission or violation by the cardholder;

(3) the conduct of the cardholder; and

(4) such other factors as the Bureau may deem necessary or appropriate.

(d) Differentiation permitted

In issuing rules required by this subsection, the Bureau may establish different standards for different types of fees and charges, as appropriate.

(e) Safe harbor rule authorized

The Bureau, in consultation with the Comptroller of the Currency, the Board of Directors of the Federal Deposit Insurance Corporation, the Director of the Office of Thrift Supervision, and the National Credit Union Administration Board, may issue rules to provide an amount for any penalty fee or charge described under subsection (a) that is presumed to be reasonable and proportional to the omission or violation to which the fee or charge relates.

§ 1665e [CCPA § 150]. Consideration of Ability to Repay

A card issuer may not open any credit card account for any consumer under an open end consumer credit plan, or increase any credit limit applicable to such account, unless the card issuer considers the ability of the consumer to make the required payments under the terms of such account.

PART D—CREDIT BILLING

§ 1666 [CCPA § 161]. Correction of Billing Errors

(a) Written notice by obligor to creditor; time for and contents of notice; procedure upon receipt of notice by creditor

If a creditor, within sixty days after having transmitted to an obligor a statement of the obligor's account in connection with an extension of consumer credit, receives at the address disclosed under section 1637(b)(10) of this title a written notice (other than notice on a payment stub or other payment medium supplied by the creditor if the creditor so stipulates with the disclosure required under section 1637(a)(7) of this title) from the obligor in which the obligor—

(1) sets forth or otherwise enables the creditor to identify the name and account number (if any) of the obligor,

(2) indicates the obligor's belief that the statement contains a billing error and the amount of such billing error, and

(3) sets forth the reasons for the obligor's belief (to the extent applicable) that the statement contains a billing error,

the creditor shall, unless the obligor has, after giving such written notice and before the expiration of the time limits herein specified, agreed that the statement was correct—

(A) not later than thirty days after the receipt of the notice, send a written acknowledgment thereof to the obligor, unless the action required in subparagraph (B) is taken within such thirty-day period, and

(B) not later than two complete billing cycles of the creditor (in no event later than ninety days) after the receipt of the notice and prior to taking any action to collect the amount, or any part thereof, indicated by the obligor under paragraph (2) either—

(i) make appropriate corrections in the account of the obligor, including the crediting of any finance charges on amounts erroneously billed, and transmit to the obligor a notification of such corrections and the creditor's explanation of any change in the amount indicated by the obligor under paragraph (2) and, if any such change is made and the obligor so requests, copies of documentary evidence of the obligor's indebtedness; or

(ii) send a written explanation or clarification to the obligor, after having conducted an investigation, setting forth to the extent applicable the reasons why the creditor believes the account of the obligor was correctly shown in the statement and, upon request of the obligor, provide copies of documentary evidence of the obligor's indebtedness. In the case of a billing error where the obligor alleges that the creditor's billing statement reflects goods not delivered to the obligor or his designee in accordance with the agreement made at the time of the transaction, a creditor may not construe such amount to be correctly shown unless he determines that such goods were actually delivered, mailed, or otherwise sent to the obligor and provides the obligor with a statement of such determination.

After complying with the provisions of this subsection with respect to an alleged billing error, a creditor has no further responsibility under this section if the obligor continues to make substantially the same allegation with respect to such error.

(b) Billing error

For the purpose of this section, a "billing error" consists of any of the following:

(1) A reflection on a statement of an extension of credit which was not made to the obligor or, if made, was not in the amount reflected on such statement.

(2) A reflection on a statement of an extension of credit for which the obligor requests additional clarification including documentary evidence thereof.

(3) A reflection on a statement of goods or services not accepted by the obligor or his designee or not delivered to the obligor or his designee in accordance with the agreement made at the time of a transaction.

(4) The creditor's failure to reflect properly on a statement a payment made by the obligor or a credit issued to the obligor.

(5) A computation error or similar error of an accounting nature of the creditor on a statement.

(6) Failure to transmit the statement required under section 1637(b) of this title to the last address of the obligor which has been disclosed to the creditor, unless that address was furnished less than twenty days before the end of the billing cycle for which the statement is required.

(7) Any other error described in regulations of the Bureau.

(c) Action by creditor to collect amount or any part thereof regarded by obligor to be a billing error

For the purposes of this section, "action to collect the amount, or any part thereof, indicated by an obligor under paragraph (2)" does not include the sending of statements of account, which may include finance charges on amounts in dispute, to the obligor following written notice from the obligor as specified under subsection (a), if—

(1) the obligor's account is not restricted or closed because of the failure of the obligor to pay the amount indicated under paragraph (2) of subsection (a), and

(2) the creditor indicates the payment of such amount is not required pending the creditor's compliance with this section.

Nothing in this section shall be construed to prohibit any action by a creditor to collect any amount which has not been indicated by the obligor to contain a billing error.

(d) Restricting or closing by creditor of account regarded by obligor to contain a billing error

Pursuant to regulations of the Bureau, a creditor operating an open end consumer credit plan may not, prior to the sending of the written explanation or clarification required under paragraph (B)(ii), restrict or close an account with respect to which the obligor has indicated pursuant to subsection (a) that he believes such account to contain a billing error solely because of the obligor's failure to pay the amount indicated to be in error. Nothing in this subsection shall be deemed to prohibit a creditor from applying against the credit limit on the obligor's account the amount indicated to be in error.

(e) Effect of noncompliance with requirements by creditor

Any creditor who fails to comply with the requirements of this section or section 1666a of this title forfeits any right to collect from the obligor the amount indicated by the obligor under paragraph (2) of subsection (a), and any finance charges thereon, except that the amount required to be forfeited under this subsection may not exceed $50.

§ 1666a [CCPA § 162]. Regulation of Credit Reports

(a) Reports by creditor on obligor's failure to pay amount regarded as billing error

After receiving a notice from an obligor as provided in section 1666(a) of this title, a creditor or his agent may not directly or indirectly threaten to report to any person adversely on the obligor's credit rating or credit standing because of the obligor's failure to pay the amount indicated by the obligor under section 1666(a)(2) of this title, and such amount may not be reported as delinquent to any third party until the creditor has met the requirements of section 1666 of this title and has allowed the obligor the same number of days (not less than ten) thereafter to make payment as is provided under the credit agreement with the obligor for the payment of undisputed amounts.

(b) Reports by creditor on delinquent amounts in dispute; notification of obligor of parties notified of delinquency

If a creditor receives a further written notice from an obligor that an amount is still in dispute within the time allowed for payment under subsection (a) of this section, a creditor may not report to any third party that the amount of the obligor is delinquent because the obligor has failed to pay an amount which he has indicated under section 1666(a)(2) of this title, unless the creditor also reports that the amount is in dispute and, at the same time, notifies the obligor of the name and address of each party to whom the creditor is reporting information concerning the delinquency.

(c) Reports by creditor of subsequent resolution of delinquent amounts

A creditor shall report any subsequent resolution of any delinquencies reported pursuant to subsection (b) to the parties to whom such delinquencies were initially reported.

§ 1666b [CCPA § 163]. Timing of Payments

(a) Time To Make Payments

A creditor may not treat a payment on an open end consumer credit plan as late for any purpose, unless the creditor has adopted reasonable procedures designed to ensure that each periodic statement including the information required by section 1637(b) of this title is mailed or delivered to the consumer not later than 21 days before the payment due date.

(b) Grace Period

If an open end consumer credit plan provides a time period within which an obligor may repay any portion of the credit extended without incurring an additional finance charge, such additional finance charge may not be imposed with respect to such portion of the credit extended for the billing cycle of which such period is a part, unless a statement which includes the amount upon which the finance charge for the period is based was mailed or delivered to the consumer not later than 21 days before the date specified in the statement by which payment must be made in order to avoid imposition of that finance charge.

§ 1666c [CCPA § 164]. Prompt and Fair Crediting of Payments

(a) In General

Payments received from an obligor under an open end consumer credit plan by the creditor shall be posted promptly to the obligor's account as specified in regulations of the Bureau. Such regulations shall prevent a finance charge from being imposed on any obligor if the creditor has received the obligor's payment in readily identifiable form, by 5:00 p.m. on the date on which such payment is due, in the amount, manner, and location indicated by the creditor to avoid the imposition thereof.

(b) Application of Payments

(1) In general.—Upon receipt of a payment from a cardholder, the card issuer shall apply amounts in excess of the minimum payment amount first to the card balance bearing the highest rate of interest, and then to each successive balance bearing the next highest rate of interest, until the payment is exhausted.

(2) Clarification relating to certain deferred interest arrangements.—A creditor shall allocate the entire amount paid by the consumer in excess of the minimum payment amount to a balance on which interest is deferred during the last 2 billing cycles immediately preceding the expiration of the period during which interest is deferred.

(c) Changes by Card Issuer

If a card issuer makes a material change in the mailing address, office, or procedures for handling cardholder payments, and such change causes a material delay in the crediting of a cardholder payment made during the 60-day period following the date on which such change took effect, the card issuer may not impose any late fee or finance charge for a late payment on the credit card account to which such payment was credited.

§ 1666d [CCPA § 165]. Treatment of Credit Balances

Whenever a credit balance in excess of $1 is created in connection with a consumer credit transaction through (1) transmittal of funds to a creditor in excess of the total balance due on an account, (2) rebates of unearned finance charges or insurance premiums, or (3) amounts otherwise owed to or held for the benefit of an obligor, the creditor shall—

(A) credit the amount of the credit balance to the consumer's account;

(B) refund any part of the amount of the remaining credit balance, upon request of the consumer; and

(C) make a good faith effort to refund to the consumer by cash, check, or money order any part of the amount of the credit balance remaining in the account for more than six months, except that no further action is required in any case in which the consumer's current location is not known by the creditor and cannot be traced through the consumer's last known address or telephone number.

§ 1666e [CCPA § 166]. Notification of Credit Card Issuer by Seller of Return of Goods, etc., by Obligor; Credit for Account of Obligor

With respect to any sales transaction where a credit card has been used to obtain credit, where the seller is a person other than the card issuer, and where the seller accepts or allows a return of the goods or forgiveness of a debit for services which were the subject of such sale, the seller shall promptly transmit to the credit card issuer, a credit statement with respect thereto and the credit card issuer shall credit the account of the obligor for the amount of the transaction.

§ 1666f [CCPA § 167]. Inducements to Cardholders by Sellers of Cash Discounts for Payments by Cash, Check or Similar Means; Finance Charge for Sales Transactions Involving Cash Discounts

(a) Cash discounts

With respect to credit card which may be used for extensions of credit in sales transactions in which the seller is a person other than the card issuer, the card issuer may not, by contract, or otherwise, prohibit any such seller from offering a discount to a cardholder to induce the cardholder to pay by cash, check, or similar means rather than use a credit card.

(b) Finance charge

With respect to any sales transaction, any discount from the regular price offered by the seller for the purpose of inducing payment by cash, checks, or other means not involving the use of an open-end credit plan or a credit card shall not constitute a finance charge as determined under section 1605 of this title if such discount is offered to all prospective buyers and its availability is disclosed clearly and conspicuously.

§ 1666g [CCPA § 168]. Tie-In Services Prohibited for Issuance of Credit Card

Notwithstanding any agreement to the contrary, a card issuer may not require a seller, as a condition to participating in a credit card plan, to open an account with or procure any other service from the card issuer or its subsidiary or agent.

§ 1666h [CCPA § 169]. Offset of Cardholder's Indebtedness by Issuer of Credit Card with Funds Deposited with Issuer by Cardholder; Remedies of Creditors Under State Law Not Affected

(a) Offset against consumer's funds

A card issuer may not take any action to offset a cardholder's indebtedness arising in connection with a consumer credit transaction under the relevant credit card plan against funds of the cardholder held on deposit with the card issuer unless—

(1) such action was previously authorized in writing by the cardholder in accordance with a credit plan whereby the cardholder agrees periodically to pay debts incurred in his open end credit account by permitting the card issuer periodically to deduct all or a portion of such debt from the cardholder's deposit account, and

(2) such action with respect to any outstanding disputed amount not be taken by the card issuer upon request of the cardholder.

In the case of any credit card account in existence on the effective date of this section, the previous written authorization referred to in clause (1) shall not be required until the date (after such effective date) when such account is renewed, but in no case later than one year after such effective date. Such written authorization shall be deemed to exist if the card issuer has previously notified the cardholder that the use of his credit card account will subject any funds which the card issuer holds in deposit accounts of such cardholder to offset against any amounts due and payable on his credit card account which have not been paid in accordance with the terms of the agreement between the card issuer and the cardholder.

(b) Attachments and levies

This section does not alter or affect the right under State law of a card issuer to attach or otherwise levy upon funds of a cardholder held on deposit with the card issuer if that remedy is constitutionally available to creditors generally.

§ 1666i [CCPA § 170]. Assertion by Cardholder Against Card Issuer of Claims and Defenses Arising Out of Credit Card Transaction; Prerequisites; Limitation on Amount of Claims or Defenses

(a) Claims and defenses assertible

Subject to the limitation contained in subsection (b), a card issuer who has issued a credit card to a cardholder pursuant to an open end consumer credit plan shall be subject to all claims (other than tort claims) and defenses arising out of any transaction in which the credit card is used as a method of payment or extension of credit if (1) the obligor has made a good faith attempt to obtain satisfactory resolution of a disagreement or problem relative to the transaction from the person honoring the credit card; (2) the amount of the initial transaction exceeds $50; and (3) the place where the initial transaction occurred was in the same State as the mailing address previously provided by the cardholder or was within 100 miles from such address, except that the limitations set forth in clauses (2) and (3) with respect to an obligor's right to assert claims and defenses against a card issuer shall not be applicable to any transaction in which the person honoring the credit card (A) is the same person as the card issuer, (B) is controlled by the card issuer, (C) is under direct or indirect common control with the card issuer, (D) is a franchised dealer in the card issuer's products or services, or (E) has obtained the order for such transaction through a mail solicitation made by or participated in by the card issuer in which the cardholder is solicited to enter into such transaction by using the credit card issued by the card issuer.

(b) Amount of claims and defenses assertible

The amount of claims or defenses asserted by the cardholder may not exceed the amount of credit outstanding with respect to such transaction at the time the cardholder first notifies the card issuer or the person honoring the credit card of such claim or defense. For the purpose of determining the amount of credit outstanding in the preceding sentence, payments and credits to the cardholder's account are deemed to have been applied, in the order indicated, to the payment of: (1) late charges in the order of their entry to the account; (2) finance charges in order of their entry to the account; and (3) debits to the account other than those set forth above, in the order in which each debit entry to the account was made.

§ 1666i–1 [CCPA § 171.] Limits on Interest Rate, Fee, and Finance Charge Increases Applicable to Outstanding Balances

(a) In General

In the case of any credit card account under an open end consumer credit plan, no creditor may increase any annual percentage rate, fee, or finance charge applicable to any outstanding balance, except as permitted under subsection (b).

(b) Exceptions

The prohibition under subsection (a) shall not apply to—

(1) an increase in an annual percentage rate upon the expiration of a specified period of time, provided that—

(A) prior to commencement of that period, the creditor disclosed to the consumer, in a clear and conspicuous manner, the length of the period and the annual percentage rate that would apply after expiration of the period;

(B) the increased annual percentage rate does not exceed the rate disclosed pursuant to subparagraph (A); and

(C) the increased annual percentage rate is not applied to transactions that occurred prior to commencement of the period;

(2) an increase in a variable annual percentage rate in accordance with a credit card agreement that provides for changes in the rate according to operation of an index that is not under the control of the creditor and is available to the general public;

(3) an increase due to the completion of a workout or temporary hardship arrangement by the obligor or the failure of the obligor to comply with the terms of a workout or temporary hardship arrangement, provided that—

(A) the annual percentage rate, fee, or finance charge applicable to a category of transactions following any such increase does not exceed the rate, fee, or finance charge that applied to that category of transactions prior to commencement of the arrangement; and

(B) the creditor has provided the obligor, prior to the commencement of such arrangement, with clear and conspicuous disclosure of the terms of the arrangement (including any increases due to such completion or failure); or

(4) an increase due solely to the fact that a minimum payment by the obligor has not been received by the creditor within 60 days after the due date for such payment, provided that the creditor shall—

(A) include, together with the notice of such increase required under section 1637(i) of this title, a clear and conspicuous written statement of the reason for the increase and that the increase will terminate not later than 6 months after the date on which it is imposed, if the creditor receives the required minimum payments on time from the obligor during that period; and

(B) terminate such increase not later than 6 months after the date on which it is imposed, if the creditor receives the required minimum payments on time during that period.

(c) Repayment of outstanding balance.—

(1) In general

The creditor shall not change the terms governing the repayment of any outstanding balance, except that the creditor may provide the obligor with one of the methods described in paragraph (2) of repaying any outstanding balance, or a method that is no less beneficial to the obligor than one of those methods.

(2) Methods

The methods described in this paragraph are—

(A) an amortization period of not less than 5 years, beginning on the effective date of the increase set forth in the notice required under section 1637(i) of this title; or

(B) a required minimum periodic payment that includes a percentage of the outstanding balance that is equal to not more than twice the percentage required before the effective date of the increase set forth in the notice required under section 1637(i) of this title.

(d) Outstanding balance defined

For purposes of this section, the term "outstanding balance" means the amount owed on a credit card account under an open end consumer credit plan as of the end of the 14th day after the date on which the creditor provides notice of an increase in the annual percentage rate, fee, or finance charge in accordance with section 1637(i) of this title.

§ 1666i–2 [CCPA § 172.] Additional Limits on Interest Rate Increases[2]

(a) Limitation on increases within first year

Except in the case of an increase described in paragraph (1), (2), (3), or (4) of section 1666i–1(b) of this title, no increase in any annual percentage rate, fee, or finance charge on any credit card account under an open end consumer credit plan shall be effective before the end of the 1-year period beginning on the date on which the account is opened.

(b) Promotional rate minimum term

No increase in any annual percentage rate applicable to a credit card account under an open end consumer credit plan that is a promotional rate (as that term is defined by the Bureau) shall be effective before the end of the 6-month period beginning on the date on which the promotional rate takes effect, subject to such reasonable exceptions as the Bureau may establish, by rule.

§ 1666j [CCPA § 173]. Applicability of State Laws[3]

(a) Consistency of provisions

This part does not annul, alter, or affect, or exempt any person subject to the provisions of this part from complying with, the laws of any State with respect to credit billing practices, except to the extent that those laws are inconsistent with any provision of this part, and then only to the extent of the inconsistency. The Bureau is authorized to determine whether such inconsistencies exist. The Bureau may not determine that any State law is inconsistent with any provision of this part if the Bureau determines that such law gives greater protection to the consumer.

(b) Exemptions by Bureau from credit billing requirements

---

[2] In the Credit CARD Act of 2009, this section is at §§ 101(d) and (e) captioned as stated in the text and at § 106(c)(2) captioned "Unilateral Changes in credit card agreement prohibited."

[3] **[Editor's Note.** Until Feb. 21, 2010, this section was numbered CCPA § 170; effective Feb. 22, 2010, it was renumbered CCPA § 173].

The Bureau shall by regulation exempt from the requirements of this part any class of credit transactions within any State if it determines that under the law of that State that class of transactions is subject to requirements substantially similar to those imposed under this part or that such law gives greater protection to the consumer, and that there is adequate provision for enforcement.

(c) Finance charge or other charge for credit for sales transactions involving cash discounts

Notwithstanding any other provisions of this subchapter, any discount offered under section 1666f(b) of this title shall not be considered a finance charge or other charge for credit under the usury laws of any State or under the laws of any State relating to disclosure of information in connection with credit transactions, or relating to the types, amounts or rates of charges, or to any element or elements of charges permissible under such laws in connection with the extension or use of credit.

PART E—CONSUMER LEASES

§ 1667 [CCPA § 181]. Definitions

For purposes of this part—

(1) The term "consumer lease" means a contract in the form of a lease or bailment for the use of personal property by a natural person for a period of time exceeding four months, and for a total contractual obligation not exceeding $50,000, primarily for personal, family, or household purposes, whether or not the lessee has the option to purchase or otherwise become the owner of the property at the expiration of the lease, except that such term shall not include any credit sale as defined in section 1602(g) of this title. Such term does not include a lease for agricultural, business, or commercial purposes, or to a government or governmental agency or instrumentality, or to an organization.

(2) The term "lessee" means a natural person who leases or is offered a consumer lease.

(3) The term "lessor" means a person who is regularly engaged in leasing, offering to lease, or arranging to lease under a consumer lease.

(4) The term "personal property" means any property which is not real property under the laws of the State where situated at the time offered or otherwise made available for lease.

(5) The terms "security" and "security interest" mean any interest in property which secures payment or performance of an obligation.

§ 1667a [CCPA § 182]. Consumer Lease Disclosures

Each lessor shall give a lessee prior to the consummation of the lease a dated written statement on which the lessor and lessee are identified setting out accurately and in a clear and conspicuous manner the following information with respect to that lease, as applicable:

(1) A brief description or identification of the leased property;

(2) The amount of any payment by the lessee required at the inception of the lease;

(3) The amount paid or payable by the lessee for official fees, registration, certificate of title, or license fees or taxes;

(4) The amount of other charges payable by the lessee not included in the periodic payments, a description of the charges and that the lessee shall be liable for the differential, if any, between the anticipated fair market value of the leased property and its appraised actual value at the termination of the lease, if the lessee has such liability;

(5) A statement of the amount or method of determining the amount of any liabilities the lease imposes upon the lessee at the end of the term and whether or not the lessee has the option to purchase the leased property and at what price and time;

(6) A statement identifying all express warranties and guarantees made by the manufacturer or lessor with respect to the leased property, and identifying the party responsible for maintaining or servicing the leased property together with a description of the responsibility;

(7) A brief description of insurance provided or paid for by the lessor or required of the lessee, including the types and amounts of the coverages and costs;

(8) A description of any security interest held or to be retained by the lessor in connection with the lease and a clear identification of the property to which the security interest relates;

(9) The number, amount, and due dates or periods of payments under the lease and the total amount of such periodic payments;

(10) Where the lease provides that the lessee shall be liable for the anticipated fair market value of the property on expiration of the lease, the fair market value of the property at the inception of the lease, the aggregate cost of the lease on expiration, and the differential between them; and

(11) A statement of the conditions under which the lessee or lessor may terminate the lease prior to the end of the term and the amount or method of determining any penalty or other charge for delinquency, default, late payments, or early termination.

The disclosures required under this section may be made in the lease contract to be signed by the lessee. The Bureau may provide by regulation that any portion of the information required to be disclosed under this section may be given in the form of estimates where the lessor is not in a position to know exact information.

§ 1667b [CCPA § 183]. Lessee's Liability on Expiration or Termination of Lease

(a) Estimated residual value of property as basis; presumptions; action by lessor for excess liability; mutually agreeable final adjustment

Where the lessee's liability on expiration of a consumer lease is based on the estimated residual value of the property such estimated residual value shall be a reasonable approximation of the anticipated actual fair market value of the property on lease expiration. There shall be a rebuttable presumption that the estimated residual value is unreasonable to the extent that the estimated residual value exceeds the actual residual value by more than three times the average payment allocable to a monthly period under the lease. In addition, where the lessee has such liability on expiration of a consumer lease there shall be a rebuttable presumption that the lessor's estimated residual value is not in good faith to the extent that the estimated residual value exceeds the actual residual value by more than three times the average payment allocable to a monthly period under the lease and such lessor shall not collect from the lessee the amount of such excess liability on expiration of a consumer lease unless the lessor brings a successful action with respect to such excess liability. In all actions, the lessor shall pay the lessee's reasonable attorney's fees. The presumptions stated in this section shall not apply to the extent the excess of estimated over actual residual value is due to physical damage to the property beyond reasonable wear and use, or to excessive use, and the lease may set standards for such wear and use if such standards are not unreasonable. Nothing in this subsection shall preclude the right of a willing lessee to make any mutually agreeable final adjustment with respect to such excess residual liability, provided such an agreement is reached after termination of the lease.

(b) Penalties and charges for delinquency, default, or early termination

Penalties or other charges for delinquency, default, or early termination may be specified in the lease but only at an amount which is reasonable in the light of the anticipated or actual harm caused by the delinquency, default, or early termination, the difficulties of proof of loss, and the inconvenience or nonfeasibility of otherwise obtaining an adequate remedy.

(c) Independent professional appraisal of residual value of property at termination of lease; finality

If a lease has a residual value provision at the termination of the lease, the lessee may obtain at his expense, a professional appraisal of the leased property by an independent third party agreed to by both parties. Such appraisal shall be final and binding on the parties.

§ 1667c [CCPA § 184]. Consumer Lease Advertising; Liability of Advertising Media

(a) In general

If an advertisement for a consumer lease includes a statement of the amount of any payment or a statement that any or no initial payment is required, the advertisement shall clearly and conspicuously state, as applicable—

(1) the transaction advertised is a lease;

(2) the total amount of any initial payments required on or before consummation of the lease or delivery of the property, whichever is later;

(3) that a security deposit is required;

(4) the number, amount, and timing of scheduled payments; and

(5) with respect to a lease in which the liability of the consumer at the end of the lease term is based on the anticipated residual value of the property, that an extra charge may be imposed at the end of the lease term.

(b) Advertising medium not liable

No owner or employee of any entity that serves as a medium in which an advertisement appears or through which an advertisement is disseminated, shall be liable under this section.

(c) Radio advertisements

(1) In general

An advertisement by radio broadcast to aid, promote, or assist, directly or indirectly, any consumer lease shall be deemed to be in compliance with the requirements of subsection (a) if such advertisement clearly and conspicuously—

(A) states the information required by paragraphs (1) and (2) of subsection (a);

(B) states the number, amounts, due dates or periods of scheduled payments, and the total of such payments under the lease;

(C) includes—

(i) a referral to—

(I) a toll-free telephone number established in accordance with paragraph (2) that may be used by consumers to obtain the information required under subsection (a); or

(II) a written advertisement that—

(aa) appears in a publication in general circulation in the community served by the radio station on which such advertisement is broadcast during the period beginning 3 days before any such broadcast and ending 10 days after such broadcast; and

(bb) includes the information required to be disclosed under subsection (a); and

(ii) the name and dates of any publication referred to in clause (i)(II); and

(D) includes any other information which the Bureau determines necessary to carry out this part.

(2) Establishment of toll-free number

(A) In general

In the case of a radio broadcast advertisement described in paragraph (1) that includes a referral to a toll-free telephone number, the lessor who offers the consumer lease shall—

(i) establish such a toll-free telephone number not later than the date on which the advertisement including the referral is broadcast;

(ii) maintain such telephone number for a period of not less than 10 days, beginning on the date of any such broadcast; and

(iii) provide the information required under subsection (a) with respect to the lease to any person who calls such number.

(B) Form of information

The information required to be provided under subparagraph (A)(iii) shall be provided verbally or, if requested by the consumer, in written form.

(3) No effect on other law

Nothing in this subsection shall affect the requirements of Federal law as such requirements apply to advertisement by any medium other than radio broadcast.

§ 1667d [CCPA § 185]. Civil liability of Lessors

(a) Grounds for maintenance of action

Any lessor who fails to comply with any requirement imposed under section 1667a or 1667b of this title with respect to any person is liable to such person as provided in section 1640 of this title.

(b) Additional grounds for maintenance of action; "creditor" defined

Any lessor who fails to comply with any requirement imposed under section 1667c of this title with respect to any person who suffers actual damage from the violation is liable to such person as provided in section 1640 of this title. For the purposes of this section, the term "creditor" as used in sections 1640 and 1641 of this title shall include a lessor as defined in this part.

(c) Jurisdiction of courts; time limitation

Notwithstanding section 1640(e) of this title, any action under this section may be brought in any United States district court or in any other court of competent jurisdiction. Such actions alleging a failure to disclose or otherwise comply with the requirements of this part shall be brought within one year of the termination of the lease agreement.

§ 1667e [CCPA § 186]. Applicability of State Laws; Exemptions by Bureau From Leasing Requirements

(a) This part does not annul, alter, or affect, or exempt any person subject to the provisions of this part from complying with, the laws of any State with respect to consumer leases, except to the extent that those laws are inconsistent with any provision of this part, and then only to the extent of the inconsistency. The Bureau is authorized to determine whether such inconsistencies exist. The Bureau may not determine that any State law is inconsistent with any provision of this part if the Bureau determines that such law gives greater protection and benefit to the consumer.

(b) The Bureau shall by regulation exempt from the requirements of this part any class of lease transactions within any State if it determines that under the law of that State that class of transactions is subject to requirements substantially similar to those imposed under this part or that such law gives greater protection and benefit to the consumer, and that there is adequate provision for enforcement.

§ 1667f [CCPA § 187]. Regulations

(a) Regulations authorized

(1) In general

The Bureau shall prescribe regulations to update and clarify the requirements and definitions applicable to lease disclosures and contracts, and any other issues specifically related to consumer leasing, to the extent that the Bureau determines such action to be necessary—

(A) to carry out this part;

(B) to prevent any circumvention of this part; or

(C) to facilitate compliance with the requirements of the[1] part.

(2) Classifications, adjustments

Any regulations prescribed under paragraph (1) may contain classifications and differentiations, and may provide for adjustments and exceptions for any class of transactions, as the Bureau considers appropriate.

(b) Model disclosure

(1) Publication

The Bureau shall establish and publish model disclosure forms to facilitate compliance with the disclosure requirements of this part and to aid the consumer in understanding the transaction to which the subject disclosure form relates.

(2) Use of automated equipment

In establishing model forms under this subsection, the Bureau shall consider the use by lessors of data processing or similar automated equipment.

(3) Use optional

A lessor may utilize a model disclosure form established by the Bureau under this subsection for purposes of compliance with this part, at the discretion of the lessor.

(4) Effect of use

Any lessor who properly uses the material aspects of any model disclosure form established by the Bureau under this subsection shall be deemed to be in compliance with the disclosure requirements to which the form relates.

SUBCHAPTER II—RESTRICTIONS ON GARNISHMENT

Table of Sections

Sec.

---

[1] So in original. Probably should be "this."

§ 1671 [CCPA § 301]. Congressional Findings and Declaration of Purpose

(a) Disadvantages of garnishment

The Congress finds:

(1) The unrestricted garnishment of compensation due for personal services encourages the making of predatory extensions of credit. Such extensions of credit divert money into excessive credit payments and thereby hinder the production and flow of goods in interstate commerce.

(2) The application of garnishment as a creditors' remedy frequently results in loss of employment by the debtor, and the resulting disruption of employment, production, and consumption constitutes a substantial burden on interstate commerce.

(3) The great disparities among the laws of the several States relating to garnishment have, in effect, destroyed the uniformity of the bankruptcy laws and frustrated the purposes thereof in many areas of the country.

(b) Necessity for regulation

On the basis of the findings stated in subsection (a) of this section, the Congress determines that the provisions of this subchapter are necessary and proper for the purpose of carrying into execution the powers of the Congress to regulate commerce and to establish uniform bankruptcy laws.

§ 1672 [CCPA § 302]. Definitions

For the purposes of this subchapter:

(a) The term "earnings" means compensation paid or payable for personal services, whether denominated as wages, salary, commission, bonus, or otherwise, and includes periodic payments pursuant to a pension or retirement program.

(b) The term "disposable earnings" means that part of the earnings of any individual remaining after the deduction from those earnings of any amounts required by law to be withheld.

(c) The term "garnishment" means any legal or equitable procedure through which the earnings of any individual are required to be withheld for payment of any debt.

§ 1673 [CCPA § 303]. Restriction on Garnishment

(a) Maximum allowable garnishment

Except as provided in subsection (b) and in section 1675 of this title, the maximum part of the aggregate disposable earnings of an individual for any workweek which is subjected to garnishment may not exceed

(1) 25 per centum of his disposable earnings for that week, or

(2) the amount by which his disposable earnings for that week exceed thirty times the Federal minimum hourly wage prescribed by section 206(a)(1) of Title 29 in effect at the time the earnings are payable,

whichever is less. In the case of earnings for any pay period other than a week, the Secretary of Labor shall by regulation prescribe a multiple of the Federal minimum hourly wage equivalent in effect to that set forth in paragraph (2).

(b) Exceptions

(1) The restrictions of subsection (a) do not apply in the case of

(A) any order for the support of any person issued by a court of competent jurisdiction or in accordance with an administrative procedure, which is established by State law, which affords substantial due process, and which is subject to judicial review.

(B) any order of any court of the United States having jurisdiction over cases under chapter 13 of Title 11.

(C) any debt due for any State or Federal tax.

(2) The maximum part of the aggregate disposable earnings of an individual for any workweek which is subject to garnishment to enforce any order for the support of any person shall not exceed—

(A) where such individual is supporting his spouse or dependent child (other than a spouse or child with respect to whose support such order is used), 50 per centum of such individual's disposable earnings for that week; and

(B) where such individual is not supporting such a spouse or dependent child described in clause (A), 60 per centum of such individual's disposable earnings for that week; except that, with respect to the disposable earnings of any individual for any workweek, the 50 per centum specified in clause (A) shall be deemed to be 55 per centum and the 60 per centum specified in clause (B) shall be deemed to be 65 per centum, if and to the extent that such earnings are subject to garnishment to enforce a support order with respect to a period which is prior to the twelve-week period which ends with the beginning of such workweek.

(c) Execution or enforcement of garnishment order or process prohibited

No court of the United States or any State, and no State (or officer or agency thereof), may make, execute, or enforce any order or process in violation of this section.

§ 1674 [CCPA § 304]. Restriction on Discharge From Employment by Reason of Garnishment

(a) Termination of employment

No employer may discharge any employee by reason of the fact that his earnings have been subjected to garnishment for any one indebtedness.

(b) Penalties

Whoever willfully violates subsection (a) of this section shall be fined not more than $1,000, or imprisoned not more than one year, or both.

§ 1675 [CCPA § 305]. Exemption for State-Regulated Garnishments

The Secretary of Labor may by regulation exempt from the provisions of section 1673(a) and (b)(2) of this title garnishments issued under the laws of any State if he determines that the laws of that State provide restrictions on garnishment which are substantially similar to those provided in section 1673(a) and (b)(2) of this title.

§ 1676 [CCPA § 306]. Enforcement by Secretary of Labor

The Secretary of Labor, acting through the Wage and Hour Division of the Department of Labor, shall enforce the provisions of this subchapter.

§ 1677 [CCPA § 307]. Effect on State Laws

This subchapter does not annul, alter, or affect, or exempt any person from complying with, the laws of any State

(1) prohibiting garnishments or providing for more limited garnishment than are allowed under this subchapter, or

(2) prohibiting the discharge of any employee by reason of the fact that his earnings have been subjected to garnishment for more than one indebtedness.

SUBCHAPTER II-A-CREDIT REPAIR ORGANIZATIONS

Table of Sections

§ 1679 [CCPA 402]. Findings and purposes

(a) Findings

The Congress makes the following findings:

(1) Consumers have a vital interest in establishing and maintaining their credit worthiness and credit standing in order to obtain and use credit. As a result, consumers who have experienced credit problems may seek assistance from credit repair organizations which offer to improve the credit standing of such consumers.

(2) Certain advertising and business practices of some companies engaged in the business of credit repair services have worked a financial hardship upon consumers, particularly those of limited economic means and who are inexperienced in credit matters.

(b) Purposes

The purposes of this subchapter are—

(1) to ensure that prospective buyers of the services of credit repair organizations are provided with the information necessary to make an informed decision regarding the purchase of such services; and

(2) to protect the public from unfair or deceptive advertising and business practices by credit repair organizations.

§ 1679a [CCPA § 403]. Definitions

For purposes of this subchapter, the following definitions apply:

(1) Consumer

The term "consumer" means an individual.

(2) Consumer credit transaction

The term "consumer credit transaction" means any transaction in which credit is offered or extended to an individual for personal, family, or household purposes.

(3) Credit repair organization

The term "credit repair organization"—

(A) means any person who uses any instrumentality of interstate commerce or the mails to sell, provide, or perform (or represent that such person can or will sell, provide, or perform) any service, in return for the payment of money or other valuable consideration, for the express or implied purpose of—

(i) improving any consumer's credit record, credit history, or credit rating; or

(ii) providing advice or assistance to any consumer with regard to any activity or service described in clause (i); and

(B) does not include—

(i) any nonprofit organization which is exempt from taxation under section 501(c)(3) of Title 26;

(ii) any creditor (as defined in section 1602 of this title), with respect to any consumer, to the extent the creditor is assisting the consumer to restructure any debt owed by the consumer to the creditor; or

(iii) any depository institution (as that term is defined in section 1813 of Title 12) or any Federal or State credit union (as those terms are defined in section 1752 of Title 12), or any affiliate or subsidiary of such a depository institution or credit union.

(4) Credit

The term "credit" has the meaning given to such term in section 1602(e) of this title.

§ 1679b [CCPA § 404]. Prohibited practices

(a) In general

No person may—

(1) make any statement, or counsel or advise any consumer to make any statement, which is untrue or misleading (or which, upon the exercise of reasonable care, should be known by the credit repair organization, officer, employee, agent, or other person to be untrue or misleading) with respect to any consumer's credit worthiness, credit standing, or credit capacity to—

(A) any consumer reporting agency (as defined in section 1681a(f) of this title); or

(B) any person—

(i) who has extended credit to the consumer; or

(ii) to whom the consumer has applied or is applying for an extension of credit;

(2) make any statement, or counsel or advise any consumer to make any statement, the intended effect of which is to alter the consumer's identification to prevent the display of the consumer's credit record, history, or rating for the purpose of concealing adverse information that is accurate and not obsolete to—

(A) any consumer reporting agency;

(B) any person—

(i) who has extended credit to the consumer; or

(ii) to whom the consumer has applied or is applying for an extension of credit;

(3) make or use any untrue or misleading representation of the services of the credit repair organization; or

(4) engage, directly or indirectly, in any act, practice, or course of business that constitutes or results in the commission of, or an attempt to commit, a fraud or deception on any person in connection with the offer or sale of the services of the credit repair organization.

(b) Payment in advance

No credit repair organization may charge or receive any money or other valuable consideration for the performance of any service which the credit repair organization has agreed to perform for any consumer before such service is fully performed.

§ 1679c [CCPA § 405]. Disclosures

(a) Disclosure required

Any credit repair organization shall provide any consumer with the following written statement before any contract or agreement between the consumer and the credit repair organization is executed:

"Consumer Credit File Rights Under State and Federal Law

"You have a right to dispute inaccurate information in your credit report by contacting the credit bureau directly. However, neither you nor any 'credit repair' company or credit repair organization has the right to have accurate, current, and verifiable information removed from your credit report. The credit bureau must remove accurate, negative information from your report only if it is over 7 years old. Bankruptcy information can be reported for 10 years.

"You have a right to obtain a copy of your credit report from a credit bureau. You may be charged a reasonable fee. There is no fee, however, if you have been turned down for credit, employment, insurance, or a rental dwelling because of information in your credit report within the preceding 60 days. The credit bureau must provide someone to help you interpret the information in your credit file. You are entitled to receive a free copy of your credit report if you are unemployed and intend to apply for employment in the next 60 days, if you are a recipient of public welfare assistance, or if you have reason to believe that there is inaccurate information in your credit report due to fraud.

"You have a right to sue a credit repair organization that violates the Credit Repair Organization Act. This law prohibits deceptive practices by credit repair organizations.

"You have the right to cancel your contract with any credit repair organization for any reason within 3 business days from the date you signed it.

"Credit bureaus are required to follow reasonable procedures to ensure that the information they report is accurate. However, mistakes may occur.

"You may, on your own, notify a credit bureau in writing that you dispute the accuracy of information in your credit file. The credit bureau must then reinvestigate and modify or remove inaccurate or incomplete information. The credit bureau may not charge any fee for this service. Any pertinent information and copies of all documents you have concerning an error should be given to the credit bureau.

"If the credit bureau's reinvestigation does not resolve the dispute to your satisfaction, you may send a brief statement to the credit bureau, to be kept in your file, explaining why you think the record is inaccurate. The credit bureau must include a summary of your statement about disputed information with any report it issues about you.

"The Federal Trade Commission regulates credit bureaus and credit repair organizations. For more information contact:

"The Public Reference Branch
"Federal Trade Commission
"Washington, D.C. 20580".

(b) Separate statement requirement

The written statement required under this section shall be provided as a document which is separate from any written contract or other agreement between the credit repair organization and the consumer or any other written material provided to the consumer.

(c) Retention of compliance records

(1) In general

The credit repair organization shall maintain a copy of the statement signed by the consumer acknowledging receipt of the statement.

(2) Maintenance for 2 years

The copy of any consumer's statement shall be maintained in the organization's files for 2 years after the date on which the statement is signed by the consumer.

§ 1679d [CCPA § 406]. Credit repair organizations contracts

(a) Written contracts required

No services may be provided by any credit repair organization for any consumer—

(1) unless a written and dated contract (for the purchase of such services) which meets the requirements of subsection (b) has been signed by the consumer; or

(2) before the end of the 3-business-day period beginning on the date the contract is signed.

(b) Terms and conditions of contract

No contract referred to in subsection (a) meets the requirements of this subsection unless such contract includes (in writing)—

(1) the terms and conditions of payment, including the total amount of all payments to be made by the consumer to the credit repair organization or to any other person;

(2) a full and detailed description of the services to be performed by the credit repair organization for the consumer, including—

(A) all guarantees of performance; and

(B) an estimate of—

(i) the date by which the performance of the services (to be performed by the credit repair organization or any other person) will be complete; or

(ii) the length of the period necessary to perform such services;

(3) the credit repair organization's name and principal business address; and

(4) a conspicuous statement in bold face type, in immediate proximity to the space reserved for the consumer's signature on the contract, which reads as follows: "You may cancel this contract without penalty or obligation at any time before midnight of the 3rd business day after the date on which you signed the contract. See the attached notice of cancellation form for an explanation of this right.".

§ 1679e [CCPA § 407]. Right to cancel contract

(a) In general

Any consumer may cancel any contract with any credit repair organization without penalty or obligation by notifying the credit repair organization of the consumer's intention to do so at any time before midnight of the 3rd business day which begins after the date on which the contract or agreement between the consumer and the credit repair organization is executed or would, but for this subsection, become enforceable against the parties.

(b) Cancellation form and other information

Each contract shall be accompanied by a form, in duplicate, which has the heading "Notice of Cancellation" and contains in bold face type the following statement:

"You may cancel this contract, without any penalty or obligation, at any time before midnight of the 3rd day which begins after the date the contract is signed by you.

"To cancel this contract, mail or deliver a signed, dated copy of this cancellation notice, or any other written notice to [name of credit repair organization] at [address of credit repair organization] before midnight on [date]

"I hereby cancel this transaction,

[date]

[purchaser's signature].".

(c) Consumer copy of contract required

Any consumer who enters into any contract with any credit repair organization shall be given, by the organization—

(1) a copy of the completed contract and the disclosure statement required under section 1679c of this title; and

(2) a copy of any other document the credit repair organization requires the consumer to sign,

at the time the contract or the other document is signed.

§ 1679f [CCPA § 408]. Noncompliance with this subchapter

(a) Consumer waivers invalid

Any waiver by any consumer of any protection provided by or any right of the consumer under this subchapter—

(1) shall be treated as void; and

(2) may not be enforced by any Federal or State court or any other person.

(b) Attempt to obtain waiver

Any attempt by any person to obtain a waiver from any consumer of any protection provided by or any right of the consumer under this subchapter shall be treated as a violation of this subchapter.

(c) Contracts not in compliance

Any contract for services which does not comply with the applicable provisions of this subchapter—

(1) shall be treated as void; and

(2) may not be enforced by any Federal or State court or any other person.

§ 1679g [CCPA § 409]. Civil liability

(a) Liability established

Any person who fails to comply with any provision of this subchapter with respect to any other person shall be liable to such person in an amount equal to the sum of the amounts determined under each of the following paragraphs:

(1) Actual damages

The greater of—

(A) the amount of any actual damage sustained by such person as a result of such failure; or

(B) any amount paid by the person to the credit repair organization.

(2) Punitive damages

(A) Individual actions

In the case of any action by an individual, such additional amount as the court may allow.

(B) Class actions

In the case of a class action, the sum of—

(i) the aggregate of the amount which the court may allow for each named plaintiff; and

(ii) the aggregate of the amount which the court may allow for each other class member, without regard to any minimum individual recovery.

(3) Attorneys' fees

In the case of any successful action to enforce any liability under paragraph (1) or (2), the costs of the action, together with reasonable attorneys' fees.

(b) Factors to be considered in awarding punitive damages

In determining the amount of any liability of any credit repair organization under subsection (a)(2), the court shall consider, among other relevant factors—

(1) the frequency and persistence of noncompliance by the credit repair organization;

(2) the nature of the noncompliance;

(3) the extent to which such noncompliance was intentional; and

(4) in the case of any class action, the number of consumers adversely affected.

§ 1679h [CCPA § 410]. Administrative enforcement

(a) In general

Compliance with the requirements imposed under this subchapter with respect to credit repair organizations shall be enforced under the Federal Trade Commission Act [15 U.S.C.A. § 41 et seq.] by the Federal Trade Commission.

(b) Violations of this subchapter treated as violations of Federal Trade Commission Act

(1) In general

For the purpose of the exercise by the Federal Trade Commission of the Commission's functions and powers under the Federal Trade Commission Act [15 U.S.C.A. § 41 et seq.], any violation of any requirement or prohibition imposed under this subchapter with respect to credit repair organizations shall constitute an unfair or deceptive act or practice in commerce in violation of section 5(a) of the Federal Trade Commission Act [15 U.S.C.A. § 45(a)].

(2) Enforcement authority under other law

All functions and powers of the Federal Trade Commission under the Federal Trade Commission Act [15 U.S.C.A. § 41 et seq.] shall be available to the Commission to enforce compliance with this subchapter by any person subject to enforcement by the Federal Trade Commission pursuant to this subsection, including the power to enforce the provisions of this subchapter in the same manner as if the violation had been a violation of any Federal Trade Commission trade regulation rule, without regard to whether the credit repair organization—

(A) is engaged in commerce; or

(B) meets any other jurisdictional tests in the Federal Trade Commission Act [15 U.S.C.A. § 41 et seq.].

(c) State action for violations

(1) Authority of States

In addition to such other remedies as are provided under State law, whenever the chief law enforcement officer of a State, or an official or agency designated by a State, has reason to believe that any person has violated or is violating this subchapter, the State—

(A) may bring an action to enjoin such violation;

(B) may bring an action on behalf of its residents to recover damages for which the person is liable to such residents under section 1679g of this title as a result of the violation; and

(C) in the case of any successful action under subparagraph (A) or (B), shall be awarded the costs of the action and reasonable attorney fees as determined by the court.

(2) Rights of Commission

(A) Notice to Commission

The State shall serve prior written notice of any civil action under paragraph (1) upon the Federal Trade Commission and provide the Commission with a copy of its complaint, except in any case where such prior notice is not feasible, in which case the State shall serve such notice immediately upon instituting such action.

(B) Intervention

The Commission shall have the right—

(i) to intervene in any action referred to in subparagraph (A);

(ii) upon so intervening, to be heard on all matters arising in the action; and

(iii) to file petitions for appeal.

(3) Investigatory powers

For purposes of bringing any action under this subsection, nothing in this subsection shall prevent the chief law enforcement officer, or an official or agency designated by a State, from exercising the powers conferred on the chief law enforcement officer or such official by the laws of such State to conduct investigations or to administer oaths or affirmations or to compel the attendance of witnesses or the production of documentary and other evidence.

(4) Limitation

Whenever the Federal Trade Commission has instituted a civil action for violation of this subchapter, no State may, during the pendency of such action, bring an action under this section against any defendant named in the complaint of the Commission for any violation of this subchapter that is alleged in that complaint.

§ 1679i [CCPA § 411]. Statute of limitations

Any action to enforce any liability under this subchapter may be brought before the later of—

(1) the end of the 5-year period beginning on the date of the occurrence of the violation involved; or

(2) in any case in which any credit repair organization has materially and willfully misrepresented any information which—

(A) the credit repair organization is required, by any provision of this subchapter, to disclose to any consumer; and

(B) is material to the establishment of the credit repair organization's liability to the consumer under this subchapter,

the end of the 5-year period beginning on the date of the discovery by the consumer of the misrepresentation.

§ 1679j [CCPA § 412]. Relation to State law

This subchapter shall not annul, alter, affect, or exempt any person subject to the provisions of this subchapter from complying with any law of any State except to the extent that such law is inconsistent with any provision of this subchapter, and then only to the extent of the inconsistency.

SUBCHAPTER III—CREDIT REPORTING AGENCIES

Table of Sections

§ 1681 [CCPA § 602]. Congressional findings and statement of purpose

(a) Accuracy and fairness of credit reporting

The Congress makes the following findings:

(1) The banking system is dependent upon fair and accurate credit reporting. Inaccurate credit reports directly impair the efficiency of the banking system, and unfair credit reporting methods undermine the public confidence which is essential to the continued functioning of the banking system.

(2) An elaborate mechanism has been developed for investigating and evaluating the credit worthiness, credit standing, credit capacity, character, and general reputation of consumers.

(3) Consumer reporting agencies have assumed a vital role in assembling and evaluating consumer credit and other information on consumers.

(4) There is a need to insure that consumer reporting agencies exercise their grave responsibilities with fairness, impartiality, and a respect for the consumer's right to privacy.

(b) Reasonable procedures

It is the purpose of this subchapter to require that consumer reporting agencies adopt reasonable procedures for meeting the needs of commerce for consumer credit, personnel, insurance, and other information in a manner which is fair and equitable to the consumer, with regard to the confidentiality, accuracy, relevancy, and proper utilization of such information in accordance with the requirements of this subchapter.

§ 1681a [CCPA § 603]. Definitions; rules of construction

(a) Definitions and rules of construction set forth in this section are applicable for the purposes of this subchapter.

(b) The term "person" means any individual, partnership, corporation, trust, estate, cooperative, association, government or governmental subdivision or agency, or other entity.

(c) The term "consumer" means an individual.

(d) Consumer report.

(1) In general.

The term "consumer report" means any written, oral, or other communication of any information by a consumer reporting agency bearing on a consumer's credit worthiness, credit standing, credit capacity, character, general reputation, personal characteristics, or mode of living which is used or expected to be used or collected in whole or in part for the purpose of serving as a factor in establishing the consumer's eligibility for—

(A) credit or insurance to be used primarily for personal, family, or household purposes;

(B) employment purposes; or

(C) any other purpose authorized under section 1681b of this title.

(2) Exclusions.

Except as provided in paragraph (3), the term "consumer report" does not include—

(A) subject to section 1681s–3 of this title, any—

(i) report containing information solely as to transactions or experiences between the consumer and the person making the report;

(ii) communication of that information among persons related by common ownership or affiliated by corporate control; or

(iii) communication of other information among persons related by common ownership or affiliated by corporate control, if it is clearly and conspicuously disclosed to the consumer that the information may be communicated among such persons and the consumer is given the opportunity, before the time that the information is initially communicated, to direct that such information not be communicated among such persons;

(B) any authorization or approval of a specific extension of credit directly or indirectly by the issuer of a credit card or similar device;

(C) any report in which a person who has been requested by a third party to make a specific extension of credit directly or indirectly to a consumer conveys his or her decision with respect to such request, if the third party advises the consumer of the name and address of the person to whom the request was made, and such person makes the disclosures to the consumer required under section 1681m of this title; or

(D) a communication described in subsection (*o*) or (x).

(3) Restriction on sharing of medical information

Except for information or any communication of information disclosed as provided in section 1681b(g)(3) of this title, the exclusions in paragraph (2) shall not apply with respect to information disclosed to any person related by common ownership or affiliated by corporate control, if the information is—

(A) medical information;

(B) an individualized list or description based on the payment transactions of the consumer for medical products or services; or

(C) an aggregate list of identified consumers based on payment transactions for medical products or services.

(e) The term "investigative consumer report" means a consumer report or portion thereof in which information on a consumer's character, general reputation, personal characteristics, or mode of living is obtained through personal interviews with neighbors, friends, or associates of the consumer reported on or with others with whom he is acquainted or who may have knowledge concerning any such items of information. However, such information shall not include specific factual information on a consumer's credit record obtained directly from a creditor of the consumer or from a consumer reporting agency when such information was obtained directly from a creditor of the consumer or from the consumer.

(f) The term "consumer reporting agency" means any person which, for monetary fees, dues, or on a cooperative nonprofit basis, regularly engages in whole or in part in the practice of assembling or evaluating consumer credit information or other information on consumers for the purpose of furnishing consumer reports to third parties, and which uses any means or facility of interstate commerce for the purpose of preparing or furnishing consumer reports.

(g) The term "file", when used in connection with information on any consumer, means all of the information on that consumer recorded and retained by a consumer reporting agency regardless of how the information is stored.

(h) The term "employment purposes" when used in connection with a consumer report means a report used for the purpose of evaluating a consumer for employment, promotion, reassignment or retention as an employee.

(i) Medical information

The term "medical information"—

(1) means information or data, whether oral or recorded, in any form or medium, created by or derived from a health care provider or the consumer, that relates to—

(A) the past, present, or future physical, mental, or behavioral health or condition of an individual;

(B) the provision of health care to an individual; or

(C) the payment for the provision of health care to an individual.[1]

(2) does not include the age or gender of a consumer, demographic information about the consumer, including a consumer's residence address or e-mail address, or any other information about a consumer that does not relate to the physical, mental, or behavioral health or condition of a consumer, including the existence or value of any insurance policy.

(j) Definitions relating to child support obligations

(1) Overdue support

The term "overdue support" has the meaning given to such term in section 666(e) of Title 42.

(2) State or local child support enforcement agency

The term "State or local child support enforcement agency" means a State or local agency which administers a State or local program for establishing and enforcing child support obligations.

(k) Adverse action.

(1) Actions included.

The term "adverse action"—

(A) has the same meaning as in section 1691(d)(6) of this title; and

(B) means—

(i) a denial or cancellation of, an increase in any charge for, or a reduction or other adverse or unfavorable change in the terms of coverage or amount of, any insurance, existing or applied for, in connection with the underwriting of insurance;

(ii) a denial of employment or any other decision for employment purposes that adversely affects any current or prospective employee;

(iii) a denial or cancellation of, an increase in any charge for, or any other adverse or unfavorable change in the terms of, any license or benefit described in section 1681b(a)(3)(D) of this title; and

(iv) an action taken or determination that is—

(I) made in connection with an application that was made by, or a transaction that was initiated by, any consumer, or in connection with a review of an account under section 1681b(a)(3)(F)(ii) of this title; and

(II) adverse to the interests of the consumer.

(2) Applicable findings, decisions, commentary, and orders.

For purposes of any determination of whether an action is an adverse action under paragraph (1)(A), all appropriate final findings, decisions, commentary, and orders issued under section 1691(d)(6) of this title by the Bureau or any court shall apply.

---

1 So in original. The period probably should be "; and".

(*l*) Firm offer of credit or insurance.

The term "firm offer of credit or insurance" means any offer of credit or insurance to a consumer that will be honored if the consumer is determined, based on information in a consumer report on the consumer, to meet the specific criteria used to select the consumer for the offer, except that the offer may be further conditioned on one or more of the following:

(1) The consumer being determined, based on information in the consumer's application for the credit or insurance, to meet specific criteria bearing on credit worthiness or insurability, as applicable, that are established—

(A) before selection of the consumer for the offer; and

(B) for the purpose of determining whether to extend credit or insurance pursuant to the offer.

(2) Verification

(A) that the consumer continues to meet the specific criteria used to select the consumer for the offer, by using information in a consumer report on the consumer, information in the consumer's application for the credit or insurance, or other information bearing on the credit worthiness or insurability of the consumer; or

(B) of the information in the consumer's application for the credit or insurance, to determine that the consumer meets the specific criteria bearing on credit worthiness or insurability.

(3) The consumer furnishing any collateral that is a requirement for the extension of the credit or insurance that was—

(A) established before selection of the consumer for the offer of credit or insurance; and

(B) disclosed to the consumer in the offer of credit or insurance.

(m) Credit or insurance transaction that is not initiated by the consumer.

The term "credit or insurance transaction that is not initiated by the consumer" does not include the use of a consumer report by a person with which the consumer has an account or insurance policy, for purposes of—

(1) reviewing the account or insurance policy; or

(2) collecting the account.

(n) State.

The term "State" means any State, the Commonwealth of Puerto Rico, the District of Columbia, and any territory or possession of the United States.

(*o*) Excluded communications.

A communication is described in this subsection if it is a communication—

(1) that, but for subsection (d)(2)(D), would be an investigative consumer report;

(2) that is made to a prospective employer for the purpose of—

(A) procuring an employee for the employer; or

(B) procuring an opportunity for a natural person to work for the employer;

(3) that is made by a person who regularly performs such procurement;

(4) that is not used by any person for any purpose other than a purpose described in subparagraph (A) or (B) of paragraph (2); and

(5) with respect to which—

(A) the consumer who is the subject of the communication—

(i) consents orally or in writing to the nature and scope of the communication, before the collection of any information for the purpose of making the communication;

(ii) consents orally or in writing to the making of the communication to a prospective employer, before the making of the communication; and

(iii) in the case of consent under clause (i) or (ii) given orally, is provided written confirmation of that consent by the person making the communication, not later than 3 business days after the receipt of the consent by that person;

(B) the person who makes the communication does not, for the purpose of making the communication, make any inquiry that if made by a prospective employer of the consumer who is the subject of the communication would violate any applicable Federal or State equal employment opportunity law or regulation; and

(C) the person who makes the communication—

(i) discloses in writing to the consumer who is the subject of the communication, not later than 5 business days after receiving any request from the consumer for such disclosure, the nature and substance of all information in the consumer's file at the time of the request, except that the sources of any information that is acquired solely for use in making the communication and is actually used for no other purpose, need not be disclosed other than under appropriate discovery procedures in any court of competent jurisdiction in which an action is brought; and

(ii) notifies the consumer who is the subject of the communication, in writing, of the consumer's right to request the information described in clause (i).

(p) Consumer reporting agency that compiles and maintains files on consumers on a nationwide basis.

The term "consumer reporting agency that compiles and maintains files on consumers on a nationwide basis" means a consumer reporting agency that regularly engages in the practice of assembling or evaluating, and maintaining, for the purpose of furnishing consumer reports to third parties bearing on a consumer's credit worthiness, credit standing, or credit capacity, each of the following regarding consumers residing nationwide:

(1) Public record information.

(2) Credit account information from persons who furnish that information regularly and in the ordinary course of business.

(q) Definitions relating to fraud alerts

(1) Active duty military consumer

The term "active duty military consumer" means a consumer in military service who—

(A) is on active duty (as defined in section 101(d)(1) of Title 10) or is a reservist performing duty under a call or order to active duty under a provision of law referred to in section 101(a)(13) of Title 10; and

(B) is assigned to service away from the usual duty station of the consumer.

(2) Fraud alert; active duty alert

The terms "fraud alert" and "active duty alert" mean a statement in the file of a consumer that—

(A) notifies all prospective users of a consumer report relating to the consumer that the consumer may be a victim of fraud, including identity theft, or is an active duty military consumer, as applicable; and

(B) is presented in a manner that facilitates a clear and conspicuous view of the statement described in subparagraph (A) by any person requesting such consumer report.

(3) Identity theft

The term "identity theft" means a fraud committed using the identifying information of another person, subject to such further definition as the Bureau may prescribe, by regulation.

(4) Identity theft report

The term "identity theft report" has the meaning given that term by rule of the Bureau, and means, at a minimum, a report—

(A) that alleges an identity theft;

(B) that is a copy of an official, valid report filed by a consumer with an appropriate Federal, State, or local law enforcement agency, including the United States Postal Inspection Service, or such other government agency deemed appropriate by the Bureau; and

(C) the filing of which subjects the person filing the report to criminal penalties relating to the filing of false information if, in fact, the information in the report is false.

(5) New credit plan

The term "new credit plan" means a new account under an open end credit plan (as defined in section 1602(i) of this title) or a new credit transaction not under an open end credit plan.

(r) Credit and debit related terms

(1) Card issuer

The term "card issuer" means—

(A) a credit card issuer, in the case of a credit card; and

(B) a debit card issuer, in the case of a debit card.

(2) Credit card

The term "credit card" has the same meaning as in section 1602 of this title.

(3) Debit card

The term "debit card" means any card issued by a financial institution to a consumer for use in initiating an electronic fund transfer from the account of the consumer at such financial institution, for the purpose of transferring money between accounts or obtaining money, property, labor, or services.

(4) Account and electronic fund transfer

The terms "account" and "electronic fund transfer" have the same meanings as in section 1693a of this title.

(5) Credit and creditor

The terms "credit" and "creditor" have the same meanings as in section 1691a of this title.

(s) Federal banking agency

The term "Federal banking agency" has the same meaning as in section 1813 of Title 12.

(t) Financial institution

The term "financial institution" means a State or National bank, a State or Federal savings and loan association, a mutual savings bank, a State or Federal credit union, or any other person that, directly or indirectly, holds a transaction account (as defined in section 461(b) of Title 12) belonging to a consumer.

(u) Reseller

The term "reseller" means a consumer reporting agency that—

(1) assembles and merges information contained in the database of another consumer reporting agency or multiple consumer reporting agencies concerning any consumer for purposes of furnishing such information to any third party, to the extent of such activities; and

(2) does not maintain a database of the assembled or merged information from which new consumer reports are produced.

(v) Commission

The term "Commission" means the Bureau.[2]

(w) The term "Bureau" means the Bureau of Consumer Financial Protection.

(x) Nationwide specialty consumer reporting agency

The term "nationwide specialty consumer reporting agency" means a consumer reporting agency that compiles and maintains files on consumers on a nationwide basis relating to—

(1) medical records or payments;

(2) residential or tenant history;

(3) check writing history;

(4) employment history; or

(5) insurance claims.

(y) Exclusion of certain communications for employee investigations

(1) Communications described in this subsection

A communication is described in this subsection if—

(A) but for subsection (d)(2)(D), the communication would be a consumer report;

(B) the communication is made to an employer in connection with an investigation of—

(i) suspected misconduct relating to employment; or

(ii) compliance with Federal, State, or local laws and regulations, the rules of a self-regulatory organization, or any preexisting written policies of the employer;

(C) the communication is not made for the purpose of investigating a consumer's credit worthiness, credit standing, or credit capacity; and

(D) the communication is not provided to any person except—

(i) to the employer or an agent of the employer;

(ii) to any Federal or State officer, agency, or department, or any officer, agency, or department of a unit of general local government;

(iii) to any self-regulatory organization with regulatory authority over the activities of the employer or employee;

---

[2] So in original.

(iv) as otherwise required by law; or

(v) pursuant to section 1681f of this title.

(2) Subsequent disclosure

After taking any adverse action based in whole or in part on a communication described in paragraph (1), the employer shall disclose to the consumer a summary containing the nature and substance of the communication upon which the adverse action is based, except that the sources of information acquired solely for use in preparing what would be but for subsection (d)(2)(D) an investigative consumer report need not be disclosed.

(3) Self-regulatory organization defined

For purposes of this subsection, the term "self-regulatory organization" includes any self-regulatory organization (as defined in section 78c(a)(26) of this title), any entity established under title I of the Sarbanes-Oxley Act of 2002, any board of trade designated by the Commodity Futures Trading Commission, and any futures association registered with such Commission.

(z) Veteran

The term "veteran" has the meaning given the term in section 101 of title 38, United States Code.

(aa) Veteran's medical debt

The term "veteran's medical debt"—

(1) means a medical collection debt of a veteran owed to a non-Department of Veterans Affairs health care provider that was submitted to the Department for payment for health care authorized by the Department of Veterans Affairs; and

(2) includes medical collection debt that the Department of Veterans Affairs has wrongfully charged a veteran.

§ 1681b [CCPA § 604]. Permissible purposes of consumer reports

(a) In general

Subject to subsection (c), any consumer reporting agency may furnish a consumer report under the following circumstances and no other:

(1) In response to the order of a court having jurisdiction to issue such an order, or a subpoena issued in connection with proceedings before a Federal grand jury.

(2) In accordance with the written instructions of the consumer to whom it relates.

(3) To a person which it has reason to believe—

(A) intends to use the information in connection with a credit transaction involving the consumer on whom the information is to be furnished and involving the extension of credit to, or review or collection of an account of, the consumer; or

(B) intends to use the information for employment purposes; or

(C) intends to use the information in connection with the underwriting of insurance involving the consumer; or

(D) intends to use the information in connection with a determination of the consumer's eligibility for a license or other benefit granted by a governmental instrumentality required by law to consider an applicant's financial responsibility or status; or

(E) intends to use the information, as a potential investor or servicer, or current insurer, in connection with a valuation of, or an assessment of the credit or prepayment risks associated with, an existing credit obligation; or

(F) otherwise has a legitimate business need for the information—

(i) in connection with a business transaction that is initiated by the consumer; or

(ii) to review an account to determine whether the consumer continues to meet the terms of the account.

(G) executive departments and agencies in connection with the issuance of government-sponsored individually-billed travel charge cards.

(4) In response to a request by the head of a State or local child support enforcement agency (or a State or local government official authorized by the head of such an agency), if the person making the request certifies to the consumer reporting agency that—

(A) the consumer report is needed for the purpose of establishing an individual's capacity to make child support payments or determining the appropriate level of such payments, or enforcing a child support order, award, agreement, or judgment;

(B) the parentage of the consumer for the child to which the obligation relates has been established or acknowledged by the consumer in accordance with State laws under which the obligation arises (if required by those laws); and

(C) the consumer report will be kept confidential, will be used solely for a purpose described in subparagraph (A), and will not be used in connection with any other civil, administrative, or criminal proceeding, or for any other purpose.

(D) Redesignated (C)

(5) To an agency administering a State plan under section 654 of Title 42 for use to set an initial or modified child support award.

(6) To the Federal Deposit Insurance Corporation or the National Credit Union Administration as part of its preparation for its appointment or as part of its exercise of powers, as conservator, receiver, or liquidating agent for an insured depository institution or insured credit union under the Federal Deposit Insurance Act or the Federal Credit Union Act, or other applicable Federal or State law, or in connection with the resolution or liquidation of a failed or failing insured depository institution or insured credit union, as applicable.

(b) Conditions for furnishing and using consumer reports for employment purposes

(1) Certification from user

A consumer reporting agency may furnish a consumer report for employment purposes only if—

(A) the person who obtains such report from the agency certifies to the agency that—

(i) the person has complied with paragraph (2) with respect to the consumer report, and the person will comply with paragraph (3) with respect to the consumer report if paragraph (3) becomes applicable; and

(ii) information from the consumer report will not be used in violation of any applicable Federal or State equal employment opportunity law or regulation; and

(B) the consumer reporting agency provides with the report, or has previously provided, a summary of the consumer's rights under this subchapter, as prescribed by the Bureau under section 1681g(c)(3) of this title.

(2) Disclosure to consumer

(A) In general

Except as provided in subparagraph (B), a person may not procure a consumer report, or cause a consumer report to be procured, for employment purposes with respect to any consumer, unless—

(i) a clear and conspicuous disclosure has been made in writing to the consumer at any time before the report is procured or caused to be procured, in a document that consists solely of the disclosure, that a consumer report may be obtained for employment purposes; and

(ii) the consumer has authorized in writing (which authorization may be made on the document referred to in clause (i)) the procurement of the report by that person.

(B) Application by mail, telephone, computer, or other similar means

If a consumer described in subparagraph (C) applies for employment by mail, telephone, computer, or other similar means, at any time before a consumer report is procured or caused to be procured in connection with that application—

(i) the person who procures the consumer report on the consumer for employment purposes shall provide to the consumer, by oral, written, or electronic means, notice that a consumer report may be obtained for employment purposes, and a summary of the consumer's rights under section 1681m(a)(3) of this title; and

(ii) the consumer shall have consented, orally, in writing, or electronically to the procurement of the report by that person.

(C) Scope

Subparagraph (B) shall apply to a person procuring a consumer report on a consumer in connection with the consumer's application for employment only if—

(i) the consumer is applying for a position over which the Secretary of Transportation has the power to establish qualifications and maximum hours of service pursuant to the provisions of section 31502 of Title 49, or a position subject to safety regulation by a State transportation agency; and

(ii) as of the time at which the person procures the report or causes the report to be procured the only interaction between the consumer and the person in connection with that employment application has been by mail, telephone, computer, or other similar means.

(3) Conditions on use for adverse actions

(A) In general

Except as provided in subparagraph (B), in using a consumer report for employment purposes, before taking any adverse action based in whole or in part on the report, the person intending to take such adverse action shall provide to the consumer to whom the report relates—

(i) a copy of the report; and

(ii) a description in writing of the rights of the consumer under this subchapter, as prescribed by the Bureau under section 1681g(c)(3) of this title.

(B) Application by mail, telephone, computer, or other similar means

(i) If a consumer described in subparagraph (C) applies for employment by mail, telephone, computer, or other similar means, and if a person who has procured a consumer report on the consumer for employment purposes takes adverse action on the employment application based in whole or in part on the report, then the person must provide to the consumer to whom the report relates, in lieu of the notices required under subparagraph (A) of this section and under section 1681m(a) of this title, within 3 business days of taking such action, an oral, written or electronic notification—

(I) that adverse action has been taken based in whole or in part on a consumer report received from a consumer reporting agency;

(II) of the name, address and telephone number of the consumer reporting agency that furnished the consumer report (including a toll-free telephone number established by the agency if the agency compiles and maintains files on consumers on a nationwide basis);

(III) that the consumer reporting agency did not make the decision to take the adverse action and is unable to provide to the consumer the specific reasons why the adverse action was taken; and

(IV) that the consumer may, upon providing proper identification, request a free copy of a report and may dispute with the consumer reporting agency the accuracy or completeness of any information in a report.

(ii) If, under clause (B)(i)(IV), the consumer requests a copy of a consumer report from the person who procured the report, then, within 3 business days of receiving the consumer's request, together with proper identification, the person must send or provide to the consumer a copy of a report and a copy of the consumer's rights as prescribed by the Bureau under section 1681g(c)(3) of this title.

(C) Scope

Subparagraph (B) shall apply to a person procuring a consumer report on a consumer in connection with the consumer's application for employment only if—

(i) the consumer is applying for a position over which the Secretary of Transportation has the power to establish qualifications and maximum hours of service pursuant to the provisions of section 31502 of Title 49, or a position subject to safety regulation by a State transportation agency; and

(ii) as of the time at which the person procures the report or causes the report to be procured the only interaction between the consumer and the person in connection with that employment application has been by mail, telephone, computer, or other similar means.

(4) Exception for national security investigations

(A) In general

In the case of an agency or department of the United States Government which seeks to obtain and use a consumer report for employment purposes, paragraph (3) shall not apply to any adverse action by such agency or department which is based in part on such consumer report, if the head of such agency or department makes a written finding that—

(i) the consumer report is relevant to a national security investigation of such agency or department;

(ii) the investigation is within the jurisdiction of such agency or department;

(iii) there is reason to believe that compliance with paragraph (3) will—

(I) endanger the life or physical safety of any person;

(II) result in flight from prosecution;

(III) result in the destruction of, or tampering with, evidence relevant to the investigation;

(IV) result in the intimidation of a potential witness relevant to the investigation;

(V) result in the compromise of classified information; or

(VI) otherwise seriously jeopardize or unduly delay the investigation or another official proceeding.

(B) Notification of consumer upon conclusion of investigation

Upon the conclusion of a national security investigation described in subparagraph (A), or upon the determination that the exception under subparagraph (A) is no longer required for the reasons set forth in such subparagraph, the official exercising the authority in such subparagraph shall provide to the consumer who is the subject of the consumer report with regard to which such finding was made—

(i) a copy of such consumer report with any classified information redacted as necessary;

(ii) notice of any adverse action which is based, in part, on the consumer report; and

(iii) the identification with reasonable specificity of the nature of the investigation for which the consumer report was sought.

(C) Delegation by head of agency or department

For purposes of subparagraphs (A) and (B), the head of any agency or department of the United States Government may delegate his or her authorities under this paragraph to an official of such agency or department who has personnel security responsibilities and is a member of the Senior Executive Service or equivalent civilian or military rank.

(D) Definitions

For purposes of this paragraph, the following definitions shall apply:

(i) Classified information.—The term "classified information" means information that is protected from unauthorized disclosure under Executive Order No. 12958 or successor orders.

(ii) National security investigation.—The term "national security investigation" means any official inquiry by an agency or department of the United States Government to determine the eligibility of a consumer to receive access or continued access to classified information or to determine whether classified information has been lost or compromised.

(E) Repealed. Pub.L. 108–177, Title III, § 361(j), Dec. 13, 2003, 117 Stat. 2625

(F) Redesignated (D)

(c) Furnishing reports in connection with credit or insurance transactions that are not initiated by the consumer

(1) In general

A consumer reporting agency may furnish a consumer report relating to any consumer pursuant to subparagraph (A) or (C) of subsection (a)(3) of this section in connection with any credit or insurance transaction that is not initiated by the consumer only if—

(A) the consumer authorizes the agency to provide such report to such person; or

(B)(i) the transaction consists of a firm offer of credit or insurance;

(ii) the consumer reporting agency has complied with subsection (e);

(iii) there is not in effect an election by the consumer, made in accordance with subsection (e) of this section, to have the consumer's name and address excluded from lists of names provided by the agency pursuant to this paragraph; and

(iv) the consumer report does not contain a date of birth that shows that the consumer has not attained the age of 21, or, if the date of birth on the consumer report shows that the consumer has not attained the age of 21, such consumer consents to the consumer reporting agency to such furnishing.

(2) Limits on information received under paragraph (1)(B)

A person may receive pursuant to paragraph (1)(B) only—

(A) the name and address of a consumer;

(B) an identifier that is not unique to the consumer and that is used by the person solely for the purpose of verifying the identity of the consumer; and

(C) other information pertaining to a consumer that does not identify the relationship or experience of the consumer with respect to a particular creditor or other entity.

(3) Information regarding inquiries

Except as provided in section 1681g(a)(5) of this title, a consumer reporting agency shall not furnish to any person a record of inquiries in connection with a credit or insurance transaction that is not initiated by a consumer.

(d) Reserved

(e) Election of consumer to be excluded from lists

(1) In general

A consumer may elect to have the consumer's name and address excluded from any list provided by a consumer reporting agency under subsection (c)(1)(B) in connection with a credit or insurance transaction that is not initiated by the consumer, by notifying the agency in accordance with paragraph (2) that the consumer does not consent to any use of a consumer report relating to the consumer in connection with any credit or insurance transaction that is not initiated by the consumer.

(2) Manner of notification

A consumer shall notify a consumer reporting agency under paragraph (1)—

(A) through the notification system maintained by the agency under paragraph (5); or

(B) by submitting to the agency a signed notice of election form issued by the agency for purposes of this subparagraph.

(3) Response of agency after notification through system

Upon receipt of notification of the election of a consumer under paragraph (1) through the notification system maintained by the agency under paragraph (5), a consumer reporting agency shall—

(A) inform the consumer that the election is effective only for the 5-year period following the election if the consumer does not submit to the agency a signed notice of election form issued by the agency for purposes of paragraph (2)(B); and

(B) provide to the consumer a notice of election form, if requested by the consumer, not later than 5 business days after receipt of the notification of the election through the system established under paragraph (5), in the case of a request made at the time the consumer provides notification through the system.

(4) Effectiveness of election

An election of a consumer under paragraph (1)—

(A) shall be effective with respect to a consumer reporting agency beginning 5 business days after the date on which the consumer notifies the agency in accordance with paragraph (2);

(B) shall be effective with respect to a consumer reporting agency—

(i) subject to subparagraph (C), during the 5-year period beginning 5 business days after the date on which the consumer notifies the agency of the election, in the case of an election for which a consumer notifies the agency only in accordance with paragraph (2)(A); or

(ii) until the consumer notifies the agency under subparagraph (C), in the case of an election for which a consumer notifies the agency in accordance with paragraph (2)(B);

(C) shall not be effective after the date on which the consumer notifies the agency, through the notification system established by the agency under paragraph (5), that the election is no longer effective; and

(D) shall be effective with respect to each affiliate of the agency.

(5) Notification system

(A) In general

Each consumer reporting agency that, under subsection (c)(1)(B), furnishes a consumer report in connection with a credit or insurance transaction that is not initiated by a consumer, shall—

(i) establish and maintain a notification system, including a toll-free telephone number, which permits any consumer whose consumer report is maintained by the agency to notify the agency, with appropriate identification, of the consumer's election to have the consumer's name and address excluded from any such list of names and addresses provided by the agency for such a transaction; and

(ii) publish by not later than 365 days after September 30, 1996, and not less than annually thereafter, in a publication of general circulation in the area served by the agency—

(I) a notification that information in consumer files maintained by the agency may be used in connection with such transactions; and

(II) the address and toll-free telephone number for consumers to use to notify the agency of the consumer's election under clause (i).

(B) Establishment and maintenance as compliance

Establishment and maintenance of a notification system (including a toll-free telephone number) and publication by a consumer reporting agency on the agency's own behalf and on behalf of any of its affiliates in accordance with this paragraph is deemed to be compliance with this paragraph by each of those affiliates.

(6) Notification system by agencies that operate nationwide

Each consumer reporting agency that compiles and maintains files on consumers on a nationwide basis shall establish and maintain a notification system for purposes of paragraph (5) jointly with other such consumer reporting agencies.

(f) Certain use or obtaining of information prohibited

A person shall not use or obtain a consumer report for any purpose unless—

(1) the consumer report is obtained for a purpose for which the consumer report is authorized to be furnished under this section; and

(2) the purpose is certified in accordance with section 1681e of this title by a prospective user of the report through a general or specific certification.

(g) Protection of medical information

(1) Limitation on consumer reporting agencies

A consumer reporting agency shall not furnish for employment purposes, or in connection with a credit or insurance transaction, a consumer report that contains medical information (other than medical contact information treated in the manner required under section 605(a)(6) of this title) about a consumer, unless—

(A) if furnished in connection with an insurance transaction, the consumer affirmatively consents to the furnishing of the report;

(B) if furnished for employment purposes or in connection with a credit transaction—

(i) the information to be furnished is relevant to process or effect the employment or credit transaction; and

(ii) the consumer provides specific written consent for the furnishing of the report that describes in clear and conspicuous language the use for which the information will be furnished; or

(C) the information to be furnished pertains solely to transactions, accounts, or balances relating to debts arising from the receipt of medical services, products, or devises, where such information, other than account status or amounts, is restricted or reported using codes that do not identify, or do not provide information sufficient to infer, the specific provider or the nature of such services, products, or devices, as provided in section 1681c(a)(6) of this title.

(2) Limitation on creditors

Except as permitted pursuant to paragraph (3)(C) or regulations prescribed under paragraph (5)(A), a creditor shall not obtain or use medical information (other than medical information treated in the manner required under section 605(a)(6) of this title) pertaining to a consumer in connection with any determination of the consumer's eligibility, or continued eligibility, for credit.

(3) Actions authorized by Federal law, insurance activities and regulatory determinations

Section 1681a(d)(3) of this title shall not be construed so as to treat information or any communication of information as a consumer report if the information or communication is disclosed—

(A) in connection with the business of insurance or annuities, including the activities described in section 18B of the model Privacy of Consumer Financial and Health Information Regulation issued by the National Association of Insurance Commissioners (as in effect on January 1, 2003);

(B) for any purpose permitted without authorization under the Standards for Individually Identifiable Health Information promulgated by the Department of Health and Human Services pursuant to the Health Insurance Portability and Accountability Act of 1996, or referred to under section 1179 of such Act, or described in section 6802(e) of this title; or

(C) as otherwise determined to be necessary and appropriate, by regulation or order, by the Bureau or the applicable State insurance authority (with respect to any person engaged in providing insurance or annuities).

(4) Limitation on redisclosure of medical information

Any person that receives medical information pursuant to paragraph (1) or (3) shall not disclose such information to any other person, except as necessary to carry out the purpose for which the information was initially disclosed, or as otherwise permitted by statute, regulation, or order.

(5) Regulations and effective date for paragraph (2)

(A)[1] Regulations required

The Bureau may, after notice and opportunity for comment, prescribe regulations that permit transactions under paragraph (2) that are determined to be necessary and appropriate to protect legitimate operational, transactional, risk, consumer, and other needs (and which shall include permitting actions necessary for administrative verification purposes), consistent with the intent of paragraph (2) to restrict the use of medical information for inappropriate purposes.

(6) Coordination with other laws

No provision of this subsection shall be construed as altering, affecting, or superseding the applicability of any other provision of Federal law relating to medical confidentiality.

§ 1681c [CCPA § 605]. Requirements relating to information contained in consumer reports

(a) Information excluded from consumer reports

Except as authorized under subsection (b), no consumer reporting agency may make any consumer report containing any of the following items of information:

(1) Cases under Title 11 or under the Bankruptcy Act that, from the date of entry of the order for relief or the date of adjudication, as the case may be, antedate the report by more than 10 years.

(2) Civil suits, civil judgments, and records of arrest that, from date of entry, antedate the report by more than seven years or until the governing statute of limitations has expired, whichever is the longer period.

(3) Paid tax liens which, from date of payment, antedate the report by more than seven years.

(4) Accounts placed for collection or charged to profit and loss which antedate the report by more than seven years.

(5) Any other adverse item of information, other than records of convictions of crimes which antedates the report by more than seven years.

(6) The name, address, and telephone number of any medical information furnisher that has notified the agency of its status, unless—

(A) such name, address, and telephone number are restricted or reported using codes that do not identify, or provide information sufficient to infer, the specific provider or the nature of such services, products, or devices to a person other than the consumer; or

(B) the report is being provided to an insurance company for a purpose relating to engaging in the business of insurance other than property and casualty insurance.

---

1 *So in original. No subpar. (B) has been enacted.*

(7) With respect to a consumer reporting agency described in section 1681a(p) of this title, any information related to a veteran's medical debt if the date on which the hospital care, medical services, or extended care services was rendered relating to the debt antedates the report by less than 1 year if the consumer reporting agency has actual knowledge that the information is related to a veteran's medical debt and the consumer reporting agency is in compliance with its obligation under section 302(c)(5) of the Economic Growth, Regulatory Relief, and Consumer Protection Act.

(8) With respect to a consumer reporting agency described in section 1681a(p) of this title, any information related to a fully paid or settled veteran's medical debt that had been characterized as delinquent, charged off, or in collection if the consumer reporting agency has actual knowledge that the information is related to a veteran's medical debt and the consumer reporting agency is in compliance with its obligation under section 302(c)(5) of the Economic Growth, Regulatory Relief, and Consumer Protection Act.

(b) Exempted cases

The provisions of paragraphs (1) through (5) of subsection (a) are not applicable in the case of any consumer credit report to be used in connection with—

(1) a credit transaction involving, or which may reasonably be expected to involve, a principal amount of $150,000 or more;

(2) the underwriting of life insurance involving, or which may reasonably be expected to involve, a face amount of $150,000 or more; or

(3) the employment of any individual at an annual salary which equals, or which may reasonably be expected to equal $75,000, or more.

(c) Running of reporting period

(1) In general—The 7-year period referred to in paragraphs (4) and (6) of subsection (a) shall begin, with respect to any delinquent account that is placed for collection (internally or by referral to a third party, whichever is earlier), charged to profit and loss, or subjected to any similar action, upon the expiration of the 180-day period beginning on the date of the commencement of the delinquency which immediately preceded the collection activity, charge to profit and loss, or similar action.

(2) Effective date—Paragraph (1) shall apply only to items of information added to the file of a consumer on or after the date that is 455 days after September 30, 1996.

(d) Information required to be disclosed

(1) Title 11 information

Any consumer reporting agency that furnishes a consumer report that contains information regarding any case involving the consumer that arises under Title 11 shall include in the report an identification of the chapter of such Title 11 under which such case arises if provided by the source of the information. If any case arising or filed under Title 11 is withdrawn by the consumer before a final judgment, the consumer reporting agency shall include in the report that such case or filing was withdrawn upon receipt of documentation certifying such withdrawal.

(2) Key factor in credit score information

Any consumer reporting agency that furnishes a consumer report that contains any credit score or any other risk score or predictor on any consumer shall include in the report a clear and conspicuous statement that a key factor (as defined in section 1681g(f)(2)(B) of this title) that adversely affected such score or predictor was the number of enquiries, if such a predictor was in fact a key factor that adversely affected such score. This paragraph shall not apply to a check services company, acting as such, which issues authorizations for the purpose of approving or processing negotiable instruments, electronic fund transfers, or similar methods of payments, but only to the extent that such company is engaged in such activities.

(e) Indication of closure of account by consumer

If a consumer reporting agency is notified pursuant to section 1681s–2(a)(4) of this title that a credit account of a consumer was voluntarily closed by the consumer, the agency shall indicate that fact in any consumer report that includes information related to the account.

(f) Indication of dispute by consumer

If a consumer reporting agency is notified pursuant to section 1681s–2(a)(3) of this title that information regarding a consumer who[3] was furnished to the agency is disputed by the consumer, the agency shall indicate that fact in each consumer report that includes the disputed information.

(g) Truncation of credit card and debit card numbers

(1) In general

Except as otherwise provided in this subsection, no person that accepts credit cards or debit cards for the transaction of business shall print more than the last 5 digits of the card number or the expiration date upon any receipt provided to the cardholder at the point of the sale or transaction.

(2) Limitation

This subsection shall apply only to receipts that are electronically printed, and shall not apply to transactions in which the sole means of recording a credit card or debit card account number is by handwriting or by an imprint or copy of the card.

(3) Effective date

This subsection shall become effective—

(A) 3 years after December 4, 2003, with respect to any cash register or other machine or device that electronically prints receipts for credit card or debit card transactions that is in use before January 1, 2005; and

(B) 1 year after December 4, 2003, with respect to any cash register or other machine or device that electronically prints receipts for credit card or debit card transactions that is first put into use on or after January 1, 2005.

(h) Notice of discrepancy in address

(1) In general

If a person has requested a consumer report relating to a consumer from a consumer reporting agency described in section 1681a(p) of this title, the request includes an address for the consumer that substantially differs from the addresses in the file of the consumer, and the agency provides a consumer report in response to the request, the consumer reporting agency shall notify the requester of the existence of the discrepancy.

(2) Regulations

(A) Regulations required

The Bureau shall, in consultation with the Federal banking agencies, the National Credit Union Administration, and the Federal Trade Commission, prescribe regulations providing guidance regarding reasonable policies and procedures that a user of a consumer report should employ when such user has received a notice of discrepancy under paragraph (1).

(B) Policies and procedures to be included

---

3 So in original. Probably should be "which".

The regulations prescribed under subparagraph (A) shall describe reasonable policies and procedures for use by a user of a consumer report—

(i) to form a reasonable belief that the user knows the identity of the person to whom the consumer report pertains; and

(ii) if the user establishes a continuing relationship with the consumer, and the user regularly and in the ordinary course of business furnishes information to the consumer reporting agency from which the notice of discrepancy pertaining to the consumer was obtained, to reconcile the address of the consumer with the consumer reporting agency by furnishing such address to such consumer reporting agency as part of information regularly furnished by the user for the period in which the relationship is established.

§ 1681c–1 [CCPA § 605A]. Identity theft prevention; fraud alerts and active duty alerts

(a) One-call fraud alerts

(1) Initial alerts

Upon the direct request of a consumer, or an individual acting on behalf of or as a personal representative of a consumer, who asserts in good faith a suspicion that the consumer has been or is about to become a victim of fraud or related crime, including identity theft, a consumer reporting agency described in section 1681a(p) of this title that maintains a file on the consumer and has received appropriate proof of the identity of the requester shall—

(A) include a fraud alert in the file of that consumer, and also provide that alert along with any credit score generated in using that file, for a period of not less than 1 year, beginning on the date of such request, unless the consumer or such representative requests that such fraud alert be removed before the end of such period, and the agency has received appropriate proof of the identity of the requester for such purpose; and

(B) refer the information regarding the fraud alert under this paragraph to each of the other consumer reporting agencies described in section 1681a(p) of this title, in accordance with procedures developed under section 1681s(f) of this title.

(2) Access to free reports

In any case in which a consumer reporting agency includes a fraud alert in the file of a consumer pursuant to this subsection, the consumer reporting agency shall—

(A) disclose to the consumer that the consumer may request a free copy of the file of the consumer pursuant to section 1681j(d) of this title; and

(B) provide to the consumer all disclosures required to be made under section 1681g of this title, without charge to the consumer, not later than 3 business days after any request described in subparagraph (A).

(b) Extended alerts

(1) In general

Upon the direct request of a consumer, or an individual acting on behalf of or as a personal representative of a consumer, who submits an identity theft report to a consumer reporting agency described in section 1681a(p) of this title that maintains a file on the consumer, if the agency has received appropriate proof of the identity of the requester, the agency shall—

(A) include a fraud alert in the file of that consumer, and also provide that alert along with any credit score generated in using that file, during the 7-year period beginning on the date of such request, unless the consumer or such representative requests that such fraud alert be removed before the end of such period and the agency has received appropriate proof of the identity of the requester for such purpose;

(B) during the 5-year period beginning on the date of such request, exclude the consumer from any list of consumers prepared by the consumer reporting agency and provided to any third party to offer credit or insurance to the consumer as part of a transaction that was not initiated by the consumer, unless the consumer or such representative requests that such exclusion be rescinded before the end of such period; and

(C) refer the information regarding the extended fraud alert under this paragraph to each of the other consumer reporting agencies described in section 1681a(p) of this title, in accordance with procedures developed under section 1681s(f) of this title.

(2) Access to free reports

In any case in which a consumer reporting agency includes a fraud alert in the file of a consumer pursuant to this subsection, the consumer reporting agency shall—

(A) disclose to the consumer that the consumer may request 2 free copies of the file of the consumer pursuant to section 1681j(d) of this title during the 12-month period beginning on the date on which the fraud alert was included in the file; and

(B) provide to the consumer all disclosures required to be made under section 1681g of this title, without charge to the consumer, not later than 3 business days after any request described in subparagraph (A).

(c) Active duty alerts

Upon the direct request of an active duty military consumer, or an individual acting on behalf of or as a personal representative of an active duty military consumer, a consumer reporting agency described in section 1681a(p) of this title that maintains a file on the active duty military consumer and has received appropriate proof of the identity of the requester shall—

(1) include an active duty alert in the file of that active duty military consumer, and also provide that alert along with any credit score generated in using that file, during a period of not less than 12 months, or such longer period as the Bureau shall determine, by regulation, beginning on the date of the request, unless the active duty military consumer or such representative requests that such fraud alert be removed before the end of such period, and the agency has received appropriate proof of the identity of the requester for such purpose;

(2) during the 2-year period beginning on the date of such request, exclude the active duty military consumer from any list of consumers prepared by the consumer reporting agency and provided to any third party to offer credit or insurance to the consumer as part of a transaction that was not initiated by the consumer, unless the consumer requests that such exclusion be rescinded before the end of such period; and

(3) refer the information regarding the active duty alert to each of the other consumer reporting agencies described in section 1681a(p) of this title, in accordance with procedures developed under section 1681s(f) of this title.

(d) Procedures

Each consumer reporting agency described in section 1681a(p) of this title shall establish policies and procedures to comply with this section, including procedures that inform consumers of the availability of initial, extended, and active duty alerts and procedures that allow consumers and active duty military consumers to request initial, extended, or active duty alerts (as applicable) in a simple and easy manner, including by telephone.

(e) Referrals of alerts

Each consumer reporting agency described in section 1681a(p) of this title that receives a referral of a fraud alert or active duty alert from another consumer reporting agency pursuant to this section shall, as though the agency received the request from the consumer directly, follow the procedures required under—

(1) paragraphs (1)(A) and (2) of subsection (a), in the case of a referral under subsection (a)(1)(B);

(2) paragraphs (1)(A), (1)(B), and (2) of subsection (b), in the case of a referral under subsection (b)(1)(C); and

(3) paragraphs (1) and (2) of subsection (c), in the case of a referral under subsection (c)(3).

(f) Duty of reseller to reconvey alert

A reseller shall include in its report any fraud alert or active duty alert placed in the file of a consumer pursuant to this section by another consumer reporting agency.

(g) Duty of other consumer reporting agencies to provide contact information

If a consumer contacts any consumer reporting agency that is not described in section 1681a(p) of this title to communicate a suspicion that the consumer has been or is about to become a victim of fraud or related crime, including identity theft, the agency shall provide information to the consumer on how to contact the Bureau and the consumer reporting agencies described in section 1681a(p) of this title to obtain more detailed information and request alerts under this section.

(h) Limitations on use of information for credit extensions

(1) Requirements for initial and active duty alerts

(A) Notification

Each initial fraud alert and active duty alert under this section shall include information that notifies all prospective users of a consumer report on the consumer to which the alert relates that the consumer does not authorize the establishment of any new credit plan or extension of credit, other than under an open-end credit plan (as defined in section 1602(i) of this title), in the name of the consumer, or issuance of an additional card on an existing credit account requested by a consumer, or any increase in credit limit on an existing credit account requested by a consumer, except in accordance with subparagraph (B).

(B) Limitation on users

(i) In general

No prospective user of a consumer report that includes an initial fraud alert or an active duty alert in accordance with this section may establish a new credit plan or extension of credit, other than under an open-end credit plan (as defined in section 1602(i) of this title), in the name of the consumer, or issue an additional card on an existing credit account requested by a consumer, or grant any increase in credit limit on an existing credit account requested by a consumer, unless the user utilizes reasonable policies and procedures to form a reasonable belief that the user knows the identity of the person making the request.

(ii) Verification

If a consumer requesting the alert has specified a telephone number to be used for identity verification purposes, before authorizing any new credit plan or extension described in clause (i) in the name of such consumer, a user of such consumer report shall contact the consumer using that telephone number or take reasonable steps to verify the consumer's identity and confirm that the application for a new credit plan is not the result of identity theft.

(2) Requirements for extended alerts

(A) Notification

Each extended alert under this section shall include information that provides all prospective users of a consumer report relating to a consumer with—

(i) notification that the consumer does not authorize the establishment of any new credit plan or extension of credit described in clause (i), other than under an open-end credit plan (as defined in section 1602(i) of this title), in the name of the consumer, or issuance of an additional card on an existing credit account requested by a consumer, or any increase in credit limit on an existing credit account requested by a consumer, except in accordance with subparagraph (B); and

(ii) a telephone number or other reasonable contact method designated by the consumer.

(B) Limitation on users

No prospective user of a consumer report or of a credit score generated using the information in the file of a consumer that includes an extended fraud alert in accordance with this section may establish a new credit plan or extension of credit, other than under an open-end credit plan (as defined in section 1602(i) of this title), in the name of the consumer, or issue an additional card on an existing credit account requested by a consumer, or any increase in credit limit on an existing credit account requested by a consumer, unless the user contacts the consumer in person or using the contact method described in subparagraph (A)(ii) to confirm that the application for a new credit plan or increase in credit limit, or request for an additional card is not the result of identity theft.

(i) National security freeze

(1) Definitions

For purposes of this subsection:

(A) The term "consumer reporting agency" means a consumer reporting agency described in section 1681a(p) of this title.

(B) The term "proper identification" has the meaning of such term as used under section 1681h of this title.

(C) The term "security freeze" means a restriction that prohibits a consumer reporting agency from disclosing the contents of a consumer report that is subject to such security freeze to any person requesting the consumer report.

(2) Placement of security freeze

(A) In general

Upon receiving a direct request from a consumer that a consumer reporting agency place a security freeze, and upon receiving proper identification from the consumer, the consumer reporting agency shall, free of charge, place the security freeze not later than—

(i) in the case of a request that is by toll-free telephone or secure electronic means, 1 business day after receiving the request directly from the consumer; or

(ii) in the case of a request that is by mail, 3 business days after receiving the request directly from the consumer.

(B) Confirmation and additional information

Not later than 5 business days after placing a security freeze under subparagraph (A), a consumer reporting agency shall—

(i) send confirmation of the placement to the consumer; and

(ii) inform the consumer of—

(I) the process by which the consumer may remove the security freeze, including a mechanism to authenticate the consumer; and

(II) the consumer's right described in section 1681m(d)(1)(D) of this title.

(C) Notice to third parties

A consumer reporting agency may advise a third party that a security freeze has been placed with respect to a consumer under subparagraph (A).

(3) Removal of security freeze

(A) In general

A consumer reporting agency shall remove a security freeze placed on the consumer report of a consumer only in the following cases:

(i) Upon the direct request of the consumer.

(ii) The security freeze was placed due to a material misrepresentation of fact by the consumer.

(B) Notice if removal not by request

If a consumer reporting agency removes a security freeze under subparagraph (A)(ii), the consumer reporting agency shall notify the consumer in writing prior to removing the security freeze.

(C) Removal of security freeze by consumer request

Except as provided in subparagraph (A)(ii), a security freeze shall remain in place until the consumer directly requests that the security freeze be removed. Upon receiving a direct request from a consumer that a consumer reporting agency remove a security freeze, and upon receiving proper identification from the consumer, the consumer reporting agency shall, free of charge, remove the security freeze not later than—

(i) in the case of a request that is by toll-free telephone or secure electronic means, 1 hour after receiving the request for removal; or

(ii) in the case of a request that is by mail, 3 business days after receiving the request for removal.

(D) Third-party requests

If a third party requests access to a consumer report of a consumer with respect to which a security freeze is in effect, where such request is in connection with an application for credit, and the consumer does not allow such consumer report to be accessed, the third party may treat the application as incomplete.

(E) Temporary removal of security freeze

Upon receiving a direct request from a consumer under subparagraph (A)(i), if the consumer requests a temporary removal of a security freeze, the consumer reporting agency shall, in accordance with subparagraph (C), remove the security freeze for the period of time specified by the consumer.

(4) Exceptions

A security freeze shall not apply to the making of a consumer report for use of the following:

(A) A person or entity, or a subsidiary, affiliate, or agent of that person or entity, or an assignee of a financial obligation owed by the consumer to that person or entity, or a prospective assignee of a financial obligation owed by the consumer to that person or entity in conjunction with the proposed purchase of the financial obligation, with which the consumer has or had prior to assignment an account or contract including a demand deposit account, or to whom the consumer issued a negotiable instrument, for the purposes of reviewing the account or collecting the financial obligation owed for the account, contract, or negotiable instrument. For purposes of this subparagraph, "reviewing the account" includes activities related to account maintenance, monitoring, credit line increases, and account upgrades and enhancements.

(B) Any Federal, State, or local agency, law enforcement agency, trial court, or private collection agency acting pursuant to a court order, warrant, or subpoena.

(C) A child support agency acting pursuant to part D of title IV of the Social Security Act (42 U.S.C. 651 et seq.).

(D) A Federal agency or a State or its agents or assigns acting to investigate fraud or acting to investigate or collect delinquent taxes or unpaid court orders or to fulfill any of its other statutory responsibilities, provided such responsibilities are consistent with a permissible purpose under section 1681b of this title.

(E) By a person using credit information for the purposes described under section 1681b(c) of this title.

(F) Any person or entity administering a credit file monitoring subscription or similar service to which the consumer has subscribed.

(G) Any person or entity for the purpose of providing a consumer with a copy of the consumer's consumer report or credit score, upon the request of the consumer.

(H) Any person using the information in connection with the underwriting of insurance.

(I) Any person using the information for employment, tenant, or background screening purposes.

(J) Any person using the information for assessing, verifying, or authenticating a consumer's identity for purposes other than the granting of credit, or for investigating or preventing actual or potential fraud.

(5) Notice of rights

At any time a consumer is required to receive a summary of rights required under section 1681g of this title, the following notice shall be included:

"CONSUMERS HAVE THE RIGHT TO OBTAIN A SECURITY FREEZE

"You have a right to place a 'security freeze' on your credit report, which will prohibit a consumer reporting agency from releasing information in your credit report without your express authorization. The security freeze is designed to prevent credit, loans, and services from being approved in your name without your consent. However, you should be aware that using a security freeze to take control over who gets access to the personal and financial information in your credit report may delay, interfere with, or prohibit the timely approval of any subsequent request or application you make regarding a new loan, credit, mortgage, or any other account involving the extension of credit.

"As an alternative to a security freeze, you have the right to place an initial or extended fraud alert on your credit file at no cost. An initial fraud alert is a 1-year alert that is placed on a consumer's credit file. Upon seeing a fraud alert display on a consumer's credit file, a business is required to take steps to verify the consumer's identity before extending new credit. If you are a victim of identity theft, you are entitled to an extended fraud alert, which is a fraud alert lasting 7 years.

"A security freeze does not apply to a person or entity, or its affiliates, or collection agencies acting on behalf of the person or entity, with which you have an existing account that requests information in your credit report for the purposes of reviewing or collecting the account. Reviewing the account includes activities related to account maintenance, monitoring, credit line increases, and account upgrades and enhancements.".

(6) Webpage

(A) Consumer reporting agencies

A consumer reporting agency shall establish a webpage that—

(i) allows a consumer to request a security freeze;

(ii) allows a consumer to request an initial fraud alert;

(iii) allows a consumer to request an extended fraud alert;

(iv) allows a consumer to request an active duty fraud alert;

(v) allows a consumer to opt-out of the use of information in a consumer report to send the consumer a solicitation of credit or insurance, in accordance with section 1681m(d) of this title; and

(vi) shall not be the only mechanism by which a consumer may request a security freeze.

(B) FTC

The Federal Trade Commission shall establish a single webpage that includes a link to each webpage established under subparagraph (A) within the Federal Trade Commission's website www.Identitytheft.gov, or a successor website.

(j) National protection for files and credit records of protected consumers

(1) Definitions

As used in this subsection:

(A) The term "consumer reporting agency" means a consumer reporting agency described in section 1681a(p) of this title.

(B) The term "protected consumer" means an individual who is—

(i) under the age of 16 years at the time a request for the placement of a security freeze is made; or

(ii) an incapacitated person or a protected person for whom a guardian or conservator has been appointed.

(C) The term "protected consumer's representative" means a person who provides to a consumer reporting agency sufficient proof of authority to act on behalf of a protected consumer.

(D) The term "record" means a compilation of information that—

(i) identifies a protected consumer;

(ii) is created by a consumer reporting agency solely for the purpose of complying with this subsection; and

(iii) may not be created or used to consider the protected consumer's credit worthiness, credit standing, credit capacity, character, general reputation, personal characteristics, or mode of living.

(E) The term "security freeze" means a restriction that prohibits a consumer reporting agency from disclosing the contents of a consumer report that is the subject of such security freeze or, in the case of a protected consumer for whom the consumer reporting agency does not have a file, a record that is subject to such security freeze to any person requesting the consumer report for the purpose of opening a new account involving the extension of credit.

(F) The term "sufficient proof of authority" means documentation that shows a protected consumer's representative has authority to act on behalf of a protected consumer and includes—

(i) an order issued by a court of law;

(ii) a lawfully executed and valid power of attorney;

(iii) a document issued by a Federal, State, or local government agency in the United States showing proof of parentage, including a birth certificate; or

(iv) with respect to a protected consumer who has been placed in a foster care setting, a written communication from a county welfare department or its agent or designee, or a county probation department or its agent or designee, certifying that the protected consumer is in a foster care setting under its jurisdiction.

(G) The term "sufficient proof of identification" means information or documentation that identifies a protected consumer and a protected consumer's representative and includes—

(i) a social security number or a copy of a social security card issued by the Social Security Administration;

(ii) a certified or official copy of a birth certificate issued by the entity authorized to issue the birth certificate; or

(iii) a copy of a driver's license, an identification card issued by the motor vehicle administration, or any other government issued identification.

(2) Placement of security freeze for a protected consumer

(A) In general

Upon receiving a direct request from a protected consumer's representative that a consumer reporting agency place a security freeze, and upon receiving sufficient proof of identification and sufficient proof of authority, the consumer reporting agency shall, free of charge, place the security freeze not later than—

(i) in the case of a request that is by toll-free telephone or secure electronic means, 1 business day after receiving the request directly from the protected consumer's representative; or

(ii) in the case of a request that is by mail, 3 business days after receiving the request directly from the protected consumer's representative.

(B) Confirmation and additional information

Not later than 5 business days after placing a security freeze under subparagraph (A), a consumer reporting agency shall—

(i) send confirmation of the placement to the protected consumer's representative; and

(ii) inform the protected consumer's representative of the process by which the protected consumer may remove the security freeze, including a mechanism to authenticate the protected consumer's representative.

(C) Creation of file

If a consumer reporting agency does not have a file pertaining to a protected consumer when the consumer reporting agency receives a direct request under subparagraph (A), the consumer reporting agency shall create a record for the protected consumer.

(3) Prohibition on release of record or file of protected consumer

After a security freeze has been placed under paragraph (2)(A), and unless the security freeze is removed in accordance with this subsection, a consumer reporting agency may not release the protected consumer's consumer report, any information derived from the protected consumer's consumer report, or any record created for the protected consumer.

(4) Removal of a protected consumer security freeze

(A) In general

A consumer reporting agency shall remove a security freeze placed on the consumer report of a protected consumer only in the following cases:

(i) Upon the direct request of the protected consumer's representative.

(ii) Upon the direct request of the protected consumer, if the protected consumer is not under the age of 16 years at the time of the request.

(iii) The security freeze was placed due to a material misrepresentation of fact by the protected consumer's representative.

(B) Notice if removal not by request

If a consumer reporting agency removes a security freeze under subparagraph (A)(iii), the consumer reporting agency shall notify the protected consumer's representative in writing prior to removing the security freeze.

(C) Removal of freeze by request

Except as provided in subparagraph (A)(iii), a security freeze shall remain in place until a protected consumer's representative or protected consumer described in subparagraph (A)(ii) directly requests that the security freeze be removed. Upon receiving a direct request from the protected consumer's representative or protected consumer described in subparagraph (A)(ii) that a consumer reporting agency remove a security freeze, and upon receiving sufficient proof of identification and sufficient proof of authority, the consumer reporting agency shall, free of charge, remove the security freeze not later than—

(i) in the case of a request that is by toll-free telephone or secure electronic means, 1 hour after receiving the request for removal; or

(ii) in the case of a request that is by mail, 3 business days after receiving the request for removal.

(D) Temporary removal of security freeze

Upon receiving a direct request from a protected consumer or a protected consumer's representative under subparagraph (A)(i), if the protected consumer or protected consumer's representative requests a temporary removal of a security freeze, the consumer reporting agency shall, in accordance with subparagraph (C), remove the security freeze for the period of time specified by the protected consumer or protected consumer's representative.

(k) Credit monitoring

(1) Definitions

In this subsection:

(A) The term "active duty military consumer" includes a member of the National Guard.

(B) The term "National Guard" has the meaning given the term in section 101(c) of title 10, United States Code.

(2) Credit monitoring

A consumer reporting agency described in section 1681a(p) of this title shall provide a free electronic credit monitoring service that, at a minimum, notifies a consumer of material additions or modifications to the file of the consumer at the consumer reporting agency to any consumer who provides to the consumer reporting agency—

(A) appropriate proof that the consumer is an active duty military consumer; and

(B) contact information of the consumer.

(3) Rulemaking

Not later than 1 year after May 24, 2018, the Federal Trade Commission shall promulgate regulations regarding the requirements of this subsection, which shall at a minimum include—

(A) a definition of an electronic credit monitoring service and material additions or modifications to the file of a consumer; and

(B) what constitutes appropriate proof.

(4) Applicability

(A) Sections 1681n and 1681*o* of this title shall not apply to any violation of this subsection.

(B) This subsection shall be enforced exclusively under section 1681s of this title by the Federal agencies and Federal and State officials identified in that section.

§ 1681c–2 [CCPA § 605B]. Block of information resulting from identity theft

(a) Block

Except as otherwise provided in this section, a consumer reporting agency shall block the reporting of any information in the file of a consumer that the consumer identifies as information that resulted from an alleged identity theft, not later than 4 business days after the date of receipt by such agency of—

(1) appropriate proof of the identity of the consumer;

(2) a copy of an identity theft report;

(3) the identification of such information by the consumer; and

(4) a statement by the consumer that the information is not information relating to any transaction by the consumer.

(b) Notification

A consumer reporting agency shall promptly notify the furnisher of information identified by the consumer under subsection (a)—

(1) that the information may be a result of identity theft;

(2) that an identity theft report has been filed;

(3) that a block has been requested under this section; and

(4) of the effective dates of the block.

(c) Authority to decline or rescind

(1) In general

A consumer reporting agency may decline to block, or may rescind any block, of information relating to a consumer under this section, if the consumer reporting agency reasonably determines that—

(A) the information was blocked in error or a block was requested by the consumer in error;

(B) the information was blocked, or a block was requested by the consumer, on the basis of a material misrepresentation of fact by the consumer relevant to the request to block; or

(C) the consumer obtained possession of goods, services, or money as a result of the blocked transaction or transactions.

(2) Notification to consumer

If a block of information is declined or rescinded under this subsection, the affected consumer shall be notified promptly, in the same manner as consumers are notified of the reinsertion of information under section 1681i(a)(5)(B) of this title.

(3) Significance of block

For purposes of this subsection, if a consumer reporting agency rescinds a block, the presence of information in the file of a consumer prior to the blocking of such information is not evidence of whether the consumer knew or should have known that the consumer obtained possession of any goods, services, or money as a result of the block.

(d) Exception for resellers

(1) No reseller file

This section shall not apply to a consumer reporting agency, if the consumer reporting agency—

(A) is a reseller;

(B) is not, at the time of the request of the consumer under subsection (a) of this section, otherwise furnishing or reselling a consumer report concerning the information identified by the consumer; and

(C) informs the consumer, by any means, that the consumer may report the identity theft to the Bureau to obtain consumer information regarding identity theft.

(2) Reseller with file

The sole obligation of the consumer reporting agency under this section, with regard to any request of a consumer under this section, shall be to block the consumer report maintained by the consumer reporting agency from any subsequent use, if—

(A) the consumer, in accordance with the provisions of subsection (a), identifies, to a consumer reporting agency, information in the file of the consumer that resulted from identity theft; and

(B) the consumer reporting agency is a reseller of the identified information.

(3) Notice

In carrying out its obligation under paragraph (2), the reseller shall promptly provide a notice to the consumer of the decision to block the file. Such notice shall contain the name, address, and telephone number of each consumer reporting agency from which the consumer information was obtained for resale.

(e) Exception for verification companies

The provisions of this section do not apply to a check services company, acting as such, which issues authorizations for the purpose of approving or processing negotiable instruments, electronic fund transfers, or similar methods of payments, except that, beginning 4 business days after receipt of information described in paragraphs (1) through (3) of subsection (a), a check services company shall not report to a national consumer reporting agency described in section 1681a(p) of this title, any information identified in the subject identity theft report as resulting from identity theft.

(f) Access to blocked information by law enforcement agencies

No provision of this section shall be construed as requiring a consumer reporting agency to prevent a Federal, State, or local law enforcement agency from accessing blocked information in a consumer file to which the agency could otherwise obtain access under subchapter.

§ 1681d [CCPA § 606]. Disclosure of investigative consumer reports

(a) Disclosure of fact of preparation

A person may not procure or cause to be prepared an investigative consumer report on any consumer unless—

(1) it is clearly and accurately disclosed to the consumer that an investigative consumer report including information as to his character, general reputation, personal characteristics, and mode of living, whichever are applicable, may be made, and such disclosure (A) is made in a writing mailed, or otherwise delivered, to the consumer, not later than three days after the date on which the report was first requested, and (B) includes a statement informing the consumer of his right to request the additional disclosures provided for under subsection (b) of this section and the written summary of the rights of the consumer prepared pursuant to section 1681g(c) of this title; and

(2) the person certifies or has certified to the consumer reporting agency that—

(A) the person has made the disclosures to the consumer required by paragraph (1); and

(B) the person will comply with subsection (b).

(b) Disclosure on request of nature and scope of investigation

Any person who procures or causes to be prepared an investigative consumer report on any consumer shall, upon written request made by the consumer within a reasonable period of time after the receipt by him of the disclosure required by subsection (a)(1), make a complete and accurate disclosure of the nature and scope of the investigation requested. This disclosure shall be made in a writing mailed, or otherwise delivered, to the consumer not later than five days after the date on which the request for such disclosure was received from the consumer or such report was first requested, whichever is the later.

(c) Limitation on liability upon showing of reasonable procedures for compliance with provisions

No person may be held liable for any violation of subsection (a) or (b) if he shows by a preponderance of the evidence that at the time of the violation he maintained reasonable procedures to assure compliance with subsection (a) or (b).

(d) Prohibitions

(1) Certification.—A consumer reporting agency shall not prepare or furnish an investigative consumer report unless the agency has received a certification under subsection (a)(2) of this section from the person who requested the report.

(2) Inquiries.—A consumer reporting agency shall not make an inquiry for the purpose of preparing an investigative consumer report on a consumer for employment purposes if the making of the inquiry by an employer or prospective employer of the consumer would violate any applicable Federal or State equal employment opportunity law or regulation.

(3) Certain public record information.—Except as otherwise provided in section 1681k of this title, a consumer reporting agency shall not furnish an investigative consumer report that includes information that is a matter of public record and that relates to an arrest, indictment, conviction, civil judicial action, tax lien, or outstanding judgment, unless the agency has verified the accuracy of the information during the 30-day period ending on the date on which the report is furnished.

(4) Certain adverse information.—A consumer reporting agency shall not prepare or furnish an investigative consumer report on a consumer that contains information that is adverse to the interest of the consumer and that is obtained through a personal interview with a neighbor, friend, or associate of the consumer or with another person with whom the consumer is acquainted or who has knowledge of such item of information, unless—

(A) the agency has followed reasonable procedures to obtain confirmation of the information, from an additional source that has independent and direct knowledge of the information; or

(B) the person interviewed is the best possible source of the information.

§ 1681e [CCPA § 607]. Compliance procedures

(a) Identity and purposes of credit users

Every consumer reporting agency shall maintain reasonable procedures designed to avoid violations of section 1681c of this title and to limit the furnishing of consumer reports to the purposes listed under section 1681b of this title. These procedures shall require that prospective users of the information identify themselves, certify the purposes for which the information is sought, and certify that the information will be used for no other purpose. Every consumer reporting agency shall make a reasonable effort to verify the identity of a new prospective user and the uses certified by such prospective user prior to furnishing such user a consumer report. No consumer reporting agency may furnish a consumer report to any person if it has reasonable grounds for believing that the consumer report will not be used for a purpose listed in section 1681b of this title.

(b) Accuracy of report

Whenever a consumer reporting agency prepares a consumer report it shall follow reasonable procedures to assure maximum possible accuracy of the information concerning the individual about whom the report relates.

(c) Disclosure of consumer reports by users allowed

A consumer reporting agency may not prohibit a user of a consumer report furnished by the agency on a consumer from disclosing the contents of the report to the consumer, if adverse action against the consumer has been taken by the user based in whole or in part on the report.

(d) Notice to users and furnishers of information

(1) Notice requirement.—A consumer reporting agency shall provide to any person—

(A) who regularly and in the ordinary course of business furnishes information to the agency with respect to any consumer; or

(B) to whom a consumer report is provided by the agency;

a notice of such person's responsibilities under this subchapter.

(2) Content of notice.—The Bureau shall prescribe the content of notices under paragraph (1), and a consumer reporting agency shall be in compliance with this subsection if it provides a notice under paragraph (1) that is substantially similar to the Bureau prescription under this paragraph.

(e) Procurement of consumer report for resale

(1) Disclosure.—A person may not procure a consumer report for purposes of reselling the report (or any information in the report) unless the person discloses to the consumer reporting agency that originally furnishes the report—

(A) the identity of the end-user of the report (or information); and

(B) each permissible purpose under section 1681b of this title for which the report is furnished to the end-user of the report (or information).

(2) Responsibilities of procurers for resale.—A person who procures a consumer report for purposes of reselling the report (or any information in the report) shall—

(A) establish and comply with reasonable procedures designed to ensure that the report (or information) is resold by the person only for a purpose for which the report may be furnished under section 1681b of this title, including by requiring that each person to which the report (or information) is resold and that resells or provides the report (or information) to any other person—

(i) identifies each end user of the resold report (or information);

(ii) certifies each purpose for which the report (or information) will be used; and

(iii) certifies that the report (or information) will be used for no other purpose; and

(B) before reselling the report, make reasonable efforts to verify the identifications and certifications made under subparagraph (A).

(3) Resale of consumer report to a Federal agency or department.—Notwithstanding paragraph (1) or (2), a person who procures a consumer report for purposes of reselling the report (or any information in the report) shall not disclose the identity of the end-user of the report under paragraph (1) or (2) if—

(A) the end user is an agency or department of the United States Government which procures the report from the person for purposes of determining the eligibility of the consumer concerned to receive access or continued access to classified information (as defined in section 1681b(b)(4)(E)(i) of this title); and

(B) the agency or department certifies in writing to the person reselling the report that nondisclosure is necessary to protect classified information or the safety of persons employed by or contracting with, or undergoing investigation for work or contracting with the agency or department.

§ 1681f [CCPA § 608]. Disclosures to governmental agencies

Notwithstanding the provisions of section 1681b of this title, a consumer reporting agency may furnish identifying information respecting any consumer, limited to his name, address, former addresses, places of employment, or former places of employment, to a governmental agency.

§ 1681g [CCPA § 609]. Disclosures to consumers

(a) Information on file; sources; report recipients

Every consumer reporting agency shall, upon request, and subject to section 1681h(a)(1) of this title, clearly and accurately disclose to the consumer:

(1) All information in the consumer's file at the time of the request, except that—

(A) if the consumer to whom the file relates requests that the first 5 digits of the social security number (or similar identification number) of the consumer not be included in the disclosure and the consumer reporting agency has received appropriate proof of the identity of the requester, the consumer reporting agency shall so truncate such number in such disclosure; and

(B) nothing in this paragraph shall be construed to require a consumer reporting agency to disclose to a consumer any information concerning credit scores or any other risk scores or predictors relating to the consumer.

(2) The sources of the information; except that the sources of information acquired solely for use in preparing an investigative consumer report and actually used for no other purpose need not be disclosed: *Provided,* That in the event an action is brought under this subchapter, such sources shall be available to the plaintiff under appropriate discovery procedures in the court in which the action is brought.

(3)(A) Identification of each person (including each end-user identified under section 1681e(e)(1) of this title) that procured a consumer report—

(i) for employment purposes, during the 2-year period preceding the date on which the request is made; or

(ii) for any other purpose, during the 1-year period preceding the date on which the request is made.

(B) An identification of a person under subparagraph (A) shall include—

(i) the name of the person or, if applicable, the trade name (written in full) under which such person conducts business; and

(ii) upon request of the consumer, the address and telephone number of the person.

(C) Subparagraph (A) does not apply if—

(i) the end user is an agency or department of the United States Government that procures the report from the person for purposes of determining the eligibility of the consumer to whom the report relates to receive access or continued access to classified information (as defined in section 1681b(b)(4)(E)(i) of this title); and

(ii) the head of the agency or department makes a written finding as prescribed under section 1681b(b)(4)(A) of this title.

(4) The dates, original payees, and amounts of any checks upon which is based any adverse characterization of the consumer, included in the file at the time of the disclosure.

(5) A record of all inquiries received by the agency during the 1-year period preceding the request that identified the consumer in connection with a credit or insurance transaction that was not initiated by the consumer.

(6) If the consumer requests the credit file and not the credit score, a statement that the consumer may request and obtain a credit score.

(b) Exempt information

The requirements of subsection (a) respecting the disclosure of sources of information and the recipients of consumer reports do not apply to information received or consumer reports furnished prior to the effective date of this subchapter except to the extent that the matter involved is contained in the files of the consumer reporting agency on that date.

(c) Summary of rights to obtain and dispute information in consumer reports and to obtain credit scores

(1) Commission[1] summary of rights required

---

[1] So in original.

(A) In general

The Commission[1] shall prepare a model summary of the rights of consumers under this subchapter.

(B) Content of summary

The summary of rights prepared under subparagraph (A) shall include a description of—

(i) the right of a consumer to obtain a copy of a consumer report under subsection (a) from each consumer reporting agency;

(ii) the frequency and circumstances under which a consumer is entitled to receive a consumer report without charge under section 1681j of this title;

(iii) the right of a consumer to dispute information in the file of the consumer under section 1681i of this title;

(iv) the right of a consumer to obtain a credit score from a consumer reporting agency, and a description of how to obtain a credit score;

(v) the method by which a consumer can contact, and obtain a consumer report from, a consumer reporting agency without charge, as provided in the regulations of the Bureau prescribed under section 211(c) of the Fair and Accurate Credit Transactions Act of 2003; and

(vi) the method by which a consumer can contact, and obtain a consumer report from, a consumer reporting agency described in section 1681a(w) of this title, as provided in the regulations of the Bureau prescribed under section 1681j(a)(1)(C) of this title.

(C) Availability of summary of rights

The Commission[1] shall—

(i) actively publicize the availability of the summary of rights prepared under this paragraph;

(ii) conspicuously post on its Internet website the availability of such summary of rights; and

(iii) promptly make such summary of rights available to consumers, on request.

(2) Summary of rights required to be included with agency disclosures

A consumer reporting agency shall provide to a consumer, with each written disclosure by the agency to the consumer under this section—

(A) the summary of rights prepared by the Bureau under paragraph (1);

(B) in the case of a consumer reporting agency described in section 1681a(p) of this title, a toll-free telephone number established by the agency, at which personnel are accessible to consumers during normal business hours;

(C) a list of all Federal agencies responsible for enforcing any provision of this subchapter, and the address and any appropriate phone number of each such agency, in a form that will assist the consumer in selecting the appropriate agency;

(D) a statement that the consumer may have additional rights under State law, and that the consumer may wish to contact a State or local consumer protection agency or a State attorney general (or the equivalent thereof) to learn of those rights; and

(E) a statement that a consumer reporting agency is not required to remove accurate derogatory information from the file of a consumer, unless the information is outdated under section 1681c of this title or cannot be verified.

(d) Summary of rights of identity theft victims

(1) In general

The Commission[1], in consultation with the Federal banking agencies and the National Credit Union Administration, shall prepare a model summary of the rights of consumers under this subchapter with respect to the procedures for remedying the effects of fraud or identity theft involving credit, an electronic fund transfer, or an account or transaction at or with a financial institution or other creditor.

(2) Summary of rights and contact information

Beginning 60 days after the date on which the model summary of rights is prescribed in final form by the Bureau pursuant to paragraph (1), if any consumer contacts a consumer reporting agency and expresses a belief that the consumer is a victim of fraud or identity theft involving credit, an electronic fund transfer, or an account or transaction at or with a financial institution or other creditor, the consumer reporting agency shall, in addition to any other action that the agency may take, provide the consumer with a summary of rights that contains all of the information required by the Bureau under paragraph (1), and information on how to contact the Bureau to obtain more detailed information.

(e) Information available to victims

(1) In general

For the purpose of documenting fraudulent transactions resulting from identity theft, not later than 30 days after the date of receipt of a request from a victim in accordance with paragraph (3), and subject to verification of the identity of the victim and the claim of identity theft in accordance with paragraph (2), a business entity that has provided credit to, provided for consideration products, goods, or services to, accepted payment from, or otherwise entered into a commercial transaction for consideration with, a person who has allegedly made unauthorized use of the means of identification of the victim, shall provide a copy of application and business transaction records in the control of the business entity, whether maintained by the business entity or by another person on behalf of the business entity, evidencing any transaction alleged to be a result of identity theft to—

(A) the victim;

(B) any Federal, State, or local government law enforcement agency or officer specified by the victim in such a request; or

(C) any law enforcement agency investigating the identity theft and authorized by the victim to take receipt of records provided under this subsection.

(2) Verification of identity and claim

Before a business entity provides any information under paragraph (1), unless the business entity, at its discretion, otherwise has a high degree of confidence that it knows the identity of the victim making a request under paragraph (1), the victim shall provide to the business entity—

(A) as proof of positive identification of the victim, at the election of the business entity—

(i) the presentation of a government-issued identification card;

[1] So in original.

(ii) personally identifying information of the same type as was provided to the business entity by the unauthorized person; or

(iii) personally identifying information that the business entity typically requests from new applicants or for new transactions, at the time of the victim's request for information, including any documentation described in clauses (i) and (ii); and

(B) as proof of a claim of identity theft, at the election of the business entity—

(i) a copy of a police report evidencing the claim of the victim of identity theft; and

(ii) a properly completed—

(I) copy of a standardized affidavit of identity theft developed and made available by the Bureau; or

(II) an[4] affidavit of fact that is acceptable to the business entity for that purpose.

(3) Procedures

The request of a victim under paragraph (1) shall—

(A) be in writing;

(B) be mailed to an address specified by the business entity, if any; and

(C) if asked by the business entity, include relevant information about any transaction alleged to be a result of identity theft to facilitate compliance with this section including—

(i) if known by the victim (or if readily obtainable by the victim), the date of the application or transaction; and

(ii) if known by the victim (or if readily obtainable by the victim), any other identifying information such as an account or transaction number.

(4) No charge to victim

Information required to be provided under paragraph (1) shall be so provided without charge.

(5) Authority to decline to provide information

A business entity may decline to provide information under paragraph (1) if, in the exercise of good faith, the business entity determines that—

(A) this subsection does not require disclosure of the information;

(B) after reviewing the information provided pursuant to paragraph (2), the business entity does not have a high degree of confidence in knowing the true identity of the individual requesting the information;

(C) the request for the information is based on a misrepresentation of fact by the individual requesting the information relevant to the request for information; or

(D) the information requested is Internet navigational data or similar information about a person's visit to a website or online service.

(6) Limitation on liability

Except as provided in section 1681s of this title, sections 1681n and 1681*o* of this title do not apply to any violation of this subsection.

---

[4] So in original. The word "an" probably should not appear.

(7) Limitation on civil liability

No business entity may be held civilly liable under any provision of Federal, State, or other law for disclosure, made in good faith pursuant to this subsection.

(8) No new recordkeeping obligation

Nothing in this subsection creates an obligation on the part of a business entity to obtain, retain, or maintain information or records that are not otherwise required to be obtained, retained, or maintained in the ordinary course of its business or under other applicable law.

(9) Rule of construction

(A) In general

No provision of subtitle A of title V of Public Law 106–102, prohibiting the disclosure of financial information by a business entity to third parties shall be used to deny disclosure of information to the victim under this subsection.

(B) Limitation

Except as provided in subparagraph (A), nothing in this subsection permits a business entity to disclose information, including information to law enforcement under subparagraphs (B) and (C) of paragraph (1), that the business entity is otherwise prohibited from disclosing under any other applicable provision of Federal or State law.

(10) Affirmative defense

In any civil action brought to enforce this subsection, it is an affirmative defense (which the defendant must establish by a preponderance of the evidence) for a business entity to file an affidavit or answer stating that—

(A) the business entity has made a reasonably diligent search of its available business records; and

(B) the records requested under this subsection do not exist or are not reasonably available.

(11) Definition of victim

For purposes of this subsection, the term "victim" means a consumer whose means of identification or financial information has been used or transferred (or has been alleged to have been used or transferred) without the authority of that consumer, with the intent to commit, or to aid or abet, an identity theft or a similar crime.

(12) Effective date

This subsection shall become effective 180 days after December 4, 2003.

(13) Effectiveness study

Not later than 18 months after December 4, 2003, the Comptroller General of the United States shall submit a report to Congress assessing the effectiveness of this provision.

(f) Disclosure of credit scores

(1) In general

Upon the request of a consumer for a credit score, a consumer reporting agency shall supply to the consumer a statement indicating that the information and credit scoring model may be different than the credit score that may be used by the lender, and a notice which shall include—

(A) the current credit score of the consumer or the most recent credit score of the consumer that was previously calculated by the credit reporting agency for a purpose related to the extension of credit;

(B) the range of possible credit scores under the model used;

(C) all of the key factors that adversely affected the credit score of the consumer in the model used, the total number of which shall not exceed 4, subject to paragraph (9);

(D) the date on which the credit score was created; and

(E) the name of the person or entity that provided the credit score or credit file upon which the credit score was created.

(2) Definitions

For purposes of this subsection, the following definitions shall apply:

(A) Credit score

The term "credit score"—

(i) means a numerical value or a categorization derived from a statistical tool or modeling system used by a person who makes or arranges a loan to predict the likelihood of certain credit behaviors, including default (and the numerical value or the categorization derived from such analysis may also be referred to as a "risk predictor" or "risk score"); and

(ii) does not include—

(I) any mortgage score or rating of an automated underwriting system that considers one or more factors in addition to credit information, including the loan to value ratio, the amount of down payment, or the financial assets of a consumer; or

(II) any other elements of the underwriting process or underwriting decision.

(B) Key factors

The term "key factors" means all relevant elements or reasons adversely affecting the credit score for the particular individual, listed in the order of their importance based on their effect on the credit score.

(3) Timeframe and manner of disclosure

The information required by this subsection shall be provided in the same timeframe and manner as the information described in subsection (a) of this section.

(4) Applicability to certain uses

This subsection shall not be construed so as to compel a consumer reporting agency to develop or disclose a score if the agency does not—

(A) distribute scores that are used in connection with residential real property loans; or

(B) develop scores that assist credit providers in understanding the general credit behavior of a consumer and predicting the future credit behavior of the consumer.

(5) Applicability to credit scores developed by another person

(A) In general

This subsection shall not be construed to require a consumer reporting agency that distributes credit scores developed by another person or entity to provide a further explanation of them, or to process a dispute arising pursuant to section 1681i of this title, except that the consumer reporting agency shall provide the consumer with the name and address and website for contacting the person or entity who developed the score or developed the methodology of the score.

(B) Exception

This paragraph shall not apply to a consumer reporting agency that develops or modifies scores that are developed by another person or entity.

(6) Maintenance of credit scores not required

This subsection shall not be construed to require a consumer reporting agency to maintain credit scores in its files.

(7) Compliance in certain cases

In complying with this subsection, a consumer reporting agency shall—

(A) supply the consumer with a credit score that is derived from a credit scoring model that is widely distributed to users by that consumer reporting agency in connection with residential real property loans or with a credit score that assists the consumer in understanding the credit scoring assessment of the credit behavior of the consumer and predictions about the future credit behavior of the consumer; and

(B) a statement indicating that the information and credit scoring model may be different than that used by the lender.

(8) Fair and reasonable fee

A consumer reporting agency may charge a fair and reasonable fee, as determined by the Bureau, for providing the information required under this subsection.

(9) Use of enquiries as a key factor

If a key factor that adversely affects the credit score of a consumer consists of the number of enquiries made with respect to a consumer report, that factor shall be included in the disclosure pursuant to paragraph (1)(C) without regard to the numerical limitation in such paragraph.

(g) Disclosure of credit scores by certain mortgage lenders

(1) In general

Any person who makes or arranges loans and who uses a consumer credit score, as defined in subsection (f), in connection with an application initiated or sought by a consumer for a closed end loan or the establishment of an open end loan for a consumer purpose that is secured by 1 to 4 units of residential real property (hereafter in this subsection referred to as the "lender") shall provide the following to the consumer as soon as reasonably practicable:

(A) Information required under subsection (f)—

(i) In general

A copy of the information identified in subsection (f) that was obtained from a consumer reporting agency or was developed and used by the user of the information.

(ii) Notice under subparagraph (D)

In addition to the information provided to it by a third party that provided the credit score or scores, a lender is only required to provide the notice contained in subparagraph (D).

(B) Disclosures in case of automated underwriting system

(i) In general

If a person that is subject to this subsection uses an automated underwriting system to underwrite a loan, that person may satisfy the obligation to provide a credit score by disclosing a credit score and associated key factors supplied by a consumer reporting agency.

(ii) Numerical credit score

However, if a numerical credit score is generated by an automated underwriting system used by an enterprise, and that score is disclosed to the person, the score shall be disclosed to the consumer consistent with subparagraph (C).

(iii) Enterprise defined

For purposes of this subparagraph, the term "enterprise" has the same meaning as in paragraph (6) of section 4502 of Title 12.

(C) Disclosures of credit scores not obtained from a consumer reporting agency

A person that is subject to the provisions of this subsection and that uses a credit score, other than a credit score provided by a consumer reporting agency, may satisfy the obligation to provide a credit score by disclosing a credit score and associated key factors supplied by a consumer reporting agency.

(D) Notice to home loan applicants

A copy of the following notice, which shall include the name, address, and telephone number of each consumer reporting agency providing a credit score that was used:

NOTICE TO THE HOME LOAN APPLICANT

"In connection with your application for a home loan, the lender must disclose to you the score that a consumer reporting agency distributed to users and the lender used in connection with your home loan, and the key factors affecting your credit scores.

"The credit score is a computor generated summary calculated at the time of the request and based on information that a consumer reporting agency or lender has on file. The scores are based on data about your credit history and payment patterns. Credit scores are important because they are used to assist the lender in determining whether you will obtain a loan. They may also be used to determine what interest rate you may be offered on the mortgage. Credit scores can change over time, depending on your conduct, how your credit history and payment patterns change, and how credit scoring technologies change.

"Because the score is based on information in your credit history, it is very important that you review the credit-related information that is being furnished to make sure it is accurate. Credit records may vary from one company to another.

"If you have questions about your credit score or the credit information that is furnished to you, contact the consumer reporting agency at the address and telephone number provided with this notice, or contact the lender, if the lender developed or generated the credit score. The consumer reporting agency plays no part in the decision to take any action on the loan application and is unable to provide you with specific reasons for the decision on a loan application.

"If you have questions concerning the terms of the loan, contact the lender.

(E) Actions not required under this subsection

This subsection shall not require any person to—

(i) explain the information provided pursuant to subsection (f);

(ii) disclose any information other than a credit score or key factors, as defined in subsection (f) of this section;

(iii) disclose any credit score or related information obtained by the user after a loan has closed;

(iv) provide more than 1 disclosure per loan transaction; or

(v) provide the disclosure required by this subsection when another person has made the disclosure to the consumer for that loan transaction.

(F) No obligation for content

(i) In general

The obligation of any person pursuant to this subsection shall be limited solely to providing a copy of the information that was received from the consumer reporting agency.

(ii) Limit on liability

No person has liability under this subsection for the content of that information or for the omission of any information within the report provided by the consumer reporting agency.

(G) Person defined as excluding enterprise

As used in this subsection, the term "person" does not include an enterprise (as defined in paragraph (6) of section 4502 of Title 12).

(2) Prohibition on disclosure clauses null and void

(A) In general

Any provision in a contract that prohibits the disclosure of a credit score by a person who makes or arranges loans or a consumer reporting agency is void.

(B) No liability for disclosure under this subsection

A lender shall not have liability under any contractual provision for disclosure of a credit score pursuant to this subsection.

§ 1681h [CCPA § 610]. Conditions and form of disclosure to consumers

(a) In general

(1) Proper identification.—A consumer reporting agency shall require, as a condition of making the disclosures required under section 1681g of this title, that the consumer furnish proper identification.

(2) Disclosure in writing.—Except as provided in subsection (b), the disclosures required to be made under section 1681g of this title shall be provided under that section in writing.

(b) Other forms of disclosure

(1) In general.—If authorized by a consumer, a consumer reporting agency may make the disclosures required under[5] 1681g of this title—

(A) other than in writing; and

(B) in such form as may be—

(i) specified by the consumer in accordance with paragraph (2); and

(ii) available from the agency.

(2) Form.—A consumer may specify pursuant to paragraph (1) that disclosures under section 1681g of this title shall be made—

(A) in person, upon the appearance of the consumer at the place of business of the consumer reporting agency where disclosures are regularly provided, during normal business hours, and on reasonable notice;

---

[5] So in original. Probably should be followed by "section."

(B) by telephone, if the consumer has made a written request for disclosure by telephone;

(C) by electronic means, if available from the agency; or

(D) by any other reasonable means that is available from the agency.

(c) Trained personnel

Any consumer reporting agency shall provide trained personnel to explain to the consumer any information furnished to him pursuant to section 1681g of this title.

(d) Persons accompanying consumer

The consumer shall be permitted to be accompanied by one other person of his choosing, who shall furnish reasonable identification. A consumer reporting agency may require the consumer to furnish a written statement granting permission to the consumer reporting agency to discuss the consumer's file in such person's presence.

(e) Limitation of liability

Except as provided in sections 1681n and 1681*o* of this title, no consumer may bring any action or proceeding in the nature of defamation, invasion of privacy, or negligence with respect to the reporting of information against any consumer reporting agency, any user of information, or any person who furnishes information to a consumer reporting agency, based on information disclosed pursuant to section 1681g, 1681h, or 1681m of this title, or based on information disclosed by a user of a consumer report to or for a consumer against whom the user has taken adverse action, based in whole or in part on the report[6] except as to false information furnished with malice or willful intent to injure such consumer.

§ 1681i [CCPA § 611]. Procedure in case of disputed accuracy

(a) Reinvestigations of disputed information

(1) Reinvestigation required.—

(A) In general.—Subject to subsection (f) and except as provided in subsection (g), if the completeness or accuracy of any item of information contained in a consumer's file at a consumer reporting agency is disputed by the consumer and the consumer notifies the agency directly, or indirectly through a reseller, of such dispute, the agency shall, free of charge, conduct a reasonable reinvestigation to determine whether the disputed information is inaccurate and record the current status of the disputed information, or delete the item from the file in accordance with paragraph (5), before the end of the 30-day period beginning on the date on which the agency receives the notice of the dispute from the consumer or reseller.

(B) Extension of period to reinvestigate.—Except as provided in subparagraph (C), the 30-day period described in subparagraph (A) may be extended for not more than 15 additional days if the consumer reporting agency receives information from the consumer during that 30-day period that is relevant to the reinvestigation.

(C) Limitations on extension of period to reinvestigate.—Subparagraph (B) shall not apply to any reinvestigation in which, during the 30-day period described in subparagraph (A), the information that is the subject of the reinvestigation is found to be inaccurate or incomplete or the consumer reporting agency determines that the information cannot be verified.

(2) Prompt notice of dispute to furnisher of information.—

6 So in original. Probably should be followed by a comma.

(A) In general.—Before the expiration of the 5-business-day period beginning on the date on which a consumer reporting agency receives notice of a dispute from any consumer or a reseller in accordance with paragraph (1), the agency shall provide notification of the dispute to any person who provided any item of information in dispute, at the address and in the manner established with the person. The notice shall include all relevant information regarding the dispute that the agency has received from the consumer or reseller.

(B) Provision of other information.—The consumer reporting agency shall promptly provide to the person who provided the information in dispute all relevant information regarding the dispute that is received by the agency from the consumer or the reseller after the period referred to in subparagraph (A) and before the end of the period referred to in paragraph (1)(A).

(3) Determination that dispute is frivolous or irrelevant.—

(A) In general.—Notwithstanding paragraph (1), a consumer reporting agency may terminate a reinvestigation of information disputed by a consumer under that paragraph if the agency reasonably determines that the dispute by the consumer is frivolous or irrelevant, including by reason of a failure by a consumer to provide sufficient information to investigate the disputed information.

(B) Notice of determination.—Upon making any determination in accordance with subparagraph (A) that a dispute is frivolous or irrelevant, a consumer reporting agency shall notify the consumer of such determination not later than 5 business days after making such determination, by mail or, if authorized by the consumer for that purpose, by any other means available to the agency.

(C) Contents of notice.—A notice under subparagraph (B) shall include—

(i) the reasons for the determination under subparagraph (A); and

(ii) identification of any information required to investigate the disputed information, which may consist of a standardized form describing the general nature of such information.

(4) Consideration of consumer information.—In conducting any reinvestigation under paragraph (1) with respect to disputed information in the file of any consumer, the consumer reporting agency shall review and consider all relevant information submitted by the consumer in the period described in paragraph (1)(A) with respect to such disputed information.

(5) Treatment of inaccurate or unverifiable information.—

(A) In general.—If, after any reinvestigation under paragraph (1) of any information disputed by a consumer, an item of the information is found to be inaccurate or incomplete or cannot be verified, the consumer reporting agency shall—

(i) promptly delete that item of information from the file of the consumer, or modify that item of information, as appropriate, based on the results of the reinvestigation; and

(ii) promptly notify the furnisher of that information that the information has been modified or deleted from the file of the consumer.

(B) Requirements relating to reinsertion of previously deleted material.—

(i) Certification of accuracy of information.—If any information is deleted from a consumer's file pursuant to subparagraph (A), the information may not be reinserted in the file by the consumer reporting agency unless the person who furnishes the information certifies that the information is complete and accurate.

(ii) Notice to consumer.—If any information that has been deleted from a consumer's file pursuant to subparagraph (A) is reinserted in the file, the consumer reporting agency shall notify the consumer of the reinsertion in writing not later than 5 business days after the reinsertion or, if authorized by the consumer for that purpose, by any other means available to the agency.

(iii) Additional information.—As part of, or in addition to, the notice under clause (ii), a consumer reporting agency shall provide to a consumer in writing not later than 5 business days after the date of the reinsertion—

(I) a statement that the disputed information has been reinserted;

(II) the business name and address of any furnisher of information contacted and the telephone number of such furnisher, if reasonably available, or of any furnisher of information that contacted the consumer reporting agency, in connection with the reinsertion of such information; and

(III) a notice that the consumer has the right to add a statement to the consumer's file disputing the accuracy or completeness of the disputed information.

(C) Procedures to prevent reappearance.—A consumer reporting agency shall maintain reasonable procedures designed to prevent the reappearance in a consumer's file, and in consumer reports on the consumer, of information that is deleted pursuant to this paragraph (other than information that is reinserted in accordance with subparagraph (B)(i)).

(D) Automated reinvestigation system.—Any consumer reporting agency that compiles and maintains files on consumers on a nationwide basis shall implement an automated system through which furnishers of information to that consumer reporting agency may report the results of a reinvestigation that finds incomplete or inaccurate information in a consumer's file to other such consumer reporting agencies.

(6) Notice of results of reinvestigation.—

(A) In general.—A consumer reporting agency shall provide written notice to a consumer of the results of a reinvestigation under this subsection not later than 5 business days after the completion of the reinvestigation, by mail or, if authorized by the consumer for that purpose, by other means available to the agency.

(B) Contents.—As part of, or in addition to, the notice under subparagraph (A), a consumer reporting agency shall provide to a consumer in writing before the expiration of the 5-day period referred to in subparagraph (A)—

(i) a statement that the reinvestigation is completed;

(ii) a consumer report that is based upon the consumer's file as that file is revised as a result of the reinvestigation;

(iii) a notice that, if requested by the consumer, a description of the procedure used to determine the accuracy and completeness of the information shall be provided to the consumer by the agency, including the business name and address of any furnisher of information contacted in connection with such information and the telephone number of such furnisher, if reasonably available;

(iv) a notice that the consumer has the right to add a statement to the consumer's file disputing the accuracy or completeness of the information; and

(v) a notice that the consumer has the right to request under subsection (d) that the consumer reporting agency furnish notifications under that subsection.

(7) Description of reinvestigation procedure.—A consumer reporting agency shall provide to a consumer a description referred to in paragraph (6)(B)(iii) by not later than 15 days after receiving a request from the consumer for that description.

(8) Expedited dispute resolution.—If a dispute regarding an item of information in a consumer's file at a consumer reporting agency is resolved in accordance with paragraph (5)(A) by the deletion of the disputed information by not later than 3 business days after the date on which the agency receives notice of the dispute from the consumer in accordance with paragraph (1)(A), then the agency shall not be required to comply with paragraphs (2), (6), and (7) with respect to that dispute if the agency—

(A) provides prompt notice of the deletion to the consumer by telephone;

(B) includes in that notice, or in a written notice that accompanies a confirmation and consumer report provided in accordance with subparagraph (C), a statement of the consumer's right to request under subsection (d) that the agency furnish notifications under that subsection; and

(C) provides written confirmation of the deletion and a copy of a consumer report on the consumer that is based on the consumer's file after the deletion, not later than 5 business days after making the deletion.

(b) Statement of dispute

If the reinvestigation does not resolve the dispute, the consumer may file a brief statement setting forth the nature of the dispute. The consumer reporting agency may limit such statements to not more than one hundred words if it provides the consumer with assistance in writing a clear summary of the dispute.

(c) Notification of consumer dispute in subsequent consumer reports

Whenever a statement of a dispute is filed, unless there is reasonable grounds to believe that it is frivolous or irrelevant, the consumer reporting agency shall, in any subsequent consumer report containing the information in question, clearly note that it is disputed by the consumer and provide either the consumer's statement or a clear and accurate codification or summary thereof.

(d) Notification of deletion of disputed information

Following any deletion of information which is found to be inaccurate or whose accuracy can no longer be verified or any notation as to disputed information, the consumer reporting agency shall, at the request of the consumer, furnish notification that the item has been deleted or the statement, codification or summary pursuant to subsection (b) or (c) to any person specifically designated by the consumer who has within two years prior thereto received a consumer report for employment purposes, or within six months prior thereto received a consumer report for any other purpose, which contained the deleted or disputed information.

(e) Treatment of complaints and report to Congress

(1) In general

The Commission[1] shall—

(A) compile all complaints that it receives that a file of a consumer that is maintained by a consumer reporting agency described in section 1681a(p) of this title contains incomplete or inaccurate information, with respect to which, the consumer appears to have disputed the completeness or accuracy with the consumer reporting agency or otherwise utilized the procedures provided by subsection (a); and

(B) transmit each such complaint to each consumer reporting agency involved.

(2) Exclusion

Complaints received or obtained by the Bureau pursuant to its investigative authority under the Consumer Financial Protection Act of 2010 shall not be subject to paragraph (1).

---

1 So in original. Probably should be "Bureau."

(3) Agency responsibilities

Each consumer reporting agency described in section 1681a(p) of this title that receives a complaint transmitted by the Bureau pursuant to paragraph (1) shall—

(A) review each such complaint to determine whether all legal obligations imposed on the consumer reporting agency under this subchapter (including any obligation imposed by an applicable court or administrative order) have been met with respect to the subject matter of the complaint;

(B) provide reports on a regular basis to the Bureau regarding the determinations of and actions taken by the consumer reporting agency, if any, in connection with its review of such complaints; and

(C) maintain, for a reasonable time period, records regarding the disposition of each such complaint that is sufficient to demonstrate compliance with this subsection.

(4) Rulemaking authority

The Commission[1] may prescribe regulations, as appropriate to implement this subsection.

(5) Annual report

The Commission[1] shall submit to the Committee on Banking, Housing, and Urban Affairs of the Senate and the Committee on Financial Services of the House of Representatives an annual report regarding information gathered by the Bureau under this subsection.

(f) Reinvestigation requirement applicable to resellers

(1) Exemption from general reinvestigation requirement

Except as provided in paragraph (2), a reseller shall be exempt from the requirements of this section.

(2) Action required upon receiving notice of a dispute

If a reseller receives a notice from a consumer of a dispute concerning the completeness or accuracy of any item of information contained in a consumer report on such consumer produced by the reseller, the reseller shall, within 5 business days of receiving the notice, and free of charge—

(A) determine whether the item of information is incomplete or inaccurate as a result of an act or omission of the reseller; and

(B) if—

(i) the reseller determines that the item of information is incomplete or inaccurate as a result of an act or omission of the reseller, not later than 20 days after receiving the notice, correct the information in the consumer report or delete it; or

(ii) if the reseller determines that the item of information is not incomplete or inaccurate as a result of an act or omission of the reseller, convey the notice of the dispute, together with all relevant information provided by the consumer, to each consumer reporting agency that provided the reseller with the information that is the subject of the dispute, using an address or a notification mechanism specified by the consumer reporting agency for such notices.

(3) Responsibility of consumer reporting agency to notify consumer through reseller

Upon the completion of a reinvestigation under this section of a dispute concerning the completeness or accuracy of any information in the file of a consumer by a consumer reporting agency that received notice of the dispute from a reseller under paragraph (2)—

(A) the notice by the consumer reporting agency under paragraph (6), (7), or (8) of subsection (a) shall be provided to the reseller in lieu of the consumer; and

(B) the reseller shall immediately reconvey such notice to the consumer, including any notice of a deletion by telephone in the manner required under paragraph (8)(A).

(4) Reseller reinvestigations

No provision of this subsection shall be construed as prohibiting a reseller from conducting a reinvestigation of a consumer dispute directly.

(g) Dispute process for veteran's medical debt

(1) In general

With respect to a veteran's medical debt, the veteran may submit a notice described in paragraph (2), proof of liability of the Department of Veterans Affairs for payment of that debt, or documentation that the Department of Veterans Affairs is in the process of making payment for authorized hospital care, medical services, or extended care services rendered to a consumer reporting agency or a reseller to dispute the inclusion of that debt on a consumer report of the veteran.

(2) Notification to veteran

The Department of Veterans Affairs shall submit to a veteran a notice that the Department of Veterans Affairs has assumed liability for part or all of a veteran's medical debt.

(3) Deletion of information from file

If a consumer reporting agency receives notice, proof of liability, or documentation under paragraph (1), the consumer reporting agency shall delete all information relating to the veteran's medical debt from the file of the veteran and notify the furnisher and the veteran of that deletion.

§ 1681j [CCPA § 612]. Charges for certain disclosures

(a) Free annual disclosure

(1) Nationwide consumer reporting agencies

(A) In general

All consumer reporting agencies described in subsections (p) and (w) of section 1681a of this title shall make all disclosures pursuant to section 1681g of this title once during any 12-month period upon request of the consumer and without charge to the consumer.

(B) Centralized source

Subparagraph (A) shall apply with respect to a consumer reporting agency described in section 1681a(p) of this title only if the request from the consumer is made using the centralized source established for such purpose in accordance with section 211(c) of the Fair and Accurate Credit Transactions Act of 2003.

(C) Nationwide specialty consumer reporting agency

(i) In general

The Commission[1] shall prescribe regulations applicable to each consumer reporting agency described in section 1681a(w) of this title to require the establishment of a streamlined process for consumers to request consumer reports under subparagraph (A), which shall include, at a minimum, the establishment by each such agency of a toll-free telephone number for such requests.

---

1 So in original. Probably should be "Bureau."

(ii) Considerations

In prescribing regulations under clause (i), the Bureau shall consider—

(I) the significant demands that may be placed on consumer reporting agencies in providing such consumer reports;

(II) appropriate means to ensure that consumer reporting agencies can satisfactorily meet those demands, including the efficacy of a system of staggering the availability to consumers of such consumer reports; and

(III) the ease by which consumers should be able to contact consumer reporting agencies with respect to access to such consumer reports.

(iii) Date of issuance

The Commission[1] shall issue the regulations required by this subparagraph in final form not later than 6 months after December 4, 2003.

(iv) Consideration of ability to comply

The regulations of the Bureau under this subparagraph shall establish an effective date by which each nationwide specialty consumer reporting agency (as defined in section 1681a(w) of this title) shall be required to comply with subsection (a), which effective date—

(I) shall be established after consideration of the ability of each nationwide specialty consumer reporting agency to comply with subsection (a); and

(II) shall be not later than 6 months after the date on which such regulations are issued in final form (or such additional period not to exceed 3 months, as the Bureau determines appropriate).

(2) Timing

A consumer reporting agency shall provide a consumer report under paragraph (1) not later than 15 days after the date on which the request is received under paragraph (1).

(3) Reinvestigations

Notwithstanding the time periods specified in section 1681i(a)(1) of this title, a reinvestigation under that section by a consumer reporting agency upon a request of a consumer that is made after receiving a consumer report under this subsection shall be completed not later than 45 days after the date on which the request is received.

(4) Exception for first 12 months of operation

This subsection shall not apply to a consumer reporting agency that has not been furnishing consumer reports to third parties on a continuing basis during the 12-month period preceding a request under paragraph (1), with respect to consumers residing nationwide.

(b) Free disclosure after adverse notice to consumer

Each consumer reporting agency that maintains a file on a consumer shall make all disclosures pursuant to section 1681g of this title without charge to the consumer if, not later than 60 days after receipt by such consumer of a notification pursuant to section 1681m of this title, or of a notification from a debt collection agency affiliated with that consumer reporting agency stating that the consumer's credit rating may be or has been adversely affected, the consumer makes a request under section 1681g of this title.

(c) Free disclosure under certain other circumstances

Upon the request of the consumer, a consumer reporting agency shall make all disclosures pursuant to section 1681g of this title once during any 12-month period without charge to that consumer if the consumer certifies in writing that the consumer—

(1) is unemployed and intends to apply for employment in the 60-day period beginning on the date on which the certification is made;

(2) is a recipient of public welfare assistance; or

(3) has reason to believe that the file on the consumer at the agency contains inaccurate information due to fraud.

(d) Free disclosures in connection with fraud alerts

Upon the request of a consumer, a consumer reporting agency described in section 1681a(p) of this title shall make all disclosures pursuant to section 1681g of this title without charge to the consumer, as provided in subsections (a)(2) and (b)(2) of section 1681c–1 of this title, as applicable.

(e) Other charges prohibited

A consumer reporting agency shall not impose any charge on a consumer for providing any notification required by this subchapter or making any disclosure required by this subchapter, except as authorized by subsection (f).

(f) Reasonable charges allowed for certain disclosures

(1) In general.—In the case of a request from a consumer other than a request that is covered by any of subsections (a) through (d), a consumer reporting agency may impose a reasonable charge on a consumer—

(A) for making a disclosure to the consumer pursuant to section 1681g of this title, which charge—

(i) shall not exceed $8; and

(ii) shall be indicated to the consumer before making the disclosure; and

(B) for furnishing, pursuant to section 1681i(d) of this title, following a reinvestigation under section 1681i(a) of this title, a statement, codification, or summary to a person designated by the consumer under that section after the 30-day period beginning on the date of notification of the consumer under paragraph (6) or (8) of section 1681i(a) of this title with respect to the reinvestigation, which charge—

(i) shall not exceed the charge that the agency would impose on each designated recipient for a consumer report; and

(ii) shall be indicated to the consumer before furnishing such information.

(2) Modification of amount.—The Bureau shall increase the amount referred to in paragraph (1)(A)(i) on January 1 of each year, based proportionally on changes in the Consumer Price Index, with fractional changes rounded to the nearest fifty cents.

(g) Prevention of Deceptive Marketing of Credit Reports.—

(1) In general.—Subject to rulemaking pursuant to section 205(b) of the Credit CARD Act of 2009, any advertisement for a free credit report in any medium shall prominently disclose in such advertisement that free credit reports are available under Federal law at: "AnnualCreditReport.com"(or such other source as may be authorized under Federal law).

(2) Television and radio advertisement.—In the case of an advertisement broadcast by television, the disclosures required under paragraph (1) shall be included in the audio and visual part of such advertisement. In the case of an advertisement broadcast by television or radio, the disclosure required under paragraph (1) shall consist only of the following: 'This is not the free credit report provided for by Federal law'.

§ 1681k [CCPA § 613]. Public record information for employment purposes

(a) In general

A consumer reporting agency which furnishes a consumer report for employment purposes and which for that purpose compiles and reports items of information on consumers which are matters of public record and are likely to have an adverse effect upon a consumer's ability to obtain employment shall—

(1) at the time such public record information is reported to the user of such consumer report, notify the consumer of the fact that public record information is being reported by the consumer reporting agency, together with the name and address of the person to whom such information is being reported; or

(2) maintain strict procedures designed to insure that whenever public record information which is likely to have an adverse effect on a consumer's ability to obtain employment is reported it is complete and up to date. For purposes of this paragraph, items of public record relating to arrests, indictments, convictions, suits, tax liens, and outstanding judgments shall be considered up to date if the current public record status of the item at the time of the report is reported.

(b) Exemption for National security investigations

Subsection (a) does not apply in the case of an agency or department of the United States Government that seeks to obtain and use a consumer report for employment purposes, if the head of the agency or department makes a written finding as prescribed under section 1681b(b)(4)(A) of this title.

§ 1681*l* [CCPA § 614]. Restrictions on investigative consumer reports

Whenever a consumer reporting agency prepares an investigative consumer report, no adverse information in the consumer report (other than information which is a matter of public record) may be included in a subsequent consumer report unless such adverse information has been verified in the process of making such subsequent consumer report, or the adverse information was received within the three-month period preceding the date the subsequent report is furnished.

§ 1681m [CCPA § 615]. Requirements on users of consumer reports

(a) Duties of users taking adverse actions on basis of information contained in consumer reports

If any person takes any adverse action with respect to any consumer that is based in whole or in part on any information contained in a consumer report, the person shall—

(1) provide oral, written, or electronic notice of the adverse action to the consumer;

(2) provide to the consumer written or electronic disclosure—

(A) of a numerical credit score as defined in section 1681g(f)(2)(A) of this title used by such person in taking any adverse action based in whole or in part on any information in a consumer report; and

(B) of the information set forth in subparagraphs (B) through (E) of section 1681g(f)(1) of this title;

(3) provide to the consumer orally, in writing, or electronically—

(A) the name, address, and telephone number of the consumer reporting agency (including a toll-free telephone number established by the agency if the agency compiles and maintains files on consumers on a nationwide basis) that furnished the report to the person; and

(B) a statement that the consumer reporting agency did not make the decision to take the adverse action and is unable to provide the consumer the specific reasons why the adverse action was taken; and

(4) provide to the consumer an oral, written, or electronic notice of the consumer's right—

(A) to obtain, under section 1681j of this title, a free copy of a consumer report on the consumer from the consumer reporting agency referred to in paragraph (3), which notice shall include an indication of the 60-day period under that section for obtaining such a copy; and

(B) to dispute, under section 1681i of this title, with a consumer reporting agency the accuracy or completeness of any information in a consumer report furnished by the agency.

(b) Adverse action based on information obtained from third parties other than consumer reporting agencies

(1) In general.—Whenever credit for personal, family, or household purposes involving a consumer is denied or the charge for such credit is increased either wholly or partly because of information obtained from a person other than a consumer reporting agency bearing upon the consumer's credit worthiness, credit standing, credit capacity, character, general reputation, personal characteristics, or mode of living, the user of such information shall, within a reasonable period of time, upon the consumer's written request for the reasons for such adverse action received within sixty days after learning of such adverse action, disclose the nature of the information to the consumer. The user of such information shall clearly and accurately disclose to the consumer his right to make such written request at the time such adverse action is communicated to the consumer.

(2) Duties of person taking certain actions based on information provided by affiliate.—

(A) Duties, generally.—If a person takes an action described in subparagraph (B) with respect to a consumer, based in whole or in part on information described in subparagraph (C), the person shall—

(i) notify the consumer of the action, including a statement that the consumer may obtain the information in accordance with clause (ii); and

(ii) upon a written request from the consumer received within 60 days after transmittal of the notice required by clause (i), disclose to the consumer the nature of the information upon which the action is based by not later than 30 days after receipt of the request.

(B) Action described.—An action referred to in subparagraph (A) is an adverse action described in section 1681a(k)(1)(A) of this title, taken in connection with a transaction initiated by the consumer, or any adverse action described in clause (i) or (ii) of section 1681a(k)(1)(B) of this title.

(C) Information described.—Information referred to in subparagraph (A)—

(i) except as provided in clause (ii), is information that—

(I) is furnished to the person taking the action by a person related by common ownership or affiliated by common corporate control to the person taking the action; and

(II) bears on the credit worthiness, credit standing, credit capacity, character, general reputation, personal characteristics, or mode of living of the consumer; and

(ii) does not include—

(I) information solely as to transactions or experiences between the consumer and the person furnishing the information; or

(II) information in a consumer report.

(c) Reasonable procedures to assure compliance

No person shall be held liable for any violation of this section if he shows by a preponderance of the evidence that at the time of the alleged violation he maintained reasonable procedures to assure compliance with the provisions of this section.

(d) Duties of users making written credit or insurance solicitations on basis of information contained in consumer files

(1) In general.—Any person who uses a consumer report on any consumer in connection with any credit or insurance transaction that is not initiated by the consumer, that is provided to that person under section 1681b(c)(1)(B) of this title, shall provide with each written solicitation made to the consumer regarding the transaction a clear and conspicuous statement that—

(A) information contained in the consumer's consumer report was used in connection with the transaction;

(B) the consumer received the offer of credit or insurance because the consumer satisfied the criteria for credit worthiness or insurability under which the consumer was selected for the offer;

(C) if applicable, the credit or insurance may not be extended if, after the consumer responds to the offer, the consumer does not meet the criteria used to select the consumer for the offer or any applicable criteria bearing on credit worthiness or insurability or does not furnish any required collateral;

(D) the consumer has a right to prohibit information contained in the consumer's file with any consumer reporting agency from being used in connection with any credit or insurance transaction that is not initiated by the consumer; and

(E) the consumer may exercise the right referred to in subparagraph (D) by notifying a notification system established under section 1681b(e) of this title.

(2) Disclosure of address and telephone number; format

A statement under paragraph (1) shall—

(A) include the address and toll-free telephone number of the appropriate notification system established under section 1681b(e) of this title; and

(B) be presented in such format and in such type size and manner as to be simple and easy to understand, as established by the Bureau, by rule, in consultation with the Federal Trade Commission, the Federal banking agencies, and the National Credit Union Administration.

(3) Maintaining criteria on file.—A person who makes an offer of credit or insurance to a consumer under a credit or insurance transaction described in paragraph (1) shall maintain on file the criteria used to select the consumer to receive the offer, all criteria bearing on credit worthiness or insurability, as applicable, that are the basis for determining whether or not to extend credit or insurance pursuant to the offer, and any requirement for the furnishing of collateral as a condition of the extension of credit or insurance, until the expiration of the 3-year period beginning on the date on which the offer is made to the consumer.

(4) Authority of Federal agencies regarding unfair or deceptive acts or practices not affected.—This section is not intended to affect the authority of any Federal or State agency to enforce a prohibition against unfair or deceptive acts or practices, including the making of false or misleading statements in connection with a credit or insurance transaction that is not initiated by the consumer.

(e) Red flag guidelines and regulations required

(1) Guidelines

The Federal banking agencies, the National Credit Union Administration, the Federal Trade Commission, the Commodity Futures Trading Commission, and the Securities and Exchange Commission shall jointly, with respect to the entities that are subject to their respective enforcement authority under section 1681s of this title—

(A) establish and maintain guidelines for use by each financial institution and each creditor regarding identity theft with respect to account holders at, or customers of, such entities, and update such guidelines as often as necessary;

(B) prescribe regulations requiring each financial institution and each creditor to establish reasonable policies and procedures for implementing the guidelines established pursuant to subparagraph (A), to identify possible risks to account holders or customers or to the safety and soundness of the institution or customers; and

(C) prescribe regulations applicable to card issuers to ensure that, if a card issuer receives notification of a change of address for an existing account, and within a short period of time (during at least the first 30 days after such notification is received) receives a request for an additional or replacement card for the same account, the card issuer may not issue the additional or replacement card, unless the card issuer, in accordance with reasonable policies and procedures—

(i) notifies the cardholder of the request at the former address of the cardholder and provides to the cardholder a means of promptly reporting incorrect address changes;

(ii) notifies the cardholder of the request by such other means of communication as the cardholder and the card issuer previously agreed to; or

(iii) uses other means of assessing the validity of the change of address, in accordance with reasonable policies and procedures established by the card issuer in accordance with the regulations prescribed under subparagraph (B).

(2) Criteria

(A) In general

In developing the guidelines required by paragraph (1)(A), the agencies described in paragraph (1) shall identify patterns, practices, and specific forms of activity that indicate the possible existence of identity theft.

(B) Inactive accounts

In developing the guidelines required by paragraph (1)(A), the agencies described in paragraph (1) shall consider including reasonable guidelines providing that when a transaction occurs with respect to a credit or deposit account that has been inactive for more than 2 years, the creditor or financial institution shall follow reasonable policies and procedures that provide for notice to be given to a consumer in a manner reasonably designed to reduce the likelihood of identity theft with respect to such account.

(3) Consistency with verification requirements

Guidelines established pursuant to paragraph (1) shall not be inconsistent with the policies and procedures required under section 5318(*l*) of Title 31.

(4) Definitions

As used in this subsection, the term "creditor"—

(A) means a creditor, as defined in section 1691a of this title, that regularly and in the ordinary course of business—

(i) obtains or uses consumer reports, directly or indirectly, in connection with a credit transaction;

(ii) furnishes information to consumer reporting agencies, as described in section 1681s–2 of this title, in connection with a credit transaction; or

(iii) advances funds to or on behalf of a person, based on an obligation of the person to repay the funds or repayable from specific property pledged by or on behalf of the person;

(B) does not include a creditor described in subparagraph (A)(iii) that advances funds on behalf of a person for expenses incidental to a service provided by the creditor to that person; and

(C) includes any other type of creditor, as defined in that section 1691a of this title, as the agency described in paragraph (1) having authority over that creditor may determine appropriate by rule promulgated by that agency, based on a determination that such creditor offers or maintains accounts that are subject to a reasonably foreseeable risk of identity theft.

(f) Prohibition on sale or transfer of debt caused by identity theft

(1) In general

No person shall sell, transfer for consideration, or place for collection a debt that such person has been notified under section 1681c–2 of this title has resulted from identity theft.

(2) Applicability

The prohibitions of this subsection shall apply to all persons collecting a debt described in paragraph (1) after the date of a notification under paragraph (1).

(3) Rule of construction

Nothing in this subsection shall be construed to prohibit—

(A) the repurchase of a debt in any case in which the assignee of the debt requires such repurchase because the debt has resulted from identity theft;

(B) the securitization of a debt or the pledging of a portfolio of debt as collateral in connection with a borrowing; or

(C) the transfer of debt as a result of a merger, acquisition, purchase and assumption transaction, or transfer of substantially all of the assets of an entity.

(g) Debt collector communications concerning identity theft

If a person acting as a debt collector (as that term is defined in subchapter V) on behalf of a third party that is a creditor or other user of a consumer report is notified that any information relating to a debt that the person is attempting to collect may be fraudulent or may be the result of identity theft, that person shall—

(1) notify the third party that the information may be fraudulent or may be the result of identity theft; and

(2) upon request of the consumer to whom the debt purportedly relates, provide to the consumer all information to which the consumer would otherwise be entitled if the consumer were not a victim of identity theft, but wished to dispute the debt under provisions of law applicable to that person.

(h) Duties of users in certain credit transactions

(1) In general

Subject to rules prescribed as provided in paragraph (6), if any person uses a consumer report in connection with an application for, or a grant, extension, or other provision of, credit on material terms that are materially less favorable than the most favorable terms available to a substantial proportion of consumers from or through that person, based in whole or in part on a consumer report, the person shall provide an oral, written, or electronic notice to the consumer in the form and manner required by regulations prescribed in accordance with this subsection.

(2) Timing

The notice required under paragraph (1) may be provided at the time of an application for, or a grant, extension, or other provision of, credit or the time of communication of an approval of an application for, or grant, extension, or other provision of, credit, except as provided in the regulations prescribed under paragraph (6).

(3) Exceptions

No notice shall be required from a person under this subsection if—

(A) the consumer applied for specific material terms and was granted those terms, unless those terms were initially specified by the person after the transaction was initiated by the consumer and after the person obtained a consumer report; or

(B) the person has provided or will provide a notice to the consumer under subsection (a) in connection with the transaction.

(4) Other notice not sufficient

A person that is required to provide a notice under subsection (a) cannot meet that requirement by providing a notice under this subsection.

(5) Content and delivery of notice

A notice under this subsection shall, at a minimum—

(A) include a statement informing the consumer that the terms offered to the consumer are set based on information from a consumer report;

(B) identify the consumer reporting agency furnishing the report;

(C) include a statement informing the consumer that the consumer may obtain a copy of a consumer report from that consumer reporting agency without charge;

(D) include the contact information specified by that consumer reporting agency for obtaining such consumer reports (including a toll-free telephone number established by the agency in the case of a consumer reporting agency described in section 1681a(p) of this title); and;

(E) include a statement informing the consumer of—

(i) a numerical credit score as defined in section 1681g(f)(2)(A) of this title, used by such person in making the credit decision described in paragraph (1) based in whole or in part on any information in a consumer report; and

(ii) the information set forth in subparagraphs (B) through (E) of section 1681g(f)(1) of this title.

(6) Rulemaking

(A) Rules Required

The Bureau shall prescribe rules to carry out this subsection.

(B) Content

Rules required by subparagraph (A) shall address, but are not limited to—

(i) the form, content, time, and manner of delivery of any notice under this subsection;

(ii) clarification of the meaning of terms used in this subsection, including what credit terms are material, and when credit terms are materially less favorable;

(iii) exceptions to the notice requirement under this subsection for classes of persons or transactions regarding which the agencies determine that notice would not significantly benefit consumers;

(iv) a model notice that may be used to comply with this subsection; and

(v) the timing of the notice required under paragraph (1), including the circumstances under which the notice must be provided after the terms offered to the consumer were set based on information from a consumer report.

(7) Compliance

A person shall not be liable for failure to perform the duties required by this section if, at the time of the failure, the person maintained reasonable policies and procedures to comply with this section.

(8) Enforcement

(A) No civil actions

Sections 1681n and 1681*o* of this title shall not apply to any failure by any person to comply with this section.

(B) Administrative enforcement

This section shall be enforced exclusively under section 1681s of this title by the Federal agencies and officials identified in that section.

§ 1681n [CCPA § 616]. Civil liability for willful noncompliance

(a) In general

Any person who willfully fails to comply with any requirement imposed under this subchapter with respect to any consumer is liable to that consumer in an amount equal to the sum of—

(1)(A) any actual damages sustained by the consumer as a result of the failure or damages of not less than $100 and not more than $1,000; or

(B) in the case of liability of a natural person for obtaining a consumer report under false pretenses or knowingly without a permissible purpose, actual damages sustained by the consumer as a result of the failure or $1,000, whichever is greater;

(2) such amount of punitive damages as the court may allow; and

(3) in the case of any successful action to enforce any liability under this section, the costs of the action together with reasonable attorney's fees as determined by the court.

(b) Civil liability for knowing noncompliance

Any person who obtains a consumer report from a consumer reporting agency under false pretenses or knowingly without a permissible purpose shall be liable to the consumer reporting agency for actual damages sustained by the consumer reporting agency or $1,000, whichever is greater.

(c) Attorney's fees

Upon a finding by the court that an unsuccessful pleading, motion, or other paper filed in connection with an action under this section was filed in bad faith or for purposes of harassment, the court shall award to the prevailing party attorney's fees reasonable in relation to the work expended in responding to the pleading, motion, or other paper.

(d) Clarification of willful noncompliance

For the purposes of this section, any person who printed an expiration date on any receipt provided to a consumer cardholder at a point of sale or transaction between December 4, 2004, and June 3, 2008, but otherwise complied with the requirements of section 1681c(g) of this title for such receipt shall not be in willful noncompliance with section 1681c(g) of this title by reason of printing such expiration date on the receipt.

§ 1681*o* [CCPA § 617]. Civil Liability for Negligent Noncompliance

(a) In general

Any person who is negligent in failing to comply with any requirement imposed under this subchapter with respect to any consumer is liable to that consumer in an amount equal to the sum of—

(1) any actual damages sustained by the consumer as a result of the failure; and

(2) in the case of any successful action to enforce any liability under this section, the costs of the action together with reasonable attorney's fees as determined by the court.

(b) Attorney's fees

On a finding by the court that an unsuccessful pleading, motion, or other paper filed in connection with an action under this section was filed in bad faith or for purposes of harassment, the court shall award to the prevailing party attorney's fees reasonable in relation to the work expended in responding to the pleading, motion, or other paper.

§ 1681p [CCPA § 618]. Jurisdiction of courts; limitation of actions

An action to enforce any liability created under this subchapter may be brought in any appropriate United States district court, without regard to the amount in controversy, or in any other court of competent jurisdiction, not later than the earlier of—

(1) 2 years after the date of discovery by the plaintiff of the violation that is the basis for such liability; or

(2) 5 years after the date on which the violation that is the basis for such liability occurs.

§ 1681q [CCPA § 619]. Obtaining information under false pretenses

Any person who knowingly and willfully obtains information on a consumer from a consumer reporting agency under false pretenses shall be fined under Title 18, imprisoned for not more than 2 years, or both.

§ 1681r [CCPA § 620]. Unauthorized disclosures by officers or employees

Any officer or employee of a consumer reporting agency who knowingly and willfully provides information concerning an individual from the agency's files to a person not authorized to receive that information shall be fined under Title 18, imprisoned for not more than 2 years, or both.

§ 1681s [CCPA § 621]. Administrative enforcement

(a) Enforcement by Federal Trade Commission

(1) In general

The Federal Trade Commission shall be authorized to enforce compliance with the requirements imposed by this subchapter under the Federal Trade Commission Act (15 U.S.C. 41 et seq.), with respect to consumer reporting agencies and all other persons subject thereto, except to the extent that enforcement of the requirements imposed under this subchapter is specifically committed to some other Government agency under any of subparagraphs (A) through (G) of subsection (b)(1), and subject to subtitle B of the Consumer Financial Protection Act of 2010, subsection (b).[1] For the purpose of the exercise by the Federal Trade Commission of its functions and powers under the Federal Trade Commission Act, a violation of any requirement or prohibition imposed under this subchapter shall constitute an unfair or deceptive act or practice in commerce, in violation of section 5(a) of the Federal Trade Commission Act (15 U.S.C. 45(a)), and shall be subject to enforcement by the Federal Trade Commission under section 5(b) of that Act with respect to any consumer reporting agency or person that is subject to enforcement by the Federal Trade Commission pursuant to this subsection, irrespective of whether that person is engaged in commerce or meets any other jurisdictional tests under the Federal Trade Commission Act. The Federal Trade Commission shall have such procedural, investigative, and enforcement powers, including the power to issue procedural rules in enforcing compliance with the requirements imposed under this subchapter and to require the filing of reports, the production of documents, and the appearance of witnesses, as though the applicable terms and conditions of the Federal Trade Commission Act were part of this subchapter. Any person violating any of the provisions of this subchapter shall be subject to the penalties and entitled to the privileges and immunities provided in the Federal Trade Commission Act as though the applicable terms and provisions of such Act are part of this subchapter.

(2) Penalties

(A) Knowing violations

Except as otherwise provided by subtitle B of the Consumer Financial Protection Act of 2010, in the event of a knowing violation, which constitutes a pattern or practice of violations of this subchapter, the Federal Trade Commission may commence a civil action to recover a civil penalty in a district court of the United States against any person that violates this subchapter. In such action, such person shall be liable for a civil penalty of not more than $2,500 per violation.

(B) Determining penalty amount

In determining the amount of a civil penalty under subparagraph (A), the court shall take into account the degree of culpability, any history of such prior conduct, ability to pay, effect on ability to continue to do business, and such other matters as justice may require.

(C) Limitation

Notwithstanding paragraph (2), a court may not impose any civil penalty on a person for a violation of section 1681s–2(a)(1) of this title, unless the person has been enjoined from committing the violation, or ordered not to commit the violation, in an action or proceeding brought by or on behalf of the Federal Trade Commission, and has violated the injunction or order, and the court may not impose any civil penalty for any violation occurring before the date of the violation of the injunction or order.

(b) Enforcement by other agencies

(1) In general

Subject to subtitle B of the Consumer Financial Protection Act of 2010, compliance with the requirements imposed under this subchapter with respect to consumer reporting agencies, persons who use consumer reports from such agencies, persons who furnish information to such

---

1 So in original.

agencies, and users of information that are subject to section 1681m(d) of this title shall be enforced under—

(A) section 8 of the Federal Deposit Insurance Act (12 U.S.C. 1818), by the appropriate Federal banking agency, as defined in section 3(q) of the Federal Deposit Insurance Act (12 U.S.C. 1813(q)), with respect to—

(i) any national bank or State savings association, and any Federal branch or Federal agency of a foreign bank;

(ii) any member bank of the Federal Reserve System (other than a national bank), a branch or agency of a foreign bank (other than a Federal branch, Federal agency, or insured State branch of a foreign bank), a commercial lending company owned or controlled by a foreign bank, and any organization operating under section 25 or 25A of the Federal Reserve Act; and

(iii) any bank or Federal savings association insured by the Federal Deposit Insurance Corporation (other than a member of the Federal Reserve System) and any insured State branch of a foreign bank;

(B) the Federal Credit Union Act (12 U.S.C. 1751 et seq.), by the Administrator of the National Credit Union Administration with respect to any Federal credit union;

(C) subtitle IV of Title 49, by the Secretary of Transportation, with respect to all carriers subject to the jurisdiction of the Surface Transportation Board;

(D) part A of subtitle VII of Title 49, by the Secretary of Transportation, with respect to any air carrier or foreign air carrier subject to that Act;

(E) the Packers and Stockyards Act, 1921 (7 U.S.C. 181 et seq.) (except as provided in section 406 of that Act), by the Secretary of Agriculture, with respect to any activities subject to that Act;

(F) the Commodity Exchange Act, with respect to a person subject to the jurisdiction of the Commodity Futures Trading Commission;

(G) the Federal securities laws, and any other laws that are subject to the jurisdiction of the Securities and Exchange Commission, with respect to a person that is subject to the jurisdiction of the Securities and Exchange Commission; and

(H) subtitle E of the Consumer Financial Protection Act of 2010, by the Bureau, with respect to any person subject to this subchapter.

(2) Incorporated definitions

The terms used in paragraph (1) that are not defined in this subchapter or otherwise defined in section 3(s) of the Federal Deposit Insurance Act (12 U.S.C. 1813(s)) have the same meanings as in section 1(b) of the International Banking Act of 1978 (12 U.S.C. 3101).

(c) State action for violations

(1) Authority of States.—In addition to such other remedies as are provided under State law, if the chief law enforcement officer of a State, or an official or agency designated by a State, has reason to believe that any person has violated or is violating this subchapter, the State—

(A) may bring an action to enjoin such violation in any appropriate United States district court or in any other court of competent jurisdiction;

(B) subject to paragraph (5), may bring an action on behalf of the residents of the State to recover—

(i) damages for which the person is liable to such residents under sections 1681n and 1681*o* of this title as a result of the violation;

(ii) in the case of a violation described in any of paragraphs (1) through (3) of section 1681s–2(c) of this title, damages for which the person would, but for section 1681s–2(c) of this title, be liable to such residents as a result of the violation; or

(iii) damages of not more than $1,000 for each willful or negligent violation; and

(C) in the case of any successful action under subparagraph (A) or (B), shall be awarded the costs of the action and reasonable attorney fees as determined by the court.

(2) Rights of Federal regulators.—The State shall serve prior written notice of any action under paragraph (1) upon the Bureau and the Federal Trade Commission or the appropriate Federal regulator determined under subsection (b) and provide the Bureau and the Federal Trade Commission or appropriate Federal regulator with a copy of its complaint, except in any case in which such prior notice is not feasible, in which case the State shall serve such notice immediately upon instituting such action. The Bureau and the Federal Trade Commission or appropriate Federal regulator shall have the right—

(A) to intervene in the action;

(B) upon so intervening, to be heard on all matters arising therein;

(C) to remove the action to the appropriate United States district court; and

(D) to file petitions for appeal.

(3) Investigatory powers.—For purposes of bringing any action under this subsection, nothing in this subsection shall prevent the chief law enforcement officer, or an official or agency designated by a State, from exercising the powers conferred on the chief law enforcement officer or such official by the laws of such State to conduct investigations or to administer oaths or affirmations or to compel the attendance of witnesses or the production of documentary and other evidence.

(4) Limitation on State action while Federal action pending.—If the Bureau, the Federal Trade Commission, or the appropriate Federal regulator has instituted a civil action or an administrative action under section 8 of the Federal Deposit Insurance Act [12 U.S.C.A. § 1818] for a violation of this subchapter, no State may, during the pendency of such action, bring an action under this section against any defendant named in the complaint of the Bureau, the Federal Trade Commission, or the appropriate Federal regulator for any violation of this subchapter that is alleged in that complaint.

(5) Limitations on State actions for certain violations

(A) Violation of injunction required.—A State may not bring an action against a person under paragraph (1)(B) for a violation described in any of paragraphs (1) through (3) of section 1681s–2(c) of this title, unless—

(i) the person has been enjoined from committing the violation, in an action brought by the State under paragraph (1)(A); and

(ii) the person has violated the injunction.

(B) Limitation on damages recoverable.—In an action against a person under paragraph (1)(B) for a violation described in any of paragraphs (1) through (3) of section 1681s–2(c) of this title, a State may not recover any damages incurred before the date of the violation of an injunction on which the action is based.

(d) Enforcement under other authority

For the purpose of the exercise by any agency referred to in subsection (b) of its powers under any Act referred to in that subsection, a violation of any requirement imposed under this subchapter shall be deemed to be a violation of a requirement imposed under that Act. In addition to its powers under any provision of law specifically referred to in subsection (b), each of the agencies referred to in that subsection may exercise, for the purpose of enforcing compliance with any requirement imposed under this subchapter any other authority conferred on it by law.

(e) Regulatory authority

(1) In general

The Bureau shall prescribe such regulations as are necessary to carry out the purposes of this subchapter, except with respect to sections 1681m(e) and 1681w of this title. The Bureau may prescribe regulations as may be necessary or appropriate to administer and carry out the purposes and objectives of this subchapter, and to prevent evasions thereof or to facilitate compliance therewith. Except as provided in section 1029(a) of the Consumer Financial Protection Act of 2010, the regulations prescribed by the Bureau under this subchapter shall apply to any person that is subject to this subchapter, notwithstanding the enforcement authorities granted to other agencies under this section.

(2) Deference

Notwithstanding any power granted to any Federal agency under this subchapter, the deference that a court affords to a Federal agency with respect to a determination made by such agency relating to the meaning or interpretation of any provision of this subchapter that is subject to the jurisdiction of such agency shall be applied as if that agency were the only agency authorized to apply, enforce, interpret, or administer the provisions of this subchapter[2] The regulations prescribed by the Bureau under this subchapter shall apply to any person that is subject to this subchapter, notwithstanding the enforcement authorities granted to other agencies under this section.

(f) Coordination of consumer complaint investigations

(1) In general

Each consumer reporting agency described in section 1681a(p) of this title shall develop and maintain procedures for the referral to each other such agency of any consumer complaint received by the agency alleging identity theft, or requesting a fraud alert under section 1681c–1 of this title or a block under section 1681c–2 of this title.

(2) Model form and procedure for reporting identity theft

The Commission[3], in consultation with the Federal Trade Commission, the Federal banking agencies, and the National Credit Union Administration, shall develop a model form and model procedures to be used by consumers who are victims of identity theft for contacting and informing creditors and consumer reporting agencies of the fraud.

(3) Annual summary reports

Each consumer reporting agency described in section 1681a(p) of this title shall submit an annual summary report to the Bureau on consumer complaints received by the agency on identity theft or fraud alerts.

(g) Bureau regulation of coding of trade names

If the Bureau determines that a person described in paragraph (9) of section 1681s–2(a) of this title has not met the requirements of such paragraph, the Bureau shall take action to ensure the person's compliance with such paragraph, which may include issuing model guidance or prescribing reasonable policies and procedures, as necessary to ensure that such person complies with such paragraph.

---

[2] So in original. Probably should be followed by a period.

[3] So in original. Probably should be "Bureau."

§ 1681s–1 [CCPA § 622]. Information on overdue child support obligations

Notwithstanding any other provision of this subchapter, a consumer reporting agency shall include in any consumer report furnished by the agency in accordance with section 1681b of this title, any information on the failure of the consumer to pay overdue support which—

(1) is provided—

(A) to the consumer reporting agency by a State or local child support enforcement agency; or

(B) to the consumer reporting agency and verified by any local, State, or Federal Government agency; and

(2) antedates the report by 7 years or less.

§ 1681s–2 [CCPA § 623]. Responsibilities of furnishers of information to consumer reporting agencies

(a) Duty of furnishers of information to provide accurate information

(1) Prohibition

(A) Reporting information with actual knowledge of errors

A person shall not furnish any information relating to a consumer to any consumer reporting agency if the person knows or has reasonable cause to believe that the information is inaccurate.

(B) Reporting information after notice and confirmation of errors

A person shall not furnish information relating to a consumer to any consumer reporting agency if—

(i) the person has been notified by the consumer, at the address specified by the person for such notices, that specific information is inaccurate; and

(ii) the information is, in fact, inaccurate.

(C) No address requirement

A person who clearly and conspicuously specifies to the consumer an address for notices referred to in subparagraph (B) shall not be subject to subparagraph (A); however, nothing in subparagraph (B) shall require a person to specify such an address.

(D) Definition

For purposes of subparagraph (A), the term "reasonable cause to believe that the information is inaccurate" means having specific knowledge, other than solely allegations by the consumer, that would cause a reasonable person to have substantial doubts about the accuracy of the information.

(E) Rehabilitation of private education loans

(i) In general

Notwithstanding any other provision of this section, a consumer may request a financial institution to remove from a consumer report a reported default regarding a private education loan, and such information shall not be considered inaccurate, if—

(I) the financial institution chooses to offer a loan rehabilitation program which includes, without limitation, a requirement of the consumer to make consecutive on-time monthly payments in a number that demonstrates, in the assessment of the financial institution offering the loan rehabilitation program, a renewed ability and willingness to repay the loan; and

(II) the requirements of the loan rehabilitation program described in subclause (I) are successfully met.

(ii) Banking agencies

(I) In general

If a financial institution is supervised by a Federal banking agency, the financial institution shall seek written approval concerning the terms and conditions of the loan rehabilitation program described in clause (i) from the appropriate Federal banking agency.

(II) Feedback

An appropriate Federal banking agency shall provide feedback to a financial institution within 120 days of a request for approval under subclause (i).

(iii) Limitation

(I) In general

A consumer may obtain the benefits available under this subsection with respect to rehabilitating a loan only 1 time per loan.

(II) Rule of construction

Nothing in this subparagraph may be construed to require a financial institution to offer a loan rehabilitation program or to remove any reported default from a consumer report as a consideration of a loan rehabilitation program, except as described in clause (i).

(iv) Definitions

For purposes of this subparagraph—

(I) the term "appropriate Federal banking agency" has the meaning given the term in section 1813 of Title 12; and

(II) the term "private education loan" has the meaning given the term in section 1650(a) of this title.

(2) Duty to correct and update information

A person who—

(A) regularly and in the ordinary course of business furnishes information to one or more consumer reporting agencies about the person's transactions or experiences with any consumer; and

(B) has furnished to a consumer reporting agency information that the person determines is not complete or accurate,

shall promptly notify the consumer reporting agency of that determination and provide to the agency any corrections to that information, or any additional information, that is necessary to make the information provided by the person to the agency complete and accurate, and shall not thereafter furnish to the agency any of the information that remains not complete or accurate.

(3) Duty to provide notice of dispute

If the completeness or accuracy of any information furnished by any person to any consumer reporting agency is disputed to such person by a consumer, the person may not furnish the information to any consumer reporting agency without notice that such information is disputed by the consumer.

(4) Duty to provide notice of closed accounts

A person who regularly and in the ordinary course of business furnishes information to a consumer reporting agency regarding a consumer who has a credit account with that person shall notify the agency of the voluntary closure of the account by the consumer, in information regularly furnished for the period in which the account is closed.

(5) Duty to provide notice of delinquency of accounts

(A) In general

A person who furnishes information to a consumer reporting agency regarding a delinquent account being placed for collection, charged to profit or loss, or subjected to any similar action shall, not later than 90 days after furnishing the information, notify the agency of the date of delinquency on the account, which shall be the month and year of the commencement of the delinquency on the account that immediately preceded the action.

(B) Rule of construction

For purposes of this paragraph only, and provided that the consumer does not dispute the information, a person that furnishes information on a delinquent account that is placed for collection, charged for profit or loss, or subjected to any similar action, complies with this paragraph, if—

(i) the person reports the same date of delinquency as that provided by the creditor to which the account was owed at the time at which the commencement of the delinquency occurred, if the creditor previously reported that date of delinquency to a consumer reporting agency;

(ii) the creditor did not previously report the date of delinquency to a consumer reporting agency, and the person establishes and follows reasonable procedures to obtain the date of delinquency from the creditor or another reliable source and reports that date to a consumer reporting agency as the date of delinquency; or

(iii) the creditor did not previously report the date of delinquency to a consumer reporting agency and the date of delinquency cannot be reasonably obtained as provided in clause (ii), the person establishes and follows reasonable procedures to ensure the date reported as the date of delinquency precedes the date on which the account is placed for collection, charged to profit or loss, or subjected to any similar action, and reports such date to the credit reporting agency.

(6) Duties of furnishers upon notice of identity theft-related information

(A) Reasonable procedures

A person that furnishes information to any consumer reporting agency shall have in place reasonable procedures to respond to any notification that it receives from a consumer reporting agency under section 1681c–2 of this title relating to information resulting from identity theft, to prevent that person from refurnishing such blocked information.

(B) Information alleged to result from identity theft

If a consumer submits an identity theft report to a person who furnishes information to a consumer reporting agency at the address specified by that person for receiving such reports stating that information maintained by such person that purports to relate to the consumer resulted from identity theft, the person may not furnish such information that purports to relate to the consumer to any consumer reporting agency, unless the person subsequently knows or is informed by the consumer that the information is correct.

(7) Negative information

(A) Notice to consumer required

(i) In general

If any financial institution that extends credit and regularly and in the ordinary course of business furnishes information to a consumer reporting agency described in section 1681a(p) of this title furnishes negative information to such an agency regarding credit extended to a customer, the financial institution shall provide a notice of such furnishing of negative information, in writing, to the customer.

(ii) Notice effective for subsequent submissions

After providing such notice, the financial institution may submit additional negative information to a consumer reporting agency described in section 1681a(p) of this title with respect to the same transaction, extension of credit, account, or customer without providing additional notice to the customer.

(B) Time of notice

(i) In general

The notice required under subparagraph (A) shall be provided to the customer prior to, or no later than 30 days after, furnishing the negative information to a consumer reporting agency described in section 1681a(p) of this title.

(ii) Coordination with new account disclosures

If the notice is provided to the customer prior to furnishing the negative information to a consumer reporting agency, the notice may not be included in the initial disclosures provided under section 1637(a) of this title.

(C) Coordination with other disclosures

The notice required under subparagraph (A)—

(i) may be included on or with any notice of default, any billing statement, or any other materials provided to the customer; and

(ii) must be clear and conspicuous.

(D) Model disclosure

(i) Duty of Bureau

The Bureau shall prescribe a brief model disclosure that a financial institution may use to comply with subparagraph (A), which shall not exceed 30 words.

(ii) Use of model not required

No provision of this paragraph may be construed to require a financial institution to use any such model form prescribed by the Bureau.

(iii) Compliance using model

A financial institution shall be deemed to be in compliance with subparagraph (A) if the financial institution uses any model form prescribed by the Bureau under this subparagraph, or the financial institution uses any such model form and rearranges its format.

(E) Use of notice without submitting negative information

No provision of this paragraph shall be construed as requiring a financial institution that has provided a customer with a notice described in subparagraph (A) to furnish negative information about the customer to a consumer reporting agency.

(F) Safe harbor

A financial institution shall not be liable for failure to perform the duties required by this paragraph if, at the time of the failure, the financial institution maintained reasonable policies and procedures to comply with this paragraph or the financial institution reasonably believed that the institution is prohibited, by law, from contacting the consumer.

(G) Definitions

For purposes of this paragraph, the following definitions shall apply:

(i) Negative information

The term "negative information" means information concerning a customer's delinquencies, late payments, insolvency, or any form of default.

(ii) Customer; financial institution

The terms "customer" and "financial institution" have the same meanings as in section 6809 of this title.

(8) Ability of consumer to dispute information directly with furnisher

(A) In general

The Bureau, in consultation with the Federal Trade Commission, the Federal banking agencies, and the National Credit Union Administration, shall prescribe regulations that shall identify the circumstances under which a furnisher shall be required to reinvestigate a dispute concerning the accuracy of information contained in a consumer report on the consumer, based on a direct request of a consumer.

(B) Considerations

In prescribing regulations under subparagraph (A), the agencies shall weigh—

(i) the benefits to consumers with the costs on furnishers and the credit reporting system;

(ii) the impact on the overall accuracy and integrity of consumer reports of any such requirements;

(iii) whether direct contact by the consumer with the furnisher would likely result in the most expeditious resolution of any such dispute; and

(iv) the potential impact on the credit reporting process if credit repair organizations, as defined in section 1679a(3) of this title, including entities that would be a credit repair organization, but for section 1679a(3)(B)(i) of this title, are able to circumvent the prohibition in subparagraph (G).

(C) Applicability

Subparagraphs (D) through (G) shall apply in any circumstance identified under the regulations promulgated under subparagraph (A).

(D) Submitting a notice of dispute

A consumer who seeks to dispute the accuracy of information shall provide a dispute notice directly to such person at the address specified by the person for such notices that—

(i) identifies the specific information that is being disputed;

(ii) explains the basis for the dispute; and

(iii) includes all supporting documentation required by the furnisher to substantiate the basis of the dispute.

(E) Duty of person after receiving notice of dispute

After receiving a notice of dispute from a consumer pursuant to subparagraph (D), the person that provided the information in dispute to a consumer reporting agency shall—

(i) conduct an investigation with respect to the disputed information;

(ii) review all relevant information provided by the consumer with the notice;

(iii) complete such person's investigation of the dispute and report the results of the investigation to the consumer before the expiration of the period under section 1681i(a)(1) of this title within which a consumer reporting agency would be required to complete its action if the consumer had elected to dispute the information under that section; and

(iv) if the investigation finds that the information reported was inaccurate, promptly notify each consumer reporting agency to which the person furnished the inaccurate information of that determination and provide to the agency any correction to that information that is necessary to make the information provided by the person accurate.

(F) Frivolous or irrelevant dispute

(i) In general

This paragraph shall not apply if the person receiving a notice of a dispute from a consumer reasonably determines that the dispute is frivolous or irrelevant, including—

(I) by reason of the failure of a consumer to provide sufficient information to investigate the disputed information; or

(II) the submission by a consumer of a dispute that is substantially the same as a dispute previously submitted by or for the consumer, either directly to the person or through a consumer reporting agency under subsection (b), with respect to which the person has already performed the person's duties under this paragraph or subsection (b), as applicable.

(ii) Notice of determination

Upon making any determination under clause (i) that a dispute is frivolous or irrelevant, the person shall notify the consumer of such determination not later than 5 business days after making such determination, by mail or, if authorized by the consumer for that purpose, by any other means available to the person.

(iii) Contents of notice

A notice under clause (ii) shall include—

(I) the reasons for the determination under clause (i); and

(II) identification of any information required to investigate the disputed information, which may consist of a standardized form describing the general nature of such information.

(G) Exclusion of credit repair organizations

This paragraph shall not apply if the notice of the dispute is submitted by, is prepared on behalf of the consumer by, or is submitted on a form supplied to the consumer by, a credit repair organization, as defined in section 1679a(3) of this title, or an entity that would be a credit repair organization, but for section 1679a(3)(B)(i) of this title.

(9) Duty to provide notice of status as medical information furnisher

A person whose primary business is providing medical services, products, or devices, or the person's agent or assignee, who furnishes information to a consumer reporting agency on a consumer shall be considered a medical information furnisher for purposes of this subchapter, and shall notify the agency of such status.

(b) Duties of furnishers of information upon notice of dispute

(1) In general

After receiving notice pursuant to section 1681i(a)(2) of this title of a dispute with regard to the completeness or accuracy of any information provided by a person to a consumer reporting agency, the person shall—

(A) conduct an investigation with respect to the disputed information;

(B) review all relevant information provided by the consumer reporting agency pursuant to section 1681i(a)(2) of this title;

(C) report the results of the investigation to the consumer reporting agency;

(D) if the investigation finds that the information is incomplete or inaccurate, report those results to all other consumer reporting agencies to which the person furnished the information and that compile and maintain files on consumers on a nationwide basis; and

(E) if an item of information disputed by a consumer is found to be inaccurate or incomplete or cannot be verified after any reinvestigation under paragraph (1), for purposes of reporting to a consumer reporting agency only, as appropriate, based on the results of the reinvestigation promptly—

(i) modify that item of information;

(ii) delete that item of information; or

(iii) permanently block the reporting of that item of information.

(2) Deadline

A person shall complete all investigations, reviews, and reports required under paragraph (1) regarding information provided by the person to a consumer reporting agency, before the expiration of the period under section 1681i(a)(1) of this title within which the consumer reporting agency is required to complete actions required by that section regarding that information.

(c) Limitation on liability

Except as provided in section 1681s(c)(1)(B) of this title, sections 1681n and 1681*o* of this title do not apply to any violation of—

(1) subsection (a) of this section, including any regulations issued thereunder;

(2) subsection (e) of this section, except that nothing in this paragraph shall limit, expand, or otherwise affect liability under section 1681n or 1681*o* of this title, as applicable, for violations of subsection (b) of this section; or

(3) subsection (e) of section 1681m of this title.

(d) Limitation on enforcement

The provisions of law described in paragraphs (1) through (3) of subsection (c)(other than with respect to the exception described in paragraph (2) of subsection (c)) shall be enforced exclusively as provided under section 1681s of this title by the Federal agencies and officials and the State officials identified in section 1681s of this title.

(e) Accuracy guidelines and regulations required

(1) Guidelines

The Bureau shall, with respect to persons or entities that are subject to the enforcement authority of the Bureau under section 1681s of this title—

(A) establish and maintain guidelines for use by each person that furnishes information to a consumer reporting agency regarding the accuracy and integrity of the information relating to consumers that such entities furnish to consumer reporting agencies, and update such guidelines as often as necessary; and

(B) prescribe regulations requiring each person that furnishes information to a consumer reporting agency to establish reasonable policies and procedures for implementing the guidelines established pursuant to subparagraph (A).

(2) Criteria

In developing the guidelines required by paragraph (1)(A), the Bureau shall—

(A) identify patterns, practices, and specific forms of activity that can compromise the accuracy and integrity of information furnished to consumer reporting agencies;

(B) review the methods (including technological means) used to furnish information relating to consumers to consumer reporting agencies;

(C) determine whether persons that furnish information to consumer reporting agencies maintain and enforce policies to ensure the accuracy and integrity of information furnished to consumer reporting agencies; and

(D) examine the policies and processes that persons that furnish information to consumer reporting agencies employ to conduct reinvestigations and correct inaccurate information relating to consumers that has been furnished to consumer reporting agencies.

§ 1681s–3 [CCPA § 624]. Affiliate sharing

(a) Special rule for solicitation for purposes of marketing

(1) Notice

Any person that receives from another person related to it by common ownership or affiliated by corporate control a communication of information that would be a consumer report, but for clauses (i), (ii), and (iii) of section 1681a(d)(2)(A) of this title, may not use the information to make a solicitation for marketing purposes to a consumer about its products or services, unless—

(A) it is clearly and conspicuously disclosed to the consumer that the information may be communicated among such persons for purposes of making such solicitations to the consumer; and

(B) the consumer is provided an opportunity and a simple method to prohibit the making of such solicitations to the consumer by such person.

(2) Consumer choice

(A) In general

The notice required under paragraph (1) shall allow the consumer the opportunity to prohibit all solicitations referred to in such paragraph, and may allow the consumer to choose from different options when electing to prohibit the sending of such solicitations, including options regarding the types of entities and information covered, and which methods of delivering solicitations the consumer elects to prohibit.

(B) Format

Notwithstanding subparagraph (A), the notice required under paragraph (1) shall be clear, conspicuous, and concise, and any method provided under paragraph (1)(B) shall be simple. The regulations prescribed to implement this section shall provide specific guidance regarding how to comply with such standards.

(3) Duration

(A) In general

The election of a consumer pursuant to paragraph (1)(B) to prohibit the making of solicitations shall be effective for at least 5 years, beginning on the date on which the person receives the election of the consumer, unless the consumer requests that such election be revoked.

(B) Notice upon expiration of effective period

At such time as the election of a consumer pursuant to paragraph (1)(B) is no longer effective, a person may not use information that the person receives in the manner described in paragraph (1) to make any solicitation for marketing purposes to the consumer, unless the consumer receives a notice and an opportunity, using a simple method, to extend the opt-out for another period of at least 5 years, pursuant to the procedures described in paragraph (1).

(4) Scope

This section shall not apply to a person—

(A) using information to make a solicitation for marketing purposes to a consumer with whom the person has a pre-existing business relationship;

(B) using information to facilitate communications to an individual for whose benefit the person provides employee benefit or other services pursuant to a contract with an employer related to and arising out of the current employment relationship or status of the individual as a participant or beneficiary of an employee benefit plan;

(C) using information to perform services on behalf of another person related by common ownership or affiliated by corporate control, except that this subparagraph shall not be construed as permitting a person to send solicitations on behalf of another person, if such other person would not be permitted to send the solicitation on its own behalf as a result of the election of the consumer to prohibit solicitations under paragraph (1)(B),

(D) using information in response to a communication initiated by the consumer;

(E) using information in response to solicitations authorized or requested by the consumer; or

(F) if compliance with this section by that person would prevent compliance by that person with any provision of State insurance laws pertaining to unfair discrimination in any State in which the person is lawfully doing business.

(5) No retroactivity

This subsection shall not prohibit the use of information to send a solicitation to a consumer if such information was received prior to the date on which persons are required to comply with regulations implementing this subsection.

(b) Notice for other purposes permissible

A notice or other disclosure under this section may be coordinated and consolidated with any other notice required to be issued under any other provision of law by a person that is subject to this section, and a notice or other disclosure that is equivalent to the notice required by subsection (a), and that is provided by a person described in subsection (a) to a consumer together with disclosures required by any other provision of law, shall satisfy the requirements of subsection (a).

(c) User requirements

Requirements with respect to the use by a person of information received from another person related to it by common ownership or affiliated by corporate control, such as the requirements of this section, constitute requirements with respect to the exchange of information among persons affiliated by common ownership or common corporate control, within the meaning of section 1681t(b)(2) of this title.

(d) Definitions

For purposes of this section, the following definitions shall apply:

(1) Pre-existing business relationship

The term "pre-existing business relationship" means a relationship between a person, or a person's licensed agent, and a consumer, based on—

(A) a financial contract between a person and a consumer which is in force;

(B) the purchase, rental, or lease by the consumer of that person's goods or services, or a financial transaction (including holding an active account or a policy in force or having another continuing relationship) between the consumer and that person during the 18-month period immediately preceding the date on which the consumer is sent a solicitation covered by this section;

(C) an inquiry or application by the consumer regarding a product or service offered by that person, during the 3-month period immediately preceding the date on which the consumer is sent a solicitation covered by this section; or

(D) any other pre-existing customer relationship defined in the regulations implementing this section.

(2) Solicitation

The term "solicitation" means the marketing of a product or service initiated by a person to a particular consumer that is based on an exchange of information described in subsection (a), and is intended to encourage the consumer to purchase such product or service, but does not include communications that are directed at the general public or determined not to be a solicitation by the regulations prescribed under this section.

§ 1681t [CCPA § 625]. Relation to State laws

(a) In general

Except as provided in subsections (b) and (c), this subchapter does not annul, alter, affect, or exempt any person subject to the provisions of this subchapter from complying with the laws of any State with respect to the collection, distribution, or use of any information on consumers, or for the prevention or mitigation of identity theft, except to the extent that those laws are inconsistent with any provision of this subchapter, and then only to the extent of the inconsistency.

(b) General exceptions

No requirement or prohibition may be imposed under the laws of any State—

(1) with respect to any subject matter regulated under—

(A) subsection (c) or (e) of section 1681b of this title, relating to the prescreening of consumer reports;

(B) section 1681i of this title, relating to the time by which a consumer reporting agency must take any action, including the provision of notification to a consumer or other person, in any procedure related to the disputed accuracy of information in a consumer's file, except that this subparagraph shall not apply to any State law in effect on September 30, 1996;

(C) subsections (a) and (b) of section 1681m of this title, relating to the duties of a person who takes any adverse action with respect to a consumer;

(D) section 1681m(d) of this title, relating to the duties of persons who use a consumer report of a consumer in connection with any credit or insurance transaction that is not initiated by the consumer and that consists of a firm offer of credit or insurance;

(E) section 1681c of this title, relating to information contained in consumer reports, except that this subparagraph shall not apply to any State law in effect on September 30, 1996;

(F) section 1681s–2 of this title, relating to the responsibilities of persons who furnish information to consumer reporting agencies, except that this paragraph shall not apply—

(i) with respect to section 54A(a) of chapter 93 of the Massachusetts Annotated Laws (as in effect on September 30, 1996); or

(ii) with respect to section 1785.25(a) of the California Civil Code (as in effect on September 30, 1996);

(G) section 1681g(e) of this title, relating to information available to victims under section 1681g(e) of this title;

(H) section 1681s–3 of this title, relating to the exchange and use of information to make a solicitation for marketing purposes; or

(I) section 1681m(h) of this title, relating to the duties of users of consumer reports to provide notice with respect to terms in certain credit transactions;

(J) subsections (i) and (j) of section 1681–1 of this title relating to security freezes; or

(K) subsection (k) of section 1681c–1 of this title, relating to credit monitoring for active duty military consumers, as defined in that subsection;

(2) with respect to the exchange of information among persons affiliated by common ownership or common corporate control, except that this paragraph shall not apply with respect to subsection (a) or (c)(1) of section 2480e of title 9, Vermont Statutes Annotated (as in effect on September 30, 1996);

(3) with respect to the disclosures required to be made under subsection (c), (d), (e), or (g) of section 1681g of this title, or subsection (f) of section 1681g of this title relating to the disclosure of credit scores for credit granting purposes, except that this paragraph—

(A) shall not apply with respect to sections 1785.10, 1785.16, and 1785.20.2 of the California Civil Code (as in effect on December 4, 2003) and section 1785.15 through section 1785.15.2 of such Code (as in effect on such date);

(B) shall not apply with respect to sections 5–3–106(2) and 212–14.3–104.3 of the Colorado Revised Statutes (as in effect on December 4, 2003); and

(C) shall not be construed as limiting, annulling, affecting, or superseding any provision of the laws of any State regulating the use in an insurance activity, or regulating disclosures concerning such use, of a credit-based insurance score of a consumer by any person engaged in the business of insurance;

(4) with respect to the frequency of any disclosure under section 1681j(a) of this title, except that this paragraph shall not apply—

(A) with respect to section 12–14.3–105(1)(d) of the Colorado Revised Statutes (as in effect on December 4, 2003);

(B) with respect to section 10–1–393(29)(C) of the Georgia Code (as in effect on December 4, 2003);

(C) with respect to section 1316.2 of title 10 of the Maine Revised Statutes (as in effect on December 4, 2003);

(D) with respect to sections 14–1209(a)(1) and 14–1209(b)(1)(i) of the Commercial Law Article of the Code of Maryland (as in effect on December 4, 2003);

(E) with respect to section 59(d) and section 59(e) of chapter 93 of the General Laws of Massachusetts (as in effect December 4, 2003);

(F) with respect to section 56:11–37.10(a)(1) of the New Jersey Revised Statutes (as in effect on December 4, 2003); or

(G) with respect to section 2480c(a)(1) of title 9 of the Vermont Statutes Annotated (as in effect on December 4, 2003); or

(5) with respect to the conduct required by the specific provisions of—

(A) section 1681c(g) of this title;

(B) section 1681c–1 of this title;

(C) section 1681c–2 of this title;

(D) section 1681g(a)(1)(A) of this title;

(E) section 1681j(a) of this title;

(F) subsections (e), (f), and (g) of section 1681m of this title;

(G) section 1681s(f) of this title;

(H) section 1681s–2(a)(6) of this title; or

(I) section 1681w of this title.

(c) "Firm offer of credit or insurance" defined

Notwithstanding any definition of the term "firm offer of credit or insurance" (or any equivalent term) under the laws of any State, the definition of that term contained in section 1681a(*l*) of this title shall be construed to apply in the enforcement and interpretation of the laws of any State governing consumer reports.

(d) Limitations

Subsections (b) and (c) do not affect any settlement, agreement, or consent judgment between any State Attorney General and any consumer reporting agency in effect on September 30, 1996.

§ 1681u [CCPA § 626]. Disclosures to FBI for counterintelligence purposes

(a) Identity of financial institutions

Notwithstanding section 1681b of this title or any other provision of this subchapter, a consumer reporting agency shall furnish to the Federal Bureau of Investigation the names and addresses of all financial institutions (as that term is defined in section 3401 of Title 12) at which a consumer maintains or has maintained an account, to the extent that information is in the files of the agency, when presented with a written request for that information that includes a term that specifically identifies a consumer or account to be used as the basis for the production of that information, signed by the Director of the Federal Bureau of Investigation, or the Director's designee in a position not lower than Deputy Assistant Director at Bureau headquarters or a Special Agent in Charge of a Bureau field office designated by the Director, which certifies compliance with this section. The Director or the Director's designee may make such a certification only if the Director or the Director's designee has determined in writing, that such information is sought for the conduct of an authorized investigation to protect against international terrorism or clandestine intelligence activities, provided that such an investigation of a United States person is not conducted solely upon the basis of activities protected by the first amendment to the Constitution of the United States.

(b) Identifying information

Notwithstanding the provisions of section 1681b of this title or any other provision of this subchapter, a consumer reporting agency shall furnish identifying information respecting a consumer, limited to name, address, former addresses, places of employment, or former places of employment, to the Federal Bureau of Investigation when presented with a written request that includes a term that specifically identifies a consumer or account to be used as the basis for the production of that information, signed by the Director or the Director's designee in a position not lower than Deputy Assistant Director at Bureau headquarters or a Special Agent in Charge of a Bureau field office designated by the Director, which certifies compliance with this subsection. The Director or the Director's designee may make such a certification only if the Director or the Director's designee has determined in writing that such information is sought for the conduct of an authorized investigation to protect against international terrorism or clandestine intelligence activities, provided that such an investigation of a United States person is not conducted solely upon the basis of activities protected by the first amendment to the Constitution of the United States.

(c) Court order for disclosure of consumer reports

Notwithstanding section 1681b of this title or any other provision of this subchapter, if requested in writing by the Director of the Federal Bureau of Investigation, or a designee of the Director in a position not lower than Deputy Assistant Director at Bureau headquarters or a Special Agent in Charge in a Bureau field office designated by the Director, a court may issue an order ex parte, which shall include a term that specifically identifies a consumer or account to be used as the basis for the production of the information, directing a consumer reporting agency to furnish a consumer report to the Federal Bureau of Investigation, upon a showing in camera that the consumer report is sought for the conduct of an authorized investigation to protect against international terrorism or clandestine intelligence activities, provided that such an investigation of a United States person is not conducted solely upon the basis of activities protected by the first amendment to the Constitution of the United States. The terms of an order issued under this subsection shall not disclose that the order is issued for purposes of a counterintelligence investigation.

(d) Prohibition of certain disclosure

(1) Prohibition

(A) In general

If a certification is issued under subparagraph (B) and notice of the right to judicial review under subsection (e) is provided, no consumer reporting agency that receives a request under subsection (a) or (b) or an order under subsection (c), or officer, employee, or agent thereof, shall disclose or specify in any consumer report, that the Federal Bureau of Investigation has sought or obtained access to information or records under subsection (a), (b), or (c).

(B) Certification

The requirements of subparagraph (A) shall apply if the Director of the Federal Bureau of Investigation, or a designee of the Director whose rank shall be no lower than Deputy Assistant Director at Bureau headquarters or a Special Agent in Charge of a Bureau field office, certifies that the absence of a prohibition of disclosure under this subsection may result in—

(i) a danger to the national security of the United States;

(ii) interference with a criminal, counterterrorism, or counterintelligence investigation;

(iii) interference with diplomatic relations; or

(iv) danger to the life or physical safety of any person.

(2) Exception

(A) In general

A consumer reporting agency that receives a request under subsection (a) or (b) or an order under subsection (c), or officer, employee, or agent thereof, may disclose information otherwise subject to any applicable nondisclosure requirement to—

(i) those persons to whom disclosure is necessary in order to comply with the request;

(ii) an attorney in order to obtain legal advice or assistance regarding the request; or

(iii) other persons as permitted by the Director of the Federal Bureau of Investigation or the designee of the Director.

(B) Application

A person to whom disclosure is made under subparagraph (A) shall be subject to the nondisclosure requirements applicable to a person to whom a request under subsection (a) or (b) or an order under subsection (c) is issued in the same manner as the person to whom the request is issued.

(C) Notice

Any recipient that discloses to a person described in subparagraph (A) information otherwise subject to a nondisclosure requirement shall inform the person of the applicable nondisclosure requirement.

(D) Identification of disclosure recipients

At the request of the Director of the Federal Bureau of Investigation or the designee of the Director, any person making or intending to make a disclosure under clause (i) or (iii) of subparagraph (A) shall identify to the Director or such designee the person to whom such disclosure will be made or to whom such disclosure was made prior to the request.

(e) Judicial review

(1) In general

A request under subsection (a) or (b) or an order under subsection (c) or a non-disclosure requirement imposed in connection with such request under subsection (d) shall be subject to judicial review under section 3511 of Title 18.

(2) Notice

A request under subsection (a) or (b) or an order under subsection (c) shall include notice of the availability of judicial review described in paragraph (1).

(e) Payment of fees

The Federal Bureau of Investigation shall, subject to the availability of appropriations, pay to the consumer reporting agency assembling or providing report or information in accordance with procedures established under this section a fee for reimbursement for such costs as are reasonably necessary and which have been directly incurred in searching, reproducing, or transporting books, papers, records, or other data required or requested to be produced under this section.

(f) Limit on dissemination

The Federal Bureau of Investigation may not disseminate information obtained pursuant to this section outside of the Federal Bureau of Investigation, except to other Federal agencies as may be necessary for the approval or conduct of a foreign counterintelligence investigation, or, where the information concerns a person subject to the Uniform Code of Military Justice, to appropriate investigative authorities within the military department concerned as may be necessary for the conduct of a joint foreign counterintelligence investigation.

(g) Rules of construction

Nothing in this section shall be construed to prohibit information from being furnished by the Federal Bureau of Investigation pursuant to a subpoena or court order, in connection with a judicial or administrative proceeding to enforce the provisions of this subchapter. Nothing in this section shall be construed to authorize or permit the withholding of information from the Congress.

(h) Reports to Congress

(1) On a semiannual basis, the Attorney General shall fully inform the Permanent Select Committee on Intelligence and the Committee on Banking, Finance and Urban Affairs of the House of Representatives, and the Select Committee on Intelligence and the Committee on Banking, Housing, and Urban Affairs of the Senate concerning all requests made pursuant to subsections (a), (b), and (c) of this section.

(2) In the case of the semiannual reports required to be submitted under paragraph (1) to the Permanent Select Committee on Intelligence of the House of Representatives and the Select Committee on Intelligence of the Senate, the submittal dates for such reports shall be as provided in section 415b of Title 50.

(i) Damages

Any agency or department of the United States obtaining or disclosing any consumer reports, records, or information contained therein in violation of this section is liable to the consumer to whom such consumer reports, records, or information relate in an amount equal to the sum of—

(1) $100, without regard to the volume of consumer reports, records, or information involved;

(2) any actual damages sustained by the consumer as a result of the disclosure;

(3) if the violation is found to have been willful or intentional, such

punitive damages as a court may allow; and

(4) in the case of any successful action to enforce liability under this subsection, the costs of the action, together with reasonable attorney fees, as determined by the court.

(j) Disciplinary actions for violations

If a court determines that any agency or department of the United States has violated any provision of this section and the court finds that the circumstances surrounding the violation raise questions of whether or not an officer or employee of the agency or department acted willfully or intentionally with respect to the violation, the agency or department shall promptly initiate a proceeding to determine whether or not disciplinary action is warranted against the officer or employee who was responsible for the violation.

(k) Good-faith exception

Notwithstanding any other provision of this subchapter, any consumer reporting agency or agent or employee thereof making disclosure of consumer reports or identifying information pursuant to this subsection in good-faith reliance upon a certification of the Federal Bureau of Investigation pursuant to provisions of this section shall not be liable to any person for such disclosure under this subchapter, the constitution of any State, or any law or regulation of any State or any political subdivision of any State.

(*l*) Limitation of remedies

Notwithstanding any other provision of this subchapter, the remedies and sanctions set forth in this section shall be the only judicial remedies and sanctions for violation of this section.

(m) Injunctive relief

In addition to any other remedy contained in this section, injunctive relief shall be available to require compliance with the procedures of this section. In the event of any successful action under this subsection, costs together with reasonable attorney fees, as determined by the court, may be recovered.

§ 1681v [CCPA § 627]. Disclosures to governmental agencies for counterterrorism purposes

(a) Disclosure

Notwithstanding section 1681b of this title or any other provision of this subchapter, a consumer reporting agency shall furnish a consumer report of a consumer and all other information in a consumer's file to a government agency authorized to conduct investigations of, or intelligence or counterintelligence activities or analysis related to, international terrorism when presented with a written certification by such government agency that such information is necessary for the agency's conduct or such investigation, activity or analysis and that includes a term that specifically identifies a consumer or account to be used as the basis for the production of such information.

(b) Form of certification

The certification described in subsection (a) shall be signed by a supervisory official designated by the head of a Federal agency or an officer of a Federal agency whose appointment to office is required to be made by the President, by and with the advice and consent of the Senate.

(c) Prohibition of certain disclosure

(1) Prohibition

(A) In general

If a certification is issued under subparagraph (B) and notice of the right to judicial review under subsection (d) is provided, no consumer reporting agency that receives a request under subsection (a), or officer, employee, or agent thereof, shall disclose or specify in any consumer report, that a government agency described in subsection (a) has sought or obtained access to information or records under subsection (a).

(B) Certification

The requirements of subparagraph (A) shall apply if the head of the government agency described in subsection (a), or a designee, certifies that the absence of a prohibition of disclosure under this subsection may result in—

(i) a danger to the national security of the United States;

(ii) interference with a criminal, counterterrorism, or counterintelligence investigation;

(iii) interference with diplomatic relations; or

(iv) danger to the life or physical safety of any person.

(2) Exception

(A) In general

A consumer reporting agency that receives a request under subsection (a), or officer, employee, or agent thereof, may disclose information otherwise subject to any applicable nondisclosure requirement to—

(i) those persons to whom disclosure is necessary in order to comply with the request;

(ii) an attorney in order to obtain legal advice or assistance regarding the request; or

(iii) other persons as permitted by the head of the government agency described in subsection (a) or a designee.

(B) Application

A person to whom disclosure is made under subparagraph (A) shall be subject to the nondisclosure requirements applicable to a person to whom a request under subsection (a) is issued in the same manner as the person to whom the request is issued.

(C) Notice

Any recipient that discloses to a person described in subparagraph (A) information otherwise subject to a nondisclosure requirement shall inform the person of the applicable nondisclosure requirement.

(D) Identification of disclosure recipients

At the request of the head of the government agency described in subsection (a) or a designee, any person making or intending to make a disclosure under clause (i) or (iii) of subparagraph (A) shall identify to the head or such designee the person to whom such disclosure will be made or to whom such disclosure was made prior to the request.

(d) Judicial review

(1) In general

A request under subsection (a) or a non-disclosure requirement imposed in connection with such request under subsection (c) shall be subject to judicial review under section 3511 of Title 18.

(2) Notice

A request under subsection (a) shall include notice of the availability of judicial review described in paragraph (1).

(e) Rule of construction

Nothing in section 1681u of this title shall be construed to limit the authority of the Director of the Federal Bureau of Investigation under this section.

(f) Safe harbor

Notwithstanding any other provision of this subchapter, any consumer reporting agency or agent or employee thereof making disclosure of consumer reports or other information pursuant to this section in good-faith reliance upon a certification of a government agency pursuant to the provisions of this section shall not be liable to any person for such disclosure under this subchapter, the constitution of any State, or any law or regulation of any State or any political subdivision of any State.

(g) Reports to Congress

(1) On a semi-annual basis, the Attorney General shall fully inform the Committee on the Judiciary, the Committee on Financial Services, and the Permanent Select Committee on Intelligence of the House of Representatives and the Committee on the Judiciary, the Committee on Banking, Housing, and Urban Affairs, and the Select Committee on Intelligence of the Senate concerning all requests made pursuant to subsection (a).

(2) In the case of the semiannual reports required to be submitted under paragraph (1) to the Permanent Select Committee on Intelligence of the House of Representatives and the Select Committee on Intelligence of the Senate, the submittal dates for such reports shall be as provided in section 3106 of Title 50.

§ 1681w [CCPA § 628]. Disposal of records

(a) Regulations

(1) In general

The Federal Trade Commission, the Securities and Exchange Commission, the Commodity Futures Trading Commission, the Federal banking agencies, and the National Credit Union Administration, with respect to the entities that are subject to their respective enforcement authority under section 1681s of this title, and in coordination as described in paragraph (2), shall issue final regulations requiring any person that maintains or otherwise possesses consumer information, or any compilation of consumer information, derived from consumer reports for a business purpose to properly dispose of any such information or compilation.

(2) Coordination

Each agency required to prescribe regulations under paragraph (1) shall—

(A) consult and coordinate with each other such agency so that, to the extent possible, the regulations prescribed by each such agency are consistent and comparable with the regulations by each such other agency; and

(B) ensure that such regulations are consistent with the requirements and regulations issued pursuant to Public Law 106–102 and other provisions of Federal law.

(3) Exemption authority

In issuing regulations under this section, the agencies identified in paragraph (1) may exempt any person or class of persons from application of those regulations, as such agency deems appropriate to carry out the purpose of this section.

(b) Rule of construction

Nothing in this section shall be construed—

(1) to require a person to maintain or destroy any record pertaining to a consumer that is not imposed under other law; or

(2) to alter or affect any requirement imposed under any other provision of law to maintain or destroy such a record.

§ 1681x [CCPA § 629]. Corporate and technological circumvention prohibited

The Commission shall prescribe regulations, to become effective not later than 90 days after December 4, 2003, to prevent a consumer reporting agency from circumventing or evading treatment as a consumer reporting agency described in section 1681a(p) of this title for purposes of this subchapter, including—

(1) by means of a corporate reorganization or restructuring, including a merger, acquisition, dissolution, divestiture, or asset sale of a consumer reporting agency; or

(2) by maintaining or merging public record and credit account information in a manner that is substantially equivalent to that described in paragraphs (1) and (2) of section 1681a(p) of this title, in the manner described in section 1681a(p) of this title.

SUBCHAPTER IV—EQUAL CREDIT OPPORTUNITY

Table of Sections

§ 1691 [CCPA § 701]. Scope of prohibition

(a) Activities constituting discrimination

It shall be unlawful for any creditor to discriminate against any applicant, with respect to any aspect of a credit transaction—

(1) on the basis of race, color, religion, national origin, sex or marital status, or age (provided the applicant has the capacity to contract);

(2) because all or part of the applicant's income derives from any public assistance program; or

(3) because the applicant has in good faith exercised any right under this chapter.

(b) Activities not constituting discrimination

It shall not constitute discrimination for purposes of this subchapter for a creditor—

(1) to make an inquiry of marital status if such inquiry is for the purpose of ascertaining the creditor's rights and remedies applicable to the particular extension of credit and not to discriminate in a determination of credit-worthiness;[8]

(2) to make an inquiry of the applicant's age or of whether the applicant's income derives from any public assistance program if such inquiry is for the purpose of determining the amount and probable continuance of income levels, credit history, or other pertinent element of credit-worthiness as provided in regulations of the Bureau;

(3) to use any empirically derived credit system which considers age if such system is demonstrably and statistically sound in accordance with regulations of the Bureau, except that in the operation of such system the age of an elderly applicant may not be assigned a negative factor or value;

(4) to make an inquiry or to consider the age of an elderly applicant when the age of such applicant is to be used by the creditor in the extension of credit in favor of such applicant; or

(5) to make an inquiry under section 1691c–2 of this title, in accordance with the requirements of that section.

(c) Additional activities not constituting discrimination

It is not a violation of this section for a creditor to refuse to extend credit offered pursuant to—

(1) any credit assistance program expressly authorized by law for an economically disadvantaged class of persons;

(2) any credit assistance program administered by a nonprofit organization for its members or an economically disadvantaged class of persons; or

(3) any special purpose credit program offered by a profit-making organization to meet special social needs which meets standards prescribed in regulations by the Bureau;

if such refusal is required by or made pursuant to such program.

(d) Reason for adverse action; procedure applicable; "adverse action" defined

---

8 So in original. Probably should not be hyphenated.

(1) Within thirty days (or such longer reasonable time as specified in regulations of the Bureau for any class of credit transaction) after receipt of a completed application for credit, a creditor shall notify the applicant of its action on the application.

(2) Each applicant against whom adverse action is taken shall be entitled to a statement of reasons for such action from the creditor. A creditor satisfies this obligation by—

(A) providing statements of reasons in writing as a matter of course to applicants against whom adverse action is taken; or

(B) giving written notification of adverse action which discloses (i) the applicant's right to a statement of reasons within thirty days after receipt by the creditor of a request made within sixty days after such notification, and (ii) the identity of the person or office from which such statement may be obtained. Such statement may be given orally if the written notification advises the applicant of his right to have the statement of reasons confirmed in writing on written request.

(3) A statement of reasons meets the requirements of this section only if it contains the specific reasons for the adverse action taken.

(4) Where a creditor has been requested by a third party to make a specific extension of credit directly or indirectly to an applicant, the notification and statement of reasons required by this subsection may be made directly by such creditor, or indirectly through the third party, provided in either case that the identity of the creditor is disclosed.

(5) The requirements of paragraph (2), (3), or (4) may be satisfied by verbal statements or notifications in the case of any creditor who did not act on more than one hundred and fifty applications during the calendar year preceding the calendar year in which the adverse action is taken, as determined under regulations of the Bureau.

(6) For purposes of this subsection, the term "adverse action" means a denial or revocation of credit, a change in the terms of an existing credit arrangement, or a refusal to grant credit in substantially the amount or on substantially the terms requested. Such term does not include a refusal to extend additional credit under an existing credit arrangement where the applicant is delinquent or otherwise in default, or where such additional credit would exceed a previously established credit limit.

(e) Copies furnished to applicants

(1) In general

Each creditor shall furnish to an applicant a copy of any and all written appraisals and valuations developed in connection with the applicant's application for a loan that is secured or would have been secured by a first lien on a dwelling promptly upon completion, but in no case later than 3 days prior to the closing of the loan, whether the creditor grants or denies the applicant's request for credit or the application is incomplete or withdrawn.

(2) Waiver

The applicant may waive the 3 day requirement provided for in paragraph (1), except where otherwise required in law.

(3) Reimbursement

The applicant may be required to pay a reasonable fee to reimburse the creditor for the cost of the appraisal, except where otherwise required in law.

(4) Free copy

Notwithstanding paragraph (3), the creditor shall provide a copy of each written appraisal or valuation at no additional cost to the applicant.

(5) Notification to applicants

At the time of application, the creditor shall notify an applicant in writing of the right to receive a copy of each written appraisal and valuation under this subsection.

(6) Valuation defined

For purposes of this subsection, the term "valuation" shall include any estimate of the value of a dwelling developed in connection with a creditor's decision to provide credit, including those values developed pursuant to a policy of a government sponsored enterprise or by an automated valuation model, a broker price opinion, or other methodology or mechanism.

§ 1691a [CCPA § 702]. Definitions; rules of construction

(a) The definitions and rules of construction set forth in this section are applicable for the purposes of this subchapter.

(b) The term "applicant" means any person who applies to a creditor directly for an extension, renewal, or continuation of credit, or applies to a creditor indirectly by use of an existing credit plan for an amount exceeding a previously established credit limit.

(c) The term "Bureau" means the Bureau of Consumer Financial Protection.

(d) The term "credit" means the right granted by a creditor to a debtor to defer payment of debt or to incur debts and defer its payment or to purchase property or services and defer payment therefor.

(e) The term "creditor" means any person who regularly extends, renews, or continues credit; any person who regularly arranges for the extension, renewal, or continuation of credit; or any assignee of an original creditor who participates in the decision to extend, renew, or continue credit.

(f) The term "person" means a natural person, a corporation, government or governmental subdivision or agency, trust, estate, partnership, cooperative, or association.

(g) Any reference to any requirement imposed under this subchapter or any provision thereof includes reference to the regulations of the Bureau under this subchapter or the provision thereof in question.

§ 1691b [CCPA § 703]. Promulgation of regulations by Bureau

(a) In general

The Bureau shall prescribe regulations to carry out the purposes of this subchapter. These regulations may contain but are not limited to such classifications, differentiation, or other provision, and may provide for such adjustments and exceptions for any class of transactions, as in the judgment of the Bureau are necessary or proper to effectuate the purposes of this subchapter, to prevent circumvention or evasion thereof, or to facilitate or substantiate compliance therewith.

(b) Exempt transactions

Such regulations may exempt from the provisions of this subchapter any class of transactions that are not primarily for personal, family, or household purposes, or business or commercial loans made available by a financial institution, except that a particular type within a class of such transactions may be exempted if the Bureau determines, after making an express finding that the application of this subchapter or of any provision of this subchapter of such transaction would not contribute substantially to effecting the purposes of this subchapter.

(c) Limitation on exemptions

An exemption granted pursuant to subsection (b) shall be for no longer than five years and shall be extended only if the Bureau makes a subsequent determination, in the manner described by such paragraph,[1] that such exemption remains appropriate.

---

[1] So in original. Probably should be "subsection."

(d) Maintenance of records

Pursuant to Bureau regulations, entities making business or commercial loans shall maintain such records or other data relating to such loans as may be necessary to evidence compliance with this subsection or enforce any action pursuant to the authority of this chapter. In no event shall such records or data be maintained for a period of less than one year. The Bureau shall promulgate regulations to implement this paragraph[1] in the manner prescribed by chapter 5 of Title 5.

(e) Notice of denial of loan

The Bureau shall provide in regulations that an applicant for a business or commercial loan shall be provided a written notice of such applicant's right to receive a written statement of the reasons for the denial of such loan.

(f) Board authority

Notwithstanding subsection (a), the Board shall prescribe regulations to carry out the purposes of this subchapter with respect to a person described in section 5519(a) of Title 12. These regulations may contain but are not limited to such classifications, differentiation, or other provision, and may provide for such adjustments and exceptions for any class of transactions, as in the judgment of the Board are necessary or proper to effectuate the purposes of this subchapter, to prevent circumvention or evasion thereof, or to facilitate or substantiate compliance therewith.

(g) Deference

Notwithstanding any power granted to any Federal agency under this subchapter, the deference that a court affords to a Federal agency with respect to a determination made by such agency relating to the meaning or interpretation of any provision of this subchapter that is subject to the jurisdiction of such agency shall be applied as if that agency were the only agency authorized to apply, enforce, interpret, or administer the provisions of this subchapter[2]

§ 1691c [CCPA § 704]. Administrative enforcement

(a) Enforcing agencies

Subject to subtitle B of the Consumer Protection Financial Protection Act of 2010[3] with[4] the requirements imposed under this subchapter shall be enforced under:

(1) section 8 of the Federal Deposit Insurance Act, by the appropriate Federal banking agency, as defined in section 3(q) of the Federal Deposit Insurance Act, with respect to—

(A) national banks, Federal savings associations, and Federal branches and Federal agencies of foreign banks;

(B) member banks of the Federal Reserve System (other than national banks), branches and agencies of foreign banks (other than Federal branches, Federal agencies, and insured State branches of foreign banks), commercial lending companies owned or controlled by foreign banks, and organizations operating under section 25 or 25A of the Federal Reserve Act; and

(C) banks and State savings associations insured by the Federal Deposit Insurance Corporation (other than members of the Federal Reserve System), and insured State branches of foreign banks;

(2) The Federal Credit Union Act [12 U.S.C.A. § 1751 et seq.], by the Administrator of the National Credit Union Administration with respect to any Federal Credit Union.

---

2 So in original. Probably should be followed by a period.

3 So in original. Probably should read the Consumer Financial Protection Act.

4 So in original. Probably should be ", compliance with".

(3) Subtitle IV of Title 49, by the Secretary of Transportation, with respect to all carriers subject to the jurisdiction of the Surface Transportation Board.

(4) Part A of subtitle VII of title 49, by the Secretary of Transportation with respect to any air carrier or foreign air carrier subject to that part.

(5) The Packers and Stockyards Act, 1921 [7 U.S.C.A. § 181 et seq.] (except as provided in section 406 of that Act [7 U.S.C.A. §§ 226, 227]), by the Secretary of Agriculture with respect to any activities subject to that Act.

(6) The Farm Credit Act of 1971 [12 U.S.C.A. § 2001 et seq.], by the Farm Credit Administration with respect to any Federal land bank, Federal land bank association, Federal intermediate credit bank, and production credit association;

(7) The Securities Exchange Act of 1934 [15 U.S.C.A. § 78a et seq.], by the Securities and Exchange Commission with respect to brokers and dealers;

(8) The Small Business Investment Act of 1958 [15 U.S.C.A. § 661 et seq.], by the Small Business Administration, with respect to small business investment companies; and

(9) Subtitle E of the Consumer Financial Protection Act of 2010, by the Bureau, with respect to any person subject to this subchapter.

The terms used in paragraph (1) that are not defined in this subchapter or otherwise defined in section 3(s) of the Federal Deposit Insurance Act (12 U.S.C. 1813(s)) shall have the meaning given to them in section 1(b) of the International Banking Act of 1978 (12 U.S.C. 3101).

(b) Violations of subchapter deemed violations of preexisting statutory requirements; additional agency powers

For the purpose of the exercise by any agency referred to in subsection (a) of its powers under any Act referred to in that subsection, a violation of any requirement imposed under this subchapter shall be deemed to be a violation of a requirement imposed under that Act. In addition to its powers under any provision of law specifically referred to in subsection (a), each of the agencies referred to in that subsection may exercise for the purpose of enforcing compliance with any requirement imposed under this subchapter, any other authority conferred on it by law. The exercise of the authorities of any of the agencies referred to in subsection (a) for the purpose of enforcing compliance with any requirement imposed under this subchapter shall in no way preclude the exercise of such authorities for the purpose of enforcing compliance with any other provision of law not relating to the prohibition of discrimination on the basis of sex or marital status with respect to any aspect of a credit transaction.

(c) Overall enforcement authority of Federal Trade Commission

Except to the extent that enforcement of the requirements imposed under this subchapter is specifically committed to some other Government agency under any of paragraphs (1) through (8) of subsection (a), and subject to subtitle B of the Consumer Financial Protection Act of 2010, the Federal Trade Commission shall be authorized to enforce such requirements. For the purpose of the exercise by the Federal Trade Commission of its functions and powers under the Federal Trade Commission Act (15 U.S.C. 41 et seq.), a violation of any requirement imposed under this subchapter shall be deemed a violation of a requirement imposed under that Act. All of the functions and powers of the Federal Trade Commission under the Federal Trade Commission Act are available to the Federal Trade Commission to enforce compliance by any person with the requirements imposed under this subchapter, irrespective of whether that person is engaged in commerce or meets any other jurisdictional tests under the Federal Trade Commission Act, including the power to enforce any rule prescribed by the Bureau under this subchapter in the same manner as if the violation had been a violation of a Federal Trade Commission trade regulation rule.

(d) Rules and regulations by enforcing agencies

The authority of the Bureau to issue regulations under this subchapter does not impair the authority of any other agency designated in this section to make rules respecting its own procedures in enforcing compliance with requirements imposed under this subchapter.

§ 1691c–1 [CCPA § 704A]. Incentives for self-testing and self-correction

(a) Privileged information

(1) Conditions for privilege

A report or result of a self-test (as that term is defined by regulations of the Bureau) shall be considered to be privileged under paragraph (2) if a creditor—

(A) conducts, or authorizes an independent third party to conduct, a self-test of any aspect of a credit transaction by a creditor, in order to determine the level or effectiveness of compliance with this subchapter by the creditor; and

(B) has identified any possible violation of this subchapter by the creditor and has taken, or is taking, appropriate corrective action to address any such possible violation.

(2) Privileged self-test

If a creditor meets the conditions specified in subparagraphs (A) and (B) of paragraph (1) with respect to a self-test described in that paragraph, any report or results of that self-test—

(A) shall be privileged; and

(B) may not be obtained or used by any applicant, department, or agency in any—

(i) proceeding or civil action in which one or more violations of this subchapter are alleged; or

(ii) examination or investigation relating to compliance with this subchapter.

(b) Results of self-testing

(1) In general

No provision of this section may be construed to prevent an applicant, department, or agency from obtaining or using a report or results of any self-test in any proceeding or civil action in which a violation of this subchapter is alleged, or in any examination or investigation of compliance with this subchapter if—

(A) the creditor or any person with lawful access to the report or results—

(i) voluntarily releases or discloses all, or any part of, the report or results to the applicant, department, or agency, or to the general public; or

(ii) refers to or describes the report or results as a defense to charges of violations of this subchapter against the creditor to whom the self-test relates; or

(B) the report or results are sought in conjunction with an adjudication or admission of a violation of this subchapter for the sole purpose of determining an appropriate penalty or remedy.

(2) Disclosure for determination of penalty or remedy

Any report or results of a self-test that are disclosed for the purpose specified in paragraph (1)(B)—

(A) shall be used only for the particular proceeding in which the adjudication or admission referred to in paragraph (1)(B) is made; and

(B) may not be used in any other action or proceeding.

(c) Adjudication

An applicant, department, or agency that challenges a privilege asserted under this section may seek a determination of the existence and application of that privilege in—

(1) a court of competent jurisdiction; or

(2) an administrative law proceeding with appropriate jurisdiction.

§ 1691c–2 [CCPA § 704B]. Small business loan data collection

(a) Purpose

The purpose of this section is to facilitate enforcement of fair lending laws and enable communities, governmental entities, and creditors to identify business and community development needs and opportunities of women-owned, minority-owned, and small businesses.

(b) Information gathering

Subject to the requirements of this section, in the case of any application to a financial institution for credit for women-owned, minority-owned, or small business, the financial institution shall—

(1) inquire whether the business is a women-owned, minority-owned, or small business, without regard to whether such application is received in person, by mail, by telephone, by electronic mail or other form of electronic transmission, or by any other means, and whether or not such application is in response to a solicitation by the financial institution; and

(2) maintain a record of the responses to such inquiry, separate from the application and accompanying information.

(c) Right to refuse

Any applicant for credit may refuse to provide any information requested pursuant to subsection (b) in connection with any application for credit.

(d) No access by underwriters

(1) Limitation

Where feasible, no loan underwriter or other officer or employee of a financial institution, or any affiliate of a financial institution, involved in making any determination concerning an application for credit shall have access to any information provided by the applicant pursuant to a request under subsection (b) in connection with such application.

(2) Limited access

If a financial institution determines that a loan underwriter or other officer or employee of a financial institution, or any affiliate of a financial institution, involved in making any determination concerning an application for credit should have access to any information provided by the applicant pursuant to a request under subsection (b), the financial institution shall provide notice to the applicant of the access of the underwriter to such information, along with notice that the financial institution may not discriminate on the basis of such information.

(e) Form and manner of information

(1) In general

Each financial institution shall compile and maintain, in accordance with regulations of the Bureau, a record of the information provided by any loan applicant pursuant to a request under subsection (b).

(2) Itemization

Information compiled and maintained under paragraph (1) shall be itemized in order to clearly and conspicuously disclose—

(A) the number of the application and the date on which the application was received;

(B) the type and purpose of the loan or other credit being applied for;

(C) the amount of the credit or credit limit applied for, and the amount of the credit transaction or the credit limit approved for such applicant;

(D) the type of action taken with respect to such application, and the date of such action;

(E) the census tract in which is located the principal place of business of the women-owned, minority-owned, or small business loan applicant;

(F) the gross annual revenue of the business in the last fiscal year of the women-owned, minority-owned, or small business loan applicant preceding the date of the application;

(G) the race, sex, and ethnicity of the principal owners of the business; and

(H) any additional data that the Bureau determines would aid in fulfilling the purposes of this section.

(3) No personally identifiable information

In compiling and maintaining any record of information under this section, a financial institution may not include in such record the name, specific address (other than the census tract required under paragraph (1)(E)),[1] telephone number, electronic mail address, or any other personally identifiable information concerning any individual who is, or is connected with, the women-owned, minority-owned, or small business loan applicant.

(4) Discretion to delete or modify publicly available data

The Bureau may, at its discretion, delete or modify data collected under this section which is or will be available to the public, if the Bureau determines that the deletion or modification of the data would advance a privacy interest.

(f) Availability of information

(1) Submission to Bureau

The data required to be compiled and maintained under this section by any financial institution shall be submitted annually to the Bureau.

(2) Availability of information

Information compiled and maintained under this section shall be—

(A) retained for not less than 3 years after the date of preparation;

(B) made available to any member of the public, upon request, in the form required under regulations prescribed by the Bureau;

(C) annually made available to the public generally by the Bureau, in such form and in such manner as is determined by the Bureau, by regulation.

(3) Compilation of aggregate data

The Bureau may, at its discretion—

(A) compile and aggregate data collected under this section for its own use; and

(B) make public such compilations of aggregate data.

(g) Bureau action

(1) In general

---

1 So in original. Probably should be "(2)(E),".

The Bureau shall prescribe such rules and issue such guidance as may be necessary to carry out, enforce, and compile data pursuant to this section.

(2) Exceptions

The Bureau, by rule or order, may adopt exceptions to any requirement of this section and may, conditionally or unconditionally, exempt any financial institution or class of financial institutions from the requirements of this section, as the Bureau deems necessary or appropriate to carry out the purposes of this section.

(3) Guidance

The Bureau shall issue guidance designed to facilitate compliance with the requirements of this section, including assisting financial institutions in working with applicants to determine whether the applicants are women-owned, minority-owned, or small businesses for purposes of this section.

(h) Definitions

For purposes of this section, the following definitions shall apply:

(1) Financial institution

The term "financial institution" means any partnership, company, corporation, association (incorporated or unincorporated), trust, estate, cooperative organization, or other entity that engages in any financial activity.

(2) Small business

The term "small business" has the same meaning as the term "small business concern" in section 632 of this title.

(3) Small business loan

The term "small business loan" means a loan made to a small business.

(4) Minority

The term "minority" has the same meaning as in section 1204(c)(3) of the Financial Institutions Reform, Recovery, and Enforcement Act of 1989.

(5) Minority-owned business

The term "minority-owned business" means a business—

(A) more than 50 percent of the ownership or control of which is held by 1 or more minority individuals; and

(B) more than 50 percent of the net profit or loss of which accrues to 1 or more minority individuals.

(6) Women-owned business

The term "women-owned business" means a business—

(A) more than 50 percent of the ownership or control of which is held by 1 or more women; and

(B) more than 50 percent of the net profit or loss of which accrues to 1 or more women.

§ 1691d [CCPA § 705]. Applicability of other laws

(a) Requests for signature of husband and wife for creation of valid lien, etc.

A request for the signature of both parties to a marriage for the purpose of creating a valid lien, passing clear title, waiving inchoate rights to property, or assigning earnings, shall not constitute discrimination under this subchapter: *Provided, however,* That this provision shall not be construed to permit a creditor to take sex or marital status into account in connection with the evaluation of creditworthiness of any applicant.

(b) State property laws affecting creditworthiness

Consideration or application of State property laws directly or indirectly affecting creditworthiness shall not constitute discrimination for purposes of this subchapter.

(c) State laws prohibiting separate extension of consumer credit to husband and wife

Any provision of State law which prohibits the separate extension of consumer credit to each party to a marriage shall not apply in any case where each party to a marriage voluntarily applies for separate credit from the same creditor: *Provided,* That in any case where such a State law is so preempted, each party to the marriage shall be solely responsible for the debt so contracted.

(d) Combining credit accounts of husband and wife with same creditor to determine permissible finance charges or loan ceilings under Federal or State laws

When each party to a marriage separately and voluntarily applies for and obtains separate credit accounts with the same creditor, those accounts shall not be aggregated or otherwise combined for purposes of determining permissible finance charges or permissible loan ceilings under the laws of any State or of the United States.

(e) Election of remedies under subchapter or State law; nature of relief determining applicability

Where the same act or omission constitutes a violation of this subchapter and of applicable State law, a person aggrieved by such conduct may bring a legal action to recover monetary damages either under this subchapter or under such State law, but not both. This election of remedies shall not apply to court actions in which the relief sought does not include monetary damages or to administrative actions.

(f) Compliance with inconsistent State laws; determination of inconsistency

This subchapter does not annul, alter, or affect, or exempt any person subject to the provisions of this subchapter from complying with, the laws of any State with respect to credit discrimination, except to the extent that those laws are inconsistent with any provision of this subchapter, and then only to the extent of the inconsistency. The Bureau is authorized to determine whether such inconsistencies exist. The Bureau may not determine that any State law is inconsistent with any provision of this subchapter if the Bureau determines that such law gives greater protection to the applicant.

(g) Exemption by regulation of credit transactions covered by State law; failure to comply with State law

The Bureau shall by regulation exempt from the requirements of sections 1691 and 1691a of this title any class of credit transactions within any State if it determines that under the law of that State that class of transactions is subject to requirements substantially similar to those imposed under this subchapter or that such law gives greater protection to the applicant, and that there is adequate provision for enforcement. Failure to comply with any requirement of such State law in any transaction so exempted shall constitute a violation of this subchapter for the purposes of section 1691e of this title.

§ 1691e [CCPA § 706]. Civil liability

(a) Individual or class action for actual damages

Any creditor who fails to comply with any requirement imposed under this subchapter shall be liable to the aggrieved applicant for any actual damages sustained by such applicant acting either in an individual capacity or as a member of a class.

(b) Recovery of punitive damages in individual and class action for actual damages; exemptions; maximum amount of punitive damages in individual actions; limitation on total recovery in class actions; factors determining amount of award

Any creditor, other than a government or governmental subdivision or agency, who fails to comply with any requirement imposed under this subchapter shall be liable to the aggrieved applicant for punitive damages in an amount not greater than $10,000, in addition to any actual damages provided in subsection (a), except that in the case of a class action the total recovery under this subsection shall not exceed the lesser of $500,000 or 1 per centum of the net worth of the creditor. In determining the amount of such damages in any action, the court shall consider, among other relevant factors, the amount of any actual damages awarded, the frequency and persistence of failures of compliance by the creditor, the resources of the creditor, the number of persons adversely affected, and the extent to which the creditor's failure of compliance was intentional.

(c) Action for equitable and declaratory relief

Upon application by an aggrieved applicant, the appropriate United States district court or any other court of competent jurisdiction may grant such equitable and declaratory relief as is necessary to enforce the requirements imposed under this subchapter.

(d) Recovery of costs and attorney fees

In the case of any successful action under subsection (a), (b), or (c), the costs of the action, together with a reasonable attorney's fee as determined by the court, shall be added to any damages awarded by the court under such subsection.

(e) Good faith compliance with rule, regulation, or interpretation of Bureau or interpretation or approval by an official or employee of Bureau of Consumer Financial Protection duly authorized by Bureau

No provision of this subchapter imposing liability shall apply to any act done or omitted in good faith in conformity with any official rule, regulation, or interpretation thereof by the Bureau or in conformity with any interpretation or approval by an official or employee of the Bureau of Consumer Financial Protection duly authorized by the Bureau to issue such interpretations or approvals under such procedures as the Bureau may prescribe therefor, notwithstanding that after such act or omission has occurred, such rule, regulation, interpretation, or approval is amended, rescinded, or determined by judicial or other authority to be invalid for any reason.

(f) Jurisdiction of courts; time for maintenance of action; exceptions

Any action under this section may be brought in the appropriate United States district court without regard to the amount in controversy, or in any other court of competent jurisdiction. No such action shall be brought later than 5 years after the date of the occurrence of the violation, except that—

(1) whenever any agency having responsibility for administrative enforcement under section 1691c of this title commences an enforcement proceeding within 5 years after the date of the occurrence of the violation,

(2) whenever the Attorney General commences a civil action under this section within 5 years after the date of the occurrence of the violation,

then any applicant who has been a victim of the discrimination which is the subject of such proceeding or civil action may bring an action under this section not later than one year after the commencement of that proceeding or action.

(g) Request by responsible enforcement agency to Attorney General for civil action

The agencies having responsibility for administrative enforcement under section 1691c of this title, if unable to obtain compliance with section 1691 of this title, are authorized to refer the matter to the Attorney General with a recommendation that an appropriate civil action be instituted. Each agency referred to in paragraphs (1), (2), and (9) of section 1691c(a) of this title shall refer the matter to the Attorney General whenever the agency has reason to believe that 1 or more creditors has engaged in a pattern or practice of discouraging or denying applications for credit in violation of section 1691(a) of this title. Each such agency may refer the matter to the Attorney General whenever the agency has reason to believe that 1 or more creditors has violated section 1691(a) of this title.

(h) Authority for Attorney General to bring civil action; jurisdiction

When a matter is referred to the Attorney General pursuant to subsection (g), or whenever he has reason to believe that one or more creditors are engaged in a pattern or practice in violation of this subchapter, the Attorney General may bring a civil action in any appropriate United States district court for such relief as may be appropriate, including actual and punitive damages and injunctive relief.

(i) Recovery under both subchapter and fair housing enforcement provisions prohibited for violation based on same transaction

No person aggrieved by a violation of this subchapter and by a violation of section 3605 of Title 42 shall recover under this subchapter and section 3612 of Title 42, if such violation is based on the same transaction.

(j) Discovery of creditor's granting standards

Nothing in this subchapter shall be construed to prohibit the discovery of a creditor's credit granting standards under appropriate discovery procedures in the court or agency in which an action or proceeding is brought.

(k) Notice to HUD of violations

Whenever an agency referred to in paragraph (1), (2), or (3) of section 1691c(a) of this title—

(1) has reason to believe, as a result of receiving a consumer complaint, conducting a consumer compliance examination, or otherwise, that a violation of this subchapter has occurred;

(2) has reason to believe that the alleged violation would be a violation of the Fair Housing Act [42 U.S.C.A. § 3601 et seq.]; and

(3) does not refer the matter to the Attorney General pursuant to subsection (g),

the agency shall notify the Secretary of Housing and Urban Development of the violation, and shall notify the applicant that the Secretary of Housing and Urban Development has been notified of the alleged violation and that remedies for the violation may be available under the Fair Housing Act.

§ 1691f [CCPA § 707]. Annual reports to Congress; contents

Each year, the Bureau and the Attorney General shall, respectively, make reports to the Congress concerning the administration of their functions under this subchapter, including such recommendations as the Bureau and the Attorney General, respectively, deem necessary or appropriate. In addition, each report of the Bureau shall include its assessment of the extent to which compliance with the requirements of this subchapter is being achieved, and a summary of the enforcement actions taken by each of the agencies assigned administrative enforcement responsibilities under section 1691c of this title.

SUBCHAPTER V—DEBT COLLECTION PRACTICES

Table of Sections

Sec.

§ 1692 [CCPA § 802]. Congressional findings and declaration of purpose

(a) Abusive practices

There is abundant evidence of the use of abusive, deceptive, and unfair debt collection practices by many debt collectors. Abusive debt collection practices contribute to the number of personal bankruptcies, to marital instability, to the loss of jobs, and to invasions of individual privacy.

(b) Inadequacy of laws

Existing laws and procedures for redressing these injuries are inadequate to protect consumers.

(c) Available non-abusive collection methods

Means other than misrepresentation or other abusive debt collection practices are available for the effective collection of debts.

(d) Interstate commerce

Abusive debt collection practices are carried on to a substantial extent in interstate commerce and through means and instrumentalities of such commerce. Even where abusive debt collection practices are purely intrastate in character, they nevertheless directly affect interstate commerce.

(e) Purposes

It is the purpose of this subchapter to eliminate abusive debt collection practices by debt collectors, to insure that those debt collectors who refrain from using abusive debt collection practices are not competitively disadvantaged, and to promote consistent State action to protect consumers against debt collection abuses.

§ 1692a [CCPA § 803]. Definitions

As used in this subchapter—

(1) The term "Bureau" means the Bureau of Consumer Financial Protection.

(2) The term "communication" means the conveying of information regarding a debt directly or indirectly to any person through any medium.

(3) The term "consumer" means any natural person obligated or allegedly obligated to pay any debt.

(4) The term "creditor" means any person who offers or extends credit creating a debt or to whom a debt is owed, but such term does not include any person to the extent that he receives an assignment or transfer of a debt in default solely for the purpose of facilitating collection of such debt for another.

(5) The term "debt" means any obligation or alleged obligation of a consumer to pay money arising out of a transaction in which the money, property, insurance, or services which are the subject of the transaction are primarily for personal, family, or household purposes, whether or not such obligation has been reduced to judgment.

(6) The term "debt collector" means any person who uses any instrumentality of interstate commerce or the mails in any business the principal purpose of which is the collection of any debts, or who regularly collects or attempts to collect, directly or indirectly, debts owed or due or asserted to be owed or due another. Notwithstanding the exclusion provided by clause (F) of the last sentence of this paragraph, the term includes any creditor who, in the process of collecting his own debts, uses any name other than his own which would indicate that a third person is collecting or attempting to collect such debts. For the purpose of section 1692f(6) of this title, such term also includes any person who uses any instrumentality of interstate commerce or the mails in any business the principal purpose of which is the enforcement of security interests. The term does not include—

(A) any officer or employee of a creditor while, in the name of the creditor, collecting debts for such creditor;

(B) any person while acting as a debt collector for another person, both of whom are related by common ownership or affiliated by corporate control, if the person acting as a debt collector does so only for persons to whom it is so related or affiliated and if the principal business of such person is not the collection of debts;

(C) any officer or employee of the United States or any State to the extent that collecting or attempting to collect any debt is in the performance of his official duties;

(D) any person while serving or attempting to serve legal process on any other person in connection with the judicial enforcement of any debt;

(E) any nonprofit organization which, at the request of consumers, performs bona fide consumer credit counseling and assists consumers in the liquidation of their debts by receiving payments from such consumers and distributing such amounts to creditors; and

(F) any person collecting or attempting to collect any debt owed or due or asserted to be owed or due another to the extent such activity (i) is incidental to a bona fide fiduciary obligation or a bona fide escrow arrangement; (ii) concerns a debt which was originated by such person; (iii) concerns a debt which was not in default at the time it was obtained by such person; or (iv) concerns a debt obtained by such person as a secured party in a commercial credit transaction involving the creditor.

(7) The term "location information" means a consumer's place of abode and his telephone number at such place, or his place of employment.

(8) The term "State" means any State, territory, or possession of the United States, the District of Columbia, the Commonwealth of Puerto Rico, or any political subdivision of any of the foregoing.

§ 1692b [CCPA § 804]. Acquisition of location information

Any debt collector communicating with any person other than the consumer for the purpose of acquiring location information about the consumer shall—

(1) identify himself, state that he is confirming or correcting location information concerning the consumer, and, only if expressly requested, identify his employer;

(2) not state that such consumer owes any debt;

(3) not communicate with any such person more than once unless requested to do so by such person or unless the debt collector reasonably believes that the earlier response of such person is erroneous or incomplete and that such person now has correct or complete location information;

(4) not communicate by post card;

(5) not use any language or symbol on any envelope or in the contents of any communication effected by the mails or telegram that indicates that the debt collector is in the debt collection business or that the communication relates to the collection of a debt; and

(6) after the debt collector knows the consumer is represented by an attorney with regard to the subject debt and has knowledge of, or can readily ascertain, such attorney's name and address, not communicate with any person other than that attorney, unless the attorney fails to respond within a reasonable period of time to communication from the debt collector.

§ 1692c [CCPA § 805]. Communication in connection with debt collection

(a) Communication with the consumer generally

Without the prior consent of the consumer given directly to the debt collector or the express permission of a court of competent jurisdiction, a debt collector may not communicate with a consumer in connection with the collection of any debt—

(1) at any unusual time or place or a time or place known or which should be known to be inconvenient to the consumer. In the absence of knowledge of circumstances to the contrary, a debt collector shall assume that the convenient time for communicating with a consumer is after 8 o'clock antemeridian and before 9 o'clock postmeridian, local time at the consumer's location;

(2) if the debt collector knows the consumer is represented by an attorney with respect to such debt and has knowledge of, or can readily ascertain, such attorney's name and address, unless the attorney fails to respond within a reasonable period of time to a communication from the debt collector or unless the attorney consents to direct communication with the consumer; or

(3) at the consumer's place of employment if the debt collector knows or has reason to know that the consumer's employer prohibits the consumer from receiving such communication.

(b) Communication with third parties

Except as provided in section 1692b of this title, without the prior consent of the consumer given directly to the debt collector, or the express permission of a court of competent jurisdiction, or as reasonably necessary to effectuate a postjudgment judicial remedy, a debt collector may not communicate, in connection with the collection of any debt, with any person other than the consumer, his attorney, a consumer reporting agency if otherwise permitted by law, the creditor, the attorney of the creditor, or the attorney of the debt collector.

(c) Ceasing communication

If a consumer notifies a debt collector in writing that the consumer refuses to pay a debt or that the consumer wishes the debt collector to cease further communication with the consumer, the debt collector shall not communicate further with the consumer with respect to such debt, except—

(1) to advise the consumer that the debt collector's further efforts are being terminated;

(2) to notify the consumer that the debt collector or creditor may invoke specified remedies which are ordinarily invoked by such debt collector or creditor; or

(3) where applicable, to notify the consumer that the debt collector or creditor intends to invoke a specified remedy.

If such notice from the consumer is made by mail, notification shall be complete upon receipt.

(d) "Consumer" defined

For the purpose of this section, the term "consumer" includes the consumer's spouse, parent (if the consumer is a minor), guardian, executor, or administrator.

§ 1692d [CCPA § 806]. Harassment or abuse

A debt collector may not engage in any conduct the natural consequence of which is to harass, oppress, or abuse any person in connection with the collection of a debt. Without limiting the general application of the foregoing, the following conduct is a violation of this section:

(1) The use or threat of use of violence or other criminal means to harm the physical person, reputation, or property of any person.

(2) The use of obscene or profane language or language the natural consequence of which is to abuse the hearer or reader.

(3) The publication of a list of consumers who allegedly refuse to pay debts, except to a consumer reporting agency or to persons meeting the requirements of section 1681a(f) or 1681b(3) of this title.

(4) The advertisement for sale of any debt to coerce payment of the debt.

(5) Causing a telephone to ring or engaging any person in telephone conversation repeatedly or continuously with intent to annoy, abuse, or harass any person at the called number.

(6) Except as provided in section 1692b of this title, the placement of telephone calls without meaningful disclosure of the caller's identity.

§ 1692e [CCPA § 807]. False or misleading representations

A debt collector may not use any false, deceptive, or misleading representation or means in connection with the collection of any debt. Without limiting the general application of the foregoing, the following conduct is a violation of this section:

(1) The false representation or implication that the debt collector is vouched for, bonded by, or affiliated with the United States or any State, including the use of any badge, uniform, or facsimile thereof.

(2) The false representation of—

(A) the character, amount, or legal status of any debt; or

(B) any services rendered or compensation which may be lawfully received by any debt collector for the collection of a debt.

(3) The false representation or implication that any individual is an attorney or that any communication is from an attorney.

(4) The representation or implication that nonpayment of any debt will result in the arrest or imprisonment of any person or the seizure, garnishment, attachment, or sale of any property or wages of any person unless such action is lawful and the debt collector or creditor intends to take such action.

(5) The threat to take any action that cannot legally be taken or that is not intended to be taken.

(6) The false representation or implication that a sale, referral, or other transfer of any interest in a debt shall cause the consumer to—

(A) lose any claim or defense to payment of the debt; or

(B) become subject to any practice prohibited by this subchapter.

(7) The false representation or implication that the consumer committed any crime or other conduct in order to disgrace the consumer.

(8) Communicating or threatening to communicate to any person credit information which is known or which should be known to be false, including the failure to communicate that a disputed debt is disputed.

(9) The use or distribution of any written communication which simulates or is falsely represented to be a document authorized, issued, or approved by any court, official, or agency of the United States or any State, or which creates a false impression as to its source, authorization, or approval.

(10) The use of any false representation or deceptive means to collect or attempt to collect any debt or to obtain information concerning a consumer.

(11) The failure to disclose in the initial written communication with the consumer and, in addition, if the initial communication with the consumer is oral, in that initial oral communication, that the debt collector is attempting to collect a debt and that any information obtained will be used for that purpose, and the failure to disclose in subsequent communications that the communication is from a debt collector, except that this paragraph shall not apply to a formal pleading made in connection with a legal action.

(12) The false representation or implication that accounts have been turned over to innocent purchasers for value.

(13) The false representation or implication that documents are legal process.

(14) The use of any business, company, or organization name other than the true name of the debt collector's business, company, or organization.

(15) The false representation or implication that documents are not legal process forms or do not require action by the consumer.

(16) The false representation or implication that a debt collector operates or is employed by a consumer reporting agency as defined by section 1681a(f) of this title.

§ 1692f [CCPA § 808]. Unfair practices

A debt collector may not use unfair or unconscionable means to collect or attempt to collect any debt. Without limiting the general application of the foregoing, the following conduct is a violation of this section:

(1) The collection of any amount (including any interest, fee, charge, or expense incidental to the principal obligation) unless such amount is expressly authorized by the agreement creating the debt or permitted by law.

(2) The acceptance by a debt collector from any person of a check or other payment instrument postdated by more than five days unless such person is notified in writing of the debt collector's intent to deposit such check or instrument not more than ten nor less than three business days prior to such deposit.

(3) The solicitation by a debt collector of any postdated check or other postdated payment instrument for the purpose of threatening or instituting criminal prosecution.

(4) Depositing or threatening to deposit any postdated check or other postdated payment instrument prior to the date on such check or instrument.

(5) Causing charges to be made to any person for communications by concealment of the true purpose of the communication. Such charges include, but are not limited to, collect telephone calls and telegram fees.

(6) Taking or threatening to take any nonjudicial action to effect dispossession or disablement of property if—

(A) there is no present right to possession of the property claimed as collateral through an enforceable security interest;

(B) there is no present intention to take possession of the property; or

(C) the property is exempt by law from such dispossession or disablement.

(7) Communicating with a consumer regarding a debt by post card.

(8) Using any language or symbol, other than the debt collector's address, on any envelope when communicating with a consumer by use of the mails or by telegram, except that a debt collector may use his business name if such name does not indicate that he is in the debt collection business.

§ 1692g [CCPA § 809]. Validation of debts

(a) Notice of debt; contents

Within five days after the initial communication with a consumer in connection with the collection of any debt, a debt collector shall, unless the following information is contained in the initial communication or the consumer has paid the debt, send the consumer a written notice containing—

(1) the amount of the debt;

(2) the name of the creditor to whom the debt is owed;

(3) a statement that unless the consumer, within thirty days after receipt of the notice, disputes the validity of the debt, or any portion thereof, the debt will be assumed to be valid by the debt collector;

(4) a statement that if the consumer notifies the debt collector in writing within the thirty-day period that the debt, or any portion thereof, is disputed, the debt collector will obtain verification of the debt or a copy of a judgment against the consumer and a copy of such verification or judgment will be mailed to the consumer by the debt collector; and

(5) a statement that, upon the consumer's written request within the thirty-day period, the debt collector will provide the consumer with the name and address of the original creditor, if different from the current creditor.

(b) Disputed debts

If the consumer notifies the debt collector in writing within the thirty-day period described in subsection (a) that the debt, or any portion thereof, is disputed, or that the consumer requests the name and address of the original creditor, the debt collector shall cease collection of the debt, or any disputed portion thereof, until the debt collector obtains verification of the debt or a copy of a judgment, or the name and address of the original creditor, and a copy of such verification or judgment, or name and address of the original creditor, is mailed to the consumer by the debt collector. Collection activities and communications that do not otherwise violate this subchapter may continue during the 30-day period referred to in subsection (a) unless the consumer has notified the debt collector in writing that the debt, or any portion of the debt, is disputed or that the consumer requests the name and address of the original creditor. Any collection activities and communication during the 30-day period may not overshadow or be inconsistent with the disclosure of the consumer's right to dispute the debt or request the name and address of the original creditor.

(c) Admission of liability

The failure of a consumer to dispute the validity of a debt under this section may not be construed by any court as an admission of liability by the consumer.

(d) Legal pleadings

A communication in the form of a formal pleading in a civil action shall not be treated as an initial communication for purposes of subsection (a).

(e) Notice provisions

The sending or delivery of any form or notice which does not relate to the collection of a debt and is expressly required by Title 26, title V of Gramm-Leach-Bliley Act, or any provision of Federal or State law relating to notice of data security breach or privacy, or any regulation prescribed under any such provision of law, shall not be treated as an initial communication in connection with debt collection for purposes of this section.

§ 1692h [CCPA § 810]. Multiple debts

If any consumer owes multiple debts and makes any single payment to any debt collector with respect to such debts, such debt collector may not apply such payment to any debt which is disputed by the consumer and, where applicable, shall apply such payment in accordance with the consumer's directions.

§ 1692i [CCPA § 811]. Legal actions by debt collectors

(a) Venue

Any debt collector who brings any legal action on a debt against any consumer shall—

(1) in the case of an action to enforce an interest in real property securing the consumer's obligation, bring such action only in a judicial district or similar legal entity in which such real property is located; or

(2) in the case of an action not described in paragraph (1), bring such action only in the judicial district or similar legal entity—

(A) in which such consumer signed the contract sued upon; or

(B) in which such consumer resides at the commencement of the action.

(b) Authorization of actions

Nothing in this subchapter shall be construed to authorize the bringing of legal actions by debt collectors.

§ 1692j [CCPA § 812]. Furnishing certain deceptive forms

(a) It is unlawful to design, compile, and furnish any form knowing that such form would be used to create the false belief in a consumer that a person other than the creditor of such consumer is participating in the collection of or in an attempt to collect a debt such consumer allegedly owes such creditor, when in fact such person is not so participating.

(b) Any person who violates this section shall be liable to the same extent and in the same manner as a debt collector is liable under section 1692k of this title for failure to comply with a provision of this subchapter.

§ 1692k [CCPA § 813]. Civil liability

(a) Amount of damages

Except as otherwise provided by this section, any debt collector who fails to comply with any provision of this subchapter with respect to any person is liable to such person in an amount equal to the sum of—

(1) any actual damage sustained by such person as a result of such failure;

(2)(A) in the case of any action by an individual, such additional damages as the court may allow, but not exceeding $1,000; or

(B) in the case of a class action, (i) such amount for each named plaintiff as could be recovered under subparagraph (A), and (ii) such amount as the court may allow for all other class members, without regard to a minimum individual recovery, not to exceed the lesser of $500,000 or 1 per centum of the net worth of the debt collector; and

(3) in the case of any successful action to enforce the foregoing liability, the costs of the action, together with a reasonable attorney's fee as determined by the court. On a finding by the court that an action under this section was brought in bad faith and for the purpose of harassment, the court may award to the defendant attorney's fees reasonable in relation to the work expended and costs.

(b) Factors considered by court

In determining the amount of liability in any action under subsection (a), the court shall consider, among other relevant factors—

(1) in any individual action under subsection (a)(2)(A), the frequency and persistence of noncompliance by the debt collector, the nature of such noncompliance, and the extent to which such noncompliance was intentional; or

(2) in any class action under subsection (a)(2)(B), the frequency and persistence of noncompliance by the debt collector, the nature of such noncompliance, the resources of the debt collector, the number of persons adversely affected, and the extent to which the debt collector's noncompliance was intentional.

(c) Intent

A debt collector may not be held liable in any action brought under this subchapter if the debt collector shows by a preponderance of evidence that the violation was not intentional and resulted from a bona fide error notwithstanding the maintenance of procedures reasonably adapted to avoid any such error.

(d) Jurisdiction

An action to enforce any liability created by this subchapter may be brought in any appropriate United States district court without regard to the amount in controversy, or in any other court of competent jurisdiction, within one year from the date on which the violation occurs.

(e) Advisory opinions of Bureau

No provision of this section imposing any liability shall apply to any act done or omitted in good faith in conformity with any advisory opinion of the Bureau, notwithstanding that after such act or omission has occurred, such opinion is amended, rescinded, or determined by judicial or other authority to be invalid for any reason.

§ 1692*l* [CCPA § 814]. Administrative enforcement

(a) Federal trade Commission

The Federal Trade Commission shall be authorized to enforce compliance with this subchapter, except to the extent that enforcement of the requirements imposed under this subchapter is specifically committed to another Government agency under any of paragraphs (1) through (5) of subsection (b), subject to subtitle B of the Consumer Financial Protection Act of 2010. For purpose of the exercise by the Federal Trade Commission of its functions and powers under the Federal Trade Commission Act (15 U.S.C. 41 et seq.), a violation of this subchapter shall be deemed an unfair or deceptive act or practice in violation of that Act. All of the functions and powers of the Federal Trade Commission under the Federal Trade Commission Act are available to the Federal Trade Commission to enforce compliance by any person with this subchapter, irrespective of whether that person is engaged in commerce or meets any other jurisdictional tests under the Federal Trade Commission Act, including the power to enforce the provisions of this subchapter, in the same manner as if the violation had been a violation of a Federal Trade Commission trade regulation rule.

(b) Applicable provisions of law

Subject to subtitle B of the Consumer Financial Protection Act of 2010, compliance with any requirements imposed under this subchapter shall be enforced under—

(1) section 8 of the Federal Deposit Insurance Act, by the appropriate Federal banking agency, as defined in section 3(q) of the Federal Deposit Insurance Act (12 U.S.C.A. § 1813(q)), with respect to—

(A) national banks, Federal savings associations, and Federal branches and Federal agencies of foreign banks;

(B) member banks of the Federal Reserve System (other than national banks), branches and agencies of foreign banks (other than Federal branches, Federal agencies, and insured State branches of foreign banks), commercial lending companies owned or controlled by foreign banks, and organizations operating under section 25 or 25A of the Federal Reserve Act; and

(C) banks and State savings associations insured by the Federal Deposit Insurance Corporation (other than members of the Federal Reserve System), and insured State branches of foreign banks;

(2) the Federal Credit Union Act, by the Administrator of the National Credit Union Administration with respect to any Federal credit union;

(3) subtitle IV of Title 49, by the Secretary of Transportation, with respect to all carriers subject to the jurisdiction of the Surface Transportation Board;

(4) part A of subtitle VII of Title 49, by the Secretary of Transportation with respect to any air carrier or any foreign air carrier subject to that part;

(5) the Packers and Stockyards Act, 1921 [7 U.S.C.A. § 181 et seq.] (except as provided in section 406 of that Act [7 U.S.C.A. §§ 226, 227]), by the Secretary of Agriculture with respect to any activities subject to that Act; and

(6) subtitle E of the Consumer Financial Protection Act of 2010, by the Bureau, with respect to any person subject to this subchapter.

The terms used in paragraph (1) that are not defined in this subchapter or otherwise defined in section 3(s) of the Federal Deposit Insurance Act (12 U.S.C. 1813(s)) shall have the meaning given to them in section 1(b) of the International Banking Act of 1978 (12 U.S.C. 3101).

(c) Agency powers

For the purpose of the exercise by any agency referred to in subsection (b) of its powers under any Act referred to in that subsection, a violation of any requirement imposed under this subchapter shall be deemed to be a violation of a requirement imposed under that Act. In addition to its powers under any provision of law specifically referred to in subsection (b), each of the agencies referred to in that subsection may exercise, for the purpose of enforcing compliance with any requirement imposed under this subchapter any other authority conferred on it by law, except as provided in subsection (d).

(d) Rules and regulations

Except as provided in section 1029(a) of the Consumer Financial Protection Act of 2010, the Bureau may prescribe rules with respect to the collection of debts by debt collectors, as defined in this subchapter.

§ 1692m [CCPA § 815]. Reports to Congress by the Commission; views of other Federal agencies

(a) Not later than one year after the effective date of this subchapter and at one-year intervals thereafter, the Bureau shall make reports to the Congress concerning the administration of its functions under this subchapter, including such recommendations as the Bureau deems necessary or appropriate. In addition, each report of the Bureau shall include its assessment of the extent to which compliance with this subchapter is being achieved and a summary of the enforcement actions taken by the Bureau under section 1692*l* of this title.

(b) In the exercise of its functions under this subchapter, the Bureau may obtain upon request the views of any other Federal agency which exercises enforcement functions under section 1692*l* of this title.

§ 1692n [CCPA § 816]. Relation to State laws

This subchapter does not annul, alter, or affect, or exempt any person subject to the provisions of this subchapter from complying with the laws of any State with respect to debt collection practices, except to the extent that those laws are inconsistent with any provision of this subchapter, and then only to the extent of the inconsistency. For purposes of this section, a State law is not inconsistent with this subchapter if the protection such law affords any consumer is greater than the protection provided by this subchapter.

§ 1692*o* [CCPA § 817]. Exemption for State regulation

The Bureau shall by regulation exempt from the requirements of this subchapter any class of debt collection practices within any State if the Bureau determines that under the law of that State that class of debt collection practices is subject to requirements substantially similar to those imposed by this subchapter, and that there is adequate provision for enforcement.

§ 1692p [CCPA § 818]. Exception for certain bad check enforcement programs operated by private entities

(a) In general

(1) Treatment of certain private entities. Subject to paragraph (2), a private entity shall be excluded from the definition of a debt collector, pursuant to the exception provided in section 1692a(6) of this title, with respect to the operation by the entity of a program described in paragraph (2)(A) under a contract described in paragraph (2)(B).

(2) Conditions of applicability. Paragraph (1) shall apply if—

(A) a State or district attorney establishes, within the jurisdiction of such State or district attorney and with respect to alleged bad check violations that do not involve a check described in subsection (b), a pretrial diversion program for alleged bad check offenders who agree to participate voluntarily in such program to avoid criminal prosecution;

(B) a private entity, that is subject to an administrative support services contract with a State or district attorney and operates under the direction, supervision, and control of such State or district attorney, operates the pretrial diversion program described in subparagraph (A); and

(C) in the course of performing duties delegated to it by a State or district attorney under the contract, the private entity referred to in subparagraph (B)—

(i) complies with the penal laws of the State;

(ii) conforms with the terms of the contract and directives of the State or district attorney;

(iii) does not exercise independent prosecutorial discretion;

(iv) contacts any alleged offender referred to in subparagraph (A) for purposes of participating in a program referred to in such paragraph—

(I) only as a result of any determination by the State or district attorney that probable cause of a bad check violation under State penal law exists, and that contact with the alleged offender for purposes of participation in the program is appropriate; and

(II) the alleged offender has failed to pay the bad check after demand for payment, pursuant to State law, is made for payment of the check amount;

(v) includes as part of an initial written communication with an alleged offender a clear and conspicuous statement that—

(I) the alleged offender may dispute the validity of any alleged bad check violation;

(II) where the alleged offender knows, or has reasonable cause to believe, that the alleged bad check violation is the result of theft or forgery of the check, identity theft, or other fraud that is not the result of the conduct of the alleged offender, the alleged offender may file a crime report with the appropriate law enforcement agency; and

(III) if the alleged offender notifies the private entity or the district attorney in writing, not later than 30 days after being contacted for the first time pursuant to clause (iv), that there is a dispute pursuant to this subsection, before further restitution efforts are pursued, the district attorney or an employee of the district attorney authorized to make such a determination makes a determination that there is probable cause to believe that a crime has been committed; and

(vi) charges only fees in connection with services under the contract that have been authorized by the contract with the State or district attorney.

(b) Certain checks excluded. A check is described in this subsection if the check involves, or is subsequently found to involve—

(1) a postdated check presented in connection with a payday loan, or other similar transaction, where the payee of the check knew that the issuer had insufficient funds at the time the check was made, drawn, or delivered;

(2) a stop payment order where the issuer acted in good faith and with reasonable cause in stopping payment on the check;

(3) a check dishonored because of an adjustment to the issuer's account by the financial institution holding such account without providing notice to the person at the time the check was made, drawn, or delivered;

(4) a check for partial payment of a debt where the payee had previously accepted partial payment for such debt;

(5) a check issued by a person who was not competent, or was not of legal age, to enter into a legal contractual obligation at the time the check was made, drawn, or delivered; or

(6) a check issued to pay an obligation arising from a transaction that was illegal in the jurisdiction of the State or district attorney at the time the check was made, drawn, or delivered.

(c) Definitions. For purposes of this section, the following definitions shall apply:

(1) State or district attorney. The term "State or district attorney" means the chief elected or appointed prosecuting attorney in a district, county (as defined in section 2 of Title 1,), municipality, or comparable jurisdiction, including State attorneys general who act as chief elected or appointed prosecuting attorneys in a district, county (as so defined), municipality or comparable jurisdiction, who may be referred to by a variety of titles such as district attorneys, prosecuting attorneys, commonwealth's attorneys, solicitors, county attorneys, and state's attorneys, and who are responsible for the prosecution of State crimes and violations of jurisdiction-specific local ordinances.

(2) Check. The term "check" has the same meaning as in section 5002(6) of Title 12.

(3) Bad check violation. The term "bad check violation" means a violation of the applicable State criminal law relating to the writing of dishonored checks.

SUBCHAPTER VI—ELECTRONIC FUND TRANSFERS

Table of Sections

§ 1693 [CCPA § 902]. Congressional Findings and Declaration of Purpose

(a) Rights and liabilities undefined

The Congress finds that the use of electronic systems to transfer funds provides the potential for substantial benefits to consumers. However, due to the unique characteristics of such systems, the application of existing consumer protection legislation is unclear, leaving the rights and liabilities of consumers, financial institutions, and intermediaries in electronic fund transfers undefined.

(b) Purposes

It is the purpose of this subchapter to provide a basic framework establishing the rights, liabilities, and responsibilities of participants in electronic fund and remittance transfer systems. The primary objective of this subchapter, however, is the provision of individual consumer rights.

§ 1693a [CCPA § 903]. Definitions

As used in this subchapter—

(1) the term "accepted card or other means of access" means a card, code, or other means of access to a consumer's account for the purpose of initiating electronic fund transfers when the person to whom such card or other means of access was issued has requested and received or has signed or has used, or authorized another to use, such card or other means of access for the purpose of transferring money between accounts or obtaining money, property, labor, or services;

(2) the term "account" means a demand deposit, savings deposit, or other asset account (other than an occasional or incidental credit balance in an open end credit plan as defined in section 1602(i) of this title), as described in regulations of the Bureau, established primarily for personal, family, or household purposes, but such term does not include an account held by a financial institution pursuant to a bona fide trust agreement;

(4)[1] the term "Board" means the Board of Governors of the Federal Reserve System;

(4) the term "Bureau" means the Bureau of Consumer Financial Protection;

(5) the term "business day" means any day on which the offices of the consumer's financial institution involved in an electronic fund transfer are open to the public for carrying on substantially all of its business functions;

(6) the term "consumer" means a natural person;

(7) the term "electronic fund transfer" means any transfer of funds, other than a transaction originated by check, draft, or similar paper instrument, which is initiated through an electronic terminal, telephonic instrument, or computer or magnetic tape so as to order, instruct, or authorize a financial institution to debit or credit an account. Such term includes, but is not limited to, point-of-sale transfers, automated teller machine transactions, direct deposits or withdrawals of funds, and transfers initiated by telephone. Such term does not include—

(A) any check guarantee or authorization service which does not directly result in a debit or credit to a consumer's account:[2]

(B) any transfer of funds, other than those processed by automated clearinghouse, made by a financial institution on behalf of a consumer by means of a service that transfers funds held at either Federal Reserve banks or other depository institutions and which is not designed primarily to transfer funds on behalf of a consumer;

(C) any transaction the primary purpose of which is the purchase or sale of securities or commodities through a broker-dealer registered with or regulated by the Securities and Exchange Commission;

(D) any automatic transfer from a savings account to a demand deposit account pursuant to an agreement between a consumer and a financial institution for the purpose of covering an overdraft or maintaining an agreed upon minimum balance in the consumer's demand deposit account; or

(E) any transfer of funds which is initiated by a telephone conversation between a consumer and an officer or employee of a financial institution which is not pursuant to a prearranged plan and under which periodic or recurring transfers are not contemplated;

as determined under regulations of the Bureau;

(8) the term "electronic terminal" means an electronic device, other than a telephone operated by a consumer, through which a consumer may initiate an electronic fund transfer. Such term includes, but is not limited to, point-of-sale terminals, automated teller machines, and cash dispensing machines;

---

1 So in original. There are 2 paragraphs designated "(4)" and no paragraph "3."

2 So in original. The colon probably should be a semi-colon.

(9) the term "financial institution" means a State or National bank, a State or Federal savings and loan association, a mutual savings bank, a State or Federal credit union, or any other person who, directly or indirectly, holds an account belonging to a consumer;

(10) the term "preauthorized electronic fund transfer" means an electronic fund transfer authorized in advance to recur at substantially regular intervals;

(11) the term "State" means any State, territory, or possession of the United States, the District of Columbia, the Commonwealth of Puerto Rico, or any political subdivision of any of the foregoing; and

(12) the term "unauthorized electronic fund transfer" means an electronic fund transfer from a consumer's account initiated by a person other than the consumer without actual authority to initiate such transfer and from which the consumer receives no benefit, but the term does not include any electronic fund transfer (A) initiated by a person other than the consumer who was furnished with the card, code, or other means of access to such consumer's account by such consumer, unless the consumer has notified the financial institution involved that transfers by such other person are no longer authorized, (B) initiated with fraudulent intent by the consumer or any person acting in concert with the consumer, or (C) which constitutes an error committed by a financial institution.

§ 1693b [CCPA § 904]. Regulations

(a) Prescription by the Bureau and the Board

(1) In general

Except as provided in paragraph (2), the Bureau shall prescribe rules to carry out the purposes of this subchapter.

(2) Authority of the Board

The Board shall have sole authority to prescribe rules—

(A) to carry out the purposes of this subchapter with respect to a person described in section 5519(a) of Title 12; and

(B) to carry out the purposes of section 1693*o*–2 of this title

In prescribing such regulations, the Board shall:

(1) consult with the other agencies referred to in section 1693*o* of this title and take into account, and allow for, the continuing evolution of electronic banking services and the technology utilized in such services,

(2) prepare an analysis of economic impact which considers the costs and benefits to financial institutions, consumers, and other users of electronic fund transfers, including the extent to which additional documentation, reports, records, or other paper work would be required, and the effects upon competition in the provision of electronic banking services among large and small financial institutions and the availability of such services to different classes of consumers, particularly low income consumers,

(3) to the extent practicable, the Board shall demonstrate that the consumer protections of the proposed regulations outweigh the compliance costs imposed upon consumers and financial institutions, and

(4) any proposed regulations and accompanying analyses shall be sent promptly to Congress by the Board.

(b) Issuance of model clauses

The Bureau shall issue model clauses for optional use by financial institutions to facilitate compliance with the disclosure requirements of section 1693c of this title and to aid consumers in understanding the rights and responsibilities of participants in electronic fund transfers by utilizing readily understandable language. Such model clauses shall be adopted after notice duly given in the Federal Register and opportunity for public comment in accordance with section 553 of Title 5. With respect to the disclosures required by section 1693c(a)(3) and (4) of this title, the Bureau shall take account of variations in the services and charges under different electronic fund transfer systems and, as appropriate, shall issue alternative model clauses for disclosure of these differing account terms.

(c) Criteria; modification of requirements

Regulations prescribed hereunder may contain such classifications, differentiations, or other provisions, and may provide for such adjustments and exceptions for any class of electronic fund transfers or remittance transfers, as in the judgment of the Bureau are necessary or proper to effectuate the purposes of this subchapter, to prevent circumvention or evasion thereof, or to facilitate compliance therewith. The Bureau shall by regulation modify the requirements imposed by this subchapter on small financial institutions if the Bureau determines that such modifications are necessary to alleviate any undue compliance burden on small financial institutions and such modifications are consistent with the purpose and objective of this subchapter.

(d) Applicability to service providers other than certain financial institutions

(1) In general

If electronic fund transfer services are made available to consumers by a person other than a financial institution holding a consumer's account, the Bureau shall by regulation assure that the disclosures, protections, responsibilities, and remedies created by this subchapter are made applicable to such persons and services.

(2) State and local government electronic benefit transfer systems

(A) "Electronic benefit transfer system" defined

In this paragraph, the term "electronic benefit transfer system"—

(i) means a system under which a government agency distributes needs-tested benefits by establishing accounts that may be accessed by recipients electronically, such as through automated teller machines or point-of-sale terminals; and

(ii) does not include employment-related payments, including salaries and pension, retirement, or unemployment benefits established by a Federal, State, or local government agency.

(B) Exemption generally

The disclosures, protections, responsibilities, and remedies established under this subchapter, and any regulation prescribed or order issued by the Bureau in accordance with this subchapter, shall not apply to any electronic benefit transfer system established under State or local law or administered by a State or local government.

(C) Exception for direct deposit into recipient's account

Subparagraph (B) shall not apply with respect to any electronic funds transfer under an electronic benefit transfer system for a deposit directly into a consumer account held by the recipient of the benefit.

(D) Rule of construction

No provision of this paragraph—

(i) affects or alters the protections otherwise applicable with respect to benefits established by any other provision[1] Federal, State, or local law; or

---

1 So in original. Probably should be followed by "of".

(ii) otherwise supersedes the application of any State or local law.

(3) Fee disclosures at automated teller machines

(A) In general

The regulations prescribed under paragraph (1) shall require any automated teller machine operator who imposes a fee on any consumer for providing host transfer services to such consumer to provide notice in accordance with subparagraph (B) to the consumer (at the time the service is provided) of—

(i) the fact that a fee is imposed by such operator for providing the service; and

(ii) the amount of any such fee.

(B) Notice requirement

The notice required under clauses (i) and (ii) of subparagraph (A) with respect to any fee described in such subparagraph shall appear on the screen of the automated teller machine, or on a paper notice issued from such machine, after the transaction is initiated and before the consumer is irrevocably committed to completing the transaction.

(C) Prohibition on fees not properly disclosed and explicitly assumed by consumer

No fee may be imposed by any automated teller machine operator in connection with any electronic fund transfer initiated by a consumer for which a notice is required under subparagraph (A), unless—

(i) the consumer receives such notice in accordance with subparagraph (B); and

(ii) the consumer elects to continue in the manner necessary to effect the transaction after receiving such notice.

(D) Definitions

For purposes of this paragraph, the following definitions shall apply:

(i) Automated teller machine operator

The term "automated teller machine operator" means any person who—

(I) operates an automated teller machine at which consumers initiate electronic fund transfers; and

(II) is not the financial institution that holds the account of such consumer from which the transfer is made.

(ii) Electronic fund transfer

The term "electronic fund transfer" includes a transaction that involves a balance inquiry initiated by a consumer in the same manner as an electronic fund transfer, whether or not the consumer initiates a transfer of funds in the course of the transaction.

(iii) Host transfer services

The term "host transfer services" means any electronic fund transfer made by an automated teller machine operator in connection with a transaction initiated by a consumer at an automated teller machine operated by such operator.

(e) Deference

No provision of this subchapter may be construed as altering, limiting, or otherwise affecting the deference that a court affords to—

(1) the Bureau in making determinations regarding the meaning or interpretation of any provision of this subchapter for which the Bureau has authority to prescribe regulations; or

(2) the Board in making determinations regarding the meaning or interpretation of section 1693*o*–2 of this title.

§ 1693c [CCPA § 905]. Terms and Conditions of Transfers

(a) Disclosures; time; form; contents

The terms and conditions of electronic fund transfers involving a consumer's account shall be disclosed at the time the consumer contracts for an electronic fund transfer service, in accordance with regulations of the Bureau. Such disclosures shall be in readily understandable language and shall include, to the extent applicable—

(1) the consumer's liability for unauthorized electronic fund transfers and, at the financial institution's option, notice of the advisability of prompt reporting of any loss, theft, or unauthorized use of a card, code, or other means of access;

(2) the telephone number and address of the person or office to be notified in the event the consumer believes than[1] an unauthorized electronic fund transfer has been or may be effected;

(3) the type and nature of electronic fund transfers which the consumer may initiate, including any limitations on the frequency or dollar amount of such transfers, except that the details of such limitations need not be disclosed if their confidentiality is necessary to maintain the security of an electronic fund transfer system, as determined by the Bureau;

(4) any charges for electronic fund transfers or for the right to make such transfers;

(5) the consumer's right to stop payment of a preauthorized electronic fund transfer and the procedure to initiate such a stop payment order;

(6) the consumer's right to receive documentation of electronic fund transfers under section 1693d of this title;

(7) a summary, in a form prescribed by regulations of the Bureau, of the error resolution provisions of section 1693f of this title and the consumer's rights thereunder. The financial institution shall thereafter transmit such summary at least once per calendar year;

(8) the financial institution's liability to the consumer under section 1693h of this title;

(9) under what circumstances the financial institution will in the ordinary course of business disclose information concerning the consumer's account to third persons; and

(10) a notice to the consumer that a fee may be imposed by—

(A) an automated teller machine operator (as defined in section 1693b(d)(3)(D)(i) of this title) if the consumer initiates a transfer from an automated teller machine that is not operated by the person issuing the card or other means of access; and

(B) any national, regional, or local network utilized to effect the transaction.

(b) Notification of changes to consumer

A financial institution shall notify a consumer in writing at least twenty-one days prior to the effective date of any change in any term or condition of the consumer's account required to be disclosed under subsection (a) if such change would result in greater cost or liability for such consumer or decreased access to the consumer's account. A financial institution may, however, implement a change in the terms or conditions of an account without prior notice when such change is immediately necessary to maintain or restore the security of an electronic fund transfer system or a consumer's

[1] So in original. Probably should be "that".

account. Subject to subsection (a)(3), the Bureau shall require subsequent notification if such a change is made permanent.

(c) Time for disclosures respecting accounts accessible prior to effective date of this subchapter

For any account of a consumer made accessible to electronic fund transfers prior to the effective date of this subchapter, the information required to be disclosed to the consumer under subsection (a) shall be disclosed not later than the earlier of—

(1) the first periodic statement required by section 1693d(c) of this title after the effective date of this subchapter; or

(2) thirty days after the effective date of this subchapter.

§ 1693d [CCPA § 906]. Documentation of Transfers

(a) Availability of written documentation to consumer; contents

For each electronic fund transfer initiated by a consumer from an electronic terminal, the financial institution holding such consumer's account shall, directly or indirectly, at the time the transfer is initiated, make available to the consumer written documentation of such transfer. The documentation shall clearly set forth to the extent applicable—

(1) the amount involved and date the transfer is initiated;

(2) the type of transfer;

(3) the identity of the consumer's account with the financial institution from which or to which funds are transferred;

(4) the identity of any third party to whom or from whom funds are transferred; and

(5) the location or identification of the electronic terminal involved.

(b) Notice of credit to consumer

For a consumer's account which is scheduled to be credited by a preauthorized electronic fund transfer from the same payor at least once in each successive sixty-day period, except where the payor provides positive notice of the transfer to the consumer, the financial institution shall elect to provide promptly either positive notice to the consumer when the credit is made as scheduled, or negative notice to the consumer when the credit is not made as scheduled, in accordance with regulations of the Bureau. The means of notice elected shall be disclosed to the consumer in accordance with section 1693c of this title.

(c) Periodic statement; contents

A financial institution shall provide each consumer with a periodic statement for each account of such consumer that may be accessed by means of an electronic fund transfer. Except as provided in subsections (d) and (e), such statement shall be provided at least monthly for each monthly or shorter cycle in which an electronic fund transfer affecting the account has occurred, or every three months, whichever is more frequent. The statement, which may include information regarding transactions other than electronic fund transfers, shall clearly set forth—

(1) with regard to each electronic fund transfer during the period, the information described in subsection (a), which may be provided on an accompanying document;

(2) the amount of any fee or charge assessed by the financial institution during the period for electronic fund transfers or for account maintenance;

(3) the balances in the consumer's account at the beginning of the period and at the close of the period; and

(4) the address and telephone number to be used by the financial institution for the purpose of receiving any statement inquiry or notice of account error from the consumer. Such address and telephone number shall be preceded by the caption "Direct Inquiries To:" or other similar language indicating that the address and number are to be used for such inquiries or notices.

(d) Consumer passbook accounts

In the case of a consumer's passbook account which may not be accessed by electronic fund transfers other than preauthorized electronic fund transfers crediting the account, a financial institution may, in lieu of complying with the requirements of subsection (c), upon presentation of the passbook provide the consumer in writing with the amount and date of each such transfer involving the account since the passbook was last presented.

(e) Accounts other than passbook accounts

In the case of a consumer's account, other than a passbook account, which may not be accessed by electronic fund transfers other than preauthorized electronic fund transfers crediting the account, the financial institution may provide a periodic statement on a quarterly basis which otherwise complies with the requirements of subsection (c).

(f) Documentation as evidence

In any action involving a consumer, any documentation required by this section to be given to the consumer which indicates that an electronic fund transfer was made to another person shall be admissible as evidence of such transfer and shall constitute prima facie proof that such transfer was made.

§ 1693e [CCPA § 907]. Preauthorized Transfers

(a) A preauthorized electronic fund transfer from a consumer's account may be authorized by the consumer only in writing, and a copy of such authorization shall be provided to the consumer when made. A consumer may stop payment of a preauthorized electronic fund transfer by notifying the financial institution orally or in writing at any time up to three business days preceding the scheduled date of such transfer. The financial institution may require written confirmation to be provided to it within fourteen days of an oral notification if, when the oral notification is made, the consumer is advised of such requirement and the address to which such confirmation should be sent.

(b) In the case of preauthorized transfers from a consumer's account to the same person which may vary in amount, the financial institution or designated payee shall, prior to each transfer, provide reasonable advance notice to the consumer, in accordance with regulations of the Bureau, of the amount to be transferred and the scheduled date of the transfer.

§ 1693f [CCPA § 908]. Error Resolution

(a) Notification to financial institution of error

If a financial institution, within sixty days after having transmitted to a consumer documentation pursuant to section 1693d(a), (c), or (d) of this title or notification pursuant to section 1693d(b) of this title, receives oral or written notice in which the consumer—

(1) sets forth or otherwise enables the financial institution to identify the name and account number of the consumer;

(2) indicates the consumer's belief that the documentation, or, in the case of notification pursuant to section 1693d(b) of this title, the consumer's account, contains an error and the amount of such error; and

(3) sets forth the reasons for the consumer's belief (where applicable) that an error has occurred, the financial institution shall investigate the alleged error, determine whether an error has occurred, and report or mail the results of such investigation and determination to the consumer within ten business days. The financial institution may require written confirmation to be provided to it within ten business days of an oral notification of error if, when the oral notification is made, the consumer is advised of such requirement and the address to which such confirmation should be sent. A financial institution which requires written confirmation in accordance with the previous sentence need not provisionally recredit a consumer's account in accordance with subsection (c), nor shall the financial institution be liable under subsection (e) if the written confirmation is not received within the ten-day period referred to in the previous sentence.

(b) Correction of error; interest

If the financial institution determines that an error did occur, it shall promptly, but in no event more than one business day after such determination, correct the error, subject to section 1693g of this title, including the crediting of interest where applicable.

(c) Provisional recredit of consumer's account

If a financial institution receives notice of an error in the manner and within the time period specified in subsection (a), it may, in lieu of the requirements of subsections (a) and (b), within ten business days after receiving such notice provisionally recredit the consumer's account for the amount alleged to be in error, subject to section 1693g of this title, including interest where applicable, pending the conclusion of its investigation and its determination of whether an error has occurred. Such investigation shall be concluded not later than forty-five days after receipt of notice of the error. During the pendency of the investigation, the consumer shall have full use of the funds provisionally recredited.

(d) Absence of error; finding; explanation

If the financial institution determines after its investigation pursuant to subsection (a) or (c) that an error did not occur, it shall deliver or mail to the consumer an explanation of its findings within 3 business days after the conclusion of its investigation, and upon request of the consumer promptly deliver or mail to the consumer reproductions of all documents which the financial institution relied on to conclude that such error did not occur. The financial institution shall include notice of the right to request reproductions with the explanation of its findings.

(e) Treble damages

If in any action under section 1693m of this title, the court finds that—

(1) the financial institution did not provisionally recredit a consumer's account within the ten-day period specified in subsection (c), and the financial institution (A) did not make a good faith investigation of the alleged error, or (B) did not have a reasonable basis for believing that the consumer's account was not in error; or

(2) the financial institution knowingly and willfully concluded that the consumer's account was not in error when such conclusion could not reasonably have been drawn from the evidence available to the financial institution at the time of its investigation,

then the consumer shall be entitled to treble damages determined under section 1693m(a)(1) of this title.

(f) Acts constituting error

For the purpose of this section, an error consists of—

(1) an unauthorized electronic fund transfer;

(2) an incorrect electronic fund transfer from or to the consumer's account;

(3) the omission from a periodic statement of an electronic fund transfer affecting the consumer's account which should have been included;

(4) a computational error by the financial institution;

(5) the consumer's receipt of an incorrect amount of money from an electronic terminal;

(6) a consumer's request for additional information or clarification concerning an electronic fund transfer or any documentation required by this subchapter; or

(7) any other error described in regulations of the Bureau.

§ 1693g [CCPA § 909]. Consumer Liability

(a) Unauthorized electronic fund transfers; limit

A consumer shall be liable for any unauthorized electronic fund transfer involving the account of such consumer only if the card or other means of access utilized for such transfer was an accepted card or other meanas[1] of access and if the issuer of such card, code, or other means of access has provided a means whereby the user of such card, code, or other means of access can be identified as the person authorized to use it, such as by signature, photograph, or fingerprint or by electronic or mechanical confirmation. In no event, however, shall a consumer's liability for an unauthorized transfer exceed the lesser of—

(1) $50; or

(2) the amount of money or value of property or services obtained in such unauthorized electronic fund transfer prior to the time the financial institution is notified of, or otherwise becomes aware of, circumstances which lead to the reasonable belief that an unauthorized electronic fund transfer involving the consumer's account has been or may be effected. Notice under this paragraph is sufficient when such steps have been taken as may be reasonably required in the ordinary course of business to provide the financial institution with the pertinent information, whether or not any particular officer, employee, or agent of the financial institution does in fact receive such information.

Notwithstanding the foregoing, reimbursement need not be made to the consumer for losses the financial institution establishes would not have occurred but for the failure of the consumer to report within sixty days of transmittal of the statement (or in extenuating circumstances such as extended travel or hospitalization, within a reasonable time under the circumstances) any unauthorized electronic fund transfer or account error which appears on the periodic statement provided to the consumer under section 1693d of this title. In addition, reimbursement need not be made to the consumer for losses which the financial institution establishes would not have occurred but for the failure of the consumer to report any loss or theft of a card or other means of access within two business days after the consumer learns of the loss or theft (or in extenuating circumstances such as extended travel or hospitalization, within a longer period which is reasonable under the circumstances), but the consumer's liability under this subsection in any such case may not exceed a total of $500, or the amount of unauthorized electronic fund transfers which occur following the close of two business days (or such longer period) after the consumer learns of the loss or theft but prior to notice to the financial institution under this subsection, whichever is less.

(b) Burden of proof

In any action which involves a consumer's liability for an unauthorized electronic fund transfer, the burden of proof is upon the financial institution to show that the electronic fund transfer was authorized or, if the electronic fund transfer was unauthorized, then the burden of proof is upon the financial institution to establish that the conditions of liability set forth in subsection (a) have been met, and, if the transfer was initiated after the effective date of section 1693c of this title, that the disclosures required to be made to the consumer under section 1693c(a)(1) and (2) of this title were in fact made in accordance with such section.

---

1 So in original. Probably should be "means."

(c) Determination of limitation on liability

In the event of a transaction which involves both an unauthorized electronic fund transfer and an extension of credit as defined in section 1602(e) of this title pursuant to an agreement between the consumer and the financial institution to extend such credit to the consumer in the event the consumer's account is overdrawn, the limitation on the consumer's liability for such transaction shall be determined solely in accordance with this section.

(d) Restriction on liability

Nothing in this section imposes liability upon a consumer for an unauthorized electronic fund transfer in excess of his liability for such a transfer under other applicable law or under any agreement with the consumer's financial institution.

(e) Scope of liability

Except as provided in this section, a consumer incurs no liability from an unauthorized electronic fund transfer.

§ 1693h [CCPA § 910]. Liability of Financial Institutions

(a) Action or failure to act proximately causing damages

Subject to subsections (b) and (c), a financial institution shall be liable to a consumer for all damages proximately caused by—

(1) the financial institution's failure to make an electronic fund transfer, in accordance with the terms and conditions of an account, in the correct amount or in a timely manner when properly instructed to do so by the consumer, except where—

(A) the consumer's account has insufficient funds;

(B) the funds are subject to legal process or other encumbrance restricting such transfer;

(C) such transfer would exceed an established credit limit;

(D) an electronic terminal has insufficient cash to complete the transaction; or

(E) as otherwise provided in regulations of the Bureau;

(2) the financial institution's failure to make an electronic fund transfer due to insufficient funds when the financal[1] institution failed to credit, in accordance with the terms and conditions of an account, a deposit of funds to the consumer's account which would have provided sufficient funds to make the transfer, and

(3) the financial institution's failure to stop payment of a preauthorized transfer from a consumer's account when instructed to do so in accordance with the terms and conditions of the account.

(b) Acts of God and technical malfunctions

A financial institution shall not be liable under subsection (a)(1) or (2) if the financial institution shows by a preponderance of the evidence that its action or failure to act resulted from—

(1) an act of God or other circumstance beyond its control, that it exercised reasonable care to prevent such an occurrence, and that it exercised such diligence as the circumstances required; or

---

[1] So in original. Probably should be "financial".

(2) a technical malfunction which was known to the consumer at the time he attempted to initiate an electronic fund transfer or, in the case of a preauthorized transfer, at the time such transfer should have occurred.

(c) Intent

In the case of a failure described in subsection (a) which was not intentional and which resulted from a bona fide error, notwithstanding the maintenance of procedures reasonably adapted to avoid any such error, the financial institution shall be liable for actual damages proved.

(d) Exception for damaged notices

If the notice required to be posted pursuant to section 1693b(d)(3)(B)(i) of this title by an automated teller machine operator has been posted by such operator in compliance with such section and the notice is subsequently removed, damaged, or altered by any person other than the operator of the automated teller machine, the operator shall have no liability under this section for failure to comply with section 1693b(d)(3)(B)(i) of this title.

§ 1693i [CCPA § 911]. Issuance of Cards or Other Means of Access

(a) Prohibition; proper issuance

No person may issue to a consumer any card, code, or other means of access to such consumer's account for the purpose of initiating an electronic fund transfer other than—

(1) in response to a request or application therefor; or

(2) as a renewal of, or in substitution for, an accepted card, code, or other means of access, whether issued by the initial issuer or a successor.

(b) Exceptions

Notwithstanding the provisions of subsection (a), a person may distribute to a consumer on an unsolicited basis a card, code, or other means of access for use in initiating an electronic fund transfer from such consumer's account, if—

(1) such card, code, or other means of access is not validated;

(2) such distribution is accompanied by a complete disclosure, in accordance with section 1693c of this title, of the consumer's rights and liabilities which will apply if such card, code, or other means of access is validated;

(3) such distribution is accompanied by a clear explanation, in accordance with regulations of the Bureau, that such card, code, or other means of access is not validated and how the consumer may dispose of such code, card, or other means of access if validation is not desired; and

(4) such card, code, or other means of access is validated only in response to a request or application from the consumer, upon verification of the consumer's identity.

(c) Validation

For the purpose of subsection (b), a card, code, or other means of access is validated when it may be used to initiate an electronic fund transfer.

§ 1693j [CCPA § 912]. Suspension of Obligations

If a system malfunction prevents the effectuation of an electronic fund transfer initiated by a consumer to another person, and such other person has agreed to accept payment by such means, the consumer's obligation to the other person shall be suspended until the malfunction is corrected and the electronic fund transfer may be completed, unless such other person has subsequently, by written request, demanded payment by means other than an electronic fund transfer.

§ 1693k [CCPA § 913]. Compulsory Use of Electronic Fund Transfers

No person may—

(1) condition the extension of credit to a consumer on such consumer's repayment by means of preauthorized electronic fund transfers; or

(2) require a consumer to establish an account for receipt of electronic fund transfers with a particular financial institution as a condition of employment or receipt of a government benefit.

§ 1693*l* [CCPA § 914]. Waiver of Rights

No writing or other agreement between a consumer and any other person may contain any provision which constitutes a waiver of any right conferred or cause of action created by this subchapter. Nothing in this section prohibits, however, any writing or other agreement which grants to a consumer a more extensive right or remedy or greater protection than contained in this subchapter or a waiver given in settlement of a dispute or action.

§ 1693*l*–1 [CCPA § 915] General-Use Prepaid Cards, Gift Certificates, and Store Gift Cards

(a) Definitions

In this section, the following definitions shall apply:

(1) Dormancy fee; inactivity charge or fee

The terms "dormancy fee" and "inactivity charge or fee" mean a fee, charge, or penalty for non-use or inactivity of a gift certificate, store gift card, or general-use prepaid card.

(2) General use[1] prepaid card, gift certificate, and store gift card

(A) General-use prepaid card

The term "general-use prepaid card" means a card or other payment code or device issued by any person that is—

(i) redeemable at multiple, unaffiliated merchants or service providers, or automated teller machines;

(ii) issued in a requested amount, whether or not that amount may, at the option of the issuer, be increased in value or reloaded if requested by the holder;

(iii) purchased or loaded on a prepaid basis; and

(iv) honored, upon presentation, by merchants for goods or services, or at automated teller machines.

(B) Gift certificate

The term "gift certificate" means an electronic promise that is—

(i) redeemable at a single merchant or an affiliated group of merchants that share the same name, mark, or logo;

(ii) issued in a specified amount that may not be increased or reloaded;

(iii) purchased on a prepaid basis in exchange for payment; and

(iv) honored upon presentation by such single merchant or affiliated group of merchants for goods or services.

(C) Store gift card

---

1 So in original. Probably should be "General-use".

The term “store gift card” means an electronic promise, plastic card, or other payment code or device that is—

(i) redeemable at a single merchant or an affiliated group of merchants that share the same name, mark, or logo;

(ii) issued in a specified amount, whether or not that amount may be increased in value or reloaded at the request of the holder;

(iii) purchased on a prepaid basis in exchange for payment; and

(iv) honored upon presentation by such single merchant or affiliated group of merchants for goods or services.

(D) Exclusions

The terms “general-use prepaid card”, “gift certificate”, and “store gift card” do not include an electronic promise, plastic card, or payment code or device that is—

(i) used solely for telephone services;

(ii) reloadable and not marketed or labeled as a gift card or gift certificate;

(iii) a loyalty, award, or promotional gift card, as defined by the Bureau;

(iv) not marketed to the general public;

(v) issued in paper form only (including for tickets and events); or

(vi) redeemable solely for admission to events or venues at a particular location or group of affiliated locations, which may also include services or goods obtainable—

(I) at the event or venue after admission; or

(II) in conjunction with admission to such events or venues, at specific locations affiliated with and in geographic proximity to the event or venue.

(3) Service fee

(A) In general

The term “service fee” means a periodic fee, charge, or penalty for holding or use of a gift certificate, store gift card, or general-use prepaid card.

(B) Exclusion

With respect to a general-use prepaid card, the term ‘service fee’ does not include a one-time initial issuance fee.

(b) Prohibition on Imposition of Fees or Charges

(1) In general

Except as provided under paragraphs (2) through (4), it shall be unlawful for any person to impose a dormancy fee, an inactivity charge or fee, or a service fee with respect to a gift certificate, store gift card, or general-use prepaid card.

(2) Exceptions

A dormancy fee, inactivity charge or fee, or service fee may be charged with respect to a gift certificate, store gift card, or general-use prepaid card, if—

(A) there has been no activity with respect to the certificate or card in the 12-month period ending on the date on which the charge or fee is imposed;

(B) the disclosure requirements of paragraph (3) have been met;

(C) not more than one fee may be charged in any given month; and

(D) any additional requirements that the Bureau may establish through rulemaking under subsection (d) have been met.

(3) Disclosure requirements

The disclosure requirements of this paragraph are met if—

(A) the gift certificate, store gift card, or general-use prepaid card clearly and conspicuously states—

(i) that a dormancy fee, inactivity charge or fee, or service fee may be charged;

(ii) the amount of such fee or charge;

(iii) how often such fee or charge may be assessed; and

(iv) that such fee or charge may be assessed for inactivity; and

(B) the issuer or vendor of such certificate or card informs the purchaser of such charge or fee before such certificate or card is purchased, regardless of whether the certificate or card is purchased in person, over the Internet, or by telephone.

(4) Exclusion

The prohibition under paragraph (1) shall not apply to any gift certificate—

(A) that is distributed pursuant to an award, loyalty, or promotional program, as defined by the Bureau; and

(B) with respect to which, there is no money or other value exchanged.

(c) Prohibition on sale of gift cards with expiration dates

(1) In general

Except as provided under paragraph (2), it shall be unlawful for any person to sell or issue a gift certificate, store gift card, or general-use prepaid card that is subject to an expiration date.

(2) Exceptions

A gift certificate, store gift card, or general-use prepaid card may contain an expiration date if—

(A) the expiration date is not earlier than 5 years after the date on which the gift certificate was issued, or the date on which card funds were last loaded to a store gift card or general-use prepaid card; and

(B) the terms of expiration are clearly and conspicuously stated.

(d) Additional Rulemaking

(1) In general

The Bureau shall—

(A) prescribe regulations to carry out this section, in addition to any other rules or regulations required by this title, including such additional requirements as appropriate relating to the amount of dormancy fees, inactivity charges or fees, or service fees that may be assessed and the amount of remaining value of a gift certificate, store gift card, or general-use prepaid card below which such charges or fees may be assessed; and

(B) shall determine the extent to which the individual definitions and provisions of the Electronic Fund Transfer Act or Regulation E should apply to general-use prepaid cards, gift certificates, and store gift cards.

(2) Consultation

In prescribing regulations under this subsection, the Bureau shall consult with the Federal Trade Commission.

(3) Timing; effective date

The regulations required by this subsection shall be issued in final form not later than 9 months after May 22, 2009.

§ 1693m [CCPA § 916]. Civil Liability

(a) Individual or class action for damages; amount of award

Except as otherwise provided by this section and section 1693h of this title, any person who fails to comply with any provision of this subchapter with respect to any consumer, except for an error resolved in accordance with section 1693f of this title, is liable to such consumer in an amount equal to the sum of—

(1) any actual damage sustained by such consumer as a result of such failure;

(2)(A) in the case of an individual action, an amount not less than $100 nor greater than $1,000; or

(B) in the case of a class action, such amount as the court may allow, except that (i) as to each member of the class no minimum recovery shall be applicable, and (ii) the total recovery under this subparagraph in any class action or series of class actions arising out of the same failure to comply by the same person shall not be more than the lesser of $500,000 or 1 per centum of the net worth of the defendant; and

(3) in the case of any successful action to enforce the foregoing liability, the costs of the action, together with a reasonable attorney's fee as determined by the court.

(b) Factors determining amount of award

In determining the amount of liability in any action under subsection (a), the court shall consider, among other relevant factors—

(1) in any individual action under subsection (a)(2)(A), the frequency and persistence of noncompliance, the nature of such noncompliance, and the extent to which the noncompliance was intentional; or

(2) in any class action under subsection (a)(2)(B), the frequency and persistence of noncompliance, the nature of such noncompliance, the resources of the defendant, the number of persons adversely affected, and the extent to which the noncompliance was intentional.

(c) Unintentional violations; bona fide error

Except as provided in section 1693h of this title, a person may not be held liable in any action brought under this section for a violation of this subchapter if the person shows by a preponderance of evidence that the violation was not intentional and resulted from a bona fide error notwithstanding the maintenance of procedures reasonably adapted to avoid any such error.

(d) Good faith compliance with rule, regulation, or interpretation

No provision of this section or section 1693n of this title imposing any liability shall apply to—

(1) any act done or omitted in good faith in conformity with any rule, regulation, or interpretation thereof by the Bureau or the Board or in conformity with any interpretation or approval by an official or employee of the Bureau of Consumer Financial Protection or the Federal Reserve System duly authorized by the Bureau or the Board to issue such interpretations or approvals under such procedures as the Bureau or the Board may prescribe therefor; or

(2) any failure to make disclosure in proper form if a financial institution utilized an appropriate model clause issued by the Bureau or the Board, notwithstanding that after such act, omission, or failure has occurred, such rule, regulation, approval, or model clause is amended, rescinded, or determined by judicial or other authority to be invalid for any reason.

(e) Notification to consumer prior to action; adjustment of consumer's account

A person has no liability under this section for any failure to comply with any requirement under this subchapter if, prior to the institution of an action under this section, the person notifies the consumer concerned of the failure, complies with the requirements of this subchapter, and makes an appropriate adjustment to the consumer's account and pays actual damages or, where applicable, damages in accordance with section 1693h of this title.

(f) Action in bad faith or for harassment; attorney's fees

On a finding by the court that an unsuccessful action under this section was brought in bad faith or for purposes of harassment, the court shall award to the defendant attorney's fees reasonable in relation to the work expended and costs.

(g) Jurisdiction of courts; time for maintenance of action

Without regard to the amount in controversy, any action under this section may be brought in any United States district court, or in any other court of competent jurisdiction, within one year from the date of the occurrence of the violation.

§ 1693n [CCPA § 917]. Criminal Liability

(a) Violations respecting giving of false or inaccurate information, failure to provide information, and failure to comply with provisions of this subchapter

Whoever knowingly and willfully—

(1) gives false or inaccurate information or fails to provide information which he is required to disclose by this subchapter or any regulation issued thereunder; or

(2) otherwise fails to comply with any provision of this subchapter;

shall be fined not more than $5,000 or imprisoned not more than one year, or both.

(b) Violations affecting interstate or foreign commerce

Whoever—

(1) knowingly, in a transaction affecting interstate or foreign commerce, uses or attempts or conspires to use any counterfeit, fictitious, altered, forged, lost, stolen, or fraudulently obtained debit instrument to obtain money, goods, services, or anything else of value which within any one-year period has a value aggregating $1,000 or more; or

(2) with unlawful or fraudulent intent, transports or attempts or conspires to transport in interstate or foreign commerce a counterfeit, fictitious, altered, forged, lost, stolen, or fraudulently obtained debit instrument knowing the same to be counterfeit, fictitious, altered, forged, lost, stolen, or fraudulently obtained; or

(3) with unlawful or fraudulent intent, uses any instrumentality of interstate or foreign commerce to sell or transport a counterfeit, fictitious, altered, forged, lost, stolen, or fraudulently obtained debit instrument knowing the same to be counterfeit, fictitious, altered, forged, lost, stolen, or fraudulently obtained; or

(4) knowingly receives, conceals, uses, or transports money, goods, services, or anything else of value (except tickets for interstate or foreign transportation) which (A) within any one-year period has a value aggregating $1,000 or more, (B) has moved in or is part of, or which constitutes interstate or foreign commerce, and (C) has been obtained with a counterfeit, fictitious, altered, forged, lost, stolen, or fraudulently obtained debit instrument; or

(5) knowingly receives, conceals, uses, sells, or transports in interstate or foreign commerce one or more tickets for interstate or foreign transportation, which (A) within any one-year period have a value aggregating $500 or more, and (B) have been purchased or obtained with one or more counterfeit, fictitious, altered, forged, lost, stolen, or fraudulently obtained debit instrument; or

(6) in a transaction affecting interstate or foreign commerce, furnishes money, property, services, or anything else of value, which within any one-year period has a value aggregating $1,000 or more, through the use of any counterfeit, fictitious, altered, forged, lost, stolen, or fraudulently obtained debit instrument knowing the same to be counterfeit, fictitious, altered, forged, lost, stolen, or fraudulently obtained—

shall be fined not more than $10,000 or imprisoned not more than ten years, or both.

(c) "Debit instrument" defined

As used in this section, the term "debit instrument" means a card, code, or other device, other than a check, draft, or similar paper instrument, by the use of which a person may initiate an electronic fund transfer.

§ 1693*o* [CCPA § 918]. Administrative Enforcement

(a) Enforcing agencies

Subject to subtitle B of the Consumer Financial Protection Act of 2010, compliance with the requirements imposed under this subchapter shall be enforced under—

(1) section 8 of the Federal Deposit Insurance Act, by the appropriate Federal banking agency, as defined in section 1813(q) of Title 12, with respect to—

(A) national banks, Federal savings associations, and Federal branches and Federal agencies of foreign banks;

(B) member banks of the Federal Reserve System (other than national banks), branches and agencies of foreign banks (other than Federal branches, Federal agencies, and insured State branches of foreign banks), commercial lending companies owned or controlled by foreign banks, and organizations operating under section 25 or 25A of the Federal Reserve Act; and

(C) banks and State savings associations insured by the Federal Deposit Insurance Corporation (other than members of the Federal Reserve System), and insured State branches of foreign banks;

(2) the Federal Credit Union Act [12 U.S.C.A. § 1751 et seq.], by the Administrator of the National Credit Union Administration with respect to any Federal credit union;

(3) part A of subtitle VII of title 49, by the Secretary of Transportation, with respect to any air carrier or foreign air carrier subject to that part;

(4) the Securities Exchange Act of 1934 [15 U.S.C.A. § 78a et seq.], by the Securities and Exchange Commission, with respect to any broker or dealer subject to that Act and[1]

(5) subtitle E of the Consumer Financial Protection Act of 2010, by the Bureau, with respect to any person subject to this subchapter, except that the Bureau shall not have authority to enforce the requirements of section 1693*o*–2 of this title or any regulations prescribed by the Board under section 1693*o*–2 of this title.

[1] So in original. Probably should be "; and".

The terms used in paragraph (1) that are not defined in this subchapter or otherwise defined in section 3(s) of the Federal Deposit Insurance Act (12 U.S.C. 1813(s)) shall have the meaning given to them in section 1(b) of the International Banking Act of 1978 (12 U.S.C. 3101).

(b) Violations of subchapter deemed violations of pre-existing statutory requirements; additional powers

For the purpose of the exercise by any agency referred to in any of paragraphs (1) through (4) of subsection (a) of its powers under any Act referred to in that subsection, a violation of any requirement imposed under this subchapter shall be deemed to be a violation of a requirement imposed under that Act. In addition to its powers under any provision of law specifically referred to in any of paragraphs (1) through (4) of subsection (a), each of the agencies referred to in that subsection may exercise, for the purpose of enforcing compliance with any requirement imposed under this subchapter, any other authority conferred on it by law.

(c) Overall enforcement authority of the Federal Trade Commission

Except to the extent that enforcement of the requirements imposed under this subchapter is specifically committed to some other Government agency under any of paragraphs (1) through (4) of subsection (a), and subject to subtitle B of the Consumer Financial Protection Act of 2010, the Federal Trade Commission shall be authorized to enforce such requirements. For the purpose of the exercise by the Federal Trade Commission of its functions and powers under the Federal Trade Commission Act, a violation of any requirement imposed under this subchapter shall be deemed a violation of a requirement imposed under that Act. All of the functions and powers of the Federal Trade Commission under the Federal Trade Commission Act are available to the Federal Trade Commission to enforce compliance by any person subject to the jurisdiction of the Federal Trade Commission with the requirements imposed under this subchapter, irrespective of whether that person is engaged in commerce or meets any other jurisdictional tests under the Federal Trade Commission Act.

§ 1693*o*–1. Remittance transfers

(a) Disclosures required for remittance transfers

(1) In general

Each remittance transfer provider shall make disclosures as required under this section and in accordance with rules prescribed by the Bureau. Disclosures required under this section shall be in addition to any other disclosures applicable under this subchapter.

(2) Disclosures

Subject to rules prescribed by the Bureau a remittance transfer provider shall provide, in writing and in a form that the sender may keep, to each sender requesting a remittance transfer, as applicable to the transaction—

(A) at the time at which the sender requests a remittance transfer to be initiated, and prior to the sender making any payment in connection with the remittance transfer, a disclosure describing—

(i) the amount of currency that will be received by the designated recipient, using the values of the currency into which the funds will be exchanged;

(ii) the amount of transfer and any other fees charged by the remittance transfer provider for the remittance transfer; and

(iii) any exchange rate to be used by the remittance transfer provider for the remittance transfer, to the nearest 1/100th of a point; and

(B) at the time at which the sender makes payment in connection with the remittance transfer—

(i) a receipt showing—

(I) the information described in subparagraph (A);

(II) the promised date of delivery to the designated recipient; and

(III) the name and either the telephone number or the address of the designated recipient, if either the telephone number or the address of the designated recipient is provided by the sender; and

(ii) a statement containing—

(I) information about the rights of the sender under this section regarding the resolution of errors; and

(II) appropriate contact information for—

(aa) the remittance transfer provider; and

(bb) the State agency that regulates the remittance transfer provider and the Bureau, including the toll-free telephone number established under section 5493 of Title 12.

(3) Requirements relating to disclosures

With respect to each disclosure required to be provided under paragraph (2) a remittance transfer provider shall—

(A) provide an initial notice and receipt, as required by subparagraphs (A) and (B) of paragraph (2), and an error resolution statement, as required by subsection (d), that clearly and conspicuously describe the information required to be disclosed therein; and

(B) with respect to any transaction that a sender conducts electronically, comply with the Electronic Signatures in Global and National Commerce Act (15 U.S.C. 7001 et seq.).

(4) Exception for disclosures of amount received

(A) In general

Subject to the rules prescribed by the Bureau, and except as provided under subparagraph (B), the disclosures required regarding the amount of currency that will be received by the designated recipient shall be deemed to be accurate, so long as the disclosures provide a reasonably accurate estimate of the foreign currency to be received. This paragraph shall apply only to a remittance transfer provider who is an insured depository institution, (as defined in section 1813 of Title 12), or an insured credit union, as defined in section 1752 of Title 12, and if—

(i) a remittance transfer is conducted through a demand deposit, savings deposit, or other asset account that the sender holds with such remittance transfer provider; and

(ii) at the time at which the sender requests the transaction, the remittance transfer provider is unable to know, for reasons beyond its control, the amount of currency that will be made available to the designated recipient.

(B) Deadline

The application of subparagraph (A) shall terminate 5 years after July 21, 2010, unless the Bureau determines that termination of such provision would negatively affect the ability of remittance transfer providers described in subparagraph (A) to send remittances to locations in foreign countries, in which case, the Bureau may, by rule, extend the application of subparagraph (A) to not longer than 10 years after July 21, 2010.

(5) Exemption authority

The Bureau may, by rule, permit a remittance transfer provider to satisfy the requirements of—

(A) paragraph (2)(A) orally, if the transaction is conducted entirely by telephone;

(B) paragraph (2)(B), in the case of a transaction conducted entirely by telephone, by mailing the disclosures required under such subparagraph to the sender, not later than 1 business day after the date on which the transaction is conducted, or by including such documents in the next periodic statement, if the telephone transaction is conducted through a demand deposit, savings deposit, or other asset account that the sender holds with the remittance transfer provider;

(C) subparagraphs (A) and (B) of paragraph (2) together in one written disclosure, but only to the extent that the information provided in accordance with paragraph (3)(A) is accurate at the time at which payment is made in connection with the subject remittance transfer; and

(D) paragraph (2)(A), without compliance with section 101(c) of the Electronic Signatures in Global Commerce Act, if a sender initiates the transaction electronically and the information is displayed electronically in a manner that the sender can keep.

(6) Storefront and Internet notices

(A) In general

(i) Prominent posting

Subject to subparagraph (B), the Bureau may prescribe rules to require a remittance transfer provider to prominently post, and timely update, a notice describing a model remittance transfer for one or more amounts, as the Bureau may determine, which notice shall show the amount of currency that will be received by the designated recipient, using the values of the currency into which the funds will be exchanged.

(ii) Onsite displays

The Bureau may require the notice prescribed under this subparagraph to be displayed in every physical storefront location owned or controlled by the remittance transfer provider.

(iii) Internet notices

Subject to paragraph (3), the Bureau shall prescribe rules to require a remittance transfer provider that provides remittance transfers via the Internet to provide a notice, comparable to a storefront notice described in this subparagraph, located on the home page or landing page (with respect to such remittance transfer services) owned or controlled by the remittance transfer provider.

(iv) Rulemaking authority

In prescribing rules under this subparagraph, the Bureau may impose standards or requirements regarding the provision of the storefront and Internet notices required under this subparagraph and the provision of the disclosures required under paragraphs (2) and (3).

(B) Study and analysis

Prior to proposing rules under subparagraph (A), the Bureau shall undertake appropriate studies and analyses, which shall be consistent with section 1693b(a)(2) of this title, and may include an advanced notice of proposed rulemaking, to determine whether a storefront notice or Internet notice facilitates the ability of a consumer—

(i) to compare prices for remittance transfers; and

(ii) to understand the types and amounts of any fees or costs imposed on remittance transfers.

(b) Foreign language disclosures

The disclosures required under this section shall be made in English and in each of the foreign languages principally used by the remittance transfer provider, or any of its agents, to advertise, solicit, or market, either orally or in writing, at that office.

(c) Regulations regarding transfers to certain nations

If the Bureau determines that a recipient nation does not legally allow, or the method by which transactions are made in the recipient country do not allow, a remittance transfer provider to know the amount of currency that will be received by the designated recipient, the Bureau may prescribe rules (not later than 18 months after July 21, 2010) addressing the issue, which rules shall include standards for a remittance transfer provider to provide—

(1) a receipt that is consistent with subsections (a) and (b); and

(2) a reasonably accurate estimate of the foreign currency to be received, based on the rate provided to the sender by the remittance transfer provider at the time at which the transaction was initiated by the sender.

(d) Remittance transfer errors

(1) Error resolution

(A) In general

If a remittance transfer provider receives oral or written notice from the sender within 180 days of the promised date of delivery that an error occurred with respect to a remittance transfer, including the amount of currency designated in subsection (a)(3)(A) that was to be sent to the designated recipient of the remittance transfer, using the values of the currency into which the funds should have been exchanged, but was not made available to the designated recipient in the foreign country, the remittance transfer provider shall resolve the error pursuant to this subsection and investigate the reason for the error.

(B) Remedies

Not later than 90 days after the date of receipt of a notice from the sender pursuant to subparagraph (A), the remittance transfer provider shall, as applicable to the error and as designated by the sender—

(i) refund to the sender the total amount of funds tendered by the sender in connection with the remittance transfer which was not properly transmitted;

(ii) make available to the designated recipient, without additional cost to the designated recipient or to the sender, the amount appropriate to resolve the error;

(iii) provide such other remedy, as determined appropriate by rule of the Bureau for the protection of senders; or

(iv) provide written notice to the sender that there was no error with an explanation responding to the specific complaint of the sender.

(2) Rules

The Bureau shall establish, by rule issued not later than 18 months after July 21, 2010, clear and appropriate standards for remittance transfer providers with respect to error resolution relating to remittance transfers, to protect senders from such errors. Standards prescribed under this paragraph shall include appropriate standards regarding record keeping, as required, including documentation—

(A) of the complaint of the sender;

(B) that the sender provides the remittance transfer provider with respect to the alleged error; and

(C) of the findings of the remittance transfer provider regarding the investigation of the alleged error that the sender brought to their attention.

(3) Cancellation and refund policy rules

Not later than 18 months after July 21, 2010, the Bureau shall issue final rules regarding appropriate remittance transfer cancellation and refund policies for consumers.

(e) Applicability of this subchapter

(1) In general

A remittance transfer that is not an electronic fund transfer, as defined in section 1693a of this title, shall not be subject to any of the provisions of sections 1693c through 1693k of this title. A remittance transfer that is an electronic fund transfer, as defined in section 1693a of this title, shall be subject to all provisions of this subchapter, except for section 1693f of this title, that are otherwise applicable to electronic fund transfers under this subchapter.

(2) Rule of construction

Nothing in this section shall be construed—

(A) to affect the application to any transaction, to any remittance provider, or to any other person of any of the provisions of subchapter II of chapter 53 of Title 31, section 1829b of Title 12, or chapter 2 of title 1 of Public Law 91–508 (12 U.S.C. 1951–1959), or any regulations promulgated thereunder; or

(B) to cause any fund transfer that would not otherwise be treated as such under paragraph (1) to be treated as an electronic fund transfer, or as otherwise subject to this subchapter, for the purposes of any of the provisions referred to in subparagraph (A) or any regulations promulgated thereunder.

(f) Acts of agents

(1) In general

A remittance transfer provider shall be liable for any violation of this section by any agent, authorized delegate, or person affiliated with such provider, when such agent, authorized delegate, or affiliate acts for that remittance transfer provider.

(2) Obligations of remittance transfer providers

The Bureau shall prescribe rules to implement appropriate standards or conditions of, liability of a remittance transfer provider, including a provider who acts through an agent or authorized delegate. An agency charged with enforcing the requirements of this section, or rules prescribed by the Bureau under this section, may consider, in any action or other proceeding against a remittance transfer provider, the extent to which the provider had established and maintained policies or procedures for compliance, including policies, procedures, or other appropriate oversight measures designed to assure compliance by an agent or authorized delegate acting for such provider.

(g) Definitions

As used in this section—

(1) the term "designated recipient" means any person located in a foreign country and identified by the sender as the authorized recipient of a remittance transfer to be made by a remittance transfer provider, except that a designated recipient shall not be deemed to be a consumer for purposes of this chapter;

(2) the term "remittance transfer"—

(A) means the electronic (as defined in section 106(2) of the Electronic Signatures in Global and National Commerce Act (15 U.S.C. 7006(2))) transfer of funds requested by a sender located in any State to a designated recipient that is initiated by a remittance transfer provider, whether or not the sender holds an account with the remittance transfer provider or whether or not the remittance transfer is also an electronic fund transfer, as defined in section 1693a of this title; and

(B) does not include a transfer described in subparagraph (A) in an amount that is equal to or lesser than the amount of a small-value transaction determined, by rule, to be excluded from the requirements under section 1693d(a) of this title;

(3) the term "remittance transfer provider" means any person or financial institution that provides remittance transfers for a consumer in the normal course of its business, whether or not the consumer holds an account with such person or financial institution; and

(4) the term "sender" means a consumer who requests a remittance provider to send a remittance transfer for the consumer to a designated recipient.

§ 1693*o*–2. Reasonable fees and rules for payment card transactions

(a) Reasonable interchange transaction fees for electronic debit transactions

(1) Regulatory authority over interchange transaction fees

The Board may prescribe regulations, pursuant to section 553 of Title 5, regarding any interchange transaction fee that an issuer may receive or charge with respect to an electronic debit transaction, to implement this subsection (including related definitions), and to prevent circumvention or evasion of this subsection.

(2) Reasonable interchange transaction fees

The amount of any interchange transaction fee that an issuer may receive or charge with respect to an electronic debit transaction shall be reasonable and proportional to the cost incurred by the issuer with respect to the transaction.

(3) Rulemaking required

(A) In general

The Board shall prescribe regulations in final form not later than 9 months after July 21, 2010, to establish standards for assessing whether the amount of any interchange transaction fee described in paragraph (2) is reasonable and proportional to the cost incurred by the issuer with respect to the transaction.

(B) Information collection

The Board may require any issuer (or agent of an issuer) or payment card network to provide the Board with such information as may be necessary to carry out the provisions of this subsection and the Board, in issuing rules under subparagraph (A) and on at least a bi-annual basis thereafter, shall disclose such aggregate or summary information concerning the costs incurred, and interchange transaction fees charged or received, by issuers or payment card networks in connection with the authorization, clearance or settlement of electronic debit transactions as the Board considers appropriate and in the public interest.

(4) Considerations; consultation

In prescribing regulations under paragraph (3)(A), the Board shall—

(A) consider the functional similarity between—

(i) electronic debit transactions; and

(ii) checking transactions that are required within the Federal Reserve bank system to clear at par;

(B) distinguish between—

(i) the incremental cost incurred by an issuer for the role of the issuer in the authorization, clearance, or settlement of a particular electronic debit transaction, which cost shall be considered under paragraph (2); and

(ii) other costs incurred by an issuer which are not specific to a particular electronic debit transaction, which costs shall not be considered under paragraph (2); and

(C) consult, as appropriate, with the Comptroller of the Currency, the Board of Directors of the Federal Deposit Insurance Corporation, the Director of the Office of Thrift Supervision, the National Credit Union Administration Board, the Administrator of the Small Business Administration, and the Director of the Bureau of Consumer Financial Protection.

(5) Adjustments to interchange transaction fees for fraud prevention costs

(A) Adjustments

The Board may allow for an adjustment to the fee amount received or charged by an issuer under paragraph (2), if—

(i) such adjustment is reasonably necessary to make allowance for costs incurred by the issuer in preventing fraud in relation to electronic debit transactions involving that issuer; and

(ii) the issuer complies with the fraud-related standards established by the Board under subparagraph (B), which standards shall—

(I) be designed to ensure that any fraud-related adjustment of the issuer is limited to the amount described in clause (i) and takes into account any fraud-related reimbursements (including amounts from charge-backs) received from consumers, merchants, or payment card networks in relation to electronic debit transactions involving the issuer; and

(II) require issuers to take effective steps to reduce the occurrence of, and costs from, fraud in relation to electronic debit transactions, including through the development and implementation of cost-effective fraud prevention technology.

(B) Rulemaking required

(i) In general

The Board shall prescribe regulations in final form not later than 9 months after July 21, 2010, to establish standards for making adjustments under this paragraph.

(ii) Factors for consideration

In issuing the standards and prescribing regulations under this paragraph, the Board shall consider—

(I) the nature, type, and occurrence of fraud in electronic debit transactions;

(II) the extent to which the occurrence of fraud depends on whether authorization in an electronic debit transaction is based on signature, PIN, or other means;

(III) the available and economical means by which fraud on electronic debit transactions may be reduced;

(IV) the fraud prevention and data security costs expended by each party involved in electronic debit transactions (including consumers, persons who accept debit cards as a form of payment, financial institutions, retailers and payment card networks);

(V) the costs of fraudulent transactions absorbed by each party involved in such transactions (including consumers, persons who accept debit cards as a form of payment, financial institutions, retailers and payment card networks);

(VI) the extent to which interchange transaction fees have in the past reduced or increased incentives for parties involved in electronic debit transactions to reduce fraud on such transactions; and

(VII) such other factors as the Board considers appropriate.

(6) Exemption for small issuers

(A) In general

This subsection shall not apply to any issuer that, together with its affiliates, has assets of less than $10,000,000,000, and the Board shall exempt such issuers from regulations prescribed under paragraph (3)(A).

(B) Definition

For purposes of this paragraph, the term "issuer" shall be limited to the person holding the asset account that is debited through an electronic debit transaction.

(7) Exemption for government-administered payment programs and reloadable prepaid cards

(A) In general

This subsection shall not apply to an interchange transaction fee charged or received with respect to an electronic debit transaction in which a person uses—

(i) a debit card or general-use prepaid card that has been provided to a person pursuant to a Federal, State or local government-administered payment program, in which the person may only use the debit card or general-use prepaid card to transfer or debit funds, monetary value, or other assets that have been provided pursuant to such program; or

(ii) a plastic card, payment code, or device that is—

(I) linked to funds, monetary value, or assets which are purchased or loaded on a prepaid basis;

(II) not issued or approved for use to access or debit any account held by or for the benefit of the card holder (other than a subaccount or other method of recording or tracking funds purchased or loaded on the card on a prepaid basis);

(III) redeemable at multiple, unaffiliated merchants or service providers, or automated teller machines;

(IV) used to transfer or debit funds, monetary value, or other assets; and

(V) reloadable and not marketed or labeled as a gift card or gift certificate.

(B) Exception

Notwithstanding subparagraph (A), after the end of the 1-year period beginning on the effective date provided in paragraph (9), this subsection shall apply to an interchange transaction fee charged or received with respect to an electronic debit transaction described in subparagraph (A)(i) in which a person uses a general-use prepaid card, or an electronic debit transaction described in subparagraph (A)(ii), if any of the following fees may be charged to a person with respect to the card:

(i) A fee for an overdraft, including a shortage of funds or a transaction processed for an amount exceeding the account balance.

(ii) A fee imposed by the issuer for the first withdrawal per month from an automated teller machine that is part of the issuer's designated automated teller machine network.

(C) Definition

For purposes of subparagraph (B), the term "designated automated teller machine network" means either—

(i) all automated teller machines identified in the name of the issuer; or

(ii) any network of automated teller machines identified by the issuer that provides reasonable and convenient access to the issuer's customers.

(D) Reporting

Beginning 12 months after July 21, 2010, the Board shall annually provide a report to the Congress regarding—

(i) the prevalence of the use of general-use prepaid cards in Federal, State or local government-administered payment programs; and

(ii) the interchange transaction fees and cardholder fees charged with respect to the use of such general-use prepaid cards.

(8) Regulatory authority over network fees

(A) In general

The Board may prescribe regulations, pursuant to section 553 of Title 5, regarding any network fee.

(B) Limitation

The authority under subparagraph (A) to prescribe regulations shall be limited to regulations to ensure that—

(i) a network fee is not used to directly or indirectly compensate an issuer with respect to an electronic debit transaction; and

(ii) a network fee is not used to circumvent or evade the restrictions of this subsection and regulations prescribed under such subsection.

(C) Rulemaking required

The Board shall prescribe regulations in final form before the end of the 9-month period beginning on July 21, 2010, to carry out the authorities provided under subparagraph (A).

(9) Effective date

This subsection shall take effect at the end of the 12-month period beginning on July 21, 2010.

(b) Limitation on payment card network restrictions

(1) Prohibitions against exclusivity arrangements

(A) No exclusive network

The Board shall, before the end of the 1-year period beginning on July 21, 2010, prescribe regulations providing that an issuer or payment card network shall not directly or through any agent, processor, or licensed member of a payment card network, by contract, requirement, condition, penalty, or otherwise, restrict the number of payment card networks on which an electronic debit transaction may be processed to—

(i) 1 such network; or

(ii) 2 or more such networks which are owned, controlled, or otherwise operated by—

(I) affiliated persons; or

(II) networks affiliated with such issuer.

(B) No routing restrictions

The Board shall, before the end of the 1-year period beginning on July 21, 2010, prescribe regulations providing that an issuer or payment card network shall not, directly or through any agent, processor, or licensed member of the network, by contract, requirement, condition, penalty, or otherwise, inhibit the ability of any person who accepts debit cards for payments to direct the routing of electronic debit transactions for processing over any payment card network that may process such transactions.

(2) Limitation on restrictions on offering discounts for use of a form of payment

(A) In general

A payment card network shall not, directly or through any agent, processor, or licensed member of the network, by contract, requirement, condition, penalty, or otherwise, inhibit the ability of any person to provide a discount or in-kind incentive for payment by the use of cash, checks, debit cards, or credit cards to the extent that—

(i) in the case of a discount or in-kind incentive for payment by the use of debit cards, the discount or in-kind incentive does not differentiate on the basis of the issuer or the payment card network;

(ii) in the case of a discount or in-kind incentive for payment by the use of credit cards, the discount or in-kind incentive does not differentiate on the basis of the issuer or the payment card network; and

(iii) to the extent required by Federal law and applicable State law, such discount or in-kind incentive is offered to all prospective buyers and disclosed clearly and conspicuously.

(B) Lawful discounts

For purposes of this paragraph, the network may not penalize any person for the providing of a discount that is in compliance with Federal law and applicable State law.

(3) Limitation on restrictions on setting transaction minimums or maximums

(A) In general

A payment card network shall not, directly or through any agent, processor, or licensed member of the network, by contract, requirement, condition, penalty, or otherwise, inhibit the ability—

(i) of any person to set a minimum dollar value for the acceptance by that person of credit cards, to the extent that—

(I) such minimum dollar value does not differentiate between issuers or between payment card networks; and

(II) such minimum dollar value does not exceed $10.00; or

(ii) of any Federal agency or institution of higher education to set a maximum dollar value for the acceptance by that Federal agency or institution of higher education of credit cards, to the extent that such maximum dollar value does not differentiate between issuers or between payment card networks.

(B) Increase in minimum dollar amount

The Board may, by regulation prescribed pursuant to section 553 of Title 5, increase the amount of the dollar value listed in subparagraph (A)(i)(II).

(4) Rule of construction:

No provision of this subsection shall be construed to authorize any person—

(A) to discriminate between debit cards within a payment card network on the basis of the issuer that issued the debit card; or

(B) to discriminate between credit cards within a payment card network on the basis of the issuer that issued the credit card.

(c) Definitions

For purposes of this section, the following definitions shall apply:

(1) Affiliate

The term "affiliate" means any company that controls, is controlled by, or is under common control with another company.

(2) Debit card

The term "debit card"—

(A) means any card, or other payment code or device, issued or approved for use through a payment card network to debit an asset account (regardless of the purpose for which the account is established), whether authorization is based on signature, PIN, or other means;

(B) includes a general-use prepaid card, as that term is defined in section 1693*l*–1(a)(2)(A) of this title; and

(C) does not include paper checks.

(3) Credit card

The term "credit card" has the same meaning as in section 1602 of this title.

(4) Discount

The term "discount"—

(A) means a reduction made from the price that customers are informed is the regular price; and

(B) does not include any means of increasing the price that customers are informed is the regular price.

(5) Electronic debit transaction

The term "electronic debit transaction" means a transaction in which a person uses a debit card.

(6) Federal agency

The term "Federal agency" means—

(A) an agency (as defined in section 101 of Title 31); and

(B) a Government corporation (as defined in section 103 of Title 5).

(7) Institution of higher education

The term "institution of higher education" has the same meaning as in[1] 1001 and 1002 of Title 20.

(8) Interchange transaction fee

The term "interchange transaction fee" means any fee established, charged or received by a payment card network for the purpose of compensating an issuer for its involvement in an electronic debit transaction.

(9) Issuer

The term "issuer" means any person who issues a debit card, or credit card, or the agent of such person with respect to such card.

(10) Network fee

The term "network fee" means any fee charged and received by a payment card network with respect to an electronic debit transaction, other than an interchange transaction fee.

(11) Payment card network

The term "payment card network" means an entity that directly, or through licensed members, processors, or agents, provides the proprietary services, infrastructure, and software that route information and data to conduct debit card or credit card transaction authorization, clearance, and settlement, and that a person uses in order to accept as a form of payment a brand of debit card, credit card or other device that may be used to carry out debit or credit transactions.

(d) Enforcement

(1) In general

Compliance with the requirements imposed under this section shall be enforced under section 1693*o* of this title.

(2) Exception

Sections 1693m and 1693n of this title shall not apply with respect to this section or the requirements imposed pursuant to this section.

§ 1693p [CCPA § 921]. Reports to Congress

(a) Not later than twelve months after the effective date of this subchapter and at one-year intervals thereafter, the Bureau shall make reports to the Congress concerning the administration of its functions under this subchapter, including such recommendations as the Bureau deems necessary and appropriate. In addition, each report of the Bureau shall include its assessment of the extent to which compliance with this subchapter is being achieved, and a summary of the enforcement actions taken under section 1693*o* of this title. In such report, the Bureau shall particularly address the effects of this subchapter on the costs and benefits to financial institutions and consumers, on competition, on the introduction of new technology, on the operations of financial institutions, and on the adequacy of consumer protection.

(b) In the exercise of its functions under this subchapter, the Bureau may obtain upon request the views of any other Federal agency which, in the judgment of the Bureau, exercises regulatory or supervisory functions with respect to any class of persons subject to this subchapter.

---

1 So in original. Probably should say "Sections".

§ 1693q [CCPA § 922]. Relation to State laws

This subchapter does not annul, alter, or affect the laws of any State relating to electronic fund transfers, dormancy fees, inactivity charges or fees, service fees, or expiration dates of gift certificates, store gift cards, or general-use prepaid cards, except to the extent that those laws are inconsistent with the provisions of this subchapter, and then only to the extent of the inconsistency. A State law is not inconsistent with this subchapter if the protection such law affords any consumer is greater than the protection afforded by this subchapter. The Bureau shall, upon its own motion or upon the request of any financial institution, State, or other interested party, submitted in accordance with procedures prescribed in regulations of the Bureau, determine whether a State requirement is inconsistent or affords greater protection. If the Bureau determines that a State requirement is inconsistent, financial institutions shall incur no liability under the law of that State for a good faith failure to comply with that law, notwithstanding that such determination is subsequently amended, rescinded, or determined by judicial or other authority to be invalid for any reason. This subchapter does not extend the applicability of any such law to any class of persons or transactions to which it would not otherwise apply.

§ 1693r [CCPA § 923]. Exemption for State regulation

The Bureau shall by regulation exempt from the requirements of this subchapter any class of electronic fund transfers within any State if the Bureau determines that under the law of that State that class of electronic fund transfers is subject to requirements substantially similar to those imposed by this subchapter, and that there is adequate provision for enforcement.

TRUTH IN LENDING (REGULATION Z)

12 C.F.R. Part 1026

Table of Sections

SUBPART A: GENERAL

§ 1026.1. Authority, purpose, coverage, organization, enforcement, and liability

(a) Authority. This part, known as Regulation Z, is issued by the Bureau of Consumer Financial Protection to implement the Federal Truth in Lending Act, which is contained in title I of the Consumer Credit Protection Act, as amended (15 U.S.C. 1601 et seq.). This part also implements title XII, section 1204 of the Competitive Equality Banking Act of 1987 (Pub.L. 100–86, 101 Stat. 552). Furthermore, this part implements certain provisions of the Real Estate Settlement Procedures Act of 1974, as amended (12 U.S.C. 2601 et seq.). In addition, this part implements certain provisions of the Financial Institutions Reform, Recovery, and Enforcement Act, as amended (12 U.S.C. 3331 et seq.).The Bureau's information-collection requirements contained in this part have been approved by the Office of Management and Budget (OMB) under the provisions of 44 U.S.C. 3501 et seq. and have been assigned OMB No. 3170–0015 (Truth in Lending).

(b) Purpose. The purpose of this part is to promote the informed use of consumer credit by requiring disclosures about its terms and cost, to ensure that consumers are provided with greater and more timely information on the nature and costs of the residential real estate settlement process, and to effect certain changes in the settlement process for residential real estate that will result in more effective advance disclosure to home buyers and sellers of settlement costs. The regulation also includes substantive protections. It gives consumers the right to cancel certain credit transactions that involve a lien on a consumer's principal dwelling, regulates certain credit card practices, and provides a means for fair and timely resolution of credit billing disputes. The regulation does not generally govern charges for consumer credit, except that several provisions in subpart G set forth special rules addressing certain charges applicable to credit card accounts under an open-end (not home-secured) consumer credit plan. The regulation requires a maximum interest rate to be stated in variable-rate contracts secured by the consumer's dwelling. It also imposes limitations on home-equity plans that are subject to the requirements of § 1026.40 and mortgages that are subject to the requirements of § 1026.32. The regulation prohibits certain acts or practices in connection with credit secured by a dwelling in § 1026.36, and credit secured by a consumer's principal dwelling in § 1026.35. The regulation also regulates certain practices of creditors who extend private education loans as defined in § 1026.46(b)(5). In addition, it imposes certain limitations on increases in costs for mortgage transactions subject to § 1026.19(e) and (f).

(c) Coverage.

(1) In general, this part applies to each individual or business that offers or extends credit, other than a person excluded from coverage of this part by section 1029 of the Consumer Financial Protection Act of 2010, Title X of the Dodd-Frank Wall Street Reform and Consumer Protection Act, Public Law 111–203, 124 Stat. 1376, when four conditions are met:

(i) The credit is offered or extended to consumers;

(ii) The offering or extension of credit is done regularly;

(iii) The credit is subject to a finance charge or is payable by a written agreement in more than four installments; and

(iv) The credit is primarily for personal, family, or household purposes.

(2) If a credit card is involved, however, certain provisions apply even if the credit is not subject to a finance charge, or is not payable by a written agreement in more than four installments, or if the credit card is to be used for business purposes.

(3) In addition, certain requirements of § 1026.40 apply to persons who are not creditors but who provide applications for home-equity plans to consumers.

(4) Furthermore, certain requirements of § 1026.57 apply to institutions of higher education.

(5) Except in transactions subject to § 1026.19(e) and (f), no person is required to provide the disclosures required by sections 128(a)(16) through (19), 128(b)(4), 129C(f)(1), 129C(g)(2) and (3), 129D(h), or 129D(j)(1)(A) of the Truth in Lending Act, section 4(c) of the Real Estate Settlement Procedures Act, or the disclosure required prior to settlement by section 129C(h) of the Truth in Lending Act. Except in transactions subject to § 1026.20(e), no person is required to provide the disclosure required by section 129D(j)(1)(B) of the Truth in Lending Act. Except in transactions subject to § 1026.39(d)(5), no person becoming a creditor with respect to an existing residential mortgage loan is required to provide the disclosure required by section 129C(h) of the Truth in Lending Act.

(d) Organization. The regulation is divided into subparts and appendices as follows:

(1) Subpart A contains general information. It sets forth:

(i) The authority, purpose, coverage, and organization of the regulation;

(ii) The definitions of basic terms;

(iii) The transactions that are exempt from coverage; and

(iv) The method of determining the finance charge.

(2) Subpart B contains the rules for open-end credit. It requires that account-opening disclosures and periodic statements be provided, as well as additional disclosures for credit and charge card applications and solicitations and for home-equity plans subject to the requirements of § 1026.60 and § 1026.40, respectively. It also describes special rules that apply to credit card transactions, treatment of payments and credit balances, procedures for resolving credit billing errors, annual percentage rate calculations, rescission requirements, and advertising.

(3) Subpart C relates to closed-end credit. It contains rules on disclosures, treatment of credit balances, annual percentage rate calculations, rescission requirements, and advertising.

(4) Subpart D contains rules on oral disclosures, disclosures in languages other than English, record retention, effect on state laws, state exemptions, and rate limitations.

(5) Subpart E contains special rules for mortgage transactions. Section 1026.32 requires certain disclosures and provides limitations for closed-end credit transactions and open-end credit plans that have rates or fees above specified amounts or certain prepayment penalties. Section 1026.33 requires special disclosures, including the total annual loan cost rate, for reverse mortgage transactions. Section 1026.34 prohibits specific acts and practices in connection with high-cost mortgages, as defined in § 1026.32(a). Section 1026.35 prohibits specific acts and practices in connection with closed-end higher-priced mortgage loans, as defined in § 1026.35(a). Section 1026.36 prohibits specific acts and practices in connection with an extension of credit secured by a dwelling. Sections 1026.37 and 1026.38 set forth special disclosure requirements for certain closed-end transactions secured by real property or a cooperative unit, as required by § 1026.19(e) and (f).

(6) Subpart F relates to private education loans. It contains rules on disclosures, limitations on changes in terms after approval, the right to cancel the loan, and limitations on co-branding in the marketing of private education loans.

(7) Subpart G relates to credit card accounts under an open-end (not home-secured) consumer credit plan (except for § 1026.57(c), which applies to all open-end credit plans). Section 1026.51 contains rules on evaluation of a consumer's ability to make the required payments under the terms of an account. Section 1026.52 limits the fees that a consumer can be required to pay with respect to an open-end (not home-secured) consumer credit plan during the first year after account opening. Section 1026.53 contains rules on allocation of payments in excess of the minimum payment. Section 1026.54 sets forth certain limitations on the imposition of finance charges as the result of a loss of a grace period. Section 1026.55 contains limitations on increases in annual percentage rates, fees, and charges for credit card accounts. Section 1026.56 prohibits the assessment of fees or charges for over-the-limit transactions unless the consumer affirmatively consents to the creditor's payment of over-the-limit transactions. Section 1026.57 sets forth rules for reporting and marketing of college student open-end credit. Section 1026.58 sets forth requirements for the Internet posting of credit card accounts under an open-end (not home-secured) consumer credit plan.

(8) Several appendices contain information such as the procedures for determinations about state laws, state exemptions and issuance of official interpretations, special rules for certain kinds of credit plans, and the rules for computing annual percentage rates in closed-end credit transactions and total-annual-loan-cost rates for reverse mortgage transactions.

(e) Enforcement and liability. Section 108 of the Truth in Lending Act contains the administrative enforcement provisions for that Act. Sections 112, 113, 130, 131, and 134 contain provisions relating to liability for failure to comply with the requirements of the Truth in Lending Act and the regulation. Section 1204(c) of title XII of the Competitive Equality Banking Act of 1987, Public Law 100–86, 101 Stat. 552, incorporates by reference administrative enforcement and civil liability provisions of sections 108 and 130 of the Truth in Lending Act. Section 19 of the Real Estate Settlement Procedures Act contains the administrative enforcement provisions for that Act.

§ 1026.2. Definitions and Rules of Construction

(a) Definitions. For purposes of this part, the following definitions apply:

(1) Act means the Truth in Lending Act (15 U.S.C. 1601 et seq.).

(2) Advertisement means a commercial message in any medium that promotes, directly or indirectly, a credit transaction.

(3)(i) Application means the submission of a consumer's financial information for the purposes of obtaining an extension of credit.

(ii) For transactions subject to § 1026.19(e), (f), or (g) of this part, an application consists of the submission of the consumer's name, the consumer's income, the consumer's social security number to obtain a credit report, the property address, an estimate of the value of the property, and the mortgage loan amount sought.

(4) Billing cycle or cycle means the interval between the days or dates of regular periodic statements. These intervals shall be equal and no longer than a quarter of a year. An interval will be considered equal if the number of days in the cycle does not vary more than four days from the regular day or date of the periodic statement.

(5) Bureau means the Bureau of Consumer Financial Protection.

(6) Business day means a day on which the creditor's offices are open to the public for carrying on substantially all of its business functions. However, for purposes of rescission under §§ 1026.15 and 1026.23, and for purposes of §§ 1026.19(a)(1)(ii), 1026.19(a)(2), 1026.19(e)(1)(iii)(B), 1026.19(e)(1)(iv), 1026.19(e)(2)(i)(A), 1026.19(e)(4)(ii), 1026.19(f)(1)(ii), 1026.19(f)(1)(iii), 1026.20(e)(5), 1026.31, and 1026.46(d)(4), the term means all calendar days except Sundays and the legal public holidays specified in 5 U.S.C. 6103(a), such as New Year's Day, the Birthday of Martin Luther King, Jr., Washington's Birthday, Memorial Day, Independence Day, Labor Day, Columbus Day, Veterans Day, Thanksgiving Day, and Christmas Day.

(7) Card issuer means a person that issues a credit card or that person's agent with respect to the card.

(8) Cardholder means a natural person to whom a credit card is issued for consumer credit purposes, or a natural person who has agreed with the card issuer to pay consumer credit obligations arising from the issuance of a credit card to another natural person. For purposes of § 1026.12(a) and (b), the term includes any person to whom a credit card is issued for any purpose, including business, commercial or agricultural use, or a person who has agreed with the card issuer to pay obligations arising from the issuance of such a credit card to another person.

(9) Cash price means the price at which a creditor, in the ordinary course of business, offers to sell for cash property or service that is the subject of the transaction. At the creditor's option, the term may include the price of accessories, services related to the sale, service contracts and taxes and fees for license, title, and registration. The term does not include any finance charge.

(10) Closed-end credit means consumer credit other than "open-end credit" as defined in this section.

(11) Consumer means a cardholder or natural person to whom consumer credit is offered or extended. However, for purposes of rescission under §§ 1026.15 and 1026.23, the term also includes a natural person in whose principal dwelling a security interest is or will be retained or acquired, if that person's ownership interest in the dwelling is or will be subject to the security interest. For purposes of §§ 1026.20(c) through (e), 1026.36(c), 1026.39, and 1026.41, the term includes a confirmed successor in interest.

(12) Consumer credit means credit offered or extended to a consumer primarily for personal, family, or household purposes.

(13) Consummation means the time that a consumer becomes contractually obligated on a credit transaction.

(14) Credit means the right to defer payment of debt or to incur debt and defer its payment.

(15)(i) Credit card means any card, plate, or other single credit device that may be used from time to time to obtain credit. The term credit card includes a hybrid prepaid-credit card as defined in § 1026.61.

(ii) Credit card account under an open-end (not home-secured) consumer credit plan means any open-end credit account that is accessed by a credit card, except:

(A) A home-equity plan subject to the requirements of § 1026.40 that is accessed by a credit card;

(B) An overdraft line of credit that is accessed by a debit card; or

(C) An overdraft line of credit that is accessed by an account number, except if the account number is a hybrid prepaid-credit card that can access a covered separate credit feature as defined in § 1026.61.

(iii) Charge card means a credit card on an account for which no periodic rate is used to compute a finance charge.

(iv) Debit card means any card, plate, or other single device that may be used from time to time to access an asset account other than a prepaid account as defined in § 1026.61. The term debit card does not include a prepaid card as defined in § 1026.61.

(16) Credit sale means a sale in which the seller is a creditor. The term includes a bailment or lease (unless terminable without penalty at any time by the consumer) under which the consumer:

(i) Agrees to pay as compensation for use a sum substantially equivalent to, or in excess of, the total value of the property and service involved; and

(ii) Will become (or has the option to become), for no additional consideration or for nominal consideration, the owner of the property upon compliance with the agreement.

(17) Creditor means:

(i) A person who regularly extends consumer credit that is subject to a finance charge or is payable by written agreement in more than four installments (not including a down payment), and to whom the obligation is initially payable, either on the face of the note or contract, or by agreement when there is no note or contract.

(ii) For purposes of §§ 1026.4(c)(8) (Discounts), 1026.9(d) (Finance charge imposed at time of transaction), and 1026.12(e) (Prompt notification of returns and crediting of refunds), a person that honors a credit card.

(iii) For purposes of subpart B, any card issuer that extends either open-end credit or credit that is not subject to a finance charge and is not payable by written agreement in more than four installments.

(iv) For purposes of subpart B (except for the credit and charge card disclosures contained in §§ 1026.60 and 1026.9(e) and (f), the finance charge disclosures contained in § 1026.6(a)(1) and (b)(3)(i) and § 1026.7(a)(4) through (7) and (b)(4) through (6) and the right of rescission set forth in § 1026.15) and subpart C, any card issuer that extends closed-end credit that is subject to a finance charge or is payable by written agreement in more than four installments.

(v) A person regularly extends consumer credit only if it extended credit (other than credit subject to the requirements of § 1026.32) more than 25 times (or more than 5 times for transactions secured by a dwelling) in the preceding calendar year. If a person did not meet these numerical standards in the preceding calendar year, the numerical standards shall be applied to the current calendar year. A person regularly extends consumer credit if, in any 12-month period, the person originates more than one credit extension that is subject to the requirements of § 1026.32 or one or more such credit extensions through a mortgage broker.

(18) Downpayment means an amount, including the value of property used as a trade-in, paid to a seller to reduce the cash price of goods or services purchased in a credit sale transaction. A deferred portion of a downpayment may be treated as part of the downpayment if it is payable not later than the due date of the second otherwise regularly scheduled payment and is not subject to a finance charge.

(19) Dwelling means a residential structure that contains one to four units, whether or not that structure is attached to real property. The term includes an individual condominium unit, cooperative unit, mobile home, and trailer, if it is used as a residence.

(20) Open-end credit means consumer credit extended by a creditor under a plan in which:

(i) The creditor reasonably contemplates repeated transactions;

(ii) The creditor may impose a finance charge from time to time on an outstanding unpaid balance; and

(iii) The amount of credit that may be extended to the consumer during the term of the plan (up to any limit set by the creditor) is generally made available to the extent that any outstanding balance is repaid.

(21) Periodic rate means a rate of finance charge that is or may be imposed by a creditor on a balance for a day, week, month, or other subdivision of a year.

(22) Person means a natural person or an organization, including a corporation, partnership, proprietorship, association, cooperative, estate, trust, or government unit.

(23) Prepaid finance charge means any finance charge paid separately in cash or by check before or at consummation of a transaction, or withheld from the proceeds of the credit at any time.

(24) Residential mortgage transaction means a transaction in which a mortgage, deed of trust, purchase money security interest arising under an installment sales contract, or equivalent consensual security interest is created or retained in the consumer's principal dwelling to finance the acquisition or initial construction of that dwelling.

(25) Security interest means an interest in property that secures performance of a consumer credit obligation and that is recognized by State or Federal law. It does not include incidental interests such as interests in proceeds, accessions, additions, fixtures, insurance proceeds (whether or not the creditor is a loss payee or beneficiary), premium rebates, or interests in after-acquired property. For purposes of disclosures under §§ 1026.6, 1026.18, 1026.19(e) and (f), and 1026.38(*l*)(6), the term does not include an interest that arises solely by operation of law. However, for purposes of the right of rescission under §§ 1026.15 and 1026.23, the term does include interests that arise solely by operation of law.

(26) State means any state, the District of Columbia, the Commonwealth of Puerto Rico, and any territory or possession of the United States.

(27)(i) Successor in interest means a person to whom an ownership interest in a dwelling securing a closed-end consumer credit transaction is transferred from a consumer, provided that the transfer is:

(A) A transfer by devise, descent, or operation of law on the death of a joint tenant or tenant by the entirety;

(B) A transfer to a relative resulting from the death of the consumer;

(C) A transfer where the spouse or children of the consumer become an owner of the property;

(D) A transfer resulting from a decree of a dissolution of marriage, legal separation agreement, or from an incidental property settlement agreement, by which the spouse of the consumer becomes an owner of the property; or

(E) A transfer into an inter vivos trust in which the consumer is and remains a beneficiary and which does not relate to a transfer of rights of occupancy in the property.

(ii) Confirmed successor in interest means a successor in interest once a servicer has confirmed the successor in interest's identity and ownership interest in the dwelling.

(b) Rules of construction. For purposes of this part, the following rules of construction apply:

(1) Where appropriate, the singular form of a word includes the plural form and plural includes singular.

(2) Where the words obligation and transaction are used in the regulation, they refer to a consumer credit obligation or transaction, depending upon the context. Where the word credit is used in the regulation, it means consumer credit unless the context clearly indicates otherwise.

(3) Unless defined in this part, the words used have the meanings given to them by state law or contract.

(4) Where the word amount is used in this part to describe disclosure requirements, it refers to a numerical amount.

§ 1026.3. Exempt transactions

The following transactions are not subject to this part or, if the exemption is limited to specified provisions of this part, are not subject to those provisions:

(a) Business, commercial, agricultural, or organizational credit.

(1) An extension of credit primarily for a business, commercial or agricultural purpose.

(2) An extension of credit to other than a natural person, including credit to government agencies or instrumentalities.

(b) Credit over applicable threshold amount.

(1) Exemption.

(i) Requirements. An extension of credit in which the amount of credit extended exceeds the applicable threshold amount or in which there is an express written commitment to extend credit in excess of the applicable threshold amount, unless the extension of credit is:

(A) Secured by any real property, or by personal property used or expected to be used as the principal dwelling of the consumer; or

(B) A private education loan as defined in § 1026.46(b)(5).

(ii) Annual adjustments. The threshold amount in paragraph (b)(1)(i) of this section is adjusted annually to reflect increases in the Consumer Price Index for Urban Wage Earners and Clerical Workers, as applicable. See the official commentary to this paragraph (b) for the threshold amount applicable to a specific extension of credit or express written commitment to extend credit.

(2) Transition rule for open-end accounts exempt prior to July 21, 2011. An open-end account that is exempt on July 20, 2011 based on an express written commitment to extend credit in excess of $25,000 remains exempt until December 31, 2011 unless:

(i) The creditor takes a security interest in any real property, or in personal property used or expected to be used as the principal dwelling of the consumer; or

(ii) The creditor reduces the express written commitment to extend credit to $25,000 or less.

(c) Public utility credit. An extension of credit that involves public utility services provided through pipe, wire, other connected facilities, or radio or similar transmission (including extensions of such facilities), if the charges for service, delayed payment, or any discounts for prompt payment are filed with or regulated by any government unit. The financing of durable goods or home improvements by a public utility is not exempt.

(d) Securities or commodities accounts. Transactions in securities or commodities accounts in which credit is extended by a broker-dealer registered with the Securities and Exchange Commission or the Commodity Futures Trading Commission.

(e) Home fuel budget plans. An installment agreement for the purchase of home fuels in which no finance charge is imposed.

(f) Student loan programs. Loans made, insured, or guaranteed pursuant to a program authorized by Title IV of the Higher Education Act of 1965 (20 U.S.C. 1070 et seq.).

(g) Employer-sponsored retirement plans. An extension of credit to a participant in an employer-sponsored retirement plan qualified under section 401(a) of the Internal Revenue Code, a tax-sheltered annuity under section 403(b) of the Internal Revenue Code, or an eligible governmental deferred compensation plan under section 457(b) of the Internal Revenue Code (26 U.S.C. 401(a); 26 U.S.C. 403(b); 26 U.S.C. 457(b)), provided that the extension of credit is comprised of fully vested funds from such participant's account and is made in compliance with the Internal Revenue Code (26 U.S.C. 1 et seq.).

(h) Partial exemption for certain mortgage loans. The special disclosure requirements in § 1026.19(g) and, unless the creditor chooses to provide the disclosures described in § 1026.19(e) and (f), in § 1026.19(e) and (f) do not apply to a transaction that satisfies all of the following criteria:

(1) The transaction is secured by a subordinate lien;

(2) The transaction is for the purpose of:

(i) Downpayment, closing costs, or other similar home buyer assistance, such as principal or interest subsidies;

(ii) Property rehabilitation assistance;

(iii) Energy efficiency assistance; or

(iv) Foreclosure avoidance or prevention;

(3) The credit contract does not require the payment of interest;

(4) The credit contract provides that repayment of the amount of credit extended is:

(i) Forgiven either incrementally or in whole, at a date certain, and subject only to specified ownership and occupancy conditions, such as a requirement that the consumer maintain the property as the consumer's principal dwelling for five years;

(ii) Deferred for a minimum of 20 years after consummation of the transaction;

(iii) Deferred until sale of the property securing the transaction; or

(iv) Deferred until the property securing the transaction is no longer the principal dwelling of the consumer;

(5)(i) The costs payable by the consumer in connection with the transaction at consummation are limited to:

(A) Recording fees;

(B) Transfer taxes;

(C) A bona fide and reasonable application fee; and

(D) A bona fide and reasonable fee for housing counseling services; and

(ii) The total of costs payable by the consumer under paragraph (h)(5)(i)(C) and (D) of this section is less than 1 percent of the amount of credit extended; and

(6) The following disclosures are provided:

(i) Disclosures described in § 1026.18 that comply with this part; or

(ii) Alternatively, disclosures described in § 1026.19(e) and (f) that comply with this part.

§ 1026.4. Finance Charge

(a) Definition. The finance charge is the cost of consumer credit as a dollar amount. It includes any charge payable directly or indirectly by the consumer and imposed directly or indirectly by the creditor as an incident to or a condition of the extension of credit. It does not include any charge of a type payable in a comparable cash transaction.

(1) Charges by third parties. The finance charge includes fees and amounts charged by someone other than the creditor, unless otherwise excluded under this section, if the creditor:

(i) Requires the use of a third party as a condition of or an incident to the extension of credit, even if the consumer can choose the third party; or

(ii) Retains a portion of the third-party charge, to the extent of the portion retained.

(2) Special rule; closing agent charges. Fees charged by a third party that conducts the loan closing (such as a settlement agent, attorney, or escrow or title company) are finance charges only if the creditor:

(i) Requires the particular services for which the consumer is charged;

(ii) Requires the imposition of the charge; or

(iii) Retains a portion of the third-party charge, to the extent of the portion retained.

(3) Special rule; mortgage broker fees. Fees charged by a mortgage broker (including fees paid by the consumer directly to the broker or to the creditor for delivery to the broker) are finance charges even if the creditor does not require the consumer to use a mortgage broker and even if the creditor does not retain any portion of the charge.

(b) Examples of finance charges. The finance charge includes the following types of charges, except for charges specifically excluded by paragraphs (c) through (e) of this section:

(1) Interest, time price differential, and any amount payable under an add-on or discount system of additional charges.

(2) Service, transaction, activity, and carrying charges, including any charge imposed on a checking or other transaction account (except a prepaid account as defined in § 1026.61) to the extent that the charge exceeds the charge for a similar account without a credit feature.

(3) Points, loan fees, assumption fees, finder's fees, and similar charges.

(4) Appraisal, investigation, and credit report fees.

(5) Premiums or other charges for any guarantee or insurance protecting the creditor against the consumer's default or other credit loss.

(6) Charges imposed on a creditor by another person for purchasing or accepting a consumer's obligation, if the consumer is required to pay the charges in cash, as an addition to the obligation, or as a deduction from the proceeds of the obligation.

(7) Premiums or other charges for credit life, accident, health, or loss-of-income insurance, written in connection with a credit transaction.

(8) Premiums or other charges for insurance against loss of or damage to property, or against liability arising out of the ownership or use of property, written in connection with a credit transaction.

(9) Discounts for the purpose of inducing payment by a means other than the use of credit.

(10) Charges or premiums paid for debt cancellation or debt suspension coverage written in connection with a credit transaction, whether or not the coverage is insurance under applicable law.

(11) With regard to a covered separate credit feature and an asset feature on a prepaid account that are both accessible by a hybrid prepaid-credit card as defined in § 1026.61:

(i) Any fee or charge described in paragraphs (b)(1) through (10) of this section imposed on the covered separate credit feature, whether it is structured as a credit subaccount of the prepaid account or a separate credit account.

(ii) Any fee or charge imposed on the asset feature of the prepaid account to the extent that the amount of the fee or charge exceeds comparable fees or charges imposed on prepaid accounts in the same prepaid account program that do not have a covered separate credit feature accessible by a hybrid prepaid-credit card.

(c) Charges excluded from the finance charge. The following charges are not finance charges:

(1) Application fees charged to all applicants for credit, whether or not credit is actually extended.

(2) Charges for actual unanticipated late payment, for exceeding a credit limit, or for delinquency, default, or a similar occurrence.

(3) Charges imposed by a financial institution for paying items that overdraw an account, unless the payment of such items and the imposition of the charge were previously agreed upon in writing. This paragraph does not apply to credit offered in connection with a prepaid account as defined in § 1026.61.

(4) Fees charged for participation in a credit plan, whether assessed on an annual or other periodic basis. This paragraph does not apply to a fee to participate in a covered separate credit feature accessible by a hybrid prepaid-credit card as defined in § 1026.61, regardless of whether this fee is imposed on the credit feature or on the asset feature of the prepaid account.

(5) Seller's points.

(6) Interest forfeited as a result of an interest reduction required by law on a time deposit used as security for an extension of credit.

(7) Real-estate related fees. The following fees in a transaction secured by real property or in a residential mortgage transaction, if the fees are bona fide and reasonable in amount:

(i) Fees for title examination, abstract of title, title insurance, property survey, and similar purposes.

(ii) Fees for preparing loan-related documents, such as deeds, mortgages, and reconveyance or settlement documents.

(iii) Notary and credit-report fees.

(iv) Property appraisal fees or fees for inspections to assess the value or condition of the property if the service is performed prior to closing, including fees related to pest-infestation or flood-hazard determinations.

(v) Amounts required to be paid into escrow or trustee accounts if the amounts would not otherwise be included in the finance charge.

(8) Discounts offered to induce payment for a purchase by cash, check, or other means, as provided in section 167(b) of the Act.

(d) Insurance and debt cancellation and debt suspension coverage—

(1) Voluntary credit insurance premiums. Premiums for credit life, accident, health, or loss-of-income insurance may be excluded from the finance charge if the following conditions are met:

(i) The insurance coverage is not required by the creditor, and this fact is disclosed in writing.

(ii) The premium for the initial term of insurance coverage is disclosed in writing. If the term of insurance is less than the term of the transaction, the term of insurance also shall be disclosed. The premium may be disclosed on a unit-cost basis only in open-end credit transactions, closed-end credit transactions by mail or telephone under § 1026.17(g), and certain closed-end credit transactions involving an insurance plan that limits the total amount of indebtedness subject to coverage.

(iii) The consumer signs or initials an affirmative written request for the insurance after receiving the disclosures specified in this paragraph, except as provided in paragraph (d)(4) of this section. Any consumer in the transaction may sign or initial the request.

(2) Property insurance premiums. Premiums for insurance against loss of or damage to property, or against liability arising out of the ownership or use of property, including single interest insurance if the insurer waives all right of subrogation against the consumer, may be excluded from the finance charge if the following conditions are met:

(i) The insurance coverage may be obtained from a person of the consumer's choice, and this fact is disclosed. (A creditor may reserve the right to refuse to accept, for reasonable cause, an insurer offered by the consumer.)

(ii) If the coverage is obtained from or through the creditor, the premium for the initial term of insurance coverage shall be disclosed. If the term of insurance is less than the term of the transaction, the term of insurance shall also be disclosed. The premium may be disclosed on a unit-cost basis only in open-end credit transactions, closed-end credit transactions by mail or telephone under § 1026.17(g), and certain closed-end credit transactions involving an insurance plan that limits the total amount of indebtedness subject to coverage.

(3) Voluntary debt cancellation or debt suspension fees. Charges or premiums paid for debt cancellation coverage for amounts exceeding the value of the collateral securing the obligation or for debt cancellation or debt suspension coverage in the event of the loss of life, health, or income or in case of accident may be excluded from the finance charge, whether or not the coverage is insurance, if the following conditions are met:

(i) The debt cancellation or debt suspension agreement or coverage is not required by the creditor, and this fact is disclosed in writing;

(ii) The fee or premium for the initial term of coverage is disclosed in writing. If the term of coverage is less than the term of the credit transaction, the term of coverage also shall be disclosed. The fee or premium may be disclosed on a unit-cost basis only in open-end credit transactions, closed-end credit transactions by mail or telephone under

§ 1026.17(g), and certain closed-end credit transactions involving a debt cancellation agreement that limits the total amount of indebtedness subject to coverage;

(iii) The following are disclosed, as applicable, for debt suspension coverage: That the obligation to pay loan principal and interest is only suspended, and that interest will continue to accrue during the period of suspension.

(iv) The consumer signs or initials an affirmative written request for coverage after receiving the disclosures specified in this paragraph, except as provided in paragraph (d)(4) of this section. Any consumer in the transaction may sign or initial the request.

(4) Telephone purchases. If a consumer purchases credit insurance or debt cancellation or debt suspension coverage for an open-end (not home-secured) plan by telephone, the creditor must make the disclosures under paragraphs (d)(1)(i) and (ii) or (d)(3)(i) through (iii) of this section, as applicable, orally. In such a case, the creditor shall:

(i) Maintain evidence that the consumer, after being provided the disclosures orally, affirmatively elected to purchase the insurance or coverage; and

(ii) Mail the disclosures under paragraphs (d)(1)(i) and (ii) or (d)(3)(i) through (iii) of this section, as applicable, within three business days after the telephone purchase.

(e) Certain security interest charges. If itemized and disclosed, the following charges may be excluded from the finance charge:

(1) Taxes and fees prescribed by law that actually are or will be paid to public officials for determining the existence of or for perfecting, releasing, or satisfying a security interest.

(2) The premium for insurance in lieu of perfecting a security interest to the extent that the premium does not exceed the fees described in paragraph (e)(1) of this section that otherwise would be payable.

(3) Taxes on security instruments. Any tax levied on security instruments or on documents evidencing indebtedness if the payment of such taxes is a requirement for recording the instrument securing the evidence of indebtedness.

(f) Prohibited offsets. Interest, dividends, or other income received or to be received by the consumer on deposits or investments shall not be deducted in computing the finance charge.

SUBPART B: OPEN-END CREDIT

§ 1026.5. General disclosure requirements

(a) Form of disclosures—

(1) General.

(i) The creditor shall make the disclosures required by this subpart clearly and conspicuously.

(ii) The creditor shall make the disclosures required by this subpart in writing, in a form that the consumer may keep, except that:

(A) The following disclosures need not be written: Disclosures under § 1026.6(b)(3) of charges that are imposed as part of an open-end (not home-secured) plan that are not required to be disclosed under § 1026.6(b)(2) and related disclosures of charges under § 1026.9(c)(2)(iii)(B); disclosures under § 1026.9(c)(2)(vi); disclosures under § 1026.9(d) when a finance charge is imposed at the time of the transaction; and disclosures under § 1026.56(b)(1)(i).

(B) The following disclosures need not be in a retainable form: Disclosures that need not be written under paragraph (a)(1)(ii)(A) of this section; disclosures for credit and charge card applications and solicitations under § 1026.60; home-equity disclosures under § 1026.40(d); the alternative summary billing-rights statement under § 1026.9(a)(2); the credit and charge card renewal disclosures required under § 1026.9(e); and the payment requirements under § 1026.10(b), except as provided in § 1026.7(b)(13).

(iii) The disclosures required by this subpart may be provided to the consumer in electronic form, subject to compliance with the consumer consent and other applicable provisions of the Electronic Signatures in Global and National Commerce Act (E-Sign Act) (15 U.S.C. 7001 et seq.). The disclosures required by §§ 1026.60, 1026.40, and 1026.16 may be provided to the consumer in electronic form without regard to the consumer consent or other provisions of the E-Sign Act in the circumstances set forth in those sections.

(2) Terminology.

(i) Terminology used in providing the disclosures required by this subpart shall be consistent.

(ii) For home-equity plans subject to § 1026.40, the terms finance charge and annual percentage rate, when required to be disclosed with a corresponding amount or percentage rate, shall be more conspicuous than any other required disclosure. The terms need not be more conspicuous when used for periodic statement disclosures under § 1026.7(a)(4) and for advertisements under § 1026.16.

(iii) If disclosures are required to be presented in a tabular format pursuant to paragraph (a)(3) of this section, the term penalty APR shall be used, as applicable. The term penalty APR need not be used in reference to the annual percentage rate that applies with the loss of a promotional rate, assuming the annual percentage rate that applies is not greater than the annual percentage rate that would have applied at the end of the promotional period; or if the annual percentage rate that applies with the loss of a promotional rate is a variable rate, the annual percentage rate is calculated using the same index and margin as would have been used to calculate the annual percentage rate that would have applied at the end of the promotional period. If credit insurance or debt cancellation or debt suspension coverage is required as part of the plan, the term required shall be used and the program shall be identified by its name. If an annual percentage rate is required to be presented in a tabular format pursuant to paragraph (a)(3)(i) or (a)(3)(iii) of this section, the term fixed, or a similar term, may not be used to describe such rate unless the creditor also specifies a time period that the rate will be fixed and the rate will not increase during that period, or if no such time period is provided, the rate will not increase while the plan is open.

(3) Specific formats.

(i) Certain disclosures for credit and charge card applications and solicitations must be provided in a tabular format in accordance with the requirements of § 1026.60(a)(2).

(ii) Certain disclosures for home-equity plans must precede other disclosures and must be given in accordance with the requirements of § 1026.40(a).

(iii) Certain account-opening disclosures must be provided in a tabular format in accordance with the requirements of § 1026.6(b)(1).

(iv) Certain disclosures provided on periodic statements must be grouped together in accordance with the requirements of § 1026.7(b)(6) and (b)(13).

(v) Certain disclosures provided on periodic statements must be given in accordance with the requirements of § 1026.7(b)(12).

(vi) Certain disclosures accompanying checks that access a credit card account must be provided in a tabular format in accordance with the requirements of § 1026.9(b)(3).

(vii) Certain disclosures provided in a change-in-terms notice must be provided in a tabular format in accordance with the requirements of § 1026.9(c)(2)(iv)(D).

(viii) Certain disclosures provided when a rate is increased due to delinquency, default or as a penalty must be provided in a tabular format in accordance with the requirements of § 1026.9(g)(3)(ii).

(b) Time of disclosures—

(1) Account-opening disclosures—

(i) General rule. The creditor shall furnish account-opening disclosures required by § 1026.6 before the first transaction is made under the plan.

(ii) Charges imposed as part of an open-end (not home-secured) plan. Charges that are imposed as part of an open-end (not home-secured) plan and are not required to be disclosed under § 1026.6(b)(2) may be disclosed after account opening but before the consumer agrees to pay or becomes obligated to pay for the charge, provided they are disclosed at a time and in a manner that a consumer would be likely to notice them. This provision does not apply to charges imposed as part of a home-equity plan subject to the requirements of § 1026.40.

(iii) Telephone purchases. Disclosures required by § 1026.6 may be provided as soon as reasonably practicable after the first transaction if:

(A) The first transaction occurs when a consumer contacts a merchant by telephone to purchase goods and at the same time the consumer accepts an offer to finance the purchase by establishing an open-end plan with the merchant or third-party creditor;

(B) The merchant or third-party creditor permits consumers to return any goods financed under the plan and provides consumers with a sufficient time to reject the plan and return the goods free of cost after the merchant or third-party creditor has provided the written disclosures required by § 1026.6; and

(C) The consumer's right to reject the plan and return the goods is disclosed to the consumer as a part of the offer to finance the purchase.

(iv) Membership fees—

(A) General. In general, a creditor may not collect any fee before account-opening disclosures are provided. A creditor may collect, or obtain the consumer's agreement to pay, membership fees, including application fees excludable from the finance charge under § 1026.4(c)(1), before providing account-opening disclosures if, after receiving the disclosures, the consumer may reject the plan and have no obligation to pay these fees (including application fees) or any other fee or charge. A membership fee for purposes of this paragraph has the same meaning as a fee for the issuance or availability of credit described in § 1026.60(b)(2). If the consumer rejects the plan, the creditor must promptly refund the membership fee if it has been paid, or take other action necessary to ensure the consumer is not obligated to pay that fee or any other fee or charge.

(B) Home-equity plans. Creditors offering home-equity plans subject to the requirements of § 1026.40 are not subject to the requirements of paragraph (b)(1)(iv)(A) of this section.

(v) Application fees. A creditor may collect an application fee excludable from the finance charge under § 1026.4(c)(1) before providing account-opening disclosures. However, if a consumer rejects the plan after receiving account-opening disclosures, the consumer must have no obligation to pay such an application fee, or if the fee was paid, it must be refunded. See § 1026.5(b)(1)(iv)(A).

(2) Periodic statements—

(i) Statement required. The creditor shall mail or deliver a periodic statement as required by § 1026.7 for each billing cycle at the end of which an account has a debit or credit balance of more than $1 or on which a finance charge has been imposed. A periodic statement need not be sent for an account if the creditor deems it uncollectible, if delinquency collection proceedings have been instituted, if the creditor has charged off the account in accordance with loan-loss provisions and will not charge any additional fees or interest on the account, or if furnishing the statement would violate Federal law.

(ii) Timing requirements—

(A) Credit card accounts under an open-end (not home-secured) consumer credit plan. For credit card accounts under an open-end (not home-secured) consumer credit plan, a card issuer must adopt reasonable procedures designed to ensure that:

(1) Periodic statements are mailed or delivered at least 21 days prior to the payment due date disclosed on the statement pursuant to § 1026.7(b)(11)(i)(A); and

(2) The card issuer does not treat as late for any purpose a required minimum periodic payment received by the card issuer within 21 days after mailing or delivery of the periodic statement disclosing the due date for that payment.

(B) Open-end consumer credit plans. For accounts under an open-end consumer credit plan, a creditor must adopt reasonable procedures designed to ensure that:

(1) If a grace period applies to the account:

(i) Periodic statements are mailed or delivered at least 21 days prior to the date on which the grace period expires; and

(ii) The creditor does not impose finance charges as a result of the loss of the grace period if a payment that satisfies the terms of the grace period is received by the creditor within 21 days after mailing or delivery of the periodic statement.

(2) Regardless of whether a grace period applies to the account:

(i) Periodic statements are mailed or delivered at least 14 days prior to the date on which the required minimum periodic payment must be received in order to avoid being treated as late for any purpose; and

(ii) The creditor does not treat as late for any purpose a required minimum periodic payment received by the creditor within 14 days after mailing or delivery of the periodic statement.

(3) For purposes of paragraph (b)(2)(ii)(B) of this section, "grace period" means a period within which any credit extended may be repaid without incurring a finance charge due to a periodic interest rate.

(3) Credit and charge card application and solicitation disclosures. The card issuer shall furnish the disclosures for credit and charge card applications and solicitations in accordance with the timing requirements of § 1026.60.

(4) Home-equity plans. Disclosures for home-equity plans shall be made in accordance with the timing requirements of § 1026.40(b).

(c) Basis of disclosures and use of estimates. Disclosures shall reflect the terms of the legal obligation between the parties. If any information necessary for accurate disclosure is unknown to the creditor, it shall make the disclosure based on the best information reasonably available and shall state clearly that the disclosure is an estimate.

(d) Multiple creditors; multiple consumers. If the credit plan involves more than one creditor, only one set of disclosures shall be given, and the creditors shall agree among themselves which creditor must comply with the requirements that this part imposes on any or all of them. If there is more than one consumer, the disclosures may be made to any consumer who is primarily liable on the account. If the right of rescission under § 1026.15 is applicable, however, the disclosures required by §§ 1026.6 and 1026.15(b) shall be made to each consumer having the right to rescind.

(e) Effect of subsequent events. If a disclosure becomes inaccurate because of an event that occurs after the creditor mails or delivers the disclosures, the resulting inaccuracy is not a violation of this part, although new disclosures may be required under § 1026.9(c).

§ 1026.6. Account-Opening Disclosures

(a) Rules affecting home-equity plans. The requirements of this paragraph (a) apply only to home-equity plans subject to the requirements of § 1026.40. A creditor shall disclose the items in this section, to the extent applicable:

(1) Finance charge. The circumstances under which a finance charge will be imposed and an explanation of how it will be determined, as follows:

(i) A statement of when finance charges begin to accrue, including an explanation of whether or not any time period exists within which any credit extended may be repaid without incurring a finance charge. If such a time period is provided, a creditor may, at its option and without disclosure, impose no finance charge when payment is received after the time period's expiration.

(ii) A disclosure of each periodic rate that may be used to compute the finance charge, the range of balances to which it is applicable, and the corresponding annual percentage rate. If a creditor offers a variable-rate plan, the creditor shall also disclose: The circumstances under which the rate(s) may increase; any limitations on the increase; and the effect(s) of an increase. When different periodic rates apply to different types of transactions, the types of transactions to which the periodic rates shall apply shall also be disclosed. A creditor is not required to adjust the range of balances disclosure to reflect the balance below which only a minimum charge applies.

(iii) An explanation of the method used to determine the balance on which the finance charge may be computed.

(iv) An explanation of how the amount of any finance charge will be determined, including a description of how any finance charge other than the periodic rate will be determined.

(2) Other charges. The amount of any charge other than a finance charge that may be imposed as part of the plan, or an explanation of how the charge will be determined.

(3) Home-equity plan information. The following disclosures described in § 1026.40(d), as applicable:

(i) A statement of the conditions under which the creditor may take certain action, as described in § 1026.40(d)(4)(i), such as terminating the plan or changing the terms.

(ii) The payment information described in § 1026.40(d)(5)(i) and (ii) for both the draw period and any repayment period.

(iii) A statement that negative amortization may occur as described in § 1026.40(d)(9).

(iv) A statement of any transaction requirements as described in § 1026.40(d)(10).

(v) A statement regarding the tax implications as described in § 1026.40(d)(11).

(vi) A statement that the annual percentage rate imposed under the plan does not include costs other than interest as described in § 1026.40(d)(6) and (d)(12)(ii).

(vii) The variable-rate disclosures described in § 1026.40(d)(12)(viii), (d)(12)(x), (d)(12)(xi), and (d)(12)(xii), as well as the disclosure described in § 1026.40(d)(5)(iii), unless the disclosures provided with the application were in a form the consumer could keep and included a representative payment example for the category of payment option chosen by the consumer.

(4) Security interests. The fact that the creditor has or will acquire a security interest in the property purchased under the plan, or in other property identified by item or type.

(5) Statement of billing rights. A statement that outlines the consumer's rights and the creditor's responsibilities under §§ 1026.12(c) and 1026.13 and that is substantially similar to the statement found in Model Form G-3 or, at the creditor's option, G-3(A), in appendix G to this part.

(b) Rules affecting open-end (not home-secured) plans. The requirements of paragraph (b) of this section apply to plans other than home-equity plans subject to the requirements of § 1026.40.

(1) Form of disclosures; tabular format for open-end (not home-secured) plans. Creditors must provide the account-opening disclosures specified in paragraph (b)(2)(i) through (b)(2)(v) (except for (b)(2)(i)(D)(2)) and (b)(2)(vii) through (b)(2)(xiv) of this section in the form of a table with the headings, content, and format substantially similar to any of the applicable tables in G-17 in appendix G.

(i) Highlighting. In the table, any annual percentage rate required to be disclosed pursuant to paragraph (b)(2)(i) of this section; any introductory rate permitted to be disclosed pursuant to paragraph (b)(2)(i)(B) or required to be disclosed under paragraph (b)(2)(i)(F) of this section, any rate that will apply after a premium initial rate expires permitted to be disclosed pursuant to paragraph (b)(2)(i)(C) or required to be disclosed pursuant to paragraph (b)(2)(i)(F), and any fee or percentage amounts or maximum limits on fee amounts disclosed pursuant to paragraphs (b)(2)(ii), (b)(2)(iv), (b)(2)(vii) through (b)(2)(xii) of this section must be disclosed in bold text. However, bold text shall not be used for: The amount of any periodic fee disclosed pursuant to paragraph (b)(2) of this section that is not an annualized amount; and other annual percentage rates or fee amounts disclosed in the table.

(ii) Location. Only the information required or permitted by paragraphs (b)(2)(i) through (v) (except for (b)(2)(i)(D)(2)) and (b)(2)(vii) through (xiv) of this section shall be in the table. Disclosures required by paragraphs (b)(2)(i)(D)(2), (b)(2)(i)(D)(3), (b)(2)(vi), and (b)(2)(xv) of this section shall be placed directly below the table. Disclosures required by paragraphs (b)(3) through (5) of this section that are not otherwise required to be in the table and other information may be presented with the account agreement or account-opening disclosure statement, provided such information appears outside the required table.

(iii) Fees that vary by state. Creditors that impose fees referred to in paragraphs (b)(2)(vii) through (b)(2)(xi) of this section that vary by state and that provide the disclosures required by paragraph (b) of this section in person at the time the open-end (not home-secured) plan is established in connection with financing the purchase of goods or services may, at the creditor's option, disclose in the account-opening table the specific fee applicable to the consumer's account, or the range of the fees, if the disclosure includes a statement that the amount of the fee varies by state and refers the consumer to the account agreement or other disclosure provided with the account-opening table where the amount of the fee applicable to the consumer's account is disclosed. A creditor may not list fees for multiple states in the account-opening summary table.

(iv) Fees based on a percentage. If the amount of any fee required to be disclosed under this section is determined on the basis of a percentage of another amount, the percentage used and the identification of the amount against which the percentage is applied may be disclosed instead of the amount of the fee.

(2) Required disclosures for account-opening table for open-end (not home-secured) plans. A creditor shall disclose the items in this section, to the extent applicable:

(i) Annual percentage rate. Each periodic rate that may be used to compute the finance charge on an outstanding balance for purchases, a cash advance, or a balance transfer, expressed as an annual percentage rate (as determined by § 1026.14(b)). When more than one rate applies for a category of transactions, the range of balances to which each rate is applicable shall also be disclosed. The annual percentage rate for purchases disclosed pursuant to this paragraph shall be in at least 16-point type, except for the following: A penalty rate that may apply upon the occurrence of one or more specific events.

(A) Variable-rate information. If a rate disclosed under paragraph (b)(2)(i) of this section is a variable rate, the creditor shall also disclose the fact that the rate may vary and how the rate is determined. In describing how the applicable rate will be determined, the creditor must identify the type of index or formula that is used in setting the rate. The value of the index and the amount of the margin that are used to calculate the variable rate shall not be disclosed in the table. A disclosure of any applicable limitations on rate increases or decreases shall not be included in the table.

(B) Discounted initial rates. If the initial rate is an introductory rate, as that term is defined in § 1026.16(g)(2)(ii), the creditor must disclose the rate that would otherwise apply to the account pursuant to paragraph (b)(2)(i) of this section. Where the rate is not tied to an index or formula, the creditor must disclose the rate that will apply after the introductory rate expires. In a variable-rate account, the creditor must disclose a rate based on the applicable index or formula in accordance with the accuracy requirements of paragraph (b)(4)(ii)(G) of this section. Except as provided in paragraph (b)(2)(i)(F) of this section, the creditor is not required to, but may disclose in the table the introductory rate along with the rate that would otherwise apply to the account if the creditor also discloses the time period during which the introductory rate will remain in effect, and uses the term "introductory" or "intro" in immediate proximity to the introductory rate.

(C) Premium initial rate. If the initial rate is temporary and is higher than the rate that will apply after the temporary rate expires, the creditor must disclose the premium initial rate pursuant to paragraph (b)(2)(i) of this section. Consistent with paragraph (b)(2)(i) of this section, the premium initial rate for purchases must be in at least 16-point type. Except as provided in paragraph (b)(2)(i)(F) of this section, the creditor is not required to, but may disclose in the table the rate that will apply after the premium initial rate expires if the creditor also discloses the time period during which the premium initial rate will remain in effect. If the creditor also discloses in the table the rate that will apply after the premium initial rate for purchases expires, that rate also must be in at least 16-point type.

(D) Penalty rates—

(1) In general. Except as provided in paragraph (b)(2)(i)(D)(2) and (b)(2)(i)(D)(3) of this section, if a rate may increase as a penalty for one or more events specified in the account agreement, such as a late payment or an extension of credit that exceeds the credit limit, the creditor must disclose pursuant to paragraph (b)(2)(i) of this section the increased rate that may apply, a brief description of the event or events that may result in the increased rate, and a brief description of how long the increased rate will remain in effect. If more than one penalty rate may apply, the creditor at its option may disclose the highest rate that could apply, instead of disclosing the specific rates or the range of rates that could apply.

(2) Introductory rates. If the creditor discloses in the table an introductory rate, as that term is defined in § 1026.16(g)(2)(ii), creditors must briefly disclose directly beneath the table the circumstances under which the introductory rate may be revoked, and the rate that will apply after the introductory rate is revoked.

(3) Employee preferential rates. If a creditor discloses in the table a preferential annual percentage rate for which only employees of the creditor, employees of a third party, or other individuals with similar affiliations with the creditor or third party, such as executive officers, directors, or principal shareholders are eligible, the creditor must briefly disclose directly beneath the table the circumstances under which such preferential rate may be revoked, and the rate that will apply after such preferential rate is revoked.

(E) Point of sale where APRs vary by state or based on creditworthiness. Creditors imposing annual percentage rates that vary by state or based on the consumer's creditworthiness and providing the disclosures required by paragraph (b) of this section in person at the time the open-end (not home-secured) plan is established in connection with financing the purchase of goods or services may, at the creditor's option, disclose pursuant to paragraph (b)(2)(i) of this section in the account-opening table:

(1) The specific annual percentage rate applicable to the consumer's account; or

(2) The range of the annual percentage rates, if the disclosure includes a statement that the annual percentage rate varies by state or will be determined based on the consumer's creditworthiness and refers the consumer to the account agreement or other disclosure provided with the account-opening table where the annual percentage rate applicable to the consumer's account is disclosed. A creditor may not list annual percentage rates for multiple states in the account-opening table.

(F) Credit card accounts under an open-end (not home-secured) consumer credit plan. Notwithstanding paragraphs (b)(2)(i)(B) and (b)(2)(i)(C) of this section, for credit card accounts under an open-end (not home-secured) plan, issuers must disclose in the table:

(1) Any introductory rate as that term is defined in § 1026.16(g)(2)(ii) that would apply to the account, consistent with the requirements of paragraph (b)(2)(i)(B) of this section, and

(2) Any rate that would apply upon the expiration of a premium initial rate, consistent with the requirements of paragraph (b)(2)(i)(C) of this section.

(ii) Fees for issuance or availability.

(A) Any annual or other periodic fee that may be imposed for the issuance or availability of an open-end plan, including any fee based on account activity or inactivity; how frequently it will be imposed; and the annualized amount of the fee.

(B) Any non-periodic fee that relates to opening the plan. A creditor must disclose that the fee is a one-time fee.

(iii) Fixed finance charge; minimum interest charge. Any fixed finance charge and a brief description of the charge. Any minimum interest charge if it exceeds $1.00 that could be imposed during a billing cycle, and a brief description of the charge. The $1.00

threshold amount shall be adjusted periodically by the Bureau to reflect changes in the Consumer Price Index. The Bureau shall calculate each year a price level adjusted minimum interest charge using the Consumer Price Index in effect on the June 1 of that year. When the cumulative change in the adjusted minimum value derived from applying the annual Consumer Price level to the current minimum interest charge threshold has risen by a whole dollar, the minimum interest charge will be increased by $1.00. The creditor may, at its option, disclose in the table minimum interest charges below this threshold.

(iv) Transaction charges. Any transaction charge imposed by the creditor for use of the open-end plan for purchases.

(v) Grace period. The date by which or the period within which any credit extended may be repaid without incurring a finance charge due to a periodic interest rate and any conditions on the availability of the grace period. If no grace period is provided, that fact must be disclosed. If the length of the grace period varies, the creditor may disclose the range of days, the minimum number of days, or the average number of the days in the grace period, if the disclosure is identified as a range, minimum, or average. In disclosing in the tabular format a grace period that applies to all features on the account, the phrase "How to Avoid Paying Interest" shall be used as the heading for the row describing the grace period. If a grace period is not offered on all features of the account, in disclosing this fact in the tabular format, the phrase "Paying Interest" shall be used as the heading for the row describing this fact.

(vi) Balance computation method. The name of the balance computation method listed in § 1026.60(g) that is used to determine the balance on which the finance charge is computed for each feature, or an explanation of the method used if it is not listed, along with a statement that an explanation of the method(s) required by paragraph (b)(4)(i)(D) of this section is provided with the account-opening disclosures. In determining which balance computation method to disclose, the creditor shall assume that credit extended will not be repaid within any grace period, if any.

(vii) Cash advance fee. Any fee imposed for an extension of credit in the form of cash or its equivalent.

(viii) Late payment fee. Any fee imposed for a late payment.

(ix) Over-the-limit fee. Any fee imposed for exceeding a credit limit.

(x) Balance transfer fee. Any fee imposed to transfer an outstanding balance.

(xi) Returned-payment fee. Any fee imposed by the creditor for a returned payment.

(xii) Required insurance, debt cancellation or debt suspension coverage.

(A) A fee for insurance described in § 1026.4(b)(7) or debt cancellation or suspension coverage described in § 1026.4(b)(10), if the insurance, or debt cancellation or suspension coverage is required as part of the plan; and

(B) A cross reference to any additional information provided about the insurance or coverage, as applicable.

(xiii) Available credit. If a creditor requires fees for the issuance or availability of credit described in paragraph (b)(2)(ii) of this section, or requires a security deposit for such credit, and the total amount of those required fees and/or security deposit that will be imposed and charged to the account when the account is opened is 15 percent or more of the minimum credit limit for the plan, a creditor must disclose the available credit remaining after these fees or security deposit are debited to the account. The determination whether the 15 percent threshold is met must be based on the minimum credit limit for the plan. However, the disclosure provided under this paragraph must be based on the actual initial credit limit provided on the account. In determining whether the 15 percent threshold test is met, the creditor must only consider fees for issuance or availability of credit, or a security deposit, that are required. If fees for issuance or availability are optional, these fees should not be considered in determining whether the disclosure must be given. Nonetheless, if the 15 percent threshold test is met, the creditor in providing the disclosure must disclose the amount of available credit calculated by excluding those optional fees, and the available credit including those optional fees. The creditor shall also disclose that the consumer has the right to reject the plan and not be obligated to pay those fees or any other fee or charges until the consumer has used the account or made a payment on the account after receiving a periodic statement. This paragraph does not apply with respect to fees or security deposits that are not debited to the account.

(xiv) Web site reference. For issuers of credit cards that are not charge cards, a reference to the Web site established by the Bureau and a statement that consumers may obtain on the Web site information about shopping for and using credit cards. Until January 1, 2013, issuers may substitute for this reference a reference to the Web site established by the Board of Governors of the Federal Reserve System.

(xv) Billing error rights reference. A statement that information about consumers' right to dispute transactions is included in the account-opening disclosures.

(3) Disclosure of charges imposed as part of open-end (not home-secured) plans. A creditor shall disclose, to the extent applicable:

(i) For charges imposed as part of an open-end (not home-secured) plan, the circumstances under which the charge may be imposed, including the amount of the charge or an explanation of how the charge is determined. For finance charges, a statement of when the charge begins to accrue and an explanation of whether or not any time period exists within which any credit that has been extended may be repaid without incurring the charge. If such a time period is provided, a creditor may, at its option and without disclosure, elect not to impose a finance charge when payment is received after the time period expires.

(ii) Charges imposed as part of the plan are:

(A) Finance charges identified under § 1026.4(a) and § 1026.4(b).

(B) Charges resulting from the consumer's failure to use the plan as agreed, except amounts payable for collection activity after default, attorney's fees whether or not automatically imposed, and post-judgment interest rates permitted by law.

(C) Taxes imposed on the credit transaction by a state or other governmental body, such as documentary stamp taxes on cash advances.

(D) Charges for which the payment, or nonpayment, affect the consumer's access to the plan, the duration of the plan, the amount of credit extended, the period for which credit is extended, or the timing or method of billing or payment.

(E) Charges imposed for terminating a plan.

(F) Charges for voluntary credit insurance, debt cancellation or debt suspension.

(iii) Charges that are not imposed as part of the plan include:

(A) Charges imposed on a cardholder by an institution other than the card issuer for the use of the other institution's ATM in a shared or interchange system.

(B) A charge for a package of services that includes an open-end credit feature, if the fee is required whether or not the open-end credit feature is included and the non-credit services are not merely incidental to the credit feature.

(C) Charges under § 1026.4(e) disclosed as specified.

(D) With regard to a covered separate credit feature and an asset feature on a prepaid account that are both accessible by a hybrid prepaid-credit card as defined in § 1026.61, any fee or charge imposed on the asset feature of the prepaid account to the extent that the amount of the fee or charge does not exceed comparable fees or charges imposed on prepaid accounts in the same prepaid account program that do not have a covered separate credit feature accessible by a hybrid prepaid-credit card.

(E) With regard to a non-covered separate credit feature accessible by a prepaid card as defined in § 1026.61, any fee or charge imposed on the asset feature of the prepaid account.

(4) Disclosure of rates for open-end (not home-secured) plans. A creditor shall disclose, to the extent applicable:

(i) For each periodic rate that may be used to calculate interest:

(A) Rates. The rate, expressed as a periodic rate and a corresponding annual percentage rate.

(B) Range of balances. The range of balances to which the rate is applicable; however, a creditor is not required to adjust the range of balances disclosure to reflect the balance below which only a minimum charge applies.

(C) Type of transaction. The type of transaction to which the rate applies, if different rates apply to different types of transactions.

(D) Balance computation method. An explanation of the method used to determine the balance to which the rate is applied.

(ii) Variable-rate accounts. For interest rate changes that are tied to increases in an index or formula (variable-rate accounts) specifically set forth in the account agreement:

(A) The fact that the annual percentage rate may increase.

(B) How the rate is determined, including the margin.

(C) The circumstances under which the rate may increase.

(D) The frequency with which the rate may increase.

(E) Any limitation on the amount the rate may change.

(F) The effect(s) of an increase.

(G) Except as specified in paragraph (b)(4)(ii)(H) of this section, a rate is accurate if it is a rate as of a specified date and this rate was in effect within the last 30 days before the disclosures are provided.

(H) Creditors imposing annual percentage rates that vary according to an index that is not under the creditor's control that provide the disclosures required by paragraph (b) of this section in person at the time the open-end (not home-secured) plan is established in connection with financing the purchase of goods or services may disclose in the table a rate, or range of rates to the extent permitted by § 1026.6(b)(2)(i)(E), that was in effect within the last 90 days before the disclosures are provided, along with a reference directing the consumer to the account agreement or other disclosure provided with the account-opening table where an annual percentage rate applicable to the consumer's account in effect within the last 30 days before the disclosures are provided is disclosed.

(iii) Rate changes not due to index or formula. For interest rate changes that are specifically set forth in the account agreement and not tied to increases in an index or formula:

(A) The initial rate (expressed as a periodic rate and a corresponding annual percentage rate) required under paragraph (b)(4)(i)(A) of this section.

(B) How long the initial rate will remain in effect and the specific events that cause the initial rate to change.

(C) The rate (expressed as a periodic rate and a corresponding annual percentage rate) that will apply when the initial rate is no longer in effect and any limitation on the time period the new rate will remain in effect.

(D) The balances to which the new rate will apply.

(E) The balances to which the current rate at the time of the change will apply.

(5) Additional disclosures for open-end (not home-secured) plans. A creditor shall disclose, to the extent applicable:

(i) Voluntary credit insurance, debt cancellation or debt suspension. The disclosures in §§ 1026.4(d)(1)(i) and (d)(1)(ii) and (d)(3)(i) through (d)(3)(iii) if the creditor offers optional credit insurance or debt cancellation or debt suspension coverage that is identified in § 1026.4(b)(7) or (b)(10).

(ii) Security interests. The fact that the creditor has or will acquire a security interest in the property purchased under the plan, or in other property identified by item or type.

(iii) Statement of billing rights. A statement that outlines the consumer's rights and the creditor's responsibilities under §§ 1026.12(c) and 1026.13 and that is substantially similar to the statement found in Model Form G-3(A) in Appendix G to this part.

§ 1026.7. Periodic Statement

The creditor shall furnish the consumer with a periodic statement that discloses the following items, to the extent applicable:

(a) Rules affecting home-equity plans. The requirements of paragraph (a) of this section apply only to home-equity plans subject to the requirements of § 1026.40. Alternatively, a creditor subject to this paragraph may, at its option, comply with any of the requirements of paragraph (b) of this section; however, any creditor that chooses not to provide a disclosure under paragraph (a)(7) of this section must comply with paragraph (b)(6) of this section.

(1) Previous balance. The account balance outstanding at the beginning of the billing cycle.

(2) Identification of transactions. An identification of each credit transaction in accordance with § 1026.8.

(3) Credits. Any credit to the account during the billing cycle, including the amount and the date of crediting. The date need not be provided if a delay in accounting does not result in any finance or other charge.

(4) Periodic rates.

(i) Except as provided in paragraph (a)(4)(ii) of this section, each periodic rate that may be used to compute the finance charge, the range of balances to which it is applicable, and the corresponding annual percentage rate. If no finance charge is imposed when the outstanding balance is less than a certain amount, the creditor is not required to disclose that fact, or the balance below which no finance charge will be imposed. If different periodic rates apply to different types of transactions, the types of transactions to which the periodic rates apply shall also be disclosed. For variable-rate plans, the fact that the periodic rate(s) may vary.

(ii) Exception. An annual percentage rate that differs from the rate that would otherwise apply and is offered only for a promotional period need not be disclosed except in periods in which the offered rate is actually applied.

(5) Balance on which finance charge computed. The amount of the balance to which a periodic rate was applied and an explanation of how that balance was determined. When a balance is determined without first deducting all credits and payments made during the billing cycle, the fact and the amount of the credits and payments shall be disclosed.

(6) Amount of finance charge and other charges. Creditors may comply with paragraphs (a)(6) of this section, or with paragraph (b)(6) of this section, at their option.

(i) Finance charges. The amount of any finance charge debited or added to the account during the billing cycle, using the term finance charge. The components of the finance charge shall be individually itemized and identified to show the amount(s) due to the application of any periodic rates and the amounts(s) of any other type of finance charge. If there is more than one periodic rate, the amount of the finance charge attributable to each rate need not be separately itemized and identified.

(ii) Other charges. The amounts, itemized and identified by type, of any charges other than finance charges debited to the account during the billing cycle.

(7) Annual percentage rate. At a creditor's option, when a finance charge is imposed during the billing cycle, the annual percentage rate(s) determined under § 1026.14(c) using the term annual percentage rate.

(8) Grace period. The date by which or the time period within which the new balance or any portion of the new balance must be paid to avoid additional finance charges. If such a time period is provided, a creditor may, at its option and without disclosure, impose no finance charge if payment is received after the time period's expiration.

(9) Address for notice of billing errors. The address to be used for notice of billing errors. Alternatively, the address may be provided on the billing rights statement permitted by § 1026.9(a)(2).

(10) Closing date of billing cycle; new balance. The closing date of the billing cycle and the account balance outstanding on that date.

(b) Rules affecting open-end (not home-secured) plans. The requirements of paragraph (b) of this section apply only to plans other than home-equity plans subject to the requirements of § 1026.40.

(1) Previous balance. The account balance outstanding at the beginning of the billing cycle.

(2) Identification of transactions. An identification of each credit transaction in accordance with § 1026.8.

(3) Credits. Any credit to the account during the billing cycle, including the amount and the date of crediting. The date need not be provided if a delay in crediting does not result in any finance or other charge.

(4) Periodic rates.

(i) Except as provided in paragraph (b)(4)(ii) of this section, each periodic rate that may be used to compute the interest charge expressed as an annual percentage rate and using the term Annual Percentage Rate, along with the range of balances to which it is applicable. If no interest charge is imposed when the outstanding balance is less than a certain amount, the creditor is not required to disclose that fact, or the balance below which no interest charge will be imposed. The types of transactions to which the periodic rates apply shall also be disclosed. For variable-rate plans, the fact that the annual percentage rate may vary.

(ii) Exception. A promotional rate, as that term is defined in § 1026.16(g)(2)(i), is required to be disclosed only in periods in which the offered rate is actually applied.

(5) Balance on which finance charge computed. The amount of the balance to which a periodic rate was applied and an explanation of how that balance was determined, using the term Balance Subject to Interest Rate. When a balance is determined without first deducting all credits and payments made during the billing cycle, the fact and the amount of the credits and payments shall be disclosed. As an alternative to providing an explanation of how the balance was determined, a creditor that uses a balance computation method identified in § 1026.60(g) may, at the creditor's option, identify the name of the balance computation method and provide a toll-free telephone number where consumers may obtain from the creditor more information about the balance computation method and how resulting interest charges were determined. If the method used is not identified in § 1026.60(g), the creditor shall provide a brief explanation of the method used.

(6) Charges imposed.

(i) The amounts of any charges imposed as part of a plan as stated in § 1026.6(b)(3), grouped together, in proximity to transactions identified under paragraph (b)(2) of this section, substantially similar to Sample G-18(A) in Appendix G to this part.

(ii) Interest. Finance charges attributable to periodic interest rates, using the term Interest Charge, must be grouped together under the heading Interest Charged, itemized and totaled by type of transaction, and a total of finance charges attributable to periodic interest rates, using the term Total Interest, must be disclosed for the statement period and calendar year to date, using a format substantially similar to Sample G-18(A) in Appendix G to this part.

(iii) Fees. Charges imposed as part of the plan other than charges attributable to periodic interest rates must be grouped together under the heading Fees, identified consistent with the feature or type, and itemized, and a total of charges, using the term Fees, must be disclosed for the statement period and calendar year to date, using a format substantially similar to Sample G-18(A) in Appendix G to this part.

(7) Change-in-terms and increased penalty rate summary for open-end (not home-secured) plans. Creditors that provide a change-in-terms notice required by § 1026.9(c), or a rate increase notice required by § 1026.9(g), on or with the periodic statement, must disclose the information in § 1026.9(c)(2)(iv)(A) and (c)(2)(iv)(B) (if applicable) or § 1026.9(g)(3)(i) on the periodic statement in accordance with the format requirements in § 1026.9(c)(2)(iv)(D), and § 1026.9(g)(3)(ii). See Forms G-18(F) and G-18(G) in Appendix G to this part.

(8) Grace period. The date by which or the time period within which the new balance or any portion of the new balance must be paid to avoid additional finance charges. If such a time period is provided, a creditor may, at its option and without disclosure, impose no finance charge if payment is received after the time period's expiration.

(9) Address for notice of billing errors. The address to be used for notice of billing errors. Alternatively, the address may be provided on the billing rights statement permitted by § 1026.9(a)(2).

(10) Closing date of billing cycle; new balance. The closing date of the billing cycle and the account balance outstanding on that date. The new balance must be disclosed in accordance with the format requirements of paragraph (b)(13) of this section.

(11) Due date; late payment costs.

(i) Except as provided in paragraph (b)(11)(ii) of this section and in accordance with the format requirements in paragraph (b)(13) of this section, for a credit card account under an open-end (not home-secured) consumer credit plan, a card issuer must provide on each periodic statement:

(A) The due date for a payment. The due date disclosed pursuant to this paragraph shall be the same day of the month for each billing cycle.

(B) The amount of any late payment fee and any increased periodic rate(s) (expressed as an annual percentage rate(s)) that may be imposed on the account as a result of a late payment. If a range of late payment fees may be assessed, the card issuer may state the range of fees, or the highest fee and an indication that the fee imposed could be lower. If the rate may be increased for more than one feature or balance, the card issuer may state the range of rates or the highest rate that could apply and at the issuer's option an indication that the rate imposed could be lower.

(ii) Exception. The requirements of paragraph (b)(11)(i) of this section do not apply to the following:

(A) Periodic statements provided solely for charge card accounts, other than covered separate credit features that are charge card accounts accessible by hybrid prepaid-credit cards as defined in § 1026.61; and

(B) Periodic statements provided for a charged-off account where payment of the entire account balance is due immediately.

(12) Repayment disclosures.

(i) In general. Except as provided in paragraphs (b)(12)(ii) and (b)(12)(v) of this section, for a credit card account under an open-end (not home-secured) consumer credit plan, a card issuer must provide the following disclosures on each periodic statement:

(A) The following statement with a bold heading: "Minimum Payment Warning: If you make only the minimum payment each period, you will pay more in interest and it will take you longer to pay off your balance;"

(B) The minimum payment repayment estimate, as described in appendix M1 to this part. If the minimum payment repayment estimate is less than 2 years, the card issuer must disclose the estimate in months. Otherwise, the estimate must be disclosed in years and rounded to the nearest whole year;

(C) The minimum payment total cost estimate, as described in appendix M1 to this part. The minimum payment total cost estimate must be rounded either to the nearest whole dollar or to the nearest cent, at the card issuer's option;

(D) A statement that the minimum payment repayment estimate and the minimum payment total cost estimate are based on the current outstanding balance shown on the periodic statement. A statement that the minimum payment repayment estimate and the minimum payment total cost estimate are based on the assumption that only minimum payments are made and no other amounts are added to the balance;

(E) A toll-free telephone number where the consumer may obtain from the card issuer information about credit counseling services consistent with paragraph (b)(12)(iv) of this section; and

(F)(1) Except as provided in paragraph (b)(12)(i)(F)(2) of this section, the following disclosures:

(i) The estimated monthly payment for repayment in 36 months, as described in appendix M1 to this part. The estimated monthly payment for repayment in 36 months must be rounded either to the nearest whole dollar or to the nearest cent, at the card issuer's option;

(ii) A statement that the card issuer estimates that the consumer will repay the outstanding balance shown on the periodic statement in 3 years if the consumer pays the estimated monthly payment each month for 3 years;

(iii) The total cost estimate for repayment in 36 months, as described in appendix M1 to this part. The total cost estimate for repayment in 36 months must be rounded either to the nearest whole dollar or to the nearest cent, at the card issuer's option; and

(iv) The savings estimate for repayment in 36 months, as described in appendix M1 to this part. The savings estimate for repayment in 36 months must be rounded either to the nearest whole dollar or to the nearest cent, at the card issuer's option.

(2) The requirements of paragraph (b)(12)(i)(F)(1) of this section do not apply to a periodic statement in any of the following circumstances:

(i) The minimum payment repayment estimate that is disclosed on the periodic statement pursuant to paragraph (b)(12)(i)(B) of this section after rounding is three years or less;

(ii) The estimated monthly payment for repayment in 36 months, as described in appendix M1 to this part, after rounding as set forth in paragraph (b)(12)(i)(F)(1)(i) of this section that is calculated for a particular billing cycle is less than the minimum payment required for the plan for that billing cycle; and

(iii) A billing cycle where an account has both a balance in a revolving feature where the required minimum payments for this feature will not amortize that balance in a fixed amount of time specified in the account agreement and a balance in a fixed repayment feature where the required minimum payment for this fixed repayment feature will amortize that balance in a fixed amount of time specified in the account agreement which is less than 36 months.

(ii) Negative or no amortization. If negative or no amortization occurs when calculating the minimum payment repayment estimate as described in appendix M1 of this part, a card issuer must provide the following disclosures on the periodic statement instead of the disclosures set forth in paragraph (b)(12)(i) of this section:

(A) The following statement: "Minimum Payment Warning: Even if you make no more charges using this card, if you make only the minimum payment each month we estimate you will never pay off the balance shown on this statement because your payment will be less than the interest charged each month";

(B) The following statement: "If you make more than the minimum payment each period, you will pay less in interest and pay off your balance sooner";

(C) The estimated monthly payment for repayment in 36 months, as described in appendix M1 to this part. The estimated monthly payment for repayment in 36 months must be rounded either to the nearest whole dollar or to the nearest cent, at the issuer's option;

(D) A statement that the card issuer estimates that the consumer will repay the outstanding balance shown on the periodic statement in 3 years if the consumer pays the estimated monthly payment each month for 3 years; and

(E) A toll-free telephone number where the consumer may obtain from the card issuer information about credit counseling services consistent with paragraph (b)(12)(iv) of this section.

(iii) Format requirements. A card issuer must provide the disclosures required by paragraph (b)(12)(i) or (b)(12)(ii) of this section in accordance with the format requirements of paragraph (b)(13) of this section, and in a format substantially similar to Samples G-18(C)(1), G-18(C)(2) and G-18(C)(3) in appendix G to this part, as applicable.

(iv) Provision of information about credit counseling services.

(A) Required information. To the extent available from the United States Trustee or a bankruptcy administrator, a card issuer must provide through the toll-free telephone number disclosed pursuant to paragraphs (b)(12)(i) or (b)(12)(ii) of this section the name, street address, telephone number, and Web site address for at least three organizations that have been approved by the United States Trustee or a bankruptcy administrator pursuant to 11 U.S.C. 111(a)(1) to provide credit counseling services in, at the card issuer's option, either the state in which the billing address for the account is located or the state specified by the consumer.

(B) Updating required information. At least annually, a card issuer must update the information provided pursuant to paragraph (b)(12)(iv)(A) of this section for consistency with the information available from the United States Trustee or a bankruptcy administrator.

(v) Exemptions. Paragraph (b)(12) of this section does not apply to:

(A) Charge card accounts that require payment of outstanding balances in full at the end of each billing cycle;

(B) A billing cycle immediately following two consecutive billing cycles in which the consumer paid the entire balance in full, had a zero outstanding balance or had a credit balance; and

(C) A billing cycle where paying the minimum payment due for that billing cycle will pay the entire outstanding balance on the account for that billing cycle.

(13) Format requirements. The due date required by paragraph (b)(11) of this section shall be disclosed on the front of the first page of the periodic statement. The amount of the late payment fee and the annual percentage rate(s) required by paragraph (b)(11) of this section shall be stated in close proximity to the due date. The ending balance required by paragraph (b)(10) of this section and the disclosures required by paragraph (b)(12) of this section shall be disclosed closely proximate to the minimum payment due. The due date, late payment fee and annual percentage rate, ending balance, minimum payment due, and disclosures required by paragraph (b)(12) of this section shall be grouped together. Sample G-18(D) in appendix G to this part sets forth an example of how these terms may be grouped.

(14) Deferred interest or similar transactions. For accounts with an outstanding balance subject to a deferred interest or similar program, the date by which that outstanding balance must be paid in full in order to avoid the obligation to pay finance charges on such balance must be disclosed on the front of any page of each periodic statement issued during the deferred interest period beginning with the first periodic statement issued during the deferred interest period that reflects the deferred interest or similar transaction. The disclosure provided pursuant to this paragraph must be substantially similar to Sample G-18(H) in appendix G to this part.

§ 1026.8. Identifying Transactions on Periodic Statements

The creditor shall identify credit transactions on or with the first periodic statement that reflects the transaction by furnishing the following information, as applicable:

(a) Sale credit.

(1) Except as provided in paragraph (a)(2) of this section, for each credit transaction involving the sale of property or services, the creditor must disclose the amount and date of the transaction, and either:

(i) A brief identification of the property or services purchased, for creditors and sellers that are the same or related; or

(ii) The seller's name; and the city and state or foreign country where the transaction took place. The creditor may omit the address or provide any suitable designation that helps the consumer to identify the transaction when the transaction took place at a location that is not fixed; took place in the consumer's home; or was a mail, Internet, or telephone order.

(2) Creditors need not comply with paragraph (a)(1) of this section if an actual copy of the receipt or other credit document is provided with the first periodic statement reflecting the transaction, and the amount of the transaction and either the date of the transaction to the consumer's account or the date of debiting the transaction are disclosed on the copy or on the periodic statement.

(b) Nonsale credit. For each credit transaction not involving the sale of property or services, the creditor must disclose a brief identification of the transaction; the amount of the transaction; and at least one of the following dates: The date of the transaction, the date the transaction was debited to the consumer's account, or, if the consumer signed the credit document, the date appearing on the document. If an actual copy of the receipt or other credit document is provided and that copy shows the amount and at least one of the specified dates, the brief identification may be omitted.

(c) Alternative creditor procedures; consumer inquiries for clarification or documentation. The following procedures apply to creditors that treat an inquiry for clarification or documentation as a notice of a billing error, including correcting the account in accordance with § 1026.13(e):

(1) Failure to disclose the information required by paragraphs (a) and (b) of this section is not a failure to comply with the regulation, provided that the creditor also maintains procedures reasonably designed to obtain and provide the information. This applies to transactions that take place outside a state, as defined in § 1026.2(a)(26), whether or not the creditor maintains procedures reasonably adapted to obtain the required information.

(2) As an alternative to the brief identification for sale or nonsale credit, the creditor may disclose a number or symbol that also appears on the receipt or other credit document given to the consumer, if the number or symbol reasonably identifies that transaction with that creditor.

§ 1026.9. Subsequent Disclosure Requirements

(a) Furnishing statement of billing rights—

(1) Annual statement. The creditor shall mail or deliver the billing rights statement required by § 1026.6(a)(5) and (b)(5)(iii) at least once per calendar year, at intervals of not less than 6 months nor more than 18 months, either to all consumers or to each consumer entitled to receive a periodic statement under § 1026.5(b)(2) for any one billing cycle.

(2) Alternative summary statement. As an alternative to paragraph (a)(1) of this section, the creditor may mail or deliver, on or with each periodic statement, a statement substantially similar to Model Form G-4 or Model Form G-4(A) in appendix G to this part, as applicable. Creditors offering home-equity plans subject to the requirements of § 1026.40 may use either Model Form, at their option.

(b) Disclosures for supplemental credit access devices and additional features.

(1) If a creditor, within 30 days after mailing or delivering the account-opening disclosures under § 1026.6(a)(1) or (b)(3)(ii)(A), as applicable, adds a credit feature to the consumer's account or mails or delivers to the consumer a credit access device, including but not limited to checks that access a credit card account, for which the finance charge terms are the same as those previously disclosed, no additional disclosures are necessary. Except as provided in paragraph (b)(3) of this section, after 30 days, if the creditor adds a credit feature or furnishes a credit access device (other than as a renewal, resupply, or the original issuance of a credit card) on the same finance charge terms, the creditor shall disclose, before the consumer uses the feature or device for the first time, that it is for use in obtaining credit under the terms previously disclosed.

(2) Except as provided in paragraph (b)(3) of this section, whenever a credit feature is added or a credit access device is mailed or delivered to the consumer, and the finance charge terms for the feature or device differ from disclosures previously given, the disclosures required by § 1026.6(a)(1) or (b)(3)(ii)(A), as applicable, that are applicable to the added feature or device shall be given before the consumer uses the feature or device for the first time.

(3) Checks that access a credit card account.

(i) Disclosures. For open-end plans not subject to the requirements of § 1026.40, if checks that can be used to access a credit card account are provided more than 30 days after account-opening disclosures under § 1026.6(b) are mailed or delivered, or are provided within 30 days of the account-opening disclosures and the finance charge terms for the checks differ from the finance charge terms previously disclosed, the creditor shall disclose on the front of the page containing the checks the following terms in the form of a table with the headings, content, and form substantially similar to Sample G-19 in appendix G to this part:

(A) If a promotional rate, as that term is defined in § 1026.16(g)(2)(i) applies to the checks:

(1) The promotional rate and the time period during which the promotional rate will remain in effect;

(2) The type of rate that will apply (such as whether the purchase or cash advance rate applies) after the promotional rate expires, and the annual percentage rate that will apply after the promotional rate expires. For a variable-rate account, a creditor must disclose an annual percentage rate based on the applicable index or formula in accordance with the accuracy requirements set forth in paragraph (b)(3)(ii) of this section; and

(3) The date, if any, by which the consumer must use the checks in order to qualify for the promotional rate. If the creditor will honor checks used after such date but will apply an annual percentage rate other than the promotional rate, the creditor must disclose this fact and the type of annual percentage rate that will apply if the consumer uses the checks after such date.

(B) If no promotional rate applies to the checks:

(1) The type of rate that will apply to the checks and the applicable annual percentage rate. For a variable-rate account, a creditor must disclose an annual percentage rate based on the applicable index or formula in accordance with the accuracy requirements set forth in paragraph (b)(3)(ii) of this section.

(2) [Reserved]

(C) Any transaction fees applicable to the checks disclosed under § 1026.6(b)(2)(iv); and

(D) Whether or not a grace period is given within which any credit extended by use of the checks may be repaid without incurring a finance charge due to a periodic interest rate. When disclosing whether there is a grace period, the phrase "How to Avoid Paying Interest on Check Transactions" shall be used as the row heading when a grace period applies to credit extended by the use of the checks. When disclosing the fact that no grace period exists for credit extended by use of the checks, the phrase "Paying Interest" shall be used as the row heading.

(ii) Accuracy. The disclosures in paragraph (b)(3)(i) of this section must be accurate as of the time the disclosures are mailed or delivered. A variable annual percentage rate is accurate if it was in effect within 60 days of when the disclosures are mailed or delivered.

(iii) Variable rates. If any annual percentage rate required to be disclosed pursuant to paragraph (b)(3)(i) of this section is a variable rate, the card issuer shall also disclose the fact that the rate may vary and how the rate is determined. In describing how the applicable rate will be determined, the card issuer must identify the type of index or formula that is used in setting the rate. The value of the index and the amount of the margin that are used to calculate the variable rate shall not be disclosed in the table. A disclosure of any applicable limitations on rate increases shall not be included in the table.

(c) Change in terms—

(1) Rules affecting home-equity plans—

(i) Written notice required—

For home-equity plans subject to the requirements of § 1026.40, whenever any term required to be disclosed under § 1026.6(a) is changed or the required minimum periodic payment is increased, the creditor shall mail or deliver written notice of the change to each consumer who may be affected. The notice shall be mailed or delivered at least 15 days prior to the effective date of the change. The 15-day timing requirement does not apply if the change has been agreed to by the consumer; the notice shall be given, however, before the effective date of the change.

(ii) Notice not required. For home-equity plans subject to the requirements of § 1026.40, a creditor is not required to provide notice under this section when the change involves a reduction of any component of a finance or other charge or when the change results from an agreement involving a court proceeding.

(iii) Notice to restrict credit. For home-equity plans subject to the requirements of § 1026.40, if the creditor prohibits additional extensions of credit or reduces the credit limit pursuant to § 1026.40(f)(3)(i) or (f)(3)(vi), the creditor shall mail or deliver written notice of the action to each consumer who will be affected. The notice must be provided not later than three business days after the action is taken and shall contain specific reasons for the action. If the creditor requires the consumer to request reinstatement of credit privileges, the notice also shall state that fact.

(2) Rules affecting open-end (not home-secured) plans.

(i) Changes where written advance notice is required.

(A) General. For plans other than home-equity plans subject to the requirements of § 1026.40, except as provided in paragraphs (c)(2)(i)(B), (c)(2)(iii) and (c)(2)(v) of this section, when a significant change in account terms as described in paragraph (c)(2)(ii) of this section is made, a creditor must provide a written notice of the change at least 45 days prior to the effective date of the change to each consumer who may be affected. The 45-day timing requirement does not apply if the consumer has agreed to a particular change as described in paragraph (c)(2)(i)(B) of this section; for such changes, notice must be given in accordance with the timing requirements of paragraph (c)(2)(i)(B) of this section. Increases in the rate applicable to a consumer's account due to delinquency, default or as a penalty described in paragraph (g) of this section that are not due to a change in the contractual terms of the consumer's account must be disclosed pursuant to paragraph (g) of this section instead of paragraph (c)(2) of this section.

(B) Changes agreed to by the consumer. A notice of change in terms is required, but it may be mailed or delivered as late as the effective date of the change if the consumer agrees to the particular change. This paragraph (c)(2)(i)(B) applies only when a consumer substitutes collateral or when the creditor can advance additional credit only if a change relatively unique to that consumer is made, such as the consumer's providing additional security or paying an increased minimum payment amount. The following are not considered agreements between the consumer and the creditor for purposes of this paragraph (c)(2)(i)(B): The consumer's general acceptance of the creditor's contract reservation of the right to change terms; the consumer's use of the account (which might imply acceptance of its terms under state law); the consumer's acceptance of a unilateral term change that is not particular to that consumer, but rather is of general applicability to consumers with that type of account; and the consumer's request to reopen a closed account or to upgrade an existing account to another account offered by the creditor with different credit or other features.

(ii) Significant changes in account terms. For purposes of this section, a "significant change in account terms" means a change to a term required to be disclosed under § 1026.6(b)(1) and (b)(2), an increase in the required minimum periodic payment, a change to a term required to be disclosed under § 1026.6(b)(4), or the acquisition of a security interest.

(iii) Charges not covered by § 1026.6(b)(1) and (b)(2). Except as provided in paragraph (c)(2)(vi) of this section, if a creditor increases any component of a charge, or introduces a new charge, required to be disclosed under § 1026.6(b)(3) that is not a significant change in account terms as described in paragraph (c)(2)(ii) of this section, a creditor must either, at its option:

(A) Comply with the requirements of paragraph (c)(2)(i) of this section; or

(B) Provide notice of the amount of the charge before the consumer agrees to or becomes obligated to pay the charge, at a time and in a manner that a consumer would be likely to notice the disclosure of the charge. The notice may be provided orally or in writing.

(iv) Disclosure requirements—

(A) Significant changes in account terms. If a creditor makes a significant change in account terms as described in paragraph (c)(2)(ii) of this section, the notice provided pursuant to paragraph (c)(2)(i) of this section must provide the following information:

(1) A summary of the changes made to terms required by § 1026.6(b)(1) and (b)(2) or § 1026.6(b)(4), a description of any increase in the required minimum periodic payment, and a description of any security interest being acquired by the creditor;

(2) A statement that changes are being made to the account;

(3) For accounts other than credit card accounts under an open-end (not home-secured) consumer credit plan subject to § 1026.9(c)(2)(iv)(B), a statement indicating the consumer has the right to opt out of these changes, if applicable, and a reference to additional information describing the opt-out right provided in the notice, if applicable;

(4) The date the changes will become effective;

(5) If applicable, a statement that the consumer may find additional information about the summarized changes, and other changes to the account, in the notice;

(6) If the creditor is changing a rate on the account, other than a penalty rate, a statement that if a penalty rate currently applies to the consumer's account, the new rate described in the notice will not apply to the consumer's account until the consumer's account balances are no longer subject to the penalty rate;

(7) If the change in terms being disclosed is an increase in an annual percentage rate, the balances to which the increased rate will be applied. If applicable, a statement identifying the balances to which the current rate will continue to apply as of the effective date of the change in terms; and

(8) If the change in terms being disclosed is an increase in an annual percentage rate for a credit card account under an open-end (not home-secured) consumer credit plan, a statement of no more than four principal reasons for the rate increase, listed in their order of importance.

(B) Right to reject for credit card accounts under an open-end (not home-secured) consumer credit plan. In addition to the disclosures in paragraph (c)(2)(iv)(A) of this section, if a card issuer makes a significant change in account terms on a credit card account under an open-end (not home-secured) consumer credit plan, the creditor must generally provide the following information on the notice provided pursuant to paragraph (c)(2)(i) of this section. This information is not required to be provided in the case of an increase in the required minimum periodic payment, an increase in a fee as a result of a reevaluation of a determination made under § 1026.52(b)(1)(i) or an adjustment to the safe harbors in § 1026.52(b)(1)(ii) to reflect changes in the Consumer Price Index, a change in an annual percentage rate applicable to a consumer's account, an increase in a fee previously reduced consistent with 50 U.S.C. app. 527 or a similar Federal or state statute or regulation if the amount of the increased fee does not exceed the amount of that fee prior to the reduction, or when the change results from the creditor not receiving the consumer's required minimum periodic payment within 60 days after the due date for that payment:

(1) A statement that the consumer has the right to reject the change or changes prior to the effective date of the changes, unless the consumer fails to make a required minimum periodic payment within 60 days after the due date for that payment;

(2) Instructions for rejecting the change or changes, and a toll-free telephone number that the consumer may use to notify the creditor of the rejection; and

(3) If applicable, a statement that if the consumer rejects the change or changes, the consumer's ability to use the account for further advances will be terminated or suspended.

(C) Changes resulting from failure to make minimum periodic payment within 60 days from due date for credit card accounts under an open-end (not home-secured) consumer credit plan. For a credit card account under an open-end (not home-secured) consumer credit plan:

(1) If the significant change required to be disclosed pursuant to paragraph (c)(2)(i) of this section is an increase in an annual percentage rate or a fee or charge required to be disclosed under § 1026.6(b)(2)(ii), (b)(2)(iii), or (b)(2)(xii) based on the consumer's failure to make a minimum periodic payment within 60 days from the due date for that payment, the notice provided pursuant to paragraph (c)(2)(i) of this section must state that the increase will cease to apply to transactions that occurred prior to or within 14 days of provision of the notice, if the creditor receives six consecutive required minimum periodic payments on or before the payment due date, beginning with the first payment due following the effective date of the increase.

(2) If the significant change required to be disclosed pursuant to paragraph (c)(2)(i) of this section is an increase in a fee or charge required to be disclosed under § 1026.6(b)(2)(ii), (b)(2)(iii), or (b)(2)(xii) based on the consumer's failure to make a minimum periodic payment within 60 days from the due date for that payment, the notice provided pursuant to paragraph (c)(2)(i) of this section must also state the reason for the increase.

(D) Format requirements—

(1) Tabular format. The summary of changes described in paragraph (c)(2)(iv)(A)(1) of this section must be in a tabular format (except for a summary of any increase in the required minimum periodic payment, a summary of a term required to be disclosed under § 1026.6(b)(4) that is not required to be disclosed under § 1026.6(b)(1) and (b)(2), or a description of any security interest being acquired by the creditor), with headings and format substantially similar to any of the account-opening tables found in G-17 in appendix G to this part. The table must disclose the changed term and information relevant to the change, if that relevant information is required by § 1026.6(b)(1) and (b)(2). The new terms shall be described in the same level of detail as required when disclosing the terms under § 1026.6(b)(2).

(2) Notice included with periodic statement. If a notice required by paragraph (c)(2)(i) of this section is included on or with a periodic statement, the information described in paragraph (c)(2)(iv)(A)(1) of this section must be disclosed on the front of any page of the statement. The summary of changes described in paragraph (c)(2)(iv)(A)(1) of this section must immediately follow the information described in paragraph (c)(2)(iv)(A)(2) through (c)(2)(iv)(A)(7) and, if applicable, paragraphs (c)(2)(iv)(A)(8), (c)(2)(iv)(B), and (c)(2)(iv)(C) of this section, and be substantially similar to the format shown in Sample G-20 or G-21 in appendix G to this part.

(3) Notice provided separately from periodic statement. If a notice required by paragraph (c)(2)(i) of this section is not included on or with a periodic statement, the information described in paragraph (c)(2)(iv)(A)(1) of this section must, at the creditor's option, be disclosed on the front of the first page of the notice or segregated on a separate page from other information given with the notice. The summary of changes required to be in a table pursuant to paragraph (c)(2)(iv)(A)(1) of this section may be on more than one page, and may use both the front and reverse sides, so long as the table begins on the front of the first page of the notice and there is a reference on the first page indicating that the table continues on the following page. The summary of changes described in paragraph (c)(2)(iv)(A)(1) of this section must immediately follow the information described in paragraph (c)(2)(iv)(A)(2) through (c)(2)(iv)(A)(7) and, if applicable, paragraphs (c)(2)(iv)(A)(8), (c)(2)(iv)(B), and (c)(2)(iv)(C), of this section, substantially similar to the format shown in Sample G-20 or G-21 in appendix G to this part.

(v) Notice not required. For open-end plans (other than home equity plans subject to the requirements of § 1026.40) a creditor is not required to provide notice under this section:

(A) When the change involves charges for documentary evidence; a reduction of any component of a finance or other charge; suspension of future credit privileges (except as provided in paragraph (c)(2)(vi) of this section) or termination of an account or plan; when the change results from an agreement involving a court proceeding; when the change is an extension of the grace period; or if the change is applicable only to checks that access a credit card account and the changed terms are disclosed on or with the checks in accordance with paragraph (b)(3) of this section;

(B) When the change is an increase in an annual percentage rate or fee upon the expiration of a specified period of time, provided that:

(1) Prior to commencement of that period, the creditor disclosed in writing to the consumer, in a clear and conspicuous manner, the length of the period and the annual percentage rate or fee that would apply after expiration of the period;

(2) The disclosure of the length of the period and the annual percentage rate or fee that would apply after expiration of the period are set forth in close proximity and in equal prominence to the first listing of the disclosure of the rate or fee that applies during the specified period of time; and

(3) The annual percentage rate or fee that applies after that period does not exceed the rate or fee disclosed pursuant to paragraph (c)(2)(v)(B)(1) of this paragraph or, if the rate disclosed pursuant to paragraph (c)(2)(v)(B)(1) of this section was a variable rate, the rate following any such increase is a variable rate determined by the same formula (index and margin) that was used to calculate the variable rate disclosed pursuant to paragraph (c)(2)(v)(B)(1);

(C) When the change is an increase in a variable annual percentage rate in accordance with a credit card or other account agreement that provides for changes in the rate according to operation of an index that is not under the control of the creditor and is available to the general public; or

(D) When the change is an increase in an annual percentage rate, a fee or charge required to be disclosed under § 1026.6(b)(2)(ii), (b)(2)(iii), (b)(2)(viii), (b)(2)(ix), (b)(2)(ix) or (b)(2)(xii), or the required minimum periodic payment due to the completion of a workout or temporary hardship arrangement by the consumer or the consumer's failure to comply with the terms of such an arrangement, provided that:

(1) The annual percentage rate or fee or charge applicable to a category of transactions or the required minimum periodic payment following any such increase does not exceed the rate or fee or charge or required minimum periodic payment that applied to that category of transactions prior to commencement of the arrangement or, if the rate that applied to a category of transactions prior to the commencement of the workout or temporary hardship arrangement was a variable rate, the rate following any such increase is a variable rate determined by the same formula (index and margin) that applied to the category of transactions prior to commencement of the workout or temporary hardship arrangement; and

(2) The creditor has provided the consumer, prior to the commencement of such arrangement, with a clear and conspicuous disclosure of the terms of the arrangement (including any increases due to such completion or failure). This disclosure must generally be provided in writing. However, a creditor may provide the disclosure of the terms of the arrangement orally by telephone, provided that the creditor mails or delivers a written disclosure of the terms of the arrangement to the consumer as soon as reasonably practicable after the oral disclosure is provided.

(vi) Reduction of the credit limit. For open-end plans that are not subject to the requirements of § 1026.40, if a creditor decreases the credit limit on an account, advance notice of the decrease must be provided before an over-the-limit fee or a penalty rate can be imposed solely as a result of the consumer exceeding the newly decreased credit limit. Notice shall be provided in writing or orally at least 45 days prior to imposing the over-the-limit fee or penalty rate and shall state that the credit limit on the account has been or will be decreased.

(d) Finance charge imposed at time of transaction.

(1) Any person, other than the card issuer, who imposes a finance charge at the time of honoring a consumer's credit card, shall disclose the amount of that finance charge prior to its imposition.

(2) The card issuer, other than the person honoring the consumer's credit card, shall have no responsibility for the disclosure required by paragraph (d)(1) of this section, and shall not consider any such charge for the purposes of §§ 1026.60, 1026.6 and 1026.7.

(e) Disclosures upon renewal of credit or charge card—

(1) Notice prior to renewal. A card issuer that imposes any annual or other periodic fee to renew a credit or charge card account of the type subject to § 1026.60, including any fee based on account activity or inactivity or any card issuer that has changed or amended any term of a cardholder's account required to be disclosed under § 1026.6(b)(1) and (b)(2) that has not previously been disclosed to the consumer, shall mail or deliver written notice of the renewal to the cardholder. If the card issuer imposes any annual or other periodic fee for renewal, the notice shall be provided at least 30 days or one billing cycle, whichever is less, before the mailing or the delivery of the periodic statement on which any renewal fee is initially charged to the account. If the card issuer has changed or amended any term required to be disclosed under § 1026.6(b)(1) and (b)(2) and such changed or amended term has not previously been disclosed to the consumer, the notice shall be provided at least 30 days prior to the scheduled renewal date of the consumer's credit or charge card. The notice shall contain the following information:

(i) The disclosures contained in § 1026.60(b)(1) through (b)(7) that would apply if the account were renewed; and

(ii) How and when the cardholder may terminate credit availability under the account to avoid paying the renewal fee, if applicable.

(2) Notification on periodic statements. The disclosures required by this paragraph may be made on or with a periodic statement. If any of the disclosures are provided on the back of a periodic statement, the card issuer shall include a reference to those disclosures on the front of the statement.

(f) Change in credit card account insurance provider—

(1) Notice prior to change. If a credit card issuer plans to change the provider of insurance for repayment of all or part of the outstanding balance of an open-end credit card account of the type subject to § 1026.60, the card issuer shall mail or deliver to the cardholder written notice of the change not less than 30 days before the change in provider occurs. The notice shall also include the following items, to the extent applicable:

(i) Any increase in the rate that will result from the change;

(ii) Any substantial decrease in coverage that will result from the change; and

(iii) A statement that the cardholder may discontinue the insurance.

(2) Notice when change in provider occurs. If a change described in paragraph (f)(1) of this section occurs, the card issuer shall provide the cardholder with a written notice no later than 30 days after the change, including the following items, to the extent applicable:

(i) The name and address of the new insurance provider;

(ii) A copy of the new policy or group certificate containing the basic terms of the insurance, including the rate to be charged; and

(iii) A statement that the cardholder may discontinue the insurance.

(3) Substantial decrease in coverage. For purposes of this paragraph, a substantial decrease in coverage is a decrease in a significant term of coverage that might reasonably be expected to affect the cardholder's decision to continue the insurance. Significant terms of coverage include, for example, the following:

(i) Type of coverage provided;

(ii) Age at which coverage terminates or becomes more restrictive;

(iii) Maximum insurable loan balance, maximum periodic benefit payment, maximum number of payments, or other term affecting the dollar amount of coverage or benefits provided;

(iv) Eligibility requirements and number and identity of persons covered;

(v) Definition of a key term of coverage such as disability;

(vi) Exclusions from or limitations on coverage; and

(vii) Waiting periods and whether coverage is retroactive.

(4) Combined notification. The notices required by paragraph (f)(1) and (2) of this section may be combined provided the timing requirement of paragraph (f)(1) of this section is met. The notices may be provided on or with a periodic statement.

(g) Increase in rates due to delinquency or default or as a penalty—

(1) Increases subject to this section. For plans other than home-equity plans subject to the requirements of § 1026.40, except as provided in paragraph (g)(4) of this section, a creditor must provide a written notice to each consumer who may be affected when:

(i) A rate is increased due to the consumer's delinquency or default; or

(ii) A rate is increased as a penalty for one or more events specified in the account agreement, such as making a late payment or obtaining an extension of credit that exceeds the credit limit.

(2) Timing of written notice. Whenever any notice is required to be given pursuant to paragraph (g)(1) of this section, the creditor shall provide written notice of the increase in rates at least 45 days prior to the effective date of the increase. The notice must be provided after the occurrence of the events described in paragraphs (g)(1)(i) and (g)(1)(ii) of this section that trigger the imposition of the rate increase.

(3)(i) Disclosure requirements for rate increases.

(A) General—

If a creditor is increasing the rate due to delinquency or default or as a penalty, the creditor must provide the following information on the notice sent pursuant to paragraph (g)(1) of this section:

(1) A statement that the delinquency or default rate or penalty rate, as applicable, has been triggered;

(2) The date on which the delinquency or default rate or penalty rate will apply;

(3) The circumstances under which the delinquency or default rate or penalty rate, as applicable, will cease to apply to the consumer's account, or that the delinquency or default rate or penalty rate will remain in effect for a potentially indefinite time period;

(4) A statement indicating to which balances the delinquency or default rate or penalty rate will be applied;

(5) If applicable, a description of any balances to which the current rate will continue to apply as of the effective date of the rate increase, unless a consumer fails to make a minimum periodic payment within 60 days from the due date for that payment; and

(6) For a credit card account under an open-end (not home-secured) consumer credit plan, a statement of no more than four principal reasons for the rate increase, listed in their order of importance.

(B) Rate increases resulting from failure to make minimum periodic payment within 60 days from due date. For a credit card account under an open-end (not home-secured) consumer credit plan, if the rate increase required to be disclosed pursuant to paragraph (g)(1) of this section is an increase pursuant to § 1026.55(b)(4) based on the consumer's failure to make a minimum periodic payment within 60 days from the due date for that payment, the notice provided pursuant to paragraph (g)(1) of this section must also state that the increase will cease to apply to transactions that occurred prior to or within 14 days of provision of the notice, if the creditor receives six consecutive required minimum periodic payments on or before the payment due date, beginning with the first payment due following the effective date of the increase.

(ii) Format requirements.

(A) If a notice required by paragraph (g)(1) of this section is included on or with a periodic statement, the information described in paragraph (g)(3)(i) of this section must be in the form of a table and provided on the front of any page of the periodic statement, above the notice described in paragraph (c)(2)(iv) of this section if that notice is provided on the same statement.

(B) If a notice required by paragraph (g)(1) of this section is not included on or with a periodic statement, the information described in paragraph (g)(3)(i) of this section must be disclosed on the front of the first page of the notice. Only information related to the increase in the rate to a penalty rate may be included with the notice, except that this notice may be combined with a notice described in paragraph (c)(2)(iv) or (g)(4) of this section.

(4) Exception for decrease in credit limit. A creditor is not required to provide a notice pursuant to paragraph (g)(1) of this section prior to increasing the rate for obtaining an extension of credit that exceeds the credit limit, provided that:

(i) The creditor provides at least 45 days in advance of imposing the penalty rate a notice, in writing, that includes:

(A) A statement that the credit limit on the account has been or will be decreased.

(B) A statement indicating the date on which the penalty rate will apply, if the outstanding balance exceeds the credit limit as of that date;

(C) A statement that the penalty rate will not be imposed on the date specified in paragraph (g)(4)(i)(B) of this section, if the outstanding balance does not exceed the credit limit as of that date;

(D) The circumstances under which the penalty rate, if applied, will cease to apply to the account, or that the penalty rate, if applied, will remain in effect for a potentially indefinite time period;

(E) A statement indicating to which balances the penalty rate may be applied; and

(F) If applicable, a description of any balances to which the current rate will continue to apply as of the effective date of the rate increase, unless the consumer fails to make a minimum periodic payment within 60 days from the due date for that payment; and

(ii) The creditor does not increase the rate applicable to the consumer's account to the penalty rate if the outstanding balance does not exceed the credit limit on the date set forth in the notice and described in paragraph (g)(4)(i)(B) of this section.

(iii)(A) If a notice provided pursuant to paragraph (g)(4)(i) of this section is included on or with a periodic statement, the information described in paragraph (g)(4)(i) of this section must be in the form of a table and provided on the front of any page of the periodic statement; or

(B) If a notice required by paragraph (g)(4)(i) of this section is not included on or with a periodic statement, the information described in paragraph (g)(4)(i) of this section must be disclosed on the front of the first page of the notice. Only information related to the reduction in credit limit may be included with the notice, except that this notice may be combined with a notice described in paragraph (c)(2)(iv) or (g)(1) of this section.

(h) Consumer rejection of certain significant changes in terms—

(1) Right to reject. If paragraph (c)(2)(iv)(B) of this section requires disclosure of the consumer's right to reject a significant change to an account term, the consumer may reject that change by notifying the creditor of the rejection before the effective date of the change.

(2) Effect of rejection. If a creditor is notified of a rejection of a significant change to an account term as provided in paragraph (h)(1) of this section, the creditor must not:

(i) Apply the change to the account;

(ii) Impose a fee or charge or treat the account as in default solely as a result of the rejection; or

(iii) Require repayment of the balance on the account using a method that is less beneficial to the consumer than one of the methods listed in § 1026.55(c)(2).

(3) Exception. Section 1026.9(h) does not apply when the creditor has not received the consumer's required minimum periodic payment within 60 days after the due date for that payment.

§ 1026.10. Payments

(a) General rule. A creditor shall credit a payment to the consumer's account as of the date of receipt, except when a delay in crediting does not result in a finance or other charge or except as provided in paragraph (b) of this section.

(b) Specific requirements for payments—

(1) General rule. A creditor may specify reasonable requirements for payments that enable most consumers to make conforming payments.

(2) Examples of reasonable requirements for payments. Reasonable requirements for making payment may include:

(i) Requiring that payments be accompanied by the account number or payment stub;

(ii) Setting reasonable cut-off times for payments to be received by mail, by electronic means, by telephone, and in person (except as provided in paragraph (b)(3) of this section), provided that such cut-off times shall be no earlier than 5 p.m. on the payment due date at the location specified by the creditor for the receipt of such payments;

(iii) Specifying that only checks or money orders should be sent by mail;

(iv) Specifying that payment is to be made in U.S. dollars; or

(v) Specifying one particular address for receiving payments, such as a post office box.

(3) In-person payments on credit card accounts—

(i) General. Notwithstanding § 1026.10(b), payments on a credit card account under an open-end (not home-secured) consumer credit plan made in person at a branch or office of a card issuer that is a financial institution prior to the close of business of that branch or office shall be considered received on the date on which the consumer makes the payment. A card issuer that is a financial institution shall not impose a cut-off time earlier than the close of business for any such payments made in person at any branch or office of the card issuer at which such payments are accepted. Notwithstanding § 1026.10(b)(2)(ii), a card issuer may impose a cut-off time earlier than 5 p.m. for such payments, if the close of business of the branch or office is earlier than 5 p.m.

(ii) Financial institution. For purposes of paragraph (b)(3) of this section, "financial institution" shall mean a bank, savings association, or credit union.

(4) Nonconforming payments—

(i) In general. Except as provided in paragraph (b)(4)(ii) of this section, if a creditor specifies, on or with the periodic statement, requirements for the consumer to follow in making payments as permitted under this § 1026.10, but accepts a payment that does not conform to the requirements, the creditor shall credit the payment within five days of receipt.

(ii) Payment methods promoted by creditor. If a creditor promotes a method for making payments, such payments shall be considered conforming payments in accordance with this paragraph (b) and shall be credited to the consumer's account as of the date of receipt, except when a delay in crediting does not result in a finance or other charge.

(c) Adjustment of account. If a creditor fails to credit a payment, as required by paragraphs (a) or (b) of this section, in time to avoid the imposition of finance or other charges, the creditor shall adjust the consumer's account so that the charges imposed are credited to the consumer's account during the next billing cycle.

(d) Crediting of payments when creditor does not receive or accept payments on due date—

(1) General. Except as provided in paragraph (d)(2) of this section, if a creditor does not receive or accept payments by mail on the due date for payments, the creditor may generally not treat a payment received the next business day as late for any purpose. For purposes of this paragraph (d), the "next business day" means the next day on which the creditor accepts or receives payments by mail.

(2) Payments accepted or received other than by mail. If a creditor accepts or receives payments made on the due date by a method other than mail, such as electronic or telephone payments, the creditor is not required to treat a payment made by that method on the next business day as timely, even if it does not accept mailed payments on the due date.

(e) Limitations on fees related to method of payment. For credit card accounts under an open-end (not home-secured) consumer credit plan, a creditor may not impose a separate fee to allow consumers to make a payment by any method, such as mail, electronic, or telephone payments, unless such payment method involves an expedited service by a customer service representative of the creditor. For purposes of paragraph (e) of this section, the term "creditor" includes a third party that collects, receives, or processes payments on behalf of a creditor.

(f) Changes by card issuer. If a card issuer makes a material change in the address for receiving payments or procedures for handling payments, and such change causes a material delay in the crediting of a payment to the consumer's account during the 60-day period following the date on which such change took effect, the card issuer may not impose any late fee or finance charge for a late payment on the credit card account during the 60-day period following the date on which the change took effect.

§ 1026.11. Treatment of Credit Balances, Account Termination

(a) Credit balances. When a credit balance in excess of $1 is created on a credit account (through transmittal of funds to a creditor in excess of the total balance due on an account, through rebates of unearned finance charges or insurance premiums, or through amounts otherwise owed to or held for the benefit of the consumer), the creditor shall:

(1) Credit the amount of the credit balance to the consumer's account;

(2) Refund any part of the remaining credit balance within seven business days from receipt of a written request from the consumer;

(3) Make a good faith effort to refund to the consumer by cash, check, or money order, or credit to a deposit account of the consumer, any part of the credit balance remaining in the account for more than six months. No further action is required if the consumer's current location is not known to the creditor and cannot be traced through the consumer's last known address or telephone number.

(b) Account termination.

(1) A creditor shall not terminate an account prior to its expiration date solely because the consumer does not incur a finance charge.

(2) Nothing in paragraph (b)(1) of this section prohibits a creditor from terminating an account that is inactive for three or more consecutive months. An account is inactive for purposes of this paragraph if no credit has been extended (such as by purchase, cash advance or balance transfer) and if the account has no outstanding balance.

(c) Timely settlement of estate debts—

(1) General rule.

(i) Reasonable policies and procedures required. For credit card accounts under an open-end (not home-secured) consumer credit plan, card issuers must adopt reasonable written policies and procedures designed to ensure that an administrator of an estate of a deceased accountholder can determine the amount of and pay any balance on the account in a timely manner.

(ii) Application to joint accounts. Paragraph (c) of this section does not apply to the account of a deceased consumer if a joint accountholder remains on the account.

(2) Timely statement of balance—

(i) Requirement. Upon request by the administrator of an estate, a card issuer must provide the administrator with the amount of the balance on a deceased consumer's account in a timely manner.

(ii) Safe harbor. For purposes of paragraph (c)(2)(i) of this section, providing the amount of the balance on the account within 30 days of receiving the request is deemed to be timely.

(3) Limitations after receipt of request from administrator—

(i) Limitation on fees and increases in annual percentage rates. After receiving a request from the administrator of an estate for the amount of the balance on a deceased consumer's account, a card issuer must not impose any fees on the account (such as a late fee, annual fee, or over-the-limit fee) or increase any annual percentage rate, except as provided by § 1026.55(b)(2).

(ii) Limitation on trailing or residual interest. A card issuer must waive or rebate any additional finance charge due to a periodic interest rate if payment in full of the balance disclosed pursuant to paragraph (c)(2) of this section is received within 30 days after disclosure.

§ 1026.12. Special Credit Card Provisions

(a) Issuance of credit cards. Regardless of the purpose for which a credit card is to be used, including business, commercial, or agricultural use, no credit card shall be issued to any person except:

(1) In response to an oral or written request or application for the card; or

(2) As a renewal of, or substitute for, an accepted credit card.

(b) Liability of cardholder for unauthorized use—

(1)(i) Definition of unauthorized use. For purposes of this section, the term "unauthorized use" means the use of a credit card by a person, other than the cardholder, who does not have actual, implied, or apparent authority for such use, and from which the cardholder receives no benefit.

(ii) Limitation on amount. The liability of a cardholder for unauthorized use of a credit card shall not exceed the lesser of $50 or the amount of money, property, labor, or services obtained by the unauthorized use before notification to the card issuer under paragraph (b)(3) of this section.

(2) Conditions of liability. A cardholder shall be liable for unauthorized use of a credit card only if:

(i) The credit card is an accepted credit card;

(ii) The card issuer has provided adequate notice of the cardholder's maximum potential liability and of means by which the card issuer may be notified of loss or theft of the card. The notice shall state that the cardholder's liability shall not exceed $50 (or any lesser amount) and that the cardholder may give oral or written notification, and shall describe a means of notification (for example, a telephone number, an address, or both); and

(iii) The card issuer has provided a means to identify the cardholder on the account or the authorized user of the card.

(3) Notification to card issuer. Notification to a card issuer is given when steps have been taken as may be reasonably required in the ordinary course of business to provide the card issuer with the pertinent information about the loss, theft, or possible unauthorized use of a credit card, regardless of whether any particular officer, employee, or agent of the card issuer does, in fact, receive the information. Notification may be given, at the option of the person giving it, in person, by telephone, or in writing. Notification in writing is considered given at the time of receipt or, whether or not received, at the expiration of the time ordinarily required for transmission, whichever is earlier.

(4) Effect of other applicable law or agreement. If state law or an agreement between a cardholder and the card issuer imposes lesser liability than that provided in this paragraph, the lesser liability shall govern.

(5) Business use of credit cards. If 10 or more credit cards are issued by one card issuer for use by the employees of an organization, this section does not prohibit the card issuer and the organization from agreeing to liability for unauthorized use without regard to this section.

However, liability for unauthorized use may be imposed on an employee of the organization, by either the card issuer or the organization, only in accordance with this section.

(c) Right of cardholder to assert claims or defenses against card issuer—

(1) General rule. When a person who honors a credit card fails to resolve satisfactorily a dispute as to property or services purchased with the credit card in a consumer credit transaction, the cardholder may assert against the card issuer all claims (other than tort claims) and defenses arising out of the transaction and relating to the failure to resolve the dispute. The cardholder may withhold payment up to the amount of credit outstanding for the property or services that gave rise to the dispute and any finance or other charges imposed on that amount.

(2) Adverse credit reports prohibited. If, in accordance with paragraph (c)(1) of this section, the cardholder withholds payment of the amount of credit outstanding for the disputed transaction, the card issuer shall not report that amount as delinquent until the dispute is settled or judgment is rendered.

(3) Limitations.

(i) General. The rights stated in paragraphs (c)(1) and (c)(2) of this section apply only if:

(A) The cardholder has made a good faith attempt to resolve the dispute with the person honoring the credit card; and

(B) The amount of credit extended to obtain the property or services that result in the assertion of the claim or defense by the cardholder exceeds $50, and the disputed transaction occurred in the same state as the cardholder's current designated address or, if not within the same state, within 100 miles from that address.

(ii) Exclusion. The limitations stated in paragraph (c)(3)(i)(B) of this section shall not apply when the person honoring the credit card:

(A) Is the same person as the card issuer;

(B) Is controlled by the card issuer directly or indirectly;

(C) Is under the direct or indirect control of a third person that also directly or indirectly controls the card issuer;

(D) Controls the card issuer directly or indirectly;

(E) Is a franchised dealer in the card issuer's products or services; or

(F) Has obtained the order for the disputed transaction through a mail solicitation made or participated in by the card issuer.

(d) Offsets by card issuer prohibited—

(1) A card issuer may not take any action, either before or after termination of credit card privileges, to offset a cardholder's indebtedness arising from a consumer credit transaction under the relevant credit card plan against funds of the cardholder held on deposit with the card issuer.

(2) Rights of the card issuer. This paragraph does not alter or affect the right of a card issuer acting under state or Federal law to do any of the following with regard to funds of a cardholder held on deposit with the card issuer if the same procedure is constitutionally available to creditors generally: Obtain or enforce a consensual security interest in the funds; attach or otherwise levy upon the funds; or obtain or enforce a court order relating to the funds.

(3) Periodic deductions.

(i) This paragraph does not prohibit a plan, if authorized in writing by the cardholder, under which the card issuer may periodically deduct all or part of the cardholder's credit card debt from a deposit account held with the card issuer (subject to the limitations in § 1026.13(d)(1)).

(ii) With respect to a covered separate credit feature accessible by a hybrid prepaid-credit card as defined in § 1026.61, for purposes of this paragraph (d)(3), "periodically" means no more frequently than once per calendar month, such as on a monthly due date disclosed on the applicable periodic statement in accordance with the requirements of § 1026.7(b)(11)(i)(A) or on an earlier date in each calendar month in accordance with a written authorization signed by the consumer.

(e) Prompt notification of returns and crediting of refunds.

(1) When a creditor other than the card issuer accepts the return of property or forgives a debt for services that is to be reflected as a credit to the consumer's credit card account, that creditor shall, within 7 business days from accepting the return or forgiving the debt, transmit a credit statement to the card issuer through the card issuer's normal channels for credit statements.

(2) The card issuer shall, within 3 business days from receipt of a credit statement, credit the consumer's account with the amount of the refund.

(3) If a creditor other than a card issuer routinely gives cash refunds to consumers paying in cash, the creditor shall also give credit or cash refunds to consumers using credit cards, unless it discloses at the time the transaction is consummated that credit or cash refunds for returns are not given. This section does not require refunds for returns nor does it prohibit refunds in kind.

(f) Discounts; tie-in arrangements. No card issuer may, by contract or otherwise:

(1) Prohibit any person who honors a credit card from offering a discount to a consumer to induce the consumer to pay by cash, check, or similar means rather than by use of a credit card or its underlying account for the purchase of property or services; or

(2) Require any person who honors the card issuer's credit card to open or maintain any account or obtain any other service not essential to the operation of the credit card plan from the card issuer or any other person, as a condition of participation in a credit card plan. If maintenance of an account for clearing purposes is determined to be essential to the operation of the credit card plan, it may be required only if no service charges or minimum balance requirements are imposed.

(g) Relation to Electronic Fund Transfer Act and Regulation E. For guidance on whether Regulation Z (12 CFR part 1026) or Regulation E (12 CFR part 1005) applies in instances involving both credit and electronic fund transfer aspects, refer to Regulation E, 12 CFR 1005.12(a) regarding issuance and liability for unauthorized use. On matters other than issuance and liability, this section applies to the credit aspects of combined credit/electronic fund transfer transactions, as applicable.

§ 1026.13. Billing Error Resolution

(a) Definition of billing error. For purposes of this section, the term billing error means:

(1) A reflection on or with a periodic statement of an extension of credit that is not made to the consumer or to a person who has actual, implied, or apparent authority to use the consumer's credit card or open-end credit plan.

(2) A reflection on or with a periodic statement of an extension of credit that is not identified in accordance with the requirements of §§ 1026.7(a)(2) or (b)(2), as applicable, and 1026.8.

(3) A reflection on or with a periodic statement of an extension of credit for property or services not accepted by the consumer or the consumer's designee, or not delivered to the consumer or the consumer's designee as agreed.

(4) A reflection on a periodic statement of the creditor's failure to credit properly a payment or other credit issued to the consumer's account.

(5) A reflection on a periodic statement of a computational or similar error of an accounting nature that is made by the creditor.

(6) A reflection on a periodic statement of an extension of credit for which the consumer requests additional clarification, including documentary evidence.

(7) The creditor's failure to mail or deliver a periodic statement to the consumer's last known address if that address was received by the creditor, in writing, at least 20 days before the end of the billing cycle for which the statement was required.

(b) Billing error notice. A billing error notice is a written notice from a consumer that:

(1) Is received by a creditor at the address disclosed under § 1026.7(a)(9) or (b)(9), as applicable, no later than 60 days after the creditor transmitted the first periodic statement that reflects the alleged billing error;

(2) Enables the creditor to identify the consumer's name and account number; and

(3) To the extent possible, indicates the consumer's belief and the reasons for the belief that a billing error exists, and the type, date, and amount of the error.

(c) Time for resolution; general procedures.

(1) The creditor shall mail or deliver written acknowledgment to the consumer within 30 days of receiving a billing error notice, unless the creditor has complied with the appropriate resolution procedures of paragraphs (e) and (f) of this section, as applicable, within the 30-day period; and

(2) The creditor shall comply with the appropriate resolution procedures of paragraphs (e) and (f) of this section, as applicable, within 2 complete billing cycles (but in no event later than 90 days) after receiving a billing error notice.

(d) Rules pending resolution. Until a billing error is resolved under paragraph (e) or (f) of this section, the following rules apply:

(1) Consumer's right to withhold disputed amount; collection action prohibited. The consumer need not pay (and the creditor may not try to collect) any portion of any required payment that the consumer believes is related to the disputed amount (including related finance or other charges). If the cardholder has enrolled in an automatic payment plan offered by the card issuer and has agreed to pay the credit card indebtedness by periodic deductions from the cardholder's deposit account, the card issuer shall not deduct any part of the disputed amount or related finance or other charges if a billing error notice is received any time up to 3 business days before the scheduled payment date.

(2) Adverse credit reports prohibited. The creditor or its agent shall not (directly or indirectly) make or threaten to make an adverse report to any person about the consumer's credit standing, or report that an amount or account is delinquent, because the consumer failed to pay the disputed amount or related finance or other charges.

(3) Acceleration of debt and restriction of account prohibited. A creditor shall not accelerate any part of the consumer's indebtedness or restrict or close a consumer's account solely because the consumer has exercised in good faith rights provided by this section. A creditor may be subject to the forfeiture penalty under 15 U.S.C. 1666(e) for failure to comply with any of the requirements of this section.

(4) **Permitted creditor actions.** A creditor is not prohibited from taking action to collect any undisputed portion of the item or bill; from deducting any disputed amount and related finance or other charges from the consumer's credit limit on the account; or from reflecting a disputed amount and related finance or other charges on a periodic statement, provided that the creditor indicates on or with the periodic statement that payment of any disputed amount and related finance or other charges is not required pending the creditor's compliance with this section.

(e) Procedures if billing error occurred as asserted. If a creditor determines that a billing error occurred as asserted, it shall within the time limits in paragraph (c)(2) of this section:

(1) Correct the billing error and credit the consumer's account with any disputed amount and related finance or other charges, as applicable; and

(2) Mail or deliver a correction notice to the consumer.

(f) Procedures if different billing error or no billing error occurred. If, after conducting a reasonable investigation, a creditor determines that no billing error occurred or that a different billing error occurred from that asserted, the creditor shall within the time limits in paragraph (c)(2) of this section:

(1) Mail or deliver to the consumer an explanation that sets forth the reasons for the creditor's belief that the billing error alleged by the consumer is incorrect in whole or in part;

(2) Furnish copies of documentary evidence of the consumer's indebtedness, if the consumer so requests; and

(3) If a different billing error occurred, correct the billing error and credit the consumer's account with any disputed amount and related finance or other charges, as applicable.

(g) Creditor's rights and duties after resolution. If a creditor, after complying with all of the requirements of this section, determines that a consumer owes all or part of the disputed amount and related finance or other charges, the creditor:

(1) Shall promptly notify the consumer in writing of the time when payment is due and the portion of the disputed amount and related finance or other charges that the consumer still owes;

(2) Shall allow any time period disclosed under § 1026.6(a)(1) or (b)(2)(v), as applicable, and § 1026.7(a)(8) or (b)(8), as applicable, during which the consumer can pay the amount due under paragraph (g)(1) of this section without incurring additional finance or other charges;

(3) May report an account or amount as delinquent because the amount due under paragraph (g)(1) of this section remains unpaid after the creditor has allowed any time period disclosed under § 1026.6(a)(1) or (b)(2)(v), as applicable, and § 1026.7(a)(8) or (b)(8), as applicable or 10 days (whichever is longer) during which the consumer can pay the amount; but

(4) May not report that an amount or account is delinquent because the amount due under paragraph (g)(1) of the section remains unpaid, if the creditor receives (within the time allowed for payment in paragraph (g)(3) of this section) further written notice from the consumer that any portion of the billing error is still in dispute, unless the creditor also:

(i) Promptly reports that the amount or account is in dispute;

(ii) Mails or delivers to the consumer (at the same time the report is made) a written notice of the name and address of each person to whom the creditor makes a report; and

(iii) Promptly reports any subsequent resolution of the reported delinquency to all persons to whom the creditor has made a report.

(h) Reassertion of billing error. A creditor that has fully complied with the requirements of this section has no further responsibilities under this section (other than as provided in paragraph (g)(4) of this section) if a consumer reasserts substantially the same billing error.

(i) Relation to Electronic Fund Transfer Act and Regulation E. A creditor shall comply with the requirements of Regulation E, 12 CFR 1005.11, and 1005.18(e) as applicable, governing error resolution rather than those of paragraphs (a), (b), (c), (e), (f), and (h) of this section if:

(1) Except with respect to a prepaid account as defined in § 1026.61, an extension of credit that is incident to an electronic fund transfer occurs under an agreement between the consumer and a financial institution to extend credit when the consumer's account is overdrawn or to maintain a specified minimum balance in the consumer's account; or

(2) With regard to a covered separate credit feature and an asset feature of a prepaid account where both are accessible by a hybrid prepaid-credit card as defined in § 1026.61, an extension of credit that is incident to an electronic fund transfer occurs when the hybrid prepaid-credit card accesses both funds in the asset feature of the prepaid account and a credit extension from the credit feature with respect to a particular transaction.

§ 1026.14. Determination of Annual Percentage Rate

(a) General rule. The annual percentage rate is a measure of the cost of credit, expressed as a yearly rate. An annual percentage rate shall be considered accurate if it is not more than $^1/_8$th of 1 percentage point above or below the annual percentage rate determined in accordance with this section. An error in disclosure of the annual percentage rate or finance charge shall not, in itself, be considered a violation of this part if:

(1) The error resulted from a corresponding error in a calculation tool used in good faith by the creditor; and

(2) Upon discovery of the error, the creditor promptly discontinues use of that calculation tool for disclosure purposes, and notifies the Bureau in writing of the error in the calculation tool.

(b) Annual percentage rate—in general. Where one or more periodic rates may be used to compute the finance charge, the annual percentage rate(s) to be disclosed for purposes of §§ 1026.60, 1026.40, 1026.6, 1026.7(a)(4) or (b)(4), 1026.9, 1026.15, 1026.16, 1026.26, 1026.55, and 1026.56 shall be computed by multiplying each periodic rate by the number of periods in a year.

(c) Optional effective annual percentage rate for periodic statements for creditors offering open-end credit plans secured by a consumer's dwelling. A creditor offering an open-end plan subject to the requirements of § 1026.40 need not disclose an effective annual percentage rate. Such a creditor may, at its option, disclose an effective annual percentage rate(s) pursuant to § 1026.7(a)(7) and compute the effective annual percentage rate as follows:

(1) Solely periodic rates imposed. If the finance charge is determined solely by applying one or more periodic rates, at the creditor's option, either:

(i) By multiplying each periodic rate by the number of periods in a year; or

(ii) By dividing the total finance charge for the billing cycle by the sum of the balances to which the periodic rates were applied and multiplying the quotient (expressed as a percentage) by the number of billing cycles in a year.

(2) Minimum or fixed charge, but not transaction charge, imposed. If the finance charge imposed during the billing cycle is or includes a minimum, fixed, or other charge not due to the application of a periodic rate, other than a charge with respect to any specific transaction during the billing cycle, by dividing the total finance charge for the billing cycle by the amount of the balance(s) to which it is applicable and multiplying the quotient (expressed as a percentage) by the number of billing cycles in a year. If there is no balance to which the finance charge is applicable, an annual percentage rate cannot be determined under this section. Where the finance charge imposed during the billing cycle is or includes a loan fee, points, or similar charge that relates to opening, renewing, or continuing an account, the amount of such charge shall not be included in the calculation of the annual percentage rate.

(3) Transaction charge imposed. If the finance charge imposed during the billing cycle is or includes a charge relating to a specific transaction during the billing cycle (even if the total finance charge also includes any other minimum, fixed, or other charge not due to the application of a periodic rate), by dividing the total finance charge imposed during the billing cycle by the total of all balances and other amounts on which a finance charge was imposed during the billing cycle without duplication, and multiplying the quotient (expressed as a percentage) by the number of billing cycles in a year, except that the annual percentage rate shall not be less than the largest rate determined by multiplying each periodic rate imposed during the billing cycle by the number of periods in a year. Where the finance charge imposed during the billing cycle is or includes a loan fee, points, or similar charge that relates to the opening, renewing, or continuing an account, the amount of such charge shall not be included in the calculation of the annual percentage rate. See Appendix F to this part regarding determination of the denominator of the fraction under this paragraph.

(4) If the finance charge imposed during the billing cycle is or includes a minimum, fixed, or other charge not due to the application of a periodic rate and the total finance charge imposed during the billing cycle does not exceed 50 cents for a monthly or longer billing cycle, or the pro rata part of 50 cents for a billing cycle shorter than monthly, at the creditor's option, by multiplying each applicable periodic rate by the number of periods in a year, notwithstanding the provisions of paragraphs (c)(2) and (c)(3) of this section.

(d) Calculations where daily periodic rate applied. If the provisions of paragraph (c)(1)(ii) or (c)(2) of this section apply and all or a portion of the finance charge is determined by the application of one or more daily periodic rates, the annual percentage rate may be determined either:

(1) By dividing the total finance charge by the average of the daily balances and multiplying the quotient by the number of billing cycles in a year; or

(2) By dividing the total finance charge by the sum of the daily balances and multiplying the quotient by 365.

§ 1026.15. Right of Rescission

(a) Consumer's right to rescind.

(1)(i) Except as provided in paragraph (a)(1)(ii) of this section, in a credit plan in which a security interest is or will be retained or acquired in a consumer's principal dwelling, each consumer whose ownership interest is or will be subject to the security interest shall have the right to rescind: each credit extension made under the plan; the plan when the plan is opened; a security interest when added or increased to secure an existing plan; and the increase when a credit limit on the plan is increased.

(ii) As provided in section 125(e) of the Act, the consumer does not have the right to rescind each credit extension made under the plan if such extension is made in accordance with a previously established credit limit for the plan.

(2) To exercise the right to rescind, the consumer shall notify the creditor of the rescission by mail, telegram, or other means of written communication. Notice is considered given when mailed, or when filed for telegraphic transmission, or, if sent by other means, when delivered to the creditor's designated place of business.

(3) The consumer may exercise the right to rescind until midnight of the third business day following the occurrence described in paragraph (a)(1) of this section that gave rise to the right of rescission, delivery of the notice required by paragraph (b) of this section, or delivery of all material disclosures, whichever occurs last. If the required notice and material disclosures are not delivered, the right to rescind shall expire 3 years after the occurrence giving rise to the right of rescission, or upon transfer of all of the consumer's interest in the property, or upon sale of the property, whichever occurs first. In the case of certain administrative proceedings, the rescission period shall be extended in accordance with section 125(f) of the Act. The term material disclosures means the information that must be provided to satisfy the requirements in § 1026.6 with regard to the method of determining the finance charge and the balance upon which a finance charge will be imposed, the annual percentage rate, the amount or method of determining the amount of any membership or participation fee that may be imposed as part of the plan, and the payment information described in § 1026.40(d)(5)(i) and (ii) that is required under § 1026.6(e)(2).

(4) When more than one consumer has the right to rescind, the exercise of the right by one consumer shall be effective as to all consumers.

(b) Notice of right to rescind. In any transaction or occurrence subject to rescission, a creditor shall deliver two copies of the notice of the right to rescind to each consumer entitled to rescind (one copy to each if the notice is delivered in electronic form in accordance with the consumer consent and other applicable provisions of the E-Sign Act). The notice shall identify the transaction or occurrence and clearly and conspicuously disclose the following:

(1) The retention or acquisition of a security interest in the consumer's principal dwelling.

(2) The consumer's right to rescind, as described in paragraph (a)(1) of this section.

(3) How to exercise the right to rescind, with a form for that purpose, designating the address of the creditor's place of business.

(4) The effects of rescission, as described in paragraph (d) of this section.

(5) The date the rescission period expires.

(c) Delay of creditor's performance. Unless a consumer waives the right to rescind under paragraph (e) of this section, no money shall be disbursed other than in escrow, no services shall be performed, and no materials delivered until after the rescission period has expired and the creditor is reasonably satisfied that the consumer has not rescinded. A creditor does not violate this section if a third party with no knowledge of the event activating the rescission right does not delay in providing materials or services, as long as the debt incurred for those materials or services is not secured by the property subject to rescission.

(d) Effects of rescission.

(1) When a consumer rescinds a transaction, the security interest giving rise to the right of rescission becomes void, and the consumer shall not be liable for any amount, including any finance charge.

(2) Within 20 calendar days after receipt of a notice of rescission, the creditor shall return any money or property that has been given to anyone in connection with the transaction and shall take any action necessary to reflect the termination of the security interest.

(3) If the creditor has delivered any money or property, the consumer may retain possession until the creditor has met its obligation under paragraph (d)(2) of this section. When the creditor has complied with that paragraph, the consumer shall tender the money or property to the creditor or, where the latter would be impracticable or inequitable, tender its reasonable value. At the consumer's option, tender of property may be made at the location of the property or at the consumer's residence. Tender of money must be made at the creditor's designated place of business. If the creditor does not take possession of the money or property within 20 calendar days after the consumer's tender, the consumer may keep it without further obligation.

(4) The procedures outlined in paragraphs (d)(2) and (3) of this section may be modified by court order.

(e) Consumer's waiver of right to rescind. The consumer may modify or waive the right to rescind if the consumer determines that the extension of credit is needed to meet a bona fide personal financial emergency. To modify or waive the right, the consumer shall give the creditor a dated written statement that describes the emergency, specifically modifies or waives the right to rescind, and bears the signature of all the consumers entitled to rescind. Printed forms for this purpose are prohibited.

(f) Exempt transactions. The right to rescind does not apply to the following:

(1) A residential mortgage transaction.

(2) A credit plan in which a state agency is a creditor.

§ 1026.16. Advertising

(a) Actually available terms. If an advertisement for credit states specific credit terms, it shall state only those terms that actually are or will be arranged or offered by the creditor.

(b) Advertisement of terms that require additional disclosures.

(1) Any term required to be disclosed under § 1026.6(b)(3) set forth affirmatively or negatively in an advertisement for an open-end (not home-secured) credit plan triggers additional disclosures under this section. Any term required to be disclosed under § 1026.6(a)(1) or (a)(2) set forth affirmatively or negatively in an advertisement for a home-equity plan subject to the requirements of § 1026.40 triggers additional disclosures under this section. If any of the terms that trigger additional disclosures under this paragraph is set forth in an advertisement, the advertisement shall also clearly and conspicuously set forth the following:

(i) Any minimum, fixed, transaction, activity or similar charge that is a finance charge under § 1026.4 that could be imposed.

(ii) Any periodic rate that may be applied expressed as an annual percentage rate as determined under § 1026.14(b). If the plan provides for a variable periodic rate, that fact shall be disclosed.

(iii) Any membership or participation fee that could be imposed.

(2) If an advertisement for credit to finance the purchase of goods or services specified in the advertisement states a periodic payment amount, the advertisement shall also state the total of payments and the time period to repay the obligation, assuming that the consumer pays only the periodic payment amount advertised. The disclosure of the total of payments and the time period to repay the obligation must be equally prominent to the statement of the periodic payment amount.

(c) Catalogs or other multiple-page advertisements; electronic advertisements.

(1) If a catalog or other multiple-page advertisement, or an electronic advertisement (such as an advertisement appearing on an Internet Web site), gives information in a table or schedule in sufficient detail to permit determination of the disclosures required by paragraph (b) of this section, it shall be considered a single advertisement if:

(i) The table or schedule is clearly and conspicuously set forth; and

(ii) Any statement of terms set forth in § 1026.6 appearing anywhere else in the catalog or advertisement clearly refers to the page or location where the table or schedule begins.

(2) A catalog or other multiple-page advertisement or an electronic advertisement (such as an advertisement appearing on an Internet Web site) complies with this paragraph if the table or schedule of terms includes all appropriate disclosures for a representative scale of amounts up to the level of the more commonly sold higher-priced property or services offered.

(d) Additional requirements for home-equity plans—

(1) Advertisement of terms that require additional disclosures. If any of the terms required to be disclosed under § 1026.6(a)(1) or (a)(2) or the payment terms of the plan are set forth, affirmatively or negatively, in an advertisement for a home-equity plan subject to the requirements of § 1026.40, the advertisement also shall clearly and conspicuously set forth the following:

(i) Any loan fee that is a percentage of the credit limit under the plan and an estimate of any other fees imposed for opening the plan, stated as a single dollar amount or a reasonable range.

(ii) Any periodic rate used to compute the finance charge, expressed as an annual percentage rate as determined under § 1026.14(b).

(iii) The maximum annual percentage rate that may be imposed in a variable-rate plan.

(2) Discounted and premium rates. If an advertisement states an initial annual percentage rate that is not based on the index and margin used to make later rate adjustments in a variable-rate plan, the advertisement also shall state with equal prominence and in close proximity to the initial rate:

(i) The period of time such initial rate will be in effect; and

(ii) A reasonably current annual percentage rate that would have been in effect using the index and margin.

(3) Balloon payment. If an advertisement contains a statement of any minimum periodic payment and a balloon payment may result if only the minimum periodic payments are made, even if such a payment is uncertain or unlikely, the advertisement also shall state with equal prominence and in close proximity to the minimum periodic payment statement that a balloon payment may result, if applicable. A balloon payment results if paying the minimum periodic payments does not fully amortize the outstanding balance by a specified date or time, and the consumer is required to repay the entire outstanding balance at such time. If a balloon payment will occur when the consumer makes only the minimum payments required under the plan, an advertisement for such a program which contains any statement of any minimum periodic payment shall also state with equal prominence and in close proximity to the minimum periodic payment statement:

(i) That a balloon payment will result; and

(ii) The amount and timing of the balloon payment that will result if the consumer makes only the minimum payments for the maximum period of time that the consumer is permitted to make such payments.

(4) Tax implications. An advertisement that states that any interest expense incurred under the home-equity plan is or may be tax deductible may not be misleading in this regard. If an advertisement distributed in paper form or through the Internet (rather than by radio or television) is for a home-equity plan secured by the consumer's principal dwelling, and the advertisement states that the advertised extension of credit may exceed the fair market value of the dwelling, the advertisement shall clearly and conspicuously state that:

(i) The interest on the portion of the credit extension that is greater than the fair market value of the dwelling is not tax deductible for Federal income tax purposes; and

(ii) The consumer should consult a tax adviser for further information regarding the deductibility of interest and charges.

(5) Misleading terms. An advertisement may not refer to a home-equity plan as "free money" or contain a similarly misleading term.

(6) Promotional rates and payments.

(i) Definitions. The following definitions apply for purposes of paragraph (d)(6) of this section:

(A) Promotional rate. The term "promotional rate" means, in a variable-rate plan, any annual percentage rate that is not based on the index and margin that will be used to make rate adjustments under the plan, if that rate is less than a reasonably current annual percentage rate that would be in effect under the index and margin that will be used to make rate adjustments under the plan.

(B) Promotional payment. The term "promotional payment" means:

(1) For a variable-rate plan, any minimum payment applicable for a promotional period that:

(i) Is not derived by applying the index and margin to the outstanding balance when such index and margin will be used to determine other minimum payments under the plan; and

(ii) Is less than other minimum payments under the plan derived by applying a reasonably current index and margin that will be used to determine the amount of such payments, given an assumed balance.

(2) For a plan other than a variable-rate plan, any minimum payment applicable for a promotional period if that payment is less than other payments required under the plan given an assumed balance.

(C) Promotional period. A "promotional period" means a period of time, less than the full term of the loan, that the promotional rate or promotional payment may be applicable.

(ii) Stating the promotional period and post-promotional rate or payments. If any annual percentage rate that may be applied to a plan is a promotional rate, or if any payment applicable to a plan is a promotional payment, the following must be disclosed in any advertisement, other than television or radio advertisements, in a clear and conspicuous manner with equal prominence and in close proximity to each listing of the promotional rate or payment:

(A) The period of time during which the promotional rate or promotional payment will apply;

(B) In the case of a promotional rate, any annual percentage rate that will apply under the plan. If such rate is variable, the annual percentage rate must be disclosed in accordance with the accuracy standards in §§ 1026.40 or 1026.16(b)(1)(ii) as applicable; and

(C) In the case of a promotional payment, the amounts and time periods of any payments that will apply under the plan. In variable-rate transactions, payments that will be determined based on application of an index and margin shall be disclosed based on a reasonably current index and margin.

(iii) Envelope excluded. The requirements in paragraph (d)(6)(ii) of this section do not apply to an envelope in which an application or solicitation is mailed, or to a banner advertisement or pop-up advertisement linked to an application or solicitation provided electronically.

(e) Alternative disclosures—television or radio advertisements. An advertisement made through television or radio stating any of the terms requiring additional disclosures under paragraphs (b)(1) or (d)(1) of this section may alternatively comply with paragraphs (b)(1) or (d)(1) of this section by stating the information required by paragraphs (b)(1)(ii) or (d)(1)(ii) of this section, as applicable, and listing a toll-free telephone number, or any telephone number that allows a consumer to reverse the phone charges when calling for information, along with a reference that such number may be used by consumers to obtain the additional cost information.

(f) Misleading terms. An advertisement may not refer to an annual percentage rate as "fixed," or use a similar term, unless the advertisement also specifies a time period that the rate will be fixed and the rate will not increase during that period, or if no such time period is provided, the rate will not increase while the plan is open.

(g) Promotional rates and fees—

(1) Scope. The requirements of this paragraph apply to any advertisement of an open-end (not home-secured) plan, including promotional materials accompanying applications or solicitations subject to § 1026.60(c) or accompanying applications or solicitations subject to § 1026.60(e).

(2) Definitions.

(i) Promotional rate means any annual percentage rate applicable to one or more balances or transactions on an open-end (not home-secured) plan for a specified period of time that is lower than the annual percentage rate that will be in effect at the end of that period on such balances or transactions.

(ii) Introductory rate means a promotional rate offered in connection with the opening of an account.

(iii) Promotional period means the maximum time period for which a promotional rate or promotional fee may be applicable.

(iv) Promotional fee means a fee required to be disclosed under § 1026.6(b)(1) and (2) applicable to an open-end (not home-secured) plan, or to one or more balances or transactions on an open-end (not home-secured) plan, for a specified period of time that is lower than the fee that will be in effect at the end of that period for such plan or types of balances or transactions.

(v) Introductory fee means a promotional fee offered in connection with the opening of an account.

(3) Stating the term "introductory". If any annual percentage rate or fee that may be applied to the account is an introductory rate or introductory fee, the term introductory or intro must be in immediate proximity to each listing of the introductory rate or introductory fee in a written or electronic advertisement.

(4) Stating the promotional period and post-promotional rate or fee. If any annual percentage rate that may be applied to the account is a promotional rate under paragraph (g)(2)(i) of this section or any fee that may be applied to the account is a promotional fee under paragraph (g)(2)(iv) of this section, the information in paragraphs (g)(4)(i) and, as applicable, (g)(4)(ii) or (iii) of this section must be stated in a clear and conspicuous manner in the advertisement. If the rate or fee is stated in a written or electronic advertisement, the information in paragraphs (g)(4)(i) and, as applicable, (g)(4)(ii) or (iii) of this section must also be stated in a prominent location closely proximate to the first listing of the promotional rate or promotional fee.

(i) When the promotional rate or promotional fee will end;

(ii) The annual percentage rate that will apply after the end of the promotional period. If such rate is variable, the annual percentage rate must comply with the accuracy standards in §§ 1026.60(c)(2), 1026.60(d)(3), 1026.60(e)(4), or 1026.16(b)(1)(ii), as applicable. If such rate cannot be determined at the time disclosures are given because the rate depends at least in part on a later determination of the consumer's creditworthiness, the advertisement must disclose the specific rates or the range of rates that might apply; and

(iii) The fee that will apply after the end of the promotional period.

(5) Envelope excluded. The requirements in paragraph (g)(4) of this section do not apply to an envelope or other enclosure in which an application or solicitation is mailed, or to a banner advertisement or pop-up advertisement, linked to an application or solicitation provided electronically.

(h) Deferred interest or similar offers—

(1) Scope. The requirements of this paragraph apply to any advertisement of an open-end credit plan not subject to § 1026.40, including promotional materials accompanying applications or solicitations subject to § 1026.60(c) or accompanying applications or solicitations subject to § 1026.60(e).

(2) Definitions. "Deferred interest" means finance charges, accrued on balances or transactions, that a consumer is not obligated to pay or that will be waived or refunded to a consumer if those balances or transactions are paid in full by a specified date. The maximum period from the date the consumer becomes obligated for the balance or transaction until the specified date by which the consumer must pay the balance or transaction in full in order to avoid finance charges, or receive a waiver or refund of finance charges, is the "deferred interest period." "Deferred interest" does not include any finance charges the consumer avoids paying in connection with any recurring grace period.

(3) Stating the deferred interest period. If a deferred interest offer is advertised, the deferred interest period must be stated in a clear and conspicuous manner in the advertisement. If the phrase "no interest" or similar term regarding the possible avoidance of interest obligations under the deferred interest program is stated, the term "if paid in full" must also be stated in a clear and conspicuous manner preceding the disclosure of the deferred interest period in the advertisement. If the deferred interest offer is included in a written or electronic advertisement, the deferred interest period and, if applicable, the term "if paid in full" must also be stated in immediate proximity to each statement of "no interest," "no payments," "deferred interest," "same as cash," or similar term regarding interest or payments during the deferred interest period.

(4) Stating the terms of the deferred interest or similar offer. If any deferred interest offer is advertised, the information in paragraphs (h)(4)(i) and (h)(4)(ii) of this section must be stated in the advertisement, in language similar to Sample G-24 in appendix G to this part. If the deferred interest offer is included in a written or electronic advertisement, the information in paragraphs (h)(4)(i) and (h)(4)(ii) of this section must also be stated in a prominent location closely proximate to the first statement of "no interest," "no payments," "deferred interest," "same as cash," or similar term regarding interest or payments during the deferred interest period.

(i) A statement that interest will be charged from the date the consumer becomes obligated for the balance or transaction subject to the deferred interest offer if the balance or transaction is not paid in full within the deferred interest period; and

(ii) A statement, if applicable, that interest will be charged from the date the consumer incurs the balance or transaction subject to the deferred interest offer if the account is in default before the end of the deferred interest period.

(5) Envelope excluded. The requirements in paragraph (h)(4) of this section do not apply to an envelope or other enclosure in which an application or solicitation is mailed, or to a banner advertisement or pop-up advertisement linked to an application or solicitation provided electronically.

SUBPART C: CLOSED-END CREDIT

§ 1026.17. General Disclosure Requirements

(a) Form of disclosures. Except for the disclosures required by § 1026.19(e), (f), and (g):

(1) The creditor shall make the disclosures required by this subpart clearly and conspicuously in writing, in a form that the consumer may keep. The disclosures required by this subpart may be provided to the consumer in electronic form, subject to compliance with the consumer consent and other applicable provisions of the Electronic Signatures in Global and National Commerce Act (E-Sign Act) (15 U.S.C. 7001 et seq.). The disclosures required by §§ 1026.17(g), 1026.19(b), and 1026.24 may be provided to the consumer in electronic form without regard to the consumer consent or other provisions of the E-Sign Act in the circumstances set forth in those sections. The disclosures shall be grouped together, shall be segregated from everything else, and shall not contain any information not directly related to the disclosures required under § 1026.18, § 1026.20(c) and (d), or § 1026.47. The disclosures required by § 1026.20(d) shall be provided as a separate document from all other written materials. The disclosures may include an acknowledgment of receipt, the date of the transaction, and the consumer's name, address, and account number. The following disclosures may be made together with or separately from other required disclosures: The creditor's identity under § 1026.18(a), the variable rate example under § 1026.18(f)(1)(iv), insurance or debt cancellation under § 1026.18(n), and certain security interest charges under § 1026.18(*o*). The itemization of the amount financed under § 1026.18(c)(1) must be separate from the other disclosures under § 1026.18, except for private education loan disclosures made in compliance with § 1026.47.

(2) Except for private education loan disclosures made in compliance with § 1026.47, the terms "finance charge" and "annual percentage rate," when required to be disclosed under § 1026.18(d) and (e) together with a corresponding amount or percentage rate, shall be more conspicuous than any other disclosure, except the creditor's identity under § 1026.18(a). For private education loan disclosures made in compliance with § 1026.47, the term "annual percentage rate," and the corresponding percentage rate must be less conspicuous than the term "finance charge" and corresponding amount under § 1026.18(d), the interest rate under §§ 1026.47(b)(1)(i) and (c)(1), and the notice of the right to cancel under § 1026.47(c)(4).

(b) Time of disclosures. The creditor shall make disclosures before consummation of the transaction. In certain residential mortgage transactions, special timing requirements are set forth in § 1026.19(a). In certain variable-rate transactions, special timing requirements for variable-rate disclosures are set forth in §§ 1026.19(b) and 1026.20(c) and (d). For private education loan disclosures made in compliance with § 1026.47, special timing requirements are set forth in § 1026.46(d). In certain transactions involving mail or telephone orders or a series of sales, the timing of disclosures may be delayed in accordance with paragraphs (g) and (h) of this section. This paragraph (b) does not apply to the disclosures required by §§ 1026.19(e), (f), and (g) and 1026.20(e).

(c) Basis of disclosures and use of estimates.

(1) The disclosures shall reflect the terms of the legal obligation between the parties.

(2)(i) If any information necessary for an accurate disclosure is unknown to the creditor, the creditor shall make the disclosure based on the best information reasonably available at the time the disclosure is provided to the consumer, and shall state clearly that the disclosure is an estimate.

(ii) For a transaction in which a portion of the interest is determined on a per-diem basis and collected at consummation, any disclosure affected by the per-diem interest shall be considered accurate if the disclosure is based on the information known to the creditor at the time that the disclosure documents are prepared for consummation of the transaction.

(3) The creditor may disregard the effects of the following in making calculations and disclosures.

(i) That payments must be collected in whole cents.

(ii) That dates of scheduled payments and advances may be changed because the scheduled date is not a business day.

(iii) That months have different numbers of days.

(iv) The occurrence of leap year.

(4) In making calculations and disclosures, the creditor may disregard any irregularity in the first period that falls within the limits described below and any payment schedule irregularity that results from the irregular first period:

(i) For transactions in which the term is less than 1 year, a first period not more than 6 days shorter or 13 days longer than a regular period;

(ii) For transactions in which the term is at least 1 year and less than 10 years, a first period not more than 11 days shorter or 21 days longer than a regular period; and

(iii) For transactions in which the term is at least 10 years, a first period shorter than or not more than 32 days longer than a regular period.

(5) If an obligation is payable on demand, the creditor shall make the disclosures based on an assumed maturity of 1 year. If an alternate maturity date is stated in the legal obligation between the parties, the disclosures shall be based on that date.

(6)(i) A series of advances under an agreement to extend credit up to a certain amount may be considered as one transaction.

(ii) When a multiple-advance loan to finance the construction of a dwelling may be permanently financed by the same creditor, the construction phase and the permanent phase may be treated as either one transaction or more than one transaction.

(d) Multiple creditors; multiple consumers. If a transaction involves more than one creditor, only one set of disclosures shall be given and the creditors shall agree among themselves which creditor must comply with the requirements that this part imposes on any or all of them. If there is more than one consumer, the disclosures may be made to any consumer who is primarily liable on the obligation. If the transaction is rescindable under § 1026.23, however, the disclosures shall be made to each consumer who has the right to rescind.

(e) Effect of subsequent events. If a disclosure becomes inaccurate because of an event that occurs after the creditor delivers the required disclosures, the inaccuracy is not a violation of this part, although new disclosures may be required under paragraph (f) of this section, § 1026.19, § 1026.20, or § 1026.48(c)(4).

(f) Early disclosures. Except for private education loan disclosures made in compliance with § 1026.47, if disclosures required by this subpart are given before the date of consummation of a transaction and a subsequent event makes them inaccurate, the creditor shall disclose before consummation (subject to the provisions of § 1026.19(a)(2), (e), and (f)):

(1) Any changed term unless the term was based on an estimate in accordance with § 1026.17(c)(2) and was labeled an estimate;

(2) All changed terms, if the annual percentage rate at the time of consummation varies from the annual percentage rate disclosed earlier by more than 1/8 of 1 percentage point in a regular transaction, or more than ¼ of 1 percentage point in an irregular transaction, as defined in § 1026.22(a).

(g) Mail or telephone orders—delay in disclosures. Except for private education loan disclosures made in compliance with § 1026.47 and mortgage disclosures made in compliance with § 1026.19(a) or (e), (f), and (g), if a creditor receives a purchase order or a request for an extension of credit by mail, telephone, or facsimile machine without face-to-face or direct telephone solicitation, the creditor may delay the disclosures until the due date of the first payment, if the following information for representative amounts or ranges of credit is made available in written form or in electronic form to the consumer or to the public before the actual purchase order or request:

(1) The cash price or the principal loan amount.

(2) The total sale price.

(3) The finance charge.

(4) The annual percentage rate, and if the rate may increase after consummation, the following disclosures:

(i) The circumstances under which the rate may increase.

(ii) Any limitations on the increase.

(iii) The effect of an increase.

(5) The terms of repayment.

(h) Series of sales—delay in disclosures. Except for mortgage disclosures made in compliance with § 1026.19(a) or (e), (f), and (g), if a credit sale is one of a series made under an agreement providing that subsequent sales may be added to an outstanding balance, the creditor may delay the required disclosures until the due date of the first payment for the current sale, if the following two conditions are met:

(1) The consumer has approved in writing the annual percentage rate or rates, the range of balances to which they apply, and the method of treating any unearned finance charge on an existing balance.

(2) The creditor retains no security interest in any property after the creditor has received payments equal to the cash price and any finance charge attributable to the sale of that property. For purposes of this provision, in the case of items purchased on different dates, the first purchased is deemed the first item paid for; in the case of items purchased on the same date, the lowest priced is deemed the first item paid for.

(i) Interim student credit extensions. For transactions involving an interim credit extension under a student credit program for which an application is received prior to the mandatory compliance date of §§ 1026.46, 47, and 48, the creditor need not make the following disclosures: the finance charge under § 1026.18(d), the payment schedule under § 1026.18(g), the total of payments under § 1026.18(h), or the total sale price under § 1026.18(j) at the time the credit is actually extended. The creditor must make complete disclosures at the time the creditor and consumer agree upon the repayment schedule for the total obligation. At that time, a new set of disclosures must be made of all applicable items under § 1026.18.

§ 1026.18. Content of Disclosures

For each transaction other than a mortgage transaction subject to § 1026.19(e) and (f), the creditor shall disclose the following information as applicable:

(a) Creditor. The identity of the creditor making the disclosures.

(b) Amount financed. The amount financed, using that term, and a brief description such as the amount of credit provided to you or on your behalf. The amount financed is calculated by:

(1) Determining the principal loan amount or the cash price (subtracting any downpayment);

(2) Adding any other amounts that are financed by the creditor and are not part of the finance charge; and

(3) Subtracting any prepaid finance charge.

(c) Itemization of amount financed.

(1) Except as provided in paragraphs (c)(2) and (c)(3) of this section, a separate written itemization of the amount financed, including:

(i) The amount of any proceeds distributed directly to the consumer.

(ii) The amount credited to the consumer's account with the creditor.

(iii) Any amounts paid to other persons by the creditor on the consumer's behalf. The creditor shall identify those persons. The following payees may be described using generic or other general terms and need not be further identified: public officials or government agencies, credit reporting agencies, appraisers, and insurance companies.

(iv) The prepaid finance charge.

(2) The creditor need not comply with paragraph (c)(1) of this section if the creditor provides a statement that the consumer has the right to receive a written itemization of the amount financed, together with a space for the consumer to indicate whether it is desired, and the consumer does not request it.

(3) Good faith estimates of settlement costs provided for transactions subject to the Real Estate Settlement Procedures Act (12 U.S.C. 2601 et seq.) may be substituted for the disclosures required by paragraph (c)(1) of this section.

(d) Finance charge. The finance charge, using that term, and a brief description such as "the dollar amount the credit will cost you."

(1) Mortgage loans. In a transaction secured by real property or a dwelling, the disclosed finance charge and other disclosures affected by the disclosed finance charge (including the amount financed and the annual percentage rate) shall be treated as accurate if the amount disclosed as the finance charge:

(i) Is understated by no more than $100; or

(ii) Is greater than the amount required to be disclosed.

(2) Other credit. In any other transaction, the amount disclosed as the finance charge shall be treated as accurate if, in a transaction involving an amount financed of $1,000 or less, it is not more than $5 above or below the amount required to be disclosed; or, in a transaction involving an amount financed of more than $1,000, it is not more than $10 above or below the amount required to be disclosed.

(e) Annual percentage rate. The annual percentage rate, using that term, and a brief description such as "the cost of your credit as a yearly rate." For any transaction involving a finance charge of $5 or less on an amount financed of $75 or less, or a finance charge of $7.50 or less on an amount financed of more than $75, the creditor need not disclose the annual percentage rate.

(f) Variable rate.

(1) Except as provided in paragraph (f)(3) of this section, if the annual percentage rate may increase after consummation in a transaction not secured by the consumer's principal dwelling or in a transaction secured by the consumer's principal dwelling with a term of one year or less, the following disclosures:

(i) The circumstances under which the rate may increase.

(ii) Any limitations on the increase.

(iii) The effect of an increase.

(iv) An example of the payment terms that would result from an increase.

(2) If the annual percentage rate may increase after consummation in a transaction secured by the consumer's principal dwelling with a term greater than one year, the following disclosures:

(i) The fact that the transaction contains a variable-rate feature.

(ii) A statement that variable-rate disclosures have been provided earlier.

(3) Information provided in accordance with §§ 1026.18(f)(2) and 1026.19(b) may be substituted for the disclosures required by paragraph (f)(1) of this section.

(g) Payment schedule. Other than for a transaction that is subject to paragraph (s) of this section, the number, amounts, and timing of payments scheduled to repay the obligation.

(1) In a demand obligation with no alternate maturity date, the creditor may comply with this paragraph by disclosing the due dates or payment periods of any scheduled interest payments for the first year.

(2) In a transaction in which a series of payments varies because a finance charge is applied to the unpaid principal balance, the creditor may comply with this paragraph by disclosing the following information:

(i) The dollar amounts of the largest and smallest payments in the series.

(ii) A reference to the variations in the other payments in the series.

(h) Total of payments. The total of payments, using that term, and a descriptive explanation such as "the amount you will have paid when you have made all scheduled payments." In any transaction involving a single payment, the creditor need not disclose the total of payments.

(i) Demand feature. If the obligation has a demand feature, that fact shall be disclosed. When the disclosures are based on an assumed maturity of 1 year as provided in § 1026.17(c)(5), that fact shall also be disclosed.

(j) Total sale price. In a credit sale, the total sale price, using that term, and a descriptive explanation (including the amount of any downpayment) such as "the total price of your purchase on credit, including your downpayment of $__." The total sale price is the sum of the cash price, the items described in paragraph (b)(2), and the finance charge disclosed under paragraph (d) of this section.

(k) Prepayment.

(1) When an obligation includes a finance charge computed from time to time by application of a rate to the unpaid principal balance, a statement indicating whether or not a charge may be imposed for paying all or part of a loan's principal balance before the date on which the principal is due.

(2) When an obligation includes a finance charge other than the finance charge described in paragraph (k)(1) of this section, a statement indicating whether or not the consumer is entitled to a rebate of any finance charge if the obligation is prepaid in full or in part.

(*l*) Late payment. Any dollar or percentage charge that may be imposed before maturity due to a late payment, other than a deferral or extension charge.

(m) Security interest. The fact that the creditor has or will acquire a security interest in the property purchased as part of the transaction, or in other property identified by item or type.

(n) Insurance and debt cancellation. The items required by § 1026.4(d) in order to exclude certain insurance premiums and debt cancellation fees from the finance charge.

(*o*) Certain security interest charges. The disclosures required by § 1026.4(e) in order to exclude from the finance charge certain fees prescribed by law or certain premiums for insurance in lieu of perfecting a security interest.

(p) Contract reference. A statement that the consumer should refer to the appropriate contract document for information about nonpayment, default, the right to accelerate the maturity of the obligation, and prepayment rebates and penalties. At the creditor's option, the statement may also include a reference to the contract for further information about security interests and, in a residential mortgage transaction, about the creditor's policy regarding assumption of the obligation.

(q) Assumption policy. In a residential mortgage transaction, a statement whether or not a subsequent purchaser of the dwelling from the consumer may be permitted to assume the remaining obligation on its original terms.

(r) Required deposit. If the creditor requires the consumer to maintain a deposit as a condition of the specific transaction, a statement that the annual percentage rate does not reflect the effect of the required deposit. A required deposit need not include, for example:

(1) An escrow account for items such as taxes, insurance or repairs;

(2) A deposit that earns not less than 5 percent per year; or

(3) Payments under a Morris Plan.

(s) Interest rate and payment summary for mortgage transactions. For a closed-end transaction secured by real property or a dwelling, other than a transaction that is subject to § 1026.19(e) and (f), the creditor shall disclose the following information about the interest rate and payments:

(1) Form of disclosures. The information in paragraphs (s)(2)–(4) of this section shall be in the form of a table, with no more than five columns, with headings and format substantially similar to Model Clause H-4(E), H-4(F), H-4(G), or H-4(H) in appendix H to this part. The table shall contain only the information required in paragraphs (s)(2)–(4) of this section, shall be placed in a prominent location, and shall be in a minimum 10-point font.

(2) Interest rates—

(i) Amortizing loans.

(A) For a fixed-rate mortgage, the interest rate at consummation.

(B) For an adjustable-rate or step-rate mortgage:

(1) The interest rate at consummation and the period of time until the first interest rate adjustment may occur, labeled as the "introductory rate and monthly payment";

(2) The maximum interest rate that may apply during the first five years after the date on which the first regular periodic payment will be due and the earliest date on which that rate may apply, labeled as "maximum during first five years"; and

(3) The maximum interest rate that may apply during the life of the loan and the earliest date on which that rate may apply, labeled as "maximum ever."

(C) If the loan provides for payment increases as described in paragraph (s)(3)(i)(B) of this section, the interest rate in effect at the time the first such payment increase is scheduled to occur and the date on which the increase will occur, labeled as "first adjustment" if the loan is an adjustable-rate mortgage or, otherwise, labeled as "first increase."

(ii) Negative amortization loans. For a negative amortization loan:

(A) The interest rate at consummation and, if it will adjust after consummation, the length of time until it will adjust, and the label "introductory" or "intro";

(B) The maximum interest rate that could apply when the consumer must begin making fully amortizing payments under the terms of the legal obligation;

(C) If the minimum required payment will increase before the consumer must begin making fully amortizing payments, the maximum interest rate that could apply at the time of the first payment increase and the date the increase is scheduled to occur; and

(D) If a second increase in the minimum required payment may occur before the consumer must begin making fully amortizing payments, the maximum interest rate that could apply at the time of the second payment increase and the date the increase is scheduled to occur.

(iii) Introductory rate disclosure for amortizing adjustable-rate mortgages. For an amortizing adjustable-rate mortgage, if the interest rate at consummation is less than the fully-indexed rate, placed in a box directly beneath the table required by paragraph (s)(1) of this section, in a format substantially similar to Model Clause H-4(I) in appendix H to this part:

(A) The interest rate that applies at consummation and the period of time for which it applies;

(B) A statement that, even if market rates do not change, the interest rate will increase at the first adjustment and a designation of the place in sequence of the month or year, as applicable, of such rate adjustment; and

(C) The fully-indexed rate.

(3) Payments for amortizing loans—

(i) Principal and interest payments. If all periodic payments will be applied to accrued interest and principal, for each interest rate disclosed under paragraph (s)(2)(i) of this section:

(A) The corresponding periodic principal and interest payment, labeled as "principal and interest;"

(B) If the periodic payment may increase without regard to an interest rate adjustment, the payment that corresponds to the first such increase and the earliest date on which the increase could occur;

(C) If an escrow account will be established, an estimate of the amount of taxes and insurance, including any mortgage insurance or any functional equivalent, payable with each periodic payment; and

(D) The sum of the amounts disclosed under paragraphs (s)(3)(i)(A) and (C) of this section or (s)(3)(i)(B) and (C) of this section, as applicable, labeled as "total estimated monthly payment."

(ii) Interest-only payments. If the loan is an interest-only loan, for each interest rate disclosed under paragraph (s)(2)(i) of this section, the corresponding periodic payment and:

(A) If the payment will be applied to only accrued interest, the amount applied to interest, labeled as "interest payment," and a statement that none of the payment is being applied to principal;

(B) If the payment will be applied to accrued interest and principal, an itemization of the amount of the first such payment applied to accrued interest and to principal, labeled as "interest payment" and "principal payment," respectively;

(C) The escrow information described in paragraph (s)(3)(i)(C) of this section; and

(D) The sum of all amounts required to be disclosed under paragraphs (s)(3)(ii)(A) and (C) of this section or (s)(3)(ii)(B) and (C) of this section, as applicable, labeled as "total estimated monthly payment."

(4) Payments for negative amortization loans. For negative amortization loans:

(i)(A) The minimum periodic payment required until the first payment increase or interest rate increase, corresponding to the interest rate disclosed under paragraph (s)(2)(ii)(A) of this section;

(B) The minimum periodic payment that would be due at the first payment increase and the second, if any, corresponding to the interest rates described in paragraphs (s)(2)(ii)(C) and (D) of this section; and

(C) A statement that the minimum payment pays only some interest, does not repay any principal, and will cause the loan amount to increase;

(ii) The fully amortizing periodic payment amount at the earliest time when such a payment must be made, corresponding to the interest rate disclosed under paragraph (s)(2)(ii)(B) of this section; and

(iii) If applicable, in addition to the payments in paragraphs (s)(4)(i) and (ii) of this section, for each interest rate disclosed under paragraph (s)(2)(ii) of this section, the amount of the fully amortizing periodic payment, labeled as the "full payment option," and a statement that these payments pay all principal and all accrued interest.

(5) Balloon payments.

(i) Except as provided in paragraph (s)(5)(ii) of this section, if the transaction will require a balloon payment, defined as a payment that is more than two times a regular periodic payment, the balloon payment shall be disclosed separately from other periodic payments disclosed in the table under this paragraph (s), outside the table and in a manner substantially similar to Model Clause H-4(J) in appendix H to this part.

(ii) If the balloon payment is scheduled to occur at the same time as another payment required to be disclosed in the table pursuant to paragraph (s)(3) or (s)(4) of this section, then the balloon payment must be disclosed in the table.

(6) Special disclosures for loans with negative amortization. For a negative amortization loan, the following information, in close proximity to the table required in paragraph (s)(1) of this section, with headings, content, and format substantially similar to Model Clause H-4(G) in appendix H to this part:

(i) The maximum interest rate, the shortest period of time in which such interest rate could be reached, the amount of estimated taxes and insurance included in each payment disclosed, and a statement that the loan offers payment options, two of which are shown.

(ii) The dollar amount of the increase in the loan's principal balance if the consumer makes only the minimum required payments for the maximum possible time and the earliest date on which the consumer must begin making fully amortizing payments, assuming that the maximum interest rate is reached at the earliest possible time.

(7) Definitions. For purposes of this § 1026.18(s):

(i) The term "adjustable-rate mortgage" means a transaction secured by real property or a dwelling for which the annual percentage rate may increase after consummation.

(ii) The term "step-rate mortgage" means a transaction secured by real property or a dwelling for which the interest rate will change after consummation, and the rates that will apply and the periods for which they will apply are known at consummation.

(iii) The term "fixed-rate mortgage" means a transaction secured by real property or a dwelling that is not an adjustable-rate mortgage or a step-rate mortgage.

(iv) The term "interest-only" means that, under the terms of the legal obligation, one or more of the periodic payments may be applied solely to accrued interest and not to loan principal; an "interest-only loan" is a loan that permits interest-only payments.

(v) The term "amortizing loan" means a loan in which payment of the periodic payments does not result in an increase in the principal balance under the terms of the legal obligation; the term "negative amortization" means payment of periodic payments that will result in an increase in the principal balance under the terms of the legal obligation; the term "negative amortization loan" means a loan, other than a reverse mortgage subject to § 1026.33, that provides for a minimum periodic payment that covers only a portion of the accrued interest, resulting in negative amortization.

(vi) The term "fully-indexed rate" means the interest rate calculated using the index value and margin at the time of consummation.

(t) "No-guarantee-to-refinance" statement—

(1) Disclosure. For a closed-end transaction secured by real property or a dwelling, other than a transaction that is subject to § 1026.19(e) and (f), the creditor shall disclose a statement that there is no guarantee the consumer can refinance the transaction to lower the interest rate or periodic payments.

(2) Format. The statement required by paragraph (t)(1) of this section must be in a form substantially similar to Model Clause H-4(K) in appendix H to this part.

§ 1026.19. Certain Mortgage and Variable-Rate Transactions

(a) Mortgage transactions subject to RESPA—

(1)(i) Time of disclosures. In a reverse mortgage transaction subject to both § 1026.33 and the Real Estate Settlement Procedures Act (12 U.S.C. 2601 et seq.) that is secured by the consumer's dwelling, the creditor shall provide the consumer with good faith estimates of the disclosures required by § 1026.18 and shall deliver or place them in the mail not later than the third business day after the creditor receives the consumer's written application.

(ii) Imposition of fees. Except as provided in paragraph (a)(1)(iii) of this section, neither a creditor nor any other person may impose a fee on a consumer in connection with the consumer's application for a reverse mortgage transaction subject to paragraph (a)(1)(i) of this section before the consumer has received the disclosures required by paragraph (a)(1)(i) of this section. If the disclosures are mailed to the consumer, the consumer is considered to have received them three business days after they are mailed.

(iii) Exception to fee restriction. A creditor or other person may impose a fee for obtaining the consumer's credit history before the consumer has received the disclosures required by paragraph (a)(1)(i) of this section, provided the fee is bona fide and reasonable in amount.

(2) Waiting periods for early disclosures and corrected disclosures.

(i) The creditor shall deliver or place in the mail the good faith estimates required by paragraph (a)(1)(i) of this section not later than the seventh business day before consummation of the transaction.

(ii) If the annual percentage rate disclosed under paragraph (a)(1)(i) of this section becomes inaccurate, as defined in § 1026.22, the creditor shall provide corrected disclosures with all changed terms. The consumer must receive the corrected disclosures no later than three business days before consummation. If the corrected disclosures are mailed to the consumer or delivered to the consumer by means other than delivery in person, the consumer is deemed to have received the corrected disclosures three business days after they are mailed or delivered.

(3) Consumer's waiver of waiting period before consummation. If the consumer determines that the extension of credit is needed to meet a bona fide personal financial emergency, the consumer may modify or waive the seven-business-day waiting period or the three-business-day waiting period required by paragraph (a)(2) of this section, after receiving the disclosures required by § 1026.18. To modify or waive a waiting period, the consumer shall give the creditor a dated written statement that describes the emergency, specifically modifies or waives the waiting period, and bears the signature of all the consumers who are primarily liable on the legal obligation. Printed forms for this purpose are prohibited.

(4) Notice. Disclosures made pursuant to paragraph (a)(1) or paragraph (a)(2) of this section shall contain the following statement: "You are not required to complete this agreement merely because you have received these disclosures or signed a loan application." The disclosure required by this paragraph shall be grouped together with the disclosures required by paragraphs (a)(1) or (a)(2) of this section.

(b) Certain variable-rate transactions. Except as provided in paragraph (d) of this section, if the annual percentage rate may increase after consummation in a transaction secured by the consumer's principal dwelling with a term greater than one year, the following disclosures must be provided at the time an application form is provided or before the consumer pays a non-refundable fee, whichever is earlier (except that the disclosures may be delivered or placed in the mail not later than three business days following receipt of a consumer's application when the application reaches the creditor by telephone, or through an intermediary agent or broker):

(1) The booklet titled Consumer Handbook on Adjustable Rate Mortgages, or a suitable substitute.

(2) A loan program disclosure for each variable-rate program in which the consumer expresses an interest. The following disclosures, as applicable, shall be provided:

(i) The fact that the interest rate, payment, or term of the loan can change.

(ii) The index or formula used in making adjustments, and a source of information about the index or formula.

(iii) An explanation of how the interest rate and payment will be determined, including an explanation of how the index is adjusted, such as by the addition of a margin.

(iv) A statement that the consumer should ask about the current margin value and current interest rate.

(v) The fact that the interest rate will be discounted, and a statement that the consumer should ask about the amount of the interest rate discount.

(vi) The frequency of interest rate and payment changes.

(vii) Any rules relating to changes in the index, interest rate, payment amount, and outstanding loan balance including, for example, an explanation of interest rate or payment limitations, negative amortization, and interest rate carryover.

(viii) At the option of the creditor, either of the following:

(A) A historical example, based on a $10,000 loan amount, illustrating how payments and the loan balance would have been affected by interest rate changes implemented according to the terms of the loan program disclosure. The example shall reflect the most recent 15 years of index values. The example shall reflect all significant loan program terms, such as negative amortization, interest rate carryover, interest rate discounts, and interest rate and payment limitations, that would have been affected by the index movement during the period.

(B) The maximum interest rate and payment for a $10,000 loan originated at the initial interest rate (index value plus margin, adjusted by the amount of any discount or premium) in effect as of an identified month and year for the loan program disclosure assuming the maximum periodic increases in rates and payments under the program; and the initial interest rate and payment for that loan and a statement that the periodic payment may increase or decrease substantially depending on changes in the rate.

(ix) An explanation of how the consumer may calculate the payments for the loan amount to be borrowed based on either:

(A) The most recent payment shown in the historical example in paragraph (b)(2)(viii)(A) of this section; or

(B) The initial interest rate used to calculate the maximum interest rate and payment in paragraph (b)(2)(viii)(B) of this section.

(x) The fact that the loan program contains a demand feature.

(xi) The type of information that will be provided in notices of adjustments and the timing of such notices.

(xii) A statement that disclosure forms are available for the creditor's other variable-rate loan programs.

(c) Electronic disclosures. For an application that is accessed by the consumer in electronic form, the disclosures required by paragraph (b) of this section may be provided to the consumer in electronic form on or with the application.

(d) Information provided in accordance with variable-rate regulations of other Federal agencies may be substituted for the disclosures required by paragraph (b) of this section.

(e) Mortgage loans—early disclosures—

(1) Provision of disclosures—

(i) Creditor. In a closed-end consumer credit transaction secured by real property or a cooperative unit, other than a reverse mortgage subject to § 1026.33, the creditor shall provide the consumer with good faith estimates of the disclosures in § 1026.37.

(ii) Mortgage broker.

(A) If a mortgage broker receives a consumer's application, either the creditor or the mortgage broker shall provide a consumer with the disclosures required under paragraph (e)(1)(i) of this section in accordance with paragraph (e)(1)(iii) of this section. If the mortgage broker provides the required disclosures, the mortgage broker shall comply with all relevant requirements of this paragraph (e). The creditor shall ensure that such disclosures are provided in accordance with all requirements of this paragraph (e). Disclosures provided by a mortgage broker in accordance with the requirements of this paragraph (e) satisfy the creditor's obligation under this paragraph (e).

(B) If a mortgage broker provides any disclosure under § 1026.19(e), the mortgage broker shall also comply with the requirements of § 1026.25(c).

(iii) Timing.

(A) The creditor shall deliver or place in the mail the disclosures required under paragraph (e)(1)(i) of this section not later than the third business day after the creditor receives the consumer's application, as defined in § 1026.2(a)(3).

(B) Except as set forth in paragraph (e)(1)(iii)(C) of this section, the creditor shall deliver or place in the mail the disclosures required under paragraph (e)(1)(i) of this section not later than the seventh business day before consummation of the transaction.

(C) For a transaction secured by a consumer's interest in a timeshare plan described in 11 U.S.C. 101(53D), paragraph (e)(1)(iii)(B) of this section does not apply.

(iv) Receipt of early disclosures. If any disclosures required under paragraph (e)(1)(i) of this section are not provided to the consumer in person, the consumer is considered to have received the disclosures three business days after they are delivered or placed in the mail.

(v) Consumer's waiver of waiting period before consummation. If the consumer determines that the extension of credit is needed to meet a bona fide personal financial emergency, the consumer may modify or waive the seven-business-day waiting period for early disclosures required under paragraph (e)(1)(iii)(B) of this section, after receiving the disclosures required under paragraph (e)(1)(i) of this section. To modify or waive the waiting period, the consumer shall give the creditor a dated written statement that describes the emergency, specifically modifies or waives the waiting period, and bears the signature of all the consumers who are primarily liable on the legal obligation. Printed forms for this purpose are prohibited.

(vi) Shopping for settlement service providers—

(A) Shopping permitted. A creditor permits a consumer to shop for a settlement service if the creditor permits the consumer to select the provider of that service, subject to reasonable requirements.

(B) Disclosure of services. The creditor shall identify the settlement services for which the consumer is permitted to shop in the disclosures required under paragraph (e)(1)(i) of this section.

(C) Written list of providers. If the consumer is permitted to shop for a settlement service, the creditor shall provide the consumer with a written list identifying available providers of that settlement service and stating that the consumer may choose a different provider for that service. The creditor must identify at least one available provider for each settlement service for which the consumer is permitted to shop. The creditor shall provide this written list of settlement service providers separately from the disclosures required by paragraph (e)(1)(i) of this section but in accordance with the timing requirements in paragraph (e)(1)(iii) of this section.

(2) Predisclosure activity—

(i) Imposition of fees on consumer—

(A) Fee restriction. Except as provided in paragraph (e)(2)(i)(B) of this section, neither a creditor nor any other person may impose a fee on a consumer in connection with the consumer's application for a mortgage transaction subject to paragraph (e)(1)(i) of this section before the consumer has received the disclosures required under paragraph (e)(1)(i) of this section and indicated to the creditor an intent to proceed with the transaction described by those disclosures. A consumer may indicate an intent to proceed with a transaction in any manner the consumer chooses, unless a particular manner of communication is required by the creditor. The creditor must document this communication to satisfy the requirements of § 1026.25.

(B) Exception to fee restriction. A creditor or other person may impose a bona fide and reasonable fee for obtaining the consumer's credit report before the consumer has received the disclosures required under paragraph (e)(1)(i) of this section.

(ii) Written information provided to consumer. If a creditor or other person provides a consumer with a written estimate of terms or costs specific to that consumer before the consumer receives the disclosures required under paragraph (e)(1)(i) of this section, the creditor or such person shall clearly and conspicuously state at the top of the front of the first page of the estimate in a font size that is no smaller than 12-point font: "Your actual rate, payment, and costs could be higher. Get an official Loan Estimate before choosing a loan." The written estimate of terms or costs may not be made with headings, content, and format substantially similar to form H-24 or H-25 of appendix H to this part.

(iii) Verification of information. The creditor or other person shall not require a consumer to submit documents verifying information related to the consumer's application before providing the disclosures required by paragraph (e)(1)(i) of this section.

(3) Good faith determination for estimates of closing costs—

(i) General rule. An estimated closing cost disclosed pursuant to paragraph (e) of this section is in good faith if the charge paid by or imposed on the consumer does not exceed the amount originally disclosed under paragraph (e)(1)(i) of this section, except as otherwise provided in paragraphs (e)(3)(ii) through (iv) of this section.

(ii) Limited increases permitted for certain charges. An estimate of a charge for a third-party service or a recording fee is in good faith if:

(A) The aggregate amount of charges for third-party services and recording fees paid by or imposed on the consumer does not exceed the aggregate amount of such charges disclosed under paragraph (e)(1)(i) of this section by more than 10 percent;

(B) The charge for the third-party service is not paid to the creditor or an affiliate of the creditor; and

(C) The creditor permits the consumer to shop for the third-party service, consistent with paragraph (e)(1)(vi) of this section.

(iii) Variations permitted for certain charges. An estimate of any of the charges specified in this paragraph (e)(3)(iii) is in good faith if it is consistent with the best information reasonably available to the creditor at the time it is disclosed, regardless of whether the amount paid by the consumer exceeds the amount disclosed under paragraph (e)(1)(i) of this section. For purposes of paragraph (e)(1)(i) of this section, good faith is determined under this paragraph (e)(3)(iii) even if such charges are paid to the creditor or affiliates of the creditor, so long as the charges are bona fide:

(A) Prepaid interest;

(B) Property insurance premiums;

(C) Amounts placed into an escrow, impound, reserve, or similar account;

(D) Charges paid to third-party service providers selected by the consumer consistent with paragraph (e)(1)(vi)(A) of this section that are not on the list provided under paragraph (e)(1)(vi)(C) of this section; and

(E) Property taxes and other charges paid for third-party services not required by the creditor.

(iv) Revised estimates. For the purpose of determining good faith under paragraph (e)(3)(i) and (ii) of this section, a creditor may use a revised estimate of a charge instead of the estimate of the charge originally disclosed under paragraph (e)(1)(i) of this section if the revision is due to any of the following reasons:

(A) Changed circumstance affecting settlement charges. Changed circumstances cause the estimated charges to increase or, in the case of estimated charges identified in paragraph (e)(3)(ii) of this section, cause the aggregate amount of such charges to increase by more than 10 percent. For purposes of this paragraph, "changed circumstance" means:

(1) An extraordinary event beyond the control of any interested party or other unexpected event specific to the consumer or transaction;

(2) Information specific to the consumer or transaction that the creditor relied upon when providing the disclosures required under paragraph (e)(1)(i) of this section and that was inaccurate or changed after the disclosures were provided; or

(3) New information specific to the consumer or transaction that the creditor did not rely on when providing the original disclosures required under paragraph (e)(1)(i) of this section.

(B) Changed circumstance affecting eligibility. The consumer is ineligible for an estimated charge previously disclosed because a changed circumstance, as defined under paragraph (e)(3)(iv)(A) of this section, affected the consumer's creditworthiness or the value of the security for the loan.

(C) Revisions requested by the consumer. The consumer requests revisions to the credit terms or the settlement that cause an estimated charge to increase.

(D) Interest rate dependent charges. The points or lender credits change because the interest rate was not locked when the disclosures required under paragraph (e)(1)(i) of this section were provided. No later than three business days after the date the interest rate is locked, the creditor shall provide a revised version of the disclosures required under paragraph (e)(1)(i) of this section to the consumer with the revised interest rate, the points disclosed pursuant to § 1026.37(f)(1), lender credits, and any other interest rate dependent charges and terms.

(E) Expiration. The consumer indicates an intent to proceed with the transaction more than 10 business days, or more than any additional number of days specified by the credit or before the offer expires, after the disclosures required under paragraph (e)(1)(i) of this section are provided pursuant to paragraph (e)(1)(iii) of this section.

(F) Delayed settlement date on a construction loan. In transactions involving new construction, where the creditor reasonably expects that settlement will occur more than 60 days after the disclosures required under paragraph (e)(1)(i) of this section are provided pursuant to paragraph (e)(1)(iii) of this section, the creditor may provide revised disclosures to the consumer if the original disclosures required under paragraph (e)(1)(i) of this section state clearly and conspicuously that at any time prior to 60 days before consummation, the creditor may issue revised disclosures. If no such statement is provided, the creditor may not issue revised disclosures, except as otherwise provided in paragraph (e)(3)(iv) of this section.

(4) Provision and receipt of revised disclosures.

(i) General rule. Subject to the requirements of paragraph (e)(4)(ii) of this section, if a creditor uses a revised estimate pursuant to paragraph (e)(3)(iv) of this section for the purpose of determining good faith under paragraphs (e)(3)(i) and (ii) of this section, the creditor shall provide a revised version of the disclosures required under paragraph (e)(1)(i) of this section or the disclosures required under paragraph (f)(1)(i) of this section (including any corrected disclosures provided under paragraph (f)(2)(i) or (ii) of this section) reflecting the revised estimate within three business days of receiving information sufficient to establish that one of the reasons for revision provided under paragraphs (e)(3)(iv)(A) through (F) of this section applies.

(ii) Relationship between revised Loan Estimates and Closing Disclosures. The creditor shall not provide a revised version of the disclosures required under paragraph (e)(1)(i) of this section on or after the date on which the creditor provides the disclosures required under paragraph (f)(1)(i) of this section. The consumer must receive any revised version of the disclosures required under paragraph (e)(1)(i) of this section not later than four business days prior to consummation. If the revised version of the disclosures required under paragraph (e)(1)(i) of this section is not provided to the consumer in person, the consumer is considered to have received such version three business days after the creditor delivers or places such version in the mail.

(f) Mortgage loans—final disclosures—

(1) Provision of disclosures—

(i) Scope. In a transaction subject to paragraph (e)(1)(i) of this section, the creditor shall provide the consumer with the disclosures required under § 1026.38 reflecting the actual terms of the transaction.

(ii) Timing—

(A) In general. Except as provided in paragraphs (f)(1)(ii)(B), (f)(2)(i), (f)(2)(iii), (f)(2)(iv), and (f)(2)(v) of this section, the creditor shall ensure that the consumer receives the disclosures required under paragraph (f)(1)(i) of this section no later than three business days before consummation.

(B) Timeshares. For transactions secured by a consumer's interest in a timeshare plan described in 11 U.S.C. 101(53D), the creditor shall ensure that the consumer receives the disclosures required under paragraph (f)(1)(i) of this section no later than consummation.

(iii) Receipt of disclosures. If any disclosures required under paragraph (f)(1)(i) of this section are not provided to the consumer in person, the consumer is considered to have received the disclosures three business days after they are delivered or placed in the mail.

(iv) Consumer's waiver of waiting period before consummation. If the consumer determines that the extension of credit is needed to meet a bona fide personal financial emergency, the consumer may modify or waive the three-business-day waiting period under paragraph (f)(1)(ii)(A) or (f)(2)(ii) of this section, after receiving the disclosures required under paragraph (f)(1)(i) of this section. To modify or waive the waiting period, the consumer shall give the creditor a dated written statement that describes the emergency, specifically modifies or waives the waiting period, and bears the signature of all consumers who are primarily liable on the legal obligation. Printed forms for this purpose are prohibited.

(v) Settlement agent. A settlement agent may provide a consumer with the disclosures required under paragraph (f)(1)(i) of this section, provided the settlement agent complies with all relevant requirements of this paragraph (f). The creditor shall ensure that such disclosures are provided in accordance with all requirements of this paragraph (f). Disclosures provided by a settlement agent in accordance with the requirements of this paragraph (f) satisfy the creditor's obligation under this paragraph (f).

(2) Subsequent changes—

(i) Changes before consummation not requiring a new waiting period. Except as provided in paragraph (f)(2)(ii), if the disclosures provided under paragraph (f)(1)(i) of this section become inaccurate before consummation, the creditor shall provide corrected disclosures reflecting any changed terms to the consumer so that the consumer receives the corrected disclosures at or before consummation. Notwithstanding the requirement to provide corrected disclosures at or before consummation, the creditor shall permit the consumer to inspect the disclosures provided under this paragraph, completed to set forth those items that are known to the creditor at the time of inspection, during the business day immediately preceding consummation, but the creditor may omit from inspection items related only to the seller's transaction.

(ii) Changes before consummation requiring a new waiting period. If one of the following disclosures provided under paragraph (f)(1)(i) of this section becomes inaccurate in the following manner before consummation, the creditor shall ensure that the consumer receives corrected disclosures containing all changed terms in accordance with the requirements of paragraph (f)(1)(ii)(A) of this section:

(A) The annual percentage rate disclosed under § 1026.38(*o*)(4) becomes inaccurate, as defined in § 1026.22.

(B) The loan product is changed, causing the information disclosed under § 1026.38(a)(5)(iii) to become inaccurate.

(C) A prepayment penalty is added, causing the statement regarding a prepayment penalty required under § 1026.38(b) to become inaccurate.

(iii) Changes due to events occurring after consummation. If during the 30-day period following consummation, an event in connection with the settlement of the transaction occurs that causes the disclosures required under paragraph (f)(1)(i) of this section to become inaccurate, and such inaccuracy results in a change to an amount actually paid by the consumer from that amount disclosed under paragraph (f)(1)(i) of this section, the creditor shall deliver or place in the mail corrected disclosures not later than 30 days after receiving information sufficient to establish that such event has occurred.

(iv) Changes due to clerical errors. A creditor does not violate paragraph (f)(1)(i) of this section if the disclosures provided under paragraph (f)(1)(i) contain non-numeric clerical errors, provided the creditor delivers or places in the mail corrected disclosures no later than 60 days after consummation.

(v) Refunds related to the good faith analysis. If amounts paid by the consumer exceed the amounts specified under paragraph (e)(3)(i) or (ii) of this section, the creditor complies with paragraph (e)(1)(i) of this section if the creditor refunds the excess to the consumer no later than 60 days after consummation, and the creditor complies with paragraph (f)(1)(i) of this section if the creditor delivers or places in the mail corrected disclosures that reflect such refund no later than 60 days after consummation.

(3) Charges disclosed—

(i) Actual charge. The amount imposed upon the consumer for any settlement service shall not exceed the amount actually received by the settlement service provider for that service, except as otherwise provided in paragraph (f)(3)(ii) of this section.

(ii) Average charge. A creditor or settlement service provider may charge a consumer or seller the average charge for a settlement service if the following conditions are satisfied:

(A) The average charge is no more than the average amount paid for that service by or on behalf of all consumers and sellers for a class of transactions;

(B) The creditor or settlement service provider defines the class of transactions based on an appropriate period of time, geographic area, and type of loan;

(C) The creditor or settlement service provider uses the same average charge for every transaction within the defined class; and

(D) The creditor or settlement service provider does not use an average charge:

(1) For any type of insurance;

(2) For any charge based on the loan amount or property value; or

(3) If doing so is otherwise prohibited by law.

(4) Transactions involving a seller—

(i) Provision to seller. In a transaction subject to paragraph (e)(1)(i) of this section that involves a seller, the settlement agent shall provide the seller with the disclosures in § 1026.38 that relate to the seller's transaction reflecting the actual terms of the seller's transaction.

(ii) Timing. The settlement agent shall provide the disclosures required under paragraph (f)(4)(i) of this section no later than the day of consummation. If during the 30-day period following consummation, an event in connection with the settlement of the transaction occurs that causes disclosures required under paragraph (f)(4)(i) of this section to become inaccurate, and such inaccuracy results in a change to the amount actually paid by the seller from that amount disclosed under paragraph (f)(4)(i) of this section, the settlement agent shall deliver or place in the mail corrected disclosures not later than 30 days after receiving information sufficient to establish that such event has occurred.

(iii) Charges disclosed. The amount imposed on the seller for any settlement service shall not exceed the amount actually received by the service provider for that service, except as otherwise provided in paragraph (f)(3)(ii) of this section.

(iv) Creditor's copy. When the consumer's and seller's disclosures under this paragraph (f) are provided on separate documents, as permitted under § 1026.38(t)(5), the settlement agent shall provide to the creditor (if the creditor is not the settlement agent) a copy of the disclosures provided to the seller under paragraph (f)(4)(i) of this section.

(5) No fee. No fee may be imposed on any person, as a part of settlement costs or otherwise, by a creditor or by a servicer (as that term is defined under 12 U.S.C. 2605(i)(2)) for the preparation or delivery of the disclosures required under paragraph (f)(1)(i) of this section.

(g) Special information booklet at time of application—

(1) Creditor to provide special information booklet. Except as provided in paragraphs (g)(1)(ii) and (iii) of this section, the creditor shall provide a copy of the special information booklet (required pursuant to section 5 of the Real Estate Settlement Procedures Act (12 U.S.C. 2604) to help consumers applying for federally related mortgage loans understand the nature and cost of real estate settlement services) to a consumer who applies for a consumer credit transaction secured by real property or a cooperative unit.

(i) The creditor shall deliver or place in the mail the special information booklet not later than three business days after the consumer's application is received. However, if the creditor denies the consumer's application before the end of the three-business-day period, the creditor need not provide the booklet. If a consumer uses a mortgage broker, the mortgage broker shall provide the special information booklet and the creditor need not do so.

(ii) In the case of a home equity line of credit subject to § 1026.40, a creditor or mortgage broker that provides the consumer with a copy of the brochure entitled "When Your Home is On the Line: What You Should Know About Home Equity Lines of Credit," or any successor brochure issued by the Bureau, is deemed to be in compliance with this section.

(iii) The creditor or mortgage broker need not provide the booklet to the consumer for a transaction, the purpose of which is not the purchase of a one-to-four family residential property, including, but not limited to, the following:

(A) Refinancing transactions;

(B) Closed-end loans secured by a subordinate lien; and

(C) Reverse mortgages.

(2) Permissible changes. Creditors may not make changes to, deletions from, or additions to the special information booklet other than the changes specified in paragraphs (g)(2)(i) through (iv) of this section.

(i) In the "Complaints" section of the booklet, "the Bureau of Consumer Financial Protection" may be substituted for "HUD's Office of RESPA" and "the RESPA office."

(ii) In the "Avoiding Foreclosure" section of the booklet, it is permissible to inform homeowners that they may find information on and assistance in avoiding foreclosures at http://www.consumerfinance.gov. The reference to the HUD Web site, http://www.hud.gov/foreclosure/, in the "Avoiding Foreclosure" section of the booklet shall not be deleted.

(iii) In the "No Discrimination" section of the appendix to the booklet, "the Bureau of Consumer Financial Protection" may be substituted for the reference to the "Board of Governors of the Federal Reserve System." In the Contact Information section of the appendix to the booklet, the following contact information for the Bureau may be added: "Bureau of Consumer Financial Protection, 1700 G Street NW., Washington, DC 20552; www.consumerfinance.gov/learnmore." The contact information for HUD's Office of RESPA and Interstate Land Sales may be removed from the "Contact Information" section of the appendix to the booklet.

(iv) The cover of the booklet may be in any form and may contain any drawings, pictures or artwork, provided that the title appearing on the cover shall not be changed. Names, addresses, and telephone numbers of the creditor or others and similar information may appear on the cover, but no discussion of the matters covered in the booklet shall appear on the cover. References to HUD on the cover of the booklet may be changed to references to the Bureau.

§ 1026.20. Disclosure Requirements Regarding Post-Consummation Events

(a) Refinancings. A refinancing occurs when an existing obligation that was subject to this subpart is satisfied and replaced by a new obligation undertaken by the same consumer. A refinancing is a new transaction requiring new disclosures to the consumer. The new finance charge shall include any unearned portion of the old finance charge that is not credited to the existing obligation. The following shall not be treated as a refinancing:

(1) A renewal of a single payment obligation with no change in the original terms.

(2) A reduction in the annual percentage rate with a corresponding change in the payment schedule.

(3) An agreement involving a court proceeding.

(4) A change in the payment schedule or a change in collateral requirements as a result of the consumer's default or delinquency, unless the rate is increased, or the new amount financed exceeds the unpaid balance plus earned finance charge and premiums for continuation of insurance of the types described in § 1026.4(d).

(5) The renewal of optional insurance purchased by the consumer and added to an existing transaction, if disclosures relating to the initial purchase were provided as required by this subpart.

(b) Assumptions. An assumption occurs when a creditor expressly agrees in writing with a subsequent consumer to accept that consumer as a primary obligor on an existing residential mortgage transaction. Before the assumption occurs, the creditor shall make new disclosures to the subsequent consumer, based on the remaining obligation. If the finance charge originally imposed on the existing obligation was an add-on or discount finance charge, the creditor need only disclose:

(1) The unpaid balance of the obligation assumed.

(2) The total charges imposed by the creditor in connection with the assumption.

(3) The information required to be disclosed under § 1026.18(k), (*l*), (m), and (n).

(4) The annual percentage rate originally imposed on the obligation.

(5) The payment schedule under § 1026.18(g) and the total of payments under § 1026.18(h) based on the remaining obligation.

(c) Rate adjustments with a corresponding change in payment. The creditor, assignee, or servicer of an adjustable-rate mortgage shall provide consumers with disclosures, as described in this paragraph (c), in connection with the adjustment of interest rates pursuant to the loan contract that results in a corresponding adjustment to the payment. To the extent that other provisions of this subpart C govern the disclosures required by this paragraph (c), those provisions apply to assignees and servicers as well as to creditors. The disclosures required by this paragraph (c) also shall be provided for an interest rate adjustment resulting from the conversion of an adjustable-rate mortgage to a fixed-rate transaction, if that interest rate adjustment results in a corresponding payment change.

(1) Coverage—

(i) In general. For purposes of this paragraph (c), an adjustable-rate mortgage or "ARM" is a closed-end consumer credit transaction secured by the consumer's principal dwelling in which the annual percentage rate may increase after consummation.

(ii) Exemptions. The requirements of this paragraph (c) do not apply to:

(A) ARMs with terms of one year or less; or

(B) The first interest rate adjustment to an ARM if the first payment at the adjusted level is due within 210 days after consummation and the new interest rate disclosed at consummation pursuant to § 1026.20(d) was not an estimate.

(C) The creditor, assignee or servicer of an adjustable-rate mortgage when the servicer on the loan is subject to the Fair Debt Collections Practices Act (FDCPA) (15 U.S.C. 1692 et seq.) with regard to the loan and the consumer has sent a notification pursuant to FDCPA section 805(c) (15 U.S.C. 1692c(c)).

(2) Timing and content. Except as otherwise provided in paragraph (c)(2) of this section, the disclosures required by this paragraph (c) shall be provided to consumers at least 60, but no more than 120, days before the first payment at the adjusted level is due. The disclosures shall be provided to consumers at least 25, but no more than 120, days before the first payment at the adjusted level is due for ARMs with uniformly scheduled interest rate adjustments occurring every 60 days or more frequently and for ARMs originated prior to January 10, 2015 in which the loan contract requires the adjusted interest rate and payment to be calculated based on the index figure available as of a date that is less than 45 days prior to the adjustment date. The disclosures shall be provided to consumers as soon as practicable, but not less than 25 days before the first payment at the adjusted level is due, for the first adjustment to an ARM if it occurs within 60 days of consummation and the new interest rate disclosed at consummation pursuant to § 1026.20(d) was an estimate. The disclosures required by this paragraph (c) shall include:

(i) A statement providing:

(A) An explanation that under the terms of the consumer's adjustable-rate mortgage, the specific time period in which the current interest rate has been in effect is ending and the interest rate and mortgage payment will change;

(B) The effective date of the interest rate adjustment and when additional future interest rate adjustments are scheduled to occur; and

(C) Any other changes to loan terms, features, or options taking effect on the same date as the interest rate adjustment, such as the expiration of interest-only or payment-option features.

(ii) A table containing the following information:

(A) The current and new interest rates;

(B) The current and new payments and the date the first new payment is due; and

(C) For interest-only or negatively-amortizing payments, the amount of the current and new payment allocated to principal, interest, and taxes and insurance in escrow, as applicable. The current payment allocation disclosed shall be the payment allocation for the last payment prior to the date of the disclosure. The new payment allocation disclosed shall be the expected payment allocation for the first payment for which the new interest rate will apply.

(iii) An explanation of how the interest rate is determined, including:

(A) The specific index or formula used in making interest rate adjustments and a source of information about the index or formula; and

(B) The type and amount of any adjustment to the index, including any margin and an explanation that the margin is the addition of a certain number of percentage points to the index, and any application of previously foregone interest rate increases from past interest rate adjustments.

(iv) Any limits on the interest rate or payment increases at each interest rate adjustment and over the life of the loan, as applicable, including the extent to which such limits result in the creditor, assignee, or servicer foregoing any increase in the interest rate and the earliest date that such foregone interest rate increases may apply to future interest rate adjustments, subject to those limits.

(v) An explanation of how the new payment is determined, including:

(A) The index or formula used;

(B) Any adjustment to the index or formula, such as the addition of a margin or the application of any previously foregone interest rate increases from past interest rate adjustments;

(C) The loan balance expected on the date of the interest rate adjustment; and

(D) The length of the remaining loan term expected on the date of the interest rate adjustment and any change in the term of the loan caused by the adjustment.

(vi) If applicable, a statement that the new payment will not be allocated to pay loan principal and will not reduce the loan balance. If the new payment will result in negative amortization, a statement that the new payment will not be allocated to pay loan principal and will pay only part of the loan interest, thereby adding to the balance of the loan. If the new payment will result in negative amortization as a result of the interest rate adjustment, the statement shall set forth the payment required to amortize fully the remaining balance at the new interest rate over the remainder of the loan term.

(vii) The circumstances under which any prepayment penalty, as defined in § 1026.32(b)(6)(i), may be imposed, such as when paying the loan in full or selling or refinancing the principal dwelling; the time period during which such a penalty may be imposed; and a statement that the consumer may contact the servicer for additional information, including the maximum amount of the penalty.

(3) Format. (i) The disclosures required by this paragraph (c) shall be provided in the form of a table and in the same order as, and with headings and format substantially similar to, forms H-4(D)(1) and (2) in appendix H to this part; and

(ii) The disclosures required by paragraph (c)(2)(ii) of this section shall be in the form of a table located within the table described in paragraph (c)(3)(i) of this section. These disclosures shall appear in the same order as, and with headings and format substantially similar to, the table inside the larger table in forms H-4(D)(1) and (2) in appendix H to this part.

(d) Initial rate adjustment. The creditor, assignee, or servicer of an adjustable-rate mortgage shall provide consumers with disclosures, as described in this paragraph (d), in connection with the initial interest rate adjustment pursuant to the loan contract. To the extent that other provisions of this subpart C govern the disclosures required by this paragraph (d), those provisions apply to assignees and servicers as well as to creditors. The disclosures required by this paragraph (d) shall be provided as a separate document from other documents provided by the creditor, assignee, or servicer. The disclosures shall be provided to consumers at least 210, but no more than 240, days before the first payment at the adjusted level is due. If the first payment at the adjusted level is due within the first 210 days after consummation, the disclosures shall be provided at consummation.

(1) Coverage—

(i) In general. For purposes of this paragraph (d), an adjustable-rate mortgage or "ARM" is a closed-end consumer credit transaction secured by the consumer's principal dwelling in which the annual percentage rate may increase after consummation.

(ii) Exemptions. The requirements of this paragraph (d) do not apply to ARMs with terms of one year or less.

(2) Content. If the new interest rate (or the new payment calculated from the new interest rate) is not known as of the date of the disclosure, an estimate shall be disclosed and labeled as such. This estimate shall be based on the calculation of the index reported in the source of information described in paragraph (d)(2)(iv)(A) of this section within fifteen business days prior to the date of the disclosure. The disclosures required by this paragraph (d) shall include:

(i) The date of the disclosure.

(ii) A statement providing:

(A) An explanation that under the terms of the consumer's adjustable-rate mortgage, the specific time period in which the current interest rate has been in effect is ending and that any change in the interest rate may result in a change in the mortgage payment;

(B) The effective date of the interest rate adjustment and when additional future interest rate adjustments are scheduled to occur; and

(C) Any other changes to loan terms, features, or options taking effect on the same date as the interest rate adjustment, such as the expiration of interest-only or payment-option features.

(iii) A table containing the following information:

(A) The current and new interest rates;

(B) The current and new payments and the date the first new payment is due; and

(C) For interest-only or negatively-amortizing payments, the amount of the current and new payment allocated to principal, interest, and taxes and insurance in escrow, as applicable. The current payment allocation disclosed shall be the payment allocation for the last payment prior to the date of the disclosure. The new payment allocation disclosed shall be the expected payment allocation for the first payment for which the new interest rate will apply.

(iv) An explanation of how the interest rate is determined, including:

(A) The specific index or formula used in making interest rate adjustments and a source of information about the index or formula; and

(B) The type and amount of any adjustment to the index, including any margin and an explanation that the margin is the addition of a certain number of percentage points to the index.

(v) Any limits on the interest rate or payment increases at each interest rate adjustment and over the life of the loan, as applicable, including the extent to which such limits result in the creditor, assignee, or servicer foregoing any increase in the interest rate and the earliest date that such foregone interest rate increases may apply to future interest rate adjustments, subject to those limits.

(vi) An explanation of how the new payment is determined, including:

(A) The index or formula used;

(B) Any adjustment to the index or formula, such as the addition of a margin;

(C) The loan balance expected on the date of the interest rate adjustment;

(D) The length of the remaining loan term expected on the date of the interest rate adjustment and any change in the term of the loan caused by the adjustment; and

(E) If the new interest rate or new payment provided is an estimate, a statement that another disclosure containing the actual new interest rate and new payment will be provided to the consumer between two and four months before the first payment at the adjusted level is due for interest rate adjustments that result in a corresponding payment change.

(vii) If applicable, a statement that the new payment will not be allocated to pay loan principal and will not reduce the loan balance. If the new payment will result in negative amortization, a statement that the new payment will not be allocated to pay loan principal and will pay only part of the loan interest, thereby adding to the balance of the loan. If the new payment will result in negative amortization as a result of the interest rate adjustment, the statement shall set forth the payment required to amortize fully the remaining balance at the new interest rate over the remainder of the loan term.

(viii) The circumstances under which any prepayment penalty, as defined in § 1026.32(b)(6)(i), may be imposed, such as when paying the loan in full or selling or refinancing the principal dwelling; the time period during which such a penalty may be imposed; and a statement that the consumer may contact the servicer for additional information, including the maximum amount of the penalty.

(ix) The telephone number of the creditor, assignee, or servicer for consumers to call if they anticipate not being able to make their new payments.

(x) The following alternatives to paying at the new rate that consumers may be able to pursue and a brief explanation of each alternative, expressed in simple and clear terms:

(A) Refinancing the loan with the current or another creditor or assignee;

(B) Selling the property and using the proceeds to pay the loan in full;

(C) Modifying the terms of the loan with the creditor, assignee, or servicer; and

(D) Arranging payment forbearance with the creditor, assignee, or servicer.

(xi) The Web site to access either the Bureau list or the HUD list of homeownership counselors and counseling organizations, the HUD toll-free telephone number to access the HUD list of homeownership counselors and counseling organizations, and the Bureau Web site to access contact information for State housing finance authorities (as defined in § 1301 of the Financial Institutions Reform, Recovery, and Enforcement Act of 1989).

(3) Format. (i) Except for the disclosures required by paragraph (d)(2)(i) of this section, the disclosures required by this paragraph (d) shall be provided in the form of a table and in the same order as, and with headings and format substantially similar to, forms H-4(D)(3) and (4) in appendix H to this part;

(ii) The disclosures required by paragraph (d)(2)(i) of this section shall appear outside of and above the table required in paragraph (d)(3)(i) of this section; and

(iii) The disclosures required by paragraph (d)(2)(iii) of this section shall be in the form of a table located within the table described in paragraph (d)(3)(i) of this section. These disclosures shall appear in the same order as, and with headings and format substantially similar to, the table inside the larger table in forms H-4(D)(3) and (4) in appendix H to this part.

(e) Escrow account cancellation notice for certain mortgage transactions—

(1) Scope. In a closed-end consumer credit transaction secured by a first lien on real property or a dwelling, other than a reverse mortgage subject to § 1026.33, for which an escrow account was established in connection with the transaction and will be cancelled, the creditor or servicer shall disclose the information specified in paragraph (e)(2) of this section in accordance with the form requirements in paragraph (e)(4) of this section, and the timing requirements in paragraph (e)(5) of this section. For purposes of this paragraph (e), the term "escrow account" has the same meaning as under 12 CFR 1024.17(b), and the term "servicer" has the same meaning as under 12 CFR 1024.2(b).

(2) Content requirements. If an escrow account was established in connection with a transaction subject to this paragraph (e) and the escrow account will be cancelled, the creditor or servicer shall clearly and conspicuously disclose, under the heading "Escrow Closing Notice," the following information:

(i) A statement informing the consumer of the date on which the consumer will no longer have an escrow account; a statement that an escrow account may also be called an impound or trust account; a statement of the reason why the escrow account will be closed; a statement that without an escrow account, the consumer must pay all property costs, such as taxes and homeowner's insurance, directly, possibly in one or two large payments a year; and a table, titled "Cost to you," that contains an itemization of the amount of any fee the creditor or servicer imposes on the consumer in connection with the closure of the consumer's escrow account, labeled "Escrow Closing Fee," and a statement that the fee is for closing the escrow account.

(ii) Under the reference "In the future":

(A) A statement of the consequences if the consumer fails to pay property costs, including the actions that a State or local government may take if property taxes are not paid and the actions the creditor or servicer may take if the consumer does not pay some or all property costs, such as adding amounts to the loan balance, adding an escrow account to the loan, or purchasing a property insurance policy on the consumer's behalf that may be more expensive and provide fewer benefits than a policy that the consumer could obtain directly;

(B) A statement with a telephone number that the consumer can use to request additional information about the cancellation of the escrow account;

(C) A statement of whether the creditor or servicer offers the option of keeping the escrow account open and, as applicable, a telephone number the consumer can use to request that the account be kept open; and

(D) A statement of whether there is a cut-off date by which the consumer can request that the account be kept open.

(3) Optional information. The creditor or servicer may, at its option, include its name or logo, the consumer's name, phone number, mailing address and property address, the issue date of the notice, the loan number, or the consumer's account number on the notice required by this paragraph (e). Except for the name and logo of the creditor or servicer, the information described in this paragraph may be placed between the heading required by paragraph (e)(2) of this section and the disclosures required by paragraphs (e)(2)(i) and (ii) of this section. The name and logo may be placed above the heading required by paragraph (e)(2) of this section.

(4) Form of disclosures. The disclosures required by paragraph (e)(2) of this section shall be provided in a minimum 10-point font, grouped together on the front side of a one-page document, separate from all other materials, with the headings, content, order, and format substantially similar to model form H-29 in appendix H to this part. The disclosure of the heading required by paragraph (e)(2) of this section shall be more conspicuous than, and shall precede, the other disclosures required by paragraph (e)(2) of this section.

(5) Timing—

(i) Cancellation upon consumer's request. If the creditor or servicer cancels the escrow account at the consumer's request, the creditor or servicer shall ensure that the consumer receives the disclosures required by paragraph (e)(2) of this section no later than three business days before the closure of the consumer's escrow account.

(ii) Cancellations other than upon the consumer's request. If the creditor or servicer cancels the escrow account and the cancellation is not at the consumer's request, the creditor or servicer shall ensure that the consumer receives the disclosures required by paragraph (e)(2) of this section no later than 30 business days before the closure of the consumer's escrow account.

(iii) Receipt of disclosure. If the disclosures required by paragraph (e)(2) of this section are not provided to the consumer in person, the consumer is considered to have received the disclosures three business days after they are delivered or placed in the mail.

(f) Successor in interest. If, upon confirmation, a servicer provides a confirmed successor in interest who is not liable on the mortgage loan obligation with a written notice and acknowledgment form in accordance with Regulation X, § 1024.32(c)(1) of this chapter, the servicer is not required to provide to the confirmed successor in interest any written disclosure required by paragraphs (c), (d), and (e) of this section unless and until the confirmed successor in interest either assumes the mortgage loan obligation under State law or has provided the servicer an executed acknowledgment in accordance with Regulation X, § 1024.32(c)(1)(iv) of this chapter, that the confirmed successor in interest has not revoked.

§ 1026.21. Treatment of Credit Balances

When a credit balance in excess of $1 is created in connection with a transaction (through transmittal of funds to a creditor in excess of the total balance due on an account, through rebates of unearned finance charges or insurance premiums, or through amounts otherwise owed to or held for the benefit of a consumer), the creditor shall:

(a) Credit the amount of the credit balance to the consumer's account;

(b) Refund any part of the remaining credit balance, upon the written request of the consumer; and

(c) Make a good faith effort to refund to the consumer by cash, check, or money order, or credit to a deposit account of the consumer, any part of the credit balance remaining in the account for more than 6 months, except that no further action is required if the consumer's current location is not known to the creditor and cannot be traced through the consumer's last known address or telephone number.

§ 1026.22. Determination of Annual Percentage Rate

(a) Accuracy of annual percentage rate.

(1) The annual percentage rate is a measure of the cost of credit, expressed as a yearly rate, that relates the amount and timing of value received by the consumer to the amount and timing of payments made. The annual percentage rate shall be determined in accordance with either the actuarial method or the United States Rule method. Explanations, equations and instructions for determining the annual percentage rate in accordance with the actuarial method are set forth in appendix J to this part. An error in disclosure of the annual percentage rate or finance charge shall not, in itself, be considered a violation of this part if:

(i) The error resulted from a corresponding error in a calculation tool used in good faith by the creditor; and

(ii) Upon discovery of the error, the creditor promptly discontinues use of that calculation tool for disclosure purposes and notifies the Bureau in writing of the error in the calculation tool.

(2) As a general rule, the annual percentage rate shall be considered accurate if it is not more than 1/8 of 1 percentage point above or below the annual percentage rate determined in accordance with paragraph (a)(1) of this section.

(3) In an irregular transaction, the annual percentage rate shall be considered accurate if it is not more than ¼ of 1 percentage point above or below the annual percentage rate determined in accordance with paragraph (a)(1) of this section. For purposes of this paragraph (a)(3), an irregular transaction is one that includes one or more of the following features: multiple advances, irregular payment periods, or irregular payment amounts (other than an irregular first period or an irregular first or final payment).

(4) Mortgage loans. If the annual percentage rate disclosed in a transaction secured by real property or a dwelling varies from the actual rate determined in accordance with paragraph (a)(1) of this section, in addition to the tolerances applicable under paragraphs (a)(2) and (3) of this section, the disclosed annual percentage rate shall also be considered accurate if:

(i) The rate results from the disclosed finance charge; and

(ii)(A) The disclosed finance charge would be considered accurate under **§ 1026.18(d)(1)** or **§ 1026.38(*o*)(2)**, as applicable; or

(B) For purposes of rescission, if the disclosed finance charge would be considered accurate under **§ 1026.23(g)** or (h), whichever applies.

(5) Additional tolerance for mortgage loans. In a transaction secured by real property or a dwelling, in addition to the tolerances applicable under paragraphs (a)(2) and (3) of this section, if the disclosed finance charge is calculated incorrectly but is considered accurate under **§ 1026.18(d)(1)** or **§ 1026.38(*o*)(2)**, as applicable, or **§ 1026.23(g)** or (h), the disclosed annual percentage rate shall be considered accurate:

(i) If the disclosed finance charge is understated, and the disclosed annual percentage rate is also understated but it is closer to the actual annual percentage rate than the rate that would be considered accurate under paragraph (a)(4) of this section;

(ii) If the disclosed finance charge is overstated, and the disclosed annual percentage rate is also overstated but it is closer to the actual annual percentage rate than the rate that would be considered accurate under paragraph (a)(4) of this section.

(b) Computation tools.

(1) The Regulation Z Annual Percentage Rate Tables produced by the Bureau may be used to determine the annual percentage rate, and any rate determined from those tables in accordance with the accompanying instructions complies with the requirements of this section. Volume I of the tables applies to single advance transactions involving up to 480 monthly payments or 104 weekly payments. It may be used for regular transactions and for transactions with any of the following irregularities: an irregular first period, an irregular first payment, and an irregular final payment. Volume II of the tables applies to transactions involving multiple advances and any type of payment or period irregularity.

(2) Creditors may use any other computation tool in determining the annual percentage rate if the rate so determined equals the rate determined in accordance with appendix J to this part, within the degree of accuracy set forth in paragraph (a) of this section.

(c) Single add-on rate transactions. If a single add-on rate is applied to all transactions with maturities up to 60 months and if all payments are equal in amount and period, a single annual percentage rate may be disclosed for all those transactions, so long as it is the highest annual percentage rate for any such transaction.

(d) Certain transactions involving ranges of balances. For purposes of disclosing the annual percentage rate referred to in § 1026.17(g)(4) (Mail or telephone orders—delay in disclosures) and (h) (Series of sales—delay in disclosures), if the same finance charge is imposed on all balances within a specified range of balances, the annual percentage rate computed for the median balance may be disclosed for all the balances. However, if the annual percentage rate computed for the median balance understates the annual percentage rate computed for the lowest balance by more than 8 percent of the latter rate, the annual percentage rate shall be computed on whatever lower balance will produce an annual percentage rate that does not result in an understatement of more than 8 percent of the rate determined on the lowest balance.

§ 1026.23. Right of Rescission

(a) Consumer's right to rescind.

(1) In a credit transaction in which a security interest is or will be retained or acquired in a consumer's principal dwelling, each consumer whose ownership interest is or will be subject to the security interest shall have the right to rescind the transaction, except for transactions described in paragraph (f) of this section. For purposes of this section, the addition to an existing obligation of a security interest in a consumer's principal dwelling is a transaction. The right of rescission applies only to the addition of the security interest and not the existing obligation. The creditor shall deliver the notice required by paragraph (b) of this section but need not deliver new material disclosures. Delivery of the required notice shall begin the rescission period.

(2) To exercise the right to rescind, the consumer shall notify the creditor of the rescission by mail, telegram or other means of written communication. Notice is considered given when mailed, when filed for telegraphic transmission or, if sent by other means, when delivered to the creditor's designated place of business.

(3)(i) The consumer may exercise the right to rescind until midnight of the third business day following consummation, delivery of the notice required by paragraph (b) of this section, or delivery of all material disclosures, whichever occurs last. If the required notice or material disclosures are not delivered, the right to rescind shall expire 3 years after consummation, upon transfer of all of the consumer's interest in the property, or upon sale of the property, whichever occurs first. In the case of certain administrative proceedings, the rescission period shall be extended in accordance with section 125(f) of the Act.

(ii) For purposes of this paragraph (a)(3), the term "material disclosures" means the required disclosures of the annual percentage rate, the finance charge, the amount financed, the total of payments, the payment schedule, and the disclosures and limitations referred to in §§ 1026.32(c) and (d) and 1026.43(g).

(4) When more than one consumer in a transaction has the right to rescind, the exercise of the right by one consumer shall be effective as to all consumers.

(b)(1) Notice of right to rescind. In a transaction subject to rescission, a creditor shall deliver two copies of the notice of the right to rescind to each consumer entitled to rescind (one copy to each if the notice is delivered in electronic form in accordance with the consumer consent and other applicable provisions of the E-Sign Act). The notice shall be on a separate document that identifies the transaction and shall clearly and conspicuously disclose the following:

(i) The retention or acquisition of a security interest in the consumer's principal dwelling.

(ii) The consumer's right to rescind the transaction.

(iii) How to exercise the right to rescind, with a form for that purpose, designating the address of the creditor's place of business.

(iv) The effects of rescission, as described in paragraph (d) of this section.

(v) The date the rescission period expires.

(2) Proper form of notice. To satisfy the disclosure requirements of paragraph (b)(1) of this section, the creditor shall provide the appropriate model form in appendix H of this part or a substantially similar notice.

(c) Delay of creditor's performance. Unless a consumer waives the right of rescission under paragraph (e) of this section, no money shall be disbursed other than in escrow, no services shall be performed and no materials delivered until the rescission period has expired and the creditor is reasonably satisfied that the consumer has not rescinded.

(d) Effects of rescission.

(1) When a consumer rescinds a transaction, the security interest giving rise to the right of rescission becomes void and the consumer shall not be liable for any amount, including any finance charge.

(2) Within 20 calendar days after receipt of a notice of rescission, the creditor shall return any money or property that has been given to anyone in connection with the transaction and shall take any action necessary to reflect the termination of the security interest.

(3) If the creditor has delivered any money or property, the consumer may retain possession until the creditor has met its obligation under paragraph (d)(2) of this section. When the creditor has complied with that paragraph, the consumer shall tender the money or property to the creditor or, where the latter would be impracticable or inequitable, tender its reasonable value. At the consumer's option, tender of property may be made at the location of the property or at the consumer's residence. Tender of money must be made at the creditor's designated place of business. If the creditor does not take possession of the money or property within 20 calendar days after the consumer's tender, the consumer may keep it without further obligation.

(4) The procedures outlined in paragraphs (d)(2) and (3) of this section may be modified by court order.

(e) Consumer's waiver of right to rescind. The consumer may modify or waive the right to rescind if the consumer determines that the extension of credit is needed to meet a bona fide personal financial emergency. To modify or waive the right, the consumer shall give the creditor a dated written statement that describes the emergency, specifically modifies or waives the right to rescind, and bears the signature of all the consumers entitled to rescind. Printed forms for this purpose are prohibited.

(f) Exempt transactions. The right to rescind does not apply to the following:

(1) A residential mortgage transaction.

(2) A refinancing or consolidation by the same creditor of an extension of credit already secured by the consumer's principal dwelling. The right of rescission shall apply, however, to the extent the new amount financed exceeds the unpaid principal balance, any earned unpaid finance charge on the existing debt, and amounts attributed solely to the costs of the refinancing or consolidation.

(3) A transaction in which a state agency is a creditor.

(4) An advance, other than an initial advance, in a series of advances or in a series of single-payment obligations that is treated as a single transaction under § 1026.17(c)(6), if the notice required by paragraph (b) of this section and all material disclosures have been given to the consumer.

(5) A renewal of optional insurance premiums that is not considered a refinancing under § 1026.20(a)(5).

(g) Tolerances for accuracy—

(1) One-half of 1 percent tolerance. Except as provided in paragraphs (g)(2) and (h)(2) of this section:

(i) The finance charge and other disclosures affected by the finance charge (such as the amount financed and the annual percentage rate) shall be considered accurate for purposes of this section if the disclosed finance charge:

(A) Is understated by no more than ½ of 1 percent of the face amount of the note or $100, whichever is greater; or

(B) Is greater than the amount required to be disclosed.

(ii) The total of payments for each transaction subject to § 1026.19(e) and (f) shall be considered accurate for purposes of this section if the disclosed total of payments:

(A) Is understated by no more than ½ of 1 percent of the face amount of the note or $100, whichever is greater; or

(B) Is greater than the amount required to be disclosed.

(2) One percent tolerance. In a refinancing of a residential mortgage transaction with a new creditor (other than a transaction covered by § 1026.32), if there is no new advance and no consolidation of existing loans

(i) The finance charge and other disclosures affected by the finance charge (such as the amount financed and the annual percentage rate) shall be considered accurate for purposes of this section if the disclosed finance charge:

(A) Is understated by no more than 1 percent of the face amount of the note or $100, whichever is greater; or

(B) Is greater than the amount required to be disclosed.

(ii) The total of payments for each transaction subject to § 1026.19(e) and (f) shall be considered accurate for purposes of this section if the disclosed total of payments:

(A) Is understated by no more than 1 percent of the face amount of the note or $100, whichever is greater; or

(B) Is greater than the amount required to be disclosed.

(h) Special rules for foreclosures—

(1) Right to rescind. After the initiation of foreclosure on the consumer's principal dwelling that secures the credit obligation, the consumer shall have the right to rescind the transaction if:

(i) A mortgage broker fee that should have been included in the finance charge was not included; or

(ii) The creditor did not provide the properly completed appropriate model form in appendix H of this part, or a substantially similar notice of rescission.

(2) Tolerance for disclosures. After the initiation of foreclosure on the consumer's principal dwelling that secures the credit obligation:

(i) The finance charge and other disclosures affected by the finance charge (such as the amount financed and the annual percentage rate) shall be considered accurate for purposes of this section if the disclosed finance charge:

(A) Is understated by no more than $35; or

(B) Is greater than the amount required to be disclosed.

(ii) The total of payments for each transaction subject to § 1026.19(e) and (f) shall be considered accurate for purposes of this section if the disclosed total of payments:

(A) Is understated by no more than $35; or

(B) Is greater than the amount required to be disclosed.

§ 1026.24. Advertising

(a) Actually available terms. If an advertisement for credit states specific credit terms, it shall state only those terms that actually are or will be arranged or offered by the creditor.

(b) Clear and conspicuous standard. Disclosures required by this section shall be made clearly and conspicuously.

(c) Advertisement of rate of finance charge. If an advertisement states a rate of finance charge, it shall state the rate as an "annual percentage rate," using that term. If the annual percentage rate may be increased after consummation, the advertisement shall state that fact. If an advertisement is for credit not secured by a dwelling, the advertisement shall not state any other rate, except that a simple annual rate or periodic rate that is applied to an unpaid balance may be stated in conjunction with, but not more conspicuously than, the annual percentage rate. If an advertisement is for credit secured by a dwelling, the advertisement shall not state any other rate, except that a simple annual rate that is applied to an unpaid balance may be stated in conjunction with, but not more conspicuously than, the annual percentage rate.

(d) Advertisement of terms that require additional disclosures—

(1) Triggering terms. If any of the following terms is set forth in an advertisement, the advertisement shall meet the requirements of paragraph (d)(2) of this section:

(i) The amount or percentage of any downpayment.

(ii) The number of payments or period of repayment.

(iii) The amount of any payment.

(iv) The amount of any finance charge.

(2) Additional terms. An advertisement stating any of the terms in paragraph (d)(1) of this section shall state the following terms, as applicable (an example of one or more typical extensions of credit with a statement of all the terms applicable to each may be used):

(i) The amount or percentage of the downpayment.

(ii) The terms of repayment, which reflect the repayment obligations over the full term of the loan, including any balloon payment.

(iii) The "annual percentage rate," using that term, and, if the rate may be increased after consummation, that fact.

(e) Catalogs or other multiple-page advertisements; electronic advertisements.

(1) If a catalog or other multiple-page advertisement, or an electronic advertisement (such as an advertisement appearing on an Internet Web site), gives information in a table or schedule in sufficient detail to permit determination of the disclosures required by paragraph (d)(2) of this section, it shall be considered a single advertisement if:

(i) The table or schedule is clearly and conspicuously set forth; and

(ii) Any statement of the credit terms in paragraph (d)(1) of this section appearing anywhere else in the catalog or advertisement clearly refers to the page or location where the table or schedule begins.

(2) A catalog or other multiple-page advertisement or an electronic advertisement (such as an advertisement appearing on an Internet Web site) complies with paragraph (d)(2) of this section if the table or schedule of terms includes all appropriate disclosures for a representative scale of amounts up to the level of the more commonly sold higher-priced property or services offered.

(f) Disclosure of rates and payments in advertisements for credit secured by a dwelling—

(1) Scope. The requirements of this paragraph apply to any advertisement for credit secured by a dwelling, other than television or radio advertisements, including promotional materials accompanying applications.

(2) Disclosure of rates.

(i) In general. If an advertisement for credit secured by a dwelling states a simple annual rate of interest and more than one simple annual rate of interest will apply over the term of the advertised loan, the advertisement shall disclose in a clear and conspicuous manner:

(A) Each simple annual rate of interest that will apply. In variable-rate transactions, a rate determined by adding an index and margin shall be disclosed based on a reasonably current index and margin;

(B) The period of time during which each simple annual rate of interest will apply; and

(C) The annual percentage rate for the loan. If such rate is variable, the annual percentage rate shall comply with the accuracy standards in §§ 1026.17(c) and 1026.22.

(ii) Clear and conspicuous requirement. For purposes of paragraph (f)(2)(i) of this section, clearly and conspicuously disclosed means that the required information in paragraphs (f)(2)(i)(A) through (C) shall be disclosed with equal prominence and in close proximity to any advertised rate that triggered the required disclosures. The required information in paragraph (f)(2)(i)(C) may be disclosed with greater prominence than the other information.

(3) Disclosure of payments—

(i) In general. In addition to the requirements of paragraph (c) of this section, if an advertisement for credit secured by a dwelling states the amount of any payment, the advertisement shall disclose in a clear and conspicuous manner:

(A) The amount of each payment that will apply over the term of the loan, including any balloon payment. In variable-rate transactions, payments that will be determined based on the application of the sum of an index and margin shall be disclosed based on a reasonably current index and margin;

(B) The period of time during which each payment will apply; and

(C) In an advertisement for credit secured by a first lien on a dwelling, the fact that the payments do not include amounts for taxes and insurance premiums, if applicable, and that the actual payment obligation will be greater.

(ii) Clear and conspicuous requirement. For purposes of paragraph (f)(3)(i) of this section, a clear and conspicuous disclosure means that the required information in paragraphs (f)(3)(i)(A) and (B) shall be disclosed with equal prominence and in close proximity to any advertised payment that triggered the required disclosures, and that the required information in paragraph (f)(3)(i)(C) shall be disclosed with prominence and in close proximity to the advertised payments.

(4) Envelope excluded. The requirements in paragraphs (f)(2) and (f)(3) of this section do not apply to an envelope in which an application or solicitation is mailed, or to a banner advertisement or pop-up advertisement linked to an application or solicitation provided electronically.

(g) Alternative disclosures—television or radio advertisements. An advertisement made through television or radio stating any of the terms requiring additional disclosures under paragraph (d)(2) of this section may comply with paragraph (d)(2) of this section either by:

(1) Stating clearly and conspicuously each of the additional disclosures required under paragraph (d)(2) of this section; or

(2) Stating clearly and conspicuously the information required by paragraph (d)(2)(iii) of this section and listing a toll-free telephone number, or any telephone number that allows a consumer to reverse the phone charges when calling for information, along with a reference that such number may be used by consumers to obtain additional cost information.

(h) Tax implications. If an advertisement distributed in paper form or through the Internet (rather than by radio or television) is for a loan secured by the consumer's principal dwelling, and the advertisement states that the advertised extension of credit may exceed the fair market value of the dwelling, the advertisement shall clearly and conspicuously state that:

(1) The interest on the portion of the credit extension that is greater than the fair market value of the dwelling is not tax deductible for Federal income tax purposes; and

(2) The consumer should consult a tax adviser for further information regarding the deductibility of interest and charges.

(i) Prohibited acts or practices in advertisements for credit secured by a dwelling. The following acts or practices are prohibited in advertisements for credit secured by a dwelling:

(1) Misleading advertising of "fixed" rates and payments. Using the word "fixed" to refer to rates, payments, or the credit transaction in an advertisement for variable-rate transactions or other transactions where the payment will increase, unless:

(i) In the case of an advertisement solely for one or more variable-rate transactions,

(A) The phrase "Adjustable-Rate Mortgage," "Variable-Rate Mortgage," or "ARM" appears in the advertisement before the first use of the word "fixed" and is at least as conspicuous as any use of the word "fixed" in the advertisement; and

(B) Each use of the word "fixed" to refer to a rate or payment is accompanied by an equally prominent and closely proximate statement of the time period for which the rate or payment is fixed, and the fact that the rate may vary or the payment may increase after that period;

(ii) In the case of an advertisement solely for non-variable-rate transactions where the payment will increase (e.g., a stepped-rate mortgage transaction with an initial lower payment), each use of the word "fixed" to refer to the payment is accompanied by an equally prominent and closely proximate statement of the time period for which the payment is fixed, and the fact that the payment will increase after that period; or

(iii) In the case of an advertisement for both variable-rate transactions and non-variable-rate transactions,

(A) The phrase "Adjustable-Rate Mortgage," "Variable-Rate Mortgage," or "ARM" appears in the advertisement with equal prominence as any use of the term "fixed," "Fixed-Rate Mortgage," or similar terms; and

(B) Each use of the word "fixed" to refer to a rate, payment, or the credit transaction either refers solely to the transactions for which rates are fixed and complies with paragraph (i)(1)(ii) of this section, if applicable, or, if it refers to the variable-rate transactions, is accompanied by an equally prominent and closely proximate statement of the time period for which the rate or payment is fixed, and the fact that the rate may vary or the payment may increase after that period.

(2) Misleading comparisons in advertisements. Making any comparison in an advertisement between actual or hypothetical credit payments or rates and any payment or simple annual rate that will be available under the advertised product for a period less than the full term of the loan, unless:

(i) In general. The advertisement includes a clear and conspicuous comparison to the information required to be disclosed under § 1026.24(f)(2) and (3); and

(ii) Application to variable-rate transactions. If the advertisement is for a variable-rate transaction, and the advertised payment or simple annual rate is based on the index and margin that will be used to make subsequent rate or payment adjustments over the term of the loan, the advertisement includes an equally prominent statement in close proximity to the payment or rate that the payment or rate is subject to adjustment and the time period when the first adjustment will occur.

(3) Misrepresentations about government endorsement. Making any statement in an advertisement that the product offered is a "government loan program", "government-supported loan", or is otherwise endorsed or sponsored by any Federal, state, or local government entity, unless the advertisement is for an FHA loan, VA loan, or similar loan program that is, in fact, endorsed or sponsored by a Federal, state, or local government entity.

(4) Misleading use of the current lender's name. Using the name of the consumer's current lender in an advertisement that is not sent by or on behalf of the consumer's current lender, unless the advertisement:

(i) Discloses with equal prominence the name of the person or creditor making the advertisement; and

(ii) Includes a clear and conspicuous statement that the person making the advertisement is not associated with, or acting on behalf of, the consumer's current lender.

(5) Misleading claims of debt elimination. Making any misleading claim in an advertisement that the mortgage product offered will eliminate debt or result in a waiver or forgiveness of a consumer's existing loan terms with, or obligations to, another creditor.

(6) Misleading use of the term "counselor". Using the term "counselor" in an advertisement to refer to a for-profit mortgage broker or mortgage creditor, its employees, or persons working for the broker or creditor that are involved in offering, originating or selling mortgages.

(7) Misleading foreign-language advertisements. Providing information about some trigger terms or required disclosures, such as an initial rate or payment, only in a foreign language in an advertisement, but providing information about other trigger terms or required disclosures, such as information about the fully-indexed rate or fully amortizing payment, only in English in the same advertisement.

SUBPART D: MISCELLANEOUS

§ 1026.25. Record Retention

(a) General rule. A creditor shall retain evidence of compliance with this part (other than advertising requirements under §§ 1026.16 and 1026.24, and other than the requirements under § 1026.19(e) and (f)) for two years after the date disclosures are required to be made or action is required to be taken. The administrative agencies responsible for enforcing the regulation may require creditors under their jurisdictions to retain records for a longer period if necessary to carry out their enforcement responsibilities under section 108 of the Act.

(b) Inspection of records. A creditor shall permit the agency responsible for enforcing this part with respect to that creditor to inspect its relevant records for compliance.

(c) Records related to certain requirements for mortgage loans—

(1) Records related to requirements for loans secured by real property—

(i) General rule. Except as provided under paragraph (c)(1)(ii) of this section, a creditor shall retain evidence of compliance with the requirements of § 1026.19(e) and (f) for three years after the later of the date of consummation, the date disclosures are required to be made, or the date the action is required to be taken.

(ii) Closing disclosures.

(A) A creditor shall retain each completed disclosure required under § 1026.19(f)(1)(i) or (f)(4)(i), and all documents related to such disclosures, for five years after consummation, notwithstanding paragraph (c)(1)(ii)(B) of this section.

(B) If a creditor sells, transfers, or otherwise disposes of its interest in a mortgage loan subject to § 1026.19(f) and does not service the mortgage loan, the creditor shall provide a copy of the disclosures required under § 1026.19(f)(1)(i) or (f)(4)(i) to the owner or servicer of the mortgage as a part of the transfer of the loan file. Such owner or servicer shall retain such disclosures for the remainder of the five-year period described under paragraph (c)(1)(ii)(A) of this section.

(C) The Bureau shall have the right to require provision of copies of records related to the disclosures required under § 1026.19(f)(1)(i) and (f)(4)(i).

(2) Records related to requirements for loan originator compensation. Notwithstanding paragraph (a) of this section, for transactions subject to § 1026.36:

(i) A creditor shall maintain records sufficient to evidence all compensation it pays to a loan originator, as defined in § 1026.36(a)(1), and the compensation agreement that governs those payments for three years after the date of payment.

(ii) A loan originator organization, as defined in § 1026.36(a)(1)(iii), shall maintain records sufficient to evidence all compensation it receives from a creditor, a consumer, or another person; all compensation it pays to any individual loan originator, as defined in § 1026.36(a)(1)(ii); and the compensation agreement that governs each such receipt or payment, for three years after the date of each such receipt or payment.

(3) Records related to minimum standards for transactions secured by a dwelling. Notwithstanding paragraph (a) of this section, a creditor shall retain evidence of compliance with § 1026.43 of this regulation for three years after consummation of a transaction covered by that section.

§ 1026.26. Use of Annual Percentage Rate in Oral Disclosures

(a) Open-end credit. In an oral response to a consumer's inquiry about the cost of open-end credit, only the annual percentage rate or rates shall be stated, except that the periodic rate or rates also may be stated. If the annual percentage rate cannot be determined in advance because there are finance charges other than a periodic rate, the corresponding annual percentage rate shall be stated, and other cost information may be given.

(b) Closed-end credit. In an oral response to a consumer's inquiry about the cost of closed-end credit, only the annual percentage rate shall be stated, except that a simple annual rate or periodic rate also may be stated if it is applied to an unpaid balance. If the annual percentage rate cannot be determined in advance, the annual percentage rate for a sample transaction shall be stated, and other cost information for the consumer's specific transaction may be given.

§ 1026.27. Language of Disclosures

Disclosures required by this part may be made in a language other than English, provided that the disclosures are made available in English upon the consumer's request. This requirement for providing English disclosures on request does not apply to advertisements subject to §§ 1026.16 and 1026.24.

§ 1026.28. Effect on State Laws

(a) Inconsistent disclosure requirements.

(1) Except as provided in paragraph (d) of this section, State law requirements that are inconsistent with the requirements contained in chapter 1 (General Provisions), chapter 2 (Credit Transactions), or chapter 3 (Credit Advertising) of the Act and the implementing provisions of this part are preempted to the extent of the inconsistency. A State law is inconsistent if it requires a creditor to make disclosures or take actions that contradict the requirements of the Federal law. A State law is contradictory if it requires the use of the same term to represent a different amount or a different meaning than the Federal law, or if it requires the use of a term different from that required in the Federal law to describe the same item. A creditor, State, or other interested party may request the Bureau to determine whether a State law requirement is inconsistent. After the Bureau determines that a State law is inconsistent, a creditor may not make disclosures using the inconsistent term or form. A determination as to whether a State law is inconsistent with the requirements of sections 4 and 5 of RESPA (other than the RESPA section 5(c) requirements regarding provision of a list of certified homeownership counselors) and §§ 1026.19(e) and (f), 1026.37, and 1026.38 shall be made in accordance with this section and not 12 CFR 1024.13.

(2)(i) State law requirements are inconsistent with the requirements contained in sections 161 (Correction of billing errors) or 162 (Regulation of credit reports) of the Act and the implementing provisions of this part and are preempted if they provide rights, responsibilities, or procedures for consumers or creditors that are different from those required by the Federal law. However, a state law that allows a consumer to inquire about an open-end credit account and imposes on the creditor an obligation to respond to such inquiry after the time allowed in the Federal law for the consumer to submit written notice of a billing error shall not be preempted in any situation where the time period for making written notice under this part has expired. If a creditor gives written notice of a consumer's rights under such state law, the notice shall state that reliance on the longer time period available under state law may result in the loss of important rights that could be preserved by acting more promptly under Federal law; it shall also explain that the state law provisions apply only after expiration of the time period for submitting a proper written notice of a billing error under the Federal law. If the state disclosures are made on the same side of a page as the required Federal disclosures, the state disclosures shall appear under a demarcation line below the Federal disclosures, and the Federal disclosures shall be identified by a heading indicating that they are made in compliance with Federal law.

(ii) State law requirements are inconsistent with the requirements contained in chapter 4 (Credit billing) of the Act (other than section 161 or 162) and the implementing provisions of this part and are preempted if the creditor cannot comply with state law without violating Federal law.

(iii) A state may request the Bureau to determine whether its law is inconsistent with chapter 4 of the Act and its implementing provisions.

(b) Equivalent disclosure requirements. If the Bureau determines that a disclosure required by state law (other than a requirement relating to the finance charge, annual percentage rate, or the disclosures required under § 1026.32) is substantially the same in meaning as a disclosure required under the Act or this part, creditors in that state may make the state disclosure in lieu of the Federal disclosure. A creditor, state, or other interested party may request the Bureau to determine whether a state disclosure is substantially the same in meaning as a Federal disclosure.

(c) Request for determination. The procedures under which a request for a determination may be made under this section are set forth in appendix A.

(d) Special rule for credit and charge cards. State law requirements relating to the disclosure of credit information in any credit or charge card application or solicitation that is subject to the requirements of section 127(c) of chapter 2 of the Act (§ 1026.60 of the regulation) or in any renewal notice for a credit or charge card that is subject to the requirements of section 127(d) of chapter 2 of the Act (§ 1026.9(e) of the regulation) are preempted. State laws relating to the enforcement of section 127(c) and (d) of the Act are not preempted.

§ 1026.29. State Exemptions

(a) General rule. Any state may apply to the Bureau to exempt a class of transactions within the state from the requirements of chapter 2 (Credit transactions) or chapter 4 (Credit billing) of the Act and the corresponding provisions of this part. The Bureau shall grant an exemption if it determines that:

(1) The state law is substantially similar to the Federal law or, in the case of chapter 4, affords the consumer greater protection than the Federal law; and

(2) There is adequate provision for enforcement.

(b) Civil liability.

(1) No exemptions granted under this section shall extend to the civil liability provisions of sections 130 and 131 of the Act.

(2) If an exemption has been granted, the disclosures required by the applicable state law (except any additional requirements not imposed by Federal law) shall constitute the disclosures required by the Act.

(c) Applications. The procedures under which a state may apply for an exemption under this section are set forth in appendix B to this part.

§ 1026.30. Limitation on Rates

A creditor shall include in any consumer credit contract secured by a dwelling and subject to the Act and this part the maximum interest rate that may be imposed during the term of the obligation when:

(a) In the case of closed-end credit, the annual percentage rate may increase after consummation, or

(b) In the case of open-end credit, the annual percentage rate may increase during the plan.

SUBPART E: SPECIAL RULES FOR CERTAIN HOME MORTGAGE TRANSACTIONS

§ 1026.31. General Rules

(a) Relation to other subparts in this part. The requirements and limitations of this subpart are in addition to and not in lieu of those contained in other subparts of this part.

(b) Form of disclosures. The creditor shall make the disclosures required by this subpart clearly and conspicuously in writing, in a form that the consumer may keep. The disclosures required by this subpart may be provided to the consumer in electronic form, subject to compliance with the consumer consent and other applicable provisions of the Electronic Signatures in Global and National Commerce Act (E-Sign Act) (15 U.S.C. 7001 et seq.).

(c) Timing of disclosure—

(1) Disclosures for high-cost mortgages. The creditor shall furnish the disclosures required by § 1026.32 at least three business days prior to consummation or account opening of a high-cost mortgage as defined in § 1026.32(a).

(i) Change in terms. After complying with this paragraph (c)(1) and prior to consummation or account opening, if the creditor changes any term that makes the disclosures inaccurate, new disclosures shall be provided in accordance with the requirements of this subpart.

(ii) Telephone disclosures. A creditor may provide new disclosures required by paragraph (c)(1)(i) of this section by telephone if the consumer initiates the change and if, prior to or at consummation or account opening:

(A) The creditor provides new written disclosures; and

(B) The consumer and creditor sign a statement that the new disclosures were provided by telephone at least three days prior to consummation or account opening, as applicable.

(iii) Consumer's waiver of waiting period before consummation or account opening. The consumer may, after receiving the disclosures required by this paragraph (c)(1), modify or waive the three-day waiting period between delivery of those disclosures and consummation or account opening if the consumer determines that the extension of credit is needed to meet a bona fide personal financial emergency. To modify or waive the right, the consumer shall give the creditor a dated written statement that describes the emergency, specifically modifies or waives the waiting period, and bears the signature of all the consumers entitled to the waiting period. Printed forms for this purpose are prohibited, except when creditors are permitted to use printed forms pursuant to § 1026.23(e)(2).

(2) Disclosures for reverse mortgages. The creditor shall furnish the disclosures required by § 1026.33 at least three business days prior to:

(i) Consummation of a closed-end credit transaction; or

(ii) The first transaction under an open-end credit plan.

(d) Basis of disclosures and use of estimates—

(1) Legal Obligation. Disclosures shall reflect the terms of the legal obligation between the parties.

(2) Estimates. If any information necessary for an accurate disclosure is unknown to the creditor, the creditor shall make the disclosure based on the best information reasonably available at the time the disclosure is provided, and shall state clearly that the disclosure is an estimate.

(3) Per-diem interest. For a transaction in which a portion of the interest is determined on a per-diem basis and collected at consummation, any disclosure affected by the per-diem interest shall be considered accurate if the disclosure is based on the information known to the creditor at the time that the disclosure documents are prepared.

(e) Multiple creditors; multiple consumers. If a transaction involves more than one creditor, only one set of disclosures shall be given and the creditors shall agree among themselves which creditor must comply with the requirements that this part imposes on any or all of them. If there is more than one consumer, the disclosures may be made to any consumer who is primarily liable on the obligation. If the transaction is rescindable under § 1026.15 or § 1026.23, however, the disclosures shall be made to each consumer who has the right to rescind.

(f) Effect of subsequent events. If a disclosure becomes inaccurate because of an event that occurs after the creditor delivers the required disclosures, the inaccuracy is not a violation of Regulation Z (12 CFR part 1026), although new disclosures may be required for mortgages covered by § 1026.32 under paragraph (c) of this section, § 1026.9(c), § 1026.19, or § 1026.20.

(g) Accuracy of annual percentage rate. For purposes of section 1026.32, the annual percentage rate shall be considered accurate, and may be used in determining whether a transaction is covered by section 1026.32, if it is accurate according to the requirements and within the tolerances under section 1026.22 for closed-end credit transactions or 1026.6(a) for open-end credit plans. The finance charge tolerances for rescission under section 1026.23(g) or (h) shall not apply for this purpose.

(h) Corrections and unintentional violations. A creditor or assignee in a high-cost mortgage, as defined in § 1026.32(a), who, when acting in good faith, failed to comply with any requirement under section 129 of the Act will not be deemed to have violated such requirement if the creditor or assignee satisfies either of the following sets of conditions:

(1)(i) Within 30 days of consummation or account opening and prior to the institution of any action, the consumer is notified of or discovers the violation;

(ii) Appropriate restitution is made within a reasonable time; and

(iii) Within a reasonable time, whatever adjustments are necessary are made to the loan or credit plan to either, at the choice of the consumer:

(A) Make the loan or credit plan satisfy the requirements of 15 U.S.C. 1631–1651; or

(B) Change the terms of the loan or credit plan in a manner beneficial to the consumer so that the loan or credit plan will no longer be a high-cost mortgage.

(2)(i) Within 60 days of the creditor's discovery or receipt of notification of an unintentional violation or bona fide error and prior to the institution of any action, the consumer is notified of the compliance failure;

(ii) Appropriate restitution is made within a reasonable time; and

(iii) Within a reasonable time, whatever adjustments are necessary are made to the loan or credit plan to either, at the choice of the consumer:

(A) Make the loan or credit plan satisfy the requirements of 15 U.S.C. 1631–1651; or

(B) Change the terms of the loan or credit plan in a manner beneficial to the consumer so that the loan or credit plan will no longer be a high-cost mortgage.

§ 1026.32. Requirements for High-Cost Mortgages

(a) Coverage.

(1) The requirements of this section apply to a high-cost mortgage, which is any consumer credit transaction that is secured by the consumer's principal dwelling, other than as provided in paragraph (a)(2) of this section, and in which:

(i) The annual percentage rate applicable to the transaction, as determined in accordance with paragraph (a)(3) of this section, will exceed the average prime offer rate, as defined in § 1026.35(a)(2), for a comparable transaction by more than:

(A) 6.5 percentage points for a first-lien transaction, other than as described in paragraph (a)(1)(i)(B) of this section;

(B) 8.5 percentage points for a first-lien transaction if the dwelling is personal property and the loan amount is less than $50,000; or

(C) 8.5 percentage points for a subordinate-lien transaction; or

(ii) The transaction's total points and fees, as defined in paragraphs (b)(1) and (2) of this section, will exceed:

(A) 5 percent of the total loan amount for a transaction with a loan amount of $20,000 or more; the $20,000 figure shall be adjusted annually on January 1 by the annual percentage change in the Consumer Price Index that was reported on the preceding June 1; or

(B) The lesser of 8 percent of the total loan amount or $1,000 for a transaction with a loan amount of less than $20,000; the $1,000 and $20,000 figures shall be adjusted annually on January 1 by the annual percentage change in the Consumer Price Index that was reported on the preceding June 1; or

(iii) Under the terms of the loan contract or open-end credit agreement, the creditor can charge a prepayment penalty, as defined in paragraph (b)(6) of this section, more than 36 months after consummation or account opening, or prepayment penalties that can exceed, in total, more than 2 percent of the amount prepaid.

(2) Exemptions. This section does not apply to the following:

(i) A reverse mortgage transaction subject to § 1026.33;

(ii) A transaction to finance the initial construction of a dwelling;

(iii) A transaction originated by a Housing Finance Agency, where the Housing Finance Agency is the creditor for the transaction; or

(iv) A transaction originated pursuant to the United States Department of Agriculture's Rural Development Section 502 Direct Loan Program.

(3) Determination of annual percentage rate. For purposes of paragraph (a)(1)(i) of this section, a creditor shall determine the annual percentage rate for a closed-or open-end credit transaction based on the following:

(i) For a transaction in which the annual percentage rate will not vary during the term of the loan or credit plan, the interest rate in effect as of the date the interest rate for the transaction is set;

(ii) For a transaction in which the interest rate may vary during the term of the loan or credit plan in accordance with an index, the interest rate that results from adding the maximum margin permitted at any time during the term of the loan or credit plan to the value of the index rate in effect as of the date the interest rate for the transaction is set, or the introductory interest rate, whichever is greater; and

(iii) For a transaction in which the interest rate may or will vary during the term of the loan or credit plan, other than a transaction described in paragraph (a)(3)(ii) of this section, the maximum interest rate that may be imposed during the term of the loan or credit plan.

(b) Definitions. For purposes of this subpart, the following definitions apply:

(1) In connection with a closed-end credit transaction, points and fees means the following fees or charges that are known at or before consummation:

(i) All items included in the finance charge under § 1026.4(a) and (b), except that the following items are excluded:

(A) Interest or the time-price differential;

(B) Any premium or other charge imposed in connection with any Federal or State agency program for any guaranty or insurance that protects the creditor against the consumer's default or other credit loss;

(C) For any guaranty or insurance that protects the creditor against the consumer's default or other credit loss and that is not in connection with any Federal or State agency program:

(1) If the premium or other charge is payable after consummation, the entire amount of such premium or other charge; or

(2) If the premium or other charge is payable at or before consummation, the portion of any such premium or other charge that is not in excess of the amount payable under policies in effect at the time of origination under section 203(c)(2)(A) of the National Housing Act (12 U.S.C. 1709(c)(2)(A)), provided that the premium or charge is required to be refundable on a pro rata basis and the refund is automatically issued upon notification of the satisfaction of the underlying mortgage loan;

(D) Any bona fide third-party charge not retained by the creditor, loan originator, or an affiliate of either, unless the charge is required to be included in points and fees under paragraph (b)(1)(i)(C), (iii), or (iv) of this section;

(E) Up to two bona fide discount points paid by the consumer in connection with the transaction, if the interest rate without any discount does not exceed:

(1) The average prime offer rate, as defined in § 1026.35(a)(2), by more than one percentage point; or

(2) For purposes of paragraph (a)(1)(ii) of this section, for transactions that are secured by personal property, the average rate for a loan insured under Title I of the National Housing Act (12 U.S.C. 1702 et seq.) by more than one percentage point; and

(F) If no discount points have been excluded under paragraph (b)(1)(i)(E) of this section, then up to one bona fide discount point paid by the consumer in connection with the transaction, if the interest rate without any discount does not exceed:

(1) The average prime offer rate, as defined in § 1026.35(a)(2), by more than two percentage points; or

(2) For purposes of paragraph (a)(1)(ii) of this section, for transactions that are secured by personal property, the average rate for a loan insured under Title I of the National Housing Act (12 U.S.C. 1702 et seq.) by more than two percentage points;

(ii) All compensation paid directly or indirectly by a consumer or creditor to a loan originator, as defined in § 1026.36(a)(1), that can be attributed to that transaction at the time the interest rate is set unless:

(A) That compensation is paid by a consumer to a mortgage broker, as defined in § 1026.36(a)(2), and already has been included in points and fees under paragraph (b)(1)(i) of this section;

(B) That compensation is paid by a mortgage broker, as defined in § 1026.36(a)(2), to a loan originator that is an employee of the mortgage broker;

(C) That compensation is paid by a creditor to a loan originator that is an employee of the creditor; or

(D) That compensation is paid by a retailer of manufactured homes to its employee.

(iii) All items listed in § 1026.4(c)(7) (other than amounts held for future payment of taxes), unless:

(A) The charge is reasonable;

(B) The creditor receives no direct or indirect compensation in connection with the charge; and

(C) The charge is not paid to an affiliate of the creditor;

(iv) Premiums or other charges payable at or before consummation for any credit life, credit disability, credit unemployment, or credit property insurance, or any other life, accident, health, or loss-of-income insurance for which the creditor is a beneficiary, or any payments directly or indirectly for any debt cancellation or suspension agreement or contract;

(v) The maximum prepayment penalty, as defined in paragraph (b)(6)(i) of this section, that may be charged or collected under the terms of the mortgage loan; and

(vi) The total prepayment penalty, as defined in paragraph (b)(6)(i) or (ii) of this section, as applicable, incurred by the consumer if the consumer refinances the existing mortgage loan, or terminates an existing open-end credit plan in connection with obtaining a new mortgage loan, with the current holder of the existing loan or plan, a servicer acting on behalf of the current holder, or an affiliate of either.

(2) In connection with an open-end credit plan, points and fees means the following fees or charges that are known at or before account opening:

(i) All items included in the finance charge under § 1026.4(a) and (b), except that the following items are excluded:

(A) Interest or the time-price differential;

(B) Any premium or other charge imposed in connection with any Federal or State agency program for any guaranty or insurance that protects the creditor against the consumer's default or other credit loss;

(C) For any guaranty or insurance that protects the creditor against the consumer's default or other credit loss and that is not in connection with any Federal or State agency program:

(1) If the premium or other charge is payable after account opening, the entire amount of such premium or other charge; or

(2) If the premium or other charge is payable at or before account opening, the portion of any such premium or other charge that is not in excess of the amount payable under policies in effect at the time of account opening under section 203(c)(2)(A) of the National Housing Act (12 U.S.C. 1709(c)(2)(A)), provided that the premium or charge is required to be refundable on a pro rata basis and the refund is automatically issued upon notification of the satisfaction of the underlying mortgage transaction;

(D) Any bona fide third-party charge not retained by the creditor, loan originator, or an affiliate of either, unless the charge is required to be included in points and fees under paragraphs (b)(2)(i)(C), (b)(2)(iii) or (b)(2)(iv) of this section;

(E) Up to two bona fide discount points payable by the consumer in connection with the transaction, provided that the conditions specified in paragraph (b)(1)(i)(E) of this section are met; and

(F) Up to one bona fide discount point payable by the consumer in connection with the transaction, provided that no discount points have been excluded under paragraph (b)(2)(i)(E) of this section and the conditions specified in paragraph (b)(1)(i)(F) of this section are met;

(ii) All compensation paid directly or indirectly by a consumer or creditor to a loan originator, as defined in § 1026.36(a)(1), that can be attributed to that transaction at the time the interest rate is set unless:

(A) That compensation is paid by a consumer to a mortgage broker, as defined in § 1026.36(a)(2), and already has been included in points and fees under paragraph (b)(2)(i) of this section;

(B) That compensation is paid by a mortgage broker, as defined in § 1026.36(a)(2), to a loan originator that is an employee of the mortgage broker;

(C) That compensation is paid by a creditor to a loan originator that is an employee of the creditor; or

(D) That compensation is paid by a retailer of manufactured homes to its employee.

(iii) All items listed in § 1026.4(c)(7) (other than amounts held for future payment of taxes) unless:

(A) The charge is reasonable;

(B) The creditor receives no direct or indirect compensation in connection with the charge; and

(C) The charge is not paid to an affiliate of the creditor;

(iv) Premiums or other charges payable at or before account opening for any credit life, credit disability, credit unemployment, or credit property insurance, or any other life, accident, health, or loss-of-income insurance for which the creditor is a beneficiary, or any payments directly or indirectly for any debt cancellation or suspension agreement or contract;

(v) The maximum prepayment penalty, as defined in paragraph (b)(6)(ii) of this section, that may be charged or collected under the terms of the open-end credit plan;

(vi) The total prepayment penalty, as defined in paragraph (b)(6)(i) or (ii) of this section, as applicable, incurred by the consumer if the consumer refinances an existing closed-end credit transaction with an open-end credit plan, or terminates an existing open-end credit plan in connection with obtaining a new open-end credit transaction, with the current holder of the existing transaction or plan, a servicer acting on behalf of the current holder, or an affiliate of either;

(vii) Any fees charged for participation in an open-end credit plan, payable at or before account opening, as described in § 1026.4(c)(4); and

(viii) Any transaction fee, including any minimum fee or per-transaction fee, that will be charged for a draw on the credit line, where the creditor must assume that the consumer will make at least one draw during the term of the plan.

(3) Bona fide discount point—(i) Closed-end credit. The term bona fide discount point means an amount equal to 1 percent of the loan amount paid by the consumer that reduces the interest rate or time-price differential applicable to the transaction based on a calculation that is consistent with established industry practices for determining the amount of reduction in the interest rate or time-price differential appropriate for the amount of discount points paid by the consumer.

(ii) Open-end credit. The term bona fide discount point means an amount equal to 1 percent of the credit limit for the plan when the account is opened, paid by the consumer, and that reduces the interest rate or time-price differential applicable to the transaction based on a calculation that is consistent with established industry practices for determining the amount of reduction in the interest rate or time-price differential appropriate for the amount of discount points paid by the consumer. See comment 32(b)(3)(i)–1 for additional guidance in determining whether a discount point is bona fide.

(4) Total loan amount—(i) Closed-end credit. The total loan amount for a closed-end credit transaction is calculated by taking the amount financed, as determined according to § 1026.18(b), and deducting any cost listed in § 1026.32(b)(1)(iii), (iv), or (vi) that is both included as points and fees under § 1026.32(b)(1) and financed by the creditor.

(ii) Open-end credit. The total loan amount for an open-end credit plan is the credit limit for the plan when the account is opened.

(5) Affiliate means any company that controls, is controlled by, or is under common control with another company, as set forth in the Bank Holding Company Act of 1956 (12 U.S.C. 1841 et seq.).

(6) Prepayment penalty—(i) Closed-end credit transactions. For a closed-end credit transaction, prepayment penalty means a charge imposed for paying all or part of the transaction's principal before the date on which the principal is due, other than a waived, bona fide third-party charge that the creditor imposes if the consumer prepays all of the transaction's principal sooner than 36 months after consummation, provided, however, that interest charged consistent with the monthly interest accrual amortization method is not a prepayment penalty for extensions of credit insured by the Federal Housing Administration that are consummated before January 21, 2015.

(ii) Open-end credit. For an open-end credit plan, prepayment penalty means a charge imposed by the creditor if the consumer terminates the open-end credit plan prior to the end of its term, other than a waived bona fide third-party charge that the creditor imposes if the consumer terminates the open-end credit plan sooner than 36 months after account opening.

(c) Disclosures. In addition to other disclosures required by this part, in a mortgage subject to this section, the creditor shall disclose the following in conspicuous type size:

(1) Notices. The following statement: "You are not required to complete this agreement merely because you have received these disclosures or have signed a loan application. If you obtain this loan, the lender will have a mortgage on your home. You could lose your home, and any money you have put into it, if you do not meet your obligations under the loan."

(2) Annual percentage rate. The annual percentage rate.

(3) Regular payment; minimum periodic payment example; balloon payment. (i) For a closed-end credit transaction, the amount of the regular monthly (or other periodic) payment and the amount of any balloon payment provided in the credit contract, if permitted under paragraph (d)(1) of this section. The regular payment disclosed under this paragraph shall be treated as accurate if it is based on an amount borrowed that is deemed accurate and is disclosed under paragraph (c)(5) of this section.

(ii) For an open-end credit plan:

(A) An example showing the first minimum periodic payment for the draw period, the first minimum periodic payment for any repayment period, and the balance outstanding at the beginning of any repayment period. The example must be based on the following assumptions:

(1) The consumer borrows the full credit line, as disclosed in paragraph (c)(5) of this section, at account opening and does not obtain any additional extensions of credit;

(2) The consumer makes only minimum periodic payments during the draw period and any repayment period; and

(3) The annual percentage rate used to calculate the example payments remains the same during the draw period and any repayment period. The creditor must provide the minimum periodic payment example based on the annual percentage rate for the plan, as described in paragraph (c)(2) of this section, except that if an introductory annual percentage rate applies, the creditor must use the rate that will apply to the plan after the introductory rate expires.

(B) If the credit contract provides for a balloon payment under the plan as permitted under paragraph (d)(1) of this section, a disclosure of that fact and an example showing the amount of the balloon payment based on the assumptions described in paragraph (c)(3)(ii)(A) of this section.

(C) A statement that the example payments show the first minimum periodic payments at the current annual percentage rate if the consumer borrows the maximum credit available when the account is opened and does not obtain any additional extensions of credit, or a substantially similar statement.

(D) A statement that the example payments are not the consumer's actual payments and that the actual minimum periodic payments will depend on the amount the consumer borrows, the interest rate applicable to that period, and whether the consumer pays more than the required minimum periodic payment, or a substantially similar statement.

(4) Variable-rate. For variable-rate transactions, a statement that the interest rate and monthly payment may increase, and the amount of the single maximum monthly payment, based on the maximum interest rate required to be included in the contract by § 1026.30.

(5) Amount borrowed; credit limit. (i) For a closed-end credit transaction, the total amount the consumer will borrow, as reflected by the face amount of the note. Where the amount borrowed includes financed charges that are not prohibited under § 1026.34(a)(10), that fact shall be stated, grouped together with the disclosure of the amount borrowed. The disclosure of the amount borrowed shall be treated as accurate if it is not more than $100 above or below the amount required to be disclosed.

(ii) For an open-end credit plan, the credit limit for the plan when the account is opened.

(d) Limitations. A high-cost mortgage shall not include the following terms:

(1)(i) Balloon payment. Except as provided by paragraphs (d)(1)(ii) and (iii) of this section, a payment schedule with a payment that is more than two times a regular periodic payment.

(ii) Exceptions. The limitations in paragraph (d)(1)(i) of this section do not apply to:

(A) A mortgage transaction with a payment schedule that is adjusted to the seasonal or irregular income of the consumer;

(B) A loan with maturity of 12 months or less, if the purpose of the loan is a "bridge" loan connected with the acquisition or construction of a dwelling intended to become the consumer's principal dwelling; or

(C) A loan that meets the criteria set forth in §§ 1026.43(f)(1)(i) through (vi) and 1026.43(f)(2), or the conditions set forth in § 1026.43(e)(6).

(iii) Open-end credit plans. If the terms of an open-end credit plan provide for a repayment period during which no further draws may be taken, the limitations in paragraph (d)(1)(i) of this section do not apply to any adjustment in the regular periodic payment that results solely from the credit plan's transition from the draw period to the repayment period.

If the terms of an open-end credit plan do not provide for any repayment period, the limitations in paragraph (d)(1)(i) of this section apply to all periods of the credit plan.

(2) Negative amortization. A payment schedule with regular periodic payments that cause the principal balance to increase.

(3) Advance payments. A payment schedule that consolidates more than two periodic payments and pays them in advance from the proceeds.

(4) Increased interest rate. An increase in the interest rate after default.

(5) Rebates. A refund calculated by a method less favorable than the actuarial method (as defined by section 933(d) of the Housing and Community Development Act of 1992, 15 U.S.C. 1615(d)), for rebates of interest arising from a loan acceleration due to default.

(6) Prepayment penalties. A prepayment penalty, as defined in paragraph (b)(6) of this section.

(7) [Reserved]

(8) Acceleration of debt. A demand feature that permits the creditor to accelerate the indebtedness by terminating the high-cost mortgage in advance of the original maturity date and to demand repayment of the entire outstanding balance, except in the following circumstances:

(i) There is fraud or material misrepresentation by the consumer in connection with the loan or open-end credit agreement;

(ii) The consumer fails to meet the repayment terms of the agreement for any outstanding balance that results in a default in payment under the loan; or

(iii) There is any action or inaction by the consumer that adversely affects the creditor's security for the loan, or any right of the creditor in such security.

§ 1026.33. Requirements for Reverse Mortgages

(a) Definition. For purposes of this subpart, reverse mortgage transaction means a nonrecourse consumer credit obligation in which:

(1) A mortgage, deed of trust, or equivalent consensual security interest securing one or more advances is created in the consumer's principal dwelling; and

(2) Any principal, interest, or shared appreciation or equity is due and payable (other than in the case of default) only after:

(i) The consumer dies;

(ii) The dwelling is transferred; or

(iii) The consumer ceases to occupy the dwelling as a principal dwelling.

(b) Content of disclosures. In addition to other disclosures required by this part, in a reverse mortgage transaction the creditor shall provide the following disclosures in a form substantially similar to the model form found in paragraph (d) of appendix K of this part:

(1) Notice. A statement that the consumer is not obligated to complete the reverse mortgage transaction merely because the consumer has received the disclosures required by this section or has signed an application for a reverse mortgage loan.

(2) Total annual loan cost rates. A good-faith projection of the total cost of the credit, determined in accordance with paragraph (c) of this section and expressed as a table of "total annual loan cost rates," using that term, in accordance with Appendix K of this part.

(3) Itemization of pertinent information. An itemization of loan terms, charges, the age of the youngest borrower and the appraised property value.

(4) Explanation of table. An explanation of the table of total annual loan cost rates as provided in the model form found in paragraph (d) of appendix K of this part.

(c) Projected total cost of credit. The projected total cost of credit shall reflect the following factors, as applicable:

(1) Costs to consumer. All costs and charges to the consumer, including the costs of any annuity the consumer purchases as part of the reverse mortgage transaction.

(2) Payments to consumer. All advances to and for the benefit of the consumer, including annuity payments that the consumer will receive from an annuity that the consumer purchases as part of the reverse mortgage transaction.

(3) Additional creditor compensation. Any shared appreciation or equity in the dwelling that the creditor is entitled by contract to receive.

(4) Limitations on consumer liability. Any limitation on the consumer's liability (such as nonrecourse limits and equity conservation agreements).

(5) Assumed annual appreciation rates. Each of the following assumed annual appreciation rates for the dwelling:

(i) 0 percent.

(ii) 4 percent.

(iii) 8 percent.

(6) Assumed loan period.

(i) Each of the following assumed loan periods, as provided in appendix L of this part:

(A) Two years.

(B) The actuarial life expectancy of the consumer to become obligated on the reverse mortgage transaction (as of that consumer's most recent birthday). In the case of multiple consumers, the period shall be the actuarial life expectancy of the youngest consumer (as of that consumer's most recent birthday).

(C) The actuarial life expectancy specified by paragraph (c)(6)(i)(B) of this section, multiplied by a factor of 1.4 and rounded to the nearest full year.

(ii) At the creditor's option, the actuarial life expectancy specified by paragraph (c)(6)(i)(B) of this section, multiplied by a factor of .5 and rounded to the nearest full year.

§ 1026.34. Prohibited Acts or Practices in Connection with High-Cost Mortgages

(a) Prohibited acts or practices for high-cost mortgages.

(1) Home improvement contracts. A creditor shall not pay a contractor under a home improvement contract from the proceeds of a high-cost mortgage, other than:

(i) By an instrument payable to the consumer or jointly to the consumer and the contractor; or

(ii) At the election of the consumer, through a third-party escrow agent in accordance with terms established in a written agreement signed by the consumer, the creditor, and the contractor prior to the disbursement.

(2) Notice to assignee. A creditor may not sell or otherwise assign a high-cost mortgage without furnishing the following statement to the purchaser or assignee: "Notice: This is a mortgage subject to special rules under the Federal Truth in Lending Act. Purchasers or assignees of this mortgage could be liable for all claims and defenses with respect to the mortgage that the consumer could assert against the creditor."

(3) Refinancings within one-year period. Within one year of having extended a high-cost mortgage, a creditor shall not refinance any high-cost mortgage to the same consumer into another high-cost mortgage, unless the refinancing is in the consumer's interest. An assignee holding or servicing a high-cost mortgage shall not, for the remainder of the one-year period following the date of origination of the credit, refinance any high-cost mortgage to the same consumer into another high-cost mortgage, unless the refinancing is in the consumer's interest. A creditor (or assignee) is prohibited from engaging in acts or practices to evade this provision, including a pattern or practice of arranging for the refinancing of its own loans by affiliated or unaffiliated creditors.

(4) Repayment ability for high-cost mortgages. In connection with an open-end, high-cost mortgage, a creditor shall not open a plan for a consumer where credit is or will be extended without regard to the consumer's repayment ability as of account opening, including the consumer's current and reasonably expected income, employment, assets other than the collateral, and current obligations including any mortgage-related obligations that are required by another credit obligation undertaken prior to or at account opening, and are secured by the same dwelling that secures the high-cost mortgage transaction. The requirements set forth in § 1026.34(a)(4)(i) through (iv) apply to open-end high-cost mortgages, but do not apply to closed-end high-cost mortgages. In connection with a closed-end, high-cost mortgage, a creditor must comply with the repayment ability requirements set forth in § 1026.43. Temporary or "bridge" loans with terms of twelve months or less, such as a loan to purchase a new dwelling where the consumer plans to sell a current dwelling within twelve months, are exempt from this repayment ability requirement.

(i) Mortgage-related obligations. For purposes of this paragraph (a)(4), mortgage-related obligations are property taxes; premiums and similar charges identified in § 1026.4(b)(5), (7), (8), and (10) that are required by the creditor; fees and special assessments imposed by a condominium, cooperative, or homeowners association; ground rent; and leasehold payments.

(ii) Basis for determination of repayment ability. Under this paragraph (a)(4) a creditor must determine the consumer's repayment ability in connection with an open-end, high cost mortgage as follows:

(A) A creditor must verify amounts of income or assets that it relies on to determine repayment ability, including expected income or assets, by the consumer's Internal Revenue Service Form W-2, tax returns, payroll receipts, financial institution records, or other third-party documents that provide reasonably reliable evidence of the consumer's income or assets.

(B) A creditor must verify the consumer's current obligations, including any mortgage-related obligations that are required by another credit obligation undertaken prior to or at account opening, and are secured by the same dwelling that secures the high-cost mortgage transaction.

(iii) Presumption of compliance. For an open-end, high cost mortgage, a creditor is presumed to have complied with this paragraph (a)(4) with respect to a transaction if the creditor:

(A) Determines the consumer's repayment ability as provided in paragraph (a)(4)(ii);

(B) Determines the consumer's repayment ability taking into account current obligations and mortgage-related obligations as defined in paragraph (a)(4)(i) of this section, and using the largest required minimum periodic payment based on the following assumptions:

(1) The consumer borrows the full credit line at account opening with no additional extensions of credit;

(2) The consumer makes only required minimum periodic payments during the draw period and any repayment period;

(3) If the annual percentage rate may increase during the plan, the maximum annual percentage rate that is included in the contract, as required by § 1026.30, applies to the plan at account opening and will apply during the draw period and any repayment period.

(C) Assesses the consumer's repayment ability taking into account at least one of the following: The ratio of total current obligations, including any mortgage-related obligations that are required by another credit obligation undertaken prior to or at account opening, and are secured by the same dwelling that secures the high-cost mortgage transaction, to income, or the income the consumer will have after paying current obligations.

(iv) Exclusions from presumption of compliance. Notwithstanding the previous paragraph, no presumption of compliance is available for an open-end, high-cost mortgage transaction for which the regular periodic payments when aggregated do not fully amortize the outstanding principal balance except as otherwise provided by § 1026.32(d)(1)(ii).

(5) Pre-loan counseling. (i) Certification of counseling required. A creditor shall not extend a high-cost mortgage to a consumer unless the creditor receives written certification that the consumer has obtained counseling on the advisability of the mortgage from a counselor that is approved to provide such counseling by the Secretary of the U.S. Department of Housing and Urban Development or, if permitted by the Secretary, by a State housing finance authority.

(ii) Timing of counseling. The counseling required under this paragraph (a)(5) must occur after:

(A) The consumer receives either the disclosure required by section 5(c) of the Real Estate Settlement Procedures Act of 1974 (12 U.S.C. 2604(c)) or the disclosures required by § 1026.40; or

(B) The consumer receives the disclosures required by § 1026.32(c), for transactions in which neither of the disclosures listed in paragraph (a)(5)(ii)(A) of this section are provided.

(iii) Affiliation prohibited. The counseling required under this paragraph (a)(5) shall not be provided by a counselor who is employed by or affiliated with the creditor.

(iv) Content of certification. The certification of counseling required under paragraph (a)(5)(i) must include:

(A) The name(s) of the consumer(s) who obtained counseling;

(B) The date(s) of counseling;

(C) The name and address of the counselor;

(D) A statement that the consumer(s) received counseling on the advisability of the high-cost mortgage based on the terms provided in either the good faith estimate required by section 5(c) of the Real Estate Settlement Procedures Act of 1974 (12 U.S.C. 2604(c)) or the disclosures required by § 1026.40; and

(E) For transactions for which neither of the disclosures listed in paragraph (a)(5)(ii)(A) of this section are provided, a statement that the consumer(s) received counseling on the advisability of the high-cost mortgage based on the terms provided in the disclosures required by § 1026.32(c); and

(F) A statement that the counselor has verified that the consumer(s) received the disclosures required by either § 1026.32(c) or the Real Estate Settlement Procedures Act of 1974 (12 U.S.C. 2601 et seq.) with respect to the transaction.

(v) Counseling fees. A creditor may pay the fees of a counselor or counseling organization for providing counseling required under this paragraph (a)(5) but may not condition the payment of such fees on the consummation or account-opening of a mortgage transaction. If the consumer withdraws the application that would result in the extension of a high-cost mortgage, a creditor may not condition the payment of such fees on the receipt of certification from the counselor required by paragraph (a)(5)(i) of this section. A creditor may, however, confirm that a counselor has provided counseling to the consumer pursuant to this paragraph (a)(5) prior to paying the fee of a counselor or counseling organization.

(vi) Steering prohibited. A creditor that extends a high-cost mortgage shall not steer or otherwise direct a consumer to choose a particular counselor or counseling organization for the counseling required under this paragraph (a)(5).

(6) Recommended default. A creditor or mortgage broker, as defined in section 1026.36(a)(2), may not recommend or encourage default on an existing loan or other debt prior to and in connection with the consummation or account opening of a high-cost mortgage that refinances all or any portion of such existing loan or debt.

(7) Modification and deferral fees. A creditor, successor-in-interest, assignee, or any agent of such parties may not charge a consumer any fee to modify, renew, extend or amend a high-cost mortgage, or to defer any payment due under the terms of such mortgage.

(8) Late fees—

(i) General. Any late payment charge imposed in connection with a high-cost mortgage must be specifically permitted by the terms of the loan contract or open-end credit agreement and may not exceed 4 percent of the amount of the payment past due. No such charge may be imposed more than once for a single late payment.

(ii) Timing. A late payment charge may be imposed in connection with a high-cost mortgage only if the payment is not received by the end of the 15-day period beginning on the date the payment is due or, in the case of a high-cost mortgage on which interest on each installment is paid in advance, the end of the 30-day period beginning on the date the payment is due.

(iii) Multiple late charges assessed on payment subsequently paid. A late payment charge may not be imposed in connection with a high-cost mortgage payment if any delinquency is attributable only to a late payment charge imposed on an earlier payment, and the payment otherwise is a full payment for the applicable period and is paid by the due date or within any applicable grace period.

(iv) Failure to make required payment. The terms of a high-cost mortgage agreement may provide that any payment shall first be applied to any past due balance. If the consumer fails to make a timely payment by the due date and subsequently resumes making payments but has not paid all past due payments, the creditor may impose a separate late payment charge for any payment(s) outstanding (without deduction due to late fees or related fees) until the default is cured.

(9) Payoff statements. (i) Fee prohibition. In general, a creditor or servicer (as defined in 12 CFR 1024.2(b)) may not charge a fee for providing to a consumer, or a person authorized by the consumer to obtain such information, a statement of the amount due to pay off the outstanding balance of a high-cost mortgage.

(ii) Processing fee. A creditor or servicer may charge a processing fee to cover the cost of providing a payoff statement, as described in paragraph (a)(9)(i) of this section, by fax or courier, provided that such fee may not exceed an amount that is comparable to fees imposed for similar services provided in connection with consumer credit transactions that are secured by the consumer's principal dwelling and are not high-cost mortgages. A creditor or servicer shall make a payoff statement available to a consumer, or a person authorized by the consumer to obtain such information, by a method other than by fax or courier and without charge pursuant to paragraph (a)(9)(i) of this section.

(iii) Processing fee disclosure. Prior to charging a processing fee for provision of a payoff statement by fax or courier, as permitted pursuant to paragraph (a)(9)(ii) of this section, a creditor or servicer shall disclose to a consumer or a person authorized by the consumer to obtain the consumer's payoff statement that payoff statements, as described in paragraph (a)(9)(i) of this section, are available by a method other than by fax or courier without charge.

(iv) Fees permitted after multiple requests. A creditor or servicer that has provided a payoff statement, as described in paragraph (a)(9)(i) of this section, to a consumer, or a person authorized by the consumer to obtain such information, without charge, other than the processing fee permitted under paragraph (a)(9)(ii) of this section, four times during a calendar year, may thereafter charge a reasonable fee for providing such statements during the remainder of the calendar year. Fees for payoff statements provided to a consumer, or a person authorized by the consumer to obtain such information, in a subsequent calendar year are subject to the requirements of this section.

(v) Timing of delivery of payoff statements. A payoff statement, as described in paragraph (a)(9)(i) of this section, for a high-cost mortgage shall be provided by a creditor or servicer within five business days after receiving a request for such statement by a consumer or a person authorized by the consumer to obtain such statement.

(10) Financing of points and fees. A creditor that extends credit under a high-cost mortgage may not finance charges that are required to be included in the calculation of points and fees, as that term is defined in § 1026.32(b)(1) and (2). Credit insurance premiums or debt cancellation or suspension fees that are required to be included in points and fees under § 1026.32(b)(1)(iv) or (2)(iv) shall not be considered financed by the creditor when they are calculated and paid in full on a monthly basis.

(b) Prohibited acts or practices for dwelling-secured loans; structuring loans to evade high-cost mortgage requirements. A creditor shall not structure any transaction that is otherwise a high-cost mortgage in a form, for the purpose, and with the intent to evade the requirements of a high-cost mortgage subject to this subpart, including by dividing any loan transaction into separate parts.

§ 1026.35. Requirements for higher-priced mortgage loans

(a) Definitions. For purposes of this section:

(1) "Higher-priced mortgage loan" means a closed-end consumer credit transaction secured by the consumer's principal dwelling with an annual percentage rate that exceeds the average prime offer rate for a comparable transaction as of the date the interest rate is set:

(i) By 1.5 or more percentage points for loans secured by a first lien with a principal obligation at consummation that does not exceed the limit in effect as of the date the transaction's interest rate is set for the maximum principal obligation eligible for purchase by Freddie Mac;

(ii) By 2.5 or more percentage points for loans secured by a first lien with a principal obligation at consummation that exceeds the limit in effect as of the date the transaction's interest rate is set for the maximum principal obligation eligible for purchase by Freddie Mac; or

(iii) By 3.5 or more percentage points for loans secured by a subordinate lien.

(2) "Average prime offer rate" means an annual percentage rate that is derived from average interest rates, points, and other loan pricing terms currently offered to consumers by a representative sample of creditors for mortgage transactions that have low-risk pricing characteristics. The Bureau publishes average prime offer rates for a broad range of types of transactions in a table updated at least weekly as well as the methodology the Bureau uses to derive these rates.

(b) Escrow accounts—

(1) Requirement to escrow for property taxes and insurance. Except as provided in paragraph (b)(2) of this section, a creditor may not extend a higher-priced mortgage loan secured by a first lien on a consumer's principal dwelling unless an escrow account is established before consummation for payment of property taxes and premiums for mortgage-related insurance required by the creditor, such as insurance against loss of or damage to property, or against liability arising out of the ownership or use of the property, or insurance protecting the creditor against the consumer's default or other credit loss. For purposes of this paragraph (b), the term "escrow account" has the same meaning as under Regulation X (12 CFR 1024.17(b)), as amended.

(2) Exemptions. Notwithstanding paragraph (b)(1) of this section:

(i) An escrow account need not be established for:

(A) A transaction secured by shares in a cooperative;

(B) A transaction to finance the initial construction of a dwelling;

(C) A temporary or "bridge" loan with a loan term of twelve months or less, such as a loan to purchase a new dwelling where the consumer plans to sell a current dwelling within twelve months; or

(D) A reverse mortgage transaction subject to § 1026.33.

(ii) Insurance premiums described in paragraph (b)(1) of this section need not be included in escrow accounts for loans secured by dwellings in condominiums, planned unit developments, or other common interest communities in which dwelling ownership requires participation in a governing association, where the governing association has an obligation to the dwelling owners to maintain a master policy insuring all dwellings.

(iii) Except as provided in paragraph (b)(2)(v) of this section, an escrow account need not be established for a transaction if, at the time of consummation:

(A) During the preceding calendar year, or, if the application for the transaction was received before April 1 of the current calendar year, during either of the two preceding calendar years, the creditor extended a covered transaction, as defined by § 1026.43(b)(1), secured by a first lien on a property that is located in an area that is either "rural" or "underserved," as set forth in paragraph (b)(2)(iv) of this section;

(B) During the preceding calendar year, or, if the application for the transaction was received before April 1 of the current calendar year, during either of the two preceding calendar years, the creditor and its affiliates together extended no more than 2,000 covered transactions, as defined by § 1026.43(b)(1), secured by first liens, that were sold, assigned, or otherwise transferred to another person, or that were subject at the time of consummation to a commitment to be acquired by another person;

(C) As of the preceding December 31st, or, if the application for the transaction was received before April 1 of the current calendar year, as of either of the two preceding December 31sts, the creditor and its affiliates that regularly extended covered transactions, as defined by § 1026.43(b)(1), secured by first liens, together, had total assets of less than $2,000,000,000; this asset threshold shall adjust automatically each year, based on the year-to-year change in the average of the Consumer Price Index for Urban Wage Earners and Clerical Workers, not seasonally adjusted, for each 12-month period ending in November, with rounding to the nearest million dollars (see comment 35(b)(2)(iii)–1.iii for the applicable threshold); and

(D) Neither the creditor nor its affiliate maintains an escrow account of the type described in paragraph (b)(1) of this section for any extension of consumer credit secured by real property or a dwelling that the creditor or its affiliate currently services, other than:

(1) Escrow accounts established for first-lien higher-priced mortgage loans on or after April 1, 2010, and before May 1, 2016; or

(2) Escrow accounts established after consummation as an accommodation to distressed consumers to assist such consumers in avoiding default or foreclosure.

(iv) For purposes of paragraph (b)(2)(iii)(A) of this section:

(A) An area is "rural" during a calendar year if it is:

(1) A county that is neither in a metropolitan statistical area nor in a micropolitan statistical area that is adjacent to a metropolitan statistical area, as those terms are defined by the U.S. Office of Management and Budget and as they are applied under currently applicable Urban Influence Codes (UICs), established by the United States Department of Agriculture's Economic Research Service (USDA-ERS).

(2) A census block that is not in an urban area, as defined by the U.S. Census Bureau using the latest decennial census of the United States; or

(3) A county or a census block that has been designated as rural by the Bureau pursuant to the application process established under section 89002 of the Helping Expand Lending Practices in Rural Communities Act, Public Law 114–94, title LXXXIX (2015). The provisions of this paragraph (b)(2)(iv)(A)(3) shall cease to have any force or effect on December 4, 2017.

(B) An area is "underserved" during a calendar year if, according to Home Mortgage Disclosure Act (HMDA) data for the preceding calendar year, it is a county in which no more than two creditors extended covered transactions, as defined in § 1026.43(b)(1), secured by first liens on properties in the county five or more times.

(C) A property shall be deemed to be in an area that is rural or underserved in a particular calendar year if the property is:

(1) Located in a county that appears on the lists published by the Bureau of counties that are rural or underserved, as defined by § 1026.35(b)(2)(iv)(A)(1) or § 1026.35(b)(2)(iv)(B), for that calendar year,

(2) Designated as rural or underserved for that calendar year by any automated tool that the Bureau provides on its public Web site, or

(3) Not designated as located in an urban area, as defined by the most recent delineation of urban areas announced by the Census Bureau, by any automated address search tool that the U.S. Census Bureau provides on its public Web site for that purpose and that specifically indicates the urban or rural designations of properties.

(v) Notwithstanding paragraph (b)(2)(iii) of this section, an escrow account must be established pursuant to paragraph (b)(1) of this section for any first-lien higher-priced mortgage loan that, at consummation, is subject to a commitment to be acquired by a person that does not satisfy the conditions in paragraph (b)(2)(iii) of this section, unless otherwise exempted by this paragraph (b)(2).

(3) Cancellation—

(i) General. Except as provided in paragraph (b)(3)(ii) of this section, a creditor or servicer may cancel an escrow account required in paragraph (b)(1) of this section only upon the earlier of:

(A) Termination of the underlying debt obligation; or

(B) Receipt no earlier than five years after consummation of a consumer's request to cancel the escrow account.

(ii) Delayed cancellation. Notwithstanding paragraph (b)(3)(i) of this section, a creditor or servicer shall not cancel an escrow account pursuant to a consumer's request described in paragraph (b)(3)(i)(B) of this section unless the following conditions are satisfied:

(A) The unpaid principal balance is less than 80 percent of the original value of the property securing the underlying debt obligation; and

(B) The consumer currently is not delinquent or in default on the underlying debt obligation.

(c) Appraisals for higher-priced mortgage loans—

(1) Definitions. For purposes of this section:

(i) Certified or licensed appraiser means a person who is certified or licensed by the State agency in the State in which the property that secures the transaction is located, and who performs the appraisal in conformity with the Uniform Standards of Professional Appraisal Practice and the requirements applicable to appraisers in title XI of the Financial Institutions Reform, Recovery, and Enforcement Act of 1989, as amended (12 U.S.C. 3331 et seq.), and any implementing regulations in effect at the time the appraiser signs the appraiser's certification.

(ii) Credit risk means the financial risk that a consumer will default on a loan.

(iii) Manufactured home has the same meaning as in 24 CFR 3280.2.

(iv) Manufacturer's invoice means a document issued by a manufacturer and provided with a manufactured home to a retail dealer that separately details the wholesale (base) prices at the factory for specific models or series of manufactured homes and itemized options (large appliances, built-in items and equipment), plus actual itemized charges for freight from the factory to the dealer's lot or the homesite (including any rental of wheels and axles) and for any sales taxes to be paid by the dealer. The invoice may recite such prices and charges on an itemized basis or by stating an aggregate price or charge, as appropriate, for each category.

(v) National Registry means the database of information about State certified and licensed appraisers maintained by the Appraisal Subcommittee of the Federal Financial Institutions Examination Council.

(vi) New manufactured home means a manufactured home that has not been previously occupied.

(vii) State agency means a "State appraiser certifying and licensing agency" recognized in accordance with section 1118(b) of the Financial Institutions Reform, Recovery, and Enforcement Act of 1989 (12 U.S.C. 3347(b)) and any implementing regulations.

(2) Exemptions. Unless otherwise specified, the requirements in paragraphs (c)(3) through (6) of this section do not apply to the following types of transactions:

(i) A loan that satisfies the criteria of a qualified mortgage as defined pursuant to 15 U.S.C. 1639c;

(ii) An extension of credit for which the amount of credit extended is equal to or less than the applicable threshold amount, which is adjusted every year to reflect increases in the Consumer Price Index for Urban Wage Earners and Clerical Workers, as applicable, and published in the official staff commentary to this paragraph (c)(2)(ii);

(iii) A transaction secured by a mobile home, boat, or trailer.

(iv) A transaction to finance the initial construction of a dwelling.

(v) A loan with a maturity of 12 months or less, if the purpose of the loan is a "bridge" loan connected with the acquisition of a dwelling intended to become the consumer's principal dwelling.

(vi) A reverse-mortgage transaction subject to 12 CFR 1026.33(a).

(vii) An extension of credit that is a refinancing secured by a first lien, with refinancing defined as in § 1026.20(a) (except that the creditor need not be the original creditor or a holder or servicer of the original obligation), provided that the refinancing meets the following criteria:

(A) Either—

(1) The credit risk of the refinancing is retained by the person that held the credit risk of the existing obligation and there is no commitment, at consummation, to transfer the credit risk to another person; or

(2) The refinancing is insured or guaranteed by the same Federal government agency that insured or guaranteed the existing obligation;

(B) The regular periodic payments under the refinance loan do not—

(1) Cause the principal balance to increase;

(2) Allow the consumer to defer repayment of principal; or

(3) Result in a balloon payment, as defined in § 1026.18(s)(5)(i); and

(C) The proceeds from the refinancing are used solely to satisfy the existing obligation and amounts attributed solely to the costs of the refinancing; and

(viii) A transaction secured by:

(A) A new manufactured home and land, but the exemption shall only apply to the requirement in paragraph (c)(3)(i) of this section that the appraiser conduct a physical visit of the interior of the new manufactured home; or

(B) A manufactured home and not land, for which the creditor obtains one of the following and provides a copy to the consumer no later than three business days prior to consummation of the transaction—

(1) For a new manufactured home, the manufacturer's invoice for the manufactured home securing the transaction, provided that the date of manufacture is no earlier than 18 months prior to the creditor's receipt of the consumer's application for credit;

(2) A cost estimate of the value of the manufactured home securing the transaction obtained from an independent cost service provider; or

(3) A valuation, as defined in § 1026.42(b)(3), of the manufactured home performed by a person who has no direct or indirect interest, financial or otherwise, in the property or transaction for which the valuation is performed and has training in valuing manufactured homes.

(3) Appraisals required—

(i) In general. Except as provided in paragraph (c)(2) of this section, a creditor shall not extend a higher-priced mortgage loan to a consumer without obtaining, prior to consummation, a written appraisal of the property to be mortgaged. The appraisal must be performed by a certified or licensed appraiser who conducts a physical visit of the interior of the property that will secure the transaction.

(ii) Safe harbor. A creditor obtains a written appraisal that meets the requirements for an appraisal required under paragraph (c)(3)(i) of this section if the creditor:

(A) Orders that the appraiser perform the appraisal in conformity with the Uniform Standards of Professional Appraisal Practice and title XI of the Financial Institutions Reform, Recovery, and Enforcement Act of 1989, as amended (12 U.S.C. 3331 et seq.), and any implementing regulations in effect at the time the appraiser signs the appraiser's certification;

(B) Verifies through the National Registry that the appraiser who signed the appraiser's certification was a certified or licensed appraiser in the State in which the appraised property is located as of the date the appraiser signed the appraiser's certification;

(C) Confirms that the elements set forth in appendix N to this part are addressed in the written appraisal; and

(D) Has no actual knowledge contrary to the facts or certifications contained in the written appraisal.

(4) Additional appraisal for certain higher-priced mortgage loans—

(i) In general. Except as provided in paragraphs (c)(2) and (c)(4)(vii) of this section, a creditor shall not extend a higher-priced mortgage loan to a consumer to finance the acquisition of the consumer's principal dwelling without obtaining, prior to consummation, two written appraisals, if:

(A) The seller acquired the property 90 or fewer days prior to the date of the consumer's agreement to acquire the property and the price in the consumer's agreement to acquire the property exceeds the seller's acquisition price by more than 10 percent; or

(B) The seller acquired the property 91 to 180 days prior to the date of the consumer's agreement to acquire the property and the price in the consumer's agreement to acquire the property exceeds the seller's acquisition price by more than 20 percent.

(ii) Different certified or licensed appraisers. The two appraisals required under paragraph (c)(4)(i) of this section may not be performed by the same certified or licensed appraiser.

(iii) Relationship to general appraisal requirements. If two appraisals must be obtained under paragraph (c)(4)(i) of this section, each appraisal shall meet the requirements of paragraph (c)(3)(i) of this section.

(iv) Required analysis in the additional appraisal. One of the two required appraisals must include an analysis of:

(A) The difference between the price at which the seller acquired the property and the price that the consumer is obligated to pay to acquire the property, as specified in the consumer's agreement to acquire the property from the seller;

(B) Changes in market conditions between the date the seller acquired the property and the date of the consumer's agreement to acquire the property; and

(C) Any improvements made to the property between the date the seller acquired the property and the date of the consumer's agreement to acquire the property.

(v) No charge for the additional appraisal. If the creditor must obtain two appraisals under paragraph (c)(4)(i) of this section, the creditor may charge the consumer for only one of the appraisals.

(vi) Creditor's determination of prior sale date and price—

(A) Reasonable diligence. A creditor must obtain two written appraisals under paragraph (c)(4)(i) of this section unless the creditor can demonstrate by exercising reasonable diligence that the requirement to obtain two appraisals does not apply. A creditor acts with reasonable diligence if the creditor bases its determination on information contained in written source documents, such as the documents listed in Appendix O to this part.

(B) Inability to determine prior sale date or price—modified requirements for additional appraisal. If, after exercising reasonable diligence, a creditor cannot determine whether the conditions in paragraphs (c)(4)(i)(A) and (c)(4)(i)(B) are present and therefore must obtain two written appraisals in accordance with paragraphs (c)(4)(i) through (v) of this section, one of the two appraisals shall include an analysis of the factors in paragraph (c)(4)(iv) of this section only to the extent that the information necessary for the appraiser to perform the analysis can be determined.

(vii) Exemptions from the additional appraisal requirement. The additional appraisal required under paragraph (c)(4)(i) of this section shall not apply to extensions of credit that finance a consumer's acquisition of property:

(A) From a local, State or Federal government agency;

(B) From a person who acquired title to the property through foreclosure, deed-in-lieu of foreclosure, or other similar judicial or non-judicial procedure as a result of the person's exercise of rights as the holder of a defaulted mortgage loan;

(C) From a non-profit entity as part of a local, State, or Federal government program under which the non-profit entity is permitted to acquire title to single-family properties for resale from a seller who acquired title to the property through the process of foreclosure, deed-in-lieu of foreclosure, or other similar judicial or non-judicial procedure;

(D) From a person who acquired title to the property by inheritance or pursuant to a court order of dissolution of marriage, civil union, or domestic partnership, or of partition of joint or marital assets to which the seller was a party;

(E) From an employer or relocation agency in connection with the relocation of an employee;

(F) From a servicemember, as defined in 50 U.S.C. App. 511(1), who received a deployment or permanent change of station order after the servicemember purchased the property;

(G) Located in an area designated by the President as a federal disaster area, if and for as long as the Federal financial institutions regulatory agencies, as defined in 12 U.S.C. 3350(6), waive the requirements in title XI of the Financial Institutions Reform, Recovery, and Enforcement Act of 1989, as amended (12 U.S.C. 3331 et seq.), and any implementing regulations in that area; or

(H) Located in a rural county, as defined in 12 CFR 1026.35(b)(2)(iv)(A).

(5) Required disclosure—

(i) In general. Except as provided in paragraph (c)(2) of this section, a creditor shall disclose the following statement, in writing, to a consumer who applies for a higher-priced mortgage loan: "We may order an appraisal to determine the property's value and charge you for this appraisal. We will give you a copy of any appraisal, even if your loan does not close. You can pay for an additional appraisal for your own use at your own cost." Compliance with the disclosure requirement in Regulation B, 12 CFR 1002.14(a)(2), satisfies the requirements of this paragraph.

(ii) Timing of disclosure. The disclosure required by paragraph (c)(5)(i) of this section shall be delivered or placed in the mail no later than the third business day after the creditor receives the consumer's application for a higher-priced mortgage loan subject to paragraph (c) of this section. In the case of a loan that is not a higher-priced mortgage loan subject to paragraph (c) of this section at the time of application, but becomes a higher-priced mortgage loan subject to paragraph (c) of this section after application, the disclosure shall be delivered or placed in the mail not later than the third business day after the creditor determines that the loan is a higher-priced mortgage loan subject to paragraph (c) of this section.

(6) Copy of appraisals—

(i) In general. Except as provided in paragraph (c)(2) of this section, a creditor shall provide to the consumer a copy of any written appraisal performed in connection with a higher-priced mortgage loan pursuant to paragraphs (c)(3) and (c)(4) of this section.

(ii) Timing. A creditor shall provide to the consumer a copy of each written appraisal pursuant to paragraph (c)(6)(i) of this section:

(A) No later than three business days prior to consummation of the loan; or

(B) In the case of a loan that is not consummated, no later than 30 days after the creditor determines that the loan will not be consummated.

(iii) Form of copy. Any copy of a written appraisal required by paragraph (c)(6)(i) of this section may be provided to the applicant in electronic form, subject to compliance with the consumer consent and other applicable provisions of the Electronic Signatures in Global and National Commerce Act (E-Sign Act) (15 U.S.C. 7001 et seq.).

(iv) No charge for copy of appraisal. A creditor shall not charge the consumer for a copy of a written appraisal required to be provided to the consumer pursuant to paragraph (c)(6)(i) of this section.

(7) Relation to other rules. The rules in this paragraph (c) were adopted jointly by the Federal Reserve Board (Board), the Office of the Comptroller of the Currency (OCC), the Federal Deposit Insurance Corporation, the National Credit Union Administration, the Federal Housing Finance Agency, and the Bureau. These rules are substantively identical to the Board's and the OCC's higher-priced mortgage loan appraisal rules published separately in 12 CFR 226.43 (for the Board) and in 12 CFR part 34, subpart G and 12 CFR part 164, subpart B (for the OCC).

(d) Evasion; open-end credit. In connection with credit secured by a consumer's principal dwelling that does not meet the definition of open-end credit in § 1026.2(a)(20), a creditor shall not structure a home-secured loan as an open-end plan to evade the requirements of this section.

(e) [Reserved by 78 FR 30745]

§ 1026.36. Prohibited Acts or Practices and Certain Requirements for Credit Secured by a Dwelling

(a) Definitions.

(1) Loan originator.

(i) For purposes of this section, the term "loan originator" means a person who, in expectation of direct or indirect compensation or other monetary gain or for direct or indirect compensation or other monetary gain, performs any of the following activities: takes an application, offers, arranges, assists a consumer in obtaining or applying to obtain, negotiates, or otherwise obtains or makes an extension of consumer credit for another person; or through advertising or other means of communication represents to the public that such person can or will perform any of these activities. The term "loan originator" includes an employee, agent, or contractor of the creditor or loan originator organization if the employee, agent, or contractor meets this definition. The term "loan originator" includes a creditor that engages in loan origination activities if the creditor does not finance the transaction at consummation out of the creditor's own resources, including by drawing on a bona fide warehouse line of credit or out of deposits held by the creditor. All creditors that engage in any of the foregoing loan origination activities are loan originators for purposes of paragraphs (f) and (g) of this section. The term does not include:

(A) A person who does not take a consumer credit application or offer or negotiate credit terms available from a creditor, but who performs purely administrative or clerical tasks on behalf of a person who does engage in such activities.

(B) An employee of a manufactured home retailer who does not take a consumer credit application, offer or negotiate credit terms available from a creditor, or advise a consumer on credit terms (including rates, fees, and other costs) available from a creditor.

(C) A person that performs only real estate brokerage activities and is licensed or registered in accordance with applicable State law, unless such person is compensated by a creditor or loan originator or by any agent of such creditor or loan originator for a particular consumer credit transaction subject to this section.

(D) A seller financer that meets the criteria in paragraph (a)(4) or (a)(5) of this section, as applicable.

(E) A servicer or servicer's employees, agents, and contractors who offer or negotiate terms for purposes of renegotiating, modifying, replacing, or subordinating principal of existing mortgages where consumers are behind in their payments, in default, or have a reasonable likelihood of defaulting or falling behind. This exception does not apply, however, to a servicer or servicer's employees, agents, and contractors who offer or negotiate a transaction that constitutes a refinancing under § 1026.20(a) or obligates a different consumer on the existing debt.

(ii) An "individual loan originator" is a natural person who meets the definition of "loan originator" in paragraph (a)(1)(i) of this section.

(iii) A "loan originator organization" is any loan originator, as defined in paragraph (a)(1)(i) of this section, that is not an individual loan originator.

(2) Mortgage broker. For purposes of this section, a mortgage broker with respect to a particular transaction is any loan originator that is not an employee of the creditor.

(3) Compensation. The term "compensation" includes salaries, commissions, and any financial or similar incentive.

(4) Seller financers; three properties. A person (as defined in § 1026.2(a)(22)) that meets all of the following criteria is not a loan originator under paragraph (a)(1) of this section:

(i) The person provides seller financing for the sale of three or fewer properties in any 12-month period to purchasers of such properties, each of which is owned by the person and serves as security for the financing.

(ii) The person has not constructed, or acted as a contractor for the construction of, a residence on the property in the ordinary course of business of the person.

(iii) The person provides seller financing that meets the following requirements:

(A) The financing is fully amortizing.

(B) The financing is one that the person determines in good faith the consumer has a reasonable ability to repay.

(C) The financing has a fixed rate or an adjustable rate that is adjustable after five or more years, subject to reasonable annual and lifetime limitations on interest rate increases. If the financing agreement has an adjustable rate, the rate is determined by the addition of a margin to an index rate and is subject to reasonable rate adjustment limitations. The index the adjustable rate is based on is a widely available index such as indices for U.S. Treasury securities or LIBOR.

(5) Seller financers; one property. A natural person, estate, or trust that meets all of the following criteria is not a loan originator under paragraph (a)(1) of this section:

(i) The natural person, estate, or trust provides seller financing for the sale of only one property in any 12-month period to purchasers of such property, which is owned by the natural person, estate, or trust and serves as security for the financing.

(ii) The natural person, estate, or trust has not constructed, or acted as a contractor for the construction of, a residence on the property in the ordinary course of business of the person.

(iii) The natural person, estate, or trust provides seller financing that meets the following requirements:

(A) The financing has a repayment schedule that does not result in negative amortization.

(B) The financing has a fixed rate or an adjustable rate that is adjustable after five or more years, subject to reasonable annual and lifetime limitations on interest rate increases. If the financing agreement has an adjustable rate, the rate is determined by the addition of a margin to an index rate and is subject to reasonable rate adjustment limitations. The index the adjustable rate is based on is a widely available index such as indices for U.S. Treasury securities or LIBOR.

(6) Credit terms. For purposes of this section, the term "credit terms" includes rates, fees, and other costs. Credit terms are selected based on the consumer's financial characteristics when those terms are selected based on any factors that may influence a credit decision, such as debts, income, assets, or credit history.

(b) Scope. Paragraphs (c)(1) and (2) of this section apply to closed-end consumer credit transactions secured by a consumer's principal dwelling. Paragraph (c)(3) of this section applies to a consumer credit transaction secured by a dwelling. Paragraphs (d) through (i) of this section apply to closed-end consumer credit transactions secured by a dwelling. This section does not apply to a home equity line of credit subject to § 1026.40, except that paragraphs (h) and (i) of this section apply to such credit when secured by the consumer's principal dwelling and paragraph (c)(3) applies to such credit when secured by a dwelling. Paragraphs (d) through (i) of this section do not apply to a loan that is secured by a consumer's interest in a timeshare plan described in 11 U.S.C. 101(53D).

(c) Servicing practices. For purposes of this paragraph (c), the terms "servicer" and "servicing" have the same meanings as provided in 12 CFR 1024.2(b).

(1) Payment processing. In connection with a closed-end consumer credit transaction secured by a consumer's principal dwelling:

(i) Periodic payments. No servicer shall fail to credit a periodic payment to the consumer's loan account as of the date of receipt, except when a delay in crediting does not result in any charge to the consumer or in the reporting of negative information to a consumer reporting agency, or except as provided in paragraph (c)(1)(iii) of this section. A periodic payment, as used in this paragraph (c), is an amount sufficient to cover principal, interest, and escrow (if applicable) for a given billing cycle. A payment qualifies as a periodic payment even if it does not include amounts required to cover late fees, other fees, or non-escrow payments a servicer has advanced on a consumer's behalf.

(ii) Partial payments. Any servicer that retains a partial payment, meaning any payment less than a periodic payment, in a suspense or unapplied funds account shall:

(A) Disclose to the consumer the total amount of funds held in such suspense or unapplied funds account on the periodic statement as required by § 1026.41(d)(3), if a periodic statement is required; and

(B) On accumulation of sufficient funds to cover a periodic payment in any suspense or unapplied funds account, treat such funds as a periodic payment received in accordance with paragraph (c)(1)(i) of this section.

(iii) Non-conforming payments. If a servicer specifies in writing requirements for the consumer to follow in making payments, but accepts a payment that does not conform to the requirements, the servicer shall credit the payment as of five days after receipt.

(2) No pyramiding of late fees. In connection with a closed-end consumer credit transaction secured by a consumer's principal dwelling, a servicer shall not impose any late fee or delinquency charge for a payment if:

(i) Such a fee or charge is attributable solely to failure of the consumer to pay a late fee or delinquency charge on an earlier payment; and

(ii) The payment is otherwise a periodic payment received on the due date, or within any applicable courtesy period.

(3) Payoff statements. In connection with a consumer credit transaction secured by a consumer's dwelling, a creditor, assignee or servicer, as applicable, must provide an accurate statement of the total outstanding balance that would be required to pay the consumer's obligation in full as of a specified date. The statement shall be sent within a reasonable time, but in no case more than seven business days, after receiving a written request from the consumer or any person acting on behalf of the consumer. When a creditor, assignee, or servicer, as applicable, is not able to provide the statement within seven business days of such a request because a loan is in bankruptcy or foreclosure, because the loan is a reverse mortgage or shared appreciation mortgage, or because of natural disasters or other similar circumstances, the payoff statement must be provided within a reasonable time. A creditor or assignee that does not currently own the mortgage loan or the mortgage servicing rights is not subject to the requirement in this paragraph (c)(3) to provide a payoff statement.

(d) Prohibited payments to loan originators—

(1) Payments based on a term of a transaction.

(i) Except as provided in paragraph (d)(1)(iii) or (iv) of this section, in connection with a consumer credit transaction secured by a dwelling, no loan originator shall receive and no person shall pay to a loan originator, directly or indirectly, compensation in an amount that is based on a term of a transaction, the terms of multiple transactions by an individual loan originator, or the terms of multiple transactions by multiple individual loan originators. If a loan originator's compensation is based in whole or in part on a factor that is a proxy for a term of a transaction, the loan originator's compensation is based on a term of a transaction. A factor that is not itself a term of a transaction is a proxy for a term of the transaction if the factor consistently varies with that term over a significant number of transactions, and the loan originator has the ability, directly or indirectly, to add, drop, or change the factor in originating the transaction.

(ii) For purposes of this paragraph (d)(1) only, a "term of a transaction" is any right or obligation of the parties to a credit transaction. The amount of credit extended is not a term of a transaction or a proxy for a term of a transaction, provided that compensation received by or paid to a loan originator, directly or indirectly, is based on a fixed percentage of the amount of credit extended; however, such compensation may be subject to a minimum or maximum dollar amount.

(iii) An individual loan originator may receive, and a person may pay to an individual loan originator, compensation in the form of a contribution to a defined contribution plan that is a designated tax-advantaged plan or a benefit under a defined benefit plan that is a designated tax-advantaged plan. In the case of a contribution to a defined contribution plan, the contribution shall not be directly or indirectly based on the terms of that individual loan originator's transactions. As used in this paragraph (d)(1)(iii), "designated tax-advantaged plan" means any plan that meets the requirements of Internal Revenue Code section 401(a), 26 U.S.C. 401(a); employee annuity plan described in Internal Revenue Code section 403(a), 26 U.S.C. 403(a); simple retirement account, as defined in Internal Revenue Code section 408(p), 26 U.S.C. 408(p); simplified employee pension described in Internal Revenue Code section 408(k), 26 U.S.C. 408(k); annuity contract described in Internal Revenue Code section 403(b), 26 U.S.C. 403(b); or eligible deferred compensation plan, as defined in Internal Revenue Code section 457(b), 26 U.S.C. 457(b).

(iv) An individual loan originator may receive, and a person may pay to an individual loan originator, compensation under a non-deferred profits-based compensation plan (i.e., any arrangement for the payment of non-deferred compensation that is determined with reference to the profits of the person from mortgage-related business), provided that:

(A) The compensation paid to an individual loan originator pursuant to this paragraph (d)(1)(iv) is not directly or indirectly based on the terms of that individual loan originator's transactions that are subject to this paragraph (d); and

(B) At least one of the following conditions is satisfied:

(1) The compensation paid to an individual loan originator pursuant to this paragraph (d)(1)(iv) does not, in the aggregate, exceed 10 percent of the individual loan originator's total compensation corresponding to the time period for which the compensation under the non-deferred profits-based compensation plan is paid; or

(2) The individual loan originator was a loan originator for ten or fewer transactions subject to this paragraph (d) consummated during the 12-month period preceding the date of the compensation determination.

(2) Payments by persons other than consumer—

(i) Dual compensation.

(A) Except as provided in paragraph (d)(2)(i)(C) of this section, if any loan originator receives compensation directly from a consumer in a consumer credit transaction secured by a dwelling:

(1) No loan originator shall receive compensation, directly or indirectly, from any person other than the consumer in connection with the transaction; and

(2) No person who knows or has reason to know of the consumer-paid compensation to the loan originator (other than the consumer) shall pay any compensation to a loan originator, directly or indirectly, in connection with the transaction.

(B) Compensation received directly from a consumer includes payments to a loan originator made pursuant to an agreement between the consumer and a person other than the creditor or its affiliates, under which such other person agrees to provide funds toward the consumer's costs of the transaction (including loan originator compensation).

(C) If a loan originator organization receives compensation directly from a consumer in connection with a transaction, the loan originator organization may pay compensation to an individual loan originator, and the individual loan originator may receive compensation from the loan originator organization, subject to paragraph (d)(1) of this section.

(ii) Exemption. A payment to a loan originator that is otherwise prohibited by section 129B(c)(2)(A) of the Truth in Lending Act is nevertheless permitted pursuant to section 129B(c)(2)(B) of the Act, regardless of whether the consumer makes any upfront payment of discount points, origination points, or fees, as described in section 129B(c)(2)(B)(ii) of the Act, as long as the loan originator does not receive any compensation directly from the consumer as described in section 129B(c)(2)(B)(i) of the Act.

(3) Affiliates. For purposes of this paragraph (d), affiliates shall be treated as a single "person."

(e) Prohibition on steering—

(1) General. In connection with a consumer credit transaction secured by a dwelling, a loan originator shall not direct or "steer" a consumer to consummate a transaction based on the fact that the originator will receive greater compensation from the creditor in that transaction than in other transactions the originator offered or could have offered to the consumer, unless the consummated transaction is in the consumer's interest.

(2) Permissible transactions. A transaction does not violate paragraph (e)(1) of this section if the consumer is presented with loan options that meet the conditions in paragraph (e)(3) of this section for each type of transaction in which the consumer expressed an interest. For purposes of paragraph (e) of this section, the term "type of transaction" refers to whether:

(i) A loan has an annual percentage rate that cannot increase after consummation;

(ii) A loan has an annual percentage rate that may increase after consummation; or

(iii) A loan is a reverse mortgage.

(3) Loan options presented. A transaction satisfies paragraph (e)(2) of this section only if the loan originator presents the loan options required by that paragraph and all of the following conditions are met:

(i) The loan originator must obtain loan options from a significant number of the creditors with which the originator regularly does business and, for each type of transaction in which the consumer expressed an interest, must present the consumer with loan options that include:

(A) The loan with the lowest interest rate;

(B) The loan with the lowest interest rate without negative amortization, a prepayment penalty, interest-only payments, a balloon payment in the first 7 years of the life of the loan, a demand feature, shared equity, or shared appreciation; or, in the case of a reverse mortgage, a loan without a prepayment penalty, or shared equity or shared appreciation; and

(C) The loan with the lowest total dollar amount of discount points, origination points or origination fees (or, if two or more loans have the same total dollar amount of discount points, origination points or origination fees, the loan with the lowest interest rate that has the lowest total dollar amount of discount points, origination points or origination fees).

(ii) The loan originator must have a good faith belief that the options presented to the consumer pursuant to paragraph (e)(3)(i) of this section are loans for which the consumer likely qualifies.

(iii) For each type of transaction, if the originator presents to the consumer more than three loans, the originator must highlight the loans that satisfy the criteria specified in paragraph (e)(3)(i) of this section.

(4) Number of loan options presented. The loan originator can present fewer than three loans and satisfy paragraphs (e)(2) and (e)(3)(i) of this section if the loan(s) presented to the consumer satisfy the criteria of the options in paragraph (e)(3)(i) of this section and the provisions of paragraph (e)(3) of this section are otherwise met.

(f) Loan originator qualification requirements. A loan originator for a consumer credit transaction secured by a dwelling must, when required by applicable State or Federal law, be registered and licensed in accordance with those laws, including the Secure and Fair Enforcement for Mortgage Licensing Act of 2008 (SAFE Act, 12 U.S.C. 5102 et seq.), its implementing regulations (12 CFR part 1007 or part 1008), and State SAFE Act implementing law. To comply with this paragraph (f), a loan originator organization that is not a government agency or State housing finance agency must:

(1) Comply with all applicable State law requirements for legal existence and foreign qualification;

(2) Ensure that each individual loan originator who works for the loan originator organization is licensed or registered to the extent the individual is required to be licensed or registered under the SAFE Act, its implementing regulations, and State SAFE Act implementing law before the individual acts as a loan originator in a consumer credit transaction secured by a dwelling; and

(3) For each of its individual loan originator employees who is not required to be licensed and is not licensed as a loan originator pursuant to § 1008.103 of this chapter or State SAFE Act implementing law:

(i) Obtain for any individual whom the loan originator organization hired on or after January 1, 2014 (or whom the loan originator organization hired before this date but for whom there were no applicable statutory or regulatory background standards in effect at the time of hire or before January 1, 2014, used to screen the individual) and for any individual regardless of when hired who, based on reliable information known to the loan originator organization, likely does not meet the standards under § 1026.36(f)(3)(ii), before the individual acts as a loan originator in a consumer credit transaction secured by a dwelling:

(A) A criminal background check through the Nationwide Mortgage Licensing System and Registry (NMLSR) or, in the case of an individual loan originator who is not a registered loan originator under the NMLSR, a criminal background check from a law enforcement agency or commercial service;

(B) A credit report from a consumer reporting agency described in section 603(p) of the Fair Credit Reporting Act (15 U.S.C. 1681a(p)) secured, where applicable, in compliance with the requirements of section 604(b) of the Fair Credit Reporting Act, 15 U.S.C. 1681b(b); and

(C) Information from the NMLSR about any administrative, civil, or criminal findings by any government jurisdiction or, in the case of an individual loan originator who is not a registered loan originator under the NMLSR, such information from the individual loan originator;

(ii) Determine on the basis of the information obtained pursuant to paragraph (f)(3)(i) of this section and any other information reasonably available to the loan originator organization, for any individual whom the loan originator organization hired on or after January 1, 2014 (or whom the loan originator organization hired before this date but for whom there were no applicable statutory or regulatory background standards in effect at the time of hire or before January 1, 2014, used to screen the individual) and for any individual regardless of when hired who, based on reliable information known to the loan originator organization, likely does not meet the standards under this paragraph (f)(3)(ii), before the individual acts as a loan originator in a consumer credit transaction secured by a dwelling, that the individual loan originator:

(A)(1) Has not been convicted of, or pleaded guilty or nolo contendere to, a felony in a domestic or military court during the preceding seven-year period or, in the case of a felony involving an act of fraud, dishonesty, a breach of trust, or money laundering, at any time;

(2) For purposes of this paragraph (f)(3)(ii)(A):

(i) A crime is a felony only if at the time of conviction it was classified as a felony under the law of the jurisdiction under which the individual was convicted;

(ii) Expunged convictions and pardoned convictions do not render an individual unqualified; and

(iii) A conviction or plea of guilty or nolo contendere does not render an individual unqualified under this § 1026.36(f) if the loan originator organization has obtained consent to employ the individual from the Federal Deposit Insurance Corporation (or the Board of Governors of the Federal Reserve System, as applicable) pursuant to section 19 of the Federal Deposit Insurance Act (FDIA), 12 U.S.C. 1829, the National Credit Union Administration pursuant to section 205 of the Federal Credit Union Act (FCUA), 12 U.S.C. 1785(d), or the Farm Credit Administration pursuant to section 5.65(d) of the Farm Credit Act of 1971 (FCA), 12 U.S.C. 227a–14(d), notwithstanding the bars posed with respect to that conviction or plea by the FDIA, FCUA, and FCA, as applicable; and

(B) Has demonstrated financial responsibility, character, and general fitness such as to warrant a determination that the individual loan originator will operate honestly, fairly, and efficiently; and

(iii) Provide periodic training covering Federal and State law requirements that apply to the individual loan originator's loan origination activities.

(g) Name and NMLSR ID on loan documents. (1) For a consumer credit transaction secured by a dwelling, a loan originator organization must include on the loan documents described in paragraph (g)(2) of this section, whenever each such loan document is provided to a consumer or presented to a consumer for signature, as applicable:

(i) Its name and NMLSR ID, if the NMLSR has provided it an NMLSR ID; and

(ii) The name of the individual loan originator (as the name appears in the NMLSR) with primary responsibility for the origination and, if the NMLSR has provided such person an NMLSR ID, that NMLSR ID.

(2) The loan documents that must include the names and NMLSR IDs pursuant to paragraph (g)(1) of this section are:

(i) The credit application;

(ii) The disclosures required by § 1026.19 (e) and (f);

(iii) The note or loan contract; and

(iv) The security instrument.

(3) For purposes of this section, NMLSR ID means a number assigned by the Nationwide Mortgage Licensing System and Registry to facilitate electronic tracking and uniform identification of loan originators and public access to the employment history of, and the publicly adjudicated disciplinary and enforcement actions against, loan originators.

(h) Prohibition on mandatory arbitration clauses and waivers of certain consumer rights—

(1) Arbitration. A contract or other agreement for a consumer credit transaction secured by a dwelling (including a home equity line of credit secured by the consumer's principal dwelling) may not include terms that require arbitration or any other non-judicial procedure to resolve any controversy or settle any claims arising out of the transaction. This prohibition does not limit a consumer and creditor or any assignee from agreeing, after a dispute or claim under the transaction arises, to settle or use arbitration or other non-judicial procedure to resolve that dispute or claim.

(2) No waivers of Federal statutory causes of action. A contract or other agreement relating to a consumer credit transaction secured by a dwelling (including a home equity line of credit secured by the consumer's principal dwelling) may not be applied or interpreted to bar a consumer from bringing a claim in court pursuant to any provision of law for damages or other relief in connection with any alleged violation of any Federal law. This prohibition does not limit a consumer and creditor or any assignee from agreeing, after a dispute or claim under the transaction arises, to settle or use arbitration or other non-judicial procedure to resolve that dispute or claim.

(i) Prohibition on financing credit insurance.

(1) A creditor may not finance, directly or indirectly, any premiums or fees for credit insurance in connection with a consumer credit transaction secured by a dwelling (including a home equity line of credit secured by the consumer's principal dwelling). This prohibition does not apply to credit insurance for which premiums or fees are calculated and paid in full on a monthly basis.

(2) For purposes of this paragraph (i):

i. "Credit insurance":

(A) Means credit life, credit disability, credit unemployment, or credit property insurance, or any other accident, loss-of-income, life, or health insurance, or any payments directly or indirectly for any debt cancellation or suspension agreement or contract, but

(B) Excludes credit unemployment insurance for which the unemployment insurance premiums are reasonable, the creditor receives no direct or indirect compensation in connection with the unemployment insurance premiums, and the unemployment insurance premiums are paid pursuant to a separate insurance contract and are not paid to an affiliate of the creditor;

ii. A creditor finances premiums or fees for credit insurance if it provides a consumer the right to defer payment of a credit insurance premium or fee owed by the consumer beyond the monthly period in which the premium or fee is due; and

iii. Credit insurance premiums or fees are calculated on a monthly basis if they are determined mathematically by multiplying a rate by the actual monthly outstanding balance.

(j) Policies and procedures to ensure and monitor compliance.

(1) A depository institution must establish and maintain written policies and procedures reasonably designed to ensure and monitor the compliance of the depository institution, its employees, its subsidiaries, and its subsidiaries' employees with the requirements of paragraphs (d), (e), (f), and (g) of this section. These written policies and procedures must be appropriate to the nature, size, complexity, and scope of the mortgage lending activities of the depository institution and its subsidiaries.

(2) For purposes of this paragraph (j), "depository institution" has the meaning in section 1503(3) of the SAFE Act, 12 U.S.C. 5102(3). For purposes of this paragraph (j), "subsidiary" has the meaning in section 3 of the Federal Deposit Insurance Act, 12 U.S.C. 1813.

(k) Negative amortization counseling.

(1) Counseling required. A creditor shall not extend credit to a first-time borrower in connection with a closed-end transaction secured by a dwelling, other than a reverse mortgage transaction subject to § 1026.33 or a transaction secured by a consumer's interest in a timeshare plan described in 11 U.S.C. 101(53D), that may result in negative amortization, unless the creditor receives documentation that the consumer has obtained homeownership counseling from a counseling organization or counselor certified or approved by the U.S. Department of Housing and Urban Development to provide such counseling.

(2) Definitions. For the purposes of this paragraph (k), the following definitions apply:

(i) A "first-time borrower" means a consumer who has not previously received a closed-end credit transaction or open-end credit plan secured by a dwelling.

(ii) "Negative amortization" means a payment schedule with regular periodic payments that cause the principal balance to increase.

(3) Steering prohibited. A creditor that extends credit to a first-time borrower in connection with a closed-end transaction secured by a dwelling, other than a reverse mortgage transaction subject to § 1026.33 or a transaction secured by a consumer's interest in a timeshare plan described in 11 U.S.C. 101(53D), that may result in negative amortization shall not steer or otherwise direct a consumer to choose a particular counselor or counseling organization for the counseling required under this paragraph (k).

§ 1026.37 Content of disclosures for certain mortgage transactions (Loan Estimate)

For each transaction subject to § 1026.19(e), the creditor shall disclose the information in this section:

(a) General information—

(1) Form title. The title of the form, "Loan Estimate," using that term.

(2) Form purpose. The statement, "Save this Loan Estimate to compare with your Closing Disclosure."

(3) Creditor. The name and address of the creditor making the disclosures.

(4) Date issued. The date the disclosures are mailed or delivered to the consumer by the creditor, labeled "Date Issued."

(5) Applicants. The name and mailing address of the consumer(s) applying for the credit, labeled "Applicants."

(6) Property. The address including the zip code of the property that secures or will secure the transaction, or if the address is unavailable, the location of such property including a zip code, labeled "Property."

(7) Sale price.

(i) For transactions that involve a seller, the contract sale price of the property identified in paragraph (a)(6) of this section, labeled "Sale Price."

(ii) For transactions that do not involve a seller, the estimated value of the property identified in paragraph (a)(6), labeled "Prop. Value."

(8) Loan term. The term to maturity of the credit transaction, stated in years or months, or both, as applicable, labeled "Loan Term."

(9) Purpose. The consumer's intended use for the credit, labeled "Purpose," using one of the following terms:

(i) Purchase. If the credit is to finance the acquisition of the property identified in paragraph (a)(6) of this section, the creditor shall disclose that the loan is for a "Purchase."

(ii) Refinance. If the credit is not for the purpose described in paragraph (a)(9)(i) of this section, and if the credit will be used to refinance an existing obligation, as defined in § 1026.20(a) (but without regard to whether the creditor is the original creditor or a holder or servicer of the original obligation), that is secured by the property identified in paragraph (a)(6) of this section, the creditor shall disclose that the loan is for a "Refinance."

(iii) Construction. If the credit is not for one of the purposes described in paragraphs (a)(9)(i) or (ii) of this section and the credit will be used to finance the initial construction of a dwelling on the property identified in paragraph (a)(6) of this section, the creditor shall disclose that the loan is for "Construction."

(iv) Home equity loan. If the credit is not for one of the purposes described in paragraphs (a)(9)(i) through (iii) of this section, the creditor shall disclose that the loan is a "Home Equity Loan."

(10) Product. A description of the loan product, labeled "Product."

(i) The description of the loan product shall include one of the following terms:

(A) Adjustable rate. If the interest rate may increase after consummation, but the rates that will apply or the periods for which they will apply are not known at consummation, the creditor shall disclose the loan product as an "Adjustable Rate."

(B) Step rate. If the interest rate will change after consummation, and the rates that will apply and the periods for which they will apply are known at consummation, the creditor shall disclose the loan product as a "Step Rate."

(C) Fixed rate. If the loan product is not an Adjustable Rate or a Step Rate, as described in paragraphs (a)(10)(i)(A) and (B) of this section, respectively, the creditor shall disclose the loan product as a "Fixed Rate."

(ii) The description of the loan product shall include the features that may change the periodic payment using the following terms, subject to paragraph (a)(10)(iii) of this section, as applicable:

(A) Negative amortization. If the principal balance may increase due to the addition of accrued interest to the principal balance, the creditor shall disclose that the loan product has a "Negative Amortization" feature.

(B) Interest only. If one or more regular periodic payments may be applied only to interest accrued and not to the loan principal, the creditor shall disclose that the loan product has an "Interest Only" feature.

(C) Step payment. If scheduled variations in regular periodic payment amounts occur that are not caused by changes to the interest rate during the loan term, the creditor shall disclose that the loan product has a "Step Payment" feature.

(D) Balloon payment. If the terms of the legal obligation include a "balloon payment," as that term is defined in paragraph (b)(5) of this section, the creditor shall disclose that the loan has a "Balloon Payment" feature.

(E) Seasonal payment. If the terms of the legal obligation expressly provide that regular periodic payments are not scheduled between specified unit-periods on a regular basis, the creditor shall disclose that the loan product has a "Seasonal Payment" feature.

(iii) The disclosure of a loan feature under paragraph (a)(10)(ii) of this section shall precede the disclosure of the loan product under paragraph (a)(10)(i) of this section. If a transaction has more than one of the loan features described in paragraph (a)(10)(ii) of this section, the creditor shall disclose only the first applicable feature in the order the features are listed in paragraph (a)(10)(ii) of this section.

(iv) The disclosures required by paragraphs (a)(10)(i)(A) and (B), and (a)(10)(ii)(A) through (D) of this section must each be preceded by the duration of any introductory rate or payment period, and the first adjustment period, as applicable.

(11) Loan type. The type of loan, labeled "Loan Type," offered to the consumer using one of the following terms, as applicable:

(i) Conventional. If the loan is not guaranteed or insured by a Federal or State government agency, the creditor shall disclose that the loan is a "Conventional."

(ii) FHA. If the loan is insured by the Federal Housing Administration, the creditor shall disclose that the loan is an "FHA."

(iii) VA. If the loan is guaranteed by the U.S. Department of Veterans Affairs, the creditor shall disclose that the loan is a "VA."

(iv) Other. For federally-insured or guaranteed loans other than those described in paragraphs (a)(11)(ii) and (iii) of this section, and for loans insured or guaranteed by a State agency, the creditor shall disclose the loan type as "Other," and provide a brief description of the loan type.

(12) Loan identification number (Loan ID #). A number that may be used by the creditor, consumer, and other parties to identify the transaction, labeled "Loan ID #."

(13) Rate lock. A statement of whether the interest rate disclosed pursuant to paragraph (b)(2) of this section is locked for a specific period of time, labeled "Rate Lock."

(i) For transactions in which the interest rate is locked for a specific period of time, the creditor must provide the date and time (including the applicable time zone) when that period ends.

(ii) The "Rate Lock" statement required by this paragraph (a)(13) shall be accompanied by a statement that the interest rate, any points, and any lender credits may change unless the interest rate has been locked, and the date and time (including the applicable time zone) at which estimated closing costs expire.

(b) Loan terms. A separate table under the heading "Loan Terms" that contains the following information and satisfies the following requirements:

(1) Loan amount. The total amount the consumer will borrow, as reflected by the face amount of the note, labeled "Loan Amount."

(2) Interest rate. The interest rate that will be applicable to the transaction at consummation, labeled "Interest Rate." For an adjustable rate transaction, if the interest rate at consummation is not known, the rate disclosed shall be the fully-indexed rate, which, for purposes of this paragraph, means the interest rate calculated using the index value and margin at the time of consummation.

(3) Principal and interest payment. The initial periodic payment amount that will be due under the terms of the legal obligation, labeled "Principal & Interest," immediately preceded by the applicable unit-period, and a statement referring to the payment amount that includes any mortgage insurance and escrow payments that is required to be disclosed pursuant to paragraph (c) of this section. If the interest rate at consummation is not known, the amount disclosed shall be calculated using the fully-indexed rate disclosed under paragraph (b)(2) of this section.

(4) Prepayment penalty. A statement of whether the transaction includes a prepayment penalty, labeled "Prepayment Penalty." For purposes of this paragraph (b)(4), "prepayment penalty" means a charge imposed for paying all or part of a transaction's principal before the date on which the principal is due, other than a waived, bona fide third-party charge that the creditor imposes if the consumer prepays all of the transaction's principal sooner than 36 months after consummation.

(5) Balloon payment. A statement of whether the transaction includes a balloon payment, labeled "Balloon Payment." For purposes of this paragraph (b)(5), "balloon payment" means a payment that is more than two times a regular periodic payment. "Balloon payment" includes the payment or payments under a transaction that requires only one or two payments during the loan term.

(6) Adjustments after consummation. For each amount required to be disclosed by paragraphs (b)(1) through (3) of this section, a statement of whether the amount may increase after consummation as an affirmative or negative answer to the question, and under such question disclosed as a subheading, "Can this amount increase after closing?" and, in the case of an affirmative answer, the following additional information, as applicable:

(i) Adjustment in loan amount. The maximum principal balance for the transaction and the due date of the last payment that may cause the principal balance to increase. The disclosure further shall indicate whether the maximum principal balance is potential or is scheduled to occur under the terms of the legal obligation.

(ii) Adjustment in interest rate. The frequency of interest rate adjustments, the date when the interest rate may first adjust, the maximum interest rate, and the first date when the interest rate can reach the maximum interest rate, followed by a reference to the disclosure required by paragraph (j) of this section. If the loan term, as defined under paragraph (a)(8) of this section, may increase based on an interest rate adjustment, the disclosure required by this paragraph (b)(6)(ii) shall also state that fact and the maximum possible loan term determined in accordance with paragraph (a)(8) of this section.

(iii) Increase in periodic payment. The scheduled frequency of adjustments to the periodic principal and interest payment, the due date of the first adjusted principal and interest payment, the maximum possible periodic principal and interest payment, and the date when the periodic principal and interest payment may first equal the maximum principal and interest payment. If any adjustments to the principal and interest payment are not the result of a change to the interest rate, a reference to the disclosure required by paragraph (i) of this section. If there is a period during which only interest is required to be paid, the disclosure required by this paragraph (b)(6)(iii) shall also state that fact and the due date of the last periodic payment of such period.

(7) Details about prepayment penalty and balloon payment. The information required to be disclosed by paragraphs (b)(4) and (5) of this section shall be disclosed as an affirmative or negative answer to the question, and under such question disclosed as a subheading, "Does the loan have these features?" If an affirmative answer for a prepayment penalty or balloon payment is required to be disclosed, the following information shall be included, as applicable:

(i) The maximum amount of the prepayment penalty that may be imposed and the date when the period during which the penalty may be imposed terminates; and

(ii) The maximum amount of the balloon payment and the due date of such payment.

(8) Timing.

(i) The dates required to be disclosed by paragraph (b)(6)(ii) of this section shall be disclosed as the year in which the event occurs, counting from the date that interest for the first scheduled periodic payment begins to accrue after consummation.

(ii) The dates required to be disclosed by paragraphs (b)(6)(i), (b)(6)(iii) and (b)(7)(ii) of this section shall be disclosed as the year in which the event occurs, counting from the due date of the initial periodic payment.

(iii) The date required to be disclosed by paragraph (b)(7)(i) of this section shall be disclosed as the year in which the event occurs, counting from the date of consummation.

(c) Projected payments. In a separate table under the heading "Projected Payments," an itemization of each separate periodic payment or range of payments, together with an estimate of taxes, insurance, and assessments and the payments to be made with escrow account funds.

(1) Periodic payment or range of payments.

(i) The initial periodic payment or range of payments is a separate periodic payment or range of payments and, except as otherwise provided in paragraph (c)(1)(ii) and (iii) of this section, the following events require the disclosure of additional separate periodic payments or ranges of payments:

(A) The periodic principal and interest payment or range of such payments may change;

(B) A scheduled balloon payment, as defined in paragraph (b)(5) of this section;

(C) The creditor must automatically terminate mortgage insurance or any functional equivalent under applicable law; and

(D) The anniversary of the due date of the initial periodic payment or range of payments that immediately follows the occurrence of multiple events described in paragraph (c)(1)(i)(A) of this section during a single year.

(ii) The table required by this paragraph (c) shall not disclose more than four separate periodic payments or ranges of payments. For all events requiring disclosure of additional separate periodic payments or ranges of payments described in paragraph (c)(1)(i)(A) through (D) of this section occurring after the third separate periodic payment or range of payments disclosed, the separate periodic payments or ranges of payments shall be disclosed as a single range of payments, subject to the following exceptions:

(A) A balloon payment that is scheduled as a final payment under the terms of the legal obligation shall always be disclosed as a separate periodic payment or range of payments, in which case all events requiring disclosure of additional separate periodic payments or ranges of payments described in paragraph (c)(1)(i)(A) through (D) of this section occurring after the second separate periodic payment or range of payments disclosed, other than the balloon payment that is scheduled as a final payment, shall be disclosed as a single range of payments.

(B) The automatic termination of mortgage insurance or any functional equivalent under applicable law shall require disclosure of an additional separate periodic payment or range of payments only if the total number of separate periodic payments or ranges of payments otherwise disclosed pursuant to this paragraph (c)(1) does not exceed three.

(iii) When a range of payments is required to be disclosed under this paragraph (c)(1), the creditor must disclose the minimum and maximum amount for both the principal and interest payment under paragraph (c)(2)(i) of this section and the total periodic payment under paragraph (c)(2)(iv) of this section. A range of payments is required to be disclosed under this paragraph (c)(1) when:

(A) Multiple events described in paragraph (c)(1)(i) of this section are combined in a single range of payments pursuant to paragraph (c)(1)(ii) of this section;

(B) Multiple events described in paragraph (c)(1)(i)(A) of this section occur during a single year or an event described in paragraph (c)(1)(i)(A) of this section occurs during the same year as the initial periodic payment or range of payments, in which case the creditor discloses the range of payments that would apply during the year in which the events occur; or

(C) The periodic principal and interest payment may adjust based on index rates at the time an interest rate adjustment may occur.

(2) Itemization. Each separate periodic payment or range of payments disclosed on the table required by this paragraph (c) shall be itemized as follows:

(i) The amount payable for principal and interest, labeled "Principal & Interest," including the term "only interest" if the payment or range of payments includes any interest only payment.

(A) In the case of a loan that has an adjustable interest rate, the maximum principal and interest payment amounts are determined by assuming that the interest rate in effect throughout the loan term is the maximum possible interest rate, and the minimum amounts are determined by assuming that the interest rate in effect throughout the loan term is the minimum possible interest rate;

(B) In the case of a loan that has an adjustable interest rate and also contains a negative amortization feature, the maximum principal and interest payment amounts after the end of the period of the loan's term during which the loan's principal balance may increase due to the addition of accrued interest are determined by assuming the maximum principal amount permitted under the terms of the legal obligation at the end of such period, and the minimum amounts are determined pursuant to paragraph (c)(2)(i)(A) of this section;

(ii) The maximum amount payable for mortgage insurance premiums corresponding to the principal and interest payment disclosed pursuant to paragraph (c)(2)(i) of this section, labeled "Mortgage Insurance";

(iii) The amount payable into an escrow account to pay some or all of the charges described in paragraph (c)(4)(ii), as applicable, labeled "Escrow," together with a statement that the amount disclosed can increase over time; and

(iv) The total periodic payment, calculated as the sum of the amounts disclosed pursuant to paragraphs (c)(2)(i) through (iii) of this section, labeled "Total Monthly Payment."

(3) Subheadings.

(i) The labels required pursuant to paragraph (c)(2) of this section must be listed under the subheading "Payment Calculation."

(ii) Except as provided in paragraph (c)(3)(iii) of this section, each separate periodic payment or range of payments to be disclosed under this paragraph (c) must be disclosed under a subheading that states the years of the loan during which that payment or range of payments will apply. The subheadings must be stated in a sequence of whole years from the due date of the initial periodic payment.

(iii) A balloon payment that is scheduled as a final payment under the terms of the legal obligation must be disclosed under the subheading "Final Payment."

(4) Taxes, insurance, and assessments. Under the information required by paragraphs (c)(1) through (3) of this section:

(i) The label "Taxes, Insurance & Assessments";

(ii) The sum of the charges identified in § 1026.43(b)(8), other than amounts identified in § 1026.4(b)(5), expressed as a monthly amount, even if no escrow account for the payment of some or any of such charges will be established;

(iii) A statement that the amount disclosed pursuant to paragraph (c)(4)(ii) of this section can increase over time;

(iv) A statement of whether the amount disclosed pursuant to paragraph (c)(4)(ii) of this section includes payments for property taxes, amounts identified in § 1026.4(b)(8), and other amounts described in paragraph (c)(4)(ii) of this section, along with a description of any such other amounts, and an indication of whether such amounts will be paid by the creditor using escrow account funds;

(v) A statement that the consumer must pay separately any amounts described in paragraph (c)(4)(ii) of this section that are not paid by the creditor using escrow account funds; and

(vi) A reference to the information disclosed pursuant to paragraph (g)(3) of this section.

(5) Calculation of taxes and insurance. For purposes of paragraphs (c)(2)(iii) and (c)(4)(ii) of this section, estimated property taxes and homeowner's insurance shall reflect:

(i) The taxable assessed value of the real property or cooperative unit securing the transaction after consummation, including the value of any improvements on the property or to be constructed on the property, if known, whether or not such construction will be financed from the proceeds of the transaction, for property taxes; and

(ii) The replacement costs of the property during the initial year after the transaction, for amounts identified in § 1026.4(b)(8).

(d) Costs at closing—

(1) Costs at closing table. In a separate table, under the heading "Costs at Closing":

(i) Labeled "Closing Costs," the dollar amount disclosed pursuant to paragraph (g)(6) of this section, together with:

(A) A statement that the amount disclosed pursuant to paragraph (d)(1)(i) of this section includes the amounts disclosed pursuant to paragraphs (f)(4), (g)(5), and (g)(6)(ii);

(B) The dollar amount disclosed pursuant to paragraph (f)(4) of this section, labeled "Loan Costs";

(C) The dollar amount disclosed pursuant to paragraph (g)(5) of this section, labeled "Other Costs":

(D) The dollar amount disclosed pursuant to paragraph (g)(6)(ii) of this section, labeled "Lender Credits"; and

(E) A statement referring the consumer to the tables disclosed pursuant to paragraphs (f) and (g) of this section for details.

(ii) Labeled "Cash to Close," the dollar amount calculated in accordance with paragraph (h)(1)(viii) of this section, together with:

(A) A statement that the amount includes the amount disclosed pursuant to paragraph (d)(1)(i) of this section, and

(B) A statement referring the consumer to the location of the table required pursuant to paragraph (h) of this section for details.

(2) Optional alternative table for transactions without a seller or for simultaneous subordinate financing. For transactions that do not involve a seller or for simultaneous subordinate financing, instead of the amount and statements described in paragraph (d)(1)(ii) of this section, the creditor may alternatively disclose, using the label "Cash to Close":

(i) The amount calculated in accordance with paragraph (h)(2)(iv) of this section;

(ii) A statement of whether the disclosed estimated amount is due from or to the consumer; and

(iii) A statement referring the consumer to the alternative table disclosed pursuant to paragraph (h)(2) of this section for details.

(e) Web site reference. A statement that the consumer may obtain general information and tools at the Web site of the Bureau, and the link or uniform resource locator address to the Web site: www.consumerfinance.gov/mortgage-estimate.

(f) Closing cost details; loan costs. Under the master heading "Closing Cost Details," in a table under the heading "Loan Costs," all loan costs associated with the transaction. The table shall contain the items and amounts listed under four subheadings, described in paragraphs (f)(1) through (4) of this section.

(1) Origination charges. Under the subheading "Origination Charges," an itemization of each amount, and a subtotal of all such amounts, that the consumer will pay to each creditor and loan originator for originating and extending the credit.

(i) The points paid to the creditor to reduce the interest rate shall be itemized separately, as both a percentage of the amount of credit extended and a dollar amount, and using the label "__% of Loan Amount (Points)." If points to reduce the interest rate are not paid, the disclosure required by this paragraph (f)(1)(i) must be blank.

(ii) The number of items disclosed under this paragraph (f)(1), including the points disclosed under paragraph (f)(1)(i) of this section, shall not exceed 13.

(2) Services you cannot shop for. Under the subheading "Services You Cannot Shop For," an itemization of each amount, and a subtotal of all such amounts, the consumer will pay for settlement services for which the consumer cannot shop in accordance with § 1026.19(e)(1)(vi)(A) and that are provided by persons other than the creditor or mortgage broker.

(i) For any item that is a component of title insurance or is for conducting the closing, the introductory description "Title—" shall appear at the beginning of the label for that item.

(ii) The number of items disclosed under this paragraph (f)(2) shall not exceed 13.

(3) Services you can shop for. Under the subheading "Services You Can Shop For," an itemization of each amount and a subtotal of all such amounts the consumer will pay for settlement services for which the consumer can shop in accordance with § 1026.19(e)(1)(vi)(A) and that are provided by persons other than the creditor or mortgage broker.

(i) For any item that is a component of title insurance or is for conducting the closing, the introductory description "Title—" shall appear at the beginning of the label for that item.

(ii) The number of items disclosed under this paragraph (f)(3) shall not exceed 14.

(4) Total loan costs. Under the subheading "Total Loan Costs," the sum of the subtotals disclosed under paragraphs (f)(1) through (3) of this section.

(5) Item descriptions and ordering. The items listed as loan costs pursuant to this paragraph (f) shall be labeled using terminology that describes each item, subject to the requirements of paragraphs (f)(1)(i), (f)(2)(i), and (f)(3)(i) of this section.

(i) The item prescribed in paragraph (f)(1)(i) of this section for points shall be the first item listed in the disclosure pursuant to paragraph (f)(1) of this section.

(ii) All other items must be listed in alphabetical order by their labels under the applicable subheading.

(6) Use of addenda.

(i) An addendum to a form of disclosures prescribed by this section may not be used for items described in paragraph (f)(1) or (2) of this section. If the creditor is not able to itemize every service and every corresponding charge required to be disclosed in the number of lines provided by paragraph (f)(1)(ii) or (f)(2)(ii) of this section, the remaining charges shall be disclosed as an aggregate amount in the last line permitted under paragraph (f)(1)(ii) or (f)(2)(ii), as applicable, labeled "Additional Charges."

(ii) An addendum to a form of disclosures prescribed by this section may be used for items described in paragraph (f)(3) of this section. If the creditor is not able to itemize all of the charges required to be disclosed in the number of lines provided by paragraph (f)(3)(ii), the remaining charges shall be disclosed as follows:

(A) Label the last line permitted under paragraph (f)(3)(ii) with an appropriate reference to an addendum and list the remaining items on the addendum in accordance with the requirements in paragraphs (f)(3) and (5) of this section; or

(B) Disclose the remaining charges as an aggregate amount in the last line permitted under paragraph (f)(3)(ii), labeled "Additional Charges."

(g) Closing cost details; other costs. Under the master heading "Closing Cost Details," in a table under the heading "Other Costs," all costs associated with the transaction that are in addition to the costs disclosed under paragraph (f) of this section. The table shall contain the items and amounts listed under six subheadings, described in paragraphs (g)(1) through (6) of this section.

(1) Taxes and other government fees. Under the subheading "Taxes and Other Government Fees," the amounts to be paid to State and local governments for taxes and other government fees, and the subtotal of all such amounts, as follows:

(i) On the first line, the sum of all recording fees and other government fees and taxes, except for transfer taxes paid by the consumer and disclosed pursuant to paragraph (g)(1)(ii) of this section, labeled "Recording Fees and Other Taxes."

(ii) On the second line, the sum of all transfer taxes paid by the consumer, labeled "Transfer Taxes."

(iii) If an amount required to be disclosed by this paragraph (g)(1) is not charged to the consumer, the amount disclosed on the applicable line required by this paragraph (g)(1) must be blank.

(2) Prepaids. Under the subheading "Prepaids," an itemization of the amounts to be paid by the consumer in advance of the first scheduled payment, and the subtotal of all such amounts, as follows:

(i) On the first line, the number of months for which homeowner's insurance premiums are to be paid by the consumer at consummation and the total dollar amount to be paid by the consumer at consummation for such premiums, labeled "Homeowner's Insurance Premium (__ months)."

(ii) On the second line, the number of months for which mortgage insurance premiums are to be paid by the consumer at consummation and the total dollar amount to be paid by the consumer at consummation for such premiums, labeled "Mortgage Insurance Premium (__ months)."

(iii) On the third line, the amount of prepaid interest to be paid per day, the number of days for which prepaid interest will be collected, the interest rate, and the total dollar amount to be paid by the consumer at consummation for such interest, labeled "Prepaid Interest (___ per day for __ days @__ %)."

(iv) On the fourth line, the number of months for which property taxes are to be paid by the consumer at consummation and the total dollar amount to be paid by the consumer at consummation for such taxes, labeled "Property Taxes (__ months)."

(v) If an amount is not charged to the consumer for any item for which this paragraph (g)(2) prescribes a label, each of the amounts required to be disclosed on that line must be blank.

(vi) A maximum of three additional items may be disclosed under this paragraph (g)(2), and each additional item must be identified and include the applicable time period covered by the amount to be paid by the consumer at consummation and the total amount to be paid.

(3) Initial escrow payment at closing. Under the subheading "Initial Escrow Payment at Closing," an itemization of the amounts that the consumer will be expected to place into a reserve or escrow account at consummation to be applied to recurring periodic charges, and the subtotal of all such amounts, as follows:

(i) On the first line, the amount escrowed per month, the number of months covered by an escrowed amount collected at consummation, and the total amount to be paid into the escrow account by the consumer at consummation for homeowner's insurance premiums, labeled "Homeowner's Insurance __ per month for __ mo."

(ii) On the second line, the amount escrowed per month, the number of months covered by an escrowed amount collected at consummation, and the total amount to be paid into the escrow account by the consumer at consummation for mortgage insurance premiums, labeled "Mortgage Insurance __ per month for __ mo."

(iii) On the third line, the amount escrowed per month, the number of months covered by an escrowed amount collected at consummation, and the total amount to be paid into the escrow account by the consumer at consummation for property taxes, labeled "Property Taxes __ per month for __ mo."

(iv) If an amount is not charged to the consumer for any item for which this paragraph (g)(3) prescribes a label, each of the amounts required to be disclosed on that line must be blank.

(v) A maximum of five items may be disclosed pursuant to this paragraph (g)(3) in addition to the items described in paragraph (g)(3)(i) through (iii) of this section, and each such additional item must be identified with a descriptive label and include the applicable amount per month, the number of months collected at consummation, and the total amount to be paid.

(4) Other. Under the subheading "Other," an itemization of any other amounts in connection with the transaction that the consumer is likely to pay or has contracted with a person other than the creditor or loan originator to pay at closing and of which the creditor is aware at the time of issuing the Loan Estimate, a descriptive label of each such amount, and the subtotal of all such amounts.

(i) For any item that is a component of title insurance, the introductory description "Title—" shall appear at the beginning of the label for that item.

(ii) The parenthetical description "(optional)" shall appear at the end of the label for items disclosing any premiums paid for separate insurance, warranty, guarantee, or event-coverage products.

(iii) The number of items disclosed under this paragraph (g)(4) shall not exceed five.

(5) Total other costs. Under the subheading "Total Other Costs," the sum of the subtotals disclosed pursuant to paragraphs (g)(1) through (4) of this section.

(6) Total closing costs. Under the subheading "Total Closing Costs," the component amounts and their sum, as follows:

(i) The sum of the amounts disclosed as loan costs and other costs under paragraphs (f)(4) and (g)(5) of this section, labeled "D + I"; and

(ii) The amount of any lender credits, disclosed as a negative number with the label "Lender Credits" provided that, if no such amount is disclosed, the amount must be blank.

(7) Item descriptions and ordering. The items listed as other costs pursuant to this paragraph (g) shall be labeled using terminology that describes each item.

(i) The items prescribed in paragraphs (g)(1)(i) and (ii), (g)(2)(i) through (iv), and (g)(3)(i) through (iii) of this section must be listed in the order prescribed as the initial items under the applicable subheading, with any additional items to follow.

(ii) All additional items must be listed in alphabetical order under the applicable subheading.

(8) Use of addenda. An addendum to a form of disclosures prescribed by this section may not be used for items required to be disclosed by this paragraph (g). If the creditor is not able to itemize all of the charges described in this paragraph (g) in the number of lines provided by paragraphs (g)(2)(vi), (3)(v), or (4)(iii) of this section, the remaining charges shall be disclosed as an aggregate amount in the last line permitted under paragraphs (g)(2)(vi), (g)(3)(v), or (g)(4)(iii), as applicable, using the label "Additional Charges."

(h) Calculating cash to close—

(1) For all transactions. Under the master heading "Closing Cost Details," under the heading "Calculating Cash to Close," the total amount of cash or other funds that must be provided by the consumer at consummation, with an itemization of that amount into the following component amounts:

(i) Total closing costs. The amount disclosed under paragraph (g)(6) of this section, labeled "Total Closing Costs";

(ii) Closing costs to be financed. The amount of any closing costs to be paid out of loan proceeds, disclosed as a negative number, labeled "Closing Costs Financed (Paid from your Loan Amount)";

(iii) Downpayment and other funds from borrower. Labeled "Down Payment/Funds from Borrower":

(A)(1) In a purchase transaction as defined in paragraph (a)(9)(i) of this section, the amount determined by subtracting the sum of the loan amount disclosed under paragraph (b)(1) of this section and any amount of existing loans assumed or taken subject to that will be disclosed under § 1026.38(j)(2)(iv) from the sale price of the property disclosed under paragraph (a)(7)(i) of this section, except as required by paragraph (h)(1)(iii)(A)(2) of this section;

(2) In a purchase transaction as defined in paragraph (a)(9)(i) of this section that is a simultaneous subordinate financing transaction or that involves improvements to be made on the property, or when the sum of the loan amount disclosed under paragraph (b)(1) of this section and any amount of existing loans assumed or taken subject to that will be disclosed under § 1026.38(j)(2)(iv) exceeds the sale price of the property disclosed under paragraph (a)(7)(i) of this section, the amount of estimated funds from the consumer as determined in accordance with paragraph (h)(1)(v) of this section; or

(B) In all transactions other than purchase transactions as defined in paragraph (a)(9)(i) of this section, the estimated funds from the consumer as determined in accordance with paragraph (h)(1)(v) of this section;

(iv) Deposit.

(A) In a purchase transaction as defined in paragraph (a)(9)(i) of this section, the amount that is paid to the seller or held in trust or escrow by an attorney or other party under the terms of the agreement for the sale of the property, disclosed as a negative number, labeled "Deposit";

(B) In all transactions other than purchase transactions as defined in paragraph (a)(9)(i) of this section, the amount of $0, labeled "Deposit";

(v) Funds for borrower. The amount of funds for the consumer, labeled "Funds for Borrower." The amount of the down payment and other funds from the consumer disclosed under paragraph (h)(1)(iii)(A)(2) or (h)(1)(iii)(B) of this section, as applicable, and of funds for the consumer disclosed under this paragraph (h)(1)(v), are determined by subtracting the sum of the loan amount disclosed under paragraph (b)(1) of this section and any amount of existing loans assumed or taken subject to that will be disclosed under § 1026.38(j)(2)(iv) (excluding any closing costs financed disclosed under paragraph (h)(1)(ii) of this section) from the total amount of all existing debt being satisfied in the transaction;

(A) If the calculation under this paragraph (h)(1)(v) yields an amount that is a positive number, such amount is disclosed under paragraph (h)(1)(iii)(A)(2) or (h)(1)(iii)(B) of this section, as applicable, and $0 is disclosed under this paragraph (h)(1)(v);

(B) If the calculation under this paragraph (h)(1)(v) yields an amount that is a negative number, such amount is disclosed under this paragraph (h)(1)(v) as a negative number, and $0 is disclosed under paragraph (h)(1)(iii)(B) of this section;

(C) If the calculation under this paragraph (h)(1)(v) yields $0, then $0 is disclosed under paragraph (h)(1)(iii)(A)(2) or (h)(1)(iii)(B) of this section, as applicable, and under this paragraph (h)(1)(v);

(vi) Seller credits. The total amount that the seller will pay for total loan costs as determined by paragraph (f)(4) of this section and total other costs as determined by paragraph (g)(5) of this section, to the extent known, disclosed as a negative number, labeled "Seller Credits";

(vii) Adjustments and other credits. The amount of all loan costs determined under paragraph (f) of this section and other costs determined under paragraph (g) of this section that are paid by persons other than the loan originator, creditor, consumer, or seller, together with any other amounts not otherwise disclosed under paragraph (f) or (g) of this section that are required to be paid by the consumer at closing in a transaction disclosed under paragraph (h)(1)(iii)(A)(1) of this section or pursuant to a purchase and sale contract, labeled "Adjustments and Other Credits"; and

(viii) Estimated Cash to Close. The sum of the amounts disclosed under paragraphs (h)(1)(i) through (vii) of this section labeled "Cash to Close."

(2) Optional alternative calculating cash to close table for transactions without a seller or for simultaneous subordinate financing. For transactions that do not involve a seller or for simultaneous subordinate financing, instead of the table described in paragraph (h)(1) above, the creditor may alternatively provide, in a separate table, under the master heading "Closing Cost Details," under the heading "Calculating Cash to Close," the total amount of cash or other funds that must be provided by the consumer at consummation with an itemization of that amount into the following component amounts:

(i) Loan amount. The amount disclosed under paragraph (b)(1) of this section, labeled "Loan Amount";

(ii) Total closing costs. The amount disclosed under paragraph (g)(6) of this section, disclosed as a negative number if the amount disclosed under paragraph (g)(6) of this section is a positive number and disclosed as a positive number if the amount disclosed under paragraph (g)(6) of this section is a negative number, labeled "Total Closing Costs";

(iii) Payoffs and payments. The total amount of payoffs and payments to be made to third parties not otherwise disclosed under paragraphs (f) and (g) of this section, labeled "Total Payoffs and Payments";

(iv) Cash to or from consumer. The amount of cash or other funds due from or to the consumer and a statement of whether the disclosed estimated amount is due from or to the consumer, calculated by the sum of the amounts disclosed under paragraphs (h)(2)(i) through (iii) of this section, labeled "Cash to Close"; and

(v) Closing costs financed. The sum of the amounts disclosed under paragraphs (h)(2)(i) and (iii) of this section, but only to the extent that the sum is greater than zero and less than or equal to the sum disclosed under paragraph (g)(6) of this section, labeled "Closing Costs Financed (Paid from your Loan Amount)."

(i) Adjustable payment table. If the periodic principal and interest payment may change after consummation but not based on an adjustment to the interest rate, or if the transaction is a seasonal payment product as described in paragraph (a)(10)(ii)(E) of this section, a separate table under the master heading "Closing Cost Details" required by paragraph (f) of this section and under the heading "Adjustable Payment (AP) Table" that contains the following information and satisfies the following requirements:

(1) Interest only payments. Whether the transaction is an interest only product pursuant to paragraph (a)(10)(ii)(B) of this section as an affirmative or negative answer to the question "Interest Only Payments?" and, if an affirmative answer is disclosed, the period during which interest only periodic payments are scheduled.

(2) Optional payments. Whether the terms of the legal obligation expressly provide that the consumer may elect to pay a specified periodic principal and interest payment in an amount other than the scheduled amount of the payment, as an affirmative or negative answer to the question "Optional Payments?" and, if an affirmative answer is disclosed, the period during which the consumer may elect to make such payments.

(3) Step payments. Whether the transaction is a step payment product pursuant to paragraph (a)(10)(ii)(C) of this section as an affirmative or negative answer to the question "Step

Payments?" and, if an affirmative answer is disclosed, the period during which the regular periodic payments are scheduled to increase.

(4) Seasonal payments. Whether the transaction is a seasonal payment product pursuant to paragraph (a)(10)(ii)(E) of this section as an affirmative or negative answer to the question "Seasonal Payments?" and, if an affirmative answer is disclosed, the period during which periodic payments are not scheduled.

(5) Principal and interest payments. Under the subheading "Principal and Interest Payments," which subheading is immediately preceded by the applicable unit-period, the following information:

(i) The number of the payment of the first periodic principal and interest payment that may change under the terms of the legal obligation disclosed under this paragraph (i), counting from the first periodic payment due after consummation, and the amount or range of the periodic principal and interest payment for such payment, labeled "First Change/Amount";

(ii) The frequency of subsequent changes to the periodic principal and interest payment, labeled "Subsequent Changes"; and

(iii) The maximum periodic principal and interest payment that may occur during the term of the transaction, and the first periodic principal and interest payment that can reach such maximum, counting from the first periodic payment due after consummation, labeled "Maximum Payment."

(j) Adjustable interest rate table. If the interest rate may increase after consummation, a separate table under the master heading "Closing Cost Details" required by paragraph (f) of this section and under the heading "Adjustable Interest Rate (AIR) Table" that contains the following information and satisfies the following requirements:

(1) Index and margin. If the interest rate may adjust and the product type is not a "Step Rate" under paragraph (a)(10)(i)(B) of this section, the index upon which the adjustments to the interest rate are based and the margin that is added to the index to determine the interest rate, if any, labeled "Index + Margin."

(2) Increases in interest rate. If the product type is a "Step Rate" and not also an "Adjustable Rate" under paragraph (a)(10)(i)(A) of this section, the maximum amount of any adjustments to the interest rate that are scheduled and pre-determined, labeled "Interest Rate Adjustments."

(3) Initial interest rate. The interest rate at consummation of the loan transaction, labeled "Initial Interest Rate."

(4) Minimum and maximum interest rate. The minimum and maximum interest rates for the loan, after any introductory period expires, labeled "Minimum/Maximum Interest Rate."

(5) Frequency of adjustments. The following information, under the subheading "Change Frequency":

(i) The month when the interest rate after consummation may first change, calculated from the date interest for the first scheduled periodic payment begins to accrue, labeled "First Change"; and

(ii) The frequency of interest rate adjustments after the initial adjustment to the interest rate, labeled, "Subsequent Changes."

(6) Limits on interest rate changes. The following information, under the subheading "Limits on Interest Rate Changes":

(i) The maximum possible change for the first adjustment of the interest rate after consummation, labeled "First Change"; and

(ii) The maximum possible change for subsequent adjustments of the interest rate after consummation, labeled "Subsequent Changes."

(k) Contact information. Under the master heading, "Additional Information About This Loan," the following information:

(1) The name and Nationwide Mortgage Licensing System and Registry identification number (NMLSR ID) (labeled "NMLS ID/License ID") for the creditor (labeled "Lender") and the mortgage broker (labeled "Mortgage Broker"), if any. In the event the creditor or the mortgage broker has not been assigned an NMLSR ID, the license number or other unique identifier issued by the applicable jurisdiction or regulating body with which the creditor or mortgage broker is licensed and/or registered shall be disclosed, with the abbreviation for the State of the applicable jurisdiction or regulatory body stated before the word "License" in the label, if any;

(2) The name and NMLSR ID of the individual loan officer (labeled "Loan Officer" and "NMLS ID/License ID," respectively) of the creditor and the mortgage broker, if any, who is the primary contact for the consumer. In the event the individual loan officer has not been assigned an NMLSR ID, the license number or other unique identifier issued by the applicable jurisdiction or regulating body with which the loan officer is licensed and/or registered shall be disclosed with the abbreviation for the State of the applicable jurisdiction or regulatory body stated before the word "License" in the label, if any; and

(3) The email address and telephone number of the loan officer (labeled "Email" and "Phone," respectively).

(l) **Comparisons.** Under the master heading, "Additional Information About This Loan" required by paragraph (k) of this section, in a separate table under the heading "Comparisons" along with the statement "Use these measures to compare this loan with other loans":

(1) In five years. Using the label "In 5 Years":

(i) The total principal, interest, mortgage insurance, and loan costs scheduled to be paid through the end of the 60th month after the due date of the first periodic payment, expressed as a dollar amount, along with the statement "Total you will have paid in principal, interest, mortgage insurance, and loan costs"; and

(ii) The principal scheduled to be paid through the end of the 60th month after the due date of the first periodic payment, expressed as a dollar amount, along with the statement "Principal you will have paid off."

(2) Annual percentage rate. The "Annual Percentage Rate," using that term and the abbreviation "APR" and expressed as a percentage, and the following statement: "Your costs over the loan term expressed as a rate. This is not your interest rate."

(3) Total interest percentage. The total amount of interest that the consumer will pay over the life of the loan, expressed as a percentage of the amount of credit extended, using the term "Total Interest Percentage," the abbreviation "TIP," and the statement "The total amount of interest that you will pay over the loan term as a percentage of your loan amount."

(m) Other considerations. Under the master heading "Additional Information About This Loan" required by paragraph (k) of this section and under the heading "Other Considerations":

(1) Appraisal. For transactions subject to 15 U.S.C. 1639h or 1691(e), as implemented in this part or Regulation B, 12 CFR part 1002, respectively, a statement, labeled "Appraisal," that:

(i) The creditor may order an appraisal to determine the value of the property identified in paragraph (a)(6) of this section and may charge the consumer for that appraisal;

(ii) The creditor will promptly provide the consumer a copy of any appraisal, even if the transaction is not consummated; and

(iii) The consumer may choose to pay for an additional appraisal of the property for the consumer's use.

(2) Assumption. A statement of whether a subsequent purchaser of the property may be permitted to assume the remaining loan obligation on its original terms, labeled "Assumption."

(3) Homeowner's insurance. At the option of the creditor, a statement that homeowner's insurance is required on the property and that the consumer may choose the insurance provider, labeled "Homeowner's Insurance."

(4) Late payment. A statement detailing any charge that may be imposed for a late payment, stated as a dollar amount or percentage charge of the late payment amount, and the number of days that a payment must be late to trigger the late payment fee, labeled "Late Payment."

(5) Refinance. The following statement, labeled "Refinance": "Refinancing this loan will depend on your future financial situation, the property value, and market conditions. You may not be able to refinance this loan."

(6) Servicing. A statement of whether the creditor intends to service the loan or transfer the loan to another servicer, labeled "Servicing."

(7) Liability after foreclosure. If the purpose of the credit transaction is to refinance an extension of credit as described in paragraph (a)(9)(ii) of this section, a brief statement that certain State law protections against liability for any deficiency after foreclosure may be lost, the potential consequences of the loss of such protections, and a statement that the consumer should consult an attorney for additional information, labeled "Liability after Foreclosure."

(8) Construction loans. In transactions involving new construction, where the creditor reasonably expects that settlement will occur more than 60 days after the provision of the loan estimate, at the creditor's option, a clear and conspicuous statement that the creditor may issue a revised disclosure any time prior to 60 days before consummation, pursuant to § 1026.19(e)(3)(iv)(F).

(n) Signature statement.

(1) At the creditor's option, under the master heading required by paragraph (k) of this section and under the heading "Confirm Receipt," a line for the signatures of the consumers in the transaction. If the creditor includes a line for the consumer's signature, the creditor must disclose the following above the signature line: "By signing, you are only confirming that you have received this form. You do not have to accept this loan because you have signed or received this form."

(2) If the creditor does not include a line for the consumer's signature, the creditor must disclose the following statement under the heading "Other Considerations" required by paragraph (m) of this section, labeled "Loan Acceptance": "You do not have to accept this loan because you have received this form or signed a loan application."

(*o*) Form of disclosures—

(1) General requirements.

(i) The creditor shall make the disclosures required by this section clearly and conspicuously in writing, in a form that the consumer may keep. The disclosures also shall be grouped together and segregated from everything else.

(ii) Except as provided in paragraph (*o*)(5) of this section, the disclosures shall contain only the information required by paragraphs (a) through (n) of this section and shall be made in the same order, and positioned relative to the master headings, headings, subheadings, labels, and similar designations in the same manner, as shown in form H-24, set forth in appendix H to this part.

(2) Headings and labels. If a master heading, heading, subheading, label, or similar designation contains the word "estimated" or a capital letter designation in form H-24, set forth in appendix H to this part, that heading, label, or similar designation shall contain the word "estimated" and the applicable capital letter designation.

(3) Form. Except as provided in paragraph (*o*)(5) of this section:

(i) For a transaction subject to § 1026.19(e) that is a federally related mortgage loan, as defined in Regulation X, 12 CFR 1024.2, the disclosures must be made using form H-24, set forth in appendix H to this part.

(ii) For any other transaction subject to this section, the disclosures must be made with headings, content, and format substantially similar to form H-24, set forth in appendix H to this part.

(iii) The disclosures required by this section may be provided to the consumer in electronic form, subject to compliance with the consumer consent and other applicable provisions of the Electronic Signatures in Global and National Commerce Act (15 U.S.C. 7001 et seq.).

(4) Rounding—

(i) Nearest dollar.

(A) The dollar amounts required to be disclosed by paragraphs (b)(6) and (7), (c)(1)(iii), (c)(2)(ii) and (iii), (c)(4)(ii), (f), (g), (h), (i), and (*l*) of this section shall be rounded to the nearest whole dollar, except that the per diem amount required to be disclosed by paragraph (g)(2)(iii) of this section and the monthly amounts required to be disclosed by paragraphs (g)(3)(i) through (iii) and (g)(3)(v) of this section shall not be rounded.

(B) The dollar amount required to be disclosed by paragraph (b)(1) of this section shall not be rounded, and if the amount is a whole number then the amount disclosed shall be truncated at the decimal point.

(C) The dollar amounts required to be disclosed by paragraph (c)(2)(iv) of this section shall be rounded to the nearest whole dollar, if any of the component amounts are required by paragraph (*o*)(4)(i)(A) of this section to be rounded to the nearest whole dollar.

(ii) Percentages. The percentage amounts required to be disclosed under paragraphs (b)(2) and (6), (f)(1)(i), (g)(2)(iii), (j), and (*l*)(2) and (3) of this section shall be disclosed by rounding the exact amounts to three decimal places and then dropping any trailing zeros that occur to the right of the decimal place.

(5) Exceptions—

(i) Unit-period. Wherever the form or this section uses "monthly" to describe the frequency of any payments or uses "month" to describe the applicable unit-period, the creditor shall substitute the appropriate term to reflect the fact that the transaction's terms provide for other than monthly periodic payments, such as bi-weekly or quarterly payments.

(ii) Translation. The form may be translated into languages other than English, and creditors may modify form H-24 of appendix H to this part to the extent that translation prevents the headings, labels, designations, and required disclosure items under this section from fitting in the space provided on form H-24.

(iii) Logo or slogan. The creditor providing the form may use a logo for, and include a slogan with, the information required by paragraph (a)(3) of this section in any font size or type, provided that such logo or slogan does not cause the information required by paragraph (a)(3) of this section to exceed the space provided for that information, as illustrated in form H-24 of appendix H to this part. If the creditor does not use a logo for the information required by paragraph (a)(3) of this section, the information shall be disclosed in a similar format as form H-24.

(iv) Business card. The creditor may physically attach a business card over the information required to be disclosed by paragraph (a)(3) of this section.

(v) Administrative information. The creditor may insert at the bottom of each page under the disclosures required by this section as illustrated by form H-24 of appendix H to this part, any administrative information, text, or codes that assist in identification of the form or the information disclosed on the form, provided that the space provided on form H-24 of appendix H to this part for any of the information required by this section is not altered.

§ 1026.38. Content of Disclosures for Certain Mortgage Transactions (Closing Disclosure)

For each transaction subject to § 1026.19(f), the creditor shall disclose the information in this section:

(a) General information—

(1) Form title. The title of the form, "Closing Disclosure," using that term.

(2) Form purpose. The following statement: "This form is a statement of final loan terms and closing costs. Compare this document with your Loan Estimate."

(3) Closing information. Under the heading "Closing Information":

(i) Date issued. The date the disclosures required by this section are delivered to the consumer, labeled "Date Issued."

(ii) Closing date. The date of consummation, labeled "Closing Date."

(iii) Disbursement date. The date the amount disclosed under paragraph (j)(3)(iii) (cash to close from or to borrower) or (k)(3)(iii) (cash from or to seller) of this section is expected to be paid in a purchase transaction under § 1026.37(a)(9)(i) to the consumer or seller, respectively, as applicable, except as provided in comment 38(a)(3)(iii)–1, or the date some or all of the loan amount disclosed under paragraph (b) of this section is expected to be paid to the consumer or a third party other than a settlement agent in a transaction that is not a purchase transaction under § 1026.37(a)(9)(i), labeled "Disbursement Date."

(iv) Settlement agent. The name of the settlement agent conducting the closing, labeled "Settlement Agent."

(v) File number. The number assigned to the transaction by the settlement agent for identification purposes, labeled "File #."

(vi) Property. The address or location of the property required to be disclosed under § 1026.37(a)(6), labeled "Property."

(vii) Sale price.

(A) In credit transactions where there is a seller, the contract sale price of the property identified in paragraph (a)(3)(vi) of this section, labeled "Sale Price."

(B) In credit transactions where there is no seller, the appraised value of the property identified in paragraph (a)(3)(vi) of this section, labeled "Appraised Prop. Value."

(4) Transaction information. Under the heading "Transaction Information":

(i) Borrower. The consumer's name and mailing address, labeled "Borrower."

(ii) Seller. Where applicable, the seller's name and mailing address, labeled "Seller."

(iii) Lender. The name of the creditor making the disclosure, labeled "Lender."

(5) Loan information. Under the heading "Loan Information":

(i) Loan term. The information required to be disclosed under § 1026.37(a)(8), labeled "Loan Term."

(ii) Purpose. The information required to be disclosed under § 1026.37(a)(9), labeled "Purpose."

(iii) Product. The information required to be disclosed under § 1026.37(a)(10), labeled "Product."

(iv) Loan type. The information required to be disclosed under § 1026.37(a)(11), labeled "Loan Type."

(v) Loan identification number. The information required to be disclosed under § 1026.37(a)(12), labeled "Loan ID #."

(vi) Mortgage insurance case number. The case number for any mortgage insurance policy, if required by the creditor, labeled "MIC #."

(b) Loan terms. A separate table under the heading "Loan Terms" that includes the information required by § 1026.37(b).

(c) Projected payments. A separate table, under the heading "Projected Payments," that includes and satisfies the following information and requirements:

(1) Projected payments or range of payments. The information required to be disclosed pursuant to § 1026.37(c)(1) through (4), other than § 1026.37(c)(4)(vi). In disclosing estimated escrow payments as described in § 1026.37(c)(2)(iii) and (c)(4)(ii), the amount disclosed on the Closing Disclosure:

(i) For transactions subject to RESPA, is determined under the escrow account analysis described in Regulation X, 12 CFR 1024.17;

(ii) For transactions not subject to RESPA, may be determined under the escrow account analysis described in Regulation X, 12 CFR 1024.17 or in the manner set forth in § 1026.37(c)(5).

(2) Estimated taxes, insurance, and assessments. A reference to the disclosure required by paragraph (*l*)(7) of this section.

(d) Costs at closing—

(1) Costs at closing table. In a separate table, under the heading "Costs at Closing":

(i) Labeled "Closing Costs," the sum of the dollar amounts disclosed pursuant to paragraphs (f)(4), (g)(5), and (h)(3) of this section, together with:

(A) A statement that the amount disclosed pursuant to paragraph (d)(1)(i) of this section includes the amounts disclosed pursuant to paragraphs (f)(4), (g)(5), and (h)(3) of this section;

(B) The dollar amount disclosed pursuant to paragraph (f)(4) of this section, labeled "Loan Costs";

(C) The dollar amount disclosed pursuant to paragraph (g)(5) of this section, labeled "Other Costs";

(D) The dollar amount disclosed pursuant to paragraph (h)(3) of this section, labeled "Lender Credits"; and

(E) A statement referring the consumer to the tables disclosed pursuant to paragraphs (f) and (g) of this section for details.

(ii) Labeled "Cash to Close," the sum of the dollar amounts calculated in accordance with paragraph (i)(9)(ii) of this section, together with:

(A) A statement that the amount disclosed pursuant to paragraph (d)(1)(ii) of this section includes the amount disclosed pursuant to paragraph (d)(1)(i) of this section; and

(B) A statement referring the consumer to the table required pursuant to paragraph (i) of this section for details.

(2) Alternative table for transactions without a seller or for simultaneous subordinate financing. For transactions that do not involve a seller or for simultaneous subordinate financing, if the creditor disclosed the optional alternative table under § 1026.37(d)(2), the creditor shall disclose, with the label "Cash to Close," instead of the sum of the dollar amounts described in paragraph (d)(1)(ii) of this section:

(i) The amount calculated in accordance with paragraph (e)(5)(ii) of this section;

(ii) A statement of whether the disclosed amount is due from or to the consumer; and

(iii) A statement referring the consumer to the table required pursuant to paragraph (e) of this section for details.

(e) Alternative calculating cash to close table for transactions without a seller or for simultaneous subordinate financing. For transactions that do not involve a seller or for simultaneous subordinate financing, if the creditor disclosed the optional alternative table under § 1026.37(h)(2), the creditor shall disclose, instead of the table described in paragraph (i) of this section, in a separate table, under the heading "Calculating Cash to Close," together with the statement "Use this table to see what has changed from your Loan Estimate":

(1) Loan amount. Labeled "Loan Amount:"

(i) Under the subheading "Loan Estimate," the loan amount disclosed on the Loan Estimate under § 1026.37(b)(1);

(ii) Under the subheading "Final," the loan amount disclosed under paragraph (b) of this section;

(iii) Disclosed more prominently than the other disclosures under paragraph (e)(1)(i) and (ii) of this section, under the subheading "Did this change?":

(A) If the amount disclosed under paragraph (e)(1)(ii) of this section is different than the amount disclosed under paragraph (e)(1)(i) of this section (unless the difference is due to rounding), a statement of that fact along with a statement of whether this amount increased or decreased; or

(B) If the amount disclosed under paragraph (e)(1)(i) of this section is equal to the amount disclosed under paragraph (e)(1)(ii) of this section a statement of that fact.

(2) Total closing costs. Labeled "Total Closing Costs":

(i) Under the subheading "Loan Estimate," the amount disclosed on the Loan Estimate under § 1026.37(h)(2)(ii);

(ii) Under the subheading "Final," the amount disclosed under paragraph (h)(1) of this section, disclosed as a negative number if the amount disclosed under paragraph (h)(1) of this section is a positive number and disclosed as a positive number if the amount disclosed under paragraph (h)(1) of this section is a negative number; and

(iii) Disclosed more prominently than the other disclosures under this paragraph (e)(2)(i) and (ii) of this section, under the subheading "Did this change?":

(A) If the amount disclosed under paragraph (e)(2)(ii) of this section is different than the amount disclosed under paragraph (e)(2)(i) of this section (unless the difference is due to rounding):

(1) A statement of that fact;

(2) If the difference in the amounts disclosed under paragraphs (e)(2)(i) and (e)(2)(ii) is attributable to differences in itemized charges that are included in either or both subtotals, a statement that the consumer should see the total loan costs and total other costs subtotals disclosed under paragraphs (f)(4) and (g)(5) of this section (together with references to such disclosures), as applicable; and

(3) If the increase exceeds the limitations on increases in closing costs under § 1026.19(e)(3), a statement that such increase exceeds the legal limits by the dollar amount of the excess and, if any refund is provided under § 1026.19(f)(2)(v), a statement directing the consumer to the disclosure required under paragraph (h)(3) of this section or, if applicable, a statement directing the consumer to the principal reduction disclosure under paragraph (t)(5)(vii)(B) of this section. Such dollar amount shall equal the sum total of all excesses of the limitations on increases in closing costs under § 1026.19(e)(3), taking into account the different methods of calculating excesses of the limitations on increases in closing costs under § 1026.19(e)(3)(i) and (ii).

(B) If the amount disclosed under paragraph (e)(2)(i) of this section is equal to the amount disclosed under paragraph (e)(2)(ii) of this section, a statement of that fact.

(3) Closing costs paid before closing. Labeled "Closing Costs Paid Before Closing:"

(i) Under the subheading "Loan Estimate," the amount of $0;

(ii) Under the subheading "Final," any amount designated as borrower-paid before closing under paragraph (h)(2) of this section, disclosed as a positive number; and

(iii) Disclosed more prominently than the other disclosures under this paragraph (e)(3)(i) and (ii) of this section, under the subheading "Did this change?":

(A) If the amount disclosed under paragraph (e)(3)(ii) of this section is different than the amount disclosed under paragraph (e)(3)(i) of this section (unless the difference is due to rounding), a statement of that fact, along with a statement that the consumer paid such amounts prior to consummation of the transaction; or

(B) If the amount disclosed under paragraph (e)(3)(ii) of this section is equal to the amount disclosed under paragraph (e)(3)(i) of this section, a statement of that fact.

(4) Payoffs and payments. Labeled "Total Payoffs and Payments,"

(i) Under the subheading "Loan Estimate," the total payoffs and payments disclosed on the Loan Estimate under § 1026.37(h)(2)(iii);

(ii) Under the subheading "Final," the amount due from or to the consumer, calculated by the sum of the amounts disclosed under paragraphs (e)(1)(ii), (e)(2)(ii), (e)(3)(ii), and (e)(4)(ii) of this section, disclosed as a positive number, together with a statement of whether the disclosed amount is due from or to the consumer.

(iii) Disclosed more prominently than the other disclosures under this paragraph (e)(4)(i) and (ii), under the subheading "Did this change?":

(A) If the amount disclosed under paragraph (e)(4)(ii) of this section is different than the amount disclosed under paragraph (e)(4)(i) of this section (unless the difference is due to rounding), a statement of that fact along with a reference to the table disclosed under paragraph (t)(5)(vii)(B) of this section; or

(B) If the amount disclosed under paragraph (e)(4)(ii) of this section is equal to the amount disclosed under paragraph (e)(4)(i) of this section, a statement of that fact.

(5) Cash to or from consumer. Labeled "Cash to Close:"

(i) Under the subheading "Loan Estimate," the estimated cash to close on the Loan Estimate together with the statement of whether the estimated amount is due from or to the consumer as disclosed under § 1026.37(h)(2)(iv);

(ii) Under the subheading "Final," the amount due from or to the consumer, calculated by the sum of the amounts disclosed under paragraphs (e)(1)(ii), (e)(2)(ii), (e)(3)(ii), and (e)(4)(ii) of this section, disclosed as a positive number, together with a statement of whether the disclosed amount is due from or to the consumer.

(6) Closing costs financed. Labeled "Closing Costs Financed (Paid from your Loan Amount)," the sum of the amounts disclosed under paragraphs (e)(1)(ii) and (e)(4)(ii) of this section, but only to the extent that the sum is greater than zero and less than or equal to the sum disclosed under paragraph (h)(1) of this section minus the sum disclosed under paragraph (h)(2) of this section designated borrower-paid before closing.

(f) Closing cost details; loan costs. Under the master heading "Closing Cost Details" with columns stating whether the charge was borrower-paid at or before closing, seller-paid at or before closing, or paid by others, all loan costs associated with the transaction, listed in a table under the heading "Loan Costs." The table shall contain the items and amounts listed under four subheadings, described in paragraphs (f)(1) through (5) of this section.

(1) Origination charges. Under the subheading "Origination Charges," and in the applicable columns as described in paragraph (f) of this section, an itemization of each amount paid for charges described in § 1026.37(f)(1), the amount of compensation paid by the creditor to a third-party loan originator along with the name of the loan originator ultimately receiving the payment, and the total of all such itemized amounts that are designated borrower-paid at or before closing.

(2) Services borrower did not shop for. Under the subheading "Services Borrower Did Not Shop For" and in the applicable columns as described in paragraph (f) of this section, an itemization of the services and corresponding costs for each of the settlement services required by the creditor for which the consumer did not shop in accordance with § 1026.19(e)(1)(vi)(A) and that are provided by persons other than the creditor or mortgage broker, the name of the person ultimately receiving the payment for each such amount, and the total of all such itemized amounts that are designated borrower-paid at or before closing. Items that were disclosed pursuant to § 1026.37(f)(3) must be disclosed under this paragraph (f)(2) if the consumer was provided a written list of settlement service providers under § 1026.19(e)(1)(vi)(C) and the consumer selected a settlement service provider contained on that written list.

(3) Services borrower did shop for. Under the subheading "Services Borrower Did Shop For" and in the applicable column as described in paragraph (f) of this section, an itemization of the services and corresponding costs for each of the settlement services required by the creditor for which the consumer shopped in accordance with § 1026.19(e)(1)(vi)(A) and that are provided by persons other than the creditor or mortgage broker, the name of the person ultimately receiving the payment for each such amount, and the total of all such itemized costs that are designated borrower-paid at or before closing. Items that were disclosed pursuant to § 1026.37(f)(3) must be disclosed under this paragraph (f)(3) if the consumer was provided a written list of settlement service providers under § 1026.19(e)(1)(vi)(C) and the consumer did not select a settlement service provider contained on that written list.

(4) Total loan costs. Under the subheading "Total Loan Costs (Borrower-Paid)," the sum of the amounts disclosed as borrower-paid pursuant to paragraph (f)(5) of this section.

(5) Subtotal of loan costs. The sum of loan costs, calculated by totaling the amounts described in paragraphs (f)(1) through (3) of this section for costs designated borrower-paid at or before closing, labeled "Loan Costs Subtotals."

(g) Closing cost details; other costs. Under the master heading "Closing Cost Details" disclosed pursuant to paragraph (f) of this section, with columns stating whether the charge was borrower-paid at or before closing, seller-paid at or before closing, or paid by others, all costs in connection with the transaction, other than those disclosed under paragraph (f) of this section, listed in a table with a heading disclosed as "Other Costs." The table shall contain the items and amounts listed under five subheadings, described in paragraphs (g)(1) through (6) of this section.

(1) Taxes and other government fees. Under the subheading "Final," the amount due from or to the consumer, calculated by the sum of the amounts disclosed under paragraphs (e)(1)(ii), (e)(2)(ii), (e)(3)(ii), and (e)(4)(ii) of this section, disclosed as a positive number, together with a statement of whether the disclosed amount is due from or to the consumer.

(i) On the first line:

(A) Before the columns described in paragraph (g) of this section, the total amount of fees for recording deeds and, separately, the total amount of fees for recording security instruments; and

(B) In the applicable column as described in paragraph (g) of this section, the total amounts paid for recording fees (including, but not limited to, the amounts in paragraph (g)(1)(i)(A) of this section); and

(ii) On subsequent lines, in the applicable column as described in paragraph (g) of this section, an itemization of transfer taxes, with the name of the government entity assessing the transfer tax.

(2) Prepaids. Under the subheading "Prepaids" and in the applicable column as described in paragraph (g) of this section, an itemization of each amount for charges described in § 1026.37(g)(2), the name of the person ultimately receiving the payment or government entity assessing the property tax, provided that the person ultimately receiving the payment need not be disclosed for the disclosure required by § 1026.37(g)(2)(iii) when disclosed pursuant to this paragraph, and the total of all such itemized amounts that are designated borrower-paid at or before closing.

(3) Initial escrow payment at closing. Under the subheading "Initial escrow payment at closing" and in the applicable column as described in paragraph (g) of this section, an itemization of each amount for charges described in § 1026.37(g)(3), the applicable aggregate adjustment pursuant to 12 CFR 1024.17(d)(2) along with the label "aggregate adjustment," and the total of all such itemized amounts that are designated borrower-paid at or before closing.

(4) Other. Under the subheading "Other" and in the applicable column as described in paragraph (g) of this section, an itemization of each amount for charges in connection with the transaction that are in addition to the charges disclosed under paragraphs (f) and (g)(1) through (3) for services that are required or obtained in the real estate closing by the consumer, the seller, or other party, the name of the person ultimately receiving the payment, and the total of all such itemized amounts that are designated borrower-paid at or before closing.

(i) For any cost that is a component of title insurance services, the introductory description "Title—" shall appear at the beginning of the label for that actual cost.

(ii) The parenthetical description "(optional)" shall appear at the end of the label for costs designated borrower-paid at or before closing for any premiums paid for separate insurance, warranty, guarantee, or event-coverage products.

(5) Total other costs. Under the subheading "Total Other Costs (Borrower-Paid)," the sum of the amounts disclosed as borrower-paid pursuant to paragraph (g)(6) of this section.

(6) Subtotal of costs. The sum of other costs, calculated by totaling the costs disclosed in paragraphs (g)(1) through (4) of this section designated borrower-paid at or before closing, labeled "Other Costs Subtotals."

(h) Closing cost totals.

(1) The sum of the costs disclosed as borrower-paid pursuant to paragraph (h)(2) of this section and the amount disclosed in paragraph (h)(3) of this section, under the subheading "Total Closing Costs (Borrower-Paid)."

(2) The sum of the amounts disclosed in paragraphs (f)(5) and (g)(6) of this section, designated borrower-paid at or before closing, and the sum of the costs designated seller-paid at or before closing or paid by others disclosed pursuant to paragraphs (f) and (g) of this section, labeled "Closing Costs Subtotals."

(3) The amount of lender credits as a negative number, labeled "Lender Credits" and designated borrower-paid at closing, and if a refund is provided pursuant to § 1026.19(f)(2)(v), a statement that this amount includes a credit for an amount that exceeds the limitations on increases in closing costs under § 1026.19(e)(3), and the amount of such credit under § 1026.19(f)(2)(v).

(4) The services and costs disclosed pursuant to paragraphs (f) and (g) of this section on the Closing Disclosure shall be labeled using terminology that describes the item disclosed, in a manner that is consistent with the descriptions or prescribed labels, as applicable, used for such items on the Loan Estimate pursuant to § 1026.37. The creditor must also list the items on the Closing Disclosure in the same sequential order as on the Loan Estimate pursuant to § 1026.37.

(i) Calculating cash to close. In a separate table, under the heading "Calculating Cash to Close," together with the statement "Use this table to see what has changed from your Loan Estimate":

(1) Total closing costs.

(i) Under the subheading "Loan Estimate," the "Total Closing Costs" disclosed on the Loan Estimate under § 1026.37(h)(1)(i), labeled using that term.

(ii) Under the subheading "Final," the amount disclosed under paragraph (h)(1) of this section.

(iii) Under the subheading "Did this change?," disclosed more prominently than the other disclosures under this paragraph (i)(1):

(A) If the amount disclosed under paragraph (i)(1)(ii) of this section is different than the amount disclosed under paragraph (i)(1)(i) of this section (unless the difference is due to rounding):

(1) A statement of that fact;

(2) If the difference in the "Total Closing Costs" is attributable to differences in itemized charges that are included in either or both subtotals, a statement that the consumer should see the total loan costs and total other costs subtotals disclosed under paragraphs (f)(4) and (g)(5) of this section (together with references to such disclosures), as applicable; and

(3) If the increase exceeds the limitations on increases in closing costs under § 1026.19(e)(3), a statement that such increase exceeds the legal limits by the dollar amount of the excess, and if any refund is provided under § 1026.19(f)(2)(v), a statement directing the consumer to the disclosure required under paragraph (h)(3) of this section or, if a principal reduction is used to provide the refund, a statement directing the consumer to the principal reduction disclosure under paragraph (j)(1)(v) of this section. Such dollar amount shall equal the sum total of all excesses of the limitations on increases in closing costs under § 1026.19(e)(3), taking into account the different methods of calculating excesses of the limitations on increases in closing costs under § 1026.19(e)(3)(i) and (ii).

(B) If the amount disclosed under paragraph (i)(1)(ii) of this section is equal to the amount disclosed under paragraph (i)(1)(i) of this section, a statement of that fact.

(2) Closing costs paid before closing.

(i) Under the subheading "Loan Estimate," the dollar amount "$0," labeled "Closing Costs Paid Before Closing."

(ii) Under the subheading "Final," the amount of "Total Closing Costs" disclosed under paragraph (h)(2) of this section and designated as borrower-paid before closing, stated as a negative number.

(iii) Under the subheading "Did this change?," disclosed more prominently than the other disclosures under this paragraph (i)(2):

(A) If the amount disclosed under paragraph (i)(2)(ii) of this section is different than the amount disclosed under paragraph (i)(2)(i) of this section (unless the difference is due to rounding), a statement of that fact, along with a statement that the consumer paid such amounts prior to consummation of the transaction; or

(B) If the amount disclosed under paragraph (i)(2)(ii) of this section is equal to the amount disclosed under paragraph (i)(2)(i) of this section, a statement of that fact.

(3) Closing costs financed.

(i) Under the subheading "Loan Estimate," the amount disclosed under § 1026.37(h)(1)(ii), labeled "Closing Costs Financed (Paid from your Loan Amount)."

(ii) Under the subheading "Final," the actual amount of the closing costs that are to be paid out of loan proceeds, if any, stated as a negative number.

(iii) Under the subheading "Did this change?," disclosed more prominently than the other disclosures under this paragraph (i)(3):

(A) If the amount disclosed under paragraph (i)(3)(ii) of this section is different than the amount disclosed under paragraph (i)(3)(i) of this section (unless the difference is due to rounding), a statement of that fact, along with a statement that the consumer included the closing costs in the loan amount, which increased the loan amount; or

(B) If the amount disclosed under paragraph (i)(3)(ii) of this section is equal to the amount disclosed under paragraph (i)(3)(i) of this section, a statement of that fact.

(4) Down payment/funds from borrower.

(i) Under the subheading "Loan Estimate," the amount disclosed under § 1026.37(h)(1)(iii), labeled "Down Payment/Funds from Borrower."

(ii) Under the subheading "Final":

(A)(1) In a purchase transaction as defined in § 1026.37(a)(9)(i), the amount determined by subtracting the sum of the loan amount disclosed under paragraph (b) of this section and any amount of existing loans assumed or taken subject to that is disclosed under paragraph (j)(2)(iv) of this section from the sale price of the property disclosed under paragraph (a)(3)(vii)(A) of this section, labeled "Down Payment/Funds from Borrower," except as required by paragraph (i)(4)(ii)(A)(2) of this section;

(2) In a purchase transaction as defined in § 1026.37(a)(9)(i) that is a simultaneous subordinate financing transaction or that involves improvements to be made on the property, or when the sum of the loan amount disclosed under paragraph (b) of this section and any amount of existing loans assumed or taken subject to that is disclosed under paragraph (j)(2)(iv) of this section exceeds the sale price disclosed under paragraph (a)(3)(vii)(A) of this section, the amount of funds from the consumer as determined in accordance with paragraph (i)(6)(iv) of this section labeled "Down Payment/Funds from Borrower;" or

(B) In all transactions not subject to paragraph (i)(4)(ii)(A) of this section, the amount of funds from the consumer as determined in accordance with paragraph (i)(6)(iv) of this section, labeled "Down Payment/Funds from Borrower."

(iii) Under the subheading "Did this change?," disclosed more prominently than the other disclosures under this paragraph (i)(4):

(A) If the amount disclosed under paragraph (i)(4)(ii) of this section is different than the amount disclosed under paragraph (i)(4)(i) of this section (unless the difference is due to rounding), a statement of that fact, along with a statement that the consumer increased or decreased this payment and that the consumer should see the details disclosed under paragraph (j)(1) or (j)(2) of this section, as applicable; or

(B) If the amount disclosed under paragraph (i)(4)(ii) of this section is equal to the amount disclosed under paragraph (i)(4)(i) of this section, a statement of that fact.

(5) Deposit.

(i) Under the subheading "Loan Estimate," the amount disclosed under § 1026.37(h)(1)(iv), labeled "Deposit."

(ii) Under the subheading "Final," the amount disclosed under paragraph (j)(2)(ii) of this section, stated as a negative number.

(iii) Under the subheading "Did this change?," disclosed more prominently than the other disclosures under this paragraph (i)(5):

(A) If the amount disclosed under paragraph (i)(5)(ii) of this section is different than the amount disclosed under paragraph (i)(5)(i) of this section (unless the difference is due to rounding), a statement of that fact, along with a statement that the consumer increased or decreased this payment, as applicable, and that the consumer should see the details disclosed under paragraph (j)(2)(ii) of this section; or

(B) If the amount disclosed under paragraph (i)(5)(ii) of this section is equal to the amount disclosed under paragraph (i)(5)(i) of this section, a statement of that fact.

(6) Funds for borrower.

(i) Under the subheading "Loan Estimate," the amount disclosed under § 1026.37(h)(1)(v), labeled "Funds for Borrower."

(ii) Under the subheading "Final," the "Funds for Borrower," labeled using that term, as determined in accordance with paragraph (i)(6)(iv) of this section.

(iii) Under the subheading "Did this change?," disclosed more prominently than the other disclosures under this paragraph (i)(6):

(A) If the amount disclosed under paragraph (i)(6)(ii) of this section is different than the amount disclosed under paragraph (i)(6)(i) of this section (unless the difference is due to rounding), a statement of that fact, along with a statement that the consumer's available funds from the loan amount have increased or decreased, as applicable; or

(B) If the amount disclosed under paragraph (i)(6)(ii) of this section is equal to the amount disclosed under paragraph (i)(6)(i) of this section, a statement of that fact.

(iv) The "Down Payment/Funds from Borrower" to be disclosed under paragraph (i)(4)(ii)(A)(2) or (B) of this section, as applicable, and "Funds for Borrower" to be disclosed under paragraph (i)(6)(ii) of this section are determined by subtracting the sum of the loan amount disclosed under paragraph (b) of this section and any amount for existing loans assumed or taken subject to that is disclosed under paragraph (j)(2)(iv) of this section (excluding any closing costs financed disclosed under paragraph (i)(3)(ii) of this section) from the total amount of all existing debt being satisfied in the transaction disclosed under paragraphs (j)(1)(ii), (iii), and (v) of this section.

(A) If the calculation under this paragraph (i)(6)(iv) yields an amount that is a positive number, such amount shall be disclosed under paragraph (i)(4)(ii)(A)(2) or (B) of this section, as applicable, and $0 shall be disclosed under paragraph (i)(6)(ii) of this section.

(B) If the calculation under this paragraph (i)(6)(iv) yields an amount that is a negative number, such amount shall be disclosed under paragraph (i)(6)(ii) of this section, stated as a negative number, and $0 shall be disclosed under paragraph (i)(4)(ii)(A)(2) or (i)(4)(ii)(B) of this section, as applicable.

(C) If the calculation under this paragraph (i)(6)(iv) yields $0, $0 shall be disclosed under paragraph (i)(4)(ii)(A)(2) or (i)(4)(ii)(B) of this section, as applicable, and under paragraph (i)(6)(ii) of this section.

(7) Seller credits.

(i) Under the subheading "Loan Estimate," the amount disclosed under § 1026.37(h)(1)(vi), labeled "Seller Credits."

(ii) Under the subheading "Final," the amount disclosed under paragraph (j)(2)(v) of this section, stated as a negative number.

(iii) Under the subheading "Did this change?," disclosed more prominently than the other disclosures under this paragraph (i)(7):

(A) If the amount disclosed under paragraph (i)(7)(ii) of this section is different than the amount disclosed under paragraph (i)(7)(i) of this section (unless the difference is due to rounding), a statement of that fact, along with a statement that the consumer should see the details disclosed:

(1) Under paragraph (j)(2)(v) of this section and in the seller-paid column under paragraphs (f) and (g) of this section; or

(2) Under either paragraph (j)(2)(v) of this section or in the seller-paid column under paragraphs (f) or (g) of this section, if the details are only disclosed under paragraph (j)(2)(v) or paragraph (f) or (g); or

(B) If the amount disclosed under paragraph (i)(7)(ii) of this section is equal to the amount disclosed under paragraph (i)(7)(i) of this section, a statement of that fact.

(8) Adjustments and other credits.

(i) Under the subheading "Loan Estimate," the amount disclosed on the Loan Estimate under § 1026.37(h)(1)(vii), labeled "Adjustments and Other Credits."

(ii) Under the subheading "Final," the amount equal to the total of the amounts disclosed under paragraphs (j)(1)(iii) and (v) of this section, to the extent amounts in paragraphs (j)(1)(iii) and (v) were not included in the calculation required by paragraph (i)(4) or (6) of this section, and paragraphs (j)(1)(vi) through (x) of this section, reduced by the total of the amounts disclosed under paragraphs (j)(2)(vi) through (xi) of this section.

(iii) Under the subheading "Did this change?," disclosed more prominently than the other disclosures under this paragraph (i)(8):

(A) If the amount disclosed under paragraph (i)(8)(ii) of this section is different than the amount disclosed under paragraph (i)(8)(i) of this section (unless the difference is due to rounding), a statement of that fact, along with a statement that the consumer should see the details disclosed under paragraphs (j)(1)(iii) and (v) through (x) and (j)(2)(vi) through (xi) of this section, as applicable; or

(B) If the amount disclosed under paragraph (i)(8)(ii) of this section is equal to the amount disclosed under paragraph (i)(8)(i) of this section, a statement of that fact.

(9) Cash to close.

(i) Under the subheading "Loan Estimate," the amount disclosed on the Loan Estimate under § 1026.37(h)(1)(viii), labeled "Cash to Close" and disclosed more prominently than the other disclosures under this paragraph (i).

(ii) Under the subheading "Final," the sum of the amounts disclosed under paragraphs (i)(1) through (i)(8) of this section under the subheading "Final," and disclosed more prominently than the other disclosures under this paragraph (i).

(j) Summary of borrower's transaction. Under the heading "Summaries of Transactions," with a statement to "Use this table to see a summary of your transaction," two separate tables are disclosed. The first table shall include, under the subheading "Borrower's Transaction," the following information and shall satisfy the following requirements:

(1) Itemization of amounts due from borrower.

(i) The total amount due from the consumer at closing, calculated as the sum of items required to be disclosed by paragraph (j)(1)(ii) through (x) of this section, excluding items paid from funds other than closing funds as described in paragraph (j)(4)(i) of this section, labeled "Due from Borrower at Closing";

(ii) The amount of the contract sales price of the property being sold in a purchase real estate transaction, excluding the price of any tangible personal property if the consumer and seller have agreed to a separate price for such items, labeled "Sale Price of Property";

(iii) The amount of the sales price of any tangible personal property excluded from the contract sales price pursuant to paragraph (j)(1)(ii) of this section, labeled "Sale Price of Any Personal Property Included in Sale";

(iv) The total amount of closing costs disclosed that are designated borrower-paid at closing, as the sum of the amounts calculated pursuant to paragraphs (h)(2) and (3) of this section, labeled "Closing Costs Paid at Closing";

(v) A description and the amount of any additional items that the seller has paid prior to the real estate closing, but reimbursed by the consumer at the real estate closing, and a description and the amount of any other items owed by the consumer at the real estate closing not otherwise disclosed pursuant to paragraph (f), (g), or (j) of this section;

(vi) The description "Adjustments for Items Paid by Seller in Advance";

(vii) The prorated amount of any prepaid taxes due from the consumer to reimburse the seller at the real estate closing, and the time period corresponding to that amount, labeled "City/Town Taxes";

(viii) The prorated amount of any prepaid taxes due from the consumer to reimburse the seller at the real estate closing, and the time period corresponding to that amount, labeled "County Taxes";

(ix) The prorated amount of any prepaid assessments due from the consumer to reimburse the seller at the real estate closing, and the time period corresponding to that amount, labeled "Assessments"; and

(x) A description and the amount of any additional items paid by the seller prior to the real estate closing that are due from the consumer at the real estate closing.

(2) Itemization of amounts already paid by or on behalf of borrower.

(i) The sum of the amounts disclosed in this paragraphs (j)(2)(ii) through (xi) of this section, excluding items paid from funds other than closing funds as described in paragraph (j)(4)(i) of this section, labeled "Paid Already by or on Behalf of Borrower at Closing";

(ii) Any amount that is paid to the seller or held in trust or escrow by an attorney or other party under the terms of the agreement for the sale of the property, labeled "Deposit";

(iii) The amount of the consumer's new loan amount or first user loan as disclosed pursuant to paragraph (b) of this section, labeled "Loan Amount";

(iv) The amount of any existing loans that the consumer is assuming, or any loans subject to which the consumer is taking title to the property, labeled "Existing Loan(s) Assumed or Taken Subject to";

(v) The total amount of money that the seller will provide at the real estate closing as a lump sum not otherwise itemized to pay for loan costs as determined by paragraph (f) of this section and other costs as determined by paragraph (g) of this section and any other obligations of the seller to be paid directly to the consumer, labeled "Seller Credit";

(vi) Descriptions and amounts of other items paid by or on behalf of the consumer and not otherwise disclosed under paragraphs (f), (g), (h), and (j)(2) of this section, labeled "Other Credits," and descriptions and the amounts of any additional amounts owed the consumer but payable to the seller before the real estate closing, under the heading "Adjustments";

(vii) The description "Adjustments for Items Unpaid by Seller";

(viii) The prorated amount of any unpaid taxes due from the seller to reimburse the consumer at the real estate closing, and the time period corresponding to that amount, labeled "City/Town Taxes";

(ix) The prorated amount of any unpaid taxes due from the seller to reimburse the consumer at the real estate closing, and the time period corresponding to that amount, labeled "County Taxes";

(x) The prorated amount of any unpaid assessments due from the seller to reimburse the consumer at the real estate closing, and the time period corresponding to that amount, labeled "Assessments"; and

(xi) A description and the amount of any additional items which have not yet been paid and which the consumer is expected to pay after the real estate closing, but which are attributable in part to a period of time prior to the real estate closing.

(3) Calculation of borrower's transaction. Under the label "Calculation":

(i) The amount disclosed pursuant to paragraph (j)(1)(i) of this section, labeled "Total Due from Borrower at Closing";

(ii) The amount disclosed pursuant to paragraph (j)(2)(i) of this section, if any, disclosed as a negative number, labeled "Total Paid Already by or on Behalf of Borrower at Closing"; and

(iii) A statement that the disclosed amount is due from or to the consumer, and the amount due from or to the consumer at the real estate closing, calculated by the sum of the amounts disclosed under paragraphs (j)(3)(i) and (ii) of this section, labeled "Cash to Close."

(4) Items paid outside of closing funds.

(i) Costs that are not paid from closing funds but that would otherwise be disclosed in the table required pursuant to paragraph (j) of this section, should be marked with the phrase "Paid Outside of Closing" or the abbreviation "P.O.C." and include the name of the party making the payment.

(ii) For purposes of this paragraph (j), "closing funds" means funds collected and disbursed at real estate closing.

(k) Summary of seller's transaction. Under the heading "Summaries of Transactions" required by paragraph (j) of this section, a separate table under the subheading "Seller's Transaction," that includes the following information and satisfies the following requirements:

(1) Itemization of amounts due to seller.

(i) The total amount due to the seller at the real estate closing, calculated as the sum of items required to be disclosed pursuant to paragraphs (k)(1)(ii) through (ix) of this section, excluding items paid from funds other than closing funds as described in paragraph (k)(4)(i) of this section, labeled "Due to Seller at Closing";

(ii) The amount of the contract sales price of the property being sold, excluding the price of any tangible personal property if the consumer and seller have agreed to a separate price for such items, labeled "Sale Price of Property";

(iii) The amount of the sales price of any tangible personal property excluded from the contract sales price pursuant to paragraph (k)(1)(ii) of this section, labeled "Sale Price of Any Personal Property Included in Sale";

(iv) A description and the amount of other items paid to the seller by the consumer pursuant to the contract of sale or other agreement, such as charges that were not disclosed pursuant to § 1026.37 on the Loan Estimate or items paid by the seller prior to the real estate closing but reimbursed by the consumer at the real estate closing;

(v) The description "Adjustments for Items Paid by Seller in Advance";

(vi) The prorated amount of any prepaid taxes due from the consumer to reimburse the seller at the real estate closing, and the time period corresponding to that amount, labeled "City/Town Taxes";

(vii) The prorated amount of any prepaid taxes due from the consumer to reimburse the seller at the real estate closing, and the time period corresponding to that amount, labeled "County Taxes";

(viii) The prorated amount of any prepaid assessments due from the consumer to reimburse the seller at the real estate closing, and the time period corresponding to that amount, labeled "Assessments"; and

(ix) A description and the amount of additional items paid by the seller prior to the real estate closing that are reimbursed by the consumer at the real estate closing.

(2) Itemization of amounts due from seller.

(i) The total amount due from the seller at the real estate closing, calculated as the sum of items required to be disclosed pursuant to paragraphs (k)(2)(ii) through (xiii) of this section, excluding items paid from funds other than closing funds as described in paragraph (k)(4)(i) of this section, labeled "Due from Seller at Closing";

(ii) The amount of any excess deposit disbursed to the seller prior to the real estate closing, labeled "Excess Deposit";

(iii) The amount of closing costs designated seller-paid at closing disclosed pursuant to paragraph (h)(2) of this section, labeled "Closing Costs Paid at Closing";

(iv) The amount of any existing loans that the consumer is assuming, or any loans subject to which the consumer is taking title to the property, labeled "Existing Loan(s) Assumed or Taken Subject to";

(v) The amount of any loan secured by a first lien on the property that will be paid off as part of the real estate closing, labeled "Payoff of First Mortgage Loan";

(vi) The amount of any loan secured by a second lien on the property that will be paid off as part of the real estate closing, labeled "Payoff of Second Mortgage Loan";

(vii) The total amount of money that the seller will provide at the real estate closing as a lump sum not otherwise itemized to pay for loan costs as determined by paragraph (f) of this section and other costs as determined by paragraph (g) of this section and any other obligations of the seller to be paid directly to the consumer, labeled "Seller Credit";

(viii) A description and amount of any and all other obligations required to be paid by the seller at the real estate closing, including any lien-related payoffs, fees, or obligations;

(ix) The description "Adjustments for Items Unpaid by Seller";

(x) The prorated amount of any unpaid taxes due from the seller to reimburse the consumer at the real estate closing, and the time period corresponding to that amount, labeled "City/Town Taxes";

(xi) The prorated amount of any unpaid taxes due from the seller to the consumer at the real estate closing, and the time period corresponding to that amount, labeled "County Taxes";

(xii) The prorated amount of any unpaid assessments due from the seller to reimburse the consumer at the real estate closing, and the time period corresponding to that amount, labeled "Assessments"; and

(xiii) A description and the amount of any additional items which have not yet been paid and which the consumer is expected to pay after the real estate closing, but which are attributable in part to a period of time prior to the real estate closing.

(3) Calculation of seller's transaction. Under the label "Calculation":

(i) The amount described in paragraph (k)(1)(i) of this section, labeled "Total Due to Seller at Closing";

(ii) The amount described in paragraph (k)(2)(i) of this section, disclosed as a negative number, labeled "Total Due from Seller at Closing"; and

(iii) A statement that the disclosed amount is due from or to the seller, and the amount due from or to the seller at closing, calculated by the sum of the amounts disclosed pursuant to paragraphs (k)(3)(i) and (ii) of this section, labeled "Cash."

(4) Items paid outside of closing funds.

(i) Charges that are not paid from closing funds but that would otherwise be disclosed in the table described in paragraph (k) of this section, should be marked with the phrase "Paid Outside of Closing" or the acronym "P.O.C." and include a statement of the party making the payment.

(ii) For purposes of this paragraph (k), "closing funds" are defined as funds collected and disbursed at real estate closing.

(*l*) Loan disclosures. Under the master heading "Additional Information About This Loan" and under the heading "Loan Disclosures":

(1) Assumption. Under the subheading "Assumption," the information required by § 1026.37(m)(2).

(2) Demand feature. Under the subheading "Demand Feature," a statement of whether the legal obligation permits the creditor to demand early repayment of the loan and, if the statement is affirmative, a reference to the note or other loan contract for details.

(3) Late payment. Under the subheading "Late Payment," the information required by § 1026.37(m)(4).

(4) Negative amortization. Under the subheading "Negative Amortization (Increase in Loan Amount)," a statement of whether the regular periodic payments may cause the principal balance to increase.

(i) If the regular periodic payments do not cover all of the interest due, the creditor must provide a statement that the principal balance will increase, such balance will likely become larger than the original loan amount, and increases in such balance lower the consumer's equity in the property.

(ii) If the consumer may make regular periodic payments that do not cover all of the interest due, the creditor must provide a statement that, if the consumer chooses a monthly payment option that does not cover all of the interest due, the principal balance may become larger than the original loan amount and the increases in the principal balance lower the consumer's equity in the property.

(5) Partial payment policy. Under the subheading "Partial Payments":

(i) If periodic payments that are less than the full amount due are accepted, a statement that the creditor, using the term "lender," may accept partial payments and apply such payments to the consumer's loan;

(ii) If periodic payments that are less than the full amount due are accepted but not applied to a consumer's loan until the consumer pays the remainder of the full amount due, a statement that the creditor, using the term "lender," may hold partial payments in a separate account until the consumer pays the remainder of the payment and then apply the full periodic payment to the consumer's loan;

(iii) If periodic payments that are less than the full amount due are not accepted, a statement that the creditor, using the term "lender," does not accept any partial payments; and

(iv) A statement that, if the loan is sold, the new creditor, using the term "lender," may have a different policy.

(6) Security interest. Under the subheading "Security Interest," a statement that the consumer is granting a security interest in the property securing the transaction, the property address including a zip code, and a statement that the consumer may lose the property if the consumer does not make the required payments or satisfy other requirements under the legal obligation.

(7) Escrow account. Under the subheading "Escrow Account":

(i) Under the reference "For now," a statement that an escrow account may also be called an impound or trust account, a statement of whether the creditor has established or will establish (at or before consummation) an escrow account in connection with the transaction, and the information required under paragraphs (*l*)(7)(i)(A) and (B) of this section:

(A) A statement that the creditor may be liable for penalties and interest if it fails to make a payment for any cost for which the escrow account is established, a statement that the consumer would have to pay such costs directly in the absence of the escrow account, and a table, titled "Escrow," that contains, if an escrow account is or will be established, an itemization of the amounts listed in paragraphs (*l*)(7)(i)(A)(1) through (4) of this section;

(1) The total amount the consumer will be required to pay into an escrow account over the first year after consummation, labeled "Escrowed Property Costs over Year 1," together with a descriptive name of each charge to be paid (in whole or in part) from the escrow account, calculated as the amount disclosed under paragraph (*l*)(7)(i)(A)(4) of this section multiplied by the number of periodic payments scheduled to be made to the escrow account during the first year after consummation;

(2) The estimated amount the consumer is likely to pay during the first year after consummation for the mortgage-related obligations described in § 1026.43(b)(8) that are known to the creditor and that will not be paid using escrow account funds, labeled "Non-Escrowed Property Costs over Year 1," together with a descriptive name of each such charge and a statement that the consumer may have to pay other costs that are not listed;

(3) The total amount disclosed under paragraph (g)(3) of this section, a statement that the payment is a cushion for the escrow account, labeled "Initial Escrow Payment," and a reference to the information disclosed under paragraph (g)(3) of this section;

(4) The amount the consumer will be required to pay into the escrow account with each periodic payment during the first year after consummation, labeled "Monthly Escrow Payment."

(5) A creditor complies with the requirements of paragraphs (*l*)(7)(i)(A)(1) and (4) of this section if the creditor bases the numerical disclosures required by those paragraphs on amounts derived from the escrow account analysis required under Regulation X, 12 CFR 1024.17.

(B) A statement of whether the consumer will not have an escrow account, the reason why an escrow account will not be established, a statement that the consumer must pay all property costs, such as taxes and homeowner's insurance, directly, a statement that the consumer may contact the creditor to inquire about the availability of an escrow account, and a table, titled "No Escrow," that contains, if an escrow account will not be established, an itemization of the following:

(1) The estimated total amount the consumer will pay directly for the mortgage-related obligations described in § 1026.43(b)(8) during the first year after consummation that are known to the creditor and a statement that, without an escrow account, the consumer must pay the identified costs, possibly in one or two large payments, labeled "Property Costs over Year 1"; and

(2) The amount of any fee the creditor imposes on the consumer for not establishing an escrow account in connection with the transaction, labeled "Escrow Waiver Fee."

(ii) Under the reference "In the future":

(A) A statement that the consumer's property costs may change and that, as a result, the consumer's escrow payment may change;

(B) A statement that the consumer may be able to cancel any escrow account that has been established, but that the consumer is responsible for directly paying all property costs in the absence of an escrow account; and

(C) A description of the consequences if the consumer fails to pay property costs, including the actions that a State or local government may take if property taxes are not paid and the actions the creditor may take if the consumer does not pay some or all property costs, such as adding amounts to the loan balance, adding an escrow account to the loan, or purchasing a property insurance policy on the consumer's behalf that may be more expensive and provide fewer benefits than what the consumer could obtain directly.

(m) Adjustable payment table. Under the master heading "Additional Information About This Loan" required by paragraph (*l*) of this section, and under the heading "Adjustable Payment (AP) Table," the table required to be disclosed by § 1026.37(i).

(n) Adjustable interest rate table. Under the master heading "Additional Information About This Loan" required by paragraph (*l*) of this section, and under the heading "Adjustable Interest Rate (AIR) Table," the table required to be disclosed by § 1026.37(j).

(*o*) Loan calculations. In a separate table under the heading "Loan Calculations":

(1) Total of payments. The "Total of Payments," using that term and expressed as a dollar amount, and a statement that the disclosure is the total the consumer will have paid after making all payments of principal, interest, mortgage insurance, and loan costs, as scheduled. The disclosed total of payments shall be treated as accurate if the amount disclosed as the total of payments:

(i) Is understated by no more than $100; or

(ii) Is greater than the amount required to be disclosed.

(2) Finance charge. The "Finance Charge," using that term and expressed as a dollar amount, and the following statement: "The dollar amount the loan will cost you." The disclosed finance charge and other disclosures affected by the disclosed financed charge (including the amount financed and the annual percentage rate) shall be treated as accurate if the amount disclosed as the finance charge:

(i) Is understated by no more than $100; or

(ii) Is greater than the amount required to be disclosed.

(3) Amount financed. The "Amount Financed," using that term and expressed as a dollar amount, and the following statement: "The loan amount available after paying your upfront finance charge."

(4) Annual percentage rate. The "Annual Percentage Rate," using that term and the abbreviation "APR" and expressed as a percentage, and the following statement: "Your costs over the loan term expressed as a rate. This is not your interest rate."

(5) Total interest percentage. The "Total Interest Percentage," using that term and the abbreviation "TIP" and expressed as a percentage, and the following statement: "The total amount of interest that you will pay over the loan term as a percentage of your loan amount."

(p) Other disclosures. Under the heading "Other Disclosures":

(1) Appraisal. For transactions subject to 15 U.S.C. 1639h or 1691(e), as implemented in this part or Regulation B, 12 CFR part 1002, respectively, under the subheading "Appraisal," that:

(i) If there was an appraisal of the property in connection with the loan, the creditor is required to provide the consumer with a copy at no additional cost to the consumer at least three days prior to consummation; and

(ii) If the consumer has not yet received a copy of the appraisal, the consumer should contact the creditor using the information disclosed pursuant to paragraph (r) of this section.

(2) Contract details. A statement that the consumer should refer to the appropriate loan document and security instrument for information about nonpayment, what constitutes a default under the legal obligation, circumstances under which the creditor may accelerate the maturity of the obligation, and prepayment rebates and penalties, under the subheading "Contract Details."

(3) Liability after foreclosure. A brief statement of whether, and the conditions under which, the consumer may remain responsible for any deficiency after foreclosure under applicable

State law, a brief statement that certain protections may be lost if the consumer refinances or incurs additional debt on the property, and a statement that the consumer should consult an attorney for additional information, under the subheading "Liability after Foreclosure."

(4) Refinance. Under the subheading "Refinance," the statement required by § 1026.37(m)(5).

(5) Tax deductions. Under the subheading "Tax Deductions," a statement that, if the extension of credit exceeds the fair market value of the property, the interest on the portion of the credit extension that is greater than the fair market value of the property is not tax deductible for Federal income tax purposes and a statement that the consumer should consult a tax adviser for further information.

(q) Questions notice. In a separate notice labeled "Questions?":

(1) A statement directing the consumer to use the contact information disclosed under paragraph (r) of this section if the consumer has any questions about the disclosures required pursuant to § 1026.19(f);

(2) A reference to the Bureau's Web site to obtain more information or to submit a complaint; and the link or uniform resource locator address to the Web site: www.consumer finance.gov/mortgage-closing; and

(3) A prominent question mark.

(r) Contact information. In a separate table, under the heading "Contact Information," the following information for each creditor (under the subheading "Lender"), mortgage broker (under the subheading "Mortgage Broker"), consumer's real estate broker (under the subheading "Real Estate Broker (B)"), seller's real estate broker (under the subheading "Real Estate Broker (S)"), and settlement agent (under the subheading "Settlement Agent") participating in the transaction:

(1) Name of the person, labeled "Name";

(2) Address, using that label;

(3) Nationwide Mortgage Licensing System & Registry (NMLSR ID) identification number, labeled "NMLS ID," or, if none, license number or other unique identifier issued by the applicable jurisdiction or regulating body with which the person is licensed and/or registered, labeled "License ID," with the abbreviation for the State of the applicable jurisdiction or regulatory body stated before the word "License" in the label, for the persons identified in paragraph (r)(1) of this section;

(4) Name of the natural person who is the primary contact for the consumer with the person identified in paragraph (r)(1) of this section, labeled "Contact";

(5) NMLSR ID, labeled "Contact NMLS ID," or, if none, license number or other unique identifier issued by the applicable jurisdiction or regulating body with which the person is licensed and/or registered, labeled "Contact License ID," with the abbreviation for the State of the applicable jurisdiction or regulatory body stated before the word "License" in the label, for the natural person identified in paragraph (r)(4) of this section,

(6) Email address for the person identified in paragraph (r)(4) of this section, labeled "Email"; and

(7) Telephone number for the person identified in paragraph (r)(4) of this section, labeled "Phone."

(s) Signature statement.

(1) At the creditor's option, under the heading "Confirm Receipt," a line for the signatures of the consumers in the transaction. If the creditor provides a line for the consumer's signature, the creditor must disclose above the signature line the statement required to be disclosed under § 1026.37(n)(1).

(2) If the creditor does not provide a line for the consumer's signature, the statement required to be disclosed under § 1026.37(n)(2) under the heading "Other Disclosures" required by paragraph (p) of this section.

(t) Form of disclosures—

(1) General requirements.

(i) The creditor shall make the disclosures required by this section clearly and conspicuously in writing, in a form that the consumer may keep. The disclosures also shall be grouped together and segregated from everything else.

(ii) Except as provided in paragraph (t)(5), the disclosures shall contain only the information required by paragraphs (a) through (s) of this section and shall be made in the same order, and positioned relative to the master headings, headings, subheadings, labels, and similar designations in the same manner, as shown in form H-25, set forth in appendix H to this part.

(2) Headings and labels. If a master heading, heading, subheading, label, or similar designation contains the word "estimated" or a capital letter designation in form H-25, set forth in appendix H to this part, that heading, label, or similar designation shall contain the word "estimated" and the applicable capital letter designation.

(3) Form. Except as provided in paragraph (t)(5) of this section:

(i) For a transaction subject to § 1026.19(f) that is a federally related mortgage loan, as defined in Regulation X, 12 CFR 1024.2, the disclosures must be made using form H-25, set forth in appendix H to this part.

(ii) For any other transaction subject to this section, the disclosures must be made with headings, content, and format substantially similar to form H-25, set forth in appendix H to this part.

(iii) The disclosures required by this section may be provided to the consumer in electronic form, subject to compliance with the consumer consent and other applicable provisions of the Electronic Signatures in Global and National Commerce Act (15 U.S.C. 7001 et seq.).

(4) Rounding—

(i) Nearest dollar. The following dollar amounts are required to be rounded to the nearest whole dollar:

(A) The dollar amounts required to be disclosed by paragraph (b) of this section that are required to be rounded by § 1026.37(*o*)(4)(i)(A) when disclosed under § 1026.37(b)(6) and (7);

(B) The dollar amounts required to be disclosed by paragraph (c) of this section that are required to be rounded by § 1026.37(*o*)(4)(i)(A) when disclosed under § 1026.37(c)(1)(iii);

(C) The dollar amounts required to be disclosed by paragraphs (e) and (i) of this section under the subheading "Loan Estimate";

(D) The dollar amounts required to be disclosed by paragraph (m) of this section; and

(E) The dollar amounts required to be disclosed by paragraph (c) of this section that are required to be rounded by § 1026.37(*o*)(4)(i)(C) when disclosed under § 1026.37(c)(2)(iv).

(ii) Percentages. The percentage amounts required to be disclosed under paragraphs (b), (f)(1), (n), and (*o*)(4) and (5) of this section shall be disclosed by rounding the exact amounts to three decimal places and then dropping any trailing zeros to the right of the decimal point.

(iii) Loan amount. The dollar amount required to be disclosed by paragraph (b) of this section as required by § 1026.37(b)(1) shall be disclosed as an unrounded number, except that if the amount is a whole number then the amount disclosed shall be truncated at the decimal point.

(5) Exceptions—

(i) Unit-period. Wherever the form or this section uses "monthly" to describe the frequency of any payments or uses "month" to describe the applicable unit-period, the creditor shall substitute the appropriate term to reflect the fact that the transaction's terms provide for other than monthly periodic payments, such as bi-weekly or quarterly payments.

(ii) Lender credits. The amount required to be disclosed by paragraph (d)(1)(i)(D) of this section may be omitted from the form if the amount is zero.

(iii) Administrative information. The creditor may insert at the bottom of each page under the disclosures required by this section as illustrated by form H-25 of appendix H to this part, any administrative information, text, or codes that assist in identification of the form or the information disclosed on the form, provided that the space provided on form H-25 for any of the information required by this section is not altered.

(iv) Closing cost details—

(A) Additional line numbers. Line numbers provided on form H-25 of appendix H to this part for the disclosure of the information required by paragraphs (f)(1) through (3) and (g)(1) through (4) of this section that are not used may be deleted and the deleted line numbers added to the space provided for any other of those paragraphs as necessary to accommodate the disclosure of additional items.

(B) Two pages. To the extent that adding or deleting line numbers provided on form H-25 of appendix H to this part, as permitted by paragraph (t)(5)(iv)(A) of this section, does not accommodate an itemization of all information required to be disclosed by paragraphs (f) through (h) on one page, the information required to be disclosed by paragraphs (f) through (h) of this section may be disclosed on two pages, provided that the information required by paragraph (f) is disclosed on a page separate from the information required by paragraph (g). The information required by paragraph (g), if disclosed on a page separate from paragraph (f), shall be disclosed on the same page as the information required by paragraph (h).

(v) Separation of consumer and seller information. The creditor or settlement agent preparing the form may use form H-25 of appendix H to this part for the disclosure provided to both the consumer and the seller, with the following modifications to separate the information of the consumer and seller, as necessary:

(A) The information required to be disclosed by paragraphs (j) and (k) of this section may be disclosed on separate pages to the consumer and the seller, respectively, with the information required by the other paragraph left blank. The information disclosed to the consumer pursuant to paragraph (j) of this section must be disclosed on the same page as the information required by paragraph (i) of this section.

(B) The information required to be disclosed by paragraphs (f) and (g) of this section with respect to costs paid by the consumer may be left blank on the disclosure provided to the seller.

(C) The information required by paragraphs (a)(2), (a)(4)(iii), (a)(5), (b) through (d), (i), (*l*) through (p), (r) with respect to the creditor and mortgage broker, and (s)(2) of this section may be left blank on the disclosure provided to the seller.

(vi) Modified version of the form for a seller or third-party. The information required by paragraphs (a)(2), (a)(4)(iii), (a)(5), (b) through (d), (f), and (g) with respect to costs paid by the consumer, (i), (j), (*l*) through (p), (q)(1), and (r) with respect to the creditor and mortgage broker, and (s) of this section may be deleted from the form provided to the seller or a third-party, as illustrated by form H-25(I) of appendix H to this part.

(vii) Transaction without a seller. The following modifications to form H-25 of appendix H to this part may be made for a transaction that does not involve a seller or for simultaneous subordinate financing, and for which the alternative tables are disclosed under paragraphs (d)(2) and (e) of this section, as illustrated by form H-25(J) of appendix H to this part:

(A) The information required by paragraph (a)(4)(ii), and paragraphs (f), (g), and (h) of this section with respect to costs paid by the seller, may be deleted.

(B) A table under the master heading "Closing Cost Details" required by paragraph (f) of this section may be added with the heading "Payoffs and Payments" that itemizes the amounts of payments made at closing to other parties from the credit extended to the consumer or funds provided by the consumer in connection with the transaction, including designees of the consumer; the payees and a description of the purpose of such disbursements under the subheading "To"; and the total amount of such payments labeled "Total Payoffs and Payments."

(C) The tables required to be disclosed by paragraphs (j) and (k) of this section may be deleted.

(viii) Translation. The form may be translated into languages other than English, and creditors may modify form H-25 of appendix H to this part to the extent that translation prevents the headings, labels, designations, and required disclosure items under this section from fitting in the space provided on form H-25.

(ix) Customary recitals and information. An additional page may be attached to the form for the purpose of including customary recitals and information used locally in real estate settlements.

§ 1026.39. Mortgage Transfer Disclosures

(a) Scope. The disclosure requirements of this section apply to any covered person except as otherwise provided in this section. For purposes of this section:

(1) A "covered person" means any person, as defined in § 1026.2(a)(22), that becomes the owner of an existing mortgage loan by acquiring legal title to the debt obligation, whether through a purchase, assignment or other transfer, and who acquires more than one mortgage loan in any twelve-month period. For purposes of this section, a servicer of a mortgage loan shall not be treated as the owner of the obligation if the servicer holds title to the loan, or title is assigned to the servicer, solely for the administrative convenience of the servicer in servicing the obligation.

(2) A "mortgage loan" means:

(i) An open-end consumer credit transaction that is secured by the principal dwelling of a consumer; and

(ii) A closed-end consumer credit transaction secured by a dwelling or real property.

(b) Disclosure required. Except as provided in paragraph (c) of this section, each covered person is subject to the requirements of this section and shall mail or deliver the disclosures required by this section to the consumer on or before the 30th calendar day following the date of transfer.

(1) Form of disclosures. The disclosures required by this section shall be provided clearly and conspicuously in writing, in a form that the consumer may keep. The disclosures required by this section may be provided to the consumer in electronic form, subject to compliance with the consumer consent and other applicable provisions of the Electronic Signatures in Global and National Commerce Act (E-Sign Act) (15 U.S.C. 7001 et seq.).

(2) The date of transfer. For purposes of this section, the date of transfer to the covered person may, at the covered person's option, be either the date of acquisition recognized in the books and records of the acquiring party, or the date of transfer recognized in the books and records of the transferring party.

(3) Multiple consumers. If more than one consumer is liable on the obligation, a covered person may mail or deliver the disclosures to any consumer who is primarily liable.

(4) Multiple transfers. If a mortgage loan is acquired by a covered person and subsequently sold, assigned, or otherwise transferred to another covered person, a single disclosure may be provided on behalf of both covered persons if the disclosure satisfies the timing and content requirements applicable to each covered person.

(5) Multiple covered persons. If an acquisition involves multiple covered persons who jointly acquire the loan, a single disclosure must be provided on behalf of all covered persons.

(c) Exceptions. Notwithstanding paragraph (b) of this section, a covered person is not subject to the requirements of this section with respect to a particular mortgage loan if:

(1) The covered person sells, or otherwise transfers or assigns legal title to the mortgage loan on or before the 30th calendar day following the date that the covered person acquired the mortgage loan which shall be the date of transfer recognized for purposes of paragraph (b)(2) of this section;

(2) The mortgage loan is transferred to the covered person in connection with a repurchase agreement that obligates the transferor to repurchase the loan. However, if the transferor does not repurchase the loan, the covered person must provide the disclosures required by this section within 30 days after the date that the transaction is recognized as an acquisition on its books and records; or

(3) The covered person acquires only a partial interest in the loan and the party authorized to receive the consumer's notice of the right to rescind and resolve issues concerning the consumer's payments on the loan does not change as a result of the transfer of the partial interest.

(d) Content of required disclosures. The disclosures required by this section shall identify the mortgage loan that was sold, assigned or otherwise transferred, and state the following, except that the information required by paragraph (d)(5) of this section shall be stated only for a mortgage loan that is a closed-end consumer credit transaction secured by a dwelling or real property other than a reverse mortgage transaction subject to § 1026.33 of this part:

(1) The name, address, and telephone number of the covered person.

(i) If a single disclosure is provided on behalf of more than one covered person, the information required by this paragraph shall be provided for each of them unless paragraph (d)(1)(ii) of this section applies.

(ii) If a single disclosure is provided on behalf of more than one covered person and one of them has been authorized in accordance with paragraph (d)(3) of this section to receive the consumer's notice of the right to rescind and resolve issues concerning the consumer's payments on the loan, the information required by paragraph (d)(1) of this section may be provided only for that covered person.

(2) The date of transfer.

(3) The name, address and telephone number of an agent or party authorized to receive notice of the right to rescind and resolve issues concerning the consumer's payments on the loan. However, no information is required to be provided under this paragraph if the consumer can use the information provided under paragraph (d)(1) of this section for these purposes.

(4) Where transfer of ownership of the debt to the covered person is or may be recorded in public records, or, alternatively, that the transfer of ownership has not been recorded in public records at the time the disclosure is provided.

(5) Partial payment policy. Under the subheading "Partial Payment":

(i) If periodic payments that are less than the full amount due are accepted, a statement that the covered person, using the term "lender," may accept partial payments and apply such payments to the consumer's loan;

(ii) If periodic payments that are less than the full amount due are accepted but not applied to a consumer's loan until the consumer pays the remainder of the full amount due, a statement that the covered person, using the term "lender," may hold partial payments in a separate account until the consumer pays the remainder of the payment and then apply the full periodic payment to the consumer's loan;

(iii) If periodic payments that are less than the full amount due are not accepted, a statement that the covered person, using the term "lender," does not accept any partial payments; and

(iv) A statement that, if the loan is sold, the new covered person, using the term "lender," may have a different policy.

(e) Optional disclosures. In addition to the information required to be disclosed under paragraph (d) of this section, a covered person may, at its option, provide any other information regarding the transaction.

(f) Successor in interest. If, upon confirmation, a servicer provides a confirmed successor in interest who is not liable on the mortgage loan obligation with a written notice and acknowledgment form in accordance with Regulation X, § 1024.32(c)(1) of this chapter, the servicer is not required to provide to the confirmed successor in interest any written disclosure required by paragraph (b) of this section unless and until the confirmed successor in interest either assumes the mortgage loan obligation under State law or has provided the servicer an executed acknowledgment in accordance with Regulation X, § 1024.32(c)(1)(iv) of this chapter, that the confirmed successor in interest has not revoked.

§ 1026.40 [Former Section 226.5b]. Requirements for Home Equity Plans

The requirements of this section apply to open-end credit plans secured by the consumer's dwelling. For purposes of this section, an annual percentage rate is the annual percentage rate corresponding to the periodic rate as determined under § 1026.14(b).

(a) Form of disclosures—

(1) General. The disclosures required by paragraph (d) of this section shall be made clearly and conspicuously and shall be grouped together and segregated from all unrelated information. The disclosures may be provided on the application form or on a separate form. The disclosure described in paragraph (d)(4)(iii), the itemization of third-party fees described in paragraph (d)(8), and the variable-rate information described in paragraph (d)(12) of this section may be provided separately from the other required disclosures.

(2) Precedence of certain disclosures. The disclosures described in paragraph (d)(1) through (4)(ii) of this section shall precede the other required disclosures.

(3) For an application that is accessed by the consumer in electronic form, the disclosures required under this section may be provided to the consumer in electronic form on or with the application.

(b) Time of disclosures. The disclosures and brochure required by paragraphs (d) and (e) of this section shall be provided at the time an application is provided to the consumer. The disclosures and the brochure may be delivered or placed in the mail not later than three business days following receipt of a consumer's application in the case of applications contained in magazines or other publications, or when the application is received by telephone or through an intermediary agent or broker.

(c) Duties of third parties. Persons other than the creditor who provide applications to consumers for home equity plans must provide the brochure required under paragraph (e) of this section at the time an application is provided. If such persons have the disclosures required under paragraph (d) of this section for a creditor's home equity plan, they also shall provide the disclosures at such time. The disclosures and the brochure may be delivered or placed in the mail not later than three business days following receipt of a consumer's application in the case of applications contained in magazines or other publications, or when the application is received by telephone or through an intermediary agent or broker.

(d) Content of disclosures. The creditor shall provide the following disclosures, as applicable:

(1) Retention of information. A statement that the consumer should make or otherwise retain a copy of the disclosures.

(2) Conditions for disclosed terms.

(i) A statement of the time by which the consumer must submit an application to obtain specific terms disclosed and an identification of any disclosed term that is subject to change prior to opening the plan.

(ii) A statement that, if a disclosed term changes (other than a change due to fluctuations in the index in a variable-rate plan) prior to opening the plan and the consumer therefore elects not to open the plan, the consumer may receive a refund of all fees paid in connection with the application.

(3) Security interest and risk to home. A statement that the creditor will acquire a security interest in the consumer's dwelling and that loss of the dwelling may occur in the event of default.

(4) Possible actions by creditor.

(i) A statement that, under certain conditions, the creditor may terminate the plan and require payment of the outstanding balance in full in a single payment and impose fees upon termination; prohibit additional extensions of credit or reduce the credit limit; and, as specified in the initial agreement, implement certain changes in the plan.

(ii) A statement that the consumer may receive, upon request, information about the conditions under which such actions may occur.

(iii) In lieu of the disclosure required under paragraph (d)(4)(ii) of this section, a statement of such conditions.

(5) Payment terms. The payment terms of the plan. If different payment terms may apply to the draw and any repayment period, or if different payment terms may apply within either period, the disclosures shall reflect the different payment terms. The payment terms of the plan include:

(i) The length of the draw period and any repayment period.

(ii) An explanation of how the minimum periodic payment will be determined and the timing of the payments. If paying only the minimum periodic payments may not repay any of the principal or may repay less than the outstanding balance, a statement of this fact, as well as a statement that a balloon payment may result. A balloon payment results if paying the minimum periodic payments does not fully amortize the outstanding balance by a specified date or time, and the consumer must repay the entire outstanding balance at such time.

(iii) An example, based on a $10,000 outstanding balance and a recent annual percentage rate, showing the minimum periodic payment, any balloon payment, and the time it would take to repay the $10,000 outstanding balance if the consumer made only those payments and obtained no additional extensions of credit. For fixed-rate plans, a recent annual percentage rate is a rate that has been in effect under the plan within the twelve months preceding the date the disclosures are provided to the consumer. For variable-rate plans, a recent annual percentage rate is the most recent rate provided in the historical example described in paragraph (d)(12)(xi) of this section or a rate that has been in effect under the plan since the date of the most recent rate in the table.

(6) Annual percentage rate. For fixed-rate plans, a recent annual percentage rate imposed under the plan and a statement that the rate does not include costs other than interest. A recent annual percentage rate is a rate that has been in effect under the plan within the twelve months preceding the date the disclosures are provided to the consumer.

(7) Fees imposed by creditor. An itemization of any fees imposed by the creditor to open, use, or maintain the plan, stated as a dollar amount or percentage, and when such fees are payable.

(8) Fees imposed by third parties to open a plan. A good faith estimate, stated as a single dollar amount or range, of any fees that may be imposed by persons other than the creditor to open the plan, as well as a statement that the consumer may receive, upon request, a good faith itemization of such fees. In lieu of the statement, the itemization of such fees may be provided.

(9) Negative amortization. A statement that negative amortization may occur and that negative amortization increases the principal balance and reduces the consumer's equity in the dwelling.

(10) Transaction requirements. Any limitations on the number of extensions of credit and the amount of credit that may be obtained during any time period, as well as any minimum outstanding balance and minimum draw requirements, stated as dollar amounts or percentages.

(11) Tax implications. A statement that the consumer should consult a tax advisor regarding the deductibility of interest and charges under the plan.

(12) Disclosures for variable-rate plans. For a plan in which the annual percentage rate is variable, the following disclosures, as applicable:

(i) The fact that the annual percentage rate, payment, or term may change due to the variable-rate feature.

(ii) A statement that the annual percentage rate does not include costs other than interest.

(iii) The index used in making rate adjustments and a source of information about the index.

(iv) An explanation of how the annual percentage rate will be determined, including an explanation of how the index is adjusted, such as by the addition of a margin.

(v) A statement that the consumer should ask about the current index value, margin, discount or premium, and annual percentage rate.

(vi) A statement that the initial annual percentage rate is not based on the index and margin used to make later rate adjustments, and the period of time such initial rate will be in effect.

(vii) The frequency of changes in the annual percentage rate.

(viii) Any rules relating to changes in the index value and the annual percentage rate and resulting changes in the payment amount, including, for example, an explanation of payment limitations and rate carryover.

(ix) A statement of any annual or more frequent periodic limitations on changes in the annual percentage rate (or a statement that no annual limitation exists), as well as a statement of the maximum annual percentage rate that may be imposed under each payment option.

(x) The minimum periodic payment required when the maximum annual percentage rate for each payment option is in effect for a $10,000 outstanding balance, and a statement of the earliest date or time the maximum rate may be imposed.

(xi) An historical example, based on a $10,000 extension of credit, illustrating how annual percentage rates and payments would have been affected by index value changes implemented according to the terms of the plan. The historical example shall be based on the most recent 15 years of index values (selected for the same time period each year) and shall reflect all significant plan terms, such as negative amortization, rate carryover, rate discounts, and rate and payment limitations, that would have been affected by the index movement during the period.

(xii) A statement that rate information will be provided on or with each periodic statement.

(e) Brochure. The home equity brochure entitled "What You Should Know About Home Equity Lines of Credit" or a suitable substitute shall be provided.

(f) Limitations on home equity plans. No creditor may, by contract or otherwise:

(1) Change the annual percentage rate unless:

(i) Such change is based on an index that is not under the creditor's control; and

(ii) Such index is available to the general public.

(2) Terminate a plan and demand repayment of the entire outstanding balance in advance of the original term (except for reverse mortgage transactions that are subject to paragraph (f)(4) of this section) unless:

(i) There is fraud or material misrepresentation by the consumer in connection with the plan;

(ii) The consumer fails to meet the repayment terms of the agreement for any outstanding balance;

(iii) Any action or inaction by the consumer adversely affects the creditor's security for the plan, or any right of the creditor in such security; or

(iv) Federal law dealing with credit extended by a depository institution to its executive officers specifically requires that as a condition of the plan the credit shall become due and payable on demand, provided that the creditor includes such a provision in the initial agreement.

(3) Change any term, except that a creditor may:

(i) Provide in the initial agreement that it may prohibit additional extensions of credit or reduce the credit limit during any period in which the maximum annual percentage rate is reached. A creditor also may provide in the initial agreement that specified changes will occur if a specified event takes place (for example, that the annual percentage rate will increase a specified amount if the consumer leaves the creditor's employment).

(ii) Change the index and margin used under the plan if the original index is no longer available, the new index has an historical movement substantially similar to that of the original index, and the new index and margin would have resulted in an annual percentage rate substantially similar to the rate in effect at the time the original index became unavailable.

(iii) Make a specified change if the consumer specifically agrees to it in writing at that time.

(iv) Make a change that will unequivocally benefit the consumer throughout the remainder of the plan.

(v) Make an insignificant change to terms.

(vi) Prohibit additional extensions of credit or reduce the credit limit applicable to an agreement during any period in which:

(A) The value of the dwelling that secures the plan declines significantly below the dwelling's appraised value for purposes of the plan;

(B) The creditor reasonably believes that the consumer will be unable to fulfill the repayment obligations under the plan because of a material change in the consumer's financial circumstances;

(C) The consumer is in default of any material obligation under the agreement;

(D) The creditor is precluded by government action from imposing the annual percentage rate provided for in the agreement;

(E) The priority of the creditor's security interest is adversely affected by government action to the extent that the value of the security interest is less than 120 percent of the credit line; or

(F) The creditor is notified by its regulatory agency that continued advances constitute an unsafe and unsound practice.

(4) For reverse mortgage transactions that are subject to § 1026.33, terminate a plan and demand repayment of the entire outstanding balance in advance of the original term except:

(i) In the case of default;

(ii) If the consumer transfers title to the property securing the note;

(iii) If the consumer ceases using the property securing the note as the primary dwelling; or

(iv) Upon the consumer's death.

(g) Refund of fees. A creditor shall refund all fees paid by the consumer to anyone in connection with an application if any term required to be disclosed under paragraph (d) of this section changes (other than a change due to fluctuations in the index in a variable-rate plan) before the plan is opened and, as a result, the consumer elects not to open the plan.

(h) Imposition of nonrefundable fees. Neither a creditor nor any other person may impose a nonrefundable fee in connection with an application until three business days after the consumer receives the disclosures and brochure required under this section. If the disclosures and brochure are mailed to the consumer, the consumer is considered to have received them three business days after they are mailed.

§ 1026.41. Periodic statements for residential mortgage loans

(a) In general—

(1) Scope. This section applies to a closed-end consumer credit transaction secured by a dwelling, unless an exemption in paragraph (e) of this section applies. A closed-end consumer credit transaction secured by a dwelling is referred to as a mortgage loan for purposes of this section.

(2) Periodic statements. A servicer of a transaction subject to this section shall provide the consumer, for each billing cycle, a periodic statement meeting the requirements of paragraphs (b), (c), and (d) of this section. If a mortgage loan has a billing cycle shorter than a period of 31 days (for example, a bi-weekly billing cycle), a periodic statement covering an entire month may be used. For the purposes of this section, servicer includes the creditor, assignee, or servicer, as applicable. A creditor or assignee that does not currently own the mortgage loan or the mortgage servicing rights is not subject to the requirement in this section to provide a periodic statement.

(b) Timing of the periodic statement. The periodic statement must be delivered or placed in the mail within a reasonably prompt time after the payment due date or the end of any courtesy period provided for the previous billing cycle.

(c) Form of the periodic statement. The servicer must make the disclosures required by this section clearly and conspicuously in writing, or electronically if the consumer agrees, and in a form that the consumer may keep. Sample forms for periodic statements are provided in appendix H-30. Proper use of these forms complies with the requirements of this paragraph (c) and the layout requirements in paragraph (d) of this section.

(d) Content and layout of the periodic statement. The periodic statement required by this section shall include:

(1) Amount due. Grouped together in close proximity to each other and located at the top of the first page of the statement:

(i) The payment due date;

(ii) The amount of any late payment fee, and the date on which that fee will be imposed if payment has not been received; and

(iii) The amount due, shown more prominently than other disclosures on the page and, if the transaction has multiple payment options, the amount due under each of the payment options.

(2) Explanation of amount due. The following items, grouped together in close proximity to each other and located on the first page of the statement:

(i) The monthly payment amount, including a breakdown showing how much, if any, will be applied to principal, interest, and escrow and, if a mortgage loan has multiple payment options, a breakdown of each of the payment options along with information on whether the principal balance will increase, decrease, or stay the same for each option listed;

(ii) The total sum of any fees or charges imposed since the last statement; and

(iii) Any payment amount past due.

(3) Past Payment Breakdown. The following items, grouped together in close proximity to each other and located on the first page of the statement:

(i) The total of all payments received since the last statement, including a breakdown showing the amount, if any, that was applied to principal, interest, escrow, fees and charges, and the amount, if any, sent to any suspense or unapplied funds account; and

(ii) The total of all payments received since the beginning of the current calendar year, including a breakdown of that total showing the amount, if any, that was applied to principal, interest, escrow, fees and charges, and the amount, if any, currently held in any suspense or unapplied funds account.

(4) Transaction activity. A list of all the transaction activity that occurred since the last statement. For purposes of this paragraph (d)(4), transaction activity means any activity that causes a credit or debit to the amount currently due. This list must include the date of the transaction, a brief description of the transaction, and the amount of the transaction for each activity on the list.

(5) Partial payment information. If a statement reflects a partial payment that was placed in a suspense or unapplied funds account, information explaining what must be done for the funds to be applied. The information must be on the front page of the statement or, alternatively, may be included on a separate page enclosed with the periodic statement or in a separate letter.

(6) Contact information. A toll-free telephone number and, if applicable, an electronic mailing address that may be used by the consumer to obtain information about the consumer's account, located on the front page of the statement.

(7) Account information. The following information:

(i) The amount of the outstanding principal balance;

(ii) The current interest rate in effect for the mortgage loan;

(iii) The date after which the interest rate may next change;

(iv) The existence of any prepayment penalty, as defined in § 1026.32(b)(6)(i), that may be charged;

(v) The Web site to access either the Bureau list or the HUD list of homeownership counselors and counseling organizations and the HUD toll-free telephone number to access contact information for homeownership counselors or counseling organizations; and

(8) Delinquency information. If the consumer is more than 45 days delinquent, the following items, grouped together in close proximity to each other and located on the first page of the statement or, alternatively, on a separate page enclosed with the periodic statement or in a separate letter:

(i) The length of the consumer's delinquency;

(ii) A notification of possible risks, such as foreclosure, and expenses, that may be incurred if the delinquency is not cured;

(iii) An account history showing, for the previous six months or the period since the last time the account was current, whichever is shorter, the amount remaining past due from each billing cycle or, if any such payment was fully paid, the date on which it was credited as fully paid;

(iv) A notice indicating any loss mitigation program to which the consumer has agreed, if applicable;

(v) A notice of whether the servicer has made the first notice or filing required by applicable law for any judicial or non-judicial foreclosure process, if applicable;

(vi) The total payment amount needed to bring the account current; and

(vii) A reference to the homeownership counselor information disclosed pursuant to paragraph (d)(7)(v) of this section.

(e) Exemptions—

(1) Reverse mortgages. Reverse mortgage transactions, as defined by § 1026.33(a), are exempt from the requirements of this section.

(2) Timeshare plans. Transactions secured by consumers' interests in timeshare plans, as defined by 11 U.S.C. 101(53D), are exempt from the requirements of this section.

(3) Coupon books. The requirements of paragraph (a) of this section do not apply to fixed-rate loans if the servicer:

(i) Provides the consumer with a coupon book that includes on each coupon the information listed in paragraph (d)(1) of this section;

(ii) Provides the consumer with a coupon book that includes anywhere in the coupon book:

(A) The account information listed in paragraph (d)(7) of this section;

(B) The contact information for the servicer, listed in paragraph (d)(6) of this section; and

(C) Information on how the consumer can obtain the information listed in paragraph (e)(3)(iii) of this section;

(iii) Makes available upon request to the consumer by telephone, in writing, in person, or electronically, if the consumer consents, the information listed in paragraph (d)(2) through (5) of this section; and

(iv) Provides the consumer the information listed in paragraph (d)(8) of this section in writing, for any billing cycle during which the consumer is more than 45 days delinquent.

(4) Small servicers—

(i) Exemption. A creditor, assignee, or servicer is exempt from the requirements of this section for mortgage loans serviced by a small servicer.

(ii) Small servicer defined. A small servicer is a servicer that:

(A) Services, together with any affiliates, 5,000 or fewer mortgage loans, for all of which the servicer (or an affiliate) is the creditor or assignee;

(B) Is a Housing Finance Agency, as defined in 24 CFR 266.5; or

(C) Is a nonprofit entity that services 5,000 or fewer mortgage loans, including any mortgage loans serviced on behalf of associated nonprofit entities, for all of which the servicer or an associated nonprofit entity is the creditor. For purposes of this paragraph (e)(4)(ii)(C), the following definitions apply:

(1) The term "nonprofit entity" means an entity having a tax exemption ruling or determination letter from the Internal Revenue Service under section 501(c)(3) of the Internal Revenue Code of 1986 (26 U.S.C. 501(c)(3); 26 CFR 1.501(c)(3)–1), and;

(2) The term "associated nonprofit entities" means nonprofit entities that by agreement operate using a common name, trademark, or servicemark to further and support a common charitable mission or purpose.

(iii) Small servicer determination. In determining whether a servicer satisfies paragraph (e)(4)(ii)(A) of this section, the servicer is evaluated based on the mortgage loans serviced by the servicer and any affiliates as of January 1 and for the remainder of the calendar year. In determining whether a servicer satisfies paragraph (e)(4)(ii)(C) of this section, the servicer is evaluated based on the mortgage loans serviced by the servicer as of January 1 and for the remainder of the calendar year. A servicer that ceases to qualify as a small servicer will have six months from the time it ceases to qualify or until the next January 1, whichever is later, to comply with any requirements from which the servicer is no longer exempt as a small servicer. The following mortgage loans are not considered in determining whether a servicer qualifies as a small servicer:

(A) Mortgage loans voluntarily serviced by the servicer for a non-affiliate of the servicer and for which the servicer does not receive any compensation or fees.

(B) Reverse mortgage transactions.

(C) Mortgage loans secured by consumers' interests in timeshare plans.

(D) Transactions serviced by the servicer for a seller financer that meets all of the criteria identified in § 1026.36(a)(5).

(5) Certain consumers in bankruptcy—

(i) Exemption. Except as provided in paragraph (e)(5)(ii) of this section, a servicer is exempt from the requirements of this section with regard to a mortgage loan if:

(A) Any consumer on the mortgage loan is a debtor in bankruptcy under title 11 of the United States Code or has discharged personal liability for the mortgage loan pursuant to 11 U.S.C. 727, 1141, 1228, or 1328; and

(B) With regard to any consumer on the mortgage loan:

(1) The consumer requests in writing that the servicer cease providing a periodic statement or coupon book;

(2) The consumer's bankruptcy plan provides that the consumer will surrender the dwelling securing the mortgage loan, provides for the avoidance of the lien securing the mortgage loan, or otherwise does not provide for, as applicable, the payment of pre-bankruptcy arrearage or the maintenance of payments due under the mortgage loan;

(3) A court enters an order in the bankruptcy case providing for the avoidance of the lien securing the mortgage loan, lifting the automatic stay pursuant to 11 U.S.C. 362 with regard to the dwelling securing the mortgage loan, or requiring the servicer to cease providing a periodic statement or coupon book; or

(4) The consumer files with the court overseeing the bankruptcy case a statement of intention pursuant to 11 U.S.C. 521(a) identifying an intent to surrender the dwelling securing the mortgage loan and a consumer has not made any partial or periodic payment on the mortgage loan after the commencement of the consumer's bankruptcy case.

(ii) Reaffirmation or consumer request to receive statement or coupon book. A servicer ceases to qualify for an exemption pursuant to paragraph (e)(5)(i) of this section with respect to a mortgage loan if the consumer reaffirms personal liability for the loan or any consumer on the loan requests in writing that the servicer provide a periodic statement or coupon book, unless a court enters an order in the bankruptcy case requiring the servicer to cease providing a periodic statement or coupon book.

(iii) Exclusive address. A servicer may establish an address that a consumer must use to submit a written request under paragraph (e)(5)(i)(B)(1) or (e)(5)(ii) of this section, provided that the servicer notifies the consumer of the address in a manner that is reasonably designed to inform the consumer of the address. If a servicer designates a specific address for requests under paragraph (e)(5)(i)(B)(1) or (e)(5)(ii) of this section, the servicer shall designate the same address for purposes of both paragraphs (e)(5)(i)(B)(1) and (e)(5)(ii) of this section.

(iv) Timing of compliance following transition—

(A) Triggering events for transitioning to modified and unmodified periodic statements. A servicer transitions to providing a periodic statement or coupon book with the modifications set forth in paragraph (f) of this section or to providing a periodic statement or coupon book without such modifications when one of the following three events occurs:

(1) A mortgage loan becomes subject to the requirements of paragraph (f) of this section;

(2) A mortgage loan ceases to be subject to the requirements of paragraph (f) of this section; or

(3) A servicer ceases to qualify for an exemption pursuant to paragraph (e)(5)(i) of this section with respect to a mortgage loan.

(B) Single-statement exemption. As of the date on which one of the events listed in paragraph (e)(5)(iv)(A) of this section occurs, a servicer is exempt from the requirements of this section with respect to the next periodic statement or coupon book that would otherwise be required but thereafter must provide modified or unmodified periodic statements or coupon books that comply with the requirements of this section.

(6) Charged-off loans.

(i) A servicer is exempt from the requirements of this section for a mortgage loan if the servicer:

(A) Has charged off the loan in accordance with loan-loss provisions and will not charge any additional fees or interest on the account; and

(B) Provides, within 30 days of charge-off or the most recent periodic statement, a periodic statement, clearly and conspicuously labeled "Suspension of Statements & Notice of Charge Off—Retain This Copy for Your Records." The periodic statement must clearly and conspicuously explain that, as applicable, the mortgage loan has been charged off and the servicer will not charge any additional fees or interest on the account; the servicer will no longer provide the consumer a periodic statement for each billing cycle; the lien on the property remains in place and the consumer remains liable for the mortgage loan obligation and any obligations arising from or related to the property, which may include property taxes; the consumer may be required to pay the balance on the account in the future, for example, upon sale of the property; the balance on the account is not being canceled or forgiven; and the loan may be purchased, assigned, or transferred.

(ii) Resuming compliance.

(A) If a servicer fails at any time to treat a mortgage loan that is exempt under paragraph (e)(6)(i) of this section as charged off or charges any additional fees or interest on the account, the obligation to provide a periodic statement pursuant to this section resumes.

(B) Prohibition on retroactive fees. A servicer may not retroactively assess fees or interest on the account for the period of time during which the exemption in paragraph (e)(6)(i) of this section applied.

(f) Modified periodic statements and coupon books for certain consumers in bankruptcy. While any consumer on a mortgage loan is a debtor in bankruptcy under title 11 of the United States Code, or if such consumer has discharged personal liability for the mortgage loan pursuant to 11 U.S.C. 727, 1141, 1228, or 1328, the requirements of this section are subject to the following modifications with regard to that mortgage loan:

(1) Requirements not applicable. The periodic statement may omit the information set forth in paragraphs (d)(1)(ii) and (d)(8)(i), (ii), and (v) of this section. The requirement in paragraph (d)(1)(iii) of this section that the amount due must be shown more prominently than other disclosures on the page shall not apply.

(2) Bankruptcy notices. The periodic statement must include the following:

(i) A statement identifying the consumer's status as a debtor in bankruptcy or the discharged status of the mortgage loan; and

(ii) A statement that the periodic statement is for informational purposes only.

(3) Chapter 12 and chapter 13 consumers. In addition to any other provisions of this paragraph (f) that may apply, with regard to a mortgage loan for which any consumer with primary liability is a debtor in a chapter 12 or chapter 13 bankruptcy case, the requirements of this section are subject to the following modifications:

(i) Requirements not applicable. In addition to omitting the information set forth in paragraph (f)(1) of this section, the periodic statement may also omit the information set forth in paragraphs (d)(8)(iii), (iv), (vi), and (vii) of this section.

(ii) Amount due. The amount due information set forth in paragraph (d)(1) of this section may be limited to the date and amount of the post-petition payments due and any post-petition fees and charges imposed by the servicer.

(iii) Explanation of amount due. The explanation of amount due information set forth in paragraph (d)(2) of this section may be limited to:

(A) The monthly post-petition payment amount, including a breakdown showing how much, if any, will be applied to principal, interest, and escrow;

(B) The total sum of any post-petition fees or charges imposed since the last statement; and

(C) Any post-petition payment amount past due.

(iv) Transaction activity. The transaction activity information set forth in paragraph (d)(4) of this section must include all payments the servicer has received since the last statement, including all post-petition and pre-petition payments and payments of post-petition fees and charges, and all post-petition fees and charges the servicer has imposed since the last statement. The brief description of the activity need not identify the source of any payments.

(v) Pre-petition arrearage. If applicable, a servicer must disclose, grouped in close proximity to each other and located on the first page of the statement or, alternatively, on a separate page enclosed with the periodic statement or in a separate letter:

(A) The total of all pre-petition payments received since the last statement;

(B) The total of all pre-petition payments received since the beginning of the consumer's bankruptcy case; and

(C) The current balance of the consumer's pre-petition arrearage.

(vi) Additional disclosures. The periodic statement must include, as applicable:

(A) A statement that the amount due includes only post-petition payments and does not include other payments that may be due under the terms of the consumer's bankruptcy plan;

(B) If the consumer's bankruptcy plan requires the consumer to make the post-petition mortgage payments directly to a bankruptcy trustee, a statement that the consumer should send the payment to the trustee and not to the servicer;

(C) A statement that the information disclosed on the periodic statement may not include payments the consumer has made to the trustee and may not be consistent with the trustee's records;

(D) A statement that encourages the consumer to contact the consumer's attorney or the trustee with questions regarding the application of payments; and

(E) If the consumer is more than 45 days delinquent on post-petition payments, a statement that the servicer has not received all the payments that became due since the consumer filed for bankruptcy.

(4) Multiple obligors. If this paragraph (f) applies in connection with a mortgage loan with more than one primary obligor, the servicer may provide the modified statement to any or all of the primary obligors, even if a primary obligor to whom the servicer provides the modified statement is not a debtor in bankruptcy.

(5) Coupon books. A servicer that provides a coupon book instead of a periodic statement under paragraph (e)(3) of this section must include in the coupon book the disclosures set forth in paragraphs (f)(2) and (f)(3)(vi) of this section, as applicable. The servicer may include these disclosures anywhere in the coupon book provided to the consumer or on a separate page enclosed with the coupon book. The servicer must make available upon request to the consumer by telephone, in writing, in person, or electronically, if the consumer consents, the information listed in paragraph (f)(3)(v) of this section, as applicable. The modifications set forth in paragraphs (f)(1) and (f)(3)(i) through (iv) and (vi) of this section apply to a coupon book and other information a servicer provides to the consumer under paragraph (e)(3) of this section.

(g) Successor in interest. If, upon confirmation, a servicer provides a confirmed successor in interest who is not liable on the mortgage loan obligation with a written notice and acknowledgment form in accordance with Regulation X, § 1024.32(c)(1) of this chapter, the servicer is not required to provide to the confirmed successor in interest any written disclosure required by this section unless and until the confirmed successor in interest either assumes the mortgage loan obligation under State law or has provided the servicer an executed acknowledgment in accordance with Regulation X, § 1024.32(c)(1)(iv) of this chapter, that the confirmed successor in interest has not revoked.

§ 1026.42. Valuation Independence

(a) Scope. This section applies to any consumer credit transaction secured by the consumer's principal dwelling.

(b) Definitions. For purposes of this section:

(1) "Covered person" means a creditor with respect to a covered transaction or a person that provides "settlement services," as defined in 12 U.S.C. 2602(3) and implementing regulations, in connection with a covered transaction.

(2) "Covered transaction" means an extension of consumer credit that is or will be secured by the consumer's principal dwelling, as defined in § 1026.2(a)(19).

(3) "Valuation" means an estimate of the value of the consumer's principal dwelling in written or electronic form, other than one produced solely by an automated model or system.

(4) "Valuation management functions" means:

(i) Recruiting, selecting, or retaining a person to prepare a valuation;

(ii) Contracting with or employing a person to prepare a valuation;

(iii) Managing or overseeing the process of preparing a valuation, including by providing administrative services such as receiving orders for and receiving a valuation, submitting a completed valuation to creditors and underwriters, collecting fees from creditors and underwriters for services provided in connection with a valuation, and compensating a person that prepares valuations; or

(iv) Reviewing or verifying the work of a person that prepares valuations.

(c) Valuation of consumer's principal dwelling.

(1) Coercion. In connection with a covered transaction, no covered person shall or shall attempt to directly or indirectly cause the value assigned to the consumer's principal dwelling to be based on any factor other than the independent judgment of a person that prepares valuations, through coercion, extortion, inducement, bribery, or intimidation of, compensation or instruction to, or collusion with a person that prepares valuations or performs valuation management functions.

(i) Examples of actions that violate paragraph (c)(1) include:

(A) Seeking to influence a person that prepares a valuation to report a minimum or maximum value for the consumer's principal dwelling;

(B) Withholding or threatening to withhold timely payment to a person that prepares a valuation or performs valuation management functions because the person does not value the consumer's principal dwelling at or above a certain amount;

(C) Implying to a person that prepares valuations that current or future retention of the person depends on the amount at which the person estimates the value of the consumer's principal dwelling;

(D) Excluding a person that prepares a valuation from consideration for future engagement because the person reports a value for the consumer's principal dwelling that does not meet or exceed a predetermined threshold; and

(E) Conditioning the compensation paid to a person that prepares a valuation on consummation of the covered transaction.

(2) Mischaracterization of value.

(i) Misrepresentation. In connection with a covered transaction, no person that prepares valuations shall materially misrepresent the value of the consumer's principal dwelling in a valuation. A misrepresentation is material for purposes of this paragraph (c)(2)(i) if it is likely to significantly affect the value assigned to the consumer's principal dwelling. A bona fide error shall not be a misrepresentation.

(ii) Falsification or alteration. In connection with a covered transaction, no covered person shall falsify and no covered person other than a person that prepares valuations shall materially alter a valuation. An alteration is material for purposes of this paragraph (c)(2)(ii) if it is likely to significantly affect the value assigned to the consumer's principal dwelling.

(iii) Inducement of mischaracterization. In connection with a covered transaction, no covered person shall induce a person to violate paragraph (c)(2)(i) or (ii) of this section.

(3) Permitted actions. Examples of actions that do not violate paragraph (c)(1) or (c)(2) include:

(i) Asking a person that prepares a valuation to consider additional, appropriate property information, including information about comparable properties, to make or support a valuation;

(ii) Requesting that a person that prepares a valuation provide further detail, substantiation, or explanation for the person's conclusion about the value of the consumer's principal dwelling;

(iii) Asking a person that prepares a valuation to correct errors in the valuation;

(iv) Obtaining multiple valuations for the consumer's principal dwelling to select the most reliable valuation;

(v) Withholding compensation due to breach of contract or substandard performance of services; and

(vi) Taking action permitted or required by applicable Federal or state statute, regulation, or agency guidance.

(d) Prohibition on conflicts of interest.

(1)(i) In general. No person preparing a valuation or performing valuation management functions for a covered transaction may have a direct or indirect interest, financial or otherwise, in the property or transaction for which the valuation is or will be performed.

(ii) Employees and affiliates of creditors; providers of multiple settlement services. In any covered transaction, no person violates paragraph (d)(1)(i) of this section based solely on the fact that the person:

(A) Is an employee or affiliate of the creditor; or

(B) Provides a settlement service in addition to preparing valuations or performing valuation management functions, or based solely on the fact that the person's affiliate performs another settlement service.

(2) Employees and affiliates of creditors with assets of more than $250 million for both of the past two calendar years. For any covered transaction in which the creditor had assets of more than $250 million as of December 31st for both of the past two calendar years, a person subject to paragraph (d)(1)(i) of this section who is employed by or affiliated with the creditor does not have a conflict of interest in violation of paragraph (d)(1)(i) of this section based on the person's employment or affiliate relationship with the creditor if:

(i) The compensation of the person preparing a valuation or performing valuation management functions is not based on the value arrived at in any valuation;

(ii) The person preparing a valuation or performing valuation management functions reports to a person who is not part of the creditor's loan production function, as defined in paragraph (d)(5)(i) of this section, and whose compensation is not based on the closing of the transaction to which the valuation relates; and

(iii) No employee, officer or director in the creditor's loan production function, as defined in paragraph (d)(5)(i) of this section, is directly or indirectly involved in selecting, retaining, recommending or influencing the selection of the person to prepare a valuation or perform valuation management functions, or to be included in or excluded from a list of approved persons who prepare valuations or perform valuation management functions.

(3) Employees and affiliates of creditors with assets of $250 million or less for either of the past two calendar years. For any covered transaction in which the creditor had assets of $250 million or less as of December 31st for either of the past two calendar years, a person subject to paragraph (d)(1)(i) of this section who is employed by or affiliated with the creditor does not have a conflict of interest in violation of paragraph (d)(1)(i) of this section based on the person's employment or affiliate relationship with the creditor if:

(i) The compensation of the person preparing a valuation or performing valuation management functions is not based on the value arrived at in any valuation; and

(ii) The creditor requires that any employee, officer or director of the creditor who orders, performs, or reviews a valuation for a covered transaction abstain from participating in any decision to approve, not approve, or set the terms of that transaction.

(4) Providers of multiple settlement services. For any covered transaction, a person who prepares a valuation or performs valuation management functions in addition to performing another settlement service for the transaction, or whose affiliate performs another settlement service for the transaction, does not have a conflict of interest in violation of paragraph (d)(1)(i) of this section as a result of the person or the person's affiliate performing another settlement service for the transaction if:

(i) The creditor had assets of more than $250 million as of December 31st for both of the past two calendar years and the conditions in paragraph (d)(2)(i)–(iii) are met; or

(ii) The creditor had assets of $250 million or less as of December 31st for either of the past two calendar years and the conditions in paragraph (d)(3)(i)–(ii) are met.

(5) Definitions. For purposes of this paragraph (d), the following definitions apply:

(i) Loan production function. The term "loan production function" means an employee, officer, director, department, division, or other unit of a creditor with responsibility for generating covered transactions, approving covered transactions, or both.

(ii) Settlement service. The term "settlement service" has the same meaning as in the Real Estate Settlement Procedures Act, 12 U.S.C. 2601 et seq.

(iii) Affiliate. The term "affiliate" has the same meaning as in Regulation Y of the Board of Governors of the Federal Reserve System, 12 CFR 225.2(a).

(e) When extension of credit prohibited. In connection with a covered transaction, a creditor that knows, at or before consummation, of a violation of paragraph (c) or (d) of this section in connection with a valuation shall not extend credit based on the valuation, unless the creditor documents that it has acted with reasonable diligence to determine that the valuation does not materially misstate or misrepresent the value of the consumer's principal dwelling. For purposes of this paragraph (e), a valuation materially misstates or misrepresents the value of the consumer's principal dwelling if the valuation contains a misstatement or misrepresentation that affects the credit decision or the terms on which credit is extended.

(f) Customary and reasonable compensation.

(1) Requirement to provide customary and reasonable compensation to fee appraisers. In any covered transaction, the creditor and its agents shall compensate a fee appraiser for performing appraisal services at a rate that is customary and reasonable for comparable appraisal services performed in the geographic market of the property being appraised. For purposes of paragraph (f) of this section, "agents" of the creditor do not include any fee appraiser as defined in paragraph (f)(4)(i) of this section.

(2) Presumption of compliance. A creditor and its agents shall be presumed to comply with paragraph (f)(1) of this section if:

(i) The creditor or its agents compensate the fee appraiser in an amount that is reasonably related to recent rates paid for comparable appraisal services performed in the geographic market of the property being appraised. In determining this amount, a creditor or its agents shall review the factors below and make any adjustments to recent rates paid in the relevant geographic market necessary to ensure that the amount of compensation is reasonable:

(A) The type of property,

(B) The scope of work,

(C) The time in which the appraisal services are required to be performed,

(D) Fee appraiser qualifications,

(E) Fee appraiser experience and professional record, and

(F) Fee appraiser work quality; and

(ii) The creditor and its agents do not engage in any anticompetitive acts in violation of state or Federal law that affect the compensation paid to fee appraisers, including:

(A) Entering into any contracts or engaging in any conspiracies to restrain trade through methods such as price fixing or market allocation, as prohibited under section 1 of the Sherman Antitrust Act, 15 U.S.C. 1, or any other relevant antitrust laws; or

(B) Engaging in any acts of monopolization such as restricting any person from entering the relevant geographic market or causing any person to leave the relevant geographic market, as prohibited under section 2 of the Sherman Antitrust Act, 15 U.S.C. 2, or any other relevant antitrust laws.

(3) Alternative presumption of compliance. A creditor and its agents shall be presumed to comply with paragraph (f)(1) of this section if the creditor or its agents determine the amount of compensation paid to the fee appraiser by relying on information about rates that:

(i) Is based on objective third-party information, including fee schedules, studies, and surveys prepared by independent third parties such as government agencies, academic institutions, and private research firms;

(ii) Is based on recent rates paid to a representative sample of providers of appraisal services in the geographic market of the property being appraised or the fee schedules of those providers; and

(iii) In the case of information based on fee schedules, studies, and surveys, such fee schedules, studies, or surveys, or the information derived therefrom, excludes compensation paid to fee appraisers for appraisals ordered by appraisal management companies, as defined in paragraph (f)(4)(iii) of this section.

(4) Definitions. For purposes of this paragraph (f), the following definitions apply:

(i) Fee appraiser. The term "fee appraiser" means:

(A) A natural person who is a state-licensed or state-certified appraiser and receives a fee for performing an appraisal, but who is not an employee of the person engaging the appraiser; or

(B) An organization that, in the ordinary course of business, employs state-licensed or state-certified appraisers to perform appraisals, receives a fee for performing appraisals, and is not subject to the requirements of section 1124 of the Financial Institutions Reform, Recovery, and Enforcement Act of 1989 (12 U.S.C. 3353).

(ii) Appraisal services. The term "appraisal services" means the services required to perform an appraisal, including defining the scope of work, inspecting the property, reviewing necessary and appropriate public and private data sources (for example, multiple listing services, tax assessment records and public land records), developing and rendering an opinion of value, and preparing and submitting the appraisal report.

(iii) Appraisal management company. The term "appraisal management company" means any person authorized to perform one or more of the following actions on behalf of the creditor:

(A) Recruit, select, and retain fee appraisers;

(B) Contract with fee appraisers to perform appraisal services;

(C) Manage the process of having an appraisal performed, including providing administrative services such as receiving appraisal orders and appraisal reports, submitting completed appraisal reports to creditors and underwriters, collecting fees from creditors and underwriters for services provided, and compensating fee appraisers for services performed; or

(D) Review and verify the work of fee appraisers.

(g) Mandatory reporting.

(1) Reporting required. Any covered person that reasonably believes an appraiser has not complied with the Uniform Standards of Professional Appraisal Practice or ethical or professional requirements for appraisers under applicable state or Federal statutes or regulations shall refer the matter to the appropriate state agency if the failure to comply is material. For purposes of this paragraph (g)(1), a failure to comply is material if it is likely to significantly affect the value assigned to the consumer's principal dwelling.

(2) Timing of reporting. A covered person shall notify the appropriate state agency within a reasonable period of time after the person determines that there is a reasonable basis to believe that a failure to comply required to be reported under paragraph (g)(1) of this section has occurred.

(3) Definition. For purposes of this paragraph (g), "state agency" means "state appraiser certifying and licensing agency" under 12 U.S.C. 3350(1) and any implementing regulations. The appropriate state agency to which a covered person must refer a matter under paragraph (g)(1) of this section is the agency for the state in which the consumer's principal dwelling is located.

(h) The Bureau issued a joint rule to implement the appraisal management company minimum requirements in the Financial Institutions Reform, Recovery, and Enforcement Act, as amended by section 1473 of the Dodd-Frank Wall Street Reform and Consumer Protection Act. See 12 CFR part 34.

§ 1026.43. Minimum Standards for Transactions Secured by a Dwelling

(a) Scope. This section applies to any consumer credit transaction that is secured by a dwelling, as defined in § 1026.2(a)(19), including any real property attached to a dwelling, other than:

(1) A home equity line of credit subject to § 1026.40;

(2) A mortgage transaction secured by a consumer's interest in a timeshare plan, as defined in 11 U.S.C. 101(53(D)); or

(3) For purposes of paragraphs (c) through (f) of this section:

(i) A reverse mortgage subject to § 1026.33;

(ii) A temporary or "bridge" loan with a term of 12 months or less, such as a loan to finance the purchase of a new dwelling where the consumer plans to sell a current dwelling within 12 months or a loan to finance the initial construction of a dwelling; or

(iii) A construction phase of 12 months or less of a construction-to-permanent loan.

(iv) An extension of credit made pursuant to a program administered by a Housing Finance Agency, as defined under 24 CFR 266.5;

(v) An extension of credit made by:

(A) A creditor designated as a Community Development Financial Institution, as defined under 12 CFR 1805.104(h);

(B) A creditor designated as a Downpayment Assistance through Secondary Financing Provider, pursuant to 24 CFR 200.194(a), operating in accordance with regulations prescribed by the U.S. Department of Housing and Urban Development applicable to such persons;

(C) A creditor designated as a Community Housing Development Organization provided that the creditor has entered into a commitment with a participating jurisdiction and is undertaking a project under the HOME program, pursuant to the provisions of 24 CFR 92.300(a), and as the terms community housing development organization, commitment, participating jurisdiction, and project are defined under 24 CFR 92.2; or

(D) A creditor with a tax exemption ruling or determination letter from the Internal Revenue Service under section 501(c)(3) of the Internal Revenue Code of 1986 (26 U.S.C. 501(c)(3); 26 CFR 1.501(c)(3)–1), provided that:

(1) During the calendar year preceding receipt of the consumer's application, the creditor extended credit secured by a dwelling no more than 200 times, except as provided in paragraph (a)(3)(vii) of this section;

(2) During the calendar year preceding receipt of the consumer's application, the creditor extended credit secured by a dwelling only to consumers with income that did not exceed the low- and moderate-income household limit as established pursuant to section 102 of the Housing and Community Development Act of 1974 (42 U.S.C. 5302(a)(20)) and amended from time to time by the U.S. Department of Housing and Urban Development, pursuant to 24 CFR 570.3;

(3) The extension of credit is to a consumer with income that does not exceed the household limit specified in paragraph (a)(3)(v)(D)(2) of this section; and

(4) The creditor determines, in accordance with written procedures, that the consumer has a reasonable ability to repay the extension of credit.

(vi) An extension of credit made pursuant to a program authorized by sections 101 and 109 of the Emergency Economic Stabilization Act of 2008 (12 U.S.C. 5211; 5219);

(vii) Consumer credit transactions that meet the following criteria are not considered in determining whether a creditor exceeds the credit extension limitation in paragraph (a)(3)(v)(D)(1) of this section:

(A) The transaction is secured by a subordinate lien;

(B) The transaction is for the purpose of:

(1) Downpayment, closing costs, or other similar home buyer assistance, such as principal or interest subsidies;

(2) Property rehabilitation assistance;

(3) Energy efficiency assistance; or

(4) Foreclosure avoidance or prevention;

(C) The credit contract does not require payment of interest;

(D) The credit contract provides that repayment of the amount of the credit extended is:

(1) Forgiven either incrementally or in whole, at a date certain, and subject only to specified ownership and occupancy conditions, such as a requirement that the consumer maintain the property as the consumer's principal dwelling for five years;

(2) Deferred for a minimum of 20 years after consummation of the transaction;

(3) Deferred until sale of the property securing the transaction; or

(4) Deferred until the property securing the transaction is no longer the principal dwelling of the consumer;

(E) The total of costs payable by the consumer in connection with the transaction at consummation is less than 1 percent of the amount of credit extended and includes no charges other than:

(1) Fees for recordation of security instruments, deeds, and similar documents;

(2) A bona fide and reasonable application fee; and

(3) A bona fide and reasonable fee for housing counseling services; and

(F) The creditor complies with all other applicable requirements of this part in connection with the transaction.

(b) Definitions. For purposes of this section:

(1) Covered transaction means a consumer credit transaction that is secured by a dwelling, as defined in § 1026.2(a)(19), including any real property attached to a dwelling, other than a transaction exempt from coverage under paragraph (a) of this section.

(2) Fully amortizing payment means a periodic payment of principal and interest that will fully repay the loan amount over the loan term.

(3) Fully indexed rate means the interest rate calculated using the index or formula that will apply after recast, as determined at the time of consummation, and the maximum margin that can apply at any time during the loan term.

(4) Higher-priced covered transaction means a covered transaction with an annual percentage rate that exceeds the average prime offer rate for a comparable transaction as of the date the interest rate is set by 1.5 or more percentage points for a first-lien covered transaction, other than a qualified mortgage under paragraph (e)(5), (e)(6), or (f) of this section; by 3.5 or more percentage points for a first-lien covered transaction that is a qualified mortgage under paragraph (e)(5), (e)(6), or (f) of this section; or by 3.5 or more percentage points for a subordinate-lien covered transaction.

(5) Loan amount means the principal amount the consumer will borrow as reflected in the promissory note or loan contract.

(6) Loan term means the period of time to repay the obligation in full.

(7) Maximum loan amount means the loan amount plus any increase in principal balance that results from negative amortization, as defined in § 1026.18(s)(7)(v), based on the terms of the legal obligation assuming:

(i) The consumer makes only the minimum periodic payments for the maximum possible time, until the consumer must begin making fully amortizing payments; and

(ii) The maximum interest rate is reached at the earliest possible time.

(8) Mortgage-related obligations mean property taxes; premiums and similar charges identified in § 1026.4(b)(5), (7), (8), and (10) that are required by the creditor; fees and special assessments imposed by a condominium, cooperative, or homeowners association; ground rent; and leasehold payments.

(9) Points and fees has the same meaning as in § 1026.32(b)(1).

(10) Prepayment penalty has the same meaning as in § 1026.32(b)(6).

(11) Recast means:

(i) For an adjustable-rate mortgage, as defined in § 1026.18(s)(7)(i), the expiration of the period during which payments based on the introductory fixed interest rate are permitted under the terms of the legal obligation;

(ii) For an interest-only loan, as defined in § 1026.18(s)(7)(iv), the expiration of the period during which interest-only payments are permitted under the terms of the legal obligation; and

(iii) For a negative amortization loan, as defined in § 1026.18(s)(7)(v), the expiration of the period during which negatively amortizing payments are permitted under the terms of the legal obligation.

(12) Simultaneous loan means another covered transaction or home equity line of credit subject to § 1026.40 that will be secured by the same dwelling and made to the same consumer at or before consummation of the covered transaction or, if to be made after consummation, will cover closing costs of the first covered transaction.

(13) Third-party record means:

(i) A document or other record prepared or reviewed by an appropriate person other than the consumer, the creditor, or the mortgage broker, as defined in § 1026.36(a)(2), or an agent of the creditor or mortgage broker;

(ii) A copy of a tax return filed with the Internal Revenue Service or a State taxing authority;

(iii) A record the creditor maintains for an account of the consumer held by the creditor; or

(iv) If the consumer is an employee of the creditor or the mortgage broker, a document or other record maintained by the creditor or mortgage broker regarding the consumer's employment status or employment income.

(c) Repayment ability—

(1) General requirement. A creditor shall not make a loan that is a covered transaction unless the creditor makes a reasonable and good faith determination at or before consummation that the consumer will have a reasonable ability to repay the loan according to its terms.

(2) Basis for determination. Except as provided otherwise in paragraphs (d), (e), and (f) of this section, in making the repayment ability determination required under paragraph (c)(1) of this section, a creditor must consider the following:

(i) The consumer's current or reasonably expected income or assets, other than the value of the dwelling, including any real property attached to the dwelling, that secures the loan;

(ii) If the creditor relies on income from the consumer's employment in determining repayment ability, the consumer's current employment status;

(iii) The consumer's monthly payment on the covered transaction, calculated in accordance with paragraph (c)(5) of this section;

(iv) The consumer's monthly payment on any simultaneous loan that the creditor knows or has reason to know will be made, calculated in accordance with paragraph (c)(6) of this section;

(v) The consumer's monthly payment for mortgage-related obligations;

(vi) The consumer's current debt obligations, alimony, and child support;

(vii) The consumer's monthly debt-to-income ratio or residual income in accordance with paragraph (c)(7) of this section; and

(viii) The consumer's credit history.

(3) Verification using third-party records. A creditor must verify the information that the creditor relies on in determining a consumer's repayment ability under § 1026.43(c)(2) using reasonably reliable third-party records, except that:

(i) For purposes of paragraph (c)(2)(i) of this section, a creditor must verify a consumer's income or assets that the creditor relies on in accordance with § 1026.43(c)(4);

(ii) For purposes of paragraph (c)(2)(ii) of this section, a creditor may verify a consumer's employment status orally if the creditor prepares a record of the information obtained orally; and

(iii) For purposes of paragraph (c)(2)(vi) of this section, if a creditor relies on a consumer's credit report to verify a consumer's current debt obligations and a consumer's application states a current debt obligation not shown in the consumer's credit report, the creditor need not independently verify such an obligation.

(4) Verification of income or assets. A creditor must verify the amounts of income or assets that the creditor relies on under § 1026.43(c)(2)(i) to determine a consumer's ability to repay a covered transaction using third-party records that provide reasonably reliable evidence of the consumer's income or assets. A creditor may verify the consumer's income using a tax-return transcript issued by the Internal Revenue Service (IRS). Examples of other records the creditor may use to verify the consumer's income or assets include:

(i) Copies of tax returns the consumer filed with the IRS or a State taxing authority;

(ii) IRS Form W-2s or similar IRS forms used for reporting wages or tax withholding;

(iii) Payroll statements, including military Leave and Earnings Statements;

(iv) Financial institution records;

(v) Records from the consumer's employer or a third party that obtained information from the employer;

(vi) Records from a Federal, State, or local government agency stating the consumer's income from benefits or entitlements;

(vii) Receipts from the consumer's use of check cashing services; and

(viii) Receipts from the consumer's use of a funds transfer service.

(5) Payment calculation—

(i) General rule. Except as provided in paragraph (c)(5)(ii) of this section, a creditor must make the consideration required under paragraph (c)(2)(iii) of this section using:

(A) The fully indexed rate or any introductory interest rate, whichever is greater; and

(B) Monthly, fully amortizing payments that are substantially equal.

(ii) Special rules for loans with a balloon payment, interest-only loans, and negative amortization loans. A creditor must make the consideration required under paragraph (c)(2)(iii) of this section for:

(A) A loan with a balloon payment, as defined in § 1026.18(s)(5)(i), using:

(1) The maximum payment scheduled during the first five years after the date on which the first regular periodic payment will be due for a loan that is not a higher-priced covered transaction; or

(2) The maximum payment in the payment schedule, including any balloon payment, for a higher-priced covered transaction;

(B) An interest-only loan, as defined in § 1026.18(s)(7)(iv), using:

(1) The fully indexed rate or any introductory interest rate, whichever is greater; and

(2) Substantially equal, monthly payments of principal and interest that will repay the loan amount over the term of the loan remaining as of the date the loan is recast.

(C) A negative amortization loan, as defined in § 1026.18(s)(7)(v), using:

(1) The fully indexed rate or any introductory interest rate, whichever is greater; and

(2) Substantially equal, monthly payments of principal and interest that will repay the maximum loan amount over the term of the loan remaining as of the date the loan is recast.

(6) Payment calculation for simultaneous loans. For purposes of making the evaluation required under paragraph (c)(2)(iv) of this section, a creditor must consider, taking into account any mortgage-related obligations, a consumer's payment on a simultaneous loan that is:

(i) A covered transaction, by following paragraph (c)(5)of this section; or

(ii) A home equity line of credit subject to § 1026.40, by using the periodic payment required under the terms of the plan and the amount of credit to be drawn at or before consummation of the covered transaction.

(7) Monthly debt-to-income ratio or residual income—

(i) Definitions. For purposes of this paragraph (c)(7), the following definitions apply:

(A) Total monthly debt obligations. The term total monthly debt obligations means the sum of: the payment on the covered transaction, as required to be calculated by paragraphs (c)(2)(iii) and (c)(5) of this section; simultaneous loans, as required by paragraphs (c)(2)(iv) and (c)(6) of this section; mortgage-related obligations, as required by paragraph (c)(2)(v) of this section; and current debt obligations, alimony, and child support, as required by paragraph (c)(2)(vi) of this section.

(B) Total monthly income. The term total monthly income means the sum of the consumer's current or reasonably expected income, including any income from assets, as required by paragraphs (c)(2)(i) and (c)(4) of this section.

(ii) Calculations—

(A) Monthly debt-to-income ratio. If a creditor considers the consumer's monthly debt-to-income ratio under paragraph (c)(2)(vii) of this section, the creditor must consider the ratio of the consumer's total monthly debt obligations to the consumer's total monthly income.

(B) Monthly residual income. If a creditor considers the consumer's monthly residual income under paragraph (c)(2)(vii) of this section, the creditor must consider the consumer's remaining income after subtracting the consumer's total monthly debt obligations from the consumer's total monthly income.

(d) Refinancing of non-standard mortgages—

(1) Definitions. For purposes of this paragraph (d), the following definitions apply:

(i) Non-standard mortgage. The term non-standard mortgage means a covered transaction that is:

(A) An adjustable-rate mortgage, as defined in § 1026.18(s)(7)(i), with an introductory fixed interest rate for a period of one year or longer;

(B) An interest-only loan, as defined in § 1026.18(s)(7)(iv); or

(C) A negative amortization loan, as defined in § 1026.18(s)(7)(v).

(ii) Standard mortgage. The term standard mortgage means a covered transaction:

(A) That provides for regular periodic payments that do not:

(1) Cause the principal balance to increase;

(2) Allow the consumer to defer repayment of principal; or

(3) Result in a balloon payment, as defined in § 1026.18(s)(5)(i);

(B) For which the total points and fees payable in connection with the transaction do not exceed the amounts specified in paragraph (e)(3) of this section;

(C) For which the term does not exceed 40 years;

(D) For which the interest rate is fixed for at least the first five years after consummation; and

(E) For which the proceeds from the loan are used solely for the following purposes:

(1) To pay off the outstanding principal balance on the non-standard mortgage; and

(2) To pay closing or settlement charges required to be disclosed under the Real Estate Settlement Procedures Act, 12 U.S.C. 2601 et seq.

(iii) Refinancing. The term refinancing has the same meaning as in § 1026.20(a).

(2) Scope. The provisions of this paragraph (d) apply to the refinancing of a non-standard mortgage into a standard mortgage when the following conditions are met:

(i) The creditor for the standard mortgage is the current holder of the existing non-standard mortgage or the servicer acting on behalf of the current holder;

(ii) The monthly payment for the standard mortgage is materially lower than the monthly payment for the non-standard mortgage, as calculated under paragraph (d)(5) of this section.

(iii) The creditor receives the consumer's written application for the standard mortgage no later than two months after the non-standard mortgage has recast.

(iv) The consumer has made no more than one payment more than 30 days late on the non-standard mortgage during the 12 months immediately preceding the creditor's receipt of the consumer's written application for the standard mortgage.

(v) The consumer has made no payments more than 30 days late during the six months immediately preceding the creditor's receipt of the consumer's written application for the standard mortgage; and

(vi) If the non-standard mortgage was consummated on or after January 10, 2014, the non-standard mortgage was made in accordance with paragraph (c) or (e) of this section, as applicable.

(3) Exemption from repayment ability requirements. A creditor is not required to comply with the requirements of paragraph (c) of this section if:

(i) The conditions in paragraph (d)(2) of this section are met; and

(ii) The creditor has considered whether the standard mortgage likely will prevent a default by the consumer on the non-standard mortgage once the loan is recast.

(4) Offer of rate discounts and other favorable terms. A creditor making a covered transaction under this paragraph (d) may offer to the consumer rate discounts and terms that are the same as, or better than, the rate discounts and terms that the creditor offers to new consumers, consistent with the creditor's documented underwriting practices and to the extent not prohibited by applicable State or Federal law.

(5) Payment calculations. For purposes of determining whether the consumer's monthly payment for a standard mortgage will be materially lower than the monthly payment for the non-standard mortgage, the following provisions shall be used:

(i) Non-standard mortgage. For purposes of the comparison conducted pursuant to paragraph (d)(2)(ii) of this section, the creditor must calculate the monthly payment for a non-standard mortgage based on substantially equal, monthly, fully amortizing payments of principal and interest using:

(A) The fully indexed rate as of a reasonable period of time before or after the date on which the creditor receives the consumer's written application for the standard mortgage;

(B) The term of the loan remaining as of the date on which the recast occurs, assuming all scheduled payments have been made up to the recast date and the payment due on the recast date is made and credited as of that date; and

(C) A remaining loan amount that is:

(1) For an adjustable-rate mortgage under paragraph (d)(1)(i)(A) of this section, the outstanding principal balance as of the date of the recast, assuming all scheduled payments have been made up to the recast date and the payment due on the recast date is made and credited as of that date;

(2) For an interest-only loan under paragraph (d)(1)(i)(B) of this section, the outstanding principal balance as of the date of the recast, assuming all scheduled payments have been made up to the recast date and the payment due on the recast date is made and credited as of that date; or

(3) For a negative amortization loan under paragraph (d)(1)(i)(C) of this section, the maximum loan amount, determined after adjusting for the outstanding principal balance.

(ii) Standard mortgage. For purposes of the comparison conducted pursuant to paragraph (d)(2)(ii) of this section, the monthly payment for a standard mortgage must be based on substantially equal, monthly, fully amortizing payments based on the maximum interest rate that may apply during the first five years after consummation.

(e) Qualified mortgages—

(1) Safe harbor and presumption of compliance—

(i) Safe harbor for loans that are not higher-priced covered transactions. A creditor or assignee of a qualified mortgage, as defined in paragraphs (e)(2), (e)(4), (e)(5), (e)(6), or (f) of this section, that is not a higher-priced covered transaction, as defined in paragraph (b)(4) of this section, complies with the repayment ability requirements of paragraph (c) of this section.

(ii) Presumption of compliance for higher-priced covered transactions.

(A) A creditor or assignee of a qualified mortgage, as defined in paragraph (e)(2), (e)(4), (e)(5), (e)(6), or (f) of this section, that is a higher-priced covered transaction, as defined in paragraph (b)(4) of this section, is presumed to comply with the repayment ability requirements of paragraph (c) of this section.

(B) To rebut the presumption of compliance described in paragraph (e)(1)(ii)(A) of this section, it must be proven that, despite meeting the prerequisites of paragraph (e)(2), (e)(4), (e)(5), (e)(6), or (f) of this section, the creditor did not make a reasonable and good faith determination of the consumer's repayment ability at the time of consummation, by showing that the consumer's income, debt obligations, alimony, child support, and the consumer's monthly payment (including mortgage-related obligations) on the covered transaction and on any simultaneous loans of which the creditor was aware at consummation would leave the consumer with insufficient residual income or assets other than the value of the dwelling (including any real property attached to the dwelling) that secures the loan with which to meet living expenses, including any recurring and material non-debt obligations of which the creditor was aware at the time of consummation.

(2) Qualified mortgage defined—general. Except as provided in paragraph (e)(4), (e)(5), (e)(6), or (f) of this section, a qualified mortgage is a covered transaction:

(i) That provides for regular periodic payments that are substantially equal, except for the effect that any interest rate change after consummation has on the payment in the case of an adjustable-rate or step-rate mortgage, that do not:

(A) Result in an increase of the principal balance;

(B) Allow the consumer to defer repayment of principal, except as provided in paragraph (f) of this section; or

(C) Result in a balloon payment, as defined in § 1026.18(s)(5)(i), except as provided in paragraph (f) of this section;

(ii) For which the loan term does not exceed 30 years;

(iii) For which the total points and fees payable in connection with the loan do not exceed the amounts specified in paragraph (e)(3) of this section;

(iv) For which the creditor underwrites the loan, taking into account the monthly payment for mortgage-related obligations, using:

(A) The maximum interest rate that may apply during the first five years after the date on which the first regular periodic payment will be due; and

(B) Periodic payments of principal and interest that will repay either:

(1) The outstanding principal balance over the remaining term of the loan as of the date the interest rate adjusts to the maximum interest rate set forth in paragraph (e)(2)(iv)(A) of this section, assuming the consumer will have made all required payments as due prior to that date; or

(2) The loan amount over the loan term;

(v) For which the creditor considers and verifies at or before consummation the following:

(A) The consumer's current or reasonably expected income or assets other than the value of the dwelling (including any real property attached to the dwelling) that secures the loan, in accordance with appendix Q and paragraphs (c)(2)(i) and (c)(4) of this section; and

(B) The consumer's current debt obligations, alimony, and child support in accordance with appendix Q and paragraphs (c)(2)(vi) and (c)(3) of this section; and

(vi) For which the ratio of the consumer's total monthly debt to total monthly income at the time of consummation does not exceed 43 percent. For purposes of this paragraph (e)(2)(vi), the ratio of the consumer's total monthly debt to total monthly income is determined:

(A) Except as provided in paragraph (e)(2)(vi)(B) of this section, in accordance with the standards in appendix Q;

(B) Using the consumer's monthly payment on:

(1) The covered transaction, including the monthly payment for mortgage-related obligations, in accordance with paragraph (e)(2)(iv) of this section; and

(2) Any simultaneous loan that the creditor knows or has reason to know will be made, in accordance with paragraphs (c)(2)(iv) and (c)(6) of this section.

(3) Limits on points and fees for qualified mortgages.

(i) Except as provided in paragraph (e)(3)(iii) of this section, a covered transaction is not a qualified mortgage unless the transaction's total points and fees, as defined in § 1026.32(b)(1), do not exceed:

(A) For a loan amount greater than or equal to $100,000 (indexed for inflation): 3 percent of the total loan amount;

(B) For a loan amount greater than or equal to $60,000 (indexed for inflation) but less than $100,000 (indexed for inflation): $3,000 (indexed for inflation);

(C) For a loan amount greater than or equal to $20,000 (indexed for inflation) but less than $60,000 (indexed for inflation): 5 percent of the total loan amount;

(D) For a loan amount greater than or equal to $12,500 (indexed for inflation) but less than $20,000 (indexed for inflation): $1,000 (indexed for inflation);

(E) For a loan amount less than $12,500 (indexed for inflation): 8 percent of the total loan amount.

(ii) The dollar amounts, including the loan amounts, in paragraph (e)(3)(i) of this section shall be adjusted annually on January 1 by the annual percentage change in the Consumer Price Index for All Urban Consumers (CPI-U) that was reported on the preceding June 1. See the official commentary to this paragraph (e)(3)(ii) for the current dollar amounts.

(iii) For covered transactions consummated on or before January 10, 2021, if the creditor or assignee determines after consummation that the transaction's total points and fees exceed the applicable limit under paragraph (e)(3)(i) of this section, the loan is not precluded from being a qualified mortgage, provided:

(A) The loan otherwise meets the requirements of paragraphs (e)(2), (e)(4), (e)(5), (e)(6), or (f) of this section, as applicable;

(B) The creditor or assignee pays to the consumer the amount described in paragraph (e)(3)(iv) of this section within 210 days after consummation and prior to the occurrence of any of the following events:

(1) The institution of any action by the consumer in connection with the loan;

(2) The receipt by the creditor, assignee, or servicer of written notice from the consumer that the transaction's total points and fees exceed the applicable limit under paragraph (e)(3)(i) of this section; or

(3) The consumer becoming 60 days past due on the legal obligation; and

(C) The creditor or assignee, as applicable, maintains and follows policies and procedures for post-consummation review of points and fees and for making payments to consumers in accordance with paragraphs (e)(3)(iii)(B) and (e)(3)(iv) of this section.

(iv) For purposes of paragraph (e)(3)(iii) of this section, the creditor or assignee must pay to the consumer an amount that is not less than the sum of the following:

(A) The dollar amount by which the transaction's total points and fees exceeds the applicable limit under paragraph (e)(3)(i) of this section; and

(B) Interest on the dollar amount described in paragraph (e)(3)(iv)(A) of this section, calculated using the contract interest rate applicable during the period from consummation until the payment described in this paragraph (e)(3)(iv) is made to the consumer.

(4) Qualified mortgage defined—special rules—

(i) General. Notwithstanding paragraph (e)(2) of this section, a qualified mortgage is a covered transaction that satisfies:

(A) The requirements of paragraphs (e)(2)(i) through (iii) of this section; and

(B) One or more of the criteria in paragraph (e)(4)(ii) of this section.

(ii) Eligible loans. A qualified mortgage under this paragraph (e)(4) must be one of the following at consummation:

(A) A loan that is eligible, except with regard to matters wholly unrelated to ability to repay:

(1) To be purchased or guaranteed by the Federal National Mortgage Association or the Federal Home Loan Mortgage Corporation operating under the conservatorship or receivership of the Federal Housing Finance Agency pursuant to section 1367(a) of the Federal Housing Enterprises Financial Safety and Soundness Act of 1992 (12 U.S.C. 4617(a)); or

(2) To be purchased or guaranteed by any limited-life regulatory entity succeeding the charter of either the Federal National Mortgage Association or the Federal Home Loan Mortgage Corporation pursuant to section 1367(i) of the Federal Housing Enterprises Financial Safety and Soundness Act of 1992 (12 U.S.C. 4617(i));

(B) A loan that is eligible to be insured, except with regard to matters wholly unrelated to ability to repay, by the U.S. Department of Housing and Urban Development under the National Housing Act (12 U.S.C. 1707 et seq.);

(C) A loan that is eligible to be guaranteed, except with regard to matters wholly unrelated to ability to repay, by the U.S. Department of Veterans Affairs;

(D) A loan that is eligible to be guaranteed, except with regard to matters wholly unrelated to ability to repay, by the U.S. Department of Agriculture pursuant to 42 U.S.C. 1472(h); or

(E) A loan that is eligible to be insured, except with regard to matters wholly unrelated to ability to repay, by the Rural Housing Service.

(iii) Sunset of special rules.

(A) Each respective special rule described in paragraph (e)(4)(ii)(B), (C), (D), or (E) of this section shall expire on the effective date of a rule issued by each respective agency pursuant to its authority under TILA section 129C(b)(3)(ii) to define a qualified mortgage.

(B) Unless otherwise expired under paragraph (e)(4)(iii)(A) of this section, the special rules in this paragraph (e)(4) are available only for covered transactions consummated on or before January 10, 2021.

(5) Qualified mortgage defined—small creditor portfolio loans.

(i) Notwithstanding paragraph (e)(2) of this section, a qualified mortgage is a covered transaction:

(A) That satisfies the requirements of paragraph (e)(2) of this section other than the requirements of paragraph (e)(2)(vi) and without regard to the standards in appendix Q to this part;

(B) For which the creditor considers at or before consummation the consumer's monthly debt-to-income ratio or residual income and verifies the debt obligations and income used to determine that ratio in accordance with paragraph (c)(7) of this section, except that the calculation of the payment on the covered transaction for purposes of determining the consumer's total monthly debt obligations in paragraph (c)(7)(i)(A) shall be determined in accordance with paragraph (e)(2)(iv) of this section instead of paragraph (c)(5) of this section;

(C) That is not subject, at consummation, to a commitment to be acquired by another person, other than a person that satisfies the requirements of paragraph (e)(5)(i)(D) of this section; and

(D) For which the creditor satisfies the requirements stated in § 1026.35(b)(2)(iii)(B) and (C).

(ii) A qualified mortgage extended pursuant to paragraph (e)(5)(i) of this section immediately loses its status as a qualified mortgage under paragraph (e)(5)(i) if legal title to the qualified mortgage is sold, assigned, or otherwise transferred to another person except when:

(A) The qualified mortgage is sold, assigned, or otherwise transferred to another person three years or more after consummation of the qualified mortgage;

(B) The qualified mortgage is sold, assigned, or otherwise transferred to a creditor that satisfies the requirements of paragraph (e)(5)(i)(D) of this section;

(C) The qualified mortgage is sold, assigned, or otherwise transferred to another person pursuant to a capital restoration plan or other action under 12 U.S.C. 1831*o*, actions or instructions of any person acting as conservator, receiver, or bankruptcy trustee, an order of a State or Federal government agency with jurisdiction to examine the creditor pursuant to State or Federal law, or an agreement between the creditor and such an agency; or

(D) The qualified mortgage is sold, assigned, or otherwise transferred pursuant to a merger of the creditor with another person or acquisition of the creditor by another person or of another person by the creditor.

(6) Qualified mortgage defined—temporary balloon-payment qualified mortgage rules.

(i) Notwithstanding paragraph (e)(2) of this section, a qualified mortgage is a covered transaction:

(A) That satisfies the requirements of paragraph (f) of this section other than the requirements of paragraph (f)(1)(vi); and

(B) For which the creditor satisfies the requirements stated in § 1026.35(b)(2)(iii)(B) and (C).

(ii) The provisions of this paragraph (e)(6) apply only to covered transactions for which the application was received before April 1, 2016.

(f) Balloon-payment qualified mortgages made by certain creditors—

(1) Exemption. Notwithstanding paragraph (e)(2) of this section, a qualified mortgage may provide for a balloon payment, provided:

(i) The loan satisfies the requirements for a qualified mortgage in paragraphs (e)(2)(i)(A), (e)(2)(ii), (e)(2)(iii), and (e)(2)(v) of this section, but without regard to the standards in appendix Q;

(ii) The creditor determines at or before consummation that the consumer can make all of the scheduled payments under the terms of the legal obligation, as described in paragraph (f)(1)(iv) of this section, together with the consumer's monthly payments for all mortgage-related obligations and excluding the balloon payment, from the consumer's current or reasonably expected income or assets other than the dwelling that secures the loan;

(iii) The creditor considers at or before consummation the consumer's monthly debt-to-income ratio or residual income and verifies the debt obligations and income used to determine that ratio in accordance with paragraph (c)(7) of this section, except that the calculation of the payment on the covered transaction for purposes of determining the consumer's total monthly debt obligations in (c)(7)(i)(A) shall be determined in accordance with paragraph (f)(iv)(A) of this section, together with the consumer's monthly payments for all mortgage-related obligations and excluding the balloon payment;

(iv) The legal obligation provides for:

(A) Scheduled payments that are substantially equal, calculated using an amortization period that does not exceed 30 years;

(B) An interest rate that does not increase over the term of the loan; and

(C) A loan term of five years or longer.

(v) The loan is not subject, at consummation, to a commitment to be acquired by another person, other than a person that satisfies the requirements of paragraph (f)(1)(vi) of this section; and

(vi) The creditor satisfies the requirements stated in § 1026.35(b)(2)(iii)(A), (B), and (C).

(2) Post-consummation transfer of balloon-payment qualified mortgage. A balloon-payment qualified mortgage, extended pursuant to paragraph (f)(1), immediately loses its status as a qualified mortgage under paragraph (f)(1) if legal title to the balloon-payment qualified mortgage is sold, assigned, or otherwise transferred to another person except when:

(i) The balloon-payment qualified mortgage is sold, assigned, or otherwise transferred to another person three years or more after consummation of the balloon-payment qualified mortgage;

(ii) The balloon-payment qualified mortgage is sold, assigned, or otherwise transferred to a creditor that satisfies the requirements of paragraph (f)(1)(vi) of this section;

(iii) The balloon-payment qualified mortgage is sold, assigned, or otherwise transferred to another person pursuant to a capital restoration plan or other action under 12 U.S.C. 1831*o*, actions or instructions of any person acting as conservator, receiver or bankruptcy trustee, an order of a State or Federal governmental agency with jurisdiction to examine the creditor pursuant to State or Federal law, or an agreement between the creditor and such an agency; or

(iv) The balloon-payment qualified mortgage is sold, assigned, or otherwise transferred pursuant to a merger of the creditor with another person or acquisition of the creditor by another person or of another person by the creditor.

(g) Prepayment penalties—

(1) When permitted. A covered transaction must not include a prepayment penalty unless:

(i) The prepayment penalty is otherwise permitted by law; and

(ii) The transaction:

(A) Has an annual percentage rate that cannot increase after consummation;

(B) Is a qualified mortgage under paragraph (e)(2), (e)(4), (e)(5), (e)(6), or (f) of this section; and

(C) Is not a higher-priced mortgage loan, as defined in § 1026.35(a).

(2) Limits on prepayment penalties. A prepayment penalty:

(i) Must not apply after the three-year period following consummation; and

(ii) Must not exceed the following percentages of the amount of the outstanding loan balance prepaid:

(A) 2 percent, if incurred during the first two years following consummation; and

(B) 1 percent, if incurred during the third year following consummation.

(3) Alternative offer required. A creditor must not offer a consumer a covered transaction with a prepayment penalty unless the creditor also offers the consumer an alternative covered transaction without a prepayment penalty and the alternative covered transaction:

(i) Has an annual percentage rate that cannot increase after consummation and has the same type of interest rate as the covered transaction with a prepayment penalty; for purposes of this paragraph (g), the term "type of interest rate" refers to whether a transaction:

(A) Is a fixed-rate mortgage, as defined in § 1026.18(s)(7)(iii); or

(B) Is a step-rate mortgage, as defined in § 1026.18(s)(7)(ii);

(ii) Has the same loan term as the loan term for the covered transaction with a prepayment penalty;

(iii) Satisfies the periodic payment conditions under paragraph (e)(2)(i) of this section;

(iv) Satisfies the points and fees conditions under paragraph (e)(2)(iii) of this section, based on the information known to the creditor at the time the transaction is offered; and

(v) Is a transaction for which the creditor has a good faith belief that the consumer likely qualifies, based on the information known to the creditor at the time the creditor offers the covered transaction without a prepayment penalty.

(4) Offer through a mortgage broker. If the creditor offers a covered transaction with a prepayment penalty to the consumer through a mortgage broker, as defined in § 1026.36(a)(2), the creditor must:

(i) Present the mortgage broker an alternative covered transaction without a prepayment penalty that satisfies the requirements of paragraph (g)(3) of this section; and

(ii) Establish by agreement that the mortgage broker must present the consumer an alternative covered transaction without a prepayment penalty that satisfies the requirements of paragraph (g)(3) of this section, offered by:

(A) The creditor; or

(B) Another creditor, if the transaction offered by the other creditor has a lower interest rate or a lower total dollar amount of discount points and origination points or fees.

(5) Creditor that is a loan originator. If the creditor is a loan originator, as defined in § 1026.36(a)(1), and the creditor presents the consumer a covered transaction offered by a person to which the creditor would assign the covered transaction after consummation, the creditor must present the consumer an alternative covered transaction without a prepayment penalty that satisfies the requirements of paragraph (g)(3) of this section, offered by:

(i) The assignee; or

(ii) Another person, if the transaction offered by the other person has a lower interest rate or a lower total dollar amount of origination discount points and points or fees.

(6) Applicability. This paragraph (g) applies only if a covered transaction is consummated with a prepayment penalty and is not violated if:

(i) A covered transaction is consummated without a prepayment penalty; or

(ii) The creditor and consumer do not consummate a covered transaction.

(h) Evasion; open-end credit. In connection with credit secured by a consumer's dwelling that does not meet the definition of open-end credit in § 1026.2(a)(20), a creditor shall not structure the loan as an open-end plan to evade the requirements of this section.

§§ 1026.44, 1026.45. [Reserved]

SUBPART F: SPECIAL RULES FOR PRIVATE EDUCATION LOANS

§ 1026.46. Special Disclosure Requirements for Private Education Loans

(a) Coverage. The requirements of this subpart apply to private education loans as defined in § 1026.46(b)(5). A creditor may, at its option, comply with the requirements of this subpart for an extension of credit subject to §§ 1026.17 and 1026.18 that is extended to a consumer for expenses incurred after graduation from a law, medical, dental, veterinary, or other graduate school and related to relocation, study for a bar or other examination, participation in an internship or residency program, or similar purposes.

(1) Relation to other subparts in this part. Except as otherwise specifically provided, the requirements and limitations of this subpart are in addition to and not in lieu of those contained in other subparts of this Part.

(2) [Reserved]

(b) Definitions. For purposes of this subpart, the following definitions apply:

(1) Covered educational institution means:

(i) An educational institution that meets the definition of an institution of higher education, as defined in paragraph (b)(2) of this section, without regard to the institution's accreditation status; and

(ii) Includes an agent, officer, or employee of the institution of higher education. An agent means an institution-affiliated organization as defined by section 151 of the Higher Education Act of 1965 (20 U.S.C. 1019) or an officer or employee of an institution-affiliated organization.

(2) Institution of higher education has the same meaning as in sections 101 and 102 of the Higher Education Act of 1965 (20 U.S.C. 1001–1002) and the implementing regulations published by the U.S. Department of Education.

(3) Postsecondary educational expenses means any of the expenses that are listed as part of the cost of attendance, as defined under section 472 of the Higher Education Act of 1965 (20 U.S.C. 1087*ll*), of a student at a covered educational institution. These expenses include tuition and fees, books, supplies, miscellaneous personal expenses, room and board, and an allowance for any loan fee, origination fee, or insurance premium charged to a student or parent for a loan incurred to cover the cost of the student's attendance.

(4) Preferred lender arrangement has the same meaning as in section 151 of the Higher Education Act of 1965 (20 U.S.C. 1019).

(5) Private education loan means an extension of credit that:

(i) Is not made, insured, or guaranteed under title IV of the Higher Education Act of 1965 (20 U.S.C. 1070 et seq.);

(ii) Is extended to a consumer expressly, in whole or in part, for postsecondary educational expenses, regardless of whether the loan is provided by the educational institution that the student attends;

(iii) Does not include open-end credit or any loan that is secured by real property or a dwelling; and

(iv) Does not include an extension of credit in which the covered educational institution is the creditor if:

(A) The term of the extension of credit is 90 days or less; or

(B) an interest rate will not be applied to the credit balance and the term of the extension of credit is one year or less, even if the credit is payable in more than four installments.

(c) Form of disclosures—

(1) Clear and conspicuous. The disclosures required by this subpart shall be made clearly and conspicuously.

(2) Transaction disclosures.

(i) The disclosures required under §§ 1026.47(b) and (c) shall be made in writing, in a form that the consumer may keep. The disclosures shall be grouped together, shall be segregated from everything else, and shall not contain any information not directly related to the disclosures required under §§ 1026.47(b) and (c), which include the disclosures required under § 1026.18.

(ii) The disclosures may include an acknowledgement of receipt, the date of the transaction, and the consumer's name, address, and account number. The following disclosures may be made together with or separately from other required disclosures: the creditor's identity under § 1026.18(a), insurance or debt cancellation under § 1026.18(n), and certain security interest charges under § 1026.18(*o*).

(iii) The term "finance charge" and corresponding amount, when required to be disclosed under § 1026.18(d), and the interest rate required to be disclosed under §§ 1026.47(b)(1)(i) and (c)(1), shall be more conspicuous than any other disclosure, except the creditor's identity under § 1026.18(a).

(3) Electronic disclosures. The disclosures required under §§ 1026.47(b) and (c) may be provided to the consumer in electronic form, subject to compliance with the consumer consent and other applicable provisions of the Electronic Signatures in Global and National Commerce Act (E-Sign Act) (15 U.S.C. 7001 et seq.). The disclosures required by § 1026.47(a) may be provided to the consumer in electronic form on or with an application or solicitation that is accessed by the consumer in electronic form without regard to the consumer consent or other provisions of the E-Sign Act. The form required to be received under § 1026.48(e) may be accepted by the creditor in electronic form as provided for in that section.

(d) Timing of disclosures—

(1) Application or solicitation disclosures.

(i) The disclosures required by § 1026.47(a) shall be provided on or with any application or solicitation. For purposes of this subpart, the term solicitation means an offer of credit that does not require the consumer to complete an application. A "firm offer of credit" as defined in section 603(*l*) of the Fair Credit Reporting Act (15 U.S.C. 1681a(*l*)) is a solicitation for purposes of this section.

(ii) The creditor may, at its option, disclose orally the information in § 1026.47(a) in a telephone application or solicitation. Alternatively, if the creditor does not disclose orally the information in § 1026.47(a), the creditor must provide the disclosures or place them in the mail no later than three business days after the consumer has applied for the credit, except that, if the creditor either denies the consumer's application or provides or places in the mail the disclosures in § 1026.47(b) no later than three business days after the consumer requests the credit, the creditor need not also provide the § 1026.47(a) disclosures.

(iii) Notwithstanding paragraph (d)(1)(i) of this section, for a loan that the consumer may use for multiple purposes including, but not limited to, postsecondary educational expenses, the creditor need not provide the disclosures required by § 1026.47(a).

(2) Approval disclosures. The creditor shall provide the disclosures required by § 1026.47(b) before consummation on or with any notice of approval provided to the consumer. If the creditor mails notice of approval, the disclosures must be mailed with the notice. If the creditor communicates notice of approval by telephone, the creditor must mail the disclosures within three business days of providing the notice of approval. If the creditor communicates notice of approval electronically, the creditor may provide the disclosures in electronic form in accordance with § 1026.46(d)(3); otherwise the creditor must mail the disclosures within three business days of communicating the notice of approval. If the creditor communicates approval in person, the creditor must provide the disclosures to the consumer at that time.

(3) Final disclosures. The disclosures required by § 1026.47(c) shall be provided after the consumer accepts the loan in accordance with § 1026.48(c)(1).

(4) Receipt of mailed disclosures. If the disclosures under paragraphs (d)(1), (d)(2) or (d)(3) of this section are mailed to the consumer, the consumer is considered to have received them three business days after they are mailed.

(e) Basis of disclosures and use of estimates—

(1) Legal obligation. Disclosures shall reflect the terms of the legal obligation between the parties.

(2) Estimates. If any information necessary for an accurate disclosure is unknown to the creditor, the creditor shall make the disclosure based on the best information reasonably available at the time the disclosure is provided, and shall state clearly that the disclosure is an estimate.

(f) Multiple creditors; multiple consumers. If a transaction involves more than one creditor, only one set of disclosures shall be given and the creditors shall agree among themselves which creditor will comply with the requirements that this part imposes on any or all of them. If there is more than one consumer, the disclosures may be made to any consumer who is primarily liable on the obligation.

(g) Effect of subsequent events—

(1) Approval disclosures. If a disclosure under § 1026.47(b) becomes inaccurate because of an event that occurs after the creditor delivers the required disclosures, the inaccuracy is not a violation of Regulation Z (12 CFR part 1026), although new disclosures may be required under § 1026.48(c).

(2) Final disclosures. If a disclosure under § 1026.47(c) becomes inaccurate because of an event that occurs after the creditor delivers the required disclosures, the inaccuracy is not a violation of Regulation Z (12 CFR part 1026).

§ 1026.47. Content of Disclosures

(a) Application or solicitation disclosures. A creditor shall provide the disclosures required under paragraph (a) of this section on or with a solicitation or an application for a private education loan.

(1) Interest Rates.

(i) The interest rate or range of interest rates applicable to the loan and actually offered by the creditor at the time of application or solicitation. If the rate will depend, in part, on a later determination of the consumer's creditworthiness or other factors, a statement that the rate for which the consumer may qualify will depend on the consumer's creditworthiness and other factors, if applicable.

(ii) Whether the interest rates applicable to the loan are fixed or variable.

(iii) If the interest rate may increase after consummation of the transaction, any limitations on the interest rate adjustments, or lack thereof; a statement that the consumer's actual rate could be higher or lower than the rates disclosed under paragraph (a)(1)(i) of this section, if applicable; and, if the limitation is determined by applicable law, that fact.

(iv) Whether the applicable interest rates typically will be higher if the loan is not co-signed or guaranteed.

(2) Fees and default or late payment costs.

(i) An itemization of the fees or range of fees required to obtain the private education loan.

(ii) Any fees, changes to the interest rate, and adjustments to principal based on the consumer's defaults or late payments.

(3) Repayment terms.

(i) The term of the loan, which is the period during which regularly scheduled payments of principal and interest will be due.

(ii) A description of any payment deferral options, or, if the consumer does not have the option to defer payments, that fact.

(iii) For each payment deferral option applicable while the student is enrolled at a covered educational institution:

(A) Whether interest will accrue during the deferral period; and

(B) If interest accrues, whether payment of interest may be deferred and added to the principal balance.

(iv) A statement that if the consumer files for bankruptcy, the consumer may still be required to pay back the loan.

(4) Cost estimates. An example of the total cost of the loan calculated as the total of payments over the term of the loan:

(i) Using the highest rate of interest disclosed under paragraph (a)(1) of this section and including all finance charges applicable to loans at that rate;

(ii) Using an amount financed of $10,000, or $5000 if the creditor only offers loans of this type for less than $10,000; and

(iii) Calculated for each payment option.

(5) Eligibility. Any age or school enrollment eligibility requirements relating to the consumer or cosigner.

(6) Alternatives to private education loans.

(i) A statement that the consumer may qualify for Federal student financial assistance through a program under Title IV of the Higher Education Act of 1965 (20 U.S.C. 1070 et seq.).

(ii) The interest rates available under each program under title IV of the Higher Education Act of 1965 (20 U.S.C. 1070 et seq.) and whether the rates are fixed or variable.

(iii) A statement that the consumer may obtain additional information concerning Federal student financial assistance from the institution of higher education that the student attends, or at the Web site of the U.S. Department of Education, including an appropriate Web site address.

(iv) A statement that a covered educational institution may have school-specific education loan benefits and terms not detailed on the disclosure form.

(7) Rights of the consumer. A statement that if the loan is approved, the terms of the loan will be available and will not change for 30 days except as a result of adjustments to the interest rate and other changes permitted by law.

(8) Self-certification information. A statement that, before the loan may be consummated, the consumer must complete the self-certification form and that the form may be obtained from the institution of higher education that the student attends.

(b) Approval disclosures. On or with any notice of approval provided to the consumer, the creditor shall disclose the information required under § 1026.18 and the following information:

(1) Interest rate.

(i) The interest rate applicable to the loan.

(ii) Whether the interest rate is fixed or variable.

(iii) If the interest rate may increase after consummation of the transaction, any limitations on the rate adjustments, or lack thereof.

(2) Fees and default or late payment costs.

(i) An itemization of the fees or range of fees required to obtain the private education loan.

(ii) Any fees, changes to the interest rate, and adjustments to principal based on the consumer's defaults or late payments.

(3) Repayment terms.

(i) The principal amount of the loan for which the consumer has been approved.

(ii) The term of the loan, which is the period during which regularly scheduled payments of principal and interest will be due.

(iii) A description of the payment deferral option chosen by the consumer, if applicable, and any other payment deferral options that the consumer may elect at a later time.

(iv) Any payments required while the student is enrolled at a covered educational institution, based on the deferral option chosen by the consumer.

(v) The amount of any unpaid interest that will accrue while the student is enrolled at a covered educational institution, based on the deferral option chosen by the consumer.

(vi) A statement that if the consumer files for bankruptcy, the consumer may still be required to pay back the loan.

(vii) An estimate of the total amount of payments calculated based on:

(A) The interest rate applicable to the loan. Compliance with § 1026.18(h) constitutes compliance with this requirement.

(B) The maximum possible rate of interest for the loan or, if a maximum rate cannot be determined, a rate of 25%.

(C) If a maximum rate cannot be determined, the estimate of the total amount for repayment must include a statement that there is no maximum rate and that the total amount for repayment disclosed under paragraph (b)(3)(vii)(B) of this section is an estimate and will be higher if the applicable interest rate increases.

(viii) The maximum monthly payment based on the maximum rate of interest for the loan or, if a maximum rate cannot be determined, a rate of 25%. If a maximum cannot be determined, a statement that there is no maximum rate and that the monthly payment amount disclosed is an estimate and will be higher if the applicable interest rate increases.

(4) Alternatives to private education loans.

(i) A statement that the consumer may qualify for Federal student financial assistance through a program under Title IV of the Higher Education Act of 1965 (20 U.S.C. 1070 et seq.).

(ii) The interest rates available under each program under Title IV of the Higher Education Act of 1965 (20 U.S.C. 1070 et seq.), and whether the rates are fixed or variable.

(iii) A statement that the consumer may obtain additional information concerning Federal student financial assistance from the institution of higher education that the student attends, or at the Web site of the U.S. Department of Education, including an appropriate Web site address.

(5) Rights of the consumer.

(i) A statement that the consumer may accept the terms of the loan until the acceptance period under § 1026.48(c)(1) has expired. The statement must include the specific date on which the acceptance period expires, based on the date upon which the consumer receives the disclosures required under this subsection for the loan. The disclosure must also specify the method or methods by which the consumer may communicate acceptance.

(ii) A statement that, except for changes to the interest rate and other changes permitted by law, the rates and terms of the loan may not be changed by the creditor during the period described in paragraph (b)(5)(i) of this section.

(c) Final disclosures. After the consumer has accepted the loan in accordance with § 1026.48(c)(1), the creditor shall disclose to the consumer the information required by § 1026.18 and the following information:

(1) Interest rate. Information required to be disclosed under § 1026.47(b)(1).

(2) Fees and default or late payment costs. Information required to be disclosed under § 1026.47(b)(2).

(3) Repayment terms. Information required to be disclosed under § 1026.47(b)(3).

(4) Cancellation right. A statement that:

(i) The consumer has the right to cancel the loan, without penalty, at any time before the cancellation period under § 1026.48(d) expires, and

(ii) Loan proceeds will not be disbursed until after the cancellation period under § 1026.48(d) expires. The statement must include the specific date on which the cancellation period expires and state that the consumer may cancel by that date. The statement must also specify the method or methods by which the consumer may cancel. If the creditor permits cancellation by mail, the statement must specify that the consumer's mailed request will be deemed timely if placed in the mail not later than the cancellation date specified on the disclosure. The disclosures required by this paragraph (c)(4) must be made more conspicuous than any other disclosure required under this section, except for the finance charge, the interest rate, and the creditor's identity, which must be disclosed in accordance with the requirements of § 1026.46(c)(2)(iii).

§ 1026.48. Limitations on Private Education Loans

(a) Co-branding prohibited.

(1) Except as provided in paragraph (b) of this section, a creditor, other than the covered educational institution itself, shall not use the name, emblem, mascot, or logo of a covered educational institution, or other words, pictures, or symbols identified with a covered educational institution, in the marketing of private education loans in a way that implies that the covered education institution endorses the creditor's loans.

(2) A creditor's marketing of private education loans does not imply that the covered education institution endorses the creditor's loans if the marketing includes a clear and conspicuous disclosure that is equally prominent and closely proximate to the reference to the covered educational institution that the covered educational institution does not endorse the creditor's loans and that the creditor is not affiliated with the covered educational institution.

(b) Endorsed lender arrangements. If a creditor and a covered educational institution have entered into an arrangement where the covered educational institution agrees to endorse the creditor's private education loans, and such arrangement is not prohibited by other applicable law or regulation, paragraph (a)(1) of this section does not apply if the private education loan marketing includes a clear and conspicuous disclosure that is equally prominent and closely proximate to the reference to the covered educational institution that the creditor's loans are not offered or made by the covered educational institution, but are made by the creditor.

(c) Consumer's right to accept.

(1) The consumer has the right to accept the terms of a private education loan at any time within 30 calendar days following the date on which the consumer receives the disclosures required under § 1026.47(b).

(2) Except for changes permitted under paragraphs (c)(3) and (c)(4), the rate and terms of the private education loan that are required to be disclosed under §§ 1026.47(b) and (c) may not be changed by the creditor prior to the earlier of:

(i) The date of disbursement of the loan; or

(ii) The expiration of the 30 calendar day period described in paragraph (c)(1) of this section if the consumer has not accepted the loan within that time.

(3) Exceptions not requiring re-disclosure.

(i) Notwithstanding paragraph (c)(2) of this section, nothing in this section prevents the creditor from:

(A) Withdrawing an offer before consummation of the transaction if the extension of credit would be prohibited by law or if the creditor has reason to believe that the consumer has committed fraud in connection with the loan application;

(B) Changing the interest rate based on adjustments to the index used for a loan;

(C) Changing the interest rate and terms if the change will unequivocally benefit the consumer; or

(D) Reducing the loan amount based upon a certification or other information received from the covered educational institution, or from the consumer, indicating that the student's cost of attendance has decreased or the consumer's other financial aid has increased. A creditor may make corresponding changes to the rate and other terms only to the extent that the consumer would have received the terms if the consumer had applied for the reduced loan amount.

(ii) If the creditor changes the rate or terms of the loan under this paragraph (c)(3), the creditor need not provide the disclosures required under § 1026.47(b) for the new loan terms, nor need the creditor provide an additional 30-day period to the consumer to accept the new terms of the loan under paragraph (c)(1) of this section.

(4) Exceptions requiring re-disclosure.

(i) Notwithstanding paragraphs (c)(2) or (c)(3) of this section, nothing in this section prevents the creditor, at its option, from changing the rate or terms of the loan to accommodate a specific request by the consumer. For example, if the consumer requests a different repayment option, the creditor may, but need not, offer to provide the requested repayment option and make any other changes to the rate and terms.

(ii) If the creditor changes the rate or terms of the loan under this paragraph (c)(4), the creditor shall provide the disclosures required under § 1026.47(b) and shall provide the consumer the 30-day period to accept the loan under paragraph (c)(1) of this section. The creditor shall not make further changes to the rates and terms of the loan, except as specified in paragraphs (c)(3) and (4) of this section. Except as permitted under § 1026.48(c)(3), unless the consumer accepts the loan offered by the creditor in response to the consumer's request, the creditor may not withdraw or change the rates or terms of the loan for which the consumer was approved prior to the consumer's request for a change in loan terms.

(d) Consumer's right to cancel. The consumer may cancel a private education loan, without penalty, until midnight of the third business day following the date on which the consumer receives the disclosures required by § 1026.47(c). No funds may be disbursed for a private education loan until the three-business day period has expired.

(e) Self-certification form. For a private education loan intended to be used for the postsecondary educational expenses of a student while the student is attending an institution of higher education, the creditor shall obtain from the consumer or the institution of higher education the form developed by the Secretary of Education under section 155 of the Higher Education Act of 1965, signed by the consumer, in written or electronic form, before consummating the private education loan.

(f) Provision of information by preferred lenders. A creditor that has a preferred lender arrangement with a covered educational institution shall provide to the covered educational institution the information required under §§ 1026.47(a)(1) through (5), for each type of private education loan that the lender plans to offer to consumers for students attending the covered educational institution for the period beginning July 1 of the current year and ending June 30 of the following year. The creditor shall provide the information annually by the later of the 1st day of April, or within 30 days after entering into, or learning the creditor is a party to, a preferred lender arrangement.

SUBPART G: SPECIAL RULES APPLICABLE TO CREDIT CARD ACCOUNTS AND OPEN-END CREDIT OFFERED TO COLLEGE STUDENTS

§ 1026.51. Ability to Pay

(a) General rule—

(1)(i) Consideration of ability to pay. A card issuer must not open a credit card account for a consumer under an open-end (not home-secured) consumer credit plan, or increase any credit limit applicable to such account, unless the card issuer considers the consumer's ability to make the required minimum periodic payments under the terms of the account based on the consumer's income or assets and current obligations.

(ii) Reasonable policies and procedures. Card issuers must establish and maintain reasonable written policies and procedures to consider the consumer's ability to make the required minimum payments under the terms of the account based on a consumer's income or assets and a consumer's current obligations. Reasonable policies and procedures include treating any income and assets to which the consumer has a reasonable expectation of access as the consumer's income or assets, or limiting consideration of the consumer's income or assets to the consumer's independent income and assets. Reasonable policies and procedures also include consideration of at least one of the following: The ratio of debt obligations to income; the ratio of debt obligations to assets; or the income the consumer will have after paying debt obligations. It would be unreasonable for a card issuer not to review any information about a consumer's income or assets and current obligations, or to issue a credit card to a consumer who does not have any income or assets.

(2) Minimum periodic payments.

(i) Reasonable method. For purposes of paragraph (a)(1) of this section, a card issuer must use a reasonable method for estimating the minimum periodic payments the consumer would be required to pay under the terms of the account.

(ii) Safe harbor. A card issuer complies with paragraph (a)(2)(i) of this section if it estimates required minimum periodic payments using the following method:

(A) The card issuer assumes utilization, from the first day of the billing cycle, of the full credit line that the issuer is considering offering to the consumer; and

(B) The card issuer uses a minimum payment formula employed by the issuer for the product the issuer is considering offering to the consumer or, in the case of an existing account, the minimum payment formula that currently applies to that account, provided that:

(1) If the applicable minimum payment formula includes interest charges, the card issuer estimates those charges using an interest rate that the issuer is considering offering to the consumer for purchases or, in the case of an existing account, the interest rate that currently applies to purchases; and

(2) If the applicable minimum payment formula includes mandatory fees, the card issuer must assume that such fees have been charged to the account.

(b) Rules affecting young consumers—

(1) Applications from young consumers. A card issuer may not open a credit card account under an open-end (not home-secured) consumer credit plan for a consumer less than 21 years old, unless the consumer has submitted a written application and the card issuer has:

(i) Financial information indicating the consumer has an independent ability to make the required minimum periodic payments on the proposed extension of credit in connection with the account; or

(ii)(A) A signed agreement of a cosigner, guarantor, or joint applicant who is at least 21 years old to be either secondarily liable for any debt on the account incurred by the consumer before the consumer has attained the age of 21 or jointly liable with the consumer for any debt on the account, and

(B) Financial information indicating such cosigner, guarantor, or joint applicant has the independent ability to make the required minimum periodic payments on such debts, consistent with paragraph (a) of this section.

(2) ***Credit line increases for young consumers.*** **(i)** If a credit card account has been opened pursuant to paragraph (b)(1)(i) of this section, no increase in the credit limit may be made on such account before the consumer attains the age of 21 unless:

(A) At the time of the contemplated increase, the consumer has an independent ability to make the required minimum periodic payments on the increased limit consistent with paragraph (b)(1)(i) of this section; or

(B) A cosigner, guarantor, or joint applicant who is at least 21 years old agrees in writing to assume liability for any debt incurred on the account, consistent with paragraph (b)(1)(ii) of this section.

(ii) If a credit card account has been opened pursuant to paragraph (b)(1)(ii) of this section, no increase in the credit limit may be made on such account before the consumer attains the age of 21 unless the cosigner, guarantor, or joint accountholder who assumed liability at account opening agrees in writing to assume liability on the increase.

§ 1026.52. Limitations on Fees

(a) Limitations during first year after account opening—

(1) General rule. Except as provided in paragraph (a)(2) of this section, the total amount of fees a consumer is required to pay with respect to a credit card account under an open-end (not home-secured) consumer credit plan during the first year after account opening must not exceed 25 percent of the credit limit in effect when the account is opened. For purposes of this paragraph, an account is considered open no earlier than the date on which the account may first be used by the consumer to engage in transactions.

(2) Fees not subject to limitations. Paragraph (a) of this section does not apply to:

(i) Late payment fees, over-the-limit fees, and returned-payment fees; or

(ii) Fees that the consumer is not required to pay with respect to the account.

(3) Rule of construction. Paragraph (a) of this section does not authorize the imposition or payment of fees or charges otherwise prohibited by law.

(b) Limitations on penalty fees. A card issuer must not impose a fee for violating the terms or other requirements of a credit card account under an open-end (not home-secured) consumer credit plan unless the dollar amount of the fee is consistent with paragraphs (b)(1) and (b)(2) of this section.

(1) General rule. Except as provided in paragraph (b)(2) of this section, a card issuer may impose a fee for violating the terms or other requirements of a credit card account under an open-end (not home-secured) consumer credit plan if the dollar amount of the fee is consistent with either paragraph (b)(1)(i) or (b)(1)(ii) of this section.

(i) Fees based on costs. A card issuer may impose a fee for violating the terms or other requirements of an account if the card issuer has determined that the dollar amount of the fee represents a reasonable proportion of the total costs incurred by the card issuer as a result of that type of violation. A card issuer must reevaluate this determination at least once every twelve months. If as a result of the reevaluation the card issuer determines that a lower fee represents a reasonable proportion of the total costs incurred by the card issuer as a result of that type of violation, the card issuer must begin imposing the lower fee within 45 days after completing the reevaluation. If as a result of the reevaluation the card issuer determines that a higher fee represents a reasonable proportion of the total costs incurred by the card issuer as a result of that type of violation, the card issuer may begin imposing the higher fee after complying with the notice requirements in § 1026.9.

(ii) Safe harbors. A card issuer may impose a fee for violating the terms or other requirements of an account if the dollar amount of the fee does not exceed, as applicable:

(A) $28;

(B) $39 if the card issuer previously imposed a fee pursuant to paragraph (b)(1)(ii)(A) of this section for a violation of the same type that occurred during the same billing cycle or one of the next six billing cycles; or

(C) Three percent of the delinquent balance on a charge card account that requires payment of outstanding balances in full at the end of each billing cycle if the card issuer has not received the required payment for two or more consecutive billing cycles.

(D) The amounts in paragraphs (b)(1)(ii)(A) and (b)(1)(ii)(B) of this section will be adjusted annually by the Bureau to reflect changes in the Consumer Price Index.

(2) Prohibited fees—

(i) Fees that exceed dollar amount associated with violation—

(A) Generally. A card issuer must not impose a fee for violating the terms or other requirements of a credit card account under an open-end (not home-secured) consumer credit plan that exceeds the dollar amount associated with the violation.

(B) No dollar amount associated with violation. A card issuer must not impose a fee for violating the terms or other requirements of a credit card account under an open-end (not home-secured) consumer credit plan when there is no dollar amount associated with the violation. For purposes of paragraph (b)(2)(i) of this section, there is no dollar amount associated with the following violations:

(1) Transactions that the card issuer declines to authorize;

(2) Account inactivity; and

(3) The closure or termination of an account.

(ii) Multiple fees based on a single event or transaction. A card issuer must not impose more than one fee for violating the terms or other requirements of a credit card account under an open-end (not home-secured) consumer credit plan based on a single event or transaction. A card issuer may, at its option, comply with this prohibition by imposing no more than one fee for violating the terms or other requirements of an account during a billing cycle.

§ 1026.53. Allocation of Payments

(a) General rule. Except as provided in paragraph (b) of this section, when a consumer makes a payment in excess of the required minimum periodic payment for a credit card account under an open-end (not home-secured) consumer credit plan, the card issuer must allocate the excess amount first to the balance with the highest annual percentage rate and any remaining portion to the other balances in descending order based on the applicable annual percentage rate.

(b) Special rules—

(1) Accounts with balances subject to deferred interest or similar program. When a balance on a credit card account under an open-end (not home-secured) consumer credit plan is subject to a deferred interest or similar program that provides that a consumer will not be obligated to pay interest that accrues on the balance if the balance is paid in full prior to the expiration of a specified period of time:

(i) Last two billing cycles. The card issuer must allocate any amount paid by the consumer in excess of the required minimum periodic payment consistent with paragraph (a) of this section, except that, during the two billing cycles immediately preceding expiration of the specified period, the excess amount must be allocated first to the balance subject to the deferred interest or similar program and any remaining portion allocated to any other balances consistent with paragraph (a) of this section; or

(ii) Consumer request. The card issuer may at its option allocate any amount paid by the consumer in excess of the required minimum periodic payment among the balances on the account in the manner requested by the consumer.

(2) Accounts with secured balances. When a balance on a credit card account under an open-end (not home-secured) consumer credit plan is secured, the card issuer may at its option allocate any amount paid by the consumer in excess of the required minimum periodic payment to that balance if requested by the consumer.

§ 1026.54. Limitations on the Imposition of Finance Charges

(a) Limitations on imposing finance charges as a result of the loss of a grace period—

(1) General rule. Except as provided in paragraph (b) of this section, a card issuer must not impose finance charges as a result of the loss of a grace period on a credit card account under an open-end (not home-secured) consumer credit plan if those finance charges are based on:

(i) Balances for days in billing cycles that precede the most recent billing cycle; or

(ii) Any portion of a balance subject to a grace period that was repaid prior to the expiration of the grace period.

(2) Definition of grace period. For purposes of paragraph (a)(1) of this section, "grace period" has the same meaning as in § 1026.5(b)(2)(ii)(B)(3).

(b) Exceptions. Paragraph (a) of this section does not apply to:

(1) Adjustments to finance charges as a result of the resolution of a dispute under § 1026.12 or § 1026.13; or

(2) Adjustments to finance charges as a result of the return of a payment.

§ 1026.55. Limitations on Increasing Annual Percentage Rates, Fees, and Charges

(a) General rule. Except as provided in paragraph (b) of this section, a card issuer must not increase an annual percentage rate or a fee or charge required to be disclosed under § 1026.6(b)(2)(ii), (b)(2)(iii), or (b)(2)(xii) on a credit card account under an open-end (not home-secured) consumer credit plan.

(b) Exceptions. A card issuer may increase an annual percentage rate or a fee or charge required to be disclosed under § 1026.6(b)(2)(ii), (b)(2)(iii), or (b)(2)(xii) pursuant to an exception set forth in this paragraph even if that increase would not be permitted under a different exception.

(1) Temporary rate, fee, or charge exception. A card issuer may increase an annual percentage rate or a fee or charge required to be disclosed under § 1026.6(b)(2)(ii), (b)(2)(iii), or (b)(2)(xii) upon the expiration of a specified period of six months or longer, provided that:

(i) Prior to the commencement of that period, the card issuer disclosed in writing to the consumer, in a clear and conspicuous manner, the length of the period and the annual percentage rate, fee, or charge that would apply after expiration of the period; and

(ii) Upon expiration of the specified period:

(A) The card issuer must not apply an annual percentage rate, fee, or charge to transactions that occurred prior to the period that exceeds the annual percentage rate, fee, or charge that applied to those transactions prior to the period;

(B) If the disclosures required by paragraph (b)(1)(i) of this section are provided pursuant to § 1026.9(c), the card issuer must not apply an annual percentage rate, fee, or charge to transactions that occurred within 14 days after provision of the notice that exceeds the annual percentage rate, fee, or charge that applied to that category of transactions prior to provision of the notice; and

(C) The card issuer must not apply an annual percentage rate, fee, or charge to transactions that occurred during the period that exceeds the increased annual percentage rate, fee, or charge disclosed pursuant to paragraph (b)(1)(i) of this section.

(2) Variable rate exception. A card issuer may increase an annual percentage rate when:

(i) The annual percentage rate varies according to an index that is not under the card issuer's control and is available to the general public; and

(ii) The increase in the annual percentage rate is due to an increase in the index.

(3) Advance notice exception. A card issuer may increase an annual percentage rate or a fee or charge required to be disclosed under § 1026.6(b)(2)(ii), (b)(2)(iii), or (b)(2)(xii) after complying with the applicable notice requirements in § 1026.9(b), (c), or (g), provided that:

(i) If a card issuer discloses an increased annual percentage rate, fee, or charge pursuant to § 1026.9(b), the card issuer must not apply that rate, fee, or charge to transactions that occurred prior to provision of the notice;

(ii) If a card issuer discloses an increased annual percentage rate, fee, or charge pursuant to § 1026.9(c) or (g), the card issuer must not apply that rate, fee, or charge to transactions that occurred prior to or within 14 days after provision of the notice; and

(iii) This exception does not permit a card issuer to increase an annual percentage rate or a fee or charge required to be disclosed under § 1026.6(b)(2)(ii), (iii), or (xii) during the first year after the account is opened, while the account is closed, or while the card issuer does not permit the consumer to use the account for new transactions. For purposes of this paragraph, an account is considered open no earlier than the date on which the account may first be used by the consumer to engage in transactions.

(4) Delinquency exception. A card issuer may increase an annual percentage rate or a fee or charge required to be disclosed under § 1026.6(b)(2)(ii), (b)(2)(iii), or (b)(2)(xii) due to the card issuer not receiving the consumer's required minimum periodic payment within 60 days after the due date for that payment, provided that:

(i) The card issuer must disclose in a clear and conspicuous manner in the notice of the increase pursuant to § 1026.9(c) or (g):

(A) A statement of the reason for the increase; and

(B) That the increased annual percentage rate, fee, or charge will cease to apply if the card issuer receives six consecutive required minimum periodic payments on or before the payment due date beginning with the first payment due following the effective date of the increase; and

(ii) If the card issuer receives six consecutive required minimum periodic payments on or before the payment due date beginning with the first payment due following the effective date of the increase, the card issuer must reduce any annual percentage rate, fee, or charge increased pursuant to this exception to the annual percentage rate, fee, or charge that applied prior to the increase with respect to transactions that occurred prior to or within 14 days after provision of the § 1026.9(c) or (g) notice.

(5) Workout and temporary hardship arrangement exception. A card issuer may increase an annual percentage rate or a fee or charge required to be disclosed under § 1026.6(b)(2)(ii), (b)(2)(iii), or (b)(2)(xii) due to the consumer's completion of a workout or temporary hardship arrangement or the consumer's failure to comply with the terms of such an arrangement, provided that:

(i) Prior to commencement of the arrangement (except as provided in § 1026.9(c)(2)(v)(D)), the card issuer has provided the consumer with a clear and conspicuous written disclosure of the terms of the arrangement (including any increases due to the completion or failure of the arrangement); and

(ii) Upon the completion or failure of the arrangement, the card issuer must not apply to any transactions that occurred prior to commencement of the arrangement an annual percentage rate, fee, or charge that exceeds the annual percentage rate, fee, or charge that applied to those transactions prior to commencement of the arrangement.

(6) Servicemembers Civil Relief Act exception. If an annual percentage rate or a fee or charge required to be disclosed under § 1026.6(b)(2)(ii), (iii), or (xii) has been decreased pursuant to 50 U.S.C. app. 527 or a similar Federal or state statute or regulation, a card issuer may increase that annual percentage rate, fee, or charge once 50 U.S.C. app. 527 or the similar statute or regulation no longer applies, provided that the card issuer must not apply to any transactions that occurred prior to the decrease an annual percentage rate, fee, or charge that exceeds the annual percentage rate, fee, or charge that applied to those transactions prior to the decrease.

(c) Treatment of protected balances.

(1) Definition of protected balance. For purposes of this paragraph, "protected balance" means the amount owed for a category of transactions to which an increased annual percentage rate or an increased fee or charge required to be disclosed under § 1026.6(b)(2)(ii), (b)(2)(iii), or (b)(2)(xii) cannot be applied after the annual percentage rate, fee, or charge for that category of transactions has been increased pursuant to paragraph (b)(3) of this section.

(2) Repayment of protected balance. The card issuer must not require repayment of the protected balance using a method that is less beneficial to the consumer than one of the following methods:

(i) The method of repayment for the account before the effective date of the increase;

(ii) An amortization period of not less than five years, beginning no earlier than the effective date of the increase; or

(iii) A required minimum periodic payment that includes a percentage of the balance that is equal to no more than twice the percentage required before the effective date of the increase.

(d) Continuing application. This section continues to apply to a balance on a credit card account under an open-end (not home-secured) consumer credit plan after:

(1) The account is closed or acquired by another creditor; or

(2) The balance is transferred from a credit card account under an open-end (not home-secured) consumer credit plan issued by a creditor to another credit account issued by the same creditor or its affiliate or subsidiary (unless the account to which the balance is transferred is subject to § 1026.40).

(e) Promotional waivers or rebates of interest, fees, and other charges. If a card issuer promotes the waiver or rebate of finance charges due to a periodic interest rate or fees or charges required to be disclosed under § 1026.6(b)(2)(ii), (iii), or (xii) and applies the waiver or rebate to a credit card account under an open-end (not home-secured) consumer credit plan, any cessation of the waiver or rebate on that account constitutes an increase in an annual percentage rate, fee, or charge for purposes of this section.

§ 1026.56. Requirements for Over-the-Limit Transactions

(a) Definition. For purposes of this section, the term "over-the-limit transaction" means any extension of credit by a card issuer to complete a transaction that causes a consumer's credit card account balance to exceed the credit limit.

(b) Opt-in requirement—

(1) General. A card issuer shall not assess a fee or charge on a consumer's credit card account under an open-end (not home-secured) consumer credit plan for an over-the-limit transaction unless the card issuer:

(i) Provides the consumer with an oral, written or electronic notice, segregated from all other information, describing the consumer's right to affirmatively consent, or opt in, to the card issuer's payment of an over-the-limit transaction;

(ii) Provides a reasonable opportunity for the consumer to affirmatively consent, or opt in, to the card issuer's payment of over-the-limit transactions;

(iii) Obtains the consumer's affirmative consent, or opt-in, to the card issuer's payment of such transactions;

(iv) Provides the consumer with confirmation of the consumer's consent in writing, or if the consumer agrees, electronically; and

(v) Provides the consumer notice in writing of the right to revoke that consent following the assessment of an over-the-limit fee or charge.

(2) Completion of over-the-limit transactions without consumer consent. Notwithstanding the absence of a consumer's affirmative consent under paragraph (b)(1)(iii) of this section, a card issuer may pay any over-the-limit transaction on a consumer's account provided that the card issuer does not impose any fee or charge on the account for paying that over-the-limit transaction.

(c) Method of election. A card issuer may permit a consumer to consent to the card issuer's payment of any over-the-limit transaction in writing, orally, or electronically, at the card issuer's option. The card issuer must also permit the consumer to revoke his or her consent using the same methods available to the consumer for providing consent.

(d) Timing and placement of notices—

(1) Initial notice—

(i) General. The notice required by paragraph (b)(1)(i) of this section shall be provided prior to the assessment of any over-the-limit fee or charge on a consumer's account.

(ii) Oral or electronic consent. If a consumer consents to the card issuer's payment of any over-the-limit transaction by oral or electronic means, the card issuer must provide the notice required by paragraph (b)(1)(i) of this section immediately prior to obtaining that consent.

(2) Confirmation of opt-in. The notice required by paragraph (b)(1)(iv) of this section may be provided no later than the first periodic statement sent after the consumer has consented to the card issuer's payment of over-the-limit transactions.

(3) Notice of right of revocation. The notice required by paragraph (b)(1)(v) of this section shall be provided on the front of any page of each periodic statement that reflects the assessment of an over-the-limit fee or charge on a consumer's account.

(e) Content—

(1) Initial notice. The notice required by paragraph (b)(1)(i) of this section shall include all applicable items in this paragraph (e)(1) and may not contain any information not specified in or otherwise permitted by this paragraph.

(i) Fees. The dollar amount of any fees or charges assessed by the card issuer on a consumer's account for an over-the-limit transaction;

(ii) APRs. Any increased periodic rate(s) (expressed as an annual percentage rate(s)) that may be imposed on the account as a result of an over-the-limit transaction; and

(iii) Disclosure of opt-in right. An explanation of the consumer's right to affirmatively consent to the card issuer's payment of over-the-limit transactions, including the method(s) by which the consumer may consent.

(2) Subsequent notice. The notice required by paragraph (b)(1)(v) of this section shall describe the consumer's right to revoke any consent provided under paragraph (b)(1)(iii) of this section, including the method(s) by which the consumer may revoke.

(3) Safe harbor. Use of Model Forms G-25(A) or G-25(B) of appendix G to this part, or substantially similar notices, constitutes compliance with the notice content requirements of paragraph (e) of this section.

(f) Joint relationships. If two or more consumers are jointly liable on a credit card account under an open-end (not home-secured) consumer credit plan, the card issuer shall treat the affirmative consent of any of the joint consumers as affirmative consent for that account. Similarly, the card issuer shall treat a revocation of consent by any of the joint consumers as revocation of consent for that account.

(g) Continuing right to opt in or revoke opt-in. A consumer may affirmatively consent to the card issuer's payment of over-the-limit transactions at any time in the manner described in the notice required by paragraph (b)(1)(i) of this section. Similarly, the consumer may revoke the consent at any time in the manner described in the notice required by paragraph (b)(1)(v) of this section.

(h) Duration of opt-in. A consumer's affirmative consent to the card issuer's payment of over-the-limit transactions is effective until revoked by the consumer, or until the card issuer decides for any reason to cease paying over-the-limit transactions for the consumer.

(i) Time to comply with revocation request. A card issuer must comply with a consumer's revocation request as soon as reasonably practicable after the card issuer receives it.

(j) Prohibited practices. Notwithstanding a consumer's affirmative consent to a card issuer's payment of over-the-limit transactions, a card issuer is prohibited from engaging in the following practices:

(1) Fees or charges imposed per cycle—

(i) General rule. A card issuer may not impose more than one over-the-limit fee or charge on a consumer's credit card account per billing cycle, and, in any event, only if the credit limit was exceeded during the billing cycle. In addition, except as provided in paragraph (j)(1)(ii) of this section, a card issuer may not impose an over-the-limit fee or charge on the consumer's credit card account for more than three billing cycles for the same over-the-limit transaction where the consumer has not reduced the account balance below the credit limit by the payment due date for either of the last two billing cycles.

(ii) Exception. The prohibition in paragraph (j)(1)(i) of this section on imposing an over-the-limit fee or charge in more than three billing cycles for the same over-the-limit transaction(s) does not apply if another over-the-limit transaction occurs during either of the last two billing cycles.

(2) Failure to promptly replenish. A card issuer may not impose an over-the-limit fee or charge solely because of the card issuer's failure to promptly replenish the consumer's available credit following the crediting of the consumer's payment under § 1026.10.

(3) Conditioning. A card issuer may not condition the amount of a consumer's credit limit on the consumer affirmatively consenting to the card issuer's payment of over-the-limit transactions if the card issuer assesses a fee or charge for such service.

(4) Over-the-limit fees attributed to fees or interest. A card issuer may not impose an over-the-limit fee or charge for a billing cycle if a consumer exceeds a credit limit solely because of fees or interest charged by the card issuer to the consumer's account during that billing cycle. For purposes of this paragraph (j)(4), the relevant fees or interest charges are charges imposed as part of the plan under § 1026.6(b)(3).

§ 1026.57. Reporting and Marketing Rules for College Student Open-End Credit

(a) Definitions—

(1) College student credit card. The term "college student credit card" as used in this section means a credit card issued under a credit card account under an open-end (not home-secured) consumer credit plan to any college student.

(2) College student. The term "college student" as used in this section means a consumer who is a full-time or part-time student of an institution of higher education.

(3) Institution of higher education. The term "institution of higher education" as used in this section has the same meaning as in sections 101 and 102 of the Higher Education Act of 1965 (20 U.S.C. 1001 and 1002).

(4) Affiliated organization. The term "affiliated organization" as used in this section means an alumni organization or foundation affiliated with or related to an institution of higher education.

(5) College credit card agreement. The term "college credit card agreement" as used in this section means any business, marketing or promotional agreement between a card issuer and an institution of higher education or an affiliated organization in connection with which college student credit cards are issued to college students currently enrolled at that institution.

(b) Public disclosure of agreements. An institution of higher education shall publicly disclose any contract or other agreement made with a card issuer or creditor for the purpose of marketing a credit card.

(c) Prohibited inducements. No card issuer or creditor may offer a college student any tangible item to induce such student to apply for or open an open-end consumer credit plan offered by such card issuer or creditor, if such offer is made:

(1) On the campus of an institution of higher education;

(2) Near the campus of an institution of higher education; or

(3) At an event sponsored by or related to an institution of higher education.

(d) Annual report to the Bureau—

(1) Requirement to report. Any card issuer that was a party to one or more college credit card agreements in effect at any time during a calendar year must submit to the Bureau an annual report regarding those agreements in the form and manner prescribed by the Bureau.

(2) Contents of report. The annual report to the Bureau must include the following:

(i) Identifying information about the card issuer and the agreements submitted, including the issuer's name, address, and identifying number (such as an RSSD ID number or tax identification number);

(ii) A copy of any college credit card agreement to which the card issuer was a party that was in effect at any time during the period covered by the report;

(iii) A copy of any memorandum of understanding in effect at any time during the period covered by the report between the card issuer and an institution of higher education or affiliated organization that directly or indirectly relates to the college credit card agreement or that controls or directs any obligations or distribution of benefits between any such entities;

(iv) The total dollar amount of any payments pursuant to a college credit card agreement from the card issuer to an institution of higher education or affiliated organization during the period covered by the report, and the method or formula used to determine such amounts;

(v) The total number of credit card accounts opened pursuant to any college credit card agreement during the period covered by the report; and

(vi) The total number of credit card accounts opened pursuant to any such agreement that were open at the end of the period covered by the report.

(3) Timing of reports. Except for the initial report described in this paragraph (d)(3), a card issuer must submit its annual report for each calendar year to the Bureau by the first business day on or after March 31 of the following calendar year.

§ 1026.58 Internet posting of credit card agreements

(a) Applicability. The requirements of this section apply to any card issuer that issues credit cards under a credit card account under an open-end (not home-secured) consumer credit plan.

(b) Definitions—

(1) Agreement. For purposes of this section, "agreement" or "credit card agreement" means the written document or documents evidencing the terms of the legal obligation, or the prospective legal obligation, between a card issuer and a consumer for a credit card account under an open-end (not home-secured) consumer credit plan. "Agreement" or "credit card agreement" also includes the pricing information, as defined in § 1026.58(b)(7).

(2) Amends. For purposes of this section, an issuer "amends" an agreement if it makes a substantive change (an "amendment") to the agreement. A change is substantive if it alters the rights or obligations of the card issuer or the consumer under the agreement. Any change in the pricing information, as defined in § 1026.58(b)(7), is deemed to be substantive.

(3) Business day. For purposes of this section, "business day" means a day on which the creditor's offices are open to the public for carrying on substantially all of its business functions.

(4) Card issuer. For purposes of this section, "card issuer" or "issuer" means the entity to which a consumer is legally obligated, or would be legally obligated, under the terms of a credit card agreement.

(5) Offers. For purposes of this section, an issuer "offers" or "offers to the public" an agreement if the issuer is soliciting or accepting applications for accounts that would be subject to that agreement.

(6) Open account. For purposes of this section, an account is an "open account" or "open credit card account" if it is a credit card account under an open-end (not home-secured) consumer credit plan and either:

(i) The cardholder can obtain extensions of credit on the account; or

(ii) There is an outstanding balance on the account that has not been charged off. An account that has been suspended temporarily (for example, due to a report by the cardholder of unauthorized use of the card) is considered an "open account" or "open credit card account."

(7) Pricing information. For purposes of this section, "pricing information" means the information listed in § 1026.6(b)(2)(i) through (b)(2)(xii). Pricing information does not include temporary or promotional rates and terms or rates and terms that apply only to protected balances.

(8) Private label credit card account and private label credit card plan. For purposes of this section:

(i) "private label credit card account" means a credit card account under an open-end (not home-secured) consumer credit plan with a credit card that can be used to make purchases only at a single merchant or an affiliated group of merchants; and

(ii) "private label credit card plan" means all of the private label credit card accounts issued by a particular issuer with credit cards usable at the same single merchant or affiliated group of merchants.

(c) Submission of agreements to Bureau—

(1) Quarterly submissions. A card issuer must make quarterly submissions to the Bureau, in the form and manner specified by the Bureau. Quarterly submissions must be sent to the Bureau no later than the first business day on or after January 31, April 30, July 31, and October 31 of each year. Each submission must contain:

(i) Identifying information about the card issuer and the agreements submitted, including the issuer's name, address, and identifying number (such as an RSSD ID number or tax identification number);

(ii) The credit card agreements that the card issuer offered to the public as of the last business day of the preceding calendar quarter that the card issuer has not previously submitted to the Bureau;

(iii) Any credit card agreement previously submitted to the Bureau that was amended during the preceding calendar quarter and that the card issuer offered to the public as of the last business day of the preceding calendar quarter, as described in § 1026.58(c)(3); and

(iv) Notification regarding any credit card agreement previously submitted to the Bureau that the issuer is withdrawing, as described in § 1026.58(c)(4), (c)(5), (c)(6), and (c)(7).

(2) [Reserved]

(3) Amended agreements. If a credit card agreement has been submitted to the Bureau, the agreement has not been amended and the card issuer continues to offer the agreement to the public, no additional submission regarding that agreement is required. If a credit card agreement that previously has been submitted to the Bureau is amended and the card issuer offered the amended agreement to the public as of the last business day of the calendar quarter in which the change became effective, the card issuer must submit the entire amended agreement to the Bureau, in the form and manner specified by the Bureau, by the first quarterly submission deadline after the last day of the calendar quarter in which the change became effective.

(4) Withdrawal of agreements. If a card issuer no longer offers to the public a credit card agreement that previously has been submitted to the Bureau, the card issuer must notify the Bureau, in the form and manner specified by the Bureau, by the first quarterly submission deadline after the last day of the calendar quarter in which the issuer ceased to offer the agreement.

(5) De minimis exception.

(i) A card issuer is not required to submit any credit card agreements to the Bureau if the card issuer had fewer than 10,000 open credit card accounts as of the last business day of the calendar quarter.

(ii) If an issuer that previously qualified for the de minimis exception ceases to qualify, the card issuer must begin making quarterly submissions to the Bureau no later than the first quarterly submission deadline after the date as of which the issuer ceased to qualify.

(iii) If a card issuer that did not previously qualify for the de minimis exception qualifies for the de minimis exception, the card issuer must continue to make quarterly submissions to the Bureau until the issuer notifies the Bureau that the card issuer is withdrawing all agreements it previously submitted to the Bureau.

(6) Private label credit card exception.

(i) A card issuer is not required to submit to the Bureau a credit card agreement if, as of the last business day of the calendar quarter, the agreement:

(A) Is offered for accounts under one or more private label credit card plans each of which has fewer than 10,000 open accounts; and

(B) Is not offered to the public other than for accounts under such a plan.

(ii) If an agreement that previously qualified for the private label credit card exception ceases to qualify, the card issuer must submit the agreement to the Bureau no later than the first quarterly submission deadline after the date as of which the agreement ceased to qualify.

(iii) If an agreement that did not previously qualify for the private label credit card exception qualifies for the exception, the card issuer must continue to make quarterly submissions to the Bureau with respect to that agreement until the issuer notifies the Bureau that the agreement is being withdrawn.

(7) Product testing exception.

(i) A card issuer is not required to submit to the Bureau a credit card agreement if, as of the last business day of the calendar quarter, the agreement:

(A) Is offered as part of a product test offered to only a limited group of consumers for a limited period of time;

(B) Is used for fewer than 10,000 open accounts; and

(C) Is not offered to the public other than in connection with such a product test.

(ii) If an agreement that previously qualified for the product testing exception ceases to qualify, the card issuer must submit the agreement to the Bureau no later than the first quarterly submission deadline after the date as of which the agreement ceased to qualify.

(iii) If an agreement that did not previously qualify for the product testing exception qualifies for the exception, the card issuer must continue to make quarterly submissions to the Bureau with respect to that agreement until the issuer notifies the Bureau that the agreement is being withdrawn.

(8) Form and content of agreements submitted to the Bureau—

(i) Form and content generally.

(A) Each agreement must contain the provisions of the agreement and the pricing information in effect as of the last business day of the preceding calendar quarter.

(B) Agreements must not include any personally identifiable information relating to any cardholder, such as name, address, telephone number, or account number.

(C) The following are not deemed to be part of the agreement for purposes of § 1026.58, and therefore are not required to be included in submissions to the Bureau:

(1) Disclosures required by state or Federal law, such as affiliate marketing notices, privacy policies, billing rights notices, or disclosures under the E-Sign Act;

(2) Solicitation materials;

(3) Periodic statements;

(4) Ancillary agreements between the issuer and the consumer, such as debt cancellation contracts or debt suspension agreements;

(5) Offers for credit insurance or other optional products and other similar advertisements; and

(6) Documents that may be sent to the consumer along with the credit card or credit card agreement such as a cover letter, a validation sticker on the card, or other information about card security.

(D) Agreements must be presented in a clear and legible font.

(ii) Pricing information.

(A) Pricing information must be set forth in a single addendum to the agreement. The addendum must contain all of the pricing information, as defined by § 1026.58(b)(7). The addendum may, but is not required to, contain any other information listed in § 1026.6(b), provided that information is complete and accurate as of the applicable date under § 1026.58. The addendum may not contain any other information.

(B) Pricing information that may vary from one cardholder to another depending on the cardholder's creditworthiness or state of residence or other factors must be disclosed either by setting forth all the possible variations (such as purchase APRs of 13 percent, 15 percent, 17 percent, and 19 percent) or by providing a range of possible variations (such as purchase APRs ranging from 13 percent to 19 percent).

(C) If a rate included in the pricing information is a variable rate, the issuer must identify the index or formula used in setting the rate and the margin. Rates that may vary from one cardholder to another must be disclosed by providing the index and the possible margins (such as the prime rate plus 5 percent, 8 percent, 10 percent, or 12 percent) or range of margins (such as the prime rate plus from 5 to 12 percent). The value of the rate and the value of the index are not required to be disclosed.

(iii) Optional variable terms addendum. Provisions of the agreement other than the pricing information that may vary from one cardholder to another depending on the cardholder's creditworthiness or state of residence or other factors may be set forth in a single addendum to the agreement separate from the pricing information addendum.

(iv) Integrated agreement. Issuers may not provide provisions of the agreement or pricing information in the form of change-in-terms notices or riders (other than the pricing information addendum and the optional variable terms addendum). Changes in provisions or pricing information must be integrated into the text of the agreement, the pricing information addendum or the optional variable terms addendum, as appropriate.

(d) Posting of agreements offered to the public.

(1) Except as provided below, a card issuer must post and maintain on its publicly available Web site the credit card agreements that the issuer is required to submit to the Bureau under § 1026.58(c). With respect to an agreement offered solely for accounts under one or more private label credit card plans, an issuer may fulfill this requirement by posting and maintaining the agreement in accordance with the requirements of this section on the publicly available Web site of at least one of the merchants at which credit cards issued under each private label credit card plan with 10,000 or more open accounts may be used.

(2) Except as provided in § 1026.58(d), agreements posted pursuant to § 1026.58(d) must conform to the form and content requirements for agreements submitted to the Bureau specified in § 1026.58(c)(8).

(3) Agreements posted pursuant to § 1026.58(d) may be posted in any electronic format that is readily usable by the general public. Agreements must be placed in a location that is prominent and readily accessible by the public and must be accessible without submission of personally identifiable information.

(4) The card issuer must update the agreements posted on its Web site pursuant to § 1026.58(d) at least as frequently as the quarterly schedule required for submission of agreements to the Bureau under § 1026.58(c). If the issuer chooses to update the agreements on its Web site more frequently, the agreements posted on the issuer's Web site may contain the provisions of the agreement and the pricing information in effect as of a date other than the last business day of the preceding calendar quarter.

(e) Agreements for all open accounts—

(1) Availability of individual cardholder's agreement. With respect to any open credit card account, a card issuer must either:

(i) Post and maintain the cardholder's agreement on its Web site; or

(ii) Promptly provide a copy of the cardholder's agreement to the cardholder upon the cardholder's request. If the card issuer makes an agreement available upon request, the issuer must provide the cardholder with the ability to request a copy of the agreement both by using the issuer's Web site (such as by clicking on a clearly identified box to make the request) and by calling a readily available telephone line the number for which is displayed on the issuer's Web site and clearly identified as to purpose. The card issuer must send to the cardholder or otherwise make available to the cardholder a copy of the cardholder's agreement in electronic or paper form no later than 30 days after the issuer receives the cardholder's request.

(2) Special rule for issuers without interactive Web sites. An issuer that does not maintain a Web site from which cardholders can access specific information about their individual accounts, instead of complying with § 1026.58(e)(1), may make agreements available upon request by providing the cardholder with the ability to request a copy of the agreement by calling a readily available telephone line, the number for which is displayed on the issuer's Web site and clearly identified as to purpose or included on each periodic statement sent to the cardholder and clearly identified as to purpose. The issuer must send to the cardholder or otherwise make available to the cardholder a copy of the cardholder's agreement in electronic or paper form no later than 30 days after the issuer receives the cardholder's request.

(3) Form and content of agreements.

(i) Except as provided in § 1026.58(e), agreements posted on the card issuer's Web site pursuant to § 1026.58(e)(1)(i) or made available upon the cardholder's request pursuant to § 1026.58(e)(1)(ii) or (e)(2) must conform to the form and content requirements for agreements submitted to the Bureau specified in § 1026.58(c)(8).

(ii) If the card issuer posts an agreement on its Web site or otherwise provides an agreement to a cardholder electronically under § 1026.58(e), the agreement may be posted or provided in any electronic format that is readily usable by the general public and must be placed in a location that is prominent and readily accessible to the cardholder.

(iii) Agreements posted or otherwise provided pursuant to § 1026.58(e) may contain personally identifiable information relating to the cardholder, such as name, address, telephone number, or account number, provided that the issuer takes appropriate measures to make the agreement accessible only to the cardholder or other authorized persons.

(iv) Agreements posted or otherwise provided pursuant to § 1026.58(e) must set forth the specific provisions and pricing information applicable to the particular cardholder. Provisions and pricing information must be complete and accurate as of a date no more than 60 days prior to:

(A) The date on which the agreement is posted on the card issuer's Web site under § 1026.58(e)(1)(i); or

(B) The date the cardholder's request is received under § 1026.58(e)(1)(ii) or (e)(2).

(v) Agreements provided upon cardholder request pursuant to § 1026.58(e)(1)(ii) or (e)(2) may be provided by the issuer in either electronic or paper form, regardless of the form of the cardholder's request.

(f) E-Sign Act requirements. Card issuers may provide credit card agreements in electronic form under § 1026.58(d) and (e) without regard to the consumer notice and consent requirements of section 101(c) of the Electronic Signatures in Global and National Commerce Act (E-Sign Act) (15 U.S.C. 7001 et seq.).

(g) Temporary suspension of agreement submission requirement—

(1) Quarterly submissions. The quarterly submission requirement in paragraph (c) of this section is suspended for the submissions that would otherwise be due to the Bureau by the first business day on or after April 30, 2015; July 31, 2015; October 31, 2015; and January 31, 2016.

(2) Posting of agreements offered to the public. Nothing in paragraph (g)(1) of this section shall affect the agreement posting requirements in paragraph (d) of this section.

§ 1026.59 Reevaluation of rate increases

(a) General rule—

(1) Evaluation of increased rate. If a card issuer increases an annual percentage rate that applies to a credit card account under an open-end (not home-secured) consumer credit plan, based on the credit risk of the consumer, market conditions, or other factors, or increased such a rate on or after January 1, 2009, and 45 days' advance notice of the rate increase is required pursuant to § 1026.9(c)(2) or (g), the card issuer must:

(i) Evaluate the factors described in paragraph (d) of this section; and

(ii) Based on its review of such factors, reduce the annual percentage rate applicable to the consumer's account, as appropriate.

(2) Rate reductions—

(i) Timing. If a card issuer is required to reduce the rate applicable to an account pursuant to paragraph (a)(1) of this section, the card issuer must reduce the rate not later than 45 days after completion of the evaluation described in paragraph (a)(1).

(ii) Applicability of rate reduction. Any reduction in an annual percentage rate required pursuant to paragraph (a)(1) of this section shall apply to:

(A) Any outstanding balances to which the increased rate described in paragraph (a)(1) of this section has been applied; and

(B) New transactions that occur after the effective date of the rate reduction that would otherwise have been subject to the increased rate.

(b) Policies and procedures. A card issuer must have reasonable written policies and procedures in place to conduct the review described in paragraph (a) of this section.

(c) Timing. A card issuer that is subject to paragraph (a) of this section must conduct the review described in paragraph (a)(1) of this section not less frequently than once every six months after the rate increase.

(d) Factors—

(1) In general. Except as provided in paragraph (d)(2) of this section, a card issuer must review either:

(i) The factors on which the increase in an annual percentage rate was originally based; or

(ii) The factors that the card issuer currently considers when determining the annual percentage rates applicable to similar new credit card accounts under an open-end (not home-secured) consumer credit plan.

(2) Rate increases imposed between January 1, 2009 and February 21, 2010. For rate increases imposed between January 1, 2009 and February 21, 2010, an issuer must consider the factors described in paragraph (d)(1)(ii) when conducting the first two reviews required under paragraph (a) of this section, unless the rate increase subject to paragraph (a) of this section was based solely upon factors specific to the consumer, such as a decline in the consumer's credit risk, the consumer's delinquency or default, or a violation of the terms of the account.

(e) Rate increases due to delinquency. If an issuer increases a rate applicable to a consumer's account pursuant to § 1026.55(b)(4) based on the card issuer not receiving the consumer's required minimum periodic payment within 60 days after the due date, the issuer is not required to perform the review described in paragraph (a) of this section prior to the sixth payment due date after the effective date of the increase. However, if the annual percentage rate applicable to the consumer's account is not reduced pursuant to § 1026.55(b)(4)(ii), the card issuer must perform the review described in paragraph (a) of this section. The first such review must occur no later than six months after the sixth payment due following the effective date of the rate increase.

(f) Termination of obligation to review factors. The obligation to review factors described in paragraph (a) and (d) of this section ceases to apply:

(1) If the issuer reduces the annual percentage rate applicable to a credit card account under an open-end (not home-secured) consumer credit plan to the rate applicable immediately prior to the increase, or, if the rate applicable immediately prior to the increase was a variable rate, to a variable rate determined by the same formula (index and margin) that was used to calculate the rate applicable immediately prior to the increase; or

(2) If the issuer reduces the annual percentage rate to a rate that is lower than the rate described in paragraph (f)(1) of this section.

(g) Acquired accounts—

(1) General. Except as provided in paragraph (g)(2) of this section, this section applies to credit card accounts that have been acquired by the card issuer from another card issuer. A card issuer that complies with this section by reviewing the factors described in paragraph (d)(1)(i) must review the factors considered by the card issuer from which it acquired the accounts in connection with the rate increase.

(2) Review of acquired portfolio. If, not later than six months after the acquisition of such accounts, a card issuer reviews all of the credit card accounts it acquires in accordance with the factors that it currently considers in determining the rates applicable to its similar new credit card accounts:

(i) Except as provided in paragraph (g)(2)(iii), the card issuer is required to conduct reviews described in paragraph (a) of this section only for rate increases that are imposed as a result of its review under this paragraph. See §§ 1026.9 and 1026.55 for additional requirements regarding rate increases on acquired accounts.

(ii) Except as provided in paragraph (g)(2)(iii) of this section, the card issuer is not required to conduct reviews in accordance with paragraph (a) of this section for any rate increases made prior to the card issuer's acquisition of such accounts.

(iii) If as a result of the card issuer's review, an account is subject to, or continues to be subject to, an increased rate as a penalty, or due to the consumer's delinquency or default, the requirements of paragraph (a) of this section apply.

(h) Exceptions—

(1) Servicemembers Civil Relief Act exception. The requirements of this section do not apply to increases in an annual percentage rate that was previously decreased pursuant to 50 U.S.C. app. 527, provided that such a rate increase is made in accordance with § 1026.55(b)(6).

(2) Charged off accounts. The requirements of this section do not apply to accounts that the card issuer has charged off in accordance with loan-loss provisions.

§ 1026.60 [Former Section 226.5a]. Credit and Charge Card Applications and Solicitations

(a) General rules. The card issuer shall provide the disclosures required under this section on or with a solicitation or an application to open a credit or charge card account.

(1) Definition of solicitation. For purposes of this section, the term solicitation means an offer by the card issuer to open a credit or charge card account that does not require the consumer to complete an application. A "firm offer of credit" as defined in section 603(*l*) of the Fair Credit Reporting Act (15 U.S.C. 1681a(*l*)) for a credit or charge card is a solicitation for purposes of this section.

(2) Form of disclosures; tabular format.

(i) The disclosures in paragraphs (b)(1) through (5) (except for (b)(1)(iv)(B)) and (b)(7) through (15) of this section made pursuant to paragraph (c), (d)(2), (e)(1) or (f) of this section generally shall be in the form of a table with headings, content, and format substantially similar to any of the applicable tables found in G-10 in appendix G to this part.

(ii) The table described in paragraph (a)(2)(i) of this section shall contain only the information required or permitted by this section. Other information may be presented on or with an application or solicitation, provided such information appears outside the required table.

(iii) Disclosures required by paragraphs (b)(1)(iv)(B), (b)(1)(iv)(C) and (b)(6) of this section must be placed directly beneath the table.

(iv) When a tabular format is required, any annual percentage rate required to be disclosed pursuant to paragraph (b)(1) of this section, any introductory rate required to be disclosed pursuant to paragraph (b)(1)(ii) of this section, any rate that will apply after a premium initial rate expires required to be disclosed under paragraph (b)(1)(iii) of this section, and any fee or percentage amounts or maximum limits on fee amounts disclosed pursuant to paragraphs (b)(2), (b)(4), (b)(8) through (b)(13) of this section must be disclosed in bold text. However, bold text shall not be used for: The amount of any periodic fee disclosed pursuant to paragraph (b)(2) of this section that is not an annualized amount; and other annual percentage rates or fee amounts disclosed in the table.

(v) For an application or a solicitation that is accessed by the consumer in electronic form, the disclosures required under this section may be provided to the consumer in electronic form on or with the application or solicitation.

(vi)(A) Except as provided in paragraph (a)(2)(vi)(B) of this section, the table described in paragraph (a)(2)(i) of this section must be provided in a prominent location on or with an application or a solicitation.

(B) If the table described in paragraph (a)(2)(i) of this section is provided electronically, it must be provided in close proximity to the application or solicitation.

(3) Fees based on a percentage. If the amount of any fee required to be disclosed under this section is determined on the basis of a percentage of another amount, the percentage used and the identification of the amount against which the percentage is applied may be disclosed instead of the amount of the fee.

(4) Fees that vary by state. Card issuers that impose fees referred to in paragraphs (b)(8) through (12) of this section that vary by state may, at the issuer's option, disclose in the table required by paragraph (a)(2)(i) of this section: The specific fee applicable to the consumer's account; or the range of the fees, if the disclosure includes a statement that the amount of the fee varies by state and refers the consumer to a disclosure provided with the table where the amount of the fee applicable to the consumer's account is disclosed. A card issuer may not list fees for multiple states in the table.

(5) Exceptions. This section does not apply to:

(i) Home-equity plans accessible by a credit or charge card that are subject to the requirements of § 1026.40;

(ii) Overdraft lines of credit tied to asset accounts accessed by check-guarantee cards or by debit cards;

(iii) Lines of credit accessed by check-guarantee cards or by debit cards that can be used only at automated teller machines;

(iv) Lines of credit accessed solely by account numbers except for a covered separate credit feature solely accessible by an account number that is a hybrid prepaid-credit card as defined in § 1026.61;

(v) Additions of a credit or charge card to an existing open-end plan;

(vi) General purpose applications unless the application, or material accompanying it, indicates that it can be used to open a credit or charge card account; or

(vii) Consumer-initiated requests for applications.

(b) Required disclosures. The card issuer shall disclose the items in this paragraph on or with an application or a solicitation in accordance with the requirements of paragraphs (c), (d), (e)(1), or (f) of this section. A credit card issuer shall disclose all applicable items in this paragraph except for paragraph (b)(7) of this section. A charge card issuer shall disclose the applicable items in paragraphs (b)(2), (4), (7) through (12), and (15) of this section. With respect to a covered separate credit feature that is a charge card account accessible by a hybrid prepaid-credit card as defined in § 1026.61, a charge card issuer also shall disclose the applicable items in paragraphs (b)(3), (13), and (14) of this section.

(1) Annual percentage rate. Each periodic rate that may be used to compute the finance charge on an outstanding balance for purchases, a cash advance, or a balance transfer, expressed as an annual percentage rate (as determined by § 1026.14(b)). When more than one rate applies for a category of transactions, the range of balances to which each rate is applicable shall also be disclosed. The annual percentage rate for purchases disclosed pursuant to this paragraph shall be in at least 16-point type, except for the following: Oral disclosures of the annual percentage rate for purchases; or a penalty rate that may apply upon the occurrence of one or more specific events.

(i) Variable rate information. If a rate disclosed under paragraph (b)(1) of this section is a variable rate, the card issuer shall also disclose the fact that the rate may vary and how the rate is determined. In describing how the applicable rate will be determined, the card issuer must identify the type of index or formula that is used in setting the rate. The value of the index and the amount of the margin that are used to calculate the variable rate shall not be disclosed in the table. A disclosure of any applicable limitations on rate increases shall not be included in the table.

(ii) Discounted initial rate. If the initial rate is an introductory rate, as that term is defined in § 1026.16(g)(2)(ii), the card issuer must disclose in the table the introductory rate, the time period during which the introductory rate will remain in effect, and must use the term "introductory" or "intro" in immediate proximity to the introductory rate. The card issuer also must disclose the rate that would otherwise apply to the account pursuant to paragraph (b)(1) of this section. Where the rate is not tied to an index or formula, the card issuer must disclose the rate that will apply after the introductory rate expires. In a variable-rate account, the card issuer must disclose a rate based on the applicable index or formula in accordance with the accuracy requirements set forth in paragraphs (c)(2), (d)(3), or (e)(4) of this section, as applicable.

(iii) Premium initial rate. If the initial rate is temporary and is higher than the rate that will apply after the temporary rate expires, the card issuer must disclose the premium initial rate pursuant to paragraph (b)(1) of this section and the time period during which the premium initial rate will remain in effect. Consistent with paragraph (b)(1) of this section, the premium initial rate for purchases must be in at least 16-point type. The issuer must also disclose in the table the rate that will apply after the premium initial rate expires, in at least 16-point type.

(iv) Penalty rates—

(A) In general. Except as provided in paragraph (b)(1)(iv)(B) and (C) of this section, if a rate may increase as a penalty for one or more events specified in the account agreement, such as a late payment or an extension of credit that exceeds the credit limit, the card issuer must disclose pursuant to this paragraph (b)(1) the increased rate that may apply, a brief description of the event or events that may result in the increased rate, and a brief description of how long the increased rate will remain in effect.

(B) Introductory rates. If the issuer discloses an introductory rate, as that term is defined in § 1026.16(g)(2)(ii), in the table or in any written or electronic promotional materials accompanying applications or solicitations subject to paragraph (c) or (e) of this section, the issuer must briefly disclose directly beneath the table the circumstances, if any, under which the introductory rate may be revoked, and the type of rate that will apply after the introductory rate is revoked.

(C) Employee preferential rates. If a card issuer discloses in the table a preferential annual percentage rate for which only employees of the card issuer, employees of a third party, or other individuals with similar affiliations with the card issuer or third party, such as executive officers, directors, or principal shareholders are eligible, the card issuer must briefly disclose directly beneath the table the circumstances under which such preferential rate may be revoked, and the rate that will apply after such preferential rate is revoked.

(v) Rates that depend on consumer's creditworthiness. If a rate cannot be determined at the time disclosures are given because the rate depends, at least in part, on a later determination of the consumer's creditworthiness, the card issuer must disclose the specific rates or the range of rates that could apply and a statement that the rate for which the consumer may qualify at account opening will depend on the consumer's creditworthiness, and other factors if applicable. If the rate that depends, at least in part, on a later determination of the consumer's creditworthiness is a penalty rate, as described in paragraph (b)(1)(iv) of this section, the card issuer at its option may disclose the highest rate that could apply, instead of disclosing the specific rates or the range of rates that could apply.

(vi) APRs that vary by state. Issuers imposing annual percentage rates that vary by state may, at the issuer's option, disclose in the table: the specific annual percentage rate applicable to the consumer's account; or the range of the annual percentage rates, if the disclosure includes a statement that the annual percentage rate varies by state and refers the consumer to a disclosure provided with the table where the annual percentage rate applicable to the consumer's account is disclosed. A card issuer may not list annual percentage rates for multiple states in the table.

(2) Fees for issuance or availability.

(i) Any annual or other periodic fee that may be imposed for the issuance or availability of a credit or charge card, including any fee based on account activity or inactivity; how frequently it will be imposed; and the annualized amount of the fee.

(ii) Any non-periodic fee that relates to opening an account. A card issuer must disclose that the fee is a one-time fee.

(3) Fixed finance charge; minimum interest charge. Any fixed finance charge and a brief description of the charge. Any minimum interest charge if it exceeds $1.00 that could be imposed during a billing cycle, and a brief description of the charge. The $1.00 threshold amount shall be adjusted periodically by the Bureau to reflect changes in the Consumer Price Index. The Bureau shall calculate each year a price level adjusted minimum interest charge using the Consumer Price Index in effect on June 1 of that year. When the cumulative change in the adjusted minimum value derived from applying the annual Consumer Price level to the current minimum interest charge threshold has risen by a whole dollar, the minimum interest charge will be increased by $1.00. The issuer may, at its option, disclose in the table minimum interest charges below this threshold.

(4) Transaction charges. Any transaction charge imposed by the card issuer for the use of the card for purchases.

(5) Grace period. The date by which or the period within which any credit extended for purchases may be repaid without incurring a finance charge due to a periodic interest rate and any conditions on the availability of the grace period. If no grace period is provided, that fact must be disclosed. If the length of the grace period varies, the card issuer may disclose the range of days, the minimum number of days, or the average number of days in the grace period, if the disclosure is identified as a range, minimum, or average. In disclosing in the tabular format a grace period that applies to all types of purchases, the phrase "How to Avoid Paying Interest on Purchases" shall be used as the heading for the row describing the grace period. If a grace period is not offered on all types of purchases, in disclosing this fact in the tabular format, the phrase "Paying Interest" shall be used as the heading for the row describing this fact.

(6) Balance computation method. The name of the balance computation method listed in paragraph (g) of this section that is used to determine the balance for purchases on which the finance charge is computed, or an explanation of the method used if it is not listed. In determining which balance computation method to disclose, the card issuer shall assume that credit extended for purchases will not be repaid within the grace period, if any.

(7) Statement on charge card payments. A statement that charges incurred by use of the charge card are due when the periodic statement is received.

(8) Cash advance fee. Any fee imposed for an extension of credit in the form of cash or its equivalent.

(9) Late payment fee. Any fee imposed for a late payment.

(10) Over-the-limit fee. Any fee imposed for exceeding a credit limit.

(11) Balance transfer fee. Any fee imposed to transfer an outstanding balance.

(12) Returned-payment fee. Any fee imposed by the card issuer for a returned payment.

(13) Required insurance, debt cancellation or debt suspension coverage.

(i) A fee for insurance described in § 1026.4(b)(7) or debt cancellation or suspension coverage described in § 1026.4(b)(10), if the insurance or debt cancellation or suspension coverage is required as part of the plan; and

(ii) A cross reference to any additional information provided about the insurance or coverage accompanying the application or solicitation, as applicable.

(14) Available credit. If a card issuer requires fees for the issuance or availability of credit described in paragraph (b)(2) of this section, or requires a security deposit for such credit, and the total amount of those required fees and/or security deposit that will be imposed and charged to the account when the account is opened is 15 percent or more of the minimum credit limit for the card, a card issuer must disclose the available credit remaining after these fees or security deposit are debited to the account, assuming that the consumer receives the minimum credit limit. In determining whether the 15 percent threshold test is met, the issuer must only consider fees for issuance or availability of credit, or a security deposit, that are required. If fees for issuance or availability are optional, these fees should not be considered in determining whether the disclosure must be given. Nonetheless, if the 15 percent threshold test is met, the issuer in providing the disclosure must disclose the amount of available credit calculated by excluding those optional fees, and the available credit including those optional fees. This paragraph does not apply with respect to fees or security deposits that are not debited to the account.

(15) Web site reference. A reference to the Web site established by the Bureau and a statement that consumers may obtain on the Web site information about shopping for and using credit cards. Until January 1, 2013, issuers may substitute for this reference a reference to the Web site established by the Board of Governors of the Federal Reserve System.

(c) Direct mail and electronic applications and solicitations—

(1) General. The card issuer shall disclose the applicable items in paragraph (b) of this section on or with an application or solicitation that is mailed to consumers or provided to consumers in electronic form.

(2) Accuracy.

(i) Disclosures in direct mail applications and solicitations must be accurate as of the time the disclosures are mailed. An accurate variable annual percentage rate is one in effect within 60 days before mailing.

(ii) Disclosures provided in electronic form must be accurate as of the time they are sent, in the case of disclosures sent to a consumer's email address, or as of the time they are viewed by the public, in the case of disclosures made available at a location such as a card issuer's Web site. An accurate variable annual percentage rate provided in electronic form is one in effect within 30 days before it is sent to a consumer's email address, or viewed by the public, as applicable.

(d) Telephone applications and solicitations—

(1) Oral disclosure. The card issuer shall disclose orally the information in paragraphs (b)(1) through (7) and (b)(14) of this section, to the extent applicable, in a telephone application or solicitation initiated by the card issuer.

(2) Alternative disclosure. The oral disclosure under paragraph (d)(1) of this section need not be given if the card issuer either:

(i)(A) Does not impose a fee described in paragraph (b)(2) of this section; or

(B) Imposes such a fee but provides the consumer with a right to reject the plan consistent with § 1026.5(b)(1)(iv); and

(ii) The card issuer discloses in writing within 30 days after the consumer requests the card (but in no event later than the delivery of the card) the following:

(A) The applicable information in paragraph (b) of this section; and

(B) As applicable, the fact that the consumer has the right to reject the plan and not be obligated to pay fees described in paragraph (b)(2) or any other fees or charges until the consumer has used the account or made a payment on the account after receiving a billing statement.

(3) Accuracy.

(i) The oral disclosures under paragraph (d)(1) of this section must be accurate as of the time they are given.

(ii) The alternative disclosures under paragraph (d)(2) of this section generally must be accurate as of the time they are mailed or delivered. A variable annual percentage rate is one that is accurate if it was:

(A) In effect at the time the disclosures are mailed or delivered; or

(B) In effect as of a specified date (which rate is then updated from time to time, but no less frequently than each calendar month).

(e) Applications and solicitations made available to general public. The card issuer shall provide disclosures, to the extent applicable, on or with an application or solicitation that is made available to the general public, including one contained in a catalog, magazine, or other generally available publication. The disclosures shall be provided in accordance with paragraph (e)(1) or (e)(2) of this section.

(1) Disclosure of required credit information. The card issuer may disclose in a prominent location on the application or solicitation the following:

(i) The applicable information in paragraph (b) of this section;

(ii) The date the required information was printed, including a statement that the required information was accurate as of that date and is subject to change after that date; and

(iii) A statement that the consumer should contact the card issuer for any change in the required information since it was printed, and a toll-free telephone number or a mailing address for that purpose.

(2) No disclosure of credit information. If none of the items in paragraph (b) of this section is provided on or with the application or solicitation, the card issuer may state in a prominent location on the application or solicitation the following:

(i) There are costs associated with the use of the card; and

(ii) The consumer may contact the card issuer to request specific information about the costs, along with a toll-free telephone number and a mailing address for that purpose.

(3) Prompt response to requests for information. Upon receiving a request for any of the information referred to in this paragraph, the card issuer shall promptly and fully disclose the information requested.

(4) Accuracy. The disclosures given pursuant to paragraph (e)(1) of this section must be accurate as of the date of printing. A variable annual percentage rate is accurate if it was in effect within 30 days before printing.

(f) In-person applications and solicitations. A card issuer shall disclose the information in paragraph (b) of this section, to the extent applicable, on or with an application or solicitation that is initiated by the card issuer and given to the consumer in person. A card issuer complies with the requirements of this paragraph if the issuer provides disclosures in accordance with paragraph (c)(1) or (e)(1) of this section.

(g) Balance computation methods defined. The following methods may be described by name. Methods that differ due to variations such as the allocation of payments, whether the finance charge begins to accrue on the transaction date or the date of posting the transaction, the existence or length of a grace period, and whether the balance is adjusted by charges such as late payment fees, annual fees and unpaid finance charges do not constitute separate balance computation methods.

(1)(i) Average daily balance (including new purchases). This balance is figured by adding the outstanding balance (including new purchases and deducting payments and credits) for each day in the billing cycle, and then dividing by the number of days in the billing cycle.

(ii) Average daily balance (excluding new purchases). This balance is figured by adding the outstanding balance (excluding new purchases and deducting payments and credits) for each day in the billing cycle, and then dividing by the number of days in the billing cycle.

(2) Adjusted balance. This balance is figured by deducting payments and credits made during the billing cycle from the outstanding balance at the beginning of the billing cycle.

(3) Previous balance. This balance is the outstanding balance at the beginning of the billing cycle.

(4) Daily balance. For each day in the billing cycle, this balance is figured by taking the beginning balance each day, adding any new purchases, and subtracting any payment and credits.

§ 1026.61. Hybrid prepaid-credit cards

(a) Hybrid prepaid-credit card—

(1) In general.

(i) Credit offered in connection with a prepaid account is subject to this section and this regulation as specified below.

(ii) For purposes of this regulation, except as provided in paragraph (a)(4) of this section, a prepaid card is a hybrid prepaid-credit card with respect to a separate credit feature as described in paragraph (a)(2)(i) of this section when it can access credit from that credit feature, or with respect to a credit feature structured as a negative balance on the asset feature of the prepaid account as described in paragraph (a)(3) of this section when it can access credit from that credit feature. A hybrid prepaid-credit card is a credit card for purposes of this regulation with respect to those credit features.

(iii) With respect to a credit feature structured as a negative balance on the asset feature of the prepaid account as described in paragraph (a)(3) of this section, a prepaid card is not a hybrid prepaid-credit card or a credit card for purposes of this regulation if the conditions set forth in paragraph (a)(4) of this section are met.

(2) Prepaid card can access credit from a covered separate credit feature—

(i) Covered separate credit feature.

(A) A separate credit feature that can be accessed by a hybrid prepaid-credit card as described in this paragraph (a)(2)(i) is defined as a covered separate credit feature. A prepaid card is a hybrid prepaid-credit card with respect to a separate credit feature when it is a single device that can be used from time to time to access the separate credit feature where the following two conditions are both satisfied:

(1) The card can be used to draw, transfer, or authorize the draw or transfer of credit from the separate credit feature in the course of authorizing, settling, or otherwise completing transactions conducted with the card to obtain goods or services, obtain cash, or conduct person-to-person transfers; and

(2) The separate credit feature is offered by the prepaid account issuer, its affiliate, or its business partner.

(B) A separate credit feature that meets the conditions set forth in paragraph (a)(2)(i)(A) of this section is a covered separate credit feature accessible by a hybrid prepaid-credit card even with respect to credit that is drawn or transferred, or authorized to be drawn or transferred, from the credit feature outside the course of a transaction conducted with the card to obtain goods or services, obtain cash, or conduct person-to-person transfers.

(ii) Non-covered separate credit feature. A separate credit feature that does not meet the two conditions set forth in paragraph (a)(2)(i) of this section is defined as a non-covered separate credit feature. A prepaid card is not a hybrid prepaid-credit card with respect to a non-covered separate credit feature, even if the prepaid card is a hybrid prepaid-credit card with respect to a covered separate credit feature as described in paragraph (a)(2)(i) of this section. A non-covered separate credit feature is not subject to the rules applicable to hybrid prepaid-credit cards; however, it may be subject to this regulation depending on its own terms and conditions, independent of the connection to the prepaid account.

(3) Prepaid card can access credit extended through a negative balance on the asset feature of the prepaid account—

(i) In general. Except as provided in paragraph (a)(4) of this section, a prepaid card is a hybrid prepaid-credit card when it is a single device that can be used from time to time to access credit extended through a negative balance on the asset feature of the prepaid account.

(ii) Negative asset balances. Notwithstanding paragraph (a)(3)(i) of this section with regard to coverage under this regulation, structuring a hybrid prepaid-credit card to access credit through a negative balance on the asset feature violates paragraph (b) of this section. A prepaid account issuer can use a negative asset balance structure to extend credit on an asset feature of a prepaid account only if the prepaid card is not a hybrid prepaid-credit card with respect to that credit as described in paragraph (a)(4) of this section.

(4) Exception for credit extended through a negative balance. A prepaid card is not a hybrid prepaid-credit card with respect to credit extended through a negative balance on the asset feature of the prepaid account and is not a credit card for purposes of this regulation with respect to that credit where:

(i) The prepaid card cannot access credit from a covered separate credit feature as described in paragraph (a)(2)(i) of this section that is offered by a prepaid account issuer or its affiliate; and

(ii) The prepaid card only can access credit extended through a negative balance on the asset feature of the prepaid account where both paragraphs (a)(4)(ii)(A) and (B) of this section are satisfied.

(A) The prepaid account issuer has an established policy and practice of either declining to authorize any transaction for which it reasonably believes the consumer has insufficient or unavailable funds in the asset feature of the prepaid account at the time the transaction is authorized to cover the amount of the transaction, or declining to authorize any such transactions except in one or more of the following circumstances:

(1) The amount of the transaction will not cause the asset feature balance to become negative by more than $10 at the time of the authorization; or

(2) In cases where the prepaid account issuer has received an instruction or confirmation for an incoming electronic fund transfer originated from a separate asset account to load funds to the prepaid account or where the prepaid account issuer has received a request from the consumer to load funds to the prepaid account from a separate asset account but in either case the funds from the separate asset account have not yet settled, the amount of the transaction will not cause the asset feature balance to become negative at the time of the authorization by more than the incoming or requested load amount, as applicable.

(B) The following fees or charges are not imposed on the asset feature of the prepaid account:

(1) Any fees or charges for opening, issuing, or holding a negative balance on the asset feature, or for the availability of credit, whether imposed on a one-time or periodic basis. This paragraph does not include fees or charges to open, issue, or hold the prepaid account where the amount of the fee or charge imposed on the asset feature is not higher based on whether credit might be offered or has been accepted, whether or how much credit the consumer has accessed, or the amount of credit available;

(2) Any fees or charges that will be imposed only when credit is extended on the asset feature or when there is a negative balance on the asset feature, except that a prepaid account issuer may impose fees or charges for the actual costs of collecting the credit extended if otherwise permitted by law; or

(3) Any fees or charges where the amount of the fee or charge is higher when credit is extended on the asset feature or when there is a negative balance on the asset feature.

(C) A prepaid account issuer may still satisfy the exception in paragraph (a)(4) of this section even if it debits fees or charges from the asset feature when there are insufficient or unavailable funds in the asset feature to cover those fees or charges at the time they are imposed, so long as those fees or charges are not the type of fees or charges enumerated in paragraph (a)(4)(ii)(B) of this section.

(5) Definitions. For purposes of this section and other provisions in the regulation that relate to hybrid prepaid-credit cards:

(i) Affiliate means any company that controls, is controlled by, or is under common control with another company, as set forth in the Bank Holding Company Act of 1956 (12 U.S.C. 1841 et seq.).

(ii) Asset feature means an asset account that is a prepaid account, or an asset subaccount of a prepaid account.

(iii) Business partner means a person (other than the prepaid account issuer or its affiliates) that can extend credit through a separate credit feature where the person or its affiliate has an arrangement with a prepaid account issuer or its affiliate except as provided in paragraph (a)(5)(iii)(D) of this section.

(A) Arrangement defined. For purposes of paragraph (a)(5)(iii) of this section, a person that can extend credit through a separate credit feature or the person's affiliate has an arrangement with a prepaid account issuer or its affiliate if the circumstances in either paragraph (a)(5)(iii)(B) or (C) of this section are met.

(B) Arrangement by agreement. A person that can extend credit through a separate credit feature or its affiliate has an arrangement with a prepaid account issuer or its affiliate if the parties have an agreement that allows the prepaid card from time to time to draw, transfer, or authorize a draw or transfer of credit in the course of authorizing, settling, or otherwise completing transactions conducted with the card to obtain goods or services, obtain cash, or conduct person-to-person transfers.

(C) Marketing arrangement. A person that can extend credit through a separate credit feature or its affiliate has an arrangement with a prepaid account issuer or its affiliate if:

(1) The parties have a business, marketing, or promotional agreement or other arrangement which provides that prepaid accounts offered by the prepaid account issuer will be marketed to the customers of the person that can extend credit; or the separate credit feature offered by the person who can extend credit will be marketed to the holders of prepaid accounts offered by the prepaid account issuer (including any marketing to customers to encourage them to authorize the prepaid card to access the separate credit feature as described in paragraph (a)(5)(iii)(C)(2) of this section); and

(2) At the time of the marketing agreement or arrangement described in paragraph (a)(5)(iii)(C)(1) of this section, or at any time afterwards, the prepaid card from time to time can draw, transfer, or authorize the draw or transfer of credit from the separate credit feature offered by the person that can extend credit in the course of authorizing, settling, or otherwise completing transactions conducted with the card to obtain goods or services, obtain cash, or conduct person-to-person transfers. This requirement is satisfied even if there is no specific agreement between the parties that the card can access the credit feature, as described in paragraph (a)(5)(iii)(B) of this section.

(D) Exception for certain credit card account arrangements. For purposes of paragraph (a)(5)(iii) of this section, a person that can extend credit through a credit card account is not a business partner of a prepaid account issuer with which it has an arrangement as defined in paragraphs (a)(5)(iii)(A) through (C) of this section with regard to such credit card account if all of the following conditions are met:

(1) The credit card account is a credit card account under an open-end (not home-secured) consumer credit plan that a consumer can access through a traditional credit card.

(2) The prepaid account issuer and the card issuer do not allow the prepaid card to draw, transfer, or authorize the draw or transfer of credit from the credit card account from time to time in the course of authorizing, settling, or otherwise completing transactions conducted with the card to obtain goods or services, obtain cash, or conduct person-to-person transfers, except where the prepaid account issuer or the card issuer has received from the consumer a written request that is separately signed or initialized to authorize the prepaid card to access the credit card account as described above. If the credit card account is linked to the prepaid account prior to April 1, 2019, or prior to the arrangement between the prepaid account issuer and the card issuer as described in paragraphs (a)(5)(iii)(A) through (C) of this section, the prepaid account issuer and the card issuer will be deemed to have satisfied this condition even if they have not received from the consumer a written request that is separately signed or initialized to authorize the prepaid card to access the credit card account as described in this paragraph.

(3) The prepaid account issuer and the card issuer do not condition the acquisition or retention of the prepaid account or the credit card account on whether a consumer authorizes the prepaid card to access the credit card account as described in paragraph (a)(5)(iii)(D)(2) of this section. If the credit card account is linked to the prepaid account prior to April 1, 2019, this condition only applies to the retention of the prepaid account and the credit card account on or after April 1, 2019.

(4) The prepaid account issuer applies the same terms, conditions, or features to the prepaid account when a consumer authorizes linking the prepaid card to the credit card account as described in paragraph (a)(5)(iii)(D)(2) of this section as it applies to the consumer's prepaid account when the consumer does not authorize such a linkage. In addition, the prepaid account issuer applies the same fees to load funds from the credit card account that is linked to the prepaid account as described above as it charges for a comparable load on the consumer's prepaid account to access a credit feature offered by a person that is not the prepaid account issuer, its affiliate, or a person with which the prepaid account issuer has an arrangement as described in paragraphs (a)(5)(iii)(A) through (C) of this section.

(5) The card issuer applies the same specified terms and conditions to the credit card account when a consumer authorizes linking the prepaid card to the credit card account as described in paragraph (a)(5)(iii)(D)(2) of this section as it applies to the consumer's credit card account when the consumer does not authorize such a linkage. In addition, the card issuer applies the same specified terms and conditions to extensions of credit accessed by the prepaid card from the credit card account as it applies to extensions of credit accessed by the traditional credit card. For purposes of this paragraph, "specified terms and conditions" means the terms and conditions required to be disclosed under § 1026.6(b), any repayment terms and conditions, and the limits on liability for unauthorized credit transactions.

(iv) Credit feature means a separate credit account or a credit subaccount of a prepaid account through which credit can be extended in connection with a prepaid card, or a negative balance on an asset feature of a prepaid account through which credit can be extended in connection with a prepaid card.

(v) Prepaid account means a prepaid account as defined in Regulation E, 12 CFR 1005.2(b)(3).

(vi) Prepaid account issuer means a financial institution as defined in Regulation E, 12 CFR 1005.2(i), with respect to a prepaid account.

(vii) Prepaid card means any card, code, or other device that can be used to access a prepaid account.

(viii) Separate credit feature means a credit account or a credit subaccount of a prepaid account through which credit can be extended in connection with a prepaid card that is separate from the asset feature of the prepaid account. This term does not include a negative balance on an asset feature of a prepaid account.

(b) Structure of credit features accessible by hybrid prepaid-credit cards. With respect to a credit feature that is accessible by a hybrid prepaid-credit card, a card issuer shall not structure the credit feature as a negative balance on the asset feature of a prepaid account. A card issuer shall structure the credit feature as a separate credit feature, either as a separate credit account, or as a credit subaccount of a prepaid account that is separate from the asset feature of the prepaid account. The separate credit feature is a covered separate credit feature accessible by a hybrid prepaid-credit card under § 1026.61(a)(2)(i).

(c) Timing requirement for credit card solicitation or application with respect to hybrid prepaid-credit cards.

(1) With respect to a covered separate credit feature that could be accessible by a hybrid prepaid-credit card at any point, a card issuer must not do any of the following until 30 days after the prepaid account has been registered:

(i) Open a covered separate credit feature that could be accessible by the hybrid prepaid-credit card;

(ii) Make a solicitation or provide an application to open a covered separate credit feature that could be accessible by the hybrid prepaid-credit card; or

(iii) Allow an existing credit feature that was opened prior to the consumer obtaining the prepaid account to become a covered separate credit feature accessible by the hybrid prepaid-credit card.

(2) For purposes of paragraph (c) of this section, the term solicitation has the meaning set forth in § 1026.60(a)(1).

APPENDIX H TO PART 1026

H-24(A) Mortgage Loan Transaction Loan Estimate—Model Form

Description: This is a blank model Loan Estimate that illustrates the application of the content requirements in § 1026.37. This form provides two variations of page one, four variations of page two, and four variations of page three, reflecting the variable content requirements in § 1026.37.

Save this Loan Estimate to compare with your Closing Disclosure.

Loan Estimate

DATE ISSUED		**LOAN TERM**	
APPLICANTS		**PURPOSE**	
		PRODUCT	
		LOAN TYPE	☐ Conventional ☐ FHA ☐ VA ☐ ______
PROPERTY		**LOAN ID #**	
SALE PRICE		**RATE LOCK**	☐ NO ☐ YES, until *Before closing, your interest rate, points, and lender credits can change unless you lock the interest rate. All other estimated closing costs expire on*

Loan Terms

Loan Terms		Can this amount increase after closing?
Loan Amount		
Interest Rate		
Monthly Principal & Interest *See Projected Payments below for your Estimated Total Monthly Payment*		
		Does the loan have these features?
Prepayment Penalty		
Balloon Payment		

Projected Payments

Payment Calculation	
Principal & Interest	
Mortgage Insurance	
Estimated Escrow *Amount can increase over time*	
Estimated Total Monthly Payment	
Estimated Taxes, Insurance & Assessments *Amount can increase over time*	**This estimate includes** / **In escrow?** ☐ Property Taxes ☐ Homeowner's Insurance ☐ Other: *See Section G on page 2 for escrowed property costs. You must pay for other property costs separately.*

Costs at Closing

Estimated Closing Costs	Includes in Loan Costs + in Other Costs – in Lender Credits. *See page 2 for details.*
Estimated Cash to Close	Includes Closing Costs. *See Calculating Cash to Close on page 2 for details.*

Visit **www.consumerfinance.gov/mortgage-estimate** for general information and tools.

Save this Loan Estimate to compare with your Closing Disclosure.

Loan Estimate

DATE ISSUED
APPLICANTS

PROPERTY
EST. PROP. VALUE

LOAN TERM
PURPOSE
PRODUCT
LOAN TYPE ☐ Conventional ☐ FHA ☐ VA ☐ ___________
LOAN ID #
RATE LOCK ☐ NO ☐ YES, until
Before closing, your interest rate, points, and lender credits can change unless you lock the interest rate. All other estimated closing costs expire on

Loan Terms

Loan Terms	Can this amount increase after closing?
Loan Amount	
Interest Rate	
Monthly Principal & Interest *See Projected Payments below for your Estimated Total Monthly Payment*	
	Does the loan have these features?
Prepayment Penalty	
Balloon Payment	

Projected Payments

Payment Calculation	
Principal & Interest Mortgage Insurance Estimated Escrow *Amount can increase over time*	
Estimated Total Monthly Payment	
Estimated Taxes, Insurance & Assessments *Amount can increase over time*	**This estimate includes** **In escrow?** ☐ Property Taxes ☐ Homeowner's Insurance ☐ Other: *See Section G on page 2 for escrowed property costs. You must pay for other property costs separately.*

Costs at Closing

Estimated Closing Costs	Includes in Loan Costs + in Other Costs – in Lender Credits. *See page 2 for details.*
Estimated Cash to Close	Includes Closing Costs. *See Calculating Cash to Close on page 2 for details.*

Visit **www.consumerfinance.gov/mortgage-estimate** for general information and tools.

LOAN ESTIMATE PAGE 1 OF 3 • LOAN ID #

Closing Cost Details

Loan Costs

A. Origination Charges

% of Loan Amount (Points)

B. Services You Cannot Shop For

C. Services You Can Shop For

D. TOTAL LOAN COSTS (A + B + C)

Other Costs

E. Taxes and Other Government Fees

Recording Fees and Other Taxes
Transfer Taxes

F. Prepaids

Homeowner's Insurance Premium (months)
Mortgage Insurance Premium (months)
Prepaid Interest (per day for days @)
Property Taxes (months)

G. Initial Escrow Payment at Closing

Homeowner's Insurance	per month for	mo.
Mortgage Insurance	per month for	mo.
Property Taxes	per month for	mo.

H. Other

I. TOTAL OTHER COSTS (E + F + G + H)

J. TOTAL CLOSING COSTS

D + I
Lender Credits

Calculating Cash to Close

Total Closing Costs (J)
Closing Costs Financed (Paid from your Loan Amount)
Down Payment/Funds from Borrower
Deposit
Funds for Borrower
Seller Credits
Adjustments and Other Credits
Estimated Cash to Close

LOAN ESTIMATE PAGE 2 OF 3 • LOAN ID #

Closing Cost Details

Loan Costs

A. Origination Charges

% of Loan Amount (Points)

B. Services You Cannot Shop For

C. Services You Can Shop For

D. TOTAL LOAN COSTS (A + B + C)

Other Costs

E. Taxes and Other Government Fees

Recording Fees and Other Taxes
Transfer Taxes

F. Prepaids

Homeowner's Insurance Premium (months)
Mortgage Insurance Premium (months)
Prepaid Interest (per day for days @)
Property Taxes (months)

G. Initial Escrow Payment at Closing

Homeowner's Insurance	per month for	mo.
Mortgage Insurance	per month for	mo.
Property Taxes	per month for	mo.

H. Other

I. TOTAL OTHER COSTS (E + F + G + H)

J. TOTAL CLOSING COSTS

D + I
Lender Credits

Calculating Cash to Close

Total Closing Costs (J)	
Closing Costs Financed (Paid from your Loan Amount)	
Down Payment/Funds from Borrower	
Deposit	
Funds for Borrower	
Seller Credits	
Adjustments and Other Credits	
Estimated Cash to Close	

Adjustable Payment (AP) Table

Interest Only Payments?	
Optional Payments?	
Step Payments?	
Seasonal Payments?	
Monthly Principal and Interest Payments	
First Change/Amount	
Subsequent Changes	
Maximum Payment	

Adjustable Interest Rate (AIR) Table

Index + Margin	
Initial Interest Rate	
Minimum/Maximum Interest Rate	
Change Frequency	
First Change	
Subsequent Changes	
Limits on Interest Rate Changes	
First Change	
Subsequent Changes	

LOAN ESTIMATE PAGE 2 OF 3 • LOAN ID #

Closing Cost Details

Loan Costs

A. Origination Charges

% of Loan Amount (Points)

B. Services You Cannot Shop For

C. Services You Can Shop For

D. TOTAL LOAN COSTS (A + B + C)

Adjustable Payment (AP) Table

Interest Only Payments?	
Optional Payments?	
Step Payments?	
Seasonal Payments?	
Monthly Principal and Interest Payments	
First Change/Amount	
Subsequent Changes	
Maximum Payment	

Other Costs

E. Taxes and Other Government Fees

Recording Fees and Other Taxes
Transfer Taxes

F. Prepaids

Homeowner's Insurance Premium (months)
Mortgage Insurance Premium (months)
Prepaid Interest (per day for days @)
Property Taxes (months)

G. Initial Escrow Payment at Closing

Homeowner's Insurance per month for mo.
Mortgage Insurance per month for mo.
Property Taxes per month for mo.

H. Other

I. TOTAL OTHER COSTS (E + F + G + H)

J. TOTAL CLOSING COSTS

D + I
Lender Credits

Calculating Cash to Close

Total Closing Costs (J)	
Closing Costs Financed (Paid from your Loan Amount)	
Down Payment/Funds from Borrower	
Deposit	
Funds for Borrower	
Seller Credits	
Adjustments and Other Credits	
Estimated Cash to Close	

LOAN ESTIMATE PAGE 2 OF 3 • LOAN ID #

Closing Cost Details

Loan Costs

A. Origination Charges

% of Loan Amount (Points)

B. Services You Cannot Shop For

C. Services You Can Shop For

D. TOTAL LOAN COSTS (A + B + C)

Other Costs

E. Taxes and Other Government Fees

Recording Fees and Other Taxes
Transfer Taxes

F. Prepaids

Homeowner's Insurance Premium (months)
Mortgage Insurance Premium (months)
Prepaid Interest (per day for days @)
Property Taxes (months)

G. Initial Escrow Payment at Closing

Homeowner's Insurance	per month for	mo.
Mortgage Insurance	per month for	mo.
Property Taxes	per month for	mo.

H. Other

I. TOTAL OTHER COSTS (E + F + G + H)

J. TOTAL CLOSING COSTS

D + I
Lender Credits

Calculating Cash to Close

Total Closing Costs (J)
Closing Costs Financed (Paid from your Loan Amount)
Down Payment/Funds from Borrower
Deposit
Funds for Borrower
Seller Credits
Adjustments and Other Credits
Estimated Cash to Close

Adjustable Interest Rate (AIR) Table

Index + Margin
Initial Interest Rate
Minimum/Maximum Interest Rate
Change Frequency
First Change
Subsequent Changes
Limits on Interest Rate Changes
First Change
Subsequent Changes

LOAN ESTIMATE PAGE 2 OF 3 • LOAN ID #

Additional Information About This Loan

LENDER
NMLS/___ LICENSE ID
LOAN OFFICER
NMLS/___ LICENSE ID
EMAIL
PHONE

MORTGAGE BROKER
NMLS/___ LICENSE ID
LOAN OFFICER
NMLS/___ LICENSE ID
EMAIL
PHONE

Comparisons	**Use these measures to compare this loan with other loans.**
In 5 Years	Total you will have paid in principal, interest, mortgage insurance, and loan costs. Principal you will have paid off.
Annual Percentage Rate (APR)	Your costs over the loan term expressed as a rate. This is not your interest rate.
Total Interest Percentage (TIP)	The total amount of interest that you will pay over the loan term as a percentage of your loan amount.

Other Considerations

Appraisal	We may order an appraisal to determine the property's value and charge you for this appraisal. We will promptly give you a copy of any appraisal, even if your loan does not close. You can pay for an additional appraisal for your own use at your own cost.
Assumption	If you sell or transfer this property to another person, we ☐ will allow, under certain conditions, this person to assume this loan on the original terms. ☐ will not allow assumption of this loan on the original terms.
Homeowner's Insurance	This loan requires homeowner's insurance on the property, which you may obtain from a company of your choice that we find acceptable.
Late Payment	If your payment is more than ___ days late, we will charge a late fee of ______________
Refinance	Refinancing this loan will depend on your future financial situation, the property value, and market conditions. You may not be able to refinance this loan.
Servicing	We intend ☐ to service your loan. If so, you will make your payments to us. ☐ to transfer servicing of your loan.

Confirm Receipt

By signing, you are only confirming that you have received this form. You do not have to accept this loan because you have signed or received this form.

Applicant Signature	Date	Co-Applicant Signature	Date

LOAN ESTIMATE PAGE 3 OF 3 • LOAN ID #

Additional Information About This Loan

LENDER
NMLS/___ LICENSE ID
LOAN OFFICER
NMLS/___ LICENSE ID
EMAIL
PHONE

MORTGAGE BROKER
NMLS/___ LICENSE ID
LOAN OFFICER
NMLS/___ LICENSE ID
EMAIL
PHONE

Comparisons	Use these measures to compare this loan with other loans.
In 5 Years	Total you will have paid in principal, interest, mortgage insurance, and loan costs. Principal you will have paid off.
Annual Percentage Rate (APR)	Your costs over the loan term expressed as a rate. This is not your interest rate.
Total Interest Percentage (TIP)	The total amount of interest that you will pay over the loan term as a percentage of your loan amount.

Other Considerations

Appraisal	We may order an appraisal to determine the property's value and charge you for this appraisal. We will promptly give you a copy of any appraisal, even if your loan does not close. You can pay for an additional appraisal for your own use at your own cost.
Assumption	If you sell or transfer this property to another person, we ☐ will allow, under certain conditions, this person to assume this loan on the original terms. ☐ will not allow assumption of this loan on the original terms.
Homeowner's Insurance	This loan requires homeowner's insurance on the property, which you may obtain from a company of your choice that we find acceptable.
Late Payment	If your payment is more than ___ days late, we will charge a late fee of ____________
Loan Acceptance	You do not have to accept this loan because you have received this form or signed a loan application.
Refinance	Refinancing this loan will depend on your future financial situation, the property value, and market conditions. You may not be able to refinance this loan.
Servicing	We intend ☐ to service your loan. If so, you will make your payments to us. ☐ to transfer servicing of your loan.

LOAN ESTIMATE PAGE 3 OF 3 • LOAN ID #

Additional Information About This Loan

LENDER	**MORTGAGE BROKER**
NMLS/___ LICENSE ID	**NMLS/___ LICENSE ID**
LOAN OFFICER	**LOAN OFFICER**
NMLS/___ LICENSE ID	**NMLS/___ LICENSE ID**
EMAIL	**EMAIL**
PHONE	**PHONE**

Comparisons	**Use these measures to compare this loan with other loans.**
In 5 Years	Total you will have paid in principal, interest, mortgage insurance, and loan costs. Principal you will have paid off.
Annual Percentage Rate (APR)	Your costs over the loan term expressed as a rate. This is not your interest rate.
Total Interest Percentage (TIP)	The total amount of interest that you will pay over the loan term as a percentage of your loan amount.

Other Considerations

Assumption	If you sell or transfer this property to another person, we ☐ will allow, under certain conditions, this person to assume this loan on the original terms. ☐ will not allow assumption of this loan on the original terms.
Late Payment	If your payment is more than ___ days late, we will charge a late fee of ___________
Refinance	Refinancing this loan will depend on your future financial situation, the property value, and market conditions. You may not be able to refinance this loan.
Servicing	We intend ☐ to service your loan. If so, you will make your payments to us. ☐ to transfer servicing of your loan.

Confirm Receipt

By signing, you are only confirming that you have received this form. You do not have to accept this loan because you have signed or received this form.

Applicant Signature	Date	Co-Applicant Signature	Date

LOAN ESTIMATE PAGE 3 OF 3 • LOAN ID #

Additional Information About This Loan

LENDER	**MORTGAGE BROKER**
NMLS/___ LICENSE ID	**NMLS/___ LICENSE ID**
LOAN OFFICER	**LOAN OFFICER**
NMLS/___ LICENSE ID	**NMLS/___ LICENSE ID**
EMAIL	**EMAIL**
PHONE	**PHONE**

Comparisons	Use these measures to compare this loan with other loans.
In 5 Years	Total you will have paid in principal, interest, mortgage insurance, and loan costs. Principal you will have paid off.
Annual Percentage Rate (APR)	Your costs over the loan term expressed as a rate. This is not your interest rate.
Total Interest Percentage (TIP)	The total amount of interest that you will pay over the loan term as a percentage of your loan amount.

Other Considerations

Assumption	If you sell or transfer this property to another person, we ☐ will allow, under certain conditions, this person to assume this loan on the original terms. ☐ will not allow assumption of this loan on the original terms.
Late Payment	If your payment is more than ___ days late, we will charge a late fee of ______________
Loan Acceptance	You do not have to accept this loan because you have received this form or signed a loan application.
Refinance	Refinancing this loan will depend on your future financial situation, the property value, and market conditions. You may not be able to refinance this loan.
Servicing	We intend ☐ to service your loan. If so, you will make your payments to us. ☐ to transfer servicing of your loan.

LOAN ESTIMATE PAGE 3 OF 3 • LOAN ID #

H-25(A) Mortgage Loan Transaction Closing Disclosure—Model Form

Description: This is a blank model Closing Disclosure that illustrates the content requirements in § 1026.38. This form provides three variations of page one, one page two, one page three, four variations of page four, and four variations of page five, reflecting the variable content requirements in § 1026.38. This form does not reflect modifications permitted under § 1026.38(t).

Closing Disclosure

This form is a statement of final loan terms and closing costs. Compare this document with your Loan Estimate.

Closing Information	Transaction Information	Loan Information
Date Issued	**Borrower**	**Loan Term**
Closing Date		**Purpose**
Disbursement Date		**Product**
Settlement Agent	**Seller**	
File #		**Loan Type** ☐ Conventional ☐ FHA ☐ VA ☐ ______
Property	**Lender**	**Loan ID #**
Sale Price		**MIC #**

Loan Terms	Can this amount increase after closing?
Loan Amount	
Interest Rate	
Monthly Principal & Interest *See Projected Payments below for your Estimated Total Monthly Payment*	
	Does the loan have these features?
Prepayment Penalty	
Balloon Payment	

Projected Payments	
Payment Calculation	
Principal & Interest	
Mortgage Insurance	
Estimated Escrow *Amount can increase over time*	
Estimated Total Monthly Payment	
Estimated Taxes, Insurance & Assessments *Amount can increase over time* *See page 4 for details*	**This estimate includes** **In escrow?** ☐ Property Taxes ☐ Homeowner's Insurance ☐ Other: *See Escrow Account on page 4 for details. You must pay for other property costs separately.*

Costs at Closing	
Closing Costs	Includes in Loan Costs + in Other Costs – in Lender Credits. *See page 2 for details.*
Cash to Close	Includes Closing Costs. *See Calculating Cash to Close on page 3 for details.*

CLOSING DISCLOSURE PAGE 1 OF 5 • LOAN ID #

Closing Disclosure

This form is a statement of final loan terms and closing costs. Compare this document with your Loan Estimate.

Closing Information	Transaction Information	Loan Information
Date Issued	**Borrower**	**Loan Term**
Closing Date		**Purpose**
Disbursement Date		**Product**
Settlement Agent	**Seller**	
File #		**Loan Type** ☐ Conventional ☐ FHA ☐ VA ☐ ___________
Property		
	Lender	**Loan ID #**
Appraised Prop. Value		**MIC #**

Loan Terms

		Can this amount increase after closing?
Loan Amount		
Interest Rate		
Monthly Principal & Interest *See Projected Payments below for your Estimated Total Monthly Payment*		
		Does the loan have these features?
Prepayment Penalty		
Balloon Payment		

Projected Payments

Payment Calculation	
Principal & Interest	
Mortgage Insurance	
Estimated Escrow *Amount can increase over time*	
Estimated Total Monthly Payment	
Estimated Taxes, Insurance & Assessments *Amount can increase over time* *See page 4 for details*	**This estimate includes** **In escrow?** ☐ Property Taxes ☐ Homeowner's Insurance ☐ Other: *See Escrow Account on page 4 for details. You must pay for other property costs separately.*

Costs at Closing

Closing Costs	Includes in Loan Costs + in Other Costs – in Lender Credits. *See page 2 for details.*
Cash to Close	Includes Closing Costs. *See Calculating Cash to Close on page 3 for details.*

CLOSING DISCLOSURE PAGE 1 OF 5 • LOAN ID #

Closing Disclosure

This form is a statement of final loan terms and closing costs. Compare this document with your Loan Estimate.

Closing Information		Transaction Information		Loan Information	
Date Issued		**Borrower**		**Loan Term**	
Closing Date				**Purpose**	
Disbursement Date				**Product**	
Settlement Agent		**Seller**			
File #				**Loan Type**	☐ Conventional ☐ FHA ☐ VA ☐ ______
Property					
		Lender		**Loan ID #**	
Estimated Prop. Value				**MIC #**	

Loan Terms		**Can this amount increase after closing?**
Loan Amount		
Interest Rate		
Monthly Principal & Interest *See Projected Payments below for your Estimated Total Monthly Payment*		
		Does the loan have these features?
Prepayment Penalty		
Balloon Payment		

Projected Payments	
Payment Calculation	
Principal & Interest	
Mortgage Insurance	
Estimated Escrow *Amount can increase over time*	
Estimated Total Monthly Payment	
Estimated Taxes, Insurance & Assessments *Amount can increase over time* *See page 4 for details*	**This estimate includes** **In escrow?** ☐ Property Taxes ☐ Homeowner's Insurance ☐ Other: *See Escrow Account on page 4 for details. You must pay for other property costs separately.*

Costs at Closing	
Closing Costs	Includes in Loan Costs + in Other Costs – in Lender Credits. *See page 2 for details.*
Cash to Close	Includes Closing Costs. *See Calculating Cash to Close on page 3 for details.*

Closing Cost Details

Loan Costs	Borrower-Paid At Closing	Borrower-Paid Before Closing	Seller-Paid At Closing	Seller-Paid Before Closing	Paid by Others
A. Origination Charges					
01 % of Loan Amount (Points)					
02					
03					
04					
05					
06					
07					
08					
B. Services Borrower Did Not Shop For					
01					
02					
03					
04					
05					
06					
07					
08					
09					
10					
C. Services Borrower Did Shop For					
01					
02					
03					
04					
05					
06					
07					
08					
D. TOTAL LOAN COSTS (Borrower-Paid)					
Loan Costs Subtotals (A + B + C)					

Other Costs	Borrower-Paid At Closing	Borrower-Paid Before Closing	Seller-Paid At Closing	Seller-Paid Before Closing	Paid by Others
E. Taxes and Other Government Fees					
01 Recording Fees Deed: Mortgage:					
02					
F. Prepaids					
01 Homeowner's Insurance Premium (mo.)					
02 Mortgage Insurance Premium (mo.)					
03 Prepaid Interest (per day from to)					
04 Property Taxes (mo.)					
05					
G. Initial Escrow Payment at Closing					
01 Homeowner's Insurance per month for mo.					
02 Mortgage Insurance per month for mo.					
03 Property Taxes per month for mo.					
04					
05					
06					
07					
08 Aggregate Adjustment					
H. Other					
01					
02					
03					
04					
05					
06					
07					
08					
I. TOTAL OTHER COSTS (Borrower-Paid)					
Other Costs Subtotals (E + F + G + H)					

J. TOTAL CLOSING COSTS (Borrower-Paid)					
Closing Costs Subtotals (D + I)					
Lender Credits					

CLOSING DISCLOSURE PAGE 2 OF 5 • LOAN ID #

Calculating Cash to Close

Use this table to see what has changed from your Loan Estimate.

	Loan Estimate	Final	Did this change?
Total Closing Costs (J)			
Closing Costs Paid Before Closing			
Closing Costs Financed (Paid from your Loan Amount)			
Down Payment/Funds from Borrower			
Deposit			
Funds for Borrower			
Seller Credits			
Adjustments and Other Credits			
Cash to Close			

Summaries of Transactions

Use this table to see a summary of your transaction.

BORROWER'S TRANSACTION

K. Due from Borrower at Closing	
01 Sale Price of Property	
02 Sale Price of Any Personal Property Included in Sale	
03 Closing Costs Paid at Closing (J)	
04	
Adjustments	
05	
06	
07	
Adjustments for Items Paid by Seller in Advance	
08 City/Town Taxes to	
09 County Taxes to	
10 Assessments to	
11	
12	
13	
14	
15	
L. Paid Already by or on Behalf of Borrower at Closing	
01 Deposit	
02 Loan Amount	
03 Existing Loan(s) Assumed or Taken Subject to	
04	
05 Seller Credit	
Other Credits	
06	
07	
Adjustments	
08	
09	
10	
11	
Adjustments for Items Unpaid by Seller	
12 City/Town Taxes to	
13 County Taxes to	
14 Assessments to	
15	
16	
17	
CALCULATION	
Total Due from Borrower at Closing (K)	
Total Paid Already by or on Behalf of Borrower at Closing (L)	
Cash to Close ☐ From ☐ To Borrower	

SELLER'S TRANSACTION

M. Due to Seller at Closing	
01 Sale Price of Property	
02 Sale Price of Any Personal Property Included in Sale	
03	
04	
05	
06	
07	
08	
Adjustments for Items Paid by Seller in Advance	
09 City/Town Taxes to	
10 County Taxes to	
11 Assessments to	
12	
13	
14	
15	
16	
N. Due from Seller at Closing	
01 Excess Deposit	
02 Closing Costs Paid at Closing (J)	
03 Existing Loan(s) Assumed or Taken Subject to	
04 Payoff of First Mortgage Loan	
05 Payoff of Second Mortgage Loan	
06	
07	
08 Seller Credit	
09	
10	
11	
12	
13	
Adjustments for Items Unpaid by Seller	
14 City/Town Taxes to	
15 County Taxes to	
16 Assessments to	
17	
18	
19	
CALCULATION	
Total Due to Seller at Closing (M)	
Total Due from Seller at Closing (N)	
Cash ☐ From ☐ To Seller	

CLOSING DISCLOSURE PAGE 3 OF 5 • LOAN ID #

Additional Information About This Loan

Loan Disclosures

Assumption
If you sell or transfer this property to another person, your lender
☐ will allow, under certain conditions, this person to assume this loan on the original terms.
☐ will not allow assumption of this loan on the original terms.

Demand Feature
Your loan
☐ has a demand feature, which permits your lender to require early repayment of the loan. You should review your note for details.
☐ does not have a demand feature.

Late Payment
If your payment is more than ___ days late, your lender will charge a late fee of ______________________

Negative Amortization (Increase in Loan Amount)
Under your loan terms, you
☐ are scheduled to make monthly payments that do not pay all of the interest due that month. As a result, your loan amount will increase (negatively amortize), and your loan amount will likely become larger than your original loan amount. Increases in your loan amount lower the equity you have in this property.
☐ may have monthly payments that do not pay all of the interest due that month. If you do, your loan amount will increase (negatively amortize), and, as a result, your loan amount may become larger than your original loan amount. Increases in your loan amount lower the equity you have in this property.
☐ do not have a negative amortization feature.

Partial Payments
Your lender
☐ may accept payments that are less than the full amount due (partial payments) and apply them to your loan.
☐ may hold them in a separate account until you pay the rest of the payment, and then apply the full payment to your loan.
☐ does not accept any partial payments.
If this loan is sold, your new lender may have a different policy.

Security Interest
You are granting a security interest in ______________________

____

____

You may lose this property if you do not make your payments or satisfy other obligations for this loan.

Escrow Account
For now, your loan
☐ will have an escrow account (also called an "impound" or "trust" account) to pay the property costs listed below. Without an escrow account, you would pay them directly, possibly in one or two large payments a year. Your lender may be liable for penalties and interest for failing to make a payment.

Escrow		
Escrowed Property Costs over Year 1		Estimated total amount over year 1 for your escrowed property costs:
Non-Escrowed Property Costs over Year 1		Estimated total amount over year 1 for your non-escrowed property costs: You may have other property costs.
Initial Escrow Payment		A cushion for the escrow account you pay at closing. See Section G on page 2.
Monthly Escrow Payment		The amount included in your total monthly payment.

☐ will not have an escrow account because ☐ you declined it ☐ your lender does not offer one. You must directly pay your property costs, such as taxes and homeowner's insurance. Contact your lender to ask if your loan can have an escrow account.

No Escrow		
Estimated Property Costs over Year 1		Estimated total amount over year 1. You must pay these costs directly, possibly in one or two large payments a year.
Escrow Waiver Fee		

In the future,
Your property costs may change and, as a result, your escrow payment may change. You may be able to cancel your escrow account, but if you do, you must pay your property costs directly. If you fail to pay your property taxes, your state or local government may (1) impose fines and penalties or (2) place a tax lien on this property. If you fail to pay any of your property costs, your lender may (1) add the amounts to your loan balance, (2) add an escrow account to your loan, or (3) require you to pay for property insurance that the lender buys on your behalf, which likely would cost more and provide fewer benefits than what you could buy on your own.

CLOSING DISCLOSURE PAGE 4 OF 5 • LOAN ID #

Additional Information About This Loan

Loan Disclosures

Assumption
If you sell or transfer this property to another person, your lender
☐ will allow, under certain conditions, this person to assume this loan on the original terms.
☐ will not allow assumption of this loan on the original terms.

Demand Feature
Your loan
☐ has a demand feature, which permits your lender to require early repayment of the loan. You should review your note for details.
☐ does not have a demand feature.

Late Payment
If your payment is more than ___ days late, your lender will charge a late fee of ______________________

Negative Amortization (Increase in Loan Amount)
Under your loan terms, you
☐ are scheduled to make monthly payments that do not pay all of the interest due that month. As a result, your loan amount will increase (negatively amortize), and your loan amount will likely become larger than your original loan amount. Increases in your loan amount lower the equity you have in this property.
☐ may have monthly payments that do not pay all of the interest due that month. If you do, your loan amount will increase (negatively amortize), and, as a result, your loan amount may become larger than your original loan amount. Increases in your loan amount lower the equity you have in this property.
☐ do not have a negative amortization feature.

Partial Payments
Your lender
☐ may accept payments that are less than the full amount due (partial payments) and apply them to your loan.
☐ may hold them in a separate account until you pay the rest of the payment, and then apply the full payment to your loan.
☐ does not accept any partial payments.
If this loan is sold, your new lender may have a different policy.

Security Interest
You are granting a security interest in ______________________

____

____

You may lose this property if you do not make your payments or satisfy other obligations for this loan.

Escrow Account
For now, your loan
☐ will have an escrow account (also called an "impound" or "trust" account) to pay the property costs listed below. Without an escrow account, you would pay them directly, possibly in one or two large payments a year. Your lender may be liable for penalties and interest for failing to make a payment.

Escrow		
Escrowed Property Costs over Year 1		Estimated total amount over year 1 for your escrowed property costs:
Non-Escrowed Property Costs over Year 1		Estimated total amount over year 1 for your non-escrowed property costs: You may have other property costs.
Initial Escrow Payment		A cushion for the escrow account you pay at closing. See Section G on page 2.
Monthly Escrow Payment		The amount included in your total monthly payment.

☐ will not have an escrow account because ☐ you declined it ☐ your lender does not offer one. You must directly pay your property costs, such as taxes and homeowner's insurance. Contact your lender to ask if your loan can have an escrow account.

No Escrow		
Estimated Property Costs over Year 1		Estimated total amount over year 1. You must pay these costs directly, possibly in one or two large payments a year.
Escrow Waiver Fee		

In the future,
Your property costs may change and, as a result, your escrow payment may change. You may be able to cancel your escrow account, but if you do, you must pay your property costs directly. If you fail to pay your property taxes, your state or local government may (1) impose fines and penalties or (2) place a tax lien on this property. If you fail to pay any of your property costs, your lender may (1) add the amounts to your loan balance, (2) add an escrow account to your loan, or (3) require you to pay for property insurance that the lender buys on your behalf, which likely would cost more and provide fewer benefits than what you could buy on your own.

Adjustable Payment (AP) Table

Interest Only Payments?	
Optional Payments?	
Step Payments?	
Seasonal Payments?	
Monthly Principal and Interest Payments	
First Change/Amount	
Subsequent Changes	
Maximum Payment	

Adjustable Interest Rate (AIR) Table

Index + Margin	
Initial Interest Rate	
Minimum/Maximum Interest Rate	
Change Frequency	
First Change	
Subsequent Changes	
Limits on Interest Rate Changes	
First Change	
Subsequent Changes	

CLOSING DISCLOSURE PAGE 4 OF 5 • LOAN ID #

Additional Information About This Loan

Loan Disclosures

Assumption
If you sell or transfer this property to another person, your lender

☐ will allow, under certain conditions, this person to assume this loan on the original terms.
☐ will not allow assumption of this loan on the original terms.

Demand Feature
Your loan

☐ has a demand feature, which permits your lender to require early repayment of the loan. You should review your note for details.
☐ does not have a demand feature.

Late Payment
If your payment is more than ___ days late, your lender will charge a late fee of ______________________

Negative Amortization (Increase in Loan Amount)
Under your loan terms, you

☐ are scheduled to make monthly payments that do not pay all of the interest due that month. As a result, your loan amount will increase (negatively amortize), and your loan amount will likely become larger than your original loan amount. Increases in your loan amount lower the equity you have in this property.
☐ may have monthly payments that do not pay all of the interest due that month. If you do, your loan amount will increase (negatively amortize), and, as a result, your loan amount may become larger than your original loan amount. Increases in your loan amount lower the equity you have in this property.
☐ do not have a negative amortization feature.

Partial Payments
Your lender

☐ may accept payments that are less than the full amount due (partial payments) and apply them to your loan.
☐ may hold them in a separate account until you pay the rest of the payment, and then apply the full payment to your loan.
☐ does not accept any partial payments.

If this loan is sold, your new lender may have a different policy.

Security Interest
You are granting a security interest in ______________________

____

____

You may lose this property if you do not make your payments or satisfy other obligations for this loan.

Escrow Account
For now, your loan

☐ will have an escrow account (also called an "impound" or "trust" account) to pay the property costs listed below. Without an escrow account, you would pay them directly, possibly in one or two large payments a year. Your lender may be liable for penalties and interest for failing to make a payment.

Escrow		
Escrowed Property Costs over Year 1		Estimated total amount over year 1 for your escrowed property costs:
Non-Escrowed Property Costs over Year 1		Estimated total amount over year 1 for your non-escrowed property costs: You may have other property costs.
Initial Escrow Payment		A cushion for the escrow account you pay at closing. See Section G on page 2.
Monthly Escrow Payment		The amount included in your total monthly payment.

☐ will not have an escrow account because ☐ you declined it ☐ your lender does not offer one. You must directly pay your property costs, such as taxes and homeowner's insurance. Contact your lender to ask if your loan can have an escrow account.

No Escrow		
Estimated Property Costs over Year 1		Estimated total amount over year 1. You must pay these costs directly, possibly in one or two large payments a year.
Escrow Waiver Fee		

In the future,
Your property costs may change and, as a result, your escrow payment may change. You may be able to cancel your escrow account, but if you do, you must pay your property costs directly. If you fail to pay your property taxes, your state or local government may (1) impose fines and penalties or (2) place a tax lien on this property. If you fail to pay any of your property costs, your lender may (1) add the amounts to your loan balance, (2) add an escrow account to your loan, or (3) require you to pay for property insurance that the lender buys on your behalf, which likely would cost more and provide fewer benefits than what you could buy on your own.

Adjustable Payment (AP) Table

Interest Only Payments?	
Optional Payments?	
Step Payments?	
Seasonal Payments?	
Monthly Principal and Interest Payments	
First Change/Amount	
Subsequent Changes	
Maximum Payment	

CLOSING DISCLOSURE PAGE 4 OF 5 • LOAN ID #

Additional Information About This Loan

Loan Disclosures

Assumption
If you sell or transfer this property to another person, your lender

☐ will allow, under certain conditions, this person to assume this loan on the original terms.
☐ will not allow assumption of this loan on the original terms.

Demand Feature
Your loan

☐ has a demand feature, which permits your lender to require early repayment of the loan. You should review your note for details.
☐ does not have a demand feature.

Late Payment
If your payment is more than ___ days late, your lender will charge a late fee of ______

Negative Amortization (Increase in Loan Amount)
Under your loan terms, you

☐ are scheduled to make monthly payments that do not pay all of the interest due that month. As a result, your loan amount will increase (negatively amortize), and your loan amount will likely become larger than your original loan amount. Increases in your loan amount lower the equity you have in this property.
☐ may have monthly payments that do not pay all of the interest due that month. If you do, your loan amount will increase (negatively amortize), and, as a result, your loan amount may become larger than your original loan amount. Increases in your loan amount lower the equity you have in this property.
☐ do not have a negative amortization feature.

Partial Payments
Your lender

☐ may accept payments that are less than the full amount due (partial payments) and apply them to your loan.
☐ may hold them in a separate account until you pay the rest of the payment, and then apply the full payment to your loan.
☐ does not accept any partial payments.

If this loan is sold, your new lender may have a different policy.

Security Interest
You are granting a security interest in ______

______

______

You may lose this property if you do not make your payments or satisfy other obligations for this loan.

Escrow Account
For now, your loan

☐ will have an escrow account (also called an "impound" or "trust" account) to pay the property costs listed below. Without an escrow account, you would pay them directly, possibly in one or two large payments a year. Your lender may be liable for penalties and interest for failing to make a payment.

Escrow		
Escrowed Property Costs over Year 1		Estimated total amount over year 1 for your escrowed property costs:
Non-Escrowed Property Costs over Year 1		Estimated total amount over year 1 for your non-escrowed property costs: You may have other property costs.
Initial Escrow Payment		A cushion for the escrow account you pay at closing. See Section G on page 2.
Monthly Escrow Payment		The amount included in your total monthly payment.

☐ will not have an escrow account because ☐ you declined it ☐ your lender does not offer one. You must directly pay your property costs, such as taxes and homeowner's insurance. Contact your lender to ask if your loan can have an escrow account.

No Escrow		
Estimated Property Costs over Year 1		Estimated total amount over year 1. You must pay these costs directly, possibly in one or two large payments a year.
Escrow Waiver Fee		

In the future,
Your property costs may change and, as a result, your escrow payment may change. You may be able to cancel your escrow account, but if you do, you must pay your property costs directly. If you fail to pay your property taxes, your state or local government may (1) impose fines and penalties or (2) place a tax lien on this property. If you fail to pay any of your property costs, your lender may (1) add the amounts to your loan balance, (2) add an escrow account to your loan, or (3) require you to pay for property insurance that the lender buys on your behalf, which likely would cost more and provide fewer benefits than what you could buy on your own.

Adjustable Interest Rate (AIR) Table

Index + Margin	
Initial Interest Rate	
Minimum/Maximum Interest Rate	
Change Frequency	
First Change	
Subsequent Changes	
Limits on Interest Rate Changes	
First Change	
Subsequent Changes	

CLOSING DISCLOSURE PAGE 4 OF 5 • LOAN ID #

Loan Calculations

Total of Payments. Total you will have paid after you make all payments of principal, interest, mortgage insurance, and loan costs, as scheduled.	
Finance Charge. The dollar amount the loan will cost you.	
Amount Financed. The loan amount available after paying your upfront finance charge.	
Annual Percentage Rate (APR). Your costs over the loan term expressed as a rate. This is not your interest rate.	
Total Interest Percentage (TIP). The total amount of interest that you will pay over the loan term as a percentage of your loan amount.	

? **Questions?** If you have questions about the loan terms or costs on this form, use the contact information below. To get more information or make a complaint, contact the Consumer Financial Protection Bureau at **www.consumerfinance.gov/mortgage-closing**

Other Disclosures

Appraisal
If the property was appraised for your loan, your lender is required to give you a copy at no additional cost at least 3 days before closing. If you have not yet received it, please contact your lender at the information listed below.

Contract Details
See your note and security instrument for information about
- what happens if you fail to make your payments,
- what is a default on the loan,
- situations in which your lender can require early repayment of the loan, and
- the rules for making payments before they are due.

Liability after Foreclosure
If your lender forecloses on this property and the foreclosure does not cover the amount of unpaid balance on this loan,

☐ state law may protect you from liability for the unpaid balance. If you refinance or take on any additional debt on this property, you may lose this protection and have to pay any debt remaining even after foreclosure. You may want to consult a lawyer for more information.

☐ state law does not protect you from liability for the unpaid balance.

Refinance
Refinancing this loan will depend on your future financial situation, the property value, and market conditions. You may not be able to refinance this loan.

Tax Deductions
If you borrow more than this property is worth, the interest on the loan amount above this property's fair market value is not deductible from your federal income taxes. You should consult a tax advisor for more information.

Contact Information

	Lender	Mortgage Broker	Real Estate Broker (B)	Real Estate Broker (S)	Settlement Agent
Name					
Address					
NMLS ID					
__ License ID					
Contact					
Contact NMLS ID					
Contact __ License ID					
Email					
Phone					

Confirm Receipt

By signing, you are only confirming that you have received this form. You do not have to accept this loan because you have signed or received this form.

Applicant Signature   Date   Co-Applicant Signature   Date

Loan Calculations

Total of Payments. Total you will have paid after you make all payments of principal, interest, mortgage insurance, and loan costs, as scheduled.	
Finance Charge. The dollar amount the loan will cost you.	
Amount Financed. The loan amount available after paying your upfront finance charge.	
Annual Percentage Rate (APR). Your costs over the loan term expressed as a rate. This is not your interest rate.	
Total Interest Percentage (TIP). The total amount of interest that you will pay over the loan term as a percentage of your loan amount.	

?

Questions? If you have questions about the loan terms or costs on this form, use the contact information below. To get more information or make a complaint, contact the Consumer Financial Protection Bureau at **www.consumerfinance.gov/mortgage-closing**

Other Disclosures

Appraisal
If the property was appraised for your loan, your lender is required to give you a copy at no additional cost at least 3 days before closing. If you have not yet received it, please contact your lender at the information listed below.

Contract Details
See your note and security instrument for information about
- what happens if you fail to make your payments,
- what is a default on the loan,
- situations in which your lender can require early repayment of the loan, and
- the rules for making payments before they are due.

Liability after Foreclosure
If your lender forecloses on this property and the foreclosure does not cover the amount of unpaid balance on this loan,

☐ state law may protect you from liability for the unpaid balance. If you refinance or take on any additional debt on this property, you may lose this protection and have to pay any debt remaining even after foreclosure. You may want to consult a lawyer for more information.

☐ state law does not protect you from liability for the unpaid balance.

Loan Acceptance
You do not have to accept this loan because you have received this form or signed a loan application.

Refinance
Refinancing this loan will depend on your future financial situation, the property value, and market conditions. You may not be able to refinance this loan.

Tax Deductions
If you borrow more than this property is worth, the interest on the loan amount above this property's fair market value is not deductible from your federal income taxes. You should consult a tax advisor for more information.

Contact Information

	Lender	Mortgage Broker	Real Estate Broker (B)	Real Estate Broker (S)	Settlement Agent
Name					
Address					
NMLS ID					
__ License ID					
Contact					
Contact NMLS ID					
Contact __ License ID					
Email					
Phone					

Loan Calculations

Total of Payments. Total you will have paid after you make all payments of principal, interest, mortgage insurance, and loan costs, as scheduled.	
Finance Charge. The dollar amount the loan will cost you.	
Amount Financed. The loan amount available after paying your upfront finance charge.	
Annual Percentage Rate (APR). Your costs over the loan term expressed as a rate. This is not your interest rate.	
Total Interest Percentage (TIP). The total amount of interest that you will pay over the loan term as a percentage of your loan amount.	

? **Questions?** If you have questions about the loan terms or costs on this form, use the contact information below. To get more information or make a complaint, contact the Consumer Financial Protection Bureau at **www.consumerfinance.gov/mortgage-closing**

Other Disclosures

Contract Details
See your note and security instrument for information about
- what happens if you fail to make your payments,
- what is a default on the loan,
- situations in which your lender can require early repayment of the loan, and
- the rules for making payments before they are due.

Liability after Foreclosure
If your lender forecloses on this property and the foreclosure does not cover the amount of unpaid balance on this loan,

☐ state law may protect you from liability for the unpaid balance. If you refinance or take on any additional debt on this property, you may lose this protection and have to pay any debt remaining even after foreclosure. You may want to consult a lawyer for more information.

☐ state law does not protect you from liability for the unpaid balance.

Refinance
Refinancing this loan will depend on your future financial situation, the property value, and market conditions. You may not be able to refinance this loan.

Tax Deductions
If you borrow more than this property is worth, the interest on the loan amount above this property's fair market value is not deductible from your federal income taxes. You should consult a tax advisor for more information.

Contact Information

	Lender	Mortgage Broker	Real Estate Broker (B)	Real Estate Broker (S)	Settlement Agent
Name					
Address					
NMLS ID					
__ License ID					
Contact					
Contact NMLS ID					
Contact __ License ID					
Email					
Phone					

Confirm Receipt

By signing, you are only confirming that you have received this form. You do not have to accept this loan because you have signed or received this form.

Applicant Signature Date Co-Applicant Signature Date

CLOSING DISCLOSURE PAGE 5 OF 5 • LOAN ID #

Loan Calculations

Total of Payments. Total you will have paid after you make all payments of principal, interest, mortgage insurance, and loan costs, as scheduled.	
Finance Charge. The dollar amount the loan will cost you.	
Amount Financed. The loan amount available after paying your upfront finance charge.	
Annual Percentage Rate (APR). Your costs over the loan term expressed as a rate. This is not your interest rate.	
Total Interest Percentage (TIP). The total amount of interest that you will pay over the loan term as a percentage of your loan amount.	

?

Questions? If you have questions about the loan terms or costs on this form, use the contact information below. To get more information or make a complaint, contact the Consumer Financial Protection Bureau at **www.consumerfinance.gov/mortgage-closing**

Other Disclosures

Contract Details
See your note and security instrument for information about
- what happens if you fail to make your payments,
- what is a default on the loan,
- situations in which your lender can require early repayment of the loan, and
- the rules for making payments before they are due.

Liability after Foreclosure
If your lender forecloses on this property and the foreclosure does not cover the amount of unpaid balance on this loan,

☐ state law may protect you from liability for the unpaid balance. If you refinance or take on any additional debt on this property, you may lose this protection and have to pay any debt remaining even after foreclosure. You may want to consult a lawyer for more information.

☐ state law does not protect you from liability for the unpaid balance.

Loan Acceptance
You do not have to accept this loan because you have received this form or signed a loan application.

Refinance
Refinancing this loan will depend on your future financial situation, the property value, and market conditions. You may not be able to refinance this loan.

Tax Deductions
If you borrow more than this property is worth, the interest on the loan amount above this property's fair market value is not deductible from your federal income taxes. You should consult a tax advisor for more information.

Contact Information

	Lender	Mortgage Broker	Real Estate Broker (B)	Real Estate Broker (S)	Settlement Agent
Name					
Address					
NMLS ID					
__ License ID					
Contact					
Contact NMLS ID					
Contact __ License ID					
Email					
Phone					

EXCERPT FROM REGULATION DD: TRUTH IN SAVINGS

12 C.F.R. Part 1030

§ 1030.5 Subsequent disclosures

(a) Change in terms—

(1) Advance notice required. A depository institution shall give advance notice to affected consumers of any change in a term required to be disclosed under § 1030.4(b) of this part if the change may reduce the annual percentage yield or adversely affect the consumer. The notice shall include the effective date of the change. The notice shall be mailed or delivered at least 30 calendar days before the effective date of the change.

(2) No notice required. No notice under this section is required for:

(i) Variable-rate changes. Changes in the interest rate and corresponding changes in the annual percentage yield in variable-rate accounts.

(ii) Check printing fees. Changes in fees assessed for check printing.

(iii) Short-term time accounts. Changes in any term for time accounts with maturities of one month or less.

(b) Notice before maturity for time accounts longer than one month that renew automatically. For time accounts with a maturity longer than one month that renew automatically at maturity, institutions shall provide the disclosures described below before maturity. The disclosures shall be mailed or delivered at least 30 calendar days before maturity of the existing account. Alternatively, the disclosures may be mailed or delivered at least 20 calendar days before the end of the grace period on the existing account, provided a grace period of at least five calendar days is allowed.

(1) Maturities of longer than one year. If the maturity is longer than one year, the institution shall provide account disclosures set forth in § 1030.4(b) of this part for the new account, along with the date the existing account matures. If the interest rate and annual percentage yield that will be paid for the new account are unknown when disclosures are provided, the institution shall state that those rates have not yet been determined, the date when they will be determined, and a telephone number consumers may call to obtain the interest rate and the annual percentage yield that will be paid for the new account.

(2) Maturities of one year or less but longer than one month. If the maturity is one year or less but longer than one month, the institution shall either:

(i) Provide disclosures as set forth in paragraph (b)(1) of this section; or

(ii) Disclose to the consumer:

(A) The date the existing account matures and the new maturity date if the account is renewed;

(B) The interest rate and the annual percentage yield for the new account if they are known (or that those rates have not yet been determined, the date when they will be determined, and a telephone number the consumer may call to obtain the interest rate and the annual percentage yield that will be paid for the new account); and

(C) Any difference in the terms of the new account as compared to the terms required to be disclosed under § 1030.4(b) of this part for the existing account.

(c) Notice before maturity for time accounts longer than one year that do not renew automatically. For time accounts with a maturity longer than one year that do not renew automatically at maturity, institutions shall disclose to consumers the maturity date and whether interest will be paid after maturity. The disclosures shall be mailed or delivered at least 10 calendar days before maturity of the existing account.

§ 1030.11. Additional Disclosure Requirements for Overdraft Services

(a) Disclosure of total fees on periodic statements—

(1) General. A depository institution must separately disclose on each periodic statement, as applicable:

(i) The total dollar amount for all fees or charges imposed on the account for paying checks or other items when there are insufficient or unavailable funds and the account becomes overdrawn, using the term "Total Overdraft Fees"; and

(ii) The total dollar amount for all fees or charges imposed on the account for returning items unpaid.

(2) Totals required. The disclosures required by paragraph (a)(1) of this section must be provided for the statement period and for the calendar year-to-date;

(3) Format requirements. The aggregate fee disclosures required by paragraph (a) of this section must be disclosed in close proximity to fees identified under § 1030.6(a)(3), using a format substantially similar to Sample Form B-10 in appendix B to this part.

(b) Advertising disclosures for overdraft services—

(1) Disclosures. Except as provided in paragraphs (b)(2) through (4) of this section, any advertisement promoting the payment of overdrafts shall disclose in a clear and conspicuous manner:

(i) The fee or fees for the payment of each overdraft;

(ii) The categories of transactions for which a fee for paying an overdraft may be imposed;

(iii) The time period by which the consumer must repay or cover any overdraft; and

(iv) The circumstances under which the institution will not pay an overdraft.

(2) Communications about the payment of overdrafts not subject to additional advertising disclosures. Paragraph (b)(1) of this section does not apply to:

(i) An advertisement promoting a service where the institution's payment of overdrafts will be agreed upon in writing and subject to the Board's Regulation Z (12 CFR part 1026);

(ii) A communication by an institution about the payment of overdrafts in response to a consumer-initiated inquiry about deposit accounts or overdrafts. Providing information about the payment of overdrafts in response to a balance inquiry made through an automated system, such as a telephone response machine, ATM, or an institution's Internet site, is not a response to a consumer-initiated inquiry for purposes of this paragraph;

(iii) An advertisement made through broadcast or electronic media, such as television or radio;

(iv) An advertisement made on outdoor media, such as billboards;

(v) An ATM receipt;

(vi) An in-person discussion with a consumer;

(vii) Disclosures required by federal or other applicable law;

(viii) Information included on a periodic statement or a notice informing a consumer about a specific overdrawn item or the amount the account is overdrawn;

(ix) A term in a deposit account agreement discussing the institution's right to pay overdrafts;

(x) A notice provided to a consumer, such as at an ATM, that completing a requested transaction may trigger a fee for overdrawing an account, or a general notice that items overdrawing an account may trigger a fee;

(xi) Informational or educational materials concerning the payment of overdrafts if the materials do not specifically describe the institution's overdraft service; or

(xii) An opt-out or opt-in notice regarding the institution's payment of overdrafts or provision of discretionary overdraft services.

(3) Exception for ATM screens and telephone response machines. The disclosures described in paragraphs (b)(1)(ii) and (iv) of this section are not required in connection with any advertisement made on an ATM screen or using a telephone response machine.

(4) Exception for indoor signs. Paragraph (b)(1) of this section does not apply to advertisements for the payment of overdrafts on indoor signs as described by § 1030.8(e)(2) of this part, provided that the sign contains a clear and conspicuous statement that fees may apply and that consumers should contact an employee for further information about applicable fees and terms. For purposes of this paragraph (b)(4), an indoor sign does not include an ATM screen.

(c) Disclosure of account balances. If an institution discloses balance information to a consumer through an automated system, the balance may not include additional amounts that the institution may provide to cover an item when there are insufficient or unavailable funds in the consumer's account, whether under a service provided in its discretion, a service subject to Regulation Z (12 CFR part 1026), or a service to transfer funds from another account of the consumer. The institution may, at its option, disclose additional account balances that include such additional amounts, if the institution prominently states that any such balance includes such additional amounts and, if applicable, that additional amounts are not available for all transactions.

CONSUMER LEASING
(REGULATION M)

---

12 C.F.R. Part 1013

Table of Sections

§ 1013.1. Authority, Scope, Purpose, and Enforcement

(a) Authority. The regulation in this part, known as Regulation M, is issued by the Bureau of Consumer Financial Protection to implement the consumer leasing provisions of the Truth in Lending Act, which is title I of the Consumer Credit Protection Act, as amended (15 U.S.C. 1601 et seq.). Information collection requirements contained in this part have been approved by the Office of Management and Budget under the provisions of 44 U.S.C. 3501 et seq. and have been assigned OMB control number 3170–0006.

(b) Scope and purpose. This part applies to all persons that are lessors of personal property under consumer leases as those terms are defined in § 1013.2(e)(1) and (h), except persons excluded from coverage of this part by section 1029 of the Consumer Financial Protection Act of 2010, title X of the Dodd-Frank Wall Street Reform and Consumer Protection Act (Dodd-Frank Act), Public Law 111–203, 124 Stat. 1376. The purpose of this part is:

(1) To ensure that lessees of personal property receive meaningful disclosures that enable them to compare lease terms with other leases and, where appropriate, with credit transactions;

(2) To limit the amount of balloon payments in consumer lease transactions; and

(3) To provide for the accurate disclosure of lease terms in advertising.

(c) Enforcement and liability. Section 108 of the Act contains the administrative enforcement provisions. Sections 112, 130, 131, and 185 of the Act contain the liability provisions for failing to comply with the requirements of the Act and this part.

§ 1013.2. Definitions

For the purposes of this part the following definitions apply:

(a) Act means the Truth in Lending Act (15 U.S.C. 1601 et seq.) and the Consumer Leasing Act is Chapter 5 of the Truth in Lending Act.

(b) Advertisement means a commercial message in any medium that directly or indirectly promotes a consumer lease transaction.

(c) Bureau refers to the Bureau of Consumer Financial Protection.

(d) Closed-end lease means a consumer lease other than an open-end lease as defined in this section.

(e)(1) Consumer lease means a contract in the form of a bailment or lease for the use of personal property by a natural person primarily for personal, family, or household purposes, for a period exceeding four months and for a total contractual obligation not exceeding the applicable threshold amount, whether or not the lessee has the option to purchase or otherwise become the owner of the property at the expiration of the lease. The threshold amount is adjusted annually to reflect increases in the Consumer Price Index for Urban Wage Earners and Clerical Workers, as applicable. See the official commentary to this paragraph (e) for the threshold amount applicable to a specific consumer lease. Unless the context indicates otherwise, in this part "lease" means "consumer lease."

(2) The term does not include a lease that meets the definition of a credit sale in Regulation Z (12 CFR 226.2(a)). It also does not include a lease for agricultural, business, or commercial purposes or a lease made to an organization.

(3) This part does not apply to a lease transaction of personal property which is incident to the lease of real property and which provides that:

(i) The lessee has no liability for the value of the personal property at the end of the lease term except for abnormal wear and tear; and

(ii) The lessee has no option to purchase the leased property.

(f) Gross capitalized cost means the amount agreed upon by the lessor and the lessee as the value of the leased property and any items that are capitalized or amortized during the lease term, including but not limited to taxes, insurance, service agreements, and any outstanding prior credit or lease balance. Capitalized cost reduction means the total amount of any rebate, cash payment, net trade-in allowance, and noncash credit that reduces the gross capitalized cost. The adjusted capitalized cost equals the gross capitalized cost less the capitalized cost reduction, and is the amount used by the lessor in calculating the base periodic payment.

(g) Lessee means a natural person who enters into or is offered a consumer lease.

(h) Lessor means a person who regularly leases, offers to lease, or arranges for the lease of personal property under a consumer lease. A person who has leased, offered, or arranged to lease personal property more than five times in the preceding calendar year or more than five times in the current calendar year is subject to the Act and this part.

(i) Open-end lease means a consumer lease in which the lessee's liability at the end of the lease term is based on the difference between the residual value of the leased property and its realized value.

(j) Organization means a corporation, trust, estate, partnership, cooperative, association, or government entity or instrumentality.

(k) Person means a natural person or an organization.

(*l*) Personal property means any property that is not real property under the law of the state where the property is located at the time it is offered or made available for lease.

(m) Realized value means:

(1) The price received by the lessor for the leased property at disposition;

(2) The highest offer for disposition of the leased property; or

(3) The fair market value of the leased property at the end of the lease term.

(n) Residual value means the value of the leased property at the end of the lease term, as estimated or assigned at consummation by the lessor, used in calculating the base periodic payment.

(*o*) Security interest and security mean any interest in property that secures the payment or performance of an obligation.

(p) State means any state, the District of Columbia, the Commonwealth of Puerto Rico, and any territory or possession of the United States.

§ 1013.3. General Disclosure Requirements

(a) General requirements. A lessor shall make the disclosures required by § 1013.4, as applicable. The disclosures shall be made clearly and conspicuously in writing in a form the consumer may keep, in accordance with this section. The disclosures required by this part may be provided to the lessee in electronic form, subject to compliance with the consumer consent and other applicable provisions of the Electronic Signatures in Global and National Commerce Act (E-Sign Act) (15 U.S.C. 7001 et seq.). For an advertisement accessed by the consumer in electronic form, the disclosures required by § 1013.7 may be provided to the consumer in electronic form in the advertisement, without regard to the consumer consent or other provisions of the E-Sign Act.

(1) Form of disclosures. The disclosures required by § 1013.4 shall be given to the lessee together in a dated statement that identifies the lessor and the lessee; the disclosures may be made either in a separate statement that identifies the consumer lease transaction or in the contract or other document evidencing the lease. Alternatively, the disclosures required to be segregated from other information under paragraph (a)(2) of this section may be provided in a separate dated statement that identifies the lease, and the other required disclosures may be provided in the lease contract or other document evidencing the lease. In a lease of multiple items, the property description required by § 1013.4(a) may be given in a separate statement that is included in the disclosure statement required by this paragraph.

(2) Segregation of certain disclosures. The following disclosures shall be segregated from other information and shall contain only directly related information: §§ 1013.4(b) through (f), (g)(2), (h)(3), (i)(1), (j), and (m)(1). The headings, content, and format for the disclosures referred to in this paragraph (a)(2) shall be provided in a manner substantially similar to the applicable model form in appendix A of this part.

(3) Timing of disclosures. A lessor shall provide the disclosures to the lessee prior to the consummation of a consumer lease.

(4) Language of disclosures. The disclosures required by § 1013.4 may be made in a language other than English provided that they are made available in English upon the lessee's request.

(b) Additional information; nonsegregated disclosures. Additional information may be provided with any disclosure not listed in paragraph (a)(2) of this section, but it shall not be stated, used, or placed so as to mislead or confuse the lessee or contradict, obscure, or detract attention from any disclosure required by this part.

(c) Multiple lessors or lessees. When a transaction involves more than one lessor, the disclosures required by this part may be made by one lessor on behalf of all the lessors. When a lease involves more than one lessee, the lessor may provide the disclosures to any lessee who is primarily liable on the lease.

(d) Use of estimates. If an amount or other item needed to comply with a required disclosure is unknown or unavailable after reasonable efforts have been made to ascertain the information, the lessor may use a reasonable estimate that is based on the best information available to the lessor, is clearly identified as an estimate, and is not used to circumvent or evade any disclosures required by this part.

(e) Effect of subsequent occurrence. If a required disclosure becomes inaccurate because of an event occurring after consummation, the inaccuracy is not a violation of this part.

(f) Minor variations. A lessor may disregard the effects of the following in making disclosures:

(1) That payments must be collected in whole cents;

(2) That dates of scheduled payments may be different because a scheduled date is not a business day;

(3) That months have different numbers of days; and

(4) That February 29 occurs in a leap year.

§ 1013.4. Content of Disclosures

For any consumer lease subject to this part, the lessor shall disclose the following information, as applicable:

(a) **Description of property.** A brief description of the leased property sufficient to identify the property to the lessee and lessor.

(b) **Amount due at lease signing or delivery.** The total amount to be paid prior to or at consummation or by delivery, if delivery occurs after consummation, using the term "amount due at lease signing or delivery." The lessor shall itemize each component by type and amount, including any refundable security deposit, advance monthly or other periodic payment, and capitalized cost reduction; and in motor vehicle leases, shall itemize how the amount due will be paid, by type and amount, including any net trade-in allowance, rebates, noncash credits, and cash payments in a format substantially similar to the model forms in appendix A of this part.

(c) **Payment schedule and total amount of periodic payments.** The number, amount, and due dates or periods of payments scheduled under the lease, and the total amount of the periodic payments.

(d) **Other charges.** The total amount of other charges payable to the lessor, itemized by type and amount, that are not included in the periodic payments. Such charges include the amount of any liability the lease imposes upon the lessee at the end of the lease term; the potential difference between the residual and realized values referred to in paragraph (k) of this section is excluded.

(e) **Total of payments.** The total of payments, with a description such as "the amount you will have paid by the end of the lease." This amount is the sum of the amount due at lease signing (less any refundable amounts), the total amount of periodic payments (less any portion of the periodic payment paid at lease signing), and other charges under paragraphs (b), (c), and (d) of this section. In an open-end lease, a description such as "you will owe an additional amount if the actual value of the vehicle is less than the residual value" shall accompany the disclosure.

(f) **Payment calculation.** In a motor vehicle lease, a mathematical progression of how the scheduled periodic payment is derived, in a format substantially similar to the applicable model form in appendix A of this part, which shall contain the following:

(1) **Gross capitalized cost.** The gross capitalized cost, including a disclosure of the agreed upon value of the vehicle, a description such as "the agreed upon value of the vehicle [state the amount] and any items you pay for over the lease term (such as service contracts, insurance, and any outstanding prior credit or lease balance)," and a statement of the lessee's option to receive a separate written itemization of the gross capitalized cost. If requested by the lessee, the itemization shall be provided before consummation.

(2) **Capitalized cost reduction.** The capitalized cost reduction, with a description such as "the amount of any net trade-in allowance, rebate, noncash credit, or cash you pay that reduces the gross capitalized cost."

(3) **Adjusted capitalized cost.** The adjusted capitalized cost, with a description such as "the amount used in calculating your base [periodic] payment."

(4) **Residual value.** The residual value, with a description such as "the value of the vehicle at the end of the lease used in calculating your base [periodic] payment."

(5) **Depreciation and any amortized amounts.** The depreciation and any amortized amounts, which is the difference between the adjusted capitalized cost and the residual value, with a description such as "the amount charged for the vehicle's decline in value through normal use and for any other items paid over the lease term."

(6) **Rent charge.** The rent charge, with a description such as "the amount charged in addition to the depreciation and any amortized amounts." This amount is the difference between the total of the base periodic payments over the lease term minus the depreciation and any amortized amounts.

(7) **Total of base periodic payments.** The total of base periodic payments with a description such as "depreciation and any amortized amounts plus the rent charge."

(8) **Lease payments.** The lease payments with a description such as "the number of payments in your lease."

(9) **Base periodic payment.** The total of the base periodic payments divided by the number of payment periods in the lease.

(10) **Itemization of other charges.** An itemization of any other charges that are part of the periodic payment.

(11) **Total periodic payment.** The sum of the base periodic payment and any other charges that are part of the periodic payment.

(g) **Early termination**—

(1) **Conditions and disclosure of charges.** A statement of the conditions under which the lessee or lessor may terminate the lease prior to the end of the lease term; and the amount or a description of the method for determining the amount of any penalty or other charge for early termination, which must be reasonable.

(2) **Early termination notice.** In a motor vehicle lease, a notice substantially similar to the following: "Early Termination. You may have to pay a substantial charge if you end this lease early. The charge may be up to several thousand dollars. The actual charge will depend on when the lease is terminated. The earlier you end the lease, the greater this charge is likely to be."

(h) **Maintenance responsibilities.** The following provisions are required:

(1) **Statement of responsibilities**. A statement specifying whether the lessor or the lessee is responsible for maintaining or servicing the leased property, together with a brief description of the responsibility;

(2) **Wear and use standard.** A statement of the lessor's standards for wear and use (if any), which must be reasonable; and

(3) **Notice of wear and use standard.** In a motor vehicle lease, a notice regarding wear and use substantially similar to the following: "Excessive Wear and Use. You may be charged for excessive wear based on our standards for normal use." The notice shall also specify the amount or method for determining any charge for excess mileage.

(i) **Purchase option.** A statement of whether or not the lessee has the option to purchase the leased property, and:

(1) **End of lease term.** If at the end of the lease term, the purchase price; and

(2) **During lease term.** If prior to the end of the lease term, the purchase price or the method for determining the price and when the lessee may exercise this option.

(j) **Statement referencing nonsegregated disclosures.** A statement that the lessee should refer to the lease documents for additional information on early termination, purchase options and maintenance responsibilities, warranties, late and default charges, insurance, and any security interests, if applicable.

(k) Liability between residual and realized values. A statement of the lessee's liability, if any, at early termination or at the end of the lease term for the difference between the residual value of the leased property and its realized value.

(l) **Right of appraisal.** If the lessee's liability at early termination or at the end of the lease term is based on the realized value of the leased property, a statement that the lessee may obtain, at the lessee's expense, a professional appraisal by an independent third party (agreed to by the lessee and the lessor) of the value that could be realized at sale of the leased property. The appraisal shall be final and binding on the parties.

(m) Liability at end of lease term based on residual value. If the lessee is liable at the end of the lease term for the difference between the residual value of the leased property and its realized value:

(1) Rent and other charges. The rent and other charges, paid by the lessee and required by the lessor as an incident to the lease transaction, with a description such as "the total amount of rent and other charges imposed in connection with your lease [state the amount]."

(2) Excess liability. A statement about a rebuttable presumption that, at the end of the lease term, the residual value of the leased property is unreasonable and not in good faith to the extent that the residual value exceeds the realized value by more than three times the base monthly payment (or more than three times the average payment allocable to a monthly period, if the lease calls for periodic payments other than monthly); and that the lessor cannot collect the excess amount unless the lessor brings a successful court action and pays the lessee's reasonable attorney's fees, or unless the excess of the residual value over the realized value is due to unreasonable or excessive wear or use of the leased property (in which case the rebuttable presumption does not apply).

(3) Mutually agreeable final adjustment. A statement that the lessee and lessor are permitted, after termination of the lease, to make any mutually agreeable final adjustment regarding excess liability.

(n) Fees and taxes. The total dollar amount for all official and license fees, registration, title, or taxes required to be paid in connection with the lease.

(o) **Insurance.** A brief identification of insurance in connection with the lease including:

(1) Through the lessor. If the insurance is provided by or paid through the lessor, the types and amounts of coverage and the cost to the lessee; or

(2) Through a third party. If the lessee must obtain the insurance, the types and amounts of coverage required of the lessee.

(p) Warranties or guarantees. A statement identifying all express warranties and guarantees from the manufacturer or lessor with respect to the leased property that apply to the lessee.

(q) Penalties and other charges for delinquency. The amount or the method of determining the amount of any penalty or other charge for delinquency, default, or late payments, which must be reasonable.

(r) Security interest. A description of any security interest, other than a security deposit disclosed under paragraph (b) of this section, held or to be retained by the lessor; and a clear identification of the property to which the security interest relates.

(s) Limitations on rate information. If a lessor provides a percentage rate in an advertisement or in documents evidencing the lease transaction, a notice stating that "this percentage may not measure the overall cost of financing this lease" shall accompany the rate disclosure. The lessor shall not use the term "annual percentage rate," "annual lease rate," or any equivalent term.

(t) Non-motor vehicle open-end leases. Non-motor vehicle open-end leases remain subject to section 182(10) of the Act regarding end of term liability.

§ 1013.5. Renegotiations, Extensions, and Assumptions

(a) Renegotiation. A renegotiation occurs when a consumer lease subject to this part is satisfied and replaced by a new lease undertaken by the same consumer. A renegotiation requires new disclosures, except as provided in paragraph (d) of this section.

(b) Extension. An extension is a continuation, agreed to by the lessor and the lessee, of an existing consumer lease beyond the originally scheduled end of the lease term, except when the continuation is the result of a renegotiation. An extension that exceeds six months requires new disclosures, except as provided in paragraph (d) of this section.

(c) Assumption. New disclosures are not required when a consumer lease is assumed by another person, whether or not the lessor charges an assumption fee.

(d) Exceptions. New disclosures are not required for the following, even if they meet the definition of a renegotiation or an extension:

(1) A reduction in the rent charge;

(2) The deferment of one or more payments, whether or not a fee is charged;

(3) The extension of a lease for not more than six months on a month-to-month basis or otherwise;

(4) A substitution of leased property with property that has a substantially equivalent or greater economic value, provided no other lease terms are changed;

(5) The addition, deletion, or substitution of leased property in a multiple-item lease, provided the average periodic payment does not change by more than 25 percent; or

(6) An agreement resulting from a court proceeding.

§ 1013.6. [Reserved]

§ 1013.7. Advertising

(a) General rule. An advertisement for a consumer lease may state that a specific lease of property at specific amounts or terms is available only if the lessor usually and customarily leases or will lease the property at those amounts or terms.

(b) Clear and conspicuous standard. Disclosures required by this section shall be made clearly and conspicuously.

(1) Amount due at lease signing or delivery. Except for the statement of a periodic payment, any affirmative or negative reference to a charge that is a part of the disclosure required under paragraph (d)(2)(ii) of this section shall not be more prominent than that disclosure.

(2) Advertisement of a lease rate. If a lessor provides a percentage rate in an advertisement, the rate shall not be more prominent than any of the disclosures in § 1013.4, with the exception of the notice in § 1013.4(s) required to accompany the rate; and the lessor shall not use the term "annual percentage rate," "annual lease rate," or equivalent term.

(c) Catalogs or other multipage advertisements; electronic advertisements. A catalog or other multipage advertisement, or an electronic advertisement (such as an advertisement appearing on an Internet Web site), that provides a table or schedule of the required disclosures shall be considered a single advertisement if, for lease terms that appear without all the required disclosures, the advertisement refers to the page or pages on which the table or schedule appears.

(d) Advertisement of terms that require additional disclosure.

(1) Triggering terms. An advertisement that states any of the following items shall contain the disclosures required by paragraph (d)(2) of this section, except as provided in paragraphs (e) and (f) of this section:

(i) The amount of any payment; or

(ii) A statement of any capitalized cost reduction or other payment (or that no payment is required) prior to or at consummation or by delivery, if delivery occurs after consummation.

(2) Additional terms. An advertisement stating any item listed in paragraph (d)(1) of this section shall also state the following items:

(i) That the transaction advertised is a lease;

(ii) The total amount due prior to or at consummation or by delivery, if delivery occurs after consummation;

(iii) The number, amounts, and due dates or periods of scheduled payments under the lease;

(iv) A statement of whether or not a security deposit is required; and

(v) A statement that an extra charge may be imposed at the end of the lease term where the lessee's liability (if any) is based on the difference between the residual value of the leased property and its realized value at the end of the lease term.

(e) Alternative disclosures—merchandise tags. A merchandise tag stating any item listed in paragraph (d)(1) of this section may comply with paragraph (d)(2) of this section by referring to a sign or display prominently posted in the lessor's place of business that contains a table or schedule of the required disclosures.

(f) Alternative disclosures—television or radio advertisements—

(1) Toll-free number or print advertisement. An advertisement made through television or radio stating any item listed in paragraph (d)(1) of this section complies with paragraph (d)(2) of this section if the advertisement states the items listed in paragraphs (d)(2)(i) through (iii) of this section, and:

(i) Lists a toll-free telephone number along with a reference that such number may be used by consumers to obtain the information required by paragraph (d)(2) of this section; or

(ii) Directs the consumer to a written advertisement in a publication of general circulation in the community served by the media station, including the name and the date of the publication, with a statement that information required by paragraph (d)(2) of this section is included in the advertisement. The written advertisement shall be published beginning at least three days before and ending at least ten days after the broadcast.

(2) Establishment of toll-free number.

(i) The toll-free telephone number shall be available for no fewer than ten days, beginning on the date of the broadcast.

(ii) The lessor shall provide the information required by paragraph (d)(2) of this section orally, or in writing upon request.

§ 1013.8. Record Retention

A lessor shall retain evidence of compliance with the requirements imposed by this part, other than the advertising requirements under § 1013.7, for a period of not less than two years after the date the disclosures are required to be made or an action is required to be taken.

§ 1013.9. Relation to State Laws

(a) Inconsistent state law. A state law that is inconsistent with the requirements of the Act and this part is preempted to the extent of the inconsistency. If a lessor cannot comply with a state law without violating a provision of this part, the state law is inconsistent within the meaning of section 186(a) of the Act and is preempted, unless the state law gives greater protection and benefit to the consumer. A state, through an official having primary enforcement or interpretative responsibilities for the state consumer leasing law, may apply to the Bureau for a preemption determination.

(b) Exemptions—

(1) Application. A state may apply to the Bureau for an exemption from the requirements of the Act and this part for any class of lease transactions within the state. The Bureau will grant such an exemption if the Bureau determines that:

(i) The class of leasing transactions is subject to state law requirements substantially similar to the Act and this part or that lessees are afforded greater protection under state law; and

(ii) There is adequate provision for state enforcement.

(2) Enforcement and liability. After an exemption has been granted, the requirements of the applicable state law (except for additional requirements not imposed by Federal law) will constitute the requirements of the Act and this part. No exemption will extend to the civil liability provisions of sections 130, 131, and 185 of the Act.

EQUAL CREDIT OPPORTUNITY (REGULATION B)

---

12 C.F.R. Part 1002

Table of Sections

§ 1002.1. Authority, Scope, and Purpose

(a) Authority and scope. This part, known as Regulation B, is issued by the Bureau of Consumer Financial Protection (Bureau) pursuant to title VII (Equal Credit Opportunity Act) of the Consumer Credit Protection Act, as amended (15 U.S.C. 1601 et seq.). Except as otherwise provided herein, this part applies to all persons who are creditors, as defined in § 1002.2(*l*), other than a person excluded from coverage of this part by section 1029 of the Consumer Financial Protection Act of 2010, title X of the Dodd-Frank Wall Street Reform and Consumer Protection Act, Public Law 111–203, 124 Stat. 1376. Information collection requirements contained in this part have been approved by the Office of Management and Budget under the provisions of 44 U.S.C. 3501 et seq. and have been assigned OMB No. 3170–0013.

(b) Purpose. The purpose of this part is to promote the availability of credit to all creditworthy applicants without regard to race, color, religion, national origin, sex, marital status, or age (provided the applicant has the capacity to contract); to the fact that all or part of the applicant's income derives from a public assistance program; or to the fact that the applicant has in good faith exercised any right under the Consumer Credit Protection Act. The regulation prohibits creditor practices that discriminate on the basis of any of these factors. The regulation also requires creditors to notify applicants of action taken on their applications; to report credit history in the names of both spouses on an account; to retain records of credit applications; to collect information about the applicant's race and other personal characteristics in applications for certain dwelling-related loans; and to provide applicants with copies of appraisal reports used in connection with credit transactions.

§ 1002.2. Definitions

For the purposes of this part, unless the context indicates otherwise, the following definitions apply.

(a) Account means an extension of credit. When employed in relation to an account, the word use refers only to open-end credit.

(b) Act means the Equal Credit Opportunity Act (Title VII of the Consumer Credit Protection Act).

(c) Adverse action.

(1) The term means:

(i) A refusal to grant credit in substantially the amount or on substantially the terms requested in an application unless the creditor makes a counteroffer (to grant credit in a different amount or on other terms) and the applicant uses or expressly accepts the credit offered;

(ii) A termination of an account or an unfavorable change in the terms of an account that does not affect all or substantially all of a class of the creditor's accounts; or

(iii) A refusal to increase the amount of credit available to an applicant who has made an application for an increase.

(2) The term does not include:

(i) A change in the terms of an account expressly agreed to by an applicant;

(ii) Any action or forbearance relating to an account taken in connection with inactivity, default, or delinquency as to that account;

(iii) A refusal or failure to authorize an account transaction at point of sale or loan, except when the refusal is a termination or an unfavorable change in the terms of an account that does not affect all or substantially all of a class of the creditor's accounts, or when the refusal is a denial of an application for an increase in the amount of credit available under the account;

(iv) A refusal to extend credit because applicable law prohibits the creditor from extending the credit requested; or

(v) A refusal to extend credit because the creditor does not offer the type of credit or credit plan requested.

(3) An action that falls within the definition of both paragraphs (c)(1) and (c)(2) of this section is governed by paragraph (c)(2) of this section.

(d) Age refers only to the age of natural persons and means the number of fully elapsed years from the date of an applicant's birth.

(e) Applicant means any person who requests or who has received an extension of credit from a creditor, and includes any person who is or may become contractually liable regarding an extension of credit. For purposes of § 1002.7(d), the term includes guarantors, sureties, endorsers, and similar parties.

(f) Application means an oral or written request for an extension of credit that is made in accordance with procedures used by a creditor for the type of credit requested. The term application does not include the use of an account or line of credit to obtain an amount of credit that is within a previously established credit limit. A completed application means an application in connection with which a creditor has received all the information that the creditor regularly obtains and considers in evaluating applications for the amount and type of credit requested (including, but not limited to, credit reports, any additional information requested from the applicant, and any approvals or reports by governmental agencies or other persons that are necessary to guarantee, insure, or provide security for the credit or collateral). The creditor shall exercise reasonable diligence in obtaining such information.

(g) Business credit refers to extensions of credit primarily for business or commercial (including agricultural) purposes, but excluding extensions of credit of the types described in §§ 1002.3(a)–(d).

(h) Consumer credit means credit extended to a natural person primarily for personal, family, or household purposes.

(i) Contractually liable means expressly obligated to repay all debts arising on an account by reason of an agreement to that effect.

(j) Credit means the right granted by a creditor to an applicant to defer payment of a debt, incur debt and defer its payment, or purchase property or services and defer payment therefor.

(k) Credit card means any card, plate, coupon book, or other single credit device that may be used from time to time to obtain money, property, or services on credit.

(*l*) Creditor means a person who, in the ordinary course of business, regularly participates in a credit decision, including setting the terms of the credit. The term creditor includes a creditor's assignee, transferee, or subrogee who so participates. For purposes of §§ 1002.4(a) and (b), the term creditor also includes a person who, in the ordinary course of business, regularly refers applicants or prospective applicants to creditors, or selects or offers to select creditors to whom requests for credit may be made. A person is not a creditor regarding any violation of the Act or this part committed by another creditor unless the person knew or had reasonable notice of the act, policy, or practice that constituted the violation before becoming involved in the credit transaction. The term does not include a person whose only participation in a credit transaction involves honoring a credit card.

(m) Credit transaction means every aspect of an applicant's dealings with a creditor regarding an application for credit or an existing extension of credit (including, but not limited to, information requirements; investigation procedures; standards of creditworthiness; terms of credit; furnishing of credit information; revocation, alteration, or termination of credit; and collection procedures).

(n) Discriminate against an applicant means to treat an applicant less favorably than other applicants.

(*o*) Elderly means age 62 or older.

(p) Empirically derived and other credit scoring systems—

(1) A credit scoring system is a system that evaluates an applicant's creditworthiness mechanically, based on key attributes of the applicant and aspects of the transaction, and that determines, alone or in conjunction with an evaluation of additional information about the applicant, whether an applicant is deemed creditworthy. To qualify as an empirically derived, demonstrably and statistically sound, credit scoring system, the system must be:

(i) Based on data that are derived from an empirical comparison of sample groups or the population of creditworthy and non-creditworthy applicants who applied for credit within a reasonable preceding period of time;

(ii) Developed for the purpose of evaluating the creditworthiness of applicants with respect to the legitimate business interests of the creditor utilizing the system (including, but not limited to, minimizing bad debt losses and operating expenses in accordance with the creditor's business judgment);

(iii) Developed and validated using accepted statistical principles and methodology; and

(iv) Periodically revalidated by the use of appropriate statistical principles and methodology and adjusted as necessary to maintain predictive ability.

(2) A creditor may use an empirically derived, demonstrably and statistically sound, credit scoring system obtained from another person or may obtain credit experience from which to develop such a system. Any such system must satisfy the criteria set forth in paragraph (p)(1)(i) through (iv) of this section; if the creditor is unable during the development process to validate the system based on its own credit experience in accordance with paragraph (p)(1) of this section, the system must be validated when sufficient credit experience becomes available. A system that fails this validity test is no longer an empirically derived, demonstrably and statistically sound, credit scoring system for that creditor.

(q) Extend credit and extension of credit mean the granting of credit in any form (including, but not limited to, credit granted in addition to any existing credit or credit limit; credit granted pursuant to an open-end credit plan; the refinancing or other renewal of credit, including the issuance of a new credit card in place of an expiring credit card or in substitution for an existing credit card; the consolidation of two or more obligations; or the continuance of existing credit without any special effort to collect at or after maturity).

(r) Good faith means honesty in fact in the conduct or transaction.

(s) Inadvertent error means a mechanical, electronic, or clerical error that a creditor demonstrates was not intentional and occurred notwithstanding the maintenance of procedures reasonably adapted to avoid such errors.

(t) Judgmental system of evaluating applicants means any system for evaluating the creditworthiness of an applicant other than an empirically derived, demonstrably and statistically sound, credit scoring system.

(u) Marital status means the state of being unmarried, married, or separated, as defined by applicable state law. The term "unmarried" includes persons who are single, divorced, or widowed.

(v) Negative factor or value, in relation to the age of elderly applicants, means utilizing a factor, value, or weight that is less favorable regarding elderly applicants than the creditor's experience warrants or is less favorable than the factor, value, or weight assigned to the class of applicants that are not classified as elderly and are most favored by a creditor on the basis of age.

(w) Open-end credit means credit extended under a plan in which a creditor may permit an applicant to make purchases or obtain loans from time to time directly from the creditor or indirectly by use of a credit card, check, or other device.

(x) Person means a natural person, corporation, government or governmental subdivision or agency, trust, estate, partnership, cooperative, or association.

(y) Pertinent element of creditworthiness, in relation to a judgmental system of evaluating applicants, means any information about applicants that a creditor obtains and considers and that has a demonstrable relationship to a determination of creditworthiness.

(z) Prohibited basis means race, color, religion, national origin, sex, marital status, or age (provided that the applicant has the capacity to enter into a binding contract); the fact that all or part of the applicant's income derives from any public assistance program; or the fact that the applicant has in good faith exercised any right under the Consumer Credit Protection Act or any state law upon which an exemption has been granted by the Bureau.

(aa) State means any state, the District of Columbia, the Commonwealth of Puerto Rico, or any territory or possession of the United States.

Editorial Note: PL 115–172, 2018 SJRes 57, approved May 21, 2018 resolved that "Congress disapproves the rule submitted by the Bureau of Consumer Financial Protection relating to "Indirect Auto Lending and Compliance with the Equal Credit Opportunity Act" (CFPB Bulletin 2013–02 (March 21, 2013), and printed in the Congressional Record on December 6, 2017, on pages S7888–S7889, along with a letter of opinion from the Government Accountability Office dated December 5,

2017, that the Bulletin is a rule under the Congressional Review Act), and such rule shall have no force or effect."

§ 1002.3. Limited Exceptions for Certain Classes of Transactions

(a) Public utilities credit.

(1) Definition. Public utilities credit refers to extensions of credit that involve public utility services provided through pipe, wire, or other connected facilities, or radio or similar transmission (including extensions of such facilities), if the charges for service, delayed payment, and any discount for prompt payment are filed with or regulated by a government unit.

(2) Exceptions. The following provisions of this part do not apply to public utilities credit:

(i) Section 1002.5(d)(1) concerning information about marital status; and

(ii) Section 1002.12(b) relating to record retention.

(b) Securities credit.

(1) Definition. Securities credit refers to extensions of credit subject to regulation under section 7 of the Securities Exchange Act of 1934 or extensions of credit by a broker or dealer subject to regulation as a broker or dealer under the Securities Exchange Act of 1934.

(2) Exceptions. The following provisions of this part do not apply to securities credit:

(i) Section 1002.5(b) concerning information about the sex of an applicant;

(ii) Section 1002.5(c) concerning information about a spouse or former spouse;

(iii) Section 1002.5(d)(1) concerning information about marital status;

(iv) Section 1002.7(b) relating to designation of name to the extent necessary to comply with rules regarding an account in which a broker or dealer has an interest, or rules regarding the aggregation of accounts of spouses to determine controlling interests, beneficial interests, beneficial ownership, or purchase limitations and restrictions;

(v) Section 1002.7(c) relating to action concerning open-end accounts, to the extent the action taken is on the basis of a change of name or marital status;

(vi) Section 1002.7(d) relating to the signature of a spouse or other person;

(vii) Section 1002.10 relating to furnishing of credit information; and

(viii) Section 1002.12(b) relating to record retention.

(c) Incidental credit.

(1) Definition. Incidental credit refers to extensions of consumer credit other than the types described in paragraphs (a) and (b) of this section:

(i) That are not made pursuant to the terms of a credit card account;

(ii) That are not subject to a finance charge (as defined in Regulation Z, 12 CFR 1026.4); and

(iii) That are not payable by agreement in more than four installments.

(2) Exceptions. The following provisions of this part do not apply to incidental credit:

(i) Section 1002.5(b) concerning information about the sex of an applicant, but only to the extent necessary for medical records or similar purposes;

(ii) Section 1002.5(c) concerning information about a spouse or former spouse;

(iii) Section 1002.5(d)(1) concerning information about marital status;

(iv) Section 1002.5(d)(2) concerning information about income derived from alimony, child support, or separate maintenance payments;

(v) Section 1002.7(d) relating to the signature of a spouse or other person;

(vi) Section 1002.9 relating to notifications;

(vii) Section 1002.10 relating to furnishing of credit information; and

(viii) Section 1002.12(b) relating to record retention.

(d) Government credit.

(1) Definition. Government credit refers to extensions of credit made to governments or governmental subdivisions, agencies, or instrumentalities.

(2) Applicability of regulation. Except for § 1002.4(a), the general rule against discrimination on a prohibited basis, the requirements of this part do not apply to government credit.

§ 1002.4. General Rules

(a) Discrimination. A creditor shall not discriminate against an applicant on a prohibited basis regarding any aspect of a credit transaction.

(b) Discouragement. A creditor shall not make any oral or written statement, in advertising or otherwise, to applicants or prospective applicants that would discourage on a prohibited basis a reasonable person from making or pursuing an application.

(c) Written applications. A creditor shall take written applications for the dwelling-related types of credit covered by § 1002.13(a).

(d) Form of disclosures.

(1) General rule. A creditor that provides in writing any disclosures or information required by this part must provide the disclosures in a clear and conspicuous manner and, except for the disclosures required by §§ 1002.5 and 1002.13, in a form the applicant may retain.

(2) Disclosures in electronic form. The disclosures required by this part that are required to be given in writing may be provided to the applicant in electronic form, subject to compliance with the consumer consent and other applicable provisions of the Electronic Signatures in Global and National Commerce Act (E-Sign Act) (15 U.S.C. 7001 et seq.). Where the disclosures under §§ 1002.5(b)(1), 1002.5(b)(2), 1002.5(d)(1), 1002.5(d)(2), 1002.13, and 1002.14(a)(2) accompany an application accessed by the applicant in electronic form, these disclosures may be provided to the applicant in electronic form on or with the application form, without regard to the consumer consent or other provisions of the E-Sign Act.

(e) Foreign-language disclosures. Disclosures may be made in languages other than English, provided they are available in English upon request.

§ 1002.5. Rules Concerning Requests for Information

(a) General rules.

(1) Requests for information. Except as provided in paragraphs (b) through (d) of this section, a creditor may request any information in connection with a credit transaction. This paragraph does not limit or abrogate any Federal or state law regarding privacy, privileged information, credit reporting limitations, or similar restrictions on obtainable information.

(2) Required collection of information. Notwithstanding paragraphs (b) through (d) of this section, a creditor shall request information for monitoring purposes as required by § 1002.13 for credit secured by the applicant's dwelling. In addition, a creditor may obtain information required by a regulation, order, or agreement issued by, or entered into with, a court or an enforcement agency (including the Attorney General of the United States or a similar state official) to monitor or enforce compliance with the Act, this part, or other Federal or state statutes or regulations.

(3) Special-purpose credit. A creditor may obtain information that is otherwise restricted to determine eligibility for a special purpose credit program, as provided in §§ 1002.8(b), (c), and (d).

(4) Other permissible collection of information. Notwithstanding paragraph (b) of this section, a creditor may collect information under the following circumstances provided that the creditor collects the information in compliance with appendix B to 12 CFR part 1003:

(i) A creditor that is a financial institution under 12 CFR 1003.2(g) may collect information regarding the ethnicity, race, and sex of an applicant for a closed-end mortgage loan that is an excluded transaction under 12 CFR 1003.3(c)(11) if it submits HMDA data concerning such closed-end mortgage loans and applications or if it submitted HMDA data concerning closed-end mortgage loans for any of the preceding five calendar years;

(ii) A creditor that is a financial institution under 12 CFR 1003.2(g) may collect information regarding the ethnicity, race, and sex of an applicant for an open-end line of credit that is an excluded transaction under 12 CFR 1003.3(c)(12) if it submits HMDA data concerning such open-end lines of credit and applications or if it submitted HMDA data concerning open-end lines of credit for any of the preceding five calendar years;

(iii) A creditor that submitted HMDA data for any of the preceding five calendar years but is not currently a financial institution under 12 CFR 1003.2(g) may collect information regarding the ethnicity, race, and sex of an applicant for a loan that would otherwise be a covered loan under 12 CFR 1003.2(e) if not excluded by 12 CFR 1003.3(c)(11) or (12);

(iv) A creditor that exceeded an applicable loan volume threshold in the first year of the two-year threshold period provided in 12 CFR 1003.2(g), 1003.3(c)(11), or 1003.3(c)(12) may, in the second year, collect information regarding the ethnicity, race, and sex of an applicant for a loan that would otherwise be a covered loan under 12 CFR 1003.2(e) if the loan were not excluded by 12 CFR 1003.3(c)(11) or (12);

(v) A creditor that is a financial institution under 12 CFR 1003.2(g), or that submitted HMDA data for any of the preceding five calendar years but is not currently a financial institution under 12 CFR 1003.2(g), may collect information regarding the ethnicity, race, and sex of an applicant for a loan that would otherwise be a covered loan under 12 CFR 1003.2(e) if the loan were not excluded by 12 CFR 1003.3(c)(10).

(vi) A creditor that is collecting information regarding the ethnicity, race, and sex of an applicant or first co-applicant may collect information regarding the ethnicity, race, and sex of a second or additional co-applicant for a covered loan under 12 CFR 1003.2(e) or for a second or additional co-applicant for a loan described in paragraphs (a)(4)(i) through (v) of this section.

(b) Limitation on information about race, color, religion, national origin, or sex. A creditor shall not inquire about the race, color, religion, national origin, or sex of an applicant or any other person in connection with a credit transaction, except as provided in paragraphs (b)(1) and (b)(2) of this section.

(1) Self-test. A creditor may inquire about the race, color, religion, national origin, or sex of an applicant or any other person in connection with a credit transaction for the purpose of conducting a self-test that meets the requirements of § 1002.15. A creditor that makes such an inquiry shall disclose orally or in writing, at the time the information is requested, that:

(i) The applicant will not be required to provide the information;

(ii) The creditor is requesting the information to monitor its compliance with the Federal Equal Credit Opportunity Act;

(iii) Federal law prohibits the creditor from discriminating on the basis of this information, or on the basis of an applicant's decision not to furnish the information; and

(iv) If applicable, certain information will be collected based on visual observation or surname if not provided by the applicant or other person.

(2) Sex. An applicant may be requested to designate a title on an application form (such as Ms., Miss, Mr., or Mrs.) if the form discloses that the designation of a title is optional. An application form shall otherwise use only terms that are neutral as to sex.

(c) Information about a spouse or former spouse.

(1) General rule. Except as permitted in this paragraph, a creditor may not request any information concerning the spouse or former spouse of an applicant.

(2) Permissible inquiries. A creditor may request any information concerning an applicant's spouse (or former spouse under paragraph (c)(2)(v) of this section) that may be requested about the applicant if:

(i) The spouse will be permitted to use the account;

(ii) The spouse will be contractually liable on the account;

(iii) The applicant is relying on the spouse's income as a basis for repayment of the credit requested;

(iv) The applicant resides in a community property state or is relying on property located in such a state as a basis for repayment of the credit requested; or

(v) The applicant is relying on alimony, child support, or separate maintenance payments from a spouse or former spouse as a basis for repayment of the credit requested.

(3) Other accounts of the applicant. A creditor may request that an applicant list any account on which the applicant is contractually liable and to provide the name and address of the person in whose name the account is held. A creditor may also ask an applicant to list the names in which the applicant has previously received credit.

(d) Other limitations on information requests.

(1) Marital status. If an applicant applies for individual unsecured credit, a creditor shall not inquire about the applicant's marital status unless the applicant resides in a community property state or is relying on property located in such a state as a basis for repayment of the credit requested. If an application is for other than individual unsecured credit, a creditor may inquire about the applicant's marital status, but shall use only the terms married, unmarried, and separated. A creditor may explain that the category unmarried includes single, divorced, and widowed persons.

(2) Disclosure about income from alimony, child support, or separate maintenance. A creditor shall not inquire whether income stated in an application is derived from alimony, child support, or separate maintenance payments unless the creditor discloses to the applicant that such income need not be revealed if the applicant does not want the creditor to consider it in determining the applicant's creditworthiness.

(3) Childbearing, childrearing. A creditor shall not inquire about birth control practices, intentions concerning the bearing or rearing of children, or capability to bear children. A creditor may inquire about the number and ages of an applicant's dependents or about dependent-related financial obligations or expenditures, provided such information is requested without regard to sex, marital status, or any other prohibited basis.

(e) Permanent residency and immigration status. A creditor may inquire about the permanent residency and immigration status of an applicant or any other person in connection with a credit transaction.

§ 1002.6. Rules Concerning Evaluation of Applications

(a) General rule concerning use of information. Except as otherwise provided in the Act and this part, a creditor may consider any information obtained, so long as the information is not used to discriminate against an applicant on a prohibited basis. The legislative history of the Act indicates that the Congress intended an "effects test" concept, as outlined in the employment field by the Supreme Court in the cases of *Griggs v. Duke Power Co.*, 401 U.S. 424 (1971), and *Albemarle Paper Co. v. Moody*, 422 U.S. 405 (1975), to be applicable to a creditor's determination of creditworthiness.

(b) Specific rules concerning use of information.

(1) Except as provided in the Act and this part, a creditor shall not take a prohibited basis into account in any system of evaluating the creditworthiness of applicants.

(2) Age, receipt of public assistance.

(i) Except as permitted in this paragraph, a creditor shall not take into account an applicant's age (provided that the applicant has the capacity to enter into a binding contract) or whether an applicant's income derives from any public assistance program.

(ii) In an empirically derived, demonstrably and statistically sound, credit scoring system, a creditor may use an applicant's age as a predictive variable, provided that the age of an elderly applicant is not assigned a negative factor or value.

(iii) In a judgmental system of evaluating creditworthiness, a creditor may consider an applicant's age or whether an applicant's income derives from any public assistance program only for the purpose of determining a pertinent element of creditworthiness.

(iv) In any system of evaluating creditworthiness, a creditor may consider the age of an elderly applicant when such age is used to favor the elderly applicant in extending credit.

(3) Childbearing, childrearing. In evaluating creditworthiness, a creditor shall not make assumptions or use aggregate statistics relating to the likelihood that any category of persons will bear or rear children or will, for that reason, receive diminished or interrupted income in the future.

(4) Telephone listing. A creditor shall not take into account whether there is a telephone listing in the name of an applicant for consumer credit but may take into account whether there is a telephone in the applicant's residence.

(5) Income. A creditor shall not discount or exclude from consideration the income of an applicant or the spouse of an applicant because of a prohibited basis or because the income is derived from part-time employment or is an annuity, pension, or other retirement benefit; a creditor may consider the amount and probable continuance of any income in evaluating an applicant's creditworthiness. When an applicant relies on alimony, child support, or separate maintenance payments in applying for credit, the creditor shall consider such payments as income to the extent that they are likely to be consistently made.

(6) Credit history. To the extent that a creditor considers credit history in evaluating the creditworthiness of similarly qualified applicants for a similar type and amount of credit, in evaluating an applicant's creditworthiness a creditor shall consider:

(i) The credit history, when available, of accounts designated as accounts that the applicant and the applicant's spouse are permitted to use or for which both are contractually liable;

(ii) On the applicant's request, any information the applicant may present that tends to indicate the credit history being considered by the creditor does not accurately reflect the applicant's creditworthiness; and

(iii) On the applicant's request, the credit history, when available, of any account reported in the name of the applicant's spouse or former spouse that the applicant can demonstrate accurately reflects the applicant's creditworthiness.

(7) Immigration status. A creditor may consider the applicant's immigration status or status as a permanent resident of the United States, and any additional information that may be necessary to ascertain the creditor's rights and remedies regarding repayment.

(8) Marital status. Except as otherwise permitted or required by law, a creditor shall evaluate married and unmarried applicants by the same standards; and in evaluating joint applicants, a creditor shall not treat applicants differently based on the existence, absence, or likelihood of a marital relationship between the parties.

(9) Race, color, religion, national origin, sex. Except as otherwise permitted or required by law, a creditor shall not consider race, color, religion, national origin, or sex (or an applicant's or other person's decision not to provide the information) in any aspect of a credit transaction.

(c) State property laws. A creditor's consideration or application of state property laws directly or indirectly affecting creditworthiness does not constitute unlawful discrimination for the purposes of the Act or this part.

§ 1002.7. Rules Concerning Extensions of Credit

(a) Individual accounts. A creditor shall not refuse to grant an individual account to a creditworthy applicant on the basis of sex, marital status, or any other prohibited basis.

(b) Designation of name. A creditor shall not refuse to allow an applicant to open or maintain an account in a birth-given first name and a surname that is the applicant's birth-given surname, the spouse's surname, or a combined surname.

(c) Action concerning existing open-end accounts.

(1) Limitations. In the absence of evidence of the applicant's inability or unwillingness to repay, a creditor shall not take any of the following actions regarding an applicant who is contractually liable on an existing open-end account on the basis of the applicant's reaching a certain age or retiring or on the basis of a change in the applicant's name or marital status:

(i) Require a reapplication, except as provided in paragraph (c)(2) of this section;

(ii) Change the terms of the account; or

(iii) Terminate the account.

(2) Requiring reapplication. A creditor may require a reapplication for an open-end account on the basis of a change in the marital status of an applicant who is contractually liable if the credit granted was based in whole or in part on income of the applicant's spouse and if information available to the creditor indicates that the applicant's income may not support the amount of credit currently available.

(d) Signature of spouse or other person.

(1) Rule for qualified applicant. Except as provided in this paragraph, a creditor shall not require the signature of an applicant's spouse or other person, other than a joint applicant, on any credit instrument if the applicant qualifies under the creditor's standards of creditworthiness for the amount and terms of the credit requested. A creditor shall not deem the submission of a joint financial statement or other evidence of jointly held assets as an application for joint credit.

(2) Unsecured credit. If an applicant requests unsecured credit and relies in part upon property that the applicant owns jointly with another person to satisfy the creditor's standards of creditworthiness, the creditor may require the signature of the other person only on the instrument(s) necessary, or reasonably believed by the creditor to be necessary, under the law of the state in which the property is located, to enable the creditor to reach the property being relied upon in the event of the death or default of the applicant.

(3) Unsecured credit—community property states. If a married applicant requests unsecured credit and resides in a community property state, or if the applicant is relying on property located in such a state, a creditor may require the signature of the spouse on any instrument necessary, or reasonably believed by the creditor to be necessary, under applicable state law to make the community property available to satisfy the debt in the event of default if:

(i) Applicable state law denies the applicant power to manage or control sufficient community property to qualify for the credit requested under the creditor's standards of creditworthiness; and

(ii) The applicant does not have sufficient separate property to qualify for the credit requested without regard to community property.

(4) Secured credit. If an applicant requests secured credit, a creditor may require the signature of the applicant's spouse or other person on any instrument necessary, or reasonably believed by the creditor to be necessary, under applicable state law to make the property being offered as security available to satisfy the debt in the event of default, for example, an instrument to create a valid lien, pass clear title, waive inchoate rights, or assign earnings.

(5) Additional parties. If, under a creditor's standards of creditworthiness, the personal liability of an additional party is necessary to support the credit requested, a creditor may request a cosigner, guarantor, endorser, or similar party. The applicant's spouse may serve as an additional party, but the creditor shall not require that the spouse be the additional party.

(6) Rights of additional parties. A creditor shall not impose requirements upon an additional party that the creditor is prohibited from imposing upon an applicant under this section.

(e) Insurance. A creditor shall not refuse to extend credit and shall not terminate an account because credit life, health, accident, disability, or other credit-related insurance is not available on the basis of the applicant's age.

§ 1002.8. Special Purpose Credit Programs

(a) Standards for programs. Subject to the provisions of paragraph (b) of this section, the Act and this part permit a creditor to extend special purpose credit to applicants who meet eligibility requirements under the following types of credit programs:

(1) Any credit assistance program expressly authorized by Federal or state law for the benefit of an economically disadvantaged class of persons;

(2) Any credit assistance program offered by a not-for-profit organization, as defined under section 501(c) of the Internal Revenue Code of 1954, as amended, for the benefit of its members or for the benefit of an economically disadvantaged class of persons; or

(3) Any special purpose credit program offered by a for-profit organization, or in which such an organization participates to meet special social needs, if:

(i) The program is established and administered pursuant to a written plan that identifies the class of persons that the program is designed to benefit and sets forth the procedures and standards for extending credit pursuant to the program; and

(ii) The program is established and administered to extend credit to a class of persons who, under the organization's customary standards of creditworthiness, probably would not receive such credit or would receive it on less favorable terms than are ordinarily available to other applicants applying to the organization for a similar type and amount of credit.

(b) Rules in other sections—

(1) General applicability. All the provisions of this part apply to each of the special purpose credit programs described in paragraph (a) of this section except as modified by this section.

(2) Common characteristics. A program described in paragraph (a)(2) or (a)(3) of this section qualifies as a special purpose credit program only if it was established and is administered so as not to discriminate against an applicant on any prohibited basis; however, all program participants may be required to share one or more common characteristics (for example, race, national origin, or sex) so long as the program was not established and is not administered with the purpose of evading the requirements of the Act or this part.

(c) Special rule concerning requests and use of information. If participants in a special purpose credit program described in paragraph (a) of this section are required to possess one or more common characteristics (for example, race, national origin, or sex) and if the program otherwise satisfies the requirements of paragraph (a) of this section, a creditor may request and consider information regarding the common characteristic(s) in determining the applicant's eligibility for the program.

(d) Special rule in the case of financial need. If financial need is one of the criteria under a special purpose credit program described in paragraph (a) of this section, the creditor may request and consider, in determining an applicant's eligibility for the program, information regarding the applicant's marital status; alimony, child support, and separate maintenance income; and the spouse's financial resources. In addition, a creditor may obtain the signature of an applicant's spouse or other person on an application or credit instrument relating to a special purpose credit program if the signature is required by Federal or state law.

§ 1002.9. Notifications

(a) Notification of action taken, ECOA notice, and statement of specific reasons.

(1) When notification is required. A creditor shall notify an applicant of action taken within:

(i) 30 days after receiving a completed application concerning the creditor's approval of, counteroffer to, or adverse action on the application;

(ii) 30 days after taking adverse action on an incomplete application, unless notice is provided in accordance with paragraph (c) of this section;

(iii) 30 days after taking adverse action on an existing account; or

(iv) 90 days after notifying the applicant of a counteroffer if the applicant does not expressly accept or use the credit offered.

(2) Content of notification when adverse action is taken. A notification given to an applicant when adverse action is taken shall be in writing and shall contain a statement of the action taken; the name and address of the creditor; a statement of the provisions of section 701(a) of the Act; the name and address of the Federal agency that administers compliance with respect to the creditor; and either:

(i) A statement of specific reasons for the action taken; or

(ii) A disclosure of the applicant's right to a statement of specific reasons within 30 days, if the statement is requested within 60 days of the creditor's notification. The disclosure shall include the name, address, and telephone number of the person or office from which the statement of reasons can be obtained. If the creditor chooses to provide the reasons orally, the creditor shall also disclose the applicant's right to have them confirmed in writing within 30 days of receiving the applicant's written request for confirmation.

(3) Notification to business credit applicants. For business credit, a creditor shall comply with the notification requirements of this section in the following manner:

(i) With regard to a business that had gross revenues of $1 million or less in its preceding fiscal year (other than an extension of trade credit, credit incident to a factoring agreement, or other similar types of business credit), a creditor shall comply with paragraphs (a)(1) and (2) of this section, except that:

(A) The statement of the action taken may be given orally or in writing, when adverse action is taken;

(B) Disclosure of an applicant's right to a statement of reasons may be given at the time of application, instead of when adverse action is taken, provided the disclosure contains the information required by paragraph (a)(2)(ii) of this section and the ECOA notice specified in paragraph (b)(1) of this section;

(C) For an application made entirely by telephone, a creditor satisfies the requirements of paragraph (a)(3)(i) of this section by an oral statement of the action taken and of the applicant's right to a statement of reasons for adverse action.

(ii) With regard to a business that had gross revenues in excess of $1 million in its preceding fiscal year or an extension of trade credit, credit incident to a factoring agreement, or other similar types of business credit, a creditor shall:

(A) Notify the applicant, within a reasonable time, orally or in writing, of the action taken; and

(B) Provide a written statement of the reasons for adverse action and the ECOA notice specified in paragraph (b)(1) of this section if the applicant makes a written request for the reasons within 60 days of the creditor's notification.

(b) Form of ECOA notice and statement of specific reasons.

(1) ECOA notice. To satisfy the disclosure requirements of paragraph (a)(2) of this section regarding section 701(a) of the Act, the creditor shall provide a notice that is substantially similar to the following: The Federal Equal Credit Opportunity Act prohibits creditors from discriminating against credit applicants on the basis of race, color, religion, national origin, sex, marital status, age (provided the applicant has the capacity to enter into a binding contract); because all or part of the applicant's income derives from any public assistance program; or because the applicant has in good faith exercised any right under the Consumer Credit Protection Act. The Federal agency that administers compliance with this law concerning this creditor is [name and address as specified by the appropriate agency or agencies listed in appendix A of this part]. Until January 1, 2013, a creditor may comply with this paragraph (b)(1) and paragraph (a)(2) of this section by including in the notice the name and address as specified by the appropriate agency in appendix A to 12 CFR Part 202, as in effect on October 1, 2011.

(2) Statement of specific reasons. The statement of reasons for adverse action required by paragraph (a)(2)(i) of this section must be specific and indicate the principal reason(s) for the adverse action. Statements that the adverse action was based on the creditor's internal standards or policies or that the applicant, joint applicant, or similar party failed to achieve a qualifying score on the creditor's credit scoring system are insufficient.

(c) Incomplete applications.

(1) Notice alternatives. Within 30 days after receiving an application that is incomplete regarding matters that an applicant can complete, the creditor shall notify the applicant either:

(i) Of action taken, in accordance with paragraph (a) of this section; or

(ii) Of the incompleteness, in accordance with paragraph (c)(2) of this section.

(2) Notice of incompleteness. If additional information is needed from an applicant, the creditor shall send a written notice to the applicant specifying the information needed, designating a reasonable period of time for the applicant to provide the information, and informing the applicant that failure to provide the information requested will result in no further consideration being given to the application. The creditor shall have no further obligation under this section if the applicant fails to respond within the designated time period. If the applicant supplies the requested information within the designated time period, the creditor shall take action on the application and notify the applicant in accordance with paragraph (a) of this section.

(3) Oral request for information. At its option, a creditor may inform the applicant orally of the need for additional information. If the application remains incomplete the creditor shall send a notice in accordance with paragraph (c)(1) of this section.

(d) Oral notifications by small-volume creditors. In the case of a creditor that did not receive more than 150 applications during the preceding calendar year, the requirements of this section (including statements of specific reasons) are satisfied by oral notifications.

(e) Withdrawal of approved application. When an applicant submits an application and the parties contemplate that the applicant will inquire about its status, if the creditor approves the application and the applicant has not inquired within 30 days after applying, the creditor may treat the application as withdrawn and need not comply with paragraph (a)(1) of this section.

(f) Multiple applicants. When an application involves more than one applicant, notification need only be given to one of them but must be given to the primary applicant where one is readily apparent.

(g) Applications submitted through a third party. When an application is made on behalf of an applicant to more than one creditor and the applicant expressly accepts or uses credit offered by one of the creditors, notification of action taken by any of the other creditors is not required. If no credit is offered or if the applicant does not expressly accept or use the credit offered, each creditor taking adverse action must comply with this section, directly or through a third party. A notice given by a third party shall disclose the identity of each creditor on whose behalf the notice is given.

§ 1002.10. Furnishing of Credit Information

(a) Designation of accounts. A creditor that furnishes credit information shall designate:

(1) Any new account to reflect the participation of both spouses if the applicant's spouse is permitted to use or is contractually liable on the account (other than as a guarantor, surety, endorser, or similar party); and

(2) Any existing account to reflect such participation, within 90 days after receiving a written request to do so from one of the spouses.

(b) Routine reports to consumer reporting agency. If a creditor furnishes credit information to a consumer reporting agency concerning an account designated to reflect the participation of both spouses, the creditor shall furnish the information in a manner that will enable the agency to provide access to the information in the name of each spouse.

(c) Reporting in response to inquiry. If a creditor furnishes credit information in response to an inquiry, concerning an account designated to reflect the participation of both spouses, the creditor shall furnish the information in the name of the spouse about whom the information is requested.

§ 1002.11. Relation to State Law

(a) Inconsistent state laws. Except as otherwise provided in this section, this part alters, affects, or preempts only those state laws that are inconsistent with the Act and this part and then only to the extent of the inconsistency. A state law is not inconsistent if it is more protective of an applicant.

(b) Preempted provisions of state law.

(1) A state law is deemed to be inconsistent with the requirements of the Act and this part and less protective of an applicant within the meaning of section 705(f) of the Act to the extent that the law:

(i) Requires or permits a practice or act prohibited by the Act or this part;

(ii) Prohibits the individual extension of consumer credit to both parties to a marriage if each spouse individually and voluntarily applies for such credit;

(iii) Prohibits inquiries or collection of data required to comply with the Act or this part;

(iv) Prohibits asking about or considering age in an empirically derived, demonstrably and statistically sound, credit scoring system to determine a pertinent element of creditworthiness, or to favor an elderly applicant; or

(v) Prohibits inquiries necessary to establish or administer a special purpose credit program as defined by § 1002.8.

(2) A creditor, state, or other interested party may request that the Bureau determine whether a state law is inconsistent with the requirements of the Act and this part.

(c) Laws on finance charges, loan ceilings. If married applicants voluntarily apply for and obtain individual accounts with the same creditor, the accounts shall not be aggregated or otherwise combined for purposes of determining permissible finance charges or loan ceilings under any Federal or state law. Permissible loan ceiling laws shall be construed to permit each spouse to become individually liable up to the amount of the loan ceilings, less the amount for which the applicant is jointly liable.

(d) State and Federal laws not affected. This section does not alter or annul any provision of state property laws, laws relating to the disposition of decedents' estates, or Federal or state banking regulations directed only toward insuring the solvency of financial institutions.

(e) Exemption for state-regulated transactions—

(1) Applications. A state may apply to the Bureau for an exemption from the requirements of the Act and this part for any class of credit transactions within the state. The Bureau will grant such an exemption if the Bureau determines that:

(i) The class of credit transactions is subject to state law requirements substantially similar to those of the Act and this part or that applicants are afforded greater protection under state law; and

(ii) There is adequate provision for state enforcement.

(2) Liability and enforcement.

(i) No exemption will extend to the civil liability provisions of section 706 of the Act or the administrative enforcement provisions of section 704 of the Act.

(ii) After an exemption has been granted, the requirements of the applicable state law (except for additional requirements not imposed by Federal law) will constitute the requirements of the Act and this part.

§ 1002.12. Record Retention

(a) Retention of prohibited information. A creditor may retain in its files information that is prohibited by the Act or this part for use in evaluating applications, without violating the Act or this part, if the information was obtained:

(1) From any source prior to March 23, 1977;

(2) From consumer reporting agencies, an applicant, or others without the specific request of the creditor; or

(3) As required to monitor compliance with the Act and this part or other Federal or state statutes or regulations.

(b) Preservation of records—

(1) Applications. For 25 months (12 months for business credit, except as provided in paragraph (b)(5) of this section) after the date that a creditor notifies an applicant of action taken on an application or of incompleteness, the creditor shall retain in original form or a copy thereof:

(i) Any application that it receives, any information required to be obtained concerning characteristics of the applicant to monitor compliance with the Act and this part or other similar law, any information obtained pursuant to § 1002.5(a)(4), and any other written or recorded information used in evaluating the application and not returned to the applicant at the applicant's request;

(ii) A copy of the following documents if furnished to the applicant in written form (or, if furnished orally, any notation or memorandum made by the creditor):

(A) The notification of action taken; and

(B) The statement of specific reasons for adverse action; and

(iii) Any written statement submitted by the applicant alleging a violation of the Act or this part.

(2) Existing accounts. For 25 months (12 months for business credit, except as provided in paragraph (b)(5) of this section) after the date that a creditor notifies an applicant of adverse action regarding an existing account, the creditor shall retain as to that account, in original form or a copy thereof:

(i) Any written or recorded information concerning the adverse action; and

(ii) Any written statement submitted by the applicant alleging a violation of the Act or this part.

(3) Other applications. For 25 months (12 months for business credit, except as provided in paragraph (b)(5) of this section) after the date that a creditor receives an application for which the creditor is not required to comply with the notification requirements of § 1002.9, the creditor shall retain all written or recorded information in its possession concerning the applicant, including any notation of action taken.

(4) Enforcement proceedings and investigations. A creditor shall retain the information beyond 25 months (12 months for business credit, except as provided in paragraph (b)(5) of this section) if the creditor has actual notice that it is under investigation or is subject to an enforcement proceeding for an alleged violation of the Act or this part, by the Attorney General of the United States or by an enforcement agency charged with monitoring that creditor's compliance with the Act and this part, or if it has been served with notice of an action filed pursuant to section 706 of the Act and § 1002.16 of this part. The creditor shall retain the information until final disposition of the matter, unless an earlier time is allowed by order of the agency or court.

(5) Special rule for certain business credit applications. With regard to a business that had gross revenues in excess of $1 million in its preceding fiscal year, or an extension of trade credit, credit incident to a factoring agreement, or other similar types of business credit, the creditor shall retain records for at least 60 days after notifying the applicant of the action taken. If within that time period the applicant requests in writing the reasons for adverse action or that records be retained, the creditor shall retain records for 12 months.

(6) Self-tests. For 25 months after a self-test (as defined in § 1002.15) has been completed, the creditor shall retain all written or recorded information about the self-test. A creditor shall retain information beyond 25 months if it has actual notice that it is under investigation or is subject to an enforcement proceeding for an alleged violation, or if it has been served with notice of a civil action. In such cases, the creditor shall retain the information until final disposition of the matter, unless an earlier time is allowed by the appropriate agency or court order.

(7) Prescreened solicitations. For 25 months after the date on which an offer of credit is made to potential customers (12 months for business credit, except as provided in paragraph (b)(5) of this section), the creditor shall retain in original form or a copy thereof:

(i) The text of any prescreened solicitation;

(ii) The list of criteria the creditor used to select potential recipients of the solicitation; and

(iii) Any correspondence related to complaints (formal or informal) about the solicitation.

§ 1002.13. Information for Monitoring Purposes

(a) Information to be requested.

(1) A creditor that receives an application for credit primarily for the purchase or refinancing of a dwelling occupied or to be occupied by the applicant as a principal residence, where the extension of credit will be secured by the dwelling, shall request as part of the application the following information regarding the applicant(s):

(i) Ethnicity and race using either:

(A) For ethnicity, the aggregate categories Hispanic or Latino and not Hispanic or Latino; and, for race, the aggregate categories American Indian or Alaska Native, Asian, Black or African American, Native Hawaiian or Other Pacific Islander, and White; or

(B) The categories and subcategories for the collection of ethnicity and race set forth in appendix B to 12 CFR part 1003.

(ii) Sex;

(iii) Marital status, using the categories married, unmarried, and separated; and

(iv) Age.

(2) Dwelling means a residential structure that contains one to four units, whether or not that structure is attached to real property. The term includes, but is not limited to, an individual condominium or cooperative unit and a mobile or other manufactured home.

(b) Obtaining information. Questions regarding ethnicity, race, sex, marital status, and age may be listed, at the creditor's option, on the application form or on a separate form that refers to the application. The applicant(s) shall be asked but not required to supply the requested information. If the applicant(s) chooses not to provide the information or any part of it, that fact shall be noted on the form. The creditor shall then also note on the form, to the extent possible, the ethnicity, race, and sex of the applicant(s) on the basis of visual observation or surname. When a creditor collects ethnicity and race information pursuant to § 1002.13(a)(1)(i)(B), the creditor must comply with any restrictions on the collection of an applicant's ethnicity or race on the basis of visual observation or surname set forth in appendix B to 12 CFR part 1003. If there is more than one co-applicant, a creditor is permitted, but is not required, to collect the information set forth in paragraph (a) of this section from a second or additional co-applicant.

(c) Disclosure to applicant(s). The creditor shall inform the applicant(s) that the information regarding ethnicity, race, sex, marital status, and age is being requested by the Federal Government for the purpose of monitoring compliance with Federal statutes that prohibit creditors from discriminating against applicants on those bases. The creditor shall also inform the applicant(s) that if the applicant(s) chooses not to provide the information, the creditor is required to note the ethnicity, race and sex on the basis of visual observation or surname.

(d) Substitute monitoring program. A monitoring program required by an agency charged with administrative enforcement under section 704 of the Act may be substituted for the requirements contained in paragraphs (a), (b), and (c) of this section.

§ 1002.14. Rules on Providing Appraisals and Other Valuations

(a) Providing appraisals and other valuations—

(1) In general. A creditor shall provide an applicant a copy of all appraisals and other written valuations developed in connection with an application for credit that is to be secured by a first lien on a dwelling. A creditor shall provide a copy of each such appraisal or other written valuation promptly upon completion, or three business days prior to consummation of the transaction (for closed-end credit) or account opening (for open-end credit), whichever is earlier. An applicant may waive the timing requirement in this paragraph (a)(1) and agree to receive any copy at or before consummation or account opening, except where otherwise prohibited by law. Any such waiver must be obtained at least three business days prior to consummation or account opening, unless the waiver pertains solely to the applicant's receipt of a copy of an appraisal or other written valuation that contains only clerical changes from a previous version of the appraisal or other written valuation provided to the applicant three or more business days prior to consummation or account opening. If the applicant provides a waiver and the transaction is not consummated or the account is not opened, the creditor must provide these copies no later than 30 days after the creditor determines consummation will not occur or the account will not be opened.

(2) Disclosure. For applications subject to paragraph (a)(1) of this section, a creditor shall mail or deliver to an applicant, not later than the third business day after the creditor receives an application for credit that is to be secured by a first lien on a dwelling, a notice in writing of the applicant's right to receive a copy of all written appraisals developed in connection with the application. In the case of an application for credit that is not to be secured by a first lien on a dwelling at the time of application, if the creditor later determines the credit will be secured by a first lien on a dwelling, the creditor shall mail or deliver the same notice in writing not later than the third business day after the creditor determines that the loan is to be secured by a first lien on a dwelling.

(3) Reimbursement. A creditor shall not charge an applicant for providing a copy of appraisals and other written valuations as required under this section, but may require applicants to pay a reasonable fee to reimburse the creditor for the cost of the appraisal or other written valuation unless otherwise provided by law.

(4) Withdrawn, denied, or incomplete applications. The requirements set forth in paragraph (a)(1) of this section apply whether credit is extended or denied or if the application is incomplete or withdrawn.

(5) Copies in electronic form. The copies required by § 1002.14(a)(1) may be provided to the applicant in electronic form, subject to compliance with the consumer consent and other applicable provisions of the Electronic Signatures in Global and National Commerce Act (E-Sign Act) (15 U.S.C. 7001 et seq.).

(b) Definitions. For purposes of paragraph (a) of this section:

(1) Consummation. The term "consummation" means the time that a consumer becomes contractually obligated on a closed-end credit transaction.

(2) Dwelling. The term "dwelling" means a residential structure that contains one to four units whether or not that structure is attached to real property. The term includes, but is not limited to, an individual condominium or cooperative unit, and a mobile or other manufactured home.

(3) Valuation. The term "valuation" means any estimate of the value of a dwelling developed in connection with an application for credit.

§ 1002.15. Incentives for Self-Testing and Self-Correction

(a) General rules—

(1) Voluntary self-testing and correction. The report or results of a self-test that a creditor voluntarily conducts (or authorizes) are privileged as provided in this section. Data collection required by law or by any governmental authority is not a voluntary self-test.

(2) Corrective action required. The privilege in this section applies only if the creditor has taken or is taking appropriate corrective action.

(3) Other privileges. The privilege created by this section does not preclude the assertion of any other privilege that may also apply.

(b) Self-test defined—

(1) Definition. A self-test is any program, practice, or study that:

(i) Is designed and used specifically to determine the extent or effectiveness of a creditor's compliance with the Act or this part; and

(ii) Creates data or factual information that is not available and cannot be derived from loan or application files or other records related to credit transactions.

(2) Types of information privileged. The privilege under this section applies to the report or results of the self-test, data or factual information created by the self-test, and any analysis, opinions, and conclusions pertaining to the self-test report or results. The privilege covers workpapers or draft documents as well as final documents.

(3) Types of information not privileged. The privilege under this section does not apply to:

(i) Information about whether a creditor conducted a self-test, the methodology used or the scope of the self-test, the time period covered by the self-test, or the dates it was conducted; or

(ii) Loan and application files or other business records related to credit transactions, and information derived from such files and records, even if the information has been aggregated, summarized, or reorganized to facilitate analysis.

(c) Appropriate corrective action—

(1) General requirement. For the privilege in this section to apply, appropriate corrective action is required when the self-test shows that it is more likely than not that a violation occurred, even though no violation has been formally adjudicated.

(2) Determining the scope of appropriate corrective action. A creditor must take corrective action that is reasonably likely to remedy the cause and effect of a likely violation by:

(i) Identifying the policies or practices that are the likely cause of the violation; and

(ii) Assessing the extent and scope of any violation.

(3) Types of relief. Appropriate corrective action may include both prospective and remedial relief, except that to establish a privilege under this section:

(i) A creditor is not required to provide remedial relief to a tester used in a self-test;

(ii) A creditor is only required to provide remedial relief to an applicant identified by the self-test as one whose rights were more likely than not violated; and

(iii) A creditor is not required to provide remedial relief to a particular applicant if the statute of limitations applicable to the violation expired before the creditor obtained the results of the self-test or the applicant is otherwise ineligible for such relief.

(4) No admission of violation. Taking corrective action is not an admission that a violation occurred.

(d) Scope of privilege—

(1) General rule. The report or results of a privileged self-test may not be obtained or used:

(i) By a government agency in any examination or investigation relating to compliance with the Act or this part; or

(ii) By a government agency or an applicant (including a prospective applicant who alleges a violation of § 1002.4(b)) in any proceeding or civil action in which a violation of the Act or this part is alleged.

(2) Loss of privilege. The report or results of a self-test are not privileged under paragraph (d)(1) of this section if the creditor or a person with lawful access to the report or results:

(i) Voluntarily discloses any part of the report or results, or any other information privileged under this section, to an applicant or government agency or to the public;

(ii) Discloses any part of the report or results, or any other information privileged under this section, as a defense to charges that the creditor has violated the Act or regulation; or

(iii) Fails or is unable to produce written or recorded information about the self-test that is required to be retained under § 1002.12(b)(6) when the information is needed to determine whether the privilege applies. This paragraph does not limit any other penalty or remedy that may be available for a violation of § 1002.12.

(3) Limited use of privileged information. Notwithstanding paragraph (d)(1) of this section, the self-test report or results and any other information privileged under this section may be obtained and used by an applicant or government agency solely to determine a penalty or remedy after a violation of the Act or this part has been adjudicated or admitted. Disclosures for this limited purpose may be used only for the particular proceeding in which the adjudication or admission was made. Information disclosed under this paragraph (d)(3) remains privileged under paragraph (d)(1) of this section.

§ 1002.16. Enforcement, Penalties, and Liabilities

(a) Administrative enforcement.

(1) As set forth more fully in section 704 of the Act, administrative enforcement of the Act and this part regarding certain creditors is assigned to the Comptroller of the Currency, Board of Governors of the Federal Reserve System, Board of Directors of the Federal Deposit Insurance Corporation, National Credit Union Administration, Surface Transportation Board, Civil

Aeronautics Board, Secretary of Agriculture, Farm Credit Administration, Securities and Exchange Commission, Small Business Administration, Secretary of Transportation, and Bureau of Consumer Financial Protection.

(2) Except to the extent that administrative enforcement is specifically assigned to some government agency other than the Bureau, and subject to subtitle B of the Consumer Financial Protection Act of 2010, the Federal Trade Commission is authorized to enforce the requirements imposed under the Act and this part.

(b) Penalties and liabilities.

(1) Sections 702(g) and 706(a) and (b) of the Act provide that any creditor that fails to comply with a requirement imposed by the Act or this part is subject to civil liability for actual and punitive damages in individual or class actions. Pursuant to sections 702(g) and 704(b), (c), and (d) of the Act, violations of the Act or this part also constitute violations of other Federal laws. Liability for punitive damages can apply only to nongovernmental entities and is limited to $10,000 in individual actions and the lesser of $500,000 or 1 percent of the creditor's net worth in class actions. Section 706(c) provides for equitable and declaratory relief and section 706(d) authorizes the awarding of costs and reasonable attorney's fees to an aggrieved applicant in a successful action.

(2) As provided in section 706(f) of the Act, a civil action under the Act or this part may be brought in the appropriate United States district court without regard to the amount in controversy or in any other court of competent jurisdiction within five years after the date of the occurrence of the violation, or within one year after the commencement of an administrative enforcement proceeding or of a civil action brought by the Attorney General of the United States within five years after the alleged violation.

(3) If an agency responsible for administrative enforcement is unable to obtain compliance with the Act or this part, it may refer the matter to the Attorney General of the United States. If the Bureau, the Comptroller of the Currency, the Federal Deposit Insurance Corporation, the Board of Governors of the Federal Reserve System, or the National Credit Union Administration has reason to believe that one or more creditors have engaged in a pattern or practice of discouraging or denying applications in violation of the Act or this part, the agency shall refer the matter to the Attorney General. If the agency has reason to believe that one or more creditors violated section 701(a) of the Act, the agency may refer a matter to the Attorney General.

(4) On referral, or whenever the Attorney General has reason to believe that one or more creditors have engaged in a pattern or practice in violation of the Act or this part, the Attorney General may bring a civil action for such relief as may be appropriate, including actual and punitive damages and injunctive relief.

(5) If the Comptroller of the Currency, the Federal Deposit Insurance Corporation, the Board of Governors of the Federal Reserve System, or the National Credit Union Administration has reason to believe (as a result of a consumer complaint, a consumer compliance examination, or some other basis) that a violation of the Act or this part has occurred which is also a violation of the Fair Housing Act, and the matter is not referred to the Attorney General, the agency shall:

(i) Notify the Secretary of Housing and Urban Development; and

(ii) Inform the applicant that the Secretary of Housing and Urban Development has been notified and that remedies may be available under the Fair Housing Act.

(c) Failure of compliance. A creditor's failure to comply with §§ 1002.6(b)(6), 1002.9, 1002.10, 1002.12 or 1002.13 is not a violation if it results from an inadvertent error. On discovering an error under §§ 1002.9 and 1002.10, the creditor shall correct it as soon as possible. If a creditor inadvertently obtains the monitoring information regarding the ethnicity, race, and sex of the applicant in a dwelling-related transaction not covered by § 1002.13, the creditor may retain information and act on the application without violating the regulation.

APPENDIX C TO PART 1002—SAMPLE NOTIFICATION FORMS

1. This Appendix contains ten sample notification forms. Forms C-1 through C-4 are intended for use in notifying an applicant that adverse action has been taken on an application or account under §§ 1002.9(a)(1) and (2)(i) of this part. Form C-5 is a notice of disclosure of the right to request specific reasons for adverse action under §§ 1002.9(a)(1) and (2)(ii). Form C-6 is designed for use in notifying an applicant, under § 1002.9(c)(2), that an application is incomplete. Forms C-7 and C-8 are intended for use in connection with applications for business credit under § 1002.9(a)(3). Form C-9 is designed for use in notifying an applicant of the right to receive a copy of appraisals under § 1002.14. Form C-10 is designed for use in notifying an applicant for nonmortgage credit that the creditor is requesting applicant characteristic information.

2. Form C-1 contains the Fair Credit Reporting Act disclosure as required by sections 615(a) and (b) of that act. Forms C-2 through C-5 contain only the section 615(a) disclosure (that a creditor obtained information from a consumer reporting agency that was considered in the credit decision). A creditor must provide the section 615(a) disclosure when adverse action is taken against a consumer based on information from a consumer reporting agency. A creditor must provide the section 615(b) disclosure when adverse action is taken based on information from an outside source other than a consumer reporting agency. In addition, a creditor must provide the section 615(b) disclosure if the creditor obtained information from an affiliate other than information in a consumer report or other than information concerning the affiliate's own transactions or experiences with the consumer. Creditors may comply with the disclosure requirements for adverse action based on information in a consumer report obtained from an affiliate by providing either the section 615(a) or section 615(b) disclosure. Optional language in Forms C-1 through C-5 may be used to direct the consumer to the entity that provided the credit score for any questions about the credit score, along with the entity's contact information. Creditors may use or not use this additional language without losing the safe harbor, since the language is optional.

3. The sample forms are illustrative and may not be appropriate for all creditors. They were designed to include some of the factors that creditors most commonly consider. If a creditor chooses to use the checklist of reasons provided in one of the sample forms in this appendix and if reasons commonly used by the creditor are not provided on the form, the creditor should modify the checklist by substituting or adding other reasons. For example, if "inadequate down payment" or "no deposit relationship with us" are common reasons for taking adverse action on an application, the creditor ought to add or substitute such reasons for those presently contained on the sample forms.

4. If the reasons listed on the forms are not the factors actually used, a creditor will not satisfy the notice requirement by simply checking the closest identifiable factor listed. For example, some creditors consider only references from banks or other depository institutions and disregard finance company references altogether; their statement of reasons should disclose "insufficient bank references," not "insufficient credit references." Similarly, a creditor that considers bank references and other credit references as distinct factors should treat the two factors separately and disclose them as appropriate. The creditor should either add such other factors to the form or check "other" and include the appropriate explanation. The creditor need not, however, describe how or why a factor adversely affected the application. For example, the notice may say "length of residence" rather than "too short a period of residence."

5. A creditor may design its own notification forms or use all or a portion of the forms contained in this Appendix. Proper use of Forms C-1 through C-4 will satisfy the requirement of § 1002.9(a)(2)(i). Proper use of Forms C-5 and C-6 constitutes full compliance with §§ 1002.9(a)(2)(ii) and 1002.9(c)(2), respectively. Proper use of Forms C-7 and C-8 will satisfy the requirements of §§ 1002.9(a)(2)(i) and (ii), respectively, for applications for business credit. Proper use of Form C-9 will satisfy the requirements of § 1002.14 of this part. Proper use of Form C-10 will satisfy the requirements of § 1002.5(b)(1).

Form C-1—Sample Notice of Action Taken and Statement of Reasons

Statement of Credit Denial, Termination or Change

Date: ____________

Applicant's Name: ____________

Applicant's Address: ____________

Description of Account, Transaction, or Requested Credit: ____________

Description of Action Taken: ____________

Part I—Principal Reason(s) for Credit Denial, Termination, or Other Action Taken Concerning Credit

This section must be completed in all instances.

___ Credit application incomplete

___ Insufficient number of credit references provided

___ Unacceptable type of credit references provided

___ Unable to verify credit references

___ Temporary or irregular employment

___ Unable to verify employment

___ Length of employment

___ Income insufficient for amount of credit requested

___ Excessive obligations in relation to income

___ Unable to verify income

___ Length of residence

___ Temporary residence

___ Unable to verify residence

___ No credit file

___ Limited credit experience

___ Poor credit performance with us

___ Delinquent past or present credit obligations with others

___ Collection action or judgment

___ Garnishment or attachment

___ Foreclosure or repossession

___ Bankruptcy

___ Number of recent inquiries on credit bureau report

___ Value or type of collateral not sufficient

___ Other, specify: ______

Part II—Disclosure of Use of Information Obtained From an Outside Source

This section should be completed if the credit decision was based in whole or in part on information that has been obtained from an outside source.

___ Our credit decision was based in whole or in part on information obtained in a report from the consumer reporting agency listed below. You have a right under the Fair Credit Reporting Act to know the information contained in your credit file at the consumer reporting agency. The reporting agency played no part in our decision and is unable to supply specific reasons why we have denied credit to you. You also have a right to a free copy of your report from the reporting agency, if you request it no later than 60 days after you receive this notice. In addition, if you find that any information contained in the report you receive is inaccurate or incomplete, you have the right to dispute the matter with the reporting agency.

Name: ___________

Address: ___________

[Toll-free] Telephone number: ___________

[We also obtained your credit score from the consumer reporting agency and used it in making our credit decision. Your credit score is a number that reflects the information in your consumer report. Your credit score can change, depending on how the information in your consumer report changes.

Your credit score: ___________

Date: ___________

Scores range from a low of ____ to a high of ____.

Key factors that adversely affected your credit score: ___________

[Number of recent inquiries on consumer report, as a key factor]

[If you have any questions regarding your credit score, you should contact [entity that provided the credit score] at:

Address: ___________

[[Toll-free] Telephone number: ___________]

___ Our credit decision was based in whole or in part on information obtained from an affiliate or from an outside source other than a consumer reporting agency. Under the Fair Credit Reporting Act, you have the right to make a written request, no later than 60 days after you receive this notice, for disclosure of the nature of this information.

If you have any questions regarding this notice, you should contact:

Creditor's name: ___________

Creditor's address: ___________

Creditor's telephone number: ___________

Notice: The Federal Equal Credit Opportunity Act prohibits creditors from discriminating against credit applicants on the basis of race, color, religion, national origin, sex, marital status, age (provided the applicant has the capacity to enter into a binding contract); because all or part of the applicant's income derives from any public assistance program; or because the applicant has in good faith exercised any right under the Consumer Credit Protection Act. The Federal agency that administers compliance with this law concerning this creditor is (name and address as specified by the appropriate agency listed in appendix A).

Form C-2—Sample Notice of Action Taken and Statement of Reasons

Date: ___________

Dear Applicant: Thank you for your recent application. Your request for [a loan/a credit card/an increase in your credit limit] was carefully considered, and we regret that we are unable to approve your application at this time, for the following reason(s):

Your Income:

___ is below our minimum requirement.

___ is insufficient to sustain payments on the amount of credit requested.

___ could not be verified.

Your Employment:

___ is not of sufficient length to qualify.

___ could not be verified.

Your Credit History:

___ of making payments on time was not satisfactory.

___ could not be verified.

Your Application:

___ lacks a sufficient number of credit references.

___ lacks acceptable types of credit references.

___ reveals that current obligations are excessive in relation to income.

Other: _______

The consumer reporting agency contacted that provided information that influenced our decision in whole or in part was [name, address and [toll-free] telephone number of the reporting agency]. The reporting agency played no part in our decision and is unable to supply specific reasons why we have denied credit to you. You have a right under the Fair Credit Reporting Act to know the information contained in your credit file at the consumer reporting agency. You also have a right to a free copy of your report from the reporting agency, if you request it no later than 60 days after you receive this notice. In addition, if you find that any information contained in the report you receive is inaccurate or incomplete, you have the right to dispute the matter with the reporting agency. Any questions regarding such information should be directed to [consumer reporting agency]. If you have any questions regarding this letter, you should contact us at [creditor's name, address and telephone number].

[We also obtained your credit score from the consumer reporting agency and used it in making our credit decision. Your credit score is a number that reflects the information in your consumer report. Your credit score can change, depending on how the information in your consumer report changes.

Your credit score: _____________

Date: _____________

Scores range from a low of ____ to a high of ____.

Key factors that adversely affected your credit score:

[Number of recent inquiries on consumer report, as a key factor]

[If you have any questions regarding your credit score, you should contact [entity that provided the credit score] at:

Address: _____________

[[Toll-free] Telephone number: _________]

Notice: The Federal Equal Credit Opportunity Act prohibits creditors from discriminating against credit applicants on the basis of race, color, religion, national origin, sex, marital status, age (provided the applicant has the capacity to enter into a binding contract); because all or part of the applicant's income derives from any public assistance program; or because the applicant has in good faith exercised any right under the Consumer Credit Protection Act. The Federal agency that administers compliance with this law concerning this creditor is (name and address as specified by the appropriate agency listed in appendix A).

Form C-3—Sample Notice of Action Taken and Statement of Reasons (Credit Scoring)

Date: __________

Dear Applicant: Thank you for your recent application for ____. We regret that we are unable to approve your request.

[Reasons for Denial of Credit]

Your application was processed by a [credit scoring] system that assigns a numerical value to the various items of information we consider in evaluating an application. These numerical values are based upon the results of analyses of repayment histories of large numbers of customers. The information you provided in your application did not score a sufficient number of points for approval of the application. The reasons you did not score well compared with other applicants were:

- Insufficient bank references
- Type of occupation
- Insufficient credit experience
- Number of recent inquiries on credit bureau report

[Your Right to Get Your Consumer Report]

In evaluating your application the consumer reporting agency listed below provided us with information that in whole or in part influenced our decision. The consumer reporting agency played no part in our decision and is unable to supply specific reasons why we have denied credit to you. You have a right under the Fair Credit Reporting Act to know the information contained in your credit file at the consumer reporting agency. It can be obtained by contacting: [Name, address, and [toll-free] telephone number of the consumer reporting agency]. You also have a right to a free copy of your report from the reporting agency, if you request it no later than 60 days after you receive this notice. In addition, if you find that any information contained in the report you receive is inaccurate or incomplete, you have the right to dispute the matter with the reporting agency.

[Information about Your Credit Score]

We also obtained your credit score from the consumer reporting agency and used it in making our credit decision. Your credit score is a number that reflects the information in your consumer report. Your credit score can change, depending on how the information in your consumer report changes.

Your credit score: __________

Date: ______________

Scores range from a low of ____ to a high of ____.

Key factors that adversely affected your credit score:

[Number of recent inquiries on consumer report, as a key factor]

[If you have any questions regarding your credit score, you should contact [entity that provided the credit score] at:

Address: ______________

[Toll-free] Telephone number: ______________]

If you have any questions regarding this letter, you should contact us at

Creditor's Name: ______________

Address: ______________

Telephone: ______________

Sincerely,

Notice: The Federal Equal Credit Opportunity Act prohibits creditors from discriminating against credit applicants on the basis of race, color, religion, national origin, sex, marital status, age (with certain limited exceptions); because all or part of the applicant's income derives from any public assistance program; or because the applicant has in good faith exercised any right under the Consumer Credit Protection Act. The Federal agency that administers compliance with this law concerning this creditor is (name and address as specified by the appropriate agency listed in appendix A).

Form C-4—Sample Notice of Action Taken, Statement of Reasons and Counteroffer

Date: ______________

Dear Applicant: Thank you for your application for ____. We are unable to offer you credit on the terms that you requested for the following reason(s): ____

We can, however, offer you credit on the following terms: ____

If this offer is acceptable to you, please notify us within [amount of time] at the following address: ____.

Our credit decision on your application was based in whole or in part on information obtained in a report from [name, address and [toll-free] telephone number of the consumer reporting agency]. You have a right under the Fair Credit Reporting Act to know the information contained in your credit file at the consumer reporting agency. The reporting agency played no part in our decision and is unable to supply specific reasons why we have denied credit to you. You also have a right to a free copy of your report from the reporting agency, if you request it no later than 60 days after you receive this notice. In addition, if you find that any information contained in the report you receive is inaccurate or incomplete, you have the right to dispute the matter with the reporting agency.

[We also obtained your credit score from the consumer reporting agency and used it in making our credit decision. Your credit score is a number that reflects the information in your consumer report. Your credit score can change, depending on how the information in your consumer report changes.

Your credit score: __________

Date: ______________

Scores range from a low of ____ to a high of ____.

Key factors that adversely affected your credit score:

[Number of recent inquiries on consumer report, as a key factor]

[If you have any questions regarding your credit score, you should contact [entity that provided the credit score] at:

Address: ______________

[Toll-free] Telephone number:—______________]

You should know that the Federal Equal Credit Opportunity Act prohibits creditors, such as ourselves, from discriminating against credit applicants on the basis of their race, color, religion, national origin, sex, marital status, age (provided the applicant has the capacity to enter into a binding contract), because they receive income from a public assistance program, or because they may have exercised their rights under the Consumer Credit Protection Act. If you believe there has been discrimination in handling your application you should contact the [name and address of the appropriate Federal enforcement agency listed in appendix A].

Sincerely,

Form C-5—Sample Disclosure of Right To Request Specific Reasons for Credit Denial

Date: ______________

Dear Applicant: Thank you for applying to us for ____.

After carefully reviewing your application, we are sorry to advise you that we cannot [open an account for you/grant a loan to you/increase your credit limit] at this time. If you would like a statement of specific reasons why your application was denied, please contact [our credit service manager] shown below within 60 days of the date of this letter. We will provide you with the statement of reasons within 30 days after receiving your request.

Creditor's name: ______________

Address: ______________

Telephone number: ______________

If we obtained information from a consumer reporting agency as part of our consideration of your application, its name, address, and [toll-free] telephone number is shown below. The reporting agency played no part in our decision and is unable to supply specific reasons why we have denied credit to you. [You have a right under the Fair Credit Reporting Act to know the information contained in your credit file at the consumer reporting agency.] You have a right to a free copy of your report from the reporting agency, if you request it no later than 60 days after you receive this notice. In addition, if you find that any information contained in the report you received is inaccurate or incomplete, you have the right to dispute the matter with the reporting agency. You can find out about the information contained in your file (if one was used) by contacting:

Consumer reporting agency's name: ______________

Address: ______________

[Toll-free] Telephone number: ______________

[We also obtained your credit score from the consumer reporting agency and used it in making our credit decision. Your credit score is a number that reflects the information in your consumer report. Your credit score can change, depending on how the information in your consumer report changes.

Your credit score: ______________

Date: ______________

Scores range from a low of ____ to a high of ____.

Key factors that adversely affected your credit score:

[Number of recent inquiries on consumer report, as a key factor]

[If you have any questions regarding your credit score, you should contact [entity that provided the credit score] at:

Address: ______________

[Toll-free] Telephone number: ______________]

Sincerely,

Notice: The Federal Equal Credit Opportunity Act prohibits creditors from discriminating against credit applicants on the basis of race, color, religion, national origin, sex, marital status, age (provided the applicant has the capacity to enter into a binding contract); because all or part of the applicant's income derives from any public assistance program; or because the applicant has in good faith exercised any right under the Consumer Credit Protection Act. The Federal agency that administers compliance with this law concerning this creditor is (name and address as specified by the appropriate agency listed in appendix A).

Form C-6—Sample Notice of Incomplete Application and Request for Additional Information

Creditor's name: __________

Address: __________

Telephone number: __________

Date: __________

Dear Applicant: Thank you for your application for credit. The following information is needed to make a decision on your application: ____

We need to receive this information by ____ (date). If we do not receive it by that date, we will regrettably be unable to give further consideration to your credit request.

Sincerely,

Form C-7—Sample Notice of Action Taken and Statement of Reasons (Business Credit)

Creditor's name: __________

Creditor's address: __________

Date: __________

Dear Applicant: Thank you for applying to us for credit. We have given your request careful consideration, and regret that we are unable to extend credit to you at this time for the following reasons:

(Insert appropriate reason, such as: Value or type of collateral not sufficient; Lack of established earnings record; Slow or past due in trade or loan payments)

Sincerely,

Notice: The Federal Equal Credit Opportunity Act prohibits creditors from discriminating against credit applicants on the basis of race, color, religion, national origin, sex, marital status, age (provided the applicant has the capacity to enter into a binding contract); because all or part of the applicant's income derives from any public assistance program; or because the applicant has in good faith exercised any right under the Consumer Credit Protection Act. The Federal agency that administers compliance with this law concerning this creditor is [name and address as specified by the appropriate agency listed in Appendix A].

Form C-8—Sample Disclosure of Right To Request Specific Reasons for Credit Denial Given at Time of Application (Business Credit)

Creditor's name: __________

Creditor's address: __________

If your application for business credit is denied, you have the right to a written statement of the specific reasons for the denial. To obtain the statement, please contact [name, address and telephone number of the person or office from which the statement of reasons can be obtained] within 60 days from the date you are notified of our decision. We will send you a written statement of reasons for the denial within 30 days of receiving your request for the statement.

Notice: The Federal Equal Credit Opportunity Act prohibits creditors from discriminating against credit applicants on the basis of race, color, religion, national origin, sex, marital status, age (provided the applicant has the capacity to enter into a binding contract); because all or part of the applicant's income derives from any public assistance program; or because the applicant has in good faith exercised any right under the Consumer Credit Protection Act. The Federal agency that administers compliance with this law concerning this creditor is [name and address as specified by the appropriate agency listed in appendix A].

Form C-9—Sample Disclosure of Right to Receive a Copy of Appraisals

We may order an appraisal to determine the property's value and charge you for this appraisal. We will promptly give you a copy of any appraisal, even if your loan does not close. You can pay for an additional appraisal for your own use at your own cost.

Form C-10—Sample Disclosure About Voluntary Data Notation

We are requesting the following information to monitor our compliance with the Federal Equal Credit Opportunity Act, which prohibits unlawful discrimination. You are not required to provide this information. We will not take this information (or your decision not to provide this information) into account in connection with your application or credit transaction. The law provides that a creditor may not discriminate based on this information, or based on whether or not you choose to provide it. [If you choose not to provide the information, we will note it by visual observation or surname].

ELECTRONIC FUND TRANSFERS (REGULATION E)

12 C.F.R. Part 1005

Table of Sections

Sec.

SUBPART A. GENERAL

§ 1005.1. Authority and Purpose

(a) Authority. The regulation in this part, known as Regulation E, is issued by the Bureau of Consumer Financial Protection (Bureau) pursuant to the Electronic Fund Transfer Act (15 U.S.C. 1693 et seq.). The information-collection requirements have been approved by the Office of Management and Budget under 44 U.S.C. 3501 et seq. and have been assigned OMB No. 3170–0014.

(b) Purpose. This part carries out the purposes of the Electronic Fund Transfer Act, which establishes the basic rights, liabilities, and responsibilities of consumers who use electronic fund transfer and remittance transfer services and of financial institutions or other persons that offer these services. The primary objective of the act and this part is the protection of individual consumers engaging in electronic fund transfers and remittance transfers.

§ 1005.2. Definitions [proposed amendments pending]

Except as otherwise provided in Subpart B, for purposes of this part, the following definitions apply:

(a)(1) "Access device" means a card, code, or other means of access to a consumer's account, or any combination thereof, that may be used by the consumer to initiate electronic fund transfers.

(2) An access device becomes an "accepted access device" when the consumer:

(i) Requests and receives, or signs, or uses (or authorizes another to use) the access device to transfer money between accounts or to obtain money, property, or services;

(ii) Requests validation of an access device issued on an unsolicited basis; or

(iii) Receives an access device in renewal of, or in substitution for, an accepted access device from either the financial institution that initially issued the device or a successor.

(b)(1) "Account" means a demand deposit (checking), savings, or other consumer asset account (other than an occasional or incidental credit balance in a credit plan) held directly or indirectly by a financial institution and established primarily for personal, family, or household purposes.

(2) The term does not include an account held by a financial institution under a bona fide trust agreement.

(3) The term includes a prepaid account.

(i) "Prepaid account" means:

(A) A "payroll card account," which is an account that is directly or indirectly established through an employer and to which electronic fund transfers of the consumer's wages, salary, or other employee compensation (such as commissions) are made on a recurring basis, whether the account is operated or managed by the employer, a third-party payroll processor, a depository institution, or any other person; or

(B) A "government benefit account," as defined in § 1005.15(a)(2); or

(C) An account that is marketed or labeled as "prepaid" and that is redeemable upon presentation at multiple, unaffiliated merchants for goods or services or usable at automated teller machines; or

(D) An account:

(1) That is issued on a prepaid basis in a specified amount or not issued on a prepaid basis but capable of being loaded with funds thereafter,

(2) Whose primary function is to conduct transactions with multiple, unaffiliated merchants for goods or services, or at automated teller machines, or to conduct person-to-person transfers, and

(3) That is not a checking account, share draft account, or negotiable order of withdrawal account.

(ii) For purposes of paragraphs (b)(3)(i)(C) and (D) of this section, the term "prepaid account" does not include:

(A) An account that is loaded only with funds from a health savings account, flexible spending arrangement, medical savings account, health reimbursement arrangement, dependent care assistance program, or transit or parking reimbursement arrangement;

(B) An account that is directly or indirectly established through a third party and loaded only with qualified disaster relief payments;

(C) The person-to-person functionality of an account established by or through the United States government whose primary function is to conduct closed-loop transactions on U.S. military installations or vessels, or similar government facilities;

(D)(1) A gift certificate as defined in § 1005.20(a)(1) and (b);

(2) A store gift card as defined in § 1005.20(a)(2) and (b);

(3) A loyalty, award, or promotional gift card as defined in § 1005.20(a)(4), or that satisfies the criteria in § 1005.20(a)(4)(i) and (ii) and is excluded from § 1005.20 pursuant to § 1005.20(b)(4); or

(4) A general-use prepaid card as defined in § 1005.20(a)(3) and (b) that is both marketed and labeled as a gift card or gift certificate; or

(E) An account established for distributing needs-tested benefits in a program established under state or local law or administered by a state or local agency, as set forth in § 1005.15(a)(2).

(c) "Act" means the Electronic Fund Transfer Act (Title IX of the Consumer Credit Protection Act, 15 U.S.C. 1693 et seq.).

(d) "Business day" means any day on which the offices of the consumer's financial institution are open to the public for carrying on substantially all business functions.

(e) "Consumer" means a natural person.

(f) "Credit" means the right granted by a financial institution to a consumer to defer payment of debt, incur debt and defer its payment, or purchase property or services and defer payment therefor.

(g) "Electronic fund transfer" is defined in § 1005.3.

(h) "Electronic terminal" means an electronic device, other than a telephone operated by a consumer, through which a consumer may initiate an electronic fund transfer. The term includes, but is not limited to, point-of-sale terminals, automated teller machines (ATMs), and cash dispensing machines.

(i) "Financial institution" means a bank, savings association, credit union, or any other person that directly or indirectly holds an account belonging to a consumer, or that issues an access device and agrees with a consumer to provide electronic fund transfer services, other than a person excluded from coverage of this part by section 1029 of the Consumer Financial Protection Act of 2010, title X of the Dodd-Frank Wall Street Reform and Consumer Protection Act, Public Law 111–203, 124 Stat. 1376.

(j) "Person" means a natural person or an organization, including a corporation, government agency, estate, trust, partnership, proprietorship, cooperative, or association.

(k) "Preauthorized electronic fund transfer" means an electronic fund transfer authorized in advance to recur at substantially regular intervals.

(*l*) "State" means any state, territory, or possession of the United States; the District of Columbia; the Commonwealth of Puerto Rico; or any political subdivision of the thereof in this paragraph (*l*).

(m) "Unauthorized electronic fund transfer" means an electronic fund transfer from a consumer's account initiated by a person other than the consumer without actual authority to initiate the transfer and from which the consumer receives no benefit. The term does not include an electronic fund transfer initiated:

(1) By a person who was furnished the access device to the consumer's account by the consumer, unless the consumer has notified the financial institution that transfers by that person are no longer authorized;

(2) With fraudulent intent by the consumer or any person acting in concert with the consumer; or

(3) By the financial institution or its employee.

§ 1005.3. Coverage

(a) General. This part applies to any electronic fund transfer that authorizes a financial institution to debit or credit a consumer's account. Generally, this part applies to financial institutions. For purposes of §§ 1005.3(b)(2) and (3), 1005.10(b), (d), and (e), 1005.13, and 1005.20, this part applies to any person, other than a person excluded from coverage of this part by section 1029 of the Consumer Financial Protection Act of 2010, Title X of the Dodd-Frank Wall Street Reform and Consumer Protection Act, Pub. L. 111–203, 124 Stat. 1376. The requirements of subpart B apply to remittance transfer providers.

(b) Electronic fund transfer.

(1) Definition. The term "electronic fund transfer" means any transfer of funds that is initiated through an electronic terminal, telephone, computer, or magnetic tape for the purpose of ordering, instructing, or authorizing a financial institution to debit or credit a consumer's account. The term includes, but is not limited to:

(i) Point-of-sale transfers;

(ii) Automated teller machine transfers;

(iii) Direct deposits or withdrawals of funds;

(iv) Transfers initiated by telephone; and

(v) Transfers resulting from debit card transactions, whether or not initiated through an electronic terminal.

(2) Electronic fund transfer using information from a check.

(i) This part applies where a check, draft, or similar paper instrument is used as a source of information to initiate a one-time electronic fund transfer from a consumer's account. The consumer must authorize the transfer.

(ii) The person initiating an electronic fund transfer using the consumer's check as a source of information for the transfer must provide a notice that the transaction will or may be processed as an electronic fund transfer, and obtain a consumer's authorization for each transfer. A consumer authorizes a one-time electronic fund transfer (in providing a check to a merchant or other payee for the MICR encoding, that is, the routing number of the financial institution, the consumer's account number and the serial number) when the consumer receives notice and goes forward with the underlying transaction. For point-of-sale transfers, the notice must be posted in a prominent and conspicuous location, and a copy thereof, or a substantially similar notice, must be provided to the consumer at the time of the transaction.

(iii) A person may provide notices that are substantially similar to those set forth in appendix A-6 to comply with the requirements of this paragraph (b)(2).

(3) Collection of returned item fees via electronic fund transfer.

(i) General. The person initiating an electronic fund transfer to collect a fee for the return of an electronic fund transfer or a check that is unpaid, including due to insufficient or uncollected funds in the consumer's account, must obtain the consumer's authorization for each transfer. A consumer authorizes a one-time electronic fund transfer from his or her account to pay the fee for the returned item or transfer if the person collecting the fee provides notice to the consumer stating that the person may electronically collect the fee, and the consumer goes forward with the underlying transaction. The notice must state that the fee will be collected by means of an electronic fund transfer from the consumer's account if the payment is returned unpaid and must disclose the dollar amount of the fee. If the fee may vary due to the amount of the transaction or due to other factors, then, except as otherwise provided in paragraph (b)(3)(ii) of this section, the person collecting the fee may disclose, in place of the dollar amount of the fee, an explanation of how the fee will be determined.

(ii) Point-of-sale transactions. If a fee for an electronic fund transfer or check returned unpaid may be collected electronically in connection with a point-of-sale transaction, the person initiating an electronic fund transfer to collect the fee must post the notice described in paragraph (b)(3)(i) of this section in a prominent and conspicuous location. The person also must either provide the consumer with a copy of the posted notice (or a substantially similar notice) at the time of the transaction, or mail the copy (or a substantially similar notice) to the consumer's address as soon as reasonably practicable after the person initiates the electronic fund transfer to collect the fee. If the amount of the fee may vary due to the amount of the transaction or due to other factors, the posted notice may explain how the fee will be determined, but the notice provided to the consumer must state the dollar amount of the fee if the amount can be calculated at the time the notice is provided or mailed to the consumer.

(c) Exclusions from coverage. The term "electronic fund transfer" does not include:

(1) Checks. Any transfer of funds originated by check, draft, or similar paper instrument; or any payment made by check, draft, or similar paper instrument at an electronic terminal.

(2) Check guarantee or authorization. Any transfer of funds that guarantees payment or authorizes acceptance of a check, draft, or similar paper instrument but that does not directly result in a debit or credit to a consumer's account.

(3) Wire or other similar transfers. Any transfer of funds through Fedwire or through a similar wire transfer system that is used primarily for transfers between financial institutions or between businesses.

(4) Securities and commodities transfers. Any transfer of funds the primary purpose of which is the purchase or sale of a security or commodity, if the security or commodity is:

(i) Regulated by the Securities and Exchange Commission or the Commodity Futures Trading Commission;

(ii) Purchased or sold through a broker-dealer regulated by the Securities and Exchange Commission or through a futures commission merchant regulated by the Commodity Futures Trading Commission; or

(iii) Held in book-entry form by a Federal Reserve Bank or Federal agency.

(5) Automatic transfers by account-holding institution. Any transfer of funds under an agreement between a consumer and a financial institution which provides that the institution will initiate individual transfers without a specific request from the consumer:

(i) Between a consumer's accounts within the financial institution;

(ii) From a consumer's account to an account of a member of the consumer's family held in the same financial institution; or

(iii) Between a consumer's account and an account of the financial institution, except that these transfers remain subject to § 1005.10(e) regarding compulsory use and sections 916 and 917 of the Act regarding civil and criminal liability.

(6) Telephone-initiated transfers. Any transfer of funds that:

(i) Is initiated by a telephone communication between a consumer and a financial institution making the transfer; and

(ii) Does not take place under a telephone bill-payment or other written plan in which periodic or recurring transfers are contemplated.

(7) Small institutions. Any preauthorized transfer to or from an account if the assets of the account-holding financial institution were $100 million or less on the preceding December 31. If assets of the account-holding institution subsequently exceed $100 million, the institution's exemption for preauthorized transfers terminates one year from the end of the calendar year in which the assets exceed $100 million. Preauthorized transfers exempt under this paragraph (c)(7) remain subject to § 1005.10(e) regarding compulsory use and sections 916 and 917 of the Act regarding civil and criminal liability.

§ 1005.4. General Disclosure Requirements; Jointly Offered Services

(a)(1) Form of disclosures. Disclosures required under this part shall be clear and readily understandable, in writing, and in a form the consumer may keep, except as otherwise provided in this part. The disclosures required by this part may be provided to the consumer in electronic form, subject to compliance with the consumer-consent and other applicable provisions of the Electronic Signatures in Global and National Commerce Act (E-Sign Act) (15 U.S.C. 7001 et seq.). A financial institution may use commonly accepted or readily understandable abbreviations in complying with the disclosure requirements of this part.

(2) Foreign language disclosures. Disclosures required under this part may be made in a language other than English, provided that the disclosures are made available in English upon the consumer's request.

(b) Additional information; disclosures required by other laws. A financial institution may include additional information and may combine disclosures required by other laws (such as the Truth in Lending Act (15 U.S.C. 1601 et seq.) or the Truth in Savings Act (12 U.S.C. 4301 et seq.) with the disclosures required by this part.

(c) Multiple accounts and account holders.

(1) Multiple accounts. A financial institution may combine the required disclosures into a single statement for a consumer who holds more than one account at the institution.

(2) Multiple account holders. For joint accounts held by two or more consumers, a financial institution need provide only one set of the required disclosures and may provide them to any of the account holders.

(d) Services offered jointly. Financial institutions that provide electronic fund transfer services jointly may contract among themselves to comply with the requirements that this part imposes on any or all of them. An institution need make only the disclosures required by §§ 1005.7 and 1005.8 that are within its knowledge and within the purview of its relationship with the consumer for whom it holds an account.

§ 1005.5. Issuance of Access Devices

(a) Solicited issuance. Except as provided in paragraph (b) of this section, a financial institution may issue an access device to a consumer only:

(1) In response to an oral or written request for the device; or

(2) As a renewal of, or in substitution for, an accepted access device whether issued by the institution or a successor.

(b) Unsolicited issuance. A financial institution may distribute an access device to a consumer on an unsolicited basis if the access device is:

(1) Not validated, meaning that the institution has not yet performed all the procedures that would enable a consumer to initiate an electronic fund transfer using the access device;

(2) Accompanied by a clear explanation that the access device is not validated and how the consumer may dispose of it if validation is not desired;

(3) Accompanied by the disclosures required by § 1005.7, of the consumer's rights and liabilities that will apply if the access device is validated; and

(4) Validated only in response to the consumer's oral or written request for validation, after the institution has verified the consumer's identity by a reasonable means.

§ 1005.6. Liability of Consumer for Unauthorized Transfers

(a) Conditions for liability. A consumer may be held liable, within the limitations described in paragraph (b) of this section, for an unauthorized electronic fund transfer involving the consumer's account only if the financial institution has provided the disclosures required by § 1005.7(b)(1), (2), and (3). If the unauthorized transfer involved an access device, it must be an accepted access device and the financial institution must have provided a means to identify the consumer to whom it was issued.

(b) Limitations on amount of liability. A consumer's liability for an unauthorized electronic fund transfer or a series of related unauthorized transfers shall be determined as follows:

(1) Timely notice given. If the consumer notifies the financial institution within two business days after learning of the loss or theft of the access device, the consumer's liability shall not exceed the lesser of $50 or the amount of unauthorized transfers that occur before notice to the financial institution.

(2) Timely notice not given. If the consumer fails to notify the financial institution within two business days after learning of the loss or theft of the access device, the consumer's liability shall not exceed the lesser of $500 or the sum of:

(i) $50 or the amount of unauthorized transfers that occur within the two business days, whichever is less; and

(ii) The amount of unauthorized transfers that occur after the close of two business days and before notice to the institution, provided the institution establishes that these transfers would not have occurred had the consumer notified the institution within that two-day period.

(3) Periodic statement; timely notice not given. A consumer must report an unauthorized electronic fund transfer that appears on a periodic statement within 60 days of the financial institution's transmittal of the statement to avoid liability for subsequent transfers. If the consumer fails to do so, the consumer's liability shall not exceed the amount of the unauthorized transfers that occur after the close of the 60 days and before notice to the institution, and that the institution establishes would not have occurred had the consumer notified the institution within the 60-day period. When an access device is involved in the unauthorized transfer, the consumer may be liable for other amounts set forth in paragraphs (b)(1) or (b)(2) of this section, as applicable.

(4) Extension of time limits. If the consumer's delay in notifying the financial institution was due to extenuating circumstances, the institution shall extend the times specified above to a reasonable period.

(5) Notice to financial institution.

(i) Notice to a financial institution is given when a consumer takes steps reasonably necessary to provide the institution with the pertinent information, whether or not a particular employee or agent of the institution actually receives the information.

(ii) The consumer may notify the institution in person, by telephone, or in writing.

(iii) Written notice is considered given at the time the consumer mails the notice or delivers it for transmission to the institution by any other usual means. Notice may be considered constructively given when the institution becomes aware of circumstances leading to the reasonable belief that an unauthorized transfer to or from the consumer's account has been or may be made.

(6) Liability under state law or agreement. If state law or an agreement between the consumer and the financial institution imposes less liability than is provided by this section, the consumer's liability shall not exceed the amount imposed under the state law or agreement.

§ 1005.7. Initial Disclosures

(a) Timing of disclosures. A financial institution shall make the disclosures required by this section at the time a consumer contracts for an electronic fund transfer service or before the first electronic fund transfer is made involving the consumer's account.

(b) Content of disclosures. A financial institution shall provide the following disclosures, as applicable:

(1) Liability of consumer. A summary of the consumer's liability, under § 1005.6 or under state or other applicable law or agreement, for unauthorized electronic fund transfers.

(2) Telephone number and address. The telephone number and address of the person or office to be notified when the consumer believes that an unauthorized electronic fund transfer has been or may be made.

(3) Business days. The financial institution's business days.

(4) Types of transfers; limitations. The type of electronic fund transfers that the consumer may make and any limitations on the frequency and dollar amount of transfers. Details of the limitations need not be disclosed if confidentiality is essential to maintain the security of the electronic fund transfer system.

(5) Fees. Any fees imposed by the financial institution for electronic fund transfers or for the right to make transfers.

(6) Documentation. A summary of the consumer's right to receipts and periodic statements, as provided in § 1005.9 of this part, and notices regarding preauthorized transfers as provided in § 1005.10(a) and (d).

(7) Stop payment. A summary of the consumer's right to stop payment of a preauthorized electronic fund transfer and the procedure for placing a stop-payment order, as provided in § 1005.10(c).

(8) Liability of institution. A summary of the financial institution's liability to the consumer under section 910 of the Act for failure to make or to stop certain transfers.

(9) Confidentiality. The circumstances under which, in the ordinary course of business, the financial institution may provide information concerning the consumer's account to third parties.

(10) Error resolution. A notice that is substantially similar to Model Form A-3 as set out in appendix A of this part concerning error resolution.

(11) ATM fees. A notice that a fee may be imposed by an automated teller machine operator as defined in § 1005.16(a), when the consumer initiates an electronic fund transfer or makes a balance inquiry, and by any network used to complete the transaction.

(c) Addition of electronic fund transfer services. If an electronic fund transfer service is added to a consumer's account and is subject to terms and conditions different from those described in the initial disclosures, disclosures for the new service are required.

§ 1005.8. Change in Terms Notice; Error Resolution Notice

(a) Change in terms notice.

(1) Prior notice required. A financial institution shall mail or deliver a written notice to the consumer, at least 21 days before the effective date, of any change in a term or condition required to be disclosed under § 1005.7(b) of this part if the change would result in:

(i) Increased fees for the consumer;

(ii) Increased liability for the consumer;

(iii) Fewer types of available electronic fund transfers; or

(iv) Stricter limitations on the frequency or dollar amount of transfers.

(2) Prior notice exception. A financial institution need not give prior notice if an immediate change in terms or conditions is necessary to maintain or restore the security of an account or an electronic fund transfer system. If the institution makes such a change permanent and disclosure would not jeopardize the security of the account or system, the institution shall notify the consumer in writing on or with the next regularly scheduled periodic statement or within 30 days of making the change permanent.

(b) Error resolution notice. For accounts to or from which electronic fund transfers can be made, a financial institution shall mail or deliver to the consumer, at least once each calendar year, an error resolution notice substantially similar to the model form set forth in Appendix A of this part (Model Form A-3). Alternatively, an institution may include an abbreviated notice substantially similar to the model form error resolution notice set forth in Appendix A of this part (Model Form A-3), on or with each periodic statement required by § 1005.9(b).

§ 1005.9. Receipts at Electronic Terminals; Periodic Statements

(a) Receipts at electronic terminals—General. Except as provided in paragraph (e) of this section, a financial institution shall make a receipt available to a consumer at the time the consumer initiates an electronic fund transfer at an electronic terminal. The receipt shall set forth the following information, as applicable:

(1) Amount. The amount of the transfer. A transaction fee may be included in this amount, provided the amount of the fee is disclosed on the receipt and displayed on or at the terminal.

(2) Date. The date the consumer initiates the transfer.

(3) Type. The type of transfer and the type of the consumer's account(s) to or from which funds are transferred. The type of account may be omitted if the access device used is able to access only one account at that terminal.

(4) Identification. A number or code that identifies the consumer's account or accounts, or the access device used to initiate the transfer. The number or code need not exceed four digits or letters to comply with the requirements of this paragraph (a)(4).

(5) Terminal location. The location of the terminal where the transfer is initiated, or an identification such as a code or terminal number. Except in limited circumstances where all terminals are located in the same city or state, if the location is disclosed, it shall include the city and state or foreign country and one of the following:

(i) The street address; or

(ii) A generally accepted name for the specific location; or

(iii) The name of the owner or operator of the terminal if other than the account-holding institution.

(6) Third party transfer. The name of any third party to or from whom funds are transferred.

(b) Periodic statements. For an account to or from which electronic fund transfers can be made, a financial institution shall send a periodic statement for each monthly cycle in which an electronic fund transfer has occurred; and shall send a periodic statement at least quarterly if no transfer has occurred. The statement shall set forth the following information, as applicable:

(1) Transaction information. For each electronic fund transfer occurring during the cycle:

(i) The amount of the transfer;

(ii) The date the transfer was credited or debited to the consumer's account;

(iii) The type of transfer and type of account to or from which funds were transferred;

(iv) For a transfer initiated by the consumer at an electronic terminal (except for a deposit of cash or a check, draft, or similar paper instrument), the terminal location described in paragraph (a)(5) of this section; and

(v) The name of any third party to or from whom funds were transferred.

(2) Account number. The number of the account.

(3) Fees. The amount of any fees assessed against the account during the statement period for electronic fund transfers, the right to make transfers, or account maintenance.

(4) Account balances. The balance in the account at the beginning and at the close of the statement period.

(5) Address and telephone number for inquiries. The address and telephone number to be used for inquiries or notice of errors, preceded by "Direct inquiries to" or similar language. The address and telephone number provided on an error resolution notice under § 1005.8(b) given on or with the statement satisfies this requirement.

(6) Telephone number for preauthorized transfers. A telephone number the consumer may call to ascertain whether preauthorized transfers to the consumer's account have occurred, if the financial institution uses the telephone-notice option under § 1005.10(a)(1)(iii).

(c) Exceptions to the periodic statement requirement for certain accounts.

(1) Preauthorized transfers to accounts. For accounts that may be accessed only by preauthorized transfers to the account the following rules apply:

(i) Passbook accounts. For passbook accounts, the financial institution need not provide a periodic statement if the institution updates the passbook upon presentation or enters on a separate document the amount and date of each electronic fund transfer since the passbook was last presented.

(ii) Other accounts. For accounts other than passbook accounts, the financial institution must send a periodic statement at least quarterly.

(2) Intra-institutional transfers. For an electronic fund transfer initiated by the consumer between two accounts of the consumer in the same institution, documenting the transfer on a periodic statement for one of the two accounts satisfies the periodic statement requirement.

(3) Relationship between paragraphs (c)(1) and (2) of this section. An account that is accessed by preauthorized transfers to the account described in paragraph (c)(1) of this section and by intra-institutional transfers described in paragraph (c)(2) of this section, but by no other type of electronic fund transfers, qualifies for the exceptions provided by paragraph (c)(1) of this section.

(d) Documentation for foreign-initiated transfers. The failure by a financial institution to provide a terminal receipt for an electronic fund transfer or to document the transfer on a periodic statement does not violate this part if:

(1) The transfer is not initiated within a state; and

(2) The financial institution treats an inquiry for clarification or documentation as a notice of error in accordance with § 1005.11.

(e) Exception for receipts in small-value transfers. A financial institution is not subject to the requirement to make available a receipt under paragraph (a) of this section if the amount of the transfer is $15 or less.

§ 1005.10. Preauthorized Transfers [proposed amendments pending]

(a) Preauthorized transfers to consumer's account.

(1) Notice by financial institution. When a person initiates preauthorized electronic fund transfers to a consumer's account at least once every 60 days, the account-holding financial institution shall provide notice to the consumer by:

(i) Positive notice. Providing oral or written notice of the transfer within two business days after the transfer occurs; or

(ii) Negative notice. Providing oral or written notice, within two business days after the date on which the transfer was scheduled to occur, that the transfer did not occur; or

(iii) Readily-available telephone line. Providing a readily available telephone line that the consumer may call to determine whether the transfer occurred and disclosing the telephone number on the initial disclosure of account terms and on each periodic statement.

(2) Notice by payor. A financial institution need not provide notice of a transfer if the payor gives the consumer positive notice that the transfer has been initiated.

(3) Crediting. A financial institution that receives a preauthorized transfer of the type described in paragraph (a)(1) of this section shall credit the amount of the transfer as of the date the funds for the transfer are received.

(b) Written authorization for preauthorized transfers from consumer's account. Preauthorized electronic fund transfers from a consumer's account may be authorized only by a writing signed or similarly authenticated by the consumer. The person that obtains the authorization shall provide a copy to the consumer.

(c) Consumer's right to stop payment.

(1) Notice. A consumer may stop payment of a preauthorized electronic fund transfer from the consumer's account by notifying the financial institution orally or in writing at least three business days before the scheduled date of the transfer.

(2) Written confirmation. The financial institution may require the consumer to give written confirmation of a stop-payment order within 14 days of an oral notification. An institution that requires written confirmation shall inform the consumer of the requirement and provide the address where confirmation must be sent when the consumer gives the oral notification. An oral stop-payment order ceases to be binding after 14 days if the consumer fails to provide the required written confirmation.

(d) Notice of transfers varying in amount.

(1) Notice. When a preauthorized electronic fund transfer from the consumer's account will vary in amount from the previous transfer under the same authorization or from the preauthorized amount, the designated payee or the financial institution shall send the consumer written notice of the amount and date of the transfer at least 10 days before the scheduled date of transfer.

(2) Range. The designated payee or the institution shall inform the consumer of the right to receive notice of all varying transfers, but may give the consumer the option of receiving notice only when a transfer falls outside a specified range of amounts or only when a transfer differs from the most recent transfer by more than an agreed-upon amount.

(e) Compulsory use.

(1) Credit. No financial institution or other person may condition an extension of credit to a consumer on the consumer's repayment by preauthorized electronic fund transfers, except for credit extended under an overdraft credit plan or extended to maintain a specified minimum balance in the consumer's account. This exception does not apply to a covered separate credit feature accessible by a hybrid prepaid-credit card as defined in Regulation Z, 12 CFR 1026.61.

(2) Employment or government benefit. No financial institution or other person may require a consumer to establish an account for receipt of electronic fund transfers with a particular institution as a condition of employment or receipt of a government benefit.

§ 1005.11. Procedures for Resolving Errors

(a) Definition of error.

(1) Types of transfers or inquiries covered. The term "error" means:

(i) An unauthorized electronic fund transfer;

(ii) An incorrect electronic fund transfer to or from the consumer's account;

(iii) The omission of an electronic fund transfer from a periodic statement;

(iv) A computational or bookkeeping error made by the financial institution relating to an electronic fund transfer;

(v) The consumer's receipt of an incorrect amount of money from an electronic terminal;

(vi) An electronic fund transfer not identified in accordance with § 1005.9 or § 1005.10(a); or

(vii) The consumer's request for documentation required by § 1005.9 or § 1005.10(a) or for additional information or clarification concerning an electronic fund transfer, including a request the consumer makes to determine whether an error exists under paragraphs (a)(1)(i) through (vi) of this section.

(2) Types of inquiries not covered. The term "error" does not include:

(i) A routine inquiry about the consumer's account balance;

(ii) A request for information for tax or other recordkeeping purposes; or

(iii) A request for duplicate copies of documentation.

(b) Notice of error from consumer.

(1) Timing; contents. A financial institution shall comply with the requirements of this section with respect to any oral or written notice of error from the consumer that:

(i) Is received by the institution no later than 60 days after the institution sends the periodic statement or provides the passbook documentation, required by § 1005.9, on which the alleged error is first reflected;

(ii) Enables the institution to identify the consumer's name and account number; and

(iii) Indicates why the consumer believes an error exists and includes to the extent possible the type, date, and amount of the error, except for requests described in paragraph (a)(1)(vii) of this section.

(2) Written confirmation. A financial institution may require the consumer to give written confirmation of an error within 10 business days of an oral notice. An institution that requires written confirmation shall inform the consumer of the requirement and provide the address where confirmation must be sent when the consumer gives the oral notification.

(3) Request for documentation or clarifications. When a notice of error is based on documentation or clarification that the consumer requested under paragraph (a)(1)(vii) of this section, the consumer's notice of error is timely if received by the financial institution no later than 60 days after the institution sends the information requested.

(c) Time limits and extent of investigation.

(1) Ten-day period. A financial institution shall investigate promptly and, except as otherwise provided in this paragraph (c), shall determine whether an error occurred within 10 business days of receiving a notice of error. The institution shall report the results to the consumer within three business days after completing its investigation. The institution shall correct the error within one business day after determining that an error occurred.

(2) Forty-five day period. If the financial institution is unable to complete its investigation within 10 business days, the institution may take up to 45 days from receipt of a notice of error to investigate and determine whether an error occurred, provided the institution does the following:

(i) Provisionally credits the consumer's account in the amount of the alleged error (including interest where applicable) within 10 business days of receiving the error notice. If the financial institution has a reasonable basis for believing that an unauthorized electronic fund transfer has occurred and the institution has satisfied the requirements of § 1005.6(a), the institution may withhold a maximum of $50 from the amount credited. An institution need not provisionally credit the consumer's account if:

(A) The institution requires but does not receive written confirmation within 10 business days of an oral notice of error; or

(B) The alleged error involves an account that is subject to Regulation T of the Board of Governors of the Federal Reserve System (Securities Credit by Brokers and Dealers, 12 CFR part 220).

(ii) Informs the consumer, within two business days after the provisional crediting, of the amount and date of the provisional crediting and gives the consumer full use of the funds during the investigation;

(iii) Corrects the error, if any, within one business day after determining that an error occurred; and

(iv) Reports the results to the consumer within three business days after completing its investigation (including, if applicable, notice that a provisional credit has been made final).

(3) Extension of time periods. The time periods in paragraphs (c)(1) and (c)(2) of this section are extended as follows:

(i) The applicable time is 20 business days in place of 10 business days under paragraphs (c)(1) and (2) of this section if the notice of error involves an electronic fund transfer to or from the account within 30 days after the first deposit to the account was made.

(ii) The applicable time is 90 days in place of 45 days under paragraph (c)(2) of this section, for completing an investigation, if a notice of error involves an electronic fund transfer that:

(A) Was not initiated within a state;

(B) Resulted from a point-of-sale debit card transaction; or

(C) Occurred within 30 days after the first deposit to the account was made.

(4) Investigation. With the exception of transfers covered by § 1005.14 of this part, a financial institution's review of its own records regarding an alleged error satisfies the requirements of this section if:

(i) The alleged error concerns a transfer to or from a third party; and

(ii) There is no agreement between the institution and the third party for the type of electronic fund transfer involved.

(d) Procedures if financial institution determines no error or different error occurred. In addition to following the procedures specified in paragraph (c) of this section, the financial institution shall follow the procedures set forth in this paragraph (d) if it determines that no error occurred or that an error occurred in a manner or amount different from that described by the consumer:

(1) Written explanation. The institution's report of the results of its investigation shall include a written explanation of the institution's findings and shall note the consumer's right to request the documents that the institution relied on in making its determination. Upon request, the institution shall promptly provide copies of the documents.

(2) Debiting provisional credit. Upon debiting a provisionally credited amount, the financial institution shall:

(i) Notify the consumer of the date and amount of the debiting;

(ii) Notify the consumer that the institution will honor checks, drafts, or similar instruments payable to third parties and preauthorized transfers from the consumer's account (without charge to the consumer as a result of an overdraft) for five business days after the notification. The institution shall honor items as specified in the notice, but need honor only items that it would have paid if the provisionally credited funds had not been debited.

(e) Reassertion of error. A financial institution that has fully complied with the error resolution requirements has no further responsibilities under this section should the consumer later reassert the same error, except in the case of an error asserted by the consumer following receipt of information provided under paragraph (a)(1)(vii) of this section.

§ 1005.12. Relation to Other Laws [proposed amendments pending]

(a) Relation to Truth in Lending.

(1) The Electronic Fund Transfer Act and this part govern:

(i) The addition to an accepted credit card, as defined in Regulation Z (12 CFR 1026.12, comment 12–2), of the capability to initiate electronic fund transfers;

(ii) The issuance of an access device (other than an access device for a prepaid account) that permits credit extensions (under a preexisting agreement between a consumer and a financial institution) only when the consumer's account is overdrawn or to maintain a specified minimum balance in the consumer's account, or under an overdraft service, as defined in § 1005.17(a) of this part;

(iii) The addition of an overdraft service, as defined in § 1005.17(a), to an accepted access device; and

(iv) A consumer's liability for an unauthorized electronic fund transfer and the investigation of errors involving:

(A) Except with respect to a prepaid account, an extension of credit that is incident to an electronic fund transfer that occurs under an agreement between the consumer and a financial institution to extend credit when the consumer's account is overdrawn or to maintain a specified minimum balance in the consumer's account, or under an overdraft service, as defined in § 1005.17(a);

(B) With respect to transactions that involve a covered separate credit feature and an asset feature on a prepaid account that are both accessible by a hybrid prepaid-credit card as those terms are defined in Regulation Z, 12 CFR 1026.61, an extension of credit that is incident to an electronic fund transfer that occurs when the hybrid prepaid-credit card accesses both funds in the asset feature of the prepaid account and a credit extension from the credit feature with respect to a particular transaction;

(C) Transactions that involves credit extended through a negative balance to the asset feature of a prepaid account that meets the conditions set forth in Regulation Z, 12 CFR 1026.61(a)(4); and

(D) With respect to transactions involving a prepaid account and a non-covered separate credit feature as defined in Regulation Z, 12 CFR 1026.61, transactions that access the prepaid account, as applicable.

(2) The Truth in Lending Act and Regulation Z (12 CFR part 1026), which prohibit the unsolicited issuance of credit cards, govern:

(i) The addition of a credit feature or plan to an accepted access device, including an access device for a prepaid account, that would make the access device into a credit card under Regulation Z (12 CFR part 1026);

(ii) Except as provided in paragraph (a)(1)(ii) of this section, the issuance of a credit card that is also an access device.

(iii) With respect to transactions involving a prepaid account and a non-covered separate credit feature as defined in Regulation Z, 12 CFR 1026.61, a consumer's liability for unauthorized use and the investigation of errors involving transactions that access the non-covered separate credit feature, as applicable.

(b) Preemption of inconsistent state laws.

(1) Inconsistent requirements. The Bureau shall determine, upon its own motion or upon the request of a state, financial institution, or other interested party, whether the Act and this part preempt state law relating to electronic fund transfers, or dormancy, inactivity, or service fees, or expiration dates in the case of gift certificates, store gift cards, or general-use prepaid cards.

(2) Standards for determination. State law is inconsistent with the requirements of the Act and this part if state law:

(i) Requires or permits a practice or act prohibited by the Federal law;

(ii) Provides for consumer liability for unauthorized electronic fund transfers that exceeds the limits imposed by the Federal law;

(iii) Allows longer time periods than the Federal law for investigating and correcting alleged errors, or does not require the financial institution to credit the consumer's account during an error investigation in accordance with § 1005.11(c)(2)(i) of this part; or

(iv) Requires initial disclosures, periodic statements, or receipts that are different in content from those required by the Federal law except to the extent that the disclosures relate to consumer rights granted by the state law and not by the Federal law.

(c) State exemptions

(1) General rule. Any state may apply for an exemption from the requirements of the Act or this part for any class of electronic fund transfers within the state. The Bureau shall grant an exemption if it determines that:

(i) Under state law the class of electronic fund transfers is subject to requirements substantially similar to those imposed by the Federal law; and

(ii) There is adequate provision for state enforcement.

(2) Exception. To assure that the Federal and state courts continue to have concurrent jurisdiction, and to aid in implementing the Act:

(i) No exemption shall extend to the civil liability provisions of section 916 of the Act; and

(ii) When the Bureau grants an exemption, the state law requirements shall constitute the requirements of the Federal law for purposes of section 916 of the Act, except for state law requirements not imposed by the Federal law.

§ 1005.13. Administrative Enforcement; Record Retention

(a) Enforcement by Federal agencies. Compliance with this part is enforced in accordance with section 918 of the Act.

(b) Record retention.

(1) Any person subject to the Act and this part shall retain evidence of compliance with the requirements imposed by the Act and this part for a period of not less than two years from the date disclosures are required to be made or action is required to be taken.

(2) Any person subject to the Act and this part having actual notice that it is the subject of an investigation or an enforcement proceeding by its enforcement agency, or having been served with notice of an action filed under sections 910, 916, or 917(a) of the Act, shall retain the records that pertain to the investigation, action, or proceeding until final disposition of the matter unless an earlier time is allowed by court or agency order.

§ 1005.14. Electronic Fund Transfer Service Provider Not Holding Consumer's Account

(a) Provider of electronic fund transfer service. A person that provides an electronic fund transfer service to a consumer but that does not hold the consumer's account is subject to all requirements of this part if the person:

(1) Issues a debit card (or other access device) that the consumer can use to access the consumer's account held by a financial institution; and

(2) Has no agreement with the account-holding institution regarding such access.

(b) Compliance by service provider. In addition to the requirements generally applicable under this part, the service provider shall comply with the following special rules:

(1) Disclosures and documentation. The service provider shall give the disclosures and documentation required by §§ 1005.7, 1005.8, and 1005.9 of this part that are within the purview of its relationship with the consumer. The service provider need not furnish the periodic statement required by § 1005.9(b) if the following conditions are met:

(i) The debit card (or other access device) issued to the consumer bears the service provider's name and an address or telephone number for making inquiries or giving notice of error;

(ii) The consumer receives a notice concerning use of the debit card that is substantially similar to the notice contained in appendix A of this part;

(iii) The consumer receives, on or with the receipts required by § 1005.9(a), the address and telephone number to be used for an inquiry, to give notice of an error, or to report the loss or theft of the debit card;

(iv) The service provider transmits to the account-holding institution the information specified in § 1005.9(b)(1), in the format prescribed by the automated clearinghouse (ACH) system used to clear the fund transfers;

(v) The service provider extends the time period for notice of loss or theft of a debit card, set forth in § 1005.6(b)(1) and (2), from two business days to four business days after the consumer learns of the loss or theft; and extends the time periods for reporting unauthorized transfers or errors, set forth in §§ 1005.6(b)(3) and 1005.11(b)(1)(i), from 60 days to 90 days following the transmittal of a periodic statement by the account-holding institution.

(2) Error resolution.

(i) The service provider shall extend by a reasonable time the period in which notice of an error must be received, specified in § 1005.11(b)(1)(i), if a delay resulted from an initial attempt by the consumer to notify the account-holding institution.

(ii) The service provider shall disclose to the consumer the date on which it initiates a transfer to effect a provisional credit in accordance with § 1005.11(c)(2)(ii).

(iii) If the service provider determines an error occurred, it shall transfer funds to or from the consumer's account, in the appropriate amount and within the applicable time period, in accordance with § 1005.11(c)(2)(i).

(iv) If funds were provisionally credited and the service provider determines no error occurred, it may reverse the credit. The service provider shall notify the account-holding institution of the period during which the account-holding institution must honor debits to the account in accordance with § 1005.11(d)(2)(ii). If an overdraft results, the service provider shall promptly reimburse the account-holding institution in the amount of the overdraft.

(c) Compliance by account-holding institution. The account-holding institution need not comply with the requirements of the Act and this part with respect to electronic fund transfers initiated through the service provider except as follows:

(1) Documentation. The account-holding institution shall provide a periodic statement that describes each electronic fund transfer initiated by the consumer with the access device issued by the service provider. The account-holding institution has no liability for the failure to comply with this requirement if the service provider did not provide the necessary information; and

(2) Error resolution. Upon request, the account-holding institution shall provide information or copies of documents needed by the service provider to investigate errors or to furnish copies of documents to the consumer. The account-holding institution shall also honor debits to the account in accordance with § 1005.11(d)(2)(ii).

§ 1005.15. Electronic Fund Transfer of Government Benefits [proposed amendments pending]

(a) Government agency subject to regulation.

(1) A government agency is deemed to be a financial institution for purposes of the Act and this part if directly or indirectly it issues an access device to a consumer for use in initiating an electronic fund transfer of government benefits from an account, other than needs-tested benefits in a program established under state or local law or administered by a state or local agency. The agency shall comply with all applicable requirements of the Act and this part, except as provided in this section.

(2) For purposes of this section, the term "account" or "government benefit account" means an account established by a government agency for distributing government benefits to a consumer electronically, such as through automated teller machines or point-of-sale terminals, but does not include an account for distributing needs-tested benefits in a program established under state or local law or administered by a state or local agency.

(b) Issuance of access devices. For purposes of this section, a consumer is deemed to request an access device when the consumer applies for government benefits that the agency disburses or will disburse by means of an electronic fund transfer. The agency shall verify the identity of the consumer receiving the device by reasonable means before the device is activated.

(c) Pre-acquisition disclosure requirements.

(1) Before a consumer acquires a government benefit account, a government agency shall comply with the pre-acquisition disclosure requirements applicable to prepaid accounts as set forth in § 1005.18(b).

(2) Additional content for government benefit accounts—

(i) Statement regarding consumer's payment options. As part of its short form pre-acquisition disclosures, the agency must provide a statement that the consumer does not have to accept the government benefit account and directing the consumer to ask about other ways to receive their benefit payments from the agency instead of receiving them via the account, using the following clause or a substantially similar clause: "You do not have to accept this benefits card. Ask about other ways to receive your benefits." Alternatively, an agency may provide a statement that the consumer has several options to receive benefit payments, followed by a list of the options available to the consumer, and directing the consumer to indicate which option the consumer chooses using the following clause or a substantially similar clause: "You have several options to receive your payments: [list of options available to the consumer]; or this benefits card. Tell the benefits office which option you choose." This statement must be located above the information required by § 1005.18(b)(2)(i) through (iv). This statement must appear in a minimum type size of eight points (or 11 pixels) and appear in no larger a type size than what is used for the fee headings required by § 1005.18(b)(2)(i) through (iv).

(ii) Statement regarding state-required information or other fee discounts and waivers. An agency may, but is not required to, include a statement in one additional line of text in the short form disclosure directing the consumer to a particular location outside the short form disclosure for information on ways the consumer may access government benefit account funds and balance information for free or for a reduced fee. This statement must be located directly below any statements disclosed pursuant to § 1005.18(b)(3)(i) and (ii), or, if no such statements are disclosed, above the statement required by § 1005.18(b)(2)(x). This statement must appear in the same type size used to disclose variable fee information pursuant to § 1005.18(b)(3)(i) and (ii), or, if none, the same type size used for the information required by § 1005.18(b)(2)(x) through (xiii).

(3) Form of disclosures. When a short form disclosure required by paragraph (c) of this section is provided in writing or electronically, the information required by § 1005.18(b)(2)(i) through (ix) shall be provided in the form of a table. Except as provided in § 1005.18(b)(6)(iii)(B), the short form disclosure required by § 1005.18(b)(2) shall be provided in a form substantially similar to Model form A-10(a) of appendix A of this part. Sample form A-10(f) in appendix a of this part provides an example of the long form disclosure required by § 1005.18(b)(4) when the agency does not offer multiple service plans.

(d) Access to account information—

(1) Periodic statement alternative. A government agency need not furnish periodic statements required by § 1005.9(b) if the agency makes available to the consumer:

(i) The consumer's account balance, through a readily available telephone line and at a terminal (such as by providing balance information at a balance-inquiry terminal or providing it, routinely or upon request, on a terminal receipt at the time of an electronic fund transfer);

(ii) An electronic history of the consumer's account transactions, such as through a Web site, that covers at least 12 months preceding the date the consumer electronically accesses the account; and

(iii) A written history of the consumer's account transactions that is provided promptly in response to an oral or written request and that covers at least 24 months preceding the date the agency receives the consumer's request.

(2) Additional access to account information requirements. For government benefit accounts, a government agency shall comply with the account information requirements applicable to prepaid accounts as set forth in § 1005.18(c)(3) through (5).

(e) Modified disclosure, limitations on liability, and error resolution requirements. A government agency that provides information under paragraph (d)(1) of this section shall comply with the following:

(1) Initial disclosures. The agency shall modify the disclosures under § 1005.7(b) by disclosing:

(i) Access to account information. A telephone number that the consumer may call to obtain the account balance, the means by which the consumer can obtain an electronic account history, such as the address of a Web site, and a summary of the consumer's right to receive a written account history upon request (in place of the summary of the right to receive a periodic statement required by § 1005.7(b)(6)), including a telephone number to call to request a history. The disclosure required by this paragraph (e)(1)(i) may be made by providing a notice substantially similar to the notice contained in paragraph (a) of appendix A-5 of this part.

(ii) Error resolution. A notice concerning error resolution that is substantially similar to the notice contained in paragraph (b) of appendix A-5 of this part, in place of the notice required by § 1005.7(b)(10).

(2) Annual error resolution notice. The agency shall provide an annual notice concerning error resolution that is substantially similar to the notice contained in paragraph (b) of appendix A-5 of this part, in place of the notice required by § 1005.8(b). Alternatively, the agency may include on or with each electronic or written history provided in accordance with paragraph (d)(1) of this section, a notice substantially similar to the abbreviated notice for periodic statements contained in paragraph (b) in appendix A-3 of this part, modified as necessary to reflect the error resolution provisions set forth in this section.

(3) Modified limitations on liability requirements.

(i) For purposes of § 1005.6(b)(3), the 60-day period for reporting any unauthorized transfer shall begin on the earlier of:

(A) The date the consumer electronically accesses the consumer's account under paragraph (d)(1)(ii) of this section, provided that the electronic history made available to the consumer reflects the unauthorized transfer; or

(B) The date the agency sends a written history of the consumer's account transactions requested by the consumer under paragraph (d)(1)(iii) of this section in which the unauthorized transfer is first reflected.

(ii) An agency may comply with paragraph (e)(3)(i) of this section by limiting the consumer's liability for an unauthorized transfer as provided under § 1005.6(b)(3) for any transfer reported by the consumer within 120 days after the transfer was credited or debited to the consumer's account.

(4) Modified error resolution requirements.

(i) The agency shall comply with the requirements of § 1005.11 in response to an oral or written notice of an error from the consumer that is received by the earlier of:

(A) Sixty days after the date the consumer electronically accesses the consumer's account under paragraph (d)(1)(ii) of this section, provided that the electronic history made available to the consumer reflects the alleged error; or

(B) Sixty days after the date the agency sends a written history of the consumer's account transactions requested by the consumer under paragraph (d)(1)(iii) of this section in which the alleged error is first reflected.

(ii) In lieu of following the procedures in paragraph (e)(4)(i) of this section, an agency complies with the requirements for resolving errors in § 1005.11 if it investigates any oral or written notice of an error from the consumer that is received by the agency within 120 days after the transfer allegedly in error was credited or debited to the consumer's account.

(f) Disclosure of fees and other information. For government benefit accounts, a government agency shall comply with the disclosure and change-in-terms requirements applicable to prepaid accounts as set forth in § 1005.18(f).

(g) Government benefit accounts accessible by hybrid prepaid-credit cards. For government benefit accounts accessible by hybrid prepaid-credit cards as defined in Regulation Z, 12 CFR 1026.61, a government agency shall comply with prohibitions and requirements applicable to prepaid accounts as set forth in § 1005.18(g).

§ 1005.16. Disclosures at Automated Teller Machines

(a) Definition. "Automated teller machine operator" means any person that operates an automated teller machine at which a consumer initiates an electronic fund transfer or a balance inquiry and that does not hold the account to or from which the transfer is made, or about which an inquiry is made.

(b) General. An automated teller machine operator that imposes a fee on a consumer for initiating an electronic fund transfer or a balance inquiry must provide a notice that a fee will be imposed for providing electronic fund transfer services or a balance inquiry that discloses the amount of the fee.

(c) Notice requirement. An automated teller machine operator must provide the notice required by paragraph (b) of this section either by showing it on the screen of the automated teller machine or by providing it on paper, before the consumer is committed to paying a fee.

(d) Imposition of fee. An automated teller machine operator may impose a fee on a consumer for initiating an electronic fund transfer or a balance inquiry only if:

(1) The consumer is provided the notice required under paragraph (c) of this section, and

(2) The consumer elects to continue the transaction or inquiry after receiving such notice.

§ 1005.17. Requirements for Overdraft Services [proposed amendments pending]

(a) Definition. For purposes of this section, the term "overdraft service" means a service under which a financial institution assesses a fee or charge on a consumer's account held by the institution for paying a transaction (including a check or other item) when the consumer has insufficient or unavailable funds in the account. The term "overdraft service" does not include any payment of overdrafts pursuant to:

(1) A line of credit subject to Regulation Z (12 CFR part 1026), including transfers from a credit card account, home equity line of credit, or overdraft line of credit;

(2) A service that transfers funds from another account held individually or jointly by a consumer, such as a savings account;

(3) A line of credit or other transaction exempt from Regulation Z (12 CFR part 1026) pursuant to 12 CFR 1026.3(d); or

(4) A covered separate credit feature accessible by a hybrid prepaid-credit card as defined in Regulation Z, 12 CFR 1026.61; or credit extended through a negative balance on the asset feature of the prepaid account that meets the conditions of 12 CFR 1026.61(a)(4).

(b) Opt-in requirement.

(1) General. Except as provided under paragraph (c) of this section, a financial institution holding a consumer's account shall not assess a fee or charge on a consumer's account for paying an ATM or one-time debit card transaction pursuant to the institution's overdraft service, unless the institution:

(i) Provides the consumer with a notice in writing, or if the consumer agrees, electronically, segregated from all other information, describing the institution's overdraft service;

(ii) Provides a reasonable opportunity for the consumer to affirmatively consent, or opt in, to the service for ATM and one-time debit card transactions;

(iii) Obtains the consumer's affirmative consent, or opt-in, to the institution's payment of ATM or one-time debit card transactions; and

(iv) Provides the consumer with confirmation of the consumer's consent in writing, or if the consumer agrees, electronically, which includes a statement informing the consumer of the right to revoke such consent.

(2) Conditioning payment of other overdrafts on consumer's affirmative consent. A financial institution shall not:

(i) Condition the payment of any overdrafts for checks, ACH transactions, and other types of transactions on the consumer affirmatively consenting to the institution's payment of ATM and one-time debit card transactions pursuant to the institution's overdraft service; or

(ii) Decline to pay checks, ACH transactions, and other types of transactions that overdraw the consumer's account because the consumer has not affirmatively consented to the institution's overdraft service for ATM and one-time debit card transactions.

(3) Same account terms, conditions, and features. A financial institution shall provide to consumers who do not affirmatively consent to the institution's overdraft service for ATM and one-time debit card transactions the same account terms, conditions, and features that it provides to consumers who affirmatively consent, except for the overdraft service for ATM and one-time debit card transactions.

(c) Timing.

(1) Existing account holders. For accounts opened prior to July 1, 2010, the financial institution must not assess any fees or charges on a consumer's account on or after August 15, 2010, for paying an ATM or one-time debit card transaction pursuant to the overdraft service, unless the institution has complied with § 1005.17(b)(1) and obtained the consumer's affirmative consent.

(2) New account holders. For accounts opened on or after July 1, 2010, the financial institution must comply with § 1005.17(b)(1) and obtain the consumer's affirmative consent before the institution assesses any fee or charge on the consumer's account for paying an ATM or one-time debit card transaction pursuant to the institution's overdraft service.

(d) Content and format. The notice required by paragraph (b)(1)(i) of this section shall be substantially similar to Model Form A-9 set forth in appendix A of this part, include all applicable items in this paragraph, and may not contain any information not specified in or otherwise permitted by this paragraph.

(1) Overdraft service. A brief description of the financial institution's overdraft service and the types of transactions for which a fee or charge for paying an overdraft may be imposed, including ATM and one-time debit card transactions.

(2) Fees imposed. The dollar amount of any fees or charges assessed by the financial institution for paying an ATM or one-time debit card transaction pursuant to the institution's overdraft service, including any daily or other overdraft fees. If the amount of the fee is determined on the basis of the number of times the consumer has overdrawn the account, the amount of the overdraft, or other factors, the institution must disclose the maximum fee that may be imposed.

(3) Limits on fees charged. The maximum number of overdraft fees or charges that may be assessed per day, or, if applicable, that there is no limit.

(4) Disclosure of opt-in right. An explanation of the consumer's right to affirmatively consent to the financial institution's payment of overdrafts for ATM and one-time debit card transactions pursuant to the institution's overdraft service, including the methods by which the consumer may consent to the service; and

(5) Alternative plans for covering overdrafts. If the institution offers a line of credit subject to Regulation Z (12 CFR part 1026) or a service that transfers funds from another account of the consumer held at the institution to cover overdrafts, the institution must state that fact. An institution may, but is not required to, list additional alternatives for the payment of overdrafts.

(6) Permitted modifications and additional content. If applicable, the institution may modify the content required by § 1005.17(d) to indicate that the consumer has the right to opt into, or opt out of, the payment of overdrafts under the institution's overdraft service for other types of transactions, such as checks, ACH transactions, or automatic bill payments; to provide a means for the consumer to exercise this choice; and to disclose the associated returned item fee and that additional merchant fees may apply. The institution may also disclose the consumer's right to revoke consent. For notices provided to consumers who have opened accounts prior to July 1, 2010, the financial institution may describe the institution's overdraft service with respect to ATM and one-time debit card transactions with a statement such as "After August 15, 2010, we will not authorize and pay overdrafts for the following types of transactions unless you ask us to (see below)."

(e) Joint relationships. If two or more consumers jointly hold an account, the financial institution shall treat the affirmative consent of any of the joint consumers as affirmative consent for that account. Similarly, the financial institution shall treat a revocation of affirmative consent by any of the joint consumers as revocation of consent for that account.

(f) Continuing right to opt in or to revoke the opt-in. A consumer may affirmatively consent to the financial institution's overdraft service at any time in the manner described in the notice required by paragraph (b)(1)(i) of this section. A consumer may also revoke consent at any time in the manner made available to the consumer for providing consent. A financial institution must implement a consumer's revocation of consent as soon as reasonably practicable.

(g) Duration and revocation of opt-in. A consumer's affirmative consent to the institution's overdraft service is effective until revoked by the consumer, or unless the financial institution terminates the service.

§ 1005.18. Requirements for Financial Institutions Offering Payroll Card Accounts

(a) Coverage. A financial institution shall comply with all applicable requirements of the Act and this part with respect to prepaid accounts except as modified by this section. For rules governing government benefit accounts, see § 1005.15.

(b) Pre-acquisition disclosure requirements—

(1) Timing of disclosures—

(i) General. Except as provided in paragraph (b)(1)(ii) or (iii) of this section, a financial institution shall provide the disclosures required by paragraph (b) of this section before a consumer acquires a prepaid account. When a prepaid account is used for disbursing funds to a consumer, and the financial institution or third party making the disbursement does not offer any alternative means for the consumer to receive those funds in lieu of accepting the prepaid account, for purposes of this paragraph, the disclosures required by paragraph (b) of this section may be provided at the time the consumer receives the prepaid account.

(ii) Disclosures for prepaid accounts acquired in retail locations. A financial institution is not required to provide the long form disclosure required by paragraph (b)(4) of this section before a consumer acquires a prepaid account in person at a retail location if the following conditions are met:

(A) The prepaid account access device is contained inside the packaging material.

(B) The disclosure required by paragraph (b)(2) of this section is provided on or are visible through an outward-facing, external surface of a prepaid account access device's packaging material.

(C) The disclosure required by paragraph (b)(2) of this section includes the information set forth in paragraph (b)(2)(xiii) of this section that allows a consumer to access the information required to be disclosed by paragraph (b)(4) of this section by telephone and via a website.

(D) The long form disclosure required by paragraph (b)(4) of this section is provided after the consumer acquires the prepaid account. If a financial institution does not provide the long form disclosure inside the prepaid account packaging material, and it is not otherwise already mailing or delivering to the consumer written account-related communications within 30 days of obtaining the consumer's contact information, it may provide the long form disclosure pursuant to this paragraph in electronic form without regard to the consumer notice and consent requirements of section 101(c) of the Electronic Signatures in Global and National Commerce Act (E-Sign Act) (15 U.S.C. 7001 et seq.).

(iii) Disclosures for prepaid accounts acquired orally by telephone. A financial institution is not required to provide the long form disclosure required by paragraph (b)(4) of this section before a consumer acquires a prepaid account orally by telephone if the following conditions are met:

(A) The financial institution communicates to the consumer orally, before the consumer acquires the prepaid account, that the information required to be disclosed by paragraph (b)(4) of this section is available both by telephone and on a Web site.

(B) The financial institution makes the information required to be disclosed by paragraph (b)(4) of this section available both by telephone and on a Web site.

(C) The long form disclosure required by paragraph (b)(4) of this section is provided after the consumer acquires the prepaid account.

(2) Short form disclosure content. In accordance with paragraph (b)(1) of this section, a financial institution shall provide a disclosure setting forth the following fees and information for a prepaid account, as applicable:

(i) Periodic fee. The periodic fee charged for holding the prepaid account, assessed on a monthly or other periodic basis, using the term "Monthly fee," "Annual fee," or a substantially similar term.

(ii) Per purchase fee. The fee for making a purchase using the prepaid account, using the term "Per purchase" or a substantially similar term.

(iii) ATM withdrawal fees. Two fees for using an automated teller machine to initiate a withdrawal of cash in the United States from the prepaid account, both within and outside of the financial institution's network or a network affiliated with the financial institution, using the term "ATM withdrawal" or a substantially similar term, and "in-network" or "out-of-network," respectively, or substantially similar terms.

(iv) Cash reload fee. The fee for reloading cash into the prepaid account using the term "Cash reload" or a substantially similar term. The fee disclosed must be the total of all charges from the financial institution and any third parties for a cash reload.

(v) ATM balance inquiry fees. Two fees for using an automated teller machine to check the balance of the prepaid account in the United States, both within and outside of the financial institution's network or a network affiliated with the financial institution, using the term "ATM balance inquiry" or a substantially similar term, and "in-network" or "out-of-network," respectively, or substantially similar terms.

(vi) Customer service fees. Two fees for calling the financial institution about the prepaid account, both for calling an interactive voice response system and a live customer service agent, using the term "Customer service" or a substantially similar term, and "automated" or "live agent," or substantially similar terms, respectively, and "per call" or a substantially similar term. When providing a short form disclosure for multiple service plans pursuant to paragraph (b)(6)(iii)(B)(2) of this section, disclose only the fee for calling the live agent customer service about the prepaid account, using the term "Live customer service" or a substantially similar term and "per call" or a substantially similar term.

(vii) Inactivity fee. The fee for non-use, dormancy, or inactivity of the prepaid account, using the term "Inactivity" or a substantially similar term, as well as the conditions that trigger the financial institution to impose that fee.

(viii) Statements regarding additional fee types—

(A) Statement regarding number of additional fee types charged. A statement disclosing the number of additional fee types the financial institution may charge consumers with respect to the prepaid account, using the following clause or a substantially similar clause: "We charge [x] other types of fees." The number of additional fee types disclosed must reflect the total number of fee types under which the financial institution may charge fees, excluding:

(1) Fees required to be disclosed pursuant to paragraphs (b)(2)(i) through (vii) and (b)(5) of this section; and

(2) Any finance charges as described in Regulation Z, 12 CFR 1026.4(b)(11), imposed in connection with a covered separate credit feature accessible by a hybrid prepaid-credit card as defined in 12 CFR 1026.61.

(B) Statement directing consumers to disclosure of additional fee types. If a financial institution makes a disclosure pursuant to paragraph (b)(2)(ix) of this section, a statement directing consumers to that disclosure, located after but on the same line of text as the statement regarding the number of additional fee types required by paragraph (b)(2)(viii)(A) of this section, using the following clause or a substantially similar clause: "Here are some of them:".

(ix) Disclosure of additional fee types—

(A) Determination of which additional fee types to disclose. The two fee types that generate the highest revenue from consumers for the prepaid account program or across prepaid account programs that share the same fee schedule during the time period provided in paragraphs (b)(2)(ix)(D) and (E) of this section, excluding:

(1) Fees required to be disclosed pursuant to paragraphs (b)(2)(i) through (vii) and (b)(5) of this section;

(2) Any fee types that generated less than 5 percent of the total revenue from consumers for the prepaid account program or across prepaid account programs that share the same fee schedule during the time period provided in paragraphs (b)(2)(ix)(D) and (E) of this section; and

(3) Any finance charges as described in Regulation Z, 12 CFR 1026.4(b)(11), imposed in connection with a covered separate credit feature accessible by a hybrid prepaid-credit card as defined in 12 CFR 1026.61.

(B) Disclosure of fewer than two additional fee types. A financial institution that has only one additional fee type that satisfies the criteria in paragraph (b)(2)(ix)(A) of this section must disclose that one additional fee type; it may, but is not required to, also disclose another additional fee type of its choice. A financial institution that has no additional fee types that satisfy the criteria in paragraph (b)(2)(ix)(A) of this section is not required to make a disclosure under this paragraph (b)(2)(ix); it may, but is not required to, disclose one or two fee types of its choice.

(C) Fee variations in additional fee types. If an additional fee type required to be disclosed pursuant to paragraph (b)(2)(ix)(A) of this section has more than two fee variations, or when providing a short form disclosure for multiple service plans pursuant to paragraph (b)(6)(iii)(B)(2) of this section, the financial institution must disclose the name of the additional fee type and the highest fee amount in accordance with paragraph (b)(3)(i) of this section; for disclosures other than for multiple service plans, it may, but is not required to, consolidate the fee variations into two categories and disclose the names of those two fee variation categories and the fee amounts in a format substantially similar to that used to disclose the two-tier fees required by paragraphs (b)(2)(v) and (vi) of this section and in accordance with paragraphs (b)(3)(i) and (b)(7)(ii)(B)(1) of this section. Except when providing a short form disclosure for multiple service plans pursuant to paragraph (b)(6)(iii)(B)(2) of this section, if an additional fee type has two fee variations, the financial institution must disclose the name of the additional fee type together with the names of the two fee variations and the fee amounts in a format substantially similar to that used to disclose the two-tier fees required by paragraphs (b)(2)(v) and (vi) of this section and in accordance with paragraph (b)(7)(ii)(B)(1) of this section. If a financial institution only charges one fee under a particular fee type, the financial institution must disclose the name of the additional fee type and the fee amount; it may, but is not required to, disclose also the name of the one fee variation for which the fee amount is charged, in a format substantially similar to that used to disclose the two-tier fees required by paragraphs (b)(2)(v) and (vi) of this section, except that the financial institution would disclose only the one fee variation name and fee amount instead of two.

(D) Timing of initial assessment of additional fee types disclosure—

(1) Existing prepaid account programs as of April 1, 2019. For a prepaid account program in effect as of April 1, 2019, the financial institution must disclose the additional fee types based on revenue for a 24-month period that begins no earlier than October 1, 2014.

(2) Existing prepaid account programs as of April 1, 2019 with unavailable data. If a financial institution does not have 24 months of fee revenue data for a particular prepaid account program from which to calculate the additional fee types disclosure in advance of April 1, 2019, the financial institution must disclose the additional fee types based on revenue it reasonably anticipates the prepaid account program will generate over the 24-month period that begins on April 1, 2019.

(3) New prepaid account programs created on or after April 1, 2019. For a prepaid account program created on or after April 1, 2019, the financial institution must disclose the additional fee types based on revenue it reasonably anticipates the prepaid account program will generate over the first 24 months of the program.

(E) Timing of periodic reassessment and update of additional fee types disclosure—

(1) General. A financial institution must reassess its additional fee types disclosure periodically as described in paragraph (b)(2)(ix)(E)(2) of this section and upon a fee schedule change as described in paragraph (b)(2)(ix)(E)(3) of this section. The financial institution must update its additional fee types disclosure if the previous disclosure no longer complies with the requirements of this paragraph (b)(2)(ix).

(2) Periodic reassessment. A financial institution must reassess whether its previously disclosed additional fee types continue to comply with the requirements of this paragraph (b)(2)(ix) every 24 months based on revenue for the previous 24-month period. The financial institution must complete this reassessment and update its disclosure, if applicable, within three months of the end of the 24-month period, except as provided in the update printing exception in paragraph (b)(2)(ix)(E)(4) of this section. A financial institution may, but is not required to, carry out this reassessment and update, if applicable, more frequently than every 24 months, at which time a new 24-month period commences.

(3) Fee schedule change. If a financial institution revises the fee schedule for a prepaid account program, it must determine whether it reasonably anticipates that the previously disclosed additional fee types will continue to comply with the requirements of this paragraph (b)(2)(ix) for the 24 months following implementation of the fee schedule change. If the financial institution reasonably anticipates that the previously disclosed additional fee types will not comply with the requirements of this paragraph (b)(2)(ix), it must update the disclosure based on its reasonable anticipation of what those additional fee types will be at the time the fee schedule change goes into effect, except as provided in the update printing exception in paragraph (b)(2)(ix)(E)(4) of this section. If an immediate change in terms and conditions is necessary to maintain or restore the security of an account or an electronic fund transfer system as described in § 1005.8(a)(2) and that change affects the prepaid account program's fee schedule, the financial institution must complete its reassessment and update its disclosure, if applicable, within three months of the date it makes the change permanent, except as provided in the update printing exception in paragraph (b)(2)(ix)(E)(4) of this section.

(4) Update printing exception. Notwithstanding the requirements to update an additional fee types disclosure in paragraph (b)(2)(ix)(E) of this section, a financial institution is not required to update the listing of additional fee types that are provided on, in, or with prepaid account packaging materials that were manufactured, printed, or otherwise produced prior to a periodic reassessment and update pursuant to paragraph (b)(2)(ix)(E)(2) of this section or prior to a fee schedule change pursuant to paragraph (b)(2)(ix)(E)(3) of this section.

(x) Statement regarding overdraft credit features. If a covered separate credit feature accessible by a hybrid prepaid-credit card as defined in Regulation Z, 12 CFR 1026.61, may be offered at any point to a consumer in connection with the prepaid account, a statement that overdraft/credit may be offered, the time period after which it may be offered, and that fees would apply, using the following clause or a substantially similar clause: "You may be offered overdraft/credit after [x] days. Fees would apply." If no such credit feature will be offered at any point to a consumer in connection with the prepaid account, a statement that no overdraft credit feature is offered, using the following clause or a substantially similar clause: "No overdraft/credit feature."

(xi) Statement regarding registration and FDIC or NCUA insurance. A statement regarding the prepaid account program's eligibility for FDIC deposit insurance or NCUA share insurance, as appropriate, and directing the consumer to register the prepaid account for insurance and other account protections, where applicable, as follows:

(A) Account is insurance eligible and does not have pre-acquisition consumer identification/verification. If a prepaid account program is set up to be eligible for FDIC deposit or NCUA share insurance, and consumer identification and verification does not occur before the account is opened, using the following clause or a substantially similar clause: "Register your card for [FDIC insurance eligibility] [NCUA insurance, if eligible,] and other protections."

(B) Account is not insurance eligible and does not have pre-acquisition consumer identification/verification. If a prepaid account program is not set up to be eligible for FDIC deposit or NCUA share insurance, and consumer identification and verification does not occur before the account is opened, using the following clause or a substantially similar clause: "Not [FDIC] [NCUA] insured. Register your card for other protections."

(C) Account is insurance eligible and has pre-acquisition consumer identification/verification. If a prepaid account program is set up to be eligible for FDIC deposit or NCUA share insurance, and consumer identification and verification occurs for all prepaid accounts within the prepaid program before the account is opened, using the following clause or a substantially similar clause: "Your funds are [eligible for FDIC insurance] [NCUA insured, if eligible]."

(D) Account is not insurance eligible and has pre-acquisition consumer identification/verification. If a prepaid account program is not set up to be eligible for FDIC deposit or NCUA share insurance, and consumer identification and verification occurs for all prepaid accounts within the prepaid account program before the account is opened, using the following clause or a substantially similar clause: "Your funds are not [FDIC] [NCUA] insured."

(E) No consumer identification/verification. If a prepaid account program is set up such that there is no consumer identification and verification process for any prepaid accounts within the prepaid account program, using the following clause or a substantially similar clause: "Treat this card like cash. Not [FDIC] [NCUA] insured."

(xii) Statement regarding CFPB Web site. A statement directing the consumer to a Web site URL of the Consumer Financial Protection Bureau (cfpb.gov/prepaid) for general information about prepaid accounts, using the following clause or a substantially similar clause: "For general information about prepaid accounts, visit cfpb.gov/prepaid."

(xiii) Statement regarding information on all fees and services. A statement directing the consumer to the location of the long form disclosure required by paragraph (b)(4) of this section to find details and conditions for all fees and services. For a financial institution offering prepaid accounts at a retail location pursuant to the retail location exception in paragraph (b)(1)(ii) of this section, this statement must also include a telephone number and a Web site URL that a consumer may use to directly access, respectively, an oral and an electronic version of the long form disclosure required under paragraph (b)(4) of this section. The disclosure required by this paragraph must be made using the following clause or a substantially similar clause: "Find details and conditions for all fees and services in [location]" or, for prepaid accounts offered at retail locations pursuant to paragraph (b)(1)(ii) of this section, made using the following clause or a substantially similar clause: "Find details and conditions for all fees and services inside the package, or call [telephone number] or visit [Web site]." The Web site URL may not exceed 22 characters and must be meaningfully named. A financial institution may, but is not required to, disclose an SMS code at the end of the statement disclosing the telephone number and Web site URL, if the SMS code can be accommodated on the same line of text as the statement required by this paragraph.

(xiv) Additional content for payroll card accounts—

(A) Statement regarding wage or salary payment options. For payroll card accounts, a statement that the consumer does not have to accept the payroll card account and directing the consumer to ask about other ways to receive wages or salary from the employer instead of receiving them via the payroll card account using the following clause or a substantially similar clause: "You do not have to accept this payroll card. Ask your employer about other ways to receive your wages." Alternatively, a financial institution may provide a statement that the consumer has several options to receive wages or salary, followed by a list of the options available to the consumer, and directing the consumer to tell the employer which option the consumer chooses using the following clause or a substantially similar clause: "You have several options to receive your wages: [list of options available to the consumer]; or this payroll card. Tell your employer which option you choose." This statement must be located above the information required by paragraphs (b)(2)(i) through (iv).

(B) Statement regarding state-required information or other fee discounts and waivers. For payroll card accounts, a financial institution may, but is not required to, include a statement in one additional line of text directing the consumer to a particular location outside the short form disclosure for information on ways the consumer may access payroll card account funds and balance information for free or for a reduced fee. This statement must be located directly below any statements disclosed pursuant to paragraphs (b)(3)(i) and (ii) of this section, or, if no such statements are disclosed, above the statement required by paragraph (b)(2)(x) of this section.

(3) Short form disclosure of variable fees and third-party fees and prohibition on disclosure of finance charges—

(i) General disclosure of variable fees. If the amount of any fee that is required to be disclosed in the short form disclosure pursuant to paragraphs (b)(2)(i) through (vii) and (ix) of this section could vary, a financial institution shall disclose the highest amount it may impose for that fee, followed by a symbol, such as an asterisk, linked to a statement explaining that the fee could be lower depending on how and where the prepaid account is used, using the following clause or a substantially similar clause: "This fee can be lower depending on how and where this card is used." Except as provided in paragraph (b)(3)(ii) of this section, a financial institution must use the same symbol and statement for all fees that could vary. The linked statement must be located above the statement required by paragraph (b)(2)(x) of this section.

(ii) Disclosure of variable periodic fee. If the amount of the periodic fee disclosed in the short form disclosure pursuant to paragraph (b)(2)(i) of this section could vary, as an alternative to the disclosure required by paragraph (b)(3)(i) of this section, the financial institution may disclose the highest amount it may impose for the periodic fee, followed by a symbol, such as a dagger, that is different from the symbol the financial institution uses pursuant to paragraph (b)(3)(i) of this section, to indicate that a waiver of the fee or a lower fee might apply, linked to a statement in one additional line of text disclosing the waiver or reduced fee amount and explaining the circumstances under which the fee waiver or reduction may occur. The linked statement must be located directly above or in place of the linked statement required by paragraph (b)(3)(i) of this section, as applicable.

(iii) Single disclosure for like fees. As an alternative to the two-tier fee disclosure required by paragraphs (b)(2)(iii), (v), and (vi) of this section and any two-tier fee required by paragraph (b)(2)(ix) of this section, a financial institution may disclose a single fee amount when the amount is the same for both fees.

(iv) Third-party fees in general. Except as provided in paragraph (b)(3)(v) of this section, a financial institution may not include any third-party fees in a disclosure made pursuant to paragraph (b)(2) of this section.

(v) Third-party cash reload fees. Any third-party fee included in the cash reload fee disclosed in the short form pursuant to paragraph (b)(2)(iv) of this section must be the highest fee known by the financial institution at the time it prints, or otherwise prepares, the short form disclosure required by paragraph (b)(2) of this section. A financial institution is not required to revise its short form disclosure to reflect a cash reload fee change by a third party until such time that the financial institution manufactures, prints, or otherwise produces new prepaid account packaging materials or otherwise updates the short form disclosure.

(vi) Prohibition on disclosure of finance charges. A financial institution may not include in a disclosure made pursuant to paragraphs (b)(2)(i) through (ix) of this section any finance charges as described in Regulation Z, 12 CFR 1026.4(b)(11), imposed in connection with a covered separate credit feature accessible by a hybrid prepaid-credit card as defined in 12 CFR 1026.61.

(4) Long form disclosure content. In accordance with paragraph (b)(1) of this section, a financial institution shall provide a disclosure setting forth the following fees and information for a prepaid account, as applicable:

(i) Title for long form disclosure. A heading stating the name of the prepaid account program and that the long form disclosure contains a list of all fees for that particular prepaid account program.

(ii) Fees. All fees that may be imposed in connection with a prepaid account. For each fee, the financial institution must disclose the amount of the fee and the conditions, if any, under which the fee may be imposed, waived, or reduced. A financial institution may not use any symbols, such as an asterisk, to explain conditions under which any fee may be imposed. A financial institution may, but is not required to, include in the long form disclosure any service or feature it provides or offers at no charge to the consumer. The financial institution must also disclose any third-party fee amounts known to the financial institution that may apply. For any such third-party fee disclosed, the financial institution may, but is not required to, include either or both a statement that the fee is accurate as of or through a specific date or that the third-party fee is subject to change. If a third-party fee may apply but the amount of that fee is not known by the financial institution, it must include a statement indicating that the third-party fee may apply without specifying the fee amount. A financial institution is not required to revise the long form disclosure required by paragraph (b)(4) of this section to reflect a fee change by a third party until such time that the financial institution manufactures, prints, or otherwise produces new prepaid account packaging materials or otherwise updates the long form disclosure.

(iii) Statement regarding registration and FDIC or NCUA insurance. The statement required by paragraph (b)(2)(xi) of this section, together with an explanation of FDIC or NCUA insurance coverage and the benefit of such coverage or the consequence of the lack of such coverage, as applicable.

(iv) Statement regarding overdraft credit features. The statement required by paragraph (b)(2)(x) of this section.

(v) Statement regarding financial institution contact information. A statement directing the consumer to a telephone number, mailing address, and Web site URL of the person or office that a consumer may contact to learn about the terms and conditions of the prepaid account, to obtain prepaid account balance information, to request a copy of transaction history pursuant to paragraph (c)(1)(iii) of this section if the financial institution does not provide periodic statements pursuant to § 1005.9(b), or to notify the financial institution when the consumer believes that an unauthorized electronic fund transfer occurred as required by § 1005.7(b)(2) and paragraph (d)(1)(ii) of this section.

(vi) Statement regarding CFPB Web site and telephone number. A statement directing the consumer to a Web site URL of the Consumer Financial Protection Bureau (cfpb.gov/prepaid) for general information about prepaid accounts, and a statement directing the consumer to a Consumer Financial Protection Bureau telephone number (1–855–411–2372) and Web site URL (cfpb.gov/complaint) to submit a complaint about a prepaid account, using the following clause or a substantially similar clause: "For general information about prepaid accounts, visit cfpb.gov/prepaid. If you have a complaint about a prepaid account, call the Consumer Financial Protection Bureau at 1–855–411–2372 or visit cfpb.gov/complaint."

(vii) Regulation Z disclosures for overdraft credit features. The disclosures described in Regulation Z, 12 CFR 1026.60(e)(1), in accordance with the requirements for such disclosures in 12 CFR 1026.60, if, at any point, a covered separate credit feature accessible by a hybrid prepaid-credit card as defined in 12 CFR 1026.61, may be offered in connection with the prepaid account. A financial institution may, but is not required to, include above the Regulation Z disclosures required by this paragraph a heading and other explanatory information introducing the overdraft credit feature. A financial institution is not required to revise the disclosure required by this paragraph to reflect a change in the fees or other terms disclosed therein until such time as the financial institution manufactures, prints, or otherwise produces new prepaid account packaging materials or otherwise updates the long form disclosure.

(5) Disclosure requirements outside the short form disclosure. At the time a financial institution provides the short form disclosure, it must also disclose the following information: the name of the financial institution; the name of the prepaid account program; the purchase price for the prepaid account, if any; and the fee for activating the prepaid account, if any. In a setting other than in a retail location, this information must be disclosed in close proximity to the short form. In a retail location, this information, other than the purchase price, must be disclosed on the exterior of the access device's packaging material. In a retail location, the purchase price must be disclosed either on the exterior of or in close proximity to the prepaid account access device's packaging material.

(6) Form of pre-acquisition disclosures—

(i) General—

(A) Written disclosures. Except as provided in paragraphs (b)(6)(i)(B) and (C) of this section, disclosures required by paragraph (b) of this section must be in writing.

(B) Electronic disclosures. Unless provided in written form prior to acquisition pursuant to paragraph (b)(1)(i) of this section, the disclosures required by paragraph (b) of this section must be provided in electronic form when a consumer acquires a prepaid account through electronic means, including via a website or mobile application, and must be viewable across all screen sizes. The long form disclosure must be provided electronically through a website when a financial institution is offering prepaid accounts at a retail location pursuant to the retail location exception in paragraph (b)(1)(ii) of this section. Electronic disclosures must be provided in a manner which is reasonably expected to be accessible in light of how a consumer is acquiring the prepaid account, in a responsive form, and using machine-readable text that is accessible via Web browsers or mobile applications, as applicable, and via screen readers. Electronic disclosures provided pursuant to paragraph (b) of this section need not meet the consumer consent and other applicable provisions of the Electronic Signatures in Global and National Commerce Act (E-Sign Act) (15 U.S.C. 7001 et seq.).

(C) Oral disclosures. Unless provided in written form prior to acquisition pursuant to paragraph (b)(1)(i) of this section, disclosures required by paragraphs (b)(2) and (5) of this section must be provided orally when a consumer acquires a prepaid account orally by telephone pursuant to the exception in paragraph (b)(1)(iii) of this section. For prepaid accounts acquired in retail locations or orally by telephone, the disclosure required by paragraph (b)(4) of this section provided by telephone pursuant to paragraph (b)(1)(ii)(C) or (b)(1)(iii)(B) of this section also must be made orally.

(ii) Retainable form. Pursuant to § 1005.4(a)(1), disclosures required by paragraph (b) of this section must be made in a form that a consumer may keep, except for disclosures provided orally pursuant to paragraphs (b)(1)(ii) or (iii) of this section, a long form disclosure provided via SMS as permitted by paragraph (b)(2)(xiii) of this section for a prepaid account sold at retail locations pursuant to the retail location exception in paragraph (b)(1)(ii) of this section, and the disclosure of a purchase price pursuant to paragraph (b)(5) of this section that is not disclosed on the exterior of the packaging material for a prepaid account sold at a retail location pursuant to the retail location exception in paragraph (b)(1)(ii) of this section.

(iii) Tabular format—

(A) General. When a short form disclosure is provided in writing or electronically, the information required by paragraphs (b)(2)(i) through (ix) of this section shall be provided in the form of a table. Except as provided in paragraph (b)(6)(iii)(B) of this section, the short form disclosure required by paragraph (b)(2) of this section shall be provided in a form substantially similar to Model Forms A-10(a) through (d) in appendix A of this part, as applicable. When a long form disclosure is provided in writing or electronically, the information required by paragraph (b)(4)(ii) of this section shall be provided in the form of a table. Sample Form A-10(f) in appendix A of this part provides an example of the long form disclosure required by paragraph (b)(4) of this section when the financial institution does not offer multiple service plans.

(B) Multiple service plans—

(1) Short form disclosure for default service plan. When a financial institution offers multiple service plans within a particular prepaid account program and each plan has a different fee schedule, the information required by paragraphs (b)(2)(i) through (ix) of this section may be provided in the tabular format described in paragraph (b)(6)(iii)(A) of this section for the service plan in which a consumer is initially enrolled by default upon acquiring the prepaid account.

(2) Short form disclosure for multiple service plans. As an alternative to disclosing the default service plan pursuant to paragraph (b)(6)(iii)(B)(1) of this section, when a financial institution offers multiple service plans within a particular prepaid account program and each plan has a different fee schedule, fee disclosures required by paragraphs (b)(2)(i) through (vii) and (ix) of this section may be provided in the form of a table with separate columns for each service plan, in a form substantially similar to Model Form A-10(e) in appendix A of this part. Column headings must describe each service plan included in the table, using the terms "Pay-as-you-go plan," "Monthly plan," "Annual plan," or substantially similar terms; or, for multiple service plans offering preferred rates or fees for the prepaid accounts of consumers who also use another non-prepaid service, column headings must describe each service plan included in the table for the preferred and non-preferred service plans, as applicable.

(3) Long form disclosure. The information in the long form disclosure required by paragraph (b)(4)(ii) of this section must be presented in the form of a table for all service plans.

(7) Specific formatting requirements for pre-acquisition disclosures—

(i) Grouping—

(A) Short form disclosure. The information required in the short form disclosure by paragraphs (b)(2)(i) through (iv) of this section must be grouped together and provided in that order. The information required by paragraphs (b)(2)(v) through (ix) of this section must be generally grouped together and provided in that order. The information required by paragraphs (b)(3)(i) and (ii) of this section, as applicable, must be generally grouped together and in the location described by paragraphs (b)(3)(i) and (ii) of this section. The information required by paragraphs (b)(2)(x) through (xiii) of this section must be generally grouped together and provided in that order. The statement regarding wage or salary payment options for payroll card accounts required by paragraph (b)(2)(xiv)(A) of this section must be located above the information required by paragraphs (b)(2)(i) through (iv) of this section, as described in paragraph (b)(2)(xiv)(A) of this section. The statement regarding state-required information or other fee discounts or waivers permitted by paragraph (b)(2)(xiv)(B) of this section, when applicable, must appear in the location described by paragraph (b)(2)(xiv)(B) of this section.

(B) Long form disclosure. The information required by paragraph (b)(4)(i) of this section must be located in the first line of the long form disclosure. The information required by paragraph (b)(4)(ii) of this section must be generally grouped together and organized under subheadings by the categories of function for which a financial institution may impose the fee. Text describing the conditions under which a fee may be imposed must appear in the table required by paragraph (b)(6)(iii)(A) of this section in close proximity to the fee amount. The statements in the long form disclosure required by paragraphs (b)(4)(iii) through (vi) of this section must be generally grouped together, provided in that order, and appear below the information required by paragraph (b)(4)(ii) of this section. If, pursuant to paragraph (b)(4)(vii) of this section, the financial institution includes the disclosures described in Regulation Z, 12 CFR 1026.60(e)(1), such disclosures must appear below the statements required by paragraph (b)(4)(vi) of this section.

(C) Multiple service plan disclosure. When providing a short form disclosure for multiple service plans pursuant to paragraph (b)(6)(iii)(B)(2) of this section, in lieu of the requirements in paragraph (b)(7)(i)(A) of this section for grouping of the disclosures required by paragraphs (b)(2)(i) through (iv) and (v) through (ix) of this section, the information required by paragraphs (b)(2)(i) through (ix) of this section must be grouped together and provided in that order.

(ii) Prominence and size—

(A) General. All text used to disclose information in the short form or in the long form disclosure pursuant to paragraphs (b)(2), (b)(3)(i) and (ii), and (b)(4) of this section must be in a single, easy-to-read type that is all black or one color and printed on a background that provides a clear contrast.

(B) Short form disclosure—

(1) Fees and other information. The information required in the short form disclosure by paragraphs (b)(2)(i) through (iv) of this section must appear as follows. Fee amounts in bold-faced type; single fee amounts in a minimum type size of 15 points (or 21 pixels); two tier fee amounts for ATM withdrawal in a minimum type size of 11 points (or 16 pixels) and in no larger a type size than what is used for the single fee amounts; and fee headings in a minimum type size of eight points (or 11 pixels) and in no larger a type size than what is used for the single fee amounts. The information required by paragraphs (b)(2)(v) through (ix) of this section must appear in a minimum type size of eight points (or 11 pixels) and appear in the same or a smaller type size than what is used for the fee headings required by paragraphs (b)(2)(i) through (iv) of this section. The information required by paragraphs (b)(2)(x) through (xiii) of this section must appear in a minimum type size of seven points (or nine pixels) and appear in no larger a type size than what is used for the information required to be disclosed by paragraphs (b)(2)(v) through (ix) of this section. Additionally, the statements disclosed pursuant to paragraphs (b)(2)(viii)(A) and (b)(2)(x) of this section and the telephone number and URL disclosed pursuant to paragraph (b)(2)(xiii) of this section, where applicable, must appear in bold-faced type. The following information must appear in a minimum type size of six points (or eight pixels) and appear in no larger a type size that what is used for the information required by paragraphs (b)(2)(x) through (xiii) of this section: text used to distinguish each of the two-tier fees pursuant to paragraphs (b)(2)(iii), (v), (vi), and (ix) of this section; text used to explain that the fee required by paragraph (b)(2)(vi) of this section applies "per call," where applicable; and text used to explain the conditions that trigger an inactivity fee and that the fee applies monthly or for the applicable time period, pursuant to paragraph (b)(2)(vii) of this section.

(2) Variable fees. The symbols and corresponding statements regarding variable fees disclosed in the short form pursuant to paragraphs (b)(3)(i) and (ii) of this section, when applicable, must appear in a minimum type size of seven points (or nine pixels) and appear in no larger a type size than what is used for the information required by paragraphs (b)(2)(x) through (xiii) of this section. A symbol required next to the fee amount pursuant to paragraphs (b)(3)(i) and (ii) of this section must appear in the same type size or pixel size as what is used for the corresponding fee amount.

(3) Payroll card account additional content. The statement regarding wage or salary payment options for payroll card accounts required by paragraph (b)(2)(xiv)(A) of this section, when applicable, must appear in a minimum type size of eight points (or 11 pixels) and appear in no larger a type size than what is used for the fee headings required by paragraphs (b)(2)(i) through (iv) of this section. The statement regarding state-required information and other fee discounts or waivers permitted by paragraph (b)(2)(xiv)(B) of this section must appear in the same type size used to disclose variable fee information pursuant to paragraph (b)(3)(i) and (ii) of this section, or, if none, the same type size used for the information required by paragraphs (b)(2)(x) through (xiii) of this section.

(C) Long form disclosure. The long form disclosure required by paragraph (b)(4) of this section must appear in a minimum type size of eight points (or 11 pixels).

(D) Multiple service plan short form disclosure. When providing a short form disclosure for multiple service plans pursuant to paragraph (b)(6)(iii)(B)(2) of this section, the fee headings required by paragraphs (b)(2)(i) through (iv) of this section must appear in bold-faced type. The information required by paragraphs (b)(2)(i) through (xiii) of this section must appear in a minimum type size of seven points (or nine pixels), except the following must appear in a minimum type size of six points (or eight pixels) and appear in no larger a type size than what is used for the information required by paragraphs (b)(2)(i) through (xiii) of this section: Text used to distinguish each of the two-tier fees required by paragraphs (b)(2)(iii) and (v) of this section; text used to explain that the fee required by paragraph (b)(2)(vi) of this section applies "per call," where applicable; text used to explain the conditions that trigger an inactivity fee pursuant to paragraph (b)(2)(vii) of this section; and text used to distinguish that fees required by paragraphs (b)(2)(i) and (vii) of this section apply monthly or for the applicable time period.

(iii) Segregation. Short form and long form disclosures required by paragraphs (b)(2) and (4) of this section must be segregated from other information and must contain only information that is required or permitted for those disclosures by paragraph (b) of this section.

(8) Terminology of pre-acquisition disclosures. Fee names and other terms must be used consistently within and across the disclosures required by paragraph (b) of this section.

(9) Prepaid accounts acquired in foreign languages—

(i) General. A financial institution must provide the pre-acquisition disclosures required by paragraph (b) of this section in a foreign language, if the financial institution uses that same foreign language in connection with the acquisition of a prepaid account in the following circumstances:

(A) The financial institution principally uses a foreign language on the prepaid account packaging material;

(B) The financial institution principally uses a foreign language to advertise, solicit, or market a prepaid account and provides a means in the advertisement, solicitation, or marketing material that the consumer uses to acquire the prepaid account by telephone or electronically; or

(C) The financial institution provides a means for the consumer to acquire a prepaid account by telephone or electronically principally in a foreign language. However, foreign language pre-acquisition disclosures are not required for payroll card accounts and government benefit accounts where the foreign language is offered by telephone via a real-time language interpretation service provided by a third party or by the employer or government agency on an informal or ad hoc basis as an accommodation to prospective payroll card account or government benefit account holders.

(ii) Long form disclosures in English upon request. A financial institution required to provide pre-acquisition disclosures in a foreign language pursuant to paragraph (b)(9)(i) of this section must also provide the information required to be disclosed in its pre-acquisition long form disclosure pursuant to paragraph (b)(4) of this section in English upon a consumer's request and on any part of the Web site where it discloses this information in a foreign language.

(c) Access to prepaid account information—

(1) Periodic statement alternative. A financial institution need not furnish periodic statements required by § 1005.9(b) if the financial institution makes available to the consumer:

(i) The consumer's account balance, through a readily available telephone line;

(ii) An electronic history of the consumer's account transactions, such as through a Web site, that covers at least 12 months preceding the date the consumer electronically accesses the account; and

(iii) A written history of the consumer's account transactions that is provided promptly in response to an oral or written request and that covers at least 24 months preceding the date the financial institution receives the consumer's request.

(2) Periodic statement alternative for unverified prepaid accounts. For prepaid accounts that are not payroll card accounts or government benefit accounts, a financial institution is not required to provide a written history of the consumer's account transactions pursuant to paragraph (c)(1)(iii) of this section for any prepaid account for which the financial institution has not completed its consumer identification and verification process as described in paragraph (e)(3)(i)(A) through (C) of this section.

(3) Information included on electronic or written histories. The history of account transactions provided under paragraphs (c)(1)(ii) and (iii) of this section must include the information set forth in § 1005.9(b).

(4) Inclusion of all fees charged. A financial institution must disclose the amount of any fees assessed against the account, whether for electronic fund transfers or otherwise, on any periodic statement provided pursuant to § 1005.9(b) and on any history of account transactions provided or made available by the financial institution.

(5) Summary totals of fees. A financial institution must display a summary total of the amount of all fees assessed by the financial institution against the consumer's prepaid account for the prior calendar month and for the calendar year to date on any periodic statement provided pursuant to § 1005.9(b) and on any history of account transactions provided or made available by the financial institution.

(d) Modified disclosure requirements. A financial institution that provides information under paragraph (c)(1) of this section shall comply with the following:

(1) Initial disclosures. The financial institution shall modify the disclosures under § 1005.7(b) by disclosing:

(i) Access to account information. A telephone number that the consumer may call to obtain the account balance, the means by which the consumer can obtain an electronic account transaction history, such as the address of a Web site, and a summary of the consumer's right to receive a written account transaction history upon request (in place of the summary of the right to receive a periodic statement required by § 1005.7(b)(6)), including a telephone number to call to request a history. The disclosure required by this paragraph may be made by providing a notice substantially similar to the notice contained in paragraph (a) of appendix A-7 of this part.

(ii) Error resolution. A notice concerning error resolution that is substantially similar to the notice contained in paragraph (b) of appendix A-7 of this part, in place of the notice required by § 1005.7(b)(10). Alternatively, for prepaid account programs for which the financial institution does not have a consumer identification and verification process, the financial institution must describe its error resolution process and limitations on consumers' liability for unauthorized transfers or, if none, state that there are no such protections.

(2) Annual error resolution notice. The financial institution shall provide an annual notice concerning error resolution that is substantially similar to the notice contained in paragraph (b) of appendix A-7 of this part, in place of the notice required by § 1005.8(b). Alternatively, a financial institution may include on or with each electronic and written account transaction history provided in accordance with paragraph (c)(1) of this section, a notice substantially similar to the abbreviated notice for periodic statements contained in paragraph (b) of appendix A-3 of this part, modified as necessary to reflect the error resolution provisions set forth in paragraph (e) of this section.

(e) Modified limitations on liability and error resolution requirements—

(1) Modified limitations on liability requirements. A financial institution that provides information under paragraph (c)(1) of this section shall comply with the following:

(i) For purposes of § 1005.6(b)(3), the 60-day period for reporting any unauthorized transfer shall begin on the earlier of:

(A) The date the consumer electronically accesses the consumer's account under paragraph (c)(1)(ii) of this section, provided that the electronic account transaction history made available to the consumer reflects the unauthorized transfer; or

(B) The date the financial institution sends a written history of the consumer's account transactions requested by the consumer under paragraph (c)(1)(iii) of this section in which the unauthorized transfer is first reflected.

(ii) A financial institution may comply with paragraph (e)(1)(i) of this section by limiting the consumer's liability for an unauthorized transfer as provided under § 1005.6(b)(3) for any transfer reported by the consumer within 120 days after the transfer was credited or debited to the consumer's account.

(2) Modified error resolution requirements. A financial institution that provides information under paragraph (c)(1) of this section shall comply with the following:

(i) The financial institution shall comply with the requirements of § 1005.11 in response to an oral or written notice of an error from the consumer that is received by the earlier of:

(A) Sixty days after the date the consumer electronically accesses the consumer's account under paragraph (c)(1)(ii) of this section, provided that the electronic account transaction history made available to the consumer reflects the alleged error; or

(B) Sixty days after the date the financial institution sends a written history of the consumer's account transactions requested by the consumer under paragraph (c)(1)(iii) of this section in which the alleged error is first reflected.

(ii) In lieu of following the procedures in paragraph (e)(2)(i) of this section, a financial institution complies with the requirements for resolving errors in § 1005.11 if it investigates any oral or written notice of an error from the consumer that is received by the institution within 120 days after the transfer allegedly in error was credited or debited to the consumer's account.

(3) Limitations on liability and error resolution for unverified accounts.

(i) For prepaid accounts that are not payroll card accounts or government benefit accounts, a financial institution is not required to comply with the liability limits and error resolution requirements in §§ 1005.6 and 1005.11 for any prepaid account for which it has not successfully completed its consumer identification and verification process.

(ii) For purposes of paragraph (e)(3)(i) of this section, a financial institution has not successfully completed its consumer identification and verification process where:

(A) The financial institution has not concluded its consumer identification and verification process with respect to a particular prepaid account, provided that it has disclosed to the consumer the risks of not registering and verifying the account using a notice that is substantially similar to the model notice contained in paragraph (c) of appendix A-7 of this part.

(B) The financial institution has concluded its consumer identification and verification process with respect to a particular prepaid account, but could not verify the identity of the consumer, provided that it has disclosed to the consumer the risks of not registering and verifying the account using a notice that is substantially similar to the model notice contained in paragraph (c) of appendix A-7 of this part; or

(C) The financial institution does not have a consumer identification and verification process for the prepaid account program, provided that it has made the alternative disclosure described in paragraph (d)(1)(ii) of this section and complies with the process it has disclosed.

(iii) Resolution of errors following successful verification. Once a financial institution successfully completes its consumer identification and verification process with respect to a prepaid account, the financial institution must limit the consumer's liability for unauthorized transfers and resolve errors that occur following verification in accordance with § 1005.6 or § 1005.11, or the modified timing requirements in this paragraph (e), as applicable.

(f) Disclosure of fees and other information—

(1) Initial disclosure of fees and other information. A financial institution must include, as part of the initial disclosures given pursuant to § 1005.7, all of the information required to be disclosed in its pre-acquisition long form disclosure pursuant to paragraph (b)(4) of this section.

(2) Change-in-terms notice. The change-in-terms notice provisions in § 1005.8(a) apply to any change in a term or condition that is required to be disclosed under § 1005.7 or paragraph (f)(1) of this section. If a financial institution discloses the amount of a third-party fee in its pre-acquisition long form disclosure pursuant to paragraph (b)(4)(ii) of this section and initial disclosures pursuant to paragraph (f)(1) of this section, the financial institution is not required to provide a change-in-terms notice solely to reflect a change in that fee amount imposed by the third party. If a financial institution provides pursuant to paragraph (f)(1) of this section the Regulation Z disclosures required by paragraph (b)(4)(vii) of this section for an overdraft credit feature, the financial institution is not required to provide a change-in-terms notice solely to reflect a change in the fees or other terms disclosed therein.

(3) Disclosures on prepaid account access devices. The name of the financial institution and the Web site URL and a telephone number a consumer can use to contact the financial institution about the prepaid account must be disclosed on the prepaid account access device. If a financial institution does not provide a physical access device in connection with a prepaid account, the disclosure must appear on the Web site, mobile application, or other entry point a consumer must visit to access the prepaid account electronically.

(g) Prepaid accounts accessible by hybrid prepaid-credit cards—

(1) In general. Except as provided in paragraph (g)(2) of this section, with respect to a prepaid account program where consumers may be offered a covered separate credit feature accessible by a hybrid prepaid-credit card as defined by Regulation Z, 12 CFR 1026.61, a financial institution must provide to any prepaid account without a covered separate credit feature the same account terms, conditions, and features that it provides on prepaid accounts in the same prepaid account program that have such a credit feature.

(2) Exception for higher fees or charges. A financial institution is not prohibited under paragraph (g)(1) of this section from imposing a higher fee or charge on the asset feature of a prepaid account with a covered separate credit feature accessible by a hybrid prepaid-credit card than the amount of a comparable fee or charge that it imposes on any prepaid account in the same prepaid account program that does not have such a credit feature.

(h) Effective date and special transition rules for disclosure provisions—

(1) Effective date generally. Except as provided in paragraphs (h)(2) and (3) of this section, the requirements of this subpart, as modified by this section, apply to prepaid accounts as defined in § 1005.2(b)(3), including government benefit accounts subject to § 1005.15, beginning April 1, 2019.

(2) Early disclosures—

(i) Exception for disclosures on existing prepaid account access devices and prepaid account packaging materials. The disclosure requirements of this subpart, as modified by this section, shall not apply to any disclosures that are provided, or that would otherwise be required to be provided, on prepaid account access devices, or on, in, or with prepaid account packaging materials that were manufactured, printed, or otherwise produced in the normal course of business prior to April 1, 2019.

(ii) Disclosures for prepaid accounts acquired on or after April 1, 2019. This paragraph applies to prepaid accounts acquired by consumers on or after April 1, 2019 via packaging materials that were manufactured, printed, or otherwise produced prior to April 1, 2019.

(A) Notices of certain changes. If a financial institution has changed a prepaid account's terms and conditions as a result of paragraph (h)(1) of this section taking effect such that a change-in-terms notice would have been required under § 1005.8(a) or paragraph (f)(2) of this section for existing customers, the financial institution must provide to the consumer a notice of the change within 30 days of obtaining the consumer's contact information.

(B) Initial disclosures. The financial institution must mail or deliver to the consumer initial disclosures pursuant to § 1005.7 and paragraph (f)(1) of this section that have been updated as a result of paragraph (h)(1) of this section taking effect, within 30 days of obtaining the consumer's contact information.

(iii) Disclosures for prepaid accounts acquired before April 1, 2019. This paragraph applies to prepaid accounts acquired by consumers before April 1, 2019. If a financial institution has changed a prepaid account's terms and conditions as a result of paragraph (h)(1) of this section taking effect such that a change-in-terms notice would have been required under § 1005.8(a) or paragraph (f)(2) of this section for existing customers, the financial institution must provide to the consumer a notice of the change at least 21 days in advance of the change becoming effective, provided the financial institution has the consumer's contact information. If the financial institution obtains the consumer's contact information less than 30 days in advance of the change becoming effective or after it has become effective, the financial institution is permitted instead to notify the consumer of the change in accordance with the timing requirements set forth in paragraph (h)(2)(ii)(A) of this section.

(iv) Method of providing notice to consumers. With respect to prepaid accounts governed by paragraph (h)(2)(ii) or (iii) of this section, if a financial institution has not obtained a consumer's consent to provide disclosures in electronic form pursuant to the Electronic Signatures in Global and National Commerce Act (E-Sign Act) (15 U.S.C. 7001 et seq.), or is not otherwise already mailing or delivering to the consumer written account-related communications within the respective time periods specified in paragraphs (h)(2)(ii) or (iii) of this section, the financial institution may provide to the consumer a notice of a change in terms and conditions pursuant to paragraph (h)(2)(ii) or (iii) of this section or required or voluntary updated initial disclosures as a result of paragraph (h)(1) of this section taking effect in electronic form without regard to the consumer notice and consent requirements of section 101(c) of the E-Sign Act.

(3) Account information not available on April 1, 2019—

(i) Electronic and written account transaction history. If, on April 1, 2019, a financial institution does not have readily accessible the data necessary to make available 12 months of electronic account transaction history pursuant to paragraph (c)(1)(ii) of this section or to provide 24 months of written account transaction history upon request pursuant to paragraph (c)(1)(iii) of this section, the financial institution may make available or provide such histories using the data for the time period it has until the financial institution has accumulated the data necessary to comply in full with the requirements set forth in paragraphs (c)(1)(ii) and (iii) of this section.

(ii) Summary totals of fees. If, on April 1, 2019, the financial institution does not have readily accessible the data necessary to calculate the summary totals of the amount of all fees assessed by the financial institution on the consumer's prepaid account for the prior calendar month and for the calendar year to date pursuant to paragraph (c)(5) of this section, the financial institution may display the summary totals using the data it has until the financial institution has accumulated the data necessary to display the summary totals as required by paragraph (c)(5) of this section.

§ 1005.19. Internet posting of prepaid account agreements

(a) Definitions—

(1) Agreement. For purposes of this section, "agreement" or "prepaid account agreement" means the written document or documents evidencing the terms of the legal obligation, or the prospective legal obligation, between a prepaid account issuer and a consumer for a prepaid account. "Agreement" or "prepaid account agreement" also includes fee information, as defined in paragraph (a)(3) of this section.

(2) Amends. For purposes of this section, an issuer "amends" an agreement if it makes a substantive change (an "amendment") to the agreement. A change is substantive if it alters the rights or obligations of the issuer or the consumer under the agreement. Any change in the fee information, as defined in paragraph (a)(3) of this section, is deemed to be substantive.

(3) Fee information. For purposes of this section, "fee information" means the short form disclosure for the prepaid account pursuant to § 1005.18(b)(2) and the fee information and statements required to be disclosed in the pre-acquisition long form disclosure for the prepaid account pursuant to § 1005.18(b)(4).

(4) Issuer. For purposes of this section, "issuer" or "prepaid account issuer" means the entity to which a consumer is legally obligated, or would be legally obligated, under the terms of a prepaid account agreement.

(5) Offers. For purposes of this section, an issuer "offers" an agreement if the issuer markets, solicits applications for, or otherwise makes available a prepaid account that would be subject to that agreement, regardless of whether the issuer offers the prepaid account to the general public.

(6) Offers to the general public. For purposes of this section, an issuer "offers to the general public" an agreement if the issuer markets, solicits applications for, or otherwise makes available to the general public a prepaid account that would be subject to that agreement.

(7) Open account. For purposes of this section, a prepaid account is an "open account" or "open prepaid account" if: There is an outstanding balance in the account; the consumer can load funds to the account even if the account does not currently hold a balance; or the consumer can access credit from a covered separate credit feature accessible by a hybrid prepaid-credit card as defined in Regulation Z, 12 CFR 1026.61, in connection with the account. A prepaid account that has been suspended temporarily (for example, due to a report by the consumer of unauthorized use of the card) is considered an "open account" or "open prepaid account."

(8) Prepaid account. For purposes of this section, "prepaid account" means a prepaid account as defined in § 1005.2(b)(3).

(b) Submission of agreements to the Bureau—

(1) Submissions on a rolling basis. An issuer must make submissions of prepaid account agreements to the Bureau on a rolling basis, in the form and manner specified by the Bureau. Rolling submissions must be sent to the Bureau no later than 30 days after an issuer offers, amends, or ceases to offer any prepaid account agreement as described in paragraphs (b)(1)(ii) through (iv) of this section. Each submission must contain:

(i) Identifying information about the issuer and the agreements submitted, including the issuer's name, address, and identifying number (such as an RSSD ID number or tax identification number), the effective date of the prepaid account agreement, the name of the program manager, if any, and the list of names of other relevant parties, if applicable (such as the employer for a payroll card program or the agency for a government benefit program);

(ii) Any prepaid account agreement offered by the issuer that has not been previously submitted to the Bureau;

(iii) Any prepaid account agreement previously submitted to the Bureau that has been amended, as described in paragraph (b)(2)(i) of this section; and

(iv) Notification regarding any prepaid account agreement previously submitted to the Bureau that the issuer is withdrawing, as described in paragraphs (b)(3), (b)(4)(ii), and (b)(5)(ii) of this section.

(2) Amended agreements—

(i) Submission of amended agreements generally. If a prepaid account agreement previously submitted to the Bureau is amended, the issuer must submit the entire amended agreement to the Bureau, in the form and manner specified by the Bureau, no later than 30 days after the change becomes effective. If other identifying information about the issuer and its submitted agreements pursuant to paragraph (b)(1)(i) of this section previously submitted to the Bureau is amended, the issuer must submit updated information to the Bureau, in the form and manner specified by the Bureau, no later than 30 days after the change becomes effective.

(ii) Submission of updated list of names of other relevant parties. Notwithstanding paragraph (b)(2)(i) of this section, an issuer may delay submitting a change to the list of names of other relevant parties to a particular agreement until the earlier of:

(A) Such time as the issuer is otherwise submitting an amended agreement or changes to other identifying information about the issuer and its submitted agreements pursuant to paragraph (b)(1)(i) of this section; or

(B) May 1 of each year, for any updates to the list of names of other relevant parties for that agreement that occurred between the issuer's last submission of relevant party information and April 1 of that year.

(3) Withdrawal of agreements no longer offered. If an issuer no longer offers a prepaid account agreement that was previously submitted to the Bureau, the issuer must notify the Bureau, in the form and manner specified by the Bureau, no later than 30 days after the issuer ceases to offer the agreement, that it is withdrawing the agreement.

(4) De minimis exception.

(i) An issuer is not required to submit any prepaid account agreements to the Bureau if the issuer has fewer than 3,000 open prepaid accounts. If the issuer has 3,000 or more open prepaid accounts as of the last day of the calendar quarter, the issuer must submit to the Bureau its prepaid account agreements no later than 30 days after the last day of that calendar quarter.

(ii) If an issuer that did not previously qualify for the de minimis exception newly qualifies for the de minimis exception, the issuer must continue to make submissions to the Bureau on a rolling basis until the issuer notifies the Bureau that the issuer is withdrawing all agreements it previously submitted to the Bureau.

(5) Product testing exception.

(i) An issuer is not required to submit a prepaid account agreement to the Bureau if the agreement meets the criteria set forth in paragraphs (b)(5)(i)(A) through (C) of this section. If the agreement fails to meet the criteria set forth in paragraphs (b)(5)(i)(A) through (C) of this section as of the last day of the calendar quarter, the issuer must submit to the Bureau that prepaid account agreement no later than 30 days after the last day of that calendar quarter. An agreement qualifies for the product testing exception if the agreement:

(A) Is offered as part of a product test offered to only a limited group of consumers for a limited period of time;

(B) Is used for fewer than 3,000 open prepaid accounts; and

(C) Is not offered other than in connection with such a product test.

(ii) If an agreement that did not previously qualify for the product testing exception newly qualifies for the exception, the issuer must continue to make submissions to the Bureau on a rolling basis with respect to that agreement until the issuer notifies the Bureau that the issuer is withdrawing the agreement.

(6) Form and content of agreements submitted to the Bureau—

(i) Form and content generally.

(A) Each agreement must contain the provisions of the agreement and the fee information currently in effect.

(B) Agreements must not include any personally identifiable information relating to any consumer, such as name, address, telephone number, or account number.

(C) The following are not deemed to be part of the agreement for purposes of this section, and therefore are not required to be included in submissions to the Bureau:

(1) Ancillary disclosures required by state or Federal law, such as affiliate marketing notices, privacy policies, or disclosures under the E-Sign Act;

(2) Solicitation or marketing materials;

(3) Periodic statements; and

(4) Documents that may be sent to the consumer along with the prepaid account or prepaid account agreement such as a cover letter, a validation sticker on the card, or other information about card security.

(D) Agreements must be presented in a clear and legible font.

(ii) Fee information. Fee information must be set forth either in the prepaid account agreement or in addenda to that agreement that attach either or both the short form disclosure for the prepaid account pursuant to § 1005.18(b)(2) and the fee information and statements required to be disclosed in the long form disclosure for the prepaid account pursuant to § 1005.18(b)(4). The agreement or addenda thereto must contain all of the fee information, as defined by paragraph (a)(3) of this section.

(iii) Integrated agreement. An issuer may not provide provisions of the agreement or fee information to the Bureau in the form of change-in-terms notices or riders (other than the optional fee information addenda described in paragraph (b)(6)(ii) of this section). Changes in provisions or fee information must be integrated into the text of the agreement, or the optional fee information addenda, as appropriate.

(c) Posting of agreements offered to the general public.

(1) An issuer must post and maintain on its publicly available Web site any prepaid account agreements offered to the general public that the issuer is required to submit to the Bureau under paragraph (b) of this section.

(2) Agreements posted pursuant to this paragraph (c) must conform to the form and content requirements for agreements submitted to the Bureau set forth in paragraph (b)(6) of this section.

(3) The issuer must post and update the agreements posted on its Web site pursuant to this paragraph (c) as frequently as the issuer is required to submit new or amended agreements to the Bureau pursuant to paragraph (b)(2)(i) of this section.

(4) Agreements posted pursuant to this paragraph (c) may be posted in any electronic format that is readily usable by the general public. Agreements must be placed in a location that is prominent and readily accessible to the public and must be accessible without submission of personally identifiable information.

(d) Agreements for all open accounts—

(1) Availability of an individual consumer's prepaid account agreement. With respect to any open prepaid account, an issuer must either:

(i) Post and maintain the consumer's agreement on its Web site; or

(ii) Promptly provide a copy of the consumer's agreement to the consumer upon the consumer's request. If the issuer makes an agreement available upon request, the issuer must provide the consumer with the ability to request a copy of the agreement by telephone. The issuer must send to the consumer a copy of the consumer's prepaid account agreement no later than five business days after the issuer receives the consumer's request.

(2) Form and content of agreements.

(i) Except as provided in this paragraph (d), agreements posted on the issuer's Web site pursuant to paragraph (d)(1)(i) of this section or sent to the consumer upon the consumer's request pursuant to paragraph (d)(1)(ii) of this section must conform to the form and content requirements for agreements submitted to the Bureau as set forth in paragraph (b)(6) of this section.

(ii) If the issuer posts an agreement on its Web site under paragraph (d)(1)(i) of this section, the agreement may be posted in any electronic format that is readily usable by the general public and must be placed in a location that is prominent and readily accessible to the consumer.

(iii) Agreements posted or otherwise provided pursuant to this paragraph (d) may contain personally identifiable information relating to the consumer, such as name, address, telephone number, or account number, provided that the issuer takes appropriate measures to make the agreement accessible only to the consumer or other authorized persons.

(iv) Agreements posted or otherwise provided pursuant to this paragraph (d) must set forth the specific provisions and fee information applicable to the particular consumer.

(v) Agreements posted pursuant to paragraph (d)(1)(i) of this section must be updated as frequently as the issuer is required to submit amended agreements to the Bureau pursuant to paragraph (b)(2)(i) of this section. Agreements provided upon consumer request pursuant to paragraph (d)(1)(ii) of this section must be accurate as of the date the agreement is sent to the consumer.

(vi) Agreements provided upon consumer request pursuant to paragraph (d)(1)(ii) of this section must be provided by the issuer in paper form, unless the consumer agrees to receive the agreement electronically.

(e) E-Sign Act requirements. Except as otherwise provided in this section, issuers may provide prepaid account agreements in electronic form under paragraphs (c) and (d) of this section without regard to the consumer notice and consent requirements of section 101(c) of the Electronic Signatures in Global and National Commerce Act (E-Sign Act) (15 U.S.C. 7001 et seq.).

(f) Initial submission date. The requirements of this section apply to prepaid accounts beginning on April 1, 2019. An issuer must submit to the Bureau no later than May 1, 2019 all prepaid account agreements it offers as of April 1, 2019.

§ 1005.20 Requirements for Gift Cards and Gift Certificates

(a) Definitions. For purposes of this section, except as excluded under paragraph (b), the following definitions apply:

(1) "Gift certificate" means a card, code, or other device that is:

(i) Issued on a prepaid basis primarily for personal, family, or household purposes to a consumer in a specified amount that may not be increased or reloaded in exchange for payment; and

(ii) Redeemable upon presentation at a single merchant or an affiliated group of merchants for goods or services.

(2) "Store gift card" means a card, code, or other device that is:

(i) Issued on a prepaid basis primarily for personal, family, or household purposes to a consumer in a specified amount, whether or not that amount may be increased or reloaded, in exchange for payment; and

(ii) Redeemable upon presentation at a single merchant or an affiliated group of merchants for goods or services.

(3) "General-use prepaid card" means a card, code, or other device that is:

(i) Issued on a prepaid basis primarily for personal, family, or household purposes to a consumer in a specified amount, whether or not that amount may be increased or reloaded, in exchange for payment; and

(ii) Redeemable upon presentation at multiple, unaffiliated merchants for goods or services, or usable at automated teller machines.

(4) "Loyalty, award, or promotional gift card" means a card, code, or other device that:

(i) Is issued on a prepaid basis primarily for personal, family, or household purposes to a consumer in connection with a loyalty, award, or promotional program;

(ii) Is redeemable upon presentation at one or more merchants for goods or services, or usable at automated teller machines; and

(iii) Sets forth the following disclosures, as applicable:

(A) A statement indicating that the card, code, or other device is issued for loyalty, award, or promotional purposes, which must be included on the front of the card, code, or other device;

(B) The expiration date for the underlying funds, which must be included on the front of the card, code, or other device;

(C) The amount of any fees that may be imposed in connection with the card, code, or other device, and the conditions under which they may be imposed, which must be provided on or with the card, code, or other device; and

(D) A toll-free telephone number and, if one is maintained, a Web site, that a consumer may use to obtain fee information, which must be included on the card, code, or other device.

(5) **Dormancy or inactivity fee.** The terms "dormancy fee" and "inactivity fee" mean a fee for non-use of or inactivity on a gift certificate, store gift card, or general-use prepaid card.

(6) **Service fee.** The term "service fee" means a periodic fee for holding or use of a gift certificate, store gift card, or general-use prepaid card. A periodic fee includes any fee that may be imposed on a gift certificate, store gift card, or general-use prepaid card from time to time for holding or using the certificate or card.

(7) **Activity.** The term "activity" means any action that results in an increase or decrease of the funds underlying a certificate or card, other than the imposition of a fee, or an adjustment due to an error or a reversal of a prior transaction.

(b) **Exclusions.** The terms "gift certificate," "store gift card," and "general-use prepaid card", as defined in paragraph (a) of this section, do not include any card, code, or other device that is:

(1) Useable solely for telephone services;

(2) Reloadable and not marketed or labeled as a gift card or gift certificate. For purposes of this paragraph (b)(2), the term "reloadable" includes a temporary non-reloadable card issued solely in connection with a reloadable card, code, or other device;

(3) A loyalty, award, or promotional gift card;

(4) Not marketed to the general public;

(5) Issued in paper form only; or

(6) Redeemable solely for admission to events or venues at a particular location or group of affiliated locations, or to obtain goods or services in conjunction with admission to such events or venues, either at the event or venue or at specific locations affiliated with and in geographic proximity to the event or venue.

(c) **Form of disclosures**

(1) Clear and conspicuous. Disclosures made under this section must be clear and conspicuous. The disclosures may contain commonly accepted or readily understandable abbreviations or symbols.

(2) Format. Disclosures made under this section generally must be provided to the consumer in written or electronic form. Except for the disclosures in paragraphs (c)(3) and (h)(2) of this section, written and electronic disclosures made under this section must be in a retainable form. Only disclosures provided under paragraphs (c)(3) and (h)(2) may be given orally.

(3) Disclosures prior to purchase. Before a gift certificate, store gift card, or general-use prepaid card is purchased, a person that issues or sells such certificate or card must disclose to the consumer the information required by paragraphs (d)(2), (e)(3), and (f)(1) of this section. The fees and terms and conditions of expiration that are required to be disclosed prior to purchase may not be changed after purchase.

(4) Disclosures on the certificate or card. Disclosures required by paragraphs (a)(4)(iii), (d)(2), (e)(3), and (f)(2) of this section must be made on the certificate or card, or in the case of a loyalty, award, or promotional gift card, on the card, code, or other device. A disclosure made in an accompanying terms and conditions document, on packaging surrounding a certificate or card, or on a sticker or other label affixed to the certificate or card does not constitute a disclosure on the certificate or card. For an electronic certificate or card, disclosures must be provided electronically on the certificate or card provided to the consumer. An issuer that provides a code or confirmation to a consumer orally must provide to the consumer a written or electronic copy of the code or confirmation promptly, and the applicable disclosures must be provided on the written copy of the code or confirmation.

(d) Prohibition on imposition of fees or charges. No person may impose a dormancy, inactivity, or service fee with respect to a gift certificate, store gift card, or general-use prepaid card, unless:

(1) There has been no activity with respect to the certificate or card, in the one-year period ending on the date on which the fee is imposed;

(2) The following are stated, as applicable, clearly and conspicuously on the gift certificate, store gift card, or general-use prepaid card:

(i) The amount of any dormancy, inactivity, or service fee that may be charged;

(ii) How often such fee may be assessed; and

(iii) That such fee may be assessed for inactivity; and

(3) Not more than one dormancy, inactivity, or service fee is imposed in any given calendar month.

(e) Prohibition on sale of gift certificates or cards with expiration dates. No person may sell or issue a gift certificate, store gift card, or general-use prepaid card with an expiration date, unless:

(1) The person has established policies and procedures to provide consumers with a reasonable opportunity to purchase a certificate or card with at least five years remaining until the certificate or card expiration date;

(2) The expiration date for the underlying funds is at least the later of:

(i) Five years after the date the gift certificate was initially issued, or the date on which funds were last loaded to a store gift card or general-use prepaid card; or

(ii) The certificate or card expiration date, if any;

(3) The following disclosures are provided on the certificate or card, as applicable:

(i) The expiration date for the underlying funds or, if the underlying funds do not expire, that fact;

(ii) A toll-free telephone number and, if one is maintained, a Web site that a consumer may use to obtain a replacement certificate or card after the certificate or card expires if the underlying funds may be available; and

(iii) Except where a non-reloadable certificate or card bears an expiration date that is at least seven years from the date of manufacture, a statement, disclosed with equal prominence and in close proximity to the certificate or card expiration date, that:

(A) The certificate or card expires, but the underlying funds either do not expire or expire later than the certificate or card, and;

(B) The consumer may contact the issuer for a replacement card; and

(4) No fee or charge is imposed on the cardholder for replacing the gift certificate, store gift card, or general-use prepaid card or for providing the certificate or card holder with the remaining balance in some other manner prior to the funds expiration date, unless such certificate or card has been lost or stolen.

(f) Additional disclosure requirements for gift certificates or cards. The following disclosures must be provided in connection with a gift certificate, store gift card, or general-use prepaid card, as applicable:

(1) Fee disclosures. For each type of fee that may be imposed in connection with the certificate or card (other than a dormancy, inactivity, or service fee subject to the disclosure requirements under paragraph (d)(2) of this section), the following information must be provided on or with the certificate or card:

(i) The type of fee;

(ii) The amount of the fee (or an explanation of how the fee will be determined); and

(iii) The conditions under which the fee may be imposed.

(2) Telephone number for fee information. A toll-free telephone number and, if one is maintained, a Web site, that a consumer may use to obtain information about fees described in paragraphs (d)(2) and (f)(1) of this section must be disclosed on the certificate or card.

(g) Compliance dates.

(1) Effective date for gift certificates, store gift cards, and general-use prepaid cards. Except as provided in paragraph (h) of this section, the requirements of this section apply to any gift certificate, store gift card, or general-use prepaid card sold to a consumer on or after August 22, 2010, or provided to a consumer as a replacement for such certificate or card.

(2) Effective date for loyalty, award, or promotional gift cards. The requirements in paragraph (a)(4)(iii) of this section apply to any card, code, or other device provided to a consumer in connection with a loyalty, award, or promotional program if the period of eligibility for such program began on or after August 22, 2010.

(h) Temporary exemption.

(1) Delayed mandatory compliance date. For any gift certificate, store gift card, or general-use prepaid card produced prior to April 1, 2010, the mandatory compliance date of the requirements of paragraphs (c)(3), (d)(2), (e)(1), (e)(3), and (f) of this section is January 31, 2011, provided that an issuer of such certificate or card:

(i) Complies with all other provisions of this section;

(ii) Does not impose an expiration date with respect to the funds underlying such certificate or card;

(iii) At the consumer's request, replaces such certificate or card if it has funds remaining at no cost to the consumer; and

(iv) Satisfies the requirements of paragraph (h)(2) of this section.

(2) Additional disclosures. Issuers relying on the delayed effective date in § 1005.20(h)(1) must disclose through in-store signage, messages during customer service calls, Web sites, and general advertising, that:

(i) The underlying funds of such certificate or card do not expire;

(ii) Consumers holding such certificate or card have a right to a free replacement certificate or card, which must be accompanied by the packaging and materials typically associated with such certificate or card; and

(iii) Any dormancy, inactivity, or service fee for such certificate or card that might otherwise be charged will not be charged if such fees do not comply with section 916 of the Act.

(3) Expiration of additional disclosure requirements. The disclosures in paragraph (h)(2) of this section:

(i) Are not required to be provided on or after January 31, 2011, with respect to in-store signage and general advertising.

(ii) Are not required to be provided on or after January 31, 2013, with respect to messages during customer service calls and Web sites.

SUBPART B. REQUIREMENTS FOR REMITTANCE TRANSFERS

12 C.F.R. § 1005.30. Remittance Transfer Definitions

Except as otherwise provided for purposes of this subpart, the following definitions apply:

(a) "Agent" means an agent, authorized delegate, or person affiliated with a remittance transfer provider, as defined under State or other applicable law, when such agent, authorized delegate, or affiliate acts for that remittance transfer provider.

(b) "Business day" means any day on which the offices of a remittance transfer provider are open to the public for carrying on substantially all business functions.

(c) "Designated recipient" means any person specified by the sender as the authorized recipient of a remittance transfer to be received at a location in a foreign country.

(d) "Preauthorized remittance transfer" means a remittance transfer authorized in advance to recur at substantially regular intervals.

(e) Remittance transfer—

(1) General definition. A "remittance transfer" means the electronic transfer of funds requested by a sender to a designated recipient that is sent by a remittance transfer provider. The term applies regardless of whether the sender holds an account with the remittance transfer provider, and regardless of whether the transaction is also an electronic fund transfer, as defined in § 1005.3(b).

(2) Exclusions from coverage. The term "remittance transfer" does not include:

(i) Small value transactions. Transfer amounts, as described in § 1005.31(b)(1)(i), of $15 or less.

(ii) Securities and commodities transfers. Any transfer that is excluded from the definition of electronic fund transfer under § 1005.3(c)(4).

(f) Remittance transfer provider—

(1) General definition. "Remittance transfer provider" or "provider" means any person that provides remittance transfers for a consumer in the normal course of its business, regardless of whether the consumer holds an account with such person.

(2) Normal course of business—

(i) Safe harbor. For purposes of paragraph (f)(1) of this section, a person is deemed not to be providing remittance transfers for a consumer in the normal course of its business if the person:

(A) Provided 100 or fewer remittance transfers in the previous calendar year; and

(B) Provides 100 or fewer remittance transfers in the current calendar year.

(ii) Transition period. If a person that provided 100 or fewer remittance transfers in the previous calendar year provides more than 100 remittance transfers in the current calendar year, and if that person is then providing remittance transfers for a consumer in the normal course of its business pursuant to paragraph (f)(1) of this section, the person has a reasonable period of time, not to exceed six months, to begin complying with this subpart. Compliance with this subpart will not be required for any remittance transfers for which payment is made during that reasonable period of time.

(g) "Sender" means a consumer in a State who primarily for personal, family, or household purposes requests a remittance transfer provider to send a remittance transfer to a designated recipient.

(h) Third-party fees. (1) "Covered third-party fees." The term "covered third-party fees" means any fees imposed on the remittance transfer by a person other than the remittance transfer provider except for fees described in paragraph (h)(2) of this section.

(2) "Non-covered third-party fees." The term "non-covered third-party fees" means any fees imposed by the designated recipient's institution for receiving a remittance transfer into an account except if the institution acts as an agent of the remittance transfer provider.

12 C.F.R. § 1005.31. Disclosures

(a) General form of disclosures—

(1) Clear and conspicuous. Disclosures required by this subpart or permitted by paragraph (b)(1)(viii) of this section or § 1005.33(h)(3) must be clear and conspicuous. Disclosures required by this subpart or permitted by paragraph (b)(1)(viii) of this section or § 1005.33(h)(3) may contain commonly accepted or readily understandable abbreviations or symbols.

(2) Written and electronic disclosures. Disclosures required by this subpart generally must be provided to the sender in writing. Disclosures required by paragraph (b)(1) of this section may be provided electronically, if the sender electronically requests the remittance transfer provider to send the remittance transfer. Written and electronic disclosures required by this subpart generally must be made in a retainable form. Disclosures provided via mobile application or text message, to the extent permitted by paragraph (a)(5) of this section, need not be retainable.

(3) Disclosures for oral telephone transactions. The information required by paragraph (b)(1) of this section may be disclosed orally if:

(i) The transaction is conducted orally and entirely by telephone;

(ii) The remittance transfer provider complies with the requirements of paragraph (g)(2) of this section;

(iii) The provider discloses orally a statement about the rights of the sender regarding cancellation required by paragraph (b)(2)(iv) of this section pursuant to the timing requirements in paragraph (e)(1) of this section; and

(iv) The provider discloses orally, as each is applicable, the information required by paragraph (b)(2)(vii) of this section and the information required by § 1005.36(d)(1)(i)(A), with respect to transfers subject to § 1005.36(d)(2)(ii), pursuant to the timing requirements in paragraph (e)(1) of this section.

(4) Oral disclosures for certain error resolution notices. The information required by § 1005.33(c)(1) may be disclosed orally if:

(i) The remittance transfer provider determines that an error occurred as described by the sender; and

(ii) The remittance transfer provider complies with the requirements of paragraph (g)(2) of this section.

(5) Disclosures for mobile application or text message transactions. The information required by paragraph (b)(1) of this section may be disclosed orally or via mobile application or text message if:

(i) The transaction is conducted entirely by telephone via mobile application or text message;

(ii) The remittance transfer provider complies with the requirements of paragraph (g)(2) of this section;

(iii) The provider discloses orally or via mobile application or text message a statement about the rights of the sender regarding cancellation required by paragraph (b)(2)(iv) of this section pursuant to the timing requirements in paragraph (e)(1) of this section; and

(iv) The provider discloses orally or via mobile application or text message, as each is applicable, the information required by paragraph (b)(2)(vii) of this section and the information required by § 1005.36(d)(1)(i)(A), with respect to transfers subject to § 1005.36(d)(2)(ii), pursuant to the timing requirements in paragraph (e)(1) of this section.

(b) Disclosure requirements—

(1) Pre-payment disclosure. A remittance transfer provider must disclose to a sender, as applicable:

(i) The amount that will be transferred to the designated recipient, in the currency in which the remittance transfer is funded, using the term "Transfer Amount" or a substantially similar term;

(ii) Any fees imposed and any taxes collected on the remittance transfer by the provider, in the currency in which the remittance transfer is funded, using the terms "Transfer Fees" for fees and "Transfer Taxes" for taxes, or substantially similar terms;

(iii) The total amount of the transaction, which is the sum of paragraphs (b)(1)(i) and (ii) of this section, in the currency in which the remittance transfer is funded, using the term "Total" or a substantially similar term;

(iv) The exchange rate used by the provider for the remittance transfer, rounded consistently for each currency to no fewer than two decimal places and no more than four decimal places, using the term "Exchange Rate" or a substantially similar term;

(v) The amount in paragraph (b)(1)(i) of this section, in the currency in which the funds will be received by the designated recipient, but only if covered third-party fees are imposed under paragraph (b)(1)(vi) of this section, using the term "Transfer Amount" or a substantially similar term. The exchange rate used to calculate this amount is the exchange rate in paragraph (b)(1)(iv) of this section, including an estimated exchange rate to the extent permitted by § 1005.32, prior to any rounding of the exchange rate;

(vi) Any covered third-party fees, in the currency in which the funds will be received by the designated recipient, using the term "Other Fees," or a substantially similar term. The exchange rate used to calculate any covered third-party fees is the exchange rate in paragraph (b)(1)(iv) of this section, including an estimated exchange rate to the extent permitted by § 1005.32, prior to any rounding of the exchange rate;

(vii) The amount that will be received by the designated recipient, in the currency in which the funds will be received, using the term "Total to Recipient" or a substantially similar term except that this amount shall not include non-covered third party fees or taxes collected on the remittance transfer by a person other than the provider regardless of whether such fees or taxes are disclosed pursuant to paragraph (b)(1)(viii) of this section. The exchange rate used to calculate this amount is the exchange rate in paragraph (b)(1)(iv) of this section, including an estimated exchange rate to the extent permitted by § 1005.32, prior to any rounding of the exchange rate.

(viii) A statement indicating that non-covered third-party fees or taxes collected on the remittance transfer by a person other than the provider may apply to the remittance transfer and result in the designated recipient receiving less than the amount disclosed pursuant to paragraph (b)(1)(vii) of this section. A provider may only include this statement to the extent that such fees or taxes do or may apply to the transfer, using the language set forth in Model Forms A-30(a) through (c) of Appendix A to this part, as appropriate, or substantially similar language. In this statement, a provider also may, but is not required, to disclose any applicable non-covered third-party fees or taxes collected by a person other than the provider. Any such figure must be disclosed in the currency in which the funds will be received, using the language set forth in Model Forms A-30(b) through (d) of Appendix A to this part, as appropriate, or substantially similar language. The exchange rate used to calculate any disclosed non-covered third-party fees or taxes collected on the remittance transfer by a person other than the provider is the exchange rate in paragraph (b)(1)(iv) of this section, including an estimated exchange rate to the extent permitted by § 1005.32, prior to any rounding of the exchange rate:

(2) Receipt. A remittance transfer provider must disclose to a sender, as applicable:

(i) The disclosures described in paragraphs (b)(1)(i) through (viii) of this section;

(ii) The date in the foreign country on which funds will be available to the designated recipient, using the term "Date Available" or a substantially similar term. A provider may provide a statement that funds may be available to the designated recipient earlier than the date disclosed, using the term "may be available sooner" or a substantially similar term;

(iii) The name and, if provided by the sender, the telephone number and/or address of the designated recipient, using the term "Recipient" or a substantially similar term;

(iv) A statement about the rights of the sender regarding the resolution of errors and cancellation, using language set forth in Model Form A-37 of Appendix A to this part or substantially similar language. For any remittance transfer scheduled by the sender at least three business days before the date of the transfer, the statement about the rights of the sender regarding cancellation must instead reflect the requirements of § 1005.36(c);

(v) The name, telephone number(s), and Web site of the remittance transfer provider;

(vi) A statement that the sender can contact the State agency that licenses or charters the remittance transfer provider with respect to the remittance transfer and the Consumer Financial Protection Bureau for questions or complaints about the remittance transfer provider, using language set forth in Model Form A-37 of Appendix A to this part or substantially similar language. The disclosure must provide the name, telephone number(s), and Web site of the State agency that licenses or charters the remittance transfer provider with respect to the remittance transfer and the name, toll-free telephone number(s), and Web site of the Consumer Financial Protection Bureau; and

(vii) For any remittance transfer scheduled by the sender at least three business days before the date of the transfer, or the first transfer in a series of preauthorized remittance transfers, the date the remittance transfer provider will make or made the remittance transfer, using the term "Transfer Date," or a substantially similar term.

(3) Combined disclosure—

(i) In general. As an alternative to providing the disclosures described in paragraph (b)(1) and (2) of this section, a remittance transfer provider may provide the disclosures described in paragraph (b)(2) of this section, as applicable, in a single disclosure pursuant to the timing requirements in paragraph (e)(1) of this section. Except as provided in paragraph (b)(3)(ii) of this section, if the remittance transfer provider provides the combined disclosure and the sender completes the transfer, the remittance transfer provider must provide the sender with proof of payment when payment is made for the remittance transfer. The proof of payment must be clear and conspicuous, provided in writing or electronically, and provided in a retainable form.

(ii) Transfers scheduled before the date of transfer. If the disclosure described in paragraph (b)(3)(i) of this section is provided in accordance with § 1005.36(a)(1)(i) and payment is not processed by the remittance transfer provider at the time the remittance transfer is scheduled, a remittance transfer provider may provide confirmation that the transaction has been scheduled in lieu of the proof of payment otherwise required by paragraph (b)(3)(i) of this section. The confirmation of scheduling must be clear and conspicuous, provided in writing or electronically, and provided in a retainable form.

(4) Long form error resolution and cancellation notice. Upon the sender's request, a remittance transfer provider must promptly provide to the sender a notice describing the sender's error resolution and cancellation rights, using language set forth in Model Form A-36 of Appendix A to this part or substantially similar language. For any remittance transfer scheduled by the sender at least three business days before the date of the transfer, the description of the rights of the sender regarding cancellation must instead reflect the requirements of § 1005.36(c).

(c) Specific format requirements—

(1) Grouping. The information required by paragraphs (b)(1)(i), (ii), and (iii) of this section generally must be grouped together. The information required by paragraphs (b)(1)(v), (vi), (vii), and (viii) of this section generally must be grouped together. Disclosures provided via mobile application or text message, to the extent permitted by paragraph (a)(5) of this section, generally need not comply with the grouping requirements of this paragraph, however information required or permitted by paragraph (b)(1)(viii) of this section must be grouped with information required by paragraph (b)(1)(vii) of this section.

(2) Proximity. The information required by paragraph (b)(1)(iv) of this section generally must be disclosed in close proximity to the other information required by paragraph (b)(1) of this section. The information required by paragraph (b)(2)(iv) of this section generally must be disclosed in close proximity to the other information required by paragraph (b)(2) of this section. The information required or permitted by paragraph (b)(1)(viii) must be in close proximity to the information required by paragraph (b)(1)(vii) of this section. Disclosures provided via mobile application or text message, to the extent permitted by paragraph (a)(5) of this section, generally need not comply with the proximity requirements of this paragraph, however information required or permitted by paragraph (b)(1)(viii) of this section must follow the information required by paragraph (b)(1)(vii) of this section.

(3) Prominence and size. Written disclosures required by this subpart or permitted by paragraph (b)(1)(viii) of this section must be provided on the front of the page on which the disclosure is printed. Disclosures required by this subpart or permitted by paragraph (b)(1)(viii) of this section that are provided in writing or electronically must be in a minimum eight-point font, except for disclosures provided via mobile application or text message, to the extent permitted by paragraph (a)(5) of this section. Disclosures required by paragraph (b) of this section or permitted by paragraph (b)(1)(viii) of this section that are provided in writing or electronically must be in equal prominence to each other.

(4) Segregation. Except for disclosures provided via mobile application or text message, to the extent permitted by paragraph (a)(5) of this section, disclosures required by this subpart that are provided in writing or electronically must be segregated from everything else and must contain only information that is directly related to the disclosures required under this subpart.

(d) Estimates. Estimated disclosures may be provided to the extent permitted by § 1005.32. Estimated disclosures must be described using the term "Estimated" or a substantially similar term in close proximity to the estimated term or terms.

(e) Timing.

(1) Except as provided in § 1005.36(a), a pre-payment disclosure required by paragraph (b)(1) of this section or a combined disclosure required by paragraph (b)(3) of this section must be provided to the sender when the sender requests the remittance transfer, but prior to payment for the transfer.

(2) Except as provided in § 1005.36(a), a receipt required by paragraph (b)(2) of this section generally must be provided to the sender when payment is made for the remittance transfer. If a transaction is conducted entirely by telephone, a receipt required by paragraph (b)(2) of this section may be mailed or delivered to the sender no later than one business day after the date on which payment is made for the remittance transfer. If a transaction is conducted entirely by telephone and involves the transfer of funds from the sender's account held by the provider, the receipt required by paragraph (b)(2) of this section may be provided on or with the next regularly scheduled periodic statement for that account or within 30 days after payment is made for the remittance transfer if a periodic statement is not provided. The statement about the rights of the sender regarding cancellation required by paragraph (b)(2)(iv) of this section may, but need not, be disclosed pursuant to the timing requirements of this paragraph if a provider discloses this information pursuant to paragraphs (a)(3)(iii) or (a)(5)(iii) of this section.

(f) Accurate when payment is made. Except as provided in § 1005.36(b), disclosures required by this section or permitted by paragraph (b)(1)(viii) of this section must be accurate when a sender makes payment for the remittance transfer, except to the extent estimates are permitted by § 1005.32.

(g) Foreign language disclosures—

(1) General. Except as provided in paragraph (g)(2) of this section, disclosures required by this subpart or permitted by paragraph (b)(1)(viii) of this section or § 1005.33(h)(3) must be made in English and, if applicable, either in:

(i) Each of the foreign languages principally used by the remittance transfer provider to advertise, solicit, or market remittance transfer services, either orally, in writing, or electronically, at the office in which a sender conducts a transaction or asserts an error; or

(ii) The foreign language primarily used by the sender with the remittance transfer provider to conduct the transaction (or for written or electronic disclosures made pursuant to § 1005.33, in the foreign language primarily used by the sender with the remittance transfer provider to assert the error), provided that such foreign language is principally used by the remittance transfer provider to advertise, solicit, or market remittance transfer services, either orally, in writing, or electronically, at the office in which a sender conducts a transaction or asserts an error, respectively.

(2) Oral, mobile application, or text message disclosures. Disclosures provided orally for transactions conducted orally and entirely by telephone under paragraph (a)(3) of this section or orally or via mobile application or text message for transactions conducted via mobile application or text message under paragraph (a)(5) of this section shall be made in the language primarily used by the sender with the remittance transfer provider to conduct the transaction. Disclosures provided orally under paragraph (a)(4) of this section for error resolution purposes shall be made in the language primarily used by the sender with the remittance transfer provider to assert the error.

12 C.F.R. § 1005.32. Estimates

(a) Temporary exception for insured institutions—

(1) General. For disclosures described in §§ 1005.31(b)(1) through (3) and 1005.36(a)(1) and (2), estimates may be provided in accordance with paragraph (c) of this section for the amounts required to be disclosed under § 1005.31(b)(1)(iv) through (vii), if:

(i) A remittance transfer provider cannot determine the exact amounts for reasons beyond its control;

(ii) A remittance transfer provider is an insured institution; and

(iii) The remittance transfer is sent from the sender's account with the institution; provided however, for the purposes of this paragraph, a sender's account does not include a prepaid account, unless the prepaid account is a payroll card account or a government benefit account.

(2) Sunset date. Paragraph (a)(1) of this section expires on July 21, 2020.

(3) Insured institution. For purposes of this section, the term "insured institution" means insured depository institutions (which includes uninsured U.S. branches and agencies of foreign depository institutions) as defined in section 3 of the Federal Deposit Insurance Act (12 U.S.C. 1813), and insured credit unions as defined in section 101 of the Federal Credit Union Act (12 U.S.C. 1752).

(b) Permanent exceptions—

(1) Permanent exception for transfers to certain countries.

(i) General. For disclosures described in §§ 1005.31(b)(1) through (b)(3) and 1005.36(a)(1) and (a)(2), estimates may be provided for transfers to certain countries in accordance with paragraph (c) of this section for the amounts required to be disclosed under § 1005.31(b)(1)(iv) through (b)(1)(vii), if a remittance transfer provider cannot determine the exact amounts when the disclosure is required because:

(A) The laws of the recipient country do not permit such a determination, or

(B) The method by which transactions are made in the recipient country does not permit such determination.

(ii) Safe harbor. A remittance transfer provider may rely on the list of countries published by the Bureau to determine whether estimates may be provided under paragraph (b)(1) of this section, unless the provider has information that a country's laws or the method by which transactions are conducted in that country permits a determination of the exact disclosure amount.

(2) Permanent exception for transfers scheduled before the date of transfer.

(i) Except as provided in paragraph (b)(2)(ii) of this section, for disclosures described in §§ 1005.36(a)(1)(i) and (a)(2)(i), estimates may be provided in accordance with paragraph (d) of this section for the amounts to be disclosed under §§ 1005.31(b)(1)(iv) through (vii) if the remittance transfer is scheduled by a sender five or more business days before the date of the transfer. In addition, if, at the time the sender schedules such a transfer, the provider agrees to a sender's request to fix the amount to be transferred in the currency in which the remittance transfer will be received and not the currency in which it is funded, estimates may also be provided for the amounts to be disclosed under §§ 1005.31(b)(1)(i) through (iii), except as provided in paragraph (b)(2)(iii) of this section.

(ii) Covered third-party fees described in § 1005.31(b)(1)(vi) may be estimated under paragraph (b)(2)(i) of this section only if the exchange rate is also estimated under paragraph (b)(2)(i) and the estimated exchange rate affects the amount of such fees.

(iii) Fees and taxes described in § 1005.31(b)(1)(ii) may be estimated under paragraph (b)(2)(i) of this section only if the amount that will be transferred in the currency in which it is funded is also estimated under paragraph (b)(2)(i) of this section, and the estimated amount affects the amount of such fees and taxes.

(3) Permanent exception for optional disclosure of non-covered third-party fees and taxes collected by a person other than the provider. For disclosures described in §§ 1005.31(b)(1) through (3) and 1005.36(a)(1) and (2), estimates may be provided for applicable non-covered third-party fees and taxes collected on the remittance transfer by a person other than the provider, which are permitted to be disclosed under § 1005.31(b)(1)(viii), provided such estimates are based on reasonable sources of information.

(c) Bases for estimates generally. Estimates provided pursuant to the exceptions in paragraph (a) or (b)(1) of this section must be based on the below-listed approach or approaches, except as otherwise permitted by this paragraph. If a remittance transfer provider bases an estimate on an approach that is not listed in this paragraph, the provider is deemed to be in compliance with this paragraph so long as the designated recipient receives the same, or greater, amount of funds than the remittance transfer provider disclosed under § 1005.31(b)(1)(vii).

(1) Exchange rate. In disclosing the exchange rate as required under § 1005.31(b)(1)(iv), an estimate must be based on one of the following:

(i) For remittance transfers sent via international ACH that qualify for the exception in paragraph (b)(1)(ii) of this section, the most recent exchange rate set by the recipient country's central bank or other governmental authority and reported by a Federal Reserve Bank;

(ii) The most recent publicly available wholesale exchange rate and, if applicable, any spread that the remittance transfer provider or its correspondent typically applies to such a wholesale rate for remittance transfers for that currency; or

(iii) The most recent exchange rate offered or used by the person making funds available directly to the designated recipient or by the person setting the exchange rate.

(2) Transfer amount in the currency in which the funds will be received by the designated recipient. In disclosing the transfer amount in the currency in which the funds will be received by the designated recipient, as required under § 1005.31(b)(1)(v), an estimate must be based on the estimated exchange rate provided in accordance with paragraph (c)(1) of this section, prior to any rounding of the estimated exchange rate.

(3) Covered third-party fees.

(i) Imposed as percentage of amount transferred. In disclosing covered third-party fees as described under § 1005.31(b)(1)(vi), that are a percentage of the amount transferred to the designated recipient, an estimated exchange rate must be based on the estimated exchange rate provided in accordance with paragraph (c)(1) of this section, prior to any rounding of the estimated exchange rate.

(ii) Imposed by intermediary or final institution. In disclosing covered third-party fees pursuant to § 1005.31(b)(1)(vi), an estimate must be based on one of the following:

(A) The remittance transfer provider's most recent remittance transfer to the designated recipient's institution, or

(B) A representative transmittal route identified by the remittance transfer provider.

(4) Amount of currency that will be received by the designated recipient. In disclosing the amount of currency that will be received by the designated recipient as required under § 1005.31(b)(1)(vii), an estimate must be based on the information provided in accordance with paragraphs (c)(1) through (3) of this section, as applicable.

(d) Bases for estimates for transfers scheduled before the date of transfer. Estimates provided pursuant to paragraph (b)(2) of this section must be based on the exchange rate or, where applicable, the estimated exchange rate based on an estimation methodology permitted under paragraph (c) of this section that the provider would have used or did use that day in providing disclosures to a sender requesting such a remittance transfer to be made on the same day. If, in accordance with this paragraph, a remittance transfer provider uses a basis described in paragraph (c) of this section but not listed in paragraph (c)(1) of this section, the provider is deemed to be in compliance with this paragraph regardless of the amount received by the designated recipient, so long as the estimation methodology is the same that the provider would have used or did use in providing disclosures to a sender requesting such a remittance transfer to be made on the same day.

12 C.F.R. § 1005.33. Procedures for Resolving Errors

(a) Definition of error.

(1) Types of transfers or inquiries covered. For purposes of this section, the term error means:

(i) An incorrect amount paid by a sender in connection with a remittance transfer unless the disclosure stated an estimate of the amount paid by a sender in accordance with § 1005.32(b)(2) and the difference results from application of the actual exchange rate, fees, and taxes, rather than any estimated amount;

(ii) A computational or bookkeeping error made by the remittance transfer provider relating to a remittance transfer;

(iii) The failure to make available to a designated recipient the amount of currency disclosed pursuant to § 1005.31(b)(1)(vii) and stated in the disclosure provided to the sender under § 1005.31(b)(2) or (3) for the remittance transfer, unless:

(A) The disclosure stated an estimate of the amount to be received in accordance with § 1005.32(a), (b)(1) or (b)(2) and the difference results from application of the actual exchange rate, fees, and taxes, rather than any estimated amounts; or

(B) The failure resulted from extraordinary circumstances outside the remittance transfer provider's control that could not have been reasonably anticipated; or

(C) The difference results from the application of non-covered third-party fees or taxes collected on the remittance transfer by a person other than the provider and the provider provided the disclosure required by § 1005.31(b)(1)(viii).

(iv) The failure to make funds available to a designated recipient by the date of availability stated in the disclosure provided to the sender under § 1005.31(b)(2) or (3) for the remittance transfer, unless the failure to make the funds available resulted from:

(A) Extraordinary circumstances outside the remittance transfer provider's control that could not have been reasonably anticipated;

(B) Delays related to a necessary investigation or other special action by the remittance transfer provider or a third party as required by the provider's fraud screening procedures or in accordance with the Bank Secrecy Act, 31 U.S.C. 5311 et seq., Office of Foreign Assets Control requirements, or similar laws or requirements;

(C) The remittance transfer being made with fraudulent intent by the sender or any person acting in concert with the sender; or

(D) The sender having provided the remittance transfer provider an incorrect account number or recipient institution identifier for the designated recipient's account or institution, provided that the remittance transfer provider meets the conditions set forth in paragraph (h) of this section;

(v) The sender's request for documentation required by § 1005.31 or for additional information or clarification concerning a remittance transfer, including a request a sender makes to determine whether an error exists under paragraphs (a)(1)(i) through (iv) of this section.

(2) Types of transfers or inquiries not covered. The term error does not include:

(i) An inquiry about the status of a remittance transfer, except where the funds from the transfer were not made available to a designated recipient by the disclosed date of availability as described in paragraph (a)(1)(iv) of this section;

(ii) A request for information for tax or other recordkeeping purposes;

(iii) A change requested by the designated recipient; or

(iv) A change in the amount or type of currency received by the designated recipient from the amount or type of currency stated in the disclosure provided to the sender under § 1005.31(b)(2) or (3) if the remittance transfer provider relied on information provided by the sender as permitted under § 1005.31 in making such disclosure.

(b) Notice of error from sender.

(1) Timing; contents. A remittance transfer provider shall comply with the requirements of this section with respect to any oral or written notice of error from a sender that:

(i) Is received by the remittance transfer provider no later than 180 days after the disclosed date of availability of the remittance transfer;

(ii) Enables the provider to identify:

(A) The sender's name and telephone number or address;

(B) The recipient's name, and if known, the telephone number or address of the recipient; and

(C) The remittance transfer to which the notice of error applies; and

(iii) Indicates why the sender believes an error exists and includes to the extent possible the type, date, and amount of the error, except for requests for documentation, additional information, or clarification described in paragraph (a)(1)(v) of this section.

(2) Request for documentation or clarification. When a notice of error is based on documentation, additional information, or clarification that the sender previously requested under paragraph (a)(1)(v) of this section, the sender's notice of error is timely if received by the remittance transfer provider the later of 180 days after the disclosed date of availability of the remittance transfer or 60 days after the provider sent the documentation, information, or clarification that had been requested.

(c) Time limits and extent of investigation.

(1) Time limits for investigation and report to consumer of error. A remittance transfer provider shall investigate promptly and determine whether an error occurred within 90 days of receiving a notice of error. The remittance transfer provider shall report the results to the sender, including notice of any remedies available for correcting any error that the provider determines has occurred, within three business days after completing its investigation.

(2) Remedies. Except as provided in paragraph (c)(2)(iii) of this section, if, following an assertion of an error by a sender, the remittance transfer provider determines an error occurred, the provider shall, within one business day of, or as soon as reasonably practicable after, receiving the sender's instructions regarding the appropriate remedy, correct the error as designated by the sender by:

(i) In the case of any error under paragraphs (a)(1)(i) through (iii) of this section, as applicable, either:

(A) Refunding to the sender the amount of funds provided by the sender in connection with a remittance transfer which was not properly transmitted, or the amount appropriate to resolve the error; or

(B) Making available to the designated recipient, without additional cost to the sender or to the designated recipient, the amount appropriate to resolve the error;

(ii) Except as provided in paragraph (c)(2)(iii) of this section, in the case of an error under paragraph (a)(1)(iv) of this section:

(A) As applicable, either:

(1) Refunding to the sender the amount of funds provided by the sender in connection with a remittance transfer which was not properly transmitted, or the amount appropriate to resolve the error; or

(2) Making available to the designated recipient the amount appropriate to resolve the error. Such amount must be made available to the designated recipient without additional cost to the sender or to the designated recipient; and

(B) Refunding to the sender any fees imposed and, to the extent not prohibited by law, taxes imposed for the remittance transfer;

(iii) In the case of an error under paragraph (a)(1)(iv) of this section that occurred because the sender provided incorrect or insufficient information in connection with the remittance transfer, the remittance transfer provider shall provide the remedies required by paragraphs (c)(2)(ii)(A)(1) and (c)(2)(ii)(B) of this section within three business days of providing the report required by paragraph (c)(1) or (d)(1) of this section except that the provider may agree to the sender's request, upon receiving the results of the error investigation, that the funds be applied towards a new remittance transfer, rather than be refunded, if the provider has not yet processed a refund. The provider may deduct from the amount refunded or applied towards a new transfer any fees actually imposed on or, to the extent not prohibited by law, taxes actually collected on the remittance transfer as part of the first unsuccessful remittance transfer attempt except that the provider shall not deduct its own fee.

(iv) In the case of a request under paragraph (a)(1)(v) of this section, providing the requested documentation, information, or clarification.

(d) Procedures if remittance transfer provider determines no error or different error occurred. In addition to following the procedures specified in paragraph (c) of this section, the remittance transfer provider shall follow the procedures set forth in this paragraph (d) if it determines that no error occurred or that an error occurred in a manner or amount different from that described by the sender.

(1) Explanation of results of investigation. The remittance transfer provider's report of the results of the investigation shall include a written explanation of the provider's findings and shall note the sender's right to request the documents on which the provider relied in making its determination. The explanation shall also address the specific complaint of the sender.

(2) Copies of documentation. Upon the sender's request, the remittance transfer provider shall promptly provide copies of the documents on which the provider relied in making its error determination.

(e) Reassertion of error. A remittance transfer provider that has fully complied with the error resolution requirements of this section has no further responsibilities under this section should the sender later reassert the same error, except in the case of an error asserted by the sender following receipt of information provided under paragraph (a)(1)(v) of this section.

(f) Relation to other laws—

(1) Relation to Regulation E § 1005.11 for incorrect EFTs from a sender's account. If an alleged error involves an incorrect electronic fund transfer from a sender's account in connection with a remittance transfer, and the sender provides a notice of error to the account-holding institution, the account-holding institution shall comply with the requirements of § 1005.11 governing error resolution rather than the requirements of this section, provided that the account-holding institution is not also the remittance transfer provider. If the remittance transfer provider is also the financial institution that holds the consumer's account, then the error-resolution provisions of this section apply when the sender provides such notice of error.

(2) Relation to Truth in Lending Act and Regulation Z. If an alleged error involves an incorrect extension of credit in connection with a remittance transfer, an incorrect amount received by the designated recipient under paragraph (a)(1)(iii) of this section that is an extension of credit for property or services not delivered as agreed, or the failure to make funds available by the disclosed date of availability under paragraph (a)(1)(iv) of this section that is an extension of credit for property or services not delivered as agreed, and the sender provides a notice of error to the creditor extending the credit, the provisions of Regulation Z, 12 CFR 1026.13, governing error resolution apply to the creditor, rather than the requirements of this section, even if the creditor is the remittance transfer provider. However, if the creditor is the remittance transfer provider, paragraph (b) of this section will apply instead of 12 CFR 1026.13(b). If the sender instead provides a notice of error to the remittance transfer provider that is not also the creditor, then the error-resolution provisions of this section apply to the remittance transfer provider.

(3) Unauthorized remittance transfers. If an alleged error involves an unauthorized electronic fund transfer for payment in connection with a remittance transfer, §§ 1005.6 and 1005.11 apply with respect to the account-holding institution. If an alleged error involves an unauthorized use of a credit account for payment in connection with a remittance transfer, the provisions of Regulation Z, 12 CFR 1026.12(b), if applicable, and § 1026.13, apply with respect to the creditor.

(g) Error resolution standards and recordkeeping requirements—

(1) Compliance program. A remittance transfer provider shall develop and maintain written policies and procedures that are designed to ensure compliance with the error resolution requirements applicable to remittance transfers under this section.

(2) Retention of error-related documentation. The remittance transfer provider's policies and procedures required under paragraph (g)(1) of this section shall include policies and procedures regarding the retention of documentation related to error investigations. Such policies and procedures must ensure, at a minimum, the retention of any notices of error submitted by a sender, documentation provided by the sender to the provider with respect to the alleged error, and the findings of the remittance transfer provider regarding the investigation of the alleged error. Remittance transfer providers are subject to the record retention requirements under § 1005.13.

(h) Incorrect account number or recipient institution identifier provided by the sender. The exception in paragraph (a)(1)(iv)(D) of this section applies if:

(1) The remittance transfer provider can demonstrate that the sender provided an incorrect account number or recipient institution identifier to the provider in connection with the remittance transfer;

(2) For any instance in which the sender provided the incorrect recipient institution identifier, prior to or when sending the transfer, the provider used reasonably available means to verify that the recipient institution identifier provided by the sender corresponded to the recipient institution name provided by the sender;

(3) The provider provided notice to the sender before the sender made payment for the remittance transfer that, in the event the sender provided an incorrect account number or recipient institution identifier, the sender could lose the transfer amount. For purposes of providing this disclosure, § 1005.31(a)(2) applies to this notice unless the notice is given at the same time as other disclosures required by this subpart for which information is permitted to be disclosed orally or via mobile application or text message, in which case this disclosure may be given in the same medium as those other disclosures;

(4) The incorrect account number or recipient institution identifier resulted in the deposit of the remittance transfer into a customer's account that is not the designated recipient's account; and

(5) The provider promptly used reasonable efforts to recover the amount that was to be received by the designated recipient.

12 C.F.R. § 1005.34. Procedures for Cancellation and Refund for Remittance Transfers

(a) Sender right of cancellation and refund. Except as provided in § 1005.36(c), a remittance transfer provider shall comply with the requirements of this section with respect to any oral or written request to cancel a remittance transfer from the sender that is received by the provider no later than 30 minutes after the sender makes payment in connection with the remittance transfer if:

(1) The request to cancel enables the provider to identify the sender's name and address or telephone number and the particular transfer to be cancelled; and

(2) The transferred funds have not been picked up by the designated recipient or deposited into an account of the designated recipient.

(b) Time limits and refund requirements. A remittance transfer provider shall refund, at no additional cost to the sender, the total amount of funds provided by the sender in connection with a remittance transfer, including any fees and, to the extent not prohibited by law, taxes imposed in connection with the remittance transfer, within three business days of receiving a sender's request to cancel the remittance transfer.

12 C.F.R. § 1005.35. Acts of Agents

A remittance transfer provider is liable for any violation of this subpart by an agent when such agent acts for the provider.

12 C.F.R. § 1005.36. Transfers Scheduled Before the Date of Transfer

(a) Timing. (1) For a one-time transfer scheduled five or more business days before the date of transfer or for the first in a series of preauthorized remittance transfers, the remittance transfer provider must:

(i) Provide either the pre-payment disclosure described in § 1005.31(b)(1) and the receipt described in § 1005.31(b)(2) or the combined disclosure described in § 1005.31(b)(3), in accordance with the timing requirements set forth in § 1005.31(e); and

(ii) If any of the disclosures provided pursuant to paragraph (a)(1)(i) of this section contain estimates as permitted by § 1005.32(b)(2), mail or deliver to the sender an additional receipt meeting the requirements described in § 1005.31(b)(2) no later than one business day after the date of the transfer. If the transfer involves the transfer of funds from the sender's account held by the provider, the receipt required by this paragraph may be provided on or with the next periodic statement for that account, or within 30 days after the date of the transfer if a periodic statement is not provided.

(2) For each subsequent preauthorized remittance transfer:

(i) If any of the information on the most recent receipt provided pursuant to paragraph (a)(1)(i) of this section, or by this paragraph (a)(2)(i), other than the temporal disclosures required by § 1005.31(b)(2)(ii) and (b)(2)(vii), is no longer accurate with respect to a subsequent preauthorized remittance transfer for reasons other than as permitted by § 1005.32, then the remittance transfer provider must provide an updated receipt meeting the requirements described in § 1005.31(b)(2) to the sender. The provider must mail or deliver this receipt to the sender within a reasonable time prior to the scheduled date of the next subsequent preauthorized remittance transfer. Such receipt must clearly and conspicuously indicate that it contains updated disclosures.

(ii) Unless a receipt was provided in accordance with paragraph (a)(2)(i) of this section that contained no estimates pursuant to § 1005.32, the remittance transfer provider must mail or deliver to the sender a receipt meeting the requirements described in § 1005.31(b)(2) no later than one business day after the date of the transfer. If the remittance transfer involves the transfer of funds from the sender's account held by the provider, the receipt required by this paragraph may be provided on or with the next periodic statement for that account, or within 30 days after the date of the transfer if a periodic statement is not provided.

(iii) A remittance transfer provider must provide the disclosures required by paragraph (d) of this section in accordance with the timing requirements of that section.

(b) Accuracy. (1) For a one-time transfer scheduled five or more business days in advance or for the first in a series of preauthorized remittance transfers, disclosures provided pursuant to paragraph (a)(1)(i) of this section must comply with § 1005.31(f) by being accurate when a sender makes payment except to the extent estimates are permitted by § 1005.32.

(2) For each subsequent preauthorized remittance transfer, the most recent receipt provided pursuant to paragraph (a)(1)(i) or (a)(2)(i) of this section must be accurate as of when such transfer is made, except:

(i) The temporal elements required by § 1005.31(b)(2)(ii) and (b)(2)(vii) must be accurate only if the transfer is the first transfer to occur after the disclosure was provided; and

(ii) To the extent estimates are permitted by § 1005.32.

(3) Disclosures provided pursuant to paragraph (a)(1)(ii) or (a)(2)(ii) of this section must be accurate as of when the remittance transfer to which it pertains is made, except to the extent estimates are permitted by § 1005.32(a) or (b)(1).

(c) Cancellation. For any remittance transfer scheduled by the sender at least three business days before the date of the transfer, a remittance transfer provider shall comply with any oral or written request to cancel the remittance transfer from the sender if the request to cancel:

(1) Enables the provider to identify the sender's name and address or telephone number and the particular transfer to be cancelled; and

(2) Is received by the provider at least three business days before the scheduled date of the remittance transfer.

(d) Additional requirements for subsequent preauthorized remittance transfers

(1) Disclosure requirement. (i) For any subsequent transfer in a series of preauthorized remittance transfers, the remittance transfer provider must disclose to the sender:

(A) The date the provider will make the subsequent transfer, using the term "Future Transfer Date," or a substantially similar term;

(B) A statement about the rights of the sender regarding cancellation as described in § 1005.31(b)(2)(iv); and

(C) The name, telephone number(s), and Web site of the remittance transfer provider.

(ii) If the future date or dates of transfer are described as occurring in regular periodic intervals, *e.g.*, the 15th of every month, rather than as a specific calendar date or dates, the remittance transfer provider must disclose any future date or dates of transfer that do not conform to the described interval.

(2) Notice requirements. (i) Except as described in paragraph (d)(2)(ii) of this section, the disclosures required by paragraph (d)(1) of this section must be received by the sender no more than 12 months, and no less than five business days prior to the date of any subsequent transfer to which it pertains. The disclosures required by paragraph (d)(1) of this section may be provided in a separate disclosure or may be provided on one or more disclosures required by this subpart related to the same series of preauthorized transfers, so long as the consumer receives the required information for each subsequent preauthorized remittance transfer in accordance with the timing requirements of this paragraph (d)(2)(i).

(ii) For any subsequent preauthorized remittance transfer for which the date of transfer is four or fewer business days after the date payment is made for that transfer, the information required by paragraph (d)(1) of this section must be provided on or with the receipt described in § 1005.31(b)(2), or disclosed as permitted by § 1005.31(a)(3) or (a)(5), for the initial transfer in that series in accordance with paragraph (a)(1)(i) of this section.

(3) Specific format requirement. The information required by paragraph (d)(1)(i)(A) of this section generally must be disclosed in close proximity to the other information required by paragraph (d)(1)(i)(B) of this section.

(4) Accuracy. Any disclosure required by paragraph (d)(1) of this section must be accurate as of the date the preauthorized remittance transfer to which it pertains is made.

MORTGAGE ASSISTANCE RELIEF SERVICES (REGULATION O)

---

12 C.F.R. Part 1015

Table of Sections

§ 1015.1. Scope of Regulations in this Part

This part, known as Regulation O, is issued by the Bureau of Consumer Financial Protection to implement the 2009 Omnibus Appropriations Act, Public Law 111–8, section 626, 123 Stat. 524 (Mar. 11, 2009), as clarified by the Credit Card Accountability Responsibility and Disclosure Act of 2009, Public Law 111–24, section 511, 123 Stat. 1734 (May 22, 2009), and as amended by the Dodd-Frank Wall Street Reform and Consumer Financial Protection Act of 2010, Public Law 111–203, section 1097, 124 Stat. 1376 (July 21, 2010). *This part applies to persons over which the Federal Trade Commission has jurisdiction under the Federal Trade Commission Act.*

§ 1015.2. Definitions

For the purposes of this part:

Clear and prominent means:

(1) In textual communications, the required disclosures shall be easily readable; in a high degree of contrast from the immediate background on which it appears; in the same languages that are substantially used in the commercial communication; in a format so that the disclosure is distinct from other text, such as inside a border; in a distinct type style, such as bold; parallel to the base of the commercial communication, and, except as otherwise provided in this rule, each letter of the disclosure shall be, at a minimum, the larger of 12-point type or one-half the size of the largest letter or numeral used in the name of the advertised Web site or telephone number to which consumers are referred to receive information relating to any mortgage assistance relief service. Textual communications include any communications in a written or printed form such as print publications or words displayed on the screen of a computer;

(2) In communications disseminated orally or through audible means, such as radio or streaming audio, the required disclosures shall be delivered in a slow and deliberate manner and in a reasonably understandable volume and pitch;

(3) In communications disseminated through video means, such as television or streaming video, the required disclosures shall appear simultaneously in the audio and visual parts of the commercial communication and be delivered in a manner consistent with paragraphs (1) and (2) of this definition. The visual disclosure shall be at least four percent of the vertical picture or screen height and appear for the duration of the oral disclosure;

(4) In communications made through interactive media, such as the internet, online services, and software, the required disclosures shall:

(i) Be consistent with paragraphs (1) through (3) of this definition;

(ii) Be made on, or immediately prior to, the page on which the consumer takes any action to incur any financial obligation;

(iii) Be unavoidable, i.e., visible to consumers without requiring them to scroll down a Web page; and

(iv) Appear in type at least the same size as the largest character of the advertisement;

(5) In all instances, the required disclosures shall be presented in an understandable language and syntax, and with nothing contrary to, inconsistent with, or in mitigation of the disclosures used in any communication of them; and

(6) For program-length television, radio, or internet-based multimedia commercial communications, the required disclosures shall be made at the beginning, near the middle, and at the end of the commercial communication.

Client trust account means a separate account created by a licensed attorney for the purpose of holding client funds, which is:

(1) Maintained in compliance with all applicable state laws and regulations, including licensing regulations; and

(2) Located in the state where the attorney's office is located, or elsewhere in the United States with the consent of the consumer on whose behalf the funds are held.

Commercial communication means any written or oral statement, illustration, or depiction, whether in English or any other language, that is designed to effect a sale or create interest in purchasing any service, plan, or program, whether it appears on or in a label, package, package insert, radio, television, cable television, brochure, newspaper, magazine, pamphlet, leaflet, circular, mailer, book insert, free standing insert, letter, catalogue, poster, chart, billboard, public transit card, point of purchase display, film, slide, audio program transmitted over a telephone system, telemarketing script, onhold script, upsell script, training materials provided to telemarketing firms, program-length commercial ("infomercial"), the internet, cellular network, or any other medium. Promotional materials and items and Web pages are included in the term "commercial communication."

(1) ***General Commercial Communication*** means a commercial communication that occurs prior to the consumer agreeing to permit the provider to seek offers of mortgage assistance relief on behalf of the consumer, or otherwise agreeing to use the mortgage assistance relief service, and that is not directed at a specific consumer.

(2) ***Consumer-Specific Commercial Communication*** means a commercial communication that occurs prior to the consumer agreeing to permit the provider to seek offers of mortgage assistance relief on behalf of the consumer, or otherwise agreeing to use the mortgage assistance relief service, and that is directed at a specific consumer.

Consumer means any natural person who is obligated under any loan secured by a dwelling.

Dwelling means a residential structure containing four or fewer units, whether or not that structure is attached to real property, that is primarily for personal, family, or household purposes. The term includes any of the following if used as a residence: An individual condominium unit, cooperative unit, mobile home, manufactured home, or trailer.

Dwelling loan means any loan secured by a dwelling, and any associated deed of trust or mortgage.

Dwelling Loan Holder means any individual or entity who holds the dwelling loan that is the subject of the offer to provide mortgage assistance relief services.

Material means likely to affect a consumer's choice of, or conduct regarding, any mortgage assistance relief service.

Mortgage Assistance Relief Service means any service, plan, or program, offered or provided to the consumer in exchange for consideration, that is represented, expressly or by implication, to assist or attempt to assist the consumer with any of the following:

(1) Stopping, preventing, or postponing any mortgage or deed of trust foreclosure sale for the consumer's dwelling, any repossession of the consumer's dwelling, or otherwise saving the consumer's dwelling from foreclosure or repossession;

(2) Negotiating, obtaining, or arranging a modification of any term of a dwelling loan, including a reduction in the amount of interest, principal balance, monthly payments, or fees;

(3) Obtaining any forbearance or modification in the timing of payments from any dwelling loan holder or servicer on any dwelling loan;

(4) Negotiating, obtaining, or arranging any extension of the period of time within which the consumer may:

(i) Cure his or her default on a dwelling loan,

(ii) Reinstate his or her dwelling loan,

(iii) Redeem a dwelling, or

(iv) Exercise any right to reinstate a dwelling loan or redeem a dwelling;

(5) Obtaining any waiver of an acceleration clause or balloon payment contained in any promissory note or contract secured by any dwelling; or

(6) Negotiating, obtaining or arranging:

(i) A short sale of a dwelling,

(ii) A deed-in-lieu of foreclosure, or

(iii) Any other disposition of a dwelling other than a sale to a third party who is not the dwelling loan holder.

Mortgage Assistance Relief Service Provider or ***Provider*** means any person that provides, offers to provide, or arranges for others to provide, any mortgage assistance relief service. This term does not include:

(1) The dwelling loan holder, or any agent or contractor of such individual or entity.

(2) The servicer of a dwelling loan, or any agent or contractor of such individual or entity.

Person means any individual, group, unincorporated association, limited or general partnership, corporation, or other business entity, except to the extent that any person is specifically excluded from the Federal Trade Commission's jurisdiction pursuant to 15 U.S.C. 44 and 45(a)(2).

Servicer means the individual or entity responsible for:

(1) Receiving any scheduled periodic payments from a consumer pursuant to the terms of the dwelling loan that is the subject of the offer to provide mortgage assistance relief services, including amounts for escrow accounts under section 10 of the Real Estate Settlement Procedures Act (12 U.S.C. 2609); and

(2) Making the payments of principal and interest and such other payments with respect to the amounts received from the consumer as may be required pursuant to the terms of the mortgage servicing loan documents or servicing contract.

Telemarketing means a plan, program, or campaign which is conducted to induce the purchase of any service, by use of one or more telephones and which involves more than one interstate telephone call.

§ 1015.3. Prohibited Representations

It is a violation of this rule for any mortgage assistance relief service provider to engage in the following conduct:

(a) Representing, expressly or by implication, in connection with the advertising, marketing, promotion, offering for sale, sale, or performance of any mortgage assistance relief service, that a consumer cannot or should not contact or communicate with his or her lender or servicer.

(b) Misrepresenting, expressly or by implication, any material aspect of any mortgage assistance relief service, including but not limited to:

(1) The likelihood of negotiating, obtaining, or arranging any represented service or result, such as those set forth in the definition of Mortgage Assistance Relief Service in § 1015.2;

(2) The amount of time it will take the mortgage assistance relief service provider to accomplish any represented service or result, such as those set forth in the definition of Mortgage Assistance Relief Service in § 1015.2;

(3) That a mortgage assistance relief service is affiliated with, endorsed or approved by, or otherwise associated with:

(i) The United States government,

(ii) Any governmental homeowner assistance plan,

(iii) Any Federal, State, or local government agency, unit, or department,

(iv) Any nonprofit housing counselor agency or program,

(v) The maker, holder, or servicer of the consumer's dwelling loan, or

(vi) Any other individual, entity, or program;

(4) The consumer's obligation to make scheduled periodic payments or any other payments pursuant to the terms of the consumer's dwelling loan;

(5) The terms or conditions of the consumer's dwelling loan, including but not limited to the amount of debt owed;

(6) The terms or conditions of any refund, cancellation, exchange, or repurchase policy for a mortgage assistance relief service, including but not limited to the likelihood of obtaining a full or partial refund, or the circumstances in which a full or partial refund will be granted, for a mortgage assistance relief service;

(7) That the mortgage assistance relief service provider has completed the represented services or has a right to claim, demand, charge, collect, or receive payment or other consideration;

(8) That the consumer will receive legal representation;

(9) The availability, performance, cost, or characteristics of any alternative to for-profit mortgage assistance relief services through which the consumer can obtain mortgage assistance relief, including negotiating directly with the dwelling loan holder or servicer, or using any nonprofit housing counselor agency or program;

(10) The amount of money or the percentage of the debt amount that a consumer may save by using the mortgage assistance relief service;

(11) The total cost to purchase the mortgage assistance relief service; or

(12) The terms, conditions, or limitations of any offer of mortgage assistance relief the provider obtains from the consumer's dwelling loan holder or servicer, including the time period in which the consumer must decide to accept the offer;

(c) Making a representation, expressly or by implication, about the benefits, performance, or efficacy of any mortgage assistance relief service unless, at the time such representation is made, the provider possesses and relies upon competent and reliable evidence that substantiates that the representation is true. For the purposes of this paragraph, *competent and reliable evidence* means tests, analyses, research, studies, or other evidence based on the expertise of professionals in the relevant area, that have been conducted and evaluated in an objective manner by individuals qualified to do so, using procedures generally accepted in the profession to yield accurate and reliable results.

§ 1015.4. Disclosures Required in Commercial Communications

It is a violation of this rule for any mortgage assistance relief service provider to engage in the following conduct:

(a) Disclosures in All General Commercial Communications—Failing to place the following statements in every general commercial communication for any mortgage assistance relief service:

(1) "(Name of company) is not associated with the government, and our service is not approved by the government or your lender."

(2) In cases where the mortgage assistance relief service provider has represented, expressly or by implication, that consumers will receive any service or result set forth in paragraphs (2) through (6) of the definition of Mortgage Assistance Relief Service in § 1015.2, "Even if you accept this offer and use our service, your lender may not agree to change your loan."

(3) The disclosures required by this paragraph must be made in a clear and prominent manner, and—

(i) In textual communications the disclosures must appear together and be preceded by the heading "IMPORTANT NOTICE," which must be in bold face font that is two point-type larger than the font size of the required disclosures; and

(ii) In communications disseminated orally or through audible means, wholly or in part, the audio component of the required disclosures must be preceded by the statement "Before using this service, consider the following information."

(b) Disclosures in All Consumer-Specific Commercial Communications—Failing to disclose the following information in every consumer-specific commercial communication for any mortgage assistance relief service:

(1) "You may stop doing business with us at any time. You may accept or reject the offer of mortgage assistance we obtain from your lender [or servicer]. If you reject the offer, you do not have to pay us. If you accept the offer, you will have to pay us (insert amount or method for calculating the amount) for our services." For the purposes of this paragraph (b)(1), the amount "you will have to pay" shall consist of the total amount the consumer must pay to purchase, receive, and use all of the mortgage assistance relief services that are the subject of the sales offer, including, but not limited to, all fees and charges.

(2) "(Name of company) is not associated with the government, and our service is not approved by the government or your lender."

(3) In cases where the mortgage assistance relief service provider has represented, expressly or by implication, that consumers will receive any service or result set forth in paragraphs (2) through (6) of the definition of Mortgage Assistance Relief Service in § 1015.2, "Even if you accept this offer and use our service, your lender may not agree to change your loan."

(4) The disclosures required by this paragraph must be made in a clear and prominent manner, and—

(i) In textual communications the disclosures must appear together and be preceded by the heading "IMPORTANT NOTICE," which must be in bold face font that is two point-type larger than the font size of the required disclosures; and

(ii) In communications disseminated orally or through audible means, wholly or in part, the audio component of the required disclosures must be preceded by the statement "Before using this service, consider the following information" and, in telephone communications, must be made at the beginning of the call.

(c) Disclosures in All General Commercial Communications, Consumer-Specific Commercial Communications, and Other Communications—In cases where the mortgage assistance relief service provider has represented, expressly or by implication, in connection with the advertising, marketing, promotion, offering for sale, sale, or performance of any mortgage assistance relief service, that the consumer should temporarily or permanently discontinue payments, in whole or in part, on a dwelling loan, failing to disclose, clearly and prominently, and in close proximity to any such representation that "If you stop paying your mortgage, you could lose your home and damage your credit rating."

§ 1015.5. Prohibition on Collection of Advance Payments and Related Disclosures

It is a violation of this rule for any mortgage assistance relief service provider to:

(a) Request or receive payment of any fee or other consideration until the consumer has executed a written agreement between the consumer and the consumer's dwelling loan holder or servicer incorporating the offer of mortgage assistance relief the provider obtained from the consumer's dwelling loan holder or servicer;

(b) Fail to disclose, at the time the mortgage assistance relief service provider furnishes the consumer with the written agreement specified in paragraph (a) of this section, the following information: "This is an offer of mortgage assistance we obtained from your lender [or servicer]. You may accept or reject the offer. If you reject the offer, you do not have to pay us. If you accept the offer, you will have to pay us [same amount as disclosed pursuant to § 1015.4(b)(1)] for our services." The disclosure required by this paragraph must be made in a clear and prominent manner, on a separate written page, and preceded by the heading: "IMPORTANT NOTICE: Before buying this service, consider the following information." The heading must be in bold face font that is two point-type larger than the font size of the required disclosure; or

(c)(1) Fail to provide, at the time the mortgage assistance relief service provider furnishes the consumer with the written agreement specified in paragraph (a) of this section, a notice from the consumer's dwelling loan holder or servicer that describes all material differences between the terms, conditions, and limitations associated with the consumer's current mortgage loan and the terms, conditions, and limitations associated with the consumer's mortgage loan if he or she accepts the dwelling loan holder's or servicer's offer, including but not limited to differences in the loan's:

(i) Principal balance;

(ii) Contract interest rate, including the maximum rate and any adjustable rates, if applicable;

(iii) Amount and number of the consumer's scheduled periodic payments on the loan;

(iv) Monthly amounts owed for principal, interest, taxes, and any mortgage insurance on the loan;

(v) Amount of any delinquent payments owing or outstanding;

(vi) Assessed fees or penalties; and

(vii) Term.

(2) The notice must be made in a clear and prominent manner, on a separate written page, and preceded by heading: "IMPORTANT INFORMATION FROM YOUR [name of lender or servicer] ABOUT THIS OFFER." The heading must be in bold face font that is two-point-type larger than the font size of the required disclosure.

(d) Fail to disclose in the notice specified in paragraph (c) of this section, in cases where the offer of mortgage assistance relief the provider obtained from the consumer's dwelling loan holder or servicer is a trial mortgage loan modification, the terms, conditions, and limitations of this offer, including but not limited to:

(1) The fact that the consumer may not qualify for a permanent mortgage loan modification; and

(2) The likely amount of the scheduled periodic payments and any arrears, payments, or fees that the consumer would owe in failing to qualify.

§ 1015.6. Assisting and Facilitating

It is a violation of this rule for a person to provide substantial assistance or support to any mortgage assistance relief service provider when that person knows or consciously avoids knowing that the provider is engaged in any act or practice that violates this rule.

§ 1015.7. Exemptions

(a) An attorney is exempt from this part, with the exception of § 1015.5, if the attorney:

(1) Provides mortgage assistance relief services as part of the practice of law;

(2) Is licensed to practice law in the state in which the consumer for whom the attorney is providing mortgage assistance relief services resides or in which the consumer's dwelling is located; and

(3) Complies with state laws and regulations that cover the same type of conduct the rule requires.

(b) An attorney who is exempt pursuant to paragraph (a) of this section is also exempt from § 1015.5 if the attorney:

(1) Deposits any funds received from the consumer prior to performing legal services in a client trust account; and

(2) Complies with all state laws and regulations, including licensing regulations, applicable to client trust accounts.

§ 1015.8. Waiver Not Permitted

It is a violation of this rule for any person to obtain, or attempt to obtain, a waiver from any consumer of any protection provided by or any right of the consumer under this rule.

§ 1015.9. Recordkeeping and Compliance Requirements

(a) Any mortgage assistance relief provider must keep, for a period of twenty-four (24) months from the date the record is created, the following records:

(1) All contracts or other agreements between the provider and any consumer for any mortgage assistance relief service;

(2) Copies of all written communications between the provider and any consumer occurring prior to the date on which the consumer entered into an agreement with the provider for any mortgage assistance relief service;

(3) Copies of all documents or telephone recordings created in connection with compliance with paragraph (b) of this section;

(4) All consumer files containing the names, phone numbers, dollar amounts paid, and descriptions of mortgage assistance relief services purchased, to the extent the mortgage assistance relief service provider keeps such information in the ordinary course of business;

(5) Copies of all materially different sales scripts, training materials, commercial communications, or other marketing materials, including Web sites and weblogs, for any mortgage assistance relief service; and

(6) Copies of the documentation provided to the consumer as specified in § 1015.5 of this rule;

(b) A mortgage assistance relief service provider also must:

(1) Take reasonable steps sufficient to monitor and ensure that all employees and independent contractors comply with this rule. Such steps shall include the monitoring of communications directed at specific consumers, and shall also include, at a minimum, the following:

(i) If the mortgage assistance relief service provider is engaged in the telemarketing of mortgage assistance relief services, performing random, blind recording and testing of the oral representations made by individuals engaged in sales or other customer service functions;

(ii) Establishing a procedure for receiving and responding to all consumer complaints; and

(iii) Ascertaining the number and nature of consumer complaints regarding transactions in which all employees and independent contractors are involved;

(2) Investigate promptly and fully each consumer complaint received;

(3) Take corrective action with respect to any employee or contractor whom the mortgage assistance relief service provider determines is not complying with this rule, which may include training, disciplining, or terminating such individual; and

(4) Maintain any information and material necessary to demonstrate its compliance with paragraphs (b)(1) through (3) of this section.

(c) A mortgage assistance relief provider may keep the records required by paragraphs (a) and (b) of this section in any form, and in the same manner, format, or place as it keeps such records in the ordinary course of business.

(d) It is a violation of this rule for a mortgage assistance relief service provider not to comply with this section.

§ 1015.10. Actions by States

Any attorney general or other officer of a state authorized by the state to bring an action under this part may do so pursuant to section 626(b) of the 2009 Omnibus Appropriations Act, Public Law 111–8, section 626, 123 Stat. 524 (Mar. 11, 2009), as amended by Public Law 111–24, section 511, 123 Stat. 1734 (May 22, 2009), and as amended by Public Law 111–203, section 1097, 124 Stat. 2102 (July 21, 2010).

§ 1015.11. Severability

The provisions of this rule are separate and severable from one another. If any provision is stayed or determined to be invalid, it is the Bureau of Consumer Financial Protection's intention that the remaining provisions shall continue in effect.

FCRA REGULATIONS (REGULATION V)[1]

12 C.F.R. Part 1022

Table of Sections

Subpart A—General Provisions

Subpart C—Affiliate Marketing

Subpart D—Medical Information

Subpart E—Duties of Furnishers of Information

Subpart F—Duties of Users Regarding Obtaining and Using Consumer Reports

Subpart H—Duties of Users Regarding Risk-Based Pricing

---

[1] Regulation V, as adopted by different regulators, is codified in the C.F.R. at different points. Only the version adopted by the CFPB is set forth here.

12 C.F.R. Part 1022

Subpart A. General Provisions

§ 1022.1. Purpose, scope, and model forms and disclosures

(a) Purpose. The purpose of this part is to implement the Fair Credit Reporting Act (FCRA). This part generally applies to persons that obtain and use information about consumers to determine the consumer's eligibility for products, services, or employment, share such information among affiliates, and furnish information to consumer reporting agencies.

(b) Scope.

(1) [Reserved]

(2) Institutions covered.

(i) Except as otherwise provided in this part, this part applies to any person subject to the FCRA except for a person excluded from coverage of this part by section 1029 of the Consumer Financial Protection Act of 2010, Title X of the Dodd-Frank Wall Street Reform and Consumer Protection Act, Public Law 111–203, 124 Stat. 1376.

(ii) For purposes of Appendix B to this part, financial institutions as defined in section 509 of the Gramm-Leach-Bliley Act (12 U.S.C. 6809), may use the model notices in Appendix B to this part to comply with the notice requirement in section 623(a)(7) of the FCRA (15 U.S.C. 1681s–2(a)(7)).

(c) Model forms and disclosures.

(1) Use. Appendices D, H, I, K, L, M, and N contain model forms and disclosures. These appendices carry out the directive in FCRA that the Bureau prescribe such model forms and disclosures. Use or distribution of these model forms and disclosures, or substantially similar forms and disclosures, will constitute compliance with any section or subsection of the FCRA requiring that such forms and disclosures be used by or supplied to any person.

(2) Definition. Substantially similar means that all information in the Bureau's prescribed model is included in the document that is distributed, and that the document distributed is formatted in a way consistent with the format prescribed by the Bureau. The document that is distributed shall not include anything that interferes with, detracts from, or otherwise undermines the information contained in the Bureau's prescribed model. Until January 1, 2013, the model forms in Appendices B, E, F, G, and H to 16 CFR part 698, as those appendices existed as of October 1, 2011, are deemed substantially similar to the corresponding model forms in Appendices H, I, K, M, and N to this part, and the model forms in Appendix H to 12 CFR part 222, as that appendix existed as of October 1, 2011, are deemed substantially similar to the corresponding model forms in Appendix H to this part.

§ 1022.2. Examples

The examples in this part are not exclusive. Compliance with an example, to the extent applicable, constitutes compliance with this part. Examples in a paragraph illustrate only the issue described in the paragraph and do not illustrate any other issue that may arise in this part.

§ 1022.3. Definitions

For purposes of this part, unless explicitly stated otherwise:

(a) Act means the FCRA (15 U.S.C. 1681 et seq.).

(b) Affiliate means any company that is related by common ownership or common corporate control with another company. For example, an affiliate of a Federal credit union is a credit union service corporation, as provided in 12 CFR part 712, that is controlled by the Federal credit union.

(c) [Reserved]

(d) Common ownership or common corporate control means a relationship between two companies under which:

(1) One company has, with respect to the other company:

(i) Ownership, control, or power to vote 25 percent or more of the outstanding shares of any class of voting security of a company, directly or indirectly, or acting through one or more other persons;

(ii) Control in any manner over the election of a majority of the directors, trustees, or general partners (or individuals exercising similar functions) of a company; or

(iii) The power to exercise, directly or indirectly, a controlling influence over the management or policies of a company, as determined by the applicable prudential regulator (as defined in 12 U.S.C. 5481(24)) (a credit union is presumed to have a controlling influence over the management or policies of a credit union service corporation if the credit union service corporation is 67% owned by credit unions) or, where there is no prudential regulator, by the Bureau; or

(2) Any other person has, with respect to both companies, a relationship described in paragraphs (d)(1)(i) through (d)(1)(ii).

(e) Company means any corporation, limited liability company, business trust, general or limited partnership, association, or similar organization.

(f) Consumer means an individual.

(g) Identifying information means any name or number that may be used, alone or in conjunction with any other information, to identify a specific person, including any:

(1) Name, social security number, date of birth, official state or government issued driver's license or identification number, alien registration number, government passport number, employer or taxpayer identification number;

(2) Unique biometric data, such as fingerprint, voice print, retina or iris image, or other unique physical representation;

(3) Unique electronic identification number, address, or routing code; or

(4) Telecommunication identifying information or access device (as defined in 18 U.S.C. 1029(e)).

(h) Identity theft means a fraud committed or attempted using the identifying information of another person without authority.

(i)(1) Identity theft report means a report:

(i) That alleges identity theft with as much specificity as the consumer can provide;

(ii) That is a copy of an official, valid report filed by the consumer with a Federal, state, or local law enforcement agency, including the United States Postal Inspection Service, the filing of which subjects the person filing the report to criminal penalties relating to the filing of false information, if, in fact, the information in the report is false; and

(iii) That may include additional information or documentation that an information furnisher or consumer reporting agency reasonably requests for the purpose of determining the validity of the alleged identity theft, provided that the information furnisher or consumer reporting agency:

(A) Makes such request not later than fifteen days after the date of receipt of the copy of the report form identified in Paragraph (i)(1)(ii) of this section or the request by the consumer for the particular service, whichever shall be the later;

(B) Makes any supplemental requests for information or documentation and final determination on the acceptance of the identity theft report within another fifteen days after its initial request for information or documentation; and

(C) Shall have five days to make a final determination on the acceptance of the identity theft report, in the event that the consumer reporting agency or information furnisher receives any such additional information or documentation on the eleventh day or later within the fifteen day period set forth in Paragraph (i)(1)(iii)(B) of this section.

(2) Examples of the specificity referenced in Paragraph (i)(1)(i) of this section are provided for illustrative purposes only, as follows:

(i) Specific dates relating to the identity theft such as when the loss or theft of personal information occurred or when the fraud(s) using the personal information occurred, and how the consumer discovered or otherwise learned of the theft.

(ii) Identification information or any other information about the perpetrator, if known.

(iii) Name(s) of information furnisher(s), account numbers, or other relevant account information related to the identity theft.

(iv) Any other information known to the consumer about the identity theft.

(3) Examples of when it would or would not be reasonable to request additional information or documentation referenced in Paragraph (i)(1)(iii) of this section are provided for illustrative purposes only, as follows:

(i) A law enforcement report containing detailed information about the identity theft and the signature, badge number or other identification information of the individual law enforcement official taking the report should be sufficient on its face to support a victim's request. In this case, without an identifiable concern, such as an indication that the report was fraudulent, it would not be reasonable for an information furnisher or consumer reporting agency to request additional information or documentation.

(ii) A consumer might provide a law enforcement report similar to the report in Paragraph (i)(1) of this section but certain important information such as the consumer's date of birth or Social Security number may be missing because the consumer chose not to provide it. The information furnisher or consumer reporting agency could accept this report, but it would be reasonable to require that the consumer provide the missing information. The Bureau's Identity Theft Affidavit is available on the Bureau's Web site (consumerfinance.gov/learnmore). The version of this form developed by the Federal Trade Commission, available on the FTC's Web site (ftc.gov/idtheft), remains valid and sufficient for this purpose.

(iii) A consumer might provide a law enforcement report generated by an automated system with a simple allegation that an identity theft occurred to support a request for a tradeline block or cessation of information furnishing. In such a case, it would be reasonable for an information furnisher or consumer reporting agency to ask that the consumer fill out and have notarized the Bureau's Identity Theft Affidavit or a similar form and provide some form of identification documentation.

(iv) A consumer might provide a law enforcement report generated by an automated system with a simple allegation that an identity theft occurred to support a request for an extended fraud alert. In this case, it would not be reasonable for a consumer reporting agency to require additional documentation or information, such as a notarized affidavit.

(j) [Reserved]

(k) Medical information means:

(1) Information or data, whether oral or recorded, in any form or medium, created by or derived from a health care provider or the consumer, that relates to:

(i) The past, present, or future physical, mental, or behavioral health or condition of an individual;

(ii) The provision of health care to an individual; or

(iii) The payment for the provision of health care to an individual.

(2) The term does not include:

(i) The age or gender of a consumer;

(ii) Demographic information about the consumer, including a consumer's residence address or email address;

(iii) Any other information about a consumer that does not relate to the physical, mental, or behavioral health or condition of a consumer, including the existence or value of any insurance policy; or

(iv) Information that does not identify a specific consumer.

(*l*) Person means any individual, partnership, corporation, trust, estate cooperative, association, government or governmental subdivision or agency, or other entity.

Subpart C. Affiliate Marketing

§ 1022.20. Coverage and definitions

(a) Coverage. Subpart C of this part applies to any person that uses information from its affiliates for the purpose of marketing solicitations, or provides information to its affiliates for that purpose, other than a person excluded from coverage of this part by section 1029 of the Consumer Financial Protection Act of 2010, Title X of the Dodd-Frank Wall Street Reform and Consumer Protection Act, Public Law 111–203, 124 Stat. 137.

(b) Definitions. For purposes of this subpart:

(1) Clear and conspicuous. The term "clear and conspicuous" means reasonably understandable and designed to call attention to the nature and significance of the information presented.

(2) Concise.

(i) In general. The term "concise" means a reasonably brief expression or statement.

(ii) Combination with other required disclosures. A notice required by this subpart may be concise even if it is combined with other disclosures required or authorized by Federal or state law.

(3) Eligibility information. The term "eligibility information" means any information the communication of which would be a consumer report if the exclusions from the definition of "consumer report" in section 603(d)(2)(A) of the Act did not apply. Eligibility information does not include aggregate or blind data that does not contain personal identifiers such as account numbers, names, or addresses.

(4) Pre-existing business relationship.

(i) In general. The term "pre-existing business relationship" means a relationship between a person, or a person's licensed agent, and a consumer based on:

(A) A financial contract between the person and the consumer which is in force on the date on which the consumer is sent a solicitation covered by this subpart;

(B) The purchase, rental, or lease by the consumer of the person's goods or services, or a financial transaction (including holding an active account or a policy in force or having another continuing relationship) between the consumer and the person, during the 18-month period immediately preceding the date on which the consumer is sent a solicitation covered by this subpart; or

(C) An inquiry or application by the consumer regarding a product or service offered by that person during the three-month period immediately preceding the date on which the consumer is sent a solicitation covered by this subpart.

(ii) Examples of pre-existing business relationships.

(A) If a consumer has a time deposit account, such as a certificate of deposit, at a financial institution that is currently in force, the financial institution has a pre-existing business relationship with the consumer and can use eligibility information it receives from its affiliates to make solicitations to the consumer about its products or services.

(B) If a consumer obtained a certificate of deposit from a financial institution, but did not renew the certificate at maturity, the financial institution has a pre-existing business relationship with the consumer and can use eligibility information it receives from its affiliates to make solicitations to the consumer about its products or services for 18 months after the date of maturity of the certificate of deposit.

(C) If a consumer obtains a mortgage, the mortgage lender has a pre-existing business relationship with the consumer. If the mortgage lender sells the consumer's entire loan to an investor, the mortgage lender has a pre-existing business relationship with the consumer and can use eligibility information it receives from its affiliates to make solicitations to the consumer about its products or services for 18 months after the date it sells the loan, and the investor has a pre-existing business relationship with the consumer upon purchasing the loan. If, however, the mortgage lender sells a fractional interest in the consumer's loan to an investor but also retains an ownership interest in the loan, the mortgage lender continues to have a pre-existing business relationship with the consumer, but the investor does not have a pre-existing business relationship with the consumer. If the mortgage lender retains ownership of the loan, but sells ownership of the servicing rights to the consumer's loan, the mortgage lender continues to have a pre-existing business relationship with the consumer. The purchaser of the servicing rights also has a pre-existing business relationship with the consumer as of the date it purchases ownership of the servicing rights, but only if it collects payments from or otherwise deals directly with the consumer on a continuing basis.

(D) If a consumer applies to a financial institution for a product or service that it offers, but does not obtain a product or service from or enter into a financial contract or transaction with the institution, the financial institution has a pre-existing business relationship with the consumer and can therefore use eligibility information it receives from an affiliate to make solicitations to the consumer about its products or services for three months after the date of the application.

(E) If a consumer makes a telephone inquiry to a financial institution about its products or services and provides contact information to the institution, but does not obtain a product or service from or enter into a financial contract or transaction with the institution, the financial institution has a pre-existing business relationship with the consumer and can therefore use eligibility information it receives from an affiliate to make solicitations to the consumer about its products or services for three months after the date of the inquiry.

(F) If a consumer makes an inquiry to a financial institution by email about its products or services, but does not obtain a product or service from or enter into a financial contract or transaction with the institution, the financial institution has a pre-existing business relationship with the consumer and can therefore use eligibility information it receives from an affiliate to make solicitations to the consumer about its products or services for three months after the date of the inquiry.

(G) If a consumer has an existing relationship with a financial institution that is part of a group of affiliated companies, makes a telephone call to the centralized call center for the group of affiliated companies to inquire about products or services offered by the insurance affiliate, and provides contact information to the call center, the call constitutes an inquiry to the insurance affiliate that offers those products or services. The insurance affiliate has a pre-existing business relationship with the consumer and can therefore use eligibility information it receives from its affiliated financial institution to make solicitations to the consumer about its products or services for three months after the date of the inquiry.

(iii) Examples where no pre-existing business relationship is created.

(A) If a consumer makes a telephone call to a centralized call center for a group of affiliated companies to inquire about the consumer's existing account at a financial institution, the call does not constitute an inquiry to any affiliate other than the financial institution that holds the consumer's account and does not establish a pre-existing business relationship between the consumer and any affiliate of the account-holding financial institution.

(B) If a consumer who has a deposit account with a financial institution makes a telephone call to an affiliate of the institution to ask about the affiliate's retail locations and hours, but does not make an inquiry about the affiliate's products or services, the call does not constitute an inquiry and does not establish a pre-existing business relationship between the consumer and the affiliate. Also, the affiliate's capture of the consumer's telephone number does not constitute an inquiry and does not establish a pre-existing business relationship between the consumer and the affiliate.

(C) If a consumer makes a telephone call to a financial institution in response to an advertisement that offers a free promotional item to consumers who call a toll-free number, but the advertisement does not indicate that the financial institution's products or services will be marketed to consumers who call in response, the call does not create a pre-existing business relationship between the consumer and the financial institution because the consumer has not made an inquiry about a product or service offered by the institution, but has merely responded to an offer for a free promotional item.

(5) Solicitation.

(i) In general. The term "solicitation" means the marketing of a product or service initiated by a person to a particular consumer that is:

(A) Based on eligibility information communicated to that person by its affiliate as described in this subpart; and

(B) Intended to encourage the consumer to purchase or obtain such product or service.

(ii) Exclusion of marketing directed at the general public. A solicitation does not include marketing communications that are directed at the general public. For example, television, general circulation magazine, and billboard advertisements do not constitute solicitations, even if those communications are intended to encourage consumers to purchase products and services from the person initiating the communications.

(iii) Examples of solicitations. A solicitation would include, for example, a telemarketing call, direct mail, email, or other form of marketing communication directed to a particular consumer that is based on eligibility information received from an affiliate.

(6) You means a person described in paragraph (a) of this section.

§ 1022.21. Affiliate marketing opt-out and exceptions

(a) Initial notice and opt-out requirement.

(1) In general. You may not use eligibility information about a consumer that you receive from an affiliate to make a solicitation for marketing purposes to the consumer, unless:

(i) It is clearly and conspicuously disclosed to the consumer in writing or, if the consumer agrees, electronically, in a concise notice that you may use eligibility information about that consumer received from an affiliate to make solicitations for marketing purposes to the consumer;

(ii) The consumer is provided a reasonable opportunity and a reasonable and simple method to "opt out," or prohibit you from using eligibility information to make solicitations for marketing purposes to the consumer; and

(iii) The consumer has not opted out.

(2) Example. A consumer has a homeowner's insurance policy with an insurance company. The insurance company furnishes eligibility information about the consumer to its affiliated creditor. Based on that eligibility information, the creditor wants to make a solicitation to the consumer about its home equity loan products. The creditor does not have a pre-existing business relationship with the consumer and none of the other exceptions apply. The creditor is prohibited from using eligibility information received from its insurance affiliate to make solicitations to the consumer about its home equity loan products unless the consumer is given a notice and opportunity to opt out and the consumer does not opt out.

(3) Affiliates who may provide the notice. The notice required by this paragraph must be provided:

(i) By an affiliate that has or has previously had a pre-existing business relationship with the consumer; or

(ii) As part of a joint notice from two or more members of an affiliated group of companies, provided that at least one of the affiliates on the joint notice has or has previously had a pre-existing business relationship with the consumer.

(b) Making solicitations.

(1) In general. For purposes of this subpart, you make a solicitation for marketing purposes if:

(i) You receive eligibility information from an affiliate;

(ii) You use that eligibility information to do one or more of the following:

(A) Identify the consumer or type of consumer to receive a solicitation;

(B) Establish criteria used to select the consumer to receive a solicitation; or

(C) Decide which of your products or services to market to the consumer or tailor your solicitation to that consumer; and

(iii) As a result of your use of the eligibility information, the consumer is provided a solicitation.

(2) Receiving eligibility information from an affiliate, including through a common database. You may receive eligibility information from an affiliate in various ways, including when the affiliate places that information into a common database that you may access.

(3) Receipt or use of eligibility information by your service provider. Except as provided in paragraph (b)(5) of this section, you receive or use an affiliate's eligibility information if a service provider acting on your behalf (whether an affiliate or a nonaffiliated third party) receives or uses that information in the manner described in paragraphs (b)(1)(i) or (b)(1)(ii) of this section. All relevant facts and circumstances will determine whether a person is acting as your service provider when it receives or uses an affiliate's eligibility information in connection with marketing your products and services.

(4) Use by an affiliate of its own eligibility information. Unless you have used eligibility information that you receive from an affiliate in the manner described in paragraph (b)(1)(ii) of this section, you do not make a solicitation subject to this subpart if your affiliate:

(i) Uses its own eligibility information that it obtained in connection with a pre-existing business relationship it has or had with the consumer to market your products or services to the consumer; or

(ii) Directs its service provider to use the affiliate's own eligibility information that it obtained in connection with a pre-existing business relationship it has or had with the consumer to market your products or services to the consumer, and you do not communicate directly with the service provider regarding that use.

(5) Use of eligibility information by a service provider.

(i) In general. You do not make a solicitation subject to Subpart C of this part if a service provider (including an affiliated or third-party service provider that maintains or accesses a common database that you may access) receives eligibility information from your affiliate that your affiliate obtained in connection with a pre-existing business relationship it has or had with the consumer and uses that eligibility information to market your products or services to the consumer, so long as:

(A) Your affiliate controls access to and use of its eligibility information by the service provider (including the right to establish the specific terms and conditions under which the service provider may use such information to market your products or services);

(B) Your affiliate establishes specific terms and conditions under which the service provider may access and use the affiliate's eligibility information to market your products and services (or those of affiliates generally) to the consumer, such as the identity of the affiliated companies whose products or services may be marketed to the consumer by the service provider, the types of products or services of affiliated companies that may be marketed, and the number of times the consumer may receive marketing materials, and periodically evaluates the service provider's compliance with those terms and conditions;

(C) Your affiliate requires the service provider to implement reasonable policies and procedures designed to ensure that the service provider uses the affiliate's eligibility information in accordance with the terms and conditions established by the affiliate relating to the marketing of your products or services;

(D) Your affiliate is identified on or with the marketing materials provided to the consumer; and

(E) You do not directly use your affiliate's eligibility information in the manner described in paragraph (b)(1)(ii) of this section.

(ii) Writing requirements.

(A) The requirements of paragraphs (b)(5)(i)(A) and (C) of this section must be set forth in a written agreement between your affiliate and the service provider; and

(B) The specific terms and conditions established by your affiliate as provided in paragraph (b)(5)(i)(B) of this section must be set forth in writing.

(6) Examples of making solicitations.

(i) A consumer has a deposit account with a financial institution, which is affiliated with an insurance company. The insurance company receives eligibility information about the consumer from the financial institution. The insurance company uses that eligibility information to identify the consumer to receive a solicitation about insurance products, and, as a result, the insurance company provides a solicitation to the consumer about its insurance products. Pursuant to paragraph (b)(1) of this section, the insurance company has made a solicitation to the consumer.

(ii) The same facts as in the example in paragraph (b)(6)(i) of this section, except that after using the eligibility information to identify the consumer to receive a solicitation about insurance products, the insurance company asks the financial institution to send the solicitation to the consumer and the financial institution does so. Pursuant to paragraph (b)(1) of this section, the insurance company has made a solicitation to the consumer because it used eligibility information about the consumer that it received from an affiliate to identify the consumer to receive a solicitation about its products or services, and, as a result, a solicitation was provided to the consumer about the insurance company's products.

(iii) The same facts as in the example in paragraph (b)(6)(i) of this section, except that eligibility information about consumers that have deposit accounts with the financial institution is placed into a common database that all members of the affiliated group of companies may independently access and use. Without using the financial institution's eligibility information, the insurance company develops selection criteria and provides those criteria, marketing materials, and related instructions to the financial institution. The financial institution reviews eligibility information about its own consumers using the selection criteria provided by the insurance company to determine which consumers should receive the insurance company's marketing materials and sends marketing materials about the insurance company's products to those consumers. Even though the insurance company has received eligibility information through the common database as provided in paragraph (b)(2) of this section, it did not use that information to identify consumers or establish selection criteria; instead, the financial institution used its own eligibility information. Therefore, pursuant to paragraph (b)(4)(i) of this section, the insurance company has not made a solicitation to the consumer.

(iv) The same facts as in the example in paragraph (b)(6)(iii) of this section, except that the financial institution provides the insurance company's criteria to the financial institution's service provider and directs the service provider to use the financial institution's eligibility information to identify financial institution consumers who meet the criteria and to send the insurance company's marketing materials to those consumers. The insurance company does not communicate directly with the service provider regarding the use of the financial institution's information to market its products to the financial institution's consumers. Pursuant to paragraph (b)(4)(ii) of this section, the insurance company has not made a solicitation to the consumer.

(v) An affiliated group of companies includes a financial institution, an insurance company, and a service provider. Each affiliate in the group places information about its consumers into a common database. The service provider has access to all information in the common database. The financial institution controls access to and use of its eligibility information by the service provider. This control is set forth in a written agreement between the financial institution and the service provider. The written agreement also requires the service provider to establish reasonable policies and procedures designed to ensure that the service provider uses the financial institution's eligibility information in accordance with specific terms and conditions established by the financial institution relating to the marketing of the products and services of all affiliates, including the insurance company. In a separate written communication, the financial institution specifies the terms and conditions under which the service provider may use the financial institution's eligibility information to market the insurance company's products and services to the financial institution's consumers. The specific terms and conditions are: a list of affiliated companies (including the insurance company) whose products or services may be marketed to the financial institution's consumers by the service provider; the specific products or types of products that may be marketed to the financial institution's consumers by the service provider; the categories of eligibility information that may be used by the service provider in marketing products or services to the financial institution's consumers; the types or categories of the financial institution's consumers to whom the service provider may market products or services of financial institution affiliates; the number and/or types of marketing communications that the service provider may send to the financial institution's consumers; and the length of time during which the service provider may market the products or services of the financial institution's affiliates to its consumers. The financial institution periodically evaluates the service provider's compliance with these terms and conditions. The insurance company asks the service provider to market insurance products to certain consumers who have deposit accounts with the financial institution. Without using the financial institution's eligibility information, the insurance company develops selection criteria and provides those criteria, marketing materials, and related instructions to the service provider. The service provider uses the financial institution's eligibility information from the common database to identify the financial institution's consumers to whom insurance products will be marketed. When the insurance company's marketing materials are provided to the identified consumers, the name of the financial institution is displayed on the insurance marketing materials, an introductory letter that accompanies the marketing materials, an account statement that accompanies the marketing materials, or the envelope containing the marketing materials. The requirements of paragraph (b)(5) of this section have been satisfied, and the insurance company has not made a solicitation to the consumer.

(vi) The same facts as in the example in paragraph (b)(6)(v) of this section, except that the terms and conditions permit the service provider to use the financial institution's eligibility information to market the products and services of other affiliates to the financial institution's consumers whenever the service provider deems it appropriate to do so. The service provider uses the financial institution's eligibility information in accordance with the discretion afforded to it by the terms and conditions. Because the terms and conditions are not specific, the requirements of paragraph (b)(5) of this section have not been satisfied.

(c) Exceptions. The provisions of this subpart do not apply to you if you use eligibility information that you receive from an affiliate:

(1) To make a solicitation for marketing purposes to a consumer with whom you have a pre-existing business relationship;

(2) To facilitate communications to an individual for whose benefit you provide employee benefit or other services pursuant to a contract with an employer related to and arising out of the current employment relationship or status of the individual as a participant or beneficiary of an employee benefit plan;

(3) To perform services on behalf of an affiliate, except that this subparagraph shall not be construed as permitting you to send solicitations on behalf of an affiliate if the affiliate would not be permitted to send the solicitation as a result of the election of the consumer to opt out under this subpart;

(4) In response to a communication about your products or services initiated by the consumer;

(5) In response to an authorization or request by the consumer to receive solicitations; or

(6) If your compliance with this subpart would prevent you from complying with any provision of state insurance laws pertaining to unfair discrimination in any state in which you are lawfully doing business.

(d) Examples of exceptions.

(1) Example of the pre-existing business relationship exception. A consumer has a deposit account with a financial institution. The consumer also has a relationship with the financial institution's securities affiliate for management of the consumer's securities portfolio. The financial institution receives eligibility information about the consumer from its securities affiliate and uses that information to make a solicitation to the consumer about the financial institution's wealth management services. The financial institution may make this solicitation even if the consumer has not been given a notice and opportunity to opt out because the financial institution has a pre-existing business relationship with the consumer.

(2) Examples of service provider exception.

(i) A consumer has an insurance policy issued by an insurance company. The insurance company furnishes eligibility information about the consumer to its affiliated financial institution. Based on that eligibility information, the financial institution wants to make a solicitation to the consumer about its deposit products. The financial institution does not have a pre-existing business relationship with the consumer and none of the other exceptions in paragraph (c) of this section apply. The consumer has been given an opt-out notice and has elected to opt out of receiving such solicitations. The financial institution asks a service provider to send the solicitation to the consumer on its behalf. The service provider may not send the solicitation on behalf of the financial institution because, as a result of the consumer's opt-out election, the financial institution is not permitted to make the solicitation.

(ii) The same facts as in paragraph (d)(2)(i) of this section, except the consumer has been given an opt-out notice, but has not elected to opt out. The financial institution asks a service provider to send the solicitation to the consumer on its behalf. The service provider may send the solicitation on behalf of the financial institution because, as a result of the consumer's not opting out, the financial institution is permitted to make the solicitation.

(3) Examples of consumer-initiated communications.

(i) A consumer who has a deposit account with a financial institution initiates a communication with the financial institution's credit card affiliate to request information about a credit card. The credit card affiliate may use eligibility information about the consumer it obtains from the financial institution or any other affiliate to make solicitations regarding credit card products in response to the consumer-initiated communication.

(ii) A consumer who has a deposit account with a financial institution contacts the institution to request information about how to save and invest for a child's college education without specifying the type of product in which the consumer may be interested. Information about a range of different products or services offered by the financial institution and one or more affiliates of the institution may be responsive to that communication. Such products or services may include the following: mutual funds offered by the institution's mutual fund affiliate; section 529 plans offered by the institution, its mutual fund affiliate, or another securities affiliate; or trust services offered by a different financial institution in the affiliated group. Any affiliate offering investment products or services that would be responsive to the consumer's request for information about saving and investing for a child's college education may use eligibility information to make solicitations to the consumer in response to this communication.

(iii) A credit card issuer makes a marketing call to the consumer without using eligibility information received from an affiliate. The issuer leaves a voice-mail message that invites the consumer to call a toll-free number to apply for the issuer's credit card. If the consumer calls the toll-free number to inquire about the credit card, the call is a consumer-initiated communication about a product or service and the credit card issuer may now use eligibility information it receives from its affiliates to make solicitations to the consumer.

(iv) A consumer calls a financial institution to ask about retail locations and hours, but does not request information about products or services. The institution may not use eligibility information it receives from an affiliate to make solicitations to the consumer about its products or services because the consumer-initiated communication does not relate to the financial institution's products or services. Thus, the use of eligibility information received from an affiliate would not be responsive to the communication and the exception does not apply.

(v) A consumer calls a financial institution to ask about retail locations and hours. The customer service representative asks the consumer if there is a particular product or service about which the consumer is seeking information. The consumer responds that the consumer wants to stop in and find out about certificates of deposit. The customer service representative offers to provide that information by telephone and mail additional information and application materials to the consumer. The consumer agrees and provides or confirms contact information for receipt of the materials to be mailed. The financial institution may use eligibility information it receives from an affiliate to make solicitations to the consumer about certificates of deposit because such solicitations would respond to the consumer-initiated communication about products or services.

(4) Examples of consumer authorization or request for solicitations.

(i) A consumer who obtains a mortgage from a mortgage lender authorizes or requests information about homeowner's insurance offered by the mortgage lender's insurance affiliate. Such authorization or request, whether given to the mortgage lender or to the insurance affiliate, would permit the insurance affiliate to use eligibility information about the consumer it obtains from the mortgage lender or any other affiliate to make solicitations to the consumer about homeowner's insurance.

(ii) A consumer completes an online application to apply for a credit card from a credit card issuer. The issuer's online application contains a blank check box that the consumer may check to authorize or request information from the credit card issuer's affiliates. The consumer checks the box. The consumer has authorized or requested solicitations from the card issuer's affiliates.

(iii) A consumer completes an online application to apply for a credit card from a credit card issuer. The issuer's online application contains a pre-selected check box indicating that the consumer authorizes or requests information from the issuer's affiliates. The consumer does not deselect the check box. The consumer has not authorized or requested solicitations from the card issuer's affiliates.

(iv) The terms and conditions of a credit card account agreement contain preprinted boilerplate language stating that by applying to open an account the consumer authorizes or requests to receive solicitations from the credit card issuer's affiliates. The consumer has not authorized or requested solicitations from the card issuer's affiliates.

(e) Relation to affiliate-sharing notice and opt-out. Nothing in this subpart limits the responsibility of a person to comply with the notice and opt-out provisions of section 603(d)(2)(A)(iii) of the Act where applicable.

§ 1022.22. Scope and duration of opt-out

(a) Scope of opt-out.

(1) In general. Except as otherwise provided in this section, the consumer's election to opt out prohibits any affiliate covered by the opt-out notice from using eligibility information received from another affiliate as described in the notice to make solicitations to the consumer.

(2) Continuing relationship.

(i) In general. If the consumer establishes a continuing relationship with you or your affiliate, an opt-out notice may apply to eligibility information obtained in connection with:

(A) A single continuing relationship or multiple continuing relationships that the consumer establishes with you or your affiliates, including continuing relationships established subsequent to delivery of the opt-out notice, so long as the notice adequately describes the continuing relationships covered by the opt-out; or

(B) Any other transaction between the consumer and you or your affiliates as described in the notice.

(ii) Examples of continuing relationships. A consumer has a continuing relationship with you or your affiliate if the consumer:

(A) Opens a deposit or investment account with you or your affiliate;

(B) Obtains a loan for which you or your affiliate owns the servicing rights;

(C) Purchases an insurance product from you or your affiliate;

(D) Holds an investment product through you or your affiliate, such as when you act or your affiliate acts as a custodian for securities or for assets in an individual retirement arrangement;

(E) Enters into an agreement or understanding with you or your affiliate whereby you or your affiliate undertakes to arrange or broker a home mortgage loan for the consumer;

(F) Enters into a lease of personal property with you or your affiliate; or

(G) Obtains financial, investment, or economic advisory services from you or your affiliate for a fee.

(3) No continuing relationship.

(i) In general. If there is no continuing relationship between a consumer and you or your affiliate, and you or your affiliate obtain eligibility information about a consumer in connection with a transaction with the consumer, such as an isolated transaction or a credit application that is denied, an opt-out notice provided to the consumer only applies to eligibility information obtained in connection with that transaction.

(ii) Examples of isolated transactions. An isolated transaction occurs if:

(A) The consumer uses your or your affiliate's ATM to withdraw cash from an account at another financial institution; or

(B) You or your affiliate sells the consumer a cashier's check or money order, airline tickets, travel insurance, or traveler's checks in isolated transactions.

(4) Menu of alternatives. A consumer may be given the opportunity to choose from a menu of alternatives when electing to prohibit solicitations, such as by electing to prohibit solicitations from certain types of affiliates covered by the opt-out notice but not other types of affiliates covered by the notice, electing to prohibit solicitations based on certain types of eligibility information but not other types of eligibility information, or electing to prohibit solicitations by certain methods of delivery but not other methods of delivery. However, one of the alternatives must allow the consumer to prohibit all solicitations from all of the affiliates that are covered by the notice.

(5) Special rule for a notice following termination of all continuing relationships.

(i) In general. A consumer must be given a new opt-out notice if, after all continuing relationships with you or your affiliate(s) are terminated, the consumer subsequently establishes another continuing relationship with you or your affiliate(s) and the consumer's eligibility information is to be used to make a solicitation. The new opt-out notice must apply, at a minimum, to eligibility information obtained in connection with the new continuing relationship. Consistent with paragraph (b) of this section, the consumer's decision not to opt out after receiving the new opt-out notice would not override a prior opt-out election by the consumer that applies to eligibility information obtained in connection with a terminated relationship, regardless of whether the new opt-out notice applies to eligibility information obtained in connection with the terminated relationship.

(ii) Example. A consumer has a checking account with a financial institution that is part of an affiliated group. The consumer closes the checking account. One year after closing the checking account, the consumer opens a savings account with the same financial institution. The consumer must be given a new notice and opportunity to opt out before the financial institution's affiliates may make solicitations to the consumer using eligibility information obtained by the financial institution in connection with the new savings account relationship, regardless of whether the consumer opted out in connection with the checking account.

(b) Duration of opt-out. The election of a consumer to opt out must be effective for a period of at least five years (the "opt-out period") beginning when the consumer's opt-out election is received and implemented, unless the consumer subsequently revokes the opt-out in writing or, if the consumer agrees, electronically. An opt-out period of more than five years may be established, including an opt-out period that does not expire unless revoked by the consumer.

(c) Time of opt-out. A consumer may opt out at any time.

§ 1022.23. Contents of opt-out notice; consolidated and equivalent notices

(a) Contents of opt-out notice.

(1) In general. A notice must be clear, conspicuous, and concise, and must accurately disclose:

(i) The name of the affiliate(s) providing the notice. If the notice is provided jointly by multiple affiliates and each affiliate shares a common name, such as "ABC," then the notice may indicate that it is being provided by multiple companies with the ABC name or multiple companies in the ABC group or family of companies, for example, by stating that the notice is provided by "all of the ABC companies," "the ABC banking, credit card, insurance, and securities companies," or by listing the name of each affiliate providing the notice. But if the affiliates providing the joint notice do not all share a common name, then the notice must either separately identify each affiliate by name or identify each of the common names used by those affiliates, for example, by stating that the notice is provided by "all of the ABC and XYZ companies" or by "the ABC banking and credit card companies and the XYZ insurance companies;"

(ii) A list of the affiliates or types of affiliates whose use of eligibility information is covered by the notice, which may include companies that become affiliates after the notice is provided to the consumer. If each affiliate covered by the notice shares a common name, such as "ABC," then the notice may indicate that it applies to multiple companies with the ABC name or multiple companies in the ABC group or family of companies, for example, by stating that the notice is provided by "all of the ABC companies," "the ABC banking, credit card, insurance, and securities companies," or by listing the name of each affiliate providing the notice. But if the affiliates covered by the notice do not all share a common name, then the notice must either separately identify each covered affiliate by name or identify each of the common names used by those affiliates, for example, by stating that the notice applies to "all of the ABC and XYZ companies" or to "the ABC banking and credit card companies and the XYZ insurance companies;"

(iii) A general description of the types of eligibility information that may be used to make solicitations to the consumer;

(iv) That the consumer may elect to limit the use of eligibility information to make solicitations to the consumer;

(v) That the consumer's election will apply for the specified period of time stated in the notice and, if applicable, that the consumer will be allowed to renew the election once that period expires;

(vi) If the notice is provided to consumers who may have previously opted out, such as if a notice is provided to consumers annually, that the consumer who has chosen to limit solicitations does not need to act again until the consumer receives a renewal notice; and

(vii) A reasonable and simple method for the consumer to opt out.

(2) Joint relationships.

(i) If two or more consumers jointly obtain a product or service, a single opt-out notice may be provided to the joint consumers. Any of the joint consumers may exercise the right to opt out.

(ii) The opt-out notice must explain how an opt-out direction by a joint consumer will be treated. An opt-out direction by a joint consumer may be treated as applying to all of the associated joint consumers, or each joint consumer may be permitted to opt out separately. If each joint consumer is permitted to opt out separately, one of the joint consumers must be permitted to opt out on behalf of all of the joint consumers and the joint consumers must be permitted to exercise their separate rights to opt out in a single response.

(iii) It is impermissible to require *all* joint consumers to opt out before implementing *any* opt-out direction.

(3) Alternative contents. If the consumer is afforded a broader right to opt out of receiving marketing than is required by this subpart, the requirements of this section may be satisfied by providing the consumer with a clear, conspicuous, and concise notice that accurately discloses the consumer's opt-out rights.

(4) Model notices. Model notices are provided in Appendix C of this part.

(b) Coordinated and consolidated notices. A notice required by this subpart may be coordinated and consolidated with any other notice or disclosure required to be issued under any other provision of law by the entity providing the notice, including but not limited to the notice described in section 603(d)(2)(A)(iii) of the Act and the Gramm-Leach-Bliley Act privacy notice.

(c) Equivalent notices. A notice or other disclosure that is equivalent to the notice required by this subpart, and that is provided to a consumer together with disclosures required by any other provision of law, satisfies the requirements of this section.

§ 1022.24. Reasonable opportunity to opt out

(a) In general. You must not use eligibility information about a consumer that you receive from an affiliate to make a solicitation to the consumer about your products or services, unless the consumer is provided a reasonable opportunity to opt out, as required by § 1022.21(a)(1)(ii) of this part.

(b) Examples of a reasonable opportunity to opt out. The consumer is given a reasonable opportunity to opt out if:

(1) By mail. The opt-out notice is mailed to the consumer. The consumer is given 30 days from the date the notice is mailed to elect to opt out by any reasonable means.

(2) By electronic means.

(i) The opt-out notice is provided electronically to the consumer, such as by posting the notice at a Web site at which the consumer has obtained a product or service. The consumer acknowledges receipt of the electronic notice. The consumer is given 30 days after the date the consumer acknowledges receipt to elect to opt out by any reasonable means.

(ii) The opt-out notice is provided to the consumer by email where the consumer has agreed to receive disclosures by email from the person sending the notice. The consumer is given 30 days after the email is sent to elect to opt out by any reasonable means.

(3) At the time of an electronic transaction. The opt-out notice is provided to the consumer at the time of an electronic transaction, such as a transaction conducted on a Web site. The consumer is required to decide, as a necessary part of proceeding with the transaction, whether to opt out before completing the transaction. There is a simple process that the consumer may use to opt out at that time using the same mechanism through which the transaction is conducted.

(4) At the time of an in-person transaction. The opt-out notice is provided to the consumer in writing at the time of an in-person transaction. The consumer is required to decide, as a necessary part of proceeding with the transaction, whether to opt out before completing the transaction, and is not permitted to complete the transaction without making a choice. There is a simple process that the consumer may use during the course of the in-person transaction to opt out, such as completing a form that requires consumers to write a "yes" or "no" to indicate their opt-out preference or that requires the consumer to check one of two blank check boxes; one that allows consumers to indicate that they want to opt out and one that allows consumers to indicate that they do not want to opt out.

(5) By including in a privacy notice. The opt-out notice is included in a Gramm-Leach-Bliley Act privacy notice. The consumer is allowed to exercise the opt-out within a reasonable period of time and in the same manner as the opt-out under that privacy notice.

§ 1022.25. Reasonable and simple methods of opting out

(a) In general. You must not use eligibility information about a consumer that you receive from an affiliate to make a solicitation to the consumer about your products or services, unless the consumer is provided a reasonable and simple method to opt out, as required by § 1022.21(a)(1)(ii) of this part.

(b) Examples.

(1) Reasonable and simple opt-out methods. Reasonable and simple methods for exercising the opt-out right include:

(i) Designating a check-off box in a prominent position on the opt-out form;

(ii) Including a reply form and a self-addressed envelope together with the opt-out notice;

(iii) Providing an electronic means to opt out, such as a form that can be electronically mailed or processed at a Web site, if the consumer agrees to the electronic delivery of information;

(iv) Providing a toll-free telephone number that consumers may call to opt out; or

(v) Allowing consumers to exercise all of their opt-out rights described in a consolidated opt-out notice that includes the privacy opt-out under the Gramm-Leach-Bliley Act, 15 U.S.C. 6801 et seq., the affiliate sharing opt-out under the Act, and the affiliate marketing opt-out under the Act, by a single method, such as by calling a single toll-free telephone number.

(2) Opt-out methods that are not reasonable and simple. Reasonable and simple methods for exercising an opt-out right do not include—

(i) Requiring the consumer to write his or her own letter;

(ii) Requiring the consumer to call or write to obtain a form for opting out, rather than including the form with the opt-out notice;

(iii) Requiring the consumer who receives the opt-out notice in electronic form only, such as through posting at a Web site, to opt out solely by paper mail or by visiting a different Web site without providing a link to that site.

(c) Specific opt-out means. Each consumer may be required to opt out through a specific means, as long as that means is reasonable and simple for that consumer.

§ 1022.26. Delivery of opt-out notices

(a) In general. The opt-out notice must be provided so that each consumer can reasonably be expected to receive actual notice. For opt-out notices provided electronically, the notice may be provided in compliance with either the electronic disclosure provisions in this subpart or the provisions in section 101 of the Electronic Signatures in Global and National Commerce Act, 15 U.S.C. 7001 et seq.

(b) Examples of reasonable expectation of actual notice. A consumer may reasonably be expected to receive actual notice if the affiliate providing the notice:

(1) Hand-delivers a printed copy of the notice to the consumer;

(2) Mails a printed copy of the notice to the last known mailing address of the consumer;

(3) Provides a notice by email to a consumer who has agreed to receive electronic disclosures by email from the affiliate providing the notice; or

(4) Posts the notice on the Web site at which the consumer obtained a product or service electronically and requires the consumer to acknowledge receipt of the notice.

(c) Examples of no reasonable expectation of actual notice. A consumer may *not* reasonably be expected to receive actual notice if the affiliate providing the notice:

(1) Only posts the notice on a sign in a branch or office or generally publishes the notice in a newspaper;

(2) Sends the notice via email to a consumer who has not agreed to receive electronic disclosures by email from the affiliate providing the notice; or

(3) Posts the notice on a Web site without requiring the consumer to acknowledge receipt of the notice.

§ 1022.27. Renewal of opt-out

(a) Renewal notice and opt-out requirement.

(1) In general. After the opt-out period expires, you may not make solicitations based on eligibility information you receive from an affiliate to a consumer who previously opted out, unless:

(i) The consumer has been given a renewal notice that complies with the requirements of this section and §§ 1022.24 through 1022.26 of this part, and a reasonable opportunity and a reasonable and simple method to renew the opt-out, and the consumer does not renew the opt-out; or

(ii) An exception in § 1022.21(c) of this part applies.

(2) Renewal period. Each opt-out renewal must be effective for a period of at least five years as provided in § 1022.22(b) of this part.

(3) Affiliates who may provide the notice. The notice required by this paragraph must be provided:

(i) By the affiliate that provided the previous opt-out notice, or its successor; or

(ii) As part of a joint renewal notice from two or more members of an affiliated group of companies, or their successors, that jointly provided the previous opt-out notice.

(b) Contents of renewal notice. The renewal notice must be clear, conspicuous, and concise, and must accurately disclose:

(1) The name of the affiliate(s) providing the notice. If the notice is provided jointly by multiple affiliates and each affiliate shares a common name, such as "ABC," then the notice may indicate that it is being provided by multiple companies with the ABC name or multiple companies in the ABC group or family of companies, for example, by stating that the notice is provided by "all of the ABC companies," "the ABC banking, credit card, insurance, and securities companies," or by listing the name of each affiliate providing the notice. But if the affiliates providing the joint notice do not all share a common name, then the notice must either separately identify each affiliate by name or identify each of the common names used by those affiliates, for example, by stating that the notice is provided by "all of the ABC and XYZ companies" or by "the ABC banking and credit card companies and the XYZ insurance companies";

(2) A list of the affiliates or types of affiliates whose use of eligibility information is covered by the notice, which may include companies that become affiliates after the notice is provided to the consumer. If each affiliate covered by the notice shares a common name, such as "ABC," then the notice may indicate that it applies to multiple companies with the ABC name or multiple companies in the ABC group or family of companies, for example, by stating that the notice is provided by "all of the ABC companies," "the ABC banking, credit card, insurance, and securities companies," or by listing the name of each affiliate providing the notice. But if the affiliates covered by the notice do not all share a common name, then the notice must either separately identify each covered affiliate by name or identify each of the common names used by those affiliates, for example, by stating that the notice applies to "all of the ABC and XYZ companies" or to "the ABC banking and credit card companies and the XYZ insurance companies;"

(3) A general description of the types of eligibility information that may be used to make solicitations to the consumer;

(4) That the consumer previously elected to limit the use of certain information to make solicitations to the consumer;

(5) That the consumer's election has expired or is about to expire;

(6) That the consumer may elect to renew the consumer's previous election;

(7) If applicable, that the consumer's election to renew will apply for the specified period of time stated in the notice and that the consumer will be allowed to renew the election once that period expires; and

(8) A reasonable and simple method for the consumer to opt out.

(c) Timing of the renewal notice.

(1) In general. A renewal notice may be provided to the consumer either:

(i) A reasonable period of time before the expiration of the opt-out period; or

(ii) Any time after the expiration of the opt-out period but before solicitations that would have been prohibited by the expired opt-out are made to the consumer.

(2) Combination with annual privacy notice. If you provide an annual privacy notice under the Gramm-Leach-Bliley Act, 15 U.S.C. 6801 et seq., providing a renewal notice with the last annual privacy notice provided to the consumer before expiration of the opt-out period is a reasonable period of time before expiration of the opt-out in all cases.

(d) No effect on opt-out period. An opt-out period may not be shortened by sending a renewal notice to the consumer before expiration of the opt-out period, even if the consumer does not renew the opt out.

Subpart D. Medical Information

§ 1022.30. Obtaining or using medical information in connection with a determination of eligibility for credit

(a) Scope. This section applies to any person that participates as a creditor in a transaction, except for a person excluded from coverage of this part by section 1029 of the Consumer Financial Protection Act of 2010, Title X of the Dodd-Frank Wall Street Reform and Consumer Protection Act, Public Law 111–203, 124 Stat. 137.

(b) General prohibition on obtaining or using medical information.

(1) In general. A creditor may not obtain or use medical information pertaining to a consumer in connection with any determination of the consumer's eligibility, or continued eligibility, for credit, except as provided in this section.

(2) Definitions.

(i) Credit has the same meaning as in section 702 of the Equal Credit Opportunity Act, 15 U.S.C. 1691a.

(ii) Creditor has the same meaning as in section 702 of the Equal Credit Opportunity Act, 15 U.S.C. 1691a.

(iii) Eligibility, or continued eligibility, for credit means the consumer's qualification or fitness to receive, or continue to receive, credit, including the terms on which credit is offered. The term does not include:

(A) Any determination of the consumer's qualification or fitness for employment, insurance (other than a credit insurance product), or other non-credit products or services;

(B) Authorizing, processing, or documenting a payment or transaction on behalf of the consumer in a manner that does not involve a determination of the consumer's eligibility, or continued eligibility, for credit; or

(C) Maintaining or servicing the consumer's account in a manner that does not involve a determination of the consumer's eligibility, or continued eligibility, for credit.

(c) Rule of construction for obtaining and using unsolicited medical information.

(1) In general. A creditor does not obtain medical information in violation of the prohibition if it receives medical information pertaining to a consumer in connection with any determination of the consumer's eligibility, or continued eligibility, for credit without specifically requesting medical information.

(2) Use of unsolicited medical information. A creditor that receives unsolicited medical information in the manner described in paragraph (c)(1) of this section may use that information in connection with any determination of the consumer's eligibility, or continued eligibility, for credit to the extent the creditor can rely on at least one of the exceptions in § 1022.30(d) or (e).

(3) Examples. A creditor does not obtain medical information in violation of the prohibition if, for example:

(i) In response to a general question regarding a consumer's debts or expenses, the creditor receives information that the consumer owes a debt to a hospital.

(ii) In a conversation with the creditor's loan officer, the consumer informs the creditor that the consumer has a particular medical condition.

(iii) In connection with a consumer's application for an extension of credit, the creditor requests a consumer report from a consumer reporting agency and receives medical information in the consumer report furnished by the agency even though the creditor did not specifically request medical information from the consumer reporting agency.

(d) Financial information exception for obtaining and using medical information.

(1) In general. A creditor may obtain and use medical information pertaining to a consumer in connection with any determination of the consumer's eligibility, or continued eligibility, for credit so long as:

(i) The information is the type of information routinely used in making credit eligibility determinations, such as information relating to debts, expenses, income, benefits, assets, collateral, or the purpose of the loan, including the use of proceeds;

(ii) The creditor uses the medical information in a manner and to an extent that is no less favorable than it would use comparable information that is not medical information in a credit transaction; and

(iii) The creditor does not take the consumer's physical, mental, or behavioral health, condition or history, type of treatment, or prognosis into account as part of any such determination.

(2) Examples.

(i) Examples of the types of information routinely used in making credit eligibility determinations. Paragraph (d)(1)(i) of this section permits a creditor, for example, to obtain and use information about:

(A) The dollar amount, repayment terms, repayment history, and similar information regarding medical debts to calculate, measure, or verify the repayment ability of the consumer, the use of proceeds, or the terms for granting credit;

(B) The value, condition, and lien status of a medical device that may serve as collateral to secure a loan;

(C) The dollar amount and continued eligibility for disability income, workers' compensation income, or other benefits related to health or a medical condition that is relied on as a source of repayment; or

(D) The identity of creditors to whom outstanding medical debts are owed in connection with an application for credit, including but not limited to, a transaction involving the consolidation of medical debts.

(ii) Examples of uses of medical information consistent with the exception.

(A) A consumer includes on an application for credit information about two $20,000 debts. One debt is to a hospital; the other debt is to a retailer. The creditor contacts the hospital and the retailer to verify the amount and payment status of the debts. The creditor learns that both debts are more than 90 days past due. Any two debts of this size that are more than 90 days past due would disqualify the consumer under the creditor's established underwriting criteria. The creditor denies the application on the basis that the consumer has a poor repayment history on outstanding debts. The creditor has used medical information in a manner and to an extent no less favorable than it would use comparable non-medical information.

(B) A consumer indicates on an application for a $200,000 mortgage loan that she receives $15,000 in long-term disability income each year from her former employer and has no other income. Annual income of $15,000, regardless of source, would not be sufficient to support the requested amount of credit. The creditor denies the application on the basis that the projected debt-to-income ratio of the consumer does not meet the creditor's underwriting criteria. The creditor has used medical information in a manner and to an extent that is no less favorable than it would use comparable non-medical information.

(C) A consumer includes on an application for a $10,000 home equity loan that he has a $50,000 debt to a medical facility that specializes in treating a potentially terminal disease. The creditor contacts the medical facility to verify the debt and obtain the repayment history and current status of the loan. The creditor learns that the debt is current. The applicant meets the income and other requirements of the creditor's underwriting guidelines. The creditor grants the application. The creditor has used medical information in accordance with the exception.

(iii) Examples of uses of medical information inconsistent with the exception.

(A) A consumer applies for $25,000 of credit and includes on the application information about a $50,000 debt to a hospital. The creditor contacts the hospital to verify the amount and payment status of the debt, and learns that the debt is current and that the consumer has no delinquencies in her repayment history. If the existing debt were instead owed to a retail department store, the creditor would approve the application and extend credit based on the amount and repayment history of the outstanding debt. The creditor, however, denies the application because the consumer is indebted to a hospital. The creditor has used medical information, here the identity of the medical creditor, in a manner and to an extent that is less favorable than it would use comparable non-medical information.

(B) A consumer meets with a loan officer of a creditor to apply for a mortgage loan. While filling out the loan application, the consumer informs the loan officer orally that she has a potentially terminal disease. The consumer meets the creditor's established requirements for the requested mortgage loan. The loan officer recommends to the credit committee that the consumer be denied credit because the consumer has that disease. The credit committee follows the loan officer's recommendation and denies the application because the consumer has a potentially terminal disease. The creditor has used medical information in a manner inconsistent with the exception by taking into account the consumer's physical, mental, or behavioral health, condition, or history, type of treatment, or prognosis as part of a determination of eligibility or continued eligibility for credit.

(C) A consumer who has an apparent medical condition, such as a consumer who uses a wheelchair or an oxygen tank, meets with a loan officer to apply for a home equity loan. The consumer meets the creditor's established requirements for the requested home equity loan and the creditor typically does not require consumers to obtain a debt cancellation contract, debt suspension agreement, or credit insurance product in connection with such loans. However, based on the consumer's apparent medical condition, the loan officer recommends to the credit committee that credit be extended to the consumer only if the consumer obtains a debt cancellation contract, debt suspension agreement, or credit insurance product from a nonaffiliated third party. The credit committee agrees with the loan officer's recommendation. The loan officer informs the consumer that the consumer must obtain a debt cancellation contract, debt suspension agreement, or credit insurance product from a nonaffiliated third party to qualify for the loan. The consumer obtains one of these products and the creditor approves the loan. The creditor has used medical information in a manner inconsistent with the exception by taking into account the consumer's physical, mental, or behavioral health, condition, or history, type of treatment, or prognosis in setting conditions on the consumer's eligibility for credit.

(e) Specific exceptions for obtaining and using medical information.

(1) In general. A creditor may obtain and use medical information pertaining to a consumer in connection with any determination of the consumer's eligibility, or continued eligibility, for credit:

(i) To determine whether the use of a power of attorney or legal representative that is triggered by a medical condition or event is necessary and appropriate or whether the consumer has the legal capacity to contract when a person seeks to exercise a power of attorney or act as legal representative for a consumer based on an asserted medical condition or event;

(ii) To comply with applicable requirements of local, state, or Federal laws;

(iii) To determine, at the consumer's request, whether the consumer qualifies for a legally permissible special credit program or credit-related assistance program that is:

(A) Designed to meet the special needs of consumers with medical conditions; and

(B) Established and administered pursuant to a written plan that:

(1) Identifies the class of persons that the program is designed to benefit; and

(2) Sets forth the procedures and standards for extending credit or providing other credit-related assistance under the program;

(iv) To the extent necessary for purposes of fraud prevention or detection;

(v) In the case of credit for the purpose of financing medical products or services, to determine and verify the medical purpose of a loan and the use of proceeds;

(vi) Consistent with safe and sound practices, if the consumer or the consumer's legal representative specifically requests that the creditor use medical information in determining the consumer's eligibility, or continued eligibility, for credit, to accommodate the consumer's particular circumstances, and such request is documented by the creditor;

(vii) Consistent with safe and sound practices, to determine whether the provisions of a forbearance practice or program that is triggered by a medical condition or event apply to a consumer;

(viii) To determine the consumer's eligibility for, the triggering of, or the reactivation of a debt cancellation contract or debt suspension agreement if a medical condition or event is a triggering event for the provision of benefits under the contract or agreement; or

(ix) To determine the consumer's eligibility for, the triggering of, or the reactivation of a credit insurance product if a medical condition or event is a triggering event for the provision of benefits under the product.

(2) Example of determining eligibility for a special credit program or credit assistance program. A not-for-profit organization establishes a credit assistance program pursuant to a written plan that is designed to assist disabled veterans in purchasing homes by subsidizing the down payment for the home purchase mortgage loans of qualifying veterans. The organization works through mortgage lenders and requires mortgage lenders to obtain medical information about the disability of any consumer that seeks to qualify for the program, use that information to verify the consumer's eligibility for the program, and forward that information to the organization. A consumer who is a veteran applies to a creditor for a home purchase mortgage loan. The creditor informs the consumer about the credit assistance program for disabled veterans and the consumer seeks to qualify for the program. Assuming that the program complies with all applicable law, including applicable fair lending laws, the creditor may obtain and use medical information about the medical condition and disability, if any, of the consumer to determine whether the consumer qualifies for the credit assistance program.

(3) Examples of verifying the medical purpose of the loan or the use of proceeds.

(i) If a consumer applies for $10,000 of credit for the purpose of financing vision correction surgery, the creditor may verify with the surgeon that the procedure will be performed. If the surgeon reports that surgery will not be performed on the consumer, the creditor may use that medical information to deny the consumer's application for credit, because the loan would not be used for the stated purpose.

(ii) If a consumer applies for $10,000 of credit for the purpose of financing cosmetic surgery, the creditor may confirm the cost of the procedure with the surgeon. If the surgeon reports that the cost of the procedure is $5,000, the creditor may use that medical information to offer the consumer only $5,000 of credit.

(iii) A creditor has an established medical loan program for financing particular elective surgical procedures. The creditor receives a loan application from a consumer requesting $10,000 of credit under the established loan program for an elective surgical procedure. The consumer indicates on the application that the purpose of the loan is to finance an elective surgical procedure not eligible for funding under the guidelines of the established loan program. The creditor may deny the consumer's application because the purpose of the loan is not for a particular procedure funded by the established loan program.

(4) Examples of obtaining and using medical information at the request of the consumer.

(i) If a consumer applies for a loan and specifically requests that the creditor consider the consumer's medical disability at the relevant time as an explanation for adverse payment history information in his credit report, the creditor may consider such medical information in evaluating the consumer's willingness and ability to repay the requested loan to accommodate the consumer's particular circumstances, consistent with safe and sound practices. The creditor may also decline to consider such medical information to accommodate the consumer, but may evaluate the consumer's application in accordance with its otherwise applicable underwriting criteria. The creditor may not deny the consumer's application or otherwise treat the consumer less favorably because the consumer specifically requested a medical accommodation, if the creditor would have extended the credit or treated the consumer more favorably under the creditor's otherwise applicable underwriting criteria.

(ii) If a consumer applies for a loan by telephone and explains that his income has been and will continue to be interrupted on account of a medical condition and that he expects to repay the loan by liquidating assets, the creditor may, but is not required to, evaluate the application using the sale of assets as the primary source of repayment, consistent with safe and sound practices, provided that the creditor documents the consumer's request by recording the oral conversation or making a notation of the request in the consumer's file.

(iii) If a consumer applies for a loan and the application form provides a space where the consumer may provide any other information or special circumstances, whether medical or non-medical, that the consumer would like the creditor to consider in evaluating the consumer's application, the creditor may use medical information provided by the consumer in that space on that application to accommodate the consumer's application for credit, consistent with safe and sound practices, or may disregard that information.

(iv) If a consumer specifically requests that the creditor use medical information in determining the consumer's eligibility, or continued eligibility, for credit and provides the creditor with medical information for that purpose, and the creditor determines that it needs additional information regarding the consumer's circumstances, the creditor may request, obtain, and use additional medical information about the consumer as necessary to verify the information provided by the consumer or to determine whether to make an accommodation for the consumer. The consumer may decline to provide additional information, withdraw the request for an accommodation, and have the application considered under the creditor's otherwise applicable underwriting criteria.

(v) If a consumer completes and signs a credit application that is not for medical purpose credit and the application contains boilerplate language that routinely requests medical information from the consumer or that indicates that by applying for credit the consumer authorizes or consents to the creditor obtaining and using medical information in connection with a determination of the consumer's eligibility, or continued eligibility, for credit, the consumer has not specifically requested that the creditor obtain and use medical information to accommodate the consumer's particular circumstances.

(5) Example of a forbearance practice or program. After an appropriate safety and soundness review, a creditor institutes a program that allows consumers who are or will be hospitalized to defer payments as needed for up to three months, without penalty, if the credit account has been open for more than one year and has not previously been in default, and the consumer provides confirming documentation at an appropriate time. A consumer is hospitalized and does not pay her bill for a particular month. This consumer has had a credit account with the creditor for more than one year and has not previously been in default. The creditor attempts to contact the consumer and speaks with the consumer's adult child, who is not the consumer's legal representative. The adult child informs the creditor that the consumer is hospitalized and is unable to pay the bill at that time. The creditor defers payments for up to three months, without penalty, for the hospitalized consumer and sends the consumer a letter confirming this practice and the date on which the next payment will be due. The creditor has obtained and used medical information to determine whether the provisions of a medically-triggered forbearance practice or program apply to a consumer.

§ 1022.31. Limits on redisclosure of information

(a) Scope. This section applies to any person, except for a person excluded from coverage of this part by section 1029 of the Consumer Financial Protection Act of 2010, Title X of the Dodd-Frank Wall Street Reform and Consumer Protection Act, Public Law 111–203, 124 Stat. 137.

(b) Limits on redisclosure. If a person described in paragraph (a) of this section receives medical information about a consumer from a consumer reporting agency or its affiliate, the person must not disclose that information to any other person, except as necessary to carry out the purpose for which the information was initially disclosed, or as otherwise permitted by statute, regulation, or order.

§ 1022.32. Sharing medical information with affiliates

(a) Scope. This section applies to any person, except for a person excluded from coverage of this part by section 1029 of the Consumer Financial Protection Act of 2010, Title X of the Dodd-Frank Wall Street Reform and Consumer Protection Act, Public Law 111–203, 124 Stat. 137.

(b) In general. The exclusions from the term "consumer report" in section 603(d)(2) of the Act that allow the sharing of information with affiliates do not apply to a person described in paragraph (a) of this section if that person communicates to an affiliate:

(1) Medical information;

(2) An individualized list or description based on the payment transactions of the consumer for medical products or services; or

(3) An aggregate list of identified consumers based on payment transactions for medical products or services.

(c) Exceptions. A person described in paragraph (a) of this section may rely on the exclusions from the term "consumer report" in section 603(d)(2) of the Act to communicate the information in paragraph (b) of this section to an affiliate:

(1) In connection with the business of insurance or annuities (including the activities described in section 18B of the model Privacy of Consumer Financial and Health Information Regulation issued by the National Association of Insurance Commissioners, as in effect on January 1, 2003);

(2) For any purpose permitted without authorization under the regulations promulgated by the Department of Health and Human Services pursuant to the Health Insurance Portability and Accountability Act of 1996 (HIPAA);

(3) For any purpose referred to in section 1179 of HIPAA;

(4) For any purpose described in section 502(e) of the Gramm-Leach-Bliley Act;

(5) In connection with a determination of the consumer's eligibility, or continued eligibility, for credit consistent with § 1022.30 of this part; or

(6) As otherwise permitted by order of the Bureau.

Subpart E. Duties of Furnishers of Information

§ 1022.40. Scope

Subpart E of this part applies to any person that furnishes information to a consumer reporting agency, except for a person excluded from coverage of this part by section 1029 of the Consumer Financial Protection Act of 2010, Title X of the Dodd-Frank Wall Street Reform and Consumer Protection Act, Public Law 111–203, 124 Stat. 1376.

§ 1022.41. Definitions

For purposes of this subpart and Appendix E of this part, the following definitions apply:

(a) Accuracy means that information that a furnisher provides to a consumer reporting agency about an account or other relationship with the consumer correctly:

(1) Reflects the terms of and liability for the account or other relationship;

(2) Reflects the consumer's performance and other conduct with respect to the account or other relationship; and

(3) Identifies the appropriate consumer.

(b) Direct dispute means a dispute submitted directly to a furnisher (including a furnisher that is a debt collector) by a consumer concerning the accuracy of any information contained in a consumer report and pertaining to an account or other relationship that the furnisher has or had with the consumer.

(c) Furnisher means an entity that furnishes information relating to consumers to one or more consumer reporting agencies for inclusion in a consumer report. An entity is not a furnisher when it:

(1) Provides information to a consumer reporting agency solely to obtain a consumer report in accordance with sections 604(a) and (f) of the FCRA;

(2) Is acting as a "consumer reporting agency" as defined in section 603(f) of the FCRA;

(3) Is a consumer to whom the furnished information pertains; or

(4) Is a neighbor, friend, or associate of the consumer, or another individual with whom the consumer is acquainted or who may have knowledge about the consumer, and who provides information about the consumer's character, general reputation, personal characteristics, or mode of living in response to a specific request from a consumer reporting agency.

(d) Integrity means that information that a furnisher provides to a consumer reporting agency about an account or other relationship with the consumer:

(1) Is substantiated by the furnisher's records at the time it is furnished;

(2) Is furnished in a form and manner that is designed to minimize the likelihood that the information may be incorrectly reflected in a consumer report; and

(3) Includes the information in the furnisher's possession about the account or other relationship that the Bureau has:

(i) Determined that the absence of which would likely be materially misleading in evaluating a consumer's creditworthiness, credit standing, credit capacity, character, general reputation, personal characteristics, or mode of living; and

(ii) Listed in section I.(b)(2)(iii) of Appendix E of this part.

§ 1022.42. Reasonable policies and procedures concerning the accuracy and integrity of furnished information

(a) Policies and procedures. Each furnisher must establish and implement reasonable written policies and procedures regarding the accuracy and integrity of the information relating to consumers that it furnishes to a consumer reporting agency. The policies and procedures must be appropriate to the nature, size, complexity, and scope of each furnisher's activities.

(b) Guidelines. Each furnisher must consider the guidelines in Appendix E of this part in developing its policies and procedures required by this section, and incorporate those guidelines that are appropriate.

(c) Reviewing and updating policies and procedures. Each furnisher must review its policies and procedures required by this section periodically and update them as necessary to ensure their continued effectiveness.

§ 1022.43. Direct disputes

(a) General rule. Except as otherwise provided in this section, a furnisher must conduct a reasonable investigation of a direct dispute if it relates to:

(1) The consumer's liability for a credit account or other debt with the furnisher, such as direct disputes relating to whether there is or has been identity theft or fraud against the consumer, whether there is individual or joint liability on an account, or whether the consumer is an authorized user of a credit account;

(2) The terms of a credit account or other debt with the furnisher, such as direct disputes relating to the type of account, principal balance, scheduled payment amount on an account, or the amount of the credit limit on an open-end account;

(3) The consumer's performance or other conduct concerning an account or other relationship with the furnisher, such as direct disputes relating to the current payment status, high balance, date a payment was made, the amount of a payment made, or the date an account was opened or closed; or

(4) Any other information contained in a consumer report regarding an account or other relationship with the furnisher that bears on the consumer's creditworthiness, credit standing, credit capacity, character, general reputation, personal characteristics, or mode of living.

(b) Exceptions. The requirements of paragraph (a) of this section do not apply to a furnisher if:

(1) The direct dispute relates to:

(i) The consumer's identifying information (other than a direct dispute relating to a consumer's liability for a credit account or other debt with the furnisher, as provided in paragraph (a)(1) of this section) such as name(s), date of birth, Social Security number, telephone number(s), or address(es);

(ii) The identity of past or present employers;

(iii) Inquiries or requests for a consumer report;

(iv) Information derived from public records, such as judgments, bankruptcies, liens, and other legal matters (unless provided by a furnisher with an account or other relationship with the consumer);

(v) Information related to fraud alerts or active duty alerts; or

(vi) Information provided to a consumer reporting agency by another furnisher; or

(2) The furnisher has a reasonable belief that the direct dispute is submitted by, is prepared on behalf of the consumer by, or is submitted on a form supplied to the consumer by, a credit repair organization, as defined in 15 U.S.C. 1679a(3), or an entity that would be a credit repair organization, but for 15 U.S.C. 1679a(3)(B)(i).

(c) Direct dispute address. A furnisher is required to investigate a direct dispute only if a consumer submits a dispute notice to the furnisher at:

(1) The address of a furnisher provided by a furnisher and set forth on a consumer report relating to the consumer;

(2) An address clearly and conspicuously specified by the furnisher for submitting direct disputes that is provided to the consumer in writing or electronically (if the consumer has agreed to the electronic delivery of information from the furnisher); or

(3) Any business address of the furnisher if the furnisher has not so specified and provided an address for submitting direct disputes under paragraphs (c)(1) or (2) of this section.

(d) Direct dispute notice contents. A dispute notice must include:

(1) Sufficient information to identify the account or other relationship that is in dispute, such as an account number and the name, address, and telephone number of the consumer, if applicable;

(2) The specific information that the consumer is disputing and an explanation of the basis for the dispute; and

(3) All supporting documentation or other information reasonably required by the furnisher to substantiate the basis of the dispute. This documentation may include, for example: a copy of the relevant portion of the consumer report that contains the allegedly inaccurate information; a police report; a fraud or identity theft affidavit; a court order; or account statements.

(e) Duty of furnisher after receiving a direct dispute notice. After receiving a dispute notice from a consumer pursuant to paragraphs (c) and (d) of this section, the furnisher must:

(1) Conduct a reasonable investigation with respect to the disputed information;

(2) Review all relevant information provided by the consumer with the dispute notice;

(3) Complete its investigation of the dispute and report the results of the investigation to the consumer before the expiration of the period under section 611(a)(1) of the FCRA (15 U.S.C. 1681i(a)(1)) within which a consumer reporting agency would be required to complete its action if the consumer had elected to dispute the information under that section; and

(4) If the investigation finds that the information reported was inaccurate, promptly notify each consumer reporting agency to which the furnisher provided inaccurate information of that determination and provide to the consumer reporting agency any correction to that information that is necessary to make the information provided by the furnisher accurate.

(f) Frivolous or irrelevant disputes.

(1) A furnisher is not required to investigate a direct dispute if the furnisher has reasonably determined that the dispute is frivolous or irrelevant. A dispute qualifies as frivolous or irrelevant if:

(i) The consumer did not provide sufficient information to investigate the disputed information as required by paragraph (d) of this section;

(ii) The direct dispute is substantially the same as a dispute previously submitted by or on behalf of the consumer, either directly to the furnisher or through a consumer reporting agency, with respect to which the furnisher has already satisfied the applicable requirements of the Act or this section; provided, however, that a direct dispute is not substantially the same as a dispute previously submitted if the dispute includes information listed in paragraph (d) of this section that had not previously been provided to the furnisher; or

(iii) The furnisher is not required to investigate the direct dispute because one or more of the exceptions listed in paragraph (b) of this section applies.

(2) Notice of determination. Upon making a determination that a dispute is frivolous or irrelevant, the furnisher must notify the consumer of the determination not later than five business days after making the determination, by mail or, if authorized by the consumer for that purpose, by any other means available to the furnisher.

(3) Contents of notice of determination that a dispute is frivolous or irrelevant. A notice of determination that a dispute is frivolous or irrelevant must include the reasons for such determination and identify any information required to investigate the disputed information, which notice may consist of a standardized form describing the general nature of such information.

Subpart F. Duties of Users Regarding Obtaining and Using Consumer Reports

§§ 1022.50 to 1022.53. [Reserved]

§ 1022.54. Duties of users making written firm offers of credit or insurance based on information contained in consumer files

(a) Scope. This subpart applies to any person who uses a consumer report on any consumer in connection with any credit or insurance transaction that is not initiated by the consumer, and that is provided to that person under section 604(c)(1)(B) of the FCRA (15 U.S.C. 1681b(c)(1)(B)), except for a person excluded from coverage of this part by section 1029 of the Consumer Financial Protection Act of 2010, Title X of the Dodd-Frank Wall Street Reform and Consumer Protection Act, Public Law 111–203, 124 Stat. 137.

(b) Definitions. For purposes of this section and Appendix D of this part, the following definitions apply:

(1) Simple and easy to understand means:

(i) A layered format as described in paragraph (c) of this section;

(ii) Plain language designed to be understood by ordinary consumers; and

(iii) Use of clear and concise sentences, paragraphs, and sections.

(iv) Examples. For purposes of this part, examples of factors to be considered in determining whether a statement is in plain language and uses clear and concise sentences, paragraphs, and sections include:

(A) Use of short explanatory sentences;

(B) Use of definite, concrete, everyday words;

(C) Use of active voice;

(D) Avoidance of multiple negatives;

(E) Avoidance of legal and technical business terminology;

(F) Avoidance of explanations that are imprecise and reasonably subject to different interpretations; and

(G) Use of language that is not misleading.

(2) Principal promotional document means the document designed to be seen first by the consumer, such as the cover letter.

(c) Prescreen opt-out notice. Any person who uses a consumer report on any consumer in connection with any credit or insurance transaction that is not initiated by the consumer, and that is provided to that person under section 604(c)(1)(B) of the FCRA (15 U.S.C. 1681b(c)(1)(B)), shall, with each written solicitation made to the consumer about the transaction, provide the consumer with the following statement, consisting of a short portion and a long portion, which shall be in the same language as the offer of credit or insurance:

(1) Short notice. The short notice shall be a clear and conspicuous, and simple and easy to understand statement as follows:

(i) Content. The short notice shall state that the consumer has the right to opt out of receiving prescreened solicitations, and shall provide the toll-free number the consumer can call to exercise that right. The short notice also shall direct the consumer to the existence and location of the long notice, and shall state the heading for the long notice. The short notice shall not contain any other information.

(ii) Form. The short notice shall be:

(A) In a type size that is larger than the type size of the principal text on the same page, but in no event smaller than 12 point type, or if provided by electronic means, then reasonable steps shall be taken to ensure that the type size is larger than the type size of the principal text on the same page;

(B) On the front side of the first page of the principal promotional document in the solicitation, or, if provided electronically, on the same page and in close proximity to the principal marketing message;

(C) Located on the page and in a format so that the statement is distinct from other text, such as inside a border; and

(D) In a type style that is distinct from the principal type style used on the same page, such as bolded, italicized, underlined, and/or in a color that contrasts with the color of the principal text on the page, if the solicitation is in more than one color.

(2) Long notice. The long notice shall be a clear and conspicuous, and simple and easy to understand statement as follows:

(i) Content. The long notice shall state the information required by section 615(d) of the Fair Credit Reporting Act (15 U.S.C. 1681m(d)). The long notice shall not include any other information that interferes with, detracts from, contradicts, or otherwise undermines the purpose of the notice.

(ii) Form. The long notice shall:

(A) Appear in the solicitation;

(B) Be in a type size that is no smaller than the type size of the principal text on the same page, and, for solicitations provided other than by electronic means, the type size shall in no event be smaller than 8 point type;

(C) Begin with a heading in capital letters and underlined, and identifying the long notice as the "PRESCREEN & OPT-OUT NOTICE;"

(D) Be in a type style that is distinct from the principal type style used on the same page, such as bolded, italicized, underlined, and/or in a color that contrasts with the color of the principal text on the page, if the solicitation is in more than one color; and

(E) Be set apart from other text on the page, such as by including a blank line above and below the statement, and by indenting both the left and right margins from other text on the page.

§§ 1022.55 to 1022.59. [Reserved]

Subpart H. Duties of Users Regarding Risk-Based Pricing

§ 1022.70. Scope

(a) Coverage.

(1) In general. This subpart applies to any person, except for a person excluded from coverage of this part by section 1029 of the Consumer Financial Protection Act of 2010, Title X of the Dodd-Frank Wall Street Reform and Consumer Protection Act, Public Law 111–203, 124 Stat. 137, that both:

(i) Uses a consumer report in connection with an application for, or a grant, extension, or other provision of, credit to a consumer that is primarily for personal, family, or household purposes; and

(ii) Based in whole or in part on the consumer report, grants, extends, or otherwise provides credit to the consumer on material terms that are materially less favorable than the most favorable material terms available to a substantial proportion of consumers from or through that person.

(2) Business credit excluded. This subpart does not apply to an application for, or a grant, extension, or other provision of, credit to a consumer or to any other applicant primarily for a business purpose.

(b) Enforcement. The provisions of this subpart will be enforced in accordance with the enforcement authority set forth in sections 621(a) and (b) of the FCRA.

§ 1022.71. Definitions

For purposes of this subpart, the following definitions apply:

(a) Adverse action has the same meaning as in 15 U.S.C. 1681a(k)(1)(A).

(b) Annual percentage rate has the same meaning as in 12 CFR 1026.14(b) with respect to an open-end credit plan and as in 12 CFR 1026.22 with respect to closed-end credit.

(c) Closed-end credit has the same meaning as in 12 CFR 1026.2(a)(10).

(d) Consumer has the same meaning as in 15 U.S.C. 1681a(c).

(e) Consummation has the same meaning as in 12 CFR 1026.2(a)(13).

(f) Consumer report has the same meaning as in 15 U.S.C. 1681a(d).

(g) Consumer reporting agency has the same meaning as in 15 U.S.C. 1681a(f).

(h) Credit has the same meaning as in 15 U.S.C. 1681a(r)(5).

(i) Creditor has the same meaning as in 15 U.S.C. 1681a(r)(5).

(j) Credit card has the same meaning as in 15 U.S.C. 1681a(r)(2).

(k) Credit card issuer has the same meaning as card issuer, as defined in 15 U.S.C. 1681a(r)(1)(A).

(*l*) Credit score has the same meaning as in 15 U.S.C. 1681g(f)(2)(A).

(m) Firm offer of credit has the same meaning as in 15 U.S.C. 1681a(*l*).

(n) Material terms means:

(1)(i) Except as otherwise provided in paragraphs (n)(1)(ii) and (n)(3) of this section, in the case of credit extended under an open-end credit plan, the annual percentage rate required to be disclosed under 12 CFR 1026.6(a)(1)(ii) or 12 CFR 1026.6(b)(2)(i), excluding any temporary initial rate that is lower than the rate that will apply after the temporary rate expires, any penalty rate that will apply upon the occurrence of one or more specific events, such as a late payment or an extension of credit that exceeds the credit limit, and any fixed annual percentage rate option for a home equity line of credit;

(ii) In the case of a credit card (other than a credit card that is used to access a home equity line of credit or a charge card), the annual percentage rate required to be disclosed under 12 CFR 1026.6(b)(2)(i) that applies to purchases ("purchase annual percentage rate") and no other annual percentage rate, or in the case of a credit card that has no purchase annual percentage rate, the annual percentage rate that varies based on information in a consumer report and that has the most significant financial impact on consumers;

(2) In the case of closed-end credit, the annual percentage rate required to be disclosed under 12 CFR 1026.17(c) and 1026.18(e); and

(3) In the case of credit for which there is no annual percentage rate, the financial term that varies based on information in a consumer report and that has the most significant financial impact on consumers, such as a deposit required in connection with credit extended by a telephone company or utility or an annual membership fee for a charge card.

(*o*) Materially less favorable means, when applied to material terms, that the terms granted, extended, or otherwise provided to a consumer differ from the terms granted, extended, or otherwise provided to another consumer from or through the same person such that the cost of credit to the first consumer would be significantly greater than the cost of credit granted, extended, or otherwise provided to the other consumer. For purposes of this definition, factors relevant to determining the significance of a difference in cost include the type of credit product, the term of the credit extension, if any, and the extent of the difference between the material terms granted, extended, or otherwise provided to the two consumers.

(p) Open-end credit plan has the same meaning as in 15 U.S.C. 1602(i), as interpreted by the Bureau in Regulation Z (12 CFR part 1026) and the Official Interpretations to Regulation Z (Supplement I to 12 CFR part 1026).

(q) Person has the same meaning as in 15 U.S.C. 1681a(b).

§ 1022.72. General requirements for risk-based pricing notices

(a) In general. Except as otherwise provided in this subpart, a person must provide to a consumer a notice ("risk-based pricing notice") in the form and manner required by this subpart if the person both:

(1) Uses a consumer report in connection with an application for, or a grant, extension, or other provision of, credit to that consumer that is primarily for personal, family, or household purposes; and

(2) Based in whole or in part on the consumer report, grants, extends, or otherwise provides credit to that consumer on material terms that are materially less favorable than the most favorable material terms available to a substantial proportion of consumers from or through that person.

(b) Determining which consumers must receive a notice. A person may determine whether paragraph (a) of this section applies by directly comparing the material terms offered to each consumer and the material terms offered to other consumers for a specific type of credit product. For purposes of this section, a "specific type of credit product" means one or more credit products with similar features that are designed for similar purposes. Examples of a specific type of credit product include student loans, unsecured credit cards, secured credit cards, new automobile loans, used automobile loans, fixed-rate mortgage loans, and variable-rate mortgage loans. As an alternative to making this direct comparison, a person may make the determination by using one of the following methods:

(1) Credit score proxy method.

(i) In general. A person that sets the material terms of credit granted, extended, or otherwise provided to a consumer, based in whole or in part on a credit score, may comply with the requirements of paragraph (a) of this section by:

(A) Determining the credit score (hereafter referred to as the "cutoff score") that represents the point at which approximately 40 percent of the consumers to whom it grants, extends, or provides credit have higher credit scores and approximately 60 percent of the consumers to whom it grants, extends, or provides credit have lower credit scores; and

(B) Providing a risk-based pricing notice to each consumer to whom it grants, extends, or provides credit whose credit score is lower than the cutoff score.

(ii) Alternative to the 40/60 cutoff score determination. In the case of credit that has been granted, extended, or provided on the most favorable material terms to more than 40 percent of consumers, a person may, at its option, set its cutoff score at a point at which the approximate percentage of consumers who historically have been granted, extended, or provided credit on material terms other than the most favorable terms would receive risk-based pricing notices under this section.

(iii) Determining the cutoff score.

(A) Sampling approach. A person that currently uses risk-based pricing with respect to the credit products it offers must calculate the cutoff score by considering the credit scores of all or a representative sample of the consumers to whom it has granted, extended, or provided credit for a specific type of credit product.

(B) Secondary source approach in limited circumstances. A person that is a new entrant into the credit business, introduces new credit products, or starts to use risk-based pricing with respect to the credit products it currently offers may initially determine the cutoff score based on information derived from appropriate market research or relevant third-party sources for a specific type of credit product, such as research or data from companies that develop credit scores. A person that acquires a credit portfolio as a result of a merger or acquisition may determine the cutoff score based on information from the party which it acquired, with which it merged, or from which it acquired the portfolio.

(C) Recalculation of cutoff scores. A person using the credit score proxy method must recalculate its cutoff score(s) no less than every two years in the manner described in paragraph (b)(1)(iii)(A) of this section. A person using the credit score proxy method using market research, third-party data, or information from a party which it acquired, with which it merged, or from which it acquired the portfolio as permitted by paragraph (b)(1)(iii)(B) of this section generally must calculate a cutoff score(s) based on the scores of its own consumers in the manner described in paragraph (b)(1)(iii)(A) of this section within one year after it begins using a cutoff score derived from market research, third-party data, or information from a party which it acquired, with which it merged, or from which it acquired the portfolio. If such a person does not grant, extend, or provide credit to new consumers during that one-year period such that it lacks sufficient data with which to recalculate a cutoff score based on the credit scores of its own consumers, the person may continue to use a cutoff score derived from market research, third-party data, or information from a party which it acquired, with which it merged, or from which it acquired the portfolio as provided in paragraph (b)(1)(iii)(B) until it obtains sufficient data on which to base the recalculation. However, the person must recalculate its cutoff score(s) in the manner described in paragraph (b)(1)(iii)(A) of this section within two years, if it has granted, extended, or provided credit to some new consumers during that two-year period.

(D) Use of two or more credit scores. A person that generally uses two or more credit scores in setting the material terms of credit granted, extended, or provided to a consumer must determine the cutoff score using the same method the person uses to evaluate multiple scores when making credit decisions. These evaluation methods may include, but are not limited to, selecting the low, median, high, most recent, or average credit score of each consumer to whom it grants, extends, or provides credit. If a person that uses two or more credit scores does not consistently use the same method for evaluating multiple credit scores (e.g., if the person sometimes chooses the median score and other times calculates the average score), the person must determine the cutoff score using a reasonable means. In such cases, use of any one of the methods that the person regularly uses or the average credit score of each consumer to whom it grants, extends, or provides credit is deemed to be a reasonable means of calculating the cutoff score.

(iv) Credit score not available. For purposes of this section, a person using the credit score proxy method who grants, extends, or provides credit to a consumer for whom a credit score is not available must assume that the consumer receives credit on material terms that are materially less favorable than the most favorable credit terms offered to a substantial proportion of consumers from or through that person and must provide a risk-based pricing notice to the consumer.

(v) Examples.

(A) A credit card issuer engages in risk-based pricing and the annual percentage rates it offers to consumers are based in whole or in part on a credit score. The credit card issuer takes a representative sample of the credit scores of consumers to whom it issued credit cards within the preceding three months. The credit card issuer determines that approximately 40 percent of the sampled consumers have a credit score at or above 720 (on a scale of 350 to 850) and approximately 60 percent of the sampled consumers have a credit score below 720. Thus, the card issuer selects 720 as its cutoff score. A consumer applies to the credit card issuer for a credit card. The card issuer obtains a credit score for the consumer. The consumer's credit score is 700. Since the consumer's 700 credit score falls below the 720 cutoff score, the credit card issuer must provide a risk-based pricing notice to the consumer.

(B) A credit card issuer engages in risk-based pricing, and the annual percentage rates it offers to consumers are based in whole or in part on a credit score. The credit card issuer takes a representative sample of the consumers to whom it issued credit cards over the preceding six months. The credit card issuer determines that approximately 80 percent of the sampled consumers received credit at its lowest annual percentage rate, and 20 percent received credit at a higher annual percentage rate. Approximately 80 percent of the sampled consumers have a credit score at or above 750 (on a scale of 350 to 850), and 20 percent have a credit score below 750. Thus, the card issuer selects 750 as its cutoff score. A consumer applies to the credit card issuer for a credit card. The card issuer obtains a credit score for the consumer. The consumer's credit score is 740. Since the consumer's 740 credit score falls below the 750 cutoff score, the credit card issuer must provide a risk-based pricing notice to the consumer.

(C) An auto lender engages in risk-based pricing, obtains credit scores from one of the nationwide consumer reporting agencies, and uses the credit score proxy method to determine which consumers must receive a risk-based pricing notice. A consumer applies to the auto lender for credit to finance the purchase of an automobile. A credit score about that consumer is not available from the consumer reporting agency from which the lender obtains credit scores. The lender nevertheless grants, extends, or provides credit to the consumer. The lender must provide a risk-based pricing notice to the consumer.

(2) Tiered pricing method.

(i) In general. A person that sets the material terms of credit granted, extended, or provided to a consumer by placing the consumer within one of a discrete number of pricing tiers for a specific type of credit product, based in whole or in part on a consumer report, may comply with the requirements of paragraph (a) of this section by providing a risk-based pricing notice to each consumer who is not placed within the top pricing tier or tiers, as described below.

(ii) Four or fewer pricing tiers. If a person using the tiered pricing method has four or fewer pricing tiers, the person complies with the requirements of paragraph (a) of this section by providing a risk-based pricing notice to each consumer to whom it grants, extends, or provides credit who does not qualify for the top tier (that is, the lowest-priced tier). For example, a person that uses a tiered pricing structure with annual percentage rates of 8, 10, 12, and 14 percent would provide the risk-based pricing notice to each consumer to whom it grants, extends, or provides credit at annual percentage rates of 10, 12, and 14 percent.

(iii) Five or more pricing tiers. If a person using the tiered pricing method has five or more pricing tiers, the person complies with the requirements of paragraph (a) of this section by providing a risk-based pricing notice to each consumer to whom it grants, extends, or provides credit who does not qualify for the top two tiers (that is, the two lowest-priced tiers) and any other tier that, together with the top tiers, comprise no less than the top 30 percent but no more than the top 40 percent of the total number of tiers. Each consumer placed within the remaining tiers must receive a risk-based pricing notice. For example, if a person has nine pricing tiers, the top three tiers (that is, the three lowest-priced tiers) comprise no less than the top 30 percent but no more than the top 40 percent of the tiers. Therefore, a person using this method would provide a risk-based pricing notice to each consumer to whom it grants, extends, or provides credit who is placed within the bottom six tiers.

(c) Application to credit card issuers.

(1) In general. A credit card issuer subject to the requirements of paragraph (a) of this section may use one of the methods set forth in paragraph (b) of this section to identify consumers to whom it must provide a risk-based pricing notice. Alternatively, a credit card issuer may satisfy its obligations under paragraph (a) of this section by providing a risk-based pricing notice to a consumer when:

(i) A consumer applies for a credit card either in connection with an application program, such as a direct-mail offer or a take-one application, or in response to a solicitation under 12 CFR 1026.60, and more than a single possible purchase annual percentage rate may apply under the program or solicitation; and

(ii) Based in whole or in part on a consumer report, the credit card issuer provides a credit card to the consumer with an annual percentage rate referenced in § 1022.71(n)(1)(ii) that is greater than the lowest annual percentage rate referenced in § 1022.71(n)(1)(ii) available in connection with the application or solicitation.

(2) No requirement to compare different offers. A credit card issuer is not subject to the requirements of paragraph (a) of this section and is not required to provide a risk-based pricing notice to a consumer if:

(i) The consumer applies for a credit card for which the card issuer provides a single annual percentage rate referenced in § 1022.71(n)(1)(ii), excluding a temporary initial rate that is lower than the rate that will apply after the temporary rate expires and a penalty rate that will apply upon the occurrence of one or more specific events, such as a late payment or an extension of credit that exceeds the credit limit; or

(ii) The credit card issuer offers the consumer the lowest annual percentage rate referenced in § 1022.71(n)(1)(ii) available under the credit card offer for which the consumer applied, even if a lower annual percentage rate referenced in § 1022.71(n)(1)(ii) is available under a different credit card offer issued by the card issuer.

(3) Examples.

(i) A credit card issuer sends a solicitation to the consumer that discloses several possible purchase annual percentage rates that may apply, such as 10, 12, or 14 percent, or a range of purchase annual percentage rates from 10 to 14 percent. The consumer applies for a credit card in response to the solicitation. The card issuer provides a credit card to the consumer with a purchase annual percentage rate of 12 percent based in whole or in part on a consumer report. Unless an exception applies under § 1022.74, the card issuer may satisfy its obligations under paragraph (a) of this section by providing a risk-based pricing notice to the consumer because the consumer received credit at a purchase annual percentage rate greater than the lowest purchase annual percentage rate available under that solicitation.

(ii) The same facts as in the example in paragraph (c)(3)(i) of this section, except that the card issuer provides a credit card to the consumer at a purchase annual percentage rate of 10 percent. The card issuer is not required to provide a risk-based pricing notice to the consumer even if, under a different credit card solicitation, that consumer or other consumers might qualify for a purchase annual percentage rate of 8 percent.

(d) Account review.

(1) In general. Except as otherwise provided in this subpart, a person is subject to the requirements of paragraph (a) of this section and must provide a risk-based pricing notice to a consumer in the form and manner required by this subpart if the person:

(i) Uses a consumer report in connection with a review of credit that has been extended to the consumer; and

(ii) Based in whole or in part on the consumer report, increases the annual percentage rate (the annual percentage rate referenced in § 1022.71(n)(1)(ii) in the case of a credit card).

(2) Example. A credit card issuer periodically obtains consumer reports for the purpose of reviewing the terms of credit it has extended to consumers in connection with credit cards. As a result of this review, the credit card issuer increases the purchase annual percentage rate applicable to a consumer's credit card based in whole or in part on information in a consumer report. The credit card issuer is subject to the requirements of paragraph (a) of this section and must provide a risk-based pricing notice to the consumer.

§ 1022.73. Content, form, and timing of risk-based pricing notices

(a) Content of the notice.

(1) In general. The risk-based pricing notice required by § 1022.72(a) or (c) must include:

(i) A statement that a consumer report (or credit report) includes information about the consumer's credit history and the type of information included in that history;

(ii) A statement that the terms offered, such as the annual percentage rate, have been set based on information from a consumer report;

(iii) A statement that the terms offered may be less favorable than the terms offered to consumers with better credit histories;

(iv) A statement that the consumer is encouraged to verify the accuracy of the information contained in the consumer report and has the right to dispute any inaccurate information in the report;

(v) The identity of each consumer reporting agency that furnished a consumer report used in the credit decision;

(vi) A statement that Federal law gives the consumer the right to obtain a copy of a consumer report from the consumer reporting agency or agencies identified in the notice without charge for 60 days after receipt of the notice;

(vii) A statement informing the consumer how to obtain a consumer report from the consumer reporting agency or agencies identified in the notice and providing contact information (including a toll-free telephone number, where applicable) specified by the consumer reporting agency or agencies;

(viii) A statement directing consumers to the Web site of the Bureau to obtain more information about consumer reports; and

(ix) If a credit score of the consumer to whom a person grants, extends, or otherwise provides credit is used in setting the material terms of credit:

(A) A statement that a credit score is a number that takes into account information in a consumer report, that the consumer's credit score was used to set the terms of credit offered, and that a credit score can change over time to reflect changes in the consumer's credit history;

(B) The credit score used by the person in making the credit decision;

(C) The range of possible credit scores under the model used to generate the credit score;

(D) All of the key factors that adversely affected the credit score, which shall not exceed four key factors, except that if one of the key factors is the number of enquiries made with respect to the consumer report, the number of key factors shall not exceed five;

(E) The date on which the credit score was created; and

(F) The name of the consumer reporting agency or other person that provided the credit score.

(2) Account review. The risk-based pricing notice required by § 1022.72(d) must include:

(i) A statement that a consumer report (or credit report) includes information about the consumer's credit history and the type of information included in that credit history;

(ii) A statement that the person has conducted a review of the account using information from a consumer report;

(iii) A statement that as a result of the review, the annual percentage rate on the account has been increased based on information from a consumer report;

(iv) A statement that the consumer is encouraged to verify the accuracy of the information contained in the consumer report and has the right to dispute any inaccurate information in the report;

(v) The identity of each consumer reporting agency that furnished a consumer report used in the account review;

(vi) A statement that Federal law gives the consumer the right to obtain a copy of a consumer report from the consumer reporting agency or agencies identified in the notice without charge for 60 days after receipt of the notice;

(vii) A statement informing the consumer how to obtain a consumer report from the consumer reporting agency or agencies identified in the notice and providing contact information (including a toll-free telephone number, where applicable) specified by the consumer reporting agency or agencies;

(viii) A statement directing consumers to the Web site of the Bureau to obtain more information about consumer reports; and

(ix) If a credit score of the consumer whose extension of credit is under review is used in increasing the annual percentage rate:

(A) A statement that a credit score is a number that takes into account information in a consumer report, that the consumer's credit score was used to set the terms of credit offered, and that a credit score can change over time to reflect changes in the consumer's credit history;

(B) The credit score used by the person in making the credit decision;

(C) The range of possible credit scores under the model used to generate the credit score;

(D) All of the key factors that adversely affected the credit score, which shall not exceed four key factors, except that if one of the key factors is the number of enquires made with respect to the consumer report, the number of key factors shall not exceed five;

(E) The date on which the credit score was created; and

(F) The name of the consumer reporting agency or other person that provided the credit score.

(b) Form of the notice.

(1) In general. The risk-based pricing notice required by § 1022.72(a), (c), or (d) must be:

(i) Clear and conspicuous; and

(ii) Provided to the consumer in oral, written, or electronic form.

(2) Model forms. Model forms of the risk-based pricing notice required by § 1022.72(a) and (c) are contained in Appendices H-1 and H-6 of this part. Appropriate use of Model Form H-1 or H-6 is deemed to comply with the requirements of § 1022.72(a) and (c). Model forms of the risk-based pricing notice required by § 1022.72(d) are contained in Appendices H-2 and H-7 of this part. Appropriate use of Model Form H-2 or H-7 is deemed to comply with the requirements of § 1022.72(d). Use of the model forms is optional.

(c) Timing.

(1) General. Except as provided in paragraph (c)(3) of this section, a risk-based pricing notice must be provided to the consumer:

(i) In the case of a grant, extension, or other provision of closed-end credit, before consummation of the transaction, but not earlier than the time the decision to approve an application for, or a grant, extension, or other provision of, credit, is communicated to the consumer by the person required to provide the notice;

(ii) In the case of credit granted, extended, or provided under an open-end credit plan, before the first transaction is made under the plan, but not earlier than the time the decision to approve an application for, or a grant, extension, or other provision of, credit is communicated to the consumer by the person required to provide the notice; or

(iii) In the case of a review of credit that has been extended to the consumer, at the time the decision to increase the annual percentage rate (annual percentage rate referenced in § 1022.71(n)(1)(ii) in the case of a credit card) based on a consumer report is communicated to the consumer by the person required to provide the notice, or if no notice of the increase in the annual percentage rate is provided to the consumer prior to the effective date of the change in the annual percentage rate (to the extent permitted by law), no later than five days after the effective date of the change in the annual percentage rate.

(2) Application to certain automobile lending transactions. When a person to whom a credit obligation is initially payable grants, extends, or provides credit to a consumer for the purpose of financing the purchase of an automobile from an auto dealer or other party that is not affiliated with the person, any requirement to provide a risk-based pricing notice pursuant to this subpart is satisfied if the person:

(i) Provides a notice described in §§ 1022.72(a), 1022.74(e), or 1022.74(f) to the consumer within the time periods set forth in paragraph (c)(1)(i) of this section, § 1022.74(e)(3), or § 1022.74(f)(4), as applicable; or

(ii) Arranges to have the auto dealer or other party provide a notice described in §§ 1022.72(a), 1022.74(e), or 1022.74(f) to the consumer on its behalf within the time periods set forth in paragraph (c)(1)(i) of this section, § 1022.74(e)(3), or § 1022.74(f)(4), as applicable, and maintains reasonable policies and procedures to verify that the auto dealer or other party provides such notice to the consumer within the applicable time periods. If the person arranges to have the auto dealer or other party provide a notice described in § 1022.74(e), the person's obligation is satisfied if the consumer receives a notice containing a credit score obtained by the dealer or other party, even if a different credit score is obtained and used by the person on whose behalf the notice is provided.

(3) Timing requirements for contemporaneous purchase credit. When credit under an open-end credit plan is granted, extended, or provided to a consumer in person or by telephone for the purpose of financing the contemporaneous purchase of goods or services, any risk-based pricing notice required to be provided pursuant to this subpart (or the disclosures permitted under § 1022.74(e) or (f)) may be provided at the earlier of:

(i) The time of the first mailing by the person to the consumer after the decision is made to approve the grant, extension, or other provision of open-end credit, such as in a mailing containing the account agreement or a credit card; or

(ii) Within 30 days after the decision to approve the grant, extension, or other provision of credit.

(d) Multiple credit scores.

(1) In general. When a person obtains or creates two or more credit scores and uses one of those credit scores in setting the material terms of credit, for example, by using the low, middle, high, or most recent score, the notices described in paragraphs (a)(1) and (2) of this section must include that credit score and information relating to that credit score required by paragraphs (a)(1)(ix) and (a)(2)(ix). When a person obtains or creates two or more credit scores and uses multiple credit scores in setting the material terms of credit by, for example, computing the average of all the credit scores obtained or created, the notices described in paragraphs (a)(1) and (2) of this section must include one of those credit scores and information relating to credit scores required by paragraphs (a)(1)(ix) and (a)(2)(ix). The notice may, at the person's option, include more than one credit score, along with the additional information specified in paragraphs (a)(1)(ix) and (a)(2)(ix) of this section for each credit score disclosed.

(2) Examples.

(i) A person that uses consumer reports to set the material terms of credit cards granted, extended, or provided to consumers regularly requests credit scores from several consumer reporting agencies and uses the low score when determining the material terms it will offer to the consumer. That person must disclose the low score in the notices described in paragraphs (a)(1) and (2) of this section.

(ii) A person that uses consumer reports to set the material terms of automobile loans granted, extended, or provided to consumers regularly requests credit scores from several consumer reporting agencies, each of which it uses in an underwriting program in order to determine the material terms it will offer to the consumer. That person may choose one of these scores to include in the notices described in paragraph (a)(1) and (2) of this section.

§ 1022.74. Exceptions

(a) Application for specific terms.

(1) In general. A person is not required to provide a risk-based pricing notice to the consumer under § 1022.72(a) or (c) if the consumer applies for specific material terms and is granted those terms, unless those terms were specified by the person using a consumer report after the consumer applied for or requested credit and after the person obtained the consumer report. For purposes of this section, "specific material terms" means a single material term, or set of material terms, such as an annual percentage rate of 10 percent, and not a range of alternatives, such as an annual percentage rate that may be 8, 10, or 12 percent, or between 8 and 12 percent.

(2) Example. A consumer receives a firm offer of credit from a credit card issuer. The terms of the firm offer are based in whole or in part on information from a consumer report that the credit card issuer obtained under the FCRA's firm offer of credit provisions. The solicitation offers the consumer a credit card with a single purchase annual percentage rate of 12 percent. The consumer applies for and receives a credit card with an annual percentage rate of 12 percent. Other customers with the same credit card have a purchase annual percentage rate of 10 percent. The exception applies because the consumer applied for specific material terms and was granted those terms. Although the credit card issuer specified the annual percentage rate in the firm offer of credit based in whole or in part on a consumer report, the credit card issuer specified that material term *before*, not *after*, the consumer applied for or requested credit.

(b) Adverse action notice. A person is not required to provide a risk-based pricing notice to the consumer under § 1022.72(a), (c), or (d) if the person provides an adverse action notice to the consumer under section 615(a) of the FCRA.

(c) Prescreened solicitations.

(1) In general. A person is not required to provide a risk-based pricing notice to the consumer under § 1022.72(a) or (c) if the person:

(i) Obtains a consumer report that is a prescreened list as described in section 604(c)(2) of the FCRA; and

(ii) Uses the consumer report for the purpose of making a firm offer of credit to the consumer.

(2) More favorable material terms. This exception applies to any firm offer of credit offered by a person to a consumer, even if the person makes other firm offers of credit to other consumers on more favorable material terms.

(3) Example. A credit card issuer obtains two prescreened lists from a consumer reporting agency. One list includes consumers with high credit scores. The other list includes consumers with low credit scores. The issuer mails a firm offer of credit to the high credit score consumers with a single purchase annual percentage rate of 10 percent. The issuer also mails a firm offer of credit to the low credit score consumers with a single purchase annual percentage rate of 14 percent. The credit card issuer is not required to provide a risk-based pricing notice to the low credit score consumers who receive the 14 percent offer because use of a consumer report to make a firm offer of credit does not trigger the risk-based pricing notice requirement.

(d) Loans secured by residential real property—credit score disclosure.

(1) In general. A person is not required to provide a risk-based pricing notice to a consumer under § 1022.72(a) or (c) if:

(i) The consumer requests from the person an extension of credit that is or will be secured by one to four units of residential real property; and

(ii) The person provides to each consumer described in paragraph (d)(1)(i) of this section a notice that contains the following:

(A) A statement that a consumer report (or credit report) is a record of the consumer's credit history and includes information about whether the consumer pays his or her obligations on time and how much the consumer owes to creditors;

(B) A statement that a credit score is a number that takes into account information in a consumer report and that a credit score can change over time to reflect changes in the consumer's credit history;

(C) A statement that the consumer's credit score can affect whether the consumer can obtain credit and what the cost of that credit will be;

(D) The information required to be disclosed to the consumer pursuant to section 609(g) of the FCRA;

(E) The distribution of credit scores among consumers who are scored under the same scoring model that is used to generate the consumer's credit score using the same scale as that of the credit score that is provided to the consumer, presented in the form of a bar graph containing a minimum of six bars that illustrates the percentage of consumers with credit scores within the range of scores reflected in each bar or by other clear and readily understandable graphical means, or a clear and readily understandable statement informing the consumer how his or her credit score compares to the scores of other consumers. Use of a graph or statement obtained from the person providing the credit score that meets the requirements of this paragraph (d)(1)(ii)(E) is deemed to comply with this requirement;

(F) A statement that the consumer is encouraged to verify the accuracy of the information contained in the consumer report and has the right to dispute any inaccurate information in the report;

(G) A statement that Federal law gives the consumer the right to obtain copies of his or her consumer reports directly from the consumer reporting agencies, including a free report from each of the nationwide consumer reporting agencies once during any 12-month period;

(H) Contact information for the centralized source from which consumers may obtain their free annual consumer reports; and

(I) A statement directing consumers to the Web site of the Bureau to obtain more information about consumer reports.

(2) Form of the notice. The notice described in paragraph (d)(1)(ii) of this section must be:

(i) Clear and conspicuous;

(ii) Provided on or with the notice required by section 609(g) of the FCRA;

(iii) Segregated from other information provided to the consumer, except for the notice required by section 609(g) of the FCRA; and

(iv) Provided to the consumer in writing and in a form that the consumer may keep.

(3) Timing. The notice described in paragraph (d)(1)(ii) of this section must be provided to the consumer at the time the disclosure required by section 609(g) of the FCRA is provided to the consumer, but in any event at or before consummation in the case of closed-end credit or before the first transaction is made under an open-end credit plan.

(4) Multiple credit scores.

(i) In general. When a person obtains two or more credit scores from consumer reporting agencies and uses one of those credit scores in setting the material terms of credit granted, extended, or otherwise provided to a consumer, for example, by using the low, middle, high, or most recent score, the notice described in paragraph (d)(1)(ii) of this section must include that credit score and the other information required by that paragraph. When a person obtains two or more credit scores from consumer reporting agencies and uses multiple credit scores in setting the material terms of credit granted, extended, or otherwise provided to a consumer, for example, by computing the average of all the credit scores obtained, the notice described in paragraph (d)(1)(ii) of this section must include one of those credit scores and the other information required by that paragraph. The notice may, at the person's option, include more than one credit score, along with the additional information specified in paragraph (d)(1)(ii) of this section for each credit score disclosed.

(ii) Examples.

(A) A person that uses consumer reports to set the material terms of mortgage credit granted, extended, or provided to consumers regularly requests credit scores from several consumer reporting agencies and uses the low score when determining the material terms it will offer to the consumer. That person must disclose the low score in the notice described in paragraph (d)(1)(ii) of this section.

(B) A person that uses consumer reports to set the material terms of mortgage credit granted, extended, or provided to consumers regularly requests credit scores from several consumer reporting agencies, each of which it uses in an underwriting program in order to determine the material terms it will offer to the consumer. That person may choose one of these scores to include in the notice described in paragraph (d)(1)(ii) of this section.

(5) Model form. A model form of the notice described in paragraph (d)(1)(ii) of this section consolidated with the notice required by section 609(g) of the FCRA is contained in Appendix H-3 of this part. Appropriate use of Model Form H-3 is deemed to comply with the requirements of § 1022.74(d). Use of the model form is optional.

(e) Other extensions of credit—credit score disclosure.

(1) In general. A person is not required to provide a risk-based pricing notice to a consumer under § 1022.72(a) or (c) if:

(i) The consumer requests from the person an extension of credit other than credit that is or will be secured by one to four units of residential real property; and

(ii) The person provides to each consumer described in paragraph (e)(1)(i) of this section a notice that contains the following:

(A) A statement that a consumer report (or credit report) is a record of the consumer's credit history and includes information about whether the consumer pays his or her obligations on time and how much the consumer owes to creditors;

(B) A statement that a credit score is a number that takes into account information in a consumer report and that a credit score can change over time to reflect changes in the consumer's credit history;

(C) A statement that the consumer's credit score can affect whether the consumer can obtain credit and what the cost of that credit will be;

(D) The current credit score of the consumer or the most recent credit score of the consumer that was previously calculated by the consumer reporting agency for a purpose related to the extension of credit;

(E) The range of possible credit scores under the model used to generate the credit score;

(F) The distribution of credit scores among consumers who are scored under the same scoring model that is used to generate the consumer's credit score using the same scale as that of the credit score that is provided to the consumer, presented in the form of a bar graph containing a minimum of six bars that illustrates the percentage of consumers with credit scores within the range of scores reflected in each bar, or by other clear and readily understandable graphical means, or a clear and readily understandable statement informing the consumer how his or her credit score compares to the scores of other consumers. Use of a graph or statement obtained from the person providing the credit score that meets the requirements of this paragraph (e)(1)(ii)(F) is deemed to comply with this requirement;

(G) The date on which the credit score was created;

(H) The name of the consumer reporting agency or other person that provided the credit score;

(I) A statement that the consumer is encouraged to verify the accuracy of the information contained in the consumer report and has the right to dispute any inaccurate information in the report;

(J) A statement that Federal law gives the consumer the right to obtain copies of his or her consumer reports directly from the consumer reporting agencies, including a free report from each of the nationwide consumer reporting agencies once during any 12-month period;

(K) Contact information for the centralized source from which consumers may obtain their free annual consumer reports; and

(L) A statement directing consumers to the Web site of the Bureau to obtain more information about consumer reports.

(2) Form of the notice. The notice described in paragraph (e)(1)(ii) of this section must be:

(i) Clear and conspicuous;

(ii) Segregated from other information provided to the consumer; and

(iii) Provided to the consumer in writing and in a form that the consumer may keep.

(3) Timing. The notice described in paragraph (e)(1)(ii) of this section must be provided to the consumer as soon as reasonably practicable after the credit score has been obtained, but in any event at or before consummation in the case of closed-end credit or before the first transaction is made under an open-end credit plan.

(4) Multiple credit scores.

(i) In general. When a person obtains two or more credit scores from consumer reporting agencies and uses one of those credit scores in setting the material terms of credit granted, extended, or otherwise provided to a consumer, for example, by using the low, middle, high, or most recent score, the notice described in paragraph (e)(1)(ii) of this section must include that credit score and the other information required by that paragraph. When a person obtains two or more credit scores from consumer reporting agencies and uses multiple credit scores in setting the material terms of credit granted, extended, or otherwise provided to a consumer, for example, by computing the average of all the credit scores obtained, the notice described in paragraph (e)(1)(ii) of this section must include one of those credit scores and the other information required by that paragraph. The notice may, at the person's option, include more than one credit score, along with the additional information specified in paragraph (e)(1)(ii) of this section for each credit score disclosed.

(ii) Examples. The manner in which multiple credit scores are to be disclosed under this section are substantially identical to the manner set forth in the examples contained in paragraph (d)(4)(ii) of this section.

(5) Model form. A model form of the notice described in paragraph (e)(1)(ii) of this section is contained in Appendix H-4 of this part. Appropriate use of Model Form H-4 is deemed to comply with the requirements of § 1022.74(e). Use of the model form is optional.

(f) Credit score not available.

(1) In general. A person is not required to provide a risk-based pricing notice to a consumer under § 1022.72(a) or (c) if the person:

(i) Regularly obtains credit scores from a consumer reporting agency and provides credit score disclosures to consumers in accordance with paragraphs (d) or (e) of this section, but a credit score is not available from the consumer reporting agency from which the person regularly obtains credit scores for a consumer to whom the person grants, extends, or provides credit;

(ii) Does not obtain a credit score from another consumer reporting agency in connection with granting, extending, or providing credit to the consumer; and

(iii) Provides to the consumer a notice that contains the following:

(A) A statement that a consumer report (or credit report) includes information about the consumer's credit history and the type of information included in that history;

(B) A statement that a credit score is a number that takes into account information in a consumer report and that a credit score can change over time in response to changes in the consumer's credit history;

(C) A statement that credit scores are important because consumers with higher credit scores generally obtain more favorable credit terms;

(D) A statement that not having a credit score can affect whether the consumer can obtain credit and what the cost of that credit will be;

(E) A statement that a credit score about the consumer was not available from a consumer reporting agency, which must be identified by name, generally due to insufficient information regarding the consumer's credit history;

(F) A statement that the consumer is encouraged to verify the accuracy of the information contained in the consumer report and has the right to dispute any inaccurate information in the consumer report;

(G) A statement that Federal law gives the consumer the right to obtain copies of his or her consumer reports directly from the consumer reporting agencies, including a free consumer report from each of the nationwide consumer reporting agencies once during any 12-month period;

(H) The contact information for the centralized source from which consumers may obtain their free annual consumer reports; and

(I) A statement directing consumers to the Web site of the Bureau to obtain more information about consumer reports.

(2) Example. A person that uses consumer reports to set the material terms of non-mortgage credit granted, extended, or provided to consumers regularly requests credit scores from a particular consumer reporting agency and provides those credit scores and additional information to consumers to satisfy the requirements of paragraph (e) of this section. That consumer reporting agency provides to the person a consumer report on a particular consumer that contains one trade line, but does not provide the person with a credit score on that consumer. If the person does not obtain a credit score from another consumer reporting agency and, based in whole or in part on information in a consumer report, grants, extends, or provides credit to the consumer, the person may provide the notice described in paragraph (f)(1)(iii) of this section. If, however, the person obtains a credit score from another consumer reporting agency, the person may not rely upon the exception in paragraph (f) of this section, but may satisfy the requirements of paragraph (e) of this section.

(3) Form of the notice. The notice described in paragraph (f)(1)(iii) of this section must be:

(i) Clear and conspicuous;

(ii) Segregated from other information provided to the consumer; and

(iii) Provided to the consumer in writing and in a form that the consumer may keep.

(4) Timing. The notice described in paragraph (f)(1)(iii) of this section must be provided to the consumer as soon as reasonably practicable after the person has requested the credit score, but in any event not later than consummation of a transaction in the case of closed-end credit or when the first transaction is made under an open-end credit plan.

(5) Model form. A model form of the notice described in paragraph (f)(1)(iii) of this section is contained in Appendix H-5 of this part. Appropriate use of Model Form H-5 is deemed to comply with the requirements of § 1022.74(f). Use of the model form is optional.

§ 1022.75. Rules of construction

For purposes of this subpart, the following rules of construction apply:

(a) One notice per credit extension. A consumer is entitled to no more than one risk-based pricing notice under § 1022.72(a) or (c), or one notice under § 1022.74(d), (e), or (f), for each grant, extension, or other provision of credit. Notwithstanding the foregoing, even if a consumer has previously received a risk-based pricing notice in connection with a grant, extension, or other provision of credit, another risk-based pricing notice is required if the conditions set forth in § 1022.72(d) have been met.

(b) Multi-party transactions.

(1) Initial creditor. The person to whom a credit obligation is initially payable must provide the risk-based pricing notice described in § 1022.72(a) or (c), or satisfy the requirements for and provide the notice required under one of the exceptions in § 1022.74(d), (e), or (f), even if that person immediately assigns the credit agreement to a third party and is not the source of funding for the credit.

(2) Purchasers or assignees. A purchaser or assignee of a credit contract with a consumer is not subject to the requirements of this subpart and is not required to provide the risk-based pricing notice described in § 1022.72(a) or (c), or satisfy the requirements for and provide the notice required under one of the exceptions in § 1022.74(d), (e), or (f).

(3) Example. A consumer obtains credit to finance the purchase of an automobile. If a bank or finance company is the person to whom the loan obligation is initially payable, the bank or finance company must provide the risk-based pricing notice to the consumer (or satisfy the requirements for and provide the notice required under one of the exceptions noted above) based on the terms offered by that bank or finance company only. The auto dealer has no duty to provide a risk-based pricing notice to the consumer. However, the bank or finance company may comply with this rule if the auto dealer has agreed to provide notices to consumers before consummation pursuant to an arrangement with the bank or finance company, as permitted under § 1022.73(c).

(c) Multiple consumers.

(1) Risk-based pricing notices. In a transaction involving two or more consumers who are granted, extended, or otherwise provided credit, a person must provide a notice to each consumer to satisfy the requirements of § 1022.72(a) or (c). Whether the consumers have the same address or not, the person must provide a separate notice to each consumer if a notice includes a credit score(s). Each separate notice that includes a credit score(s) must contain only the credit score(s) of the consumer to whom the notice is provided, and not the credit score(s) of the other consumer. If the consumers have the same address, and the notice does not include a credit score(s), a person may satisfy the requirements by providing a single notice addressed to both consumers.

(2) Credit score disclosure notices. In a transaction involving two or more consumers who are granted, extended, or otherwise provided credit, a person must provide a separate notice to each consumer to satisfy the exceptions in § 1022.74(d), (e), or (f). Whether the consumers have the same address or not, the person must provide a separate notice to each consumer. Each separate notice must contain only the credit score(s) of the consumer to whom the notice is provided, and not the credit score(s) of the other consumer.

(3) Examples.

(i) Two consumers jointly apply for credit with a creditor. The creditor obtains credit scores on both consumers. Based in part on the credit scores, the creditor grants credit to the consumers on material terms that are materially less favorable than the most favorable terms available to other consumers from the creditor. The creditor provides risk-based pricing notices to satisfy its obligations under this subpart. The creditor must provide a separate risk-based pricing notice to each consumer whether the consumers have the same address or not. Each risk-based pricing notice must contain only the credit score(s) of the consumer to whom the notice is provided.

(ii) Two consumers jointly apply for credit with a creditor. The two consumers reside at the same address. The creditor obtains credit scores on each of the two consumer applicants. The creditor grants credit to the consumers. The creditor provides credit score disclosure notices to satisfy its obligations under this subpart. Even though the two consumers reside at the same address, the creditor must provide a separate credit score disclosure notice to each of the consumers. Each notice must contain only the credit score of the consumer to whom the notice is provided.

Subpart I. Duties of Users of Consumer Reports Regarding Identity Theft

§§ 1022.80, 1022.81. [Reserved]

§ 1022.82. Duties of users regarding address discrepancies

(a) Scope. This section applies to a user of consumer reports (user) that receives a notice of address discrepancy from a consumer reporting agency described in 15 U.S.C. 1681a(p), except for a person excluded from coverage of this part by section 1029 of the Consumer Financial Protection Act of 2010, Title X of the Dodd-Frank Wall Street Reform and Consumer Protection Act, Public Law 111–203, 124 Stat. 137.

(b) Definition. For purposes of this section, a notice of address discrepancy means a notice sent to a user by a consumer reporting agency described in 15 U.S.C. 1681a(p) pursuant to 15 U.S.C. 1681c(h)(1), that informs the user of a substantial difference between the address for the consumer that the user provided to request the consumer report and the address(es) in the agency's file for the consumer.

(c) Reasonable belief.

(1) Requirement to form a reasonable belief. A user must develop and implement reasonable policies and procedures designed to enable the user to form a reasonable belief that a consumer report relates to the consumer about whom it has requested the report, when the user receives a notice of address discrepancy.

(2) Examples of reasonable policies and procedures.

(i) Comparing the information in the consumer report provided by the consumer reporting agency with information the user:

(A) Obtains and uses to verify the consumer's identity in accordance with the requirements of the Customer Identification Program (CIP) rules implementing 31 U.S.C. 5318(*l*) (31 CFR 1020.220);

(B) Maintains in its own records, such as applications, change of address notifications, other customer account records, or retained CIP documentation; or

(C) Obtains from third-party sources; or

(ii) Verifying the information in the consumer report provided by the consumer reporting agency with the consumer.

(d) Consumer's address.

(1) Requirement to furnish consumer's address to a consumer reporting agency. A user must develop and implement reasonable policies and procedures for furnishing an address for the consumer that the user has reasonably confirmed is accurate to the consumer reporting agency described in 15 U.S.C. 1681a(p) from whom it received the notice of address discrepancy when the user:

(i) Can form a reasonable belief that the consumer report relates to the consumer about whom the user requested the report;

(ii) Establishes a continuing relationship with the consumer; and

(iii) Regularly and in the ordinary course of business furnishes information to the consumer reporting agency from which the notice of address discrepancy relating to the consumer was obtained.

(2) Examples of confirmation methods. The user may reasonably confirm an address is accurate by:

(i) Verifying the address with the consumer about whom it has requested the report;

(ii) Reviewing its own records to verify the address of the consumer;

(iii) Verifying the address through third-party sources; or

(iv) Using other reasonable means.

(3) Timing. The policies and procedures developed in accordance with paragraph (d)(1) of this section must provide that the user will furnish the consumer's address that the user has reasonably confirmed is accurate to the consumer reporting agency described in 15 U.S.C. 1681a(p) as part of the information it regularly furnishes for the reporting period in which it establishes a relationship with the consumer.

Subpart M. Duties of Consumer Reporting Agencies Regarding Identity Theft

§ 1022.120. [Reserved]

§ 1022.121. Active duty alerts

(a) Duration. The duration of an active duty alert shall be twelve months.

§ 1022.122. [Reserved]

§ 1022.123. Appropriate proof of identity

(a) Consumer reporting agencies shall develop and implement reasonable requirements for what information consumers shall provide to constitute proof of identity for purposes of sections 605A, 605B, and 609(a)(1) of the FCRA. In developing these requirements, the consumer reporting agencies must:

(1) Ensure that the information is sufficient to enable the consumer reporting agency to match consumers with their files; and

(2) Adjust the information to be commensurate with an identifiable risk of harm arising from misidentifying the consumer.

(b) Examples of information that might constitute reasonable information requirements for proof of identity are provided for illustrative purposes only, as follows:

(1) Consumer file match. The identification information of the consumer including his or her full name (first, middle initial, last, suffix), any other or previously used names, current and/or recent full address (street number and name, apt. no., city, state, and zip code), full nine digits of Social Security number, and/or date of birth.

(2) Additional proof of identity. Copies of government issued identification documents, utility bills, and/or other methods of authentication of a person's identity which may include, but would not be limited to, answering questions to which only the consumer might be expected to know the answer.

§§ 1022.124 to 1022.129. [Reserved]

Subpart N. Duties of Consumer Reporting Agencies Regarding Disclosures to Consumers

§ 1022.130. Definitions

For purposes of this subpart, the following definitions apply:

(a) Annual file disclosure means a file disclosure that is provided to a consumer, upon consumer request and without charge, once in any twelve month period, in compliance with section 612(a) of the FCRA, 15 U.S.C. 1681j(a).

(b) Associated consumer reporting agency means a consumer reporting agency that owns or maintains consumer files housed within systems operated by one or more nationwide consumer reporting agencies.

(c) Consumer report has the meaning provided in section 603(d) of the FCRA, 15 U.S.C. 1681a(d).

(d) Consumer reporting agency has the meaning provided in section 603(f) of the FCRA, 15 U.S.C. 1681a(f).

(e) Extraordinary request volume occurs when the number of consumers requesting or attempting to request file disclosures during any twenty-four hour period is more than 175 percent of the rolling ninety-day daily average of consumers requesting or attempting to request file disclosures. For example, if over the previous ninety days an average of one hundred consumers per day requested or attempted to request file disclosures, then extraordinary request volume would be any volume greater than 175 percent of one hundred, i.e., 176 or more requests in a single twenty-four hour period.

(f) File disclosure means a disclosure by a consumer reporting agency pursuant to section 609 of the FCRA, 15 U.S.C. 1681g.

(g) High request volume occurs when the number of consumers requesting or attempting to request file disclosures during any twenty-four hour period is more than 125 percent of the rolling ninety-day daily average of consumers requesting or attempting to request file disclosures. For example, if over the previous ninety days an average of one hundred consumers per day requested or attempted to request file disclosures, then high request volume would be any volume greater than 125 percent of one hundred, i.e., 126 or more requests in a single twenty-four hour period.

(h) Nationwide consumer reporting agency means a consumer reporting agency that compiles and maintains files on consumers on a nationwide basis as defined in section 603(p) of the FCRA, 15 U.S.C. 1681a(p).

(i) Nationwide specialty consumer reporting agency has the meaning provided in section 603(w) of the FCRA, 15 U.S.C. 1681a(w).

(j) Request method means the method by which a consumer chooses to communicate a request for an annual file disclosure.

§§ 1022.131 to 1022.135. [Reserved]

§ 1022.136. Centralized source for requesting annual file disclosures from nationwide consumer reporting agencies

(a) Purpose. The purpose of the centralized source is to enable consumers to make a single request to obtain annual file disclosures from all nationwide consumer reporting agencies, as required under section 612(a) of the FCRA, 15 U.S.C. 1681j(a).

(b) Establishment and operation. All nationwide consumer reporting agencies shall jointly design, fund, implement, maintain, and operate a centralized source for the purpose described in Paragraph (a) of this section. The centralized source required by this part shall:

(1) Enable consumers to request annual file disclosures by any of the following request methods, at the consumers' option:

(i) A single, dedicated Web site,

(ii) A single, dedicated toll-free telephone number; and

(iii) Mail directed to a single address;

(2) Be designed, funded, implemented, maintained, and operated in a manner that:

(i) Has adequate capacity to accept requests from the reasonably anticipated volume of consumers contacting the centralized source through each request method, as determined in accordance with Paragraph (c) of this section;

(ii) Collects only as much personally identifiable information as is reasonably necessary to properly identify the consumer as required under the FCRA, section 610(a)(1), 15 U.S.C. 1681h(a)(1), and other applicable laws and regulations, and to process the transaction(s) requested by the consumer;

(iii) Provides information through the centralized source Web site and telephone number regarding how to make a request by all request methods required under paragraph (b)(1) of this section; and

(iv) Provides clear and easily understandable information and instructions to consumers, including, but not necessarily limited to:

(A) Providing information on the progress of the consumer's request while the consumer is engaged in the process of requesting a file disclosure,

(B) For a Web site request method, providing access to a "help" or "frequently asked questions" screen, which includes specific information that consumers might reasonably need to request file disclosures, the answers to questions that consumers might reasonably ask, and instructions whereby a consumer may file a complaint with the centralized source and with the Bureau;

(C) In the event that a consumer requesting a file disclosure through the centralized source cannot be properly identified in accordance with the FCRA, section 610(a)(1), 15 U.S.C. 1681h(a)(1), and other applicable laws and regulations, providing a statement that the consumers' identity cannot be verified; and directions on how to complete the request, including what additional information or documentation will be required to complete the request, and how to submit such information; and

(D) A statement indicating that the consumer has reached the Web site or telephone number for ordering free annual credit reports as required by Federal law; and

(3) Make available to consumers a standardized form established jointly by the nationwide consumer reporting agencies, which consumers may use to make a request for an annual file disclosure, either by mail or on the Web site required under paragraph (b)(1) of this section, from the centralized source required by this part. The form provided at Appendix L to part 1022, may be used to comply with this section.

(c) Requirement to anticipate. The nationwide consumer reporting agencies shall implement reasonable procedures to anticipate, and to respond to, the volume of consumers who will contact the centralized source through each request method, to request, or attempt to request, a file disclosure, including developing and implementing contingency plans to address circumstances that are reasonably likely to occur and that may materially and adversely impact the operation of the nationwide consumer reporting agency, a centralized source request method, or the centralized source.

(1) The contingency plans required by this section shall include reasonable measures to minimize the impact of such circumstances on the operation of the centralized source and on consumers contacting, or attempting to contact, the centralized source.

(i) Such reasonable measures to minimize impact shall include, but are not necessarily limited to:

(A) The extent reasonably practicable under the circumstances, providing information to consumers on how to use another available request method;

(B) The extent reasonably practicable under the circumstances, communicating, to a consumer who attempts but is unable to make a request, the fact that a condition exists that has precluded the centralized source from accepting all requests, and the period of time after which the centralized source is reasonably anticipated to be able to accept the consumers' request for an annual file disclosure; and

(C) Taking all reasonable steps to restore the centralized source to normal operating status as quickly as reasonably practicable under the circumstances.

(ii) Reasonable measures to minimize impact may also include, as appropriate, collecting request information but declining to accept the request for processing until a reasonable later time, provided that the consumer is clearly and prominently informed, to the extent reasonably practicable under the circumstances, of when the request will be accepted for processing.

(2) A nationwide consumer reporting agency shall not be deemed in violation of paragraph (b)(2)(i) of this section if a centralized source request method is unavailable to accept requests for a reasonable period of time for purposes of conducting maintenance on the request method, provided that the other required request methods remain available during such time.

(d) Disclosures required. If a nationwide consumer reporting agency has the ability to provide a consumer report to a third party relating to a consumer, regardless of whether the consumer report is owned by that nationwide consumer reporting agency or by an associated consumer reporting agency, that nationwide consumer reporting agency shall, upon proper identification in compliance with section 610(a)(1) of the FCRA, 15 U.S.C. 1681h(a)(1), provide an annual file disclosure to such consumer if the consumer makes a request through the centralized source.

(e) High request volume and extraordinary request volume.

(1) High request volume. Provided that a nationwide consumer reporting agency has implemented reasonable procedures developed in accordance with Paragraph (c) of this section, entitled "requirement to anticipate," the nationwide consumer reporting agency shall not be deemed in violation of Paragraph (b)(2)(i) of this section for any period of time in which a centralized source request method, the centralized source, or the nationwide consumer reporting agency experiences high request volume, if the nationwide consumer reporting agency:

(i) Collects all consumer request information and delays accepting the request for processing until a reasonable later time; and

(ii) Clearly and prominently informs the consumer of when the request will be accepted for processing.

(2) Extraordinary request volume. Provided that the nationwide consumer reporting agency has implemented reasonable procedures developed in compliance with Paragraph (c) of this section, entitled "requirement to anticipate," the nationwide consumer reporting agency shall not be deemed in violation of Paragraph (b)(2)(i) of this section for any period of time during which a particular centralized source request method, the centralized source, or the nationwide consumer reporting agency experiences extraordinary request volume.

(f) Information use and disclosure. Any personally identifiable information collected from consumers as a result of a request for annual file disclosure, or other disclosure required by the FCRA, made through the centralized source, may be used or disclosed by the centralized source or a nationwide consumer reporting agency only:

(1) To provide the annual file disclosure or other disclosure required under the FCRA requested by the consumer;

(2) To process a transaction requested by the consumer at the same time as a request for annual file disclosure or other disclosure;

(3) To comply with applicable legal requirements, including those imposed by the FCRA and this part; and

(4) To update personally identifiable information already maintained by the nationwide consumer reporting agency for the purpose of providing consumer reports, provided that the nationwide consumer reporting agency uses and discloses the updated personally identifiable information subject to the same restrictions that would apply, under any applicable provision of law or regulation, to the information updated or replaced.

(g) Communications provided through centralized source.

(1) Any advertising or marketing for products or services, any communications or instructions that advertise or market any products or services, or any request to establish an account through the centralized source must be delayed until after the consumer has obtained his or her annual file disclosure.

(i) In the case of requests made by mail or telephone, the consumer "has obtained his or her annual file disclosure" when the file disclosure is mailed, and the nationwide consumer reporting agency may include advertising for other products or services with the file disclosure.

(ii) In the case of requests made through the centralized source Web site, the consumer "has obtained his or her annual file disclosure" when the file disclosure is delivered to the consumer through the Internet, and the nationwide consumer reporting agency may include advertising for other products or services with the file disclosure.

(2) Any communications, instructions, or permitted advertising or marketing shall not interfere with, detract from, contradict, or otherwise undermine the purpose of the centralized source stated in Paragraph (a) of this section.

(3) Examples of interfering, detracting, inconsistent, and/or undermining communications include:

(i) Centralized source materials that represent, expressly or by implication, that a consumer must purchase a paid product or service in order to receive or to understand the annual file disclosure;

(ii) Centralized source materials that represent, expressly or by implication, that annual file disclosures are not free, or that obtaining an annual file disclosure will have a negative impact on the consumers' credit standing; and

(iii) Centralized source materials that falsely represent, expressly or by implication, that a product or service offered ancillary to receipt of a file disclosure, such as a credit score or credit monitoring service, is free, or fail to clearly and prominently disclose that consumers must cancel a service, advertised as free for an initial period of time, to avoid being charged, if such is the case.

(h) Other practices prohibited through the centralized source. The centralized source shall not:

(1) Contain hyperlinks to commercial or proprietary Web sites until after the consumer has obtained his or her annual file disclosure, except for technical transfers to a Web page on which consumers can request their free annual file disclosure; provided, however, that no hyperlinks to commercial Web sites shall appear on the initial page of the centralized source.

(2) Require consumers to set up an account in connection with obtaining an annual file disclosure; or

(3) Ask or require consumers to agree to terms or conditions in connection with obtaining an annual file disclosure.

§ 1022.137. Streamlined process for requesting annual file disclosures from nationwide specialty consumer reporting agencies

(a) Streamlined process requirements. Any nationwide specialty consumer reporting agency shall have a streamlined process for accepting and processing consumer requests for annual file disclosures. The streamlined process required by this part shall:

(1) Enable consumers to request annual file disclosures by a toll-free telephone number that:

(i) Provides clear and prominent instructions for requesting disclosures by any additional available request methods, that do not interfere with, detract from, contradict, or otherwise undermine the ability of consumers to obtain annual file disclosures through the streamlined process required by this part;

(ii) Is published, in conjunction with all other published numbers for the nationwide specialty consumer reporting agency, in any telephone directory in which any telephone number for the nationwide specialty consumer reporting agency is published; and

(iii) Is clearly and prominently posted on any Web site owned or maintained by the nationwide specialty consumer reporting agency that is related to consumer reporting, along with instructions for requesting disclosures by any additional available request methods; and

(2) Be designed, funded, implemented, maintained, and operated in a manner that:

(i) Has adequate capacity to accept requests from the reasonably anticipated volume of consumers contacting the nationwide specialty consumer reporting agency through the streamlined process, as determined in compliance with Paragraph (b) of this section;

(ii) Collects only as much personal information as is reasonably necessary to properly identify the consumer as required under the FCRA, section 610(a)(1), 15 U.S.C. 1681h(a)(1), and other applicable laws and regulations; and

(iii) Provides clear and easily understandable information and instructions to consumers, including but not necessarily limited to:

(A) Providing information on the status of the consumers request while the consumer is in the process of making a request;

(B) For a Web site request method, providing access to a "help" or "frequently asked questions" screen, which includes more specific information that consumers might reasonably need to order their file disclosure, the answers to questions that consumers might reasonably ask, and instructions whereby a consumer may file a complaint with the nationwide specialty consumer reporting agency and with the Bureau; and

(C) In the event that a consumer requesting a file disclosure cannot be properly identified in accordance with the FCRA, section 610(a)(1), 15 U.S.C. 1681h(a)(1), and other applicable laws and regulations, providing a statement that the consumers identity cannot be verified; and directions on how to complete the request, including what additional information or documentation will be required to complete the request, and how to submit such information.

(b) Requirement to anticipate. A nationwide specialty consumer reporting agency shall implement reasonable procedures to anticipate, and respond to, the volume of consumers who will contact the nationwide specialty consumer reporting agency through the streamlined process to request, or attempt to request, file disclosures, including developing and implementing contingency plans to address circumstances that are reasonably likely to occur and that may materially and adversely impact the operation of the nationwide specialty consumer reporting agency, a request method, or the streamlined process.

(1) The contingency plans required by this section shall include reasonable measures to minimize the impact of such circumstances on the operation of the streamlined process and on consumers contacting, or attempting to contact, the nationwide specialty consumer reporting agency through the streamlined process.

(i) Such reasonable measures to minimize impact shall include, but are not necessarily limited to:

(A) To the extent reasonably practicable under the circumstances, providing information to consumers on how to use another available request method;

(B) To the extent reasonably practicable under the circumstances, communicating, to a consumer who attempts but is unable to make a request, the fact that a condition exists that has precluded the nationwide specialty consumer reporting agency from accepting all requests, and the period of time after which the agency is reasonably anticipated to be able to accept the consumers request for an annual file disclosure; and

(C) Taking all reasonable steps to restore the streamlined process to normal operating status as quickly as reasonably practicable under the circumstances.

(ii) Measures to minimize impact may also include, as appropriate, collecting request information but declining to accept the request for processing until a reasonable later time, provided that the consumer is clearly and prominently informed, to the extent reasonably practicable under the circumstances, of when the request will be accepted for processing.

(2) A nationwide specialty consumer reporting agency shall not be deemed in violation of paragraph (a)(2)(i) of this section if the toll-free telephone number required by this part is unavailable to accept requests for a reasonable period of time for purposes of conducting maintenance on the request method, provided that the nationwide specialty consumer reporting agency makes other request methods available to consumers during such time.

(c) High request volume and extraordinary request volume.

(1) High request volume. Provided that the nationwide specialty consumer reporting agency has implemented reasonable procedures developed in accordance with Paragraph (b) of this section, entitled "requirement to anticipate," a nationwide specialty consumer reporting agency shall not be deemed in violation of Paragraph (a)(2)(i) of this section for any period of time during which a streamlined process request method or the nationwide specialty consumer reporting agency experiences high request volume, if the nationwide specialty consumer reporting agency:

(i) Collects all consumer request information and delays accepting the request for processing until a reasonable later time; and

(ii) Clearly and prominently informs the consumer of when the request will be accepted for processing.

(2) Extraordinary request volume. Provided that the nationwide specialty consumer reporting agency has implemented reasonable procedures developed in accordance with Paragraph (b) of this section, entitled "requirement to anticipate," a nationwide specialty consumer reporting agency shall not be deemed in violation of Paragraph (a)(2)(i) of this section for any period of time during which a streamlined process request method or the nationwide specialty consumer reporting agency experiences extraordinary request volume.

(d) Information use and disclosure. Any personally identifiable information collected from consumers as a result of a request for annual file disclosure, or other disclosure required by the FCRA, made through the streamlined process, may be used or disclosed by the nationwide specialty consumer reporting agency only:

(1) To provide the annual file disclosure or other disclosure required under the FCRA requested by the consumer;

(2) To process a transaction requested by the consumer at the same time as a request for annual file disclosure or other disclosure;

(3) To comply with applicable legal requirements, including those imposed by the FCRA and this part; and

(4) To update personally identifiable information already maintained by the nationwide specialty consumer reporting agency for the purpose of providing consumer reports, provided that the nationwide specialty consumer reporting agency uses and discloses the updated personally identifiable information subject to the same restrictions that would apply, under any applicable provision of law or regulation, to the information updated or replaced.

(e) Requirement to accept or redirect requests. If a consumer requests an annual file disclosure through a method other than the streamlined process established by the nationwide specialty consumer reporting agency in compliance with this part, a nationwide specialty consumer reporting agency shall:

(1) Accept the consumers request; or

(2) Instruct the consumer how to make the request using the streamlined process required by this part.

§ 1022.138. Prevention of deceptive marketing of free credit reports

(a) For purposes of this section:

(1) AnnualCreditReport.com and (877) 322–8228 means the Uniform Resource Locator address "AnnualCreditReport.com" and toll-free telephone number, (877) 322–8228. These are the locator address and toll-free telephone number currently used by the centralized source. If the locator address or toll-free telephone number changes in the future, the new address or telephone number shall be substituted within a reasonable time.

(2) Free credit report means a file disclosure prepared by or obtained from, directly or indirectly, a nationwide consumer reporting agency (as defined in section 603(p) of the FCRA), that is represented, either expressly or impliedly, to be available to the consumer at no cost if the consumer purchases a product or service, or agrees to purchase a product or service subject to cancellation.

(3) General requirements for disclosures. The disclosures covered by Paragraph (b) of this section shall contain only the prescribed content and comply with the following requirements:

(i) All disclosures shall be prominent;

(ii) All disclosures shall be made in the same language as that principally used in the advertisement;

(iii) Visual disclosures shall be easily readable; in a high degree of contrast from the immediate background on which it appears; in a format so that the disclosure is distinct from other text, such as inside a border; in a distinct type style, such as bold; and parallel to the base of the advertisement or screen;

(iv) Audio disclosures shall be delivered in a slow and deliberate manner and in a reasonably understandable volume and pitch;

(v) Program-length television, radio, or Internet-hosted multimedia advertisement disclosures shall be made at the beginning, near the middle, and at the end of the advertisement; and

(vi) Nothing contrary to, inconsistent with, or that undermines the required disclosures shall be used in any advertisement in any medium, nor shall any audio, visual, or print technique be used that is likely to detract significantly from the communication of any disclosure.

(b) Medium-specific disclosures. All offers of free credit reports shall prominently include the disclosures required by this section.

(1) Television advertisements.

(i) All advertisements for free credit reports broadcast on television shall include the following disclosure in close proximity to the first mention of a free credit report: "This is not the free credit report provided for by Federal law."

(ii) The disclosure shall appear at the same time in the audio and visual part of the advertisement. The visual disclosure shall be at least four percent of the vertical picture height and appear for a minimum of four seconds.

(2) Radio advertisements. All advertisements for free credit reports broadcast on radio shall include the following disclosure in close proximity to the first mention of a free credit report: "This is not the free credit report provided for by Federal law."

(3) Print advertisements. All advertisements for free credit reports in print shall include the following disclosure in the form specified below and in close proximity to the first mention of a free credit report. The first line of the disclosure shall be centered and contain only the following language: "THIS NOTICE IS REQUIRED BY LAW." Immediately below the first line of the disclosure the following language shall appear: "You have the right to a free credit report from AnnualCreditReport.com or (877) 322–8228, the ONLY authorized source under Federal law." Each letter of the disclosure text shall be, at minimum, one-half the size of the largest character used in the advertisement.

(4) Web sites. Any Web site offering free credit reports must display the disclosure set forth in paragraphs (b)(4)(i), (ii), and (v) of this section on each page that mentions a free credit report and on each page of the ordering process. This disclosure shall be visible across the top of each page where the disclosure is required to appear; shall appear inside a box; and shall appear in the form specified below:

(i) The first element of the disclosure shall be a header that is centered and shall consist of the following text: "THIS NOTICE IS REQUIRED BY LAW. Read more at consumerfinance.gov/learnmore." Each letter of the header shall be one-half the size of the largest character of the disclosure text required by paragraph (b)(4)(ii) of this section. The reference to consumerfinance.gov/learnmore shall be an operational hyperlink, underlined, and in a color that is a high degree of contrast from the color of the other disclosure text and background color of the box. Until January 1, 2013, "www.ftc.gov" and the corresponding hyperlink may be substituted for "consumerfinance.gov/learmore" and the corresponding hyperlink;

(ii) The second element of the disclosure shall appear below the header required by paragraph (b)(4)(i) and shall consist of the following text: "You have the right to a free credit report from AnnualCreditReport.com or (877) 322–8228, the ONLY authorized source under Federal law." The reference to AnnualCreditReport.com shall be an operational hyperlink to the centralized source, underlined, and in the same color as the hyperlink to consumerfinance.gov/learnmore required in § 1022.138(b)(4)(i);

(iii) The color of the text required by § 1022.138(b)(4)(i) and (ii) shall be in a high degree of contrast with the background color of the box;

(iv) The background of the box shall be a solid color in a high degree of contrast from the background of the page and the color shall not appear elsewhere on the page;

(v) The third element of the disclosure shall appear below the text required by paragraph (b)(4)(ii) and shall be an operational hyperlink to AnnualCreditReport.com that appears as a centered button containing the following language: "Take me to the authorized source." The background of this button shall be the same color as the hyperlinks required by § 1022.138(b)(4)(i) and (ii) and the text shall be in a high degree of contrast to the background of the button;

(vi) Each character of the text required in paragraph (b)(4)(ii) and (v) of this section shall be, at minimum, the same size as the largest character on the page, including characters in an image or graphic banner;

(vii) Each character of the disclosure shall be displayed as plain text and in a sans serif font, such as Arial; and

(viii) The space between each element of the disclosure required in paragraph (b)(i), (ii), and (v) of this section shall be, at minimum, the same size as the largest character on the page, including characters in an image or graphic banner. The space between the boundaries of the box and the text or button required in § 1022.138(b)(i), (ii), and (v) shall be, at minimum, twice the size of the vertical height of the largest character on the page, including characters in an image or graphic banner.

(5) Internet-hosted multimedia advertising. All advertisements for free credit reports disseminated through Internet-hosted multimedia in both audio and visual formats shall include the following disclosure in the form specified below and in close proximity to the first mention of a free credit report. The first line of the disclosure shall be centered and contain only the following language: "THIS NOTICE IS REQUIRED BY LAW." Immediately below the first line of the disclosure the following language shall appear: "You have the right to a free credit report from AnnualCreditReport.com or (877) 322–8228, the ONLY authorized source under Federal law." The disclosure shall appear at the same time in the audio and visual part of the advertisement. If the advertisement contains characters, the visual disclosure shall be, at minimum, the same size as the largest character on the advertisement.

(6) Telephone requests. When consumers call any telephone number, other than the number of the centralized source, appearing in an advertisement that represents free credit reports are available at the number, consumers must receive the following audio disclosure at the first mention of a free credit report: "The following notice is required by law. You have the right to a free credit report from AnnualCreditReport.com or (877) 322–8228, the only authorized source under Federal law."

(7) Telemarketing solicitations. When telemarketing sales calls are made that include offers of free credit reports, the call must include at the first mention of a free credit report the following disclosure: "The following notice is required by law. You have the right to a free credit report from AnnualCreditReport.com or (877) 322–8228, the only authorized source under Federal law."

§ 1022.139. [Reserved]

Subpart O. Miscellaneous Duties of Consumer Reporting Agencies

§ 1022.140. Prohibition against circumventing or evading treatment as a consumer reporting agency

(a) A consumer reporting agency shall not circumvent or evade treatment as a "consumer reporting agency that compiles and maintains files on consumers on a nationwide basis," as defined under section 603(p) of the FCRA, 15 U.S.C. 1681a(p), by any means, including, but not limited to:

(1) Corporate organization, reorganization, structure, or restructuring, including merger, acquisition, dissolution, divestiture, or asset sale of a consumer reporting agency; or

(2) Maintaining or merging public record and credit account information in a manner that is substantially equivalent to that described in Paragraphs (1) and (2) of section 603(p) of the FCRA, 15 U.S.C. 1681a(p).

(b) Examples:

(1) Circumvention through reorganization by data type. XYZ Inc. is a consumer reporting agency that compiles and maintains files on consumers on a nationwide basis. It restructures its operations so that public record information is assembled and maintained only by its corporate affiliate, ABC Inc. XYZ continues operating as a consumer reporting agency but ceases to comply with the FCRA obligations of a consumer reporting agency that compiles and maintains files on consumers on a nationwide basis, asserting that it no longer meets the definition found in FCRA section 603(p), because it no longer maintains public record information. XYZ's conduct is a circumvention or evasion of treatment as a consumer reporting agency that compiles and maintains files on consumers on a nationwide basis, and thus violates this section.

(2) Circumvention through reorganization by regional operations. PDQ Inc. is a consumer reporting agency that compiles and maintains files on consumers on a nationwide basis. It restructures its operations so that corporate affiliates separately assemble and maintain all information on consumers residing in each state. PDQ continues to operate as a consumer reporting agency but ceases to comply with the FCRA obligations of a consumer reporting agency that compiles and maintains files on consumers on a nationwide basis, asserting that it no longer meets the definition found in FCRA section 603(p), because it no longer operates on a nationwide basis. PDQ's conduct is a circumvention or evasion of treatment as a consumer reporting agency that compiles and maintains files on consumers on a nationwide basis, and thus violates this section.

(3) Circumvention by a newly formed entity. Smith Co. is a new entrant in the marketplace for consumer reports that bear on a consumer's credit worthiness, standing and capacity. Smith Co. organizes itself into two affiliated companies: Smith Credit Co. and Smith Public Records Co. Smith Credit Co. assembles and maintains credit account information from persons who furnish that information regularly and in the ordinary course of business on consumers residing nationwide. Smith Public Records Co. assembles and maintains public record information on consumers nationwide. Neither Smith Co. nor its affiliated organizations comply with FCRA obligations of consumer reporting agencies that compile and maintain files on consumers on a nationwide basis. Smith Co.'s conduct is a circumvention or evasion of treatment as a consumer reporting agency that compiles and maintains files on consumers on a nationwide basis, and thus violates this section.

(4) Bona fide, arm's length transaction with unaffiliated party. Foster Ltd. is a consumer reporting agency that compiles and maintains files on consumers on a nationwide basis. Foster Ltd. sells its public record information business to an unaffiliated company in a bona fide, arm's length transaction. Foster Ltd. ceases to assemble, evaluate and maintain public record information on consumers residing nationwide, and ceases to offer reports containing public record information. Foster Ltd.'s conduct is not a circumvention or evasion of treatment as a consumer reporting agency that compiles and maintains files on consumers on a nationwide basis. Foster Ltd.'s conduct does not violate this part.

(c) Limitation on applicability. Any person who is otherwise in violation of paragraph (a) of this section shall be deemed to be in compliance with this part if such person is in compliance with all obligations imposed upon consumer reporting agencies that compile and maintain files on consumers on a nationwide basis under the FCRA, 15 U.S.C. 1681 et seq.

§ 1022.141. Reasonable charges for certain disclosures

Pursuant to section 612(f) of the FCRA, 15 U.S.C. 1681j(f), the charge imposed by a consumer reporting agency for a disclosure to the consumer pursuant to section 609 of the FCRA, 15 U.S.C. 1681g, shall not exceed the maximum allowable charge set by the Bureau.

APPENDIX A TO PART 1022 [RESERVED]

APPENDIX B—TO PART 1022—MODEL NOTICES OF FURNISHING NEGATIVE INFORMATION

a. Although use of the model notices is not required, a financial institution that is subject to section 623(a)(7) of the FCRA shall be deemed to be in compliance with the notice requirement in section 623(a)(7) of the FCRA if the institution properly uses the model notices in this appendix (as applicable).

b. A financial institution may use Model Notice B-1 if the institution provides the notice prior to furnishing negative information to a nationwide consumer reporting agency.

c. A financial institution may use Model Notice B-2 if the institution provides the notice after furnishing negative information to a nationwide consumer reporting agency.

d. Financial institutions may make certain changes to the language or format of the model notices without losing the safe harbor from liability provided by the model notices. The changes to the model notices may not be so extensive as to affect the substance, clarity, or meaningful sequence of the language in the model notices. Financial institutions making such extensive revisions will lose the safe harbor from liability that this appendix provides. Acceptable changes include, for example,

1. Rearranging the order of the references to "late payment(s)," or "missed payment(s)."

2. Pluralizing the terms "credit bureau," "credit report," and "account."

3. Specifying the particular type of account on which information may be furnished, such as "credit card account."

4. Rearranging in Model Notice B-1 the phrases "information about your account" and "to credit bureaus" such that it would read "We may report to credit bureaus information about your account."

Model Notice B-1

We may report information about your account to credit bureaus. Late payments, missed payments, or other defaults on your account may be reflected in your credit report.

Model Notice B-2

We have told a credit bureau about a late payment, missed payment or other default on your account. This information may be reflected in your credit report.

APPENDIX C—TO PART 1022—MODEL FORMS FOR OPT-OUT NOTICES

a. Although use of the model forms is not required, use of the model forms in this appendix (as applicable) complies with the requirement in section 624 of the Act for clear, conspicuous, and concise notices.

b. Certain changes may be made to the language or format of the model forms without losing the protection from liability afforded by use of the model forms. These changes may not be so extensive as to affect the substance, clarity, or meaningful sequence of the language in the model forms. Persons making such extensive revisions will lose the safe harbor that this appendix provides. Acceptable changes include, for example:

1. Rearranging the order of the references to "your income," "your account history," and "your credit score."

2. Substituting other types of information for "income," "account history," or "credit score" for accuracy, such as "payment history," "credit history," "payoff status," or "claims history."

3. Substituting a clearer and more accurate description of the affiliates providing or covered by the notice for phrases such as "the [ABC] group of companies," including without limitation a statement that the entity providing the notice recently purchased the consumer's account.

4. Substituting other types of affiliates covered by the notice for "credit card," "insurance," or "securities" affiliates.

5. Omitting items that are not accurate or applicable. For example, if a person does not limit the duration of the opt-out period, the notice may omit information about the renewal notice.

6. Adding a statement informing consumers how much time they have to opt out before shared eligibility information may be used to make solicitations to them.

7. Adding a statement that the consumer may exercise the right to opt out at any time.

8. Adding the following statement, if accurate: "If you previously opted out, you do not need to do so again."

9. Providing a place on the form for the consumer to fill in identifying information, such as his or her name and address.

10. Adding disclosures regarding the treatment of opt-outs by joint consumers to comply with § 1022.23(a)(2) of this part.

C-1 Model Form for Initial Opt-out Notice (Single-Affiliate Notice)

C-2 Model Form for Initial Opt-out Notice (Joint Notice)

C-3 Model Form for Renewal Notice (Single-Affiliate Notice)

C-4 Model Form for Renewal Notice (Joint Notice)

C-5 Model Form for Voluntary "No Marketing" Notice

C-1—Model Form for Initial Opt-Out Notice (Single-Affiliate Notice)—[Your Choice To Limit Marketing]/[Marketing Opt-Out]

- [Name of Affiliate] is providing this notice.
- [Optional: Federal law gives you the right to limit some but not all marketing from our affiliates. Federal law also requires us to give you this notice to tell you about your choice to limit marketing from our affiliates.]
- You may limit our affiliates in the [ABC] group of companies, such as our [credit card, insurance, and securities] affiliates, from marketing their products or services to you based

on your personal information that we collect and share with them. This information includes your [income], your [account history with us], and your [credit score].

- Your choice to limit marketing offers from our affiliates will apply [until you tell us to change your choice]/[for x years from when you tell us your choice]/[for at least 5 years from when you tell us your choice]. [Include if the opt-out period expires.] Once that period expires, you will receive a renewal notice that will allow you to continue to limit marketing offers from our affiliates for [another x years]/[at least another 5 years].
- [Include, if applicable, in a subsequent notice, including an annual notice, for consumers who may have previously opted out.] If you have already made a choice to limit marketing offers from our affiliates, you do not need to act again until you receive the renewal notice.

To limit marketing offers, contact us [include all that apply]:

- By telephone: 1–(877) ###-####
- On the Web: www.—.com
- By mail: Check the box and complete the form below, and send the form to:

[Company name]

[Company address]

—Do not allow your affiliates to use my personal information to market to me.

C-2—Model Form for Initial Opt-Out Notice (Joint Notice)—[Your Choice To Limit Marketing]/[Marketing Opt-Out]

- The [ABC group of companies] is providing this notice.
- [Optional: Federal law gives you the right to limit some but not all marketing from the [ABC] companies. Federal law also requires us to give you this notice to tell you about your choice to limit marketing from the [ABC] companies.]
- You may limit the [ABC] companies, such as the [ABC credit card, insurance, and securities] affiliates, from marketing their products or services to you based on your personal information that they receive from other [ABC] companies. This information includes your [income], your [account history], and your [credit score].
- Your choice to limit marketing offers from the [ABC] companies will apply [until you tell us to change your choice]/[for x years from when you tell us your choice]/[for at least 5 years from when you tell us your choice]. [Include if the opt-out period expires.] Once that period expires, you will receive a renewal notice that will allow you to continue to limit marketing offers from the [ABC] companies for [another x years]/[at least another 5 years].
- [Include, if applicable, in a subsequent notice, including an annual notice, for consumers who may have previously opted out.] If you have already made a choice to limit marketing offers from the [ABC] companies, you do not need to act again until you receive the renewal notice.

To limit marketing offers, contact us [include all that apply]:

- By telephone: 1–(877) ###-####
- On the Web: www.—.com
- By mail: Check the box and complete the form below, and send the form to:

[Company name]

[Company address]

—Do not allow any company [in the ABC group of companies] to use my personal information to market to me.

C-3—Model Form for Renewal Notice (Single-Affiliate Notice)—[Renewing Your Choice To Limit Marketing]/[Renewing Your Marketing Opt-Out]

- [Name of Affiliate] is providing this notice.
- [Optional: Federal law gives you the right to limit some but not all marketing from our affiliates. Federal law also requires us to give you this notice to tell you about your choice to limit marketing from our affiliates.]
- You previously chose to limit our affiliates in the [ABC] group of companies, such as our [credit card, insurance, and securities] affiliates, from marketing their products or services to you based on your personal information that we share with them. This information includes your [income], your [account history with us], and your [credit score].
- Your choice has expired or is about to expire.

To renew your choice to limit marketing for [x] more years, contact us [include all that apply]:

- By telephone: 1–(877) ###-####
- On the Web: www.—.com
- By mail: Check the box and complete the form below, and send the form to:

  [Company name]

  [Company address]

—Renew my choice to limit marketing for [x] more years.

C-4—Model Form for Renewal Notice (Joint Notice)—[Renewing Your Choice To Limit Marketing]/[Renewing Your Marketing Opt-Out]

- The [ABC group of companies] is providing this notice.
- [Optional: Federal law gives you the right to limit some but not all marketing from the [ABC] companies. Federal law also requires us to give you this notice to tell you about your choice to limit marketing from the [ABC] companies.]
- You previously chose to limit the [ABC] companies, such as the [ABC credit card, insurance, and securities] affiliates, from marketing their products or services to you based on your personal information that they receive from other ABC companies. This information includes your [income], your [account history], and your [credit score].
- Your choice has expired or is about to expire.

To renew your choice to limit marketing for [x] more years, contact us [include all that apply]:

- By telephone: 1–(877) ###-####
- On the Web: www.—.com
- By mail: Check the box and complete the form below, and send the form to:

  [Company name]

  [Company address]

—Renew my choice to limit marketing for [x] more years.

C-5—Model Form for Voluntary “No Marketing” Notice—[Your Choice To Stop Marketing]

- [Name of Affiliate] is providing this notice.
- You may choose to stop all marketing from us and our affiliates.

- [Your choice to stop marketing from us and our affiliates will apply until you tell us to change your choice.]

  To stop all marketing, contact us [include all that apply]:

- By telephone: 1 (877) ###-####
- On the Web: www.—.com
- By mail: Check the box and complete the form below, and send the form to:

  [Company name]

  [Company address]

  —Do not market to me.

APPENDIX D—TO PART 1022—MODEL FORMS FOR FIRM OFFERS OF CREDIT OR INSURANCE

In order to comply with § 1022.54, the following model notices may be used:

(a) English language model notice. **(1)** Short notice.

Here's a Line About Credit

J.S. Name
12345 Friendly Street
City, ST 12345

PFOR 00 MON
FIXED ABC

■

BALANCE TR
FOR 00 MONTHS

■

NO MONTHS FEE

■

INTERNET SECURITY
SECURITY

■

ONLINE FRAUD PRO
GUARANTEE

■

YOUR BALANCE
PAY YOUR BILL

■

FEE-FREE REWARDS
PROGRAM

Dear Ms. Name,

Back in the last century, we saw how technology was changing the way people do things. So we set out to create a the last century, we saw how technology was changing the way people do things. Back in the last century, we saw how technology was changing the way people do things. So we set out to create a the last century, we saw how technology was changing the way people do things.

Back in the last century, we saw how technology was changing the way people do things. So we set out to create a smart kind of credit card. Back in the last century, we saw how technology was changing the way. Back in the last century, we saw how technology was changing the way people do things. So we set out to create a the last century, we saw how technology was changing the way people do things.

Back in the last century, we saw how technology was changing the way people do things. So we set out to create a smart kind of credit card. Back in the last century, we saw how technology was changing the way peop. So we set out to create a smart kind of credit card. Back in the last century, we saw how technology was changing the way people do things. So we set out to create a smart kind of credit a smart kind of credit card.

So we set out to create a smart kind of credit card. Back in the last century, we saw how technology was changing the way people. Back in the last century, we saw how technology was changing the way people do things. So we set out to create a smart kind of credit card.

We saw how technology was changing the way people do things. So we set out to create a smart kind of credit card. Back in the last century, we saw how technology.

Sincerely,

John W. Doe
President, Credit Card Company

You can choose to stop receiving "prescreened" offers of [credit or insurance] from this and other companies by calling toll-free [toll-free number]. See <u>PRESCREEN & OPT-OUT NOTICE</u> on other side [or other location] for more information about prescreened offers.

(2) Long notice.

Back in the last century, we saw how technology was changing the way people do things. So we set out to create a smart kind of credit card. Back in the last century, we saw how technology was changing the way. Back in the last century, we saw how technology was changing the way people do things. So we set out to create a the last century, we saw how technology was changing the way people do things.

HEADER

Percent Rate for	Other ABCs	Variable info material	Grace or repases Are placed here	Computing the balast	Annual Fee	Usual Place Finance Charge
Back in the last century, we saw how technology was changing the way people do things. So we set out to create a smart kind of credit card.	Back in the last century, we saw how technology was changing the way people do things. So we set out to create a smart kind of credit card. Back in the last century, we saw how technology was changing the way.	Back in the last century, we saw how technology was changing the way people do things. So we set out to create a smart kind of credit card.	Back in the last century, we saw how technology was changing.	Back in the last century, we saw how technology was changing the way people do things. So we set out to create a smart kind of credit card.	Back long ago.	Back in the last century, we saw how technology.

Back in the last century, we saw how technology was changing the way people do things. So we set out to create a smart kind of credit card. Back in the last century, we saw how technology was changing the way. Back in the last century, we saw how technology was changing the way people do things. So we set out to create a smart kind of credit card. Back in the last century, we saw how technology was changing the way. Back in the last century, we saw how technology was changing the way people do things. So we set out to create a smart kind of credit card. Back in the last century, we saw how technology was changing the way.

Back in the last century, we saw how technology was changing the way people do things. So we set out to create a smart kind of credit card. Back in the last century, we saw how technology was changing the way. Back in the last century, we saw how technology was changing the way people do things. So we set out to create a smart kind of credit card. Back in the last century, we saw how technology was changing the way. Back in the last century, we saw how technology was changing the way people do things. So we set out to create a smart kind of credit card. Back in the last century, we saw how technology was changing the way. Back in the last century, we saw how technology was changing the way people do things. So we set out to create a smart kind of credit card. Back in the last century, we saw how technology was changing the way. Back in the last century, we saw how technology was changing the way people do things. So we set out to create a smart kind of credit card. Back in the last century, we saw how technology was changing the way.

Back in the last century, we saw how technology was changing the way. Back in the last century, we saw how technology was changing the way people do things. So we set out to create a smart kind of credit card. Back in the last century, we saw how technology was changing the way.

Back in the last century, we saw how technology was changing the way. Back in the last century, we saw how technology was changing the way people do things. So we set out to create a smart kind of credit card. Back in the last century, we saw how technology was changing the way.

TERMS AND CONDITIONS

Back in the last century, we saw how technology was changing the way people do things. So we set out to create a smart kind of credit card. Back in the last century, we saw how technology was changing the way. Back in the last century, we saw how technology was changing the way people do things. So we set out to create a smart kind of credit card. Back in the last century, we saw how technology was changing the way. Back in the last century, we saw how technology was changing the way people do things. So we set out to create a smart kind of credit card. Back in the last century, we saw how technology was changing the way. Back in the last century, we saw how technology was changing the way people do things. So we set out to create a smart kind of credit card. Back in the last century, we saw how technology was changing the way. Back in the last century, we saw how technology was changing the way people do things. So we set out to create a smart kind of credit card. Back in the last century, we saw how technology was changing the way. Back in the last century, we saw how technology was changing the way people do things. So we set out to create a smart kind of credit card. Back in the last century, we saw how technology was changing the way. Back in the last century, we saw how technology was changing the way people do things. So we set out to create a smart kind of credit card. Back in the last century, we saw how technology was changing the way. Back in the last century, we saw how technology was changing the way people do things. So we set out to create a smart kind of credit card. Back in the last century, we saw how technology was changing the way. Back in the last century, we saw how technology was changing the way. Back in the last century, we saw how technology was changing the way people do things. So we set out to create a smart kind of credit card. Back in the last century, we saw how technology was changing the way. Back in the last century, we saw how technology was changing the way people do things. So we set out to create a smart kind of credit card. Back in the last century, we saw how technology was changing the way. Back in the last century, we saw how technology was changing the way people do things. Back in the last century, we saw how technology was changing the way. Back in the last century, we saw y, we saw how technology was changing the way. Back in the last century, we saw how technology was changing the way people do things.

Act Notice: the a smart kind of credit card. Back in the last century, we saw how technology was changing the way people do things. So we set out to create a smart kind of credit card. Back in the last century, we saw how technology was changing the way. Back in the last century, we saw.

__PRESCREEN & OPT-OUT NOTICE__: This "prescreened" offer of [credit or insurance] is based on information in your credit report indicating that you meet certain criteria. This offer is not guaranteed if you do not meet our criteria [including providing acceptable property as collateral]. If you do not want to receive prescreened offers of [credit or insurance] from this and other companies, call the consumer reporting agencies [or name of consumer reporting agency] toll-free, [toll-free number]; or write: [consumer reporting agency name and mailing address].

Notice to Some Residents: te a smart kind of credit card. Back in the last century, we saw how technology was changing the way. Back in the last century, we saw how technology was changing the way people do things. So we set out to create a smart kind of credit card. Back in the last century, we saw how technology was changing the way. Back in the last century. So we set out to create a smart kind of credit card. Back in the last century, we saw how technology was changing the way.

(b) Spanish language model notice. **(1)** Short notice.

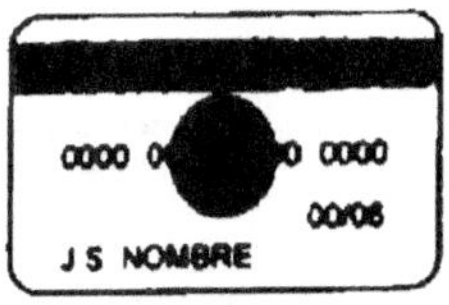

Aquí están líneas crédito

J.S. Nombre
1234 Calle Amistosa
Ciudad, ST 12345

Estimada Señora Nombre:

En el siglo pasado vimos como la tecnología estaba cambiando la manera en que la gente hace las cosas. Así que creamos una tarjeta de crédito inteligente, vimos como la tecnología estaba cambiando la manera en que la gente hace las cosas. En el siglo pasado vimos como la tecnología estaba cambiando la manera en que la gente hace las cosas. Así que creamos una tarjeta de crédito inteligente. Vimos como la tecnología estaba cambiando la manera en que la gente hace las cosas.

Así que creamos una tarjeta de crédito inteligente. Vimos como la tecnología estaba cambiando la manera en que la gente hace las cosas. En el siglo pasado vimos como la tecnología estaba cambiando la manera en que la gente hace las cosas. Así que creamos una tarjeta de crédito inteligente, vimos como la tecnología estaba cambiando la manera en que la gente hace las cosas.

Vimos como la tecnología estaba cambiando la manera en que la gente hace las cosas. En el siglo pasado vimos como la tecnología estaba cambiando la manera en que la gente hace las cosas. Así que creamos una tarjeta de crédito inteligente, vimos como la tecnología estaba cambiando la manera en que la gente hace las cosas. En el siglo pasado vimos como la tecnología estaba cambiando la manera en que la gente hace las cosas.

Así que creamos una tarjeta de crédito inteligente. Vimos como la tecnología estaba cambiando la manera en que la gente hace las cosas. En el siglo pasado vimos como la tecnología estaba cambiando la manera en que la gente hace las cosas. Así que creamos una tarjeta de crédito inteligente. Vimos como la tecnología estaba cambiando la manera en que la gente hace las cosas.

Sinceramente,

John W. Doe
Presidente, Compañía

PFOR 00 MON FIJO ABC

■

TRANSFERENCIA DE BALANCE POR MESES

■

SIN CUOTA MENSUAL

■

PAGO ELECTRÓNICO SEGURO

■

PROTECCIÓN CONTRA FRAUDE EN LÍNEA GARANTIZADO

■

SU BALANCE PAGA SU CUENTA

■

PROGRAMA DE RECOMPENSAS SIN CUENTA

Usted puede elegir no recibir más "ofertas de [crédito o seguro] pre-investigadas" de esta y otras compañías llamando sin cargos al [número sin cargo]. Ver la <u>NOTIFICACIÓN DE PRE-INVESTIGACIÓN Y EXCLUSIÓN VOLUNTARIA</u> al otro lado de esta página [o en otro lugar] para más información sobre ofertas pre-investigadas.

(2) Long notice.

En el siglo pasado vimos como la tecnologia estaba cambiando la manera en que la gente hace las cosas. Así que creamos una tarjeta de crédito inteligente, vimos como la tecnología estaba cambiando la manera en que la gente hace las cosas. En el siglo pasado vimos como la tecnología estaba cambiando la manera en que la gente hace las cosas. Así que creamos una tarjeta de crédito inteligente.

AQUÍ ESTÁN

Protección Contra Fraude	Programa de Recompensas	Su Balance Paga	Sin Cuota Mensual	Protección Contra Fraude	Recompensas Sin Cuenta	Sin Cuota Mensual
En el siglo pasado vimos como la tecnologia estaba cambiando la manera en que la gente hace las cosas.	Vimos como la tecnologia estaba cambiando la manera en que la gente hace las cosas. Vimos como la tecnología estaba cambiando la manera en que la gente hace las cosas.	En el siglo pasado vimos como la tecnología estaba cambiando la manera en que la gente hace las cosas. En el siglo pasado vimos como la gente hace las cosas. Así que cremos.	Así que creamos una tarjeta de crédito inteligente.	En el siglo pasado vimos como la tecnología estaba cambiando la manera en que la gente hace las cosas.	Así que cremos.	Vimos como la tecnología estaba cambiando la manera en que la gente hace las cosas.

En el siglo pasado vimos como la tecnologia estaba cambiando la manera en que la gente hace las cosas. Así que creamos una tarjeta de crédito inteligente, vimos como la tecnología estaba cambiando la manera en que la gente hace las cosas. En el siglo pasado vimos como la tecnologia estaba cambiando la manera en que la gente hace las cosas. Así que creamos una tarjeta de crédito inteligente. Vimos como la tecnologia estaba cambiando la manera en que la gente hace las cosas. Así que creamos una tarjeta de crédito inteligente. Vimos como la tecnologia estaba cambiando la manera en que la gente hace las cosas.

Así que creamos una tarjeta de crédito inteligente; vimos como la tecnología estaba cambiando la manera en que la gente hace las cosas. En el siglo pasado vimos como la tecnología estaba cambiando la manera en que le gente hace las cosas. Así que creamos una tarjeta de crédito inteligente. Vimos como la tecnologia estaba cambiando la manera en que la gente hace las cosas. Así que creamos una tarjeta de crédito inteligente. Vimos como la tecnologia estaba cambiando la manera en que la gente hace las cosas. En el siglo pasado vimos como la tecnología estaba cambiando la manera en que la gente hace las cosas. Así que creamos una tarjeta de crédito inteligente, vimos como la tecnología estaba cambiando la manera en que la gente hace las cosas.

Vimos como la tecnologia estaba cambiando la manera en que la gente hace las cosas. En el siglo pasado vimos como la tecnologie estaba cambiando la manera en que la gente hace las cosas. Así que creamos una tarjeta de crédito inteligente, vimos como la tecnología estaba cambiando la manera en que la gente hace las cosas. En el siglo pasado vimos como la tecnologia estaba cambiando la manera en que la gente hace las cosas. Así que creamos una tarjeta de crédito inteligente. Vimos como la tecnología estaba cambiando la manera en que la gente hace las cosas. En el siglo pasado vimos como la tecnología estaba cambiando la manera en que la gente hace las cosas. En el siglo pasado vimos como la tecnología estaba cambiando la manera en que la gente hace las cosas.

TERMINOS Y CONDICIONA

En el siglo pasado vimos como la tecnologia estaba cambiando la manera en que la gente hace las cosas. Así que creamos una tarjeta de crédito inteligente, vimos como la tecnología estaba cambiando la manera en que la gente hace las cosas. En el siglo pasado vimos como la tecnología estaba cambiando la manera en que la gente hace las cosas. Así que creamos una tarjeta de crédito inteligente. Vimos como la tecnologia estaba cambiando la manera en que la gente hace las cosas.

Así que creamos una tarjeta de crédito inteligente. Vimos como la tecnologia estaba cambiando la manera en que la gente hace las cosas. En el siglo pasado vimos como la tecnologia estaba cambiando la manera en que la gente hace las cosas. Así que creamos una tarjeta de crédito inteligente, vimos como la tecnología estaba cambiando la manera en que la gente hace las cosas.

Vimos como la tecnología estaba cambiando la manera en que la gente hace las cosas. En el siglo pasado vimos como la tecnologia estaba cambiando la manera en que la gente hace las cosas. Así que creamos una tarjeta de crédito inteligente, vimos como la tecnología estaba cambiando la manera en que la gente hace las cosas. En el siglo pasado vimos como la tecnología estaba cambiando la manera en que la gente hace las cosas.

Así que creamos una tarjeta de crédito inteligente. Vimos como la tecnología estaba cambiando la manera en que la gente hace las cosas. En el siglo pasado vimos como la tecnologia estaba cambiando la manera en que le gente hace las cosas. Así que creamos una tarjeta de crédito inteligente. Vimos como la tecnología estaba cambiando la manera en que la gente hace las cosas.

En el siglo pasado vimos como la tecnologia estaba cambiando la manera en que la gente hace las cosas. Así que creamos una tarjeta de crédito inteligente, vimos como la tecnologia estaba cambiando la manera en que la gente hace las cosas. En el siglo pasado vimos como la tecnología estaba cambiando la manera en que la gente hace las cosas. Así que creamos una tarjeta de crédito inteligente. Vimos como la tecnologia estaba cambiando la manera en que la gente hace las cosas. Así que creamos una tarjeta de crédito inteligente. Vimos como la tecnología estaba cambiando la manera en que la gente hace las cosas. En el siglo pasado vimos como la tecnología estaba cambiando la manera en que la gente hace las cosas. Así que creamos una tarjeta de crédito inteligente. Vimos como la tecnología estaba cambiando la manera en que le gente hace las cosas. Vimos como la tecnología estaba cambiando la manera en qua la gente hace las cosas. Vimos como la tecnología estaba cambiando la manera en que la gente hace las cosas. Vimos como la tecnologia estaba cambiando la manera en que la gente hace las cosas.

NOTIFICACIÓN DE PRE-INVESTIGACIÓN Y EXCLUSIÓN VOLUNTARIA: Esta oferta de [crédito o seguro] está basada en información contenida en su informe de crédito que indica que usted cumple con ciertos criterios [incluyendo la condición de tener propiedades aceptables como colateral]. Si usted no cumple con nuestros criterios, esta oferta no está garantizada. Si usted no desea recibir ofertas de [crédito o seguro] pre-investigadas de ésta y otras compañias, llame a las agencias de información del consumidor [o nombre de la agencia de información del consumidor] sin cargos, [número sin cargo]; o escriba a: [nombre de la agencia de información del consumidor y dirección de correo].

En el siglo pasado vimos como; la tecnologia estaba cambiando la manera en que la gente hace las cosas. Así que creamos una tarjeta de crédito inteligente. Vimos como la tecnologia estaba cambiando la manera en que la gente hace las cosas. Vimos como la tecnologia estaba cambiando la manera en que la gente hace las cosas. Vimos como la tecnología estaba cambiando la manera en que la gente hace las cosas. Vimos como la tecnología estaba cambiando la manera en que la gente hace las cosas.

APPENDIX E—TO PART 1022—INTERAGENCY GUIDELINES CONCERNING THE ACCURACY AND INTEGRITY OF INFORMATION FURNISHED TO CONSUMER REPORTING AGENCIES

The Bureau encourages voluntary furnishing of information to consumer reporting agencies. Section 1022.42 of this part requires each furnisher to establish and implement reasonable written policies and procedures concerning the accuracy and integrity of the information it furnishes to consumer reporting agencies. Under § 1022.42(b) of this part, a furnisher must consider the guidelines set forth below in developing its policies and procedures. In establishing these policies and procedures, a furnisher may include any of its existing policies and procedures that are relevant and appropriate. Section 1022.42(c) requires each furnisher to review its policies and procedures periodically and update them as necessary to ensure their continued effectiveness.

I. Nature, Scope, and Objectives of Policies and Procedures

(a) Nature and Scope. Section 1022.42(a) of this part requires that a furnisher's policies and procedures be appropriate to the nature, size, complexity, and scope of the furnisher's activities. In developing its policies and procedures, a furnisher should consider, for example:

(1) The types of business activities in which the furnisher engages;

(2) The nature and frequency of the information the furnisher provides to consumer reporting agencies; and

(3) The technology used by the furnisher to furnish information to consumer reporting agencies.

(b) Objectives. A furnisher's policies and procedures should be reasonably designed to promote the following objectives:

(1) To furnish information about accounts or other relationships with a consumer that is accurate, such that the furnished information:

(i) Identifies the appropriate consumer;

(ii) Reflects the terms of and liability for those accounts or other relationships; and

(iii) Reflects the consumer's performance and other conduct with respect to the account or other relationship;

(2) To furnish information about accounts or other relationships with a consumer that has integrity, such that the furnished information:

(i) Is substantiated by the furnisher's records at the time it is furnished;

(ii) Is furnished in a form and manner that is designed to minimize the likelihood that the information may be incorrectly reflected in a consumer report; thus, the furnished information should:

(A) Include appropriate identifying information about the consumer to whom it pertains; and

(B) Be furnished in a standardized and clearly understandable form and manner and with a date specifying the time period to which the information pertains; and

(iii) Includes the credit limit, if applicable and in the furnisher's possession;

(3) To conduct reasonable investigations of consumer disputes and take appropriate actions based on the outcome of such investigations; and

(4) To update the information it furnishes as necessary to reflect the current status of the consumer's account or other relationship, including, for example:

(i) Any transfer of an account (e.g., by sale or assignment for collection) to a third party; and

(ii) Any cure of the consumer's failure to abide by the terms of the account or other relationship.

II. Establishing and Implementing Policies and Procedures

In establishing and implementing its policies and procedures, a furnisher should:

(a) Identify practices or activities of the furnisher that can compromise the accuracy or integrity of information furnished to consumer reporting agencies, such as by:

(1) Reviewing its existing practices and activities, including the technological means and other methods it uses to furnish information to consumer reporting agencies and the frequency and timing of its furnishing of information;

(2) Reviewing its historical records relating to accuracy or integrity or to disputes; reviewing other information relating to the accuracy or integrity of information provided by the furnisher to consumer reporting agencies; and considering the types of errors, omissions, or other problems that may have affected the accuracy or integrity of information it has furnished about consumers to consumer reporting agencies;

(3) Considering any feedback received from consumer reporting agencies, consumers, or other appropriate parties;

(4) Obtaining feedback from the furnisher's staff; and

(5) Considering the potential impact of the furnisher's policies and procedures on consumers.

(b) Evaluate the effectiveness of existing policies and procedures of the furnisher regarding the accuracy and integrity of information furnished to consumer reporting agencies; consider whether new, additional, or different policies and procedures are necessary; and consider whether implementation of existing policies and procedures should be modified to enhance the accuracy and integrity of information about consumers furnished to consumer reporting agencies.

(c) Evaluate the effectiveness of specific methods (including technological means) the furnisher uses to provide information to consumer reporting agencies; how those methods may affect the accuracy and integrity of the information it provides to consumer reporting agencies; and whether new, additional, or different methods (including technological means) should be used to provide information to consumer reporting agencies to enhance the accuracy and integrity of that information.

III. Specific Components of Policies and Procedures

In developing its policies and procedures, a furnisher should address the following, as appropriate:

(a) Establishing and implementing a system for furnishing information about consumers to consumer reporting agencies that is appropriate to the nature, size, complexity, and scope of the furnisher's business operations.

(b) Using standard data reporting formats and standard procedures for compiling and furnishing data, where feasible, such as the electronic transmission of information about consumers to consumer reporting agencies.

(c) Maintaining records for a reasonable period of time, not less than any applicable recordkeeping requirement, in order to substantiate the accuracy of any information about consumers it furnishes that is subject to a direct dispute.

(d) Establishing and implementing appropriate internal controls regarding the accuracy and integrity of information about consumers furnished to consumer reporting agencies, such as by implementing standard procedures and verifying random samples of information provided to consumer reporting agencies.

(e) Training staff that participates in activities related to the furnishing of information about consumers to consumer reporting agencies to implement the policies and procedures.

(f) Providing for appropriate and effective oversight of relevant service providers whose activities may affect the accuracy or integrity of information about consumers furnished to consumer reporting agencies to ensure compliance with the policies and procedures.

(g) Furnishing information about consumers to consumer reporting agencies following mergers, portfolio acquisitions or sales, or other acquisitions or transfers of accounts or other obligations in a manner that prevents re-aging of information, duplicative reporting, or other problems that may similarly affect the accuracy or integrity of the information furnished.

(h) Deleting, updating, and correcting information in the furnisher's records, as appropriate, to avoid furnishing inaccurate information.

(i) Conducting reasonable investigations of disputes.

(j) Designing technological and other means of communication with consumer reporting agencies to prevent duplicative reporting of accounts, erroneous association of information with the wrong consumer(s), and other occurrences that may compromise the accuracy or integrity of information provided to consumer reporting agencies.

(k) Providing consumer reporting agencies with sufficient identifying information in the furnisher's possession about each consumer about whom information is furnished to enable the consumer reporting agency properly to identify the consumer.

(*l*) Conducting a periodic evaluation of its own practices, consumer reporting agency practices of which the furnisher is aware, investigations of disputed information, corrections of inaccurate information, means of communication, and other factors that may affect the accuracy or integrity of information furnished to consumer reporting agencies.

(m) Complying with applicable requirements under the FCRA and its implementing regulations.

APPENDIX F, G—TO PART 1022—[RESERVED]

APPENDIX H—TO PART 1022—MODEL FORMS FOR RISK-BASED PRICING AND CREDIT SCORE DISCLOSURE EXCEPTION NOTICES

1. This appendix contains four model forms for risk-based pricing notices and three model forms for use in connection with the credit score disclosure exceptions. Each of the model forms is designated for use in a particular set of circumstances as indicated by the title of that model form.

2. Model form H-1 is for use in complying with the general risk-based pricing notice requirements in Sec. 1022.72 if a credit score is not used in setting the material terms of credit. Model form H-2 is for risk-based pricing notices given in connection with account review if a credit score is not used in increasing the annual percentage rate. Model form H-3 is for use in connection with the credit score disclosure exception for loans secured by residential real property. Model form H-4 is for use in connection with the credit score disclosure exception for loans that are not secured by residential real property. Model form H-5 is for use in connection with the credit score disclosure exception when no credit score is available for a consumer. Model form H-6 is for use in complying with the general risk-based pricing notice requirements in Sec. 1022.72 if a credit score is used in setting the material terms of credit. Model form H-7 is for risk-based pricing notices given in connection with account review if a credit score is used in increasing the annual percentage rate. All forms contained in this appendix are models; their use is optional.

3. A person may change the forms by rearranging the format or by making technical modifications to the language of the forms, in each case without modifying the substance of the disclosures. Any such rearrangement or modification of the language of the model forms may not be so extensive as to materially affect the substance, clarity, comprehensibility, or meaningful sequence of the forms. Persons making revisions with that effect will lose the benefit of the safe harbor for appropriate use of Appendix H model forms. A person is not required to conduct consumer testing when rearranging the format of the model forms.

a. Acceptable changes include, for example:

i. Corrections or updates to telephone numbers, mailing addresses, or Web site addresses that may change over time.

ii. The addition of graphics or icons, such as the person's corporate logo.

iii. Alteration of the shading or color contained in the model forms.

iv. Use of a different form of graphical presentation to depict the distribution of credit scores.

v. Substitution of the words "credit" and "creditor" or "finance" and "finance company" for the terms "loan" and "lender."

vi. Including pre-printed lists of the sources of consumer reports or consumer reporting agencies in a "check-the-box" format.

vii. Including the name of the consumer, transaction identification numbers, a date, and other information that will assist in identifying the transaction to which the form pertains.

viii. Including the name of an agent, such as an auto dealer or other party, when providing the "Name of the Entity Providing the Notice."

ix. Until January 1, 2013, substituting "For more information about credit reports and your rights under Federal law, visit the Federal Reserve Board's Web site at www.federalreserve.gov, or the Federal Trade Commission's Web site at www.ftc.gov." for "For more information about credit reports and your rights under Federal law, visit the Consumer Financial Protection Bureau's Web site at www.consumerfinance.gov/learnmore."

b. Unacceptable changes include, for example:

i. Providing model forms on register receipts or interspersed with other disclosures.

ii. Eliminating empty lines and extra spaces between sentences within the same section.

4. If a person uses an appropriate Appendix H model form, or modifies a form in accordance with the above instructions, that person shall be deemed to be acting in compliance with the provisions of § 1022.73 or § 1022.74, as applicable, of this part. It is intended that appropriate use of Model Form H-3 also will comply with the disclosure that may be required under section 609(g) of the FCRA. Optional language in model forms H-6 and H-7 may be used to direct the consumer to the entity (which may be a consumer reporting agency or the creditor itself, for a proprietary score that meets the definition of a credit score) that provided the credit score for any questions about the credit score, along with the entity's contact information. Creditors may use or not use the additional language without losing the safe harbor, since the language is optional.

H-1 Model form for risk-based pricing notice.

H-2 Model form for account review risk-based pricing notice.

H-3 Model form for credit score disclosure exception for credit secured by one to four units of residential real property.

H-4 Model form for credit score disclosure exception for loans not secured by residential real property.

H-5 Model form for credit score disclosure exception for loans where credit score is not available.

H-6 Model form for risk-based pricing notice with credit score information.

H-7 Model form for account review risk-based pricing notice with credit score information.

H-1. Model form for risk-based pricing notice

[Name of Entity Providing the Notice]
Your Credit Report[s] and the Price You Pay for Credit

What is a credit report?	A credit report is a record of your credit history. It includes information about whether you pay your bills on time and how much you owe to creditors.
How did we use your credit report[s]?	We used information from your credit report[s] to set the terms of the credit we are offering you, such as the [Annual Percentage Rate/down payment]. The terms offered to you may be less favorable than the terms offered to consumers who have better credit histories.
What if there are mistakes in your credit report[s]?	You have a right to dispute any inaccurate information in your credit report[s]. If you find mistakes on your credit report[s], contact **[insert name of CRA(s)]**, which [is/are] the [consumer reporting agency/consumer reporting agencies] from which we obtained your credit report[s]. It is a good idea to check your credit report[s] to make sure the information [it contains/they contain] is accurate.
How can you obtain a copy of your credit report[s]?	Under Federal law, you have the right to obtain a copy of your credit report[s] without charge for 60 days after you receive this notice. To obtain your free report[s], contact **[insert name of CRA(s)]**: *By telephone:* Call toll-free: 1-877-xxx-xxxx *By mail:* Mail your written request to: **[Insert address]** *On the web:* Visit **[insert website address]**
How can you get more information about credit reports?	For more information about credit reports and your rights under Federal law, visit the Consumer Financial Protection Bureau's website at www.consumerfinance.gov/learnmore.

H-2. Model form for account review risk-based pricing notice

[Name of Entity Providing the Notice]
Your Credit Report[s] and the Pricing of Your Account

What is a credit report?	A credit report is a record of your credit history. It includes information about whether you pay your bills on time and how much you owe to creditors.
How did we use your credit report[s]?	We have used information from your credit report[s] to review the terms of your account with us. Based on our review of your credit report[s], we have increased the annual percentage rate on your account.
What if there are mistakes in your credit report[s]?	You have a right to dispute any inaccurate information in your credit report[s]. If you find mistakes on your credit report[s], contact **[insert name of CRA(s)]**, which [is/are] [a consumer reporting agency/consumer reporting agencies] from which we obtained your credit report[s]. It is a good idea to check your credit report[s] to make sure the information [it contains/they contain] is accurate.
How can you obtain a copy of your credit report[s]?	Under Federal law, you have the right to obtain a copy of your credit report[s] without charge for 60 days after you receive this notice. To obtain your free report[s], contact **[insert name of CRA(s)]**: *By telephone:* Call toll-free: 1-877-xxx-xxxx *By mail:* Mail your written request to: **[Insert address]** *On the web:* Visit **[insert website address]**
How can you get more information about credit reports?	For more information about credit reports and your rights under Federal law, visit the Consumer Financial Protection Bureau's website at www.consumerfinance.gov/learnmore.

H-3. Model form for credit score disclosure exception for loans secured by one to four units of residential real property

[Name of Entity Providing the Notice]
Your Credit Score and the Price You Pay for Credit

Your Credit Score	
Your credit score	**[Insert credit score]** Source **[Insert source]** Date **[Insert date score was created]**

Understanding Your Credit Score	
What you should know about credit scores	Your credit score is a number that reflects the information in your credit report. Your credit report is a record of your credit history. It includes information about whether you pay your bills on time and how much you owe to creditors. Your credit score can change, depending on how your credit history changes.
How we use your credit score	Your credit score can affect whether you can get a loan and how much you will have to pay for that loan.
The range of scores	Scores range from a low of **[Insert bottom number in the range]** to a high of **[Insert top number in the range]**. Generally, the higher your score, the more likely you are to be offered better credit terms.

How your score compares to the scores of other consumers

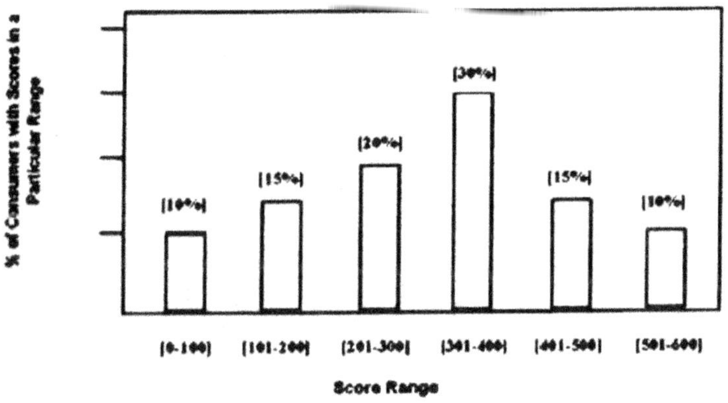

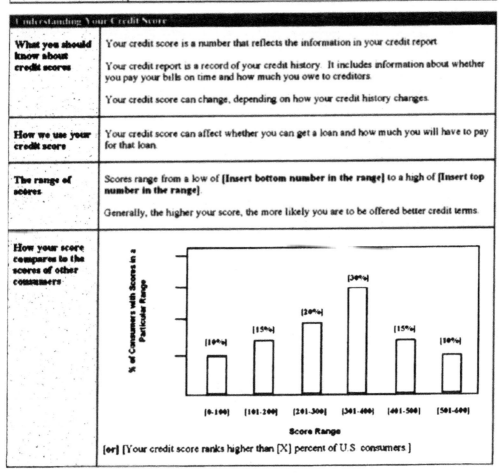

[or] [Your credit score ranks higher than [X] percent of U.S. consumers.]

Understanding Your Credit Score (continued)	
Key factors that adversely affected your credit score	**[Insert first factor]** **[Insert second factor]** **[Insert third factor]** **[Insert fourth factor]** **[Insert fifth factor, if applicable]**

Checking Your Credit Report	
What if there are mistakes in your credit report?	You have a right to dispute any inaccurate information in your credit report. If you find mistakes on your credit report, contact the consumer reporting agency. It is a good idea to check your credit report to make sure the information it contains is accurate.
How can you obtain a copy of your credit report?	Under Federal law, you have the right to obtain a free copy of your credit report from each of the nationwide consumer reporting agencies once a year. To order your free annual credit report— *By telephone:* Call toll-free: 1-877-322-8228 *On the web:* Visit www.annualcreditreport.com *By mail:* Mail your completed Annual Credit Report Request Form (which you can obtain from the Federal Trade Commission's website at http://www.ftc.gov/bcp/conline/include/requestformfinal.pdf) to: Annual Credit Report Request Service P.O. Box 105281 Atlanta, GA 30348-5281
How can you get more information?	For more information about credit reports and your rights under Federal law, visit the Consumer Financial Protection Bureau's website at www.consumerfinance.gov/learnmore.

Notice to the Home Loan Applicant

In connection with your application for a home loan, the lender must disclose to you the score that a consumer reporting agency distributed to users and the lender used in connection with your home loan, and the key factors affecting your credit scores.

The credit score is a computer generated summary calculated at the time of the request and based on information that a consumer reporting agency or lender has on file. The scores are based on data about your credit history and payment patterns. Credit scores are important because they are used to assist the lender in determining whether you will obtain a loan. They may also be used to determine what interest rate you may be offered on the mortgage. Credit scores can change over time, depending on your conduct, how your credit history and payment patterns change, and how credit scoring technologies change.

Because the score is based on information in your credit history, it is very important that you review the credit-related information that is being furnished to make sure it is accurate. Credit records may vary from one company to another.

If you have questions about your credit score or the credit information that is furnished to you, contact the consumer reporting agency at the address and telephone number provided with this notice, or contact the lender, if the lender developed or generated the credit score. The consumer reporting agency plays no part in the decision to take any action on the loan application and is unable to provide you with specific reasons for the decision on a loan application.

If you have questions concerning the terms of the loan, contact the lender.

H-4. Model form for credit score disclosure exception for loans not secured by residential real property

[Name of Entity Providing the Notice]
Your Credit Score and the Price You Pay for Credit

Your Credit Score	
Your credit score	**[Insert credit score]** Source: **[Insert source]** Date: **[Insert date score was created]**

Understanding Your Credit Score	
What you should know about credit scores	Your credit score is a number that reflects the information in your credit report. Your credit report is a record of your credit history. It includes information about whether you pay your bills on time and how much you owe to creditors. Your credit score can change, depending on how your credit history changes.
How we use your credit score	Your credit score can affect whether you can get a loan and how much you will have to pay for that loan.
The range of scores	Scores range from a low of **[Insert bottom number in the range]** to a high of **[Insert top number in the range]**. Generally, the higher your score, the more likely you are to be offered better credit terms.
How your score compares to the scores of other consumers	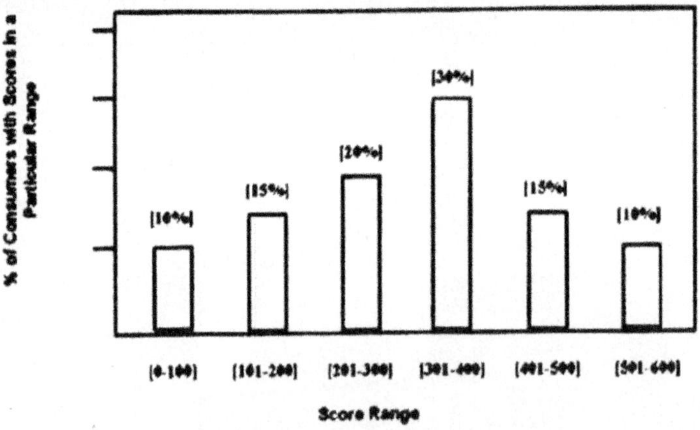 **[or]** [Your credit score ranks higher than [X] percent of U.S. consumers.]

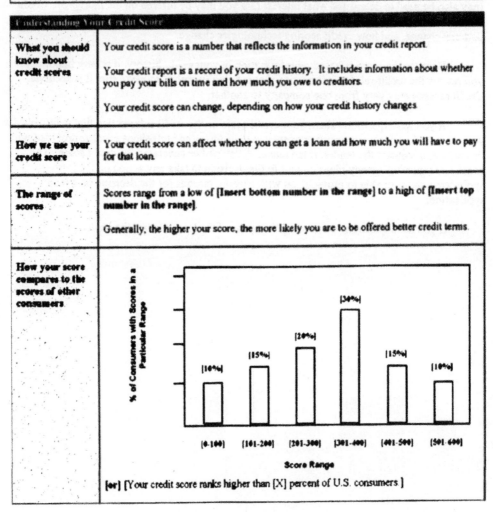

Checking Your Credit Report	
What if there are mistakes in your credit report?	You have a right to dispute any inaccurate information in your credit report. If you find mistakes on your credit report, contact the consumer reporting agency. It is a good idea to check your credit report to make sure the information it contains is accurate.
How can you obtain a copy of your credit report?	Under Federal law, you have the right to obtain a free copy of your credit report from each of the nationwide consumer reporting agencies once a year. To order your free annual credit report— *By telephone:* Call toll-free: 1-877-322-8228 *On the web:* Visit www.annualcreditreport.com *By mail:* Mail your completed Annual Credit Report Request Form (which you can obtain from the Federal Trade Commission's website at http://www.ftc.gov/bcp/conline/include/requestformfinal.pdf) to: Annual Credit Report Request Service P.O. Box 105281 Atlanta, GA 30348-5281
How can you get more information?	For more information about credit reports and your rights under Federal law, visit the Consumer Financial Protection Bureau's website at www.consumerfinance.gov/learnmore.

H-5. Model form for loans where credit score is not available

[Name of Entity Providing the Notice]
Credit Scores and the Price You Pay for Credit

Your Credit Score	
Your credit score	Your credit score is not available from **[insert name of CRA]**, which is a consumer reporting agency, because they may not have enough information about your credit history to calculate a score.
What you should know about credit scores	A credit score is a number that reflects the information in a credit report. A credit report is a record of your credit history. It includes information about whether you pay your bills on time and how much you owe to creditors. A credit score can change, depending on how a consumer's credit history changes.
Why credit scores are important	Credit scores are important because consumers who have higher credit scores generally will get more favorable credit terms. Not having a credit score can affect whether you can get a loan and how much you will have to pay for that loan.
Checking Your Credit Report	
What if there are mistakes in your credit report?	You have a right to dispute any inaccurate information in your credit report. If you find mistakes on your credit report, contact the consumer reporting agency. It is a good idea to check your credit report to make sure the information it contains is accurate.
How can you obtain a copy of your credit report?	Under Federal law, you have the right to obtain a free copy of your credit report from each of the nationwide consumer reporting agencies once a year. To order your free annual credit report— *By telephone:* Call toll-free: 1-877-322-8228 *On the web:* Visit www.annualcreditreport.com *By mail:* Mail your completed Annual Credit Report Request

	Form (which you can obtain from the Federal Trade Commission's website at http://www.ftc.gov/bcp/conline/include/requestformfinal.pdf) to: Annual Credit Report Request Service P.O. Box 105281 Atlanta, GA 30348-5281
How can you get more information?	For more information about credit reports and your rights under Federal law, visit the Consumer Financial Protection Bureau's website at www.consumerfinance.gov/learnmore.

H-6. Model form for risk-based pricing notice with credit score information

[Name of Entity Providing the Notice]
Your Credit Report[s] and the Price You Pay for Credit

What is a credit report?	A credit report is a record of your credit history. It includes information about whether you pay your bills on time and how much you owe to creditors.
How did we use your credit report[s]?	We used information from your credit report[s] to set the terms of the credit we are offering you, such as the [Annual Percentage Rate/down payment]. The terms offered to you may be less favorable than the terms offered to consumers who have better credit histories.
What if there are mistakes in your credit report[s]?	You have a right to dispute any inaccurate information in your credit report[s]. If you find mistakes on your credit report[s], contact **[insert name of CRA(s)]**, which [is/are] the [consumer reporting agency/consumer reporting agencies] from which we obtained your credit report[s]. It is a good idea to check your credit report[s] to make sure the information [it contains/they contain] is accurate.
How can you obtain a copy of your credit report[s]?	Under Federal law, you have the right to obtain a copy of your credit report[s] without charge for 60 days after you receive this notice. To obtain your free report[s], contact **[insert name of CRA(s)]**: *By telephone:* Call toll-free: 1-877-xxx-xxxx *By mail:* Mail your written request to: **[insert address]** *On the web:* Visit **[insert website address]**
How can you get more information about credit reports?	For more information about credit reports and your rights under Federal law, visit the Consumer Financial Protection Bureau's website at www.consumerfinance.gov/learnmore.

Your Credit Score and Understanding Your Credit Score

Your credit score	**[Insert credit score]** Source: **[Insert source]** Date: **[Insert date score was created]**
What you should know about credit scores	Your credit score is a number that reflects the information in your credit report. We used your credit score to set the terms of credit we are offering you. Your credit score can change, depending on how your credit history changes.
The range of scores	Scores range from a low of **[insert bottom number in the range]** to a high of **[insert top number in the range]**.
Key <u>factors</u> that adversely affected your credit score	**[Insert first factor]** **[Insert second factor]** **[Insert third factor]** **[Insert fourth factor]** **[Insert number of enquiries as a key factor, if applicable]**
[How can you get more information about your credit score?]	[If you have any questions regarding your credit score, you should contact [entity that provided the credit score] at: Address: ______________________________ ________ ______________________________ ________ [Toll-free] Telephone number:______________________________]

H-7. Model form for account review risk-based pricing notice with credit score information

[Name of Entity Providing the Notice]
Your Credit Report[s] and the Pricing of Your Account

What is a credit report?	A credit report is a record of your credit history. It includes information about whether you pay your bills on time and how much you owe to creditors.
How did we use your credit report[s]?	We have used information from your credit report[s] to review the terms of your account with us. Based on our review of your credit report[s], we have increased the annual percentage rate on your account.
What if there are mistakes in your credit report[s]?	You have a right to dispute any inaccurate information in your credit report[s]. If you find mistakes on your credit report[s], contact **[insert name of CRA(s)]**, which [is/are] [a consumer reporting agency/consumer reporting agencies] from which we obtained your credit report[s]. It is a good idea to check your credit report[s] to make sure the information [it contains/they contain] is accurate.
How can you obtain a copy of your credit report[s]?	Under Federal law, you have the right to obtain a copy of your credit report[s] without charge for 60 days after you receive this notice. To obtain your free report[s], contact **[insert name of CRA(s)]**: *By telephone:* Call toll-free: 1-877-xxx-xxxx *By mail:* Mail your written request to: **[insert address]** *On the web:* Visit **[insert website address]**
How can you get more information about credit reports?	For more information about credit reports and your rights under Federal law, visit the Consumer Financial Protection Bureau's website at www.consumerfinance.gov/learnmore.

Your Credit Score and Understanding Your Credit Score

Your credit score	**[Insert credit score]** Source: **[Insert source]** Date: **[Insert date score was created]**
What you should know about credit scores	Your credit score is a number that reflects the information in your credit report. We used your credit score to set the terms of credit we are offering you. Your credit score can change, depending on how your credit history changes.
The range of scores	Scores range from a low of **[insert bottom number in the range]** to a high of **[insert top number in the range]**.
Key factors that adversely affected your credit score	**[Insert first factor]** **[Insert second factor]** **[Insert third factor]** **[Insert fourth factor]** **[Insert number of enquiries as a key factor, if applicable]**
[How can you get more information about your credit score?]	[If you have any questions regarding your credit score, you should contact [entity that provided the credit score] at: Address: ______________________________ ________ ______________________________ ________ [Toll-free] Telephone number:______________________________]

APPENDIX I—TO PART 1022—SUMMARY OF CONSUMER IDENTITY THEFT RIGHTS

The prescribed form for this summary is a disclosure that is substantially similar to the Bureau's model summary with all information clearly and prominently displayed. A summary should accurately reflect changes to those items that may change over time (such as telephone numbers) to remain in compliance. Translations of this summary will be in compliance with the Bureau's prescribed model, provided that the translation is accurate and that it is provided in a language used by the recipient consumer.

Para información en español, visite www.consumerfinance.gov/learnmore o escribe a la Consumer Financial Protection Bureau, 1700 G Street N.W., Washington, DC 20552.

Remedying the Effects of Identity Theft

You are receiving this information because you have notified a consumer reporting agency that you believe that you are a victim of identity theft. Identity theft occurs when someone uses your name, Social Security number, date of birth, or other identifying information, without authority, to commit fraud. For example, someone may have committed identity theft by using your personal information to open a credit card account or get a loan in your name. For more information, visit www.consumerfinance.gov/learnmore or write to: Consumer Financial Protection Bureau, 1700 G Street N.W., Washington, DC 20552.

The Fair Credit Reporting Act (FCRA) gives you specific rights when you are, or believe that you are, the victim of identity theft. Here is a brief summary of the rights designed to help you recover from identity theft.

1. **You have the right to ask that nationwide consumer reporting agencies place "fraud alerts" in your file to let potential creditors and others know that you may be a victim of identity theft.** A fraud alert can make it more difficult for someone to get credit in your name because it tells creditors to follow certain procedures to protect you. It also may delay your ability to obtain credit. You may place a fraud alert in your file by calling just one of the three nationwide consumer reporting agencies. As soon as that agency processes your fraud alert, it will notify the other two, which then also must place fraud alerts in your file.

   - Equifax: 1-800-XXX-XXXX; www.equifax.com
   - Experian: 1-800-XXX-XXXX; www.experian.com
   - TransUnion: 1-800-XXX-XXXX; www.transunion.com

   An initial fraud alert stays in your file for at least 90 days. An extended alert stays in your file for seven years. To place either of these alerts, a consumer reporting agency will require you to provide appropriate proof of your identity, which may include your Social Security number. If you ask for an extended alert, you will have to provide an identity theft report. An identity theft report includes a copy of a report you have filed with a federal, state, or local law enforcement agency, and additional information a consumer reporting agency may require you to submit. For more detailed information about the identity theft report, visit www.consumerfinance.gov/learnmore.

2. **You have the right to free copies of the information in your file (your "file disclosure").** An initial fraud alert entitles you to a copy of all the information in your file at each of the three nationwide agencies, and an extended alert entitles you to two free file disclosures in a 12-month period following the placing of the alert. These additional disclosures may help you detect signs of fraud, for example, whether fraudulent accounts have been opened in your name or whether someone has reported a change in your address. Once a year, you also have the right to a free copy of the information in your file at any consumer reporting agency, if you believe it has inaccurate information due to fraud, such as identity theft. You also

have the ability to obtain additional free file disclosures under other provisions of the FCRA. See www.consumerfinance.gov/learnmore.

3. **You have the right to obtain documents relating to fraudulent transactions made or accounts opened using your personal information.** A creditor or other business must give you copies of applications and other business records relating to transactions and accounts that resulted from the theft of your identity, if you ask for them in writing. A business may ask you for proof of your identity, a police report, and an affidavit before giving you the documents. It may also specify an address for you to send your request. Under certain circumstances, a business can refuse to provide you with these documents. See www.consumerfinance.gov/learnmore.

4. **You have the right to obtain information from a debt collector.** If you ask, a debt collector must provide you with certain information about the debt you believe was incurred in your name by an identity thief – like the name of the creditor and the amount of the debt.

5. **If you believe information in your file results from identity theft, you have the right to ask that a consumer reporting agency block that information from your file.** An identity thief may run up bills in your name and not pay them. Information about the unpaid bills may appear on your consumer report. Should you decide to ask a consumer reporting agency to block the reporting of this information, you must identify the information to block, and provide the consumer reporting agency with proof of your identity and a copy of your identity theft report. The consumer reporting agency can refuse or cancel your request for a block if, for example, you don't provide the necessary documentation, or where the block results from an error or a material misrepresentation of fact made by you. If the agency declines or rescinds the block, it must notify you. Once a debt resulting from identity theft has been blocked, a person or business with notice of the block may not sell, transfer, or place the debt for collection.

6. **You also may prevent businesses from reporting information about you to consumer reporting agencies if you believe the information is a result of identity theft.** To do so, you must send your request to the address specified by the business that reports the information to the consumer reporting agency. The business will expect you to identify what information you do not want reported and to provide an identity theft report.

To learn more about identity theft and how to deal with its consequences, visit www.consumerfinance.gov/learnmore, or write to the Consumer Financial Protection Bureau. You may have additional rights under state law. For more information, contact your local consumer protection agency or your state Attorney General.

In addition to the new rights and procedures to help consumers deal with the effects of identity theft, the FCRA has many other important consumer protections. They are described in more detail at www.consumerfinance.gov/learnmore.

APPENDIX J—TO PART 1022—[RESERVED]

APPENDIX K—TO PART 1022—SUMMARY OF CONSUMER RIGHTS

The prescribed form for this summary is a disclosure that is substantially similar to the Bureau's model summary with all information clearly and prominently displayed. The list of Federal regulators that is included in the Bureau's prescribed summary may be provided separately so long as this is done in a clear and conspicuous way. A summary should accurately reflect changes to those items that may change over time (e.g., dollar amounts, or telephone numbers and addresses of Federal agencies) to remain in compliance. Translations of this summary will be in compliance with the Bureau's prescribed model, provided that the translation is accurate and that it is provided in a language used by the recipient consumer.

Para información en español, visite www.consumerfinance.gov/learnmore o escribe a la Consumer Financial Protection Bureau, 1700 G Street N.W., Washington, DC 20552.

A Summary of Your Rights Under the Fair Credit Reporting Act

The federal Fair Credit Reporting Act (FCRA) promotes the accuracy, fairness, and privacy of information in the files of consumer reporting agencies. There are many types of consumer reporting agencies, including credit bureaus and specialty agencies (such as agencies that sell information about check writing histories, medical records, and rental history records). Here is a summary of your major rights under the FCRA. **For more information, including information about additional rights, go to www.consumerfinance.gov/learnmore or write to: Consumer Financial Protection Bureau, 1700 G Street N.W., Washington, DC 20552.**

- **You must be told if information in your file has been used against you.** Anyone who uses a credit report or another type of consumer report to deny your application for credit, insurance, or employment – or to take another adverse action against you – must tell you, and must give you the name, address, and phone number of the agency that provided the information.

- **You have the right to know what is in your file.** You may request and obtain all the information about you in the files of a consumer reporting agency (your "file disclosure"). You will be required to provide proper identification, which may include your Social Security number. In many cases, the disclosure will be free. You are entitled to a free file disclosure if:
  - a person has taken adverse action against you because of information in your credit report;
  - you are the victim of identity theft and place a fraud alert in your file;
  - your file contains inaccurate information as a result of fraud;
  - you are on public assistance;
  - you are unemployed but expect to apply for employment within 60 days.

  In addition, all consumers are entitled to one free disclosure every 12 months upon request from each nationwide credit bureau and from nationwide specialty consumer reporting agencies. See www.consumerfinance.gov/learnmore for additional information.

- **You have the right to ask for a credit score.** Credit scores are numerical summaries of your credit-worthiness based on information from credit bureaus. You may request a credit score from consumer reporting agencies that create scores or distribute scores used in residential real property loans, but you will have to pay for it. In some mortgage transactions, you will receive credit score information for free from the mortgage lender.

- **You have the right to dispute incomplete or inaccurate information.** If you identify information in your file that is incomplete or inaccurate, and report it to the consumer reporting agency, the agency must investigate unless your dispute is frivolous. See www.consumerfinance.gov/learnmore for an explanation of dispute procedures.

- **Consumer reporting agencies must correct or delete inaccurate, incomplete, or unverifiable information.** Inaccurate, incomplete, or unverifiable information must be removed or corrected, usually within 30 days. However, a consumer reporting agency may continue to report information it has verified as accurate.

- **Consumer reporting agencies may not report outdated negative information.** In most cases, a consumer reporting agency may not report negative information that is more than seven years old, or bankruptcies that are more than 10 years old.

- **Access to your file is limited.** A consumer reporting agency may provide information about you only to people with a valid need – usually to consider an application with a creditor, insurer, employer, landlord, or other business. The FCRA specifies those with a valid need for access.

- **You must give your consent for reports to be provided to employers.** A consumer reporting agency may not give out information about you to your employer, or a potential employer, without your written consent given to the employer. Written consent generally is not required in the trucking industry. For more information, go to www.consumerfinance.gov/learnmore.

- **You many limit "prescreened" offers of credit and insurance you get based on information in your credit report.** Unsolicited "prescreened" offers for credit and insurance must include a toll-free phone number you can call if you choose to remove your name and address from the lists these offers are based on. You may opt out with the nationwide credit bureaus at 1-800-XXX-XXXX.

- **You may seek damages from violators.** If a consumer reporting agency, or, in some cases, a user of consumer reports or a furnisher of information to a consumer reporting agency violates the FCRA, you may be able to sue in state or federal court.

- **Identity theft victims and active duty military personnel have additional rights.** For more information, visit www.consumerfinance.gov/learnmore.

States may enforce the FCRA, and many states have their own consumer reporting laws. In some cases, you may have more rights under state law. For more information, contact your state or local consumer protection agency or your state Attorney General. For information about your federal rights, contact:

TYPE OF BUSINESS:	CONTACT:
1.a. Banks, savings associations, and credit unions with total assets of over $10 billion and their affiliates b. Such affiliates that are not banks, savings associations, or credit unions also should list, in addition to the CFPB:	a. Consumer Financial Protection Bureau 1700 G Street, N.W. Washington, DC 20552 b. Federal Trade Commission: Consumer Response Center - FCRA Washington, DC 20580 (877) 382-4357
2. To the extent not included in item 1 above: a. National banks, federal savings associations, and federal branches and federal agencies of foreign banks b. State member banks, branches and agencies of foreign banks (other than federal branches, federal agencies, and Insured State Branches of Foreign Banks), commercial lending companies owned or controlled by foreign banks, and organizations operating under section 25 or 25A of the Federal Reserve Act c. Nonmember Insured Banks, Insured State Branches of Foreign Banks, and insured state savings associations d. Federal Credit Unions	 a. Office of the Comptroller of the Currency Customer Assistance Group 1301 McKinney Street, Suite 3450 Houston, TX 77010-9050 b. Federal Reserve Consumer Help Center P.O. Box. 1200 Minneapolis, MN 55480 c. FDIC Consumer Response Center 1100 Walnut Street, Box #11 Kansas City, MO 64106 d. National Credit Union Administration Office of Consumer Protection (OCP) Division of Consumer Compliance and Outreach (DCCO) 1775 Duke Street Alexandria, VA 22314
3. Air carriers	Asst. General Counsel for Aviation Enforcement & Proceedings Aviation Consumer Protection Division Department of Transportation 1200 New Jersey Avenue, S.E. Washington, DC 20590
4. Creditors Subject to the Surface Transportation Board	Office of Proceedings, Surface Transportation Board Department of Transportation 395 E Street, S.W. Washington, DC 20423
5. Creditors Subject to the Packers and Stockyards Act, 1921	Nearest Packers and Stockyards Administration area supervisor
6. Small Business Investment Companies	Associate Deputy Administrator for Capital Access United States Small Business Administration 409 Third Street, SW, 8th Floor Washington, DC 20416
7. Brokers and Dealers	Securities and Exchange Commission 100 F Street, N.E. Washington, DC 20549
8. Federal Land Banks, Federal Land Bank Associations, Federal Intermediate Credit Banks, and Production Credit Associations	Farm Credit Administration 1501 Farm Credit Drive McLean, VA 22102-5090
9. Retailers, Finance Companies, and All Other Creditors Not Listed Above	FTC Regional Office for region in which the creditor operates or Federal Trade Commission: Consumer Response Center - FCRA Washington, DC 20580 (877) 382-4357

APPENDIX L—TO PART 1022—STANDARDIZED FORM FOR REQUESTING ANNUAL FILE DISCLOSURES

REQUEST FOR FREE CREDIT REPORT

Note to Consumers: **You have the right to obtain a free copy of your credit report once every 12 months (also known as an "annual file disclosure"), from each of the nationwide consumer reporting agencies. Your report may contain information on where you work and live, the credit accounts that have been opened in your name, if you've paid your bills on time, and whether you have been sued, arrested, or have filed for bankruptcy. Businesses use this information in making decisions about whether to offer you credit, insurance, or employment, and on what terms.**

Use this form to request your credit report from any, or all, of the nationwide consumer reporting agencies.

The following information is required to process your request:

Your Full Name: ________________________________

Your Street Address: ________________________________

Your City, State & Zip Code: ________________________________

Your Telephone Numbers (with area code): Day: ____________________
Evening: ____________________

Your Social Security number: ______________ Your Date of Birth______________

Place a check next to each credit report you want.

_____ I want a credit report from each of the nationwide consumer reporting agencies

OR

_____ I want a credit report from:
_____ [name of nationwide consumer reporting agency]
_____ [name of nationwide consumer reporting agency]
_____ [name of nationwide consumer reporting agency]

Please check how you would like to receive your report. (Note: because of the need to accurately identify you before we send you your credit report, we may not be able to offer every delivery method to every consumer. We will try to honor your preference.)

_____ [available delivery method]
_____ [available delivery method]
_____ [available delivery method]

_____ Check here if, for security purposes, you want your copy of your credit report to include only the last four digits of your Social Security number (SSN), rather than your entire SSN.

For more information on obtaining your free credit report, visit [insert appropriate website address], call [insert appropriate telephone number], or write to [insert appropriate address].

Mail this form to:
[insert appropriate address]

Your report(s) will be sent within 15 days after we receive your request.

APPENDIX M—TO PART 1022—NOTICE OF FURNISHER RESPONSIBILITIES

The prescribed form for this disclosure is a separate document that is substantially similar to the Bureau's model notice with all information clearly and prominently displayed. Consumer reporting agencies may limit the disclosure to only those items that they know are relevant to the furnisher that will receive the notice.

All furnishers of information to consumer reporting agencies must comply with all applicable regulations. Information about applicable regulations currently in effect can be found at the Consumer Financial Protection Bureau's website, www.consumerfinance.gov/learnmore.

NOTICE TO FURNISHERS OF INFORMATION: OBLIGATIONS OF FURNISHERS UNDER THE FCRA

The federal Fair Credit Reporting Act (FCRA), 15 U.S.C 1681-1681y, imposes responsibilities on all persons who furnish information to consumer reporting agencies (CRAs). These responsibilities are found in Section 623 of the FCRA, 15 U.S.C 1681s-2. State law may impose additional requirements on furnishers. All furnishers of information to CRAs should become familiar with the applicable laws and may want to consult with their counsel to ensure that they are in compliance. The text of the FCRA is available at the website of the Consumer Financial Protection Bureau (CFPB): www.consumerfinance.gov/learnmore. A list of the sections of the FCRA cross-referenced to the U.S Code is at the end of this document.

Section 623 imposes the following duties upon furnishers:

Accuracy Guidelines

The FCRA requires furnishers to comply with federal guidelines and regulations dealing with the accuracy of information provided to CRAs by furnishers. Federal regulations and guidelines are available at www.consumerfinance.gov/learnmore. Section 623(e).

General Prohibition on Reporting Inaccurate Information

The FCRA prohibits information furnishers from providing information to a CRA that they know or have reasonable cause to believe is inaccurate. However, the furnisher is not subject to this general prohibition if it clearly and conspicuously specifies an address to which consumers may write to notify the furnisher that certain information is inaccurate. Sections 623(a)(1)(A) and (a)(1)(C).

Duty to Correct and Update Information

If at any time a person who regularly and in the ordinary course of business furnishes information to one or more CRAs determines that the information provided is not complete or accurate, the furnisher must promptly provide complete and accurate information to the CRA. In addition, the furnisher must notify all CRAs that received the information of any corrections, and must thereafter report only the complete and accurate information. Section 623(a)(2).

Duties After Notice of Dispute from Consumer

If a consumer notifies a furnisher, at an address specified for the furnisher for such notices, that specific information is inaccurate, and the information is, in fact, inaccurate, the furnisher must thereafter report the correct information to CRAs. Section 623(a)(1)(B).

If a consumer notifies a furnisher that the consumer disputes the completeness or accuracy of any information reported by the furnisher, the furnisher may not subsequently report that information to a CRA without providing notice of the dispute. Section 623(a)(3).

Furnishers must comply with federal regulations that identify when an information furnisher must investigate a dispute made directly to the furnisher by a consumer. Under these regulations, furnishers must complete an investigation within 30 days (or 45 days, if the consumer later provides relevant additional information) unless the dispute is frivolous or irrelevant or comes from a "credit repair organization." Section 623(a)(8). Federal regulations are available at www.consumerfinance.gov/learnmore. Section 623(a)(8)

Duties After Notice of Dispute from Consumer Reporting Agency

If a CRA notifies a furnisher that a consumer disputes the completeness or accuracy of information provided by the furnisher, the furnisher has a duty to follow certain procedures. The furnisher must:

- Conduct an investigation and review all relevant information provided by the CRA, including information given to the CRA by the consumer. Sections 623(b)(1)(A) and (b)(1)(B).
- Report the results to the CRA that referred the dispute, and, if the investigation establishes that the information was, in fact, incomplete or inaccurate, report the results to all CRAs to which the furnisher provided the information that compile and maintain files on a nationwide basis. Section 623(b)(1)(C) and (b)(1)(D).
- Complete the above steps within 30 days from the date the CRA receives the dispute (or 45 days, if the consumer later provides relevant additional information to the CRA). Section 623(b)(2).
- Promptly modify or delete the information, or block its reporting. Section 623(b)(1)(E).

Duty to Report Voluntary Closing of Credit Accounts

If a consumer voluntarily closes a credit account, any person who regularly and in the ordinary course of business furnished information to one or more CRAs must report this fact when it provides information to CRAs for the time period in which the account was closed. Section 623(a)(4).

Duty to Report Dates of Delinquencies

If a furnisher reports information concerning a delinquent account placed for collection, charged to profit or loss, or subject to any similar action, the furnisher must, within 90 days after reporting the information, provide the CRA with the month and the year of the commencement of the delinquency that immediately preceded the action, so that the agency will know how long to keep the information in the consumer's file. Section 623(a)(5).

Any person, such as a debt collector, that has acquired or is responsible for collecting delinquent accounts and that reports information to CRAs may comply with the requirements of Section 623(a)(5) (until there is a consumer dispute) by reporting the same delinquency date previously reported by the creditor. If the creditor did not report this date, they may comply with the FCRA by establishing reasonable procedures to obtain and report delinquency dates, or, if a delinquency date cannot be reasonably obtained, by following reasonable procedures to ensure that the date reported precedes the date when the account was placed for collection, charged to profit or loss, or subjected to any similar action. Section 623(a)(5).

Duties of Financial Institutions When Reporting Negative Information

Financial institutions that furnish information to "nationwide" consumer reporting agencies, as defined in Section 603(p), must notify consumers in writing if they may furnish or have furnished negative information to a CRA. Section 623(a)(7). The CFPB has prescribed model disclosures, 12 CFR Part 1022, App. B.

Duties When Furnishing Medical Information

A furnisher whose primary business is providing medical services, products, or devices (and such furnisher's agents or assignees) is a medical information furnisher for the purposes of the FCRA and must notify all CRAs to which it reports of this fact. Section 623(a)(9). This notice will enable CRAs to comply with their duties under Section 604(g) when reporting medical information.

Duties When ID Theft Occurs

All furnishers must have in place reasonable procedures to respond to notifications from CRAs that information furnished is the result of identity theft, and to prevent refurnishing the information in the future. A furnisher may not furnish information that a consumer has identified as resulting from identity theft unless the furnisher subsequently knows or is informed by the consumer that the information is correct. Section 623 (a)(6). If a furnisher learns that it has furnished inaccurate information due to identity theft, it must notify each CRA of the correct information and must thereafter report only complete and accurate information. Section 623(a)(2). When any furnisher of information is notified pursuant to the procedures set forth in Section 605B that a debt has resulted from identity theft, the furnisher many not sell, transfer, or place for collection the debt except in certain limited circumstances. Section 615(f).

The CFPB's website, www.consumerfinance.gov/learnmore, has more information about the FCRA, including publications for businesses and the full text of the FCRA.

Citations for FCRA sections in the U.S. Code, 15 U.S.C. § 1681 et seq.:

Section 602	15 U.S.C. 1681	Section 615	15 U.S.C. 1681m
Section 603	15 U.S.C. 1681a	Section 616	15 U.S.C. 1681n
Section 604	15 U.S.C. 1681b	Section 617	15 U.S.C. 1681o
Section 605	15 U.S.C. 1681c	Section 618	15 U.S.C. 1681p
Section 605A	15 U.S.C. 1681cA	Section 619	15 U.S.C. 1681q
Section 605B	15 U.S.C. 1681cB	Section 620	15 U.S.C. 1681r
Section 606	15 U.S.C. 1681d	Section 621	15 U.S.C. 1681s
Section 607	15 U.S.C. 1681e	Section 622	15 U.S.C. 1681s-1
Section 608	15 U.S.C. 1681f	Section 623	15 U.S.C. 1681s-2
Section 609	15 U.S.C. 1681g	Section 624	15 U.S.C. 1681t
Section 610	15 U.S.C. 1681h	Section 625	15 U.S.C. 1681u
Section 611	15 U.S.C. 1681i	Section 626	15 U.S.C. 1681v
Section 612	15 U.S.C. 1681j	Section 627	15 U.S.C. 1681w
Section 613	15 U.S.C. 1681k	Section 628	15 U.S.C. 1681x
Section 614	15 U.S.C. 1681l	Section 629	15 U.S.C. 1681y

APPENDIX N—TO PART 1022—NOTICE OF USER RESPONSIBILITIES

The prescribed form for this disclosure is a separate document that is substantially similar to the Bureau's notice with all information clearly and prominently displayed. Consumer reporting agencies may limit the disclosure to only those items that they know are relevant to the user that will receive the notice.

All users of consumer reports must comply with all applicable regulations. Information about applicable regulations currently in effect can be found at the Consumer Financial Protection Bureau's website, www.consumerfinance.gov/learnmore.

NOTICE TO USERS OF CONSUMER REPORTS:
OBLIGATIONS OF USERS UNDER THE FCRA

The Fair Credit Reporting Act (FCRA), 15 U.S.C. 1681-1681y, requires that this notice be provided to inform users of consumer reports of their legal obligations. State law may impose additional requirements. The text of the FCRA is set forth in full at the Consumer Financial Protection Bureau's (CFPB) website at www.consumerfinance.gov/learnmore. At the end of this document is a list of United States Code citations for the FCRA. Other information about user duties is also available at the CFPB's website. **Users must consult the relevant provisions of the FCRA for details about their obligations under the FCRA.**

The first section of this summary sets forth the responsibilities imposed by the FCRA on all users of consumer reports. The subsequent sections discuss the duties of users of reports that contain specific types of information, or that are used for certain purposes, and the legal consequences of violations. If you are a furnisher of information to a consumer reporting agency (CRA), you have additional obligations and will receive a separate notice from the CRA describing your duties as a furnisher.

I. OBLIGATIONS OF ALL USERS OF CONSUMER REPORTS

A. Users Must Have a Permissible Purpose

Congress has limited the use of consumer reports to protect consumers' privacy. All users must have a permissible purpose under the FCRA to obtain a consumer report. Section 604 contains a list of the permissible purposes under the law. These are:

- As ordered by a court or a federal grand jury subpoena. Section 604(a)(1)
- As instructed by the consumer in writing. Section 604(a)(2)
- For the extension of credit as a result of an application from a consumer, or the review or collection of a consumer's account. Section 604(a)(3)(A)
- For employment purposes, including hiring and promotion decisions, where the consumer has given written permission. Sections 604(a)(3)(B) and 604(b)

- For the underwriting of insurance as a result of an application from a consumer. Section 604(a)(3)(C)
- When there is a legitimate business need, in connection with a business transaction that is initiated by the consumer. Section 604(a)(3)(F)(i)
- To review a consumer's account to determine whether the consumer continues to meet the terms of the account. Section 604(a)(3)(F)(ii)
- To determine a consumer's eligibility for a license or other benefit granted by a governmental instrumentality required by law to consider an applicant's financial responsibility or status. Section 604(a)(3)(D)
- For use by a potential investor or servicer, or current insurer, in a valuation or assessment of the credit or prepayment risks associated with an existing credit obligation. Section 604(a)(3)(E)
- For use by state and local officials in connection with the determination of child support payments, or modifications and enforcement thereof. Sections 604(a)(4) and 604(a)(5)

In addition, creditors and insurers may obtain certain consumer report information for the purpose of making "prescreened" unsolicited offers of credit or insurance. Section 604(c). The particular obligations of users of "prescreened" information are described in Section VII below.

B. Users Must Provide Certifications

Section 604(f) prohibits any person from obtaining a consumer report from a consumer reporting agency (CRA) unless the person has certified to the CRA the permissible purpose(s) for which the report is being obtained and certifies that the report will not be used for any other purpose.

C. Users Must Notify Consumers When Adverse Actions Are Taken

The term "adverse action" is defined very broadly by Section 603. "Adverse actions" include all business, credit, and employment actions affecting consumers that can be considered to have a negative impact as defined by Section 603(k) of the FCRA – such as denying or canceling credit or insurance, or denying employment or promotion. No adverse action occurs in a credit transaction where the creditor makes a counteroffer that is accepted by the consumer.

1. Adverse Actions Based on Information Obtained From a CRA

If a user takes any type of adverse action as defined by the FCRA that is based at least in part on information contained in a consumer report, Section 615(a) requires the user to notify the consumer. The notification may be done in writing, orally, or by electronic means. It must include the following:

- The name, address, and telephone number of the CRA (including a toll-free telephone number, if it is a nationwide CRA) that provided the report.
- A statement that the CRA did not make the adverse decision and is not able to explain why the decision was made.
- A statement setting forth the consumer's right to obtain a free disclosure of the consumer's file from the CRA if the consumer makes a request within 60 days.
- A statement setting forth the consumer's right to dispute directly with the CRA the accuracy or completeness of any information provided by the CRA.

2. Adverse Actions Based on Information Obtained From Third Parties Who Are Not Consumer Reporting Agencies

If a person denies (or increases the charge for) credit for personal, family, or household purposes based either wholly or partly upon information from a person other than a CRA, and the information is the type of consumer information covered by the FCRA, Section 615(b)(1) requires that the user clearly and accurately disclose to the consumer his or her right to be told the nature of the information that was relied upon if the consumer makes a written request within 60 days of notification. The user must provide the disclosure within a reasonable period of time following the consumer's written request.

3. Adverse Actions Based on Information Obtained From Affiliates

If a person takes an adverse action involving insurance, employment, or a credit transaction initiated by the consumer, based on information of the type covered by the FCRA, and this information was obtained from an entity affiliated with the user of the information by common ownership or control, Section 615(b)(2) requires the user to notify the consumer of the adverse action. The notice must inform the consumer that he or she may obtain a disclosure of the nature of the information relied upon by making a written request within 60 days of receiving the adverse action notice. If the consumer makes such a request, the user must disclose the nature of the information not later than 30 days after receiving the request. If consumer report information is shared among affiliates and then used for an adverse action, the user must make an adverse action disclosure as set forth in I.C.1 above.

D. Users Have Obligations When Fraud and Active Duty Military Alerts are in Files

When a consumer has placed a fraud alert, including one relating to identity theft, or an active duty military alert with a nationwide consumer reporting agency as defined in Section 603(p) and resellers, Section 605A(h) imposes limitations on users of reports obtained from the consumer reporting agency in certain circumstances, including the establishment of a new credit plan and the issuance of additional credit cards. For initial fraud alerts and active duty alerts, the user must have reasonable policies and procedures in place to form a belief that the user knows the identity of the applicant or contact the consumer at a telephone number specified by the consumer; in the case of extended fraud alerts, the user must contact the consumer in accordance with the contact information provided in the consumer's alert.

E. Users Have Obligations When Notified of an Address Discrepancy

Section 605(h) requires nationwide CRAs, as defined in Section 603(p), to notify users that request reports when the address for a consumer provided by the user in requesting the report is substantially different from the addresses in the consumer's file. When this occurs, users must comply with regulations specifying the procedures to be followed. Federal regulations are available at www.consumerfinance.gov/learnmore.

F. Users Have Obligations When Disposing of Records

Section 628 requires that all users of consumer report information have in place procedures to properly dispose of records containing this information. Federal regulations have been issued that cover disposal.

II. CREDITORS MUST MAKE ADDITIONAL DISCLOSURES

If a person uses a consumer report in connection with an application for, or a grant, extension, or provision of, credit to a consumer on material terms that are materially less favorable than the most favorable terms available to a substantial proportion of consumers from or through that person, based in whole or in part on a consumer report, the person must provide a risk-based pricing notice to the consumer in accordance with regulations prescribed by the CFPB.

Section 609(g) requires a disclosure by all persons that make or arrange loans secured by residential real property (one to four units) and that use credit scores. These persons must provide credit scores and other information about credit scores to applicants, including the disclosure set forth in Section 609(g)(1)(D) ("Notice to the Home Loan Applicant").

III. OBLIGATIONS OF USERS WHEN CONSUMER REPORTS ARE OBTAINED FOR EMPLOYMENT PURPOSES

A. Employment Other Than in the Trucking Industry

If information from a CRA is used for employment purposes, the user has specific duties, which are set forth in Section 604(b) of the FCRA. The user must:

- Make a clear and conspicuous written disclosure to the consumer before the report is obtained, in a document that consists solely of the disclosure, that a consumer report may be obtained.
- Obtain from the consumer prior written authorization. Authorization to access reports during the term of employment may be obtained at the time of employment.
- Certify to the CRA that the above steps have been followed, that the information being obtained will not be used in violation of any federal or state equal opportunity law or regulation, and that, if any adverse action is to be taken based on the consumer report, a copy of the report and a summary of the consumer's rights will be provided to the consumer.
- **Before** taking an adverse action, the user must provide a copy of the report to the consumer as well as the summary of consumer's rights. (The user should receive this summary from the CRA.) A Section 615(a) adverse action notice should be sent after the adverse action is taken.

An adverse action notice also is required in employment situations if credit information (other than transactions and experience data) obtained from an affiliate is used to deny employment. Section 615(b)(2)

The procedures for investigative consumer reports and employee misconduct investigations are set forth below.

B. Employment in the Trucking Industry

Special rules apply for truck drivers where the only interaction between the consumer and the potential employer is by mail, telephone, or computer. In this case, the consumer may provide consent orally or electronically, and an adverse action may be made orally, in writing, or electronically. The consumer may obtain a copy of any report relied upon by the trucking company by contacting the company.

IV. OBLIGATIONS WHEN INVESTIGATIVE CONSUMER REPORTS ARE USED

Investigative consumer reports are a special type of consumer report in which information about a consumer's character, general reputation, personal characteristics, and mode of living is obtained through personal interviews by an entity or person that is a consumer reporting agency. Consumers who are the subjects of such reports are given special rights under the FCRA. If a user intends to obtain an investigative consumer report, Section 606 requires the following:

- The user must disclose to the consumer that an investigative consumer report may be obtained. This must be done in a written disclosure that is mailed, or otherwise delivered, to the consumer at some time before or not later than three days after the date on which the report was first requested. The disclosure must include a statement informing the consumer of his or her right to request additional disclosures of the nature and scope of the investigation as described below, and the summary of consumer rights required by Section 609 of the FCRA. (The summary of consumer rights will be provided by the CRA that conducts the investigation.)

- The user must certify to the CRA that the disclosures set forth above have been made and that the user will make the disclosure described below.

- Upon the written request of a consumer made within a reasonable period of time after the disclosures required above, the user must make a complete disclosure of the nature and scope of the investigation. This must be made in a written statement that is mailed, or otherwise delivered, to the consumer no later than five days after the date on which the request was received from the consumer or the report was first requested, whichever is later in time.

V. SPECIAL PROCEDURES FOR EMPLOYEE INVESTIGATIONS

Section 603(x) provides special procedures for investigations of suspected misconduct by an employee or for compliance with Federal, state or local laws and regulations or the rules of a self-regulatory organization, and compliance with written policies of the employer. These investigations are not treated as consumer reports so long as the employer or its agent complies with the procedures set forth in Section 603(x), and a summary describing the nature and scope of the inquiry is made to the employee if an adverse action is taken based on the investigation.

VI. OBLIGATIONS OF USERS OF MEDICAL INFORMATION

Section 604(g) limits the use of medical information obtained from consumer reporting agencies (other than payment information that appears in a coded form that does not identify the medical provider). If the information is to be used for an insurance transaction, the consumer must give consent to the user of the report or the information must be coded. If the report is to be used for employment purposes – or in connection with a credit transaction (except as provided in federal regulations) – the consumer must provide specific written consent and the medical information must be relevant. Any user who receives medical information shall not disclose the information to any other person (except where necessary to carry out the purpose for which the information was disclosed, or as permitted by statute, regulation, or order).

VII. OBLIGATIONS OF USERS OF "PRESCREENED" LISTS

The FCRA permits creditors and insurers to obtain limited consumer report information for use in connection with unsolicited offers of credit or insurance under certain circumstances. Sections 603(1), 604(c), 604(e), and 615(d). This practice is known as "prescreening" and typically involves obtaining from a CRA a list of consumers who meet certain preestablished criteria. If any person intends to use prescreened lists, that person must (1) before the offer is made, establish the criteria that will be relied upon to make the offer and to grant credit or insurance, and (2) maintain such criteria on file for a three-year period beginning on the date on which the offer is made to each consumer. In addition, any user must provide with each written solicitation a clear and conspicuous statement that:

- Information contained in a consumer's CRA file was used in connection with the transaction.
- The consumer received the offer because he or she satisfied the criteria for credit worthiness or insurability used to screen for the offer.
- Credit or insurance may not be extended if, after the consumer responds, it is determined that the consumer does not meet the criteria used for screening or any applicable criteria bearing on credit worthiness or insurability, or the consumer does not furnish required collateral.
- The consumer may prohibit the use of information in his or her file in connection with future prescreened offers of credit or insurance by contacting the notification system established by the CRA that provided the report. The statement must include the address and toll-free telephone number of the appropriate notification system.

In addition, the CFPB has established the format, type size, and manner of the disclosure required by Section 615(d), with which users must comply. The relevant regulation is 12 CFR 1022.54.

VIII. OBLIGATIONS OF RESELLERS

A. Disclosure and Certification Requirements

Section 607(e) requires any person who obtains a consumer report for resale to take the following steps:

- Disclose the identity of the end-user to the source CRA.
- Identify to the source CRA each permissible purpose for which the report will be furnished to the end-user.
- Establish and follow reasonable procedures to ensure that reports are resold only for permissible purposes, including procedures to obtain:
  (1) the identity of all end-users;
  (2) certifications from all users of each purpose for which reports will be used; and
  (3) certifications that reports will not be used for any purpose other than the purpose(s) specified to the reseller. Resellers must make reasonable efforts to verify this information before selling the report.

B. Reinvestigations by Resellers

Under Section 611(f), if a consumer disputes the accuracy or completeness of information in a report prepared by a reseller, the reseller must determine whether this is a result of an action or omission on its part and, if so, correct or delete the information. If not, the reseller must send the dispute to the source CRA for reinvestigation. When any CRA notifies the reseller of the results of an investigation, the reseller must immediately convey the information to the consumer.

C. Fraud Alerts and Resellers

Section 605A(f) requires resellers who receive fraud alerts or active duty alerts from another consumer reporting agency to include these in their reports.

IX. LIABILITY FOR VIOLATIONS OF THE FCRA

Failure to comply with the FCRA can result in state government or federal government enforcement actions, as well as private lawsuits. Sections 616, 617, and 621. In addition, any person who knowingly and willfully obtains a consumer report under false pretenses may face criminal prosecution. Section 619.

The CFPB's website, www.consumerfinance.gov/learnmore, has more information about the FCRA, including publications for businesses and the full text of the FCRA.

Citations for FCRA sections in the U.S. Code, 15 U.S.C. § 1681 et seq.:

Section 602	15 U.S.C. 1681	Section 615	15 U.S.C. 1681m
Section 603	15 U.S.C. 1681a	Section 616	15 U.S.C. 1681n
Section 604	15 U.S.C. 1681b	Section 617	15 U.S.C. 1681o
Section 605	15 U.S.C. 1681c	Section 618	15 U.S.C. 1681p
Section 605A	15 U.S.C. 1681cA	Section 619	15 U.S.C. 1681q
Section 605B	15 U.S.C. 1681cB	Section 620	15 U.S.C. 1681r
Section 606	15 U.S.C. 1681d	Section 621	15 U.S.C. 1681s
Section 607	15 U.S.C. 1681e	Section 622	15 U.S.C. 1681s-1
Section 608	15 U.S.C. 1681f	Section 623	15 U.S.C. 1681s-2
Section 609	15 U.S.C. 1681g	Section 624	15 U.S.C. 1681t
Section 610	15 U.S.C. 1681h	Section 625	15 U.S.C. 1681u
Section 611	15 U.S.C. 1681i	Section 626	15 U.S.C. 1681v
Section 612	15 U.S.C. 1681j	Section 627	15 U.S.C. 1681w
Section 613	15 U.S.C. 1681k	Section 628	15 U.S.C. 1681x
Section 614	15 U.S.C. 1681l	Section 629	15 U.S.C. 1681y

ADDITIONAL FCRA REGULATIONS

12 C.F.R. Part 41

Table of Sections

Subpart I. Proper Disposal of Records Containing Consumer Information

Sec.

Subpart J. Identity Theft Red Flags

Appendix J to Part 41—Interagency Guidelines on Identity Theft Detection, Prevention and Mitigation

12 CFR Part 41

Subpart I. Proper Disposal of Records Containing Consumer Information

§ 41.83. Proper disposal of records containing consumer information

(a) Definitions as used in this section.

(1) Consumer means an individual.

(2) Federal savings association means a Federal savings association or an operating subsidiary of a Federal savings association.

(3) National bank means a national bank, an operating subsidiary of a national bank, or a Federal branch or agency of a foreign bank.

(b) In general. Each national bank or Federal savings association must properly dispose of any consumer information that it maintains or otherwise possesses in accordance with the Interagency

Guidelines Establishing Information Security Standards, as set forth in Appendix B to 12 CFR part 30, to the extent that the bank or savings association is covered by the scope of the Guidelines.

(c) Rule of construction. Nothing in this section shall be construed to:

(1) Require a national bank or Federal savings association to maintain or destroy any record pertaining to a consumer that is not imposed under any other law; or

(2) Alter or affect any requirement imposed under any other provision of law to maintain or destroy such a record.

Subpart J. Identity Theft Red Flags

§ 41.90. Duties regarding the detection, prevention, and mitigation of identity theft

(a) Scope. This section applies to a financial institution or creditor that is a national bank; a Federal savings association; a Federal branch or agency of a foreign bank; or an operating subsidiary of any of these institutions that is not a functionally regulated subsidiary within the meaning of section 5(c)(5) of the Bank Holding Company Act of 1956, as amended (12 U.S.C. 1844(c)(5)).

(b) Definitions. For purposes of this section and Appendix J, the following definitions apply:

(1) Account means a continuing relationship established by a person with a financial institution or creditor to obtain a product or service for personal, family, household or business purposes. Account includes:

(i) An extension of credit, such as the purchase of property or services involving a deferred payment; and

(ii) A deposit account.

(2) The term board of directors includes:

(i) In the case of a branch or agency of a foreign bank, the managing official in charge of the branch or agency; and

(ii) In the case of any other creditor that does not have a board of directors, a designated employee at the level of senior management.

(3) Covered account means:

(i) An account that a financial institution or creditor offers or maintains, primarily for personal, family, or household purposes, that involves or is designed to permit multiple payments or transactions, such as a credit card account, mortgage loan, automobile loan, margin account, cell phone account, utility account, checking account, or savings account; and

(ii) Any other account that the financial institution or creditor offers or maintains for which there is a reasonably foreseeable risk to customers or to the safety and soundness of the financial institution or creditor from identity theft, including financial, operational, compliance, reputation, or litigation risks.

(4) Credit has the same meaning as in 15 U.S.C. 1681a(r)(5).

(5) Creditor has the same meaning as in 15 U.S.C. 1681m(e)(4).

(6) Customer means a person that has a covered account with a financial institution or creditor.

(7) Financial institution has the same meaning as in 15 U.S.C. 1681a(t).

(8) Identity theft has the same meaning as in 12 CFR 1022.3(h).

(9) Person means any individual, partnership, corporation, trust, estate, cooperative, association, government, or governmental subdivision or agency, or other entity.

(10) Red Flag means a pattern, practice, or specific activity that indicates the possible existence of identity theft.

(11) Service provider means a person that provides a service directly to the financial institution or creditor.

(c) Periodic Identification of Covered Accounts. Each financial institution or creditor must periodically determine whether it offers or maintains covered accounts. As a part of this determination, a financial institution or creditor must conduct a risk assessment to determine whether it offers or maintains covered accounts described in paragraph (b)(3)(ii) of this section, taking into consideration:

(1) The methods it provides to open its accounts;

(2) The methods it provides to access its accounts; and

(3) Its previous experiences with identity theft.

(d) Establishment of an Identity Theft Prevention Program.

(1) Program requirement. Each financial institution or creditor that offers or maintains one or more covered accounts must develop and implement a written Identity Theft Prevention Program (Program) that is designed to detect, prevent, and mitigate identity theft in connection with the opening of a covered account or any existing covered account. The Program must be appropriate to the size and complexity of the financial institution or creditor and the nature and scope of its activities.

(2) Elements of the Program. The Program must include reasonable policies and procedures to:

(i) Identify relevant Red Flags for the covered accounts that the financial institution or creditor offers or maintains, and incorporate those Red Flags into its Program;

(ii) Detect Red Flags that have been incorporated into the Program of the financial institution or creditor;

(iii) Respond appropriately to any Red Flags that are detected pursuant to paragraph (d)(2)(ii) of this section to prevent and mitigate identity theft; and

(iv) Ensure the Program (including the Red Flags determined to be relevant) is updated periodically, to reflect changes in risks to customers and to the safety and soundness of the financial institution or creditor from identity theft.

(e) Administration of the Program. Each financial institution or creditor that is required to implement a Program must provide for the continued administration of the Program and must:

(1) Obtain approval of the initial written Program from either its board of directors or an appropriate committee of the board of directors;

(2) Involve the board of directors, an appropriate committee thereof, or a designated employee at the level of senior management in the oversight, development, implementation and administration of the Program;

(3) Train staff, as necessary, to effectively implement the Program; and

(4) Exercise appropriate and effective oversight of service provider arrangements.

(f) Guidelines. Each financial institution or creditor that is required to implement a Program must consider the guidelines in Appendix J of this part and include in its Program those guidelines that are appropriate.

§ 41.91. Duties of card issuers regarding changes of address

(a) Scope. This section applies to an issuer of a debit or credit card (card issuer) that is a national bank; a Federal savings association; a Federal branch or agency of a foreign bank; or any of these institutions that is not a functionally regulated subsidiary within the meaning of section 5(c)(5) of the Bank Holding Company Act of 1956, as amended (12 U.S.C. 1844(c)(5)).

(b) Definitions. For purposes of this section:

(1) Cardholder means a consumer who has been issued a credit or debit card.

(2) Clear and conspicuous means reasonably understandable and designed to call attention to the nature and significance of the information presented.

(3) Consumer means an individual.

(c) Address validation requirements. A card issuer must establish and implement reasonable policies and procedures to assess the validity of a change of address if it receives notification of a change of address for a consumer's debit or credit card account and, within a short period of time afterwards (during at least the first 30 days after it receives such notification), the card issuer receives a request for an additional or replacement card for the same account. Under these circumstances, the card issuer may not issue an additional or replacement card, until, in accordance with its reasonable policies and procedures and for the purpose of assessing the validity of the change of address, the card issuer:

(1)(i) Notifies the cardholder of the request:

(A) At the cardholder's former address; or

(B) By any other means of communication that the card issuer and the cardholder have previously agreed to use; and

(ii) Provides to the cardholder a reasonable means of promptly reporting incorrect address changes; or

(2) Otherwise assesses the validity of the change of address in accordance with the policies and procedures the card issuer has established pursuant to § 41.90 of this part.

(d) Alternative timing of address validation. A card issuer may satisfy the requirements of paragraph (c) of this section if it validates an address pursuant to the methods in paragraph (c)(1) or (c)(2) of this section when it receives an address change notification, before it receives a request for an additional or replacement card.

(e) Form of notice. Any written or electronic notice that the card issuer provides under this paragraph must be clear and conspicuous and provided separately from its regular correspondence with the cardholder.

§ 41.92. Examples

The examples in appendix J and supplement A to appendix J are not exclusive. Compliance with an example, to the extent applicable, constitutes compliance with this subpart. Examples in a paragraph illustrate only the issue described in the paragraph and do not illustrate any other issue that may arise in this subpart.

APPENDIX J—TO PART 41—INTERAGENCY GUIDELINES ON IDENTITY THEFT DETECTION, PREVENTION, AND MITIGATION

Section 41.90 of this part requires each financial institution and creditor that offers or maintains one or more covered accounts, as defined in § 41.90(b)(3) of this part, to develop and provide for the continued administration of a written Program to detect, prevent, and mitigate identity theft in connection with the opening of a covered account or any existing covered account. These guidelines are intended to assist financial institutions and creditors in the formulation and maintenance of a Program that satisfies the requirements of § 41.90 of this part.

I. The Program

In designing its Program, a financial institution or creditor may incorporate, as appropriate, its existing policies, procedures, and other arrangements that control reasonably foreseeable risks to customers or to the safety and soundness of the financial institution or creditor from identity theft.

II. Identifying Relevant Red Flags

(a) Risk Factors. A financial institution or creditor should consider the following factors in identifying relevant Red Flags for covered accounts, as appropriate:

(1) The types of covered accounts it offers or maintains;

(2) The methods it provides to open its covered accounts;

(3) The methods it provides to access its covered accounts; and

(4) Its previous experiences with identity theft.

(b) Sources of Red Flags. Financial institutions and creditors should incorporate relevant Red Flags from sources such as:

(1) Incidents of identity theft that the financial institution or creditor has experienced;

(2) Methods of identity theft that the financial institution or creditor has identified that reflect changes in identity theft risks; and

(3) Applicable supervisory guidance.

(c) Categories of Red Flags. The Program should include relevant Red Flags from the following categories, as appropriate. Examples of Red Flags from each of those categories are appended as Supplement A to this Appendix J.

(1) Alerts, notifications, or other warnings received from consumer reporting agencies or service providers, such as fraud detection services;

(2) The presentation of suspicious documents;

(3) The presentation of suspicious personal identifying information, such as a suspicious address change;

(4) The unusual use of, or other suspicious activity related to, a covered account; and

(5) Notice from customers, victims of identity theft, law enforcement authorities, or other persons regarding possible identity theft in connection with covered accounts held by the financial institution or creditor.

III. Detecting Red Flags

The Program's policies and procedures should address the detection of Red Flags in connection with the opening of covered accounts and existing covered accounts, such as by:

(a) Obtaining identifying information about, and verifying the identity of, a person opening a covered account, for example, using the policies and procedures regarding identification and verification set forth in the Customer Identification Program rules implementing 31 U.S.C. 5318(*l*); and

(b) Authenticating customers, monitoring transactions, and verifying the validity of change of address requests, in the case of existing covered accounts.

IV. Preventing and Mitigating Identity Theft

The Program's policies and procedures should provide for appropriate responses to the Red Flags the financial institution or creditor has detected that are commensurate with the degree of risk posed.

In determining an appropriate response, a financial institution or creditor should consider aggravating factors that may heighten the risk of identity theft, such as a data security incident that results in unauthorized access to a customer's account records held by the financial institution, creditor, or third party, or notice that a customer has provided information related to a covered account held by the financial institution or creditor to someone fraudulently claiming to represent the financial institution or creditor or to a fraudulent website. Appropriate responses may include the following:

(a) Monitoring a covered account for evidence of identity theft;

(b) Contacting the customer;

(c) Changing any passwords, security codes, or other security devices that permit access to a covered account;

(d) Reopening a covered account with a new account number;

(e) Not opening a new covered account;

(f) Closing an existing covered account;

(g) Not attempting to collect on a covered account or not selling a covered account to a debt collector;

(h) Notifying law enforcement; or

(i) Determining that no response is warranted under the particular circumstances.

V. Updating the Program

Financial institutions and creditors should update the Program (including the Red Flags determined to be relevant) periodically, to reflect changes in risks to customers or to the safety and soundness of the financial institution or creditor from identity theft, based on factors such as:

(a) The experiences of the financial institution or creditor with identity theft;

(b) Changes in methods of identity theft;

(c) Changes in methods to detect, prevent, and mitigate identity theft;

(d) Changes in the types of accounts that the financial institution or creditor offers or maintains; and

(e) Changes in the business arrangements of the financial institution or creditor, including mergers, acquisitions, alliances, joint ventures, and service provider arrangements.

VI. Methods for Administering the Program

(a) Oversight by the board of directors, an appropriate committee of the board, or a designated employee at the level of senior management should include:

(1) Assigning specific responsibility for the Program's implementation;

(2) Reviewing reports prepared by staff regarding compliance by the financial institution or creditor with § 41.90 of this part; and

(3) Approving material changes to the Program as necessary to address changing identity theft risks.

(b) Reports. (1) In general. Staff of the financial institution or creditor responsible for development, implementation, and administration of its Program should report to the board of directors, an appropriate committee of the board, or a designated employee at the level of senior management, at least annually, on compliance by the financial institution or creditor with § 41.90 of this part.

(2) Contents of report. The report should address material matters related to the Program and evaluate issues such as: the effectiveness of the policies and procedures of the financial institution or creditor in addressing the risk of identity theft in connection with the opening of covered accounts and with respect to existing covered accounts; service provider arrangements; significant incidents involving identity theft and management's response; and recommendations for material changes to the Program.

(c) Oversight of service provider arrangements. Whenever a financial institution or creditor engages a service provider to perform an activity in connection with one or more covered accounts the financial institution or creditor should take steps to ensure that the activity of the service provider is conducted in accordance with reasonable policies and procedures designed to detect, prevent, and mitigate the risk of identity theft. For example, a financial institution or creditor could require the service provider by contract to have policies and procedures to detect relevant Red Flags that may arise in the performance of the service provider's activities, and either report the Red Flags to the financial institution or creditor, or to take appropriate steps to prevent or mitigate identity theft.

VII. Other Applicable Legal Requirements

Financial institutions and creditors should be mindful of other related legal requirements that may be applicable, such as:

(a) For financial institutions and creditors that are subject to 31 U.S.C. 5318(g), filing a Suspicious Activity Report in accordance with applicable law and regulation;

(b) Implementing any requirements under 15 U.S.C. 1681c–1(h) regarding the circumstances under which credit may be extended when the financial institution or creditor detects a fraud or active duty alert;

(c) Implementing any requirements for furnishers of information to consumer reporting agencies under 15 U.S.C. 1681s–2, for example, to correct or update inaccurate or incomplete information, and to not report information that the furnisher has reasonable cause to believe is inaccurate; and

(d) Complying with the prohibitions in 15 U.S.C. 1681m on the sale, transfer, and placement for collection of certain debts resulting from identity theft.

Supplement A to Appendix J

In addition to incorporating Red Flags from the sources recommended in section II.b. of the Guidelines in Appendix J of this part, each financial institution or creditor may consider incorporating into its Program, whether singly or in combination, Red Flags from the following illustrative examples in connection with covered accounts:

Alerts, Notifications or Warnings from a Consumer Reporting Agency

1. A fraud or active duty alert is included with a consumer report.

2. A consumer reporting agency provides a notice of credit freeze in response to a request for a consumer report.

3. A consumer reporting agency provides a notice of address discrepancy, as defined in 12 CFR 1022.82(b) of this part.

4. A consumer report indicates a pattern of activity that is inconsistent with the history and usual pattern of activity of an applicant or customer, such as:

a. A recent and significant increase in the volume of inquiries;

b. An unusual number of recently established credit relationships;

c. A material change in the use of credit, especially with respect to recently established credit relationships; or

d. An account that was closed for cause or identified for abuse of account privileges by a financial institution or creditor.

Suspicious Documents

5. Documents provided for identification appear to have been altered or forged.

6. The photograph or physical description on the identification is not consistent with the appearance of the applicant or customer presenting the identification.

7. Other information on the identification is not consistent with information provided by the person opening a new covered account or customer presenting the identification.

8. Other information on the identification is not consistent with readily accessible information that is on file with the financial institution or creditor, such as a signature card or a recent check.

9. An application appears to have been altered or forged, or gives the appearance of having been destroyed and reassembled.

Suspicious Personal Identifying Information

10. Personal identifying information provided is inconsistent when compared against external information sources used by the financial institution or creditor. For example:

a. The address does not match any address in the consumer report; or

b. The Social Security Number (SSN) has not been issued, or is listed on the Social Security Administration's Death Master File.

11. Personal identifying information provided by the customer is not consistent with other personal identifying information provided by the customer. For example, there is a lack of correlation between the SSN range and date of birth.

12. Personal identifying information provided is associated with known fraudulent activity as indicated by internal or third-party sources used by the financial institution or creditor. For example:

a. The address on an application is the same as the address provided on a fraudulent application; or

b. The phone number on an application is the same as the number provided on a fraudulent application.

13. Personal identifying information provided is of a type commonly associated with fraudulent activity as indicated by internal or third-party sources used by the financial institution or creditor. For example:

a. The address on an application is fictitious, a mail drop, or a prison; or

b. The phone number is invalid, or is associated with a pager or answering service.

14. The SSN provided is the same as that submitted by other persons opening an account or other customers.

15. The address or telephone number provided is the same as or similar to the address or telephone number submitted by an unusually large number of other persons opening accounts or by other customers.

16. The person opening the covered account or the customer fails to provide all required personal identifying information on an application or in response to notification that the application is incomplete.

17. Personal identifying information provided is not consistent with personal identifying information that is on file with the financial institution or creditor.

18. For financial institutions and creditors that use challenge questions, the person opening the covered account or the customer cannot provide authenticating information beyond that which generally would be available from a wallet or consumer report.

Unusual Use of, or Suspicious Activity Related to, the Covered Account

19. Shortly following the notice of a change of address for a covered account, the institution or creditor receives a request for a new, additional, or replacement card or a cell phone, or for the addition of authorized users on the account.

20. A new revolving credit account is used in a manner commonly associated with known patterns of fraud. For example:

a. The majority of available credit is used for cash advances or merchandise that is easily convertible to cash (e.g., electronics equipment or jewelry); or

b. The customer fails to make the first payment or makes an initial payment but no subsequent payments.

21. A covered account is used in a manner that is not consistent with established patterns of activity on the account. There is, for example:

a. Nonpayment when there is no history of late or missed payments;

b. A material increase in the use of available credit;

c. A material change in purchasing or spending patterns;

d. A material change in electronic fund transfer patterns in connection with a deposit account; or

e. A material change in telephone call patterns in connection with a cellular phone account.

22. A covered account that has been inactive for a reasonably lengthy period of time is used (taking into consideration the type of account, the expected pattern of usage and other relevant factors).

23. Mail sent to the customer is returned repeatedly as undeliverable although transactions continue to be conducted in connection with the customer's covered account.

24. The financial institution or creditor is notified that the customer is not receiving paper account statements.

25. The financial institution or creditor is notified of unauthorized charges or transactions in connection with a customer's covered account.

Notice From Customers, Victims of Identity Theft, Law Enforcement Authorities, or Other Persons Regarding Possible Identity Theft in Connection With Covered Accounts Held by the Financial Institution or Creditor

26. The financial institution or creditor is notified by a customer, a victim of identity theft, a law enforcement authority, or any other person that it has opened a fraudulent account for a person engaged in identity theft.

PROPOSED CONSUMER FINANCIAL PROTECTION BUREAU DEBT COLLECTION REGULATIONS

PART 1006—DEBT COLLECTION PRACTICES (REGULATION F)

Subpart A—General

§ 1006.1 Authority, purpose, and coverage

(a) Authority. This part, known as Regulation F, is issued by the Bureau of Consumer Financial Protection pursuant to sections 814(d) and 817 of the Fair Debt Collection Practices Act (FDCPA or Act), 15 U.S.C. 1692*l*(d), 1692*o*; title X of the Dodd-Frank Wall Street Reform and Consumer Protection Act (Dodd-Frank Act), 12 U.S.C. 5481 et seq.; and paragraphs (b)(1) and (d)(1) of section 104 of the Electronic Signatures in Global and National Commerce Act (E-SIGN Act), 15 U.S.C. 7004.

(b) Purpose. This part carries out the purposes of the FDCPA, which include eliminating abusive debt collection practices by debt collectors, ensuring that debt collectors who refrain from using abusive debt collection practices are not competitively disadvantaged, and promoting consistent State action to protect consumers against debt collection abuses. This part also prescribes requirements to ensure that certain features of debt collection are disclosed fully, accurately, and effectively to consumers in a manner that permits consumers to understand the costs, benefits, and risks associated with debt collection, in light of the facts and circumstances. Finally, this part sets record retention requirements to enable the Bureau to administer and carry out the purposes of the FDCPA, the Dodd-Frank Act, and this part, as well as to prevent evasions thereof. The record retention requirements also will facilitate supervision of debt collectors and the assessment and detection of risks to consumers.

(c) Coverage. (1) Except as provided in § 1006.108 and appendix A of this part regarding applications for State exemptions from the FDCPA, this part applies to debt collectors, as defined in § 1006.2(i), other than a person excluded from coverage by section 1029(a) of the Consumer Financial Protection Act of 2010, title X of the Dodd-Frank Act (12 U.S.C. 5519(a)).

(2) Certain provisions of this part apply to debt collectors only when they are collecting consumer financial product or service debt as defined in § 1006.2(f). These provisions are §§ 1006.14(b)(1)(ii), 1006.34(c)(2)(iv) and (3)(iv), and 1006.30(b)(1)(ii).

§ 1006.2 Definitions

For purposes of this part, the following definitions apply:

(a) *Act* or *FDCPA* means the Fair Debt Collection Practices Act (15 U.S.C. 1692 et seq.).

(b) *Attempt to communicate* means any act to initiate a communication or other contact with any person through any medium, including by soliciting a response from such person. An attempt to communicate includes providing a limited-content message, as defined in paragraph (j) of this section.

(c) *Bureau* means the Bureau of Consumer Financial Protection.

(d) *Communicate or communication* means the conveying of information regarding a debt directly or indirectly to any person through any medium. A debt collector does not convey information regarding a debt directly or indirectly to any person if the debt collector provides only a limited-content message, as defined in paragraph (j) of this section.

(e) *Consumer* means any natural person, whether living or deceased, obligated or allegedly obligated to pay any debt. For purposes of §§ 1006.6 and 1006.14(h), the term consumer includes the persons described in § 1006.6(a).

(f) *Consumer financial product or service debt* means any debt related to any consumer financial product or service, as that term is defined in section 1002(5) of the Dodd-Frank Act (12 U.S.C. 5481(5)).

(g) *Creditor* means any person who offers or extends credit creating a debt or to whom a debt is owed. The term creditor does not, however, include any person to the extent that such person receives an assignment or transfer of a debt in default solely to facilitate collection of the debt for another.

(h) *Debt,* except for the purpose of paragraph (f) of this section, means any obligation or alleged obligation of a consumer to pay money arising out of a transaction in which the money, property, insurance, or services that are the subject of the transaction are primarily for personal, family, or household purposes, whether or not the obligation has been reduced to judgment. For the purpose of paragraph (f) of this section, debt means debt as that term is used in the Dodd-Frank Act.

(i)(1) *Debt collector* means any person who uses any instrumentality of interstate commerce or mail in any business the principal purpose of which is the collection of debts, or who regularly collects or attempts to collect, directly or indirectly, debts owed or due, or asserted to be owed or due, to another. Notwithstanding paragraph (h)(2)(vi) of this section, the term debt collector includes any creditor that, in the process of collecting its own debts, uses any name other than its own that would indicate that a third person is collecting or attempting to collect such debts. For the purpose of § 1006.22(e), the term also includes any person who uses any instrumentality of interstate commerce or mail in any business the principal purpose of which is the enforcement of security interests.

(2) The term debt collector excludes:

(i) Any officer or employee of a creditor while the officer or employee is collecting debts for the creditor in the creditor's name;

(ii) Any person while acting as a debt collector for another person if:

(A) The person acting as a debt collector does so only for persons with whom the person acting as a debt collector is related by common ownership or affiliated by corporate control; and

(B) The principal business of the person acting as a debt collector is not the collection of debts;

(iii) Any officer or employee of the United States or any State to the extent that collecting or attempting to collect any debt is in the performance of the officer's or employee's official duties;

(iv) Any person while serving or attempting to serve legal process on any other person in connection with the judicial enforcement of any debt;

(v) Any nonprofit organization that, at the request of consumers, performs bona fide consumer credit counseling and assists consumers in liquidating their debts by receiving payment from such consumers and distributing such amounts to creditors;

(vi) Any person collecting or attempting to collect any debt owed or due, or asserted to be owed or due to another, to the extent such debt collection activity:

(A) Is incidental to a bona fide fiduciary obligation or a bona fide escrow arrangement;

(B) Concerns a debt that such person originated;

(C) Concerns a debt that was not in default at the time such person obtained it; or

(D) Concerns a debt that such person obtained as a secured party in a commercial credit transaction involving the creditor; and

(vii) A private entity, to the extent such private entity is operating a bad check enforcement program that complies with section 818 of the Act.

(j) *Limited-content message* means a message for a consumer that includes all of the content described in paragraph (j)(1) of this section, that may include any of the content described in paragraph (j)(2) of this section, and that includes no other content.

(1) *Required content.* A limited-content message is a message for a consumer that includes all of the following:

(i) The consumer's name;

(ii) A request that the consumer reply to the message;

(iii) The name or names of one or more natural persons whom the consumer can contact to reply to the debt collector;

(iv) A telephone number that the consumer can use to reply to the debt collector; and

(v) If applicable, the disclosure required by § 1006.6(e).

(2) *Optional content.* In addition to the content described in paragraph (j)(1) of this section, a limited-content message may include one or more of the following:

(i) A salutation;

(ii) The date and time of the message;

(iii) A generic statement that the message relates to an account; and

(iv) Suggested dates and times for the consumer to reply to the message.

(k) *Person* includes natural persons, corporations, companies, associations, firms, partnerships, societies, and joint stock companies.

(*l*) *State* means any State, territory, or possession of the United States, the District of Columbia, the Commonwealth of Puerto Rico, or any political subdivision of any of the foregoing.

Subpart B—Rules for FDCPA Debt Collectors

§ 1006.6 Communications in connection with debt collection

(a) *Definition.* For purposes of this section, the term consumer includes:

(1) The consumer's spouse;

(2) The consumer's parent, if the consumer is a minor;

(3) The consumer's legal guardian;

(4) The executor or administrator of the consumer's estate, if the consumer is deceased; and

(5) A confirmed successor in interest, as defined in Regulation X, 12 CFR 1024.31, and Regulation Z, 12 CFR 1026.2(a)(27)(ii).

(b) *Communications with a consumer—in general.* Except as provided in paragraph (b)(4) of this section, a debt collector must not communicate or attempt to communicate with a consumer in connection with the collection of any debt as prohibited by paragraphs (b)(1) through (3) of this section.

(1) *Prohibitions regarding unusual or inconvenient times or places.* A debt collector must not communicate or attempt to communicate with a consumer in connection with the collection of any debt:

(i) At any unusual time, or at a time that the debt collector knows or should know is inconvenient to the consumer. In the absence of the debt collector's knowledge of circumstances to the contrary, a time before 8:00 a.m. and after 9:00 p.m. local time at the consumer's location is inconvenient; or

(ii) At any unusual place, or at a place that the debt collector knows or should know is inconvenient to the consumer.

(2) *Prohibitions regarding consumer represented by an attorney.* A debt collector must not communicate or attempt to communicate with a consumer in connection with the collection of any debt if the debt collector knows the consumer is represented by an attorney with respect to the debt and knows, or can readily ascertain, the attorney's name and address, unless the attorney:

(i) Fails to respond within a reasonable period of time to a communication from the debt collector; or

(ii) Consents to the debt collector communicating directly with the consumer.

(3) *Prohibitions regarding consumer's place of employment.* A debt collector must not communicate or attempt to communicate with a consumer in connection with the collection of any debt at the consumer's place of employment, if the debt collector knows or has reason to know that the consumer's employer prohibits the consumer from receiving such communication.

(4) *Exceptions.* The prohibitions in paragraphs (b)(1) through (3) of this section do not apply when a debt collector communicates or attempts to communicate with a consumer in connection with the collection of any debt with:

(i) The prior consent of the consumer, given directly to the debt collector during a communication that does not violate paragraphs (b)(1) through (3) of this section; or

(ii) The express permission of a court of competent jurisdiction.

(c) *Communications with a consumer—after refusal to pay or cease communication notice.*

(1) *Prohibitions.* Except as provided in paragraph (c)(2) of this section, a debt collector must not communicate or attempt to communicate further with a consumer with respect to a debt if the consumer notifies the debt collector in writing that:

(i) The consumer refuses to pay the debt; or

(ii) The consumer wants the debt collector to cease further communication with the consumer.

(2) *Exceptions.* The prohibitions in paragraph (c)(1) of this section do not apply when a debt collector communicates or attempts to communicate further with a consumer with respect to the debt:

(i) To advise the consumer that the debt collector's further efforts are being terminated;

(ii) To notify the consumer that the debt collector or creditor may invoke specified remedies that the debt collector or creditor ordinarily invokes; or

(iii) Where applicable, to notify the consumer that the debt collector or creditor intends to invoke a specified remedy.

(d) *Communications with third parties.* **(1)** *Prohibitions.* Except as provided in paragraph (d)(2) of this section, a debt collector must not communicate, in connection with the collection of any debt, with any person other than:

(i) The consumer;

(ii) The consumer's attorney;

(iii) A consumer reporting agency, if otherwise permitted by law;

(iv) The creditor;

(v) The creditor's attorney; or

(vi) The debt collector's attorney.

(2) *Exceptions.* The prohibition in paragraph (d)(1) of this section does not apply when a debt collector communicates, in connection with the collection of any debt, with a person:

(i) For the purpose of acquiring location information, as provided in § 1006.10;

(ii) With the prior consent of the consumer given directly to the debt collector;

(iii) With the express permission of a court of competent jurisdiction; or

(iv) As reasonably necessary to effectuate a postjudgment judicial remedy.

(3) *Reasonable procedures for email and text message communications.* A debt collector maintains procedures that are reasonably adapted, for purposes of FDCPA section 813(c), to avoid a bona fide error in sending an email or text message communication that would result in a violation of paragraph (d)(1) of this section if the debt collector, when communicating with a consumer using an email address or, in the case of a text message, a telephone number, maintains procedures that include steps to reasonably confirm and document that:

(i) The debt collector communicated with the consumer using:

(A) An email address or, in the case of a text message, a telephone number that the consumer recently used to contact the debt collector for purposes other than opting out of electronic communications;

(B) A non-work email address or, in the case of a text message, a non-work telephone number, if:

(1) The creditor or the debt collector notified the consumer clearly and conspicuously, other than through the specific non-work email address or non-work telephone number, that the debt collector might use that non-work email address or non-work telephone number for debt collection communications by email or text message, where the creditor or debt collector provided the notification no more than 30 days before the debt collector's first such communication, and the notification identified the legal name of the debt collector and the non-work email address or non-work telephone number the debt collector proposed to use, described one or more ways the consumer could opt out of such communications, and provided the consumer with a specified reasonable period in which to opt out before beginning such communications; and

(2) The opt-out period specified in the notice described in paragraph (d)(3)(i)(B)(*1*) of this section has expired and the consumer has not opted out of receiving debt collection communications at the specific non-work email address or non-work telephone number, as applicable; or

(C) A non-work email address or, in the case of a text message, a non-work telephone number that the creditor or a prior debt collector obtained from the consumer to communicate about the debt if, before the debt was placed with the debt collector, the creditor or the prior debt collector recently sent communications about the debt to that non-work email address or non-work telephone number, and the consumer did not request the creditor or the prior debt collector to stop using that non-work email address or non-work telephone number to communicate about the debt; and

(ii) The debt collector took additional steps to prevent communications using an email address or telephone number that the debt collector knows has led to a disclosure prohibited by paragraph (d)(1) of this section.

(e) *Opt-out notice for electronic communications or attempts to communicate.* A debt collector who communicates or attempts to communicate with a consumer electronically in connection with the collection of a debt using a specific email address, telephone number for text messages, or other electronic-medium address must include in such communication or attempt to communicate a clear and conspicuous statement describing one or more ways the consumer can opt out of further electronic communications or attempts to communicate by the debt collector to that address or telephone number. The debt collector may not require, directly or indirectly, that the consumer, in order to opt out, pay any fee to the debt collector or provide any information other than the email address, telephone number for text messages, or other electronic-medium address subject to the opt out.

§ 1006.10 Acquisition of location information

(a) *Definition.* The term *location information* means a consumer's:

(1) Place of abode and telephone number at such place; or

(2) Place of employment.

(b) *Form and content of location communications.* A debt collector communicating with a person other than the consumer for the purpose of acquiring location information must:

(1) Identify himself or herself individually by name, state that he or she is confirming or correcting the consumer's location information, and, only if expressly requested, identify his or her employer;

(2) Not state that the consumer owes any debt;

(3) Not communicate by postcard;

(4) Not use any language or symbol on any envelope or in the contents of any communication by mail indicating that the debt collector is in the debt collection business or that the communication relates to the collection of a debt; and

(5) After the debt collector knows the consumer is represented by an attorney with regard to the subject debt and has knowledge of, or can readily ascertain, such attorney's name and address, not communicate with any person other than that attorney, unless the attorney fails to respond to the debt collector's communication within a reasonable period of time.

(c) *Frequency of location communications.* In addition to complying with the frequency limits in § 1006.14(b), a debt collector communicating with any person other than the consumer for the purpose of acquiring location information about the consumer must not communicate more than once with such person unless requested to do so by such person, or unless the debt collector reasonably believes that the earlier response of such person is erroneous or incomplete and that such person now has correct or complete location information.

§ 1006.14 Harassing, oppressive, or abusive conduct

(a) *In general.* A debt collector must not engage in any conduct the natural consequence of which is to harass, oppress, or abuse any person in connection with the collection of any debt, including, but not limited to, the conduct described in paragraphs (b) through (h) of this section.

(b) *Repeated or continuous telephone calls or telephone conversations.*

(1) *In general.*

(i) *FDCPA prohibition.* In connection with the collection of a debt, a debt collector must not place telephone calls or engage any person in telephone conversation repeatedly or continuously with intent to annoy, abuse, or harass any person at the called number.

(ii) *Identification and prevention of Dodd-Frank Act unfair act or practice.* With respect to a debt collector who is collecting a consumer financial product or service debt, as defined in § 1006.2(f), it is an unfair act or practice under section 1031 of the Dodd-Frank Act to place telephone calls or engage any person in telephone conversation repeatedly or continuously in connection with the collection of such debt, such that the natural consequence is to harass, oppress, or abuse any person at the called number. To prevent this unfair act or practice, such a debt collector must not exceed the frequency limits in paragraph (b)(2) of this section.

(2) *Frequency limits.* Subject to paragraph (b)(3) of this section, a debt collector violates paragraphs (b)(1)(i) and (ii) of this section, as applicable, by placing a telephone call to a particular person in connection with the collection of a particular debt either:

(i) More than seven times within seven consecutive days; or

(ii) Within a period of seven consecutive days after having had a telephone conversation with the person in connection with the collection of such debt. The date of the telephone conversation is the first day of the seven-consecutive-day period.

(3) *Certain telephone calls excluded from the frequency limits.* Telephone calls placed to a person do not count toward, and are permitted in excess of, the frequency limits in paragraph (b)(2) of this section if they are:

(i) Made to respond to a request for information from such person;

(ii) Made with such person's prior consent given directly to the debt collector;

(iii) Not connected to the dialed number; or

(iv) With the persons described in § 1006.6(d)(1)(ii) through (vi).

(4) *Effect of complying with frequency limits.* A debt collector who does not exceed the frequency limits in paragraph (b)(2) of this section complies with paragraph (b)(1) of this section and section 806(5) of the FDCPA (15 U.S.C. 1692d(5)), and does not, based on the frequency of its telephone calls, violate paragraph (a) of this section, section 806 of the FDCPA (15 U.S.C. 1692d), or sections 1031 or 1036(a)(1)(B) of the Dodd-Frank Act (12 U.S.C. 5531 or 5536(a)(1)(B)).

(5) *Definition.* For purposes of this paragraph (b), *particular debt* means each of a consumer's debts in collection. However, in the case of student loan debts, the term particular debt means all student loan debts that a consumer owes or allegedly owes that were serviced under a single account number at the time the debts were obtained by the debt collector.

(c) *Violence or other criminal means.* In connection with the collection of a debt, a debt collector must not use or threaten to use violence or other criminal means to harm the physical person, reputation, or property of any person.

(d) *Obscene or profane language.* In connection with the collection of a debt, a debt collector must not use obscene or profane language, or language the natural consequence of which is to abuse the hearer or reader.

(e) *Debtor's list.* In connection with the collection of a debt, a debt collector must not publish a list of consumers who allegedly refuse to pay debts, except to a consumer reporting agency or to persons meeting the requirements of sections 603(f) or 604(a)(3) of the Fair Credit Reporting Act (15 U.S.C. 1681a(f) or 1681b(a)(3)).

(f) *Coercive advertisements.* In connection with the collection of a debt, a debt collector must not advertise for sale any debt to coerce payment of the debt.

(g) *Meaningful disclosure of identity.* In connection with the collection of a debt, a debt collector must not place telephone calls without meaningfully disclosing the caller's identity, except as provided in § 1006.10.

(h) *Prohibited communication media.*

(1) *In general.* In connection with the collection of any debt, a debt collector must not communicate or attempt to communicate with a consumer through a medium of communication if the consumer has requested that the debt collector not use that medium to communicate with the consumer. For purposes of this paragraph, the term "consumer" has the meaning given to it in § 1006.6(a).

(2) *Exceptions.* Notwithstanding the prohibition in paragraph (h)(1) of this section:

(i) If a consumer opts out in writing of receiving electronic communications from a debt collector, a debt collector may reply once to confirm the consumer's request to opt out, provided that the reply contains no information other than a statement confirming the consumer's request; or

(ii) If a consumer initiates contact with a debt collector using an address or a telephone number that the consumer previously requested the debt collector not use, the debt collector may respond once to that consumer-initiated communication.

§ 1006.18 False, deceptive, or misleading representations or means

(a) *In general.* A debt collector must not use any false, deceptive, or misleading representation or means in connection with the collection of any debt, including, but not limited to, the conduct described in paragraphs (b) through (d) of this section.

(b) *False, deceptive, or misleading representations.*

(1) A debt collector must not falsely represent or imply that:

(i) The debt collector is vouched for, bonded by, or affiliated with the United States or any State, including through the use of any badge, uniform, or facsimile thereof.

(ii) The debt collector operates or is employed by a consumer reporting agency, as defined by section 603(f) of the Fair Credit Reporting Act (15 U.S.C. 1681a(f)).

(iii) Any individual is an attorney or that any communication is from an attorney.

(iv) The consumer committed any crime or other conduct in order to disgrace the consumer.

(v) A sale, referral, or other transfer of any interest in a debt causes or will cause the consumer to:

(A) Lose any claim or defense to payment of the debt; or

(B) Become subject to any practice prohibited by this part.

(vi) Accounts have been turned over to innocent purchasers for value.

(vii) Documents are legal process.

(viii) Documents are not legal process forms or do not require action by the consumer.

(2) A debt collector must not falsely represent:

(i) The character, amount, or legal status of any debt.

(ii) Any services rendered, or compensation that may be lawfully received, by any debt collector for the collection of a debt.

(3) A debt collector must not represent or imply that nonpayment of any debt will result in the arrest or imprisonment of any person or the seizure, garnishment, attachment, or sale of any property or wages of any person unless such action is lawful and the debt collector or creditor intends to take such action.

(c) *False, deceptive, or misleading collection means.* A debt collector must not:

(1) Threaten to take any action that cannot legally be taken or that is not intended to be taken.

(2) Communicate or threaten to communicate to any person credit information that the debt collector knows or should know is false, including the failure to communicate that a disputed debt is disputed.

(3) Use or distribute any written communication that simulates or that the debt collector falsely represents to be a document authorized, issued, or approved by any court, official, or agency of the United States or any State, or that creates a false impression about its source, authorization, or approval.

(4) Use any business, company, or organization name other than the true name of the debt collector's business, company, or organization.

(d) *False representations or deceptive means.* A debt collector must not use any false representation or deceptive means to collect or attempt to collect any debt or to obtain information concerning a consumer.

(e) *Disclosures required.*

(1) *Initial communications.* A debt collector must disclose in its initial communication with a consumer that the debt collector is attempting to collect a debt and that any information obtained will be used for that purpose. If the debt collector's initial communication with the consumer is oral, the debt collector must make the disclosure required by this paragraph again in its initial written communication with the consumer.

(2) *Subsequent communications.* In each communication with the consumer subsequent to the communications described in paragraph (e)(1) of this section, the debt collector must disclose that the communication is from a debt collector.

(3) *Exception.* Disclosures under paragraphs (e)(1) and (2) of this section are not required in a formal pleading made in connection with a legal action.

(f) *Assumed names.* This section does not prohibit a debt collector's employee from using an assumed name when communicating or attempting to communicate with a person, provided that the employee uses the assumed name consistently and that the employer can readily identify any employee using an assumed name.

(g) *Safe harbor for meaningful attorney involvement in debt collection litigation submissions.* A debt collector that is a law firm or who is an attorney complies with § 1006.18 when submitting a pleading, written motion, or other paper submitted to the court during debt collection litigation if an attorney personally:

(1) Drafts or reviews the pleading, written motion, or other paper; and

(2) Reviews information supporting such pleading, written motion, or other paper and determines, to the best of the attorney's knowledge, information, and belief, that, as applicable:

(A) The claims, defenses, and other legal contentions are warranted by existing law;

(B) The factual contentions have evidentiary support; and

(C) The denials of factual contentions are warranted on the evidence or, if specifically so identified, are reasonably based on belief or lack of information.

§ 1006.22 Unfair or unconscionable means

(a) *In general.* A debt collector must not use unfair or unconscionable means to collect or attempt to collect any debt, including, but not limited to, the conduct described in paragraphs (b) through (f) of this section.

(b) *Collection of unauthorized amounts.* A debt collector must not collect any amount unless such amount is expressly authorized by the agreement creating the debt or permitted by law. For purposes of this paragraph, the term "any amount" includes any interest, fee, charge, or expense incidental to the principal obligation.

(c) *Postdated payment instruments.* A debt collector must not:

(1) Accept from any person a check or other payment instrument postdated by more than five days unless such person is notified in writing of the debt collector's intent to deposit such check or instrument not more than ten, nor less than three, days (excluding legal public holidays, Saturdays, and Sundays) prior to such deposit.

(2) Solicit any postdated check or other postdated payment instrument for the purpose of threatening or instituting criminal prosecution.

(3) Deposit or threaten to deposit any postdated check or other postdated payment instrument prior to the date on such check or instrument.

(d) *Charges resulting from concealment of purpose.* A debt collector must not cause charges to be made to any person for communications by concealment of the true purpose of the communication. Such charges include, but are not limited to, collect telephone calls and telegram fees.

(e) *Nonjudicial action regarding property.* A debt collector must not take or threaten to take any nonjudicial action to effect dispossession or disablement of property if:

(1) There is no present right to possession of the property claimed as collateral through an enforceable security interest;

(2) There is no present intention to take possession of the property; or

(3) The property is exempt by law from such dispossession or disablement.

(f) *Restrictions on use of certain media.* A debt collector must not:

(1) Communicate with a consumer regarding a debt by postcard.

(2) Use any language or symbol, other than the debt collector's address, on any envelope when communicating with a consumer by mail, except that a debt collector may use the debt collector's business name on an envelope if such name does not indicate that the debt collector is in the debt collection business.

(3) Communicate or attempt to communicate with a consumer using an email address that the debt collector knows or should know is provided to the consumer by the consumer's employer, unless the debt collector has received directly from the consumer either prior consent to use that email address or an email from that email address.

(4) Communicate or attempt to communicate with a consumer in connection with the collection of a debt by a social media platform that is viewable by a person other than the persons described in § 1006.6(d)(1)(i) through (vi).

(g) *Safe harbor for certain emails and text messages relating to the collection of a debt.* A debt collector who communicates with a consumer using an email address or telephone number and following the procedures described in § 1006.6(d)(3) does not violate paragraph (a) of this section by revealing in the email or text message the debt collector's name or other information indicating that the communication relates to the collection of a debt.

§ 1006.26 Collection of time-barred debts

(a) *Definitions.* For purposes of this section:

(1) *Statute of limitations* means the period prescribed by applicable law for bringing a legal action against the consumer to collect a debt.

(2) *Time-barred debt* means a debt for which the applicable statute of limitations has expired.

(b) *Suits and threats of suit prohibited.* A debt collector must not bring or threaten to bring a legal action against a consumer to collect a debt that the debt collector knows or should know is a time-barred debt.

(c) *[Reserved]*

§ 1006.30 Other prohibited practices

(a) *Communication prior to furnishing information.* A debt collector must not furnish to a consumer reporting agency, as defined in section 603(f) of the Fair Credit Reporting Act (15 U.S.C. 1681a(f)), information regarding a debt before communicating with the consumer about the debt.

(b) *Prohibition on the sale, transfer, or placement of certain debts.*

(1) In general.

(i) *FDCPA prohibition.* Except as provided in paragraph (b)(2) of this section, a debt collector must not sell, transfer, or place for collection a debt if the debt collector knows or should know that:

(A) The debt has been paid or settled;

(B) The debt has been discharged in bankruptcy; or

(C) An identity theft report, as defined in section 603(q)(4) of the Fair Credit Reporting Act (15 U.S.C. 1681a(q)(4)), was filed with respect to the debt.

(ii) *Identification of Dodd-Frank Act unfair act or practice.* With respect to a debt collector who is collecting a consumer financial product or service debt, as defined in § 1006.2(f), it is an unfair act or practice under section 1031 of the Dodd-Frank Act to sell, transfer, or place for collection a debt described in paragraph (b)(1)(i) of this section.

(2) *Exceptions.* A debt collector may sell, transfer, or place for collection a debt described in paragraph (b)(1)(i) of this section if the debt collector:

(i) Transfers the debt to the debt's owner;

(ii) Transfers the debt to a previous owner of the debt if transfer is authorized under the terms of the original contract between the debt collector and the previous owner;

(iii) Securitizes the debt or pledges a portfolio of such debt as collateral in connection with a borrowing; or

(iv) Transfers the debt as a result of a merger, acquisition, purchase and assumption transaction, or transfer of substantially all of the debt collector's assets.

(c) *Multiple debts.* If a consumer makes any single payment to a debt collector with respect to multiple debts owed by the consumer, the debt collector:

(1) Must apply the payment in accordance with the directions given by the consumer, if any; and

(2) Must not apply the payment to any debt that is disputed by the consumer.

(d) *Legal actions by debt collectors.* (1) *Action to enforce interest in real property.* A debt collector who brings a legal action against a consumer to enforce an interest in real property securing the consumer's debt must bring the action only in a judicial district or similar legal entity in which such real property is located.

(2) *Other legal actions.* A debt collector who brings a legal action against a consumer other than to enforce an interest in real property securing the consumer's debt must bring such action only in the judicial district or similar legal entity in which the consumer:

(i) Signed the contract sued upon; or

(ii) Resides at the commencement of the action.

(3) *Authorization of actions.* Nothing in this part authorizes debt collectors to bring legal actions.

(e) *Furnishing certain deceptive forms.* A debt collector must not design, compile, and furnish any form that the debt collector knows would be used to cause a consumer falsely to believe that a person other than the consumer's creditor is participating in collecting or attempting to collect a debt that the consumer allegedly owes to the creditor.

§ 1006.34 Notice for validation of debts

(a)(1) *Validation information required.* Except as provided in paragraph (a)(2) of this section, a debt collector must provide a consumer with the validation information described in paragraph (c) of this section either:

(i) By sending the consumer a validation notice in a manner permitted by § 1006.42:

(A) In the initial communication, as defined in paragraph (b)(2) of this section; or

(B) Within five days of that initial communication; or

(ii) By providing the validation information orally in the initial communication.

(2) *Exception.* A debt collector who otherwise would be required to send a validation notice pursuant to paragraph (a)(1)(i)(B) of this section is not required to do so if the consumer has paid the debt prior to the time that paragraph (a)(1)(i)(B) of this section would require the validation notice to be sent.

(b) *Definitions.* For purposes of this section:

(1) *Clear and conspicuous* means disclosures that are readily understandable. In the case of written and electronic disclosures, the location and type size also must be readily noticeable to consumers. In the case of oral disclosures, the disclosures also must be given at a volume and speed sufficient for the consumer to hear and comprehend them.

(2) *Initial communication* means the first time that, in connection with the collection of a debt, a debt collector conveys information, directly or indirectly, regarding the debt to the consumer, other than a communication in the form of a formal pleading in a civil action, or any form or notice that does not relate to the collection of the debt and is expressly required by:

(i) The Internal Revenue Code of 1986 (26 U.S.C. 1 et seq.);

(ii) Title V of the Gramm-Leach-Bliley Act (15 U.S.C. 6801 through 6827); or

(iii) Any provision of Federal or State law or regulation mandating notice of a data security breach or privacy risk.

(3) *Itemization date* means any one of the following four reference dates for which a debt collector can ascertain the amount of the debt:

(i) The last statement date, which is the date of the last periodic statement or written account statement or invoice provided to the consumer;

(ii) The charge-off date, which is the date the debt was charged off;

(iii) The last payment date, which is the date the last payment was applied to the debt; or

(iv) The transaction date, which is the date of the transaction that gave rise to the debt.

(4) *Validation notice* means a written or electronic notice that provides the validation information described in paragraph (c) of this section.

(5) *Validation period* means the period starting on the date that a debt collector provides the validation information described in paragraph (c) of this section and ending 30 days after the consumer receives or is assumed to receive the validation information. For purposes of determining the end of the validation period, the debt collector may assume that a consumer receives the validation information on any date that is at least five days (excluding legal public holidays, Saturdays, and Sundays) after the debt collector provides it.

(c) *Validation information.*

(1) *Debt collector communication disclosure.* The statement required by § 1006.18(e).

(2) *Information about the debt.* Except as provided in paragraph (c)(5) of this section:

(i) The debt collector's name and mailing address.

(ii) The consumer's name and mailing address.

(iii) If the debt is a credit card debt, the merchant brand, if any, associated with the debt, to the extent available to the debt collector.

(iv) If the debt collector is collecting consumer financial product or service debt as defined in § 1006.2(f), the name of the creditor to whom the debt was owed on the itemization date.

(v) The account number, if any, associated with the debt on the itemization date, or a truncated version of that number.

(vi) The name of the creditor to whom the debt currently is owed.

(vii) The itemization date.

(viii) The amount of the debt on the itemization date.

(ix) An itemization of the current amount of the debt in a tabular format reflecting interest, fees, payments, and credits since the itemization date.

(x) The current amount of the debt.

(3) *Information about consumer protections.* (i) A statement that specifies what date the debt collector will consider the end date of the validation period and states that, if the consumer notifies the debt collector in writing before the end of the validation period that the debt, or any portion of the debt, is disputed, the debt collector must cease collection of the debt, or the disputed portion of the debt, until the debt collector sends the consumer either the verification of the debt or a copy of a judgment.

(ii) A statement that specifies what date the debt collector will consider the end date of the validation period and states that, if the consumer requests in writing before the end of the validation period the name and address of the original creditor, the debt collector must cease collection of the debt until the debt collector sends the consumer the name and address of the original creditor, if different from the current creditor.

(iii) A statement that specifies what date the debt collector will consider the end date of the validation period and states that, unless the consumer contacts the debt collector to dispute the validity of the debt, or any portion of the debt, before the end of the validation period, the debt collector will assume that the debt is valid.

(iv) If the debt collector is collecting consumer financial product or service debt as defined in § 1006.2(f), a statement that informs the consumer that additional information regarding consumer protections in debt collection is available on the Bureau's website at https://www.consumerfinance.gov.

(v) A statement explaining how a consumer can take the actions described in paragraphs (c)(4) and (d)(3), as applicable, of this section electronically, if the debt collector sends a validation notice electronically.

(vi) For a validation notice delivered in the body of an email pursuant to § 1006.42(b)(1) or (c)(2)(i), the opt-out statement required by § 1006.6(e).

(4) *Consumer response information.* The following information, segregated from the validation information described in paragraphs (c)(1) through (3) of this section and from any optional information included pursuant to paragraphs (d)(3)(i), (ii), (iv), and (v) of this section, and, if provided in a validation notice, located at the bottom of the notice under the headings, "How do you want to respond?" and "Check all that apply:":

(i) *Dispute prompts.* The following statements, listed in the following order, and using the following phrasing or substantially similar phrasing, each next to a prompt:

(A) "I want to dispute the debt because I think:;"

(B) "This is not my debt;"

(C) "The amount is wrong;" and

(D) "Other (please describe on reverse or attach additional information)."

(ii) *Original-creditor information prompt.* The statement, "I want you to send me the name and address of the original creditor," using that phrase or a substantially similar phrase, next to a prompt.

(iii) *Mailing addresses.* Mailing addresses for the consumer and the debt collector, which include the debt collector's and the consumer's names.

(5) *Special rule for certain residential mortgage debt.* For residential mortgage debt subject to Regulation Z, 12 CFR 1026.41, a debt collector need not provide the validation information described in paragraphs (c)(2)(vii) through (ix) of this section if the debt collector:

(i) Provides the consumer at the same time as the validation notice, a copy of the most recent periodic statement provided to the consumer under Regulation Z, 12 CFR 1026.41(b); and

(ii) Refers to that periodic statement in the validation notice.

(d) *Form of validation information.*

(1) *In general.*

(i) The validation information described in paragraph (c) of this section must be clear and conspicuous.

(ii) If provided in a validation notice, the content, format, and placement of the validation information described in § 1006.34(c) and of the optional disclosures permitted by paragraph (d)(3) of this section must be substantially similar to Model Form B-3 in appendix B of this part.

(2) *Safe harbor.* A debt collector who uses Model Form B-3 in appendix B of this part complies with the requirements of paragraphs (a)(1)(i) and (d)(1) of this section.

(3) *Optional disclosures.* A debt collector may, at its option, include any of the following information if providing the validation information required by paragraph (a)(1) of this section.

(i) *Telephone contact information.* The debt collector's telephone contact information, including telephone number and the times that the debt collector accepts consumer telephone calls.

(ii) *Reference code.* A number or code that the debt collector uses to identify the debt or the consumer.

(iii) *Payment disclosures.*

(A) The statement, "Contact us about your payment options," using that phrase or a substantially similar phrase. The optional payment disclosure permitted by this paragraph must be no more prominent than any of the validation information described in paragraph (c) of this section; and

(B) With the consumer response information described in paragraph (c)(4) of this section, the statement "I enclosed this amount," using that phrase or a substantially similar phrase, payment instructions after that statement, and a prompt. The optional payment disclosure permitted by this paragraph must be no more prominent than the validation information described in paragraph (c) of this section.

(iv) *Disclosures required by applicable law.* On the front of a validation notice, a statement that other disclosures required by applicable law appear on the reverse of the validation notice and, on the reverse of the validation notice, any such required disclosures.

(v) *Information about electronic communications.* The following information:

(A) The debt collector's website and email address.

(B) If validation information is not provided electronically, the statement described in paragraph (c)(3)(v) of this section explaining how a consumer can take the actions described in paragraphs (c)(4) and (d)(3) of this section electronically.

(vi) *Spanish-language translation disclosures.* The following disclosures regarding a consumer's ability to request a Spanish-language translation of a validation notice:

(A) The statement, "Póngase en contacto con nosotros para solicitar una copia de este formulario en español" (which means "Contact us to request a copy of the form in Spanish"), using that phrase or a substantially similar phrase in Spanish. If providing this optional disclosure, a debt collector may include supplemental information in Spanish that specifies how a consumer may request a Spanish-language validation notice.

(B) With the consumer response information described in paragraph (c)(4) of this section, the statement "Quiero esta forma en español" (which means "I want this form in Spanish"), using that phrase or a substantially similar phrase in Spanish, next to a prompt.

(4) *Validation notices delivered electronically.* If a debt collector delivers a validation notice electronically pursuant to § 1006.42, a debt collector may, at its option, format the validation notice as follows:

(i) *Prompts.* Any prompt described in paragraphs (c)(4)(i) or (ii) or paragraphs (d)(3)(iii)(B) or (vi)(B) of this section may be displayed electronically as a fillable field.

(ii) *Hyperlinks.* Hyperlinks may be embedded that, when clicked:

(A) Connect consumers to the debt collector's website; or

(B) Permit consumers to respond to the dispute and original-creditor information prompts described in paragraphs (c)(4)(i) and (ii) of this section.

(e) *Translation into other languages.* A debt collector may send the consumer a validation notice completely and accurately translated into any language if the debt collector also sends an English-language validation notice in the same communication that satisfies paragraph (a)(1) of this section. If a debt collector has already provided an English-language validation notice that satisfies paragraph (a)(1) of this section and subsequently provides the consumer a validation notice translated into any another language, the debt collector need not provide an additional copy of the English-language notice.

§ 1006.38 Disputes and requests for original-creditor information

(a) *Definitions.* For purposes of this section, the following definitions apply:

(1) *Duplicative dispute* means a dispute submitted by the consumer in writing within the validation period that:

(i) Is substantially the same as a dispute previously submitted by the consumer in writing within the validation period for which the debt collector already has satisfied the requirements of paragraph (d)(2)(i) of this section; and

(ii) Does not include new and material information to support the dispute.

(2) *Validation period* has the same meaning given to it in § 1006.34(b)(5).

(b) *Overshadowing of rights to dispute or request original-creditor information.* During the validation period, a debt collector must not engage in any collection activities or communications that overshadow or are inconsistent with the disclosure of the consumer's rights to dispute the debt and to request the name and address of the original creditor.

(c) *Requests for original-creditor information.* Upon receipt of a request for the name and address of the original creditor submitted by the consumer in writing within the validation period, a debt collector must cease collection of the debt until the debt collector provides the name and address of the original creditor to the consumer in writing or electronically in a manner permitted by § 1006.42.

(d) *Disputes.*

(1) *Failure to dispute.* The failure of a consumer to dispute the validity of a debt does not constitute a legal admission of liability by the consumer.

(2) *Response to disputes.* Upon receipt of a dispute submitted by the consumer in writing within the validation period, a debt collector must cease collection of the debt, or any disputed portion of the debt, until the debt collector:

(i) Provides a copy either of verification of the debt or of a judgment to the consumer in writing or electronically in a manner permitted by § 1006.42; or

(ii) In the case of a dispute that the debt collector reasonably determines is a duplicative dispute, either:

(A) Notifies the consumer in writing or electronically in a manner permitted by § 1006.42 that the dispute is duplicative, provides a brief statement of the reasons for the determination, and refers the consumer to the debt collector's response to the earlier dispute; or

(B) Satisfies paragraph (d)(2)(i) of this section.

§ 1006.42 Providing required disclosures

(a) *Providing required disclosures.*

(1) *In general.* A debt collector who provides disclosures required by this part in writing or electronically must do so in a manner that is reasonably expected to provide actual notice and in a form that the consumer may keep and access later.

(2) *Exceptions.* A debt collector need not comply with paragraph (a)(1) of this section when providing the disclosure required by § 1006.6(e) or § 1006.18(e) in writing or electronically, unless the disclosure is included on a notice required by § 1006.34(a)(1)(i) or § 1006.38(c) or (d)(2), or in an electronic communication containing a hyperlink to such notice.

(b) *Requirements for certain disclosures provided electronically.* To comply with paragraph (a) of this section, a debt collector who provides the validation notice described in § 1006.34(a)(1)(i)(B), or the disclosures described in § 1006.38(c) or (d)(2), electronically must

(1) Except as provided in paragraph (c) of this section, provide the disclosure in accordance with section 101(c) of the Electronic Signatures in Global and National Commerce Act (E-SIGN Act) (15 U.S.C. 7001(c)) after the consumer provides affirmative consent directly to the debt collector;

(2) Identify the purpose of the communication by including, in the subject line of an email or in the first line of a text message transmitting the disclosure, the name of the creditor to whom the debt currently is owed or allegedly is owed and one additional piece of information identifying the debt, other than the amount;

(3) Permit receipt of notifications of undeliverability from communications providers, monitor for any such notifications, and treat any such notifications as precluding a reasonable expectation of actual notice for that delivery attempt; and

(4) When providing the validation notice described in § 1006.34(a)(1)(i)(B), provide the disclosure in a responsive format that is reasonably expected to be accessible on a screen of any commercially available size and via commercially available screen readers.

(c) *Alternative procedures for providing certain disclosures electronically.* A debt collector who provides the validation notice described in § 1006.34(a)(1)(i)(B), or the disclosures described in § 1006.38(c) or (d)(2), electronically need not comply with paragraph (b)(1) of this section if the debt collector:

(1) Provides the disclosure by sending an electronic communication to an email address or, in the case of a text message, a telephone number that the creditor or a prior debt collector could have used to provide electronic disclosures related to that debt in accordance with section 101(c) of the E-SIGN Act; and

(2) Places the disclosure either:

(i) In the body of an email sent to an email address described in paragraph (c)(1) of this section; or

(ii) On a secure website that is accessible by clicking on a clear and conspicuous hyperlink included within an electronic communication sent to an email address or a telephone number described in paragraph (c)(1) of this section, provided that:

(A) The disclosure is accessible on the website for a reasonable period of time and can be saved or printed;

(B) The consumer receives notice and an opportunity to opt out of hyperlinked delivery as described in paragraph (d) of this section; and

(C) The consumer, during the opt-out period, has not opted out.

(d) *Notice and opportunity to opt out of hyperlinked delivery.* For a consumer to receive notice and an opportunity to opt out of hyperlinked delivery as required by paragraph (c)(2)(ii)(B) of this section, the debt collector must, before providing the disclosure, either:

(1) *Communication by the debt collector.* Inform the consumer, in a communication with the consumer, of:

(i) The name of the consumer who owes or allegedly owes the debt;

(ii) The name of the creditor to whom the debt currently is owed or allegedly owed;

(iii) The email address or telephone number from which the debt collector intends to send the electronic communication containing the hyperlink to the disclosure;

(iv) The email address or telephone number to which the debt collector intends to send the electronic communication containing the hyperlink to the disclosure;

(v) The consumer's ability to opt out of hyperlinked delivery of disclosures to such email address or telephone number; and

(vi) Instructions for opting out, including a reasonable period within which to opt out; or

(2) *Communication by the creditor.* Confirm that, no more than 30 days before the debt collector's electronic communication containing the hyperlink to the disclosure, the creditor communicated with the consumer using the email address or, in the case of a text message, the telephone number to which the debt collector intends to send the electronic communication and informed the consumer of:

(i) The placement or sale of the debt to the debt collector;

(ii) The name the debt collector uses when collecting debts;

(iii) The debt collector's option to use the consumer's email address or, in the case of a text message, the consumer's telephone number to provide any legally required debt collection disclosures in a manner that is consistent with Federal law; and

(iv) The information in paragraphs (d)(1)(iii), (v), and (vi) of this section.

(e) *Safe harbors.* (1) *Disclosures provided by mail.* A debt collector satisfies paragraph (a) of this section if the debt collector mails a printed copy of a disclosure to the consumer's residential address, unless the debt collector receives a notification from the entity or person responsible for delivery that the disclosure was not delivered.

(2) *Validation notice contained in the initial communication.* A debt collector who provides the validation notice described in § 1006.34(a)(1)(i)(A) within the body of an email that is the initial communication with the consumer satisfies paragraph (a)(1) of this section if the debt collector satisfies the requirements of paragraph (b) of this section for validation notices described in § 1006.34(a)(1)(i)(B). If such a debt collector follows the procedures described in paragraph (c) of this section, the debt collector may, in lieu of sending the validation notice to an email address that the creditor or a prior debt collector could use for delivery of electronic disclosures in accordance with section 101(c) of the E-SIGN Act (as described in paragraph (c)(1) of this section), send the validation notice to an email address selected through the procedures described in § 1006.6(d)(3).

Subpart C—[Reserved]

Subpart D—Miscellaneous

§ 1006.100 Record retention

(a) A debt collector must retain evidence of compliance with this part starting on the date that the debt collector begins collection activity on a debt until three years after:

(1) The debt collector's last communication or attempted communication in connection with the collection of the debt; or

(2) The debt is settled, discharged, or transferred to the debt owner or to another debt collector.

§ 1006.104 Relation to State laws

Neither the Act nor the corresponding provisions of this part annul, alter, affect, or exempt any person subject to the provisions of the Act or the corresponding provisions of this part from complying with the laws of any State with respect to debt collection practices, except to the extent that those laws are inconsistent with any provision of the Act or the corresponding provisions of this part, and then only to the extent of the inconsistency. For purposes of this section, a State law is not inconsistent with the Act or the corresponding provisions of this part if the protection such law affords any consumer is greater than the protection provided by the Act or the corresponding provisions of this part.

§ 1006.108 Exemption for State regulation

(a) *Exemption for State regulation.* Any State may apply to the Bureau for a determination that, under the laws of that State, any class of debt collection practices within that State is subject to requirements that are substantially similar to, or provide greater protection for consumers than, those imposed under sections 803 through 812 of the Act (15 U.S.C. 1692a through 1692j) and the corresponding provisions of this part, and that there is adequate provision for State enforcement of such requirements.

(b) *Procedures and criteria.* The procedures and criteria whereby States may apply to the Bureau for exemption of a class of debt collection practices within the applying State from the provisions of the Act and the corresponding provisions of this part as provided in section 817 of the Act (15 U.S.C. 1692*o*) are set forth in appendix A of this part.

North South Group
P.O. Box 121212
Pasadena, CA 91111-2222
(800) 123-4567 from 8am to 8pm EST, Monday to Saturday
www.example.com

To: Person A
2323 Park Street
Apartment 342
Bethesda, MD 20815

Reference: 584-345

North South Group is a debt collector. We are trying to collect a debt that you owe to Bank of Rockville. We will use any information you give us to help collect the debt.

Our information shows:

You had a Main Street Department Store credit card from Bank of Rockville with account number 123-456-789.

As of January 2, 2017, you owed:		$	2,234.56
Between January 2, 2017 and today:			
You were charged this amount in interest:	+	$	75.00
You were charged this amount in fees:	+	$	25.00
You paid or were credited this amount toward the debt:	–	$	50.00
Total amount of the debt now:		**$**	**2,284.56**

How can you dispute the debt?

- **Call or write to us by November 12, 2019, to dispute all or part of the debt.** If you do not, we will assume that our information is correct. If you write to us by November 12, 2019, we must stop collection on any amount you dispute until we send you information that shows you owe the debt.
- You may use the form below or you may write to us without the form. You may also include supporting documents. We accept disputes electronically at www.example.com/dispute.

What else can you do?

- **Write to ask for the name and address of the original creditor.** If you write by November 12, 2019, we will stop collection until we send you that information. You may use the form below or write to us without the form. We accept such requests electronically at www.example.com/request.
- **Learn more about your rights under federal law.** For instance, you have the right to stop or limit how we contact you. Go to www.consumerfinance.gov.
- Contact us about your payment options.
- Review state law disclosures on reverse side, if applicable.
- Póngase en contacto con nosotros para solicitar una copia de este formulario en español.

Mail this form to:
North South Group
P.O. Box 121212
Pasadena, CA 91111-2222

Person A
2323 Park Street
Apartment 342
Bethesda, MD 20815

How do you want to respond?

Check all that apply.

☐ **I want to dispute the debt because I think:**

- ☐ This is not my debt.
- ☐ The amount is wrong.
- ☐ Other (please describe on reverse or attach additional information).

☐ **I want you to send me the name and address of the original creditor.**

☐ **I enclosed this amount:** $

Make your check payable to *North South Group*. Include the reference number 584-345.

☐ **Quiero esta forma en español.**

CFPB BULLETIN 2013–07

Date: July 10, 2013

Subject: Prohibition of Unfair, Deceptive, or Abusive Acts or Practices in the Collection of Consumer Debts

Under the Dodd-Frank Wall Street Reform and Consumer Protection Act (Dodd-Frank Act), all covered persons or service providers are legally required to refrain from committing unfair, deceptive, or abusive acts or practices (collectively, UDAAPs) in violation of the Act. The Consumer Financial Protection Bureau (CFPB or Bureau) is issuing this bulletin to clarify the contours of that obligation in the context of collecting consumer debts.

This bulletin describes certain acts or practices related to the collection of consumer debt that could, depending on the facts and circumstances, constitute UDAAPs prohibited by the Dodd-Frank Act. Whether conduct like that described in this bulletin constitutes a UDAAP may depend on additional facts and analysis. The examples described in this bulletin are not exhaustive of all potential UDAAPs. The Bureau may closely review any covered person or service provider's consumer debt collection efforts for potential violations of Federal consumer financial laws.

A. Background

UDAAPs can cause significant financial injury to consumers, erode consumer confidence, and undermine fair competition in the financial marketplace. Original creditors and other covered persons and service providers under the Dodd-Frank Act involved in collecting debt related to any consumer financial product or service are subject to the prohibition against UDAAPs in the Dodd-Frank Act.[1]

In addition to the prohibition of UDAAPs under the Dodd-Frank Act, the Fair Debt Collection Practices Act (FDCPA) also makes it illegal for a person defined as a "debt collector" from engaging in conduct "the natural consequence of which is to harass, oppress, or abuse any person in connection with the collection of a debt,"[2] to "use any false, deceptive, or misleading representation or means in connection with the collection of any debt,"[3] or to "use any unfair or unconscionable means to collect or attempt to collect any debt."[4] The FDCPA generally applies to third-party debt collectors, such as collection agencies, debt purchasers, and attorneys who are regularly engaged in debt collection.[5] All parties covered by the FDCPA must comply with any obligations they have under the FDCPA, in addition to any obligations to refrain from UDAAPs in violation of the Dodd-Frank Act.

---

1 *See* Dodd-Frank Act, §§ 1002, 1031 & 1036(a), codified at 12 U.S.C. §§ 5481, 5531 & 5536(a). It is also prohibited for any person, even if not a covered person or service provider, to knowingly or recklessly provide substantial assistance to a covered person or service provider in violating section 1031 of the Dodd-Frank Act. *See* Dodd-Frank Act, § 1036(a)(3), 12 U.S.C. § 5536(a)(3). The principles of "unfair" and "deceptive" practices in the Act are informed by the standards for the same terms under Section 5 of the Federal Trade Commission Act (FTC Act). *See* CFPB Examination Manual v.2 (Oct. 2012) at UDAAP 1 (CFPB Exam Manual). To the extent that this Bulletin cites FTC guidance or authority, such references reflect the views of the FTC, and are not binding upon the Bureau in interpreting the Dodd-Frank Act's prohibition on UDAAPs.

2 FDCPA § 806, 15 U.S.C. § 1692d.

3 FDCPA § 807, 15 U.S.C. § 1692e. This provision also imposes affirmative obligations on "debt collectors" under the FDCPA when collecting consumer debts.

4 FDCPA § 808, 15 U.S.C. § 1692f. This provision also imposes affirmative obligations on "debt collectors" under the FDCPA when collecting consumer debts.

5 *See* FDCPA § 803(6), 15 U.S.C. § 1692a(6). The FDCPA also covers, as a "debt collector," a creditor who, in collecting its own debts, uses any name other than its own which would indicate that a third person is attempting to collect the debts.

Although the FDCPA's definition of "debt collector" does not include some persons who collect consumer debt, all covered persons and service providers must refrain from committing UDAAPs in violation of the Dodd-Frank Act. [6]

B. Summary of Applicable Standards for UDAAPs

1. *Unfair Acts or Practices*

The Dodd-Frank Act prohibits conduct that constitutes an unfair act or practice. An act or practice is unfair when:

(1) It causes or is likely to cause substantial injury to consumers;

(2) The injury is not reasonably avoidable by consumers; and

(3) The injury is not outweighed by countervailing benefits to consumers or to competition.[7]

A "substantial injury" typically takes the form of monetary harm, such as fees or costs paid by consumers because of the unfair act or practice. However, the injury does not have to be monetary.[8] Although emotional impact and other subjective types of harm will not ordinarily amount to substantial injury, in certain circumstances emotional impacts may amount to or contribute to substantial injury.[9] In addition, actual injury is not required; a significant risk of concrete harm is sufficient.[10]

An injury is not reasonably avoidable by consumers when an act or practice interferes with or hinders a consumer's ability to make informed decisions or take action to avoid that injury.[11] Injury caused by transactions that occur without a consumer's knowledge or consent is not reasonably avoidable.[12] Injuries that can only be avoided by spending large amounts of money or other significant resources also may not be reasonably avoidable.[13] Finally, an act or practice is not unfair if the injury it causes or is likely to cause is outweighed by its consumer or competitive benefits.[14]

Established public policy may be considered with all other evidence to determine whether an act or practice is unfair, but may not serve as the primary basis for such determination.[15]

2. *Deceptive Acts or Practices*

The Dodd-Frank Act also prohibits conduct that constitutes a deceptive act or practice. An act or practice is deceptive when:

(1) The act or practice misleads or is likely to mislead the consumer;

(2) The consumer's interpretation is reasonable under the circumstances; and

(3) The misleading act or practice is material.[16]

---

[6] The FDCPA also reaches any person who designs, compiles, or furnishes forms knowing such forms would be used to create the false belief in a consumer that a person other than the creditor is participating in collecting the creditor's debts. See FDCPA § 812, 15 U.S.C. § 1692j.

[7] Dodd-Frank Act §§ 1031, 1036, 12 U.S.C. §§ 5531, 5536.

[8] CFPB Exam Manual at UDAAP 2; *see also FTC v. Accusearch, Inc.*, 06-cv-105-D, 2007 WL 4356786, at *7–8 (D. Wyo. Sept. 28, 2007); FTC Policy Statement on Unfairness (Dec. 17, 1980), *available at* http://www.ftc.gov/bcp/policystmt/ad-unfair.htm.

[9] CFPB Exam Manual at UDAAP 2.

[10] *Id.*

[11] *Id.*

[12] *Id.*

[13] *See id.* at 2–3.

[14] Dodd-Frank Act § 1031(c)(1)(B), 12 U.S.C. § 5531(c)(1)(B); *see also* CFPB Exam Manual at UDAAP 2.

[15] Dodd-Frank Act § 1031(c)(2), 12 U.S.C. § 5531(c)(2); *see also* CFPB Exam Manual at UDAAP 3.

[16] The standard for "deceptive" practices in the Dodd-Frank Act is informed by the standards for the same terms under Section 5 of the FTC Act. *See* CFPB Exam Manual at UDAAP 5.

To determine whether an act or practice has actually misled or is likely to mislead a consumer, the totality of the circumstances is considered.[17] Deceptive acts or practices can take the form of a representation or omission.[18] The Bureau also looks at implied representations, including any implications that statements about the consumer's debt can be supported. Ensuring that claims are supported before they are made will minimize the risk of omitting material information and/or making false statements that could mislead consumers.

To determine if the consumer's interpretation of the information was reasonable under the circumstances when representations target a specific audience, such as older Americans or financially distressed consumers, the communication may be considered from the perspective of a reasonable member of the target audience.[19] A statement or information can be misleading even if not all consumers, or not all consumers in the targeted group, would be misled, so long as a significant minority would be misled.[20] Likewise, if a representation conveys more than one meaning to reasonable consumers, one of which is false, the speaker may still be liable for the misleading interpretation.[21] Material information is information that is likely to affect a consumer's choice of, or conduct regarding, the product or service. Information that is likely important to consumers is material.[22]

Sometimes, a person may make a disclosure or other qualifying statement that might prevent consumers from being misled by a representation or omission that, on its own, would be deceptive. The Bureau looks to the following factors in assessing whether the disclosure or other qualifying statement is adequate to prevent the deception: whether the disclosure is prominent enough for a consumer to notice; whether the information is presented in a clear and easy to understand format; the placement of the information; and the proximity of the information to the other claims it qualifies.[23]

3. Abusive Acts or Practices

The Dodd-Frank Act also prohibits conduct that constitutes an abusive act or practice. An act or practice is abusive when it:

(1) Materially interferes with the ability of a consumer to understand a term or condition of a consumer financial product or service; or

(2) Takes unreasonable advantage of—

(A) a consumer's lack of understanding of the material risks, costs, or conditions of the product or service;

(B) a consumer's inability to protect his or her interests in selecting or using a consumer financial product or service; or

(C) a consumer's reasonable reliance on a covered person to act in his or her interests.[24]

---

17 CFPB Exam Manual at UDAAP 5.

18 *Id.*

19 *See id.* at 6.

20 *Id.*

21 *Id.*

22 *Id.*

23 *Id.*; *see also* CFPB Bulletin 12–06, Marketing of Credit Card Add-On Products (July 12, 2012), *available at* http://files.consumerfinance.gov/f/201207_cfpb_bulletin_marketing_of_credit_card_addon_products.pdf.

24 Dodd-Frank Act § 1031(d), 12 U.S.C. § 5531(d); *see also* CFPB Exam Manual at UDAAP 9; Stipulated Final Judgment and Order, Conclusions of Law ¶ 12, 9:13-cv-80548 and Compl. ¶¶ 55–63, *CFPB v. Am. Debt Settlement Solutions, Inc.*, 9:13-cv-80548 (S.D. Fla. May 30, 2013), *available at* http://files.consumerfinance.gov/f/201305_cfpb_proposed-order_adss.pdf and http://files.consumerfinance.gov/f/201305_cfpb_complaint_adss.pdf. The Stipulated Final Judgment and Order was signed by U.S. District Judge Middlebrooks and entered on the court docket on June 6, 2013. *See* Stipulated Final J. & Order [ECF Docket Entry No. 5], 9:13-cv-80548 (S.D. Fla.).

It is important to note that, although abusive acts or practices may also be unfair or deceptive, each of these prohibitions are separate and distinct, and are governed by separate legal standards.[25]

C. Examples of Unfair, Deceptive and/or Abusive Acts or Practices

Depending on the facts and circumstances, the following non-exhaustive list of examples of conduct related to the collection of consumer debt could constitute UDAAPs. Accordingly, the Bureau will be watching these practices closely.

- **Collecting or assessing a debt and/or any additional amounts in connection with a debt (including interest, fees, and charges) not expressly authorized by the agreement creating the debt or permitted by law.**[26]
- **Failing to post payments timely or properly or to credit a consumer's account with payments that the consumer submitted on time and then charging late fees to that consumer.**[27]
- **Taking possession of property without the legal right to do so.**
- **Revealing the consumer's debt, without the consumer's consent, to the consumer's employer and/or co-workers.**[28]
- **Falsely representing the character, amount, or legal status of the debt.**
- **Misrepresenting that a debt collection communication is from an attorney.**
- **Misrepresenting that a communication is from a government source or that the source of the communication is affiliated with the government.**
- **Misrepresenting whether information about a payment or non-payment would be furnished to a credit reporting agency.**[29]
- **Misrepresenting to consumers that their debts would be waived or forgiven if they accepted a settlement offer, when the company does not, in fact, forgive or waive the debt.**[30]
- **Threatening any action that is not intended or the covered person or service provider does not have the authorization to pursue, including false threats of lawsuits, arrest, prosecution, or imprisonment for non-payment of a debt.**

Again, the obligation to avoid UDAAPs under the Dodd-Frank Act is in addition to any obligations that may arise under the FDCPA. Original creditors and other covered persons and service providers involved in collecting debt related to any consumer financial product or service are subject to the prohibition against UDAAPs in the Dodd-Frank Act. The CFPB will continue to review closely the

---

[25] CFPB Exam Manual at UDAAP 9.

[26] *See* Compl. ¶¶ 34–38 & 43–44, *FTC v. Fairbanks Capital Corp.*, 03–12219 (D. Mass. Nov. 12, 2003) (alleging that the charging of late fees and other associated charges was unfair practice under Section 5 of the FTC Act and a violation of §§ 807 and 808 of the FDCPA), *available at* http://www.ftc.gov/os/2003/11/0323014comp.pdf.

[27] *Id.* ¶¶ 22–25.

[28] *See, e.g.*, Compl. ¶¶ 24 & 30–31, *FTC v. Cash Today, Ltd.*, 3:08-cv-590 (D. Nev. Nov. 12, 2008), *available at* http://www.ftc.gov/os/caselist/0723093/081112cmp0923093.pdf, (asserting that Cash Today engaged in unfair collection practices in violation of Section 5 of the FTC Act by, among other things, disclosing the existence of consumer's debt to employers, co-workers, and other third parties despite being told by consumers not to contact their workplaces); *FTC v. LoanPointe*, LLC., 2:10 CV 00225-DAK, 2011 WL 4348304, at *5–6 (D. Utah Sept. 16, 2011) (finding that disclosure of existence and amount of debt to consumer's employer without consumer's prior approval constitutes an unfair practice under the FTC Act).

[29] *See, e.g.*, *In re Am. Express Centurion Bank*, Joint Consent Order at 3 (Oct. 1, 2012), *available at* http://files.consumerfinance.gov/f/2012-CFPB-0002-American-Express-Centurion-Consent-Order.pdf.

[30] *Id.*

practices of those engaged in the collection of consumer debts for potential UDAAPs, including the practices described above. The Bureau will use all appropriate tools to assess whether supervisory, enforcement, or other actions may be necessary.

MISCELLANEOUS STATUTES

Selections from the Fair Housing Act

42 U.S.C.A. §§ 3604–3605

Table of Sections

§ 3604. Discrimination in the sale or rental of housing and other prohibited practices

As made applicable by section 3603 of this title and except as exempted by sections 3603(b) and 3607 of this title, it shall be unlawful—

(a) To refuse to sell or rent after the making of a bona fide offer, or to refuse to negotiate for the sale or rental of, or otherwise make unavailable or deny, a dwelling to any person because of race, color, religion, sex, familial status, or national origin.

(b) To discriminate against any person in the terms, conditions, or privileges of sale or rental of a dwelling, or in the provision of services or facilities in connection therewith, because of race, color, religion, sex, familial status, or national origin.

(c) To make, print, or publish, or cause to be made, printed, or published any notice, statement, or advertisement, with respect to the sale or rental of a dwelling that indicates any preference, limitation, or discrimination based on race, color, religion, sex, handicap, familial status, or national origin, or an intention to make any such preference, limitation, or discrimination.

(d) To represent to any person because of race, color, religion, sex, handicap, familial status, or national origin that any dwelling is not available for inspection, sale, or rental when such dwelling is in fact so available.

(e) For profit, to induce or attempt to induce any person to sell or rent any dwelling by representations regarding the entry or prospective entry into the neighborhood of a person or persons of a particular race, color, religion, sex, handicap, familial status, or national origin.

(f)(1) To discriminate in the sale or rental, or to otherwise make unavailable or deny, a dwelling to any buyer or renter because of a handicap of—

(A) that buyer or renter,[1]

(B) a person residing in or intending to reside in that dwelling after it is so sold, rented, or made available; or

(C) any person associated with that buyer or renter.

(2) To discriminate against any person in the terms, conditions, or privileges of sale or rental of a dwelling, or in the provision of services or facilities in connection with such dwelling, because of a handicap of—

(A) that person; or

(B) a person residing in or intending to reside in that dwelling after it is so sold, rented, or made available; or

---

1 So in original. The comma probably should be a semicolon.

(C) any person associated with that person.

(3) For purposes of this subsection, discrimination includes—

(A) a refusal to permit, at the expense of the handicapped person, reasonable modifications of existing premises occupied or to be occupied by such person if such modifications may be necessary to afford such person full enjoyment of the premises except that, in the case of a rental, the landlord may where it is reasonable to do so condition permission for a modification on the renter agreeing to restore the interior of the premises to the condition that existed before the modification, reasonable wear and tear excepted.[2]

(B) a refusal to make reasonable accommodations in rules, policies, practices, or services, when such accommodations may be necessary to afford such person equal opportunity to use and enjoy a dwelling; or

(C) in connection with the design and construction of covered multifamily dwellings for first occupancy after the date that is 30 months after September 13, 1988, a failure to design and construct those dwellings in such a manner that—

(i) the public use and common use portions of such dwellings are readily accessible to and usable by handicapped persons;

(ii) all the doors designed to allow passage into and within all premises within such dwellings are sufficiently wide to allow passage by handicapped persons in wheelchairs; and

(iii) all premises within such dwellings contain the following features of adaptive design:

(I) an accessible route into and through the dwelling;

(II) light switches, electrical outlets, thermostats, and other environmental controls in accessible locations;

(III) reinforcements in bathroom walls to allow later installation of grab bars; and

(IV) usable kitchens and bathrooms such that an individual in a wheelchair can maneuver about the space.

(4) Compliance with the appropriate requirements of the American National Standard for buildings and facilities providing accessibility and usability for physically handicapped people (commonly cited as "ANSI A117.1") suffices to satisfy the requirements of paragraph (3)(C)(iii).

(5)(A) If a State or unit of general local government has incorporated into its laws the requirements set forth in paragraph (3)(C), compliance with such laws shall be deemed to satisfy the requirements of that paragraph.

(B) A State or unit of general local government may review and approve newly constructed covered multifamily dwellings for the purpose of making determinations as to whether the design and construction requirements of paragraph (3)(C) are met.

(C) The Secretary shall encourage, but may not require, States and units of local government to include in their existing procedures for the review and approval of newly constructed covered multifamily dwellings, determinations as to whether the design and construction of such dwellings are consistent with paragraph (3)(C), and shall provide technical assistance to States and units of local government and other persons to implement the requirements of paragraph (3)(C).

---

2 So in original. The period probably should be a semicolon.

(D) Nothing in this subchapter shall be construed to require the Secretary to review or approve the plans, designs or construction of all covered multifamily dwellings, to determine whether the design and construction of such dwellings are consistent with the requirements of paragraph 3(C).

(6)(A) Nothing in paragraph (5) shall be construed to affect the authority and responsibility of the Secretary or a State or local public agency certified pursuant to section 3610(f)(3) of this title to receive and process complaints or otherwise engage in enforcement activities under this subchapter.

(B) Determinations by a State or a unit of general local government under paragraphs (5)(A) and (B) shall not be conclusive in enforcement proceedings under this subchapter.

(7) As used in this subsection, the term "covered multifamily dwellings" means—

(A) buildings consisting of 4 or more units if such buildings have one or more elevators; and

(B) ground floor units in other buildings consisting of 4 or more units.

(8) Nothing in this subchapter shall be construed to invalidate or limit any law of a State or political subdivision of a State, or other jurisdiction in which this subchapter shall be effective, that requires dwellings to be designed and constructed in a manner that affords handicapped persons greater access than is required by this subchapter.

(9) Nothing in this subsection requires that a dwelling be made available to an individual whose tenancy would constitute a direct threat to the health or safety of other individuals or whose tenancy would result in substantial physical damage to the property of others.

§ 3605. Discrimination in residential real estate-related transactions

(a) In general

It shall be unlawful for any person or other entity whose business includes engaging in residential real estate-related transactions to discriminate against any person in making available such a transaction, or in the terms or conditions of such a transaction, because of race, color, religion, sex, handicap, familial status, or national origin.

(b) "Residential real estate-related transaction" defined

As used in this section, the term "residential real estate-related transaction" means any of the following:

(1) The making or purchasing of loans or providing other financial assistance—

(A) for purchasing, constructing, improving, repairing, or maintaining a dwelling; or

(B) secured by residential real estate.

(2) The selling, brokering, or appraising of residential real property.

(c) Appraisal exemption

Nothing in this subchapter prohibits a person engaged in the business of furnishing appraisals of real property to take into consideration factors other than race, color, religion, national origin, sex, handicap, or familial status.

Excerpt from the Americans with Disabilities Act

42 U.S.C. § 12181. Definitions.

As used in this subchapter:

* * *

(7) Public accommodation

The following private entities are considered public accommodations for purposes of this subchapter, if the operations of such entities affect commerce—

(A) an inn, hotel, motel, or other place of lodging, except for an establishment located within a building that contains not more than five rooms for rent or hire and that is actually occupied by the proprietor of such establishment as the residence of such proprietor;

(B) a restaurant, bar, or other establishment serving food or drink;

(C) a motion picture house, theater, concert hall, stadium, or other place of exhibition or entertainment;

(D) an auditorium, convention center, lecture hall, or other place of public gathering;

(E) a bakery, grocery store, clothing store, hardware store, shopping center, or other sales or rental establishment;

(F) a laundromat, dry-cleaner, bank, barber shop, beauty shop, travel service, shoe repair service, funeral parlor, gas station, office of an accountant or lawyer, pharmacy, insurance office, professional office of a health care provider, hospital, or other service establishment;

(G) a terminal, depot, or other station used for specified public transportation;

(H) a museum, library, gallery, or other place of public display or collection;

(I) a park, zoo, amusement park, or other place of recreation;

(J) a nursery, elementary, secondary, undergraduate, or postgraduate private school, or other place of education;

(K) a day care center, senior citizen center, homeless shelter, food bank, adoption agency, or other social service center establishment; and

(L) a gymnasium, health spa, bowling alley, golf course, or other place of exercise or recreation.

* * *

42 U.S.C. § 12182. Prohibition of discrimination by public accommodations.

(a) General rule

No individual shall be discriminated against on the basis of disability in the full and equal enjoyment of the goods, services, facilities, privileges, advantages, or accommodations of any place of public accommodation by any person who owns, leases (or leases to), or operates a place of public accommodation.

(b) Construction

(1) General prohibition

(A) Activities

(i) Denial of participation

It shall be discriminatory to subject an individual or class of individuals on the basis of a disability or disabilities of such individual or class, directly, or through contractual, licensing, or other arrangements, to a denial of the opportunity of the individual or class to participate in or benefit from the goods, services, facilities, privileges, advantages, or accommodations of an entity.

(ii) Participation in unequal benefit

It shall be discriminatory to afford an individual or class of individuals, on the basis of a disability or disabilities of such individual or class, directly, or through contractual, licensing, or other arrangements with the opportunity to participate in or benefit from a good, service, facility, privilege, advantage, or accommodation that is not equal to that afforded to other individuals.

(iii) Separate benefit

It shall be discriminatory to provide an individual or class of individuals, on the basis of a disability or disabilities of such individual or class, directly, or through contractual, licensing, or other arrangements with a good, service, facility, privilege, advantage, or accommodation that is different or separate from that provided to other individuals, unless such action is necessary to provide the individual or class of individuals with a good, service, facility, privilege, advantage, or accommodation, or other opportunity that is as effective as that provided to others.

(iv) Individual or class of individuals

For purposes of clauses (i) through (iii) of this subparagraph, the term "individual or class of individuals" refers to the clients or customers of the covered public accommodation that enters into the contractual, licensing or other arrangement.

(B) Integrated settings

Goods, services, facilities, privileges, advantages, and accommodations shall be afforded to an individual with a disability in the most integrated setting appropriate to the needs of the individual.

(C) Opportunity to participate

Notwithstanding the existence of separate or different programs or activities provided in accordance with this section, an individual with a disability shall not be denied the opportunity to participate in such programs or activities that are not separate or different.

(D) Administrative methods

An individual or entity shall not, directly or through contractual or other arrangements, utilize standards or criteria or methods of administration—

(i) that have the effect of discriminating on the basis of disability; or

(ii) that perpetuate the discrimination of others who are subject to common administrative control.

(E) Association

It shall be discriminatory to exclude or otherwise deny equal goods, services, facilities, privileges, advantages, accommodations, or other opportunities to an individual or entity because of the known disability of an individual with whom the individual or entity is known to have a relationship or association.

(2) Specific prohibitions

(A) Discrimination

For purposes of subsection (a) of this section, discrimination includes—

(i) the imposition or application of eligibility criteria that screen out or tend to screen out an individual with a disability or any class of individuals with disabilities from fully and equally enjoying any goods, services, facilities, privileges, advantages, or accommodations, unless such criteria can be shown to be necessary for the provision of the goods, services, facilities, privileges, advantages, or accommodations being offered;

(ii) a failure to make reasonable modifications in policies, practices, or procedures, when such modifications are necessary to afford such goods, services, facilities, privileges, advantages, or accommodations to individuals with disabilities, unless the entity can demonstrate that making such modifications would fundamentally alter the nature of such goods, services, facilities, privileges, advantages, or accommodations;

(iii) a failure to take such steps as may be necessary to ensure that no individual with a disability is excluded, denied services, segregated or otherwise treated differently than other individuals because of the absence of auxiliary aids and services, unless the entity can demonstrate that taking such steps would fundamentally alter the nature of the good, service, facility, privilege, advantage, or accommodation being offered or would result in an undue burden;

(iv) a failure to remove architectural barriers, and communication barriers that are structural in nature, in existing facilities, and transportation barriers in existing vehicles and rail passenger cars used by an establishment for transporting individuals (not including barriers that can only be removed through the retrofitting of vehicles or rail passenger cars by the installation of a hydraulic or other lift), where such removal is readily achievable; and

(v) where an entity can demonstrate that the removal of a barrier under clause (iv) is not readily achievable, a failure to make such goods, services, facilities, privileges, advantages, or accommodations available through alternative methods if such methods are readily achievable.

* * *

Excerpt from the Civil Rights Act of 1866

42 U.S.C.A. § 1982

Property rights of citizens. All citizens of the United States shall have the same right, in every State and Territory, as is enjoyed by white citizens thereof to inherit, purchase, lease, sell, hold and convey real and personal property.

Selected Privacy Materials

18 U.S.C.A. § 2710. Wrongful disclosure of video tape rental or sale records

(a) Definitions.—For purposes of this section—

(1) the term "consumer" means any renter, purchaser, or subscriber of goods or services from a video tape service provider;

(2) the term "ordinary course of business" means only debt collection activities, order fulfillment, request processing, and the transfer of ownership;

(3) the term "personally identifiable information" includes information which identifies a person as having requested or obtained specific video materials or services from a video tape service provider; and

(4) the term "video tape service provider" means any person, engaged in the business, in or affecting interstate or foreign commerce, of rental, sale, or delivery of prerecorded video cassette tapes or similar audio visual materials, or any person or other entity to whom a disclosure is made under subparagraph (D) or (E) of subsection (b)(2), but only with respect to the information contained in the disclosure.

(b) Video tape rental and sale records.—(1) A video tape service provider who knowingly discloses, to any person, personally identifiable information concerning any consumer of such provider shall be liable to the aggrieved person for the relief provided in subsection (d).

(2) A video tape service provider may disclose personally identifiable information concerning any consumer—

(A) to the consumer;

(B) to any person with the informed, written consent (including through an electronic means using the Internet) of the consumer that—

(i) is in a form distinct and separate from any form setting forth other legal or financial obligations of the consumer;

(ii) at the election of the consumer—

(I) is given at the time the disclosure is sought; or

(II) is given in advance for a set period of time, not to exceed 2 years or until consent is withdrawn by the consumer, whichever is sooner; and

(iii) the video tape service provider has provided an opportunity, in a clear and conspicuous manner, for the consumer to withdraw on a case-by-case basis or to withdraw from ongoing disclosures, at the consumer's election;

(C) to a law enforcement agency pursuant to a warrant issued under the Federal Rules of Criminal Procedure, an equivalent State warrant, a grand jury subpoena, or a court order;

(D) to any person if the disclosure is solely of the names and addresses of consumers and if—

(i) the video tape service provider has provided the consumer with the opportunity, in a clear and conspicuous manner, to prohibit such disclosure; and

(ii) the disclosure does not identify the title, description, or subject matter of any video tapes or other audio visual material; however, the subject matter of such materials may be disclosed if the disclosure is for the exclusive use of marketing goods and services directly to the consumer;

(E) to any person if the disclosure is incident to the ordinary course of business of the video tape service provider; or

(F) pursuant to a court order, in a civil proceeding upon a showing of compelling need for the information that cannot be accommodated by any other means, if—

(i) the consumer is given reasonable notice, by the person seeking the disclosure, of the court proceeding relevant to the issuance of the court order; and

(ii) the consumer is afforded the opportunity to appear and contest the claim of the person seeking the disclosure.

If an order is granted pursuant to subparagraph (C) or (F), the court shall impose appropriate safeguards against unauthorized disclosure.

(3) Court orders authorizing disclosure under subparagraph (C) shall issue only with prior notice to the consumer and only if the law enforcement agency shows that there is probable cause to believe that the records or other information sought are relevant to a legitimate law enforcement inquiry. In the case of a State government authority, such a court order shall not issue if prohibited by the law of such State. A court issuing an order pursuant to this section, on a motion made promptly by the video tape service provider, may quash or modify such order if the information or records requested are unreasonably voluminous in nature or if compliance with such order otherwise would cause an unreasonable burden on such provider.

(c) Civil action.—**(1)** Any person aggrieved by any act of a person in violation of this section may bring a civil action in a United States district court.

(2) The court may award—

(A) actual damages but not less than liquidated damages in an amount of $2,500;

(B) punitive damages;

(C) reasonable attorneys' fees and other litigation costs reasonably incurred; and

(D) such other preliminary and equitable relief as the court determines to be appropriate.

(3) No action may be brought under this subsection unless such action is begun within 2 years from the date of the act complained of or the date of discovery.

(4) No liability shall result from lawful disclosure permitted by this section.

(d) Personally identifiable information.—Personally identifiable information obtained in any manner other than as provided in this section shall not be received in evidence in any trial, hearing, arbitration, or other proceeding in or before any court, grand jury, department, officer, agency, regulatory body, legislative committee, or other authority of the United States, a State, or a political subdivision of a State.

(e) Destruction of old records.—A person subject to this section shall destroy personally identifiable information as soon as practicable, but no later than one year from the date the information is no longer necessary for the purpose for which it was collected and there are no pending requests or orders for access to such information under subsection (b)(2) or (c)(2) or pursuant to a court order.

(f) Preemption.—The provisions of this section preempt only the provisions of State or local law that require disclosure prohibited by this section.

California Consumer Privacy Act of 2018*

Cal.Civ.Code §§ 1798.100 et seq.

Table of Sections

§ 1798.100. Consumer rights regarding personal information collection by businesses; disclosure; information requests; retention of personal information collected for single, one-time use transaction

(a) A consumer shall have the right to request that a business that collects a consumer's personal information disclose to that consumer the categories and specific pieces of personal information the business has collected.

(b) A business that collects a consumer's personal information shall, at or before the point of collection, inform consumers as to the categories of personal information to be collected and the purposes for which the categories of personal information shall be used. A business shall not collect additional categories of personal information or use personal information collected for additional purposes without providing the consumer with notice consistent with this section.

(c) A business shall provide the information specified in subdivision (a) to a consumer only upon receipt of a verifiable consumer request.

(d) A business that receives a verifiable consumer request from a consumer to access personal information shall promptly take steps to disclose and deliver, free of charge to the consumer, the personal information required by this section. The information may be delivered by mail or electronically, and if provided electronically, the information shall be in a portable and, to the extent technically feasible, readily useable format that allows the consumer to transmit this information to another entity without hindrance. A business may provide personal information to a consumer at any time, but shall not be required to provide personal information to a consumer more than twice in a 12-month period.

(e) This section shall not require a business to retain any personal information collected for a single, one-time transaction, if such information is not sold or retained by the business or to reidentify or otherwise link information that is not maintained in a manner that would be considered personal information.

§ 1798.105. Consumer rights regarding deletion of personal information collected by businesses; disclosure; deletion requests; exceptions

(a) A consumer shall have the right to request that a business delete any personal information about the consumer which the business has collected from the consumer.

(b) A business that collects personal information about consumers shall disclose, pursuant to Section 1798.130, the consumer's rights to request the deletion of the consumer's personal information.

(c) A business that receives a verifiable consumer request from a consumer to delete the consumer's personal information pursuant to subdivision (a) of this section shall delete the consumer's personal information from its records and direct any service providers to delete the consumer's personal information from their records.

(d) A business or a service provider shall not be required to comply with a consumer's request to delete the consumer's personal information if it is necessary for the business or service provider to maintain the consumer's personal information in order to:

(1) Complete the transaction for which the personal information was collected, fulfill the terms of a written warranty or product recall conducted in accordance with federal law, provide a good or service requested by the consumer, or reasonably anticipated within the context of a business' ongoing business relationship with the consumer, or otherwise perform a contract between the business and the consumer.

(2) Detect security incidents, protect against malicious, deceptive, fraudulent, or illegal activity; or prosecute those responsible for that activity.

(3) Debug to identify and repair errors that impair existing intended functionality.

(4) Exercise free speech, ensure the right of another consumer to exercise that consumer's right of free speech, or exercise another right provided for by law.

(5) Comply with the California Electronic Communications Privacy Act pursuant to Chapter 3.6 (commencing with Section 1546) of Title 12 of Part 2 of the Penal Code.

(6) Engage in public or peer-reviewed scientific, historical, or statistical research in the public interest that adheres to all other applicable ethics and privacy laws, when the business' deletion of the information is likely to render impossible or seriously impair the achievement of such research, if the consumer has provided informed consent.

(7) To enable solely internal uses that are reasonably aligned with the expectations of the consumer based on the consumer's relationship with the business.

(8) Comply with a legal obligation.

(9) Otherwise use the consumer's personal information, internally, in a lawful manner that is compatible with the context in which the consumer provided the information.

§ 1798.110. Businesses collecting personal information; consumer rights regarding disclosure of categories and uses of personal information; duties of business

(a) A consumer shall have the right to request that a business that collects personal information about the consumer disclose to the consumer the following:

(1) The categories of personal information it has collected about that consumer.

(2) The categories of sources from which the personal information is collected.

(3) The business or commercial purpose for collecting or selling personal information.

(4) The categories of third parties with whom the business shares personal information.

(5) The specific pieces of personal information it has collected about that consumer.

(b) A business that collects personal information about a consumer shall disclose to the consumer, pursuant to paragraph (3) of subdivision (a) of Section 1798.130, the information specified in subdivision (a) upon receipt of a verifiable consumer request from the consumer.

(c) A business that collects personal information about consumers shall disclose, pursuant to subparagraph (B) of paragraph (5) of subdivision (a) of Section 1798.130:

(1) The categories of personal information it has collected about consumers.

(2) The categories of sources from which the personal information is collected.

(3) The business or commercial purpose for collecting or selling personal information.

(4) The categories of third parties with whom the business shares personal information.

(5) That a consumer has the right to request the specific pieces of personal information the business has collected about that consumer.

(d) This section does not require a business to do the following:

(1) Retain any personal information about a consumer collected for a single one-time transaction if, in the ordinary course of business, that information about the consumer is not retained.

(2) Reidentify or otherwise link any data that, in the ordinary course of business, is not maintained in a manner that would be considered personal information.

§ 1798.115. Businesses selling personal information or disclosing for business purpose; consumer rights regarding disclosure of categories and uses of personal information; duties of business

(a) A consumer shall have the right to request that a business that sells the consumer's personal information, or that discloses it for a business purpose, disclose to that consumer:

(1) The categories of personal information that the business collected about the consumer.

(2) The categories of personal information that the business sold about the consumer and the categories of third parties to whom the personal information was sold, by category or categories of personal information for each category of third parties to whom the personal information was sold.

(3) The categories of personal information that the business disclosed about the consumer for a business purpose.

(b) A business that sells personal information about a consumer, or that discloses a consumer's personal information for a business purpose, shall disclose, pursuant to paragraph (4) of subdivision (a) of Section 1798.130, the information specified in subdivision (a) to the consumer upon receipt of a verifiable consumer request from the consumer.

(c) A business that sells consumers' personal information, or that discloses consumers' personal information for a business purpose, shall disclose, pursuant to subparagraph (C) of paragraph (5) of subdivision (a) of Section 1798.130:

(1) The category or categories of consumers' personal information it has sold, or if the business has not sold consumers' personal information, it shall disclose that fact.

(2) The category or categories of consumers' personal information it has disclosed for a business purpose, or if the business has not disclosed the consumers' personal information for a business purpose, it shall disclose that fact.

(d) A third party shall not sell personal information about a consumer that has been sold to the third party by a business unless the consumer has received explicit notice and is provided an opportunity to exercise the right to opt-out pursuant to Section 1798.120.

§ 1798.120. Consumer right to opt-out; notice to consumer; sale of personal information prohibited; consumers less than 16 years of age

(a) A consumer shall have the right, at any time, to direct a business that sells personal information about the consumer to third parties not to sell the consumer's personal information. This right may be referred to as the right to opt-out.

(b) A business that sells consumers' personal information to third parties shall provide notice to consumers, pursuant to subdivision (a) of Section 1798.135, that this information may be sold and that consumers have the "right to opt-out" of the sale of their personal information.

(c) Notwithstanding subdivision (a), a business shall not sell the personal information of consumers if the business has actual knowledge that the consumer is less than 16 years of age, unless the consumer, in the case of consumers at least 13 years of age and less than 16 years of age, or the consumer's parent or guardian, in the case of consumers who are less than 13 years of age, has affirmatively authorized the sale of the consumer's personal information. A business that willfully disregards the consumer's age shall be deemed to have had actual knowledge of the consumer's age. This right may be referred to as the "right to opt-in."

(d) A business that has received direction from a consumer not to sell the consumer's personal information or, in the case of a minor consumer's personal information has not received consent to sell the minor consumer's personal information shall be prohibited, pursuant to paragraph (4) of subdivision (a) of Section 1798.135, from selling the consumer's personal information after its receipt of the consumer's direction, unless the consumer subsequently provides express authorization for the sale of the consumer's personal information.

§ 1798.125. Discrimination prohibited; financial incentives

(a)(1) A business shall not discriminate against a consumer because the consumer exercised any of the consumer's rights under this title, including, but not limited to, by:

(A) Denying goods or services to the consumer.

(B) Charging different prices or rates for goods or services, including through the use of discounts or other benefits or imposing penalties.

(C) Providing a different level or quality of goods or services to the consumer.

(D) Suggesting that the consumer will receive a different price or rate for goods or services or a different level or quality of goods or services.

(2) Nothing in this subdivision prohibits a business from charging a consumer a different price or rate, or from providing a different level or quality of goods or services to the consumer, if that difference is reasonably related to the value provided to the business by the consumer's data.

(b)(1) A business may offer financial incentives, including payments to consumers as compensation, for the collection of personal information, the sale of personal information, or the deletion of personal information. A business may also offer a different price, rate, level, or quality of goods or services to the consumer if that price or difference is directly related to the value provided to the business by the consumer's data.

(2) A business that offers any financial incentives pursuant to this subdivision shall notify consumers of the financial incentives pursuant to Section 1798.130

(3) A business may enter a consumer into a financial incentive program only if the consumer gives the business prior opt-in consent pursuant to Section 1798.130 that clearly describes the material terms of the financial incentive program, and which may be revoked by the consumer at any time.

(4) A business shall not use financial incentive practices that are unjust, unreasonable, coercive, or usurious in nature.

§ 1798.130. Businesses collecting personal information; compliance requirements

(a) In order to comply with Sections 1798.100, 1798.105, 1798.110, 1798.115, and 1798.125, a business shall, in a form that is reasonably accessible to consumers:

(1)(A) Make available to consumers two or more designated methods for submitting requests for information required to be disclosed pursuant to Sections 1798.110 and 1798.115, including, at a minimum, a toll-free telephone number. A business that operates exclusively online and has a direct relationship with a consumer from whom it collects personal information shall only be required to provide an email address for submitting requests for information required to be disclosed pursuant to Sections 1798.110 and 1798.115.

(B) If the business maintains an internet website, make the internet website available to consumers to submit requests for information required to be disclosed pursuant to Sections 1798.110 and 1798.115.

(2) Disclose and deliver the required information to a consumer free of charge within 45 days of receiving a verifiable consumer request from the consumer. The business shall promptly take steps to determine whether the request is a verifiable consumer request, but this shall not extend the business' duty to disclose and deliver the information within 45 days of receipt of the consumer's request. The time period to provide the required information may be extended once by an additional 45 days when reasonably necessary, provided the consumer is provided notice of the extension within the first 45-day period. The disclosure shall cover the 12-month period preceding the business' receipt of the verifiable consumer request and shall be made in writing and delivered through the consumer's account with the business, if the consumer maintains an account with the business, or by mail or electronically at the consumer's option if the consumer does not maintain an account with the business, in a readily useable format that allows the consumer to transmit this information from one entity to another entity without hindrance. The business may require authentication of the consumer that is reasonable in light of the nature of the personal information requested, but shall not require the consumer to create an account with the business in order to make a verifiable consumer request. If the consumer maintains an account with the business, the business may require the consumer to submit the request through that account.

(3) For purposes of subdivision (b) of Section 1798.110:

(A) To identify the consumer, associate the information provided by the consumer in the verifiable consumer request to any personal information previously collected by the business about the consumer.

(B) Identify by category or categories the personal information collected about the consumer in the preceding 12 months by reference to the enumerated category or categories in subdivision (c) that most closely describes the personal information collected.

(4) For purposes of subdivision (b) of Section 1798.115

(A) Identify the consumer and associate the information provided by the consumer in the verifiable consumer request to any personal information previously collected by the business about the consumer.

(B) Identify by category or categories the personal information of the consumer that the business sold in the preceding 12 months by reference to the enumerated category in subdivision (c) that most closely describes the personal information, and provide the categories of third parties to whom the consumer's personal information was sold in the preceding 12 months by reference to the enumerated category or categories in subdivision (c) that most closely describes the personal information sold. The business shall disclose the information in a list that is separate from a list generated for the purposes of subparagraph (C).

(C) Identify by category or categories the personal information of the consumer that the business disclosed for a business purpose in the preceding 12 months by reference to the enumerated category or categories in subdivision (c) that most closely describes the personal information, and provide the categories of third parties to whom the consumer's personal information was disclosed for a business purpose in the preceding 12 months by reference to the enumerated category or categories in subdivision (c) that most closely describes the personal information disclosed. The business shall disclose the information in a list that is separate from a list generated for the purposes of subparagraph (B).

(5) Disclose the following information in its online privacy policy or policies if the business has an online privacy policy or policies and in any California-specific description of consumers' privacy rights, or if the business does not maintain those policies, on its internet website and update that information at least once every 12 months:

(A) A description of a consumer's rights pursuant to Sections 1798.100, 1798.105, 1798.110, 1798.115, and 1798.125 and one or more designated methods for submitting requests.

(B) For purposes of subdivision (c) of Section 1798.110, a list of the categories of personal information it has collected about consumers in the preceding 12 months by reference to the enumerated category or categories in subdivision (c) that most closely describe the personal information collected.

(C) For purposes of paragraphs (1) and (2) of subdivision (c) of Section 1798.115, two separate lists:

(i) A list of the categories of personal information it has sold about consumers in the preceding 12 months by reference to the enumerated category or categories in subdivision (c) that most closely describe the personal information sold, or if the business has not sold consumers' personal information in the preceding 12 months, the business shall disclose that fact.

(ii) A list of the categories of personal information it has disclosed about consumers for a business purpose in the preceding 12 months by reference to the enumerated category in subdivision (c) that most closely describe the personal information disclosed, or if the business has not disclosed consumers' personal information for a business purpose in the preceding 12 months, the business shall disclose that fact.

(6) Ensure that all individuals responsible for handling consumer inquiries about the business' privacy practices or the business' compliance with this title are informed of all requirements in Sections 1798.100, 1798.105, 1798.110, 1798.115, and 1798.125, and this section, and how to direct consumers to exercise their rights under those sections.

(7) Use any personal information collected from the consumer in connection with the business' verification of the consumer's request solely for the purposes of verification.

(b) A business is not obligated to provide the information required by Sections 1798.110 and 1798.115 to the same consumer more than twice in a 12-month period.

(c) The categories of personal information required to be disclosed pursuant to Sections 1798.110 and 1798.115 shall follow the definition of personal information in Section 1798.140.

§ 1798.135. Businesses subject to consumer right to opt-out; compliance requirements

(a) A business that is required to comply with Section 1798.120 shall, in a form that is reasonably accessible to consumers:

(1) Provide a clear and conspicuous link on the business's Internet homepage, titled "Do Not Sell My Personal Information," to an Internet Web page that enables a consumer, or a person authorized by the consumer, to opt-out of the sale of the consumer's personal information. A business shall not require a consumer to create an account in order to direct the business not to sell the consumer's personal information.

(2) Include a description of a consumer's rights pursuant to Section 1798.120, along with a separate link to the "Do Not Sell My Personal Information" Internet Web page in:

(A) Its online privacy policy or policies if the business has an online privacy policy or policies.

(B) Any California-specific description of consumers' privacy rights.

(3) Ensure that all individuals responsible for handling consumer inquiries about the business's privacy practices or the business's compliance with this title are informed of all requirements in Section 1798.120 and this section and how to direct consumers to exercise their rights under those sections.

(4) For consumers who exercise their right to opt-out of the sale of their personal information, refrain from selling personal information collected by the business about the consumer.

(5) For a consumer who has opted-out of the sale of the consumer's personal information, respect the consumer's decision to opt-out for at least 12 months before requesting that the consumer authorize the sale of the consumer's personal information.

(6) Use any personal information collected from the consumer in connection with the submission of the consumer's opt-out request solely for the purposes of complying with the opt-out request.

(b) Nothing in this title shall be construed to require a business to comply with the title by including the required links and text on the homepage that the business makes available to the public generally, if the business maintains a separate and additional homepage that is dedicated to California consumers and that includes the required links and text, and the business takes reasonable steps to ensure that California consumers are directed to the homepage for California consumers and not the homepage made available to the public generally.

(c) A consumer may authorize another person solely to opt-out of the sale of the consumer's personal information on the consumer's behalf, and a business shall comply with an opt-out request received from a person authorized by the consumer to act on the consumer's behalf, pursuant to regulations adopted by the Attorney General.

§ 1798.140. Definitions

For purposes of this title:

(a) "Aggregate consumer information" means information that relates to a group or category of consumers, from which individual consumer identities have been removed, that is not linked or reasonably linkable to any consumer or household, including via a device. "Aggregate consumer information" does not mean one or more individual consumer records that have been de-identified.

(b) "Biometric information" means an individual's physiological, biological, or behavioral characteristics, including an individual's deoxyribonucleic acid (DNA), that can be used, singly or in combination with each other or with other identifying data, to establish individual identity. Biometric information includes, but is not limited to, imagery of the iris, retina, fingerprint, face, hand, palm, vein patterns, and voice recordings, from which an identifier template, such as a faceprint, a minutiae template, or a voiceprint, can be extracted, and keystroke patterns or rhythms, gait patterns or rhythms, and sleep, health, or exercise data that contain identifying information.

(c) "Business" means:

(1) A sole proprietorship, partnership, limited liability company, corporation, association, or other legal entity that is organized or operated for the profit or financial benefit of its shareholders or other owners that collects consumers' personal information or on the behalf of which that information is collected and that alone, or jointly with others, determines the purposes and means of the processing of consumers' personal information, that does business in the State of California, and that satisfies one or more of the following thresholds:

(A) Has annual gross revenues in excess of twenty-five million dollars ($25,000,000), as adjusted pursuant to paragraph (5) of subdivision (a) of Section 1798.185.

(B) Alone or in combination, annually buys, receives for the business's commercial purposes, sells, or shares for commercial purposes, alone or in combination, the personal information of 50,000 or more consumers, households, or devices.

(C) Derives 50 percent or more of its annual revenues from selling consumers' personal information.

(2) Any entity that controls or is controlled by a business as defined in paragraph (1) and that shares common branding with the business. "Control" or "controlled" means ownership of, or the power to vote, more than 50 percent of the outstanding shares of any class of voting security of a business; control in any manner over the election of a majority of the directors, or of individuals exercising similar functions; or the power to exercise a controlling influence over the management of a company. "Common branding" means a shared name, servicemark, or trademark.

(d) "Business purpose" means the use of personal information for the business's or a service provider's operational purposes, or other notified purposes, provided that the use of personal information shall be reasonably necessary and proportionate to achieve the operational purpose for which the personal information was collected or processed or for another operational purpose that is compatible with the context in which the personal information was collected. Business purposes are:

(1) Auditing related to a current interaction with the consumer and concurrent transactions, including, but not limited to, counting ad impressions to unique visitors, verifying positioning and quality of ad impressions, and auditing compliance with this specification and other standards.

(2) Detecting security incidents, protecting against malicious, deceptive, fraudulent, or illegal activity, and prosecuting those responsible for that activity.

(3) Debugging to identify and repair errors that impair existing intended functionality.

(4) Short-term, transient use, provided that the personal information is not disclosed to another third party and is not used to build a profile about a consumer or otherwise alter an individual consumer's experience outside the current interaction, including, but not limited to, the contextual customization of ads shown as part of the same interaction.

(5) Performing services on behalf of the business or service provider, including maintaining or servicing accounts, providing customer service, processing or fulfilling orders and transactions, verifying customer information, processing payments, providing financing, providing advertising or marketing services, providing analytic services, or providing similar services on behalf of the business or service provider.

(6) Undertaking internal research for technological development and demonstration.

(7) Undertaking activities to verify or maintain the quality or safety of a service or device that is owned, manufactured, manufactured for, or controlled by the business, and to improve, upgrade, or enhance the service or device that is owned, manufactured, manufactured for, or controlled by the business.

(e) "Collects," "collected," or "collection" means buying, renting, gathering, obtaining, receiving, or accessing any personal information pertaining to a consumer by any means. This includes receiving information from the consumer, either actively or passively, or by observing the consumer's behavior.

(f) "Commercial purposes" means to advance a person's commercial or economic interests, such as by inducing another person to buy, rent, lease, join, subscribe to, provide, or exchange products, goods, property, information, or services, or enabling or effecting, directly or indirectly, a commercial transaction. "Commercial purposes" do not include for the purpose of engaging in speech that state or federal courts have recognized as noncommercial speech, including political speech and journalism.

(g) "Consumer" means a natural person who is a California resident, as defined in Section 17014 of Title 18 of the California Code of Regulations, as that section read on September 1, 2017, however identified, including by any unique identifier.

(h) "Deidentified" means information that cannot reasonably identify, relate to, describe, be capable of being associated with, or be linked, directly or indirectly, to a particular consumer, provided that a business that uses deidentified information:

(1) Has implemented technical safeguards that prohibit reidentification of the consumer to whom the information may pertain.

(2) Has implemented business processes that specifically prohibit reidentification of the information.

(3) Has implemented business processes to prevent inadvertent release of deidentified information.

(4) Makes no attempt to reidentify the information.

(i) "Designated methods for submitting requests" means a mailing address, email address, internet web page, internet web portal, toll-free telephone number, or other applicable contact information, whereby consumers may submit a request or direction under this title, and any new, consumer-friendly means of contacting a business, as approved by the Attorney General pursuant to Section 1798.185.

(j) "Device" means any physical object that is capable of connecting to the internet, directly or indirectly, or to another device.

(k) "Health insurance information" means a consumer's insurance policy number or subscriber identification number, any unique identifier used by a health insurer to identify the consumer, or any information in the consumer's application and claims history, including any appeals records, if the information is linked or reasonably linkable to a consumer or household, including via a device, by a business or service provider.

(l) **"Homepage"** means the introductory page of an internet website and any internet web page where personal information is collected. In the case of an online service, such as a mobile application, homepage means the application's platform page or download page, a link within the application, such as from the application configuration, "About," "Information," or settings page, and any other location that allows consumers to review the notice required by subdivision (a) of Section 1798.135, including, but not limited to, before downloading the application.

(m) "Infer" or "inference" means the derivation of information, data, assumptions, or conclusions from facts, evidence, or another source of information or data.

(n) "Person" means an individual, proprietorship, firm, partnership, joint venture, syndicate, business trust, company, corporation, limited liability company, association, committee, and any other organization or group of persons acting in concert.

(*o*)(1) "Personal information" means information that identifies, relates to, describes, is reasonably capable of being associated with, or could reasonably be linked, directly or indirectly, with a particular consumer or household. Personal information includes, but is not limited to, the following if it identifies, relates to, describes, is reasonably capable of being associated with, or could be reasonably linked, directly or indirectly, with a particular consumer or household:

(A) Identifiers such as a real name, alias, postal address, unique personal identifier, online identifier, internet protocol address, email address, account name, social security number, driver's license number, passport number, or other similar identifiers.

(B) Any categories of personal information described in subdivision (e) of Section 1798.80.

(C) Characteristics of protected classifications under California or federal law.

(D) Commercial information, including records of personal property, products or services purchased, obtained, or considered, or other purchasing or consuming histories or tendencies.

(E) Biometric information

(F) Internet or other electronic network activity information, including, but not limited to, browsing history, search history, and information regarding a consumer's interaction with an internet website, application, or advertisement.

(G) Geolocation data.

(H) Audio, electronic, visual, thermal, olfactory, or similar information.

(I) Professional or employment-related information.

(J) Education information, defined as information that is not publicly available personally identifiable information as defined in the Family Educational Rights and Privacy Act (20 U.S.C. Sec. 1232g; 34 C.F.R. Part 99).

(K) Inferences drawn from any of the information identified in this subdivision to create a profile about a consumer reflecting the consumer's preferences, characteristics, psychological trends, predispositions, behavior, attitudes, intelligence, abilities, and aptitudes.

(2) "Personal information" does not include publicly available information. For purposes of this paragraph, "publicly available" means information that is lawfully made available from federal, state, or local government records. "Publicly available" does not mean biometric information collected by a business about a consumer without the consumer's knowledge.

(3) "Personal information" does not include consumer information that is deidentified or aggregate consumer information.

(p) "Probabilistic identifier" means the identification of a consumer or a device to a degree of certainty of more probable than not based on any categories of personal information included in, or similar to, the categories enumerated in the definition of personal information.

(q) "Processing" means any operation or set of operations that are performed on personal data or on sets of personal data, whether or not by automated means.

(r) "Pseudonymize" or "Pseudonymization" means the processing of personal information in a manner that renders the personal information no longer attributable to a specific consumer without the use of additional information, provided that the additional information is kept separately and is subject to technical and organizational measures to ensure that the personal information is not attributed to an identified or identifiable consumer.

(s) "Research" means scientific, systematic study and observation, including basic research or applied research that is in the public interest and that adheres to all other applicable ethics and privacy laws or studies conducted in the public interest in the area of public health. Research with personal information that may have been collected from a consumer in the course of the consumer's interactions with a business's service or device for other purposes shall be:

(1) Compatible with the business purpose for which the personal information was collected.

(2) Subsequently pseudonymized and deidentified, or deidentified and in the aggregate, such that the information cannot reasonably identify, relate to, describe, be capable of being associated with, or be linked, directly or indirectly, to a particular consumer.

(3) Made subject to technical safeguards that prohibit reidentification of the consumer to whom the information may pertain.

(4) Subject to business processes that specifically prohibit reidentification of the information.

(5) Made subject to business processes to prevent inadvertent release of deidentified information.

(6) Protected from any reidentification attempts.

(7) Used solely for research purposes that are compatible with the context in which the personal information was collected.

(8) Not be used for any commercial purpose.

(9) Subjected by the business conducting the research to additional security controls that limit access to the research data to only those individuals in a business as are necessary to carry out the research purpose.

(t)(1) "Sell," "selling," "sale," or "sold," means selling, renting, releasing, disclosing, disseminating, making available, transferring, or otherwise communicating orally, in writing, or by electronic or other means, a consumer's personal information by the business to another business or a third party for monetary or other valuable consideration.

(2) For purposes of this title, a business does not sell personal information when:

(A) A consumer uses or directs the business to intentionally disclose personal information or uses the business to intentionally interact with a third party, provided the third party does not also sell the personal information, unless that disclosure would be consistent with the provisions of this title. An intentional interaction occurs when the consumer intends to interact with the third party, via one or more deliberate interactions. Hovering over, muting, pausing, or closing a given piece of content does not constitute a consumer's intent to interact with a third party.

(B) The business uses or shares an identifier for a consumer who has opted out of the sale of the consumer's personal information for the purposes of alerting third parties that the consumer has opted out of the sale of the consumer's personal information.

(C) The business uses or shares with a service provider personal information of a consumer that is necessary to perform a business purpose if both of the following conditions are met:

(i) The business has provided notice of that information being used or shared in its terms and conditions consistent with Section 1798.135.

(ii) The service provider does not further collect, sell, or use the personal information of the consumer except as necessary to perform the business purpose.

(D) The business transfers to a third party the personal information of a consumer as an asset that is part of a merger, acquisition, bankruptcy, or other transaction in which the third party assumes control of all or part of the business, provided that information is used or shared consistently with Sections 1798.110 and 1798.115. If a third party materially alters how it uses or shares the personal information of a consumer in a manner that is materially inconsistent with the promises made at the time of collection, it shall provide prior notice of the new or changed practice to the consumer. The notice shall be sufficiently prominent and robust to ensure that existing consumers can easily exercise their choices consistently with Section 1798.120. This subparagraph does not authorize a business to make material, retroactive privacy policy changes or make other changes in their privacy policy in a manner that would violate the Unfair and Deceptive Practices Act (Chapter 5 (commencing with Section 17200) of Part 2 of Division 7 of the Business and Professions Code).

(u) "Service" or "services" means work, labor, and services, including services furnished in connection with the sale or repair of goods.

(v) "Service provider" means a sole proprietorship, partnership, limited liability company, corporation, association, or other legal entity that is organized or operated for the profit or financial benefit of its shareholders or other owners, that processes information on behalf of a business and to which the business discloses a consumer's personal information for a business purpose pursuant to a written contract, provided that the contract prohibits the entity receiving the information from retaining, using, or disclosing the personal information for any purpose other than for the specific purpose of performing the services specified in the contract for the business, or as otherwise permitted by this title, including retaining, using, or disclosing the personal information for a commercial purpose other than providing the services specified in the contract with the business.

(w) "Third party" means a person who is not any of the following:

(1) The business that collects personal information from consumers under this title.

(2)(A) A person to whom the business discloses a consumer's personal information for a business purpose pursuant to a written contract, provided that the contract:

(i) Prohibits the person receiving the personal information from:

(I) Selling the personal information.

(II) Retaining, using, or disclosing the personal information for any purpose other than for the specific purpose of performing the services specified in the contract, including retaining, using, or disclosing the personal information for a commercial purpose other than providing the services specified in the contract.

(III) Retaining, using, or disclosing the information outside of the direct business relationship between the person and the business.

(ii) Includes a certification made by the person receiving the personal information that the person understands the restrictions in subparagraph (A) and will comply with them.

(B) A person covered by this paragraph that violates any of the restrictions set forth in this title shall be liable for the violations. A business that discloses personal information to a person covered by this paragraph in compliance with this paragraph shall not be liable under this title if the person receiving the personal information uses it in violation of the restrictions set forth in this title, provided that, at the time of disclosing the personal information, the business does not have actual knowledge, or reason to believe, that the person intends to commit such a violation.

(x) "Unique identifier" or "Unique personal identifier" means a persistent identifier that can be used to recognize a consumer, a family, or a device that is linked to a consumer or family, over time and across different services, including, but not limited to, a device identifier; an Internet Protocol address; cookies, beacons, pixel tags, mobile ad identifiers, or similar technology; customer number, unique pseudonym, or user alias; telephone numbers, or other forms of persistent or probabilistic identifiers that can be used to identify a particular consumer or device. For purposes of this subdivision, "family" means a custodial parent or guardian and any minor children over which the parent or guardian has custody.

(y) "Verifiable consumer request" means a request that is made by a consumer, by a consumer on behalf of the consumer's minor child, or by a natural person or a person registered with the Secretary of State, authorized by the consumer to act on the consumer's behalf, and that the business can reasonably verify, pursuant to regulations adopted by the Attorney General pursuant to paragraph (7) of subdivision (a) of Section 1798.185 to be the consumer about whom the business has collected personal information. A business is not obligated to provide information to the consumer pursuant to Sections 1798.100, 1798.105, 1798.110, and 1798.115 if the business cannot verify, pursuant to this subdivision and regulations adopted by the Attorney General pursuant to paragraph (7) of subdivision (a) of Section 1798.185, that the consumer making the request is the consumer about whom the business has collected information or is a person authorized by the consumer to act on such consumer's behalf.

§ 1798.145. Effect of obligations imposed on businesses; application of title

(a) The obligations imposed on businesses by this title shall not restrict a business' ability to:

(1) Comply with federal, state, or local laws.

(2) Comply with a civil, criminal, or regulatory inquiry, investigation, subpoena, or summons by federal, state, or local authorities.

(3) Cooperate with law enforcement agencies concerning conduct or activity that the business, service provider, or third party reasonably and in good faith believes may violate federal, state, or local law.

(4) Exercise or defend legal claims.

(5) Collect, use, retain, sell, or disclose consumer information that is deidentified or in the aggregate consumer information.

(6) Collect or sell a consumer's personal information if every aspect of that commercial conduct takes place wholly outside of California. For purposes of this title, commercial conduct takes place wholly outside of California if the business collected that information while the consumer was outside of California, no part of the sale of the consumer's personal information occurred in California, and no personal information collected while the consumer was in California is sold. This paragraph shall not permit a business from storing, including on a device, personal information about a consumer when the consumer is in California and then collecting that personal information when the consumer and stored personal information is outside of California.

(b) The obligations imposed on businesses by Sections 1798.110 to 1798.135, inclusive, shall not apply where compliance by the business with the title would violate an evidentiary privilege under California law and shall not prevent a business from providing the personal information of a consumer to a person covered by an evidentiary privilege under California law as part of a privileged communication.

(c)(1) This title shall not apply to any of the following:

(A) Medical information governed by the Confidentiality of Medical Information Act (Part 2.6 (commencing with Section 56) of Division 1) or protected health information that is collected by a covered entity or business associate governed by the privacy, security, and breach notification rules issued by the United States Department of Health and Human Services, Parts 160 and 164 of Title 45 of the Code of Federal Regulations, established pursuant to the Health Insurance Portability and Accountability Act of 1996 (Public Law 104-191) and the Health Information Technology for Economic and Clinical Health Act (Public Law 111-5).

(B) A provider of health care governed by the Confidentiality of Medical Information Act (Part 2.6 (commencing with Section 56) of Division 1) or a covered entity governed by the privacy, security, and breach notification rules issued by the United States Department of Health and Human Services, Parts 160 and 164 of Title 45 of the Code of Federal Regulations, established pursuant to the Health Insurance Portability and Accountability Act of 1996 (Public Law 104-191), to the extent the provider or covered entity maintains patient information in the same manner as medical information or protected health information as described in subparagraph (A) of this section.

(C) Information collected as part of a clinical trial subject to the Federal Policy for the Protection of Human Subjects, also known as the Common Rule, pursuant to good clinical practice guidelines issued by the International Council for Harmonisation or pursuant to human subject protection requirements of the United States Food and Drug Administration.

(2) For purposes of this subdivision, the definitions of "medical information" and "provider of health care" in Section 56.05 shall apply and the definitions of "business associate," "covered entity," and "protected health information" in Section 160.103 of Title 45 of the Code of Federal Regulations shall apply.

(d)(1) This title shall not apply to an activity involving the collection, maintenance, disclosure, sale, communication, or use of any personal information bearing on a consumer's credit worthiness, credit standing, credit capacity, character, general reputation, personal characteristics, or mode of living by a consumer reporting agency, as defined in subdivision (f) of Section 1681a of Title 15 of the United States Code, by a furnisher of information, as set forth in Section 1681s-2 of Title 15 of the United States Code, who provides information for use in a consumer report, as defined in subdivision (d) of Section 1681a of Title 15 of the United States Code, and by a user of a consumer report as set forth in Section 1681b of Title 15 of the United States Code.

(2) Paragraph (1) shall apply only to the extent that such activity involving the collection, maintenance, disclosure, sale, communication, or use of such information by that agency, furnisher, or user is subject to regulation under the Fair Credit Reporting Act, section 1681 et seq., Title 15 of the United States Code and the information is not used, communicated, disclosed, or sold except as authorized by the Fair Credit Reporting Act.

(3) This subdivision shall not apply to Section 1798.150.

(e) This title shall not apply to personal information collected, processed, sold, or disclosed pursuant to the federal Gramm-Leach-Bliley Act (Public Law 106-102), and implementing regulations, or the California Financial Information Privacy Act (Division 1.4 (commencing with Section 4050) of the Financial Code). This subdivision shall not apply to Section 1798.150.

(f) This title shall not apply to personal information collected, processed, sold, or disclosed pursuant to the Driver's Privacy Protection Act of 1994 (18 U.S.C. Sec. 2721 et seq.). This subdivision shall not apply to Section 1798.150.

(g)(1) Section 1798.120 shall not apply to vehicle information or ownership information retained or shared between a new motor vehicle dealer, as defined in Section 426 of the Vehicle Code, and the vehicle's manufacturer, as defined in Section 672 of the Vehicle Code, if the vehicle or ownership information is shared for the purpose of effectuating, or in anticipation of effectuating, a vehicle repair covered by a vehicle warranty or a recall conducted pursuant to Sections 30118 to 30120, inclusive, of Title 49 of the United States Code, provided that the new motor vehicle dealer or vehicle manufacturer with which that vehicle information or ownership information is shared does not sell, share, or use that information for any other purpose.

(2) For purposes of this subdivision:

(A) **"Vehicle information"** means the vehicle information number, make, model, year, and odometer reading.

(B) **"Ownership information"** means the name or names of the registered owner or owners and the contact information for the owner or owners.

(h)(1) This title shall not apply to any of the following:

(A) Personal information that is collected by a business about a natural person in the course of the natural person acting as a job applicant to, an employee of, owner of, director of, officer of, medical staff member of, or contractor of that business to the extent that the natural person's personal information is collected and used by the business solely within the context of the natural person's role or former role as a job applicant to, an employee of, owner of, director of, officer of, medical staff member of, or a contractor of that business.

(B) Personal information that is collected by a business that is emergency contact information of the natural person acting as a job applicant to, an employee of, owner of, director of, officer of, medical staff member of, or contractor of that business to the extent that the personal information is collected and used solely within the context of having an emergency contact on file.

(C) Personal information that is necessary for the business to retain to administer benefits for another natural person relating to the natural person acting as a job applicant to, an employee of, owner of, director of, officer of, medical staff member of, or contractor of that business to the extent that the personal information is collected and used solely within the context of administering those benefits.

(2) For purposes of this subdivision:

(A) **"Contractor"** means a natural person who provides any service to a business pursuant to a written contract.

(B) **"Director"** means a natural person designated in the articles of incorporation as such or elected by the incorporators and natural persons designated, elected, or appointed by any other name or title to act as directors, and their successors.

(C) **"Medical staff member"** means a licensed physician and surgeon, dentist, or podiatrist, licensed pursuant to Division 2 (commencing with Section 500) of the Business and Professions Code and a clinical psychologist as defined in Section 1316.5 of the Health and Safety Code.

(D) "Officer" means a natural person elected or appointed by the board of directors to manage the daily operations of a corporation, such as a chief executive officer, president, secretary, or treasurer.

(E) "Owner" means a natural person who meets one of the following:

(i) Has ownership of, or the power to vote, more than 50 percent of the outstanding shares of any class of voting security of a business.

(ii) Has control in any manner over the election of a majority of the directors or of individuals exercising similar functions.

(iii) Has the power to exercise a controlling influence over the management of a company.

(3) This subdivision shall not apply to subdivision (b) of Section 1798.100 or Section 1798.150.

(4) This subdivision shall become inoperative on January 1, 2021.

(i) Notwithstanding a business' obligations to respond to and honor consumer rights requests pursuant to this title:

(1) A time period for a business to respond to any verified consumer request may be extended by up to 90 additional days where necessary, taking into account the complexity and number of the requests. The business shall inform the consumer of any such extension within 45 days of receipt of the request, together with the reasons for the delay.

(2) If the business does not take action on the request of the consumer, the business shall inform the consumer, without delay and at the latest within the time period permitted of response by this section, of the reasons for not taking action and any rights the consumer may have to appeal the decision to the business.

(3) If requests from a consumer are manifestly unfounded or excessive, in particular because of their repetitive character, a business may either charge a reasonable fee, taking into account the administrative costs of providing the information or communication or taking the action requested, or refuse to act on the request and notify the consumer of the reason for refusing the request. The business shall bear the burden of demonstrating that any verified consumer request is manifestly unfounded or excessive.

(j) A business that discloses personal information to a service provider shall not be liable under this title if the service provider receiving the personal information uses it in violation of the restrictions set forth in the title, provided that, at the time of disclosing the personal information, the business does not have actual knowledge, or reason to believe, that the service provider intends to commit such a violation. A service provider shall likewise not be liable under this title for the obligations of a business for which it provides services as set forth in this title.

(k) This title shall not be construed to require a business to collect personal information that it would not otherwise collect in the ordinary course of its business, retain personal information for longer than it would otherwise retain such information in the ordinary course of its business, or reidentify or otherwise link information that is not maintained in a manner that would be considered personal information.

(*l*) The rights afforded to consumers and the obligations imposed on the business in this title shall not adversely affect the rights and freedoms of other consumers.

(m) The rights afforded to consumers and the obligations imposed on any business under this title shall not apply to the extent that they infringe on the noncommercial activities of a person or entity described in subdivision (b) of Section 2 of Article I of the California Constitution.

(n)(1) The obligations imposed on businesses by Sections 1798.100, 1798.105, 1798.110, 1798.115, 1798.130, and 1798.135 shall not apply to personal information reflecting a written or verbal communication or a transaction between the business and the consumer, where the consumer is a natural person who is acting as an employee, owner, director, officer, or contractor of a company, partnership, sole proprietorship, nonprofit, or government agency and whose communications or transaction with the business occur solely within the context of the business conducting due diligence regarding, or providing or receiving a product or service to or from such company, partnership, sole proprietorship, nonprofit, or government agency.

(2) For purposes of this subdivision:

(A) **"Contractor"** means a natural person who provides any service to a business pursuant to a written contract.

(B) **"Director"** means a natural person designated in the articles of incorporation as such or elected by the incorporators and natural persons designated, elected, or appointed by any other name or title to act as directors, and their successors.

(C) **"Officer"** means a natural person elected or appointed by the board of directors to manage the daily operations of a corporation, such as a chief executive officer, president, secretary, or treasurer.

(D) **"Owner"** means a natural person who meets one of the following:

(i) Has ownership of, or the power to vote, more than 50 percent of the outstanding shares of any class of voting security of a business.

(ii) Has control in any manner over the election of a majority of the directors or of individuals exercising similar functions.

(iii) Has the power to exercise a controlling influence over the management of a company

(3) This subdivision shall become inoperative on January 1, 2021.

1798.150. Civil actions for violations of duty to implement and maintain reasonable security procedures and practices; remedies; requirements

(a)(1) Any consumer whose nonencrypted and nonredacted personal information, as defined in subparagraph (A) of paragraph (1) of subdivision (d) of Section 1798.81.5, is subject to an unauthorized access and exfiltration, theft, or disclosure as a result of the business's violation of the duty to implement and maintain reasonable security procedures and practices appropriate to the nature of the information to protect the personal information may institute a civil action for any of the following:

(A) To recover damages in an amount not less than one hundred dollars ($100) and not greater than seven hundred and fifty ($750) per consumer per incident or actual damages, whichever is greater.

(B) Injunctive or declaratory relief.

(C) Any other relief the court deems proper.

(2) In assessing the amount of statutory damages, the court shall consider any one or more of the relevant circumstances presented by any of the parties to the case, including, but not limited to, the nature and seriousness of the misconduct, the number of violations, the persistence of the misconduct, the length of time over which the misconduct occurred, the willfulness of the defendant's misconduct, and the defendant's assets, liabilities, and net worth.

(b) Actions pursuant to this section may be brought by a consumer if, prior to initiating any action against a business for statutory damages on an individual or class-wide basis, a consumer provides a business 30 days' written notice identifying the specific provisions of this title the consumer alleges have been or are being violated. In the event a cure is possible, if within the 30 days the business actually cures the noticed violation and provides the consumer an express written statement that the violations have been cured and that no further violations shall occur, no action for individual statutory damages or class-wide statutory damages may be initiated against the business. No notice shall be required prior to an individual consumer initiating an action solely for actual pecuniary damages suffered as a result of the alleged violations of this title. If a business continues to violate this title in breach of the express written statement provided to the consumer under this section, the consumer may initiate an action against the business to enforce the written statement and may pursue statutory damages for each breach of the express written statement, as well as any other violation of the title that postdates the written statement.

(c) The cause of action established by this section shall apply only to violations as defined in subdivision (a) and shall not be based on violations of any other section of this title. Nothing in this title shall be interpreted to serve as the basis for a private right of action under any other law. This shall not be construed to relieve any party from any duties or obligations imposed under other law or the United States or California Constitution.

§ 1798.155. Attorney General guidance; civil action brought by Attorney General; amount and allocation of penalties

(a) Any business or third party may seek the opinion of the Attorney General for guidance on how to comply with the provisions of this title.

(b) A business shall be in violation of this title if it fails to cure any alleged violation within 30 days after being notified of alleged noncompliance. Any business, service provider, or other person that violates this title shall be subject to an injunction and liable for a civil penalty of not more than two thousand five hundred dollars ($2,500) for each violation or seven thousand five hundred dollars ($7,500) for each intentional violation, which shall be assessed and recovered in a civil action brought in the name of the people of the State of California by the Attorney General. The civil penalties provided for in this section shall be exclusively assessed and recovered in a civil action brought in the name of the people of the State of California by the Attorney General.

(c) Any civil penalty assessed for a violation of this title, and the proceeds of any settlement of an action brought pursuant to subdivision (b), shall be deposited in the Consumer Privacy Fund, created within the General Fund pursuant to subdivision (a) of Section 1798.160 with the intent to fully offset any costs incurred by the state courts and the Attorney General in connection with this title.

§ 1798.160. Consumer Privacy Fund; use of funds

(a) A special fund to be known as the "Consumer Privacy Fund" is hereby created within the General Fund in the State Treasury, and is available upon appropriation by the Legislature to offset any costs incurred by the state courts in connection with actions brought to enforce this title and any costs incurred by the Attorney General in carrying out the Attorney General's duties under this title.

(b) Funds transferred to the Consumer Privacy Fund shall be used exclusively to offset any costs incurred by the state courts and the Attorney General in connection with this title. These funds shall not be subject to appropriation or transfer by the Legislature for any other purpose, unless the Director of Finance determines that the funds are in excess of the funding needed to fully offset the costs incurred by the state courts and the Attorney General in connection with this title, in which case the Legislature may appropriate excess funds for other purposes.

§ 1798.175. Intent, scope, and construction of title

This title is intended to further the constitutional right of privacy and to supplement existing laws relating to consumers' personal information, including, but not limited to, Chapter 22 (commencing with Section 22575) of Division 8 of the Business and Professions Code and Title 1.81 (commencing with Section 1798.80). The provisions of this title are not limited to information collected electronically or over the Internet, but apply to the collection and sale of all personal information collected by a business from consumers. Wherever possible, law relating to consumers' personal information should be construed to harmonize with the provisions of this title, but in the event of a conflict between other laws and the provisions of this title, the provisions of the law that afford the greatest protection for the right of privacy for consumers shall control.

§ 1798.180. Supersedure and preemption

This title is a matter of statewide concern and supersedes and preempts all rules, regulations, codes, ordinances, and other laws adopted by a city, county, city and county, municipality, or local agency regarding the collection and sale of consumers' personal information by a business.

§ 1798.185. Adoption of regulations; public participation; subject matter; enforcement actions

(a) On or before July 1, 2020, the Attorney General shall solicit broad public participation and adopt regulations to further the purposes of this title, including, but not limited to, the following areas:

(1) Updating as needed additional categories of personal information to those enumerated in subdivision (c) of Section 1798.130 and subdivision (o) of Section 1798.140 in order to address changes in technology, data collection practices, obstacles to implementation, and privacy concerns.

(2) Updating as needed the definition of unique identifiers to address changes in technology, data collection, obstacles to implementation, and privacy concerns, and additional categories to the definition of designated methods for submitting requests to facilitate a consumer's ability to obtain information from a business pursuant to Section 1798.130.

(3) Establishing any exceptions necessary to comply with state or federal law, including, but not limited to, those relating to trade secrets and intellectual property rights, within one year of passage of this title and as needed thereafter.

(4) Establishing rules and procedures for the following:

(A) To facilitate and govern the submission of a request by a consumer to opt-out of the sale of personal information pursuant to Section 1798.120.

(B) To govern business compliance with a consumer's opt-out request.

(C) For the development and use of a recognizable and uniform opt-out logo or button by all businesses to promote consumer awareness of the opportunity to opt-out of the sale of personal information.

(5) Adjusting the monetary threshold in subparagraph (A) of paragraph (1) of subdivision (c) of Section 1798.140 in January of every odd-numbered year to reflect any increase in the Consumer Price Index.

(6) Establishing rules, procedures, and any exceptions necessary to ensure that the notices and information that businesses are required to provide pursuant to this title are provided in a manner that may be easily understood by the average consumer, are accessible to consumers with disabilities, and are available in the language primarily used to interact with the consumer, including establishing rules and guidelines regarding financial incentive offerings, within one year of passage of this title and as needed thereafter.

(7) Establishing rules and procedures to further the purposes of Sections 1798.110 and 1798.115 and to facilitate a consumer's or the consumer's authorized agent's ability to obtain information pursuant to Section 1798.130, with the goal of minimizing the administrative burden on consumers, taking into account available technology, security concerns, and the burden on the business, to govern a business's determination that a request for information received from a consumer is a verifiable consumer request, including treating a request submitted through a password-protected account maintained by the consumer with the business while the consumer is logged into the account as a verifiable consumer request and providing a mechanism for a consumer who does not maintain an account with the business to request information through the business's authentication of the consumer's identity, within one year of passage of this title and as needed thereafter.

(b) The Attorney General may adopt additional regulations as follows:

(1) To establish rules and procedures on how to process and comply with verifiable consumer requests for specific pieces of personal information relating to a household in order to address obstacles to implementation and privacy concerns.

(2) As necessary to further the purposes of this title.

(c) The Attorney General shall not bring an enforcement action under this title until six months after the publication of the final regulations issued pursuant to this section or July 1, 2020, whichever is sooner.

§ 1798.190. Intermediate steps or transactions to be disregarded

If a series of steps or transactions were component parts of a single transaction intended from the beginning to be taken with the intention of avoiding the reach of this title, including the disclosure of information by a business to a third party in order to avoid the definition of sell, a court shall disregard the intermediate steps or transactions for purposes of effectuating the purposes of this title.

§ 1798.192. Void and unenforceable provisions of contract or agreement

Any provision of a contract or agreement of any kind that purports to waive or limit in any way a consumer's rights under this title, including, but not limited to, any right to a remedy or means of enforcement, shall be deemed contrary to public policy and shall be void and unenforceable. This section shall not prevent a consumer from declining to request information from a business, declining to opt-out of a business's sale of the consumer's personal information, or authorizing a business to sell the consumer's personal information after previously opting out.

§ 1798.194. Liberal construction of title

This title shall be liberally construed to effectuate its purposes.

§ 1798.196. Construction with federal law, United States Constitution, and California Constitution

This title is intended to supplement federal and state law, if permissible, but shall not apply if such application is preempted by, or in conflict with, federal law or the United States or California Constitution.

§ 1798.198. Operative date of title

(a) Subject to limitation provided in subdivision (b), and in Section 1798.199, this title shall be operative January 1, 2020.

(b) This title shall become operative only if initiative measure No. 17-0039, The Consumer Right to Privacy Act of 2018, is withdrawn from the ballot pursuant to Section 9604 of the Elections Code.*

§ 1798.199. Operative date of Section 1798.180

Notwithstanding Section 1798.198, Section 1798.180 shall be operative on the effective date of the act[1] adding this section.

---

* Initiative measure No. 17-0039 was withdrawn from the ballot June 28, 2018.

[1] Stats.2018, c. 735 (S.B.1121), eff. Sept. 23, 2018.

SELECTED TELEMARKETING STATUTES AND REGULATIONS

Telephone Consumer Protection Act

47 U.S.C.A. § 227

§ 227. Restrictions on use of telephone equipment

(a) Definitions

As used in this section—

(1) The term "automatic telephone dialing system" means equipment which has the capacity—

(A) to store or produce telephone numbers to be called, using a random or sequential number generator; and

(B) to dial such numbers.

(2) The term "established business relationship", for purposes only of subsection (b)(1)(C)(i) of this section, shall have the meaning given the term in section 64.1200 of title 47, Code of Federal Regulations, as in effect on January 1, 2003, except that—

(A) such term shall include a relationship between a person or entity and a business subscriber subject to the same terms applicable under such section to a relationship between a person or entity and a residential subscriber; and

(B) an established business relationship shall be subject to any time limitation established pursuant to paragraph (2)(G)).[1]

(3) The term "telephone facsimile machine" means equipment which has the capacity (A) to transcribe text or images, or both, from paper into an electronic signal and to transmit that signal over a regular telephone line, or (B) to transcribe text or images (or both) from an electronic signal received over a regular telephone line onto paper.

(4) The term "telephone solicitation" means the initiation of a telephone call or message for the purpose of encouraging the purchase or rental of, or investment in, property, goods, or services, which is transmitted to any person, but such term does not include a call or message (A) to any person with that person's prior express invitation or permission, (B) to any person with whom the caller has an established business relationship, or (C) by a tax exempt nonprofit organization.

(5) The term "unsolicited advertisement" means any material advertising the commercial availability or quality of any property, goods, or services which is transmitted to any person without that person's prior express invitation or permission, in writing or otherwise.

(b) Restrictions on use of automated telephone equipment

(1) Prohibitions

It shall be unlawful for any person within the United States, or any person outside the United States if the recipient is within the United States—

[1] So in original. The second closing parenthesis probably should not appear.

(A) to make any call (other than a call made for emergency purposes or made with the prior express consent of the called party) using any automatic telephone dialing system or an artificial or prerecorded voice—

(i) to any emergency telephone line (including any "911" line and any emergency line of a hospital, medical physician or service office, health care facility, poison control center, or fire protection or law enforcement agency);

(ii) to the telephone line of any guest room or patient room of a hospital, health care facility, elderly home, or similar establishment; or

(iii) to any telephone number assigned to a paging service, cellular telephone service, specialized mobile radio service, or other radio common carrier service, or any service for which the called party is charged for the call, unless such call is made solely to collect a debt owed to or guaranteed by the United States;

(B) to initiate any telephone call to any residential telephone line using an artificial or prerecorded voice to deliver a message without the prior express consent of the called party, unless the call is initiated for emergency purposes, is made solely pursuant to the collection of a debt owed to or guaranteed by the United States, or is exempted by rule or order by the Commission under paragraph (2)(B);

(C) to use any telephone facsimile machine, computer, or other device to send, to a telephone facsimile machine, an unsolicited advertisement, unless—

(i) the unsolicited advertisement is from a sender with an established business relationship with the recipient;

(ii) the sender obtained the number of the telephone facsimile machine through—

(I) the voluntary communication of such number, within the context of such established business relationship, from the recipient of the unsolicited advertisement, or

(II) a directory, advertisement, or site on the Internet to which the recipient voluntarily agreed to make available its facsimile number for public distribution, except that this clause shall not apply in the case of an unsolicited advertisement that is sent based on an established business relationship with the recipient that was in existence before July 9, 2005, if the sender possessed the facsimile machine number of the recipient before July 9, 2005; and

(iii) the unsolicited advertisement contains a notice meeting the requirements under paragraph (2)(D),

except that the exception under clauses (i) and (ii) shall not apply with respect to an unsolicited advertisement sent to a telephone facsimile machine by a sender to whom a request has been made not to send future unsolicited advertisements to such telephone facsimile machine that complies with the requirements under paragraph (2)(E); or

(D) to use an automatic telephone dialing system in such a way that two or more telephone lines of a multi-line business are engaged simultaneously.

(2) Regulations; exemptions and other provisions

The Commission shall prescribe regulations to implement the requirements of this subsection. In implementing the requirements of this subsection, the Commission—

(A) shall consider prescribing regulations to allow businesses to avoid receiving calls made using an artificial or prerecorded voice to which they have not given their prior express consent;

(B) may, by rule or order, exempt from the requirements of paragraph (1)(B) of this subsection, subject to such conditions as the Commission may prescribe—

(i) calls that are not made for a commercial purpose; and

(ii) such classes or categories of calls made for commercial purposes as the Commission determines—

(I) will not adversely affect the privacy rights that this section is intended to protect; and

(II) do not include the transmission of any unsolicited advertisement;

(C) may, by rule or order, exempt from the requirements of paragraph (1)(A)(iii) of this subsection calls to a telephone number assigned to a cellular telephone service that are not charged to the called party, subject to such conditions as the Commission may prescribe as necessary in the interest of the privacy rights this section is intended to protect;

(D) shall provide that a notice contained in an unsolicited advertisement complies with the requirements under this subparagraph only if—

(i) the notice is clear and conspicuous and on the first page of the unsolicited advertisement;

(ii) the notice states that the recipient may make a request to the sender of the unsolicited advertisement not to send any future unsolicited advertisements to a telephone facsimile machine or machines and that failure to comply, within the shortest reasonable time, as determined by the Commission, with such a request meeting the requirements under subparagraph (E) is unlawful;

(iii) the notice sets forth the requirements for a request under subparagraph (E);

(iv) the notice includes—

(I) a domestic contact telephone and facsimile machine number for the recipient to transmit such a request to the sender; and

(II) a cost-free mechanism for a recipient to transmit a request pursuant to such notice to the sender of the unsolicited advertisement; the Commission shall by rule require the sender to provide such a mechanism and may, in the discretion of the Commission and subject to such conditions as the Commission may prescribe, exempt certain classes of small business senders, but only if the Commission determines that the costs to such class are unduly burdensome given the revenues generated by such small businesses;

(v) the telephone and facsimile machine numbers and the cost-free mechanism set forth pursuant to clause (iv) permit an individual or business to make such a request at any time on any day of the week; and

(vi) the notice complies with the requirements of subsection (d) of this section;

(E) shall provide, by rule, that a request not to send future unsolicited advertisements to a telephone facsimile machine complies with the requirements under this subparagraph only if—

(i) the request identifies the telephone number or numbers of the telephone facsimile machine or machines to which the request relates;

(ii) the request is made to the telephone or facsimile number of the sender of such an unsolicited advertisement provided pursuant to subparagraph (D)(iv) or by any other method of communication as determined by the Commission; and

(iii) the person making the request has not, subsequent to such request, provided express invitation or permission to the sender, in writing or otherwise, to send such advertisements to such person at such telephone facsimile machine;

(F) may, in the discretion of the Commission and subject to such conditions as the Commission may prescribe, allow professional or trade associations that are tax-exempt nonprofit organizations to send unsolicited advertisements to their members in furtherance of the association's tax-exempt purpose that do not contain the notice required by paragraph (1)(C)(iii), except that the Commission may take action under this subparagraph only—

(i) by regulation issued after public notice and opportunity for public comment; and

(ii) if the Commission determines that such notice required by paragraph (1)(C)(iii) is not necessary to protect the ability of the members of such associations to stop such associations from sending any future unsolicited advertisements;

(G)(i) may, consistent with clause (ii), limit the duration of the existence of an established business relationship, however, before establishing any such limits, the Commission shall—

(I) determine whether the existence of the exception under paragraph (1)(C) relating to an established business relationship has resulted in a significant number of complaints to the Commission regarding the sending of unsolicited advertisements to telephone facsimile machines;

(II) determine whether a significant number of any such complaints involve unsolicited advertisements that were sent on the basis of an established business relationship that was longer in duration than the Commission believes is consistent with the reasonable expectations of consumers;

(III) evaluate the costs to senders of demonstrating the existence of an established business relationship within a specified period of time and the benefits to recipients of establishing a limitation on such established business relationship; and

(IV) determine whether with respect to small businesses, the costs would not be unduly burdensome; and

(ii) may not commence a proceeding to determine whether to limit the duration of the existence of an established business relationship before the expiration of the 3-month period that begins on July 9, 2005; and

(H) may restrict or limit the number and duration of calls made to a telephone number assigned to a cellular telephone service to collect a debt owed to or guaranteed by the United States.

(3) Private right of action

A person or entity may, if otherwise permitted by the laws or rules of court of a State, bring in an appropriate court of that State—

(A) an action based on a violation of this subsection or the regulations prescribed under this subsection to enjoin such violation,

(B) an action to recover for actual monetary loss from such a violation, or to receive $500 in damages for each such violation, whichever is greater, or

(C) both such actions.

If the court finds that the defendant willfully or knowingly violated this subsection or the regulations prescribed under this subsection, the court may, in its discretion, increase the amount of the award to an amount equal to not more than 3 times the amount available under subparagraph (B) of this paragraph.

(c) Protection of subscriber privacy rights

(1) Rulemaking proceeding required

Within 120 days after December 20, 1991, the Commission shall initiate a rulemaking proceeding concerning the need to protect residential telephone subscribers' privacy rights to avoid receiving telephone solicitations to which they object. The proceeding shall—

(A) compare and evaluate alternative methods and procedures (including the use of electronic databases, telephone network technologies, special directory markings, industry-based or company-specific "do not call" systems, and any other alternatives, individually or in combination) for their effectiveness in protecting such privacy rights, and in terms of their cost and other advantages and disadvantages;

(B) evaluate the categories of public and private entities that would have the capacity to establish and administer such methods and procedures;

(C) consider whether different methods and procedures may apply for local telephone solicitations, such as local telephone solicitations of small businesses or holders of second class mail permits;

(D) consider whether there is a need for additional Commission authority to further restrict telephone solicitations, including those calls exempted under subsection (a)(3) of this section, and, if such a finding is made and supported by the record, propose specific restrictions to the Congress; and

(E) develop proposed regulations to implement the methods and procedures that the Commission determines are most effective and efficient to accomplish the purposes of this section.

(2) Regulations

Not later than 9 months after December 20, 1991, the Commission shall conclude the rulemaking proceeding initiated under paragraph (1) and shall prescribe regulations to implement methods and procedures for protecting the privacy rights described in such paragraph in an efficient, effective, and economic manner and without the imposition of any additional charge to telephone subscribers.

(3) Use of database permitted

The regulations required by paragraph (2) may require the establishment and operation of a single national database to compile a list of telephone numbers of residential subscribers who object to receiving telephone solicitations, and to make that compiled list and parts thereof available for purchase. If the Commission determines to require such a database, such regulations shall—

(A) specify a method by which the Commission will select an entity to administer such database;

(B) require each common carrier providing telephone exchange service, in accordance with regulations prescribed by the Commission, to inform subscribers for telephone exchange service of the opportunity to provide notification, in accordance with regulations established under this paragraph, that such subscriber objects to receiving telephone solicitations;

(C) specify the methods by which each telephone subscriber shall be informed, by the common carrier that provides local exchange service to that subscriber, of (i) the subscriber's right to give or revoke a notification of an objection under subparagraph (A), and (ii) the methods by which such right may be exercised by the subscriber;

(D) specify the methods by which such objections shall be collected and added to the database;

(E) prohibit any residential subscriber from being charged for giving or revoking such notification or for being included in a database compiled under this section;

(F) prohibit any person from making or transmitting a telephone solicitation to the telephone number of any subscriber included in such database;

(G) specify (i) the methods by which any person desiring to make or transmit telephone solicitations will obtain access to the database, by area code or local exchange prefix, as required to avoid calling the telephone numbers of subscribers included in such database; and (ii) the costs to be recovered from such persons;

(H) specify the methods for recovering, from persons accessing such database, the costs involved in identifying, collecting, updating, disseminating, and selling, and other activities relating to, the operations of the database that are incurred by the entities carrying out those activities;

(I) specify the frequency with which such database will be updated and specify the method by which such updating will take effect for purposes of compliance with the regulations prescribed under this subsection;

(J) be designed to enable States to use the database mechanism selected by the Commission for purposes of administering or enforcing State law;

(K) prohibit the use of such database for any purpose other than compliance with the requirements of this section and any such State law and specify methods for protection of the privacy rights of persons whose numbers are included in such database; and

(L) require each common carrier providing services to any person for the purpose of making telephone solicitations to notify such person of the requirements of this section and the regulations thereunder.

(4) Considerations required for use of database method

If the Commission determines to require the database mechanism described in paragraph (3), the Commission shall—

(A) in developing procedures for gaining access to the database, consider the different needs of telemarketers conducting business on a national, regional, State, or local level;

(B) develop a fee schedule or price structure for recouping the cost of such database that recognizes such differences and—

(i) reflect the relative costs of providing a national, regional, State, or local list of phone numbers of subscribers who object to receiving telephone solicitations;

(ii) reflect the relative costs of providing such lists on paper or electronic media; and

(iii) not place an unreasonable financial burden on small businesses; and

(C) consider (i) whether the needs of telemarketers operating on a local basis could be met through special markings of area white pages directories, and (ii) if such directories are needed as an adjunct to database lists prepared by area code and local exchange prefix.

(5) Private right of action

A person who has received more than one telephone call within any 12-month period by or on behalf of the same entity in violation of the regulations prescribed under this subsection may, if otherwise permitted by the laws or rules of court of a State bring in an appropriate court of that State—

(A) an action based on a violation of the regulations prescribed under this subsection to enjoin such violation,

(B) an action to recover for actual monetary loss from such a violation, or to receive up to $500 in damages for each such violation, whichever is greater, or

(C) both such actions.

It shall be an affirmative defense in any action brought under this paragraph that the defendant has established and implemented, with due care, reasonable practices and procedures to effectively prevent telephone solicitations in violation of the regulations prescribed under this subsection. If the court finds that the defendant willfully or knowingly violated the regulations prescribed under this subsection, the court may, in its discretion, increase the amount of the award to an amount equal to not more than 3 times the amount available under subparagraph (B) of this paragraph.

(6) Relation to subsection (b)

The provisions of this subsection shall not be construed to permit a communication prohibited by subsection (b).

(d) Technical and procedural standards

(1) Prohibition

It shall be unlawful for any person within the United States—

(A) to initiate any communication using a telephone facsimile machine, or to make any telephone call using any automatic telephone dialing system, that does not comply with the technical and procedural standards prescribed under this subsection, or to use any telephone facsimile machine or automatic telephone dialing system in a manner that does not comply with such standards; or

(B) to use a computer or other electronic device to send any message via a telephone facsimile machine unless such person clearly marks, in a margin at the top or bottom of each transmitted page of the message or on the first page of the transmission, the date and time it is sent and an identification of the business, other entity, or individual sending the message and the telephone number of the sending machine or of such business, other entity, or individual.

(2) Telephone facsimile machines

The Commission shall revise the regulations setting technical and procedural standards for telephone facsimile machines to require that any such machine which is manufactured after one year after December 20, 1991, clearly marks, in a margin at the top or bottom of each transmitted page or on the first page of each transmission, the date and time sent, an identification of the business, other entity, or individual sending the message, and the telephone number of the sending machine or of such business, other entity, or individual.

(3) Artificial or prerecorded voice systems

The Commission shall prescribe technical and procedural standards for systems that are used to transmit any artificial or prerecorded voice message via telephone. Such standards shall require that—

(A) all artificial or prerecorded telephone messages (i) shall, at the beginning of the message, state clearly the identity of the business, individual, or other entity initiating the call, and (ii) shall, during or after the message, state clearly the telephone number or address of such business, other entity, or individual; and

(B) any such system will automatically release the called party's line within 5 seconds of the time notification is transmitted to the system that the called party has hung up, to allow the called party's line to be used to make or receive other calls.

(e) Prohibition on provision of inaccurate caller identification information

(1) In general

It shall be unlawful for any person within the United States, in connection with any telecommunications service or IP-enabled voice service, to cause any caller identification service to knowingly transmit misleading or inaccurate caller identification information with the intent to defraud, cause harm, or wrongfully obtain anything of value, unless such transmission is exempted pursuant to paragraph (3)(B).

(2) Protection for blocking caller identification information

Nothing in this subsection may be construed to prevent or restrict any person from blocking the capability of any caller identification service to transmit caller identification information.

(3) Regulations

(A) In general

Not later than 6 months after December 22, 2010, the Commission shall prescribe regulations to implement this subsection.

(B) Content of regulations

(i) In general

The regulations required under subparagraph (A) shall include such exemptions from the prohibition under paragraph (1) as the Commission determines is appropriate.

(ii) Specific exemption for law enforcement agencies or court orders

The regulations required under subparagraph (A) shall exempt from the prohibition under paragraph (1) transmissions in connection with—

(I) any authorized activity of a law enforcement agency; or

(II) a court order that specifically authorizes the use of caller identification manipulation.

(4) Repealed. Pub.L. 115–141, Div. P, Title IV, § 402(i)(3), Mar. 23, 2018, 132 Stat. 1089

(5) Penalties

(A) Civil forfeiture

(i) In general

Any person that is determined by the Commission, in accordance with paragraphs (3) and (4) of section 503(b) of this title, to have violated this subsection shall be liable to the United States for a forfeiture penalty. A forfeiture penalty under this paragraph shall be in addition to any other penalty provided for by this chapter. The amount of the forfeiture penalty determined under this paragraph shall not exceed $10,000 for each violation, or 3 times that amount for each day of a continuing violation, except that the amount assessed for any continuing violation shall not exceed a total of $1,000,000 for any single act or failure to act.

(ii) Recovery

Any forfeiture penalty determined under clause (i) shall be recoverable pursuant to section 504(a) of this title.

(iii) Procedure

No forfeiture liability shall be determined under clause (i) against any person unless such person receives the notice required by section 503(b)(3) of this title or section 503(b)(4) of this title.

(iv) 2-year statute of limitations

No forfeiture penalty shall be determined or imposed against any person under clause (i) if the violation charged occurred more than 2 years prior to the date of issuance of the required notice or notice or apparent liability.

(B) Criminal fine

Any person who willfully and knowingly violates this subsection shall upon conviction thereof be fined not more than $10,000 for each violation, or 3 times that amount for each day of a continuing violation, in lieu of the fine provided by section 501 of this title for such a violation. This subparagraph does not supersede the provisions of section 501 of this title relating to imprisonment or the imposition of a penalty of both fine and imprisonment.

(6) Enforcement by States

(A) In general

The chief legal officer of a State, or any other State officer authorized by law to bring actions on behalf of the residents of a State, may bring a civil action, as parens patriae, on behalf of the residents of that State in an appropriate district court of the United States to enforce this subsection or to impose the civil penalties for violation of this subsection, whenever the chief legal officer or other State officer has reason to believe that the interests of the residents of the State have been or are being threatened or adversely affected by a violation of this subsection or a regulation under this subsection.

(B) Notice

The chief legal officer or other State officer shall serve written notice on the Commission of any civil action under subparagraph (A) prior to initiating such civil action. The notice shall include a copy of the complaint to be filed to initiate such civil action, except that if it is not feasible for the State to provide such prior notice, the State shall provide such notice immediately upon instituting such civil action.

(C) Authority to intervene

Upon receiving the notice required by subparagraph (B), the Commission shall have the right—

(i) to intervene in the action;

(ii) upon so intervening, to be heard on all matters arising therein; and

(iii) to file petitions for appeal.

(D) Construction

For purposes of bringing any civil action under subparagraph (A), nothing in this paragraph shall prevent the chief legal officer or other State officer from exercising the powers conferred on that officer by the laws of such State to conduct investigations or to administer oaths or affirmations or to compel the attendance of witnesses or the production of documentary and other evidence.

(E) Venue; service or process

(i) Venue

An action brought under subparagraph (A) shall be brought in a district court of the United States that meets applicable requirements relating to venue under section 1391 of Title 28.

(ii) Service of process

In an action brought under subparagraph (A)—

(I) process may be served without regard to the territorial limits of the district or of the State in which the action is instituted; and

(II) a person who participated in an alleged violation that is being litigated in the civil action may be joined in the civil action without regard to the residence of the person.

(7) Effect on other laws

This subsection does not prohibit any lawfully authorized investigative, protective, or intelligence activity of a law enforcement agency of the United States, a State, or a political subdivision of a State, or of an intelligence agency of the United States.

(8) Definitions

For purposes of this subsection:

(A) Caller identification information

The term "caller identification information" means information provided by a caller identification service regarding the telephone number of, or other information regarding the origination of, a call made using a telecommunications service or IP-enabled voice service.

(B) Caller identification service

The term "caller identification service" means any service or device designed to provide the user of the service or device with the telephone number of, or other information regarding the origination of, a call made using a telecommunications service or IP-enabled voice service. Such term includes automatic number identification services.

(C) IP-enabled voice service

The term "IP-enabled voice service" has the meaning given that term by section 9.3 of the Commission's regulations (47 C.F.R. 9.3), as those regulations may be amended by the Commission from time to time.

(9) Limitation

Notwithstanding any other provision of this section, subsection (f) shall not apply to this subsection or to the regulations under this subsection.

(f) Effect on State law

(1) State law not preempted

Except for the standards prescribed under subsection (d) of this section and subject to paragraph (2) of this subsection, nothing in this section or in the regulations prescribed under this section shall preempt any State law that imposes more restrictive intrastate requirements or regulations on, or which prohibits—

(A) the use of telephone facsimile machines or other electronic devices to send unsolicited advertisements;

(B) the use of automatic telephone dialing systems;

(C) the use of artificial or prerecorded voice messages; or

(D) the making of telephone solicitations.

(2) State use of databases

If, pursuant to subsection (c)(3) of this section, the Commission requires the establishment of a single national database of telephone numbers of subscribers who object to receiving telephone solicitations, a State or local authority may not, in its regulation of telephone solicitations, require the use of any database, list, or listing system that does not include the part of such single national database that relates to such State.

(g) Actions by States

(1) Authority of States

Whenever the attorney general of a State, or an official or agency designated by a State, has reason to believe that any person has engaged or is engaging in a pattern or practice of telephone calls or other transmissions to residents of that State in violation of this section or the regulations prescribed under this section, the State may bring a civil action on behalf of its residents to enjoin such calls, an action to recover for actual monetary loss or receive $500 in damages for each violation, or both such actions. If the court finds the defendant willfully or knowingly violated such regulations, the court may, in its discretion, increase the amount of the award to an amount equal to not more than 3 times the amount available under the preceding sentence.

(2) Exclusive jurisdiction of Federal courts

The district courts of the United States, the United States courts of any territory, and the District Court of the United States for the District of Columbia shall have exclusive jurisdiction over all civil actions brought under this subsection. Upon proper application, such courts shall also have jurisdiction to issue writs of mandamus, or orders affording like relief, commanding the defendant to comply with the provisions of this section or regulations prescribed under this section, including the requirement that the defendant take such action as is necessary to remove the danger of such violation. Upon a proper showing, a permanent or temporary injunction or restraining order shall be granted without bond.

(3) Rights of Commission

The State shall serve prior written notice of any such civil action upon the Commission and provide the Commission with a copy of its complaint, except in any case where such prior notice is not feasible, in which case the State shall serve such notice immediately upon instituting such action. The Commission shall have the right (A) to intervene in the action, (B) upon so intervening, to be heard on all matters arising therein, and (C) to file petitions for appeal.

(4) Venue; service of process

Any civil action brought under this subsection in a district court of the United States may be brought in the district wherein the defendant is found or is an inhabitant or transacts business or wherein the violation occurred or is occurring, and process in such cases may be served in any district in which the defendant is an inhabitant or where the defendant may be found.

(5) Investigatory powers

For purposes of bringing any civil action under this subsection, nothing in this section shall prevent the attorney general of a State, or an official or agency designated by a State, from exercising the powers conferred on the attorney general or such official by the laws of such State to conduct investigations or to administer oaths or affirmations or to compel the attendance of witnesses or the production of documentary and other evidence.

(6) Effect on State court proceedings

Nothing contained in this subsection shall be construed to prohibit an authorized State official from proceeding in State court on the basis of an alleged violation of any general civil or criminal statute of such State.

(7) Limitation

Whenever the Commission has instituted a civil action for violation of regulations prescribed under this section, no State may, during the pendency of such action instituted by the

Commission, subsequently institute a civil action against any defendant named in the Commission's complaint for any violation as alleged in the Commission's complaint.

(8) "Attorney general" defined

As used in this subsection, the term "attorney general" means the chief legal officer of a State.

(h) Junk fax enforcement report

The Commission shall submit an annual report to Congress regarding the enforcement during the past year of the provisions of this section relating to sending of unsolicited advertisements to telephone facsimile machines, which report shall include—

(1) the number of complaints received by the Commission during such year alleging that a consumer received an unsolicited advertisement via telephone facsimile machine in violation of the Commission's rules;

(2) the number of citations issued by the Commission pursuant to section 503 of this title during the year to enforce any law, regulation, or policy relating to sending of unsolicited advertisements to telephone facsimile machines;

(3) the number of notices of apparent liability issued by the Commission pursuant to section 503 of this title during the year to enforce any law, regulation, or policy relating to sending of unsolicited advertisements to telephone facsimile machines;

(4) for each notice referred to in paragraph (3)—

(A) the amount of the proposed forfeiture penalty involved;

(B) the person to whom the notice was issued;

(C) the length of time between the date on which the complaint was filed and the date on which the notice was issued; and

(D) the status of the proceeding;

(5) the number of final orders imposing forfeiture penalties issued pursuant to section 503 of this title during the year to enforce any law, regulation, or policy relating to sending of unsolicited advertisements to telephone facsimile machines;

(6) for each forfeiture order referred to in paragraph (5)—

(A) the amount of the penalty imposed by the order;

(B) the person to whom the order was issued;

(C) whether the forfeiture penalty has been paid; and

(D) the amount paid;

(7) for each case in which a person has failed to pay a forfeiture penalty imposed by such a final order, whether the Commission referred such matter for recovery of the penalty; and

(8) for each case in which the Commission referred such an order for recovery—

(A) the number of days from the date the Commission issued such order to the date of such referral;

(B) whether an action has been commenced to recover the penalty, and if so, the number of days from the date the Commission referred such order for recovery to the date of such commencement; and

(C) whether the recovery action resulted in collection of any amount, and if so, the amount collected.

The Telemarketing and Consumer Fraud and Abuse Prevention Act

15 U.S.C. § 6101 et seq.

Table of Sections

§ 6101. Findings

The Congress makes the following findings:

(1) Telemarketing differs from other sales activities in that it can be carried out by sellers across State lines without direct contact with the consumer. Telemarketers also can be very mobile, easily moving from State to State.

(2) Interstate telemarketing fraud has become a problem of such magnitude that the resources of the Federal Trade Commission are not sufficient to ensure adequate consumer protection from such fraud.

(3) Consumers and others are estimated to lose $40 billion a year in telemarketing fraud.

(4) Consumers are victimized by other forms of telemarketing deception and abuse.

(5) Consequently, Congress should enact legislation that will offer consumers necessary protection from telemarketing deception and abuse.

§ 6102. Telemarketing rules

(a) In general

(1) The Commission shall prescribe rules prohibiting deceptive telemarketing acts or practices and other abusive telemarketing acts or practices.

(2) The Commission shall include in such rules respecting deceptive telemarketing acts or practices a definition of deceptive telemarketing acts or practices which shall include fraudulent charitable solicitations, and which may include acts or practices of entities or individuals that assist or facilitate deceptive telemarketing, including credit card laundering.

(3) The Commission shall include in such rules respecting other abusive telemarketing acts or practices—

(A) a requirement that telemarketers may not undertake a pattern of unsolicited telephone calls which the reasonable consumer would consider coercive or abusive of such consumer's right to privacy,

(B) restrictions on the hours of the day and night when unsolicited telephone calls can be made to consumers,

(C) a requirement that any person engaged in telemarketing for the sale of goods or services shall promptly and clearly disclose to the person receiving the call that the purpose of the call is to sell goods or services and make such other disclosures as the Commission deems appropriate, including the nature and price of the goods and services;[1] and

(D) a requirement that any person engaged in telemarketing for the solicitation of charitable contributions, donations, or gifts of money or any other thing of value, shall promptly and clearly disclose to the person receiving the call that the purpose of the call is to solicit charitable contributions, donations, or gifts, and make such other disclosures as the Commission considers appropriate, including the name and mailing address of the charitable organization on behalf of which the solicitation is made.

In prescribing the rules described in this paragraph, the Commission shall also consider recordkeeping requirements.

(b) Rulemaking authority

The Commission shall have authority to prescribe rules under subsection (a), in accordance with section 553 of Title 5. In prescribing a rule under this section that relates to the provision of a consumer financial product or service that is subject to the Consumer Financial Protection Act of 2010, including any enumerated consumer law thereunder, the Commission shall consult with the Bureau of Consumer Financial Protection regarding the consistency of a proposed rule with standards, purposes, or objectives administered by the Bureau of Consumer Financial Protection.

(c) Violations

Any violation of any rule prescribed under subsection (a)—

(1) shall be treated as a violation of a rule under section 57a of this title regarding unfair or deceptive acts or practices; and

(2) that is committed by a person subject to the Consumer Financial Protection Act of 2010 shall be treated as a violation of a rule under section 1031 of that Act regarding unfair, deceptive, or abusive acts or practices.

(d) Securities and Exchange Commission rules

(1) Promulgation

(A) In general

Except as provided in subparagraph (B), not later than 6 months after the effective date of rules promulgated by the Federal Trade Commission under subsection (a), the Securities and Exchange Commission shall promulgate, or require any national securities exchange or registered securities association to promulgate, rules substantially similar to such rules to prohibit deceptive and other abusive telemarketing acts or practices by persons described in paragraph (2).

(B) Exception

The Securities and Exchange Commission is not required to promulgate a rule under subparagraph (A) if it determines that—

(i) Federal securities laws or rules adopted by the Securities and Exchange Commission thereunder provide protection from deceptive and other abusive telemarketing by persons described in paragraph (2) substantially similar to that provided by rules promulgated by the Federal Trade Commission under subsection (a); or

(ii) such a rule promulgated by the Securities and Exchange Commission is not necessary or appropriate in the public interest, or for the protection of investors, or would be inconsistent with the maintenance of fair and orderly markets.

---

1 So in original. The semicolon probably should be a comma.

If the Securities and Exchange Commission determines that an exception described in clause (i) or (ii) applies, the Securities and Exchange Commission shall publish in the Federal Register its determination with the reasons for it.

(2) Application

(A) In general

The rules promulgated by the Securities and Exchange Commission under paragraph (1)(A) shall apply to a broker, dealer, transfer agent, municipal securities dealer, municipal securities broker, government securities broker, government securities dealer, investment adviser or investment company, or any individual associated with a broker, dealer, transfer agent, municipal securities dealer, municipal securities broker, government securities broker, government securities dealer, investment adviser or investment company. The rules promulgated by the Federal Trade Commission under subsection (a) shall not apply to persons described in the preceding sentence.

(B) Definitions

For purposes of subparagraph (A)—

(i) the terms "broker", "dealer", "transfer agent", "municipal securities dealer", "municipal securities broker", "government securities broker", and "government securities dealer" have the meanings given such terms by paragraphs (4), (5), (25), (30), (31), (43), and (44) of section 78c(a) of this title;

(ii) the term "investment adviser" has the meaning given such term by section 80b–2(a)(11) of this title; and

(iii) the term "investment company" has the meaning given such term by section 80a–3(a) of this title.

(e) Commodity Futures Trading Commission rules

(1) Application

The rules promulgated by the Federal Trade Commission under subsection (a) shall not apply to persons described in section 9b(1) of Title 7.

(2) Omitted

§ 6103. Actions by States

(a) In general

Whenever an attorney general of any State has reason to believe that the interests of the residents of that State have been or are being threatened or adversely affected because any person has engaged or is engaging in a pattern or practice of telemarketing which violates any rule of the Commission under section 6102 of this title, the State, as parens patriae, may bring a civil action on behalf of its residents in an appropriate district court of the United States to enjoin such telemarketing, to enforce compliance with such rule of the Commission, to obtain damages, restitution, or other compensation on behalf of residents of such State, or to obtain such further and other relief as the court may deem appropriate.

(b) Notice

The State shall serve prior written notice of any civil action under subsection (a) or (f)(2) upon the Commission and provide the Commission with a copy of its complaint, except that if it is not feasible for the State to provide such prior notice, the State shall serve such notice immediately upon instituting such action. Upon receiving a notice respecting a civil action, the Commission shall have the right (1) to intervene in such action, (2) upon so intervening, to be heard on all matters arising therein, and (3) to file petitions for appeal.

(c) Construction

For purposes of bringing any civil action under subsection (a) of this section, nothing in this chapter shall prevent an attorney general from exercising the powers conferred on the attorney general by the laws of such State to conduct investigations or to administer oaths or affirmations or to compel the attendance of witnesses or the production of documentary and other evidence.

(d) Actions by Commission

Whenever a civil action has been instituted by or on behalf of the Commission or the Bureau of Consumer Financial Protection for violation of any rule prescribed under section 6102 of this title, no State may, during the pendency of such action instituted by or on behalf of the Commission or the Bureau of Consumer Financial Protection, institute a civil action under subsection (a) or (f)(2) against any defendant named in the complaint in such action for violation of any rule as alleged in such complaint.

(e) Venue; service of process

Any civil action brought under subsection (a) in a district court of the United States may be brought in the district in which the defendant is found, is an inhabitant, or transacts business or wherever venue is proper under section 1391 of Title 28. Process in such an action may be served in any district in which the defendant is an inhabitant or in which the defendant may be found.

(f) Actions by other State officials

(1) Nothing contained in this section shall prohibit an authorized State official from proceeding in State court on the basis of an alleged violation of any civil or criminal statute of such State.

(2) In addition to actions brought by an attorney general of a State under subsection (a), such an action may be brought by officers of such State who are authorized by the State to bring actions in such State on behalf of its residents.

§ 6104. Actions by private persons

(a) In general

Any person adversely affected by any pattern or practice of telemarketing which violates any rule of the Commission under section 6102 of this title, or an authorized person acting on such person's behalf, may, within 3 years after discovery of the violation, bring a civil action in an appropriate district court of the United States against a person who has engaged or is engaging in such pattern or practice of telemarketing if the amount in controversy exceeds the sum or value of $50,000 in actual damages for each person adversely affected by such telemarketing. Such an action may be brought to enjoin such telemarketing, to enforce compliance with any rule of the Commission under section 6102 of this title, to obtain damages, or to obtain such further and other relief as the court may deem appropriate.

(b) Notice

The plaintiff shall serve prior written notice of the action upon the Commission and provide the Commission with a copy of its complaint, except in any case where such prior notice is not feasible, in which case the person shall serve such notice immediately upon instituting such action. The Commission shall have the right (A) to intervene in the action, (B) upon so intervening, to be heard on all matters arising therein, and (C) to file petitions for appeal.

(c) Action by Commission or Bureau of Consumer Financial Protection

Whenever a civil action has been instituted by or on behalf of the Commission or the Bureau of Consumer Financial Protection for violation of any rule prescribed under section 6102 of this title, no person may, during the pendency of such action instituted by or on behalf of the Commission or the

Bureau of Consumer Financial Protection, institute a civil action against any defendant named in the complaint in such action for violation of any rule as alleged in such complaint.

(d) Cost and fees

The court, in issuing any final order in any action brought under subsection (a), may award costs of suit and reasonable fees for attorneys and expert witnesses to the prevailing party.

(e) Construction

Nothing in this section shall restrict any right which any person may have under any statute or common law.

(f) Venue; service of process

Any civil action brought under subsection (a) in a district court of the United States may be brought in the district in which the defendant is found, is an inhabitant, or transacts business or wherever venue is proper under section 1391 of Title 28. Process in such an action may be served in any district in which the defendant is an inhabitant or in which the defendant may be found.

§ 6105. Administration and applicability of chapter

(a) In general

Except as otherwise provided in sections 6102(d), 6102(e), 6103, and 6104 of this title, this chapter shall be enforced by the Commission under the Federal Trade Commission Act (15 U.S.C. 41 et seq.). Consequently, no activity which is outside the jurisdiction of that Act shall be affected by this chapter.

(b) Actions by Commission

The Commission shall prevent any person from violating a rule of the Commission under section 6102 of this title in the same manner, by the same means, and with the same jurisdiction, powers, and duties as though all applicable terms and provisions of the Federal Trade Commission Act (15 U.S.C. 41 et seq.) were incorporated into and made a part of this chapter. Any person who violates such rule shall be subject to the penalties and entitled to the privileges and immunities provided in the Federal Trade Commission Act in the same manner, by the same means, and with the same jurisdiction, power, and duties as though all applicable terms and provisions of the Federal Trade Commission Act were incorporated into and made a part of this chapter.

(c) Effect on other laws

Nothing contained in this chapter shall be construed to limit the authority of the Commission under any other provision of law.

(d) Enforcement by Bureau of Consumer Financial Protection

Except as otherwise provided in sections 6102(d), 6102(e), 6103, and 6104 of this title, and subject to subtitle B of the Consumer Financial Protection Act of 2010, this chapter shall be enforced by the Bureau of Consumer Financial Protection under subtitle E of the Consumer Financial Protection Act of 2010, with respect to the offering or provision of a consumer financial product or service subject to that Act.

§ 6106. Definitions

For purposes of this chapter:

(1) The term "attorney general" means the chief legal officer of a State.

(2) The term "Commission" means the Federal Trade Commission.

(3) The term "State" means any State of the United States, the District of Columbia, Puerto Rico, the Northern Mariana Islands, and any territory or possession of the United States.

(4) The term "telemarketing" means a plan, program, or campaign which is conducted to induce purchases of goods or services, or a charitable contribution, donation, or gift of money or any other thing of value, by use of one or more telephones and which involves more than one interstate telephone call. The term does not include the solicitation of sales through the mailing of a catalog which—

(A) contains a written description, or illustration of the goods or services offered for sale,

(B) includes the business address of the seller,

(C) includes multiple pages of written material or illustrations, and

(D) has been issued not less frequently than once a year,

where the person making the solicitation does not solicit customers by telephone but only receives calls initiated by customers in response to the catalog and during those calls takes orders only without further solicitation.

§ 6107. Enforcement of orders

(a) General authority

Subject to subsections (b) and (c), the Federal Trade Commission may bring a criminal contempt action for violations of orders of the Commission obtained in cases brought under section 53(b) of this title.

(b) Appointment

An action authorized by subsection (a) may be brought by the Federal Trade Commission only after, and pursuant to, the appointment by the Attorney General of an attorney employed by the Commission, as a special assistant United States Attorney.

(c) Request for appointment

(1) Appointment upon request or motion

A special assistant United States Attorney may be appointed under subsection (b) upon the request of the Federal Trade Commission or the court which has entered the order for which contempt is sought or upon the Attorney General's own motion.

(2) Timing

The Attorney General shall act upon any request made under paragraph (1) within 45 days of the receipt of the request.

(d) Termination of authority

The authority of the Federal Trade Commission to bring a criminal contempt action under subsection (a) expires 2 years after the date of the first promulgation of rules under section 6102 of this title. The expiration of such authority shall have no effect on an action brought before the expiration date.

§ 6108. Review

Upon the expiration of 5 years following the date of the first promulgation of rules under section 6102 of this title, the Commission shall review the implementation of this chapter and its effect on deceptive telemarketing acts or practices and report the results of the review to the Congress.

Telemarketing Regulations

16 C.F.R. Part 310

Table of Sections

§ 310.1. Scope of regulations in this part

This part implements the Telemarketing and Consumer Fraud and Abuse Prevention Act, 15 U.S.C. 6101–6108, as amended.

§ 310.2. Definitions

(a) Acquirer means a business organization, financial institution, or an agent of a business organization or financial institution that has authority from an organization that operates or licenses a credit card system to authorize merchants to accept, transmit, or process payment by credit card through the credit card system for money, goods or services, or anything else of value.

(b) Attorney General means the chief legal officer of a state.

(c) Billing information means any data that enables any person to access a customer's or donor's account, such as a credit card, checking, savings, share or similar account, utility bill, mortgage loan account, or debit card.

(d) Caller identification service means a service that allows a telephone subscriber to have the telephone number, and, where available, name of the calling party transmitted contemporaneously with the telephone call, and displayed on a device in or connected to the subscriber's telephone.

(e) Cardholder means a person to whom a credit card is issued or who is authorized to use a credit card on behalf of or in addition to the person to whom the credit card is issued.

(f) Cash-to-cash money transfer means the electronic (as defined in section 106(2) of the Electronic Signatures in Global and National Commerce Act (15 U.S.C. 7006(2)) transfer of the value of cash received from one person to another person in a different location that is sent by a money transfer provider and received in the form of cash. For purposes of this definition, money transfer provider means any person or financial institution that provides cash-to-cash money transfers for a person in the normal course of its business, whether or not the person holds an account with such person or financial institution. The term cash-to-cash money transfer includes a remittance transfer, as defined in section 919(g)(2) of the Electronic Fund Transfer Act ("EFTA"), 15 U.S.C. 1693a, that is a cash-to-cash transaction; however it does not include any transaction that is:

(1) An electronic fund transfer as defined in section 903 of the EFTA;

(2) Covered by Regulation E, 12 CFR 1005.20, pertaining to gift cards; or

(3) Subject to the Truth in Lending Act, 15 U.S.C. 1601 et seq.

(g) Cash reload mechanism is a device, authorization code, personal identification number, or other security measure that makes it possible for a person to convert cash into an electronic (as defined in section 106(2) of the Electronic Signatures in Global and National Commerce Act (15 U.S.C. 7006(2)) form that can be used to add funds to a general-use prepaid card, as defined in Regulation E, 12 CFR 1005.2, or an account with a payment intermediary. For purposes of this definition, a cash reload mechanism is not itself a general-use prepaid debit card or a swipe reload process or similar method in which funds are added directly onto a person's own general-use prepaid card or account with a payment intermediary.

(h) Charitable contribution means any donation or gift of money or any other thing of value.

(i) Commission means the Federal Trade Commission.

(j) Credit means the right granted by a creditor to a debtor to defer payment of debt or to incur debt and defer its payment.

(k) Credit card means any card, plate, coupon book, or other credit device existing for the purpose of obtaining money, property, labor, or services on credit.

(*l*) Credit card sales draft means any record or evidence of a credit card transaction.

(m) Credit card system means any method or procedure used to process credit card transactions involving credit cards issued or licensed by the operator of that system.

(n) Customer means any person who is or may be required to pay for goods or services offered through telemarketing.

(*o*) Debt relief service means any program or service represented, directly or by implication, to renegotiate, settle, or in any way alter the terms of payment or other terms of the debt between a person and one or more unsecured creditors or debt collectors, including, but not limited to, a reduction in the balance, interest rate, or fees owed by a person to an unsecured creditor or debt collector.

(p) Donor means any person solicited to make a charitable contribution.

(q) Established business relationship means a relationship between a seller and a consumer based on:

(1) the consumer's purchase, rental, or lease of the seller's goods or services or a financial transaction between the consumer and seller, within the eighteen (18) months immediately preceding the date of a telemarketing call; or

(2) the consumer's inquiry or application regarding a product or service offered by the seller, within the three (3) months immediately preceding the date of a telemarketing call.

(r) Free-to-pay conversion means, in an offer or agreement to sell or provide any goods or services, a provision under which a customer receives a product or service for free for an initial period and will incur an obligation to pay for the product or service if he or she does not take affirmative action to cancel before the end of that period.

(s) Investment opportunity means anything, tangible or intangible, that is offered, offered for sale, sold, or traded based wholly or in part on representations, either express or implied, about past, present, or future income, profit, or appreciation.

(t) Material means likely to affect a person's choice of, or conduct regarding, goods or services or a charitable contribution.

(u) Merchant means a person who is authorized under a written contract with an acquirer to honor or accept credit cards, or to transmit or process for payment credit card payments, for the purchase of goods or services or a charitable contribution.

(v) Merchant agreement means a written contract between a merchant and an acquirer to honor or accept credit cards, or to transmit or process for payment credit card payments, for the purchase of goods or services or a charitable contribution.

(w) Negative option feature means, in an offer or agreement to sell or provide any goods or services, a provision under which the customer's silence or failure to take an affirmative action to reject goods or services or to cancel the agreement is interpreted by the seller as acceptance of the offer.

(x) Outbound telephone call means a telephone call initiated by a telemarketer to induce the purchase of goods or services or to solicit a charitable contribution.

(y) Person means any individual, group, unincorporated association, limited or general partnership, corporation, or other business entity.

(z) Preacquired account information means any information that enables a seller or telemarketer to cause a charge to be placed against a customer's or donor's account without obtaining the account number directly from the customer or donor during the telemarketing transaction pursuant to which the account will be charged.

(aa) Prize means anything offered, or purportedly offered, and given, or purportedly given, to a person by chance. For purposes of this definition, chance exists if a person is guaranteed to receive an item and, at the time of the offer or purported offer, the telemarketer does not identify the specific item that the person will receive.

(bb) Prize promotion means:

(1) A sweepstakes or other game of chance; or

(2) An oral or written express or implied representation that a person has won, has been selected to receive, or may be eligible to receive a prize or purported prize.

(cc) Remotely created payment order means any payment instruction or order drawn on a person's account that is created by the payee or the payee's agent and deposited into or cleared through the check clearing system. The term includes, without limitation, a "remotely created check," as defined in Regulation CC, Availability of Funds and Collection of Checks, 12 CFR 229.2(fff), but does not include a payment order cleared through an Automated Clearinghouse (ACH) Network or subject to the Truth in Lending Act, 15 U.S.C. 1601 et seq., and Regulation Z, 12 CFR part 1026.

(dd) Seller means any person who, in connection with a telemarketing transaction, provides, offers to provide, or arranges for others to provide goods or services to the customer in exchange for consideration.

(ee) State means any state of the United States, the District of Columbia, Puerto Rico, the Northern Mariana Islands, and any territory or possession of the United States.

(ff) Telemarketer means any person who, in connection with telemarketing, initiates or receives telephone calls to or from a customer or donor.

(gg) Telemarketing means a plan, program, or campaign which is conducted to induce the purchase of goods or services or a charitable contribution, by use of one or more telephones and which involves more than one interstate telephone call. The term does not include the solicitation of sales through the mailing of a catalog which: contains a written description or illustration of the goods or services offered for sale; includes the business address of the seller; includes multiple pages of written material or illustrations; and has been issued not less frequently than once a year, when the person making the solicitation does not solicit customers by telephone but only receives calls initiated by customers in response to the catalog and during those calls takes orders only without further solicitation. For purposes of the previous sentence, the term "further solicitation" does not include providing the customer with information about, or attempting to sell, any other item included in the same catalog which prompted the customer's call or in a substantially similar catalog.

(hh) Upselling means soliciting the purchase of goods or services following an initial transaction during a single telephone call. The upsell is a separate telemarketing transaction, not a continuation of the initial transaction. An "external upsell" is a solicitation made by or on behalf of a seller different from the seller in the initial transaction, regardless of whether the initial transaction and the subsequent solicitation are made by the same telemarketer. An "internal upsell" is a solicitation made by or on behalf of the same seller as in the initial transaction, regardless of whether the initial transaction and subsequent solicitation are made by the same telemarketer.

§ 310.3. Deceptive telemarketing acts or practices

(a) Prohibited deceptive telemarketing acts or practices. It is a deceptive telemarketing act or practice and a violation of this Rule for any seller or telemarketer to engage in the following conduct:

(1) Before a customer consents to pay[659] for goods or services offered, failing to disclose truthfully, in a clear and conspicuous manner, the following material information:

(i) The total costs to purchase, receive, or use, and the quantity of, any goods or services that are the subject of the sales offer;[660]

(ii) All material restrictions, limitations, or conditions to purchase, receive, or use the goods or services that are the subject of the sales offer;

(iii) If the seller has a policy of not making refunds, cancellations, exchanges, or repurchases, a statement informing the customer that this is the seller's policy; or, if the seller or telemarketer makes a representation about a refund, cancellation, exchange, or repurchase policy, a statement of all material terms and conditions of such policy;

(iv) In any prize promotion, the odds of being able to receive the prize, and, if the odds are not calculable in advance, the factors used in calculating the odds; that no purchase or payment is required to win a prize or to participate in a prize promotion and that any purchase or payment will not increase the person's chances of winning; and the no-purchase/no-payment method of participating in the prize promotion with either instructions on how to participate or an address or local or toll-free telephone number to which customers may write or call for information on how to participate;

(v) All material costs or conditions to receive or redeem a prize that is the subject of the prize promotion;

(vi) In the sale of any goods or services represented to protect, insure, or otherwise limit a customer's liability in the event of unauthorized use of the customer's credit card, the limits on a cardholder's liability for unauthorized use of a credit card pursuant to 15 U.S.C. 1643;

(vii) If the offer includes a negative option feature, all material terms and conditions of the negative option feature, including, but not limited to, the fact that the customer's account will be charged unless the customer takes an affirmative action to avoid the charge(s), the date(s) the charge(s) will be submitted for payment, and the specific steps the customer must take to avoid the charge(s); and

(viii) In the sale of any debt relief service:

(A) the amount of time necessary to achieve the represented results, and to the extent that the service may include a settlement offer to any of the customer's creditors

---

[659] When a seller or telemarketer uses, or directs a customer to use, a courier to transport payment, the seller or telemarketer must make the disclosures required by § 310.3(a)(1) before sending a courier to pick up payment or authorization for payment, or directing a customer to have a courier pick up payment or authorization for payment. In the case of debt relief services, the seller or telemarketer must make the disclosures required by § 310.3(a)(1) before the consumer enrolls in an offered program.

[660] For offers of consumer credit products subject to the Truth in Lending Act, 15 U.S.C. 1601 et seq., and Regulation Z, 12 CFR 226, compliance with the disclosure requirements under the Truth in Lending Act and Regulation Z shall constitute compliance with § 310.3(a)(1)(i) of this Rule.

or debt collectors, the time by which the debt relief service provider will make a bona fide settlement offer to each of them;

(B) to the extent that the service may include a settlement offer to any of the customer's creditors or debt collectors, the amount of money or the percentage of each outstanding debt that the customer must accumulate before the debt relief service provider will make a bona fide settlement offer to each of them;

(C) to the extent that any aspect of the debt relief service relies upon or results in the customer's failure to make timely payments to creditors or debt collectors, that the use of the debt relief service will likely adversely affect the customer's creditworthiness, may result in the customer being subject to collections or sued by creditors or debt collectors, and may increase the amount of money the customer owes due to the accrual of fees and interest; and

(D) to the extent that the debt relief service requests or requires the customer to place funds in an account at an insured financial institution, that the customer owns the funds held in the account, the customer may withdraw from the debt relief service at any time without penalty, and, if the customer withdraws, the customer must receive all funds in the account, other than funds earned by the debt relief service in compliance with § 310.4(a)(5)(i)(A) through (C).

(2) Misrepresenting, directly or by implication, in the sale of goods or services any of the following material information:

(i) The total costs to purchase, receive, or use, and the quantity of, any goods or services that are the subject of a sales offer;

(ii) Any material restriction, limitation, or condition to purchase, receive, or use goods or services that are the subject of a sales offer;

(iii) Any material aspect of the performance, efficacy, nature, or central characteristics of goods or services that are the subject of a sales offer;

(iv) Any material aspect of the nature or terms of the seller's refund, cancellation, exchange, or repurchase policies;

(v) Any material aspect of a prize promotion including, but not limited to, the odds of being able to receive a prize, the nature or value of a prize, or that a purchase or payment is required to win a prize or to participate in a prize promotion;

(vi) Any material aspect of an investment opportunity including, but not limited to, risk, liquidity, earnings potential, or profitability;

(vii) A seller's or telemarketer's affiliation with, or endorsement or sponsorship by, any person or government entity;

(viii) That any customer needs offered goods or services to provide protections a customer already has pursuant to 15 U.S.C. 1643;

(ix) Any material aspect of a negative option feature including, but not limited to, the fact that the customer's account will be charged unless the customer takes an affirmative action to avoid the charge(s), the date(s) the charge(s) will be submitted for payment, and the specific steps the customer must take to avoid the charge(s); or

(x) Any material aspect of any debt relief service, including, but not limited to, the amount of money or the percentage of the debt amount that a customer may save by using such service; the amount of time necessary to achieve the represented results; the amount of money or the percentage of each outstanding debt that the customer must accumulate before the provider of the debt relief service will initiate attempts with the customer's creditors or debt collectors or make a bona fide offer to negotiate, settle, or modify the terms of the customer's debt; the effect of the service on a customer's creditworthiness; the effect of the service on collection efforts of the customer's creditors or debt collectors; the percentage or number of customers who attain the represented results; and whether a debt relief service is offered or provided by a non-profit entity.

(3) Causing billing information to be submitted for payment, or collecting or attempting to collect payment for goods or services or a charitable contribution, directly or indirectly, without the customer's or donor's express verifiable authorization, except when the method of payment used is a credit card subject to protections of the Truth in Lending Act and Regulation Z,[661] or a debit card subject to the protections of the Electronic Fund Transfer Act and Regulation E.[662] Such authorization shall be deemed verifiable if any of the following means is employed:

(i) Express written authorization by the customer or donor, which includes the customer's or donor's signature;[663]

(ii) Express oral authorization which is audio-recorded and made available upon request to the customer or donor, and the customer's or donor's bank or other billing entity, and which evidences clearly both the customer's or donor's authorization of payment for the goods or services or charitable contribution that are the subject of the telemarketing transaction and the customer's or donor's receipt of all of the following information:

(A) An accurate description, clearly and conspicuously stated, of the goods or services or charitable contribution for which payment authorization is sought;

(B) The number of debits, charges, or payments (if more than one);

(C) The date(s) the debit(s), charge(s), or payment(s) will be submitted for payment;

(D) The amount(s) of the debit(s), charge(s), or payment(s);

(E) The customer's or donor's name;

(F) The customer's or donor's billing information, identified with sufficient specificity such that the customer or donor understands what account will be used to collect payment for the goods or services or charitable contribution that are the subject of the telemarketing transaction;

(G) A telephone number for customer or donor inquiry that is answered during normal business hours; and

(H) The date of the customer's or donor's oral authorization; or

(iii) Written confirmation of the transaction, identified in a clear and conspicuous manner as such on the outside of the envelope, sent to the customer or donor via first class mail prior to the submission for payment of the customer's or donor's billing information, and that includes all of the information contained in §§ 310.3(a)(3)(ii)(A)–(G) and a clear and conspicuous statement of the procedures by which the customer or donor can obtain a refund from the seller or telemarketer or charitable organization in the event the confirmation is inaccurate; provided, however, that this means of authorization shall not be deemed verifiable in instances in which goods or services are offered in a transaction involving a free-to-pay conversion and preacquired account information.

(4) Making a false or misleading statement to induce any person to pay for goods or services or to induce a charitable contribution.

---

[661] Truth in Lending Act, 15 U.S.C. 1601 et seq., and Regulation Z, 12 CFR part 226.

[662] Electronic Fund Transfer Act, 15 U.S.C. 1693 et seq., and Regulation E, 12 CFR part 205.

[663] For purposes of this Rule, the term "signature" shall include an electronic or digital form of signature, to the extent that such form of signature is recognized as a valid signature under applicable federal law or state contract law.

(b) Assisting and facilitating. It is a deceptive telemarketing act or practice and a violation of this Rule for a person to provide substantial assistance or support to any seller or telemarketer when that person knows or consciously avoids knowing that the seller or telemarketer is engaged in any act or practice that violates §§ 310.3(a), (c) or (d), or § 310.4 of this Rule.

(c) Credit card laundering. Except as expressly permitted by the applicable credit card system, it is a deceptive telemarketing act or practice and a violation of this Rule for:

(1) A merchant to present to or deposit into, or cause another to present to or deposit into, the credit card system for payment, a credit card sales draft generated by a telemarketing transaction that is not the result of a telemarketing credit card transaction between the cardholder and the merchant;

(2) Any person to employ, solicit, or otherwise cause a merchant, or an employee, representative, or agent of the merchant, to present to or deposit into the credit card system for payment, a credit card sales draft generated by a telemarketing transaction that is not the result of a telemarketing credit card transaction between the cardholder and the merchant; or

(3) Any person to obtain access to the credit card system through the use of a business relationship or an affiliation with a merchant, when such access is not authorized by the merchant agreement or the applicable credit card system.

(d) Prohibited deceptive acts or practices in the solicitation of charitable contributions. It is a fraudulent charitable solicitation, a deceptive telemarketing act or practice, and a violation of this Rule for any telemarketer soliciting charitable contributions to misrepresent, directly or by implication, any of the following material information:

(1) The nature, purpose, or mission of any entity on behalf of which a charitable contribution is being requested;

(2) That any charitable contribution is tax deductible in whole or in part;

(3) The purpose for which any charitable contribution will be used;

(4) The percentage or amount of any charitable contribution that will go to a charitable organization or to any particular charitable program;

(5) Any material aspect of a prize promotion including, but not limited to: the odds of being able to receive a prize; the nature or value of a prize; or that a charitable contribution is required to win a prize or to participate in a prize promotion; or

(6) A charitable organization's or telemarketer's affiliation with, or endorsement or sponsorship by, any person or government entity.

§ 310.4. Abusive telemarketing acts or practices

(a) Abusive conduct generally. It is an abusive telemarketing act or practice and a violation of this Rule for any seller or telemarketer to engage in the following conduct:

(1) Threats, intimidation, or the use of profane or obscene language;

(2) Requesting or receiving payment of any fee or consideration for goods or services represented to remove derogatory information from, or improve, a person's credit history, credit record, or credit rating until:

(i) The time frame in which the seller has represented all of the goods or services will be provided to that person has expired; and

(ii) The seller has provided the person with documentation in the form of a consumer report from a consumer reporting agency demonstrating that the promised results have been achieved, such report having been issued more than six months after the results were achieved. Nothing in this Rule should be construed to affect the requirement in the Fair

Credit Reporting Act, 15 U.S.C. 1681, that a consumer report may only be obtained for a specified permissible purpose;

(3) Requesting or receiving payment of any fee or consideration from a person for goods or services represented to recover or otherwise assist in the return of money or any other item of value paid for by, or promised to, that person in a previous transaction, until seven (7) business days after such money or other item is delivered to that person. This provision shall not apply to goods or services provided to a person by a licensed attorney;

(4) Requesting or receiving payment of any fee or consideration in advance of obtaining a loan or other extension of credit when the seller or telemarketer has guaranteed or represented a high likelihood of success in obtaining or arranging a loan or other extension of credit for a person;

(5)(i) Requesting or receiving payment of any fee or consideration for any debt relief service until and unless:

(A) The seller or telemarketer has renegotiated, settled, reduced, or otherwise altered the terms of at least one debt pursuant to a settlement agreement, debt management plan, or other such valid contractual agreement executed by the customer;

(B) The customer has made at least one payment pursuant to that settlement agreement, debt management plan, or other valid contractual agreement between the customer and the creditor or debt collector; and

(C) To the extent that debts enrolled in a service are renegotiated, settled, reduced, or otherwise altered individually, the fee or consideration either:

(1) Bears the same proportional relationship to the total fee for renegotiating, settling, reducing, or altering the terms of the entire debt balance as the individual debt amount bears to the entire debt amount. The individual debt amount and the entire debt amount are those owed at the time the debt was enrolled in the service; or

(2) Is a percentage of the amount saved as a result of the renegotiation, settlement, reduction, or alteration. The percentage charged cannot change from one individual debt to another. The amount saved is the difference between the amount owed at the time the debt was enrolled in the service and the amount actually paid to satisfy the debt.

(ii) Nothing in § 310.4(a)(5)(i) prohibits requesting or requiring the customer to place funds in an account to be used for the debt relief provider's fees and for payments to creditors or debt collectors in connection with the renegotiation, settlement, reduction, or other alteration of the terms of payment or other terms of a debt, provided that:

(A) The funds are held in an account at an insured financial institution;

(B) The customer owns the funds held in the account and is paid accrued interest on the account, if any;

(C) The entity administering the account is not owned or controlled by, or in any way affiliated with, the debt relief service;

(D) The entity administering the account does not give or accept any money or other compensation in exchange for referrals of business involving the debt relief service; and

(E) The customer may withdraw from the debt relief service at any time without penalty, and must receive all funds in the account, other than funds earned by the debt relief service in compliance with § 310.4(a)(5)(i)(A) through (C), within seven (7) business days of the customer's request.

(6) Disclosing or receiving, for consideration, unencrypted consumer account numbers for use in telemarketing; provided, however, that this paragraph shall not apply to the disclosure or receipt of a customer's or donor's billing information to process a payment for goods or services or a charitable contribution pursuant to a transaction;

(7) Causing billing information to be submitted for payment, directly or indirectly, without the express informed consent of the customer or donor. In any telemarketing transaction, the seller or telemarketer must obtain the express informed consent of the customer or donor to be charged for the goods or services or charitable contribution and to be charged using the identified account. In any telemarketing transaction involving preacquired account information, the requirements in paragraphs (a)(7)(i) through (ii) of this section must be met to evidence express informed consent.

(i) In any telemarketing transaction involving preacquired account information and a free-to-pay conversion feature, the seller or telemarketer must:

(A) Obtain from the customer, at a minimum, the last four (4) digits of the account number to be charged;

(B) Obtain from the customer his or her express agreement to be charged for the goods or services and to be charged using the account number pursuant to paragraph (a)(7)(i)(A) of this section; and,

(C) Make and maintain an audio recording of the entire telemarketing transaction.

(ii) In any other telemarketing transaction involving preacquired account information not described in paragraph (a)(7)(i) of this section, the seller or telemarketer must:

(A) At a minimum, identify the account to be charged with sufficient specificity for the customer or donor to understand what account will be charged; and

(B) Obtain from the customer or donor his or her express agreement to be charged for the goods or services and to be charged using the account number identified pursuant to paragraph (a)(7)(ii)(A) of this section;

(8) Failing to transmit or cause to be transmitted the telephone number, and, when made available by the telemarketer's carrier, the name of the telemarketer, to any caller identification service in use by a recipient of a telemarketing call; provided that it shall not be a violation to substitute (for the name and phone number used in, or billed for, making the call) the name of the seller or charitable organization on behalf of which a telemarketing call is placed, and the seller's or charitable organization's customer or donor service telephone number, which is answered during regular business hours;

(9) Creating or causing to be created, directly or indirectly, a remotely created payment order as payment for goods or services offered or sold through telemarketing or as a charitable contribution solicited or sought through telemarketing; or

(10) Accepting from a customer or donor, directly or indirectly, a cash-to-cash money transfer or cash reload mechanism as payment for goods or services offered or sold through telemarketing or as a charitable contribution solicited or sought through telemarketing.

(b) Pattern of calls.

(1) It is an abusive telemarketing act or practice and a violation of this Rule for a telemarketer to engage in, or for a seller to cause a telemarketer to engage in, the following conduct:

(i) Causing any telephone to ring, or engaging any person in telephone conversation, repeatedly or continuously with intent to annoy, abuse, or harass any person at the called number;

(ii) Denying or interfering in any way, directly or indirectly, with a person's right to be placed on any registry of names and/or telephone numbers of persons who do not wish to receive outbound telephone calls established to comply with paragraph (b)(1)(iii)(A) of this section, including, but not limited to, harassing any person who makes such a request; hanging up on that person; failing to honor the request; requiring the person to listen to a sales pitch before accepting the request; assessing a charge or fee for honoring the request; requiring a person to call a different number to submit the request; and requiring the person to identify the seller making the call or on whose behalf the call is made;

(iii) Initiating any outbound telephone call to a person when:

(A) That person previously has stated that he or she does not wish to receive an outbound telephone call made by or on behalf of the seller whose goods or services are being offered or made on behalf of the charitable organization for which a charitable contribution is being solicited; or

(B) That person's telephone number is on the "do-not-call" registry, maintained by the Commission, of persons who do not wish to receive outbound telephone calls to induce the purchase of goods or services unless the seller or telemarketer:

(1) Can demonstrate that the seller has obtained the express agreement in writing, of such person to place calls to that person. Such written agreement shall clearly evidence such person's authorization that calls made by or on behalf of a specific party may be placed to that person, and shall include the telephone number to which the calls may be placed and the signature[664] of that person; or

(2) Can demonstrate that the seller has an established business relationship with such person, and that person has not stated that he or she does not wish to receive outbound telephone calls under paragraph (b)(1)(iii)(A) of this section; or

(iv) Abandoning any outbound telephone call. An outbound telephone call is "abandoned" under this section if a person answers it and the telemarketer does not connect the call to a sales representative within two (2) seconds of the person's completed greeting.

(v) Initiating any outbound telephone call that delivers a prerecorded message, other than a prerecorded message permitted for compliance with the call abandonment safe harbor in § 310.4(b)(4)(iii), unless:

(A) In any such call to induce the purchase of any good or service, the seller has obtained from the recipient of the call an express agreement, in writing, that:

(i) The seller obtained only after a clear and conspicuous disclosure that the purpose of the agreement is to authorize the seller to place prerecorded calls to such person;

(ii) The seller obtained without requiring, directly or indirectly, that the agreement be executed as a condition of purchasing any good or service;

(iii) Evidences the willingness of the recipient of the call to receive calls that deliver prerecorded messages by or on behalf of a specific seller; and

(iv) Includes such person's telephone number and signature;[665] and

---

[664] For purposes of this Rule, the term "signature" shall include an electronic or digital form of signature, to the extent that such form of signature is recognized as a valid signature under applicable federal law or state contract law.

[665] For purposes of this Rule, the term "signature" shall include an electronic or digital form of signature, to the extent that such form of signature is recognized as a valid signature under applicable federal law or state contract law.

(B) In any such call to induce the purchase of any good or service, or to induce a charitable contribution from a member of, or previous donor to, a non-profit charitable organization on whose behalf the call is made, the seller or telemarketer:

(i) Allows the telephone to ring for at least fifteen (15) seconds or four (4) rings before disconnecting an unanswered call; and

(ii) Within two (2) seconds after the completed greeting of the person called, plays a prerecorded message that promptly provides the disclosures required by § 310.4(d) or (e), followed immediately by a disclosure of one or both of the following:

(A) In the case of a call that could be answered in person by a consumer, that the person called can use an automated interactive voice and/or keypress-activated opt-out mechanism to assert a Do Not Call request pursuant to § 310.4(b)(1)(iii)(A) at any time during the message. The mechanism must:

(1) Automatically add the number called to the seller's entity-specific Do Not Call list;

(2) Once invoked, immediately disconnect the call; and

(3) Be available for use at any time during the message; and

(B) In the case of a call that could be answered by an answering machine or voicemail service, that the person called can use a toll-free telephone number to assert a Do Not Call request pursuant to § 310.4(b)(1)(iii)(A). The number provided must connect directly to an automated interactive voice or keypress-activated opt-out mechanism that:

(1) Automatically adds the number called to the seller's entity-specific Do Not Call list;

(2) Immediately thereafter disconnects the call; and

(3) Is accessible at any time throughout the duration of the telemarketing campaign; and

(iii) Complies with all other requirements of this part and other applicable federal and state laws.

(C) Any call that complies with all applicable requirements of this paragraph (v) shall not be deemed to violate § 310.4(b)(1)(iv) of this part.

(D) This paragraph (v) shall not apply to any outbound telephone call that delivers a prerecorded healthcare message made by, or on behalf of, a covered entity or its business associate, as those terms are defined in the HIPAA Privacy Rule, 45 CFR 160.103.

(2) It is an abusive telemarketing act or practice and a violation of this Rule for any person to sell, rent, lease, purchase, or use any list established to comply with § 310.4(b)(1)(iii)(A), or maintained by the Commission pursuant to § 310.4(b)(1)(iii)(B), for any purpose except compliance with the provisions of this Rule or otherwise to prevent telephone calls to telephone numbers on such lists.

(3) A seller or telemarketer will not be liable for violating § 310.4(b)(1)(ii) and (iii) if it can demonstrate that, as part of the seller's or telemarketer's routine business practice:

(i) It has established and implemented written procedures to comply with § 310.4(b)(1)(ii) and (iii);

(ii) It has trained its personnel, and any entity assisting in its compliance, in the procedures established pursuant to § 310.4(b)(3)(i);

(iii) The seller, or a telemarketer or another person acting on behalf of the seller or charitable organization, has maintained and recorded a list of telephone numbers the seller or charitable organization may not contact, in compliance with § 310.4(b)(1)(iii)(A);

(iv) The seller or a telemarketer uses a process to prevent telemarketing to any telephone number on any list established pursuant to § 310.4(b)(3)(iii) or 310.4(b)(1)(iii)(B), employing a version of the "do-not-call" registry obtained from the Commission no more than thirty-one (31) days prior to the date any call is made, and maintains records documenting this process;

(v) The seller or a telemarketer or another person acting on behalf of the seller or charitable organization, monitors and enforces compliance with the procedures established pursuant to § 310.4(b)(3)(i); and

(vi) Any subsequent call otherwise violating paragraph (b)(1)(ii) or (iii) of this section is the result of error and not of failure to obtain any information necessary to comply with a request pursuant to paragraph (b)(1)(iii)(A) of this section not to receive further calls by or on behalf of a seller or charitable organization.

(4) A seller or telemarketer will not be liable for violating § 310.4(b)(1)(iv) if:

(i) The seller or telemarketer employs technology that ensures abandonment of no more than three (3) percent of all calls answered by a person, measured over the duration of a single calling campaign, if less than 30 days, or separately over each successive 30-day period or portion thereof that the campaign continues.

(ii) The seller or telemarketer, for each telemarketing call placed, allows the telephone to ring for at least fifteen (15) seconds or four (4) rings before disconnecting an unanswered call;

(iii) Whenever a sales representative is not available to speak with the person answering the call within two (2) seconds after the person's completed greeting, the seller or telemarketer promptly plays a recorded message that states the name and telephone number of the seller on whose behalf the call was placed[666]; and

(iv) The seller or telemarketer, in accordance with § 310.5(b)–(d), retains records establishing compliance with § 310.4(b)(4)(i)–(iii).

(c) Calling time restrictions. Without the prior consent of a person, it is an abusive telemarketing act or practice and a violation of this Rule for a telemarketer to engage in outbound telephone calls to a person's residence at any time other than between 8:00 a.m. and 9:00 p.m. local time at the called person's location.

(d) Required oral disclosures in the sale of goods or services. It is an abusive telemarketing act or practice and a violation of this Rule for a telemarketer in an outbound telephone call or internal or external upsell to induce the purchase of goods or services to fail to disclose truthfully, promptly, and in a clear and conspicuous manner to the person receiving the call, the following information:

(1) The identity of the seller;

(2) That the purpose of the call is to sell goods or services;

(3) The nature of the goods or services; and

---

[666] This provision does not affect any seller's or telemarketer's obligation to comply with relevant state and federal laws, including but not limited to the TCPA, 47 U.S.C. 227, and 47 CFR part 64.1200.

(4) That no purchase or payment is necessary to be able to win a prize or participate in a prize promotion if a prize promotion is offered and that any purchase or payment will not increase the person's chances of winning. This disclosure must be made before or in conjunction with the description of the prize to the person called. If requested by that person, the telemarketer must disclose the no-purchase/no-payment entry method for the prize promotion; provided, however, that, in any internal upsell for the sale of goods or services, the seller or telemarketer must provide the disclosures listed in this section only to the extent that the information in the upsell differs from the disclosures provided in the initial telemarketing transaction.

(e) Required oral disclosures in charitable solicitations. It is an abusive telemarketing act or practice and a violation of this Rule for a telemarketer, in an outbound telephone call to induce a charitable contribution, to fail to disclose truthfully, promptly, and in a clear and conspicuous manner to the person receiving the call, the following information:

(1) The identity of the charitable organization on behalf of which the request is being made; and

(2) That the purpose of the call is to solicit a charitable contribution.

§ 310.5. Recordkeeping requirements

(a) Any seller or telemarketer shall keep, for a period of 24 months from the date the record is produced, the following records relating to its telemarketing activities:

(1) All substantially different advertising, brochures, telemarketing scripts, and promotional materials;

(2) The name and last known address of each prize recipient and the prize awarded for prizes that are represented, directly or by implication, to have a value of $25.00 or more;

(3) The name and last known address of each customer, the goods or services purchased, the date such goods or services were shipped or provided, and the amount paid by the customer for the goods or services; [667]

(4) The name, any fictitious name used, the last known home address and telephone number, and the job title(s) for all current and former employees directly involved in telephone sales or solicitations; provided, however, that if the seller or telemarketer permits fictitious names to be used by employees, each fictitious name must be traceable to only one specific employee; and

(5) All verifiable authorizations or records of express informed consent or express agreement required to be provided or received under this Rule.

(b) A seller or telemarketer may keep the records required by § 310.5(a) in any form, and in the same manner, format, or place as they keep such records in the ordinary course of business. Failure to keep all records required by § 310.5(a) shall be a violation of this Rule.

(c) The seller and the telemarketer calling on behalf of the seller may, by written agreement, allocate responsibility between themselves for the recordkeeping required by this Section. When a seller and telemarketer have entered into such an agreement, the terms of that agreement shall govern, and the seller or telemarketer, as the case may be, need not keep records that duplicate those of the other. If the agreement is unclear as to who must maintain any required record(s), or if no such agreement exists, the seller shall be responsible for complying with §§ 310.5(a)(1)–(3) and (5); the telemarketer shall be responsible for complying with § 310.5(a)(4).

---

[667] For offers of consumer credit products subject to the Truth in Lending Act, 15 U.S.C. 1601 et seq., and Regulation Z, 12 CFR 226, compliance with the recordkeeping requirements under the Truth in Lending Act, and Regulation Z, shall constitute compliance with § 310.5(a)(3) of this Rule.

(d) In the event of any dissolution or termination of the seller's or telemarketer's business, the principal of that seller or telemarketer shall maintain all records as required under this section. In the event of any sale, assignment, or other change in ownership of the seller's or telemarketer's business, the successor business shall maintain all records required under this section.

§ 310.6. Exemptions

(a) Solicitations to induce charitable contributions via outbound telephone calls are not covered by § 310.4(b)(1)(iii)(B) of this Rule.

(b) The following acts or practices are exempt from this Rule:

(1) The sale of pay-per-call services subject to the Commission's Rule entitled "Trade Regulation Rule Pursuant to the Telephone Disclosure and Dispute Resolution Act of 1992," 16 CFR Part 308, provided, however, that this exemption does not apply to the requirements of §§ 310.4(a)(1), (a)(7), (b), and (c);

(2) The sale of franchises subject to the Commission's Rule entitled "Disclosure Requirements and Prohibitions Concerning Franchising," ("Franchise Rule") 16 CFR part 436, and the sale of business opportunities subject to the Commission's Rule entitled "Disclosure Requirements and Prohibitions Concerning Business Opportunities," ("Business Opportunity Rule") 16 CFR part 437, provided, however, that this exemption does not apply to the requirements of §§ 310.4(a)(1), (a)(7), (b), and (c);

(3) Telephone calls in which the sale of goods or services or charitable solicitation is not completed, and payment or authorization of payment is not required, until after a face-to-face sales or donation presentation by the seller or charitable organization, provided, however, that this exemption does not apply to the requirements of §§ 310.4(a)(1), (a)(7), (b), and (c);

(4) Telephone calls initiated by a customer or donor that are not the result of any solicitation by a seller, charitable organization, or telemarketer, provided, however, that this exemption does not apply to any instances of upselling included in such telephone calls;

(5) Telephone calls initiated by a customer or donor in response to an advertisement through any medium, other than direct mail solicitation, provided, however, that this exemption does not apply to:

(i) Calls initiated by a customer or donor in response to an advertisement relating to investment opportunities, debt relief services, business opportunities other than business arrangements covered by the Franchise Rule or Business Opportunity Rule, or advertisements involving offers for goods or services described in § 310.3(a)(1)(vi) or § 310.4(a)(2) through (4);

(ii) The requirements of § 310.4(a)(9) or (10); or

(iii) Any instances of upselling included in such telephone calls;

(6) Telephone calls initiated by a customer or donor in response to a direct mail solicitation, including solicitations via the U.S. Postal Service, facsimile transmission, electronic mail, and other similar methods of delivery in which a solicitation is directed to specific address(es) or person(s), that clearly, conspicuously, and truthfully discloses all material information listed in § 310.3(a)(1), for any goods or services offered in the direct mail solicitation, and that contains no material misrepresentation regarding any item contained in § 310.3(d) for any requested charitable contribution; *provided,* however, that this exemption does not apply to:

(i) Calls initiated by a customer in response to a direct mail solicitation relating to prize promotions, investment opportunities, debt relief services, business opportunities other than business arrangements covered by the Franchise Rule or Business Opportunity Rule, or goods or services described in § 310.3(a)(1)(vi) or § 310.4(a)(2) through (4);

(ii) The requirements of § 310.4(a)(9) or (10); or

(iii) Any instances of upselling included in such telephone calls; and

(7) Telephone calls between a telemarketer and any business to induce the purchase of goods or services or a charitable contribution by the business, except calls to induce the retail sale of nondurable office or cleaning supplies; provided, however, that §§ 310.4(b)(1)(iii)(B) and 310.5 shall not apply to sellers or telemarketers of nondurable office or cleaning supplies.

§ 310.7. Actions by states and private persons

(a) Any attorney general or other officer of a state authorized by the state to bring an action under the Telemarketing and Consumer Fraud and Abuse Prevention Act, and any private person who brings an action under that Act, shall serve written notice of its action on the Commission, if feasible, prior to its initiating an action under this Rule. The notice shall be sent to the Office of the Director, Bureau of Consumer Protection, Federal Trade Commission, Washington, D.C. 20580, and shall include a copy of the state's or private person's complaint and any other pleadings to be filed with the court. If prior notice is not feasible, the state or private person shall serve the Commission with the required notice immediately upon instituting its action.

(b) Nothing contained in this Section shall prohibit any attorney general or other authorized state official from proceeding in state court on the basis of an alleged violation of any civil or criminal statute of such state.

§ 310.8. Fee for access to the National Do Not Call Registry

(a) It is a violation of this Rule for any seller to initiate, or cause any telemarketer to initiate, an outbound telephone call to any person whose telephone number is within a given area code unless such seller, either directly or through another person, first has paid the annual fee, required by § 310.8(c), for access to telephone numbers within that area code that are included in the National Do Not Call Registry maintained by the Commission under § 310.4(b)(1)(iii)(B); provided, however, that such payment is not necessary if the seller initiates, or causes a telemarketer to initiate, calls solely to persons pursuant to §§ 310.4(b)(1)(iii)(B)(i) or (ii), and the seller does not access the National Do Not Call Registry for any other purpose.

(b) It is a violation of this Rule for any telemarketer, on behalf of any seller, to initiate an outbound telephone call to any person whose telephone number is within a given area code unless that seller, either directly or through another person, first has paid the annual fee, required by § 310.8(c), for access to the telephone numbers within that area code that are included in the National Do Not Call Registry; provided, however, that such payment is not necessary if the seller initiates, or causes a telemarketer to initiate, calls solely to persons pursuant to §§ 310.4(b)(1)(iii)(B)(i) or (ii), and the seller does not access the National Do Not Call Registry for any other purpose.

(c) The annual fee, which must be paid by any person prior to obtaining access to the National Do Not Call Registry, is $65 for each area code of data accessed, up to a maximum of $17,765; *provided, however*, that there shall be no charge to any person for accessing the first five area codes of data, and *provided further*, that there shall be no charge to any person engaging in or causing others to engage in outbound telephone calls to consumers and who is accessing area codes of data in the National Do Not Call Registry if the person is permitted to access, but is not required to access, the National Do Not Call Registry under this Rule, 47 CFR 64.1200, or any other Federal regulation or law. No person may participate in any arrangement to share the cost of accessing the National Do Not Call Registry, including any arrangement with any telemarketer or service provider to divide the costs to access the registry among various clients of that telemarketer or service provider.

(d) Each person who pays, either directly or through another person, the annual fee set forth in paragraph (c) of this section, each person excepted under paragraph (c) from paying the annual fee, and each person excepted from paying an annual fee under § 310.4(b)(1)(iii)(B), will be provided a unique account number that will allow that person to access the registry data for the selected area codes at any time for the twelve month period beginning on the first day of the month in which the person paid the fee ("the annual period"). To obtain access to additional area codes of data during the first six months of the annual period, each person required to pay the fee under paragraph (c) of this section must first pay $65 for each additional area code of data not initially selected. To obtain access to additional area codes of data during the second six months of the annual period, each person required to pay the fee under paragraph (c) of this section must first pay $32 for each additional area code of data not initially selected. The payment of the additional fee will permit the person to access the additional area codes of data for the remainder of the annual period.

(e) Access to the National Do Not Call Registry is limited to telemarketers, sellers, others engaged in or causing others to engage in telephone calls to consumers, service providers acting on behalf of such persons, and any government agency that has law enforcement authority. Prior to accessing the National Do Not Call Registry, a person must provide the identifying information required by the operator of the registry to collect the fee, and must certify, under penalty of law, that the person is accessing the registry solely to comply with the provisions of this Rule or to otherwise prevent telephone calls to telephone numbers on the registry. If the person is accessing the registry on behalf of sellers, that person also must identify each of the sellers on whose behalf it is accessing the registry, must provide each seller's unique account number for access to the national registry, and must certify, under penalty of law, that the sellers will be using the information gathered from the registry solely to comply with the provisions of this Rule or otherwise to prevent telephone calls to telephone numbers on the registry.

§ 310.9. Severability

The provisions of this Rule are separate and severable from one another. If any provision is stayed or determined to be invalid, it is the Commission's intention that the remaining provisions shall continue in effect.

RESTORE ONLINE SHOPPERS' CONFIDENCE ACT (ROSCA)

15 U.S.C.A. §§ 8401–8405

Table of Sections

§ 8401. Findings; declaration of policy

The Congress finds the following:

(1) The Internet has become an important channel of commerce in the United States, accounting for billions of dollars in retail sales every year. Over half of all American adults have now either made an online purchase or an online travel reservation.

(2) Consumer confidence is essential to the growth of online commerce. To continue its development as a marketplace, the Internet must provide consumers with clear, accurate information and give sellers an opportunity to fairly compete with one another for consumers' business.

(3) An investigation by the Senate Committee on Commerce, Science, and Transportation found abundant evidence that the aggressive sales tactics many companies use against their online customers have undermined consumer confidence in the Internet and thereby harmed the American economy.

(4) The Committee showed that, in exchange for "bounties" and other payments, hundreds of reputable online retailers and websites shared their customers' billing information, including credit card and debit card numbers, with third party sellers through a process known as "data pass". These third party sellers in turn used aggressive, misleading sales tactics to charge millions of American consumers for membership clubs the consumers did not want.

(5) Third party sellers offered membership clubs to consumers as they were in the process of completing their initial transactions on hundreds of websites. These third party "post-transaction" offers were designed to make consumers think the offers were part of the initial purchase, rather than a new transaction with a new seller.

(6) Third party sellers charged millions of consumers for membership clubs without ever obtaining consumers' billing information, including their credit or debit card information, directly from the consumers. Because third party sellers acquired consumers' billing information from the initial merchant through "data pass", millions of consumers were unaware they had been enrolled in membership clubs.

(7) The use of a "data pass" process defied consumers' expectations that they could only be charged for a good or a service if they submitted their billing information, including their complete credit or debit card numbers.

(8) Third party sellers used a free trial period to enroll members, after which they periodically charged consumers until consumers affirmatively canceled the memberships. This use of "free-to-pay conversion" and "negative option" sales took advantage of consumers' expectations that they would have an opportunity to accept or reject the membership club offer at the end of the trial period.

§ 8402. Prohibitions against certain unfair and deceptive Internet sales practices

(a) Requirements for certain Internet-based sales

It shall be unlawful for any post-transaction third party seller to charge or attempt to charge any consumer's credit card, debit card, bank account, or other financial account for any good or service sold in a transaction effected on the Internet, unless—

(1) before obtaining the consumer's billing information, the post-transaction third party seller has clearly and conspicuously disclosed to the consumer all material terms of the transaction, including—

(A) a description of the goods or services being offered;

(B) the fact that the post-transaction third party seller is not affiliated with the initial merchant, which may include disclosure of the name of the post-transaction third party in a manner that clearly differentiates the post-transaction third party seller from the initial merchant; and

(C) the cost of such goods or services; and

(2) the post-transaction third party seller has received the express informed consent for the charge from the consumer whose credit card, debit card, bank account, or other financial account will be charged by—

(A) obtaining from the consumer—

(i) the full account number of the account to be charged; and

(ii) the consumer's name and address and a means to contact the consumer; and

(B) requiring the consumer to perform an additional affirmative action, such as clicking on a confirmation button or checking a box that indicates the consumer's consent to be charged the amount disclosed.

(b) Prohibition on data-pass used to facilitate certain deceptive Internet sales transactions

It shall be unlawful for an initial merchant to disclose a credit card, debit card, bank account, or other financial account number, or to disclose other billing information that is used to charge a customer of the initial merchant, to any post-transaction third party seller for use in an Internet-based sale of any goods or services from that post-transaction third party seller.

(c) Application with other law

Nothing in this chapter shall be construed to supersede, modify, or otherwise affect the requirements of the Electronic Funds[34] Transfer Act (15 U.S.C. 1693 et seq.) or any regulation promulgated thereunder.

(d) Definitions

In this section:

(1) Initial merchant

The term "initial merchant" means a person that has obtained a consumer's billing information directly from the consumer through an Internet transaction initiated by the consumer.

(2) Post-transaction third party seller

The term "post-transaction third party seller" means a person that—

(A) sells, or offers for sale, any good or service on the Internet;

---

[34] So in original. Probably should be "Fund".

(B) solicits the purchase of such goods or services on the Internet through an initial merchant after the consumer has initiated a transaction with the initial merchant; and

(C) is not—

(i) the initial merchant;

(ii) a subsidiary or corporate affiliate of the initial merchant; or

(iii) a successor of an entity described in clause (i) or (ii).

§ 8403. Negative option marketing on the Internet

It shall be unlawful for any person to charge or attempt to charge any consumer for any goods or services sold in a transaction effected on the Internet through a negative option feature (as defined in the Federal Trade Commission's Telemarketing Sales Rule in part 310 of title 16, Code of Federal Regulations), unless the person—

(1) provides text that clearly and conspicuously discloses all material terms of the transaction before obtaining the consumer's billing information;

(2) obtains a consumer's express informed consent before charging the consumer's credit card, debit card, bank account, or other financial account for products or services through such transaction; and

(3) provides simple mechanisms for a consumer to stop recurring charges from being placed on the consumer's credit card, debit card, bank account, or other financial account.

§ 8404. Enforcement by Federal Trade Commission

(a) In general

Violation of this chapter or any regulation prescribed under this chapter shall be treated as a violation of a rule under section 18 of the Federal Trade Commission Act (15 U.S.C. 57a) regarding unfair or deceptive acts or practices. The Federal Trade Commission shall enforce this chapter in the same manner, by the same means, and with the same jurisdiction, powers, and duties as though all applicable terms and provisions of the Federal Trade Commission Act (15 U.S.C. 41 et seq.) were incorporated into and made a part of this chapter.

(b) Penalties

Any person who violates this chapter or any regulation prescribed under this chapter shall be subject to the penalties and entitled to the privileges and immunities provided in the Federal Trade Commission Act as though all applicable terms and provisions of the Federal Trade Commission Act were incorporated in and made part of this chapter.

(c) Authority preserved

Nothing in this section shall be construed to limit the authority of the Commission under any other provision of law.

§ 8405. Enforcement by State attorneys general

(a) Right of action

Except as provided in subsection (e), the attorney general of a State, or other authorized State officer, alleging a violation of this chapter or any regulation issued under this chapter that affects or may affect such State or its residents may bring an action on behalf of the residents of the State in any United States district court for the district in which the defendant is found, resides, or transacts business, or wherever venue is proper under section 1391 of Title 28, to obtain appropriate injunctive relief.

(b) Notice to Commission required

A State shall provide prior written notice to the Federal Trade Commission of any civil action under subsection (a) together with a copy of its complaint, except that if it is not feasible for the State to provide such prior notice, the State shall provide such notice immediately upon instituting such action.

(c) Intervention by the Commission

The Commission may intervene in such civil action and upon intervening—

(1) be heard on all matters arising in such civil action; and

(2) file petitions for appeal of a decision in such civil action.

(d) Construction

Nothing in this section shall be construed—

(1) to prevent the attorney general of a State, or other authorized State officer, from exercising the powers conferred on the attorney general, or other authorized State officer, by the laws of such State; or

(2) to prohibit the attorney general of a State, or other authorized State officer, from proceeding in State or Federal court on the basis of an alleged violation of any civil or criminal statute of that State.

(e) Limitation

No separate suit shall be brought under this section if, at the time the suit is brought, the same alleged violation is the subject of a pending action by the Federal Trade Commission or the United States under this chapter.

UNSOLICITED COMMERCIAL EMAIL MATERIALS

Controlling the Assault of Non-Solicited Pornography and Marketing ("CANSPAM") Act of 2003, 15 U.S.C. § 7701 et seq.

Table of Sections

Sec.

§ 7701. Congressional findings and policy

(a) Findings

The Congress finds the following:

(1) Electronic mail has become an extremely important and popular means of communication, relied on by millions of Americans on a daily basis for personal and commercial purposes. Its low cost and global reach make it extremely convenient and efficient, and offer unique opportunities for the development and growth of frictionless commerce.

(2) The convenience and efficiency of electronic mail are threatened by the extremely rapid growth in the volume of unsolicited commercial electronic mail. Unsolicited commercial electronic mail is currently estimated to account for over half of all electronic mail traffic, up from an estimated 7 percent in 2001, and the volume continues to rise. Most of these messages are fraudulent or deceptive in one or more respects.

(3) The receipt of unsolicited commercial electronic mail may result in costs to recipients who cannot refuse to accept such mail and who incur costs for the storage of such mail, or for the time spent accessing, reviewing, and discarding such mail, or for both.

(4) The receipt of a large number of unwanted messages also decreases the convenience of electronic mail and creates a risk that wanted electronic mail messages, both commercial and noncommercial, will be lost, overlooked, or discarded amidst the larger volume of unwanted messages, thus reducing the reliability and usefulness of electronic mail to the recipient.

(5) Some commercial electronic mail contains material that many recipients may consider vulgar or pornographic in nature.

(6) The growth in unsolicited commercial electronic mail imposes significant monetary costs on providers of Internet access services, businesses, and educational and nonprofit institutions that carry and receive such mail, as there is a finite volume of mail that such providers, businesses, and institutions can handle without further investment in infrastructure.

(7) Many senders of unsolicited commercial electronic mail purposefully disguise the source of such mail.

(8) Many senders of unsolicited commercial electronic mail purposefully include misleading information in the messages' subject lines in order to induce the recipients to view the messages.

(9) While some senders of commercial electronic mail messages provide simple and reliable ways for recipients to reject (or "opt-out" of) receipt of commercial electronic mail from such senders in the future, other senders provide no such "opt-out" mechanism, or refuse to honor the requests of recipients not to receive electronic mail from such senders in the future, or both.

(10) Many senders of bulk unsolicited commercial electronic mail use computer programs to gather large numbers of electronic mail addresses on an automated basis from Internet websites or online services where users must post their addresses in order to make full use of the website or service.

(11) Many States have enacted legislation intended to regulate or reduce unsolicited commercial electronic mail, but these statutes impose different standards and requirements. As a result, they do not appear to have been successful in addressing the problems associated with unsolicited commercial electronic mail, in part because, since an electronic mail address does not specify a geographic location, it can be extremely difficult for law-abiding businesses to know with which of these disparate statutes they are required to comply.

(12) The problems associated with the rapid growth and abuse of unsolicited commercial electronic mail cannot be solved by Federal legislation alone. The development and adoption of technological approaches and the pursuit of cooperative efforts with other countries will be necessary as well.

(b) Congressional determination of public policy

On the basis of the findings in subsection (a) of this section, the Congress determines that—

(1) there is a substantial government interest in regulation of commercial electronic mail on a nationwide basis;

(2) senders of commercial electronic mail should not mislead recipients as to the source or content of such mail; and

(3) recipients of commercial electronic mail have a right to decline to receive additional commercial electronic mail from the same source.

§ 7702. Definitions

In this chapter:

(1) Affirmative consent

The term "affirmative consent", when used with respect to a commercial electronic mail message, means that—

(A) the recipient expressly consented to receive the message, either in response to a clear and conspicuous request for such consent or at the recipient's own initiative; and

(B) if the message is from a party other than the party to which the recipient communicated such consent, the recipient was given clear and conspicuous notice at the time the consent was communicated that the recipient's electronic mail address could be transferred to such other party for the purpose of initiating commercial electronic mail messages.

(2) Commercial electronic mail message

(A) In general

The term "commercial electronic mail message" means any electronic mail message the primary purpose of which is the commercial advertisement or promotion of a commercial product or service (including content on an Internet website operated for a commercial purpose).

(B) Transactional or relationship messages

The term "commercial electronic mail message" does not include a transactional or relationship message.

(C) Regulations regarding primary purpose

Not later than 12 months after December 16, 2003, the Commission shall issue regulations pursuant to section 7711 of this title defining the relevant criteria to facilitate the determination of the primary purpose of an electronic mail message.

(D) Reference to company or website

The inclusion of a reference to a commercial entity or a link to the website of a commercial entity in an electronic mail message does not, by itself, cause such message to be treated as a commercial electronic mail message for purposes of this chapter if the contents or circumstances of the message indicate a primary purpose other than commercial advertisement or promotion of a commercial product or service.

(3) Commission

The term "Commission" means the Federal Trade Commission.

(4) Domain name

The term "domain name" means any alphanumeric designation which is registered with or assigned by any domain name registrar, domain name registry, or other domain name registration authority as part of an electronic address on the Internet.

(5) Electronic mail address

The term "electronic mail address" means a destination, commonly expressed as a string of characters, consisting of a unique user name or mailbox (commonly referred to as the "local part") and a reference to an Internet domain (commonly referred to as the "domain part"), whether or not displayed, to which an electronic mail message can be sent or delivered.

(6) Electronic mail message

The term "electronic mail message" means a message sent to a unique electronic mail address.

(7) FTC Act

The term "FTC Act" means the Federal Trade Commission Act (15 U.S.C. 41 et seq.).

(8) Header information

The term "header information" means the source, destination, and routing information attached to an electronic mail message, including the originating domain name and originating electronic mail address, and any other information that appears in the line identifying, or purporting to identify, a person initiating the message.

(9) Initiate

The term "initiate", when used with respect to a commercial electronic mail message, means to originate or transmit such message or to procure the origination or transmission of such message, but shall not include actions that constitute routine conveyance of such message. For purposes of this paragraph, more than one person may be considered to have initiated a message.

(10) Internet

The term "Internet" has the meaning given that term in the Internet Tax Freedom Act (47 U.S.C. 151 nt).

(11) Internet access service

The term "Internet access service" has the meaning given that term in section 231(e)(4) of Title 47.

(12) Procure

The term "procure", when used with respect to the initiation of a commercial electronic mail message, means intentionally to pay or provide other consideration to, or induce, another person to initiate such a message on one's behalf.

(13) Protected computer

The term "protected computer" has the meaning given that term in section 1030(e)(2)(B) of Title 18.

(14) Recipient

The term "recipient", when used with respect to a commercial electronic mail message, means an authorized user of the electronic mail address to which the message was sent or delivered. If a recipient of a commercial electronic mail message has one or more electronic mail addresses in addition to the address to which the message was sent or delivered, the recipient shall be treated as a separate recipient with respect to each such address. If an electronic mail address is reassigned to a new user, the new user shall not be treated as a recipient of any commercial electronic mail message sent or delivered to that address before it was reassigned.

(15) Routine conveyance

The term "routine conveyance" means the transmission, routing, relaying, handling, or storing, through an automatic technical process, of an electronic mail message for which another person has identified the recipients or provided the recipient addresses.

(16) Sender

(A) In general

Except as provided in subparagraph (B), the term "sender", when used with respect to a commercial electronic mail message, means a person who initiates such a message and whose product, service, or Internet web site is advertised or promoted by the message.

(B) Separate lines of business or divisions

If an entity operates through separate lines of business or divisions and holds itself out to the recipient throughout the message as that particular line of business or division rather than as the entity of which such line of business or division is a part, then the line of business or the division shall be treated as the sender of such message for purposes of this chapter.

(17) Transactional or relationship message

(A) In general

The term "transactional or relationship message" means an electronic mail message the primary purpose of which is—

(i) to facilitate, complete, or confirm a commercial transaction that the recipient has previously agreed to enter into with the sender;

(ii) to provide warranty information, product recall information, or safety or security information with respect to a commercial product or service used or purchased by the recipient;

(iii) to provide—

(I) notification concerning a change in the terms or features of;

(II) notification of a change in the recipient's standing or status with respect to; or

(III) at regular periodic intervals, account balance information or other type of account statement with respect to, a subscription, membership, account, loan, or comparable ongoing commercial relationship involving the ongoing purchase or use by the recipient of products or services offered by the sender;

(iv) to provide information directly related to an employment relationship or related benefit plan in which the recipient is currently involved, participating, or enrolled; or

(v) to deliver goods or services, including product updates or upgrades, that the recipient is entitled to receive under the terms of a transaction that the recipient has previously agreed to enter into with the sender.

(B) Modification of definition

The Commission by regulation pursuant to section 7711 of this title may modify the definition in subparagraph (A) to expand or contract the categories of messages that are treated as transactional or relationship messages for purposes of this chapter to the extent that such modification is necessary to accommodate changes in electronic mail technology or practices and accomplish the purposes of this chapter.

§ 7703. Prohibition against predatory and abusive commercial e-mail

(a) Omitted

(b) United States Sentencing Commission

(1) Directive

Pursuant to its authority under section 994(p) of Title 28 and in accordance with this section, the United States Sentencing Commission shall review and, as appropriate, amend the sentencing guidelines and policy statements to provide appropriate penalties for violations of section 1037 of Title 18, as added by this section, and other offenses that may be facilitated by the sending of large quantities of unsolicited electronic mail.

(2) Requirements

In carrying out this subsection, the Sentencing Commission shall consider providing sentencing enhancements for—

(A) those convicted under section 1037 of Title 18 who—

(i) obtained electronic mail addresses through improper means, including—

(I) harvesting electronic mail addresses of the users of a website, proprietary service, or other online public forum operated by another person, without the authorization of such person; and

(II) randomly generating electronic mail addresses by computer; or

(ii) knew that the commercial electronic mail messages involved in the offense contained or advertised an Internet domain for which the registrant of the domain had provided false registration information; and

(B) those convicted of other offenses, including offenses involving fraud, identity theft, obscenity, child pornography, and the sexual exploitation of children, if such offenses involved the sending of large quantities of electronic mail.

(c) Sense of Congress

It is the sense of Congress that—

(1) Spam has become the method of choice for those who distribute pornography, perpetrate fraudulent schemes, and introduce viruses, worms, and Trojan horses into personal and business computer systems; and

(2) the Department of Justice should use all existing law enforcement tools to investigate and prosecute those who send bulk commercial e-mail to facilitate the commission of Federal crimes, including the tools contained in chapters 47 and 63 of Title 18 (relating to fraud and false statements); chapter 71 of Title 18 (relating to obscenity); chapter 110 of Title 18 (relating to the sexual exploitation of children); and chapter 95 of Title 18 (relating to racketeering), as appropriate.

§ 7704. Other protections for users of commercial electronic mail

(a) Requirements for transmission of messages

(1) Prohibition of false or misleading transmission information

It is unlawful for any person to initiate the transmission, to a protected computer, of a commercial electronic mail message, or a transactional or relationship message, that contains, or is accompanied by, header information that is materially false or materially misleading. For purposes of this paragraph—

(A) header information that is technically accurate but includes an originating electronic mail address, domain name, or Internet Protocol address the access to which for purposes of initiating the message was obtained by means of false or fraudulent pretenses or representations shall be considered materially misleading;

(B) a "from" line (the line identifying or purporting to identify a person initiating the message) that accurately identifies any person who initiated the message shall not be considered materially false or materially misleading; and

(C) header information shall be considered materially misleading if it fails to identify accurately a protected computer used to initiate the message because the person initiating the message knowingly uses another protected computer to relay or retransmit the message for purposes of disguising its origin.

(2) Prohibition of deceptive subject headings

It is unlawful for any person to initiate the transmission to a protected computer of a commercial electronic mail message if such person has actual knowledge, or knowledge fairly implied on the basis of objective circumstances, that a subject heading of the message would be likely to mislead a recipient, acting reasonably under the circumstances, about a material fact regarding the contents or subject matter of the message (consistent with the criteria used in enforcement of section 45 of this title).

(3) Inclusion of return address or comparable mechanism in commercial electronic mail—

(A) In general

It is unlawful for any person to initiate the transmission to a protected computer of a commercial electronic mail message that does not contain a functioning return electronic mail address or other Internet-based mechanism, clearly and conspicuously displayed, that—

(i) a recipient may use to submit, in a manner specified in the message, a reply electronic mail message or other form of Internet-based communication requesting not to receive future commercial electronic mail messages from that sender at the electronic mail address where the message was received; and

(ii) remains capable of receiving such messages or communications for no less than 30 days after the transmission of the original message.

(B) More detailed options possible

The person initiating a commercial electronic mail message may comply with subparagraph (A)(i) by providing the recipient a list or menu from which the recipient may choose the specific types of commercial electronic mail messages the recipient wants to receive or does not want to receive from the sender, if the list or menu includes an option under which the recipient may choose not to receive any commercial electronic mail messages from the sender.

(C) Temporary inability to receive messages or process requests

A return electronic mail address or other mechanism does not fail to satisfy the requirements of subparagraph (A) if it is unexpectedly and temporarily unable to receive messages or process requests due to a technical problem beyond the control of the sender if the problem is corrected within a reasonable time period.

(4) Prohibition of transmission of commercial electronic mail after objection

(A) In general

If a recipient makes a request using a mechanism provided pursuant to paragraph (3) not to receive some or any commercial electronic mail messages from such sender, then it is unlawful—

(i) for the sender to initiate the transmission to the recipient, more than 10 business days after the receipt of such request, of a commercial electronic mail message that falls within the scope of the request;

(ii) for any person acting on behalf of the sender to initiate the transmission to the recipient, more than 10 business days after the receipt of such request, of a commercial electronic mail message with actual knowledge, or knowledge fairly implied on the basis of objective circumstances, that such message falls within the scope of the request;

(iii) for any person acting on behalf of the sender to assist in initiating the transmission to the recipient, through the provision or selection of addresses to which the message will be sent, of a commercial electronic mail message with actual knowledge, or knowledge fairly implied on the basis of objective circumstances, that such message would violate clause (i) or (ii); or

(iv) for the sender, or any other person who knows that the recipient has made such a request, to sell, lease, exchange, or otherwise transfer or release the electronic mail address of the recipient (including through any transaction or other transfer involving mailing lists bearing the electronic mail address of the recipient) for any purpose other than compliance with this chapter or other provision of law.

(B) Subsequent affirmative consent

A prohibition in subparagraph (A) does not apply if there is affirmative consent by the recipient subsequent to the request under subparagraph (A).

(5) Inclusion of identifier, opt-out, and physical address in commercial electronic mail

(A) It is unlawful for any person to initiate the transmission of any commercial electronic mail message to a protected computer unless the message provides—

(i) clear and conspicuous identification that the message is an advertisement or solicitation;

(ii) clear and conspicuous notice of the opportunity under paragraph (3) to decline to receive further commercial electronic mail messages from the sender; and

(iii) a valid physical postal address of the sender.

(B) Subparagraph (A)(i) does not apply to the transmission of a commercial electronic mail message if the recipient has given prior affirmative consent to receipt of the message.

(6) Materially

For purposes of paragraph (1), the term "materially", when used with respect to false or misleading header information, includes the alteration or concealment of header information in a manner that would impair the ability of an Internet access service processing the message on behalf of a recipient, a person alleging a violation of this section, or a law enforcement agency to identify, locate, or respond to a person who initiated the electronic mail message or to investigate the alleged violation, or the ability of a recipient of the message to respond to a person who initiated the electronic message.

(b) Aggravated violations relating to commercial electronic mail

(1) Address harvesting and dictionary attacks—

(A) In general

It is unlawful for any person to initiate the transmission, to a protected computer, of a commercial electronic mail message that is unlawful under subsection (a), or to assist in the origination of such message through the provision or selection of addresses to which the message will be transmitted, if such person had actual knowledge, or knowledge fairly implied on the basis of objective circumstances, that—

(i) the electronic mail address of the recipient was obtained using an automated means from an Internet website or proprietary online service operated by another person, and such website or online service included, at the time the address was obtained, a notice stating that the operator of such website or online service will not give, sell, or otherwise transfer addresses maintained by such website or online service to any other party for the purposes of initiating, or enabling others to initiate, electronic mail messages; or

(ii) the electronic mail address of the recipient was obtained using an automated means that generates possible electronic mail addresses by combining names, letters, or numbers into numerous permutations.

(B) Disclaimer

Nothing in this paragraph creates an ownership or proprietary interest in such electronic mail addresses.

(2) Automated creation of multiple electronic mail accounts

It is unlawful for any person to use scripts or other automated means to register for multiple electronic mail accounts or online user accounts from which to transmit to a protected computer, or enable another person to transmit to a protected computer, a commercial electronic mail message that is unlawful under subsection (a).

(3) Relay or retransmission through unauthorized access

It is unlawful for any person knowingly to relay or retransmit a commercial electronic mail message that is unlawful under subsection (a) from a protected computer or computer network that such person has accessed without authorization.

(c) Supplementary rulemaking authority

The Commission shall by regulation, pursuant to section 7711 of this title—

(1) modify the 10-business-day period under subsection (a)(4)(A) or subsection (a)(4)(B), or both, if the Commission determines that a different period would be more reasonable after taking into account—

(A) the purposes of subsection (a);

(B) the interests of recipients of commercial electronic mail; and

(C) the burdens imposed on senders of lawful commercial electronic mail; and

(2) specify additional activities or practices to which subsection (b) applies if the Commission determines that those activities or practices are contributing substantially to the proliferation of commercial electronic mail messages that are unlawful under subsection (a).

(d) Requirement to place warning labels on commercial electronic mail containing sexually oriented material

(1) In general

No person may initiate in or affecting interstate commerce the transmission, to a protected computer, of any commercial electronic mail message that includes sexually oriented material and—

(A) fail to include in subject heading for the electronic mail message the marks or notices prescribed by the Commission under this subsection; or

(B) fail to provide that the matter in the message that is initially viewable to the recipient, when the message is opened by any recipient and absent any further actions by the recipient, includes only—

(i) to the extent required or authorized pursuant to paragraph (2), any such marks or notices;

(ii) the information required to be included in the message pursuant to subsection (a)(5); and

(iii) instructions on how to access, or a mechanism to access, the sexually oriented material.

(2) Prior affirmative consent

Paragraph (1) does not apply to the transmission of an electronic mail message if the recipient has given prior affirmative consent to receipt of the message.

(3) Prescription of marks and notices

Not later than 120 days after December 16, 2003, the Commission in consultation with the Attorney General shall prescribe clearly identifiable marks or notices to be included in or associated with commercial electronic mail that contains sexually oriented material, in order to inform the recipient of that fact and to facilitate filtering of such electronic mail. The Commission shall publish in the Federal Register and provide notice to the public of the marks or notices prescribed under this paragraph.

(4) Definition

In this subsection, the term "sexually oriented material" means any material that depicts sexually explicit conduct (as that term is defined in section 2256 of Title 18), unless the depiction constitutes a small and insignificant part of the whole, the remainder of which is not primarily devoted to sexual matters.

(5) Penalty

Whoever knowingly violates paragraph (1) shall be fined under Title 18 or imprisoned not more than 5 years, or both.

§ 7705. Businesses knowingly promoted by electronic mail with false or misleading transmission information

(a) In general

It is unlawful for a person to promote, or allow the promotion of, that person's trade or business, or goods, products, property, or services sold, offered for sale, leased or offered for lease, or otherwise made available through that trade or business, in a commercial electronic mail message the transmission of which is in violation of section 7704(a)(1) of this title if that person—

(1) knows, or should have known in the ordinary course of that person's trade or business, that the goods, products, property, or services sold, offered for sale, leased or offered for lease, or otherwise made available through that trade or business were being promoted in such a message;

(2) received or expected to receive an economic benefit from such promotion; and

(3) took no reasonable action—

(A) to prevent the transmission; or

(B) to detect the transmission and report it to the Commission.

(b) Limited enforcement against third parties

(1) In general

Except as provided in paragraph (2), a person (hereinafter referred to as the "third party") that provides goods, products, property, or services to another person that violates subsection (a) shall not be held liable for such violation.

(2) Exception

Liability for a violation of subsection (a) shall be imputed to a third party that provides goods, products, property, or services to another person that violates subsection (a) if that third party—

(A) owns, or has a greater than 50 percent ownership or economic interest in, the trade or business of the person that violated subsection (a); or

(B)(i) has actual knowledge that goods, products, property, or services are promoted in a commercial electronic mail message the transmission of which is in violation of section 7704(a)(1) of this title; and

(ii) receives, or expects to receive, an economic benefit from such promotion.

(c) Exclusive enforcement by FTC

Subsections (f) and (g) of section 7706 of this title do not apply to violations of this section.

(d) Savings provision

Except as provided in section 7706(f)(8) of this title, nothing in this section may be construed to limit or prevent any action that may be taken under this chapter with respect to any violation of any other section of this chapter.

§ 7706. Enforcement generally

(a) Violation is unfair or deceptive act or practice

Except as provided in subsection (b), this chapter shall be enforced by the Commission as if the violation of this chapter were an unfair or deceptive act or practice proscribed under section 57a(a)(1)(B) of this title.

(b) Enforcement by certain other agencies

Compliance with this chapter shall be enforced—

(1) under section 1818 of Title 12, in the case of—

(A) national banks, and Federal branches and Federal agencies of foreign banks, by the Office of the Comptroller of the Currency;

(B) member banks of the Federal Reserve System (other than national banks), branches and agencies of foreign banks (other than Federal branches, Federal agencies, and insured State branches of foreign banks), commercial lending companies owned or controlled by foreign banks, organizations operating under section 25 or 25A of the Federal Reserve Act (12 U.S.C. 601 and 611), and bank holding companies, by the Board;

(C) banks insured by the Federal Deposit Insurance Corporation (other than members of the Federal Reserve System) and insured State branches of foreign banks, by the Board of Directors of the Federal Deposit Insurance Corporation; and

(D) savings associations the deposits of which are insured by the Federal Deposit Insurance Corporation, by the Director of the Office of Thrift Supervision;

(2) under the Federal Credit Union Act (12 U.S.C. 1751 et seq.) by the Board of the National Credit Union Administration with respect to any Federally insured credit union;

(3) under the Securities Exchange Act of 1934 (15 U.S.C. 78a et seq.) by the Securities and Exchange Commission with respect to any broker or dealer;

(4) under the Investment Company Act of 1940 (15 U.S.C. 80a–1 et seq.) by the Securities and Exchange Commission with respect to investment companies;

(5) under the Investment Advisers Act of 1940 (15 U.S.C. 80b–1 et seq.) by the Securities and Exchange Commission with respect to investment advisers registered under that Act;

(6) under State insurance law in the case of any person engaged in providing insurance, by the applicable State insurance authority of the State in which the person is domiciled, subject to section 6701 of this title, except that in any State in which the State insurance authority elects not to exercise this power, the enforcement authority pursuant to this chapter shall be exercised by the Commission in accordance with subsection (a);

(7) under part A of subtitle VII of Title 49 by the Secretary of Transportation with respect to any air carrier or foreign air carrier subject to that part;

(8) under the Packers and Stockyards Act, 1921 (7 U.S.C. 181 et seq.) (except as provided in section 406 of that Act (7 U.S.C. 226, 227)), by the Secretary of Agriculture with respect to any activities subject to that Act;

(9) under the Farm Credit Act of 1971 (12 U.S.C. 2001 et seq.) by the Farm Credit Administration with respect to any Federal land bank, Federal land bank association, Federal intermediate credit bank, or production credit association; and

(10) under the Communications Act of 1934 (47 U.S.C. 151 et seq.) by the Federal Communications Commission with respect to any person subject to the provisions of that Act.

(c) Exercise of certain powers

For the purpose of the exercise by any agency referred to in subsection (b) of its powers under any Act referred to in that subsection, a violation of this chapter is deemed to be a violation of a Federal Trade Commission trade regulation rule. In addition to its powers under any provision of law specifically referred to in subsection (b), each of the agencies referred to in that subsection may exercise, for the purpose of enforcing compliance with any requirement imposed under this chapter, any other authority conferred on it by law.

(d) Actions by the Commission

The Commission shall prevent any person from violating this chapter in the same manner, by the same means, and with the same jurisdiction, powers, and duties as though all applicable terms and provisions of the Federal Trade Commission Act (15 U.S.C. 41 et seq.) were incorporated into and made a part of this chapter. Any entity that violates any provision of that subtitle is subject to the penalties and entitled to the privileges and immunities provided in the Federal Trade Commission Act in the same manner, by the same means, and with the same jurisdiction, power, and duties as though all applicable terms and provisions of the Federal Trade Commission Act were incorporated into and made a part of that subtitle.[1]

(e) Availability of cease-and-desist orders and injunctive relief without showing of knowledge

Notwithstanding any other provision of this chapter, in any proceeding or action pursuant to subsection (a), (b), (c), or (d) of this section to enforce compliance, through an order to cease and desist or an injunction, with section 7704(a)(1)(C) of this title, section 7704(a)(2) of this title, clause (ii), (iii), or (iv) of section 7704(a)(4)(A) of this title, section 7704(b)(1)(A) of this title, or section 7704(b)(3) of this title, neither the Commission nor the Federal Communications Commission shall be required to allege or prove the state of mind required by such section or subparagraph.

(f) Enforcement by States

(1) Civil action

---

1 So in original.

In any case in which the attorney general of a State, or an official or agency of a State, has reason to believe that an interest of the residents of that State has been or is threatened or adversely affected by any person who violates paragraph (1) or (2) of section 7704(a), who violates section 7704(d), or who engages in a pattern or practice that violates paragraph (3), (4), or (5) of section 7704(a) of this title, the attorney general, official, or agency of the State, as parens patriae, may bring a civil action on behalf of the residents of the State in a district court of the United States of appropriate jurisdiction—

(A) to enjoin further violation of section 7704 of this title by the defendant; or

(B) to obtain damages on behalf of residents of the State, in an amount equal to the greater of—

(i) the actual monetary loss suffered by such residents; or

(ii) the amount determined under paragraph (3).

(2) Availability of injunctive relief without showing of knowledge

Notwithstanding any other provision of this chapter, in a civil action under paragraph (1)(A) of this subsection, the attorney general, official, or agency of the State shall not be required to allege or prove the state of mind required by section 7704(a)(1)(C) of this title, section 7704(a)(2) of this title, clause (ii), (iii), or (iv) of section 7704(a)(4)(A) of this title, section 7704(b)(1)(A) of this title, or section 7704(b)(3) of this title.

(3) Statutory damages

(A) In general

For purposes of paragraph (1)(B)(ii), the amount determined under this paragraph is the amount calculated by multiplying the number of violations (with each separately addressed unlawful message received by or addressed to such residents treated as a separate violation) by up to $250.

(B) Limitation

For any violation of section 7704 of this title (other than section 7704(a)(1) of this title), the amount determined under subparagraph (A) may not exceed $2,000,000.

(C) Aggravated damages

The court may increase a damage award to an amount equal to not more than three times the amount otherwise available under this paragraph if—

(i) the court determines that the defendant committed the violation willfully and knowingly; or

(ii) the defendant's unlawful activity included one or more of the aggravating violations set forth in section 7704(b) of this title.

(D) Reduction of damages

In assessing damages under subparagraph (A), the court may consider whether—

(i) the defendant has established and implemented, with due care, commercially reasonable practices and procedures designed to effectively prevent such violations; or

(ii) the violation occurred despite commercially reasonable efforts to maintain compliance the practices and procedures to which reference is made in clause (i).

(4) Attorney fees

In the case of any successful action under paragraph (1), the court, in its discretion, may award the costs of the action and reasonable attorney fees to the State.

(5) Rights of Federal regulators

The State shall serve prior written notice of any action under paragraph (1) upon the Federal Trade Commission or the appropriate Federal regulator determined under subsection (b) and provide the Commission or appropriate Federal regulator with a copy of its complaint, except in any case in which such prior notice is not feasible, in which case the State shall serve such notice immediately upon instituting such action. The Federal Trade Commission or appropriate Federal regulator shall have the right—

(A) to intervene in the action;

(B) upon so intervening, to be heard on all matters arising therein;

(C) to remove the action to the appropriate United States district court; and

(D) to file petitions for appeal.

(6) Construction

For purposes of bringing any civil action under paragraph (1), nothing in this chapter shall be construed to prevent an attorney general of a State from exercising the powers conferred on the attorney general by the laws of that State to—

(A) conduct investigations;

(B) administer oaths or affirmations; or

(C) compel the attendance of witnesses or the production of documentary and other evidence.

(7) Venue; service of process

(A) Venue

Any action brought under paragraph (1) may be brought in the district court of the United States that meets applicable requirements relating to venue under section 1391 of Title 28.

(B) Service of process

In an action brought under paragraph (1), process may be served in any district in which the defendant—

(i) is an inhabitant; or

(ii) maintains a physical place of business.

(8) Limitation on State action while Federal action is pending

If the Commission, or other appropriate Federal agency under subsection (b), has instituted a civil action or an administrative action for violation of this chapter, no State attorney general, or official or agency of a State, may bring an action under this subsection during the pendency of that action against any defendant named in the complaint of the Commission or the other agency for any violation of this chapter alleged in the complaint.

(9) Requisite scienter for certain civil actions

Except as provided in section 7704(a)(1)(C) of this title, section 7704(a)(2) of this title, clause (ii), (iii), or (iv) of section 7704(a)(4)(A) of this title, section 7704(b)(1)(A) of this title, or section 7704(b)(3) of this title, in a civil action brought by a State attorney general, or an official or agency of a State, to recover monetary damages for a violation of this chapter, the court shall not grant the relief sought unless the attorney general, official, or agency establishes that the defendant acted with actual knowledge, or knowledge fairly implied on the basis of objective circumstances, of the act or omission that constitutes the violation.

(g) Action by provider of Internet access service

(1) Action authorized

A provider of Internet access service adversely affected by a violation of section 7704(a)(1), (b), (d) of this title, or a pattern or practice that violates paragraph (2), (3), (4), or (5) of section 7704(a) of this title, may bring a civil action in any district court of the United States with jurisdiction over the defendant—

(A) to enjoin further violation by the defendant; or

(B) to recover damages in an amount equal to the greater of—

(i) actual monetary loss incurred by the provider of Internet access service as a result of such violation; or

(ii) the amount determined under paragraph (3).

(2) Special definition of "procure"

In any action brought under paragraph (1), this chapter shall be applied as if the definition of the term "procure" in section 7702(12) of this title contained, after "behalf" the words "with actual knowledge, or by consciously avoiding knowing, whether such person is engaging, or will engage, in a pattern or practice that violates this chapter".

(3) Statutory damages

(A) In general

For purposes of paragraph (1)(B)(ii), the amount determined under this paragraph is the amount calculated by multiplying the number of violations (with each separately addressed unlawful message that is transmitted or attempted to be transmitted over the facilities of the provider of Internet access service, or that is transmitted or attempted to be transmitted to an electronic mail address obtained from the provider of Internet access service in violation of section 7704(b)(1)(A)(i) of this title, treated as a separate violation) by—

(i) up to $100, in the case of a violation of section 7704(a)(1) of this title; or

(ii) up to $25, in the case of any other violation of section 7704 of this title.

(B) Limitation

For any violation of section 7704 of this title (other than section 7704(a)(1) of this title), the amount determined under subparagraph (A) may not exceed $1,000,000.

(C) Aggravated damages

The court may increase a damage award to an amount equal to not more than three times the amount otherwise available under this paragraph if—

(i) the court determines that the defendant committed the violation willfully and knowingly; or

(ii) the defendant's unlawful activity included one or more of the aggravated violations set forth in section 7704(b) of this title.

(D) Reduction of damages

In assessing damages under subparagraph (A), the court may consider whether—

(i) the defendant has established and implemented, with due care, commercially reasonable practices and procedures designed to effectively prevent such violations; or

(ii) the violation occurred despite commercially reasonable efforts to maintain compliance with the practices and procedures to which reference is made in clause (i).

(4) Attorney fees

In any action brought pursuant to paragraph (1), the court may, in its discretion, require an undertaking for the payment of the costs of such action, and assess reasonable costs, including reasonable attorneys' fees, against any party.

§ 7707. Effect on other laws

(a) Federal law

(1) Nothing in this chapter shall be construed to impair the enforcement of section 223 or 231 of Title 47, chapter 71 (relating to obscenity) or 110 (relating to sexual exploitation of children) of Title 18, or any other Federal criminal statute.

(2) Nothing in this chapter shall be construed to affect in any way the Commission's authority to bring enforcement actions under FTC Act for materially false or deceptive representations or unfair practices in commercial electronic mail messages.

(b) State law

(1) In general

This chapter supersedes any statute, regulation, or rule of a State or political subdivision of a State that expressly regulates the use of electronic mail to send commercial messages, except to the extent that any such statute, regulation, or rule prohibits falsity or deception in any portion of a commercial electronic mail message or information attached thereto.

(2) State law not specific to electronic mail

This chapter shall not be construed to preempt the applicability of—

(A) State laws that are not specific to electronic mail, including State trespass, contract, or tort law; or

(B) other State laws to the extent that those laws relate to acts of fraud or computer crime.

(c) No effect on policies of providers of Internet access service

Nothing in this chapter shall be construed to have any effect on the lawfulness or unlawfulness, under any other provision of law, of the adoption, implementation, or enforcement by a provider of Internet access service of a policy of declining to transmit, route, relay, handle, or store certain types of electronic mail messages.

§ 7708. Do-Not-E-Mail registry

(a) In general

Not later than 6 months after December 16, 2003, the Commission shall transmit to the Senate Committee on Commerce, Science, and Transportation and the House of Representatives Committee on Energy and Commerce a report that—

(1) sets forth a plan and timetable for establishing a nationwide marketing Do-Not-E-Mail registry;

(2) includes an explanation of any practical, technical, security, privacy, enforceability, or other concerns that the Commission has regarding such a registry; and

(3) includes an explanation of how the registry would be applied with respect to children with e-mail accounts.

(b) Authorization to implement

The Commission may establish and implement the plan, but not earlier than 9 months after December 16, 2003.

§ 7709. Study of effects of commercial electronic mail

(a) In general

Not later than 24 months after December 16, 2003, the Commission, in consultation with the Department of Justice and other appropriate agencies, shall submit a report to the Congress that provides a detailed analysis of the effectiveness and enforcement of the provisions of this chapter and the need (if any) for the Congress to modify such provisions.

(b) Required analysis

The Commission shall include in the report required by subsection (a)—

(1) an analysis of the extent to which technological and marketplace developments, including changes in the nature of the devices through which consumers access their electronic mail messages, may affect the practicality and effectiveness of the provisions of this chapter;

(2) analysis and recommendations concerning how to address commercial electronic mail that originates in or is transmitted through or to facilities or computers in other nations, including initiatives or policy positions that the Federal Government could pursue through international negotiations, fora, organizations, or institutions; and

(3) analysis and recommendations concerning options for protecting consumers, including children, from the receipt and viewing of commercial electronic mail that is obscene or pornographic.

§ 7710. Improving enforcement by providing rewards for information about violations; labeling

The Commission shall transmit to the Senate Committee on Commerce, Science, and Transportation and the House of Representatives Committee on Energy and Commerce—

(1) a report, within 9 months after December 16, 2003, that sets forth a system for rewarding those who supply information about violations of this chapter, including—

(A) procedures for the Commission to grant a reward of not less than 20 percent of the total civil penalty collected for a violation of this chapter to the first person that—

(i) identifies the person in violation of this chapter; and

(ii) supplies information that leads to the successful collection of a civil penalty by the Commission; and

(B) procedures to minimize the burden of submitting a complaint to the Commission concerning violations of this chapter, including procedures to allow the electronic submission of complaints to the Commission; and

(2) a report, within 18 months after December 16, 2003, that sets forth a plan for requiring commercial electronic mail to be identifiable from its subject line, by means of compliance with Internet Engineering Task Force Standards, the use of the characters "ADV" in the subject line, or other comparable identifier, or an explanation of any concerns the Commission has that cause the Commission to recommend against the plan.

§ 7711. Regulations

(a) In general

The Commission may issue regulations to implement the provisions of this Act (not including the amendments made by sections 4 and 12). Any such regulations shall be issued in accordance with section 553 of Title 5.

(b) Limitation

Subsection (a) may not be construed to authorize the Commission to establish a requirement pursuant to section 7704(a)(5)(A) of this title to include any specific words, characters, marks, or labels in a commercial electronic mail message, or to include the identification required by section 7704(a)(5)(A) of this title in any particular part of such a mail message (such as the subject line or body).

§ 7712. Application to wireless

(a) Effect on other law

Nothing in this chapter shall be interpreted to preclude or override the applicability of section 227 of Title 47 or the rules prescribed under section 6102 of this title.

(b) FCC rulemaking

The Federal Communications Commission, in consultation with the Federal Trade Commission, shall promulgate rules within 270 days to protect consumers from unwanted mobile service commercial messages. The Federal Communications Commission, in promulgating the rules, shall, to the extent consistent with subsection (c)—

(1) provide subscribers to commercial mobile services the ability to avoid receiving mobile service commercial messages unless the subscriber has provided express prior authorization to the sender, except as provided in paragraph (3);

(2) allow recipients of mobile service commercial messages to indicate electronically a desire not to receive future mobile service commercial messages from the sender;

(3) take into consideration, in determining whether to subject providers of commercial mobile services to paragraph (1), the relationship that exists between providers of such services and their subscribers, but if the Commission determines that such providers should not be subject to paragraph (1), the rules shall require such providers, in addition to complying with the other provisions of this chapter, to allow subscribers to indicate a desire not to receive future mobile service commercial messages from the provider—

(A) at the time of subscribing to such service; and

(B) in any billing mechanism; and

(4) determine how a sender of mobile service commercial messages may comply with the provisions of this chapter, considering the unique technical aspects, including the functional and character limitations, of devices that receive such messages.

(c) Other factors considered

The Federal Communications Commission shall consider the ability of a sender of a commercial electronic mail message to reasonably determine that the message is a mobile service commercial message.

(d) Mobile service commercial message defined

In this section, the term "mobile service commercial message" means a commercial electronic mail message that is transmitted directly to a wireless device that is utilized by a subscriber of commercial mobile service (as such term is defined in section 332(d) of Title 47) in connection with such service.

§ 7713. Separability

If any provision of this chapter or the application thereof to any person or circumstance is held invalid, the remainder of this chapter and the application of such provision to other persons or circumstances shall not be affected.

Fraud and related activity in connection with electronic mail

18 U.S.C. § 1037

(a) In general.—Whoever, in or affecting interstate or foreign commerce, knowingly—

(1) accesses a protected computer without authorization, and intentionally initiates the transmission of multiple commercial electronic mail messages from or through such computer,

(2) uses a protected computer to relay or retransmit multiple commercial electronic mail messages, with the intent to deceive or mislead recipients, or any Internet access service, as to the origin of such messages,

(3) materially falsifies header information in multiple commercial electronic mail messages and intentionally initiates the transmission of such messages,

(4) registers, using information that materially falsifies the identity of the actual registrant, for five or more electronic mail accounts or online user accounts or two or more domain names, and intentionally initiates the transmission of multiple commercial electronic mail messages from any combination of such accounts or domain names, or

(5) falsely represents oneself to be the registrant or the legitimate successor in interest to the registrant of 5 or more Internet Protocol addresses, and intentionally initiates the transmission of multiple commercial electronic mail messages from such addresses,

or conspires to do so, shall be punished as provided in subsection (b).

(b) Penalties.—The punishment for an offense under subsection (a) is—[a fine or imprisonment or both] * * *

(d) Definitions.—In this section: * * *

(2) Materially.—For purposes of paragraphs (3) and (4) of subsection (a), header information or registration information is materially falsified if it is altered or concealed in a manner that would impair the ability of a recipient of the message, an Internet access service processing the message on behalf of a recipient, a person alleging a violation of this section, or a law enforcement agency to identify, locate, or respond to a person who initiated the electronic mail message or to investigate the alleged violation.

(3) Multiple.—The term "multiple" means more than 100 electronic mail messages during a 24-hour period, more than 1,000 electronic mail messages during a 30-day period, or more than 10,000 electronic mail messages during a 1-year period. * * *

REGULATIONS IMPLEMENTING THE CANSPAM ACT, 16 C.F.R. PART 316

Table of Sections

§ 316.1. Scope

This part implements the Controlling the Assault of Non-Solicited Pornography and Marketing Act of 2003 ("CAN-SPAM Act"), 15 U.S.C. 7701–7713.

§ 316.2. Definitions

(a) The definition of the term "affirmative consent" is the same as the definition of that term in the CAN-SPAM Act, 15 U.S.C. 7702(1).

(b) "Character" means an element of the American Standard Code for Information Interchange ("ASCII") character set.

(c) The definition of the term "commercial electronic mail message" is the same as the definition of that term in the CAN-SPAM Act, 15 U.S.C. 7702(2).

(d) The definition of the term "electronic mail address" is the same as the definition of that term in the CAN-SPAM Act, 15 U.S.C. 7702(5).

(e) The definition of the term "electronic mail message" is the same as the definition of that term in the CAN-SPAM Act, 15 U.S.C. 7702(6).

(f) The definition of the term "initiate" is the same as the definition of that term in the CAN-SPAM Act, 15 U.S.C. 7702(9).

(g) The definition of the term "Internet" is the same as the definition of that term in the CAN-SPAM Act, 15 U.S.C. 7702(10).

(h) "Person" means any individual, group, unincorporated association, limited or general partnership, corporation, or other business entity.

(i) The definition of the term "procure" is the same as the definition of that term in the CAN-SPAM Act, 15 U.S.C. 7702(12).

(j) The definition of the term "protected computer" is the same as the definition of that term in the CAN-SPAM Act, 15 U.S.C. 7702(13).

(k) The definition of the term "recipient" is the same as the definition of that term in the CAN-SPAM Act, 15 U.S.C. 7702(14).

(*l*) The definition of the term "routine conveyance" is the same as the definition of that term in the CAN-SPAM Act, 15 U.S.C. 7702(15).

(m) The definition of the term "sender" is the same as the definition of that term in the CAN-SPAM Act, 15 U.S.C. 7702(16), provided that, when more than one person's products, services, or Internet website are advertised or promoted in a single electronic mail message, each such person who is within the Act's definition will be deemed to be a "sender," except that, only one person will be deemed to be the "sender" of that message if such person: (A) is within the Act's definition of "sender"; (B) is identified in the "from" line as the sole sender of the message; and (C) is in compliance with 15

U.S.C. 7704(a)(1), 15 U.S.C. 7704(a)(2), 15 U.S.C. 7704(a)(3)(A)(i), 15 U.S.C. 7704(a)(5)(A), and 16 CFR 316.4.

(n) The definition of the term "sexually oriented material" is the same as the definition of that term in the CAN-SPAM Act, 15 U.S.C. 7704(d)(4).

(*o*) The definition of the term "transactional or relationship messages" is the same as the definition of that term in the CAN-SPAM Act, 15 U.S.C. 7702(17).

(p) "Valid physical postal address" means the sender's current street address, a Post Office box the sender has accurately registered with the United States Postal Service, or a private mailbox the sender has accurately registered with a commercial mail receiving agency that is established pursuant to United States Postal Service regulations.

§ 316.3. Primary purpose

(a) In applying the term "commercial electronic mail message" defined in the CAN-SPAM Act, 15 U.S.C. 7702(2), the "primary purpose" of an electronic mail message shall be deemed to be commercial based on the criteria in paragraphs (a)(1) through (3) and (b) of this section:[1]

(1) If an electronic mail message consists exclusively of the commercial advertisement or promotion of a commercial product or service, then the "primary purpose" of the message shall be deemed to be commercial.

(2) If an electronic mail message contains both the commercial advertisement or promotion of a commercial product or service as well as transactional or relationship content as set forth in paragraph (c) of this section, then the "primary purpose" of the message shall be deemed to be commercial if:

(i) A recipient reasonably interpreting the subject line of the electronic mail message would likely conclude that the message contains the commercial advertisement or promotion of a commercial product or service; or

(ii) The electronic mail message's transactional or relationship content as set forth in paragraph (c) of this section does not appear, in whole or in substantial part, at the beginning of the body of the message.

(3) If an electronic mail message contains both the commercial advertisement or promotion of a commercial product or service as well as other content that is not transactional or relationship content as set forth in paragraph (c) of this section, then the "primary purpose" of the message shall be deemed to be commercial if:

(i) A recipient reasonably interpreting the subject line of the electronic mail message would likely conclude that the message contains the commercial advertisement or promotion of a commercial product or service; or

(ii) A recipient reasonably interpreting the body of the message would likely conclude that the primary purpose of the message is the commercial advertisement or promotion of a commercial product or service. Factors illustrative of those relevant to this interpretation include the placement of content that is the commercial advertisement or promotion of a commercial product or service, in whole or in substantial part, at the beginning of the body of the message; the proportion of the message dedicated to such content; and how color, graphics, type size, and style are used to highlight commercial content.

(b) In applying the term "transactional or relationship message" defined in the CAN-SPAM Act, 15 U.S.C. § 7702(17), the "primary purpose" of an electronic mail message shall be deemed to be

[1] The Commission does not intend for these criteria to treat as a "commercial electronic mail message" anything that is not commercial speech.

transactional or relationship if the electronic mail message consists exclusively of transactional or relationship content as set forth in paragraph (c) of this section.

(c) Transactional or relationship content of email messages under the CAN-SPAM Act is content:

(1) To facilitate, complete, or confirm a commercial transaction that the recipient has previously agreed to enter into with the sender;

(2) To provide warranty information, product recall information, or safety or security information with respect to a commercial product or service used or purchased by the recipient;

(3) With respect to a subscription, membership, account, loan, or comparable ongoing commercial relationship involving the ongoing purchase or use by the recipient of products or services offered by the sender, to provide—

(i) Notification concerning a change in the terms or features;

(ii) Notification of a change in the recipient's standing or status; or

(iii) At regular periodic intervals, account balance information or other type of account statement;

(4) To provide information directly related to an employment relationship or related benefit plan in which the recipient is currently involved, participating, or enrolled; or

(5) To deliver goods or services, including product updates or upgrades, that the recipient is entitled to receive under the terms of a transaction that the recipient has previously agreed to enter into with the sender.

§ 316.4. Requirement to place warning labels on commercial electronic mail that contains sexually oriented material

(a) Any person who initiates, to a protected computer, the transmission of a commercial electronic mail message that includes sexually oriented material must:

(1) Exclude sexually oriented materials from the subject heading for the electronic mail message and include in the subject heading the phrase "SEXUALLY-EXPLICIT:" in capital letters as the first nineteen (19) characters at the beginning of the subject line;[2]

(2) Provide that the content of the message that is initially viewable by the recipient, when the message is opened by any recipient and absent any further actions by the recipient, include only the following information:

(i) The phrase "SEXUALLY-EXPLICIT: "in a clear and conspicuous manner;[3]

(ii) Clear and conspicuous identification that the message is an advertisement or solicitation;

(iii) Clear and conspicuous notice of the opportunity of a recipient to decline to receive further commercial electronic mail messages from the sender;

(iv) A functioning return electronic mail address or other Internet-based mechanism, clearly and conspicuously displayed, that

(A) A recipient may use to submit, in a manner specified in the message, a reply electronic mail message or other form of Internet-based communication requesting not

---

2 The phrase "SEXUALLY-EXPLICIT" comprises 17 characters, including the dash between the two words. The colon (:) and the space following the phrase are the 18th and 19th characters.

3 This phrase consists of nineteen (19) characters and is identical to the phrase required in 316.5(a)(1) of this Rule.

to receive future commercial electronic mail messages from that sender at the electronic mail address where the message was received; and

(B) Remains capable of receiving such messages or communications for no less than 30 days after the transmission of the original message;

(v) Clear and conspicuous display of a valid physical postal address of the sender; and

(vi) Any needed instructions on how to access, or activate a mechanism to access, the sexually oriented material, preceded by a clear and conspicuous statement that to avoid viewing the sexually oriented material, a recipient should delete the email message without following such instructions.

(b) Prior affirmative consent. Paragraph (a) does not apply to the transmission of an electronic mail message if the recipient has given prior affirmative consent to receipt of the message.

§ 316.5. Prohibition on charging a fee or imposing other requirements on recipients who wish to opt out

Neither a sender nor any person acting on behalf of a sender may require that any recipient pay any fee, provide any information other than the recipient's electronic mail address and opt-out preferences, or take any other steps except sending a reply electronic mail message or visiting a single Internet Web page, in order to:

(a) Use a return electronic mail address or other Internet-based mechanism, required by 15 U.S.C. 7704(a)(3), to submit a request not to receive future commercial electronic mail messages from a sender; or

(b) Have such a request honored as required by 15 U.S.C. 7704(a)(3)(B) and (a)(4).

§ 316.6. Severability

The provisions of this Part are separate and severable from one another. If any provision is stayed or determined to be invalid, it is the Commission's intention that the remaining provisions shall continue in effect.

EXCERPTS FROM FINANCIAL PRIVACY LAWS

EXCERPTS FROM THE GRAMM-LEACH-BLILEY ACT, 15 U.S.C. § 6801 ET SEQ.

Table of Sections

§ 6801. Protection of nonpublic personal information

(a) Privacy obligation policy

It is the policy of the Congress that each financial institution has an affirmative and continuing obligation to respect the privacy of its customers and to protect the security and confidentiality of those customers' nonpublic personal information.

(b) Financial institutions safeguards

In furtherance of the policy in subsection (a) of this section, each agency or authority described in section 6805(a) of this title, other than the Bureau of Consumer Financial Protection, shall establish appropriate standards for the financial institutions subject to their jurisdiction relating to administrative, technical, and physical safeguards—

(1) to insure the security and confidentiality of customer records and information;

(2) to protect against any anticipated threats or hazards to the security or integrity of such records; and

(3) to protect against unauthorized access to or use of such records or information which could result in substantial harm or inconvenience to any customer.

§ 6802. Obligations with respect to disclosures of personal information

(a) Notice requirements

Except as otherwise provided in this subchapter, a financial institution may not, directly or through any affiliate, disclose to a nonaffiliated third party any nonpublic personal information, unless such financial institution provides or has provided to the consumer a notice that complies with section 6803 of this title.

(b) Opt out

(1) In general

A financial institution may not disclose nonpublic personal information to a nonaffiliated third party unless—

(A) such financial institution clearly and conspicuously discloses to the consumer, in writing or in electronic form or other form permitted by the regulations prescribed under section 6804 of this title, that such information may be disclosed to such third party;

(B) the consumer is given the opportunity, before the time that such information is initially disclosed, to direct that such information not be disclosed to such third party; and

(C) the consumer is given an explanation of how the consumer can exercise that nondisclosure option.

(2) Exception

This subsection shall not prevent a financial institution from providing nonpublic personal information to a nonaffiliated third party to perform services for or functions on behalf of the financial institution, including marketing of the financial institution's own products or services, or financial products or services offered pursuant to joint agreements between two or more financial institutions that comply with the requirements imposed by the regulations prescribed under section 6804 of this title, if the financial institution fully discloses the providing of such information and enters into a contractual agreement with the third party that requires the third party to maintain the confidentiality of such information.

(c) Limits on reuse of information

Except as otherwise provided in this subchapter, a nonaffiliated third party that receives from a financial institution nonpublic personal information under this section shall not, directly or through an affiliate of such receiving third party, disclose such information to any other person that is a nonaffiliated third party of both the financial institution and such receiving third party, unless such disclosure would be lawful if made directly to such other person by the financial institution.

(d) Limitations on the sharing of account number information for marketing purposes

A financial institution shall not disclose, other than to a consumer reporting agency, an account number or similar form of access number or access code for a credit card account, deposit account, or transaction account of a consumer to any nonaffiliated third party for use in telemarketing, direct mail marketing, or other marketing through electronic mail to the consumer.

(e) General exceptions

Subsections (a) and (b) shall not prohibit the disclosure of nonpublic personal information—

(1) as necessary to effect, administer, or enforce a transaction requested or authorized by the consumer, or in connection with—

(A) servicing or processing a financial product or service requested or authorized by the consumer;

(B) maintaining or servicing the consumer's account with the financial institution, or with another entity as part of a private label credit card program or other extension of credit on behalf of such entity; or

(C) a proposed or actual securitization, secondary market sale (including sales of servicing rights), or similar transaction related to a transaction of the consumer;

(2) with the consent or at the direction of the consumer;

(3)(A) to protect the confidentiality or security of the financial institution's records pertaining to the consumer, the service or product, or the transaction therein; (B) to protect against or prevent actual or potential fraud, unauthorized transactions, claims, or other liability; (C) for required institutional risk control, or for resolving customer disputes or inquiries; (D) to persons holding a legal or beneficial interest relating to the consumer; or (E) to persons acting in a fiduciary or representative capacity on behalf of the consumer;

(4) to provide information to insurance rate advisory organizations, guaranty funds or agencies, applicable rating agencies of the financial institution, persons assessing the institution's compliance with industry standards, and the institution's attorneys, accountants, and auditors;

(5) to the extent specifically permitted or required under other provisions of law and in accordance with the Right to Financial Privacy Act of 1978 [12 U.S.C.A. § 3401 et seq.], to law enforcement agencies (including the Bureau of Consumer Financial Protection[1] a Federal functional regulator, the Secretary of the Treasury with respect to subchapter II of chapter 53 of Title 31, and chapter 2 of Title I of Public Law 91–508 (12 U.S.C. 1951–1959), a State insurance authority, or the Federal Trade Commission), self-regulatory organizations, or for an investigation on a matter related to public safety;

(6)(A) to a consumer reporting agency in accordance with the Fair Credit Reporting Act [15 U.S.C.A. § 1681 et seq.], or **(B)** from a consumer report reported by a consumer reporting agency;

(7) in connection with a proposed or actual sale, merger, transfer, or exchange of all or a portion of a business or operating unit if the disclosure of nonpublic personal information concerns solely consumers of such business or unit; or

(8) to comply with Federal, State, or local laws, rules, and other applicable legal requirements; to comply with a properly authorized civil, criminal, or regulatory investigation or subpoena or summons by Federal, State, or local authorities; or to respond to judicial process or government regulatory authorities having jurisdiction over the financial institution for examination, compliance, or other purposes as authorized by law.

§ 6803. Disclosure of institution privacy policy

(a) Disclosure required

At the time of establishing a customer relationship with a consumer and not less than annually during the continuation of such relationship, a financial institution shall provide a clear and conspicuous disclosure to such consumer, in writing or in electronic form or other form permitted by the regulations prescribed under section 6804 of this title, of such financial institution's policies and practices with respect to—

(1) disclosing nonpublic personal information to affiliates and nonaffiliated third parties, consistent with section 6802 of this title, including the categories of information that may be disclosed;

(2) disclosing nonpublic personal information of persons who have ceased to be customers of the financial institution; and

(3) protecting the nonpublic personal information of consumers.

(b) Regulations

Disclosures required by subsection (a) shall be made in accordance with the regulations prescribed under section 6804 of this title.

(c) Information to be included

The disclosure required by subsection (a) shall include—

(1) the policies and practices of the institution with respect to disclosing nonpublic personal information to nonaffiliated third parties, other than agents of the institution, consistent with section 6802 of this title, and including—

(A) the categories of persons to whom the information is or may be disclosed, other than the persons to whom the information may be provided pursuant to section 6802(e) of this title; and

---

1 So in original. Probably should be followed by a comma.

(B) the policies and practices of the institution with respect to disclosing of nonpublic personal information of persons who have ceased to be customers of the financial institution;

(2) the categories of nonpublic personal information that are collected by the financial institution;

(3) the policies that the institution maintains to protect the confidentiality and security of nonpublic personal information in accordance with section 6801 of this title; and

(4) the disclosures required, if any, under section 1681a(d)(2)(A)(iii) of this title.

(d) Exemption for certified public accountants

(1) In general

The disclosure requirements of subsection (a) do not apply to any person, to the extent that the person is—

(A) a certified public accountant;

(B) certified or licensed for such purpose by a State; and

(C) subject to any provision of law, rule, or regulation issued by a legislative or regulatory body of the State, including rules of professional conduct or ethics, that prohibits disclosure of nonpublic personal information without the knowing and expressed consent of the consumer.

(2) Limitation

Nothing in this subsection shall be construed to exempt or otherwise exclude any financial institution that is affiliated or becomes affiliated with a certified public accountant described in paragraph (1) from any provision of this section.

(3) Definitions

For purposes of this subsection, the term "State" means any State or territory of the United States, the District of Columbia, Puerto Rico, Guam, American Samoa, the Trust Territory of the Pacific Islands, the Virgin Islands, or the Northern Mariana Islands.

(e) Model forms

(1) In general

The agencies referred to in section 6804(a)(1) of this title shall jointly develop a model form which may be used, at the option of the financial institution, for the provision of disclosures under this section.

(2) Format

A model form developed under paragraph (1) shall—

(A) be comprehensible to consumers, with a clear format and design;

(B) provide for clear and conspicuous disclosures;

(C) enable consumers easily to identify the sharing practices of a financial institution and to compare privacy practices among financial institutions; and

(D) be succinct, and use an easily readable type font.

(3) Timing

A model form required to be developed by this subsection shall be issued in proposed form for public comment not later than 180 days after October 13, 2006.

(4) Safe harbor

Any financial institution that elects to provide the model form developed by the agencies under this subsection shall be deemed to be in compliance with the disclosures required under this section.

(f) Exception to annual notice requirement

A financial institution that—

(1) provides nonpublic personal information only in accordance with the provisions of subsection (b)(2) or (e) of section 6802 of this title or regulations prescribed under section 6804(b) of this title, and

(2) has not changed its policies and practices with regard to disclosing nonpublic personal information from the policies and practices that were disclosed in the most recent disclosure sent to consumers in accordance with this section,

shall not be required to provide an annual disclosure under this section until such time as the financial institution fails to comply with any criteria described in paragraph (1) or (2).

§ 6804. Rulemaking

(a) Regulatory authority

(1) Rulemaking

(A) In general

Except as provided in subparagraph (C), the Bureau of Consumer Financial Protection and the Securities and Exchange Commission shall have authority to prescribe such regulations as may be necessary to carry out the purposes of this subchapter with respect to financial institutions and other persons subject to their respective jurisdiction under section 6805 of this title (and notwithstanding subtitle B of the Consumer Financial Protection Act of 2010), except that the Bureau of Consumer Financial Protection shall not have authority to prescribe regulations with respect to the standards under section 6801 of this title.

(B) CFTC

The Commodity Futures Trading Commission shall have authority to prescribe such regulations as may be necessary to carry out the purposes of this subchapter with respect to financial institutions and other persons subject to the jurisdiction of the Commodity Futures Trading Commission under section 7b–2 of Title 7.

(C) Federal Trade Commission authority

Notwithstanding the authority of the Bureau of Consumer Financial Protection under subparagraph (A), the Federal Trade Commission shall have authority to prescribe such regulations as may be necessary to carry out the purposes of this subchapter with respect to any financial institution that is a person described in section 5519(a) of the Consumer Financial Protection Act of 2010.

(D) Rule of construction

Nothing in this paragraph shall be construed to alter, affect, or otherwise limit the authority of a State insurance authority to adopt regulations to carry out this subchapter.

(2) Coordination, consistency, and comparability

Each of the agencies authorized under paragraph (1) to prescribe regulations shall consult and coordinate with the other such agencies and, as appropriate, and with[35] representatives of State insurance authorities designated by the National Association of Insurance Commissioners,

---

35 So in original. Probably should be "and, as appropriate, with".

for the purpose of assuring, to the extent possible, that the regulations prescribed by each agency are consistent and comparable with the regulations prescribed by the other such agencies.

(3) Procedures and deadline

Such regulations shall be prescribed in accordance with applicable requirements of Title 5.

(b) Authority to grant exceptions

The regulations prescribed under subsection (a) may include such additional exceptions to subsections (a) through (d) of section 6802 of this title as are deemed consistent with the purposes of this subchapter.

§ 6805. Enforcement

(a) In general

Subject to subtitle B of the Consumer Financial Protection Act of 2010, this subchapter and the regulations prescribed thereunder shall be enforced by the Bureau of Consumer Financial Protection, the Federal functional regulators, the State insurance authorities, and the Federal Trade Commission with respect to financial institutions and other persons subject to their jurisdiction under applicable law, as follows:

(1) Under section 1818 of Title 12 by the appropriate Federal banking agency, as defined in section 1813(q) of Title 12, in the case of—

(A) national banks, Federal branches and Federal agencies of foreign banks, and any subsidiaries of such entities (except brokers, dealers, persons providing insurance, investment companies, and investment advisers);

(B) member banks of the Federal Reserve System (other than national banks), branches and agencies of foreign banks (other than Federal branches, Federal agencies, and insured State branches of foreign banks), commercial lending companies owned or controlled by foreign banks, organizations operating under section 25 or 25A of the Federal Reserve Act [12 U.S.C.A. § 601 et seq. or 611 et seq.], and bank holding companies and their nonbank subsidiaries or affiliates (except brokers, dealers, persons providing insurance, investment companies, and investment advisers);

(C) banks insured by the Federal Deposit Insurance Corporation (other than members of the Federal Reserve System), insured State branches of foreign banks, and any subsidiaries of such entities (except brokers, dealers, persons providing insurance, investment companies, and investment advisers); and

(D) savings associations the deposits of which are insured by the Federal Deposit Insurance Corporation, and any subsidiaries of such savings associations (except brokers, dealers, persons providing insurance, investment companies, and investment advisers).

(2) Under the Federal Credit Union Act [12 U.S.C.A. § 1751 et seq.], by the Board of the National Credit Union Administration with respect to any federally insured credit union, and any subsidiaries of such an entity.

(3) Under the Securities Exchange Act of 1934 [15 U.S.C.A. § 78a et seq.], by the Securities and Exchange Commission with respect to any broker or dealer.

(4) Under the Investment Company Act of 1940 [15 U.S.C.A. § 80a–1 et seq.], by the Securities and Exchange Commission with respect to investment companies.

(5) Under the Investment Advisers Act of 1940 [15 U.S.C.A. § 80b–1 et seq.], by the Securities and Exchange Commission with respect to investment advisers registered with the Commission under such Act.

(6) Under State insurance law, in the case of any person engaged in providing insurance, by the applicable State insurance authority of the State in which the person is domiciled, subject to section 6701 of this title.

(7) Under the Federal Trade Commission Act [15 U.S.C.A. § 41 et seq.], by the Federal Trade Commission for any other financial institution or other person that is not subject to the jurisdiction of any agency or authority under paragraphs (1) through (6) of this subsection.

(8) Under subtitle E of the Consumer Financial Protection Act of 2010, by the Bureau of Consumer Financial Protection, in the case of any financial institution and other covered person or service provider that is subject to the jurisdiction of the Bureau and any person subject to this subchapter, but not with the respect to the standards under section 6801 of this title.

(b) Enforcement of section 6801

(1) In general

Except as provided in paragraph (2), the agencies and authorities described in subsection (a), other than the Bureau of Consumer Financial Protection, shall implement the standards prescribed under section 6801(b) of this title in the same manner, to the extent practicable, as standards prescribed pursuant to section 1831p–1(a) of Title 12 are implemented pursuant to such section.

(2) Exception

The agencies and authorities described in paragraphs (3), (4), (5), (6), and (7) of subsection (a) shall implement the standards prescribed under section 6801(b) of this title by rule with respect to the financial institutions and other persons subject to their respective jurisdictions under subsection (a).

(c) Absence of State action

If a State insurance authority fails to adopt regulations to carry out this subchapter, such State shall not be eligible to override, pursuant to section 1831x(g)(2)(B)(iii) of Title 12, the insurance customer protection regulations prescribed by a Federal banking agency under section 1831x(a) of Title 12.

(d) Definitions

The terms used in subsection (a)(1) that are not defined in this subchapter or otherwise defined in section 1813(s) of Title 12 shall have the same meaning as given in section 3101 of Title 12.

§ 6806. Relation to other provisions

Except for the amendments made of subsections (a) and (b), nothing in this chapter shall be construed to modify, limit, or supersede the operation of the Fair Credit Reporting Act [15 U.S.C.A. § 1681 et seq.], and no inference shall be drawn on the basis of the provisions of this chapter regarding whether information is transaction or experience information under section 603 of such Act [15 U.S.C.A. § 1681a].

§ 6807. Relation to State laws

(a) In general

This subchapter and the amendments made to this subchapter shall not be construed as superseding, altering, or affecting any statute, regulation, order, or interpretation in effect in any State, except to the extent that such statute, regulation, order, or interpretation is inconsistent with the provisions of this subchapter, and then only to the extent of the inconsistency.

(b) Greater protection under State law

For purposes of this section, a State statute, regulation, order, or interpretation is not inconsistent with the provisions of this subchapter if the protection such statute, regulation, order, or interpretation affords any person is greater than the protection provided under this subchapter and the amendments made by this subchapter, as determined by the Bureau of Consumer Financial Protection, after consultation with the agency or authority with jurisdiction under section 6805(a) of this title of either the person that initiated the complaint or that is the subject of the complaint, on its own motion or upon the petition of any interested party.

§ 6808. Study of information sharing among financial affiliates

(a) In general

The Secretary of the Treasury, in conjunction with the Federal functional regulators and the Federal Trade Commission, shall conduct a study of information sharing practices among financial institutions and their affiliates. Such study shall include—

(1) the purposes for the sharing of confidential customer information with affiliates or with nonaffiliated third parties;

(2) the extent and adequacy of security protections for such information;

(3) the potential risks for customer privacy of such sharing of information;

(4) the potential benefits for financial institutions and affiliates of such sharing of information;

(5) the potential benefits for customers of such sharing of information;

(6) the adequacy of existing laws to protect customer privacy;

(7) the adequacy of financial institution privacy policy and privacy rights disclosure under existing law;

(8) the feasibility of different approaches, including opt-out and opt-in, to permit customers to direct that confidential information not be shared with affiliates and nonaffiliated third parties; and

(9) the feasibility of restricting sharing of information for specific uses or of permitting customers to direct the uses for which information may be shared.

(b) Consultation

The Secretary shall consult with representatives of State insurance authorities designated by the National Association of Insurance Commissioners, and also with financial services industry, consumer organizations and privacy groups, and other representatives of the general public, in formulating and conducting the study required by subsection (a).

(c) Report

On or before January 1, 2002, the Secretary shall submit a report to the Congress containing the findings and conclusions of the study required under subsection (a), together with such recommendations for legislative or administrative action as may be appropriate.

§ 6809. Definitions

As used in this subchapter:

(1) Federal banking agency

The term "Federal banking agency" has the same meaning as given in section 1813 of Title 12.

(2) Federal functional regulator

The term "Federal functional regulator" means—

(A) the Board of Governors of the Federal Reserve System;

(B) the Office of the Comptroller of the Currency;

(C) the Board of Directors of the Federal Deposit Insurance Corporation;

(D) the Director of the Office of Thrift Supervision;

(E) the National Credit Union Administration Board; and

(F) the Securities and Exchange Commission.

(3) Financial institution

(A) In general

The term "financial institution" means any institution the business of which is engaging in financial activities as described in section 1843(k) of Title 12.

(B) Persons subject to CFTC regulation

Notwithstanding subparagraph (A), the term "financial institution" does not include any person or entity with respect to any financial activity that is subject to the jurisdiction of the Commodity Futures Trading Commission under the Commodity Exchange Act [7 U.S.C.A. § 1 et seq.].

(C) Farm credit institutions

Notwithstanding subparagraph (A), the term "financial institution" does not include the Federal Agricultural Mortgage Corporation or any entity chartered and operating under the Farm Credit Act of 1971 [12 U.S.C.A. § 2001 et seq.].

(D) Other secondary market institutions

Notwithstanding subparagraph (A), the term "financial institution" does not include institutions chartered by Congress specifically to engage in transactions described in section 6802(e)(1)(C) of this title, as long as such institutions do not sell or transfer nonpublic personal information to a nonaffiliated third party.

(4) Nonpublic personal information

(A) The term "nonpublic personal information" means personally identifiable financial information—

(i) provided by a consumer to a financial institution;

(ii) resulting from any transaction with the consumer or any service performed for the consumer; or

(iii) otherwise obtained by the financial institution.

(B) Such term does not include publicly available information, as such term is defined by the regulations prescribed under section 6804 of this title.

(C) Notwithstanding subparagraph (B), such term—

(i) shall include any list, description, or other grouping of consumers (and publicly available information pertaining to them) that is derived using any nonpublic personal information other than publicly available information; but

(ii) shall not include any list, description, or other grouping of consumers (and publicly available information pertaining to them) that is derived without using any nonpublic personal information.

(5) Nonaffiliated third party

The term "nonaffiliated third party" means any entity that is not an affiliate of, or related by common ownership or affiliated by corporate control with, the financial institution, but does not include a joint employee of such institution.

(6) Affiliate

The term "affiliate" means any company that controls, is controlled by, or is under common control with another company.

(7) Necessary to effect, administer, or enforce

The term "as necessary to effect, administer, or enforce the transaction" means—

(A) the disclosure is required, or is a usual, appropriate, or acceptable method, to carry out the transaction or the product or service business of which the transaction is a part, and record or service or maintain the consumer's account in the ordinary course of providing the financial service or financial product, or to administer or service benefits or claims relating to the transaction or the product or service business of which it is a part, and includes—

(i) providing the consumer or the consumer's agent or broker with a confirmation, statement, or other record of the transaction, or information on the status or value of the financial service or financial product; and

(ii) the accrual or recognition of incentives or bonuses associated with the transaction that are provided by the financial institution or any other party;

(B) the disclosure is required, or is one of the lawful or appropriate methods, to enforce the rights of the financial institution or of other persons engaged in carrying out the financial transaction, or providing the product or service;

(C) the disclosure is required, or is a usual, appropriate, or acceptable method, for insurance underwriting at the consumer's request or for reinsurance purposes, or for any of the following purposes as they relate to a consumer's insurance: Account administration, reporting, investigating, or preventing fraud or material misrepresentation, processing premium payments, processing insurance claims, administering insurance benefits (including utilization review activities), participating in research projects, or as otherwise required or specifically permitted by Federal or State law; or

(D) the disclosure is required, or is a usual, appropriate or acceptable method, in connection with—

(i) the authorization, settlement, billing, processing, clearing, transferring, reconciling, or collection of amounts charged, debited, or otherwise paid using a debit, credit or other payment card, check, or account number, or by other payment means;

(ii) the transfer of receivables, accounts or interests therein; or

(iii) the audit of debit, credit or other payment information.

(8) State insurance authority

The term "State insurance authority" means, in the case of any person engaged in providing insurance, the State insurance authority of the State in which the person is domiciled.

(9) Consumer

The term "consumer" means an individual who obtains, from a financial institution, financial products or services which are to be used primarily for personal, family, or household purposes, and also means the legal representative of such an individual.

(10) Joint agreement

The term "joint agreement" means a formal written contract pursuant to which two or more financial institutions jointly offer, endorse, or sponsor a financial product or service, and as may be further defined in the regulations prescribed under section 6804 of this title.

(11) Customer relationship

The term "time of establishing a customer relationship" shall be defined by the regulations prescribed under section 6804 of this title, and shall, in the case of a financial institution engaged in extending credit directly to consumers to finance purchases of goods or services, mean the time of establishing the credit relationship with the consumer.

EXCERPTS FROM THE REGULATIONS IMPLEMENTING THE GRAMM-LEACH-BLILEY ACT, 12 C.F.R. PART 1016

(REGULATION P)

Table of Sections

§ 1016.1 Purpose and scope

(a) Purpose. This part governs the treatment of nonpublic personal information about consumers by the financial institutions listed in paragraph (b) of this section. This part:

(1) Requires a financial institution to provide notice to customers about its privacy policies and practices;

(2) Describes the conditions under which a financial institution may disclose nonpublic personal information about consumers to nonaffiliated third parties; and

(3) Provides a method for consumers to prevent a financial institution from disclosing that information to most nonaffiliated third parties by "opting out" of that disclosure, subject to the exceptions in §§ 1016.13, 1016.14, and 1016.15.

(b) Scope. (1) This part applies only to nonpublic personal information about individuals who obtain financial products or services primarily for personal, family, or household purposes from the institutions listed below. This part does not apply to information about companies or about individuals who obtain financial products or services for business, commercial, or agricultural purposes. This part applies to those financial institutions and other persons for which the Bureau of Consumer Financial

Protection (Bureau) has rulemaking authority pursuant to section 504(a)(1)(A) of the Gramm-Leach-Bliley Act (GLB Act) (15 U.S.C. 6804(a)(1)(A)). Specifically, this part applies to any financial institution and other covered person or service provider that is subject to Subtitle A of Title V of the GLB Act, including third parties that are not financial institutions but that receive nonpublic personal information from financial institutions with whom they are not affiliated. This part does not apply to certain motor vehicle dealers described in 12 U.S.C. 5519 or to entities for which the Securities and Exchange Commission or the Commodity Futures Trading Commission has rulemaking authority pursuant to sections 504(a)(1)(A)–(B) of the GLB Act (15 U.S.C. 6804(a)(1)(A)–(B)). Except as otherwise specifically provided herein, entities to which this part applies are referred to in this part as "you."

(2)(i) Nothing in this part modifies, limits, or supersedes the standards governing individually identifiable health information promulgated by the Secretary of Health and Human Services under the authority of sections 262 and 264 of the Health Insurance Portability and Accountability Act of 1996 (42 U.S.C. 1320d–1320d–8).

(ii) Any institution of higher education that complies with the Federal Educational Rights and Privacy Act (FERPA), 20 U.S.C. 1232g, and its implementing regulations, 34 CFR part 99, and that is also a financial institution described in § 1016.3(*l*)(3) of this part, shall be deemed to be in compliance with this part if it is in compliance with FERPA.

(3) Nothing in this part shall apply to:

(i) A financial institution that is a person described in section 1029(a) of the Consumer Financial Protection Act of 2010, title X of the Dodd-Frank Wall Street Reform and Consumer Protection Act (Dodd-Frank Act), Public Law 111–203, 124 Stat. 1376 (12 U.S.C. 5519(a));

(ii) A financial institution or other person subject to the jurisdiction on the Commodity Futures Trading Commission under 7 U.S.C. 7b–2;

(iii) A broker or dealer that is registered under the Securities Exchange Act of 1934 (15 U.S.C. 78a *et seq.*;)

(iv) A registered investment adviser, properly registered by or on behalf of either the Securities Exchange Commission or any state, with respect to its investment advisory activities and its activities incidental to those investment advisory activities;

(v) An investment company that is registered under the Investment Company Act of 1940 (15 U.S.C. 80a–1 *et seq.*;) or

(vi) An insurance company, with respect to its insurance activities and its activities incidental to those insurance activities, that is subject to supervision by a state insurance regulator.

§ 1016.2 Model privacy form and examples

(a) Model privacy form. Use of the model privacy form in the appendix to this part, consistent with the instructions in the appendix constitutes compliance with the notice content requirements of §§ 1016.6 and 1016.7 of this part, although use of the model privacy form is not required.

(b) Examples. The examples in this part are not exclusive. Compliance with an example, to the extent applicable, constitutes compliance with this part.

§ 1016.3 Definitions

As used in this part, unless the context requires otherwise:

(a)(1) Affiliate means any company that controls, is controlled by, or is under common control with another company.

(2) Examples in the case of a credit union.

(i) An affiliate of a Federal credit union is a credit union service organization (CUSO), as provided in 12 CFR part 712, that is controlled by the Federal credit union.

(ii) An affiliate of a federally-insured, state-chartered credit union is a company that is controlled by the credit union.

(b)(1) Clear and conspicuous means that a notice is reasonably understandable and designed to call attention to the nature and significance of the information in the notice.

(2) Examples—

(i) Reasonably understandable. You make your notice reasonably understandable if you:

(A) Present the information in the notice in clear, concise sentences, paragraphs, and sections;

(B) Use short explanatory sentences or bullet lists whenever possible;

(C) Use definite, concrete, everyday words and active voice whenever possible;

(D) Avoid multiple negatives;

(E) Avoid legal and highly technical business terminology whenever possible; and

(F) Avoid explanations that are imprecise and readily subject to different interpretations.

(ii) Designed to call attention. You design your notice to call attention to the nature and significance of the information in it if you:

(A) Use a plain-language heading to call attention to the notice;

(B) Use a typeface and type size that are easy to read;

(C) Provide wide margins and ample line spacing;

(D) Use boldface or italics for key words; and

(E) In a form that combines your notice with other information, use distinctive type size, style, and graphic devices, such as shading or sidebars, when you combine your notice with other information.

(iii) Notices on Web sites. If you provide a notice on a Web site, you design your notice to call attention to the nature and significance of the information in it if you use text or visual cues to encourage scrolling down the page if necessary to view the entire notice and ensure that other elements on the Web site (such as text, graphics, hyperlinks, or sound) do not distract attention from the notice, and you either:

(A) Place the notice on a screen that consumers frequently access, such as a page on which transactions are conducted; or

(B) Place a link on a screen that consumers frequently access, such as a page on which transactions are conducted, that connects directly to the notice and is labeled appropriately to convey the importance, nature, and relevance of the notice.

(c) Collect means to obtain information that you organize or can retrieve by the name of an individual or by identifying number, symbol, or other identifying particular assigned to the individual, irrespective of the source of the underlying information.

(d) Company means any corporation, limited liability company, business trust, general or limited partnership, association, or similar organization.

(e)(1) Consumer means an individual who obtains or has obtained a financial product or service from you that is to be used primarily for personal, family, or household purposes, or that individual's legal representative.

(2) Examples in the case of a financial institution other than a credit union. For purposes of this paragraph (e)(2), "you" is limited to financial institutions other than credit unions.

(i) An individual who applies to you for credit for personal, family, or household purposes is a consumer of a financial service, regardless of whether the credit is extended.

(ii) An individual who provides nonpublic personal information to you in order to obtain a determination about whether he or she may qualify for a loan to be used primarily for personal, family, or household purposes is a consumer of a financial service, regardless of whether the loan is extended.

(iii) An individual who provides nonpublic personal information to you in connection with obtaining or seeking to obtain financial, investment, or economic advisory services is a consumer regardless of whether you establish a continuing advisory relationship.

(iv) If you hold ownership or servicing rights to an individual's loan that is used primarily for personal, family, or household purposes, the individual is your consumer, even if you hold those rights in conjunction with one or more other institutions. (The individual is also a consumer with respect to the other financial institutions involved.) An individual who has a loan in which you have ownership or servicing rights is your consumer, even if you, or another institution with those rights, hire an agent to collect on the loan.

(v) An individual who is a consumer of another financial institution is not your consumer solely because you act as agent for, or provide processing or other services to, that financial institution.

(vi) An individual is not your consumer solely because he or she has designated you as trustee for a trust.

(vii) An individual is not your consumer solely because he or she is a beneficiary of a trust for which you are a trustee.

(viii) An individual is not your consumer solely because he or she is a participant or a beneficiary of an employee benefit plan that you sponsor or for which you act as a trustee or fiduciary.

(3) Examples in the case of a credit union. For purposes of this paragraph (e)(3), "you" is limited to credit unions.

(i) An individual who provides nonpublic personal information to you in connection with obtaining or seeking to obtain credit union membership is your consumer regardless of whether you establish a customer relationship.

(ii) An individual who provides nonpublic personal information to you in connection with using your ATM is your consumer.

(iii) If you hold ownership or servicing rights to an individual's loan, the individual is your consumer, even if you hold those rights in conjunction with one or more financial institutions. The individual is also a consumer with respect to the other financial institutions involved. This applies even if you, or another financial institution with those rights, hire an agent to collect on the loan or to provide processing or other services.

(iv) An individual who is a consumer of another financial institution is not your consumer solely because you act as agent for, or provide processing or other services to, that financial institution.

(v) An individual is not your consumer solely because he or she is a participant or a beneficiary of an employee benefit plan that you sponsor or for which you act as a trustee or fiduciary.

(f) **Consumer reporting agency** has the same meaning as in section 603(f) of the Fair Credit Reporting Act (15 U.S.C. 1681a(f)).

(g) **Control** of a company means:

(1) Ownership, control, or power to vote 25 percent or more of the outstanding shares of any class of voting security of the company, directly or indirectly, or acting through one or more other persons;

(2) Control in any manner over the election of a majority of the directors, trustees, or general partners (or individuals exercising similar functions) of the company; or

(3) The power to exercise, directly or indirectly, a controlling influence over the management or policies of the company as determined by the applicable prudential regulator (as defined in 12 U.S.C. 5481(24)), if any.

(4) *Example in the case of credit unions.* A credit union is presumed to have a controlling influence over the management or policies of a CUSO, if the CUSO is 67% owned by credit unions.

(h) **Credit union** means a Federal or state-chartered credit union that the National Credit Union Share Insurance Fund insures.

(i) **Customer** means a consumer who has a customer relationship with you.

(j)(1) **Customer relationship** means a continuing relationship between a consumer and you under which you provide one or more financial products or services to the consumer that are to be used primarily for personal, family, or household purposes. As noted in the examples, and for purposes of this part only, in the case of a credit union, a customer relationship will exist between a credit union and certain consumers that are not the credit union's members.

(2) **Examples in the case of financial institutions other than credit unions and covered entities subject to FTC enforcement jurisdiction.** For purposes of this paragraph (j)(2), "you" is limited to financial institutions other than credit unions and financial institutions described in paragraph (*l*)(3) of this section.

(i) **Continuing relationship**. A consumer has a continuing relationship with you if the consumer:

(A) Has a deposit or investment account with you;

(B) Obtains a loan from you;

(C) Has a loan for which you own the servicing rights;

(D) Purchases an insurance product from you;

(E) Holds an investment product through you, such as when you act as a custodian for securities or for assets in an Individual Retirement Arrangement;

(F) Enters into an agreement or understanding with you whereby you undertake to arrange or broker a home mortgage loan for the consumer;

(G) Enters into a lease of personal property with you; or

(H) Obtains financial, investment, or economic advisory services from you for a fee.

(ii) **No continuing relationship**. A consumer does not, however, have a continuing relationship with you if:

(A) The consumer obtains a financial product or service only in isolated transactions, such as using your ATM to withdraw cash from an account at another financial institution or purchasing a cashier's check or money order;

(B) You sell the consumer's loan and do not retain the rights to service that loan; or

(C) You sell the consumer airline tickets, travel insurance, or traveler's checks in isolated transactions.

(3) Examples in the case of covered entities subject to FTC enforcement jurisdiction. For purposes of this paragraph (j)(3), "you" is limited to financial institutions described in paragraph (*l*)(3) of this section.

(i) Continuing relationship. A consumer has a continuing relationship with you if the consumer:

(A) Has a credit or investment account with you;

(B) Obtains a loan from you;

(C) Purchases an insurance product from you;

(D) Holds an investment product through you, such as when you act as a custodian for securities or for assets in an Individual Retirement Arrangement;

(E) Enters into an agreement or understanding with you whereby you undertake to arrange or broker a home mortgage loan, or credit to purchase a vehicle, for the consumer;

(F) Enters into a lease of personal property on a non-operating basis with you;

(G) Obtains financial, investment, or economic advisory services from you for a fee;

(H) Becomes your client for the purpose of obtaining tax preparation or credit counseling services from you;

(I) Obtains career counseling while seeking employment with a financial institution or the finance, accounting, or audit department of any company (or while employed by such a financial institution or department of any company);

(J) Is obligated on an account that you purchase from another financial institution, regardless of whether the account is in default when purchased, unless you do not locate the consumer or attempt to collect any amount from the consumer on the account;

(K) Obtains real estate settlement services from you; or

(L) Has a loan for which you own the servicing rights.

(ii) No continuing relationship. A consumer does not, however, have a continuing relationship with you if:

(A) The consumer obtains a financial product or service from you only in isolated transactions, such as using your ATM to withdraw cash from an account at another financial institution; purchasing a money order from you; cashing a check with you; or making a wire transfer through you;

(B) You sell the consumer's loan and do not retain the rights to service that loan;

(C) You sell the consumer airline tickets, travel insurance, or traveler's checks in isolated transactions;

(D) The consumer obtains one-time personal or real property appraisal services from you; or

(E) The consumer purchases checks for a personal checking account from you.

(4) Examples in the case of a credit union.

(i) Continuing relationship. A consumer has a continuing relationship with a credit union if the consumer:

(A) Is a member as defined in the credit union's bylaws;

(B) Is a nonmember who has a share, share draft, or credit card account with the credit union jointly with a member;

(C) Is a nonmember who has a loan that the credit union services;

(D) Is a nonmember who has an account with a credit union that has been designated as a low-income credit union; or

(E) Is a nonmember who has an account in a federally-insured, state-chartered credit union pursuant to state law

(ii) No continuing relationship. A consumer does not, however, have a continuing relationship with a credit union if the consumer is a nonmember and:

(A) The consumer only obtains a financial product or service in isolated transactions, such as using the credit union's ATM to withdraw cash from an account maintained at another financial institution or purchasing travelers checks; or

(B) The credit union sells the consumer's loan and does not retain the rights to service that loan.

(k) Federal functional regulator means:

(1) The Board of Governors of the Federal Reserve System;

(2) The Office of the Comptroller of the Currency;

(3) The Board of Directors of the Federal Deposit Insurance Corporation;

(4) The National Credit Union Administration Board; and

(5) The Securities and Exchange Commission.

(*l*)(1) Except for entities described in paragraph (*l*)(3) of this section, *financial institution* means any institution the business of which is engaging in activities that are financial in nature or incidental to such financial activities as described in section 4(k) of the Bank Holding Company Act of 1956 (12 U.S.C. 1843(k)).

(2) For purposes of paragraph (*l*)(1) of this section, *financial institution* does not include:

(i) Any person or entity with respect to any financial activity that is subject to the jurisdiction of the Commodity Futures Trading Commission under the Commodity Exchange Act (7 U.S.C. 1 *et seq.*);

(ii) The Federal Agricultural Mortgage Corporation or any entity chartered and operating under the Farm Credit Act of 1971 (12 U.S.C. 2001 *et seq.*); or

(iii) Institutions chartered by Congress specifically to engage in securitizations, secondary market sales (including sales of servicing rights), or similar transactions related to a transaction of a consumer, as long as such institutions do not sell or transfer nonpublic personal information to a nonaffiliated third party.

(3)(i) Special definition for entities subject to the Federal Trade Commission's enforcement jurisdiction. In the case of an entity described in section 505(a)(7) of the GLB Act (other than such an entity described in section 504(a)(1)(C) of that Act), *financial institution* means any institution the business of which is engaging in financial activities as described in section 4(k) of the Bank Holding Company Act of 1956 (12 U.S.C. 1843(k)). For purposes of this paragraph (*l*)(3), an institution that is significantly engaged in financial activities is a financial institution.

(ii) Examples of financial institution. For purposes of this paragraph (*l*)(3):

(A) A retailer that extends credit by issuing its own credit card directly to consumers is a financial institution because extending credit is a financial activity listed in 12 CFR 225.28(b)(1) and referenced in section 4(k)(4)(F) of the Bank Holding Company Act and issuing that extension of credit through a proprietary credit card demonstrates that a retailer is significantly engaged in extending credit.

(B) A personal property or real estate appraiser is a financial institution because real and personal property appraisal is a financial activity listed in 12 CFR 225.28(b)(2)(i) and referenced in section 4(k)(4)(F) of the Bank Holding Company Act.

(C) An automobile dealership that is not described in section 1029(a) of the Dodd-Frank Act (12 U.S.C. 5519(a)) and that, as a usual part of its business, leases automobiles on a nonoperating basis for longer than 90 days is a financial institution with respect to its leasing business because leasing personal property on a nonoperating basis where the initial term of the lease is at least 90 days is a financial activity listed in 12 CFR 225.28(b)(3) and referenced in section 4(k)(4)(F) of the Bank Holding Company Act.

(D) A career counselor that specializes in providing career counseling services to individuals currently employed by or recently displaced from a financial organization, individuals who are seeking employment with a financial organization, or individuals who are currently employed by or seeking placement with the finance, accounting or audit departments of any company is a financial institution because such career counseling activities are financial activities listed in 12 CFR 225.28(b)(9)(iii) and referenced in section 4(k)(4)(F) of the Bank Holding Company Act.

(E) A business that prints and sells checks for consumers, either as its sole business or as one of its product lines, is a financial institution because printing and selling checks is a financial activity that is listed in 12 CFR 225.28(b)(10)(ii) and referenced in section 4(k)(4)(F) of the Bank Holding Company Act.

(F) A business that regularly wires money to and from consumers is a financial institution because transferring money is a financial activity referenced in section 4(k)(4)(A) of the Bank Holding Company Act and regularly providing that service demonstrates that the business is significantly engaged in that activity.

(G) A check cashing business is a financial institution because cashing a check is exchanging money, which is a financial activity listed in section 4(k)(4)(A) of the Bank Holding Company Act.

(H) An accountant or other tax preparation service that is in the business of completing income tax returns is a financial institution because tax preparation services is a financial activity listed in 12 CFR 225.28(b)(6)(vi) and referenced in section 4(k)(4)(G) of the Bank Holding Company Act.

(I) A business that operates a travel agency in connection with financial services is a financial institution because operating a travel agency in connection with financial services is a financial activity listed in 12 CFR 211.5(d)(15) and referenced in section 4(k)(4)(G) of the Bank Holding Company Act.

(J) An entity that provides real estate settlement services is a financial institution because providing real estate settlement services is a financial activity listed in 12 CFR 225.28(b)(2)(viii) and referenced in section 4(k)(4)(F) of the Bank Holding Company Act.

(K) A mortgage broker is a financial institution because brokering loans is a financial activity listed in 12 CFR 225.28(b)(1) and referenced in section 4(k)(4)(F) of the Bank Holding Company Act.

(L) An investment advisory company and a credit counseling service are each financial institutions because providing financial and investment advisory services are financial activities referenced in section 4(k)(4)(C) of the Bank Holding Company Act.

(iii) For purposes of this paragraph (*l*)(3), *financial institution* does not include:

(A) Any person or entity with respect to any financial activity that is subject to the jurisdiction of the Commodity Futures Trading Commission under the Commodity Exchange Act (7 U.S.C. 1 *et seq.*);

(B) The Federal Agricultural Mortgage Corporation or any entity chartered and operating under the Farm Credit Act of 1971 (12 U.S.C. 2001 *et seq.*); or

(C) Institutions chartered by Congress specifically to engage in securitizations, secondary market sales (including sales of servicing rights) or similar transactions related to a transaction of a consumer, as long as such institutions do not sell or transfer nonpublic personal information to a nonaffiliated third party other than as permitted by §§ 1016.14 and 1016.15 of this part.

(D) Entities that engage in financial activities but that are not significantly engaged in those financial activities.

(iv) Examples of entities that are not significantly engaged in financial activities.

(A) A retailer is not a financial institution if its only means of extending credit are occasional "lay away" and deferred payment plans or accepting payment by means of credit cards issued by others.

(B) A retailer is not a financial institution merely because it accepts payment in the form of cash, checks, or credit cards that it did not issue.

(C) A merchant is not a financial institution merely because it allows an individual to "run a tab."

(D) A grocery store is not a financial institution merely because it allows individuals to whom it sells groceries to cash a check, or write a check for a higher amount than the grocery purchase and obtain cash in return.

(m)(1) Financial product or service means any product or service that a financial holding company could offer by engaging in an activity that is financial in nature or incidental to such a financial activity under section 4(k) of the Bank Holding Company Act of 1956 (12 U.S.C. 1843(k)).

(2) Special definition for entities subject to the Federal Trade Commission's enforcement jurisdiction. In the case of an entity described in section 505(a)(7) of the GLB Act (other than such an entity described in section 504(a)(1)(C) of that Act), *financial product or service* means any product or service that a financial holding company could offer by engaging in a financial activity under section 4(k) of the Bank Holding Company Act of 1956 (12 U.S.C. 1843(k)).

(3) Financial service includes your evaluation or brokerage of information that you collect in connection with a request or an application from a consumer for a financial product or service.

(n) Member means a consumer who is a member of a credit union, as defined in the credit union's bylaws.

***(o)*(1) Nonaffiliated third party** means any person except:

(i) Your affiliate; or

(ii) A person employed jointly by you and any company that is not your affiliate (but *nonaffiliated third party* includes the other company that jointly employs the person).

(2) Nonaffiliated third party includes, for financial institutions other than credit unions, any company that is an affiliate solely by virtue of your or your affiliate's direct or indirect ownership or control of the company in conducting merchant banking or investment banking activities of the type described in section 4(k)(4)(H) or insurance company investment activities of the type described in section 4(k)(4)(I) of the Bank Holding Company Act of 1956 (12 U.S.C. 1843(k)(4)(H) and (I)).

(p)(1) Nonpublic personal information means:

(i) Personally identifiable financial information; and

(ii) Any list, description, or other grouping of consumers (and publicly available information pertaining to them) that is derived using any personally identifiable financial information that is not publicly available.

(2) Nonpublic personal information does not include:

(i) Publicly available information, except as included on a list described in paragraph (p)(1)(ii) of this section; or

(ii) Any list, description, or other grouping of consumers (and publicly available information pertaining to them) that is derived without using any personally identifiable financial information that is not publicly available.

(3) Examples of lists.

(i) Nonpublic personal information includes any list of individuals' names and street addresses that is derived in whole or in part using personally identifiable financial information that is not publicly available, such as account numbers.

(ii) Nonpublic personal information does not include any list of individuals' names and addresses that contains only publicly available information, is not derived in whole or in part using personally identifiable financial information that is not publicly available, and is not disclosed in a manner that indicates that any of the individuals on the list is a consumer of a financial institution.

(q)(1) Personally identifiable financial information means any information:

(i) A consumer provides to you to obtain a financial product or service from you;

(ii) About a consumer resulting from any transaction involving a financial product or service between you and a consumer; or

(iii) You otherwise obtain about a consumer in connection with providing a financial product or service to that consumer.

(2) Examples—

(i) Information included. Personally identifiable financial information includes:

(A) Information a consumer provides to you on an application to obtain a loan, a credit card, a credit union membership, or other financial product or service;

(B) Account balance information, payment history, overdraft history, and credit or debit card purchase information;

(C) The fact that an individual is or has been one of your customers or has obtained a financial product or service from you;

(D) Any information about your consumer if it is disclosed in a manner that indicates that the individual is or has been your consumer;

(E) Any information that a consumer provides to you or that you or your agent otherwise obtain in connection with collecting on, or servicing, a loan or a credit account;

(F) Any information you collect through an internet "cookie" (an information collecting device from a Web server); and

(G) Information from a consumer report.

(ii) Information not included. Personally identifiable financial information does not include:

(A) A list of names and addresses of customers of an entity that is not a financial institution; and

(B) Information that does not identify a consumer, such as aggregate information or blind data that does not contain personal identifiers such as account numbers, names, or addresses.

(r)(1) Publicly available information means any information that you have a reasonable basis to believe is lawfully made available to the general public from:

(i) Federal, state, or local government records;

(ii) Widely distributed media; or

(iii) Disclosures to the general public that are required to be made by Federal, state, or local law.

(2) Reasonable basis. You have a reasonable basis to believe that information is lawfully made available to the general public if you have taken steps to determine:

(i) That the information is of the type that is available to the general public; and

(ii) Whether an individual can direct that the information not be made available to the general public and, if so, that your consumer has not done so.

(3) Examples—

(i) Government records. Publicly available information in government records includes information in government real estate records and security interest filings.

(ii) Widely distributed media. Publicly available information from widely distributed media includes information from a telephone book, a television or radio program, a newspaper, or a Web site that is available to the general public on an unrestricted basis. A Web site is not restricted merely because an Internet service provider or a site operator requires a fee or a password, so long as access is available to the general public.

(iii) Reasonable basis.

(A) You have a reasonable basis to believe that mortgage information is lawfully made available to the general public if you have determined that the information is of the type included on the public record in the jurisdiction where the mortgage would be recorded.

(B) You have a reasonable basis to believe that an individual's telephone number is lawfully made available to the general public if you have located the telephone number in the telephone book or the consumer has informed you that the telephone number is not unlisted.

(s)(1) You means a financial institution for which the Bureau has rulemaking authority under section 504(a)(1)(A) of the GLB Act (15 U.S.C. 6804(a)(1)(A)).

(2) You does not include:

(i) A financial institution that is a person described in section 1029(a) of the Consumer Financial Protection Act of 2010 (12 U.S.C. 5519(a));

(ii) A financial institution or other person subject to the jurisdiction on the Commodity Futures Trading Commission under 7 U.S.C. 7b–2;

(iii) A broker or dealer that is registered under the Securities Exchange Act of 1934 (15 U.S.C. 78a *et seq.*);

(iv) A registered investment adviser, properly registered by or on behalf of either the Securities Exchange Commission or any State, with respect to its investment advisory activities and its activities incidental to those investment advisory activities;

(v) An investment company that is registered under the Investment Company Act of 1940 (15 U.S.C. 80a–1 *et seq.*); or

(vi) An insurance company, with respect to its insurance activities and its activities incidental to those insurance activities, that is subject to supervision by a State insurance regulator.

Subpart A: Privacy and Opt-out Notices

§ 1016.4 Initial privacy notice to consumers required

(a) Initial notice requirement. You must provide a clear and conspicuous notice that accurately reflects your privacy policies and practices to:

(1) Customer. An individual who becomes your customer, not later than when you establish a customer relationship, except as provided in paragraph (e) of this section; and

(2) Consumer. A consumer, before you disclose any nonpublic personal information about the consumer to any nonaffiliated third party, if you make such a disclosure other than as authorized by §§ 1016.14 and 1016.15 of this part.

(b) When initial notice to a consumer is not required. You are not required to provide an initial notice to a consumer under paragraph (a) of this section if:

(1) You do not disclose any nonpublic personal information about the consumer to any nonaffiliated third party, other than as authorized by §§ 1016.14 and 1016.15; and

(2) You do not have a customer relationship with the consumer.

(c) When you establish a customer relationship—

(1) General rule. You establish a customer relationship when you and the consumer enter into a continuing relationship.

(2) Special rule for loans. You establish a customer relationship with a consumer when you originate or acquire the servicing rights to a loan to the consumer for personal, family, or household purposes. If you subsequently transfer the servicing rights to that loan to another financial institution, the customer relationship transfers with the servicing rights.

(3) Examples—

(i) Examples of establishing customer relationship by financial institutions other than credit unions and covered entities subject to FTC enforcement

jurisdiction. For purposes of this paragraph (c)(3)(i), "you" is limited to financial institutions other than credit unions and financial institutions described in § 1016.3(*l*)(3). You establish a customer relationship when the consumer:

(A) Opens a credit card account with you;

(B) Executes the contract to open a deposit account with you, obtains credit from you, or purchases insurance from you;

(C) Agrees to obtain financial, economic, or investment advisory services from you for a fee; or

(D) Becomes your client for the purpose of your providing credit counseling or tax preparation services.

(ii) Examples of establishing customer relationship by covered entities subject to FTC enforcement jurisdiction. For purposes of this paragraph (c)(3)(ii), "you" is limited to financial institutions described in § 1016.3(*l*)(3) of this part. You establish a customer relationship when the consumer:

(A) Opens a credit card account with you;

(B) Executes the contract to obtain credit from you or purchases insurance from you;

(C) Agrees to obtain financial, economic, or investment advisory services from you for a fee;

(D) Becomes your client for the purpose of your providing credit counseling or tax preparation services or to obtain career counseling while seeking employment with a financial institution or the finance, accounting, or audit department of any company (or while employed by such a company or financial institution);

(E) Provides any personally identifiable financial information to you in an effort to obtain a mortgage loan through you;

(F) Executes the lease for personal property with you;

(G) Is an obligor on an account that you purchased from another financial institution and whom you have located and begun attempting to collect amounts owed on the account; or

(H) Provides you with the information necessary for you to compile and provide access to all of the consumer's online financial accounts at your Web site.

(iii) Examples of establishing customer relationship by credit unions. For purposes of this paragraph (c)(3)(iii), "you" is limited to a credit union. You establish a customer relationship when the consumer:

(A) Becomes your member under your bylaws;

(B) Is a nonmember and opens a credit card account with you jointly with a member under your procedures;

(C) Is a nonmember and executes the contract to open a share or share draft account with you or obtains credit from you jointly with a member, including an individual acting as a guarantor;

(D) Is a nonmember and opens an account with you and you are a credit union designated as a low-income credit union;

(E) Is a nonmember and opens an account with you pursuant to State law and you are a State-chartered credit union.

(iv) Examples of loan rule. You establish a customer relationship with a consumer who obtains a loan for personal, family, or household purposes when you:

(A) Originate the loan to the consumer; or

(B) Purchase the servicing rights to the consumer's loan.

(d) Existing customers. When an existing customer obtains a new financial product or service from you that is to be used primarily for personal, family, or household purposes, you satisfy the initial notice requirements of paragraph (a) of this section as follows:

(1) You may provide a revised privacy notice, under § 1016.8 of this part, that covers the customer's new financial product or service; or

(2) If the initial, revised, or annual notice that you most recently provided to that customer was accurate with respect to the new financial product or service, you do not need to provide a new privacy notice under paragraph (a) of this section.

(e) Exceptions to allow subsequent delivery of notice.

(1) You may provide the initial notice required by paragraph (a)(1) of this section within a reasonable time after you establish a customer relationship if:

(i) Establishing the customer relationship is not at the customer's election; or

(ii) Providing notice not later than when you establish a customer relationship would substantially delay the customer's transaction and the customer agrees to receive the notice at a later time.

(2) Examples of exceptions—

(i) Not at customer's election.

(A) In the case of financial institutions other than credit unions and financial institutions described in § 1016.3(*l*)(3), establishing a customer relationship is not at the customer's election if you acquire a customer's deposit liability or the servicing rights to a customer's loan from another financial institution and the customer does not have a choice about your acquisition.

(B) In the case of financial institutions described in § 1016.3(*l*)(3), establishing a customer relationship is not at the customer's election if you acquire a customer's loan or the servicing rights from another financial institution and the customer does not have a choice about your acquisition.

(C) In the case of credit unions, establishing a customer relationship is not at the customer's election if you acquire a customer's deposit liability from another financial institution and the customer does not have a choice about your acquisition.

(ii) Substantial delay of customer's transaction. Providing notice not later than when you establish a customer relationship would substantially delay the customer's transaction when:

(A) You and the individual agree over the telephone to enter into a customer relationship involving prompt delivery of the financial product or service; or

(B) You establish a customer relationship with an individual under a program authorized by title IV of the Higher Education Act of 1965 (20 U.S.C. 1070 *et seq.*) or similar student loan programs where loan proceeds are disbursed promptly without prior communication between you and the customer.

(iii) No substantial delay of customer's transaction. Providing notice not later than when you establish a customer relationship would not substantially delay the customer's transaction when the relationship is initiated in person at your office or through other means by which the customer may view the notice, such as on a Web site.

(f) Delivery. When you are required to deliver an initial privacy notice by this section, you must deliver it according to § 1016.9 of this part. If you use a short-form initial notice for non-customers according to § 1016.6(d) of this part, you may deliver your privacy notice according to § 1016.6(d)(3).

§ 1016.5 Annual privacy notice to customers required

(a)(1) General rule. Except as provided by paragraph (e) of this section, you must provide a clear and conspicuous notice to customers that accurately reflects your privacy policies and practices not less than annually during the continuation of the customer relationship. Annually means at least once in any period of 12 consecutive months during which that relationship exists. You may define the 12-consecutive-month period, but you must apply it to the customer on a consistent basis.

(2) Example. You provide a notice annually if you define the 12-consecutive-month period as a calendar year and provide the annual notice to the customer once in each calendar year following the calendar year in which you provided the initial notice. For example, if a customer opens an account on any day of year 1, you must provide an annual notice to that customer by December 31 of year 2.

(b)(1) Termination of customer relationship. You are not required to provide an annual notice to a former customer.

(2) Examples in the case of financial institutions other than credit unions and covered entities subject to FTC enforcement jurisdiction. For purposes of this paragraph (b)(2), "you" is limited to financial institutions other than credit unions and financial institutions described in § 1016.3(*l*)(3). Your customer becomes a former customer when:

(i) In the case of a deposit account, the account is inactive under your policies;

(ii) In the case of a closed-end loan, the customer pays the loan in full, you charge off the loan, or you sell the loan without retaining servicing rights;

(iii) In the case of a credit card relationship or other open-end credit relationship, you no longer provide any statements or notices to the customer concerning that relationship or you sell the credit card receivables without retaining servicing rights; or

(iv) You have not communicated with the customer about the relationship for a period of 12 consecutive months, other than to provide annual privacy notices or promotional material.

(3) Examples in the case of covered entities subject to FTC enforcement jurisdiction. For purposes of this paragraph (b)(3), "you" is limited to financial institutions described in § 1016.3(*l*)(3) of this part. Your customer becomes a former customer when:

(i) In the case of a closed-end loan, the customer pays the loan in full, you charge off the loan, or you sell the loan without retaining servicing rights;

(ii) In the case of a credit card relationship or other open-end credit relationship, you sell the receivables without retaining servicing rights;

(iii) In the case of credit counseling services, the customer has failed to make required payments under a debt management plan, has been notified that the plan is terminated, and you no longer provide any statements or notices to the customer concerning that relationship;

(iv) In the case of mortgage or vehicle loan brokering services, your customer has obtained a loan through you (and you no longer provide any statements or notices to the customer concerning that relationship), or has ceased using your services for such purposes;

(v) In the case of tax preparation services, you have provided and received payment for the service and no longer provide any statements or notices to the customer concerning that relationship;

(vi) In the case of providing real estate settlement services, at the time the customer completes execution of all documents related to the real estate closing, you have received payment, or you have completed all of your responsibilities with respect to the settlement, including filing documents on the public record, whichever is later; or

(vii) In cases where there is no definitive time at which the customer relationship has terminated, you have not communicated with the customer about the relationship for a period of 12 consecutive months, other than to provide annual privacy notices or promotional material.

(4) Examples in the case of a credit union. An individual becomes a former customer of a credit union when:

(i) The individual is no longer the credit union's member as defined in the credit union's bylaws;

(ii) In the case of a nonmember's share or share draft account, the account is inactive under the credit union's policies;

(iii)[1]In the case of a nonmember's closed-end loan, the loan is paid in full, the credit union charges off the loan, or the credit union sells the loan without retaining servicing rights;

(iii)[1]In the case of a credit card relationship or other open-end credit relationship with a nonmember, the credit union no longer provides any statements or notices to the nonmember concerning that relationship, or the credit union sells the credit card receivables without retaining servicing rights; or

(v)[1] The credit union has not communicated with the nonmember about the relationship for a period of 12 consecutive months, other than to provide annual privacy notices or promotional material.

(c) Special rule for loans in the case of a financial institution other than a credit union. If a financial institution other than a credit union does not have a customer relationship with a consumer under the special rule for loans in § 1016.4(c)(2) of this part, then it need not provide an annual notice to that consumer under this section.

(d) Delivery. When you are required to deliver an annual privacy notice by this section, you must deliver it according to § 1016.9 of this part.

(e) Exception to annual privacy notice requirement.

(1) When exception available. You are not required to deliver an annual privacy notice if you:

(i) Provide nonpublic personal information to nonaffiliated third parties only in accordance with the provisions of § 1016.13, § 1016.14, or § 1016.15; and

(ii) Have not changed your policies and practices with regard to disclosing nonpublic personal information from the policies and practices that were disclosed to the customer under § 1016.6(a)(2) through (5) and (9) in the most recent privacy notice provided pursuant to this part.

---

1 So in original; there are two subsections (b)(4)(iii). See 76 FR 79035.

1 So in original; there are two subsections (b)(4)(iii). See 76 FR 79035.

1 So in original; there is no subsection (b)(4)(iv). See 76 FR 79035.

(2) Delivery of annual privacy notice after financial institution no longer meets requirements for exception. If you have been excepted from delivering an annual privacy notice pursuant to paragraph (e)(1) of this section and change your policies or practices in such a way that you no longer meet the requirements for that exception, you must comply with paragraph (e)(2)(i) or (e)(2)(ii) of this section, as applicable.

(i) Changes preceded by a revised privacy notice. If you no longer meet the requirements of paragraph (e)(1) of this section because you change your policies or practices in such a way that § 1016.8 requires you to provide a revised privacy notice, you must provide an annual privacy notice in accordance with the timing requirements in paragraph (a) of this section, treating the revised privacy notice as an initial privacy notice.

(ii) Changes not preceded by a revised privacy notice. If you no longer meet the requirements of paragraph (e)(1) of this section because you change your policies or practices in such a way that § 1016.8 does not require you to provide a revised privacy notice, you must provide an annual privacy notice within 100 days of the change in your policies or practices that causes you to no longer meet the requirements of paragraph (e)(1) of this section.

(iii) Examples.

(A) You change your policies and practices in such a way that you no longer meet the requirements of paragraph (e)(1) of this section effective April 1 of year 1. Assuming you define the 12-consecutive-month period pursuant to paragraph (a) of this section as a calendar year, if you were required to provide a revised privacy notice under § 1016.8 and you provided that notice on March 1 of year 1, you must provide an annual privacy notice by December 31 of year 2. If you were not required to provide a revised privacy notice under § 1016.8, you must provide an annual privacy notice by July 9 of year 1.

(B) You change your policies and practices in such a way that you no longer meet the requirements of paragraph (e)(1) of this section, and so provide an annual notice to your customers. After providing the annual notice to your customers, you once again meet the requirements of paragraph (e)(1) of this section for an exception to the annual notice requirement. You do not need to provide additional annual notices to your customers until such time as you no longer meet the requirements of paragraph (e)(1) of this section.

§ 1016.6 Information to be included in privacy notices

(a) General rule. The initial, annual, and revised privacy notices that you provide under §§ 1016.4, 1016.5, and 1016.8 of this part must include each of the following items of information, in addition to any other information you wish to provide, that applies to you and to the consumers to whom you send your privacy notice:

(1) The categories of nonpublic personal information that you collect;

(2) The categories of nonpublic personal information that you disclose;

(3) The categories of affiliates and nonaffiliated third parties to whom you disclose nonpublic personal information, other than those parties to whom you disclose information under §§ 1016.14 and 1016.15 of this part;

(4) The categories of nonpublic personal information about your former customers that you disclose and the categories of affiliates and nonaffiliated third parties to whom you disclose nonpublic personal information about your former customers, other than those parties to whom you disclose information under §§ 1016.14 and 1016.15;

(5) If you disclose nonpublic personal information to a nonaffiliated third party under § 1016.13 (and no other exception in § 1016.14 or § 1016.15 applies to that disclosure), a separate statement of the categories of information you disclose and the categories of third parties with whom you have contracted;

(6) An explanation of the consumer's right under § 1016.10(a) of this part to opt out of the disclosure of nonpublic personal information to nonaffiliated third parties, including the method(s) by which the consumer may exercise that right at that time;

(7) Any disclosures that you make under section 603(d)(2)(A)(iii) of the Fair Credit Reporting Act (15 U.S.C. 1681a(d)(2)(A)(iii)) (that is, notices regarding the ability to opt out of disclosures of information among affiliates);

(8) Your policies and practices with respect to protecting the confidentiality and security of nonpublic personal information; and

(9) Any disclosure that you make under paragraph (b) of this section.

(b) Description of nonaffiliated third parties subject to exceptions. If you disclose nonpublic personal information to third parties as authorized under §§ 1016.14 and 1016.15, you are not required to list those exceptions in the initial or annual privacy notices required by §§ 1016.4 and 1016.5. When describing the categories with respect to those parties, it is sufficient to state that you make disclosures to other nonaffiliated companies:

(1) For your everyday business purposes, such as [*include all that apply*] to process transactions, maintain account(s), respond to court orders and legal investigations, or report to credit bureaus; or

(2) As permitted by law.

(c) Examples—

(1) Categories of nonpublic personal information that you collect. You satisfy the requirement to categorize the nonpublic personal information that you collect if you list the following categories, as applicable:

(i) Information from the consumer;

(ii) Information about the consumer's transactions with you or your affiliates;

(iii) Information about the consumer's transactions with nonaffiliated third parties; and

(iv) Information from a consumer reporting agency.

(2) Categories of nonpublic personal information you disclose.

(i) You satisfy the requirement to categorize the nonpublic personal information that you disclose if you list the categories described in paragraph (c)(1) of this section, as applicable, and a few examples to illustrate the types of information in each category.

(ii) If you reserve the right to disclose all of the nonpublic personal information about consumers that you collect, you may simply state that fact without describing the categories or examples of the nonpublic personal information you disclose.

(3) Categories of affiliates and nonaffiliated third parties to whom you disclose. You satisfy the requirement to categorize the affiliates and nonaffiliated third parties to whom you disclose nonpublic personal information if you list the following categories, as applicable, and a few examples to illustrate the types of third parties in each category.

(i) Financial service providers, followed by illustrative examples such as mortgage bankers, securities broker-dealers, and insurance agents;

(ii) Non-financial companies, followed by illustrative examples such as retailers, magazine publishers, airlines, and direct marketers; and

(iii) Others, followed by examples such as nonprofit organizations.

(4) Disclosures under exception for service providers and joint marketers. If you disclose nonpublic personal information under the exception in § 1016.13 of this part to a nonaffiliated third party to market products or services that you offer alone or jointly with another financial institution, you satisfy the disclosure requirement of paragraph (a)(5) of this section if you:

(i) List the categories of nonpublic personal information you disclose, using the same categories and examples you used to meet the requirements of paragraph (a)(2) of this section, as applicable; and

(ii) State whether the third party is:

(A) A service provider that performs marketing services on your behalf or on behalf of you and another financial institution; or

(B) A financial institution with whom you have a joint marketing agreement.

(5) Simplified notices. If you do not disclose, and do not wish to reserve the right to disclose, nonpublic personal information about customers or former customers to affiliates or nonaffiliated third parties except as authorized under §§ 1016.14 and 1016.15, you may simply state that fact, in addition to the information you must provide under paragraphs (a)(1), (a)(8), (a)(9), and (b) of this section.

(6) Confidentiality and security. You describe your policies and practices with respect to protecting the confidentiality and security of nonpublic personal information if you do both of the following:

(i) Describe in general terms who is authorized to have access to the information; and

(ii) State whether you have security practices and procedures in place to ensure the confidentiality of the information in accordance with your policy. You are not required to describe technical information about the safeguards you use.

(d) Short-form initial notice with opt out notice for non-customers.

(1) You may satisfy the initial notice requirements in §§ 1016.4(a)(2), 1016.7(b), and 1016.7(c) of this part for a consumer who is not a customer by providing a short-form initial notice at the same time as you deliver an opt out notice as required in § 1016.7.

(2) A short-form initial notice must:

(i) Be clear and conspicuous;

(ii) State that your privacy notice is available upon request; and

(iii) Explain a reasonable means by which the consumer may obtain that notice.

(3) You must deliver your short-form initial notice according to § 1016.9. You are not required to deliver your privacy notice with your short-form initial notice. You instead may simply provide the consumer a reasonable means to obtain your privacy notice. If a consumer who receives your short-form notice requests your privacy notice, you must deliver your privacy notice according to § 1016.9.

(4) Examples of obtaining privacy notice. You provide a reasonable means by which a consumer may obtain a copy of your privacy notice if you:

(i) Provide a toll-free telephone number that the consumer may call to request the notice; or

(ii) For a consumer who conducts business in person at your office, maintain copies of the notice on hand that you provide to the consumer immediately upon request.

(e) Future disclosures. Your notice may include:

(1) Categories of nonpublic personal information that you reserve the right to disclose in the future, but do not currently disclose; and

(2) Categories of affiliates or nonaffiliated third parties to whom you reserve the right in the future to disclose, but to whom you do not currently disclose, nonpublic personal information.

(f) Model privacy form. Pursuant to § 1016.2(a) of this part, a model privacy form that meets the notice content requirements of this section is included in the appendix to this part.

§ 1016.7 Form of opt out notice to consumers; opt out methods

(a)(1) Form of opt out notice. If you are required to provide an opt out notice under § 1016.10(a), you must provide a clear and conspicuous notice to each of your consumers that accurately explains the right to opt out under that section. The notice must state:

(i) That you disclose or reserve the right to disclose nonpublic personal information about your consumer to a nonaffiliated third party;

(ii) That the consumer has the right to opt out of that disclosure; and

(iii) A reasonable means by which the consumer may exercise the opt out right.

(2) Examples—

(i) Adequate opt out notice. You provide adequate notice that the consumer can opt out of the disclosure of nonpublic personal information to a nonaffiliated third party if you:

(A) Identify all of the categories of nonpublic personal information that you disclose or reserve the right to disclose, and all of the categories of nonaffiliated third parties to which you disclose the information, as described in § 1016.6(a)(2) and (3) of this part, and state that the consumer can opt out of the disclosure of that information; and

(B) Identify the financial products or services that the consumer obtains from you, either singly or jointly, to which the opt out direction would apply.

(ii) Reasonable opt out means. You provide a reasonable means to exercise an opt out right if you:

(A) Designate check-off boxes in a prominent position on the relevant forms with the opt out notice;

(B) Include a reply form together with the opt out notice that, in the case of financial institutions described in § 1016.3(*l*)(3) of this part, includes the address to which the form should be mailed;

(C) Provide an electronic means to opt out, such as a form that can be sent via electronic mail or a process at your Web site, if the consumer agrees to the electronic delivery of information; or

(D) Provide a toll-free telephone number that consumers may call to opt out.

(iii) Unreasonable opt out means. You *do not* provide a reasonable means of opting out if:

(A) The only means of opting out is for the consumer to write his or her own letter to exercise that opt out right; or

(B) The only means of opting out as described in any notice subsequent to the initial notice is to use a check-off box that you provided with the initial notice but did not include with the subsequent notice.

(iv) Specific opt out means. You may require each consumer to opt out through a specific means, as long as that means is reasonable for that consumer.

(b) Same form as initial notice permitted. You may provide the opt out notice together with or on the same written or electronic form as the initial notice you provide in accordance with § 1016.4.

(c) Initial notice required when opt out notice delivered subsequent to initial notice. If you provide the opt out notice later than required for the initial notice in accordance with § 1016.4 of this part, you must also include a copy of the initial notice with the opt out notice in writing or, if the consumer agrees, electronically.

(d) Joint relationships in the case of financial institutions other than credit unions and covered entities subject to FTC enforcement jurisdiction. For purposes of this paragraph (d), "you" is limited to financial institutions other than credit unions and financial institutions described in § 1016.3(*l*)(3) of this part.

(1) If two or more consumers jointly obtain a financial product or service from you, you may provide a single opt out notice. Your opt out notice must explain how you will treat an opt out direction by a joint consumer (as explained in paragraph (d)(5) of this section).

(2) Any of the joint consumers may exercise the right to opt out. You may either:

(i) Treat an opt out direction by a joint consumer as applying to all of the associated joint consumers; or

(ii) Permit each joint consumer to opt out separately.

(3) If you permit each joint consumer to opt out separately, you must permit one of the joint consumers to opt out on behalf of all of the joint consumers.

(4) You may not require *all* joint consumers to opt out before you implement *any* opt out direction.

(5) Example. If John and Mary have a joint checking account with you and arrange for you to send statements to John's address, you may do any of the following, but you must explain in your opt out notice which opt out policy you will follow:

(i) Send a single opt out notice to John's address, but you must accept an opt out direction from either John or Mary.

(ii) Treat an opt out direction by either John or Mary as applying to the entire account. If you do so, and John opts out, you may not require Mary to opt out as well before implementing John's opt out direction.

(iii) Permit John and Mary to make different opt out directions. If you do so:

(A) You must permit John and Mary to opt out for each other;

(B) If both opt out, you must permit both to notify you in a single response (such as on a form or through a telephone call); and

(C) If John opts out and Mary does not, you may only disclose nonpublic personal information about Mary, but not about John and not about John and Mary jointly.

(e) Joint relationships in the case of credit unions.

(1) If two or more consumers jointly obtain a financial product or service, other than a loan, from a credit union, the credit union may provide only a single opt out notice. The opt out notice must explain how the credit union will treat an opt out direction by a joint consumer (as explained in the examples in paragraph (e)(5) of this section).

(2) Any of the joint consumers may exercise the right to opt out. A credit union may either:

(i) Treat an opt out direction by a joint consumer to apply to all of the associated joint consumers; or

(ii) Permit each joint consumer to opt out separately.

(3) If a credit union permits each joint consumer to opt out separately, the credit union must permit one of the joint consumers to opt out on behalf of all of the joint consumers.

(4) A credit union may not require all joint consumers to opt out before the credit union implements any opt out direction.

(5) Example. If John and Mary have a joint share account with a credit union and arrange for the credit union to send statements to John's address, the credit union may do any of the following, but it must explain in its opt out notice which opt out policy it will follow:

(i) Send a single opt out notice to John's address, but it must accept an opt out direction from either John or Mary.

(ii) Treat an opt out direction by either John or Mary as applying to the entire account. If it does so, and John opts out, it may not require Mary to opt out as well before implementing John's opt out direction.

(iii) Permit John and Mary to make different opt out directions. If it does so, and if John and Mary both opt out, it must permit one or both of them to notify it in a single response (such as on a form or through a telephone call).

(6) Special rule for loans.

(i) A credit union is required to provide an initial opt out notice to a borrower or guarantor on a loan if it shares his or her nonpublic personal information with nonaffiliated third parties other than for purposes under §§ 1016.13, 1016.14, and 1016.15.

(ii) A credit union may satisfy its annual opt out notice requirement by providing one notice to those borrowers and guarantors jointly.

(f) Joint relationships in the case of covered entities subject to FTC enforcement jurisdiction. For purposes of this paragraph (f), "you" is limited to the financial institutions described in § 1016.3(*l*)(3).

(1) If two or more consumers jointly obtain a financial product or service from you, you may provide a single opt out notice, unless one or more of those consumers requests a separate opt out notice. Your opt out notice must explain how you will treat an opt out direction by a joint consumer (as explained in paragraph (f)(5) of this section).

(2) Any of the joint consumers may exercise the right to opt out. You may either:

(i) Treat an opt out direction by a joint consumer as applying to all of the associated joint consumers; or

(ii) Permit each joint consumer to opt out separately.

(3) If you permit each joint consumer to opt out separately, you must permit one of the joint consumers to opt out on behalf of all of the joint consumers.

(4) You may not require *all* joint consumers to opt out before you implement *any* opt out direction.

(5) Example. If John and Mary have a joint credit card account with you and arrange for you to send statements to John's address, you may do any of the following, but you must explain in your opt out notice which opt out policy you will follow:

(i) Send a single opt out notice to John's address, but you must accept an opt out direction from either John or Mary.

(ii) Treat an opt out direction by either John or Mary as applying to the entire account. If you do so, and John opts out, you may not require Mary to opt out as well before implementing John's opt out direction.

(iii) Permit John and Mary to make different opt out directions. If you do so:

(A) You must permit John and Mary to opt out for each other;

(B) If both opt out, you must permit both to notify you in a single response (such as on a form or through a telephone call); and

(C) If John opts out and Mary does not, you may only disclose nonpublic personal information about Mary, but not about John and not about John and Mary jointly.

(g) Time to comply with opt out. You must comply with a consumer's opt out direction as soon as reasonably practicable after you receive it.

(h) Continuing right to opt out. A consumer may exercise the right to opt out at any time.

(i) Duration of consumer's opt out direction.

(1) A consumer's direction to opt out under this section is effective until the consumer revokes it in writing or, if the consumer agrees, electronically.

(2) When a customer relationship terminates, the customer's opt out direction continues to apply to the nonpublic personal information that you collected during or related to that relationship. If the individual subsequently establishes a new customer relationship with you, the opt out direction that applied to the former relationship does not apply to the new relationship.

(j) Delivery. When you are required to deliver an opt out notice by this section, you must deliver it according to § 1016.9 of this part.

(k) Model privacy form. Pursuant to § 1016.2(a) of this part, a model privacy form that meets the notice content requirements of this section is included in the appendix to this part.

§ 1016.8 Revised privacy notices

(a) General rule. Except as otherwise authorized in this part, you must not, directly or through any affiliate, disclose any nonpublic personal information about a consumer to a nonaffiliated third party other than as described in the initial notice that you provided to that consumer under § 1016.4 of this part, unless:

(1) You have provided to the consumer a clear and conspicuous revised notice that accurately describes your policies and practices;

(2) You have provided to the consumer a new opt out notice;

(3) You have given the consumer a reasonable opportunity, before you disclose the information to the nonaffiliated third party, to opt out of the disclosure; and

(4) The consumer does not opt out.

(b) Examples.

(1) Except as otherwise permitted by §§ 1016.13, 1016.14, and 1016.15 of this part, you must provide a revised notice before you:

(i) Disclose a new category of nonpublic personal information to any nonaffiliated third party;

(ii) Disclose nonpublic personal information to a new category of nonaffiliated third party; or

(iii) Disclose nonpublic personal information about a former customer to a nonaffiliated third party, if that former customer has not had the opportunity to exercise an opt out right regarding that disclosure.

(2) A revised notice is not required if you disclose nonpublic personal information to a new nonaffiliated third party that you adequately described in your prior notice.

(c) Delivery. When you are required to deliver a revised privacy notice by this section, you must deliver it according to § 1016.9 of this part.

§ 1016.9 Delivering privacy and opt out notices

(a) How to provide notices. You must provide any privacy notices and opt out notices, including short-form initial notices, that this part requires so that each consumer can reasonably be expected to receive actual notice in writing or, if the consumer agrees, electronically.

(b)(1) Examples of reasonable expectation of actual notice. You may reasonably expect that a consumer will receive actual notice if you:

(i) Hand-deliver a printed copy of the notice to the consumer;

(ii) Mail a printed copy of the notice to the last known address of the consumer;

(iii) For the consumer who conducts transactions electronically:

(A) In the case of financial institutions other than those described in § 1016.3(*l*)(3) of this part, post the notice on the electronic site and require the consumer to acknowledge receipt of the notice as a necessary step to obtaining a particular financial product or service; or

(B) In the case of financial institutions described in § 1016.3(*l*)(3), clearly and conspicuously post the notice on the electronic site and require the consumer to acknowledge receipt of the notice as a necessary step to obtaining a particular financial product or service;

(iv) For an isolated transaction with the consumer, such as an ATM transaction, post the notice on the ATM screen and require the consumer to acknowledge receipt of the notice as a necessary step to obtaining the particular financial product or service.

(2) Examples of unreasonable expectation of actual notice. You may *not,* however, reasonably expect that a consumer will receive actual notice of your privacy policies and practices if you:

(i) Only post a sign in your branch or office or generally publish advertisements of your privacy policies and practices; or

(ii) Send the notice via electronic mail to a consumer who does not obtain a financial product or service from you electronically.

(c) Annual notices only. You may reasonably expect that a customer will receive actual notice of your annual privacy notice if:

(1) The customer uses your website to access financial products and services electronically and agrees to receive notices at the website, and you post your current privacy notice continuously in a clear and conspicuous manner on the website; or

(2) The customer has requested that you refrain from sending any information regarding the customer relationship, and your current privacy notice remains available to the customer upon request.

(d) Oral description of notice insufficient. You may not provide any notice required by this part solely by orally explaining the notice, either in person or over the telephone.

(e) Retention or accessibility of notices for customers.

(1) For customers only, you must provide the initial notice required by § 1016.4(a)(1), the annual notice required by § 1016.5(a), and the revised notice required by § 1016.8 so that the customer can retain them or obtain them later in writing or, if the customer agrees, electronically.

(2) Examples of retention or accessibility. You provide a privacy notice to the customer so that the customer can retain it or obtain it later if you:

(i) Hand-deliver a printed copy of the notice to the customer;

(ii) Mail a printed copy of the notice to the last known address of the customer, or, in the case of credit unions, mail a printed copy of the notice to the last known address of the customer upon request of the customer; or

(iii) Make your current privacy notice available on a Web site (or a link to another Web site) for the customer who obtains a financial product or service electronically and agrees to receive the notice at the Web site.

(f) Joint notice with other financial institutions. You may provide a joint notice from you and one or more of your affiliates or other financial institutions, as identified in the notice, as long as the notice is accurate with respect to you and the other institutions.

(g) Joint relationships in the case of financial institutions other than credit unions and covered entities subject to FTC enforcement jurisdiction. For purposes of this paragraph (g), "you" is limited to financial institutions other than credit unions and the financial institutions described in § 1016.3(*l*)(3). If two or more consumers jointly obtain a financial product or service from you, you may satisfy the initial, annual, and revised notice requirements of §§ 1016.4(a), 1016.5(a), and 1016.8(a), respectively, by providing one notice to those consumers jointly.

(h) Joint relationships in the case of covered entities subject to FTC enforcement jurisdiction. For purposes of this paragraph (h), "you" is limited to the financial institutions described in § 1016.3(*l*)(3). If two or more consumers jointly obtain a financial product or service from you, you may satisfy the initial, annual, and revised notice requirements of §§ 1016.4(a), 1016.5(a), and 1016.8(a) by providing one notice to those consumers jointly, unless one or more of those consumers requests separate notices.

(i) Joint relationships in the case of credit unions.

(1) If two or more consumers jointly obtain a financial product or service, other than a loan, from a credit union, the credit union may satisfy the requirements of § 1016.4(a) by providing one initial notice to those consumers jointly.

(2) Special rule for loans in the case of credit unions.

(i) A credit union is required to provide an initial notice to a borrower or guarantor on a loan if the credit union shares his or her nonpublic personal information with nonaffiliated third parties other than for purposes under §§ 1016.13, 1016.14, and 1016.15.

(ii) A credit union may satisfy the annual notice requirements of § 1016.5 by providing one notice to those borrowers and guarantors jointly.

Subpart B: Limits on Disclosures

§ 1016.10 Limits on disclosure of nonpublic personal information to nonaffiliated third parties

(a)(1) Conditions for disclosure. Except as otherwise authorized in this part, you may not, directly or through any affiliate, disclose any nonpublic personal information about a consumer to a nonaffiliated third party unless:

(i) You have provided to the consumer an initial notice as required under § 1016.4 of this part;

(ii) You have provided to the consumer an opt out notice as required in § 1016.7 of this part;

(iii) You have given the consumer a reasonable opportunity, before you disclose the information to the nonaffiliated third party, to opt out of the disclosure; and

(iv) The consumer does not opt out.

(2) Opt out definition. Opt out means a direction by the consumer that you not disclose nonpublic personal information about that consumer to a nonaffiliated third party, other than as permitted by §§ 1016.13, 1016.14, and 1016.15.

(3) Examples of reasonable opportunity to opt out. You provide a consumer with a reasonable opportunity to opt out if:

(i) By mail. You mail the notices required in paragraph (a)(1) of this section to the consumer and allow the consumer to opt out by mailing a form, calling a toll-free telephone number, or any other reasonable means within 30 days from the date you mailed the notices.

(ii) By electronic means. A customer opens an online account with you and agrees to receive the notices required in paragraph (a)(1) of this section electronically, and you allow the customer to opt out by any reasonable means within 30 days after the date that the customer acknowledges receipt of the notices in conjunction with opening the account.

(iii) Isolated transaction with consumer. For an isolated transaction, such as the purchase of a cashier's check by a consumer, you provide the consumer with a reasonable opportunity to opt out if you provide the notices required in paragraph (a)(1) of this section at the time of the transaction and request that the consumer decide, as a necessary part of the transaction, whether to opt out before completing the transaction.

(b) Application of opt out to all consumers and all nonpublic personal information.

(1) You must comply with this section, regardless of whether you and the consumer have established a customer relationship.

(2) Unless you comply with this section, you may not, directly or through any affiliate, disclose any nonpublic personal information about a consumer that you have collected, regardless of whether you collected it before or after receiving the direction to opt out from the consumer.

(c) Partial opt out. You may allow a consumer to select certain nonpublic personal information or certain nonaffiliated third parties with respect to which the consumer wishes to opt out.

§ 1016.11 Limits on redisclosure and reuse of information

(a)(1) Information you receive under an exception. If you receive nonpublic personal information from a nonaffiliated financial institution under an exception in § 1016.14 or § 1016.15 of this part, your disclosure and use of that information is limited as follows:

(i) You may disclose the information to the affiliates of the financial institution from which you received the information;

(ii) You may disclose the information to your affiliates, but your affiliates may, in turn, disclose and use the information only to the extent that you may disclose and use the information; and

(iii) You may disclose and use the information pursuant to an exception in § 1016.14 or § 1016.15 in the ordinary course of business to carry out the activity covered by the exception under which you received the information.

(2) Example. If you receive a customer list from a nonaffiliated financial institution in order to provide account processing services under the exception in § 1016.14(a), you may disclose that information under any exception in § 1016.14 or § 1016.15 in the ordinary course of business in order to provide those services. For example, you could disclose the information in response to a properly authorized subpoena or, in the case of financial institutions other than those described in § 1016.3(*l*)(3), to your attorneys, accountants, and auditors. You could not disclose that information to a third party for marketing purposes or use that information for your own marketing purposes.

(b)(1) Information you receive outside of an exception. If you receive nonpublic personal information from a nonaffiliated financial institution other than under an exception in § 1016.14 or § 1016.15 of this part, you may disclose the information only:

(i) To the affiliates of the financial institution from which you received the information;

(ii) To your affiliates, but your affiliates may, in turn, disclose the information only to the extent that you can disclose the information; and

(iii) To any other person, if the disclosure would be lawful if made directly to that person by the financial institution from which you received the information.

(2) Example. If you obtain a customer list from a nonaffiliated financial institution outside of the exceptions in §§ 1016.14 and 1016.15:

(i) You may use that list for your own purposes; and

(ii) You may disclose that list to another nonaffiliated third party only if the financial institution from which you purchased the list could have lawfully disclosed the list to that third party. That is, you may disclose the list in accordance with the privacy policy of the financial institution from which you received the list, as limited by the opt out direction of each consumer whose nonpublic personal information you intend to disclose, and you may disclose the list in accordance with an exception in § 1016.14 or § 1016.15, such as to your attorneys or accountants.

(c) Information you disclose under an exception. If you disclose nonpublic personal information to a nonaffiliated third party under an exception in § 1016.14 or § 1016.15 of this part, the third party may disclose and use that information only as follows:

(1) The third party may disclose the information to your affiliates;

(2) The third party may disclose the information to its affiliates, but its affiliates may, in turn, disclose and use the information only to the extent that the third party may disclose and use the information; and

(3) The third party may disclose and use the information pursuant to an exception in § 1016.14 or § 1016.15 in the ordinary course of business to carry out the activity covered by the exception under which it received the information.

(d) Information you disclose outside of an exception. If you disclose nonpublic personal information to a nonaffiliated third party other than under an exception in § 1016.14 or § 1016.15 of this part, the third party may disclose the information only:

(1) To your affiliates;

(2) To its affiliates, but its affiliates, in turn, may disclose the information only to the extent the third party can disclose the information; and

(3) To any other person, if the disclosure would be lawful if you made it directly to that person.

§ 1016.12 Limits on sharing account number information for marketing purposes

(a) General prohibition on disclosure of account numbers. You must not, directly or through an affiliate, disclose, other than to a consumer reporting agency, an account number or similar form of access number or access code for a consumer's credit card account, deposit account, share account, or transaction account to any nonaffiliated third party for use in telemarketing, direct mail marketing, or other marketing through electronic mail to the consumer.

(b) Exceptions. Paragraph (a) of this section does not apply if you disclose an account number or similar form of access number or access code:

(1) To your agent or service provider solely in order to perform marketing for your own products or services, as long as the agent or service provider is not authorized to directly initiate charges to the account; or

(2) To a participant in a private label credit card program or an affinity or similar program where the participants in the program are identified to the customer when the customer enters into the program.

(c) Examples—

(1) Account number. An account number, or similar form of access number or access code, does not include a number or code in an encrypted form, as long as you do not provide the recipient with a means to decode the number or code.

(2) Transaction account. A transaction account is an account other than a deposit account, a share account, or a credit card account. A transaction account does not include an account to which third parties cannot initiate charges.

Subpart C: Exceptions

§ 1016.13 Exception to opt out requirements for service providers and joint marketing

(a) General rule.

(1) The opt out requirements in §§ 1016.7 and 1016.10 of this part do not apply when you provide nonpublic personal information to a nonaffiliated third party to perform services for you or functions on your behalf, if you:

(i) Provide the initial notice in accordance with § 1016.4; and

(ii) Enter into a contractual agreement with the third party that prohibits the third party from disclosing or using the information other than to carry out the purposes for which you disclosed the information, including use under an exception in § 1016.14 or § 1016.15 in the ordinary course of business to carry out those purposes.

(2) Example. If you disclose nonpublic personal information under this section to a financial institution with which you perform joint marketing, your contractual agreement with that institution meets the requirements of paragraph (a)(1)(ii) of this section if it prohibits the institution from disclosing or using the nonpublic personal information except as necessary to carry out the joint marketing or under an exception in § 1016.14 or § 1016.15 in the ordinary course of business to carry out that joint marketing.

(b) Service may include joint marketing. The services a nonaffiliated third party performs for you under paragraph (a) of this section may include marketing of your own products or services or marketing of financial products or services offered pursuant to joint agreements between you and one or more financial institutions.

(c) Definition of joint agreement. For purposes of this section, joint agreement means a written contract pursuant to which you and one or more financial institutions jointly offer, endorse, or sponsor a financial product or service.

§ 1016.14 Exceptions to notice and opt out requirements for processing and servicing transactions

(a) Exceptions for processing transactions at consumer's request. The requirements for initial notice in § 1016.4(a)(2), for the opt out in §§ 1016.7 and 1016.10, and for service providers and joint marketing in § 1016.13 do not apply if you disclose nonpublic personal information as necessary to effect, administer, or enforce a transaction that a consumer requests or authorizes, or in connection with:

(1) Servicing or processing a financial product or service that a consumer requests or authorizes;

(2) Maintaining or servicing the consumer's account with you, or with another entity as part of a private label credit card program or other extension of credit on behalf of such entity; or

(3) A proposed or actual securitization, secondary market sale (including sales of servicing rights), or similar transaction related to a transaction of the consumer.

(b) Necessary to effect, administer, or enforce a transaction means that the disclosure is:

(1) Required, or is one of the lawful or appropriate methods, to enforce your rights or the rights of other persons engaged in carrying out the financial transaction or providing the product or service; or

(2) Required, or is a usual, appropriate or acceptable method:

(i) To carry out the transaction or the product or service business of which the transaction is a part, and record, service, or maintain the consumer's account in the ordinary course of providing the financial service or financial product;

(ii) To administer or service benefits or claims relating to the transaction or the product or service business of which it is a part;

(iii) To provide a confirmation, statement, or other record of the transaction, or information on the status or value of the financial service or financial product to the consumer or the consumer's agent or broker;

(iv) To accrue or recognize incentives or bonuses associated with the transaction that are provided by you or any other party;

(v) To underwrite insurance at the consumer's request or for reinsurance purposes, or for any of the following purposes as they relate to a consumer's insurance: account administration, reporting, investigating, or preventing fraud or material misrepresentation, processing premium payments, processing insurance claims, administering insurance benefits (including utilization review activities), participating in research projects, or as otherwise required or specifically permitted by Federal or state law; or

(vi) In connection with:

(A) The authorization, settlement, billing, processing, clearing, transferring, reconciling or collection of amounts charged, debited, or otherwise paid using a debit, credit, or other payment card, check, or account number, or by other payment means;

(B) The transfer of receivables, accounts, or interests therein; or

(C) The audit of debit, credit, or other payment information.

§ 1016.15 Other exceptions to notice and opt out requirements

(a) Exceptions to opt out requirements. The requirements for initial notice in § 1016.4(a)(2), for the opt out in §§ 1016.7 and 1016.10, and for service providers and joint marketing in § 1016.13 do not apply when you disclose nonpublic personal information:

(1) With the consent or at the direction of the consumer, provided that the consumer has not revoked the consent or direction;

(2)(i) To protect the confidentiality or security of your records pertaining to the consumer, service, product, or transaction;

(ii) To protect against or prevent actual or potential fraud, unauthorized transactions, claims, or other liability;

(iii) For required institutional risk control or for resolving consumer disputes or inquiries;

(iv) To persons holding a legal or beneficial interest relating to the consumer; or

(v) To persons acting in a fiduciary or representative capacity on behalf of the consumer;

(3) To provide information to insurance rate advisory organizations, guaranty funds or agencies, agencies that are rating you, persons that are assessing your compliance with industry standards, and your attorneys, accountants, and auditors;

(4) To the extent specifically permitted or required under other provisions of law and in accordance with the Right to Financial Privacy Act of 1978 (12 U.S.C. 3401 *et seq.*) to law enforcement agencies (including the Bureau, a Federal functional regulator, the Secretary of the Treasury, with respect to 31 U.S.C. Chapter 53, Subchapter II (Records and Reports on Monetary Instruments and Transactions) and 12 U.S.C. Chapter 21 (Financial Recordkeeping), a state insurance authority, with respect to any person domiciled in that insurance authority's state that is engaged in providing insurance, and the Federal Trade Commission), self-regulatory organizations, or for an investigation on a matter related to public safety;

(5)(i) To a consumer reporting agency in accordance with the Fair Credit Reporting Act (15 U.S.C. 1681 *et seq.*); or

(ii) From a consumer report reported by a consumer reporting agency;

(6) In connection with a proposed or actual sale, merger, transfer, or exchange of all or a portion of a business or operating unit if the disclosure of nonpublic personal information concerns solely consumers of such business or unit; or

(7)(i) To comply with Federal, state, or local laws, rules and other applicable legal requirements;

(ii) To comply with a properly authorized civil, criminal, or regulatory investigation, or subpoena or summons by Federal, state, or local authorities; or

(iii) To respond to judicial process or government regulatory authorities having jurisdiction over you for examination, compliance, or other purposes as authorized by law.

(b) Examples of consent and revocation of consent.

(1) A consumer may specifically consent to your disclosure to a nonaffiliated insurance company of the fact that the consumer has applied to you for a mortgage so that the insurance company can offer homeowner's insurance to the consumer.

(2) A consumer may revoke consent by subsequently exercising the right to opt out of future disclosures of nonpublic personal information as permitted under § 1016.7(h) of this part.

Subpart D: Relation to Other Laws

§ 1016.16 Protection of Fair Credit Reporting Act

Nothing in this part shall be construed to modify, limit, or supersede the operation of the Fair Credit Reporting Act (15 U.S.C. 1681 *et seq.*), and no inference shall be drawn on the basis of the provisions of this part regarding whether information is transaction or experience information under section 603 of that Act.

§ 1016.17 Relation to state laws

(a) In general. This part shall not be construed as superseding, altering, or affecting any statute, regulation, order, or interpretation in effect in any state, except to the extent that such state statute, regulation, order, or interpretation is inconsistent with the provisions of this part, and then only to the extent of the inconsistency.

(b) Greater protection under state law. For purposes of this section, a state statute, regulation, order, or interpretation is not inconsistent with the provisions of this part if the protection such statute, regulation, order, or interpretation affords any consumer is greater than the protection provided under this part, as determined by the Bureau, on its own motion or upon the petition of any interested party, after consultation with the agency or authority with jurisdiction under section 505(a) of the GLB Act (15 U.S.C. 6805(a)) over either the person that initiated the complaint or that is the subject of the complaint.

Appendix to Part 1016—Model Privacy Form

A. The Model Privacy Form

Version 1: Model Form With No Opt-Out.

Rev. [insert date]

FACTS	**WHAT DOES [NAME OF FINANCIAL INSTITUTION] DO WITH YOUR PERSONAL INFORMATION?**
Why?	Financial companies choose how they share your personal information. Federal law gives consumers the right to limit some but not all sharing. Federal law also requires us to tell you how we collect, share, and protect your personal information. Please read this notice carefully to understand what we do.
What?	The types of personal information we collect and share depend on the product or service you have with us. This information can include: ■ Social Security number and [income] ■ [account balances] and [payment history] ■ [credit history] and [credit scores] When you are *no longer* our customer, we continue to share your information as described in this notice.
How?	All financial companies need to share customers' personal information to run their everyday business. In the section below, we list the reasons financial companies can share their customers' personal information; the reasons [name of financial institution] chooses to share; and whether you can limit this sharing.

Reasons we can share your personal information	Does [name of financial institution] share?	Can you limit this sharing?
For our everyday business purposes— such as to process your transactions, maintain your account(s), respond to court orders and legal investigations, or report to credit bureaus		
For our marketing purposes— to offer our products and services to you		
For joint marketing with other financial companies		
For our affiliates' everyday business purposes— information about your transactions and experiences		
For our affiliates' everyday business purposes— information about your creditworthiness		
For our affiliates to market to you		
For nonaffiliates to market to you		

Questions?	Call [phone number] or go to [website]

Page 2

Who we are	
Who is providing this notice?	[insert]
What we do	
How does [name of financial institution] protect my personal information?	To protect your personal information from unauthorized access and use, we use security measures that comply with federal law. These measures include computer safeguards and secured files and buildings. [insert]
How does [name of financial institution] collect my personal information?	We collect your personal information, for example, when you ■ [open an account] or [deposit money] ■ [pay your bills] or [apply for a loan] ■ [use your credit or debit card] [We also collect your personal information from other companies.] OR [We also collect your personal information from others, such as credit bureaus, affiliates, or other companies.]
Why can't I limit all sharing?	Federal law gives you the right to limit only ■ sharing for affiliates' everyday business purposes – information about your creditworthiness ■ affiliates from using your information to market to you ■ sharing for nonaffiliates to market to you State laws and individual companies may give you additional rights to limit sharing. [See below for more on your rights under state law.]
Definitions	
Affiliates	Companies related by common ownership or control. They can be financial and nonfinancial companies. ■ *[affiliate information]*
Nonaffiliates	Companies not related by common ownership or control. They can be financial and nonfinancial companies. ■ *[nonaffiliate information]*
Joint marketing	A formal agreement between nonaffiliated financial companies that together market financial products or services to you. ■ *[joint marketing information]*
Other important information	
[insert other important information]	

Version 2: Model Form with Opt-Out by Telephone and/or Online.

Rev. [insert date]

FACTS	WHAT DOES [NAME OF FINANCIAL INSTITUTION] DO WITH YOUR PERSONAL INFORMATION?
Why?	Financial companies choose how they share your personal information. Federal law gives consumers the right to limit some but not all sharing. Federal law also requires us to tell you how we collect, share, and protect your personal information. Please read this notice carefully to understand what we do.
What?	The types of personal information we collect and share depend on the product or service you have with us. This information can include: ▪ Social Security number and [income] ▪ [account balances] and [payment history] ▪ [credit history] and [credit scores]
How?	All financial companies need to share customers' personal information to run their everyday business. In the section below, we list the reasons financial companies can share their customers' personal information; the reasons [name of financial institution] chooses to share; and whether you can limit this sharing.

Reasons we can share your personal information	Does [name of financial institution] share?	Can you limit this sharing?
For our everyday business purposes — such as to process your transactions, maintain your account(s), respond to court orders and legal investigations, or report to credit bureaus		
For our marketing purposes — to offer our products and services to you		
For joint marketing with other financial companies		
For our affiliates' everyday business purposes — information about your transactions and experiences		
For our affiliates' everyday business purposes — information about your creditworthiness		
For our affiliates to market to you		
For nonaffiliates to market to you		

To limit our sharing	▪ Call **[phone number]**—our menu will prompt you through your choice(s) or ▪ Visit us online: **[website]** **Please note:** If you are a *new* customer, we can begin sharing your information [30] days from the date we sent this notice. When you are *no longer* our customer, we continue to share your information as described in this notice. However, you can contact us at any time to limit our sharing.
Questions?	Call [phone number] or go to [website]

Page 2

Who we are	
Who is providing this notice?	[insert]
What we do	
How does [name of financial institution] protect my personal information?	To protect your personal information from unauthorized access and use, we use security measures that comply with federal law. These measures include computer safeguards and secured files and buildings. [insert]
How does [name of financial institution] collect my personal information?	We collect your personal information, for example, when you ■ [open an account] or [deposit money] ■ [pay your bills] or [apply for a loan] ■ [use your credit or debit card] [We also collect your personal information from other companies.] **OR** [We also collect your personal information from others, such as credit bureaus, affiliates, or other companies.]
Why can't I limit all sharing?	Federal law gives you the right to limit only ■ sharing for affiliates' everyday business purposes – information about your creditworthiness ■ affiliates from using your information to market to you ■ sharing for nonaffiliates to market to you State laws and individual companies may give you additional rights to limit sharing. [See below for more on your rights under state law.]
What happens when I limit sharing for an account I hold jointly with someone else?	[Your choices will apply to everyone on your account.] **OR** [Your choices will apply to everyone on your account—unless you tell us otherwise.]
Definitions	
Affiliates	Companies related by common ownership or control. They can be financial and nonfinancial companies. ■ *[affiliate information]*
Nonaffiliates	Companies not related by common ownership or control. They can be financial and nonfinancial companies. ■ *[nonaffiliate information]*
Joint marketing	A formal agreement between nonaffiliated financial companies that together market financial products or services to you. ■ *[joint marketing information]*
Other important information	
[insert other important information]	

Version 3: Model Form with Mail-In Opt-Out Form.

Rev. [insert date]

FACTS	WHAT DOES [NAME OF FINANCIAL INSTITUTION] DO WITH YOUR PERSONAL INFORMATION?
Why?	Financial companies choose how they share your personal information. Federal law gives consumers the right to limit some but not all sharing. Federal law also requires us to tell you how we collect, share, and protect your personal information. Please read this notice carefully to understand what we do.
What?	The types of personal information we collect and share depend on the product or service you have with us. This information can include: ■ Social Security number and [income] ■ [account balances] and [payment history] ■ [credit history] and [credit scores]
How?	All financial companies need to share customers' personal information to run their everyday business. In the section below, we list the reasons financial companies can share their customers' personal information; the reasons [name of financial institution] chooses to share; and whether you can limit this sharing.

Reasons we can share your personal information	Does [name of financial institution] share?	Can you limit this sharing?
For our everyday business purposes— such as to process your transactions, maintain your account(s), respond to court orders and legal investigations, or report to credit bureaus		
For our marketing purposes— to offer our products and services to you		
For joint marketing with other financial companies		
For our affiliates' everyday business purposes— information about your transactions and experiences		
For our affiliates' everyday business purposes— information about your creditworthiness		
For our affiliates to market to you		
For nonaffiliates to market to you		

To limit our sharing	■ Call [phone number]—our menu will prompt you through your choice(s) ■ Visit us online: [website] or ■ Mail the form below **Please note:** If you are a *new* customer, we can begin sharing your information [30] days from the date we sent this notice. When you are *no longer* our customer, we continue to share your information as described in this notice. However, you can contact us at any time to limit our sharing.
Questions?	Call [phone number] or go to [website]

Mail-in Form

Leave Blank OR [If you have a joint account, your choice(s) will apply to everyone on your account unless you mark below. ❑ Apply my choices only to me]	Mark any/all you want to limit: ❑ Do not share information about my creditworthiness with your affiliates for their everyday business purposes. ❑ Do not allow your affiliates to use my personal information to market to me. ❑ Do not share my personal information with nonaffiliates to market their products and services to me. Name Address City, State, Zip [Account #]	**Mail to:** [Name of Financial Institution] [Address1] [Address2] [City], [ST] [ZIP]

Version 4. Optional Mail-in Form.

Mail-in Form

Leave Blank OR [If you have a joint account, your choice(s) will apply to everyone on your account unless you mark below. ❑ Apply my choices only to me]	Mark any/all you want to limit: ❑ Do not share information about my creditworthiness with your affiliates for their everyday business purposes. ❑ Do not allow your affiliates to use my personal information to market to me. ❑ Do not share my personal information with nonaffiliates to market their products and services to me.	
	Name	
	Address	
	City, State, Zip	
	[Account #]	

Mail To: [Name of Financial Institution], [Address1] [Address2], [City], [ST] [ZIP]

B. General Instructions

1. *How the Model Privacy Form Is Used*

(a) The model form may be used, at the option of a financial institution, including a group of financial institutions that use a common privacy notice, to meet the content requirements of the privacy notice and opt-out notice set forth in §§ 1016.6 and 1016.7 of this part.

(b) The model form is a standardized form, including page layout, content, format, style, pagination, and shading. Institutions seeking to obtain the safe harbor through use of the model form may modify it only as described in these Instructions.

(c) Note that disclosure of certain information, such as assets, income, and information from a consumer reporting agency, may give rise to obligations under the Fair Credit Reporting Act [15 U.S.C. 1681–1681x] (FCRA), such as a requirement to permit a consumer to opt out of disclosures to affiliates or designation as a consumer reporting agency if disclosures are made to nonaffiliated third parties.

(d) The word "customer" may be replaced by the word "member" whenever it appears in the model form, as appropriate.

2. *The Contents of the Model Privacy Form*

The model form consists of two pages, which may be printed on both sides of a single sheet of paper, or may appear on two separate pages. Where an institution provides a long list of institutions at the end of the model form in accordance with Instruction C.3(a)(1), or provides additional information in accordance with Instruction C.3(c), and such list or additional information exceeds the space available on page two of the model form, such list or additional information may extend to a third page.

(a) Page One. The first page consists of the following components:

(1) Date last revised (upper right-hand corner).

(2) Title.

(3) Key frame (Why?, What?, How?).

(4) Disclosure table ("Reasons we can share your personal information").

(5) "To limit our sharing" box, as needed, for the financial institution's opt-out information.

(6) "Questions" box, for customer service contact information.

(7) Mail-in opt-out form, as needed.

(b) Page Two. The second page consists of the following components:

(1) Heading (Page 2).

(2) Frequently Asked Questions ("Who we are" and "What we do").

(3) Definitions.

(4) "Other important information" box, as needed.

3. The Format of the Model Privacy Form

The format of the model form may be modified only as described below.

(a) Easily readable type font. Financial institutions that use the model form must use an easily readable type font. While a number of factors together produce easily readable type font, institutions are required to use a minimum of 10-point font (unless otherwise expressly permitted in these Instructions) and sufficient spacing between the lines of type.

(b) Logo. A financial institution may include a corporate logo on any page of the notice, so long as it does not interfere with the readability of the model form or the space constraints of each page.

(c) Page size and orientation. Each page of the model form must be printed on paper in portrait orientation, the size of which must be sufficient to meet the layout and minimum font size requirements, with sufficient white space on the top, bottom, and sides of the content.

(d) Color. The model form must be printed on white or light color paper (such as cream) with black or other contrasting ink color. Spot color may be used to achieve visual interest, so long as the color contrast is distinctive and the color does not detract from the readability of the model form. Logos may also be printed in color.

(e) Languages. The model form may be translated into languages other than English.

C. INFORMATION REQUIRED IN THE MODEL PRIVACY FORM

The information in the model form may be modified only as described below:

1. Name of the Institution or Group of Affiliated Institutions Providing the Notice

Insert the name of the financial institution providing the notice or a common identity of affiliated institutions jointly providing the notice on the form wherever [name of financial institution] appears.

2. Page One

(a) Last revised date. The financial institution must insert in the upper right-hand corner the date on which the notice was last revised. The information shall appear in minimum 8-point font as "rev. [month/year]" using either the name or number of the month, such as "rev. July 2009" or "rev. 7/09".

(b) General instructions for the "What?" box.

(1) The bulleted list identifies the types of personal information that the institution collects and shares. All institutions must use the term "Social Security number" in the first bullet.

(2) Institutions must use five (5) of the following terms to complete the bulleted list: Income; account balances; payment history; transaction history; transaction or loss history; credit history; credit scores; assets; investment experience; credit-based insurance scores; insurance claim history; medical information; overdraft history; purchase history; account transactions; risk tolerance; medical-related debts; credit card or other debt; mortgage rates and payments; retirement assets; checking account information; employment information; wire transfer instructions.

(c) General instructions for the disclosure table. The left column lists reasons for sharing or using personal information. Each reason correlates to a specific legal provision described in paragraph C.2(d) of this Instruction. In the middle column, each institution must provide a "Yes" or "No" response that accurately reflects its information sharing policies and practices with respect to the reason listed on the left. In the right column, each institution must provide in each box one of the following three (3) responses, as applicable, that reflects whether a consumer can limit such sharing: "Yes" if it is required to or voluntarily provides an opt-out; "No" if it does not provide an opt-out; or "We don't share" if it answers "No" in the middle column. Only the sixth row ("For our affiliates to market to you") may be omitted at the option of the institution. *See* paragraph C.2(d)(6) of this Instruction.

(d) Specific disclosures and corresponding legal provisions.

(1) **For our everyday business purposes.** This reason incorporates sharing information under §§ 1016.14 and 1016.15 and with service providers pursuant to § 1016.13 of this part other than the purposes specified in paragraphs C.2(d)(2) or C.2(d)(3) of these Instructions.

(2) **For our marketing purposes.** This reason incorporates sharing information with service providers by an institution for its own marketing pursuant to § 1016.13 of this part. An institution that shares for this reason may choose to provide an opt-out.

(3) **For joint marketing with other financial companies.** This reason incorporates sharing information under joint marketing agreements between two or more financial institutions and with any service provider used in connection with such agreements pursuant to § 1016.13 of this part. An institution that shares for this reason may choose to provide an opt-out.

(4) **For our affiliates' everyday business purposes—information about transactions and experiences.** This reason incorporates sharing information specified in sections 603(d)(2)(A)(i) and (ii) of the FCRA. An institution that shares for this reason may choose to provide an opt-out.

(5) **For our affiliates' everyday business purposes—information about creditworthiness.** This reason incorporates sharing information pursuant to section 603(d)(2)(A)(iii) of the FCRA. An institution that shares for this reason must provide an opt-out.

(6) **For our affiliates to market to you.** This reason incorporates sharing information specified in section 624 of the FCRA. This reason may be omitted from the disclosure table when: the institution does not have affiliates (or does not disclose personal information to its affiliates); the institution's affiliates do not use personal information in a manner that requires an opt-out; or the institution provides the affiliate marketing notice separately. Institutions that include this reason must provide an opt-out of indefinite duration. An institution that is required to provide an affiliate marketing opt-out, but does not include that opt-out in the model form under this part, must comply with section 624 of the FCRA and 12 CFR part 1022, subpart C, with respect to the initial notice and opt-out and any subsequent renewal notice and opt-out. An institution not required to provide an opt-out under this subparagraph may elect to include this reason in the model form.

(7) **For nonaffiliates to market to you.** This reason incorporates sharing described in §§ 1016.7 and 1016.10(a) of this part. An institution that shares personal information for this reason must provide an opt-out.

(e) To limit our sharing: A financial institution must include this section of the model form *only* if it provides an opt-out. The word "choice" may be written in either the singular or plural, as appropriate. Institutions must select one or more of the applicable opt-out methods described: Telephone, such as by a toll-free number; a Web site; or use of a mail-in opt-out form. Institutions may include the words "toll-free" before telephone, as appropriate. An institution that allows consumers to opt out online must provide either a specific Web address that takes consumers directly to the opt-out page or a general Web address that provides a clear and conspicuous direct link to the opt-out page. The opt-out choices made available to the consumer who contacts the institution through these methods must correspond accurately to the "Yes" responses in the third column of the disclosure table. In the part titled "Please note," institutions may insert a number that is 30 or greater in the space marked "[30]." Instructions on voluntary or state privacy law opt-out information are in paragraph C.2(g)(5) of these Instructions.

(f) Questions box. Customer service contact information must be inserted as appropriate, where [phone number] or [Web site] appear. Institutions may elect to provide either a phone number, such as a toll-free number, or a web address, or both. Institutions may include the words "toll-free" before the telephone number, as appropriate.

(g) Mail-in opt-out form. Financial institutions must include this mail-in form *only* if they state in the "To limit our sharing" box that consumers can opt out by mail. The mail-in form must provide opt-out options that correspond accurately to the "Yes" responses in the third column in the disclosure table. Institutions that require customers to provide only name and address may omit the section identified as "[account #]." Institutions that require additional or different information, such as a random opt-out number or a truncated account number, to implement an opt-out election should modify the "[account #]" reference accordingly. This includes institutions that require customers with multiple accounts to identify each account to which the opt-out should apply. An institution must enter its opt-out mailing address: in the far right of this form (*see* version 3); or below the form (*see* version 4). The reverse side of the mail-in opt-out form must not include any content of the model form.

(1) **Joint accountholder**. Only institutions that provide their joint accountholders the choice to opt out for only one accountholder, in accordance with paragraph C.3(a)(5) of these Instructions, must include in the far left column of the mail-in form the following statement: "If you have a joint account, your choice(s) will apply to everyone on your account unless you mark below. Apply my choice(s) only to me." The word "choice" may be written in either the singular or plural, as appropriate. Financial institutions that provide insurance products or services, provide this option, and elect to use the model form may substitute the word "policy" for "account" in this statement. Institutions that do not provide this option may eliminate this left column from the mail-in form.

(2) **FCRA section 603(d)(2)(A)(iii) opt-out**. If the institution shares personal information pursuant to section 603(d)(2)(A)(iii) of the FCRA, it must include in the mail-in opt-out form the following statement: " Do not share information about my creditworthiness with your affiliates for their everyday business purposes."

(3) **FCRA section 624 opt-out**. If the institution incorporates section 624 of the FCRA in accord with paragraph C.2(d)(6) of these Instructions, it must include in the mail-in opt-out form the following statement: "Do not allow your affiliates to use my personal information to market to me."

(4) **Nonaffiliate opt-out**. If the financial institution shares personal information pursuant to § 1016.10(a) of this part, it must include in the mail-in opt-out form the following statement: " Do not share my personal information with nonaffiliates to market their products and services to me."

(5) **Additional opt-outs**. Financial institutions that use the disclosure table to provide opt-out options beyond those required by Federal law must provide those opt-outs in this section of the model form. A financial institution that chooses to offer an opt-out for its own marketing in the mail-in opt-out form must include one of the two following statements: " Do not share my personal information to market to me." *or* "Do not use my personal information to market to me." A financial institution that chooses to offer an opt-out for joint marketing must include the following statement: "Do not share my personal information with other financial institutions to jointly market to me."

(h) Barcodes. A financial institution may elect to include a barcode and/or "tagline" (an internal identifier) in 6-point font at the bottom of page one, as needed for information internal to the institution, so long as these do not interfere with the clarity or text of the form.

3. Page Two

(a) General Instructions for the Questions. Certain of the Questions may be customized as follows:

(1) **"Who is providing this notice?"** This question may be omitted where only one financial institution provides the model form and that institution is clearly identified in the title on page one. Two or more financial institutions that jointly provide the model form must use this question to identify themselves as required by § 1016.9(f) of this part. Where the list of institutions exceeds four (4) lines, the institution must describe in the response to this question the general types of institutions jointly providing the notice and must separately identify those institutions, in minimum 8-point font, directly following the "Other important information" box, or, if that box is not included in the institution's form, directly following the "Definitions." The list may appear in a multi-column format.

(2) **"How does [name of financial institution] protect my personal information?"** The financial institution may only provide additional information pertaining to its safeguards practices following the designated response to this question. Such information may include information about the institution's use of cookies or other measures it uses to safeguard personal information. Institutions are limited to a maximum of 30 additional words.

(3) **"How does [name of financial institution] collect my personal information?"** Institutions must use five (5) of the following terms to complete the bulleted list for this question: Open an account; deposit money; pay your bills; apply for a loan; use your credit or debit card; seek financial or tax advice; apply for insurance; pay insurance premiums; file an insurance claim; seek advice about your investments; buy securities from us; sell securities to us; direct us to buy securities; direct us to sell your securities; make deposits or withdrawals from your account; enter into an investment advisory contract; give us your income information; provide employment information; give us your employment history; tell us about your investment or retirement portfolio; tell us about your investment or retirement earnings; apply for financing; apply for a lease; provide account information; give us your contact information; pay us by check; give us your wage statements; provide your mortgage information; make a wire transfer; tell us who receives the money; tell us where to send the money; show your government-issued ID; show your driver's license; order a commodity futures or option trade. Institutions that collect personal information from their affiliates and/or credit bureaus must include after the bulleted list the following statement: "We also collect your personal information from others, such as credit bureaus, affiliates, or other companies." Institutions that do not collect personal information from their affiliates or credit bureaus but do collect information from other companies must include the following statement instead: "We also collect your personal information from other companies." Only institutions that do not collect any personal information from affiliates, credit bureaus, or other companies can omit both statements.

(4) **"Why can't I limit all sharing?"** Institutions that describe state privacy law provisions in the *"Other important information"* box must use the bracketed sentence: "See below for more on your rights under state law." Other institutions must omit this sentence.

(5) **"What happens when I limit sharing for an account I hold jointly with someone else?"** Only financial institutions that provide opt-out options must use this question. Other institutions must omit this question. Institutions must choose one of the following two statements to respond to this question: "Your choices will apply to everyone on your account." or "Your choices will apply to everyone on your account—unless you tell us otherwise." Financial institutions that provide insurance products or services and elect to use the model form may substitute the word "policy" for "account" in these statements.

(b) General Instructions for the Definitions. The financial institution must customize the space below the responses to the three definitions in this section. This specific information must be in italicized lettering to set off the information from the standardized definitions.

(1) **Affiliates.** As required by § 1016.6(a)(3) of this part, where [*affiliate information*] appears, the financial institution must:

(i) If it has no affiliates, state: "[name of financial institution] has no affiliates";

(ii) If it has affiliates but does not share personal information, state: "[name of financial institution] does not share with our affiliates"; or

(iii) If it shares with its affiliates, state, as applicable: "Our affiliates include companies with a [common corporate identity of financial institution] name; financial companies such as [insert illustrative list of companies]; nonfinancial companies, such as [insert illustrative list of companies]; and others, such as [insert illustrative list]."

(2) **Nonaffiliates.** As required by § 1016.6(c)(3) of this part, where [*nonaffiliate information*] appears, the financial institution must:

(i) If it does not share with nonaffiliated third parties, state: "[name of financial institution] does not share with nonaffiliates so they can market to you"; or

(ii) If it shares with nonaffiliated third parties, state, as applicable: "Nonaffiliates we share with can include [list categories of companies such as mortgage companies, insurance companies, direct marketing companies, and nonprofit organizations]."

(3) **Joint Marketing.** As required by § 1016.13 of this part, where [*joint marketing*] appears, the financial institution must:

(i) If it does not engage in joint marketing, state: "*[name of financial institution] doesn't jointly market*"; or

(ii) If it shares personal information for joint marketing, state, as applicable: "*Our joint marketing partners include [list categories of companies such as credit card companies].*"

(c) General instructions for the "Other important information" box. This box is optional. The space provided for information in this box is not limited. Only the following types of information can appear in this box.

(1) State and/or international privacy law information; and/or

(2) Acknowledgment of receipt form.

Illinois Biometric Information Privacy Act 740 ILCS 14/1 *et seq.*

§ 1. Short title. This Act may be cited as the Biometric Information Privacy Act.

§ 5. Legislative findings; intent. The General Assembly finds all of the following:

(a) The use of biometrics is growing in the business and security screening sectors and appears to promise streamlined financial transactions and security screenings.

(b) Major national corporations have selected the City of Chicago and other locations in this State as pilot testing sites for new applications of biometric-facilitated financial transactions, including finger-scan technologies at grocery stores, gas stations, and school cafeterias.

(c) Biometrics are unlike other unique identifiers that are used to access finances or other sensitive information. For example, social security numbers, when compromised, can be changed. Biometrics, however, are biologically unique to the individual; therefore, once compromised, the individual has no recourse, is at heightened risk for identity theft, and is likely to withdraw from biometric-facilitated transactions.

(d) An overwhelming majority of members of the public are weary of the use of biometrics when such information is tied to finances and other personal information.

(e) Despite limited State law regulating the collection, use, safeguarding, and storage of biometrics, many members of the public are deterred from partaking in biometric identifier-facilitated transactions.

(f) The full ramifications of biometric technology are not fully known.

(g) The public welfare, security, and safety will be served by regulating the collection, use, safeguarding, handling, storage, retention, and destruction of biometric identifiers and information.

§ 10. Definitions. In this Act:

"Biometric identifier" means a retina or iris scan, fingerprint, voiceprint, or scan of hand or face geometry. Biometric identifiers do not include writing samples, written signatures, photographs, human biological samples used for valid scientific testing or screening, demographic data, tattoo descriptions, or physical descriptions such as height, weight, hair color, or eye color. Biometric identifiers do not include donated organs, tissues, or parts as defined in the Illinois Anatomical Gift Act or blood or serum stored on behalf of recipients or potential recipients of living or cadaveric transplants and obtained or stored by a federally designated organ procurement agency. Biometric identifiers do not include biological materials regulated under the Genetic Information Privacy Act. Biometric identifiers do not include information captured from a patient in a health care setting or information collected, used, or stored for health care treatment, payment, or operations under the federal Health Insurance Portability and Accountability Act of 1996. Biometric identifiers do not include an X-ray, roentgen process, computed tomography, MRI, PET scan, mammography, or other image or film of the human anatomy used to diagnose, prognose, or treat an illness or other medical condition or to further validate scientific testing or screening.

"Biometric information" means any information, regardless of how it is captured, converted, stored, or shared, based on an individual's biometric identifier used to identify an individual. Biometric information does not include information derived from items or procedures excluded under the definition of biometric identifiers.

"Confidential and sensitive information" means personal information that can be used to uniquely identify an individual or an individual's account or property. Examples of confidential and sensitive information include, but are not limited to, a genetic marker, genetic testing information, a unique identifier number to locate an account or property, an account number, a PIN number, a pass code, a driver's license number, or a social security number.

"Private entity" means any individual, partnership, corporation, limited liability company, association, or other group, however organized. A private entity does not include a State or local government agency. A private entity does not include any court of Illinois, a clerk of the court, or a judge or justice thereof.

"Written release" means informed written consent or, in the context of employment, a release executed by an employee as a condition of employment.

§ 15. Retention; collection; disclosure; destruction.

(a) A private entity in possession of biometric identifiers or biometric information must develop a written policy, made available to the public, establishing a retention schedule and guidelines for permanently destroying biometric identifiers and biometric information when the initial purpose for collecting or obtaining such identifiers or information has been satisfied or within 3 years of the individual's last interaction with the private entity, whichever occurs first. Absent a valid warrant or subpoena issued by a court of competent jurisdiction, a private entity in possession of biometric identifiers or biometric information must comply with its established retention schedule and destruction guidelines.

(b) No private entity may collect, capture, purchase, receive through trade, or otherwise obtain a person's or a customer's biometric identifier or biometric information, unless it first:

(1) informs the subject or the subject's legally authorized representative in writing that a biometric identifier or biometric information is being collected or stored;

(2) informs the subject or the subject's legally authorized representative in writing of the specific purpose and length of term for which a biometric identifier or biometric information is being collected, stored, and used; and

(3) receives a written release executed by the subject of the biometric identifier or biometric information or the subject's legally authorized representative.

(c) No private entity in possession of a biometric identifier or biometric information may sell, lease, trade, or otherwise profit from a person's or a customer's biometric identifier or biometric information.

(d) No private entity in possession of a biometric identifier or biometric information may disclose, redisclose, or otherwise disseminate a person's or a customer's biometric identifier or biometric information unless:

(1) the subject of the biometric identifier or biometric information or the subject's legally authorized representative consents to the disclosure or redisclosure;

(2) the disclosure or redisclosure completes a financial transaction requested or authorized by the subject of the biometric identifier or the biometric information or the subject's legally authorized representative;

(3) the disclosure or redisclosure is required by State or federal law or municipal ordinance; or

(4) the disclosure is required pursuant to a valid warrant or subpoena issued by a court of competent jurisdiction.

(e) A private entity in possession of a biometric identifier or biometric information shall:

(1) store, transmit, and protect from disclosure all biometric identifiers and biometric information using the reasonable standard of care within the private entity's industry; and

(2) store, transmit, and protect from disclosure all biometric identifiers and biometric information in a manner that is the same as or more protective than the manner in which the private entity stores, transmits, and protects other confidential and sensitive information.

§ 20. Right of action. Any person aggrieved by a violation of this Act shall have a right of action in a State circuit court or as a supplemental claim in federal district court against an offending party. A prevailing party may recover for each violation:

(1) against a private entity that negligently violates a provision of this Act, liquidated damages of $1,000 or actual damages, whichever is greater;

(2) against a private entity that intentionally or recklessly violates a provision of this Act, liquidated damages of $5,000 or actual damages, whichever is greater;

(3) reasonable attorneys' fees and costs, including expert witness fees and other litigation expenses; and

(4) other relief, including an injunction, as the State or federal court may deem appropriate.

§ 25. Construction.

(a) Nothing in this Act shall be construed to impact the admission or discovery of biometric identifiers and biometric information in any action of any kind in any court, or before any tribunal, board, agency, or person.

(b) Nothing in this Act shall be construed to conflict with the X-Ray Retention Act, the federal Health Insurance Portability and Accountability Act of 1996 and the rules promulgated under either Act.

(c) Nothing in this Act shall be deemed to apply in any manner to a financial institution or an affiliate of a financial institution that is subject to Title V of the federal Gramm-Leach-Bliley Act of 1999 and the rules promulgated thereunder.

(d) Nothing in this Act shall be construed to conflict with the Private Detective, Private Alarm, Private Security, Fingerprint Vendor, and Locksmith Act of 2004 and the rules promulgated thereunder.

(e) Nothing in this Act shall be construed to apply to a contractor, subcontractor,

EXCERPT FROM ELECTRONIC SIGNATURES IN GLOBAL AND NATIONAL COMMERCE ACT (E-SIGN), 15 U.S.C. §§ 7001 ET SEQ.

§ 7001. General Rule of Validity

(a) In general

Notwithstanding any statute, regulation, or other rule of law (other than this subchapter and subchapter II), with respect to any transaction in or affecting interstate or foreign commerce—

(1) a signature, contract, or other record relating to such transaction may not be denied legal effect, validity, or enforceability solely because it is in electronic form; and

(2) a contract relating to such transaction may not be denied legal effect, validity, or enforceability solely because an electronic signature or electronic record was used in its formation.

(b) Preservation of rights and obligations

This subchapter does not—

(1) limit, alter, or otherwise affect any requirement imposed by a statute, regulation, or rule of law relating to the rights and obligations of persons under such statute, regulation, or rule of law other than a requirement that contracts or other records be written, signed, or in nonelectronic form; or

(2) require any person to agree to use or accept electronic records or electronic signatures, other than a governmental agency with respect to a record other than a contract to which it is a party.

(c) Consumer disclosures

(1) Consent to electronic records

Notwithstanding subsection (a), if a statute, regulation, or other rule of law requires that information relating to a transaction or transactions in or affecting interstate or foreign commerce be provided or made available to a consumer in writing, the use of an electronic record to provide or make available (whichever is required) such information satisfies the requirement that such information be in writing if—

(A) the consumer has affirmatively consented to such use and has not withdrawn such consent;

(B) the consumer, prior to consenting, is provided with a clear and conspicuous statement—

(i) informing the consumer of (I) any right or option of the consumer to have the record provided or made available on paper or in nonelectronic form, and (II) the right of the consumer to withdraw the consent to have the record provided or made available in an electronic form and of any conditions, consequences (which may include termination of the parties' relationship), or fees in the event of such withdrawal;

(ii) informing the consumer of whether the consent applies (I) only to the particular transaction which gave rise to the obligation to provide the record, or (II) to identified categories of records that may be provided or made available during the course of the parties' relationship;

(iii) describing the procedures the consumer must use to withdraw consent as provided in clause (i) and to update information needed to contact the consumer electronically; and

(iv) informing the consumer (I) how, after the consent, the consumer may, upon request, obtain a paper copy of an electronic record, and (II) whether any fee will be charged for such copy;

(C) the consumer—

(i) prior to consenting, is provided with a statement of the hardware and software requirements for access to and retention of the electronic records; and

(ii) consents electronically, or confirms his or her consent electronically, in a manner that reasonably demonstrates that the consumer can access information in the electronic form that will be used to provide the information that is the subject of the consent; and

(D) after the consent of a consumer in accordance with subparagraph (A), if a change in the hardware or software requirements needed to access or retain electronic records creates a material risk that the consumer will not be able to access or retain a subsequent electronic record that was the subject of the consent, the person providing the electronic record—

(i) provides the consumer with a statement of (I) the revised hardware and software requirements for access to and retention of the electronic records, and (II) the right to withdraw consent without the imposition of any fees for such withdrawal and without the imposition of any condition or consequence that was not disclosed under subparagraph (B)(i); and

(ii) again complies with subparagraph (C).

(2) Other rights

(A) Preservation of consumer protections

Nothing in this subchapter affects the content or timing of any disclosure or other record required to be provided or made available to any consumer under any statute, regulation, or other rule of law.

(B) Verification or acknowledgment

If a law that was enacted prior to this chapter expressly requires a record to be provided or made available by a specified method that requires verification or acknowledgment of receipt, the record may be provided or made available electronically only if the method used provides verification or acknowledgment of receipt (whichever is required).

(3) Effect of failure to obtain electronic consent or confirmation of consent

The legal effectiveness, validity, or enforceability of any contract executed by a consumer shall not be denied solely because of the failure to obtain electronic consent or confirmation of consent by that consumer in accordance with paragraph (1)(C)(ii).

(4) Prospective effect

Withdrawal of consent by a consumer shall not affect the legal effectiveness, validity, or enforceability of electronic records provided or made available to that consumer in accordance with paragraph (1) prior to implementation of the consumer's withdrawal of consent. A consumer's withdrawal of consent shall be effective within a reasonable period of time after receipt of the withdrawal by the provider of the record. Failure to comply with paragraph (1)(D) may, at the election of the consumer, be treated as a withdrawal of consent for purposes of this paragraph.

(5) Prior consent

This subsection does not apply to any records that are provided or made available to a consumer who has consented prior to the effective date of this subchapter to receive such records in electronic form as permitted by any statute, regulation, or other rule of law.

(6) Oral communications

An oral communication or a recording of an oral communication shall not qualify as an electronic record for purposes of this subsection except as otherwise provided under applicable law.

(d) Retention of contracts and records

(1) Accuracy and accessibility

If a statute, regulation, or other rule of law requires that a contract or other record relating to a transaction in or affecting interstate or foreign commerce be retained, that requirement is met by retaining an electronic record of the information in the contract or other record that—

(A) accurately reflects the information set forth in the contract or other record; and

(B) remains accessible to all persons who are entitled to access by statute, regulation, or rule of law, for the period required by such statute, regulation, or rule of law, in a form that is capable of being accurately reproduced for later reference, whether by transmission, printing, or otherwise.

(2) Exception

A requirement to retain a contract or other record in accordance with paragraph (1) does not apply to any information whose sole purpose is to enable the contract or other record to be sent, communicated, or received.

(3) Originals

If a statute, regulation, or other rule of law requires a contract or other record relating to a transaction in or affecting interstate or foreign commerce to be provided, available, or retained in its original form, or provides consequences if the contract or other record is not provided, available, or retained in its original form, that statute, regulation, or rule of law is satisfied by an electronic record that complies with paragraph (1).

(4) Checks

If a statute, regulation, or other rule of law requires the retention of a check, that requirement is satisfied by retention of an electronic record of the information on the front and back of the check in accordance with paragraph (1).

(e) Accuracy and ability to retain contracts and other records

Notwithstanding subsection (a), if a statute, regulation, or other rule of law requires that a contract or other record relating to a transaction in or affecting interstate or foreign commerce be in writing, the legal effect, validity, or enforceability of an electronic record of such contract or other record may be denied if such electronic record is not in a form that is capable of being retained and accurately reproduced for later reference by all parties or persons who are entitled to retain the contract or other record.

(f) Proximity

Nothing in this subchapter affects the proximity required by any statute, regulation, or other rule of law with respect to any warning, notice, disclosure, or other record required to be posted, displayed, or publicly affixed.

(g) Notarization and acknowledgment

If a statute, regulation, or other rule of law requires a signature or record relating to a transaction in or affecting interstate or foreign commerce to be notarized, acknowledged, verified, or made under oath, that requirement is satisfied if the electronic signature of the person authorized to perform those acts, together with all other information required to be included by other applicable statute, regulation, or rule of law, is attached to or logically associated with the signature or record.

(h) Electronic agents

A contract or other record relating to a transaction in or affecting interstate or foreign commerce may not be denied legal effect, validity, or enforceability solely because its formation, creation, or delivery involved the action of one or more electronic agents so long as the action of any such electronic agent is legally attributable to the person to be bound.

(i) Insurance

It is the specific intent of the Congress that this subchapter and subchapter II of this chapter apply to the business of insurance.

(j) Insurance agents and brokers

An insurance agent or broker acting under the direction of a party that enters into a contract by means of an electronic record or electronic signature may not be held liable for any deficiency in the electronic procedures agreed to by the parties under that contract if—

(1) the agent or broker has not engaged in negligent, reckless, or intentional tortious conduct;

(2) the agent or broker was not involved in the development or establishment of such electronic procedures; and

(3) the agent or broker did not deviate from such procedures.

EXCERPTS FROM REGULATION CC, AVAILABILITY OF FUNDS AND COLLECTION OF CHECKS 12 C.F.R. PART 229

Table of Sections

Subpart D: Substitute Checks

Subpart D: Substitute Checks

§ 229.51 General provisions governing substitute checks

(a) Legal equivalence. A substitute check for which a bank has provided the warranties described in § 229.52 is the legal equivalent of an original check for all persons and all purposes, including any provision of federal or state law, if the substitute check—

(1) Accurately represents all of the information on the front and back of the original check as of the time the original check was truncated; and

(2) Bears the legend, "This is a legal copy of your check. You can use it the same way you would use the original check."

(b) Reconverting bank duties. A bank shall ensure that a substitute check for which it is the reconverting bank—

(1) Bears all indorsements applied by parties that previously handled the check in any form (including the original check, a substitute check, or another paper or electronic representation of such original check or substitute check) for forward collection or return;

(2) Identifies the reconverting bank in a manner that preserves any previous reconverting bank identifications, in accordance with ANS X9.100–140 and

(3) Identifies the bank that truncated the original check, in accordance with ANS X9.100–140.

(c) Applicable law. A substitute check that is the legal equivalent of an original check under paragraph (a) of this section shall be subject to any provision, including any provision relating to the protection of customers, of this part, the U.C.C., and any other applicable federal or state law as if such substitute check were the original check, to the extent such provision of law is not inconsistent with the Check 21 Act or this subpart.

§ 229.52 Substitute check warranties

(a) Content and provision of substitute-check warranties.

(1) A bank that transfers, presents, or returns a substitute check (or a paper or electronic representation of a substitute check) for which it receives consideration warrants to the parties listed in paragraph (b) of this section that—

(i) The substitute check meets the requirements for legal equivalence described in § 229.51(a)(1)–(2); and

(ii) No depositary bank, drawee, drawer, or indorser will receive presentment or return of, or otherwise be charged for, the substitute check, the original check, or a paper or electronic representation of the substitute check or original check such that that person will be asked to make a payment based on a check that it already has paid.

(2) A bank that rejects a check submitted for deposit and returns to its customer a substitute check (or a paper or electronic representation of a substitute check) makes the warranties in paragraph (a)(1) of this section regardless of whether the bank received consideration.

(b) Warranty recipients. A bank makes the warranties described in paragraph (a) of this section to the person to which the bank transfers, presents, or returns the substitute check or a paper or electronic representation of such substitute check and to any subsequent recipient, which could include a collecting or returning bank, the depositary bank, the drawer, the drawee, the payee, the depositor, and any indorser. These parties receive the warranties regardless of whether they received the substitute check or a paper or electronic representation of a substitute check.

§ 229.53 Substitute check indemnity

(a) Scope of indemnity.

(1) A bank that transfers, presents, or returns a substitute check or a paper or electronic representation of a substitute check for which it receives consideration shall indemnify the recipient and any subsequent recipient (including a collecting or returning bank, the depositary bank, the drawer, the drawee, the payee, the depositor, and any indorser) for any loss incurred by any recipient of a substitute check if that loss occurred due to the receipt of a substitute check instead of the original check.

(2) A bank that rejects a check submitted for deposit and returns to its customer a substitute check (or a paper or electronic representation of a substitute check) shall indemnify the recipient as described in paragraph (a)(1) of this section regardless of whether the bank received consideration.

(b) Indemnity amount—

(1) In general. Unless otherwise indicated by paragraph (b)(2) or (b)(3) of this section, the amount of the indemnity under paragraph (a) of this section is as follows:

(i) If the loss resulted from a breach of a substitute check warranty provided under § 229.52, the amount of the indemnity shall be the amount of any loss (including interest, costs, reasonable attorney's fees, and other expenses of representation) proximately caused by the warranty breach.

(ii) If the loss did not result from a breach of a substitute check warranty provided under § 229.52, the amount of the indemnity shall be the sum of—

(A) The amount of the loss, up to the amount of the substitute check; and

(B) Interest and expenses (including costs and reasonable attorney's fees and other expenses of representation) related to the substitute check.

(2) Comparative negligence.

(i) If a loss described in paragraph (a) of this section results in whole or in part from the indemnified person's negligence or failure to act in good faith, then the indemnity amount described in paragraph (b)(1) of this section shall be reduced in proportion to the amount of negligence or bad faith attributable to the indemnified person.

(ii) Nothing in this paragraph (b)(2) reduces the rights of a consumer or any other person under the U.C.C. or other applicable provision of state or federal law.

(3) Effect of producing the original check or a sufficient copy—

(i) If an indemnifying bank produces the original check or a sufficient copy, the indemnifying bank shall—

(A) Be liable under this section only for losses that are incurred up to the time that the bank provides that original check or sufficient copy to the indemnified person; and

(B) Have a right to the return of any funds it has paid under this section in excess of those losses.

(ii) The production by the indemnifying bank of the original check or a sufficient copy under paragraph (b)(3)(i) of this section shall not absolve the indemnifying bank from any liability under any warranty that the bank has provided under § 229.52 or other applicable law.

(c) Subrogation of rights—

(1) In general. An indemnifying bank shall be subrogated to the rights of the person that it indemnifies to the extent of the indemnity it has provided and may attempt to recover from another person based on a warranty or other claim.

(2) Duty of indemnified person for subrogated claims. Each indemnified person shall have a duty to comply with all reasonable requests for assistance from an indemnifying bank in connection with any claim the indemnifying bank brings against a warrantor or other person related to a check that forms the basis for the indemnification.

§ 229.54 Expedited recredit for consumers

(a) Circumstances giving rise to a claim. A consumer may make a claim under this section for a recredit with respect to a substitute check if the consumer asserts in good faith that—

(1) The bank holding the consumer's account charged that account for a substitute check that was provided to the consumer (although the consumer need not be in possession of that substitute check at the time he or she submits a claim);

(2) The substitute check was not properly charged to the consumer account or the consumer has a warranty claim with respect to the substitute check;

(3) The consumer suffered a resulting loss; and

(4) Production of the original check or a sufficient copy is necessary to determine whether or not the substitute check in fact was improperly charged or whether the consumer's warranty claim is valid.

(b) Procedures for making claims. A consumer shall make his or her claim for a recredit under this section with the bank that holds the consumer's account in accordance with the timing, content, and form requirements of this section.

(1) Timing of claim.

(i) The consumer shall submit his or her claim such that the bank receives the claim by the end of the 40th calendar day after the later of the calendar day on which the bank mailed or delivered, by a means agreed to by the consumer—

(A) The periodic account statement that contains information concerning the transaction giving rise to the claim; or

(B) The substitute check giving rise to the claim.

(ii) If the consumer cannot submit his or her claim by the time specified in paragraph (b)(1)(i) of this section because of extenuating circumstances, the bank shall extend the 40-calendar-day period by an additional reasonable amount of time.

(iii) If a consumer makes a claim orally and the bank requires the claim to be in writing, the consumer's claim is timely if the oral claim was received within the time described in paragraphs (b)(1)(i)–(ii) of this section and the written claim was received within the time described in paragraph (b)(3)(ii) of this section.

(2) Content of claim.

(i) The consumer's claim shall include the following information:

(A) A description of the consumer's claim, including the reason why the consumer believes his or her account was improperly charged for the substitute check or the nature of his or her warranty claim with respect to such check;

(B) A statement that the consumer suffered a loss and an estimate of the amount of that loss;

(C) The reason why production of the original check or a sufficient copy is necessary to determine whether or not the charge to the consumer's account was proper or the consumer's warranty claim is valid; and

(D) Sufficient information to allow the bank to identify the substitute check and investigate the claim.

(ii) If a consumer attempts to make a claim but fails to provide all the information in paragraph (b)(2)(i) of this section that is required to constitute a claim, the bank shall inform the consumer that the claim is not complete and identify the information that is missing.

(3) Form and submission of claim; computation of time for bank action. The bank holding the account that is the subject of the consumer's claim may, in its discretion, require the consumer to submit the information required by this section in writing. A bank that requires a written submission—

(i) May permit the consumer to submit the written claim electronically;

(ii) Shall inform a consumer who submits a claim orally of the written claim requirement at the time of the oral claim and may require such consumer to submit the written claim such that the bank receives the written claim by the 10th business day after the banking day on which the bank received the oral claim; and

(iii) Shall compute the time periods for acting on the consumer's claim described in paragraph (c) of this section from the date on which the bank received the written claim.

(c) Action on claims. A bank that receives a claim that meets the requirements of paragraph (b) of this section shall act as follows:

(1) Valid consumer claim. If the bank determines that the consumer's claim is valid, the bank shall—

(i) Recredit the consumer's account for the amount of the consumer's loss, up to the amount of the substitute check, plus interest if the account is an interest-bearing account, no later than the end of the business day after the banking day on which the bank makes that determination; and

(ii) Send to the consumer the notice required by paragraph (e)(1) of this section.

(2) Invalid consumer claim. If a bank determines that the consumer's claim is not valid, the bank shall send to the consumer the notice described in paragraph (e)(2) of this section.

(3) Recredit pending investigation. If the bank has not taken an action described in paragraph (c)(1) or (c)(2) of this section before the end of the 10th business day after the banking day on which the bank received the claim, the bank shall—

(i) By the end of that business day—

(A) Recredit the consumer's account for the amount of the consumer's loss, up to the lesser of the amount of the substitute check or $2,500, plus interest on that amount if the account is an interest-bearing account; and

(B) Send to the consumer the notice required by paragraph (e)(1) of this section; and

(ii) Recredit the consumer's account for the remaining amount of the consumer's loss, if any, up to the amount of the substitute check, plus interest if the account is an interest-bearing account, no later than the end of the 45th calendar day after the banking day on which the bank received the claim and send to the consumer the notice required by paragraph (e)(1) of this section, unless the bank prior to that time has determined that the consumer's claim is or is not valid in accordance with paragraph (c)(1) or (c)(2) of this section.

(4) Reversal of recredit. A bank may reverse a recredit that it has made to a consumer account under paragraph (c)(1) or (c)(3) of this section, plus interest that the bank has paid, if any, on that amount, if the bank—

(i) Determines that the consumer's claim was not valid; and

(ii) Notifies the consumer in accordance with paragraph (e)(3) of this section.

(d) Availability of recredit—

(1) Next-day availability. Except as provided in paragraph (d)(2) of this section, a bank shall make any amount that it recredits to a consumer account under this section available for withdrawal no later than the start of the business day after the banking day on which the bank provides the recredit.

(2) Safeguard exceptions. A bank may delay availability to a consumer of a recredit provided under paragraph (c)(3)(i) of this section until the start of the earlier of the business day after the banking day on which the bank determines the consumer's claim is valid or the 45th calendar day after the banking day on which the bank received the oral or written claim, as required by paragraph (b) of this section, if—

(i) The consumer submits the claim during the 30-calendar-day period beginning on the banking day on which the consumer account was established;

(ii) Without regard to the charge that gave rise to the recredit claim—

(A) On six or more business days during the six-month period ending on the calendar day on which the consumer submitted the claim, the balance in the consumer account was negative or would have become negative if checks or other charges to the account had been paid; or

(B) On two or more business days during such six-month period, the balance in the consumer account was negative or would have become negative in the amount of $5,000 or more if checks or other charges to the account had been paid; or

(iii) The bank has reasonable cause to believe that the claim is fraudulent, based on facts that would cause a well-grounded belief in the mind of a reasonable person that the claim is fraudulent. The fact that the check in question or the consumer is of a particular class may not be the basis for invoking this exception.

(3) Overdraft fees. A bank that delays availability as permitted in paragraph (d)(2) of this section may not impose an overdraft fee with respect to drafts drawn by the consumer on such recredited funds until the fifth calendar day after the calendar day on which the bank sent the notice required by paragraph (e)(1) of this section.

(e) Notices relating to consumer expedited recredit claims—

(1) Notice of recredit. A bank that recredits a consumer account under paragraph (c) of this section shall send notice to the consumer of the recredit no later than the business day after the banking day on which the bank recredits the consumer account. This notice shall describe—

(i) The amount of the recredit; and

(ii) The date on which the recredited funds will be available for withdrawal.

(2) Notice that the consumer's claim is not valid. If a bank determines that a substitute check for which a consumer made a claim under this section was in fact properly charged to the consumer account or that the consumer's warranty claim for that substitute check was not valid, the bank shall send notice to the consumer no later than the business day after the banking day on which the bank makes that determination. This notice shall—

(i) Include the original check or a sufficient copy, except as provided in § 229.58;

(ii) Demonstrate to the consumer that the substitute check was properly charged or the consumer's warranty claim is not valid; and

(iii) Include the information or documents (in addition to the original check or sufficient copy), if any, on which the bank relied in making its determination or a statement that the consumer may request copies of such information or documents.

(3) Notice of a reversal of recredit. A bank that reverses an amount it previously recredited to a consumer account shall send notice to the consumer no later than the business day after the banking day on which the bank made the reversal. This notice shall include the information listed in paragraph (e)(2) of this section and also describe—

(i) The amount of the reversal, including both the amount of the recredit (including the interest component, if any) and the amount of interest paid on the recredited amount, if any, being reversed; and

(ii) The date on which the bank made the reversal.

(f) Other claims not affected. Providing a recredit in accordance with this section shall not absolve the bank from liability for a claim made under any other provision of law, such as a claim for wrongful dishonor of a check under the U.C.C., or from liability for additional damages, such as damages under § 229.53 or § 229.56 of this subpart or U.C.C. 4–402.

§ 229.55 Expedited recredit for banks

(a) Circumstances giving rise to a claim. A bank that has an indemnity claim under § 229.53 with respect to a substitute check may make an expedited recredit claim against an indemnifying bank if—

(1) The claimant bank or a bank that the claimant bank has indemnified—

(i) Has received a claim for expedited recredit from a consumer under § 229.54; or

(ii) Would have been subject to such a claim if the consumer account had been charged for the substitute check;

(2) The claimant bank is obligated to provide an expedited recredit with respect to such substitute check under § 229.54 or otherwise has suffered a resulting loss; and

(3) The production of the original check or a sufficient copy is necessary to determine the validity of the charge to the consumer account or the validity of any warranty claim connected with such substitute check.

(b) Procedures for making claims. A claimant bank shall send its claim to the indemnifying bank, subject to the timing, content, and form requirements of this section.

(1) Timing of claim. The claimant bank shall submit its claim such that the indemnifying bank receives the claim by the end of the 120th calendar day after the date of the transaction that gave rise to the claim.

(2) Content of claim. The claimant bank's claim shall include the following information—

(i) A description of the consumer's claim or the warranty claim related to the substitute check, including why the bank believes that the substitute check may not be properly charged to the consumer account;

(ii) A statement that the claimant bank is obligated to recredit a consumer account under § 229.54 or otherwise has suffered a loss and an estimate of the amount of that recredit or loss, including interest if applicable;

(iii) The reason why production of the original check or a sufficient copy is necessary to determine the validity of the charge to the consumer account or the warranty claim; and

(iv) Sufficient information to allow the indemnifying bank to identify the substitute check and investigate the claim.

(3) Requirements relating to copies of substitute checks. If the information submitted by a claimant bank under paragraph (b)(2) of this section includes a copy of any substitute check, the claimant bank shall take reasonable steps to ensure that the copy cannot be mistaken for the legal equivalent of the check under § 229.51(a) or sent or handled by any bank, including the indemnifying bank, for forward collection or return.

(4) Form and submission of claim; computation of time. The indemnifying bank may, in its discretion, require the claimant bank to submit the information required by this section in writing, including a copy of the paper or electronic claim submitted by the consumer, if any. An indemnifying bank that requires a written submission—

(i) May permit the claimant bank to submit the written claim electronically;

(ii) Shall inform a claimant bank that submits a claim orally of the written claim requirement at the time of the oral claim; and

(iii) Shall compute the 10-day time period for acting on the claim described in paragraph (c) of this section from the date on which the bank received the written claim.

(c) Action on claims. No later than the 10th business day after the banking day on which the indemnifying bank receives a claim that meets the requirements of paragraph (b) of this section, the indemnifying bank shall—

(1) Recredit the claimant bank for the amount of the claim, up to the amount of the substitute check, plus interest if applicable;

(2) Provide to the claimant bank the original check or a sufficient copy; or

(3) Provide information to the claimant bank regarding why the indemnifying bank is not obligated to comply with paragraph (c)(1) or (c)(2) of this section.

(d) Recredit does not abrogate other liabilities. Providing a recredit to a claimant bank under this section does not absolve the indemnifying bank from liability for claims brought under any other law or from additional damages under § 229.53 or § 229.56.

(e) Indemnifying bank's right to a refund.

(1) If a claimant bank reverses a recredit it previously made to a consumer account under § 229.54 or otherwise receives reimbursement for a substitute check that formed the basis of its claim under this section, the claimant bank shall provide a refund promptly to any indemnifying bank that previously advanced funds to the claimant bank. The amount of the refund to the indemnifying bank shall be the amount of the reversal or reimbursement obtained by the claimant bank, up to the amount previously advanced by the indemnifying bank.

(2) If the indemnifying bank provides the claimant bank with the original check or a sufficient copy under paragraph (c)(2) of this section, § 229.53(b)(3) governs the indemnifying bank's entitlement to repayment of any amount provided to the claimant bank that exceeds the amount of losses the claimant bank incurred up to that time.

§ 229.56 Liability

(a) Measure of damages—

(1) In general. Except as provided in paragraph (a)(2) or (a)(3) of this section or § 229.53, any person that breaches a warranty described in § 229.52 or fails to comply with any requirement of this subpart with respect to any other person shall be liable to that person for an amount equal to the sum of—

(i) The amount of the loss suffered by the person as a result of the breach or failure, up to the amount of the substitute check; and

(ii) Interest and expenses (including costs and reasonable attorney's fees and other expenses of representation) related to the substitute check.

(2) Offset of recredits. The amount of damages a person receives under paragraph (a)(1) of this section shall be reduced by any amount that the person receives and retains as a recredit under § 229.54 or § 229.55.

(3) Comparative negligence.

(i) If a person incurs damages that resulted in whole or in part from that person's negligence or failure to act in good faith, then the amount of any damages due to that person under paragraph (a)(1) of this section shall be reduced in proportion to the amount of negligence or bad faith attributable to that person.

(ii) Nothing in this paragraph (a)(3) reduces the rights of a consumer or any other person under the U.C.C. or other applicable provision of federal or state law.

(b) Timeliness of action. Delay by a bank beyond any time limits prescribed or permitted by this subpart is excused if the delay is caused by interruption of communication or computer facilities, suspension of payments by another bank, war, emergency conditions, failure of equipment, or other circumstances beyond the control of the bank and if the bank uses such diligence as the circumstances require.

(c) Jurisdiction. A person may bring an action to enforce a claim under this subpart in any United States district court or in any other court of competent jurisdiction. Such claim shall be brought within one year of the date on which the person's cause of action accrues. For purposes of this paragraph, a cause of action accrues as of the date on which the injured person first learns, or by which such person reasonably should have learned, of the facts and circumstances giving rise to the cause of action, including the identity of the warranting or indemnifying bank against which the action is brought.

(d) Notice of claims. Except as otherwise provided in this paragraph (d), unless a person gives notice of a claim under this section to the warranting or indemnifying bank within 30 calendar days after the person has reason to know of both the claim and the identity of the warranting or indemnifying bank, the warranting or indemnifying bank is discharged from liability in an action to enforce a claim under this subpart to the extent of any loss caused by the delay in giving notice of the claim. A timely recredit claim by a consumer under § 229.54 constitutes timely notice under this paragraph.

§ 229.57 Consumer awareness

(a) General disclosure requirement and content. Each bank shall provide, in accordance with paragraph (b) of this section, a brief disclosure to each of its consumer customers that describes—

(1) That a substitute check is the legal equivalent of an original check; and

(2) The consumer recredit rights that apply when a consumer in good faith believes that a substitute check was not properly charged to his or her account.

(b) Distribution—

(1) Disclosure to consumers who receive paid checks with periodic account statements. A bank shall provide the disclosure described in paragraph (a) of this section to a consumer customer who receives paid original checks or paid substitute checks with his or her periodic account statement—

(i) No later than the first regularly scheduled communication with the consumer after October 28, 2004, for each consumer who is a customer of the bank on that date; and

(ii) At the time the customer relationship is initiated, for each customer relationship established after October 28, 2004.

(2) Disclosure to consumers who receive substitute checks on an occasional basis.

(i) The bank shall provide the disclosure described in paragraph (a) of this section to a consumer customer of the bank who requests an original check or a copy of a check and receives a substitute check. If feasible, the bank shall provide this disclosure at the time of the consumer's request; otherwise, the bank shall provide this disclosure no later than the time at which the bank provides a substitute check in response to the consumer's request.

(ii) The bank shall provide the disclosure described in paragraph (a) of this section to a consumer customer of the bank who receives a returned substitute check, at the time the bank provides such substitute check.

(3) Multiple account holders. A bank need not give separate disclosures to each customer on a jointly held account.

§ 229.58 Mode of delivery of information

A bank may deliver any notice or other information that it is required to provide under this subpart by United States mail or by any other means through which the recipient has agreed to receive account information. If a bank is required to provide an original check or a sufficient copy, the bank instead may provide an electronic image of the original check or sufficient copy if the recipient has agreed to receive that information electronically.

§ 229.59 Relation to other law

The Check 21 Act and this subpart supersede any provision of federal or state law, including the Uniform Commercial Code, that is inconsistent with the Check 21 Act or this subpart, but only to the extent of the inconsistency.

§ 229.60 Variation by agreement

Any provision of § 229.55 may be varied by agreement of the banks involved. No other provision of this subpart may be varied by agreement by any person or persons.

MAGNUSON-MOSS WARRANTY—FEDERAL TRADE COMMISSION IMPROVEMENT ACT

15 U.S.C. §§ 2301–2312 Selected Sections

Title 1. Consumer Product Warranties

Table of Sections

§ 2301 [MMWA § 101]. Definitions

For the purposes of this chapter:

(1) The term "consumer product" means any tangible personal property which is distributed in commerce and which is normally used for personal, family, or household purposes (including any such property intended to be attached to or installed in any real property without regard to whether it is so attached or installed).

(2) The term "Commission" means the Federal Trade Commission.

(3) The term "consumer" means a buyer (other than for purposes of resale) of any consumer product, any person to whom such product is transferred during the duration of an implied or written warranty (or service contract) applicable to the product, and any other person who is entitled by the terms of such warranty (or service contract) or under applicable State law to enforce against the warrantor (or service contractor) the obligations of the warranty (or service contract).

(4) The term "supplier" means any person engaged in the business of making a consumer product directly or indirectly available to consumers.

(5) The term "warrantor" means any supplier or other person who gives or offers to give a written warranty or who is or may be obligated under an implied warranty.

(6) The term "written warranty" means—

(A) any written affirmation of fact or written promise made in connection with the sale of a consumer product by a supplier to a buyer which relates to the nature of the material or workmanship and affirms or promises that such material or workmanship is defect free or will meet a specified level of performance over a specified period of time, or

(B) any undertaking in writing in connection with the sale by a supplier of a consumer product to refund, repair, replace, or take other remedial action with respect to such product in the event that such product fails to meet the specifications set forth in the undertaking, which written affirmation, promise, or undertaking becomes part of the basis of the bargain between a supplier and a buyer for purposes other than resale of such product.

(7) The term "implied warranty" means an implied warranty arising under State law (as modified by sections 2308 and 2304(a) of this title) in connection with the sale by a supplier of a consumer product.

(8) The term "service contract" means a contract in writing to perform, over a fixed period of time or for a specified duration, services relating to the maintenance or repair (or both) of a consumer product.

(9) The term "reasonable and necessary maintenance" consists of those operations (A) which the consumer reasonably can be expected to perform or have performed and (B) which are necessary to keep any consumer product performing its intended function and operating at a reasonable level of performance.

(10) The term "remedy" means whichever of the following actions the warrantor elects:

(A) repair,

(B) replacement, or

(C) refund;

except that the warrantor may not elect refund unless (i) the warrantor is unable to provide replacement and repair is not commercially practicable or cannot be timely made, or (ii) the consumer is willing to accept such refund.

(11) The term "replacement" means furnishing a new consumer product which is identical or reasonably equivalent to the warranted consumer product.

(12) The term "refund" means refunding the actual purchase price (less reasonable depreciation based on actual use where permitted by rules of the Commission).

(13) The term "distributed in commerce" means sold in commerce, introduced or delivered for introduction into commerce, or held for sale or distribution after introduction into commerce.

(14) The term "commerce" means trade, traffic, commerce, or transportation—

(A) between a place in a State and any place outside thereof, or

(B) which affects trade, traffic, commerce, or transportation described in subparagraph (A).

(15) The term "State" means a State, the District of Columbia, the Commonwealth of Puerto Rico, the Virgin Islands, Guam, the Canal Zone, or American Samoa. The term "State law" includes a law of the United States applicable only to the District of Columbia or only to a territory or possession of the United States; and the term "Federal law" excludes any State law.

§ 2302 [MMWA § 102]. Rules governing contents of warranties

(a) Full and conspicuous disclosure of terms and conditions; additional requirements for contents

In order to improve the adequacy of information available to consumers, prevent deception, and improve competition in the marketing of consumer products, any warrantor warranting a consumer product to a consumer by means of a written warranty shall, to the extent required by rules of the Commission, fully and conspicuously disclose in simple and readily understood language the terms and conditions of such warranty. Such rules may require inclusion in the written warranty of any of the following items among others:

(1) The clear identification of the names and addresses of the warrantors.

(2) The identity of the party or parties to whom the warranty is extended.

(3) The products or parts covered.

(4) A statement of what the warrantor will do in the event of a defect, malfunction, or failure to conform with such written warranty—at whose expense—and for what period of time.

(5) A statement of what the consumer must do and expenses he must bear.

(6) Exceptions and exclusions from the terms of the warranty.

(7) The step-by-step procedure which the consumer should take in order to obtain performance of any obligation under the warranty, including the identification of any person or class of persons authorized to perform the obligations set forth in the warranty.

(8) Information respecting the availability of any informal dispute settlement procedure offered by the warrantor and a recital, where the warranty so provides, that the purchaser may be required to resort to such procedure before pursuing any legal remedies in the courts.

(9) A brief, general description of the legal remedies available to the consumer.

(10) The time at which the warrantor will perform any obligations under the warranty.

(11) The period of time within which, after notice of a defect, malfunction, or failure to conform with the warranty, the warrantor will perform any obligations under the warranty.

(12) The characteristics or properties of the products, or parts thereof, that are not covered by the warranty.

(13) The elements of the warranty in words or phrases which would not mislead a reasonable, average consumer as to the nature or scope of the warranty.

(b) Availability of terms to consumer; manner and form for presentation and display of information; duration; extension of period for written warranty or service contract

(1)(A) The Commission shall prescribe rules requiring that the terms of any written warranty on a consumer product be made available to the consumer (or prospective consumer) prior to the sale of the product to him.

(B) The Commission may prescribe rules for determining the manner and form in which information with respect to any written warranty of a consumer product shall be clearly and conspicuously presented or displayed so as not to mislead the reasonable, average consumer, when such information is contained in advertising, labeling, point-of-sale material, or other representations in writing.

(2) Nothing in this chapter (other than paragraph (3) of this subsection) shall be deemed to authorize the Commission to prescribe the duration of written warranties given or to require that a consumer product or any of its components be warranted.

(3) The Commission may prescribe rules for extending the period of time a written warranty or service contract is in effect to correspond with any period of time in excess of a reasonable period (not less than 10 days) during which the consumer is deprived of the use of such consumer product by reason of failure of the product to conform with the written warranty or by reason of the failure of the warrantor (or service contractor) to carry out such warranty (or service contract) within the period specified in the warranty (or service contract).

(c) Prohibition on conditions for written or implied warranty; waiver by Commission

No warrantor of a consumer product may condition his written or implied warranty of such product on the consumer's using, in connection with such product, any article or service (other than article or service provided without charge under the terms of the warranty) which is identified by brand, trade, or corporate name; except that the prohibition of this subsection may be waived by the Commission if—

(1) the warrantor satisfies the Commission that the warranted product will function properly only if the article or service so identified is used in connection with the warranted product, and

(2) the Commission finds that such a waiver is in the public interest.

The Commission shall identify in the Federal Register, and permit public comment on, all applications for waiver of the prohibition of this subsection, and shall publish in the Federal Register its disposition of any such application, including the reasons therefor.

(d) Incorporation by reference of detailed substantive warranty provisions

The Commission may by rule devise detailed substantive warranty provisions which warrantors may incorporate by reference in their warranties.

(e) Applicability to consumer products costing more than $5

The provisions of this section apply only to warranties which pertain to consumer products actually costing the consumer more than $5.

§ 2303 [MMWA § 103]. Designation of written warranties

(a) Full (statement of duration) or limited warranty

Any warrantor warranting a consumer product by means of a written warranty shall clearly and conspicuously designate such warranty in the following manner, unless exempted from doing so by the Commission pursuant to subsection (c) of this section:

(1) If the written warranty meets the Federal minimum standards for warranty set forth in section 2304 of this title, then it shall be conspicuously designated a "full (statement of duration) warranty".

(2) If the written warranty does not meet the Federal minimum standards for warranty set forth in section 2304 of this title, then it shall be conspicuously designated a "limited warranty".

(b) Applicability of requirements, standards, etc., to representations or statements of customer satisfaction

This section and sections 2302 and 2304 of this title shall not apply to statements or representations which are similar to expressions of general policy concerning customer satisfaction and which are not subject to any specific limitations.

(c) Exemptions by Commission

In addition to exercising the authority pertaining to disclosure granted in section 2302 of this title, the Commission may by rule determine when a written warranty does not have to be designated either "full (statement of duration)" or "limited" in accordance with this section.

(d) Applicability to consumer products costing more than $10 and not designated as full warranties

The provisions of subsections (a) and (c) of this section apply only to warranties which pertain to consumer products actually costing the consumer more than $10 and which are not designated "full (statement of duration) warranties".

§ 2304 [MMWA § 104]. Federal minimum standards for warranties

(a) Remedies under written warranty; duration of implied warranty; exclusion or limitation on consequential damages for breach of written or implied warranty; election of refund or replacement

In order for a warrantor warranting a consumer product by means of a written warranty to meet the Federal minimum standards for warranty—

(1) such warrantor must as a minimum remedy such consumer product within a reasonable time and without charge, in the case of a defect, malfunction, or failure to conform with such written warranty;

(2) notwithstanding section 2308(b) of this title, such warrantor may not impose any limitation on the duration of any implied warranty on the product;

(3) such warrantor may not exclude or limit consequential damages for breach of any written or implied warranty on such product, unless such exclusion or limitation conspicuously appears on the face of the warranty; and

(4) if the product (or a component part thereof) contains a defect or malfunction after a reasonable number of attempts by the warrantor to remedy defects or malfunctions in such product, such warrantor must permit the consumer to elect either a refund for, or replacement without charge of, such product or part (as the case may be). The Commission may by rule specify for purposes of this paragraph, what constitutes a reasonable number of attempts to remedy particular kinds of defects or malfunctions under different circumstances. If the warrantor replaces a component part of a consumer product, such replacement shall include installing the part in the product without charge.

(b) Duties and conditions imposed on consumer by warrantor

(1) In fulfilling the duties under subsection (a) of this section respecting a written warranty, the warrantor shall not impose any duty other than notification upon any consumer as a condition of securing remedy of any consumer product which malfunctions, is defective, or does not conform to the written warranty, unless the warrantor has demonstrated in a rulemaking proceeding, or can demonstrate in an administrative or judicial enforcement proceeding (including private enforcement), or in an informal dispute settlement proceeding, that such a duty is reasonable.

(2) Notwithstanding paragraph (1), a warrantor may require, as a condition to replacement of, or refund for, any consumer product under subsection (a) of this section, that such consumer product shall be made available to the warrantor free and clear of liens and other encumbrances, except as otherwise provided by rule or order of the Commission in cases in which such a requirement would not be practicable.

(3) The Commission may, by rule define in detail the duties set forth in subsection (a) of this section and the applicability of such duties to warrantors of different categories of consumer products with "full (statement of duration)" warranties.

(4) The duties under subsection (a) of this section extend from the warrantor to each person who is a consumer with respect to the consumer product.

(c) Waiver of standards

The performance of the duties under subsection (a) of this section shall not be required of the warrantor if he can show that the defect, malfunction, or failure of any warranted consumer product to conform with a written warranty, was caused by damage (not resulting from defect or malfunction) while in the possession of the consumer, or unreasonable use (including failure to provide reasonable and necessary maintenance).

(d) Remedy without charge

For purposes of this section and of section 2302(c) of this title, the term "without charge" means that the warrantor may not assess the consumer for any costs the warrantor or his representatives incur in connection with the required remedy of a warranted consumer product. An obligation under subsection (a)(1)(A) of this section to remedy without charge does not necessarily require the warrantor to compensate the consumer for incidental expenses; however, if any incidental expenses are incurred because the remedy is not made within a reasonable time or because the warrantor imposed an unreasonable duty upon the consumer as a condition of securing remedy, then the consumer shall be entitled to recover reasonable incidental expenses which are so incurred in any action against the warrantor.

(e) Incorporation of standards to products designated with full warranty for purposes of judicial actions

If a supplier designates a warranty applicable to a consumer product as a "full (statement of duration)" warranty, then the warranty on such product shall, for purposes of any action under section 2310(d) of this title or under any State law, be deemed to incorporate at least the minimum requirements of this section and rules prescribed under this section.

§ 2305 [MMWA § 105]. Full and limited warranting of a consumer product

Nothing in this chapter shall prohibit the selling of a consumer product which has both full and limited warranties if such warranties are clearly and conspicuously differentiated.

§ 2306 [MMWA § 106]. Service contracts; rules for full, clear and conspicuous disclosure of terms and conditions; addition to or in lieu of written warranty

(a) The Commission may prescribe by rule the manner and form in which the terms and conditions of service contracts shall be fully, clearly, and conspicuously disclosed.

(b) Nothing in this chapter shall be construed to prevent a supplier or warrantor from entering into a service contract with the consumer in addition to or in lieu of a written warranty if such contract fully, clearly, and conspicuously discloses its terms and conditions in simple and readily understood language.

§ 2307 [MMWA § 107]. Designation of representatives by warrantor to perform duties under written or implied warranty

Nothing in this chapter shall be construed to prevent any warrantor from designating representatives to perform duties under the written or implied warranty: *Provided*, That such warrantor shall make reasonable arrangements for compensation of such designated representatives, but no such designation shall relieve the warrantor of his direct responsibilities to the consumer or make the representative a cowarrantor.

§ 2308 [MMWA § 108]. Implied warranties

(a) Restrictions on disclaimers or modifications

No supplier may disclaim or modify (except as provided in subsection (b) of this section) any implied warranty to a consumer with respect to such consumer product if (1) such supplier makes any written warranty to the consumer with respect to such consumer product, or (2) at the time of sale, or within 90 days thereafter, such supplier enters into a service contract with the consumer which applies to such consumer product.

(b) Limitation on duration

For purposes of this chapter (other than section 2304(a)(2) of this title), implied warranties may be limited in duration to the duration of a written warranty of reasonable duration, if such limitation is conscionable and is set forth in clear and unmistakable language and prominently displayed on the face of the warranty.

(c) Effectiveness of disclaimers, modifications, or limitations

A disclaimer, modification, or limitation made in violation of this section shall be ineffective for purposes of this chapter and State law.

§ 2309 [MMWA § 109]. Procedures applicable to promulgation of rules by Commission

(a) Oral presentation

Any rule prescribed under this chapter shall be prescribed in accordance with section 553 of Title 5; except that the Commission shall give interested persons an opportunity for oral presentations of data, views, and arguments, in addition to written submissions. A transcript shall be kept of any oral presentation. Any such rule shall be subject to judicial review under section 57a(e) of this title in the same manner as rules prescribed under section 57a(a)(1)(B) of this title, except that section 57a(e)(3)(B) of this title shall not apply.

(b) Warranties and warranty practices involved in sale of used motor vehicles

The Commission shall initiate within one year after January 4, 1975, a rulemaking proceeding dealing with warranties and warranty practices in connection with the sale of used motor vehicles; and, to the extent necessary to supplement the protections offered the consumer by this chapter, shall prescribe rules dealing with such warranties and practices. In prescribing rules under this subsection, the Commission may exercise any authority it may have under this chapter, or other law, and in addition it may require disclosure that a used motor vehicle is sold without any warranty and specify the form and content of such disclosure.

§ 2310 [MMWA § 110]. Remedies in consumer disputes

(a) Informal dispute settlement procedures; establishment; rules setting forth minimum requirements; effect of compliance by warrantor; review of informal procedures or implementation by Commission; application to existing informal procedures

(1) Congress hereby declares it to be its policy to encourage warrantors to establish procedures whereby consumer disputes are fairly and expeditiously settled through informal dispute settlement mechanisms.

(2) The Commission shall prescribe rules setting forth minimum requirements for any informal dispute settlement procedure which is incorporated into the terms of a written warranty to which any provision of this chapter applies. Such rules shall provide for participation in such procedure by independent or governmental entities.

(3) One or more warrantors may establish an informal dispute settlement procedure which meets the requirements of the Commission's rules under paragraph (2). If—

(A) a warrantor establishes such a procedure,

(B) such procedure, and its implementation, meets the requirements of such rules, and

(C) he incorporates in a written warranty a requirement that the consumer resort to such procedure before pursuing any legal remedy under this section respecting such warranty,

then (i) the consumer may not commence a civil action (other than a class action) under subsection (d) of this section unless he initially resorts to such procedure; and (ii) a class of consumers may not proceed in a class action under subsection (d) of this section except to the extent the court determines necessary to establish the representative capacity of the named plaintiffs, unless the named plaintiffs (upon notifying the defendant that they are named plaintiffs in a class action with respect to a warranty obligation) initially resort to such procedure. In the case of such a class action which is brought in a district court of the United States, the representative capacity of the named plaintiffs shall be established in the application of rule 23 of the Federal Rules of Civil

Procedure. In any civil action arising out of a warranty obligation and relating to a matter considered in such a procedure, any decision in such procedure shall be admissible in evidence.

(4) The Commission on its own initiative may, or upon written complaint filed by any interested person shall, review the bona fide operation of any dispute settlement procedure resort to which is stated in a written warranty to be a prerequisite to pursuing a legal remedy under this section. If the Commission finds that such procedure or its implementation fails to comply with the requirements of the rules under paragraph (2), the Commission may take appropriate remedial action under any authority it may have under this chapter or any other provision of law.

(5) Until rules under paragraph (2) take effect, this subsection shall not affect the validity of any informal dispute settlement procedure respecting consumer warranties, but in any action under subsection (d) of this section, the court may invalidate any such procedure if it finds that such procedure is unfair.

(b) Prohibited acts

It shall be a violation of section 45(a)(1) of this title for any person to fail to comply with any requirement imposed on such person by this chapter (or a rule thereunder) or to violate any prohibition contained in this chapter (or a rule thereunder).

(c) Injunction proceedings by Attorney General or Commission for deceptive warranty, noncompliance with requirements, or violating prohibitions; procedures; definitions

(1) The district courts of the United States shall have jurisdiction of any action brought by the Attorney General (in his capacity as such), or by the Commission by any of its attorneys designated by it for such purpose, to restrain (A) any warrantor from making a deceptive warranty with respect to a consumer product, or (B) any person from failing to comply with any requirement imposed on such person by or pursuant to this chapter or from violating any prohibition contained in this chapter. Upon proper showing that, weighing the equities and considering the Commission's or Attorney General's likelihood of ultimate success, such action would be in the public interest and after notice to the defendant, a temporary restraining order or preliminary injunction may be granted without bond. In the case of an action brought by the Commission, if a complaint under section 45 of this title is not filed within such period (not exceeding 10 days) as may be specified by the court after the issuance of the temporary restraining order or preliminary injunction, the order or injunction shall be dissolved by the court and be of no further force and effect. Any suit shall be brought in the district in which such person resides or transacts business. Whenever it appears to the court that the ends of justice require that other persons should be parties in the action, the court may cause them to be summoned whether or not they reside in the district in which the court is held, and to that end process may be served in any district.

(2) For the purposes of this subsection, the term "deceptive warranty" means (A) a written warranty which (i) contains an affirmation, promise, description, or representation which is either false or fraudulent, or which, in light of all of the circumstances, would mislead a reasonable individual exercising due care; or (ii) fails to contain information which is necessary in light of all of the circumstances, to make the warranty not misleading to a reasonable individual exercising due care; or (B) a written warranty created by the use of such terms as "guaranty" or "warranty", if the terms and conditions of such warranty so limit its scope and application as to deceive a reasonable individual.

(d) Civil action by consumer for damages, etc.; jurisdiction; recovery of costs and expenses; cognizable claims

(1) Subject to subsections (a)(3) and (e) of this section, a consumer who is damaged by the failure of a supplier, warrantor, or service contractor to comply with any obligation under this chapter, or under a written warranty, implied warranty, or service contract, may bring suit for damages and other legal and equitable relief—

(A) in any court of competent jurisdiction in any State or the District of Columbia; or

(B) in an appropriate district court of the United States, subject to paragraph (3) of this subsection.

(2) If a consumer finally prevails in any action brought under paragraph (1) of this subsection, he may be allowed by the court to recover as part of the judgment a sum equal to the aggregate amount of cost and expenses (including attorneys' fees based on actual time expended) determined by the court to have been reasonably incurred by the plaintiff for or in connection with the commencement and prosecution of such action, unless the court in its discretion shall determine that such an award of attorneys' fees would be inappropriate.

(3) No claim shall be cognizable in a suit brought under paragraph (1)(B) of this subsection—

(A) if the amount in controversy of any individual claim is less than the sum or value of $25;

(B) if the amount in controversy is less than the sum or value of $50,000 (exclusive of interests and costs) computed on the basis of all claims to be determined in this suit; or

(C) if the action is brought as a class action, and the number of named plaintiffs is less than one hundred.

(e) Class actions; conditions; procedures applicable

No action (other than a class action or an action respecting a warranty to which subsection (a)(3) of this section applies) may be brought under subsection (d) of this section for failure to comply with any obligation under any written or implied warranty or service contract, and a class of consumers may not proceed in a class action under such subsection with respect to such a failure except to the extent the court determines necessary to establish the representative capacity of the named plaintiffs, unless the person obligated under the warranty or service contract is afforded a reasonable opportunity to cure such failure to comply. In the case of such a class action (other than a class action respecting a warranty to which subsection (a)(3) of this section applies) brought under subsection (d) of this section for breach of any written or implied warranty or service contract, such reasonable opportunity will be afforded by the named plaintiffs and they shall at that time notify the defendant that they are acting on behalf of the class. In the case of such a class action which is brought in a district court of the United States, the representative capacity of the named plaintiffs shall be established in the application of rule 23 of the Federal Rules of Civil Procedure.

(f) Warrantors subject to enforcement of remedies

For purposes of this section, only the warrantor actually making a written affirmation of fact, promise, or undertaking shall be deemed to have created a written warranty, and any rights arising thereunder may be enforced under this section only against such warrantor and no other person.

§ 2311 [MMWA § 111]. Applicability to other laws

(a) Federal Trade Commission Act and Federal Seed Act

(1) Nothing contained in this chapter shall be construed to repeal, invalidate, or supersede the Federal Trade Commission Act [15 U.S.C.A. § 41 et seq.] or any statute defined therein as an Antitrust Act.

(2) Nothing in this chapter shall be construed to repeal, invalidate, or supersede the Federal Seed Act [7 U.S.C.A. § 1551 et seq.] and nothing in this chapter shall apply to seed for planting.

(b) Rights, remedies, and liabilities

(1) Nothing in this chapter shall invalidate or restrict any right or remedy of any consumer under State law or any other Federal law.

(2) Nothing in this chapter (other than sections 2308 and 2304(a)(2) and (4) of this title) shall (A) affect the liability of, or impose liability on, any person for personal injury, or (B) supersede any provision of State law regarding consequential damages for injury to the person or other injury.

(c) State warranty laws

(1) Except as provided in subsection (b) of this section and in paragraph (2) of this subsection, a State requirement—

(A) which relates to labeling or disclosure with respect to written warranties or performance thereunder;

(B) which is within the scope of an applicable requirement of sections 2302, 2303, and 2304 of this title (and rules implementing such sections), and

(C) which is not identical to a requirement of section 2302, 2303, or 2304 of this title (or a rule thereunder),

shall not be applicable to written warranties complying with such sections (or rules thereunder).

(2) If, upon application of an appropriate State agency, the Commission determines (pursuant to rules issued in accordance with section 2309 of this title) that any requirement of such State covering any transaction to which this chapter applies (A) affords protection to consumers greater than the requirements of this chapter and (B) does not unduly burden interstate commerce, then such State requirement shall be applicable (notwithstanding the provisions of paragraph (1) of this subsection) to the extent specified in such determination for so long as the State administers and enforces effectively any such greater requirement.

(d) Other Federal warranty laws

This chapter (other than section 2302(c) of this title) shall be inapplicable to any written warranty the making or content of which is otherwise governed by Federal law. If only a portion of a written warranty is so governed by Federal law, the remaining portion shall be subject to this chapter.

§ 2312 [MMWA § 112]. Effective dates [Omitted]

MAGNUSON-MOSS WARRANTY ACT (MMWA) REGULATIONS

16 C.F.R. Parts 700–703

PART 700

Table of Sections

PART 700. INTERPRETATIONS OF MAGNUSON-MOSS WARRANTY ACT

PART 701. DISCLOSURE OF WRITTEN CONSUMER PRODUCT WARRANTY TERMS AND CONDITIONS

PART 702. PRE-SALE AVAILABILITY OF WRITTEN WARRANTY TERMS

PART 703. INFORMAL DISPUTE SETTLEMENT PROCEDURES

§ 700.1. Products covered

(a) The Act applies to written warranties on tangible personal property which is normally used for personal, family, or household purposes. This definition includes property which is intended to be attached to or installed in any real property without regard to whether it is so attached or installed. This means that a product is a "consumer product" if the use of that type of product is not uncommon. The percentage of sales or the use to which a product is put by any individual buyer is not determinative. For example, products such as automobiles and typewriters which are used for both personal and commercial purposes come within the definition of consumer product. Where it is unclear whether a particular product is covered under the definition of consumer product, any ambiguity will be resolved in favor of coverage.

(b) Agricultural products such as farm machinery, structures and implements used in the business or occupation of farming are not covered by the Act where their personal, family, or household use is uncommon. However, those agricultural products normally used for personal or household gardening (for example, to produce goods for personal consumption, and not for resale) are consumer products under the Act.

(c) The definition of "Consumer product" limits the applicability of the Act to personal property, "including any such property intended to be attached to or installed in any real property without regard to whether it is so attached or installed." This provision brings under the Act separate items of equipment attached to real property, such as air conditioners, furnaces, and water heaters.

(d) The coverage of separate items of equipment attached to real property includes, but is not limited to, appliances and other thermal, mechanical, and electrical equipment. (It does not extend to the wiring, plumbing, ducts, and other items which are integral component parts of the structure.) State law would classify many such products as fixtures to, and therefore a part of, realty. The statutory definition is designed to bring such products under the Act regardless of whether they may be considered fixtures under state law.

(e) The coverage of building materials which are not separate items of equipment is based on the nature of the purchase transaction. An analysis of the transaction will determine whether the goods are real or personal property. The numerous products which go into the construction of a consumer dwelling are all consumer products when sold "over the counter," as by hardware and building supply retailers. This is also true where a consumer contracts for the purchase of such materials in connection with the improvement, repair, or modification of a home (for example, paneling, dropped ceilings, siding, roofing, storm windows, remodeling). However, where such products are at the time of sale integrated into the structure of a dwelling they are not consumer products as they cannot be practically distinguished from realty. Thus, for example, the beams, wallboard, wiring, plumbing, windows, roofing, and other structural components of a dwelling are not consumer products when they are sold as part of real estate covered by a written warranty.

(f) In the case where a consumer contracts with a builder to construct a home, a substantial addition to a home, or other realty (such as a garage or an in-ground swimming pool) the building materials to be used are not consumer products. Although the materials are separately identifiable at the time the contract is made, it is the intention of the parties to contract for the construction of realty which will integrate the component materials. Of course, as noted above, any separate items of equipment to be attached to such realty are consumer products under the Act.

(g) Certain provisions of the Act apply only to products actually costing the consumer more than a specified amount. Section 103 applies to consumer products actually costing the consumer more than $10, excluding tax. The $10 minimum will be interpreted to include multiple-packaged items which may individually sell for less than $10, but which have been packaged in a manner that does not permit breaking the package to purchase an item or items at a price less than $10. Thus, a written warranty on a dozen items packaged and priced for sale at $12 must be designated, even though identical items may be offered in smaller quantities at under $10. This interpretation applies in the same manner to the minimum dollar limits in section 102 and rules promulgated under that section.

(h) Warranties on replacement parts and components used to repair consumer products are covered; warranties on services are not covered. Therefore, warranties which apply solely to a repairer's workmanship in performing repairs are not subject to the Act. Where a written agreement warrants both the parts provided to effect a repair and the workmanship in making that repair, the warranty must comply with the Act and the rules thereunder.

(i) The Act covers written warranties on consumer products "distributed in commerce" as that term is defined in section 101(3). Thus, by its terms the Act arguably applies to products exported to foreign jurisdictions. However, the public interest would not be served by the use of Commission resources to enforce the Act with respect to such products. Moreover, the legislative intent to apply the requirements of the Act to such products is not sufficiently clear to justify such an extraordinary result. The Commission does not contemplate the enforcement of the Act with respect to consumer products exported to foreign jurisdictions. Products exported for sale at military post exchanges remain subject to the same enforcement standards as products sold within the United States, its territories and possessions.

§ 700.2. Date of manufacture

Section 112 of the Act provides that the Act shall apply only to those consumer products manufactured after July 4, 1975. When a consumer purchases repair of a consumer product the date of manufacture of any replacement parts used is the measuring date for determining coverage under the Act. The date of manufacture of the consumer product being repaired is in this instance not relevant. Where a consumer purchases or obtains on an exchange basis a rebuilt consumer product, the date that the rebuilding process is completed determines the Act's applicability.

§ 700.3. Written warranty

(a) The Act imposes specific duties and liabilities on suppliers who offer written warranties on consumer products. Certain representations, such as energy efficiency ratings for electrical appliances, care labeling of wearing apparel, and other product information disclosures may be express warranties under the Uniform Commercial Code. However, these disclosures alone are not written warranties under this Act. Section 101(6) provides that a written affirmation of fact or a written promise of a specified level of performance must relate to a specified period of time in order to be considered a "written warranty."[1] A product information disclosure without a specified time period to which the disclosure relates is therefore not a written warranty. In addition, section 111(d) exempts from the Act (except section 102(c)) any written warranty the making or content of which is required by federal law. The Commission encourages the disclosure of product information which is not deceptive and which may benefit consumers, and will not construe the Act to impede information disclosure in product advertising or labeling.

(b) Certain terms, or conditions, of sale of a consumer product may not be "written warranties" as that term is defined in Section 101(6), and should not be offered or described in a manner that may deceive consumers as to their enforceability under the Act. For example, a seller of consumer products may give consumers an unconditional right to revoke acceptance of goods within a certain number of days after delivery without regard to defects or failure to meet a specified level of performance. Or a seller may permit consumers to return products for any reason for credit toward purchase of another item. Such terms of sale taken alone are not written warranties under the Act. Therefore, suppliers should avoid any characterization of such terms of sale as warranties. The use of such terms as "free trial period" and "trade-in credit policy" in this regard would be appropriate. Furthermore, such terms

1 A "written warranty" is also created by a written affirmation of fact or a written promise that the product is defect free, or by a written undertaking of remedial action within the meaning of section 101(6)(B).

of sale should be stated separately from any written warranty. Of course, the offering and performance of such terms of sale remain subject to section 5 of the Federal Trade Commission Act, 15 U.S.C. 45.

(c) The Magnuson-Moss Warranty Act generally applies to written warranties covering consumer products. Many consumer products are covered by warranties which are neither intended for, nor enforceable by, consumers. A common example is a warranty given by a component supplier to a manufacturer of consumer products. (The manufacturer may, in turn, warrant these components to consumers.) The component supplier's warranty is generally given solely to the product manufacturer, and is neither intended to be conveyed to the consumer nor brought to the consumer's attention in connection with the sale. Such warranties are not subject to the Act, since a written warranty under section 101(6) of the Act must become "part of the basis of the bargain between a supplier and a buyer for purposes other than resale." However, the Act applies to a component supplier's warranty in writing which is given to the consumer. An example is a supplier's written warranty to the consumer covering a refrigerator that is sold installed in a boat or recreational vehicle. The supplier of the refrigerator relies on the boat or vehicle assembler to convey the written agreement to the consumer. In this case, the supplier's written warranty is to a consumer, and is covered by the Act.

§ 700.4. Parties "actually making" a written warranty

Section 110(f) of the Act provides that only the supplier "actually making" a written warranty is liable for purposes of FTC and private enforcement of the Act. A supplier who does no more than distribute or sell a consumer product covered by a written warranty offered by another person or business and which identifies that person or business as the warrantor is not liable for failure of the written warranty to comply with the Act or rules thereunder. However, other actions and written and oral representations of such a supplier in connection with the offer or sale of a warranted product may obligate that supplier under the Act. If under state law the supplier is deemed to have "adopted" the written affirmation of fact, promise, or undertaking, the supplier is also obligated under the Act. Suppliers are advised to consult state law to determine those actions and representations which may make them co-warrantors, and therefore obligated under the warranty of the other person or business.

§ 700.5. Expressions of general policy

(a) Under section 103(b), statements or representations of general policy concerning customer satisfaction which are not subject to any specific limitation need not be designated as full or limited warranties, and are exempt from the requirements of sections 102, 103, and 104 of the Act and rules thereunder. However, such statements remain subject to the enforcement provisions of section 110 of the Act, and to section 5 of the Federal Trade Commission Act, 15 U.S.C. 45.

(b) The section 103(b) exemption applies only to general policies, not to those which are limited to specific consumer products manufactured or sold by the supplier offering such a policy. In addition, to qualify for an exemption under section 103(b) such policies may not be subject to any specific limitations. For example, policies which have an express limitation of duration or a limitation of the amount to be refunded are not exempted. This does not preclude the imposition of reasonable limitations based on the circumstances in each instance a consumer seeks to invoke such an agreement. For instance, a warrantor may refuse to honor such an expression of policy where a consumer has used a product for 10 years without previously expressing any dissatisfaction with the product. Such a refusal would not be a specific limitation under this provision.

§ 700.6. Designation of warranties

(a) Section 103 of the Act provides that written warranties on consumer products manufactured after July 4, 1975, and actually costing the consumer more than $10, excluding tax, must be designated either "Full (statement of duration) Warranty" or "Limited Warranty". Warrantors may include a statement of duration in a limited warranty designation. The designation or designations should appear clearly and conspicuously as a caption, or prominent title, clearly separated from the text of the warranty. The full (statement of duration) warranty and limited warranty are the exclusive designations permitted under the Act, unless a specific exception is created by rule.

(b) Section 104(b)(4) states that "the duties under subsection (a)(of section 104) extend from the warrantor to each person who is a consumer with respect to the consumer product." Section 101(3) defines a consumer as "a buyer (other than for purposes of resale) of any consumer product, any person to whom such product is transferred during the duration of an implied or written warranty (or service contract) applicable to the product. * * *." Therefore, a full warranty may not expressly restrict the warranty rights of a transferee during its stated duration. However, where the duration of a full warranty is defined solely in terms of first purchaser ownership there can be no violation of section 104(b)(4), since the duration of the warranty expires, by definition, at the time of transfer. No rights of a subsequent transferee are cut off as there is no transfer of ownership "during the duration of (any) warranty." Thus, these provisions do not preclude the offering of a full warranty with its duration determined exclusively by the period during which the first purchaser owns the product, or uses it in conjunction with another product. For example, an automotive battery or muffler warranty may be designated as "full warranty for as long as you own your car." Because this type of warranty leads the consumer to believe that proof of purchase is not needed so long as he or she owns the product a duty to furnish documentary proof may not be reasonably imposed on the consumer under this type of warranty. The burden is on the warrantor to prove that a particular claimant under this type of warranty is not the original purchaser or owner of the product. Warrantors or their designated agents may, however, ask consumers to state or affirm that they are the first purchaser of the product.

§ 700.7. Use of warranty registration cards

(a) Under section 104(b)(1) of the Act a warrantor offering a full warranty may not impose on consumers any duty other than notification of a defect as a condition of securing remedy of the defect or malfunction, unless such additional duty can be demonstrated by the warrantor to be reasonable. Warrantors have in the past stipulated the return of a "warranty registration" or similar card. By "warranty registration card" the Commission means a card which must be returned by the consumer shortly after purchase of the product and which is stipulated or implied in the warranty to be a condition precedent to warranty coverage and performance.

(b) A requirement that the consumer return a warranty registration card or a similar notice as a condition of performance under a full warranty is an unreasonable duty. Thus, a provision such as, "This warranty is void unless the warranty registration card is returned to the warrantor" is not permissible in a full warranty, nor is it permissible to imply such a condition in a full warranty.

(c) This does not prohibit the use of such registration cards where a warrantor suggests use of the card as one possible means of proof of the date the product was purchased. For example, it is permissible to provide in a full warranty that a consumer may fill out and return a card to place on file proof of the date the product was purchased. Any such suggestion to the consumer must include notice that failure to return the card will not affect rights under the warranty, so long as the consumer can show in a reasonable manner the date the product was purchased. Nor does this interpretation prohibit a seller from obtaining from purchasers at the time of sale information requested by the warrantor.

§ 700.8. Warrantor's decision as final

A warrantor shall not indicate in any written warranty or service contract either directly or indirectly that the decision of the warrantor, service contractor, or any designated third party is final or binding in any dispute concerning the warranty or service contract. Nor shall a warrantor or service contractor state that it alone shall determine what is a defect under the agreement. Such statements are deceptive since section 110(d) of the Act gives state and federal courts jurisdiction over suits for breach of warranty and service contract.

§ 700.9. Duty to install under a full warranty

Under section 104(a)(1) of the Act, the remedy under a full warranty must be provided to the consumer without charge. If the warranted product has utility only when installed, a full warranty must provide such installation without charge regardless of whether or not the consumer originally paid for installation by the warrantor or his agent. However, this does not preclude the warrantor from imposing on the consumer a duty to remove, return, or reinstall where such duty can be demonstrated by the warrantor to meet the standard of reasonableness under section 104(b)(1).

§ 700.10. Section 102(c)

(a) Section 102(c) prohibits tying arrangements that condition coverage under a written warranty on the consumer's use of an article or service identified by brand, trade, or corporate name unless that article or service is provided without charge to the consumer.

(b) Under a limited warranty that provides only for replacement of defective parts and no portion of labor charges, section 102(c) prohibits a condition that the consumer use only service (labor) identified by the warrantor to install the replacement parts. A warrantor or his designated representative may not provide parts under the warranty in a manner which impedes or precludes the choice by the consumer of the person or business to perform necessary labor to install such parts.

(c) No warrantor may condition the continued validity of a warranty on the use of only authorized repair service and/or authorized replacement parts for non-warranty service and maintenance. For example, provisions such as, "This warranty is void if service is performed by anyone other than an authorized 'ABC' dealer and all replacement parts must be genuine 'ABC' parts," and the like, are prohibited where the service or parts are not covered by the warranty. These provisions violate the Act in two ways. First, they violate the section 102 (c) ban against tying arrangements. Second, such provisions are deceptive under section 110 of the Act, because a warrantor cannot, as a matter of law, avoid liability under a written warranty where a defect is unrelated to the use by a consumer of "unauthorized" articles or service. This does not preclude a warrantor from expressly excluding liability for defects or damage caused by such "unauthorized" articles or service; nor does it preclude the warrantor from denying liability where the warrantor can demonstrate that the defect or damage was so caused.

§ 700.11. Written warranty, service contract, and insurance distinguished for purposes of compliance under the Act

(a) The Act recognizes two types of agreements which may provide similar coverage of consumer products, the written warranty, and the service contract. In addition, other agreements may meet the statutory definitions of either "written warranty" or "service contract," but are sold and regulated under state law as contracts of insurance. One example is the automobile breakdown insurance policies sold in many jurisdictions and regulated by the state as a form of casualty insurance. The McCarran-Ferguson Act, 15 U.S.C. 1011 et seq., precludes jurisdiction under federal law over "the business of insurance" to the extent an agreement is regulated by state law as insurance. Thus, such agreements are subject to the Magnuson-Moss Warranty Act only to the extent they are not regulated in a particular state as the business of insurance.

(b) "Written warranty" and "service contract" are defined in sections 101(6) and 101(8) of the Act, respectively. A written warranty must be "part of the basis of the bargain." This means that it must be conveyed at the time of sale of the consumer product and the consumer must not give any consideration beyond the purchase price of the consumer product in order to benefit from the agreement. It is not a requirement of the Act that an agreement obligate a supplier of the consumer product to a written warranty, but merely that it be part of the basis of the bargain between a supplier and a consumer. This contemplates written warranties by third-party non-suppliers.

(c) A service contract under the Act must meet the definitions of section 101(8). An agreement which would meet the definition of written warranty in section 101(6)(A) or (B) but for its failure to satisfy the basis of the bargain test is a service contract. For example, an agreement which calls for some consideration in addition to the purchase price of the consumer product, or which is entered into at some date after the purchase of the consumer product to which it applies, is a service contract. An agreement which relates only to the performance of maintenance and/or inspection services and which is not an undertaking, promise, or affirmation with respect to a specified level of performance, or that the product is free of defects in materials or workmanship, is a service contract. An agreement to perform periodic cleaning and inspection of a product over a specified period of time, even when offered at the time of sale and without charge to the consumer, is an example of such a service contract.

§ 700.12. Effective date of 16 CFR parts 701 and 702

The Statement of Basis and Purpose of the final rules promulgated on December 31, 1975, provides that parts 701 and 702 of this chapter will become effective one year after the date of promulgation, December 31, 1976. The Commission intends this to mean that these rules apply only to written warranties on products manufactured after December 31, 1976.

PART 701

§ 701.1. Definitions

(a) The Act means the Magnuson-Moss Warranty Federal Trade Commission Improvement Act, 15 U.S.C. 2301, et seq.

(b) Consumer product means any tangible personal property which is distributed in commerce and which is normally used for personal, family, or household purposes (including any such property intended to be attached to or installed in any real property without regard to whether it is so attached or installed. Products which are purchased solely for commercial or industrial use are excluded solely for purposes of this Part).

(c) Written warranty means:

(1) Any written affirmation of fact or written promise made in connection with the sale of a consumer product by a supplier to a buyer which relates to the nature of the material or workmanship and affirms or promises that such material or workmanship is defect free or will meet a specified level of performance over a specified period of time, or

(2) Any undertaking in writing in connection with the sale by a supplier of a consumer product to refund, repair, replace, or take other remedial action with respect to such product in the event that such product fails to meet the specifications set forth in the undertaking, which written affirmation, promise or undertaking becomes part of the basis of the bargain between a supplier and a buyer for purposes other than resale of such product.

(d) Implied warranty means an implied warranty arising under State law (as modified by sections 104(a) and 108 of the Act) in connection with the sale by a supplier of a consumer product.

(e) Remedy means whichever of the following actions the warrantor elects:

(1) Repair,

(2) Replacement, or

(3) Refund; except that the warrantor may not elect refund unless:

(i) The warrantor is unable to provide replacement and repair is not commercially practicable or cannot be timely made, or

(ii) The consumer is willing to accept such refund.

(f) Supplier means any person engaged in the business of making a consumer product directly or indirectly available to consumers.

(g) Warrantor means any supplier or other person who gives or offers to give a written warranty.

(h) Consumer means a buyer (other than for purposes of resale or use in the ordinary course of the buyer's business) of any consumer product, any person to whom such product is transferred during the duration of an implied or written warranty applicable to the product, and any other such person who is entitled by the terms of such warranty or under applicable State law to enforce against the warrantor the obligations of the warranty.

(i) On the face of the warranty means:

(1) Where the warranty is a single sheet with printing on both sides of the sheet or where the warranty is comprised of more than one sheet, the page on which the warranty text begins;

(2) Where the warranty is included as part of a larger document, such as a use and care manual, the page in such document on which the warranty text begins.

§ 701.2. Scope

The regulations in this part establish requirements for warrantors for disclosing the terms and conditions of written warranties on consumer products actually costing the consumer more than $15.00.

§ 701.3. Written warranty terms

(a) Any warrantor warranting to a consumer by means of a written warranty a consumer product actually costing the consumer more than $15.00 shall clearly and conspicuously disclose in a single document in simple and readily understood language, the following items of information:

(1) The identity of the party or parties to whom the written warranty is extended, if the enforceability of the written warranty is limited to the original consumer purchaser or is otherwise limited to persons other than every consumer owner during the term of the warranty;

(2) A clear description and identification of products, or parts, or characteristics, or components or properties covered by and where necessary for clarification, excluded from the warranty;

(3) A statement of what the warrantor will do in the event of a defect, malfunction or failure to conform with the written warranty, including the items or services the warrantor will pay for or provide, and, where necessary for clarification, those which the warrantor will not pay for or provide;

(4) The point in time or event on which the warranty term commences, if different from the purchase date, and the time period or other measurement of warranty duration;

(5) A step-by-step explanation of the procedure which the consumer should follow in order to obtain performance of any warranty obligation, including the persons or class of persons authorized to perform warranty obligations. This includes the name(s) of the warrantor(s), together with: The mailing address(es) of the warrantor(s), and/or the name or title and the address of any employee or department of the warrantor responsible for the performance of warranty obligations, and/or a telephone number which consumers may use without charge to obtain information on warranty performance;

(6) Information respecting the availability of any informal dispute settlement mechanism elected by the warrantor in compliance with part 703 of this subchapter;

(7) Any limitations on the duration of implied warranties, disclosed on the face of the warranty as provided in section 108 of the Act, accompanied by the following statement:

Some States do not allow limitations on how long an implied warranty lasts, so the above limitation may not apply to you.

(8) Any exclusions of or limitations on relief such as incidental or consequential damages, accompanied by the following statement, which may be combined with the statement required in paragraph (a)(7) of this section:

Some States do not allow the exclusion or limitation of incidental or consequential damages, so the above limitation or exclusion may not apply to you.

(9) A statement in the following language:

This warranty gives you specific legal rights, and you may also have other rights which vary from State to State.

(b) Paragraphs (a)(1) through (9) of this section shall not be applicable with respect to statements of general policy on emblems, seals or insignias issued by third parties promising replacement or refund if a consumer product is defective, which statements contain no representation or assurance of the quality or performance characteristics of the product; Provided That: (1) The disclosures required by paragraphs (a)(1) through (9) of this section are published by such third parties in each issue of a publication with a general circulation, and (2) such disclosures are provided free of charge to any consumer upon written request.

§ 701.4. Owner registration cards

When a warrantor employs any card such as an owner's registration card, a warranty registration card, or the like, and the return of such card is a condition precedent to warranty coverage and performance, the warrantor shall disclose this fact in the warranty. If the return of such card reasonably appears to be a condition precedent to warranty coverage and performance, but is not such a condition, that fact shall be disclosed in the warranty.

PART 702

§ 702.1. Definitions

(a) The Act means the Magnuson-Moss Warranty Federal Trade Commission Improvement Act, 15 U.S.C. 2301, et seq.

(b) Consumer product means any tangible personal property which is distributed in commerce and which is normally used for personal, family, or household purposes (including any such property intended to be attached to or installed in any real property without regard to whether it is so attached or installed). Products which are purchased solely for commercial or industrial use are excluded solely for purposes of this Part.

(c) Written warranty means—

(1) Any written affirmation of fact or written promise made in connection with the sale of a consumer product by a supplier to a buyer which relates to the nature of the material or workmanship and affirms or promises that such material or workmanship is defect free or will meet a specified level of performance over a specified period of time, or

(2) Any undertaking in writing in connection with the sale by a supplier of a consumer product to refund, repair, replace or take other remedial action with respect to such product in the event that such product fails to meet the specifications set forth in the undertaking, which written affirmation, promise, or undertaking becomes part of the basis of the bargain between a supplier and a buyer for purposes other than resale of such product.

(d) Warrantor means any supplier or other person who gives or offers to give a written warranty.

(e) Seller means any person who sells or offers for sale for purposes other than resale or use in the ordinary course of the buyer's business any consumer product.

(f) Supplier means any person engaged in the business of making a consumer product directly or indirectly available to consumers.

§ 702.2. Scope

The regulations in this part establish requirements for sellers and warrantors for making the terms of any written warranty on a consumer product available to the consumer prior to sale.

§ 702.3. Pre-sale availability of written warranty terms

The following requirements apply to consumer products actually costing the consumer more than $15.00:

(a) Duties of seller. Except as provided in paragraphs (c) through (d) of this section, the seller of a consumer product with a written warranty shall make a text of the warranty readily available for examination by the prospective buyer by:

(1) Displaying it in close proximity to the warranted product, or

(2) Furnishing it upon request prior to sale and placing signs reasonably calculated to elicit the prospective buyer's attention in prominent locations in the store or department advising such prospective buyers of the availability of warranties upon request.

(b) Duties of the warrantor.

(1) A warrantor who gives a written warranty warranting to a consumer a consumer product actually costing the consumer more than $15.00 shall:

(i) Provide sellers with warranty materials necessary for such sellers to comply with the requirements set forth in paragraph (a) of this section, by the use of one or more by the following means:

(A) Providing a copy of the written warranty with every warranted consumer product; and/or

(B) Providing a tag, sign, sticker, label, decal or other attachment to the product, which contains the full text of the written warranty; and/or

(C) Printing on or otherwise attaching the text of the written warranty to the package, carton, or other container if that package, carton or other container is normally used for display purposes. If the warrantor elects this option a copy of the written warranty must also accompany the warranted product; and/or

(D) Providing a notice, sign, or poster disclosing the text of a consumer product warranty. If the warrantor elects this option, a copy of the written warranty must also accompany each warranted product.

(ii) Provide catalog, mail order, and door-to-door sellers with copies of written warranties necessary for such sellers to comply with the requirements set forth in paragraphs (c) and (d) of this section.

(2) Paragraph (a)(1) of this section shall not be applicable with respect to statements of general policy on emblems, seals or insignias issued by third parties promising replacement or refund if a consumer product is defective, which statements contain no representation or assurance of the quality or performance characteristics of the product; provided that

(i) The disclosures required by § 701.3(a)(1) through (9) of this part are published by such third parties in each issue of a publication with a general circulation, and

(ii) Such disclosures are provided free of charge to any consumer upon written request.

(c) Catalog and mail order sales.

(1) For purposes of this paragraph:

(i) Catalog or mail order sales means any offer for sale, or any solicitation for an order for a consumer product with a written warranty, which includes instructions for ordering the product which do not require a personal visit to the seller's establishment.

(ii) Close conjunction means on the page containing the description of the warranted product, or on the page facing that page.

(2) Any seller who offers for sale to consumers consumer products with written warranties by means of a catalog or mail order solicitation shall:

(i) Clearly and conspicuously disclose in such catalog or solicitation in close conjunction to the description of warranted product, or in an information section of the catalog or solicitation clearly referenced, including a page number, in close conjunction to the description of the warranted product, either:

(A) The full text of the written warranty; or

(B) That the written warranty can be obtained free upon specific written request, and the address where such warranty can be obtained. If this option is elected, such seller shall promptly provide a copy of any written warranty requested by the consumer.

(d) Door-to-door sales.

(1) For purposes of this paragraph:

(i) Door-to-door sale means a sale of consumer products in which the seller or his representative personally solicits the sale, including those in response to or following an invitation by a buyer, and the buyer's agreement to offer to purchase is made at a place other than the place of business of the seller.

(ii) Prospective buyer means an individual solicited by a door-to-door seller to buy a consumer product who indicates sufficient interest in that consumer product or maintains sufficient contact with the seller for the seller reasonably to conclude that the person solicited is considering purchasing the product.

(2) Any seller who offers for sale to consumers consumer products with written warranties by means of door-to-door sales shall, prior to the consummation of the sale, disclose the fact that the sales representative has copies of the warranties for the warranted products being offered for sale, which may be inspected by the prospective buyer at any time during the sales presentation. Such disclosure shall be made orally and shall be included in any written materials shown to prospective buyers.

PART 703

§ 703.1. Definitions

(a) The Act means the Magnuson-Moss Warranty—Federal Trade Commission Improvement Act, 15 U.S.C. 2301, et seq.

(b) Consumer product means any tangible personal property which is distributed in commerce and which is normally used for personal, family, or household purposes (including any such property intended to be attached to or installed in any real property without regard to whether it is so attached or installed).

(c) Written warranty means:

(1) Any written affirmation of fact or written promise made in connection with the sale of a consumer product by a supplier to a buyer which relates to the nature of the material or workmanship and affirms or promises that such material or workmanship is defect free or will meet a specified level of performance over a specified period of time, or

(2) Any undertaking in writing in connection with the sale by a supplier of a consumer product to refund, repair, replace, or take other remedial action with respect to such product in the event that such product fails to meet the specifications set forth in the undertaking, which written affirmation, promise or undertaking becomes part of the basis of the bargain between a supplier and a buyer for purposes other than resale of such product.

(d) Warrantor means any person who gives or offers to give a written warranty which incorporates an informal dispute settlement mechanism.

(e) Mechanism means an informal dispute settlement procedure which is incorporated into the terms of a written warranty to which any provision of Title I of the Act applies, as provided in Section 110 of the Act.

(f) Members means the person or persons within a Mechanism actually deciding disputes.

(g) Consumer means a buyer (other than for purposes of resale) of any consumer product, any person to whom such product is transferred during the duration of a written warranty applicable to the product, and any other person who is entitled by the terms of such warranty or under applicable state law to enforce against the warrantor the obligations of the warranty.

(h) On the face of the warranty means:

(1) If the warranty is a single sheet with printing on both sides of the sheet, or if the warranty is comprised of more than one sheet, the page on which the warranty text begins;

(2) If the warranty is included as part of a longer document, such as a use and care manual, the page in such document on which the warranty text begins.

§ 703.2. Duties of warrantor

(a) The warrantor shall not incorporate into the terms of a written warranty a Mechanism that fails to comply with the requirements contained in §§ 703.3 through 703.8 of this part. This paragraph shall not prohibit a warrantor from incorporating into the terms of a written warranty the step-by-step procedure which the consumer should take in order to obtain performance of any obligation under the warranty as described in section 102(a)(7) of the Act and required by part 701 of this subchapter.

(b) The warrantor shall disclose clearly and conspicuously at least the following information on the face of the written warranty:

(1) A statement of the availability of the informal dispute settlement mechanism;

(2) The name and address of the Mechanism, or the name and a telephone number of the Mechanism which consumers may use without charge;

(3) A statement of any requirement that the consumer resort to the Mechanism before exercising rights or seeking remedies created by Title I of the Act; together with the disclosure that if a consumer chooses to seek redress by pursuing rights and remedies not created by Title I of the Act, resort to the Mechanism would not be required by any provision of the Act; and

(4) A statement, if applicable, indicating where further information on the Mechanism can be found in materials accompanying the product, as provided in § 703.2(c) of this section.

(c) The warrantor shall include in the written warranty or in a separate section of materials accompanying the product, the following information:

(1) Either (i) a form addressed to the Mechanism containing spaces requesting the information which the Mechanism may require for prompt resolution of warranty disputes; or (ii) a telephone number of the Mechanism which consumers may use without charge;

(2) The name and address of the Mechanism;

(3) A brief description of Mechanism procedures;

(4) The time limits adhered to by the Mechanism; and

(5) The types of information which the Mechanism may require for prompt resolution of warranty disputes.

(d) The warrantor shall take steps reasonably calculated to make consumers aware of the Mechanism's existence at the time consumers experience warranty disputes. Nothing contained in paragraphs (b), (c), or (d) of this section shall limit the warrantor's option to encourage consumers to seek redress directly from the warrantor as long as the warrantor does not expressly require consumers to seek redress directly from the warrantor. The warrantor shall proceed fairly and expeditiously to attempt to resolve all disputes submitted directly to the warrantor.

(e) Whenever a dispute is submitted directly to the warrantor, the warrantor shall, within a reasonable time, decide whether, and to what extent, it will satisfy the consumer, and inform the consumer of its decision. In its notification to the consumer of its decision, the warrantor shall include the information required in § 703.2(b) and (c) of this section.

(f) The warrantor shall:

(1) Respond fully and promptly to reasonable requests by the Mechanism for information relating to disputes;

(2) Upon notification of any decision of the Mechanism that would require action on the part of the warrantor, immediately notify the Mechanism whether, and to what extent, warrantor will abide by the decision; and

(3) Perform any obligations it has agreed to.

(g) The warrantor shall act in good faith in determining whether, and to what extent, it will abide by a Mechanism decision.

(h) The warrantor shall comply with any reasonable requirements imposed by the Mechanism to fairly and expeditiously resolve warranty disputes.

MINIMUM REQUIRMENTS OF THE MECHANISM

§ 703.3. Mechanism organization

(a) The Mechanism shall be funded and competently staffed at a level sufficient to ensure fair and expeditious resolution of all disputes, and shall not charge consumers any fee for use of the Mechanism.

(b) The warrantor and the sponsor of the Mechanism (if other than the warrantor) shall take all steps necessary to ensure that the Mechanism, and its members and staff, are sufficiently insulated from the warrantor and the sponsor, so that the decisions of the members and the performance of the staff are not influenced by either the warrantor or the sponsor. Necessary steps shall include, at a minimum, committing funds in advance, basing personnel decisions solely on merit, and not assigning conflicting warrantor or sponsor duties to Mechanism staff persons.

(c) The Mechanism shall impose any other reasonable requirements necessary to ensure that the members and staff act fairly and expeditiously in each dispute.

§ 703.4. Qualification of members

(a) No member deciding a dispute shall be:

(1) A party to the dispute, or an employee or agent of a party other than for purposes of deciding disputes; or

(2) A person who is or may become a party in any legal action, including but not limited to class actions, relating to the product or complaint in dispute, or an employee or agent of such person other than for purposes of deciding disputes. For purposes of this paragraph (a) a person shall not be considered a "party" solely because he or she acquires or owns an interest in a party solely for investment, and the acquisition or ownership of an interest which is offered to the general public shall be prima facie evidence of its acquisition or ownership solely for investment.

(b) When one or two members are deciding a dispute, all shall be persons having no direct involvement in the manufacture, distribution, sale or service of any product. When three or more members are deciding a dispute, at least two-thirds shall be persons having no direct involvement in the manufacture, distribution, sale or service of any product. "Direct involvement" shall not include acquiring or owning an interest solely for investment, and the acquisition or ownership of an interest which is offered to the general public shall be prima facie evidence of its acquisition or ownership solely for investment. Nothing contained in this section shall prevent the members from consulting with any persons knowledgeable in the technical, commercial or other areas relating to the product which is the subject of the dispute.

(c) Members shall be persons interested in the fair and expeditious settlement of consumer disputes.

§ 703.5. Operation of the Mechanism

(a) The Mechanism shall establish written operating procedures which shall include at least those items specified in paragraphs (b) through (j) of this section. Copies of the written procedures shall be made available to any person upon request.

(b) Upon notification of a dispute, the Mechanism shall immediately inform both the warrantor and the consumer of receipt of the dispute.

(c) The Mechanism shall investigate, gather and organize all information necessary for a fair and expeditious decision in each dispute. When any evidence gathered by or submitted to the Mechanism raises issues relating to the number of repair attempts, the length of repair periods, the possibility of unreasonable use of the product, or any other issues relevant in light of Title I of the Act (or rules thereunder), including issues relating to consequential damages, or any other remedy under the Act (or rules thereunder), the Mechanism shall investigate these issues. When information which will or may be used in the decision, submitted by one party, or a consultant under § 703.4(b) of this part, or any other source tends to contradict facts submitted by the other party, the Mechanism shall clearly, accurately, and completely disclose to both parties the contradictory information (and its source) and shall provide both parties an opportunity to explain or rebut the information and to submit additional materials. The Mechanism shall not require any information not reasonably necessary to decide the dispute.

(d) If the dispute has not been settled, the Mechanism shall, as expeditiously as possible but at least within 40 days of notification of the dispute, except as provided in paragraph (e) of this section:

(1) Render a fair decision based on the information gathered as described in paragraph (c) of this section, and on any information submitted at an oral presentation which conforms to the requirements of paragraph (f) of this section (A decision shall include any remedies appropriate under the circumstances, including repair, replacement, refund, reimbursement for expenses, compensation for damages, and any other remedies available under the written warranty or the Act (or rules thereunder); and a decision shall state a specified reasonable time for performance);

(2) Disclose to the warrantor its decision and the reasons therefor;

(3) If the decision would require action on the part of the warrantor, determine whether, and to what extent, warrantor will abide by its decision; and

(4) Disclose to the consumer its decision, the reasons therefor, warrantor's intended actions (if the decision would require action on the part of the warrantor), and the information described in paragraph (g) of this section. For purposes of paragraph (d) of this section a dispute shall be deemed settled when the Mechanism has ascertained from the consumer that:

(i) The dispute has been settled to the consumer's satisfaction; and

(ii) The settlement contains a specified reasonable time for performance.

(e) The Mechanism may delay the performance of its duties under paragraph (d) of this section beyond the 40 day time limit:

(1) Where the period of delay is due solely to failure of a consumer to provide promptly his or her name and address, brand name and model number of the product involved, and a statement as to the nature of the defect or other complaint; or

(2) For a 7 day period in those cases where the consumer has made no attempt to seek redress directly from the warrantor.

(f) The Mechanism may allow an oral presentation by a party to a dispute (or a party's representative) only if:

(1) Both warrantor and consumer expressly agree to the presentation;

(2) Prior to agreement the Mechanism fully discloses to the consumer the following information:

(i) That the presentation by either party will take place only if both parties so agree, but that if they agree, and one party fails to appear at the agreed upon time and place, the presentation by the other party may still be allowed;

(ii) That the members will decide the dispute whether or not an oral presentation is made,

(iii) The proposed date, time and place for the presentation; and

(iv) A brief description of what will occur at the presentation including, if applicable, parties' rights to bring witnesses and/or counsel; and

(3) Each party has the right to be present during the other party's oral presentation. Nothing contained in this paragraph (b) of this section shall preclude the Mechanism from allowing an oral presentation by one party, if the other party fails to appear at the agreed upon time and place, as long as all of the requirements of this paragraph have been satisfied.

(g) The Mechanism shall inform the consumer, at the time of disclosure required in paragraph (d) of this section that:

(1) If he or she is dissatisfied with its decision or warrantor's intended actions, or eventual performance, legal remedies, including use of small claims court, may be pursued;

(2) The Mechanism's decision is admissible in evidence as provided in section 110(a)(3) of the Act; and

(3) The consumer may obtain, at reasonable cost, copies of all Mechanism records relating to the consumer's dispute.

(h) If the warrantor has agreed to perform any obligations, either as part of a settlement agreed to after notification to the Mechanism of the dispute or as a result of a decision under paragraph (d) of this section, the Mechanism shall ascertain from the consumer within 10 working days of the date for performance whether performance has occurred.

(i) A requirement that a consumer resort to the Mechanism prior to commencement of an action under section 110(d) of the Act shall be satisfied 40 days after notification to the Mechanism of the dispute or when the Mechanism completes all of its duties under paragraph (d) of this section, whichever occurs sooner. Except that, if the Mechanism delays performance of its paragraph (d) of this section duties as allowed by paragraph (e) of this section, the requirement that the consumer initially resort to the Mechanism shall not be satisfied until the period of delay allowed by paragraph (e) of this section has ended.

(j) Decisions of the Mechanism shall not be legally binding on any person. However, the warrantor shall act in good faith, as provided in § 703.2(g) of this part. In any civil action arising out of a warranty obligation and relating to a matter considered by the Mechanism, any decision of the Mechanism shall be admissible in evidence, as provided in section 110(a)(3) of the Act.

§ 703.6. Recordkeeping

(a) The Mechanism shall maintain records on each dispute referred to it which shall include:

(1) Name, address and telephone number of the consumer;

(2) Name, address, telephone number and contact person of the warrantor;

(3) Brand name and model number of the product involved;

(4) The date of receipt of the dispute and the date of disclosure to the consumer of the decision;

(5) All letters or other written documents submitted by either party;

(6) All other evidence collected by the Mechanism relating to the dispute, including summaries of relevant and material portions of telephone calls and meetings between the Mechanism and any other person (including consultants described in § 703.4(b) of this part);

(7) A summary of any relevant and material information presented by either party at an oral presentation;

(8) The decision of the members including information as to date, time and place of meeting, and the identity of members voting; or information on any other resolution;

(9) A copy of the disclosure to the parties of the decision;

(10) A statement of the warrantor's intended action(s);

(11) Copies of follow-up letters (or summaries of relevant and material portions of follow-up telephone calls) to the consumer, and responses thereto; and

(12) Any other documents and communications (or summaries of relevant and material portions of oral communications) relating to the dispute.

(b) The Mechanism shall maintain an index of each warrantor's disputes grouped under brand name and sub-grouped under product model.

(c) The Mechanism shall maintain an index for each warrantor as will show:

(1) All disputes in which the warrantor has promised some performance (either by settlement or in response to a Mechanism decision) and has failed to comply; and

(2) All disputes in which the warrantor has refused to abide by a Mechanism decision.

(d) The Mechanism shall maintain an index as will show all disputes delayed beyond 40 days.

(e) The Mechanism shall compile semi-annually and maintain statistics which show the number and percent of disputes in each of the following categories:

(1) Resolved by staff of the Mechanism and warrantor has complied;

(2) Resolved by staff of the Mechanism, time for compliance has occurred, and warrantor has not complied;

(3) Resolved by staff of the Mechanism and time for compliance has not yet occurred;

(4) Decided by members and warrantor has complied;

(5) Decided by members, time for compliance has occurred, and warrantor has not complied;

(6) Decided by members and time for compliance has not yet occurred;

(7) Decided by members adverse to the consumer;

(8) No jurisdiction;

(9) Decision delayed beyond 40 days under § 703.5(e)(1) of this part;

(10) Decision delayed beyond 40 days under § 703.5(e)(2) of this part;

(11) Decision delayed beyond 40 days for any other reason; and

(12) Pending decision.

(f) The Mechanism shall retain all records specified in paragraphs (a) through (e) of this section for at least 4 years after final disposition of the dispute.

§ 703.7. Audits

(a) The Mechanism shall have an audit conducted at least annually, to determine whether the Mechanism and its implementation are in compliance with this part. All records of the Mechanism required to be kept under § 703.6 of this part shall be available for audit.

(b) Each audit provided for in paragraph (a) of this section shall include at a minimum the following:

(1) Evaluation of warrantors' efforts to make consumers aware of the Mechanism's existence as required in § 703.2(d) of this part;

(2) Review of the indexes maintained pursuant to § 703.6(b), (c), and (d) of this part; and

(3) Analysis of a random sample of disputes handled by the Mechanism to determine the following:

(i) Adequacy of the Mechanism's complaint and other forms, investigation, mediation and follow-up efforts, and other aspects of complaint handling; and

(ii) Accuracy of the Mechanism's statistical compilations under § 703.6(e) of this part. (For purposes of this subparagraph "analysis" shall include oral or written contact with the consumers involved in each of the disputes in the random sample.)

(c) A report of each audit under this section shall be submitted to the Federal Trade Commission, and shall be made available to any person at reasonable cost. The Mechanism may direct its auditor to delete names of parties to disputes, and identity of products involved, from the audit report.

(d) Auditors shall be selected by the Mechanism. No auditor may be involved with the Mechanism as a warrantor, sponsor or member, or employee or agent thereof, other than for purposes of the audit.

§ 703.8. Openness of records and proceedings

(a) The statistical summaries specified in § 703.6(e) of this part shall be available to any person for inspection and copying.

(b) Except as provided under paragraphs (a) and (e) of this section, and paragraph (c) of § 703.7 of this part, all records of the Mechanism may be kept confidential, or made available only on such terms and conditions, or in such form, as the Mechanism shall permit.

(c) The policy of the Mechanism with respect to records made available at the Mechanism's option shall be set out in the procedures under § 703.5(a) of this part; the policy shall be applied uniformly to all requests for access to or copies of such records.

(d) Meetings of the members to hear and decide disputes shall be open to observers on reasonable and nondiscriminatory terms. The identity of the parties and products involved in disputes need not be disclosed at meetings.

(e) Upon request the Mechanism shall provide to either party to a dispute:

(1) Access to all records relating to the dispute; and

(2) Copies of any records relating to the dispute, at reasonable cost.

(f) The Mechanism shall make available to any person upon request, information relating to the qualifications of Mechanism staff and members.

EXCERPTS FROM TITLE 12 OF THE CODE OF FEDERAL REGULATIONS OCC REGULATIONS

---

12 C.F.R. 34 and 7

Table of Sections

§ 34.3. General rule

(a) A national bank may make, arrange, purchase, or sell loans or extensions of credit, or interests therein, that are secured by liens on, or interests in, real estate (real estate loans), subject to 12 U.S.C. 1828(*o*) and such restrictions and requirements as the Comptroller of the Currency may prescribe by regulation or order.

(b) A national bank shall not make a consumer loan subject to this subpart based predominantly on the bank's realization of the foreclosure or liquidation value of the borrower's collateral, without regard to the borrower's ability to repay the loan according to its terms. A bank may use any reasonable method to determine a borrower's ability to repay, including, for example, the borrower's current and expected income, current and expected cash flows, net worth, other relevant financial resources, current financial obligations, employment status, credit history, or other relevant factors.

(c) A national bank shall not engage in unfair or deceptive practices within the meaning of section 5 of the Federal Trade Commission Act, 15 U.S.C. 45(a)(1), and regulations promulgated thereunder in connection with loans made under this part.

§ 34.4. Applicability of state law

(a) A national bank may make real estate loans under 12 U.S.C. 371 and § 34.3, without regard to state law limitations concerning:

(1) Licensing, registration (except for purposes of service of process), filings, or reports by creditors;

(2) The ability of a creditor to require or obtain private mortgage insurance, insurance for other collateral, or other credit enhancements or risk mitigants, in furtherance of safe and sound banking practices;

(3) Loan-to-value ratios;

(4) The terms of credit, including schedule for repayment of principal and interest, amortization of loans, balance, payments due, minimum payments, or term to maturity of the loan, including the circumstances under which a loan may be called due and payable upon the passage of time or a specified event external to the loan;

(5) The aggregate amount of funds that may be loaned upon the security of real estate;

(6) Escrow accounts, impound accounts, and similar accounts;

(7) Security property, including leaseholds;

(8) Access to, and use of, credit reports;

(9) Disclosure and advertising, including laws requiring specific statements, information, or other content to be included in credit application forms, credit solicitations, billing statements, credit contracts, or other credit-related documents;

(10) Processing, origination, servicing, sale or purchase of, or investment or participation in, mortgages;

(11) Disbursements and repayments;

(12) Rates of interest on loans;[1]

(13) Due-on-sale clauses except to the extent provided in 12 U.S.C. 1701j–3 and 12 CFR part 591; and

(14) Covenants and restrictions that must be contained in a lease to qualify the leasehold as acceptable security for a real estate loan.

(b) State laws on the following subjects are not inconsistent with the real estate lending powers of national banks and apply to national banks to the extent consistent with the decision of the Supreme Court in Barnett Bank of Marion County, N.A. v. Nelson, Florida Insurance Commissioner, et al., 517 U.S. 25 (1996):

(1) Contracts;

(2) Torts;

(3) Criminal law;[2]

(4) Homestead laws specified in 12 U.S.C. 1462a(f);

(5) Rights to collect debts;

(6) Acquisition and transfer of real property;

(7) Taxation;

(8) Zoning; and

(9) Any other law that the OCC determines to be applicable to national banks in accordance with the decision of the Supreme Court in Barnett Bank of Marion County, N.A. v. Nelson, Florida Insurance Commissioner, et al., 517 U.S. 25 (1996), or that is made applicable by Federal law.

§ 7.4000. Visitorial Powers with respect to national banks

(a) General rule.

(1) Under 12 U.S.C. 484, only the OCC or an authorized representative of the OCC may exercise visitorial powers with respect to national banks. State officials may not exercise visitorial powers with respect to national banks, such as conducting examinations, inspecting or requiring

[1] The limitations on charges that comprise rates of interest on loans by national banks are determined under Federal law. See 12 U.S.C. 85 and 1735f–7a; 12 CFR 7.4001. State laws purporting to regulate national bank fees and charges that do not constitute interest are addressed in 12 CFR 7.4002.

[2] But see the distinction drawn by the Supreme Court in Easton v. Iowa, 188 U.S. 220, 238 (1903), where the Court stated that "[u]ndoubtedly a state has the legitimate power to define and punish crimes by general laws applicable to all persons within its jurisdiction * * *. But it is without lawful power to make such special laws applicable to banks organized and operating under the laws of the United States." Id. at 239 (holding that Federal law governing the operations of national banks preempted a state criminal law prohibiting insolvent banks from accepting deposits).

the production of books or records of national banks, or prosecuting enforcement actions, except in limited circumstances authorized by federal law. However, production of a bank's records (other than non-public OCC information under 12 CFR part 4, subpart C) may be required under normal judicial procedures.

(2) For purposes of this section, visitorial powers include:

(i) Examination of a bank;

(ii) Inspection of a bank's books and records;

(iii) Regulation and supervision of activities authorized or permitted pursuant to federal banking law; and

(iv) Enforcing compliance with any applicable Federal or state laws concerning those activities, including through investigations that seek to ascertain compliance through production of non-public information by the bank, except as otherwise provided in paragraphs (a), (b), and (c) of this section.

(3) Unless otherwise provided by Federal law, the OCC has exclusive visitorial authority with respect to the content and conduct of activities authorized for national banks under Federal law.

(b) Exclusion. In accordance with the decision of the Supreme Court in Cuomo v. Clearing House Assn., L.L.C., 129 S. Ct. 2710 (2009), an action against a national bank in a court of appropriate jurisdiction brought by a state attorney general (or other chief law enforcement officer) to enforce an applicable law against a national bank and to seek relief as authorized by such law is not an exercise of visitorial powers under 12 U.S.C. 484.

(c) Exceptions to the general rule. Under 12 U.S.C. 484, the OCC's exclusive visitorial powers are subject to the following exceptions.

(1) Exceptions authorized by Federal law. National banks are subject to such visitorial powers as are provided by Federal law. Examples of laws vesting visitorial power in other governmental entities include laws authorizing state or other Federal officials to:

(i) Inspect the list of shareholders, provided that the official is authorized to assess taxes under state authority (12 U.S.C. 62; this section also authorizes inspection of the shareholder list by shareholders and creditors of a national bank);

(ii) Review, at reasonable times and upon reasonable notice to a bank, the bank's records solely to ensure compliance with applicable state unclaimed property or escheat laws upon reasonable cause to believe that the bank has failed to comply with those laws (12 U.S.C. 484(b));

(iii) Verify payroll records for unemployment compensation purposes (26 U.S.C. 3305(c));

(iv) Ascertain the correctness of Federal tax returns (26 U.S.C. 7602);

(v) Enforce the Fair Labor Standards Act (29 U.S.C. 211); and

(vi) Functionally regulate certain activities, as provided under the Gramm-Leach-Bliley Act, Pub.L. 106–102, 113 Stat. 1338 (Nov. 12, 1999).

(2) Exception for courts of justice. National banks are subject to such visitorial powers as are vested in the courts of justice. This exception pertains to the powers inherent in the judiciary.

(3) Exception for Congress. National banks are subject to such visitorial powers as shall be, or have been, exercised or directed by Congress or by either House thereof or by any committee of Congress or of either House duly authorized.

(d) Report of examination. The report of examination made by an OCC examiner is designated solely for use in the supervision of the bank. The bank's copy of the report is the property of the OCC and is loaned to the bank and any holding company thereof solely for its confidential use. The bank's directors, in keeping with their responsibilities both to depositors and to shareholders, should thoroughly review the report. The report may be made available to other persons only in accordance with the rules on disclosure in 12 CFR part 4.

§ 7.4002. National bank charges

(a) Authority to impose charges and fees. A national bank may charge its customers non-interest charges and fees, including deposit account service charges.

(b) Considerations.

(1) All charges and fees should be arrived at by each bank on a competitive basis and not on the basis of any agreement, arrangement, undertaking, understanding, or discussion with other banks or their officers.

(2) The establishment of non-interest charges and fees, their amounts, and the method of calculating them are business decisions to be made by each bank, in its discretion, according to sound banking judgment and safe and sound banking principles. A national bank establishes non-interest charges and fees in accordance with safe and sound banking principles if the bank employs a decision-making process through which it considers the following factors, among others:

(i) The cost incurred by the bank in providing the service;

(ii) The deterrence of misuse by customers of banking services;

(iii) The enhancement of the competitive position of the bank in accordance with the bank's business plan and marketing strategy; and

(iv) The maintenance of the safety and soundness of the institution.

(c) Interest. Charges and fees that are "interest" within the meaning of 12 U.S.C. 85 are governed by § 7.4001 and not by this section.

(d) State law. The OCC applies preemption principles derived from the United States Constitution, as interpreted through judicial precedent, when determining whether State laws apply that purport to limit or prohibit charges and fees described in this section.

(e) National bank as fiduciary. This section does not apply to charges imposed by a national bank in its capacity as a fiduciary, which are governed by 12 CFR part 9.

§ 7.4007 Deposit-taking by national banks

(a) Authority of national banks. A national bank may receive deposits and engage in any activity incidental to receiving deposits, including issuing evidence of accounts, subject to such terms, conditions, and limitations prescribed by the Comptroller of the Currency and any other applicable Federal law.

(b) Applicability of state law. A national bank may exercise its deposit-taking powers without regard to state law limitations concerning:

(1) Abandoned and dormant accounts;[3]

(2) Checking accounts;

---

[3] This does not apply to state laws of the type upheld by the United States Supreme Court in Anderson Nat'l Bank v. Luckett, 321 U.S. 233 (1944), which obligate a national bank to "pay [deposits] to the persons entitled to demand payment according to the law of the state where it does business." Id. at 248–249.

(3) Disclosure requirements;

(4) Funds availability;

(5) Savings account orders of withdrawal;

(6) State licensing or registration requirements (except for purposes of service of process); and

(7) Special purpose savings services;[4]

(c) State laws that are not preempted. State laws on the following subjects are not inconsistent with the deposit-taking powers of national banks and apply to national banks to the extent consistent with the decision of the Supreme Court in Barnett Bank of Marion County, N.A. v. Nelson, Florida Insurance Commissioner, et al. 517 U.S. 25 (1996):

(1) Contracts;

(2) Torts;

(3) Criminal law;[5]

(4) Rights to collect debts;

(5) Acquisition and transfer of property;

(6) Taxation;

(7) Zoning; and

(8) Any other law that the OCC determines to be applicable to national banks in accordance with the decision of the Supreme Court in Barnett Bank of Marion County, N.A. v. Nelson, Florida Insurance Commissioner, et al. 517 U.S. 25 (1996), or that is made applicable by Federal law.

§ 7.4008 Lending by national banks

(a) Authority of national banks. A national bank may make, sell, purchase, participate in, or otherwise deal in loans and interests in loans that are not secured by liens on, or interests in, real estate, subject to such terms, conditions, and limitations prescribed by the Comptroller of the Currency and any other applicable Federal law.

(b) Standards for loans. A national bank shall not make a consumer loan subject to this § 7.4008 based predominantly on the bank's realization of the foreclosure or liquidation value of the borrower's collateral, without regard to the borrower's ability to repay the loan according to its terms. A bank may use any reasonable method to determine a borrower's ability to repay, including, for example, the borrower's current and expected income, current and expected cash flows, net worth, other relevant financial resources, current financial obligations, employment status, credit history, or other relevant factors.

(c) Unfair and deceptive practices. A national bank shall not engage in unfair or deceptive practices within the meaning of section 5 of the Federal Trade Commission Act, 15 U.S.C. 45(a)(1), and regulations promulgated thereunder in connection with loans made under this § 7.4008.

(d) Applicability of state law. A national bank may make non-real estate loans without regard to state law limitations concerning:

---

4 State laws purporting to regulate national bank fees and charges are addressed in 12 CFR 7.4002.

5 But see the distinction drawn by the Supreme Court in Easton v. Iowa, 188 U.S. 220, 238 (1903), where the Court stated that "[u]ndoubtedly a state has the legitimate power to define and punish crimes by general laws applicable to all persons within its jurisdiction * * *. But it is without lawful power to make such special laws applicable to banks organized and operating under the laws of the United States." Id. at 239 (holding that Federal law governing the operations of national banks preempted a state criminal law prohibiting insolvent banks from accepting deposits).

(1) Licensing, registration (except for purposes of service of process), filings, or reports by creditors;

(2) The ability of a creditor to require or obtain insurance for collateral or other credit enhancements or risk mitigants, in furtherance of safe and sound banking practices;

(3) Loan-to-value ratios;

(4) The terms of credit, including the schedule for repayment of principal and interest, amortization of loans, balance, payments due, minimum payments, or term to maturity of the loan, including the circumstances under which a loan may be called due and payable upon the passage of time or a specified event external to the loan;

(5) Escrow accounts, impound accounts, and similar accounts;

(6) Security property, including leaseholds;

(7) Access to, and use of, credit reports;

(8) Disclosure and advertising, including laws requiring specific statements, information, or other content to be included in credit application forms, credit solicitations, billing statements, credit contracts, or other credit-related documents;

(9) Disbursements and repayments; and

(10) Rates of interest on loans.[6]

(e) State laws that are not preempted. State laws on the following subjects are not inconsistent with the non-real estate lending powers of national banks and apply to national banks to the extent consistent with the decision of the Supreme Court in Barnett Bank of Marion County, N.A. v. Nelson, Florida Insurance Commissioner, et al., 517 U.S. 25 (1996):

(1) Contracts;

(2) Torts;

(3) Criminal law;[7]

(4) Rights to collect debts;

(5) Acquisition and transfer of property;

(6) Taxation;

(7) Zoning; and

(8) Any other law that the OCC determines to be applicable to national banks in accordance with the decision of the Supreme Court in Barnett Bank of Marion County, N.A. v. Nelson, Florida Insurance Commissioner, et al., 517 U.S. 25 (1996) or that is made applicable by Federal law.

§ 7.4009 [Reserved]

§ 7.4010 Applicability of state law and visitorial powers to federal savings associations and subsidiaries

(a) In accordance with section 1046 of the Dodd-Frank Wall Street Reform and Consumer Protection Act (12 U.S.C. 25b), Federal savings associations and their subsidiaries shall be subject to

---

[6] The limitations on charges that comprise rates of interest on loans by national banks are determined under Federal law. See 12 U.S.C. 85; 12 CFR 7.4001. State laws purporting to regulate national bank fees and charges that do not constitute interest are addressed in 12 CFR 7.4002.

[7] .See supra note 5 regarding the distinction drawn by the Supreme Court in Easton v. Iowa, 188 U.S. 220, 238 (1903).

the same laws and legal standards, including regulations of the OCC, as are applicable to national banks and their subsidiaries, regarding the preemption of state law.

(b) In accordance with section 1047 of the Dodd-Frank Wall Street Reform and Consumer Protection Act (12 U.S.C. 1465), the provisions of section 5136C(i) of the Revised Statutes regarding visitorial powers apply to Federal savings associations and their subsidiaries to the same extent and in the same manner as if they were national banks or national bank subsidiaries.

12 U.S.C. § 25b. State Law Preemption Standards for National Banks and Subsidiaries Clarified

(a) Definitions

For purposes of this section, the following definitions shall apply:

(1) National bank

The term "national bank" includes—

(A) any bank organized under the laws of the United States; and

(B) any Federal branch established in accordance with the International Banking Act of 1978.

(2) State consumer financial laws

The term "State consumer financial law" means a State law that does not directly or indirectly discriminate against national banks and that directly and specifically regulates the manner, content, or terms and conditions of any financial transaction (as may be authorized for national banks to engage in), or any account related thereto, with respect to a consumer.

(3) Other definitions

The terms "affiliate", "subsidiary", "includes", and "including" have the same meanings as in section 1813 of this title.

(b) Preemption standard

(1) In general

State consumer financial laws are preempted, only if—

(A) application of a State consumer financial law would have a discriminatory effect on national banks, in comparison with the effect of the law on a bank chartered by that State;

(B) in accordance with the legal standard for preemption in the decision of the Supreme Court of the United States in Barnett Bank of Marion County, N. A. v. Nelson, Florida Insurance Commissioner, et al., 517 U.S. 25 (1996), the State consumer financial law prevents or significantly interferes with the exercise by the national bank of its powers; and any preemption determination under this subparagraph may be made by a court, or by regulation or order of the Comptroller of the Currency on a case-by-case basis, in accordance with applicable law; * * *

EXCERPTS FROM THE REAL ESTATE SETTLEMENT PROCEDURES ACT AND IMPLEMENTING REGULATIONS

Analysis

12 U.S.C. § 2607. [RESPA § 8]. Prohibition against kickbacks and unearned fees

(a) Business referrals

No person shall give and no person shall accept any fee, kickback, or thing of value pursuant to any agreement or understanding, oral or otherwise, that business incident to or a part of a real estate settlement service involving a federally related mortgage loan shall be referred to any person.

(b) Splitting charges

No person shall give and no person shall accept any portion, split, or percentage of any charge made or received for the rendering of a real estate settlement service in connection with a transaction involving a federally related mortgage loan other than for services actually performed.

(c) Fees, salaries, compensation, or other payments

Nothing in this section shall be construed as prohibiting (1) the payment of a fee (A) to attorneys at law for services actually rendered or (B) by a title company to its duly appointed agent for services actually performed in the issuance of a policy of title insurance or (C) by a lender to its duly appointed agent for services actually performed in the making of a loan, (2) the payment to any person of a bona fide salary or compensation or other payment for goods or facilities actually furnished or for services actually performed, (3) payments pursuant to cooperative brokerage and referral arrangements or agreements between real estate agents and brokers, (4) affiliated business arrangements so long as (A) a disclosure is made of the existence of such an arrangement to the person being referred and, in connection with such referral, such person is provided a written estimate of the charge or range of charges generally made by the provider to which the person is referred (i) in the case of a face-to-face referral or a referral made in writing or by electronic media, at or before the time of the referral (and compliance with this requirement in such case may be evidenced by a notation in a written, electronic, or similar system of records maintained in the regular course of business); (ii) in the case of a referral made by telephone, within 3 business days after the referral by telephone,[1] (and in such case an abbreviated verbal disclosure of the existence of the arrangement and the fact that a written disclosure will be provided within 3 business days shall be made to the person being referred during the telephone referral); or (iii) in the case of a referral by a lender (including a referral by a lender to an affiliated lender), at the time the estimates required under section 2604(c) of this title are provided (notwithstanding clause (i) or (ii)); and any required written receipt of such disclosure (without regard to the manner of the disclosure under clause (i), (ii), or (iii)) may be obtained at the closing or settlement (except that a person making a face-to-face referral who provides the written disclosure at or before the time of the referral shall attempt to obtain any required written receipt of such disclosure at such time and if the person being referred chooses not to acknowledge the receipt of the disclosure at that time, that fact shall be noted in the written, electronic, or similar system of records maintained in the regular course of business by the person making the referral), (B) such person is not required to use any particular provider of settlement services, and (C) the only thing of value that is received from the arrangement, other than the payments permitted under this subsection, is a return on the ownership interest or franchise relationship, or (5) such other payments or classes of payments or other transfers as are specified in regulations prescribed by the Bureau, after consultation with the Attorney General, the Secretary of Veterans Affairs, the Federal Home Loan Bank Board, the Federal Deposit Insurance Corporation, the Board of Governors of the Federal Reserve System, and the Secretary of Agriculture. For purposes of the preceding sentence, the following shall not be considered a violation of clause (4)(B): (i) any arrangement that requires a buyer, borrower, or seller to pay for the services of an attorney, credit reporting agency, or real estate appraiser chosen by the lender to represent the lender's interest in a real estate transaction, or (ii) any arrangement where an attorney or law firm represents a client in a real estate transaction and issues or arranges for the issuance of a policy of title insurance in the transaction directly as agent or through a separate corporate title insurance agency that may be established by that attorney or law firm and operated as an adjunct to his or its law practice.

---

1 So in original. The comma probably should not appear.

(d) Penalties for violations; joint and several liability; treble damages; actions for injunction by Bureau and Secretary and by State officials; costs and attorney fees; construction of State laws

(1) Any person or persons who violate the provisions of this section shall be fined not more than $10,000 or imprisoned for not more than one year, or both.

(2) Any person or persons who violate the prohibitions or limitations of this section shall be jointly and severally liable to the person or persons charged for the settlement service involved in the violation in an amount equal to three times the amount of any charge paid for such settlement service.

(3) No person or persons shall be liable for a violation of the provisions of subsection (c)(4)(A) if such person or persons proves by a preponderance of the evidence that such violation was not intentional and resulted from a bona fide error notwithstanding maintenance of procedures that are reasonably adapted to avoid such error.

(4) The Bureau, the Secretary, or the attorney general or the insurance commissioner of any State may bring an action to enjoin violations of this section. Except, to the extent that a person is subject to the jurisdiction of the Bureau, the Secretary, or the attorney general or the insurance commissioner of any State, the Bureau shall have primary authority to enforce or administer this section, subject to subtitle B of the Consumer Financial Protection Act of 2010.

(5) In any private action brought pursuant to this subsection, the court may award to the prevailing party the court costs of the action together with reasonable attorneys fees.

(6) No provision of State law or regulation that imposes more stringent limitations on affiliated business arrangements shall be construed as being inconsistent with this section.

REGULATIONS IMPLEMENTING REAL ESTATE SETTLEMENT PROCEDURES ACT

REGULATION X REGULATIONS IMPLEMENTING REAL ESTATE SETTLEMENT PROCEDURES ACT (REGULATION X)

EXCERPTS FROM 12 C.F.R. PART 1024

Table of Sections

Subpart A-General

Subpart B—Mortgage Settlement and Escrow Accounts

Subpart C—Mortgage Servicing

§ 1024.1. Designation

This part, known as Regulation X, is issued by the Bureau of Consumer Financial Protection to implement the Real Estate Settlement Procedures Act of 1974, as amended, 12 U.S.C. 2601 *et. seq.*

§ 1024.2. Definitions

(a) Statutory terms. All terms defined in RESPA (12 U.S.C. 2602) are used in accordance with their statutory meaning unless otherwise defined in paragraph (b) of this section or elsewhere in this part.

(b) Other terms. As used in this part:

Application means the submission of a borrower's financial information in anticipation of a credit decision relating to a federally related mortgage loan, which shall include the borrower's name, the borrower's monthly income, the borrower's social security number to obtain a credit report, the property address, an estimate of the value of the property, the mortgage loan amount sought, and any other information deemed necessary by the loan originator. An application may either be in writing or electronically submitted, including a written record of an oral application.

Balloon payment has the same meaning as "balloon payment" under Regulation Z (12 CFR part 1026).

Bureau means the Bureau of Consumer Financial Protection.

Business day means a day on which the offices of the business entity are open to the public for carrying on substantially all of the entity's business functions.

Changed circumstances means:

(1)(i) Acts of God, war, disaster, or other emergency;

(ii) Information particular to the borrower or transaction that was relied on in providing the GFE and that changes or is found to be inaccurate after the GFE has been provided. This may include information about the credit quality of the borrower, the amount of the loan, the estimated value of the property, or any other information that was used in providing the GFE;

(iii) New information particular to the borrower or transaction that was not relied on in providing the GFE; or

(iv) Other circumstances that are particular to the borrower or transaction, including boundary disputes, the need for flood insurance, or environmental problems.

(2) Changed circumstances do not include:

(i) The borrower's name, the borrower's monthly income, the property address, an estimate of the value of the property, the mortgage loan amount sought, and any information contained in any credit report obtained by the loan originator prior to providing the GFE, unless the information changes or is found to be inaccurate after the GFE has been provided; or

(ii) Market price fluctuations by themselves.

Dealer means, in the case of property improvement loans, a seller, contractor, or supplier of goods or services. In the case of manufactured home loans, "dealer" means one who engages in the business of manufactured home retail sales.

Dealer loan or dealer consumer credit contract means, generally, any arrangement in which a dealer assists the borrower in obtaining a federally related mortgage loan from the funding lender and then assigns the dealer's legal interests to the funding lender and receives the net proceeds of the loan. The funding lender is the lender for the purposes of the disclosure requirements of this part. If a dealer is a "creditor" as defined under the definition of "federally related mortgage loan" in this part, the dealer is the lender for purposes of this part.

Effective date of transfer is defined in section 6(i)(1) of RESPA (12 U.S.C. 2605(i)(1)). In the case of a home equity conversion mortgage or reverse mortgage as referenced in this section, the effective date of transfer is the transfer date agreed upon by the transferee servicer and the transferor servicer.

Federally related mortgage loan means:

(1) Any loan (other than temporary financing, such as a construction loan):

(i) That is secured by a first or subordinate lien on residential real property, including a refinancing of any secured loan on residential real property, upon which there is either:

(A) Located or, following settlement, will be constructed using proceeds of the loan, a structure or structures designed principally for occupancy of from one to four families (including individual units of condominiums and cooperatives and including any related interests, such as a share in the cooperative or right to occupancy of the unit); or

(B) Located or, following settlement, will be placed using proceeds of the loan, a manufactured home; and

(ii) For which one of the following paragraphs applies. The loan:

(A) Is made in whole or in part by any lender that is either regulated by or whose deposits or accounts are insured by any agency of the Federal Government;

(B) Is made in whole or in part, or is insured, guaranteed, supplemented, or assisted in any way:

(1) By the Secretary of the Department of Housing and Urban Development (HUD) or any other officer or agency of the Federal Government; or

(2) Under or in connection with a housing or urban development program administered by the Secretary of HUD or a housing or related program administered by any other officer or agency of the Federal Government;

(C) Is intended to be sold by the originating lender to the Federal National Mortgage Association, the Government National Mortgage Association, the Federal Home Loan Mortgage Corporation (or its successors), or a financial institution from which the loan is to be purchased by the Federal Home Loan Mortgage Corporation (or its successors);

(D) Is made in whole or in part by a "creditor," as defined in section 103(g) of the Consumer Credit Protection Act (15 U.S.C. 1602(g)), that makes or invests in residential real estate loans aggregating more than $1,000,000 per year. For purposes of this definition, the term "creditor" does not include any agency or instrumentality of any State, and the term "residential real estate loan" means any loan secured by residential real property, including single-family and multifamily residential property;

(E) Is originated either by a dealer or, if the obligation is to be assigned to any maker of mortgage loans specified in paragraphs (1)(ii)(A) through (D) of this definition, by a mortgage broker; or

(F) Is the subject of a home equity conversion mortgage, also frequently called a "reverse mortgage," issued by any maker of mortgage loans specified in paragraphs (1)(ii) (A) through (D) of this definition.

(2) Any installment sales contract, land contract, or contract for deed on otherwise qualifying residential property is a federally related mortgage loan if the contract is funded in whole or in part by proceeds of a loan made by any maker of mortgage loans specified in paragraphs (1)(ii) (A) through (D) of this definition.

(3) If the residential real property securing a mortgage loan is not located in a State, the loan is not a federally related mortgage loan.

Good faith estimate or GFE means an estimate of settlement charges a borrower is likely to incur, as a dollar amount, and related loan information, based upon common practice and experience in the locality of the mortgaged property, as provided on the form prescribed in § 1024.7 and prepared in accordance with the Instructions in appendix C to this part.

HUD means the Department of Housing and Urban Development.

HUD-1 or HUD-1A settlement statement (also *HUD-1 or HUD-1A*) means the statement that is prescribed in this part for setting forth settlement charges in connection with either the purchase or the refinancing (or other subordinate lien transaction) of 1- to 4-family residential property.

Lender means, generally, the secured creditor or creditors named in the debt obligation and document creating the lien. For loans originated by a mortgage broker that closes a federally related mortgage loan in its own name in a table funding transaction, the lender is the person to whom the obligation is initially assigned at or after settlement. A lender, in connection with dealer loans, is the lender to whom the loan is assigned, unless the dealer meets the definition of creditor as defined under "federally related mortgage loan" in this section. See also § 1024.5(b)(7), secondary market transactions.

Loan originator means a lender or mortgage broker.

Manufactured home is defined in HUD regulation 24 CFR 3280.2.

Mortgage broker means a person (other than an employee of a lender) that renders origination services and serves as an intermediary between a borrower and a lender in a transaction involving a federally related mortgage loan, including such a person that closes the loan in its own name in a table-funded transaction.

Mortgaged property means the real property that is security for the federally related mortgage loan.

Origination service means any service involved in the creation of a federally related mortgage loan, including but not limited to the taking of the loan application, loan processing, the underwriting and funding of the loan, and the processing and administrative services required to perform those functions.

Person is defined in section 3(5) of RESPA (12 U.S.C. 2602(5)).

Prepayment penalty has the same meaning as "prepayment penalty" under Regulation Z (12 CFR part 1026).

Public Guidance Documents means Federal Register documents adopted or published, that the Bureau may amend from time-to-time by publication in the Federal Register. These documents are also available from the Bureau. Requests for copies of Public Guidance Documents should be directed to the Associate Director, Research, Markets and Regulations, Bureau of Consumer Financial Protection, 1700 G Street, NW, Washington, DC 20552.

Refinancing means a transaction in which an existing obligation that was subject to a secured lien on residential real property is satisfied and replaced by a new obligation undertaken by the same borrower and with the same or a new lender. The following shall not be treated as a refinancing, even when the existing obligation is satisfied and replaced by a new obligation with the same lender (this definition of "refinancing" as to transactions with the same lender is similar to Regulation Z, 12 CFR 1026.20(a)):

(1) A renewal of a single payment obligation with no change in the original terms;

(2) A reduction in the annual percentage rate as computed under the Truth in Lending Act with a corresponding change in the payment schedule;

(3) An agreement involving a court proceeding;

(4) A workout agreement, in which a change in the payment schedule or change in collateral requirements is agreed to as a result of the consumer's default or delinquency, unless the rate is increased or the new amount financed exceeds the unpaid balance plus earned finance charges and premiums for continuation of allowable insurance; and

(5) The renewal of optional insurance purchased by the consumer that is added to an existing transaction, if disclosures relating to the initial purchase were provided.

Regulation Z means the regulations issued by the Bureau (12 CFR part 1026) to implement the Federal Truth in Lending Act (15 U.S.C. 1601 *et seq.*), and includes the Commentary on Regulation Z.

Required use means a situation in which a person must use a particular provider of a settlement service in order to have access to some distinct service or property, and the person will pay for the settlement service of the particular provider or will pay a charge attributable, in whole or in part, to the settlement service. However, the offering of a package (or combination of settlement services) or the offering of discounts or rebates to consumers for the purchase of multiple settlement services does not constitute a required use. Any package or discount must be optional to the purchaser. The discount must be a true discount below the prices that are otherwise generally available, and must not be made up by higher costs elsewhere in the settlement process.

RESPA means the Real Estate Settlement Procedures Act of 1974 (12 U.S.C. 2601 *et seq.*).

Servicer means a person responsible for the servicing of a federally related mortgage loan (including the person who makes or holds such loan if such person also services the loan). The term does not include:

(1) The Federal Deposit Insurance Corporation (FDIC), in connection with assets acquired, assigned, sold, or transferred pursuant to section 13(c) of the Federal Deposit Insurance Act or as receiver or conservator of an insured depository institution;

(2) The National Credit Union Administration (NCUA), in connection with assets acquired, assigned, sold, or transferred pursuant to section 208 of the Federal Credit Union Act or as conservator or liquidating agent of an insured credit union; and

(3) The Federal National Mortgage Corporation (FNMA); the Federal Home Loan Mortgage Corporation (Freddie Mac); the FDIC; HUD, including the Government National Mortgage Association (GNMA) and the Federal Housing Administration (FHA) (including cases in which a mortgage insured under the National Housing Act (12 U.S.C. 1701 *et seq.*) is assigned to HUD); the NCUA; the Farm Service Agency; and the Department of Veterans Affairs (VA), in any case in which the assignment, sale, or transfer of the servicing of the federally related mortgage loan is preceded by termination of the contract for servicing the loan for cause, commencement of proceedings for bankruptcy of the servicer, commencement of proceedings by the FDIC for conservatorship or receivership of the servicer (or an entity by which the servicer is owned or controlled), or commencement of proceedings by the NCUA for appointment of a conservator or liquidating agent of the servicer (or an entity by which the servicer is owned or controlled).

Servicing means receiving any scheduled periodic payments from a borrower pursuant to the terms of any federally related mortgage loan, including amounts for escrow accounts under section 10 of RESPA (12 U.S.C. 2609), and making the payments to the owner of the loan or other third parties of principal and interest and such other payments with respect to the amounts received from the borrower as may be required pursuant to the terms of the mortgage servicing loan documents or servicing contract. In the case of a home equity conversion mortgage or reverse mortgage as referenced in this section, servicing includes making payments to the borrower.

Settlement means the process of executing legally binding documents regarding a lien on property that is subject to a federally related mortgage loan. This process may also be called "closing" or "escrow" in different jurisdictions.

Settlement service means any service provided in connection with a prospective or actual settlement, including, but not limited to, any one or more of the following:

(1) Origination of a federally related mortgage loan (including, but not limited to, the taking of loan applications, loan processing, and the underwriting and funding of such loans);

(2) Rendering of services by a mortgage broker (including counseling, taking of applications, obtaining verifications and appraisals, and other loan processing and origination services, and communicating with the borrower and lender);

(3) Provision of any services related to the origination, processing or funding of a federally related mortgage loan;

(4) Provision of title services, including title searches, title examinations, abstract preparation, insurability determinations, and the issuance of title commitments and title insurance policies;

(5) Rendering of services by an attorney;

(6) Preparation of documents, including notarization, delivery, and recordation;

(7) Rendering of credit reports and appraisals;

(8) Rendering of inspections, including inspections required by applicable law or any inspections required by the sales contract or mortgage documents prior to transfer of title;

(9) Conducting of settlement by a settlement agent and any related services;

(10) Provision of services involving mortgage insurance;

(11) Provision of services involving hazard, flood, or other casualty insurance or homeowner's warranties;

(12) Provision of services involving mortgage life, disability, or similar insurance designed to pay a mortgage loan upon disability or death of a borrower, but only if such insurance is required by the lender as a condition of the loan;

(13) Provision of services involving real property taxes or any other assessments or charges on the real property;

(14) Rendering of services by a real estate agent or real estate broker; and

(15) Provision of any other services for which a settlement service provider requires a borrower or seller to pay.

Special information booklet means the booklet adopted pursuant to section 5 of RESPA (12 U.S.C. 2604) to help persons understand the nature and costs of settlement services. The Bureau publishes the form of the special information booklet in the Federal Register or by other public notice. The Bureau may issue or approve additional booklets or alternative booklets by publication of a Notice in the Federal Register .

State means any state of the United States, the District of Columbia, the Commonwealth of Puerto Rico, and any territory or possession of the United States.

Table funding means a settlement at which a loan is funded by a contemporaneous advance of loan funds and an assignment of the loan to the person advancing the funds. A table-funded transaction is not a secondary market transaction (see § 1024.5(b)(7)).

Third party means a settlement service provider other than a loan originator.

Title company means any institution, or its duly authorized agent, that is qualified to issue title insurance.

Title service means any service involved in the provision of title insurance (lender's or owner's policy), including but not limited to: Title examination and evaluation; preparation and issuance of title commitment; clearance of underwriting objections; preparation and issuance of a title insurance policy or policies; and the processing and administrative services required to perform these functions. The term also includes the service of conducting a settlement.

Tolerance means the maximum amount by which the charge for a category or categories of settlement costs may exceed the amount of the estimate for such category or categories on a GFE.

§ 1024.3. E-Sign applicability

The disclosures required by this part may be provided in electronic form, subject to compliance with the consumer consent and other applicable provisions of the Electronic Signatures in Global and National Commerce Act (E-Sign Act) (15 U.S.C. 7001 *et seq.*).

§ 1024.4. Reliance upon rule, regulation or interpretation by the Bureau

(a) Rule, regulation or interpretation.

(1) For purposes of sections 19(a) and (b) of RESPA (12 U.S.C. 2617(a) and (b)), only the following constitute a rule, regulation or interpretation of the Bureau:

(i) All provisions, including appendices and supplements, of this part. Any other document referred to in this part is not incorporated in this part unless it is specifically set out in this part;

(ii) Any other document that is published in the *Federal Register* by the Bureau and states that it is an "interpretation," "interpretive rule," "commentary," or a "statement of policy" for purposes of section 19(a) of RESPA. Except in unusual circumstances, interpretations will not be issued separately but will be incorporated in an official interpretation to this part, which will be amended periodically.

(2) A "rule, regulation, or interpretation thereof by the Bureau" for purposes of section 19(b) of RESPA (12 U.S.C. 2617(b)) shall not include the special information booklet prescribed by the Bureau or any other statement or issuance, whether oral or written, by an officer or representative of the Bureau, letter or memorandum by the Director, General Counsel, or other officer or employee of the Bureau, preamble to a regulation or other issuance of the Bureau, Public Guidance Document, report to Congress, pleading, affidavit or other document in litigation, pamphlet, handbook, guide, telegraphic communication, explanation, instructions to forms, speech or other material of any nature which is not specifically included in paragraph (a)(1) of this section.

(b) All informal counsel's opinions and staff interpretations issued by HUD before November 2, 1992, were withdrawn as of that date. Courts and administrative agencies, however, may use previous opinions to determine the validity of conduct under the previous Regulation X.

§ 1024.5. Coverage of RESPA

(a) Applicability. RESPA and this part apply to all federally related mortgage loans, except as provided in paragraphs (b) and (d) of this section.

(b) Exemptions.

(1) [Reserved]

(2) Business purpose loans. An extension of credit primarily for a business, commercial, or agricultural purpose, as defined by 12 CFR 1026.3(a)(1) of Regulation Z. Persons may rely on Regulation Z in determining whether the exemption applies.

(3) Temporary financing. Temporary financing, such as a construction loan. The exemption for temporary financing does not apply to a loan made to finance construction of 1- to 4-family residential property if the loan is used as, or may be converted to, permanent financing by the same lender or is used to finance transfer of title to the first user. If a lender issues a commitment for permanent financing, with or without conditions, the loan is covered by this part. Any construction loan for new or rehabilitated 1- to 4-family residential property, other than a loan to a *bona fide* builder (a person who regularly constructs 1- to 4-family residential structures for sale or lease), is subject to this part if its term is for two years or more. A "bridge loan" or "swing loan" in which a lender takes a security interest in otherwise covered 1- to 4-family residential property is not covered by RESPA and this part.

(4) Vacant land. Any loan secured by vacant or unimproved property, unless within two years from the date of the settlement of the loan, a structure or a manufactured home will be constructed or placed on the real property using the loan proceeds. If a loan for a structure or manufactured home to be placed on vacant or unimproved property will be secured by a lien on that property, the transaction is covered by this part.

(5) Assumption without lender approval. Any assumption in which the lender does not have the right expressly to approve a subsequent person as the borrower on an existing federally related mortgage loan. Any assumption in which the lender's permission is both required and obtained is covered by RESPA and this part, whether or not the lender charges a fee for the assumption.

(6) Loan conversions. Any conversion of a federally related mortgage loan to different terms that are consistent with provisions of the original mortgage instrument, as long as a new note is not required, even if the lender charges an additional fee for the conversion.

(7) Secondary market transactions. A bona fide transfer of a loan obligation in the secondary market is not covered by RESPA and this part, except with respect to RESPA (12 U.S.C. 2605) and subpart C of this part (§§ 1024.30–1024.41). In determining what constitutes a *bona fide* transfer, the Bureau will consider the real source of funding and the real interest of the funding lender. Mortgage broker transactions that are table-funded are not secondary market transactions. Neither the creation of a dealer loan or dealer consumer credit contract, nor the first assignment of such loan or contract to a lender, is a secondary market transaction (see § 1024.2).

(c) Relation to State laws.

(1) State laws that are inconsistent with RESPA or this part are preempted to the extent of the inconsistency. However, RESPA and these regulations do not annul, alter, affect, or exempt any person subject to their provisions from complying with the laws of any State with respect to settlement practices, except to the extent of the inconsistency.

(2) Upon request by any person, the Bureau is authorized to determine if inconsistencies with State law exist; in doing so, the Bureau shall consult with appropriate Federal agencies.

(i) The Bureau may not determine that a State law or regulation is inconsistent with any provision of RESPA or this part, if the Bureau determines that such law or regulation gives greater protection to the consumer.

(ii) In determining whether provisions of State law or regulations concerning affiliated business arrangements are inconsistent with RESPA or this part, the Bureau may not construe those provisions that impose more stringent limitations on affiliated business arrangements as inconsistent with RESPA so long as they give more protection to consumers and/or competition.

(3) Any person may request the Bureau to determine whether an inconsistency exists by submitting to the address established by the Bureau to request an official interpretation, a copy of the State law in question, any other law or judicial or administrative opinion that implements, interprets or applies the relevant provision, and an explanation of the possible inconsistency. A determination by the Bureau that an inconsistency with State law exists will be made by publication of a notice in the Federal Register. "Law" as used in this section includes regulations and any enactment which has the force and effect of law and is issued by a State or any political subdivision of a State.

(4) A specific preemption of conflicting State laws regarding notices and disclosures of mortgage servicing transfers is set forth in § 1024.33(d).

(d) Partial exemptions for certain mortgage loans. Sections 1024.6, 1024.7, 1024.8, 1024.10, and 1024.33(a) do not apply to a federally related mortgage loan:

(1) That is subject to the special disclosure requirements for certain consumer credit transactions secured by real property set forth in Regulation Z, 12 CFR 1026.19(e), (f), and (g); or

(2) That satisfies the criteria in Regulation Z, 12 CFR 1026.3(h).

§ 1024.6. Special information booklet at time of loan application

(a) Lender to provide special information booklet. Subject to the exceptions set forth in this paragraph, the lender shall provide a copy of the special information booklet to a person from whom the lender receives, or for whom the lender prepares, a written application for a federally related mortgage loan. When two or more persons apply together for a loan, the lender is in compliance if the lender provides a copy of the booklet to one of the persons applying.

(1) The lender shall provide the special information booklet by delivering it or placing it in the mail to the applicant not later than three business days (as that term is defined in § 1024.2) after the application is received or prepared. However, if the lender denies the borrower's application for credit before the end of the three-business-day period, then the lender need not provide the booklet to the borrower. If a borrower uses a mortgage broker, the mortgage broker shall distribute the special information booklet and the lender need not do so. The intent of this provision is that the applicant receive the special information booklet at the earliest possible date.

(2) In the case of a federally related mortgage loan involving an open-ended credit plan, as defined in Regulation Z, 12 CFR 1026.2(a)(20), a lender or mortgage broker that provides the borrower with a copy of the brochure entitled "When Your Home is On the Line: What You Should Know About Home Equity Lines of Credit", or any successor brochure issued by the Bureau, is deemed to be in compliance with this section.

(3) In the categories of transactions set forth at the end of this paragraph, the lender or mortgage broker does not have to provide the booklet to the borrower. Under the authority of section 19(a) of RESPA (12 U.S.C. 2617(a)), the Bureau may issue a revised or separate special information booklet that deals with these transactions, or the Bureau may choose to endorse the forms or booklets of other Federal agencies. In such an event, the requirements for delivery by lenders and the availability of the booklet or alternate materials for these transactions will be set forth in a Notice in the Federal Register. This paragraph shall apply to the following transactions:

(i) Refinancing transactions;

(ii) Closed-end loans, as defined in 12 CFR 1026.2(a)(10) of Regulation Z, when the lender takes a subordinate lien;

(iii) Reverse mortgages; and

(iv) Any other federally related mortgage loan whose purpose is not the purchase of a 1- to 4-family residential property.

(b) Revision. The Bureau may from time to time revise the special information booklet, publishing a notice in the Federal Register .

(c) Reproduction. The special information booklet may be reproduced in any form, provided that no change is made other than as provided under paragraph (d) of this section. The special information booklet may not be made a part of a larger document for purposes of distribution under

RESPA and this section. Any color, size and quality of paper, type of print, and method of reproduction may be used so long as the booklet is clearly legible.

(d) Permissible changes.

(1) No changes to, deletions from, or additions to the special information booklet currently prescribed by the Bureau shall be made other than the permissible changes specified in paragraphs (d)(2) and (3) of this section or changes as otherwise approved in writing by the Bureau in accordance with the procedures described in this paragraph (d). A request to the Bureau for approval of any changes other than the permissible changes specified in paragraphs (d)(2) and (3) of this section shall be submitted in writing to the address indicated in the definition of Public Guidance Documents in § 1024.2, stating the reasons why the applicant believes such changes, deletions, or additions are necessary.

(2) The cover of the booklet may be in any form and may contain any drawings, pictures or artwork, provided that the words "settlement costs" are used in the title. Names, addresses and telephone numbers of the lender or others and similar information may appear on the cover, but no discussion of the matters covered in the booklet shall appear on the cover. References to HUD on the cover of the booklet may be changed to references to the Bureau.

(3) The special information booklet may be translated into languages other than English.

§ 1024.7. Good faith estimate

(a) Lender to provide.

(1) Except as otherwise provided in paragraphs (a), (b), or (h) of this section, not later than 3 business days after a lender receives an application, or information sufficient to complete an application, the lender must provide the applicant with a GFE. In the case of dealer loans, the lender must either provide the GFE or ensure that the dealer provides the GFE.

(2) The lender must provide the GFE to the loan applicant by hand delivery, by placing it in the mail, or, if the applicant agrees, by fax, email, or other electronic means.

(3) The lender is not required to provide the applicant with a GFE if, before the end of the 3-business-day period:

(i) The lender denies the application; or

(ii) The applicant withdraws the application.

(4) The lender is not permitted to charge, as a condition for providing a GFE, any fee for an appraisal, inspection, or other similar settlement service. The lender may, at its option, charge a fee limited to the cost of a credit report. The lender may not charge additional fees until after the applicant has received the GFE and indicated an intention to proceed with the loan covered by that GFE. If the GFE is mailed to the applicant, the applicant is considered to have received the GFE 3 calendar days after it is mailed, not including Sundays and the legal public holidays specified in 5 U.S.C. 6103(a).

(5) The lender may at any time collect from the loan applicant any information that it requires in addition to the required application information. However, the lender is not permitted to require, as a condition for providing a GFE, that an applicant submit supplemental documentation to verify the information provided on the application.

(b) Mortgage broker to provide.

(1) Except as otherwise provided in paragraphs (a), (b), or (h) of this section, either the lender or the mortgage broker must provide a GFE not later than 3 business days after a mortgage broker receives either an application or information sufficient to complete an application. The lender is responsible for ascertaining whether the GFE has been provided. If the mortgage broker has provided a GFE, the lender is not required to provide an additional GFE.

(2) The mortgage broker must provide the GFE by hand delivery, by placing it in the mail, or, if the applicant agrees, by fax, email, or other electronic means.

(3) The mortgage broker is not required to provide the applicant with a GFE if, before the end of the 3-business-day period:

(i) The mortgage broker or lender denies the application; or

(ii) The applicant withdraws the application.

(4) The mortgage broker is not permitted to charge, as a condition for providing a GFE, any fee for an appraisal, inspection, or other similar settlement service. The mortgage broker may, at its option, charge a fee limited to the cost of a credit report. The mortgage broker may not charge additional fees until after the applicant has received the GFE and indicated an intention to proceed with the loan covered by that GFE. If the GFE is mailed to the applicant, the applicant is considered to have received the GFE 3 calendar days after it is mailed, not including Sundays and the legal public holidays specified in 5 U.S.C. 6103(a).

(5) The mortgage broker may at any time collect from the loan applicant any information that it requires in addition to the required application information. However, the mortgage broker is not permitted to require, as a condition for providing a GFE, that an applicant submit supplemental documentation to verify the information provided on the application.

(c) Availability of GFE terms. Except as provided in this paragraph, the estimate of the charges and terms for all settlement services must be available for at least 10 business days from when the GFE is provided, but it may remain available longer, if the loan originator extends the period of availability. The estimate for the following charges are excepted from this requirement: the interest rate, charges and terms dependent upon the interest rate, which includes the charge or credit for the interest rate chosen, the adjusted origination charges, and per diem interest.

(d) Content and form of GFE. The GFE form is set out in appendix C to this part. The loan originator must prepare the GFE in accordance with the requirements of this section and the Instructions in appendix C to this part. The instructions in appendix C to this part allow for flexibility in the preparation and distribution of the GFE in hard copy and electronic format.

(e) Tolerances for amounts included on GFE.

(1) Except as provided in paragraph (f) of this section, the actual charges at settlement may not exceed the amounts included on the GFE for:

(i) The origination charge;

(ii) While the borrower's interest rate is locked, the credit or charge for the interest rate chosen;

(iii) While the borrower's interest rate is locked, the adjusted origination charge; and

(iv) Transfer taxes.

(2) Except as provided in paragraph (f) of this section, the sum of the charges at settlement for the following services may not be greater than 10 percent above the sum of the amounts included on the GFE:

(i) Lender-required settlement services, where the lender selects the third party settlement service provider;

(ii) Lender-required services, title services and required title insurance, and owner's title insurance, when the borrower uses a settlement service provider identified by the loan originator; and

(iii) Government recording charges.

(3) The amounts charged for all other settlement services included on the GFE may change at settlement.

(f) Binding GFE. The loan originator is bound, within the tolerances provided in paragraph (e) of this section, to the settlement charges and terms listed on the GFE provided to the borrower, unless a revised GFE is provided prior to settlement consistent with this paragraph (f) or the GFE expires in accordance with paragraph (f)(4) of this section. If a loan originator provides a revised GFE consistent with this paragraph, the loan originator must document the reason that a revised GFE was provided. Loan originators must retain documentation of any reason for providing a revised GFE for no less than 3 years after settlement.

(1) Changed circumstances affecting settlement costs. If changed circumstances result in increased costs for any settlement services such that the charges at settlement would exceed the tolerances for those charges, the loan originator may provide a revised GFE to the borrower. If a revised GFE is to be provided, the loan originator must do so within 3 business days of receiving information sufficient to establish changed circumstances. The revised GFE may increase charges for services listed on the GFE only to the extent that the changed circumstances actually resulted in higher charges.

(2) Changed circumstances affecting loan. If changed circumstances result in a change in the borrower's eligibility for the specific loan terms identified in the GFE, the loan originator may provide a revised GFE to the borrower. If a revised GFE is to be provided, the loan originator must do so within 3 business days of receiving information sufficient to establish changed circumstances. The revised GFE may increase charges for services listed on the GFE only to the extent that the changed circumstances affecting the loan actually resulted in higher charges.

(3) Borrower requested changes. If a borrower requests changes to the federally related mortgage loan identified in the GFE that change the settlement charges or the terms of the loan, the loan originator may provide a revised GFE to the borrower. If a revised GFE is to be provided, the loan originator must do so within three business days of the borrower's request. The revised GFE may increase charges for services listed on the GFE only to the extent that the borrower-requested changes to the mortgage loan identified on the GFE actually resulted in higher charges.

(4) Expiration of GFE. If a borrower does not express an intent to continue with an application within 10 business days after the GFE is provided, or such longer time specified by the loan originator pursuant to paragraph (c) of this section, the loan originator is no longer bound by the GFE.

(5) Interest rate-dependent charges and terms. If the interest rate has not been locked, or a locked interest rate has expired, the charge or credit for the interest rate chosen, the adjusted origination charges, per diem interest, and loan terms related to the interest rate may change. When the interest rate is later locked, a revised GFE must be provided showing the revised interest rate-dependent charges and terms. The loan originator must provide the revised GFE within 3 business days of the interest rate being locked or, for an expired interest rate, re-locked. All other charges and terms must remain the same as on the original GFE, except as otherwise provided in paragraph (f) of this section.

(6) New construction home purchases. In transactions involving new construction home purchases, where settlement is anticipated to occur more than 60 calendar days from the time a GFE is provided, the loan originator may provide the GFE to the borrower with a clear and conspicuous disclosure stating that at any time up until 60 calendar days prior to closing, the loan originator may issue a revised GFE. If no such separate disclosure is provided, the loan originator cannot issue a revised GFE, except as otherwise provided in paragraph (f) of this section.

(g) GFE is not a loan commitment. Nothing in this section shall be interpreted to require a loan originator to make a loan to a particular borrower. The loan originator is not required to provide a GFE if the loan originator does not have available a loan for which the borrower is eligible.

(h) Open-end lines of credit (home-equity plans) under Truth in Lending Act. In the case of a federally related mortgage loan involving an open-end line of credit (home-equity plan) covered under the Truth in Lending Act and Regulation Z, a lender or mortgage broker that provides the borrower with the disclosures required by 12 CFR 1026.40 of Regulation Z at the time the borrower applies for such loan shall be deemed to satisfy the requirements of this section.

(i) Violations of section 5 of RESPA (12 U.S.C. 2604). A loan originator that violates the requirements of this section shall be deemed to have violated section 5 of RESPA. If any charges at settlement exceed the charges listed on the GFE by more than the permitted tolerances, the loan originator may cure the tolerance violation by reimbursing to the borrower the amount by which the tolerance was exceeded, at settlement or within 30 calendar days after settlement. A borrower will be deemed to have received timely reimbursement if the loan originator delivers or places the payment in the mail within 30 calendar days after settlement.

§ 1024.8. Use of HUD-1 or HUD-1A settlement statements

(a) Use by settlement agent. The settlement agent shall use the HUD-1 settlement statement in every settlement involving a federally related mortgage loan in which there is a borrower and a seller. For transactions in which there is a borrower and no seller, such as refinancing loans or subordinate lien loans, the HUD-1 may be utilized by using the borrower's side of the HUD-1 statement. Alternatively, the form HUD-1A may be used for these transactions. The HUD-1 or HUD-1A may be modified as permitted under this part. Either the HUD-1 or the HUD-1A, as appropriate, shall be used for every RESPA-covered transaction, unless its use is specifically exempted. The use of the HUD-1 or HUD-1A is exempted for open-end lines of credit (home-equity plans) covered by the Truth in Lending Act and Regulation Z.

(b) Charges to be stated. The settlement agent shall complete the HUD-1 or HUD-1A, in accordance with the instructions set forth in appendix A to this part. The loan originator must transmit to the settlement agent all information necessary to complete the HUD-1 or HUD-1A.

(1) In general. The settlement agent shall state the actual charges paid by the borrower and seller on the HUD-1, or by the borrower on the HUD-1A. The settlement agent must separately itemize each third party charge paid by the borrower and seller. All origination services performed by or on behalf of the loan originator must be included in the loan originator's own charge. Administrative and processing services related to title services must be included in the title underwriter's or title agent's own charge. The amount stated on the HUD-1 or HUD-1A for any itemized service cannot exceed the amount actually received by the settlement service provider for that itemized service, unless the charge is an average charge in accordance with paragraph (b)(2) of this section.

(2) Use of average charge.

(i) The average charge for a settlement service shall be no more than the average amount paid for a settlement service by one settlement service provider to another settlement service provider on behalf of borrowers and sellers for a particular class of transactions involving federally related mortgage loans. The total amounts paid by borrowers and sellers for a settlement service based on the use of an average charge may not exceed the total amounts paid to the providers of that service for the particular class of transactions.

(ii) The settlement service provider shall define the particular class of transactions for purposes of calculating the average charge as all transactions involving federally related mortgage loans for:

(A) A period of time as determined by the settlement service provider, but not less than 30 calendar days and not more than 6 months;

(B) A geographic area as determined by the settlement service provider; and

(C) A type of loan as determined by the settlement service provider.

(iii) A settlement service provider may use an average charge in the same class of transactions for which the charge was calculated. If the settlement service provider uses the average charge for any transaction in the class, the settlement service provider must use the same average charge in every transaction within that class for which a GFE was provided.

(iv) The use of an average charge is not permitted for any settlement service if the charge for the service is based on the loan amount or property value. For example, an average charge may not be used for transfer taxes, interest charges, reserves or escrow, or any type of insurance, including mortgage insurance, title insurance, or hazard insurance.

(v) The settlement service provider must retain all documentation used to calculate the average charge for a particular class of transactions for at least 3 years after any settlement for which that average charge was used.

(c) Violations of section 4 of RESPA (12 U.S.C. 2603). A violation of any of the requirements of this section will be deemed to be a violation of section 4 of RESPA. An inadvertent or technical error in completing the HUD-1 or HUD-1A shall not be deemed a violation of section 4 of RESPA if a revised HUD-1 or HUD-1A is provided in accordance with the requirements of this section within 30 calendar days after settlement.

§ 1024.9. Reproduction of settlement statements

(a) Permissible changes—HUD-1. The following changes and insertions are permitted when the HUD-1 settlement statement is reproduced:

(1) The person reproducing the HUD-1 may insert its business name and logo in section A and may rearrange, but not delete, the other information that appears in section A.

(2) The name, address, and other information regarding the lender and settlement agent may be printed in sections F and H, respectively.

(3) Reproduction of the HUD-1 must conform to the terminology, sequence, and numbering of line items as presented in lines 100–1400. However, blank lines or items listed in lines 100–1400 that are not used locally or in connection with mortgages by the lender may be deleted, except for the following: Lines 100, 120, 200, 220, 300, 301, 302, 303, 400, 420, 500, 520, 600, 601, 602, 603, 700, 800, 900, 1000, 1100, 1200, 1300, and 1400. The form may be shortened correspondingly. The number of a deleted item shall not be used for a substitute or new item, but the number of a blank space on the HUD-1 may be used for a substitute or new item.

(4) Charges not listed on the HUD-1, but that are customary locally or pursuant to the lender's practice, may be inserted in blank spaces. Where existing blank spaces on the HUD-1 are insufficient, additional lines and spaces may be added and numbered in sequence with spaces on the HUD-1.

(5) The following variations in layout and format are within the discretion of persons reproducing the HUD-1 and do not require prior Bureau approval: Size of pages; tint or color of pages; size and style of type or print; vertical spacing between lines or provision for additional horizontal space on lines (for example, to provide sufficient space for recording time periods used in prorations); printing of the HUD-1 contents on separate pages, on the front and back of a single page, or on one continuous page; use of multicopy tear-out sets; printing on rolls for computer purposes; reorganization of sections B through I, when necessary to accommodate computer printing; and manner of placement of the HUD number, but not the OMB approval number, neither of which may be deleted. The expiration date associated with the OMB number listed on the form may be deleted. Any changes in the HUD number or OMB approval number may be announced by notice in the Federal Register, rather than by amendment of this part.

(6) The borrower's information and the seller's information may be provided on separate pages.

(7) Signature lines may be added.

(8) The HUD-1 may be translated into languages other than English.

(9) An additional page may be attached to the HUD-1 for the purpose of including customary recitals and information used locally in real estate settlements; for example, breakdown of payoff figures, a breakdown of the borrower's total monthly mortgage payments, check disbursements, a statement indicating receipt of funds, applicable special stipulations between buyer and seller, and the date funds are transferred. If space permits, such information may be added at the end of the HUD-1.

(10) As required by HUD/FHA in FHA-insured loans.

(11) As allowed by § 1024.17, relating to an initial escrow account statement.

(b) Permissible changes—HUD-1A. The changes and insertions on the HUD-1 permitted under paragraph (a) of this section are also permitted when the HUD-1A settlement statement is reproduced, except the changes described in paragraphs (a)(3) and (6) of this section.

(c) Written approval. Any other deviation in the HUD-1 or HUD-1A forms is permissible only upon receipt of written approval of the Bureau; provided, however, that notwithstanding contrary instructions in this section or appendix A of this part, reproducing the HUD-1 or HUD-1A forms with the Bureau's OMB approval number displayed in place of HUD's OMB approval number does not require the written approval of the Bureau. A request to the Bureau for approval shall be submitted in writing to the address indicated in the definition of Public Guidance Documents in § 1024.2 and shall state the reasons why the applicant believes such deviation is needed. The prescribed form(s) must be used until approval is received.

§ 1024.10. One-day advance inspection of HUD-1 or HUD-1A settlement statement; delivery; recordkeeping

(a) Inspection one day prior to settlement upon request by the borrower. The settlement agent shall permit the borrower to inspect the HUD-1 or HUD-1A settlement statement, completed to set forth those items that are known to the settlement agent at the time of inspection, during the business day immediately preceding settlement. Items related only to the seller's transaction may be omitted from the HUD-1.

(b) Delivery. The settlement agent shall provide a completed HUD-1 or HUD-1A to the borrower, the seller (if there is one), the lender (if the lender is not the settlement agent), and/or their agents. When the borrower's and seller's copies of the HUD-1 or HUD-1A differ as permitted by the instructions in appendix A to this part, both copies shall be provided to the lender (if the lender is not the settlement agent). The settlement agent shall deliver the completed HUD-1 or HUD-1A at or before the settlement, except as provided in paragraphs (c) and (d) of this section.

(c) Waiver. The borrower may waive the right to delivery of the completed HUD-1 or HUD-1A no later than at settlement by executing a written waiver at or before settlement. In such case, the completed HUD-1 or HUD-1A shall be mailed or delivered to the borrower, seller, and lender (if the lender is not the settlement agent) as soon as practicable after settlement.

(d) Exempt transactions. When the borrower or the borrower's agent does not attend the settlement, or when the settlement agent does not conduct a meeting of the parties for that purpose, the transaction shall be exempt from the requirements of paragraphs (a) and (b) of this section, except that the HUD-1 or HUD-1A shall be mailed or delivered as soon as practicable after settlement.

(e) Recordkeeping. The lender shall retain each completed HUD-1 or HUD-1A and related documents for five years after settlement, unless the lender disposes of its interest in the mortgage and does not service the mortgage. In that case, the lender shall provide its copy of the HUD-1 or HUD-1A to the owner or servicer of the mortgage as a part of the transfer of the loan file. Such owner or servicer shall retain the HUD-1 or HUD-1A for the remainder of the five-year period. The Bureau shall have the right to inspect or require copies of records covered by this paragraph (e).

§ 1024.11. Mailing

The provisions of this part requiring or permitting mailing of documents shall be deemed to be satisfied by placing the document in the mail (whether or not received by the addressee) addressed to the addresses stated in the loan application or in other information submitted to or obtained by the lender at the time of loan application or submitted or obtained by the lender or settlement agent, except that a revised address shall be used where the lender or settlement agent has been expressly informed in writing of a change in address.

§ 1024.12. No fee

No fee shall be imposed or charge made upon any other person, as a part of settlement costs or otherwise, by a lender in connection with a federally related mortgage loan made by it (or a loan for the purchase of a manufactured home), or by a servicer (as that term is defined under 12 U.S.C. 2605(i)(2)) for or on account of the preparation and distribution of the HUD-1 or HUD-1A settlement statement, escrow account statements required pursuant to section 10 of RESPA (12 U.S.C. 2609), or statements required by the Truth in Lending Act (15 U.S.C. 1601 *et seq.*).

§ 1024.13. [Reserved]

§ 1024.14. Prohibition against kickbacks and unearned fees

(a) Section 8 violation. Any violation of this section is a violation of section 8 of RESPA (12 U.S.C. 2607).

(b) No referral fees. No person shall give and no person shall accept any fee, kickback or other thing of value pursuant to any agreement or understanding, oral or otherwise, that business incident to or part of a settlement service involving a federally related mortgage loan shall be referred to any person. Any referral of a settlement service is not a compensable service, except as set forth in § 1024.14(g)(1). A company may not pay any other company or the employees of any other company for the referral of settlement service business.

(c) No split of charges except for actual services performed. No person shall give and no person shall accept any portion, split, or percentage of any charge made or received for the rendering of a settlement service in connection with a transaction involving a federally related mortgage loan other than for services actually performed. A charge by a person for which no or nominal services are performed or for which duplicative fees are charged is an unearned fee and violates this section. The source of the payment does not determine whether or not a service is compensable. Nor may the prohibitions of this part be avoided by creating an arrangement wherein the purchaser of services splits the fee.

(d) Thing of value. This term is broadly defined in section 3(2) of RESPA (12 U.S.C. 2602(2)). It includes, without limitation, monies, things, discounts, salaries, commissions, fees, duplicate payments of a charge, stock, dividends, distributions of partnership profits, franchise royalties, credits representing monies that may be paid at a future date, the opportunity to participate in a money-making program, retained or increased earnings, increased equity in a parent or subsidiary entity, special bank deposits or accounts, special or unusual banking terms, services of all types at special or free rates, sales or rentals at special prices or rates, lease or rental payments based in whole or in part on the amount of business referred, trips and payment of another person's expenses, or reduction in credit against an existing obligation. The term "payment" is used throughout §§ 1024.14 and 1024.15

as synonymous with the giving or receiving of any "thing of value" and does not require transfer of money.

(e) Agreement or understanding. An agreement or understanding for the referral of business incident to or part of a settlement service need not be written or verbalized but may be established by a practice, pattern or course of conduct. When a thing of value is received repeatedly and is connected in any way with the volume or value of the business referred, the receipt of the thing of value is evidence that it is made pursuant to an agreement or understanding for the referral of business.

(f) Referral.

(1) A referral includes any oral or written action directed to a person which has the effect of affirmatively influencing the selection by any person of a provider of a settlement service or business incident to or part of a settlement service when such person will pay for such settlement service or business incident thereto or pay a charge attributable in whole or in part to such settlement service or business.

(2) A referral also occurs whenever a person paying for a settlement service or business incident thereto is required to use (see § 1024.2, "required use") a particular provider of a settlement service or business incident thereto.

(g) Fees, salaries, compensation, or other payments.

(1) Section 8 of RESPA permits:

(i) A payment to an attorney at law for services actually rendered;

(ii) A payment by a title company to its duly appointed agent for services actually performed in the issuance of a policy of title insurance;

(iii) A payment by a lender to its duly appointed agent or contractor for services actually performed in the origination, processing, or funding of a loan;

(iv) A payment to any person of a *bona fide* salary or compensation or other payment for goods or facilities actually furnished or for services actually performed;

(v) A payment pursuant to cooperative brokerage and referral arrangements or agreements between real estate agents and real estate brokers. (The statutory exemption restated in this paragraph refers only to fee divisions within real estate brokerage arrangements when all parties are acting in a real estate brokerage capacity, and has no applicability to any fee arrangements between real estate brokers and mortgage brokers or between mortgage brokers.);

(vi) Normal promotional and educational activities that are not conditioned on the referral of business and that do not involve the defraying of expenses that otherwise would be incurred by persons in a position to refer settlement services or business incident thereto; or

(vii) An employer's payment to its own employees for any referral activities.

(2) The Bureau may investigate high prices to see if they are the result of a referral fee or a split of a fee. If the payment of a thing of value bears no reasonable relationship to the market value of the goods or services provided, then the excess is not for services or goods actually performed or provided. These facts may be used as evidence of a violation of section 8 and may serve as a basis for a RESPA investigation. High prices standing alone are not proof of a RESPA violation. The value of a referral (*i.e.*, the value of any additional business obtained thereby) is not to be taken into account in determining whether the payment exceeds the reasonable value of such goods, facilities or services. The fact that the transfer of the thing of value does not result in an increase in any charge made by the person giving the thing of value is irrelevant in determining whether the act is prohibited.

(3) Multiple services. When a person in a position to refer settlement service business, such as an attorney, mortgage lender, real estate broker or agent, or developer or builder, receives a payment for providing additional settlement services as part of a real estate transaction, such payment must be for services that are actual, necessary and distinct from the primary services provided by such person. For example, for an attorney of the buyer or seller to receive compensation as a title agent, the attorney must perform core title agent services (for which liability arises) separate from attorney services, including the evaluation of the title search to determine the insurability of the title, the clearance of underwriting objections, the actual issuance of the policy or policies on behalf of the title insurance company, and, where customary, issuance of the title commitment, and the conducting of the title search and closing.

(h) Recordkeeping. Any documents provided pursuant to this section shall be retained for five (5) years from the date of execution.

(i) Appendix B of this part. Illustrations in appendix B of this part demonstrate some of the requirements of this section.

§ 1024.15. Affiliated business arrangements

(a) General. An affiliated business arrangement is defined in section 3(7) of RESPA (12 U.S.C. 2602(7)).

(b) Violation and exemption. An affiliated business arrangement is not a violation of section 8 of RESPA (12 U.S.C. 2607) and of § 1024.14 if the conditions set forth in this section are satisfied. Paragraph (b)(1) of this section shall not apply to the extent it is inconsistent with section 8(c)(4)(A) of RESPA (12 U.S.C. 2607(c)(4)(A)).

(1) The person making each referral has provided to each person whose business is referred a written disclosure, in the format of the Affiliated Business Arrangement Disclosure Statement set forth in appendix D of this part, of the nature of the relationship (explaining the ownership and financial interest) between the provider of settlement services (or business incident thereto) and the person making the referral and of an estimated charge or range of charges generally made by such provider (which describes the charge using the same terminology, as far as practical, as section L of the HUD-1 settlement statement). The disclosures must be provided on a separate piece of paper no later than the time of each referral or, if the lender requires use of a particular provider, the time of loan application, except that:

(i) Where a lender makes the referral to a borrower, the condition contained in paragraph (b)(1) of this section may be satisfied at the time that the good faith estimate or a statement under § 1024.7(d) is provided; and

(ii) Whenever an attorney or law firm requires a client to use a particular title insurance agent, the attorney or law firm shall provide the disclosures no later than the time the attorney or law firm is engaged by the client.

(iii) Failure to comply with the disclosure requirements of this section may be overcome if the person making a referral can prove by a preponderance of the evidence that procedures reasonably adopted to result in compliance with these conditions have been maintained and that any failure to comply with these conditions was unintentional and the result of a *bona fide* error. An error of legal judgment with respect to a person's obligations under RESPA is not a *bona fide* error. Administrative and judicial interpretations of section 130(c) of the Truth in Lending Act shall not be binding interpretations of the preceding sentence or section 8(d)(3) of RESPA (12 U.S.C. 2607(d)(3)).

(2) No person making a referral has required (as defined in § 1024.2, "required use") any person to use any particular provider of settlement services or business incident thereto, except if such person is a lender, for requiring a buyer, borrower or seller to pay for the services of an attorney, credit reporting agency, or real estate appraiser chosen by the lender to represent the lender's interest in a real estate transaction, or except if such person is an attorney or law firm for arranging for issuance of a title insurance policy for a client, directly as agent or through a separate corporate title insurance agency that may be operated as an adjunct to the law practice of the attorney or law firm, as part of representation of that client in a real estate transaction.

(3) The only thing of value that is received from the arrangement other than payments listed in § 1024.14(g) is a return on an ownership interest or franchise relationship.

(i) In an affiliated business arrangement:

(A) *Bona fide* dividends, and capital or equity distributions, related to ownership interest or franchise relationship, between entities in an affiliate relationship, are permissible; and

(B) *Bona fide* business loans, advances, and capital or equity contributions between entities in an affiliate relationship (in any direction), are not prohibited—so long as they are for ordinary business purposes and are not fees for the referral of settlement service business or unearned fees.

(ii) A return on an ownership interest does not include:

(A) Any payment which has as a basis of calculation no apparent business motive other than distinguishing among recipients of payments on the basis of the amount of their actual, estimated or anticipated referrals;

(B) Any payment which varies according to the relative amount of referrals by the different recipients of similar payments; or

(C) A payment based on an ownership, partnership or joint venture share which has been adjusted on the basis of previous relative referrals by recipients of similar payments.

(iii) Neither the mere labeling of a thing of value, nor the fact that it may be calculated pursuant to a corporate or partnership organizational document or a franchise agreement, will determine whether it is a *bona fide* return on an ownership interest or franchise relationship. Whether a thing of value is such a return will be determined by analyzing facts and circumstances on a case by case basis.

(iv) A return on franchise relationship may be a payment to or from a franchisee but it does not include any payment which is not based on the franchise agreement, nor any payment which varies according to the number or amount of referrals by the franchisor or franchisee or which is based on a franchise agreement which has been adjusted on the basis of a previous number or amount of referrals by the franchiser or franchisees. A franchise agreement may not be constructed to insulate against kickbacks or referral fees.

(c) Definitions. As used in this section:

Associate is defined in section 3(8) of RESPA (12 U.S.C. 2602(8)).

Affiliate relationship means the relationship among business entities where one entity has effective control over the other by virtue of a partnership or other agreement or is under common control with the other by a third entity or where an entity is a corporation related to another corporation as parent to subsidiary by an identity of stock ownership.

Beneficial ownership means the effective ownership of an interest in a provider of settlement services or the right to use and control the ownership interest involved even though legal ownership or title may be held in another person's name.

Control, as used in the definitions of "associate" and "affiliate relationship," means that a person:

(i) Is a general partner, officer, director, or employer of another person;

(ii) Directly or indirectly or acting in concert with others, or through one or more subsidiaries, owns, holds with power to vote, or holds proxies representing, more than 20 percent of the voting interests of another person;

(iii) Affirmatively influences in any manner the election of a majority of the directors of another person; or

(iv) Has contributed more than 20 percent of the capital of the other person.

Direct ownership means the holding of legal title to an interest in a provider of settlement service except where title is being held for the beneficial owner.

Franchise is defined in FTC regulation 16 CFR 436.1(h).

Franchisor is defined in FTC regulation 16 CFR 436.1(k).

Franchisee is defined in FTC regulation 16 CFR 436.1(i).

FTC means the Federal Trade Commission.

Person who is in a position to refer settlement service business means any real estate broker or agent, lender, mortgage broker, builder or developer, attorney, title company, title agent, or other person deriving a significant portion of his or her gross income from providing settlement services.

(d) Recordkeeping. Any documents provided pursuant to this section shall be retained for 5 years after the date of execution.

(e) Appendix B of this part. Illustrations in appendix B of this part demonstrate some of the requirements of this section.

§ 1024.16. Title companies

No seller of property that will be purchased with the assistance of a federally related mortgage loan shall violate section 9 of RESPA (12 U.S.C. 2608). Section 1024.2 defines "required use" of a provider of a settlement service.

§ 1024.20. List of homeownership counseling organizations

(a) Provision of list.

(1) Except as otherwise provided in this section, not later than three business days after a lender, mortgage broker, or dealer receives an application, or information sufficient to complete an application, the lender must provide the loan applicant with a clear and conspicuous written list of homeownership counseling organizations that provide relevant counseling services in the loan applicant's location. The list of homeownership counseling organizations distributed to each loan applicant under this section shall be obtained no earlier than 30 days prior to the time when the list is provided to the loan applicant from either:

(i) The website maintained by the Bureau for lenders to use in complying with the requirements of this section; or

(ii) Data made available by the Bureau or HUD for lenders to use in complying with the requirements of this section, provided that the data is used in accordance with instructions provided with the data.

(2) The list of homeownership counseling organizations provided under this section may be combined and provided with other mortgage loan disclosures required pursuant to Regulation Z, 12 CFR part 1026, or this part unless prohibited by Regulation Z or this part.

(3) A mortgage broker or dealer may provide the list of homeownership counseling organizations required under this section to any loan applicant from whom it receives or for whom it prepares an application. If the mortgage broker or dealer has provided the required list of homeownership counseling organizations, the lender is not required to provide an additional list. The lender is responsible for ensuring that the list of homeownership counseling organizations is provided to a loan applicant in accordance with this section.

(4) If the lender, mortgage broker, or dealer does not provide the list of homeownership counseling organizations required under this section to the loan applicant in person, the lender must mail or deliver the list to the loan applicant by other means. The list may be provided in electronic form, subject to compliance with the consumer consent and other applicable provisions of the Electronic Signatures in Global and National Commerce Act (E-Sign Act), 15 U.S.C. 7001 *et seq*.

(5) The lender is not required to provide the list of homeownership counseling organizations required under this section if, before the end of the three-business-day period provided in paragraph (a)(1) of this section, the lender denies the application or the loan applicant withdraws the application.

(6) If a mortgage loan transaction involves more than one lender, only one list of homeownership counseling organizations required under this section shall be given to the loan applicant and the lenders shall agree among themselves which lender will comply with the requirements that this section imposes on any or all of them. If there is more than one loan applicant, the required list of homeownership counseling organizations may be provided to any loan applicant with primary liability on the mortgage loan obligation.

(b) Open-end lines of credit (home-equity plans) under Regulation Z. For a federally related mortgage loan that is a home-equity line of credit subject to Regulation Z, 12 CFR 1026.40, a lender or mortgage broker that provides the loan applicant with the list of homeownership organizations required under this section may comply with the timing and delivery requirements set out in either paragraph (a) of this section or 12 CFR 1026.40(b).

(c) Exemptions.

(1) Reverse mortgage transactions. A lender is not required to provide an applicant for a reverse mortgage transaction subject to 12 CFR 1026.33(a) the list of homeownership counseling organizations required under this section.

(2) Timeshare plans. A lender is not required to provide an applicant for a mortgage loan secured by a timeshare, as described under 11 U.S.C. 101(53D), the list of homeownership counseling organizations required under this section.

§ 1024.30. Scope

(a) In general. Except as provided in paragraph (b) and (c) of this section, this subpart applies to any mortgage loan, as that term is defined in § 1024.31.

(b) Exemptions. Except as otherwise provided in § 1024.41(j), §§ 1024.38 through 41 of this subpart shall not apply to the following:

(1) A servicer that qualifies as a small servicer pursuant to 12 CFR 1026.41(e)(4);

(2) A servicer with respect to any reverse mortgage transaction as that term is defined in § 1024.31; and

(3) A servicer with respect to any mortgage loan for which the servicer is a qualified lender as that term is defined in 12 CFR 617.7000.

(c) Scope of certain sections.

(1) § 1024.33(a) only applies to reverse mortgage transactions.

(2) The procedures set forth in §§ 1024.39 through 41 of this subpart only apply to a mortgage loan that is secured by a property that is a borrower's principal residence.

(d) Successors in interest. A confirmed successor in interest shall be considered a borrower for purposes of § 1024.17 and this subpart.

§ 1024.31. Definitions

For purposes of this subpart:

Confirmed successor in interest means a successor in interest once a servicer has confirmed the successor in interest's identity and ownership interest in a property that secures a mortgage loan subject to this subpart.

Consumer reporting agency has the meaning set forth in section 603 of the Fair Credit Reporting Act, 15 U.S.C. 1681a.

Day means calendar day.

Delinquency means a period of time during which a borrower and a borrower's mortgage loan obligation are delinquent. A borrower and a borrower's mortgage loan obligation are delinquent beginning on the date a periodic payment sufficient to cover principal, interest, and, if applicable, escrow becomes due and unpaid, until such time as no periodic payment is due and unpaid.

Hazard insurance means insurance on the property securing a mortgage loan that protects the property against loss caused by fire, wind, flood, earthquake, theft, falling objects, freezing, and other similar hazards for which the owner or assignee of such loan requires insurance.

Loss mitigation application means an oral or written request for a loss mitigation option that is accompanied by any information required by a servicer for evaluation for a loss mitigation option.

Loss mitigation option means an alternative to foreclosure offered by the owner or assignee of a mortgage loan that is made available through the servicer to the borrower.

Master servicer means the owner of the right to perform servicing. A master servicer may perform the servicing itself or do so through a subservicer.

Mortgage loan means any federally related mortgage loan, as that term is defined in § 1024.2 subject to the exemptions in § 1024.5(b), but does not include open-end lines of credit (home equity plans).

Qualified written request means a written correspondence from the borrower to the servicer that includes, or otherwise enables the servicer to identify, the name and account of the borrower, and either:

(1) States the reasons the borrower believes the account is in error; or

(2) Provides sufficient detail to the servicer regarding information relating to the servicing of the mortgage loan sought by the borrower.

Reverse mortgage transaction has the meaning set forth in 12 CFR 1026.33(a).

Service provider means any party retained by a servicer that interacts with a borrower or provides a service to the servicer for which a borrower may incur a fee.

Subservicer means a servicer that does not own the right to perform servicing, but that performs servicing on behalf of the master servicer.

Successor in interest means a person to whom an ownership interest in a property securing a mortgage loan subject to this subpart is transferred from a borrower, provided that the transfer is:

(1) A transfer by devise, descent, or operation of law on the death of a joint tenant or tenant by the entirety;

(2) A transfer to a relative resulting from the death of a borrower;

(3) A transfer where the spouse or children of the borrower become an owner of the property;

(4) A transfer resulting from a decree of a dissolution of marriage, legal separation agreement, or from an incidental property settlement agreement, by which the spouse of the borrower becomes an owner of the property; or

(5) A transfer into an inter vivos trust in which the borrower is and remains a beneficiary and which does not relate to a transfer of rights of occupancy in the property.

Transferee servicer means a servicer that obtains or will obtain the right to perform servicing pursuant to an agreement or understanding.

Transferor servicer means a servicer, including a table-funding mortgage broker or dealer on a first-lien dealer loan, that transfers or will transfer the right to perform servicing pursuant to an agreement or understanding.

§ 1024.32. General disclosure requirements

(a) Disclosure requirements—

(1) Form of disclosures. Except as otherwise provided in this subpart, disclosures required under this subpart must be clear and conspicuous, in writing, and in a form that a recipient may keep. The disclosures required by this subpart may be provided in electronic form, subject to compliance with the consumer consent and other applicable provisions of the E-Sign Act, as set forth in § 1024.3. A servicer may use commonly accepted or readily understandable abbreviations in complying with the disclosure requirements of this subpart.

(2) Foreign language disclosures. Disclosures required under this subpart may be made in a language other than English, provided that the disclosures are made available in English upon a recipient's request.

(b) Additional information; disclosures required by other laws. Unless expressly prohibited in this subpart, by other applicable law, such as the Truth in Lending Act (15 U.S.C. 1601 *et seq.*) or the Truth in Savings Act (12 U.S.C. 4301 *et seq.*), or by the terms of an agreement with a Federal or State regulatory agency, a servicer may include additional information in a disclosure required under this subpart or combine any disclosure required under this subpart with any disclosure required by such other law.

(c) Successors in interest—

(1) Optional notice with acknowledgment form. Upon confirmation, a servicer may provide a confirmed successor in interest who is not liable on the mortgage loan obligation with a written notice together with a separate acknowledgment form that meets the requirements of paragraph (c)(1)(iv) of this section and that does not require acknowledgment of any items other than those identified in paragraph (c)(1)(iv) of this section. The written notice must clearly and conspicuously explain that:

(i) The servicer has confirmed the successor in interest's identity and ownership interest in the property;

(ii) Unless the successor in interest assumes the mortgage loan obligation under State law, the successor in interest is not liable for the mortgage debt and cannot be required to use the successor in interest's assets to pay the mortgage debt, except that the lender has a security interest in the property and a right to foreclose on the property, when permitted by law and authorized under the mortgage loan contract;

(iii) The successor in interest may be entitled to receive certain notices and communications about the mortgage loan if the servicer is not providing them to another confirmed successor in interest or borrower on the account;

(iv) In order to receive such notices and communications, the successor in interest must execute and provide to the servicer an acknowledgment form that:

(A) Requests receipt of such notices and communications if the servicer is not providing them to another confirmed successor in interest or borrower on the account; and

(B) Indicates that the successor in interest understands that such notices do not make the successor in interest liable for the mortgage debt and that the successor in interest is only liable for the mortgage debt if the successor in interest assumes the mortgage loan obligation under State law; and

(C) Informs the successor in interest that there is no time limit to return the acknowledgment but that the servicer will not begin sending such notices and communications to the confirmed successor in interest until the acknowledgment is returned; and

(v) Whether or not the successor in interest executes the acknowledgment described in paragraph (c)(1)(iv) of this section, the successor in interest is entitled to submit notices of error under § 1024.35, requests for information under § 1024.36, and requests for a payoff statement under § 1026.36 with respect to the mortgage loan account, with a brief explanation of those rights and how to exercise them, including appropriate address information.

(2) Effect of failure to execute acknowledgment. If, upon confirmation, a servicer provides a confirmed successor in interest who is not liable on the mortgage loan obligation with a written notice and acknowledgment form in accordance with paragraph (c)(1) of this section, the servicer is not required to provide to the confirmed successor in interest any written disclosure required by § 1024.17, § 1024.33, § 1024.34, § 1024.37, or § 1024.39 or to comply with the live contact requirements in § 1024.39(a) with respect to the confirmed successor in interest until the confirmed successor in interest either assumes the mortgage loan obligation under State law or executes an acknowledgment that complies with paragraph (c)(1)(iv) of this section and provides it to the servicer.

(3) Additional copies of acknowledgment form. If a servicer provides a confirmed successor in interest with a written notice and acknowledgment form in accordance with paragraph (c)(1) of this section, the servicer must make additional copies of the written notice and acknowledgment form available to the confirmed successor in interest upon written or oral request.

(4) Multiple notices unnecessary. Except as required by § 1024.36, a servicer is not required to provide to a confirmed successor in interest any written disclosure required by § 1024.17, § 1024.33, § 1024.34, § 1024.37, or § 1024.39(b) if the servicer is providing the same specific disclosure to another borrower on the account. A servicer is also not required to comply with the live contact requirements set forth in § 1024.39(a) with respect to a confirmed successor in interest if the servicer is complying with those requirements with respect to another borrower on the account.

§ 1024.33. Mortgage servicing transfers

(a) Servicing disclosure statement. Within three days (excluding legal public holidays, Saturdays, and Sundays) after a person applies for a reverse mortgage transaction, the lender, mortgage broker who anticipates using table funding, or dealer in a first-lien dealer loan shall provide to the person a servicing disclosure statement that states whether the servicing of the mortgage loan may be assigned, sold, or transferred to any other person at any time. Appendix MS-1 of this part contains a model form for the disclosures required under this paragraph (a). If a person who applies for a reverse mortgage transaction is denied credit within the three-day period, a servicing disclosure statement is not required to be delivered.

(b) Notices of transfer of loan servicing—

(1) Requirement for notice. Except as provided in paragraph (b)(2) of this section, each transferor servicer and transferee servicer of any mortgage loan shall provide to the borrower a notice of transfer for any assignment, sale, or transfer of the servicing of the mortgage loan. The notice must contain the information described in paragraph (b)(4) of this section. Appendix MS-2 of this part contains a model form for the disclosures required under this paragraph (b).

(2) Certain transfers excluded.

(i) The following transfers are not assignments, sales, or transfers of mortgage loan servicing for purposes of this section if there is no change in the payee, address to which payment must be delivered, account number, or amount of payment due:

(A) A transfer between affiliates;

(B) A transfer that results from mergers or acquisitions of servicers or subservicers;

(C) A transfer that occurs between master servicers without changing the subservicer;

(ii) The Federal Housing Administration (FHA) is not required to provide to the borrower a notice of transfer where a mortgage insured under the National Housing Act is assigned to the FHA.

(3) Time of notice—

(i) In general. Except as provided in paragraphs (b)(3)(ii) and (b)(3)(iii) of this section, the transferor servicer shall provide the notice of transfer to the borrower not less than 15 days before the effective date of the transfer of the servicing of the mortgage loan. The transferee servicer shall provide the notice of transfer to the borrower not more than 15 days after the effective date of the transfer. The transferor and transferee servicers may provide a single notice, in which case the notice shall be provided not less than 15 days before the effective date of the transfer of the servicing of the mortgage loan.

(ii) Extended time. The notice of transfer shall be provided to the borrower by the transferor servicer or the transferee servicer not more than 30 days after the effective date of the transfer of the servicing of the mortgage loan in any case in which the transfer of servicing is preceded by:

(A) Termination of the contract for servicing the loan for cause;

(B) Commencement of proceedings for bankruptcy of the servicer;

(C) Commencement of proceedings by the FDIC for conservatorship or receivership of the servicer or an entity that owns or controls the servicer; or

(D) Commencement of proceedings by the NCUA for appointment of a conservator or liquidating agent of the servicer or an entity that owns or controls the servicer.

(iii) Notice provided at settlement. Notices of transfer provided at settlement by the transferor servicer and transferee servicer, whether as separate notices or as a combined notice, satisfy the timing requirements of paragraph (b)(3) of this section.

(4) Contents of notice. The notices of transfer shall include the following information:

(i) The effective date of the transfer of servicing;

(ii) The name, address, and a collect call or toll-free telephone number for an employee or department of the transferee servicer that can be contacted by the borrower to obtain answers to servicing transfer inquiries;

(iii) The name, address, and a collect call or toll-free telephone number for an employee or department of the transferor servicer that can be contacted by the borrower to obtain answers to servicing transfer inquiries;

(iv) The date on which the transferor servicer will cease to accept payments relating to the loan and the date on which the transferee servicer will begin to accept such payments. These dates shall either be the same or consecutive days;

(v) Whether the transfer will affect the terms or the continued availability of mortgage life or disability insurance, or any other type of optional insurance, and any action the borrower must take to maintain such coverage; and

(vi) A statement that the transfer of servicing does not affect any term or condition of the mortgage loan other than terms directly related to the servicing of the loan.

(c) Borrower payments during transfer of servicing—

(1) Payments not considered late. During the 60-day period beginning on the effective date of transfer of the servicing of any mortgage loan, if the transferor servicer (rather than the transferee servicer that should properly receive payment on the loan) receives payment on or before the applicable due date (including any grace period allowed under the mortgage loan instruments), a payment may not be treated as late for any purpose.

(2) Treatment of payments. Beginning on the effective date of transfer of the servicing of any mortgage loan, with respect to payments received incorrectly by the transferor servicer (rather than the transferee servicer that should properly receive the payment on the loan), the transferor servicer shall promptly either:

(i) Transfer the payment to the transferee servicer for application to a borrower's mortgage loan account, or

(ii) Return the payment to the person that made the payment and notify such person of the proper recipient of the payment.

(d) Preemption of State laws. A lender who makes a mortgage loan or a servicer shall be considered to have complied with the provisions of any State law or regulation requiring notice to a borrower at the time of application for a loan or transfer of servicing of a loan if the lender or servicer complies with the requirements of this section. Any State law requiring notice to the borrower at the time of application or at the time of transfer of servicing of the loan is preempted, and there shall be no additional borrower disclosure requirements. Provisions of State law, such as those requiring additional notices to insurance companies or taxing authorities, are not preempted by section 6 of RESPA or this section, and this additional information may be added to a notice provided under this section, if permitted under State law.

§ 1024.34. Timely escrow payments and treatment of escrow account balances

(a) Timely escrow disbursements required. If the terms of a mortgage loan require the borrower to make payments to the servicer of the mortgage loan for deposit into an escrow account to pay taxes, insurance premiums, and other charges for the mortgaged property, the servicer shall make payments from the escrow account in a timely manner, that is, on or before the deadline to avoid a penalty, as governed by the requirements in § 1024.17(k).

(b) Refund of escrow balance—

(1) In general. Except as provided in paragraph (b)(2) of this section, within 20 days (excluding legal public holidays, Saturdays, and Sundays) of a borrower's payment of a mortgage loan in full, a servicer shall return to the borrower any amounts remaining in an escrow account that is within the servicer's control.

(2) Servicer may credit funds to a new escrow account. Notwithstanding paragraph (b)(1) of this section, if the borrower agrees, a servicer may credit any amounts remaining in an escrow account that is within the servicer's control to an escrow account for a new mortgage loan as of the date of the settlement of the new mortgage loan if the new mortgage loan is provided to the borrower by a lender that:

(i) Was also the lender to whom the prior mortgage loan was initially payable;

(ii) Is the owner or assignee of the prior mortgage loan; or

(iii) Uses the same servicer that serviced the prior mortgage loan to service the new mortgage loan.

§ 1024.35. Error resolution procedures

(a) Notice of error. A servicer shall comply with the requirements of this section for any written notice from the borrower that asserts an error and that includes the name of the borrower, information that enables the servicer to identify the borrower's mortgage loan account, and the error the borrower believes has occurred. A notice on a payment coupon or other payment form supplied by the servicer need not be treated by the servicer as a notice of error. A qualified written request that asserts an error relating to the servicing of a mortgage loan is a notice of error for purposes of this section, and a servicer must comply with all requirements applicable to a notice of error with respect to such qualified written request.

(b) Scope of error resolution. For purposes of this section, the term "error" refers to the following categories of covered errors:

(1) Failure to accept a payment that conforms to the servicer's written requirements for the borrower to follow in making payments.

(2) Failure to apply an accepted payment to principal, interest, escrow, or other charges under the terms of the mortgage loan and applicable law.

(3) Failure to credit a payment to a borrower's mortgage loan account as of the date of receipt in violation of 12 CFR 1026.36(c)(1).

(4) Failure to pay taxes, insurance premiums, or other charges, including charges that the borrower and servicer have voluntarily agreed that the servicer should collect and pay, in a timely manner as required by § 1024.34(a), or to refund an escrow account balance as required by § 1024.34(b).

(5) Imposition of a fee or charge that the servicer lacks a reasonable basis to impose upon the borrower.

(6) Failure to provide an accurate payoff balance amount upon a borrower's request in violation of section 12 CFR 1026.36(c)(3).

(7) Failure to provide accurate information to a borrower regarding loss mitigation options and foreclosure, as required by § 1024.39.

(8) Failure to transfer accurately and timely information relating to the servicing of a borrower's mortgage loan account to a transferee servicer.

(9) Making the first notice or filing required by applicable law for any judicial or non-judicial foreclosure process in violation of § 1024.41(f) or (j).

(10) Moving for foreclosure judgment or order of sale, or conducting a foreclosure sale in violation of § 1024.41(g) or (j).

(11) Any other error relating to the servicing of a borrower's mortgage loan.

(c) Contact information for borrowers to assert errors. A servicer may, by written notice provided to a borrower, establish an address that a borrower must use to submit a notice of error in accordance with the procedures in this section. The notice shall include a statement that the borrower must use the established address to assert an error. If a servicer designates a specific address for receiving notices of error, the servicer shall designate the same address for receiving information requests pursuant to § 1024.36(b). A servicer shall provide a written notice to a borrower before any change in the address used for receiving a notice of error. A servicer that designates an address for receipt of notices of error must post the designated address on any Web site maintained by the servicer if the Web site lists any contact address for the servicer.

(d) Acknowledgment of receipt. Within five days (excluding legal public holidays, Saturdays, and Sundays) of a servicer receiving a notice of error from a borrower, the servicer shall provide to the borrower a written response acknowledging receipt of the notice of error.

(e) Response to notice of error—

(1) Investigation and response requirements—

(i) In general. Except as provided in paragraphs (f) and (g) of this section, a servicer must respond to a notice of error by either:

(A) Correcting the error or errors identified by the borrower and providing the borrower with a written notification of the correction, the effective date of the correction, and contact information, including a telephone number, for further assistance; or

(B) Conducting a reasonable investigation and providing the borrower with a written notification that includes a statement that the servicer has determined that no error occurred, a statement of the reason or reasons for this determination, a statement of the borrower's right to request documents relied upon by the servicer in reaching its determination, information regarding how the borrower can request such documents, and contact information, including a telephone number, for further assistance.

(ii) Different or additional error. If during a reasonable investigation of a notice of error, a servicer concludes that errors occurred other than, or in addition to, the error or errors alleged by the borrower, the servicer shall correct all such additional errors and provide the borrower with a written notification that describes the errors the servicer identified, the action taken to correct the errors, the effective date of the correction, and contact information, including a telephone number, for further assistance.

(2) Requesting information from borrower. A servicer may request supporting documentation from a borrower in connection with the investigation of an asserted error, but may not:

(i) Require a borrower to provide such information as a condition of investigating an asserted error; or

(ii) Determine that no error occurred because the borrower failed to provide any requested information without conducting a reasonable investigation pursuant to paragraph (e)(1)(i)(B) of this section.

(3) Time limits—

(i) In general. A servicer must comply with the requirements of paragraph (e)(1) of this section:

(A) Not later than seven days (excluding legal public holidays, Saturdays, and Sundays) after the servicer receives the notice of error for errors asserted under paragraph (b)(6) of this section.

(B) Prior to the date of a foreclosure sale or within 30 days (excluding legal public holidays, Saturdays, and Sundays) after the servicer receives the notice of error, whichever is earlier, for errors asserted under paragraphs (b)(9) and (10) of this section.

(C) For all other asserted errors, not later than 30 days (excluding legal public holidays, Saturdays, and Sundays) after the servicer receives the applicable notice of error.

(ii) Extension of time limit. For asserted errors governed by the time limit set forth in paragraph (e)(3)(i)(C) of this section, a servicer may extend the time period for responding by an additional 15 days (excluding legal public holidays, Saturdays, and Sundays) if, before the end of the 30-day period, the servicer notifies the borrower of the extension and the reasons for the extension in writing. A servicer may not extend the time period for responding to errors asserted under paragraph (b)(6), (9), or (10) of this section.

(4) Copies of documentation. A servicer shall provide to the borrower, at no charge, copies of documents and information relied upon by the servicer in making its determination that no error occurred within 15 days (excluding legal public holidays, Saturdays, and Sundays) of receiving the borrower's request for such documents. A servicer is not required to provide documents relied upon that constitute confidential, proprietary or privileged information. If a servicer withholds documents relied upon because it has determined that such documents constitute confidential, proprietary or privileged information, the servicer must notify the borrower of its determination in writing within 15 days (excluding legal public holidays, Saturdays, and Sundays) of receipt of the borrower's request for such documents.

(5) Omissions in responses to requests for documentation. In its response to a request for documentation under paragraph (e)(4) of this section, a servicer may omit location and contact information and personal financial information (other than information about the terms, status, and payment history of the mortgage loan) if:

(i) The information pertains to a potential or confirmed successor in interest who is not the requester; or

(ii) The requester is a confirmed successor in interest and the information pertains to any borrower who is not the requester.

(f) Alternative compliance—

(1) Early correction. A servicer is not required to comply with paragraphs (d) and (e) of this section if the servicer corrects the error or errors asserted by the borrower and notifies the borrower of that correction in writing within five days (excluding legal public holidays, Saturdays, and Sundays) of receiving the notice of error.

(2) Error asserted before foreclosure sale. A servicer is not required to comply with the requirements of paragraphs (d) and (e) of this section for errors asserted under paragraph (b)(9) or (10) of this section if the servicer receives the applicable notice of an error seven or fewer days before a foreclosure sale. For any such notice of error, a servicer shall make a good faith attempt to respond to the borrower, orally or in writing, and either correct the error or state the reason the servicer has determined that no error has occurred.

(g) Requirements not applicable—

(1) In general. A servicer is not required to comply with the requirements of paragraphs (d), (e) and (i) of this section if the servicer reasonably determines that any of the following apply:

(i) Duplicative notice of error. The asserted error is substantially the same as an error previously asserted by the borrower for which the servicer has previously complied with its obligation to respond pursuant to paragraphs (d) and (e) of this section, unless the borrower provides new and material information to support the asserted error. New and material information means information that was not reviewed by the servicer in connection with investigating a prior notice of the same error and is reasonably likely to change the servicer's prior determination about the error.

(ii) Overbroad notice of error. The notice of error is overbroad. A notice of error is overbroad if the servicer cannot reasonably determine from the notice of error the specific error that the borrower asserts has occurred on a borrower's account. To the extent a servicer can reasonably identify a valid assertion of an error in a notice of error that is otherwise overbroad, the servicer shall comply with the requirements of paragraphs (d), (e) and (i) of this section with respect to that asserted error.

(iii) Untimely notice of error. A notice of error is delivered to the servicer more than one year after:

(A) Servicing for the mortgage loan that is the subject of the asserted error was transferred from the servicer receiving the notice of error to a transferee servicer; or

(B) The mortgage loan balance was paid in full.

(2) Notice to borrower. If a servicer determines that, pursuant to this paragraph (g), the servicer is not required to comply with the requirements of paragraphs (d), (e), and (i) of this section, the servicer shall notify the borrower of its determination in writing not later than five days (excluding legal public holidays, Saturdays, and Sundays) after making such determination. The notice to the borrower shall set forth the basis under paragraph (g)(1) of this section upon which the servicer has made such determination.

(h) Payment requirements prohibited. A servicer shall not charge a fee, or require a borrower to make any payment that may be owed on a borrower's account, as a condition of responding to a notice of error.

(i) Effect on servicer remedies—

(1) Adverse information. After receipt of a notice of error, a servicer may not, for 60 days, furnish adverse information to any consumer reporting agency regarding any payment that is the subject of the notice of error.

(2) Remedies permitted. Except as set forth in this section with respect to an assertion of error under paragraph (b)(9) or (10) of this section, nothing in this section shall limit or restrict a lender or servicer from pursuing any remedy it has under applicable law, including initiating foreclosure or proceeding with a foreclosure sale.

§ 1024.36. Requests for information

(a) Information request. A servicer shall comply with the requirements of this section for any written request for information from a borrower that includes the name of the borrower, information that enables the servicer to identify the borrower's mortgage loan account, and states the information the borrower is requesting with respect to the borrower's mortgage loan. A request on a payment coupon or other payment form supplied by the servicer need not be treated by the servicer as a request for information. A request for a payoff balance need not be treated by the servicer as a request for information. A qualified written request that requests information relating to the servicing of the mortgage loan is a request for information for purposes of this section, and a servicer must comply with all requirements applicable to a request for information with respect to such qualified written request.

(b) Contact information for borrowers to request information. A servicer may, by written notice provided to a borrower, establish an address that a borrower must use to request information in accordance with the procedures in this section. The notice shall include a statement that the borrower must use the established address to request information. If a servicer designates a specific address for receiving information requests, a servicer shall designate the same address for receiving notices of error pursuant to § 1024.35(c). A servicer shall provide a written notice to a borrower before any change in the address used for receiving an information request. A servicer that designates an address for receipt of information requests must post the designated address on any Web site maintained by the servicer if the Web site lists any contact address for the servicer.

(c) Acknowledgment of receipt. Within five days (excluding legal public holidays, Saturdays, and Sundays) of a servicer receiving an information request from a borrower, the servicer shall provide to the borrower a written response acknowledging receipt of the information request.

(d) Response to information request—

(1) Investigation and response requirements. Except as provided in paragraphs (e) and (f) of this section, a servicer must respond to an information request by either:

(i) Providing the borrower with the requested information and contact information, including a telephone number, for further assistance in writing; or

(ii) Conducting a reasonable search for the requested information and providing the borrower with a written notification that states that the servicer has determined that the requested information is not available to the servicer, provides the basis for the servicer's determination, and provides contact information, including a telephone number, for further assistance.

(2) Time limits—

(i) In general. A servicer must comply with the requirements of paragraph (d)(1) of this section:

(A) Not later than 10 days (excluding legal public holidays, Saturdays, and Sundays) after the servicer receives an information request for the identity of, and address or other relevant contact information for, the owner or assignee of a mortgage loan; and

(B) For all other requests for information, not later than 30 days (excluding legal public holidays, Saturdays, and Sundays) after the servicer receives the information request.

(ii) Extension of time limit. For requests for information governed by the time limit set forth in paragraph (d)(2)(i)(B) of this section, a servicer may extend the time period for responding by an additional 15 days (excluding legal public holidays, Saturdays, and Sundays) if, before the end of the 30-day period, the servicer notifies the borrower of the extension and the reasons for the extension in writing. A servicer may not extend the time period for requests for information governed by paragraph (d)(2)(i)(A)of this section.

(3) Omissions in responses to requests. In its response to a request for information, a servicer may omit location and contact information and personal financial information (other than information about the terms, status, and payment history of the mortgage loan) if:

(i) The information pertains to a potential or confirmed successor in interest who is not the requester; or

(ii) The requester is a confirmed successor and the information pertains to any borrower who is not the requester.

(e) Alternative compliance. A servicer is not required to comply with paragraphs (c) and (d) of this section if the servicer provides the borrower with the information requested and contact information, including a telephone number, for further assistance in writing within five days (excluding legal public holidays, Saturdays, and Sundays) of receiving an information request.

(f) Requirements not applicable—

(1) In general. A servicer is not required to comply with the requirements of paragraphs (c) and (d) of this section if the servicer reasonably determines that any of the following apply:

(i) Duplicative information. The information requested is substantially the same as information previously requested by the borrower for which the servicer has previously complied with its obligation to respond pursuant to paragraphs (c) and (d) of this section.

(ii) Confidential, proprietary or privileged information. The information requested is confidential, proprietary or privileged.

(iii) Irrelevant information. The information requested is not directly related to the borrower's mortgage loan account.

(iv) Overbroad or unduly burdensome information request. The information request is overbroad or unduly burdensome. An information request is overbroad if a borrower requests that the servicer provide an unreasonable volume of documents or information to a borrower. An information request is unduly burdensome if a diligent servicer could not respond to the information request without either exceeding the maximum time limit permitted by paragraph (d)(2) of this section or incurring costs (or dedicating resources) that would be unreasonable in light of the circumstances. To the extent a servicer can reasonably identify a valid information request in a submission that is otherwise overbroad or unduly burdensome, the servicer shall comply with the requirements of paragraphs (c) and (d) of this section with respect to that requested information.

(v) Untimely information request. The information request is delivered to a servicer more than one year after:

(A) Servicing for the mortgage loan that is the subject of the information request was transferred from the servicer receiving the request for information to a transferee servicer; or

(B) The mortgage loan is discharged.

(2) ***Notice to borrower.*** If a servicer determines that, pursuant to this paragraph (f), the servicer is not required to comply with the requirements of paragraphs (c) and (d) of this section, the servicer shall notify the borrower of its determination in writing not later than five days (excluding legal public holidays, Saturdays, and Sundays) after making such determination. The notice to the borrower shall set forth the basis under paragraph (f)(1) of this section upon which the servicer has made such determination.

(g) Payment requirement limitations—

(1) Fees prohibited. Except as set forth in paragraph (g)(2) of this section, a servicer shall not charge a fee, or require a borrower to make any payment that may be owed on a borrower's account, as a condition of responding to an information request.

(2) Fee permitted. Nothing in this section shall prohibit a servicer from charging a fee for providing a beneficiary notice under applicable State law, if such a fee is not otherwise prohibited by applicable law.

(h) Servicer remedies. Nothing in this section shall prohibit a servicer from furnishing adverse information to any consumer reporting agency or pursuing any of its remedies, including initiating foreclosure or proceeding with a foreclosure sale, allowed by the underlying mortgage loan instruments, during the time period that response to an information request notice is outstanding.

(i) Potential successors in interest.

(1) With respect to any written request from a person that indicates that the person may be a successor in interest and that includes the name of the transferor borrower from whom the person received an ownership interest and information that enables the servicer to identify the mortgage loan account, a servicer shall respond by providing the potential successor in interest with a written description of the documents the servicer reasonably requires to confirm the person's identity and ownership interest in the property and contact information, including a telephone number, for further assistance. With respect to the written request, a servicer shall treat the potential successor in interest as a borrower for purposes of the requirements of paragraphs (c) through (g) of this section.

(2) If a written request under paragraph (i)(1) of this section does not provide sufficient information to enable the servicer to identify the documents the servicer reasonably requires to confirm the person's identity and ownership interest in the property, the servicer may provide a response that includes examples of documents typically accepted to establish identity and ownership interest in a property; indicates that the person may obtain a more individualized description of required documents by providing additional information; specifies what additional information is required to enable the servicer to identify the required documents; and provides contact information, including a telephone number, for further assistance. A servicer's response under this paragraph (i)(2) must otherwise comply with the requirements of paragraph (i)(1). Notwithstanding paragraph (f)(1)(i) of this section, if a potential successor in interest subsequently provides orally or in writing the required information specified by the servicer pursuant to this paragraph (i)(2), the servicer must treat the new information, together with the original request, as a new, non-duplicative request under paragraph (i)(1), received as of the date the required information was received, and must respond accordingly.

(3) In responding to a request under paragraph (i)(1) of this section prior to confirmation, the servicer is not required to provide any information other than the information specified in paragraphs (i)(1) and (2) of this section. In responding to a written request under paragraph (i)(1) that requests other information, the servicer must indicate that the potential successor in interest may resubmit any request for information once confirmed as a successor in interest.

(4) If a servicer has established an address that a borrower must use to request information pursuant to paragraph (b) of this section, a servicer must comply with the requirements of paragraph (i)(1) of this section only for requests received at the established address.

§ 1024.37. Force-placed insurance

(a) Definition of force-placed insurance—

(1) In general. For the purposes of this section, the term "force-placed insurance" means hazard insurance obtained by a servicer on behalf of the owner or assignee of a mortgage loan that insures the property securing such loan.

(2) Types of insurance not considered force-placed insurance. The following insurance does not constitute "force-placed insurance" under this section:

(i) Hazard insurance required by the Flood Disaster Protection Act of 1973.

(ii) Hazard insurance obtained by a borrower but renewed by the borrower's servicer as described in § 1024.17(k)(1), (2), or (5).

(iii) Hazard insurance obtained by a borrower but renewed by the borrower's servicer at its discretion, if the borrower agrees.

(b) Basis for charging borrower for force-placed insurance. A servicer may not assess on a borrower a premium charge or fee related to force-placed insurance unless the servicer has a reasonable basis to believe that the borrower has failed to comply with the mortgage loan contract's requirement to maintain hazard insurance.

(c) Requirements before charging borrower for force-placed insurance—

(1) In general. Before a servicer assesses on a borrower any premium charge or fee related to force-placed insurance, the servicer must:

(i) Deliver to a borrower or place in the mail a written notice containing the information required by paragraph (c)(2) of this section at least 45 days before a servicer assesses on a borrower such charge or fee;

(ii) Deliver to the borrower or place in the mail a written notice in accordance with paragraph (d)(1) of this section; and

(iii) By the end of the 15-day period beginning on the date the written notice described in paragraph (c)(1)(ii) of this section was delivered to the borrower or placed in the mail, not have received, from the borrower or otherwise, evidence demonstrating that the borrower has had in place, continuously, hazard insurance coverage that complies with the loan contract's requirements to maintain hazard insurance.

(2) Content of notice. The notice required by paragraph (c)(1)(i) of this section shall set forth the following information:

(i) The date of the notice;

(ii) The servicer's name and mailing address;

(iii) The borrower's name and mailing address;

(iv) A statement that requests the borrower to provide hazard insurance information for the borrower's property and identifies the property by its physical address;

(v) A statement that:

(A) The borrower's hazard insurance is expiring, has expired, or provides insufficient coverage, as applicable;

(B) The servicer does not have evidence that the borrower has hazard insurance coverage past the expiration date or evidence that the borrower has hazard insurance that provides sufficient coverage, as applicable; and

(C) If applicable, identifies the type of hazard insurance for which the servicer lacks evidence of coverage;

(vi) A statement that hazard insurance is required on the borrower's property, and that the servicer has purchased or will purchase, as applicable, such insurance at the borrower's expense;

(vii) A statement requesting the borrower to promptly provide the servicer with insurance information;

(viii) A description of the requested insurance information and how the borrower may provide such information, and if applicable, a statement that the requested information must be in writing;

(ix) A statement that insurance the servicer has purchased or purchases:

(A) May cost significantly more than hazard insurance purchased by the borrower;

(B) Not provide as much coverage as hazard insurance purchased by the borrower;

(x) The servicer's telephone number for borrower inquiries; and

(xi) If applicable, a statement advising the borrower to review additional information provided in the same transmittal.

(3) Format. A servicer must set the information required by paragraphs (c)(2)(iv), (vi), and (ix)(A) and (B) in bold text, except that the information about the physical address of the borrower's property required by paragraph (c)(2)(iv) of this section may be set in regular text. A servicer may use form MS-3A in appendix MS-3 of this part to comply with the requirements of paragraphs (c)(1)(i) and (2) of this section.

(4) Additional information. Except for the mortgage loan account number, a servicer may not include any information other than information required by paragraph (c)(2) of this section in the written notice required by paragraph (c)(1)(i) of this section. However, a servicer may provide such additional information to a borrower on separate pieces of paper in the same transmittal.

(d) Reminder notice—

(1) In general. The notice required by paragraph (c)(1)(ii) of this section shall be delivered to the borrower or placed in the mail at least 15 days before a servicer assesses on a borrower a premium charge or fee related to force-placed insurance. A servicer may not deliver to a borrower or place in the mail the notice required by paragraph (c)(1)(ii) of this section until at least 30 days after delivering to the borrower or placing in the mail the written notice required by paragraph (c)(1)(i) of this section.

(2) Content of the reminder notice—

(i) *Servicer receiving no insurance information.* A servicer that receives no hazard insurance information after delivering to the borrower or placing in the mail the notice required by paragraph (c)(1)(i) of this section must set forth in the notice required by paragraph (c)(1)(ii) of this section:

(A) The date of the notice;

(B) A statement that the notice is the second and final notice;

(C) The information required by paragraphs (c)(2)(ii) through (xi) of this section; and

(D) The cost of the force-placed insurance, stated as an annual premium, except if a servicer does not know the cost of force-placed insurance, a reasonable estimate shall be disclosed and identified as such.

(ii) Servicer not receiving demonstration of continuous coverage. A servicer that has received hazard insurance information after delivering to a borrower or placing in the mail the notice required by paragraph (c)(1)(i) of this section, but has not received, from the borrower or otherwise, evidence demonstrating that the borrower has had sufficient hazard insurance coverage in place continuously, must set forth in the notice required by paragraph (c)(1)(ii) of this section the following information:

(A) The date of the notice;

(B) The information required by paragraphs (c)(2)(ii) through (iv) and (xi) through (xi) and (d)(2)(i)(B) and (D) of this section;

(C) A statement that the servicer has received the hazard insurance information that the borrower provided;

(D) A statement that requests the borrower to provide the information that is missing;

(E) A statement that the borrower will be charged for insurance the servicer has purchased or purchases for the period of time during which the servicer is unable to verify coverage;

(3) Format. A servicer must set the information required by paragraphs (d)(2)(i)(B) and (D) of this section in bold text. The requirements of paragraph (c)(3) of this section apply to the information required by paragraph (d)(2)(i)(C) of this section. A servicer may use form MS-3B in appendix MS-3 of this part to comply with the requirements of paragraphs (d)(1) and (d)(2)(i) of this section. A servicer may use form MS-3C in appendix MS-3 of this part to comply with the requirements of paragraphs (d)(1) and (d)(2)(ii) of this section.

(4) Additional information. Except for the borrower's mortgage loan account number, a servicer may not include any information other than information required by paragraph (d)(2)(i) or (ii) of this section, as applicable, in the written notice required by paragraph (c)(1)(ii) of this section. However, a servicer may provide such additional information to a borrower on separate pieces of paper in the same transmittal.

(5) Updating notice with borrower information. If a servicer receives new information about a borrower's hazard insurance after a written notice required by paragraph (c)(1)(ii) of this section has been put into production, the servicer is not required to update such notice based on the new information so long as the notice was put into production a reasonable time prior to the servicer delivering the notice to the borrower or placing the notice in the mail.

(e) Renewing or replacing force-placed insurance—

(1) In general. Before a servicer assesses on a borrower a premium charge or fee related to renewing or replacing existing force-placed insurance, a servicer must:

(i) Deliver to the borrower or place in the mail a written notice containing the information set forth in paragraph (e)(2) of this section at least 45 days before assessing on a borrower such charge or fee; and

(ii) By the end of the 45-day period beginning on the date the written notice required by paragraph (e)(1)(i) of this section was delivered to the borrower or placed in the mail, not have received, from the borrower or otherwise, evidence demonstrating that the borrower has purchased hazard insurance coverage that complies with the loan contract's requirements to maintain hazard insurance.

(iii) Charging a borrower before end of notice period. Notwithstanding paragraphs (e)(1)(i) and (ii) of this section, if not prohibited by State or other applicable law, if a servicer has renewed or replaced existing force-placed insurance and receives evidence demonstrating that the borrower lacked insurance coverage for some period of time following the expiration of the existing force-placed insurance (including during the notice period prescribed by paragraph (e)(1), of this section), the servicer may, promptly upon receiving such evidence, assess on the borrower a premium charge or fee related to renewing or replacing existing force-placed insurance for that period of time.

(2) Content of renewal notice. The notice required by paragraph (e)(1)(i) of this section shall set forth the following information:

(i) The date of the notice;

(ii) The servicer's name and mailing address;

(iii) The borrower's name and mailing address;

(iv) A statement that requests the borrower to update the hazard insurance information for the borrower's property and identifies the borrower's property by its physical address;

(v) A statement that the servicer previously purchased insurance on the borrower's property and assessed the cost of the insurance to the borrower because the servicer did not have evidence that the borrower had hazard insurance coverage for the property;

(vi) A statement that:

(A) The insurance the servicer purchased previously has expired or is expiring, as applicable; and

(B) Because hazard insurance is required on the borrower's property, the servicer intends to maintain insurance on the property by renewing or replacing the insurance it previously purchased;

(vii) A statement informing the borrower:

(A) That insurance the servicer purchases may cost significantly more than hazard insurance purchased by the borrower;

(B) That such insurance may not provide as much coverage as hazard insurance purchased by the borrower; and

(C) The cost of the force-placed insurance, stated as an annual premium, except if a servicer does not know the cost of force-placed insurance, a reasonable estimate shall be disclosed and identified as such.

(viii) A statement that if the borrower purchases hazard insurance, the borrower should promptly provide the servicer with insurance information.

(ix) A description of the requested insurance information and how the borrower may provide such information, and if applicable, a statement that the requested information must be in writing;

(x) The servicer's telephone number for borrower inquiries; and

(xi) If applicable, a statement advising a borrower to review additional information provided in the same transmittal.

(3) Format. A servicer must set the information required by paragraphs (e)(2)(iv), (vi)(B), and (vii)(A) through (C) of this section in bold text, except that the information about the physical address of the borrower's property required by paragraph (e)(2)(iv) may be set in regular text. A servicer may use form MS-3D in appendix MS-3 of this part to comply with the requirements of paragraphs (e)(1)(i) and (2) of this section.

(4) Additional information. Except for the borrower's mortgage loan account number, a servicer may not include any information other than information required by paragraph (e)(2) of this section in the written notice required by paragraph (e)(1) of this section. However, a servicer may provide such additional information to a borrower on separate pieces of paper in the same transmittal.

(5) Frequency of renewal notices. Before each anniversary of a servicer purchasing force-placed insurance on a borrower's property, the servicer shall deliver to the borrower or place in the mail the written notice required by paragraph (e)(1) of this section. A servicer is not required to provide the written notice required by paragraph (e)(1) of this section more than once a year.

(f) Mailing the notices. If a servicer mails a written notice required by paragraphs (c)(1)(i), (c)(1)(ii), or (e)(1) of this section, the servicer must use a class of mail not less than first-class mail.

(g) Cancellation of force-placed insurance. Within 15 days of receiving, from the borrower or otherwise, evidence demonstrating that the borrower has had in place hazard insurance coverage that complies with the loan contract's requirements to maintain hazard insurance, a servicer must:

(1) Cancel the force-placed insurance the servicer purchased to insure the borrower's property; and

(2) Refund to such borrower all force-placed insurance premium charges and related fees paid by such borrower for any period of overlapping insurance coverage and remove from the borrower's account all force-placed insurance charges and related fees for such period that the servicer has assessed to the borrower.

(h) Limitations on force-placed insurance charges—

(1) In general. Except for charges subject to State regulation as the business of insurance and charges authorized by the Flood Disaster Protection Act of 1973, all charges related to force-placed insurance assessed to a borrower by or through the servicer must be bona fide and reasonable.

(2) Bona fide and reasonable charge. A bona fide and reasonable charge is a charge for a service actually performed that bears a reasonable relationship to the servicer's cost of providing the service, and is not otherwise prohibited by applicable law.

(i) Relationship to Flood Disaster Protection Act of 1973. If permitted by regulation under section 102(e) of the Flood Disaster Protection Act of 1973, a servicer subject to the requirements of this section may deliver to the borrower or place in the mail any notice required by this section and the notice required by section 102(e) of the Flood Disaster Protection Act of 1973 on separate pieces of paper in the same transmittal.

§ 1024.38. General servicing policies, procedures, and requirements

(a) Reasonable policies and procedures. A servicer shall maintain policies and procedures that are reasonably designed to achieve the objectives set forth in paragraph (b) of this section.

(b) Objectives—

(1) Accessing and providing timely and accurate information. The policies and procedures required by paragraph (a) of this section shall be reasonably designed to ensure that the servicer can:

(i) Provide accurate and timely disclosures to a borrower as required by this subpart or other applicable law;

(ii) Investigate, respond to, and, as appropriate, make corrections in response to complaints asserted by a borrower;

(iii) Provide a borrower with accurate and timely information and documents in response to the borrower's requests for information with respect to the borrower's mortgage loan;

(iv) Provide owners or assignees of mortgage loans with accurate and current information and documents about all mortgage loans they own;

(v) Submit documents or filings required for a foreclosure process, including documents or filings required by a court of competent jurisdiction, that reflect accurate and current information and that comply with applicable law; and

(vi)(A) Upon receiving notice of the death of a borrower or of any transfer of the property securing a mortgage loan, promptly facilitate communication with any potential or confirmed successors in interest regarding the property;

(B) Upon receiving notice of the existence of a potential successor in interest, promptly determine the documents the servicer reasonably requires to confirm that person's identity and ownership interest in the property and promptly provide to the potential successor in interest a description of those documents and how the person may submit a written request under § 1024.36(i) (including the appropriate address); and

(C) Upon the receipt of such documents, promptly make a confirmation determination and promptly notify the person, as applicable, that the servicer has confirmed the person's status, has determined that additional documents are required (and what those documents are), or has determined that the person is not a successor in interest.

(2) Properly evaluating loss mitigation applications. The policies and procedures required by paragraph (a) of this section shall be reasonably designed to ensure that the servicer can:

(i) Provide accurate information regarding loss mitigation options available to a borrower from the owner or assignee of the borrower's mortgage loan;

(ii) Identify with specificity all loss mitigation options for which borrowers may be eligible pursuant to any requirements established by an owner or assignee of the borrower's mortgage loan;

(iii) Provide prompt access to all documents and information submitted by a borrower in connection with a loss mitigation option to servicer personnel that are assigned to assist the borrower pursuant to § 1024.40;

(iv) Identify documents and information that a borrower is required to submit to complete a loss mitigation application and facilitate compliance with the notice required pursuant to § 1024.41(b)(2)(i)(B); and

(v) Properly evaluate a borrower who submits an application for a loss mitigation option for all loss mitigation options for which the borrower may be eligible pursuant to any requirements established by the owner or assignee of the borrower's mortgage loan and, where applicable, in accordance with the requirements of § 1024.41.

(vi) Promptly identify and obtain documents or information not in the borrower's control that the servicer requires to determine which loss mitigation options, if any, to offer the borrower in accordance with the requirements of § 1024.41(c)(4).

(3) Facilitating oversight of, and compliance by, service providers. The policies and procedures required by paragraph (a) of this section shall be reasonably designed to ensure that the servicer can:

(i) Provide appropriate servicer personnel with access to accurate and current documents and information reflecting actions performed by service providers;

(ii) Facilitate periodic reviews of service providers, including by providing appropriate servicer personnel with documents and information necessary to audit compliance by service providers with the servicer's contractual obligations and applicable law; and

(iii) Facilitate the sharing of accurate and current information regarding the status of any evaluation of a borrower's loss mitigation application and the status of any foreclosure proceeding among appropriate servicer personnel, including any personnel assigned to a borrower's mortgage loan account as described in § 1024.40, and appropriate service provider personnel, including service provider personnel responsible for handling foreclosure proceedings.

(4) Facilitating transfer of information during servicing transfers. The policies and procedures required by paragraph (a) of this section shall be reasonably designed to ensure that the servicer can:

(i) As a transferor servicer, timely transfer all information and documents in the possession or control of the servicer relating to a transferred mortgage loan to a transferee servicer in a form and manner that ensures the accuracy of the information and documents transferred and that enables a transferee servicer to comply with the terms of the transferee servicer's obligations to the owner or assignee of the mortgage loan and applicable law; and

(ii) As a transferee servicer, identify necessary documents or information that may not have been transferred by a transferor servicer and obtain such documents from the transferor servicer.

(iii) For the purposes of paragraph (b)(4) of this section, transferee servicer means a servicer, including a master servicer or a subservicer, that performs or will perform servicing of a mortgage loan and transferor servicer means a servicer, including a master servicer or a subservicer, that transfers or will transfer the servicing of a mortgage loan.

(5) Informing borrowers of the written error resolution and information request procedures. The policies and procedures required by paragraph (a) of this section shall be reasonably designed to ensure that the servicer informs borrowers of the procedures for submitting written notices of error set forth in § 1024.35 and written information requests set forth in § 1024.36.

(c) Standard requirements—

(1) Record retention. A servicer shall retain records that document actions taken with respect to a borrower's mortgage loan account until one year after the date a mortgage loan is discharged or servicing of a mortgage loan is transferred by the servicer to a transferee servicer.

(2) Servicing file. A servicer shall maintain the following documents and data on each mortgage loan account serviced by the servicer in a manner that facilitates compiling such documents and data into a servicing file within five days:

(i) A schedule of all transactions credited or debited to the mortgage loan account, including any escrow account as defined in § 1024.17(b) and any suspense account;

(ii) A copy of the security instrument that establishes the lien securing the mortgage loan;

(iii) Any notes created by servicer personnel reflecting communications with the borrower about the mortgage loan account;

(iv) To the extent applicable, a report of the data fields relating to the borrower's mortgage loan account created by the servicer's electronic systems in connection with servicing practices; and

(v) Copies of any information or documents provided by the borrower to the servicer in accordance with the procedures set forth in §§ 1024.35 or 1024.41.

§ 1024.39. Early intervention requirements for certain borrowers

(a) Live contact. Except as otherwise provided in this section, a servicer shall establish or make good faith efforts to establish live contact with a delinquent borrower no later than the 36th day of a borrower's delinquency and again no later than 36 days after each payment due date so long as the borrower remains delinquent. Promptly after establishing live contact with a borrower, the servicer shall inform the borrower about the availability of loss mitigation options, if appropriate.

(b) Written notice—

(1) Notice required. Except as otherwise provided in this section, a servicer shall provide to a delinquent borrower a written notice with the information set forth in paragraph (b)(2) of this section no later than the 45th day of the borrower's delinquency and again no later than 45 days after each payment due date so long as the borrower remains delinquent. A servicer is not required to provide the written notice, however, more than once during any 180-day period. If a borrower is 45 days or more delinquent at the end of any 180-day period after the servicer has provided the written notice, a servicer must provide the written notice again no later than 180 days after the provision of the prior written notice. If a borrower is less than 45 days delinquent at the end of any 180-day period after the servicer has provided the written notice, a servicer must provide the written notice again no later than 45 days after the payment due date for which the borrower remains delinquent.

(2) Content of the written notice. The notice required by paragraph (b)(1) of this section shall include:

(i) A statement encouraging the borrower to contact the servicer;

(ii) The telephone number to access servicer personnel assigned pursuant to § 1024.40(a) and the servicer's mailing address;

(iii) If applicable, a statement providing a brief description of examples of loss mitigation options that may be available from the servicer;

(iv) If applicable, either application instructions or a statement informing the borrower how to obtain more information about loss mitigation options from the servicer; and

(v) The Web site to access either the Bureau list or the HUD list of homeownership counselors or counseling organizations, and the HUD toll-free telephone number to access homeownership counselors or counseling organizations.

(3) Model clauses. Model clauses MS-4(A), MS-4(B), and MS-4(C), in appendix MS-4 to this part may be used to comply with the requirements of paragraph (b).

(c) Borrowers in bankruptcy—

(1) Partial exemption. While any borrower on a mortgage loan is a debtor in bankruptcy under title 11 of the United States Code, a servicer, with regard to that mortgage loan:

(i) Is exempt from the requirements of paragraph (a) of this section;

(ii) Is exempt from the requirements of paragraph (b) of this section if no loss mitigation option is available, or if any borrower on the mortgage loan has provided a notification pursuant to the Fair Debt Collection Practices Act (FDCPA) section 805(c) (15 U.S.C. 1692c(c)) with respect to that mortgage loan as referenced in paragraph (d) of this section; and

(iii) If the conditions of paragraph (c)(1)(ii) of this section are not met, must comply with the requirements of paragraph (b)of this section, as modified by this paragraph (c)(1)(iii):

(A) If a borrower is delinquent when the borrower becomes a debtor in bankruptcy, a servicer must provide the written notice required by paragraph (b) of this section not later than the 45th day after the borrower files a bankruptcy petition under title 11 of the United States Code. If the borrower is not delinquent when the borrower files a bankruptcy petition, but subsequently becomes delinquent while a debtor in bankruptcy, the servicer must provide the written notice not later than the 45th day of the borrower's delinquency. A servicer must comply with these timing requirements regardless of whether the servicer provided the written notice in the preceding 180-day period.

(B) The written notice required by paragraph (b) of this section may not contain a request for payment.

(C) A servicer is not required to provide the written notice required by paragraph (b) of this section more than once during a single bankruptcy case.

(2) Resuming compliance.

(i) Except as provided in paragraph (c)(2)(ii) of this section, a servicer that was exempt from paragraphs (a) and (b) of this section pursuant to paragraph (c)(1) of this section must resume compliance with paragraphs (a) and (b) of this section after the next payment due date that follows the earliest of the following events:

(A) The bankruptcy case is dismissed;

(B) The bankruptcy case is closed; and

(C) The borrower reaffirms personal liability for the mortgage loan.

(ii) With respect to a mortgage loan for which the borrower has discharged personal liability pursuant to 11 U.S.C. 727, 1141, 1228, or 1328, a servicer:

(A) Is not required to resume compliance with paragraph (a) of this section; and

(B) Must resume compliance with paragraph (b) of this section if the borrower has made any partial or periodic payment on the mortgage loan after the commencement of the borrower's bankruptcy case.

(d) Fair Debt Collection Practices Act—partial exemption. With regard to a mortgage loan for which any borrower has provided a notification pursuant to the Fair Debt Collection Practices Act (FDCPA) section 805(c) (15 U.S.C. 1692c(c)), a servicer subject to the FDCPA with respect to that borrower's loan:

(1) Is exempt from the requirements of paragraph (a) of this section;

(2) Is exempt from the requirements of paragraph (b) of this section if no loss mitigation option is available, or while any borrower on that mortgage loan is a debtor in bankruptcy under title 11 of the United States Code as referenced in paragraph (c) of this section; and

(3) If the conditions of paragraph (d)(2) of this section are not met, must comply with the requirements of paragraph (b) of this section, as modified by this paragraph (d)(3):

(i) In addition to the information required pursuant to paragraph (b)(2) of this section, the written notice must include a statement that the servicer may or intends to invoke its specified remedy of foreclosure. Model clause MS-4(D) in appendix MS-4 to this part may be used to comply with this requirement.

(ii) The written notice may not contain a request for payment.

(iii) A servicer is prohibited from providing the written notice more than once during any 180-day period. If a borrower is 45 days or more delinquent at the end of any 180-day period after the servicer has provided the written notice, a servicer must provide the written notice again no later than 190 days after the provision of the prior written notice. If a borrower is less than 45 days delinquent at the end of any 180-day period after the servicer has provided the written notice, a servicer must provide the written notice again no later than 45 days after the payment due date for which the borrower remains delinquent or 190 days after the provision of the prior written notice, whichever is later.

§ 1024.40. Continuity of contact

(a) In general. A servicer shall maintain policies and procedures that are reasonably designed to achieve the following objectives:

(1) Assign personnel to a delinquent borrower by the time the servicer provides the borrower with the written notice required by § 1024.39(b), but in any event, not later than the 45th day of the borrower's delinquency.

(2) Make available to a delinquent borrower, via telephone, personnel assigned to the borrower as described in paragraph (a)(1) of this section to respond to the borrower's inquiries, and as applicable, assist the borrower with available loss mitigation options until the borrower has made, without incurring a late charge, two consecutive mortgage payments in accordance with the terms of a permanent loss mitigation agreement.

(3) If a borrower contacts the personnel assigned to the borrower as described in paragraph (a)(1) of this section and does not immediately receive a live response from such personnel, ensure that the servicer can provide a live response in a timely manner.

(b) Functions of servicer personnel. A servicer shall maintain policies and procedures reasonably designed to ensure that servicer personnel assigned to a delinquent borrower as described in paragraph (a) of this section perform the following functions:

(1) Provide the borrower with accurate information about:

(i) Loss mitigation options available to the borrower from the owner or assignee of the borrower's mortgage loan;

(ii) Actions the borrower must take to be evaluated for such loss mitigation options, including actions the borrower must take to submit a complete loss mitigation application, as defined in § 1024.41, and, if applicable, actions the borrower must take to appeal the servicer's determination to deny a borrower's loss mitigation application for any trial or permanent loan modification program offered by the servicer;

(iii) The status of any loss mitigation application that the borrower has submitted to the servicer;

(iv) The circumstances under which the servicer may make a referral to foreclosure; and

(v) Applicable loss mitigation deadlines established by an owner or assignee of the borrower's mortgage loan or § 1024.41.

(2) Retrieve, in a timely manner:

(i) A complete record of the borrower's payment history; and

(ii) All written information the borrower has provided to the servicer, and if applicable, to prior servicers, in connection with a loss mitigation application;

(3) Provide the documents and information identified in paragraph (b)(2) of this section to other persons required to evaluate a borrower for loss mitigation options made available by the servicer, if applicable; and

(4) Provide a delinquent borrower with information about the procedures for submitting a notice of error pursuant to § 1024.35 or an information request pursuant to § 1024.36.

§ 1024.41. Loss mitigation procedures

(a) Enforcement and limitations. A borrower may enforce the provisions of this section pursuant to section 6(f) of RESPA (12 U.S.C. 2605(f)). Nothing in § 1024.41 imposes a duty on a servicer to provide any borrower with any specific loss mitigation option. Nothing in section 1024.41 should be construed to create a right for a borrower to enforce the terms of any agreement between a servicer and the owner or assignee of a mortgage loan, including with respect to the evaluation for, or offer of, any loss mitigation option or to eliminate any such right that may exist pursuant to applicable law.

(b) Receipt of a loss mitigation application—

(1) Complete loss mitigation application. A complete loss mitigation application means an application in connection with which a servicer has received all the information that the servicer requires from a borrower in evaluating applications for the loss mitigation options available to the borrower. A servicer shall exercise reasonable diligence in obtaining documents and information to complete a loss mitigation application.

(2) Review of loss mitigation application submission—

(i) Requirements. If a servicer receives a loss mitigation application 45 days or more before a foreclosure sale, a servicer shall:

(A) Promptly upon receipt of a loss mitigation application, review the loss mitigation application to determine if the loss mitigation application is complete; and

(B) Notify the borrower in writing within 5 days (excluding legal public holidays, Saturdays, and Sundays) after receiving the loss mitigation application that the servicer acknowledges receipt of the loss mitigation application and that the servicer has determined that the loss mitigation application is either complete or incomplete. If a loss mitigation application is incomplete, the notice shall state the additional documents and information the borrower must submit to make the loss mitigation application complete and the applicable date pursuant to paragraph (2)(ii) of this section. The notice to the borrower shall include a statement that the borrower should consider contacting servicers of any other mortgage loans secured by the same property to discuss available loss mitigation options.

(ii) Time period disclosure. The notice required pursuant to paragraph (b)(2)(i)(B) of this section must include a reasonable date by which the borrower should submit the documents and information necessary to make the loss mitigation application complete.

(3) Determining protections. To the extent a determination of whether protections under this section apply to a borrower is made on the basis of the number of days between when a complete loss mitigation application is received and when a foreclosure sale occurs, such determination shall be made as of the date a complete loss mitigation application is received.

(c) Evaluation of loss mitigation applications—

(1) Complete loss mitigation application. Except as provided in paragraph (c)(4)(ii) of this section, if a servicer receives a complete loss mitigation application more than 37 days before a foreclosure sale, then, within 30 days of receiving the complete loss mitigation application, a servicer shall:

(i) Evaluate the borrower for all loss mitigation options available to the borrower; and

(ii) Provide the borrower with a notice in writing stating the servicer's determination of which loss mitigation options, if any, it will offer to the borrower on behalf of the owner or assignee of the mortgage. The servicer shall include in this notice the amount of time the borrower has to accept or reject an offer of a loss mitigation program as provided for in paragraph (e) of this section, if applicable, and a notification, if applicable, that the borrower has the right to appeal the denial of any loan modification option as well as the amount of time the borrower has to file such an appeal and any requirements for making an appeal, as provided for in paragraph (h) of this section.

(2) Incomplete loss mitigation application evaluation—

(i) In general. Except as set forth in paragraph (c)(2)(ii) of this section, a servicer shall not evade the requirement to evaluate a complete loss mitigation option for all loss mitigation options available to the borrower by offering a loss mitigation option based upon an evaluation of any information provided by a borrower in connection with an incomplete loss mitigation application.

(ii) Reasonable time. Notwithstanding paragraph (c)(2)(i) of this section, if a servicer has exercised reasonable diligence in obtaining documents and information to complete a loss mitigation application, but a loss mitigation application remains incomplete for a significant period of time under the circumstances without further progress by a borrower to make the loss mitigation application complete, a servicer may, in its discretion, evaluate an incomplete loss mitigation application and offer a borrower a loss mitigation option. Any such evaluation and offer is not subject to the requirements of this section and shall not constitute an evaluation of a single complete loss mitigation application for purposes of paragraph (i)of this section.

(iii) Short-term loss mitigation options. Notwithstanding paragraph (c)(2)(i) of this section, a servicer may offer a short-term payment forbearance program or a short-term repayment plan to a borrower based upon an evaluation of an incomplete loss mitigation application. Promptly after offering a payment forbearance program or a repayment plan under this paragraph (c)(2)(iii), unless the borrower has rejected the offer, the servicer must provide the borrower a written notice stating the specific payment terms and duration of the program or plan, that the servicer offered the program or plan based on an evaluation of an incomplete application, that other loss mitigation options may be available, and that the borrower has the option to submit a complete loss mitigation application to receive an evaluation for all loss mitigation options available to the borrower regardless of whether the borrower accepts the program or plan. A servicer shall not make the first notice or filing required by applicable law for any judicial or non-judicial foreclosure process, and shall not move for foreclosure judgment or order of sale or conduct a foreclosure sale, if a borrower is performing pursuant to the terms of a payment forbearance program or repayment plan offered pursuant to this paragraph (c)(2)(iii). A servicer may offer a short-term payment forbearance program in conjunction with a short-term repayment plan pursuant to this paragraph (c)(2)(iii).

(iv) Facially complete application. A loss mitigation application shall be considered facially complete when a borrower submits all the missing documents and information as stated in the notice required under paragraph (b)(2)(i)(B) of this section, when no additional information is requested in such notice, or once the servicer is required to provide the borrower a written notice pursuant to paragraph (c)(3)(i) of this section. If the servicer later discovers that additional information or corrections to a previously submitted document are required to complete the application, the servicer must promptly request the missing information or corrected documents and treat the application as complete for the purposes of paragraphs (f)(2) and (g) of this section until the borrower is given a reasonable opportunity to complete the application. If the borrower completes the application within this period, the application shall be considered complete as of the date it first became facially complete, for the purposes of paragraphs (d), (e), (f)(2), (g), and (h) of this section, and as of the date the application was actually complete for the purposes of this paragraph (c). A servicer that complies with this paragraph (c)(2)(iv) will be deemed to have fulfilled its obligation to provide an accurate notice under paragraph (b)(2)(i)(B) of this section.

(3) Notice of complete application.

(i) Except as provided in paragraph (c)(3)(ii) of this section, within 5 days (excluding legal public holidays, Saturdays, and Sundays) after receiving a borrower's complete loss mitigation application, a servicer shall provide the borrower a written notice that sets forth the following information:

(A) That the loss mitigation application is complete;

(B) The date the servicer received the complete application;

(C) That the servicer expects to complete its evaluation within 30 days of the date it received the complete application;

(D) That the borrower is entitled to certain foreclosure protections because the servicer has received the complete application, and, as applicable, either:

(1) If the servicer has not made the first notice or filing required by applicable law for any judicial or non-judicial foreclosure process, that the servicer cannot make the first notice or filing required to commence or initiate the foreclosure process under applicable law before evaluating the borrower's complete application; or

(2) If the servicer has made the first notice or filing required by applicable law for any judicial or non-judicial foreclosure process, that the servicer has begun the foreclosure process, and that the servicer cannot conduct a foreclosure sale before evaluating the borrower's complete application;

(E) That the servicer may need additional information at a later date to evaluate the application, in which case the servicer will request that information from the borrower and give the borrower a reasonable opportunity to submit it, the evaluation process may take longer, and the foreclosure protections could end if the servicer does not receive the information as requested; and

(F) That the borrower may be entitled to additional protections under State or Federal law.

(ii) A servicer is not required to provide a notice pursuant to paragraph (c)(3)(i) of this section if:

(A) The servicer has already provided the borrower a notice under paragraph (b)(2)(i)(B) of this section informing the borrower that the application is complete and the servicer has not subsequently requested additional information or a corrected version of a previously submitted document from the borrower pursuant to paragraph (c)(2)(iv) of this section;

(B) The application was not complete or facially complete more than 37 days before a foreclosure sale; or

(C) The servicer has already provided the borrower a notice regarding the application under paragraph (c)(1)(ii) of this section.

(4) Information not in the borrower's control—

(i) Reasonable diligence. If a servicer requires documents or information not in the borrower's control to determine which loss mitigation options, if any, it will offer to the borrower, the servicer must exercise reasonable diligence in obtaining such documents or information.

(ii) Effect in case of delay.

(A)(1) Except as provided in paragraph (c)(4)(ii)(A)(2) of this section, a servicer must not deny a complete loss mitigation application solely because the servicer lacks required documents or information not in the borrower's control.

(2) If a servicer has exercised reasonable diligence to obtain required documents or information from a party other than the borrower or the servicer, but the servicer has been unable to obtain such documents or information for a significant period of time following the 30-day period identified in paragraph (c)(1) of this section, and the servicer, in accordance with applicable requirements established by the owner or assignee of the borrower's mortgage loan, is unable to determine which loss mitigation options, if any, it will offer the borrower without such documents or information, the servicer may deny the application and provide the borrower with a written notice in accordance with paragraph (c)(1)(ii) of this section. When providing the written notice in accordance with paragraph (c)(1)(ii) of this section, the servicer must also provide the borrower with a copy of the written notice required by paragraph (c)(4)(ii)(B) of this section.

(B) If a servicer is unable to make a determination within the 30-day period identified in paragraph (c)(1) of this section as to which loss mitigation options, if any, it will offer to the borrower because the servicer lacks required documents or information from a party other than the borrower or the servicer, the servicer must, within such 30-day period or promptly thereafter, provide the borrower a written notice, informing the borrower:

(1) That the servicer has not received documents or information not in the borrower's control that the servicer requires to determine which loss mitigation options, if any, it will offer to the borrower on behalf of the owner or assignee of the mortgage;

(2) Of the specific documents or information that the servicer lacks;

(3) That the servicer has requested such documents or information; and

(4) That the servicer will complete its evaluation of the borrower for all available loss mitigation options promptly upon receiving the documents or information.

(C) If a servicer must provide a notice required by paragraph (c)(4)(ii)(B) of this section, the servicer must not provide the borrower a written notice pursuant to paragraph (c)(1)(ii) of this section until the servicer receives the required documents or information referenced in paragraph (c)(4)(ii)(B)(2) of this section, except as provided in paragraph (c)(4)(ii)(A)(2) of this section. Upon receiving such required documents or information, the servicer must promptly provide the borrower with the written notice pursuant to paragraph (c)(1)(ii) of this section.

(d) Denial of loan modification options. If a borrower's complete loss mitigation application is denied for any trial or permanent loan modification option available to the borrower pursuant to paragraph (c) of this section, a servicer shall state in the notice sent to the borrower pursuant to paragraph (c)(1)(ii) of this section the specific reason or reasons for the servicer's determination for each such trial or permanent loan modification option and, if applicable, that the borrower was not evaluated on other criteria.

(e) Borrower response—

(1) In general. Subject to paragraphs (e)(2)(ii) and (iii) of this section, if a complete loss mitigation application is received 90 days or more before a foreclosure sale, a servicer may require that a borrower accept or reject an offer of a loss mitigation option no earlier than 14 days after the servicer provides the offer of a loss mitigation option to the borrower. If a complete loss mitigation application is received less than 90 days before a foreclosure sale, but more than 37 days before a foreclosure sale, a servicer may require that a borrower accept or reject an offer of a loss mitigation option no earlier than 7 days after the servicer provides the offer of a loss mitigation option to the borrower.

(2) Rejection—

(i) In general. Except as set forth in paragraphs (e)(2)(ii) and (iii) of this section, a servicer may deem a borrower that has not accepted an offer of a loss mitigation option within the deadline established pursuant to paragraph (e)(1) of this section to have rejected the offer of a loss mitigation option.

(ii) Trial Loan Modification Plan. A borrower who does not satisfy the servicer's requirements for accepting a trial loan modification plan, but submits the payments that would be owed pursuant to any such plan within the deadline established pursuant to paragraph (e)(1) of this section, shall be provided a reasonable period of time to fulfill any remaining requirements of the servicer for acceptance of the trial loan modification plan beyond the deadline established pursuant to paragraph (e)(1) of this section.

(iii) Interaction with appeal process. If a borrower makes an appeal pursuant to paragraph (h) of this section, the borrower's deadline for accepting a loss mitigation option offered pursuant to paragraph (c)(1)(ii) of this section shall be extended until 14 days after the servicer provides the notice required pursuant to paragraph (h)(4) of this section.

(f) Prohibition on foreclosure referral—

(1) Pre-foreclosure review period. A servicer shall not make the first notice or filing required by applicable law for any judicial or non-judicial foreclosure process unless:

(i) A borrower's mortgage loan obligation is more than 120 days delinquent;

(ii) The foreclosure is based on a borrower's violation of a due-on-sale clause; or

(iii) The servicer is joining the foreclosure action of a superior or subordinate lienholder.

(2) Application received before foreclosure referral. If a borrower submits a complete loss mitigation application during the pre-foreclosure review period set forth in paragraph (f)(1) of this section or before a servicer has made the first notice or filing required by applicable law for any judicial or non-judicial foreclosure process, a servicer shall not make the first notice or filing required by applicable law for any judicial or non-judicial foreclosure process unless:

(i) The servicer has sent the borrower a notice pursuant to paragraph (c)(1)(ii) of this section that the borrower is not eligible for any loss mitigation option and the appeal process in paragraph (h) of this section is not applicable, the borrower has not requested an appeal within the applicable time period for requesting an appeal, or the borrower's appeal has been denied;

(ii) The borrower rejects all loss mitigation options offered by the servicer; or

(iii) The borrower fails to perform under an agreement on a loss mitigation option.

(g) Prohibition on foreclosure sale. If a borrower submits a complete loss mitigation application after a servicer has made the first notice or filing required by applicable law for any judicial or non-judicial foreclosure process but more than 37 days before a foreclosure sale, a servicer shall not move for foreclosure judgment or order of sale, or conduct a foreclosure sale, unless:

(1) The servicer has sent the borrower a notice pursuant to paragraph (c)(1)(ii) of this section that the borrower is not eligible for any loss mitigation option and the appeal process in paragraph (h) of this section is not applicable, the borrower has not requested an appeal within the applicable time period for requesting an appeal, or the borrower's appeal has been denied;

(2) The borrower rejects all loss mitigation options offered by the servicer; or

(3) The borrower fails to perform under an agreement on a loss mitigation option.

(h) Appeal process—

(1) Appeal process required for loan modification denials. If a servicer receives a complete loss mitigation application 90 days or more before a foreclosure sale or during the period set forth in paragraph (f) of this section, a servicer shall permit a borrower to appeal the servicer's determination to deny a borrower's loss mitigation application for any trial or permanent loan modification program available to the borrower.

(2) Deadlines. A servicer shall permit a borrower to make an appeal within 14 days after the servicer provides the offer of a loss mitigation option to the borrower pursuant to paragraph (c)(1)(ii) of this section.

(3) Independent evaluation. An appeal shall be reviewed by different personnel than those responsible for evaluating the borrower's complete loss mitigation application.

(4) Appeal determination. Within 30 days of a borrower making an appeal, the servicer shall provide a notice to the borrower stating the servicer's determination of whether the servicer will offer the borrower a loss mitigation option based upon the appeal and, if applicable, how long the borrower has to accept or reject such an offer or a prior offer of a loss mitigation option.. A servicer may require that a borrower accept or reject an offer of a loss mitigation option after an appeal no earlier than 14 days after the servicer provides the notice to a borrower. A servicer's determination under this paragraph is not subject to any further appeal.

(i) Duplicative requests. A servicer must comply with the requirements of this section for a borrower's loss mitigation application, unless the servicer has previously complied with the requirements of this section for a complete loss mitigation application submitted by the borrower and the borrower has been delinquent at all times since submitting the prior complete application.

(j) Small servicer requirements. A small servicer shall be subject to the prohibition on foreclosure referral in paragraph (f)(1) of this section. A small servicer shall not make the first notice or filing required by applicable law for any judicial or non-judicial foreclosure process and shall not move for foreclosure judgment or order of sale, or conduct a foreclosure sale, if a borrower is performing pursuant to the terms of an agreement on a loss mitigation option.

(k) Servicing transfers—

(1) In general—

(i) Timing of compliance. Except as provided in paragraphs (k)(2) through (4) of this section, if a transferee servicer acquires the servicing of a mortgage loan for which a loss mitigation application is pending as of the transfer date, the transferee servicer must comply with the requirements of this section for that loss mitigation application within the timeframes that were applicable to the transferor servicer based on the date the transferor servicer received the loss mitigation application. All rights and protections under paragraphs (c) through (h) of this section to which a borrower was entitled before a transfer continue to apply notwithstanding the transfer.

(ii) Transfer date defined. For purposes of this paragraph (k), the transfer date is the date on which the transferee servicer will begin accepting payments relating to the mortgage loan, as disclosed on the notice of transfer of loan servicing pursuant to § 1024.33(b)(4)(iv).

(2) Acknowledgment notices—

(i) Transferee servicer timeframes. If a transferee servicer acquires the servicing of a mortgage loan for which the period to provide the notice required by paragraph (b)(2)(i)(B) of this section has not expired as of the transfer date and the transferor servicer has not provided such notice, the transferee servicer must provide the notice within 10 days (excluding legal public holidays, Saturdays, and Sundays) of the transfer date.

(ii) Prohibitions. A transferee servicer that must provide the notice required by paragraph (b)(2)(i)(B) of this section under this paragraph (k)(2):

(A) Shall not make the first notice or filing required by applicable law for any judicial or non-judicial foreclosure process until a date that is after the reasonable date disclosed to the borrower pursuant to paragraph (b)(2)(ii) of this section, notwithstanding paragraph (f)(1) of this section. For purposes of paragraph (f)(2) of this section, a borrower who submits a complete loss mitigation application on or before the reasonable date disclosed to the borrower pursuant to paragraph (b)(2)(ii) of this section shall be treated as having done so during the pre-foreclosure review period set forth in paragraph (f)(1) of this section.

(B) Shall comply with paragraphs (c), (d), and (g) of this section if the borrower submits a complete loss mitigation application to the transferee or transferor servicer 37 or fewer days before the foreclosure sale but on or before the reasonable date disclosed to the borrower pursuant to paragraph (b)(2)(ii) of this section.

(3) Complete loss mitigation applications pending at transfer. If a transferee servicer acquires the servicing of a mortgage loan for which a complete loss mitigation application is pending as of the transfer date, the transferee servicer must comply with the applicable requirements of paragraphs (c)(1) and (4) of this section within 30 days of the transfer date.

(4) Applications subject to appeal process. If a transferee servicer acquires the servicing of a mortgage loan for which an appeal of a transferor servicer's determination pursuant to paragraph (h) of this section has not been resolved by the transferor servicer as of the transfer date or is timely filed after the transfer date, the transferee servicer must make a determination on the appeal if it is able to do so or, if it is unable to do so, must treat the appeal as a pending complete loss mitigation application.

(i) Determining appeal. If a transferee servicer is required under this paragraph (k)(4) to make a determination on an appeal, the transferee servicer must complete the determination and provide the notice required by paragraph (h)(4) of this section within 30 days of the transfer date or 30 days of the date the borrower made the appeal, whichever is later.

(ii) Servicer unable to determine appeal. A transferee servicer that is required to treat a borrower's appeal as a pending complete loss mitigation application under this paragraph (k)(4) must comply with the requirements of this section for such application, including evaluating the borrower for all loss mitigation options available to the borrower from the transferee servicer. For purposes of paragraph (c) or (k)(3) of this section, as applicable, such a pending complete loss mitigation application shall be considered complete as of the date the appeal was received by the transferor servicer or the transferee servicer, whichever occurs first. For purposes of paragraphs (e) through (h) of this section, the transferee servicer must treat such a pending complete loss mitigation application as facially complete under paragraph (c)(2)(iv) as of the date it was first facially complete or complete, as applicable, with respect to the transferor servicer.

(5) Pending loss mitigation offers. A transfer does not affect a borrower's ability to accept or reject a loss mitigation option offered under paragraph (c) or (h) of this section. If a transferee servicer acquires the servicing of a mortgage loan for which the borrower's time period under paragraph (e) or (h) of this section for accepting or rejecting a loss mitigation option offered by the transferor servicer has not expired as of the transfer date, the transferee servicer must allow the borrower to accept or reject the offer during the unexpired balance of the applicable time period.

MILITARY LENDING ACT

10 U.S.C.A. § 987. Terms of consumer credit extended to members and dependents; limitations.

(a) Interest.—A creditor who extends consumer credit to a covered member of the armed forces or a dependent of such a member shall not require the member or dependent to pay interest with respect to the extension of such credit, except as—

(1) agreed to under the terms of the credit agreement or promissory note;

(2) authorized by applicable State or Federal law; and

(3) not specifically prohibited by this section.

(b) Annual percentage rate.—A creditor described in subsection (a) may not impose an annual percentage rate of interest greater than 36 percent with respect to the consumer credit extended to a covered member or a dependent of a covered member.

(c) Mandatory loan disclosures.—

(1) Information required.—With respect to any extension of consumer credit (including any consumer credit originated or extended through the internet) to a covered member or a dependent of a covered member, a creditor shall provide to the member or dependent the following information orally and in writing before the issuance of the credit:

(A) A statement of the annual percentage rate of interest applicable to the extension of credit.

(B) Any disclosures required under the Truth in Lending Act (15 U.S.C. 1601 et seq.).

(C) A clear description of the payment obligations of the member or dependent, as applicable.

(2) Terms.—Such disclosures shall be presented in accordance with terms prescribed by the regulations issued by the Board of Governors of the Federal Reserve System to implement the Truth in Lending Act (15 U.S.C. 1601 et seq.).

(d) Preemption.—

(1) Inconsistent laws.—Except as provided in subsection (f)(2), this section preempts any State or Federal law, rule, or regulation, including any State usury law, to the extent that such law, rule, or regulation is inconsistent with this section, except that this section shall not preempt any such law, rule, or regulation that provides protection to a covered member or a dependent of such a member in addition to the protection provided by this section.

(2) Different treatment under State law of members and dependents prohibited.—States shall not—

(A) authorize creditors to charge covered members and their dependents annual percentage rates of interest for any consumer credit or loans higher than the legal limit for residents of the State; or

(B) permit violation or waiver of any State consumer lending protections covering consumer credit for the benefit of residents of the State on the basis of nonresident or military status of a covered member or dependent of such a member, regardless of the member's or dependent's domicile or permanent home of record.

(e) Limitations.—It shall be unlawful for any creditor to extend consumer credit to a covered member or a dependent of such a member with respect to which—

(1) the creditor rolls over, renews, repays, refinances, or consolidates any consumer credit extended to the borrower by the same creditor with the proceeds of other credit extended to the same covered member or a dependent;

(2) the borrower is required to waive the borrower's right to legal recourse under any otherwise applicable provision of State or Federal law, including any provision of the Servicemembers Civil Relief Act (50 U.S.C. 3901 et seq.);

(3) the creditor requires the borrower to submit to arbitration or imposes onerous legal notice provisions in the case of a dispute;

(4) the creditor demands unreasonable notice from the borrower as a condition for legal action;

(5) the creditor uses a check or other method of access to a deposit, savings, or other financial account maintained by the borrower, or the title of a vehicle as security for the obligation;

(6) the creditor requires as a condition for the extension of credit that the borrower establish an allotment to repay an obligation; or

(7) the borrower is prohibited from prepaying the loan or is charged a penalty or fee for prepaying all or part of the loan.

(f) Penalties and remedies.—

(1) Misdemeanor.—A creditor who knowingly violates this section shall be fined as provided in title 18, or imprisoned for not more than one year, or both.

(2) Preservation of other remedies.—The remedies and rights provided under this section are in addition to and do not preclude any remedy otherwise available under law to the person claiming relief under this section, including any award for consequential and punitive damages.

(3) Contract void.—Any credit agreement, promissory note, or other contract prohibited under this section is void from the inception of such contract.

(4) Arbitration.—Notwithstanding section 2 of title 9, or any other Federal or State law, rule, or regulation, no agreement to arbitrate any dispute involving the extension of consumer credit shall be enforceable against any covered member or dependent of such a member, or any person who was a covered member or dependent of that member when the agreement was made.

(5) Civil Liability.—

(A) In General.—A person who violates this section with respect to any person is civilly liable to such person for—

(i) any actual damage sustained as a result, but not less than $500 for each violation;

(ii) appropriate punitive damages;

(iii) appropriate equitable or declaratory relief; and

(iv) any other relief provided by law

(B) Costs of the Action.—In any successful action to enforce the civil liability described in subparagraph (A), the person who violated this section is also liable for the costs of the action, together with reasonable attorney fees as determined by the court.

(C) Effect of Finding of Bad Faith and Harassment.—In any successful action by a defendant under this section, if the court finds the action was brought in bad faith and for the purpose of harassment, the plaintiff is liable for the attorney fees of the defendant as determined by the court to be reasonable in relation to the work expended and costs incurred.

(D) Defenses.—A person may not be held liable for civil liability under this paragraph if the person shows by a preponderance of evidence that the violation was not intentional and resulted from a bona fide error notwithstanding the maintenance of procedures reasonably adapted to avoid any such error. Examples of a bona fide error include clerical, calculation, computer malfunction and programming, and printing errors, except that an error of legal judgment with respect to a person's obligations under this section is not a bona fide error.

(E) Jurisdiction, Venue, and Statute of Limitations.—An action for civil liability under this paragraph may be brought in any appropriate United States district court, without regard to the amount in controversy, or in any other court of competent jurisdiction, not later than the earlier of—

(i) two years after the date of discovery by the plaintiff of the violation that is the basis for such liability; or

(ii) five years after the date on which the violation that is the basis for such liability occurs.

(6) Administrative Enforcement.—The provisions of this section (other than paragraph (1) of this subsection) shall be enforced by the agencies specified in section 108 of the Truth in Lending Act (15 U.S.C. 1607) in the manner set forth in that section or under any other applicable authorities available to such agencies.

(g) Servicemembers Civil Relief Act protections unaffected.—Nothing in this section may be construed to limit or otherwise affect the applicability of section 207 of the Servicemembers Civil Relief Act (50 U.S.C. App. 527).

(h) Regulations.—**(1)** The Secretary of Defense shall prescribe regulations to carry out this section.

(2) Such regulations shall establish the following:

(A) Disclosures required of any creditor that extends consumer credit to a covered member or dependent of such a member.

(B) The method for calculating the applicable annual percentage rate of interest on such obligations, in accordance with the limit established under this section.

(C) A maximum allowable amount of all fees, and the types of fees, associated with any such extension of credit, to be expressed and disclosed to the borrower as a total amount and as a percentage of the principal amount of the obligation, at the time at which the transaction is entered into.

(D) Definitions of "creditor" under paragraph (5) and "consumer credit" under paragraph (6) of subsection (i), consistent with the provisions of this section.

(E) Such other criteria or limitations as the Secretary of Defense determines appropriate, consistent with the provisions of this section.

(3) In prescribing regulations under this subsection, and not less often than once every two years thereafter, the Secretary of Defense shall consult with the following:

(A) The Federal Trade Commission.

(B) The Board of Governors of the Federal Reserve System.

(C) The Office of the Comptroller of the Currency.

(D) The Federal Deposit Insurance Corporation.

(E) The Bureau of Consumer Financial Protection.

(F) The National Credit Union Administration.

(G) The Treasury Department.

(i) Definitions.—In this section:

(1) Covered member.—The term "covered member" means a member of the armed forces who is—

(A) on active duty under a call or order that does not specify a period of 30 days or less; or

(B) on active Guard and Reserve Duty.

(2) Dependent.—The term "dependent", with respect to a covered member, means a person described in subparagraph (A), (D), (E), or (I) of section 1072(2) of this title.

(3) Interest.—The term "interest" includes all cost elements associated with the extension of credit, including fees, service charges, renewal charges, credit insurance premiums, any ancillary product sold with any extension of credit to a servicemember or the servicemember's dependent, as applicable, and any other charge or premium with respect to the extension of consumer credit.

(4) Annual percentage rate.—The term "annual percentage rate" has the same meaning as in section 107 of the Truth and Lending Act (15 U.S.C. 1606), as implemented by regulations of the Board of Governors of the Federal Reserve System. For purposes of this section, such term includes all fees and charges, including charges and fees for single premium credit insurance and other ancillary products sold in connection with the credit transaction, and such fees and charges shall be included in the calculation of the annual percentage rate.

(5) Creditor.—The term "creditor" means a person—

(A) who—

(i) is engaged in the business of extending consumer credit; and

(ii) meets such additional criteria as are specified for such purpose in regulations prescribed under this section; or

(B) who is an assignee of a person described in subparagraph (A) with respect to any consumer credit extended.

(6) Consumer credit.—The term "consumer credit" has the meaning provided for such term in regulations prescribed under this section, except that such term does not include (A) a residential mortgage, or (B) a loan procured in the course of purchasing a car or other personal property, when that loan is offered for the express purpose of financing the purchase and is secured by the car or personal property procured.

DEPARTMENT OF DEFENSE REGULATIONS

LIMITATIONS ON TERMS OF CONSUMER CREDIT EXTENDED TO SERVICE MEMBERS AND DEPENDENTS

32 C.F.R. Part 232

Table of Sections

§ 232.1. Authority, Purpose, and Coverage

(a) Authority. This part is issued by the Department of Defense to implement 10 U.S.C. 987.

(b) Purpose. The purpose of this part is to impose limitations on the cost and terms of certain extensions of credit to Service members and their dependents, and to provide additional protections relating to such transactions in accordance with 10 U.S.C. 987.

(c) Coverage. This part defines the types of transactions involving "consumer credit," a "creditor," and a "covered borrower" that are subject to the regulation, consistent with the provisions of 10 U.S.C. 987. In addition, this part:

(1) Provides the maximum allowable amount of all charges, and the types of charges, that may be associated with a covered extension of consumer credit;

(2) Requires a creditor to provide to a covered borrower a statement of the Military Annual Percentage Rate, or MAPR, before or at the time the borrower becomes obligated on the transaction or establishes an account for the consumer credit. The statement required by § 232.6(a)(1) differs from and is in addition to the disclosures that must be provided to consumers under the Truth in Lending Act;

(3) Provides for the method creditors shall use in calculating the MAPR, and;

(4) Contains such other criteria and limitations as the Secretary of Defense has determined appropriate, consistent with the provisions of 10 U.S.C. 987.

§ 232.2. Applicability

(a)(1) Applicability. This part applies to consumer credit extended by creditors to a covered borrower, as those terms are defined in this part. Nothing in this part applies to a credit transaction or account relating to a consumer who is not a covered borrower at the time he or she becomes obligated on a credit transaction or establishes an account for credit. Nothing in this part applies to a credit transaction or account relating to a consumer (which otherwise would be consumer credit) when the consumer no longer is a covered borrower.

(2) Examples—

(i) Covered borrower. Consumer A is a member of the armed forces but not serving on active duty, and holds an account for closed-end credit with a financial institution. After establishing the closed-end credit account, Consumer A is ordered to serve on active duty, thereby becoming a covered borrower, and soon thereafter separately establishes an open-end line of credit for personal purposes (which is not subject to any exception or temporary exemption) with the financial institution. This part applies to the open-end line of credit, but not to the closed-end credit account.

(ii) Not a covered borrower. Same facts as described in paragraph (a)(2)(i) of this section. One year after establishing the open-end line of credit, Consumer A ceases to serve on active duty. This part never did apply to the closed-end credit account, and because Consumer A no longer is a covered borrower, this part no longer applies to the open-end line of credit.

(b) Examples. The examples in this part are not exclusive. To the extent that an example in this part implicates a term or provision of Regulation Z (12 CFR part 1026), issued by the Consumer Financial Protection Bureau to implement the Truth in Lending Act, Regulation Z shall control the meaning of that term or provision.

§ 232.3. Definitions

Terms used in this part are defined as follows:

(a) Affiliate means any person that controls, is controlled by, or is under common control with another person.

(b) Billing cycle has the same meaning as "billing cycle" in Regulation Z.

(c) Bureau means the Consumer Financial Protection Bureau.

(d) Closed-end credit means consumer credit (but for the conditions applicable to consumer credit under this part) other than consumer credit that is "open-end credit" as that term is defined in Regulation Z.

(e) Consumer means a natural person.

(f)(1) Consumer credit means credit offered or extended to a covered borrower primarily for personal, family, or household purposes, and that is:

(i) Subject to a finance charge; or

(ii) Payable by a written agreement in more than four installments.

(2) Exceptions. Notwithstanding paragraph (f)(1) of this section, consumer credit does not mean:

(i) A residential mortgage, which is any credit transaction secured by an interest in a dwelling, including a transaction to finance the purchase or initial construction of the dwelling, any refinance transaction, home equity loan or line of credit, or reverse mortgage;

(ii) Any credit transaction that is expressly intended to finance the purchase of a motor vehicle when the credit is secured by the vehicle being purchased;

(iii) Any credit transaction that is expressly intended to finance the purchase of personal property when the credit is secured by the property being purchased;

(iv) Any credit transaction that is an exempt transaction for the purposes of Regulation Z (other than a transaction exempt under 12 CFR 1026.29) or otherwise is not subject to disclosure requirements under Regulation Z; and

(v) Any credit transaction or account for credit for which a creditor determines that a consumer is not a covered borrower by using a method and by complying with the recordkeeping requirement set forth in § 232.5(b).

(g)(1) Covered borrower means a consumer who, at the time the consumer becomes obligated on a consumer credit transaction or establishes an account for consumer credit, is a covered member (as defined in paragraph (g)(2) of this section) or a dependent (as defined in paragraph (g)(3) of this section) of a covered member.

(2) The term "covered member" means a member of the armed forces who is serving on—

(i) Active duty pursuant to title 10, title 14, or title 32, United States Code, under a call or order that does not specify a period of 30 days or fewer; or

(ii) Active Guard and Reserve duty, as that term is defined in 10 U.S.C. 101(d)(6).

(3) The term "dependent" with respect to a covered member means a person described in subparagraph (A), (D), (E), or (I) of 10 U.S.C. 1072(2).

(4) Notwithstanding paragraph (g)(1) of this section, covered borrower does not mean a consumer who (though a covered borrower at the time he or she became obligated on a consumer credit transaction or established an account for consumer credit) no longer is a covered member (as defined in paragraph (g)(2) of this section) or a dependent (as defined in paragraph (g)(2) of this section) of a covered member.

(h) Credit means the right granted to a consumer by a creditor to defer payment of debt or to incur debt and defer its payment.

(i) Creditor, except as provided in § 232.8(a), (f), and (g), means a person who is:

(1) Engaged in the business of extending consumer credit; or

(2) An assignee of a person described in paragraph (i)(1) of this section with respect to any consumer credit extended.

(3) For the purposes of this definition, a creditor is engaged in the business of extending consumer credit if the creditor considered by itself and together with its affiliates meets the transaction standard for a "creditor" under Regulation Z with respect to extensions of consumer credit to covered borrowers.

(j) Department means the Department of Defense.

(k) Dwelling means a residential structure that contains one to four units, whether or not the structure is attached to real property. The term includes an individual condominium unit, cooperative unit, mobile home, and manufactured home.

(*l*) Electronic fund transfer has the same meaning as in the regulation issued by the Bureau to implement the Electronic Fund Transfer Act, as amended from time to time (12 CFR part 1005).

(m) Federal credit union has the same meaning as "Federal credit union" in the Federal Credit Union Act (12 U.S.C. 1752(1)).

(n) Finance charge has the same meaning as "finance charge" in Regulation Z.

(*o*) Insured depository institution has the same meaning as "insured depository institution" in the Federal Deposit Insurance Act (12 U.S.C. 1813(c)).

(p) Military annual percentage rate (MAPR). The MAPR is the cost of the consumer credit expressed as an annual rate, and shall be calculated in accordance with § 232.4(c).

(q) Open-end credit means consumer credit that (but for the conditions applicable to consumer credit under this part) is "open-end credit" under Regulation Z.

(r) Person means a natural person or organization, including any corporation, partnership, proprietorship, association, cooperative, estate, trust, or government unit.

(s) Regulation Z means any rules, or interpretations thereof, issued by the Bureau to implement the Truth in Lending Act, as amended from time to time, including any interpretation or approval issued by an official or employee duly authorized by the Bureau to issue such interpretations or approvals. However, for any provision of this part requiring a creditor to comply with Regulation Z, a creditor who is subject to Regulation Z (12 CFR part 226) issued by the Board of Governors of the Federal Reserve System must continue to comply with 12 CFR part 226. Words that are not defined in this part have the same meanings given to them in Regulation Z (12 CFR part 1026) issued by the Bureau, as amended from time to time, including any interpretation thereof by the Bureau or an official or employee of the Bureau duly authorized by the Bureau to issue such interpretations. Words that are not defined in this part or Regulation Z, or any interpretation thereof, have the meanings given to them by State or Federal law.

(t) Short-term, small amount loan means a closed-end loan that is—

(1) Subject to and made in accordance with a Federal law (other than 10 U.S.C. 987) that expressly limits the rate of interest that a Federal credit union or an insured depository institution may charge on an extension of credit, provided that the limitation set forth in that law is comparable to a limitation of an annual percentage rate of interest of 36 percent; and

(2) Made in accordance with the requirements, terms, and conditions of a rule, prescribed by the appropriate Federal regulatory agency (or jointly by such agencies), that implements the Federal law described in paragraph (t)(1) of this section, provided further that such law or rule contains—

(i) A fixed numerical limit on the maximum maturity term, which term shall not exceed 9 months; and

(ii) A fixed numerical limit on any application fee that may be charged to a consumer who applies for such closed-end loan.

§ 232.4. Terms of Consumer Credit Extended to Covered Borrowers

(a) General conditions. A creditor who extends consumer credit to a covered borrower may not require the covered borrower to pay an MAPR for the credit with respect to such extension of credit, except as:

(1) Agreed to under the terms of the credit agreement or promissory note;

(2) Authorized by applicable State or Federal law; and

(3) Not specifically prohibited by this part.

(b) Limit on cost of consumer credit. A creditor may not impose an MAPR greater than 36 percent in connection with an extension of consumer credit that is closed-end credit or in any billing cycle for open-end credit.

(c) Calculation of the MAPR.—

(1) Charges included in the MAPR. The charges for the MAPR shall include, as applicable to the extension of consumer credit:

(i) Any credit insurance premium or fee, any charge for single premium credit insurance, any fee for a debt cancellation contract, or any fee for a debt suspension agreement;

(ii) Any fee for a credit-related ancillary product sold in connection with the credit transaction for closed-end credit or an account for open-end credit; and

(iii) Except for a bona fide fee (other than a periodic rate) which may be excluded under paragraph (d) of this section:

(A) Finance charges associated with the consumer credit;

(B) Any application fee charged to a covered borrower who applies for consumer credit, other than an application fee charged by a Federal credit union or an insured depository institution when making a short-term, small amount loan, provided that the application fee is charged to the covered borrower not more than once in any rolling 12-month period; and

(C) Any fee imposed for participation in any plan or arrangement for consumer credit, subject to paragraph (c)(2)(ii)(B) of this section.

(iv) Certain exclusions of Regulation Z inapplicable. Any charge set forth in paragraphs (c)(1)(i) through (iii) of this section shall be included in the calculation of the MAPR even if that charge would be excluded from the finance charge under Regulation Z.

(2) Computing the MAPR—

(i) Closed-end credit. For closed-end credit, the MAPR shall be calculated following the rules for calculating and disclosing the "Annual Percentage Rate (APR)" for credit transactions under Regulation Z based on the charges set forth in paragraph (c)(1) of this section.

(ii) Open-end credit—

(A) In general. Except as provided in paragraph (c)(2)(ii)(B) of this section, for open-end credit, the MAPR shall be calculated following the rules for calculating the effective annual percentage rate for a billing cycle as set forth in § 1026.14(c)and (d) of Regulation Z (as if a creditor must comply with that section) based on the charges set forth in paragraph (c)(1) of this section. Notwithstanding § 1026.14(c) and (d) of Regulation Z, the amount of charges related to opening, renewing, or continuing an account must be included in the calculation of the MAPR to the extent those charges are set forth in paragraph (c)(1) of this section.

(B) No balance during a billing cycle. For open-end credit, if the MAPR cannot be calculated in a billing cycle because there is no balance in the billing cycle, a creditor may not impose any fee or charge during that billing cycle, except that the creditor may impose a fee for participation in any plan or arrangement for that open-end credit so long as the participation fee does not exceed $100 per annum, regardless of the billing cycle in which the participation fee is imposed; provided, however, that the $100-per annum limitation on the amount of the participation fee does not apply to a bona fide participation fee imposed in accordance with paragraph (d) of this section.

(d) Bona fide fee charged to a credit card account—

(1) In general. For consumer credit extended in a credit card account under an open-end (not home-secured) consumer credit plan, a bona fide fee, other than a periodic rate, is not a charge required to be included in the MAPR pursuant to paragraph (c)(1) of this section. The exclusion provided for any bona fide fee under this paragraph (d) applies only to the extent that the charge by the creditor is a bona fide fee, and must be reasonable for that type of fee.

(2) Ineligible items. The exclusion for bona fide fees in paragraph (d)(1) of this section does not apply to—

(i) Any credit insurance premium or fee, including any charge for single premium credit insurance, any fee for a debt cancellation contract, or any fee for a debt suspension agreement; or

(ii) Any fee for a credit-related ancillary product sold in connection with the credit transaction for closed-end credit or an account for open-end credit.

(3) Standards relating to bona fide fees—

(i) Like-kind fees. To assess whether a bona fide fee is reasonable under paragraph (d)(1) of this section, the fee must be compared to fees typically imposed by other creditors for the same or a substantially similar product or service. For example, when assessing a bona fide cash advance fee, that fee must be compared to fees charged by other creditors for transactions in which consumers receive extensions of credit in the form of cash or its equivalent. Conversely, when assessing a foreign transaction fee, that fee may not be compared to a cash advance fee because the foreign transaction fee involves the service of exchanging the consumer's currency (e.g., a reserve currency) for the local currency demanded by a merchant for a good or service, and does not involve the provision of cash to the consumer.

(ii) Safe harbor. A bona fide fee is reasonable under paragraph (d)(1) of this section if the amount of the fee is less than or equal to an average amount of a fee for the same or a substantially similar product or service charged by 5 or more creditors each of whose U.S. credit cards in force is at least $3 billion in an outstanding balance (or at least $3 billion in loans on U.S. credit card accounts initially extended by the creditor) at any time during the 3-year period preceding the time such average is computed.

(iii) Reasonable fee. A bona fide fee that is higher than an average amount, as calculated under paragraph (d)(3)(ii) of this section, also may be reasonable under paragraph (d)(1) of this section depending on other factors relating to the credit card account. A bona fide fee charged by a creditor is not unreasonable solely because other creditors do not charge a fee for the same or a substantially similar product or service.

(iv) Indicia of reasonableness for a participation fee. An amount of a bona fide fee for participation in a credit card account may be reasonable under paragraph (d)(1) of this section if that amount reasonably corresponds to the credit limit in effect or credit made available when the fee is imposed, to the services offered under the credit card account, or to other factors relating to the credit card account. For example, even if other creditors typically charge $100 per annum for participation in credit card accounts, a $400 fee nevertheless may be reasonable if (relative to other accounts carrying participation fees) the credit made available to the covered borrower is significantly higher or additional services or other benefits are offered under that account.

(4) Effect of charging fees on bona fide fees—

(i) Bona fide fees treated separately from charges for credit insurance products or credit-related ancillary products. If a creditor imposes a fee described in paragraph (c)(1) of this section and imposes a finance charge to a covered borrower, the total amount of the fee(s) and finance charge(s) shall be included in the MAPR pursuant to paragraph (c) of this section, and the imposition of any fee or finance charge described in paragraph (c)(1) of this section shall not affect whether another type of fee may be excluded as a bona fide fee under this paragraph (d).

(ii) Effect of charges for non-bona fide fees. If a creditor imposes any fee (other than a periodic rate or a fee that must be included in the MAPR pursuant to paragraph (c)(1) of this section) that is not a bona fide fee and imposes a finance charge to a covered borrower, the total amount of those fees, including any bona fide fees, and other finance charges shall be included in the MAPR pursuant to paragraph (c) of this section.

(iii) Examples.

(A) In a credit card account under an open-end (not home-secured) consumer credit plan during a given billing cycle, Creditor A imposes on a covered borrower a fee for a debt cancellation product (as described in paragraph (c)(1)(i) of this section), a finance charge (as described in paragraph (c)(1)(iii)(A)), and a bona fide foreign transaction fee that qualifies for the exclusion under this paragraph (d). Only the fee for the debt cancellation product and the finance charge must be included when calculating the MAPR.

(B) In a credit card account under an open-end (not home-secured) consumer credit plan during a given billing cycle, Creditor B imposes on a covered borrower a fee for a debt cancellation product (as described in paragraph (c)(1)(i) of this section), a finance charge (as described in paragraph (c)(1)(iii)(A)), a bona fide foreign transaction fee that qualifies for the exclusion under this paragraph (d), and a bona fide, but unreasonable cash advance fee. All of the fees—including the foreign transaction fee that otherwise would qualify for the exclusion under this paragraph (d)—and the finance charge must be included when calculating the MAPR.

(5) Rule of construction. Nothing in paragraph (d)(1) of this section authorizes the imposition of fees or charges otherwise prohibited by this part or by other applicable State or Federal law.

§ 232.5. Identification of Covered Borrower

(a) No restriction on method for covered-borrower check. A creditor is permitted to apply its own method to assess whether a consumer is a covered borrower.

(b) Safe harbor—

(1) In general. A creditor may conclusively determine whether credit is offered or extended to a covered borrower, and thus may be subject to 10 U.S.C. 987 and the requirements of this part, by assessing the status of a consumer in accordance with this paragraph (b).

(2) Methods to check status of consumer—

(i) Department database—

(A) In general. To determine whether a consumer is a covered borrower, a creditor may verify the status of a consumer by using information relating to that consumer, if any, obtained directly or indirectly from the database maintained by the Department, available at https://www.dmdc.osd.mil/mla/welcome.xhtml. A search of the Department's database requires the entry of the consumer's last name, date of birth, and Social Security number.

(B) Historic lookback prohibited. At any time after a consumer has entered into a transaction or established an account involving an extension of credit, a creditor (including an assignee) may not, directly or indirectly, obtain any information from any database maintained by the Department to ascertain whether a consumer had been a covered borrower as of the date of that transaction or as of the date that account was established.

(ii) Consumer report from a nationwide consumer reporting agency. To determine whether a consumer is a covered borrower, a creditor may verify the status of a consumer by using a statement, code, or similar indicator describing that status, if any, contained in a consumer report obtained from a consumer reporting agency that compiles and maintains files on consumers on a nationwide basis, or a reseller of such a consumer report (as each of those terms is defined in the Fair Credit Reporting Act (15 U.S.C. 1681a) and any implementing regulation (12 CFR part 1022)).

(3) Determination and recordkeeping; one-time determination permitted. A creditor who makes a determination regarding the status of a consumer by using one or both of the methods set forth in paragraph (b)(2) of this section shall be deemed to be conclusive with respect to that transaction or account involving consumer credit between the creditor and that consumer, so long as that creditor timely creates and thereafter maintains a record of the information so obtained. A creditor may make the determination described in this paragraph (b), and keep the record of that information obtained at that time, solely at the time—

(i) A consumer initiates the transaction or 30 days prior to that time;

(ii) A consumer applies to establish the account or 30 days prior to that time; or

(iii) The creditor develops or processes, with respect to a consumer, a firm offer of credit that (among the criteria used by the creditor for the offer) includes the status of the consumer as a covered borrower, so long as the consumer responds to that offer not later than 60 days after the time that the creditor had provided that offer to the consumer. If the consumer responds to the creditor's offer later than 60 days after the time that the creditor had provided that offer to the consumer, then the creditor may not rely upon its initial determination in developing or processing that offer, and, instead, may act on the consumer's response as if the consumer is initiating the transaction or applying to establish the account (as described in paragraph (b)(3)(i) or (ii) of this section).

§ 232.6. Mandatory Loan Disclosures

(a) Required information. With respect to any extension of consumer credit (including any consumer credit originated or extended through the internet) to a covered borrower, a creditor shall provide to the covered borrower the following information before or at the time the borrower becomes obligated on the transaction or establishes an account for the consumer credit:

(1) A statement of the MAPR applicable to the extension of consumer credit;

(2) Any disclosure required by Regulation Z, which shall be provided only in accordance with the requirements of Regulation Z that apply to that disclosure; and

(3) A clear description of the payment obligation of the covered borrower, as applicable. A payment schedule (in the case of closed-end credit) or account-opening disclosure (in the case of open-end credit) provided pursuant to paragraph (a)(2) of this section satisfies this requirement.

(b) One-time delivery; multiple creditors.

(1) The information described in paragraphs (a)(1) and (a)(3) of this section are not required to be provided to a covered borrower more than once for the transaction or the account established for consumer credit with respect to that borrower.

(2) Multiple creditors. If a transaction involves more than one creditor, then only one of those creditors must provide the disclosures in accordance with this section. The creditors may agree among themselves which creditor may provide the information described in paragraphs (a)(1) and (a)(3) of this section.

(c) Statement of the MAPR—

(1) In general. A creditor may satisfy the requirement of paragraph (a)(1) of this section by describing the charges the creditor may impose, in accordance with this part and subject to the terms and conditions of the agreement, relating to the consumer credit to calculate the MAPR. Paragraph (a)(1) of this section shall not be construed as requiring a creditor to describe the MAPR as a numerical value or to describe the total dollar amount of all charges in the MAPR that apply to the extension of consumer credit.

(2) Method of providing a statement regarding the MAPR. A creditor may include a statement of the MAPR applicable to the consumer credit in the agreement with the covered borrower involving the consumer credit transaction. Paragraph (a)(1) of this section shall not be construed as requiring a creditor to include a statement of the MAPR applicable to an extension of consumer credit in any advertisement relating to the credit.

(3) Model statement. A statement substantially similar to the following statement may be used for the purpose of paragraph (a)(1) of this section: "Federal law provides important protections to members of the Armed Forces and their dependents relating to extensions of consumer credit. In general, the cost of consumer credit to a member of the Armed Forces and his or her dependent may not exceed an annual percentage rate of 36 percent. This rate must include, as applicable to the credit transaction or account: The costs associated with credit insurance premiums; fees for ancillary products sold in connection with the credit transaction; any application fee charged (other than certain application fees for specified credit transactions or accounts); and any participation fee charged (other than certain participation fees for a credit card account)."

(d) Methods of delivery—

(1) Written disclosures. The creditor shall provide the information required by paragraphs (a)(1) and (3) of this section in writing in a form the covered borrower can keep.

(2) Oral disclosures.

(i) In general. The creditor also shall orally provide the information required by paragraphs (a)(1) and (3) of this section.

(ii) Methods to provide oral disclosures. A creditor may satisfy the requirement in paragraph (d)(2)(i) of this section if the creditor provides—

(A) The information to the covered borrower in person; or

(B) A toll-free telephone number in order to deliver the oral disclosures to a covered borrower when the covered borrower contacts the creditor for this purpose.

(iii) Toll-free telephone number on application or disclosure. If applicable, the toll-free telephone number must be included on—

(A) A form the creditor directs the consumer to use to apply for the transaction or account involving consumer credit; or

(B) A written disclosure the creditor provides to the covered borrower, pursuant to paragraph (d)(1) of this section.

(e) When disclosures are required for refinancing or renewal of covered loan. The refinancing or renewal of consumer credit requires new disclosures under this section only when the transaction for that credit would be considered a new transaction that requires disclosures under Regulation Z.

§ 232.7. Preemption

(a) Inconsistent laws. 10 U.S.C. 987 as implemented by this part preempts any State or Federal law, rule or regulation, including any State usury law, to the extent such law, rule or regulation is inconsistent with this part, except that any such law, rule or regulation is not preempted by this part to the extent that it provides protection to a covered borrower greater than those protections provided by 10 U.S.C. 987 and this part.

(b) Different treatment under State law of covered borrowers is prohibited. States may not:

(1) Authorize creditors to charge covered borrowers rates of interest for any consumer credit or loans that are higher than the legal limit for residents of the State, or

(2) Permit the violation or waiver of any State consumer lending protection covering consumer credit that is for the benefit of residents of the State on the basis of the covered borrower's nonresident or military status, regardless of the covered borrower's domicile or permanent home of record, provided that the protection would otherwise apply to the covered borrower.

§ 232.8. Limitations

Title 10 U.S.C. 987 makes it unlawful for any creditor to extend consumer credit to a covered borrower with respect to which:

(a) The creditor rolls over, renews, repays, refinances, or consolidates any consumer credit extended to the covered borrower by the same creditor with the proceeds of other consumer credit extended by that creditor to the same covered borrower. This paragraph shall not apply to a transaction when the same creditor extends consumer credit to a covered borrower to refinance or renew an extension of credit that was not covered by this paragraph because the consumer was not a covered borrower at the time of the original transaction. For the purposes of this paragraph, the term "creditor" means a person engaged in the business of extending consumer credit subject to applicable law to engage in deferred presentment transactions or similar payday loan transactions (as described in the relevant law), provided however, that the term does not include a person that is chartered or licensed under Federal or State law as a bank, savings association, or credit union.

(b) The covered borrower is required to waive the covered borrower's right to legal recourse under any otherwise applicable provision of State or Federal law, including any provision of the Servicemembers Civil Relief Act (50 U.S.C. App. 501 et seq.).

(c) The creditor requires the covered borrower to submit to arbitration or imposes other onerous legal notice provisions in the case of a dispute.

(d) The creditor demands unreasonable notice from the covered borrower as a condition for legal action.

(e) The creditor uses a check or other method of access to a deposit, savings, or other financial account maintained by the covered borrower, except that, in connection with a consumer credit transaction with an MAPR consistent with § 232.4(b), the creditor may:

(1) Require an electronic fund transfer to repay a consumer credit transaction, unless otherwise prohibited by law;

(2) Require direct deposit of the consumer's salary as a condition of eligibility for consumer credit, unless otherwise prohibited by law; or

(3) If not otherwise prohibited by applicable law, take a security interest in funds deposited after the extension of credit in an account established in connection with the consumer credit transaction.

(f) The creditor uses the title of a vehicle as security for the obligation involving the consumer credit, provided however, that for the purposes of this paragraph, the term "creditor" does not include a person that is chartered or licensed under Federal or State law as a bank, savings association, or credit union.

(g) The creditor requires as a condition for the extension of consumer credit that the covered borrower establish an allotment to repay the obligation. For the purposes of this paragraph only, the term "creditor" shall not include a "military welfare society," as defined in 10 U.S.C. 1033(b)(2), or a "service relief society," as defined in 37 U.S.C. 1007(h)(4).

(h) The covered borrower is prohibited from prepaying the consumer credit or is charged a penalty fee for prepaying all or part of the consumer credit.

§ 232.9. Penalties and Remedies

(a) Misdemeanor. A creditor or assignee who knowingly violates 10 U.S.C. 987 as implemented by this part shall be fined as provided in title 18, United States Code, or imprisoned for not more than one year, or both.

(b) Preservation of other remedies. The remedies and rights provided under 10 U.S.C. 987 as implemented by this part are in addition to and do not preclude any remedy otherwise available under State or Federal law or regulation to the person claiming relief under the statute, including any award for consequential damages and punitive damages.

(c) Contract void. Any credit agreement, promissory note, or other contract with a covered borrower that fails to comply with 10 U.S.C. 987 as implemented by this regulation or which contains one or more provisions prohibited under 10 U.S.C. 987 as implemented by this regulation is void from the inception of the contract.

(d) Arbitration. Notwithstanding 9 U.S.C. 2, or any other Federal or State law, rule, or regulation, no agreement to arbitrate any dispute involving the extension of consumer credit to a covered borrower pursuant to this part shall be enforceable against any covered borrower, or any person who was a covered borrower when the agreement was made.

(e) Civil liability—

(1) In general. A person who violates 10 U.S.C. 987 as implemented by this part with respect to any person is civilly liable to such person for:

(i) Any actual damage sustained as a result, but not less than $500 for each violation;

(ii) Appropriate punitive damages;

(iii) Appropriate equitable or declaratory relief; and

(iv) Any other relief provided by law.

(2) Costs of the action. In any successful action to enforce the civil liability described in paragraph (e)(1) of this section, the person who violated 10 U.S.C. 987 as implemented by this part is also liable for the costs of the action, together with reasonable attorney fees as determined by the court.

(3) Effect of finding of bad faith and harassment. In any successful action by a defendant under this section, if the court finds the action was brought in bad faith and for the purpose of harassment, the plaintiff is liable for the attorney fees of the defendant as determined by the court to be reasonable in relation to the work expended and costs incurred.

(4) Defenses. A person may not be held liable for civil liability under paragraph (e) of this section if the person shows by a preponderance of evidence that the violation was not intentional and resulted from a bona fide error notwithstanding the maintenance of procedures reasonably adapted to avoid any such error. Examples of a bona fide error include clerical, calculation, computer malfunction and programming, and printing errors, except that an error of legal judgment with respect to a person's obligations under 10 U.S.C. 987 as implemented by this part is not a bona fide error.

(5) Jurisdiction, venue, and statute of limitations. An action for civil liability under paragraph (e) of this section may be brought in any appropriate United States district court, without regard to the amount in controversy, or in any other court of competent jurisdiction, not later than the earlier of:

(i) Two years after the date of discovery by the plaintiff of the violation that is the basis for such liability; or

(ii) Five years after the date on which the violation that is the basis for such liability occurs.

§ 232.10. Administrative Enforcement

The provisions of this part, other than § 232.9(a), shall be enforced by the agencies specified in section 108 of the Truth in Lending Act (15 U.S.C. 1607) in the manner set forth in that section or under any other applicable authorities available to such agencies by law.

§ 232.11. Servicemembers Civil Relief Act Protections Unaffected

Nothing in this part may be construed to limit or otherwise affect the applicability of Section 207 and any other provisions of the Servicemembers Civil Relief Act (50 U.S.C. App. 527).

§ 232.12. Effective Dates

(a) In general. This regulation shall take effect October 1, 2015, except that, other than as provided in this section and in § 232.13(b)(1), nothing in this part shall apply to consumer credit that is extended to a covered borrower and consummated before October 3, 2016.

(b) Prior extensions of consumer credit. Consumer credit that is extended to a covered borrower and consummated any time between October 1, 2007, and October 3, 2016, is subject to the definitions, conditions, and requirements of this part as were established by the Department and effective on October 1, 2007.

(c) New extensions of consumer credit. Except as provided in paragraphs (d) and (e) of this section with respect to extensions of consumer credit under paragraph (b) of this section (and except as permitted by § 232.13(b)(1)), the requirements of this part that are effective as of October 1, 2015, shall apply only to a consumer credit transaction or account for consumer credit consummated or established on or after October 3, 2016.

(d) Provisions of 10 U.S.C. 987(d)(2). The amendments to 10 U.S.C. 987(d)(2) enacted in section 661(a) of the National Defense Authorization Act for Fiscal Year 2013 (Pub.L. 112–239, 126 Stat. 1785), as reflected in § 232.7(b), took effect on January 2, 2014.

(e) Civil liability remedies. The provisions set forth in § 232.9(e) shall apply with respect to consumer credit extended on or after January 2, 2013.

§ 232.13. Compliance dates

(a) In general. Except as provided in paragraph (c) of this section, a creditor must comply with the requirements of this part, as may be applicable, with respect to a consumer credit transaction or account for consumer credit consummated or established on or after October 3, 2016, not later than that date.

(b) Safe harbors for identifying a covered borrower—

(1) New safe harbors. Section 232.5 shall apply October 3, 2016.

(2) Prior safe harbor valid until general compliance date. The provisions relating to the identification of a covered borrower set forth in § 232.5(a) of the regulation established by the Department and effective on October 1, 2007 (including the interpretation by the Department that provides an exception from the safe harbor for the creditor's knowledge that the applicant is a covered borrower) shall remain in effect until October 3, 2016.

(c) Limited exemption for credit card account; reservation of authority—

(1) In general. Notwithstanding § 232.3(f)(1) and subject to paragraph (c)(2) of this section, until October 3, 2017, consumer credit does not mean credit extended in a credit card account under an open-end (not home-secured) consumer credit plan.

(2) Authority to issue an order to extend exemption. The Secretary, or an official of the Department duly authorized by the Secretary, may, by order, extend the expiration of the exemption set forth in paragraph (c)(1) of this section, until a date not later than October 3, 2018.

Excerpt from the Racketeer Influenced and Corrupt Organizations Act ("RICO")

18 U.S.C. § 1961. Definitions

As used in this chapter—

(1) "racketeering activity" means

(A) any act or threat involving murder, kidnapping, gambling, arson, robbery, bribery, extortion, dealing in obscene matter, or dealing in a controlled substance or listed chemical (as defined in section 102 of the Controlled Substances Act), which is chargeable under State law and punishable by imprisonment for more than one year;

(B) any act which is indictable under any of the following provisions of title 18, United States Code: Section 201 (relating to bribery), section 224 (relating to sports bribery), sections 471, 472, and 473 (relating to counterfeiting), section 659 (relating to theft from interstate shipment) if the act indictable under section 659 is felonious, section 664 (relating to embezzlement from pension and welfare funds), sections 891–894 (relating to extortionate credit transactions), section 1028 (relating to fraud and related activity in connection with identification documents), section 1029 (relating to fraud and related activity in connection with access devices), section 1084 (relating to the transmission of gambling information), section 1341 (relating to mail fraud), section 1343 (relating to wire fraud), section 1344 (relating to financial institution fraud), section 1351 (relating to fraud in foreign labor contracting), section 1425 (relating to the procurement of citizenship or nationalization unlawfully), section 1426 (relating to the reproduction of naturalization or citizenship papers), section 1427 (relating to the sale of naturalization or citizenship papers), sections 1461–1465 (relating to obscene matter), section 1503 (relating to obstruction of justice), section 1510 (relating to obstruction of criminal investigations), section 1511 (relating to the obstruction of State or local law enforcement), section 1512 (relating to tampering with a witness, victim, or an informant), section 1513 (relating to retaliating against a witness, victim, or an informant), section 1542 (relating to false statement in application and use of passport), section 1543 (relating to forgery or false use of passport), section 1544 (relating to misuse of passport), section 1546 (relating to fraud and misuse of visas, permits, and other documents), sections 1581–1592 (relating to peonage, slavery, and trafficking in persons).,[1] section 1951 (relating to interference with commerce, robbery, or extortion), section 1952 (relating to racketeering), section 1953 (relating to interstate transportation of wagering paraphernalia), section 1954 (relating to unlawful welfare fund payments), section 1955 (relating to the prohibition of illegal gambling businesses), section 1956 (relating to the laundering of monetary instruments), section 1957 (relating to engaging in monetary transactions in property derived from specified unlawful activity), section 1958 (relating to use of interstate commerce facilities in the commission of murder-for-hire), section 1960 (relating to illegal money transmitters), sections 2251, 2251A, 2252, and 2260 (relating to sexual exploitation of children), sections 2312 and 2313 (relating to interstate transportation of stolen motor vehicles), sections 2314 and 2315 (relating to interstate transportation of stolen property), section 2318 (relating to trafficking in counterfeit labels for phonorecords, computer programs or computer program documentation or packaging and copies of motion pictures or other audiovisual works), section 2319 (relating to criminal infringement of a copyright), section 2319A (relating to unauthorized fixation of and trafficking in sound recordings and music videos of live musical performances), section 2320 (relating to trafficking in goods or services bearing counterfeit marks), section 2321 (relating to trafficking in certain motor vehicles or motor vehicle parts), sections 2341–2346 (relating to trafficking in contraband cigarettes), sections 2421–24 (relating to white slave traffic), sections 175–178 (relating to biological weapons), sections 229–229F (relating to chemical weapons), section 831 (relating to nuclear materials),

[1] So in original.

(C) any act which is indictable under title 29, United States Code, section 186 (dealing with restrictions on payments and loans to labor organizations) or section 501(c) (relating to embezzlement from union funds),

(D) any offense involving fraud connected with a case under title 11 (except a case under section 157 of this title), fraud in the sale of securities, or the felonious manufacture, importation, receiving, concealment, buying, selling, or otherwise dealing in a controlled substance or listed chemical (as defined in section 102 of the Controlled Substances Act), punishable under any law of the United States,

(E) any act which is indictable under the Currency and Foreign Transactions Reporting Act,

(F) any act which is indictable under the Immigration and Nationality Act, section 274 (relating to bringing in and harboring certain aliens), section 277 (relating to aiding or assisting certain aliens to enter the United States), or section 278 (relating to importation of alien for immoral purpose) if the act indictable under such section of such Act was committed for the purpose of financial gain, or

(G) any act that is indictable under any provision listed in section 2332b(g)(5)(B);

* * *

(4) "enterprise" includes any individual, partnership, corporation, association, or other legal entity, and any union or group of individuals associated in fact although not a legal entity;

(5) "pattern of racketeering activity" requires at least two acts of racketeering activity, one of which occurred after the effective date of this chapter and the last of which occurred within ten years (excluding any period of imprisonment) after the commission of a prior act of racketeering activity;

(6) "unlawful debt" means a debt (A) incurred or contracted in gambling activity which was in violation of the law of the United States, a State or political subdivision thereof, or which is unenforceable under State or Federal law in whole or in part as to principal or interest because of the laws relating to usury, and (B) which was incurred in connection with the business of gambling in violation of the law of the United States, a State or political subdivision thereof, or the business of lending money or a thing of value at a rate usurious under State or Federal law, where the usurious rate is at least twice the enforceable rate;

* * *

18 U.S.C. § 1962. Prohibited Activities

(a) It shall be unlawful for any person who has received any income derived, directly or indirectly, from a pattern of racketeering activity or through collection of an unlawful debt in which such person has participated as a principal within the meaning of section 2, title 18, United States Code, to use or invest, directly or indirectly, any part of such income, or the proceeds of such income, in acquisition of any interest in, or the establishment or operation of, any enterprise which is engaged in, or the activities of which affect, interstate or foreign commerce. A purchase of securities on the open market for purposes of investment, and without the intention of controlling or participating in the control of the issuer, or of assisting another to do so, shall not be unlawful under this subsection if the securities of the issuer held by the purchaser, the members of his immediate family, and his or their accomplices in any pattern or racketeering activity or the collection of an unlawful debt after such purchase do not amount in the aggregate to one percent of the outstanding securities of any one class, and do not confer, either in law or in fact, the power to elect one or more directors of the issuer.

(b) It shall be unlawful for any person through a pattern of racketeering activity or through collection of an unlawful debt to acquire or maintain, directly or indirectly, any interest in or control of any enterprise which is engaged in, or the activities of which affect, interstate or foreign commerce.

(c) It shall be unlawful for any person employed by or associated with any enterprise engaged in, or the activities of which affect, interstate or foreign commerce, to conduct or participate, directly or indirectly, in the conduct of such enterprise's affairs through a pattern of racketeering activity or collection of unlawful debt.

(d) It shall be unlawful for any person to conspire to violate any of the provisions of subsection (a), (b), or (c) of this section.

18 U.S.C. § 1964. Civil remedies

(a) The district courts of the United States shall have jurisdiction to prevent and restrain violations of section 1962 of this chapter by issuing appropriate orders, including, but not limited to: ordering any person to divest himself of any interest, direct or indirect, in any enterprise; imposing reasonable restrictions on the future activities or investments of any person, including, but not limited to, prohibiting any person from engaging in the same type of endeavor as the enterprise engaged in, the activities of which affect interstate or foreign commerce; or ordering dissolution or reorganization of any enterprise, making due provision for the rights of innocent persons.

(b) The Attorney General may institute proceedings under this section. Pending final determination thereof, the court may at any time enter such restraining orders or prohibitions, or take such other actions, including the acceptance of satisfactory performance bonds, as it shall deem proper.

(c) Any person injured in his business or property by reason of a violation of section 1962 of this chapter may sue therefor in any appropriate United States district court and shall recover threefold the damages he sustains and the cost of the suit, including a reasonable attorney's fee, except that no person may rely upon any conduct that would have been actionable as fraud in the purchase or sale of securities to establish a violation of section 1962. The exception contained in the preceding sentence does not apply to an action against any person that is criminally convicted in connection with the fraud, in which case the statute of limitations shall start to run on the date on which the conviction becomes final.

(d) A final judgment or decree rendered in favor of the United States in any criminal proceeding brought by the United States under this chapter shall estop the defendant from denying the essential allegations of the criminal offense in any subsequent civil proceeding brought by the United States.

SELECTED MATERIALS ON CLASS ACTIONS

Federal Rules of Civil Procedure Rule 23. Class Actions

(a) Prerequisites. One or more members of a class may sue or be sued as representative parties on behalf of all members only if:

(1) the class is so numerous that joinder of all members is impracticable;

(2) there are questions of law or fact common to the class;

(3) the claims or defenses of the representative parties are typical of the claims or defenses of the class; and

(4) the representative parties will fairly and adequately protect the interests of the class.

(b) Types of Class Actions. A class action may be maintained if Rule 23(a) is satisfied and if:

(1) prosecuting separate actions by or against individual class members would create a risk of:

(A) inconsistent or varying adjudications with respect to individual class members that would establish incompatible standards of conduct for the party opposing the class; or

(B) adjudications with respect to individual class members that, as a practical matter, would be dispositive of the interests of the other members not parties to the individual adjudications or would substantially impair or impede their ability to protect their interests;

(2) the party opposing the class has acted or refused to act on grounds that apply generally to the class, so that final injunctive relief or corresponding declaratory relief is appropriate respecting the class as a whole; or

(3) the court finds that the questions of law or fact common to class members predominate over any questions affecting only individual members, and that a class action is superior to other available methods for fairly and efficiently adjudicating the controversy. The matters pertinent to these findings include:

(A) the class members' interests in individually controlling the prosecution or defense of separate actions;

(B) the extent and nature of any litigation concerning the controversy already begun by or against class members;

(C) the desirability or undesirability of concentrating the litigation of the claims in the particular forum; and

(D) the likely difficulties in managing a class action.

(c) **Certification Order**; Notice to Class Members; Judgment; Issues Classes; Subclasses.

(1) **Certification Order**.

(A) **Time to Issue**. At an early practicable time after a person sues or is sued as a class representative, the court must determine by order whether to certify the action as a class action.

(B) **Defining the Class; Appointing Class Counsel**. An order that certifies a class action must define the class and the class claims, issues, or defenses, and must appoint class counsel under Rule 23(g).

(C) **Altering or Amending the Order**. An order that grants or denies class certification may be altered or amended before final judgment.

(2) **Notice**.

(A) **For (b)(1) or (b)(2) Classes**. For any class certified under Rule 23(b)(1) or (b)(2), the court may direct appropriate notice to the class.

(B) **For (b)(3) Classes**. For any class certified under Rule 23(b)(3)—or upon ordering notice under Rule 23(e)(1) to a class proposed to be certified for purposes of settlement under Rule 23(b)(3)—the court must direct to class members the best notice that is practicable under the circumstances, including individual notice to all members who can be identified through reasonable effort. The notice may be by one or more of the following: United States mail, electronic means, or other appropriate means. The notice must clearly and concisely state in plain, easily understood language:

(i) the nature of the action;

(ii) the definition of the class certified;

(iii) the class claims, issues, or defenses;

(iv) that a class member may enter an appearance through an attorney if the member so desires;

(v) that the court will exclude from the class any member who requests exclusion;

(vi) the time and manner for requesting exclusion; and

(vii) the binding effect of a class judgment on members under Rule 23(c)(3).

(3) Judgment. Whether or not favorable to the class, the judgment in a class action must:

(A) for any class certified under Rule 23(b)(1) or (b)(2), include and describe those whom the court finds to be class members; and

(B) for any class certified under Rule 23(b)(3), include and specify or describe those to whom the Rule 23(c)(2) notice was directed, who have not requested exclusion, and whom the court finds to be class members.

(4) Particular Issues. When appropriate, an action may be brought or maintained as a class action with respect to particular issues.

(5) Subclasses. When appropriate, a class may be divided into subclasses that are each treated as a class under this rule.

(d) Conducting the Action.

(1) In General. In conducting an action under this rule, the court may issue orders that:

(A) determine the course of proceedings or prescribe measures to prevent undue repetition or complication in presenting evidence or argument;

(B) require—to protect class members and fairly conduct the action—giving appropriate notice to some or all class members of:

(i) any step in the action;

(ii) the proposed extent of the judgment; or

(iii) the members' opportunity to signify whether they consider the representation fair and adequate, to intervene and present claims or defenses, or to otherwise come into the action;

(C) impose conditions on the representative parties or on intervenors;

(D) require that the pleadings be amended to eliminate allegations about representation of absent persons and that the action proceed accordingly; or

(E) deal with similar procedural matters.

(2) Combining and Amending Orders. An order under Rule 23(d)(1) may be altered or amended from time to time and may be combined with an order under Rule 16.

(e) Settlement, Voluntary Dismissal, or Compromise. The claims, issues, or defenses of a certified class—or a class proposed to be certified for purposes of settlement—may be settled, voluntarily dismissed, or compromised only with the court's approval. The following procedures apply to a proposed settlement, voluntary dismissal, or compromise:

(1) Notice to the Class.

(A) Information That Parties Must Provide to the Court. The parties must provide the court with information sufficient to enable it to determine whether to give notice of the proposal to the class.

(B) Grounds for a Decision to Give Notice. The court must direct notice in a reasonable manner to all class members who would be bound by the proposal if giving notice is justified by the parties' showing that the court will likely be able to:

(i) approve the proposal under Rule 23(e)(2); and

(ii) certify the class for purposes of judgment on the proposal.

(2) Approval of the Proposal. If the proposal would bind class members, the court may approve it only after a hearing and only on finding that it is fair, reasonable, and adequate after considering whether:

(A) the class representatives and class counsel have adequately represented the class;

(B) the proposal was negotiated at arm's length;

(C) the relief provided for the class is adequate, taking into account:

(i) the costs, risks, and delay of trial and appeal;

(ii) the effectiveness of any proposed method of distributing relief to the class, including the method of processing class-member claims;

(iii) the terms of any proposed award of attorney's fees, including timing of payment; and

(iv) any agreement required to be identified under Rule 23(e)(3); and

(D) the proposal treats class members equitably relative to each other.

(3) Identifying Agreements. The parties seeking approval must file a statement identifying any agreement made in connection with the proposal.

(4) New Opportunity to be Excluded. If the class action was previously certified under Rule 23(b)(3), the court may refuse to approve a settlement unless it affords a new opportunity to request exclusion to individual class members who had an earlier opportunity to request exclusion but did not do so.

(5) Class-Member Objections.

(A) In General. Any class member may object to the proposal if it requires court approval under this subdivision (e). The objection must state whether it applies only to the objector, to a specific subset of the class, or to the entire class, and also state with specificity the grounds for the objection.

(B) Court Approval Required for Payment in Connection with an Objection. Unless approved by the court after a hearing, no payment or other consideration may be provided in connection with:

(i) forgoing or withdrawing an objection, or

(ii) forgoing, dismissing, or abandoning an appeal from a judgment approving the proposal.

(C) Procedure for Approval After an Appeal. If approval under Rule 23(e)(5)(B) has not been obtained before an appeal is docketed in the court of appeals, the procedure of Rule 62.1 applies while the appeal remains pending.

(f) Appeals. A court of appeals may permit an appeal from an order granting or denying class-action certification under this rule, but not from an order under Rule 23(e)(1). A party must file a petition for permission to appeal with the circuit clerk within 14 days after the order is entered, or within 45 days after the order is entered if any party is the United States, a United States agency, or a United States officer or employee sued for an act or omission occurring in connection with duties performed on the United States' behalf. An appeal does not stay proceedings in the district court unless the district judge or the court of appeals so orders.

(g) Class Counsel.

(1) Appointing Class Counsel. Unless a statute provides otherwise, a court that certifies a class must appoint class counsel. In appointing class counsel, the court:

(A) must consider:

(i) the work counsel has done in identifying or investigating potential claims in the action;

(ii) counsel's experience in handling class actions, other complex litigation, and the types of claims asserted in the action;

(iii) counsel's knowledge of the applicable law; and

(iv) the resources that counsel will commit to representing the class;

(B) may consider any other matter pertinent to counsel's ability to fairly and adequately represent the interests of the class;

(C) may order potential class counsel to provide information on any subject pertinent to the appointment and to propose terms for attorney's fees and nontaxable costs;

(D) may include in the appointing order provisions about the award of attorney's fees or nontaxable costs under Rule 23(h); and

(E) may make further orders in connection with the appointment.

(2) Standard for Appointing Class Counsel. When one applicant seeks appointment as class counsel, the court may appoint that applicant only if the applicant is adequate under Rule 23(g)(1) and (4). If more than one adequate applicant seeks appointment, the court must appoint the applicant best able to represent the interests of the class.

(3) Interim Counsel. The court may designate interim counsel to act on behalf of a putative class before determining whether to certify the action as a class action.

(4) Duty of Class Counsel. Class counsel must fairly and adequately represent the interests of the class.

(h) Attorney's Fees and Nontaxable Costs. In a certified class action, the court may award reasonable attorney's fees and nontaxable costs that are authorized by law or by the parties' agreement. The following procedures apply:

(1) A claim for an award must be made by motion under Rule 54(d)(2), subject to the provisions of this subdivision (h), at a time the court sets. Notice of the motion must be served on all parties and, for motions by class counsel, directed to class members in a reasonable manner.

(2) A class member, or a party from whom payment is sought, may object to the motion.

(3) The court may hold a hearing and must find the facts and state its legal conclusions under Rule 52(a).

(4) The court may refer issues related to the amount of the award to a special master or a magistrate judge, as provided in Rule 54(d)(2)(D).

Excerpts from Title 28, U.S. Code

28 U.S.C. § 1332, 1453, 1712

§ 1332. Diversity of citizenship; amount in controversy; costs

(a) The district courts shall have original jurisdiction of all civil actions where the matter in controversy exceeds the sum or value of $75,000, exclusive of interest and costs, and is between—

(1) citizens of different States;

(2) citizens of a State and citizens or subjects of a foreign state, except that the district courts shall not have original jurisdiction under this subsection of an action between citizens of a State and citizens or subjects of a foreign state who are lawfully admitted for permanent residence in the United States and are domiciled in the same State;

(3) citizens of different States and in which citizens or subjects of a foreign state are additional parties; and

(4) a foreign state, defined in section 1603(a) of this title, as plaintiff and citizens of a State or of different States.

(b) Except when express provision therefor is otherwise made in a statute of the United States, where the plaintiff who files the case originally in the Federal courts is finally adjudged to be entitled to recover less than the sum or value of $75,000, computed without regard to any setoff or counterclaim to which the defendant may be adjudged to be entitled, and exclusive of interest and costs, the district court may deny costs to the plaintiff and, in addition, may impose costs on the plaintiff.

(c) For the purposes of this section and section 1441 of this title—

(1) a corporation shall be deemed to be a citizen of every State and foreign state by which it has been incorporated and of the State or foreign state where it has its principal place of business, except that in any direct action against the insurer of a policy or contract of liability insurance, whether incorporated or unincorporated, to which action the insured is not joined as a party-defendant, such insurer shall be deemed a citizen of—

(A) every State and foreign state of which the insured is a citizen;

(B) every State and foreign state by which the insurer has been incorporated; and

(C) the State or foreign state where the insurer has its principal place of business; and

(2) the legal representative of the estate of a decedent shall be deemed to be a citizen only of the same State as the decedent, and the legal representative of an infant or incompetent shall be deemed to be a citizen only of the same State as the infant or incompetent.

(d)(1) In this subsection—

(A) the term "class" means all of the class members in a class action;

(B) the term "class action" means any civil action filed under rule 23 of the Federal Rules of Civil Procedure or similar State statute or rule of judicial procedure authorizing an action to be brought by 1 or more representative persons as a class action;

(C) the term "class certification order" means an order issued by a court approving the treatment of some or all aspects of a civil action as a class action; and

(D) the term "class members" means the persons (named or unnamed) who fall within the definition of the proposed or certified class in a class action.

(2) The district courts shall have original jurisdiction of any civil action in which the matter in controversy exceeds the sum or value of $5,000,000, exclusive of interest and costs, and is a class action in which—

(A) any member of a class of plaintiffs is a citizen of a State different from any defendant;

(B) any member of a class of plaintiffs is a foreign state or a citizen or subject of a foreign state and any defendant is a citizen of a State; or

(C) any member of a class of plaintiffs is a citizen of a State and any defendant is a foreign state or a citizen or subject of a foreign state.

(3) A district court may, in the interests of justice and looking at the totality of the circumstances, decline to exercise jurisdiction under paragraph (2) over a class action in which greater than one-third but less than two-thirds of the members of all proposed plaintiff classes in the aggregate and the primary defendants are citizens of the State in which the action was originally filed based on consideration of—

(A) whether the claims asserted involve matters of national or interstate interest;

(B) whether the claims asserted will be governed by laws of the State in which the action was originally filed or by the laws of other States;

(C) whether the class action has been pleaded in a manner that seeks to avoid Federal jurisdiction;

(D) whether the action was brought in a forum with a distinct nexus with the class members, the alleged harm, or the defendants;

(E) whether the number of citizens of the State in which the action was originally filed in all proposed plaintiff classes in the aggregate is substantially larger than the number of citizens from any other State, and the citizenship of the other members of the proposed class is dispersed among a substantial number of States; and

(F) whether, during the 3-year period preceding the filing of that class action, 1 or more other class actions asserting the same or similar claims on behalf of the same or other persons have been filed.

(4) A district court shall decline to exercise jurisdiction under paragraph (2)—

(A)(i) over a class action in which—

(I) greater than two-thirds of the members of all proposed plaintiff classes in the aggregate are citizens of the State in which the action was originally filed;

(II) at least 1 defendant is a defendant—

(aa) from whom significant relief is sought by members of the plaintiff class;

(bb) whose alleged conduct forms a significant basis for the claims asserted by the proposed plaintiff class; and

(cc) who is a citizen of the State in which the action was originally filed; and

(III) principal injuries resulting from the alleged conduct or any related conduct of each defendant were incurred in the State in which the action was originally filed; and

(ii) during the 3-year period preceding the filing of that class action, no other class action has been filed asserting the same or similar factual allegations against any of the defendants on behalf of the same or other persons; or

(B) two-thirds or more of the members of all proposed plaintiff classes in the aggregate, and the primary defendants, are citizens of the State in which the action was originally filed.

(5) Paragraphs (2) through (4) shall not apply to any class action in which—

(A) the primary defendants are States, State officials, or other governmental entities against whom the district court may be foreclosed from ordering relief; or

(B) the number of members of all proposed plaintiff classes in the aggregate is less than 100.

(6) In any class action, the claims of the individual class members shall be aggregated to determine whether the matter in controversy exceeds the sum or value of $5,000,000, exclusive of interest and costs.

(7) Citizenship of the members of the proposed plaintiff classes shall be determined for purposes of paragraphs (2) through (6) as of the date of filing of the complaint or amended complaint, or, if the case stated by the initial pleading is not subject to Federal jurisdiction, as of the date of service by plaintiffs of an amended pleading, motion, or other paper, indicating the existence of Federal jurisdiction.

(8) This subsection shall apply to any class action before or after the entry of a class certification order by the court with respect to that action.

(9) Paragraph (2) shall not apply to any class action that solely involves a claim—

(A) concerning a covered security as defined under 16(f)(3)[1] of the Securities Act of 1933 (15 U.S.C. 78p(f)(3)[2]) and section 28(f)(5)(E) of the Securities Exchange Act of 1934 (15 U.S.C. 78bb(f)(5)(E));

(B) that relates to the internal affairs or governance of a corporation or other form of business enterprise and that arises under or by virtue of the laws of the State in which such corporation or business enterprise is incorporated or organized; or

(C) that relates to the rights, duties (including fiduciary duties), and obligations relating to or created by or pursuant to any security (as defined under section 2(a)(1) of the Securities Act of 1933 (15 U.S.C. 77b(a)(1)) and the regulations issued thereunder).

(10) For purposes of this subsection and section 1453, an unincorporated association shall be deemed to be a citizen of the State where it has its principal place of business and the State under whose laws it is organized.

(11)(A) For purposes of this subsection and section 1453, a mass action shall be deemed to be a class action removable under paragraphs (2) through (10) if it otherwise meets the provisions of those paragraphs.

(B)(i) As used in subparagraph (A), the term "mass action" means any civil action (except a civil action within the scope of section 1711(2)) in which monetary relief claims of 100 or more persons are proposed to be tried jointly on the ground that the plaintiffs' claims involve common questions of law or fact, except that jurisdiction shall exist only over those plaintiffs whose claims in a mass action satisfy the jurisdictional amount requirements under subsection (a).

(ii) As used in subparagraph (A), the term "mass action" shall not include any civil action in which—

(I) all of the claims in the action arise from an event or occurrence in the State in which the action was filed, and that allegedly resulted in injuries in that State or in States contiguous to that State;

(II) the claims are joined upon motion of a defendant;

---

1 So in original. Reference to "16(f)(3)" probably should be preceded by "section".

2 So in original. Probably should be "77p(f)(3)".

(III) all of the claims in the action are asserted on behalf of the general public (and not on behalf of individual claimants or members of a purported class) pursuant to a State statute specifically authorizing such action; or

(IV) the claims have been consolidated or coordinated solely for pretrial proceedings.

(C)(i) Any action(s) removed to Federal court pursuant to this subsection shall not thereafter be transferred to any other court pursuant to section 1407, or the rules promulgated thereunder, unless a majority of the plaintiffs in the action request transfer pursuant to section 1407.

(ii) This subparagraph will not apply—

(I) to cases certified pursuant to rule 23 of the Federal Rules of Civil Procedure; or

(II) if plaintiffs propose that the action proceed as a class action pursuant to rule 23 of the Federal Rules of Civil Procedure.

(D) The limitations periods on any claims asserted in a mass action that is removed to Federal court pursuant to this subsection shall be deemed tolled during the period that the action is pending in Federal court.

(e) The word "States", as used in this section, includes the Territories, the District of Columbia, and the Commonwealth of Puerto Rico.

§ 1453. Removal of class actions

(a) Definitions.—In this section, the terms "class", "class action", "class certification order", and "class member" shall have the meanings given such terms under section 1332(d)(1).

(b) In general.—A class action may be removed to a district court of the United States in accordance with section 1446 (except that the 1-year limitation under section 1446(c)(1) shall not apply), without regard to whether any defendant is a citizen of the State in which the action is brought, except that such action may be removed by any defendant without the consent of all defendants.

(c) Review of remand orders.—

(1) In general.—Section 1447 shall apply to any removal of a case under this section, except that notwithstanding section 1447(d), a court of appeals may accept an appeal from an order of a district court granting or denying a motion to remand a class action to the State court from which it was removed if application is made to the court of appeals not more than 10 days after entry of the order.

(2) Time period for judgment.—If the court of appeals accepts an appeal under paragraph (1), the court shall complete all action on such appeal, including rendering judgment, not later than 60 days after the date on which such appeal was filed, unless an extension is granted under paragraph (3).

(3) Extension of time period.—The court of appeals may grant an extension of the 60-day period described in paragraph (2) if—

(A) all parties to the proceeding agree to such extension, for any period of time; or

(B) such extension is for good cause shown and in the interests of justice, for a period not to exceed 10 days.

(4) Denial of appeal.—If a final judgment on the appeal under paragraph (1) is not issued before the end of the period described in paragraph (2), including any extension under paragraph (3), the appeal shall be denied.

(d) Exception.—This section shall not apply to any class action that solely involves—

(1) a claim concerning a covered security as defined under section 16(f)(3) of the Securities Act of 1933 (15 U.S.C. 78p(f)(3)[1]) and section 28(f)(5)(E) of the Securities Exchange Act of 1934 (15 U.S.C. 78bb(f)(5)(E));

(2) a claim that relates to the internal affairs or governance of a corporation or other form of business enterprise and arises under or by virtue of the laws of the State in which such corporation or business enterprise is incorporated or organized; or

(3) a claim that relates to the rights, duties (including fiduciary duties), and obligations relating to or created by or pursuant to any security (as defined under section 2(a)(1) of the Securities Act of 1933 (15 U.S.C. 77b(a)(1)) and the regulations issued thereunder).

§ 1712. Coupon settlements

(a) Contingent fees in coupon settlements.—If a proposed settlement in a class action provides for a recovery of coupons to a class member, the portion of any attorney's fee award to class counsel that is attributable to the award of the coupons shall be based on the value to class members of the coupons that are redeemed.

(b) Other attorney's fee awards in coupon settlements.—

(1) In general.—If a proposed settlement in a class action provides for a recovery of coupons to class members, and a portion of the recovery of the coupons is not used to determine the attorney's fee to be paid to class counsel, any attorney's fee award shall be based upon the amount of time class counsel reasonably expended working on the action.

(2) Court approval.—Any attorney's fee under this subsection shall be subject to approval by the court and shall include an appropriate attorney's fee, if any, for obtaining equitable relief, including an injunction, if applicable. Nothing in this subsection shall be construed to prohibit application of a lodestar with a multiplier method of determining attorney's fees.

(c) Attorney's fee awards calculated on a mixed basis in coupon settlements.—If a proposed settlement in a class action provides for an award of coupons to class members and also provides for equitable relief, including injunctive relief—

(1) that portion of the attorney's fee to be paid to class counsel that is based upon a portion of the recovery of the coupons shall be calculated in accordance with subsection (a); and

(2) that portion of the attorney's fee to be paid to class counsel that is not based upon a portion of the recovery of the coupons shall be calculated in accordance with subsection (b).

(d) Settlement valuation expertise.—In a class action involving the awarding of coupons, the court may, in its discretion upon the motion of a party, receive expert testimony from a witness qualified to provide information on the actual value to the class members of the coupons that are redeemed.

(e) Judicial scrutiny of coupon settlements.—In a proposed settlement under which class members would be awarded coupons, the court may approve the proposed settlement only after a hearing to determine whether, and making a written finding that, the settlement is fair, reasonable, and adequate for class members. The court, in its discretion, may also require that a proposed settlement agreement provide for the distribution of a portion of the value of unclaimed coupons to 1 or more charitable or governmental organizations, as agreed to by the parties. The distribution and redemption of any proceeds under this subsection shall not be used to calculate attorneys' fees under this section.

---

1 So in original. Probably should be "77p(f)(3)".

The Federal Arbitration Act, 9 U.S.C. § 1 et seq.

Table of Sections

§ 1. "Maritime transactions" and "commerce" defined; exceptions to operation of title

"Maritime transactions", as herein defined, means charter parties, bills of lading of water carriers, agreements relating to wharfage, supplies furnished vessels or repairs to vessels, collisions, or any other matters in foreign commerce which, if the subject of controversy, would be embraced within admiralty jurisdiction; "commerce", as herein defined, means commerce among the several States or with foreign nations, or in any Territory of the United States or in the District of Columbia, or between any such Territory and another, or between any such Territory and any State or foreign nation, or between the District of Columbia and any State or Territory or foreign nation, but nothing herein contained shall apply to contracts of employment of seamen, railroad employees, or any other class of workers engaged in foreign or interstate commerce.

§ 2. Validity, irrevocability, and enforcement of agreements to arbitrate

A written provision in any maritime transaction or a contract evidencing a transaction involving commerce to settle by arbitration a controversy thereafter arising out of such contract or transaction, or the refusal to perform the whole or any part thereof, or an agreement in writing to submit to arbitration an existing controversy arising out of such a contract, transaction, or refusal, shall be valid, irrevocable, and enforceable, save upon such grounds as exist at law or in equity for the revocation of any contract.

§ 3. Stay of proceedings where issue therein referable to arbitration

If any suit or proceeding be brought in any of the courts of the United States upon any issue referable to arbitration under an agreement in writing for such arbitration, the court in which such suit is pending, upon being satisfied that the issue involved in such suit or proceeding is referable to arbitration under such an agreement, shall on application of one of the parties stay the trial of the action until such arbitration has been had in accordance with the terms of the agreement, providing the applicant for the stay is not in default in proceeding with such arbitration.

§ 4. Failure to arbitrate under agreement; petition to United States court having jurisdiction for order to compel arbitration; notice and service thereof; hearing and determination

A party aggrieved by the alleged failure, neglect, or refusal of another to arbitrate under a written agreement for arbitration may petition any United States district court which, save for such agreement, would have jurisdiction under Title 28, in a civil action or in admiralty of the subject matter of a suit arising out of the controversy between the parties, for an order directing that such arbitration proceed in the manner provided for in such agreement. Five days' notice in writing of such application shall be served upon the party in default. Service thereof shall be made in the manner provided by the Federal Rules of Civil Procedure. The court shall hear the parties, and upon being satisfied that the making of the agreement for arbitration or the failure to comply therewith is not in issue, the court shall make an order directing the parties to proceed to arbitration in accordance with the terms of the agreement. The hearing and proceedings, under such agreement, shall be within the district in which the petition for an order directing such arbitration is filed. If the making of the arbitration agreement or the failure, neglect, or refusal to perform the same be in issue, the court shall proceed summarily to the trial thereof. If no jury trial be demanded by the party alleged to be in default, or if the matter in dispute is within admiralty jurisdiction, the court shall hear and determine such issue. Where such an issue is raised, the party alleged to be in default may, except in cases of admiralty, on or before the return day of the notice of application, demand a jury trial of such issue, and upon such demand the court shall make an order referring the issue or issues to a jury in the manner provided by the Federal Rules of Civil Procedure, or may specially call a jury for that purpose. If the jury find that no agreement in writing for arbitration was made or that there is no default in proceeding thereunder, the proceeding shall be dismissed. If the jury find that an agreement for arbitration was made in writing and that there is a default in proceeding thereunder, the court shall make an order summarily directing the parties to proceed with the arbitration in accordance with the terms thereof.

§ 5. Appointment of arbitrators or umpire

If in the agreement provision be made for a method of naming or appointing an arbitrator or arbitrators or an umpire, such method shall be followed; but if no method be provided therein, or if a method be provided and any party thereto shall fail to avail himself of such method, or if for any other reason there shall be a lapse in the naming of an arbitrator or arbitrators or umpire, or in filling a vacancy, then upon the application of either party to the controversy the court shall designate and appoint an arbitrator or arbitrators or umpire, as the case may require, who shall act under the said agreement with the same force and effect as if he or they had been specifically named therein; and unless otherwise provided in the agreement the arbitration shall be by a single arbitrator.

§ 6. Application heard as motion

Any application to the court hereunder shall be made and heard in the manner provided by law for the making and hearing of motions, except as otherwise herein expressly provided.

§ 7. Witnesses before arbitrators; fees; compelling attendance

The arbitrators selected either as prescribed in this title or otherwise, or a majority of them, may summon in writing any person to attend before them or any of them as a witness and in a proper case to bring with him or them any book, record, document, or paper which may be deemed material as evidence in the case. The fees for such attendance shall be the same as the fees of witnesses before masters of the United States courts. Said summons shall issue in the name of the arbitrator or arbitrators, or a majority of them, and shall be signed by the arbitrators, or a majority of them, and shall be directed to the said person and shall be served in the same manner as subpoenas to appear and testify before the court; if any person or persons so summoned to testify shall refuse or neglect to obey said summons, upon petition the United States district court for the district in which such arbitrators, or a majority of them, are sitting may compel the attendance of such person or persons before said arbitrator or arbitrators, or punish said person or persons for contempt in the same manner provided by law for securing the attendance of witnesses or their punishment for neglect or refusal to attend in the courts of the United States.

§ 8. Proceedings begun by libel in admiralty and seizure of vessel or property

If the basis of jurisdiction be a cause of action otherwise justiciable in admiralty, then, notwithstanding anything herein to the contrary, the party claiming to be aggrieved may begin his proceeding hereunder by libel and seizure of the vessel or other property of the other party according to the usual course of admiralty proceedings, and the court shall then have jurisdiction to direct the parties to proceed with the arbitration and shall retain jurisdiction to enter its decree upon the award.

§ 9. Award of arbitrators; confirmation; jurisdiction; procedure

If the parties in their agreement have agreed that a judgment of the court shall be entered upon the award made pursuant to the arbitration, and shall specify the court, then at any time within one year after the award is made any party to the arbitration may apply to the court so specified for an order confirming the award, and thereupon the court must grant such an order unless the award is vacated, modified, or corrected as prescribed in sections 10 and 11 of this title. If no court is specified in the agreement of the parties, then such application may be made to the United States court in and for the district within which such award was made. Notice of the application shall be served upon the adverse party, and thereupon the court shall have jurisdiction of such party as though he had appeared generally in the proceeding. If the adverse party is a resident of the district within which the award was made, such service shall be made upon the adverse party or his attorney as prescribed by law for service of notice of motion in an action in the same court. If the adverse party shall be a nonresident, then the notice of the application shall be served by the marshal of any district within which the adverse party may be found in like manner as other process of the court.

§ 10. Same; vacation; grounds; rehearing

(a) In any of the following cases the United States court in and for the district wherein the award was made may make an order vacating the award upon the application of any party to the arbitration—

(1) where the award was procured by corruption, fraud, or undue means;

(2) where there was evident partiality or corruption in the arbitrators, or either of them;

(3) where the arbitrators were guilty of misconduct in refusing to postpone the hearing, upon sufficient cause shown, or in refusing to hear evidence pertinent and material to the controversy; or of any other misbehavior by which the rights of any party have been prejudiced; or

(4) where the arbitrators exceeded their powers, or so imperfectly executed them that a mutual, final, and definite award upon the subject matter submitted was not made.

(b) If an award is vacated and the time within which the agreement required the award to be made has not expired, the court may, in its discretion, direct a rehearing by the arbitrators.

(c) The United States district court for the district wherein an award was made that was issued pursuant to section 580 of title 5 may make an order vacating the award upon the application of a person, other than a party to the arbitration, who is adversely affected or aggrieved by the award, if the use of arbitration or the award is clearly inconsistent with the factors set forth in section 572 of title 5.

§ 11. Same; modification or correction; grounds; order

In either of the following cases the United States court in and for the district wherein the award was made may make an order modifying or correcting the award upon the application of any party to the arbitration—

(a) Where there was an evident material miscalculation of figures or an evident material mistake in the description of any person, thing, or property referred to in the award.

(b) Where the arbitrators have awarded upon a matter not submitted to them, unless it is a matter not affecting the merits of the decision upon the matter submitted.

(c) Where the award is imperfect in matter of form not affecting the merits of the controversy.

The order may modify and correct the award, so as to effect the intent thereof and promote justice between the parties.

§ 12. Notice of motions to vacate or modify; service; stay of proceedings

Notice of a motion to vacate, modify, or correct an award must be served upon the adverse party or his attorney within three months after the award is filed or delivered. If the adverse party is a resident of the district within which the award was made, such service shall be made upon the adverse party or his attorney as prescribed by law for service of notice of motion in an action in the same court. If the adverse party shall be a nonresident then the notice of the application shall be served by the marshal of any district within which the adverse party may be found in like manner as other process of the court. For the purposes of the motion any judge who might make an order to stay the proceedings in an action brought in the same court may make an order, to be served with the notice of motion, staying the proceedings of the adverse party to enforce the award.

§ 13. Papers filed with order on motions; judgment; docketing; force and effect; enforcement

The party moving for an order confirming, modifying, or correcting an award shall, at the time such order is filed with the clerk for the entry of judgment thereon, also file the following papers with the clerk:

(a) The agreement; the selection or appointment, if any, of an additional arbitrator or umpire; and each written extension of the time, if any, within which to make the award.

(b) The award.

(c) Each notice, affidavit, or other paper used upon an application to confirm, modify, or correct the award, and a copy of each order of the court upon such an application.

The judgment shall be docketed as if it was rendered in an action.

The judgment so entered shall have the same force and effect, in all respects, as, and be subject to all the provisions of law relating to, a judgment in an action; and it may be enforced as if it had been rendered in an action in the court in which it is entered.

§ 14. Contracts not affected

This title shall not apply to contracts made prior to January 1, 1926.

§ 15. Inapplicability of the Act of State doctrine

Enforcement of arbitral agreements, confirmation of arbitral awards, and execution upon judgments based on orders confirming such awards shall not be refused on the basis of the Act of State doctrine.

§ 16. Appeals

(a) An appeal may be taken from—

(1) an order—

(A) refusing a stay of any action under section 3 of this title,

(B) denying a petition under section 4 of this title to order arbitration to proceed,

(C) denying an application under section 206 of this title to compel arbitration,

(D) confirming or denying confirmation of an award or partial award, or

(E) modifying, correcting, or vacating an award;

(2) an interlocutory order granting, continuing, or modifying an injunction against an arbitration that is subject to this title; or

(3) a final decision with respect to an arbitration that is subject to this title.

(b) Except as otherwise provided in section 1292(b) of title 28, an appeal may not be taken from an interlocutory order—

(1) granting a stay of any action under section 3 of this title;

(2) directing arbitration to proceed under section 4 of this title;

(3) compelling arbitration under section 206 of this title; or

(4) refusing to enjoin an arbitration that is subject to this title.

Part Two

STATE STATUTES

UDAP (UNFAIR OR DECEPTIVE ACTS OR PRACTICES) STATUTES

(Selected Statutes & Sections)

CALIFORNIA

CALIFORNIA UNFAIR BUSINESS PRACTICES ACT

California Bus. & Prof. Code

Sec.

§ 17200. Unfair competition; prohibited activities

As used in this chapter, unfair competition shall mean and include any unlawful, unfair or fraudulent business act or practice and unfair, deceptive, untrue or misleading advertising and any act prohibited by Chapter 1 (commencing with Section 17500) of Part 3 of Division 7 of the Business and Professions Code.

§ 17204. Actions for Injunctions by Attorney General, District Attorney, County Counsel, and City Attorneys

Actions for any relief pursuant to this chapter shall be prosecuted exclusively in a court of competent jurisdiction by the Attorney General or a district attorney or by a county counsel authorized by agreement with the district attorney in actions involving violation of a county ordinance, or by a city attorney of a city, having a population in excess of 750,000, or by a city attorney in a city or county or, with the consent of the district attorney, by a city prosecutor in any city having a full-time city prosecutor in the name of the people of the State of California upon their own complaint or upon the complaint of a board, officer, person, corporation or association or by a person who has suffered injury in fact and has lost money or property as a result of such unfair competition.

§ 17500. False or misleading statements; penalty

It is unlawful for any person, firm, corporation or association, or any employee thereof with intent directly or indirectly to dispose of real or personal property or to perform services, professional or otherwise, or anything of any nature whatsoever or to induce the public to enter into any obligation relating thereto, to make or disseminate or cause to be made or disseminated before the public in this state, or to make or disseminate or cause to be made or disseminated from this state before the public in any state, in any newspaper or other publication, or any advertising device, or by public outcry or proclamation, or in any other manner or means whatever, including over the Internet, any statement, concerning that real or personal property or those services, professional or otherwise, or concerning any circumstance or matter of fact connected with the proposed performance or disposition thereof, which is untrue or misleading, and which is known, or which by the exercise of reasonable care should be known, to be untrue or misleading, or for any person, firm, or corporation to so make or disseminate or cause to be so made or disseminated any such statement as part of a plan or scheme with the intent not to sell that personal property or those services, professional or otherwise, so advertised at the price stated therein, or as so advertised. Any violation of the provisions of this section is a misdemeanor punishable by imprisonment in the county jail not exceeding six months, or by a fine not exceeding two thousand five hundred dollars ($2,500), or by both that imprisonment and fine.

CALIFORNIA CONSUMER LEGAL REMEDIES ACT

Cal. Civ. Code

§ 1770. List of proscribed practices

(a) The following unfair methods of competition and unfair or deceptive acts or practices undertaken by any person in a transaction intended to result or that results in the sale or lease of goods or services to any consumer are unlawful:

(1) Passing off goods or services as those of another.

(2) Misrepresenting the source, sponsorship, approval, or certification of goods or services.

(3) Misrepresenting the affiliation, connection, or association with, or certification by, another.

(4) Using deceptive representations or designations of geographic origin in connection with goods or services.

(5) Representing that goods or services have sponsorship, approval, characteristics, ingredients, uses, benefits, or quantities that they do not have or that a person has a sponsorship, approval, status, affiliation, or connection that he or she does not have.

(6) Representing that goods are original or new if they have deteriorated unreasonably or are altered, reconditioned, reclaimed, used, or secondhand.

(7) Representing that goods or services are of a particular standard, quality, or grade, or that goods are of a particular style or model, if they are of another.

(8) Disparaging the goods, services, or business of another by false or misleading representation of fact.

(9) Advertising goods or services with intent not to sell them as advertised.

(10) Advertising goods or services with intent not to supply reasonably expectable demand, unless the advertisement discloses a limitation of quantity.

(11) Advertising furniture without clearly indicating that it is unassembled if that is the case.

(12) Advertising the price of unassembled furniture without clearly indicating the assembled price of that furniture if the same furniture is available assembled from the seller.

(13) Making false or misleading statements of fact concerning reasons for, existence of, or amounts of, price reductions.

(14) Representing that a transaction confers or involves rights, remedies, or obligations that it does not have or involve, or that are prohibited by law.

(15) Representing that a part, replacement, or repair service is needed when it is not.

(16) Representing that the subject of a transaction has been supplied in accordance with a previous representation when it has not.

(17) Representing that the consumer will receive a rebate, discount, or other economic benefit, if the earning of the benefit is contingent on an event to occur subsequent to the consummation of the transaction.

(18) Misrepresenting the authority of a salesperson, representative, or agent to negotiate the final terms of a transaction with a consumer.

(19) Inserting an unconscionable provision in the contract.

(20) Advertising that a product is being offered at a specific price plus a specific percentage of that price unless (A) the total price is set forth in the advertisement, which may include, but is not limited to, shelf tags, displays, and media advertising, in a size larger than any other price in that advertisement, and (B) the specific price plus a specific percentage of that price represents a markup from the seller's costs or from the wholesale price of the product. This subdivision shall not apply to in-store advertising by businesses that are open only to members or cooperative organizations organized pursuant to Division 3 (commencing with Section 12000) of Title 1 of the Corporations Code where more than 50 percent of purchases are made at the specific price set forth in the advertisement.

(21) Selling or leasing goods in violation of Chapter 4 (commencing with Section 1797.8) of Title 1.7.

(22)(A) Disseminating an unsolicited prerecorded message by telephone without an unrecorded, natural voice first informing the person answering the telephone of the name of the caller or the organization being represented, and either the address or the telephone number of the caller, and without obtaining the consent of that person to listen to the prerecorded message.

(B) This subdivision does not apply to a message disseminated to a business associate, customer, or other person having an established relationship with the person or organization making the call, to a call for the purpose of collecting an existing obligation, or to any call generated at the request of the recipient.

(23)(A) The home solicitation, as defined in subdivision (h) of Section 1761, of a consumer who is a senior citizen where a loan is made encumbering the primary residence of that consumer for purposes of paying for home improvements and where the transaction is part of a pattern or practice in violation of either subsection (h) or (i) of Section 1639 of Title 15 of the United States Code or paragraphs (1), (2), and (4) of subdivision (a) of Section 226.34 of Title 12 of the Code of Federal Regulations.

(B) A third party shall not be liable under this subdivision unless (i) there was an agency relationship between the party who engaged in home solicitation and the third party, or (ii) the third party had actual knowledge of, or participated in, the unfair or deceptive transaction. A third party who is a holder in due course under a home solicitation transaction shall not be liable under this subdivision.

(24)(A) Charging or receiving an unreasonable fee to prepare, aid, or advise any prospective applicant, applicant, or recipient in the procurement, maintenance, or securing of public social services.

(B) For purposes of this paragraph, the following definitions shall apply:

(i) "Public social services" means those activities and functions of state and local government administered or supervised by the State Department of Health Care Services, the State Department of Public Health, or the State Department of Social Services, and involved in providing aid or services, or both, including health care services, and medical assistance, to those persons who, because of their economic circumstances or social condition, are in need of that aid or those services and may benefit from them.

(ii) "Public social services" also includes activities and functions administered or supervised by the United States Department of Veterans Affairs or the California Department of Veterans Affairs involved in providing aid or services, or both, to veterans, including pension benefits.

(iii) "Unreasonable fee" means a fee that is exorbitant and disproportionate to the services performed. Factors to be considered, if appropriate, in determining the reasonableness of a fee, are based on the circumstances existing at the time of the service and shall include, but not be limited to, all of the following:

(I) The time and effort required.

(II) The novelty and difficulty of the services.

(III) The skill required to perform the services.

(IV) The nature and length of the professional relationship.

(V) The experience, reputation, and ability of the person providing the services.

(C) This paragraph shall not apply to attorneys licensed to practice law in California, who are subject to the California Rules of Professional Conduct and to the mandatory fee arbitration provisions of Article 13 (commencing with Section 6200) of Chapter 4 of Division 3 of the Business and Professions Code, when the fees charged or received are for providing representation in administrative agency appeal proceedings or court proceedings for purposes of procuring, maintaining, or securing public social services on behalf of a person or group of persons.

* * *

(b)(1) It is an unfair or deceptive act or practice for a mortgage broker or lender, directly or indirectly, to use a home improvement contractor to negotiate the terms of any loan that is secured, whether in whole or in part, by the residence of the borrower and that is used to finance a home improvement contract or any portion of a home improvement contract. For purposes of this subdivision, "mortgage broker or lender" includes a finance lender licensed pursuant to the California Finance Lenders Law (Division 9 (commencing with Section 22000) of the Financial Code), a residential mortgage lender licensed pursuant to the California Residential Mortgage Lending Act (Division 20 (commencing with Section 50000) of the Financial Code), or a real estate broker licensed under the Real Estate Law (Division 4 (commencing with Section 10000) of the Business and Professions Code).

(2) This section shall not be construed to either authorize or prohibit a home improvement contractor from referring a consumer to a mortgage broker or lender by this subdivision. However, a home improvement contractor may refer a consumer to a mortgage lender or broker if that referral does not violate Section 7157 of the Business and Professions Code or any other law. A mortgage lender or broker may purchase an executed home improvement contract if that purchase does not violate Section 7157 of the Business and Professions Code or any other law. Nothing in this paragraph shall have any effect on the application of Chapter 1 (commencing with Section 1801) of Title 2 to a home improvement transaction or the financing of a home improvement transaction.

§ 1780. Consumer's action; relief; senior citizens or disabled persons; venue; court costs and attorney's fees

(a) Any consumer who suffers any damage as a result of the use or employment by any person of a method, act, or practice declared to be unlawful by Section 1770 may bring an action against that person to recover or obtain any of the following:

(1) Actual damages, but in no case shall the total award of damages in a class action be less than one thousand dollars ($1,000).

(2) An order enjoining the methods, acts, or practices.

(3) Restitution of property.

(4) Punitive damages.

(5) Any other relief that the court deems proper.

(b)(1) Any consumer who is a senior citizen or a disabled person, as defined in subdivisions (f) and (g) of Section 1761, as part of an action under subdivision (a), may seek and be awarded, in addition to the remedies specified therein, up to five thousand dollars ($5,000) where the trier of fact does all of the following:

(A) Finds that the consumer has suffered substantial physical, emotional, or economic damage resulting from the defendant's conduct.

(B) Makes an affirmative finding in regard to one or more of the factors set forth in subdivision (b) of Section 3345.

(C) Finds that an additional award is appropriate.

(2) Judgment in a class action by senior citizens or disabled persons under Section 1781 may award each class member that additional award if the trier of fact has made the foregoing findings.

(c) Whenever it is proven by a preponderance of the evidence that a defendant has engaged in conduct in violation of paragraph (24) of subdivision (a) of Section 1770, in addition to all other remedies otherwise provided in this section, the court shall award treble actual damages to the plaintiff. This subdivision shall not apply to attorneys licensed to practice law in California, who are subject to the California Rules of Professional Conduct and to the mandatory fee arbitration provisions of Article 13 (commencing with Section 6200) of Chapter 4 of Division 3 of the Business and Professions Code, when the fees charged or received are for providing representation in administrative agency appeal proceedings or court proceedings for purposes of procuring, maintaining, or securing public social services on behalf of a person or group of persons.

(d) An action under subdivision (a) or (b) may be commenced in the county in which the person against whom it is brought resides, has his or her principal place of business, or is doing business, or in the county where the transaction or any substantial portion thereof occurred.

In any action subject to this section, concurrently with the filing of the complaint, the plaintiff shall file an affidavit stating facts showing that the action has been commenced in a county described in this section as a proper place for the trial of the action. If a plaintiff fails to file the affidavit required by this section, the court shall, upon its own motion or upon motion of any party, dismiss the action without prejudice.

(e) The court shall award court costs and attorney's fees to a prevailing plaintiff in litigation filed pursuant to this section. Reasonable attorney's fees may be awarded to a prevailing defendant upon a finding by the court that the plaintiff's prosecution of the action was not in good faith.

CONNECTICUT

CONNECTICUT UNFAIR TRADE PRACTICES ACT

Connecticut Statutes

Table of Sections

Sec.

§ 42–110a. Definitions

As used in this chapter:

(1) "Commissioner" means the Commissioner of Consumer Protection;

(2) "Documentary material" means the original or a copy of a book, record, report, memorandum, paper, communication, tabulation, map, chart, photograph, mechanical transcription, or other tangible document or recording, wherever situate;

(3) "Person" means a natural person, corporation, limited liability company, trust, partnership, incorporated or unincorporated association, and any other legal entity;

(4) "Trade" and "commerce" means the advertising, the sale or rent or lease, the offering for sale or rent or lease, or the distribution of any services and any property, tangible or intangible, real, personal or mixed, and any other article, commodity, or thing of value in this state.

§ 42–110b. Unfair trade practices prohibited. Legislative intent

(a) No person shall engage in unfair methods of competition and unfair or deceptive acts or practices in the conduct of any trade or commerce.

(b) It is the intent of the legislature that in construing subsection (a) of this section, the commissioner and the courts of this state shall be guided by interpretations given by the Federal Trade Commission and the federal courts to Section 5(a)(1) of the Federal Trade Commission Act (15 USC 45(a)(1)), as from time to time amended.

(c) The commissioner may, in accordance with chapter 54, establish by regulation acts, practices or methods which shall be deemed to be unfair or deceptive in violation of subsection (a) of this section. Such regulations shall not be inconsistent with the rules, regulations and decisions of the federal trade commission and the federal courts in interpreting the provisions of the Federal Trade Commission Act.

(d) It is the intention of the legislature that this chapter be remedial and be so construed.

§ 42–110c. Exceptions

(a) Nothing in this chapter shall apply to: (1) Transactions or actions otherwise permitted under law as administered by any regulatory board or officer acting under statutory authority of the state or of the United States; or (2) acts done by the publisher, owner, agent or employee of a newspaper, periodical or radio or television station in the publication or dissemination of an advertisement, where the publisher, owner, agent or employee did not have knowledge of the false, misleading, unfair or deceptive character of the advertisement, and did not have direct financial interest in the sale or distribution of the advertised product or service.

(b) The burden of proving exemption, as provided in this section, from the provisions of this chapter shall be upon the person claiming the exemption.

* * *

§ 42–110e. Appeals

Any person required by an order of the commissioner to cease and desist from using any method, act or practice declared unlawful by section 42–110b or to make restitution may appeal therefrom in accordance with the provisions of section 4–183. Appeals under this section shall be privileged cases to be heard by the court as soon after the return day as shall be practicable.

* * *

§ 42–110g. Action for damages. Class actions. Costs and fees. Equitable relief. Jury trial

(a) Any person who suffers any ascertainable loss of money or property, real or personal, as a result of the use or employment of a method, act or practice prohibited by section 42–110b, may bring an action in the judicial district in which the plaintiff or defendant resides or has his principal place of business or is doing business, to recover actual damages. Proof of public interest or public injury shall not be required in any action brought under this section. The court may, in its discretion, award punitive damages and may provide such equitable relief as it deems necessary or proper.

(b) Persons entitled to bring an action under subsection (a) of this section may, pursuant to rules established by the judges of the Superior Court, bring a class action on behalf of themselves and other persons similarly situated who are residents of this state or injured in this state to recover damages.

(c) Upon commencement of any action brought under subsection (a) of this section, the plaintiff shall mail a copy of the complaint to the Attorney General and the Commissioner of Consumer Protection and, upon entry of any judgment or decree in the action, shall mail a copy of such judgment or decree to the Attorney General and the Commissioner of Consumer Protection.

(d) In any action brought by a person under this section, the court may award, to the plaintiff, in addition to the relief provided in this section, costs and reasonable attorneys' fees based on the work reasonably performed by an attorney and not on the amount of recovery. In a class action in which there is no monetary recovery, but other relief is granted on behalf of a class, the court may award, to the plaintiff, in addition to other relief provided in this section, costs and reasonable attorneys' fees. In any action brought under this section, the court may, in its discretion, order, in addition to damages or in lieu of damages, injunctive or other equitable relief.

(e) Any final order issued by the Department of Consumer Protection and any permanent injunction, final judgment or final order of the court made under section 42–110d, 42–110m, 42–110*o* or 42–110p shall be prima facie evidence in an action brought under this section that the respondent or defendant used or employed a method, act or practice prohibited by section 42–110b, provided this section shall not apply to consent orders or judgments entered before any testimony has been taken.

(f) An action under this section may not be brought more than three years after the occurrence of a violation of this chapter.

(g) In any action brought by a person under this section there shall be a right to a jury trial except with respect to the award of punitive damages under subsection (a) of this section or the award of costs, reasonable attorneys' fees and injunctive or other equitable relief under subsection (d) of this section.

§ 42–110h. Class actions

As soon as practicable after the commencement of an action brought as a class action, the court shall determine by order whether it is to be so maintained. An order under this section may be conditional, and it may be amended before decision on the merits. An order issued under this section shall be immediately appealable by either party.

* * *

§ 42–110m. Restraining orders or injunctions. Relief

(a) Whenever the commissioner has reason to believe that any person has been engaged or is engaged in an alleged violation of any provision of this chapter said commissioner may proceed as provided in sections 42–110d and 42–110e or may request the Attorney General to apply in the name of the state of Connecticut to the Superior Court for an order temporarily or permanently restraining and enjoining the continuance of such act or acts or for an order directing restitution and the appointment of a receiver in appropriate instances, or both. Proof of public interest or public injury shall not be required in any action brought pursuant to section 42–110d, section 42–110e or this section. The court may award the relief applied for or so much as it may deem proper including reasonable attorney's fees, accounting and such other relief as may be granted in equity. In such action the commissioner shall be responsible for all necessary investigative support.

* * *

§ 42–110*o*. Civil penalties

(a) Any person who violates the terms of a temporary restraining order or an injunction issued under subsection (d) of section 42–110d or subsection (a) of section 42–110m shall forfeit and pay to the state a civil penalty of not more than twenty five thousand dollars per violation. For purposes of this section the court issuing the injunction shall retain jurisdiction, and the cause shall be continued, and in such cases the Attorney General acting in the name of the state may petition for recovery of civil penalties.

(b) In any action brought under section 42–110m, if the court finds that a person is wilfully using or has wilfully used a method, act or practice prohibited by section 42–110b, the Attorney General, upon petition to the court, may recover, on behalf of the state, a civil penalty of not more than five thousand dollars for each violation. For purposes of this subsection, a wilful violation occurs when the party committing the violation knew or should have known that his conduct was a violation of section 42–110b.

* * *

NEW YORK

NEW YORK GENERAL BUSINESS LAW

N.Y. Gen. Bus. Law

Table of Sections

§ 349. Deceptive acts and practices unlawful

(a) Deceptive acts or practices in the conduct of any business, trade or commerce or in the furnishing of any service in this state are hereby declared unlawful.

(b) Whenever the attorney general shall believe from evidence satisfactory to him that any person, firm, corporation or association or agent or employee thereof has engaged in or is about to engage in any of the acts or practices stated to be unlawful he may bring an action in the name and on behalf of the people of the state of New York to enjoin such unlawful acts or practices and to obtain restitution of any moneys or property obtained directly or indirectly by any such unlawful acts or practices. In such action preliminary relief may be granted under article sixty-three of the civil practice law and rules.

(c) Before any violation of this section is sought to be enjoined, the attorney general shall be required to give the person against whom such proceeding is contemplated notice by certified mail and an opportunity to show in writing within five business days after receipt of notice why proceedings should not be instituted against him, unless the attorney general shall find, in any case in which he seeks preliminary relief, that to give such notice and opportunity is not in the public interest.

(d) In any such action it shall be a complete defense that the act or practice is, or if in interstate commerce would be, subject to and complies with the rules and regulations of, and the statutes administered by, the federal trade commission or any official department, division, commission or agency of the United States as such rules, regulations or statutes are interpreted by the federal trade commission or such department, division, commission or agency or the federal courts.

(e) Nothing in this section shall apply to any television or radio broadcasting station or to any publisher or printer of a newspaper, magazine or other form of printed advertising, who broadcasts, publishes, or prints the advertisement.

(f) In connection with any proposed proceeding under this section, the attorney general is authorized to take proof and make a determination of the relevant facts, and to issue subpoenas in accordance with the civil practice law and rules.

(g) This section shall apply to all deceptive acts or practices declared to be unlawful, whether or not subject to any other law of this state, and shall not supersede, amend or repeal any other law of this state under which the attorney general is authorized to take any action or conduct any inquiry.

(h) In addition to the right of action granted to the attorney general pursuant to this section, any person who has been injured by reason of any violation of this section may bring an action in his own name to enjoin such unlawful act or practice, an action to recover his actual damages or fifty dollars, whichever is greater, or both such actions. The court may, in its discretion, increase the award of damages to an amount not to exceed three times the actual damages up to one thousand dollars, if the court finds the defendant willfully or knowingly violated this section. The court may award reasonable attorney's fees to a prevailing plaintiff.

§ 350. False advertising unlawful

False advertising in the conduct of any business, trade or commerce or in the furnishing of any service in this state is hereby declared unlawful.

§ 350–a. False advertising

1. The term "false advertising" means advertising, including labeling, of a commodity, or of the kind, character, terms or conditions of any employment opportunity if such advertising is misleading in a material respect. In determining whether any advertising is misleading, there shall be taken into account (among other things) not only representations made by statement, word, design, device, sound or any combination thereof, but also the extent to which the advertising fails to reveal facts material in the light of such representations with respect to the commodity or employment to which the advertising relates under the conditions prescribed in said advertisement, or under such conditions as are customary or usual. For purposes of this article, with respect to the advertising of an employment opportunity, it shall be deemed "misleading in a material respect" to either fail to reveal whether the employment available or being offered requires or is conditioned upon the purchasing or leasing of supplies, material, equipment or other property or whether such employment is on a commission rather than a fixed salary basis and, if so, whether the salaries advertised are only obtainable if sufficient commissions are earned.

2. An employer shall not be liable under this section as a result of a failure to disclose all material facts relating to terms and conditions of employment if the aggrieved person has not suffered actual pecuniary damage as a result of the misleading advertising of an employment opportunity or if the employer has, prior to the aggrieved person suffering any pecuniary damage, disclosed in writing to that person a full and accurate description of the kind, character, terms and conditions of the employment opportunity.

3. It shall constitute false advertising to display or announce, in print or broadcast advertising, the price of an item after deduction of a rebate unless the actual selling price is displayed or announced, and clear and conspicuous notice is given in the advertisement that a mail-in rebate is required to achieve the lower net price.

§ 350–e. Construction

1. This article neither enlarges nor diminishes the rights of parties in private litigation except as provided in this section.

2. This article does not repeal the provisions of subdivision twelve of section sixty-three of the executive law.

3. Any person who has been injured by reason of any violation of section three hundred fifty or three hundred fifty-a of this article may bring an action in his or her own name to enjoin such unlawful act or practice, an action to recover his or her actual damages or five hundred dollars, whichever is greater, or both such actions. The court may, in its discretion, increase the award of damages to an amount not to exceed three times the actual damages, up to ten thousand dollars, if the court finds that the defendant willfully or knowingly violated this section. The court may award reasonable attorney's fees to a prevailing plaintiff.

UTAH

UTAH CONSUMER SALES PRACTICES ACT

Utah Code Ann.

Table of Sections

§ 13–11–1. Citation of act

This act shall be known and may be cited as the "Utah Consumer Sales Practices Act."

§ 13–11–2. Construction and purposes of act

This act shall be construed liberally to promote the following policies:

(1) To simplify, clarify, and modernize the law governing consumer sales practices;

(2) To protect consumers from suppliers who commit deceptive and unconscionable sales practices;

(3) To encourage the development of fair consumer sales practices;

(4) To make state regulation of consumer sales practices not inconsistent with the policies of the Federal Trade Commission Act relating to consumer protection;

(5) To make uniform the law, including the administrative rules, with respect to the subject of this act among those states which enact similar laws; and

(6) To recognize and protect suppliers who in good faith comply with the provisions of this act.

§ 13–11–3. Definitions

As used in this chapter:

* * *

(2)(a) "Consumer transaction" means a sale, lease, assignment, award by chance, or other written or oral transfer or disposition of goods, services, or other property, both tangible and intangible (except securities and insurance) to, or apparently to, a person for:

(i) primarily personal, family, or household purposes; or

(ii) purposes that relate to a business opportunity that requires:

(A) expenditure of money or property by the person described in Subsection (2)(a); and

(B) the person described in Subsection (2)(a) to perform personal services on a continuing basis and in which the person described in Subsection (2)(a) has not been previously engaged.

* * *

(3) "Enforcing authority" means the Division of Consumer Protection.

(4) "Final judgment" means a judgment, including any supporting opinion, that determines the rights of the parties and concerning which appellate remedies have been exhausted or the time for appeal has expired.

(5) "Person" means an individual, corporation, government, governmental subdivision or agency, business trust, estate, trust, partnership, association, cooperative, or any other legal entity.

(6) "Supplier" means a seller, lessor, assignor, offeror, broker, or other person who regularly solicits, engages in, or enforces consumer transactions, whether or not he deals directly with the consumer.

§ 13-11-4. Deceptive act or practice by supplier

(1) A deceptive act or practice by a supplier in connection with a consumer transaction violates this chapter whether it occurs before, during, or after the transaction.

(2) Without limiting the scope of Subsection (1), a supplier commits a deceptive act or practice if the supplier knowingly or intentionally:

(a) indicates that the subject of a consumer transaction has sponsorship, approval, performance characteristics, accessories, uses, or benefits, if it has not;

(b) indicates that the subject of a consumer transaction is of a particular standard, quality, grade, style, or model, if it is not;

(c) indicates that the subject of a consumer transaction is new, or unused, if it is not, or has been used to an extent that is materially different from the fact;

(d) indicates that the subject of a consumer transaction is available to the consumer for a reason that does not exist, including any of the following reasons falsely used in an advertisement:

(i) "going out of business";

(ii) "bankruptcy sale";

(iii) "lost our lease";

(iv) "building coming down";

(v) "forced out of business";

(vi) "final days";

(vii) "liquidation sale";

(viii) "fire sale";

(ix) "quitting business"; or

(x) an expression similar to any of the expressions in Subsections (2)(d)(i) through (ix);

(e) indicates that the subject of a consumer transaction has been supplied in accordance with a previous representation, if it has not;

(f) indicates that the subject of a consumer transaction will be supplied in greater quantity than the supplier intends;

(g) indicates that replacement or repair is needed, if it is not;

(h) indicates that a specific price advantage exists, if it does not;

(i) indicates that the supplier has a sponsorship, approval, or affiliation the supplier does not have;

(j)

(i) indicates that a consumer transaction involves or does not involve a warranty, a disclaimer of warranties, particular warranty terms, or other rights, remedies, or obligations, if the representation is false; or

(ii) fails to honor a warranty or a particular warranty term;

(k) indicates that the consumer will receive a rebate, discount, or other benefit as an inducement for entering into a consumer transaction in return for giving the supplier the names of prospective consumers or otherwise helping the supplier to enter into other consumer transactions, if receipt of the benefit is contingent on an event occurring after the consumer enters into the transaction;

(*l*) after receipt of payment for goods or services, fails to ship the goods or furnish the services within the time advertised or otherwise represented or, if no specific time is advertised or represented, fails to ship the goods or furnish the services within 30 days, unless within the applicable time period the supplier provides the buyer with the option to:

(i) cancel the sales agreement and receive a refund of all previous payments to the supplier if the refund is mailed or delivered to the buyer within ten business days after the day on which the seller receives written notification from the buyer of the buyer's intent to cancel the sales agreement and receive the refund; or

(ii) extend the shipping date to a specific date proposed by the supplier;

(m) except as provided in Subsection (3)(b), fails to furnish a notice meeting the requirements of Subsection (3)(a) of the purchaser's right to cancel a direct solicitation sale within three business days of the time of purchase if:

(i) the sale is made other than at the supplier's established place of business pursuant to the supplier's personal contact, whether through mail, electronic mail, facsimile transmission, telephone, or any other form of direct solicitation; and

(ii) the sale price exceeds $25;

(n) promotes, offers, or grants participation in a pyramid scheme as defined under Title 76, Chapter 6a, Pyramid Scheme Act;

(*o*) represents that the funds or property conveyed in response to a charitable solicitation will be donated or used for a particular purpose or will be donated to or used by a particular organization, if the representation is false;

(p) if a consumer indicates the consumer's intention of making a claim for a motor vehicle repair against the consumer's motor vehicle insurance policy:

(i) commences the repair without first giving the consumer oral and written notice of:

(A) the total estimated cost of the repair; and

(B) the total dollar amount the consumer is responsible to pay for the repair, which dollar amount may not exceed the applicable deductible or other copay arrangement in the consumer's insurance policy; or

(ii) requests or collects from a consumer an amount that exceeds the dollar amount a consumer was initially told the consumer was responsible to pay as an insurance deductible or other copay arrangement for a motor vehicle repair under Subsection (2)(p)(i), even if that amount is less than the full amount the motor vehicle insurance policy requires the insured to pay as a deductible or other copay arrangement, unless:

(A) the consumer's insurance company denies that coverage exists for the repair, in which case, the full amount of the repair may be charged and collected from the consumer; or

(B) the consumer misstates, before the repair is commenced, the amount of money the insurance policy requires the consumer to pay as a deductible or other copay arrangement, in which case, the supplier may charge and collect from the consumer an amount that does not exceed the amount the insurance policy requires the consumer to pay as a deductible or other copay arrangement;

(q) includes in any contract, receipt, or other written documentation of a consumer transaction, or any addendum to any contract, receipt, or other written documentation of a consumer transaction, any confession of judgment or any waiver of any of the rights to which a consumer is entitled under this chapter;

(r) charges a consumer for a consumer transaction that has not previously been agreed to by the consumer;

(s) solicits or enters into a consumer transaction with a person who lacks the mental ability to comprehend the nature and consequences of:

(i) the consumer transaction; or

(ii) the person's ability to benefit from the consumer transaction; or

(t) solicits for the sale of a product or service by providing a consumer with an unsolicited check or negotiable instrument the presentment or negotiation of which obligates the consumer to purchase a product or service, unless the supplier is:

(i) a depository institution under Section 7–1–103;

(ii) an affiliate of a depository institution; or

(iii) an entity regulated under Title 7, Financial Institutions Act.

(u) sends an unsolicited mailing to a person that appears to be a billing, statement, or request for payment for a product or service the person has not ordered or used, or that implies that the mailing requests payment for an ongoing product or service the person has not received or requested.

(v) issues a gift certificate, instrument, or other record in exchange for payment to provide the bearer, upon presentation, goods or services in a specified amount without printing in a readable manner on the gift certificate, instrument, packaging, or record any expiration date or information concerning a fee to be charged and deducted from the balance of the gift certificate, instrument, or other record; or

(w) misrepresents the geographical origin or location of the supplier's business in connection with the sale of cut flowers, flower arrangements, or floral products.

(3)(a) The notice required by Subsection (2)(m) shall:

(i) be a conspicuous statement written in dark bold with at least 12 point type on the first page of the purchase documentation; and

(ii) read as follows: "YOU, THE BUYER, MAY CANCEL THIS CONTRACT AT ANY TIME PRIOR TO MIDNIGHT OF THE THIRD BUSINESS DAY (or time period reflecting the supplier's cancellation policy but not less than three business days) AFTER THE DATE OF THE TRANSACTION OR RECEIPT OF THE PRODUCT, WHICHEVER IS LATER".

(b) A supplier is exempt from the requirements of Subsection (2)(m) if the supplier's cancellation policy:

(i) is communicated to the buyer; and

(ii) offers greater rights to the buyer than Subsection (2)(m).

(4)(a) A gift certificate, instrument, or other record that does not print an expiration date in accordance with Subsection (2)(v) does not expire.

(b) A gift certificate, instrument, or other record that does not include printed information concerning a fee to be charged and deducted from the balance of the gift certificate, instrument, or other record is not subject to the charging and deduction of the fee.

(c) Subsections (2)(v) and (4)(b) do not apply to a gift certificate, instrument, or other record useable at multiple, unaffiliated sellers of goods or services if an expiration date is printed on the gift certificate, instrument, or other record.

§ 13–11–5. Unconscionable act or practice by supplier

(1) An unconscionable act or practice by a supplier in connection with a consumer transaction violates this act whether it occurs before, during, or after the transaction.

(2) The unconscionability of an act or practice is a question of law for the court. If it is claimed or appears to the court that an act or practice may be unconscionable, the parties shall be given a reasonable opportunity to present evidence as to its setting, purpose, and effect to aid the court in making its determination.

(3) In determining whether an act or practice is unconscionable, the court shall consider circumstances which the supplier knew or had reason to know.

* * *

§ 13–11–7. Duties of enforcing authority—Confidentiality of identity of persons investigated—Civil penalty for violation of restraining or injunctive orders

(1) The enforcing authority shall:

(a) enforce this chapter throughout the state;

(b) cooperate with state and local officials, officials of other states, and officials of the federal government in the administration of comparable statutes;

(c) inform consumers and suppliers on a continuing basis of the provisions of this chapter and of acts or practices that violate this chapter including mailing information concerning final judgments to persons who request it, for which he may charge a reasonable fee to cover the expense;

(d) receive and act on complaints; and

(e) maintain a public file of final judgments rendered under this chapter that have been either reported officially or made available for public dissemination under Subsection (1)(c), final consent judgments, and to the extent the enforcing authority considers appropriate, assurances of voluntary compliance.

(2) In carrying out his duties, the enforcing authority may not publicly disclose the identity of a person investigated unless his identity has become a matter of public record in an enforcement proceeding or he has consented to public disclosure.

(3) On motion of the enforcing authority, or on its own motion, the court may impose a civil penalty of not more than $5,000 for each day a temporary restraining order, preliminary injunction, or permanent injunction issued under this chapter is violated, if the supplier received notice of the restraining or injunctive order. Civil penalties imposed under this section shall be paid to the General Fund.

§ 13–11–8. Powers of enforcing authority

(1) The enforcing authority may conduct research, hold public hearings, make inquiries, and publish studies relating to consumer sales acts or practices.

(2) The enforcing authority shall adopt substantive rules that prohibit with specificity acts or practices that violate section 13–11–4 and appropriate procedural rules.

* * *

§ 13–11–17. Actions by enforcing authority

(1) The enforcing authority may bring an action:

(a) to obtain a declaratory judgment that an act or practice violates this chapter;

(b) to enjoin, in accordance with the principles of equity, a supplier who has violated, is violating, or is otherwise likely to violate this chapter; and

(c) to recover, for each violation, actual damages, or obtain relief under Subsection (2)(b), on behalf of consumers who complained to the enforcing authority within a reasonable time after it instituted proceedings under this chapter.

(2)

(a) The enforcing authority may bring a class action on behalf of consumers for the actual damages caused by an act or practice specified as violating this chapter in a rule adopted by the enforcing authority under Subsection 13–11–8(2) before the consumer transactions on which the action is based, or declared to violate Section 13–11–4 or 13–11–5 by final judgment of courts of general jurisdiction and appellate courts of this state that was either reported officially or made available for public dissemination under Subsection 13–11–7(1)(c) by the enforcing authority ten days before the consumer transactions on which the action is based, or, with respect to a supplier who agreed to it, was prohibited specifically by the terms of a consent judgment that became final before the consumer transactions on which the action is based.

* * *

(d) If a supplier shows by a preponderance of the evidence that a violation of this chapter resulted from a bona fide error notwithstanding the maintenance of procedures reasonably adapted to avoid the error, recovery under this Subsection (2) is limited to the amount, if any, by which the supplier was unjustly enriched by the violation.

(e) An action may not be brought by the enforcing authority under this Subsection(2) more than two years after the occurrence of a violation of this chapter.

(3)

(a) The enforcing authority may terminate an investigation or an action other than a class action upon acceptance of the supplier's written assurance of voluntary compliance with this chapter. Acceptance of an assurance may be conditioned on a commitment to reimburse consumers or take other appropriate corrective action.

(b) An assurance is not evidence of a prior violation of this chapter. Unless an assurance has been rescinded by agreement of the parties or voided by a court for good cause, subsequent failure to comply with the terms of an assurance is prima facie evidence of a violation.

(4)

(a) In addition to other penalties and remedies set out under this chapter, and in addition to its other enforcement powers under Title 13, Chapter 2, Division of Consumer Protection, the division director may issue a cease and desist order and impose an administrative fine of up to $2,500 for each violation of this chapter.

(b) All money received through administrative fines imposed under this section shall be deposited in the Consumer Protection Education and Training Fund created by Section 13–2–8.

§ 13–11–17.5. Costs and attorney's fees

Any judgment granted in favor of the enforcing authority in connection with the enforcement of this chapter shall include, in addition to any other monetary award or injunctive relief, an award of reasonable attorney's fees, court costs, and costs of investigation.

* * *

§ 13–11–19. Actions by consumer

(1) Whether he seeks or is entitled to damages or otherwise has an adequate remedy at law, a consumer may bring an action to:

(a) obtain a declaratory judgment that an act or practice violates this chapter; and

(b) enjoin, in accordance with the principles of equity, a supplier who has violated, is violating, or is likely to violate this chapter.

(2) A consumer who suffers loss as a result of a violation of this chapter may recover, but not in a class action, actual damages or $2,000, whichever is greater, plus court costs.

(3) Whether a consumer seeks or is entitled to recover damages or has an adequate remedy at law, he may bring a class action for declaratory judgment, an injunction, and appropriate ancillary relief against an act or practice that violates this chapter.

(4)

(a) A consumer who suffers loss as a result of a violation of this chapter may bring a class action for the actual damages caused by an act or practice specified as violating this chapter by a rule adopted by the enforcing authority under Subsection 13–11–8(2) before the consumer transactions on which the action is based, or declared to violate Section 13–11–4 or 13–11–5 by a final judgment of the appropriate court or courts of general jurisdiction and appellate courts of this state that was either officially reported or made available for public dissemination under Subsection 13–11–7(1)(c) by the enforcing authority ten days before the consumer transactions on which the action is based, or with respect to a supplier who agreed to it, was prohibited specifically by the terms of a consent judgment which became final before the consumer transactions on which the action is based.

* * *

(c) If a supplier shows by a preponderance of the evidence that a violation of this chapter resulted from a bona fide error notwithstanding the maintenance of procedures reasonably adapted to avoid the error, recovery under this section is limited to the amount, if any, in which the supplier was unjustly enriched by the violation.

(5) Except for services performed by the enforcing authority, the court may award to the prevailing party a reasonable attorney's fee limited to the work reasonably performed if:

(a) the consumer complaining of the act or practice that violates this chapter has brought or maintained an action he knew to be groundless; or a supplier has committed an act or practice that violates this chapter; and

(b) an action under this section has been terminated by a judgment or required by the court to be settled under Subsection 13–11–21(1)(a).

* * *

§ 13–11–22. Exemptions from application of act

(1) This act does not apply to:

(a) An act or practice required or specifically permitted by or under federal law, or by or under state law;

(b) A publisher, broadcaster, printer, or other person engaged in the dissemination of information or the reproduction of printed or pictorial matter so far as the information or matter has been disseminated or reproduced on behalf of others without actual knowledge that it violated this act;

(c) Claim for personal injury or death or claim for damage to property other than the property that is the subject of the consumer transaction;

(d) Credit terms of a transaction otherwise subject to this act; or

(e) Any public utility subject to the regulating jurisdiction of the Public Service Commission of the state of Utah.

(2) A person alleged to have violated this act has the burden of showing the applicability of this section.

§ 13–11–23. Other remedies available—Class action only as prescribed by act

The remedies of this act are in addition to remedies otherwise available for the same conduct under state or local law, except that a class action relating to a transaction governed by this act may be brought only as prescribed by this act.

[The following Maryland and Michigan statutes serve as representatives of the state rent-to-own laws]

ANNOTATED CODE OF MARYLAND
COMMERCIAL LAW
TITLE 12. CREDIT REGULATIONS
Subtitle 11. Maryland Rental-Purchase Agreement Act

Table of Sections

§ 12–1101. Definitions

(a) In this subtitle the following words have the meanings indicated.

(b)

(1) "Advertisement" means a commercial message in any medium that aids, promotes, or assists, directly or indirectly, a rental-purchase agreement.

(2) "Advertisement" does not include in-store merchandising ads.

(c) "Cash price" means the price at which the lessor would have sold rental property covered by a rental-purchase agreement to the consumer unconditionally for cash on the date of consummation.

(d) "Consumer" means an individual who rents personal property under a rental-purchase agreement primarily for personal, family, or household purposes.

(e) "Consummation" means the time at which a consumer enters into a rental-purchase agreement.

(f) "Cost of lease services" means the difference between the final purchase price of rental property and the cash price of rental property.

(g) "Lessor" means a person who regularly provides the use of personal property through rental-purchase agreements to consumers and to whom rental payments are initially payable on the face of a rental-purchase agreement.

(h) "Rental property" means personal property that is the subject of a rental-purchase agreement.

(i) "Rental-purchase agreement" means an agreement that:

(1) Is for the use of personal property by an individual primarily for personal, family, or household purposes;

(2) Is for an initial period of 4 months or less;

(3) Is automatically renewable for a weekly or monthly period with each rental payment after the initial period; and

(4) Allows but does not obligate the consumer to become the owner of the property.

§ 12–1102. Effect and application

(a) A rental-purchase agreement that complies with this subtitle may not be deemed to be:

(1) A "retail sale", as defined in s 12–601 (s) of this title;

(2) An "installment sale agreement", as defined in s 12–601 (m) of this title; or

(3) A "security interest", as defined in s 1–201 (37) of this article.

(b) This subtitle does not apply to:

(1) A rental-purchase agreement made primarily for business, commercial, or agricultural purposes, or made with governmental agencies, instrumentalities, or organizations;

(2) A rental of a safe deposit box;

(3) A lease or bailment of personal property that:

(i) Is incidental to the rental of real property; and

(ii) Provides that the consumer has no option to purchase the rented real property; or

(4) A lease of an automobile.

§ 12–1103. Disclosures required

(a)(1) A lessor shall disclose to a consumer the information required under this subtitle.

(2) In a transaction involving more than 1 lessor, only 1 lessor need make the disclosures required under this subtitle, but all lessors shall be bound by the disclosures made.

(b) A lessor shall make the disclosures required under this subtitle before consummation of the rental-purchase agreement.

(c) A lessor shall:

(1) Make the disclosures required under this subtitle in a written form that is simple and understandable and is written or typed in a size not less than 10 point type;

(2) Make the disclosures required under this subtitle in English or in any other language used by the lessor in advertisements related to the rental-purchase transaction;

(3) Make the disclosures required under this subtitle on the face of the rental-purchase agreement and summary of costs chart above the consumer's signature lines; and

(4) Deliver a copy of the rental-purchase agreement and summary of costs chart to the consumer.

(d) If a disclosure becomes inaccurate as a result of any act, occurrence, or agreement by the consumer after delivery of the rental property, the resulting inaccuracy is not a violation of this subtitle.

§ 12–1104. Specific contents of disclosure

(a) The lessor shall disclose in each rental-purchase agreement, as applicable:

(1) The total number, total amount, and timing of all rental payments necessary to acquire ownership of the rental property;

(2) A statement that the consumer will not own the rental property until the consumer has paid the total of payments necessary to acquire ownership;

(3) A brief description of the rental property sufficient to identify the rental property to the consumer and the lessor, including an identification number and a statement indicating whether the rental property is new or used;

(4)(i) A statement of the cash price of the rental property; or

(ii) If a single rental-purchase agreement involves a lease of 2 or more items of rental property as a set, a statement of the aggregate cash price of all items;

(5) The cost of lease services of the rental property;

(6) The total of initial payments paid or required to be paid at or before consummation of the rental-purchase agreement or delivery of the rental property, whichever is later;

(7) A statement that the total of rental payments does not include other charges, such as reinstatement fees, damage fees, or pickup fees;

(8) A statement that the consumer has the right to exercise an early purchase option and the price, formula, or method for determining the early purchase option price;

(9) A statement that the consumer must pay the early purchase option price for the rental property if, and when, the rental property is lost, stolen, damaged, or destroyed;

(10)(i) A statement identifying the lessor as the party responsible for maintaining or servicing the rental property while it is being rented;

(ii) A description of that responsibility; and

(iii) A statement that if any part of a manufacturer's express warranty covers the rental property at the time the consumer acquires ownership of the rental property, it shall be transferred to the consumer, if allowed by the terms of the warranty;

(11) The date of consummation and the identities of the lessor and consumer;

(12) A statement that the consumer may terminate the rental-purchase agreement without penalty by voluntarily surrendering or returning the rental property in good repair, normal wear and tear excepted, upon expiration of any rental term and payment of any past due rental payments;

(13) Notice of the consumer's right to reinstate an agreement as provided in s 12–1106 of this subtitle; and

(14) Any other charges, including reinstatement fees, damage fees, and pickup fees.

(b) The lessor shall disclose in each summary of costs chart, as applicable:

(1) The cash price of the rental property;

(2) The timing of the payments for the rental property;

(3) The total purchase price if the payment schedule under item (2) of this subsection is completed according to the schedule; and

(4) The cost of lease services of the rental property.

(c) A lessor shall place on property which is to be leased as a part of a rental-purchase agreement and is displayed in the lessor's place of business a tag which shall indicate:

(1) The number and amount of individual renewal payments necessary to purchase the property;

(2) The total amount necessary to purchase the property; and

(3) Whether the property is new or used.

§ 12–1105. Proscribed terms

A rental-purchase agreement may not contain:

(1) A confession of judgment;

(2) A negotiable instrument;

(3) A security interest or any other claim of a property interest in any goods except the rental property delivered by the lessor pursuant to the rental-purchase agreement;

(4) A wage assignment;

(5) A waiver by the consumer of claims or defenses; or

(6) A provision authorizing the lessor or a person acting on the lessor's behalf to enter upon the consumer's premises or to commit any breach of the peace in the repossession of rental property.

§ 12–1106. Reinstatement and repossession

(a) A consumer who fails to make a timely rental payment may reinstate the rental-purchase agreement, without losing any rights or options that exist under the rental-purchase agreement, if within 5 days of the renewal date, for a consumer who renews on a monthly basis, or within 2 days of the renewal date, for a consumer who renews on a weekly basis, the consumer pays:

(1) All past due rental charges;

(2) If the rental property has been picked up or repossessed, the reasonable costs of pickup and redelivery; and

(3) Any applicable reinstatement fee, which may not exceed $5.

(b) A consumer who has paid less than two-thirds of the total of payments necessary to acquire ownership of the rental property and who has returned or voluntarily surrendered the rental property without judicial process during the applicable reinstatement period under subsection (a) of this section or who has made the property available for pickup at the request of the lessor, whichever occurs last, may reinstate the rental-purchase agreement prior to a date not less than 21 days after the date of the return of the rental property.

(c) A consumer who has paid two-thirds or more of the total of payments necessary to acquire ownership of the rental property and who has returned or voluntarily surrendered the rental property without judicial process during the applicable period set forth in subsection (a) of this section or who has made the property available for pickup at the request of the lessor, whichever occurs last, may reinstate the rental-purchase agreement prior to a date not less than 45 days after the date of the return of the rental property.

(d) Nothing in this section shall prevent a lessor from repossessing the property during the reinstatement period, but a repossession may not affect the consumer's right to reinstate. After reinstatement, the lessor shall provide the consumer with the same rental property or a substitute property of comparable quality and condition.

(e)(1) A lessor may repossess property under a rental-purchase agreement if the consumer is in default of:

(i) Any sum due under the agreement; or

(ii) The performance of any promise the breach of which is expressly made a ground for repossessing the property.

(2) A lessor may repossess property only by legal process or self-help without the use of force. Nothing in this section authorizes a violation of criminal law.

(3) At the time of repossession of the property, the lessor shall deliver to the consumer a written notice which states the right of the buyer to reinstate the rental-purchase agreement, the last date by which the consumer may reinstate the agreement, and the amount payable for reinstatement.

(4) The consumer may reinstate the rental-purchase agreement within 15 days after the date of repossession by paying:

(i) All past due rental charges;

(ii) The reasonable costs of pickup and redelivery; and

(iii) A reinstatement fee of $5.

§ 12–1106.1. Retention of a copy of the agreement

A lessor shall maintain a copy of the rental-purchase agreement for 3 years after the final payment on a rental-purchase agreement.

§ 12–1107. Receipt; Written Statement of Account

(a) A lessor shall provide the consumer with a written receipt for each payment under a rental-purchase agreement made in person by cash or money order, or, if the payment is made in any other form, on request.

(b) The written receipt shall contain the:

(1) Total amount paid;

(2) Total amount due that week or month; and

(3) Total remaining rental payments necessary to acquire ownership of the item.

(c) The lessor shall provide the consumer with a written statement of account within 3 days after the consumer's request.

§ 12–1108. New agreements

(a) When a rental-purchase agreement is satisfied and replaced by a new rental-purchase agreement between the lessor and consumer, the lessor and consumer shall negotiate a new rental-purchase agreement requiring new disclosures.

(b) The following do not require the negotiation of a new rental-purchase agreement:

(1) The addition or return of rental property under a multiple-item agreement or the substitution of the rental property, if in either case the average payment allocable to a payment period is not changed by more than 25 percent;

(2) A deferral or extension of 1 or more rental payments, or portions of a rental payment;

(3) A reduction in charges in the rental-purchase agreement; or

(4) A rental-purchase agreement involved in a court proceeding.

§ 12–1109. Advertising

(a) An advertisement for a rental-purchase agreement that refers to or states the dollar amount of any payment and the right to acquire ownership for any 1 specific item shall clearly and conspicuously state, as applicable:

(1) That the transaction advertised is a rental-purchase agreement;

(2) The total cost and the number of payments necessary to acquire ownership; and

(3) That the consumer acquires no ownership right if the total amount necessary to acquire ownership is not paid.

(b) Any owner, employee, or agent of any medium in which an advertisement appears or through which it is disseminated may not be liable for violations under this section.

(c) The requirements under subsection (a) of this section do not apply to an advertisement that:

(1) Does not refer to or state the amount of any payment; or

(2) Is published in the yellow pages of a telephone directory or in any similar directory of business.

§ 12–1110. Sanctions

(a) A person who willfully and intentionally violates any provision of this subtitle is guilty of a misdemeanor and on conviction is subject to a fine not to exceed $500 per violation.

(b) For a violation of a provision of this subtitle, a consumer under a rental-purchase agreement may recover from the lessor committing the violation, or may set off by way of a counterclaim in an action brought by the lessor or its assignee, an amount equal to:

(1) Actual damages; and

(2) $500 plus reasonable attorney's fees and court costs.

(c) A lessor or its assignee may not be held liable under this subtitle if the lessor or its assignee proves by a preponderance of the evidence:

(1) That the violation was unintentional and resulted from a bona fide error, notwithstanding the maintenance of procedures reasonably adopted to avoid that type of error; and

(2) That the lessor or its assignee corrected the error and refunded any money excessively charged due to the error, within 30 days after discovering or receiving notice of the error.

§ 12–1110.1. Notice of default, court action to recover property

(a) A lessor may not bring a court action to recover property subject to a rental-purchase agreement until 15 days after the consumer has been sent notice of a default.

(b) Notice of default sent by certified mail to the consumer's last known address constitutes notice.

(c) The notice shall include any amount the consumer must pay to reinstate the rental-purchase agreement, if applicable.

§ 12–1111. Sample form

The following is an example of a form which shall be used to satisfy the disclosure requirements of §§ 12–1103(c) and 12–1104(a) of this subtitle:

Rental-Purchase Agreement

1.	Lessor(s):	Lessee(s):
	Name ____________	Name ____________
	Address ____________	Address ____________
	Telephone no. ________	Telephone no. ________

2. Description of Rental Property:

Identification

Item	Quantity	Number	Condition
____________	____________	____________	New ________
Cash Price:	____________		Used ______

3. Total Initial Payment:

Rental Payment: $ ________________

Delivery Charge: $ ________________

Tax: $ ________________

Other (specify): $ ________________

Total: $ ________________

4. Rental Payments:

Total Weekly Rental Payment: __________ (includes tax)

Total Monthly Rental Payment: __________ (includes tax)

5. Other Charges:

In Home Pick-up Fee: $ ________________

Reinstatement Fee: $ ________________

Other (specify): $ ________________

6. Total Cost To Acquire Ownership:

If you renew this rental agreement each week/month, for ______ weeks/months, you will pay a total of $______ to own the rental property. This amount includes your total initial payment but does not include other charges such as damage, reinstatement or pick-up fees for which you may be liable.

7. Cost of Lease Services:

The cost of lease services is the difference between the final purchase price of the rental property and the cash price of the rental property. The cost of lease services for the rental property is $_________.

8. No Ownership Until Total Paid:

You will not acquire ownership of the rental property until you pay the total rental payments necessary to acquire ownership, or unless you exercise an early purchase option.

9. Early Purchase Option:

You may purchase the rental property at any time after your first rental payment.

(Describe formula or method here)

10. Maintenance:

We (lessor) are responsible for maintaining the rental property in good working condition while it is being rented. We will provide all necessary service, repair or replacement (specify if in home or in store) if you notify us by phone or mail that service is needed. We will not be responsible for repairs done by anyone other than us.

11. Warranty:

If allowed by the manufacturer, the manufacturer's express warranty covering the rental property rented under this agreement will be transferred to you if, and at the time, you acquire ownership of the rental property.

12. Damages:

You (lessee) are entirely responsible for loss, damages, theft or destruction of the rental property while it is in your possession. Your liability for such damage will not exceed the early purchase option price of the rental property as of the date it is lost, stolen, damaged or destroyed.

13. Termination:

You (lessee) may terminate this agreement without penalty at the end of any weekly or monthly term by returning the rental property to us in good condition. You will be liable for any unpaid rental payments due upon the date of return.

14. Reinstatement:

If you (lessee) fail to make a timely payment, you may reinstate the agreement without penalty, if:

(1) You pay all past due rental charges and a reinstatement fee within 2 days (weekly renters) or 5 days (monthly renters) of your renewal date; or

(2) You return or voluntarily surrender the rental property within 2 days (weekly renters) or 5 days (monthly renters) of your renewal date. If you choose to reinstate the agreement after returning the rental property, you will have up to 21 days (or longer depending on how long you have rented the rental property) to pay all past due rental charges, a reinstatement fee and a reasonable redelivery fee if we deliver the rental property.

I have read the above disclosures before signing this rental-purchase agreement.

Lessee(s): ______________________ Date: ______________________

____

(b) The following is an example of a form which shall be used to satisfy the disclosure requirements of §§ 12–1103(c) and 12–1104(b) of this subtitle:

Summary of Costs of Your Rental-Purchase Agreement

Cash Price	**Scheduled Payments**	**Final Purchase Price**	**Cost of Lease Services**
The price of the rental property if purchased in-store at the time of consummation.	The amount you pay per week/month.	The Amount you will have paid after you have made all payments as scheduled.	The cost of your rental-purchase transaction.
$________	$________	$________	$________

Timing of Payments: Payment in the amount of $ ________ is due on a (Weekly/Bi-Weekly/Semi-Monthly/Monthly) basis.

Timing of Payments: Payment in the amount of $ ________ is due on a (Weekly/Bi-Weekly/Semi-Monthly/Monthly) basis.

Termination: You have the right to terminate this rental-purchase agreement at the end of any term by surrendering the rental property to the lessor.

The disclosures above are part of the terms and conditions of your rental-purchase agreement with (company name).

Lessee(s): ______________________ Date: ______________________

____

MICHIGAN RENTAL PURCHASE AGREEMENT ACT

Table of Sections

§ 445.951. Short title

This act shall be known and may be cited as the "rental-purchase agreement act."

§ 445.952. Definitions

As used in this act:

(a) "Lessee" means a person who leases property pursuant to a rental-purchase agreement.

(b) "Lessor" means a person who, in the ordinary course of business, regularly leases, offers to lease, or arranges for the leasing of property under a rental-purchase agreement.

(c) "Period" means a day, week, 1 month, or other subdivision of a year.

(d) "Rental-purchase agreement" means an agreement for the use of personal property by a lessee primarily for personal, family, or household purposes, for an initial period of 4 months or less that is automatically renewable with each payment after the initial period and that permits the lessee to become the owner of the property. Rental-purchase agreements shall not include any of the following:

(i) A lease or agreement which constitutes a credit sale as defined in 12 C.F.R. 226.2(a)(16) and section 1602(g) of the truth in lending act, 15 U.S.C. 1602(g).

(ii) A lease which constitutes a consumer lease as defined in 12 C.F.R. 213.2(a)(6).

(iii) Any lease for agricultural, business, or commercial purposes.

(iv) Any lease made to an organization.

(v) Any lease of money or intangible personal property.

(vi) A lease or agreement which constitutes a retail installment transaction as defined in section 2 of the retail installment sales act, Act No. 224 of the Public Acts of 1966, being section 445.852 of the Michigan Compiled Laws.

§ 445.953. Rental-purchase agreement, contents

(1) A rental-purchase agreement shall be in the form of a written statement which shall include all of the following:

(a) A brief description of the leased property, sufficient to identify the property to the lessee and lessor including whether the property is new or previously rented. If a lease is for multiple items, a description of each item may be provided in a separate statement which is incorporated by reference in the primary disclosure statement.

(b) The total amount of any initial payment, including any advance payment, delivery charge, or any trade-in allowance to be paid by the lessee at or before consummation of the rental-purchase agreement.

(c) The amount and timing of payments.

(d) The amount of all other charges, individually itemized, payable by the lessee to the lessor, which are not included in the periodic payments.

(e) A statement of the party liable for loss, damage in excess of normal wear and tear, or destruction to the leased property.

(f) The lessee's right to reinstate and the amount or method of determining the amount of any penalty or other charge for reinstatement as established in section 8.

(g) The party responsible for maintaining or servicing the leased property together with a brief description of this responsibility.

(h) A statement of the conditions under which the lessee or lessor may terminate the lease.

(i) A statement of the product of the number of payments times the amount of each payment necessary to acquire ownership of the leased property.

(j) A statement that the lessee has the option to purchase the leased property during the term of the rental-purchase agreement and, at what price, formula, or by what method the price is determined.

(k) The cash price of the property if purchased rather than leased.

(*l*) A statement that if any part of a manufacturer's warranty remains on the leased property at the point that a lessee assumes ownership of the property, the warranty will be passed on to the lessee.

(m) A notice in a prominent place in type not smaller than the size of 12-point type, or in legible print with letters not smaller than 1/8 inch, in substantially the following form:

NOTICE: THIS AGREEMENT IS REGULATED BY STATE LAW AND MAY BE ENFORCED BY THE ATTORNEY GENERAL OR BY PRIVATE LEGAL ACTION.

(2) All information required by this section shall be stated in a clear and coherent manner, using words and phrases of common meaning. The information shall be appropriately divided and captioned by its sections. All numerical amounts and percentages shall be stated in figures. The information shall also be disclosed by the lessor prior to the signing of the lease by the lessee on a dated written statement which identifies the lease or rental-purchase agreement and the parties to it. The written statement shall contain all of the information required by this section and shall be provided directly on the lease contract or instrument or on a separate form. A separate form may utilize the format provided for in section 19.

(3) At the lessor's option, information in addition to that required by this section may be disclosed if the additional information is not stated, utilized, or placed in a manner which will contradict, obscure, or distract attention from the required information.

§ 445.954. Purchase price

(1) The amount to be paid by the lessee to acquire ownership as disclosed in section 3(j) shall not be greater than the cash price as disclosed under section 3(k) minus an amount equal to 45% of all periodic rental payments made by the lessee.

(2) If at any time an amount equal to 45% of the total periodic rental payments paid by the lessee to the lessor equals the cash purchase price disclosed under section 3(k), then the lessee shall acquire ownership of the rental property.

(3) This section shall not prohibit a lessor from offering a rental-purchase agreement which provides that an amount equal to 45% or more of the periodic rental payments is applied toward the purchase price disclosed in section 3(k).

§ 445.955. Advertisements; display of merchandise

(1) An advertisement for any rental-purchase agreement shall not state that a specific lease of any property at specific amounts or terms is available unless the lessor usually and customarily leases or will lease the property at those amounts or terms.

(2) An advertisement shall not state that a payment or a periodic payment is due at the start of a lease without disclosing both the payment due at the start of the lease, the periodic payment, all other charges payable by the lessee, and the total of all periodic payments necessary to obtain ownership.

(3) Every item displayed or offered under a rental purchase agreement shall have clearly and conspicuously indicated in arabic numerals, so as to be readable and understandable by visual inspection, each of the following stamped upon or affixed to the item:

(a) The cash price of the item.

(b) The amount of a periodic payment.

(c) The total number of periodic payments required for ownership.

§ 445.956. Rental-purchase agreements, prohibited provisions

A rental-purchase agreement shall not contain a provision requiring any of the following:

(a) A garnishment of wages or a power of attorney to confess a judgment.

(b) Authorization to the lessor or a person acting on the lessor's behalf to unlawfully enter upon the lessee's premises or to commit any breach of the peace in the repossession of goods.

(c) The lessee to waive any defense, counterclaim, or right of action against the lessor or a person acting on the lessor's behalf, as the lessee's agent in collection of payments under the lease or in the repossession of goods.

(d) The lessee to agree not to assert against the lessor or against an assignee a claim or defense arising out of the lease.

(e) A requirement for any collection or repossession charges in excess of those allowable under section 7(e) and applicable court rules.

§ 445.957. Lessors; prohibited practices

A lessor shall not require any of the following:

(a) The purchase of insurance by the lessee from the lessor of a leased item.

(b) A payment that is in excess or in addition to a normal periodic payment and that is required in order to purchase a leased item at the conclusion of the periodic payments necessary to acquire ownership.

(c) A penalty for early termination of a rental-purchase agreement or for the return of an item at any point.

(d) A processing fee of any sort.

(e) A fee for in home collection of a payment unless the lessee has expressly agreed to the fee and the amount of the fee is disclosed.

(f) A periodic payment or late fee for a rental period beginning after the lessee has returned or surrendered the leased property to the lessor or the lessor's agent.

(g) Any charge or fee for reinstatement of the rental-purchase agreement in addition to or in excess of those expressly permitted in section 8.

§ 445.958. Late payments; late fee; reinstatement

(1) A lessee who fails to make a timely periodic payment may reinstate the original rental-purchase agreement without losing any rights or options previously acquired under the rental-purchase agreement by paying the past due periodic payment, any applicable late fee, and, if redelivery of an item is necessary, a delivery fee not to exceed the original delivery fee, by the later of the following dates:

(a) 7 days after failing to make the timely periodic payment.

(b) 90 days after failing to make the timely periodic payment, if the lessee returns or voluntarily surrenders the item, other than through judicial process, within 7 days after failing to make the timely periodic payment.

(2) A lessee shall not be charged a late fee for failure to make a timely periodic payment unless the periodic payment is more than the following number of days past due:

(a) 5 days, if the periodic payment is due monthly or less frequently.

(b) 2 days, if the periodic payment is due more frequently than monthly.

(3) A late fee shall not exceed the greater of $10.00 or 5% of the amount of the missed payment.

(4) If reinstatement occurs pursuant to this section, the lessor shall provide the lessee with either the same item leased by the lessee prior to reinstatement or a substitute item of comparable quality and condition. If a substitute item is provided, the lessor shall provide the lessee with all of the information required in section 3.

§ 445.959. Violations; notice to attorney general; injunctions, notice; penalties

(1) When the attorney general has probable cause to believe that a person has engaged, is engaging, or is about to engage in a method, act, or practice which is unlawful pursuant to this act, and upon notice given in accordance with this section, the attorney general may bring an action in accordance with principles of equity to restrain the defendant by temporary or permanent injunction from engaging in the method, act, or practice. The action may be brought in the circuit court of the county where the defendant is established or conducts business or, if the defendant is not established in this state, in the circuit court of Ingham county. The court may award costs to the prevailing party.

For persistent and knowing violation of this act the court may assess the defendant a civil penalty of not more than $25,000.00.

(2) Unless waived by the court on good cause shown not less than 10 days before the commencement of an action under this section, the attorney general shall notify the person of the attorney general's intended action and give the person an opportunity to cease and desist from the alleged unlawful method, act, or practice or to confer with the attorney general in person, by counsel, or by other representative as to the proposed action before the proposed filing date. The notice may be given the person by mail, postage prepaid, to his or her usual place of business or, if the person does not have a usual place of business, to his or her last known address, or, with respect to a corporation, only to a resident agent who is designated to receive service of process or to an officer of the corporation.

(3) A prosecuting attorney or law enforcement officer receiving notice of an alleged violation of this act, or of a violation of an injunction, order, decree, or judgment issued in an action brought pursuant to this section, or of an assurance under this act, shall immediately forward written notice of the violation together with any information he or she may have to the office of the attorney general.

(4) A person who knowingly violates the terms of an injunction, order, decree, or judgment issued pursuant to this section shall forfeit and pay to the state a civil penalty of not more than $5,000.00 for each violation. For the purposes of this section, the court issuing an injunction, order, decree, or judgment shall retain jurisdiction, the cause shall be continued, and the attorney general may petition for recovery of a civil penalty as provided by this section.

§ 445.960. Allegedly unlawful practices; assurance of discontinuance; stipulations; form

(1) When the attorney general has authority to institute an action or proceeding pursuant to section 9, the attorney general may accept an assurance of discontinuance of a method, act, or practice which is alleged to be unlawful under this act from the person who is alleged to have engaged, be engaging, or be about to engage in the method, act, or practice. The assurance shall not constitute an admission of guilt nor be introduced in any other proceeding. The assurance may include a stipulation for any or all of the following:

(a) The voluntary payment by the person for the costs of investigation.

(b) An amount to be held in escrow pending the outcome of an action.

(c) An amount for restitution to an aggrieved person.

(2) An assurance of discontinuance shall be in writing and may be filed with the circuit court of Ingham county. The clerk of the court shall maintain a record of the filings. Unless rescinded by the parties or voided by a court for good cause, the assurance may be enforced in the circuit court by the parties to the assurance. The assurance may be modified by the parties or by a court for good cause.

§ 445.961. Appearance before attorney general; testimony, production of documents; subpoena; notice; records, disclosure

(1) Upon the ex parte application of the attorney general to the circuit court in the county where the defendant is established or conducts business or, if the defendant is not established in this state, in Ingham county, the circuit court, if it finds probable cause to believe a person has engaged, is engaging, or is about to engage in a method, act, or practice which is unlawful under this act, may, after an ex parte hearing, issue a subpoena compelling a person to appear before the attorney general and answer under oath questions relating to an alleged violation of this act. A person served with a subpoena may be accompanied by counsel when he or she appears before the attorney general. The subpoena may compel a person to produce the books, records, papers, documents, or things relating to an alleged violation of this act. During the examination of documentary material under the subpoena, the court may require a person having knowledge of the documentary material or the matters contained therein to attend and give testimony under oath or acknowledgment with respect to the documentary material.

(2) The subpoena shall include the notice of the time, place, and cause of the taking of testimony, the examination, or the attendance and shall allow not less than 10 days before the date of the taking of testimony or examination, unless for good cause shown the court shortens that period of time.

(3) Service of the notice shall be in the manner provided and subject to the provisions that apply to service of process upon a defendant in a civil action commenced in the circuit court.

(4) The notice shall:

(a) State the time and place for the taking of testimony or the examination and the name and address of the person to be examined. If the name is not known, the notice shall give a general description sufficient to identify the person or the particular class or group to which the person belongs.

(b) State a reference to this section and the general subject matter under investigation.

(c) Describe the documentary material to be produced with reasonable specificity so as to indicate fairly the material demanded.

(d) Prescribe a return date within which the documentary material shall be produced.

(e) Identify the members of the attorney general's staff to whom the documentary material shall be made available for inspection and copying.

(5) At any time before the date specified in the notice, upon motion for good cause shown, the court may extend the reporting date or modify or set aside the notice and subpoena.

(6) The documentary material or other information obtained by the attorney general pursuant to an investigation under this section shall be confidential records of the office of the attorney general and shall not be available for public inspection or copying or divulged to any person except as provided in this section. The attorney general may disclose documentary material or other information as follows:

(a) To other law enforcement officials.

(b) In connection with an enforcement action brought pursuant to this act.

(c) Upon order of the court, to a party in a private action brought pursuant to this act.

(7) A person who discloses information designated confidential by this section, except as permitted by subsection (6) or under court order, is guilty of a misdemeanor and may be fined not more than $2,500.00, or imprisoned for not more than 1 year, or both.

§ 445.962. Noncompliance; penalties

(1) A person upon whom a notice is served pursuant to section 11 shall comply with the terms of the notice unless otherwise provided by the order of the circuit court.

(2) A person who does any of the following shall be assessed a civil penalty of not more than $5,000.00:

(a) Knowingly without good cause fails to appear when served with a notice.

(b) Knowingly avoids, evades, or prevents compliance, in whole or in part, with an investigation, including the removal from any place, concealment, destruction, mutilation, alteration, or falsification of documentary material in the possession, custody, or control of a person subject to the notice.

(c) Knowingly conceals relevant information.

(3) The attorney general may file a petition in the circuit court of the county in which the person is established or conducts business or, if the person is not established in this state, in the circuit court of Ingham county for an order to enforce compliance with a subpoena or this section. A violation of a final order entered pursuant to this section shall be punished as civil contempt.

(4) Upon the petition of the attorney general, the circuit court may enjoin a person from doing business in this state if the person persistently and knowingly evades or prevents compliance with an injunction issued pursuant to this act.

§ 445.963. Class actions by attorney general; notice; damages; limitations

(1) The attorney general may bring a class action on behalf of persons residing in or injured in this state for the actual damages caused by a method, act, or practice in trade or commerce which is prohibited by this act.

(2) On motion of the attorney general and without bond in an action under this section the court may make an appropriate order: to reimburse persons who have suffered damages; to carry out a transaction in accordance with the aggrieved persons' reasonable expectations; to strike or limit the application of unconscionable clauses of contracts to avoid an unconscionable result; or to grant other appropriate relief. The court after a hearing may appoint a receiver or order sequestration of the defendant's assets if it appears to the satisfaction of the court that the defendant threatens or is about to remove, conceal, or dispose of his or her assets to the detriment of members of the class.

(3) If at any stage of the proceedings the court requires that notice be sent to the class, the attorney general may petition the court to require the defendant to bear the cost of the notice. In determining whether to impose the cost on the defendant or the state, the court shall consider the probability that the attorney general will succeed on the merits of the action.

(4) If the defendant shows by a preponderance of the evidence that a violation of this act resulted from a bona fide error notwithstanding the maintenance of procedures reasonably adapted to avoid the error, the amount of recovery shall be limited to actual damages.

(5) An action shall not be brought by the attorney general under this section more than 6 years after the occurrence of the method, act, or practice which is the subject of the action nor more than 1 year after the last payment in a transaction involving the method, act, or practice which is the subject of the action, whichever period of time ends on a later date.

§ 445.964. Private actions, class actions; orders; damages; limitations

(1) Whether or not a person seeks damages or has an adequate remedy at law, a person may bring an action to do either or both of the following:

(a) Obtain a declaratory judgment that a method, act, or practice is unlawful under this act.

(b) Enjoin in accordance with the principles of equity a person who is engaging or is about to engage in a method, act, or practice which is unlawful under this act.

(2) Except in a class action, a person who suffers loss as a result of a violation of this act may bring an action to recover actual damages or $250.00, whichever is greater, together with reasonable attorneys' fees.

(3) A person who suffers loss as a result of a violation of this act may bring a class action on behalf of persons residing or injured in this state for the actual damages caused by a method, act, or practice which is prohibited by this act.

(4) On motion of a person and without bond in an action brought under subsection (3) the court may make an appropriate order: to reimburse persons who have suffered damages; to carry out a transaction in accordance with the aggrieved persons' reasonable expectations; to strike or limit the application of unconscionable clauses of contracts to avoid an unconscionable result; or to grant other appropriate relief. The court after a hearing may appoint a receiver or order sequestration of the defendant's assets if it appears to the satisfaction of the court that the defendant threatens or is about to remove, conceal, or dispose of his or her assets to the detriment of members of the class.

(5) If at any stage of proceedings brought under subsection (3) the court requires that notice be sent to the class, a person may petition the court to require the defendant to bear the cost of notice. In determining whether to impose the cost on the defendant or the plaintiff, the court shall consider the probability that the person will succeed on the merits of his or her action.

(6) If the defendant shows by a preponderance of the evidence that a violation of this act resulted from a bona fide error notwithstanding the maintenance of procedures reasonably adapted to avoid the error, the amount of recovery shall be limited to actual damages.

(7) An action under this section shall not be brought more than 6 years after the occurrence of the method, act, or practice which is the subject of the action nor more than 1 year after the last payment in a transaction involving the method, act, or practice which is the subject of the action, whichever period of time ends at a later date. However, when a person commences an action against another person, the defendant may assert, as a defense or counterclaim, any claim under this act arising out of the transaction on which the action is brought.

. . .

§ 445.969. Effect of act; other causes of action, inconsistent ordinances or regulations

This act shall not affect any other cause of action which is available. A city, village, township, or county shall not enact an ordinance or other regulation inconsistent with this act or with a rule promulgated pursuant to this act.

§ 445.970. Rental-purchase agreement form

The following form is an example of the form which may be used to satisfy the requirements of this act:

RENTAL-PURCHASE AGREEMENT

1. Lessor(s) Lessee(s)

______________________ ______________________

______________________ ______________________

______________________ ______________________

2. Description of Leased Property:

Item	Quantity Serial #	Mfg.	Model	New/Previously Rented

3. Total Payment Due at Beginning of Contract:

Advance Payment of $______________

Delivery Charge $______________

Use Taxes $______________

Other $______________ (please specify).

Total $______________

4. Term and cost of the lease (monthly/weekly)

The first monthly/weekly payment of $______ is due on ______________.

Other regular payments of $_________ on the _________ of month/week thereafter.

Total number of monthly/weekly payments ______________.

Total amount of all other charges $______________ (please specify).

Sum total of all payments $______________.

5. Periodic Payment:

You may renew the lease weekly or monthly as you choose.

The weekly rental would be $______________.

The monthly rental would be $______________.

6. For a charge of $__________per payment, we can pick up the payment at your home.

Sign here if you want this service__________.

7. Liability:

8. Maintenance:

We will maintain the leased property in good working condition during the term of the lease and will provide all necessary service and repair (specify if in home or in store) if you notify us by phone or mail that service is needed. We are not responsible for maintenance done by anyone other than us.

9. Termination and Default:

You may terminate this lease at the end of any weekly/monthly term without paying any charges other than those previously due.

We may terminate this lease for a default in payment or breach of any other material term of the lease. If a termination occurs, we shall be entitled to all rental payments up to the date of termination and the expenses of repossessing the property if you fail to surrender it to us.

10. Reinstatement:

If you miss a payment, you may reinstate this contract within 7 days after the payment due date without losing any rights or options previously acquired. The time to reinstate will be extended to 90 days after the payment due date if you return or voluntarily surrender the property, other than through judicial process, within 7 days after the payment due date. To reinstate, you must pay the past due payment and any applicable late fee. The late fee will not exceed the greater of $10.00 or 5% of the payment that is past due. However, if the payment is due monthly or less frequently, we will not charge a late fee unless the payment is more than 5 days past due. If the payment is due more frequently than monthly, we will not charge a late fee unless the payment is more than 2 days past due. Also, we may charge a delivery fee that is not more than the original delivery fee, if we must redeliver the property.

11. Purchase Option:

You may purchase the property leased to you under this contract for the cash price minus 45% of all periodic payments made.

The property leased under this contract would cost $_______ if purchased rather than leased.

12. Warranty:

A manufacturer's warranty on the property leased under this contract shall be passed on to the lessee if the lessee purchases the property.

13. Notice:

This agreement is regulated by state law enforceable by the attorney general or by private legal action.

I have read the above statement before signing this agreement.

Date: ______________________ Lessee: ______________________

Date: ______________________ Lessee: ______________________

UNIFORM CONSUMER CREDIT CODE
(1974 ACT)

PREFATORY NOTE

In promulgating the Uniform Consumer Credit Code (the "U3C") in 1968 (the "1968 Text"), the National Conference of Commissioners on Uniform State Laws proposed a completely new approach to the law governing consumer credit.

Enactment of the Code would abolish the crazy-quilt, patch-work welter of prior laws on consumer credit and replace them by a single new comprehensive law providing a modern, theoretically and pragmatically consistent structure of legal regulation designed to provide an adequate volume of credit at reasonable cost under conditions fair to both consumers and creditors. Upon its enactment, no longer would credit regulation within a State consist of a number of separate uncoordinated statutes governing the activities of different types of creditors in disparate ways.

All creditors dealing with consumers would be covered by the same statute. Under this Act, the total consumer credit process—from advertising through collection—would be within the scope of regulation, with variations in the law based on functional differences in the kinds of transactions rather than on the kinds of creditors involved. Whether a consumer is financing an automobile with a sales finance company or borrowing money from a consumer finance or small loan company, certain basic protections would apply across-the-board to safeguard the consumer.

Thus the Conference has chosen to approach consumer credit in much the same way it did so successfully with respect to secured transactions under Article 9 of the Uniform Commercial Code: function should prevail over form.

Nine States have now adopted the U3C: Oklahoma and Utah in 1969, and Colorado, Idaho, Indiana, and Wyoming in 1971, all in substantially the form of the 1968 Text; Kansas in 1973 in substantially that of the U3C Committee's Working Redraft No. 4; and Iowa and Maine in 1974 in substantially that of the Committee's Working Redraft No. 4 or 5. The Code has had an impact on the development of consumer credit law far beyond those States in which it has been adopted. Many provisions of the Federal Truth in Lending Act and Federal Reserve Board Regulation Z are traceable to the U3C. The National Consumer Act and, later, the Model Consumer Credit Act, although taking extreme consumer positions, follow the structure of the U3C. In 1971 Congress enacted for the District of Columbia comprehensive consumer credit legislation drawn in large part from the U3C. In 1972 Wisconsin enacted similar legislation based on the U3C and the National Consumer Act. Adaptations of U3C provisions have been enacted widely in the credit laws of many States; the home solicitation sale provisions are perhaps the best illustration.

Revision of the 1968 Text

Events occurring after promulgation of the 1968 Text have made it desirable to revise it. Experience in the States which enacted the Code has proved that the Code works and that both consumers and creditors are pleased with it, but this experience has also turned up a few unforeseen problems of the kind that come to light only after a law has been in effect. The revision has dealt with these matters as well as with some of the variations from the 1968 Text that were enacted in several of the States.[1]

The late 1960's and early 1970's have seen a number of important legislative and judicial developments in consumer credit. Information gained from legal services attorneys has thrown new

---

[1] See Report No. 1 of the U3C Committee which contains comments of the Committee on the desirability of the variations in State enactments of the 1968 Text.

light on the needs of poverty-level consumers, but has also revealed that those needs cannot be met solely by consumer credit legislation of general application. The National Consumer Law Center has produced a number of legislative proposals. The United States Supreme Court revolutionized debtor-creditor law in its *Sniadach* 2 decision in 1969. Developments at both the federal level (Consumer Credit Protection Act, Regulation Z, Fair Credit Reporting Act) and the state level (Wisconsin Consumer Act) have invited a review of the U3C. Then, too, new ways of granting consumer credit appeared on the scene during this period. The concept of a nation-wide credit card was in its infancy when the 1968 Text was being prepared in the 1960's; today it is a reality.

A major factor calling for a review of the U3C is the Report of the National Commission on Consumer Finance ("NCCF"). This landmark study, the product of three years of work by a federally sponsored Commission, is the first comprehensive examination in the United States of the whole field of consumer finance. The recommendations of the Commission reflect both objectivity and understanding of the complex consumer credit process.

The National Commission on Consumer Finance was authorized under Title IV, Section 404(a) of the Consumer Credit Protection Act to ". . . study and appraise the functioning and structure of the consumer finance industry, as well as consumer credit transactions generally." It issued its Report on December 31, 1972, four weeks after the U3C Committee's Working Redraft No. 4 was published. The Report contains some 100 recommendations intended to improve the consumer credit marketplace, over 40 of which were intended exclusively for implementation by federal statute, *e.g.*, amendments to the Truth in Lending Act and to the Bankruptcy Act. Of the 60 or so recommendations requiring State action, at least 15 related to matters entirely outside the scope of the U3C, *e.g.*, bank branching and enforcement of antitrust laws. Thus only about 45 recommendations required consideration by the U3C Committee.

Of these 45 recommendations, the U3C Committee's Working Redraft No. 4 anticipated over half. The Committee's Working Redraft No. 5 and this Act substantially implement the National Commission's recommendations regarding co-signer agreements, door-to-door sales, buyer's claims and defenses in credit card and other consumer credit transactions, deficiency judgments, "sewer service," limitations on garnishment, debt collection practices, and State enforcement of the Federal Truth in Lending Act.[1] Thus, this Act reflects a conscious and, it is believed, successful effort to incorporate into a single comprehensive code the majority of the recommendations of the National Commission on Consumer Finance that were intended for implementation by state action.[2]

Price of Credit

A basic issue in any regulation in this area is the price of credit. In simplest terms, consumers want credit at the lowest possible prices, and creditors want to supply credit but can and will do so only if they may reasonably expect repayment of principal plus an adequate return on credit extended. In a free economy the prices of goods, services and land traditionally have been controlled by free operation of the marketplace. To some extent this principle has also extended to the price of credit but for a variety of historical reasons since before the time of Christ, societies have attempted to control the price of credit by executive or legislative fiat. Invariably these attempts have either dried up "legal" or legitimate credit or significantly reduced the amount of credit which would have been available in a free economy. Invariably, too, consumers have been losers by this process.

For hundreds of years in England[3] and in the American colonies and in most of the States, general usury statutes prescribed such low maximum ceilings that they materially interfered with the extension and free flow of credit. In many areas general usury statutes have prevented entirely or reduced substantially the extension of credit with the result that either the courts or legislatures found it necessary to provide a proliferation of exceptions to these statutes. The basic premises of the 1968 Text were that (1) in the business area general usury statutes should be terminated completely and control of the price of credit left solely to the free operation of the marketplace; (2) although in the

[2] Sniadach v. Family Finance Corp. (1969) 89 S.Ct. 1820, 395 U.S. 337, 23 L.Ed.2d 349.

[3] England repealed its usury laws in 1854.

consumer credit area the operation of the same free enterprise principles is equally warranted, many consumers do not have equal bargaining power with creditors and traditionally have been protected by governmental controls, including maximum rates, and the U3C should provide recommended maximum rates in a standard form more simple and understandable than a hodge podge of exceptions to general usury statutes; and (3) any rate structure provided should be of the maximum ceiling variety and not a specification of actual rates to be charged as in the regulation of public utilities.

The U3C Committee's Working Redrafts Nos. 1 through 5[4] and this Act reflect the belief, strongly buttressed by the NCCF Report, that these basic premises are sound and reaffirm them. The proposed specific ceiling rates are socially and economically sound and fit with the other provisions of the U3C and the approach used in drafting it.

This Act makes no change in the specific maximum rates included in the 1968 Text. Empirical evidence developed since 1968 and cited in the U3C Committee's Report No. 1 strongly supports the wisdom of the basic principles adopted and the specific rates suggested. Although the 1968 Text's maximum rates were lowered in some enacting States, in all these States consumer credit has been extended in most cases at rates below the ceilings permitted by the U3C. Five of the six enacting States studied in the Committee's Report No. 1 lowered the maximum ceiling on revolving sale credit from 24% per annum to 18%; however, this change is rejected because the cost studies referred to in the Committee's comment in its Report No. 1 consistently establish that in the case of substantially all sellers, the cost of extending revolving consumer sales credit exceeds 18% per year. For the reasons stated in Report No. 1, reduction in this ceiling rate is believed to be economically unsound.

The extensive studies and findings reported in Chapters 6, 7 and 8 of the NCCF Report clearly support the reasonableness of the U3C maximum ceilings. If anything, the NCCF Report indicates that if the U3C ceilings are open to criticism, the ground should be that they are too low at least for small, short term extensions of credit.

The United States is now experiencing serious inflation. In attempting to combat this inflation the federal government has imposed price controls and ceilings on some goods and services. Opinions may differ as to whether these controls or ceilings were or were not desirable, but there can be little doubt that they not only have not controlled prices significantly but also have caused severe dislocations in the supplies of some goods and services. The difficulties coming to light in these attempts to control prices of goods and services extended equally to attempts to control the price of credit by legislation. General usury statutes and other state laws limiting rates on home mortgages below free market rates have drastically reduced the availability of mortgage funds, the volume of home construction, and employment in the building trades.

Competition and Freedom of Entry

In advocating primary reliance on the marketplace to control the price of credit, the National Conference has recognized the fundamental importance of competition to permit market forces to operate most effectively, a recognition consistent with the conclusions of the National Commission on Consumer Finance. In moving away from the segmented controls of particular types of credit grantors in consumer credit laws prior to the U3C to a single comprehensive statute dealing with consumer credit generally, it is believed that competition has been and will be enhanced. In the U3C Committee's Working Redrafts Nos. 3 through 5 and in this Act, this comprehensive approach has been continued and strengthened by eliminating the separation and duplication in the treatment of sales credit and loans provided in the 1968 Text.

Licensing is a means of providing governmental control of particular kinds of activity, but it restricts freedom of entry into markets and inhibits competition. The 1968 Text avoided the extension of licensing requirements and also sought to diminish existing licensing requirements.

---

4 The U3C Committee's Working Redrafts Nos. 1 and 2 were internal; its Working Redrafts Nos. 3, 4, and 5 were distributed widely.

However, the small loan industry, accustomed to licensing under pre-Code law, in no way objected to licensing and entirely approved of its continuance under the U3C. Moreover, banks and thrift institutions contended that since they could not open offices without the approval of supervisory authorities and since all their activities were regulated and subject to close supervision and examination, small loan lenders should be subject to similar requirements. Consumer comment received on this issue favored increasing rather than decreasing licensing requirements. In response to these various views, the U3C Committee's Working Redrafts Nos. 3 through 5 and this Act have added in Section 2.302 the requirement that licensees obtain a separate license for each place of business where loans are made.

As in the 1968 Text, any lender making loans at a rate in excess of 18% per annum either must be a bank, thrift institution or other supervised financial organization (subsection (41) of Section 1.301) or obtain a license under Section 2.302. On the other hand, this Act avoids imposing on sellers or other types of organizations not engaged in lending any requirement to obtain a license, whether the business carried on is direct or through the use of credit cards. (See subsections (12), (15), (25), and (39) of Section 1.301 and Sections 2.301 and 2.302.)

Consumer Oriented Changes and Additions

Another basic issue in the regulation of consumer credit is adequate protection of consumers from creditor practices and agreements that are abusive or have a potential for abuse. Drawing upon the sources referred to in this Prefatory Note, a substantial number of consumer oriented changes from the 1968 Text have been included in this Act. It is believed that each change or addition has merit and will provide additional protection to consumers but will not interfere with the extension of consumer credit or with legitimate practices of the great majority of creditors.

In making these consumer oriented changes, the necessary relationship between these changes and the U3C rate structure has not been forgotten. In the language of the National Commission on Consumer Finance:

Recommendations regarding remedies are inextricably interwoven with Commission recommendations on rates and availability . . . It is imperative that the relationship be realistically assessed—the higher the rate the fewer the remedies needed and vice versa. States may decide to narrow or broaden Commission recommendations on remedies and contract provisions. But they should recognize that modifications are likely to affect the cost and availability of consumer credit.[5]

A summary of many of these changes and additions follows.

(1) Holder in Due Course; Sales Related Loans; Credit Cards

A major controversial area in consumer credit has been that related to the holder in due course doctrine as applied to outright transfers of retail paper, to sales related loans and to credit card transactions. Traditionally banks and others made credit judgments on purchases of consumer paper solely on the basis of the credit of the buyer and without regard to any aspects of the sale transaction being financed. Insulation of creditors from claims and defenses arising out of sale transactions was obtained in different ways: by use of negotiable notes generating the rights of a holder in due course, or by provisions in contracts freeing assignees of rights under contracts from claims or defenses of buyers against sellers. Banks and others have attempted to preserve these longstanding principles. They have argued that they are lenders of money, not sellers of goods or services, that buyers have the right and responsibility of picking sellers, and that buyers should look solely to sellers for cure of violations of sales contracts, breaches of warranty, and the like.

On the other hand, consumer advocates contend that financing institutions often have close relations with sellers from whom notes and rights under sales contracts are acquired, that these situations are better able than consumers to police sellers and to require of them reasonable standards of performance. Consequently, consumer advocates contend that creditors acquiring sales paper should *not* be free from claims and defenses of buyers against sellers. Consumer advocates have no

[5] NCCF Report, p. 24.

difficulty in providing examples of hardships suffered by aggrieved buyers when faced with contentions by assignees of their contracts that the assignees know nothing about the details of the sales and should not be affected by claims or defenses buyers might have against sellers, and that buyers are still obligated to make their installment payments.

For upward of 20 years, this underlying dispute has existed and waxed more intense. The issue has been tested in courts, with a number of courts deciding in consumer cases that waiver of defense clauses included in instalment contracts signed by buyers were not effective as contrary to public policy. Legislatures took up the issue and in a number of States enacted statutes prohibiting the use of negotiable notes in consumer sale transactions or limiting or prohibiting waiver of defense clauses in retail instalment sale contracts, and sometimes both. These statutes varied in terms of dollar amounts involved and types of transactions to which they applied.

Recognizing the existence of the controversy and that the underlying issue had not been finally resolved, the 1968 Text by Section 2.403 prohibited the taking of negotiable notes in consumer sale and lease transactions and by Section 2.404 provided alternative provisions relating to the effectiveness of waiver of defense clauses. Of the six enacting States covered by Report No. 1, all enacted the prohibition of negotiable notes in Section 2.403 of the 1968 Text, two States prohibited the waiver of defense clauses, one State took no action on the subject, and three States elected to permit these clauses with restrictions.

In Section 3.307 of this Act, the prohibition of the use of negotiable instruments in consumer sales and leases is continued and strengthened. In Section 3.404, the consumer position is substantially adopted by deleting entirely Alternative B of the 1968 Text and by strengthening the 1968 Alternative A provisions prohibiting waiver of defense clauses. It is believed that on this issue consumers have the stronger case. However, this decision reinforces the need to retain the proposed rate ceilings, since the findings of the National Commission on Consumer Finance show that restrictions on holders' rights tend to increase finance charges and reduce the availability of credit.

In more recent years, another issue has developed which is different from but closely related to transfers of sale paper. That issue is the further contention by consumers that even if the transaction is exclusively in the form of a loan but if proceeds of the loan are used to purchase goods or services, at least under certain circumstances, lenders should be subject to defenses of buyers against sellers. Banks, consumer finance companies and other lenders have objected to this type of provision even more strenuously than to provisions prohibiting waiver of defense clauses in assigned instalment sale contracts.

Notwithstanding objections of this kind by lenders, a number of legislatures have enacted provisions of this type. Section 3.405 of this Act includes such a provision, but is limited to certain prescribed situations where the relationship between the lender and the seller is close and the lender either acts in a manner or receives benefits of a kind that ties the lender closely not only to the seller but to the particular sale transaction.

Inevitably, the argument and debate with respect to these two issues led to argument and debate of the same underlying issues when goods or services are purchased with the aid of a three party credit card issued by a bank or other financing agency. Again banks have argued strenuously that in issuing credit cards and making payments to sellers upon use of the cards by the cardholders, the bank knows nothing about the sellers or the sale transactions and should be completely insulated in its rights against its cardholders from any claims or defenses the cardholder buyers might have against the sellers. Banks have further argued that making them in any way subject to claims or defenses cardholders might have against sellers could seriously interfere with the acceptability and convenience of credit cards (and, by extension, the development of the electronic funds transfer system), because not only would banks be more hesitant to issue cards but sellers would also be more reluctant to make sales in reliance on credit cards.

On the other hand, consumer advocates have contended that banks issuing credit cards are better equipped to police sellers than are consumers, banks may in agreements with sellers obtain charge back agreements from them if merchandise risks or claims arise, and in any event, as between cardholders and card-issuing banks, merchandise risks of this kind should be borne by the banks.

On this third and latest issue, argument and debate again have been intense. However, in California and in the Fair Credit Billing Act passed by the Senate as S. 2101 in the summer of 1973, a compromise solution was worked out which bids fair to provide a resolution of this third issue. The compromise solution is that the card issuing bank is subject to any claims or defenses the cardholder may have against the seller only if (1) the customer makes a good faith attempt to resolve a disagreement with the seller, (2) the credit card transaction involves more than $50, and (3) both the residence of the cardholder and the place where the sale or lease occurred are [in the same State or] within 100 miles of each other.

If the card-issuing bank is subject to claims or defenses under this solution, it may have to rely upon rights of charge-back against the seller.

The rationale of this compromise as to amount is that in smaller transactions of $50 or less, the credit card should be looked upon as basically the equivalent of cash and the transaction should have all the finality of a cash transaction.

The rationale for the geographic distinction is that the normal area for use of a credit card as a credit instrument is reasonably proximate to the residence of the cardholder and consequently card-issuing banks should be subject to claims and defenses of the cardholder against the seller only if a transaction and the seller are in this not too large area. A further reason is that any policing of merchants by banks could not reasonably be expected for unlimited geographic distances. Consequently, if and to the extent a cardholder uses his credit card in another State or at a location some distance from his residence, sellers, card-issuing banks and others in the credit card mechanism should not have to worry about credit cards giving to cardholders undue advantages in merchandise disputes by being able to withhold payments from the banks and in turn forcing banks to charge back items to sellers requiring sellers to seek collection from cardholders in distant places.

Section 3.403 of this Act adopts this basic compromise solution. Further, in each of Sections 3.403, 3.404, and 3.405 the extent to which card-issuing banks, lenders and finance companies may be subject to claims and defenses of buyers against sellers is limited to the amount outstanding for the particular transaction at the time the bank or other lender first receives notice of the dispute. Suggestions that card-issuing banks and other lenders should be responsible for the original amount of the transaction and even for product liability that might arise out of the transaction are rejected as neither feasible nor reasonable.

(2) Territorial Reach of Protection

Additional protection is afforded to residents of the enacting State with respect to mail order loans by applying the limitations on finance charges and related provisions to these transactions and giving the Administrator power over them as though the loans were entered into in the enacting State. Also prohibitions of other types of agreements limiting the jurisdiction of the enacting state have been added. See Section 1.201.

(3) Vendor's Single Interest Insurance

The conditions under which a creditor may make an additional charge for vendor's single interest insurance have been more clearly specified and tightened. See Section 2.501.

(4) Notice to Consumers of Precautions and Rights

In certain types of closed-end credit transactions, the creditor is required to furnish the consumer with a copy of the basic contract documents and to advise the consumer of this right, of the wisdom of not signing without reading, and of the right to prepay and possible right to receive a refund. See Section 3.203.

(5) Receipts, Statements and Evidence of Payment

Provisions that consumers are entitled to receipts, statements as to dates and amounts of payments, and evidence of payment in various situations have been added. See Section 3.206.

(6) Notice to Co-Signers

Provisions requiring notice to co-signers and other sureties as to the nature of their obligations have been inserted in accordance with NCCF recommendations. See Section 3.208.

(7) Restrictions on Security and its Enforcement

A potential loophole in the restrictions on security interests that might allow a creditor to take security in a wife's goods for the husband's debt has been eliminated by extending the restriction to property generally rather than only to property of the consumer. See Section 3.301. In addition, enforcement of security interests in property, exempt from execution under a judgment, to secure loans has been restricted. See Section 5.116.

(8) Revocable Deductions from Earnings

Better to assure that an authorized deduction from earnings is revocable both in law and in fact, provisions have been added to give the consumer notice of the revocable nature of any authorization of deductions. See Section 3.305.

(9) Referral Sales and Leases

Restrictions on referral sales and leases have been tightened so as to cover both referral arrangements that are not specifically bargained for in a contract sense and arrangements financed by other than the seller or lessor. In addition to the sanction provided in the section dealing with referrals, a private right of action by the consumer for violation of the prohibition is created better to deter this conduct. See Sections 3.309 and 5.201.

(10) Home Solicitation Sales

The provisions with respect to home solicitation sales have been widened to cover transactions at any residence, not just the residence of the buyer, and have been tightened to prevent evasion by the seller or lessor arranging to have someone else do the financing or by too free use of the emergency exception, and by assuring the buyer a copy of the "buyer's right to cancel" at the time he signs the agreement. Further protection to the consumer is also afforded by prohibition of any cancellation fee and clarification of the right to cancel even though goods sold have received the ordinary use or consumption contemplated by the transaction. Provisions are added that compliance with Federal Trade Commission notice requirements meets U3C requirements in this regard. See Article 3, Part 5.

(11) Refunds of Separate Charges for Insurance

To restrict the creditor's right to withhold a refund until the maturity of a contract, provisions have been added entitling a consumer to a refund at his option rather than a credit in the event of a required rebate of any separate charge for insurance. See Section 4.108.

(12) Deficiency Judgments

Following the NCCF recommendation, restrictions on deficiency judgments have been increased to apply to transactions up to $1,750 rather than $1,000 and have been widened to apply to loans in which the lender is subject to claims and defenses arising from sales as well as to consumer credit sales. See Section 5.103.

(13) Garnishment

Also following an NCCF recommendation, provisions for special court relief from garnishments after judgment on normally non-exempt earnings have been added. See Section 5.105.

(14) Unconscionability

Provisions for court determination of unconscionability in an action by the consumer have been widened to cover, in addition to a consumer credit transaction, (a) a transaction that a consumer is led to believe will give rise to a consumer credit transaction so that, for example, a seller cannot bind the consumer to a short term sale contract payable in a lump sum on the assurance he will secure financing, and then inform the consumer that financing is unavailable and keep the down payment or goods traded upon the consumer's default, (b) inducing a transaction by unconscionable conduct; and (c) unconscionable collection practices. In addition, factors that may be considered in determining unconscionability are spelled out and a provision allowing recovery of attorney's fees is included. See Section 5.108.

(15) Default

Provisions have been added that restrict the unfettered right of the creditor to determine what constitutes a default; that require as a condition to acceleration of debt or enforcement of security interest that the consumer be given notice of his right within a reasonable time to cure a default consisting of the failure to make a required payment; that further clarify the conditions under which self-help repossession is permissible; that control venue in suits against a consumer to collect; that specify what a creditor's petition or complaint must contain to establish his claim; and that provide for relief from default judgments for cause, including sewer service. See Sections 5.109 through 5.115.

(16) Consumers' Remedies

The consumer is given a right of action to recover actual damages and a penalty for the violation of all provisions of the Act which do not have an express or implicit sanction, and even for some provisions that do, better to guard against *in terrorem* uses of prohibited agreements and practices and better to assure compliance with the law. Although the question of the availability of a class action in general is left to other law, the right to recover a penalty is expressly made not enforceable in a class action. In addition, recovery of a penalty is authorized in cases of excess charges or failure to refund within a reasonable time after demand (and a presumption as to reasonable time is created), and the amount of the penalty is not tied to the excess charge, which might permit only a low recovery and therefore establish an inadequate incentive when the excess charge is small. Finally, the voidness penalty for making supervised loans without a necessary license has been deleted as unworkable, and the allowance of attorney's fees has been liberalized and clarified. See Section 5.201.

(17) Administrator's Powers

The rule making power of the Administrator has been expanded; his investigatory powers are increased; his ability to use the device of an assurance of discontinuance has been clarified; his ability to obtain injunctions or other appropriate relief has been clarified; and his powers to sue on behalf of consumers have been clarified. See Sections 6.104, 6.106, 6.109, 6.110, 6.111, 6.112, and 6.113.

Alternative Methods of Computing Finance Charges—Open-End Credit

Another issue that has caused concern in recent years is the appropriate method for computing finance charges on open-end credit. This issue is a product of evolutionary development of practices during the last 25 or more years and of the failure of protagonists for different views to recognize or openly discuss the basic questions involved. This Act deals with this problem in realistic terms.

Four general approaches in imposing finance charges have been used although there have been many variants particularly with regard to the average daily balance method.

The method used by a number of large retailers when they first established revolving accounts was the "ending balance method." The finance charge was computed on the balance in the account at the close of the monthly billing cycle (the "ending balance"). This balance reflected all amounts owed through the date the balance was determined and took into account all purchases and payments through that date.

The previous balance method is the one used by most retailers and until the advent of the modern computer was by far the prevailing method. The finance charge is computed on the same balance as under the ending balance method but the billing of the charge is deferred until the close of the next billing cycle for that customer. At the close of the cycle when the charge is billed, the balance is the "previous balance," that is the previous month's ending balance brought forward as the beginning balance of the current cycle. The billing of the finance charge is deferred to give the customer the opportunity to avoid a finance charge by paying the full amount before the next cycle's billing date. If he makes only a partial payment the finance charge is computed on the full amount of the previous balance. It is this feature which has chagrined consumer advocates who have felt that the finance charge should reflect payments made during the cycle for which the bill was received. The deferral feature of the previous balance method was designed to accommodate customers who wanted the option of using their revolving accounts like the formerly common 30-day charge accounts. Merchants found that the lack of opportunity to avoid finance charges made the ending balance system unattractive both to themselves and to consumers and led many merchants to change from the ending balance method to the previous balance method.

The adjusted balance method provides for the calculation of the finance charge on an amount equal to the previous balance minus all payments and credits during the current cycle but excludes any purchases made during the current cycle. The primary user of this method is a major retailer who did not offer revolving credit until many years after these accounts had become popular.

The average daily balance method requires computer technology and could not be utilized until recent years. The cost of this technology makes this method unavailable to many credit grantors. Under this method the finance charge is computed on the sum of the balances outstanding each day during the billing cycle, divided by the number of days in the cycle. Purchases may or may not be included in the daily balance from the day they are made and there may not be an optional feature permitting the customer to avoid finance charges by full payment.

Against this evolutionary background in the retail area, another important factor—the bank credit card—has become involved in the controversy. A cardinal principle has been that if and when a bank lends money, it is entitled to a return or interest on the money loaned from the date of the loan until the loan is paid. In various ways this principle has been followed in both closed-end and open-end credit, but one major exception has developed. When banks moved into the credit card field in the 1960's, they recognized that if credit cards were to be used in the purchase of goods and services, banks would be competing with retailers already extending credit for these same purposes. Consequently, to develop a credit card program that would be competitive with retailers, banks modelled their operations closely on revolving credit techniques of retailers and contrary to the usual principle of banking, provided for free periods to cardholders either under the previous balance or adjusted balance methods. Hence, in bank credit card operations under which banks pay to retailers the dollar amount, less a "merchant discount," of credit card purchases within a few days from the date of purchase and hence at that time advance actual funds for the account of cardholders, but make no charge to cardholders for the credit advanced for the same 30–60 day free period allowed by retailers, the basic principle of charging interest for the full period on which funds are outstanding has been abandoned, the loss of interest being compensated for by the merchant discount charged the retailer.

Against this background, both retailers and banks have vehemently contended that the previous balance method of computing finance charges is justified, legitimate, and proper and should not be outlawed. On the other hand, consumer advocates have urged the mandatory imposition of the adjusted balance method. In support of this position, they contend that it is unfair to them if they have to pay finance charges computed on balances existing at the beginning of the cycle, if these balances have been reduced by payments made during the cycle. Based upon varying possible fact situations, consumer advocates cite "horror stories" of very high percentage rates in finance charges (computed by the actuarial method) that may result if the previous balance method is utilized. In advancing these arguments, however, these advocates never suggest that if the previous balance is reduced by payments made during the cycle, it should also be increased by additional purchases made and charged to the account during the cycle. In other words, these advocates are happy to have, in both retail and bank credit card operations, the continuance of a 30–60 day free period but make the essentially one-sided argument that if the previous balance method is used, it should be reduced by payments made during the cycle.

Computation of finance charges on the average daily balances outstanding in the account of a customer during the cycle for which a bill is rendered is a legitimate, proper method. This Act authorizes the use of this method in Section 2.202(2)(a). However, since the previous balance vs. the adjusted balance argument continues, both in the Congress in its consideration of S. 2101 and throughout the country in state legislatures, Section 2.202(2)(b) of this Act provides alternative language for each of the previous balance and adjusted balance methods to permit legislatures to adopt whichever form they approve. Although a strenuous effort was made in the consideration of S. 2101 to prohibit the use of the previous balance method, this effort failed in the Senate and, as S. 2101 now stands, the previous balance method will continue to be permissible.

Changes in Provisions for Deferrals and Rebates—Sections 2.503 and 2.510

A widespread if not the prevailing practice in the credit industry is to compute both deferrals and rebates by the sum of the balances method. This practice permits single computations in precomputed transactions involving both one or more deferrals and a subsequent rebate. Subsection (6) of Section 3.210 of the 1968 Text in requiring separate calculations of deferrals and rebates casts doubt on this industry practice.

The revisions of Sections 2.503 and 2.510 of this Act are designed to provide affirmatively for this industry practice which simplifies computations and not only does not prejudice consumers but also reduces their costs. A further revision of Section 2.510 requires the use of the actuarial method of calculating refunds upon prepayment of transactions involving a large number of payments when the sum of the balances method produces higher costs to consumers.

Federal Preemption of Disclosure

Increasingly in the last decade the Congress has interested itself in various aspects of consumer credit. Particularity in the case of the Consumer Credit Protection Act (of which the Truth in Lending Act is a part) enacted in 1968 and in amendments of that Act enacted since 1968, Congress has moved into a major area of consumer credit: disclosures to be made to consumers. In that Act the Congress took pains to recognize that other areas of consumer credit continued to be subject to state law and, even in the case of disclosure, made provision for determinations by the Board of Governors of the Federal Reserve System that state law was sufficiently identical with the federal Act to warrant States applying for and obtaining exemptions from the application of the federal Act. Under these provisions, four or more States have applied for and obtained exemptions.

However, States seeking exemption found that state laws with respect to disclosure must be identical not only to the Truth in Lending Act but also to Regulation Z issued under that Act.

Entirely aside from these efforts on the part of the Congress and certain States to preserve States' rights and some measure of state control over consumer credit, actual experience from 1968 to the present time has demonstrated that in substantially all cases, creditors engaging in consumer credit look to the federal law and Regulation Z as the controlling law in the area of disclosure. Creditors have found that any additional provisions of state law on the subject constitute a nuisance in attempts to comply with federal law and frequently add confusion in these efforts to comply. Further, in those States obtaining exemptions from the Federal Reserve Board, state officials charged with the duty of enforcing state statutes and regulations designed to parallel the federal Act and Regulation Z find the task of keeping state law parallel onerous and troublesome.

Against this background, this Act evidences the conclusion that the Congress has preempted the field of disclosure and any attempt of States to remain in the field by enacting statutes and regulations of their own cause substantially more harm than good. Consequently, this Act contains few substantive disclosure provisions and in Section 3.201 provides simply that a person upon whom the federal Act imposes duties or obligations shall make or give to the consumer the disclosures required of him by the federal Act and in all respects comply with that Act. Section 3.201 allows the Administrator to enforce the disclosure provisions of the Truth in Lending Act and Regulation Z as state law. Other tracking sections of this Act include Sections 1.102(2); 1.202(5); 1.301(1); 1.301(33); 1.302; 2.201(4); 2.401(4); 2.501(1); 2.501(2); 3.209; 3.501; 5.107; 5.203; 5.302; and 6.102(3).

In adopting this basic approach the National Conference recognizes that in some States problems of delegation of legislative power may arise. However, in the ever increasing complexity of areas in which both the federal government and individual States have enacted legislation, solutions of this type are increasingly common and have been sustained. See, *e.g.*, incorporation of definition of "taxable income": by reference to Federal Internal Revenue Code, approved in City National Bank of Clinton v. Iowa State Tax Commission, 251 Iowa 603, 102 N.W.2d 381 (1960); incorporation by state legislatures of Federal Insurance Contributions Act for coverage of state and local governmental employees under Social Security; enactment of state War Emergency Acts as enforcement measures in aid of federal legislation creating the Office of Price Administration and providing for the regulation of prices during war time, approved in People v. Mailman, 182 Misc. 870 (1944); affirmed on appeal 293 N.Y. 887 (1944); incorporation of state law in Federal Assimilative Crimes Act of 1948, 17 U.S.C. § 13, approved in United States v. Sharpnack (1958) 78 S.Ct. 291, 355 U.S. 286, 2 L.Ed.2d 282. In any event, whatever difficulties may be involved, the course adopted in this Act and the abandonment of any effort to duplicate disclosure requirements by substantive provisions seem preferable to the alternative of attempting to establish and maintain parallel federal and state legislation on the subject.

Changes Resulting from Special Problems of Particular Types of Creditors

In a few instances particular types of creditors presented special problems which they considered deserved clarification of or changes from the 1968 Text. In the instances set forth below some adaptations to solve these special problems appear to be justified.

At the request of credit unions, subsection (6) of Section 1.202 has been added so that in any State enacting the U3C it will be optional with the enacting State whether ceilings on rates or limits on loan maturities provided in the U3C will be applicable to credit unions or whether these rates and maturities will be governed by other laws of the State or the United States enacted specifically for credit unions.

A widespread practice of some oil companies operating directly or through franchised filling stations is to avoid the usual revolving credit feature in their credit card agreements which gives the customer the option of paying in full or in instalments. Instead, these companies customarily require full payment of the amount of each billing statement but provide for and assess charges if payments are delinquent. Section 2.601 makes clear that transactions of this kind are not consumer credit transactions governed by the U3C; however, to make equally clear that consumer credit transactions are involved if charges for delinquency are imposed but delinquencies are ignored in practice; the definitions of "finance charge" in Section 1.301(20) and "open-end credit" in Section 1.301(28) have been revised or added.

In many States special statutes have been passed providing for insurance premium financing. To provide for the particular needs of this type of financing a definition of an "insurance premium loan" and some substantive provisions have been added and appear in this Act. See Sections 1.301(22), 2.302(2), 2.401(6), 3.207, 5.110(3) and 5.111(4). These provisions together with other general provisions of the U3C make these special statutes unnecessary and permit their repeal.

In the States that have enacted the U3C and in other States that have considered it, supervised financial organizations, *e.g.*, banks, thrift institutions and the like, have argued that they are currently supervised by agencies to whom various types of fees and charges must be paid and that they should not be required to pay the same fees as other creditors to finance the administration of the U3C. This Act reflects the belief that all creditors extending consumer credit in a State enacting the U3C are governed by the U3C and should share in financing the cost of its administration, but, responding to these arguments of supervised financial organizations, a new subsection (4) of Section 6.203 reduces by 50% the standard volume fees payable by these organizations.

Refinements and Clarifications

In addition to the above changes and additions, this Act includes many clarifications and refinements and much simplification and improvement of language. Not the least of these has been the reorganization of Articles 2 and 3 to eliminate much of the duplication in these two Articles in the 1968 Text. Although these two Articles have been substantially shortened by the changes, no important distinctions between sales credit and loans have been ignored; rather, they have been clarified, particularly in the case of credit cards. Sections referring specifically to credit cards include: Sections 1.301(12), (15), (17), (24), (25), (28), and (39) and 3.403.

ARTICLE 1. GENERAL PROVISIONS AND DEFINITIONS

Table of Sections

§ 1.101. [Short Title]

This Act shall be known and may be cited as Uniform Consumer Credit Code.

§ 1.102. [Purposes; Rules of Construction]

(1) This Act shall be liberally construed and applied to promote its underlying purposes and policies.

(2) The underlying purposes and policies of this Act are:

(a) to simplify, clarify, and modernize the law governing consumer credit and usury;

(b) to provide rate ceilings to assure an adequate supply of credit to consumers;

(c) to further consumer understanding of the terms of credit transactions and to foster competition among suppliers of consumer credit so that consumers may obtain credit at reasonable cost;

(d) to protect consumers against unfair practices by some suppliers of consumer credit, having due regard for the interests of legitimate and scrupulous creditors;

(e) to permit and encourage the development of fair and economically sound consumer credit practices;

(f) to conform the regulation of disclosure in consumer credit transactions to the Federal Truth in Lending Act; and

(g) to make uniform the law, including administrative rules, among the various jurisdictions.

(3) A reference to a requirement imposed by this Act includes reference to a related rule of the Administrator adopted pursuant to this Act.

§ 1.103. [Supplementary General Principles of Law Applicable]

Unless displaced by the particular provisions of this Act, the Uniform Commercial Code and the principles of law and equity, including the law relative to capacity to contract, principal and agent, estoppel, fraud, misrepresentation, duress, coercion, mistake, bankruptcy, or other validating or invalidating cause supplement its provisions. In the event of inconsistency between the Uniform Commercial Code and this Act the provisions of this Act control.

§ 1.104. [Construction Against Implicit Repeal]

This Act being a general act intended as a unified coverage of its subject matter, no part of it shall be construed to be impliedly repealed by subsequent legislation if that construction can reasonably be avoided.

§ 1.105. [Severability]

If any provision of this Act or the application thereof to any person or circumstances is held invalid, the invalidity does not affect other provisions or applications of this Act which can be given effect without the invalid provision or application, and to this end the provisions of this Act are severable.

§ 1.106. [Adjustment of Dollar Amounts]

(1) From time to time the dollar amounts in this Act designated as subject to change shall change, as provided in this section, according to and to the extent of changes in the Consumer Price Index for Urban Wage Earners and Clerical Workers: U.S. City Average, All Items, 1967 = 100, compiled by the Bureau of Labor Statistics, United States Department of Labor, and hereafter referred to as the Index. The Index for December of the year preceding the year in which this Act becomes effective is the Reference Base Index.

(2) The designated dollar amounts shall change on July 1 of each even-numbered year if the percentage of change, calculated to the nearest whole percentage point, between the Index and the end of the preceding year and the Reference Base Index is ten per cent or more, but

(a) the portion of the percentage change in the Index in excess of a multiple of ten per cent shall be disregarded and the dollar amounts shall change only in multiples of ten per cent of the amounts appearing in this Act on the date of enactment; and

(b) the dollar amounts shall not change if the amounts required by this section are those currently in effect pursuant to this Act as a result of earlier application of this section.

(3) If the Index is revised, the percentage of change pursuant to this section shall be calculated on the basis of the revised Index. If a revision of the Index changes the Reference Base Index, a revised Reference Base Index shall be determined by multiplying the Reference Base Index then applicable by the rebasing factor furnished by the Bureau of Labor Statistics. If the Index is superseded, the Index referred to in this section is the one represented by the Bureau of Labor Statistics as reflecting most accurately changes in the purchasing power of the dollar for consumers.

(4) The Administrator shall adopt a rule announcing

(a) on or before April 30 of each year in which dollar amounts are to change, the changes in dollar amounts required by subsection (2); and

(b) promptly after the changes occur, changes in the Index required by subsection (3) including, if applicable, the numerical equivalent of the Reference Base Index under a revised Reference Base Index and the designation or title of any index superseding the Index.

(5) A person does not violate this Act with respect to a transaction otherwise complying with this Act if he relies on dollar amounts either determined according to subsection (2) or appearing in the last rule of the Administrator announcing the then current dollar amounts.

§ 1.107. [Waiver; Agreement to Forego Rights; Settlement of Claims]

(1) Except as otherwise permitted in this Act, a consumer may waive or agree to forego rights or benefits under this Act only in settlement of a bona fide dispute.

(2) A claim by a consumer against a creditor for an excess charge, any other violation of this Act, a civil penalty, or a claim against a consumer for a default or breach of a duty imposed by this Act, if disputed in good faith, may be settled by agreement.

(3) A claim against a consumer, whether or not disputed, may be settled for less value than the amount claimed.

(4) A settlement in which the consumer waives or agrees to forego rights or benefits under this Act is invalid if the court as a matter of law finds the settlement to have been unconscionable at the time it was made. The competence of the consumer, any deception or coercion practiced upon him, the nature and extent of the legal advice received by him, and the value of the consideration are relevant to the issue of unconscionability.

§ 1.108. [Effect of Act on Powers of Organizations]

(1) This Act prescribes maximum charges for all creditors, except lessors and those excluded (Section 1.202), extending credit in consumer credit transactions (subsection (13) of Section 1.301), and displaces existing limitations on the powers of those creditors based on maximum charges.

(2) With respect to sellers of goods or services, small loan companies, licensed lenders, consumer and sales finance companies, industrial banks and loan companies, and commercial banks and trust companies, this Act displaces existing limitations on their powers based solely on amount or duration of credit.

(3) Except as provided in subsection (1) [and in the Article on Effective Date and Repealer (Article 9)], this Act does not displace the limitations on powers of credit unions, savings banks, savings and loan associations, or other thrift institutions whether organized for the profit of shareholders or as mutual organizations.

(4) Except as provided in subsections (1) and (2) [and in the Article on Effective Date and Repealer (Article 9)], this Act does not displace:

(a) limitations on powers of supervised financial organizations (subsection (41) of Section 1.301) with respect to the amount of a loan to a single borrower, the ratio of a loan to the value of collateral, the duration of a loan secured by an interest in land, or other similar restrictions designed to protect deposits, or

(b) limitations on powers an organization is authorized to exercise under the laws of this State or the United States.

§ 1.109. [Transactions Subject to Act by Agreement]

Parties to a credit transaction or modification thereof that is not a consumer credit transaction (subsection (13) of Section 1.301) may agree in a writing signed by them that the transaction is subject to the provisions of this Act applying to consumer credit transactions. If the parties so agree the transaction is a consumer credit transaction for the purposes of this Act.

§ 1.110. [Obligation of Good Faith]

(1) Every contract or duty within this Act imposes an obligation of good faith in its performance or enforcement.

(2) "Good faith" means honesty in fact in the conduct or transaction concerned.

§ 1.201. [Territorial Application]

(1) Except as otherwise provided in this section, this Act applies to a consumer credit transaction entered into in this State. For the purposes of this Act, a consumer credit transaction is entered into in this State if:

(a) pursuant to other than open-end credit, either a signed writing evidencing the obligation or offer of the consumer is received by the creditor in this State, or the creditor induces the consumer who is a resident of this State to enter into the transaction by face-to-face solicitation in this State; or

(b) pursuant to open-end credit, either the consumer's communication or his indication of intention to establish the open-end credit arrangement is received by the creditor in this State or, if no communication or indication of intention is given by the consumer before the first transaction, the creditor's communication notifying the consumer of the privilege of using the arrangement is mailed in this State.

(2) With respect to a consumer loan to which this Act does not otherwise apply, if a consumer who is a resident of this State, pursuant to solicitation in this State, sends a signed writing evidencing the obligation or offer of the consumer to a creditor in another state and receives the cash proceeds of the loan in this State:

(a) the creditor may not contract for or receive charges exceeding those permitted by the Article on Finance Charges and Related Provisions (Article 2); and

(b) the provisions on Powers and Functions of Administrator (Part 1) of the Article on Administration (Article 6) apply as though the loan were entered into in this State.

(3) The Part on Limitations on Creditors' Remedies (Part 1) of the Article on Remedies and Penalties (Article 5) applies to actions or other proceedings brought in this State to enforce rights arising from consumer credit transactions or extortionate extensions of credit, wherever entered into.

(4) Except as provided in subsection (2), a consumer credit transaction to which this Act does not apply entered into with a person who is a resident of this State at the time of the transaction is valid and enforceable in this State to the extent that it is valid and enforceable under the laws of another jurisdiction, but:

(a) a creditor may not collect through actions or other proceedings in this State an amount exceeding the total amount permitted if the Article on Finance Charges and Related Provisions (Article 2) were applicable; and

(b) a creditor may not enforce rights against the consumer in this State with respect to the provisions of agreements that violate the provisions on Limitations on Agreements and Practices (Part 3) and Limitations on Consumers' Liabilities (Part 4) of the Article on Regulation of Agreements and Practices (Article 3).

(5) Except as provided in subsections (2), (3), and (4), a consumer credit transaction entered into in another jurisdiction is valid and enforceable in this State according to its terms to the extent that it is valid and enforceable under the laws of the other jurisdiction.

(6) For the purposes of this Act, the residence of a consumer is the address given by him as his residence in a writing signed by him in connection with a consumer credit transaction until he notifies the creditor of a different address as his residence, and is then the different address.

(7) Notwithstanding other provisions of this section:

(a) except as provided in subsection (3), this Act does not apply if the consumer is not a resident of this State at the time of a consumer credit transaction and the parties have agreed that the law of his residence applies; and

(b) this Act applies if the consumer is a resident of this State at the time of a consumer credit transaction and the parties have agreed that the law of his residence applies.

(8) Each of the following agreements or provisions of an agreement by a consumer who is a resident of this State at the time of a consumer credit transaction is invalid with respect to the transaction:

(a) that the law of another jurisdiction apply;

(b) that the consumer consents to be subject to the process of another jurisdiction;

(c) that the consumer appoints an agent to receive service of process;

(d) that fixes venue; and

(e) that the consumer consents to the jurisdiction of the court that does not otherwise have jurisdiction.

(9) The following provisions of this Act specify the applicable law governing certain cases:

(a) applicability (Section 6.102) of the Part on Powers and Functions of Administrator (Part 1) of the Article on Administration (Article 6); and

(b) applicability (Section 6.201) of the Part on Notification and Fees (Part 2) of the Article on Administration (Article 6).

§ 1.202. [Exclusions]

This Act does not apply to:

(1) extensions of credit to organizations;

(2) except as otherwise provided in the Article on Insurance (Article 4), the sale of insurance if the insured is not obligated to pay instalments of the premium and the insurance may terminate or be cancelled after non-payment of an instalment of the premium;

(3) transactions under public utility or common carrier tariffs if a subdivision or agency of this State or of the United States regulates the charges for the services involved, the charges for delayed payment, and any discount allowed for early payment;

(4) transactions in securities or commodities accounts with a broker-dealer registered with the Securities and Exchange Commission; [or]

(5) except with respect to the provisions on compliance with the Federal Truth in Lending Act (Section 3.201), [civil liability for violation of disclosure provisions (Section 5.203), criminal penalties for disclosure violations (Section 5.302)], and powers and functions of the Administrator with respect to disclosure violations (Part 1 of Article 6), pawnbrokers who are licensed and whose rates and charges are regulated under or pursuant to ordinances or other statutes [;] or

(6) ceilings on rates or limits on loan maturities of credit extended by a credit union organized under the laws of this State or of the United States if these ceilings or limits are established by these laws or by applicable regulations.

Notes

1. If the enacting State wishes to apply for an exemption from the Federal Truth in Lending Act, the brackets before and after Sections 5.203 and 5.302 should be deleted and those sections enacted, and the brackets in subsection (5) preceding and following references to those sections should be omitted;

otherwise, delete the brackets and the language enclosed within them, and delete the references to Sections 5.203 and 5.302 in the Table of Articles, Parts, and Sections.

2. If subsection (6) is included by the enacting State, delete "[or]" at the end of subsection (4), the opening bracket at the end of subsection (5), and the closing bracket at the end of subsection (6). If subsection (6) is not included by the enacting State, delete the brackets before and after "or" at the end of subsection (4).

§ 1.203. [Jurisdiction [and Service of Process]]

[(1)] The [ ] court of this State may exercise jurisdiction over any creditor with respect to any conduct of the creditor subject to this Act or with respect to any claim arising from a transaction subject to this Act.

[(2) In addition to any other method provided by [rule] [statute], personal jurisdiction over a creditor may be acquired in a civil action or proceeding instituted in the [ ] court by service of process in the manner provided in this section. If a creditor is not a resident of this State or is a corporation not authorized to do business in this State and engages in any conduct in this State subject to this Act or in a transaction subject to this Act, he may designate an agent upon whom service of process may be made in this State. The agent shall be a resident of this State or a corporation authorized to do business in this State. The designation shall be in a writing and filed with the Secretary of State. If a designation is not made and filed or if process cannot be served in this State upon the designated agent, process may be served upon the Secretary of State, but service upon him is not effective unless the plaintiff or petitioner forthwith mails a copy of the process and pleading by registered or certified mail to the defendant or respondent at his last reasonably ascertainable address. An affidavit of compliance with this section shall be filed with the clerk of the court on or before the return day of the process, if any, or within any further time the court allows.]

Note

If the enacting State has an adequate long arm statute, the bracketed words "and Service of Process" in the section heading, the bracketed "(1)," and all of subsection (2) may be omitted.

§ 1.301. [General Definitions]

(1) "Actuarial method" means the method of allocating payments made on a debt between the amount financed and the finance charge pursuant to which a payment is applied first to the accumulated finance charge and any remainder is subtracted from, or any deficiency is added to, the unpaid balance of the amount financed. The Administrator may adopt rules not inconsistent with the Federal Truth in Lending Act further defining the term and prescribing its application.

(2) "Administrator" means the Administrator designated in the Article (Article 6) on Administration (Section 6.103).

(3) "Agreement" means the bargain of the parties in fact as found in their language or by implication from other circumstances including course of dealing, usage of trade, or course of performance.

(4) "Agricultural purpose" means a purpose relating to the production, harvest, exhibition, marketing, transportation, processing, or manufacture of agricultural products by a natural person who cultivates, plants, propagates, or nurtures the agricultural products. "Agricultural products" includes agricultural, horticultural, viticultural, and dairy products, livestock, wildlife, poultry, bees, forest products, fish and shellfish, and products thereof, including processed and manufactured products, and products raised or produced on farms and processed or manufactured products thereof.

(5) "Amount financed" means the total of the following items:

(a) in the case of a sale, the cash price of the goods, services, or interest in land, less the amount of any down payment made in cash or in property traded in, and the amount actually paid or to be paid by the seller pursuant to an agreement with the buyer to discharge a security interest in, a lien on, or a debt with respect to property traded in;

(b) in case of a loan, the net amount paid to, receivable by, or paid or payable for the account of the debtor, plus the amount of any discount excluded from the finance charge (paragraph (b)(iii) of subsection (20)); and

(c) in the case of a sale or loan, to the extent that payment is deferred and the amount is not otherwise included and is authorized and disclosed to the consumer as required by law:

(i) amounts actually paid or to be paid by the creditor for registration, certificate of title, or license fees, and

(ii) permitted additional charges (Section 2.501).

(6) "Billing cycle" means the time interval between periodic billing statement dates.

(7) "Card issuer" means a person who issues a credit card.

(8) "Cardholder" means a person to whom a credit card is issued or who has agreed with the card issuer to pay obligations arising from the issuance to or use of the card by another person.

(9) "Cash price" of goods, services, or an interest in land means the price at which they are offered for sale by the seller to cash buyers in the ordinary course of business and may include (1) the cash price of accessories or services related to the sale, such as delivery, installation, alterations, modifications, and improvements, and (b) taxes to the extent imposed on a cash sale of the goods, services, or interest in land. The cash price stated by the seller to the buyer in a disclosure statement required by law is presumed to be the cash price.

(10) "Conspicuous":

A term or clause is "conspicuous" when it is so written that a reasonable person against whom it is to operate ought to have noticed it. Whether or not a term or clause is conspicuous is for decision by the court.

(11) "Consumer" means the buyer, lessee, or debtor to whom credit is granted in a consumer credit transaction.

(12) "Consumer credit sale":

(a) Except as provided in paragraph (b), "consumer credit sale" means a sale of goods, services, or an interest in land in which:

(i) credit is granted either pursuant to a seller credit card or by a seller who regularly engages as a seller in credit transactions of the same kind;

(ii) the buyer is a person other than an organization;

(iii) the goods, services, or interest in land are purchased primarily for a personal, family, household, or agricultural purpose;

(iv) the debt is payable in instalments or a finance charge is made; and

(v) with respect to a sale of goods or services, the amount financed does not exceed $25,000.

(b) A "consumer credit sale" does not include:

(i) a sale in which the seller allows the buyer to purchase goods or services pursuant to a lender credit card, or

(ii) unless the sale is made subject to this Act by agreement (Section 1.109), a sale of an interest in land if the finance charge does not exceed 12 per cent per year calculated according to the actuarial method on the assumption that the debt will be paid according to the agreed terms and will not be paid before the end of the agreed term.

(c) The amount of $25,000 in paragraph (a)(v) is subject to change pursuant to the provisions on adjustment of dollar amounts (Section 1.106).

(13) "Consumer credit transaction" means a consumer credit sale or consumer loan or a refinancing or consolidation thereof, or a consumer lease.

(14) "Consumer lease":

(a) "Consumer lease" means a lease of goods:

(i) which a lessor regularly engaged in the business of leasing makes to a person, except an organization, who takes under the lease primarily for a personal, family, household, or agricultural purpose;

(ii) in which the amount payable under the lease does not exceed $25,000;

(iii) which is for a term exceeding four months; and

(iv) which is not made pursuant to a lender credit card.

(b) The amount of $25,000 in paragraph (a)(ii) is subject to change pursuant to the provisions on adjustment of dollar amounts (Section 1.106).

(15) "Consumer loan":

(a) Except as provided in paragraph (b), "consumer loan" means a loan made by a creditor regularly engaged in the business of making loans in which:

(i) the debtor is a person other than an organization;

(ii) the debt is incurred primarily for a personal, family, household, or agricultural purpose;

(iii) the debt is payable in instalments or a finance charge is made; and

(iv) the amount financed does not exceed $25,000 or the debt, other than one incurred primarily for an agricultural purpose, is secured by an interest in land.

(b) A "consumer loan" does not include:

(i) a sale or lease in which the seller or lessor allows the buyer or lessee to purchase or lease pursuant to a seller credit card, or

(ii) unless the loan is made subject to this Act by agreement (Section 1.109), a loan secured by an interest in land if the security interest is bona fide and not for the purpose of circumvention or evasion of this Act and the finance charge does not exceed 12 per cent per year calculated according to the actuarial method on the assumption that the debt will be paid according to the agreed terms and will not be paid before the end of the agreed term.

(c) A loan that would be a consumer loan if the lender were regularly engaged in the business of making loans is a consumer loan if the loan is arranged for a commission or other compensation by a person regularly engaged in the business of arranging those loans and the lender is not regularly engaged in the business of making loans. The arranger is deemed to be the creditor making the loan.

(d) The amount of $25,000 in paragraph(a)(iv) is subject to change pursuant to the provisions on adjustment of dollar amounts (Section 1.106).

(16) "Credit" means the right granted by a creditor to a consumer to defer payment of debt, to incur debt and defer its payment, or to purchase property or services and defer payment therefor.

(17) "Credit card" means a card or device issued under an arrangement pursuant to which a card issuer gives to a cardholder the privilege of obtaining credit from the card issuer or other person in purchasing or leasing property or services, obtaining loans, or otherwise. A transaction is "pursuant to a credit card" only if credit is obtained according to the terms of the arrangement by transmitting

information contained on the card or device orally, in writing, by mechanical or electronic methods, or in any other manner. A transaction is not "pursuant to a credit card" if the card or device is used solely in that transaction to:

(a) identify the cardholder or evidence his credit-worthiness and credit is not obtained according to the terms of the arrangement;

(b) obtain a guarantee of payment from the cardholder's deposit account, whether or not the payment results in a credit extension to the cardholder by the card issuer; or

(c) effect an immediate transfer of funds from the cardholder's deposit account by electronic or other means, whether or not the transfer results in a credit extension to the cardholder by the card issuer.

(18) "Creditor" means the person who grants credit in a consumer credit transaction or, except as otherwise provided, an assignee of a creditor's right to payment, but use of the term does not in itself impose on an assignee any obligation of his assignor. In case of credit granted pursuant to a credit card, "creditor" means the card issuer and not another person honoring the credit card.

(19) "Earnings" means compensation paid or payable by an employer to an employee or for his account for personal services rendered or to be rendered by him, whether denominated as wages, salary, commission, bonus, or otherwise, and includes periodic payments pursuant to a pension, retirement, or disability program.

(20) "Finance charge":

(a) Except as provided in paragraph (b), "finance charge" means the sum of all charges payable directly or indirectly by the consumer and imposed directly or indirectly by the creditor as an incident to or as a condition of the extension of credit, including any of the following types of charges which are applicable:

(i) interest or any amount payable under a point, discount, or other system of charges, however denominated;

(ii) time-price differential, credit service, service, carrying, or other charge, however denominated;

(iii) premium or other charge for any guarantee or insurance protecting the creditor against the consumer's default or other credit loss; and

(iv) charges incurred for investigating the collateral or credit-worthiness of the consumer or for commissions or brokerage for obtaining the credit, irrespective of the person to whom the charges are paid or payable, unless the creditor had no notice of the charges when the credit was granted.

(b) The term does not include:

(i) charges as a result of default or delinquency if made for actual unanticipated late payment, delinquency, default, or other like occurrence, unless the parties agree that these charges are finance charges; a charge is not made for actual unanticipated late payment, delinquency, default or other like occurrence if imposed on an account that is or may be debited from time to time for purchases or other debts and, under its terms, payment in full or of a specified amount is required when billed, and in the ordinary course of business the consumer is permitted to continue to have purchases or other debts debited to the account after imposition of the charge;

(ii) additional charges (Section 2.501) or deferral charges (Section 2.503); or

(iii) a discount, if a creditor purchases or satisfies obligations of a cardholder pursuant to a credit card and the purchase or satisfaction is made at less than the face amount of the obligation.

(21) "Goods" includes goods not in existence at the time the transaction is entered into and merchandise certificates, but excludes money, chattel paper, documents of title, and instruments.

(22) "Insurance premium loan" means a consumer loan that (a) is made for the sole purpose of financing the payment by or on behalf of an insured of the premium on one or more policies or contracts issued by or on behalf of an insurer, (b) is secured by an assignment by the insured to the lender of the unearned premium on the policy or contract, and (c) contains an authorization to cancel the policy or contract financed.

(23) Except as otherwise provided, "lender" includes an assignee of a lender's right to payment, but use of the term does not in itself impose on an assignee any obligation of the lender.

(24) "Lender credit card" means a credit card issued by a supervised lender.

(25) "Loan":

(a) Except as provided in paragraph (b), "loan" includes:

(i) the creation of debt by the lender's payment of or agreement to pay money to the debtor or to a third person for the account of the debtor;

(ii) the creation of debt pursuant to a lender credit card in any manner, including a cash advance or the card issuer's honoring a draft or similar order for the payment of money drawn or accepted by the debtor, paying or agreeing to pay the debtor's obligation, or purchasing or otherwise acquiring the debtor's obligation from the obligee or his assignees;

(iii) the creation of debt by a cash advance to a debtor pursuant to a seller credit card;

(iv) the creation of debt by a credit to an account with the lender upon which the debtor is entitled to draw immediately; and

(v) the forbearance of debt arising from a loan.

(b) "Loan" does not include:

(i) a card issuer's payment or agreement to pay money to a third person for the account of a debtor if the debt of the debtor arises from a sale or lease and results from use of a seller credit card; or

(ii) the forbearance of debt arising from a sale or lease.

(26) "Merchandise certificate" means a writing not redeemable in cash and usable in its face amount in lieu of cash in exchange for goods or services.

(27) "Official fees" means:

(a) fees and charges prescribed by law which actually are or will be paid to public officials for determining the existence of or for perfecting, releasing, terminating, or satisfying a security interest related to a consumer credit transaction; or

(b) premiums payable for insurance in lieu of perfecting a security interest otherwise required by the creditor in connection with the transaction, if the premium does not exceed the fees and charges described in paragraph (a) which would otherwise be payable.

(28) "Open-end credit" means an arrangement pursuant to which:

(a) a creditor may permit a consumer, from time to time, to purchase or lease on credit from the creditor or pursuant to a credit card, or to obtain loans from the creditor or pursuant to a credit card;

(b) the amounts financed and the finance and other appropriate charges are debited to an account;

(c) the finance charge, if made, is computed on the account periodically; and

(d) either the consumer has the privilege of paying in full or in instalments or the creditor periodically imposes charges computed on the account for delaying payment and permits the consumer to continue to purchase or lease on credit.

(29) "Organization" means a corporation, government or governmental subdivision or agency, trust, estate, partnership, cooperative, or association.

(30) "Payable in instalments" means that payment is required or permitted by agreement to be made in more than four periodic payments, excluding a downpayment. If any periodic payment other than the downpayment under an agreement requiring or permitting two or more periodic payments is more than twice the amount of any other periodic payment, excluding a downpayment, a consumer credit transaction is "payable in instalments."

(31) "Person" includes a natural person or an individual, and an organization.

(32) "Person related to" with respect to an individual means (a) the spouse of the individual, (b) a brother, brother-in-law, sister, sister-in-law of the individual, (c) an ancestor or lineal descendant of the individual or his spouse, and (d) any other relative, by blood or marriage, of the individual or his spouse who shares the same home with the individual. "Person related to" with respect to an organization means (a) a person directly or indirectly controlling, controlled by, or under common control with the organization, (b) an officer or director of the organization or a person performing similar functions with respect to the organization or to a person related to the organization, (c) the spouse of a person related to the organization, and (d) a relative by blood or marriage of a person related to the organization who shares the same home with him.

(33) "Precomputed consumer credit transaction" means a consumer credit transaction, other than a consumer lease, in which the debt is a sum comprising the amount financed and the amount of the finance charge computed in advance. A disclosure required by the Federal Truth in Lending Act does not in itself make a finance charge or transaction precomputed.

(34) "Presumed" or "presumption" means that the trier of fact must find the existence of the fact presumed unless and until evidence is introduced which would support a finding of its non-existence.

(35) "Sale of goods" includes an agreement in the form of a bailment or lease of goods if the bailee or lessee pays or agrees to pay as compensation for use a sum substantially equivalent to or in excess of the aggregate value of the goods involved and it is agreed that the bailee or lessee will become, or for no other or a nominal consideration has the option to become, the owner of the goods upon full compliance with the terms of the agreement.

(36) "Sale of an interest in land" includes a lease in which the lessee has an option to purchase the interest and all or a substantial part of the rental or other payments previously made by him are applied to the purchase price.

(37) "Sale of services" means furnishing or agreeing to furnish services and includes making arrangements to have services furnished by another.

(38) "Seller" includes, except as otherwise provided, an assignee of the seller's right to payment, but use of the term does not in itself impose on an assignee any obligation of the seller.

(39) "Seller credit card" means either:

(a) a credit card issued primarily for the purpose of giving the cardholder the privilege of using the card to purchase or lease property or services from the card issuer, persons related to the card issuer, or persons licensed or franchised to do business under the card issuer's business or trade name or designation, or both from any of these persons and from other persons; or

(b) a credit card issued by a person except a supervised lender primarily for the purpose of giving the cardholder the privilege of using the credit card to purchase or lease property or services from at least 100 persons not related to the card issuer.

(40) "Services" includes (a) work, labor, and other personal services, (b) privileges with respect to transportation, hotel and restaurant accommodations, education, entertainment, recreation, physical culture, hospital accommodations, funerals, cemetery accommodations, and the like, and (c) insurance.

(41) "Supervised financial organization" means a person, except an insurance company or other organization primarily engaged in an insurance business:

(a) organized, chartered, or holding an authorization certificate under laws of this State or of the United States that authorizes the person to make loans and to receive deposits, including a savings, share, certificate or deposit account, and

(b) subject to supervision by an official or agency of this State or of the United States.

(42) "Supervised lender" means a person authorized to make or take assignments of supervised loans, under a license issued by the Administrator (Section 2.301) or as a supervised financial organization (subsection (41)).

(43) "Supervised loan" means a consumer loan, including a loan made pursuant to open-end credit, in which the rate of the finance charge, calculated according to the actuarial method, exceeds 18 per cent per year.

§ 1.302. [Definition: "Federal Truth in Lending Act"]

In this Act, as applicable, "Federal Truth in Lending Act" means Title I of the Consumer Credit Protection Act (Public Law 90–321; 82 Stat. 146; 15 U.S.C. §§ 1601 et seq.; as amended), except for the provisions concerning issuance, liability of holders, and fraudulent use of credit cards (Sections 132–134, as added by Public Law 90–321; 84 Stat. 1126; 15 U.S.C. §§ 1642–1644), and includes regulations issued by the Board of Governors of the Federal Reserve System pursuant to that Act except those relating to the excepted provisions.

§ 1.303. [Other Defined Terms]

Other defined terms in this Act and the sections in which they appear are:

"Closing costs" Section 2.501(1)

"Computational period" Section 2.503(1)

"Deferral" Section 2.503(1)

"Deferral period" Section 2.503(1)

"Disposable earnings" Section 5.105

"Garnishment" Section 5.105

"Home solicitation sale" Section 3.501

"Interval" Section 2.503(1)

"Periodic balance" Section 2.503(1)

"Pursuant to a credit card" Section 1.301(17)

"Residence" Section 1.201(6)

"Rule of 78" Section 2.503(1)

"Standard deferral" Section 2.503(1)

"Sum of the balances method" Section 2.503(1)

"Transaction" Section 2.503(1)

ARTICLE 2. FINANCE CHARGES AND RELATED PROVISIONS

Table of Sections

§ 2.101. [Short Title]

This Article shall be known and may be cited as Uniform Consumer Credit Code—Finance Charges and Related Provisions.

§ 2.102. [Scope]

Part 2 of this Article applies to consumer credit sales. Parts 3 and 4 apply to consumer loans, including loans made by supervised lenders. Part 5 applies to other charges and modifications with respect to consumer credit transactions. Part 6 applies to other credit transactions.

§ 2.201. [Finance Charge for Consumer Credit Sales Not Pursuant to Open-End Credit]

(1) With respect to a consumer credit sale, except a sale pursuant to open-end credit, a creditor may contract for and receive a finance charge not exceeding that permitted in this section.

(2) The finance charge, calculated according to the actuarial method, may not exceed the equivalent of the greater of either of the following:

(a) the total of:

(i) 36 per cent per year on that part of the unpaid balances of the amount financed which is $300 or less;

(ii) 21 per cent per year on that part of the unpaid balances of the amount financed which exceeds $300 but does not exceed $1,000; and

(iii) 15 per cent per year on that part of the unpaid balances of the amount financed which exceeds $1,000; or

(b) 18 per cent per year on the unpaid balances of the amount financed.

(3) This section does not limit or restrict the manner of calculating the finance charge whether by way of add-on, discount, single annual percentage rate, or otherwise, so long as the rate of the finance charge does not exceed that permitted by this section. The finance charge may be contracted for and earned at the single annual percentage rate that would earn the same finance charge as the graduated rates when the debt is paid according to the agreed terms and the calculations are made according to the actuarial method. If the sale is a precomputed consumer credit transaction:

(a) the finance charge may be calculated on the assumption that all scheduled payments will be made when due, and

(b) the effect of prepayment is governed by the provisions on rebate upon prepayment (Section 2.510).

(4) For purposes of this section, the term of a sale agreement commences with the date the credit is granted or, if goods are delivered or services performed ten days or more after that date, with the date of commencement of delivery or performance. Any month may be counted as 1/12 th of a year, but a day is counted as 1/365 th of a year. Subject to classifications and differentiations the seller may reasonably establish, a part of a month in excess of 15 days may be treated as a full month if periods of 15 days or less are disregarded and that procedure is not consistently used to obtain a greater yield than would otherwise be permitted. The Administrator may adopt rules not inconsistent with the Federal Truth in Lending Act with respect to treating as regular other minor irregularities in amount or time.

(5) Subject to classifications and differentiations the seller may reasonably establish, he may make the same finance charge on all amounts financed within a specified range. A finance charge so made does not violate subsection (2) if:

(a) when applied to the median amount within each range, it does not exceed the maximum permitted by subsection (2), and

(b) when applied to the lowest amount within each range, it does not produce a rate of finance charge exceeding the rate calculated according to paragraph (a) by more than eight per cent of the rate calculated according to paragraph (a).

(6) minimum finance charge of not more than $5 when the amount financed does not exceed $75, or $7.50 when the amount financed exceeds $75.

(7) The amounts of $300 and $1,000 in subsection (2) are subject to change pursuant to the provisions on adjustment of dollar amounts (Section 1.106).

§ 2.202. [Finance Charge for Consumer Credit Sales Pursuant to Open-End Credit]

(1) With respect to a consumer credit sale pursuant to open-end credit, a creditor may contract for and receive a finance charge not exceeding that permitted in this section.

(2) For each billing cycle a finance charge may be made which is a percentage of an amount not exceeding the greatest of:

(a) the average daily balance of the open-end account in the billing cycle for which the charge is made, which is the sum of the amount unpaid each day during that cycle, divided by the number of days in that cycle; the amount unpaid on a day is determined by adding to any balance unpaid as of the beginning of that day all purchases and other debits and deducting all payments and other credits made or received as of that day;

(b) the balance of the open-end account at the beginning of the first day of the billing cycle [after deducting all payments and credits made in the cycle except credits attributable to purchases charged to the account during the cycle]; or

(c) the median amount within a specified range including the balance of the open-end account not exceeding that permitted by paragraph (a) or (b); a finance charge may be made pursuant to this paragraph only if the creditor, subject to classifications and differentiations he may reasonably establish, makes the same charge on all balances within the specified range and if the percentage when applied to the median amount within the range does not produce a charge exceeding the charge resulting from applying that percentage to the lowest amount within the range by more than eight per cent of the charge on the median amount.

(3) If the billing cycle is monthly, the finance charge may not exceed an amount equal to two per cent of that part of the maximum amount pursuant to subsection (2) which is $500 or less and one and one-half per cent of that part of the maximum amount which is more than $500. If the billing cycle is not monthly, the maximum charge for the billing cycle shall bear the same relation to the applicable monthly maximum charge as the number of days in the billing cycle bears to 365 divided by 12. A billing cycle is monthly if the closing date of the cycle is the same date each month or does not vary by more than four days from the regular date. Without regard to the length of the billing cycle, the finance charge may be computed at a daily rate that does not exceed 1/365ths of 12 times the monthly charge permitted by this section for a billing cycle that is monthly.

(4) If the finance charge determined pursuant to subsection (3) is less than 50 cents, a finance charge may be made which does not exceed 50 cents if the billing cycle is monthly or longer, or the pro rata part of 50 cents which bears the same relation to 50 cents as the number of days in the billing cycle bears to 365 divided by 12 if the billing cycle is shorter than monthly.

(5) The amounts of $500 in subsection (3) are subject to change pursuant to the provisions on adjustment of dollar amounts (Section 1.106).

§ 2.301. [Authority to Make Supervised Loans]

Unless a person is a supervised financial organization or has obtained a license from the Administrator authorizing him so to do, he may not engage in the business of:

(1) making supervised loans, or

(2) taking assignments of and undertaking direct collection of payments from or enforcement of rights against consumers arising from supervised loans, but he may collect and enforce for three months without a license if he promptly applies for a license and his application has not been denied.

§ 2.302. [License to Make Supervised Loans]

(1) The Administrator shall receive and act on all applications for licenses to make supervised loans under this Act. Applications shall be in the form and filed in the manner prescribed by the Administrator and contain or be accompanied by the information the Administrator requires by rule.

(2) The Administrator may not issue a license unless upon investigation he finds that the financial responsibility, character, and fitness of the applicant, and of the members thereof if the applicant is a partnership or association or of the officers and directors thereof if the applicant is a corporation, warrant belief that the business will be operated honestly and fairly within the purposes of this Act. In determining the financial responsibility of an applicant proposing to engage in making insurance premium loans, the Administrator shall consider the liabilities the lender may incur for erroneous cancellation of insurance.

(3) Upon written request, the applicant is entitled to a hearing on the question of his qualifications for a license if (a) the Administrator notifies the applicant in writing that his application has been denied, or (b) the Administrator does not issue a license within 60 days after the application for the license was filed. A request for a hearing may not be made more than 15 days after the

Administrator mails a writing to the applicant notifying him that the application has been denied and stating in substance the Administrator's findings supporting denial of the application.

(4) The Administrator shall issue additional licenses to the same licensee upon compliance with all the provisions of this Act governing issuance of a single license. A separate license is required for each place of business. Each license remains in full force and effect until surrendered, suspended, or revoked.

(5) A licensee may not change the location of any place of business without giving the Administrator at least 15 days prior written notice.

(6) A licensee may conduct the business of making supervised loans only at or from a place of business for which he holds a license and only under the name in the license. Credit granted pursuant to a lender credit card does not violate this subsection.

§ 2.303. [Revocation or Suspension of License]

(1) The Administrator may issue to a person licensed to make supervised loans an order to show cause why his license with respect to one or more specific places of business should not be suspended for a period not in excess of six months or be revoked. The order shall set a place for a hearing and a time therefor that is no less than ten days from the date of the order. After the hearing the Administrator shall revoke or suspend the license or, if there are mitigating circumstances, may accept an assurance of discontinuance (Section 6.109) and allow retention of the license, if he finds that:

(a) the licensee has repeatedly and intentionally violated this Act or any rule or order lawfully made pursuant to this Act, or has violated an assurance of discontinuance; or

(b) facts or conditions exist which clearly would have justified the Administrator in refusing to grant a license for that place or those places of business were these facts or conditions known to exist at the time the application for the license was made.

(2) A revocation or suspension of a license is not lawful unless the Administrator, before instituting proceedings, gives notice to the licensee of the facts or conduct which warrant the intended action, and the licensee is afforded an opportunity to show compliance with all lawful requirements for retention of the license.

(3) If the Administrator finds that probable cause for revocation of a license exists and that enforcement of this Act requires immediate suspension of the license pending investigation, he, after a hearing upon five days' written notice, may enter an order suspending the license for not more than 30 days.

(4) Whenever the Administrator revokes or suspends a license, he shall enter an order to that effect and forthwith notify the licensee of the revocation or suspension. Within five days after entry of the order he shall deliver to the licensee a copy of the order and the findings supporting the order.

(5) A person holding a license to make supervised loans may relinquish the license by notifying the Administrator in writing of its relinquishment, but the relinquishment does not affect his liability for acts previously committed.

(6) Revocation, suspension, or relinquishment of a license does not impair or affect the obligation of any preexisting lawful contract between the licensee and any consumer.

(7) The administrator may reinstate or license, terminate a suspension, or grant a new license to a person whose license has been revoked or suspended if no fact or condition then exists which clearly would have justified the Administrator in refusing to grant a license.

§ 2.304. [Records; Annual Reports]

(1) Every licensee shall maintain records in conformity with generally accepted accounting principles and practices in a manner that will enable the Administrator to determine whether the

licensee is complying with this Act. The record keeping system of a licensee is sufficient if he makes the required information reasonably available. The records need not be kept in the place of business where supervised loans are made, if the Administrator is given free access to the records wherever located. The records pertaining to any loan need not be preserved for more than two years after making the final entry relating to the loan, but in the case of open-end credit the two years are measured from the date of each entry.

(2) On or before April 15 each year every licensee shall file with the Administrator a composite annual report in the form prescribed by the Administrator relating to all supervised loans made by him. The Administrator shall consult with comparable officials in other states for the purpose of making the kinds of information required in annual reports uniform among the states. Information contained in annual reports shall be confidential and may be published only in composite form.

§ 2.305. [Examinations and Investigations]

(1) The Administrator shall examine periodically at intervals he deems appropriate the loans, business, and records of every licensee. In addition, for the purpose of discovering violations of this Act or securing information lawfully required, the Administrator or the official or agency to whose supervision the organization is subject (Section 6.105) at any time may investigate the loans, business, and records of any lender. For these purposes he shall have free and reasonable access to the offices, places of business, and records of the lender.

(2) If the lender's records are located outside this State, the lender at his option shall make them available to the Administrator at a convenient location within this State, or pay the reasonable and necessary expenses for the Administrator or his representative to examine them where they are located. The Administrator may designate representatives, including comparable officials of the state in which the records are located, to inspect them on his behalf.

(3) For purposes of this section, the Administrator may administer oaths or affirmations, and upon request of a party or his own motion may subpoena witnesses, compel their attendance, adduce evidence, and require the production of any matter which is relevant to the investigation, including the existence, description, nature, custody, condition, and location of any books, documents, or other tangible things and the identity and location of persons having knowledge of relevant facts, or any other matter reasonably calculated to lead to the discovery of admissible evidence.

(4) Upon failure without lawful excuse to obey a subpoena or to give testimony and upon reasonable notice to all persons affected thereby, the Administrator may apply to the [ ] court for an order compelling compliance.

§ 2.306. [Application of [Administrative Procedure Act] [Part on Administrative Procedure and Judicial Review] to Part]

Except as otherwise provided, the [State administrative procedure act] [Part on Administrative Procedure and Judicial Review (Part 4) of the Article on Administration (Article 6)] applies to and governs all administrative action taken by the Administrator pursuant to this Part.

§ 2.307. [Restrictions on Interest in Land as Security]

(1) A lender may contract for an interest in land as security, except to secure a supervised loan in which the amount financed is $1,000 or less. A security interest taken in violation of this section is unenforceable to the extent of that loan.

(2) The amount of $1,000 in subsection (1) is subject to change pursuant to the provisions on adjustment of dollar amounts (Section 1.106).

§ 2.308. [Regular Schedule of Payments; Maximum Loan Term]

(1) Supervised loans, not made pursuant to open-end credit and in which the amount financed is $1,000 or less, shall be scheduled to be payable in substantially equal instalments at substantially equal periodic intervals except to the extent that the schedule of payments is adjusted to the seasonal or irregular income of the debtor, and

(a) over a period not exceeding 37 months if the amount financed exceeds $300, or

(b) over a period not exceeding 25 months if the amount financed is $300 or less.

(2) The amounts of $300 and $1,000 in subsection (1) are subject to change pursuant to the provisions on adjustment of dollar amounts (Section 1.106).

§ 2.309. [No Other Business for Purpose of Evasion]

A supervised lender may not carry on other business for the purpose of evasion or violation of this Act at a location where he makes supervised loans.

§ 2.401. [Finance Charge for Consumer Loans]

(1) With respect to a consumer loan, including a loan pursuant to open-end credit, a lender who is not a supervised lender may contract for and receive a finance charge, calculated according to the actuarial method, not exceeding 18 per cent per year. With respect to a consumer loan made pursuant to open-end credit, the finance charge shall be deemed not to exceed 18 per cent per year if the finance charge contracted for and received does not exceed a charge for each monthly billing cycle which is one and one-half per cent of the average daily balance of the open-end account in the billing cycle for which the charge is made. The average daily balance of the open-end account is the sum of the amount unpaid each day during that cycle divided by the number of days in the cycle. The amount unpaid on a day is determined by adding to any balance unpaid as of the beginning of that day all purchases, loans, and other debits and deducting all payments and other credits made or received as of that day. If the billing cycle is not monthly, the finance charge shall be deemed not to exceed 18 per cent per year if the finance charge contracted for and received does not exceed a percentage which bears the same relation to one and one-half per cent as the number of days in the billing cycle bears to 365 divided by 12. A billing cycle is monthly if the closing date of the cycle is the same date each month or does not vary by more than four days from the regular date.

(2) With respect to a consumer loan, including a loan pursuant to open-end credit, a supervised lender may contract for and receive a finance charge, calculated according to the actuarial method, not exceeding the equivalent of the greater of either of the following:

(a) the total of:

(i) 36 per cent per year on that part of the unpaid balances of the amount financed which is $300 or less;

(ii) 21 per cent per year on that part of the unpaid balances of the amount financed which exceeds $300 but does not exceed $1,000; and

(iii) 15 per cent per year on that part of the unpaid balances of the amount financed which exceeds $1,000; or

(b) 18 per cent per year on the unpaid balances of the amount financed.

(3) This section does not limit or restrict the manner of calculating the finance charge, whether by way of add-on, discount, single annual percentage rate, or otherwise, so long as the rate of the finance charge does not exceed that permitted by this section. The finance charge may be contracted for and earned at the single annual percentage rate that would earn the same finance charge as the graduated rates when the debt is paid according to the agreed terms and the calculations are made according to the actuarial method. If the loan is a precomputed consumer credit transaction:

(a) the finance charge may be calculated on the assumption that all scheduled payments will be made when due, and

(b) the effect of prepayment is governed by the provisions on rebate upon prepayment (Section 2.510).

(4) Except as provided in subsection (6), the term of a loan for purposes of this section commences on the day the loan is made. Any month my be counted as 1/12th of a year, but a day is counted as 1/365 th of a year. Subject to classifications and differentiations the lender may reasonably establish, a part of a month in excess of 15 days may be treated as a full month if periods of 15 days or less are disregarded and that procedure is not consistently used to obtain a greater yield than would otherwise be permitted. The Administrator may adopt rules not inconsistent with the Federal Truth in Lending Act with respect to treating as regular other minor irregularities in amount or time.

(5) Subject to classifications and differentiations the lender may reasonably establish, he may make the same finance charge on all amounts financed within a specified range. A finance charge so made does not violate subsection (1) or (2) if:

(a) when applied to the median amount within each range, it does not exceed the maximum permitted by the applicable subsection, and

(b) when applied to the lowest amount within each range, it does not produce a rate of finance charge exceeding the rate calculated according to paragraph (a) by more than eight per cent of the rate calculated according to paragraph (a).

(6) With respect to an insurance premium loan, the term of the loan commences on the earliest inception date of a policy or contract of insurance payment of the premium on which is financed by the loan.

(7) The amounts of $300 and $1,000 in subsection (2) are subject to change pursuant to the provisions on adjustment of dollar amounts (Section 1.106).

§ 2.501. [Additional Charges]

(1) In addition to the finance charge permitted by the parts of this Article on maximum finance charges for consumer credit sales and consumer loans (Parts 2 and 4), a creditor may contract for and receive the following additional charges:

(a) official fees and taxes;

(b) charges for insurance as described in subsection (2);

(c) annual charges, payable in advance, for the privilege of using a credit card which entitles the cardholder to purchase or lease goods or services from at least 100 persons not related to the card issuer, under an arrangement pursuant to which the debts resulting from the purchases or leases are payable to the card issuer;

(d) with respect to a debt secured by an interest in land, the following "closing costs," if they are bona fide, reasonable in amount, and not for the purpose of circumvention or evasion of this Act:

(i) fees or premiums for title examination, abstract of title, title insurance, surveys, or similar purposes,

(ii) fees for preparation of a deed, settlement statement, or other documents, if not paid to the creditor or a person related to the creditor,

(iii) escrows for future payments of taxes, including assessments for improvements, insurance, and water, sewer and land rents, and

(iv) fees for notarizing deeds and other documents, if not paid to the creditor or a person related to the creditor; and

(e) charges for other benefits, including insurance, conferred on the consumer, if the benefits are of value to him and if the charges are reasonable in relation to the benefits, are of a type that is not for credit, and are authorized as permissible additional charges by rule adopted by the Administrator.

(2) An additional charge may be made for insurance written in connection with the transaction:

(a) with respect to insurance against loss of or damage to property, or against liability arising out of the ownership or use of property, if the creditor furnishes a clear, conspicuous, and specific statement in writing to the consumer setting forth the cost of the insurance if obtained from or through the creditor and stating that the consumer may choose the person through whom the insurance is to be obtained;

(b) with respect to consumer credit insurance providing life, accident, or health coverage, if the insurance coverage is not required by the creditor, and this fact is clearly and conspicuously disclosed in writing to the consumer, and if, in order to obtain the insurance in connection with the extension of credit, the consumer gives specific, dated, and separately signed affirmative written indication of his desire to do so after written disclosure to him of the cost thereof; and

(c) with respect to vendor's single interest insurance, but only (i) to the extent that the insurer has no right of subrogation against the consumer, and (ii) to the extent that the insurance does not duplicate the coverage of other insurance under which loss is payable to the creditor as his interest may appear, against loss of or damage to property for which a separate charge is made to the consumer pursuant to paragraph (a), and (iii) if a clear, conspicuous, and specific statement in writing is furnished by the creditor to the consumer setting forth the cost of the insurance if obtained from or through the creditor and stating that the consumer may choose the person through whom the insurance is to be obtained.

Comments

1. The two categories of charges a creditor is permitted to make at the inception of a credit extension are finance charges (Section 1.301(20)) and additional charges as enumerated in this section. In general, the charges designated as additional charges fall roughly into three classes: (1) those that would likely have been incurred had there been no credit extension (*e.g.*, closing costs); (2) those closely related to the extension of credit but providing valuable subsidiary benefits to the consumer (*e.g.*, the front-end credit card charge; life, accident, health, and property insurance); and (3) those ultimately payable to third parties with no portion of the charge returnable to the creditor by commission or otherwise (*e.g.*, taxes; official fees for perfecting security interests). These classes are nonexclusive; for instance property insurance would sometimes fall within class (1) and closing costs fit into class (3) as well as in (1). Paragraph (e) of subsection (1) provides the Administrator with the flexibility needed to allow him to deal with new kinds of charges as new credit transactions evolve.

2. Though this section coincides with Regulation Z Section 226.4(a) in excluding premiums for insurance from the finance charge under certain stated conditions, it varies from Regulation Z Section 226.4(e) in that it does not include appraisal fees and credit report charges as additional charges. Section 1.301(20)(a)(iv) expressly designates these charges as part of the finance charge. Another variation from Truth in Lending is the treatment of vendor's single interest insurance (V.S.I.). Federal Reserve Interpretation 226.404 allows exclusion of the premium for V.S.I. insurance from the finance charge. Paragraph (c) of subsection (2) adopts a more sophisticated test and allows the premium to be treated as an additional charge in limited situations in which the vendor's single interest coverage does not duplicate the coverage of other insurance under which loss is payable to the creditor as his interest may appear, against loss of or damage to property for which a separate charge is made to the consumer. In this case, the charge is sufficiently beneficial to the consumer to justify classifying the premium as in additional charge.

§ 2.502. [Delinquency Charges]

(1) With respect to a precomputed consumer credit transaction, the parties may contract for a delinquency charge on any instalment not paid in full within ten days after its due date, as originally

scheduled or as deferred, in an amount, not exceeding $5, which is not more than five per cent of the unpaid amount of the instalment.

(2) A delinquency charge under subsection (1) may be collected only once on an instalment however long it remains in default. No delinquency charge may be collected with respect to a deferred instalment unless the instalment is not paid in full within ten days after its deferred due date. A delinquency charge may be collected at the time it accrues or at any time thereafter.

(3) A delinquency charge under subsection (1) may not be collected on an instalment paid in full within ten days after its scheduled or deferred instalment due date even though an earlier maturing instalment or a delinquency or deferral charge on an earlier instalment has not been paid in full. For purposes of this subsection a payment is deemed to have been applied first to any instalment due in the computational period (paragraph (a) of subsection (1) of Section 2.503) in which it is received and then to delinquent instalments and charges.

(4) If two instalments or parts thereof of a precomputed consumer loan are in default for ten days or more, the lender may elect to convert the loan from a precomputed loan to one in which the finance charge is based on unpaid balances. In this event he shall make a rebate pursuant to the provisions on rebate upon prepayment (Section 2.510) as if the date of prepayment were one day before the maturity date of a delinquent instalment, and thereafter may make a finance charge as authorized by the provisions on finance charge for consumer loans by lenders not supervised lenders (subsection (1) of Section 2.401) or finance charge for consumer loans by supervised lenders (subsection (2) of Section 2.401), whichever is appropriate. The amount of the rebate shall not be reduced by the amount of any permitted minimum charge (Section 2.510). If the creditor proceeds under this subsection, any delinquency or deferral charges made with respect to instalments due at or after the maturity date of the first delinquent instalment shall be rebated, and no further delinquency or deferral charges shall be made.

(5) The amount of $5 in subsection (1) is subject to change pursuant to the provisions on adjustment of dollar amounts (Section 1.106).

Comments

1. If a consumer is late in making a payment under a precomputed credit transaction, the creditor would receive no income for the period of delay unless a delinquency charge were permitted. The alternative of not permitting delinquency charges is rejected because the result would be to enforce a lower effective ceiling on finance charge rates for delinquent consumers than for consumers who pay promptly. Delinquency charges are inapplicable to open-end credit plans under which the finance charge continues to accumulate through any period of delay thus compensating the creditor for this period.

2. The principal consumer abuse at which the section is aimed is that of precluding multiple delinquency charges stemming from a single delayed payment. Under law before this Act if the consumer's payments were due on the first of the month and the January payment of $100 was not made until the 15th, the creditor could assess a late payment of $5 (assuming that to be the correct figure under state law) and allocate the $100 payment received on February 1st, $95 to the February payment and $5 to the unpaid delinquency charge, thus causing the consumer to be delinquent in February as well. If the consumer made his $100 payment on time for each of the remaining months of the contract, he would incur a delinquency charge for each month remaining on the contract because of the rule allowing the creditor to allocate current payments to unpaid charges incurred in past periods. Subsection (3) meets this problem by compelling the creditor to apply the full $100 payment received on February 1 to the payment due that month. Hence, the creditor could collect the delinquency charge only for January if all other payments were made on time.

§ 2.503. [Deferral Charges]

(1) In this section and in the provisions on rebate upon prepayment (Section 2.510) the following defined terms apply with respect to a precomputed consumer credit transaction:

(a) "Computational period" means (i) the interval between scheduled due dates of the instalments under the transaction if the intervals are substantially equal or, (ii) if the intervals are not substantially equal, one month if the smallest interval between the scheduled due dates of instalments under the transaction is one month or more, and, otherwise, one week.

(b) "Deferral" means a postponement of the scheduled due date of an instalment as originally scheduled or as previously deferred.

(c) "Deferral period" means a period in which no instalment is scheduled to be paid by reason of a deferral.

(d) The "interval" between specified dates means the interval between them including one or the other but not both of them; if the interval between the date of a transaction and the due date of the first scheduled instalment does not exceed one month by more than 15 days when the computational period is one month, or does not exceed 11 days when the computational period is on week, the interval may be considered by the creditor as one computational period.

(e) "Periodic balance" means the amount scheduled to be outstanding on the last day of a computational period before deducting the instalment, if any, scheduled to be paid on that day.

(f) "Standard deferral" means a deferral with respect to a transaction made as of the due date of an instalment as scheduled before the deferral by which the due dates of that instalment and all subsequent instalments as scheduled before the deferral are deferred for a period equal to the deferral period. A standard deferral may be for one or more full computational periods or a portion of one computational period or a combination of any of these.

(g) "Sum of the balances method," also known as the "Rule of 78," means a method employed with respect to a transaction to determine the portion of the finance charge attributable to a period of time before the scheduled due date of the final instalment of the transaction. The amount so attributable is determined by multiplying the finance charge by a fraction the numerator of which is the sum of the periodic balances included within the period and the denominator of which is the sum of all periodic balances under the transaction. According to the sum of the balances method the portion of the finance charge attributable to a specified computational period is the difference between the portions of the finance charge attributable to the periods of time including and excluding, respectively, the computational period, both determined according to the sum of the balances method.

(h) "Transaction" means a precomputed consumer credit transaction unless the context otherwise requires.

(2) Before or after default in payment of a scheduled instalment of a transaction, the parties to the transaction may agree in writing to a deferral of all or part of one or more unpaid instalments and the creditor may make at the time of deferral and receive at that time or at any time thereafter a deferral charge not exceeding that provided in this section.

(3) A standard deferral may be made with respect to a transaction as of the due date, as originally scheduled or as deferred pursuant to a standard deferral, of an instalment with respect to which no delinquency charge (Section 2.502) has been made or, if made, is deducted from the deferral charge computed according to this subsection. The deferral charge for a standard deferral may equal but not exceed the portion of the finance charge attributable to the computational period immediately preceding the due date of the earliest maturing instalment deferred as determined according to the sum of the balances method multiplied by the whole or fractional number of computational periods in the deferral period, counting each day as 1/30 th of a month without regard to differences in lengths of months when the computational period is one month or as 1/7 th of a week when the computation period is one week. A deferral charge computed according to this subsection is earned pro rata during the deferral period and is fully earned on the last day of the deferral period.

(4) With respect to a transaction as to which a creditor elects not to make and does not make a standard deferral or a deferral charge for a standard deferral, a deferral charge computed according to this subsection may be made as of the due date, as scheduled originally or as deferred pursuant to either subsection (3) or this subsection, of an instalment with respect to which no delinquency charge

(Section 2.502) has been made or, if made, is deducted from the deferral charge computed according to this subsection. A deferral charge pursuant to this subsection may equal but not exceed the rate of finance charge required to be disclosed to the consumer pursuant to law applied to each amount deferred for the period for which it is deferred computed without regard to differences in lengths of months, but proportionately for a part of a month, counting each day as 1/30 th of a month or as 1/7 th of a week. A deferral charge computed according to this subsection is earned pro rata with respect to each amount deferred during the period for which it is deferred.

(5) In addition to the deferral charge permitted by this section, a creditor may make and receive appropriate additional charges (Section 2.501), and any amount of these charges which is not paid may be added to the deferral charge computed according to subsection (3) or to the amount deferred for the purpose of computing the deferral charge computed according to subsection (4).

(6) The parties may agree in writing at the time of a transaction that, if an instalment is not paid within ten days after its due date, the creditor may unilaterally grant a deferral and make charges as provided in this section. A deferral charge may not be made for a period after the date that the creditor elects to accelerate the maturity of the transaction.

§ 2.504. [Finance Charge on Refinancing]

With respect to a consumer credit transaction except a consumer lease, the creditor by agreement with the consumer may refinance the unpaid balance and contract for and receive a finance charge based on the amount financed resulting from the refinancing at a rate not exceeding that permitted by the provisions on finance charge for consumer credit sales other than open-end credit (Section 2.201) if a consumer credit sale is refinanced, or for consumer loans (subsection (1) or (2) of Section 2.401, whichever is appropriate) if a consumer loan is refinanced. For the purpose of determining the finance charge permitted, the amount financed resulting from the refinancing comprises the following:

(1) if the transaction was not precomputed, the total of the unpaid balance and the accrued charges on the date of the refinancing, or, if the transaction was precomputed, the amount which the consumer would have been required to pay upon prepayment pursuant to the provisions on rebate upon prepayment (Section 2.510) on the date of refinancing, but for the purpose of computing this amount no minimum charge is permitted; and

(2) appropriate additional charges (Section 2.501), payment of which is deferred.

§ 2.505. [Finance Charge on Consolidation]

(1) In this section "consumer credit transaction" does not include a consumer lease.

(2) If a consumer owes an unpaid balance to a creditor with respect to a consumer credit transaction and becomes obligated on another consumer credit transaction with the same creditor, the parties may agree to a consolidation resulting in a single schedule of payments. If the previous consumer credit transaction was not precomputed, the parties may agree to add the unpaid amount of the amount financed and accrued charges on the date of consolidation to the amount financed with respect to the subsequent consumer credit transaction. If the previous consumer credit transaction was precomputed, the parties may agree to refinance the unpaid balance pursuant to the provisions on refinancing (Section 2.504) and to consolidate the amount financed resulting from the refinancing by adding it to the amount financed with respect to the subsequent consumer credit transaction. In either case the creditor may contract for and receive a finance charge as provided in subsection (3) based on the aggregate amount financed resulting from the consolidation.

(3) If the debts consolidated arise exclusively from consumer credit sales, the transaction is a consolidation with respect to a consumer credit sale and the creditor may make a finance charge not exceeding that permitted by the provisions on finance charge for consumer credit sales other than one-end credit (Section 2.201). If the debts consolidated include a debt arising from a prior or contemporaneous consumer loan, the transaction is a consolidation with respect to a consumer loan and the creditor may make a finance charge not exceeding that permitted by the provisions on finance

charge for consumer loans by lenders not supervised lenders (subsection (1) of Section 2.401) or consumer loans by supervised lenders (subsection (2) of Section 2.401), whichever is appropriate.

(4) If a consumer owes an unpaid balance to a creditor with respect to a consumer credit transaction arising out of a consumer credit sale, and becomes obligated on another consumer credit transaction arising out of another consumer credit sale by the same seller, the parties may agree to a consolidation resulting in a single schedule of payments either pursuant to subsection (2) or by adding together the unpaid balances with respect to the two sales.

§ 2.506. [Advances to Perform Covenants of Consumer]

(1) If the agreement with respect to a consumer credit transaction other than a consumer lease contains covenants by the consumer to perform certain duties pertaining to insuring or preserving collateral and the creditor pursuant to the agreement pays for performance of the duties on behalf of the consumer, he may add the amounts paid to the debt. Within a reasonable time after advancing any sums, he shall state to the consumer in writing the amount of sums advanced, any charges with respect to this amount, and any revised payment schedule and, if the duties of the consumer performed by the creditor pertain to insurance, a brief description of the insurance paid for by the creditor including the type and amount of coverages. Further information need not be given.

(2) A finance charge may be made for sums advanced pursuant to subsection (1) at a rate not exceeding the rate of finance charge required to be stated to the consumer pursuant to law in a disclosure statement, but with respect to open-end credit the amount of the advance may be added to the unpaid balance of the debt and the creditor may make a finance charge not exceeding that permitted by the appropriate provisions on finance charge for consumer credit sales pursuant to open-end credit (Section 2.202) or for consumer loans (subsection (1) or (2) of Section 2.401), whichever is appropriate.

§ 2.507. [Attorney's Fees] [ALTERNATIVE A]

With respect to a consumer credit transaction, the agreement may not provide for payment by the consumer of attorney's fees. A provision in violation of this section is unenforceable.

§ 2.507. [Attorney's Fees] [ALTERNATIVE B]

(1) With respect to a consumer loan in which the finance charge calculated according to the actuarial method is more than 18 per cent per year, the agreement may not provide for payment by the consumer of attorney's fees:

(a) if the loan is not pursuant to open-end credit and the amount financed is $1,000 or less; or

(b) if the loan is pursuant to open-end credit and the balance of the account at the time of default is $1,000 or less.

A provision in violation of this subsection is unenforceable.

(2) With respect to any other consumer credit transaction, the agreement may provide for payment by the consumer of reasonable attorney's fees not in excess of 15 per cent of the unpaid debt after default and referral to an attorney not a salaried employee of the creditor. A provision in violation of this subsection is unenforceable.

(3) The amounts of $1,000 in subsection (1) are subject to change pursuant to the provisions on adjustment of dollar amounts (Section 1.106).

§ 2.508. [Conversion to Open-End Credit]

The parties may agree at or within ten days before the time of conversion to add the unpaid balance of a consumer credit transaction, except a consumer lease, not made pursuant to open-end credit to the consumer's open-end credit account with the creditor. The unpaid balance so added is an amount equal to the amount financed determined according to the provisions on finance charge on refinancing (Section 2.504).

§ 2.509. [Right to Prepay]

Subject to the provisions on rebate upon prepayment (Section 2.510), the consumer may prepay in full the unpaid balance of a consumer credit transaction, except a consumer lease, at any time without penalty.

§ 2.510. [Rebate Upon Prepayment]

(1) Except as otherwise provided in this section, upon prepayment in full of a precomputed consumer credit transaction, the creditor shall rebate to the consumer an amount not less than the unearned portion of the finance charge computed according to this section. If the rebate otherwise required is less than $1, no rebate need be made.

(2) Upon prepayment of a consumer credit transaction, whether or not precomputed, except a consumer lease or one pursuant to open-end credit, the creditor may collect or retain a minimum charge not exceeding $5 in a transaction which had an amount financed of $75 or less, or not exceeding $7.50 in a transaction which had an amount financed of more than $75, if the minimum charge was contracted for and the finance charge earned at the time of prepayment is less than the minimum charge contracted for.

(3) In the following subsections these terms have the meanings ascribed to them in subsection (1) of Section 2.503: computational period, deferral, deferral period, periodic balance, standard deferral, sum of the balances method, and transaction.

(4) If, with respect to a transaction payable according to its original terms in no more than [48] instalments, the creditor has made either:

(a) no deferral or deferral charge, the unearned portion of the finance charge is no less than the portion thereof attributable according to the sum of the balances method to the period from the first day of the computational period following that in which prepayment occurs to the scheduled due date of the final instalment of the transaction; or

(b) a standard deferral and a deferral charge pursuant to the provisions on a standard deferral, the unpaid balance of the transaction includes any unpaid portions of the deferral charge and any appropriate additional charges incident to the deferral, and the unearned portion of the finance charge is no less than the portion thereof attributable according to the sum of the balances method to the period from the first day of the computational period following that in which prepayment occurs except that the numerator of the fraction is the sum of the periodic balances, after rescheduling to give effect to any standard deferral, scheduled to follow the computational period in which prepayment occurs. A separate rebate of the deferral charge is not required unless the unpaid balance of the transaction is paid in full during the deferral period, in which event the creditor shall also rebate the unearned portion of the deferral charge.

(5) In lieu of computing a rebate of the unearned portion of the finance charge as provided in subsection (4) of this section, the creditor:

(a) shall, with respect to a transaction payable according to its original terms in more than [48] instalments, and a transaction payable according to its original terms in no more than [48] instalments as to which the creditor has made a deferral other than a standard deferral, and

(b) may, in other cases, recompute or redetermine the earned finance charge by applying, according to the actuarial method, the annual percentage rate of finance charge required to be disclosed to the consumer pursuant to law to the actual unpaid balances of the amount financed for the actual time that the unpaid balances were outstanding as of the date of prepayment, giving effect to each payment, including payments of any deferral and delinquency charges, as of the date of the payment. The Administrator shall adopt rules to simplify the calculation of the unearned portion of the finance charge, including allowance of the use of tables or other methods derived by application of a percentage rate which deviates by not more than one-half of one per cent from the rate of the finance charge required to be disclosed to the consumer pursuant to law, and based on the assumption that all payments were made as originally scheduled or as deferred.

(6) Except as otherwise provided in subsection (5), this section does not preclude the collection or retention by the creditor of delinquency charges (Section 2.502).

(7) If the maturity is accelerated for any reason and judgment is entered, the consumer is entitled to the same rebate as if payment had been made on the date judgment is entered.

(8) Upon prepayment in full of a precomputed consumer credit transaction by the proceeds of consumer credit insurance (Section 4.103), the consumer or his estate is entitled to the same rebate as though the consumer had prepaid the agreement on the date the proceeds of insurance are paid to the creditor, but no later than 20 business days after satisfactory proof of loss is furnished to the creditor.

§ 2.601. [Charges for Other Credit Transactions]

(1) Except as provided in subsection (2), with respect to a credit transaction other than a consumer credit transaction, the parties may contract for payment by the debtor of any finance or other charge.

(2) With respect to a credit transaction which would be a consumer credit transaction if a finance charge were made, a charge for delinquency may not exceed amounts allowed for finance charges for consumer credit sales pursuant to open-end credit (Section 2.202).

ARTICLE 3. REGULATION OF AGREEMENTS AND PRACTICES

Table of Sections

---

§ 3.101. [Short Title]

This Article shall be known and may be cited as Uniform Consumer Credit Code—Regulation of Agreements and Practices.

§ 3.102. [Scope]

Part 2 of this Article applies to disclosure with respect to consumer credit transactions. The provision on compliance with the Federal Truth in Lending Act (Section 3.201) applies to a sale of an interest in land or a loan secured by an interest in land, without regard to the rate of finance charge, if the sale or loan is otherwise a consumer credit sale or consumer loan. Parts 3 and 4 of this Article apply, respectively, to limitations on agreements and practices, and limitations on consumers' liabilities with respect to certain consumer credit transactions. Part 5 applies to home solicitation sales.

§ 3.201. [Compliance With Federal Truth in Lending Act]

(1) A person upon whom the Federal Truth in Lending Act imposes duties or obligations shall make or give to the consumer the disclosures, information, and notices required of him by that Act and in all respects comply with that Act. To the extent the Federal Truth in Lending Act does not impose duties or obligations upon a person in a credit transaction, except a consumer lease, that is a consumer credit transaction under this Act, the person shall make or give to the consumer disclosures, information, and notices in accordance with the Federal Truth in Lending Act with respect to the credit transaction.

(2) The Federal Truth in Lending Act is deemed to apply to a credit transaction which is a consumer credit transaction under this Act, notwithstanding its inclusion in a class of transactions within this State which, by regulation of the Board of Governors of the Federal Reserve System, is exempt from the Federal Truth in Lending Act.

§ 3.202. [Consumer Leases]

(1) With respect to a consumer lease the lessor shall give to the lessee the following information:

(a) brief description or identification of the goods;

(b) amount of any payment required at the inception of the lease;

(c) amount paid or payable for official fees, registration, certificate of title, or license fees or taxes;

(d) amount of other charges not included in the periodic payments and a brief description of the charges;

(e) brief description of insurance to be provided or paid for by the lessor, including the types and amounts of the coverages;

(f) number of periodic payments, the amount of each payment, the due date of the first payment, the due dates of subsequent payments or interval between payments, and the total amount payable by the lessee;

(g) statement of the conditions under which the lessee may terminate the lease before the end of the term; and

(h) statement of the liabilities the lease imposes upon the lessee at the end of the term.

(2) The disclosures required by this section:

(a) shall be made clearly and conspicuously in writing, a copy of which shall be delivered to the lessee;

(b) may be supplemented by additional information or explanations supplied by the lessor, but none shall be stated, utilized, or placed so as to mislead or confuse the lessee or contradict, obscure, or detract attention from the information required to be disclosed by this section;

(c) need be made only to the extent applicable;

(d) shall be made on the assumption that all scheduled payments will be made when due and will comply with this section although rendered inaccurate by an act, occurrence, or agreement after the required disclosure; and

(e) shall be made before the lease transaction is consummated, but may be made in the lease to be signed by the lessee.

§ 3.203. [Notice to Consumer]

The creditor shall give to the consumer a copy of any writing evidencing a consumer credit transaction, except one pursuant to open-end credit, if the writing requires or provides for the signature of the consumer. The writing evidencing the consumer's obligation to pay the debt shall contain a clear and conspicuous notice informing the consumer that he should not sign it before reading it, that he is entitled to a copy of it, and, except in case of a consumer lease, that he is entitled to prepay the unpaid balance at any time without penalty and may be entitled to receive a refund of unearned charges in accordance with law. The following notice if clear and conspicuous complies with this section:

NOTICE TO CONSUMER

1. Do not sign this paper before you read it.

2. You are entitled to a copy of this paper.

3. You may prepay the unpaid balance at any time without penalty and may be entitled to receive a refund of unearned charges in accordance with law.

§ 3.204. [Notice of Assignment]

A consumer may pay the original creditor until he receives notification of assignment of rights to payment pursuant to a consumer credit transaction and that payment is to be made to the assignee. A notification which does not reasonably identify the rights assigned is ineffective. If requested by the consumer, the assignee shall seasonably furnish reasonable proof that the assignment has been made and unless he does so the consumer may pay the original creditor.

§ 3.205. [Change in Terms of Open-End Credit Accounts]

(1) Whether or not a change is authorized by prior agreement, a creditor may change the terms of an open-end credit account applying to any balance incurred before or after the effective date of the change. If the change increases the rate of the finance charge or of additional charges, alters the method of determining the balance upon which charges are made so that increased charges may result,

or imposes or increases minimum charges, the change is effective with respect to a balance incurred before the effective date of the change only if the consumer after receiving disclosure of the change agrees to it in writing or the creditor delivers or mails to the consumer two written disclosures of the change, the first at least three months before the effective date of the change and the second at a later time before the effective date of the change.

(2) A disclosure provided for in subsection (1) is mailed to the consumer when mailed to him at his address used by the creditor for mailing him periodic billing statements.

(3) If a creditor attempts to change the terms of an open-end credit account as provided in subsection (1) without complying with this section, any additional cost or charge to the consumer resulting from the change is an excess charge and is subject to the remedies available to the consumer (Section 5.201) and to the Administrator (Section 6.113).

Comments

1. New developments in consumer credit practices may require changes in open-end credit accounts from time to time. A national department store or commercial bank issuing credit cards may have hundreds of thousands of cardholders. Insurmountable difficulties would confront such creditors were it necessary for them to obtain from each consumer his signed consent to a change in terms. Experience indicates that only a minority of customers take the trouble to return an express approval or disapproval of a change in terms. Nevertheless, merchants and banks should not be permitted to take advantage of customers by changes which are unfair, unanticipated, or inadequately communicated. This provision is designed to allow creditors to change the terms of their open-end accounts in a manner which is feasible from their standpoint but which safeguards the interests of their customers.

2. Truth in Lending requires 15-days' notice of certain changes in an open-end credit account (Regulation Z Section 226.7(e)), and if the change either does not increase credit costs or, if costs are increased, affects only balances incurred after the date of the change, the creditor need only give the 15-day Truth in Lending notice. However, under this section if the change increases credit costs for consumers and applies to balances already incurred, the creditor must either obtain the consumer's written consent to the change or comply with the notice provisions of this section, as well as comply with Truth in Lending.

§ 3.206. [Receipts; Statements of Account; Evidence of Payment]

(1) The creditor shall deliver or mail to the consumer, without request, a written receipt for each payment by coin or currency on an obligation pursuant to a consumer credit transaction. A periodic statement showing a payment received by mail complies with this subsection.

(2) Upon written request of a consumer, the person to whom an obligation is owed pursuant to a consumer credit transaction, except one pursuant to open-end credit, shall provide a written statement of the dates and amounts of payments made within the 12 months preceding the month in which the request is received and the total amount unpaid as of the end of the period covered by the statement. The statement shall be provided without charge once during each year of the term of the obligation. If additional statements are requested the creditor may charge not in excess of [$_______] for each additional statement.

(3) After a consumer has fulfilled all obligations with respect to a consumer credit transaction, except one pursuant to open-end credit, the person to whom the obligation was owed, upon request of the consumer, shall deliver or mail to the consumer written evidence acknowledging payment in full of all obligations with respect to the transaction.

§ 3.207. [Form of Insurance Premium Loan Agreement]

An agreement pursuant to which an insurance premium loan is made shall contain the names of the insurance agent or broker negotiating each policy or contract and of the insurer issuing each policy or contract, the number and inception date of, and premium for, each policy or contract, the date on which the term of the loan begins, and a clear and conspicuous notice that each policy or contract may be cancelled if payment is not made in accordance with the agreement. If a policy or contract has not been issued by the time the agreement is signed, the agreement may provide that the insurance agent or broker may insert the appropriate information in the agreement, and, if he does so, shall furnish the information promptly in writing to the insured.

§ 3.208. [Notice to Co-Signers and Similar Parties]

(1) A natural person, other than the spouse of the consumer, is not obligated as a co-signer, co-maker, guarantor, indorser, surety, or similar party with respect to a consumer credit transaction, unless before or contemporaneously with signing any separate agreement of obligation or any writing setting forth the terms of the debtor's agreement, the person receives a separate written notice that contains a completed identification of the debt he may have to pay and reasonably informs him of his obligation with respect to it.

(2) A clear and conspicuous notice in substantially the following form complies with this section:

NOTICE

You agree to pay the debt identified below although you may not personally receive any property, services, or money. You may be sued for payment although the person who receives the property, services, or money is able to pay. This notice is not the contract that obligates you to pay the debt. Read the contract for the exact terms of your obligation.

IDENTIFICATION OF DEBT YOU MAY HAVE TO PAY

(Name of Debtor)

(Name of Creditor)

(Date)

(Kind of Debt)

I have received a copy of this notice.

____

(Date)

____

(Signed)

(3) The notice required by this section need not be given to a seller, lessor, or lender who is obligated to an assignee of his rights.

(4) A person entitled to notice under this section shall also be given a copy of any writing setting forth the terms of the debtor's agreement and of any separate agreement of obligation signed by the person entitled to the notice.

§ 3.209. [Advertising]

(1) A seller, lessor, or lender may not advertise, print, display, publish, distribute, broadcast, or cause to be advertised, printed, displayed, published, distributed, or broadcast in any manner any statement or representation with regard to the rates, terms, or conditions of credit with respect to a consumer credit transaction that is false, misleading, or deceptive.

(2) Advertising that complies with the Federal Truth in Lending Act does not violate this section.

(3) This section does not apply to the owner or personnel, as such, of any medium in which an advertisement appears or through which it is disseminated.

§ 3.301. [Security in Sales and Leases]

(1) With respect to a consumer credit sale, a seller may take a security interest in the property sold. In addition, a seller may take a security interest in goods upon which services are performed or in which goods sold are installed or to which they are annexed, or in land to which the goods are affixed or which is maintained, repaired or improved as a result of the sale of the goods or services, if in the case of a security interest in land the debt secured is $1,000 or more, or, in the case of a security interest in goods the debt secured is $300 or more. The seller may also take a security interest in property to secure the debt arising from a consumer credit sale primarily for an agricultural purpose. Except as provided with respect to cross-collateral (Section 3.302) a seller may not otherwise take a security interest in property to secure the debt arising from a consumer credit sale.

(2) With respect to a consumer lease, except one primarily for an agricultural purpose, a lessor may not take a security interest in property to secure the debt arising from the lease. This subsection does not apply to a security deposit for a consumer lease.

(3) A security interest taken in violation of this section is void.

(4) The amounts of $1,000 and $300 in subsection (1) are subject to change pursuant to the provisions on adjustment of dollar amounts (Section 1.106).

Comments

This section limits sellers and lessors with respect to the manner in which they may secure the obligation arising from a consumer credit sale (Section 1.301(12)) or consumer lease (Section 1.301(14)). See Section 5.116 for limitations on the creditor's right to realize on collateral exempt under the law of this State.

1. Sales of goods. A seller may take a security interest in the goods sold but not in other goods or land unless the goods sold become closely connected with the goods or land in which the security interest is taken. Under this section an appliance dealer may retain a security interest in a washing machine sold but may not take a security interest in other appliances to secure the sale obligation unless he complies with Section 3.302. Except as provided in Section 3.302, a seller of goods may take additional security for the sale obligation in other goods or land only if the debt secured is substantial—$300 in the case of a security interest in goods, $1,000 in the case of a security interest in land—and then only if the goods or land in which the additional security interest is taken are goods in which the goods sold are installed or to which they are annexed or land to which the goods sold are annexed or which is maintained, repaired, or improved by the goods sold.

2. Sales of services. The seller may not take a security interest in goods or land to secure an obligation arising out of the sale of services unless the services are performed on the goods or are used to maintain, repair, or improve the land. Even then, the debt secured must be $300 in the case of a security interest in goods and $1,000 in the case of a security interest in land. Thus a seller of dancing lessons may not take a security interest in goods or lands, and a carpenter or painter may take a security interest in a residence only if the debt arising from the sale of services is $1,000 or more.

3. Sales of land. The seller can retain a security interest only in the land sold and not in other goods or land. It should be noted, however, that this section applies only to consumer credit sales and a sale of an interest in land in which the finance charge is 12% or less is not a consumer credit sale. Section 1.301(12).

4. Consumer leases. A lessor may not secure the lease obligation by taking a security interest in property.

5. Sales for agricultural purposes. Farmers sometimes secure the unpaid balance of a sale obligation by giving security interests in their land or farm equipment. In order not to disturb this practice, an exception in the application of this section is made for sales and leases for agricultural purposes.

§ 3.302. [Cross-Collateral]

(1) In addition to contracting for a security interest pursuant to the provisions on security in sales and leases (Section 3.301), a seller in a consumer credit sale may secure the debt arising from

the sale by contracting for a security interest in other property if as a result of a prior sale the seller has an existing security interest in the other property. The seller may also contract for a security interest in the property sold in the subsequent sale as security for the previous debt.

(2) If the seller contracts for a security interest in other property pursuant to this section, the rate of finance charge thereafter on the aggregate unpaid balances so secured may not exceed that permitted if the balances so secured were consolidated pursuant to the provisions on finance charge on consolidation (subsection (2) of Section 2.505). The seller has a reasonable time after so contracting in which to make any adjustments required by this section.

Comments

1. A seller who sells goods on credit to a buyer in more than one sale may secure the debts arising from each sale by a cross-security interest in the other goods sold so long as the seller has an existing security interest in the other goods. Section 3.303 specifies when a seller loses his security interest in goods in a cross-collateral situation.

2. Subsection (1) allows cross-collateral to be taken either for separate debts or for consolidated debts, but subsection (2) limits the rate of the finance charge that a seller may charge in the separate debt case to that chargeable had the debts been consolidated pursuant to Section 2.505(2). To illustrate, if a buyer who owes seller a $275 balance from one sale makes a subsequent $250 purchase, the seller may consolidate these debts under Section 2.505(2) so that the finance charge would be calculated on the sum of the refinanced balance of the first sale, *e.g.*, $260, and the amount financed under the second sale, $250, or a total of $510. Under Section 2.201, the seller may then charge a maximum rate of 36% on the first $300 and 21% on the next $210. However, if the debts were kept separate, the seller might charge the maximum of 36% on both the $275 and $250 balances. In effect subsection (2) prevents the seller from taking the advantages of cross-collateral without also offering the buyer the lower rates that would have resulted had the debts been consolidated pursuant to Section 2.505(2).

§ 3.303. [Debt Secured by Cross-Collateral]

(1) If debts arising from two or more consumer credit sales, except sales primarily for an agricultural purpose or pursuant to open-end credit, are secured by cross-collateral (Section 3.302) or consolidated into one debt payable on a single schedule of payments, and the debt is secured by security interests taken with respect to one or more of the sales, payments received by the seller after the taking of cross-collateral or the consolidation are deemed, for the purpose of determining the amount of the debt secured by the various security interests, to have been applied first to the payment of the debts arising from the sales first made. To the extent debts are paid according to this section, security interests in items of property terminate as the debt originally incurred with respect to each item is paid.

(2) Payments received by the seller upon an open-end credit account are deemed, for the purpose of determining the amount of the debt secured by the various security interests, to have been applied first to the payment of finance charges in the order of their entry to the account and then to the payment of debts in the order in which the entries to the account showing the debts were made.

(3) If the debts consolidated arose from two or more sales made on the same day, payments received by the seller are deemed, for the purpose of determining the amount of the debt secured by the various security interests, to have been applied first to the payment of the smallest debt.

Comments

1. When a seller consolidates debts arising from sales and secures the consolidated debt by security interests in the goods sold in these sales or when a seller secures separate debts by cross-collateral (Section 3.302), this section prevents the seller from retaining a security interest in all of the goods until the buyer's entire debt is paid. The basis of the section is that a security interest in goods terminates when the debt incurred in the sale of the goods is paid. For the purpose of determining when this debt is paid, subsection (1) allocates the buyer's payments first to the debts first incurred. Thus if the seller consolidates debts of $100, $200, and $300 arising from sales made in that order, the security interest in the goods purchased

pursuant to the $100 sale terminates when $100 of the consolidated debt is paid. If the seller does not consolidate these debts but secures them by cross-collateral, he must allocate all of the buyer's payments to the $100 debt until it is paid off, and so forth. Subsection (2) applies this first-payments-against-first-debts rule to open-end accounts.

2. Subsection (3) applies to the case in which the buyer purchases a $750 TV in one apartment at 9:30 a.m. and a $150 typewriter in another department at 10:00 a.m. Subsequently the debts are consolidated. This subsection relieves the seller of having to keep records of the exact hour a sale is made. It is derived from Regulation Z Section 226.8(h).

§ 3.304. [Use of Multiple Agreements]

(1) A creditor may not use multiple agreements with respect to a single consumer credit transaction with intent to obtain a higher finance charge than otherwise would be permitted by the provisions of the Article on Finance Charges and Related Provisions (Article 2).

(2) The excess amount of finance charge resulting from a violation of subsection (1) is an excess charge for the purposes of the provisions on rights of parties (Section 5.201) and the provisions on civil actions by Administrator (Section 6.113).

§ 3.305. [No Assignment of Earnings]

(1) A creditor may not take an assignment of earnings of the consumer for payment or as security for payment of a debt arising out of a consumer credit transaction. An assignment of earnings in violation of this section is unenforceable by the assignee of the earnings and revocable by the consumer. This section does not prohibit a consumer from authorizing deductions from his earnings in favor of his creditor if the authorization is revocable, the consumer is given a complete copy of the writing evidencing the authorization at the time he signs it, and the writing contains on its face a conspicuous notice of the consumer's right to revoke the authorization.

(2) A sale of unpaid earnings made in consideration of the payment of money to or for the account of the seller of the earnings is deemed to be a loan to him secured by an assignment of earnings.

Comments

This Act recognizes the potential for hardship for a consumer and his dependents which may result from a disruption of the steady flow of family income. Just as Section 5.104 prevents a creditor from attaching unpaid earnings of a consumer before he obtains judgment, this provision precludes a creditor from reaching the consumer's earnings pursuant to an irrevocable wage assignment obtained from the consumer. The purpose of both sections is to afford the consumer an opportunity to have his debt determined by a court before his unpaid earnings are taken against his will by a creditor. This provision prohibits a creditor from taking either an assignment of earnings as payment or as security for payment for a debt or a sale of earnings in payment of the price or rental. A revocable payroll deduction authorization in favor of a creditor is not forbidden by this section so long as the requisite notice is given to the consumer of his right to revoke.

§ 3.306. [Authorization to Confess Judgment Prohibited]

A consumer may not authorize any person to confess judgment on a claim arising out of a consumer credit transaction. An authorization in violation of this section is void.

§ 3.307. [Certain Negotiable Instruments Prohibited]

With respect to a consumer credit sale or consumer lease, [except a sale or lease primarily for an agricultural purpose,] the creditor may not take a negotiable instrument other than a check dated not later than ten days after its issuance as evidence of the obligation of the consumer.

Comments

This section, together with Sections 3.403, 3.404, and 3.405, states a major tenet of this Act: that the holder in due course doctrine should be abrogated in consumer cases. Whatever beneficial effects this doctrine may have in promoting the currency of paper is greatly outweighed by the harshness of its consequences in denying consumers the right to raise valid defenses arising out of credit transactions. The first step in abolition of the doctrine is the prohibition found in this section of the use of negotiable instruments in consumer credit sales and consumer leases. The presence of the bracketed language recognizes the strong tradition of the use of negotiable instruments in agricultural transactions in some States.

§ 3.308. [Balloon Payments]

(1) Except as provided in subsection (2), if any scheduled payment of a consumer credit transaction is more than twice as large as the average of earlier scheduled payments, the consumer has the right to refinance, without penalty, the amount of that payment at the time it is due. The terms of the refinancing shall be no less favorable to the consumer than the terms of the original transaction.

(2) This section does not apply to:

(a) a consumer lease;

(b) a transaction pursuant to open-end credit;

(c) a transaction primarily for an agricultural purpose;

(d) a transaction to the extent that the payment schedule is adjusted to the seasonal or irregular income or scheduled payments or obligations of the consumer; or

(e) a transaction of a class defined by rule of the Administrator as not requiring for the protection of the consumer his right to refinance as provided in this section.

§ 3.309. [Referral Sales and Leases]

With respect to a consumer credit sale or consumer lease, the seller or lessor may not give or offer to give a rebate or discount or otherwise pay or offer to pay value to the consumer as an inducement for a sale or lease for the consumer giving to the seller or lessor the names of prospective buyers or lessees, or otherwise aiding the seller or lessor in making a sale or lease to another person, if the earning of the rebate, discount or other value is contingent upon the occurrence of an event after the time the consumer agrees to buy or lease. If a consumer is induced by a violation of this section to enter into a consumer credit sale or consumer lease, the agreement is unenforceable by the seller or lessor and the consumer, at his option, may rescind the agreement or retain the property delivered and the benefit of any services performed, without any obligation to pay for them. A sale or lease that would be a referral sale or lease if credit were extended by the seller or lessor is nonetheless so because the property or services are paid for in whole or in part by use of a credit card or by a consumer loan with respect to which the lender is subject to claims and defenses arising from the sale or lease (Section 3.405), and the consumer has the same rights against the card issuer or lender that he has against the seller or lessor under this section.

Comments

1. The typical referral sale scheme which would be barred by this section is one in which the seller, before closing the sale, offers to reduce the price by $25 for every name of a person the buyer supplies who will agree to buy from the seller. The seller may be able to make an inflated price tag much more palatable to a buyer if he can convince the buyer that the referral plan will greatly reduce the amount he will actually have to pay. The buyer may not realize until later that his friends whose names he submitted are not as gullible as he and that he is bound to pay the original balance of the contract price.

2. The evil this section is aimed at is the raising of expectations in a buyer of benefits to accrue to him from events which are to occur in the future. This provision has no effect on a seller's agreement to

reduce at the time of the sale the price of an item in exchange for the buyer's giving the seller a list of prospective purchasers or assisting in other ways if the price reduction is not contingent on whether the purchasers do in fact buy or on whether other events occur in the future.

3. The misuse of the referral sale scheme has been so pervasive in some segments of vendor credit that this provision, in an effort to halt these practices, not only makes agreements in violation of this section unenforceable but also allows the buyer to retain the goods sold or the benefit of services rendered with no obligation to pay for them. Alternatively, the buyer may rescind the agreement, return the goods, and recover any payment. Use of a referral scheme subjects the offending seller or lessor to a penalty under Section 5.201. Creditors cannot evade this section by the use of credit cards or consumer loans.

§ 3.401. [Restriction on Liability in Consumer Lease]

The obligation of a lessee upon expiration of a consumer lease [, except one primarily for an agricultural purpose,] may not exceed twice the average payment allocable to a monthly period under the lease. This limitation does not apply to charges for damages to the leased property or for other default.

§ 3.402. [Limitation on Default Charges]

Except for reasonable expenses incurred in realizing on a security interest, the agreement with respect to a consumer credit transaction other than a consumer lease may not provide for any charges as a result of default by the consumer except those authorized by this Act. A provision in violation of this section is unenforceable.

§ 3.403. [Card Issuer Subject to Claims and Defenses]

(1) This section neither limits the liability of nor imposes liability on a card issuer as a manufacturer, supplier, seller, or lessor of property or services sold or leased pursuant to the credit card. This section may subject a card issuer to claims and defenses of a cardholder against a seller or lessor arising from sales or leases made pursuant to the credit card.

(2) A card issuer is subject to claims and defenses of a cardholder against the seller or lessor arising from the sale or lease of property or services by a seller or lessor licensed, franchised, or permitted by the card issuer or a person related to the card issuer to do business under the trade name or designation of the card issuer or a person related to the card issuer, to the extent of the original amount owing to the card issuer with respect to the sale or lease of the property or services as to which the claim or defense arose.

(3) Except as otherwise provided in this section, a card issuer, including a lender credit card issuer, is subject to all claims and defenses of a cardholder against the seller or lessor arising from the sale or lease of property or services pursuant to the credit card:

(a) if the original amount owing to the card issuer with respect to the sale or lease of the property or services as to which the claim or defense arose exceeds $50;

(b) if the residence of the cardholder and the place where the sale or lease occurred are [in the same state or] within 100 miles of each other;

(c) if the cardholder has made a good faith attempt to obtain satisfaction from the seller or lessor with respect to the claim or defense; and

(d) to the extent of the amount owing to the card issuer with respect to the sale or lease of the property or services as to which the claim or defense arose at the time the card issuer has notice of the claim or defense. Notice of the claim or defense may be given before the attempt specified in paragraph (c). Oral notice is effective unless the card issuer requests written confirmation when or promptly after oral notice is given and the cardholder fails to give the card issuer written confirmation within the period of time, not less than 14 days, stated to the cardholder when written confirmation is requested.

(4) For the purpose of determining the amount owing to the card issuer with respect to a sale or lease upon an open-end credit account, payments received for the account are deemed to have been applied first to the payment of finance charges in the order of their entry to the account and then to the payment of debts in the order in which the entries of the debts are made to the account.

(5) An agreement may not limit or waive the claims or defenses of a cardholder under this section.

Comments

1. The policies stated in Sections 3.307 and 3.404 of abolition of the holder in due course doctrine could be thwarted if the parties could deprive consumers of their claims and defenses merely by recasting assigned paper transactions into credit card transactions. Thus subsection (3) subjects credit card issuers to consumer claims and defenses in those transactions in which the credit card is more likely to be used as a true credit device (sales or leases in excess of $50) and in which the great volume of credit card use takes place (sales or leases [within the consumer's state of residence or] within 100 miles of the residence). For a discussion of the amount of the debt owing against which the claim or defense can be asserted, see Comment 2 to Section 3.404.

2. The first sentence of subsection (1) recognizes that some credit card issuers (*e.g.*, the major retail chains) are themselves the sellers or lessors of products or services, and their liability as sellers or lessors is in no way affected by their status as credit card issuers. Subsection (2) provides that when the card issuer (*e.g.*, oil distributors), allows others to sell products while operating under the issuer's name, the card issuer should be liable to the full amount of the credit extended in the sale as the financer of the transaction but should bear no further liability for products defects or the like merely because the sale was made pursuant to its credit card. If such a card issuer was in fact the manufacturer or processor of the defective products sold pursuant to its credit card by its franchised dealer, then the case would fall within the first sentence of subsection (1) and the presence of the credit card would be irrelevant to the manufacturer's or processor's liability. Subsection (3) imposes liability on the card issuer as described in Comment 1 because of the card issuer's status as the financer of the sale or lease transaction made pursuant to its card. See the second sentence of subsection (1).

§ 3.404. [Assignee Subject to Claims and Defenses]

(1) With respect to a consumer credit sale or consumer lease [, except one primarily for an agricultural purpose], an assignee of the rights of the seller or lessor is subject to all claims and defenses of the consumer against the seller or lessor arising from the sale or lease of property or services, notwithstanding that the assignee is a holder in due course of a negotiable instrument issued in violation of the provisions prohibiting certain negotiable instruments (Section 3.307).

(2) A claim or defense of a consumer specified in subsection (1) may be asserted against the assignee under this section only if the consumer has made a good faith attempt to obtain satisfaction from the seller or lessor with respect to the claim or defense and then only to the extent of the amount owing to the assignee with respect to the sale or lease of the property or services as to which the claim or defense arose at the time the assignee has notice of the claim or defense. Notice of the claim or defense may be given before the attempt specified in this subsection. Oral notice is effective unless the assignee requests written confirmation when or promptly after oral notice is given and the consumer fails to give the assignee written confirmation within the period of time, not less than 14 days, stated to the consumer when written confirmation is requested.

(3) For the purpose of determining the amount owing to the assignee with respect to the sale or lease:

(a) payments received by the assignee after the consolidation of two or more consumer credit sales, except pursuant to open-end credit, are deemed to have been applied first to the payment of the sales first made; if the sales consolidated arose from sales made on the same day, payments are deemed to have been applied first to the smallest sale; and

(b) payments received for an open-end credit account are deemed to have been applied first to the payment of finance charges in the order of their entry to the account and then to the payment of debts in the order in which the entries of the debts are made to the account.

(4) An agreement may not limit or waive the claims or defenses of a consumer under this section.

Comments

1. This section codifies a growing body of case law under UCC Section 9–206 to the effect that assignees take consumer paper subject to consumer claims and defenses. This section explicitly provides for preservation of consumer defenses even though the assignee is a holder in due course (subsection (1)) or the consumer has purported to waive his claims and defenses as against the assignee (subsection (4)). The policy justifications for the section are to protect the consumer from the harshness of the holder in due course doctrine as well as to encourage financial institutions taking assignments of consumer paper to use discretion in dealing with sellers and lessors whose transactions give rise to an unusual percentage of consumer complaints. See Section 3.307.

2. The consumer, upon making a good faith attempt to obtain satisfaction from his seller or lessor, can assert his claim or defense against the assignee to the extent of the amount still owing to the assignee at the time the assignee learns of the claim or defense. If the assignee knows of the defense before any payments are made to him, the consumer can raise his claim or defense to the full amount of the assigned debt. Orderly procedures will necessitate some written record on the part of the assignee of the consumer's notification regarding his claim or defense, but the consumer ought to be able to rely on having given oral notification unless the assignee requests written confirmation. Hence, the assignee has the option of making his own written record upon receiving oral notice from the consumer or of requesting written notice from the consumer and allowing 14 days for the consumer to send his written confirmation. Subsection (3) uses the same tests for determining the amount owing on a debt as are used in Section 3.303.

§ 3.405. [Lender Subject to Claims and Defenses Arising From Sales and Leases]

(1) A lender, except the issuer of a lender credit card, who, with respect to a particular transaction, makes a consumer loan to enable a consumer to buy or lease from a particular seller or lessor property or services [, except primarily for an agricultural purpose,] is subject to all claims and defenses of the consumer against the seller or lessor arising from that sale or lease of the property or services if:

(a) the lender knows that the seller or lessor arranged for the extension of credit by the lender for a commission, brokerage, or referral fee;

(b) the lender is a person related to the seller or lessor, unless the relationship is remote or is not a factor in the transaction;

(c) the seller or lessor guarantees the loan or otherwise assumes the risk of loss by the lender upon the loan;

(d) the lender directly supplies the seller or lessor with the contract document used by the consumer to evidence the loan, and the seller or lessor has knowledge of the credit terms and participates in preparation of the document;

(e) the loan is conditioned upon the consumer's purchase or lease of the property or services from the particular seller or lessor, but the lender's payment of proceeds of the loan to the seller or lessor does not in itself establish that the loan was so conditioned; or

(f) the lender, before he makes the consumer loan, has knowledge or, from his course of dealing with the particular seller or lessor or his records, notice of substantial complaints by other buyers or lessees of the particular seller's or lessor's failure or refusal to perform his contracts with them and of the particular seller's or lessor's failure to remedy his defaults within a reasonable time after notice to him of the complaints.

(2) A claim or defense of a consumer specified in subsection (1) may be asserted against the lender under this section only if the consumer has made a good faith attempt to obtain satisfaction

from the seller or lessor with respect to the claim or defense and then only to the extent of the amount owing to the lender with respect to the sale or lease of the property or services as to which the claim or defense arose at the time the lender has notice of the claim or defense. Notice of the claim or defense may be given before the attempt specified in this subsection. Oral notice is effective unless the lender requests written confirmation when or promptly after oral notice is given and the consumer fails to give the lender written confirmation within the period of time, not less than 14 days, stated to the consumer when written confirmation is requested.

(3) For the purpose of determining the amount owing to the lender with respect to the sale or lease:

(a) payments received by the lender after consolidation of two or more consumer loans, except pursuant to open-end credit, are deemed to have been applied first to the payment of the loans first made; if the loans consolidated arose from loans made on the same day, payments are deemed to have been applied first to the smallest loan; and

(b) payments received for an open-end credit account are deemed to have been applied first to the payment of finance charges in the order of their entry to the account and then to the payment of debts in the order in which the entries of the debts are made to the account.

(4) An agreement may not limit or waive the claims or defenses of a consumer under this section.

Comments

1. This section extends this Act's policy of preserving consumer claims and defenses to direct loan cases in those situations in which the relationship between the seller or lessor and the lender justifies allowing the consumer to raise claims or defenses against the lender. The requisite relationship exists when the seller or lessor arranges for the extension of credit in paragraphs (a) and (d) of subsection (1) within the meaning of Regulation Z Section 226.2(f), is related to the lender in paragraph (b), or guarantees the loan in paragraph (c), and in cases in which the lender conditions the loan on the purchase or lease from a particular seller or lessor in paragraph (e), or knows before he makes the loan of a history of consumer complaints about the seller or lessor in paragraph (f).

2. For a discussion of the amount of the debt owing against which the claim or defense can be asserted under subsections (2) and (3), see Comment 2 to Section 3.404.

§ 3.501. [Definition: "Home Solicitation Sale"]

"Home solicitation sale" means a consumer credit sale of goods or services, except primarily for an agricultural purpose, in which the seller or a person acting for him personally solicits the sale, and the buyer's agreement or offer to purchase is given to the seller or a person acting from him, at a residence. It does not include a sale made pursuant to a pre-existing open-end credit account with the seller or pursuant to prior negotiations between the parties at a business establishment at a fixed location where goods or services are offered or exhibited for sale, a transaction conducted and consummated entirely by mail or telephone, or a sale which is subject to the provisions of the Federal Truth in Lending Act on the consumer's right to rescind certain transactions. A sale that would be a home solicitation sale if credit were extended by the seller is nonetheless so because the goods or services are paid for in whole or in part by use of a credit card or by a consumer loan with respect to which the lender is subject to claims and defenses arising from the sale (Section 3.405), and the buyer has the same rights against the card issuer or lender that he has against the seller under this Part.

Comments

1. The Act singles out for special treatment consumer credit sales in which the buyer's order is given to the seller at a residence. An underlying consideration for Part 5 is the belief that in a significant proportion of such sales the consumer is induced to sign a sales contract by high pressure techniques. The Act recognizes that many buyers in such cases may be unwilling parties to the transaction and gives to them a limited right to cancel the sale. Section 3.502. The right of cancellation applies to "home solicitation sales."

2. The definition of "home solicitation sales" differentiates between those types of transactions which have been the subject of particular abuse and those which have not. Although high pressure salesmanship can be practiced anywhere, the underlying theory of Section 3.501 is that the sale in the home is particularly susceptible to such methods. Two elements are required to bring a transaction within the definition. First, there must be personal solicitation at a residence. Second, the act of the buyer in binding himself by agreeing or offering to purchase, must also take place at a residence. The phrase "at a residence" rather than "in a residence" is used to prevent avoidance of the Act by the expedient of having the buyer sign the contract outside of, but in the immediate vicinity of, the home.

3. Sellers who sell by means of solicitation in the home can avoid the application of Part 5 [Section 3.501 et seq.] by having the contract or offer to purchase signed by the buyer at the office of the seller or at some place other than a residence. If the buyer must go to the seller's office or some other place to sign the contract or offer there is less likelihood that he is acting because of undue pressure by the seller. Similarly, where the buyer has already established a prior relationship with the seller by having a pre-existing open-end account or by having previously negotiated with the seller with respect to the sale at the seller's business establishment the likelihood of coercion of the buyer is substantially less. This Part does not apply in these cases.

4. Sellers may not avoid operation of this Part by permitting consumers to buy by using credit cards or by using loan proceeds provided by the seller or obtained through loans arranged by the seller or with respect to which the seller and lender share one of the other relationships described by Section 3.405.

5. A seller subject to this Part may also be subject to the FTC Regulation on Cooling Off Period for Door-to-Door Sales. In the event of direct inconsistency between that Regulation and this Act, that Regulation prevails. Subsection (2) of Section 3.503 provides that the seller complies with this Act if he uses the notice of cancellation prescribed by that Regulation. With regard to other areas in which FTC Regulation overlaps with this Act, the Administrator by rule (Section 6.104(1)(e)) may prescribe the compliance required by the seller under this Act in relation to that Regulation.

§ 3.502. [Buyer's Right to Cancel]

(1) Except as provided in subsection (5), in addition to any right otherwise to revoke an offer, the buyer may cancel a home solicitation sale until midnight of the third business day after the day on which the buyer signs an agreement or offer to purchase which complies with this Part.

(2) Cancellation occurs when the buyer gives written notice of cancellation to the seller at the address stated in the agreement or offer to purchase.

(3) Notice of cancellation, if given by mail, is given when it is properly addressed with postage prepaid and deposited in a mailbox.

(4) Notice of cancellation given by the buyer need not take a particular form and is sufficient if it indicates by any form of written expression the intention of the buyer not to be bound by the home solicitation sale.

(5) The buyer may not cancel a home solicitation sale if, by a separate dated and signed statement that is not as to its material provisions a printed form and describes an emergency requiring immediate remedy, the buyer requests the seller to provide goods or services without delay in order to safeguard the health, safety, or welfare of natural persons or to prevent damage to property the buyer owns or for which he is responsible, and

(a) the seller in good faith makes a substantial beginning of performance of the contract before the buyer gives notice of cancellation, and

(b) in the case of goods, they cannot be returned to the seller in substantially as good condition as when received by the buyer.

Comments

1. The buyer has a right to cancel a home solicitation sale pursuant to this section. The notice of cancellation must be in writing, given to the seller at the address stated in the agreement signed by the

buyer, and given prior to midnight of the third business day after the day the buyer signs an agreement or offer to purchase which complies with Section 3.503. These are the only formal requirements of the Act with respect to the buyer's cancellation.

2. Although the Act does not require that a notice of cancellation be mailed it is assumed that this will be the normal method of cancellation. Notice of cancellation is given at the time of mailing. The risk of non-receipt of a mailed notice of cancellation is placed on the seller, but the buyer has the burden of proving that the notice was properly mailed.

3. Goods and services are frequently sold on credit to a buyer at his home because of an emergency. Common examples are emergency repairs to broken water pipes, furnaces, appliances and the like. Since such transactions may come within the definition of home solicitation sales, sellers may be reluctant to perform services or deliver goods before expiration of the 3-day cancellation period. Application of the right of cancellation to emergency situations would have the undesirable effect of seriously deterring credit sellers from performing in time to deal with emergencies. Subsection (5) therefore provides that the buyer may not cancel a sale if the stated conditions are met. A portion of subsection (5) is derived from Regulation Z Section 226.9(e).

4. The right to cancel provided by Section 3.502 is not exclusive. It in no way affects the right that the buyer may have independent of the Act to revoke an offer to purchase which has not been accepted by the seller, or to rescind because of fraud, duress, breach of warranty, or other causes, or under the Federal Truth in Lending Act.

§ 3.503. [Form of Agreement or Offer; Statement of Buyer's Rights]

(1) In a home solicitation sale, unless the buyer requests the seller to provide goods or services without delay in an emergency (subsection (5) of Section 3.502), the seller shall present to the buyer and obtain his signature to a written agreement or offer to purchase that designates as the date of the transaction the date on which the buyer actually signs and contains a statement of the buyer's rights that complies with subsection (2). A copy of any writing required by this subsection to be signed by the buyer, completed at least as to the date of the transaction and the name and mailing address of the seller, shall be given to the buyer at the time he signs the writing.

(2) The statement shall either:

(a) comply with any notice of cancellation or similar requirement of any trade regulation rule of the Federal Trade Commission which by its terms applies to the home solicitation sale; or

(b) appear under the conspicuous caption: "BUYER'S RIGHT TO CANCEL," and read as follows: "If you decide you do not want the goods or services, you may cancel this agreement by mailing a notice to the seller. The notice must say that you do not want the goods or services and must be mailed before midnight of the third business day after you sign this agreement. The notice must be mailed to:

_________________________________(insert name & mailing address of seller)."

(3) Until the seller has complied with this section the buyer may cancel the home solicitation sale by notifying the seller in any manner and by any means of his intention to cancel.

§ 3.504. [Restoration of Down Payment]

(1) Within ten days after a notice of cancellation has been received by the seller or an offer to purchase has been otherwise revoked, the seller shall tender to the buyer any payments made by the buyer, any note or other evidence of indebtedness, and any goods traded in. A provision permitting the seller to keep all or any part of any goods traded in, payment, note, or evidence of indebtedness is in violation of this section and unenforceable.

(2) If the down payment includes goods traded in, the goods shall be tendered in substantially as good condition as when received by the seller. If the seller fails to tender the goods as provided by

this section, the buyer may elect to recover an amount equal to the trade-in allowance stated in the agreement.

(3) Until the seller has complied with the obligations imposed by this section the buyer may retain possession of goods delivered to him by the seller and has a lien on the goods in his possession or control for any recovery to which he is entitled.

§ 3.505. [Duty of Buyer; No Compensation for Services Before Cancellation]

(1) Except as provided by the provisions on retention of goods by the buyer (subsection (3) of Section 3.504), and allowing for ordinary wear and tear or consumption of the goods contemplated by the transaction, within a reasonable time after a home solicitation sale has been cancelled or an offer to purchase revoked, the buyer upon demand shall tender to the seller any goods delivered by the seller pursuant to the sale, but he is not obligated to tender at any place other than his residence. If the seller fails to demand possession of goods within a reasonable time after cancellation or revocation, the goods become the property of the buyer without obligation to pay for them. For the purpose of this section, a reasonable time is presumed to be 40 days.

(2) The buyer shall take reasonable care of the goods in his possession before cancellation or revocation and for a reasonable time thereafter, during which time the goods are otherwise at the seller's risk.

(3) If a home solicitation sale is cancelled, the seller is not entitled to compensation for any services he performed pursuant to it.

ARTICLE 4. INSURANCE

Table of Sections

Sec.

---

§ 4.101. [Short Title]

This Article shall be known and may be cited as Uniform Consumer Credit Code—Insurance.

§ 4.102. [Scope [; Relation to Credit Insurance Act; Applicability to Parties]]

[(1)] This Article applies to insurance provided or to be provided in relation to a consumer credit transaction.

[(2) This Article supplements and does not repeal the Credit Insurance Act but to the extent of inconsistency between this Act and the Credit Insurance Act this Act controls. The provisions of this Act concerning administrative controls, liabilities, and penalties do not apply to persons acting as insurers, and the similar provisions of the Credit Insurance Act do not apply to creditors and debtors.]

§ 4.103. [Definition[s]: "Consumer Credit Insurance" [; "Credit Insurance Act"]]

In this Act:

[(1)] "Consumer credit insurance" means insurance, except insurance on property, by which the satisfaction of debt in whole or in part is a benefit provided, but does not include

(a) insurance provided in relation to a consumer credit transaction in which a payment is scheduled more than ten years after the extension of credit;

(b) insurance issued by an insurer as an isolated transaction not related to an agreement or plan for insuring consumers of or from the creditor; or

(c) insurance indemnifying the creditor against loss due to the consumer's default.

[(2) "Credit Insurance Act" means [NAIC Model Act, or any similar statute].]

§ 4.104. [Creditor's Provision of and Charge for Insurance; Excess Amount of Charge]

(1) Except as otherwise provided in this Article and subject to the provisions on additional charges (Section 2.501) and maximum finance charges (Parts 2 and 4 of Article 2), a creditor may agree to provide insurance, and may contract for and receive a charge for insurance separate from and in addition to other charges. A creditor need not make a separate charge for insurance provided or required by him. This Act does not authorize the issuance of the insurance prohibited under any statute, or rule thereunder, governing the business of insurance.

(2) The excess amount of a charge for insurance provided for in agreements in violation of this Article is an excess charge for purposes of the provisions of the Article on Remedies and Penalties (Article 5) as to effect of violations on rights of parties (Section 5.201) and of the provisions of the Article on Administration (Article 6) as to civil actions by the Administrator (Section 6.113).

§ 4.105. [Conditions Applying to Insurance to Be Provided by Creditor]

If a creditor agrees with a consumer to provide insurance:

(1) the insurance shall be evidenced by an individual policy or certificate of insurance delivered to the consumer, or mailed to him at his address as stated by him, within 30 days after the term of the insurance commences under the agreement between the creditor and consumer, or the creditor shall promptly notify the consumer of any failure or delay in providing the insurance; and

(2) the creditor shall pay to the consumer or his estate all proceeds of consumer credit or property insurance received by the creditor in excess of the amount to which the creditor is entitled within ten days after receipt by the creditor of the proceeds.

§ 4.106. [Unconscionability]

(1) In applying the provisions of this Act on unconscionability (Sections 5.108 and 6.111) to a separate charge for insurance, consideration shall be given, among other factors, to:

(a) potential benefits to the consumer including the satisfaction of his obligations;

(b) the creditor's need for the protection provided by the insurance; and

(c) the relation between the amount and terms of credit granted and the insurance benefits provided.

(2) If consumer credit insurance otherwise complies with this Article and other applicable law, neither the amount nor the term of the insurance nor the amount of a charge therefor is in itself unconscionable.

§ 4.107. [Maximum Charge by Creditor for Insurance]

(1) Except as provided in subsection (2), if a creditor contracts for or receives a separate charge for insurance, the amount charged to the consumer for the insurance may not exceed the premium to be charged by the insurer, as computed at the time the charge to the consumer is determined, conforming to any rate filings required by law and made by the insurer with the [Commissioner] of Insurance.

(2) A creditor who provides consumer credit insurance in relation to open-end credit may calculate the charge to the consumer in each billing cycle by applying the current premium rate to the balance in the manner permitted with respect to finance charges by the provisions on finance charge for consumer credit sales pursuant to open-end credit (Section 2.202).

§ 4.108. [Refund Required; Amount]

(1) Upon prepayment in full of a consumer credit transaction other than a consumer lease by the proceeds of consumer credit insurance, the consumer or his estate is entitled to a refund of any portion of a separate charge for insurance which by reason of prepayment is retained by the creditor or returned to him by the insurer, unless the charge was computed from time to time on the basis of the balances of the consumer's account.

(2) This Article does not require a creditor to grant a refund to the consumer if all refunds due to him under this Article amount to less than $1 and, except as provided in subsection (1), does not require the creditor to account to the consumer for any portion of a separate charge for insurance because:

(a) the insurance is terminated by performance of the insurer's obligation;

(b) the creditor pays or accounts for premiums to the insurer in amounts and at times determined by the agreement between them; or

(c) the creditor receives directly or indirectly under any policy of insurance a gain or advantage not prohibited by law.

(3) Except as provided in subsection (2), the creditor shall promptly make or cause to be made an appropriate refund to the consumer with respect to any separate charge made to him for insurance if:

(a) the insurance is not provided or is provided for a shorter term than that for which the charge to the consumer for insurance was computed; or

(b) the insurance terminates before the end of the term for which it was written because of prepayment in full or otherwise.

(4) A refund required by subsection (3) is appropriate as to amount if it is computed according to a method prescribed or approved by the [Commissioner] of Insurance or a formula filed by the insurer with the [Commissioner] of Insurance at least 30 days before the consumer's right to a refund becomes determinable, unless the method or formula is employed after the [Commissioner] of Insurance notifies the insurer that he disapproves it.

§ 4.109. [Existing Insurance; Choice of Insurer]

If a creditor requires insurance, upon notice to him the consumer has the option of providing the required insurance through an existing policy of insurance owned or controlled by the consumer, or through a policy to be obtained and paid for by the consumer, but the creditor for reasonable cause may decline the insurance provided by the consumer.

§ 4.110. [Charge for Insurance in Connection With a Deferral, Refinancing, or Consolidation; Duplicate Charges]

(1) A creditor may not contract for or receive a separate charge for insurance in connection with a deferral (Section 2.503), a refinancing (Section 2.504), or a consolidation (Section 2.505), unless:

(a) the consumer agrees at or before the time of the deferral, refinancing, or consolidation that the charge may be made;

(b) the consumer is or is to be provided with insurance for an amount or a term, or insurance of a kind, in addition to that to which he would have been entitled had there been no deferral, refinancing, or consolidation;

(c) the consumer receives a refund or credit on account of any unexpired term of existing insurance in the amount required if the insurance were terminated (Section 4.108); and

(d) the charge does not exceed the amount permitted by this Article (Section 4.107).

(2) A creditor may not contract for or receive a separate charge for insurance which duplicates insurance with respect to which the creditor has previously contracted for or received a separate charge.

§ 4.111. [Cooperation Between Administrator and [Commissioner] of Insurance]

The Administrator and the [Commissioner] of Insurance shall consult and assist one another in maintaining compliance with this Article. They may jointly pursue investigations, prosecute suits, and take other official action they deem appropriate if either of them is otherwise empowered to take the action. If the Administrator is informed of a violation or suspected violation by an insurer of this Article, or of the insurance laws, rules, and regulations of this State, he shall inform the [Commissioner] of Insurance of the circumstances.

§ 4.112. [Administrative Action of [Commissioner] of Insurance]

[(1) To the extent that his responsibility under this Article requires, the [Commissioner] of Insurance shall adopt rules with respect to insurers, and with respect to refunds (Section 4.108), forms, schedules of premium rates and charges (Section 4.203), and his approval or disapproval thereof and, in case of violation, may make an order for compliance.

(2)] [The State administrative procedure act] [Each provision of the Part on Administrative Procedure and Judicial Review (Part 4) of the Article on Administration (Article 6) that applies to and governs administrative action taken by the Administrator also] applies to and governs all administrative action taken by the [Commissioner] of Insurance pursuant to this section.

§ 4.201. [Term of Insurance]

(1) Consumer credit insurance provided by a creditor may be subject to the furnishing of evidence of insurability satisfactory to the insurer. Whether or not the evidence is required, the term of the insurance shall commence no later than when the consumer becomes obligated to the creditor or when the consumer applies for the insurance, whichever is later, except as follows:

(a) if any required evidence of insurability is not furnished until more than 30 days after the term otherwise would commence, the term may commence on the date the insurer determines the evidence to be satisfactory; or

(b) if the creditor provides insurance not previously provided covering debts previously created, the term may commence on the effective date of the policy.

(2) The originally scheduled term of consumer credit insurance shall extend at least until the due date of the last scheduled payment of the debt, except as follows:

(a) if the insurance relates to an open-end credit account, the term need extend only until payment of the debt under the account and may be sooner terminated after at least 30 days' notice to the consumer; or

(b) if the consumer is informed in writing that the insurance will be written for a specified shorter time, the term need extend only until the end of the specified time.

(3) The term of consumer credit insurance may not extend more than 15 days after the originally scheduled due date of the last scheduled payment of the debt, unless it is extended without additional cost to the consumer or as an incident to a deferral, refinancing, or consolidation.

§ 4.202. [Amount of Insurance]

(1) Except as provided in subsection (2):

(a) in the case of consumer credit insurance providing life coverage, the amount of insurance may not initially exceed the debt and, if the debt is payable in instalments, may not exceed at any time the greater of the scheduled or actual amount of the debt; or

(b) in the case of any other consumer credit insurance, the total amount of periodic benefits payable may not exceed the total of scheduled unpaid instalments of the debt, and the amount of any periodic benefit may not exceed the original amount of debt divided by the number of periodic instalments in which it is payable.

(2) If consumer credit insurance is provided in connection with an open-end credit account, the amounts payable as insurance benefits may be reasonably commensurate with the amount of debt as it exists from time to time. If consumer credit insurance is provided in connection with a commitment to grant credit in the future, the amounts payable as insurance benefits may be reasonably commensurate with the total from time to time of the amount of debt and the amount of the commitment. If the debt or the commitment is primarily for an agricultural purpose and there is no regular schedule of payments, the amounts payable as insurance benefits may equal the total of the initial amount of debt and the amount of the commitment.

§ 4.203. [Filing and Approval of Rates and Forms]

(1) A creditor may not use a form or a schedule of premium rates or charges, the filing of which is required by this section, if the [Commissioner] of Insurance has disapproved the form or schedule and has notified the insurer of his disapproval. A creditor may not use a form or schedule unless:

(a) the form or schedule has been on file with the [Commissioner] of Insurance for 30 days, or has earlier been approved by him; and

(b) the insurer has complied with this section with respect to the insurance.

(2) Except as provided in subsection (3), all policies, certificates of insurance, notices of proposed insurance, applications for insurance, endorsements, and riders relating to consumer credit insurance delivered or issued for delivery in this State, and the schedules of premium rates or charges pertaining thereto, shall be filed by the insurer with the [Commissioner] of Insurance. Within 30 days after the filing of any form or schedule, he shall disapprove it if the premium rates or charges are unreasonable in relation to the benefits provided under the form, or if the form contains provisions which are unjust,

unfair, inequitable, or deceptive, encourage misrepresentation of the coverage, or are contrary to any provision of the [Insurance Code] or of any rule or regulation promulgated thereunder.

(3) If a group policy of consumer credit insurance has been delivered in another state, the forms to be filed by the insurer with the [Commissioner] of Insurance are the group certificates and notices of proposed insurance. He shall approve them if:

(a) they provide the information that would be required if the group policy were delivered in this State; and

(b) the applicable premium rates or charges do not exceed those established by his rules or regulations.

§ 4.301. [Property Insurance]

(1) A creditor may not contract for or receive a separate charge for insurance against loss of or damage to property, unless:

(a) the insurance covers a substantial risk of loss of or damage to property related to the credit transaction;

(b) the amount, terms, and conditions of the insurance are reasonable in relation to the character and value of the property insured or to be insured; and

(c) the term of the insurance is reasonable in relation to the terms of credit.

(2) The term of the insurance is reasonable if it is customary and does not extend substantially beyond a scheduled maturity.

(3) With respect to a transaction, except pursuant to open-end credit, a creditor may not contract for or receive a separate charge for insurance against loss of or damage to property, unless the amount financed exclusive of charges for the insurance is $300 or more and the value of the property is $300 or more.

(4) With respect to a transaction pursuant to open-end credit, the Administrator may adopt rules consistent with the principles set out in subsections (1) and (2) prescribing whether, and the conditions under which, a creditor may contract for or receive a separate charge for insurance against loss of or damage to property.

(5) The amounts of $300 in subsection (3) are subject to change pursuant to the provisions on adjustment of dollar amounts (Section 1.106).

§ 4.302. [Insurance on Creditor's Interest Only]

If a creditor contracts for or receives a separate charge for insurance against loss of or damage to property, the risk of loss or damage not willfully caused by the consumer is on the consumer only to the extent of any deficiency in the effective coverage of the insurance, even though the insurance covers only the interest of the creditor.

§ 4.303. [Liability Insurance]

A creditor may not contract for or receive a separate charge for insurance against liability unless the insurance covers a substantial risk of liability arising out of the ownership or use of property related to the credit transaction.

§ 4.304. [Cancellation by Creditor]

This section does not apply to an insurance premium loan. A creditor may request cancellation of a policy of property or liability insurance only after the consumer's default or in accordance with a written authorization by the consumer. In either case the cancellation does not take effect until written notice is delivered to the consumer or mailed to him at his address as stated by him. The notice shall state that the policy may be cancelled on a date not less than ten days after the notice is delivered, or, if the notice is mailed, not less than 13 days after it is mailed. A cancellation may not take effect until those times.

ARTICLE 5. REMEDIES AND PENALTIES

Table of Sections

---

§ 5.101. [Short Title]

This Article shall be known and may be cited as Uniform Consumer Credit Code—Remedies and Penalties.

§ 5.102. [Scope]

This Part applies to actions or other proceedings to enforce rights arising from consumer credit transactions, to extortionate extensions of credit (Section 5.107), and to unconscionability (Section 5.108).

§ 5.103. [Restrictions on Deficiency Judgments]

(1) This section applies to a deficiency on a consumer credit sale of goods or services and on a consumer loan in which the lender is subject to claims and defenses arising from sales and leases (Section 3.405). A consumer is not liable for a deficiency unless the creditor had disposed of the goods in good faith and in a commercially reasonable manner.

(2) If the seller repossesses or voluntarily accepts surrender of goods that were the subject of the sale and in which he has a security interest, the consumer is not personally liable to the seller for the unpaid balance of the debt arising from the sale of a commercial unit of goods of which the cash sale price was $1,750 or less, and the seller is not obligated to resell the collateral unless the consumer

has paid 60 per cent or more of the cash price and has not signed after default a statement renouncing his rights in the collateral.

(3) If the seller repossesses or voluntarily accepts surrender of goods that were not the subject of the sale but in which he has a security interest to secure a debt arising from a sale of goods or services or a combined sale of goods and services and the cash price of the sale was $1,750 or less, the consumer is not personally liable to the seller for the unpaid balance of the debt arising from the sale, and the seller's duty to dispose of the collateral is governed by the provisions on disposition of collateral (Part 5 of Article 9) of the Uniform Commercial Code.

(4) If the lender takes possession or voluntarily accepts surrender of goods in which he has a purchase money security interest to secure a debt arising from a consumer loan in which the lender is subject to claims and defenses arising from sales and leases (Section 3.405) and the net proceeds of the loan paid to or for the benefit of the consumer were $1,750 or less, the consumer is not personally liable to the lender for the unpaid balance of the debt arising from that loan and the lender's duty to dispose of the collateral is governed by the provisions on disposition of collateral (Part 5 of Article 9) of the Uniform Commercial Code.

(5) For the purpose of determining the unpaid balance of consolidated debts or debts pursuant to open-end credit, the allocation of payments to a debt shall be determined in the same manner as provided for determining the amount of debt secured by various security interests (Section 3.303).

(6) The consumer may be held liable in damages to the creditor if the consumer has wrongfully damaged the collateral or if, after default and demand, the consumer has wrongfully failed to make the collateral available to the creditor.

(7) If the creditor elects to bring an action against the consumer for a debt arising from a consumer credit sale of goods or services or from a consumer loan in which the lender is subject to claims and defenses arising from sales and leases (Section 3.405), when under this section he would not be entitled to a deficiency judgment if he took possession of the collateral, and obtains judgment:

(a) he may not take possession of the collateral, and

(b) the collateral is not subject to levy or sale on execution or similar proceedings pursuant to the judgment.

(8) The amounts of $1,750 in subsections (2), (3) and (4) are subject to change pursuant to the provisions on adjustment of dollar amounts (Section 1.106).

§ 5.104. [No Garnishment Before Judgment]

Before entry of judgment in an action against a consumer for debt arising from a consumer credit transaction, the creditor may not attach unpaid earnings of the consumer by garnishment or like proceedings.

§ 5.105. [Limitation on Garnishment]

(1) For purposes of this Part:

(a) "disposable earnings" means that part of the earnings of an individual remaining after the deduction from those earnings of amounts required by law to be withheld; and

(b) "garnishment" means any legal or equitable procedure through which earnings of an individual are required to be withheld for payment of a debt.

(2) The maximum part of the aggregate disposable earnings of an individual for any workweek which is subjected to garnishment to enforce payment of a judgment arising from a consumer credit transaction may not exceed the lesser of:

(a) 25 per cent of his disposable earnings for that week, or

(b) the amount by which his disposable earnings for that week exceed 40 times the Federal minimum hourly wage prescribed by Section 6(a)(1) of the Fair Labor Standards Act of 1938, U.S.C. tit. 29, § 206(a)(1), in effect at the time the earnings are payable.

In case of earnings for a pay period other than a week, the Administrator shall prescribe by rule a multiple of the Federal minimum hourly wage equivalent in effect to that set forth in paragraph (b).

(3) No court may make, execute, or enforce an order or process in violation of this section.

(4) At any time after entry of a judgment in favor of a creditor in an action against a consumer for debt arising from a consumer credit transaction, the consumer may file with the court his verified application for an order exempting from garnishment pursuant to that judgment, for an appropriate period of time, a greater portion or all of his aggregate disposable earnings for a workweek or other applicable pay period than is provided for in subsection (2). He shall designate in the application the portion of his earnings not exempt from garnishment under this section and other law, the period of time for which the additional exemption is sought, describe the judgment with respect to which the application is made, and state that the designated portion as well as his earnings that are exempt by law are necessary for the maintenance of him or a family supported wholly or partly by the earnings. Upon filing a sufficient application under this subsection, the court may issue any temporary order necessary under the circumstances to stay enforcement of the judgment by garnishment, shall set a hearing on the application not less than [five] nor more than [ten] days after the date of filing of the application, and shall cause notice of the application and the hearing date to be served on the judgment creditor or his attorney of record. At the hearing, if it appears to the court that all or any portion of the earnings sought to be additionally exempt are necessary for the maintenance of the consumer or a family supported wholly or partly by the earnings of the consumer for all or any part of the time requested in the application, the court shall issue an order granting the application to that extent; otherwise it shall deny the application. The order is subject to modification or vacation upon further application of any party to it upon a showing of changed circumstances after a hearing upon notice to all interested parties.

§ 5.106. [No Discharge From Employment for Garnishment]

An employer may not discharge an employee for the reason that a creditor of the employee has subjected or attempted to subject unpaid earnings of the employee to garnishment or like proceedings directed to the employer for the purpose of paying a judgment arising from a consumer credit transaction.

§ 5.107. [Extortionate Extensions of Credit]

(1) If it is the understanding of the creditor and the consumer at the time an extension of credit is made that delay in making repayment or failure to make repayment could result in the use of violence or other criminal means to cause harm to the person, reputation, or property of any person, the repayment of the extension of credit is unenforceable through civil judicial processes against the consumer.

(2) If it is shown that an extension of credit was made at an annual rate exceeding 45 per cent calculated according to the actuarial method and that the creditor then had a reputation for the use or threat of use of violence or other criminal means to cause harm to the person, reputation, or property of any person to collect extensions of credit or to punish the non-repayment thereof, there is prima facie evidence that the extension of credit was unenforceable under subsection (1).

§ 5.108. [Unconscionability; Inducement by Unconscionable Conduct; Unconscionable Debt Collection]

(1) With respect to a transaction that is, gives rise to, or leads the debtor to believe will give rise to, a consumer credit transaction, if the court as a matter of law finds:

(a) the agreement or transaction to have been unconscionable at the time it was made, or to have been induced by unconscionable conduct, the court may refuse to enforce the agreement; or

(b) any term or part of the agreement or transaction to have been unconscionable at the time it was made, the court may refuse to enforce the agreement, enforce the remainder of the agreement without the unconscionable term or part, or so limit the application of any unconscionable term or part as to avoid any unconscionable result.

(2) With respect to a consumer credit transaction, if the court as a matter of law finds that a person has engaged in, is engaging in, or is likely to engage in unconscionable conduct in collecting a debt arising from that transaction, the court may grant an injunction and award the consumer any actual damages he has sustained.

(3) If it is claimed or appears to the court that the agreement or transaction or any term or part thereof may be unconscionable, or that a person has engaged in, is engaging in, or is likely to engage in unconscionable conduct in collecting a debt, the parties shall be afforded a reasonable opportunity to present evidence as to the setting, purpose, and effect of the agreement or transaction or term or part thereof, or of the conduct, to aid the court in making the determination.

(4) In applying subsection (1), consideration shall be given to each of the following factors, among others, as applicable:

(a) belief by the seller, lessor, or lender at the time a transaction is entered into that there is no reasonable probability of payment in full of the obligation by the consumer or debtor;

(b) in the case of a consumer credit sale or consumer lease, knowledge by the seller or lessor at the time of the sale or lease of the inability of the consumer to receive substantial benefits from the property or services sold or leased;

(c) in the case of a consumer credit sale or consumer lease, gross disparity between the price of the property or services sold or leased and the value of the property or services measured by the price at which similar property or services are readily obtainable in credit transactions by like consumers;

(d) the fact that the creditor contracted for or received separate charges for insurance with respect to a consumer credit sale or consumer loan with the effect of making the sale or loan, considered as a whole, unconscionable; and

(e) the fact that the seller, lessor, or lender has knowingly taken advantage of the inability of the consumer or debtor reasonably to protect his interests by reason of physical or mental infirmities, ignorance, illiteracy, inability to understand the language of the agreement, or similar factors.

(5) In applying subsection (2), consideration shall be given to each of the following factors, among others, as applicable:

(a) using or threatening to use force, violence, or criminal prosecution against the consumer or members of his family;

(b) communicating with the consumer or a member of his family at frequent intervals or at unusual hours or under other circumstances so that it is a reasonable inference that the primary purpose of the communication was to harass the consumer;

(c) using fraudulent, deceptive, or misleading representations such as a communication which simulates legal process or which gives the appearance of being authorized, issued, or approved by a government, governmental agency, or attorney at law when it is not, or threatening or attempting to enforce a right with knowledge or reason to know that the right does not exist;

(d) causing or threatening to cause injury to the consumer's reputation or economic status by disclosing information affecting the consumer's reputation for credit-worthiness with knowledge or reason to know that the information is false; communicating with the consumer's employer before obtaining a final judgment against the consumer, except as permitted by statute or to verify the consumer's employment; disclosing to a person, with knowledge or reason to know that the person does not have a legitimate business need for the information, or in any way prohibited by statute, information affecting the consumer's credit or other reputation; or disclosing information concerning the existence of a debt known to be disputed by the consumer without disclosing that fact; and

(e) engaging in conduct with knowledge that like conduct has been restrained or enjoined by a court in a civil action by the Administrator against any person pursuant to the provisions on injunctions against fraudulent or unconscionable agreements or conduct (Section 6.111).

(6) If in an action in which unconscionability is claimed the court finds unconscionability pursuant to subsection (1) or (2), the court shall award reasonable fees to the attorney for the consumer or debtor. If the court does not find unconscionability and the consumer or debtor claiming unconscionability has brought or maintained an action he knew to be groundless, the court shall award reasonable fees to the attorney for the party against whom the claim is made. In determining attorney's fees, the amount of the recovery on behalf of the consumer is not controlling.

(7) The remedies of this section are in addition to remedies otherwise available for the same conduct under law other than this Act, but double recovery of actual damages may not be had.

(8) For the purpose of this section, a charge or practice expressly permitted by this Act is not in itself unconscionable.

Comments

1. Subsections (1) and (3) are derived in significant part from UCC Section 2–302. Subsection (1), as does UCC Section 2–302, provides that a court can refuse to enforce or can adjust an agreement or part of an agreement that was unconscionable on its face at the time it was made. However, many agreements are not in and of themselves unconscionable according to their terms, but they would never have been entered into by a consumer if unconscionable means had not been employed to induce the consumer to agree to the contract. It would be a frustration of the policy against unconscionable contracts for a creditor to be able to utilize unconscionable acts or practices to obtain an agreement. Consequently subsection (1) also gives to the court the power to refuse to enforce an agreement if it finds as a matter of law that it was induced by unconscionable conduct. Finally, subsection (1) includes provisions for court determination of unconscionability in a transaction that a consumer is led to believe will give rise to a consumer credit transaction so that, for example, a seller cannot bind the consumer to a short term sale contract payable in a lump sum on the assurance the seller will secure financing for the consumer, and then inform the consumer financing is unavailable and keep the downpayment or goods traded in as a penalty for non-payment.

In subsection (3) the omission of the adjective "commercial" found in UCC Section 2–302 from the provision concerning the presentation of evidence as to the conduct's or contract's "setting, purpose, and effect" is deliberate. Unlike the UCC, this section is concerned only with transactions involving consumers, and the relevant standard of conduct for purposes of this section is not that which might be acceptable as between knowledgeable merchants but rather that which measures acceptable conduct on the part of a businessman toward a consumer.

2. Subsection (2) provides a consumer remedy for unconscionable conduct in the collection of consumer credit debts. In recent years, there has been much legislative activity in this area. In subjecting this type of creditor conduct to the concept of unconscionability, this section provides a more flexible device for halting multifarious activities than the specific and somewhat rigid treatment contained in other legislation, and follows the lead of Section 6.111 of this Act which affords the Administrator the means to deal with this type of practice. Indeed this section considered as a whole confers on the consumer the ability to obtain relief in basically the same situations the Administrator is authorized to seek relief under Section 6.111, although not necessarily under the same conditions, *e.g.*, no course of conduct is required. The section is not exclusive, however; subsection (7) stipulates that the remedies of this section are in addition to

remedies otherwise available for the same conduct under law other than this Act so as to preserve, for example, the developing remedy for abusive debt collection in tort.

3. This section is intended to make it possible for the courts to police conduct which is, and contracts or clauses which are found to be unconscionable. The basic test is whether, in the light of the background and setting of the market, the needs of the particular trade or case, and the condition of the particular parties to the conduct or contract, the conduct involved is, or the contract or clauses involved are so one-sided as to be unconscionable under the circumstances existing at the time the conduct occurs or is threatened or at the time of the making of the contract. The principle is one of the prevention of oppression and unfair surprise and not the disturbance of reasonable allocation of risks or reasonable advantage because of superior bargaining power or position. The particular facts involved in each case are of utmost importance since certain conduct, contracts or contractual provisions may be unconscionable in some situations but not in others. The following cases illustrate prior application of the doctrine of unconscionability: Williams v. Walker-Thomas Furn. Co., 350 F.2d 445, 121 U.S.App.D.C. 315 (1965); American Home Improvement, Inc. v. MacIver, 105 N.H. 435, 201 A.2d 886 (1964); Ellsworth Dobbs, Inc. v. Johnson, 50 N.J. 528, 236 A.2d 843 (1967); Unico v. Owen, 50 N.J. 101, 232 A.2d 405 (1967); Henningsen v. Bloomfield Motors, Inc., 32 N.J. 358, 161 A.2d 69 (1960); Frostifresh Corp. v. Reynoso, 54 Misc.2d 119, 281 N.Y.S.2d 964 (Sup.Ct., App.Term, 2d Dept.1967), rev'g in part 52 Misc.2d 26, 274 N.Y.S.2d 757 (Nassau Co.1966).

4. Subsections (4) and (5) list a number of specific factors to be considered on the issue of unconscionability. It is impossible to anticipate all of the factors and considerations which may support a conclusion of unconscionability in a given instance so the listing is not exclusive. The following are illustrative of individual transactions which would entitle a consumer to relief under this section:

Under subsection (4)(a), a sale of goods to a low income consumer without expectation of payment but with the expectation of repossessing the goods sold and reselling them at a profit;

Under subsection (4)(b), a sale to a Spanish speaking laborer-bachelor of an English language encyclopedia set, or the sale of two expensive vacuum cleaners to two poor families sharing the same apartment and one rug;

Under subsection (4)(c), a home solicitation sale of a set of cookware or flatware to a housewife for $375 in an area where a set of comparable quality is readily available on credit in stores for $125 or less;

Under subsection (4)(e), a sale of goods on terms known by the seller to be disadvantageous to the consumer where the written agreement is in English, the consumer is literate only in Spanish, the transaction was negotiated orally in Spanish by the seller's salesman, and the written agreement was neither translated nor explained to the consumer, but the mere fact a consumer has little education and cannot read or write and must sign with an "X" is not itself determinative of unconscionability;

Under subsection (5)(a) and (c), threatening that the creditor will have the consumer thrown in jail and her welfare checks stopped if the debt is not paid.

5. Since the remedies of this section are non-monetary in nature except for the ability to recover actual damages for unconscionable debt collection, subsection (6) authorizes an award of reasonable attorneys fees to the successful consumer or debtor. However, to discourage litigation seeking exculpation from merely bad bargains, provision is also made for recovery by a creditor if the court does not find unconscionability and the consumer's or debtor's action was known by the consumer or debtor to be groundless.

6. Subsection (8) prohibits a finding that a charge or practice expressly permitted by this Act is in itself unconscionable. However, even though a practice or charge is authorized by this Act, the totality of a particular creditor's conduct may show that the practice or charge is part of unconscionable conduct. Therefore, in determining unconscionability, the creditor's total conduct, including that part of his conduct which is in accordance with the provisions of this Act, may be considered.

§ 5.109. [Default]

An agreement of the parties to a consumer credit transaction with respect to default on the part of the consumer is enforceable only to the extent that:

(1) the consumer fails to make a payment as required by agreement; or

(2) the prospect of payment, performance, or realization of collateral is significantly impaired; the burden of establishing the prospect of significant impairment is on the creditor.

§ 5.110. [Notice of Consumer's Right to Cure]

(1) With respect to a consumer credit transaction, after a consumer has been in default for ten days for failure to make a required payment and has not voluntarily surrendered possession of goods that are collateral, a creditor may give the consumer the notice described in this section. A creditor gives notice to the consumer under this section when he delivers the notice to the consumer or mails the notice to him at his residence (subsection (6) of Section 1.201).

(2) Except as provided in subsection (3), the notice shall be in writing and conspicuously state: the name, address, and telephone number of the creditor to whom payment is to be made, a brief identification of the credit transaction, the consumer's right to cure the default, and the amount of payment and date by which payment must be made to cure the default. A notice in substantially the following form complies with this subsection:

(name, address, and telephone number of creditor) (account number, if any) (brief identification of credit transaction) (date) is the LAST DAY FOR PAYMENT (amount) is the AMOUNT NOW DUE

You are late in making your payment(s). If you pay the AMOUNT NOW DUE (above) by the LAST DAY FOR PAYMENT (above), you may continue with the contract as though you were not late. If you do not pay by that date, we may exercise our rights under the law.

If you are late again in making your payments, we may exercise our rights without sending you another notice like this one. If you have questions, write or telephone the creditor promptly.

(3) If the consumer credit transaction is an insurance premium loan, the notice shall conform to the requirements of subsection (2) and a notice in substantially the form specified in that subsection complies with this subsection, except for the following:

(a) in lieu of a brief identification of the credit transaction, the notice shall identify the transaction as an insurance premium loan and each insurance policy or contract that may be cancelled;

(b) in lieu of the statement in the form of notice specified in subsection (2) that the creditor may exercise his rights under the law, the statement that each policy or contract identified in the notice may be cancelled; and

(c) the last paragraph of the form of notice specified in subsection (2) shall be omitted.

§ 5.111. [Cure of Default]

(1) With respect to a consumer credit transaction, except as provided in subsection (2), after a default consisting only of the consumer's failure to make a required payment, a creditor, because of that default, may neither accelerate maturity of the unpaid balance of the obligation, nor take possession of or otherwise enforce a security interest in goods that are collateral until 20 days after a notice of the consumer's right to cure (Section 5.110) is given, nor, with respect to an insurance premium loan, give notice of cancellation as provided in subsection (4) until 13 days after a notice of the consumer's right to cure (Section 5.110) is given. Until expiration of the minimum applicable period after the notice is given, the consumer may cure all defaults consisting of a failure to make the required payment by tendering the amount of all unpaid sums due at the time of the tender, without acceleration, plus any unpaid delinquency or deferral charges. Cure restores the consumer to his rights under the agreement as though the defaults had not occurred.

(2) With respect to defaults on the same obligation other than an insurance premium loan and subject to subsection (1), after a creditor has once given a notice of consumer's right to cure (Section 5.110), this section gives the consumer no right to cure and imposes no limitation on the creditor's

right to proceed against the consumer or goods that are collateral. For the purpose of this section, in open-end credit, the obligation is the unpaid balance of the account and there is no right to cure and no limitation on the creditor's rights with respect to a default that occurs within 12 months after an earlier default as to which a creditor has given a notice of consumer's right to cure (Section 5.110).

(3) This section and the provisions on waiver, agreements to forego rights, and settlement of claims (Section 1.107) do not prohibit a consumer from voluntarily surrendering possession of goods which are collateral and the creditor from thereafter accelerating maturity of the obligation and enforcing the obligation and his security interest in the goods at any time after default.

(4) If a default on an insurance premium loan is not cured, the lender may give notice of cancellation of each insurance policy or contract to be cancelled. If given, the notice of cancellation shall be in writing and given to the insurer who issued the policy or contract and to the insured. The insurer, within two business days after receipt of the notice of cancellation together with a copy of the insurance premium loan agreement if not previously given to him, shall give any notice of cancellation required by the policy, contract, or law and, within ten business days after the effective date of the cancellation, pay to the lender any premium unearned on the policy or contract as of that effective date. Within ten business days after receipt of the unearned premium, the lender shall pay to the consumer indebted upon the insurance premium loan any excess of the unearned premium received over the amount owing by the consumer upon the insurance premium loan.

§ 5.112. [Creditor's Right to Take Possession After Default]

Upon default by a consumer with respect to a consumer credit transaction, unless the consumer voluntarily surrenders possession of the collateral to the creditor, the creditor may take possession of the collateral without judicial process only if possession can be taken without entry into a dwelling and without the use of force or other breach of the peace.

§ 5.113. [Venue]

An action by a creditor against a consumer arising from a consumer credit transaction shall be brought in the [county] of the consumer's residence (subsection (6) of Section 1.201), unless an action is brought to enforce an interest in land securing the consumer's obligation, in which case the action may be brought in the [county] in which the land or a part thereof is located. If the [county] of the consumer's residence has changed the consumer upon motion may have the action removed to the [county] of his current residence. If the residence of the consumer is not within this State, the action may be brought in the [county] in which the sale, lease, or loan was made. If the initial papers offered for filing in the action on their face show noncompliance with this section, the [clerk] shall not accept them.

§ 5.114. [Complaint; Proof]

(1) In an action brought by a creditor against a consumer arising from a consumer credit transaction, the complaint shall allege the facts of the consumer's default, the amount to which the creditor is entitled, and an indication of how that amount was determined.

(2) A default judgment may not be entered in the action in favor of the creditor unless the complaint is verified by the creditor or sworn testimony, by affidavit or otherwise, is adduced showing that the creditor is entitled to the relief demanded.

§ 5.115. [Stay of Enforcement of or Relief From Default Judgment]

At any time after entry of a default judgment in favor of a creditor and against a consumer in an action arising from a consumer credit transaction, the court which rendered the judgment, for cause including lack of jurisdiction to render the judgment, and upon motion of a party or its own motion, with notice as the court may direct, may stay enforcement of or relieve the consumer from the judgment by order upon just and equitable conditions.

§ 5.116. [Limitation on Enforcement of Security for Supervised Loan]

(1) Except as to a purchase money security interest, this section applies to a security interest in an item of goods other than a motor vehicle which (a) is possessed by a consumer, (b) is being used by him or a member of a family wholly or partly supported by him, (c) is or may be claimed to be exempt from execution on a money judgment under the laws of this State, and (d) is collateral for a supervised loan.

(2) Unless the consumer, after written notice to him of his rights under this section, voluntarily surrenders to the lender possession of any item of goods to which this section applies, the lender, without an order or process of the [ ] court, may not take possession of the items or otherwise enforce the security interest according to its terms. The notice to the consumer shall conform to any rule adopted by the Administrator.

(3) The court may order or authorize process respecting an item of goods to which this section applies only after a hearing upon notice to the consumer of the hearing and his rights at it. The notice shall be as directed by the court. The order or authorization may prescribe appropriate conditions as to payments upon the debt secured or otherwise. The court may not order or authorize process respecting the item if it finds upon the hearing both that the consumer lacks the means to pay all or part of the debt secured and that continued possession and use of the item is necessary to avoid undue hardship for the consumer or a member of a family wholly or partly supported by him.

(4) The court, upon application of the lender or the consumer and notice to the other, and after a hearing and a finding of changed circumstances, may vacate or modify an order or authorization pursuant to this section.

§ 5.201. [Effect of Violations on Rights of Parties]

(1) If a creditor has violated any provision of this Act applying to collection of an excess charge or amount or enforcement of rights (subsections (2) and (4) of Section 1.201), authority to make supervised loans (Section 2.301), restrictions on interests in land as security (Section 2.307), limitations on the schedule of payments on loan terms for supervised loans (Section 2.308), attorney's fees (Section 2.507), charges for other credit transactions (Section 2.601), disclosure with respect to consumer leases (Section 3.202), notice to consumers (Section 3.203), receipts, statements of account, and evidences of payment (Section 3.206), form of insurance premium loan agreement (Section 3.207), notice to co-signers and similar parties (Section 3.208), security in sales and leases (Section 3.301), no assignments of earnings (Section 3.305), authorizations to confess judgment (Section 3.306), certain negotiable instruments prohibited (Section 3.307), referral sales and leases (Section 3.309), limitations on default charges (Section 3.402), card issuer subject to claims and defenses (subsection (5) of Section 3.403), assignees subject to claims and defenses (subsection (4) of Section 3.404), lenders subject to claims and defenses arising from sales and leases (subsection (4) of Section 3.405), limitation on enforcement of security for supervised loan (Section 5.116), or assurance of discontinuance (Section 6.109), the consumer has a [claim for relief] [cause of action] to recover actual damages and also a right in an action other than a class action, to recover from the person violating this Act a penalty in an amount determined by the court not less than $100 nor more than $1,000. With respect to violations arising from sales or loans made pursuant to open-end credit, no action pursuant to this subsection may be brought more than two years after the violations occurred. With respect to violations arising from other consumer credit transactions, no action pursuant to this subsection may be brought more than one year after the scheduled or accelerated maturity of the debt.

(2) A consumer is not obligated to pay a charge in excess of that allowed by this Act and has a right of refund of any excess charge paid. A refund may not be made by reducing the consumer's obligation by the amount of the excess charge, unless the creditor has notified the consumer that the consumer may request a refund and the consumer has not so requested within 30 days thereafter. If the consumer has paid an amount in excess of the lawful obligation under the agreement, the consumer may recover the excess amount from the person who made the excess charge or from an assignee of

that person's rights who undertakes direct collection of payments from or enforcement of rights against consumers arising from the debt.

(3) If a creditor has contracted for or received a charge in excess of that allowed by this Act, or if a consumer is entitled to a refund and a person liable to the consumer refuses to make a refund within a reasonable time after demand, the consumer may recover from the creditor or the person liable in an action other than a class action a penalty in an amount determined by the court not less than $100 nor more than $1,000. With respect to excess charges arising from sales or loans made pursuant to open-end credit, no action pursuant to this subsection may be brought more than two years after the violation or passage of a reasonable time for refund occurs. With respect to excess charges arising from other consumer credit transactions no action pursuant to this subsection may be brought more than one year after the scheduled or accelerated maturity of the debt. For purposes of this subsection, a reasonable time is presumed to be 30 days.

(4) Except as otherwise provided, a violation of this Act does not impair rights on a debt.

(5) If an employer discharges an employee in violation of the provisions prohibiting discharge (Section 5.106), the employee within [ ] days may bring a civil action for recovery of wages lost as a result of the violation and for an order requiring reinstatement of the employee. Damages recoverable shall not exceed lost wages for six weeks.

(6) A creditor is not liable for a penalty under subsection (1) or (3) if he notifies the consumer of a violation before the creditor receives from the consumer written notice of the violation or the consumer has brought an action under this section, and the creditor corrects the violation within 45 days after notifying the consumer. If the violation consists of a prohibited agreement, giving the consumer a corrected copy of the writing containing the violation is sufficient notification and correction. If the violation consists of an excess charge, correction shall be made by an adjustment or refund. The Administrator and any official or agency of this State having supervisory authority over a supervised financial organization shall give prompt notice to a creditor of any violation discovered pursuant to an examination or investigation of the transactions, business, records, and acts of the creditor (Sections 2.305, 6.105 and 6.106).

(7) A creditor may not be held liable in an action brought under this section for a violation of this Act if the creditor shows by a preponderance of evidence that the violation was not intentional and resulted from a bona fide error notwithstanding the maintenance of procedures reasonably adapted to avoid the error.

(8) In an action in which it is found that a creditor has violated this Act, the court shall award to the consumer the costs of the action and to his attorneys their reasonable fees. In determining attorney's fees, the amount of the recovery on behalf of the consumer is not controlling.

§ 5.202. [Damages or Penalties as Set-Off to Obligation]

Damages or penalties to which a consumer is entitled pursuant to this Part may be set off against the consumer's obligation, and may be raised as a defense to an action on the obligation without regard to the time limitations prescribed by this Part.

§ 5.203. [Civil Liability for Violation of Disclosure Provisions]

(1) Except as otherwise provided in this section, a creditor who, in violation of the provisions of the Federal Truth in Lending Act other than its provisions concerning advertising of credit terms, fails to disclose information to a person entitled to it under this Act is liable to that person in an amount equal to the sum of:

(a) twice the amount of the finance charge in connection with the transaction, but the liability under this paragraph shall be not less than $100 or exceed $1,000; and

(b) in the case of a successful action to enforce the liability under paragraph (a), the costs of the action together with reasonable attorney's fees as determined by the court.

(2) A creditor has no liability under this section, if within 15 days after discovering an error, and before the institution of an action under this section or the receipt of written notice of the error, the creditor notifies the person concerned of the error and makes adjustments in the appropriate account as necessary to assure that the person will not be required to pay a finance charge in excess of the amount or percentage rate actually disclosed. The Administrator and any official or agency of this State having supervisory authority over a supervised financial organization shall give prompt notice to a creditor of any error discovered pursuant to an examination or investigation of the transactions, business, records, and acts of the creditor (Sections 2.305, 6.105 and 6.106).

(3) A creditor may not be held liable in any action brought under this section for a violation of this Act if the creditor shows by a preponderance of evidence that the violation was not intentional and resulted from a bona fide error notwithstanding the maintenance of procedures reasonably adapted to avoid the error.

(4) Any action which may be brought under this section against the original creditor in a credit transaction involving a security interest in land may be maintained against any subsequent assignee of the original creditor, if the assignee, its subsidiaries, or affiliates were in a continuing business relationship with the original creditor at the time the credit was extended or at the time of the assignment, unless the assignment was involuntary, or the assignee shows by a preponderance of evidence that it did not have reasonable grounds to believe that the original creditor was engaged in violations of this Act and that it maintained procedures reasonably adapted to apprise it of the existence of the violations.

(5) An obligor or consumer has all rights under this Act that he has under the Federal Truth in Lending Act concerning a right of rescission as to certain transactions. A creditor or other person has all liabilities and defenses under this section that he has under the Federal Truth in Lending Act.

(6) In this section, creditor includes a person who in the ordinary course of business regularly extends or arranges for the extension of credit, or offers to arrange for the extension of credit, and the seller of an interest in land and the lender who makes a loan secured by an interest in land if, but for the rate of the finance charge made in the transaction, the sale or loan would be a consumer credit sale or consumer loan.

(7) An action may not be brought under this section more than one year after the date of the occurrence of the violation.

(8) The liability of a creditor under this section is in lieu of and not in addition to his liability under the Federal Truth in Lending Act. An action by a person with respect to a violation may not be maintained pursuant to this section if a final judgment has been rendered for or against that person with respect to the same violation pursuant to the Federal Truth in Lending Act. If a final judgment has been rendered in favor of a person pursuant to this section and thereafter a final judgment with respect to the same violation is rendered in favor of the same person pursuant to the Federal Truth in Lending Act, a creditor liable under both judgments has a [claim for relief] [cause of action] against that person for appropriate relief to the extent necessary to avoid double liability with respect to the same violation.

(9) The Administrator shall adopt rules to keep this section in harmony with the Federal Truth in Lending Act. These rules supersede any provisions of this section which are inconsistent with the Federal Truth in Lending Act.]

§ 5.301. [Willful and Knowing Violations]

(1) A supervised lender who willfully and knowingly makes charges in excess of those permitted by the Article on Finance Charges and Related Provisions (Article 2) applying to supervised loans (Part 4) is guilty of a misdemeanor and upon conviction may be [sentenced to pay a fine not exceeding $[ ], or to imprisonment not exceeding one year, or both].

(2) A person who, in violation of the provisions of this Act applying to authority to make supervised loans (Section 2.301), willfully and knowingly engages without a license in the business of making supervised loans, or of taking assignments of and undertaking direct collection of payments from and enforcement of rights against consumers arising from supervised loans, is guilty of a misdemeanor and upon conviction may be [sentenced to pay a fine not exceeding $[ ], or to imprisonment not exceeding one year, or both].

(3) A person who willfully and knowingly engages in the business of entering into consumer credit transactions, or of taking assignments of rights against consumers arising therefrom and undertaking direct collection of payments or enforcement of these rights, without complying with the provisions of this Act concerning notification (Section 6.202) or payment of fees (Section 6.203), is guilty of a misdemeanor and upon conviction may be [sentenced to pay a fine not exceeding $100].

§ 5.302. [Disclosure Violations]

(1) A person is guilty of a [misdemeanor] and upon conviction may be sentenced to pay a fine not exceeding $5,000, or to imprisonment not exceeding one year, or both, if he willfully and knowingly:

(a) gives false or inaccurate information or fails to provide information which he is required to disclose under the Federal Truth in Lending Act;

(b) uses any rate table or chart, the use of which is authorized by the provisions of the Federal Truth in Lending Act, in a manner which consistently understates the annual percentage rate determined according to those provisions; or

(c) otherwise fails to comply with any requirement of the provisions on disclosure of the Federal Truth in Lending Act.

(2) The criminal liability of a person under this section is in lieu of and not in addition to his criminal liability under the Federal Truth in Lending Act; no prosecution of a person with respect to the same violation may be maintained pursuant to both this section and the Federal Truth in Lending Act.]

ARTICLE 6. ADMINISTRATION [OMITTED]

(2) A person who, in violation of the provisions of this Act applying to authority to make supervised loans (Section 2.301), willfully and knowingly engages without a license in the business of making supervised loans, or of taking assignments of and undertaking direct collection of payments from and enforcing rights against consumers arising from supervised loans, is guilty of a misdemeanor and upon conviction may be sentenced to pay a fine not exceeding $[ ] or to imprisonment not exceeding [one year], or both.

(3) A person who willfully and knowingly engages in the business of entering into consumer credit transactions, or of taking assignments of rights against consumers arising therefrom and undertaking direct collection of payments or enforcement of rights against consumers, without complying with the provisions of this Act concerning notification (Section 6.202) or payment of fees (Section 6.203), is guilty of a misdemeanor and upon conviction may be sentenced to pay a fine not exceeding $[100].

§ 5.302 [Disclosure Violations]

(1) A person is guilty of a misdemeanor and upon conviction may be sentenced to pay a fine not exceeding $5,000, or to imprisonment not exceeding one year, or both, if he willfully and knowingly

(a) gives false or inaccurate information or fails to provide information which he is required to disclose under the Federal Truth in Lending Act;

(b) uses any rate table or chart, the use of which is authorized by the provisions of the Federal Truth in Lending Act in a manner which consistently understates the annual percentage rate determined according to those provisions; or

(c) otherwise fails to comply with any requirement of the provisions on disclosure of the Federal Truth in Lending Act.

(2) The criminal liability of a person under this section is in lieu of and not in addition to his criminal liability under the Federal Truth in Lending Act for any violation. No prosecution of a person with respect to the same violation may be maintained pursuant to both this section and the Federal Truth in Lending Act.

ARTICLE 6. ADMINISTRATION [OMITTED]

UNIFORM COMMERCIAL CODE

(Selected Sections)

ARTICLE 1. GENERAL PROVISIONS

(2006 version)

Table of Sections

§ 1–309. Option to Accelerate at Will

A term providing that one party or that party's successor in interest may accelerate payment or performance or require collateral or additional collateral "at will" or when the party "deems itself insecure," or words of similar import, means that the party has power to do so only if that party in good faith believes that the prospect of payment or performance is impaired. The burden of establishing lack of good faith is on the party against which the power has been exercised.

Official Comment

Source: Former Section 1–208.

Changes from former law: Except for minor stylistic changes, this section is identical to former Section 1–208.

1. The common use of acceleration clauses in many transactions governed by the Uniform Commercial Code, including sales of goods on credit, notes payable at a definite time, and secured transactions, raises an issue as to the effect to be given to a clause that seemingly grants the power to accelerate at the whim and caprice of one party. This section is intended to make clear that despite language that might be so construed and which further might be held to make the agreement void as against public policy or to make the contract illusory or too indefinite for enforcement, the option is to be exercised only in the good faith belief that the prospect of payment or performance is impaired.

Obviously this section has no application to demand instruments or obligations whose very nature permits call at any time with or without reason. This section applies only to an obligation of payment or performance which in the first instance is due at a future date.

§ 1–310. Subordinated Obligations

An obligation may be issued as subordinated to performance of another obligation of the person obligated, or a creditor may subordinate its right to performance of an obligation by agreement with either the person obligated or another creditor of the person obligated. Subordination does not create a security interest as against either the common debtor or a subordinated creditor.

Official Comment

Source: Former Section 1–209.

Changes from former law: This section is substantively identical to former Section 1–209. The language in that section stating that it "shall be construed as declaring the law as it existed prior to the enactment of this section and not as modifying it" has been deleted.

1. Billions of dollars of subordinated debt are held by the public and by institutional investors. Commonly, the subordinated debt is subordinated on issue or acquisition and is evidenced by an investment

security or by a negotiable or non-negotiable note. Debt is also sometimes subordinated after it arises, either by agreement between the subordinating creditor and the debtor, by agreement between two creditors of the same debtor, or by agreement of all three parties. The subordinated creditor may be a stockholder or other "insider" interested in the common debtor; the subordinated debt may consist of accounts or other rights to payment not evidenced by any instrument. All such cases are included in the terms "subordinated obligation," "subordination," and "subordinated creditor."

2. Subordination agreements are enforceable between the parties as contracts; and in the bankruptcy of the common debtor dividends otherwise payable to the subordinated creditor are turned over to the superior creditor. This "turn-over" practice has on occasion been explained in terms of "equitable lien," "equitable assignment," or "constructive trust," but whatever the label the practice is essentially an equitable remedy and does not mean that there is a transaction "that creates a security interest in personal property . . . by contract" or a "sale of accounts, chattel paper, payment intangibles, or promissory notes" within the meaning of Section 9–109. On the other hand, nothing in this section prevents one creditor from assigning his rights to another creditor of the same debtor in such a way as to create a security interest within Article 9, where the parties so intend.

3. The enforcement of subordination agreements is largely left to supplementary principles under Section 1–103. If the subordinated debt is evidenced by a certificated security, Section 8–202(a) authorizes enforcement against purchasers on terms stated or referred to on the security certificate. If the fact of subordination is noted on a negotiable instrument, a holder under Sections 3–302 and 3–306 is subject to the term because notice precludes him from taking free of the subordination. Sections 3–302(3)(a), 3–306, and 8–317 severely limit the rights of levying creditors of a subordinated creditor in such cases.

ARTICLE 2. SALES

[**Editor's Note**. Although an amended version of Article 2 was released by the American Law Institute and the National Conference of Commissioners on Uniform State Laws in 2003, it failed to be enacted in any state and was withdrawn from the official text in 2011. This volume contains selected sections and official comment of particular interest to consumer law from the "unamended" version, which remains the official text of Article Two of the Uniform Commercial Code.]

Table of Sections

Sec.

§ 2-202. Final Written Expression: Parol or Extrinsic Evidence

Terms with respect to which the confirmatory memoranda of the parties agree or which are otherwise set forth in a writing intended by the parties as a final expression of their agreement with respect to such terms as are included therein may not be contradicted by evidence of any prior agreement or of a contemporaneous oral agreement but may be explained or supplemented

(a) by course of performance, course of dealing or usage of trade (Section 1-205 and 1-303) or by course of performance (Section 2-208); and

(b) by evidence of consistent additional terms unless the court finds the writing to have been intended also as a complete and exclusive statement of the terms of the agreement.

Official Comment

Prior Uniform Statutory Provisions: None.

Purposes:

1. This section definitely rejects:

(a) Any assumption that because a writing has been worked out which is final on some matters, it is to be taken as including all the matters agreed upon;

(b) The premise that the language used has the meaning attributable to such language by rules of construction existing in the law rather than the meaning which arises out of the commercial context in which it was used; and

(c) The requirement that a condition precedent to the admissibility of the type of evidence specified in paragraph (a) is an original determination by the court that the language used is ambiguous.

2. Paragraph (a) makes admissible evidence of course of dealing, usage of trade and course of performance to explain or supplement the terms of any writing stating the agreement of the parties in order that the true understanding of the parties as to the agreement may be reached. Such writings are to be read on the assumption that the course of prior dealings between the parties and the usages of trade were taken for granted when the document was phrased. Unless carefully negated they have become an element of the meaning of the words used. Similarly, the course of actual performance by the parties is considered the best indication of what they intended the writing to mean.

3. Under paragraph (b) consistent additional terms, not reduced to writing, may be proved unless the court finds that the writing was intended by both parties as a complete and exclusive statement of all the terms. If the additional terms are such that, if agreed upon, they would certainly have been included in the document in the view of the court, then evidence of their alleged making must be kept from the trier of fact.

§ 2-204. Formation in General

(1) A contract for sale of goods may be made in any manner sufficient to show agreement, including conduct by both parties which recognizes the existence of such a contract.

(2) An agreement sufficient to constitute a contract for sale may be found even though the moment of its making is undetermined.

(3) Even though one or more terms are left open a contract for sale does not fail for indefiniteness if the parties have intended to make a contract and there is a reasonably certain basis for giving an appropriate remedy.

Official Comment

Prior Uniform Statutory Provision: Sections 1 and 3, Uniform Sales Act.

Changes: Completely rewritten by this and other sections of this Article.

Purposes of Changes:

Subsection (1) continues without change the basic policy of recognizing any manner of expression of agreement, oral, written or otherwise. The legal effect of such an agreement is, of course, qualified by other provisions of this Article.

Under subsection (1) appropriate conduct by the parties may be sufficient to establish an agreement. Subsection (2) is directed primarily to the situation where the interchanged correspondence does not disclose the exact point at which the deal was closed, but the actions of the parties indicate that a binding obligation has been undertaken.

Subsection (3) states the principle as to "open terms" underlying later sections of the Article. If the parties intend to enter into a binding agreement, this subsection recognizes that agreement as valid in law, despite missing terms, if there is any reasonably certain basis for granting a remedy. The test is not certainty as to what the parties were to do nor as to the exact amount of damages due the plaintiff. Nor is the fact that one or more terms are left to be agreed upon enough of itself to defeat an otherwise adequate agreement. Rather, commercial standards on the point of "indefiniteness" are intended to be applied, this Act making provision elsewhere for missing terms needed for performance, open price, remedies and the like.

The more terms the parties leave open, the less likely it is that they have intended to conclude a binding agreement, but their actions may be frequently conclusive on the matter despite the omissions.

§ 2-206. Offer and Acceptance in Formation of Contract

(1) Unless otherwise unambiguously indicated by the language or circumstances

(a) an offer to make a contract shall be construed as inviting acceptance in any manner and by any medium reasonable in the circumstances;

(b) an order or other offer to buy goods for prompt or current shipment shall be construed as inviting acceptance either by a prompt promise to ship or by the prompt or current shipment of conforming or non-conforming goods, but such a shipment of non-conforming goods does not constitute an acceptance if the seller seasonably notifies the buyer that the shipment is offered only as an accommodation to the buyer.

(2) Where the beginning of a requested performance is a reasonable mode of acceptance an offeror who is not notified of acceptance within a reasonable time may treat the offer as having lapsed before acceptance.

Official Comment

Prior Uniform Statutory Provision: Sections 1 and 3, Uniform Sales Act.

Changes: Completely rewritten in this and other sections of this Article.

Purposes of Changes: To make it clear that:

1. Any reasonable manner of acceptance is intended to be regarded as available unless the offeror has made quite clear that it will not be acceptable. Former technical rules as to acceptance, such as requiring that telegraphic offers be accepted by telegraphed acceptance, etc., are rejected and a criterion that the acceptance be "in any manner and by any medium reasonable under the circumstances," is substituted. This section is intended to remain flexible and its applicability to be enlarged as new media of communication develop or as the more time-saving present day media come into general use.

2. Either shipment or a prompt promise to ship is made a proper means of acceptance of an offer looking to current shipment. In accordance with ordinary commercial understanding the section interprets an order looking to current shipment as allowing acceptance either by actual shipment or by a prompt promise to ship and rejects the artificial theory that only a single mode of acceptance is normally envisaged by an offer. This is true even though the language of the offer happens to be "ship at once" or the like. "Shipment" is here used in the same sense as in Section 2-504; it does not include the beginning of delivery by the seller's own truck or by messenger. But loading on the seller's own truck might be a beginning of performance under subsection (2).

3. The beginning of performance by an offeree can be effective as acceptance so as to bind the offeror only if followed within a reasonable time by notice to the offeror. Such a beginning of performance must unambiguously express the offeree's intention to engage himself. For the protection of both parties it is essential that notice follow in due course to constitute acceptance. Nothing in this section however bars the possibility that under the common law performance begun may have an intermediate effect of temporarily barring revocation of the offer, or at the offeror's option, final effect in constituting acceptance.

4. Subsection (1)(b) deals with the situation where a shipment made following an order is shown by a notification of shipment to be referable to that order but has a defect. Such a non-conforming shipment is normally to be understood as intended to close the bargain, even though it proves to have been at the same time a breach. However, the seller by stating that the shipment is non-conforming and is offered only as an accommodation to the buyer keeps the shipment or notification from operating as an acceptance.

§ 2–207. Additional Terms in Acceptance or Confirmation

(1) A definite and seasonable expression of acceptance or a written confirmation which is sent within a reasonable time operates as an acceptance even though it states terms additional to or different from those offered or agreed upon, unless acceptance is expressly made conditional on assent to the additional or different terms.

(2) The additional terms are to be construed as proposals for addition to the contract. Between merchants such terms become part of the contract unless:

(a) the offer expressly limits acceptance to the terms of the offer;

(b) they materially alter it; or

(c) notification of objection to them has already been given or is given within a reasonable time after notice of them is received.

(3) Conduct by both parties which recognizes the existence of a contract is sufficient to establish a contract for sale although the writings of the parties do not otherwise establish a contract. In such case the terms of the particular contract consist of those terms on which the writings of the parties agree, together with any supplementary terms incorporated under any other provisions of this Act.

Official Comment

Prior Uniform Statutory Provision: Sections 1 and 3, Uniform Sales Act.

Changes: Completely rewritten by this and other sections of this Article.

1. This section is intended to deal with two typical situations. The one is the written confirmation, where an agreement has been reached either orally or by informal correspondence between the parties and is followed by one or both of the parties sending formal memoranda embodying the terms so far as agreed upon and adding terms not discussed. The other situation is offer and acceptance, in which a wire or letter expressed and intended as an acceptance or the closing of an agreement adds further minor suggestions or proposals such as "ship by Tuesday," "rush," "ship draft against bill of lading inspection allowed," or the like. A frequent example of the second situation is the exchange of printed purchase order and acceptance (sometimes called "acknowledgment") forms. Because the forms are oriented to the thinking of the respective drafting parties, the terms contained in them often do not correspond. Often the seller's form contains terms different from or additional to those set forth in the buyer's form. Nevertheless, the parties proceed with the transaction. [Comment 1 was amended in 1966.]

2. Under this Article a proposed deal which in commercial understanding has in fact been closed is recognized as a contract. Therefore, any additional matter contained in the confirmation or in the acceptance falls within subsection (2) and must be regarded as a proposal for an added term unless the acceptance is made conditional on the acceptance of the additional or different terms. [Comment 2 was amended in 1966.]

3. Whether or not additional or different terms will become part of the agreement depends upon the provisions of subsection (2). If they are such as materially to alter the original bargain, they will not be included unless expressly agreed to by the other party. If, however, they are terms which would not so

change the bargain they will be incorporated unless notice of objection to them has already been given or is given within a reasonable time.

4. Examples of typical clauses which would normally "materially alter" the contract and so result in surprise or hardship if incorporated without express awareness by the other party are: a clause negating such standard warranties as that of merchantability or fitness for a particular purpose in circumstances in which either warranty normally attaches; a clause requiring a guaranty of 90% or 100% deliveries in a case such as a contract by cannery, where the usage of the trade allows greater quantity leeways; a clause reserving to the seller the power to cancel upon the buyer's failure to meet any invoice when due; a clause requiring that complaints be made in a time materially shorter than customary or reasonable.

5. Examples of clauses which involve no element of unreasonable surprise and which therefore are to be incorporated in the contract unless notice of objection is seasonably given are: a clause setting forth and perhaps enlarging slightly upon the seller's exemption due to supervening causes beyond his control, similar to those covered by the provision of this Article on merchant's excuse by failure of presupposed conditions or a clause fixing in advance any reasonable formula of proration under such circumstances; a clause fixing a reasonable time for complaints within customary limits, or in the case of a purchase for sub-sale, providing for inspection by the sub-purchaser; a clause providing for interest on overdue invoices or fixing the seller's standard credit terms where they are within the range of trade practice and do not limit any credit bargained for; a clause limiting the right of rejection for defects which fall within the customary trade tolerances for acceptance "with adjustment" or otherwise limiting remedy in a reasonable manner (see Sections 2–718 and 2–719).

6. If no answer is received within a reasonable time after additional terms are proposed, it is both fair and commercially sound to assume that their inclusion has been assented to. Where clauses on confirming forms sent by both parties conflict each party must be assumed to object to a clause of the other conflicting with one on the confirmation sent by himself. As a result the requirement that there be notice of objection which is found in subsection (2) is satisfied and the conflicting terms do not become a part of the contract. The contract then consists of the terms originally expressly agreed to, terms on which the confirmations agree, and terms supplied by this Act, including subsection (2). The written confirmation is also subject to Section 2–201. Under that section a failure to respond permits enforcement of a prior oral agreement; under this section a failure to respond permits additional terms to become part of the agreement. [Comment 6 was amended in 1966.]

7. In many cases, as where goods are shipped, accepted and paid for before any dispute arises, there is no question whether a contract has been made. In such cases, where the writings of the parties do not establish a contract, it is not necessary to determine which act or document constituted the offer and which the acceptance. See Section 2–204. The only question is what terms are included in the contract, and subsection (3) furnishes the governing rule. [Comment 7 was added in 1966.]

§ 2–209. Modification, Rescission and Waiver

(1) An agreement modifying a contract within this Article needs no consideration to be binding.

(2) A signed agreement which excludes modification or rescission except by a signed writing cannot be otherwise modified or rescinded, but except as between merchants such a requirement on a form supplied by the merchant must be separately signed by the other party.

(3) The requirements of the statute of frauds section of this Article (Section 2–201) must be satisfied if the contract as modified is within its provisions.

(4) Although an attempt at modification or rescission does not satisfy the requirements of subsection (2) or (3) it can operate as a waiver.

(5) A party who has made a waiver affecting an executory portion of the contract may retract the waiver by reasonable notification received by the other party that strict performance will be required of any term waived, unless the retraction would be unjust in view of a material change of position in reliance on the waiver.

Official Comment

Prior Uniform Statutory Provision: Subsection (1)—Compare Section 1, Uniform Written Obligations Act; Subsections (2) to (5)—none.

Purposes of Changes and New Matter:

1. This section seeks to protect and make effective all necessary and desirable modifications of sales contracts without regard to the technicalities which at present hamper such adjustments.

2. Subsection (1) provides that an agreement modifying a sales contract needs no consideration to be binding.

However, modifications made thereunder must meet the test of good faith imposed by this Act. The effective use of bad faith to escape performance on the original contract terms is barred, and the extortion of a "modification" without legitimate commercial reason is ineffective as a violation of the duty of good faith. Nor can a mere technical consideration support a modification made in bad faith.

The test of "good faith" between merchants or as against merchants includes "observance of reasonable commercial standards of fair dealing in the trade" (Section 2–103), and may in some situations require an objectively demonstrable reason for seeking a modification. But such matters as a market shift which makes performance come to involve a loss may provide such a reason even though there is no such unforeseen difficulty as would make out a legal excuse from performance under Sections 2–615 and 2–616.

3. Subsections (2) and (3) are intended to protect against false allegations of oral modifications. "Modification or rescission" includes abandonment or other change my mutual consent, contrary to the decision in Green v. Doniger, 300 N.Y. 238, 90 N.E.2d 56 (1949); it does not include unilateral "termination" or "cancellation" as defined in Section 2–106.

The Statute of Frauds provisions of this Article are expressly applied to modifications by subsection (3). Under those provisions the "delivery and acceptance" test is limited to the good which have been accepted, that is, to the past. "Modification" for the future cannot therefore be conjured up by oral testimony if the price involved is $500.00 or more since such modification must be shown at least by an authenticated memo. And since a memo is limited in its effect to the quantity of goods set forth in it there is safeguard against oral evidence.

Subsection (2) permits the parties in effect to make their own Statute of Frauds as regards any future modification of the contract by giving effect to a clause in a signed agreement which expressly requires any modification to be by signed writing. But note that if a consumer is to be held to such a clause on a form supplied by a merchant it must be separately signed.

4. Subsection (4) is intended, despite the provisions of subsections (2) and (3), to prevent contractual provisions excluding modification except by a signed writing from limiting in other respects the legal effect of the parties' actual later conduct. The effect of such conduct as a waiver is further regulated in subsection (5).

§ 2–302. Unconscionable Contract or Clause

(1) If the court as a matter of law finds the contract or any clause of the contract to have been unconscionable at the time it was made the court may refuse to enforce the contract, or it may enforce the remainder of the contract without the unconscionable clause, or it may so limit the application of any unconscionable clause as to avoid any unconscionable result.

(2) When it is claimed or appears to the court that the contract or any clause thereof may be unconscionable the parties shall be afforded a reasonable opportunity to present evidence as to its commercial setting, purpose and effect to aid the court in making the determination.

Official Comment

Purposes:

1. This section is intended to make it possible for the courts to police explicitly against the contracts or clauses which they find to be unconscionable. In the past such policing has been accomplished by adverse

construction of language, by manipulation of the rules of offer and acceptance or by determinations that the clause is contrary to public policy or to the dominant purpose of the contract. This section is intended to allow the court to pass directly on the unconscionability of the contract or particular clause therein and to make a conclusion of law as to its unconscionability. The basic test is whether, in the light of the general commercial background and the commercial needs of the particular trade or case, the clauses involved are so one-sided as to be unconscionable under the circumstances existing at the time of the making of the contract. Subsection (2) makes it clear that it is proper for the court to hear evidence upon these questions. The principle is one of the prevention of oppression and unfair surprise (Cf. Campbell Soup Co. v. Wentz, 172 F.2d 80, 3d Cir.1948) and not of disturbance of allocation of risks because of superior bargaining power. The underlying basis of this section is illustrated by the results in cases such as the following:

Kansas City Wholesale Grocery Co. v. Weber Packing Corporation, 93 Utah 414, 73 P.2d 1272 (1937), where a clause limiting time for complaints was held inapplicable to latent defects in a shipment of catsup which could be discovered only by microscopic analysis; Hardy v. General Motors Acceptance Corporation, 38 Ga.App. 463, 144 S.E. 327 (1928), holding that a disclaimer of warranty clause applied only to express warranties, thus letting in a fair implied warranty; Andrews Bros. v. Singer & Co. (1934 CA) 1 K.B. 17, holding that where a car with substantial mileage was delivered instead of a "new" car, a disclaimer of warranties, including those "implied," left unaffected an "express obligation" on the description, even though the Sale of Goods Act called such an implied warranty; New Prague Flouring Mill Co. v. G. A. Spears, 194 Iowa 417, 189 N.W. 815 (1922), holding that a clause permitting the seller, upon the buyer's failure to supply shipping instructions, to cancel, ship, or allow delivery date to be indefinitely postponed 30 days at a time by the inaction, does not indefinitely postpone the date of measuring damages for the buyer's breach, to the seller's advantage; and Kansas Flour Mills Co. v. Dirks, 100 Kan. 376, 164 P. 273 (1917), where under a similar clause in a rising market the court permitted the buyer to measure his damages for non-delivery at the end of only one 30 day postponement; Green v. Arcos, Ltd. (1931 CA) 47 T.L.R. 336, where a blanket clause prohibiting rejection of shipments by the buyer was restricted to apply to shipments where discrepancies represented merely mercantile variations; Meyer v. Packard Cleveland Motor Co., 106 Ohio St. 328, 140 N.E. 118 (1922), in which the court held that a "waiver" of all agreements not specified did not preclude implied warranty of fitness of a rebuilt dump truck for ordinary use as a dump truck; Austin Co. v. J. H. Tillman Co., 104 Or. 541, 209 P. 131 (1922), where a clause limiting the buyer's remedy to return was held to be applicable only if the seller had delivered a machine needed for a construction job which reasonably met the contract description; Bekkevold v. Potts, 173 Minn. 87, 216 N.W. 790, 59 A.L.R. 1164 (1927), refusing to allow warranty of fitness for purpose imposed by law to be negated by clause excluding all warranties "made" by the seller; Robert A. Munroe & Co. v. Meyer (1930) 2 K.B. 312, holding that the warranty of description overrides a clause reading "with all faults and defects" where adulterated meat not up to the contract description was delivered.

2. Under this section the court, in its discretion, may refuse to enforce the contract as a whole if it is permeated by the unconscionability, or it may strike any single clause or group of clauses which are so tainted or which are contrary to the essential purpose of the agreement, or it may simply limit unconscionable clauses so as to avoid unconscionable results.

3. The present section is addressed to the court, and the decision is to be made by it. The commercial evidence referred to in subsection (2) is for the court's consideration, not the jury's. Only the agreement which results from the court's action on these matters is to be submitted to the general triers of the facts.

§ 2-313. Express Warranties by Affirmation, Promise, Description, Sample

(1) Express warranties by the seller are created as follows:

(a) Any affirmation of fact or promise made by the seller to the buyer which relates to the goods and becomes part of the basis of the bargain creates an express warranty that the goods shall conform to the affirmation or promise.

(b) Any description of the goods which is made part of the basis of the bargain creates an express warranty that the goods shall conform to the description.

(c) Any sample or model which is made part of the basis of the bargain creates an express warranty that the whole of the goods shall conform to the sample or model.

(2) It is not necessary to the creation of an express warranty that the seller use formal words such as "warrant" or "guarantee" or that he have a specific intention to make a warranty, but an affirmation merely of the value of the goods or a statement purporting to be merely the seller's opinion or commendation of the goods does not create a warranty.

Official Comment

1. "Express" warranties rest on "dickered" aspects of the individual bargain, and go so clearly to the essence of that bargain that words of disclaimer in a form are repugnant to the basic dickered terms. "Implied" warranties rest so clearly on a common factual situation or set of conditions that no particular language or action is necessary to evidence them and they will arise in such a situation unless unmistakably negated.

This section reverts to the older case law insofar as the warranties of description and sample are designated "express" rather than "implied".

2. Although this section is limited in its scope and direct purpose to warranties made by the seller to the buyer as part of a contract for sale, the warranty sections of this Article are not designed in any way to disturb those lines of case law growth which have recognized that warranties need not be confined either to sales contracts or to the direct parties to such a contract. They may arise in other appropriate circumstances such as in the case of bailments for hire, whether such bailment is itself the main contract or is merely a supplying of containers under a contract for the sale of their contents. The provisions of Section 2–318 on third party beneficiaries expressly recognize this case law development within one particular area. Beyond that, the matter is left to the case law with the intention that the policies of this Act may offer useful guidance in dealing with further cases as they arise.

3. The present section deals with affirmations of fact by the seller, descriptions of the goods or exhibitions of samples, exactly as any other part of a negotiation which ends in a contract is dealt with. No specific intention to make a warranty is necessary if any of these factors is made part of the basis of the bargain. In actual practice affirmations of fact made by the seller about the goods during a bargain are regarded as part of the description of those goods; hence no particular reliance on such statements need be shown in order to weave them into the fabric of the agreement. Rather, any fact which is to take such affirmations, once made, out of the agreement requires clear affirmative proof. The issue normally is one of fact.

4. In view of the principle that the whole purpose of the law of warranty is to determine what it is that the seller has in essence agreed to sell, the policy is adopted of those cases which refuse except in unusual circumstances to recognize a material deletion of the seller's obligation. Thus, a contract is normally a contract for a sale of something describable and described. A clause generally disclaiming "all warranties, express or implied" cannot reduce the seller's obligation with respect to such description and therefore cannot be given literal effect under Section 2–316.

This is not intended to mean that the parties, if they consciously desire, cannot make their own bargain as they wish. But in determining what they have agreed upon good faith is a factor and consideration should be given to the fact that the probability is small that a real price is intended to be exchanged for a pseudo-obligation.

5. Paragraph (1)(b) makes specific some of the principles set forth above when a description of the goods is given by the seller.

A description need not be by words. Technical specifications, blueprints and the like can afford more exact description than mere language and if made part of the basis of the bargain goods must conform with them. Past deliveries may set the description of quality, either expressly or impliedly by course of dealing. Of course, all descriptions by merchants must be read against the applicable trade usages with the general rules as to merchantability resolving any doubts.

6. The basic situation as to statements affecting the true essence of the bargain is no different when a sample or model is involved in the transaction. This section includes both a "sample" actually drawn from the bulk of goods which is the subject matter of the sale, and a "model" which is offered for inspection when the subject matter is not at hand and which has not been drawn from the bulk of the goods.

Although the underlying principles are unchanged, the facts are often ambiguous when something is shown as illustrative, rather than as a straight sample. In general, the presumption is that any sample or model just as any affirmation of fact is intended to become a basis of the bargain. But there is no escape from the question of fact. When the seller exhibits a sample purporting to be drawn from an existing bulk, good faith of course requires that the sample be fairly drawn. But in mercantile experience the mere exhibition of a "sample" does not of itself show whether it is merely intended to "suggest" or to "be" the character of the subject-matter of the contract. The question is whether the seller has so acted with reference to the sample as to make him responsible that the whole shall have at least the values shown by it. The circumstances aid in answering this question. If the sample has been drawn from an existing bulk, it must be regarded as describing values of the goods contracted for unless it is accompanied by an unmistakable denial of such responsibility. If, on the other hand, a model of merchandise not on hand is offered, the mercantile presumption that it has become a literal description of the subject matter is not so strong, and particularly so if modification on the buyer's initiative impairs any feature of the model.

7. The precise time when words of description or affirmation are made or samples are shown is not material. The sole question is whether the language or samples or models are fairly to be regarded as part of the contract. If language is used after the closing of the deal (as when the buyer when taking delivery asks and receives an additional assurance), the warranty becomes a modification, and need not be supported by consideration if it is otherwise reasonable and in order (Section 2-209).

8. Concerning affirmations of value or a seller's opinion or commendation under subsection (2), the basic question remains the same: What statements of the seller have in the circumstances and in objective judgment become part of the basis of the bargain? As indicated above, all of the statements of the seller do so unless good reason is shown to the contrary. The provisions of subsection (2) are included, however, since common experience discloses that some statements or predictions cannot fairly be viewed as entering into the bargain. Even as to false statements of value, however, the possibility is left open that a remedy may be provided by the law relating to fraud or misrepresentation.

§ 2-314. Implied Warranty: Merchantability; Usage of Trade

(1) Unless excluded or modified (Section 2-316), a warranty that the goods shall be merchantable is implied in a contract for their sale if the seller is a merchant with respect to goods of that kind. Under this section the serving for value of food or drink to be consumed either on the premises or elsewhere is a sale.

(2) Goods to be merchantable must be at least such as

(a) pass without objection in the trade under the contract description; and

(b) in the case of fungible goods, are of fair average quality within the description; and

(c) are fit for the ordinary purposes for which such goods are used; and

(d) run, within the variations permitted by the agreement, of even kind, quality and quantity within each unit and among all units involved; and

(e) are adequately contained, packaged, and labeled as the agreement may require; and

(f) conform to the promises or affirmations of fact made on the container or label if any.

(3) Unless excluded or modified (Section 2-316) other implied warranties may arise from course of dealing or usage of trade.

Official Comment

Purposes of Changes: This section, drawn in view of the steadily developing case law on the subject, is intended to make it clear that:

1. The seller's obligation applies to present sales as well as to contracts to sell subject to the effects of any examination of specific goods. (Subsection (2) of Section 2-316). Also, the warranty of merchantability applies to sales for use as well as to sales for resale.

2. The question when the warranty is imposed turns basically on the meaning of the terms of the agreement as recognized in the trade. Goods delivered under an agreement made by a merchant in a given line of trade must be of a quality comparable to that generally acceptable in that line of trade under the description or other designation of the goods used in the agreement. The responsibility imposed rests on any merchant-seller, and the absence of the words "grower or manufacturer or not" which appeared in Section 15(2) of the Uniform Sales Act does not restrict the applicability of this section.

3. A specific designation of goods by the buyer does not exclude the seller's obligation that they be fit for the general purposes appropriate to such goods. A contract for the sale of second-hand goods, however, involves only such obligation as is appropriate to such goods for that is their contract description. A person making an isolated sale of goods is not a "merchant" within the meaning of the full scope of this section and, thus, no warranty of merchantability would apply. His knowledge of any defects not apparent on inspection would, however, without need for express agreement and in keeping with the underlying reason of the present section and the provisions on good faith, impose an obligation that known material but hidden defects be fully disclosed.

4. Although a seller may not be a "merchant" as to the goods in question, if he states generally that they are "guaranteed" the provisions of this section may furnish a guide to the content of the resulting express warranty. This has particular significance in the case of second-hand sales, and has further significance in limiting the effect of fine-print disclaimer clauses where their effect would be inconsistent with large-print assertions of "guarantee".

5. The second sentence of subsection (1) covers the warranty with respect to food and drink. Serving food or drink for value is a sale, whether to be consumed on the premises or elsewhere. Cases to the contrary are rejected. The principal warranty is that stated in subsections (1) and (2)(c) of this section.

6. Subsection (2) does not purport to exhaust the meaning of "merchantable" nor to negate any of its attributes not specifically mentioned in the text of the statute, but arising by usage of trade or through case law. The language used is "must be at least such as . . . ," and the intention is to leave open other possible attributes of merchantability.

7. Paragraphs (a) and (b) of subsection (2) are to be read together. Both refer, as indicated above, to the standards of that line of the trade which fits the transaction and the seller's business. "Fair average" is a term directly appropriate to agricultural bulk products and means goods centering around the middle belt of quality, not the least or the worst that can be understood in the particular trade by the designation, but such as can pass "without objection." Of course a fair percentage of the least is permissible but the goods are not "fair average" if they are all of the least or worst quality possible under the description. In cases of doubt as to what quality is intended, the price at which a merchant closes a contract is an excellent index of the nature and scope of his obligation under the present section.

8. Fitness for the ordinary purposes for which goods of the type are used is a fundamental concept of the present section and is covered in paragraph (c). As stated above, merchantability is also a part of the obligation owing to the purchaser for use. Correspondingly, protection, under this aspect of the warranty, of the person buying for resale to the ultimate consumer is equally necessary, and merchantable goods must therefore be "honestly" resalable in the normal course of business because they are what they purport to be.

9. Paragraph (d) on evenness of kind, quality and quantity follows case law. But precautionary language has been added as a reminder of the frequent usages of trade which permit substantial variations both with and without an allowance or an obligation to replace the varying units.

10. Paragraph (e) applies only where the nature of the goods and of the transaction require a certain type of container, package or label. Paragraph (f) applies, on the other hand, wherever there is a label or container on which representations are made, even though the original contract, either by express terms or usage of trade, may not have required either the labelling or the representation. This follows from the general obligation of good faith which requires that a buyer should not be placed in the position of reselling or using goods delivered under false representations appearing on the package or container. No problem of extra consideration arises in this connection since, under this Article, an obligation is imposed by the original contract not to deliver mislabeled articles, and the obligation is imposed where mercantile good faith so requires and without reference to the doctrine of consideration.

11. Exclusion or modification of the warranty of merchantability, or of any part of it, is dealt with in the section to which the text of the present section makes explicit precautionary references. That section must be read with particular reference to its subsection (4) on limitation of remedies. The warranty of merchantability, wherever it is normal, is so commonly taken for granted that its exclusion from the contract is a matter threatening surprise and therefore requiring special precaution.

12. Subsection (3) is to make explicit that usage of trade and course of dealing can create warranties and that they are implied rather than express warranties and thus subject to exclusion or modification under Section 2–316. A typical instance would be the obligation to provide pedigree papers to evidence conformity of the animal to the contract in the case of a pedigreed dog or blooded bull.

13. In an action based on breach of warranty, it is of course necessary to show not only the existence of the warranty but the fact that the warranty was broken and that the breach of the warranty was the proximate cause of the loss sustained. In such an action an affirmative showing by the seller that the loss resulted from some action or event following his own delivery of the goods can operate as a defense. Equally, evidence indicating that the seller exercised care in the manufacture, processing or selection of the goods is relevant to the issue of whether the warranty was in fact broken. Action by the buyer following an examination of the goods which ought to have indicated the defect complained of can be shown as matter bearing on whether the breach itself was the cause of the injury.

§ 2-315. Implied Warranty: Fitness for Particular Purpose

Where the seller at the time of contracting has reason to know any particular purpose for which the goods are required and that the buyer is relying on the seller's skill or judgment to select or furnish suitable goods, there is unless excluded or modified under the next section an implied warranty that the goods shall be fit for such purpose.

Official Comment

Purposes of Changes:

1. Whether or not this warranty arises in any individual case is basically a question of fact to be determined by the circumstances of the contracting. Under this section the buyer need not bring home to the seller actual knowledge of the particular purpose for which the goods are intended or of his reliance on the seller's skill and judgment, if the circumstances are such that the seller has reason to realize the purpose intended or that the reliance exists. The buyer, of course, must actually be relying on the seller.

2. A "particular purpose" differs from the ordinary purpose for which the goods are used in that it envisages a specific use by the buyer which is peculiar to the nature of his business whereas the ordinary purposes for which goods are used are those envisaged in the concept of merchantability and go to uses which are customarily made of the goods in question. For example, shoes are generally used for the purpose of walking upon ordinary ground, but a seller may know that a particular pair was selected to be used for climbing mountains.

A contract may of course include both a warranty of merchantability and one of fitness for a particular purpose.

The provisions of this Article on the cumulation and conflict of express and implied warranties must be considered on the question of inconsistency between or among warranties. In such a case any question of fact as to which warranty was intended by the parties to apply must be resolved in favor of the warranty of fitness for particular purpose as against all other warranties except where the buyer has taken upon himself the responsibility of furnishing the technical specifications.

3. In connection with the warranty of fitness for a particular purpose the provisions of this Article on the allocation or division of risks are particularly applicable in any transaction in which the purpose for which the goods are to be used combines requirements both as to the quality of the goods themselves and compliance with certain laws or regulations. How the risks are divided is a question of fact to be determined, where not expressly contained in the agreement, from the circumstances of contracting, usage of trade, course of performance and the like, matters which may constitute the "otherwise agreement" of the parties by which they may divide the risk or burden.

4. The absence from this section of the language used in the Uniform Sales Act in referring to the seller, "whether he be the grower or manufacturer or not," is not intended to impose any requirement that the seller be a grower or manufacturer. Although normally the warranty will arise only where the seller is a merchant with the appropriate "skill or judgment," it can arise as to nonmerchants where this is justified by the particular circumstances.

5. The elimination of the "patent or other trade name" exception constitutes the major extension of the warranty of fitness which has been made by the cases and continued in this Article. Under the present section the existence of a patent or other trade name and the designation of the article by that name, or indeed in any other definite manner, is only one of the facts to be considered on the question of whether the buyer actually relied on the seller, but it is not of itself decisive of the issue. If the buyer himself is insisting on a particular brand he is not relying on the seller's skill and judgment and so no warranty results. But the mere fact that the article purchased has a particular patent or trade name is not sufficient to indicate nonreliance if the article has been recommended by the seller as adequate for the buyer's purposes.

6. The specific reference forward in the present section to the following section on exclusion or modification of warranties is to call attention to the possibility of eliminating the warranty in any given case. However it must be noted that under the following section the warranty of fitness for a particular purpose must be excluded or modified by a conspicuous writing.

§ 2–316. Exclusion or Modification of Warranties

(1) Words or conduct relevant to the creation of an express warranty and words or conduct tending to negate or limit warranty shall be construed wherever reasonable as consistent with each other; but subject to the provisions of this Article on parol or extrinsic evidence (Section 2–202) negation or limitation is inoperative to the extent that such construction is unreasonable.

(2) Subject to subsection (3), to exclude or modify the implied warranty of merchantability or any part of it the language must mention merchantability and in case of a writing must be conspicuous, and to exclude or modify any implied warranty of fitness the exclusion must be by a writing and conspicuous. Language to exclude all implied warranties of fitness is sufficient if it states, for example, that "There are no warranties which extend beyond the description on the face hereof."

(3) Notwithstanding subsection (2)

(a) unless the circumstances indicate otherwise, all implied warranties are excluded by expressions like "as is", "with all faults" or other language which in common understanding calls the buyer's attention to the exclusion of warranties and makes plain that there is no implied warranty; and

(b) when the buyer before entering into the contract has examined the goods or the sample or model as fully as he desired or has refused to examine the goods there is no implied warranty with regard to defects which an examination ought in the circumstances to have revealed to him; and

(c) an implied warranty can also be excluded or modified by course of dealing or course of performance or usage of trade.

(4) Remedies for breach of warranty can be limited in accordance with the provisions of this Article on liquidation or limitation of damages and on contractual modification of remedy (Sections 2–718 and 2–719).

Official Comment

Purposes:

1. This section is designed principally to deal with those frequent clauses in sales contracts which seek to exclude "all warranties, express or implied." It seeks to protect a buyer from unexpected and unbargained language of disclaimer by denying effect to such language when inconsistent with language of express warranty and permitting the exclusion of implied warranties only by conspicuous language or other circumstances which protect the buyer from surprise.

2. The seller is protected under this Article against false allegations of oral warranties by its provisions on parol and extrinsic evidence and against unauthorized representations by the customary "lack of authority" clauses. This Article treats the limitation or avoidance of consequential damages as a matter of limiting remedies for breach, separate from the matter of creation of liability under a warranty. If no warranty exists, there is of course no problem of limiting remedies for breach of warranty. Under subsection (4) the question of limitation of remedy is governed by the sections referred to rather than by this section.

3. Disclaimer of the implied warranty of merchantability is permitted under subsection (2), but with the safeguard that such disclaimers must mention merchantability and in case of a writing must be conspicuous.

4. Unlike the implied warranty of merchantability, implied warranties of fitness for a particular purpose may be excluded by general language, but only if it is in writing and conspicuous.

5. Subsection (2) presupposes that the implied warranty in question exists unless excluded or modified. Whether or not language of disclaimer satisfies the requirements of this section, such language may be relevant under other sections to the question whether the warranty was ever in fact created. Thus, unless the provisions of this Article on parol and extrinsic evidence prevent, oral language of disclaimer may raise issues of fact as to whether reliance by the buyer occurred and whether the seller had "reason to know" under the section on implied warranty of fitness for a particular purpose.

6. The exceptions to the general rule set forth in paragraphs (a), (b) and (c) of subsection (3) are common factual situations in which the circumstances surrounding the transaction are in themselves sufficient to call the buyer's attention to the fact that no implied warranties are made or that a certain implied warranty is being excluded.

7. Paragraph (a) of subsection (3) deals with general terms such as "as is," "as they stand," "with all faults," and the like. Such terms in ordinary commercial usage are understood to mean that the buyer takes the entire risk as to the quality of the goods involved. The terms covered by paragraph (a) are in fact merely a particularization of paragraph (c) which provides for exclusion or modification of implied warranties by usage of trade.

8. Under paragraph (b) of subsection (3) warranties may be excluded or modified by the circumstances where the buyer examines the goods or a sample or model of them before entering into the contract. "Examination" as used in this paragraph is not synonymous with inspection before acceptance or at any other time after the contract has been made. It goes rather to the nature of the responsibility assumed by the seller at the time of the making of the contract. Of course if the buyer discovers the defect and uses the goods anyway, or if he unreasonably fails to examine the goods before he uses them, resulting injuries may be found to result from his own action rather than proximately from a breach of warranty. See Sections 2-314 and 2-715 and comments thereto.

In order to bring the transaction within the scope of "refused to examine" in paragraph (b), it is not sufficient that the goods are available for inspection. There must in addition be a demand by the seller that the buyer examine the goods fully. The seller by the demand puts the buyer on notice that he is assuming the risk of defects which the examination ought to reveal. The language "refused to examine" in this paragraph is intended to make clear the necessity for such demand.

Application of the doctrine of "caveat emptor" in all cases where the buyer examines the goods regardless of statements made by the seller is, however, rejected by this Article. Thus, if the offer of examination is accompanied by words as to their merchantability or specific attributes and the buyer indicates clearly that he is relying on those words rather than on his examination, they give rise to an "express" warranty. In such cases the question is one of fact as to whether a warranty of merchantability has been expressly incorporated in the agreement. Disclaimer of such an express warranty is governed by subsection (1) of the present section.

The particular buyer's skill and the normal method of examining goods in the circumstances determine what defects are excluded by the examination. A failure to notice defects which are obvious cannot excuse the buyer. However, an examination under circumstances which do not permit chemical or other testing of the goods would not exclude defects which could be ascertained only by such testing. Nor can latent defects be excluded by a simple examination. A professional buyer examining a product in his field will be held to have assumed the risk as to all defects which a professional in the field ought to observe, while a nonprofessional buyer will be held to have assumed the risk only for such defects as a layman might be expected to observe.

9. The situation in which the buyer gives precise and complete specifications to the seller is not explicitly covered in this section, but this is a frequent circumstance by which the implied warranties may be excluded. The warranty of fitness for a particular purpose would not normally arise since in such a situation there is usually no reliance on the seller by the buyer. The warranty of merchantability in such a transaction, however, must be considered in connection with the next section on the cumulation and conflict of warranties. Under paragraph (c) of that section in case of such an inconsistency the implied warranty of merchantability is displaced by the express warranty that the goods will comply with the specifications. Thus, where the buyer gives detailed specifications as to the goods, neither of the implied warranties as to quality will normally apply to the transaction unless consistent with the specifications.

§ 2-601. Buyer's Rights on Improper Delivery

Subject to the provisions of this Article on breach in installment contracts (Section 2-612) and unless otherwise agreed under the sections on contractual limitations of remedy (Sections 2-718 and 2-719), if the goods or the tender of delivery fail in any respect to conform to the contract, the buyer may

(a) reject the whole; or

(b) accept the whole; or

(c) accept any commercial unit or units and reject the rest.

Official Comment

Purposes of Changes: To make it clear that:

1. A buyer accepting a non-conforming tender is not penalized by the loss of any remedy otherwise open to him. This policy extends to cover and regulate the acceptance of a part of any lot improperly tendered in any case where the price can reasonably be apportioned. Partial acceptance is permitted whether the part of the goods accepted conforms or not. The only limitation on partial acceptance is that good faith and commercial reasonableness must be used to avoid undue impairment of the value of the remaining portion of the goods. This is the reason for the insistence on the "commercial unit" in paragraph (c). In this respect, the test is not only what unit has been the basis of contract, but whether the partial acceptance produces so materially adverse an effect on the remainder as to constitute bad faith.

2. Acceptance made with the knowledge of the other party is final. An original refusal to accept may be withdrawn by a later acceptance if the seller has indicated that he is holding the tender open. However, if the buyer attempts to accept, either in whole or in part, after his original rejection has caused the seller to arrange for other disposition of the goods, the buyer must answer for any ensuing damage since the next section provides that any exercise of ownership after rejection is wrongful as against the seller. Further, he is liable even though the seller may choose to treat his action as acceptance rather than conversion, since the damage flows from the misleading notice. Such arrangements for resale or other disposition of the goods by the seller must be viewed as within the normal contemplation of a buyer who has given notice of rejection. However, the buyer's attempts in good faith to dispose of defective goods where the seller has failed to give instructions within a reasonable time are not to be regarded as an acceptance.

§ 2-602. Manner and Effect of Rightful Rejection

(1) Rejection of goods must be within a reasonable time after their delivery or tender. It is ineffective unless the buyer seasonably notifies the seller.

(2) Subject to the provisions of the two following sections on rejected goods (Sections 2-603 and 2-604),

(a) after rejection any exercise of ownership by the buyer with respect to any commercial unit is wrongful as against the seller; and

(b) if the buyer has before rejection taken physical possession of goods in which he does not have a security interest under the provisions of this Article (subsection (3) of Section 2–711), he is under a duty after rejection to hold them with reasonable care at the seller's disposition for a time sufficient to permit the seller to remove them; but

(c) the buyer has no further obligations with regard to goods rightfully rejected.

(3) The seller's rights with respect to goods wrongfully rejected are governed by the provisions of this Article on Seller's remedies in general (Section 2–703).

Official Comment

Purposes of Changes: To make it clear that:

1. A tender or delivery of goods made pursuant to a contract of sale, even though wholly non-conforming, requires affirmative action by the buyer to avoid acceptance. Under subsection (1), therefore, the buyer is given a reasonable time to notify the seller of his rejection, but without such seasonable notification his rejection is ineffective. The sections of this Article dealing with inspection of goods must be read in connection with the buyer's reasonable time for action under this subsection. Contract provisions limiting the time for rejection fall within the rule of the section on "Time" and are effective if the time set gives the buyer a reasonable time for discovery of defects. What constitutes a due "notifying" of rejection by the buyer to the seller is defined in Section 1–201.

2. Subsection (2) lays down the normal duties of the buyer upon rejection, which flow from the relationship of the parties. Beyond his duty to hold the goods with reasonable care for the buyer's [seller's] disposition, this section continues the policy of prior uniform legislation in generally relieving the buyer from any duties with respect to them, except when the circumstances impose the limited obligation of salvage upon him under the next section.

3. The present section applies only to rightful rejection by the buyer. If the seller has made a tender which in all respects conforms to the contract, the buyer has a positive duty to accept and his failure to do so constitutes a "wrongful rejection" which gives the seller immediate remedies for breach. Subsection (3) is included here to emphasize the sharp distinction between the rejection of an improper tender and the non-acceptance which is a breach by the buyer.

4. The provisions of this section are to be appropriately limited or modified when a negotiation is in process.

§ 2-607. Effect of Acceptance; Notice of Breach; Burden of Establishing Breach After Acceptance; Notice of Claim or Litigation to Person Answerable Over

(1) The buyer must pay at the contract rate for any goods accepted.

(2) Acceptance of goods by the buyer precludes rejection of the goods accepted and if made with knowledge of a non-conformity cannot be revoked because of it unless the acceptance was on the reasonable assumption that the non-conformity would be seasonably cured but acceptance does not of itself impair any other remedy provided by this Article for non-conformity.

(3) Where a tender has been accepted

(a) the buyer must within a reasonable time after he discovers or should have discovered any breach notify the seller of breach or be barred from any remedy; and

(b) if the claim is one for infringement or the like (subsection (3) of Section 2–312) and the buyer is sued as a result of such a breach he must so notify the seller within a reasonable time after he receives notice of the litigation or be barred from any remedy over for liability established by the litigation.

(4) The burden is on the buyer to establish any breach with respect to the goods accepted.

(5) Where the buyer is sued for breach of a warranty or other obligation for which his seller is answerable over

(a) he may give his seller written notice of the litigation. If the notice states that the seller may come in and defend and that if the seller does not do so he will be bound in any action against him by his buyer by any determination of fact common to the two litigations, then unless the seller after seasonable receipt of the notice does come in and defend he is so bound.

(b) if the claim is one for infringement or the like (subsection (3) of Section 2-312) the original seller may demand in writing that his buyer turn over to him control of the litigation including settlement or else be barred from any remedy over and if he also agrees to bear all expense and to satisfy any adverse judgment, then unless the buyer after seasonable receipt of the demand does turn over control the buyer is so barred.

(6) The provisions of subsections (3), (4) and (5) apply to any obligation of a buyer to hold the seller harmless against infringement or the like (subsection (3) of Section 2-312).

Official Comment

1. Under subsection (1), once the buyer accepts a tender the seller acquires a right to its price on the contract terms. In cases of partial acceptance, the price of any part accepted is, if possible, to be reasonably apportioned, using the type of apportionment familiar to the courts in quantum valebat cases, to be determined in terms of "the contract rate," which is the rate determined from the bargain in fact (the agreement) after the rules and policies of this Article have been brought to bear.

2. Under subsection (2) acceptance of goods precludes their subsequent rejection. Any return of the goods thereafter must be by way of revocation of acceptance under the next section. Revocation is unavailable for a non-conformity known to the buyer at the time of acceptance, except where the buyer has accepted on the reasonable assumption that the non-conformity would be seasonably cured.

3. All other remedies of the buyer remain unimpaired under subsection (2). This is intended to include the buyer's full rights with respect to future installments despite his acceptance of any earlier non-conforming installment.

4. The time of notification is to be determined by applying commercial standards to a merchant buyer. "A reasonable time" for notification from a retail consumer is to be judged by different standards so that in his case it will be extended, for the rule of requiring notification is designed to defeat commercial bad faith, not to deprive a good faith consumer of his remedy.

The content of the notification need merely be sufficient to let the seller know that the transaction is still troublesome and must be watched. There is no reason to require that the notification which saves the buyer's rights under this section must include a clear statement of all the objections that will be relied on by the buyer, as under the section covering statements of defects upon rejection (Section 2-605). Nor is there reason for requiring the notification to be a claim for damages or of any threatened litigation or other resort to a remedy. The notification which saves the buyer's rights under this Article need only be such as informs the seller that the transaction is claimed to involve a breach, and thus opens the way for normal settlement through negotiation.

5. Under this Article various beneficiaries are given rights for injuries sustained by them because of the seller's breach of warranty. Such a beneficiary does not fall within the reason of the present section in regard to discovery of defects and the giving of notice within a reasonable time after acceptance, since he has nothing to do with acceptance. However, the reason of this section does extend to requiring the beneficiary to notify the seller that an injury has occurred. What is said above, with regard to the extended time for reasonable notification from the lay consumer after the injury is also applicable here; but even a beneficiary can be properly held to the use of good faith in notifying, once he has had time to become aware of the legal situation.

6. Subsection (4) unambiguously places the burden of proof to establish breach on the buyer after acceptance. However, this rule becomes one purely of procedure when the tender accepted was non-conforming and the buyer has given the seller notice of breach under subsection (3). For subsection (2) makes it clear that acceptance leaves unimpaired the buyer's right to be made whole, and that right can be exercised by the buyer not only by way of cross-claim for damages, but also by way of recoupment in diminution or extinction of the price.

7. Subsections (3)(b) and (5)(b) give a warrantor against infringement an opportunity to defend or compromise third-party claims or be relieved of his liability. Subsection (5)(a) codifies for all warranties the practice of voucher to defend. Compare Section 3–803. Subsection (6) makes these provisions applicable to the buyer's liability for infringement under Section 2–312.

8. All of the provisions of the present section are subject to any explicit reservation of rights.

§ 2–608. Revocation of Acceptance in Whole or in Part

(1) The buyer may revoke his acceptance of a lot or commercial unit whose non-conformity substantially impairs its value to him if he has accepted it

(a) on the reasonable assumption that its non-conformity would be cured and it has not been seasonably cured; or

(b) without discovery of such non-conformity if his acceptance was reasonably induced either by the difficulty of discovery before acceptance or by the seller's assurances.

(2) Revocation of acceptance must occur within a reasonable time after the buyer discovers or should have discovered the ground for it and before any substantial change in condition of the goods which is not caused by their own defects. It is not effective until the buyer notifies the seller of it.

(3) A buyer who so revokes has the same rights and duties with regard to the goods involved as if he had rejected them.

Official Comment

1. Although the prior basic policy is continued, the buyer is no longer required to elect between revocation of acceptance and recovery of damages for breach. Both are now available to him. The non-alternative character of the two remedies is stressed by the terms used in the present section. The section no longer speaks of "rescission," a term capable of ambiguous application either to transfer of title to the goods or to the contract of sale and susceptible also of confusion with cancellation for cause of an executed or executory portion of the contract. The remedy under this section is instead referred to simply as "revocation of acceptance" of goods tendered under a contract for sale and involves no suggestion of "election" of any sort.

2. Revocation of acceptance is possible only where the non-conformity substantially impairs the value of the goods to the buyer. For this purpose the test is not what the seller had reason to know at the time of contracting; the question is whether the non-conformity is such as will in fact cause a substantial impairment of value to the buyer though the seller had no advance knowledge as to the buyer's particular circumstances.

3. "Assurances" by the seller under paragraph (b) of subsection (1) can rest as well in the circumstances or in the contract as in explicit language used at the time of delivery. The reason for recognizing such assurances is that they induce the buyer to delay discovery. These are the only assurances involved in paragraph (b). Explicit assurances may be made either in good faith or bad faith. In either case any remedy accorded by this Article is available to the buyer under the section on remedies for fraud.

4. Subsection (2) requires notification of revocation of acceptance within a reasonable time after discovery of the grounds for such revocation. Since this remedy will be generally resorted to only after attempts at adjustment have failed, the reasonable time period should extend in most cases beyond the time in which notification of breach must be given, beyond the time for discovery of non-conformity after acceptance and beyond the time for rejection after tender. The parties may by their agreement limit the time for notification under this section, but the same sanctions and considerations apply to such agreements as are discussed in the comment on manner and effect of rightful rejection.

5. The content of the notice under subsection (2) is to be determined in this case as in others by considerations of good faith, prevention of surprise, and reasonable adjustment. More will generally be necessary than the mere notification of breach required under the preceding section. On the other hand the requirements of the section on waiver of buyer's objections do not apply here. The fact that quick notification of trouble is desirable affords good ground for being slow to bind a buyer by his first statement. Following

the general policy of this Article, the requirements of the content of notification are less stringent in the case of a non-merchant buyer.

6. Under subsection (2) the prior policy is continued of seeking substantial justice in regard to the condition of goods restored to the seller. Thus the buyer may not revoke his acceptance if the goods have materially deteriorated except by reason of their own defects. Worthless goods, however, need not be offered back and minor defects in the articles reoffered are to be disregarded.

7. The policy of the section allowing partial acceptance is carried over into the present section and the buyer may revoke his acceptance, in appropriate cases, as to the entire lot or any commercial unit thereof.

§ 2–714. Buyer's Damages for Breach in Regard to Accepted Goods

(1) Where the buyer has accepted goods and given notification (subsection (3) of Section 2–607) he may recover as damages for any non-conformity of tender the loss resulting in the ordinary course of events from the seller's breach as determined in any manner which is reasonable.

(2) The measure of damages for breach of warranty is the difference at the time and place of acceptance between the value of the goods accepted and the value they would have had if they had been as warranted, unless special circumstances show proximate damages of a different amount.

(3) In a proper case any incidental and consequential damages under the next section may also be recovered.

Official Comment

1. This section deals with the remedies available to the buyer after the goods have been accepted and the time for revocation of acceptance has gone by. In general this section adopts the rule of the prior uniform statutory provision for measuring damages where there has been a breach of warranty as to goods accepted, but goes further to lay down an explicit provision as to the time and place for determining the loss.

The section on deduction of damages from price provides an additional remedy for a buyer who still owes part of the purchase price, and frequently the two remedies will be available concurrently. The buyer's failure to notify of his claim under the section on effects of acceptance, however, operates to bar his remedies under either that section or the present section.

2. The "non-conformity" referred to in subsection (1) includes not only breaches of warranties but also any failure of the seller to perform according to his obligations under the contract. In the case of such non-conformity, the buyer is permitted to recover for his loss "in any manner which is reasonable."

3. Subsection (2) describes the usual, standard and reasonable method of ascertaining damages in the case of breach of warranty but it is not intended as an exclusive measure. It departs from the measure of damages for non-delivery in utilizing the place of acceptance rather than the place of tender. In some cases the two may coincide, as where the buyer signifies his acceptance upon the tender. If, however, the non-conformity is such as would justify revocation of acceptance, the time and place of acceptance under this section is determined as of the buyer's decision not to revoke.

4. The incidental and consequential damages referred to in subsection (3), which will usually accompany an action brought under this section, are discussed in detail in the comment on the next section.

§ 2–715. Buyer's Incidental and Consequential Damages

(1) Incidental damages resulting from the seller's breach include expenses reasonably incurred in inspection, receipt, transportation and care and custody of goods rightfully rejected, any commercially reasonable charges, expenses or commissions in connection with effecting cover and any other reasonable expense incident to the delay or other breach.

(2) Consequential damages resulting from the seller's breach include

(a) any loss resulting from general or particular requirements and needs of which the seller at the time of contracting had reason to know and which could not reasonably be prevented by cover or otherwise; and

(b) injury to person or property proximately resulting from any breach of warranty.

Official Comment

Purposes of Changes and New Matter:

1. Subsection (1) is intended to provide reimbursement for the buyer who incurs reasonable expenses in connection with the handling of rightfully rejected goods or goods whose acceptance may be justifiably revoked, or in connection with effecting cover where the breach of the contract lies in non-conformity or non-delivery of the goods. The incidental damages listed are not intended to be exhaustive but are merely illustrative of the typical kinds of incidental damage.

2. Subsection (2) operates to allow the buyer, in an appropriate case, any consequential damages which are the result of the seller's breach. The "tacit agreement" test for the recovery of consequential damages is rejected. Although the older rule at common law which made the seller liable for all consequential damages of which he had "reason to know" in advance is followed, the liberality of that rule is modified by refusing to permit recovery unless the buyer could not reasonably have prevented the loss by cover or otherwise. Subparagraph (2) carries forward the provisions of the prior uniform statutory provision as to consequential damages resulting from breach of warranty, but modifies the rule by requiring first that the buyer attempt to minimize his damages in good faith, either by cover or otherwise.

3. In the absence of excuse under the section on merchant's excuse by failure of presupposed conditions, the seller is liable for consequential damages in all cases where he had reason to know of the buyer's general or particular requirements at the time of contracting. It is not necessary that there be a conscious acceptance of an insurer's liability on the seller's part, nor is his obligation for consequential damages limited to cases in which he fails to use due effort in good faith.

Particular needs of the buyer must generally be made known to the seller while general needs must rarely be made known to charge the seller with knowledge.

Any seller who does not wish to take the risk of consequential damages has available the section on contractual limitation of remedy.

4. The burden of proving the extent of loss incurred by way of consequential damage is on the buyer, but the section on liberal administration of remedies rejects any doctrine of certainty which requires almost mathematical precision in the proof of loss. Loss may be determined in any manner which is reasonable under the circumstances.

5. Subsection (2)(b) states the usual rule as to breach of warranty, allowing recovery for injuries "proximately" resulting from the breach. Where the injury involved follows the use of goods without discovery of the defect causing the damage, the question of "proximate" cause turns on whether it was reasonable for the buyer to use the goods without such inspection as would have revealed the defects. If it was not reasonable for him to do so, or if he did in fact discover the defect prior to his use, the injury would not proximately result from the breach of warranty.

6. In the case of sale of wares to one in the business of reselling them, resale is one of the requirements of which the seller has reason to know within the meaning of subsection (2)(a).

§ 2-717. Deduction of Damages from the Price

The buyer on notifying the seller of his intention to do so may deduct all or any part of the damages resulting from any breach of the contract from any part of the price still due under the same contract.

Official Comment

Purposes:

1. This section permits the buyer to deduct from the price damages resulting from any breach by the seller and does not limit the relief to cases of breach of warranty as did the prior uniform statutory provision. To bring this provision into application the breach involved must be of the same contract under which the price in question is claimed to have been earned.

2. The buyer, however, must give notice of his intention to withhold all or part of the price if he wishes to avoid a default within the meaning of the section on insecurity and right to assurances. In conformity with the general policies of this Article, no formality of notice is required and any language which reasonably indicates the buyer's reason for holding up his payment is sufficient.

§ 2–719. Contractual Modification or Limitation of Remedy

(1) Subject to the provisions of subsections (2) and (3) of this section and of the preceding section on liquidation and limitation of damages,

(a) the agreement may provide for remedies in addition to or in substitution for those provided in this Article and may limit or alter the measure of damages recoverable under this Article, as by limiting the buyer's remedies to return of the goods and repayment of the price or to repair and replacement of non-conforming goods or parts; and

(b) resort to a remedy as provided is optional unless the remedy is expressly agreed to be exclusive, in which case it is the sole remedy.

(2) Where circumstances cause an exclusive or limited remedy to fail of its essential purpose, remedy may be had as provided in this Act.

(3) Consequential damages may be limited or excluded unless the limitation or exclusion is unconscionable. Limitation of consequential damages for injury to the person in the case of consumer goods is prima facie unconscionable but limitation of damages where the loss is commercial is not.

Official Comment

1. Under this section parties are left free to shape their remedies to their particular requirements and reasonable agreements limiting or modifying remedies are to be given effect.

However, it is of the very essence of a sales contract that at least minimum adequate remedies be available. If the parties intend to conclude a contract for sale within this Article they must accept the legal consequence that there be at least a fair quantum of remedy for breach of the obligations or duties outlined in the contract. Thus any clause purporting to modify or limit the remedial provisions of this Article in an unconscionable manner is subject to deletion and in that event the remedies made available by this Article are applicable as if the stricken clause had never existed. Similarly, under subsection (2), where an apparently fair and reasonable clause because of circumstances fails in its purpose or operates to deprive either party of the substantial value of the bargain, it must give way to the general remedy provisions of this Article.

2. Subsection (1)(b) creates a presumption that clauses prescribing remedies are cumulative rather than exclusive. If the parties intend the term to describe the sole remedy under the contract, this must be clearly expressed.

3. Subsection (3) recognizes the validity of clauses limiting or excluding consequential damages but makes it clear that they may not operate in an unconscionable manner. Actually such terms are merely an allocation of unknown or undeterminable risks. The seller in all cases is free to disclaim warranties in the manner provided in Section 2–316.

ARTICLE 2. SALES
(As Amended In 2003)

[**Editor's Note**. Although an amended version of Article 2 was released by the American Law Institute and the National Conference of Commissioners on Uniform State Laws in 2003, it failed to be enacted in any state and was withdrawn from the official text in 2011. However, some commentators have surmised that some of the provisions relating to consumer transactions might be used as guidance by courts seeking to interpret the unamended version of Article 2. Thus, we have included a few selected sections of the amended version.]

Table of Sections

§ 2–313A. Obligation to Remote Purchaser Created by Record Packaged With or Accompanying Goods

(1) In this section:

(a) "Immediate buyer" means a buyer that enters into a contract with the seller.

(b) "Remote purchaser" means a person that buys or leases goods from an immediate buyer or other person in the normal chain of distribution.

(2) This section applies only to new goods and goods sold or leased as new goods in a transaction of purchase in the normal chain of distribution.

(3) If in a record packaged with or accompanying the goods the seller makes an affirmation of fact or promise that relates to the goods, provides a description that relates to the goods, or makes a remedial promise, and the seller reasonably expects the record to be, and the record is, furnished to the remote purchaser, the seller has an obligation to the remote purchaser that:

(a) the goods will conform to the affirmation of fact, promise, or description unless a reasonable person in the position of the remote purchaser would not believe that the affirmation of fact, promise, or description created an obligation; and

(b) the seller will perform the remedial promise

(4) It is not necessary to the creation of an obligation under this section that the seller use formal words such as "warrant" or "guarantee" or that the seller have a specific intention to undertake an obligation, but an affirmation merely of the value of the goods or a statement purporting to be merely the seller's opinion or commendation of the goods does not create an obligation

(5) The following rules apply to the remedies for breach of an obligation created under this section:

(a) The seller may modify or limit the remedies available to the remote purchaser if the modification or limitation is furnished to the remote purchaser no later than the time of purchase or if the modification or limitation is contained in the record that contains the affirmation of fact, promise, or description

(b) Subject to a modification or limitation of remedy, a seller in breach is liable for incidental or consequential damages under Section 2–715, but not for lost profits.

(c) The remote purchaser may recover as damages for breach of a seller's obligation arising under subsection (3) the loss resulting in the ordinary course of events as determined in any reasonable manner.

(6) An obligation that is not a remedial promise is breached if the goods did not conform to the affirmation of fact, promise, or description creating the obligation when the goods left the seller's control.

Official Comment

1. Sections 2–313A and 2–313B are new, and they follow case law and practice in extending a seller's obligations regarding new goods to remote purchasers. Section 2–313A deals with what are commonly called "pass-through warranties". The usual transaction in which this obligation arises is when a manufacturer sells goods in a package to a retailer and include in the package a record that sets forth the obligations that the manufacturer is willing to undertake in favor of the final party in the distributive chain, who is the person that buys or leases the goods from the retailer. If the manufacturer had sold the goods directly to the final party in the distributive chain, whether the manufacturer would incur liability is determined by Section 2–313 and this section is inapplicable.

No direct contract exists between the seller and the remote purchaser, and thus the seller's obligation under this section is not referred to as an "express warranty." Use of "obligation" rather than "express warranty" avoids any inference that the obligation arises as part of the basis of the bargain as would be required to create an express warranty under Section 2–313. The test for whether an obligation other than a remedial promise arises is similar in some respects to the basis of the bargain requirement in Section 2–313, but the test set forth in this section is exclusive. Because "remedial promise" in Section 2–313 is not subject to the requirement that it arise as part of the basis of the bargain, the term is used in this section.

2. The party to which an obligation runs under this section may either buy or lease the goods, and thus the term "remote purchaser" is used. The term is more limited than "purchaser" in Article 1, however, and does not include a donee or any voluntary transferee who is not a buyer or lessee. Moreover, the remote purchaser must be part of the normal chain of distribution for the particular product. That chain will, by definition, include at least three parties and may well include more. For example, the manufacturer might sell first to a wholesaler that would then resell the goods to a retailer for sale or lease to the public. A buyer or lessee from the retailer would qualify as a remote purchaser and could invoke this section against either the manufacturer or the wholesaler (if the wholesaler provided a record to the retailer to be furnished to the final party in the distribution chain), but no subsequent transferee, such as a used-goods buyer or sublessee, would qualify. The law governing assignment and third-party beneficiary, including Section 2–318, should be consulted to determine whether a party other than the remote purchaser can enforce an obligation created under this section.

3. The application of this section is limited to new goods and goods sold or leased as new goods within the normal chain of distribution. It does not apply to goods that are sold outside the normal chain, such as "gray" goods or salvaged goods, nor does it apply if the goods are unused but sold as seconds. The concept is flexible, and to determine whether goods have been sold or leased in the normal chain of distribution requires consideration of the seller's expectations for the manner in which its goods will reach the remote purchaser. For example, a car manufacturer may be aware that certain of its dealers transfer cars among themselves, and under the particular circumstances of the case a court might find that a new car sold initially to one dealer but leased to the remote purchaser by another dealer was leased in the normal chain of distribution. The concept may also include such practices as door-to-door sales and distribution through a nonprofit organization.

The phrase "goods sold or leased as new goods" refers to goods that in the normal course of business would be considered new. There are many instances in which goods might be used for a limited purpose yet be sold or leased in the normal chain of distribution as new goods. For example, goods that have been returned to a dealer by a purchaser and placed back into the dealer's inventory might be sold or leased as new goods in the normal chain of distribution. Other examples might include goods that have been used for the purpose of inspection (*e.g.*, a car that has been test-driven) and goods that have been returned by a sale-or-return buyer (Section 2–326).

4. This section applies only to obligations set forth in a record that is packaged with the goods or otherwise accompanies them (subsection (2)). Examples include a label affixed to the outside of a container, a card inside a container, or a booklet handed to the remote purchaser at the time of purchase. In addition, the seller must be able to anticipate that the remote purchaser will acquire the record, and therefore this

section is limited to records that the seller reasonably expects to be furnished, and that are in fact furnished, to the remote purchaser.

Neither this section nor Section 2–313B are intended to overrule cases that impose liability on facts outside the direct scope of one of the sections. For example, the sections are not intended to overrule a decision imposing liability on a seller that distributes a sample to a remote purchaser.

5. Obligations other than remedial promises created under this section are analogous to express warranties and are subject to a test that is akin to the basis of the bargain test of Section 2–313(2). The seller is entitled to shape the scope of the obligation, and the seller's language tending to create an obligation must be considered in context. If a reasonable person in the position of the remote purchaser, reading the seller's language in its entirety, would not believe that an affirmation of fact, promise or description created an obligation, there is no liability under this section.

6. There is no difference between remedial promise as used in this section (and Section 2–313B) and the same term as used in Section 2–313.

7. Subsection (5)(a) makes clear that the seller may employ the provisions of Section 2–719 to modify or limit the remedies available to the remote purchaser for breach of the seller's obligation in this section. The modification or limitation may appear on the same record as the one which creates the obligation, or it may be provided to the remote purchaser separately, but in no event may it be furnished to the remote purchaser any later than the time of purchase.

The requirements and limitations set forth in Section 2–719, such as the requirement of an express statement of exclusivity and the tests for failure of essential purpose (Section 2–719(2)) and unconscionability (Section 2–719(3)) are applicable to a modification or limitation of remedy under this section.

8. As with express warranties, no specific language or intention is necessary to create an obligation, and whether an obligation exists is normally an issue of fact. Subsection (3) is virtually identical to Section 2–313(3), and the tests developed under the common law and under that section to determine whether a statement creates an obligation or is mere puffing are applicable to this section.

Just as a seller can limit the extent to which its language creates an express warranty under Section 2–313 by placing that language in a broader context, a seller under this section or Section 2–313B can limit the extent of its liability to a remote purchaser (subsection(4)(a)). In other words, the seller, in undertaking an obligation under these sections, can control the scope and limits of that obligation.

9. As a rule, a remote purchaser may recover monetary damages measured in the same manner as in the case of an aggrieved buyer under Section 2–714 as well as incidental and consequential damages under Section 2–715 to the extent they would be available to an aggrieved buyer. Subsection (5)(c) parallels Section 2–714(1) in allowing the buyer to recover for loss resulting in the ordinary course of events as determined in any manner which is reasonable. In the case of an obligation that is not a remedial promise, the normal measure of damages would be the difference between the value of the goods if they had conformed to the seller's statements and their actual value, and the normal measure of damages for breach of a remedial promise would be the difference between the value of the promised remedial performance and the value of the actual performance received.

Subsection (5)(b) precludes a remote purchaser from recovering consequential damages in the form of lost profits.

§ 2-313B. Obligation to Remote Purchaser Created by Communication to the Public

(1) In this section:

(a) "Immediate buyer" means a buyer that enters into a contract with the seller.

(b) "Remote purchaser" means a person that buys or leases goods from an immediate buyer or other person in the normal chain of distribution.

(2) This section applies only to new goods and goods sold or leased as new goods in a transaction of purchase in the normal chain of distribution.

(3) If in an advertisement or a similar communication to the public a seller makes an affirmation of fact or promise that relates to the goods, provides a description that relates to the goods, or makes a remedial promise, and the remote purchaser enters into a transaction of purchase with knowledge of and with the expectation that the goods will conform to the affirmation of fact, promise, or description, or that the seller will perform the remedial promise, the seller has an obligation to the remote purchaser that

(a) the goods will conform to the affirmation of fact, promise, or description unless a reasonable person in the position of the remote purchaser would not believe that the affirmation of fact, promise, or description created an obligation; and

(b) the seller will perform the remedial promise

(4) It is not necessary to the creation of an obligation under this section that the seller use formal words such as "warrant" or "guarantee" or that the seller have a specific intention to undertake an obligation, but an affirmation merely of the value of the goods or a statement purporting to be merely the seller's opinion or commendation of the goods does not create an obligation.

(5) The following rules apply to the remedies for breach of an obligation created under this section:

(a) The seller may modify or limit the remedies available to the remote purchaser if the modification or limitation is furnished to the remote purchaser no later than the time of purchase. The modification or limitation may be furnished as part of the communication that contains the affirmation of fact, promise, or description

(b) Subject to a modification or limitation of remedy, a seller in breach is liable for incidental or consequential damages under Section 2-715, but not for lost profits.

(c) The remote purchaser may recover as damages for breach of a seller's obligation arising under subsection (3) the loss resulting in the ordinary course of events as determined in any reasonable manner

(6) An obligation that is not a remedial promise is breached if the goods did not conform to the affirmation of fact, promise, or description creating the obligation when the goods left the seller's control.

Official Comment

1. Sections 2-313B and 2-313A are new, and they follow case law and practice in extending a seller's obligations for new goods to remote purchasers. This section deals with obligations to a remote purchaser created by advertising or a similar communication to the public. The normal situation where this obligation will arise is when a manufacturer engages in an advertising campaign directed towards all or part of the market for its product and will make statements that if made to an immediate buyer would amount to an express warranty or remedial promise under Section 2-313. The goods, however, are sold to someone other than the recipient of the advertising and are then resold or leased to the recipient. By imposing liability on the seller, this section adopts the approach of cases such as *Randy Knitwear, Inc. v. American Cyanamid Co.*, 11 N.Y.2d 5, 226 N.Y.S.2d 363, 181 N.E.2d 399 (Ct. App. 1962).

If the seller's advertisement is made to an immediate buyer, whether the seller incurs liability is determined by Section 2-313 and this section is inapplicable.

2. This section parallels Section 2-313A in most respects, and the Official Comments to that section should be consulted. In particular, the reasoning of Comment 1 (scope and terminology), Comment 2 (definition of remote purchaser), Comment 3 (new goods and goods sold as new goods in the normal chain of distribution), Comment 4 (reasonable person in the position of the remote purchaser), Comment 7 (modification or limitation of remedy), Comment 8 (puffing and limitations on extent of obligation) and Comment 9 (damages) is adopted here.

3. This section provides an additional test for enforceability not found in Section 2-313A. For the obligation to be created the remote purchaser must, at the time of purchase, have knowledge of the affirmation of fact, promise, description or remedial promise and must also have an expectation that the

goods will conform or that the seller will comply. This test is entirely subjective, while the reasonable person test in subsection (3)(a) is objective in nature. Both tests must be met.

Thus, the seller will incur no liability to the remote purchaser if: i) the purchaser did not have knowledge of the seller's statement at the time of purchase; ii) the remote purchaser knew of the seller's statement at the time of purchase but did not expect the goods to conform or the seller to comply; iii) a reasonable person in the position of the remote purchaser would not believe that the seller's statement created an obligation (this test does not apply to remedial promises), or iv) the seller's statement is puffing.

4. To determine whether the tests set forth in this section are satisfied the temporal relationship between the communication and the purchase should be considered by the court. For example, the remote purchaser may acquire the goods years after the seller's advertising campaign. In this circumstance, it would be highly unusual for the advertisement to have created the level of expectation in the remote purchaser or belief in the reasonable person in the position of the remote person necessary for the creation of an obligation under this section.

5. To determine whether an obligation arises under this Section, all information known to the remote purchaser at the time of contracting must be considered. For example, a news release by a manufacturer limiting the statements made in its advertising and which are known by the remote purchaser, or a communication to the remote purchaser by the immediate seller limiting the statements made in the manufacturer's advertising must be considered to determine whether the expectation requirement applicable to the remote purchaser and the belief requirement applicable to the reasonable person in the position of the remote purchaser are satisfied.

6. The remedies for breach of an obligation arising under this section may be modified or limited as set forth in Section 2-719. The modification or limitation may be contained in the advertisement that creates the obligation, or it may be separately furnished to the remote purchaser no later than the time of purchase.

7. Section 2-318 deals with the extension of obligations to certain third-party beneficiaries. Of course, no extension is necessary if the goods are purchased by an agent. In this case, the knowledge and expectation of the principal, not the agent, are relevant in determining whether an obligation arises under this section. Nothing in this Act precludes a court from determining that a household operates as a buying unit under the law of agency.

§ 2-316. Exclusion or Modification of Warranties

(1) Words or conduct relevant to the creation of an express warranty and words or conduct tending to negate or limit warranty shall be construed wherever reasonable as consistent with each other; but subject to Section 2-202, negation or limitation is inoperative to the extent that such construction is unreasonable.

(2) Subject to subsection (3), to exclude or modify the implied warranty of merchantability or any part of it in a consumer contract the language must be in a record, be conspicuous, and state "The seller undertakes no responsibility for the quality of the goods except as otherwise provided in this contract," and in any other contract the language must mention merchantability and in case of a record must be conspicuous. Subject to subsection (3), to exclude or modify the implied warranty of fitness, the exclusion must be in a record and be conspicuous. Language to exclude all implied warranties of fitness in a consumer contract must state "The seller assumes no responsibility that the goods will be fit for any particular purpose for which you may be buying these goods, except as otherwise provided in the contract," and in any other contract the language is sufficient if it states, for example, that "There are no warranties that extend beyond the description on the face hereof." Language that satisfies the requirements of this subsection for the exclusion or modification of a warranty in a consumer contract also satisfies the requirements for any other contract.

(3) Notwithstanding subsection (2):

(a) unless the circumstances indicate otherwise, all implied warranties are excluded by expressions like "as is", "with all faults" or other language that in common understanding calls the buyer's attention to the exclusion of warranties, makes plain that there is no implied warranty, and, in a consumer contract evidenced by a record, is set forth conspicuously in the record;

(b) if the buyer before entering into the contract has examined the goods or the sample or model as fully as desired or has refused to examine the goods after a demand by the seller there is no implied warranty with regard to defects that an examination in the circumstances should have revealed to the buyer; and

(c) an implied warranty may also be excluded or modified by course of dealing or course of performance or usage of trade.

(4) Remedies for breach of warranty may be limited in accordance with Sections 2–718 and 2–719.

Official Comment

1. Subsection (1) is designed principally to deal with those frequent clauses in sales contracts which seek to exclude "all warranties, express or implied." It seeks to protect a buyer from unexpected and unbargained language of disclaimer by denying effect to this language when inconsistent with language of express warranty and permitting the exclusion of implied warranties only by language or other circumstances which protect the buyer from surprise.

The seller is protected against false allegations of oral warranties by this Article's provisions on parol and extrinsic evidence and against unauthorized representations by the customary "lack of authority" clauses. This Article treats the limitation or avoidance of consequential damages as a matter of limiting remedies for breach, separate from the matter of creation of liability under a warranty. If no warranty exists, there is of course no problem of limiting remedies for breach of warranty. Under subsection (4), the question of limitation of remedy is governed by the sections referred to rather than by this section.

2. The general test for disclaimers of implied warranties remains in subsection (3)(a), and the more specific tests are in subsection (2). A disclaimer that satisfies the requirements of subsection (3)(a) need not also satisfy any of the requirements of subsection (2).

3. Subsection (2) distinguishes between commercial and consumer contracts. In a commercial contract, language that disclaims the implied warranty of merchantability need not be in a record, but if it is in a record it must be conspicuous. Under this subsection, a conspicuous record is required to disclaim the implied warranty of merchantability in a consumer contract and to disclaim the implied warranty of fitness in any contract. Use of the language required by this subsection for consumer contracts satisfies the language requirements for other contracts governed by this subsection.

4. Subsection (2) presupposes that the implied warranty in question exists unless excluded or modified. Whether or not language of disclaimer satisfies the requirements of this section, the language may be relevant under other sections to the question of whether the warranty was ever in fact created. Thus, unless the provisions of this Article on parol and extrinsic evidence prevent its introduction, oral language of a disclaimer may raise issues of fact about whether reliance by the buyer occurred and whether the seller had "reason to know" under the section on implied warranty of fitness for a particular purpose.

5. Subsection (3)(a) deals with general terms such as "as is," "as they stand," "with all faults," and the like. These terms in ordinary commercial usage are understood to mean that the buyer takes the entire risk as to the quality of the goods involved. The terms covered by the subsection are in fact merely a particularization of subsection (3)(c), which provides for exclusion or modification of implied warranties by usage of trade. Nothing in subsection (3)(a) prevents a term such as "there are no implied warranties" from being effective in appropriate circumstances, as when the term is a negotiated term between commercial parties.

Satisfaction of subsection (3)(a) does not require that the language be set forth in a record, but if there is a record the language must be conspicuous if the contract is a consumer contract.

6. The exceptions to the general rule set forth in subsections (3)(b) and (3)(c) are common factual situations in which the circumstances surrounding the transaction are in themselves sufficient to call the buyer's attention to the fact that no implied warranties are made or that a certain implied warranty is being excluded.

Under subsection (3)(b), warranties may be excluded or modified by the circumstances when the buyer examines the goods or a sample or model of them before entering into the contract. "Examination" as used in this paragraph is not synonymous with inspection before acceptance or at any other time after the contract has been made. Of course if the buyer discovers the defect and uses the goods anyway, or if the buyer unreasonably fails to examine the goods before using them, the resulting injuries may be found to have resulted from the buyer's own action rather than have been proximately caused by a breach of warranty. *See* Sections 2–314 and 2–715.

To bring the transaction within the scope of "refused to examine" in subsection (3)(b), it is not sufficient that the goods are available for inspection. There must in addition be an actual examination by the buyer or a demand by the seller that the buyer examine the goods fully. The seller's demand must place the buyer on notice that the buyer is assuming the risk of defects which the examination ought to reveal.

Application of the doctrine of "caveat emptor" in all cases where the buyer examines the goods regardless of statements made by the seller is, however, rejected by this Article. Thus, if the offer of examination is accompanied by words about their merchantability or specific attributes, and the buyer indicates clearly a reliance on those words rather than on the buyer's examination, the words give rise to an "express" warranty. In these cases, the question is one of fact about whether a warranty of merchantability has been expressly incorporated in the agreement.

The particular buyer's skill and the normal method of examining goods in the circumstances determine what defects are excluded by the examination. A failure to notice defects which are obvious cannot excuse the buyer because of the lack of notice. However, an examination under circumstances which do not permit chemical or other testing of the goods does not exclude defects which could be ascertained only by testing. Nor can latent defects be excluded by a simple examination. A professional buyer examining a product in the buyer's field will be held to have assumed the risk for all defects which a professional in the field ought to observe, while a nonprofessional buyer will be held to have assumed the risk only for the defects as a layperson might be expected to observe.

7. The situation in which the buyer gives precise and complete specifications to the seller is not explicitly covered in this section, but this is a frequent circumstance by which the implied warranties may be excluded. The warranty of fitness for a particular purpose would not normally arise since in this situation there is usually no reliance on the seller by the buyer. The warranty of merchantability in a transaction of this type, however, must be considered in connection with the next section on the cumulation and conflict of warranties. Under paragraph(c) of that section in case of an inconsistency the implied warranty of merchantability is displaced by the express warranty that the goods will comply with the specifications. Thus, where the buyer gives detailed specifications as to the goods, neither of the implied warranties as to quality will normally apply to the transaction unless consistent with the specifications.

§ 2–608. Revocation of Acceptance in Whole or in Part

(1) A buyer may revoke acceptance of a lot or commercial unit whose nonconformity substantially impairs its value to the buyer if the buyer has accepted it:

(a) on the reasonable assumption that its nonconformity would be cured and it has not been seasonably cured; or

(b) without discovery of the nonconformity if the buyer's acceptance was reasonably induced either by the difficulty of discovery before acceptance or by the seller's assurances.

(2) Revocation of acceptance must occur within a reasonable time after the buyer discovers or should have discovered the ground for it and before any substantial change in condition of the goods which is not caused by their own defects. The revocation is not effective until the buyer notifies the seller of it.

(3) A buyer that so revokes has the same rights and duties with regard to the goods involved as if the buyer had rejected them.

(4) If a buyer uses the goods after a rightful rejection or justifiable revocation of acceptance, the following rules apply:

(a) Any use by the buyer that is unreasonable under the circumstances is wrongful as against the seller and is an acceptance only if ratified by the seller.

(b) Any use of the goods that is reasonable under the circumstances is not wrongful as against the seller and is not an acceptance, but in an appropriate case the buyer is obligated to the seller for the value of the use to the buyer.

Official Comment

Purposes of Changes: To make it clear that:

1. Although the prior basic policy is continued, the buyer is no longer required to elect between revocation of acceptance and recovery of damages for breach. Both are now available to him. The non-alternative character of the two remedies is stressed by the terms used in the present section. The section no longer speaks of "rescission," a term capable of ambiguous application either to transfer of title to the goods or to the contract of sale and susceptible also of confusion with cancellation for cause of an executed or executory portion of the contract. The remedy under this section is instead referred to simply as "revocation of acceptance" of goods tendered under a contract for sale and involves no suggestion of "election" of any sort.

2. Revocation of acceptance is possible only where the non-conformity substantially impairs the value of the goods to the buyer. For this purpose the test is not what the seller had reason to know at the time of contracting; the question is whether the non-conformity is such as will in fact cause a substantial impairment of value to the buyer though the seller had no advance knowledge as to the buyer's particular circumstances.

3. "Assurances" by the seller under paragraph (b) of subsection (1) can rest as well in the circumstances or in the contract as in explicit language used at the time of delivery. The reason for recognizing such assurances is that they induce the buyer to delay discovery. These are the only assurances involved in paragraph (b). Explicit assurances may be made either in good faith or bad faith. In either case any remedy accorded by this Article is available to the buyer under the section on remedies for fraud.

4. Subsection (2) requires notification of revocation of acceptance within a reasonable time after discovery of the grounds for such revocation. Since this remedy will be generally resorted to only after attempts at adjustment have failed, the reasonable time period should extend in most cases beyond the time in which notification of breach must be given, beyond the time for discovery of non-conformity after acceptance and beyond the time for rejection after tender. The parties may by their agreement limit the time for notification under this section, but the same sanctions and considerations apply to such agreements as are discussed in the comment on manner and effect of rightful rejection.

5. The content of the notice under subsection (2) is to be determined in this case as in others by considerations of good faith, prevention of surprise, and reasonable adjustment. More will generally be necessary than the mere notification of breach required under the preceding section. On the other hand the requirements of the section on waiver of buyer's objections do not apply here. The fact that quick notification of trouble is desirable affords good ground for being slow to bind a buyer by his first statement. Following the general policy of this Article, the requirements of the content of notification are less stringent in the case of a non-merchant buyer.

6. Under subsection (2) the prior policy is continued of seeking substantial justice in regard to the condition of goods restored to the seller. Thus the buyer may not revoke his acceptance if the goods have materially deteriorated except by reason of their own defects. Worthless goods, however, need not be offered back and minor defects in the articles reoffered are to be disregarded.

7. The policy of the section allowing partial acceptance is carried over into the present section and the buyer may revoke his acceptance, in appropriate cases, as to the entire lot or any commercial unit thereof.

8. Subsection (4) deals with the problem of post-rejection or revocation use of the goods. The courts have developed several alternative approaches. Under original Article 2, a buyer's post-rejection or revocation use of the goods could be treated as an acceptance, thus undoing the rejection or revocation, could be a violation of the buyer's obligation of reasonable care, or could be a reasonable use for which the buyer must compensate the seller. Subsection (4) adopts the third approach.

In general, a buyer that either rejects or revokes acceptance of the goods should not subsequently use the goods in a manner that is inconsistent with the seller's ownership. In some instances, however, the use may be reasonable. For example, a consumer buyer may have incurred an unavoidable obligation to a third-party financier and, if the seller fails to refund the price as required by this Article, the buyer may have no reasonable alternative but to use the goods (e.g., a rejected mobile home that provides needed shelter). Another example might involve a commercial buyer that is unable immediately to obtain cover and must use the goods to fulfill its obligations to third parties. If circumstances change so that the buyer's use after an effective rejection or a justified revocation of acceptance is no longer reasonable, the continued use of the goods is unreasonable and is wrongful against the seller. This gives the seller the option of ratifying the use, thereby treating it as an acceptance, or pursuing a non-Code remedy for conversion.

If the buyer's use is reasonable under the circumstances, the buyer's actions cannot be treated as an acceptance. The buyer must compensate the seller for the value of the use of the goods to the buyer. Determining the appropriate level of compensation requires a consideration of the buyer's particular circumstances and should take into account the defective condition of the goods. There may be circumstances, such as where the use is solely for the purpose of protecting the buyer's security interest in the goods, where no compensation is due the seller under this section. If the seller has a right to compensation under this section that compensation must be netted out against any right of the buyer to damages for the seller's breach of contract.

ARTICLE 3. NEGOTIABLE INSTRUMENTS

Table of Sections

§ 3–302. Holder in Due Course

(1) A holder in due course is a holder who takes the instrument

(a) for value; and

(b) in good faith; and

(c) without notice that it is overdue or has been dishonored or of any defense against or claim to it on the part of any person.

(2) A payee may be a holder in due course.

(3) A holder does not become a holder in due course of an instrument:

(a) by purchase of it at judicial sale or by taking it under legal process; or

(b) by acquiring it in taking over an estate; or

(c) by purchasing it as part of a bulk transaction not in regular course of business of the transferor.

(4) A purchaser of a limited interest can be a holder in due course only to the extent of the interest purchased.

§ 3–302. Holder in Due Course (as amended in 2002)

[**Editor's Note**. This version contains subsection (g) which recognizes the state statutory and case law restricting the use of the holder in due course doctrine in consumer transactions. However, the amended version of Article 3 has been adopted in only 9 states, as of 2012: Arkansas, Indiana, Kentucky, Mississippi, Nevada, New Mexico, Oklahoma, South Carolina and Texas].

(a) Subject to subsection (c) and Section 3–106(d), "holder in due course" means the holder of an instrument if:

(1) the instrument when issued or negotiated to the holder does not bear such apparent evidence of forgery or alteration or is not otherwise so irregular or incomplete as to call into question its authenticity; and

(2) the holder took the instrument (i) for value, (ii) in good faith, (iii) without notice that the instrument is overdue or has been dishonored or that there is an uncured default with respect to payment of another instrument issued as part of the same series, (iv) without notice that the instrument contains an unauthorized signature or has been altered, (v) without notice of any claim to the instrument described in Section 3–306, and (vi) without notice that any party has a defense or claim in recoupment described in Section 3–305(a).

(b) Notice of discharge of a party, other than discharge in an insolvency proceeding, is not notice of a defense under subsection (a), but discharge is effective against a person who became a holder in due course with notice of the discharge. Public filing or recording of a document does not of itself constitute notice of a defense, claim in recoupment, or claim to the instrument.

(c) Except to the extent a transferor or predecessor in interest has rights as a holder in due course, a person does not acquire rights of a holder in due course of an instrument taken (i) by legal process or by purchase in an execution, bankruptcy, or creditor's sale or similar proceeding, (ii) by purchase as part of a bulk transaction not in ordinary course of business of the transferor, or (iii) as the successor in interest to an estate or other organization.

(d) If, under Section 3–303(a)(1), the promise of performance that is the consideration for an instrument has been partially performed, the holder may assert rights as a holder in due course of the instrument only to the fraction of the amount payable under the instrument equal to the value of the partial performance divided by the value of the promised performance.

(e) If (i) the person entitled to enforce an instrument has only a security interest in the instrument and (ii) the person obliged to pay the instrument has a defense, claim in recoupment, or claim to the instrument that may be asserted against the person who granted the security interest, the person entitled to enforce the instrument may assert rights as a holder in due course only to an amount payable under the instrument which, at the time of enforcement of the instrument, does not exceed the amount of the unpaid obligation secured.

(f) To be effective, notice must be received at a time and in a manner that gives a reasonable opportunity to act on it.

(g) This section is subject to any law limiting status as a holder in due course in particular classes of transactions.

Official Comment

1. Subsection (a)(1) is a return to the N.I.L. rule that the taker of an irregular or incomplete instrument is not a person the law should protect against defenses of the obligor or claims of prior owners. This reflects a policy choice against extending the holder in due course doctrine to an instrument that is so incomplete or irregular "as to call into question its authenticity." The term "authenticity" is used to make it clear that the irregularity or incompleteness must indicate that the instrument may not be what it purports to be. Persons who purchase or pay such instruments should do so at their own risk. Under subsection (1) of former Section 3–304, irregularity or incompleteness gave a purchaser notice of a claim or defense. But it was not clear from that provision whether the claim or defense had to be related to the irregularity or incomplete aspect of the instrument. This ambiguity is not present in subsection (a)(1).

2. Subsection (a)(2) restates subsection (1) of former Section 3–302. Section 3–305(a) makes a distinction between defenses to the obligation to pay an instrument and claims in recoupment by the maker or drawer that may be asserted to reduce the amount payable on the instrument. Because of this distinction,

which was not made in former Article 3, the reference in subsection (a)(2)(vi) is to both a defense and a claim in recoupment. Notice of forgery or alteration is stated separately because forgery and alteration are not technically defenses under subsection (a) of Section 3–305.

3. Discharge is also separately treated in the first sentence of subsection (b). Except for discharge in an insolvency proceeding, which is specifically stated to be a real defense in Section 3–305(a)(1), discharge is not expressed in Article 3 as a defense and is not included in Section 3–305(a)(2). Discharge is effective against anybody except a person having rights of a holder in due course who took the instrument without notice of the discharge. Notice of discharge does not disqualify a person from becoming a holder in due course. For example, a check certified after it is negotiated by the payee may subsequently be negotiated to a holder. If the holder had notice that the certification occurred after negotiation by the payee, the holder necessarily had notice of the discharge of the payee as indorser. Section 3–415(d). Notice of that discharge does not prevent the holder from becoming a holder in due course, but the discharge is effective against the holder. Section 3–601(b). Notice of a defense under Section 3–305(a)(1) of a maker, drawer or acceptor based on a bankruptcy discharge is different. There is no reason to give holder in due course status to a person with notice of that defense. The second sentence of subsection (b) is from former Section 3–304(5).

4. Professor Britton in his treatise Bills and Notes 309 (1961) stated: "A substantial number of decisions before the [N.I.L.] indicates that at common law there was nothing in the position of the payee as such which made it impossible for him to be a holder in due course." The courts were divided, however, about whether the payee of an instrument could be a holder in due course under the N.I.L. Some courts read N.I.L. § 52(4) to mean that a person could be a holder in due course only if the instrument was "negotiated" to that person. N.I.L. § 30 stated that "an instrument is negotiated when it is transferred from one person to another in such manner as to constitute the transferee the holder thereof." Normally, an instrument is "issued" to the payee; it is not transferred to the payee. N.I.L. § 191 defined "issue" as the "first delivery of the instrument * * * to a person who takes it as a holder." Thus, some courts concluded that the payee never could be a holder in due course. Other courts concluded that there was no evidence that the N.I.L. was intended to change the common law rule that the payee could be a holder in due course. Professor Britton states on p. 318: "The typical situations which raise the [issue] are those where the defense of a maker is interposed because of fraud by a [maker who is] principal debtor * * * against a surety co-maker, or where the defense of fraud by a purchasing remitter is interposed by the drawer of the instrument against the good faith purchasing payee."

Former Section 3–302(2) stated: "A payee may be a holder in due course." This provision was intended to resolve the split of authority under the N.I.L. It made clear that there was no intent to change the common-law rule that allowed a payee to become a holder in due course. See Comment 2 to former Section 3–302. But there was no need to put subsection (2) in former Section 3–302 because the split in authority under the N.I.L. was caused by the particular wording of N.I.L. § 52(4). The troublesome language in that section was not repeated in former Article 3 nor is it repeated in revised Article 3. Former Section 3–302(2) has been omitted in revised Article 3 because it is surplusage and may be misleading. The payee of an instrument can be a holder in due course, but use of the holder-in-due-course doctrine by the payee of an instrument is not the normal situation.

The primary importance of the concept of holder in due course is with respect to assertion of defenses or claims in recoupment (Section 3–305) and of claims to the instrument (Section 3–306). The holder-in-due-course doctrine assumes the following case as typical. Obligor issues a note or check to Obligee. Obligor is the maker of the note or drawer of the check. Obligee is the payee. Obligor has some defense to Obligor's obligation to pay the instrument. For example, Obligor issued the instrument for goods that Obligee promised to deliver. Obligee never delivered the goods. The failure of Obligee to deliver the goods is a defense. Section 3–303(b). Although Obligor has a defense against Obligee, if the instrument is negotiated to Holder and the requirements of subsection (a) are met, Holder may enforce the instrument against Obligor free of the defense. Section 3–305(b). In the typical case the holder in due course is not the payee of the instrument. Rather, the holder in due course is an immediate or remote transferee of the payee. If Obligor in our example is the only obligor on the check or note, the holder-in-due-course doctrine is irrelevant in determining rights between Obligor and Obligee with respect to the instrument.

But in a small percentage of cases it is appropriate to allow the payee of an instrument to assert rights as a holder in due course. The cases are like those referred to in the quotation from Professor Britton referred to above, or other cases in which conduct of some third party is the basis of the defense of the issuer of the instrument. The following are examples:

Case #1. Buyer pays for goods bought from Seller by giving to Seller a cashier's check bought from Bank. Bank has a defense to its obligation to pay the check because Buyer bought the check from Bank with a check known to be drawn on an account with insufficient funds to cover the check. If Bank issued the check to Buyer as payee and Buyer indorsed it over to Seller, it is clear that Seller can be a holder in due course taking free of the defense if Seller had no notice of the defense. Seller is a transferee of the check. There is no good reason why Seller's position should be any different if Bank drew the check to the order of Seller as payee. In that case, when Buyer took delivery of the check from Bank, Buyer became the owner of the check even though Buyer was not the holder. Buyer was a remitter. Section 3–103(a)<<-(11)->><<+ (15)+>>. At that point nobody was the holder. When Buyer delivered the check to Seller, ownership of the check was transferred to Seller who also became the holder. This is a negotiation. Section 3–201. The rights of Seller should not be affected by the fact that in one case the negotiation to Seller was by a holder and in the other case the negotiation was by a remitter. Moreover, it should be irrelevant whether Bank delivered the check to Buyer and Buyer delivered it to Seller or whether Bank delivered it directly to Seller. In either case Seller can be a holder in due course that takes free of Bank's defense.

Case #2. X fraudulently induces Y to join X in a spurious venture to purchase a business. The purchase is to be financed by a bank loan for part of the price. Bank lends money to X and Y by deposit in a joint account of X and Y who sign a note payable to Bank for the amount of the loan. X then withdraws the money from the joint account and absconds. Bank acted in good faith and without notice of the fraud of X against Y. Bank is payee of the note executed by Y, but its right to enforce the note against Y should not be affected by the fact that Y was induced to execute the note by the fraud of X. Bank can be a holder in due course that takes free of the defense of Y. Case #2 is similar to Case #1. In each case the payee of the instrument has given value to the person committing the fraud in exchange for the obligation of the person against whom the fraud was committed. In each case the payee was not party to the fraud and had no notice of it.

Suppose in Case #2 that the note does not meet the requirements of Section 3–104(a) and thus is not a negotiable instrument covered by Article 3. In that case, Bank cannot be a holder in due course but the result should be the same. Bank's rights are determined by general principles of contract law. Restatement Second, Contracts § 164(2) governs the case. If Y is induced to enter into a contract with Bank by a fraudulent misrepresentation by X, the contract is voidable by Y unless Bank "in good faith and without reason to know of the misrepresentation either gives value or relies materially on the transaction." Comment e to § 164(2) states:

> "This is the same principle that protects an innocent person who purchases goods or commercial paper in good faith, without notice and for value from one who obtained them from the original owner by a misrepresentation. See Uniform Commercial Code §§ 2–403(1), 3–305. In the cases that fall within [§ 164(2)], however, the innocent person deals directly with the recipient of the misrepresentation, which is made by one not a party to the contract."

The same result follows in Case #2 if Y had been induced to sign the note as an accommodation party (Section 3–419). If Y signs as co-maker of a note for the benefit of X, Y is a surety with respect to the obligation of X to pay the note but is liable as maker of the note to pay Bank. Section 3–419(b). If Bank is a holder in due course, the fraud of X cannot be asserted against Bank under Section 3–305(b). But the result is the same without resort to holder-in-due-course doctrine. If the note is not a negotiable instrument governed by Article 3, general rules of suretyship apply. Restatement, Security § 119 states that the surety (Y) cannot assert a defense against the creditor (Bank) based on the fraud of the principal (X) if the creditor "without knowledge of the fraud * * * extended credit to the principal on the security of the surety's promise * * *." The underlying principle of § 119 is the same as that of § 164(2) of Restatement Second, Contracts.

Case #3. Corporation draws a check payable to Bank. The check is given to an officer of Corporation who is instructed to deliver it to Bank in payment of a debt owed by Corporation to Bank. Instead, the officer, intending to defraud Corporation, delivers the check to Bank in payment of the officer's personal debt, or the check is delivered to Bank for deposit to the officer's personal account. If Bank obtains payment of the check, Bank has received funds of Corporation which have been used for the personal benefit of the officer. Corporation in this case will assert a claim to the proceeds of the check against Bank. If Bank was a holder in due course of the check it took the check free of Corporation's claim. Section 3–306. The issue in this case is whether Bank had notice of the claim when it took the check. If Bank knew that the officer was a fiduciary with respect to the check, the issue is governed by Section 3–307.

Case #4. Employer, who owed money to X, signed a blank check and delivered it to Secretary with instructions to complete the check by typing in X's name and the amount owed to X. Secretary fraudulently completed the check by typing in the name of Y, a creditor to whom Secretary owed money. Secretary then delivered the check to Y in payment of Secretary's debt. Y obtained payment of the check. This case is similar to Case #3. Since Secretary was authorized to complete the check, Employer is bound by Secretary's act in making the check payable to Y. The drawee bank properly paid the check. Y received funds of Employer which were used for the personal benefit of Secretary. Employer asserts a claim to these funds against Y. If Y is a holder in due course, Y takes free of the claim. Whether Y is a holder in due course depends upon whether Y had notice of Employer's claim.

5. Subsection (c) is based on former Section 3–302(3). Like former Section 3–302(3), subsection (c) is intended to state existing case law. It covers a few situations in which the purchaser takes an instrument under unusual circumstances. The purchaser is treated as a successor in interest to the prior holder and can acquire no better rights. But if the prior holder was a holder in due course, the purchaser obtains rights of a holder in due course.

Subsection (c) applies to a purchaser in an execution sale or sale in bankruptcy. It applies equally to an attaching creditor or any other person who acquires the instrument by legal process or to a representative, such as an executor, administrator, receiver or assignee for the benefit of creditors, who takes the instrument as part of an estate. Subsection (c) applies to bulk purchases lying outside of the ordinary course of business of the seller. For example, it applies to the purchase by one bank of a substantial part of the paper held by another bank which is threatened with insolvency and seeking to liquidate its assets. Subsection (c) would also apply when a new partnership takes over for value all of the assets of an old one after a new member has entered the firm, or to a reorganized or consolidated corporation taking over the assets of a predecessor.

In the absence of controlling state law to the contrary, subsection (c) applies to a sale by a state bank commissioner of the assets of an insolvent bank. However, subsection (c) may be preempted by federal law if the Federal Deposit Insurance Corporation takes over an insolvent bank. Under the governing federal law, the FDIC and similar financial institution insurers are given holder in due course status and that status is also acquired by their assignees under the shelter doctrine.

6. Subsections (d) and (e) clarify two matters not specifically addressed by former Article 3:

Case #5. Payee negotiates a $1,000 note to Holder who agrees to pay $900 for it. After paying $500, Holder learns that Payee defrauded Maker in the transaction giving rise to the note. Under subsection (d) Holder may assert rights as a holder in due course to the extent of $555.55 ($500 / $900 = .555 x $1,000 = $555.55). This formula rewards Holder with a ratable portion of the bargained for profit.

Case #6. Payee negotiates a note of Maker for $1,000 to Holder as security for payment of Payee's debt to Holder of $600. Maker has a defense which is good against Payee but of which Holder has no notice. Subsection (e) applies. Holder may assert rights as a holder in due course only to the extent of $600. Payee does not get the benefit of the holder-in-due-course status of Holder. With respect to $400 of the note, Maker may assert any rights that Maker has against Payee. A different result follows if the payee of a note negotiated it to a person who took it as a holder in due course and that person pledged the note as security for a debt. Because the defense cannot be asserted against the pledgor, the pledgee can assert rights as a holder in due course for the full amount of the note for the benefit of both the pledgor and the pledgee.

7. There is a large body of state statutory and case law restricting the use of the holder in due course doctrine in consumer transactions as well as some business transactions that raise similar issues. Subsection (g) subordinates Article 3 to that law and any other similar law that may evolve in the future. Section 3–106(d) also relates to statutory or administrative law intended to restrict use of the holder-in-due-course doctrine. See Comment 3 to Section 3–106.

8. The status of holder in due course resembles the status of protected holder under Article 29 of the Convention on International Bills of Exchange and International Promissory Notes. The requirements for being a protected holder under Article 29 generally track those of Section 3–302. *Amendments approved by the Permanent Editorial Board for Uniform Commercial Code November 2, 2002.*

§ 3–305. Rights of a Holder in Due Course

To the extent that a holder is a holder in due course he takes the instrument free from

(1) all claims to it on the part of any person; and

(2) all defenses of any party to the instrument with whom the holder has not dealt except

(a) infancy, to the extent that it is a defense to a simple contract; and

(b) such other incapacity, or duress, or illegality of the transaction, as renders the obligation of the party a nullity; and

(c) such misrepresentation as has induced the party to sign the instrument with neither knowledge nor reasonable opportunity to obtain knowledge of its character or its essential terms; and

(d) discharge in insolvency proceedings; and

(e) any other discharge of which the holder has notice when he takes the instrument.

§ 3–305. Defenses and Claims in Recoupment; Claims in Consumer Transactions [as amended in 2002]

[Editor's Note. This version contains subsections (e) and (f) which recognize the state statutory and case law restricting the use of the holder in due course doctrine in consumer transactions. However, the amended version of Article 3 has been adopted in only 9 states, as of 2012: Arkansas, Indiana, Kentucky, Mississippi, Nevada, New Mexico, Oklahoma, South Carolina and Texas].

(a) Except as otherwise provided in this section, the right to enforce the obligation of a party to pay an instrument is subject to the following:

(1) a defense of the obligor based on (i) infancy of the obligor to the extent it is a defense to a simple contract, (ii) duress, lack of legal capacity, or illegality of the transaction which, under other law, nullifies the obligation of the obligor, (iii) fraud that induced the obligor to sign the instrument with neither knowledge nor reasonable opportunity to learn of its character or its essential terms, or (iv) discharge of the obligor in insolvency proceedings;

(2) a defense of the obligor stated in another section of this Article or a defense of the obligor that would be available if the person entitled to enforce the instrument were enforcing a right to payment under a simple contract; and

(3) a claim in recoupment of the obligor against the original payee of the instrument if the claim arose from the transaction that gave rise to the instrument; but the claim of the obligor may be asserted against a transferee of the instrument only to reduce the amount owing on the instrument at the time the action is brought.

(b) The right of a holder in due course to enforce the obligation of a party to pay the instrument is subject to defenses of the obligor stated in subsection (a)(1), but is not subject to defenses of the obligor stated in subsection (a)(2) or claims in recoupment stated in subsection (a)(3) against a person other than the holder.

(c) Except as stated in subsection (d), in an action to enforce the obligation of a party to pay the instrument, the obligor may not assert against the person entitled to enforce the instrument a defense, claim in recoupment, or claim to the instrument (Section 3–306) of another person, but the other person's claim to the instrument may be asserted by the obligor if the other person is joined in the action and personally asserts the claim against the person entitled to enforce the instrument. An obligor is not obliged to pay the instrument if the person seeking enforcement of the instrument does not have rights of a holder in due course and the obligor proves that the instrument is a lost or stolen instrument.

(d) In an action to enforce the obligation of an accommodation party to pay an instrument, the accommodation party may assert against the person entitled to enforce the instrument any defense or claim in recoupment under subsection (a) that the accommodated party could assert against the person entitled to enforce the instrument, except the defenses of discharge in insolvency proceedings, infancy, and lack of legal capacity.

(e) In a consumer transaction, if law other than this article requires that an instrument include a statement to the effect that the rights of a holder or transferee are subject to a claim or defense that the issuer could assert against the original payee, and the instrument does not include such a statement:

(1) the instrument has the same effect as if the instrument included such a statement;

(2) the issuer may assert against the holder or transferee all claims and defenses that would have been available if the instrument included such a statement; and

(3) the extent to which claims may be asserted against the holder or transferee is determined as if the instrument included such a statement.

(f) This section is subject to law other than this article that establishes a different rule for consumer transactions.

Official Comment (to amended § 3-305)

1. Subsection (a) states the defenses to the obligation of a party to pay the instrument. Subsection (a)(1) states the "real defenses" that may be asserted against any person entitled to enforce the instrument.

Subsection (a)(1)(i) allows assertion of the defense of infancy against a holder in due course, even though the effect of the defense is to render the instrument voidable but not void. The policy is one of protection of the infant even at the expense of occasional loss to an innocent purchaser. No attempt is made to state when infancy is available as a defense or the conditions under which it may be asserted. In some jurisdictions it is held that an infant cannot rescind the transaction or set up the defense unless the holder is restored to the position held before the instrument was taken which, in the case of a holder in due course, is normally impossible. In other states an infant who has misrepresented age may be estopped to assert infancy. Such questions are left to other law, as an integral part of the policy of each state as to the protection of infants.

Subsection (a)(1)(ii) covers mental incompetence, guardianship, ultra vires acts or lack of corporate capacity to do business, or any other incapacity apart from infancy. Such incapacity is largely statutory. Its existence and effect is left to the law of each state. If under the state law the effect is to render the obligation of the instrument entirely null and void, the defense may be asserted against a holder in due course. If the effect is merely to render the obligation voidable at the election of the obligor, the defense is cut off.

Duress, which is also covered by subsection (a)(ii), is a matter of degree. An instrument signed at the point of a gun is void, even in the hands of a holder in due course. One signed under threat to prosecute the son of the maker for theft may be merely voidable, so that the defense is cut off. Illegality is most frequently a matter of gambling or usury, but may arise in other forms under a variety of statutes. The statutes differ in their provisions and the interpretations given them. They are primarily a matter of local concern and local policy. All such matters are therefore left to the local law. If under that law the effect of the duress or the illegality is to make the obligation entirely null and void, the defense may be asserted against a holder in due course. Otherwise it is cut off.

Subsection (a)(1)(iii) refers to "real" or "essential" fraud, sometimes called fraud in the essence or fraud in the factum, as effective against a holder in due course. The common illustration is that of the maker who is tricked into signing a note in the belief that it is merely a receipt or some other document. The theory of the defense is that the signature on the instrument is ineffective because the signer did not intend to sign such an instrument at all. Under this provision the defense extends to an instrument signed with knowledge that it is a negotiable instrument, but without knowledge of its essential terms. The test of the defense is that of excusable ignorance of the contents of the writing signed. The party must not only have been in ignorance, but must also have had no reasonable opportunity to obtain knowledge. In determining what is a reasonable opportunity all relevant factors are to be taken into account, including the intelligence, education, business experience, and ability to read or understand English of the signer. Also relevant is the nature of the representations that were made, whether the signer had good reason to rely on the representations or to have confidence in the person making them, the presence or absence of any third person who might read or explain the instrument to the signer, or any other possibility of obtaining independent information, and the apparent necessity, or lack of it, for acting without delay. Unless the misrepresentation meets this test, the defense is cut off by a holder in due course.

Subsection (a)(1)(iv) states specifically that the defense of discharge in insolvency proceedings is not cut off when the instrument is purchased by a holder in due course. "Insolvency proceedings" is defined in Section 1–201(22) and it includes bankruptcy whether or not the debtor is insolvent. Subsection (2)(e) of former Section 3–305 is omitted. The substance of that provision is stated in Section 3–601(b).

2. Subsection (a)(2) states other defenses that, pursuant to subsection (b), are cut off by a holder in due course. These defenses comprise those specifically stated in Article 3 and those based on common law contract principles. Article 3 defenses are nonissuance of the instrument, conditional issuance, and issuance for a special purpose (Section 3–105(b)); failure to countersign a traveler's check (Section 3–106(c)); modification of the obligation by a separate agreement (Section 3–117); payment that violates a restrictive indorsement (Section 3–206(f)); instruments issued without consideration or for which promised performance has not been given (Section 3–303(b)), and breach of warranty when a draft is accepted (Section 3–417(b)). The most prevalent common law defenses are fraud, misrepresentation or mistake in the issuance of the instrument. In most cases the holder in due course will be an immediate or remote transferee of the payee of the instrument. In most cases the holder-in-due-course doctrine is irrelevant if defenses are being asserted against the payee of the instrument, but in a small number of cases the payee of the instrument may be a holder in due course. Those cases are discussed in Comment 4 to Section 3–302.

Assume Buyer issues a note to Seller in payment of the price of goods that Seller fraudulently promises to deliver but which are never delivered. Seller negotiates the note to Holder who has no notice of the fraud. If Holder is a holder in due course, Holder is not subject to Buyer's defense of fraud. But in some cases an original party to the instrument is a holder in due course. For example, Buyer fraudulently induces Bank to issue a cashier's check to the order of Seller. The check is delivered by Bank to Seller, who has no notice of the fraud. Seller can be a holder in due course and can take the check free of Bank's defense of fraud. This case is discussed as Case #1 in Comment 4 to Section 3–302. Former Section 3–305 stated that a holder in due course takes free of defenses of "any party to the instrument with whom the holder has not dealt." The meaning of this language was not at all clear and if read literally could have produced the wrong result. In the hypothetical case, it could be argued that Seller "dealt" with Bank because Bank delivered the check to Seller. But it is clear that Seller should take free of Bank's defense against Buyer regardless of whether Seller took delivery of the check from Buyer or from Bank. The quoted language is not included in Section 3–305. It is not necessary. If Buyer issues an instrument to Seller and Buyer has a defense against Seller, that defense can obviously be asserted. Buyer and Seller are the only people involved. The holder-in-due-course doctrine has no relevance. The doctrine applies only to cases in which more than two parties are involved. Its essence is that the holder in due course does not have to suffer the consequences of a defense of the obligor on the instrument that arose from an occurrence with a third party.

3. Subsection (a)(3) is concerned with claims in recoupment which can be illustrated by the following example. Buyer issues a note to the order of Seller in exchange for a promise of Seller to deliver specified equipment. If Seller fails to deliver the equipment or delivers equipment that is rightfully rejected, Buyer has a defense to the note because the performance that was the consideration for the note was not rendered. Section 3–303(b). This defense is included in Section 3–305(a)(2). That defense can always be asserted against Seller. This result is the same as that reached under former Section 3–408.

But suppose Seller delivered the promised equipment and it was accepted by Buyer. The equipment, however, was defective. Buyer retained the equipment and incurred expenses with respect to its repair. In this case, Buyer does not have a defense under Section 3–303(b). Seller delivered the equipment and the equipment was accepted. Under Article 2, Buyer is obliged to pay the price of the equipment which is represented by the note. But Buyer may have a claim against Seller for breach of warranty. If Buyer has a warranty claim, the claim may be asserted against Seller as a counterclaim or as a claim in recoupment to reduce the amount owing on the note. It is not relevant whether Seller is or is not a holder in due course of the note or whether Seller knew or had notice that Buyer had the warranty claim. It is obvious that holder-in-due-course doctrine cannot be used to allow Seller to cut off a warranty claim that Buyer has against Seller. Subsection (b) specifically covers this point by stating that a holder in due course is not subject to a "claim in recoupment * * * against a person other than the holder."

Suppose Seller negotiates the note to Holder. If Holder had notice of Buyer's warranty claim at the time the note was negotiated to Holder, Holder is not a holder in due course (Section 3–302(a)(2)(iv)) and Buyer may assert the claim against Holder (Section 3–305(a)(3)) but only as a claim in recoupment, i.e. to reduce the amount owed on the note. If the warranty claim is $1,000 and the unpaid note is $10,000, Buyer owes $9,000 to Holder. If the warranty claim is more than the unpaid amount of the note, Buyer owes nothing to Holder, but Buyer cannot recover the unpaid amount of the warranty claim from Holder. If Buyer had already partially paid the note, Buyer is not entitled to recover the amounts paid. The claim can be used only as an offset to amounts owing on the note. If Holder had no notice of Buyer's claim and otherwise qualifies as a holder in due course, Buyer may not assert the claim against Holder. Section 3–305(b).

The result under Section 3–305 is consistent with the result reached under former Article 3, but the rules for reaching the result are stated differently. Under former Article 3 Buyer could assert rights against Holder only if Holder was not a holder in due course, and Holder's status depended upon whether Holder had notice of a defense by Buyer. Courts have held that Holder had that notice if Holder had notice of Buyer's warranty claim. The rationale under former Article 3 was "failure of consideration." This rationale does not distinguish between cases in which the seller fails to perform and those in which the buyer accepts the performance of seller but makes a claim against the seller because the performance is faulty. The term "failure of consideration" is subject to varying interpretations and is not used in Article 3. The use of the term "claim in recoupment" in Section 3–305(a)(3) is a more precise statement of the nature of Buyer's right against Holder. The use of the term does not change the law because the treatment of a defense under subsection (a)(2) and a claim in recoupment under subsection (a)(3) is essentially the same.

Under former Article 3, case law was divided on the issue of the extent to which an obligor on a note could assert against a transferee who is not a holder in due course a debt or other claim that the obligor had against the original payee of the instrument. Some courts limited claims to those that arose in the transaction that gave rise to the note. This is the approach taken in Section 3–305(a)(3). Other courts allowed the obligor on the note to use any debt or other claim, no matter how unrelated to the note, to offset the amount owed on the note. Under current judicial authority and non-UCC statutory law, there will be many cases in which a transferee of a note arising from a sale transaction will not qualify as a holder in due course. For example, applicable law may require the use of a note to which there cannot be a holder in due course. See Section 3–106(d) and Comment 3 to Section 3–106. It is reasonable to provide that the buyer should not be denied the right to assert claims arising out of the sale transaction. Subsection (a)(3) is based on the belief that it is not reasonable to require the transferee to bear the risk that wholly unrelated claims may also be asserted. The determination of whether a claim arose from the transaction that gave rise to the instrument is determined by law other than this Article and thus may vary as local law varies.

4. Subsection (c) concerns claims and defenses of a person other than the obligor on the instrument. It applies principally to cases in which an obligation is paid with the instrument of a third person. For example, Buyer buys goods from Seller and negotiates to Seller a cashier's check issued by Bank in payment of the price. Shortly after delivering the check to Seller, Buyer learns that Seller had defrauded Buyer in the sale transaction. Seller may enforce the check against Bank even though Seller is not a holder in due course. Bank has no defense to its obligation to pay the check and it may not assert defenses, claims in recoupment, or claims to the instrument of Buyer, except to the extent permitted by the "but" clause of the first sentence of subsection (c). Buyer may have a claim to the instrument under Section 3–306 based on a right to rescind the negotiation to Seller because of Seller's fraud. Section 3–202(b) and Comment 2 to Section 3–201. Bank cannot assert that claim unless Buyer is joined in the action in which Seller is trying to enforce payment of the check. In that case Bank may pay the amount of the check into court and the court will decide whether that amount belongs to Buyer or Seller. The last sentence of subsection (c) allows the issuer of an instrument such as a cashier's check to refuse payment in the rare case in which the issuer can prove that the instrument is a lost or stolen instrument and the person seeking enforcement does not have rights of a holder in due course.

5. Subsection (d) applies to instruments signed for accommodation (Section 3–419) and this subsection equates the obligation of the accommodation party to that of the accommodated party. The accommodation party can assert whatever defense or claim the accommodated party had against the person enforcing the instrument. The only exceptions are discharge in bankruptcy, infancy and lack of capacity. The same rule does not apply to an indorsement by a holder of the instrument in negotiating the instrument. The indorser, as transferor, makes a warranty to the indorsee, as transferee, that no defense or claim in recoupment is good against the indorser. Section 3–416(a)(4). Thus, if the indorsee sues the indorser because of dishonor of the instrument, the indorser may not assert the defense or claim in recoupment of the maker or drawer against the indorsee.

Section 3–305(d) must be read in conjunction with Section 3–605, which provides rules (usually referred to as suretyship defenses) for determining when the obligation of an accommodation party is discharged, in whole or in part, because of some act or omission of a person entitled to enforce the instrument. To the extent a rule stated in Section 3–605 is inconsistent with Section 3–305(d), the Section 3–605 rule governs. For example, Section 3–605(a) provides rules for determining when and to what extent a discharge of the accommodated party under Section 3–604 will discharge the accommodation party. As explained in Comment 2 to Section 3–605, discharge of the accommodated party is normally part of a settlement under which the holder of a note accepts partial payment from an accommodated party who is financially unable to pay the entire amount of the note. If the holder then brings an action against the accommodation party to recover the remaining unpaid amount of the note, the accommodation party cannot use Section 3–305(d) to nullify Section 3–605(a) by asserting the discharge of the accommodated party as a defense. On the other hand, suppose the accommodated party is a buyer of goods who issued the note to the seller who took the note for the buyer's obligation to pay for the goods. Suppose the buyer has a claim for breach of warranty with respect to the goods against the seller and the warranty claim may be asserted against the holder of the note. The warranty claim is a claim in recoupment. If the holder and the accommodated party reach a settlement under which the holder accepts payment less than the amount of the note in full satisfaction of the note and the warranty claim, the accommodation party could defend an action on the note by the holder by asserting the accord and satisfaction under Section 3–305(d). There is no conflict with Section 3–605(a) because that provision is not intended to apply to settlement of disputed claims.

6. Subsection (e) is added to clarify the treatment of an instrument that omits the notice currently required by the Federal Trade Commission Rule related to certain consumer credit sales and consumer purchase money loans (16 C.F.R. Part 433). This subsection adopts the view that the instrument should be treated as if the language required by the FTC Rule were present. It is based on the language describing that rule in Section 3–106(d) and the analogous provision in Section 9–404(d).

7. Subsection (f) is modeled on Sections 9–403(e) and 9–404(c). It ensures that Section 3–305 is interpreted to accommodate relevant consumer-protection laws. The absence of such a provision from other sections in Article 3 should not justify any inference about the meaning of those sections.

8. Articles 28 and 30 of the Convention on International Bills of Exchange and International Promissory Notes includes a similar dichotomy, with a narrower group of defenses available against a protected holder under Articles 28(1) and 30 than are available under Article 28(2) against a holder that is not a protected holder.

§ 3–403. Unauthorized Signature

(a) Unless otherwise provided in this Article or Article 4, an unauthorized signature is ineffective except as the signature of the unauthorized signer in favor of a person who in good faith pays the instrument or takes it for value. An unauthorized signature may be ratified for all purposes of this Article.

(b) If the signature of more than one person is required to constitute the authorized signature of an organization, the signature of the organization is unauthorized if one of the required signatures is lacking.

(c) The civil or criminal liability of a person who makes an unauthorized signature is not affected by any provision of this Article which makes the unauthorized signature effective for the purposes of this Article.

Official Comment

1. "Unauthorized" signature is defined in Section 1–201(43) as one that includes a forgery as well as a signature made by one exceeding actual or apparent authority. Former Section 3–404(1) stated that an unauthorized signature was inoperative as the signature of the person whose name was signed unless that person "is precluded from denying it." Under former Section 3–406 if negligence by the person whose name was signed contributed to an unauthorized signature, that person "is precluded from asserting the * * * lack of authority." Both of these sections were applied to cases in which a forged signature appeared on an instrument and the person asserting rights on the instrument alleged that the negligence of the purported signer contributed to the forgery. Since the standards for liability between the two sections differ, the overlap between the sections caused confusion. Section 3–403(a) deals with the problem by removing the preclusion language that appeared in former Section 3–404.

2. The except clause of the first sentence of subsection (a) states the generally accepted rule that the unauthorized signature, while it is wholly inoperative as that of the person whose name is signed, is effective to impose liability upon the signer or to transfer any rights that the signer may have in the instrument. The signer's liability is not in damages for breach of warranty of authority, but is full liability on the instrument in the capacity in which the signer signed. It is, however, limited to parties who take or pay the instrument in good faith; and one who knows that the signature is unauthorized cannot recover from the signer on the instrument.

3. The last sentence of subsection (a) allows an unauthorized signature to be ratified. Ratification is a retroactive adoption of the unauthorized signature by the person whose name is signed and may be found from conduct as well as from express statements. For example, it may be found from the retention of benefits received in the transaction with knowledge of the unauthorized signature. Although the forger is not an agent, ratification is governed by the rules and principles applicable to ratification of unauthorized acts of an agent.

Ratification is effective for all purposes of this Article. The unauthorized signature becomes valid so far as its effect as a signature is concerned. Although the ratification may relieve the signer of liability on the instrument, it does not of itself relieve the signer of liability to the person whose name is signed. It does not in any way affect the criminal law. No policy of the criminal law prevents a person whose name is forged to assume liability to others on the instrument by ratifying the forgery, but the ratification cannot affect the rights of the state. While the ratification may be taken into account with other relevant facts in determining punishment, it does not relieve the signer of criminal liability.

4. Subsection (b) clarifies the meaning of "unauthorized" in cases in which an instrument contains less than all of the signatures that are required as authority to pay a check. Judicial authority was split on the issue whether the one-year notice period under former Section 4–406(4) (now Section 4–406(f)) barred a customer's suit against a payor bank that paid a check containing less than all of the signatures required by the customer to authorize payment of the check. Some cases took the view that if a customer required that a check contain the signatures of both A and B to authorize payment and only A signed, there was no unauthorized signature within the meaning of that term in former Section 4–406(4) because A's signature was neither unauthorized nor forged. The other cases correctly pointed out that it was the customer's signature at issue and not that of A; hence, the customer's signature was unauthorized if all signatures required to authorize payment of the check were not on the check. Subsection (b) follows the latter line of cases. The same analysis applies if A forged the signature of B. Because the forgery is not effective as a signature of B, the required signature of B is lacking.

Subsection (b) refers to "the authorized signature of an organization." The definition of "organization" in Section 1–201(28) is very broad. It covers not only commercial entities but also "two or more persons having a joint or common interest." Hence subsection (b) would apply when a husband and wife are both required to sign an instrument.

§ 3–404. Impostors; Fictitious Payees

(a) If an impostor, by use of the mails or otherwise, induces the issuer of an instrument to issue the instrument to the impostor, or to a person acting in concert with the impostor, by impersonating the payee of the instrument or a person authorized to act for the payee, an indorsement of the instrument by any person in the name of the payee is effective as the indorsement of the payee in favor of a person who, in good faith, pays the instrument or takes it for value or for collection.

(b) If (i) a person whose intent determines to whom an instrument is payable (Section 3–110(a) or (b)) does not intend the person identified as payee to have any interest in the instrument, or

(ii) the person identified as payee of an instrument is a fictitious person, the following rules apply until the instrument is negotiated by special indorsement:

(1) Any person in possession of the instrument is its holder.

(2) An indorsement by any person in the name of the payee stated in the instrument is effective as the indorsement of the payee in favor of a person who, in good faith, pays the instrument or takes it for value or for collection.

(c) Under subsection (a) or (b), an indorsement is made in the name of a payee if (i) it is made in a name substantially similar to that of the payee or (ii) the instrument, whether or not indorsed, is deposited in a depositary bank to an account in a name substantially similar to that of the payee.

(d) With respect to an instrument to which subsection (a) or (b) applies, if a person paying the instrument or taking it for value or for collection fails to exercise ordinary care in paying or taking the instrument and that failure substantially contributes to loss resulting from payment of the instrument, the person bearing the loss may recover from the person failing to exercise ordinary care to the extent the failure to exercise ordinary care contributed to the loss.

Official Comment

1. Under former Article 3, the impostor cases were governed by former Section 3–405(1)(a) and the fictitious payee cases were governed by Section 3–405(1)(b). Section 3–404 replaces former Section 3–405(1)(a) and (b) and modifies the previous law in some respects. Former Section 3–405 was read by some courts to require that the indorsement be in the exact name of the named payee. Revised Article 3 rejects this result. Section 3–404(c) requires only that the indorsement be made in a name "substantially similar" to that of the payee. Subsection (c) also recognizes the fact that checks may be deposited without indorsement. Section 4–205(a).

Subsection (a) changes the former law in a case in which the impostor is impersonating an agent. Under former Section 3–405(1)(a), if Impostor impersonated Smith and induced the drawer to draw a check to the order of Smith, Impostor could negotiate the check. If Impostor impersonated Smith, the president of Smith Corporation, and the check was payable to the order of Smith Corporation, the section did not apply. See the last paragraph of Comment 2 to former Section 3–405. In revised Article 3, Section 3–404(a) gives Impostor the power to negotiate the check in both cases.

2. Subsection (b) is based in part on former Section 3–405(1)(b) and in part on N.I.L. § 9(3). It covers cases in which an instrument is payable to a fictitious or nonexisting person and to cases in which the payee is a real person but the drawer or maker does not intend the payee to have any interest in the instrument. Subsection (b) applies to any instrument, but its primary importance is with respect to checks of corporations and other organizations. It also applies to forged check cases. The following cases illustrate subsection (b):

Case #1. Treasurer is authorized to draw checks in behalf of Corporation. Treasurer fraudulently draws a check of Corporation payable to Supplier Co., a non-existent company. Subsection (b) applies because Supplier Co. is a fictitious person and because Treasurer did not intend Supplier Co. to have any interest in the check. Under subsection (b)(1) Treasurer, as the person in possession of the check, becomes the holder of the check. Treasurer indorses the check in the name "Supplier Co." and deposits it in Depositary Bank. Under subsection (b)(2) and (c)(i), the indorsement is effective to make Depositary Bank the holder and therefore a person entitled to enforce the instrument. Section 3–301.

Case #2. Same facts as Case #1 except that Supplier Co. is an actual company that does business with Corporation. If Treasurer intended to steal the check when the check was drawn, the result in Case #2 is the same as the result in Case #1. Subsection (b) applies because Treasurer did not intend Supplier Co. to have any interest in the check. It does not make any difference whether Supplier Co. was or was not a creditor of Corporation when the check was drawn. If Treasurer did not decide to steal the check until after the check was drawn, the case is covered by Section 3–405 rather than Section 3–404(b), but the result is the same. See Case #6 in Comment 3 to Section 3–405.

Case #3. Checks of Corporation must be signed by two officers. President and Treasurer both sign a check of Corporation payable to Supplier Co., a company that does business with Corporation from time to time but to which Corporation does not owe any money. Treasurer knows that no money is owed to Supplier Co. and does not intend that Supplier Co. have any interest in the check. President believes that money is owed to Supplier Co. Treasurer obtains possession of the check after it is signed. Subsection (b) applies because Treasurer is "a person whose intent determines to whom an instrument is payable" and Treasurer does not intend Supplier Co. to have any interest in the check. Treasurer becomes the holder of the check and may negotiate it by indorsing it in the name "Supplier Co."

Case #4. Checks of Corporation are signed by a check-writing machine. Names of payees of checks produced by the machine are determined by information entered into the computer that operates the machine. Thief, a person who is not an employee or other agent of Corporation, obtains access to the computer and causes the check-writing machine to produce a check payable to Supplier Co., a non-existent company. Subsection (b)(ii) applies. Thief then obtains possession of the check. At that point Thief becomes the holder of the check because Thief is the person in possession of the instrument. Subsection (b)(1). Under Section 3–301 Thief, as holder, is the "person entitled to enforce the instrument" even though Thief does not have title to the check and is in wrongful possession of it. Thief indorses the check in the name "Supplier Co." and deposits it in an account in Depositary Bank which Thief opened in the name "Supplier Co." Depositary Bank takes the check in good faith and credits the "Supplier Co." account. Under subsection (b)(2) and (c)(i), the indorsement is effective. Depositary Bank becomes the holder and the person entitled to enforce the check. The check is presented to the drawee bank for payment and payment is made. Thief then withdraws the credit to the account. Although the check was issued without authority given by Corporation, the drawee bank is entitled to pay the check and charge Corporation's account if there was an agreement with Corporation allowing the bank to debit Corporation's account for payment of checks produced by the check-writing machine whether or not authorized. The indorsement is also effective if Supplier Co. is a real person. In that case subsection (b)(i) applies. Under Section 3–110(b) Thief is the person whose intent determines to whom the check is payable, and Thief did not intend Supplier Co. to have any interest in the check. When the drawee bank pays the check, there is no breach of warranty under Section 3–417(a)(1) or 4–208(a)(1) because Depositary Bank was a person entitled to enforce the check when it was forwarded for payment.

Case #5. Thief, who is not an employee or agent of Corporation, steals check forms of Corporation. John Doe is president of Corporation and is authorized to sign checks on behalf of Corporation as drawer. Thief draws a check in the name of Corporation as drawer by forging the signature of Doe. Thief makes the check payable to the order of Supplier Co. with the intention of stealing it. Whether Supplier Co. is a fictitious person or a real person, Thief becomes the holder of the check and the person entitled to enforce it. The analysis is the same as that in Case #4. Thief deposits the check in an account in Depositary Bank which Thief opened in the name "Supplier Co." Thief either indorses the check in a name other than "Supplier Co." or does not indorse the check at all. Under Section 4–205(a) a depositary bank may become holder of a check deposited to the account of a customer if the customer was a holder, whether or not the customer indorses. Subsection (c)(ii) treats deposit to an account in a name substantially similar to that of the payee as the equivalent of indorsement in the name of the payee. Thus, the deposit is an effective indorsement of the check. Depositary Bank becomes the holder of the check and the person entitled to enforce the check. If the check is paid by the drawee bank, there is no breach of warranty under Section 3–417(a)(1) or 4–208(a)(1) because Depositary Bank was a person entitled to enforce the check when it was forwarded for payment and, unless Depositary Bank knew about the forgery of Doe's signature, there is no breach of warranty under Section 3–417(a)(3) or 4–208(a)(3). Because the check was a forged check the drawee bank is not entitled to charge Corporation's account unless Section 3–406 or Section 4–406 applies.

3. In cases governed by subsection (a) the dispute will normally be between the drawer of the check that was obtained by the impostor and the drawee bank that paid it. The drawer is precluded from obtaining recredit of the drawer's account by arguing that the check was paid on a forged indorsement so long as the drawee bank acted in good faith in paying the check. Cases governed by subsection (b) are illustrated by Cases #1 through #5 in Comment 2. In Cases #1, #2, and #3 there is no forgery of the check, thus the drawer of the check takes the loss if there is no lack of good faith by the banks involved. Cases #4 and #5 are forged check cases. Depositary Bank is entitled to retain the proceeds of the check if it didn't know about the forgery. Under Section 3–418 the drawee bank is not entitled to recover from Depositary Bank on the basis of payment by mistake because Depositary Bank took the check in good faith and gave value for the check when the credit given for the check was withdrawn. And there is no breach of warranty under Section 3–417(a)(1) or (3) or 4–208(a)(1) or (3). Unless Section 3–406 applies the loss is taken by the drawee bank if a forged check is paid, and that is the result in Case #5. In Case #4 the loss is taken by Corporation, the drawer, because an agreement between Corporation and the drawee bank allowed the bank to debit Corporation's account despite the unauthorized use of the check-writing machine.

If a check payable to an impostor, fictitious payee, or payee not intended to have an interest in the check is paid, the effect of subsections (a) and (b) is to place the loss on the drawer of the check rather than on the drawee or the depositary bank that took the check for collection. Cases governed by subsection (a) always involve fraud, and fraud is almost always involved in cases governed by subsection (b). The drawer is in the best position to avoid the fraud and thus should take the loss. This is true in Case #1, Case #2, and Case #3. But in some cases the person taking the check might have detected the fraud and thus have prevented the loss by the exercise of ordinary care. In those cases, if that person failed to exercise ordinary care, it is reasonable that that person bear loss to the extent the failure contributed to the loss. Subsection (d) is intended to reach that result. It allows the person who suffers loss as a result of payment of the check to recover from the person who failed to exercise ordinary care. In Case #1, Case #2, and Case #3, the person suffering the loss is Corporation, the drawer of the check. In each case the most likely defendant is the depositary bank that took the check and failed to exercise ordinary care. In those cases, the drawer has a cause of action against the offending bank to recover a portion of the loss. The amount of loss to be allocated to each party is left to the trier of fact. Ordinary care is defined in Section 3–103(a)(7)–(9). An example of the type of conduct by a depositary bank that could give rise to recovery under subsection (d) is discussed in Comment 4 to Section 3–405. That comment addresses the last sentence of Section 3–405(b) which is similar to Section 3–404(d).

In Case #1, Case #2, and Case #3, there was no forgery of the drawer's signature. But cases involving checks payable to a fictitious payee or a payee not intended to have an interest in the check are often forged check cases as well. Examples are Case #4 and Case #5. Normally, the loss in forged check cases is on the drawee bank that paid the check. Case #5 is an example. In Case #4 the risk with respect to the forgery is shifted to the drawer because of the agreement between the drawer and the drawee bank. The doctrine that prevents a drawee bank from recovering payment with respect to a forged check if the payment was made to a person who took the check for value and in good faith is incorporated into Section 3–418 and Sections 3–417(a)(3) and 4–208(a)(3). This doctrine is based on the assumption that the depositary bank normally has no way of detecting the forgery because the drawer is not that bank's customer. On the other hand, the drawee bank, at least in some cases, may be able to detect the forgery by comparing the signature on the check with the specimen signature that the drawee has on file. But in some forged check cases the depositary bank is in a position to detect the fraud. Those cases typically involve a check payable to a fictitious payee or a payee not intended to have an interest in the check. Subsection (d) applies to those cases. If the depositary bank failed to exercise ordinary care and the failure substantially contributed to the loss, the drawer in Case #4 or the drawee bank in Case #5 has a cause of action against the depositary bank under subsection (d). Comment 4 to Section 3–405 can be used as a guide to the type of conduct that could give rise to recovery under Section 3–404(d).

§ 3–406. Negligence Contributing to Forged Signature or Alteration of Instrument

(a) A person whose failure to exercise ordinary care substantially contributes to an alteration of an instrument or to the making of a forged signature on an instrument is precluded from asserting the alteration or the forgery against a person who, in good faith, pays the instrument or takes it for value or for collection.

(b) Under subsection (a), if the person asserting the preclusion fails to exercise ordinary care in paying or taking the instrument and that failure substantially contributes to loss, the loss is allocated between the person precluded and the person asserting the preclusion according to the extent to which the failure of each to exercise ordinary care contributed to the loss.

(c) Under subsection (a), the burden of proving failure to exercise ordinary care is on the person asserting the preclusion. Under subsection (b), the burden of proving failure to exercise ordinary care is on the person precluded.

Official Comment

1. Section 3–406(a) is based on former Section 3–406. With respect to alteration, Section 3–406 adopts the doctrine of Young v. Grote, 4 Bing. 253 (1827), which held that a drawer who so negligently draws an instrument as to facilitate its material alteration is liable to a drawee who pays the altered instrument in good faith. Under Section 3–406 the doctrine is expanded to apply not only to drafts but to all instruments. It includes in the protected class any "person who, in good faith, pays the instrument or takes it for value or for collection." Section 3–406 rejects decisions holding that the maker of a note owes no duty of care to the holder because at the time the instrument is issued there is no contract between them. By issuing the instrument and "setting it afloat upon a sea of strangers" the maker or drawer voluntarily enters into a relation with later holders which justifies imposition of a duty of care. In this respect an instrument so negligently drawn as to facilitate alteration does not differ in principle from an instrument containing blanks which may be filled. Under Section 3–407 a person paying an altered instrument or taking it for value, in good faith and without notice of the alteration may enforce rights with respect to the instrument according to its original terms. If negligence of the obligor substantially contributes to an alteration, this section gives the holder or the payor the alternative right to treat the altered instrument as though it had been issued in the altered form.

No attempt is made to define particular conduct that will constitute "failure to exercise ordinary care [that] substantially contributes to an alteration." Rather, "ordinary care" is defined in Section 3–103(a)(7)–(9) in general terms. The question is left to the court or the jury for decision in the light of the circumstances in the particular case including reasonable commercial standards that may apply.

Section 3–406 does not make the negligent party liable in tort for damages resulting from the alteration. If the negligent party is stopped from asserting the alteration the person taking the instrument is fully protected because the taker can treat the instrument as having been issued in the altered form.

2. Section 3–406 applies equally to a failure to exercise ordinary care that substantially contributes to the making of a forged signature on an instrument. Section 3–406 refers to "forged signature" rather than "unauthorized signature" that appeared in former Section 3–406 because it more accurately describes the scope of the provision. Unauthorized signature is a broader concept that includes not only forgery but also the signature of an agent which does not bind the principal under the law of agency. The agency cases are resolved independently under agency law. Section 3–406 is not necessary in those cases.

The "substantially contributes" test of former Section 3–406 is continued in this section in preference to a "direct and proximate cause" test. The "substantially contributes" test is meant to be less stringent than a "direct and proximate cause" test. Under the less stringent test the preclusion should be easier to establish. Conduct "substantially contributes" to a material alteration or forged signature if it is a contributing cause of the alteration or signature and a substantial factor in bringing it about. The analysis of "substantially contributes" in former Section 3–406 by the court in Thompson Maple Products v. Citizens National Bank of Corry, 234 A.2d 32 (Pa.Super.Ct.1967), states what is intended by the use of the same words in revised Section 3–406(b). Since Section 3–404(d) and Section 3–405(b) also use the words "substantially contributes" the analysis of these words also applies to those provisions.

3. The following cases illustrate the kind of conduct that can be the basis of a preclusion under Section 3–406(a):

Case #1. Employer signs checks drawn on Employer's account by use of a rubber stamp of Employer's signature. Employer keeps the rubber stamp along with Employer's personalized blank check forms in an unlocked desk drawer. An unauthorized person fraudulently uses the check forms to write checks on Employer's account. The checks are signed by use of the rubber stamp. If Employer demands that

Employer's account in the drawee bank be recredited because the forged check was not properly payable, the drawee bank may defend by asserting that Employer is precluded from asserting the forgery. The trier of fact could find that Employer failed to exercise ordinary care to safeguard the rubber stamp and the check forms and that the failure substantially contributed to the forgery of Employer's signature by the unauthorized use of the rubber stamp.

Case #2. An insurance company draws a check to the order of Sarah Smith in payment of a claim of a policyholder, Sarah Smith, who lives in Alabama. The insurance company also has a policyholder with the same name who lives in Illinois. By mistake, the insurance company mails the check to the Illinois Sarah Smith who indorses the check and obtains payment. Because the payee of the check is the Alabama Sarah Smith, the indorsement by the Illinois Sarah Smith is a forged indorsement. Section 3–110(a). The trier of fact could find that the insurance company failed to exercise ordinary care when it mailed the check to the wrong person and that the failure substantially contributed to the making of the forged indorsement. In that event the insurance company could be precluded from asserting the forged indorsement against the drawee bank that honored the check.

Case #3. A company writes a check for $10. The figure "10" and the word "ten" are typewritten in the appropriate spaces on the check form. A large blank space is left after the figure and the word. The payee of the check, using a typewriter with a typeface similar to that used on the check, writes the word "thousand" after the word "ten" and a comma and three zeros after the figure "10". The drawee bank in good faith pays $10,000 when the check is presented for payment and debits the account of the drawer in that amount. The trier of fact could find that the drawer failed to exercise ordinary care in writing the check and that the failure substantially contributed to the alteration. In that case the drawer is precluded from asserting the alteration against the drawee if the check was paid in good faith.

4. Subsection (b) differs from former Section 3–406 in that it adopts a concept of comparative negligence. If the person precluded under subsection (a) proves that the person asserting the preclusion failed to exercise ordinary care and that failure substantially contributed to the loss, the loss may be allocated between the two parties on a comparative negligence basis. In the case of a forged indorsement the litigation is usually between the payee of the check and the depositary bank that took the check for collection. An example is a case like Case #1 of Comment 3 to Section 3–405. If the trier of fact finds that Employer failed to exercise ordinary care in safeguarding the check and that the failure substantially contributed to the making of the forged indorsement, subsection (a) of Section 3–406 applies. If Employer brings an action for conversion against the depositary bank that took the checks from the forger, the depositary bank could assert the preclusion under subsection (a). But suppose the forger opened an account in the depositary bank in a name identical to that of Employer, the payee of the check, and then deposited the check in the account. Subsection (b) may apply. There may be an issue whether the depositary bank should have been alerted to possible fraud when a new account was opened for a corporation shortly before a very large check payable to a payee with the same name is deposited. Circumstances surrounding the opening of the account may have suggested that the corporation to which the check was payable may not be the same as the corporation for which the account was opened. If the trier of fact finds that collecting the check under these circumstances was a failure to exercise ordinary care, it could allocate the loss between the depositary bank and Employer, the payee.

§ 3–419. Instruments Signed for Accommodation

(a) If an instrument is issued for value given for the benefit of a party to the instrument ("accommodated party") and another party to the instrument ("accommodation party") signs the instrument for the purpose of incurring liability on the instrument without being a direct beneficiary of the value given for the instrument, the instrument is signed by the accommodation party "for accommodation."

(b) An accommodation party may sign the instrument as maker, drawer, acceptor, or indorser and, subject to subsection (d), is obliged to pay the instrument in the capacity in which the accommodation party signs. The obligation of an accommodation party may be enforced notwithstanding any statute of frauds and whether or not the accommodation party receives consideration for the accommodation.

(c) A person signing an instrument is presumed to be an accommodation party and there is notice that the instrument is signed for accommodation if the signature is an anomalous indorsement or is accompanied by words indicating that the signer is acting as surety or guarantor with respect to the obligation of another party to the instrument. Except as provided in Section 3–605, the obligation of an accommodation party to pay the instrument is not affected by the fact that the person enforcing the obligation had notice when the instrument was taken by that person that the accommodation party signed the instrument for accommodation.

(d) If the signature of a party to an instrument is accompanied by words indicating unambiguously that the party is guaranteeing collection rather than payment of the obligation of another party to the instrument, the signer is obliged to pay the amount due on the instrument to a person entitled to enforce the instrument only if (i) execution of judgment against the other party has been returned unsatisfied, (ii) the other party is insolvent or in an insolvency proceeding, (iii) the other party cannot be served with process, or (iv) it is otherwise apparent that payment cannot be obtained from the other party.

(e) If the signature of a party to an instrument is accompanied by words indicating that the party guarantees payment or the signer signs the instrument as an accommodation party in some other manner that does not unambiguously indicate an intention to guarantee collection rather than payment, the signer is obliged to pay the amount due on the instrument to a person entitled to enforce the instrument in the same circumstances as the accommodated party would be obliged, without prior resort to the accommodated party by the person entitled to enforce the instrument.

(f) An accommodation party who pays the instrument is entitled to reimbursement from the accommodated party and is entitled to enforce the instrument against the accommodated party. In proper circumstances, an accommodation party may obtain relief that requires the accommodated party to perform its obligations on the instrument. An accommodated party who that pays the instrument has no right of recourse against, and is not entitled to contribution from, an accommodation party.

Official Comment

1. Section 3–419 replaces former Section 3–415 and 3–416. An accommodation party is a person who signs an instrument to benefit the accommodated party either by signing at the time value is obtained by the accommodated party or later, and who is not a direct beneficiary of the value obtained. An accommodation party will usually be a co-maker or anomalous indorser. Subsection (a) distinguishes between direct and indirect benefit. For example, if X cosigns a note of Corporation that is given for a loan to Corporation, X is an accommodation party if no part of the loan was paid to X or for X's direct benefit. This is true even though X may receive indirect benefit from the loan because X is employed by Corporation or is a stockholder of Corporation, or even if X is the sole stockholder so long as Corporation and X are recognized as separate entities.

2. It does not matter whether an accommodation party signs gratuitously either at the time the instrument is issued or after the instrument is in the possession of a holder. Subsection (b) of Section 3–419 takes the view stated in Comment 3 to former Section 3–415 that there need be no consideration running to the accommodation party: "The obligation of the accommodation party is supported by any consideration for which the instrument is taken before it is due. Subsection (2) is intended to change occasional decisions holding that there is no sufficient consideration where an accommodation party signs a note after it is in the hands of a holder who has given value. The [accommodation] party is liable to the holder in such a case even though there is no extension of time or other concession."

3. As stated in Comment 1, whether a person is an accommodation party is a question of fact. But it is almost always the case that a co-maker who signs with words of guaranty after the signature is an accommodation party. The same is true of an anomalous indorser. In either case a person taking the instrument is put on notice of the accommodation status of the co-maker or indorser. This is relevant to Section 3–605(h)(e). But, under subsection (c), signing with words of guaranty or as an anomalous indorser also creates a presumption that the signer is an accommodation party. A party challenging accommodation

party status would have to rebut this presumption by producing evidence that the signer was in fact a direct beneficiary of the value given for the instrument.

An accommodation party is always a surety. A surety who is not a party to the instrument, however, is not an accommodation party. For example, if M issues a note payable to the order of P, and S signs a separate contract in which S agrees to pay P the amount of the instrument if it is dishonored, S is a surety but is not an accommodation party. In such a case, S's rights and duties are determined under the general law of suretyship. In unusual cases two parties to an instrument may have a surety relationship that is not governed by Article 3 because the requirements of Section 3–419(a) are not met. In those cases the general law of suretyship applies to the relationship. See PEB Commentary No. 11, dated February 10, 1994 [Appendix II Vol. 3A, Uniform Laws Annotated, Master Edition or ULA Database on Westlaw].

4. Subsection (b) states that an accommodation party is liable on the instrument in the capacity in which the party signed the instrument. In most cases that capacity will be either that of a maker or indorser of a note. But subsection (d) provides a limitation on subsection (b). If the signature of the accommodation party is accompanied by words indicating unambiguously that the party is guaranteeing collection rather than payment of the instrument, liability is limited to that stated in subsection (d), which is based on former Section 3–416(2).

Former Article 3 was confusing because the obligation of a guarantor was covered both in Section 3–415 and in Section 3–416. The latter section suggested that a signature accompanied by words of guaranty created an obligation distinct from that of an accommodation party. Revised Article 3 eliminates that confusion by stating in Section 3–419 the obligation of a person who uses words of guaranty. Portions of former Section 3–416 are preserved. Former Section 3–416(2) is reflected in Section 3–419(d) and former Section 3–416(4) is reflected in Section 3–419(c). Words added to an anomalous indorsement indicating that payment of the instrument is guaranteed by the indorser do not change the liability of the indorser as stated in Section 3–415. This is a change from former Section 3–416(5). See PEB Commentary No. 11, dated February 10, 1994 [Appendix II Vol. 3A, Uniform Laws Annotated, Master Edition or ULA Database on Westlaw].

5. Subsection (e)(f) like former Section 3–415(5), provides that an accommodation party that pays the instrument is entitled to enforce the instrument against the accommodated party. Since the accommodation party that pays the instrument is entitled to enforce the instrument against the accommodated party, the accommodation party also obtains rights to any security interest or other collateral that secures payment of the instrument. Subsection (e)(f) also provides that an accommodation party that pays the instrument is entitled to reimbursement from the accommodated party. See PEB Commentary No. 11, dated February 10, 1994 [Appendix II Vol. 3A, Uniform Laws Annotated, Master Edition or ULA Database on Westlaw].

6. In occasional cases, the accommodation party might pay the instrument even though the accommodated party had a defense to its obligation that was available to the accommodation party under Section 3–305(d). In such cases, the accommodation party's right to reimbursement may conflict with the accommodated party's right to raise its defense. For example, suppose the accommodation party pays the instrument without being aware of the defense. In that case the accommodation party should be entitled to reimbursement. Suppose the accommodation party paid the instrument with knowledge of the defense. In that case, to the extent of the defense, reimbursement ordinarily would not be justified, but under some circumstances reimbursement may be justified depending upon the facts of the case. The resolution of this conflict is left to the general law of suretyship. Section 1–103. See PEB Commentary No. 11, dated February 10, 1994 [Appendix II Vol. 3A, Uniform Laws Annotated, Master Edition or ULA Database on Westlaw].

7. Section 3–419, along with Section 3–116(a) and (b), Section 3–305(d) and Section 3–605, provides rules governing the rights of accommodation parties. In addition, except to the extent that it is displaced by provisions of this Article, the general law of suretyship also applies to the rights of accommodation parties. Section 1–103. See PEB Commentary No. 11, dated February 10, 1994 [Appendix II Vol. 3A, Uniform Laws Annotated, Master Edition or ULA Database on Westlaw].

ARTICLE 4. BANK DEPOSITS AND COLLECTIONS

Table of Sections

§ 4–103. Variation by Agreement; Measure of Damages; Action Constituting Ordinary Care

(a) The effect of the provisions of this Article may be varied by agreement, but the parties to the agreement cannot disclaim a bank's responsibility for its lack of good faith or failure to exercise ordinary care or limit the measure of damages for the lack or failure. However, the parties may determine by agreement the standards by which the bank's responsibility is to be measured if those standards are not manifestly unreasonable.

(b) Federal Reserve regulations and operating circulars, clearing-house rules, and the like have the effect of agreements under subsection (a), whether or not specifically assented to by all parties interested in items handled.

(c) Action or non-action approved by this Article or pursuant to Federal Reserve regulations or operating circulars is the exercise of ordinary care and, in the absence of special instructions, action or non-action consistent with clearing-house rules and the like or with a general banking usage not disapproved by this Article, is prima facie the exercise of ordinary care.

(d) The specification or approval of certain procedures by this Article is not disapproval of other procedures that may be reasonable under the circumstances.

(e) The measure of damages for failure to exercise ordinary care in handling an item is the amount of the item reduced by an amount that could not have been realized by the exercise of ordinary care. If there is also bad faith it includes any other damages the party suffered as a proximate consequence.

Official Comment

1. Section 1–102 states the general principles and rules for variation of the effect of this Act by agreement and the limitations to this power. Section 4–103 states the specific rules for variation of Article 4 by agreement and also certain standards of ordinary care. In view of the technical complexity of the field of bank collections, the enormous number of items handled by banks, the certainty that there will be variations from the normal in each day's work in each bank, the certainty of changing conditions and the possibility of developing improved methods of collection to speed the process, it would be unwise to freeze present methods of operation by mandatory statutory rules. This section, therefore, permits within wide limits variation of the effect of provisions of the Article by agreement.

2. Subsection (a) confers blanket power to vary all provisions of the Article by agreements of the ordinary kind. The agreements may not disclaim a bank's responsibility for its own lack of good faith or failure to exercise ordinary care and may not limit the measure of damages for the lack or failure, but this subsection like Section 1–102(3) approves the practice of parties determining by agreement the standards by which the responsibility is to be measured. In the absence of a showing that the standards manifestly are unreasonable, the agreement controls. Owners of items and other interested parties are not affected by agreements under this subsection unless they are parties to the agreement or are bound by adoption, ratification, estoppel or the like.

As here used "agreement" has the meaning given to it by Section 1–201(3). The agreement may be direct, as between the owner and the depositary bank; or indirect, as in the case in which the owner authorizes a particular type of procedure and any bank in the collection chain acts pursuant to such authorization. It may be with respect to a single item; or to all items handled for a particular customer, e.g., a general agreement between the depositary bank and the customer at the time a deposit account is opened.

Legends on deposit tickets, collection letters and acknowledgments of items, coupled with action by the affected party constituting acceptance, adoption, ratification, estoppel or the like, are agreements if they meet the tests of the definition of "agreement." See Section 1–201(3). First Nat. Bank of Denver v. Federal Reserve Bank, 6 F.2d 339 (8th Cir.1925) (deposit slip); Jefferson County Bldg. Ass'n v. Southern Bank & Trust Co., 225 Ala. 25, 142 So. 66 (1932) (signature card and deposit slip); Semingson v. Stock Yards Nat. Bank, 162 Minn. 424, 203 N.W. 412 (1925) (passbook); Farmers State Bank v. Union Nat. Bank, 42 N.D. 449, 454, 173 N.W. 789, 790 (1919) (acknowledgment of receipt of item).

3. Subsection (a) (subject to its limitations with respect to good faith and ordinary care) goes far to meet the requirements of flexibility. However, it does not by itself confer fully effective flexibility. Since it is recognized that banks handle a great number of items every business day and that the parties interested in each item include the owner of the item, the drawer (if it is a check), all nonbank indorsers, the payor bank and from one to five or more collecting banks, it is obvious that it is impossible, practically, to obtain direct agreements from all of these parties on all items. In total, the interested parties constitute virtually every adult person and business organization in the United States. On the other hand they may become bound to agreements on the principle that collecting banks acting as agents have authority to make binding agreements with respect to items being handled. This conclusion was assumed but was not flatly decided in Federal Reserve Bank of Richmond v. Malloy, 264 U.S. 160, at 167, 44 S.Ct. 296, at 298, 68 L.Ed. 617, 31 A.L.R. 1261 (1924).

To meet this problem subsection (b) provides that official or quasi-official rules of collection, that is Federal Reserve regulations and operating circulars, clearing-house rules, and the like, have the effect of agreements under subsection (a), whether or not specifically assented to by all parties interested in items handled. Consequently, such official or quasi-official rules may, standing by themselves but subject to the good faith and ordinary care limitations, vary the effect of the provisions of Article 4.

Federal Reserve regulations. Various sections of the Federal Reserve Act (12 U.S.C. § 221 et seq.) authorize the Board of Governors of the Federal Reserve System to direct the Federal Reserve banks to exercise bank collection functions. For example, Section 10 (12 U.S.C. § 248(*o*)) authorizes the Board to require each Federal Reserve bank to exercise the functions of a clearing house for its members and Section 13 (12 U.S.C. § 342) authorizes each Federal Reserve bank to receive deposits from nonmember banks solely for the purposes of exchange or of collection. Under this statutory authorization the Board has issued Regulation J (Subpart A—Collection of Checks and Other Items). Under the supremacy clause of the Constitution, federal regulations prevail over state statutes. Moreover, the Expedited Funds Availability Act, 12 U.S.C. Section 4007(b) provides that the Act and Regulation CC, 12 CFR 229, supersede "any provision of the law of any State, including the Uniform Commercial Code as in effect in such State, which is inconsistent with this chapter or such regulations." See Comment 1 to Section 4–102.

Federal Reserve operating circulars. The regulations of the Federal Reserve Board authorize the Federal Reserve banks to promulgate operating circulars covering operating details. Regulation J, for example, provides that "Each Reserve Bank shall receive and handle items in accordance with this subpart, and shall issue operating circulars governing the details of its handling of items and other matters deemed appropriate by the Reserve Bank." This Article recognizes that "operating circulars" issued pursuant to the regulations and concerned with operating details as appropriate may, within their proper sphere, vary the effect of the Article.

Clearing-House Rules. Local clearing houses have long issued rules governing the details of clearing; hours of clearing, media of remittance, time for return of mis-sent items and the like. The case law has recognized these rules, within their proper sphere, as binding on affected parties and as appropriate sources for the courts to look to in filling out details of bank collection law. Subsection (b) in recognizing clearing-house rules as a means of preserving flexibility continues the sensible approach indicated in the cases. Included in the term "clearing houses" are county and regional clearing houses as well as those within a single city or town. There is, of course, no intention of authorizing a local clearing house or a group of clearing houses to rewrite the basic law generally. The term "clearing-house rules" should be understood in the light of functions the clearing houses have exercised in the past.

And the like. This phrase is to be construed in the light of the foregoing. "Federal Reserve regulations and operating circulars" cover rules and regulations issued by public or quasi-public agencies under statutory authority. "Clearing-house rules" cover rules issued by a group of banks which have associated themselves to perform through a clearing house some of their collection, payment and clearing functions. Other agencies or associations of this kind may be established in the future whose rules and regulations could be appropriately looked on as constituting means of avoiding absolute statutory rigidity. The phrase "and the like" leaves open possibilities for future development. An agreement between a number of banks or even all the banks in an area simply because they are banks, would not of itself, by virtue of the phrase "and the like," meet the purposes and objectives of subsection (b).

4. Under this Article banks come under the general obligations of the use of good faith and the exercise of ordinary care. "Good faith" is defined in Section 3–103(a)(4) Section 1–201(b)(20). The term "ordinary care" is defined in Section 3–103(a)(7)(9). These definitions are made to apply to Article 4 by Section 4–104(c). Section 4–202 states respects in which collecting banks must use ordinary care. Subsection (c) of Section 4–103 provides that action or non-action approved by the Article or pursuant to Federal Reserve regulations or operating circulars constitutes the exercise of ordinary care. Federal Reserve regulations and operating circulars constitute an affirmative standard of ordinary care equally with the provisions of Article 4 itself.

Subsection (c) further provides that, absent special instructions, action or non-action consistent with clearing-house rules and the like or with a general banking usage not disapproved by the Article, prima facie constitutes the exercise of ordinary care. Clearing-house rules and the phrase "and the like" have the significance set forth above in these Comments. The term "general banking usage" is not defined but should be taken to mean a general usage common to banks in the area concerned. See Section 1–205(2). In a case in which the adjective "general" is used, the intention is to require a usage broader than a mere practice between two or three banks but it is not intended to require a usage broader than a mere practice between two or three banks but it is not intended to require anything as broad as a country-wide usage. A usage followed generally throughout a state, a substantial portion of a state, a metropolitan area or the like would certainly be sufficient. Consistently with the principle of Section 1–205(3), action or non-action consistent with clearing-house rules or the like or with banking usages prima facie constitutes the exercise of ordinary care. However, the phrase "in the absence of special instructions" affords owners of items an opportunity to prescribe other standards and although there may be no direct supervision or control of clearing houses or banking usages by official supervisory authorities, the confirmation of ordinary care by compliance with these standards is prima facie only, thus conferring on the courts the ultimate power to determine ordinary care in any case in which it should appear desirable to do so. The prima facie rule does, however, impose on the party contesting the standards to establish that they are unreasonable, arbitrary or unfair as used by the particular bank.

5. Subsection (d), in line with the flexible approach required for the bank collection process is designed to make clear that a novel procedure adopted by a bank is not to be considered unreasonable merely because that procedure is not specifically contemplated by this Article or by agreement, or because it has not yet been generally accepted as a bank usage. Changing conditions constantly call for new procedures and someone has to use the new procedure first. If this procedure is found to be reasonable under the circumstances, provided, of course, that it is not inconsistent with any provision of the Article or other law or agreement, the bank which has followed the new procedure should not be found to have failed in the exercise of ordinary care.

6. Subsection (e) sets forth a rule for determining the measure of damages for failure to exercise ordinary care which, under subsection (a), cannot be limited by agreement. In the absence of bad faith the maximum recovery is the amount of the item concerned. The term "bad faith" is not defined; the connotation is the absence of good faith (Section 3–103). When it is established that some part or all of the item could not have been collected even by the use of ordinary care the recovery is reduced by the amount that would have been in any event uncollectible. This limitation on recovery follows the case law. Finally, if bad faith is established the rule opens to allow the recovery of other damages, whose "proximateness" is to be tested by the ordinary rules applied in comparable cases. Of course, it continues to be as necessary under subsection (e) as it has been under ordinary common law principles that, before the damage rule of the subsection becomes operative, liability of the bank and some loss to the customer or owner must be established.

§ 4–208. Presentment Warranties

(a) If an unaccepted draft is presented to the drawee for payment or acceptance and the drawee pays or accepts the draft, (i) the person obtaining payment or acceptance, at the time of presentment, and (ii) a previous transferor of the draft, at the time of transfer, warrant to the drawee that pays or accepts the draft in good faith that:

(1) the warrantor is, or was, at the time the warrantor transferred the draft, a person entitled to enforce the draft or authorized to obtain payment or acceptance of the draft on behalf of a person entitled to enforce the draft;

(2) the draft has not been altered; and

(3) the warrantor has no knowledge that the signature of the purported drawer of the draft is unauthorized; and

(4) with respect to any remotely-created consumer item, that the person on whose account the item is drawn authorized the issuance of the item in the amount for which the item is drawn.

(b) A drawee making payment may recover from a warrantor damages for breach of warranty equal to the amount paid by the drawee less the amount the drawee received or is entitled to receive from the drawer because of the payment. In addition, the drawee is entitled to compensation for expenses and loss of interest resulting from the breach. The right of the drawee to recover damages under this subsection is not affected by any failure of the drawee to exercise ordinary care in making payment. If the drawee accepts the draft (i) breach of warranty is a defense to the obligation of the acceptor, and (ii) if the acceptor makes payment with respect to the draft, the acceptor is entitled to recover from a warrantor for breach of warranty the amounts stated in this subsection.

(c) If a drawee asserts a claim for breach of warranty under subsection (a) based on an unauthorized indorsement of the draft or an alteration of the draft, the warrantor may defend by proving that the indorsement is effective under Section 3–404 or 3–405 or the drawer is precluded under Section 3–406 or 4–406 from asserting against the drawee the unauthorized indorsement or alteration.

(d) If (i) a dishonored draft is presented for payment to the drawer or an indorser or (ii) any other item is presented for payment to a party obliged to pay the item, and the item is paid, the person obtaining payment and a prior transferor of the item warrant to the person making payment in good faith that the warrantor is, or was, at the time the warrantor transferred the item, a person entitled to enforce the item or authorized to obtain payment on behalf of a person entitled to enforce the item. The person making payment may recover from any warrantor for breach of warranty an amount equal to the amount paid plus expenses and loss of interest resulting from the breach.

(e) The warranties stated in subsections (a) and (d) cannot be disclaimed with respect to checks. Unless notice of a claim for breach of warranty is given to the warrantor within 30 days after the claimant has reason to know of the breach and the identity of the warrantor, the warrantor is discharged to the extent of any loss caused by the delay in giving notice of the claim.

(f) A cause of action for breach of warranty under this section accrues when the claimant has reason to know of the breach.

Official Comment

This section conforms to Section 3–417 and extends its coverage to items. The substance of this section is discussed in the Comment to Section 3–417. "Draft" is defined in Section 4–104 as including an item that is an order to pay so as to make clear that the term "draft" in Article 4 may include items that are not instruments within Section 3–104.

For an explanation of subsection (a)(4), see comment 8 to Section 3–416.

§ 4-401. When Bank May Charge Customer's Account

(a) A bank may charge against the account of a customer an item that is properly payable from the account even though the charge creates an overdraft. An item is properly payable if it is authorized by the customer and is in accordance with any agreement between the customer and bank.

(b) A customer is not liable for the amount of an overdraft if the customer neither signed the item nor benefited from the proceeds of the item.

(c) A bank may charge against the account of a customer a check that is otherwise properly payable from the account, even though payment was made before the date of the check, unless the customer has given notice to the bank of the postdating describing the check with reasonable certainty. The notice is effective for the period stated in Section 4–403(b) for stop-payment orders, and must be received at such time and in such manner as to afford the bank a reasonable opportunity to act on it before the bank takes any action with respect to the check described in Section 4–303. If a bank charges against the account of a customer a check before the date stated in the notice of postdating, the bank is liable for damages for the loss resulting from its act. The loss may include damages for dishonor of subsequent items under Section 4–402.

(d) A bank that in good faith makes payment to a holder may charge the indicated account of its customer according to:

(1) the original terms of the altered item; or

(2) the terms of the completed item, even though the bank knows the item has been completed unless the bank has notice that the completion was improper.

Official Comment

1. An item is properly payable from a customer's account if the customer has authorized the payment and the payment does not violate any agreement that may exist between the bank and its customer. For an example of a payment held to violate an agreement with a customer, see Torrance National Bank v. Enesco Federal Credit Union, 285 P.2d 737 (Cal.App.1955). An item drawn for more than the amount of a customer's account may be properly payable. Thus under subsection (a) a bank may charge the customer's account for an item even though payment results in an overdraft. An item containing a forged drawer's signature or forged indorsement is not properly payable. Concern has arisen whether a bank may require a customer to execute a stop-payment order when the customer notifies the bank of the loss of an unindorsed or specially indorsed check. Since such a check cannot be properly payable from the customer's account, it is inappropriate for a bank to require stop-payment order in such a case.

2. Subsection (b) adopts the view of case authority holding that if there is more than one customer who can draw on an account, the nonsigning customer is not liable for an overdraft unless that person benefits from the proceeds of the item.

3. Subsection (c) is added because the automated check collection system cannot accommodate postdated checks. A check is usually paid upon presentment without respect to the date of the check. Under the former law, if a payor bank paid a postdated check before its stated date, it could not charge the customer's account because the check was not "properly payable." Hence, the bank might have been liable for wrongfully dishonoring subsequent checks of the drawer that would have been paid had the postdated check not been prematurely paid. Under subsection (c) a customer wishing to postdate a check must notify the payor bank of its postdating in time to allow the bank to act on the customer's notice before the bank has to commit itself to pay the check. If the bank fails to act on the customer's timely notice, it may be liable for damages for the resulting loss which may include damages for dishonor of subsequent items. This Act does not regulate fees that banks charge their customers for a notice of postdating or other services covered by the Act, but under principles of law such as unconscionability or good faith and fair dealing, courts have reviewed fees and the bank's exercise of a discretion to set fees. Perdue v. Crocker National Bank, 38 Cal.3d 913 (1985) (unconscionability); Best v. United Bank of Oregon, 739 P.2d 554, 562–566 (1987) (good faith and fair dealing). In addition, Section 1–203 provides that every contract or duty within this Act imposes an obligation of good faith in its performance or enforcement.

4. Section 3–407(c) states that a payor bank or drawee which pays a fraudulently altered instrument in good faith and without notice of the alteration may enforce rights with respect to the instrument according to its original terms or, in the case of an incomplete instrument altered by unauthorized completion, according to its terms as completed. Section 4–401(d) follows the rule stated in Section 3–407(c) by applying it to an altered item and allows the bank to enforce rights with respect to the altered item by charging the customer's account.

§ 4–406. Customer's Duty to Discover and Report Unauthorized Signature or Alteration

(a) A bank that sends or makes available to a customer a statement of account showing payment of items for the account shall either return or make available to the customer the items paid or provide information in the statement of account sufficient to allow the customer reasonably to identify the items paid. The statement of account provides sufficient information if the item is described by item number, amount, and date of payment.

(b) If the items are not returned to the customer, the person retaining the items shall either retain the items or, if the items are destroyed, maintain the capacity to furnish legible copies of the items until the expiration of seven years after receipt of the items. A customer may request an item from the bank that paid the item, and that bank must provide in a reasonable time either the item or, if the item has been destroyed or is not otherwise obtainable, a legible copy of the item.

(c) If a bank sends or makes available a statement of account or items pursuant to subsection(a), the customer must exercise reasonable promptness in examining the statement or the items to determine whether any payment was not authorized because of an alteration of an item or because a purported signature by or on behalf of the customer was not authorized. If, based on the statement or items provided, the customer should reasonably have discovered the unauthorized payment, the customer must promptly notify the bank of the relevant facts.

(d) If the bank proves that the customer failed, with respect to an item, to comply with the duties imposed on the customer by subsection (c), the customer is precluded from asserting against the bank:

(1) the customer's unauthorized signature or any alteration on the item, if the bank also proves that it suffered a loss by reason of the failure; and

(2) the customer's unauthorized signature or alteration by the same wrongdoer on any other item paid in good faith by the bank if the payment was made before the bank received notice from the customer of the unauthorized signature or alteration and after the customer had been afforded a reasonable period of time, not exceeding 30 days, in which to examine the item or statement of account and notify the bank.

(e) If subsection (d) applies and the customer proves that the bank failed to exercise ordinary care in paying the item and that the failure substantially contributed to loss, the loss is allocated between the customer precluded and the bank asserting the preclusion according to the extent to which the failure of the customer to comply with subsection (c) and the failure of the bank to exercise ordinary care contributed to the loss. If the customer proves that the bank did not pay the item in good faith, the preclusion under subsection (d) does not apply.

(f) Without regard to care or lack of care of either the customer or the bank, a customer who does not within one year after the statement or items are made available to the customer (subsection (a)) discover and report the customer's unauthorized signature on or any alteration on the item is precluded from asserting against the bank the unauthorized signature or alteration. If there is a preclusion under this subsection, the payor bank may not recover for breach of warranty under Section 4–208 with respect to the unauthorized signature or alteration to which the preclusion applies.

Official Comment

1. Under subsection (a), if a bank that has paid a check or other item for the account of a customer makes available to the customer a statement of account showing payment of the item, the bank must either return the item to the customer or provide a description of the item sufficient to allow the customer to

identify it. Under subsection (c), the customer has a duty to exercise reasonable promptness in examining the statement or the returned item to discover any unauthorized signature of the customer or any alteration and to promptly notify the bank if the customer should reasonably have discovered the unauthorized signature or alteration.

The duty stated in subsection (c) becomes operative only if the "bank sends or makes available a statement of account or items pursuant to subsection (a)." A bank is not under a duty to send a statement of account or the paid items to the customer; but, if it does not do so, the customer does not have any duties under subsection (c).

Under subsection (a), a statement of account must provide information "sufficient to allow the customer reasonably to identify the items paid." If the bank supplies its customer with an image of the paid item, it complies with this standard. But a safe harbor rule is provided. The bank complies with the standard of providing "sufficient information" if "the item is described by item number, amount, and date of payment." This means that the customer's duties under subsection (c) are triggered if the bank sends a statement of account complying with the safe harbor rule without returning the paid items. A bank does not have to return the paid items unless it has agreed with the customer to do so. Whether there is such an agreement depends upon the particular circumstances. See Section 1–201(3). If the bank elects to provide the minimum information that is "sufficient" under subsection (a) and, as a consequence, the customer could not "reasonably have discovered the unauthorized payment," there is no preclusion under subsection (d). If the customer made a record of the issued checks on the check stub or carbonized copies furnished by the bank in the checkbook, the customer should usually be able to verify the paid items shown on the statement of account and discover any unauthorized or altered checks. But there could be exceptional circumstances. For example, if a check is altered by changing the name of the payee, the customer could not normally detect the fraud unless the customer is given the paid check or the statement of account discloses the name of the payee of the altered check. If the customer could not "reasonably have discovered the unauthorized payment" under subsection (c) there would not be a preclusion under subsection (d).

The safe harbor provided by subsection (a) serves to permit a bank, based on the state of existing technology, to trigger the customer's duties under subsection (c) by providing a "statement of account showing payment of items" without having to return the paid items, in any case in which the bank has not agreed with the customer to return the paid items. The safe harbor does not, however, preclude a customer under subsection (d) from asserting its unauthorized signature or an alteration against a bank in those circumstances in which under subsection (c) the customer should not "reasonably have discovered the unauthorized payment." Whether the customer has failed to comply with its duties under subsection (c) is determined on a case-by-case basis.

The provision in subsection (a) that a statement of account contains "sufficient information if the item is described by item number, amount, and date of payment" is based upon the existing state of technology. This information was chosen because it can be obtained by the bank's computer from the check's MICR line without examination of the items involved. The other two items of information that the customer would normally want to know—the name of the payee and the date of the item—cannot currently be obtained from the MICR line. The safe harbor rule is important in determining the feasibility of payor or collecting bank check retention plans. A customer who keeps a record of checks written, e.g., on the check stubs or carbonized copies of the checks supplied by the bank in the checkbook, will usually have sufficient information to identify the items on the basis of item number, amount, and date of payment. But customers who do not utilize these record-keeping methods may not. The policy decision is that accommodating customers who do not keep adequate records is not as desirable as accommodating customers who keep more careful records. This policy results in less cost to the check collection system and thus to all customers of the system. It is expected that technological advances such as image processing may make it possible for banks to give customers more information in the future in a manner that is fully compatible with automation or truncation systems. At that time the Permanent Editorial Board may wish to make recommendations for an amendment revising the safe harbor requirements in the light of those advances.

2. Subsection (d) states the consequences of a failure by the customer to perform its duty under subsection (c) to report an alteration or the customer's unauthorized signature. Subsection (d)(1) applies to the unauthorized payment of the item to which the duty to report under subsection (c) applies. If the bank proves that the customer "should reasonably have discovered the unauthorized payment" (See Comment 1) and did not notify the bank, the customer is precluded from asserting against the bank the alteration or the

customer's unauthorized signature if the bank proves that it suffered a loss as a result of the failure of the customer to perform its subsection (c) duty. Subsection (d)(2) applies to cases in which the customer fails to report an unauthorized signature or alteration with respect to an item in breach of the subsection (c) duty (See Comment 1) and the bank subsequently pays other items of the customer with respect to which there is an alteration or unauthorized signature of the customer and the same wrongdoer is involved. If the payment of the subsequent items occurred after the customer has had a reasonable time (not exceeding 30 days) to report with respect to the first item and before the bank received notice of the unauthorized signature or alteration of the first item, the customer is precluded from asserting the alteration or unauthorized signature with respect to the subsequent items.

If the customer is precluded in a single or multiple item unauthorized payment situation under subsection (d), but the customer proves that the bank failed to exercise ordinary care in paying the item or items and that the failure substantially contributed to the loss, subsection (e) provides a comparative negligence test for allocating loss between the customer and the bank. Subsection (e) also states that, if the customer proves that the bank did not pay the item in good faith, the preclusion under subsection (d) does not apply.

Subsection (d)(2) changes former subsection (2)(b) by adopting a 30-day period in place of a 14-day period. Although the 14-day period may have been sufficient when the original version of Article 4 was drafted in the 1950s, given the much greater volume of checks at the time of the revision, a longer period was viewed as more appropriate. The rule of subsection (d)(2) follows pre-Code case law that payment of an additional item or items bearing an unauthorized signature or alteration by the same wrongdoer is a loss suffered by the bank traceable to the customer's failure to exercise reasonable care (See Comment 1) in examining the statement and notifying the bank of objections to it. One of the most serious consequences of failure of the customer to comply with the requirements of subsection (c) is the opportunity presented to the wrongdoer to repeat the misdeeds. Conversely, one of the best ways to keep down losses in this type of situation is for the customer to promptly examine the statement and notify the bank of an unauthorized signature or alteration so that the bank will be alerted to stop paying further items. Hence, the rule of subsection (d)(2) is prescribed, and to avoid dispute a specific time limit, 30 days, is designated for cases to which the subsection applies. These considerations are not present if there are no losses resulting from the payment of additional items. In these circumstances, a reasonable period for the customer to comply with its duties under subsection (c) would depend on the circumstances (Section 1–204(2)) and the subsection (d)(2) time limit should not be imported by analogy into subsection (c).

3. Subsection (b) applies if the items are not returned to the customer. Check retention plans may include a simple payor bank check retention plan or the kind of check retention plan that would be authorized by a truncation agreement in which a collecting bank or the payee may retain the items. Even after agreeing to a check retention plan, a customer may need to see one or more checks for litigation or other purposes. The customer's request for the check may always be made to the payor bank. Under subsection (b) retaining banks may destroy items but must maintain the capacity to furnish legible copies for seven years. A legible copy may include an image of an item. This Act does not define the length of the reasonable period of time for a bank to provide the check or copy of the check. What is reasonable depends on the capacity of the bank and the needs of the customer. This Act does not specify sanctions for failure to retain or furnish the items or legible copies; this is left to other laws regulating banks. See Comment 3 to Section 4–101. Moreover, this Act does not regulate fees that banks charge their customers for furnishing items or copies or other services covered by the Act, but under principles of law such as unconscionability or good faith and fair dealing, courts have reviewed fees and the bank's exercise of a discretion to set fees. Perdue v. Crocker National Bank, 38 Cal.3d 913 (1985) (unconscionability); Best v. United Bank of Oregon, 739 P.2d 554, 562–566 (1987) (good faith and fair dealing). In addition, Section 1–203 provides that every contract or duty within this Act imposes an obligation of good faith in its performance or enforcement.

4. Subsection (e) replaces former subsection (3) and poses a modified comparative negligence test for determining liability. See the discussion on this point in the Comments to Sections 3–404, 3–405, and 3–406. The term "good faith" is defined in Section 3–103(a)(4) Section 1–201(b)(20) as including "observance of reasonable commercial standards of fair dealing." The connotation of this standard is fairness and not absence of negligence.

The term "ordinary care" used in subsection (e) is defined in Section 3–103(a)(7), made applicable to Article 4 by Section 4–104(c), to provide that sight examination by a payor bank is not required if its procedure is reasonable and is commonly followed by other comparable banks in the area. The case law is divided on this issue. The definition of "ordinary care" in Section 3–103 rejects those authorities that hold, in effect, that failure to use sight examination is negligence as a matter of law. The effect of the definition of "ordinary care" on Section 4–406 is only to provide that in the small percentage of cases in which a customer's failure to examine its statement or returned items has led to loss under subsection (d) a bank should not have to share that loss solely because it has adopted an automated collection or payment procedure in order to deal with the great volume of items at a lower cost to all customers.

5. Several changes are made in former Section 4–406(5). First, former subsection (5) is deleted and its substance is made applicable only to the one-year notice preclusion in former subsection (4) (subsection (f)). Thus if a drawer has not notified the payor bank of an unauthorized check or material alteration within the one-year period, the payor bank may not choose to recredit the drawer's account and pass the loss to the collecting banks on the theory of breach of warranty. Second, the reference in former subsection (4) to unauthorized indorsements is deleted. Section 4–406 imposes no duties on the drawer to look for unauthorized indorsements. Section 4–111 sets out a statute of limitations allowing a customer a three-year period to seek a credit to an account improperly charged by payment of an item bearing an unauthorized indorsement. Third, subsection (c) is added to Section 4–208 to assure that if a depositary bank is sued for breach of a presentment warranty, it can defend by showing that the drawer is precluded by Section 3–406 or Section 4–406(c) and (d). *Revisions approved by the Permanent Editorial Board for the Uniform Commercial Code, March 16, 1991.*

ARTICLE 9. SECURED TRANSACTIONS

Table of Sections

Sec.

§ 9-401. Alienability of Debtor's Rights

(a) **[Other law governs alienability; exceptions.]** Except as otherwise provided in subsection (b) and Sections 9–406, 9–407, 9–408, and 9–409, whether a debtor's rights in collateral may be voluntarily or involuntarily transferred is governed by law other than this article.

(b) **[Agreement does not prevent transfer.]** An agreement between the debtor and secured party which prohibits a transfer of the debtor's rights in collateral or makes the transfer a default does not prevent the transfer from taking effect.

Official Comment

1. **Source.** Former Section 9-311.

2. **Scope of This Part.** This Part deals with several issues affecting third parties (i.e., parties other than the debtor and the secured party). These issues are not addressed in Part 3, Subpart 3, which deals with priorities. This Part primarily addresses the rights and duties of account debtors and other persons obligated on collateral who are not, themselves, parties to a secured transaction.

3. **Governing Law.** There was some uncertainty under former Article 9 as to which jurisdiction's law (usually, which jurisdiction's version of Article 9) applied to the matters that this Part addresses. Part 3, Subpart 1, does not determine the law governing these matters because they do not relate to perfection, the effect of perfection or nonperfection, or priority. However, it might be inappropriate for a designation of applicable law by a debtor and secured party under Section 1–105 to control the law applicable to an independent transaction or relationship between the debtor and an account debtor.

Consider an example under Section 9–408.

Example 1: State X has adopted this Article; former Article 9 is the law of State Y. A general intangible (e.g., a franchise agreement) between a debtor-franchisee, D, and an account debtor-franchisor, AD, is governed by the law of State Y. D grants to SP a security interest in its rights under the franchise agreement. The franchise agreement contains a term prohibiting D's assignment of its rights under the agreement. D and SP agree that their secured transaction is governed by the law of State X. Under State X's Section 9–408, the restriction on D's assignment is ineffective to prevent the creation, attachment, or perfection of SP's security interest. State Y's former Section 9–318(4), however, does not address restrictions on the creation of security interests in general intangibles other than general intangibles for money due or to become due. Accordingly, it does not address restrictions on the assignment to SP of D's rights under the franchise agreement. The non-Article-9 law of State Y, which does address restrictions, provides that the prohibition on assignment is effective.

This Article does not provide a specific answer to the question of which State's law applies to the restriction on assignment in the example. However, assuming that under non-UCC choice-of-law principles the effectiveness of the restriction would be governed by the law of State Y, which governs the franchise agreement, the fact that State X's Article 9 governs the secured transaction between SP and D would not override the otherwise applicable law governing the agreement. Of course, to the extent that jurisdictions eventually adopt identical versions of this Article and courts interpret it consistently, the inability to identify the applicable law in circumstances such as those in the example may be inconsequential.

4. **Inalienability Under Other Law.** Subsection (a) addresses the question whether property necessarily is transferable by virtue of its inclusion (i.e., its eligibility as collateral) within the scope of Article 9. It gives a negative answer, subject to the identified exceptions. The substance of subsection (a) was implicit under former Article 9.

5. **Negative Pledge Covenant.** Subsection (b) is an exception to the general rule in subsection (a). It makes clear that in secured transactions under this Article the debtor has rights in collateral (whether legal title or equitable) which it can transfer and which its creditors can reach. It is best explained with an example.

Example 2: A debtor, D, grants to SP a security interest to secure a debt in excess of the value of the collateral. D agrees with SP that it will not create a subsequent security interest in the collateral and that any security interest purportedly granted in violation of the agreement will be void. Subsequently, in violation of its agreement with SP, D purports to grant a security interest in the same collateral to another secured party.

Subsection (b) validates D's creation of the subsequent (prohibited) security interest, which might even achieve priority over the earlier security interest. See Comment 7. However, unlike some other provisions of this Part, such as Section 9–406, subsection (b) does not provide that the agreement restricting assignment itself is "ineffective." Consequently, the debtor's breach may create a default.

6. **Rights of Lien Creditors.** Difficult problems may arise with respect to attachment, levy, and other judicial procedures under which a debtor's creditors may reach collateral subject to a security interest. For example, an obligation may be secured by collateral worth many times the amount of the obligation. If a lien creditor has caused all or a portion of the collateral to be seized under judicial process, it may be difficult to determine the amount of the debtor's "equity" in the collateral that has been seized. The section leaves resolution of this problem to the courts. The doctrine of marshaling may be appropriate.

7. **Sale of Receivables.** If a debtor sells an account, chattel paper, payment intangible, or promissory note outright, as against the buyer the debtor has no remaining rights to transfer. If, however, the buyer fails to perfect its interest, then solely insofar as the rights of certain third parties are concerned, the debtor is deemed to retain its rights and title. See Section 9–318. The debtor has the power to convey these rights to a subsequent purchaser. If the subsequent purchaser (buyer or secured lender) perfects its interest, it will achieve priority over the earlier, unperfected purchaser. See Section 9–322(a)(1).

§ 9–403. Agreement Not to Assert Defenses Against Assignee

(a) **["Value."]** In this section, "value" has the meaning provided in Section 3–303(a).

(b) **[Agreement not to assert claim or defense.]** Except as otherwise provided in this section, an agreement between an account debtor and an assignor not to assert against an assignee any claim or defense that the account debtor may have against the assignor is enforceable by an assignee that takes an assignment:

(1) for value;

(2) in good faith;

(3) without notice of a claim of a property or possessory right to the property assigned; and

(4) without notice of a defense or claim in recoupment of the type that may be asserted against a person entitled to enforce a negotiable instrument under Section 3–305(a).

(c) **[When subsection (b) not applicable.]** Subsection (b) does not apply to defenses of a type that may be asserted against a holder in due course of a negotiable instrument under Section 3–305(b).

(d) **[Omission of required statement in consumer transaction.]** In a consumer transaction, if a record evidences the account debtor's obligation, law other than this article requires that the record include a statement to the effect that the rights of an assignee are subject to claims or defenses that the account debtor could assert against the original obligee, and the record does not include such a statement:

(1) the record has the same effect as if the record included such a statement; and

(2) the account debtor may assert against an assignee those claims and defenses that would have been available if the record included such a statement.

(e) **[Rule for individual under other law.]** This section is subject to law other than this article which establishes a different rule for an account debtor who is an individual and who incurred the obligation primarily for personal, family, or household purposes.

(f) **[Other law not displaced.]** Except as otherwise provided in subsection (d), this section does not displace law other than this article which gives effect to an agreement by an account debtor not to assert a claim or defense against an assignee.

Official Comment

1. **Source.** Former Section 9–206.

2. **Scope and Purpose.** Subsection (b), like former Section 9–206, generally validates an agreement between an account debtor and an assignor that the account debtor will not assert against an assignee claims and defenses that it may have against the assignor. These agreements are typical in installment sale agreements and leases. However, this section expands former Section 9–206 to apply to all account debtors; it is not limited to account debtors that have bought or leased goods. This section applies only to the obligations of an "account debtor," as defined in Section 9–102. Thus, it does not determine the circumstances under which and the extent to which a person who is obligated on a negotiable instrument is disabled from asserting claims and defenses. Rather, Article 3 must be consulted. See, e.g., Sections 3–305, 3–306. Article 3 governs even when the negotiable instrument constitutes part of chattel paper. See Section 9–102 (an obligor on a negotiable instrument constituting part of chattel paper is not an "account debtor").

3. **Conditions of Validation; Relationship to Article 3.** Subsection (b) validates an account debtor's agreement only if the assignee takes an assignment for value, in good faith, and without notice of conflicting claims to the property assigned or of certain claims or defenses of the account debtor. Like former Section 9–206, this section is designed to put the assignee in a position that is no better and no worse than that of a holder in due course of a negotiable instrument under Article 3. However, former Section 9–206 left open certain issues, e.g., whether the section incorporated the special Article 3 definition of "value" in Section 3–303 or the generally applicable definition in Section 1–201(44). Subsection (a) addresses this question; it provides that "value" has the meaning specified in Section 3–303(a). Similarly, subsection (c) provides that subsection (b) does not validate an agreement with respect to defenses that could be asserted against a holder in due course under Section 3–305(b) (the so-called "real" defenses). In 1990, the definition of "holder in due course" (Section 3–302) and the articulation of the rights of a holder in due course (Sections

3–305 and 3–306) were revised substantially. This section tracks more closely the rules of Sections 3–302, 3–305, and 3–306.

4. **Relationship to Terms of Assigned Property.** Former Section 9–206(2), concerning warranties accompanying the sale of goods, has been deleted as unnecessary. This Article does not regulate the terms of the account, chattel paper, or general intangible that is assigned, except insofar as the account, chattel paper, or general intangible itself creates a security interest (as often is the case with chattel paper). Thus, Article 2, and not this Article, determines whether a seller of goods makes or effectively disclaims warranties, even if the sale is secured. Similarly, other law, and not this Article, determines the effectiveness of an account debtor's undertaking to pay notwithstanding, and not to assert, any defenses or claims against an assignor-e.g., a "hell-or-high-water" provision in the underlying agreement that is assigned. If other law gives effect to this undertaking, then, under principles of *nemo dat,* the undertaking would be enforceable by the assignee (secured party). If other law prevents the assignor from enforcing the undertaking, this section nevertheless might permit the assignee to do so. The right of the assignee to enforce would depend upon whether, under the particular facts, the account debtor's undertaking fairly could be construed as an agreement that falls within the scope of this section and whether the assignee meets the requirements of this section.

5. **Relationship to Federal Trade Commission Rule.** Subsection (d) is new. It applies to rights evidenced by a record that is required to contain, but does not contain, the notice set forth in Federal Trade Commission Rule 433, 16 C.F.R. Part 433 (the "Holder-in-Due-Course Regulations"). Under this subsection, an assignee of such a record takes subject to the consumer account debtor's claims and defenses to the same extent as it would have if the writing had contained the required notice. Thus, subsection (d) effectively renders waiver-of-defense clauses ineffective in the transactions with consumers to which it applies.

6. **Relationship to Other Law.** Like former Section 9–206(1), this section takes no position on the enforceability of waivers of claims and defenses by consumer account debtors, leaving that question to other law. However, the reference to "law other than this article" in subsection (e) encompasses administrative rules and regulations; the reference in former Section 9–206(1) that it replaces ("statute or decision") arguably did not.

This section does not displace other law that gives effect to a non-consumer account debtor's agreement not to assert defenses against an assignee, even if the agreement would not qualify under subsection (b). See subsection (f). It validates, but does not invalidate, agreements made by a non-consumer account debtor. This section also does not displace other law to the extent that the other law permits an assignee, who takes an assignment with notice of a claim of a property or possessory right, a defense, or a claim in recoupment, to enforce an account debtor's agreement not to assert claims and defenses against the assignor (e.g., a "hell-or-high-water" agreement). See Comment 4. It also does not displace an assignee's right to assert that an account debtor is estopped from asserting a claim or defense. Nor does this section displace other law with respect to waivers of potential future claims and defenses that are the subject of an agreement between the account debtor and the assignee. Finally, it does not displace Section 1–107, concerning waiver of a breach that allegedly already has occurred.

§ 9–404. Rights Acquired by Assignee; Claims and Defenses Against Assignee

(a) **[Assignee's rights subject to terms, claims, and defenses; exceptions.]** Unless an account debtor has made an enforceable agreement not to assert defenses or claims, and subject to subsections (b) through (e), the rights of an assignee are subject to:

(1) all terms of the agreement between the account debtor and assignor and any defense or claim in recoupment arising from the transaction that gave rise to the contract; and

(2) any other defense or claim of the account debtor against the assignor which accrues before the account debtor receives a notification of the assignment authenticated by the assignor or the assignee.

(b) **[Account debtor's claim reduces amount owed to assignee.]** Subject to subsection (c) and except as otherwise provided in subsection (d), the claim of an account debtor against an assignor may be asserted against an assignee under subsection (a) only to reduce the amount the account debtor owes.

(c) **[Rule for individual under other law.]** This section is subject to law other than this article which establishes a different rule for an account debtor who is an individual and who incurred the obligation primarily for personal, family, or household purposes.

(d) **[Omission of required statement in consumer transaction.]** In a consumer transaction, if a record evidences the account debtor's obligation, law other than this article requires that the record include a statement to the effect that the account debtor's recovery against an assignee with respect to claims and defenses against the assignor may not exceed amounts paid by the account debtor under the record, and the record does not include such a statement, the extent to which a claim of an account debtor against the assignor may be asserted against an assignee is determined as if the record included such a statement.

(e) **[Inapplicability to health-care-insurance receivable.]** This section does not apply to an assignment of a health-care-insurance receivable.

Official Comment

1. **Source.** Former Section 9-318(1).

2. **Purpose; Rights of Assignee in General.** Subsection (a), like former Section 9-318(1), provides that an assignee generally takes an assignment subject to defenses and claims of an account debtor. Under subsection (a)(1), if the account debtor's defenses on an assigned claim arise from the transaction that gave rise to the contract with the assignor, it makes no difference whether the defense or claim accrues before or after the account debtor is notified of the assignment. Under subsection (a)(2), the assignee takes subject to other defenses or claims only if they accrue before the account debtor has been notified of the assignment. Of course, an account debtor may waive its right to assert defenses or claims against an assignee under Section 9-403 or other applicable law. Subsection (a) tracks Section 3-305(a)(3) more closely than its predecessor.

3. **Limitation on Affirmative Claims.** Subsection (b) is new. It limits the claim that the account debtor may assert against an assignee. Borrowing from Section 3-305(a)(3) and cases construing former Section 9-318, subsection (b) generally does not afford the account debtor the right to an affirmative recovery from an assignee.

4. **Consumer Account Debtors; Relationship to Federal Trade Commission Rule.** Subsections (c) and (d) also are new. Subsection (c) makes clear that the rules of this section are subject to other law establishing special rules for consumer account debtors. An "account debtor who is an individual" as used in subsection (c) includes individuals who are jointly or jointly and severally obligated. Subsection (d) applies to rights evidenced by a record that is required to contain, but does not contain, the notice set forth in Federal Trade Commission Rule 433, 16 C.F.R. Part 433 (the "Holder-in-Due-Course Regulations"). Under subsection (d), a consumer account debtor has the same right to an affirmative recovery from an assignee of such a record as the consumer would have had against the assignee had the record contained the required notice.

5. **Scope; Application to "Account Debtor."** This section deals only with the rights and duties of "account debtors"—and for the most part only with account debtors on accounts, chattel paper, and payment intangibles. Subsection (e) provides that the obligation of an insurer with respect to a health-care-insurance receivable is governed by other law. References in this section to an "account debtor" include account debtors on collateral that is proceeds. Neither this section nor any other provision of this Article, including Sections 9-408 and 9-409, provides analogous regulation of the rights and duties of other obligors on collateral, such as the maker of a negotiable instrument (governed by Article 3), the issuer of or nominated person under a letter of credit (governed by Article 5), or the issuer of a security (governed by Article 8). Article 9 leaves those rights and duties untouched; however, Section 9-409 deals with the special case of letters of credit. When chattel paper is composed in part of a negotiable instrument, the obligor on the instrument is not an "account debtor," and Article 3 governs the rights of the assignee of the chattel paper with respect to the issues that this section addresses. See, e.g., Section 3-601 (dealing with discharge of an obligation to pay a negotiable instrument).

§ 9–601. Rights After Default; Judicial Enforcement; Consignor or Buyer of Accounts, Chattel Paper, Payment Intangibles, or Promissory Notes

(a) **[Rights of secured party after default.]** After default, a secured party has the rights provided in this part and, except as otherwise provided in Section 9–602, those provided by agreement of the parties. A secured party:

(1) may reduce a claim to judgment, foreclose, or otherwise enforce the claim, security interest, or agricultural lien by any available judicial procedure; and

(2) if the collateral is documents, may proceed either as to the documents or as to the goods they cover.

(b) **[Rights and duties of secured party in possession or control.]** A secured party in possession of collateral or control of collateral under Section 9–104, 9–105, 9–106, or 9–107 has the rights and duties provided in Section 9–207.

(c) **[Rights cumulative; simultaneous exercise.]** The rights under subsections (a) and (b) are cumulative and may be exercised simultaneously.

(d) **[Rights of debtor and obligor.]** Except as otherwise provided in subsection (g) and Section 9–605, after default, a debtor and an obligor have the rights provided in this part and by agreement of the parties.

(e) **[Lien of levy after judgment.]** If a secured party has reduced its claim to judgment, the lien of any levy that may be made upon the collateral by virtue of an execution based upon the judgment relates back to the earliest of:

(1) the date of perfection of the security interest or agricultural lien in the collateral;

(2) the date of filing a financing statement covering the collateral; or

(3) any date specified in a statute under which the agricultural lien was created.

(f) **[Execution sale.]** A sale pursuant to an execution is a foreclosure of the security interest or agricultural lien by judicial procedure within the meaning of this section. A secured party may purchase at the sale and thereafter hold the collateral free of any other requirements of this article.

(g) **[Consignor or buyer of certain rights to payment.]** Except as otherwise provided in Section 9–607(c), this part imposes no duties upon a secured party that is a consignor or is a buyer of accounts, chattel paper, payment intangibles, or promissory notes.

Official Comment

1. **Source.** Former Section 9–501(1), (2), (5).

2. **Enforcement: In General.** The rights of a secured party to enforce its security interest in collateral after the debtor's default are an important feature of a secured transaction. (Note that the term "rights," as defined in Section 1–201, includes "remedies.") This Part provides those rights as well as certain limitations on their exercise for the protection of the defaulting debtor, other creditors, and other affected persons. However, subsections (a) and (d) make clear that the rights provided in this Part do not exclude other rights provided by agreement.

3. **When Remedies Arise.** Under subsection (a) the secured party's rights arise "[a]fter default." As did former Section 9–501, this Article leaves to the agreement of the parties the circumstances giving rise to a default. This Article does not determine whether a secured party's post-default conduct can constitute a waiver of default in the face of an agreement stating that such conduct shall not constitute a waiver. Rather, it continues to leave to the parties' agreement, as supplemented by law other than this Article, the determination whether a default has occurred or has been waived. See Section 1–103.

4. **Possession of Collateral; Section 9–207.** After a secured party takes possession of collateral following a default, there is no longer any distinction between a security interest that before default was nonpossessory and a security interest that was possessory before default, as under a common-law pledge.

This Part generally does not distinguish between the rights of a secured party with a nonpossessory security interest and those of a secured party with a possessory security interest. However, Section 9–207 addresses rights and duties with respect to collateral in a secured party's possession. Under subsection (b) of this section, Section 9–207 applies not only to possession before default but also to possession after default. Subsection (b) also has been conformed to Section 9–207, which, unlike former Section 9–207, applies to secured parties having control of collateral.

5. **Cumulative Remedies.** Former Section 9–501(1) provided that the secured party's remedies were cumulative, but it did not explicitly provide whether the remedies could be exercised simultaneously. Subsection (c) permits the simultaneous exercise of remedies if the secured party acts in good faith. The liability scheme of Subpart 2 affords redress to an aggrieved debtor or obligor. Moreover, permitting the simultaneous exercise of remedies under subsection (c) does not override any non-UCC law, including the law of tort and statutes regulating collection of debts, under which the simultaneous exercise of remedies in a particular case constitutes abusive behavior or harassment giving rise to liability.

6. **Judicial Enforcement.** Under subsection (a) a secured party may reduce its claim to judgment or foreclose its interest by any available procedure outside this Article under applicable law. Subsection (e) generally follows former Section 9–501(5). It makes clear that any judicial lien that the secured party may acquire against the collateral effectively is a continuation of the original security interest (if perfected) and not the acquisition of a new interest or a transfer of property on account of a preexisting obligation. Under former Section 9–501(5), the judicial lien was stated to relate back to the date of perfection of the security interest. Subsection (e), however, provides that the lien relates back to the earlier of the date of filing or the date of perfection. This provides a secured party who enforces a security interest by judicial process with the benefit of the "first-to-file-or-perfect" priority rule of Section 9–322(a)(1).

7. **Agricultural Liens.** Part 6 provides parallel treatment for the enforcement of agricultural liens and security interests. Because agricultural liens are statutory rather than consensual, this Article does draw a few distinctions between these liens and security interests. Under subsection (e), the statute creating an agricultural lien would govern whether and the date to which an execution lien relates back. Section 9–606 explains when a "default" occurs in the agricultural lien context.

8. **Execution Sales.** Subsection (f) also follows former Section 9–501(5). It makes clear that an execution sale is an appropriate method of foreclosure contemplated by this Part. However, the sale is governed by other law and not by this Article, and the limitations under Section 9–610 on the right of a secured party to purchase collateral do not apply.

9. **Sales of Receivables; Consignments.** Subsection (g) provides that, except as provided in Section 9–607(c), the duties imposed on secured parties do not apply to buyers of accounts, chattel paper, payment intangibles, or promissory notes. Although denominated "secured parties," these buyers own the entire interest in the property sold and so may enforce their rights without regard to the seller ("debtor") or the seller's creditors. Likewise, a true consignor may enforce its ownership interest under other law without regard to the duties that this Part imposes on secured parties. Note, however, that Section 9–615 governs cases in which a consignee's secured party (other than a consignor) is enforcing a security interest that is senior to the security interest (i.e., ownership interest) of a true consignor.

§ 9-609. Secured Party's Right to Take Possession After Default

(a) **[Possession; rendering equipment unusable; disposition on debtor's premises.]** After default, a secured party:

(1) may take possession of the collateral; and

(2) without removal, may render equipment unusable and dispose of collateral on a debtor's premises under Section 9–610.

(b) **[Judicial and nonjudicial process.]** A secured party may proceed under subsection (a):

(1) pursuant to judicial process; or

(2) without judicial process, if it proceeds without breach of the peace.

(c) **[Assembly of collateral.]** If so agreed, and in any event after default, a secured party may require the debtor to assemble the collateral and make it available to the secured party at a place to be designated by the secured party which is reasonably convenient to both parties.

Official Comment

1. **Source.** Former Section 9–503.

2. **Secured Party's Right to Possession.** This section follows former Section 9–503 and earlier uniform legislation. It provides that the secured party is entitled to take possession of collateral after default.

3. **Judicial Process; Breach of Peace.** Subsection (b) permits a secured party to proceed under this section without judicial process if it does so "without breach of the peace." Although former Section 9–503 placed the same condition on a secured party's right to take possession of collateral, subsection (b) extends the condition to the right provided in subsection (a)(2) as well. Like former Section 9–503, this section does not define or explain the conduct that will constitute a breach of the peace, leaving that matter for continuing development by the courts. In considering whether a secured party has engaged in a breach of the peace, however, courts should hold the secured party responsible for the actions of others taken on the secured party's behalf, including independent contractors engaged by the secured party to take possession of collateral.

This section does not authorize a secured party who repossesses without judicial process to utilize the assistance of a law-enforcement officer. A number of cases have held that a repossessing secured party's use of a law-enforcement officer without benefit of judicial process constituted a failure to comply with former Section 9–503.

4. **Damages for Breach of Peace.** Concerning damages that may be recovered based on a secured party's breach of the peace in connection with taking possession of collateral, see Section 9–625, Comment 3.

5. **Multiple Secured Parties.** More than one secured party may be entitled to take possession of collateral under this section. Conflicting rights to possession among secured parties are resolved by the priority rules of this Article. Thus, a senior secured party is entitled to possession as against a junior claimant. Non-UCC law governs whether a junior secured party in possession of collateral is liable to the senior in conversion. Normally, a junior who refuses to relinquish possession of collateral upon the demand of a secured party having a superior possessory right to the collateral would be liable in conversion.

6. **Secured Party's Right to Disable and Dispose of Equipment on Debtor's Premises.** In the case of some collateral, such as heavy equipment, the physical removal from the debtor's plant and the storage of the collateral pending disposition may be impractical or unduly expensive. This section follows former Section 9–503 by providing that, in lieu of removal, the secured party may render equipment unusable or may dispose of collateral on the debtor's premises. Unlike former Section 9–503, however, this section explicitly conditions these rights on the debtor's default. Of course, this section does not validate unreasonable action by a secured party. Under Section 9–610, all aspects of a disposition must be commercially reasonable.

7. **Debtor's Agreement to Assemble Collateral.** This section follows former Section 9–503 also by validating a debtor's agreement to assemble collateral and make it available to a secured party at a place that the secured party designates. Similar to the treatment of agreements to permit collection prior to default under Section 9–607 and former 9–502, however, this section validates these agreements whether or not they are conditioned on the debtor's default. For example, a debtor might agree to make available to a secured party, from time to time, any instruments or negotiable documents that the debtor receives on account of collateral. A court should not infer from this section's validation that a debtor's agreement to assemble and make available collateral would not be enforceable under other applicable law.

8. **Agreed Standards.** Subject to the limitation imposed by Section 9–603(b), this section's provisions concerning agreements to assemble and make available collateral and a secured party's right to disable equipment and dispose of collateral on a debtor's premises are likely topics for agreement on standards as contemplated by Section 9–603.

§ 9-625. Remedies for Secured Party's Failure to Comply With Article

(a) **[Judicial orders concerning noncompliance.]** If it is established that a secured party is not proceeding in accordance with this article, a court may order or restrain collection, enforcement, or disposition of collateral on appropriate terms and conditions.

(b) **[Damages for noncompliance.]** Subject to subsections (c), (d), and (f), a person is liable for damages in the amount of any loss caused by a failure to comply with this article. Loss caused by a failure to comply may include loss resulting from the debtor's inability to obtain, or increased costs of, alternative financing.

(c) **[Persons entitled to recover damages; statutory damages in consumer-goods transaction.]** Except as otherwise provided in Section 9-628:

(1) a person that, at the time of the failure, was a debtor, was an obligor, or held a security interest in or other lien on the collateral may recover damages under subsection (b) for its loss; and

(2) if the collateral is consumer goods, a person that was a debtor or a secondary obligor at the time a secured party failed to comply with this part may recover for that failure in any event an amount not less than the credit service charge plus 10 percent of the principal amount of the obligation or the time-price differential plus 10 percent of the cash price.

(d) **[Recovery when deficiency eliminated or reduced.]** A debtor whose deficiency is eliminated under Section 9-626 may recover damages for the loss of any surplus. However, a debtor or secondary obligor whose deficiency is eliminated or reduced under Section 9-626 may not otherwise recover under subsection (b) for noncompliance with the provisions of this part relating to collection, enforcement, disposition, or acceptance.

(e) **[Statutory damages: noncompliance with specified provisions.]** In addition to any damages recoverable under subsection (b), the debtor, consumer obligor, or person named as a debtor in a filed record, as applicable, may recover $500 in each case from a person that:

(1) fails to comply with Section 9-208;

(2) fails to comply with Section 9-209;

(3) files a record that the person is not entitled to file under Section 9-509(a);

(4) fails to cause the secured party of record to file or send a termination statement as required by Section 9-513(a) or (c);

(5) fails to comply with Section 9-616(b)(1) and whose failure is part of a pattern, or consistent with a practice, of noncompliance; or

(6) fails to comply with Section 9-616(b)(2).

(f) **[Statutory damages: noncompliance with Section 9-210.]** A debtor or consumer obligor may recover damages under subsection (b) and, in addition, $500 in each case from a person that, without reasonable cause, fails to comply with a request under Section 9-210. A recipient of a request under Section 9-210 which never claimed an interest in the collateral or obligations that are the subject of a request under that section has a reasonable excuse for failure to comply with the request within the meaning of this subsection.

(g) **[Limitation of security interest: noncompliance with Section 9-210.]** If a secured party fails to comply with a request regarding a list of collateral or a statement of account under Section 9-210, the secured party may claim a security interest only as shown in the list or statement included in the request as against a person that is reasonably misled by the failure.

Official Comment

1. **Source.** Former Section 9-507.

2. **Remedies for Noncompliance; Scope.** Subsections (a) and (b) provide the basic remedies afforded to those aggrieved by a secured party's failure to comply with this Article. Like all provisions that create liability, they are subject to Section 9–628, which should be read in conjunction with Section 9–605. The principal limitations under this Part on a secured party's right to enforce its security interest against collateral are the requirements that it proceed in good faith (Section 1–203), in a commercially reasonable manner (Sections 9–607 and 9–610), and, in most cases, with reasonable notification (Sections 9–611 through 9–614). Following former Section 9–507, under subsection (a) an aggrieved person may seek injunctive relief, and under subsection (b) the person may recover damages for losses caused by noncompliance. Unlike former Section 9–507, however, subsections (a) and (b) are not limited to noncompliance with provisions of this Part of Article 9. Rather, they apply to noncompliance with any provision of this Article. The change makes this section applicable to noncompliance with Sections 9–207 (duties of secured party in possession of collateral), 9–208 (duties of secured party having control over deposit account), 9–209 (duties of secured party if account debtor has been notified of an assignment), 9–210 (duty to comply with request for accounting, etc.), 9–509(a) (duty to refrain from filing unauthorized financing statement), and 9–513(a) or (c) (duty to provide termination statement). Subsection (a) also modifies the first sentence of former Section 9–507(1) by adding the references to "collection" and "enforcement." Subsection (c)(2), which gives a minimum damage recovery in consumer-goods transactions, applies only to noncompliance with the provisions of this Part.

3. **Damages for Noncompliance with This Article.** Subsection (b) sets forth the basic remedy for failure to comply with the requirements of this Article: a damage recovery in the amount of loss caused by the noncompliance. Subsection (c) identifies who may recover under subsection (b). It affords a remedy to any aggrieved person who is a debtor or obligor. However, a principal obligor who is not a debtor may recover damages only for noncompliance with Section 9–616, inasmuch as none of the other rights and duties in this Article run in favor of such a principal obligor. Such a principal obligor could not suffer any loss or damage on account of noncompliance with rights or duties of which it is not a beneficiary. Subsection (c) also affords a remedy to an aggrieved person who holds a competing security interest or other lien, regardless of whether the aggrieved person is entitled to notification under Part 6. The remedy is available even to holders of senior security interests and other liens. The exercise of this remedy is subject to the normal rules of pleading and proof. A person who has delegated the duties of a secured party but who remains obligated to perform them is liable under this subsection. The last sentence of subsection (d) eliminates the possibility of double recovery or other over-compensation arising out of a reduction or elimination of a deficiency under Section 9–626, based on noncompliance with the provisions of this Part relating to collection, enforcement, disposition, or acceptance. Assuming no double recovery, a debtor whose deficiency is eliminated under Section 9–626 may pursue a claim for a surplus. Because Section 9–626 does not apply to consumer transactions, the statute is silent as to whether a double recovery or other over-compensation is possible in a consumer transaction.

Damages for violation of the requirements of this Article, including Section 9–609, are those reasonably calculated to put an eligible claimant in the position that it would have occupied had no violation occurred. See Section 1–106. Subsection (b) supports the recovery of actual damages for committing a breach of the peace in violation of Section 9–609, and principles of tort law supplement this subsection. See Section 1–103. However, to the extent that damages in tort compensate the debtor for the same loss dealt with by this Article, the debtor should be entitled to only one recovery.

4. **Minimum Damages in Consumer-Goods Transactions.** Subsection (c)(2) provides a minimum, statutory, damage recovery for a debtor and secondary obligor in a consumer-goods transaction. It is patterned on former Section 9–507(1) and is designed to ensure that every noncompliance with the requirements of Part 6 in a consumer-goods transaction results in liability, regardless of any injury that may have resulted. Subsection (c)(2) leaves the treatment of statutory damages as it was under former Article 9. A secured party is not liable for statutory damages under this subsection more than once with respect to any one secured obligation (see Section 9–628(e)), nor is a secured party liable under this subsection for failure to comply with Section 9–616 (see Section 9–628(d)).

Following former Section 9–507(1), this Article does not include a definition or explanation of the terms "credit service charge," "principal amount," "time-price differential," or "cash price," as used in subsection (c)(2). It leaves their construction and application to the court, taking into account the subsection's purpose of providing a minimum recovery in consumer-goods transactions.

5. **Supplemental Damages.** Subsections (e) and (f) provide damages that supplement the recovery, if any, under subsection (b). Subsection (e) imposes an additional $500 liability upon a person who fails to comply with the provisions specified in that subsection, and subsection (f) imposes like damages on a person who, without reasonable excuse, fails to comply with a request for an accounting or a request regarding a list of collateral or statement of account under Section 9–210. However, under subsection (f), a person has a reasonable excuse for the failure if the person never claimed an interest in the collateral or obligations that were the subject of the request.

6. **Estoppel.** Subsection (g) limits the extent to which a secured party who fails to comply with a request regarding a list of collateral or statement of account may claim a security interest.

UNIFORM COMPUTER INFORMATION TRANSACTIONS ACT (UCITA)

(Selected Sections)

Table of Sections

§ 112. Manifesting Assent

(a) **[How person manifests assent.]** A person manifests assent to a record or term if the person, acting with knowledge of, or after having an opportunity to review the record or term or a copy of it:

(1) authenticates the record or term with intent to adopt or accept it; or

(2) intentionally engages in conduct or makes statements with reason to know that the other party or its electronic agent may infer from the conduct or statement that the person assents to the record or term.

(b) **[How electronic agent manifests assent.]** An electronic agent manifests assent to a record or term if, after having an opportunity to review it, the electronic agent:

(1) authenticates the record or term; or

(2) engages in operations that in the circumstances indicate acceptance of the record or term.

(c) **[Assent to specific term.]** If this [Act] or other law requires assent to a specific term, a manifestation of assent must relate specifically to the term.

(d) **[Proof of assent.]** Conduct or operations manifesting assent may be proved in any manner, including a showing that a person or an electronic agent obtained or used the information or informational rights and that a procedure existed by which a person or an electronic agent must have engaged in the conduct or operations in order to do so. Proof of compliance with subsection 60 (a)(2) is sufficient if there is conduct that assents and subsequent conduct that reaffirms assent by electronic means.

(e) **[Agreement for future transactions.]** The effect of this section may be modified by an agreement setting out standards applicable to future transactions between the parties.

(f) **[Online services, network access, and telecommunications services.]** Providers of online services, network access, and telecommunications services, or the operators of facilities thereof, do not manifest assent to a contractual relationship simply by their provision of those services to other parties, including, without limitation, transmission, routing, or providing connections; linking; caching; hosting; information location tools; and storage of materials, at the request or initiation of a person other than the service provider.

Comment

1. **Scope of Section.** This section provides standards for "manifestation of assent." Section 113 deals with the related, important concept of an "opportunity to review". In this Act, having an opportunity to review a record is a precondition to manifesting assent.

2. **General Theme.** The term "manifesting assent" comes from *Restatement (Second) of Contracts* § 19. This section corresponds to *Restatement* § 19, but more fully explicates the concept. Codification establishes uniformity that is lacking in common law.

Restatement (Second) of Contracts § 19(1) provides: "The manifestation of assent may be made wholly or partly by written or spoken words or by other acts or by failure to act." This section adopts that view. Conduct can convey assent as clearly as words. This rule is important in electronic commerce, where most interactions involve conduct rather than words. Subsection (b) adapts that principle to electronic agent contracting.

"Manifesting assent" has several roles: 1) a method by which a party agrees to a contract; 2) a method by which a party adopts terms of a record as the terms of a contract; and 3) if required by this Act, a means of assenting to a particular term. In most cases, the same act accomplishes the results under 1 and 2.

Manifesting assent does not require any specific formality of language or conduct. In this Act, however, to manifest assent to a record or term requires meeting three conditions:

- **First**, the person must have knowledge of the record or term or an opportunity to review it before assenting. An opportunity to review requires that the record be available in a manner that ought to call it to the attention of a reasonable person and that readily permits review. Section 113 may also require a right of return if the opportunity to review comes after a person becomes obligated to pay or begins performance.
- **Second**, having had an opportunity to review, the person must manifest assent. The person may authenticate the record or term, express assent verbally, or intentionally engage in conduct with reason to know that the conduct indicates assent. *Restatement (Second) of Contracts* § 19. As in the *Restatement* this can include a failure to action if the circumstances so indicate.
- **Third**, the conduct, statement, or authentication must be attributable in law to the person. General agency law and Section 212 provide standards for attribution.

3. **Manifesting Assent.**

a. **Assent by Statements or Authentication.** A person can assent to a record or term by stating or otherwise indicating its assent or by "authenticating" the record or term. Authentication occurs if a party signs a record or does an electronic equivalent. Section 102 (a)(6).

b. **Assent by Conduct.** Assent occurs if a person acts or fails to act having reason to know its behavior will be viewed by the other party as indicating assent. Whether this occurs depends on the circumstances. As in common law, proof of assent does not require proof of a person's subjective intent or purpose, but focuses on objective indicia, including whether there was an act or a failure to act voluntarily engaged in with reason to know that an inference of assent would be drawn. Actions objectively indicating assent are assent. This follows modern contract law doctrines of objective assent. Doctrines of mistake, fraud, and duress apply in appropriate cases.

Assent does not require that a party be able to negotiate or modify terms, but the assenting behavior must be intentional (voluntary). This same rule prevails in all other contract law. Intentional conduct is satisfied if the alternative of refusing to act exists, even if refusing leaves no alternative source for the computer information. On the other hand, conduct is not assent if it is conduct which the assenting party cannot avoid doing, such as blinking one's eyes. Courts use common sense in applying this standard in common law and will do so under this Act. Actions in a context of a mutual reservation of the right to defer agreement to a contract do not manifest assent; neither party has any reason to believe that its conduct will suggest assent to the other party.

Knowledge that conduct or inaction is assent satisfies this rule. Also, conduct is assent if a person has "reason to know" the conduct will lead the other party to believe that there was assent. Factors that relate to this issue include: the ordinary expectations of similar persons in similar contexts;

language on a display, package, or otherwise made available to the party; the fact that the party can decline and return the information, but decides to use it; information communicated before the conduct occurred; and standards and practices of the business, trade or industry of which the person has reason to know.

The "reason to know" standard is not met if the computer information is sent to a recipient unsolicited under terms that purport to create a binding contract by failure to object to the unsolicited sending. In such cases, it is not reasonable for the sending party to infer assent from silence; the threshold for manifesting assent is not met.

c. **Assent by Electronic Agents.** Assent may occur through automated systems ("electronic agents"). Either or both parties (including consumers) may use electronic agents. For electronic agents, assent cannot be based on knowledge or reason to know, since computer programs are capable of neither and the automated nature of the interaction may mean that no individual is aware of it. Subsection (b) focuses on the electronic agent's acts, not knowledge or reason to know. Assent occurs if the agent's operations were an authentication or if, in the circumstances, the operations indicate assent. In this Act, manifesting assent requires a prior opportunity to review. For an electronic agent, this opportunity occurs only if the record or term was presented in such a way that a reasonably configured electronic agent could react to it. See Section 113(b). The capability of an automated system to react and an assessment of the implications of its actions are the only appropriate measures of assent.

d. **Assent to Particular Terms.** This Act distinguishes between assent to a record 62 and, when required by this Act or other law, assent to a particular term in a record. Assent to a record encompasses all terms of the record. Section 208. Assent to a particular term, if required, requires acts that specifically relate to that term. This is like a requirement that a party "initial" a clause to make it effective. One act, however, may assent to both the record and the term if the circumstances, including the language of the record, clearly indicate that this is true, such as where assent is clearly indicated as being to the record and to a term the nature of which is made clear to the assenting party.

4. **Terms of Agreement.** Manifestation of assent to a record is not the only way in which parties establish the terms of their agreement. This Act does not alter recognition in law of other methods of agreeing to terms. For example, a product description can become part of an agreement without manifestation of assent to a record repeating that description; the product description defines the bargain itself. A party that licenses a database of names of "consumer attorneys" need only provide a database of consumer attorneys since this is the bargain; the provider is not required to obtain assent to a record stating that deal. Similarly, the licensee can rely on the fact that the database must contain consumer attorneys, not other lawyers. If a product is clearly identified on the package or in representations to the licensee as for consumer use only, that term is effective without language in a record restating the description or conduct assenting to that record. Of course, if the nature of the product is not obvious and there is no assent or agreement to terms defining it, hidden conditions might not be part of the agreement.

Often, copyright or other intellectual property notices restrict use of a product without needing assent to contract terms. For example, a video rental may place a notice on screen that limits the customer's use such as by precluding commercial public performances. Enforceability of such notices does not depend on obtaining a manifestation of assent.

5. **Proof of Assent.** Many different acts can establish assent to a contract or a contract term. It is not possible to state them in a statute. In electronic commerce, one important method is by showing that a procedure existed that required an authentication or other assent in order to proceed in an automated system. This is recognized in subsection (d).

Subsection (d) also encourages use of double assent procedures as a reconfirmation showing intentional assent ("intentionally engages in conduct . . . with reason to know"). It makes clear that if the assenting party has an opportunity to confirm or deny assent before proceeding to obtain or use information, confirmation meets the requirement of subsection (a)(2). This does not alter the effectiveness of a single indication of assent. When properly set out with an opportunity to review terms and to make clear that an act such as clicking assent on-screen is assent, a single indication of assent suffices. See *Caspi v. Microsoft Network, L.L.C.*, 323 N.J.Super. 118, 732 A.2d 528 (N.J. A.D. 1999), *cert. den.*, 162 N.J. 199, 743 A.2d 851 (1999); *Register.com, Inc., v. Verio, Inc.* 126 F.Supp.2d 238 (SD NY 2000).

Illustration 1: The registration screen for NY Online prominently states: "Please read the License. It contains important terms about your use and our obligations. If you agree to the license, indicate this by clicking the 'I agree' button. If you do not agree, click 'I decline'." The on-screen buttons are clearly identified. The underlined text is a hypertext link that, if selected, promptly displays the license. A party that indicates "I agree" assents to the license and adopts its terms.

Illustration 2: The first screen of an online stock-quote service requires that the potential licensee enter its name, address and credit card number. After entering the information and striking the "enter" key, the licensee has access to the data and receives a monthly bill. Somewhere below the place to enter the information, but hidden in small print, is the statement: "Terms and conditions of service; disclaimers." The customer's attention is not called to this sentence, nor is the customer asked to react to it. Even though using the service creates a contract, there may be no assent to the terms of service and disclaimer, since there is no act indicating assent to those terms. If there is no assent 63 to those terms, the court would determine contract terms on other grounds, including the rules of this Act and usage of trade.

Illustration 3: The purchasing screen of an on-line software provider provides the terms of the license, a space to indicate the software purchased, and two on-screen buttons indicating "I agree" and "I decline" respectively. A user that completes the order and indicates "I agree" causes the system to move to a second screen. This second screen summarizes the order and asks the user to click, either confirming its order, or canceling it. This satisfies subsection (a)(2) on intentional conduct and reason to know. It also satisfies the error correction procedure in Section 213.

6. **Authority to Act.** The person manifesting assent must be one that can bind the party seeking the benefits or being charged with the obligations or restrictions of the agreement. In general, this Act treats this issue as a question of attribution: are the assent-producing acts attributable to this particular person? A person that desires to enforce terms against another must establish that it dealt with an individual or agent that had authority to bind the person or, at least, establish that the person to be bound accepted the benefits of the contract or otherwise ratified the acts. If the individual who assented did not have authority and the conduct was not ratified or otherwise adopted, there may be no assent as to the party "represented," but only as to the individual who acted. If this occurs, both the purported principal and the relying party may be at risk: the relying party (e.g., licensor) risks loss of its terms with respect to the party it intended to have bound, while the purported principal ("licensee" using information not obtained by a proper agent) risks that use of the computer information infringes a copyright or patent, since the principal does not have the benefit of the license. There must be an adequate connection between the individual who had the opportunity to review and the one whose acts constitute assent. Of course, a party with authority can delegate that authority to another and such delegation may be either express or implicit. Thus, a CEO may authorize her secretary to agree to a license when the CEO instructs the secretary to sign up for legal materials online or to install a newly acquired program that is subject to an on-screen license.

Questions of this sort arise under agency law as augmented in this Act, such as by the provision on electronic agents in Section 211 or rules in this Act on attribution. Other law governs questions of ordinary agency law, estoppel and the like.

7. **Modification of Rules.** Subsection (e) recognizes that parties, by prior agreement, may define what constitutes assent with respect to future conduct in ongoing relationships. Compare Section 113(e). The parties may call for more or less formality than set out in this Act. This is important for cases where multiple transfers in electronic commerce occur pursuant to prior agreement. Assent in such cases can just as well be found in the original agreement as in the subsequent conduct.

8. **Third Party Service Providers.** Assent requires conduct by the party to be bound or its agents. If the party is enabled to reach a system because of services provided by a third party communications or service provider, the service provider typically does not intend or enter into in a contractual relationship with the provider of the information. While the customer's acts may constitute assent by the customer, they do not bind the service provider since the service provider's actions are in the nature of transmissions and enabling access, not assent to a contractual relationship.

Subsection (f) makes clear that service providers—providers of online services, network access, or the operation of facilities thereof—do not manifest assent to a contractual relationship simply from their provision of such services, including but not limited to transmission, routing, providing connections, or linking or storage of material at the request or initiation of a person other than the service provider. If, for example, a telecommunications company provided the routing for a user to reach a particular online location, the fact that the user of the service might assent to a contract at that location does not mean that the service provider has done so. The 64 conduct of the customer does not bind the service provider.

Of course, in some on-line systems the service provider has direct contractual relationships with the content providers or may desire access to and use the information on its own behalf, and therefore may assent to terms in order to obtain access. In the absence of these circumstances, however, the mere fact that the third-party service provider enables the customer to reach the information site does not constitute assent to the terms at that site.

§ 113. Opportunity to Review

(a) [**Manner of availability generally.**] A person has an opportunity to review a record or term only if it is made available in a manner that ought to call it to the attention of a reasonable person and permit review.

(b) [**Manner of availability by electronic agent.**] An electronic agent has an opportunity to review a record or term only if it is made available in a manner that would enable a reasonably configured electronic agent to react to the record or term.

(c) [**When right of return required.**] If a record or term is available for review only after a person becomes obligated to pay or begins its performance, the person has an opportunity to review only if it has a right to a return if it rejects the record. However, a right to a return is not required if:

(1) the record proposes a modification of contract or provides particulars of performance under Section 305; or

(2) the primary performance is other than delivery or acceptance of a copy, the agreement is not a mass-market transaction, and the parties at the time of contracting had reason to know that a record or term would be presented after performance, use, or access to the information began.

(d) [**Right of return created.**] The right to a return under this section may arise by law or agreement.

(e) [**Agreement for future transactions.**] The effect of this section may be modified by an agreement setting out standards applicable to future transactions between the parties.

Comment

1. **Scope of this Section.** This section sets out the basic standards for when a party has been given an opportunity to review the terms of a record. Unless there is an opportunity to review the record, under Section 112 the party cannot manifest assent to it.

2. **Opportunity to Review.** A manifestation of assent to a record or term under this Act cannot occur unless there was an opportunity to review the record or term. Common law does not clearly establish this requirement, but the requirement of an opportunity to review terms reasonably made available reflects simple fairness and establishes concepts that curtail procedural aspects of unconscionability. Section 111. For a person, an opportunity to review requires that a record be made available in a manner that ought to call it to the attention of a reasonable person and permit review. See *Specht v. Netscape Communications Corp.*, 306 F.3d 17, 2002 WL 31166784 n. 13 (Fed. Cir. 2002). This requirement is met if the person knows of the record or has reason to know that the record or term exists in a form and location that in the circumstances permit review of it or a copy of it. For an electronic agent, an opportunity to review exists only if the record is one to which a reasonably configured electronic agent could respond. Terms made available for review during an over-the-counter transaction or otherwise in a manner required under federal law give an opportunity to review.

a. **Declining to Use the Opportunity to Review.** An opportunity to review does not require that the person use that opportunity. The condition is met even if the person does not read or actually review the record. This is not changed because the party desires to complete the transaction rapidly, is under pressure to do so, or because the party has other demands on its attention, unless the one party actively manipulates circumstances to induce the other party not to review the record. Such manipulation may vitiate the alleged opportunity to review.

b. **Permits Review.** How a record is made available for review may differ for electronic and paper records. In both, however, a record is not available for review if access to it is so time consuming or cumbersome, or if its presentation is so obscure or oblique, as to make it difficult to review. It must be presented in a way as to reasonably permit review. In an electronic system, a record promptly accessible through an electronic link ordinarily qualifies. Actions that comply with federal or other applicable consumer laws that require making contract terms or disclosure available, or that provide standards for doing so, satisfy this requirement.

c. **Right to Return.** If terms in a record are not available until after there is an initial commitment to the transaction, subsection (c) indicates that ordinarily there is no opportunity to review unless the party can return the product (or for a vendor that refuses the other party's terms, recover the product) and receive appropriate reimbursement of payments if it rejects the terms. The return right creates a situation where meaningful assent can occur. The right exists only for the first licensee. If the right to a return is created only by agreement or by an offer from the one party, rather than by law, the right must be communicated to the other person so that the person ought to become aware of it.

Computer information is frequently distributed without charge for the purpose of enabling the recipient to enter into transactions with the licensor. The "beginning of performance" under subsection (c) in such cases is typically not payment, but selection of a password or other attribution procedure or the initiation of a transaction. In such situations, with respect to a right of return, the licensor's obligation is satisfied if it provides instructions on request for destruction or return of the information and, when applicable under Section 209, reimburses the other party for costs, if any. Although the party refusing terms has a reasonable time within which to contact the licensor and destroy the information, it must do so before it uses the information to select a security procedure or initiate a transaction.

There is no distinction between software distributed at a nominal price and software that is competitively priced. Therefore, if a financial or other institution distributes software at a nominal price that enables a customer to manage its personal finances or to engage in transactions with the distributor of the software, it must offer the right of return in the same manner as a company that distributes such at a market price.

The return right provides incentive for a licensor to make the terms of the license available up-front if commercially practicable since this avoids the right of return in this section and in Sections 209 and 613. An additional incentive, under Sections 208 and 209, is that, when presentation of terms is deferred, the terms cannot become part of the contract unless the other party had reason to know that terms would be presented later. A decision to delay presentation of terms without an important commercial reason to do so may result in substantial costs and uncertainty.

Failure to provide a right to return when required does not invalidate the agreement, but creates a risk that the terms will not be assented to by the party to which they were presented. If there is no manifestation of assent to a record, the terms of the agreement are determined by considering all the circumstances, including the expectations of the parties, applicable usage of trade and course of dealing, and the property rights, if any, involved in the transaction. In such cases, courts should be careful to avoid unwarranted forfeiture or unjust enrichment. An agreement with payment and other agreed terms that reflect a right to use information for consumer purposes only cannot be transformed into an unlimited right of commercial use by a failure of assent.

3. **Modifications and Layered Contracting.** The right to a return provisions do not apply to proposals to modify an agreement or to cases where the agreement gives a party the right to specify particulars of performance. If the contract allows one party unilaterally to alter terms, no further agreement is required for the changed terms to be effective if the term is not unconscionable or otherwise made invalid. If that contractual right does not exist, however, and one party proposes in a record modifications of the contract (that can become effective only on the other person's agreement to them), there must be an opportunity to review the terms before a manifestation of assent pursuant to Section 112.

Similarly, the return right does not apply where parties begin performance in the expectation that a record containing contract terms will be presented and adopted later and the performance is more than merely tendering and accepting an existing copy of computer information. Subsection (c). This is common in software development and other complex contracts; this Act does not disturb that commercial practice.

4. **Modification of Rules.** Subsection (e) allows parties, by prior agreement, to define what constitutes assent with respect to future conduct in ongoing relationships. The parties may call for more or less formality than set out in this Act. This is important for cases where multiple transfers in electronic commerce occur pursuant to prior agreement. Assent in such cases can just as well be found in the original agreement as in the subsequent conduct.

§ 114. Pretransaction Disclosures in Internet-Type Transactions

(a) **[Scope of section.]** This section applies to a licensor that makes its computer information available to a licensee by electronic means from its Internet or similar electronic site.

(b) **[Sufficient opportunity to review.]** In such a case, the licensor affords an opportunity to review the terms of a standard form license which opportunity satisfies Section 113 with respect to a licensee that acquires the information from that site, if the licensor:

(1) makes the standard terms of the license readily available for review by the licensee before the information is delivered or the licensee becomes obligated to pay, whichever occurs first, by:

(A) displaying prominently and in close proximity to a description of the computer information, or to instructions or steps for acquiring it, the standard terms or a reference to an electronic location from which they can be readily obtained; or

(B) disclosing the availability of the standard terms in a prominent place on the site from which the computer information is offered and promptly furnishing a copy of the standard terms on request before the transfer of the computer information; and

(2) does not take affirmative acts to prevent printing or storage of the standard terms for archival or review purposes by the licensee.

(c) **[Other methods of giving opportunity to review.]** Failure to provide an opportunity to review under this section does not preclude a person from providing a person an opportunity to review by other means pursuant to Section 113 or law other than this [Act].

Comment

1. **Scope of Section.** This section deals with pre-transaction disclosures of contract terms in Internet transactions where the contract is formed on-line for an electronic delivery of information.

2. **Relation to Other Assent Rules.** This section provides guidance for Internet commerce and an incentive for use of particular types of disclosures of terms and acts as an incentive-creating, safe harbor rule. The section does not foreclose use of other procedures. Failure to comply with this section does not bear on whether a license is enforceable or whether the procedures used adequately establish an opportunity to review. Whether an opportunity to review has occurred is determined under the general standards in Section 113.

3. **Disclosure and Downloading.** The disclosure rules in this section are modeled the federal Magnuson-Moss Warranty Act. They combine actual disclosure with availability of terms. It is sufficient that standard terms be available on request. Terms might be made available by hyperlink on the particular site or through providing a potential licensee with an address (electronic or otherwise) from which the terms can be obtained. The terms to be made available are the standard terms of a license of the type involved. Supplying the terms can meet the requirements for providing an opportunity to review if the provisions of this section are met.

The terms or a reference to them must be in a prominent place in the site or in close proximity to the computer information or instructions for obtaining it. The intent of the close proximity standard is that the terms or the reference to them would be called to the attention of an ordinary reasonable person.

Given all other conditions being satisfied, this section is met if the licensor does not take affirmative steps to preclude printing or storage of the terms of the agreement. This does not require that the licensor adopt technologies that enable downloading or printing, although many technologies allow this. It does require that there be nothing affirmatively done to preclude use of one of those alternatives. For example, a licensor that uses a technology which would otherwise enable copying the contract terms and modifies it specifically to preclude copying does not qualify under the provisions of this section. However, one method of compliance is sufficient: if the terms include sensitive information that is more susceptible to unauthorized distribution if made available in electronic form, the licensor may preclude electronic copies. As long as it does not also preclude the ability to print a paper copy, this section is still satisfied. If the licensor links the person to another location under the control of a third party, knowing that affirmative steps will be taken at that location to prevent downloading or printing, there is no compliance with this section.

§ 209. Mass-Market License

(a) **[Limitation on terms.]** Adoption of the terms of a mass-market license under Section 208 is effective only if the party agrees to the license, such as by manifesting assent, before or during the party's initial performance or use of or access to the information. A term is not part of the license if:

(1) the term is unconscionable or is unenforceable under Section 105(a) or (b);

(2) subject to Section 301, the term conflicts with a term to which the parties to the license have expressly agreed;

(3) under Section 113, the licensee does not have an opportunity to review the term before agreeing to it; or

(4) the term is not available to the licensee after assent to the license in one or more of the following forms:

(A) an immediately available nonelectronic record that the licensee may keep;

(B) an immediately available electronic record that can be printed or stored by the licensee for archival and review purposes; or

(C) in a copy available at no additional cost on a seasonable request in a record by a licensee that was unable to print or store the license for archival and review purposes.

(b) **[Right of return and reimbursement.]** If a mass-market license or a copy of the license is not available in a manner permitting an opportunity to review by the licensee before the licensee becomes obligated to pay and the licensee does not agree, such as by manifesting assent, to the license after having an opportunity to review, the licensee is entitled to a return under Section 113 and, in addition, to:

(1) reimbursement of any reasonable expenses incurred in complying with the licensor's instructions for returning or destroying the computer information or, in the absence of instructions, expenses incurred for return postage or similar reasonable expense in returning the computer information; and

(2) compensation for any reasonable and foreseeable costs of restoring the licensee's information processing system to reverse changes in the system caused by the installation, if:

(A) the installation occurs because information must be installed to enable review of the license; and

(B) the installation alters the system or information in it but does not restore the system or information after removal of the installed information because the licensee rejected the license.

(c) **[Licensor's opportunity to review.]** In a mass-market transaction, if the licensor does not have an opportunity to review a record containing proposed terms from the licensee before the licensor delivers or becomes obligated to deliver the information, and if the licensor does not agree, such as by manifesting assent, to those terms after having that opportunity, the licensor is entitled to a return.

(d) **[Notice of refund.]** In a case governed by subsection (b), notice must be given in the license or otherwise that a refund may be obtained from the person to which the payment was made or other person designated in the notice if the licensee refuses the terms.

Comment

1. **Scope of Section.** Mass-market licenses are typically standard forms where the licensee either takes or leaves the license. Thus, significant protections are provided in this section. This section must be read in connection with Sections 208, 112 and 113. In addition, trade use, course of dealing, and course of performance are relevant, as are the supplementary terms of this Act on issues not resolved by express terms or practical construction. Sections 116(c), 302. Many mass-market licenses are available for review and agreed to at the outset of a transaction; but some licenses are presented later. This section deals with both and relies also on the rules in Section 208. Many mass-market transactions involve three parties and two contracts. That circumstance is addressed here and in Section 613.

2. **General Rules for Enforceability.** Several limiting concepts govern where assent to a record is relevant to establishing the terms of a mass-market license:

a. **Unconscionability and Fundamental Public Policy.** Even if a party agrees to a mass market license, paragraph (a)(1) makes clear a court may invalidate unconscionable terms or terms against fundamental public policy under rules that apply to all contracts under this Act.

Unconscionability doctrine invalidates terms that are bizarre or oppressive and hidden in boilerplate language. See Section 111. For example, a term in a mass-market license for $50 software providing that any default causes a default in all other licenses between the parties may be unconscionable, if there was no reason for the licensee to anticipate that breach of the small license would breach an unrelated larger license between the parties. Similarly, a clause in a mass-market license that grants a license-back of a licensee's trademarks or trade secrets without any discussion of the issue would ordinarily be unconscionable. This section rejects the additional test in *Restatement (Second) of Contracts* § 211(3).

b. **Conflict with Expressly Agreed Terms.** Paragraph (a)(2) provides that standard terms in a mass-market license cannot alter terms expressly agreed to between the parties to the license. A term is expressly agreed if the parties discuss and come to agreement regarding the issue and the term becomes part of the bargain. For example, if a librarian acquires software for children from a licensor under an express agreement that the software may be used in its library network, a term in the license that limits use to a single user computer system conflicts with and is overridden by the agreement for a network license. Similarly, in a consumer contract where the vendor promises a "90 day right to a refund" and the parties agree to that, the mass-market license cannot alter that term between those parties. Of course, there must be an agreement and this rule is subject to traditional parol evidence concepts. This rule is consistent with Section 613 where the terms of a publisher's license do not alter the agreement between the end user and the retailer unless expressly adopted by them.

c. **Assent and Agreement.** Under this Act, a party adopts the terms of a mass market license only if it agrees to the record, by manifesting assent or otherwise. A party cannot do so unless it had an opportunity to review the record ***before*** it agrees. Section 112. Paragraph (a)(3) makes clear that, under Section 113, the record must be available for review and called to the person's attention in a manner such that a reasonable person ought to have noticed it before assenting. See Section 113. The opportunity to review the terms must come before assent to them.

Adopting terms of a record under this section for a mass-market license is pursuant to Section 208, and is subject to the limits stated in that section. If the terms of the record are proposed after a party commences performance, they are effective only if the party had reason to know that terms would be proposed and agrees or manifests assent to the terms once proposed. For mass-market licenses, however, even if reason to know exists at the outset, under this section the terms must be made available no later than during the initial performance or use of the information and the person has a statutory right to a return if it refuses the license.

d. **Ability to Retain Terms.** Paragraph (a)(4) provides additional licensee protection not present in other law. The person presenting terms of a mass-market license must make it possible for the licensee to retain a copy of the agreed license, or to obtain a copy if the contract was presented in a context in which it originally could not have been retained (e.g., presentation at a kiosk with no printing or copying capability). The ability to retain the license terms enables the licensee to have information about its obligations on an ongoing basis. Paragraph (a)(4) provides for a right that typically is not mandated in other general contract law (such as UCC Article 2). It outlines three options in which this capability to retain the agreed record can be achieved:

- presentation in a form the licensee can keep such as on paper or diskette or in the licensed computer program;

- presentation in retainable or printable electronic form such as an electronic presentation on a web site which the licensee can print, download, copy or email to a storage device of the licensee, or in the computer program itself; or

- provision of a copy on timely request from a licensee who is unable to print or store its own copy because the presentation does not allow that to occur.

This paragraph is satisfied if a copy *can* be kept, printed or stored etc. after the licensee consents to the license, or obtained on request, whether the licensee *in fact* keeps or prints it at all or at that time, or uses a device that could do so. This is consistent with commentary to the federal Electronic Signatures in Global and National Commerce Act. See 146 Cong. Rec. S5281–06, at S5285, 106th Cong., 2d Sess. (June 16, 2000) (statement of Sen. Abraham).

3. **Relevance of a License.** The enforceability of a license is important to both the licensor and the licensee. License terms define the product by, for example, distinguishing between a right to use for a single user or with multiple users on a network, or between a right to consumer use or a right to commercial use. Often, the license benefits the licensee, giving it rights that would not be present in the absence of a license or rights that could not be exercised without permission of the owner of informational rights. See, e.g., *Green Book International Corp. v. Inunity Corp.*, 2 F.Supp.2d 112 (D. Mass. 1998). The license allows the licensee to avoid infringement.

The terms of mass-market contracts can be established in many ways. An oral agreement may suffice as would an agreement to terms in a record. Product descriptions may define the bargain without reference to any record containing contractual terms. Parties may leave terms open and agree that the terms may be specified later by a party.

4. **Terms Prior to Payment.** If a mass-market license is presented before the price is paid, this Act follows general law that enforces a standard form contract if the party assents to it. The fact that license terms are non-negotiable does not invalidate them under general contract law or this Act. A conclusion that a contract is a contract of adhesion may, however, require courts to take a closer look at *terms* to prevent unconscionability. See, e.g., *Klos v. Polske Linie Lotnicze*, 133 F.3d 164 (2d Cir. 1998); *Fireman's Fund Insurance v. M.V. DSR Atlantic*, 131 F.3d 1336 (9th Cir. 1998); *Chan v. Adventurer Cruises, Inc.*, 123 F.3d 1287 (9th Cir. 1997). This Act's concepts of manifest assent and opportunity to review also address concerns relevant to such a review.

5. **Terms after Initial Agreement.** Mass market licenses may be presented after initial general agreement from the licensee. In some distribution channels this allows a more efficient mode of contracting between end users and remote parties; this is especially important where the remote party controls copyright or similar rights in the information. Enforceability of the license is important to both parties. Under federal law, a mere sale of a copy of a copyrighted work does not give the copy owner a number of rights that it may desire. The limitations in subsection (b) impose significant costs that create incentives for licensors to present terms at the outset when practicable for the distribution channel employed.

Most courts under current law enforce contract terms that are presented and assented to after initial agreement. See, e.g., *Carnival Cruise Lines, Inc. v. Shute*, 111 S.Ct. 1522 (1991); *ProCD Inc. v. Zeidenberg*, 86 F.3d 1447 (7th Cir. 1996); *Hill vs. Gateway 2000 Inc.*, 105 F.3d 1147 (7th Cir. 1997); *Brower v. Gateway 2000, Inc.*, 676 N.Y.S.2d 569 (N.Y.A.D. 1998); *M.A. Mortenson Co., Inc. v. Timberline Software Corp.*, 998 P.2d 305 (Wash. 1999); *I.Lan Systems, Inc. v. Netscout Service Level Corp.*, 183 F.Supp.2d 328, 46 UCC Rep.Serv.2d 287 (U.S. Dis. Mass., 2002) ("*Step-Saver* once was the leading case on shrinkwrap agreements.

Today that distinction goes to ... *ProCD* ... 'Money now, terms later' is a practical way to form contracts, especially with purchasers of software").

Subsection (b) imposes some added limitations. It allows such terms to be enforceable only if there is agreement, or if there is a manifestation of assent after a chance to review terms and only pursuant to the rule that a party that rejects terms for information must be given a cost free right to say no. This does not mean that the licensee can reject the license and use or copy the information. The right to a return creates a situation equivalent to that which would have existed if the licensee had a chance to review the terms and rejected the license at the preliminary agreement. It does not apply if the licensee agrees to the license. However, a mass-market licensee who agrees to the license but receives a nonconforming product has a right to reject the copy and obtain a refund of the contract fee as a remedy for breach of the contract. See Section 704(b).

a. **Timing of Assent.** Agreement to the mass-market record must occur no later than during the initial use of the information. This limits the time during which layered contracting may occur in the mass market and reflects customary practices in software and other industries. Of course, any applicable federal law that establishes a right to rescind a contract and return a product is not altered by this Act. Section 105. Also, assent to the record does not alter the licensee's right to refuse a defective product that constitutes a breach of contract. Assent to contract terms is different from acceptance of a copy. "Acceptance" of the copy ordinarily requires a right to inspect it. See Section 608. For mass-market transactions, this Act follows U.C.C. Article 2 on this issue.

b. **Cost Free Return.** Under subsection (b), if terms are not available for review until after an initial agreement, the party being asked to assent must have a right to reject the terms return the information product. Possible liability for the expense of reinstating a customer's system after review, creates an incentive to make the license or a copy available for review before the initial obligation is created. This Act refers to a return right, rather than a right to a refund, because, under developing technologies, the right may apply to either the licensee or the licensor, whichever is asked to assent to the record. See Section 102(57) (defining the right of return).

The return right under this section includes, but expands on the return right described in Section 113. In this section, the return right is cost free in that it requires reimbursement for reasonable costs of making the return and, if installation of the information was required to review the license, the reasonable costs in returning the system to its initial condition. The fact that this section states an affirmative right in mass market licenses does not affect whether under an agreement or other law, a similar right exists in other contexts.

The expenses incurred in return relate only to the subject matter of the rejected license (the computer information) and do not include goods delivered in the same transaction. Rights regarding the goods are governed by Uniform Commercial Code Article 2 or 2A. The expenses must be reasonable and foreseeable. The costs of return do not include attorney fees or the cost of using an unreasonably expensive means of return or lost income or the like unless such expenses are required to comply with instructions of the licensor. The reimbursement right refers to ordinary expenses, such as the cost of postage.

Similarly, if expenses are incurred because the information must be installed to review the license, expenses of reversing changes caused by the installation that are chargeable to the licensor must be reasonable and foreseeable. The reference here is to actual, out-of-pocket expenses and not to compensation for lost time or lost opportunity or for consequential damages. The expenses must be foreseeable. A licensor may be reasonably charged with ordinary requirements of a licensee that are consistent with others in the same general position, but is not responsible for losses caused by the particular circumstances of the licensee of which it had no notice. A twenty-dollar mass market license should not expose the provider to significant loss unless the method of presenting the license can be said ordinarily to cause such loss. Similarly, it is ordinarily not reasonable to provide recovery of disproportionate expenses associated with eliminating minor and inconsequential changes in a system that do not affect its functionality. On the other hand, the provider is responsible for actual reasonable expenses that are foreseeable from the method used to obtain assent.

c. **Notice of the Right to Return.** Subsection (d) provides that notice must be given indicating the person from whom the refund and return can be obtained. The notice may be given in the license or otherwise at a time making it possible for the person refusing the license terms to obtain a return within any reasonable time stated for it or, if no time is stated, a reasonable time. See Section 102(57) (defining the right of return). The purpose is to allow the licensee to assert its rights within the period for a return if it chooses to refuse the license. The section does not require the notice to include address or telephone information because, in massmarket distribution, the identity of the eventual retailer or other person from which a copy was obtained cannot be known in advance. In such cases, the person can be described, for example, as "the store from which you obtained this copy." See also Section 613 (describing when a right of return is due from a dealer) and Section 102(57).

§ 406. Disclaimer or Modification of Warranty

(a) **[Express warranties and disclaimers.]** Words or conduct relevant to the creation of an express warranty and words or conduct tending to disclaim or modify an express warranty must be construed wherever reasonable as consistent with each other. Subject to Section 301 with regard to parol or extrinsic evidence, the disclaimer or modification is inoperative to the extent that such construction is unreasonable.

(b) **[Implied warranties: disclaimer or modification.]** Except as otherwise provided in subsections (c), (d), and (e), to disclaim or modify an implied warranty or any part of it, but not the warranty in Section 401, the following rules apply:

(1) **[Disclaimer of Section 403 and 404 warranties.]** Except as otherwise provided in this subsection:

(A) To disclaim or modify the implied warranty arising under Section 403, language must mention "merchantability" or "quality" or use words of similar import and, if in a record, must be conspicuous.

(B) To disclaim or modify the implied warranty arising under Section 404, language in a record must mention "accuracy" or use words of similar import.

(2) **[Disclaimer of Section 405 warranty.]** Language to disclaim or modify the implied warranty arising under Section 405 must be in a record and be conspicuous. It is sufficient to state "There is no warranty that this information, our efforts, or the system will fulfill any of your particular purposes or needs", or words of similar import.

(3) **[Disclaimer of all implied warranties.]** Language in a record is sufficient to disclaim all implied warranties if it individually disclaims each implied warranty or, except for the warranty in Section 401, if it is conspicuous and states "Except for express warranties stated in this contract, if any, this 'information' 'computer program' is provided with all faults, and the entire risk as to satisfactory quality, performance, accuracy, and effort is with the user", or words of similar import.

(4) **[Disclaimer or modification pursuant to other law.]** A disclaimer or modification sufficient under [Article 2 or 2A of the Uniform Commercial Code] to disclaim or modify an implied warranty of merchantability is sufficient to disclaim or modify the warranties under Sections 403 and 404. A disclaimer or modification sufficient under [Article 2 or 2A of the Uniform Commercial Code] to disclaim or modify an implied warranty of fitness for a particular purpose is sufficient to disclaim or modify the warranties under Section 405.

(c) **[Effect of "as is" or "with all faults".]** Unless the circumstances indicate otherwise, all implied warranties, but not the warranty under Section 401, are disclaimed by expressions like "as is" or "with all faults" or other language that in common understanding calls the licensee's attention to the disclaimer of warranties and makes plain that there are no implied warranties.

(d) **[Effect of precontract examination.]** If a licensee before entering into a contract has examined the information or the sample or model as fully as it desired or has refused to examine the information, there is no implied warranty with regard to defects that an examination ought in the circumstances to have revealed to the licensee.

(e) **[Effect of commercial context.]** An implied warranty may also be disclaimed or modified by course of performance, course of dealing, or usage of trade.

(f) **[Terms apply to all performances.]** If a contract requires ongoing performance or a series of performances by the licensor, language of disclaimer or modification which complies with this section is effective with respect to all performances under the contract.

(g) **[Limitation of remedies.]** Remedies for breach of warranty may be limited in accordance with this [Act] with respect to liquidation or limitation of damages and contractual modification of remedy.

PRINCIPLES OF THE LAW SOFTWARE CONTRACTS

American Law Institute

(Selected Section with Comments and Illustrations)

§ 2.02 Standard-Form Transfers of Generally Available Software; Enforcement of the Standard Form

(a) This Section applies to standard-form transfers of generally available software as defined in § 1.01(*l*).

(b) A transferee adopts a standard form as a contract when a reasonable transferor would believe the transferee intends to be bound to the form.

(c) A transferee will be deemed to have adopted a standard form as a contract if

(1) the standard form is reasonably accessible electronically prior to initiation of the transfer at issue;

(2) upon initiating the transfer, the transferee has reasonable notice of and access to the standard form before payment or, if there is no payment, before completion of the transfer;

(3) in the case of an electronic transfer of software, the transferee signifies agreement at the end of or adjacent to the electronic standard form, or in the case of a standard form printed on or attached to packaged software or separately wrapped from the software, the transferee does not exercise the opportunity to return the software unopened for a full refund within a reasonable time after the transfer; and

(4) the transferee can store and reproduce the standard form if presented electronically.

(d) Subject to § 1.10 (public policy), § 1.11 (unconscionability), and other invalidating defenses supplied by these Principles or outside law, a standard term is enforceable if reasonably comprehensible.

(e) If a transferee asserts that it did not adopt a standard form as a contract under subsection (b) or asserts a failure of the transferor to comply with subsection (c) or (d), the transferor has the burden of production and persuasion on the issue of compliance with the subsections.

Comment:

a. *Scope.* Section 2.02 applies to standard-form transfers of generally available software (defined in § 1.01(*l*)) only. These include electronic and prepackaged software transfers.

Section 2.02(b) adopts the general contract-law objective test of contract formation. See Comment *b*. Subsection (c) enumerates factors that ensure enforcement of a standard form under the objective test of formation. Subsection (d) requires clarity of standard terms, and subsection (e) deals with burdens of proof.

Section 2.02 applies whether the transferee is a consumer or a large-or small-business end user, so long as the software is available to the general public under substantially the same terms and the quantity of copies transferred is small, meaning consistent with a retail sale. See § 1.01(*l*), Comment *a*. Restricting the reach of this Section to consumers would create hardship for many small businesses, who essentially are in the same position as consumers downloading software over the Internet. Even large businesses (who less regularly shop for software in a retail market) may have difficulty overseeing their employees' processing of small-quantity software transactions, especially if there is no opportunity to peruse the terms prior to a transaction. Further, drawing lines between what constitutes a large or small business or between businesses in the same position as consumers and businesses with a better bargaining position would be difficult and largely arbitrary. In addition, enlarging the scope of the Section to include businesses should increase the incentive of drafters to write reasonable terms because businesses are more likely to read disclosed terms. Perhaps most important, because the elements of § 2.02 are largely in the nature of disclosure and not onerous for transferors, a "one size fits all" approach is sure to reach all of those worthy of disclosure protection without unduly burdening software transferors.

Transferees that acquire a large number of copies of software or gain the right to access software for a large number of users pursuant to a standard form do not come under § 2.02. Nor do transferees of custom software even if the quantity is small. Such transferees do not necessarily need the special considerations of this Section because they often consist of sophisticated businesses that should be expected to insist on access to and to read and understand the standard form, and even in some instances, to bargain successfully for better terms. Even if the transferee's business is small and less sophisticated, large-quantity and often expensive custom-software transactions should constitute a red flag that the standard form is important and should be read. Nonetheless, as developed more fully in Comment *b* to § 2.01, courts applying that Section should be especially vigilant about the formation process and the substantive terms on the theory that even in large-quantity, standard-form transactions or custom-software transactions transferees may have little or no bargaining power and the standard form may contain suspect terms.

Even if a party establishes the formation of a contract under § 2.02, enforcement is subject to public policy, unconscionability, and other invalidating defenses supplied by these Principles or outside law.

Illustrations:

1. B, a consumer, downloads and installs a single copy of a software transferor's word-processing software. The software is available to the general public for retail sale via the Internet. B clicks "I agree" on a computer screen presenting a standard-form licensing agreement prior to the download. Section 2.02 applies to the transaction. Same result if B acquires a copy of the software at a retail store and the software package contains a paper copy of the standard form.

2. B, a small general contractor with 18 employees, downloads three copies of software from a software developer's website to assist in assembling construction bids. An officer of B clicks "I agree" on a computer screen presenting a standard-form licensing agreement. Section 2.02 applies because the software is available to the general public and three copies of the software is consistent with a retail sale. See § 1.01(*l*), Comment *a.* If B had arranged to download 100 copies of the software or to download one copy after agreeing to a large or unlimited multiple-user license agreement, § 2.01 would apply, not § 2.02. The magnitude of the transfer would be inconsistent with a retail sale. In addition, in the case of a multiple-user agreement, the terms would be different from a typical retail sale.

b. *General rule.* Section 2.02(b) adopts the flexible contract-law approach to contract formation that bases formation on the objective test of whether a reasonable transferor would believe the transferee intends to be bound. Notwithstanding this approach, in many instances, failure to satisfy subsection (c), which consists of transferor best practices, may mean that the standard form will not be enforceable because a reasonable transferor would not believe the transferee intends to be bound to the form. In such cases, if the transfer has not been terminated, the terms of the contract consist of those terms in which the parties agree, the terms supplied by these Principles, and outside-law default rules. Cf. § 2.01(b)(2).

Subsection (b) also applies subject to other Sections of these Principles, such as § 1.11 (unconscionability), and outside law also may bar the formation of a contract or enforcement of some of its terms. Nor does subsection (b) preempt consumer-protection law. See § 1.12.

<u>Electronic transfers of software</u>

Section 2.02(b) is consistent with the general emerging approach to e-standard forms that allows for various kinds of acceptable electronic presentations of the standard form. For example, under current technology, if a transferee clicks on an "I agree" icon located at the end of a standard form, a reasonable transferor would believe the transferee intends to adopt the standard form as a contract. The same result may follow even if the terms are accessible via a hyperlink or a scroll-down window located near the "I agree" icon provided that the transferee must click "I agree" or the like. Other presentations may be more problematic. For example, mere reference to standard terms found on another page (browsewrap) may be insufficient under the reasonable-transferor test unless the transferee is already well-acquainted with the terms, for example, from previous notices and transactions.

For several reasons, § 2.02(b) does not establish a bright-line rule for enforcement requiring, for example, clicking "I agree" at the end of an electronic standard form. First, as already mentioned, case law already presents a wide variety of formation types that are not easily captured by a narrow rule and, for the most part, handle the issues in an effective manner. These include situations in which the transferee is aware of the terms because of a course of dealing or because the transferor delivered an update of previously downloaded software. The safeguard of requiring a click at the end of the form does not seem necessary in either case. Second, open-source transfers rarely follow the current click-wrap model, and these Principles should not upset an established custom unless problematic. Third, certain publishers of software, such as shareware, may have difficulty ensuring that Internet distributors of their software abide by bright-line formation requirements. Fourth, some transactions simply may be too cumbersome yet sufficiently insignificant to require scrolling through a standard form before agreeing to the form. Nevertheless, in the usual case, transferors should adopt the best practices of subsection (c) to ensure enforcement of the form, which include presenting the standard form in a manner that requires clicking "I agree" or the like at the end of or adjacent to the standard form. See Comment *c*.

Illustration:

3. B, a consumer, downloads a single copy of word-processing software manufactured by A, a software publisher. Before paying with a credit card, B clicks "I agree to the terms" on a computer screen that also states: "Please read the License because it includes important terms governing your use of the software." The quoted language constitutes a hyperlink that takes the transferee to the terms. If B was unaware of the terms because of the lack of previous dealings with A or otherwise, a court may find that a reasonable transferor would not believe B intended to be bound to the terms.

<u>**Packaged Software**</u>

In a typical transfer of packaged software, often called a "shrinkwrap transaction," the transferee acquires the packaged software either at a store or by placing an order on an Internet site or over the telephone and pays with a credit card. The first opportunity to read the terms, usually contained in the package or presented electronically upon downloading and installing the software, occurs after the transferee brings the software package home or the software is delivered. Shrinkwrap agreements obviously exacerbate the problem of standard forms by requiring payment before the transferee sees the terms.

Courts first considering the shrinkwrap process (many of the cases, both old and recent, involve hard goods such as computers) did not favor shrinkwrap terms because of their unavailability until after payment. Commentators criticized UCITA for taking a contrary position. Under UCITA § 112(a), shrinkwrap terms are enforceable if a person "manifests assent" after an "opportunity to review" the terms. Under § 113(a), "[a] person has an opportunity to review" a term if it is "made available in a manner that ought to call it to the attention of a reasonable person and permit review." Under § 113(c), in shrinkwrap situations, with some exceptions, a "person has an opportunity to review only if it has a right to a return if it rejects the record." Writers thought that copyholders who brought their software home might delay opening the package or returning the software, or might decide not to return it because of their needs, the cost of returning it, or their unhappiness with only a few terms. In any of these situations, a copyholder probably would be bound to the terms under UCITA's test. Despite these criticisms of shrinkwrap presentations, many courts and commentators note the value and popularity of the shrinkwrap method of doing business.

Subsection (b) allows for various methods of packaged-software contract formation, based on when a reasonable transferor would believe the transferee intends to be bound. For example, if a printed standard form is not separately wrapped from the software, a transferee may adopt the standard form as a contract by failing to exercise the opportunity to return the software opened or unopened for a full refund within a reasonable time after the transfer. If the transferee can read the standard form before opening the software because, for example, the standard form is printed on or attached to the package or the standard form and the software are separately wrapped within the package, a reasonable transferor may believe that the transferee intends to be bound upon opening the software wrapper.

Methods of notice and presentation of a printed standard form that fall between these examples require a case-by-case judicial analysis of what is reasonable under the circumstances. Notwithstanding the open-endedness of subsection (b), subsection (c) prescribes best practices that ensure enforcement of the standard form.

Illustration:

4. B, a consumer, acquires a copy of a word-processing program at a retail store. A is the manufacturer of the software. The software package contains a paper copy of the standard form attached to the package that is accessible without opening the software. A court may find that a reasonable transferor would believe that B intends to be bound to the standard form if B opens the software wrapper. A can ensure enforcement by following the requirements of subsection (c).

c. Best practices. Subsection (c) prescribes best practices and constitutes a safe-harbor provision for transferors. Compliance with subsection (c) should assure a transferor of the enforcement of the standard form, but failure to comply does not absolutely bar a transferor from otherwise proving transferee assent. Unsophisticated transferors who may not have knowledge of the requirements of subsection (c) or cannot prove whether or what type of standard form was posted at the time of contracting should not be precluded from establishing the transferee's intention to be bound based on subsection (b). See also Comment *b*. Further, when appropriate, an objective of the Principles is to present courts with perspectives on best practices, not to prescribe flat rules. Notwithstanding the nature of subsection (c), in many instances, failure to comply with the subsection should mean that the standard form will not be enforceable because it fails the reasonable-transferor test of subsection (b).

Subsection (c) presents several requirements. The standard form must be reasonably accessible electronically prior to any particular transaction (regardless of whether the standard form is electronic or printed); upon initiation of a transaction, the transferee must receive reasonable notice of and access to the standard form prior to payment or completion of the transaction; the transferee must signify agreement at the end of or adjacent to an e-standard form or, in the case of a standard form printed on or attached to a package or separately wrapped from the software, must fail to exercise the opportunity to return the packaged software unopened for a full refund within a reasonable time; the terms must be reasonably comprehensible; and electronic terms must be capable of storage and reproduction, such as by printing a hard copy.

Under subsection (c)(1), a standard form must be reasonably accessible electronically prior to initiation of the transaction at issue. Initiation of a transfer occurs when, viewed objectively, the transferee intends to contract and begins that process, such as by clicking on a "purchase" icon that precedes elicitation of payment information or by bringing packaged software to the check-out line in a retail store. Based on current technology, a transferor therefore can satisfy this aspect of subsection (c)(1) by maintaining an Internet presence and by posting its terms prior to the initiation of any particular transfer so that transferees can read and compare terms without entering a transaction at all. Accessibility issues under subsection (c)(1) also include the sufficiency of notice on the website of the standard form's availability, who must display the standard form, the manner of presentation, and when the standard form is available to read.

For example, notice on the transferor's homepage of the availability of the standard form should be sufficient if a visitor to the site could not help but see the notice. Based on current technology, the standard form should be reasonably accessible from the website of the party asserting enforcement of the standard form against the transferee. This will usually be the software manufacturer or access provider, but it also may be a retail vendor with a web presence. It is hard to imagine that a software manufacturer would not already have a presence on the Internet but, at any rate, creating and maintaining a homepage should not be costly. Nor should disclosure of terms on the website be expensive.

Based on current technology, reasonable accessibility with respect to the manner of presentation means, for example, that the standard form should not disappear after appearing on a computer screen and should be conspicuously displayed. In addition, standard terms should be on the homepage or only a few clicks away because transferees may become discouraged and lose interest if they must search too far to reach their Internet destination.

Reasonable accessibility with respect to time means that the standard form is on display for a reasonable time prior to initiation of a transaction. A "reasonable time" depends on the circumstances, but would ordinarily mean that the terms are available during the period a typical shopper would look for them prior to a transaction.

Subsection (c)(2)'s notice and access requirements are different from the requirements of (c)(1). Subsection (c)(1) requires a transferor to maintain a web presence and to post its terms prior to any particular transaction. A transferee could then see terms without entering any transaction at all. Subsection (c)(2), on the other hand, applies to a transaction in progress and requires a presentation so that the transferee cannot help but become aware of the terms.

In an electronic transfer of software, for example, subsection (c)(2)'s notice and access requirements require first that the notice is conspicuous both in terms of placement and size so that a transferee cannot help but see the notice. Further, the notice should constitute a hyperlink that leads directly to the standard form or, at minimum, the standard form should be only a few clicks away from the notice. The standard form itself also must be conspicuously displayed.

In the case of packaged software ordered by telephone, subsection (c)(2) would be satisfied by an announcement of the form's availability on the Internet. Although a transferee is unlikely to terminate the telephone call to access and read the standard form, a transferee should be made aware of that opportunity before payment. As mentioned in the Summary Overview to Topic 2, "[i]ncreasing the opportunity to read supports autonomy reasons for enforcing software standard forms. . . ." If the transferee is physically present in a store, the store can satisfy the requirements of subsection (c)(2) by posting or distributing the standard form or by making a computer available to view the terms online. Reasonable accessibility also requires the store to furnish adequate notice of the availability of the terms. Adequate notice requires that a reasonable shopper would understand that the terms are available on paper or by using a store computer prior to a transaction. Standard forms printed on or attached to the software package ordinarily are reasonably accessible as well. In the case of orders placed over the Internet for packaged software, the provider can present the terms electronically.

Under subsection (c)(3), to signify acceptance and to complete an electronic transfer of software, a transferee must click "I agree" or the like after terms are presented on a screen, just as a transferee must sign a paper standard form. Subsection (c)(3) would be satisfied, for example, if the "I agree" icon is adjacent to a scroll-down window that contains the standard form. This form of clickwrap closely resembles traditional modes of agreeing to paper standard forms. Under subsection (c)(3), a mere screen reference to terms that can be found somewhere else on the site would be insufficient as would a scroll-down window containing the standard form if the "I agree" icon is not at the end of or adjacent to the standard form.

In the case of packaged software, under current marketing processes, at least in theory, a transferee in a shrinkwrap transaction can return software for a full refund after opening the software package and reviewing the terms. However, in reality many, perhaps most, retailers refuse to accept returns of software if the package is opened, presumably at least in part because transferees can easily make a copy of the software before returning it. Further, monitoring and policing the transferee to deter copying is problematic. In addition, some retailers have begun charging a "restocking fee" for returns.

To satisfy subsection (c)(3), the standard form must be accessible without opening the software package. In fact, under § 2.02(c), a transferee has several opportunities to read the standard form before opening the software package. Therefore, a transferee can return packaged software and receive a refund for a reasonable time, but only if the package is unopened. Under this approach, the transferor does not have to monitor or police transferee copying before returning the software. Further, the subsection should create incentives for transferors to make their standard forms separately accessible. Section 2.02(b) governs the question of a transferee's adoption of a standard form if the transferee opens a software package in which the standard form is not separately accessible on or in the package.

* * *

Illustrations:

5. B, a consumer, downloads a single copy of word-processing software manufactured by A, a software transferor. The standard form is reasonably accessible on the homepage of A's website prior to B's selection of A's software. B clicks "I agree" at the bottom of a standard form presented on a computer screen before the download begins. Section 2.02(c)(1) through (3) are satisfied.

6. B, a consumer, downloads a single copy of word-processing software from A, a software transferor. The standard form is reasonably accessible on the homepage of A's website prior to B's selection of A's software. B clicks "I agree to the terms" on a computer screen that states: "Please read the License because it includes important terms governing your use of the software." The quoted language constitutes a hyperlink that takes the transferee to the terms. Section 2.02(c)(3) is not satisfied.

7. B, a merchant in business for herself, downloads from A, a software manufacturer, a single copy of a software "plug-in" that serves to enhance the user's browser capabilities. The standard-form licensing agreement is available on A's homepage prior to the transaction. However, the license appears in a scroll-down window for two minutes and then disappears. Further, the standard form occupies such a small part of the screen that the form is not readable without special attention. The standard form is not reasonably accessible for both reasons, and § 2.02(c)(1) is not satisfied.

8. B, a small mortgage lender with three employees, telephones A, a software manufacturer, and orders one copy of computer software to assist in the preparation and management of loan-closing documents. B pays by credit card. The software is available to the general public under the same terms. The packaged software delivered to B includes a paper copy of the standard-form licensing agreement that is accessible without opening the software. The terms are not reasonably accessible on A's website prior to the transfer. A has not satisfied § 2.02(c)(1) of these Principles.

d. *Comprehensibility*. Subsection (d) follows current law in striking incomprehensible terms. Incomprehensible terms are "unintelligible" or ambiguous, use "obscure terminology," conflict with each other, or lack certainty, even after the admission of extrinsic evidence. General contract law asks whether a reasonable person of average intelligence and education can understand the language with ordinary effort, and this test should be applied here.

Illustration:

9. B, a merchant with three employees, downloads a single copy of word-processing software from A, a software transferor. The standard form is reasonably accessible on the homepage of A's website prior to the transaction. B clicks "I agree" at the bottom of a standard form presented on a computer screen before the download begins. Nevertheless, the standard form, in garbled language, fails to clarify that A has conditioned B's access to the word-processing software on B accepting another program consisting of spyware that will monitor B's Internet activity and supply information to a third party. Under § 2.02(d), the spyware terms are not reasonably comprehensible and therefore not enforceable.

e. *Benefits of website disclosure*. These Principles adopt website disclosure as part of a package of best practices because it may be the best strategy for minimizing the problem of market failures in the retail-like, standard-form market for software. Transferors should follow the set of best practices to ensure enforcement of their standard forms and because disclosure is inexpensive. At the same time, at least in theory, transferors will be unable to ignore the increased number of readers of standard forms and shoppers for terms. Transferors will also be mindful of watchdog groups that can easily access the standard form and can spread the word about the use of unsavory terms. Transferors therefore may be moved to write fair terms to preserve their reputations and market shares. Further, website disclosure enables transferees to read and compare terms before the excitement of a particular transaction deflects their focus from the terms. Software transferors will be unable to segregate readers and offer them better terms because of the large number of readers. Businesses in noncompetitive industries also may want to write reasonable terms because of the volume of readers. In theory, prices should adequately reflect the quality of the terms.

Section 2.02(c) also supports economic-liberty reasons for enforcing contracts. The idea of individual assent is obviously more robust when transferees have a reasonable opportunity to read and compare terms. As Karl Llewellyn suggested, such transferees have given their blanket assent to reasonable standard terms, regardless of whether they decide to read and shop for terms.

As the primary strategy for dealing with market failures, website disclosure also avoids difficult questions, such as the need to distinguish transferees who should be relieved of their standard-form obligations from those who should remain bound. It is no surprise that transferees exhibit many different emotions and attitudes when they are e-shopping. The law cannot effectively distinguish those software shoppers who are capable of fending for themselves from those who, because of emotional or cognitive deficiencies, may fail to understand adverse terms.

f. *Costs of website disclosure.* Website disclosure should be relatively inexpensive. The costs of maintaining a web homepage and displaying a standard form should be insignificant, especially because virtually all software transferors have or soon will have a web page. Nor should enforcement costs be high.

* * *

h. *Will website disclosure succeed?* The website-disclosure provisions of subsection (c), if followed, will fail to motivate transferors to write reasonable standard terms if transferees still do not read and shop for terms or watchdog groups fail to spread the word or are otherwise ineffectual. Many commentators are not optimistic about disclosure as a remedy for market failures in standard-form contracting. They have observed the relative failure of truth-in-lending and other disclosure legislation. In addition, they have noted that, notwithstanding disclosure, people still have rational reasons for failing to read their forms, decisionmaking processes that deter careful reading, and a limited ability to process all of the information they do read. In the software-contract setting, transferees also exhibit impatience and exuberance that stand in the way of a measured response to disclosed terms. In fact, if a transferee is not contemplating an immediate transaction, she may find reading terms especially tedious and worthless. Further, the barrage of new information that disclosure will make available on the Internet may only increase the problem of information overload.

In addition, watchdog groups may be ill-equipped to police unsavory terms, either because they fail to identify particularly problematic terms or because they fail to spread the word adequately because of their lack of influence or the lack of exposure of their websites.

Perhaps the most ominous possibility is that website disclosure will fail to increase transferee reading of terms, but will create a safe haven for businesses to draft marginal ones. Most courts contemplating the enforcement of standard terms under doctrines such as unconscionability look for problems with the bargaining process and with the substantive unfairness of the terms. The more outrageous the bargaining process, the more likely a court will strike a substantive term, and vice versa. In light of the judicial acceptance of such a sliding scale, marginal terms that do not quite meet the test of substantive abuse may be enforceable because of their disclosure on the website. In fact, there may be some justice to this approach, especially if competitors of the transferor offered better terms so that the transferee had a choice. After all, if a term is not substantively unconscionable, is fully disclosed, and the transferee had options, on what grounds should it be stricken? Indeed, § 1.11 of these Principles adopts the traditional sliding-scale approach of unconscionability because of its soundness.

Nonetheless, increasing the enforcement of some marginal terms is a real concern. Still, affording transferees the opportunity to read and compare terms prior to a transaction as well as during or, in the case of shrinkwrap, sometimes even after a transaction is likely the most promising of many imperfect solutions. Other methods of dealing with market failures run into numerous problems of their own. See supra the Summary Overview to Topic 2 of this Chapter. Further, disclosure is inexpensive and unlikely to impede commerce even if it fails to resolve market imperfections. In addition, including businesses in the coverage of § 2.02 should increase the incentive of drafters to write reasonable terms because businesses are more likely to read disclosed terms. And even if, in the short run, software transferors rely on § 2.02(b) instead of (c) or benefit from disclosure more than transferees, eventually the word should get out about a transferor who fails to disclose terms on its website and who continues to employ unsavory terms. Such a transferor's incentives should change as it loses market share.

Illustration:

11. B, a consumer, downloads a single copy of virus-protection software from A, a software transferor. The governing standard form is reasonably accessible on the homepage of A's website prior to B's selection of A's software. B clicks "I agree," at the end of a computer screen presenting the standard form before the download begins. A standard term allows the software transferor to "collect nonpersonal information about B's web surfing and computer use." The term may be substantively suspect, but its disclosure prior to the transaction makes a determination of unconscionability problematic. Nevertheless, in the long run, A may replace the provision because of adverse publicity and the loss of market share.

SELECTED LEMON LAW STATUTES

Ohio Rev. Code §§ 1345.71—.78

Table of Sections

§ 1345.71. Definitions

As used in sections 1345.71 to 1345.78 of the Revised Code:

(A) "Consumer" means any of the following:

(1) The purchaser, other than for purposes of resale, of a motor vehicle;

(2) Any lessee of a motor vehicle in a contractual arrangement under which a charge is made for the use of the vehicle at a periodic rate for a term of thirty days or more, and title to the vehicle is in the name of a person other than the user;

(3) Any person to whom the motor vehicle is transferred during the duration of the express warranty that is applicable to the motor vehicle;

(4) Any other person who is entitled by the terms of the warranty to enforce the warranty.

(B) "Manufacturer" and "distributor" have the same meanings as in section 4517.01 of the Revised Code, and "manufacturer" includes a remanufacturer as defined in that section.

(C) "Express warranty" and "warranty" mean the written warranty of the manufacturer or distributor of a new motor vehicle concerning the condition and fitness for use of the vehicle, including any terms or conditions precedent to the enforcement of obligations under that warranty.

(D) "Motor vehicle" means any passenger car or noncommercial motor vehicle or those parts of any motor home that are not part of the permanently installed facilities for cold storage, cooking and consuming of food, and for sleeping but does not mean any mobile home or recreational vehicle, or any manufactured home as defined in section 3781.06 of the Revised Code.

(E) "Nonconformity" means any defect or condition that substantially impairs the use, value, or safety of a motor vehicle to the consumer and does not conform to the express warranty of the manufacturer or distributor.

(F) "Full purchase price" means both of the following:

(1) In the case of a sale, the contract price for the motor vehicle, including charges for transportation, undercoating, dealer-installed options and accessories, dealer services, dealer preparation, and delivery charges; all finance, credit insurance, warranty, and service contract charges incurred by the consumer; and all sales tax, license and registration fees, and other government charges.

(2) In the case of a lease, the capitalized cost reduction, security deposit, taxes, title fees, all monthly lease payments, the residual value of the vehicle, and all finance, credit insurance, warranty, and service contract charges incurred by the consumer.

(G) "Buyback" means a motor vehicle that has been replaced or repurchased by a manufacturer as the result of a court judgment, a determination of an informal dispute settlement mechanism, or a settlement agreed to by a consumer regardless of whether it is in the context of a court, an informal dispute settlement mechanism, or otherwise, in this or any other state, in which the consumer has asserted that the motor vehicle does not conform to the warranty, has presented documentation to establish that a nonconformity exists pursuant to section 1345.72 or 1345.73 of the Revised Code, and has requested replacement or repurchase of the vehicle.

(H) "Mobile home," "motor home," "noncommercial motor vehicle," "passenger car," and "recreational vehicle" have the same meanings as in section 4501.01 of the Revised Code.

§ 1345.72. Repair of new vehicle with warranty nonconformity; replacement of vehicle; return and refund of full purchase price; liability of dealer; effect on loan, retail installment sales contract, or lease

(A) If a new motor vehicle does not conform to any applicable express warranty and the consumer reports the nonconformity to the manufacturer, its agent, or its authorized dealer during the period of one year following the date of original delivery or during the first eighteen thousand miles of operation, whichever is earlier, the manufacturer, its agent, or its authorized dealer shall make any repairs as are necessary to conform the vehicle to such express warranty, notwithstanding the fact that the repairs are made after the expiration of the appropriate time period.

(B) If the manufacturer, its agent, or its authorized dealer is unable to conform the motor vehicle to any applicable express warranty by repairing or correcting any nonconformity after a reasonable number of repair attempts, the manufacturer, at the consumer's option and subject to division (D) of this section, either shall replace the motor vehicle with a new motor vehicle acceptable to the consumer or shall accept return of the vehicle from the consumer and refund each of the following:

(1) The full purchase price;

(2) All incidental damages, including, but not limited to, any fees charged by the lender or lessor for making or canceling the loan or lease, and any expenses incurred by the consumer as a result of the nonconformity, such as charges for towing, vehicle rental, meals, and lodging.

(C) Nothing in this section imposes any liability on a new motor vehicle dealer or creates a cause of action by a buyer against a new motor vehicle dealer.

(D) Sections 1345.71 to 1345.78 of the Revised Code do not affect the obligation of a consumer under a loan or retail installment sales contract or the interest of any secured party, except as follows:

(1) If the consumer elects to take a refund, the manufacturer shall forward the total sum required under division (B) of this section by an instrument jointly payable to the consumer and any lienholder that appears on the face of the certificate of title or the lessor. Prior to disbursing the funds to the consumer, the lienholder or lessor may deduct the balance owing to it, including any fees charged for canceling the loan or the lease and refunded pursuant to division (B) of this section, and shall immediately remit the balance if any, to the consumer and cancel the lien or the lease.

(2) If the consumer elects to take a new motor vehicle, the manufacturer shall notify any lienholder noted on the certificate of title under section 4505.13 of the Revised Code or the lessor. If both the lienholder or the lessor and the consumer consent to finance or lease the new motor vehicle obtained through the exchange in division (B) of this section, the lienholder or the lessor shall release the lien on or surrender the title to the nonconforming motor vehicle after it has obtained a lien on or title to the new motor vehicle. If the existing lienholder or lessor does not finance or lease the new motor vehicle, it has no obligation to discharge the note or cancel the lien on or surrender the title to the nonconforming motor vehicle until the original indebtedness or the lease terms are satisfied.

§ 1345.73. Presumption of reasonable number of attempts to conform vehicle to warranty

(A) Except as provided in division (B) of this section, it shall be presumed that a reasonable number of attempts have been undertaken by the manufacturer, its dealer, or its authorized agent to conform a motor vehicle to any applicable express warranty if, during the period of one year following the date of original delivery or during the first eighteen thousand miles of operation, whichever is earlier, any of the following apply:

(1) Substantially the same nonconformity has been subject to repair three or more times and either continues to exist or recurs;

(2) The vehicle is out of service by reason of repair for a cumulative total of thirty or more calendar days;

(3) There have been eight or more attempts to repair any nonconformity;

(4) There has been at least one attempt to repair a nonconformity that results in a condition that is likely to cause death or serious bodily injury if the vehicle is driven, and the nonconformity either continues to exist or recurs.

(B)(1) Any period of time described in division (A) of this section shall be extended by any period of time during which the vehicle could not be reasonably repaired due to war, invasion, civil unrest, strike, fire, flood, or natural disaster.

(2) If an extension of time is necessitated under division (B)(1) of this section due to the conditions described in that division, the manufacturer shall arrange for the use of a vehicle for the consumer whose vehicle is out of service at no cost to the consumer. If the manufacturer utilizes or contracts with a motor vehicle dealer or other third party to provide the vehicle, the manufacturer shall reimburse the motor vehicle dealer or other third party at a reasonable rate for the use of the vehicle.

§ 1345.74. Statement of buyer's rights; statement following service or repair of vehicle

(A) At the time of purchase, the manufacturer, either directly or through its agent or its authorized dealer, shall provide to the consumer a written statement on a separate piece of paper, in ten-point type, all capital letters, in substantially the following form: IMPORTANT: IF THIS VEHICLE IS DEFECTIVE, YOU MAY BE ENTITLED UNDER STATE LAW TO A REPLACEMENT OR TO COMPENSATION.

In the case of a leased motor vehicle, the written statement described in this division shall be provided to the consumer by the manufacturer, either directly or through the lessor, at the time of execution of the lease agreement.

(B) The manufacturer or authorized dealer shall provide to the consumer, each time the motor vehicle of the consumer is returned from being serviced or repaired, a fully itemized written statement indicating all work performed on the vehicle, including, but not limited to, parts and labor as described in the rules adopted pursuant to section 1345.77 of the Revised Code.

§ 1345.75. Action by aggrieved consumer; time limits; defenses

(A) Any consumer may bring a civil action in a court of common pleas or other court of competent jurisdiction against any manufacturer if the manufacturer fails to comply with section 1345.72 of the Revised Code and, in addition to the relief to which the consumer is entitled under that section, shall be entitled to recover reasonable attorney's fees and all court costs.

(B) The remedies in sections 1345.71 to 1345.78 of the Revised Code are in addition to remedies otherwise available to consumers under law.

(C) Any action brought under division (A) of this section shall be commenced within five years of the date of original delivery of the motor vehicle. Any period of limitation of actions under any federal or Ohio laws with respect to any consumer shall be tolled for the period that begins on the date that a complaint is filed with an informal dispute resolution mechanism established pursuant to section 1345.77 of the Revised Code and ends on the date of the decision by the informal dispute resolution mechanism.

(D) It is an affirmative defense to any claim under this section that a nonconformity is the result of abuse, neglect, or the unauthorized modification or alteration of a motor vehicle by anyone other than the manufacturer, its agent, or its authorized dealer.

§ 1345.76. Resale or lease of buyback vehicle; vehicles with dangerous defect not to be sold

(A) A buyback may not be resold or leased in this state unless each of the following applies:

(1) The manufacturer provides the same express warranty that was provided to the original consumer, except that the term of the warranty shall be the greater of either of the following:

(a) Twelve thousand miles or twelve months after the date of resale, whichever is earlier;

(b) The remaining term of any manufacturer's original warranty.

(2) The manufacturer provides to the consumer, either directly or through its agent or its authorized dealer, and prior to obtaining the signature of the consumer on any document, a written statement on a separate piece of paper, in ten-point type, all capital letters, in substantially the following form:

WARNING: THIS VEHICLE PREVIOUSLY WAS SOLD AS NEW. IT WAS RETURNED TO THE MANUFACTURER OR ITS AGENT IN EXCHANGE FOR A REPLACEMENT VEHICLE OR REFUND AS A RESULT OF THE FOLLOWING DEFECT(S) OR CONDITION(S):

1. ______________________________
2. ______________________________
3. ______________________________
4. ______________________________
5. ______________________________

____

DATE

____

BUYER'S SIGNATURE

The manufacturer shall list each defect or condition on a separate line of the written statement provided to the consumer.

(B) Notwithstanding the provisions of division (A) of this section, if a new motor vehicle has been returned under the provisions of section 1345.72 of the Revised Code or a similar law of another state because of a nonconformity likely to cause death or serious bodily injury if the vehicle is driven, the motor vehicle may not be sold, leased, or operated in this state.

(C) A manufacturer that takes possession of a buyback shall obtain the certificate of title for the buyback from the consumer, lienholder, or the lessor. The manufacturer and any subsequent transferee, within thirty days and prior to transferring title to the buyback, shall deliver the certificate of title to the clerk of the court of common pleas and shall make application for a certificate of title for the buyback. The clerk shall issue a buyback certificate of title for the vehicle on a form, prescribed by the registrar of motor vehicles, that bears or is stamped on its face with the words "BUYBACK: This vehicle was returned to the manufacturer because it may not have conformed to its warranty." in black boldface letters in an appropriate location as determined by the registrar. The buyback certificate of title shall be assigned upon transfer of the buyback, for use as evidence of ownership of the buyback and is transferable to any person. Every subsequent certificate of title, memorandum certificate of title, or duplicate copy of a certificate of title or memorandum certificate of title issued for the buyback also shall bear or be stamped on its face with the words "BUYBACK: This vehicle was returned to the manufacturer because it may not have conformed to its warranty." in black boldface letters in the appropriate location.

The clerk of the court of common pleas shall charge a fee of five dollars for each buyback certificate of title, duplicate copy of a buyback certificate of title, memorandum buyback certificate of title, and notation of any lien on a buyback certificate of title. The clerk shall retain two dollars and twenty-five cents of the fee charged for each buyback certificate of title, four dollars and seventy-five cents of the fee charged for each duplicate copy of a buyback certificate of title, all of the fees charged for each memorandum buyback certificate of title, and four dollars and twenty-five cents of the fee charged for each notation of a lien.

The remaining two dollars and seventy-five cents charged for the buyback certificate of title, the remaining twenty-five cents charged for the duplicate copy of a buyback certificate of title, and the remaining seventy-five cents charged for the notation of any lien on a buyback certificate of title shall be paid to the registrar in accordance with division (A) of section 4505.09 of the Revised Code, who shall deposit it as required by division (B) of that section.

(D) No manufacturer that applies for a certificate of title for a buyback shall fail to clearly and unequivocally inform the clerk of the court of common pleas to whom application for a buyback certificate of title for the motor vehicle is submitted that the motor vehicle for which application for a buyback certificate of title is being made is a buyback and that the manufacturer, its agent, or its authorized dealer is applying for a buyback certificate of title for the motor vehicle and not a certificate of title.

§ 1345.77. Informal dispute resolution mechanism

(A) The attorney general shall adopt rules for the establishment and qualification of an informal dispute resolution mechanism to provide for the resolution of warranty disputes between the consumer and the manufacturer, its agent, or its authorized dealer. The mechanism shall be under the supervision of the division of consumer protection of the office of the attorney general and shall meet or exceed the minimum requirements for an informal dispute resolution mechanism as provided by the "Magnuson-Moss Warranty Federal Trade Commission Improvement Act," 88 Stat. 2183, 15 U.S.C.A. 2301, and regulations adopted thereunder.

(B) If a qualified informal dispute resolution mechanism exists and the consumer receives timely notification, in writing, of the availability of the mechanism with a description of its operation and effect, the cause of action under section 1345.75 of the Revised Code may not be asserted by the consumer until after the consumer has initially resorted to the informal dispute resolution mechanism. If such a mechanism does not exist, if the consumer is dissatisfied with the decision produced by the mechanism, or if the manufacturer, its agent, or its authorized dealer fails to promptly fulfill the terms determined by the mechanism, the consumer may assert a cause of action under section 1345.75 of the Revised Code.

(C) Any violation of a rule adopted pursuant to division (A) of this section is an unfair and deceptive act or practice as defined by section 1345.02 of the Revised Code.

§ 1345.78. Unfair and deceptive acts or practices

(A) Failure to comply with section 1345.76 of the Revised Code, in connection with a consumer transaction as defined in division (A) of section 1345.01 of the Revised Code, is an unfair and deceptive act or practice in violation of division (A) of section 1345.02 of the Revised Code.

(B) The attorney general shall investigate any alleged violation of division (D) of section 1345.76 of the Revised Code and, in an appropriate case, may bring an appropriate action in a court of competent jurisdiction, charging a manufacturer with a violation of that division.

N.Y. Gen. Bus. L. § 198–a. Warranties

§ 198–a. Warranties

(a) As used in this section:

(1) "Consumer" means the purchaser, lessee or transferee, other than for purposes of resale, of a motor vehicle which is used primarily for personal, family or household purposes and any other person entitled by the terms of the manufacturer's warranty to enforce the obligations of such warranty;

(2) "Motor vehicle" means a motor vehicle excluding off-road vehicles, which was subject to a manufacturer's express warranty at the time of original delivery and either (i) was purchased, leased or transferred in this state within either the first eighteen thousand miles of operation or two years from the date of original delivery, whichever is earlier, or (ii) is registered in this state;

(3) "Manufacturer's express warranty" or "warranty" means the written warranty, so labeled, of the manufacturer of a new motor vehicle, including any terms or conditions precedent to the enforcement of obligations under that warranty.

(4) "Mileage deduction formula" means the mileage which is in excess of twelve thousand miles times the purchase price, or the lease price if applicable, of the vehicle divided by one hundred thousand miles.

(5) "Lessee" means any consumer who leases a motor vehicle pursuant to a written lease agreement which provides that the lessee is responsible for repairs to such motor vehicle.

(6) "Lease price" means the aggregate of:

(i) the lessor's actual purchase cost;

(ii) the freight cost, if applicable;

(iii) the cost for accessories, if applicable;

(iv) any fee paid to another to obtain the lease; and

(v) an amount equal to five percent of the lessor's actual purchase cost as prescribed in subparagraph (i) of this paragraph.

(7) "Service fees" means the portion of a lease payment attributable to:

(i) an amount for earned interest calculated on the rental payments previously paid to the lessor for the leased vehicle at an annual rate equal to two points above the prime rate in effect on the date of the execution of the lease; and

(ii) any insurance or other costs expended by the lessor for the benefit of the lessee.

(8) "Capitalized cost" means the aggregate deposit and rental payments previously paid to the lessor for the leased vehicle less service fees.

(b)(1) If a new motor vehicle which is sold and registered in this state does not conform to all express warranties during the first eighteen thousand miles of operation or during the period of two years following the date of original delivery of the motor vehicle to such consumer, whichever is the earlier date, the consumer shall during such period report the nonconformity, defect or condition to the manufacturer, its agent or its authorized dealer. If the notification is received by the manufacturer's agent or authorized dealer, the agent or dealer shall within seven days forward written notice thereof to the manufacturer by certified mail, return receipt requested, and shall include in such notice a statement indicating whether or not such repairs have been undertaken. The manufacturer, its agent or its authorized dealer shall correct said nonconformity, defect or condition at no charge to the consumer, notwithstanding the fact that such repairs are made after the expiration of such period of operation or such two year period.

(2) If a manufacturer's agent or authorized dealer refuses to undertake repairs within seven days of receipt of the notice by a consumer of a nonconformity, defect or condition pursuant to paragraph one of this subdivision, the consumer may immediately forward written notice of such refusal to the manufacturer by certified mail, return receipt requested. The manufacturer or its authorized agent shall have twenty days from receipt of such notice of refusal to commence such repairs. If within such twenty day period, the manufacturer or its authorized agent fails to commence such repairs, the manufacturer, at the option of the consumer, shall replace the motor vehicle with a comparable motor vehicle, or accept return of the vehicle from the consumer and refund to the consumer the full purchase price or, if applicable, the lease price and any trade-in allowance plus fees and charges. Such fees and charges shall include but not be limited to all license fees, registration fees and any similar governmental charges, less an allowance for the consumer's use of the vehicle in excess of the first twelve thousand miles of operation pursuant to the mileage deduction formula defined in paragraph four of subdivision (a) of this section, and a reasonable allowance for any damage not attributable to normal wear or improvements.

(c)(1) If, within the period specified in subdivision (b) of this section, the manufacturer or its agents or authorized dealers are unable to repair or correct any defect or condition which substantially impairs the value of the motor vehicle to the consumer after a reasonable number of attempts, the manufacturer, at the option of the consumer, shall replace the motor vehicle with a comparable motor vehicle, or accept return of the vehicle from the consumer and refund to the consumer the full purchase price or, if applicable, the lease price and any trade-in allowance plus fees and charges. Any return of a motor vehicle may, at the option of the consumer, be made to the dealer or other authorized agent of the manufacturer who sold such vehicle to the consumer or to the dealer or other authorized agent who attempted to repair or correct the defect or condition which necessitated the return and shall not be subject to any further shipping charges. Such fees and charges shall include but not be limited to all license fees, registration fees and any similar governmental charges, less an allowance for the consumer's use of the vehicle in excess of the first twelve thousand miles of operation pursuant to the mileage deduction formula defined in paragraph four of subdivision (a) of this section, and a reasonable allowance for any damage not attributable to normal wear or improvements.

(2) A manufacturer which accepts return of the motor vehicle because the motor vehicle does not conform to its warranty shall notify the commissioner of the department of motor vehicles that the motor vehicle was returned to the manufacturer for nonconformity to its warranty and shall disclose, in accordance with the provisions of section four hundred seventeen-a of the vehicle and traffic law prior to resale either at wholesale or retail, that it was previously returned to the manufacturer for nonconformity to its warranty. Refunds shall be made to the consumer and lienholder, if any, as their interests may appear on the records of ownership kept by the department of motor vehicles. Refunds shall be accompanied by the proper application for credit or refund of state and local sales taxes as published by the department of taxation and finance and by a notice that the sales tax paid on the purchase price, lease price or portion thereof being refunded is refundable by the commissioner of taxation and finance in accordance with the provisions of subdivision (f) of section eleven hundred thirty-nine of the tax law. If applicable, refunds shall be made to the lessor and lessee as their interests may appear on the records of ownership kept by the department of motor vehicles, as follows: the lessee shall receive the capitalized cost and the lessor shall receive the lease price less the aggregate deposit and rental payments previously paid to the lessor for the leased vehicle. The terms of the lease shall be deemed terminated contemporaneously with the date of the arbitrator's decision and award and no penalty for early termination shall be assessed as a result thereof. Refunds shall be accompanied by the proper application form for credit or refund of state and local sales tax as published by the department of taxation and finance and a notice that the sales tax paid on the lease price or portion thereof being refunded is refundable by the commissioner of taxation and finance in accordance with the provisions of subdivision (f) of section eleven hundred thirty-nine of the tax law.

(3) It shall be an affirmative defense to any claim under this section that:

(i) the nonconformity, defect or condition does not substantially impair such value; or

(ii) the nonconformity, defect or condition is the result of abuse, neglect or unauthorized modifications or alterations of the motor vehicle.

(d) It shall be presumed that a reasonable number of attempts have been undertaken to conform a motor vehicle to the applicable express warranties, if:

(1) the same nonconformity, defect or condition has been subject to repair four or more times by the manufacturer or its agents or authorized dealers within the first eighteen thousand miles of operation or during the period of two years following the date of original delivery of the motor vehicle to a consumer, whichever is the earlier date, but such nonconformity, defect or condition continues to exist; or

(2) the vehicle is out of service by reason of repair of one or more nonconformities, defects or conditions for a cumulative total of thirty or more calendar days during either period, whichever is the earlier date.

(e) The term of an express warranty, the two year warranty period and the thirty day out of service period shall be extended by any time during which repair services are not available to the consumer because of a war, invasion or strike, fire, flood or other natural disaster.

(f) Nothing in this section shall in any way limit the rights or remedies which are otherwise available to a consumer under any other law.

(g) If a manufacturer has established an informal dispute settlement mechanism, such mechanism shall comply in all respects with the provisions of this section and the provisions of subdivision (c) of this section concerning refunds or replacement shall not apply to any consumer who has not first resorted to such mechanism. In the event that an arbitrator in such an informal dispute mechanism awards a refund or replacement vehicle, he or she shall not reduce the award to an amount less than the full purchase price or the lease price, if applicable, or a vehicle of equal value, plus all fees and charges except to the extent such reductions are specifically permitted under subdivision (c) of this section.

(h) A manufacturer shall have up to thirty days from the date the consumer notifies the manufacturer of his or her acceptance of the arbitrator's decision to comply with the terms of that decision. Failure to comply with the thirty day limitation shall also entitle the consumer to recover a fee of twenty-five dollars for each business day of noncompliance up to five hundred dollars. Provided, however, that nothing contained in this subdivision shall impose any liability on a manufacturer where a delay beyond the thirty day period is attributable to a consumer who has requested a replacement vehicle built to order or with options that are not comparable to the vehicle being replaced or otherwise made compliance impossible within said period. In no event shall a consumer who has resorted to an informal dispute settlement mechanism be precluded from seeking the rights or remedies available by law.

(i) Any agreement entered into by a consumer for the purchase of a new motor vehicle which waives, limits or disclaims the rights set forth in this section shall be void as contrary to public policy. Said rights shall inure to a subsequent transferee of such motor vehicle.

Any provision of any agreement entered into by a consumer for the purchase of a new motor vehicle which includes as an additional cost for such motor vehicle an expense identified as being for the purpose of affording such consumer his or her rights under this section, shall be void as contrary to public policy.

(j) Any action brought pursuant to this section shall be commenced within four years of the date of original delivery of the motor vehicle to the consumer.

(k) Each consumer shall have the option of submitting any dispute arising under this section upon the payment of a prescribed filing fee to an alternate arbitration mechanism established pursuant to regulations promulgated hereunder by the New York state attorney general. Upon application of the consumer and payment of the filing fee, all manufacturers shall submit to such alternate arbitration.

Such alternate arbitration shall be conducted by a professional arbitrator or arbitration firm appointed by and under regulations established by the New York state attorney general. Such mechanism shall insure the personal objectivity of its arbitrators and the right of each party to present its case, to be in attendance during any presentation made by the other party and to rebut or refute such presentation. In all other respects, such alternate arbitration mechanism shall be governed by article seventy-five of the civil practice law and rules; provided, however, that notwithstanding paragraph (i) of subdivision (a) of section seventy-five hundred two of the civil practice law and rules, special proceedings brought before a court pursuant to such article seventy-five in relation to an arbitration hereunder shall be brought only in the county where the consumer resides or where the arbitration was held or is pending.

(*l*) A court may award reasonable attorney's fees to a prevailing plaintiff or to a consumer who prevails in any judicial action or proceeding arising out of an arbitration proceeding held pursuant to subdivision (k) of this section. In the event a prevailing plaintiff is required to retain the services of an attorney to enforce collection of an award granted pursuant to this section, the court may assess against the manufacturer reasonable attorney's fees for services rendered to enforce collection of said award.

(m)(1) Each manufacturer shall require that each informal dispute settlement mechanism used by it provide, at a minimum, the following:

(i) that the arbitrators participating in such mechanism are trained in arbitration and familiar with the provisions of this section, that the arbitrators and consumers who request arbitration are provided with a written copy of the provisions of this section, together with the notice set forth below entitled "NEW CAR LEMON LAW BILL OF RIGHTS", and that consumers, upon request, are given an opportunity to make an oral presentation to the arbitrator;

(ii) that the rights and procedures used in the mechanism comply with federal regulations promulgated by the federal trade commission relating to informal dispute settlement mechanisms; and

(iii) that the remedies set forth under subdivision (c) of this section are awarded if, after a reasonable number of attempts have been undertaken under subdivision (d) of this section to conform the vehicle to the express warranties, the defect or nonconformity still exists.

(2) The following notice shall be provided to consumers and arbitrators and shall be printed in conspicuous ten point bold face type:

NEW CAR LEMON LAW BILL OF RIGHTS

(1) IN ADDITION TO ANY WARRANTIES OFFERED BY THE MANUFACTURER, YOUR NEW CAR, IF PURCHASED AND REGISTERED IN NEW YORK STATE, IS

WARRANTED AGAINST ALL MATERIAL DEFECTS FOR EIGHTEEN THOUSAND MILES OR TWO YEARS, WHICHEVER COMES FIRST.

(2) YOU MUST REPORT ANY PROBLEMS TO THE MANUFACTURER, ITS AGENT, OR AUTHORIZED DEALER.

(3) UPON NOTIFICATION, THE PROBLEM MUST BE CORRECTED FREE OF CHARGE.

(4) IF THE SAME PROBLEM CANNOT BE REPAIRED AFTER FOUR OR MORE ATTEMPTS; OR IF YOUR CAR IS OUT OF SERVICE TO REPAIR A PROBLEM FOR A TOTAL OF THIRTY DAYS DURING THE WARRANTY PERIOD; OR IF THE MANUFACTURER OR ITS AGENT REFUSES TO REPAIR A SUBSTANTIAL DEFECT OR CONDITION WITHIN TWENTY DAYS OF RECEIPT OF NOTICE SENT BY YOU TO THE MANUFACTURER BY CERTIFIED MAIL, RETURN RECEIPT REQUESTED; THEN YOU MAY BE ENTITLED TO EITHER A COMPARABLE CAR OR A REFUND OF YOUR PURCHASE PRICE, PLUS LICENSE AND REGISTRATION FEES, MINUS A MILEAGE ALLOWANCE ONLY IF THE VEHICLE HAS BEEN DRIVEN MORE THAN 12,000 MILES. SPECIAL NOTIFICATION REQUIREMENTS MAY APPLY TO MOTOR HOMES.

(5) A MANUFACTURER MAY DENY LIABILITY IF THE PROBLEM IS CAUSED BY ABUSE, NEGLECT, OR UNAUTHORIZED MODIFICATIONS OF THE CAR.

(6) A MANUFACTURER MAY REFUSE TO EXCHANGE A COMPARABLE CAR OR REFUND YOUR PURCHASE PRICE IF THE PROBLEM DOES NOT SUBSTANTIALLY IMPAIR THE VALUE OF YOUR CAR.

(7) IF A MANUFACTURER HAS ESTABLISHED AN ARBITRATION PROCEDURE, THE MANUFACTURER MAY REFUSE TO EXCHANGE A COMPARABLE CAR OR REFUND YOUR PURCHASE PRICE UNTIL YOU FIRST RESORT TO THE PROCEDURE.

(8) IF THE MANUFACTURER DOES NOT HAVE AN ARBITRATION PROCEDURE, YOU MAY RESORT TO ANY REMEDY BY LAW AND MAY BE ENTITLED TO YOUR ATTORNEY'S FEES IF YOU PREVAIL.

(9) NO CONTRACT OR AGREEMENT CAN VOID ANY OF THESE RIGHTS.

(10) AS AN ALTERNATIVE TO THE ARBITRATION PROCEDURE MADE AVAILABLE THROUGH THE MANUFACTURER, YOU MAY INSTEAD CHOOSE TO SUBMIT YOUR CLAIM TO AN INDEPENDENT ARBITRATOR, APPROVED BY THE ATTORNEY GENERAL. YOU MAY HAVE TO PAY A FEE FOR SUCH AN ARBITRATION. CONTACT YOUR LOCAL CONSUMER OFFICE OR ATTORNEY GENERAL'S OFFICE TO FIND OUT HOW TO ARRANGE FOR INDEPENDENT ARBITRATION.

(3) All informal dispute settlement mechanisms shall maintain the following records:

(i) the number of purchase price and lease price refunds and vehicle replacements requested, the number of each awarded in arbitration, the amount of each award and the number of awards that were complied with in a timely manner;

(ii) the number of awards where additional repairs or a warranty extension was the most prominent remedy, the amount or value of each award, and the number of such awards that were complied with in a timely manner;

(iii) the number and total dollar amount of awards where some form of reimbursement for expenses or compensation for losses was the most prominent remedy, the amount or value of each award and the number of such awards that were complied with in a timely manner; and

(iv) the average number of days from the date of a consumer's initial request to arbitrate until the date of the final arbitrator's decision and the average number of days from the date of the final arbitrator's decision to the date on which performance was satisfactorily carried out.

(n) Special provisions applicable to motor homes:

(1) To the extent that the provisions of this subdivision are inconsistent with the other provisions of this section, the provisions of this subdivision shall apply.

(2) For purposes of this section, the manufacturer of a motor home is any person, partnership, corporation, factory branch, or other entity engaged in the business of manufacturing or assembling new motor homes for sale in this state.

(3) This section does not apply to the living facilities of motor homes, which are the portions thereof designed, used or maintained primarily as living quarters and shall include, but not be limited to the flooring, plumbing system and fixtures, roof air conditioner, furnace, generator, electrical systems other than automotive circuits, the side entrance door, exterior compartments, and windows other than the windshield and driver and front passenger windows.

(4) If, within the first eighteen thousand miles of operation or during the period of two years following the date of original delivery of the motor vehicle to such consumer, whichever is the earlier date, the manufacturer of a motor home or its agents or its authorized dealers or repair shops to which they refer a consumer are unable to repair or correct any covered defect or condition which substantially impairs the value of the motor home to the consumer after a reasonable number of attempts, the motor home manufacturer, at the option of the consumer, shall replace the motor home with a comparable motor home, or accept return of the motor home from the consumer and refund to the consumer the full purchase price or, if applicable, the lease price and any trade in allowance plus fees and charges as well as the other fees and charges set forth in paragraph one of subdivision (c) of this section.

(5) If an agent or authorized dealer of a motor home manufacturer or a repair shop to which they refer a consumer refuses to undertake repairs within seven days of receipt of notice by a consumer of a nonconformity, defect or condition within the first eighteen thousand miles of operation or during the period of two years following the date of original delivery of the motor home to such consumer, whichever is the earlier date, the consumer may immediately forward written notice of such refusal to the motor home manufacturer by certified mail, return receipt requested. The motor home manufacturer or its authorized agent or a repair shop to which they refer a consumer shall have twenty days from receipt of such notice of refusal to commence such repairs. If within such twenty day period, the motor home manufacturer or its authorized agent or repair shop to which they refer a consumer, fails to commence such repairs, the motor home manufacturer, at the option of the consumer, shall replace the motor home with a comparable motor home, or accept return of the motor home from the consumer and refund to the consumer the full purchase price or, if applicable, the lease price, and any trade-in allowance or other charges, fees, or allowances. Such fees and charges shall include but not be limited to all license fees, registration fees, and any similar governmental charges, less an allowance for the consumer's use of the vehicle in excess of the first twelve thousand miles of operation pursuant to the mileage deduction formula defined in paragraph four of subdivision (a) of this section, and a reasonable allowance for any damage not attributable to normal wear or improvements.

(6) If within the first eighteen thousand miles of operation or during the period of two years following the date of original delivery of the motor home to such consumer, whichever is the earlier date, the same covered nonconformity, defect or condition in a motor home has been subject to repair two times or a motor home has been out of service by reason of repair for twenty-one days, whichever occurs first, the consumer must have reported this to the motor home manufacturer or its authorized dealer by certified mail, return receipt requested, and may institute any proceeding or other action pursuant to this section if the motor home has been out of service by reason of three repair attempts or for at least thirty days. The special notification requirements of this paragraph shall only apply if the manufacturer or its authorized dealer provides a prior written copy of the requirements of this paragraph to the consumer and receipt of the notice is acknowledged by the consumer in writing. If the consumer who has received notice from the manufacturer fails to comply with the special notification requirements of this paragraph, additional repair attempts or days out of service by reason of repair shall not be taken into account in determining whether the consumer is entitled to a remedy provided in paragraph four of this subdivision. However, additional repair attempts or days out of service by reason of repair that occur after the consumer complies with such special notification requirements shall be taken into account in making that determination. It shall not count as a repair attempt if the repair facility is not authorized by the applicable motor home manufacturer to perform warranty work on the identified nonconformity. It shall count as only one repair attempt for a motor home if the same nonconformity is being addressed a second time due to the consumer's decision to continue traveling and to seek the repair of the same nonconformity at another repair facility rather than wait for the initial repair to be completed.

(7) Nothing in this section shall in any way limit any rights, remedies or causes of action that a consumer or motor home manufacturer may otherwise have against the manufacturer of the motor home's chassis, or its propulsion and other components.

(8)(A) Each manufacturer shall require that each informal dispute settlement mechanism used by it provide, at a minimum, the following:

(i) that the arbitrators participating in such mechanism are trained in arbitration and familiar with the provisions of this section, that the arbitrators and consumers who request arbitration are provided with a written copy of the provisions of this section, together with the notice set forth below entitled "NEW MOTOR HOME LEMON LAW BILL OF RIGHTS", and that consumers, upon request, are given an opportunity to make an oral presentation to the arbitrator;

(ii) that the rights and procedures used in the mechanism comply with federal regulations promulgated by the federal trade commission relating to informal dispute settlement mechanisms; and

(iii) that the remedies set forth under subdivision (c) of this section are awarded if, after a reasonable number of attempts have been undertaken under subdivision (d) of this section to conform the vehicle to the express warranties, the defect or nonconformity still exists.

(B) Notwithstanding the provisions of paragraph two of subdivision (m) of this section, the following provision shall apply for purposes of this subdivision:

The following notice shall be provided to consumers and arbitrators and shall be printed in conspicuous ten point bold face type:

NEW MOTOR HOME LEMON LAW BILL OF RIGHTS

(1) IN ADDITION TO ANY WARRANTIES OFFERED BY THE MANUFACTURER, YOUR NEW MOTOR HOME, IF PURCHASED AND REGISTERED IN NEW YORK STATE, IS WARRANTED AGAINST ALL MATERIAL DEFECTS FOR EIGHTEEN THOUSAND MILES OR TWO YEARS, WHICHEVER COMES FIRST. HOWEVER, THIS ADDITIONAL WARRANTY DOES NOT APPLY TO THE LIVING FACILITIES OF MOTOR HOMES, WHICH ARE THE PORTIONS THEREOF DESIGNED, USED OR MAINTAINED PRIMARILY AS LIVING QUARTERS AND SHALL INCLUDE, BUT NOT BE LIMITED TO THE FLOORING, PLUMBING SYSTEM AND FIXTURES, ROOF AIR CONDITIONER, FURNACE, GENERATOR, ELECTRICAL SYSTEMS OTHER THAN AUTOMOTIVE CIRCUITS, THE SIDE ENTRANCE DOOR, EXTERIOR

COMPARTMENTS, AND WINDOWS OTHER THAN THE WINDSHIELD AND DRIVER AND FRONT PASSENGER WINDOWS.

(2) YOU MUST REPORT ANY PROBLEMS TO THE MANUFACTURER, ITS AGENT, OR AUTHORIZED DEALER.

(3) UPON NOTIFICATION, THE PROBLEM MUST BE CORRECTED FREE OF CHARGE.

(4) IF, WITHIN THE FIRST EIGHTEEN THOUSAND MILES OF OPERATION OR DURING THE PERIOD OF TWO YEARS FOLLOWING THE DATE OF ORIGINAL DELIVERY OF THE MOTOR VEHICLE TO SUCH CONSUMER, WHICHEVER IS THE EARLIER DATE THE MANUFACTURER OF A MOTOR HOME OR ITS AGENTS OR ITS AUTHORIZED DEALERS OR REPAIR SHOPS TO WHICH THEY REFER A CONSUMER ARE UNABLE TO REPAIR OR CORRECT ANY COVERED DEFECT OR CONDITION WHICH SUBSTANTIALLY IMPAIRS THE VALUE OF THE MOTOR HOME TO THE CONSUMER AFTER A REASONABLE NUMBER OF ATTEMPTS, THE MOTOR HOME MANUFACTURER, AT THE OPTION OF THE CONSUMER, SHALL REPLACE THE MOTOR HOME WITH A COMPARABLE MOTOR HOME, OR ACCEPT RETURN OF THE MOTOR HOME FROM THE CONSUMER AND REFUND TO THE CONSUMER THE FULL PURCHASE PRICE OR, IF APPLICABLE, THE LEASE PRICE AND ANY TRADE-IN ALLOWANCE, PLUS FEES AND CHARGES, AS WELL AS THE OTHER FEES AND CHARGES, INCLUDING BUT NOT LIMITED TO ALL LICENSE FEES, REGISTRATION FEES, AND ANY SIMILAR GOVERNMENTAL CHARGES, LESS AN ALLOWANCE FOR THE CONSUMER'S USE OF THE VEHICLE IN EXCESS OF TWELVE THOUSAND MILES TIMES THE PURCHASE PRICE, OR THE LEASE PRICE IF APPLICABLE, OF THE VEHICLE DIVIDED BY ONE HUNDRED THOUSAND MILES, AND A REASONABLE ALLOWANCE FOR ANY DAMAGE NOT ATTRIBUTABLE TO NORMAL WEAR OR IMPROVEMENTS.

(5) SPECIAL NOTICE PROVISION: IF WITHIN EIGHTEEN THOUSAND MILES OR TWO YEARS, WHICHEVER COMES FIRST, THE SAME COVERED NONCONFORMITY, DEFECT OR CONDITION IN YOUR MOTOR HOME HAS BEEN SUBJECT TO REPAIR TWO TIMES OR YOUR MOTOR HOME HAS BEEN OUT OF SERVICE BY REASON OF REPAIR FOR TWENTY-ONE DAYS, WHICHEVER COMES FIRST, YOU MUST HAVE REPORTED THIS TO THE MOTOR HOME MANUFACTURER OR ITS AUTHORIZED DEALER BY CERTIFIED MAIL, RETURN RECEIPT REQUESTED, AND YOU MAY INSTITUTE ANY PROCEEDING OR OTHER ACTION PURSUANT TO THE LEMON LAW IF THE MOTOR HOME HAS BEEN OUT OF SERVICE BY REASON OF THREE REPAIR ATTEMPTS OR FOR AT LEAST THIRTY DAYS. THIS SPECIAL NOTICE REQUIREMENT SHALL ONLY APPLY IF THE MANUFACTURER OR ITS AUTHORIZED DEALER PROVIDES WRITTEN COPY OF THE REQUIREMENTS OF THIS PARAGRAPH TO YOU AND RECEIPT OF NOTICE IS ACKNOWLEDGED BY YOU IN WRITING. IF YOU FAIL TO COMPLY WITH THE SPECIAL NOTIFICATION REQUIREMENTS OF THIS PARAGRAPH, ADDITIONAL REPAIR ATTEMPTS OR DAYS OUT OF SERVICE BY REASON OF REPAIR SHALL NOT BE TAKEN INTO ACCOUNT IN DETERMINING WHETHER YOU ARE ENTITLED TO A REMEDY PROVIDED IN PARAGRAPH FOUR. HOWEVER, ADDITIONAL REPAIR ATTEMPTS OR DAYS OUT OF SERVICE BY REASON OF REPAIR THAT OCCUR AFTER YOU COMPLY WITH SUCH SPECIAL NOTIFICATION REQUIREMENTS SHALL BE TAKEN INTO ACCOUNT IN MAKING THAT DETERMINATION. NOTICE TO THE MANUFACTURER SHOULD BE SENT TO THE FOLLOWING: NOTICE TO THE DEALER SHOULD BE SENT TO THE FOLLOWING:

(6) A MANUFACTURER MAY DENY LIABILITY IF THE PROBLEM IS CAUSED BY ABUSE, NEGLECT, OR UNAUTHORIZED MODIFICATIONS OF THE MOTOR HOME.

(7) A MANUFACTURER MAY REFUSE TO EXCHANGE A COMPARABLE MOTOR HOME OR REFUND YOUR PURCHASE PRICE IF THE PROBLEM IS NOT COVERED BY THE LEMON LAW OR DOES NOT SUBSTANTIALLY IMPAIR THE VALUE OF YOUR MOTOR HOME.

(8) IF A MANUFACTURER HAS ESTABLISHED AN ARBITRATION PROCEDURE, THE MANUFACTURER MAY REFUSE TO EXCHANGE A COMPARABLE MOTOR HOME OR REFUND YOUR PURCHASE PRICE UNTIL YOU FIRST RESORT TO THE PROCEDURE.

(9) IF THE MANUFACTURER DOES NOT HAVE AN ARBITRATION PROCEDURE, YOU MAY RESORT TO ANY REMEDY BY LAW AND MAY BE ENTITLED TO YOUR ATTORNEY'S FEES IF YOU PREVAIL.

(10) NO CONTRACT OR AGREEMENT CAN VOID ANY OF THESE RIGHTS.

(11) AS AN ALTERNATIVE TO THE ARBITRATION PROCEDURE MADE AVAILABLE THROUGH THE MANUFACTURER, YOU MAY INSTEAD CHOOSE TO SUBMIT YOUR CLAIM TO AN INDEPENDENT ARBITRATOR, APPROVED BY THE ATTORNEY GENERAL. YOU MAY HAVE TO PAY A FEE FOR SUCH ARBITRATION. CONTACT YOUR LOCAL CONSUMER OFFICE OR ATTORNEY GENERAL'S OFFICE TO FIND OUT HOW TO ARRANGE FOR INDEPENDENT ARBITRATION.

(o) At the time of purchase or lease of a motor vehicle from an authorized dealer in this state, the manufacturer shall provide to the dealer or leaseholder, and the dealer or leaseholder shall provide to the consumer a notice, printed in not less than eight point bold face type, entitled "New Car Lemon Law Bill of Rights". The text of such notice shall be identical with the notice required by paragraph two of subdivision (m) of this section.

UNIFORM CONDOMINIUM ACT

(Selected Sections)

§ 4–114. [Implied Warranties of Quality]

(a) A declarant and any dealer warrants that a unit will be in at least as good condition at the earlier of the time of the conveyance or delivery of possession as it was at the time of contracting, reasonable wear and tear excepted.

(b) A declarant and any dealer impliedly warrants that a unit and the common elements in the condominium are suitable for the ordinary uses of real estate of its type and that any improvements made or contracted for by the declarant or dealer or made by any person before the creation of the condominium, will be:

(1) free from defective materials; and

(2) constructed in accordance with applicable law, according to sound engineering and construction standards, and in a workmanlike manner.

(c) A declarant and any dealer warrants to a purchaser of a unit that may be used for residential use that an existing use, continuation of which is contemplated by the parties, does not violate applicable law at the earlier of the time of conveyance or delivery of possession.

(d) Warranties imposed by this section may be excluded or modified as specified in Section 4–115.

(e) For purposes of this section, improvements made or contracted for by an affiliate of a declarant are made or contracted for by the declarant.

(f) Any conveyance of a unit transfers to the purchaser all of the declarant's implied warranties of quality.

§ 4–115 [Exclusion or Modification of Implied Warranties of Quality]

(a) Except as limited by subsection (b) with respect to a purchaser of a unit that may be used for residential use, implied warranties of quality:

(1) may be excluded or modified by agreement of the parties; and

(2) are excluded by expression of disclaimer, such as "as is," "with all faults," or other language which in common understanding calls the buyer's attention to the exclusion of warranties.

(b) With respect to a purchaser of a unit that may be occupied for residential use, no general disclaimer of implied warranties of quality is effective, but a declarant and any dealer may disclaim liability in an instrument signed by the purchaser for a specified defect or specified failure to comply with applicable law, if the defect or failure entered into and became a part of the basis of the bargain.

PREDATORY LENDING AND USURY STATUTES—SELECTED

New York Criminal Usury Statute

New York Penal Law § 190.40 Criminal usury in the second degree

A person is guilty of criminal usury in the second degree when, not being authorized or permitted by law to do so, he knowingly charges, takes or receives any money or other property as interest on the loan or forbearance of any money or other property, at a rate exceeding twenty-five per centum per annum or the equivalent rate for a longer or shorter period.

Criminal usury in the second degree is a class E felony.

Kentucky Deferred Deposit Service Business and Check Cashing Statute

Ky. Rev. Stat. § 286.9

§ 286.9–020 Requirement of license

Except as provided in KRS 286.9–030, no person shall engage in the business of cashing checks or accepting deferred deposit transactions for a fee or other consideration without having first obtained a license. A separate license shall be required for each location from which the business of cashing checks or accepting deferred deposit transactions is conducted. Any person engaged in that business on the effective date of this section may continue to engage in the business without a license until the commissioner shall have acted upon his or her application for a license if the application is filed within sixty (60) days after April 14, 1998.

§ 286.9–030 Exemptions from applicability of this subtitle

The provisions of this subtitle shall not apply to:

(1) Any bank, trust company, savings and loan association, savings bank, credit union, consumer loan company, or industrial loan corporation which is chartered, licensed, or organized under the laws of this Commonwealth or under federal law and authorized to do business in this Commonwealth;

(2) Any person who cashes checks without receiving, directly or indirectly, any consideration or fee therefor;

(3) Any person principally engaged in the retail sale of goods or services who, either as an incident to or independently of a retail sale, may from time to time cash checks for a fee or other consideration;

(4) The United States and any department, agency, or instrumentality thereof; and

(5) A state or any agency, department, or political subdivision of a state.

§ 286.9–100 Procedures to be followed by licensees

(1) Any fee charged by a licensee for cashing a check or entering into a deferred deposit transaction shall be disclosed in writing to the bearer of the check prior to cashing the check or entering into a deferred deposit transaction, and the fee shall be deemed a service fee and not interest. A licensee shall not charge a service fee in excess of fifteen dollars ($15) per one hundred dollars ($100) on the face amount of the deferred deposit check. A licensee shall prorate any fee, based upon the maximum fee of fifteen dollars ($15) per one hundred dollars ($100). This service fee shall be for a period of at least fourteen (14) days.

(2) Before a licensee shall deposit with any bank or other depository institution a check cashed by the licensee, the check shall be endorsed with the actual name under which the licensee is doing business.

(3) No licensee shall cash a check payable to a payee other than a natural person unless the licensee has previously obtained appropriate documentation from the board of directors or similar governing body of the payee clearly indicating the authority of the natural person or persons cashing the check, draft, or money order on behalf of the payee.

(4) No licensee shall indicate through advertising, signs, billhead, or otherwise that checks may be cashed without identification of the bearer of the check; and any person seeking to cash a check shall be required to submit reasonable identification as prescribed by the commissioner. The provisions of this subsection shall not prohibit a licensee from cashing a check simultaneously with the verification and establishment of the identity of the presenter by means other than the presentation of identification.

(5) Within two (2) business days after being advised by a financial institution that a payment instrument has been altered, forged, stolen, obtained through fraudulent or illegal means, negotiated without proper legal authority, or otherwise represents the proceeds of illegal activity, the licensee shall notify the commissioner and the prosecutor or law enforcement authority in the county in which the check was received. If a payment instrument is returned to the licensee by a financial institution for any of these reasons, the licensee shall not release the payment instrument without the written consent of the prosecutor or law enforcement authority, or a court order.

(6) No licensee shall alter or delete the date on any payment instrument accepted by the licensee.

(7) No licensee shall engage in unfair or deceptive acts, practices, or advertising in the conduct of the licensed business.

(8) No licensee shall require a customer to provide security for the transaction or require the customer to provide a guaranty from another person.

(9) A licensee shall not have more than two (2) deferred deposit transactions from any one (1) customer at any one time. The total proceeds received by the customer from all of the deferred deposit transactions shall not exceed five hundred dollars ($500).

(10)(a) Prior to the establishment of the common database of deferred deposit transactions established by KRS 286.9–140, each licensee shall inquire of any customer seeking to present a deferred deposit transaction, whether the customer has any outstanding deferred deposit transactions from any licensee.

(b) If the customer represents in writing that the customer has no more than one (1) deferred deposit transaction outstanding to any licensee and that the total proceeds received by the customer from the outstanding deferred deposit transaction issued by the customer does not equal or exceed five hundred dollars ($500), a licensee may accept a deferred deposit transaction in an amount that, when combined with the customer's other outstanding deferred deposit transaction, does not exceed five hundred dollars ($500) of total proceeds received by the customer.

(c) If the customer represents in writing that the customer has more than one (1) deferred deposit transaction outstanding to licensees or if the total proceeds received by the customer from the deferred deposit transactions equal or exceed five hundred dollars ($500), a licensee shall not enter into another deferred deposit transaction with that customer until the customer represents to the licensee in writing that the customer qualifies to enter into a new deferred deposit transaction under the requirements set forth in this subtitle.

(d) If the database described in KRS 286.9–140 is unavailable due to technical difficulties with the database, as determined by the commissioner, the licensee shall utilize the process established in this subsection to verify deferred deposit transactions.

(11) A licensee shall not use any device or agreement, including agreements with an affiliate of a licensee, with the intent to obtain greater charges than are authorized in this subtitle.

(12) No licensee shall agree to hold a deferred deposit transaction for more than sixty (60) days.

(13) Each deferred deposit transaction shall be made according to a written agreement that shall be dated and signed by the customer and the licensee or an authorized agent of the licensee at the licensed location, and made available to the commissioner upon request. The customer shall receive a copy of this agreement.

(14) A licensee or its affiliate shall not for a fee renew, roll over, or otherwise consolidate a deferred deposit transaction for a customer.

(15) No individual who enters into a deferred deposit transaction with a licensee shall be convicted under the provisions of KRS 514.040.

(16) No licensee who enters into a deferred deposit transaction with an individual shall prosecute or threaten to prosecute an individual under the provisions of KRS 514.040.

(17) Each licensee shall conspicuously display in each of its deferred deposit business locations a sign supplied by the commissioner that gives the following notice: "No person who enters into a post-dated or deferred deposit transaction with this business establishment will be prosecuted for or convicted of writing cold checks or of theft by deception under the provisions of KRS 514.040."

(18) A licensee may not enter into a deferred deposit transaction with a customer who has two (2) open deferred deposit transactions.

(19) A licensee shall verify a customer's eligibility to enter into a deferred presentment service transaction by doing one (1) of the following, as applicable:

(a) If the commissioner has not implemented a database under KRS 286.9–140 or the database described in KRS 286.9–140 is not fully operational, as determined by the commissioner, the licensee shall verify that the customer meets the eligibility requirements for a deferred presentment service transaction under this subtitle. The licensee shall maintain a database of all of the licensee's transactions at all of its locations and search that database to meet its obligation under this subtitle.

(b) If the commissioner has implemented a database under KRS 286.9–140 and the database described in that section is fully operational, as determined by the commissioner, the licensee shall promptly and accurately access the database through an Internet real-time connection, and verify that the customer meets the eligibility requirements for a deferred presentment service transaction under this subtitle.

§ 286.9–991 Civil penalty for violation of subtitle

(1) The commissioner may levy a civil penalty against a person who violates any provision of, or administrative regulation promulgated under, this subtitle or any order issued by the commissioner under this subtitle.

(2) The civil penalty shall be not less than one thousand dollars ($1,000) or more than five thousand dollars ($5,000) per violation for each day the violation is outstanding, plus the state's costs and expenses for the examination, investigation, and prosecution of this matter, including reasonable attorney's fees and court costs.

(3) Any civil penalties imposed may be in addition to any other remedy or penalty imposed in this subtitle.

North Carolina General Statutes

§ 24-1.1E. Restrictions and limitations on high-cost home loans

(a) Definitions.—The following definitions apply for the purposes of this section:

(1) "Affiliate" means any company that controls, is controlled by, or is under common control with another company, as set forth in the Bank Holding Company Act of 1956 (12 U.S.C. § 1841 et seq.), as amended from time to time.

(2) "Annual percentage rate" means the annual percentage rate for the loan calculated according to the provisions of the federal Truth-in-Lending Act (15 U.S.C. § 1601, et seq.), and the regulations promulgated thereunder by the Federal Reserve Board (as said Act and regulations are amended from time to time).

(3) "Bona fide loan discount points" means loan discount points knowingly paid by the borrower for the purpose of reducing, and which in fact result in a bona fide reduction of, the interest rate or time-price differential applicable to the loan, provided the amount of the interest rate reduction purchased by the discount points is reasonably consistent with established industry norms and practices for secondary mortgage market transactions.

(4) A "high-cost home loan" means a loan other than a reverse mortgage transaction in which:

a. The principal amount of the loan (or, in the case of an open-end credit plan, the borrower's initial maximum credit limit) does not exceed the lesser of (i) the conforming loan size limit for a single-family dwelling as established from time to time by Fannie Mae, or (ii) three hundred thousand dollars ($300,000);

b. The borrower is a natural person;

c. The debt is incurred by the borrower primarily for personal, family, or household purposes;

d. The loan is secured by either (i) a security interest in a manufactured home (as defined in G.S. 143-147(7)) which is or will be occupied by the borrower as the borrower's principal dwelling, or (ii) a mortgage or deed of trust on real estate upon which there is located or there is to be located a structure or structures designed principally for occupancy of from one to four families which is or will be occupied by the borrower as the borrower's principal dwelling; and

e. The terms of the loan exceed one or more of the thresholds as defined in subdivision (6) of this section.

(4a) "Mortgage broker" is as defined in G.S. 53-243.01.

(5) "Points and fees" is defined as provided in this subdivision.

a. The term includes all of the following:

1. All items paid by a borrower at or before closing and that are required to be disclosed under sections 226.4(a) and 226.4(b) of Title 12 of the Code of Federal Regulations, as amended from time to time, except interest or the time-price differential. However, the meaning of the term "points and fees" shall not include any up-front fees collected and paid to the Federal Housing Administration, the Veterans' Administration, or the U.S. Department of Agriculture to insure or guarantee a home loan.

2. All charges paid by a borrower at or before closing and that are for items listed under section 226.4(c)(7) of Title 12 of the Code of Federal Regulations, as amended from time to time, but only if the lender receives direct or indirect compensation in connection with the charge or the charge is paid to an affiliate of the lender; otherwise, the charges are not included within the meaning of the phrase "points and fees".

3. To the extent not otherwise included in sub-subdivision a.1. or a.2. of this subdivision, all compensation paid from any source to a mortgage broker, including compensation paid to a mortgage broker in a table-funded transaction. A bona fide sale of a loan in the secondary mortgage market shall not be considered a table-funded transaction, and a table-funded transaction shall not be considered a secondary market transaction.

4. The maximum prepayment fees and penalties which may be charged or collected under the terms of the loan documents.

b. Notwithstanding the remaining provisions of this subdivision, the term does not include (i) taxes, filing fees, recording and other charges and fees paid or to be paid to public officials for determining the existence of or for perfecting, releasing, or satisfying a security interest; and (ii) fees paid to a person other than a lender or an affiliate of the lender or to the mortgage broker or an affiliate of the mortgage broker for the following: fees for tax payment services; fees for flood certification; fees for pest infestation and flood determinations; appraisal fees; fees for inspections performed prior to closing; credit reports; surveys; attorneys' fees (if the borrower has the right to select the attorney from an approved list or otherwise); notary fees; escrow charges, so long as not otherwise included under sub-subdivision a. of this subdivision; title insurance premiums; and premiums for insurance against loss or damage to property, including hazard insurance and flood insurance premiums, provided that the conditions in section 226.4(d)(2) of Title 12 of the Code of Federal Regulations are met.

c. For open-end credit plans, the term includes those points and fees described in sub-subdivisions a.1. through a.3. of this subdivision, plus (i) the minimum additional fees the borrower would be required to pay to draw down an amount equal to the total loan amount, and (ii) the maximum prepayment fees and penalties which may be charged or collected under the terms of the loan documents.

(5a) A "table-funded transaction" is a loan transaction closed by a mortgage broker in the mortgage broker's own name with funds advanced by a person other than the mortgage broker in which the loan is assigned contemporaneously or within one business day of the funding of the loan to the person that advanced the funds.

(6) "Thresholds" means:

a. Without regard to whether the loan transaction is or may be a "residential mortgage transaction" (as the term "residential mortgage transaction" is defined in section 226.2(a)(24) of Title 12 of the Code of Federal Regulations, as amended from time to time), the annual percentage rate of the loan at the time the loan is consummated is such that the loan is considered a "mortgage" under section 152 of the Home Ownership and Equity Protection Act of 1994 (Pub. Law 103–25, [15 U.S.C. § 1602(aa)]), as the same may be amended from time to time, and regulations adopted pursuant thereto by the Federal Reserve Board, including section 226.32 of Title 12 of the Code of Federal Regulations, as the same may be amended from time to time;

b. The total points and fees, as defined in G.S. 24–1.1E(a)(5), exceed five percent (5%) of the total loan amount if the total loan amount is twenty thousand dollars ($20,000) or more, or (ii) the lesser of eight percent (8%) of the total loan amount or one thousand dollars ($1,000), if the total loan amount is less than twenty thousand dollars ($20,000); provided, the following discount points and prepayment fees and penalties shall be excluded from the calculation of the total points and fees payable by the borrower:

1. Up to and including two bona fide loan discount points payable by the borrower in connection with the loan transaction, but only if the interest rate from which the loan's interest rate will be discounted does not exceed by more than one percentage point (1%) the required net yield for a 90-day standard mandatory delivery commitment for a reasonably comparable loan from either Fannie Mae or the Federal Home Loan Mortgage Corporation, whichever is greater;

2. Up to and including one bona fide loan discount point payable by the borrower in connection with the loan transaction, but only if the interest rate from which the loan's interest rate will be discounted does not exceed by more than two percentage points (2%) the required net yield for a 90-day standard mandatory delivery commitment for a reasonably comparable loan from either Fannie Mae or the Federal Home Loan Mortgage Corporation, whichever is greater;

3. For a closed-end loan, prepayment fees and penalties which may be charged or collected under the terms of the loan documents which do not exceed one percent (1%) of the amount prepaid, provided the loan documents do not permit the lender to charge or collect any prepayment fees or penalties more than 30 months after the loan closing;

4. For an open-end credit plan, prepayment fees and penalties which may be charged or collected under the terms of the loan documents which do not exceed one percent (1%) of the amount prepaid, provided the loan documents do not permit the lender to charge or collect any prepayment fees or penalties more than (i) 30 months after the loan closing if the borrower has no right or option under the loan documents to repay all or any portion of the outstanding balance of the open-end credit plan at a fixed interest rate over a specified period of time or, (ii) if the borrower has a right or option under the loan documents to repay all or any portion of the outstanding balance of the open-end credit plan at a fixed interest rate over a specified period of time, 30 months after the date the borrower voluntarily exercises that right or option; or

c. If the loan is a closed-end loan, the loan documents permit the lender to charge or collect prepayment fees or penalties more than 30 months after the loan closing or which exceed, in the aggregate, more than two percent (2%) of the amount prepaid. If the loan is an open-end credit plan, the loan documents permit the lender to charge or collect prepayment fees or penalties (i) more than 30 months after the loan closing if the borrower has no right or option under the loan documents to repay all or any portion of the outstanding balance of the open-end credit plan at a fixed interest rate over a specified period of time or, (ii) if the borrower has a right or option under the loan documents to repay all or any portion of the outstanding balance of the open-end credit plan at a fixed interest rate over a specified period of time, more than 30 months after the date the borrower voluntarily exercises that right or option, or (iii) which exceed, in the aggregate, more than two percent (2%) of the amount prepaid.

(7) For a closed-end loan, "total loan amount" has the same meaning as the term "total loan amount" as used in section 226.32 of Title 12 of the Code of Federal Regulations, and shall be calculated in accordance with the Federal Reserve Board's Official Staff Commentary thereto. For an open-end credit plan, "total loan amount" means the borrower's initial maximum credit limit.

(b) Limitations.—A high-cost home loan shall be subject to the following limitations:

(1) No call provision.—No high-cost home loan may contain a provision which permits the lender, in its sole discretion, to accelerate the indebtedness. This provision does not apply when repayment of the loan has been accelerated by default, pursuant to a due-on-sale provision, or pursuant to some other provision of the loan documents unrelated to the payment schedule.

(2) No balloon payment.—No high-cost home loan may contain a scheduled payment that is more than twice as large as the average of earlier scheduled payments. This provision does not apply when the payment schedule is adjusted to the seasonal or irregular income of the borrower.

(3) No negative amortization.—No high-cost home loan may contain a payment schedule with regular periodic payments that cause the principal balance to increase.

(4) No increased interest rate.—No high-cost home loan may contain a provision which increases the interest rate after default. This provision does not apply to interest rate changes in a variable rate loan otherwise consistent with the provisions of the loan documents, provided the change in the interest rate is not triggered by the event of default or the acceleration of the indebtedness.

(5) No advance payments.—No high-cost home loan may include terms under which more than two periodic payments required under the loan are consolidated and paid in advance from the loan proceeds provided to the borrower.

(6) No modification or deferral fees.—A lender may not charge a borrower any fees to modify, renew, extend, or amend a high-cost home loan or to defer any payment due under the terms of a high-cost home loan.

(c) Prohibited Acts and Practices.—The following acts and practices are prohibited in the making of a high-cost home loan:

(1) No lending without home-ownership counseling.—A lender may not make a high-cost home loan without first receiving certification from a counselor approved by the North Carolina Housing Finance Agency that the borrower has received counseling on the advisability of the loan transaction and the appropriate loan for the borrower.

(2) No lending without due regard to repayment ability.—As used in this subsection, the term "obligor" refers to each borrower, co-borrower, cosigner, or guarantor obligated to repay a loan. A lender may not make a high-cost home loan unless the lender reasonably believes at the time the loan is consummated that one or more of the obligors, when considered individually or collectively, will be able to make the scheduled payments to repay the obligation based upon a consideration of their current and expected income, current obligations, employment status, and other financial resources (other than the borrower's equity in the dwelling which secures repayment of the loan). An obligor shall be presumed to be able to make the scheduled payments to repay the obligation if, at the time the loan is consummated, the obligor's total monthly debts, including amounts owed under the loan, do not exceed fifty percent (50%) of the obligor's monthly gross income as verified by the credit application, the obligor's financial statement, a credit report, financial information provided to the lender by or on behalf of the obligor, or any other reasonable means; provided, no presumption of inability to make the scheduled payments to repay the obligation shall arise solely from the fact that, at the time the loan is consummated, the obligor's total monthly debts (including amounts owed under the loan) exceed fifty percent (50%) of the obligor's monthly gross income.

(3) No financing of fees or charges.—In making a high-cost home loan, a lender may not directly or indirectly finance:

a. Any prepayment fees or penalties payable by the borrower in a refinancing transaction if the lender or an affiliate of the lender is the noteholder of the note being refinanced;

b. Any points and fees; or

c. Any other charges payable to third parties.

(4) No benefit from refinancing existing high-cost home loan with new high-cost home loan.—A lender may not charge a borrower points and fees in connection with a high-cost home loan if the proceeds of the high-cost home loan are used to refinance an existing high-cost home loan held by the same lender as noteholder.

(5) Restrictions on home-improvement contracts.—A lender may not pay a contractor under a home-improvement contract from the proceeds of a high-cost home loan other than (i) by an instrument payable to the borrower or jointly to the borrower and the contractor, or (ii) at the election of the borrower, through a third-party escrow agent in accordance with terms established in a written agreement signed by the borrower, the lender, and the contractor prior to the disbursement.

(6) No shifting of liability.—A lender is prohibited from shifting any loss, liability, or claim of any kind to the closing agent or closing attorney for any violation of this section.

(d) Unfair and Deceptive Acts or Practices.—Except as provided in subsection (e) of this section, the making of a high-cost home loan which violates any provisions of subsection (b) or (c) of this section is hereby declared usurious in violation of the provisions of this Chapter and unlawful as an unfair or deceptive act or practice in or affecting commerce in violation of the provisions of G.S. 75–1.1. The provisions of this section shall apply to any person who in bad faith attempts to avoid the application of this section by (i) the structuring of a loan transaction as an open-end credit plan for the purpose and with the intent of evading the provisions of this section when the loan would have been a high-cost home loan if the loan had been structured as a closed-end loan, or (ii) dividing any loan transaction into separate parts for the purpose and with the intent of evading the provisions of this section, or (iii) any other such subterfuge. The Attorney General, the Commissioner of Banks, or any party to a high-cost home loan may enforce the provisions of this section. Any person seeking damages or penalties under the provisions of this section may recover damages under either this Chapter or Chapter 75, but not both.

(e) Corrections and Unintentional Violations.—A lender in a high-cost home loan who, when acting in good faith, fails to comply with subsections (b) or (c) of this section, will not be deemed to have violated this section if the lender establishes that either:

(1) Within 30 days of the loan closing and prior to the institution of any action under this section, the borrower is notified of the compliance failure, appropriate restitution is made, and whatever adjustments are necessary are made to the loan to either, at the choice of the borrower, (i) make the high-cost home loan satisfy the requirements of subsections (b) and (c) of this section, or (ii) change the terms of the loan in a manner beneficial to the borrower so that the loan will no longer be considered a high-cost home loan subject to the provisions of this section; or

(2) The compliance failure was not intentional and resulted from a bona fide error notwithstanding the maintenance of procedures reasonably adapted to avoid such errors, and within 60 days after the discovery of the compliance failure and prior to the institution of any action under this section or the receipt of written notice of the compliance failure, the borrower is notified of the compliance failure, appropriate restitution is made, and whatever adjustments are necessary are made to the loan to either, at the choice of the borrower, (i) make the high-cost home loan satisfy the requirements of subsections (b) and (c) of this section, or (ii) change the terms of the loan in a manner beneficial to the borrower so that the loan will no longer be considered a high-cost home loan subject to the provisions of this section. Examples of a bona fide error include clerical, calculation, computer malfunction and programming, and printing errors. An error of legal judgment with respect to a person's obligations under this section is not a bona fide error.

(f) Severability.—The provisions of this section shall be severable, and if any phrase, clause, sentence, or provision is declared to be invalid or is preempted by federal law or regulation, the validity of the remainder of this section shall not be affected thereby. If any provision of this section is declared to be inapplicable to any specific category, type, or kind of points and fees, the provisions of this section shall nonetheless continue to apply with respect to all other points and fees.

(g) A mortgage broker who brokers a high-cost home loan that violates any provisions of subsection (b) or (c) of this section shall be jointly and severally liable with the lender.

STATE CLASS ACTION STATUTE—ILLINOIS

735 ILCS § 5/2–801. Prerequisites for the maintenance of a class action

§ 2–801. Prerequisites for the maintenance of a class action. An action may be maintained as a class action in any court of this State and a party may sue or be sued as a representative party of the class only if the court finds:

(1) The class is so numerous that joinder of all members is impracticable.

(2) There are questions of fact or law common to the class, which common questions predominate over any questions affecting only individual members.

(3) The representative parties will fairly and adequately protect the interest of the class.

(4) The class action is an appropriate method for the fair and efficient adjudication of the controversy.

Part Three

RESTATEMENT PROVISIONS

SELECTED SECTIONS FROM RESTATEMENT 2D OF TORTS

Topic 1

FRAUDULENT MISREPRESENTATION (DECEIT)

§ 525. Liability for Fraudulent Misrepresentation

One who fraudulently makes a misrepresentation of fact, opinion, intention or law for the purpose of inducing another to act or to refrain from action in reliance upon it, is subject to liability to the other in deceit for pecuniary loss caused to him by his justifiable reliance upon the misrepresentation.

TITLE A. FRAUDULENT CHARACTER OF MISREPRESENTATION

§ 526. Conditions under Which Misrepresentation is Fraudulent (Scienter)

A misrepresentation is fraudulent if the maker

(a) knows or believes that the matter is not as he represents it to be,

(b) does not have the confidence in the accuracy of his representation that he states or implies, or

(c) knows that he does not have the basis for his representation that he states or implies.

TITLE B. EXPECTATION OF INFLUENCING CONDUCT

§ 531. General Rule

One who makes a fraudulent misrepresentation is subject to liability to the persons or class of persons whom he intends or has reason to expect to act or to refrain from action in reliance upon the misrepresentation, for pecuniary loss suffered by them through their justifiable reliance in the type of transaction in which he intends or has reason to expect their conduct to be influenced.

TITLE C. JUSTIFIABLE RELIANCE

§ 537. General Rule

The recipient of a fraudulent misrepresentation can recover against its maker for pecuniary loss resulting from it if, but only if,

(a) he relies on the misrepresentation in acting or refraining from action, and

(b) his reliance is justifiable.

§ 538. Materiality of Misrepresentation

(1) Reliance upon a fraudulent misrepresentation is not justifiable unless the matter misrepresented is material.

(2) The matter is material if

(a) a reasonable man would attach importance to its existence or nonexistence in determining his choice of action in the transaction in question; or

(b) the maker of the representation knows or has reason to know that its recipient regards or is likely to regard the matter as important in determining his choice of action, although a reasonable man would not so regard it.

§ 538A. Opinion

A representation is one of opinion if it expresses only

(a) the belief of the maker, without certainty, as to the existence of a fact; or

(b) his judgment as to quality, value, authenticity, or other matters of judgment.

§ 539. Representation of Opinion Implying Justifying Facts

(1) A statement of opinion as to facts not disclosed and not otherwise known to the recipient may, if it is reasonable to do so, be interpreted by him as an implied statement

(a) that the facts known to the maker are not incompatible with his opinion; or

(b) that he knows facts sufficient to justify him in forming it.

(2) In determining whether a statement of opinion may reasonably be so interpreted, the recipient's belief as to whether the maker has an adverse interest is important.

§ 540. Duty to Investigate

The recipient of a fraudulent misrepresentation of fact is justified in relying upon its truth, although he might have ascertained the falsity of the representation had he made an investigation.

Topic 2

CONCEALMENT AND NONDISCLOSURE

§ 550. Liability for Fraudulent Concealment

One party to a transaction who by concealment or other action intentionally prevents the other from acquiring material information is subject to the same liability to the other, for pecuniary loss as though he had stated the nonexistence of the matter that the other was thus prevented from discovering.

§ 551. Liability for Nondisclosure

(1) One who fails to disclose to another a fact that he knows may justifiably induce the other to act or refrain from acting in a business transaction is subject to the same liability to the other as though he had represented the nonexistence of the matter that he has failed to disclose, if, but only if, he is under a duty to the other to exercise reasonable care to disclose the matter in question.

(2) One party to a business transaction is under a duty to exercise reasonable care to disclose to the other before the transaction is consummated,

(a) matters known to him that the other is entitled to know because of a fiduciary or other similar relation of trust and confidence between them; and

(b) matters known to him that he knows to be necessary to prevent his partial or ambiguous statement of the facts from being misleading; and

(c) subsequently acquired information that he knows will make untrue or misleading a previous representation that when made was true or believed to be so; and

(d) the falsity of a representation not made with the expectation that it would be acted upon, if he subsequently learns that the other is about to act in reliance upon it in a transaction with him; and

(e) facts basic to the transaction, if he knows that the other is about to enter into it under a mistake as to them, and that the other, because of the relationship between them, the customs of the trade or other objective circumstances, would reasonably expect a disclosure of those facts.

Topic 3

NEGLIGENT MISREPRESENTATION

§ 552. Information Negligently Supplied for the Guidance of Others

(1) One who, in the course of his business, profession or employment, or in any other transaction in which he has a pecuniary interest, supplies false information for the guidance of others in their business transactions, is subject to liability for pecuniary loss caused to them by their justifiable reliance upon the information, if he fails to exercise reasonable care or competence in obtaining or communicating the information.

(2) Except as stated in Subsection (3), the liability stated in Subsection (1) is limited to loss suffered

(a) by the person or one of a limited group of persons for whose benefit and guidance he intends to supply the information or knows that the recipient intends to supply it; and

(b) through reliance upon it in a transaction that he intends the information to influence or knows that the recipient so intends or in a substantially similar transaction.

(3) The liability of one who is under a public duty to give the information extends to loss suffered by any of the class of persons for whose benefit the duty is created, in any of the transactions in which it is intended to protect them.

§ 552A. Contributory Negligence

The recipient of a negligent misrepresentation is barred from recovery for pecuniary loss suffered in reliance upon it if he is negligent in so relying.

§ 552B. Damages for Negligent Misrepresentation

(1) The damages recoverable for a negligent misrepresentation are those necessary to compensate the plaintiff for the pecuniary loss to him of which the misrepresentation is a legal cause, including

(a) the difference between the value of what he has received in the transaction and its purchase price or other value given for it; and

(b) pecuniary loss suffered otherwise as a consequence of the plaintiff's reliance upon the misrepresentation.

(2) The damages recoverable for a negligent misrepresentation do not include the benefit of the plaintiff's contract with the defendant.

Topic 4

INNOCENT MISREPRESENTATIONS

§ 552C. Misrepresentation in Sale, Rental or Exchange Transaction

(1) One who, in a sale, rental or exchange transaction with another, makes a misrepresentation of a material fact for the purpose of inducing the other to act or to refrain from acting in reliance upon it, is subject to liability to the other for pecuniary loss caused to him by his justifiable reliance upon the misrepresentation, even though it is not made fraudulently or negligently.

(2) Damages recoverable under the rule stated in this section are limited to the difference between the value of what the other has parted with and the value of what he has received in the transaction.

SELECTED SECTIONS FROM RESTATEMENT 2D OF CONTRACTS

Topic 1

MISREPRESENTATION

§ 161. When Non-Disclosure is Equivalent to an Assertion

A person's non-disclosure of a fact known to him is equivalent to an assertion that the fact does not exist in the following cases only:

(a) Where he knows that disclosure of the fact is necessary to prevent some previous assertion from being a misrepresentation or from being fraudulent or material.

(b) Where he knows that disclosure of the fact would correct a mistake of the other party as to a basic assumption on which that party is making the contract and if non-disclosure of the fact amounts to a failure to act in good faith and in accordance with reasonable standards of fair dealing.

(c) Where he knows that disclosure of the fact would correct a mistake of the other party as to the contents or effect of a writing, evidencing or embodying an agreement in whole or in part.

(d) Where the other person is entitled to know the fact because of a relation of trust and confidence between them.

§ 162. When a Misrepresentation is Fraudulent or Material

(1) A misrepresentation is fraudulent if the maker intends his assertion to induce a party to manifest his assent and the maker

(a) knows or believes that the assertion is not in accord with the facts, or

(b) does not have the confidence that he states or implies in the truth of the assertion, or

(c) knows that he does not have the basis that he states or implies for the assertion.

(2) A misrepresentation is material if it would be likely to induce a reasonable person to manifest his assent, or if the maker knows that it would be likely to induce the recipient to do so.

§ 163. When a Misrepresentation Prevents Formation of a Contract

If a misrepresentation as to the character or essential terms of a proposed contract induces conduct that appears to be a manifestation of assent by one who neither knows nor has reasonable opportunity to know of the character or essential terms of the proposed contract, his conduct is not effective as a manifestation of assent.

§ 164. When a Misrepresentation Makes a Contract Voidable

(1) If a party's manifestation of assent is induced by either a fraudulent or a material misrepresentation by the other party upon which the recipient is justified in relying, the contract is voidable by the recipient.

(2) If a party's manifestation of assent is induced by either a fraudulent or a material misrepresentation by one who is not a party to the transaction upon which the recipient is justified in relying, the contract is voidable by the recipient, unless the other party to the transaction in good faith

and without reason to know of the misrepresentation either gives value or relies materially on the transaction.

§ 168. Reliance on Assertions of Opinion

(1) An assertion is one of opinion if it expresses only a belief, without certainty, as to the existence of a fact or expresses only a judgment as to quality, value, authenticity, or similar matters.

(2) If it is reasonable to do so, the recipient of an assertion of a person's opinion as to facts not disclosed and not otherwise known to the recipient may properly interpret it as an assertion

(a) that the facts known to that person are not incompatible with his opinion, or

(b) that he knows facts sufficient to justify him in forming it.

§ 169. When Reliance on an Assertion of Opinion is Not Justified

To the extent that an assertion is one of opinion only, the recipient is not justified in relying on it unless the recipient

(a) stands in such a relation of trust and confidence to the person whose opinion is asserted that the recipient is reasonable in relying on it, or

(b) reasonably believes that, as compared with himself, the person whose opinion is asserted has special skill, judgment or objectivity with respect to the subject matter, or

(c) is for some other special reason particularly susceptible to a misrepresentation of the type involved.

Part Four

INTERNATIONAL MATERIALS

EUROPEAN UNION DIRECTIVES

Directive 2011/83/EU of the European Parliament and of the Council of 25 October 2011 on consumer rights

* * *

SUBJECT MATTER, DEFINITIONS AND SCOPE

Article 1

Subject matter

The purpose of this Directive is, through the achievement of a high level of consumer protection, to contribute to the proper functioning of the internal market by approximating certain aspects of the laws, regulations and administrative provisions of the Member States concerning contracts concluded between consumers and traders.

Article 2

Definitions

For the purpose of this Directive, the following definitions shall apply:

(1) "consumer" means any natural person who, in contracts covered by this Directive, is acting for purposes which are outside his trade, business, craft or profession;

(2) "trader" means any natural person or any legal person, irrespective of whether privately or publicly owned, who is acting, including through any other person acting in his name or on his behalf, for purposes relating to his trade, business, craft or profession in relation to contracts covered by this Directive;

(3) "goods" means any tangible movable items, with the exception of items sold by way of execution or otherwise by authority of law; water, gas and electricity shall be considered as goods within the meaning of this Directive where they are put up for sale in a limited volume or a set quantity;

(4) "goods made to the consumer's specifications" means non-prefabricated goods made on the basis of an individual choice of or decision by the consumer;

(5) "sales contract" means any contract under which the trader transfers or undertakes to transfer the ownership of goods to the consumer and the consumer pays or undertakes to pay the price thereof, including any contract having as its object both goods and services;

(6) "service contract" means any contract other than a sales contract under which the trader supplies or undertakes to supply a service to the consumer and the consumer pays or undertakes to pay the price thereof;

(7) "distance contract" means any contract concluded between the trader and the consumer under an organised distance sales or service-provision scheme without the simultaneous physical presence of the trader and the consumer, with the exclusive use of one or more means of distance communication up to and including the time at which the contract is concluded;

(8) "off-premises contract" means any contract between the trader and the consumer:

(a) concluded in the simultaneous physical presence of the trader and the consumer, in a place which is not the business premises of the trader;

(b) for which an offer was made by the consumer in the same circumstances as referred to in point (a);

(c) concluded on the business premises of the trader or through any means of distance communication immediately after the consumer was personally and individually addressed in a place which is not the business premises of the trader in the simultaneous physical presence of the trader and the consumer; or

(d) concluded during an excursion organised by the trader with the aim or effect of promoting and selling goods or services to the consumer;

(9) "business premises" means:

(a) any immovable retail premises where the trader carries out his activity on a permanent basis; or

(b) any movable retail premises where the trader carries out his activity on a usual basis;

(10) "durable medium" means any instrument which enables the consumer or the trader to store information addressed personally to him in a way accessible for future reference for a period of time adequate for the purposes of the information and which allows the unchanged reproduction of the information stored;

(11) "digital content" means data which are produced and supplied in digital form;

(12) "financial service" means any service of a banking, credit, insurance, personal pension, investment or payment nature;

(13) "public auction" means a method of sale where goods or services are offered by the trader to consumers, who attend or are given the possibility to attend the auction in person, through a transparent, competitive bidding procedure run by an auctioneer and where the successful bidder is bound to purchase the goods or services;

(14) "commercial guarantee" means any undertaking by the trader or a producer (the guarantor) to the consumer, in addition to his legal obligation relating to the guarantee of conformity, to reimburse the price paid or to replace, repair or service goods in any way if they do not meet the specifications or any other requirements not related to conformity set out in the guarantee statement or in the relevant advertising available at the time of, or before the conclusion of the contract;

(15) "ancillary contract" means a contract by which the consumer acquires goods or services related to a distance contract or an off-premises contract and where those goods are supplied or those services are provided by the trader or by a third party on the basis of an arrangement between that third party and the trader.

Article 3

Scope

1. This Directive shall apply, under the conditions and to the extent set out in its provisions, to any contract concluded between a trader and a consumer. It shall also apply to contracts for the supply of water, gas, electricity or district heating, including by public providers, to the extent that these commodities are provided on a contractual basis.

2. If any provision of this Directive conflicts with a provision of another Union act governing specific sectors, the provision of that other Union act shall prevail and shall apply to those specific sectors.

3. This Directive shall not apply to contracts:

(a) for social services, including social housing, childcare and support of families and persons permanently or temporarily in need, including long-term care;

(b) for healthcare as defined in point (a) of Article 3 of Directive 2011/24/EU, whether or not they are provided via healthcare facilities;

(c) for gambling, which involves wagering a stake with pecuniary value in games of chance, including lotteries, casino games and betting transactions;

(d) for financial services;

(e) for the creation, acquisition or transfer of immovable property or of rights in immovable property;

(f) for the construction of new buildings, the substantial conversion of existing buildings and for rental of accommodation for residential purposes;

(g) which fall within the scope of Council Directive 90/314/EEC of 13 June 1990 on package travel, package holidays and package tours [18];

(h) which fall within the scope of Directive 2008/122/EC of the European Parliament and of the Council of 14 January 2009 on the protection of consumers in respect of certain aspects of timeshare, long-term holiday product, resale and exchange contracts [19];

(i) which, in accordance with the laws of Member States, are established by a public office-holder who has a statutory obligation to be independent and impartial and who must ensure, by providing comprehensive legal information, that the consumer only concludes the contract on the basis of careful legal consideration and with knowledge of its legal scope;

(j) for the supply of foodstuffs, beverages or other goods intended for current consumption in the household, and which are physically supplied by a trader on frequent and regular rounds to the consumer's home, residence or workplace;

(k) for passenger transport services, with the exception of Article 8(2) and Articles 19 and 22;

(l) concluded by means of automatic vending machines or automated commercial premises;

(m) concluded with telecommunications operators through public payphones for their use or concluded for the use of one single connection by telephone, Internet or fax established by a consumer.

4. Member States may decide not to apply this Directive or not to maintain or introduce corresponding national provisions to off-premises contracts for which the payment to be made by the consumer does not exceed EUR 50. Member States may define a lower value in their national legislation.

5. This Directive shall not affect national general contract law such as the rules on the validity, formation or effect of a contract, in so far as general contract law aspects are not regulated in this Directive.

6. This Directive shall not prevent traders from offering consumers contractual arrangements which go beyond the protection provided for in this Directive.

Article 4

Level of harmonisation

Member States shall not maintain or introduce, in their national law, provisions diverging from those laid down in this Directive, including more or less stringent provisions to ensure a different level of consumer protection, unless otherwise provided for in this Directive.

CHAPTER II

CONSUMER INFORMATION FOR CONTRACTS OTHER THAN DISTANCE OR OFF-PREMISES CONTRACTS

Article 5

Information requirements for contracts other than distance or off-premises contracts

1. Before the consumer is bound by a contract other than a distance or an off-premises contract, or any corresponding offer, the trader shall provide the consumer with the following information in a clear and comprehensible manner, if that information is not already apparent from the context:

(a) the main characteristics of the goods or services, to the extent appropriate to the medium and to the goods or services;

(b) the identity of the trader, such as his trading name, the geographical address at which he is established and his telephone number;

(c) the total price of the goods or services inclusive of taxes, or where the nature of the goods or services is such that the price cannot reasonably be calculated in advance, the manner in which the price is to be calculated, as well as, where applicable, all additional freight, delivery or postal charges or, where those charges cannot reasonably be calculated in advance, the fact that such additional charges may be payable;

(d) where applicable, the arrangements for payment, delivery, performance, the time by which the trader undertakes to deliver the goods or to perform the service, and the trader's complaint handling policy;

(e) in addition to a reminder of the existence of a legal guarantee of conformity for goods, the existence and the conditions of after-sales services and commercial guarantees, where applicable;

(f) the duration of the contract, where applicable, or, if the contract is of indeterminate duration or is to be extended automatically, the conditions for terminating the contract;

(g) where applicable, the functionality, including applicable technical protection measures, of digital content;

(h) where applicable, any relevant interoperability of digital content with hardware and software that the trader is aware of or can reasonably be expected to have been aware of.

2. Paragraph 1 shall also apply to contracts for the supply of water, gas or electricity, where they are not put up for sale in a limited volume or set quantity, of district heating or of digital content which is not supplied on a tangible medium.

3. Member States shall not be required to apply paragraph 1 to contracts which involve day-to-day transactions and which are performed immediately at the time of their conclusion.

4. Member States may adopt or maintain additional pre-contractual information requirements for contracts to which this Article applies.

CHAPTER III

CONSUMER INFORMATION AND RIGHT OF WITHDRAWAL FOR DISTANCE AND OFF-PREMISES CONTRACTS

Article 6

Information requirements for distance and off-premises contracts

1. Before the consumer is bound by a distance or off-premises contract, or any corresponding offer, the trader shall provide the consumer with the following information in a clear and comprehensible manner:

(a) the main characteristics of the goods or services, to the extent appropriate to the medium and to the goods or services;

(b) the identity of the trader, such as his trading name;

(c) the geographical address at which the trader is established and the trader's telephone number, fax number and e-mail address, where available, to enable the consumer to contact the trader quickly and communicate with him efficiently and, where applicable, the geographical address and identity of the trader on whose behalf he is acting;

(d) if different from the address provided in accordance with point (c), the geographical address of the place of business of the trader, and, where applicable, that of the trader on whose behalf he is acting, where the consumer can address any complaints;

(e) the total price of the goods or services inclusive of taxes, or where the nature of the goods or services is such that the price cannot reasonably be calculated in advance, the manner in which the price is to be calculated, as well as, where applicable, all additional freight, delivery or postal charges and any other costs or, where those charges cannot reasonably be calculated in advance, the fact that such additional charges may be payable. In the case of a contract of indeterminate duration or a contract containing a subscription, the total price shall include the total costs per billing period. Where such contracts are charged at a fixed rate, the total price shall also mean the total monthly costs. Where the total costs cannot be reasonably calculated in advance, the manner in which the price is to be calculated shall be provided;

(f) the cost of using the means of distance communication for the conclusion of the contract where that cost is calculated other than at the basic rate;

(g) the arrangements for payment, delivery, performance, the time by which the trader undertakes to deliver the goods or to perform the services and, where applicable, the trader's complaint handling policy;

(h) where a right of withdrawal exists, the conditions, time limit and procedures for exercising that right in accordance with Article 11(1), as well as the model withdrawal form set out in Annex I(B);

(i) where applicable, that the consumer will have to bear the cost of returning the goods in case of withdrawal and, for distance contracts, if the goods, by their nature, cannot normally be returned by post, the cost of returning the goods;

(j) that, if the consumer exercises the right of withdrawal after having made a request in accordance with Article 7(3) or Article 8(8), the consumer shall be liable to pay the trader reasonable costs in accordance with Article 14(3);

(k) where a right of withdrawal is not provided for in accordance with Article 16, the information that the consumer will not benefit from a right of withdrawal or, where applicable, the circumstances under which the consumer loses his right of withdrawal;

(l) a reminder of the existence of a legal guarantee of conformity for goods;

(m) where applicable, the existence and the conditions of after sale customer assistance, after-sales services and commercial guarantees;

(n) the existence of relevant codes of conduct, as defined in point (f) of Article 2 of Directive 2005/29/EC, and how copies of them can be obtained, where applicable;

(*o*) the duration of the contract, where applicable, or, if the contract is of indeterminate duration or is to be extended automatically, the conditions for terminating the contract;

(p) where applicable, the minimum duration of the consumer's obligations under the contract;

(q) where applicable, the existence and the conditions of deposits or other financial guarantees to be paid or provided by the consumer at the request of the trader;

(r) where applicable, the functionality, including applicable technical protection measures, of digital content;

(s) where applicable, any relevant interoperability of digital content with hardware and software that the trader is aware of or can reasonably be expected to have been aware of;

(t) where applicable, the possibility of having recourse to an out-of-court complaint and redress mechanism, to which the trader is subject, and the methods for having access to it.

2. Paragraph 1 shall also apply to contracts for the supply of water, gas or electricity, where they are not put up for sale in a limited volume or set quantity, of district heating or of digital content which is not supplied on a tangible medium.

3. In the case of a public auction, the information referred to in points (b), (c) and (d) of paragraph 1 may be replaced by the equivalent details for the auctioneer.

4. The information referred to in points (h), (i) and (j) of paragraph 1 may be provided by means of the model instructions on withdrawal set out in Annex I(A). The trader shall have fulfilled the information requirements laid down in points (h), (i) and (j) of paragraph 1 if he has supplied these instructions to the consumer, correctly filled in.

5. The information referred to in paragraph 1 shall form an integral part of the distance or off-premises contract and shall not be altered unless the contracting parties expressly agree otherwise.

6. If the trader has not complied with the information requirements on additional charges or other costs as referred to in point (e) of paragraph 1, or on the costs of returning the goods as referred to in point (i) of paragraph 1, the consumer shall not bear those charges or costs.

7. Member States may maintain or introduce in their national law language requirements regarding the contractual information, so as to ensure that such information is easily understood by the consumer.

8. The information requirements laid down in this Directive are in addition to information requirements contained in Directive 2006/123/EC and Directive 2000/31/EC and do not prevent Member States from imposing additional information requirements in accordance with those Directives.

Without prejudice to the first subparagraph, if a provision of Directive 2006/123/EC or Directive 2000/31/EC on the content and the manner in which the information is to be provided conflicts with a provision of this Directive, the provision of this Directive shall prevail.

9. As regards compliance with the information requirements laid down in this Chapter, the burden of proof shall be on the trader.

Article 7

Formal requirements for off-premises contracts

1. With respect to off-premises contracts, the trader shall give the information provided for in Article 6(1) to the consumer on paper or, if the consumer agrees, on another durable medium. That information shall be legible and in plain, intelligible language.

2. The trader shall provide the consumer with a copy of the signed contract or the confirmation of the contract on paper or, if the consumer agrees, on another durable medium, including, where applicable, the confirmation of the consumer's prior express consent and acknowledgement in accordance with point (m) of Article 16.

3. Where a consumer wants the performance of services or the supply of water, gas or electricity, where they are not put up for sale in a limited volume or set quantity, or of district heating to begin during the withdrawal period provided for in Article 9(2), the trader shall require that the consumer makes such an express request on a durable medium.

4. With respect to off-premises contracts where the consumer has explicitly requested the services of the trader for the purpose of carrying out repairs or maintenance for which the trader and the consumer immediately perform their contractual obligations and where the payment to be made by the consumer does not exceed EUR 200:

(a) the trader shall provide the consumer with the information referred to in points (b) and (c) of Article 6(1) and information about the price or the manner in which the price is to be calculated together with an estimate of the total price, on paper or, if the consumer agrees, on another durable medium. The trader shall provide the information referred to in points (a), (h) and (k) of Article 6(1), but may choose not to provide it on paper or another durable medium if the consumer expressly agrees;

(b) the confirmation of the contract provided in accordance with paragraph 2 of this Article shall contain the information provided for in Article 6(1).

Member States may decide not to apply this paragraph.

5. Member States shall not impose any further formal pre-contractual information requirements for the fulfilment of the information obligations laid down in this Directive.

Article 8

Formal requirements for distance contracts

1. With respect to distance contracts, the trader shall give the information provided for in Article 6(1) or make that information available to the consumer in a way appropriate to the means of distance communication used in plain and intelligible language. In so far as that information is provided on a durable medium, it shall be legible.

2. If a distance contract to be concluded by electronic means places the consumer under an obligation to pay, the trader shall make the consumer aware in a clear and prominent manner, and directly before the consumer places his order, of the information provided for in points (a), (e), (*o*) and (p) of Article 6(1).

The trader shall ensure that the consumer, when placing his order, explicitly acknowledges that the order implies an obligation to pay. If placing an order entails activating a button or a similar function, the button or similar function shall be labelled in an easily legible manner only with the words "order with obligation to pay" or a corresponding unambiguous formulation indicating that placing the order entails an obligation to pay the trader. If the trader has not complied with this subparagraph, the consumer shall not be bound by the contract or order.

3. Trading websites shall indicate clearly and legibly at the latest at the beginning of the ordering process whether any delivery restrictions apply and which means of payment are accepted.

4. If the contract is concluded through a means of distance communication which allows limited space or time to display the information, the trader shall provide, on that particular means prior to the conclusion of such a contract, at least the pre-contractual information regarding the main characteristics of the goods or services, the identity of the trader, the total price, the right of withdrawal, the duration of the contract and, if the contract is of indeterminate duration, the conditions for terminating the contract, as referred to in points (a), (b), (e), (h) and (*o*) of Article 6(1). The other information referred to in Article 6(1) shall be provided by the trader to the consumer in an appropriate way in accordance with paragraph 1 of this Article.

5. Without prejudice to paragraph 4, if the trader makes a telephone call to the consumer with a view to concluding a distance contract, he shall, at the beginning of the conversation with the consumer, disclose his identity and, where applicable, the identity of the person on whose behalf he makes that call, and the commercial purpose of the call.

6. Where a distance contract is to be concluded by telephone, Member States may provide that the trader has to confirm the offer to the consumer who is bound only once he has signed the offer or has sent his written consent. Member States may also provide that such confirmations have to be made on a durable medium.

7. The trader shall provide the consumer with the confirmation of the contract concluded, on a durable medium within a reasonable time after the conclusion of the distance contract, and at the latest at the time of the delivery of the goods or before the performance of the service begins. That confirmation shall include:

(a) all the information referred to in Article 6(1) unless the trader has already provided that information to the consumer on a durable medium prior to the conclusion of the distance contract; and

(b) where applicable, the confirmation of the consumer's prior express consent and acknowledgment in accordance with point (m) of Article 16.

8. Where a consumer wants the performance of services, or the supply of water, gas or electricity, where they are not put up for sale in a limited volume or set quantity, or of district heating, to begin during the withdrawal period provided for in Article 9(2), the trader shall require that the consumer make an express request.

9. This Article shall be without prejudice to the provisions on the conclusion of e-contracts and the placing of e-orders set out in Articles 9 and 11 of Directive 2000/31/EC.

10. Member States shall not impose any further formal pre-contractual information requirements for the fulfilment of the information obligations laid down in this Directive.

Article 9

Right of withdrawal

1. Save where the exceptions provided for in Article 16 apply, the consumer shall have a period of 14 days to withdraw from a distance or off-premises contract, without giving any reason, and without incurring any costs other than those provided for in Article 13(2) and Article 14.

2. Without prejudice to Article 10, the withdrawal period referred to in paragraph 1 of this Article shall expire after 14 days from:

(a) in the case of service contracts, the day of the conclusion of the contract;

(b) in the case of sales contracts, the day on which the consumer or a third party other than the carrier and indicated by the consumer acquires physical possession of the goods or:

(i) in the case of multiple goods ordered by the consumer in one order and delivered separately, the day on which the consumer or a third party other than the carrier and indicated by the consumer acquires physical possession of the last good;

(ii) in the case of delivery of a good consisting of multiple lots or pieces, the day on which the consumer or a third party other than the carrier and indicated by the consumer acquires physical possession of the last lot or piece;

(iii) in the case of contracts for regular delivery of goods during defined period of time, the day on which the consumer or a third party other than the carrier and indicated by the consumer acquires physical possession of the first good;

(c) in the case of contracts for the supply of water, gas or electricity, where they are not put up for sale in a limited volume or set quantity, of district heating or of digital content which is not supplied on a tangible medium, the day of the conclusion of the contract.

3. The Member States shall not prohibit the contracting parties from performing their contractual obligations during the withdrawal period. Nevertheless, in the case of off-premises contracts, Member States may maintain existing national legislation prohibiting the trader from collecting the payment from the consumer during the given period after the conclusion of the contract.

Article 10

Omission of information on the right of withdrawal

1. If the trader has not provided the consumer with the information on the right of withdrawal as required by point (h) of Article 6(1), the withdrawal period shall expire 12 months from the end of the initial withdrawal period, as determined in accordance with Article 9(2).

2. If the trader has provided the consumer with the information provided for in paragraph 1 of this Article within 12 months from the day referred to in Article 9(2), the withdrawal period shall expire 14 days after the day upon which the consumer receives that information.

Article 11

Exercise of the right of withdrawal

1. Before the expiry of the withdrawal period, the consumer shall inform the trader of his decision to withdraw from the contract. For this purpose, the consumer may either:

(a) use the model withdrawal form as set out in Annex I(B); or

(b) make any other unequivocal statement setting out his decision to withdraw from the contract.

Member States shall not provide for any formal requirements applicable to the model withdrawal form other than those set out in Annex I(B).

2. The consumer shall have exercised his right of withdrawal within the withdrawal period referred to in Article 9(2) and Article 10 if the communication concerning the exercise of the right of withdrawal is sent by the consumer before that period has expired.

3. The trader may, in addition to the possibilities referred to in paragraph 1, give the option to the consumer to electronically fill in and submit either the model withdrawal form set out in Annex I(B) or any other unequivocal statement on the trader's website. In those cases the trader shall communicate to the consumer an acknowledgement of receipt of such a withdrawal on a durable medium without delay.

4. The burden of proof of exercising the right of withdrawal in accordance with this Article shall be on the consumer.

Article 12

Effects of withdrawal

The exercise of the right of withdrawal shall terminate the obligations of the parties:

(a) to perform the distance or off-premises contract; or

(b) to conclude the distance or off-premises contract, in cases where an offer was made by the consumer.

Article 13

Obligations of the trader in the event of withdrawal

1. The trader shall reimburse all payments received from the consumer, including, if applicable, the costs of delivery without undue delay and in any event not later than 14 days from the day on which he is informed of the consumer's decision to withdraw from the contract in accordance with Article 11.

The trader shall carry out the reimbursement referred to in the first subparagraph using the same means of payment as the consumer used for the initial transaction, unless the consumer has expressly agreed otherwise and provided that the consumer does not incur any fees as a result of such reimbursement.

2. Notwithstanding paragraph 1, the trader shall not be required to reimburse the supplementary costs, if the consumer has expressly opted for a type of delivery other than the least expensive type of standard delivery offered by the trader.

3. Unless the trader has offered to collect the goods himself, with regard to sales contracts, the trader may withhold the reimbursement until he has received the goods back, or until the consumer has supplied evidence of having sent back the goods, whichever is the earliest.

Article 14

Obligations of the consumer in the event of withdrawal

1. Unless the trader has offered to collect the goods himself, the consumer shall send back the goods or hand them over to the trader or to a person authorised by the trader to receive the goods, without undue delay and in any event not later than 14 days from the day on which he has communicated his decision to withdraw from the contract to the trader in accordance with Article 11. The deadline shall be met if the consumer sends back the goods before the period of 14 days has expired.

The consumer shall only bear the direct cost of returning the goods unless the trader has agreed to bear them or the trader failed to inform the consumer that the consumer has to bear them.

In the case of off-premises contracts where the goods have been delivered to the consumer's home at the time of the conclusion of the contract, the trader shall at his own expense collect the goods if, by their nature, those goods cannot normally be returned by post.

2. The consumer shall only be liable for any diminished value of the goods resulting from the handling of the goods other than what is necessary to establish the nature, characteristics and functioning of the goods. The consumer shall in any event not be liable for diminished value of the goods where the trader has failed to provide notice of the right of withdrawal in accordance with point (h) of Article 6(1).

3. Where a consumer exercises the right of withdrawal after having made a request in accordance with Article 7(3) or Article 8(8), the consumer shall pay to the trader an amount which is in proportion to what has been provided until the time the consumer has informed the trader of the exercise of the right of withdrawal, in comparison with the full coverage of the contract. The proportionate amount to be paid by the consumer to the trader shall be calculated on the basis of the total price agreed in the contract. If the total price is excessive, the proportionate amount shall be calculated on the basis of the market value of what has been provided.

4. The consumer shall bear no cost for:

(a) the performance of services or the supply of water, gas or electricity, where they are not put up for sale in a limited volume or set quantity, or of district heating, in full or in part, during the withdrawal period, where:

(i) the trader has failed to provide information in accordance with points (h) or (j) of Article 6(1); or

(ii) the consumer has not expressly requested performance to begin during the withdrawal period in accordance with Article 7(3) and Article 8(8); or

(b) the supply, in full or in part, of digital content which is not supplied on a tangible medium where:

(i) the consumer has not given his prior express consent to the beginning of the performance before the end of the 14-day period referred to in Article 9;

(ii) the consumer has not acknowledged that he loses his right of withdrawal when giving his consent; or

(iii) the trader has failed to provide confirmation in accordance with Article 7(2) or Article 8(7).

5. Except as provided for in Article 13(2) and in this Article, the consumer shall not incur any liability as a consequence of the exercise of the right of withdrawal.

Article 15

Effects of the exercise of the right of withdrawal on ancillary contracts

1. Without prejudice to Article 15 of Directive 2008/48/EC of the European Parliament and of the Council of 23 April 2008 on credit agreements for consumers [20], if the consumer exercises his right of withdrawal from a distance or an off-premises contract in accordance with Articles 9 to 14 of this Directive, any ancillary contracts shall be automatically terminated, without any costs for the consumer, except as provided for in Article 13(2) and in Article 14 of this Directive.

2. The Member States shall lay down detailed rules on the termination of such contracts.

Article 16

Exceptions from the right of withdrawal

Member States shall not provide for the right of withdrawal set out in Articles 9 to 15 in respect of distance and off-premises contracts as regards the following:

(a) service contracts after the service has been fully performed if the performance has begun with the consumer's prior express consent, and with the acknowledgement that he will lose his right of withdrawal once the contract has been fully performed by the trader;

(b) the supply of goods or services for which the price is dependent on fluctuations in the financial market which cannot be controlled by the trader and which may occur within the withdrawal period;

(c) the supply of goods made to the consumer's specifications or clearly personalised;

(d) the supply of goods which are liable to deteriorate or expire rapidly;

(e) the supply of sealed goods which are not suitable for return due to health protection or hygiene reasons and were unsealed after delivery;

(f) the supply of goods which are, after delivery, according to their nature, inseparably mixed with other items;

(g) the supply of alcoholic beverages, the price of which has been agreed upon at the time of the conclusion of the sales contract, the delivery of which can only take place after 30 days and the actual value of which is dependent on fluctuations in the market which cannot be controlled by the trader;

(h) contracts where the consumer has specifically requested a visit from the trader for the purpose of carrying out urgent repairs or maintenance. If, on the occasion of such visit, the trader provides services in addition to those specifically requested by the consumer or goods other than replacement parts necessarily used in carrying out the maintenance or in making the repairs, the right of withdrawal shall apply to those additional services or goods;

(i) the supply of sealed audio or sealed video recordings or sealed computer software which were unsealed after delivery;

(j) the supply of a newspaper, periodical or magazine with the exception of subscription contracts for the supply of such publications;

(k) contracts concluded at a public auction;

(*l*) the provision of accommodation other than for residential purpose, transport of goods, car rental services, catering or services related to leisure activities if the contract provides for a specific date or period of performance;

(m) the supply of digital content which is not supplied on a tangible medium if the performance has begun with the consumer's prior express consent and his acknowledgment that he thereby loses his right of withdrawal.

CHAPTER IV

OTHER CONSUMER RIGHTS

* * *

Article 18

Delivery

1. Unless the parties have agreed otherwise on the time of delivery, the trader shall deliver the goods by transferring the physical possession or control of the goods to the consumer without undue delay, but not later than 30 days from the conclusion of the contract.

2. Where the trader has failed to fulfil his obligation to deliver the goods at the time agreed upon with the consumer or within the time limit set out in paragraph 1, the consumer shall call upon him to make the delivery within an additional period of time appropriate to the circumstances. If the trader fails to deliver the goods within that additional period of time, the consumer shall be entitled to terminate the contract.

The first subparagraph shall not be applicable to sales contracts where the trader has refused to deliver the goods or where delivery within the agreed delivery period is essential taking into account all the circumstances attending the conclusion of the contract or where the consumer informs the trader, prior to the conclusion of the contract, that delivery by or on a specified date is essential. In those cases, if the trader fails to deliver the goods at the time agreed upon with the consumer or within the time limit set out in paragraph 1, the consumer shall be entitled to terminate the contract immediately.

3. Upon termination of the contract, the trader shall, without undue delay, reimburse all sums paid under the contract.

4. In addition to the termination of the contract in accordance with paragraph 2, the consumer may have recourse to other remedies provided for by national law.

* * *

Directive 93/13/EEC: Unfair Terms

THE COUNCIL OF THE EUROPEAN COMMUNITIES, * * *

HAS ADOPTED THIS DIRECTIVE:

DIRECTIVE 93/13

Article 1

1. The purpose of this Directive is to approximate the laws, regulations and administrative provisions of the Member States relating to unfair terms in contracts concluded between a seller or supplier and a consumer.

2. The contractual terms which reflect mandatory statutory or regulatory provisions and the provisions or principles of international conventions to which the Member States or the Community are party, particularly in the transport area, shall not be subject to the provisions of this Directive.

Article 2

For the purposes of this Directive:

(a) *"unfair terms"* means the contractual terms defined in Article 3;

(b) *"consumer"* means any natural person who, in contracts covered by this Directive, is acting for purposes which are outside his trade, business or profession;

(c) *"seller or supplier"* means any natural or legal person who, in contracts covered by this Directive, is acting for purposes relating to his trade, business or profession, whether publicly owned or privately owned.

Article 3

1. A contractual term which has not been individually negotiated shall be regarded as unfair if, contrary to the requirement of good faith, it causes a significant imbalance in the parties' rights and obligations arising under the contract, to the detriment of the consumer.

2. A term shall always be regarded as not individually negotiated where it has been drafted in advance and the consumer has therefore not been able to influence the substance of the term, particularly in the context of a pre-formulated standard contract.

The fact that certain aspects of a term or one specific term have been individually negotiated shall not exclude the application of this Article to the rest of a contract if an overall assessment of the contract indicates that it is nevertheless a pre-formulated standard contract.

Where any seller or supplier claims that a standard term has been individually negotiated, the burden of proof in this respect shall be incumbent on him.

3. The Annex shall contain an indicative and non-exhaustive list of the terms which may be regarded as unfair.

Article 4

1. Without prejudice to Article 7, the unfairness of a contractual term shall be assessed, taking into account the nature of the goods or services for which the contract was concluded and by referring, at the time of conclusion of the contract, to all the circumstances attending the conclusion of the contract and to all the other terms of the contract or of another contract on which it is dependent.

2. Assessment of the unfair nature of the terms shall relate neither to the definition of the main subject matter of the contract nor to the adequacy of the price and remuneration, on the one hand, as against the services or goods supplies in exchange, on the other, in so far as these terms are in plain intelligible language.

Article 5

In the case of contracts where all or certain terms offered to the consumer are in writing, these terms must always be drafted in plain, intelligible language. Where there is doubt about the meaning of a term, the interpretation most favourable to the consumer shall prevail. This rule on interpretation shall not apply in the context of the procedures laid down in Article 7 (2).

Article 6

1. Member States shall lay down that unfair terms used in a contract concluded with a consumer by a seller or supplier shall, as provided for under their national law, not be binding on the consumer and that the contract shall continue to bind the parties upon those terms if it is capable of continuing in existence without the unfair terms.

2. Member States shall take the necessary measures to ensure that the consumer does not lose the protection granted by this Directive by virtue of the choice of the law of a non-Member country as the law applicable to the contract if the latter has a close connection with the territory of the Member States.

Article 7

1. Member States shall ensure that, in the interests of consumers and of competitors, adequate and effective means exist to prevent the continued use of unfair terms in contracts concluded with consumers by sellers or suppliers.

2. The means referred to in paragraph 1 shall include provisions whereby persons or organizations, having a legitimate interest under national law in protecting consumers, may take action according to the national law concerned before the courts or before competent administrative bodies for a decision as to whether contractual terms drawn up for general use are unfair, so that they can apply appropriate and effective means to prevent the continued use of such terms.

3. With due regard for national laws, the legal remedies referred to in paragraph 2 may be directed separately or jointly against a number of sellers or suppliers from the same economic sector or their associations which use or recommend the use of the same general contractual terms or similar terms.

Article 8

Member States may adopt or retain the most stringent provisions compatible with the Treaty in the area covered by this Directive, to ensure a maximum degree of protection for the consumer.

* * *

Article 9

The Commission shall present a report to the European Parliament and to the Council concerning the application of this Directive five years at the latest after the date in Article 10 (1).

Article 10

1. Member States shall bring into force the laws, regulations and administrative provisions necessary to comply with this Directive no later than 31 December 1994. They shall forthwith inform the Commission thereof.

These provisions shall be applicable to all contracts concluded after 31 December 1994.

2. When Member States adopt these measures, they shall contain a reference to this Directive or shall be accompanied by such reference on the occasion of their official publication. The methods of making such a reference shall be laid down by the Member States.

3. Member States shall communicate the main provisions of national law which they adopt in the field covered by this Directive to the Commission.

Article 11

This Directive is addressed to the Member States.

DIRECTIVE 93/13

ANNEX

TERMS REFERRED TO IN ARTICLE 3 (3) [terms which may be regarded as unfair]

1. Terms which have the object or effect of:

(a) excluding or limiting the legal liability of a seller or supplier in the event of the death of a consumer or personal injury to the latter resulting from an act or omission of that seller or supplier;

(b) inappropriately excluding or limiting the legal rights of the consumer vis-a-vis the seller or supplier or another party in the event of total or partial non-performance or inadequate performance by the seller or supplier of any of the contractual obligations, including the option of offsetting a debt owed to the seller or supplier against any claim which the consumer may have against him;

(c) making an agreement binding on the consumer whereas provision of services by the seller or supplier is subject to a condition whose realization depends on his own will alone;

(d) permitting the seller or supplier to retain sums paid by the consumer where the latter decides not to conclude or perform the contract, without providing for the consumer to receive compensation of an equivalent amount from the seller or supplier where the latter is the party cancelling the contract;

(e) requiring any consumer who fails to fulfill his obligation to pay a disproportionately high sum in compensation;

(f) authorizing the seller or supplier to dissolve the contract on a discretionary basis where the same facility is not granted to the consumer, or permitting the seller or supplier to retain the sums paid for services not yet supplied by him where it is the seller or supplier himself who dissolves the contract;

(g) enabling the seller or supplier to terminate a contract of indeterminate duration without reasonable notice except where there are serious grounds for doing so;

(h) automatically extending a contract of fixed duration where the consumer does not indicate otherwise, when the deadline fixed for the consumer to express this desire not to extend the contract is unreasonably early;

(i) irrevocably binding the consumer to terms with which he had no real opportunity of becoming acquainted before the conclusion of the contract;

(j) enabling the seller or supplier to alter the terms of the contract unilaterally without a valid reason which is specified in the contract;

(k) enabling the seller or supplier to alter unilaterally without a valid reason any characteristics of the product or service to be provided;

(l) providing for the price of goods to be determined at the time of delivery or allowing a seller of goods or supplier of services to increase their price without in both cases giving the consumer the corresponding right to cancel the contract if the final price is too high in relation to the price agreed when the contract was concluded;

(m) giving the seller or supplier the right to determine whether the goods or services supplied are in conformity with the contract, or giving him the exclusive right to interpret any term of the contract;

(n) limiting the seller's or supplier's obligation to respect commitments undertaken by his agents or making his commitments subject to compliance with a particular formality;

(o) obliging the consumer to fulfill all his obligations where the seller or supplier does not perform his;

(p) giving the seller or supplier the possibility of transferring his rights and obligations under the contract, where this may serve to reduce the guarantees for the consumer, without the latter's agreement;

(q) excluding or hindering the consumer's right to take legal action or exercise any other legal remedy, particularly by requiring the consumer to take disputes exclusively to arbitration not covered by legal provisions, unduly restricting the evidence available to him or imposing on him a burden of proof which, according to the applicable law, should lie with another party to the contract.

2. Scope of subparagraphs (g), (j) and (*l*)

(a) Subparagraph (g) is without hindrance to terms by which a supplier of financial services reserves the right to terminate unilaterally a contract of indeterminate duration without notice where there is a valid reason, provided that the supplier is required to inform the other contracting party or parties thereof immediately.

(b) Subparagraph (j) is without hindrance to terms under which a supplier of financial services reserves the right to alter the rate of interest payable by the consumer or due to the latter, or the amount of other charges for financial services without notice where there is a valid reason, provided that the supplier is required to inform the other contracting party or parties thereof at the earliest opportunity and that the latter are free to dissolve the contract immediately.

Subparagraph (j) is also without hindrance to terms under which a seller or supplier reserves the right to alter unilaterally the conditions of a contract of indeterminate duration, provided that he is required to inform the consumer with reasonable notice and that the consumer is free to dissolve the contract.

(c) Subparagraphs (g), (j) and (*l*) do not apply to:

—transactions in transferable securities, financial instruments and other products or services where the price is linked to fluctuations in a stock exchange quotation or index or a financial market rate that the seller or supplier does not control;

—contracts for the purchase or sale of foreign currency, traveller's cheques or international money orders denominated in foreign currency;

(d) Subparagraph (*l*) is without hindrance to price-indexation clauses, where lawful, provided that the method by which prices vary is explicitly described.

Part Five

HELPFUL INTERNET SITES[1]

Blogs

Consumer Law and Policy Blog: www.clpblog.org

Credit Slips: http://www.creditslips.org/

U.S. PIRG blog: http://www.uspirg.org/blogs/usp/eds-blog

Government Web Sites

All United States government agencies: http://www.lib.lsu.edu/collections/govdocs/directory/

Board of Governors of the Federal Reserve System: http://www.federalreserve.gov/

Comptroller of the Currency: http://www.occ.gov/

Consumer Financial Protection Bureau: http://www.consumerfinance.gov/

European Commission: Justice and Consumers: http://ec.europa.eu/consumers/index_en.htm

Federal Trade Commission: http://www.ftc.gov/

Library of Congress: http://loc.gov

National Association of Attorneys General: http://www.naag.org/.

Consumer Research and Advocacy Organizations

American Council on Consumer Interests: http://consumerinterests.org

American Enterprise Institute for Public Policy Research Liability Project: http://www.aei.org/

Center for Democracy and Technology: https://cdt.org

Center for Responsible Lending: http://www.responsiblelending.org/

Center for Science in the Public Interest: http://www.cspinet.org/

Consumer Action: http://www.consumer-action.org/

Consumer Federation of America: http://www.consumerfed.org/

Consumer Reports (subscription required for some services): http://www.consumerreports.org/

Electronic Frontier Foundation: http://www.eff.org/

Electronic Privacy Information Center: http://www.epic.org/

International Association of Consumer Law: https://www.iacl.net.au

National Association of Consumer Advocates: https://www.consumeradvocates.org

National Consumer Law Center: http://www.nclc.org/

Public Citizen: http://www.citizen.org/

Public Justice Center: http://www.publicjustice.org/

United States Public Interest Research Groups: http://www.uspirg.org/

---

1 Inclusion in this list does not imply endorsement of the views expressed by any Web site.

HELPFUL INTERNET SITES

Industry Organizations and Law Firms

American Bankers Association: http://www.aba.com/default.htm

Association of Credit and Collection Professionals: http://www.acainternational.org

Ballard Spahr's CFPB Monitor: http://www.cfpbmonitor.com/

Institute for Legal Reform (affiliated with the U.S. Chamber of Commerce): http://www.instituteforlegalreform.com/

National Chamber Litigation Center (affiliated with the U.S. Chamber of Commerce): http://www.chamberlitigation.com

Other Resources

American Bar Association site on safe cyber shopping: http://www.safeshopping.org/

Better Business Bureau: http://www.bbb.org/

Consumer World: http://www.consumerworld.org/

Free annual credit reports: https://www.annualcreditreport.com/cra/index.jsp

Privacy Exchange: http://www.privacyexchange.org/

Podcasts

Ballard Spahr's Consumer Finance Monitor Podcast

Consumer Rights Talk

Breach (about data breaches)

The Dream (about pyramid schemes)